ENCYCLOPAEDIA JUDAICA

ENCYCLOPAEDIA JUDAICA

SECOND EDITION

VOLUME 18
San–Sol

Fred Skolnik, *Editor in Chief*
Michael Berenbaum, *Executive Editor*

MACMILLAN REFERENCE USA
An imprint of Thomson Gale, a part of The Thomson Corporation

IN ASSOCIATION WITH
KETER PUBLISHING HOUSE LTD., JERUSALEM

THOMSON
GALE

Detroit • New York • San Francisco • New Haven, Conn. • Waterville, Maine • London

THOMSON
GALE

ENCYCLOPAEDIA JUDAICA, Second Edition

Fred Skolnik, *Editor in Chief*
Michael Berenbaum, *Executive Editor*
Shlomo S. (Yosh) Gafni, *Editorial Project Manager*
Rachel Gilon, *Editorial Project Planning and Control*

Thomson Gale
Gordon Macomber, *President*
Frank Menchaca, *Senior Vice President and Publisher*
Jay Flynn, *Publisher*
Hélène Potter, *Publishing Director*

Keter Publishing House
Yiphtach Dekel, *Chief Executive Officer*
Peter Tomkins, *Executive Project Director*

Complete staff listings appear in Volume 1

For more information, contact
Macmillan Reference USA
An imprint of Thomson Gale
27500 Drake Rd.
Farmington Hills, MI 48331-3535
Or you can visit our internet site at
http://www.gale.com

LIBRARY OF CONGRESS CATALOGING-IN-PUBLICATION DATA

Encyclopaedia Judaica / Fred Skolnik, editor-in-chief ; Michael Berenbaum, executive editor. -- 2nd ed.
v. cm.
Includes bibliographical references and index.
Contents: v.1. Aa-Alp.
ISBN 0-02-865928-7 (set hardcover : alk. paper) -- ISBN 0-02-865929-5 (vol. 1 hardcover : alk. paper) -- ISBN 0-02-865930-9 (vol. 2 hardcover : alk. paper) -- ISBN 0-02-865931-7 (vol. 3 hardcover : alk. paper) -- ISBN 0-02-865932-5 (vol. 4 hardcover : alk. paper) -- ISBN 0-02-865933-3 (vol. 5 hardcover : alk. paper) -- ISBN 0-02-865934-1 (vol. 6 hardcover : alk. paper) -- ISBN 0-02-865935-X (vol. 7 hardcover : alk. paper) -- ISBN 0-02-865936-8 (vol. 8 hardcover : alk. paper) -- ISBN 0-02-865937-6 (vol. 9 hardcover : alk. paper) -- ISBN 0-02-865938-4 (vol. 10 hardcover : alk. paper) -- ISBN 0-02-865939-2 (vol. 11 hardcover : alk. paper) -- ISBN 0-02-865940-6 (vol. 12 hardcover : alk. paper) -- ISBN 0-02-865941-4 (vol. 13 hardcover : alk. paper) -- ISBN 0-02-865942-2 (vol. 14 hardcover : alk. paper) -- ISBN 0-02-865943-0 (vol. 15: alk. paper) -- ISBN 0-02-865944-9 (vol. 16: alk. paper) -- ISBN 0-02-865945-7 (vol. 17: alk. paper) -- ISBN 0-02-865946-5 (vol. 18: alk. paper) -- ISBN 0-02-865947-3 (vol. 19: alk. paper) -- ISBN 0-02-865948-1 (vol. 20: alk. paper) -- ISBN 0-02-865949-X (vol. 21: alk. paper) -- ISBN 0-02-865950-3 (vol. 22: alk. paper)
1. Jews -- Encyclopedias. I. Skolnik, Fred. II. Berenbaum, Michael, 1945-
DS102.8.E496 2007
909'.04924 -- dc22

2006020426

ISBN-13:

978-0-02-865928-2 (set)
978-0-02-865929-9 (vol. 1)
978-0-02-865930-5 (vol. 2)
978-0-02-865931-2 (vol. 3)
978-0-02-865932-9 (vol. 4)
978-0-02-865933-6 (vol. 5)
978-0-02-865934-3 (vol. 6)
978-0-02-865935-0 (vol. 7)
978-0-02-865936-7 (vol. 8)
978-0-02-865937-4 (vol. 9)
978-0-02-865938-1 (vol. 10)
978-0-02-865939-8 (vol. 11)
978-0-02-865940-4 (vol. 12)
978-0-02-865941-1 (vol. 13)
978-0-02-865942-8 (vol. 14)
978-0-02-865943-5 (vol. 15)
978-0-02-865944-2 (vol. 16)
978-0-02-865945-9 (vol. 17)
978-0-02-865946-6 (vol. 18)
978-0-02-865947-3 (vol. 19)
978-0-02-865948-0 (vol. 20)
978-0-02-865949-7 (vol. 21)
978-0-02-865950-3 (vol. 22)

This title is also available as an e-book
ISBN-10: 0-02-866097-8
ISBN-13: 978-0-02-866097-4
Contact your Thomson Gale representative for ordering information.
Printed in the United States of America

10 9 8 7 6 5 4 3 2

TABLE OF CONTENTS

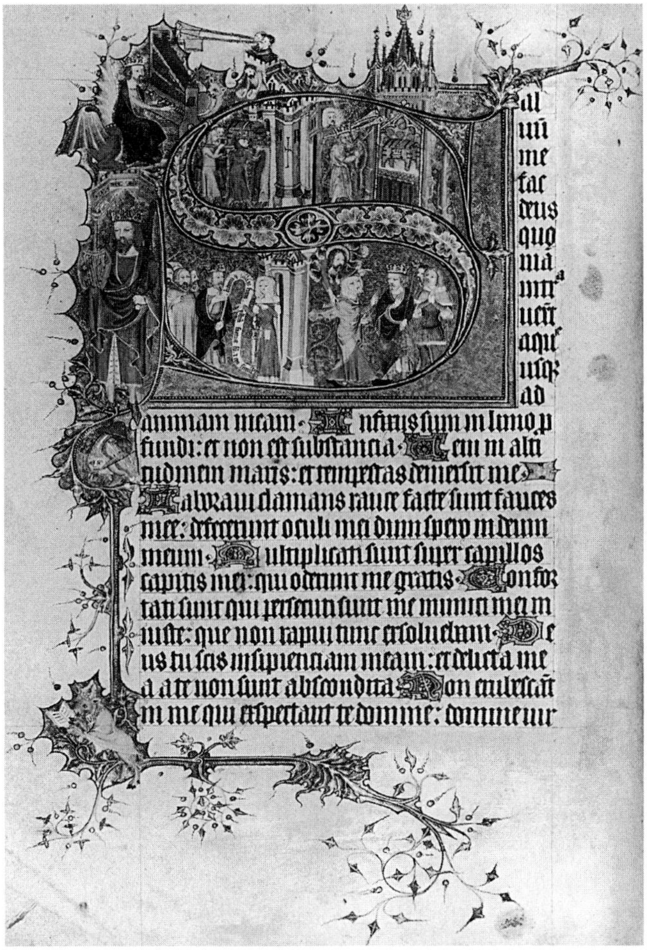

Illuminated initial letter "S" of the word Salvus *at the opening of Psalm 68 (Vulgate; 69 according to the Masoretic text) in the* Bohun Psalter, *14th century. The four scenes from the story of David are, top left, the Ark being carried up to Jerusalem (II Sam. 6:1–15); right, Michal watches David dancing before the Ark* (ibid., *16); bottom left, David reproves Michal for her criticism of him* (ibid., *20–23); right, the prophet Nathan assures David of the endurance of his kingdom (II Sam. 16). London, British Museum, EG 3277, fol. 46v.*

SAN-SOL

SAN'A (Ar. **Ṣanʿā**), capital of *Yemen with 1.85 million inhabitants (2005 estimate), 100 km from the coast of the Red Sea, on a plateau on the western slope of Jabal (Mount) Nuqūm, at an elevation of 2,200 meters above sea level. Once a small town of not more than 50,000 souls, its speedy development took place after the republican revolution of 1962. For many centuries it has been the chief economic, political, and religious center of the Yemen Highlands. It is one of the oldest continuously inhabited cities, known since the pre-Islamic Sabaean Kingdom. Most of the remains of that period have been destroyed through reuse of building material. The principal Sabaean monument in Sanʿa was the Ghumdn Palace, probably situated north of *al-Jāmiʿ al-Kabīr* (the Grand Mosque), the earliest reference to which is at the beginning of the third century C.E. This palace, according to al-Ḥamdānī 20 stories high, was destroyed under the caliph ʿUthmān (644–56 C.E.). Sanʿā has a very distinct architecture and is considered one of the world's most beautiful cities. Hence, it is high on international organizations preservation list.

The tradition of the Jews of Yemen refers to Sanʿa as *Resh Galūt*, namely one of the first places in Yemen in which they settled when they left Jerusalem 40 years before the destruction of the First Temple (586 B.C.E.), responding to *Jeremiah's prophecies about destruction. According to that tradition, the Jews first settled in Barāsh, at that time a fortified town at the top of Jabal Nuqūm, about another 550 meters above the city. Eduard *Glaser, who visited the place in 1882, found there Jewish inscriptions dated to 589 C.E. Rabbi Joseph Qāfih visited the place in 1937 and found a few vestiges of a synagogue and two ritual baths. Later on the Jews went down the mount to Qaṣr (the Citadel of) Sanʿa, the most ancient and the higher part of the city, adjacent to the quarter of *al-qaʾī*, after which many Jewish families are called *al-qaʾīʾī*, to give evidence that indeed Jews lived for some time in the Qaṣr, which was known as Qaṣr *Sām ibn Nuḥ*, according to a Jewish-Muslim tradition that it was built by that biblical figure (i.e., Shem). Al-Rāz, a Yemenite Muslim chronographer, writes that in 991 there were 1040 houses in Sanʿa, 35 of them occupied by Jews.

We have some more solid information regarding the next move of the Sanāni Jews from Barāsh and the Qaṣr to their first neighborhood in the city between the walls, in the eastern quarter today known as *al-Fulayī*. All sources attest that Jews were forcefully expelled from the heights of Jabal Nuqūm as part of anti-Jewish discriminatory and humiliating regulations. This did not take place immediately after the Muslim occupation of Yemen in 629, but many years later, probably under the rule of the Egyptian *Ayyubids (1173–1254). *Al-Fulayī* was located at the eastern end of the city, not far from the *Sā'ilah*, the wādī dividing the city from north to south. The Jews first built their new houses south of the gate leading to the close town of Shu'ūb, near the Wādī al-Marbakī. Rabbi Joseph Qāfiḥ informs us that, while he was visiting a Muslim scholar in *al-Fulayī* in the early 1940s, the latter showed him that his house was originally a Jewish one, as attested by the roof of the living room built to be removed for the Feast of Tabernacles. The Jewish origin of many houses in the city and their typical structure was determined as well by the German anthropologist Carl Rathjens, who visited Yemen in the 1920s and the 1930s. It is not known how long the Jews lived in this place, but it seems that for a certain period they still kept their synagogue in the Qaṣr, as attested by remains of a Bible on which it was noted that it belonged to the *Hanīsat al-yahūd fi Hārat al- Qaṣr* (the synagogue of the Jews in the neighborhood of *al-Qaṣr*) and dated to some years after the Jews were expelled from there by the Ayyubids.

For unknown reasons, and in an unknown year, the Jews had again to abandon their houses in the quarter of *al-Fulayī* and to move westward and build new houses on both sides of the *Sā'ilah*. There they suffered from the occasionally drastic floods of the *Sā'ilah*. From different documents one may deduce that this happened between 1615 and 1662, but from a note in a manuscript (see below) we can determine that it happened already in 1457.

The spiritual center of the Jewish Sanani community was the central synagogue, *kanīsat al-'ulamā'* or *Midrash ha-Ḥakhamim* (the Academy of the Scholars), which moved with the Jews from one place to another. It functioned as a Supreme Court of Appeal not only in regard to Jewish courts throughout Yemen, but in regard to the central Jewish court in San'a itself. From a note in a manuscript in the library of Leiden we learn that the old synagogue of San'a was destroyed in 1457 under the rule of Aḥmad 'Amir, the founder of the Dāhirī dynasty, and that the one located in the *Sā'ilah* was destroyed in 1679. This synagogue was later restored as a mosque – *Masjid al-Jalā'* (the Mosque of the Expulsion).

The destruction of the latter synagogue was part of the big tragic event of *Galut *Mawza'* in which almost all the Jews of Yemen were expelled from their neighborhoods in cities, towns, and villages to the ancient small town in the west of Yemen, not far from the port town of *Mokha. That was a result of the Jewish messianic movement in 1667, when some Jews in Yemen, headed by a Slaymān Jamāl, a Jewish Sanani scholar, followed the messianic Shabbatean movement and tried to seize control of San'a from the Muslim governor in the Qasr. The Jews were aggressively punished and, after a legal-religious debate between Muslim scholars of Yemen, Imām al-Mutawakkil Ismā'īl (1644–1676) accepted the conclusion that the Jews had lost their right to live as **dhimmis* (a protected community) under the Zaydi imamate and ordered his heir al-Mahdī Ahmad ibn al-Hasan (1676–1681) to expel all the Jews. When the expulsion edict was canceled in 1681, the Jews of San'a, like Jews in other localities throughout Yemen, were not allowed to return to their neighborhoods and houses within the walls and had to build for themselves meager new houses outside the city, close to the Muslim garden neighborhood of *Bīr al-'Azab*. This new Jewish neighborhood was called *Qā' al-Yahūd* (the valley of the Jews), which for almost 140 years was completely exposed to assaults of the tribal warriors. Only in 1818 was *Qā' al-Yahūd* annexed to the city by a protecting wall.

The houses in *Qā' al-Yahūd* were small and poor, not more than two stories high in accordance with the humiliating anti-Jewish regulations, and the streets very narrow and unpleasant. During the years of chaos in the 19th century, most of the houses were abandoned by the Jews, who moved to the periphery. But following the Turkish occupation in 1872 the Jewish neighborhood was populated and, in 1876, a new neighborhood, *al-Qaryah al-Jadīda*, was built south of the old one. During the 1930s and the 1940s, under the rule of Imām Yahyā (1904–1948), *Qā 'al-Yahūd* became very crowded, with at least 10,000 people, by the influx of Jews who left their places in towns and villages on their way to the Land of Israel or to make a better living. But the *aliyah* in the years 1949–1951 completely emptied the city of its Jews. Today nothing is left in San'a to recall its Jewish history.

BIBLIOGRAPHY: Y. Qāfiḥ in: *Maḥnayim*, 119 (1958), 36–45; C. Rathjens, *Jewish Domestic Architecture in San'ā* (1957); R.B Sergeant and R. Lewcock, *San'ā – An Arabian Islamic City* (1983); Y. Tobi, *Iyyunim bi-Megillat Teman* (1986), 56–78.

[Yosef Tobi (2nd ed.)]

SANANDAJ (Sinneh), until 1935 main town in Iranian Kurdistan, N.W. of Hamadan. It was the center of Aramaic-speaking Jewry in Persia, but little is known about it before the 17th century. It is listed as a Jewish community in the Judeo-Persian chronicles of *Babai ibn Lutf and Babai ibn Farhad. The community was visited by disciples of the Shabbatean movement. The 19th-century traveler *David d'Beth Hillel found there two small synagogues and 100 Jewish families, some of them rich merchants (engaged in commerce with Georgia) and artisans. At that time the *nasi* of the Jewish community was also treasurer of the governor of Sinneh. In 1903 the Alliance Israélite Universelle established a school there. At the time about 2,000 Jews lived in the town. The community dwindled considerably as a result of immigration to Israel after the 1979 revolution, and no Jews lived there in 2000.

BIBLIOGRAPHY: A.J. Brawer, *Avak Derakhim*, 2 (1946), 110–27. **ADD BIBLIOGRAPHY:** A. Netzer "Jews of Sanandaj," in: *Shofar* (March 2001), 22ff. (in Persian).

[Walter Joseph Fischel / Amnon Netzer (2nd ed.)]

SAN ANTONIO, city in S. central Texas; 2005 population, 1,144,646; Jewish population, 12,000. As early as 1715, three years before the founding of the city, several courageous families from northern Mexico had settled on the banks of the San Antonio River. Among them were members of the Carvajal family, of Jewish descent. Two Jewish patriots of the Texan Army fought the Mexican troops in San Antonio in 1835 – Surgeon Moses Albert Levy, and Edward Israel Johnson. With the advent of Texas statehood and the simultaneous immigration to Texas of Jews from Germany and Alsace-Lorraine, a permanent Jewish community in San Antonio was established around 1850. By 1855 Jews established their own cemetery. In 1856 they had organized the Hebrew Benevolent Society, reorganized in 1885 as the Montefiore Benevolent Society; and in 1870 the Ladies Hebrew Benevolent Society was formed. By 1874 there were enough Jews to found a formal congregation, Temple Beth-El (Reform), although Jews had been gathering for worship in private homes for years.

With the mass immigration of Central and East European Jews from the early 1880s into the 20th century, more Orthodox Jews reached San Antonio. These traditionalists founded their own cemetery in 1885, organized their own congregation, Agudas Achim, in 1889, and established a *talmud torah* in 1909. As Agudas Achim became Conservative, a third synagogue – Orthodox- Rodfei Sholom-B'nai Israel, was created in 1908. Many organizations proliferated: the first B'nai B'rith lodge was chartered in 1874; a chapter of the Zionist Organization of America was formed in 1904; a section of the National Council of Jewish Women began in 1907; and a chapter of Hadassah was organized in 1918.

In 1922 the San Antonio Jewish Social Service Federation (now the Jewish Federation of San Antonio) was created to coordinate the many community groups. During World War I the influx of Jewish military personnel in the South Texas area brought the need for extensive hospitality and services in San Antonio, a major military post. This tradition, supervised by the National Welfare Board, continued throughout the years and four wars.

In the last third of the 20th century, scores of northern Jews moved to the Sun Belt, and the Jewish population of San Antonio nearly doubled during this period. In 1985, emissaries of Chabad Lubavitch established a base in San Antonio. In 1989, a Reconstructionist congregation, Beth Am, was established, and in 2005, Temple Chai, a second Reform congregation was founded. Congregations and rabbis of all wings of Judaism have traditionally enjoyed unusually harmonious and productive relationships.

Jews have been cordially accepted in all phases of industrial, commercial, and professional life in San Antonio. However, social acceptance in its highest ranks was once limited, although today there are no barriers to such acceptance. None of the three predominately Jewish social clubs organized from 1887 onward survived. San Antonio Jews have not sought political office, by and large, but the community has produced leaders in every other phase of civic life: manufacturing, creation of department stores, agriculture, banking, and the professions.

Jews have distinguished themselves in the city's philanthropic and cultural activities. Rabbi David Jacobson, together with the local Roman Catholic archbishop and the Episcopal bishop, is credited with the peaceful racial desegregation of San Antonio in the 1960s. Other prominent leaders have included: Alexander Joske, pioneer merchant and philanthropist; Dan and Anton Oppenheim, pioneer bankers, ranchers, and Confederate officers; Mayer and Sol Halff, pioneer merchants and ranchers; Frederick Oppenheimer and his wife, pioneer art collectors and museum benefactors; Max Reiter, founder of the San Antonio Symphony Orchestra; Rabbi Samuel Stahl, Helen Jacobson, Jocelyn Straus, Richard Goldsmith, Charles Martin Wender, and Michael Beldon, civic workers; Joe and Harry Freeman, agriculturalists and philanthropists; Sylvan Lang, leader in legal education; and Perry Kallison, agriculturalist and local radio personality.

BIBLIOGRAPHY: F.C. Chabot, *With the Makers of San Antonio* (1937); S. Viener, in: AJHSP, 46 (1956/57), 101–13; AJYB, 2 (1900–01), 472–3; Temple Beth-El, San-Antonio, Texas, *Diamond Jubilee 1874–1949* (1949).

[Frances R. Kallison / Samuel Stahl (2nd ed.)]

SANBALLAT (Heb. סַנְבַּלַּט; Aram. סנאבלט (Cowley, Aramaic, 30:29); Akk. *Sin-uballiṭ*, "Sin has given life"), the name of three personalities who appear as governors of Samaria during the Persian period.

Sanballat I

Designated the Horonite, Sanballat I opposed Nehemiah's efforts to rebuild the walls of Jerusalem (445 B.C.E.). The epithet is of uncertain reference, and scholars have related it to Lower or Upper Beth-Horon on the Samarian border of Benjamin; to the village Ḥuwwāra, 1 km. (⅝ mi.) south of Shechem; or to the Moabite town of Horônaim. The first location is not far from the plain of Ono where Sanballat proposed to meet Nehemiah (Neh. 6:2). The second is in the heart of Samarian territory. The third would imply a Transjordanian origin for Sanballat, parallel to that of Tobiah "the Ammonite servant" (Neh. 2:10, 19). Whatever his origin, Sanballat must have considered himself a worshiper of the God of Israel, for his sons bore the Hebrew theophoric names Delaiah ("The Lord has drawn up, delivered") and Shelemiah ("The Lord has requited"; Cowley, Aramaic, 30:29).

In the memoirs of Nehemiah, Sanballat appears both as "enemy" (Neh. 6:1, 16) and as allied by marriage to the family of the high priest (Neh. 13:28). Nehemiah describes his mission in rebuilding the wall of Jerusalem as proceeding through seven stages, each one punctuated by a futile attempt on the part of Sanballat and his allies to thwart the effort. To Sanballat and Tobiah, Nehemiah's arrival from Susa (Shushan) to seek the welfare of Jerusalem was a bad omen (Neh. 2:10). When Sanballat, Tobiah, and Geshem the Arabian heard of his intention to rebuild the wall, they mocked and scorned and wondered whether Nehemiah was contemplating rebellion. From Nehemiah's complete rejection of their remarks it may be inferred that they had sought, and perhaps even held, some official position in the city (Neh. 2:19–20). As the work proceeded, mockery turned to disbelief and anger (Neh. 3:33–35), to the point where military steps were planned. These too were successfully blocked by Nehemiah (Neh. 4). When the wall was completed and all but the gateways fully repaired, they sought by various means to dispose of Nehemiah personally or to compromise his position within the nation. These efforts likewise failed, and Nehemiah's "enemies" were forced to concede that his task was divinely supported (Neh. 6).

Even though the high priest Eliashib was aligned with Nehemiah in rebuilding the wall (Neh. 3:1), his grandson was married to Sanballat's daughter during Nehemiah's absence from Jerusalem. Upon his return Nehemiah expelled the priest from his presence (Neh. 13:28). A subsequent governor named Bagohi, however, joined with Sanballat's son Delaiah (407 B.C.E.) in supporting the reconstruction of the Elephantine Jewish Temple, with the proviso that animal sacrifices not be offered there (Cowley, Aramaic, 32).

Sanballat II

Sanballat II is known as governor of Samaria in the early fourth century B.C.E. from an Aramaic papyrus and a clay sealing in Paleo-Hebrew discovered in Wadi Dāliya north of Jericho. Both inscriptions are of Sanballat II's elder son, whose name is to be restored as either [Jesh]ua or [Jadd]ua. The latter, also a governor, was apparently succeeded by his brother Hananiah who, in turn, was succeeded by Sanballat III. The practice of papponymy (naming a child for its grandfather) was common in the Persian and Hellenistic periods.

Sanballat III

Appointed "satrap" of Samaria by Darius III, Sanballat III married his daughter Nikaso to Manasseh brother of Jaddua, high priest in Jerusalem. When Jaddua and the Jerusalem elders ordered Manasseh to dissolve the marriage or stay away from the altar, Sanballat offered him the high priesthood in a temple he would build on Mt. Gerizim. Meanwhile, Alexander the Great advanced into Palestine and Sanballat shifted his allegiance. He pressed Alexander for permission to build the new temple by arguing that, not only did Manasseh have the support of many Jews, but that it was to the conqueror's interest to see the Jews divided. He also offered Alexander a contingent of 8,000 soldiers. The offer was accepted and the soldiers subsequently settled in Egypt. Permission to erect the temple was granted and Sanballat died shortly thereafter (Jos., Ant., 11:302–25, 340–45). This incident, recorded by Josephus, is absent from the Samaritan chronicles.

BIBLIOGRAPHY: H.H. Rowley, in: BJRL, 38 (1955/56), 166–98; F.M. Cross, in: BA, 26 (1963), 116–21; idem, in: HTR, 59 (1966), 201–11; idem, in: D.N. Freedman and J.C. Greenfield (eds.), *New Directions in Biblical Archaeology* (1969), 53–57.

[Bezalel Porten]

SANBAR (Sandberg), MOSHE (1926–), Israeli economist. Sanbar was born in Hungary, and was imprisoned in German concentration camps during World War II. He immigrated to Israel in 1948, and after studying economics, statistics, and sociology at the Hebrew University, served from 1951 to 1958 as project director and then deputy director of the Israel Institute of Applied Social Research. In 1958 he entered the civil service, serving in the Treasury successively as director of research, deputy director of state revenues, director of the budgets, and economic adviser. In 1968 he was appointed deputy chairman and from 1970 to 1971 chairman of the board of the Israel Development Bank Ltd. as well as chief economic adviser to the minister of finance (1969–71) and acting deputy minister of commerce and industry (1970–71).

In 1971 Sanbar succeeded David *Horowitz as governor of the Bank of Israel, holding the office until 1976. He represented Israel at the International Bank for Reconstruction and Development (IBRD), International Development Association (IDA), and International Finance Corporation (IFC), and was appointed by the government as chairman of the Economic Development and Refugee Rehabilitation Trust. In later years he served as chairman of the Center of Organizations of Holocaust Survivors in Israel, an umbrella organization for 29 groups and 300,000 survivors founded in 1989.

Sanbar wrote numerous articles and research studies dealing with income policy, taxation, budget policy, and central banking. His book *My Longest Year* (Hebrew and English, 1966), for which he was awarded the Yad Vashem Prize in 1967, describes his experiences during the German occupation of Hungary.

[Dov Genachowski]

SANCHES, FRANCISCO (1550/52–1623), philosopher and physician. He was born in either Braga, Portugal, or Tuy, Spain, to a Spanish New Christian family. His father, the prominent physician, Antonio Sanches, was probably from a Castilian Jewish family that included Gabriel *Sanchez, royal treasurer under Queen Isabella. Antonio and his family fled to Bordeaux around 1564, soon after the Inquisition was established in Galicia. Young Francisco apparently studied at the College de Guyenne (Montaigne, his distant cousin, also went there), in Rome and finally received his medical degree from Montpellier in 1574. He was refused a professorship there and moved to Toulouse, where he became professor of philosophy in 1585, and professor of medicine in 1612.

Sanches wrote on philosophical and medical subjects. His earliest writing is a letter to the mathematician, Father Clavius, in 1574–75, offering a skeptical criticism of the Platonic view of mathematics, and the impossibility of gaining any genuine knowledge of reality through mathematics. He wrote his most famous work, *Quod nihil sequitur* (published in 1581), presenting the best technical exposition of Renaissance philosophical skepticism, and offering the first statement of a limited empirical scientific method as the only positive way of proceeding if genuine knowledge is unattainable.

Sanches apparently coined the term "scientific method." He also wrote against astrology and other forms of Renaissance pseudoscience.

Sanches has been considered by some the first modern philosopher. They have seen him as a precursor of Descartes, because of his thoroughgoing skepticism and his method of doubt, and as a precursor of Francis Bacon because of his emphasis on empirical study. However, Sanches' skepticism is more complete than Descartes'. From an analysis of the human epistemological situation, Sanches concluded that nothing could be known about the nature or causes of reality. Human logic and science were unable to determine the real nature of things. Neither the Aristotelian nor the Platonic theories, he contended, were able to give us any genuine means of gaining knowledge. True science would give immediate, intuitive comprehension of the real features of an object. But only God could possess such knowledge. Our limitations, plus the nature of objects themselves, forever prevent us from gaining genuine knowledge. Since nothing can be known, he contended that we should instead do what we can, that is, carry on patient, careful empirical research, and cautiously judge and evaluate the data. This will not lead to knowledge, but to the best information available about the world.

Sanches saw modern science not as a new metaphysical approach to reality, but as a limited empirical way of proceeding when the quest for certainty has been abandoned. Any further information about the world can only be gained by faith. Sanches influenced the later skeptics, as well as some of the major philosophers in the 17th century. His skepticism led to a tradition of mitigated or constructive skepticism that flourished in the 17th century and has been revived in the modern positivistic and pragmatic interpretations of scientific knowledge.

BIBLIOGRAPHY: L. Gerkrath, *Franz Sanchez* (1860); A. Moreira de Sá, *Francisco Sanches filósofo e matemático*, 2 vols. (1947), includes bibliography; R.H. Popkin, *History of Scepticism from Erasmus to Descartes* (1964), 38–43; incl. bibl.; J. de Carvalho, in: F. Sanches, *Opera Philosophica* (1955), vii–liv; M. Menéndez y Pelayo, *Ensayos de Crítica Filosófica* (1948), 174–201.

[Richard H. Popkin]

SANCHEZ, ANTONIO NUÑES RIBEIRO (1699–1783), Marrano physician. Born in Penamacor, Portugal, Sanchez fled to Holland to escape persecution and studied medicine at the University of Leiden. In 1731, on the recommendation of his teacher, the noted Professor Boerhaave, he became physician to Empress Anna Ivanovna of Russia and eventually to the czar and his family. A gifted physician, and a member of the Imperial Academy of Science, Sanchez is recorded in the *Memoirs* of Empress Catherine II as having cured her of a serious illness. However, in 1747, he was forced to leave St. Petersburg after Czarina Elizabeth Petrovna, an antisemite, discovered Sanchez' Jewish origins. He then went to Paris and resumed his medical practice in the poorer sections of the city. In 1762, when Catherine II came to power, she granted him a life pension of 1,000 rubles annually in belated recognition of his faithful service to the royal court. Sanchez published *Dissertation sur l'origine de la maladie vénérienne* (Paris, 1750) and *De Cura Variolarum Vaporarii Ope apud Russos* (1768), which first informed European physicians of the medical value of Russian vapor baths.

BIBLIOGRAPHY: *Biographisches Lexikon der hervorragenden Aerzte*, 5 (1932⁴), 4–5, incl. bibl.

SÁNCHEZ, GABRIEL (d. 1505), treasurer of the kingdom of Aragon under Ferdinand and Isabella. He was a member of a distinguished family of *Conversos, which traced its origin to the Alazar (see *Eleazar) family of Saragossa; his father, Pedro Sánchez, became converted to Christianity with the rest of his family at the beginning of the 15th century. In 1475 Gabriel Sánchez was appointed assistant to his brother Luis, who served as treasurer of Aragon, and whom he later succeeded. After the murder of the inquisitor Pedro de *Arbués in 1485, Gabriel's brothers Juan de Pedro, Alonso, and Guillén were accused of complicity, and grave charges were brought against Gabriel as well. The Inquisition, however, disregarded these accusations and his position was not affected. His brothers succeeded in fleeing from Aragon. With Luis de *Santangel, Sánchez assisted Christopher *Columbus in collecting funds for his voyages, and Columbus sent him a letter in May 1493 from Portugal similar to that which he sent to Santangel, describing his first voyage.

After Gabriel's death, his son LUIS succeeded to his position, in which he served until his death in 1530, when it was transferred to his other son, GABRIEL. During the 16th century members of the Sánchez family married into several of the prominent families of Spanish aristocracy, such as the Gurrea and Mendoza families.

BIBLIOGRAPHY: Baer, Spain, 2 (1966), 370f., 375f., 498; Serrano y Sanz, *Orígenes de la dominación española en América* (1918), 152ff.; Zaforteza y Musoles, in: *Archivos de genealogía y heráldica*, 2 (1953), 156–76; Cabezudo Astrain, in: *Revista de Archivos, Bibliotecas y Museos*, 58 (1960), 81–103.

SAND, LEONARD B. (1928–), U.S. judge. Sand, a native of the Bronx, NY, who graduated from New York University and Harvard Law School, was admitted to the bar in 1953 and soon became a partner in the law firm of Robinson, Silverman, Pearce, Aronsohn, Sand and Berman. An expert on tax law, he was appointed to be a judge in Federal District Court in Manhattan in 1978. Sand presided over several important cases but two stand out: a two-decade-long case involving a desegregation lawsuit against the public schools of Yonkers, a New York City suburb, and the conviction and imprisonment of four terrorists for conspiring with Osama bin Laden in the 1998 bombings of two American embassies in East Africa. The Yonkers case, over time, stood for several things: race, class, neighborhood, the American dream. The case, brought by the United States Justice Department in 1980, then joined by the National Association for the Advancement of Colored

People, charged that race determined location and quality of education in Yonkers. The plaintiffs stated that the reason the schools were segregated was because the housing of Yonkers was segregated. Sand heard the case himself, without a jury, at the request of both sides. The trial took up most of 1983 and 1984. There were 93 days of testimony from 84 witnesses, 140 depositions, and thousands of exhibits. By the end of the trial, it was clear that Yonkers was segregated. Sand had to decide why. He saw a 40-year pattern, fueled by Yonkers city officials who approved sites for housing. Sand ordered Yonkers to redraw its districts and to move some of its poor minority residents from the poor minority side of town into public housing, to be built just for them, in the white, middle-class side of town. His ruling was appealed but subsequently upheld. In 1986 Sand ordered a federal monitor to oversee the integration of the schools through a host of court-ordered measures still in effect 20 years later, including magnet programs and busing. In the terrorism case, a jury trial, prosecutors called 92 government witnesses and introduced more than 1,300 exhibits in a four-month process. The prosecutors said the conspiracy grew out of a Muslim organization that had centers in Afghanistan and other places, including Brooklyn. Some of the members of the Brooklyn circles were convicted in the bombing of the World Trade Center in 1993 and in a plot to blow up other New York City landmarks. Sand sentenced the four men to life in prison without any chance of parole.

[Stewart Kampel (2nd ed.)]

SANDAK (Heb. סַנְדָּק; in common parlance also **sandek**), designation of the godfather who holds the male child upon his knees during the *circumcision ceremony. The name is derived either from the Greek σύνδικος (cf. Lat. *syndicus*, "patron"), or, more probably, from σύντεκνος ("companion of the father," cf. Fr. *compère*; Ger. *Gevatter*); the form *syndikos* appears in post-mishnaic Midrash literature (Yal., Ps. 723).

The function of the *sandak* probably arose from the necessity of having someone assist the *mohel* by holding the child firmly during the circumcision operation. To act as *sandak* is considered a great honor and as a meritorious religious act which, according to the kabbalists, has atoning qualities. Where a grandfather of the child is still alive, it is customary to bestow the honor of *sandak* upon him. The woman who brings the child to the circumcision and hands it over to the *sandak* is called *sandakit*. The *sandak* is also known by various other names: *ba'al berit* or *ba'al berit milah*; *tofes ha-yeled* ("holder of the child"); *av sheni* ("second father"); or *shali'aḥ* ("messenger"). Jews of European origin also use the term *kvater* (the woman, *kvaterin*), which is the corrupted form of the German *Gevatter* ("godfather"). The question is raised whether a person may be *sandak* more than once in the same family. R. *Elijah b. Solomon Zalman, the Gaon of Vilna, decided in the affirmative (Be'ur ha-Gra to YD 265), notwithstanding reservations against this practice based upon fear of the "evil eye."

BIBLIOGRAPHY: Kohut, Arukh, 6 (1922⁶), 83–84; Eisenstein, Dinim, 222.

SANDALFON, name of one of the most exalted angels. Ezekiel 1:15 was interpreted in the Babylonian Talmud (Ḥag. 13b) as referring to an angel who stood on the earth with his head reaching up to the living creatures (the *ḥayyot*). This "wheel" is called Sandalfon, who is said to stand so far above his colleague, apparently *Metatron, that a journey between them would take 500 years. His place is behind the *Merkabah, the heavenly chariot, and he fashions crowns for his creator. According to the sources of the Merkabah literature, these crowns are made from Israel's prayers, an idea widely repeated in Jewish literature. Sandalfon is also mentioned as one of the highest angels in the story of Moses' ascension to heaven, and in the Midrash *Konen* he is called a mediator or "translator" between Israel and God, obviously because he transforms the words of prayer into mystical crowns on God's head. The etymology of the name is explained, probably correctly, as *synadelphos* ("confrère" or "colleague"), namely of Metatron. He is mentioned in many hymns, and conjurations regarding him and his mystery are found in Merkabah literature; one such is "The Mystery of Sandalfon" (*Merkavah Shelemah*, 1922, fol. la). Here he has the power to nullify hostile decrees against Israel. In later sources he is frequently defined as the angel set over birds, *sar ha-ofot*, particularly in the writings of the *Ḥasidei Ashkenaz and in the Zohar. Spanish kabbalists of the 13th century interpreted the name as a composition of two elements: *sandal*, meaning in the Talmud a still unformed embryo, and *fon*, understood as a formation of a face *panim*; these two elements therefore represent matter and form, brought together in Sandalfon. Many kabbalists declared that Sandalfon was an angelic transfiguration of the prophet Elijah, just as Metatron was described in earlier sources as the transfiguration of Enoch. Since the word *sandal* has the meaning "shoe," Sandalfon was also thought of as the "shoe" of the *Shekhinah*, that is to say the angel on which the feet of the *Shekhinah* rested. Some kabbalists considered him the teacher of Moses. Later Kabbalah ascribed to him a special sphere of mystical being which was essentially more than a pure angelic host.

BIBLIOGRAPHY: R. Margalioth, *Malakhei Elyon* (1945), 148–54; M. Schwab, *Vocabulaire de l'angélologie* (1897), 201; G. Davidson, *A Dictionary of Angels* (1967), 267.

[Gershom Scholem]

SAN DANIELE DEL FRIULI, small town in Udine province, Friuli, N.E. Italy. The presence of Jews is first confirmed in a document dating from 1523 which refers to the management of a bank entrusted to one Simon Nantua and, later, to his sons. There were also Jewish physicians living in San Daniele at least from 1549.

In 1600, two Luzzatto brothers, who had come from Venice, joined the bank; in 1623–1624 the bank passed to the Luzzatto family's control alone. The Luzzattos managed the bank until 1714, when it was suppressed following the opening of a **Monte di Pieta*. Meanwhile the community had grown. The Catholic reaction reached San Daniele in the early 17th century, the Jews being compelled to wear the *badge in 1626.

The 18th century was a period of expansion for the Jewish community, although the Venetian government closed the bank. Aside from the bank, the Jews were engaged in other professions, such as raising silkworms; agriculture (mainly beekeeping); handicrafts, such as goldsmiths; industry, such as the production of bricks; and trade in tobacco. The synagogue was erected between the years 1729 and 1731. In the same period, in 1735, the community purchased an area for the cemetery. The Luzzatto family dominated the life of San Daniele. An important figure was Letizia Luzzatto. San Daniele was the birthplace of the brothers Ephraim and Isaac *Luzzatto, both poets; the latter, who studied medicine at the University of Padua, was a successful physician. He wrote a book of poetry, *Toledot Yiẓḥak*. He also satirized the local life in his parody, *Mishnayot Sandaniel*. In 1777 the Republic of Venice, on whom San Daniele was dependent, decreed the expulsion of the Jews from all places without a ghetto; San Daniele therefore had to be abandoned. It seems that the services of Isaac Luzzatto were so valued by the local population that the local authorities requested the Serenissima to exclude the latter from the decree of expulsion. Some of those expelled sought refuge in Gorizia, but the majority went to Trieste. Among the latter was Ezechia Luzzatto, father of Samuel David *Luzzatto. In the first decades of the 20th century a small community was reestablished in San Daniele, but it was short-lived.

BIBLIOGRAPHY: Milano, Bibliotheca, index; F. Luzzatto, *Chroniche storiche della Università degli ebrei di San Daniele del Friuli* (1964); Y. Luzzatto, *Toledot Yiẓḥak* (1944), 133–7; Zoller, in: REJ, 94 (1933), 50–56; E. Patriarca, in: *Atti del Congresso… Storia Patria* (1958), 33–63. **ADD. BIBLIOGRAPHY:** S.G. Cusin and P.C. Ioly Zorattini, *Friuli Venezia Giulia, Itinerari ebraici, I luoghi, la storia, l'arte* (1998), 92–100.

[Attilio Milano / Samuele Rocca (2nd ed.)]

°SANDBERG, WILLEM JACOB (1897–1984), Dutch museum curator and Righteous Among the Nations. Sandberg served as the curator of the Stedelijk (Municipal) Museum in Amsterdam, a position he held from 1938. During the occupation of the Netherlands by the Germans in World War II, Sandberg helped organize an artists' resistance movement. Shocked by the persecution of the Jews, together with several friends he began forging identity cards. His training and expertise as a graphic designer was of help to him in this clandestine endeavor, as well as his contacts in the publishing world. When young Dutch men were called up for forced labor, Sandberg's group produced numerous forged documents for people electing not to report for work in Germany. The Jewish Dorothea Hertz-Loeb was one of those who benefited from Sandberg's aid, to whom, along with three members of her family, he supplied forged identity papers, which were produced in the basement of the museum. When the deportation of Jews began on a massive scale in the summer of 1942, the artists' resistance group decided to blow up the Population Registration Office in Amsterdam. Sandberg participated in the planning of this operation, including the capture of the heavily guarded building and setting fire to the archives. The explosives to be used in this attack were temporarily stored in his home. After much preparation, the attack was carried out on March 27, 1943. Unfortunately, the Germans eventually got wind of the identity of the perpetrators of this attack and most were arrested, with 13 men condemned to death and executed in July 1943. Sandberg luckily escaped arrest. The night when his home was searched, he happened to be in the dunes near the North Sea, where the art treasures of Amsterdam had been hidden. His wife and son, however, were arrested and incarcerated for several months. Sandberg hid in the countryside for the remainder of the occupation, circulating letters to make people believe he had escaped to Switzerland. From his hideout, he sent reports on German troop movements. After the war, Sandberg served until 1963 as director of the Stedelijk Museum, which he turned into an internationally acclaimed museum of contemporary art. In 1964, he accepted the invitation to head the newly established Israel Museum in Jerusalem, a position he held until 1968. That year, Yad Vashem awarded him the title of Righteous Among the Nations.

BIBLIOGRAPHY: Yad Vashem Archives M31–504; I. Gutman (ed.), *Encyclopedia of the Righteous Among the Nations: Netherlands*, Vol. 2 (2004), 659–60.

[Mordecai Paldiel (2nd ed.)]

SANDERLING, KURT (1912–), conductor. Sanderling was born in East Prussia and began his conducting career at the age of 18, as assistant conductor at the Berlin Staatsoper. Forced to leave Nazi Germany, he was subsequently engaged to conduct the Moscow Radio Orchestra. A guest performance with the Leningrad Philharmonic Orchestra led to his becoming, with Mravinsky, its director (1941–60). In 1960, he moved to East Berlin, where he became chief conductor of the Berlin Symphony Orchestra. Sanderling also directed the Dresden Staatskapelle Orchestra between 1964 and 1967, taking it on European tours.

[Max Loppert (2nd ed.)]

SANDERS, BERNARD (1941–), independent member of Congress (1991–). Sanders was born in Brooklyn, New York, the son of a paint salesman who immigrated to the U.S. as a young man. His mother raised her two sons in a small apartment, while his father earned a steady but limited income. Sanders' family circumstances, in which money was often tight, strongly influenced his understanding of the financial difficulties that face many working class families. Sanders graduated from James Madison High School in Brooklyn and spent one year at Brooklyn College. He then transferred to the University of Chicago, where he graduated in 1964 and then bought land in Middlesex, Vermont.

In 1971 his interest in progressive politics took him to a meeting of the newly formed Liberty Union Party, a third-party alternative to the Democrats and the Republicans. He left that meeting as the party's candidate for the U.S. Senate, and ended up with two percent of the vote. He ran three more races as a Liberty Union candidate – once more for the U.S. Senate, and twice for governor. His highest statewide vote as a Liberty Union candidate was six percent.

In 1981, he ran for mayor of Burlington, the largest city in the state and a university town. His victory was far from overwhelming. He beat the six-term Democratic incumbent by 12 votes. He won reelection three more times. In 1987, he defeated the mayoral candidate that both parties supported. During his tenure, the Progressives won several seats on the City Council. He worked on a people-friendly waterfront and on creating a tax base beyond the property tax. His support came from the working class instead of the business establishment.

Sanders stepped down as mayor of Burlington after four terms, and eight years. He was followed in office by a fellow Progressive. In 1986, he ran for governor of Vermont and came in third with 14 percent of the vote. In 1988, he ran for Vermont's lone seat in the U.S. House of Representatives and lost by only three percentage points. A rematch in 1990 had Sanders a 16-point victor. He served in Congress as an independent, though he caucused with the Democrats and was given seniority by them. He was the first independent to serve in Congress since the 1940s and only the third avowed socialist to be elected to that body.

In Congress he pursued a progressive political agenda and founded the Progressive Coalition, which sought tax reform and single payer health insurance and reduced defense spending. He took on the Administration – Democratic and Republican alike – for a progressive agenda. Through 2005 he had been re-elected seven times. He was the longest-serving independent in the history of the House of Representatives.

Sanders received national recognition by helping to lead the fight to keep lower-income Vermonters and Americans warm in the wintertime, through successful efforts to increase funding for the Low-Income Home Energy Assistance (LIHEAP). He also brought funding into the state for the student-based development of a curriculum on child-labor.

He followed the politically interesting principle "act locally, think globally" and thus led a well-publicized bus trip across the Canadian border with Vermonters to buy prescription drugs. As a result, the nation learned that the pharmaceutical industry sells exactly the same medicine in Canada, and every other country, at far lower prices than they are sold in the United States. Sanders played an active role in working with Vermont IBM employees who experienced a massive cut-back in the pensions they had been promised by that company. In Congress he established the House Progressive Caucus that had grown to 56 members as of 2005. Sanders chaired the caucus for its first eight years. Unlike most of his colleagues, he refused to take PAC money and thus protected his independence. With the retirement of former Republican, and now independent, Senator Jeffords, Sanders was set to become an independent candidate for the Senate in 2006. Representing Vermont on a statewide basis, he begins the race with significant name recognition, and having run in statewide races time and again, since his seat is the only House seat Vermont has in Congress.

[Michael Berenbaum (2nd ed.)]

SANDGROUND, JACK HENRY (1899–1976), U.S. parasitologist. Born in Johannesburg, South Africa, he went to the U.S. in the early 1920s. Sandground's research dealt with a wide variety of parasitic problems, especially those involved with the helminths.

His investigations of the worms included their biology and taxonomy, as well as problems concerned with immunity and chemotherapy. He served as a member of many scientific expeditions. Sandground carried out research on the nutrition of protozoa, immunology against poliomyelitis, and the detoxication of arsenicals and other drugs utilized in treating neurosyphilis and various tropical diseases.

[Norman Levin]

SAN DIEGO, combined city-county in S. California; county population 3 million (2005), Jewish population 89,000.

Jewish life in San Diego started in what is called Old Town, near the San Diego River and just below the hill on which the Spanish built the first California mission in 1769. The first Jew arrived at this remote frontier site in 1850, the same year the city received its charter. In this town of 800, there were, perhaps, 25 Jews until the 1860s. Most were very visible for their number, both as businessmen and civic leaders. When, in the 1870s, the center of town moved southeast, to its permanent location, on San Diego Bay, the Jewish population moved also. They set up stores and lived nearby; the first synagogues were in this downtown area. In the 1920s the reform congregation, Beth Israel, moved uptown to the west side of Balboa Park, and by the mid-20th century the Conservative and Orthodox congregations had moved uptown to the north and east sides of the park. The neighborhood of North Park became the center of Jewish life with a kosher butcher, bakery, a Jewish Community Center and the homes and businesses of many of the patrons. By the late 1970s the community had migrated primarily to the east, near San Diego State University, to the South in Chula Vista, and a little to the north. With the coming of the University of California San Diego to La Jolla in the late 1960s, the Jewish community began to move there as well. Prior to that, beginning in the 1940s, the residents of La Jolla had a restrictive covenant against Jews and other minorities in their property deeds, which was enforced by the real estate agents. At the beginning of the 21st century there was no Jewish area, and the population was very spread out. Jews congregate throughout San Diego County, from the Mexican border to the northern boundary, the Marine Base at Camp Pendleton. As a matter of fact, Jews even congregate at Camp Pendleton and south of the border in Tijuana.

Religious Life

Louis Rose, the first Jewish settler, arrived in 1850. A multitalented entrepreneur, he also held various prominent government positions. He was an early benefactor to the Jewish community, and two locations, Rose Canyon and Roseville are named for him. Rose was joined by Lewis Franklin who held the first recorded Jewish religious observance (Day of Atonement) in Southern California in his home soon after he arrived in 1851. Perhaps this was Franklin's hobby, as he had held the first Jewish service in San Francisco in 1849. The Jewish population increased dramatically with the arrival of Mark Jacobs (aka Jacob Marks), his wife, Hannah, and their 12 children. One daughter, Leah, married Marcus Katz in the first Jewish marriage ceremony in Southern California in 1853; another daughter, Victoria, who married Franklin's brother, Maurice, kept a diary (1856–57), which is an important record of Jewish life at that time.

Marcus Schiller was a businessman, public official, and Jewish community leader for 40 years. During his tenure on the City Board of Trustees, along with his business partner, Joseph Mannasse, 1,400 acres were set aside for Balboa Park, the main park in the city center. In 1861, Schiller organized the first congregation, Adath Jeshurun (Orthodox), the oldest congregation in Southern California, which in 1887 incorporated as Congregation Beth Israel (Reform). The Jewish population at this time was approximately 300. In the midst of planning its synagogue, the congregation hired its first rabbi, Samuel Freuder, in 1888. Within a year he left and became a Christian missionary. Twenty years later, he realized his mistake and wrote a book called *A Missionary's Return in Judaism* (1915). Built of wood in the gothic style, Temple Beth Israel was completed in 1889 and used for 37 years. Moved to a county park in 1978, it is one of the two oldest synagogue structures extant in California. With the Jewish population of San Diego increasing to 2,000, Congregation Beth Israel built its second home, a Byzantine-style synagogue, in 1926, near Balboa Park. Its "Temple Center" became the focal point of Jewish communal life for over 25 years. When the congregation moved to its third home in 2001, its previous building was saved from demolition, because of its eligibility for the National Register of Historic Places. At the beginning of the 21st century, Beth Israel was the only congregation in the American West to have its three synagogues still in use.

In 1905, East European immigrants formed an orthodox congregation, Tifereth Israel Synagogue. When, in 1939, this congregation became Conservative, another Orthodox congregation was formed, Beth Jacob. These three congregations, which were led out of the war years by three influential rabbis – Reform, Morton J. Cohn (1946–61); Conservative, Monroe Levens (1948–74), and Orthodox, Baruch Stern (1947–77) – were the only ones until the 1950s, when the Jewish population increased to 6,000 and new congregations formed. By the beginning of the 21st century, there were over 30 congregations, including the three original ones, covering all the trends in Judaism, from Humanistic to Chabad.

Communal Life

As the Jewish community grew, so did the need for social and communal service. At the beginning, men and women took separate paths to this end.

Forty men, led by Marcus Schiller, formed the first Hebrew Benevolent Society of San Diego in 1871. Twenty-six signatories received the charter for the B'nai B'rith Eduard Lasker Lodge #370 in 1887, with Simon Levi as president. By mid-20th century there were seven men's lodges, some named for prominent citizens such as Samuel I. Fox, Edward Breitbard, and Henry Weinberger. In 1929 Anna Shelley organized the Birdie Stodel B'nai B'rith Women's Chapter which grew by mid-century into five chapters in the county. AZA Fraternity and B'nai B'rith Girls followed in 1930, and Hillel in 1947. In mid-century Zionist groups were also strong, but by the end of the century, most of the organizations, except for Hillel, were in decline.

In 1890, Mrs. Simon Levi organized the Ladies Hebrew Aid Society, with 20 members "to render relief to the sick and needy, to rehabilitate families and to aid the orphan and half-orphan." This group joined with the Jolly Sewing Circle, Hebrew Sisterhood and Junior Charity League in 1918 to form the Federated Jewish Charities. In 1936, the Charities split into two: the Jewish Welfare Society, later to become Jewish Family Service, incorporated, and the United Jewish Fund, predecessor of the United Jewish Federation of San Diego, was formed. The Jolly 16, a women's social and benevolent group, started a ten-bed San Diego Hebrew Home for the Aged which opened in 1944. A much larger facility opened in 1950, in partnership with the Jewish Community Center, and in 1989 the Hebrew Home expanded and moved to northern San Diego County. The first Jewish Community Center opened in 1946 in a storefront in North Park. Within six years a new building with a pool, gymnasium, classrooms and a library opened in the eastern part of the city, which served the community for almost 50 years. A larger facility opened in the La Jolla area in 1985 and was expanded in the late 1990s.

Mrs. Abraham Blochman started formal Jewish education for Beth Israel's children in 1887. Education remained the purview of individual congregations until the 1960s, when the San Diego Hebrew Day School and the Bureau of Jewish Education were created. The Bureau became the independent Agency for Jewish Education in 1986. In 1979 the San Diego Jewish Academy began, and 20 years later it opened as a full-time school at a large campus in northern San Diego.

In 1970, with the Jewish population at 12,000, a Judaic studies program began at San Diego State University. Fifteen years later this program grew into the Lipinsky Institute for Judaic Studies, sponsored by arts patrons Bernard and Dorris Lipinsky. Lawrence Baron, the director of the Institute since 1988, holds the Nasatir Professorship in Modern Jewish History, named for Abraham P. Nasatir, an Orthodox Jew who was the first Jewish professor at the university (1928–1974). When he arrived, most of the students and faculty had never met a Jew before, but by the end of his tenure, Nasatir Hall had been named for him. University of California, San Diego, started its Judaic Studies program in 1977, with an emphasis on biblical scholarship, attracting some of the nation's foremost scholars, such as David Noel Freedman, Richard Elliott Friedman, David Goodblatt, and Thomas Levy.

A group of women, under the direction of Irene Fine, began the Women's Institute for Continuing Jewish Education in 1977. It pioneered the teaching of Torah, Talmud and Midrash by women. *The San Diego Women's Haggadah* (1980), the first women's text for a feminist *seder*, was followed by other publications which led the way for Jewish feminists.

With the Jewish population at 30,000 in 1980, a small group led by historian Henry Schwartz founded the Jewish Historical Society of San Diego. Its archive for local Jewish history was established in 1999 by Stanley and Laurel Schwartz in cooperation with the Lipinsky Institute. The archive's opening in 2000 celebrated 150 years of San Diego Jewry.

The year 1914 saw the first weekly Jewish newspaper, *The Southwest Jewish Press*, which later became the *San Diego Jewish Press Heritage*, concluding its run in 2003. In 2005, there were two Jewish newspapers: the bi-weekly *San Diego Jewish Times*, formerly *Israel Today*, and the monthly *San Diego Jewish Journal*. Rabbi Aaron Gottesman brought the community a Jewish radio program called "Milk and Honey" during the 1980s.

Personalities

The following people are some of those who have made contributions which have had a lasting effect on the community and beyond.

French immigrant Abraham Blochman and his son Lucien started the Blochman Banking Company in 1893. By the late 20th century, it had become Security Pacific National Bank, one of the largest banks in California. The Blochman family took various leadership roles in the Jewish community and in civic and communal affairs. Lucien was a director of the Panama-California Exposition of 1915 which gave Balboa Park its Spanish architecture. He and his sister Mina Blochman Brust helped found the San Diego Chapter of the American Red Cross at the turn of the century, and Mina started the First Aid Program in 1919.

Abraham Klauber, who arrived in 1869, was an early merchant and San Diego booster whose descendants were prominent into the 21st century. Daughter Alice Klauber, an artist, directed the arts pavilion at the 1915 Exposition. A business partner of Abraham Klauber, Sigmund Steiner moved to Escondido in north San Diego County to open a store and became mayor (1894–1906). Under his leadership, the grape growing industry flourished with an annual Grape Day Festival and parade, one of the largest in Southern California. The festival at Grape Day Park was still celebrated at the beginning of the 21st century.

The five Levi brothers, two of whom had long lasting effects in San Diego county and were also business partners of Klauber, came to San Diego in the 1870s. Simon was a civic and religious leader who started the Simon Levi Company, wholesale grocery and liquor. Adolph, whose interests spread from the Pacific Ocean to the easternmost reaches of the county, was in the livery and ranching business. Also a civic and religious leader, his descendants carried on the family's communal spirit into the 21st century.

Samuel I. Fox owned the Lion Clothing Store, which was located next to the Hog and Hominy Store operated by a Mr. Baer on what was known as the "Zoo Block." From 1886 to his death in 1939, he was a civic, communal and religious leader who promoted the business community by helping to secure local control of the port and the water supply. In 1930 he was the first president of the San Diego Community Chest and was one of the organizers of the 1935 Exposition in Balboa Park which helped pull the city out of the depression.

Brothers Henry and Jacob Weinberger were communal and religious leaders. Jacob became the first federal judge in San Diego in 1946 and was the founding president of the United Jewish Fund (1936–45). The restored 1917 federal bankruptcy courthouse is named for him. Judge Edward Schwartz was appointed to the U.S. District Court by President Johnson in 1968, where he remained until his death in 2000. During his term he became chief justice, and in 1995 the U.S. Courthouse was named the Edward J. Schwartz Courthouse and Federal Building.

In the later part of the 20th century, several business people made their mark on the national scene and became local philanthropists. Sol Price, 1976 founder of the first national retail membership warehouse, The Price Club, along with his family, has funded much neighborhood redevelopment and university growth. Pioneering scientists, Irwin Jacobs and Andrew Viterbi, founded LINKABIT, in 1968, a breakthrough company in the development of digital technology. In 1985 they went on to start Qualcomm, the cell phone industry giant. Both men, their families and their companies became major philanthropists, with the Jewish Community Center, synagogues, the San Diego Symphony, Qualcomm Stadium, theaters, public broadcasting and universities as some of the beneficiaries of their gifts.

Jews have participated in the arts with internationally renowned conductor, David Amos, who directs the Jewish Community Orchestra, and Ian Campbell, the San Diego Opera director since 1983. Under his direction the opera commissioned local composer Myron Fink to write the music for *The Conquistador*, the story of a family of secret Jews during the Inquisition in Mexico, which premiered in San Diego in 1997.

Robert Breitbard founded the San Diego Hall of Champions Sports Museum, in 1961. Located in Balboa Park and with Breitbard still its driving force at the beginning of the 21st century, it was the nation's largest multi-sport museum. The Park is also host to the Museum of Photographic Arts, whose founding director, Arthur Ollman, has brought world class exhibitions to the museum since 1983 and into the 21st century.

Jack Gross started the first TV station in San Diego, KFMB, in 1949, and along with his son radio talk-show host and critic, Laurence Gross, Jews have maintained a long and steady presence on local TV news into the 21st century, with newscasters Marty Levine, Susan Taylor, and Gloria Penner.

In the national public sphere, former industrialist, Colonel Irving Salomon came to San Diego County after World War II. In 1953 President Eisenhower appointed him as a delegate to the United Nations General Assembly, for which he worked until his death in 1979. He and his wife Cecile, a classical pianist and composer of Jewish music, entertained notables at their ranch in Valley Center and were benefactors for cultural programs.

Real estate developer M. Larry Lawrence bought and restored the famous 1888 Hotel Del Coronado in 1963. His philanthropy helped create the new Jewish Community Center in 1985 which bears his family name. President Clinton made him ambassador to Switzerland (1994–96).

Jonas Salk, originator of the poliomyelitis vaccine, started the Salk Institute in La Jolla in 1963 and created a haven for world renowned research, while enabling architect Louis Kahn to design one of the world's great buildings.

Though many Jews had served the city government as elected officials, the first Jewish mayor, Susan Golding, was elected in 1992, serving for two terms. Her father, Brage Golding, was president of San Diego State University from 1972 to 1977.

In 1993 two Jews were elected to congress, Robert Filner and Lynn Schenk. Schenk later became chief of staff for Governor Gray Davis, and Filner continued his tenure in congress into the 21st century. In 2000 Susan Davis was elected to congress. In 2005, two out of the five-person county congressional delegation were Jewish.

William Kolender, a career law enforcement professional, served as the chief of the San Diego Police Department for 13 years, beginning in 1975. After a short retirement, in 1995 he was elected sheriff of San Diego County, and he held the post into the 21st century. Together with Rabbi Aaron Gottesman, he started the San Diego Police Department Chaplaincy Program in 1968.

Former U.S. attorney, Alan Bersin, completed a tenure as superintendent of San Diego City Schools in 2005 and was appointed by Governor Arnold Schwarzenegger as secretary of education for California.

At the beginning of the 21st century, as California's population swelled, so did the Jewish population, with newcomers from all parts of the U.S. and other countries such as South Africa, Iran, and especially from Latin and South America. Cousins of first generation eastern European Jewish immigrants, who came to the U.S. at the beginning of the 20th century, found themselves welcomed in Mexico and other Latin countries, and eventually, in San Diego. Proximity to Mexico provided a distinct flavor, as Jewish residents moved back and forth across the border for business, social activities and worship. The migratory inclination of the community was broadened by snowbirds in the winter, "zonies" (Arizonans), refugees from the desert heat, in the summer, a growing retirement community, and a large military presence. Many had strong ties to other places, which sometimes restrained their participation in local community life. Close-knit alliances formed, based on origins, either native or immigrant, as extended families were far away.

BIBLIOGRAPHY: N.B. Stern, "The Franklin Brothers of San Diego," in: *Journal of San Diego History* (1975); T. Casper, "The Blochman Saga in San Diego," in: *Journal of San Diego History* (1977); R.A. Burlinson, "Samuel Fox, Merchant and Civil Leader in San Diego, 1886–1939," in: *Journal of San Diego History* (1980); L.M. Klauber, "Abraham Klauber – a Pioneer Merchant (1831–1911)," in: *Western States Jewish History* (1970); H. Schwartz. "The Levi Saga: Temecula, Julian, San Diego," in: *Western States Jewish History* (1974); R.D. Gerson, "San Diego's Unusual Rabbi, Samuel Freuder," in: *Western States Jewish History* (1993); idem, "Jewish Religious Life in San Diego, California, 1851–1918" (unpublished thesis, 1974); L. Baron, "The Jews of San Diego State University, California," in: *Western States Jewish History* (1998); V. Jacobs and S. Arden (eds.), *Diary of a San Diego Girl – 1856* (1974); L.G. Stanford, *Ninety Weinberger Years: The Jacob Weinberger Story* (1971); *B'nai B'rith Centennial 1887 – 1987 Commemorative Booklet*; W.M. Kramer, L.Schwartz, S. Schwartz, *Old Town, New Town an Enjoyment of San Diego Jewish History* (1994); S. Schwartz, *A Brief History of Congregation Beth Israel.* 135th Birthday 1861–1996, booklet; M.E. Stratthaus, "Flaw in the Jewel: Housing Discrimination Against Jews in La Jolla, California," in: *American Jewish History* (1996).

[Stan Schwartz and Laurel Schwartz (2nd ed.)]

SANDLER, ADAM RICHARD (1966–), U.S. actor, screenwriter, musician. Sandler was born in Brooklyn, New York, but spent his childhood and teenage years in Manchester, N.H., where most of his family continued to reside. Sandler was discovered in a New York comedy club by *Saturday Night Live* (*SNL*) member Dennis Miller. He was a *SNL* cast member for five years, creating such notable characters as Opera Man, Canteen Boy, and Cajun Man. In 1996, his "Chanukah Song" became one of the most requested holiday songs on radio. Sandler appeared in over a dozen feature films, specializing in broad, physical comedy, from the early *Coneheads* (1993), to *Billy Madison* (1995) and *Happy Gilmore* (1996), on which he shared screenwriting credit, to the title roles in *The Wedding Singer* (1998), *The Waterboy* (1998), and *Big Daddy* (1999). He turned to dramatic roles with *Punch-Drunk Love* (2002) and in 2005 reprised the role of prison inmate/former pro quarterback Paul Crewe, originally played in 1974 by Burt Reynolds, in *The Longest Yard*. With *Adam Sandler's 8 Crazy Nights*, Sandler created the first feature length animated Chanukah musical (2002). He also appeared in *Anger Management* with Jack Nicholson (2003), James Brooks' *Spanglish* (2004), and *50 First Dates* with Drew Barrymore (2004).

[Amy Handelsman (2nd ed.)]

SANDLER, BORIS (1950–), Yiddish writer, journalist, broadcaster. Born in Beltsy (Moldova), Sandler graduated from the Kishinev Conservatory (1975) and was violinist in the Moldovian Symphony Orchestra. In 1983 he received an advanced degree in creative writing from the Gorky Literary Institute (Moscow). Having first attempted writing in Russian, Sandler soon realized that his native Yiddish was more suitable for his themes and style. Although no formal education in Yiddish existed in the Soviet Union after 1948, he was fortunate to find as a mentor the prominent Bessarabian Yiddish author Yekhiel *Shraybman. He debuted in the Moscow Yiddish monthly *Sovetish Heymland* (1981), whose editorial board he later joined (1986). He was president of the Yiddish Cultural Organization of Moldova, had a Yiddish program on Moldovan State Television, edited *Undzer Kol*, and wrote two film scripts about the fate of Bessarabian Jewry (1989–92). Immigrating to Israel (1992), he worked at The Hebrew University and edited the children's magazine *Kind un Keyt*. From 1998 he was editor-in-chief of the New York weekly *Forverts*. In addition to numerous stories, essays, and articles in periodicals, Sandler published several volumes of fiction: *Treplekh aroyf tsu a Nes: Dertseylungen un Noveln* ("Stairs up to a Miracle: Tales and Short Stories," 1986), *Der Inyen Numer 5390 (fun di KGB Arkhivn)* ("Case No. 5390, from the KGB Archives," 1992), *Der Alter Brunem: Dertseylungen, Miniatyurn, Roman* ("The Old Well: Tales, Miniatures, Novel," 1994), *Toyern* ("Gates," 1997), and *Ven der Goylem hot Farmakht di Oygn* ("When the Golem Closed his Eyes," 2004). The major theme of Sandler's fiction is the past and present of Bessarabian Jews. His style remains close to the spoken idiom, but is also influenced by recent modes, such as magical realism.

[Mikhail Krutikov (2nd ed.)]

SANDLER, JACOB KOPPEL (d. 1931), composer and music director. Sandler was born in Bielozwekvo and as a child sang in the choir of Cantor Mordecai Minkowsky (the father of Pinhas *Minkowsky). He later became choral director for Cantor Samuel Polishuk. He married and went into business, but subsequently lost his money and in 1888 went to the United States. There he became choral director for several well-known cantors and, at the same time, directed Yiddish theater choruses, first as an assistant to Zelig Mogulescu and then as an independent composer and director. In 1889 Sandler produced Goldfaden's *Dr. Almasad* and in 1896 composed the music for Joseph Lattiner's operetta *Kiddush ha-Shem or the Jewish Minieer*. He also composed for M. Horowitz' operettas *The Hero and Bracha or the Jewish King of Poland for a Night* (1896). In the latter work the song "Eli, Eli" (generally spelled Eili, Eili) with text by Boris Tomashefsky, was featured, and, because of its tremendous effect, the operetta played for many weeks. It became one of the most popular Jewish compositions in the Western world and was performed and recorded by folk and opera singers, as well as cantors. Jossele *Rosenblatt maintained that before "Eili, Eili" appeared in this American operetta, it was heard in Europe as a folksong. He further alleged that the melody was also found among the compositions for *seliḥot* by a cantor of an earlier generation. The controversy has not been resolved. In any case, the appearance of "Eili, Eili" as an anonymous "folk song" in most of the recordings and printed versions (including the publications of the *Society for Jewish Folk Music) cannot be adduced as proof of a folk origin, since all of them postdate the operetta. Sandler served for a time as composer-director of the Arch Street Theatre in Philadelphia and then withdrew from the theater to appear as a synagogue choral director for the High Holy Days.

BIBLIOGRAPHY: Z. Zylbercweig, in: *Leksikon fun Yidishn Teater*, 4 (1934), 1514–15.

[Avraham Soltes]

SANDMEL, SAMUEL (1911–1979), biblical scholar. Sandmel was born in Dayton, Ohio, and graduated from the University of Missouri in 1932 and from the Hebrew Union College in 1937, receiving his doctorate from Yale University in 1949. He served as Hillel Foundation rabbi in North Carolina from 1939 to 1942, and at Yale from 1946 to 1949. He was professor of Jewish Literature and Thought at Vanderbilt University from 1949 to 1952. In 1952 he was appointed professor of Bible and Hellenistic literature at the Hebrew Union College. Among the many honorary degrees bestowed upon him was the President's Fellowship, by Brown University. At the time of his death he was Helen A. Regenstein Professor of Religion of the Chicago Divinity School. He was also an editor of the Oxford Study Edition of the New English Bible. Sandmel was an internationally recognized authority on the relationship between Judaism and the New Testament.

Among his works are *A Jewish Understanding of the New Testament* (1957), *The Genius of Paul* (1958), *The Hebrew Scriptures* (1963), *We Jews and Jesus* (1965), *We Jews and You Christians* (1967), *Herod: Profile of a Tyrant* (1967), *The First Christian Century in Judaism and Christianity* (1969), *The Enjoyment of Scripture* (1972), *Two Living Traditions* (1972), *Judaism and Christian Beginnings* (1978), and *Anti-Semitism in the New Testament* (1978). He also published a novel about Moses, *Atop the Mountain* (1973)

[Heinz Hartman (2nd ed.)]

SANDOMIERZ (Rus. **Sandomir**; in Latin documents of the 12th century Sudomir; in early and Jewish sources **Tsoyzmir** or **Tsuzmir**), town in Kielce province, central Poland. Jews settled there at the beginning of the 13th century, making that community one of the oldest in Poland. In 1367 representatives of the Jewish communities of Sandomierz, *Cracow, and *Lvov requested King *Casimir III (the Great) to confirm the privileges of Polish Jewry. Toward the end of the 15th century the townsmen of Sandomierz waged a stubborn struggle against the local Jewish merchants, who were sometimes compelled to move to other towns. In 1550 there were 40 Jews living in Sandomierz and paying state taxes. At the beginning of the 17th century there existed a street with 16 houses owned by Jews, and the old synagogue was built. During the war with Sweden (1655/56) most of the Jews of the town were slaughtered and the rest expelled. In 1658 (see *Poland-Lithuania) King John II Casimir permitted the Jews to return to Sandomierz and granted them the right to engage in commerce. This privilege was later confirmed by King John III Sobieski (1674) and King Augustus III (1745). The struggle of the townsmen, supported by the local Catholic priests, against the Jews of Sandomierz led to a series of *blood libels at the end of the 17th century and the first half of the 18th. In the first case, which occurred in 1698, the *parnas* of the community, Aaron Berek, was accused of murdering a Christian child (see the pamphlet of the Jew-baiting priest Stefan Żuchowski, *Odgłas processów kryminalnych na Zydów…*, 1700). Considerable harm was done to the Jewish community of Sandomierz as a result of other blood libels in 1710 and 1748. In 1765, 430 Jews paying the poll tax resided in the town; they comprised 90 families (with 14 tailors, 8 hatmakers, 2 goldsmiths, and 5 butchers) owning 30 houses. Another 366 Jews who lived in the surrounding villages also paid the poll tax. During the period of Austrian rule in Sandomierz (1795–1809) the restrictions on Jewish craftsmen were abolished, and a Jewish school with German as the language of instruction was opened. In 1815 Sandomierz was included in Congress Poland. Restrictions on Jewish settlement in the town remained until 1862. In 1827, 799 Jews lived there (23% of the total population), and in 1857, 924 (29%). In the second half of the 19th century the Jewish population of the town increased considerably, reaching 2,164 (34%) in 1897. Their main livelihood was from trading in agricultural produce, leather, timber, tailoring, shoemaking, and transportation. In 1921 there were 2,641 Jews (39%) living in the town.

[Mark Wischnitzer and Arthur Cygielman]

Holocaust Period

At the outbreak of World War II there were about 2,500 Jews living in Sandomierz. The German army entered on Sept. 15, 1939 and immediately organized pogroms, during which Jews were killed. In the first half of 1942 nearly two thousand Jews from the vicinity were expelled to Sandomierz, and the town's Jewish population grew to about 5,200. On Oct. 29, 1942, about 3,200 Jews were deported from Sandomierz to the *Belzec death camp. During deportations which took place in the summer and fall of 1942, thousands of Jews from the whole *Radom district fled into the forest, where they tried to survive in hiding and to organize guerilla units. On Nov. 10, 1942, the Germans published a decree on the establishment of four new ghettos in the region (Sandomierz, *Szydlowiec, *Radomsko, and Ujazd), where Jews were promised security if they left the forests. Thousands of Jews, unable to see the possibility of surviving in the forests during the winter, responded to the German appeal. About 6,000 Jews were concentrated in the ghetto of Sandomierz, which was liquidated on Jan. 10, 1943, when almost all its inmates were deported to the *Treblinka death camp. Only 700 Jews were left; of them 300 were deported to the forced-labor camp in *Skarzysko-Kamienna, and 400 were transferred to the forced-labor camp established in Sandomierz. This camp was liquidated in January 1944 and almost all the inmates were murdered. After the war the Jewish community of Sandomierz was not reconstituted.

[Stefan Krakowski]

BIBLIOGRAPHY: Warsaw, Archiwum Głowne Akt Dawnych, *Komisja rządowa spraw wewnętrznych i policji*, 2963; *Władze centralne powstania listopadowego*, 362; *Archiwum skarbu koronnego*, 35 no. 316 (= CAHJP, 2174, 3696, and 7827, respectively); Zakład Narodowy imienia Ossolińskich, 1640/II (= CAHJP, ḤM 6650); Halpern, Pinkas, index; R. Mahler, *Yidn in Amolikn Poyln in Likht fun Tsifern* (1958), index; B. Wasiutyński, *Ludność żydowska w Polsce w wiekach XIX i XX* (1930), 31, 54, 71; L. Rotoczny, *Przewodnik po Sandomierzu* (1910); D. Kandel, in: *Kwartalnik poswięcony badaniu przeszłości Żydow w Polsce*, 1 (1912); I. Schiper, *Dzieje handlu żydowskiego na ziemiach polskich* (1937), index; M. Balaban, *Historja Żydow w Krakowie i na Kazimierzu*, 2 vols. (1931–36), index.

SÁNDOR, PÁL (1860–1936), Hungarian statesman and economist. Born in Hódmezövásárhely, Sándor entered his father's grain business. An active member of the Budapest exchange, he also founded and chaired the Hungarian trade union. In 1912 he was appointed director of the Budapest municipal tramway company. Sándor began his political career as a member of the Budapest municipal council, delegated by the governing Liberal Party. He sat in parliament as a delegate of the same party from 1901 and was a member of the Liberal Party opposition under Horthy's regime. Somewhat defensively and apologetically, Sándor attacked the antisemitic policies of the government and its first discriminatory laws, the *numerus clausus, restricting higher education for Jewish youth. He was an extreme assimilationist and outspoken opponent of Zionism.

BIBLIOGRAPHY: D. Polonyi, in: *Zsidó Évkönyv* (1928/29), 116–7; P. Sándor, in: *Egyenlőség*, no. 7 (1936), 7–8.

[Baruch Yaron]

SANDROW, EDWARD T. (1906–1975), U.S. Conservative rabbi and communal leader. Sandrow was born in Philadelphia and was ordained at the Jewish Theological Seminary of America (1933). His first rabbinical position was at the Ohavai Shalom synagogue in Portland, Oregon (1933–37). Sandrow then became rabbi at Temple Beth El in Cedarhurst, Long Island. He was a teaching fellow at New York University (1948–52). At the Jewish Theological Seminary he was visiting professor in homiletics (1954–56, 1962–63) and of pastoral psychiatry (1963 onwards). Sandrow's interest in pastoral psychiatry is expressed in some of his articles. He contributed a chapter called "Conscience and Guilt: A Jewish View" to Simon Noveck's (ed.), *Judaism and Psychiatry* (1956).

Sandrow was president of the Rabbinical Assembly of America (1960–62) and of the New York Board of Rabbis (1966–67). In the latter organization he served as chairman of the board of governors (1968–70). He was a member of the board of directors of the American Friends of the Hebrew University (1968–1975), an alternate member of the board of governors of the Hebrew University in Jerusalem, and a member of the boards of directors of the Joint Distribution Committee, the Zionist Organization of America, and the National Jewish Welfare Board. He was also chairman of the commission on Jewish chaplaincy of the latter organization. From 1960 he served as chairman of the board of *Hadoar*. He was coauthor of *Young Faith*, a prayer book with music for children.

SANDZER, ḤAYYIM BEN MENAHEM (d. 1783), talmudist and kabbalist. Ḥayyim, who was born in Sandz but should not be confused with Ḥayyim *Halberstamm of Sandz, became one of the great scholars of Brody. Aside from his great talmudic scholarship, he was considered one of the outstanding kabbalists of his time. In 1744 he was counted with Ezekiel *Landau and Moses Ostrer among the kabbalists of the *Klaus* in Brody, the famous Galician kabbalistic center. It is related that Israel Ba'al Shem Tov said that Ḥayyim's soul was a spark of the soul of *Johanan b. Zakkai, while Jacob, son of Ezekiel Landau, remarked in the preface to his father's *Noda bi-Yhudah* that Ḥayyim was his father's teacher in Kabbalah. In 1752 he condemned Jonathan *Eybeschuetz's amulets as Shabbatean. Although an outspoken adversary of the ḥasidic movement, he was highly respected in ḥasidic circles.

One of his responsa appears in *Noda bi-Yhudah* and others in Israel *Lipschutz's *Or Yisrael*. Most of his novellae and responsa on the *Arba'ah Turim*, however, remained unpublished. Many years after his death Ḥayyim's commentary on *Avot, Ne'dar ba-Kodesh*, was published (1862).

BIBLIOGRAPHY: N.M. Gelber, *Toledot Yehudei Brody* (1955), 63, 330.

[Anthony Lincoln Lavine]

SAN FRANCISCO BAY AREA, including San Francisco, a combined city-county in N. California, and surrounding area. In 2001 the San Francisco city population was 776,733, with the Jewish population 49,500; an additional 160,000 Jews lived in the surrounding area.

Following the discovery of gold in Northern California in 1848, thousands of Jews were among the quarter of a million people making the long and arduous trip to one of the most remote regions on the continent. Although a few came overland, most of the Jewish pioneers chose the sea route: The four- or five-month long, 16,000-mile journey "around the Horn" often shortened by a land crossing of malarial swamps at Panama or Nicaragua.

Gold Rush San Francisco was engulfed by peoples from all over the world, and the town's Jewish community was itself highly diverse. The majority was from the German-speaking lands of Central Europe, especially Bavaria and the Prussian province of Posen (seized from Poland in 1793). Others hailed from England or the French provinces of Alsace and Lorraine, and a few were Sephardim from the West Indies or the American South.

In the coarse mining towns of the Mother Lode, along the western foothills of the Sierras, Jews established businesses, burial societies, and synagogues. In the gateway boomtown that was San Francisco, rife with prostitution, gambling, and gunfights, about 30 Jews held High Holiday services in a wood-framed tent as early as 1849.

Despite the frequent fires, sandstorms, and epidemics that ravaged the fledgling city, a number of the pioneer Jews became immensely successful. Antisemitism was less salient than in many other parts of America, and Jews, rarely perceived as interlopers, were well represented among the early political leaders, judges, and sheriffs. Others distinguished themselves in business, amassing fortunes in dry goods, banking and utilities, real estate and insurance, mining and overseas commerce, tobacco and produce. In later generations the extensive philanthropy of these first families – Fleishhacker, Haas, Koshland, Stern, Steinhardt, Dinkelspiel, Zellerbach and others – made their names well-known in Northern California to Jew and non-Jew alike.

The most famous pioneer Jew is the Bavarian Levi Strauss, whose jeans have become one of the most recognizable symbols of America around the world. The brothers-in law Louis Sloss and Lewis Gerstle headed the enormous Alaska Commercial Company, which for decades held a highly lucrative, federally granted concession for the territory's sealskins. Another early arrival, the Westphalian engineer Adolph Sutro, designed and built a four-mile mining tunnel through the Comstock silver lode in Nevada. He invested the profits in San Francisco real estate, became one of the wealthiest men in the state, and was elected mayor in 1892, the first Jewish mayor of a major American city. At the end of the 19th century, Julius Kahn was elected to the House of Representatives from San Francisco and served 12 terms. Following his death in 1924, his wife, Florence Prag *Kahn, was elected to his seat, the first Jewish woman in the U.S. Congress.

Many of the children of the pioneers, Bay Area Jewry's second generation, distinguished themselves in the arts. David Belasco, an innovative playwright and producer, set designer and director, became one of the leading theatrical personalities in the country. Toby Rosenthal, a consummate portraitist and genre painter, was one of a half dozen gifted San Francisco Jewish painters who came of age in the late 19th century. A.L. Gump, as a purveyor and connoisseur of Far Eastern art, jewelry and furnishings, literally changed the taste of San Franciscans, even while an impenetrable social barrier existed between whites and Asians.

The religious expression of this frontier community was decidedly liberal, and the two earliest synagogues, Emanu-El and Sherith Israel, both formed in the first week of April 1851, came to embrace Reform Judaism, the former within a decade of its founding, the latter by the turn of the century. Soon after the Civil War, Emanu-El erected the magnificent Sutter Street Temple, its twin gothic towers a prominent feature of the young city's skyline. In 1925, the congregation moved to the Lake Street location it currently occupies and built another architectural masterpiece, harmoniously blending Byzantine, Moorish, and Spanish mission styles. The domed sanctuary, influenced by the Hagia Sophia in Istanbul, is one of the most noted houses of worship on the West Coast. Sherith Israel constructed its grand synagogue, even more eclectic in style and filled with vivid stained-glass windows, in 1905. It withstood the devastating earthquake and fire of the following year, unlike Emanu-El's temple and most other buildings housing San Francisco's Jewish institutions.

While San Francisco, with a Jewish population of almost 20,000, was the second largest Jewish community in the United States by 1880, Oakland, across the Bay, grew more slowly. But the city of fewer than a thousand Jews produced two extraordinary personalities: the maverick Reform rabbi Judah L. *Magnes, a passionate advocate for social justice in New York and founder and first president of The Hebrew University of Jerusalem, and the irreverent author and avant-garde art critic, Gertrude *Stein. Both attended the Sunday school of the First Hebrew Congregation, today's Temple Sinai. Magnes and Stein lived most of their adult lives abroad, but, by their own admission, their path-breaking careers owed much to their exuberant formative years in the East Bay.

Jews could be found on both sides of the violent class conflict that gripped the Bay Area during the Progressive era and later in the Depression. They included the agrarian reformers David Lubin, his son Simon Lubin, and half-brother Harris Weinstock; the socialist Anna Strunsky; the suffragette Selina Solomons; and labor organizers such as Lou Goldblatt and Rose *Pesotta. At Sherith Israel, Rabbi Jacob Nieto and his successor, the young Jacob *Weinstein, spoke out forcefully on behalf of the disadvantaged. But corporate titans such as I.W. *Hellman, Jr., and the brothers Herbert and Mortimer Fleishhacker were mainstays of the conservative, anti-union forces in the Bay Area.

The turn of the century saw an influx of thousands of Yiddish-speaking immigrants, although for many decades they accounted for a relatively low proportion of the total Jewish population compared with other major American cities. In San Francisco, shanties of East European Jews sprang up in the South of Market area before it was destroyed in the 1906 earthquake and fire. Two newer neighborhoods took its place after the disaster: the outlying San Bruno Avenue quarter, and the more populous Fillmore-MacAllister district, a vibrant Jewish neighborhood in the heart of the city until well after World War II. The Fillmore produced one of the century's greatest child prodigies, the violinist Yehudi *Menuhin, while another violinist destined for worldwide fame, Isaac *Stern, grew up in the nearby Richmond District. In Oakland, a colorful East European Jewish neighborhood arose in the aging Victorian houses west of Broadway, centered on the Orthodox Congregation Beth Jacob on Ninth and Castro Streets.

Most of the city's Jewish immigrants left the ethnic enclaves by the 1940s for more mixed, middle class neighborhoods, such as the Richmond and Sunset Districts in San Francisco and the Grand Lake District in Oakland. Still, a thick social barrier remained between them and the German-Jewish elite, many of whom lived in exclusive Pacific Heights with commanding views of the Bay. The two groups differed on the proper response to the Holocaust and fought bitterly over the merits of Zionism. During World War II, Rabbi Irving Reichert of Emanu-El, along with key lay leaders of his congregation, founded the local chapter of the American Council for Judaism, dedicated to preventing the creation of a Jewish state; it soon became the strongest branch of the ACJ in the country. The forceful young Rabbi, Saul White, a Polish immigrant who served the Conservative synagogue Beth Sholom, which was comprised largely of East Europeans, countered Reichert.

After the birth of Israel in 1948, and American recognition, a community consensus was reached, and nearly all the pioneer families transferred their full support to the Jewish state. The eloquent, new rabbi at Emanu-El, Alvin Fine, advocated Zionism from the pulpit.

Fine and his close friend Benjamin Swig, owner of the historic Fairmont Hotel, helped shift the leadership of Bay Area Jewry into the mainstream of American Judaism. Swig was the son of a Lithuanian immigrant, but two descendants of pioneers were no less active in invigorating Jewish life: Walter Haas and Daniel Koshland, cousins, brothers-in-law and co-owners of Levi Strauss and Company. Meanwhile, thousands of young Jewish newcomers from the East and Midwest, and refugees from the Nazi terror, also infused the community with a new sense of pride and unity with world Jewry. In the 1970s and 1980s, the Bay Area Jewry was especially assertive in the rescue of Jews from Ethiopia and the Soviet Union. Today, many tens of thousands of Jews from the former Soviet Union live in the region, in San Francisco and on the Peninsula in particular, having been aided by the Jewish Community Federation and its agencies.

In the post-World War II period, the Bay Area continued to be a fertile field for audacious Jewish artists such as the "beat" poet Allen *Ginsberg, the comedian Lenny *Bruce, the sculptor Jacques Schnier, and the rock impressario (and Holocaust survivor) Bill *Graham.

The Jewish community became intertwined with both the counter-culture and gay rights movement, which took hold in the Bay Area beginning in the late 1960s. The House of Love and Prayer founded by Rabbi Shlomo *Carlebach, and later the Jewish Renewal Movement of New Age rabbi Zalman *Schachter-Shalomi, drew many spiritually minded young Jews disaffected with traditional synagogue services. Jewish mysticism and mediation have remained common features of Bay Area Jewish life, both within and outside synagogues.

In 1977, one of the first synagogues in the country formed expressly for homosexuals was founded in San Francisco, Congregation Sha'ar Zahav. The following year, a member of the Board of Supervisors, Harvey Milk, a New York-born Jew and the only openly gay officeholder in the country, was assassinated in City Hall (along with Mayor George Moscone) by former supervisor Dan White. The shocking tragedy energized many homosexuals, and since then there has been an increasing number of openly gay rabbis and lay leaders in the Bay Area. The general Jewish community has shown great sensitivity to the AIDS crisis since a pivotal, widely circulated Yom Kippur sermon on the issue was delivered at Emanu-El in 1985 by its senior rabbi, Robert Kirschner.

San Francisco's and the East Bay's Jewish Community Federations and their fast-growing endowment funds, as well as family foundations such as Koret, have tried to meet the rapidly increasing and changing needs of the diverse Bay Area Jewish community. By the mid-1980s the Jewish population numbered around 223,000, 4% of the entire Bay Area. In 2004, it was estimated to have doubled (as had the general population in the past two decades) as a result of huge suburban gains: Contra Costa County, Marin and Sonoma Counties, and the Peninsula. A particularly large and vibrant Jewish community, including many immigrants from the Former Soviet Union as well as Israelis, has emerged on the Sourthern end of the Peninsula, with the city of Palo Alto as its hub. With about 72,000 Jews, the South Peninsula (essentially Santa Clara County) has passed San Francisco and contains the largest Jewish population of any region in the Bay Area. A large percentage of the Bay Area Jewish community is intermarried; a recent demographic study revealed that about a quarter of those living in Jewish households is non-Jewish.

Jews are prominent in almost every phase of the region's robust economic, cultural, and professional life. They are highly represented among the Nobel laureates of UC Berkeley and Stanford; they are leading corporate executives; they are on the cutting edge of bio-medical research and technological innovation in Silicon Valley. In 1992, two Bay Area Jewish women, Dianne *Feinstein and Barbara *Boxer were elected to the United States Senate, and they have both been twice reelected. Since 1995, Michael Tilson *Thomas (grandson of the great Yiddish actor Boris Thomashefsky) has been the music director of the San Francisco Symphony, the third Jew to serve in that capacity.

Recent decades have witnessed a virtual renaissance in Jewish education. Illustrious scholars teach in Jewish studies programs at the Bay Area's many institutions of higher learning – particularly Stanford (Steven Zipperstein and Arnold *Eisen), UC Berkeley (Robert *Alter and Daniel *Boyarin), and nearby UC Davis (David *Biale). The day school movement, moribund until the 1960s, has burgeoned in recent decades and in the early 2000s counts 13 schools in the area. Lehrhaus Judaica, a school for adult Jewish education, spans the entire Bay Area with its offerings. Public intellectuals such as Michael Lerner, founder and editor of the leftwing *Tikkun* magazine, have enlivened the debate in the Jewish community on Israel and other Jewish issues.

The recent growth of cultural and recreational centers has also been impressive. With the Judah L. Magnes Museum and the Contemporary Jewish Museum, A Traveling Jewish Theater, the Jewish Film Festival, and its myriad of new, well-equipped JCCs and residences for seniors, the Bay Area has emerged as one of the most dynamic Jewish communities in North America.

BIBLIOGRAPHY: F. Rosenbaum, *Visions of Reform: Congregation Emanu-El and the Jews of San Francisco, 1849–2000* (2000); I. Narell, *Our City: The Jews of San Francisco* (1981); A.F. Kahn, *Jewish Voices of the California Gold Rush, 1849–1880* (2002); A.F. Kahn and M. Dollinger, *California Jews* (2003); F. Rosenbaum, *Free to Choose: The Making of a Jewish Community in the American West, Oakland, California* (1976).

[Fred S. Rosenbaum (2nd ed.)]

SAN GABRIEL–POMONA VALLEYS, California. The estimated 30,000–40,000 Jews of San Gabriel–Pomona Valley in the early 21st century are spread over a significant distance with a low density of Jews in any given community. Beginning in East Los Angeles, the area covers East Los Angeles south to Whittier, east through the Pomona Valley, west of the borders of Fontanta, and includes Ontario, Alta Loma, and Pasadena. The area spans three counties: Los Angeles County, Western San Bernardino County, and a small slice of northern Orange County (including La Habra and La Puente).

Some older parts of the Los Angeles Jewish community are found within the San Gabriel Valley though the much more numerous Jewish migration from East Los Angeles was to the San Fernando Valley. The most visible Jewish institution in the community is the synagogue, primarily Conservative and Reform. There is no mainstream Orthodox presence, though Chabad is found in Pasadena and in the Inland Empire.

Pasadena is the home of one of the communities' day schools, the Weizmann Day School, which is housed at the Pasadena Jewish Temple and Center, a Conservative Synagogue. The Atid Hebrew Academy is in West Covina and is housed on the grounds of Temple Ami Shalom.

The Pasadena community has a large number of scientists employed by Cal Tech and JPL, which led the space probe to Mars. The Pomona Valley Jewish community has a large number of academics employed at the Claremont Colleges and the universities that ring the valleys. There is no Jewish Community Center, perhaps because of the distances involved and the traffic patterns of Los Angeles, so that the Federation offers programs and services somewhat like a Jewish Community Center without a major community building. Among its activities are the Festival in the Park, a Jewish Counseling Referral Network, two day camps at two locations, and a successful annual Jewish book festival.

Federation activities include the Senior Van program that brings together isolated seniors and senior groups, the Camp Gan Shalom (summer day camp) for area children, community-building programs such as the Jewish Festival, Women's Forum, Women's Business and Professionals' Association, Lunchtime Jewish Learning, and the Jewish Book Festival.

The community offers direct support to Jewish schools through its Jewish Education Consultant, Principal's Council, Special Education Consultant, Teacher In-Service programs, and direct cash grants to area schools. There are a Jewish Family Resource Service, a local counseling referral program, and scholarships for participants in organizational Israel experiences, as well as a Shabbaton program for area children. The

Jewish Community News is a monthly newspaper devoted to local Jewish activity and national and international news of Jewish interest.

There is a Conservative synagogue in Montebello, Temple B'nai Emet, and in Pasadena, Congregation B'nai Torah. Pomona has a Reform synagogue, Temple Beth Israel, that houses a pre-school. Ontario features a Conservative synagogue, Temple Sholom. The Chabad of the Inland is located in Rancho Cucamonga. West Covina also has a Conservative congregation, Temple Ami Shalom, and Whittier has a Conservative synagogue, Temple Beth Shalom. The Reconstructionist Havurah in Whittier pioneered the use of Havurot within the congregation long before they became fashionable in other sections of the country, and they have now sustained themselves and continued for a generation. Congregation Shaarei Torah in Arcadia, a Conservative congregation, also houses a Jewish pre-school called B'nai Simcha. There is also a Reform temple, B'nai David, in Temple City. Temple Beth Israel of Highland Park and Eagle Rock is a Conservative congregation. Sinai Temple of Glendale, a Reform congregation, became affiliated with the San Gabriel-Pomona Valleys Federation. Adat Re'im in the Pomona Valley has just been constituted.

There are a string of hospitals along the foothills of the Valley including *City of Hope, which is now a non-sectarian hospital but well aware of its Jewish roots, and thus the area has attracted Jewish physicians and Jews in allied medical professions. Some parts of the Jewish community are old – at least by California standards – once rooted in the Jewish community of Los Angeles areas such as Monterey Park and Montebello. Others have developed in the post-war migration to California and in the string of Jewish communities throughout Southern California.

Some areas were settled by Jewish chicken farmers; there was an area of egg farming and chicken farming in the valley. Over time the land became more valuable than the farms, and several would-be farmers found themselves prosperous real estate developers.

Because of the vastly increasing cost of housing and the shortage of housing in the Los Angeles area, the Jewish community of Los Angeles is moving westward into the western outreaches of the San Fernando Valley and eastward into the Pomona Valley-San Bernardino area. As young families mature, one suspects that there will be a growing need for Jewish institutions, Jewish education, and synagogues to meet an expanding population.

[Michael Berenbaum (2nd ed.)]

SANGUINETTI, AZARIAH ḤAYYIM (early 19th century), Italian preacher. A pupil of *Ishmael b. Abraham ha-Kohen, rabbi of Modena, Sanguinetti was the author of a book of homilies, *Olah Ḥadashah* (Leghorn, 1838). The sermons, which make use of talmudic and midrashic sources, rely especially on the Commentaries of Naḥmanides. Influenced by kabbalistic literature, Sanguinetti frequently quoted from the Zohar and used kabbalistic terms and symbols. Additional material was appended to the work in the supplement, *"Evrei Olah,"* which deals mainly with *halakhah*. The introduction to the book indicates that Sanguinetti succeeded his teacher as rabbi of Modena.

SANHEDRIN. Great Sanhedrin usually means the supreme political, religious, and judicial body in Palestine during the Roman period, both before and after the destruction of the Temple, until the abolishment of the patriarchate (c. 425 C.E.). The precise definition of the term Sanhedrin has engaged the attention of historians in the past century, owing to the apparent conflict between the Hellenistic and rabbinic sources as to its nature and functions. While in the Hellenistic sources, in Josephus and the Gospels, it appears as a political and judicial council headed by the ruler, the tannaitic sources depict it chiefly as a legislative body dealing with religious matters, and in rare cases acting as a court – for instance, to try a false prophet or high priest.

The first historical mention of the Sanhedrin is in the statement of Josephus that in 57 B.C.E. *Gabinius divided the country into five *synedria* (Ant., 14:91) or *synodoi* (Wars, 1:170). Most scholars agree that the reference is to a purely political body, as the Romans did not interfere with the religious life of conquered people. Their objective was, as Schalit points out, the prevention of uprisings. The next report describes *Hyrcanus, as ethnarch of Judea, presiding over the Sanhedrin trying Herod, the strategus of the Galilee, for political murder (Ant., 14:168–70). Subsequently, when Herod became king, he had the Sanhedrin condemn Hyrcanus for plotting against him (Ant., 15:173), though according to another account, he did so himself without the Sanhedrin (15:176). Josephus' next reference to a Sanhedrin is to one that consisted of Roman high officials, convened at the suggestion of Augustus in Syria, to try the sons of Herod for rebellion against their father (16:356ff.); according to Josephus (Wars, 1:537), this Sanhedrin consisted of Herod's "own relatives and the provincial governors." When the Sadducean high priest, Ananus, "convened the judges of the Sanhedrin" (Jos., Ant., 20:200) to condemn James, the brother of Jesus, his opponents, the Pharisees, took great pains to have him removed. Their plea before the Roman governor that Ananus "had no authority to convene the Sanhedrin without his consent" (20:202) was obviously a pretext. Ananus' Sanhedrin was no doubt a Sadducean one, so that in removing Ananus shortly after this, Agrippa II pleased the Pharisees. On the other hand, the Sanhedrin convened by Agrippa II to permit the levitical singers to wear the priestly linen garments – apparently in accord with II Chronicles 5:12 – was a Pharisaic one (Arakh. 11a–b). Josephus' objection to this ruling (Ant., 20:216–18) represents the priestly-Sadducean view. Josephus received his commission as a supreme commander from the Sanhedrin (Life, 62), though he usually refers to it as the *koinon* (*ibid.*, 190, 309) and describes it as the assembly of the leading people of Jerusalem (*ibid.*, 28, see also Wars, 2:562).

The Gospels describe three trials before the Sanhedrin, all of them presided over by the high priest, but apparently in different locations. Jesus was tried on Passover night, or on the preceding night, in the palace of the high priest (Mark 14:53ff.; John 18:13). His disciples, Peter and John Zebedee, were questioned at "eventide," "in Jerusalem" (Acts, 4:3–6). In the case of Paul, the chief priest "and all their Sanhedrin" were ordered to meet in the chief captain's quarters (Acts, 22:25–30). The tannaitic sources, however, depict the Great Sanhedrin as an assembly of sages permanently situated in the Chamber of Hewn Stone in the Temple, meeting daily, only during the daytime between the hours of the two daily sacrifices (approximately 7:30 A.M.–3:30 P.M.), and never at night, on the Sabbaths or festivals, or on their eves. It was the place "where the Law went forth to all Israel" (Sanh. 11:2; Tosef., Sanh. 7:1) and was the final authority on *halakhah*; the penalty of contravening its decisions on the part of a scholar – *zaken mamre – was death (Sanh. *ibid*.). Settling questions of priestly genealogy was also within the province of the Great Sanhedrin (Mid. 5:4; Tosef., Sanh. loc. cit.). Actual cases are recorded of questions being sent to "the sages in the Chamber of Hewn Stone" (Eduy. 7:4) and of Rabban Gamaliel going to the Chamber and receiving a reply to a question which he put (Pe'ah 2:6).

The competence of the Sanhedrin is listed in tannaitic literature. "A tribe, a false prophet, or the high priest may not be tried save by the court of seventy-one; they may not send forth the people to wage a battle of free choice save by the decision of the court of one and seventy; they may not add to the City [of Jerusalem], or the Courts of the Temple save by the decision of the court of seventy-one; they may not set up sanhedrins for the several tribes save by the decision of the court of one and seventy; and they may not proclaim [any city to be] an *Ir ha-Niddaḥat [cf. Deut. 13:13–19] save by the decision of one and seventy" (Sanh. 1:5). The Tosefta enumerates still other functions: "They may not burn the red heifer save according to the instructions of the court of 71; they may not declare one a *zaken mamre* save the court of 71; they may not set up a king or a high priest save by the decision of the court of 71" (Tos., Sanh. 3:4). Elsewhere the Mishnah rules that the rites of the water of ordeals (see *Sotah; Sot. 1:4) and the *eglah arufah – i.e., the breaking of the heifer's neck in order to atone for the sin of an anonymous murder (cf. Deut. 21: 1–9) – may be performed only under the supervision of the Great *Bet Din* in Jerusalem (Sot. 9:1).

Unlike Buechler (see bibl., pp. 56ff.) and Zeitlin (see bibl., pp. 70–71) who regard the tannaitic list of the functions of the Great *Bet Din* as merely ideal, Tchernowitz (see bibl., 242ff.) insists upon its practical reality. Thus, Simeon the Hasmonean was appointed high priest and "Prince of the people of God" (see *Asaramel) by the Great Assembly of priests and heads of the nation (I Macc., 14:27ff.; cf. Tosef., Sanh. 3:4). Again, "Jonathan, after the war with Demetrius, returned and called the elders of the people together; and took counsel with them to raise the height of the walls of Jerusalem, and to raise a great mound between the citadel and the city" (*ibid.* 12:35–36), things which could only be done, according to the Mishnah, with the consent of the Great Court (Sanh. 1:5; Shevu. 2:2). Yet, in rebuilding the ruins of the city and its walls and carrying on defensive wars, Jonathan did not consult with the Assembly; neither did Simeon take counsel with regard to the fortifying of Judea (I Macc., 13:33). These things did not require the consent of the Sanhedrin (Tchernowitz, op. cit., 243–7). Furthermore, the reference to "tribes," as Alon says, is to sections of the country; or else, the term "tribes," like "false prophet" may put into legal formulation practices current in the biblical period, as Z. Karl suggests.

Another aspect of the conflict between the sources is that, whereas the tannaitic documents represent the Sanhedrin as being composed of Pharisaic scholars, headed by the foremost men of the sect – the *nasi* and *av bet din* – the Hellenistic accounts usually make the high priest, or the king, the president of the body. Thus Samaias and Pollion (that is, probably, Shemaiah and Avtalyon, or Shammai and Hillel) and Simeon b. Gamaliel, who are mentioned in Josephus, and Gamaliel I, who is cited in the Book of Acts, are referred to in these books merely as prominent members of the Sanhedrin, though in the tannaitic documents they are represented as the presidents of that body. In the Book of Acts, moreover, the Sanhedrin is depicted as being "one part Sadducees and the other Pharisees" (Acts, 23:6).

The historians' answers may be classified into three groups. Some scholars maintain that there was a single Sanhedrin, the supreme political, religious and judicial body, but they differ among themselves as to the other aspects of the reconstruction. Schuerer, who dismisses the rabbinic sources, regards the high priest as the presiding officer. Hoffmann held the highest office to belong to the Pharisaic *nasi*, though the secular rulers often usurped the role. Jelski, following a middle course, divides the functions of the presidency between the high priest, upon whom he bestows the title *nasi*, and the Pharisaic *av bet din*. Similarly, G. Alon believes that the Sanhedrin was composed of Pharisees and Sadducees, each dominating it by turns. Chwolson thinks that the Great Sanhedrin of the rabbinic documents was nothing but a committee on religious law appointed by the Sanhedrin (so, too, Dubnow and Klausner). Common to all these theories is the erroneous assumption that there can be only one Sanhedrin in a city. In reality, a Sanhedrin can be the king's or ruler's council, a body of high officials; a congress of allies or confederates, a military war council, etc. (see Liddell-Scott, *Greek-English Lexicon*, s.v. συνέθριον).

Another group of scholars believes that there were in Jerusalem three small Sanhedrins, each of a different composition and task – priestly, Pharisaic, and aristocratic – each consisting of 23 members. A joint meeting of the three Sanhedrins, headed by a *nasi* and *av bet din*, constituted the Great Sanhedrin of 71 (Geiger, Derenbourg, etc.). This imaginary reconstruction flounders on the Tosefta (Ḥag. 2:9 and Sanh. 7:1) and the Jerusalem Talmud (Sanh. 1:7, 19c), according to which, contrary to the Babylonian Talmud (Sanh. 88b), the small Sanhedrin consisted only of three. The third group of scholars is agreed that there were two supreme bodies in Jerusalem, a political and a religious, but disagree on almost everything else. Buechler thinks that the religious body was properly called *Bet Din ha-Gadol she-be-Lishkat ha-Gazit* ("Great *Bet Din* in the Chamber of Hewn Stone"), and the application to it of the term Sanhedrin was a misnomer. Zeitlin points out that there is no evidence that the political Sanhedrin was called "Great," but his view that the division between the political and the religious authorities dates back to Simeon the Hasmonean is questionable. More likely the separation was the result of the fact that the political views of the religious Sanhedrin were not sought by Hyrcanus and Aristobulus, the sons of Salome, nor by Herod, nor by the high priests who were appointed by Romans.

The opponents of the theory of the double Sanhedrin base themselves mainly on three arguments: no proof exists that the *nasi* headed the Sanhedrin in the days of the Temple; the priests' authority to "declare" the law is scripturally prescribed (Deut. 17:9), so that the high priest must have at least formally headed the religious Sanhedrin, as he did among the Qumran sect; and in Judaism there is no division between the religious and the secular. As against these arguments, it has been pointed out: the law concerning the assignment of one's property to the *nasi* (Ned. 5:5), which dates from Temple days, assumes that the *nasi* headed the Sanhedrin, just as he did in the post-destruction era; the Pharisaic exegesis dispensed with the need of priests in issuing legal decisions, the Pharisees basing their ruling on the superfluous words "and to judge" (Deut. 17:9; see Sif., Deut. 153); and the Pharisees did not voluntarily relinquish their right to judge on political matters. The political rulers simply did not consult them. After the destruction of the Temple the religious Sanhedrin was reconvened in *Jabneh, and, under the presidency of the *nasi*, it now became also the supreme political instrument for all the Jews of the Roman Empire. When Judea was destroyed as a result of the failure of Bar Kokhba, the Sanhedrin moved to Galilee. At first it met in Usha, then in nearby Shefaram, subsequently, in Judah ha-Nasi's time, in Bet She'arim and Sepphoris, and in the end in Tiberias. The Romans apparently withdrew their recognition of the Sanhedrin when they dissolved the patriarchate.

BIBLIOGRAPHY: Geiger, Urschrift; Derenbourg, Hist; D. Hoffmann, in: *Jahres-Bericht des Rabbiner-Seminars fuer das Orthodoxe Judenthum pro 5638* (1878); Schuerer, Gesch, 2 (1907^4); I. Jelski, *Die innere Einrichtung des grossen Synedrions zu Jerusalem* (1894); A. Buechler, *Das Synedrion in Jerusalem* (1902); A. Schalit, *Ha-Mishtar ha-Roma'i be-Ereẓ Yisrael* (1937); S. Zeitlin, *Who Crucified Jesus?* (1942); Ch. Tchernowitz, *Toledot ha-Halakhah* (1935–50), especially 4 (1950), 215–61; Alon, Toledot, 2 (1961^2), 38f. and passim; S. Hoenig, *The Great Sanhedrin* (1953); H. Mantel, *Studies in the History of the Sanhedrin* (1961).

[Hugo Mantel]

SANHEDRIN (Heb. סַנְהֶדְרִין), fourth tractate in the Mishnah order of *Nezikin*. The sequence of the tractates within an order being as a rule determined by the size of the tractates, it should be remembered that the three *Bavot* originally constituted one large tractate of 30 chapters, to which *Sanhedrin*, together with *Makkot which was originally united with it, is second in size. *Sanhedrin, in the context of this tractate, means "court of justice," referring to the great *bet din*, which comprised 71 ordained scholars, and the subordinate courts, composed of 23 judges, functioning in various towns. The general term *bet din* usually referred to minor courts of three members. In general, the tractate deals with the composition and power of the courts of different kinds and degrees, with legal procedure and criminal law.

Chapter 1 defines the various courts and their competence: i.e., the "courts of three" with monetary matters; that of 23 with criminal cases which may involve the death penalty; and that of 71 with exceptional cases, like trying a high priest or a whole city accused of idolatry. Chapter 2 deals with the privileges of the high priest and the king in general. Chapter 3 describes the setting up of ad hoc "courts of three," rules concerning the qualification of judges and witnesses, and questions of judicial procedure. Chapter 4 discusses the differences between criminal and civil procedure, and Chapter 5 gives details on the way witnesses were examined. Chapter 6 gives information as to how the death penalty by stoning was carried out, and Chapter 7 enumerates the four modes of execution: stoning, burning, decapitation, and strangulation, but stoning having been discussed in the previous chapter, it proceeds with the details of the three other modes of execution. The subject of stoning is then taken up again, giving the crimes to which this mode of execution applies. Chapter 8 deals with the "stubborn and rebellious son" (Deut. 21:18–21). Chapter 9 discusses the crimes to which the penalties of burning and decapitation are applicable, and goes in detail into the various aspects of the crime of murder, especially the question of intent (premeditation). Some extraordinary modes of punishment are also discussed here. Chapter 10 opens with the well-known statement that "all Israel have a portion in the world to come," implying that even criminals put to death by order of the court will be resurrected at the end of days, but then it goes on to list certain categories of sinners (specific kinds of heretics and idolaters) to whom the comfort of resurrection is denied. Chapter 11 deals with the crimes to which the penalty of strangulation applies, discussing the case of the **zaken mamre* ("rebellious teacher") and the false prophet, in particular. In the Babylonian Talmud this last chapter is placed tenth, while the mishnaic tenth becomes the concluding chapter. The rabbis go to great lengths (90b–92a) to prove that the belief in the resurrection of the dead was rooted in the Torah. There is *Gemara* to both Babylonian and Jerusalem Talmuds. In the Tosefta, this tractate is divided into 14 chapters.

Incorporated in the Mishnah *Sanhedrin* are ancient *halakhot* and even *mishnayot* from the time of the Second Temple. "The king can neither judge nor be judged" (2:4) is an early enactment dating from the time of Alexander *Yannai, and earlier still is the statement, "when [the king] sits in judgment [the Torah scroll] shall be with him" (*ibid*). Mishnah 4:2, which deals with those who married into the priesthood, also belongs to the time when Jerusalem was at the height of its glory, and the whole order of the four capital cases certainly – by its very nature – dates from Temple times. Chapter 9:6 is connected apparently with the *Hasmonean era, and this is most certainly the case with regard to the Mishnah "Kanna'im [zealots] fall upon one who has intercourse with an Aramean woman" (9:6). The well-known Mishnah at the beginning of chapter 10 is anti-Sadducean, and this testifies to its early origin. Naturally the views of *tannaim* of a very much later period were incorporated in the final arrangement of the Mishnah. Recognizable and particularly conspicuous in *Sanhedrin* are additions from the halakhic Midrashim, most of which are from the school of Akiva. Some of them belong to the school of R. Ishmael and were apparently added by R. Simeon b. Yoḥai, since many anonymous *mishnayot* are in accordance with their view. The English translation of the tractate in the Soncino Talmud (1935) is by J. Shachter and H. Freedman.

BIBLIOGRAPHY: Epstein, Tanna'im, 417–21; Ḥ. Albeck, *Shishah Sidrei Mishnah*, 4 (1959), 163–8.

[Arnost Zvi Ehrman]

SANHEDRIN, FRENCH, Jewish assembly of 71 members convened in Paris during February–March 1807, at the request of Napoleon *Bonaparte. The object of this assembly was to convert the "secular" answers given by the Assembly of Jewish *Notables to the questions put to them by the government into doctrinal decisions, which would be binding on the Jews religiously, by drafting them as precepts based on the Bible and *halakhah*. Previously, on Oct. 6, 1806, the Assembly of Jewish Notables sent a manifesto to the Jewish communities in Europe, inviting them – in vague terms – to participate in the activities for "revival" and "freedom" which Napoleon was preparing through the Sanhedrin for the benefit of the Jewish people. The response of European Jewry to this manifesto was exceedingly poor. The Sanhedrin was constituted of two-thirds rabbis and one-third laymen (some of the rabbis and all the laymen had been members of the Assembly of Jewish Notables), all from the French Empire and the "Kingdom of Italy." David *Sinzheim of Strasbourg, one of the eminent halakhic authorities of the day, was appointed president. The nine regulations issued by the Sanhedrin were confirmed in eight solemn and magnificent sessions. The doctrinal preamble to the regulations states that the Jewish religion comprises both religious precepts which are eternal, and political precepts which had no further validity from the time Jewry ceased to be a nation.

The regulations stated that:

(1) polygamy is prohibited among Jews; (2–3) the Jewish bill of divorce or religious marriage has no validity unless it has been preceded by a civil act, and mixed marriages are binding upon Jews civilly (but not religiously); (4–5–6) the Jews of every country must treat its citizens as their own brothers according to the universalist rules of moral conduct, and Jews who have become citizens of a state must regard that country as their fatherland; (7–8–9) Jews must engage in useful professions, and the taking of interest from both Jews and gentiles shall be subject to the laws of the country. At first sight, it would appear that the drafters of the regulations subordinated Jewish law to that of the state, but in reality they did not undermine halakhic principles. It was only in subsequent generations that the declaration of the "separation of the political from the religious in Judaism" became a matter of principle among certain Jewish circles who became assimilated in the modern state.

BIBLIOGRAPHY: D. Tama, *Collection des procès-verbaux et décisions du Grand-Sanhédrin* (Paris, 1807); idem, *Transactions of the Parisian Sanhédrim* (London, 1807); A.-E. Halphen (ed.), *Recueil des lois, décrets et ordonnances concernant les Israélites* (1851), 20–34; R. Anchel, *Napoléon et les Juifs* (1928); F. Pietri, *Napoléon et les Israélites* (1965), 84–115; B. Mevorah (ed.), *Napoleon u-Tekufato* (1968), 77–132.

[Baruch Mevorah]

SANIELEVICI, HENRIC (1875–1951), Romanian literary critic and biologist. Born in Botoşani, Moldavia, Sanielevici pursued two entirely separate careers, one scientific and the other literary. His polemical gifts revealed themselves in the articles which he contributed – some under the pseudonym Hassan – to leading Romanian periodicals and newspapers. He held that literary works contained two types of phenomena: the sociological and the psychological. The former was to be clarified and coordinated on the basis of materialistic principles of history, the latter on what Sanielevici himself termed "differential psychology" and "the psycho-physiology of race." Sanielevici particularly opposed ultra-nationalistic tendencies in Romanian literary circles and from 1903 published critical essays and studies written in a vigorous and uncompromising spirit. The most important were collected in *Incercări critice* (1903), *Cercetări critice și filosofice* (1916), *Studii critice* (1920), and *Alte cercetări critice și filosofice* (1925).

Sanielevici's work as a biologist eventually led him to the issue of race. In *La vie des mammifères et des hommes fossiles déchiffrée à l'aide de l'anatomie* (1926), he examined and compared the organs of mastication and digestion in man and other mammals in order to explain the development of man and the ethnic diversity of mankind. Within a decade he had entered the fight against Nazi racial theories with his two-volume work *In slujba Satanei* ("In the Service of the Devil", 1930–35). Here he rejected the usual criteria of language and nation, and determined race solely according to anthropological type. He also endeavored to establish psychological constants that would explain national characteristics, thus setting forth a new theory of race and racial psychology. Though originally an advocate of Jewish assimilation, Sanielevici greatly modified his views after World War I.

BIBLIOGRAPHY: P.P. Negulescu, in: *Analele Academiei Române*, 2nd. ser., 38 (1915–16); E. Lovinescu, *Critice*, 8 (1923), 117; G. Călinescu, *Istoria literaturii Române…* (c. 1941), 569–70; idem, *Ulysse* (1967), 261–5.

[Dora Litani-Littman]

SAN JOSE, city in California, 40 miles S. of San Francisco, with a Jewish population of 40,000 in 2005. San Jose was the first capital of California (1849–51). Ten men organized the Jewish community of San Jose in 1861 as the Bickur Cholim Society. By 1869 the membership, made up primarily of merchants, was 35 from San Jose and the vicinity. The Jewish population in 1880 was 265. Until 1953 Congregation Bickur Cholim, now Temple Emanu-El (after a fire in 1848), was the only synagogue. Although its ritual was Reform, separate services were conducted on the High Holidays to accommodate the Orthodox members.

Congregation Sinai, today conservative, was organized in 1953, while Conservative Congregation Beth David, Saratoga, began in 1962.

In the early 21st century there were over two dozen Jewish organizations in Santa Clara Valley, 16 being synagogues with their own religious schools. There were an additional four synagogues in Monterey County. Nearby there is also Beth Torah in Fremont (Alameda County) and various synagogues along the Peninsula, from Palo Alto to Burlingame, which have a working relationship with the San Francisco Jewish Federation, as does the Hillel at Stanford University. Hillel of Silicon Valley serves San Jose State and Santa Clara Universities plus Evergreen, Mission, San Jose City, De Anza, Foothill, and West Valley Community Colleges.

In 2005 the Jewish Federation of Silicon Valley (the name changed from Jewish Federation of Greater San Jose in September, 2004) celebrated its 75th anniversary and later moved into the new Gloria and Ken Levy Family Campus on August 1, 2005. This facility houses the Yavneh Day School, Jewish Family Service, the Addison Penzak JCC and the San Jose Federation. Some additional key autonomous organizations include the JCRC, Jewish Education Council, *Jewish Community News*, Jewish Community Preschool, the Jewish Community Chaplain Program, and three cemeteries. Also within the immediate vicinity are Jewish educational institutions from preschool through high school.

The presence of national defense contractors and scientific and engineering firms brought many highly educated Jews to the area beginning in 1950. This process has intensified during the high tech boom, which has influenced Jewish existence in Santa Clara Valley in all aspects of life, and many individuals established their own prosperous firms.

BIBLIOGRAPHY: *Temple Emanu-El Centennial Anniversary 1861–1961* (1961); *Statistics of the Jews of the United States* (1880); *Jewish Federation of Silicon Valley: A Community Celebration of the Federation's 75th Anniversary* (2005)

[Robert E. Levinson / Stephen D. Kinsey (2nd ed.)]

SAN MARINO, tiny independent republic near *Rimini surrounded by Italian territory. Jewish loan-banks appeared there as early as 1369, one of them being managed by a woman. In 1442 some of the bankers were accused of conspiracy against the state, and the duke of Urbino intervened with the "regents" of the republic to prevent the Jews being further molested. The activities of Jewish moneylenders continued until the 17th century. Although in modern times any Jewish connection with San Marino was sporadic, the tiny republic obediently enacted racial laws in 1938, in imitation of Italy, against the dozen Jewish families who had drifted there in recent years; they were repealed on the fall of Mussolini in the summer of 1943. The consul general of Israel in Rome serves in the same capacity also in San Marino.

BIBLIOGRAPHY: Milano, Bibliotheca, index; Bernardi, in: REJ, 48 (1904), 241–64; 49 (1904), 80–97; 50 (1905), 129–35; Lonardo, in: *Atti e memorie della Regia deputazione di storia patria per le Marche*, 2 (1905), 93–115.

[Ariel Toaff]

SAN NICANDRO, small town near Bari, S. Italy. San Nicandro became noteworthy when 23 peasant families there adopted Judaism. About 1930 a winegrower, Danato Manduzio, inspired by a dream, began to preach the truth of the Mosaic law and the necessity of conversion to it. A self-educated man and a tenacious apostle of his new mystical beliefs, he and his followers finally adopted Judaism, despite the threats of the local clergy, the hostility of the Fascist authorities, and the dissuasion of the rabbinate in Rome, which feared that they, too, might suffer from the new anti-Jewish policy of the government. It is probable, however, that contact with members of the Jewish Brigade in the region (in Garagano and Foggia) in the 1940s and Zionist ideas reinforced the movement. The conversion of Manduzio and his followers was formally recognized in 1944. In 1948 Manduzio died. The following year the group moved to Israel where they joined the moshav *Almah in Upper Galilee. Not all of them, however, remained there and the group split up. In 1992 few of the remaining inhabitants were still adhering to Judaism and, according to a visitor to the area, it was mainly the women who continued to celebrate certain Jewish holidays in a private house that served as a synagogue (*tempio*). They tended to interpret biblical commandments rather literally, in a way that may be termed as "karaitization." But although they still observed some *kashrut* laws, they had little contact with rabbinical authorities, did not circumcise their sons, and the men declared they could not refrain from working on the Sabbath. In the early 2000s the group was not recognized as Jewish by rabbinical authorities.

BIBLIOGRAPHY: E. Cassin, *History of a Religious Phenomenon* (1959); P.E. Lapide, *The Prophet of San Nicandro* (1953); J. Ben-David, in: JJSO, 2 (1960), 244–58. **ADD. BIBLIOGRAPHY:** C. Cividalli, "Ritorno a San Nicandro," in: RMI, 39 (1973), 226–36; E. Trevisan Semi, "A Conversion Movement in Italy: Jewish Universalism and Gender in San Nicandro," in: T. Parfitt (ed.), *Judaising Movements. Studies in the Margins of Judaism* (2002), 65–85.

[Giorgio Romano / Nadia Zeldes (2nd ed.)]

SANOK (called **Sonik** by the Jews), town in Rzeszow province, S.E. Poland. From 1772 to 1918 the town was under Austrian rule (central *Galicia). The remains of an ancient Jewish cemetery in the vicinity testify to the existence of a Jewish settlement in the town in the second half of the 14th century, after Sanok had been annexed to Poland by King *Casimir III. The names of some Jewish members appear in a list of the craftsmen's guild of the town in 1514. However, a Jewish community was organized only at the end of the 16th century and was subordinate to that of Lesko. In 1570, 17 of the 200 families residing in the town were Jewish. They earned their living as traders in wine and grain, and as furriers, tailors, and tanners. At the beginning of the 18th century, the Jewish settlement at Sanok grew, receiving privileges from King Augustus II (1720) and King Augustus III (1754). A synagogue was built in the 1720s. There were 467 poll-tax paying Jews in Sanok and its environs in 1765. During the 19th century local trade in lumber, timber, and cloth manufacture was concentrated in Jewish hands. At the end of the 19th century, the Jews of Sanok initiated the development of oil production in the area. From 1868 the representatives of the local Jewish community played an important part in municipal institutions. Under Austrian rule the Jewish population grew quickly: in 1800 it numbered about 1,850 (40% of the total population); in 1880, it numbered 2,129 (42%); and in 1910, 4,073 (38%). Ḥasidism became strong in the community toward the end of the 18th century and, up to the end of the 19th, concentrated around the *kloyzn* of the Ḥasidim of *Belz, Bobob, Nowy Sacz, and *Sadgora. At the beginning of the 20th century, Zionist organizations sprang up. The teacher Ẓevi Abt founded in 1909 a Hebrew school called Safah Berurah which had 77 pupils in 1911. From 1910 to 1914, the weekly *Folksfraynd* was published. In 1921, 4,067 Jews formed 42% of the total population of the town. Between the two world wars the Jews of Sanok occupied key positions in the town economy. From 1919 to 1921, Meir *Shapira served as rabbi of Sanok. Among those born in the town was Benzion *Katz.

[Arthur Cygielman]

Holocaust Period

The number of Jews in Sanok in 1939 was over 5,000. The Germans entered the city on Sept. 8, 1939, and in the first days of the occupation the synagogues were burned. A few hundred Jews were deported to the other side of the San River, which was under Soviet rule. In 1941 the Jews were concentrated in a ghetto, which contained about 8,000 people – including Jews from nearby townlets. There they were subjected to forced labor, including work in the stone quarries of Trepcza. On Sept. 10, 1942, most of the Jews of Sanok were deported to a concentration camp at Zaslaw. Only a few succeeded in escaping. After the Germans concentrated Jews from the entire Sanok area in the Zaslaw camp, 4,000 people were sent to the *Belzec death camp. The sick and aged were shot in the nearby forests. In October 1942 two more transports were sent to Belzec. On Sept. 14, 1942, the Germans announced that those who had escaped would be allowed to return to the ghetto and live there. About 300 Jews returned to the ghetto; they were later executed or transported to concentration camps. A few hundred Sanok Jews survived the Holocaust, most of them having been in the Soviet Union during the war. Some Jews rescued from the Nazis were killed by antisemitic Polish bands.

[Aharon Weiss]

BIBLIOGRAPHY: A. Shravit (ed.), *Sanok, Sefer Zikkaron* (1969); Wroclaw, *Zakład Narodowy imienia Ossolińskich*, 2501/II 9730/II (= CAHJP, ḤM 6664, ḤM 71059); Halpern, Pinkas, index; R. Mahler, *Yidn in Amolikn Poyln in Likht fun Tsifern* (1958), index; idem, *Ha-Haskalah ve-ha-Ḥasidut* (1961), 433–5; B. Wasiutyński, *Ludność żydowska w Polsce w wiekach XIX i XX* (1930), 96, 107, 118, 147; I. Schiper, *Dzieje handlu żydowskiego na ziemiach polskich* (1937), index; N.M. Gelber, *Ha-Tenu'ah ha-Ẓiyyonit be-Galiẓyah 1875–1918* (1958), 201; S. Nobel, in: *YIVO Bleter*, 45 (1965/66); A. Fastnacht, *Zarys dziejów Sanoka* (1958).

SAN REMO CONFERENCE, a conference of the Allies in World War I (Great Britain, France, and Italy), held in San Remo, Italy, in April 1920, which confirmed the pledge contained in the *Balfour Declaration concerning the establishment of a Jewish national home in Palestine. The conference was a continuation of a previous meeting between the Allies held in London in February 1920, where it was decided, among other things, to put Palestine under British Mandatory rule. The British delegation to San Remo was headed by Prime Minister David Lloyd George and Lord Curzon, who had replaced Lord *Balfour as foreign minister in 1919. At both meetings the French expressed many reservations about the inclusion of the Balfour Declaration in the peace treaty, and it was only after the exertion of British pressure that they were gradually persuaded to agree to it. The San Remo Conference was attended by Chaim *Weizmann, Nahum *Sokolow, and Herbert *Samuel, who presented a memorandum to the British delegation on the final settlement in the Eastern Mediterranean region. Lord Balfour was called in for consultations. The article concerning Palestine was debated on April 24, and the next day it was finally resolved to incorporate the Balfour Declaration in Britain's mandate in Palestine. Thus Britain was made responsible "for putting into effect the declaration made on the 8th [sic.] November 1917 by the British Government and adopted by the other Allied Powers, in favor of the establishment in Palestine of a national home for the Jewish people; it being clearly understood that nothing should be done which may prejudice the civil and religious rights of existing non-Jewish communities in Palestine, or the rights and political status enjoyed by Jews in any other country." The resolution was celebrated by mass demonstrations throughout the Jewish world.

BIBLIOGRAPHY: L. Stein, *The Balfour Declaration* (1961), 652–63; C. Weizmann, *Trial and Error* (1949), 321–5; D. Lloyd George, *The Truth About the Peace Conference*, 2 (1938), 1167–75, 1182–90; J. Nevakivi, *Britain, France and the Arab Middle East* (1969), 240–54 and index.

[Getzel Kressel]

SANTA COLOMA DE QUERALT, town in Tarragona province, N.E. Spain. Santa Coloma de Queralt's Jewish community was a typical small community in Catalonia. There were many such small communities which were hardly mentioned in the central archive of the Kingdom of Aragon, the Arxiu de la Corona d'Aragó. The information we have on the Jews of Santa Coloma comes from the most extensive notarial protocols kept today in the Archivi Histórico Provincial de Tarragona. In the 13th century 30 Jewish families were allowed to dwell in Santa Coloma, which was under the jurisdiction of the House of Queralt. Santa Coloma de Queralt was a village of 150 houses in the 14th century. The Jews engaged in agriculture, commerce, and crafts, and at the beginning of their settlement they already owned slaves. The richest Jews, constituting less than 10% of the local Jews, were moneylenders whose activities and transactions are fully recorded. The sources offer interesting details about Jewish life and important information about some of the leading members of the community. The notarial acts contain valuable information on the internal life of the Jews, on marriage contracts, education, social welfare, and communal organization. There were two synagogues, one in Carrer Major, called Scola de Judeus, and the other was the Beth Midrash in Carrer dels Jueus. The Jewish quarter was situated in the area today known as Carrer de los Quarteres. In the Baixada de la Presó, the Jews had their *espital,* which served visitors and poor Jews. In 1328 the Jewish population numbered seven families, while by 1347 there were already 30 Jewish families. At some point in the 14th century the Jewish population reached a maximum of 100 families.

In the 1370s and 1380s a Jewish female physician, *Floreta Ca Noga, was known among the inhabitants of the town. She treated the queen in 1381 and was greatly esteemed by the royal court. In Santa Coloma lived the Jewish poet Astruc Bonafeu. Culturally, the community must have been quite developed. Contracts with private teachers and the impressive library of Solomon Samuel Azcarell are good illustrations. The persecutions of 1391 affected the town, and there were subsequent problems connected with conversions, such as the case of an apostate who appeared before a government official in 1391 and accused his wife of refusing to convert and live with him as a Christian. In the records of the local notary additional cases are noted where Jewish women demanded conversion while the husbands remained faithful to Judaism. According to the records of the notary, the couples were separated by agreement. In spite of all this, the community continued to exist until after the *Tortosa Disputation, and it may have continued until the days of the expulsion.

BIBLIOGRAPHY: J. Segura y Valls, *Historia de la villa de Santa Coloma de Queralt* (1879), 59ff., 82f.; Baer, Urkunden, 1 (1929), index; A. Cardoner Planas, in: *Sefarad*, 9 (1949), 443; F. Cantera, *Sinagogas españolas* (1955), 282ff.; A.J. Soberanas i Lleó, in: *Boletín Arqueológico de Tarragona*, 67–68 (1967–68), 191–204. **ADD. BIBLIOGRAPHY:** Y. Assis, in: *Proceedings of the 8th World Congress of Jewish Studies* (1982), 2:33–38 (Hebrew section); idem, in: Y. Kaplan (ed.), *Jews and Conversos; Studies in Society and the Inquisitiion*, (1985), 21–38; idem, *The Jews of Santa Coloma de Queralt: An Economic and Demographic Study of a community at the End of the Thirteenth Century*, (1988); G. Secall i Güell, *La comunitat hebrea de Santa Coloma de Queralt* (1986).

[Haim Beinart /Yom Tov Assis (2nd ed.)]

SANTA CRUZ, coastal city in Northern California. The county had a population of 240,880 in 2001, including an estimated 6,000 Jews. Louis Schwartz, believed to be the first Jewish settler in Santa Cruz, in 1855 opened a general store with the Brownstone brothers. The Jewish community grew slowly; it initially was comprised of single men, but eventually women came and then families. The first observance of the Jewish New Year, under lay leadership, was in 1869, with meetings in community halls or in churches.

In 1877 Home of Peace Cemetery was consecrated on land that was donated to the Jewish community. Like many Jewish communities, Santa Cruz' Jewish community's first piece of property was a cemetery. A mutual aid society followed, when in 1887 a small group of Jewish families founded a Hebrew Benevolent Society in Santa Cruz. The first known synagogue building was acquired in the early 1930s. In 1954, the still small Jewish community built a modest synagogue on Bay Street, which was named Temple Beth El, incorporated as the Jewish Community Center of Santa Cruz, California, Inc. Rabbi Richard Litvak became the first full-time rabbi of Temple Beth El in 1977. The Temple moved to new facilities in Aptos in 1990.

In the last third of the 20th century and beyond, the Jewish community of Santa Cruz was directly linked to the University of California Santa Cruz with its many Jewish students and faculty. UC Santa Cruz boasts the largest percentage of Jewish students at any Northern California campus (approximately 20% of 15,000 students are Jews: 2,600 undergrads and 250 graduate students). UC Santa Cruz has a Jewish Studies program and a Jewish Studies Research Unit. Among its faculty is Murray Baumgarten, the editor of *Judaism*.

Active in Santa Cruz are three Jewish congregations and a Havurah. Temple Beth El is the oldest and remains a Reform Congregation. Chabad by the Sea is the Orthodox congregation. Congregation Kol Tefilah is Conservative and Hadesh Yamenu is the Havurah grouping.

The Hillel serves some 4,000 Jewish college students in the region, including UC Santa Cruz, Cabrillo College, and CSU Monterey Bay.

Social Justice is a local Jewish focus, much in keeping with the ethos of the university and the community. "Out in Our Faith" is a gay and lesbian, bi-sexual, and transvestite group. There is a local chapter of the Tikkun Community, COEJL: Coalition on the Environment and Jewish Life, Eco-Jew, and Mazon chapter.

The Jewish community of Santa Cruz sponsors an annual Jewish film festival and has published *The Santa Cruz Haggadah*.

[Michael Bernbaum (2nd ed.)]

SANTA FE, the first and one of the most important provinces in *Argentina, opened for the agricultural settlement of immigrants; capital city of the province.

The Province

Jewish population above five years of age, according to the 1960 census, was 14,152 out of a total of 1,865,537. In 2005 it was estimated by the Va'ad ha-Kehilot (see *Argentina) at 2,400 families. Jewish agricultural settlement started in Santa Fe province around the towns of Vieja Monigotes and Moisésville in 1888 and 1889, respectively. Land owned in Santa Fe by the Jewish Colonization Association (ICA) included more than 147,000 hectares, mainly concentrated in Moisésville and the Montefiore colony near Ceres. Today the remaining Jewish settlers in Santa Fe deal more in cattle than in agriculture.

The disintegration of agricultural settlements brought about the creation of Jewish communities in many towns and villages in the province. A survey conducted in 1943 by ICA found 21,833 Jews in the province, of whom only 2,956 lived on the agricultural settlements; 17,422 lived in 11 cities and towns; and another 1,455 lived in 112 villages and hamlets. In the following years, because of increased migration from rural to urban areas, there was a sharp decline in the number of areas with Jewish population, as well as in the number of Jews in the rural areas generally. In 1964, 12 cities and towns had organized Jewish communities affiliated with the Va'ad ha-Kehillot, the principal ones being *Rosario (in 2005 with some 1,600 families), Rafaela, Moisésville, Ceres, Palacios, San Cristóbal, and the capital city, Santa Fe.

The City

The first Jews to reach the city of Santa Fe were immigrants who arrived from Eastern Europe and Morocco in 1888–89. The first communal organization was the Sociedad Israelita Latina del Cementerio, established by Moroccan Jews in 1895. The Ashkenazi Sociedad Unión Israelita de Socorros was founded in 1906. In 1909 there were 547 Jews in the city, most of whom were small businessmen and laborers. By 1943 the Jewish community had increased to an estimated 4,000, of whom 3,600 were Ashkenazim and the rest Sephardim from Morocco, Turkey, and Syria. At that time the Ashkenazim maintained their own *ḥevra kaddisha* which constituted the central communal institution, and over whose control a conflict ensued between the Zionist Sociedad Unión Israelita Sionista and the "progressive" (pro-Communist) Sociedad Cultural I.L. Peretz. Both groups, however, were subsidized by the *ḥevra kaddisha*, conducted separate cultural activities, and maintained their own schools. In later years, the *ḥevra kaddisha* became the Comunidad Israelita, with a membership of 742 families in 1969 that declined to 600 in 2005. In June 2005 the Comunidad Israelita, within the framework of the commemoration of its centenary, inaugurated a Jewish museum – Museo Judío de Santa Fe "*Hinenu*." The community life of the Sephardim continued to center on the common cemetery. Despite the fact that the Sephardim had formed separate synagogues according to countries of origin, in the 1950s, they established a common congregation, Sociedad Hebrea Sefaradí de Socorros Mutuos.

In addition to several welfare and women's organizations, three important financial bodies were established in Santa Fe: two credit cooperatives and a commercial cooperative founded by peddlers. In 1970 the Jewish institutions in Santa Fe comprised two Ashkenazi synagogues – one of them Conservative, one Sephardi synagogue, a *shoḥet*, a *mikveh*, the Club Israelita Macabi, and three Jewish credit institutions. The Ḥ.N. Bialik Jewish kindergarten and day school had in the 1970s an enrollment of 144 pupils. In the early 21st century there was also a Zionist youth movement, Macabi Ẓa'ir, connected with He-Ḥalutz la-Merḥav. The city's branch of *DAIA is the umbrella organization for all groups except the pro-Communists.

[Daniel Benito Rubinstein Novick]

SANTANGEL, LUIS DE (d. 1498), comptroller-general (*Escribano de Ración*) to Ferdinand and Isabella of Spain. Born in Valencia, he was a descendant of a noble Converso family, the Chinillos of Calatayud. One of its members, Azarias Chinillo, became converted to Christianity at the time of the disputation of *Tortosa and adopted the name Luis de Santangel. This Santangel, the protégé of the Catholic monarchs, was the grandson of the first Luis de Santangel, after whom he was named. He began his career as a courtier, and served as a tax collector of the Royal Treasury, until in 1481 he was appointed comptroller-general, a position which he held until his death. He was succeeded by his brother JAIME and his son FERNANDO. In 1486 he became acquainted with Christopher *Columbus and was greatly impressed by his projects. Santangel's influence with the Catholic monarchs was decisive in gaining their acceptance of Columbus' proposals. He lent 1,140,000 maravedis to finance the historic voyage which resulted in the discovery of the American continent. In recognition of this assistance, Columbus wrote his first letter on his impressions of the voyage to Santangel. Written on Feb. 18, 1493, it contains interesting descriptions of his findings. Santangel also used his influence at court to help Conversos caught in the meshes of the Inquisition. He assisted the Jews expelled from Spain in 1492 by contributing toward the hire of vessels to enable them to leave the country. He should not be confused with another Luis de Santangel, a member of the same family, who was accused of complicity in the assassination of the inquisitor Pedro de Arbués, and was burned at the stake.

BIBLIOGRAPHY: Baer, Spain, 2 (1966), index; M. Serrano y Sanz, *Orígenes de la dominación española en América* (1918), 97ff.; M. Ballesteros-Gaibrois, *Valencia y los reyes católicos* (1943), index; F. Cabezudo Astrain, in: *Sefarad*, 23 (1963), 265ff.; Suarez Fernandez, Documentos, 434–5. **ADD. BIBLIOGRAPHY:** J. Manzano Manzano, *Cristóbal colón: siete años decisivos de su vida, 1485–1492* (1989[2]), 363–81; 443–52; J. Ventura Subirats, in: *XIII Congrés d'histo'ria de la Corona d'Aragó*, vol. 4 (1990), 47–58.

SANTARÉM, city in central Portugal. An important Jewish community in the Middle Ages, Santarém was the rabbinical seat for the district of Estremadura. On his capture of the city in 1140, Affonso Henriques, the first king of Portugal, is said to have found a Jewish community and a synagogue there. The charter of Santarém and *Beja conferred by Affonso Henriques contained legislation against the Jews, stipulating among other things that, in litigation between Jews and Christians, only Christian witnesses would be accepted, and that Christians would not be accountable for offenses against Jews. Various Cortes held in Santarém issued discriminatory decrees against the Jews, that of 1461 decreeing that Jews should not wear silk, and of 1468 ordering all Jews to wear an identifying badge and to live within the Jewish quarter. Late in 1490, or early in 1491, the Jews of Santarém fulsomely greeted the Spanish princess, eldest daughter of Queen Isabella, who had been betrothed to the Portuguese prince Affonso, and regaled her with gifts as she stopped in Santarém on the way from Évora. After the forced conversion of 1497, a substantial community of New *Christians lived in Santarém, suffering grievously from the devastating earthquake of Jan. 26, 1531, and its aftermath. Fanatical monks seized on the disaster to denounce the New Christians and their friends, calling the earthquake a divine punishment for the toleration of the New Christians. New Christians were attacked and expelled from their homes, and many were compelled to seek refuge in the mountains. The distinguished dramatist Gil Vicente took up the cudgels on their behalf, and his passionate pleas for sanity and moderation restored calm. There were further disorders against the New Christians of Santarém in 1630.

BIBLIOGRAPHY: M. Kayserling, *Geschichte der Juden in Portugal* (1867), 2, 13, 52, 64, 98, 180; J Mendes dos Remedios, *Os judeus em Portugal* (1895), passim.

[Martin A. Cohen]

SANTOB DE CARRIÓN (Shem Tov ben Isaac Ardutiel; 13th–14th century), Hebrew and Spanish poet. Nothing is known of his life, except that he lived in Carrión de los Condes. Samuel *Ibn Sasson, who lived in the same town, exchanged some poems with him between 1330 and 1340, although only those sent by Ibn Sasson are preserved. By that time, Santob was already "famous in the kingdom of Spain." Santob was no longer young when he dedicated to Pedro I of Castile his *Proverbios morales* (known also as the *Consejos y documentos al rey don Pedro*), a series of poems on ethical and intellectual virtues and defects. The work itself was probably written between 1355 and 1360. This exists in five 15th-century manuscripts, one an *aljamiado* text (i.e., Spanish written in Hebrew characters), and another copy of one of them. Modern editions include 725 stanzas. The philosophical ideas in this first example of gnomic literature in Castilian are not highly original – the sources were probably Hebrew and Arabic ethical poetry – but the expression is concise and poetic. Its main themes are the golden mean in human conduct and the relativity of existence in this world. A thread of melancholic pessimism runs through the work, but it does not negate the didactic and moral elevation of the verses. Américo Castro described him as the first one who expressed in the Spanish language the bitterness of someone who considers himself worthy, even if society does not recognize him as such. He presented him as a "refined rationalist," a "good islamicized Hispano-Hebrew." With a completely different perspective, C. Sánchez Albornoz saw in Santob a model of a perfectly Castilianized Jew.

Some of the passages of the book are among the most quoted ones in Spanish literature, such as the comparison of the proverbs written by a Jewish author with the rose born on the thornbush. Taking as a literary model the wisdom sayings of the Book of Proverbs, he addresses a moral message to his contemporaries, including traditional ideas and his own perspective. Santob gives a picture of the Jews of the epoch as "loyal to the law of the land, supportive of universalistic ethical and religious codes, actively engaged in commerce, skeptical of the world and perhaps increasingly of their own social ambience, and, in coded messages, longing for final deliverance" (Perry).

The *Proverbios* enjoyed considerable popularity, both in Jewish and Christian circles. Its maxims were quoted by the kabbalist Abraham ibn Saba and by the Marquis of Santillana, who numbered Santob among the great "trovadores" of his country. *Proverbios Morales* was published several times, and a critical edition from a manuscript in the Hebrew characters of the 15th century was published by Ig. Gonzalez Llubera (1947); other, more recent editions are that of A. García Calvo (1974), S. Shepard (1986) T.A. Perry (1986) and P. Díaz-Mas and C. Mota (1998). The work has been the object of many commentaries and very different interpretations (Zemke, 1997, mentions more than 160 studies). Though other Jewish poets in Spain wrote poetry in Spanish, Santob de Carrión is the only one whose Spanish verses have survived. Although other Spanish works, such as the *Danza de la Muerte*, have been attributed to Santob, there is no basis for such attribution. The fact that a Jew wrote in Spanish was not seen with sympathy in the Jewish communities; Ibn Sasson recommended to Santob to abandon "their language" and to write in Hebrew, "the pure language, close to you."

Santob's Hebrew writings include a liturgical poem (the *viddui gadol* "*Ribbono shel olam, bi-re'oti beḥurotai*") which has been incorporated into the Sephardi ritual for the Day of Atonement. His *bakkashah*, "*Yam Kohelet*," consists of 2,000 words, each beginning with the letter *mem*; it has not yet been conveniently published. Four *pizmonim* have also been attributed to him. His rhymed narrative (*maqāma*-like) called *Milḥemet ha-Et ve-ha-Misparayim* ("The Struggle between the Pen and the Scissors," 1345), contains a debate on the importance of pen and scissors as instruments of writing (*Divrei Ḥakhamim* (Metz, 1649), 47a). A critical edition of this rhymed prose was published by Y. Nini and M. Fruchtman (1980). Santob also translated the poetic composition of Israel ha-Israeli, a disciple of Asher b. Jehiel, from Arabic into Hebrew, under the title *Mitzvot Zemanniyyot*, and wrote an extensive introduction. This work, probably written in Soria, is still in manuscript.

BIBLIOGRAPHY: Y. Baer, *MinḤah le-David* (1935), 200; Baer, Spain, 1 (1966), 358, 447; A. Castro, *España en su historia* (1948), 561–81; Davidson, *Oẓar*, 4 (1933), 476; Gonzalez Llubera, in: *Hispanic Review*, 8 (1940), 113–24; Schirmann, Sefarad, 2 (1956), 529–40;

L. Stein, *Untersuchung ueber die Proverbios morales von Santob de Carrion* (1900). **ADD. BIBLIOGRAPHY:** A. García Calvo, *Glosas de sabiduría o Proverbios morales y otras rimas* (1974); idem, in: *Raíces hebreas en Extremadura* (1996), 419–34; S. Shepard, *Shem Tov, His World and His Words* (1978); idem, *Proverbios morales* (1986); C. Colahan, in: Sefarad, 39:1 (1979), 87–107; 39:2, 265–308; Y. Nini and M. Fruchtman, *Ma'aseh ha-Rav (Milḥemet ha-Et ve-ha-Misparayim)* (1980); T.A. Perry, *Santob de Carrión, Proverbios morales* (1986); idem, *The Moral Proverbs of Santob de Carrión: Jewish Wisdom in Christian Spain* (1987); J. Zemke, in: *La Corónica*, 17:1 (1988), 76–89; idem, *Critical Approaches to the "Proverbios morales" of Shem Tov de Carrión: An Annotated Bibliography* (1997); S. Einbinder, in: HUCA, 65 (1994), 261–76; Schirmann-Fleischer, *The History of Hebrew Poetry in Christian Spain and Southern France* (Hebrew; 1997), 562–69; Sem Tob de Carrión, *Proverbios morales*, P. Díaz-Mas and C. Mota (eds.) (1998); M. Raden, in: *Hispanófila*, 135 (2002), 1–17.

[Kenneth R. Scholberg and Abraham Meir Habermann / Angel Sáenz-Badillos (2nd ed.)]

SANŪʿ, YAʿQUB OR JAMES (known as **Abu Nazzara**; 1839–1912), Egyptian playwright; one of the first authors of plays in spoken Arabic, and one of the creators of satiric journalism in modern *Egypt. He was born in Egypt and studied in Leghorn. He then returned to Egypt and earned his livelihood by giving private lessons. He began to write as a result of his interest in politics, a rare phenomenon among Egyptian Jews of that time. Sanūʿ joined the ranks of a small group which was to be the nucleus of the Egyptian nationalist movement, and from 1858 began to write articles and, later, mordant plays against the government. For several years he presented plays in spoken Arabic, until this was prohibited in 1872. Thereafter he concentrated his literary and political efforts on publishing newspapers, of which he was printing editor and (from 1876) owner. In these, he mocked the khedive Ismāʿīl and incited his readers against his rule. In 1878 he was compelled to leave Egypt. He continued his journalistic activities in Paris and his periodicals were smuggled into Egypt, each time under a different title. After 1882 he directed his attacks against the British, who had occupied Egypt, and tried to enlist support against them in *France and *Turkey. His failure in this project was the cause of his retirement from political activity a few years before his death.

BIBLIOGRAPHY: Landau, in: JJS, 3 (1952), 30–44; 5 (1954), 179–80; I.L. Gendzier, in: MEJ, 15 (1961), 16–28; idem, *Practical Visions of Yaʿqub Sanuʿ* (1966); J.M. Landau, *Jews in Nineteenth-Century Egypt* (1969). **ADD BIBLIOGRAPHY:** J.M. Landau, *Studies in the Arab Theater and Cinema* (1958), 65–67; Sh. Moreh, "Yaʿqūb Ṣanū..." in: Sh. Shamir (ed.), *The Jews of Egypt: A Mediterranean Society...* (1987), 111–29.

[Jacob M. Landau]

SÃO PAULO, the richest and most populated state in the United States of Brazil. Area: 248,209.426 km^2; population (2000): 37,032,403; state capital: São Paulo, the largest and most important city in Brazil, population (2000): 10,434,252. The Jewish population in the state in 2005 was estimated at 45,000, out of which 42,000 lived in the city of São Paulo and 3,000 in various towns in the hinterland of the state. Besides the capital, small Jewish communities are to be found in the following towns: Santos, Campinas, Santo Andre, São Caetano, and very small communities in Ribeirão Preto, Piracicaba, Taubaté, São Carlos, Sorocaba, and São José dos Campos.

The presence of Portuguese New Christians began with the colonization of Brazil, then inhabited by many groups of indigenous peoples. The city of São Paulo was founded in 1554 by Jesuit Catholic colonists. In the colonial period (1500–1822), thousands of New Christian Portuguese came to Brazil. During this period, there was a percentage of New Christians among the inhabitants of the southern "capitanias" (regions under Portuguese governors) and some rose to positions of local influence. Until the proclamation of independence in Brazil, in 1822, Catholicism was the official religion and there was no freedom regarding the practice of other religions.

Two years after Brazil declared its independence from Portugal (1822) it adopted its first constitution. Roman Catholicism remained the state religion, but the constitution proclaimed some tolerance of other religions. When Brazil became a republic (1889), the new constitution (1891) abolished all remnants of religious discrimination and ensured the civil rights of all citizens.

The city of São Paulo began its urban development in the 1860s due to the expansion of coffee plantations and immigration from Europe. Especially after the abolition of slavery (1888), until the 1940s, São Paulo City and the State welcomed a large influx of immigrants from several countries, a total of over 3,000,000 mainly from Italy, Japan, Spain, Portugal, Lebanon, and Syria, who came to work in coffee plantations. São Paulo has since then been an open city that has welcomed immigrants and foreigners, integrating them and assuming traits of each new culture. São Paulo also received Brazilian migrants from all over the country. The cultural and ethnic diversity is present in the history and identity of the city.

Contemporary Jewish presence in São Paulo started in the last quarter of the 19th century, when Jewish immigrants arrived from both Eastern and Central Europe, mainly from the Alsace-Lorraine region. It was not an organized and systematic immigration flow, but one which occurred rather on an individual basis. These first immigrants did not create a Jewish community.

It was only during World War I that a Jewish community began to be organized in the city of São Paulo, initially consisting of immigrants from Eastern Europe (most of them from Russia, Poland, Lithuania, Romania/Bessarabia, and Hungary). Restrictions on immigration to the U.S. and Canada in the 1920s made Brazil a feasible and interesting destination for East European Jewish immigrants. As a new metropolis, in the 1920s São Paulo attracted immigrants, offering freedom of religion and community association, economic, industrial, and commercial opportunities, as well as proper conditions for settlement and social betterment. São Paulo's urbanization and economic expansion rates had a decisive impact on the integration and upward social mobility of significant numbers of immigrants. The city's population grew from 240,000 in 1890 to 580,000 in 1920, reaching approximately 2,000,000 in 1954.

By the 1920s, the Jews in São Paulo had already organized a complete network of institutions, such as schools, welfare entities, synagogues, a cemetery, a burial society, credit cooperatives, political movements, press, and social and sports clubs, which molded a dynamic and well-integrated Jewish-Brazilian community supported by organizations such as JCA, HIAS, and HICEM.

The first organizations to be founded were the Kahal Israel Synagogue (1912); Sociedade Beneficente das Damas Israelitas (Froien Farein, 1915); Sociedade Beneficente Amigos dos Pobres Ezra (1916); the Zionist movement Ahavat Zion (1916); the Knesset Israel Synagogue (1916); Gymnasio Hebraico-Brasileiro Renascença – the first Jewish-Brazilian school to teach the official curricula in São Paulo (1922); the Sociedade Cemitério (1923); the burial association Chevra Kadisha (1924); Macabi (1927); Sociedade Cooperativa de Crédito Popular do Bom Retiro (1928); Policlínica Linath Hatzedek (1929); B'nai Brith (1931); and Ginásio Talmud Torá (1932). A small *talmud torah*, inaugurated in 1916, functioned as a *ḥeder*, but was only open for a short period of time.

Sephardi immigration from Lebanon, Syria, and cities in Ereẓ Israel took place in the 1920s. The Sephardim organized the Comunidade Israelita Sefaradi (1924) and founded three synagogues, Comunidade Sefardim de São Paulo (1929, later known as Sinagoga Israelita Brasileira do Rito Português and Sinagoga da Rua da Abolição) and two in the working class neighborhood of Mooca, in São Paulo – Sinagoga Israelita Brasileira (1930), linked to Jews originating from Sidon, and Sinagoga da União Israelita Paulista (1935).

After 1933, a growing number of immigrants arrived in São Paulo from Germany (and later on from Italy). In 1936 they founded the Congregação Israelita Paulista (CIP), Lar das Crianças (Children's Home), and the scouting movement Avanhandava. CIP consisted of 2,000 member families, and became the largest Jewish center in town.

In the hinterland of the State of São Paulo, small communities were formed in several townships, such as São Caetano, Santo André, São José dos Campos, Mogi das Cruzes, Sorocaba, Jundiaí, Campinas, Ribeirão Preto, and Franca, particularly following the railroad trade routes that served the export of coffee, the main State and Brazilian export product up to the 1920s. In Santos, the harbor where immigrants disembarked, an important Jewish community also flourished.

The main neighborhood of the Jewish minority in São Paulo was the district of Bom Retiro, next to the "Luz" Railroad Station, terminal of the trains coming from Santos, and main route of the export coffee cargoes going to the Santos port. Jewish immigrants used to call Bom Retiro a "little shtetl" and economic activities were basically trade and clothing manufacturing, initially as *clientelchik* (peddlers), and later on as merchants, small manufacturers, and industrialists.

In the 1940s there were Jewish nuclei in several neighborhoods besides Bom Retiro, such as Bras, Cambuci, Lapa, Mooca, and Pinheiros, and each one of them supported a school, a synagogue, and a community center.

In 1915 the Sociedade Beneficente das Damas Israelitas was founded in São Paulo. From then on, women have organized and directed diverse organizations, thus creating a tradition of engagement in Jewish public life. Women were very active in social institutions and also created Lar das Crianças das Damas Israelitas (1939) and Organização Feminina de Assistência Social (Ofidas, 1940). Zionist women's organizations were founded, such as WIZO (1926) and Naamat Pioneiras (1948). As a matter of fact, many women assumed the direction of community organizations, including Federação Israelita do Estado de São Paulo in the 1990s.

In 1940, according to official numbers, the number of Jews in the State of São Paulo reached 20,379 and in 1950 the number was 26,443. In 1941 the Asylo dos Velhos (Old Age Home) was founded, later on called Lar Golda Meir, which currently bears the name Residencial Israelita Albert Einstein – Lar Golda Meir. Between 1936 and 1966, the Sanatório Ezra – Ezra Hospital for Tuberculosis operated in São José dos Campos with 120 beds, also assisting non-Jews. In 1959 the Centro Israelita de Assistência ao Menor (Ciam) for handicapped children was established. In São Paulo, Jewish female prostitutes (exploited from the late 19th century by the Tzvi Migdal women trafficking network, centered in Buenos Aires), founded the Sociedade Feminina Religiosa e Beneficente Israelita (1924–1968, in São Paulo). There were two specific cemeteries where the prostitutes were buried, in São Paulo and in the town of Cubatão, near Santos. The graves of the São Paulo cemetery, which was located in the Santana neighborhood, are now at the Butantã cemetery, one of the three Jewish cemeteries run by Chevra Kadisha. The Cubatão cemetery is preserved next to the city's municipal cemetery. This chapter in its history carries a strong taboo among the members of the community, although it has been the subject of some literary and history works.

In the 1930s, having settled in a few cities and owing to their economic, social, and cultural public activities, the Jews became one of the "most visible" groups of immigrants, in the words of the historian Jeffrey H. Lesser. Thus, they came to be the object of local, national, and international gambling, "pawns of the powerful," especially during the Vargas regime in Brazil, when a "Jewish question" was raised in the country.

Under the Getulio Vargas regime (1930–1945), the semi-fascist Estado-Novo (1937–1945), and during World War II, immigration restrictions (after 1937) and the activities of Ação Integralista Brasileira (a fascist party that existed from 1933 to 1938) generated an environment of nationalism and xenophobia.

Thousands of immigrants from Nazi-dominated Europe were barred, but, nevertheless, Jewish immigration continued individually by a variety of means, mainly through case by case negotiations, but never organized through charitable national or international organizations.

Despite the dictatorship and the climate of nationalistic xenophobia, the Jewish organizations adjusted to the nationalist legislation and learned how to confront the restrictions (against all immigrants, not specifically antisemitic), thus allowing them to continue operating. The schools continued to teach Hebrew and Jewish culture, the synagogues maintained their religious services, radio programs played Jewish music, and innumerable organizations were established during this period, resulting in a very fertile period for the organizations and the unity of the Jewish community. The German Jews became most alarmed, especially after Brazil broke relations with Germany and Italy in August 1942, but their organizations went on as usual during the war years.

There are no records of any coercive closure of Jewish organizations in São Paulo, then the biggest Jewish community in the country, during the Estado-Novo regime and especially in the war years. The antisemitism present in governmental and intellectual circles, among diplomats and the elite, did not result in violent actions against the Jews living in São Paulo in particular or Brazil in general, or against those who managed to breach the immigration barriers. In São Paulo the community took part in campaigns in support of the war effort by Brazil, which followed a policy of alignment with the United States and the Allies. This included the sending of the Força Expedicionária Brasileira (FEB), with 30,000 soldiers, who fought in Italy in 1944 and 1945. With the restriction on imports and the naval blockade, there was important industrial and technical development in the great urban centers to supply goods which had previously been imported. This created new work opportunities for the inhabitants of the cities, among them the Jewish immigrants who had technical, commercial, and industrial abilities.

In the 1940s, intense debates about Zionism took place in São Paulo, particularly about the unified campaigns that led to the foundation of the Zionist-oriented Federação Israelita do Estado de São Paulo. Sectors of German Jews, organized within the CIP, did not initially join the Federation. Some very active Zionist youth movements were founded, such as Ha-Shomer ha-Ẓa'ir, Gordonia, Iḥud, Dror, Bnei Akiva, Netzach, Betar, scouting Avanhandava and, in the 1960s, Chazit Hanoar. Although with fewer members and a somewhat weaker ideological stand and Zionist pioneer goal, some of these organizations are still active in the early 21st century.

Leftist Jews were organized from the 1920s, when they ran a small school linked to the Bund. In 1954 the Instituto Cultural Israelita Brasileiro (known as "Casa do Povo") was founded. Together with the Teatro de Arte Israelita Brasileiro (Taib) and Scholem Aleichem school, these organizations represented the left-wing Jews, many of them involved in the Communist Party. They gave public voice to Yiddish culture and language and managed an active press.

Until the 1950s, more than 13 synagogues and six schools were founded. The schools reflected the Jewish diversity in São Paulo, both regarding religion and politics. Renascença, H.N. Bialik, and I.L. Peretz were Hebraist and Zionists; Scholem Aleichem was Yiddishist and leftist, and Talmud Torá and Beit Chinuch were orthodox. As of the 1950s and 1960s, Yiddish, which had so far been the language of the Jewish minority, was replaced by Hebrew as the main language taught in schools.

In the early 21st century the Jews of São Paulo were politically represented by the Federação Israelita do Estado de São Paulo, founded in 1946 to coordinate efforts to assist postwar Jewish immigration. After World War II, a few thousand families from the Displaced Persons' camps in Germany, and, in the 1950s, Jews from Egypt, Hungary, and Israel, settled in São Paulo, the last significant Jewish immigration to it.

In 1954, the Associação Brasileira A Hebraica was founded. With some 25,000 members, it became one of the most important sports and recreational clubs in São Paulo, and is the largest Jewish organization in Brazil. As of 1964 São Paulo was the seat of the Confederação Israelita do Brasil (Conib), founded in 1948 in Rio de Janeiro as the representative umbrella organization of the Jewish communities. The most accurate demographic and sociological survey of the Jews in São Paulo was carried out by the Federação Israelita de São Paulo in 1970 and published by the sociologist Henrique Rattner. In 1971, the Hospital Israelita Albert Einstein opened; it is regarded as one of the best private hospitals in Latin America.

In the 1969 census of the Jewish community, 28,498 people were counted in 9,086 families, with an average of 3.2 persons per family. Since the number of Jewish families is larger than that covered in the census and is about 14,000 families, the number of Jews in the capital, São Paulo, was approximately 45,000 in 1969.

In 1976, the União Brasileiro-Israelita do Bem-Estar Social – Unibes was founded, becoming the largest and most important Jewish welfare organization in São Paulo. Through several health insurance and other programs, it serves hundreds of persons within the Jewish community and the population in general.

In the Early 21st Century

Although it makes up less than 0.01 percent of the total population of the city, the Jewish community has a solid institutional network, a diverse and dynamic Jewish life, and the Jews play an important role in many different fields and activities, including the economy, the culture, the professions, the arts, and intellectual and cultural life, thus forming a minority whose participation and visibility in the city's daily life very much surpasses its minuscule percentage of population. Their integration in public life is demonstrated by the presence of Jews in the city and state governments as well as in NGO's, universities and cultural and educational institutions, public services, courts of law, etc. In the 2003 municipal elections, the Jewish community did not vote together to elect a single Jewish city counselor, despite the various Jewish candidates belonging to several political parties.

In a number of cities of the State of São Paulo – Santos, Santo André, São Caetano and Campinas – there are synagogues and Jewish activities. But the Jewish life in the small towns of São Paulo State is declining, without any regular Jewish school.

All in all, there are approximately 100 organizations; 68 of them affiliated with the Federação Israelita do Estado de São Paulo. The Jewish community in São Paulo is organized around a well-structured institutional and community life, with the A Hebraica club, synagogues, and schools as social nuclei. Some events, such as the Festival de Cinema Judaico and the Festival Carmel of Jewish Folkloric Dance, are important cultural activities taking place in the city.

In the city there are four Jewish restaurants and many shops carrying food and religious products in the neighborhoods of Higienópolis and Bom Retiro, the nucleus of the community, although the Jewish population lives in many parts of the city. Since the 1960s, Sephardi Jews have also come to live in the neighborhood of Higienópolis and founded three new Sephardi synagogues. Currently, the Bom Retiro district has become a Korean immigrant commercial center that in many cases replaced Jewish businesses.

In spite of sporadic slogans painted on walls, occasional declarations or articles in small publications, and antisemitic and Nazi sites and some rare anti-Jewish publications, generally linked to anti-Israeli political campaigns, there are no antisemitic activities that distress or alter the routine of the Jewish community in São Paulo. Although there is strong concern regarding the security of the institutions of the community, especially following the terrorist attacks in Argentina against the Israeli Embassy (1992) and AMIA (1994), Jewish life in São Paulo is entirely free and public. Governmental authorities as well as the Federação Israelita, and organizations such as the B'nai B'rith, have always kept a vigilant attitude.

In São Paulo there is an active Christian-Jewish dialog involving important authorities of both the Catholic and Protestant churches. CIP's Rabbi Henry I. Sobel was an active participant in this dialogue as well as in ecumenical religious and political events, where various religious groups also participate and which have domestic and international resonance. He was also very active in the defense of human rights (even under the Brazilian military dictatorship that ruled the country from 1964 to 1979), thus becoming the most active and renowned Jewish representative both in the city and the nation as a whole.

During the 1990s, due to the sluggish economy, some strata of the Jewish middle class suffered partial impoverishment, which made it necessary to enhance the social assistance services. Unibes, Lar das Crianças ad CIP, Ciam, Ten Yard, Department de Voluntaries do Hospital Israelita Albert Einstein, Oficina Abrigada de Trabalho (OAT), Federação Israelita, plus a series of small initiatives, have assisted the Jewish community and concluded a series of agreements with the São Paulo city and state governments to assist the poor population of the city. The Jewish organizations are regarded as a paradigm of management and assistance, and have been awarded several renowned prizes in Brazil.

In 2004, there were in São Paulo 20 regular Jewish schools, including kindergartens, with approximately 4,000 students. However, the number of students in the Jewish schools has been declining.

There are 30 synagogues in the city, including liberal CIP and Comunidade Shalom, which had the first female Brazilian rabbi. The Beit Chabad movement has grown considerably and Bnei Akiva runs a synagogue.

São Paulo is home to significant publishing activity, the largest publisher being Editora Perspectiva, founded by Jaco Guinsburg, the most important Brazilian translator and publisher of Jewish classic texts and Yiddish and Hebrew literature. Also of note are the publishers Sefer and Mayanot. Moreover, there is in the city a Jewish bookstore, Sefer.

The experience of Jewish immigration to São Paulo has been described in the pages of authors such as Samuel Rawet, J. Guinsburg, Eliezer Levin, Alberto Mograbi, and Meir Kucinsky (who wrote in Yiddish, and was published in Israel and translated into Portuguese).

Within the University of São Paulo there is a graduate course on Hebrew Language and Culture as well as a Jewish Study Center, which offers master's degree and doctoral programs, plus free courses on Jewish and Yiddish cultures. Other universities in the city and the state, such as Universidade Estadual de Campinas, Pontifícia Universidade Católica, and Universidade Presbiteriana Mackenzie, also offer courses on Hebrew and Jewish culture.

The Arquivo Histórico Judaico Brasileiro, founded in 1976, gathers and centralizes documents on Jewish immigration to the city and the nation and functions as an important center for the preservation and dissemination of Jewish memories and history, maintaining the most significant Jewish library in the country, including a Yiddish section.

With no direct link to the Jewish community, the Lasar Segall Museum, sponsored by the Instituto do Patrimônio Histórico e Artístico Nacional (Iphan), hosts the collection of the artist Lasar *Segall, an exponent of Modernism in the arts.

The Jewish communications media include a series of magazines, journals, and bulletins, geared internally to the Jewish community. There are also three TV programs, the oldest and most important being Mosaico, considered the oldest Brazilian TV program in general (not specifically Jewish). Formerly, the Jewish community published a significant number of publications, such as *Crônica Israelita*, *Revista Brasil-Israel*, *Resenha Judaica*, *Encontro*, the *Shalom* magazine plus Yiddish publications. The Jewish press is declining and covers at most social activities.

Local organizations include the Organização Sionista Unificada, the Casa de Cultura de Israel, Centro de Cultura Judaica, Associação Janusz Korczak do Brasil, three different Yiddish language clubs, Fundo Comunitário, Keren Kayemet Leisrael, Sherith Hapleitá (Holocaust survivors Association), and Câmara Brasil-Israel de Comércio e Indústria. In 2004 the Consulate General of Israel was closed in São Paulo, although Israel is a central reference point for the self-identity of Jews in São Paulo.

BIBLIOGRAPHY: Documents and publications of Arquivo Histórico Judaico Brasileiro; A.I. Hirschberg. *Desafio e Reposta. A História da Congregação Israelita Paulista* (1976); E. & F. Wolf. *Guia Histórico da Comunidade Judaica de São Paulo* (1988); J.H. Lesser, *Welcoming the Undesirables: Brazil and the Jewish Question* (1995); idem, *Pawns of the Powerful: Jewish Immigration to Brazil 1904–1945* (1989); H. Rattner, *Tradição e Ruptura (A comunidade judaica em São Paulo)* (1977); N. Falbel, *Estudos sobre a comunidade judaica no Brasil* (1984); R. Cytrynowicz, *Unibes 85 anos. Uma história do trabalho assistencial na comunidade judaica em São Paulo* (2000); R. Cytrynowicz, *Além do Estado e da ideologia: imigração judaica, Estado-Novo e Segunda Guerra Mundial* (2002).

[Roney Cytrynowicz (2nd ed.)]

SAPERSTEIN, ABRAHAM M. (Abe; 1902–1966), U.S. basketball entrepreneur; creator, promoter, and coach of the Harlem Globetrotters Basketball Team for 39 years; member of the Basketball Hall of Fame. Born in London, Saperstein came to Chicago at six with his nine brothers and sisters. He was active in basketball, baseball, track, and wrestling at Lake View High School, winning 15 letters. He then played semiprofessional baseball and basketball, earning $5 a night, and at age 24 took over the running of an all-black basketball team, the Savoy Big Five, named for Chicago's Savoy Ballroom. Saperstein changed the team's name to the Harlem Globetrotters, to indicate both a black team (Harlem), and a traveling or barnstorming team (Globetrotters). He placed his five players in a battered Model T Ford and took to the road. They played their first game on January 7, 1927, in Hinckley, Ill., before a crowd of 300 with a paycheck of $75. Saperstein, who stood five-foot-three, was the manager, coach, trainer, chauffeur, ball boy – and the team's only substitute. The Globetrotters won 397 games and lost 32 in their first three seasons, but found it difficult locating opponents willing bow to their dominating play. Saperstein then conceived the idea of a comic, razzle-dazzle style, and the team soon became a sought-after attraction on the basketball barnstorming circuit, showing off a superb blend of clowning and basketball wizardry, of vaudeville and solid basketball skill. In 1940 the team won the World Basketball Championship against the Chicago Bruins, and won the International Cup in 1943 and 1944. Over the years, the Globetrotters developed into an international entertainment attraction, meeting popes and kings and playing in bullrings, on stages, and aboard aircraft carriers and in more than 100 countries on five continents, including drawing 75,000 for a game at the Olympic Stadium in Berlin in 1951. The Globetrotters are one of the most famous sports organizations in the world, with Saperstein being called the "Barnum of Basketball" and his team known as "America's No. 1 Goodwill Ambassadors." Indeed, their flashy brand of play and the patriotic red, white, and blue uniforms became the first basketball experience for many spectators in Mexico, Belgium, Portugal, Morocco, Singapore, and Colombia. In March 1961, Saperstein announced the formation of the American Basketball League. Saperstein served as commissioner, though the league only lasted a season and a half. He was elected to the Basketball Hall of Fame in 1970.

[Elli Wohlgelernter (2nd ed.)]

SAPERSTEIN, DAVID N. (1947–), U.S. rabbi. The longtime director of the Reform Jewish Movement's Religious Action Center (RAC) in Washington, D.C., Saperstein was an influential leader in the so-called "Jewish lobby" in Washington for more than three decades. As J.J. Goldberg in his book *Jewish Power* observed: "[led] since 1974 by the savvy, charismatic Rabbi David Saperstein, the RAC has become one of the most powerful Jewish bodies in Washington [second only to AIPAC]." The son of Long Island Reform Rabbi Harold I. Saperstein, Saperstein was ordained in 1973 by the Hebrew Union College-Jewish Institute of Religion in New York. He then served as assistant rabbi at New York City's Temple Rodeph Sholom until Rabbi Maurice Eisendrath, the president of the Union of American Hebrew Congregations (now the Union for Reform Judaism), and Albert Vorspan, the director of the Commission on Social Action of Reform Judaism, invited him to Washington, D.C., to direct the center.

As coordinator of the Reform Movement's social action advocacy to Congress and the Executive branch, Saperstein became a leading spokesperson in Congressional hearings, the media, and Jewish community organizations, for the mostly liberal views of Reform Jewry. Under Saperstein's tutelage, the center built a wide-reaching social action education program that trains nearly 3,000 Jewish adults, youth, rabbinic and lay leaders each year and which provides extensive legislative and programmatic materials used by Reform synagogues and other Jewish organizations.

Well-known as a skilled coalition builder, he headed several national religious coalitions, including Interfaith Impact, the Interfaith Coalition on Energy, and the Coalition to Preserve Religious Liberty. He served on the boards and executive committees of numerous national public interest organizations, including the NAACP, Common Cause, People for the American Way, the Leadership Conference on Civil Rights, and the National Religious Partnership for the Environment. Saperstein was also credited with helping to forge groundbreaking coalitions with religious right groups, leading to successful passage of legislation on issues including religious freedom, prison rape, human trafficking, and genocide in Sudan. Among the legislation passed through this coalition's efforts was the International Religious Freedom Act of 1998, passed unanimously by Congress. This led, in 1999, to Saperstein being elected as the first chair of the U.S. Commission on International Religious Freedom.

For many years, Saperstein traveled widely, speaking in synagogues, federations, and universities, appearing on television news and talk shows as one of the leading exponents of Reform Judaism's strong views on social justice issues. His books, which have been used widely as sources for Jewish social action studies and activities, include *Jewish Dimensions of Social Justice: Tough Moral Choices of Our Time*; *Tough Choices: Jewish Perspectives on Social Justice*; *Preventing the Nuclear Holocaust: A Jewish Response*; and *Critical Issues Facing Reform Judaism* 1972.

An attorney with a specialty in church-state relations, Saperstein has taught seminars on both First Amendment Church-State Law and Jewish Law at Georgetown University Law School for more than 25 years, with articles published in legal periodicals, including the *Harvard Law Review.*

[Mark Pelavin (2nd ed.)]

SAPERSTEIN, HAROLD I. (1910–2001), a leading congregational rabbi of mid-20th century American Reform Judaism. As an undergraduate at Cornell, Saperstein was influenced by Rabbi Stephen S. *Wise to enter the Jewish Institute of Religion, from which he graduated in 1935. From 1933 (while still a student, replacing his ailing uncle Rabbi Adolph Lasker) until 1980, he served as the Rabbi of Temple Emanu-El of Lynbrook, Long Island. During his tenure, the Lynbrook synagogue grew from some seventy families to nearly one thousand.

As chaplain for the American Army from 1943 to 1946, he served in North Africa, Italy, France, Germany, and Belgium, reaching the rank of major. His report on the young Jews hidden by Father Joseph André of Namur, which appeared in *The New York Times*, was one of the first public reports of Gentiles saving Jews. In Worms, Germany, soon after the American forces entered, he recovered the priceless 13th-century illuminated Worms Mahzor from Dr. Friedrich M. Illert, a German archivist who had hidden it during the war, and facilitated its eventual transfer to the National Library in Jerusalem. (These endeavors were later described in *Rabbis in Uniform* by Louis Barish and *G.I. Jews* by Deborah Dash Moore.)

An inveterate traveler to far-flung Jewish communities, Saperstein attended the World Zionist Congress of 1939, visiting Jews in northern Poland and Palestine in the summer of 1939 (where he was injured by an Arab sniper), Russia, Poland, and Hungary in 1959, India, Ethiopia, and South Africa in 1967, and some 80 other countries on six continents. He served as the North American chair of the World Union for Progressive Judaism. A lifelong Zionist (as was his grandfather, Rabbi Hyman M. Lasker of Troy, New York), who served as chair of the Israel Committee of the Central Conference of American Rabbis, he and his wife Marcia helped pioneer youth and congregational trips to Israel, leading with the first Israel tour sponsored by the National Federation of Temple Youth in 1955.

Outspoken civil rights activists, during the summer of 1965 he and his wife did voter-registration work in Lowndes County, Alabama, with the Student Non-Violent Coordinating Committee.

During his term as president of the New York Board of Rabbis (1970–1972), he was a frequent public spokesman on behalf of Soviet Jewry, and he was on the cutting edge of the confrontation with the Jewish Defense League.

Despite these public roles, Saperstein thought of himself primarily as a congregational rabbi: as teacher, preacher, and counselor to three generations of Jews. After his formal retirement from Lynbrook he returned to full-time rabbinic service in New York City's Central Synagogue and Rodeph Sholom Congregation, and in the West London Synagogue of British Jews. He and his wife Marcia also traveled on behalf of the Union of American Hebrew Congregations through various regions of the United States, visiting small synagogues to provide rabbinic services and training for their lay leaders.

A selection of his sermons responding to historical events, *Witness from the Pulpit: Topical Sermons 1933–1980*, was edited by his son Marc, a professor of Jewish Studies at Harvard, Washington University in St. Louis, and The George Washington University. His younger son, Rabbi David *Saperstein, has headed the Religious Action Center of Reform Judaism since 1974.

[Mark Pelavin (2nd ed.)]

SAPHIR, JACOB (1822–1885), writer and traveler; born in Oshmiany in the province of *Vilna. Saphir's father, who was the *shoḥet* of the townlet, belonged to the *Perushim* – the disciples of Elijah b. Solomon Zalman, the Gaon of Vilna. In 1832 his parents immigrated to Ereẓ Israel, settling at first in Safed. A year after their arrival his father died, and when the year of mourning was just ending, he lost his mother, too. In 1836 he fled to Jerusalem with many members of the *Perushim* community because of the pogroms which the Jewish population of Safed suffered at the time. Saphir was educated under the system of the disciples of the Gaon of Vilna, which prevailed in Jerusalem at the beginning of the Ashkenazi settlement there. In addition to his religious knowledge and a rhetorical mastery of the Hebrew language, Saphir also acquired a fundamental knowledge of spoken and literary Arabic, read the *Koran, and was familiar with Latin script. He became a teacher at the *Jerusalem *talmud torah* Eẓ Ḥayyim. He later became the scribe of the *ḥevra kaddisha* of the Ashkenazim and of the *Perushim* community. As scribe of the community, it was his task to write poems in honor of important visitors, such as Moses *Montefiore when he visited Jerusalem in 1839. Saphir also wrote pamphlets and many articles, most of which were published in **Ha-Levanon*, edited by his son-in-law, R. Jehiel *Brill. Saphir was the son-in-law of R. Solomon Zalman Hacohen, one of the *Perushim* leaders in Jerusalem. In 1853 he wrote a promotional letter for Ereẓ Israel lemons, and another to R. Saul Zelig Hacohen dealing with the problem of Jerusalem's *Yishuv Yashan.*

In 1857 he traveled to the Oriental countries as the emissary of the *Perushim* community, to raise funds for the construction of the great synagogue in the courtyard of the Ḥurvah of R. Judah Ḥasid and for the *talmud torah.* He at first intended to go to *Egypt and *Aden, and from there by sea to *India, and was among the first to see the treasures of the Fostat **Genizah*, an account of which is found in his works. In Egypt he was defrauded of most of the money which was intended for his journey to India, and his financial plight brought him to *Yemen. Endangering his life, he embarked on a small sailing craft for Jedda, the port of Mecca, and from there continued to Ḥodeyda, the port of *San'a, the capital of Yemen (beginning of 1858). He first thought of proceeding to Aden in order to enter the interior of Yemen by the *Ṭariq al-Yaman* ("Road of the South"), but lacking transport, he entered the interior by the road known as *Tarīq al-Shām* ("Road of the North").

After walking for three days along the desolate coastal plain (Tihāma) to the Ḥarāz mountains, Saphir met the first Yemenite Jews, and when he reached the nearby town of Jirwāh, he was deeply impressed by them and their way of life, which he mentioned in a letter to Jerusalem. From there he went on to Ḥajara, Muḍmar, Manākha, and Yafīd in the Ḥayma mountains. Near Yafīd all his possessions, including his credentials as an emissary, were stolen from him. From Yafīd he went to Qaryat al-Qābil in the vicinity of San'a, where the Jews advised him not to visit San'a because of the severe living conditions for the Jews which prevailed there during that period. In the meantime Saphir visited Shībam, where he celebrated Purim, and from there, by way of Kawkabān, he reached San'a, staying there during the whole of Passover. With San'a as his base, he visited 'Amrān – spending Shavuot there – Ḥajjah, and Kuḥlān, which was the northernmost place that he reached. To the east of San'a, he visited Sa'wān and Tan'im. He returned by the road upon which he had come – the eastern road to Hodeyda – which he reached after a journey of eight months through the interior of Yemen. He stayed in Aden for more than a month and celebrated the Day of Atonement and Sukkot, sailing from there to India on Nov. 5, 1859. After traveling to India, Java, Australia, New Zealand, and Ceylon, Saphir once more returned to Aden, three years and four months later. On this occasion Saphir again thought of visiting the interior of Yemen, having become deeply attached to its Jews since his first visit; nonetheless, he refrained from doing this after hearing of the persecution of the Jews by the *imām* al-Mutawakkil. Saphir returned from Aden to Jerusalem by way of Jedda and Egypt (May 1863), after an absence of four years and ten months.

Upon his return to Jerusalem he recorded his travels in *Even Sappir* (2 vols., 1866, 1874, repr. 1969; condensed by A. Yaari and published as *Sefer Massa' Teiman* (1944, 1951^2). This work is outstanding for its penetrating observations and lively and fluent style. It contains valuable information on the lives of the Jews and their customs during the 19th century in the Oriental countries, particularly in Yemen. Saphir was the first to discover Yemenite Jewry in its greatness. Saphir's lifelike descriptions depict the innermost parts of the home, the village, the merchant on his business premises, the craftsman in his workshop, the elementary school teacher and his education, the synagogue and the *ḥakham mōri*. He also notes important details on their customs at circumcisions and marriages, and the version of the prayers for weekdays and festivals. He was the first to publish various Yemenite poems, and his details on the Hebrew pronunciation and syntax employed by Yemenite Jews are also of importance.

In 1869 Saphir was again sent to Egypt and the European countries, as emissary of the Bikkur Ḥolim hospital of Jerusalem, and he was once more the emissary of the above institution in 1873 when he went to *Russia. Upon his return to Jerusalem he continued to take an interest in Yemenite Jewry, and when he learned of the impostor who appeared as the pseudo-messiah Shukr *Kuhayl, he wrote an *Iggeret Teiman ha-Shenit* ("Second Epistle to Yemen") in which he warned the Jews of Yemen to beware of him (published Vilna 1873). In 1883–85 he lent his assistance to the publication of *Ḥemdat ha-Yamim* ("The Most Delightful of Days") of R. Shalom *Shabazi, the most prominent of the Yemenite poets, and wrote a foreword to it. Saphir also lived to witness the emigration from Yemen in 1882. In his last years Saphir devoted himself to the settlement of Petaḥ Tikvah. In his letter to R. Judah *Alkalai, Saphir deals with the idea of natural *ge'ulah* (redemption). He also wrote a few poems in honor of Moses *Montefiore. A village in the Judean Hills was named Even Sappir in his honor.

BIBLIOGRAPHY: J.J. Rivlin, in: *Moznayim*, 11 (1940), 74–81, 385–99. **ADD. BIBLIOGRAPHY:** A. Yaari, *Sheluḥei Ereẓ Yisrael* (1951), 820–22; idem, *Iggerot Ereẓ Yisrael*, 422–23; *Em ha-Moshavot Petaḥ Tikvah* (1953), 141–45; A.R. Malachi, in: *Areshet*, 5 (1972), 369–86; A. Morgenstern, in: *Cathedra* 24 (1982), 68; idem, *Ge'ulah be-Derekh ha-Teva* (1997), 17, 126, 128–30.

[Yehiel Nahshon / Leah Bornstein-Makovetsky (2nd ed.)]

SAPHIR, MORITZ (Moses) GOTTLIEB (1795–1858), Austrian satirist and critic. Born into a Yiddish-speaking, Orthodox family in Lovasbereny, near Budapest, Saphir, the son of a merchant, attended the Pressburg (Bratislava) yeshivah, and later the more advanced yeshivah of Rabbi Samuel *Landau in Prague. He then studied literature at Pest, and his subsequent contact with the German language, literature and culture led him to abandon traditional Judaism. Saphir then began to write German verse and Yiddish comedies. In 1823 Adolf Baeuerle, the founder-editor of the *Wiener Theater-Zeitung*, sought his collaboration, but Saphir's satirical and sensational articles were a source of scandal, and in 1825 he left Vienna for Berlin. There, too, he engaged in polemics with the literary élite and found it advisable to take refuge in Munich. From there Saphir was eventually expelled because of a satire on the Bavarian king and, for a brief time, he joined *Heine and *Boerne in Paris. In 1832 Saphir turned his back on liberalism and was baptized as a Lutheran. Five years later he founded his own periodical, *Der Humorist*, in Vienna. Saphir's biting wit, much feared in his time, was no longer directed against Metternich's reactionary policies, but rather against general human foibles and follies. His popularity and influence did not wane until after the Revolution of 1848. Saphir's works include humorous and satirical poems, essays, feuilletons, literary criticism, theater reviews, comedies, short stories, sketches, and short novels. His *Humoristischer-Volkskalender* (1850–66) had an unusually wide vogue and his *Pariser Briefe* *ueber Leben, Kunst, Gesellschaft und Industrie* (1855) was frequently reprinted. Saphir's witticisms circulated throughout the German-speaking world, and his satirical sketches were recited by actors for several decades. In later years he referred to his Jewish origin as a birth deformity, corrected by a baptismal operation. Saphir's collected works appeared from 1887 in 26 volumes. A collection of proverbs and sayings by Saphir – (*Sprichwoerter und Redensarten im Biedermeier. Prosatexte*, ed. W. Mieder) appeared in 1998.

BIBLIOGRAPHY: A. Saver, *Probleme und Gestalten* (1933), 141–94; S. Koesterich, *Saphirs Prosastil* (thesis, Frankfurt, 1934); M. Robitsek, *Saphir Gottlieb Móric* (Hung., 1938), incl. bibl.; S. Kaznelson (ed.), *Juden im deutschen Kulturbereich* (19623), 895–7, and index. **ADD. BIBLIOGRAPHY:** J. Sonnleitner, "Bauernfeld – Saphir – Nestroy: literarische Streitfaelle im oesterreichischen Vormaerz," in: W. Schmidt-Dengler et al. (eds.), *Konflikte – Skandale – Dichterfehden in der oesterreichischen Literatur* (1995), 92–117; S.P. Scheichl, "Saphir – kein Wiener Heine," in: *Les écrivains juifs autrichiens (du "Vormärz" à nos jours)*, texts collected and ed. by J. Doll (2000), 27–41; P. Wruck, "Gelegenheitsdichtung und literarische Geselligkeit. Das Beispiel der Berliner 'Mittwochsgesellschaft' und des 'Tunnel über der Spree' und ihrer Liederbuecher; *im Anhang Moritz Gottlieb Saphir: 'Der Gelegenheitsdichter,'*" in: *Berliner Hefte zur Geschichte des literarischen Lebens*, no. 4 (2001), 36–59; P. Varga, "'Magyar vagyok!' Identität und Ungarnbild von Moritz Gottlieb Saphir," in: E. Kulcsár-Szabó (ed.), *"Das rechte Maß getroffen"* (2004), 98–107.

[Sol Liptzin]

SAPHIRE, SAUL (1895–1974), Yiddish novelist. Born in Vilna and educated at the Lida *yeshivah*, he immigrated to the U.S. via Japan in 1916, settling in New York, where he devoted himself to teaching and journalism. For more than half a century, he enjoyed great popularity among Yiddish readers through his novels, serialized in the New York dailies *Tageblat*, *Morgen-Zhurnal*, and *Forverts*, and reprinted in other Yiddish organs. He is reputed to have written some 100 novels, of which more than 20 were published. His favored genre was the historical romance based on biblical and post-biblical figures, ranging from the Patriarchs, Joseph, Joshua, Deborah, Samson, Jephthah, Ruth, Saul, David, Solomon, and Esther, to the poets of Spain: Maimonides, Elijah the Gaon of Vilna, the Ba'al Shem Tov, and Solomon Maimon. Several of his novels were translated into English, such as *Der Kalif fun Kordova* (1927; *The Caliph of Cordova*, 1929), a romance of Moorish Spain during the Golden Age of 'Abd al-Raḥman II; *Tsivhn Roym un Yerusholayim* (1929; *A Challenge to Caesar*, 1938), dealing with the Jewish revolt against Rome which ended in the destruction of the Second Temple. His novel on Columbus, *Kolombus der Yid* (1934), dealing with the expulsion of the Jews from Spain and the discovery of America, was translated into Hebrew, *Kolumbus ha-Yehudi* (1948). Saphire also co-authored with Donovan Fitzpatrick *Navy Maverick* (1963), a biography in English of the controversial American-Jewish naval officer Uriah Phillips Levy.

BIBLIOGRAPHY: LNYL, 6 (1965), 310–11.

[Sol Liptzin / Jerold C. Frakes (2nd ed.)]

SAPIR, EDWARD (1884–1939), U.S. ethnographer, anthropologist, and linguist. Born in Lauenburg, Germany, Sapir, the son of an Orthodox rabbi, was taken to the U.S. in 1889. He was educated in New York and in Germany. He studied with Franz *Boas, and it was Boas' work in anthropological linguistics that stimulated Sapir to adopt this branch of anthropology as his major professional interest. For 15 years Sapir was chief of the Geological Survey of Canada, engaging in field research, and he became an expert in American-Indian languages. He taught at the universities of Toronto and Chicago, and in 1931 he was appointed professor of anthropology and linguistics at Yale University. He was fascinated by problems of language and its connections with logic, thought, and the total culture of which it was a part. He applied his early training in Indo-European comparative linguistics to the grammars of unwritten languages and their relationships. He concentrated increasingly on linguistics and its establishment as an academic discipline. It was his deep conviction that culture did not completely pattern its communicants, that diverse life experience produced different individuals within the same culture, and that therefore there are as many cultures. He produced some valuable ethnographic studies, among others on the Takelma and Nootka, and published such important essays in anthropological theory as *Time Perspective in Aboriginal American Culture: A Study in Method* (1916) and "Anthropology and Sociology" in: W.F. Ogburn and A. Goldenweiser (eds.), *The Social Sciences and their Interrelations* (1927), 97–113. The shadow of Nazism concerned him deeply, and he lent the weight of his academic prestige and personal involvement to various Jewish defensive efforts. But his primary scholarly achievement was in linguistics where, together with Leonard *Bloomfield, he is to be regarded as a founder of formal descriptive linguistics based on a phonemic theory and distributional method that analyzes the sound and utterance, the morphemes of a language, following a pattern of their environmental distribution. Sapir established in his "Sound Patterns in Language" (*Language*, 1 (1925), 37–51) the principle of structural analysis as fundamental for both anthropology and linguistics. Sapir's work as a researcher, teacher, and theorist has exerted a permanent influence on the study of language and has stimulated new work in sociolinguistics, ethnolinguistics, psycholinguistics, semantics, and semiotics. Sapir did not hesitate to evaluate his own culture. In 1924 in his essay "Culture, Genuine and Spurious" (in: *American Journal of Sociology*, 29 (1924), 401–29) he expressed his profound discontent with contemporary culture.

BIBLIOGRAPHY: R. Benedict, in: *American Anthropologist*, 41 (1939), 465–77, incl. bibl. of his writings; *International Encyclopedia of the Social Sciences* (1968) s.v., incl. bibl.

[Ephraim Fischoff]

SAPIR, ELIYAHU (1869–1911), Ereẓ Israel pioneer and pedagogue; grandson of Jacob *Saphir. He was born in *Jerusalem and from 1889 taught Arabic and, later, Hebrew in the Petaḥ Tikvah school. He was one of the first to teach Hebrew through the medium of Hebrew and to take the students into the fields, in order to foster love for the Ereẓ Israel landscape. Being the only one in the vicinity to know both Arabic and the legal rules concerning taxes, lands, and inheritance, he gave free assistance not only to Petaḥ Tikvah's settlement committee, but also to Arab neighbors, whose ignorance was exploited by the effendis. In addition, he started evening courses in Hebrew and Arabic in Petaḥ Tikvah. After 11 years he became a clerk in the *Jewish Colonization Association (ICA), where he dealt with registration of land transactions, which was a very complicated task at the time. His greatest success was in setting the borders of and obtaining purchase certificates for the lands of *Sejera. In 1904 he began to work in the Anglo-Palestine Bank in Jaffa, and he was its vice director. He tried to teach people to make use of commercial credit rather than to rely on charity. He was one of the three Jews of Ottoman citizenship in whose name the lands of Tel Aviv were purchased.

He devoted much time to the study of geography. Kippert's German wall map of Palestine, re-edited in Hebrew by Sapir, was the only one used in schools and offices until 1930. His book, *Ha-Areẓ*. published in 1911, was for many years the only comprehensive historical and geographical lexicon of Palestine.

[Abraham J. Brawer]

His son, JOSEPH SAPIR (1902–1972), public worker in Israel, was born in *Jaffa. In 1921 he participated in the defense of Petaḥ Tikvah (to which his family had moved previously). He was a member of the agricultural committee there and founded the cooperative union Ha-Ḥaklai. From 1928 he was active in the Farmers' *Federation of Israel, later becoming a member of its executive, as well as in the Pardes company (the largest cooperative company in Israel marketing citrus fruits), serving as its director in 1921–39. In 1940 he was elected on behalf of the General Zionists as mayor of Petaḥ Tikvah, and he held this post until 1951. He was elected to the first and subsequent Knessets on behalf of the General Zionists and later on behalf of the Liberal Party. In 1952–55 (Second Knesset) he served as minister of transportation. With the establishment of the national coalition government on the eve of the Six-Day War he served as a minister without portfolio (1967–69), and from 1969 to 1970 as minister of commerce and industry. In 1968 he was elected chairman of the Liberal Party and was rotating chairman of the Gaḥal Party.

BIBLIOGRAPHY: Y. Ḥurgin (ed.), in: *Mi-Yamim Rishonim*, 2, no. 2 (1944); M. Ben Hillel Ha-Cohen, in: *Koveẓ Mikhtevei Eliyahu Sapir* (1913), introd.

SAPIR, JOSEPH (1869–1935), Zionist leader. Born in *Kishinev, Sapir qualified as a doctor. A member of Ḥovevei Zion from his youth, he was one of the most prominent Zionists in Odessa, and he established a publishing house, Di Kopeke Bibliotek, which published Zionist literature in Yiddish and Russian. In 1903 he wrote a book for the general reader on the essence and history of Zionism, which was published in Russian and Hebrew and was an authoritative source for Zionist education. He edited a Russian-language Zionist weekly called *Kadimah* ("Forward," later *Yevreyskai Mysl'*, 1907). After the 1917 Bolshevik revolution, Sapir was elected chairman of the South Russia Zionist Organization and was one of the leaders of the committee that aided victims of pogroms. He left Russia soon thereafter, spending several years in Bessarabia, and reached Palestine in 1925. Sapir was director of a department of the Bikkur Ḥolim hospital in Jerusalem. He also engaged in painting and sculpture and published a book of articles and memoirs, *Ḥalutzei ha-Teḥiyyah* (1930).

BIBLIOGRAPHY: Tidhar, 3 (1958[2]), 1239–40; A. Raphaeli, *Pa'amei Ge'ullah* (1952), index.

[Yehuda Slutsky]

SAPIR (Koslowsky), PINḤAS (1907–1975), Israeli labor leader, member of the Fourth to Eighth Knessets. Born in Suwalki, Poland, Sapir went to the Tahkemoni religious school and later attended a teachers' seminary in Warsaw. Early in his youth he joined the *He-Halutz movement and served as its treasurer. He emigrated to Palestine in 1929 and settled in Kefar Saba, where he worked at first in citrus groves. At that time he organized several strikes over the issue of Jewish labor and was consequently arrested in 1932. Later on he started working as an accountant and was also instrumental in the founding of the water supply service and a popular credit bank in Kefar Saba. In the years 1937–47 he served as the deputy of Levi *Eshkol in Ḥevrat ha-Mayim, which turned into the *Mekorot Water Company and later became the national water company of the state of Israel. In 1947 he was appointed to the committee in charge of preparing the Negev settlements for the approaching *War of Independence. In February 1948 Sapir was appointed deputy head of the Civil Defense of the *Yishuv*, and was eventually granted the rank of lieutenant colonel. In August 1948 he was sent to Europe to coordinate purchases of military equipment. In 1948–53 he served as director general of the Ministry of Defense, under David *Ben-Gurion. In 1953–55 he served as director general of the Ministry of Finance under Eshkol. Sapir was appointed minister of commerce and industry in 1955 and served in this ministry until 1964. One of his main tasks in this position was to encourage domestic and foreign investment in industries – both private and public – in the new development towns. He was first elected to the Fourth Knesset on the Mapai list in 1959. Sapir was instrumental in revealing many of the facts connected with the *Lavon Affair that finally led to the resignation of Ben-Gurion from the premiership. When Eshkol replaced Ben-Gurion as prime minister in 1963, Sapir succeeded him as minister of finance, serving in this position until 1968. As minister of finance he was responsible for the controversial policy of economic slowdown in the years 1966–67, which was designed to decrease the deficit in the balance of payments, improve the structure of investments and employment, and foster productivity for export. In August 1968, Sapir succeeded Golda *Meir as secretary general of the newly founded *Israel Labor Party, serving in this position until 1970. In 1968–69 he served in the government as minister without portfolio. Following Eshkol's sudden death in February 1969, Sapir was considered as a possible heir, but Meir was chosen by the Labor Party for the post. After the elections to the Seventh Knesset in 1969, he was once again appointed by Meir as minister of finance, and served again as minister of commerce and industry in 1970–72, after Gaḥal left the coalition.

Sapir was reappointed minister of finance in the short-lived government formed by Meir after the elections to the Eighth Knesset. Following her resignation in April, he declined to stand as a candidate for the premiership or to serve in the government formed by Yitzhak *Rabin, whom he himself had nominated. In June 1974 Sapir was unanimously elected as chairman of the World Zionist Organization and the Jewish Agency, following the death of Louis *Pincus.

Sapir was one of the few Labor leaders who was disturbed by Israel's territorial expansion resulting from the Six-Day War, especially for economic reasons, and the social and demographic ramifications. He had reservations about Jewish settlement beyond the Green Line. He also acted to prevent the appointment of Ariel *Sharon as chief of staff.

Sapir's ideological rivals accused him of excessive pragmatism, and betrayal of the socialist ideals of his party. He had the image of a strong man, and the black notebook, in which he was accustomed to jot down notes, turned into a symbol. Nevertheless, there is no doubt that Sapir helped navigate the Israeli economy through stormy seas, and he was personally responsible for many of Israel's economic achievements under Labor rule.

After his death in 1975 the development center named for Pinḥas Sapir was opened at Tel Aviv University, to engage in research in economic, industrial, social, political, cultural and educational development.

BIBLIOGRAPHY: A. Avneri, *Sapir* (1970); WZO, *Pinḥas Sapir 5667–5735, 1907–1975: Ḥazon ve-Hagshamah* (1975); M. Na'or, *Ẓemiḥato shel Manhig: Pinḥas Sapir 1930–1949* (1987); M. Na'or, *Pinḥas Sapir Ish Kefar Saba* (1987); D. Levy, *Pinḥas Sapir ve-ha-Pitu'aḥ ha-Ta'asiyyati shel Yisrael* (1993); B. Karni, *Pinḥas Sapir: Shalit Be'al Korḥo* (1996).

[Susan Hattis Rolef (2nd ed.)]

SAPIRO, AARON (1884–1959), U.S. lawyer. Sapiro, born in San Francisco, California, spent most of his poverty-stricken childhood in an orphan asylum. He went on, however, to graduate from the University of Cincinnati, studied briefly for the rabbinate, and then received his law degree from the University of California. Sapiro's legal practice emphasized labor law, men's compensation, and, especially, farm cooperatives. He was the author of the California Industrial Accident laws and was chiefly responsible for the standard Cooperative Marketing Act in effect in over 40 states. In 1924 Sapiro was attacked by Henry Ford's *Dearborn Independent* in a series of articles alleging a Jewish conspiracy to control U.S. agriculture. He brought a $1,000,000 damage suit against Ford, and when the case came to trial in 1927, Ford denied antisemitic intent, but settled out of court with Sapiro. The Ford-Sapiro case set the stage for the conclusion of the *Dearborn Independent's* anti-Jewish campaign and for Ford's public apology to the Jews.

BIBLIOGRAPHY: *New York Times* (Nov. 25, 1959); G.H. Larsen and H.E. Erdman, in: *Missisippi Valley Historical Review*, 49 (1962/63), 242–68; M. Rosenstock, *Louis Marshall, Defender of Jewish Rights* (1965), 182–97.

[Morton Rosenstock]

SAPIRSTEIN-STONE-WEISS FAMILY, Cleveland, Ohio, business and philanthropic family. JACOB J. SAPIRSTEIN (1884–1987) emigrated from Poland to Cleveland, Ohio, in 1906 and began what would become the second largest greeting card company in the world, American Greetings Corporation, by selling postcards imported from Germany. Sons Irving and Morris worked with their father from a very young age. The company pioneered display stands for greeting cards and began designing and printing its own cards in 1936. In 1940 the sons changed their name to Stone, and in 1960 IRVING I. STONE (1909–2000) succeeded his father as president of the company. MORRY WEISS, married to a granddaughter of the family, joined the company in 1961 and became president in 1978. In 2003 great-grandson ZEV WEISS became chief executive officer of American Greetings.

The family has been a consistent supporter of Orthodox Jewish causes in Cleveland, the United States, and Israel, most notably the Hebrew Academy of Cleveland, the Telshe Yeshiva (Wickliffe, Ohio), Yeshiva University, and Telshe Stone in Israel. Several widely used ArtScroll publications bear the family names, including the Stone *Chumash* and *Tanach* and the Sapirstein *Rashi*. Morry Weiss is on the board of Yeshiva University and is a prime supporter of Edah. The family members' philanthropic efforts have been associated with Orthodox Zionist and modern Orthodox causes, and they have been active participants in the larger Cleveland community, both Jewish and secular.

BIBLIOGRAPHY: D. Van Tassel and J. Grabowski (eds.), "American Greetings," "Sapirstein, Jacob J.," "Stone, Irving, I.," in: *Encyclopedia of Cleveland History*, online edition, http://ech.cwru.edu.ech (1998, 1997, and 2001); MS. 4581 Jacob J. Sapirstein Papers, Western Reserve Historical Society, Cleveland, Ohio; "Irving Stone: Pioneer of Jewish Education Passes Away at 90," in: *Booknews from ArtScroll Online*, http://www.artscroll.com/mem_FEB00.htm.

SAPORTA (or **Sasporta**), **ḤANOKH** (15th century), scholar. Originally from a noble family in Catalonia, Saporta was rabbi in Adrianople after R. Isaac Ẓarefati. In addition to his Torah learning, he was also versed in the sciences. He apparently participated in an effort at that time made by the Rabbanites to reconcile the Karaites. Because of the Karaites' theological weakness, the Rabbanites sought to introduce talmudic learning among them. This explains the presence of Karaites among his pupils. His principal pupil was Mordecai *Comtino, and Saporta's system of thought and learning can be traced in Comtino's works.

BIBLIOGRAPHY: Gurland, in: *Talpioth* (1895), 8; Danon, in: JQR, 15 (1924/25), 309–10; Rosanes, Togarmah, 1 (1930²), 26, 47; Obadia, in: *Sinai*, 6 (1940), 76.

SAR, SAMUEL L. (**Shmuel Leib**; 1893–1962), educator. Sar was born on Shushan Purim in Ligmiany, in what is now Linkmenys, Lithuania. The eldest of six boys, he began his education at the nearby yeshivah of Vidz, later moving on to Ponevich (*Panevezys) yeshivah and a branch of Telz at Shaduva, where he studied for several years with Rabbi Joseph Bloch. After receiving *semikhah*, Sar was chosen by Rabbi Mayer Tzvi Jung to be trained as a rabbi for communities in the Austro-Hungarian empire and was sent to Vienna to pursue a rigorous program. He later followed Jung to London but ultimately chose to immigrate to the United States, arriving in Baltimore, Maryland, in 1914. His first job was as superintendent of a network of *talmud torahs*. Simultaneously, he began undergraduate studies at Johns Hopkins and Mount Vernon Collegiate Institute and entered law school at the University of Maryland.

In 1919 he was invited by Bernard *Revel to join the staff of the Rabbi Isaac Elchanan Theological Seminary (the forerunner of Yeshiva University) as a lecturer in Talmud and secretary of the administration. Following Revel's death in 1940 and the accession of Dr. *Belkin to the presidency, Sar was appointed dean of men, a position that reflected his multiple tasks on behalf of the student body. In practice, he was the main address for the students and was considered the institution's ultimate problem-solver, earning him the appellation "Mr. Yeshiva."

Besides his devotion to Torah learning and Jewish education, Sar played a prominent role in Jewish communal affairs in the United States, especially in the post-Holocaust relief and rehabilitation efforts sponsored by American Jewry. In fall 1945, he was sent on behalf of the American Jewish Conference to Europe to visit the displaced persons camps in Germany and present a survey of the Jewish Holocaust survivors and recommendations on how best to provide for their immediate needs. Along with Major Alfred Fleischman and Hans Lamm, Sar served as liaison between the survivors and UNRRA as part of the efforts of American Jewry to assist the survivors.

In 1948, Sar returned to Europe, this time as director of the Central Orthodox Committee of the Joint Distribution Committee, which was established in 1947 to unify American Jewry's efforts to care for the religious needs of the Orthodox survivors in Europe. A lifelong Religious Zionist, Sar was one of the leaders of the Mizrachi both in the United States and in world Jewish bodies. He served as acting president and chairman of the Vaad Hapoel of American Mizrachi and represented the movement in the Merkaz Olami (world center). He also played an important role in the creation of Bar-Ilan University in Israel with his good friend Pinchas Churgin. Sar's son, Eli Sar, was director of medical services at Yeshiva College and Stern College for close to 50 years; his daughter, Esther Zuroff, was director of student services at Stern College for three decades; and his son-in-law, Rabbi Abraham Zuroff, was the supervisor of all four YU high schools and the principal of YUHSB for 30 years.

[Efraim Zuroff 2nd ed.)]

SARACHEK, BERNARD ("**Red**"; 1912–2005), innovative U.S. basketball strategist, mentor to basketball greats, longtime Yeshiva College coach. Born in the Bronx, New York, Sarachek began his basketball career as a player at Stuyvesant High School. After playing for New York University, his first coaching job was as an assistant coach at his high school alma mater. He later moved on to a Workman's Circle team which included legendary New York Knicks coach Red *Holzman and prominent NBA referee Norm Drucker. During World War II, he coached in the military at Pearl Harbor, where his Schofield Barracks team won an armed forces title. After the war, he began coaching professionally, initially with the Scranton Miners of the American Basketball League (one of the predecessors of the National Basketball Association), where he made history by breaking the league's discriminatory practices by starting three Afro-Americans at the same time.

Sarachek achieved fame during his longtime tenure as basketball coach and athletic director at Yeshiva University. He began his career there in 1938 after he was approached by several students who sought to hire him privately to coach their team. Although plagued by the lack of a home court, no athletic scholarships, and the students' extremely demanding double schedule of Jewish and secular studies which often ended late at night, he invariably managed to field respectable, well-coached teams (nicknamed the "Mighty Mites") which enjoyed several winning seasons (the 1954–55 team went 16–2). In 39 seasons as coach at YU, his overall record was 202–263, which, given the limited talent available and the enormous problems facing the basketball program, was, to a large extent, a credit to Sarachek's coaching skills.

Despite the fact that Sarachek coached in NCAA Division III (or its equivalent) for most of his career, and his teams did not achieve outstanding success on the court, his knowledge of the game and his innovative offensive and defensive strategies were legendary, and he mentored such outstanding coaches as Lou Carnesecca (St. John's); Red Holzman (New York Knicks); and Jack Donohue (Power Memorial). He is credited with being among the first to emphasize the importance of movement on offense without the ball (going backdoor, "change of direction") and he created new alignments of the zone defense as well as innovative in-bounds plays. After coaching at Yeshiva, he worked as a scout for the Nets (ABA).

While not religiously observant, Sarachek was known for his strong sense of Jewish identity and his profound recognition of the important role sports could play in fostering Jewish pride and combating assimilation. This also explains his deep loyalty to Yeshiva or, in his words, "Yeshiva is special. It's a team for the Jewish people to be able to watch them play and be honored by them, to have pride. When you find a Jewish athlete doing something, you feel proud. That's more important to me than anything else."

Sarachek is a member of the Jewish Sports Hall of Fame in Commack, New York; the New York City Hall of Fame; and the New York City Basketball Hall of Fame. In 1992, Yeshiva University named its annual high school invitational tournament the Red Sarachek Basketball Tournament.

[Efraim Zuroff (2nd ed.)]

SARACHEK, JOSEPH (1892–1953), U.S. Conservative rabbi and scholar. Sarachek, born in New York City, was ordained by the Jewish Theological Seminary of America in 1916. He occupied various pulpits in the New York area, served as chaplain for the New York City Department of Correction, and taught at Yeshiva University. He was president of the New York Board of Rabbis in 1941–42. Sarachek devoted himself principally to research in medieval Jewish literature. He wrote *The Doctrine of the Messiah in Medieval Jewish Literature* (1923), *Faith and Reason: The Conflict Over the Rationalism of Maimonides* (1935; 1970²); and *Don Isaac Abravanel* (1938). These works are especially useful to students of the intellectual and religious history of medieval Jewry.

[Sefton D. Temkin]

SARAGOSSA (Sp. **Zaragoza**; Heb. סרקסטה, סרקרסטה), city in Aragon, N.E. Spain; capital of the former kingdom of Aragon. Jews were already living in Saragossa during the late Roman and Visigothic periods, for which, however, details are not available.

Muslim Period

There was an important Jewish community in Saragossa during the period of Muslim rule. In addition to commerce, Jews were well represented in various industries, particularly cloth and leather, tanning, and shoe making. The community was apparently influential, as the acceptance of certain Jewish practices by Saragossa Christians elicited a reaction on the part of the Mozarabic priest Evantius in the eighth century (Migne, *Patrologia Latina*, vol. 88, 719–22). It is also believed that *Bodo, the Frankish priest, converted to Judaism in 838 in Saragossa. Jews served as advisers in the court of the tolerant Tajib dynasty during the 11th century, among them, Abu Ishaq Jekuthiel b. Isaac of the wealthy *Ibn Hasan family, killed in 1039. A cultural and intellectual center in the 11th century, Saragossa was the residence of the philologist Jonah *Ibn Janaḥ, the physician and philosopher Menahem ibn al-Fawal, the poets Levi b. Jacob *Ibn Altabban and Moses *Ibn Al-Takkana, the poet and linguist Joseph ibn Ḥisdai, the talmudist and *dayyan* *David b. Saadiah, and the philosopher *Baḥya b. Joseph ibn Paquda. E. Ashtor (see bibliography) estimates that the Jews constituted 6.3% of the total population of Saragossa (which was under 20,000) during the 11th century. Saragossa also had a Karaite community.

The Jewish Quarter

From the time of Muslim rule until the eve of the expulsion of the Jews from Spain in 1492, the Jewish quarter in Saragossa continued to be situated within the city walls of the Roman period, in the southeastern section. It was formerly larger than during the final years of the Jewish settlement in Saragossa. The judería no longer exists. Its location was at the back of today's Ramiro I hotel, between the Seminar of San Carlos and Magdalena Place. There was "the enclosed" judería, and there was a second one, the new one, outside the Roman walls. The old Jewish quarter was surrounded by the Roman walls and an inner wall that separated it from the Christian districts. This quarter had six gates. It center was in today's Santo Dominguito street, which led to the Gate of the Judería. The fortress of the Jews, the slaughter-house, the Great Synagogue and the hospital were located there. In the fortress there was a prison for Jews and Muslims. As a result of the growth of the community, by the end of the 13th century a new Jewish quarter was established. This new quarter, situated to the south of the old one, between the Coso and San Miguel streets, has preserved its medieval features more or less. This quarter is known as Barrio Nuevo. The buildings of the community included a series of synagogues: the Great Synagogue (Mayor) in San Carlos place, the Small Synagogue (Menor), the Engravers' Synagogue (which appears to have been known as the Bikkur Ḥolim synagogue), the Synagogue of Cehán, the Synagogue of Bienvenist, and the Synagogue of Hevrat Talmud Torah. The only Jewish building that has remained is that of the Jewish Baths, found in Coso, nos 132–136. The community representatives were accustomed to meet in the Aljaferia fortress situated outside the city when they elected their leaders and officials. During the 14th century the king maintained a zoological garden in one of its wings, and the community was responsible for the feeding of the animals.

After the Christian Reconquest

When Saragossa was conquered by Alfonso I el Batallador in 1118, the Jews were granted various privileges. Alfonso had close relations with a Jew named Eleazar who lived in Saragossa and was employed in the service of the king. In the distribution of properties which followed the conquest, there is also mention of the *alfaquim* Benveniste and his family who received a vineyard in the outskirts of the city. When Alfonso VII of Castile occupied Saragossa for a short while (1134), he ratified the grants to the San Salvador Church in Saragossa previously made by Alfonso I of Aragon from the tithe and customs duties which were paid by the Moors and the Jews. In 1195 Alfonso II granted Maestre Jossep Aben Filca, his brother Rabi Asser, and their heirs after them, an annual income of 300 sólidos which was to be paid to them from the customs duties received from the Jews of Saragossa.

Pedro II continued to grant further personal privileges: in 1212, he granted to the Jew Alazrach, son of Abulfath Abenalazar, the members of his household and his heirs, a series of rights on their property; he exempted them from the reproof section which formed part of the text of the Jewish *oath, from the Jewish ban (*ḥerem*), and from the community's regulations. James I also adopted this policy of granting privileges to the distinguished Jewish families of Saragossa and thus favored the members of the *Alconstantini and de la *Cavallería families. Members of the Alconstantini family (Baḥya and Solomon) accompanied him as interpreters when he set out on his campaign to conquer the Balearic Isles and Valencia. Members of these families, as well as of the Benveniste family, gave their support to the counter-ban issued in 1232 by the communities of Huesca, Monzon, Calatayud, and Lérida against *Solomon b. Abraham of Montpellier and his colleagues because of their ban against those who studied the works of Maimonides and philosophy (see *Maimonidean Controversy).

One of the principal occupations of the Jews of Saragossa was garment making. The *draperos* held an important place in the community, coming directly after the personalities who had influence at court. Their shops were situated in the Jewish quarter and beyond, and they also employed Christians in spinning and weaving. They were followed in rank by craftsmen of every category: tailors, engravers, mantle-makers, furriers, goldsmiths, wool-cleaners, metal workers, blacksmiths, shoemakers, embroiderers, and cobblers, several of whom received special privileges in appreciation of their services to the crown. These craftsmen later organized their own benevolent societies. There were also landowners in the community who owned fields and vineyards outside the city, cultivated by daily workers and slaves. This occupational structure persisted until the expulsion.

The gap between the rich and the poor was very wide. The rich, including the *francos* who were exempt from contributing to the taxes paid by the community and were outside its jurisdiction, had full control of all communal affairs. The lower classes, composed of craftsmen, felt very oppressed. In 1263 they organized an opposition group called Kat ha-Ḥavurah (The People's Faction) and tried to obtain certain rights with the help of the king. This courageous act was the beginning of a social struggle that spread in the Kingdom of Aragon and caused constitutional reform in many communities. This did not always produce satisfactory results, and the members of the lower classes adopted a new method for ameliorating their position. They established many confraternities, *ḥavurot* in Hebrew, which tried to resolve their social, economic, educational, and medical problems that the establishment failed to solve. The leading confraternities were the Rodfei Zedek, Osei Hesed, Malbishe Arumim, Bikur Ḥolim, Shomrei Ḥolim, the confraternities of the craftsmen which included the shoemakers and the tanners, as well as religious groups that included Ashmoret ha-Boker, confraria fr Cefarim, and Talmud Torah.

James I granted additional privileges to the community, including rights of judicial autonomy; the *oath could be taken according to Jewish law; lawsuits between Jews and Christians could take place before a judge of the same religion as the defendant; Jewish prisoners were set free for the Sabbath. The history of the community during his reign was marked by the internal struggle for power between the de la Cavallería and Alconstantini families. Don Judah de la Cavallería, the bailiff of the city, became involved in a dispute with Solomon *Alconstantini. Don Judah remained in office until 1276 and died a short while later. Moses Alconstantini, the *alfaquim* of Pedro III, was appointed in his place. Don Moses was, however, unable to hold his position in Saragossa, and in 1277 became bailiff of Valencia. During the time of Don Judah the first *blood libel on Spanish soil was circulated in Saragossa (1250); the Jews were accused of the murder of a Christian child and the subsequent agitation reached a dangerous pitch. The community of Saragossa was among the largest in the kingdom, not of lesser size than those of Barcelona in Catalonia or Toledo in Castile, at times even surpassing them. The community administration, which was responsible to the crown for the payment of taxes, introduced internal systems of taxation. In addition to the direct tax, it levied an indirect tax on meat, wine, commercial transactions, loans, and real estate, a profit tax, a tax on dowries, and a tax on the daily wage of craftsmen (cf. Solomon b. Abraham Adret, Resp., pt. 5, nos. 279, 281).

In 1294 a rumor spread in Saragossa that some Jews had murdered a Christian child and extracted his heart and liver for magical purposes. The municipal authorities appointed an expert on magic to investigate the matter, while in the meantime the Jews succeeded in finding the "murdered" child in a neighboring city. King James II severely condemned the municipal authorities for the disaster which they had been about to bring upon the community.

In the tax regulations of 1331, the community sought to reorganize both the internal taxation system and the methods of collecting the tax for which it was responsible to the king. Particularly important were the taxes levied on commercial transactions, real estate, and movable property, the *sisa* tax on meat and wine, and the methods of measuring and assessing which were introduced to prevent evasion. In 1333 Alfonso IV issued several edicts in favor of the community connected with the registration procedure for debts and pledges. Pedro IV also issued similar laws, but apparently the community administration, which also had the support of the government, did not succeed in overcoming the irregularities persisting in taxation, its assessment and collection. In 1335 the infante Pedro informed his father Alfonso IV of the degenerate condition of the community and the irregularities found in it. By then the community was almost ruined through the accumulation of debts and the loans which it was compelled to seek in order to pay the levies and fines which the state itself imposed with such frequency. In 1342, on the basis of a privilege granted by Pedro IV, the community of Saragossa proclaimed a *ḥerem* upon anyone who obtained a tax exemption or accepted a position in the community as rabbi, *shoḥet*, scribe, *albedin*, or emissary with the assistance of a royal privilege.

The *Black Death struck a severe blow at the community of Saragossa. Hardly one-fifth of its members survived. On Oct. 27, 1348, King Pedro instructed the procurador-general of Aragon and the other royal officials in Saragossa not to compel the community to pay taxes until the plague ceased and new arrangements for tax payment were agreed upon. Members of the de la Cavallería family, whose position had diminished after the death of Don Judah, once more gained the leadership in the community administration; subsequently they maintained their position until most of them converted to Christianity after the disputation of *Tortosa (see below).

The cultural and general progress of the community in the early 1360s was largely due to the de la Cavallería family. Don Vidal de la Cavallería, one of the kingdom's notables, leased the minting of gold coins in the kingdom in conjunction with a Christian of Saragossa, an agent of the king, and leased the taxes in collaboration with another Christian. He was versed in Jewish learning, and after his death in 1373 his wife Orovida continued to manage her husband's affairs. His brother, Solomon, was also active in his town and community. The most outstanding member of the family, however, was his son and the son-in-law of Vidal: Judah Benveniste de la Cavallería, who, from the late 1370s, was involved in many of the kingdom's affairs and carried on important commerce in Barcelona and other places. His house in Saragossa was a center of Hebrew culture and he signed state documents in Hebrew. Solomon and Benveniste maintained friendly relations with *Nissim b. Reuben Gerondi and apparently supported *Isaac b. Sheshet Perfet, who arrived in Saragossa in about 1372–73 and was active there for 13 years. The responsa left by Isaac b. Sheshet yield much information on the way of life of the Jews of Saragossa.

In the relations between the king and the community of Saragossa there was no change in the attitude of the crown. In 1363 Pedro IV imposed a levy of 5,000 livres in Jaca currency toward the expenses of the war against Castile. From the 1370s the administration of the community was dominated by Solomon Abnarrabi, one of the leading *muqaddimūn*. Apparently, the members of the de la Cavallería family had ceased to take an interest in communal affairs. In the early 1380s, complaints concerning the inefficient administration of the community were submitted to the king's treasurer. It was revealed that the debts of the community amounted to 200,000 sólidos, and the *muqaddimūn* were accused of having exempted their relatives from taxes and granting them benefits.

It was only from 1386 that the community began to repay its debts, and R. Ḥasdai *Crescas, who settled in Saragossa about that time, did much to liquidate the debts and improve the community's condition. In 1387 he was appointed supreme justice in the prosecution of informers throughout the kingdom. He became the leader of the Jews in the kingdom after the anti-Jewish persecutions of 1391.

Saragossa was spared from the persecutions of 1391 because of the presence of the king in the city, which he used as a summer residence. The king and queen did not leave the city until the end of October to punish the rioters. In April 1392, John I thanked the city leaders for protecting the community and encouraged them to maintain this policy.

Activities for the rehabilitation of the communities of the kingdom after the persecutions subsequently centered in Saragossa. Ḥasdai Crescas and Moses b. Samuel Abbas, who had moved from Tudela to Saragossa during the 1370s, devoted themselves to the welfare of their coreligionists. Following the massacres in the peninsula, Ḥasdai Crescas assumed the leadership of the communities and offered financial assistance to those who suffered in the massacres. Crescas made several journeys to Navarre, probably to suggest a haven to the Jews who had suffered from the persecutions. It may be that in this context we have to understand Crescas' famous letter to the community of Avignon.

In 1396, with the consent of the government, Ḥasdai Crescas instituted regulations for the community of Saragossa. They show a pronounced tendency to strengthen the authority of the *muqaddimūn* and enable them to impose their decisions without undue delays. As early as 1399 the queen, however, found it necessary to accept the complaints of the community and change these regulations. According to the decisions of Ḥasdai Crescas, the treasurer was appointed from among the four *muqaddimūn*, while the funds of the community were supervised by one of them, and could not pass from his keeping. The queen allocated an annual sum of 8,000 sólidos to defray outstanding debts, while Ḥasdai Crescas had set no limits to the amounts which could be collected. The queen clearly intended to minimize the authoritative tendencies of his regulations, while maintaining the community in an orderly state. Ḥasdai Crescas died in 1410, Benveniste de la Cavallería in 1411, but worthy successors of these two personalities were still available. The rabbinical position of Ḥasdai Crescas was taken over by *Merahiah b. Isaac ha-Levi (en Ferrer Saladin), who was assisted by *Mattathias ha-Yiẓhari and Moses Abbas, leaders of former days.

[Haim Beinart / Yom Tov Assis (2nd ed.)]

Results of the Disputation of Tortosa

The community of Saragossa, like the other communities of the kingdom, underwent a difficult period at the time of the Disputation of *Tortosa in 1413–14. Its emissaries to the disputation were Zerahiah ha-Levi and Mattathias ha-Yiẓhari; they were accompanied by the interceder Don Vidal, the son of Don Benveniste de la Cavallería.

The consequences of the disputation of Tortosa affected the Saragossa community in the same way as it had the other communities in Spain. Some of its prominent members, including members of the de la Cavallería family, converted to Christianity, among them Benafos, who assumed the name of Fernando, and Vidal, who took the name of Gonzalo and received a position in the kingdom's administration. The conversion of Vidal had wide repercussions. His teacher, R. Solomon da Piera, also converted with him. Two poets of that generation, Solomon *Bonafed and Bonastruc Desmaestre, regarded his renunciation as marking the nation's decline. The government had already realized the undesirability of the Conversos, whose numbers were increasing, continuing to reside in the same quarter as the Jews. The Conversos, at first only a few in number, were requested to leave but refused; a commission was finally set up to assess the value of their houses which the Jews of the quarter were ordered to pay to them. Many families were broken up. In 1415 the Jews of Saragossa faced a threat of further disorders; many attacks were made on them after Vicente *Ferrer had been preaching. Ferdinand ordered that measures be taken to assure their protection. During this period, the community of Saragossa numbered about 200 families. This was also its size at the time of the expulsion in 1492, although it received Jewish refugees throughout this century.

The community nevertheless underwent a lengthy period of decline because there were no notable leaders after the Tortosa disputation; its administration was concentrated in the hands of the craftsmen and simple folk who were incompetent to manage its affairs. Alfonso v was aware of the community's situation and in 1417 ordered the *merino* of Saragossa and Vidal de la Cavalleria to take over the accounts from the appointees, to introduce order into the administration's affairs, and to appoint community leaders, *muqaddimūn*, members of the council, treasurers, and a notary. Alfonso even authorized them to defend the community against the missionary sermons of apostates. He also ordered that the books of the Talmud which had been confiscated were to be returned to the Jews of Saragossa, as they had been returned to the other Jews of the kingdom (1419). Synagogues which had been confiscated were also to be restored. He authorized Jews to take leases from Christians. However, several monks, a Christian jurist, and several apostates were delegated to make a general examination of the books of the Jews. An event that occurred on the 17th of Shevat, 5420 (1420), was subsequently celebrated by the community as the "Purim of Saragossa." The Jews of the city were accused by an informer of carrying empty Torah cases at the reception being held in honor of the king; however, they were found to contain Torah scrolls and the Jews were thus spared punishment. A special scroll describing this miracle was also written.

Despite the efforts at rehabilitation and the support of the crown, the despair which had set in among the Jews continued and there were additional conversions. According to a cautious estimate, about 200 Jews yearly converted to Christianity between 1420 and 1430. To assist the community's recovery, associations were established for the support of the poor, for Torah study, etc. Endeavors to organize relief for the poor and the persecuted brought a certain revival in community life. Saragossa was outstanding for this activity until the expulsion.

In 1438 Alfonso ordered that the community was to be administered by three *muqaddimūn*, a council of nine members, and a treasurer. Throughout this period the community existed side by side with an active group of Conversos, some of whom had abandoned the Jewish faith of their own free will (see below).

In 1457 Alfonso granted the community of Saragossa a series of alleviations: he exempted it from payment of special taxes for ten years, granted a general amnesty, and guaranteed his protection against seizures by Church tribunals and against imprisonment or seizure by officers of the kingdom. The annual tax then amounted to 12,000 sólidos in Jaca currency, as it was in 1460 and in 1482.

When Ferdinand inherited the crown of Aragon in 1479, his policy toward the Jews of Castile was also applied in Aragon. In 1481 he wrote to the prior of the Cathedral of Saragossa and reproached him for having ordered the Jews to return to their quarter and authorizing them to close off the passages to the Christian streets. He also complained that even the prior had issued orders concerning the garb of the Jews and had forbidden several crafts upon the basis of a papal bull. Ferdinand explained that even a papal bull required the consent of the crown if it was to be applied. He ordered the Jews to wear a distinctive *badge and instructed the municipal officials to see that the crown's instructions concerning the Jews were carried out, and to assure their protection, which implied that the city was not to adopt an independent policy in the treatment of the Jews living there.

In 1486 the king granted the request of Torquemada and ordered the expulsion of the Jews from Saragossa and *Albarracin (see also below). After the issue of the edict, Ferdinand, however, wrote to Torquemada and suggested that an extension of six months be given. The edict was presumably not applied because notarial documents (such as testaments and the like) are extant from the year 1491, indicating that there was still a Jewish population in Saragossa, while the general decree of expulsion of the Jews was published there on April 29, 1492.

The Inquisition officials took upon themselves to supervise the preparations for the expulsion. They issued an order prohibiting the purchase of properties from Jews, but the Jews of Saragossa apparently did not heed this prohibition and proceeded with the transfer or sale of their properties. On June 28, the bailiff general convened the municipal leaders for an urgent discussion on the problem of the property of the Jews. It was agreed that a part of the community's debts would be covered by its property, but another part of the properties, especially those in personal possession, would finance the departure of the exiles. The Jewish quarter was transferred to the municipal council. A short while before the expulsion, the Abnarrabi family, whose ancestors had held important functions in the past administration of the community, converted to Christianity. Several members of the family assumed the name of Santa Fé (Joshua Abnarrabi became Juan de Santa Fé); Ishmael Abnarrabi, known as a merchant and banker active during the 1470s, also chose this alternative; so did Vidal Abnarrabi, a renowned physician in the town (as a Christian, he took the name of Alfonso de Eimeric). None of the members of this family was tried by the Inquisition, and they apparently became integrated within Christian society. During the whole of this period, Christian notaries were fully occupied with drawing up inventories of the properties of those who were about to leave; these lists give much information on the situation of the Jews of Saragossa during the last stage of the community's existence. It is assumed that the Jews of Saragossa departed in the direction of the ports of the kingdom, but some of them presumably went to the kingdom of Navarre.

The Conversos in Saragossa

Although there were Jews in Saragossa who deliberately or willingly abandoned Judaism, many after their conversion continued to observe the Jewish precepts and were Jews in every respect. Several of the Conversos in Saragossa became renowned. In 1450 Pedro de la Cavallería completed his apologia for Christianity, *Zelus christi contra Judaeos, Sarracenos et infideles*, in Saragossa, in which he revealed a wide knowledge of Jewish affairs, while his familiarity with the Jewish community is striking. Even so, at trials held by the Inquisition during the 1480s, testimony was brought against him that he was accustomed to eat in Jewish houses, that he participated in the Grace after Meals, and that he had spoken scornfully of Christianity. It was he who brought to Castile the pearl necklace which Ferdinand had sent to his betrothed, Isabella.

At the beginning of May 1484, Torquemada appointed two inquisitors to the tribunal of Saragossa. The tribunal established its seat outside the city in the Aljaferia fortress and, on May 10, the first *auto-da-fé took place and four Conversos were burned at the stake. It nevertheless appears that the tribunal proceeded rather slowly in its task. Leading Conversos of Saragossa were related to the local nobility (including the royal family) by marriage, and in general the Conversos in the city had close social and commercial relations with the Christian population. On Nov. 29, 1484, the Council of the Estates of Aragon, influenced by the Conversos who took part in the local and national administration, sent a delegation to the king and demanded that the new inquisition be abolished because it contradicted the laws of the country, and the appointment of inquisitors by Torquemada was in direct contradiction to the charters issued in the kingdom. The king declared to the emissaries of Aragon that the former inquisitors had neglected their duties and accepted bribery, but loyal Christians had no need to fear the Inquisition because it would not molest them. In practice, the government realized that in Saragossa a cautious policy should be adopted over the Converso problem.

On Sept. 14, 1485, an incident took place in Saragossa which had repercussions throughout Spain. On that day, the inquisitor Pedro de *Arbués was assassinated in the Cathedral of Saragossa while engrossed in his prayers. The Converso community, as well as the Jews, were threatened with total annihilation, but the municipal and royal officials suppressed the riots and began an energetic search for the culprits. In December 1485 the Inquisition tribunal resumed its activities and applied justice according to the strict letter of the law. From then onward, monthly autos-da-fé were held, and many Conversos were burned at the stake. Among those sentenced was Jaime de Montesa, a respected jurist who was the leading conspirator against Pedro de Arbués. With him was sentenced Juan de Pedro Sánchez, the brother of the royal treasurer Gabriel *Sánchez, who fled and was burned in effigy. Luis de *Santangel, the father-in-law of Gabriel Sánchez, who had been raised to knighthood in appreciation of his service, was also accused of complicity in the murder and of adherence to Judaism and burned at the stake. Francisco de Santa Fé, who acted as assessor to the governor of Aragon, the grandson of the well-known apostate Jerónimo de Santa Fé, committed suicide in the Inquisition jail; his body was burned and his ashes were thrown into the R. Ebro. Even Gabriel Sanchez and Alfonso de la Cavallería did not escape suspicion. On April 30, 1492, one day after the publication of the decree of expulsion in Saragossa, R. Levi b. Shem Tov, one of the community's scholars, appeared before the investigators of heresy and testified that in 1490, upon the orders of the Inquisitor, he had called upon the members of the community, and cautioned them under the threat of the *ḥerem* to testify before the Inquisition all that was known to them on the Conversos who observed the Jewish precepts.

Just as the Inquisition sought to extirpate these important personalities, it did not spare the ordinary Conversos who adhered to their former faith and Jewish way of life. The trials of María López, the wife of Pedro de Santa Cruz, and of Francisco de Tarazona, which were held before the expulsion, provide a remarkable example of the lives led by Jews and Conversos. According to a list apparently drawn up during the 17th century, over 600 people were tried up to the beginning of the 16th century. Only a few of the dossiers of those who were sentenced, however, are extant. Most were lost when the last secretary of the Inquisition, Juan Antonio Llorente, transferred them to France at the time of the Peninsular War in the early 19th century; only a few of them have been preserved there.

[Haim Beinart]

BIBLIOGRAPHY: MUSLIM PERIOD: Ashtor, Korot, 1 (1966), 51, 218–22; 2 (1966), 153f., 160–5; idem, in: *Zion*, 28 (1963), 42; Torres-Balbas, in: *Al-Andalus*, 19 (1954), 191–2; 21 (1956), 172–90; J. Bosch Vilá, in: *Cuadernos de historia*, 10–11 (1960), 7–67. CHRISTIAN PERIOD: Baer, Spain; Baer, Urkunden; Baer, Studien; idem, in: *Devir*, 2 (1924), 310ff.; Beinart, in: *Sefunot*, 5 (1961), 77–134; B. Dinur, *ibid.*, 32 (1967), 161–74; M. Serrano y Sanz, *Orígenes de la dominacíon española en América*, 1 (1918); F. Vendrell Gallostra, in: *Sefarad*, 3 (1943), 115–54; F. Cantera, *ibid.*, 7 (1947), 147–51; L. Piles Ros, *ibid.*, 10 (1950), 75ff.; R. del Arco, *ibid.*, 14 (1954), 79–98; J. Cabezudo Astrain, *ibid.*, 372–84; 15 (1955), 103–36; 16 (1956), 136–47; 20 (1960), 407–17; F. Vendrell de Millás, *ibid.*, 326–51; 24 (1964), 81–106; F. Cantera, *Sinagogas españolas* (1955), 353–66; A. López de Meneses in: *Estudios de Edad Media de la Corona de Aragón*, 6 (1956), 48, 49, 102, 103, 141; A. Huici Miranda, *ibid.*, 7 (1962), 7–32; G. Tilander, *Documento desconocido de la aljama de Zaragoza del año 1331* (1958); M. Gual Camarena, in: *Hispania*, 82 (1961), 189–231; J. Madurell-Marimón, *ibid.*, 84 (1961), 495–548; H.C. Lea, *A History of the Inquisition of Spain* (1904), index. **ADD. BIBLIOGRAPHY:** A. Canellas, in: *Boletín municipal de Zaragoza*, 37 (1974), 85–97; J.L. Lacave, in: *Sefarad*, 35 (1975), 3–35; M.P. Gay Molíns, in: *Cuadernos de historia*, 31–32 (1978), 141–81; idem, in: *La ciudad de Zaragoza en la Corona de Aragón* (1984), 335–42; Y. Assis, in: *Proceedings of the 7th World Congress of Jewish Studies*, (1981), vol. 4, 37–7 (Hebrew section); idem, in: H. Beinart (ed.), *The Sephardi Legacy* (1992), 318–45; D. Romano, in: *La ciudad de Zara-*

goza en la Corona de Aragón (1984), 507–19; E. Gutwirth, in: *Sefarad,* 45 (1985), 23–53; A. Blasco Martínez, in: *Minorités et marginaux en France méridionale et dans la péninsule ibérique (VIIIe–XVIIIe siècles)* (1986), 177–202; idem, in: *Aragón en la edad media,* 7 (1988), 81–96; idem, in: *Michael,* 11 (1989), 99–120; idem, in: *Sefarad,* 49 (1989), 227–36; 50 (1990), 3–46; 265–88; idem, *La judería de Zaragoza en el siglo XIV* (1988); idem, *Aragón en la edad media,* 8 (1989), 113–31; idem, in: *Anuario de estudios medievales* 19 (1989), 113–31; M.A. Motis Dolader, *La expulsión de los judíos de Zaragoza,* (1985); idem, in: *Minorités et marginaux en France méridionale et dans la péninsule ibérique (VIIe–XVIIIe siècles),* (1986), 385–412; idem, in: *Proceedings of the 9th World Congress of Jewish Studies,* (1986), Division B, vol. 1, 121–28; idem, in: *Aragón en la edad media,* 6 (1987), 247–62; idem, in: *Aragón en la edad media,* 7 (1988), 97–155; J. Lomba Fuentes, *La filosofía judía en Zaragoza,* (1988).

SARAH (**Sarai**; Heb. שָׂרָה, שָׂרַי), the first of the four matriarchs; wife of *Abraham. Sarah is first mentioned in Genesis 11:29. Exceptionally, her genealogy is not given. According to Genesis 20:12, Sarah was Abraham's half-sister, the daughter of his father, but not of his mother. It is difficult, however, to reconcile this information with Genesis 11:31, from a different documentary source, where Sarah is identified as Terah's daughter-in-law. Immediately after Sarah's introduction, mention is made of her infertility (Gen. 11:30). This fact serves to emphasize Abraham's unquestioning faith and obedience to the Lord's command that he leave his native land, predicated as it was on a promise of great progeny (12:1–4).

The first incident in which Sarah figures prominently is the account of her descent to Egypt along with Abraham during a famine in Canaan (12:10–20). Immediately before entering Egypt, Abraham becomes apprehensive lest Sarah's striking beauty, which is especially noteworthy since she was 65 years old at the time (cf. 12:4; 17:17; *Genesis Apocryphon,* 20), inspire the Egyptians to kill him for the sake of acquiring her (Gen. 12:12). Thus, Abraham instructs his wife to claim that she is his sister in order to protect him. Sarah obeys Abraham's wishes, and when her beauty is reported to the pharaoh by his courtiers, she is taken into the royal palace. Abraham is apparently generously rewarded for the hand of his "sister" (12:16). When, however, the royal household is afflicted with plagues, the pharaoh apparently realizes that Sarah is Abraham's wife and that he is being punished for having intercourse with her. He forthwith returns her to Abraham, at the same time ordering them to leave his domain (12:17–20).The entire story foreshadows the plagues of Egypt and Israel's successful departure from there as already seen in the Midrash (Gen. R. (ed. Theodor and Albeck), 385).

It was once thought that this unusual account and its parallel in Genesis 20:1–18 involving the same couple but another monarch, Abimelech of Gerar (cf. also 26:6–11), were illuminated by the *Nuzi documents, which, according to *Speiser, attest to the existence in Hurrian society of a judicial status of wife-sistership, whereby a woman, in addition to becoming a man's wife, was adopted by him as his sister and thereby merited higher social status and greater privileges than an ordinary wife. Speiser's reading though was shown to be wrong (see *Genesis). Sarah's prolonged barrenness prompted her to give her handmaid Hagar to Abraham in order that she might bear him a child in her mistress' place (16:12). This unusual device, found only once again in the Bible (cf. Gen. 30:1–8), is also attested to in the Nuzi documents and elsewhere, where it is stipulated that if a wife is childless, she must provide her husband with a female slave as a concubine. Once Hagar had conceived, her arrogant attitude toward her mistress prompted Sarah to treat her so harshly that she finally fled, only to return in accordance with a divine order (16:4–9). Ultimately, however, after Sarah had given birth to Isaac, she saw to it that Hagar and her son were permanently expelled from Abraham's household (Gen. 21; in Galatians ch. 4 Paul allegorizes this story so that it predicts the displacement of Judaism by Christianity). The extraordinary fact that Sarah would bear a child at 90 years of age was first announced by God to Abraham at the same time that both his and Sarah's names were changed, the latter from Sarai (17:15–17). The promise of offspring was repeated when the angels visited their tent before the destruction of Sodom and Gomorrah (18:10). These promises were received with incredulity by the Patriarch and his wife (17:17; 18:12), who "laughed" when they heard the news, thus providing the basis for the name of the son, *Isaac.

Sarah died at the age of 127 in Kiriath-Arba, which, the text explains, is "now Hebron" (23:1–2). She was buried in the cave of *Machpelah, which was purchased by Abraham as a family grave from one of the local citizens, Ephron son of Zofar, in strict accordance with legal regulations for land purchase (23:3–20). Outside Genesis, Sarah is mentioned in the Bible only in Isaiah 51:2 as the progenitrix of the people of Israel.

The usual interpretation of the name Sarah is "princess" or "chieftainness," although it may also be connected with the Akkadian *Šārrat,* one of the designations of the moon-goddess Ishtar. Some scholars have explained that Sarah's original name, שָׂרַי, represents an early specialized feminine form, as is now known from Ugaritic, where the termination of feminine personal names is quite common. Others have pointed out that the name Sari may not be a doublet of Sarah, since the Greek translation has the expected doubling of the *r* in the case of Sarah (*Sarra*), Σάρρα, but not in the case of Sarai. The latter has been connected with the Arabic word *sharā,* "repeated flashing."

[Myra J. Siff / S. David Sperling (2nd ed.)]

In the Aggadah

Sarah is identified with Iscah, the daughter of Abraham's brother, Haran (Gen. 11:29), and thus Abraham's niece. She was called Iscah because all gazed (*sakkah,* "to look") at her beauty (Meg. 14a) which she retained throughout her journeys and even in her old age (Gen. R. 40:4). She was so beautiful that all other people were like monkeys by comparison (BB 58a). Even Abishag the Shunammite, whose beauty is extolled, never achieved half of Sarah's attractiveness (Sanh.

39b). Another interpretation for the name Iscah was that she possessed the gift of prophecy, which enabled her to discern (i.e., to look with the eyes of vision) by means of the Holy Spirit (Meg. 14a). She was one of the seven prophetesses and her prophetic gifts were superior even to those of Abraham (Ex. R. 1:1). While in Haran, Abraham converted the men and Sarah the women. The change of her name from the original Sarai ("a princess to her own people") to Sarah denoted that henceforth she would be "a princess for all mankind" (Gen. R. 47:1). When Abraham journeyed to Egypt, he concealed her in a chest lest she be ravished by the Egyptians. Nonetheless, she was discovered by customs' officials (Gen. R. 40:5). As a token of his love, Pharaoh gave the land of Goshen to her as a hereditary possession. For this reason the Israelites subsequently lived there (PdRE, 36). Sarah prayed to God to deliver her from Pharaoh and an angel was sent to whip the king at her command (Gen. R. 41:2; cf. *Genesis Apocryphon*, ed. by N. Avigad and Y. Yadin (1956) p. 43f.). It was a result of this sign of divine favor that Pharaoh gave her his daughter Hagar as a handmaid (Gen. R. 45:1). For details of the relationship between Sarah and Hagar, see *Hagar, in the *Aggadah*.

Sarah should have reached Abraham's lifespan of 175, but 48 years were taken away because of her readiness to dispute with Abraham over Hagar's misdeeds (RH 16b; Gen. R. 45:5). Sarah was originally barren, but a miracle was performed for her after her name was changed from Sarai and her youth was restored (Gen. R. 47:2). After she had given birth to Isaac, many people claimed that the Patriarch and his wife had adopted a foundling and were pretending that it was their own son. Abraham made a banquet on the day that Isaac was weaned, and Sarah invited many women. They all brought their infants with them, and Sarah suckled them all, thus convincing the guests that she was indeed the mother (BM 87a; Gen. R. 53:9). Others stated that Abimelech was the father, but it was disproved by Isaac's striking resemblance to his father (Gen. R. 53:6; BM 87a). Sarah's behavior toward Ishmael, whom she drove away from Abraham's roof, is justified on the grounds that she saw him commit idolatry, rape, and murder (Tosef., Sot. 6:6; Gen. R. 53:11). During her lifetime, the doors to her house were always hospitably open; her dough miraculously increased; a light burned from Friday evening to Friday evening; and a pillar of the divine cloud rested above her tent (Gen. R. 60:16). Her death was caused by the shock of learning about the **Akedah*. According to one version, Satan appeared to her and told her that Abraham had actually slaughtered, or was about to slaughter, Isaac (*Sefer ha-Yashar, Va-Yera*; PdRE 32). According to another text it was Isaac himself who returned and told her of the event (Lev. R. 20:2). The inhabitants of Hebron closed their places of business out of respect for her memory and as a reward did not die before they participated 38 years later in the obsequies of Abraham (Gen. R. 58:7; 62:3).

[Aaron Rothkoff]

BIBLIOGRAPHY: Skinner, *Genesis* (ICC, 1912), 237–335; K.L. Tallqvist, *Assyrian Personal Names* (1914), 193; E.A. Speiser, in: A. Altmann (ed.), *Biblical and Other Studies* (1963), 15–28; idem, *Genesis* (1964), 78ff.; L. Rost, *Gottes Wort und Gottes Land* (1965), 186–93; N.M. Sarna, *Understanding Genesis* (1966), index. IN THE AGGADAH: Ginzberg, Legends, index; G. Vermès, *Scripture and Tradition in Judaism* (1961), 96ff. **ADD. BIBLIOGRAPHY:** N. Sarna, *JPS Torah Commentary Genesis* (1989); S.D. Sperling, *The Original Torah* (1998), 78–80.

SARAH OF TURNOVO, also known as **Queen Theodora of Bulgaria**, was a 14th-century Jewish woman who lived in the city of Turnovo, then the capital of Bulgaria. Nothing is known about her life until 1346, when, according to a Greek document, Czar Ivan Alexander of Bulgaria "thrust out his former wife who was still living and substituted a Jewess …." The Jewess in question was Sarah, known for her beauty and intelligence. The Greek document makes it clear that the Czar "loved her for her beauty." He arranged for her baptism and she was renamed Theodora.

No document indicates whether Sarah objected to being converted, but there is some evidence that she did not turn her back on the Jewish people. While she was queen, she was believed to have influenced Ivan Alexander to exercise a more liberal policy toward the Jews of their land. As a result, the anti-Jewish legislation that was adopted by the Christian Church in 1352 was never fully implemented in Bulgaria. This fact has led a few historians to conclude that Queen Theodora may have had considerable impact on state affairs. Her influence, if indeed it existed, had no long-lasting effect, however, and ultimately caused a backlash. Several Jews were accused of fostering heresy, and when the czar repealed their death sentence, riots broke out and the accused were subsequently killed by a mob.

Sarah/Theodora and Ivan Alexander had a daughter named Tamar, who was married to Emperor Murad I (1360–89), ruler of the Ottoman Empire. A few generations later, knowledge of Tamar's origins gave rise to rumors of a Jewish woman in the sultan's harem and it was suggested that Mehmed II, son of Murad II, was born of a Jewish mother.

BIBLIOGRAPHY: S. Bowman, *The Jews of Byzantium: 1204–1453* (1985), 277; S. Rosanes, *Divrei Yemei Yisrael be-Togarmah* (1907), 6; E. Taitz, S. Henry, and C.Tallan, *The JPS Guide to Jewish Women: 600 B.C.E.–1900 C.E.* (2003), 86.

[Emily Taitz (2nd ed.)]

SARAJEVO (**Serajevo**; Turk. **Bosna-Serai**; Heb. שראי־בוסנה), city and capital of Bosnia-Herzegovina. The first Jews came to Sarajevo in the middle of the 16th century, spreading from there to smaller towns of Bosnia, e.g., *Travnik, Bugojno, Zenica, Tuzla, *Banja-Luka, and Mostar, capital of the twin province of Herzegovina. Although some earlier tombstones (in horizontal trunk form) were discovered in the Old Sephardi cemetery at Borak (western periphery of Sarajevo), the first documents attesting Jewish presence date from 1565.

Spanish refugees came from Salonika, but some of them may also have come directly by sea. Despite a different language (Ladino) and divergent customs, the newcomers were quickly accepted as useful city dwellers; they were mostly artisans and some were merchants. Jews were known as the early pharmacists of the region, as well as *hatchims* (from the Arabic-Turkish *Ḥakīm*, "doctor"). Muslim fanatics tried at first to prevent the settlement of Jews, forcing a few families to flee to Dubrovnik and Hungary. However, these were isolated cases which did not interfere with the good relations that developed between Muslims and Jews. There is evidence from the end of the 16th century in the so-called *sijille* (court records) that Jews appeared before the *sharīʿa* (Muslim religious tribunals) in civil cases.

A special Jewish quarter with a synagogue, near the main market of Sarajevo, was erected in 1577, authorization having been obtained from the pasha Siavush. Known to the population as *tchifut-khan*, the Jews themselves called it either *mahalla judia* (Jewish quarters) or *cortijo* (the communal yard). Later, as the community grew, Jews resided elsewhere as there were no legal restrictions. The first synagogue (constructed in 1581) was named, in the Spanish tradition, Il Cal grande, but it was destroyed by fire and restored or rebuilt several times.

Trade Activities

Jewish merchants used both main trade routes: from east to west (Sofia, Serbia, and Sarajevo to Dubrovnik, *Split, Zadar, and/or Venice and Trieste) and from south to north (i.e., Constantinople, Salonika via *Skoplje, Sjenica to Sarajevo, from where a lateral route went to Travnik, Kostajnica, Dalmatia, and Italy). Many Jews worked as blacksmiths, tailors, shoemakers, butchers, and joiners, and later as metal workers; they also operated the first sawmill and traded in iron, wood, and chemicals, in addition to articles such as textiles, furs, glass, and dyes. In Sarajevo, and in Bosnia as a whole, there were many indigent families and a Jewish proletariat.

The general situation of the Jews during the Ottoman era was good. They had their religious and juridical independence in all personal matters and civil cases, and broad autonomy in community affairs. The Ottoman authorities enforced rabbinical court sentences when they were requested to do so. However, the Jews had to pay the poll tax (*kharaj*) and were subject to various extortions and briberies. In the 17th century Ashkenazi families came to Sarajevo, fleeing European persecutions. They founded their own community, which had a separate existence until the Holocaust.

Historical Developments

During the siege and the Austrian conquest of Sarajevo by Prince Eugene of Savoy in 1679, Jews suffered along with the general population, the Jewish quarter, with its synagogue, being destroyed. About that time new settlers came from Rumelia, Bulgaria, and Serbia, as well as from Padua and Venice. The evolution of the community during the 18th century was generally undisturbed and was led by rabbis who organized a *talmud torah* and cared for the spiritual needs of the Jews, whose numbers reached 1,000 by 1800. During the first half of the 19th century further growth occurred, and official recognition of the community was granted by the Ottoman sultan. The rabbi of Sarajevo, Moses Pereira, was named by imperial firman *Ḥakham bashi* for Bosnia and Herzegovina in 1840. Some acts of ransom and discriminatory orders were decreed, but the various revolts against Ottoman rule and the influence of the European powers in Constantinople helped cause the *Tanzimāt* (reforms) program of 1840 and 1856, assuring equality for non-Turks before the law. In the face of occasional defamation, Sarajevo Jewry had to make donations in kind or money. Nevertheless, they largely maintained their cultural and religious life without outside interference, taking on new crafts and professions, as well as adding copper, zinc, glass, and dyes to their exports. By the middle of the 19th century all doctors in Sarajevo and Bosnia were Jews.

The Austrian annexation of the city in 1878 brought a new wave of Ashkenazim, who were officials, experts, and entrepreneurs. The new masters immediately demanded 100,000 ducats from the Jewish community, which was paid in several installments. On the other hand, the Austrians introduced new industries and made capital investments which created new employment and trade opportunities, largely directed toward Vienna, Prague, and Budapest. The earlier rivals – Ragusans and Venetians – were replaced by local and foreign Serbs who gradually became dominant in foreign trade, thus limiting the field of Jewish traders or pushing them out. Some Jews consequently changed their vocation, thereby contributing to the developments and modernization of the country as pioneers in optics, watchmaking, fine mechanics, printing (the first printing press belonged to Daniel Kajon), etc. The Jewish community numbered about 10,000 persons by the end of the 19th century.

After World War I the Yugoslav era began, the Jews enjoying freedom and equal treatment; their diverse economic, religious, cultural, and artistic activities continued unhindered, even though the Jewish population of 14,000 represented less than 1% of the general population of Bosnia. In 1927–31 the Sephardi synagogue, the largest in the Balkans, was constructed, only to be desecrated and plundered by the Croatian Fascists and the Germans not more than ten years later, and after the war it became a theater hall. The old Sephardi synagogue became a Jewish museum.

Rabbis and Jewish Learning

The first rabbis known to have led their community in the 17th century were Zebulun, Maẓli'aḥ Muchacho (earlier of Salonika), Samuel Baruch, Ḥayyim Shabbetai, Judah Lerma, and the famous R. Ẓevi *Ashkenazi, who was from Ofen (Buda) and known as "Ḥakham Ẓevi." The latter lived in Sarajevo from 1686 to 1697 and combated Nehemiah Ḥayon's Shabbatean views. The protocols (*pinkasim*) were kept in Hebrew and a *bet din* was set up. Very few of the documents are extant. Among later rabbis the most prominent was R. David Pardo "Morenu," author of the rabbinical commentaries: *La-Menaẓẓeaḥ le-David*, *Ḥasdei David*, and *Mizmor le-David*, and responsa. He founded a rabbinical dynasty (an exceptional phenomenon among Yugoslav Jewry), and his son Isaac and grandson Jacob succeeded him in office. Nineteenth century rabbis of note included Moses Danon; Moses Pereira, also known as Musa effendi; Meir Danon; Eliezer Shem Tov Papo; and Isaac Papo, a prolific author who wrote not only in Hebrew but also in Ladino (*Bet Tefillah, Tikkun Moda'ah*). The last rabbi under the Ottomans was Joseph Finzi, whose work *Va-Yelakket Yosef* was printed in Belgrade.

In 1928 a theological seminary was opened in Sarajevo by the federation of the Jewish communities, offering a secondary school education. The seminary's first rector, Rabbi Moritz Levi, author of the first historical study on the Sephardim in Bosnia, died in the Holocaust. Another prominent teacher and translator from Hebrew to Serbo-Croat was Jacob Maestro, who was known as "Morenu."

Jewish Life before the Holocaust

Apart from the religious field, Sarajevo Jewry had a wide range of social and cultural organizations and a thriving Jewish press. Among the institutions the senior was La Benevolencia, a mutual aid society founded in 1894; two bodies, Melacha and Geula, helped artisans and economic activities, and in 1901 a choir, Lyra-sociedad de cantar do los judíos-españoles, was established. There was a Jewish worker's union, La Matatja. The first newspaper published in Sarajevo was *La Alborada* (Aurora), a literary weekly which appeared from 1898 to 1902. The weeklies *Židovska Svijest, Jevrejska Tribuna, Narodna židovska svijest*, and *Jevrejski Glas*, with a section printed in Ladino, were published during 1928–41. Several memorial volumes were also published.

Zionist organizations were active between the two world wars. The youth movement, Ha-Shomer ha-Ẓa'ir, was well established and during the Holocaust provided, together with Matatja, a considerable number of partisans, fighters, and leaders of the resistance movement. An organization with Sephardi separatist tendencies was linked to de Picciotto's World Sephardi Union.

Jews in Literature and Arts

Isak (Isaac) Samokovlija (d. 1955), a forceful writer, lived in Sarajevo until his death. He vividly described Bosnian Jewish life, especially the problems of the porters, peddlers, beggars, and artisans. Daniel Ozmo, who did mostly woodcuts, Daniel Kabiljo-Danilus, and Yosif (Joseph) Levi-Monsino, all of whom perished during the Ustashi-Artuković era, were well-known painters. The illuminated Sarajevo Haggadah is kept in the National Museum of Sarajevo; it was acquired by the Museum (then, the Landesmuseum) in 1895 for 100 florins. Its origin, however, was in Spain and has nothing to do with Sarajevo (see *Haggadah).

Jews in Politics

The first European-educated physician in Bosnia, Isaac Shalom, better known as Isaac effendi, was the first (appointed) Jewish member of the provincial Majlis Idaret (assembly). His son Salomon "effendi" Shalom succeeded him. Javer (Xaver) "effendi" Baruch was elected as a deputy to the Ottoman parliament in 1876. During the Austrian and Yugoslav periods Jews generally abstained from active participation in politics. In the 1930s – when the economic situation deteriorated – a number of younger Jews turned to the illegal Communist Party, some of them gaining prominence in the party's ranks during the subsequent struggle against the occupiers and quislings.

Holocaust and After

Between the two world wars Sarajevo was the third-largest Jewish center of Yugoslavia (after Zagreb and Belgrade). In 1935 there were 8,318 Jews; in 1941, 10,500.

The Germans arrived on April 15, 1941, and the following day wrecked the Sephardi synagogue, which was the largest in the Balkans. This was followed by requisitions, expropriations, execution of hostages for acts of sabotage, individual arrests, and mass deportations of Jews. Members of the Jewish community were deported between September and November 1941, mostly to Jasenovac, Loborgrad (women), and Djakovo. Extermination took place in these Ustashi (Croatian) concentration camps. Only a small number of Jews survived the first wave of killings and they were later dispatched to the Auschwitz gas chambers. A limited number of Jews survived either by joining partisan units or by reaching Italy. Several scores of army officers and soldiers mobilized by the Yugoslav army upon the German invasion spent the war years in German POW camps, protected by the Geneva Convention, and thus returned to Sarajevo after the Holocaust. In all, over 9,000 Jews were murdered by the Nazis.

After the Holocaust, the community was reconstituted, but most of the survivors chose to immigrate to Israel in the years 1948–49. Religious services were organized in the Ashkenazi synagogue (which had remained more or less intact) by R. Menahem Romano, and some social and cultural activities were renewed. A monument to "the fighters and martyrs" was erected in the Jewish cemetery at Kovačica, and a celebration of the 400th anniversary of the arrival of the Jews in Bosnia and Herzegovina was held in 1970, with participation of delegates from abroad, including the U.S. and Israel. On this occasion a memorial volume was published. In 1971 the community numbered 1,000.

During the Bosnian War (1992–1994) the old Jewish cemetery was badly damaged. Nine hundred Jews were evacuated in buses to Pirovac, to the former Yugoslav summer camp near *Split, and 150 by air to *Belgrade. In 2002 the centennial of the Ashkenazi synagogue was commemorated with a stamp issued by the government of Bosnia and Herzegovina. In 2004 there were 700 Jews living in Sarajevo, including some refugees who returned home.

BIBLIOGRAPHY: M. Levy, *Die Sephardim in Bosnien* (1911); A. Hananel and E. Eškenazi, *Fontes hebraici...*, 2 (1960), 87–88, 234–5, 258–66, 334–5, 391–3; *Jevrejski Almanah* (1954–67), passim; *Omanut* (Zagreb, 1935–41), passim; *Spomenica povodom 400 godina od dolaska Jevreja u Bosnu i Hercegovinu* (1970); Savez Jevrejskih Opstina Jugoslavije, *Spomenica "50," 1919–1959* (1969).

[Zvi Loker]

SARASOHN, KASRIEL HERSCH (1835–1905), Yiddish and Hebrew newspaper publisher. Born in Suwalki province, Russia, he settled in New York in 1871, and in the following year founded a weekly paper, *Di New Yorker Yidishe Tsaytung*, which was unsuccessful. Two years later he founded the first American Yiddish weekly *Di Yidishe Gazeten*, which survived for more than half a century and paved the way for the first Yiddish daily in America, *Yidishes Tageblat*. This traditionally-oriented daily exerted a great influence upon the immigrant generation at the turn of the century and attained a circulation of 70,000 copies. Its editors included the journalist John Paley, *Tashrak and G. *Bublick. Its influence declined after World War I, and in 1928 it merged with the *Morning-Journal*. Sarasohn also founded a Hebrew weekly, *Haivri*, which he maintained from 1891 to 1898, despite annual deficits. In 1882 he organized a society for aiding Jewish immigrants, which in 1890 merged with the *Hebrew Immigrant Aid Society (HIAS).

BIBLIOGRAPHY: Rejzen, Leksikon, 4 (1929), 883–6; Starkman, in: YIVO, *Yorbukh Amopteyl* (1931), 273–95.

[Sol Liptzin]

SARASOTA, city on Florida's west coast. It is a sophisticated arts community and beach resort, ringing Sarasota Bay and the Gulf of Mexico, and offering 35 miles of beaches. During the Civil War, Judah P. Benjamin served as Attorney General, Secretary of War and Secretary of State of the Confederacy and was known as the most prominent 19th century American Jew. Benjamin was President Jefferson Davis' closest confidant and David Levy Yulee's cousin. When General Robert E. Lee surrendered in 1865, Benjamin headed south to Ellenton, FL, and sheltered at the Gamble Mansion, near Sarasota. With this exception, there is no record of Jews in this area until the 20th century. With changes in transportation and the lure of cheap land for sale, a trickle of Jews began migrating to the Sarasota area. Marcus Weinkle left Russia in 1887, was a sheepherder in Palestine, then immigrated to the U. S in 1890 to Moffit, Florida (east of Sarasota), where he ran a 2,000-acre lumber business. He brought a Torah with him and conducted services for Jews in the surrounding area. He kept kosher, married and had two children there; his daughter Charlotte became a winter resident of Sarasota decades later.

Simon Rosin came from Baltimore first to Ocala, FL, then settled in Arcadia in 1905, where he opened a store and later built an arcade, which housed the U.S. Post Office. He and his wife had one son, Aurel, in 1910. Aurel was a lawyer and cattle rancher, and he and his wife Elsie raised four sons in Arcadia, where they had over 4,000 acres for their cattle ranch. Elsie took the boys to Sarasota for religious school and bar mitzvah training; three sons remained in Sarasota.

The first Jew to permanently settle in Sarasota was Philip Levy, who fled the pogroms of Lithuania in 1905. Working for a pants manufacturing firm, he traveled to St. Petersburg, FL, in 1909, where he met and married Cecelia Tarapani. In 1913 Philip and Cecelia Levy settled in Sarasota and opened a womenswear store. They were the only Jews there until 1925. As others settled, the Levys conducted Sabbath and High Holiday services in their home. Joseph Idelson peddled dry goods; he and his wife Rose were attracted by the land boom and moved to Sarasota with their children in 1925. Idelson opened a general merchandise store, invested in banks and real estate, and was one of the founders of the Jewish Community Center (today's Temple Beth Sholom) in 1928. The first synagogue in Sarasota was built on property donated by the city, and they had their first services for Yom Kippur just prior to the hurricane. The congregation acquired a site from the city in 1932 for a Jewish burial ground. After World War II a number of Jewish soldiers who had passed through Sarasota returned to settle. Growth was gradual. By 1950, the community had expanded to 75 families. In 1956 a "break-away" group of members of Temple Beth Sholom established a Reform congregation, Temple Emanu-El. The Jewish Community Council, the forerunner of the Sarasota-Manatee Federation, was founded in 1959; Sidney Adler was the first president.

Many of these pioneers were lovers of the arts and contributed to building Sarasota's cultural infrastructure. The Van Wezel Performing Arts Hall that opened on Sarasota Bay in 1967 is named for Jews who left money for this purpose. The area began to attract Jewish writers, artists, and musicians. Author McKinley Kantor came to Sarasota around 1940; two of his books have a Florida setting: *The Noises of their Wings* (Everglades) and *Beauty Beast* (north Florida). Among other notable talents are Paul Wolfe, musical director and maestro, who served the West Coast Symphony for decades; Syd Solomon, a nationally acclaimed artist who came in 1946; Leo Rogers, a driving force to create the Sarasota Opera Association and the Sarasota Ballet of Florida; Hal Davis who was public relations manager for Benny Goodman and Columbia Records before moving to Sarasota, where, in 1980, he founded the Jazz Club of Sarasota; and Frank Eliscu, the designer of the Heisman Trophy (the highest honor in college football) and the glass panels above the doors of the Library of Congress, as well as works of sculpture for the Van Wezel, Ringling Museum of Art, Temple Emanu-El, and Temple Beth Sholom in Sarasota. Paul Rubenfeld, known to millions as Pee Wee Herman, came to Sarasota in 1960 as a child and graduated from Sarasota High School. Many Jews have contributed largely to the community in education and social services. Harry Sudakoff dedicated the Sudakoff Center at New College. Alex Schoenbaum, former All-American football player, started Shoney's Big Boy restaurant chain. In 1974 Betty and Alex Schoenbaum began spending part of the year in Sarasota and became major supporters of civic and Jewish activities. In 1990 the Schoenbaums contributed funds to help open the City of Sarasota's human services complex, which houses 19 social service agencies. Some Jews who have been involved politically are David Cohen, who served as mayor 1964–66 and played a major role in the establishment of the Florida West Coast Symphony and the Van Wezel Performing Arts Hall, and Lou Ann Rosengarten Palmer, who came to Sarasota in

1948 and was a performer with the Sailor Circus Show. She serves on the Sarasota City Commission where she sat as mayor in 1984 and 1988.

Jewish developers planted citrus groves and opened new residential districts. Jules and Jack Freeman came to Sarasota in 1953 and began planting citrus. From 1968 to 1971 they planted the "world's largest orange grove," which is three times the size of Manhattan, NYC, and has over three million citrus trees. National Geographic magazine published an aerial photo of the 27,000 acres and commented, "The grove was one of the distinguishing landmarks in Florida visible from space." Charles Lavin, sensing the plight of many elderly on fixed incomes, bought the Mira Mar Hotel in Sarasota, the Manatee River Hotel in Bradenton, and the MacArthur Beach Hotel in Venice and turned them into retirement homes. Martin Paver sailed to Sarasota with his family from New York in 1949. He and his sons developed housing subdivisions for the "snowbirds" (residents 3–7 months of the year) migrating south.

In 1979 a group established Beth Israel, a Reform Congregation, on Longboat Key. Bradenton Conservative Jewish families organized as Temple Beth El in 1975. The Jewish Community Center of Venice began in 1983. In 1984 Jewish Family Services (JFS) was granted their charter. The JCC opened the first summer camp in 1989.

The Jewish community has matured in the past three decades and agencies and organizations grew as the sensitivity for local and worldwide Jewish needs was expanded. About 17,500 Jews live in Sarasota-Manatee (2005), consisting primarily of the cities of Sarasota, Longboat Key, Bradenton, and Venice. Most are from the mid-west and the Washington-Boston corridor and are closely bonded by the cultural and Jewish life of the community. The greatest growth has been in Bradenton, and there is a significant cluster of Jews in high-rise condominiums in Longboat Key. The area attracts primarily wealthy Jews of retirement age who are in good health. Only 1% of the adults were born in the area, 32% of households affiliate with a congregation, and 21% are "snowbirds." Eighty-two percent of Jewish children (ages 6–12) are currently enrolled in formal Jewish education. The Federation's agencies include a Jewish Retirement Complex (Kobernick House) and Flanzer Jewish Community Center, and they sponsor a monthly Jewish newspaper, *The Chronicle*. There are 10 congregations of every stripe, and branches representing almost every national and international Jewish organization.

(Some of the demographic analysis comes from Ira Sheskin's 2001 Study for the Sarasota-Manatee Jewish Federation.)

[Marcia Jo Zerivitz (2nd ed.)]

SARATOV, capital of Saratov district, Russia; before the 1917 Revolution, capital of Saratov province on the west bank of the R. Volga. Until 1917 the province of Saratov was outside the bounds of the *Pale of Settlement. Shortly before the middle of the 19th century a small Jewish community was formed by Jewish soldiers stationed in Saratov. A few of these had families and even engaged in trade and crafts. By the middle of the century, there were 44 such Jewish soldiers stationed in the city. Besides these, a few Jews who were not in the army resided in Saratov, despite the restrictions. In the spring of 1853 this tiny community was projected into the forefront of Russian Jewish affairs when three Jews in Saratov, one of them an apostate, were involved in a *blood libel in which it was alleged that they had murdered two Christian children. This incident brought a renewal of the blood libel throughout Russia. When special investigators sent from St. Petersburg failed to prove the guilt of the Jews, the government appointed a legal investigation commission whose task it was not only to investigate the murders, but also to seek information about the "secret dogmas of Jewish religious extremism." This commission, too, was unable to cast guilt upon the Jews. Though its findings were confirmed by the Senate, the State Council, in May 1860, concluded that guilt had been established, even if no motive for the murders could be shown. The three found guilty were sentenced to hard labor. During the course of the investigation a large number of Jewish books were confiscated. In December 1858 a commission of experts, including Daniel *Chwolson, was appointed to examine these books and indicate whether they contained evidence of the ritual use of Christian blood by Jews. The commission concluded that the works contained nothing to support the libel.

During the second half of the century Jews were permitted to live outside the Pale of Settlement in Saratov. By 1897 there were 1,460 Jews in Saratov (1.1% of the total population). The wave of pogroms of October 1905 reached Saratov, where a number of Jews were killed. During World War I many refugees from the battle zone found sanctuary in Saratov. From 1919 to 1921 a group of *He-Ḥalutz members, calling themselves "Mishmar ha-Volga" ("The Volga Guard"), stayed in Saratov while preparing to settle in Ereẓ Israel. In 1926 Saratov had a Jewish population of 6,717 (3.1%), and in 1939 there were 6,982 Jews in the district, most of them in the city. During WWII Saratov was not occupied by the Germans. The baking of *maẓẓot* was prohibited in 1959. In the late 1960s the Jewish population was estimated at 15,000. There was one synagogue. In 2002 around 3,500 Jews remained in the entire district. The city of Saratov had a full range of community services and a chief rabbi.

BIBLIOGRAPHY: Aharoni, in: *He-Avar*, 9 (1962), 150–9; 10 (1963), 188–201; *Ha-Me'assef* (1902), 245–67; *Die Judenpogrome in Russland*, 2 (1910), 520–4; Y.J. Hessen (Gessen), *Krovavy navet v Rossii* (1912), 17–23; *Perezhitoye*, 4 (1913), 2119.

[Yehuda Slutsky]

SARAVAL, family of scholars. ABRAHAM BEN JUDAH LEIB, the most noted of them, lived in *Venice during the 16th century and wrote a commentary on *Sefer ha-Ma'amadot*. JACOB BEN LEIB lived in Cologne in the 16th century. His name is mentioned in the responsa *Naḥalat Ya'akov* of Jacob b. Elhanan Heilbronn. Judah Leib *Saraval (d. 1617) was rabbi in

Venice. NEHEMIAH BEN JUDAH LEIB (d. 1649), a rabbinic scholar in Venice, wrote a laudatory introduction to Joseph Solomon Delmedigo's *Elim* (Amsterdam, 1629). His name is mentioned approvingly in the responsa *Mayim Rabbim* of Raphael Meldola (1:11), and *Devar Shemu'el* of Samuel Aboab (no. 19). SOLOMON ḤAI BEN NEHEMIAH was a Venetian scholar of the 17th century, whose name is mentioned approvingly in *Devar Shemu'el* of Samuel Aboab (p. 375), and in *Piskei Recanati ha-Aḥaronim* (p. 24). Jacob Raphael b. Simḥah Judah *Saraval was rabbi in Mantua, author and poet. LEON ḤAI (1771–1851) lived in Trieste. He wrote *Discorsi pronunciati all' apertura degli studi della comunità israelitica di Trieste* (Trieste, 1811). He possessed a library containing many manuscripts and incunabula.

BIBLIOGRAPHY: Steinschneider, Cat Bod, 709, 1371, 2500; Benjacob, Oẓar, 351; Mortara, index, 59; Ghirondi-Neppi, 218–9, 272–3; Azulai (1852), 59 n. 11; Roth, Italy, 397, 410, 498; C. Roth, *History of the Jews in Venice* (1930), index; Zunz, Gesch, 243, 568.

[Guiseppe Laras]

SARAVAL, JACOB RAPHAEL BEN SIMḤAH JUDAH (1707?–1782), Italian rabbi, man of letters, and musician. Saraval was born in Venice. He was one of the rabbis of Venice who supported Jacob *Emden in his dispute with Jonathan *Eybeschutz. He communicated with the English scholar Kennicott on subjects of biblical philology. In 1752 he was appointed rabbi of Mantua and many of the documents in the communal archives bear his signature. During the 1760s and 1770s he traveled to Holland and England on behalf of his community. When the antisemitic lawyer Giovanni Battista Benedetti of Ferrara published his *Dissertazione della Religione e del Giuramento degli Ebrei* at the beginning of the 1770s, Saraval rejoined with *Lettera apologetica* (Mantua, 1775). He was also known as a preacher, poet, and composer of *piyyutim*, and engaged in various branches of secular culture – arts, literature, and music – in which fields he wrote many works. In addition he translated from various languages. One of his translations, the libretto of Handel's oratorio *Esther* (apparently done at the request of the Jews of England and Holland), is one of the first free verse translations from English to Hebrew without recourse to the traditional meters.

Among his translations from Hebrew to Italian are: *Avot* (Venice, 1729, with Simeon Calimani); *Ḥovot ha-Levavot* of *Baḥya ibn Paquda (*Avvertimenti all'anima*, Venice, 1806); and various *piyyutim* from the Sephardi liturgy. He wrote the *Kinat Sofedim* (Mantua, 1776) to commemorate the earthquake in Mantua which claimed 65 Jewish victims. On returning from his travels in Holland and England, he wrote *Viaggi in Olanda* (Venice, 1807) on his Dutch journey.

BIBLIOGRAPHY: Steinschneider, in: MGWJ, 43 (1899), 569f.; C. Roth, *History of the Jews in Venice* (1930), 341–3; Schirmann, Italyah, 401–7; idem, in: *Zion*, 29 (1964), 78–79; Gorali, in: *Taẓlil*, 2 (1961), 73–84; S. Simonsohn, *Toledot ha-Yehudim be-Dukkasut Mantovah*, 2 vols. (1962–64), index; I. Levi, in: *Il Vessillo Israelitico*, 53 (1905), 58f.

[Abraham David]

SARAVAL, JUDAH LEIB (d. 1617), Venetian rabbi. Saraval was a pupil of Samuel Judah *Katzenellenbogen and a member of the *bet din* of Ben Zion Sarfati, and after the latter's death was appointed chief rabbi of Venice. Taking part in the well-known dispute about the Rovigo *mikveh* (see Moses *Porto-Rafa), he was one of those to permit its use. His decision on the subject is published in the *Mashbit Milḥamot* (Venice, 1606), as well as one prohibiting the playing of tennis on the Sabbath. He was in charge of, and the treasurer for, the monies collected in Italy for Ereẓ Israel. Some of his responsa were published in *Naḥalat Ya'akov* (Padua, 1623), a collection of responsa by his pupil, Jacob b. Elhanan Heilperin, and also in the works of his contemporaries. He was on friendly terms with Leone *Modena. He translated *Saadiah Gaon's commentary to the Song of Songs (Nowydwor, 1777) from the original Arabic, the thorough knowledge of Arabic necessary for such a task being a rare accomplishment for a 17th century Italian rabbi. Saraval died in Padua.

BIBLIOGRAPHY: Steinschneider, Arab Lit, 58f.; Judah Aryeh of Modena, *Ziknei Yehudah*, ed. by S. Simonsohn (1956), 51f. (introd.); 38–39 (second pagination); L. Blau, in: *Jahresbericht der Landes-Rabbinerschule in Budapest*, 28 (1905), 105; 29 (1906), 114–6; Sonne, in: *Koveẓ al Yad*, 5 (1950), 215–7.

[Abraham David]

SARDI, SAMUEL BEN ISAAC (1185/90–1255/56), Spanish halakhist. Sardi lived in Barcelona and was well-to-do. Among the deeds written in Barcelona during the years 1073–1328 and published by Millás Vallicrosa are a number dated the beginning of the 13th century which are connected with the letting by Sardi of his lands and properties. Sardi was a pupil and colleague of Naḥmanides and sent him many halakhic queries to which he obtained detailed responsa; some of them, included in the *Sefer Ha-Terumot*, also appear in the works of the *Rishonim* (see Asaf in bibl.). Sardi also corresponded with Nathan b. Meir of Trinquetaille (*Sefer ha-Terumot*, gate 52) and began compiling his important work, *Ha-Terumot*, when he was 30 years old, finishing it in about 1225.

This work deals only with civil and commercial law and is, in fact, the first comprehensive code in Jewish law devoted solely to civil law. It had a considerable influence on Jewish law, chiefly through the *Arba'ah Turim* of *Jacob b. Asher which is often based on it in the section *Ḥoshen Mishpat*. In the introduction, and in the work itself, Sardi mentions another of his works, *Sefer Ha-Zikhronot*, which is not extant. Its scope is unknown, but from his references to it it appears to have consisted of talmudic novellae. *Ha-Terumot* was published in Salonika (1596, 1628), Prague (1608) and Venice (1643), the last with a valuable commentary by Azariah Figo, entitled *Giddulei Terumah* (2nd ed. Zolkiev 1709).

BIBLIOGRAPHY: Azulai, 1 (1852), 177, no. 129; 2 (1852), 160, n. 98; Gross, Gal Jud, 326; M. Schwab, *Rapport sur les Inscriptions Hébraïques de l'Espagne* (1907), 151f. (= *Nouvelles Archives des Missions Scientifiques*, 14 (1907), 379f.); J.M. Millás Vallicrosa, *Documents Hebraics de jueus Catalans* (1927), 21ff.; S. Assaf, *Sifran shel Rishonim*

(1935), 53–55; F. Cantera and J.M. Millás Vallicrosa, *Las inscripciones hebráicas de España* (1956), 346–8.

[Shlomoh Zalman Havlin]

SARDINIA, Mediterranean island belonging to Italy. The first authentic information regarding Jews in Sardinia is that in 19 C.E. Emperor Tiberius deported 4,000 Jewish youths to the island because a Roman Jew had defrauded a proselyte named Fulvia, wife of the senator Saturninus. Jewish inscriptions of the classical period have been found in Sardinia, in particular at San Antioco. The situation of the Jews was presumably similar to that of Jews in the other parts of the Roman Empire but deteriorated with the triumph of Christianity. In 599 a newly baptized Jew named Peter burst into the synagogue at Cagliari on Easter Sunday with a mob at his heels and deposited his baptismal robe, together with a crucifix and an image of the Virgin, in front of the Ark. When the Jews appealed to Pope Gregory I, he ordered reparation to be made. From the seventh century until 1326, when the island came under Aragonese rule, the situation of the Jews was generally good, although anti-Jewish riots occurred in Oristano and in the district of Arborea, which resulted in their expulsion from these localities. The Jewish settlement in Iglesias was prohibited temporarily after 1327.

The Jews continued to prosper during the first century of Aragonese rule and were even granted additional privileges, mainly in *Alghero; Sassari and *Cagliari also had sizable communities. Many Jews from Spain settled in Sardinia. Each community was headed by elected officers who had authority to decide in civil cases between Jews, and on minor claims between Jews and Christians. From 1430 conditions deteriorated. Except in Alghero, the Jews were obliged to wear a special *badge. They were forbidden to wear jewelry and allowed to wear only black shoes. Jews were prohibited from trading on Christian holidays and from employing Christians. No additional Jews were allowed to settle on the island. In 1485 the Jews were declared the property of the king and placed under the jurisdiction of a special royal officer. They were also forbidden to export any property or wares from the island. With the expulsion of the Jews from Spain and the Aragonese dominions in July 1492, the Jews were compelled to leave Sardinia. Many of the Sardinian exiles settled temporarily in the kingdom of Naples, others went to North Africa and to Turkey, especially Constantinople, where the surname Sardaigna is still common. Some, however, remained in Sardinia as converts to Christianity – notably the Caracassonna family, which for a while played a considerable role in Sardinian public life. A tribunal of the Inquisition was established in 1492 and remained sporadically active for some years.

From the close of the Middle Ages, no Jewish community of importance has existed in the island, and it was only in the 19th century that a few individual Jews settled here and there, generally on a temporary basis. By the Italian law regulating Jewish communal organization in 1931, Sardinia was included in the jurisdiction of the Rome community. Some historians consider that, during the tranquil period in the Middle Ages before Aragonese rule, considerable groups of Jews merged into the Christian population, instanced by the relatively small number of Jews found there in the 15th century. The absorption of the Jews into the general population is said to have left its mark on Sardinian life and institutions. Jewish elements may be found, according to some writers, in local folk customs, and in names of persons and places. However, such elements may be the result of the influence of other cultures which had a common source with Judaism or of chance resemblances.

BIBLIOGRAPHY: L. Falchi, *Gli Ebrei nella storia e nella poesia popolare dei Sardi* (1934); idem, *La dominazione ebraica in Sardegna* (1936); Milano, Bibliotheca, index, s.v. *Sardegna*; Milano, Italia, index, s.v. *Sardegune*; Roth, Italy, index; Spano, in: *Rivista Sarda*, 1 (1875), 23–52; Medina, in: RMI, 10 (1935/36), 145–6; Eliezer ben David (Bedarida), *ibid.*, 11 (1936/37), 328–58, 424–3; Levi, *ibid.*, 12 (1937/38), 129–62; Frey, Corpus, 1 (1936), nos. 656–60; Boscolo, in: *Annali della Facoltà di lettere e filosofia dell' Università di Cagliari*, 19 (1952), 162–71.

[Menachem E. Artom]

SARDIS, capital of the ancient kingdom of Lydia some 60 miles (90 km.) from the west coast of Turkey. A world capital under the Mermnad dynasty (c. 680–547 B.C.E.) whose riches culminated under Croesus, Sardis was a Hellenistic royal capital (270?–133 B.C.E.). Rebuilt after a devastating earthquake (17 C.E.), it was a prosperous Roman and Byzantine city until destroyed by Khosrau II of Persia in 616 C.E.

Sardis (Sfard in Lydian and Persian) is most probably the *Sepharad of Obadiah v. 20. If so, its Jewish community goes back to the time of the Persian Empire (547–334 B.C.E.). Although Sardis is not specifically mentioned, the historical situation makes it highly probably that some Jews were settled in the Lydian capital. After Antiochus III first destroyed, then refounded, Sardis (215–213 B.C.E.), his viceroy Zeuxis brought in Jewish settlers from Mesopotamia. A Roman decree cited by Josephus (Ant. 14:259–61) says that the Jewish community at Sardis had a place of assembly "from the beginning"; another decree makes it certain that there was a synagogue not later than the first century B.C.E. The size (probably several thousand in a city of c. 100,000) and the affluence of the Jewish community under the Roman rule have been made evident by the huge synagogue (over 130 yd. [120 m.] long and 20 yd. [18 m.] wide) discovered in 1962. Located on the main avenue of Sardis, behind a row of shops some of which were owned by Jews (Jacob, elder of the synagogue, Sabbatios, Samuel, Theoktistos), the structure formed part of the Roman gymnasium complex planned after 17 C.E. Perhaps the hall was originally intended as a Roman civil basilica but was turned over to the Jewish congregation, which changed and decorated the structure with elegant mosaics and marble revetments. It is conjectured that one of the few Hebrew inscriptions honors the emperor Lucius Verus, who visited Sardis in 166 C.E. Among the 80 inscriptions of the donors in Greek one antedates 212, and many with the family name Aurelius are of the

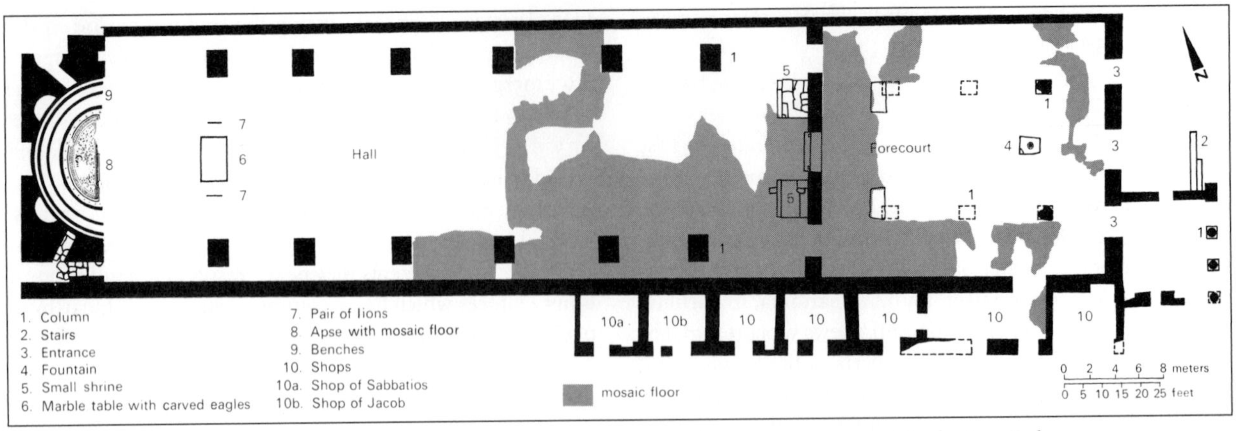

Plan of the synagogue at Sardis, late 2nd–early 3rd century C.E. *Based on D. J. Metten,* The Ancient Synagogue at Sardis, *New York, 1965.*

third century C.E. The building was renovated around 400 C.E. and destroyed in 616.

This, the largest of early synagogues preserved, consists of an entrance colonnade on the east, a peristyle forecourt with a fountain in the form of a marble crater, a prayer hall of basilican plan with six pairs of strong piers, and an apse at the western end with three rows of benches presumably for the elders of the community. Fragments of 18 candelabras (*menorot*) of marble and bronze were found. At the eastern end of the hall, between three gates, are two small shrines. At the western end a mosaic with water of life and two peacocks adorned the apse; in the bay next to the apse was a large marble table flanked by two pairs of lions, perhaps alluding to the tribe of Judah. Another donor describes himself as "of the tribe of Leontii." Traces of a light structure in the center of the hall may come from the **bimah*. A donor's mosaic inscription nearby (of the renewal period) mentions a "priest and teacher of wisdom" (i.e., rabbi?). Behind (west of) the apse two rooms belonged at one time to the synagogue; one had water installations (for the **mikveh*), the other a painted inscription: "Blessing unto the People." The prayer hall, splendidly revetted with marble, is estimated to have held up to a thousand people. The Jewish community apparently dispersed at the fall of the city in 616 C.E.

BIBLIOGRAPHY: Jos., Ant., 14:235, 259–61; 16:171; H.C. Butler, *Sardis*, 1 (1922); G.M.A. Hanfmann, *Sardis und Lydien* (1960); idem, in: BASOR, no. 170 (1963), 1–65; idem, in: *Papers of the Fourth World Congress of Jewish Studies*, 1 (1967), 37–42; L. Robert, *Nouvelles inscriptions de Sardis* (1964); Shiloh, in: BIES, 30 (1966), 245ff.; Mitten, in: BA, 29 (1966), 63ff.; EM, 5 (1968), 1100ff., s.v. *Sefarad*; Frey, Corpus, 2 (1952), nos. 750–1.

SARFATI (Ẓarefati, Sarfatti), name frequently given to Jews originating from *France, e.g., ABRAHAM SARFATI, who emigrated to Catalonia, author of *Tamid ha-Shaḥar*; Joseph ben MOSES SARFATI, mathematician; and ISAAC HA-SHAḤAR who emigrated to the East. The most important family often bearing the additional surname of Sarfati was the *Trabot or Trabotti family, who probably originated from Trévoux (France) and came to Italy in the second half of the 15th century. A *Sarfaty family were rabbis of Fez (Morocco) for several generations (16th–18th centuries).

SAMUEL SARFATI, called Gallo (d. c. 1519), a physician originating from Provence, settled in Rome in 1498. He represented the Jewish community at the coronation of Pope Julius II (1503) and a year later became the personal physician to the pope, who confirmed the privileges granted him by Pope Alexander VI, including permission to attend Christian patients, exemption from wearing the Jewish *badge, and papal protection for him and his family. In 1515 he became physician of Giuliano de' Medici. Samuel's son JOSEPH, called Josiphon, Giosifante, or Giuseppe Gallo (d. 1527), was a physician, philosopher, poet, and mathematician. An accomplished linguist, he had a good knowledge of Hebrew, Aramaic, Arabic, Greek, and Latin. The pope extended to him the privileges that had been accorded to his father; these were confirmed by Pope Leo X and Pope Clement VII in 1524. Joseph translated into Hebrew the Spanish comedy *Celestina*. He survived remarkable adventures, assisted David *Reubeni, and died as the result of his sufferings during the sack of Rome. ISAAC SARFATI was physician to Pope Clement VII (1523–34), who reconfirmed his right to the family's privileges. SAMUEL SARFATI (16th century) was a printer in Rome. JOSEPH SARFATI (16th century), a rabbi of Fez, converted to Christianity. Adopting the name of his godfather Pope Julius III (1550–55), Andrea del Monte, he became a violent anti-Jewish preacher. One of his sermons was heard by Michel de *Montaigne. Sarfati was one of the instigators of the condemnation of the Talmud and its burning in Rome in 1553. JACOB BEN SOLOMON SARFATI (14th century), a physician, was born in northern France. On the expulsion of the Jews, he moved to Avignon in the second half of the 14th century.

He was the author of *Mishkenot Ya'akov* (extant in Ms.), a work divided into three books: *Beit Ya'akov*, allegorical interpretations of some passages of the Pentateuch; *Yeshu'ot Ya'akov*, a discourse on the plagues of Egypt; and *Kehillat Ya'akov*, a theological exposition of the laws given on Mount Sinai. In a supplement, *Evel Rabbati*, he describes the deaths of his three sons who perished in the course of three months during the plague of 1395. He also wrote a medical treatise on migraine.

BIBLIOGRAPHY: U. Cassuto, *Gli Ebrei a Firenze nell' Età del Rinascimento* (1918); Hirschberg, Afrikah, 2 (1965), 156–8, 246–9.

[Renato Spiegel]

SARFATTI, GAD B. (1916–), Hebrew scholar and linguist. Born in Pisa, Italy, he studied at the University of Florence (1933–37). He immigrated to Israel in 1939, joined kibbutz Tirat Ẓevi (1940–47), and served in the Israeli army (1948–50). While Sarfatti received his academic training in mathematics in Italy, in Israel he studied Talmud in a yeshivah (1941–43), and Hebrew and linguistics at The Hebrew University of Jerusalem (1952–55). He also studied at the Laboratoire d'analyse lexicographique of the University of Besancon, France (1963). Sarfatti's major fields of research are Medieval Hebrew and Hebrew semantics. Teaching at Bar-Ilan University from 1962, he was appointed full professor in 1978, and emeritus in 1988. He was elected a member of the Hebrew Academy in 1970 and was named its vice president (1981–87). He was visiting professor at various universities in Italy and the U.S. He was awarded the Israel Prize for linguistics in 2000. Among his major publications are *Mathematical Terminology in Hebrew Scientific Literature of the Middle-Ages* (Heb., 1968) and *Hebrew Semantics* (Heb., 1985). A full list of Sarfatti's works and scientific publications appear in *Balshanut Ivrit* ("Hebrew Linguistics"), 33–35 (1992), 9–13.

[Aharon Maman (2nd ed.)]

SARFATY, family of rabbinic scholars in *Fez, *Morocco. According to a family tradition, the Sarfatys are descendants of Rabbenu Tam. R. Solomon, rabbi in Majorca, is mentioned in the responsa of R. Isaac bar Sheshet. A branch of the family settled in Fez. ISAAC (d. c. 1600) was *dayyan* in Fez. Some of his commentaries on biblical verses are quoted by his son Vidal in his works. VIDAL HA-SARFATY (c. 1550–1620) was referred to as "senior" and described as ḥasid ("pious"). He was a disciple of R. Abraham Uzziel.

His commentaries are outstanding for their originality; he quotes the Zohar and appears to have been a kabbalist. Many of the works of Spanish rabbis are cited in his works. Sarfaty's writings included: *Derekh ha-Kodesh*, a commentary to the *Sifra* (1908); *Megillat Sefarim*, on Esther, Ruth, and Lamentations; and *Oẓar Neḥmad*, on Psalms (both works were published in Amsterdam in 1718 under the title *Ẓuf Devash*); *Imrei Yosher* (1874), a commentary on *Midrash Rabbah*; and notes on R. Elijah Mizraḥi which were included in Samuel Sarfaty's *Nimmukei Shemu'el* (Amsterdam, 1718).

ISAAC (d. c. 1660), Vidal's son, was rabbi and *nagid* in Fez. The community backed him as *nagid* and appealed to the king to maintain him in this position. The king, however, appointed another in his place in 1650, nevertheless requesting that he remain in office. Isaac refused and was thereupon penalized by the king. When he secretly fled to Tetuán, he was arrested and imprisoned until he paid a fine. He wrote indexes to the *Midreshei Halakhah* and *Midreshei Aggadah*. He was his brother Abraham's business partner. His son, VIDAL (1631–1703), was *dayyan* together with R. Saadiah ibn Danān and R. Menahem Serero. He wrote decisions which have been lost. R. Jacob b. Ẓur was his son-in-law by a second marriage. His cousin, R. SAMUEL BEN ABRAHAM (1660–1713), was *dayyan* in Fez with R. Judah b. Atar. A sharp-witted talmudist and profound *posek*, he wrote *Divrei Shemu'el* (Amsterdam, 1699), novellae to the Talmud; *Nimmukei Shemu'el* (Amsterdam, 1718), a supercommentary on Rashi and Naḥmanides to the Torah; *Me'ulefet Sappirim*, which was published with *Nimmukei Shemu'el* in 1718; and decisions which are extant in manuscript. His brother, R. AARON (1665–c. 1740), was *dayyan* in Salé. He was a disciple of R. Aaron ha-Sab'uni who opposed the Shabbateans. He wrote *Misgav ha-Immahot*, which was included in the above-mentioned *Ẓuf Devash*. His cousin, R. ELIJAH BEN JOSEPH BEN ISAAC (1715–1805), was a disciple of R. Judah b. Atar. From 1770 he was the halakhic authority of the Maghreb. R. Jacob b. Ẓur was among the rabbis whom he ordained; he also educated many disciples. Intending to immigrate to Ereẓ Israel during the famine of 1738, he acquired letters of recommendation from the rabbis of Tetuán. From 1790 to 1792 he resided in Sefrou. His son, R. ISRAEL JACOB (1740–c. 1826), was appointed rabbi and *dayyan* during his father's lifetime. A leader of the community and a minister of the king, he greatly assisted the Jewish communites of Morocco. His brother, R. RAPHAEL MENAHEM HA-SARFATY (d. 1843), was one of the king's ministers and *nagid*.

R. VIDAL BEN SOLOMON BEN ISRAEL JACOB (1797–1856) was a rabbi, *dayyan*, and profound talmudist. A number of his decisions were published in the works of Moroccan *Ḥakhamim*. His son, R. ABNER ISRAEL (1827–1884), was rabbi and *dayyan* in Fez. Knowledgeable in philosophy and other sciences, he held disputations with Muslim scholars. A pietist and kabbalist, he was beloved by the masses, who continued to visit his tomb into the 20th century. He was also a bibliophile and a collector of books. He wrote legal decisions and responsa. His most important work is *Yaḥas Fez*, summaries of which have been published in Hebrew and French. His son, R. VIDAL (1862–1921), was rabbi in Fez from 1892. In 1919 he was appointed *av bet din* by the French Protectorate government. His son, R. ABNER ISRAEL (d. 1933), was appointed *dayyan* in Safi in 1932.

R. ẒEMAḤ (1647–1717), of pious character, was one of the most prominent 17th-century Tunisian *Ḥakhamim*. After living in Damascus for many years, he immigrated to Ereẓ Israel in 1656 and settled in Jerusalem. He was well known as a talmudist, and Azulai testifies in *Shem ha-Gedolim* that he saw "pages of the *Gemara* of the holy Midrash [yeshivah] Bet Ya'akov illuminated by his novellae." After Sarfaty's death his disciples held various rabbinic positions in Tunis; they also published his novellae in their works.

BIBLIOGRAPHY: J.M. Toledano, *Ner ha-Ma'arav* (1911), index; J. Ben-Naim, *Malkhei Rabbanan* (1931), s.v.; G. Vajda, *Un Recueil de Textes Historiques Judéo-Marocains* (1951), index, s.v. *Vidal ha-Sarfati.*

[Haim Bentov]

SARGON II (Heb. סַרְגּוֹן), king of Assyria and Babylonia, (722–705 B.C.E.), successor of Shalmaneser V, and father of *Sennacherib. There are conflicting opinions among scholars as to whether or not he was a son of Tiglath-Pileser III. The circumstances which brought Sargon to the throne are obscure; he may well have been an usurper, or a descendant of a secondary line of the royal house. His name, identical with that of Sargon of Akkad and Sargon I of Assyria, means: "the legitimate king" (see Tadmor, in bibl.). The beginning of his reign was marked by domestic difficulties, which he solved by giving the Assyrians and the settlers of *Haran a charter freeing them from taxes and military service. In 720 Sargon marched against *Merodach-Baladan, who had ascended the Babylonian throne the previous year. Supported by the Elamites, who were the chief opponents in the battle, Merodach-Baladan met Sargon at Dêr and defeated, or at least stopped, him. Engaged on practically all fronts in fighting rebellions – which he was able to suppress – Sargon could not take revenge against the Babylonian king until 710. This time his victory was complete. He entered Babylon, proclaiming himself king. Between 719 and 711 Sargon campaigned against the Medes, Mannai, and Ararat. In the "West" he completed the subjugation and conquest of Israel and Samaria, and, after quelling an Egyptian-sponsored revolt, rebuilt it and made it capital of his new province, Samerīna. Sargon's overall policy was the intermingling of the populations and the resources of the Near East under Assyrian leadership. For this purpose he went on to open the road to Egypt. In 716 he cleared and subjugated the western Sinai area and established an Assyrian *kārum*, a trade settlement, the purpose of this expedition being the opening up of Egyptian and Arabian trade to Assyria.

In approximately 713–712 Sargon conquered and organized Ashdod (Isa. 20:1 alludes to the first steps of this campaign). Then, under the commander in chief the *tartan*, Azuri, the plotting king of Ashdod, was deposed. Ashdod was supported by Egypt and very likely by *Hezekiah king of Judah; but the latter changed his mind after the Assyrian conquest of *Azekah. Remains of a stele of Sargon were discovered in Ashdod.

Near the modern Khorsabad he built a new capital city, Dûr-Sharrukin ("Sargon's fortress"). Sargon was killed in a campaign against the Cimmerians – newcomers in Urarṭu – and his encampment was sacked.

BIBLIOGRAPHY: H. Tadmor, in: JAOS, 12 (1955), 22–40; idem, in: *Eretz Israel*, 5 (1959), 150–62; P. Artzi, *ibid.*, 9 (1969) 28 n. 55; W.W. Hallo, in: BA, 23 (1960), 51–56.

SARID (Heb. שָׂרִיד).

(1) Town on the border of the territory of Zebulun (Josh. 19:10, 12). The original Hebrew form of the name was evidently Sadod; it appears as Sedud in the Septuagint, and scholars have accordingly located it at Tell Shadūd in the central Jezreel Valley. The pottery on the site dates from the Late Bronze to the Arabic periods, early Iron Age pottery being especially abundant.

[Michael Avi-Yonah]

(2) Kibbutz in northern Israel, in the Jezreel Valley, affiliated with Kibbutz Arẓi ha-Shomer ha-Ẓa'ir. Sarid was founded in 1926 by pioneers from Czechoslovakia, Germany, and East European countries. In 1970 Sarid had 620 inhabitants and maintained a regional high school of Ha-Shomer ha-Ẓa'ir. In the mid-1990s the population was approximately 715, dropping to 611 in 2002. The kibbutz raised field crops and fruits, poultry, and dairy cattle and also had a grindstone factory.

[Efraim Orni]

BIBLIOGRAPHY: Alt, in: PJB, 22 (1926), 59–60; 25 (1929), 38; Albright, in: BASOR, 19 (1925), 9; Abel, Geog, 2 (1938), 449; Press, Ereẓ, s.v.; Aharoni, Land, index. **WEBSITE:** www.sarid.org.il.

SARID (Schneider), YOSSI (1940–), Israeli journalist and politician, member of the Knesset since the Eighth Knesset in 1974. Born in Reḥovot, he served in the artillery corps and as a military reporter. In the course of his studies at the Hebrew University in Jerusalem in 1961–64, he worked as a reporter and news editor for the Israel Broadcasting Authority. He received a B.A. in philosophy and literature in 1964. Until 1965 he served as the spokesman of *Mapai, and, after the elections to the Sixth Knesset in 1965, served as advisor to Prime Minister Levi *Eshkol. He received an M.A. in political science and sociology from the New School for Social Research in New York in 1969. After his return to Israel, he was close to Minister of Finance Pinḥas *Sapir.

In 1970–73 Sarid ran the section for academics in the Ministry of Labor. In the elections right after the Yom Kippur War at the end of 1973, he was first elected to the Knesset on the Alignment list. In the course of 1974, after a deadly terrorist attack on Kiryat Shemonah, he moved with his family to the northern town for three years, and, in addition to his position as a Member of Knesset, worked voluntarily as a teacher in one of the local high schools. Sarid was one of the staunchest opponents of Operation Peace for Galilee in 1982, and as a result a rift opened between him and the Labor Party. When, after the elections to the Eleventh Knesset in 1984, the Labor Party decided to join a National Unity Government with the *Likud on the basis of rotation in the premiership, and agreed to Ariel *Sharon being given a ministerial position in the government despite the conclusions of the Kahane Commission, and approved the continued financial and moral support of Jewish settlements in the West Bank and Gaza Strip, Sarid decided to leave the party, and joined the Civil Rights Movement, headed by Shulamit *Aloni. Free of the constraints of membership in a leading party, Sarid became famous for his outspokenness and cynical style, and assumed the role of the "hated left-winger" among right-wing circles. In 1985 Sarid became editor of *Politika*, a left-wing political journal, which he continued to edit for several years.

In 1992, as a member of *Meretz, Sarid was appointed minister of the environment, and joined Minister for Foreign Affairs Shimon *Peres in peace talks after the signing of the Declaration of Principles with the Palestinians in 1993. When Aloni resigned from active politics prior to the elections to the Fourteenth Knesset in 1996, Sarid was elected as leader of the CRM and of Meretz. In the government formed by Ehud *Barak after the elections to the Fifteenth Knesset, Sarid was appointed minister of education and culture, a position he held until June 2000, when he decided to take Meretz out of the government several months before the outbreak of the second Intifada, owing to his dissatisfaction with Barak's attempts to pacify *Shas. In March 2000, Sarid was the first official Israeli who accepted an invitation by the Armenian Church in Jerusalem to participate in a memorial service for the genocide of the Armenians at the hands of the Turks in 1915, even though the official Israeli position was not to anger the Turkish government, which has never accepted responsibility for the event.

Following the major electoral defeat suffered by Meretz in the elections to the Sixteenth Knesset in 2003, when it lost four of its 10 seats, Sarid resigned from his position as leader of the party, but remained in the Knesset. In July 2004 he underwent brain surgery to remove a benign tumor.

In the Knesset, Sarid has served on the Foreign Affairs and Defense Committee, the House Committee, and the Education and Culture Committee.

He wrote books of poetry, *Pegishah be-Makom Aḥer* (1960) and *Shirim 2003–2005*, and *Ze ha-Nitu'aḥ Sheli* (2005), a book about his brain-surgery experience.

BIBLIOGRAPHY: Y. Ben-Porat, *Siḥot im Yossi Sarid* (1997).

[Susan Hattis Rolef (2nd ed.)]

SARKIL, *Khazar fortress, built on the Don with Byzantine help in 833 C.E. Sarkil's purpose appears to have been to defend Khazaria from enemies approaching from the west – who these were is not specifically stated, but the Pechenegs, Magyars, and Russians have been suggested – and, more particularly, to control the Don-Volga portage. This was the route by which ninth-century Russian merchants (Ibn Khurradādhbih, *Kitāb al-Masālik wa al-Mamālik*, 154) from the Black Sea reached the Volga; in the same century it was called the "Khazarian way." Sarkil is mentioned in the Long Version of the Reply of Joseph king of the *Khazars to *Ḥasdai ibn Shaprut. The name is explained as being from the Turkic (Chuvash) for "white house," hence it has been identified with Bela Vezha in the Russian Chronicle, and somewhat more doubtfully with the Arabic al-Bayḍā', "the white" (usually taken to mean *Atil). M.I. Artamonov fixes the site of Sarkil on the left bank of the lower Don near the village of Tsimlyanskaya, now covered by the waters of a reservoir. The remains on a neighboring site on the right bank of the Don are thought to be those of a forerunner of Sarkil, the name of which – corresponding to the material from which it was built (white limestone) – was transferred to the new fortress (the historic Sarkil was built of brick). Sarkil (Bela Vezha) is said to have been destroyed in the great Russian attack upon Khazaria in 965.

BIBLIOGRAPHY: D.M. Dunlop, *History of the Jewish Khazars* (1954), index; M.I. Artamonov, *Istoriya Khazar* (1962), 288–323; idem, in: *Sovetskaya Arkheologiya*, 16 (1952), 42–76; idem, in: *Materialy i issledovaniya po arkheologii S.S.S.R.*, 62 (1958); G. Moravcsik, *Byzantinoturcica*, 2 (1958), 268–9; A.N. Poliak, *Kazariyah* (1951), index s.v. *Sharkil.*

[Douglas Morton Dunlop]

SARMAD, MUHAMMAD SA'ID (d. 1661), Persian poet. Born into a rabbinical family in Kashan in the early 17th century, Sarmad became a convert to *Islam, though he is always referred to in Persian and European sources as "Sarmad the Jew," "the Hebrew pantheist," or "the Jewish mystic." Migrating to *India, he moved from Tatta to Hyderabad and in 1654 was in Delhi, capital of the Mogul empire, where he led the life of a dervish, a "naked fakir walking through the streets." A popular composer of Sufic poetry, he collaborated with the author of the *Dabistān*, a comprehensive work in Persian on comparative religion. Material for the chapter on Judaism was supplied by Sarmad, who also edited a Persian translation of the Pentateuch of which six chapters of Genesis were included in the *Dabistān*. Sarmad's association with the crown prince of the Mogul dynasty led to his downfall, and he was executed in Delhi. His *Dīwān*, containing over 300 poems, was printed in 1897.

BIBLIOGRAPHY: Fischel, in: PAAJR, 18 (1949), 137–77; A.V.W. Jackson, *The Dabistan, or School of Manners* (1901).

[Walter Joseph Fischel]

°**SARMIENTO, PEDRO** (c. 1400–1464), commander of the fortress (*alcaide del alcázar*) of Toledo, responsible for riots against the *Conversos in the town in 1449. Sarmiento came from a family of courtiers and served as chief confectioner (*repostero mayor*) to John II of Castile (1406–54), who appointed him commander of the Toledo fortress in 1445. In 1449 he incited the population of the town to attack the Conversos holding public office there. The pretext for the revolt was a heavy tax imposed by the courtier Alvaro de Luna in the name of the king. As a first step, the rioters set fire to the house of a certain Alonso Cota, of Converso origin, one of the principal tax farmers. Sarmiento took over the powers of the local authorities and arrested all the prominent Conversos. After he had carried out a judicial investigation, and they had confessed their loyalty to Judaism under torture, he condemned them to be burned at the stake.

Sarmiento then published a regulation which laid down, on the strength of an imaginary royal privilege allegedly granted to Toledo by one of the former kings, that New Christians and their issue could not hold public office. It was the first instance of racial discrimination practiced in Castile against the Conversos. A memorandum by Sarmiento's legal adviser, García de Mora, was attached to the regulation. It included severe accusations against the New Christians who, he alleged, were practicing Judaism and plotting against Christianity and the faithful. The disorders in Toledo spread as far as *Ciudad Real, where trials of Conversos were also held. Sarmiento's actions were condemned by the king, who dismissed him from his position. Pope *Nicholas V issued a bull in which he denounced the regulation. In the same year the bishop of Burgos, Alonso de Cartagena (the son of Solomon *ha-Levi who had adopted Christianity), wrote his *Defensorium Unitatis Christiana*, in which he sharply criticized the segregation between Old and New Christians introduced by Sarmiento. In 1452 Sarmiento was pardoned by the king and during the reign of his successor, Henry IV (1454–74), was reinstated in his court functions.

BIBLIOGRAPHY: Baer, Spain, 2 (1966), 279–82; E. Benito Ruano, in: *Revista de la Universidad de Madrid*, 5 (1956), 345ff.; 6 (1957), 277ff.; idem, *Hidalguía* (1957), 41ff., 314ff.; idem, in: *Hispania*, 17 (1957), 483ff.; idem, *Toledo en el siglo XV* (1961), index; H. Beinart, *Anusim be-Din ha-Inkvizizyah* (1965), index.

[Joseph Kaplan]

SARNA, EZEKIEL (1889–1969), *rosh yeshivah* in Israel. Born in Gorodok, Lithuania, Sarna was the son of Jacob Ḥayyim Sarna, the *Maggid* ("preacher") of Slonim and a close associate of Ḥayyim *Soloveitchik. At an early age Ezekiel was accepted in the famous yeshivah of Slobodka, Lithuania, where he became known as the *illui* ("child prodigy") of Gorodok. He was particularly influenced by the method of study and moral inspiration of the heads of the yeshivah – the *Sabba* of Slobodka, Nathan Ẓevi *Finkel, and Moses Mordecai *Epstein. When World War I broke out, the Slobodka yeshivah was transferred from Kovno to Kremenchug in the Ukraine. In this period Sarna studied under *Israel Meir ha-Kohen (Ḥafeẓ-Ḥayyim). His marriage to Epstein's daughter accorded Sarna, already distinguished by his talent and profound acumen, a special status. After the war the yeshivah returned to Slobodka, where Sarna was appointed a lecturer. Following the *Balfour Declaration, the third wave of *aliyah* got under way, and Epstein decided (1924) to transfer the Slobodka yeshivah to Ereẓ Israel. For this purpose he sent Sarna to choose a site. Sarna selected Hebron, where he immediately became one of the heads of the yeshivah and was mainly responsible for its development. About a year later Finkel and Epstein joined the yeshivah. On the death of his father-in-law in 1927, Sarna was appointed *rosh yeshivah*, a position he held until his death. The yeshivah attracted students from all parts of the world and, at the time of its destruction in the pogrom of 1929, had 265 students. Sarna reestablished the yeshivah in Jerusalem as the Hebron Yeshivah. Under Sarna's guidance it again flourished. His talmudic and *musar* discourses achieved a reputation in the yeshivah world, and Hebron Yeshivah developed into one of the largest and most important Torah centers in Israel, continuing the educational and *musar* methods of the great Lithuanian yeshivot. As a leader of the Va'ad ha-Yeshivot, Sarna was mainly preoccupied by his own and other yeshivot, but was also actively interested in national problems. He was a member of the Mo'eẓet Gedolei ha-Torah, the supreme religious institution of *Agudat Israel. He held independent views on political matters, both local and foreign, and on occasion addressed his opinions to the prime minister and members of the Israel government, attempting by virtue of his personality to influence the political, social, and religious life of the state. He was instrumental in obtaining exemption from military service for yeshivah students. Sarna had a unique style in *halakhah* and *musar*, and published a number of books, including commentaries on *Judah Halevi's *Kuzari* (1965), on the *Orḥot Ḥayyim* by *Asher b. Jehiel (1957, 1962), and on *Mesillat Yesharim* (1957, 1965) by Moses Ḥayyim *Luzzatto. He left many manuscripts on *halakhah* and Jewish thought. Despite an illness in his last years, he undertook the establishment of the new yeshivah center, Kiryat Ḥevron, in southern Jerusalem.

[Itzhak Goldshlag]

SARNA, JONATHAN DANIEL (1955–), university professor, author, and scholar of American Jewish history. Born in Philadelphia and raised in New York and Boston, Sarna was the son of the renowned Bible scholar Nahum M. *Sarna and Helen Horowitz, a librarian. Sarna earned degrees from Boston Hebrew College and Brandeis University before matriculating to Yale University where he pursued graduate studies in American history, modern Jewish history, and American religious history. Upon receiving his Ph.D. in 1979, Sarna was awarded a postgraduate fellowship at Hebrew Union College-Jewish Institute of Religion (HUC-JIR) in Cincinnati, Ohio, by the pioneering American Jewish historian Jacob Rader *Marcus. The following year, he joined HUC-JIR's faculty, and he quickly rose to the rank of professor. In 1990, Sarna became the Joseph H. and Belle R. Braun Professor of American Jewish History at Brandeis University.

Sarna's keen interest in American Jewish history first emerged during his teenage years. He later theorized that his strong interest in the field may have come from the fact that he was the first member of his family born in the United States. He became convinced that by synthesizing American and Jewish history, he could gain a deeper understanding of his own world.

At Yale, Sarna's historical philosophy took shape. He was influenced by many members of the university's history faculty, including Sidney Ahlstrom, the distinguished scholar of American religion. Noting that many historians tended to categorize Jews in America as an ethnic group with little reference to their religious life, Sarna set out to place American Judaism within the larger historical context of religious life in America. His doctoral dissertation was a biographical study of Mordecai Manuel *Noah, one of the first American Jews to gain prominence in both the Jewish and the general community. Sarna used Noah's life to exemplify a central theme in American Jewish history: the ongoing effort to be American and Jewish at the same time. The nature of this tension is summarized in the title of his first book, which grew out of his dissertation: *Jacksonian Jew: The Two Worlds of Mordecai Noah* (1981).

In his second major volume, *JPS, A Cultural History of the Jewish Publication Society* (1989), Sarna similarly examined the ways in which Jews have interacted with American culture. In his magnum opus, *American Judaism* (2004), a full-scale interpretive history of Jewish religious life in America, Sarna broadly demonstrated how evolving trends in American religion as a whole have repeatedly influenced the historical development of Jewish religious life in America.

A prolific author, Sarna wrote, edited, or co-edited dozens of historical publications that have influenced the field of American Jewish history. His volume *People Walk on Their Heads* (1982) illuminates the complicated and difficult nature of Jewish immigrant life in New York. Sarna's interest in the history of Jewish communities impelled him to publish several articles and books on this subject, including *The Jews of Cincinnati* (1989) and *The Jews of Boston* (1995). Many of Sarna's monographs, such as his essay on the development of mixed seating in the American synagogue and his article on the role of great awakenings in American Judaism, have spurred American Jewish historians to explore new avenues of research.

Many of Sarna's historical readers have become useful tools for the teaching of American Jewish history, such as *The American Jewish Experience* (1986, rev. ed. 1997); *Religion and State in the American Jewish Experience* (1997); *Women and American Judaism: Historical Perspectives* (2001); and *Jews and the American Public Square* (2002).

By the dawn of the 21st century, Sarna had become a senior scholar in the field. He served as chair of the Academic Advisory and Editorial Board of The Jacob Rader Marcus Center of the American Jewish Archives, where he also served as consulting scholar. He also became a consulting historian to the National Museum of American Jewish History in Philadelphia. In 2004–2005, Sarna was named chief historian for Celebrate 350, the Jewish community's national organizing committee for commemorating the 350th anniversary of Jewish life in America. He was also a consulting scholar to the congressionally recognized Commission for Commemorating 350 Years of American Jewish History.

Sarna's deep knowledge of the field attracted many scholars and researchers to consult with him and, as a faculty advisor at both HUC-JIR and Brandeis University, he influenced a significant number of graduate students who went on to fill important research and teaching positions in the field.

Sarna is married to Rabbi Ruth Langer, a professor of Jewish Studies at Boston College.

[Gary P. Zola (2nd ed.)]

SARNA, NAHUM M. (1923–2006), biblical scholar. Sarna was born in London into a family that was both traditionally observant and Zionist. After receiving an intensive elementary and secondary Jewish education, he attended Jews' College, then part of the University of London, where he earned his B.A. (1944) and M.A. (1946), studying rabbinics, Bible and Semitic languages. From Jews' College Sarna also received a Minister's Diploma (1949), a degree that certified its holders as pulpit ministers rather than legal decisors (*posekim*). He moved briefly to postwar Israel (1949), but because conditions there were not favorable for serious study, Sarna came to Dropsie College in Philadelphia and completed his Ph.D. (1955) under Cyrus *Gordon. While pursuing his studies, and shortly thereafter, Sarna taught at Gratz College in Philadelphia (1951–57). Between 1957 and 1965 Sarna served at the Jewish Theological Seminary as librarian (1957–63) and as associate professor of Bible. Not receiving promotion at JTS, Sarna moved to Brandeis University as Golding Professor, and served in that chair from 1965 to 1985. Between 1966 and 1981 Sarna was a member of the committee that translated the last section of the Jewish Bible (*Ketuvim*, or Writings) for the *Tanakh: The Holy Scriptures* of the Jewish Publication Society (1982). Sarna successfully employed both ancient Near Eastern material and the traditional Jewish sources to illuminate the Bible. He also pioneered in "inner biblical interpretation," showing how biblical writers often interpreted and reinterpreted each other. In a very active retirement, Sarna held visiting professorships and initiated and edited the JPS Torah Commentary, for which he wrote the volumes *Genesis* (1989), and *Exodus* (1991). Famed as a pedagogue and lecturer, Sarna was highly influential in training many of the current generation of Bible scholars. But Sarna wrote for intelligent laics as well. As Jeffrey Tigay observed, "No scholar has done as much as Sarna to educate English-speaking Jewry about the Bible," as exemplified in *Exploring Exodus* (1986) and in *Songs of the Heart: An Introduction to the Book of Psalms* (1993), and the aforementioned JPS Torah volumes.

BIBLIOGRAPHY: M. Brettler in: DBI, 2:438–39; J. Tigay, in: N. Sarna, *Studies in Biblical Interpretation* (2000), xiii–xxiv; bibliography of Sarna's publications, in: ibid., 431–36.

[S. David Sperling (2nd ed.)]

SARNOFF, DAVID (1891–1971), U.S. electronics pioneer and executive. Sarnoff, who was born in Uzlian, Russia, was taken to the U.S. in 1900. A self-taught telegrapher who had joined the Marconi Telegraph Company of America in 1906 as an office boy, Sarnoff was the operator on duty who picked up and relayed the *Titanic's* distress signal in 1912. When the Radio Corporation of America (RCA), formed in 1919, gained control of the Marconi Company, Sarnoff became RCA's commercial manager (1919) and subsequently its president (1930). Foreseeing the enormous growth of the radio medium, and determined to prove the practicality of coast-to-coast broadcasting, he founded the National Broadcasting Company in 1926 as an RCA subsidiary. Later, he directed RCA's efforts toward making television a practical working medium. He developed its potential as an inexpensive instrument providing entertainment and information for a mass audience. His subsequent decision to invest huge sums to develop color television was made in the face of determined opposition within the company. However, the success of color television vindicated his decision. Sarnoff's abilities built RCA into the world's largest electronic complex, doing approximately $2 billion business annually in the late 1960s, in fields ranging from radio and television to computers and earth-orbiting satellites, and employing approximately 100,000 persons in the U.S. and 43 foreign plants.

Active in Jewish affairs, Sarnoff was a member of the board of trustees of the Educational Alliance and the first honorary fellow of the Weizmann Institute of Science. He was associated with the Jewish Theological Seminary for over 25 years and served as a member of both its board of directors and its executive committee. Long active in the U.S. Army Reserve, he was appointed to the rank of brigadier general in 1944.

His son, ROBERT SARNOFF (1918–1997), who was born in New York City, served in the army during World War II. After a period as an executive with Cowles Publications (1945–48), he joined the National Broadcasting Company. Sarnoff subsequently served as that company's president (1955–58) and board chairman (1958–66). In 1966 he was appointed president of RCA and in 1967, chief executive officer. He resigned in 1975. He was married to opera singer Anna Moffo.

BIBLIOGRAPHY: E. Lyons, *David Sarnoff, A Biography* (1966). **ADD. BIBLIOGRAPHY:** E. Myers, *David Sarnoff: Radio and TV Boy* (1972); C. Dreher, *Sarnoff, an American Success* (1977); K. Bilby, *The General* (1986); T. Lewis, *Empire of the Air* (1991); D. Stashower, *The Boy Genius and the Mogul: The Untold Story of Television* (2002).

SARNY, town in Rovno district, Ukraine. It may be assumed that the first Jews settled in Sarny in 1901, with the opening of the railroad station there. As Sarny was then a village, Jews had difficulty, under the czarist restrictions on their settlement in villages, in obtaining permission to live there. After Sarny acquired the status of a town in May 1903, its Jewish community developed rapidly. During the Civil War after the end of World War I, the Jews of Sarny did not suffer from the pogroms in Ukraine, and the community aided refugees and orphans from other places. Sarny's economy was largely based on the lumber industry. In independent Poland, after Sarny was made the district capital in 1921, the city developed further. The Jewish population numbered 2,808 in 1921 (47% of the total), 3,414 (45%) in 1931, and 4,950 (45%) in 1937. A *Tarbut school was founded in 1920–21, and an *ORT school in 1923–24. There were also a *talmud torah*, and several *ḥadarim*. At the outbreak of World War II, preparations were under way for opening a Hebrew high school. Until the early 1920s *ẓaddikim* of the *Karlin-Stolin ḥasidic dynasty lived in Sarny, and later continued to visit it.

[Shmuel Spector]

Holocaust Period

After the outbreak of World War II many refugees arrived in Sarny, and by 1941 the number of Jews there had risen to 7,000. During the Soviet occupation (1939–41) the Jewish institutions were disbanded. The 2,000 refugees from German-occupied western Poland were transferred to the Soviet interior. The Germans occupied Sarny on July 5, 1941, and immediately the Ukrainians staged a three-day pogrom. There began persecution of the Jews, indiscriminate murder, seizure of able-bodied people for forced labor, and extortion of large sums of money. On the Day of Atonement (Oct. 1, 1941) they rounded up the Jews in Sarny for a census and ordered them to wear the yellow badge, instead of a white band with a blue Star of David. A ghetto was established in April 1942, packed with 6,000 persons, 15 per room, and a few weeks later the Jewish community was forced to pay a "fine" of 250,000 rubles ($50,000). In June 1942, when information of mass murders reached Sarny, armed groups were organized there. They planned to set a fire and escape into the forest. But when the Germans came, the secretary of the Judenrat convinced the groups not to act. The Germans transferred the ghetto Jews to the "Poleska" camp, where about 15,000 Jews and 1,500 gypsies Jews from near-by settlements were already concentrated. On Aug. 27–28, 1942, the Germans began to "liquidate" the community. A group headed by two Jews, Tendler and Josef Gendelman, cut the wire fence, ordered to set fire to the camp barracks, and called for a mass escape. Thousands tried to flee, many of them were shot, and only a few hundred reached the forests; there some of them joined the Soviet partisan units of Satanovski and Kaplan (both Jews).

Sarny was retaken by the Soviet army on Jan. 11, 1944. A handful of survivors returned from the Soviet interior, and about 20 Jewish partisans, some of whom had fought against the Ukrainian bands led by Stefan Bandera. The remnants of the Sarny community fenced in the local cemetery and restored the tombstones that had been used for pavements. In the late 1960s there were about 100 Jews in Sarny.

[Aharon Weiss / Shmuel Spector (2nd ed.)]

BIBLIOGRAPHY: *Sefer Yizkor li-Kehillat Sarny* (1961). **ADD. BIBLIOGRAPHY:** S. Spector (ed.), PK *Poland*, vol. 5 – *Volhynia and Polesie* (1990).

SARPHATI, SAMUEL (1813–1866), Dutch physician and social reformer. Sarphati was one of the progressive leaders of Amsterdam in the mid-19th century. At the start of his professional career he was employed part time by the Portuguese Jewish community as a physician for the poor. The social dismay he experienced made him engage in numerous social and economic development projects. He initiated the first municipal garbage-collecting service, and was involved in the building of an industrial bakery to provide quality bread for the masses as well as the establishment of the city's first school of trade and commerce. Other endeavors saw public toilets situated throughout the city and the filling in of several polluted and foul-smelling inner-city canals. Sarphati stimulated urban expansion outside the ancient city walls. To facilitate financial investors he was instrumental in establishing the Netherlands Credit and Deposits Bank, a national mortgage bank and building society. Sarphati was also responsible for the founding of the "Paleis voor Volksvlijt," a vast glass-and-steel industrial exhibition hall, and the grand Amstel Hotel to accommodate commercial entrepreneurs.

Sarphati was a co-founder of the Netherlands Pharmaceutical Society. He was a member of the North Holland Provincial Council and was decorated Knight of the Order of the Netherlands Lion. A street, a park, and a quay in Amsterdam are named after him.

BIBLIOGRAPHY: S. Bottenheim, *Dr. Samuel Sarphati…* (1945); H. van der Kooy and J. de Leeuwe, *Sarphati, een biografie* (2001)

[Henriette Boas / Daniel M. Metz (2nd ed.)]

ṢARRĀF, Arabic money changer, intendant, treasurer; *ṣarrāf bashi*, Arabic-Turkish chief money changer, chief banker. In Islamic countries Muslims were all but forbidden to work in gold and silver, not only as goldsmiths and silversmiths but also as *jahābidha* (Persian; sing. *jahbādh*), i.e., money changers, coin testers, and collectors of taxes and customs dues, who had to be capable of calculating the value of different kinds of coins in accordance with the percentage of precious metal they contained. An order by the caliph al-Muqtadir (908–932) restricted the employment of Jews and Christians in the government to physicians and *jahābidha*. Arab sources report the presence of Jewish wholesale merchants, toll farmers, and bankers at the court of the caliphs in *Baghdad. A Jew, Yaqʿūb ibn Yusūf *Ibn Killis, laid the foundation for a public tax collection system in *Egypt during the reign of al-Muʿizz (969–975), the first *Fāṭimid ruler of that country. *Ḥisdai ibn Shaprut was the chief customs collector and a physician in *Umayyad Spain during the reign of Abd al-Raḥmān III (912–961). These dignitaries indirectly influenced the attitude of the governments toward the Jews. The prominent Jacob *Ibn Jau, a merchant and the official manufacturer and supplier of silk, was appointed tax collector and *nasi* of the Jews in Spain during the rule of al-*Manṣur (977–991).

In the Ottoman Empire many Jews, Armenians, and Copts served as *ṣarrāf* at the courts of the provincial pashas and in the capital. Their positions as tax collectors, toll farmers, cashiers, and bankers, and their influence at court enabled them to act as the natural spokesmen for their communities. The Jewish representatives had titles such as *chelebi* (Turkish: gentleman), *bazirkān* (Persian: *bazargar*, merchant), *muʿallim* (Arabic: teacher). These titles were still in use in the early 19th century in *Istanbul. The Armenian equivalent bore the title *amira*. The *amira*, the banker, and the financial advisers to the viziers and various ministers of the Ottoman government were the highest secular authorities in the Armenian community until regulations for the Armenian *millet were finally drafted and approved in 1863.

A similar development occurred in *Iraq. From the early 18th century, the Jewish *ṣarrāf bashi*, the chief banker and finance minister to the pasha or *wālī* of Baghdad, assumed the position and title of **nasi*. Until the middle of the 19th century the *ṣarrāf bashi* of Baghdad acted as *nasi* of the Baghdad community. His political importance sometimes was exaggerated and compared with that of the *exilarch under the *Abbasids, e.g., in the report of the Jewish convert to Christianity and missionary J. *Wolff (author of *Narrative of a Mission to Bokhara*, 1852), who was introduced to the *nasi* Saul Laniado in 1824. The first *nasi* in Baghdad was the *ṣarrāf bashi* Moses b. Mordecai *Shindookh. One of the last to hold the office of *ṣarrāf bashi* in Baghdad was Ezra b. Joseph Gabbai. His brother Ezekiel attained the position of *ṣarrāf bashi* to the sultan Maḥmūd II (1808–39). Court intrigues and interdenominational rivalry between Jews and Armenians sometimes made the position of *ṣarrāf bashi* a very dangerous one, and the tragic deaths of some are described in various sources.

In Egypt the appointment of Joseph *Cattaui as *ṣarrāf bashi* by the khedive Saʿīd (1854–1863) was not linked with any official function in the Jewish community. The development of tourism necessitated enforcing of controls over the money changers, and this became the main task of the *ṣarrāf bashi*. E.W. Lane (in *The Manners and Customs of the Modern Egyptians* (1968), 562) wrote: "Many of the Egyptian Jews are *ṣarrāfs* (or bankers and moneylenders), others are *seyrefees* (dialect: money changers), and are esteemed men of strict probity." In 1872 a German traveler also stressed the role of the Jews in the banking (*ṣarrāf*) business: "They tend to be *ṣaraffen* (money changers) and then rise easily to a kind of banker, some indeed becoming great bankers" (M. Luettke, *Aegyptens neue Zeit*, 1 (1873), 98). According to a Christian Arabic source (Ali Mubārak, *Al-Khiṭaṭ al-Jadīda*, 12 (1305 A.H.), 95) in the middle of the 19th century, 21 out of 49 Jews in Suez were money changers.

[Haïm Z'ew Hirschberg]

Jewish Banking (Middle East)

With the growing involvement of Middle Eastern countries in the world economy during the second half of the 19th century, and the expansion of financial operations in these countries, Jewish banking families at the major commercial centers of the Ottoman Empire and Egypt reached the zenith of their economic power. Their influence on financial and economic developments was great. Among these families were the *Sassoons (Baghdad-Bombay-London), the *Camondos (Istanbul-Paris), and the Menashes (Alexandria-Vienna). The big banking families did not confine their activities to the financial sector. They were involved in foreign trade transactions and in commercial agriculture, transportation, and urban development projects. These big banker-entrepreneurs also made substantial contributions to Jewish community institutions. Their support of education was of particular significance. At times the Jewish bankers operated in fierce competition and at other times in cooperation with European banks and with other local big banking families (Greek, Armenian, and also Muslim). In the course of their activity during the last decades of the century, some of the Jewish banking families transferred their business headquarters to European capitals, especially London and Paris. The extreme changes in the political and economic conditions in the Middle East and Europe during the first half of the 20th century brought about the decline of these influential families. In some cases their assets were confiscated or nationalized, in others they were acquired by or merged with large economic concerns or multinational corporations.

[Gad Gilbar (2nd ed.)]

BIBLIOGRAPHY: Fischel, Islam; Ibn Daud, Tradition, 50–51 (Hebrew section), 69 (English section); H.Z. Hirschberg, in: A.J. Arberry (ed.), *Religion in the Middle East*, 1 (1969), 119–225; D.S. Sassoon,

History of the Jews in Baghdad (1949), 122–7; A. Ben-Ya'acov, *Yehudei Bavel* (1965), passim; Rosanes, Togarmah, 6 (1945), 71–76; E.W. Lane, *Modern Egyptians* (1908, repr. 1936), 562; J.M. Landau, *Ha-Yehudim be-Miẓrayim ba-Me'ah ha-Tesha-Esreh* (1967), index s.v. *Ḥalfanut.* **ADD. BIBLIOGRAPHY:** JEWISH BANKING: A. Wright and H.A. Cartwright, *Twentieth Century Impressions of Egypt* (1909); S. Jackson, *The Sassoons*, 1968; G. Kramer, *The Jews in Modern Egypt 1914–1952* (1989); N. Şeni, "The Camondos and their Imprint on 19th-Century Istanbul," in: *International Journal of Middle East Studies*, 26 (1994), 663–75; N. Şeni and S. Le Tarnec, *Les Camondos ou l'éclipse d'une fortune* (1997); M. Rozen (ed.), *The Last Ottoman Century and Beyond: The Jews in Turkey and the Balkans, 1808–1945* (2005).

SARRAUTE (Cherniak), NATHALIE (1900–1999), French novelist. Born in Ivanova-Vosnesensk, Russia, into an assimilated Jewish family, Nathalie Sarraute was taken to France at the age of two. She practiced as a lawyer until the Nazi occupation in 1940, when she joined the French underground. Her literary career began rather late. She had studied philology at the universities of Oxford and Berlin, and in 1938 published *Tropismes* (Eng. tr. 1967), a series of cameos which constituted a criticism of language and a condemnation of subject matter as such in the novel. Her own first novel, however, did not appear until 1944. Entitled *Portrait d'un inconnu*, it attracted much attention. particularly that of Sartre. Nathalie Sarraute is recognized as one of the initiators of the modern school known as "le nouveau roman," which counted Alain Robbe-Grillet and Michel Butor among its best-known younger members. Her novels *Martereau* (1953; Eng. 1967), *Le Planetarium* (1959, 19682), and *Les Fruits d'or* (1963), do not relate any story or describe any events, and in fact represent the trend of the anti-novel. Their aim is to reveal a reality which is both beneath and beyond the everyday, obvious reality of the traditional and existentialist novel. The author stated her views on the novel in a series of essays, *L'Ere du soupçon* (1956; *The Age of Suspicion*, 1967). For a time she abandoned the novel and wrote two radio plays, *Le Silence* and *Le Mensonge* (published in one volume, 1967); but in *Entre la vie et la mort* (1968), using literary circles as a setting, she reverted to her basic form. Later novels included *L'Usage de la parole* (1980) and *Tu ne t'aimes pas* (1989). Her autobiography, *Enfance*, appeared in 1983. Nathalie Sarraute, a liberal leftist, eventually adopted an openly pro-Israel stand and paid a lengthy visit to the country in 1969.

BIBLIOGRAPHY: M. Kranakē, *Nathalie Sarraute* (Fr., 1965), incl. bibl.; J. Jaccard, *Nathalie Sarraute* (Fr., 1967); R. Micha, *Nathalie Sarraute* (Fr., 1966). **ADD. BIBLIOGRAPHY:** S. Barbour, *Nathalie Sarraute and the Feminist Reader* (1993); H. Watson-Williams, *The Novels of Nathalie Sarraute* (1981); B. Knapp, *Nathalie Sarraute* (1994); E. O'Beirne, *Reading Nathalie Sarraute: Dialogue and Distance* (1999).

[Arnold Mandel]

SARREGUEMINES, town in the Moselle department, northeastern France. Jews have lived in Sarreguemines since the 13th century. Expelled in 1477, they reappeared at the latest in 1690 under the French occupation. One family was authorized to settle in the town in 1721, others in 1753, and still others in 1787. The synagogue, erected about 1769, was rebuilt in 1862, and again in 1959, after having been destroyed in 1940. The local rabbinate was established in 1791. Throughout the 19th and early 20th centuries, the Jewish community slowly grew. By 1939, it numbered approximately 395. It is estimated that about 89 of Sarreguemines' Jews died during the Holocaust. In 1971 the Jewish community numbered 250. In 2005, in an act of vandalism, over 60 of the Jewish cemetery's 500 tombstones were toppled and smashed.

BIBLIOGRAPHY: H. Hiegel, *Châtellenie... de Sarreguemines* (1934), 314–5; R. Weil, in: *Almanach-Calendrier des communautés israélites de la Moselle* (1956), 81–83.

[Gilbert Cahen]

SAR SHALOM BEN BOAZ (d. c. 859 or 864 C.E.), *gaon* of Sura from 838 to 848. Sar Shalom succeeded *Kohen Ẓedek and was succeeded by *Natronai b. Hilai. His personality reflects a kindly individual, profoundly learned, who exercised a benign and understanding authority. His appeal to the Jewry of the time and their admiration for him probably account for the fact that he was the most prolific writer of responsa of his time, and more than 100 of them are extant. A large number deal primarily with matters pertaining to prayer, benedictions, and the reading of the Torah; excerpts of his erudite opinions were later incorporated in the *Seder *Amram Ga'on*. Sar Shalom's responsa reveal a liberal attitude to non-Jews: he explicitly prohibited taking advantage of, or in any way infringing upon, the rights of those who were not coreligionists, even if according to the letter of the law it might be considered permissible. He ruled that even if a woman went through the ceremony of ablution for conversion against her will, she was to be considered fully Jewish, and food, including wine, served by her was permissible for use.

He never assumed an overbearing manner to his subordinates. Indeed, a generous, conciliatory tone is manifested in his epistles to leaders of Jewish communities even from distant countries, who turned to him for religious clarification in different matters. He never adopted a dogmatic view in his decisions; he would generally present both sides of a disputation, explaining the practices followed, and points of view held by the academies of both Sura and Pumbedita, the great centers of learning, and allowing the heads of congregations to make their own choice. Moreover, he admonished the people not to bind themselves with regulations to which it would be difficult to adhere. If he heard that a community had restricted itself by a vow which it later felt unable to comply with, he would use the authority of his office to rescind such an oath. He explains the reasons for his decisions in an amiable tone and often writes in his responsa how much he would prefer to have his correspondents in his presence for thorough elucidation, to make his decision acceptable to the inquirer. In his responsa Sar Shalom also deals with some of the geonic *takkanot*. Although of mild disposition, he severely punished a person who struck another, a man who maltreated his wife, and a wife who was guilty of recalcitrant behavior toward her husband.

BIBLIOGRAPHY: R.S. Weinberg, in: *Sinai*, 65 (1969), 69–99; J. Mueller, *Mafte'aḥ li-Teshuvot ha-Ge'onim* (1891), 92–100; B.M. Lewin, *Oẓar ha-Ge'onim*, 1–12 (1928–43), index; H. Tykocinski, *Takkanot ha-Ge'onim*, tr. by M. Havazelet (1959), 70, 99; S. Abramson, *Ba-Merkazim u-va-Tefuẓot bi-Tekufat ha-Ge'onim* (1965), 14; M. Havazelet, *Ha-Rambam ve-ha-Ge'onim* (1967), 155; Baron, Social^2, index.

[Meir Havazelet]

SAR SHALOM BEN MOSES HA-LEVI (12th century), the last of the Egyptian *geonim*. Sar Shalom held office in Fostat from 1171 until at least 1195. He had followed his brother, the *Gaon* *Nethanel b. Moses ha-Levi, in the position. Before then, he had held the post of *av bet din* in the Yeshivah shel Ereẓ Israel of Damascus, which, according to *Benjamin of Tudela, was headed by Sar Shalom's brother Azariah. While acting as *gaon*, Sar Shalom signed himself *rosh yeshivat Ereẓ ha-Ẓevi*, or *rosh yeshivat Ge'on Ya'akov* ("Head of the Yeshivah of the Glory of Jacob").

BIBLIOGRAPHY: Mann, Egypt, index; Mann, Texts, 1 (1931), 257f.; idem, in: HUCA, 3 (1926), 295f.; Baneth, in: *Sefer ha-Yovel... A. Marx* (1950), 77; S. Assaf, in: *Tarbiz*, 1 no. 2 (1930), 80f.; S.D. Goitein, *ibid.*, 31 (1962), 369; 33 (1964), 184.

[Abraham David]

SARṬABA (Alexandrium), fortress, probably built by Alexander *Yannai and named after him According to Josephus, it was located near Coreae in the Jordan Valley (Ant., 14:49, 83). Situated on the top of a high mountain, it was exceptionally well supplied (Jos., Wars, 1:134). Here *Aristobulus II surrendered to Pompey in 63 B.C.E. It later served as a stronghold of the nationalist opposition to Rome. Gabinus besieged *Alexander, the son of Aristobulus there (*ibid.*, 1:161ff.), after which the fortress was demolished. Pheroras, Herod's brother, refortified it (Jos., Ant., 14:419; Wars, 1:308). Under Herod it served for the safekeeping of his wife Mariamne, who later buried his sons there after they had been executed on Herod's orders (Jos., Ant., 16:394; Wars, 1:551). It apparently also served for the burial of several other members of the Hasmonean dynasty. The place is not mentioned in accounts of the Jewish War against Rome. According to the Mishnah, it was one of the stations for the transmission of signals announcing the new moon and holidays from Jerusalem to Babylonia (RH 2:4; cf. Tosef., 2:2). Alexandrium is identified with Qarn Sarṭaba, a dominating peak overlooking the Jordan Valley, S.E. of Nablus (1,244 ft. – c. 379 m. above sea level; 2,388 ft. – c. 728 m. above the Jordan Valley). The remains include walls of bossed masonry, the style typical of the Hasmonean period, a cistern, and traces of an aqueduct. Excavations at the fortress were conducted at the site by Y. Tsafrir and Y. Magen between 1981 and 1983, with the discovery of the remains of a monumental peristyle hall and other remains, including an inscribed ostraca mentioning a "Pinchas" and a "Levi." The aqueduct leading to the site and other remains in the hinterland of the fortress were investigated by D. Amit.

BIBLIOGRAPHY: Abel, in: RB, 22 (1913), 228ff.; Schmidt, in: JBL, 29 (1910), 77ff.; Moulton, in: BASOR, 62 (1936), 15ff. **ADD. BIBLIOGRAPHY:** Y. Tsafrir and Y. Magen, "Two Seasons of Excavations at the Sartaba/Alexandrium Fortress," in: *Qadmoniot*, 17 (1984), 26–32; D. Amit, "Water Supply to the Alexandrium Fortress (Sartaba)," in: D. Amit et al., *The Aqueducts of Ancient Palestine* (1989), 215–21; Y. Tsafrir, L. Di Segni, and J. Green, *Tabula Imperii Romani. Iudaea – Palaestina: Maps and Gazetteer* (1994), 60–61, s.v. "Alexandrion."

[Michael Avi-Yonah / Shimon Gibson (2nd ed.)]

SARUG (Saruk), ISRAEL (fl. 1590–1610), Egyptian kabbalist. Sarug probably belonged to an Egyptian family of rabbinic scholars with kabbalistic leanings. A manuscript written in 1565 in *Cairo (British Museum 759) was copied for Isaac Sarug; Israel Sarug, whose signature as owner appears on the manuscript, was probably his son. Sarug may have known Isaac *Luria while the latter was in *Egypt and have become acquainted then with some of his early teaching and kabbalistic behavior. Although he was not one of Luria's pupils in Safed, he later claimed to have been one of his main disciples. He had access to some of the writings of Luria's disciples (Ḥayyim *Vital, Moses *Jonah, *Joseph ibn Tabul) and from them constructed his own version of Luria's doctrine, adding important speculations of his own. His whereabouts between 1570 and 1593 are unknown, but he must have spent some time during the 1580s in Safed. Between 1594 and 1600 he disseminated his version of Lurianic Kabbalah in Italy, founding a whole school of kabbalists who accepted his teaching as authentic. Among them were the most distinguished kabbalists of that time, such as Menahem Azariah *Fano, Isaac Fano, and *Aaron Berechiah b. Moses of Modena. Several manuscripts written between 1597 and 1604 contain summaries of his oral teachings and copies of writings which he had brought with him. According to Leone *Modena, Sarug's teachings in Venice were strongly tinged with philosophic ideas; he also claimed that he could recognize the transmigrations of the souls of the people he met. After he left Italy, he taught Abraham *Herrera in Ragusa and spent some time in Salonika (before 1604). It seems improbable that Sarug is identical with the "famous Ḥasid" Israel Saruk who died in Safed in 1602, leaving his manuscripts with his daughter, who several years later became the wife of the immigrant kabbalist from Moravia, Shlimel (Solomon) Dresnitz. There is evidence that Sarug spent some time in Poland after 1600, but later legend put his stay earlier and made him the kabbalistic teacher of Solomon *Luria in Cracow.

Only four of Sarug's works have been printed. The book *Limmudei Aẓilut*, published erroneously under the name of Ḥayyim Vital (1897), contains two of these: an exposition of his version of Luria's teachings on *ẓimẓum*, which differs widely from all other known versions, and his commentary on the portion of the *Zohar called *Sifra di-Ẓeni'uta*. The book also contains a description of the world of *Beri'ah*, the angelological realm next to the world of divine emanation, *Aẓilut*. His traditions concerning specific transmigrations of biblical and talmudic personalities were published in part under the name of Menahem Azariah Fano (Prague, 1688; with a commentary by J.M. Leiner, Lublin, 1907). Sarug's commentary on the three hymns for Sabbath composed by Luria was first published in Nowy Oleksiniec in 1767. In all his writings Sarug refers to Luria as "the master" but never as "my master." Most of the first published presentations of Lurianic Kabbalah were according to Sarug's version, which exerted a profound influence, although it was attacked as inauthentic by *Ḥayyim b. Abraham ha-Kohen of Aleppo and other kabbalists.

BIBLIOGRAPHY: G. Scholem, in: *Zion*, 5 (1940), 214–43; S.A. Horodezky, *Torat ha-Kabbalah shel Rabbi Yiẓḥak Ashkenazi-Ari ve-Rabbi Ḥayyim Vital-Raḥu* (1947), 79–82; G. Scholem, in: RHR, 143 (1953), 33; D. Tamar, in: *Zion*, 19 (1954), 173.

[Gershom Scholem]

SARŪJ (Suruc), small town near the southern border of *Turkey. Sarūj was a thriving town during the rule of the *Abbasid caliphs and in the crusader period. For many years a Jewish community existed in Sarūj, and its name appears among the communities of northern *Babylonia and *Syria to which the head of the *Baghdad academy, *Samuel b. Ali, addressed an *iggeret* ("circular letter") in 1197. A letter from the middle of the 12th century gives the name of a Jewish merchant from Saruj who traveled to Sicily on business. Judah Al-Ḥarizi, who visited the town at the beginning of the 13th century, reported on his meeting with R. Eleazar ha-Bavli (Abū Manṣūr Ibn Abī Yāsir), a wealthy and hospitable philanthropist, and noted that the Jewish community was small (*Taḥkemoni*, ed. by A. Kaminka (1899), 367).

BIBLIOGRAPHY: G. Le Strange, *Lands of the Eastern Caliphate* (1930), 108, 125; S. Assaf, in: *Tarbiz*, 1 (1930), no. 1, 124; 1 (1930) no. 2, 63. **ADD. BIBLIOGRAPHY:** M. Gil, *Be-Malkhut Ishmaʿel*, 1 (1997), 295–96.

[Eliyahu Ashtor / Leah Bornstein-Makovetsky (2nd ed.)]

SĀRŪM, ABRAHAM (1878–1942), communal worker in Jerusalem. Born in *Yemen, Sārūm emigrated to Palestine in 1893 and became head of the Yemenite community in Jerusalem. After the Yemenites left the Sephardi community in Jerusalem in 1907, he became secretary of the congregation's committee. From then until his death he devoted himself to the members of his community. In 1919 he was elected chairman of the community's committee in Jerusalem. He joined the *Mizrachi movement and was elected member of its central committee in 1919. He was a delegate to the first and second Asefat ha-Nivḥarim and a member of the Va'ad Le'ummi for many years. During the riots on Passover 1921, he was an active member of the Haganah. He was one of the initiators and heads of the Association of Yemenites in Palestine, established in 1924.

BIBLIOGRAPHY: *Zikkaron le-Avraham Sarum* (1945); M.D. Gaon, *Yehudei ha-Mizraḥ be-Ereẓ Yirael*, 2 (1932), 583.

[Yehuda Ratzaby]

SASA (Heb. סַאסָא), kibbutz in Upper Galilee, near the Israel-Lebanese border, 2,550 ft. (850 m.) above sea level, affiliated with Kibbutz Arẓi ha-Shomer ha-Ẓa'ir. A Jewish village existed on the site at least from the Roman period, attested to by tomb caves typical of the time of the *amoraim and by remnants of a synagogue. Ancient Jewish travelers visited the traditional tombs of rabbis Sisi, Levi b. Sisi, and Yose b. Sisi at this place. A fortress stood on the site at the time of Ẓāhir al-Omar. In the *War of Independence, Israeli columns advancing from the west and east in Operation Hiram met near the village Sa'sa', which was then abandoned by its Arab inhabitants (Oct.–Nov. 1948). In 1949 a kibbutz was established there by pioneers from North America who were joined by Israeli-born and other members. Sasa developed hill farming methods after arduous land reclamation. Its deciduous fruit orchards and beef cattle were suited to the cool, rainy climate (40 in. annual average). In addition, it also had field crops, dairy cattle and poultry, and operated factories for plastics and chemicals as well as a guest house. In the mid-1990s the population was approximately 425, dropping to 371 in 2002.

WEBSITE: www.sasa.org.il.

[Efraim Orni]

SASKATCHEWAN, province in W. Canada; part of Canada's Northwest Territories until incorporated as a province in 1905.

Saskatchewan's first Jewish resident was Max Goldstein, a Russian-born tailor who opened a store in Fort Qu'Appelle in 1877. During the Second Riel Rebellion in 1885 he served as quartermaster. In 1882 a Jewish farm project, called New Jerusalem, was started in the Moosomin area, but adverse conditions forced the settlers to give up. Numerous Jews were among those who laid tracks for the Canadian Pacific Railroad in the early 1880s.

After 1888 farm colonies were started which survived several generations. Jewish farm colonies were sometimes utopian ventures directed from above, and sometimes independent initiatives. The first colony was established in 1888, near Wapella. In 1892 the Young Men's Hebrew and Benevolent Society, on behalf of the Jewish Colonization Association (ICA), established the colony of Hirsch (named after Baron De Hirsch) in southern Saskatchewan; its initial group consisted of 47 Russian Jewish families. The first Jews to settle in the Wapella area were John Heppner and Abraham Kleiman. By 1892 there were 20 Jewish families, and young men interested in farming came to Wapella for their training. Hirsch had the oldest Jewish cemetery in the province, and was the site of the province's first synagogue building. The town had public schools, but also a Hebrew school, a *shoḥet*, and a Jewish community structure. Forty Jewish families (a total of 100 people) founded Lipton in 1901 with the help of ICA. They were taught by nearby Indians and Metis how to erect log houses chinked with clay and roofed with sod. In Lipton, too, Jewish teachers were engaged and a cemetery laid out. Edenbridge, also helped in its founding (1906) by ICA, was so named by its settlers. The name was conceived as "Yidn-Bridge" (Jews' Bridge), after a bridge across the Carrot River. The first settlers were 56 Lithuanian Jews who had lived in South Africa. Louis Vickar responded to an advertisement of the Canadian government offering 160 acres of virgin land for ten dollars. Edenbridge also had an active Jewish community. In the Sonnenfeld colony, which was aided in its founding (1906) by ICA, the villages of Oungre and Hoffer sprang up, the latter named after Moses Hoffer, the father of two brothers who were among the founders of the Sonnenfeld colony.

As was the case with others who settled in the west, many Jews did not succeed at farming, and left for the larger Jewish communities of western Canada. In addition to personal hardships, the great drought of the 1930s and the trend to mechanization and urbanization hastened the decline of Jewish farming. Of every 100 gainfully employed Jewish men in Saskatchewan in 1936, 11 were farmers and five were farm laborers. While the great majority of Jewish farmers in Canada in previous years were in Saskatchewan, since World War II the ICA devoted most of its efforts in Canada to Ontario, particularly the Niagara peninsula. The Jewish farm colonies are now mostly alive in memory alone. The Canadian government has placed the beautiful Beth Israel synagogue at Edenbridge on its national register of historic sites.

Regina, the capital of the province, had nine Jews in 1891, but the true beginnings of the present community would have to wait about 20 years. By the time of the 1911 census there were 130 residents. That year a *shoḥet* was hired, and services were held in his home. Two years later the members of the community erected a synagogue, Beth Jacob, with the lieutenant-governor of the province laying the cornerstone. In 1914 a building was rented to serve as a *talmud torah,* and 10 years later a building was erected to house it. In 1926 a central budgeting structure was created, and the Regina Federated Community was established. In 1951 the Beth Jacob Congregation built a new synagogue, with a new annex added four years later to house the school and the community center under one roof. At its height in 1931 there were just over 1,000 Jews. By 1951 the number had fallen to 740 and the 2001 census enumerated 720 Jews in Regina. In 2006 there were two synagogues in Regina. In addition to Beth Jacob, with its Conservative-style service, there was the Reform Temple Beth Tikvah, established in 1990. Because of the relatively high rate of interfaith marriages, some members of the community took the initiative to build a burial ground where Jewish and non-Jewish partners could lie next to each other, separated by a fence deemed halakhically acceptable. It opened in the summer of 2005.

The first known settlers of Saskatoon were William and Fanny Landa, who arrived in 1907 with their two children. The first *minyan* was on Rosh ha-Shanah in 1908.The members of the congregation Agudas Israel built a synagogue in 1912 and a new one was erected in 1919. In 1958 a Jewish community center was built that also served as a house of worship. Saskatoon had a Jewish mayor, Sydney Buckwold, for several terms. Agudas Israel became a Conservative congregation, and in March, 2000 Congregation Shir Chadash, also Conservative, was established. In 1911 the census counted 77 Jews. Since 1931 the number has hovered around 700 Jews, with as many as 793 Jews in 1961. The census of 2001 enumerated 700 Jews exactly, making it roughly the same size as Regina's community.

In addition to the settlements in the farm colonies and in the large urban centers, Jews settled in many of the small towns of rural Saskatchewan in the interwar period. In their time, Jewish general stores, like Chinese cafes, were part of small-town Saskatchewan. In the 1931 census there was at least one Jew in almost 200 cities, towns, villages or hamlets in the province. Sometimes Jews constituted a remarkably high percentage of the total population. Thus, for 1931, the demographer Louis Rosenberg noted that the "urban centre with the largest percentage of Jews in its population is not Montreal, Toronto, or some larger Eastern city, but is the little village of Lipton in Saskatchewan, where the Jewish population of 53 formed 15.01 % of its total population."

In 2002, the Jewish community of Saskatchewan was unexpectedly thrust into the national spotlight. In December of that year, David Ahenakew, former president of both the Federation of Saskatchewan Indian Nations and the Chief of the Canada-wide Assembly of First Nations, gave an interview to the Saskatoon *StarPhoenix* where he explained that the Holocaust was a way of getting over a "disease" and that without the Holocaust "Jews would have owned the goddamned world." Ahenakew was arrested for willfully promoting hatred in June 2003, and was convicted in July 2005. Within days of the conviction, Ahenakew's membership in the prestigious Order of Canada was revoked. As a result of this incident, there have been the attempts to create and strengthen relations between Jews and First Nations groups. The leaders of the organizations that Ahenakew had once dominated were quick to denounce his remarks. In 2003 leaders from the Aboriginal community went to the Yom ha-Shoah ceremonies in Saskatoon and attended a Friday night dinner, and members of the Jewish community participated in ceremonies led by First Nations groups. Canadian Jewish organizations have organized missions to Israel for aboriginal leaders, and have been conducting ongoing meetings.

The Jewish population of Saskatchewan, although quite diverse because of the relatively large rural presence of its past, has never been very large. In 1911 the census counted some 2,060 Jews. At its peak in 1931, there were only 5,047 recorded, and the numbers have been declining ever since. In 1951 there were 3,017, and over the next 10 years the numbers fell to 2,710. The 2001 census enumerated 2,090 Jews in the province. Although this downward trend seemed relentless, it was hoped that an improving economy in the province would attract more Jews in the coming years.

BIBLIOGRAPHY: L. Rosenberg, *Canada's Jews* (1939). **ADD. BIBLIOGRAPHY:** G. Tulchinsky, *Taking Root* (1991); idem, *Branching Out* (1998); F. Curtis, *Our Heritage: The History of the Regina and Region Jewish Community* (1989); C. Golumb (ed.), *Heritage & History: The Saskatoon Jewish Community* (1998/9).

[Benjamin G. Kayfetz / Richard Menkis (2nd ed.)]

SASLAVSKY, LUIS SIMÓN (pseudonyms: **Simón Fourcade** and **Hugo Espinelli;** 1908–1995), Argentinean film director, author, and producer. Born in Rosario, Province of Santa Fé, Argentina, Saslavsky was drawn into the film world as a reporter for *La Nación* in Hollywood. He returned to Argentina and directed *Crimen a las tres* (1935), *La Fuga* (1937), and *Nace un Amor* (1938). He later sacrificed some of his intellectual quality to popular taste but continued to show some originality, as in *Historia de una Noche* (1941). Saslavsky was compelled to leave Argentina during the Perón government and lived in Europe for 15 years from 1948. He directed *Corona Negra* in Spain in 1951 and other films in both Spain and France, including *Les Louves* (1957) and *Première mai* (1958). Returning to Argentina, he produced *Las Ratas* and *Placeres conyugales* (1963), *La industria del matrimonio* (1964), *Vení conmigo* (1972), and *El Fausto criollo* (1979).

SASOV (Pol. **Sasów**), town in Lvov district, Ukraine; within Poland until 1772, under Austrian rule until 1919, reverted to Poland until 1945. Founded in 1615, the town was granted autonomy by King Sigismund III, who also bestowed many privileges on its merchants and instituted market days. In 1726 the Jews of Sasov were granted a privilege by the owner of the town, Jacob Sobieski, son of King John III Sobieski. Accordingly all Jewish communal institutions were exempted from taxes, Jews were permitted to trade without hindrance and to deal in alcoholic liquor, and the amount of taxes the Jews had to pay was made equal to that paid by the other townsmen. In 1764 there were 223 Jews living in Sasov. Sasov was celebrated among Ḥasidim as the residence of *Moses Leib of Sasov, also called Moses Leib of Brody (d. 1807). The community numbered 1,906 (58% of the total population) in 1880; 1,761 (52.1% of the total) in 1912; and 1,096 (35.4%) in 1921. Jews were occupied mainly with making candles and ornamental strips (*atarot*) for prayer-shawls, for the production of which Sasov was a world center. After World War I the Jews of Sasov suffered from unemployment. Their economic position deteriorated at the end of the 1920s and the beginning of the 1930s. Many starved and had to be helped by Jewish relief societies: Jewish communal life also suffered because of the poverty.

[Shimshon Leib Kirshenboim]

Holocaust Period

Before the outbreak of World War II there were about 1,500 Jews in Sasov. On Sept. 17, 1939, the Red Army entered the city, which was administered by Soviet authorities until the German-Soviet war. The Germans occupied the town on July 2, 1941; during the first two weeks they killed 22 leaders on the pretext of their being communists. Three *Aktionen* took place, the largest on July 15, 1942, when the Jews were deported to *Belzec death camp. The remaining 400 Jews were deported on Nov. 25, 1942, to *Zloczow (Zolochev) and shared the fate of that community. A forced-labor camp, established in March 1942, was liquidated in July 1943, when all its inmates were shot in the nearby woods. After the war the Jewish community of Sasov was not reconstituted.

SASPORTAS, JACOB (c. 1610–1698), rabbi, a fierce opponent of the Shabbatean movement. He was born and educated in Oran (North Africa) and became widely known for his talmudic erudition. After his appointment as rabbi of the Tlemçen community the neighboring communities also recognized his authority. However, when he was 37 years old he was dismissed by the government; he then proceeded to wander throughout Europe, visiting many communities in Germany, Italy, and England (he was offered the position of *haham* of the Sephardi community in London in 1664 but left the next year because of the plague). His main ambition was the rabbinate of Amsterdam, but he did not achieve it until 1693, when he was 83 years old. Personal bitterness deriving from his lack of a congregation which could serve as a base for his activities colored his attitude in many disputes. He was a staunch defender of the rabbinate and the traditional *halakhah* and throughout his life was involved in polemical disputes. Many of his responsa were collected in the book *Ohel Ya'akov* (Amsterdam, 1737), published by his son, Abraham.

Sasportas was largely known, however, for his collection of letters, *Ẓiẓat Novel Ẓevi*, comprising his answers to various Shabbatean letters and pamphlets, as well as the original pamphlets themselves. The work therefore became one of the main sources for the study of the Shabbatean movement during the lifetime of *Shabbetai Ẓevi. At the time of the dispute Sasportas lived in Hamburg, so that most of the material in his collection is mainly concerned with Western Europe and Italy, but he had some success in his efforts to obtain material from the East as well.

Arranged in chronological order, the work covers the years 1666–76. In the main it consists of letters received by Sasportas, his answers to them, some letters which he wrote on his own initiative, and some comments on the development of the Shabbatean movement. Nearly half of it concerns the year 1666, from the first announcements of the appearance of Shabbetai Ẓevi as Messiah until his conversion to Islam at the end of that year. The second part is dedicated to the events following the conversion, 1667–68, and describes the "failure" of the Shabbatean movement. The third part consists of letters written in 1668–69, and is mostly directed against the renewed Shabbatean propaganda, which tried to explain the conversion of the Messiah and to introduce new norms of behavior suitable for the period of messianic fulfillment. The last four pages deal with the period from 1673 to 1676, sketching some of the main events of these years.

Sasportas' bitter denunciation of the Shabbatean movement, its prophet *Nathan of Gaza, and its believers (some of whom were his former friends), is based upon various ideological concepts. First was his adherence to the traditional conception of the messianic age; in great detail he pointed out the differences between what was happening at that time and the traditional ideas concerning the messianic era. He also saw the new movement as a revolution against established institutions and rabbinic norms, fearing that they might be set aside through the influence of Nathan of Gaza and other Shabbatean thinkers who laid claim to the faith of the populace without any appeal to rabbinic tradition. His hatred was also based on his not unfounded suspicion that the new movement contained antinomian elements, revealed in some utterances of Nathan, in the "strange deeds" of Shabbetai Ẓevi, and in the behavior of their followers. He frequently compared the new movement with Christianity and feared that the Shabbateans would follow the ancient example.

Sasportas' book is the fiercest attack upon Shabbateanism written during the early years of the movement. However, I. *Tishby and R. Shatz have proved that the published work does not reflect his attitude during the period before Shabbetai Ẓevi's apostasy. By comparing Sasportas' original copies with the version prepared for publication, they demonstrated that in many instances he falsified his own letters, changing phrases and adding passages to show that his opposition was far more thorough and resolute from the beginning than it really was, and he glossed over his own hesitation and half-belief in Shabbetai Ẓevi during the months in which the movement reached its peak. The full version of *Ẓiẓat Novel Ẓevi* was first published by I. Tishby from the only complete manuscript in 1954. For a long time, however, it was known only in the shortened version (*Kiẓẓur Ẓiẓat Novel Ẓevi*) printed in Amsterdam in 1737, by Jacob Emden in Altona in 1757, and lastly in Odessa in 1867.

BIBLIOGRAPHY: I. Tishby (ed.), *Ẓiẓat Novel Ẓevi* (1954); R. Shatz, in: *Beḥinot*, 10 (1956), 50–66; Scholem, Shabbetai Ẓevi, passim.

[Joseph Dan]

SASSO, SANDY EISENBERG (1947–), Reconstructionist rabbi and author. Sasso was born and raised in Melrose Park, Penn., a suburb of Philadelphia. She received bachelors' and masters' degrees from Temple University and attended the Reconstructionist Rabbinical College (RRC) in that city. In 1974 Sasso became the first woman to graduate from RRC and the second woman rabbi in the United States. She and her fellow rabbinical student, Dennis Sasso, married in 1970, becoming the first rabbinic couple in history.

From 1974 to 1977, Sasso served as rabbi of the Manhattan Reconstructionist Havurah in New York. In 1977 Sandy and Dennis Sasso jointly accepted positions as rabbis of Congregation Beth-El Zedeck in Indianapolis, a congregation with joint Conservative and Reconstructionist affiliation. She continued in that post in 2005. In 1996, Sasso received a Doctor of Ministry degree from Christian Theological Seminary in Indianapolis. She and her husband were the first rabbinic couple to serve a congregation affiliated with the Conservative movement, and she was the first rabbi to become a mother.

Sasso undertook local and national leadership of Jewish, interfaith, and community organizations. She served as president of the Indianapolis Board of Rabbis, the Reconstructionist Rabbinical Association (1989–91), and the Gleaners Food Bank. She lectured in religion and Judaism at Butler University and Christian Theological Seminary in Indianapolis.

As one of the first female rabbis, she explored the roles of women in Judaism and the rabbinate and offered new perspectives on lifecycle events. Her "B'rit B'not Yisrael" (Covenant for the Daughters of Israel), co-authored with her husband, Dennis Sasso, was among the first of new ceremonies for infant girls paralleling the *brit milah* (circumcision) ceremony for boys. Sasso wrote liturgical poetry on the life cycle and spoke widely on women in the rabbinate and gendered language in prayer.

In writings for both parents and children, Sasso offered liberal approaches to theology and Judaism, drawing on tradition and midrash. She authored a series of award-winning children's books on religious and spiritual themes, including *God's Paintbrush* (1992); *In God's Name* (1994); *But God Remembered: Stories of Women from Creation to the Promised Land* (1995); and *Butterflies under Our Hats* (2006).

She received the 2004 Helen Keating Ott Award for Outstanding Contribution to Children's Literature and the 2005 Sugarman Family Award for Jewish Children's Literature. She co-authored, with Rabbi Jeffery Schein, *Kol Hano'ar* (Voice of the Children; 2005), the Reconstructionist movement's first children's prayer book.

BIBLIOGRAPHY: P. Nadell, *Women Who Would Be Rabbis: A History of Women's Ordination, 1889–1985* (1998).

[Robert P. Tabak (2nd ed.)]

SASSON, AARON BEN JOSEPH (1550/5–1626), rabbinic scholar in the *Ottoman Empire. Aaron was educated in *Salonika, where he lived until 1600, and died in Constantinople. He was a pupil of Mordecai Matalon and a pupil and colleague of his father-in-law, Solomon II of the *Levi (Bet ha-Levi) dynasty. Aaron had charge of a yeshivah and disseminated Torah in Salonika and then in Constantinople. The circumstances under which he left Salonika with all his family are not clear, but seem to have been connected with the death of Solomon II and the subsequent struggle that year to succeed him in the Evora community and its yeshivah. Aaron was active in teaching and the giving of halakhic rulings from c. 1585 until his death. Queries were addressed to him from many, often distant, places. His responsa, which he had already prepared for publication, were published in part after his death and show his keen mind and dialectical ability. He was a distinguished talmudist and halakhic authority. From the very beginning of his activity as a *posek*, the greatest *posekim* of Salonika turned to him for confirmation of their rulings. Aaron bases his rulings upon contemporary scholars – Joseph ibn *Lev, Samuel de *Medina, and Solomon ha-Kohen – and debates sharply with early scholars as well as with the great scholars who closely preceded him, such as Elijah *Mizraḥi, Joseph *Colon, and Joseph Caro. He was sometimes attacked for his attitude toward other scholars.

Aaron seems to have been even more important as a teacher than as a halakhic authority. He educated many students, many of whom were among the greatest scholars of the

Ottoman Empire in the first half of the 17th century, such as *Ḥayyim (b.) Shabbetai, Ḥayyim *Alfandari, Mordecai Kalai, and Shabbetai Jonah. His novellae on the Talmud (on *Ketubbot, Yevamot, Bava Kamma, Bava Meẓia*, and other isolated subjects), which remain in manuscript, mirror the learning in his yeshivah. He bases himself greatly upon the words of Joseph ibn Lev, debating them by use of *pilpul* and explaining at length the *Tosafot Gornish*. In addition he wrote a work on Jacob b. Asher's *Arba'ah Turim* and on Maimonides' *Mishneh Torah*, as well as a short work on the laws of *agunah* and other topics.

Aaron was connected by marriage with the families of the greatest scholars of Salonika. His sister was married to David ibn *Naḥmias, and his son was the brother-in-law of Meir b. Abraham di *Boton. His family was generally on close terms with the Levi dynasty, and after his departure from Salonika, a correspondence ensued between the two families, part of which has been preserved. Aaron's son Joseph saw to the publication of his father's responsa *Torat Emet* (Venice, 1626) and served as rabbi in Venice. Joseph and Aaron's grandson Aaron b. Isaac (b. 1629) were renowned talmudists (see, e.g., the responsa of Joseph of Trani, EH no. 22; the responsa *Penei Moshe*, pt. 2, no. 105). A well-known *dayyan* named JOSEPH B. MOSES SASSON of Salonika, who was active from 1580 to 1600, appears to have been a member of the same family (see the responsa of Samuel de Medina, EH no. 165; *Torat Emet* no. 2).

BIBLIOGRAPHY: A. Sasson, *Torat Emet* (Venice, 1626), introductions; Conforte, Kore, index; Michael, Or, nos. 294, 298, pp. 140–1; Steinschneider, Cat Bod, 2958, no. 8621; Ch. Hirschensohn, in: *Hamisderonah*, 2 (1888), 219–23, 340–3; Rosanes, Togarmah, 3 (1938), 55–56; S. Poznański, in: ZHB, 16 (1913), 178–9.

[Joseph Hacker]

SASSON, ELIYAHU (1902–1978), Israeli diplomat and expert on Arab affairs. Sasson was born in *Damascus, where, at the age of 18, he was the only Jewish member of the Arab Syrian National Committee and publicly greeted Feisal, the short-tenured king of *Syria, on behalf of the Damascus Jewish community. On Feisal's personal initiative he edited for several months an Arab-language Jewish newspaper to foster understanding between the Jewish and the Arab peoples in the spirit of the *Weizmann-Feisal agreement. In 1920, after Feisal's ousting from Syria by the French, Sasson settled in Palestine and soon became a recognized expert on Arab affairs, at first in various newspapers and later for the Zionist Executive, where he served from 1930 as head of its Arab department. On the Executive's behalf he maintained for years contacts with Arab leaders and traveled widely throughout the Middle East. During World War II he was instrumental in spreading British anti-Nazi propaganda in the Arab countries, and in 1948 he directed the Arab broadcasts of the clandestine *Haganah radio station. On behalf of the nascent Israeli government he negotiated with King Abdullah of Transjordan and corresponded with the secretary general of the Arab League, Azzam Pasha, and other Arab leaders. After World War II he was a member of most Zionist and Israeli delegations which negotiated the political future of Palestine or Israel-Arab relations: in 1946 in London, in 1947–48 at the United Nations, in 1949 in the armistice talks with the Arab governments in Rhodes and at the abortive peace talks at Lausanne. In 1949 he headed Israel's office in Paris which maintained unpublicized contacts with the Arabs. From 1950 to 1952 he was Israeli minister to *Turkey; afterward minister (and from 1957, ambassador) in Rome until 1960. While serving in 1961 as ambassador in Berne, Switzerland, he was recalled to become a member of the Israeli government as minister of posts, becoming minister of police in 1966 (until 1969). Sasson published many articles and political reminiscences in the Hebrew and Arab-language press in Israel, and remained a staunch supporter of the idea that an Israel-Arab understanding is feasible and the enmity between Jews and Arabs a transient phenomenon.

BIBLIOGRAPHY: Tidhar, 5 (1952), 2281–82.

[Benjamin Jaffe]

SASSOON, family of Jewish merchants, philanthropists, and men of letters, originally from *Baghdad; its members rose to great influence and affluence first in India and then in England and China. The founder of the family was SHEIKH SASSOON B. SĀLAḤ (1750–1830), who was the president (*nasi*) of the Jewish community in Baghdad for almost 40 years and chief treasurer of the Ottoman pashas of Baghdad. Through the building of textile mills and factories in Bombay on a large scale, the Sassoons exerted tremendous power in the commercial arena, and the wide ramifications of their activities earned them the reputation of the merchant-princes of the Orient, "the Rothschilds of the East." His son DAVID S. SASSOON (1792–1864), who had taken on the commercial activities of the family, escaped from the oppression and tyranny of Pasha Daud and fled in 1828 to *Bushire on the Persian Gulf, where he was joined by his father, who died there. David S. Sassoon moved with his large family in 1832 to *Bombay, where he established a business which assumed international scope. The philanthropic activities of David Sassoon and his eight sons greatly benefited Bombay as a whole, and the Jewish community in particular. In 1861 he built in Byculla, Bombay, the synagogue Magen David, and some of the most important cultural and civic institutions, including hospitals, orphanages, libraries, museums, schools, and charitable communal organizations owe their existence to Sassoon's munificence and generosity. David Sassoon was instrumental in publishing the Judeo-Arabic newspaper *Doresh Tov le-Ammo* (1855–66) and supported scholars and scholarly publications. In Poona, where he had his summer residence, he built the David S. Sassoon Hospital, noteworthy for its nonsectarian character, an infirmary and leper asylum, and in 1863 the synagogue Ohel David, whose 90-foot spire is a Poona landmark. His mausoleum, on which there is a long Hebrew inscription in both prose and poetry, is situated in the courtyard of the synagogue. His eldest son,

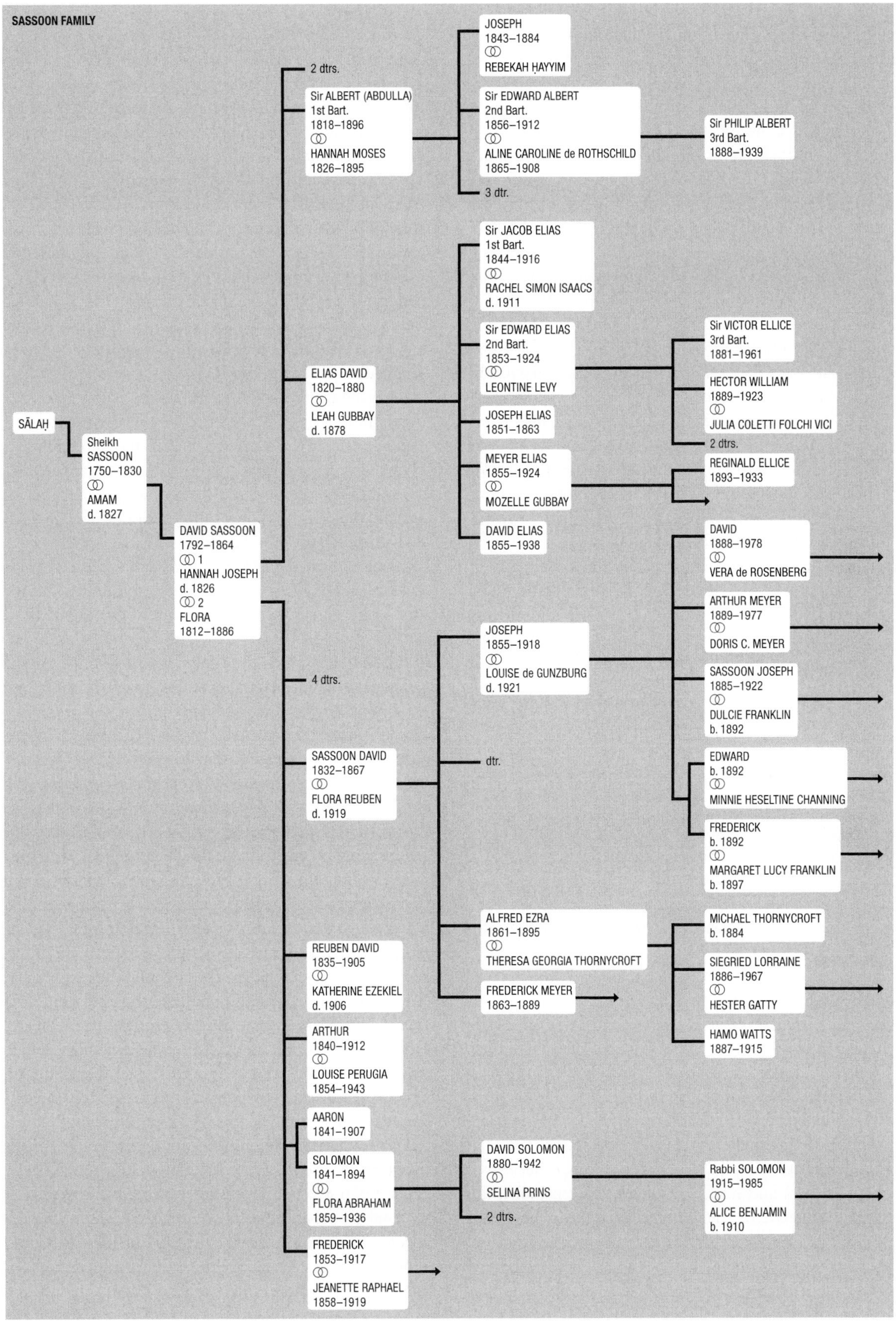
SASSOON FAMILY
SĀLAḤ
Sheikh SASSOON 1750–1830 ⚭ AMAM d. 1827
DAVID SASSOON 1792–1864 ⚭ 1 HANNAH JOSEPH d. 1826 ⚭ 2 FLORA 1812–1886
2 dtrs.
Sir ALBERT (ABDULLA) 1st Bart. 1818–1896 ⚭ HANNAH MOSES 1826–1895
JOSEPH 1843–1884 ⚭ REBEKAH ḤAYYIM
Sir EDWARD ALBERT 2nd Bart. 1856–1912 ⚭ ALINE CAROLINE de ROTHSCHILD 1865–1908
Sir PHILIP ALBERT 3rd Bart. 1888–1939
3 dtr.
ELIAS DAVID 1820–1880 ⚭ LEAH GUBBAY d. 1878
Sir JACOB ELIAS 1st Bart. 1844–1916 ⚭ RACHEL SIMON ISAACS d. 1911
Sir EDWARD ELIAS 2nd Bart. 1853–1924 ⚭ LEONTINE LEVY
Sir VICTOR ELLICE 3rd Bart. 1881–1961
HECTOR WILLIAM 1889–1923 ⚭ JULIA COLETTI FOLCHI VICI
2 dtrs.
JOSEPH ELIAS 1851–1863
MEYER ELIAS 1855–1924 ⚭ MOZELLE GUBBAY
REGINALD ELLICE 1893–1933
DAVID ELIAS 1855–1938
4 dtrs.
SASSOON DAVID 1832–1867 ⚭ FLORA REUBEN d. 1919
JOSEPH 1855–1918 ⚭ LOUISE de GUNZBURG d. 1921
DAVID 1888–1978 ⚭ VERA de ROSENBERG
ARTHUR MEYER 1889–1977 ⚭ DORIS C. MEYER
SASSOON JOSEPH 1885–1922 ⚭ DULCIE FRANKLIN b. 1892
EDWARD b. 1892 ⚭ MINNIE HESELTINE CHANNING
FREDERICK b. 1892 ⚭ MARGARET LUCY FRANKLIN b. 1897
dtr.
ALFRED EZRA 1861–1895 ⚭ THERESA GEORGIA THORNYCROFT
MICHAEL THORNYCROFT b. 1884
SIEGRIED LORRAINE 1886–1967 ⚭ HESTER GATTY
HAMO WATTS 1887–1915
FREDERICK MEYER 1863–1889
REUBEN DAVID 1835–1905 ⚭ KATHERINE EZEKIEL d. 1906
ARTHUR 1840–1912 ⚭ LOUISE PERUGIA 1854–1943
AARON 1841–1907
SOLOMON 1841–1894 ⚭ FLORA ABRAHAM 1859–1936
DAVID SOLOMON 1880–1942 ⚭ SELINA PRINS
2 dtrs.
Rabbi SOLOMON 1915–1985 ⚭ ALICE BENJAMIN b. 1910
FREDERICK 1853–1917 ⚭ JEANETTE RAPHAEL 1858–1919

SIR ABDULLA (later Albert) SASSOON (1818–1896), was similarly prominent in commerce and philanthropy in Bombay. He established one of the first large-scale textile mills in Bombay, thus extending his father's business to include industry as well as trade. In 1872–75 he constructed the first wharf on the west coast of India, the Sassoon Docks in Kolaba, which employed thousands of local workers and stimulated the Bombay government to build the larger Prince's Dock. In addition to providing the initiative for establishing Bombay as a modern port city, he contributed a new building to the Elphinstone High School, maintained a Jewish school, the David Sassoon Benevolent Institution, and supplied university scholarships. In the mid-1870s Albert settled in London, where the family's business interests were increasingly centered. In recognition of his role in the industrialization of India, he was made a baronet in 1890 and was on terms of personal friendship with the Prince of Wales, later Edward VII. But it was Albert's brothers (by David's second wife), REUBEN D. SASSOON (1835–1905) and ARTHUR SASSOON (1840–1912), who became particularly prominent in the court circle of Edward VII. Reuben, little concerned with the family's business, was a favorite traveling companion of the Prince of Wales. Arthur, a man of learning who spoke Hebrew and knew the Bible well, was a highly praised host during the late Victorian and Edwardian age. His home in Brighton was the scene of lavish entertainments, at which Edward VII was a frequent guest. Participating neither in the firm nor in society was AARON SASSOON (1841–1907), whose life remains obscure. He left most of his fortune to be distributed to the poor, wherever David Sassoon and Company did business. Aaron's twin brother, SOLOMON SASSOON (1841–1894), who remained in the Orient, was at an early age put in charge of the business interests in Shanghai and Hong Kong. The most capable businessman, after Albert, of all the brothers in the family enterprise, he controlled the company from 1877 to 1894. Solomon was a Hebraist and student of the Talmud, but his wife FLORA SASSOON (1859–1936), a great-granddaughter of the original David Sassoon, actually achieved renown as a Hebrew scholar and was often consulted on questions of Jewish law. After her husband's death, Flora managed the firm in Bombay for some years and in 1901 settled in England, where she entertained scholars and public men in a grand style. Strictly Orthodox in her observance of Judaism, she included a *shoḥet* and a *minyan* in her entourage when traveling. In 1924, at Jews' College, London, she delivered a learned discourse on the Talmud, and in 1930 she published an essay on Rashi in the *Jewish Forum*. Solomon and Flora's son DAVID SOLOMON SASSOON (1880–1942), who continued their interest in things Jewish, became an outstanding Hebraist and bibliophile. His important collection of over 1,000 Hebrew and Samaritan manuscripts, including the Farḥi Bible, written in 14th-century Provence, was cataloged in *Ohel Dawid* (2 vols., 1932). His independent publications included his pioneer edition of *Samuel ha-Nagid's *diwan* from a manuscript in his own collection (1934) and his *History of the Jews of Baghdad* (1949).

SOLOMON DAVID SASSOON (1915–1985), son of David Solomon and Selina Sassoon, was ordained as a rabbi in 1936. He lived in Letchworth outside London until 1970, when he settled in Jerusalem. He inherited his father's valuable collection of Hebrew manuscripts and increased the total collection to 1,350 items. He retained his father's scholarly tastes and published *Moshav Zekenim* (1959), a commentary of the tosafists on the Pentateuch from a manuscript in his collection; *Abraham b. Maimon's commentary on Genesis and Exodus, from a Bodleian manuscript (1965); and an elegant facsimile edition of the Mishnah commentary of Maimonides (3 vols., 1956–66), with an introduction, from manuscripts in his collection and in Oxford, which are claimed to be autographs of Maimonides. He wrote *a Critical Study of Electrical Stunning and the Jewish Method of Slaughter* (1955) and *The Spiritual Heritage of the Sephardim* (1957).

Of the original eight brothers, SASSOON DAVID SASSOON (1832–1867), the third eldest and the first to settle in England, was perhaps most active in Jewish communal life in England. In addition to advancing the company's interests there, he was warden of his synagogue, member of the council of the Jews' College, and examiner in Hebrew at the Jews' Free School. His daughter, RACHEL SASSOON *BEER (1858–1927), was the editor of the *Sunday Observer* and the *Sunday Times*. On the death of the paterfamilias David Sassoon, Albert assumed the leadership of the company. ELIAS DAVID SASSOON (1820–1880), disliking his subordinate position, left the family business and founded in 1867 a separate and rival firm, E.D. Sassoon and Company. With interests in the Orient, Africa, Europe, and America, the new company prospered even more than the original one. Elias, following the policy of his father, provided his numerous Jewish employees with schools and synagogues even in the company's remotest outposts. His son, Sir JACOB ELIAS SASSOON (1844–1916), expanded his father's business enterprise in India by building a large textile company, which comprised six mills and the country's first dye works. The company was instrumental in developing the cotton textile industry in western India, and in the peak year of 1916 the Jacob Sassoon Mill, India's largest, employed 15,000 workers. In Bombay his philanthropic activities included building the Central College of Science, a general hospital, and the Keneseth Eliyahu synagogue. SIR EDWARD ALBERT SASSOON (1856–1912), the son of Albert Sassoon, married Aline Caroline de Rothschild. Edward Albert was the first Sassoon to choose politics as his profession. In 1899 he was elected to parliament as a member of the Conservative Party, and held this seat until his death. His son, Sir PHILIP SASSOON (1888–1939), won a seat in parliament as a Conservative in 1912 and remained a member until his death. During World War I he served as military secretary to Field Marshal Douglas Haig, commander in chief of the British armies in France. Although privately horrified by the war, he publicly denounced the pacifistic sentiments of his relative, the poet Siegfried Lorraine *Sassoon. From 1924 to 1929, and from 1931 to 1937, Philip was undersecretary of state for air, in which capacity he expressed his love of aviation and his belief in the importance of air power. In *The Third Route* (1929), he related the story of his 17,000-mile flying tour of British overseas air stations. Philip was also a connoisseur of art of high repute, in recognition of which he was appointed trustee of the National Gallery, the Wallace Collection, and the Tate Gallery, and he was able to display his taste in his last public office as first commissioner (minister) of works, responsible for royal palaces, parks, and ancient monuments. His sister, SYBIL (1894–1989), married Lord Rocksavage, later Marquess of Cholmondeley, alternate hereditary Lord Great Chamberlain. She was a celebrated hostess and deputy director of the Women's Royal Naval Service in World War II. The last important businessman of the dynasty was SIR VICTOR (ELLICE) SASSOON (1881–1961), the son of Sir Edward Elias and Leontine Sassoon. Like his forebears, he contributed to the development of industry in India and served as a leader of British Indian Jewry. Victor Sassoon was an air enthusiast and served during World War I in the Royal Naval Air Service, sustaining permanent injuries from a flying accident. He was a member of the Indian Legislative Assembly in 1922–23 and from 1926 to 1929, and after 1933 worked strenuously to help refugees fleeing from Nazism. In 1931 he transferred the headquarters of the E.D. Sassoon Banking Company to Shanghai. After the interests of the company were overtaken by successive Japanese and Chinese Communist occupations, Sir Victor moved to the Bahamas in 1948 and built up new mercantile, banking, and property interests. A famous racehorse owner, he won the Derby four times. Another successful relative of the Sassoons was SIR SASSOON JACOB DAVID (1849–1926), cotton merchant and chairman of the Bank of India, who was the grandson of Elias David Sassoon. Sir Sassoon's son, SIR PERCIVAL DAVID (1892–1964), was probably the foremost collector of Chinese art of his time and the founder of the Percival David Foundation of Chinese Art, the leading British museum of its kind, in Bloomsbury, London. A noted scholar of the subject, he did much to popularize Chinese art in the West. The Sassoon family was one of the most remarkable examples of upward social mobility in British history. Wearing Oriental dress in Baghdad until the mid-19th century, and not resident in Britain until about 1870, by the Edwardian period they had become baronets, associates of royalty, and Conservative M.P.s in Kent.

BIBLIOGRAPHY: C. Roth, *Sassoon Dynasty* (1941); P.H. Emden, *Jews of Britain* (1943), 324–33; D.S. Sassoon, *History of the Jews in Baghdad* (1949), index; A. Ben-Jacob, in: L. Jung (ed.), *Jewish Leaders* (1953), 524–31; S. Jackson, *The Sassoons* (1968). **ADD. BIBLIOGRAPHY:** ODNB online for "Sassoon family" and individual members; C. Bermant, *The Cousinhood* (1971), index.

[Walter Joseph Fischel]

SASSOON, SIR EZEKIEL (1860–1932), Iraqi Jewish statesman; born in Baghdad and died in Paris. Sassoon studied in London secondary schools and was a law student in *Vienna. He served as a member of the Ottoman House of Representatives from 1909 to 1918 and as minister of finance in five independent Iraqi governments (1921–25). From 1925 he was elected to several terms in the Iraqi House of Representatives as a delegate of the Jewish community in Baghdad.

[Hayyim J. Cohen]

SASSOON, SIEGFRIED LORRAINE (1886–1967), English poet and novelist. The son of Alfred Ezra Sassoon, of the famous *Sassoon family, and his wife, the daughter of Thomas Thorneycroft, a prominent gentile sculptor, Siegfried Sassoon was educated at Marlborough and Cambridge. He published some poetry for private circulation in 1906–12. He served as an infantry officer throughout World War I, was awarded the Military Cross, and was twice wounded. It was in the hospital in 1917 that he first met the poet Wilfred Owen, an aspect of whose style he helped to revolutionize in the last phase of the younger man's life. After Owen's tragic death at the very end of World War I, Sassoon did much to popularize his work. Sassoon's own book of antiwar poems, *The Old Huntsman*, appeared in 1917. Others followed in quick succession: *Counter-Attack* in 1918 and *War Poems* and *Picture Show* in 1919. His attitude to World War II was to be a less pacifist one. After World War I he flirted with socialism, becoming literary editor of the Labour *Daily Herald* for a brief period in 1919. Sassoon's two most important prose works were the semi-autobiographical novels, *Memoirs of a Fox-Hunting Man* (1928) and *Memoirs of an Infantry Officer* (1930). These, which form part of the trilogy, *The Complete Memoirs of George Sherston* (1936), are written in a more urbane and reflective vein than his poetry. Though it uses approximately traditional forms, Sassoon's verse is filled with a direct, idiomatic language brutally descriptive of the horrors of war and the complacency of civilians. His other writings include *Siegfried's Journey (1916–20)* (1945), a biography, *Meredith* (1948), and *Collected Poems* (1961).

In *The Old Huntsman* Sassoon had written: "Religion beats me. I'm amazed at folk/Drinking the gospels in and never scratching/Their heads for questions…." His ties with Judaism were certainly negligible; raised as an Anglican, he became a convert to Roman Catholicism in 1957. Sassoon's *Diaries*, edited by Rupert Hart-Davis, were published in three volumes in 1983–85.

BIBLIOGRAPHY: G. Keynes, *Bibliography of Siegfried Sassoon* (1962); M. Thorpe, *Siegfried Sassoon, a Critical Study* (1966). **ADD. BIBLIOGRAPHY:** ODNB online.

[Jon Silkin]

SASSOON, VIDAL (1928–), British hairdresser and anti-defamation philanthropist. No relation to the famous and wealthy British family of the same name, Vidal Sassoon was born to poverty in London's East End, where he fought Fascist thugs in the street and spent much of his childhood in an orphanage. At 14 he was apprenticed to a Jewish barber in the East End and, after World War II, became one of the leading hairdressers to London's Society ladies in the West End. His innovative hair styling made him famous, and he has been called "the father of modern hairdressing." Sassoon founded a highly successful international chain of hairdressers and hair care products. He fought for Israel in the 1948 War of Independence and, in 1962, founded the Vidal Sassoon International Center for the Study of Antisemitism at The Hebrew University of Jerusalem, which is internationally known for funding research about and monitoring antisemitic activities.

[William D. Rubinstein (2nd ed.)]

SATAN (Heb. שָׂטָן). In the Bible, except perhaps for I Chronicles 21:1 (see below), Satan is not a proper name referring to a particular being and a demoniac one who is the antagonist or rival of God. In its original application, in fact, it is a common noun meaning an adversary who opposes and obstructs. It is applied to human adversaries in I Samuel 29:4; II Samuel 19:23; I Kings 5:18; 11:14, 23, 25, and its related verb is used of prosecution in a law court (Ps. 109:6) and the role of an antagonist in general (Ps. 38:20[21]; 109:4, 20, 29). The angel who was sent to obstruct Balaam (Num. 22:32) was evidently chosen ad hoc, as a satan (*le-saṭan*), and perhaps the consonants *lsṭn* are rather to be read as the infinitive *lisṭon*, "to oppose or obstruct." There is nothing here to indicate that שִׂטְנָה (*siṭnah*) was the permanent function of a particular angel. "The Satan" as the standing appellation of a particular angel first appears around 520 B.C.E. in Zechariah 3 and then in *Job 1–2. In I Chronicles 21:1, which has already been referred to, the article is disposed with, and "Satan" seems to be a real proper name. In Zechariah 3, the Satan acts as prosecutor in the celestial court; in Job 1–2, he questions Job's integrity in the latter's absence and suggests to the Lord that it be tested. He is clearly subordinate to God, a member of His suite (Heb. *bene ha-e'lohim*), who is unable to act without His permission. Nowhere is he in any sense a rival of God. In I Chronicles 21:1, in which Satan is said to have incited David to take a census of Israel which resulted in the death of 70,000 Israelites (21:14), he has obviously been secondarily substituted because of doctrinal consideration for "the Lord," who plays this part.

Post-Biblical

Satan is not prominent in the Apocrypha and Apocalypses, and, where mentioned, he is barely personalized but merely represents the forces of anti-God and of evil. Thus the Martyrdom of Isaiah (2:2) states that "Manasseh forsook the service of the God of his fathers and he served Satan and his angels and his powers." In the Testament of Gad (4:7) the warning is given that "the spirit of hatred worketh together with Satan through hastiness of spirit." Dan is told to "beware of Satan and his spirits" (6:1; cf. also 3:6 and 5:6; for other references see I En. 54:6; Assumption of Moses 10:1). The legend in the Talmud and Midrash that it was Satan who challenged God to put Abraham to the test of the *Akedah* (i.e., the sacrifice of Isaac; see below) appears in Jubilees (17:16) where, however, he is called *Mastema.

References in the tannaitic literature are even more sparse, and, with few exceptions, Satan similarly appears merely as the impersonal force of evil. Thus Tosefta *Shabbat* 17 (18):3 states: "If you see a wicked man setting out on a journey and you wish to go by the same route, anticipate your journey by three days or postpone it for three days, because Satan accompanies the wicked man." The same trend is seen in the injunction "Open not your mouth to Satan" (Ber. 9a; see later), which, though given in the name of an *amora*, is stated "also to have been taught in the name of R. Yose." R. Johanan's statement of Satan persuading God about the *Akedah* is also given in the name of a *tanna*, Yose b. Zimra. The *Sifrei* (to Deut. 218), making the rebellious son the inevitable consequence of the father succumbing to the beauty of a female captive mentioned in the previous passage, declares: "the father of this one lusted after a beautiful woman (captive) and thus brought Satan into his house." R. Joshua states that the verse "the earth is given into the hands of the wicked" (Job 9:24) refers to Satan (BB 16a). The only personification of Satan found in tannaitic literature is the story of R. Meir spending three days to bring about a reconciliation between two inveterate quarrelers, upon which Satan complained, "He has drawn me out of my home" (Git. 52a). Similarly, R. Akiva was tempted by Satan in the form of a woman, but Satan relented.

In the New Testament Satan emerges as the very personification of the spirit of evil, as an independent personality, the Antichrist. He is the author of all evil (Luke 10:19). In Revelation 12:9 there is the fullest description of him: "that old serpent called the devil and Satan which deceived the whole world. He was cast into the earth and his angels were cast out with him." He is the personal tempter of Jesus (Matt. 4), and it is this New Testament conception of Satan which has entered into popular lore. The Jews who would not accept Jesus are referred to as "the synagogue of Satan" (Rev. 2:9, 3:9).

During the amoraic period, however, Satan became much more prominent in the Talmud and Midrash. An interesting example of the development of the idea of Satan in amoraic times can be seen by a comparison between the *Sifrei* and the Midrash. The former, in its comment to Numbers 25:1, says "wherever 'dwellings' is mentioned Satan leaps in!" He is frequently referred to as *Samael, but the references which follow refer to the actual name Satan. He appears sometimes in the same impersonal guise as in the Apocrypha and among the *tannaim*. He is identified with the *yeẓer ha-ra* (the evil inclination in general) and with the angel of death (BB 16a), but in addition he emerges more and more as a distinct identity. The Satan of Job who challenges God to put Job to the test of suffering is made to play the same role with Abraham. He accuses Abraham that despite the boon of being granted a son in his old age, Abraham did not "have one turtle-dove or pigeon to sacrifice before this," and Abraham is ordered to sacrifice Isaac to prove his obedience to God (Sanh. 89b). In this connection an almost sympathetic view is taken of

Satan. His purpose in challenging Job's piety is for a worthy purpose: that God should not forget the greater loyalty of Abraham (BB 16a).

Although he appears as the tempter, he is much more to the fore as the accuser, and the phrase *Satan mekatreg* ("Satan the accuser"; Gen. R. 38:7; TJ, Ber. 1:1, Shab. 2:6) occurs with great frequency. The well-known phrase "open not thy mouth to Satan" is significant in this respect in its context. The Talmud states that when his dead lies before him a mourner should justify the divine judgment by saying: "Sovereign of the Universe, I have sinned before Thee and Thou hast not punished me a thousandth part." To this the objection was raised that he should not say so, since he thereby "gives an opening to Satan" (cf. *Rema*, YD 376:2).

Satan was responsible for all the sins in the Bible: for the fall of man (PdRE 13:1), for the people worshiping the golden calf by telling them that Moses would not return from Mount Sinai (Shab. 89a), and for David's sin with Bath-Sheba (Sanh. 107a). He is associated with the gentile nations in sneering at the *Ḥukkim*, those laws – such as *sha'atnez and the prohibition of the pig – for which no rational reason can be given, and thus weakening the religious loyalties of the Jews (Yoma 67b; for this tempting of the rabbis, see Kid. 81a–b). The purpose of the sounding of the *shofar* on Rosh Ha-Shanah is "in order to confuse Satan" (RH 16b), but on the Day of Atonement he is completely powerless. This is hinted at in the fact that the numerical equivalent of Satan is 364, i.e., there is one day in the year on which he is powerless (Yoma 20a).

References to Satan in the liturgy are few and impersonal. The *Hashkivenu prayer of the evening service includes a plea to "remove from us the enemy, pestilence… and Satan" (the adversary), while the morning blessings preceding the *Pesukei de-Zimra* conclude with R. Judah ha-Nasi's prayer (Ber. 16b) to be spared from "the corrupting Satan." The *reshut of the *ḥazzan* before *Musaf* on the High Holy Days includes the sentence "and rebuke the Satan that he accuse me not," and under the influence of the Kabbalah six biblical verses are recited before the sounding of the *shofar*, the initial letters of which form the acrostic *kera Satan* ("tear Satan"). During the Middle Ages the Church, basing itself on such passages in the New Testament as "Ye are of your father and the devil" (John 8:44), propounded the doctrine that the Jews were the "spawn of Satan," with many of his characteristics. As such they were less than human beings – sorcerers, magicians, and evildoers – and this theory was a determining factor in the denial of rights to, and persecutions of, the Jews.

BIBLIOGRAPHY: N.H. Torczyner (Tur-Sinai), *The Book of Job* (1957), xvi, 38–45; T.H. Gaster, in: IDB, 4 (1962), 224–8 (incl. bibl.). POST-BIBLICAL: *Theologisches Woerterbuch zum Neuen Testament*, 2 (1935), 71–80; L. Jung, *Fallen Angels in Jewish, Christian, and Muhammedean Literature* (1926); Ginzberg, Legends, index s.v.; H.L. Strack and P. Billerbeck, *Kommentar zum Neuen Testament aus Talmud und Midrash*, 1 (1922), 136–49; J. Trachtenberg, *The Devil and the Jews* (1943), 18–22, 59–63, 198–200; G. Scholem, *Von der mystischen Gestalt der Gottheit* (1962), index.

[Louis Isaac Rabinowitz]

SATANOV, town in Khmelnitsky district, Ukraine; until 1793 within Poland. A Jewish community was organized there in the second half of the 16th century, after Podolia was incorporated within the kingdom of Poland. The Jews of Satanov engaged in the import of goods from the east, leasing of estates and customs dues, manufacture of alcoholic beverages (see *Wine and Liquor Trade), and goldsmithery. The town and its Jewish community suffered periodically from the incursions of the Tatars and Cossacks, in particular from their combined attacks in 1651 and from the Cossacks in 1703. The magnificent synagogue in Satanov was built in the form of a fortress, so that Jews would be able to defend themselves in such attacks. During the 18th century Satanov was the leading community in Podolia. Its *dayyanim* held a trial of the *Frankists there in 1756. In 1765 there were 1,369 Jews paying the poll tax in Satanov. Until the incorporation of Satanov within Russia in 1793, the Jews there took part in the international commerce, traveling to the fairs of *Leipzig, *Breslau, and *Frankfurt.

The Hebrew writer and *maskil* Isaac *Satanow lived in the town and was active there in the second half of the 18th century, as was Menahem Mendel (Lefin) *Levin (1749–1826), among the pioneers of the *Haskalah in Eastern Europe, and Alexander b. Ẓevi Margaliot (d. 1802), author of *Teshuvot ha-Re'em*, who was rabbi of Satanov. From the end of the 18th century and during the 19th, Satanov was an important center of *Ḥasidism. Until 1862 Jewish settlement there was restricted by the authorities, owing to the proximity of the town to the Austrian border. The Jewish population numbered 2,848 (64% of the total) in 1897. In 1919 the Jews in Satanov suffered from *pogroms at the hands of the Ukrainian nationalists. Satanov probably had 2,359 Jews in 1926, then declining to 1,516 (40% of the total population). A rural Jewish council existed in the Soviet period. The Germans entered Satanov on July 6, 1941. On May 14, 1942, they locked 240 Jews in a cellar, letting them choke to death. Through 1942, 210 Jews were shot to death. Most of the 800 people officially murdered by the Germans were Jews.

BIBLIOGRAPHY: Halpern, Pinkas, 75, 94, 416f.; M. Balaban, *Żydzi lwowscy na przełomie XVIgo i XVIIgo wieku* (1906), 53f., 399; idem, *Le-Toledot ha-Tenu'ah ha-Frankit*, 1 (1934), 118–27; R. Mahler, *Yidn in Amolikn Poyln in Likht fun Tsifern* (1958), index; S. Łlastik, *Z dziejów oświecenia żydowskiego* (1961), 90f.; E. Tcherikower, *Di Ukrainer Pogromen in Yor 1919* (1965), 145.

[Shimshon Leib Kirshenboim / Shmuel Spector (2nd ed.)]

SATANOW, ISAAC (1732–1804), Hebrew writer, born in Satanov, Podolia. Satonow settled in Berlin in 1771 or 1772, where he served as the director of the printing press of the Ḥevrat Ḥinnukh Ne'arim ("Society for the Education of the Youth"). Among the most prolific of the early Haskalah writers, he did not restrict himself to any particular literary field, but wrote in most of those genres used by the later Haskalah writers. Although an exponent of the Jewish enlightenment of 18th-century Berlin, he displayed an affinity for Jewish mysticism.

Between 1780 and 1784 he traveled several times to Galicia, where he was involved in printing the kabbalistic book *Ez Ḥayyim* (1785), attributed to R. Isaac Luria. Satanow demonstrated a wealth of knowledge of the Hebrew language, ranking as a model stylist throughout the Haskalah period. He ascribed several of his works to earlier writers, and consequently used fictitious names for the authors of the recommendations for his own books and of their forewords. His books include *Sefer ha-Shorashim* or *Hebraeisch-Deutsches Lexicon*, one of his major works, which was a Hebrew-German dictionary and thesaurus in two parts; a number of books of liturgy, *Tefillah mi-Kol ha-Shanah al Pi Kelalei ha-Dikduk* (1785), *Haggadah shel Pesaḥ* (1785); and *Seliḥot* (1785); as well as *Mishlei Asaf* and *Zemirot Asaf* (4 vols., 1789–1802), collections of proverbs in imitation of the Book of Proverbs. (Satanow adopted the pseudonym "Asaf" from the acrostic for "Itzik Satanow.") In the last, his best-known work, the peak of his imitative ability is displayed, and, at the same time, the finest expression of his own sentiments and thoughts. The work, attributed to the biblical Asaph son of Berechiah, is written in the style of Proverbs and Psalms. In his *Zohar Taniana* (1783), *Nevu'at Yeled* (1793), and *Imrei Bina* (1784), he tried to build a bridge between the mystical world of Kabbalah and the rationalistic views of the Haskalah.

Satanow grappled with the problem of the use of biblical and post-biblical Hebrew. In his book *Iggeret Beit Tefillah* (1773), a work on prayers and liturgy, he classified every word that he explained as either "Hebrew" or "talmudic," and proceeded to clarify this question at other opportunities as well. He may have been the first Hebrew writer who sought to break out of the strict framework of biblical style, although he himself was very adept in the biblical style called *meliẓah*. Hence he demanded that new words be coined; in *Iggeret Beit Tefillah* he complains that the vocabulary of biblical Hebrew had not preserved its great lexical range.

BIBLIOGRAPHY: J. Klausner, Sifrut, 1 (1952), 165–77; Zinberg, Sifrut, 5 (1959), 118–22; G. Kressel, Leksikon, 2 (1967), 490–3; S. Werses, in: *Tarbiz*, 32 (1963), 370–92. **ADD. BIBLIOGRAPHY:** M. Pelli, *Isaac Satanow's "Mishlei Asaf" as Reflecting the Ideology of the German Hebrew Haskalah* (1972); idem, *Kiryat Sefer* 54 (1979), 817–24; idem, *The Age of Haskalah* (1979), 151–70; N. Rezler-Bersohn, in: YBLBI 25 (1980), 81–100; S. Werses, *Haskalah ve-Shabta'ut* (1988), 33–38; M. Pelli, *Be-Ma'avakei Temurah*, 83–139; R. Horwitz, in: YLBI 45 (2000), 3–24.

[Getzel Kressel; Noam Zadoff (2nd ed.)]

SATANOWSKI, MARCOS (1893–1957), Argentine jurist. Born in Bahia Blanca, Satanowski graduated from the University of Buenos Aires in 1928 and was appointed professor of commercial law. In 1946, he was dismissed by the Perón regime but was reinstated in 1955 and held the chair until his death. He founded and was the first president of the Sociedad Hebraica Argentinea. He published many books on legal and other subjects including *El actual Regimen Monetario Argentino* (1933) and *El Renovado Pueblo de Israel* (1954). In 1957 he was involved in a trial for the return of the newspaper *La Razón* to its former owner, Ricardo Peralta Ramos, from whom it was expropriated by Perón's regime. He was murdered by three assailants, probably in a mission of the Secretaría de Informaciones del Estado – SIDE (National Intelligence Service), while working in his office.

SATINSKY, SOL (1900–1966), U.S. manufacturer and communal leader. Satinsky was born in Philadelphia. Entering the family business, Frankford Worsted Mills, in 1920, he became its president in 1930, renaming it Frankford Woolen Mills. He was also a partner in Satinsky Brothers Realty Co. Satinsky early became active in welfare and education projects.

He was president of the Jewish Family Service and United Hebrew Schools and helped to create the Federation of Jewish Agencies of Philadelphia, which he served in several capacities. He was also president of the Philadelphia Allied Jewish Appeal and chairman of the National Council of the Joint Distribution Committee. Strongly committed to Jewish scholarship, Satinsky served as chairman of the American Jewish History Center of the Jewish Theological Seminary, president of the Jewish Publication Society, and acting president of Dropsie College. Satinsky was active in the World Affairs Council of Philadelphia; among his other interests was a collection of Lincoln memorabilia which he donated to Cornell University.

[Gladys Rosen]

SATORALJAUJHELY (in Yiddish popularly abridged to **Ujhely**), city in N.E. Hungary. Before World War I it was one of the main Jewish settlements in Hungary, excluding *Subcarpathian Ruthenia and *Transylvania. Jews first arrived there at the beginning of the 18th century, in connection with the nationalist army of F. Rákóczi. An organized community was established in 1771. The first Jewish elementary school was founded in 1836; M. *Heilprin was among its teachers. The first rabbi was S. Weil. He was succeeded by Moses *Teitelbaum (1808–40), founder of the celebrated dynasty of *ẓaddikim*. His grandson was compelled to leave the town as a result of the opposition to the Ḥasidim. Rabbinical office was then held by Jeremiah Loew (1854–73), who took part in the Hungarian General Jewish Congress of 1868–69. He endeavored to prevent a split within the community after the schism within Hungarian Jewry that followed the congress (see *Hungary), but in 1886 his son Eleazar Loew (1873–86) founded a separate Orthodox community. After the separation of the Orthodox sector, the majority of the community remained *status quo ante.

After the term of office of R. Kalman Weiss (1890–1910), a rabbi was not appointed until the arrival of S. Roth (1921–44), the last rabbi. A large synagogue was erected in 1888. The Orthodox community also built a large synagogue and established a higher yeshivah (1922–44). The Jewish population numbered 3,523 in 1869; 5,730 in 1910; 6,445 in 1920; and 4,160 in 1941. They were mainly occupied in commerce, but a number were in professions.

Holocaust and Contemporary Periods

The Jews in the city were affected by the anti-Jewish legislation, unemployment, and other difficulties that faced the rest of the Jews in Hungary in the interwar period. After the German invasion (March 19, 1944), about 4,000 Jews from Satoraljaujhely were confined in a ghetto, joined by another 11,000 from nearby villages, all crowded 20–25 to a room. All were deported to the death camp at *Auschwitz between May 16 and June 3 in four transports. Only 555 survived. There were 204 Jews living in Satoraljaujhely in 1953.

BIBLIOGRAPHY: Fodor, in: *Magyar Zsidó Almanach* (1911), 268; I. Goldberger, *Ha-Ẓofeh me-Ereẓ Hagar*, 1 (1911), 121–35; *Magyar Zsidó Szemle*, 14 (1897), 372–3; *Magyar Zsidó Lexikon* (1929), 768–9.

[Baruch Yaron]

SATRAP (Heb. pl. אֲחַשְׁדַּרְפְּנִים; Aram. אֲחַשְׁדַּרְפְּנַיָּא; Old Persian *xšaçapāvan*, "protector of the province"; Greek σατράπης), an official title during the Persian Empire of varying meaning. According to Herodotus (3:89–94) and contemporary inscriptional material, Darius I divided up his empire for administrative purposes into some 20 districts called satrapies. In the biblical passages where Persian officials are listed in descending order of importance, the satrap almost always comes first (Esth. 3:12; 8:9; Dan. 3:2–3, 27; Ezra 8:36; Esth. 9:3, a literary variation?). The one passage which defines the title, however, speaks of Darius the Mede appointing 120 satraps over his kingdom (Dan. 6:2). Such a division of the realm is reminiscent of the Esther narrative (Esth. 1:1; 8:9) where Ahasuerus (Xerxes, the successor of Darius), is said to have ruled over 127 provinces (Heb. *medinot*).

The flexibility of titles as they are translated from one language to another and transferred from official to literary sources may be seen by a comparison of three sources. The Old Persian Darius Behistun inscription calls Dadarshi "satrap" of Bactria (3:13–14). The fragmentary Aramaic text apparently refers to him as "governor" (*peḥah*; Cowley, Aramaic, p. 252, line 18). Likewise, Tattenai, head of the Trans-Euphrates, apparently a satrapy, was called "governor" (Ezra 5:3, 6; 6:6, 13). Conversely, Greek historians occasionally used "satrap" to designate lower officials.

[Bezalel Porten]

The satrap possessed very extensive authority: he supervised the administration of the districts of his province, including the imposition of taxes. He had the right to mint coins in his name, except for gold coins, the minting of which was the prerogative of the emperor. He was the supreme judge and traveled throughout the province dispensing justice. He was responsible for security inside his province and supervised the highways. He also had an army which he recruited locally, but the garrisons in the citadels and the regular army were under the direct command of the emperor. The *peḥah* was subordinate to the satrap, who in turn was subject to the representative of the emperor, but satraps frequently conducted their own foreign policy. Sometimes more than one province was under the rule of one satrap. The office of satrap at times passed by inheritance, and there were dynasties of satraps which continued for many generations. As a result of the extensive authority bestowed upon the satrap, the Persian Empire in the course of time was a united country only in theory; in practice the forces of schism and disintegration prevailed more and more. From time to time, the great satraps rebelled, and it was only with difficulty that the emperors succeeded in overpowering them. Alexander the Great continued with the division of the country into satrapies; and it was continued by the Seleucids. The satrap of Transjordan held sway also over Samaria and Judea, and when there was a governor in Judea, he was subject to the authority of this satrap.

[Abraham Schalit]

BIBLIOGRAPHY: Herodotus, 3:89ff.; P. Julien, *Zur Verwaltung der Satrapien unter Alexander dem Grossen* (1914); Pauly-Wissowa, 2nd series, 3 (1921), 82–188; O. Leuze, *Die Satrapieneinteilung in Syrien und im Zweistromlande von 520–320* (1935); E. Bickermann, *Institutions des Seleucides* (1937); J.A. Montgomery, *Daniel* (ICC, 1927), 199; B. Porten, *Archives from Elephantine* (1968), 24, no. 93; A.F. Rainey, *Australian Journal of Biblical Archaeology*, 1 (1969), 51ff.

SATU-MARE (Hung. **Szatmárnémeti** or **Szatmár**, also called **Sakmér**), city in Satu-Mare province, N.W. Romania; until World War I and between 1940 and 1944, part of Hungary. There is sporadic mention of the presence of Jews in or passing through Satu-Mare in the early 18th century. Permission was granted to the Jews to settle in the city because it was hoped by the more powerful local Hungarian landlords that they would bring economic prosperity, which they actually did for a period of centuries. Jews, too, became landlords or lessees. Some became involved in large-scale agriculture; many others contributed to the development of trade and industry.; and still others were employed in Jewish workshops at low wages. There were 11 Jews in the town in 1734 and 19 in 1746. In 1841 several Jews obtained permits to settle in Satu-Mare permanently. A community was formally established in 1849, and a synagogue erected in 1857. Benjamin Ze'ev Mendelbaum became the first rabbi in 1849, officiating until his death in 1896. Through his influence the community defined itself as Orthodox in 1869 (see *Hungary). In 1898 it split up and a *status quo ante community was established. A magnificent synagogue was erected in 1904. The Jewish population rose from 78 in 1850 to 3,427 (16% of the total population) in 1870, 7,194 (20% of the total population) in 1910, and 11,533 (21% of the total population) in 1930. There were then five large synagogues and about 20 smaller ones in the city. The first Jewish printing press was established in 1903.

From the end of the 19th century, there were conflicts among the supporters of Ḥasidism and the *Mitnaggedim*. From 1902 the status quo community was led by a Zionist rabbi, Dr. Samuel Sándor Jordán, who established the first Hebrew kindergarten in Hungary. The first Jewish schools were opened in 1866. Between 1940 and 1944 there was also a secondary school for boys and girls (four classes).

Jews took an active part in the development of industry and commerce in Satu-Mare, were prominent in the liberal professions, and contributed to the local Hungarian press. Between the two world wars, branches of the Zionist movements were active in the community; a B'nai B'rith lodge was established, as well as a branch of the Jewish party and other institutions. The rabbis of the Orthodox community were Judah Gruenwald (until 1920) and Eliezer David Gruenwald. After his death in 1928, a bitter conflict followed within the Orthodox community over the election of a new rabbi. The struggle lasted six years and was concluded in 1934 by the victory of the supporters of Joel *Teitelbaum, whose domineering personality and uncompromising anti-Zionist stand influenced Orthodox Jewry in the whole of Transylvania.

Although the influence of Neologism was extremely weak in this region, many Jewish intellectuals were drawn to the Hungarian language and culture, becoming important figures in Hungarian society. Between the two world wars the influence of the fascist Iron Guard was felt. This was the reason why in 1940 the Jews received the Hungarian Horthiite troups with open arms. They were not aware of the changes post–World War I Hungary had undergone under Admiral Horthy's rule. The first signs of what was to come manifested themselves shortly after the city was occupied by Hungary and "foreign" Jews were deported to Kamenets-Podolski, where they were murdered by Hungarian and German troops. In spring 1944 the rest of the Jews, some 20,000 including refugees, were first ghettoized and then deported to Auschwitz after the majority of men had been sent to forced labor battalions. Less than 15% survived the Holocaust and were able to make their way back to their homes.

After World War II some of the survivors returned from the camps, and about 500 Jews resettled there. They were joined by former residents and Jews from other localities, and by 1947 they numbered approximately 5,000. Subsequently many moved away or immigrated to Ereẓ Israel, and by 1970 there remained some 500 Jews in Satu-Mare, with numbers later declining.

BIBLIOGRAPHY: MHJ, 3 (1937), index s.v.; *Szatmárkerületi zsidók*, 5 pt. 1 (1959); 5 pt. 2 (1960); 7 (1963), index locorum s.v. *Szatmár*; M. Stern, *A szatmári zsidók útja* (1931).

[Yehouda Marton / Paul Schveiger (2nd ed.)]

SATZ, LUDWIG (1891–1944), Yiddish comedian. Born in Lvov, Poland, Satz joined a troupe of Yiddish actors in 1910 and played in Gordin's *Got, Mentsh und der Taivl*. He appeared in Budapest and London and achieved Broadway success as Abe Potash in *Potash and Perlmutter*, 1913. He also acted with Jacob Adler and Maurice Schwartz, and in Boris Thomashefsky's Yiddish venture on Broadway (1923–24). Later he toured Europe and South America.

SATZ, MARIO (1944–), Argentine poet, author, and essayist. He was born in Coronel Pringles, Argentina. His extensive travels had significant influence on his writing. He lived in Israel for three years and from 1978 he lived in Barcelona, Spain. Satz is a prolific author of poetry, and narrative and nonfiction works that include books about Kabbalah and Jewish history.

His early poetry is intimately connected to the natural world. In volumes such as *Los cuatro elementos* (1964), *Las frutas* (1970), *Canon de polen* (1976), *Los peces, los pájaros, las flores* (1976), and *Las redes cristalinas* (1985) he examines the beauty and power of nature in practically all its earthly manifestations. He is also the author of a vast novelistic series titled *Planetarium*, which consists of five novels that comprise a textual solar system. The novels *Sol* (1976), *Luna* (1977), and *Tierra* (1978) form a trilogy in which the author utilizes the cities of Jerusalem and Cuzco, Peru, as sites for examining Latin American history and culture together with Jewish tradition. The subsequent novels, *Marte* (1980) and *Mercurio* (1990), do not continue the story of the trilogy though they are part of the *Planetarium* project.

His book *Tres cuentos españoles* (1988) takes on a much more focused perspective with the portrayal of multicultural 13th century Spain in which Christian, Muslim, and Jewish cultures existed and thrived side by side. His attention to detail and historical accuracy is remarkable. The novel *Azahar* (1996) continues with the same focus on Iberia, this time with a focus on religious-mystical traditions from Kabbalah to *The Book of the Dead*. The author's nonfiction works reveal his interest in Jewish history and mysticism and are evidence of his capability for profound theological thinking. Representative texts in this vein include *Poética de la Kábala* (1985), *Judaísmo: 4,000 años de cultura* (1982), and *El dador alegre: ensayos de Kábala* (1997).

[Darrell B. Lockhart (2nd ed.)]

°**SAUCKEL, FRITZ** (**Ernst Friedrich Christoph**; 1894–1946), Nazi official. Born in Hassfurt to a family of minor officials, Sauckel worked in the merchant marines of Norway and Sweden prior to World War I. During World War I he was a prisoner of war. He joined the Nazi Party in 1921 and was appointed *Gauleiter* ("district leader") of the Nazi Party in Thuringia in 1925 and its governor in 1933. On March 21, 1942, he was appointed by *Hitler plenipotentiary (*Generalbevollmaechtigter*) for labor recruitment, and thus he became the most notorious slave driver of Nazi Germany. His self-described task was to make maximum use of the slave labor for the "lowest conceivable expenditure." Up to March 1, 1944, seven and a half million workers were brought on his orders to Germany from all over occupied Europe, of whom only 200,000 came voluntarily. Their working and living conditions were unbearable. Conditions among Jews were the worst. They were literally worked to death. In the fall of 1942 Sauckel, with the aid of the *RSHA, organized the drafting of Polish workers in order to replace Jews working in the armament industry, with the aim of deporting those Jews to concentration and death camps. He was convicted at the trial of major war criminals in Nuremberg and hanged on October 16, 1946.

BIBLIOGRAPHY: E. Davidson, *Trial of the Germans* (1966), index; G.M. Gilbert, *Nuremberg Diary* (1947), index; IMT, *Trial of the*

Major War Criminals, 24 (1949), index. **ADD. BIBLIOGRAPHY:** E.L. Homze, *Foreign Labor in Nazi Germany* (1967); B. Ferencz, *Less than Slaves: Jewish Forced Labor and the Quest for Compensation* (1979).

[Yehuda Reshef / Michael Berenbaum (2nd ed.)]

SAUDI ARABIA, an authoritarian monarchy, whose legal system is based on a strict interpretation of Islamic law, known in the West as Wahhabism, after the spiritual leader of the original Saudi state, Muḥammad ibn ʿAbdul Wahhāb (1703–1792). Modern Saudi Arabia was established in 1932 by King Abdul Aziz ibn Abdul Rahman Āl Saud (1880–1953), who waged a three-decade-long campaign to unify the kingdom and re-claim the patrimony that was one ruled intermittently by his family in the 18th and 19th centuries. He was also known in the West by the name King Ibn Saud. Like the earlier Saudi states, the modern Saudi Kingdom was based on a political partnership between the Āl-Saud family and the Wahhabi clerics, whom the Saudis funded and empowered with control over Saudi ministries. Today Saudi Arabia's land area is 1,960,582 square kilometers. Its longest land boundaries are with *Yemen (1,458 km.), *Iraq (814 km.), and *Jordan (744 km). But it also shares borders with Oman, the United Arab Emirates, Qatar, and Kuwait. The Saudi Kingdom is made up of a number of regions including the Najd plateau, the birthplace of the Saudi royal family, the Hijaz, where the Muslim holy cities of Mecca and *Medina are located, and the Eastern Province, where the Saudi oil fields are situated that contain 25 per cent of the world's proven petroleum reserves. Since 1953, Saudi Arabia has been ruled by the sons of Ibn Saud who were successively: Saud, Faisal, Khaled, and Fahd, and in 2005, King Abdullah, who was born in 1923, acceded to the throne.

To understand Saudi attitudes to the Jewish people and the Jewish state, Israel, it is necessary to examine Wahhabi doctrines towards the monotheistic faiths outside of *Islam. These were far harsher than those adopted under classical Islam, which defined Jews and Christians as *ahl al-kitāb* (people of the book) who were entitled to live their lives under their respective religious codes, albeit as second-class citizens, who had to pay special discriminatory taxes for non-Muslims, such as **jizya* (poll tax) and **kharāj* (land tax). In his main work, the *Kitāb al-Tawḥīd* (The Book of Monotheism) Muḥammad ibn ʿAbdul Wahhāb described Jews and Christians as sorcerers who believed in devil worship. He challenged the assertion that both groups were truly monotheistic, charging that "the ways of the people of the book are condemned as those of the polytheists." Given that there was a negligible presence of either religious group in Central Arabia in the 18th century, these theoretical distinctions would only become relevant after the establishment of the modern Saudi state, when Wahhabi doctrines would influence Saudi attitudes to Israel as well as provide the ideological underpinnings for jihadi movements, like al-Qaeda.

Saudi Arabia was implacably opposed to the creation of the State of Israel. Several years after U.S. oil companies, led by Standard Oil of California, secured oil exploration rights in Saudi Arabia, King Ibn Saud addressed a series of letters to President Franklin Delano Roosevelt, stating his opposition to the creation of a Jewish state in British Palestine, and raised the subject yet again in his historic summit meeting with Roosevelt on the USS *Quincy* in Egypt's Great Bitter Lake. But Ibn Saud's primary concern after Israel's creation came from his Arab rivals – the Hashemite Kingdoms of Transjordan and Iraq – and their British sponsors. Ibn Saud was not prepared to sacrifice his relations with the U.S. and give up on American security guarantees against his potential rivals, despite Washington's backing of the partition of Palestine and its early recognition of the State of Israel. His son, King Faisal, launched an oil embargo against the U.S. during the 1973 Yom Kippur War, but quickly sought to repair his relations with Washington, and agreed to a U.S.-sponsored buildup of Saudi military capabilities against Soviet-backed Arab rivals, from F-15 fighter aircraft to AWACS planes.

Saudi Arabia sent its ambassador in Washington, Prince Bandar, to attend the 1991 Madrid peace conference with Israel, Syria, *Lebanon, and a Jordanian-Palestinian delegation. There was a slight incremental thaw in Israeli-Saudi contacts thereafter. Saudi Arabia attended the 1992 Moscow multilateral negotiations and the various working-groups that it had established. But after the 1993 Oslo Agreements, Saudi Arabia did not follow the examples of Qatar and Oman, which allowed Israel to open quasi-diplomatic trade offices in their capitals. Nor did the Saudis follow the model of Bahrain and UAE (Dubai) which allowed Israelis to attend multilateral conferences on their soil. Saudi Foreign Minister Saud Al-Faisal attended a 1996 counter-terrorism conference in Sharm al-Sheikh, Egypt, with Israeli Prime Minister Shimon *Peres, marking the outer reaches of Saudi readiness for open, high-level contacts. The Saudi religious establishment, represented by the Saudi Grand Mufti, Sheikh Abdul Aziz bin Baz, was not willing to condone the idea of permanent peace with Israel, but was only willing to concede the idea of a *hudna* with the Jewish state, which, he explained in a formal document, was only a temporary truce until the balance of power changes. During the 1990s, despite its demand for religious identification in its visa applications, Saudi Arabia hosted several American Jewish organizations, including the American Jewish Congress and the Anti-Defamation League.

After Yasser *Arafat's Fatah movement became the dominant component of the *Palestine Liberation Organization (PLO) in the late 1960s, Saudi Arabia became its largest financial backer. Yet after the PLO allied itself with Saddam Hussein in the 1991 Gulf War, Saudi Arabia increasingly began to provide financial assistance to Hamas, despite its direct involvement in suicide bombings against Israeli civilians, through large Wahhabi charities, such as al-Haramain, the Muslim World League's International Islamic Relief Organization, and the World Assembly for Muslim Youth. The 9/11 attacks by al-Qaeda on New York and Washington brought into focus the Saudi connection to the new escalation of global terrorism, since 15 out of the 19 hijackers were Saudi citizens. Moreover, their overall commander, Osama bin Laden, was born and educated in Saudi Arabia and had worked with Saudi intelligence against the Soviet presence in *Afghanistan. In 1998, he set up the "World Islamic Front Against Crusaders and Jews." He relied heavily on Wahhabi religious scholars, such as Suleiman al-Ulwan or Hamud bin Uqla al-Shuaibi, who justified his use of mass violence against the "infidels," which, from their doctrinal standpoint, included Christians and Jews. Both scholars justified suicide bombings against Israeli civilians on the website of Hamas. Other Saudi scholars, like Nasser bin Hamed al-Fahd and Ali al-Khudeir, put out religious opinions that dovetailed with al-Qaeda strategy, since they advocated the mass murder of infidels by means of weapons of mass destruction. After 2003, Israeli officials, like Defense Minister Shaul *Mofaz, became openly concerned with al-Qaeda's penetration of the Saudi military, including the Saudi Air Force. Israel raised the possibility that Saudi F-15 fighter planes, deployed during the 2003 Iraq War at Tabuk Air Base near Eilat, might be used by al-Qaeda suicide pilots for operations against Israeli buildings in Tel Aviv.

King Abdullah, in his capacity as crown prince, floated a new peace plan between Israel and the Arab world through *New York Times* columnist Thomas Friedman on February 17, 2002. The core of the plan was the idea of exchanging a "full Israeli withdrawal" from the territories Israel captured in the Six-Day War for "full normalization" of relations with Israel. But Abdullah retreated from this formula with the Arab peace initiative that was launched at the Beirut Arab summit on March 28, 2002, when he watered down his original proposal and suggested instead granting Israel "normal relations" – a Syrian diplomatic term that was less than full peace. Given Saudi sensitivities to Western penetration, it is unlikely that Abdullah was really proposing full normalization with tourism, business ties, and cultural exchanges. Behind the scenes of the Saudi peace plan was Adel al-Jubeir, Abdullah's foreign policy advisor, who had been dispatched to Washington to repair Saudi Arabia's tarnished image in the U.S. after 9/11. It is probable that this was the context of the Saudi proposals.

BIBLIOGRAPHY: M. Abir, *Saudi Arabia: Government, Society and the Gulf Crises* (1993); M. Fandy, *Saudi Arabia and the Politics of Dissent* (1999); D. Gold, *Hatred's Kingdom: How Saudi Arabia Supports the New Global Terrorism* (2004); M Al-Rasheed, *A History of Saudi Arabia* (2002); A. Vassiliev, *The History of Saudi Arabia* (2000); J.D. Halevi, "Al-Qaeda's Intellectual Legacy: New Radical Islamic Thinking Justifying the Genocide of Infidels," in: *Jerusalem Viewpoints* (Dec. 1, 2003).

[Dore Gold (2nd ed.)]

SAUL (Heb. שָׁאוּל; "asked, requested, lent [by the Lord]"), the first king of Israel (c. 1029–1005 B.C.E.); son of Kish from the tribe of Benjamin (I Sam. 9:1, 21). Saul's home was in Gibeah (*ibid.* 10:26), i.e., Gibeath-Benjamin, also known as Gibeath-Shaul (*ibid.* 11:4), which he made his capital. After his death, his bones were buried in the tomb of his father, Kish, in Zela (II Sam. 21:24; cf. Josh. 18:28). Zela would seem to be the name of a place close to Gibeath-Benjamin where the house of Saul had its lands. According to I Chronicles 8:29–30, Saul's family came from Gibeon.

In the days of *Samuel's leadership the Israelites became increasingly aware that the time had come to replace the rule of the *Judges by a central, permanent authority capable of freeing the people from the pressure of the surrounding nations, and, in particular, from the domination of the Philistines (I Sam. 8:20; 9:16). The people therefore demanded of Samuel that he set a king over them, "to govern us like all the nations" (*ibid.* 8:5). The cycle of stories about the enthroning of Saul is made up of various divergent traditions. According to I Samuel 9:1–10: 16, Saul – "a handsome young man, and there was not a man more handsome among the people of Israel; from his shoulders and upward he was taller than all the people" – went out to look for his father's lost asses. Meanwhile the Lord revealed His will to Samuel. "Tomorrow about this time I will send to you a man from the land of Benjamin, and you shall anoint him to be a prince over my people" (9:16). Samuel carried out God's command and poured oil on Saul's head. Saul modestly expressed his amazement at being anointed ruler of Israel. On his way back to his home in Gibeah, he was suddenly seized with the spirit of the Lord and joined a group of prophets "and prophesied [i.e., went into an ecstatic trance] among them" (10:10). In I Samuel 10:17–27, in contrast, it is related that Samuel assembled the people at Mizpah and cast lots before them. The lot fell on Saul, who was acclaimed king, "and all the people shouted 'Long live the king!'" (10:24). In this tradition, too, Saul stands out as a man of modest and humble character who "hid himself among the baggage" (10:22). In chapter 11, again, it is recounted that Saul was proclaimed king in Gilgal after his defeat and rout of the *Ammonites, who were attempting to subject the inhabitants of Jabesh-Gilead, kinsmen of the tribe of Benjamin. In this story Saul appears as a charismatic leader of the same type as the Judges who had arisen to save Israel in time of trouble. His choice to lead the people was determined by his heroism on the battlefield. The interrelation of the above traditions is variously conceived by modern commentators. At all events, all the stories are agreed that Saul was chosen as king by God, and anointed by Samuel with the people's approval.

Most of Saul's years as king were spent in wars against the enemies of Israel: "When Saul had taken the kingship over Israel, he fought against all its enemies on every side, against *Moab, against the Ammonites, against *Edom, against the kings of Zobah, and against the *Philistines" (14:47). In particular, "there was hard fighting against the Philistines all the days of Saul" (14:52). The signal for the start of the struggle with the Philistines was given when *Jonathan, Saul's son, struck down the Philistine governor in Geba (i.e., Gibeah) in Benjamin (13:3). Saul mustered the Israelites at Gilgal, near Jericho, while the Philistines encamped at Michmas (13:15–16). From there troops of Philistine raiders made punitive attacks on Israel (13:17–18). Saul waited at Gilgal for Samuel to come and give the signal for the battle to begin. When Samuel failed to appear and the people were beginning to disperse, Saul of-

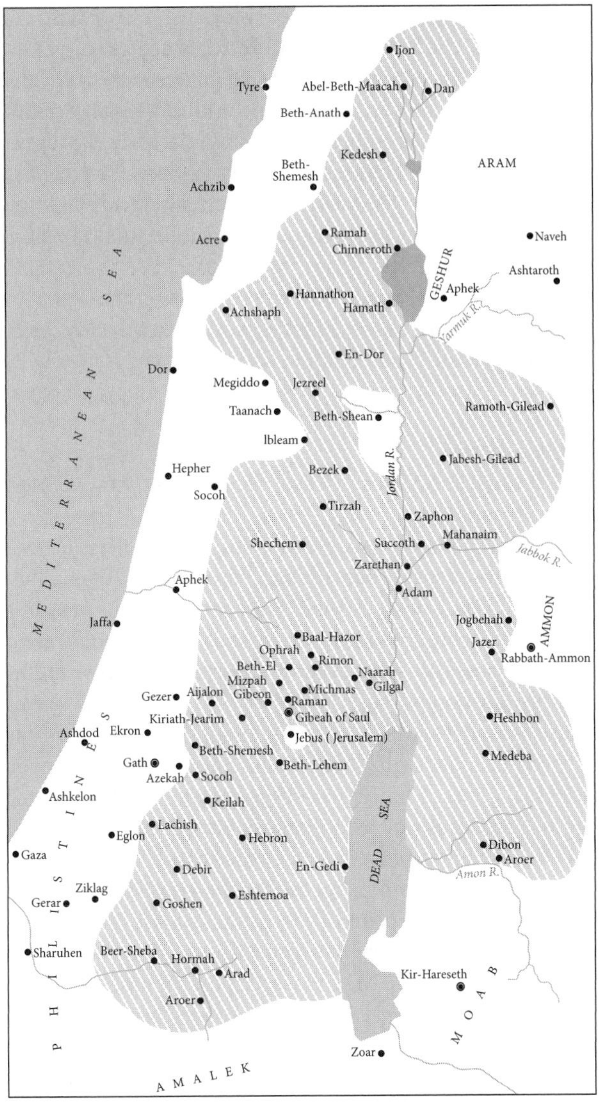

Limits of Saul's kingdom, end of the 11th century B.C.E. *After Y. Aharoni* Carta's Atlas of the Bible, *Jerusalem, 1964.*

fered up the burnt-offering and moved out to engage the Philistines, advancing on Gibeath-Benjamin with six thousand men. Jonathan took the nearby Philistine garrison by surprise, and the panic-stricken Philistines fled westward through the valley of Aijalon to Philistia (14:31). In this war the Philistines were driven out of the hill country of Ephraim. This was only the beginning of a series of wars against the Philistines. One of the engagements which is described in detail in the Bible is the battle in the Valley of Elah in the territory of Judah (I Sam. 17), in which *David killed the Philistine giant *Goliath. When the Philistines saw their hero felled in single combat by the young David, they fled to their own country. The encounter in the Valley of Elah thus liberated the hill country of Judah from Philistine rule. For his conduct of the wars against the enemies of Israel, Saul did not rely solely on the national levies but also established a regular armed force led by trained commanders, such as his own son Jonathan and *Abner son of Ner (13:2–3; 14:50, 52). Of special historical importance was the war against *Amalek, since it was in this war that the breach between Samuel and Saul first appeared (I Sam. 15). Samuel ordered Saul to smite the Amalekites and destroy them utterly, leaving no survivors (cf. Ex. 17:16). Saul mustered the people at Telaim, which is apparently identical with Telem in the Negev (Josh. 15:24). The war was fought in the southern desert regions "from Havilah as far as Shur, which is east of Egypt." The defeat of the Amalekites brought much needed relief to the people of Judah and Simeon, who had suffered greatly from the nomads' incursions. By his wars against the raiders from the desert (cf. I Chron. 5:10) Saul won the loyal support of the Israelites living in the southern border regions of Ereẓ Israel and Transjordan, since he was fighting to protect the territories on which they were settled. His kingdom then comprised the areas of Israelite settlement in Judah, Ephraim, Galilee, and also in Transjordan (as may be deduced from the extent of the kingdom of his son, Ish-Bosheth (II Sam. 2:8–9). Saul did not try to extend his rule beyond the area of Israelite settlement; nor does he appear to have attacked the non-Israelite families living within that area – apart from the Gibeonites, whom he sought to destroy "in his zeal for the people of Israel and Judah" (II Sam. 21:1ff.), i.e., in order to convert his kingdom into a solid ethnic block uninterrupted by non-Israelite enclaves. Saul does not seem to have made far-reaching changes in the tribal organization of the Israelites, or to have taken any drastic measures to establish a centralized authority, with a royal court and an elaborate bureaucratic machinery. He was thus able to avoid friction with the tribal leaders who exercised their power within the framework of the local tribal institutions.

But Saul did not succeed in remaining on good terms with Samuel. The tangled relations between the two men reflect the difficulties of the transition from the old regime of the Judges to the new monarchal rule. According to one tradition, Samuel opposed the people's demand for a king, since in his view the Lord was the King of Israel and the people's demand was thus tantamount to a rejection of God (see *Gideon). When he was commanded by God to grant the people's request, he demanded of both the people and the king absolute obedience to the Lord and to the prophet that spoke in His name (I Sam. 12:14–15; 15:22), regardless of political, military, or human considerations. This demand explains the deterioration of the relations between Samuel and Saul. The rift between them first appeared at the time of the engagement at Michmas (I Sam. 13), when Saul sacrificed the burnt-offering, instead of waiting patiently for Samuel to come and give the signal for the battle to commence. It may be that Samuel regarded Saul's offering of the sacrifice as an encroachment upon his own priestly authority and as an attempt by Saul to arrogate ritual powers to the king. Samuel declared to Saul that his rule would be short-lived: "But now your kingdom shall not continue" (13:14). The rift between Samuel and Saul became final after Saul's failure to comply with the order given him to exterminate the Amalekites (15:34–35; 28:18). The awareness that the Lord had rejected him gradually penetrated into Saul's mind in the course of his relations with David. As soon as David – who was now Saul's son-in-law – appeared at the court, Saul realized that he was the people's favorite (18:16). David's victories over the Philistines aroused Saul's envy (18:5–9, 12–16), and this envy turned into a blind hatred which drove Saul to try to kill David (18:20–29; 19:1, 4–7, 9–10). The rift between Saul and Samuel, David's growing popularity, and the suspicion that even those closest to him had traitorously joined David in a plot against him (20:30–31; 22:8) – R. Kittel suggested that there may have been a plot to depose him as mentally incompetent and to make Jonathan king in his stead – all undermined Saul's self-confidence and darkened his mind (16:14–23). His destiny now began to run its tragic course as he became more and more given to alternating fits of hatred and love, violence and depression, stubbornness and remorse. His morbid suspiciousness, his uncontrolled outbursts of passion, and his fear of David (18:15) frequently disturbed his mental balance, driving him to violent acts bordering on madness, such as hurling his spear at his son Jonathan (20:33), or killing the priests of Nob for – unless R. Kittel is right – unwittingly helping David (21:2ff.). David was compelled to flee from Saul's service into the Judean desert, where Saul tried to pursue him.

At the same time, Saul continued to bear the heavy burden of the prolonged war against the Philistines, who hoped to exploit the quarrel between Saul and David to reestablish their domination of the Israelites. When the Philistines mustered their forces in the Valley of Jezreel, Saul marched out with his army to meet them and camped near En-Harod at the foot of Mount Gilboa (28:4; 29:1). Greatly alarmed by the size and power of the Philistine army, he sought a sign from the Lord about the outcome of the impending battle, but "the Lord did not answer him, either by dreams, or by Urim, or by prophets" (28:6). In despair, he appealed to a medium to raise the spirit of the dead Samuel for him (she is commonly but inaccurately called the "witch" of *En-Dor), but according to the biblical account Samuel castigated him as before and prophesied a bitter end for him: "And tomorrow you and your sons shall be with me; The Lord will give Israel also with you into the hand of the Philistines" (28:19). Saul bravely led the Israelite host out to meet the Philistines, but in the ensuing engagement the Philistines clearly had the upper hand right from the start and the Israelites broke into flight, leaving many dead behind them on Mount Gilboa. Realizing that there was no escape from the archers pressing in around him, Saul chose to die by his own hand, "lest these uncircumcised come and make sport of me" (31:4; but cf. II Sam. 6:1–10). When the Philistines found his body, "they cut off his head, and stripped off his armor, and sent messengers throughout the land of the Philistines, to carry the good news to their idols and to the people" (31:9). The body itself they nailed to the walls of Beth-Shean. The men of Jabesh-Gilead, who still gratefully remembered how Saul had fought against Nahash the Ammonite when the latter was threatening their city (I Sam. 11), took down his body from the wall and buried his bones in Jabesh-Gilead. The bones were subsequently reinterred in the tomb of Saul's father (II Sam. 21:14). With the Israelite defeat on Mount Gilboa the Philistines were once more the dominant power in Ereẓ Israel and their pressure on the Israelites increased. A zealous Yahwist, Saul is credited with building the first altar to Yahweh (I Sam 14: 31–35) and with ridding the land of necromancers (I Sam. 28:3). K. van der Toorn finds Saul central to the formation of Yahwism as a state religion. Building on Toorn's work, Sperling argues that the historical Saul inspired the creation of the figure Moses.

[Bustanay Oded]

In the *Aggadah*

Saul, the first anointed king (Esth. R., Proem 10) was selected for many reasons:

(1) his military prowess (Mid. Sam. 11:78–79), (2) his unusual handsomeness (Ber. 48b), (3) his modesty (Tosef., Ber. 4:16; Tanḥ. B., Lev. 4), (4) his innocence since he was considered free from sin like "a one-year-old child" (Yoma 22b), and (5) the merits of his ancestors, particularly his grandfather Abiel, who was also named Ner ("candle") because he lit the streets after dark so that people might go to the houses of study (TJ, Shev. 3:10, 34d). He liberally endowed all poor brides (II Sam. 1:24; *Mishnat R. Eliezer*, 186); and during his initial successful war with Nahash, Saul displayed his zeal for the scrupulous observance of the sacrificial ordinances by rebuking his warriors for eating the sacrificial meat before the blood was sprinkled on the altar (Zev. 120a). There is a marked tendency by the rabbis to show the first king of Israel in a favorable light even when the Scriptures deprecate his actions. Even his sin during the Amalekite conflict is explained by Saul's refusal to consider the women, children, and cattle as sinners and worthy of death (Yoma 22b). It is Doeg who induces Saul to spare the Amalek king, Agag, His argument was that the law prohibits the slaying of an animal and its young on the same day; how much less permissible is it to destroy at one time old and young, men and children (Mid. Sam. 18:99–100). Saul had no selfish interest in retaining the Amalekite booty since he was so wealthy that he took a military census by giving one of his own sheep to every one of his soldiers, distributing not less than two hundred thousand sheep (Yoma 22b). His final days were filled with regrets on account of his executing the priests at Nob, and his remorse secured pardon for him (Ber. 12b; Tanḥ. B., Lev. 45).

He was even more worthy than David. David had many wives and concubines while Saul had but one wife. David remained behind, fearing to lose his life in battle with Absalom, while Saul led his troops into his final battle. Saul led the life of a saint in his own house, observing even the priestly laws of purity. God rebuked David for composing a song on the downfall of Saul, stating, "Had you been Saul and he David, I would have annihilated many a David out of regard for him" (MK 16b). David was also punished for having cut off the corner of Saul's mantle, for no amount of clothing would keep him warm (Ber. 62b). Finally, when a great famine fell upon the land during the reign of David, God told him that it had been inflicted because Saul's remains had not been buried with due honor. At that moment a heavenly voice resounded calling Saul "the elect of God" (Ber. 12b). The real reason for his loss of the monarchy was his misplaced meekness in not avenging himself against the "base fellows" who "despised him" (I Sam. 10:27; Yoma 22b). Moreover, his family was of such immaculate nobility that his descendants might have become too arrogant (Yoma 22b). However, his persecution of David was unjustified and it greatly contrasted with the humility he previously displayed. In contrast to his hesitancy in accepting the monarchy, he now sought to slay David rather than surrender his throne (ARN², 20, 43). Once, when Saul and his men surrounded David, an angel appeared and summoned him home to repulse the raid of the Philistines upon the land. Saul only gave up the pursuit of David after a majority of his officers had so decided. Some still felt that the seizure of David was even more important than defeating the Philistines (Mid. Ps. to 9:83; 18:138).

The witch of En-Dor realized that it was Saul who was summoning Samuel when he appeared upright before them. In necromancy the rule is that a spirit raised from the dead appears head downward and feet in the air, unless it is summoned by a king (Tanh. B., Lev. 82). Samuel told Saul that if he fled he would save himself; but if he would accept God's judgment and find his death in battle, his sins would be forgiven and he would join Samuel in afterlife (Lev. R. 26:7). After his death, God told the angels of his admiration for Saul's final courageous act in going into war "knowing that he will lose his life, yet he took his sons with him, and cheerfully accepted the punishment ordained" (Tanḥ. B., Lev. 82).

In Islam

The name Ṭālūt, which is given to Saul in the *Koran (2:248), is an allusion to his exceptional height (cf. I Sam. 9:2; 10:23). The form of this name was probably influenced by that of Jālūt (given to *Goliath) or *tābūt* (see below). After Mūsā's (i.e., Moses) death, the people of Israel requested of their prophet (his name is not mentioned, but see *Samuel) that he appoint a king to rule them. However, when Ṭālūt was designated as king, the people of Israel refused to accept him. The prophet then gave them a sign, that the *tābūt* (Ethiopian *tābōt*; Aramaic *tebuta*; "the Holy Ark") would come to them and in it would be *Sakīna* (Heb. *shekhinah*, "Divine Presence"). This would be the sign for believers (cf. Sot. 13a). When Ṭālūt went out to battle with his regiments, he passed by a stream, where he put his men to a trial. Only those who drew water with their hands were found worthy to pursue the campaign against the enemy (cf. the tale in Judg. 7:4–6). In that battle *David defeated Goliath (Jālūt; Sura 2:247–252). *Muhammad stops his narrative at this point. In post-Koranic literature the biblical name of Saul b. Kish is known to the commentators, and the descriptions from the Bible and the *aggadah* are added to the figure of Ṭālūt, in particular those concerning his attitude toward David and his attempts to kill him, as well as the meeting at En-Dor. Ṭālūt died in a holy war (**jihād*), after reigning for 40 years.

In the Arts

Unlike many other major figures of the Old Testament, Saul was accorded no particular significance in medieval Christian typology; and thus his first important appearance in the literature, art, and music of the West really dates from the Renaissance era. Among the earliest literary treatments of the subject were the Spanish dramatist Vasco Diaz Tanco's *Tragedia de Amon y Saul* (1552), which has not survived; *La Coronazione del Re Saul*, one of Giovan Maria Cecchi's realistic biblical plays of the same period; and an anonymous Italian work, *La Rapresentatione della distruttione di Saul…* (Florence, 1559). In Germany, the *Meistersinger* Hans Sachs wrote a *Tragedia Koenig Sauls* (1557). From this time onward the complex and tragic character of Saul attracted countless writers. Two outstanding 16th-century dramas on the theme were written by the French Protestant Jean de la Taille: *Saül le Furieux* (1572) and *La famine ou les Gabéonites* (1573). Interest was maintained in the 17th century, beginning with Claude Billard's *Saül* (1610).

The subject lent itself to more varied treatment in the 18th century. In England, *Tragedy of King Saul* (London, 1703), a verse play in five acts rejected by the censor, has been attributed to both Joseph Trapp and Roger Boyle. French tragedies entitled *Saül* were written by the abbé Nadal (1705) and *Voltaire (1763), the latter's work bearing a characteristic imprint of mockery. An outstanding 18th-century treatment of the subject was the Italian Vittorio Alfieri's tragedy, *Saul* (1782), which was later translated into English (1815) and, as *Aḥarit Sha'ul*, into Hebrew (by M.J. Lebensohn, 1870). An original Hebrew drama published in 1794 was *Melukhat Sha'ul, ha-Melekh ha-Rishon al-Yeshurun* (Vienna, 1794; often reprinted) by Joseph Troplowitz (= Joseph *Ha-Efrati c. 1770–1804). Saul appears as a tragic hero, torn by guilt, fear, and envy. From the era of Romanticism through the various movements of the 19th century, Saul continued to fascinate poets and dramatists. Lord *Byron's "Saul" poems (in: *Hebrew Melodies*, 1815) include the scene in which the king meets the witch of En-Dor and another poem on the theme was written by Robert *Browning (1845). There were two French tragedies – Alphonse de Lamartine's *Saül* (1818) and another of the same title by Alexandre Soumet (1822). There were also several tragedies in German, notably Karl Ferdinand Gutzkow's *Koenig Saul* (1839), Karl *Beck's *Saul* (1841), and Friedrich Rueckert's *Saul und David* (1843). The Cuban writer Gertrudis Gómez de Avellaneda (Peregrina), who lived mostly in Spain, was the author of a powerful drama, *Saúl* (1849), and in Romania Alexandru Macedonski and Cincinat Pavelescu wrote the tragedy, *Saul* (1893).

Literary exploitation of the subject has been heightened in the 20th century by the use of psychological motivation.

Works written before World War I include two poems by Rainer Maria Rilke, "*Saul unter den Propheten*" and "*Samuels Erscheinung vor Saul*." These were followed by dramas by the Japanese Torahiko Khori (1918), the Norwegian Jon Norstog (*Kong Saul*, 1920), and the South African (Afrikaans) writer W. Pienaar (1928). André Gide's *Saül*, a five-act drama written in the 1890s but published nearly 30 years later in 1922, portrays Saul as an old man consumed by the gratification of his lusts. The ill-fated monarch also plays a central part in the English writer D.H. Lawrence's play, *David* (1926), which was originally entitled "*Saul*."

A large proportion of modern works on the subject have, however, been written by Jews, and of these most are dramas. Plays written before World War II include Max Donkhin's Russian *Saul* (1902), dramas by Lion *Feuchtwanger and Karl *Wolfskehl (1905), Israël *Querido's Dutch tragedy, *Saul en David* (1914), and *Tsar Saul* (1937), a drama in Russian by Naum Isaakovich Shimkin. Postwar works include dramas by Abel Jacob *Herzberg (*Sauls dood*, 1959) and Max Zweig (1961), and Charles Israel's novel, *Rizpah* (1961). Some of the most interesting dramatic treatments of the Saul theme have been written in Hebrew and Yiddish. Among those in Yiddish are *Shaul* (1922) by Hirsh Brill of Kovno (1891–1925); *Der Melekh Shaul* (1948), published in Poland by Israel Ashendorf; a dramatic sketch (in *Lider un Poemen*, 1949) by the Mexican Yiddish writer Nahum Pozner; and Leizer Treister's *Der Pastekh-Kenig* ("The Shepherd King," 1955). In Hebrew, there are poems by Tchernikowsky and dramas by M. Lazebnik (1932) and by Max *Brod and Shin *Shalom (*Sha'ul Melekh Yisrael*, 1944), the latter taking the form of a *Schicksalstragoedie* (tragedy of fate).

Saul's noble son Jonathan has also inspired writers from the 17th century onward. Two early Italian tragedies, both entitled *Gionata*, were published by Bartolommeo Tortoletti Veronese (1624) and the Jesuit Saverio Bettinelli (1747); and a "Tragedy of Jonathan" was one of the plays of the 16th-century Spanish author Vasco Diaz Tanco which has been lost. In the 20th century, treatments include "Yonatan," a poem based on I Sam. 14:1–43, by the Hebrew poetess *Rachel; Arthur W. Spaulding's novel, *A Man of Valor* (1908); and S.B. Rosner's German drama, *Jonatan und Tirzah* (1912). Saul's daughter Michal, who became David's wife, has also figured in literary works of the 19th and 20th centuries. Hebrew treatments include J.L. *Gordon's epic *Ahavat David u-Mikhal* (1857) and Aharon *Ashman's three-act drama, *Mikhal Bat Sha'ul* (1941; *Michal the Daughter of Saul*, 1957); and there have also been dramas by the Italian Adolfo Isaia (*Micol*, 1898), the Yiddish writer David *Pinski (*Mikhol*, 1918), and the Dutch author J.D. van Calcar (1937). Morris Raphael *Cohen published *King Saul's Daughter* (1952), a biblical dialogue.

In art, scenes from the life of Saul are found in the third-century wall paintings from the synagogue of Dura *Europos, on the fourth-century door at St. Ambrogio, Milan, and in a variety of Carolingian and medieval manuscript illuminations. Representation of the subject during the Middle Ages was almost entirely confined to illuminated manuscripts. The main episodes to have been treated are Saul anointed by Samuel (I Sam. 10:1), David playing the harp before Saul (I Sam. 16:23), Saul casting a spear at David (I Sam. 19:10), David finding Saul in the cave (I Sam. 24:4, and Saul visiting the witch of En-Dor (I Sam. 28:8). Although David playing the harp before Saul was the subject of a copper engraving by Lucas Van Leyden (1494–1533), it was mainly *Rembrandt who depicted Saul with a degree of pathos and drama. There is an early painting by Rembrandt in the Staedel Institute, Frankfurt, and a later one in the Hague Museum. In the latter work the angry king, moved to tears, hides his face behind a curtain while David is absorbed in his music. There is a modern treatment of the theme by the Dutch artist Jozef *Israëls. In recent times, the lives of David and Saul were treated in a series of 41 lithographs by the Austrian artist Oskar Kokoschka.

In Music

Earlier musical compositions on the theme include a choral work by Heinrich Schuetz, *Saul* (for three choirs and instruments); the second of Kuhnau's "Biblical Sonatas" (1700), *Der von David mittelst der Musik curierte Saul*, for keyboard instrument; and Bononuni's anthem for the funeral of the Duke of Marlborough, *When Saul was King over Israel* (1722). Occasionally Jonathan is the main figure, as in Caldara's oratorio, *Gionata* (1728; libretto by Zeno). Handel's oratorio, *Saul* (text by Charles Jennens), was first performed at the King's Theater, London, in January 1739 and the "Death March in Saul" has entered the repertoire of standard funeral marches. Another English work was Samuel Arnold's *The Cure of Saul* (oratorio, 1767). A. Salieri left an unfinished oratorio, *Saulle*; and other works of the period were operas, oratorios, and melodramas by Seyfried (1798), Rolle (1776), and a pastiche, *Saul*, for which the music was "mixed" by Kalkbrenner and Lachnith from works by Mozart, Haydn, Cimarosa, and Paisiello (Paris, 1803). At the same time, Gossec also composed an oratorio, *Saul*. The Italian Jewish composer Michele *Bolaffi composed an opera, *Saul*, which was not staged. Byron's three poems on Saul (in *Hebrew Melodies*) were first set to music by Isaac *Nathan. There were later settings by many others, including Moussorgsky's *King Saul* (a translation by Kozlov of *Warriors and Chiefs*), song with piano, later arranged for orchestral accompaniment by Glazunov and for tenor or alto, mixed choir, piano or orchestra, trumpet, and side drum by Lazare *Saminsky (1929). Two other 19th-century compositions were Rossini's oratorio, *Saul* (1834), and a successful opera by Antonio Buzzi (1843). Among musical treatments of the late 19th century were Ferdinand Hiller's oratorio, *Saul* (1857); another by Hubert Parry, *King Saul* (1894); and Georges Enesco's cantata, *La vision de Saül* (1896). Works of the 20th century include Carl Nielsen's oratorio-like opera, *Saul og David* (1902); Arthur Honegger's incidental music to André Gide's *Saül* (1922); an orchestral work, *Saul en David* by Johann Wagenaar (1862–1941); and the opera *Saul* by Hermann Reutter, with libretto after A. Lernet-Holenia (1928; revised

1947). For Max Zweig's drama, *Saul*, in a Hebrew translation by J. Horowitz, performed by Habimah in 1949, the incidental music was written by Emanuel *Amiran. Three later compositions are *The Lamentation of Saul* by Norman dello Joio (1954) for baritone and orchestra, based on D.H. Lawrence's play, *David*; Josef *Tal's concert-opera, *Saul at Endor* (première at Ramat Gan, 1955); and Mario *Castelnuovo-Tedesco's opera, *Saul* (1960).

See also: *David in the Arts; *Samuel in the Arts.

[Bathja Bayer]

BIBLIOGRAPHY: Bright, Hist. 164–74; Tadmor, in: H.H. Ben-Sasson (ed.), *Toledot Am Yisrael bi-Ymei Kedem* (1969), 93–97; Albright, in: AASOR, 4 (1924), 160ff.; Mendelsohn, in: BASOR, 143 (1956), 17–22; Bardtke, in: BOR, 25 (1968), 289–302 (Ger.); R. Kittel, *Great Men and Movements in Israel* (1929, 1968). IN THE AGGADAH: Ginzberg, Legends, index. IN ISLAM: Tabarī, *Tafsīr*, 2 (1323 A.H.), 377–87; idem, *Taʾrīkh*, 1 (1367 A.H.), 330–8; ʿUmāra ibn Wathīma, Ms. fol. 40r–42v; Thaʿlabī; *Qiṣaṣ* (1356 A.H., 223–31; Kisāʾī, *Qiṣaṣ* (1356 A.H.), 250–8; A. Geiger, *Was hat Mohammed aus dem Judenthume aufgenommen?* (1902), 44, 53–54; M. Gruenbaum, *Neue Beiträge zur semitischen Sagenkunde* (1893), 185–9; J.W. Hirschberg (ed.), *Der Diwan des as-Samauʾal ibn Adijā…* (1931), 25, 60; H. Speyer, *Die biblischen Erzählungen im Qoran* (1961), 364–71. IN THE ARTS: J. Mueller, *König Saul in Sage und Dichtung* (1891); M. Roston, *Biblical Drama in England* (1968), index. **ADD. BIBLIOGRAPHY:** D. Edelman, in: ABD, 5:989–99; idem, *King Saul in the Historiography of Judah* (1991); K. van der Toorn, in: VT, 43 (1993), 519–42; S.D. Sperling, *The Original Torah* (1998), 121–34; A. Rainey and R. Notley, *The Sacred Bridge* (2006), 145–47.

SAUL BEN ANAN (c. 800), sectarian leader, son of *Anan b. David. He succeeded his father as head of the sect of Ananites about the end of the eighth century. In *Karaite tradition, which regards Anan as the titular founder of Karaism, Saul is listed second in the hereditary line of Karaite "princes." Nothing is known of his activity, except for his reported interpretation of the Seventh Commandment in the sense that adultery covers all illicit intimacy. He was succeeded in his princely office by his son *Josiah.

BIBLIOGRAPHY: S. Pinsker, *Likkutei Kadmoniyyot* (1860), 44 (first pagination), 53, 62, 106, 186 (second pagination); Mann, Texts, 2 (1935), index; L. Nemoy, *Karaite Anthology* (1952), 6, 21.

[Leon Nemoy]

°SAULCY, LOUIS FELICIEN DE JOSEPH CAIGNART (1807–1880), French numismatist, Orientalist, and archaeologist. Saulcy was born in Lille, France. He traveled in Syria and Palestine in 1850–51, 1863, and 1869, discovering the Shihan Stele and recognizing that the mound of Jericho was the site of an ancient city. In 1863 he cleared the Tombs of the Kings in Jerusalem, mistaking them for the Tombs of the House of David. This was the first archaeological excavation in the Holy Land. Although his archaeological work is now considered somewhat slipshod and amateurish, Saulcy was of some importance as a numismatist: he was the first to catalogue the coins of Palestine, noting many which have since disappeared, and left after him an extensive coin collection.

His works include *Numismatique des Croisades* (1847); *Recherches sur la numismatique judaïque* (1854); *Numismatique de la Terre Sainte* (1874); *Voyage autour de la Mer Morte* (2 vols., 1853); *Voyage en Terre Sainte* (2 vols., 1865; including his account of the excavation of the Tombs of the Kings in vol. 1,345–410; vol. 2, 188–9, 309–11); and *Carnets de voyage en Orient*, ed. by F. Bassan (1955).

[Michael Avi-Yonah]

SAVANNAH, city in Georgia, U.S., third oldest Jewish community in North America. A seaport, the city had a total population of 129,808, according to the 2004 U.S. Census estimates, of whom 3,500 were Jews in 2005.

On July 11, 1733, 41 Jews arrived aboard a ship chartered by London's Sephardi synagogue. Despite objections from London's Georgia trustees, the Jews won the legal right to settle and own property. Original settlers included Dr. Samuel Nunes, who rescued the colonists from an epidemic; his son-in-law Abraham de Lyon, who introduced viticulture; Abraham Minis, who became supplier for the militia of the founder of Georgia, James Edward Oglethorpe; and Benjamin Sheftall, interpreter for German Salzburger settlers. Sheftall and his son Levi kept the community's vital records from 1733 to 1809. In 1740, the Jewish population reached 100, but economic failure in Georgia, coupled with Spanish raids from Florida, gradually dispersed the community until only the Minis and Sheftall families remained.

Although ritual appurtenances had been brought from England, it was not until 1735 that Ashkenazim and Sephardim could agree to organize the congregation Mickve Israel, which conducted worship in a small hut. A ritual bath was opened in 1738. Oglethorpe granted the original settlers a cemetery, but when the town grew around it, Mordecai Sheftall, by deed of August 2, 1773, donated to Mickve Israel a portion of his farm plot for "the use of a burial ground and for erecting a synagogue." The cemetery was used until 1850. The remainder of the property was sold, and the proceeds were used in 1902 to build a school and social center, the Mordecai Sheftall Memorial, which was replaced in 1957. Fluctuation in population occasionally forced the abandonment of public worship. In 1790, Mickve Israel obtained a charter from the governor, but 30 years elapsed before Jacob de la Motta (1789–1845) prevailed upon his coreligionists to build a synagogue, which was dedicated in 1820 and consecrated the following year. In 1829, it burned down (though its Torah – brought to Savannah in 1733 – and ark were saved) and was replaced with a brick edifice that remained in use until 1878, when the present Gothic structure was dedicated. Mickve Israel preserved Sephardi traditions until 1903, when it joined the Reform movement. It is the oldest reform congregation in the United States, using an organ for services in 1820, having mixed seating in 1860, as well as having a mixed choir populated by both sexes and even non-Jews. In 2005, 300 families were members of the congregation.

Prussian-Polish immigrants of the 1850s organized what became the Orthodox Congregation B'nai B'rith Jacob. The

Eastern European immigration to the United States enlarged its membership. Organized under the leadership of Rabbi Jacob Rosenfeld after he was dismissed as rabbi at Mickve Israel over a dispute dealing with *kashrut*, the congregation built its first synagogue on the northeast corner of State and Montgomery Streets in 1866 and held services on Friday evenings and Saturday mornings. A flourishing membership prompted the community to build a new, larger synagogue with a Hebrew school on the same site in 1909; at its peak, the school boasted an enrollment of 200 students. The congregation built a third structure, in 1962, on Abercorn Street and held its first services there on Passover. In 2005, 425 families belonged to the congregation.

Congregation Agudath Achim, formed as an Orthodox group in 1901, was incorporated in 1903 and became Conservative in 1945 with the dedication of its third synagogue. The original congregation numbered 46 families; in 2005, it had 270 families. In the early 1980s, it formed a joint school with Mickve Israel, which was renamed in 1991 as the Shalom School, and in 2005 enrolled 100 students. Shalom School is a supplemental religious school that meets two weekday afternoons and on Sunday. The congregation celebrated its centennial year in 2003 and as part of that celebration, rededicated a Holocaust Torah from Kamenice, Czechoslovakia.

Established in 2002, the Hillel chapter at Savannah College of Art and Design had approximately 25 members in 2005.

The Savannah B'nai Brith was chartered in 1860. Savannah Jewry also developed many charitable societies: Hebrew Benevolent (1851); Ladies Hebrew Benevolent (1853); Harmonie Club (1865); Orphan Aid (1880), affiliated with the B'nai B'rith Atlanta Orphanage; Hebra Gemiluth Hessed (1888); Young Woman's Aid (1906); Women's Circle (1908); Hadassah (1918). A Young Men's Hebrew Association (1874) lasted several generations. These and other agencies came under the aegis of the Jewish Education Alliance (chartered 1912). Designed as an Americanizing center, the Alliance developed into a center of Jewish activities; it moved to larger premises in the 1950s. In 1990, the Alliance founded the Rambam Day School for students aged 2 through eighth grade; 2005 enrollment was 122 students. The Savannah Jewish Council, founded in 1943 and now known as the Savannah Jewish Federation, conducts the annual United Jewish Appeal campaign as well as social and educational programs.

The Savannah Jewish Archives are housed in the Georgia Historical Society in Savannah, Georgia. Established in 1994, they are administered by the Savannah Jewish Federation and are one of two Jewish archives in the state. The second is located in Atlanta.

Jews have always played an active role in all facets of Savannah life, with many holding public office. Most notable was Herman Myers (1847–1909), who served as mayor from 1895 to 1897 and from 1899 to 1907, and Kenneth Sadler, city council member (2003–). Other notable community members include Kenneth Rubin, awarded the Distinguished Service Cross in the Vietnam War in 1967, and William Wexler, international president of B'nai Brith from 1965 to 1971.

BIBLIOGRAPHY: M.H. Stern, in: AJHSP, 53 (1963/64), 169–99; 54 (1964/65), 243–77; Congregation Mickve Israel, *Contact Commemorative Issue* (March 1955); B. Postal and L. Koppman, *Jewish Tourist's Guide to the U.S.* (1954), 123–7, 131–2. **ADD. BIBLIOGRAPHY:** Savannah Jewish Archives held at the Georgia Historical Society, Savannah, Georgia (with acknowledgment to Kaye Kole for her invaluable research there).

[Malcolm H. Stern / David Weinstock (2nd ed.)]

SAVERNE (Ger. **Zabern**), town in the department of Bas-Rhin, in eastern France. The presence of Jews in Saverne is confirmed from at least 1334. The community suffered during the *Armleder persecutions in 1338. At the time of the *Black Death in 1349 there was only one Jewish family in Saverne, which was compelled to leave the town. By 1622 there were a few Jews again living in Saverne; in 1716, there were seven families and 21 in 1784. The community numbered over 300 persons at the close of the 19th century. It maintained a Jewish primary school (founded in 1857). A new synagogue was opened in 1898. Its population subsequently declined. During World War II, 30 Jews of Saverne died during deportation. The community numbered about 100 in 1970.

BIBLIOGRAPHY: D. Fischer, *Etude sur l'organisation municipale de Saverne* (1865), 30f.; O. Meyer, *La régence épiscopale de Saverne* (1935), index; L. Bachmeyer, *Pages d'histoire de Saverne* (1965), 11, 32, 39; Z. Szajkowski, *Analytical Franco-Jewish Gazetteer, 1939–1945* (1966), 250; Germ Jud, 2.2 (1968), 937f.

[Bernhard Blumenkranz]

SAVILLE, VICTOR (1897–1979), British film director and producer. Saville was born in Birmingham, the son of an Orthodox fine arts dealer, Gabriel Salberg. He was educated at King Edward VI School in Birmingham and was wounded in World War I. From 1919 Saville was a partner with Michael *Balcon, another leading film producer, in Victory Motion Pictures, and from the late 1920s was one of Britain's leading filmmakers, producing or directing such movies as *South Riding* (1937), *Goodbye Mr. Chips* (1939), *Dr. Jekyll and Mr. Hyde* (1941), and *Green Dolphin Street* (1947). In the 1950s he changed direction, producing several of Mickey Spillane's "hard-boiled" thrillers such as *I, The Jury* (1953). Saville's wife, Phoebe, was the niece of the prominent British film distributor and producer Charles M. Woolf (1879–1942). His son, SIR JOHN WOOLF (1913–1999), was also a major British film producer, responsible for such works as Lawrence Olivier's Shakespearean epic *Henry V* (1944) and, after the war, *Moulin Rouge* (1953), *Richard III* (1955), *Room At the Top* (1959), and the film version of the musical *Oliver!* (1968), which won six Oscars. Woolf was also the cofounder of Anglia Television and was responsible for the series *Tales of the Unexpected* (1979–89) and other drama productions. He was knighted in 1975.

BIBLIOGRAPHY: ODNB online.

[William D. Rubinstein (2nd ed.)]

SAVITT, RICHARD (**Dick**; 1927–), U.S. tennis player, the only Jew ever to win Wimbledon, Pete *Sampras excepted; member of the International Tennis Hall of Fame. Born in Bayonne, New Jersey, Savitt taught himself tennis as a 14-year-old, and reached the finals of the New Jersey Boys Championship. In 1944, his family moved to El Paso, Texas, where Savitt was co-captain of his high school basketball team and became an all-Texas player. At the same time, he ranked eighth nationally among junior tennis players and was the 17th ranked amateur overall. Savitt joined the Navy in 1945 and played on its basketball team, completing his tour of duty the following year. Cornell University offered him a basketball scholarship, but Savitt decided, after injuries cut short his hoop career, to concentrate on tennis. In 1947, he was national ranked 26th, and two years later he moved up to 16th. In 1950, Savitt won the Eastern Intercollegiate, East Clay Court, and New York State tournaments, and without the benefit of coaching he reached the semifinals of the U.S. Championship at Forest Hills. He then won the Australian Open, defeating the three top Aussies – John Bromwich, Frank Sedgman, and Ken McGregor – and on July 6, 1951, Savitt won the All-England championship at Wimbledon, defeating McGregor 6–4, 6–4, 6–4. After the tournament, Savitt and Herb Flam were named to the U.S. Davis Cup team, the first time that Jewish players ever made the squad. But inexplicably – and despite his being clearly the best American player at that time, even making the cover of *Time* magazine on August 27, 1951 – Savitt was passed over for the Davis Cup final against the Australian team, a controversial decision that was discussed by sports writers all over the world. The following year, Savitt was so upset at being snubbed that he announced he would retire from competitive tennis following the 1952 U.S. National Indoor Championships, which he won. He returned to tennis on a part-time basis in 1956, and won the 1958 and 1961 U.S. National Indoor Championships, making him the first to win three times. In 1961, Savitt won the singles and doubles (with Mike Franks) gold medals at the Maccabiah Games, which began a lifetime commitment to Israeli tennis. In 1981, he and his son, Robert, won the U.S. father and son doubles title. Savitt was ranked six times in the U.S. Top Ten between 1950 and 1959 (No. 2 in 1951), and four times in the World Top Ten between 1951 and 1957 (No. 2 in 1951). He was elected to the International Tennis Hall of Fame in 1976.

[Elli Wohlgelernter (2nd ed.)]

SAVORA, SAVORAIM (Aram. סָבוֹרָא, סָבוֹרָאִים), Babylonian scholars between the *amoraim and the *geonim. Very little is known of this period, the principal sources being Sherira (*Iggeret Sherira Ga'on*, ed. by B.M. Lewin (1921), 67–71, 95–99), who drew upon early geonic archival material; Abraham ibn Daud (Ibn Daud, Tradition, 43–55); and some additional geonic fragments such as *Seder Tanna'im ve-Amora'im*, etc. Traditionally, the amoraic phase ends with the death of *Ravina (BM 86a) in 499 C.E. According to *Seder Tanna'im ve-Amora'im* (ed. by Grossberg, 105–11) and Sherira, the last of the *savoraim* were Gada (Gazai) and Simuna, who died in 540, while Ibn Daud extends the savoraic period for five generations, from Mar Joseph (502) until the death of Sheshna in 689. It would appear that the transition from one period to another was so gradual that only in retrospect could the *geonim* somewhat arbitrarily fix terminal dates to the savoraic period, and different reckonings were adduced. Sherira, Ibn Daud, and *Seder Tannai'm ve-Amora'im* all give lists of *savoraim*, but the textual state of these lists is poor, and only a few major personalities can be definitely identified, e.g., Abba (Rava) Joseph (Yose), Aḥa b. Huna, Aḥai of Be-Hatim, Geviha of Argiza (Git. 7a), Mordecai, Pappias, Rabbah of Rov, and Samuel b. Abbahu (Rabbah; Ḥul. 59b).

The term *savoraim*, first found in geonic sources, and based on *savora* in the Jerusalem Talmud, *Kiddushin* 2, 63d (where it means a scholar competent to render decisions) implies those who give private subjective judgments rather than authoritative ones. According to Sherira, after Ravina there was no *hora'ah* (independent decision based on interpretation of the Mishnah), but the *savoraim* "rendered decisions similar to *hora'ah*, and gave explanations of all that had been left unsettled." This implies that they added nothing essentially new to the Talmud, merely adding explanations which in some ways were similar to amoraic decisions and coming to practical conclusions on undecided issues (hence the savoraic terminology of *ve-hilkheta* ("and the ruling is"), *pashit* ("he resolved it"), *mistabra* ("it is reasonable"), etc. Sherira adds that a number of savoraic decisions (of Ena and Simuna) and indeed complete arguments (e.g., Kid. 2a–3b) have been included in the Talmud. Analysis of these additions often demonstrates a close similarity in style and argumentation to that of the later *amoraim*, again underscoring the problem of pinpointing the moment of transition between the two periods.

According to (some versions of) *Seder Tanna'im va-Amora'im*, the *savoraim* did no more than "merely determine the arrangement of the Talmud text in all its chapters." Evidently, this represents but one (the earliest?) phase of savoraic activity, during which the redaction of the Talmud, begun in the late amoraic period, was completed. The *savoraim* completed the ordering of the Talmud, clarified certain unsettled halakhic decisions, introduced additional discussions and explanations of existing texts, and inserted brief technical guide phrases to facilitate study of the texts. Recent tendencies have been to increase the extent of their contribution to the Talmud, though this is still a subject of considerable controversy.

BIBLIOGRAPHY: Baron, Social^2, 2 (1952), 426; 6 (1958), 17f., 328f. (with a critical bibl.); B.M. Lewin, in: *Azkarah le-Nishmat… A.I. Kook*, pt. 4 (1937), 145–208; idem, in: *Ha-Tor*, 6 (1926), nos. 16, 34; A. Weiss, *Ha-Yeẓirah shel ha-Savora'im* (1953); Halevy, Dorot, 3 (1923), 1–63; M.D. Yudelivitz, *Yeshivat Pumbedita bi-Ymei ha-Amora'im* (1935), 52–54; Z. Jawitz, *Toledot Yisrael*, (1922), 213–24.

[Daniel Sperber]

SAVOY (Fr. **Savoie**), formerly a county and then a duchy, reunited with France in 1860, includes the present departments of Savoie and Haute-Savoie in S.E. France. A Jewish inscription of 688 from *Narbonne, mentioning a Jew named Sapaudus, may be the first evidence of the presence of Jews in that region. Formal proofs of Jewish settlement in Savoy date only from the second half of the 13th century (the assertion that Jews were in Savoy after the expulsion from France in 1182 has no documentary basis, not even in *Emek ha-Bakha* of *Joseph ha-Kohen). Jews were to be found not only in Chambéry, but particularly in the following places (not including those which belonged to Savoy only temporarily): Aiguebelle, Montmélian, Rumilly, Yenne, Saint-Genix. Noteworthy is the place name "Lac des Juifs" near Chambéry. In almost all these places the Jews suffered bloody persecution in 1348 on the charge of spreading the *Black Death; even those who survived were robbed of all their goods.

The expulsion of the Jews from France in 1394 led to their emigrating into Savoy again. In 1417 the first investigation of Jewish books was entrusted to two converted Jews. Moreover, for many years the dukes had favored proselytizing activities, guaranteeing comfortable subsidies to new Christians. This was probably the persecution that Joseph ha-Kohen noted in 1394 and which he attributed to the preaching of Vicente *Ferrer; in fact, he notes having seen "a book of tattered appearance because it was one of those which the Jews, in those unhappy days, kept hidden at the bottom of wells until their torment was over." There was a fresh investigation into Jewish books in 1426 (this time directed by the inquisitor Ponce Feugerons), which resulted in the Jews pledging to delete the prohibited passages he had listed. The statutes promulgated by Duke Amadeus in 1430 reflect this general hostility by forcing the Jews to reside in a separate quarter ("Judeazimus") and wear a distinctive badge, and forbidding them to mingle with Christians on Christian festivals. There was another investigation of Jewish books in 1466, as well as of a series of other accusations – committing murders, practicing abortions, magic, and sorcery, and publicly insulting the duke. The investigation of books was again entrusted to a converted Jew, the physician Louis of Nice, a man whom the duke had favored for more than 20 years. Criminal proceedings were abandoned, however, despite numerous witnesses for the prosecution, when the Jews paid a very heavy fine.

From then on there is no further evidence of the presence of Jews in Savoy, except at Chambéry; it is therefore probable that their departure – voluntary or forced – resulted from these criminal proceedings. Joseph ha-Kohen dates the banishment of the Jews from Savoy to 1461. The existence of the Jewish community of Chambéry up to the beginning of the 16th century was recorded by the Jewish scholar Gershom *Soncino, who lived there at the time. There were a number of important Jewish doctors, some of them converts.

BIBLIOGRAPHY: Gross, Gal Jud, 639f., 628; G. Sessa, *Tractatus de Judaeis* (1717); M.A. Gerson, in: REJ, 8 (1884), 235–42; A. Nordmann, *ibid.*, 83 (1927), 63–73; 84 (1927), 81–91; C.A. Costa de Beauregard, in: *Mémoires de l'Académie des Sciences, Belles-Lettres et Arts de Savoie*, series 2, 2 (1854), 81–126; S. Dufour and F. Rabut, in: *Mémoires et documents publiés par la Société d'histoire et d'archéologie*, 15 (1875), 3–28; M. Esposito, in: *Revue d'histoire ecclésiastique*, 34 (1938), 785–801; H. Merhavia, in: KS, 45 (1969/70), 590–606.

[Bernhard Blumenkranz]

SAVRAN (Bendery), ḥasidic dynasty. MOSES ẒEVI SAVRAN (d. 1838), son of R. SIMEON SOLOMON, held rabbinical posts in Berdichev, Savran (in Podolia), and Titshlinik. From boyhood he excluded from his life all activities that might distract him from his studies. Savran strongly opposed the ḥasidic followers of Naḥman of *Bratslav, whom he denounced as "sinners," and warned his followers not to intermarry with them. Azriel Dov, a disciple of Moses Ẓevi, collected the discourses of his master, which were published under the title *Likkutei Shoshanim* (1872). His son SIMEON SOLOMON (d. 1848) and his grandson DAVID (d. 1913), son-in-law of Nahum of *Chernobyl, continued the dynasty. The second son of Simeon Solomon, ARYEH LEIB OF BENDERY (d. 1854) founded a dynasty which produced four ḥasidic leaders, SIMEON SOLOMON (d. 1864), ISAAC (d. 1911), son-in-law of Joseph of Radziwillow, SIMEON SOLOMON (d. 1924), and JOSEPH (b. 1882).

BIBLIOGRAPHY: I. Berger, *Eser Atarot* (1910), 82–84.

[Harry Rabinowicz]

SAVYON (Heb. סַבְיוֹן), urban settlement, with municipal council status, in central Israel, south of Petaḥ Tikvah. Founded on the initiative of immigrants from South Africa as a garden suburb, it had a population of 1,430 in 1968 and 2,470 in 2002, occupying an area of 1.1 sq. mi. (2.9 sq. km.). Savyon is an upper middle-class community, with most residents commuting to work in Tel Aviv or elsewhere in the area. The settlement's name is that of the *senecio* plant common in the region.

[Efraim Orni / Shaked Gilboa (2nd ed.)]

SAWICKI (Reisler), JERZY (1908–1967), Polish lawyer who was a prosecuting counsel at the Polish War Crimes Tribunal and a member of the Polish delegation at the Nuremberg Trials. Born in Skole, Galicia, into an Orthodox Jewish family, Sawicki graduated and practiced as a lawyer. He went into hiding during the Nazi occupation. After the war he rapidly acquired distinction as a prosecutor in war crimes trials and other important cases. Subsequently he became professor of criminal law at Warsaw University and a member of several international institutions concerned with the reform of criminal law.

Sawicki was the author of numerous works on criminal law, genocide, and the trial of Nazi war criminals, including *Prawo norymberskie* ("The Nuremberg Judgment," 1948), with T. Cyprian, and *Przed polskim prokuratorem* ("Before the Polish Prosecutor," 1958). After 1945 he was a founder and an active member of the "Polish Friends of the Hebrew University."

[Israel (Ignacy) Isserles]

SAXON, DAVID STEPHEN (1920–2005), U.S. educator and physicist. Saxon was born in St. Paul, Minnesota. He attended the Massachusetts Institute of Technology and received his B.S. in 1941 and his Ph.D. in 1944. In 1946 he became an associate physicist with Phillips Laboratories in New York and the following year joined the faculty of the University of California at Los Angeles as an assistant professor of physics. At UCLA he became professor of physics in 1957, served as dean of physical sciences (1963–1966), vice chancellor (1968–1972), and executive vice chancellor (1974–1975). In 1975 he was elected the 14th president of the University of California and served until 1983.

Saxon's academic fields were theoretical physics, nuclear physics, quantum mechanics, and electromagnetic theory. In addition to being a renowned scholar, he was an outstanding academic administrator and a distinguished leader. In 1967 the UCLA Alumni Association presented him with the Distinguished Teaching Award. After he retired from teaching, he became professor emeritus of physics and astronomy at UCLA.

Among his publications are *Elementary Quantum Mechanics* (1968), *The Nuclear Independent Particle Model* (with A.E.S. Green and T. Sawada, 1968), *Discontinuities in Wave Guides* (with J. Schwinger, 1968), and *Physics for the Liberal Arts Student* (with W.B. Fretter, 1971).

[Frederick R. Lachman]

SAXONY (Ger. **Sachsen**), state in Germany, formerly an electorate and kingdom. Information about the first Jewish settlers in Saxony dates back to the tenth century. During the rule of the German emperor Otto I (936–973), Jews lived in the towns of *Magdeburg, *Halle, *Erfurt, and *Merseburg, among other places. Up to the end of the 12th century they were able to earn their living, primarily as merchants, without interference. In the 13th century, following persecutions during the Crusades and accusations of ritual murder (see *blood libel), the position of the Jews deteriorated. According to the medieval German law code *Sachsenspiegel* (1220–1235; see *Germany), Jews were not allowed to carry arms, build new synagogues, or keep Christian servants, nor could they hold any public office. They were not allowed to appear as witnesses or call Christian witnesses, and were thus entirely at the court's mercy. However, since the economic activities of the Jews were of interest to the margraves of Saxony, many of these restrictions were abolished as early as the middle of the 13th century and were replaced by more liberal regulations. Jews were allowed to have their tribunals and to be landowners. As may be gathered from the responsa literature and from the medieval chronicles, there was already a busy community life in those early days. The communities were collectively responsible to the authorities. A meeting at Erfurt in 1391 was attended by rabbis and community elders. Among famous talmudic scholars who resided in the communities of Saxony were *Asher b. Jehiel (the "Rosh") and *Isaac b. Moses of Vienna ("Or Zaru'a"). During the *Rindfleisch persecutions (1298), Jews in the southern cities of Saxony were affected. The large-scale persecutions and expulsions from German cities at the time of the *Black Death (1348–50) also affected the communities in Saxony.

Community life in most cities was renewed, but on a diminished scale. Moneylending had become the main occupation of the Jews, who were hard hit by the debt cancellations of Emperor Wenceslaus (1378–1400). The 15th century witnessed the expulsion of Jews from most of the cities – Erfurt (1458), Halle (1493), Aschersleben (1494), and Torgau (1432). The expulsions of *Meissen (1430), and of the 16th century from Merseburg (1514), *Zwickau, Plauen, and *Muehlhausen (1541–43) were more strictly enforced, due to the militant anti-Jewish spirit of the Protestant Reformation in Saxony. However, a few Jews were tolerated – such as Meister Baruch, the physician of the rulers Ernst (1464–85) and Albert III (1485–1500) – who, together with his two sons, received special permission to engage in moneylending. In the 16th century there were complaints about the economic activity of foreign Jews, who were mainly attracted by the Saxon silver mines. The government and the municipal authorities took steps to ensure that the presence of Jews at the Leipzig fairs should be temporary and limited to the duration of the fairs.

The first Jew to receive a *Schutzbrief* (see **Schutzjuden*) in Saxony was Behrend *Lehmann, the *Court Jew of Elector Frederick Augustus I (the Strong; 1694–1733); in 1710 Lehmann preferred to remain in *Halberstadt, while his cousin, Jonas Meyer, and his son settled as his agents in *Dresden, the capital. In 1723 they maintained households, numbering 30 and 40 respectively, to the annoyance of the burghers. The Jewish community of *Leipzig was founded in 1710 by Gerd Levi, court purveyor to the mint.

Frederick Augustus II (1733–63) in the year of his accession abolished the **Leibzoll* for the Jews passing through Saxony on business. His prime minister, Heinrich von Bruehl, was very partial to court Jews fulfilling various economic functions (military contractors, purveyors to the mint, etc.). As Frederick Augustus was, like his father, king of Poland as well, many of the court Jews originated in Poland. The *Kaskel (Kaskele) family, court Jews, bankers, and financiers, originally from Poland, played a central economic role in Saxony in the late 18th and 19th centuries.

Frederick Augustus III (1768–1827), elector and first king of Saxony, promulgated a restrictive *Judenordnung* (regulation concerning Jews) in 1772. Saxon Jewry thus remained numerically static throughout the following decades; an increase during the Napoleonic wars proved to be only temporary. The number of Jews in Dresden in 1800 (1,031) was halved by 1815. In 1832 there were 852 Jews in the kingdom, 712 in Dresden and 140 in Leipzig. The struggle for emancipation was led by Bernhard *Beer and W.T. *Krug. In 1834 Jews were allowed to learn trades and live outside Dresden proper, while Jewish affairs were placed under the supervision of the ministry of religion and education. Further slight improvements were effected in 1837 and 1838. In 1840 the Jewish *oath was amended, partially due to the urging of the **Landrabbiner* Zacharias *Frankel (1836–1854). Full equality was obtained during the 1848 Revolution, only to be repealed in 1851. It was not until 1868 and 1869 that Jews attained full legal equality. The number of Jews increased slowly from 1,022 in 1849 (0.05% of the total population) to 1,555 in 1861 and 3,346 in 1871 (0.13%). After emancipation their number leaped to 6,616 in 1880 (0.22%), 12,378 in 1900, and 17,587 in 1910 (0.53%). This increase, due in large part to immigration from Austria (Galicia) and Russia (Poland) and rapid industrialization in Saxony, had serious repercussions. Antisemites raised a cry against inundation by *Ostjuden*, while there was friction within the Jewish communities too. In 1925 there were 23,200 (0.46%, half the German average), with 5,120 in Leipzig, 5,120 in Dresden, and 2,796 in Chemnitz (*Karl-Marx-Stadt). Rural communities were nonexistent. Anti-Jewish sentiment was expressed in anti-*sheḥitah laws and the exclusion of Jews from the civil service. The only Jew elected to the *Landtag* was Emil *Lehmann, leader of the Dresden community. In October 1938 thousands of Polish Jews were expelled; on November 9–10 the synagogues were burned down, and thousands more Jews emigrated after pogroms and arrests. The remainder were deported to concentration camps. After the war new communities arose in Leipzig, Dresden, and Karl-Marx-Stadt (renamed Chemnitz in 1990). In 1945 the three communities had 563 members. The membership declined continuously. They numbered 214 in 1969; 169 in 1976; and 106 in 1989. After 1990 the membership increased due to the immigration of Jews from the former Soviet Union. In 1992 the Association of Jewish Communities in Saxony was founded as an umbrella organization of the communities in Dresden, Leipzig, and Chemnitz. They numbered 232 in 1994 and 2,314 in 2004. The association employs a rabbi who officiates in the three communities.

BIBLIOGRAPHY: K. Sidori (pseud. of I. Kaim), *Geschichte der Juden in Sachsen* (1840); A. Levy, *Geschichte der Juden in Sachsen* (1900); S. Neufeld, in: MGWJ, 69 (1925), 283–95; idem, in: AUJW (Jan. 21, 1966); idem, *Die Juden im thueringisch-saechsichen Gebiet waehrend des Mittelalters* (1917–27); J. Segall, in: *Zeitschrift fuer Demographie und Statistik der Juden*, 10 (1914), 33–46; H. Schnee, *Die Hoffinanz und der moderne Staat*, 2 (1954), 167–292; Kisch, Germany, index; S. Stern, *The Court Jew* (1950), index. **ADD. BIBLIOGRAPHY:** *Germania Judaica*, vol, 3, 1350– 1514 (1987), 2063–73; *Juden in Sachsen. Ihr Leben und Leiden* (1994); S. Hoeppner and M. Jahn, *Juedische Vereine und Organisationen in Chemnitz, Dresden und Leipzig 1918–1933* (1997); U. Offenberg, "Seid vorsichtig gegen die Machthaber," in: *Die juedischen Gemeinden in der SBZ und der DDR 1945– 1990* (1998), 50–56; F. Specht, *Zwischen Ghetto und Selbstbehauptung. Musikalisches Leben der Juden in Sachsen 1933–1941* (2000); C. Wustmann, "Geschichte juedischer Sozialarbeit in Sachsen," in: G. Stecklina (ed.), *Juedische Sozialarbeit in Deutschland* (2000), 49–99.

[Reuven Michael / Larissa Daemmig (2nd ed.)]

SCAASI, ARNOLD (1931–), U.S. fashion designer. Scaasi was born Arnold Isaacs in Montreal, Canada, the son of a local furrier. Although he never graduated from high school, he became a celebrated designer whose custom-made tailored suits and glamorous gowns were worn by movie stars, society matrons, and at least five U.S. first ladies. He changed his last name, but he never denied his heritage, often describing himself as "a Jewish kid from Montreal." When he was still a teenager, the family moved to Melbourne, Australia, where Arnold fell under the spell of his aunt Ida Wynn, a prominent fundraiser for the Women's International Zionist Organization, who was equally well known for her chic French wardrobe. His interest in fashion piqued, he returned to Montreal to study design, then moved to Paris and apprenticed to Paquin, a prestigious couture house. He came to New York City in 1953 and began working with Charles James, a brilliant but eccentric designer. Around that time, Isaacs was assigned to create dresses for a series of automobile ads. Someone suggested reversing the spelling of his last name for added glamour and Scaasi was born. As his reputation for bold colors and sculptural shapes spread, he landed a red evening coat on the cover of *Vogue* magazine in December 1955. The following May, he launched a wholesale collection. He won a Coty Fashion Award in 1958 and opened a custom-design business in 1962. His dresses turned up at glittering parties from Manhattan to Los Angeles. In 1969, Barbra *Streisand accepted her Oscar for *Funny Girl* wearing a Scaasi-designed sheer pantsuit that created a sensation. Scaasi's clients have included actresses Elizabeth *Taylor, Lauren *Bacall, and Mary Tyler Moore, soprano Joan Sutherland, sculptor Louise *Nevelson, and social doyennes such as Brooke Astor. After already designing clothing for first ladies Mamie Eisenhower, Jacqueline Kennedy, and Lady Bird Johnson, he created a royal blue velvet and satin gown that Barbara Bush wore to her husband's Inaugural Ball in 1989. It was later donated to the Smithsonian Institution and Mrs. Bush became one of Scaasi's best clients. He has also designed clothes for her daughter-in-law Laura Bush, another first lady. In 1989, Scaasi introduced a women's fragrance. Later, to broaden his reach, he stopped doing runway shows and embarked on a series of licensing ventures for products ranging from lower-price dresses to sunglasses. With writer Bernadine Morris, he produced a book entitled *A Cut Above* in 1996, released to coincide with a retrospective of his work at the New-York Historical Society. In 1997, a decade after the Council of Fashion Designers of America honored him for "creative excellence," he won the group's Lifetime Achievement Award. It was presented by Barbara Bush. In 2001, a major exhibition of Scaasi's work was mounted at Kent State University in Ohio, and the following year, a similar presentation was staged at the Fashion Institute of Technology in New York. A memoir, *Women I Have Dressed (and Undressed)*, was published in 2004.

[Mort Sheinman (2nd ed.)]

°**SCALIGER, JOSEPH JUSTUS** (1540–1609), French scholar and philologist. Scaliger was the tenth child of Julius Caesar Scaliger (Giulio Cesare Della Scala, 1484–1558), who was an outstanding humanist, well known for his controversies with Erasmus and Rabelais. He became a Protestant in 1562, and ten years later fled the Massacre of St. Bartholomew, but returned to France in 1574. From 1593 until his death he was a professor at the University of Leiden, where the prevailing liberal Calvinism was in harmony with his own views. Holding an unusually tolerant and enlightened attitude toward the Jews, he considered them the best teachers of Hebrew, particularly for students of rabbinic literature. Basing himself on the findings of Elijah *Levita, he maintained that the Hebrew vowel points were of masoretic origin and that the Zohar was post-talmudic, a stand that was later challenged by Johannes *Buxtorf (II). Scaliger's library contained a manuscript translation of the Zohar by *Egidio da Viterbo.

BIBLIOGRAPHY: L. Moréri, *Grand Dictionnaire Historique*, 9 (Paris, 1759), 224–5; J. Bernays, *Joseph Justus Scaliger* (Ger., 1855); L. Sainéan, *La Langue de Rabelais*, 2 (1923), 497ff.; F. Secret, *Le Zôhar chez les kabbalistes chrétiens de la Renaissance* (1964^2), 34ff., 100; idem, *Les Kabbalistes chrétiens de la Renaissance* (1964), 212, 334–5.

[Godfrey Edmond Silverman]

SCANDINAVIAN LITERATURE. The literary culture of the Scandinavian countries dates back about one millennium, the Danish, Faroese, Icelandic, Norwegian, and Swedish languages having developed on separate paths from the original Germanic root from about the ninth century. With rare exceptions, biblical and other Hebraic influences did not make an appearance in works by Danish, Norwegian, and Swedish writers until the Renaissance, and the contribution of Jewish authors began only very much later, from about the middle of the 19th century.

Danish Literature

BIBLICAL AND HEBRAIC INFLUENCES. Probably the earliest work of biblical inspiration written by a Dane was the *Hexaëmeron*, a 12-part, 8,000-line neo-Latin poem on the Creation by Anders Sunesøn (1164–1228), a Danish archbishop who studied in Oxford, Bologna, and Paris. It was not until the Lutheran Reformation in the early 16th century, however, that the impact of the Bible was felt on Danish language and literature. The first complete translation that has survived, the King Christian III Bible (1550), a literary monument, was continually revised and modernized until 1931 and was long the sole cultural source of the ordinary Dane. Since Christianity was, until the 19th century, the decisive cultural factor in Denmark, the Danish language and outlook were greatly influenced by stories, legends, ideas, and idioms drawn from the Old Testament; more than 300 familiar quotations in the everyday language, as well as about half of the "Christian" names, are of biblical origin. As in several other countries, Latin was the main literary language of the 17th century; several authors dealt with biblical themes in accordance with the ethical approach of Danish Protestantism, although these works were inaccessible to the unlearned majority of the population. Outstanding among these books was another *Hexaëmeron* (1661), composed in Alexandrine verse by Anders Christensen Arrebo, known as the "father of Danish poetry." Arrebo's epic, begun in 1630 and published only years after his death, was written in Danish. It was a free reworking of the French Protestant *Du Bartas' Creation epic, *La Semaine*, muting the more pagan elements of the original, and is generally regarded as the first milestone in the elevation of the Danish language to a vehicle of lofty poetic expression. Arrebo is also remembered as the author of a verse translation of Psalms into Danish (1623).

From the mid-19th century, several writers used biblical themes in drama and fiction. Frederik Paludan-Müller, an eminent poet and bishop, wrote *Abels død* (1844), and his example was followed by other Danish authors. Among later works on biblical subjects were Sven Lange's drama, *Samson og Dalila* (1909), *Jeremias* (1916), a play by Knud Gjørup; Kaj *Munk's drama, *En idealist* (1928; *Herod the King*, 1947), Harald Tandrup's novel *Profeten Jonas privat* (1937; *Jonah and the Voice*, 1937), Poul *Borchsenius' *Stjernesønnen* (1952; *Son of a Star*, 1960), a novel about Bar Kokhba; and a trilogy about Moses by Poul Hoffmann (1961–63).

THE IMAGE OF THE JEW. Perhaps the first writer in Denmark to introduce contemporary Jewish characters in his works was Ludvig Holberg (1684–1754), a pioneer of modern Danish literature. Holberg lived at a time when few Jews resided in Copenhagen, but nevertheless he encountered them during his travels in Germany and Holland. The Jewish types in his comedies are mainly theatrical figures: moneylenders, peddlers, the "Jewish priest" (complete with long beard, caftan, and fur hat); their "Jewish" language was a conglomeration of Danish and German. Nevertheless, Holberg showed a more scientific interest in the Jews, publishing a sympathetic historical study, *Den jødiske historie* (1742). Holger Paulli (b. 1644), who was influenced by pietist expectations, believed in the Jewish return to the Holy Land as a condition for the second coming of Jesus. One of the Christian forerunners of Zionism, he published books calling on the European monarchs to conquer Palestine so that the Jews might regain it as their state. In his novel, *Rigsdaler sedlens Haendelser* ("Events of a Dollar Note," 1789–93), Peter Andreas Heiberg projects a mixed image of the Jew, some being only interested in making money; but in *Kina-Farere* ("The Chinese Clippers," 1792) one Jew is honorable, his virtue promoting the play's dénouement. The poet Jens Immanuel Baggesen visited the Frankfurt ghetto, and in *Labyrinthen* ("The Labyrinth," 1792ff.), a book of travel, he presents a sympathetic picture of Jewish misery in their cramped quarter. Baggesen also wrote a statement warmly supporting Christian Wilhelm von *Dohm's book in favor of Jewish emancipation. In the early 19th century, Adam Gottlob Oehlenschläger, the "father of modern Danish literature," describes in his fairy tale play *Aladdin* (1805) a Jew who covets gold and hates Christians; but his *Sanct Hans Aftenspil* ("Midsummernight's Play," 1802) contains idyllic pictures of an old Jewish juggler and a Jewish boy in a market place.

The year 1813 was that of a notorious Jewish literary feud which began when a hack writer, Thomas Thaarup, translated Friedrich Buchholtz' violently antisemitic German book, "Moses und Jesus." The preface to this work claimed that "selfishness, indolence, and ferocity have been distinctive characteristics of the Jews from their very origin." Its publication gave rise to an uproar, and many writers and public figures in Denmark took sides in the controversy. Significant pleas in favor of the Jews came from poets of note such as Jens Baggensen and Steen Steensen Blicher, the latter maintaining that emancipation might restore dignity to the Jews. Blicher's short story *"Jøderne på Hald"* ("The Jews of the Mason Hald") portrays two sympathetic Jewish brothers named Lima and a young girl named Sulamith.

During the first half of the 19th century, the "Golden Age" of Danish literature, Jewish characters frequently appeared in Danish works. Thomasine Gyllembourg's short story *Jøden* ("The Jew," 1836) presents as its hero a "Nathan the Wise" similar to *Lessing's nobleminded Jew. Her son, Johan Ludvig Heiberg, wrote a successful comedy, *Kong Salomon og Jørgen Hattemager* ("King Solomon and George the Hatter," 1825), in which he wittily portrayed Solomon Goldkalb as a goodnatured, amusing character. Heiberg married a talented actress, Johanne Luise Pätges, whose mother was Jewish. Positive Jewish figures also appeared in the works of Hans Christian Andersen, the author of world-famous children's stories and fairy tales. In his novel *Kun en Spillemand* ("Only a Fiddler," 1837), the Jewess Naomi is the fiery, passionate heroine, and in *Denjødiske Pige* ("The Jewish Girl") Sarah remains loyal to her Jewish faith for the sake of her dead mother. Andersen also wrote a touching poem, "Rabbi Meyer." The *Wandering Jew theme also attracted several Danish poets – Bernhard Severin Ingemann, Frederik Paludan-Müller (*Ahasverus*, 1854), and Jens Christian Hostrup. The liberal Christian author and scholar Nicolai Frederik Severin Grundtvig wrote some 1,500 religious poems and hymns, many biblical in tone, in which he stresses the importance to world history of "the Hebrew people."

[Poul Borchsenius]

By the beginning of the 20th century, the Danish Jew had acquired a large measure of "naturalization" in drama and fiction. Thus the brothers Carl Edvard and Georg *Brandes appeared in Sven Lange's novel, *De første kampe* (1925), which was mainly concerned with the elder, Georg. A work of greater importance was Nobel prizewinner Henrik Pontoppidan's vast eight-volume novel *Lykke-Per* ("Lucky Peter," 1898–1904), which, with extraordinary detail and precision, conveyed the author's pessimistic view of contemporary Danish society through the Salomons, a middle-class Copenhagen family. This novel contains a moving description of the learned Aron Israel, whose "soul was as pure as his coat was dirty," and an admiring portrayal of Georg Brandes. Later, Jews also figured in works by Kaj Munk, Poul Borchsenius, Aage Bertelsen, and Sivert Gunst, whose *Hr. Menachem og Hans Hus* (1950) describes Jewish life in Copenhagen at the beginning of the 19th century. However, most of the 20th-century Danish literature dealing with Jewish themes was produced by Jewish authors.

THE JEWISH CONTRIBUTION. From the mid-19th century, Jews began to play an increasingly important role in Danish literary life. Among the pioneers were the converts Nicolai Abrahams and Henrik *Hertz; the Brandes brothers; and the novelist Meïr Aron *Goldschmidt, who frequently returned to Jewish social themes. These were followed by the playwright and novelist Poul Levin; Henri *Nathansen, who also dealt with the problem of Jewish survival in an alien environment; and Louis Levy. During the first three decades of the 20th century, Simon Koch also gained some distinction as a writer of fiction with novels such as *Digteren* (1907). Writers best known for their journalism included Herman Bing and Edvard Brandes, two of the three co-founders of the leading newspaper *Politiken*; Gottlieb Siesby; Valdemar Koppel; and Peter Nansen, a grandson of Mendel Levin *Nathanson, editor of the *Berlingske Tidende*, all of whose descendants were, however, converts to Christianity.

The Nazi occupation of Denmark, the famous rescue operation across the Øresund conducted by the Danish resistance, and the deportation of most of the Jews who remained behind were events that left their mark on postwar Danish literature. They inspired a number of books by younger authors, such as Hanne Kaufmann and Ralph Oppenhejm, and works by a Polish immigrant writer, Pinhas *Welner, which were translated from Yiddish and enjoyed considerable success in Danish editions.

Swedish Literature

BIBLICAL AND HEBRAIC INFLUENCES. In Sweden, as in other Christian lands, the Reformation inspired the first complete Swedish translation of the Old and New Testaments, which had previously been undertaken only in part, and from the Vulgate. The lead was taken by two Lutheran churchmen, Olaus Petri (1493–1552) and Laurentius Andraeae (c. 1475–1552) who, having no knowledge of Hebrew, based their work on Martin *Luther's German version. With minor stylistic changes this Gustavus I ("Gustaf Vasa") Bible remained Sweden's authorized version until 1917, when a new translation received royal sanction. Olaus Petri was also the reputed author of an early play on an apocryphal theme, *Tobiae Commedia* (1550), the earliest known drama in Swedish to have survived. Another early 16th-century Reformation drama was the anonymous *Holofernes och Judit*. The portion of the Old Testament whose influence is most evident in Swedish culture is the Book of Psalms. Many hymns of the Swedish church are no more than paraphrases of Psalms, retaining much of the Bible's phraseology. The most important poetical work of biblical inspiration written in the 17th century was the epic *Guds Werck och Hwila* ("God's Work and Rest," 1725) by Bishop Haquin Spegel, a gigantic composition using the Creation story as a basis and inspired by the French epic of Du Bartas. Two other biblical epics of the same era were *Bibliske Werlden* ("The Biblical World," ed. by J. Reenstierna, 1687) by Samuel Columbus, a series of biblical tales from the Creation to the Last Judgment; and *Biblisk Quinnospegel* ("The Biblical

Women's Mirror") by Olaf Kolmodin, a succession of monologues by famous women of the Bible. A very different use of the Bible was made by scholars of the patriotic "Gothic" trend, who set out to prove the antiquity and glory of Swedish history. This movement reached its peak in the *Atlantica* of Olaus Rudbeck, who adapted the stories of the Flood and the Tower of Babel to fit his assertions.

The 18th-century Enlightenment in Sweden brought with it skeptical and critical views of the Scriptures. Not daring to attack the New Testament, radical authors chose the Old Testament as their target. The "singing poet" Carl Mikael Bellman wrote a series of drinking songs on biblical themes, more merry than blasphemous, taking care to select the more colorful stories, such as Lot and his daughters, Joseph and Potiphar's wife, Esther and Ahasuerus, and, most famous of all, Noah as the inventor of wine. A favorite episode taken from the Apocrypha was that of Susanna and the Elders, on which Jacob Wallenberg wrote a play (1778). However, the most celebrated Swedish authors of the age did not share this attitude to the Bible. The mystic and visionary Emanuel Swedenborg used biblical material in his construction of the spiritual world; one of his works, *De cultu et amore Dei* (1745), is a very subjective paraphrase of the Genesis and Eden story. Linnaeus (Carl von Linné), the architect of botanical systems and a keen-sighted traveler, was a believer in universal Divine retribution. He expounded his creed in *Nemesis Divina*, in which he elaborated the biblical doctrine that sons are punished for their father's sins, and even quoted a talmudic parable on the theme. Among those who had a sense for the sublime in biblical poetry was the Orientalist Johan Adam Tingstadius, who, in preparation for a complete new edition of the Bible, published translations from the original sources of some lyrical portions (Song of Songs, part of Psalms, etc.). Although his works did not influence the poetess Hedvig Charlotta Nordenflycht's ode based on a passage from Exodus, he may well have inspired Johan Henric Kellgren's *Den nya skapselsen eller inbillningens värld* ("The New Creation, or the World of Imagination," 1789), the first major romantic poem in Swedish. Of the later romantic poets, two were especially inspired by the Bible. Archbishop Johan Olof Wallin was the principal editor of *Svenska psalmboken* (1819) and its major contributor; his hymns won him the nickname of "The Northern Harp of David." Erik Johan Stagnelius created a personal religious mythology from biblical, Platonic, gnostic, and Manichean elements, and was perhaps also influenced by *Milton's *Paradise Lost*, which by then had appeared in Swedish translation. He published a volume of lyrics, *Liljor i Saron* ("Lilies of Sharon," 1821).

Toward the middle of the 19th century, the liberal author Abraham Viktor Rydberg wrote a pamphlet against Lutheran orthodoxy, *Bibelns lära om Kristus* (1862), which shows knowledge of the messianic ideas of the Second Temple period and a profound respect and love for the Scriptures, although he did not accept their sanctity. In his cantata for the Uppsala University Jubilee, the desert wanderings of the Israelites symbolize mankind's striving. An amusing product of amateur Bible research may later be seen in a story about Moses, *Jahves eld* ("Jehovah's Fire," 1918) written by the skeptic Hjalmar Emil Fredrik Söderberg.

The works of the outstanding writer of the naturalist generation, August Strindberg, were steeped in the language of the Bible. He eagerly exploited the Bible to develop his favorite themes: the struggle between the sexes (the Fall, Samson and Delilah); Man's struggle with God, (one part of his *Legender* (1898) is titled "Jacob Wrestles"); and the class struggle (his autobiographical *Tjänsteqvinnans son* ("The Bondwoman's Son," 1886), alludes to the story of Ishmael and Hagar). Toward the end of his life, Strindberg studied Hebrew and speculated about its origin and relationship to other languages. In the late 19th century, the new romantic trend was also attracted to the Old Testament. Gustaf Fröding wrote exquisite poems on biblical themes; others of a naively rustic type, ranging from the humorous to the sublime, were composed by Erik Axel Karlfelt and Selma Lagerlöf, who undertook a cruise to Egypt and Palestine and published *Jerusalem* (2 vols., 1901–02), a novel about a group of Swedish peasants, who, prompted by religious yearnings, emigrate to the Holy Land. Selma Lagerlöf's work had been anticipated by Fredrika Bremer's account of a visit to Palestine in about 1861.

From the early 20th century, fewer biblical themes appeared in Swedish literature and, on the whole, New Testament subjects were preferred. The works of the Nobel prizewinner Pär Fabian Lagerkvist exemplify, in various novels loosely connected with the Christian gospels (*Barabbas*, 1950; *Sibyllan*, 1956, *Mariamne*, 1967), the non-believer's conflict with a faith he cannot share. However, the Book of Job was the inspiration for Karin Boye's unfinished cantata, *De sju dödssynderna* ("The Seven Deadly Sins," 1941), which deals with the problem of theodicy. The figure of Job also attracted the Finno-Swedish poet Rabbe Arnfinn Enckell, author of a poetic dialogue between Job and a star. An interesting work dealing with the same issues was *Kains memoaren* (Eng., *Testament of Cain*, 1967) by Lars Johan Wictor Gyllensten, which displays a knowledge not only of the Bible, but also of some tales of midrashic origin. Another 20th-century work was Olov Hartmann's modern miracle play, *Profet och timmerman* ("Prophet and Timber-Cutter," 1954). Biblical themes come into strong focus in the works of artist Bo Beskow (1906–1989), who in his old age turned his attention from the canvas and instead clothed various biblical scenes in words rather than color. He published *Och vattnet stod på jorden* ("And the Waters Covered the Earth") in 1978, followed in 1980 by *Rösten är Jakobs* ("The Voice of Jacob") and *Isebel* in 1982. His last work, published in 1984, was *Solmannen* ("The Sun Man"), which was a story about Samson.

Marianne Fredriksson (1927–) wrote several novels based on the stories of Genesis: *Evas bok* ("The Book of Eva") in 1980, *Kains bok* ("The Book of Cain") in 1981, and *Noreas saga* ("Norea's Saga") in 1986, all of them showing a remarkable gift for bringing biblical characters to life in contemporary times. Fredriksson also wrote *Simon och ekarna* ("Simon and the Oaks") in 1985, a postwar story set in Göteborg, about an adopted Jewish boy who knows nothing about his origins.

Sven Delblanc (1935–1992) was a highly productive author whose 1983 book *Jerusalems natt* ("A Night in Jerusalem") portrays Josephus Flavius and his thoughts on the situation in Jerusalem during a highly volatile period of the Roman occupation. Torgny Lindgren (1938–) wrote a highly appreciated biblical account of King David's marriage to Batsheva in a book entitled *Bat Seba* (1984).

THE IMAGE OF THE JEW. In older Swedish literature, the figure of the Jew was entirely based on traditional Christian clichés, as, for example, in *Passionstankar*, a poem about the Passion by Jacob Frese (1690–1729). The early Jewish settlers attracted scant notice in Sweden at the end of the 18th century, though an eloquent speech in parliament, favoring their admission, was made by pastor Anders Chydenius. The first important literary portrait of a Jew occurs in *Drottningens juvelsmycke* ("The Queen's Diadem," 1834) by Carl Jonas Love Almqvist, whose romantic novel includes a Jewish character of the traditionally negative type. A very different treatment was given to the Jewish family in Viktor Rydberg's *Den siste atenaren* ("The Last Athenian," 1859), a historical novel set in the era of Julian the Apostate, which violently criticizes the traditional idealization of the early Christians. The characters in this work include a young Jewess who is seduced by a heathen, and a tolerant young rabbi who, by a curious anachronism, is said to be an expert in the Kabbalah. Rydberg was also continually fascinated by the Wandering Jew, who appears in several of his poems (e.g., *Prometeus och Ahasverus*, 1877). Other Swedish authors who developed the same motif were Strindberg, Gustaf Fröding, Oscar Ivar *Levertin, Per Hallström (*Ahasverus*, 1908), Bo Hjalmar Bergman, Sigfrid Lindström, Pär Lagerkvist, (Ahasverus *död*, 1960) and, especially, Gösta Oswald, whose *Christinalegender* ("Legends about Christina") also deals with this theme.

A literary interest in the Jews was reawakened in the 1880s under the impact of rising antisemitism in Germany and of the radical movements of the time. The Jew was seen either as the cynical, rootless radical or as the "herald of a new age." The eminent Danish critic Georg Brandes became the prototype for both. In his play *John Ulfstjerna* (1907), Tor Harald Hedberg portrayed the revolutionary Jew as an intriguer; yet many Jewish intellectuals with more moderate and patriotic views scarcely accorded with this image. Strindberg, as always, was ambivalent, presenting totally contrasting pictures. In his novel *Röda rummet* ("The Red Room," 1879) and the pamphlet *Det nya riket* ("The New Kingdom," 1882) he wittily caricatured unsympathetic Jews; but elsewhere, as in the chronicle play *Gustav Vasa* (1899), he introduced a venerable Jewish patriarch from Lübeck, a complete anachronism in 16th-century Sweden. The playwright and novelist Hjalmar Frederik Elgérus Bergman displayed a great interest in the Jews, having made the acquaintance of Jewish immigrants from eastern Europe while in Berlin. In his masterly play *Patrasket* (1928), the Jew is represented as the man of imagination, and the author's use of comedy conceals the real tragedy.

There have been few aggressive antisemites among Swedish writers of the 20th century, but two of the most prominent were the poet and essayist Vilhelm Ekelung and the novelist Agnes von Krusenstjerna, whose cycle *Fröknarna von Pahlen* ("The Von Pahlen Women," 7 vols., 1930–35), contains some viciously anti-Jewish portraits and diatribes. On the other hand, two conservative authors, pro-German and even sympathetic toward the Hitler regime (though not themselves antisemitic), were among the first Swedes to discuss Zionist pioneering in Ereẓ Israel: the explorer Sven Hedin, author of the travel book *Jerusalem* (1918), and the literary historian Fredrik Böök (1883–1961), who wrote the remarkable *Resa till Jerusalem* ("Journey to Jerusalem," 1925) and attended the opening ceremony of The Hebrew University.

The Nazi persecution of the Jews is reflected in the works of the 1930s and 1940s. Among the poets who expressed anger and grief were Be Bergman and Arvid Mörne; novelists who dealt with the theme included Josef Kjellgren, in *Guldkedjan* ("The Golden Chain," 1940), and Eyvind Johnson in his *Krilon-Trilogie* (1941–43). Most deeply incensed was the half-German anti-Nazi Arvid Brenner (Fritz Helge Heerberger), who took refuge in Sweden. His novel *Kompromiss* (1934) deals with the Nazi rise to power: *Ny vardag* ("A New Weekday," 1936) and *En dag som andra* ("A Day Like Any Other") are concerned with refugee life in Sweden. After World War II, the surviving victims of Hitler's regime became a conventional literary type, and symbolic of the neutral, well-meaning Swede's bad conscience. *Tvärbalk* ("Cross Beam," 1963) by Sivar Arnér concerns a Swede who exchanges his frigid wife for a Jewess whose life was shattered by her treatment in a Nazi concentration camp. A similar theme is developed in *Legionärerna* ("The Legionaries") by Per-Olov Enquist, which also deals with the negative Swedish policies toward Jewish refugees after the war.

Eyvind Johnson (1900–1976) is remarkable for being a non-Jewish Swede with deep and accurate insight into the tribulations faced by the decimated Jewish survivors of Hitler's war of annihilation. His *Molnen over Metapontion* ("The Clouds over Metapontion," 1957) and *Favel, ensam* ("Favel All Alone," 1968) reflect acute understanding of the situation faced by the remnants of Jewish Europe.

Artur Lundkvist (1906–1991) wrote two historical novels, *Tvivla korsfarare* ("Think Again, Crusader," 1972) and *Slavar i Särkland* ("Slaves in Särkland," 1975), featuring many Jewish characters and highlighting the fruitful exchanges between cultures over the ages. Kenne Fant (1923–) wrote *R. En dokumentär roman* ("R.: A Documentary Novel," 1988) about Raoul *Wallenberg. Olle Hedberg (1899–1974) wrote *Ut med blondinerna* ("Out with the Blondes") in 1939, a stinging satire that ridiculed the Nazi race laws of contemporary Germany. Bengt Ek (1917–1990) wrote a novel for teenagers, published in 1981, titled *Hos morfar i Getapulien* ("Life with Grandpa in

Goat-Land"). It is a warm, humorously related story about two Jewish boys from Berlin who are sent by their Swedish mother to their grandfather in Sweden to escape the hardships in the aftermath of World War I. Jan Gehlin (1922–) served for many years as chair of the Swedish Authors' Association. The son of famous artist Esther Henriques, and thus a scion of one of the oldest Jewish families in Scandinavia, Gehlin wrote two partly autobiographical novels, *Enskilt område* ("Private Property," 1949) and *Gränstrakter* ("Borderlands," 1953), to counter the evils of Nazism and persecution of Jews. Paul Andersson (1930–1976) published a collection of poems in 1956 entitled *Judiska motiv* ("Jewish Subjects"), the first Swede after Ragnar Josephson to publish verse on a Jewish theme. Per Ahlmark (1939–), a former member of the Swedish Riksdag or Parliament, also led the Swedish Liberal Party for three years and served as Sweden's deputy prime minister. Fired by a deep interest in Jewish subjects, he published his first collection of poems, *Flykter* ("Escapes") in 1985. In 1991 he worked together with Lilian Edström on the publication of Yehuda *Amichai's Hebrew poems in Swedish, titled *Bombens diameter* ("The Bomb's Diameter"), followed in 1993 by *Det eviga hatet: Om nynazism, anti-semitism och Radio Islam* ("The Eternal Hatred: On Neo-Nazism, Antisemitism and Radio Islam"). Following a host of publications during the 1990s, Per Ahlmark released *Det är demokratin, dumbom!* ("It's Democracy, Stupid!") in 2004, a scathing criticism of the world's indifference to the plight of the Iraqi people under Saddam Hussein and the lessons to be learned from not speaking out for democracy and freedom.

[Viveka Heyman / Ilya Meyer (2nd ed.)]

THE JEWISH CONTRIBUTION. Jews began to play an important part in Sweden's literary life only from the last decades of the 19th century, although after the 1850s Rosa Warrens was active as a poetess and translator. The major creative author was Oskar Ivar Levertin, some of whose verse and prose works dealt with themes of Jewish interest (*Kung Salomo och Morolf*, 1905). His contemporary, the popular novelist Sophie Elkan, accompanied Selma Lagerlöf on her tour of the Near East and published an account entitled *Drömmen om Österlandet* ("The Dream of the Eastern Land," 1904). However, the major Jewish contribution was really in literary history and criticism, a field in which Johan Henrik Emil *Schück, Karl Johan *Warburg, and Martin *Lamm all excelled. An important contribution was also made by members of the eminent *Josephson family, headed by the painter Ernst Abraham *Josephson who published some poems and who appears in a novel by Strindberg. The art historian Ragnar Josephson (1891–1966) was a successful dramatist and, in his early period, published *Judiska dikter* (1916; revised 1943), a collection of poems on Jewish themes. Together with Sweden's chief rabbi Marcus *Ehrenpreis, he also issued translations of modern Hebrew verse. His nephew, the actor Erland Josephson (1923–), starred in plays by the refugee dramatist Peter *Weiss, and wrote a variety of works, in some of which – notably his novel *En Berättelse om herr Silberstein* ("The Tale of Mr. Silberstein," 1957) and the play *Benjamin* (1963) – the problem of antisemitism is analyzed. His preoccupation with this theme had been anticipated by his uncle, Ragnar Josephson, who, during the 1930s, published *Den Dubbla Loyalitaeten* ("The Dual Loyalty"), a booklet describing the predicament of Swedish Jews who were eyewitnesses to the heartless policy of driving hapless Jewish refugees back to certain death in Nazi Germany.

A more authentic note was struck by Jewish authors who were not entirely Swedish by birth or upbringing. Chief Rabbi Ehrenpreis, who had once been prominent in modern Hebrew literature, later wrote books in Swedish on the intellectual history of the Jews, and also published some interesting autobiographical works. Zenia Larsson (1922–), a Polish Jewess who survived the Holocaust and later reached Sweden, wrote three autobiographical novels, which describe the Lodz ghetto, her liberation from a Nazi concentration camp, and her first experiences in her adopted country. Her most famous works are *Skuggor vid träbron* ("Shadows by the Wooden Bridge," 1961), *Lång är gryningen* ("The Long Dawn," 1961), *Livet till motes* ("Accepting Life," 1962), *Åter till Babel* ("A Return to Babel," 1964), and *Vägen hem* ("The Return Home," 1975). Other works on similar subjects were published by two other refugees who nevertheless retained their original links with German culture – the playwright Peter Weiss and the Nobel prizewinning poet Nelly *Sachs. There are contemporary Swedish-born authors who also write in a similar vein, such as Susanne Gottfarb (1948–), Kjell Grape (1939–), and Peter Mosskin (1945–), all of whom turn the spotlight inward and retrace their Jewish heritage, in some cases a heritage that was almost lost through the events of modern European history.

Marianne Ahrne (1940–) went back to her Jewish roots in her novels *Äppelblom och ruiner* ("Apple Blossoms and Ruins," 1980) and *Katarina Horowitz drömmar* ("Katarina Horowitz's Dreams," 1990).

A new generation of Jewish writers has emerged in Sweden. Most, but not all, trace their roots in Sweden back three or four generations, yet their writings often strongly reflect the events of the first half of the last century. Tomas Böhm (1945–) was born in Stockholm to parents who fled there from Austria. Among his many books are novels with a Jewish motif, such as *Fjällturen* ("A Trip in the Swedish Alps," 1980) and *Adamsäpplen och huvudvärk* ("Adam's Apples and Headaches," 1993). Jonathan Freud (1943–) lives in Israel, where he works as a guide, journalist, teacher, and lecturer. He writes books that link history with current events and is often critical of the poor standard of journalism and analysis practiced by reporters based in Jerusalem who, he feels, provide media coverage simply to justify their presence, remarkably devoid of historical reflection or factual basis. His first book, *Från Jerusalem* ("From Jerusalem"), was published in 1986 and was followed a year later by a short novel, *Palestinsk oskuld* ("Palestinian Innocence"). *Judarnas Konung* ("King of the Jews"), which dealt with King Herod, appeared in 1988, and in 1991 he published *En judisk bosättare* ("A Jewish Settler").

Anita Goldman (1953–) is a journalist who lived for a while in Israel. She started her writing career with *Allt genast* ("Everything Right Now," 1978), followed by a number of novels with a feminist theme: *Våra bibliska mödrar* ("Our Biblical Mothers") and *Den sista kvinnan från Ur* ("The Last Woman of Ur"), both published in 1988. *Stenarnas döttrar* ("Daughters of the Stones") appeared in 1989. In 1994 she published *Orden som brändes* ("The Burning Words"), a novel about *Beruryah, represented in the Talmud as a woman of learning and wife of R. *Meir. Marianne Goldman (1951–) is a dramatist whose works have appeared on stage, TV, and on the big screen. Together with Kerstin Klein-Persky, she wrote *Kaos är granne med Finkelstein* ("Chaos Lives Next Door to Finkelstein," 1990), and she also wrote the film script for *Freud flyttar hemifrån* ("Freud Moves Away from Home"). In her *Dansa samba med mig* ("Come Dance the Samba with Me," 1994) she took up several key issues affecting second-generation children – the children of Holocaust survivors.

Salomon Schulman (1947–) focuses largely on Yiddish literature. He has translated the works of Abraham *Sutzkever, publishing his *Grönt akvarium* ("Green Aquarium," 1986). *Garva med Goldstein* ("Laugh with Goldstein," 1988) is a compilation of Jewish humor. His *Natten läser stjärnor, jiddisch-dikter från ett desperat sekel* ("The Night Reads the Stars, Yiddish Poems from a Desperate Century," 1991) is a dark account of the fate that befell so many of Europe's brilliant Yiddish writers and poets.

Another writer with an immense impact who also recounts a dark past is Hedi Fried (1924–). Born in Romania and brought to Sweden as a survivor of Hitler's death camps, she studied at university and graduated as a psychologist. However, it was only later that she finally decided to document her past, with the publication of her English-language memoir *Fragments of Life* (1990), translated later into Swedish as *Skärvor av ett liv*. The sequel, *Livet tillbaka* ("Back to Life," 1995) deals with her personal road back to life in her new country, Sweden.

Nelly *Sachs (1891–1970) was rescued and brought to Sweden through the good offices of Nobel Prize-winning Swedish authoress Selma Lagerlöf. She wrote poetry in German about the terrible fate of her people, and her work was translated into Swedish by a number of famous lyricists. In 1966 she shared the Nobel Prize in literature with Israeli author S.Y. *Agnon. Her play *Eli. Ett Mysteriespel om Israels lidande* ("Eli: A Mystery Play about Israel's Suffering," 1966) has been staged both in German and in Swedish, and she published collections of poems until the year she died.

Leif Silbersky (1938–) traces his ancestry back to the Balkans three generations ago. A renowned defense lawyer with many high-profile cases to his credit, he is also a widely read author. His writing career began with the factual *Porträtt av terrorister: intervjuer med terrorister i israeliska fängelser* ("Portrait of Terrorists: Interviews with Terrorists in Israeli Jails," 1977). He has also written a series of detective novels together with Swedish author Olov Svedelid. The first was *Sista vittnet* ("The Last Witness," 1977, followed by a new book every year until 1985, then a break until 1990 when *En röst för döden* ("A Voice for Death") was published. The main character throughout the series is an old Jewish lawyer named Rosenbaum, a survivor of the Holocaust.

[Ilya Meyer (2nd ed.)]

Norwegian Literature

BIBLICAL INFLUENCES. The first impact of the Bible on Norwegian culture has been traced to the *Stjórn*, a medieval Icelandic paraphrase of parts of the Old Testament. However, after the Reformation, the Danish translation of the Bible held sway well into the 20th century. As elsewhere, biblical terms and phrases enriched the literary Danish (*Riksmål*) spoken in educated circles and the purer Norwegian (*Landsmal*) that only gained ground much later. Although biblical themes have appeared in the works of Norwegian writers, they have been rarer than might have been expected, even in comparison with Denmark and Sweden, perhaps as a result of Norway's greater cultural isolation. In 1881, Karl Herschell, the first Jew in Bergen, wrote a book about the Pentateuch; and, in the 20th century, Haakon B. Mahrt published the novel *Jonas* (1935) and Halldis Moren Vesaas included a poem about Esther in her verse collection *Tung tids tale* ("Talk of Hard Times," 1945). In general, biblical motifs characterize the description of contemporary Jewish figures in works by modern Norwegian writers.

THE IMAGE OF THE JEW. Even before Jews first settled in the country, they provided occasional stereotypes for Norwegian authors, beginning with Ludwig Holberg, born in Bergen, but who made his name in Denmark (see above). A Jewish moneylender appears in *Aktierne eller de Rige* (1788), a play by Claus Fasting, and in one of the early works of the poet Henrik Arnold *Wergeland. One of the articles in the Norwegian Constitution of 1814 prohibited Jewish settlement, a decree which aroused the indignant opposition of several liberal writers, headed by Wergeland who, in his pamphlets and in verse collections such as the epic *Jöden* ("The Jew," 1842) and *Jödinden* ("The Jewess," 1844), was a tireless champion of the proscribed Jews, demanding that they be granted both permission to enter Norway and equal rights with the rest of the population. In this stand Wergeland had been anticipated by Andreas Munch (1811–1884), who wrote the poem *Jöderne* ("The Jews," 1836), and he was followed by the writers of two plays: Adolph Rosenkilde in *En Jöde i Mandal* ("A Jew in Mandal," 1849) and Christian Rasmus Hansson in *Den förste Jöde* ("The First Jew," 1852).

An amendment to the constitution, favoring Jewish admission, was passed in 1852. Later in the 19th century, the same sympathetic approach was displayed by Alexander Lange Kielland in his *Mennesker og dyr* ("Men and Animals," 1891), which describes the Jews of Salonika, and in John Paulsen's *Jödinden* ("The Jewess," 1892), a novel influenced by Wergeland, which deals with the problems of mixed marriage and conversion in Denmark, and which includes some characters who display the effects of political antisemitism in contemporary Germany. In his poem *Juleaftenen* ("Christmas Eve," 1842) Wergeland had portrayed a Jewish peddler in northern Sweden. By the beginning of the 20th century, some Jewish immigrants endeavored to make a living by peddling their wares at railroad and construction sites, at country fairs, and in fishing villages. Jews of this type are referred to by several novelists, notably Johan Bojer in *Den siste viking* (1921; "Last of the Vikings," 1923); Knut Hamsun in *Landstrykere* ("The Vagabonds," 1927); and Nils. A. Ytreberg in *Svarta Björn* ("The Black Bear," 1954). Hamsun had a pathological hatred of the British and Americans and, during World War II, became a prominent quisling. The Jewish peddler also appears in *Hebraerens sön* ("Son of the Hebrew," 1911), a work by Matti Aikio, a writer of Norwegian-Lapp origin. In his novel a Jew, abandoned by his Polish refugee parents, is raised by Christian foster parents in Finmark (northern Norway) and becomes an artist. He is an eyewitness to a Polish pogrom, and Aikio shows how he is torn between the conflicting Jewish and Christian traditions. The same kind of restlessness finally moves a Galician-born Danish Jew to emigrate to Ereẓ Israel in "Efraim ben Ruben," one of the stories in Sigurd Christiansen's collection *Idyllen om Sander* ("The Idyll of Sander," 1928). During the 1930s, Helge Krok showed in her play *Underveis* ("En Route," 1931) how, despite radical views in politics and religion, one of her characters experiences a revival of ancestral Jewish feeling.

A number of Norwegian novels have dealt with the Nazi persecution of Norwegian Jewry and with the deportation of the Jews or their flight to Sweden, and often discuss more general aspects of the Jewish fate and of antisemitism. They include Axel Kielland's *Lev farlig* ("Live Dangerously," 1943); Aimée Sommerfelt's *Ung front* ("Young Front," 1945) and *Miriam* (1950; Eng. 1963); and Odd Bang-Hansen's *Ringer rundt brönnen* ("Rings around the Well," 1946). The last writer also raises the issue of Norwegian-Jewish relations in his *I denne natt* ("On this Night," 1947). The postwar problem of the Jewish refugee figures in the works of several other writers, including Jens Ingvald Bjøorneboe, who deals with the question in *Jonas* (1955) and who also describes former Wehrmacht soldiers on a holiday tour of Italy in his play *Fugleelskerne* ("The Bird Fanciers," 1966). Among those who dealt with Nazi treatment of the German Jews was Ronald August Fangen, in his *En lysets Engel* ("An Angel of Light," 1945). A writer who frequently used Jewish themes was Ragnar Kvam, the author of several articles about Israel, including one about the *Exodus* affair of 1947 and the German camp to which the ship's unfortunate passengers were brutally returned. This last subject also appears in Kvam's novel, *Alle vil hjem* ("Everyone Wants to Go Home," 1950), which depicts antisemitic agitation during the years of World War II, the Nazi deportations, and the unfriendly reception that awaited a survivor when he reached his village, all of which he believed precipitated Jewish immigration to Israel. The problem of antisemitism recurs in Kvam's later novel, *Den store stillheten* ("The Great Silence," 1964), and it also dominates *Kjaerlighetsstien* ("The Path of Love," 1946), by Johan Borgen, who discussed the widespread phenomenon of antisemitism in newspaper articles. A Jewish artist, Miriam, makes several appearances in a trilogy by Borgen (*Lillelord, De mörke skogene, Vi har ham nu*, 1955–57) and a Jewish concentration camp survivor figures in another of his novels, *Blåtind* ("The Blue Peak," 1964). Finn Alnaes also introduces a Jewish war victim in his *Koloss* (1963).

Jewish suffering in Norway during the Nazi occupation also inspired several poems of the postwar era. Such works were written by Inger Hagerup, in *Den Syvende natt* ("The Seventh Night," 1947); Halldis Moren Vesaas; Andreas Graven (*Jöden*, 1945); and Olav Dalgard, in *Gjennom mörket* ("Through the Darkness," 1945). Other Norwegian poems on themes connected with the Holocaust were Leif S. Rode's *Barnemordet i Betlehem* ("The Massacre of the Infants in Bethlehem,"1945); Carl Frederik Prytz's *Ghetto* (1960), on the Warsaw Jewish revolt; and Georg Johannesen's "*Jödisk partisansang*" ("Jewish Partisan Song") from the collection *Nye dikt* ("New Poems," 1966). From 1945 poems about the Jewish plight were published in the Norwegian press, as were others on the State of Israel's battle for survival in May 1948. Though much discussed in Norway, Israel has mainly attracted more popular writers, such as the editor Victor Mogens, author of *Folket som ikke vil dø* (1954), and Kare Holt, who wrote a tale for juveniles, *Römlingen Oskar og Maria fra Hulesjöen* ("Oscar and Maria the Refugees of Lake Ḥuleh," 1959). In 1982 Sigurd Senje published *Ekko fra Skriktjenn 1942–47* ("Ecco from the Lake of Screams"), a documentary novel based on the "Feldman Case" of 1942–47). The Feldmans were a Jewish couple murdered by Norwegian border runners who were supposed to help them get to Sweden in 1942. The two border runners admitted to the murders in 1947 but were not convicted. This tragic episode was also made into a film. Many of the accounts about Jews in the Holocaust are documentary. Jahn Otto Johansen wrote *Det hendte også her* ("It Also Happened Here," 1984), an account of the Norwegian Holocaust. Per Ole Johansen wrote: *Oss selv nærmest: Norge og jødene 1914–1943* ("Closest to Ourselves: Norway and the Jews 1914–43," 1984), an account of antisemitism in the Norwegian police and courts. Kristian Ottosen, a Norwegian historian, wrote an account of the deportation of Norwegian Jews during World War II: *I slik en natt* ("On a Night Such as This," 1994). Karoline Frogner, a Norwegian film producer and author, published the book and produced the film *Mørketid: kvinners møte med nazismen* ("Time of Darkness: Women's Encounter with Nazism," 1995). There are interviews with several women who survived the Ravensbrueck concentration camp, among them four Jewish women. Ragnar Ulstein wrote *Jødar på flukt* ("Jews on the Run," 1995); Vebjørn Selbekk's *Jødehat på norsk: fra eidsvollsmennene til Boot boys* ("The Norwegian Hatred of Jews: From the Men at Eidsvoll to Boot Boys," 2001), was an account of Norwegian attitudes to the Jews through the ages. The internationally known Norwegian author Lars Saabye Christensen briefly describes a Jewish girl and her family as they are arrested in their home in Oslo in his epic novel *Halvbroren* ("The

Halfbrother," 2001), where he describes life in Oslo during and after the war through four generations.

In 2003 Einhart Lorentz published *Veien mot Holocaust* ("The Road to the Holocaust"), a chronological account of the stages that led to the mass deportations and murder of about six million Jews, and Espen Søby wrote *Kathe, alltid vært I Norge* ("Kathe Always Stayed in Norway), where he follows the fortunes of the 15-year-old Jewish schoolgirl Kathe Lasnik and her family, who were deported and murdered in Auschwitz in 1942.

THE JEWISH CONTRIBUTION. In a country with a Jewish community as small as that in Norway, the number of Jewish writers has naturally been slight. Two authors who wrote books after World War II were Elsa Dickman, whose novel *Korsveien* ("The Crossroad," 1945) first appeared in Sweden, and Eva Scheer, whose *Vi bygger i sand* ("We Build on Sand," 1948) traces the history of a Jewish family from its settlement in Norway until the Nazi deportations. Israel provides the theme for two other books by Eva Scheer: *Vi möttes i Jerusalem* ("We Met in Jerusalem," 1951) and *Israel, dobbelt löftets land* ("Israel, Land of the Twofold Covenant," 1967). Another novelist, Torborg Nedreaas, the great-granddaughter of Karl Herschell, portrays Jewish members of her family in *Musikk fra en blå brŏnn* ("Music from a Blue Well," 1960); in the title story of her collection *Bak skapet står öksen* ("Behind the Cupboard there is an Ax," 1945) she touched on the subject of German antisemitism. An outstanding figure in Norway's postwar cultural life, the refugee publisher and author Max *Tau promoted the translation and publication of works by several Israel writers and displayed his attachment to the Jewish heritage in his novels and autobiography. Øystein Wingaard Wolf (1958–) is one of few Norwegian writers with a Jewish background to have published books in the 1980s. He has written several collections of poems and novels. *Ingen kan forklare ordet "fred"* ("No One Can Explain the Word 'Peace'"), a journey through the East European world in words, music and photographs (1987), is a collection of poems and short stories from eastern Europe translated into Norwegian. The novel *Dodi Ashers død* ('The Death of Dodi Asher," 1986) won a prize.

The author Mona Levin wrote the biography of her father, the Norwegian Jewish pianist Robert Levin: *Med livet i hendene* ("With Life in my Hands," 1983).

Most of the books written by Norwegian Jews are biographies of and by concentration camp survivors written in the 1980s and 1990s; Herman Sachnowitz, *Det angår også deg* ("This Concerns You," 1976); Ernest Arberle, written by Arvid Møller, *Vi må ikke glemme* ("We Must Not Forget," 1980); Robert Savosnik with Hans Melien, *Jeg ville ikke dø* ("I Did Not Want to Die," 1986); Herman Kahan with Knut M. Hansson, *Ilden og lyset* ("The Fire and the Light," 1988); Mendel Szanjfeld with Simon Szajnfeld; *Fortell hva som skjedde med oss; erindringer fra Holocaust* ("Tell What Happened to Us: Recounting the Holocaust," 1993); Kai Feinberg with Arnt Stefansen, *Fange nr 79108 vender tilbake* ("Prisoner No. 79108 Returns," 1995); Vera Komissar with Sverre M. Nyrønning, *På tross av alt: Julius Paltiel – norsk jøde i Auschwitz* ("Despite Everything: Julius Paltiel – Norwegian Jew in Auschwitz," 1995). Vera Kommisar also wrote a book about Norwegian Jews who escaped to Sweden in 1942: *Nådetid: norske jøder på flukt 1942* ("Time of Grace: Norwegian Jews on the Run, 1942," 1992) as well as *Jødiske gleder: en bok om jødedommen, jødiske helligdager og koscher mat* ("Jewish Delights: A Book on Judaism, Jewish Holidays and Kosher Food," 1998). Ove Borøchstein wrote *J – historien om kristiansundsjødene* ("J – the Story of the Jews from Kristiansund," 2001). Abel Abrahamsen, a Norwegian Jew living in the United States, published *Jewish Life and Culture in Norway: Wergeland's Legacy* (2003), an illustrated account of Jewish life in Norway before the war.

[Oskar Mendelsohn / Lynn C. Feinberg (2nd ed.)]

BIBLIOGRAPHY: P. Borchsenius, *Historien om de danske jøder* (1969); C.S. Petersen and U. Andersen, *Dansk Litteratur-historie*, 4 vols. (1925–29); B. Balslev, *De danske Jøders Historie* (1932); H.M. Valentin, *Judarnas Historia; Sverige* (1924); P.M. Granqvist, *Det Svenska Israel* (1933); C.V. Jacobowsky, in: JBA, 19 (1962), 52–59; idem, in: *Judisk Tidskrift*, 10 (1943); idem, *"Nyare svenske-judisk litteratur (1946–51),"* in: *Judisk Krönika*, no. 2 (1952).

SCEPTER (Heb. *meḥoqeq, maṭṭeh, shevet, sharvit*), a staff symbolic of royal authority, originally conceived as power to strike down enemies (Ezek. 19:14; Ps. 110:2). Thus the Bible calls a king "scepter" (Gen. 49:10) or "scepter-bearer" (Amos 1:5, 8), while God, as king of kings, wields a scepter (Isa. 30:31). The Persian Ahasuerus extends a golden scepter to a *persona grata* (Esth. 4:11). Two main types of scepters are pictured in Near Eastern sculptures and reliefs:

(a) a long staff with an ornamental head (mainly in Egypt and Iran), and

(b) a short-handled battle mace (mainly in Assyria). The latter symbolizes royal military power (cf. Num. 24:17).

[Mayer Irwin Gruber]

SCHAALMAN, HERMAN E. (1916–), Reform rabbi. Schaalman was born in Munich, Germany, where his father – a veteran of World War I, having fought in the Battle of Verdun – was a professor of mathematics and physics and a cantor at an orphanage. His mother came from a rabbinic family. Herman was a graduate of the Maximillian Gymnasium (1935) and was but the second boy in the Liberal Gemeinde to read the entire *sidrah* for his bar mitzvah. He was taught Hebrew privately and entered the Liehranstalt fuer die Wissenschat des Judentums in 1935, when German universities were closed to Jewish students. Along with Alfred Wolfe and Guenther *Plaut and two other students, he was offered a scholarship to Hebrew Union College by its visionary president Julian *Morgenstern, who rescued five students and five scholars from Nazi Germany by bringing them to HUC. Schaalman was a student at Hebrew Union College (1935–41) and was ordained in 1941. He studied at the University of Cincinnati, receiving both his

B.A. and his M.A. (1937). He was also awarded an honorary degree of doctor of divinity from Hebrew Union College–Jewish Institute of Religion in 1966.

He served as rabbi of Temple Judah in Cedar Rapids, Iowa (1941–49), taught at nearby Coe College and Cornell College, and became director of the Chicago Federation of the Union of American Hebrew Congregations between 1949 and 1951. Under his leadership the Olin-Sang Ruby Union Institute was established and he was its first director. Olin-Sang-Ruby is a camp and retreat center that serves children and adults in Oconomowoc, Wisconsin. Despite his desperate need for the $15,000 down payment for a $63,000 purchase, Schaalman returned a $5,000 check he had received from a Chicago area gangster who had been affiliated with Al Capone and who ran a string of brothels. He received the funds elsewhere. As a regional director, he helped found four congregations in the Chicago area in the post-war boom. Schaalman came to Emanuel Congregation of Chicago in 1955. In 2006 it had more than 900 families as members.

Schaalman served on the board of directors of the Jewish Federation of Metropolitan Chicago. He served as chair of the Advisory Committee of the American Jewish Committee and was president of the Central Conference of American Rabbis (1981–83); he also served as chairman of the Ethics Committee, the Committee of Patrilineal Decent, and the Mixed Marriage Committee of the CCAR.

Schaalman was active in Chicago civic and cultural activities and was an early pioneer in interfaith work. The Chicago Archdiocese awarded him a Larueante in Ecumenicisim in 1995.

He published articles primarily in the field of theology in various journals and was co-editor of a book, *Preaching Biblical Texts.* He continued to teach throughout his rabbinate. Schaalman held the Jewish Chautauqua Society resident lectureship at the Garrett Evangelical Theological Seminary, Evanston, and the Chicago Theological Seminary.

In recognition of a career devoted to the service of others, he was cited as one of the outstanding foreign-born citizens of Chicago by the Immigrants' Service League. He was inducted into the Hall of Fame of the Jewish Community Centers.

Schaalman was president of the Chicago Board of Rabbis and of the Jewish Council on Urban Affairs. He was a long-time member of the Education Committee of National Holocaust Council.

As he reached the much honored stage of four score years, the honors for the life he led started pouring in. In September 1999, the Jewish Federation of Metropolitan Chicago bestowed on him its award, the Julius Rosenwald Medallion. In June 2000, the Catholic Theological Union at Chicago conferred on him an honorary doctorate in ministry. In October 2000, the Chicago Theological Seminary selected Rabbi Schaalman to receive their prestigious Graham Taylor Award and announced the establishment of the Rabbi Herman E. Schaalman Chair in Jewish Studies in recognition of his enormous impact on theological students, pastors, rabbis, and academics through over 14 years of teaching in Jewish-Christian Studies. The Spertus Institute of Judaic Studies granted the rabbi an honorary doctorate in October 2001. In May 2002, Schaalman was the recipient of the highest award given by the state of Illinois, the Lincoln Medal.

In May 2004 he received an honorary doctorate from Garrett – Evangelical Theological Institute at Northwestern University in Evanston, Illinois.

In June 2004 he received the Luminary Senior Award from the City of Chicago and he was inducted into the 2004 Chicago Senior Citizens Hall of Fame.

In September 2004 the Chicago City Park District dedicated a park in the rabbi's honor.

[Michael Berenbaum (2nd ed.)]

SCHAAP, RICHARD J. (**Dick**; 1934–2001), U.S. sportswriter, sports broadcaster, and author or co-author of 33 books. Schaap was the eldest of three children, born in Flatbush, Brooklyn, to Leah and Maury, a salesman. His paternal grandparents were of Dutch descent, and his maternal grandparents were from Russia. When asked if he was Jewish, Schaap would joke, "Yes, by birth and by appetite." Schaap was raised on Long Island in Freeport, New York, where at age 14 he began writing a sports column for the weekly *Freeport Leader.* He moved the following year to the *Nassau Daily Review-Star* under 20-year-old sports editor and future Pulitzer Prize-winner Jimmy Breslin. Schaap attended Cornell University (1955), where he was the starting goalie for the university's lacrosse team and editor-in-chief of the *Cornell Daily Sun.* Thereafter he attended Columbia University Graduate School of Journalism while working at the *Long Island Press* at night. After graduating in 1956, Schaap worked at *Newsweek* magazine (1956–63), and the *New York Herald Tribune* and the *World Journal Tribune* (1964–66), serving as the paper's city editor and also as a columnist. It was Schaap who coined the term "Fun City" for New York. Schaap began writing sports books, became sports anchor for WNBC-TV in New York City in 1971, and was named editor of *Sport* magazine in 1973. In the 1970s, he was a correspondent for *NBC Nightly News* and the *Today Show,* and then moved to ABC's *World News Tonight* and *20/20* in the 1980s. Schaap won five Emmy Awards, for his profiles of comedian Sid *Caesar (1983) and Olympian Tom Waddell (1988); two for sports reporting; and for writing. He was also a theater critic, leading him to quip that he was the only person ever to vote both for the Tony Awards and for the Heisman Trophy. In 1988 he began hosting *The Sports Reporters* on ESPN, hosted *Schaap One on One* on ESPN Classic, and hosted a syndicated ESPN Radio show called *The Sporting Life with Dick Schaap,* in which he discussed the week's developments in sports with his son Jeremy, who was also an ESPN sportswriter. Among his 33 books are two autobiographies which made *The New York Times* bestseller list: football star Jerry Kramer's *Instant Replay* (1968) and two-sport star Bo Jackson's *Bo Knows Bo,* which was the best-selling sports autobiography ever. He wrote "as told to" biographies of Joe Namath, Hank Aaron,

Joe Montana, Tom Seaver, Billy *Crystal, Dave DeBusschere, and others, a biography of Robert F. Kennedy, *RFK*, and co-authored *.44* with Breslin, about Son of Sam serial killer David Berkowicz. Schaap's final book was the autobiographical *Flashing Before My Eyes*, in which he recounts humorous and poignant memories of a career spanning 50 years. Schaap won the Northeastern Award for Excellence in Broadcast Sports Journalism in 1986, the Women's Sports Foundation Award for Excellence in Covering Women's Sports in 1984, and was the 2002 winner of the Associated Press Sports Editors Red Smith Award. He was the first journalist inducted into the True Heroes of Sport Hall of Fame by the Northeastern University Center for Sport and Society.

[Elli Wohlgelernter (2nd ed.)]

SCHACH, FABIUS (1868–1930), one of the first members of the Zionist movement in Germany. Born in Wexna, Lithuania, Schach studied at yeshivot and went to Riga and then Berlin, where he studied at the university. There he made the acquaintance of Max *Bodenheimer, who brought him to Cologne as a Hebrew teacher (1893). Together with Bodenheimer and David Wolffsohn, he founded a Jewish national society that formed the nucleus of the German Zionist Federation. Schach participated in the First Zionist Congress and helped to draw up the *Basle Program. Afterward he fell out with Theodor *Herzl and his associates and spent the following years in Karlsruhe and Berlin. During World War I he worked in Hamburg as the editor of newspapers and journals, including those which opposed Zionism. During his Zionist period he was one of the foremost propagandists of the Zionist cause and a prolific writer, especially in German (but also in Hebrew) on Zionism, Judaism, and the Hebrew and Yiddish languages. Among his works is *Volk-oder Salonjudentum* (1893). His sister MIRIAM (1867–1956) was a pioneer of political Zionism in France. She left her home in Lithuania in 1879, completed her studies at the Sorbonne in Paris, and taught the liberal arts and languages at various high schools in France. She played an important role, together with Max *Nordau, Alexander *Marmorek, and Bernard *Lazar, in putting Zionist ideas across to the French. She also helped to found the French Zionist newspaper, *L'Echo Sioniste* (published from 1900). During the last years of her life, she lived in Haifa. A Hebrew version by K.A. Bertini of her memoirs of the beginnings of the Zionist movement in France, titled *Asher Ittam Hithallakhti*, was published in 1951.

BIBLIOGRAPHY: L. Jaffe (ed.), *Sefer ha-Congress* (1950²), 201, 391–2; R. Lichtheim, *Toledot ha-Ẓiyyonut be-Germanyah* (1951), index.

[Getzel Kressel]

SCHACH, LEONARD LAZARUS (1918–1996), theatrical director and producer. Schach was born in Cape Town and early on showed an interest in the theater by serving as president of the amateur University Dramatic Society in 1939–42. In 1947–48 he undertook a world survey of national subsidized theater on behalf of the South African Department of Adult Education, resulting in the establishment of the National Theater Organization in 1948.

From 1948 to 1964 he directed over 200 productions in South Africa, including those of his own professional theater company (the Cockpit Players, later Leonard Schach Productions), founded in 1951.

Schach emigrated in 1965 to Israel, where he was invited to join the Cameri Theater as "resident guest director." In addition he directed for Habimah, the Haifa Municipal Theater, Zavit, Bimot, Giora Godick Productions, the Israel Philharmonic Orchestra and the Israel Chamber Ensemble Orchestra. He also directed plays and operas in England, the United States, Italy, and Belgium, and made the film *Cry in the Wind* in Greece.

Schach was the recipient of many awards, including the 1960 Cape Tercentenarian Award of Merit (1960), the Queen of England's Coronation Medal for services to the English theater (1953), the Drama Critics of Brussels award (for *After the Fall*, 1966), Israel's David's Harp award for best director of the year (*Birthday Party*, 1968), and the Breytenbach award of South Africa for best director of the year for his production of *Equus* (1976). He has also been granted the Freedom of the City of Cape Town for his theatrical activity.

BIBLIOGRAPHY: *Stage by Stage*, a biography by Donald Inskup (1977); Yearbook of National Theater and Art Councils.

[Louis Isaac Rabinowitz]

SCHACHNOWITZ, SELIG (1874–1952), Orthodox journalist and writer. Of Lithuanian origin, Schachnowitz served as cantor of the Swiss-Jewish rural community of Endingen between 1901 and 1908. In 1908 he began his work as editor of the *Israelit*, Germany's leading modern Orthodox newspaper, which appeared in Frankfurt am Main. He also taught at the Breuer yeshivah and was a prolific writer. In the main he depicted famous personalities in Jewish history, such as Don Abarbanel of Spain (1937), the leading figure at the time of the mass exodus (1492), Moses Schreiber of Pressburg (1933), Maimonides (1935), and the mystical rabbi Seckel Loeb Wormser of Michelstadt (1912). He also wrote about Jewish folkways of Galicia (1910), the Khazars (1920), the Falashas (*Beta Israel) (1923), a proselyte to Judaism in Vilna (repr. 1943), retold the Bible, and wrote a sympathetic description of Ereẓ Israel in 1932, thus attenuating the hard-line anti-Zionist approach of Agudat Israel. In 1938 he managed to receive an immigrant permit for Switzerland, where he visited the many Jewish refugees in the camps. He helped give them the steadfastness to endure the hardship of their life. In 1952 his death in Zurich was widely deplored. Some of his books were translated into Yiddish and English. His retelling of the Bible was reprinted by the Zentralrat der Juden in Deutschland (1970).

BIBLIOGRAPHY: Kaufmann, Bibliographie, No. 1449.

[Uri Kaufmann (2nd ed.)]

SCHACHT, ALEXANDER (**Al**; "The Clown Prince of Baseball"; 1892–1984), U.S. baseball player and entertainer who performed in a battered top hat and a tattered tuxedo with tails, wielding a catcher's mitt that weighed 25 pounds. Schacht was born on the Lower East Side to Russian immigrants Ida, daughter of a rabbi, and Samuel, son of a prominent farmer and a skilled locksmith, who once made a set of iron doors for the White House for Teddy Roosevelt. Schacht was a pitcher for Commerce High School, but was expelled for accepting $4 to pitch a semi-pro game. He then started his career in 1910 playing for Walton in upstate New York. Schacht played for Cleveland in the outlawed Federal League, and in the International League for Newark and the Jersey City Giants, for whom he pitched 10 shutouts. Schacht was drafted into the army in World War I before making his Major League debut for the Washington Nationals on September 18, 1919, at the age of 26. At spring training the following year, he met Nick Altrock, himself a baseball clown, and the two formed a clowning partnership, though they did not like each other and later in their partnership never spoke to each other. A sore arm curtailed Schacht's career in less than two years, and he retired from playing with a record of 14–10 with a 4.48 ERA in 53 games. He continued as a coach and clown with Altrock, until Schacht left for Boston in 1934, and afterward he performed alone in an act that was part pantomime and part anecdotes. During rain delays he would plop down in a mud puddle with two bats, and pantomime rowing as if he were in a boat. He was also known for staging mock boxing and tennis matches on the field. Schacht performed at 25 World Series and 18 All-Star Games, and by his estimation entertained more than 70 million fans in his nearly five decades as an entertainer. During World War II, Schacht made three trips overseas with the USO, entertaining thousands of troops in Europe, Africa, and Asia. After the war, Schacht gave up touring and opened a restaurant on East 52nd St. in New York. He was the author of *Clowning Through Baseball* (1941); *Al Schacht Dope Book: Diamond Facts, Figures And Fun* (1944); *GI Had Fun* (1945); and *My Own Particular Screwball* (1955).

[Elli Wohlgelernter (2nd ed.)]

SCHACHTEL, HUGO-HILLEL (1876–1949), early Zionist and one of the heads of the *Jewish National Fund (JNF) in Germany. Born in Sulnierschuetz (now Sulmierzyce, Poland), Schachtel later settled in Breslau, where he completed his studies as a dentist. He began his activities in a Breslau Zionist society and offered his services to Theodor *Herzl shortly after the appearance of *Der Judenstaat*. In his reply (dated Nov. 19, 1896), Herzl asked him to set up propaganda societies in Poland. Schachtel spent the following decades active in Zionist affairs, both in the Breslau Zionist society and in the JNF. In 1904 he published a manual of information about Ereẓ Israel and the Zionist movement which ran through several editions (the fifth edition came out in 1924 under the title *Eretz-Israel Merkbuch*). He also compiled an index to the proceedings and a collection of the resolutions of the first seven Zionist Congresses (1905–06). In 1932 he settled in Haifa.

BIBLIOGRAPHY: N. Agmon (Bistritski; ed.), *Megillat ha-Adamah*, 2 (*Demuyot*; 1951), 199–200; G. Herlitz, *Ishim ba-Ẓiyyonut* (1965).

[Getzel Kressel]

SCHACHTER, CARL (1932–), U.S. music theorist; the most important practitioner of Schenkerian theory in his generation. Born in Chicago, Schachter studied piano and conducting in New York and focused on theory following his studies with Felix Salzer. Schachter was a professor in the Mannes School of Music, Queens College, the CUNY Graduate Center, and the Juilliard School of Music, and gave lectures and classes all over North America and Europe. Schachter's profound understanding of theory is best seen in his illuminating commentary on Schenker's *Free Composition* (*Journal of Music Theory*, 1981). He is best known for the textbooks which he coauthored: *Counterpoint in Composition* (with Felix Salzer, 1969) and *Harmony and Voice Leading* (with Edward Aldwell, 1978, 1989², 2003³). Schachter developed a complementary tool to voice-leading graphs: durational graphs, which indicate the normalized time-span of each event (at a given level). His essays focus on analysis of 18th- and 19th-century music. His most important essays were collected in *Unfoldings* (1999).

BIBLIOGRAPHY: J.N. Straus, "Introduction: A Dialogue between Author and Editor," in: *Unfoldings*. (1999).

[Yossi Goldenberg (2nd ed.)]

SCHACHTER, HERSCHEL (1917–), U.S. Orthodox. rabbi. Born in Brooklyn, New York, Schachter was ordained by the Rabbi Isaac Elchanan Theological Seminary in 1941. He served as rabbi of Agudath Shalom, Stamford, Conn., in 1940. During World War II, Schachter was a U.S. army chaplain and was the first Jewish chaplain to aid the survivors of Buchenwald. He arrived there on April 12, 1945, with General George Patton's Third Army.

Going from one barracks to the next, he declared in Yiddish, "*Sholom Alecheim Yidden, ihr zint frei*" (Hello Jews, you are free). He officiated at the first Friday night service after liberation and conducted a *seder* for the survivors. He established a *ḥevra kadisha* (burial society), and acquired a plot of land for a Jewish cemetery, organized a list of Jews in the camp and others who came through, set up a mail service and a package program.

After much discussion, he convinced the military to allow young people in Buchenwald to establish a kibbutz to prepare for life in Palestine. In this he worked with Chaplain Robert Marcus, another Orthodox rabbi. Marcus and Schachter each accompanied transports of Jewish children from Buchenwald to France.

He was appointed rabbi of the Mosholu Jewish Center, New York, in 1946. The neighborhood was amid a large and thriving Jewish community of the Bronx. At its peak more than 1,000 people crowded into the synagogue on the high holidays. His sermons were the topic of discussion. In 1956–57

Schachter was religious adviser to Jews fleeing from Hungary. He served as president of the Religious Zionists of America and chairman of the Conference of Presidents of Major American Jewish organizations, the first Orthodox rabbi to hold that position. He was able to maintain unity despite vast differences of ideology and politics. One person who worked closely with him, Jerry Goodman of the National Conference on Soviet Jewry, said "he was aware of the power that he had but it never changed him. He never forgot his roots were in the Bronx. And despite his national leadership he stayed in the Bronx and served the Jewish people from that perch." As the neighborhood changed and Jews moved out, Rabbi Schachter stayed. By the mid 1990s the synagogue was almost empty even on the High Holidays. The synagogue closed in 2000, not because it lacked for funds – they could have easily be raised – but because there were no Jews. They had left for Riverdale, for Westchester, they were elsewhere.

Rabbi Schachter's son, Jacob J. *Schachter is a prominent Orthodox rabbi who for many years was the rabbi of the Jewish Center in Manhattan's West Side, a thriving Jewish community.

BIBLIOGRAPHY: A. Grobman, *Battling for Souls* (2004).

[Jeanette Friedman (2nd ed.)]

SCHACHTER, JACOB J. (1950–), U.S. Orthodox rabbi. Schachter was born into a prominent rabbinic family; his father was Rabbi Herschel *Schachter who was among the first to enter Buchenwald after liberation and who served as rabbi of the Moshula Jewish Center and as chairman of the Conference of Presidents of Major American Jewish Organizations. Jacob Schachter graduated from Brooklyn College in 1973, *summa cum laude* and Phi Beta Kappa, winning the Abraham S. Goodhartz Award for Excellence in Judaic Studies. He was ordained at Mesivta Torah Vodaath that same year. He then went to Harvard, where he was a teaching fellow from 1978 to 1980 and from which he received his Ph.D. in Near Eastern Languages in 1981. He became rabbi of the Jewish Center in Manhattan, one of the most prestigious Orthodox congregations in the world, where Rabbis Norman *Lamm and Leo *Jung had served. Mordecai *Kaplan had also been there in the early 20th century during the waning years of his service as an Orthodox rabbi. Under Schachter's leadership, the synagogue grew from almost 200 to nearly 600 families – with close to 1,000 participants in services on Sabbath mornings. Among his other activities while at the Jewish Center, he directed Yeshiva University's Torah u-Madda Project from 1986 to 1997, and was an adjunct assistant professor at the Stern College for Women at Yeshiva University from 1993 to 1999. In 1995, he was awarded the prestigious Daniel Jeremy Silver Fellowship from the department of Near Eastern languages and civilizations, Harvard University. He also served as a member of the faculties of The Wexner Heritage Foundation (from 1992) and The Wexner Foundation (from 1995). He was a member of the editorial boards of the magazines *Tradition* and *Jewish Action*, served on the board of governors of the Orthodox Union, and was the founding president of the Council of Orthodox Jewish Organizations of the Upper West Side (1994–2000).

Perhaps tired of the pulpit and seeking to move closer to academic life, he shocked many when he left the Jewish Center to become dean of the newly founded Rabbi Joseph B. Soloveitchik Institute in Boston in 2000. The institute is dedicated to perpetuating the teachings of Rabbi Soloveitchik as a force within the Orthodox community and as a model for all Jews. Guided by the integrity of *halakhah*, Jewish tradition, and meaningful engagement with general culture, the institute is intended to enhance Jewish study and actively develop Jewish leadership for the contemporary world.

He returned to New York in 2005 to become professor of Jewish History and Thought and Senior Scholar at the Center for the Jewish Future at Yeshiva University. His appointment was seen as a signal by the new president of Yeshiva University that he wanted to reinvigorate the college, and to stress the twin goals of Yeshiva University. As a university professor, Schachter was asked to develop multidisciplinary initiatives in various academic units of the university. The position of Senior Scholar enabled Schachter to play a prominent role in the new center's development and to shape the Orthodox world for contemporary Orthodox Jews who are sophisticated, intelligent, and rooted professionally and culturally in the secular world while living traditional Jewish lives.

He took up the battle for a different type of synthesis within contemporary Orthodoxy. Writing in the student newspaper, Schachter said: "By 'synthesis' we must understand not a co-existence of equals but an integrated system of religious and secular ideas based on the eternal verities of our religion. We begin our career here with the basic postulates of Orthodox Judaism. Then, as we continue our studies, we fit the secular ideas into the religious pattern, thus broadening our understanding and enriching our religious life."

As a scholar, Schachter was the founding editor of The *Torah u-Madda Journal* and editor of *Reverence, Righteousness and Rahamanut: Essays in Memory of Rabbi Dr. Leo Jung* (1992), *Jewish Tradition and the Nontraditional Jew* (1992), and the award-winning *Judaism's Encounter with Other Cultures: Rejection or Integration?* (1997). He was also the co-editor of the Orthodox Union's *Siddur Nechamas Yisrael: The Complete Service for the Period of Bereavement* (1995). He was the co-author, with fellow YU Professor Jeffrey Gurrock, of the award-winning *A Modern Heretic and a Traditional Community: Mordecai M. Kaplan, Orthodoxy, and American Judaism*, which traces Kaplan's disillusionment with Orthodoxy while rabbi at the Jewish Center (1996), and author of close to 50 articles and reviews in Hebrew and English.

[Michael Berenbaum (2nd ed.)]

SCHACHTER-SHALOMI, ZALMAN (1924–), U.S. rabbi and leader of the Jewish Renewal. Schachter-Shalomi was born in Zholkiew, Poland, and educated in Vienna, Austria, at the gymnasium Brit Bilu Agudah and Yeshiva Yesod Ha-Torah. In 1938 he and his family fled to Antwerp, Belgium, to avoid

Nazi capture, where he had his first contact with Chabad Hasidim. In April 1940 his family was interned in a labor camp in Vichy, France. In September 1940 they were freed, and he moved to Marseilles, France. In 1947 he received rabbinical ordination from Central Yeshiva Tomchei T'mimim (Chabad) in Brooklyn, New York. In 1962 he and counterculture guru Timothy Leary experimented with LSD at the Vendanta Center in Massachusetts. In 1968 he earned a DHL from Hebrew Union College in Cincinnati, Ohio. Beginning as a Chabad emissary in 1969, he founded B'nei Or (later the alliance for Jewish Renewal) and was promoted to full professor at the University of Manitoba in Saskatchewan, Canada, where he taught from 1969 to 1975, serving both as professor and Hillel director. He taught at Temple University from 1975 to 1987 and then at the Naropa Institute (later Naropa University) from 1995 to 2004.

Reb Zalman, as he became known, was a disciple of the sixth Lubavitcher Rebbe and served as one of the first emissaries of the seventh rebbe (Menachem Mendel *Schneersohn) in the late 1940s. Together with his colleague Rabbi Shlomo *Carlebach, Schachter-Shalomi revolutionized American Jewry by translating ḥasidic spirituality into a counter-cultural language.

Dissatisfied with the insular nature of post-war ḥasidic Judaism yet committed to the ḥasidic vision he gleaned from its texts, he left the formal community of Lubavitch yet transformed ḥasidic outreach into a non-Orthodox post-halakhic Jewish pietism that was at once universal, highly ritualistic, and unabashedly heterodox (some would say heretical). Kabbalistic and ḥasidic Judaism served as the groundwork for his new Judaism that advocated absorbing other spiritual disciplines into itself to enhance a contemplative Judaism for a "new age." He formulated what he called a paradigm shift, drawing from the medieval kabbalistic works of *Sefer Temunah* and *Sefer Ha-Peliah* (and their Shabbatean and ḥasidic interpreters) that presented a model of changing cosmic eons, reflected in historical epochs each of which required a "new Torah."

[Shaul Magid (2nd ed.)]

SCHACHT PLAN, Nazi plan to finance Jewish emigration from Germany, conceived in the wake of the **Kristallnacht* by Hjalmar Schacht, minister of economics and president of the Reichsbank, and Hans Fishboeck, state secretary in the Reich Ministry of Finance. The plan was in consonance with two major goals of German policy prior to the "Final Solution" – the forced emigration of Jews and the expropriation of their property. This plan was not the first suggestion of a policy of mutual interest, beneficial to both the German state and to a significantly lesser extent to the Jews – though the possibility of emigration was of inestimable value the longer the Nazis were in power. In 1933, the *Haavara agreement was struck, enabling Jews to leave Germany and go to Palestine with at least some assets. Under the Schacht plan, those German Jews wishing to emigrate could not take their property with them, for it had been confiscated by the Reich authorities, who compensated them with government bonds at the lowest interest. The planners tried to capitalize on the concern shown by foreign Jewish bodies and international refugee organizations and link the facility of transfer of Jewish assets to the promotion of German exports. They wanted foreign Jewish bodies to raise a loan of RM 1,500,000 in foreign currency (then equivalent to $600,000) to enable the resettlement of emigrants. Other essentials of the plan called for placing 25% of the Jewish property in Germany and Austria in a trust fund. The assets were to be gradually converted into cash and transferred only if Germany's foreign exchange would permit, or sooner in the form of "supplementary" exports. The remaining 75% was to remain at Germany's disposal to be used to maintain Jews before their emigration or those unable to emigrate. This fund was to finance the emigration of 150,000 able-bodied Jews and 250,000 dependents in the course of three years. Schacht claimed that *Hitler and *Goering had assented to his plan. *Ribbentrop opposed it for personal and political reasons and did his best to frustrate it. To implement it, Schacht negotiated with George Rublee, the director of the Intergovernmental Committee of Refugees, who had formerly conceived his own plan for linking emigration to German exports, with the Reich as the debtor of the foreign loan, but agreed to the emigrants being the debtors. Rublee's committee planned to proceed through two committees, one on a governmental level and the second of private individuals. Jewish leaders approached by Rublee opposed the second committee, to give the lie to the Nazi propaganda of a world Jewish financial body. They believed that the whole problem should he considered by governments exclusively. The experts of the governments concerned with Jewish immigration objected to making confiscated Jewish property the basis for increasing German exports. Rublee ran into further difficulty in finding governments that were ready to accept Jewish immigrants in great numbers. Schacht was dismissed at the beginning of 1939, but the Nazis continued the negotiations. Rublee, who sincerely believed in the plan as a means to help the Jews, resigned because of the difficulties he encountered. The negotiations between his successors and the Nazi government dragged on until their disruption with the outbreak of World War II, when emigration became impossible.

BIBLIOGRAPHY: Documents on German Foreign Policy 1918–1945, series D, vol. 5 (1953), 900–940; J. Tenenbaum in: *Yad Vashem Studies* (1958), 70–77; A.D. Morse, *While 6 Million Died* (1967), 197–203; L.L. Strauss, *Man and Decisions* (1963), 103–9; D.A. Cheson, *Morning and Noon* (1965), 126–30.

[Yehuda Reshef / Michael Berenbaum (2nd ed.)]

SCHAECHTER, JOSEPH (1901–), educator and Hebrew writer. Born in Galicia, he was ordained for the rabbinate and studied at Vienna University. Schaechter immigrated to Ereẓ Israel in 1938, and taught in secondary schools, first in Tel Aviv and then in Haifa. From 1951 he was the supervisor of secondary schools in Haifa. Disturbed by the gap between

Orthodoxy and secularism in Israel society, Schaechter tried to turn Israel non-Orthodox youth back to its Jewish heritage. He sought to achieve this by approaching the Bible and Talmud as a philosophy of life. Schaechter felt that modern man was uprooted and cynical in the technological world, because he had forgotten to invest life with meaning and to look within himself. This inner search was the heritage of Israel. In his *Pirkei Hadrakhah ba-Tanakh* (1960) he showed the failings of both the Orthodox and non-orthodox education systems, the one teaching Bible as a book of *mitzvot*, the other as an archaeological guide book. Besides contributing to various literary periodicals, he wrote books on such varied topics as logic, science and faith, Talmud, and the prayer book.

His books include *Mavo Kaẓar le-Logistikah* (1937), *Sintaksis* (1944), *Mi-Madda le-Emunah* (1953), *Mavo la-Talmud* (1954), *Mishnato shel A.D. Gordon* (1957), *Mavo la-Siddur* (1958), *Oẓar ha-Talmud* (1963), *Mavo la-Tanakh* (1968), and several works on education, including *Limmudei ha-Yahadut ba-Ḥinnukh ha-Al-Yesodi* (1968), a summary of Schaechter's teachings by his students.

BIBLIOGRAPHY: S. Kremer, *Hillufei Mishmarot be-Sifrutenu* (1959), 348–53; H. Weiner, *Wild Goats of Ein Gedi* (1961), 262–6; J.S. Diamond, in: *The Reconstructionist*, 30 (Dec. 25, 1964), 17–24. 17–24.

[Getzel Kressel]

SCHAECHTER, MORDKHE (1927–), Yiddish linguist, author, editor, and educator. Born in Cernauti, Romania (now Chernivtsy, Ukraine), Schaechter, who went to the U.S. in 1951, was a leading Yiddishist, both in promoting the maintenance of the language and in adapting it through language planning to modern life and technology. Coeditor of the Territorialist bimonthly *Oyfn Shvel*, published by the Freeland League, he contributed to various other Yiddish publications, and collaborated with M. *Weinreich in the writing of *Yidisher Ortografisher Vegvayzer* (1961). Chief interviewer of *The Language and Culture Atlas of Ashkenazic Jewry* (1992–2000), he also wrote books and articles on Yiddish dialectology, toponymy, terminology, style, and grammar. His *Elyokem Zunzer's Verk* (published by the *YIVO Institute in 1964) has been acclaimed as the best critical edition of a Yiddish writer and his works. Schaechter participated in various institutions and foundations promoting the Yiddish language, and was instrumental in organizing some: he was a prime mover in the creation of the youth movement, Yugntruf – Youth for Yiddish (1963). From 1962 he taught Yiddish at the Jewish Teachers' Seminary and, from 1968, at both Yeshiva University and Columbia University in New York.

BIBLIOGRAPHY: LNYL, vol. 8.

[Leybl Kahn]

SCHAECHTER-GOTTESMAN, BELLA (1920–), artist, Yiddish poet, and songwriter. Schaechter-Gottesman was born Beyle Schaechter in Vienna, the daughter of Lifshe Gottesman, and Benjamin Schaechter. The family moved to Cernauti, Romania (Czernowitz, now part of the Ukraine), when Beyle was 18 months old. She attended school where instruction was in Romanian, also learning French and Latin, spoke Yiddish at home, and German or Ukrainian around town. Home was full of music, as her mother knew a large folk song repertoire and had a wonderful voice. Years later, Lifshe Schaechter-Widman recorded songs in the United States and wrote a memoir, *Durkhgelebt a Velt: Zikhroynes* (1973).

In 1938, Beyle's two years of study at the Vienna art school was cut short when Hitler invaded Austria. Using her Romanian passport, she returned to her family in Cernauti, only to spend the war years in her hometown under dire circumstances. In February 1941, she married Jonas Gottesman, a physician, with whom she ultimately had three children. They wound up in the Cernauti ghetto with the other Jews, but her husband arranged authorization for them to remain in the area, and thus they survived the war. After the war, Beyle and her family settled briefly in Vienna before coming to New York City in 1951.

Schaechter-Gottesman started her theatrical and literary career with works for children, writing musical plays and puppet shows for the Scholem Aleichem Yiddish School in New York. She edited a children's magazine, *Kinder Zhurnal,* from 1972 to 1982, and founded and edited the magazine by children, *Enge Benge*. Her first book of poetry was *Mir Forn* in 1963, followed by *Stezhkes Tsvishn Moyern: Lider* ("Footpaths Amidst Stonewalls: Poems," 1972) and *Sharey Lider* ("Sunrise Poetry," 1980). Another book of poetry, *Lider* (1995), was published in both English and Yiddish. *Perpl Shlengt zikh der veg: Lider* ("Winding Purple Road," 2002) also featured her drawings.

Her outpouring of musical song started to see publication in the 1990s, with *Zumerteg: Tsvantsik Zinglider* ("Summer Days: Twenty Songs," 1990) and *Fli mayn flishlang! Kinderlider mit Musik* ("Fly My Kite!" 1999); recordings of her songs also appeared: *Zumerteg New Yiddish Songs* (1991) and *Af di Gasn Fun Shtot* ("On the Streets of the City," 2003). Her bilingual children's book *Mume blume di Makhsheyfe* ("Aunt Bluma, the Witch," 2000) has been translated into numerous languages. She performed Yiddish folk songs on *Bay Mayn Mames Shtible* ("At My Mother's House," 2004). Schaechter-Gottesman was awarded the People's Hall of Fame Award from the Museum of the City of New York (1998) and the Osher Tshushinsky Award from the Congress for Jewish Culture (1994).

With the rekindled interest in Yiddish culture and klezmer music during the 1970s and 1980s, Schaechter-Gottesman participated in popular cultural festivals and workshops such as the Yiddish Folk Arts Workshop ("Klezkamp"), Buffalo on the Roof, Klezkanada, Ashkenaz Festival, and Weimar Klezmerwochen, spreading the knowledge of her music.

[Judith S. Pinnolis (2nd ed.)]

°**SCHAEFFER, CLAUDE F.A.** (1898–1982), French archaeologist. He was curator of the French National Museums and the Museum of Antiquities (1933); director of research of the Centre National de la Recherche Scientifique (1946); and professor of European prehistory and national archaeology at the Ecole du Louvre (1951) and at the College of France (1954). He directed a number of French archaeological missions in Italy, Turkey, Egypt, and especially at Ras Shamra in Syria and Enkomia-Alasia in Cyprus.

Schaeffer is principally remembered as the excavator of Ras Shamra (see *Ugarit), one of the most remarkable archaeological discoveries of the 20th century bearing directly upon the language and literature of the Hebrew Bible. He examined the importance of Ras Shamra for the understanding of the literature, archaeology, history, and theology of Israel and its surroundings.

The religion of Ras Shamra and the form and quality of Canaanite poetry are compared with the Bible in his 1936 Schweich Lectures of the British Academy, published in 1939 as *The Cuneiform Texts of Ras Shamra-Ugarit*. The authoritative reports directly covering the expeditions at Ras Shamra published under his direction include *La… campagne de fouilles à Ras Shamra-Ugarit* (17 vols. (1929–55); *Ugaritica* (4 vols., 1939–62), and *Le Palais Royal d'Ugarit*, containing the texts from the different literary archives of the royal palace at Ras Shamra (1955).

[Zev Garber]

SCHAEFFER, HANS (1886–1967), German government official. Born in Breslau, Schaeffer began to practice law in 1912. He served with the German armed forces during World War I and, when demobilized early in 1919, was appointed to the German Ministry of Economic Affairs. At first engaged in drafting the economic provisions of the Weimar Constitution, he was promoted in 1923 to undersecretary and shifted to international economic affairs. German reparations became his principal field. In 1929, during the beginnings of the world economic depression, he joined the Ministry of Finance, where he became instrumental in overcoming the German banking crisis and relieving Germany of its war debt. In 1932 he left government service to become president of the *Ullstein publishing house, but in 1933 the Nazi government forced his dismissal. Subsequently he worked together with Allen Dulles and Jean Monnet on the liquidation of the Swedish Kreuger Match Combine, and in 1936 he became the Combine's adviser and moved to Sweden, where he lived until his death. Schaeffer took an interest in Jewish affairs, particularly after Hitler's rise to power. He participated in the formation of the *Reichsvertretung der deutschen Juden and was in contact with the Jewish representatives at the *Evian Conference. Schaeffer kept a diary which represents an important source for German economic history from the 1920s to the 1960s.

BIBLIOGRAPHY: S. Adler-Rudel, in: BLBI, 10 (1967), 159–215; S. Kaznelson, *Juden im deutschen Kulturbereich* (1959), 582; *New York Times* (March 25, 1967), 23. **ADD. BIBLIOGRAPHY:** E. Wandel, *Hans Schaeffer* (1974).

[Joachim O. Ronall]

SCHAFER, STEPHEN (1911–1976), criminologist and sociologist. Born in Hungary, Schafer was professor of criminology at Budapest University (1947–51), chairman of the Hungarian prison commission, and president of the supervising board of delinquency. He left Hungary in 1956 and became a consultant to the British Home Office research unit. In 1961, Schafer immigrated to the U.S. and taught successively at the Florida State, Ohio, and Northeastern universities, and served as a consultant to the President's Commission on Law Enforcement and Administration of Justice.

Schafer's principal book in English was *Restitution to Victims of Crime* (1960), a problem on which he became a leading expert. Some of his other works, as a preeminent researcher in the field of victimology, include *The Victim and His Criminal* (1968), *Theories in Criminology* (1969), *Juvenile Delinquency* (1970), *The Political Criminal: The Problem of Morality and Crime* (1974), *Social Problems in a Changing Society* (1975), and *Introduction to Criminology* (1976[2]).

[Zvi Hermon / Ruth Beloff (2nd ed.)]

SCHAFF, ADAM (1913–), Polish philosopher of Jewish origin; the dominant figure in Marxist philosophy in Poland from the assumption of power by the Communist government in 1945. Born in Lvov, he studied in the Soviet Union. He returned to become professor of philosophy at the Warsaw University and director of the Institute of Philosophy at the Polish Academy of Science. At first of orthodox views, he nevertheless engaged in active and mutually respectful debate and development with the eminent Polish school of logic and epistemology (Ajdukiewicz, Kotarbinski, Ingarden, among others), and later also with Marxists influenced by existentialist and other non-Marxist philosophical thought (the most important being Kolakowski). Schaff wrote many works, from initial studies in the theory of truth to later works on semantics, on the nature of historical explanation, on the role of language in cognition, on ethics in private and in social life, and on the still uncompleted tasks of Marxist philosophy, for which his chief work is *Marksyzm i jednostka ludzka* (1965; *Marxism and the Human Individual*, 1970). Other books appearing in English are *Alienation as a Social Phenomenon, Language and Cognition*, and *History and Truth*. Schaff had wide influence within the eastern European countries, and also among American and western European thinkers on sociological and philosophical matters, perhaps most practically through work with UNESCO. During the period of active pressure against Jews in Poland in 1968, Schaff's official positions in the Polish university and academy hierarchy were greatly reduced in scope and authority, and he ceased to be a member of the Central Committee of the Communist Party of Poland. However, through all the upheavals in Poland he managed to maintain his status as an influential thinker.

[Robert S. Cohen]

SCHAFFHAUSEN, canton and its capital city in N. Switzerland. The earliest record of Jews in the canton is dated 1291. The Jews were burned there during the excesses of 1349, and in 1401 all the Jews in the city were condemned to death and 30 were burned. The Jews were expelled from the canton in 1475. Individual Jews who visited the canton during the 16th to 18th centuries were refused the right of residence. Jews of nearby southern German rural communitites (Gailingen, Randegg, Worblingen and Wangen) appeared on weekdays doing business as livestock traders and peddlers. In 1865 the laws restricting Jewish settlement were repealed, and by 1874 full emancipation was granted. However, few Jews settled there. A *minyan* existed in the 1920s.

BIBLIOGRAPHY: F. Guggenheim-Gruenberg, *Die Juden in der Schweiz* (1961); A. Weldler-Steinberg, *Geschichte der Juden in der Schweiz* (1966), index; Germ Jud, 2 (1968), 740–2.

[Uri Kaufmann (2nd ed.)]

SCHAKOWSKY, JANICE D. ("**Jan**"; 1944–), member of the U.S. House of Representatives, serving the 9th District of Illinois from 1999. "We need more Jan Schakowskys," *New York Magazine* declared, noting that the congresswoman from Illinois represents the future of Democratic progressive politics.

Born in Chicago, Schakowsky, a citizen advocate, grassroots organizer, and elected public official, fought throughout her career for economic and social justice and improved quality of life for all; for an end to violence against women; and for a national investment in healthcare, public education, and housing needs.

She carried on the legacy of her predecessor, Sid Yates, representing a district that is incredibly diverse, stretching from the liberal lakefront through some of Chicago's ethnic neighborhoods, encompassing Devon Avenue and extending to O'Hare International Airport. She picked up his mantle of leadership, especially regarding his support for Israel and the United States Holocaust Memorial Museum.

Schakowsky, who served on the House Democratic Leadership team as chief deputy whip, was a member of the Energy and Commerce Committee, where she was ranking member of the Subcommittee on Commerce, Trade, and Consumer Protection; she also served on the Subcommittee on Environment and Hazardous Materials and the Subcommittee on Oversight and Investigations.

Schakowsky won major legislative victories to increase federal assistance for abused women and children and to protect the rights of battered immigrant women, to reform election laws guaranteeing that no registered voter is turned away at the poll, to expand housing opportunities for low-income people, and to assist small business owners and farmers. Schakowsky worked in Congress to safeguard the rights of victims of identity theft and to protect consumers from predatory lenders. A champion for the nation's seniors, Schakowsky was actively engaged in the campaign for seniors and persons with disabilities to access affordable prescription drugs. Schakowsky was also working to ensure that seniors receive quality home, hospice, and nursing care.

A graduate of the University of Illinois, Schakowsky was a longtime consumer rights advocate. She was responsible for a 1969 law requiring the printing of freshness dates on groceries. She was program director of Illinois Public Action, Illinois' largest public interest group, from 1976 to 1985, where she fought for energy reform and stronger protection from toxic chemicals. She then moved to the Illinois State Council of Senior Citizens as executive director, where she organized across the state for lower cost prescription drugs and tax relief for seniors, financial protection for the spouses of nursing home residents, and other benefits for the elderly. She held that position from 1985 until 1990, when she was elected to the Illinois House of Representatives. She served there for four terms until elected to the U.S. House of Representatives in 1998.

[Jill Weinberg (2nd ed.)]

SCHALIT, ABRAHAM CHAIM (1898–1979), historian. Born in Zolochev, Galicia, Schalit studied classics at Vienna University. He settled in Ereẓ Israel in 1929 and worked in various posts. In 1950 he became a lecturer in Jewish history at The Hebrew University, Jerusalem, and professor in 1957. His most important work was *Hordos ha-Melekh* ("King Herod," 1960) for which he received the Israel Prize for Jewish Studies (1960). The book was translated in an enlarged form into German, *Koenig Herodes* (1969). Not only a comprehensive study of Herod, it is also a brilliant analysis of the structure of Roman rule in Palestine, a subject to which Schalit had previously devoted his *Ha-Mishtar ha-Roma'i be-Ereẓ Yisrael* ("Roman Rule in Ereẓ Israel," 1937). Schalit's other important field of research was the writings of Josephus. In numerous articles he dealt with several aspects of the historian's method and sources; he also wrote an introduction to, and translated into Hebrew, Josephus' *Antiquities of the Jews* (Books 1–10, 1947; 11–20, 1963), as well as a concordance of all names appearing in Josephus' works, *Namenwoerterbuch zu Flavius Josephus* (1968). Schalit was divisional editor of the *Encyclopaedia Judaica* for the Second Temple period.

[Isaiah Gafni]

SCHALIT, HEINRICH (1886–1973), composer. Schalit was born in Vienna and studied at the musical conservatory there. He settled in Munich, where he worked as music teacher and as organist at the Great Synagogue. In 1933 he left Germany and was appointed organist at the Great Synagogue in Rome. He later emigrated to the U.S., where he was organist for congregations in Providence, Rhode Island, and Denver, Colorado. Among his sacred compositions are his *Friday Night Liturgy*, his *Hebrew Song of Praise*, and his setting of Psalm 98. He also wrote orchestral, chamber, and piano music, as well as songs.

SCHALIT, ISIDOR (1871–1953), first secretary of the Zionist Office and one of Herzl's first assistants. Born in Nowosolky, Ukraine, Schalit grew up in Vienna, where he qualified as a dentist. He was raised in an atmosphere of support for Ḥibbat

Zion, joined the student Zionist society *Kadimah in Vienna (1889), and was actively engaged in establishing a network of similar organizations in Austria. He was a member of the academic circle in Vienna that offered Herzl assistance on the publication of *Der Judenstaat*. On Whit Sunday 1896 Herzl wrote in his diary:

> Two fellows from the Kadimah, Schalit and Neuberger, called on me. They told me that a proposal was afoot to recruit a volunteer battalion of one or two thousand and to attempt a landing at Jaffa. Even if some might have to give up their lives in the attempt, Europe would start paying attention to the aspirations of the Jews. I advised them against this fine Garibaldian idea.

Herzl made Schalit a member of the editorial board of *Die Welt*, but shortly afterward, at the outbreak of the Turko-Greek War (1897), Schalit set out at the head of a delegation of five medical student volunteers to provide first aid on the Turkish front, a venture which was intended to gain Turkish sympathy for Herzl's proposals. Afterward Schalit was the main technical organizer of the First Zionist Congress at Basle (1897). He flew the Zionist flag from the Basle Casino and did it again at the 1937 Congress, which celebrated in Basle the 40th anniversary of the First Congress. He also signaled the opening of the First Congress by knocking with a hammer on the table of the chairman, an act which he performed at all subsequent Congresses – down to the first Congress in the State of Israel in 1951. After the First Congress he was appointed secretary of the Zionist Office, a post he filled during Herzl's lifetime. With the transfer of the Zionist center to Cologne, after Herzl's death, he was elected head of the Zionist Organization in Austria. From then on he was active in the Austrian and the World Zionist Organizations. In 1938 he settled in Palestine, where he published memoirs of the beginnings of political Zionism (in *Haolam*, *Davar*, etc.).

BIBLIOGRAPHY: T. Herzl, *Complete Diaries*, 5 (1960), index; J. Levi, *Isidor Schalit* (Heb., 1951), Tidhar, 3 (1949), 1443–46.

[Getzel Kressel]

SCHALLY, ANDREW VICTOR (1926–), medical research worker and Nobel laureate. Schally was born in Wilno, Poland (now Vilnius, Lithuania), and became a U.S. citizen in 1962. At the outset of World War II, his father, a professional soldier, left his family to fight with the Allied forces. Schally survived the war in Romania and immigrated to the U.K. in 1945. He was educated at Bridge of Allan School in Scotland and received his B.Sc. in chemistry from London University. After a period at the Medical Research Council's National Institute for Medical Research at Mill Hill, London (1950–52), he moved to Canada where he gained his Ph.D. in chemistry at McGill University under the supervision of Dr. M. Saffran (1952–57). He joined the department of physiology at Baylor University College of Medicine in Houston, Texas (1957–62). In 1962 he moved for the rest of his career to New Orleans as chief of the Endocrine and Polypeptide Laboratories at the Veterans Administration Hospital, where he became a senior medical investigator (1973), and a member of the faculty of medicine at Tulane University, where he became professor of medicine in 1967. Schally's interest in medical research in general began at Mill Hill, and in endocrinology at McGill. He was early convinced that the hypothalamus in the brain produces hormones which regulate the pituitary gland, and hence the production of hormones by the thyroid and adrenal glands, and also the hormones which control growth and reproductive capacity. His initially controversial ideas were vindicated by a long and laborious series of experiments necessary to isolate sufficient material with which to characterize hormones produced by the hypothalamus and to demonstrate their actions. His research established the central role of the brain in controlling the endocrine system through the pituitary gland. It has immense implications for devising new strategies for birth control and suppressing hormone-dependent cancers. Indeed he has been consistently motivated to find clinical applications for his discoveries. In later work he was especially interested in developing novel antitumor peptides. Schally worked with close colleagues for most of his career in New Orleans and collaborated with many scientists and clinicians worldwide, and especially with clinical endocrinologists in the U.K. By 2005 he was an author of 2,200 papers, and he continued to be scientifically productive. He was awarded the Nobel Prize in physiology or medicine jointly with Roger Guillemin and Rosalyn *Yalow (1977). His many other honors include membership of the U.S. National Academy of Sciences, the Gairdner Award (1974), and the Lasker Award in Basic Medical Science (1975). He married Dr. Ana Maria de Medeiros-Comaru (1976), a distinguished Brazilian endocrinologist and his collaborator before her death (2004). Schally had a lifelong passion for soccer and as a young man contemplated a career in this sport.

[Michael Denman (2nd ed.)]

SCHAMA, SIMON (1945–), British-American historian. Schama was educated at Cambridge University, where he taught from 1966 to 1976. He subsequently taught at Oxford and then in the United States, where he became a professor at Harvard and, later, Columbia University. He wrote important works on Dutch history, such as *Patriots and Liberators: Revolution in the Netherlands, 1780–1813* (1977) and *An Embarrassment of Riches: An Interpretation of Dutch Culture in the Golden Age* (1987), as well as a bestselling account of the French Revolution, *Citizens: A Chronicle of the French Revolution* (1989). Schama also wrote widely on art, in such works as *Rembrandt's Eyes* (1999), and was the art critic of *The New Yorker* magazine in 1995–98. He is probably best-known for the 16-part history of Britain he made for the BBC, which was watched by millions of viewers and became a bestselling three-volume work, *A History of Britain* (2000–3). Schama also wrote on Jewish history, *The Rothschilds and the Land of Israel* (1978).

[William D. Rubinstein (2nd ed.)]

SCHAMES, SAMSON (1898–1967), U.S. artist. Born in Frankfurt, Schames studied at the Staedelschule. He designed stage sets for several German theaters, and for the Jewish theater, which was founded in 1933. Although Schames had settled in Britain in 1938 to flee the Nazis, the British government interned him and other perceived potential German threats to national security in 1940 in Huyton Alien Internment Camp, near Liverpool. Other residents of the camp included Martin *Bloch and John *Heartfield. Here, Schames used debris, often grayed from bombardments, to fashion abstract collages and mosaics. In 1948 he immigrated to New York. He exhibited his work in a show in Germany in 1955. In 1989, Schames received a large posthumous exhibition at the Jewish Museum in Frankfurt. An expressionist, he endowed whatever he painted with explosive spontaneity displayed through stark, spiky strokes. He was a nephew of the Frankfurt gallery owner Ludwig Schames (1852–1922), who exhibited the Expressionists. His work has been exhibited internationally, in such institutions as the Bezalel National Museum, Jerusalem; the Leo Baeck Institute, New York; and the Walker Art Gallery, Liverpool, among other places.

BIBLIOGRAPHY: Bezalel National Museum (Jerusalem), *Samson Schames: 29.9–22.10, 1959; Watercolours and Mixed Media* (1959); Juedisches Museum (Frankfurt am Main), *Samson Schames 1898–1967. Bilder und Mosaiken* (1989).

SCHANBERG, SYDNEY H. (1934–), U.S. journalist. Born in Clinton, Massachusetts, Sydney Hillel Schanberg graduated from Harvard University. He joined the staff of *The New York Times* in the late 1950s and covered local news before becoming Albany bureau chief, where he covered the activities of Gov. Nelson A. Rockefeller and the New York State legislature. His first foreign assignment for the *Times* took him to India and Pakistan during the late 1960s and early 1970s, with side trips to cover the Vietnam War. But after the end of the war Schanberg heard about the American bombing of Cambodia, which President Richard M. Nixon and Secretary of State Henry A. *Kissinger denied. In Cambodia, Schanberg covered the emergence of the Khmer Rouge, a secretive revolutionary group that conducted genocide against the Cambodian people, particularly the educated. Schanberg chose to stay in Cambodia in 1975 after the Americans were thrown out of the country, partly to report the story and partly to help his assistant, Dith Pran, and his family survive. Schanberg failed to save Pran, who managed to elude his captors for several years by working in rice fields, but Schanberg finally had to flee. His report of the mass murders committed by the Khmer Rouge for the purpose of cleansing Cambodia provided a chilling story of a death machine. Schanberg's reports earned him the Pulitzer Prize in 1976. The dramatic story, told in the book *The Death and Life of Dith Pran*, and the reunion of Schanberg and Pran were made into a film, *The Killing Fields*, in 1984, that won three Academy Awards. Schanberg returned to the *Times* a year after the Pulitzer and shortly thereafter became metropolitan editor. But he was not an effective administrator and he was replaced, becoming a columnist. After a while, Schanberg became a columnist for *New York Newsday*, commenting on a wide variety of topics, including events in New York City. When that paper folded, Schanberg joined *The Village Voice* in New York, where he wrote the Press Clips column. He was a strong opponent of the Bush administration and its war in Iraq. He also took to task Senator John Kerry in 1993 for his alleged drive to normalize relations with Hanoi.

[Stewart Kampel (2nd ed.)]

SCHANFARBER, TOBIAS (1862–1942), U.S. Reform rabbi. Born in Cleveland, the son of Aaron and Sarah (Newman), he graduated from the University of Cincinnati (B.A.) in 1885 and received rabbinic ordination at the Hebrew Union College in 1886. Following ordination Schanfarber officiated at Shomer Emunim Congregation in Toledo (1886–87), Congregation Achduth Vesholom in Ft. Wayne (1887–88), Har Sinai Congregation in Baltimore (1888–98), and Congregation Sha'arai Shomayim in Mobile (1899–1901), before spending the bulk of his career (1901–26) at Kehilath Anshe Mayriv in Chicago. Upon his retirement he was named rabbi emeritus at KAM. During his tenure in Baltimore, from 1894 to 1898, he did post-graduate study in Semitics at Johns Hopkins University under Professor Paul Haupt. Schanfarber edited or co-edited numerous Jewish newspapers, including the *Mobile Jewish Chronicle, Baltimore Jewish Comment, Chicago Israelite, Sentinel,* and *Reform Advocate.* From 1907 to 1909 he served as corresponding secretary of the Central Conference of American Rabbis. Other organizational posts included being vice president of the Vigilance Association; a trustee of the Jewish People's Institute and the Michael Reese Hospital; and president (and later honorary life president) of the Chicago Rabbinical Association. Schanfarber was a member of the first generation of American trained rabbis and was a disciple of Isaac Mayer *Wise (1819–1900). Early in his career Schanfarber supported a radical form of Reform Judaism, including advocating Sunday instead of Sabbath services. In later years he adopted a more moderate approach to observance while rejecting what he called "secularism": i.e., removing God and Torah from Jewish life. He was called "a cultured gentleman, liberal in thought, though of great strength in his convictions, and a gifted orator on almost any subject which the public man is called upon to deal with." In 1933 he received an honorary Doctor of Hebrew Laws from HUC.

BIBLIOGRAPHY: *Who's Who in American Jewry, 1938–1939* (1938), 930–31; *The Advocate*, vol. 101, no. 6 (March 13, 1942) 1–4; *Central Conference of American Rabbis Yearbook*, vol. 52 (1942), 269–75.

[Kevin Proffitt (2nd ed.)]

SCHANKER, LOUIS (1903–1981), U.S. painter, printmaker, sculptor, and educator. Schanker's early adulthood experiences were varied: as an adolescent he worked in a circus, on farms in both the U.S. and Canada, and on the Erie Railroad. Between 1919 and 1923, he studied part-time at Cooper Union. Until 1927, he attended classes at the Art School of the Educational Alliance and the Art Students League. Working in the WPA mural division, he created wall panels in 1924 for a Long Island hospital, and exhibited murals at the Hall of Medicine and Public Health at the 1939 World's Fair. In 1931–32, he traveled to and studied in Paris and Mallorca. Between 1940 and 1941, he created woodcuts for the WPA Arts Project. He founded the group "The Ten" in 1935 with Adolph Gottlieb, Ilya Bolotowsky, and Ben-Zion, among others, with which he exhibited until 1939; The Ten concerned itself more with formal and artistic problems than with political tribulations. In 1936, Schanker assisted in the foundation of the American Abstract Artists group. The subjects of Schanker's art, including woodblock and linoleum prints and paintings, ranged among various subjects, especially sports, carnival, and religious subjects, such as St. George and the Dragon. His works of the late 1930s and 1940s, such as *Aerial Act* (1940), often featured graceful lines which coalesced into simple but expressive figures animated with flat, bright, areas of color. While the former composition owes much to Matisse and Miro, the monochromatic woodcut *Forms in Action* of the following year displays angular shapes, one perhaps dancing while another plays a keyboard or bass; this suggestion of speed and rhythm is indebted to the German and Austrian Expressionists, as well as to Japanese woodblock prints. Schanker's work reveals the artist's careful study of a variety of his contemporaries working in both the United States and Europe: Wasily Kandinsky, Arshile Gorky, Picasso, Max Ernst, Paul Klee, and George Rouault, among many others. In the 1960s, Schanker introduced the motif of a circle into his compositions, often combining it with other simple forms, and animating the whole with vibrant color. During this period, he also produced many primitivist wood sculptures influenced by Constantin Brancusi. Critics note that these sculptures were not a departure from his previous printmaking, since Schanker worked on his woodblocks with the tools of both sculptor and carpenter. Schanker taught at the New School for Social Research between 1943 and 1960. Between 1949 and 1964, he taught at Bard College. He made his home in New York City, Stamford, Connecticut, and East Hampton, New York. His art has been widely exhibited: at the Buchholz Gallery (1943), the Puma Gallery (1943), the Guggenheim Museum (1954), the Victoria and Albert Museum (1954–55), the Associated American Artists (1978), and the New York Public Library (2003). Examples of his work are in the collections of the Art Institute of Chicago, the Brooklyn Museum, the Metropolitan Museum of Art, the National Gallery of Art, the Philadelphia Museum of Art, and the Smithsonian American Art Museum.

BIBLIOGRAPHY: E. Genauer, "Quiet Pleasures of Serious Art," in: *New York Herald Tribune* (June 3, 1962), sec. 4, 6A; N. Kleeblatt and S. Chevlowe, *Painting a Place in America* (1991); O.Z. Soltes, *Fixing the World: Jewish American Painters in the Twentieth Century* (2003).

[Nancy Buchwald (2nd ed.)]

SCHANZER, CARLO (1865–1953), Italian politician. Born in Vienna, Schanzer became professor of constitutional law at the University of Rome. From 1912 to 1928 he was division chairman of the Consiglio di Stato – in Italy the main legal, administrative, and judiciary body. He was a member of Parliament and, from 1919, of the Senate. From 1906 to 1909, under the ministry of Giovanni Giolitti, Schanzer held the office of postmaster general, and he was minister of the treasury and finance in 1919 and foreign minister in 1922. From 1920 to 1924 Schanzer was the Italian representative to the League of Nations at Geneva. Between 1921 and 1922 he headed the Italian delegation to the Naval Conference in Washington, D.C., where Italy achieved naval equality with France. He died in Rome.

BIBLIOGRAPHY: *Enciclopedia Italiana*, vol. 31, 48–49.

[Massimo Longo Adorno (2nd ed.)]

SCHAPERA, ISAAC (1905–2003), South African anthropologist. Born in South Africa, Schapera taught at the London School of Economics as assistant in anthropology (1928–29), served as lecturer at the University of Witwatersrand, Johannesburg (1930), and at the University of Cape Town as senior lecturer and professor (1930–50). In 1950 he was appointed professor of anthropology at the London School of Economics. Schapera conducted several anthropological field expeditions to the Bechuanaland Protectorate between 1929 and 1950. He contributed to the discipline of applied anthropology by his study of labor migration in Bechuanaland – its causes and effects both positive and negative – and so served as a guide for colonial policy. From 1961 to 1963 he was president of the Royal Anthropological Institute.

He wrote *Government and Politics in Tribal Societies* (1956), *Handbook of Tswana Law and Custom* (1938, 1955^2), *Migrant Labour and Tribal Life* (1947), and edited *Bantu-Speaking Tribes of South Africa* (1937), and *David Livingstone's Letters and Journals*.

ADD. BIBLIOGRAPHY: S. Heald, "The Legacy of Isaac Schapira (1905–2003)," in: *Anthropology Today*, (Dec. 19, 2003), 18–19.

[Ephraim Fischoff]

SCHAPIRA, DAVID (1907–1977), Argentine politician. He was born in Carlos Casares at one of the agricultural settlements established in the province of Buenos Aires, Argentina, by the Jewish Colonization Association (ICA), founded by Baron Maurice de *Hirsch. Schapira practiced medicine and also was very active in national political life in the Unión Cívica Radical del Pueblo party. In 1958 he was elected senator in the province of Buenos Aires, serving until 1962. He was chairman of the Senate Public Health Committee. From 1963 to 1967 Schapira sat in the National Chamber of Deputies until the military regime of General Ongania closed the parliament.

SCHAPIRA, HERMANN (Ẓevi Hirsch; 1840–1898), one of the first leaders of *Ḥibbat Zion and political Zionism, originator of the ideas of the *Jewish National Fund and The Hebrew University. Born in Erswilken, Lithuania, Schapira displayed outstanding talents from early childhood. He became the rabbi and *rosh yeshivah* in a Lithuanian townlet. In 1866 he moved to Kovno, where he began his scientific and linguistic studies, and thence to Berlin in 1867 in order to pursue them further. After a period of hardship, hunger, and scholarly exertions, he was accepted as a student in a crafts' academy (Gewerbe Akademie), but was later obliged to return to Russia because of lack of means. He worked for a number of years as a clerk in commercial enterprises in Odessa and other cities to save money in order to return to his studies. The substantial sum he earned as a military supplier during the Russo-Turkish War (1877–78) finally made it possible for him to realize his ambition. Schapira went to Heidelberg, where he devoted himself to the study of mathematics and attracted academic notice by his achievements in this field. Among his publications was the mathematical work *Mishnat ha-Middot* in Hebrew ("The Study of Measures") and in German translation in 1880. In 1883 Schapira became university lecturer and in 1887 was appointed associate professor in higher mathematics.

After the pogroms in Russia in 1881, he had joined the Ḥibbat Zion movement, and published articles in *Ha-Meliẓ* in 1882 calling for the establishment of agricultural settlements in Ereẓ Israel, and the founding of a university with departments for training rabbis and secular teachers, as well as teaching theoretical and practical sciences (mathematics, astronomy, etc., and chemistry, agriculture, and industrial crafts). The language of instruction would be German, but Hebrew would be taught as much as possible so that "in the course of time Hebrew might become a spoken language as well." Schapira expressed his willingness to teach at this university and even contacted other Jewish scholars with this end in view. He was one of the founders of Ḥovevei Zion in Odessa, which became the center of all Ḥovevei Zion societies inside Russia and in other countries. In Heidelberg in 1884 he founded the Zion society for the settlement of Ereẓ Israel. The failure of the Ḥibbat Zion movement to awaken a widespread Jewish national movement or to initiate large-scale settlement in Ereẓ Israel caused Schapira to despair, and he withdrew from public and literary activities.

His status as a professor at Heidelberg University was insecure, and he felt isolated from his non-Jewish and even from his Jewish colleagues, the majority of whom were assimilated or even converted. His mathematical studies showed great talents but were unsystematically written and never fully completed. His economic circumstances were poor, and he was obliged to take on various other jobs to support himself, including watchmaking. After a period of doubt, Schapira embraced a religious philosophy and way of life. In Reuben Brainin's periodical *Mi-Mizraḥ u-mi-Ma'arav* ("From East and West") he published in 1894 two fragments from a book in which he tried to synthesize modern science with traditional Judaism. A group of Zionist students in Heidelberg roused Schapira to renewed activity. After initial hesitation he became an enthusiastic supporter of the new Zionist movement founded by *Herzl. To the First Zionist Congress (1897) he brought two proposals: the first was the creation of a "general Jewish fund," to which the whole of world Jewry, poor and rich, would contribute. Two-thirds of the fund would be assigned to purchasing land, and the remaining third would serve for the maintenance and cultivation of the land acquired. The land would not be sold but only leased for a period not exceeding 49 years. The second suggestion was the establishment of a Jewish university in Ereẓ Israel. Schapira's first proposal was accepted only by the Fifth Congress (1901), at which the Jewish National Fund was founded; his second proposal had to wait until the 11th Congress (1913).

Schapira devoted the last years of his life to the dissemination of the Zionist idea among German Jewry. He corresponded with Herzl and was active in the student group Safah Berurah in Heidelberg. In his last article, "*Shalom*," published posthumously, he wished that "God will let him live to teach the sons of His people in the school of Torah, wisdom, and labor which would be built in the Holy Land." His collected writings on Zionism, edited by B. Dinaburg (Dinur), were published in 1925. In 1953 his remains were re-interred on Mount Herzl in Jerusalem.

BIBLIOGRAPHY: L. Jaffe, *The Life of Hermann Schapira* (1939); I. Klausner, *Karka va-Ru'aḥ – Ḥayyav u-Fo'olo shel Hermann Schapira* (1966); B. Dinaburg, *Mefallesei Derekh* (1946), 62–69.

[Yehuda Slutsky]

SCHAPIRA, NOAH (1866–1931), Hebrew poet and labor leader in Ereẓ Israel before the Second Aliyah. Born in Kishinev, Schapira was an active member of the Ḥibbat Zion movement there together with Meir *Dizengoff. In 1890 he settled in Ereẓ Israel, where he became an agricultural laborer first in Reḥovot and later in Zikhron Ya'akov. He was the moving spirit behind the organization of Jewish workers that was founded at the end of the 19th century and remained in existence until the members of the Second Aliyah began to organize themselves. On behalf of this federation he negotiated both with employers and with Ḥovevei Zion leaders in Odessa, especially *Aḥad Ha-Am. He spent his last years in Tel Aviv. Schapira published articles on the affairs of the *yishuv* in the Hebrew press and was known especially for his poetry, which was, in effect, the first labor poetry to be written in Ereẓ Israel. His song "*Ya-Ḥai-Li-Li, Hah Amali*" and his Hebrew translation of E. *Zunser's song "*Ha-Maḥareshah*" were popular favorites for two generations. He signed these songs with the pseudonym "Bar-Nash."

BIBLIOGRAPHY: M. Ravina, "*Ya-Ḥai-Li-Li, Hah Amali*" *u-Meḥabbero* (1966).

[Getzel Kressel]

SCHAPIRO, ISRAEL (1882–1957), bibliographer, Orientalist, and librarian. Schapiro, born in Sejny, *Poland, was the son of R. Toviyyah Pesah Schapiro (1845–1924), a Hebrew and Yiddish writer and educator in *Russia and the U.S. Israel Schapiro studied at the Telsiai (Telz) Yeshivah, Strasbourg University, and the Hochschule (Lehranstalt) fuer die Wissenschaft des Judentums, Berlin. From 1907 to 1910 he taught at the Jerusalem Teachers' Training College and from 1911 to 1913 in New York, where he also coedited the Hebrew weekly *Ha-Deror*. From 1913 to 1944 he headed the newly created Semitic division of the Library of Congress, Washington, D.C., which he built up into a collection of over 40,000 volumes, including incunabula and other rare editions, and lectured on Semitics at George Washington University (1916–27). In 1950 he settled in Israel. Schapiro wrote extensively on subjects of Jewish history and bibliography for the Hebrew and Yiddish press.

His published work includes *Die haggadischen Elemente im erzaehlenden Teil des Korans* (1907); "Bibliography of Hebrew Translations of English Works" (in: *Studies in Jewish Bibliography in Memory of A.S. Freidus*, 1929); *Bibliography of Hebrew Translations of German Works* (1934); and "Schiller und Goethe im Hebraeischen" (in: *Festschrift fuer A. Freimann zum 60. Geburtstag* (1935)). He also edited his father's *Mashal ha-Kadmoni* (with biography, 1925) and *Pitgamim shel Ḥakhamim* (1927).

SCHAPIRO, JACOB SALWYN (1879–1973), U.S. historian. Born in New York State, Schapiro taught history at City College, N.Y. from 1909 until his retirement in 1947, and rose to the rank of full professor (1922). Schapiro's principal interest was 19th-century European history, with emphasis on intellectual history.

His major works are *Social Reform and the Reformation* (1909); *Condorcet and the Rise of Liberalism* (1934); *Liberalism and the Challenge of Fascism* (1949); and *World in Crisis* (1950), an analysis of political and social movements in the 20th century. He is also author of *Liberalism: Its Meaning and History* (1958), *Movements of Social Dissent in Modern Europe* (1962), and *Anticlericalism* (1967). His *Modern and Contemporary European History* (1918) was one of the first textbooks to treat history as the evolution of civilization, embracing social, economic, intellectual, and literary developments, and it had a marked influence on a generation of college students. Many revised editions have appeared.

[Oscar Isaiah Janowsky]

SCHAPIRO, LEONARD (1908–1983), British political scientist. Schapiro was born in Glasgow but lived in Riga and Petrograd from 1915 to 1921. His father's family had been wealthy and influential figures in Latvia before the Revolution. In 1921 the family settled in London; Schapiro was educated at St. Paul's School and London University. He practiced as a barrister from 1932 until 1955. During World War II he worked as an intelligence monitor and, with his knowledge of many languages and his Russian background, was already regarded as one of Britain's greatest experts on the Soviet Union. Schapiro then taught at the London School of Economics and was professor of political science from 1963 to 1975. His many works on the Soviet Union include *The Origins of Communist Autocracy* (1955); *The Communist Party of the Soviet Union* (1960), generally regarded as the best Western work on this subject; *Rationalism and Nationalism in Russian Nineteenth-Century Political Thought* (1967); and a biography of Turgenev (1978). He was also chairman of the editorial board of the journal *Soviet Jewish Affairs* and did much to support Soviet Jewry.

BIBLIOGRAPHY: ODNB online.

[William D. Rubinstein (2nd ed.)]

SCHAPIRO, MEYER (1904–1996), U.S. historian of art. Schapiro was born in Siauliai, Lithuania, but immigrated to the United States as a child of three. He was first introduced to art history at an evening class at the Hebrew Settlement House in Brownsville, taught by John Sloan. He graduated from Columbia University in 1924 with honors in art history and philosophy, receiving his doctorate in 1929. Schapiro taught in the department of art, history, and archaeology at Columbia from 1928 onwards, teaching at that institution as a University Professor from 1965 to 1975, when he was appointed professor emeritus. He was lecturer of fine arts at New York University from 1932 to 1936, the New School for Social Research from 1936 to 1952, London University from 1947 to 1957, the Hebrew University in 1961, Norton Professor of Fine Arts at Harvard from 1966 to 1967, Oxford University in 1968, and at the College of France in 1974. Schapiro was a Fellow of the American Academy of Arts and Sciences and of the American Philosophical Society, and was elected to the American Institute of Arts and Letters. Columbia University awarded him the Alexander Hamilton Medal for distinguished service in 1975. A professorship in Modern Art and Theory was created at Columbia in his name. He is acknowledged as one of the most distinguished American historians of art. A rigorous observer and theorist, he addressed the relationship among society, artist, and artwork, arguing that social and institutional forces mediated the actions of even the modern artist. In this way, his viewpoint differed from that of Clement Greenberg and Harold Rosenberg, two other Jewish intellectuals who contributed to the shape of modern art history in New York during this period. Schapiro was a masterful and gifted art historian of medieval art, Romanesque sculpture, and 19th and 20th century art, especially that of Cezanne, Courbet, Mondrian, and van Gogh. His friends and former students included Irving Howe, Willem de Kooning, Jacques Lipchitz, Robert Motherwell, and Barnett Newman. He also worked with Max Horkheimer and Herbert Marcuse when they moved the Frankfurt School from Germany to New York. The publisher George Baziller has published four volumes of Schapiro's work, beginning in 1977 with *Selected Papers. Romanesque Art*; the last volume *Theory and Philosophy of Art* was printed in 1994. He published his celebrated works *Van Gogh* in 1950, *Cezanne* in 1952, and *Words and Pictures* in 1973. He also contributed articles to *The Nation* and *Partisan Review*. Schapiro's research and writing continues to be instrumental to contemporary art historians, including Norman Bryson, T.J. Clark, and Linda Nochlin.

BIBLIOGRAPHY: D. Carrier, "Worldview in Painting – Art and Society. Book Review," in: *Art Bulletin*, 82 (June 2000); T. Crow, "Village Voice," in: *Artforum International*, 34 (June 1996); M. Schapiro, "The Nature of Abstract Art," in: *Modern Art: 19th and 20th Centuries. Selected Papers* (1968).

[Nancy Buchwald (2nd ed.)]

SCHAPPES, MORRIS U. (**Moise ben Haim Shapshilevich**; 1907–2004), historian and social activist. Born in Kamenets-Podolski, Ukraine, he immigrated to the U.S. with his parents in 1914. He received a B.A. from City College and an M.A. from Columbia University (1930). He began his academic career at the City University of New York, where he taught English from 1928 to 1941, when he lost his position in the anti-Communist purges of 1940–41. One of 40 faculty members who were dismissed for refusing to cooperate with the Rapp-Coudert Committee's investigation of alleged subversive activities at the university, Schappes was incarcerated on the charge of perjury, having claimed under oath that he could name only three Communists at the school, two of whom were dead. When a colleague named some 50 names, Schappes was sentenced to 13 months in prison.

In 1946 he founded *Jewish Life* (since 1957, *Jewish Currents*), a socialist, pro-Israel but non-Zionist magazine concerned with literature, political and social commentary, of which he was the editor for four decades. The magazine, which had become an unofficial organ of the Communist Party, gradually broke its ties with the Soviet Union and moved more toward Israel, especially after the Six-Day War of 1967.

In 1981, the faculty senate of City College apologized for firing Schappes and his colleagues. In 1993 he was awarded the Torchbearer Award of the American Jewish Historical Society.

His major publications include *The Letters of Emma Lazarus, 1868–1885* (1949) and two major works on American Jewish history: *A Documentary History of the Jews in the United States, 1654–1875* (1950) and *The Jews in the United States: A Pictorial History, 1654–1954* (1955). He also wrote *Resistance Is the Lesson: The Meaning of the Warsaw Ghetto Uprising* (1947); *Anti-Semitism and Reaction, 1795–1800* (1948); and *The Political Origins of the United Hebrew Trades, 1888* (1977).

ADD. BIBLIOGRAPHY: R. Boyer, *Patriot in Prison: The Story of Morris U. Schappes* (1944).

[Jack Nusan Porter / Ruth Beloff (2nd ed.)]

SCHARFSTEIN, ẒEVI (1884–1972), U.S. Hebrew educator, journalist, and publisher. Born in the Ukraine, Scharfstein devoted himself to educational work from 1903. After directing a Hebrew school in Tarnow, Galicia (1900–14), he arrived in the United States in 1914 and two years later became instructor at the Teachers Institute of the Jewish Theological Seminary, where he eventually served as professor of Jewish education until his retirement in 1960.

A prodigious contributor to the Hebrew press, his column in the American Hebrew weekly *Hadoar* dealt with political and, especially, with literary events. From 1907 Scharfstein also published educational texts embracing Hebrew literature, Jewish education, Bible, and Hebrew language.

His historical works as a Jewish educator include *Ha-Ḥeder be-Ḥayyei Ammenu* (1943) and *Toledot ha-Ḥinnukh be-Yisrael ba-Dorot ha-Aḥaronim* (5 vols., 1960–66); and his autobiographical works comprise *Arba'im Shanah ba-Amerikah* (1955–56). Among his contributions to Hebrew lexicography is *Oẓar ha-Ra'yonot ve-ha-Pitgamim* (3 vols., 1966). From 1940 Scharfstein was editor of the educational periodical *Shevilei ha-Ḥinnukh*.

BIBLIOGRAPHY: *Sefer ha-Yovel li-Khevod Ẓevi Scharfstein* (1955), 7–28 (incl. bibl.); *Sefer Scharfstein* (1944), 163–231 (incl. bibl.); *Sefer Scharfstein* (1971); Waxman, Literature, index.

[Eisig Silberschlag]

SCHARY, DORE (**Isidore**; 1905–1980), U.S. film writer and producer. Born in Newark, New Jersey, Schary acquired a reputation as a screenwriter in Hollywood before he was 30. In 1941 he became an executive producer for Metro Goldwyn Mayer (MGM), where his policy of producing scripts with a social message led to such films as *Boys Town* (1938); *Edison, the Man* (1940); *Joe Smith, American* (1942); and *Bataan* (1943). He moved to Vanguard in 1943, and to RKO in 1947, the year in which his *Crossfire* put the issue of antisemitism on the screen for the first time in the United States. In 1947 Schary returned to MGM, of which he became chief production manager in 1951. Among the more than 300 pictures he produced there were such popular successes as *Battleground* (1949); *The Asphalt Jungle* (1950); *King Solomon's Mines* (1950); *Quo Vadis?* (1951); *Lili* (1953); and *Julius Caesar* (1953). Schary was dismissed from his post in 1956 as part of a sweeping reorganization, but remained with MGM as a consultant for the next ten years. Turning to the stage, he wrote the Broadway hit *Sunrise at Campobello* (1958), which dealt with the early career of Franklin D. Roosevelt, and for which he won a Tony Award. He also wrote the successful musical *The Unsinkable Molly Brown* (1960).

Active politically in the liberal wing of the Democratic Party, Schary was also interested in Israel and Jewish affairs and served for many years as national chairman of the Anti-Defamation League of the B'nai B'rith (1963–69). In 1948 he was given the Thomas Jefferson Award by the Council Against Intolerance in America. In 1970 he was appointed New York City's first commissioner of cultural affairs. In 1982 the ADL established the annual Dore Schary Award, presented to student film and video productions on subjects that combat prejudice and promote human rights.

His autobiography, *For Special Occasions*, appeared in 1962. His final autobiography, *Heyday*, was published in 1979.

BIBLIOGRAPHY: J. (Schary) Zimmer, *With a Cast of Thousands: A Hollywood Childhood* (1963); *Current Biography 1948* (1949).

[Stewart Kampel / Ruth Beloff (2nd ed.)]

SCHATZ, BORIS (1867–1932), painter and sculptor; founder of the *Bezalel School of Art in Jerusalem. Schatz was born in

Varna, province of Kovno, Lithuania. The son of a *melammed*, he was sent to the yeshivah in Vilna but broke away from his family and religious studies and turned to art. In 1889 he went to Paris and worked under the sculptor *Antokolsky, and the painter Cormon. He was invited in 1895 to Bulgaria where he became court sculptor to Prince Ferdinand and was a founder of the Royal Academy of Art in Sofia. In 1900 he received the gold medal in the Paris Salon for his *Head of Old Woman*. After meeting Theodor Herzl in 1903, he became an enthusiastic Zionist. Schatz first proposed the idea of an art school at the 1905 Zionist Congress and when it was accepted went to Palestine to execute it. Three years later, he settled in Jerusalem, where he established the Bezalel School of Art (1906), to which he soon added a small museum. Schatz arranged exhibitions of the Bezalel crafts in Europe and the U.S. These were the first displays of the products of Ereẓ Israel exhibited abroad. During World War I, the school was closed down, and Schatz was held prisoner for ten months. He succeeded in obtaining funds in the U.S. for the reconstruction of his school and the museum. He died in Denver, Colorado, while on a successful fund-raising mission and was buried on Mount Scopus in Jerusalem. The school was closed on his death, but reestablished the following year with the aid of a government grant. Schatz was both a realist and an idealist, a product of the dying romanticism and the reawakening of national consciousness in Eastern Europe. He took this spirit with him to Palestine, and adapted it to the needs of the country. The Bezalel School gave a young generation of artists and craftsmen the opportunity to study in the country and fostered a national style of arts and crafts, based on European techniques and Near-Eastern art forms. Schatz was a prolific artist, concentrating mainly on sculpture. His work is characterized by a naturalistic romanticism. From 1903, he worked almost exclusively on Jewish themes, representing religious practices, Jewish leaders, and biblical subject. His main works include: *Mattathias*, *Blessing the Candles*, *Havdalah*, *The Scribe*, *Blowing the Shofar*, *Isaiah*, *At the Wailing Wall*, *Herzl*, *Bialik*, *Ben-Yehudah*, and *Isaac M. Wise*. His son BEZALEL (1912–1978), an expressional abstract artist, illustrated Henry Miller's silk-screen printed *Into the Night Life* and specialized in ceramic murals and metal projects combined with architecture and craft designing (including one of the two gates at the Yad Vashem memorial, Jerusalem). Bezalel's wife, LOUISE, was an artist known for her delicate abstract water colors. Boris' daughter ZAHARA (1916–) created abstract sculpture in plastics and wire. She received the Israel Prize (1954).

BIBLIOGRAPHY: B. Schatz, *31 Oil paintings* (1921); H. Gamzu, *Painting and Sculpture in Israel* (1951), 11–12. **ADD BIBLIOGRAPHY:** N. Shilo-Cohen (ed.), *Bezalel shel Schatz – 1906–1929*, Israel Museum, Jerusalem (1983); Y. Zalmona, *Boris Schatz*, Hakibbutz Hameuhad, Jerusalem (1985).

[Yona Fisher]

SCHATZ, ẒEVI (1890–1921), Hebrew writer. Born in Russia, Schatz grew up in non-Jewish surroundings. He corresponded with *Trumpeldor regarding the establishment of a commune in Palestine and later immigrated there. Between 1918 and 1920, he was a soldier in the Jewish Legion and was killed in an Arab riot along with *Brenner. Under the influence of Brenner, who was his mentor and editor, he began to write in Hebrew during the last years of his life. He wrote two novellas, of which *Be-Lo Niv* (originally entitled *Al Gevul ha-Demamah*) was published during his lifetime, and *Batyah*, along with some poetry, appeared posthumously. Schatz was the first to depict the experiences of the individual in the kibbutz in fiction as well as in his letters and conversations. All these were collected by M. Poznansky in *Al Gevul ha-Demamah* (1929; 1967; 1990).

BIBLIOGRAPHY: Kressel, Leksikon, 2 (1967), 975. **ADD. BIBLIOGRAPHY:** H. Shoham, *Ha-Kevuẓah be-Te'atron Po'alei Ereẓ Yisrael: Ha-Haẓagah "Batyah"* (1988); S. Keshet, "*Omanut ha-Ḥayyim o Omanut ha-Bitui: al Z. Schatz*," in: *Le-Sapper et ha-Kibbuẓ* (1990), 47–65; idem, "*Dov Aḥer u-Brenner Shemo: Bein Schatz le-Brenner*," in: *Alei Siaḥ*, 36 (1995), 119–26.

[Getzel Kressel]

SCHATZ-ANIN, MAX (1885–1975), left-wing Socialist ideologist and author. Born in Friedrichstadt (Jaunjelgava), Latvia, Schatz-Anin studied law at St. Petersburg and joined the *Zionist Socialist Workers' Party (territorialists). He was later arrested and deported abroad, where he contributed to the party press in Russia and Central Europe. Schatz-Anin graduated from Berne university after writing his doctoral thesis "*Zur Nationalitaetenfrage*" (1910). On the eve of the congress of the Socialist International in Copenhagen (1910), he published an essay on "The Jewish Proletariat in the Socialist International," in which he demanded that nationalities be represented at the International. Returning to Russia in 1912, he settled in Riga as a lawyer. After the February Revolution in 1917, Schatz-Anin represented his party in the Petrograd Soviet and was a co-founder of the *United Jewish Socialist Workers' Party, representing it in the executive committee of the Ukrainian *Rada*. Returning to Riga in 1919, he joined the illegal Communist party and founded the left-wing Yiddishist Kultur-Lige. Although he went blind (1928), he continued to deliver lectures and write and was appointed university professor when Latvia became a Soviet Republic.

His philosophical essays and historical works in Yiddish and Russian include *Temporalism* (1919), *Sotsiale Opozitsye in Yidisher Geshikhte* ("Social Opposition in Jewish History," 1927), and *Di Gezelshaftlikhe Bavegungen bay Yidn tsvishn der Ershter un Tsveyter Velt-Milkhome* (1941).

BIBLIOGRAPHY: Rejzen, Leksikon, 1 (1926), 117–9; *Sovetish Heymland* (June 1965), 158.

[Joseph Gar]

SCHAULSON BRODSKY, JORGE (1954–), Chilean politician. He was the son of Jacobo *Schaulson, politician and member of the Chilean Parliament. During the government of Pinochet, he studied law in the United States and graduated in 1980. Upon his return to Chile he began practicing law, maintaining offices in Santiago and in New York. He was one of the founders of the Pro Democracy Party (PPD) and in 2005 was its vice president. Schaulson was elected to Parliament in 1989 and reelected in 1993; he was president of the lower chamber. In 2004 he lost the election for the post of mayor of Santiago.

[Moshe Nes El (2nd ed.)]

SCHAULSON NUMHAUSER, JACOBO (1917–1989), Chilean lawyer and politician. Born in Santiago, he graduated in law in 1941 and was president of the Juventud Radical (Youth of the Radical Party). He practiced law and became legal adviser to the governor of Santiago province. Schaulson Numhauser was made professor of civil law at the University of Santiago in 1953. As an active figure in the Chilean Radical Party, he sat in the Chamber of Deputies from 1949 to 1965. He was secretary and later vice president of his party, president of the Chamber of Deputies (1961–62), and a member of the Constitutional Tribunal. In 1950 he represented Chile at the United Nations. After his retirement he worked as a lawyer.

[Paul Link / Moshe Nes El (2nd ed.)]

SCHAWLOW, ARTHUR L. (1921–1999), U.S. physicist and Nobel laureate. He was born in Mount Vernon, New York, to an immigrant father from Riga and a Canadian mother. When he was aged three, the family moved to Toronto, where he was educated at Vaughan Road Collegiate Institute. He won a scholarship enabling him to graduate in mathematics and physics from the University of Toronto (1941). During World War II he worked in radar development, before returning to the university to earn his Ph.D. (1951) in spectroscopy under the supervision of Malcolm Crawford. He was a postdoctoral research fellow in the physics department of Columbia University, New York, where he worked with Charles H. Townes, and then a physicist at the Bell Telephone Laboratories (1951–61), where he continued to collaborate with Townes. In 1961 he became professor of physics at Stanford University, where he was chairman of the department (1966–70), J.G. Jackson and C.J. Wood Professor of Physics from 1978, and subsequently emeritus professor. Schawlow's main research interest was spectroscopy, and he and Townes conceived the idea for, and in 1957 built, the first laser (light amplification by stimulated emission of radiation). The practical applications of these discoveries are now common knowledge. Schawlow applied these theoretical and technical advances to his research in optics, superconductivity, and fundamental problems of atomic structure. He and Townes did not benefit personally from the patent won by the Bell Telephone Company. Schawlow and Townes won the 1981 Nobel Prize in physics, shared with Kai M. Siegbahn. His many honors included election to the American Academy of Arts and Sciences and the U.S. National Academy of Sciences, the Marconi International Fellowship (1977), and the U.S. National Medal of Science (1991). He was a distinguished teacher, and his book *Microwave Spectroscopy* (1955), coauthored by Townes, was a standard text. Schawlow married Townes' sister Amelia, an outstanding musician, in 1951. She died in a road traffic accident in 1991. Their son Artie was autistic, and his parents organized the nonprofit California Vocations, a group home for autistic individuals, renamed the Arthur Schawlow Center in 1999. They also had two daughters. Schawlow was a clarinetist and jazz expert, with a legendary sense of humor manifest in his social and professional life.

[Michael Denman (2nd ed.)]

SCHAYES, ADOLPH ("**Dolph**"; 1928–), U.S. basketball player and coach, member of the NBA's 25th and 50th Anniversary teams, and member of Basketball Hall of Fame. Schayes, a native New Yorker, was an All-American standout at New York University, where he won the Haggerty Award in his senior year. Initially taken by the New York Knickerbockers in the 1948 draft, Schayes chose to join the recently formed Syracuse Nationals of the NBL. The 6′ 8″ Schayes had an immediate impact, leading the Nats in scoring en route to a much improved 40–23 finish. The following year Schayes proved even more effective, as the Nats, now officially part of the NBA, finished on top of their conference, going 51–13. For the 1950–51 season, the NBA instituted All-Star games, and Schayes, being a consistent top-ten leader in all offensive categories and rebounds, was an NBA All-Star in each of his remaining 12 seasons as a full-time player for Syracuse; in six of those seasons he was First Team All-NBA. Over the course of his 15 seasons with the Nats, Schayes led the team to an overall .572 winning percentage and the 1955 NBA Championship. In 1963, the Nats moved to Philadelphia and became the 76ers, naming Schayes as player-coach. When Schayes ended his playing career in 1964, he was the NBA's all-time leading scorer, with 19,247 points. His career scoring and 18.2 points-per-game average remain top-50 all-time records. Schayes is also one of the top free-throw shooters in NBA history, ranking 6th all-time in free throws made (6,979) and is in the top-50 in lifetime free-throw shooting percentage (84.9%). He is also 16th in rebounds-per-game (12.1) and 23rd all-time in total rebounds (11,256). During his three-year stint as coach of the 76ers, Schayes enjoyed great success as well, guiding them in his third season to a 55–25 record, while being named NBA Coach of the Year in 1966. During the early 1970s, Schayes was supervisor of NBA Officials. In 1977, he coached the U.S. team to a gold medal at the Maccabiah Games, with his son, DANNY SCHAYES (1959–), as the star player. Danny went on to play for Syracuse University and from there to a successful 18-year NBA career.

[Robert B. Klein (2nd ed.)]

SCHECHTER, ABRAHAM ISRAEL (1894–1936), rabbi and scholar. Schechter, who was born in Vizhnitsa, Bukovina, worked as a librarian in Switzerland, and then emigrated to the U.S. in 1922. From 1924 he taught at the Hebrew Theological College, Chicago, and later served as rabbi in Houston, Texas, and Providence, Rhode Island.

Among his published works are *Palaestina, seine Geschichte und Kultur* (1905, which had to be withdrawn after a court order for plagiarism); *Studies in Jewish Liturgy*, on the *Ḥibbur Berakhot* by Menahem b. Solomon (1930) which drew criticism from I. Davidson (JQR, 21, 1930–31), 241–79; Schechter's rejoinder, in: JQR, 22 (1931–32), 147–52); and *Lectures on Jewish Liturgy* (1933). Schechter's collection of Hebraica and Judaica was given to Texas University Library.

His wife EVA wrote *Symbols and Ceremonies of the Jewish Home* (1930).

SCHECHTER, MATHILDE ROTH (1857–1924), founding president of the National Women's League of the United Synagogue of America, now known as the *Women's League for Conservative Judaism. Born in Guttentag, Germany, Mathilde Roth grew up in the Breslau Jewish orphans home. A gifted student, she attended the Breslau Teacher's Seminary. In 1885, she went to England to study and to be a tutor in the home of Michael Friedlaender, principal of Jews College. In the library of that college she met the distinguished scholar Solomon *Schechter. They wed in 1887.

The Schechter home quickly became a center for Jewish intellectual life, largely thanks to Mathilde Schechter's legendary hospitality. That tradition continued in her subsequent homes, in Cambridge, after Solomon Schechter was appointed lecturer at the university, and then, after 1902, in New York, when he became president of the Jewish Theological Seminary. In Cambridge, Mathilde Schechter gave birth to their three children, a son and two daughters. Even as she raised them, she edited the works of local scholars and engaged in other literary pursuits, including translating the German poet Heinrich *Heine. Furthermore, she edited almost everything her famous husband wrote.

In the United States Mathilde Schechter complemented her husband's establishment of Conservative Judaism by laying the foundations for its women's organization in 1918. The National Women's League of the United Synagogue of America subsequently grew to become one of the largest Jewish women's organizations in the United States. Mathilde Schechter believed that the Women's League could help women deepen religious life in their homes, synagogues, and wider communities. She persuaded the Women's League to establish a Students' House in New York City in 1918, which became a home away from home for Jewish students as well as for Jewish servicemen on leave. She also founded and taught at a Jewish vocational school for girls on the Lower East Side and was national chairwoman of education for Hadassah.

Mathilde Roth Schechter extended the domestic ideal of women caring for their home and family, which she lived to the fullest, to women's caring for their synagogues and wider Jewish communities. She thus stands within a coterie of leaders of American Jewish women, who, in the early decades of the 20th century, laid out new avenues for women's activism within Jewish life.

BIBLIOGRAPHY: *They Dared to Dream: A History of the National Women's League, 1918–1968* (1967); P.S. Nadell, *Conservative Judaism in America* (1988), 221–22; M. Scult. "The Baale Boste Reconsidered: The Life of Mathilde Roth Schechter (M.R.S.)," in: *Modern Judaism* 7, 1 (February 1987), 1–27; idem. "Mathilde Schechter," in: P.E. Hyman and D. Dash Moore (eds.), *Jewish Women in America: An Historical Encyclopedia* 2 (1997), 1201–3.

[Pamela S. Nadell (2nd ed.)]

SCHECHTER, SOLOMON (Shneur Zalman; 1847–1915), rabbinic scholar and president of the *Jewish Theological Seminary of America. Schechter was born in Focsani, Romania. His father, a Chabad Ḥasid, was a ritual slaughterer (Ger. *Schaechter*). In his teens he studied with the rabbinic author Joseph Saul Nathanson in Lemberg. From about 1875 to 1879 he attended the Vienna *bet ha-midrash*. He acquired a lifelong devotion to scientific study of the tradition and developed the central notion of the community of Israel as decisive for Jewish living and thinking. He was to call it "Catholic Israel." From 1879 he studied at the Berlin Hochschule fuer die Wissenschaft des Judentums and at the University of Berlin. When, in 1882, a fellow student at the Hochschule, Claude Goldsmid Montefiore, invited him to be his tutor in rabbinics in London, Schechter accepted. In England he rose to prominence as a rabbinic scholar and spokesman for Jewish traditionalism. In 1890 he was appointed lecturer in talmudics and in 1892 reader in rabbinics at Cambridge University. In 1899 he also became professor of Hebrew at University College, London.

Schechter's first substantial work was his edition of *Avot de-Rabbi Nathan* (1887). His fame rests on the scholarly recovery of the Cairo *Genizah. It created a sensation in the world of scholarship, and in its wake Jewish history and the history of Mediterranean society have been rewritten. Over one hundred thousand manuscripts and manuscript fragments were brought to England and presented to Cambridge University by Schechter and Charles Taylor, the master of St. John's College who had made Schechter's trip possible. Together they published the newly discovered fragments of the Hebrew original of Ben *Sira (*The Wisdom of Ben Sira*, 1899).

Late in 1901 Schechter accepted an invitation by a number of leading American Jews, notably his friend, Judge Mayer Sulzberger of Philadelphia, to assume the post of president of the Jewish Theological Seminary of America. He served in this capacity from 1902 until his death. He was able to attract a distinguished faculty, including Louis Ginzberg. Alexander Marx, Israel Friedlaender, Israel Davidson, and Mordecai M. Kaplan. The Seminary became one of the most important centers of Jewish learning and of Jewish intellectual and, indeed, national revival. Schechter's *Studies in Judaism* (3 vols., 1896–1924), his *Some Aspects of Rabbinic Theology* (in book form, 1909; based on essays in the *Jewish Quarterly Review*, 1894–1896), and *Seminary Addresses and Other Papers* (1915) remain indispensable documents of American Jewish religious Conservatism. Steering a course between Orthodoxy and Reform, Schechter combined scholarliness and objectivity with piety, and piety with a measure of flexibility and innovation in doctrine and practice. In 1913 Schechter was instrumental in founding the *United Synagogue of America (his original designation read "Agudath Jeshurun – A Union for Promoting Traditional Judaism in America"), which became a major national institution of Conservative Judaism in the United States. In 1905 he acknowledged Zionism as "the great bulwark against assimilation." He felt close to religious and spiritual Zionism and in 1913 attended the 11th Zionist Congress in Vienna. Over the strenuous objections of Seminary board members Jacob H. Schiff and Louis Marshall, he opened the Seminary to Zionist activity. But he remained, essentially, a builder of religious Judaism in the American diaspora.

Schechter is considered the chief architect of Conservative Judaism in the United States. In his view, this version of Jewish religious life and thought was organically related to the Historical School, founded by Zunz, Frankel, and Graetz. Schechter defined the theological position of the school: "It is not the mere revealed Bible that is of first importance to the Jew but the Bible as it repeats itself in history, in other words, as it is interpreted by Tradition… Since then the interpretation of Scripture or the Secondary Meaning is mainly a product of changing historical influences, it follows that the center of authority is actually removed from the Bible and placed in some living body, which, by reason of its being in touch with the ideal aspirations and the religious needs of the age, is best able to determine the nature of the Secondary Meaning. This living body, however, is not represented by any section of the nation, or any corporate priesthood, or Rabbihood, but by the collective conscience of Catholic Israel, as embodied in the Universal Synagogue" (*Studies in Judaism*, Series One, JPS, 1896, xvii–xviii).

Though a staunch traditionalist, Schechter admitted the possibility of change. However, he felt that changes should not be introduced arbitrarily or deliberately. Rather, "the norm as well as the sanction of Judaism is the practice actually in vogue. Its consecration is the consecration of general use – or, in other words, of Catholic Israel" (*ibid.*, xix). Schechter insisted (*ibid.*, 180ff.) Judaism must be understood as regulating not only our actions but also our thoughts: "It is true that every great religion is a 'concentration of many ideas and ideals' which make this religion able to adapt itself to various modes of thinking and living. But there must always be a point round which all these ideas concentrate themselves. This center is Dogma."

BIBLIOGRAPHY: N. Bentwich, *Solomon Schechter: A Biography* (1938); A.S. Oko, *Solomon Schechter: A Bibliography* (1938); M. Davis, *The Emergence of Conservative Judaism* (1963); A. Marx, *Essays in Jewish Biography* (1947), 229–50; B. Mandelbaum, *The Wisdom of Solomon Schechter* (1963); M. Ben-Horin, in: JSOS, 25 (1963), 249–86; 27 (1965), 75–102; 30 (1968), 262–71; idem, in: AJHSQ, 56 (1966/67), 208–31); idem, in: *JQR Seventy-fifth Anniversary Volume* (1967), 47–59; H.H. and M.L. Rubenovitz, *The Walking Heart* (1967), 14–20; A. Parzen, *Architects of* Conservative Judaism (1964); A. Karp, in: *The Jewish Experience in America*, 5 (1969), 111–29; A. Scheiber, in: HUCA, 33 (1962), 255–75. **ADD. BIBLIOGRAPHY:** C. Adler, in: *The American Jewish Year Book*, 18 (1916–1917), 24–67; N. Bentwich, in: *Melilah*, 2 (1946), 25–36 (Heb.); G. Cohen, in: *Proceedings of the Rabbinical Assembly*, 44 (1982), 57–68; R. Fierstien and J. Waxman (eds.), *Solomon Schechter in America: A Centennial Tribute* (2002); D. Fine, in: *Judaism*, 46:1 (Winter 1997), 3–24; S. Goldman (ed.), *Schechter Memorial: JTS Students' Annual*, 3 (1916); S. Greenberg, in: *Conservative Judaism*, 39:4 (Summer 1987), 7–29; Ch.I. Hoffman in: C. Adler (ed.), *The Jewish Theological Seminary Semi-Centennial Volume* (1939), 49–64; J. Kabakoff, in: *Bitzaron*, 9 (Summer–Winter 1987–88), 70–81 (Heb.); P. Nadell, *Conservative Judaism in America: A Biographical Dictionary and Sourcebook* (1988), 222–27 with bibliography; I. Schorsch, in: *Conservative Judaism*, 55:2 (Winter 2003), 3–23; S. Siegel, in: *Proceedings of the Rabbinical Assembly*, 39 (1977), 44–55; J. Wertheimer (ed.), *Tradition Renewed: A History of the Jewish Theological Seminary* (1997), 1, 43–102, 293–326; 2, 446–449; A. Ya'ari, *Iggerot Shneior Zalman Schechter el Poznanski* (1944); Y. Zussman, in: *Mada'ei ha-Yahadut*, 38 (1998), 213–30 (Heb.).

[Meir Ben-Horon]

SCHECHTER INSTITUTE OF JEWISH STUDIES, THE (Machon Schechter L'mada'ey Hayahadut). The institute was founded in Jerusalem in 1984 as the Seminary of Judaic Studies (Bet Hamidrash L'limudey Hayahadut) to train Conservative rabbis for the Masorti Movement in Israel. It was viewed as the spiritual heir of the *Breslau Rabbinical Seminary (1854–1939) and the *Jewish Theological Seminary of America (JTS; 1887ff.). It was founded by JTS under the leadership of Chancellor Gershon *Cohen and Vice Chancellor Simon *Greenberg, and by the Masorti (Conservative) Movement in Israel represented by Prof. Reuven *Hammer, who also served as its first dean (1984–1987). It met initially at the Schocken Institute, a JTS affiliate in Jerusalem, and the founders dreamed that it would eventually have 60 students.

The Seminary grew rapidly under the leadership of Prof. Lee *Levine, who served as dean and later president (1987–94) and rector (1994–96), as the Seminary moved first to the Ma'ayanot building and then to Neve Schechter (1990), which had been a dormitory for JTS rabbinical students. The first class of four rabbinical students was ordained in July 1988, but Levine and his successors felt that it was not enough to ordain Israeli Conservative rabbis. They felt that the most effective way to bring Jewish education in general and Conservative Judaism in particular to Israel was by developing large educational programs for public school children and teachers and for new immigrants. Levine therefore founded the TALI Education Fund (1987) which funds and supervises the TALI school system in Israel, received permission from Israel's Council for Higher Education to grant an M.A. degree in Jewish Studies as a branch of JTS (1989), adopted Midreshet Yerushalayim, which became a program for Russian-speaking and Hungarian Jews (1990), and adopted the one year rabbinical programs of JTS, the *University of Judaism in Los Angeles, and the *Seminario Rabbinico in Buenos Aires (1990).

During Levine's tenure, the TALI Education Fund began to turn the TALI schools into a real school system: many schools were added, a syllabus for grades 1–9 was published, curricula were written, in-service training was developed, and agreements were reached with the Ministry of Education. The M.A. program in Jewish Studies grew rapidly from five students in 1990–91 to over 200 in 1994, and Levine began to hire full-time faculty. Together with Prof. David *Golinkin, the dean, he developed an innovative interdisciplinary M.A. program in Jewish studies for Israeli educators, with specializations such as informal education, family and community studies, and Jewish Women's Studies as well as a D.H.L. program as a branch of JTS.

Midreshet Yerushalayim had been founded in the 1980s as a post-high school yeshivah-style program for Conservative Jews from North America. Transformed under the leadership of Levine and Shmuel Glick, it founded an outreach program for Russian-speaking immigrants in Israel and a TALI school system and Ramah Camps in the former Soviet Union, and it revived the moribund *Rabbinical Seminary in Budapest by adding a Pedagogium for teachers, which eventually became the University of Jewish Studies in Budapest.

During Rabbi Benjamin Segal's tenure as president (1994–99), all of the Seminary's programs continued to grow at a rapid rate and the institution was renamed the Schechter Institute of Jewish Studies in 1998, in honor of Prof. Solomon *Schechter, one of the main founders of Conservative Judaism in North America. Segal more than doubled the budget, adopted sound fiscal and administrative policies, began the accreditation process to turn Schechter into an Israeli institution of higher learning, and endowed the Liebhaber Prize for Religious Tolerance. He founded the Institute of Applied Halakhah together with Golinkin; its goal was to publish halakhic literature in different languages for the worldwide Conservative Movement. He also developed indigenous leadership by hiring three young graduates of Schechter – Alexander Even-Chen as dean of the Graduate School, Eitan Chikli as director of the TALI Education Fund, and Yair Paz as director of Midreshet Yerushalayim in Israel.

Prof. Alice Shalvi, who served as rector (1997–2000) and acting president (1999–2000), laid the groundwork for an M.A. track in Judaism and the Arts and a Center of Jewish Art which developed curricula for the TALI schools and websites. She founded The Center for Women and Jewish Law (1999) together with Golinkin, and helped launch *Nashim: A Journal of Jewish Women's Studies and Gender Issues* (1998), which was co-published with Brandeis University and later with Indiana University Press. Shalvi also hired Gila Katz, who had founded the TALI day school in Czernowitz, as director of Midreshet Yerushalayim in Ukraine.

During Golinkin's tenure (2000ff.), the four major Schechter programs became four separate *amutot* (non-profit organizations) as The Schechter Institute achieved accreditation as an Israeli institution of higher education (2005). Annual fundraising increased dramatically, while endowments and endowed chairs were raised for the first time. The Schechter Institute hired many tenure-track faculty and undertook an ambitious program of publishing academic and popular works in Hebrew, English, Russian, French, and Spanish. The TALI school system expanded rapidly after receiving official recognition from the Ministry of Education in 2003 and began to publish at least four new TALI textbooks per year. Midreshet Yerushalayim expanded to 46 branches in Israel and to 17 schools and camps in Ukraine.

By 2006, the Schechter Rabbinical Seminary had 60 students from Israel and abroad; the Schechter Institute of Jewish Studies graduate school had 450 students and 60 full and part-time faculty; the TALI Education Fund provided enriched Jewish education to 25,000 Israeli children in almost 140 TALI schools and pre-schools; and Midreshet Yerushalayim taught Jewish studies to thousands of Russian immigrants in Israel and to Jews in Ukraine and Hungary. Golinkin stated that his dream was to provide every Israeli and eastern European Jew with a Jewish education.

BIBLIOGRAPHY: GENERAL: D. Elazar and R.M. Geffen, *The Conservative Movement in Judaism: Dilemmas and Opportunities* (2000), 138–40; N. Gillman, *Conservative Judaism: The New Century* (1993), 178–89; D. Golinkin, *Proceedings of the Rabbinical Assembly*, 62 (2000), 194–96; idem, *Women's League Outlook*, 75/3 (Spring 2005), 22–26; E. Lederhendler, in: J. Wertheimer (ed.), *Tradition Renewed: A History of the Jewish Theological Seminary of America* (1997), 2:244–48; L. Levine et al., *Et La'asot*, 2 (Summer 1989), 13–29 (Heb.); H. Meirovich, *The Shaping of Masorti Judaism in Israel* (1999); I. Schorsch, *Thoughts from 3080* (1987), 17–24; B. Segal, *Proceedings of the Rabbinical Assembly*, 62 (1995), 104–8; E. Tabory in: U. Rebhun and Ch. Waxman (eds.), *Jews in Israel* (2004), 290–92. TALI: W. Ackerman and G. Showstack, *Conservative Judaism*, 40/1 (Fall 1987), 67–80; E. Chikli, *Tali Education: The Development and Realization of an Educational Idea* (Heb., 2005); T. Horovitz, *Dor L'dor*, 15 (Heb., 1999); L. Levine, *Studies in Jewish Education*, 7 (1995), 259–77. MIDRESHET YERUSHALAYIM: Sh. Glick, *Dor L'dor* 24 (2004), 39–54 (Heb.); D. Golinkin, *Insight Israel: The View from Schechter* (2003), 138–40, 154–56.

[David Golinkin (2nd ed.)]

SCHECHTMAN, JOSEPH B. (1891–1970), Zionist leader, authority on population movements, and author. Schechtman, who was born in Odessa, served in the all-Russian Jewish Congress convened in Petrograd (1917) and the Ukrainian National Assembly convened in Kiev (1918). After leaving Russia in 1921, he became coeditor and later managing editor of *Razsvyet* (1922–32), the organ of the Federation of Russian-Ukrainian Zionists, and subsequently the leading *Revisionist weekly. Schechtman approved *Jabotinsky's resignation from the Actions Committee of the World Zionist Organization in 1923, but disagreed with his concurrent resignation from the Zionist Organization itself. However, this partial support later became total when the two men took the lead in founding the World Union of Zionist Revisionists in Paris in 1925 which elected Jabotinsky its president. Schechtman, in common with Jabotinsky, became steadily disenchanted with the subsequent actions of the Zionist leaders. He opposed the proposed enlargement of the Jewish Agency (1929) to include a 50% proportion of non-Zionists, fearing that such a move would contribute to the dilution of, and possibly betray, the aims of political Zionism. However, he and the other Revisionists were not averse to an Agency that would be elected by universal suffrage. In 1929 Schechtman became chief editor of *Nayer Veg*, a Yiddish-language Revisionist organ.

In 1935, the Revisionists left the Zionist Organization, established the New Zionist Organization in Vienna, and elected Jabotinsky its president. Schechtman continued his work in the Revisionist movement both in Europe and after going to the U.S. in 1941. From 1941 to 1943 he was a research fellow for the Institute of Jewish Affairs. He directed the Research Bureau on Population Movements (1943–44), and from 1944 to 1945 served as a consultant to the Office of Strategic Services (OSS) on population movements. Schechtman was subsequently a member of the World Zionist Organization's Actions Committee; a member of the executive of the World Jewish Congress; and chairman of the World Party Council. At his death, he was president of the United Revisionists of America and chairman of the World Council of the Zionist Revision Movement.

Schechtman's books include: a two-volume autobiography of Vladimir Jabotinsky, his best-known work, entitled *Rebel and Statesman; the Early Years* (1956), and *Fighter and Prophet; the Last Years* (1961); *On Wings of Eagles* (1961); *The United States and the Jewish State Movement* (1966); *Star in Eclipse; Russian Jewry Revisited* (1961); *European Population Transfers*, 1939–1945 (1946); and *Postwar Population Transfers in Europe*, 1945–1955 (1962).

SCHECK, BARRY (1949–), U.S. lawyer. Born in Queens, NY, and raised in Manhattan, Scheck, the son of a television producer and entertainers' representative, graduated from Yale University. He was politically active in the "Dump Johnson" movement of the late 1960s before going to the University of California Boalt Hall School of Law in Berkeley, where he worked for the United Farm Workers Union. Scheck became a lawyer for the Legal Aid Society, New York City's law firm for the poor, in the Bronx. There he met a fellow lawyer, Peter Neufeld, who would become his best friend. After three years with Legal Aid, Scheck joined the faculty of the Benjamin N. Cardozo School of Law, where he and Neufeld in 1992 founded the Innocence Project, a nonprofit legal clinic that seeks the release of wrongly convicted individuals through DNA testing. The Innocence Project relies on students to handle case work under the supervision of a team of lawyers. The lawyers screen cases to determine whether postconviction testing of DNA, the genetic material found in all human cells, can yield conclusive proof of innocence. Although DNA testing of crime scene evidence had been used since the late 1980s, it was not until the end of the 20th century that significant advances in the technology made it possible to examine minute specimens. The Innocence Project, by the early years of the 21st century, had helped to exonerate more than 80 people and was working on hundreds of other cases. Scheck was the DNA expert on the team of lawyers defending O.J. Simpson, the former football star, who was found not guilty of murder in a celebrated trial in the 1990s. Scheck and Neufeld were partners with the late Johnnie Cochran in a small civil rights law firm in Manhattan. The firm represented Abner Louima, a Haitian immigrant who was allegedly sodomized by New York City police officers in 1997. In 2003 the Innocence Project spawned the Life After Exoneration Project, to help the wrongly convicted after they were out of prison. Scheck and Neufeld, with Jim Dwyer, were the authors of *Actual Innocence* (2000), which recounted the stories of some of the people they helped free. Inspired by the Innocence Project, about 30 similar organizations formed around the country at law schools, journalism schools, undergraduate college, and public defenders' offices.

[Stewart Kampel (2nd ed.)]

SCHECKTER, JODY (1950–), race car driver, winner of the 1979 Formula One World Drivers Championship. Scheckter was born in East London, South Africa, but at the age of 20 he moved to England, where he developed his racing skills. In 1972 Scheckter qualified for his first Formula One race at Watkins Glen, finishing in ninth place. The following year Scheckter won the Formula 5000 (5 liter max. engine), while gaining a reputation for his aggressive style. A major setback occurred several months later, when he spun out of control at the end of the first lap of the 1973 British Grand Prix, taking out seven other cars in the process. However, Scheckter got back on track in 1974, finishing in third place in the Formula One standings, a feat he would repeat in 1976, and better in 1977 with a second-place finish. After dropping to seventh place in 1978, Scheckter decided to switch driving teams for the fourth time in his career, this time going with Ferrari. The move proved to be decisive, as Scheckter managed three first-place finishes (the Belgian, Monegasque, and Italian Grand Prix) over the course of the 1979 season, en route to amassing 51 points and winning the Formula One Championship. The following year, Scheckter could not find his form, accumulating only two points, and subsequently decided to retire from auto racing. Not resting on his laurels, that same year Scheckter moved to America and immediately started a business in firearms training simulators, which he sold in 1996 for approximately $100 million. He then moved back to England and began buying up plots of land near Basingstoke, and then ran a "biodynamic farming" business on an estate of over 2,500 acres. One of Scheckter's sons, Tomas, became a successful racing driver in his own right in the Indy Racing League, winning the 2005 Bombardier Learjet 500 and finishing fourth in the 2003 Indianapolis 500.

[Robert B. Klein (2nd ed.)]

SCHEFFLER, ISRAEL (1923–), U.S. philosopher and educator. Scheffler was born in New York City. He received a B.A. and an M.A. in psychology from Brooklyn College, and an M.H.L. from the Jewish Theological Seminary of America. He received his Ph.D. in philosophy from the University of Pennsylvania. Scheffler began his professional career at Harvard in 1952 and became professor of education and philosophy in 1964. His *The Language of Education* (1960) was a pioneering work in the field of linguistic analysis as applied to education. In his work, Scheffler attempted to apply philosophical methods to educational ideas. He developed the logical evaluation of assertion, namely the examination of ideas from the standpoint of clarity and the examination of arguments from the standpoint of validity. Philosophical analysis, of which Scheffler was a leading spokesman, stressed the clarification of basic notions and modes of argument rather than the synthesizing of available beliefs into some total outlook.

After he retired from teaching, he was named Victor S. Thomas Professor of Education and Philosophy, Emeritus, at Harvard University. In 2003 he became the scholar-in-residence at the Mandel Center for Studies in Jewish Education at Brandeis University.

His works include *Philosophy and Education* (1958, 1966^2), *The Anatomy of Inquiry* (1963), *Conditions of Knowledge* (1965), *Science and Subjectivity* (1967), *Beyond the Letter* (1979), *Reason and Teaching* (1988), *Of Human Potential* (1990), *Teachers of My Youth, an American Jewish Experience* (1994), *Symbolic Worlds* (1996), and *Gallery of Scholars* (2005). He co-edited *Visions of Jewish Education* (2003).

[Ernest Schwarcz / Ruth Beloff (2nd ed.)]

SCHEFTELOWITZ, ISIDOR (1876–1934), Orientalist and rabbi. Scheftelowitz was born in Sandersleben, duchy of Anhalt, Germany. He studied Sanskrit and Iranian philology and worked for a time at the British Museum and at the Bodleian Library in Oxford. During 1908–26 he served as rabbi and teacher of religion in Cologne. In 1919 he began teaching at the newly founded Cologne University, becoming professor in 1923. When the Nazis seized power, he emigrated to England and taught at Oxford University. Scheftelowitz made a considerable contribution to the study of Sanskrit and Iranian philology and history, as well as to that of comparative religion.

Among his published works are *Arisches im Alten Testament* (2 vols., 1901–03), *Apocrypha der Rigveda* (1906), *Zur Textkritik und Lautlehre der Rigveda* (1907), *Das Fisch-Symbol im Judentum und Christentum* (1911), *Die altpersische Religion und das Judentum* (1920), *Die Entstehung der manichaeischen Religion…* (1922), *Die Bewertung der aramaeischen Urkunden von Assuan und Elephantine fuer die juedische und iranische Geschichte* (Ger. and Heb., 1923), *Is Manicheism an Iranian Religion?* (1924), *Altpalaestinensischer Bauernglaube* (1925), and *Die Zeit als Schicksalsgottheit in der indischen und iranischen Religion* (1929).

SCHEIBER, ALEXANDER (1913–1985), Hungarian rabbi and scholar. Scheiber was ordained at the Landesrabbinerschule in his native Budapest. After serving as rabbi in Dunaföldvár (1940–44), he became a professor at the Landesrabbinerschule in 1945 and its director in 1950. He also joined the faculty of the University of Szeged (1949), teaching Oriental folklore. Scheiber concentrated on the spiritual survival of the remnant of Hungarian Jewry during the postwar period. Under his leadership the traditions of the rabbinical seminary were maintained, and it continued to graduate young rabbis who filled rabbinical positions in Hungary and abroad. He considered it his mission to explore the Hungarian Jewish past and perpetuate its memory, as well as to study and publish the contributions of great Hungarian-Jewish scholars, including W. Bacher, I. Loew, and B. Heller.

As a scholar, Scheiber's fields of specialization were Jewish history – especially the history of Hungarian Jewry – literature, Jewish folklore, and art. Studying and evaluating the Kaufmann *genizah*, he discovered the Rabbanite prayer book mentioned by Kirkisānī (HUCA, 22 (1949), 307–20), part of the chronicle of Obadiah (KS, 30 (1954), 93–98), and fragments of the *She'elot Attikot* (HUCA, 27 (1956), 291–303, and 36 (1965), 227–59). Together with D.S. Loewinger, Scheiber published a volume of texts (*Ginzei Kaufmann*, 1, 1949). In 1957 a facsimile edition of the Kaufman *Haggadah* was published. During several stays in England, mainly at Cambridge, he discovered many important *genizah* fragments.

His contributions to the history of Hungarian Jewry include *Corpus Inscriptionum Hungariae Judaicarum* (Hung. 1960, with Ger. summary), on Jewish inscriptions found in Hungary, and *Hebraeische Kodexueberreste in ungarlaendischen Einbandstafeln* (Hung. 1969, with Ger. summary). Together with Philipp Gruenvald he edited *Monumenta Hungariae Judaica* (vols. 5–7, 1959, and from vol. 8 by Scheiber only). He also wrote the history of Sopron's (Oedenburg's) synagogue, which dates back to the Middle Ages (REJ, 118 (1959/60), 79–93, and Hungarian (1963)). He also published studies in folklore. Scheiber edited the *Jubilee Volume in Honour of Prof. B. Heller* (1941) and *Semitic Studies in Memory of I. Loew* (1947). A complete bibliography of all Scheiber's publications has been published (Budapest, 1976). He edited the *Encyclopaedia Judaica*'s department of the history of the Jews in Hungary.

[Jeno Zsoldos]

SCHEID, ELIE (1841–1922), Jewish historian and administrator. Born in Haguenau, Alsace, he received a traditional Jewish education and studied for the rabbinate. Scheid, who contributed to the Franco-Jewish press, wrote several historical studies which were collected in his book *Histoire des Juifs d'Alsace* (1887). In 1883 Baron Edmond de *Rothschild invited him to Paris to organize the city's Ḥevrat ha-Ẓedakah ("Charitable Society") and at the end of that year he was appointed inspector of the Baron's settlement project in Ereẓ Israel, a post he held until the end of 1899. He dealt with all settlement matters and conducted political negotiations on behalf of the Baron with the Turkish authorities in Constantinople. Scheid disapproved of Herzl's diplomatic activities, regarding them as dangerous to settlement in Ereẓ Israel. On the other hand, he did not succeed in finding a common language with the settlers. They regarded him as far removed from their aspirations and identified him, perhaps more than he deserved, with the negative aspects of the paternalistic regime introduced by the Baron in the settlements and with the corruption which existed among the Baron's officials.

BIBLIOGRAPHY: JE, S.V.; Tidhar, 1 (1947), 206–7; I. Klausner, *Mi-Kattowitz ad Basel*, 2 (1965), index; T. Herzl, *Complete Diaries*, ed. by R. Patai, 5 (1960), index.

[Yehuda Slutsky]

SCHEINDLIN, RAYMOND P. (1940–), U.S. Judaic literary scholar. Born in Philadepbia and educated at Gratz College, Philadelphia, The Hebrew University of Jerusalem, the University of Pennsylvania (B.A. 1961), Jewish Theological Seminary of America (JTSA) (M.H.L. 1963; rabbinical ordination, 1965), and Columbia University (Ph.D. 1971). Scheindlin taught at McGill University, Montreal (1969–72), Cornell University (1972–74), and the Jewish Theological Seminary, New York (from 1974). He was the director of the Shalom Spiegel Institute of Medieval Hebrew Poetry at the JTSA and was a visiting professor at New York and Columbia universities and a fellow of the University of Pennsylvania Center for Judaic Studies (1993), as well as a member of the Columbia Seminar in Islamic Studies and a senior fellow of the Oxford University Centre for Postgraduate Hebrew Studies. Scheindlin was a part-time rabbi of the Kane Street Synagogue, a Conservative congregation in Brooklyn (1979–82). He was a Guggenheim Fellow in 1988 and was chosen as a Cullman Fellow of the New York Public Library for 2005–06 for a work on Judah Halevi. Scheindlin was a member of a number of professional and scholarly organizations, including the Association for Jewish Studies, the Jewish Publication Society of America, and the Society of Judeo-Arabic Studies. In addition he was a member of the editorial boards of *Jewish Quarterly Review*, *Arabic and Middle Eastern Literatures*, *Medieval Iberia*, *Prooftexts*, and *Edebiyat*.

Scheindlin is recognized as a leading authority on the poetry of medieval Spain and the encounter of Hebrew and Arabic traditions that produced it. His principal publications are *Form and Structure in the Poetry of al-Mu'tamid Ibn 'Abbad* (1974), *Wine, Women, and Death: Medieval Hebrew Poems on the Good Life* (edited and translated, 1986), *The Gazelle: Medieval Hebrew Poems on God, Israel, and the Soul* (edited and translated, 1991), *The Book of Job* (a verse translation with notes, 1998), *A Short History of the Jewish People: From Legendary Times to Modern Statehood* (1998), and *The Cambridge History of Arabic Literature: Al-Andalus* (U.S. title: *The Literature of al-Andalus*; 2000, edited with Maria Rosa Menocal and Michael Sells). He was the translator of Ismar *Elbogen's *Jewish Liturgy in Its Historical Development* (1993) and is also the author of a widely used handbook on Arabic grammar, *201 Arabic Verbs* (1978). Scheindlin wrote the libretto for an opera by Lee Goldstein, *Miriam and the Angel of Death*, based on a story by I.L. Peretz (1984), and provided translations of Hebrew texts for songs by Hugo Weisgall (*Love's Wounded*, 1987; *Psalm of the Distant Dove*, based on poems of Judah Halevi, 1995). He published numerous scholarly articles, translations from Yiddish and medieval Hebrew, and contributions to scholarly collections.

[Drew Silver (2nd ed.)]

SCHEINERT, DAVID (1916–1996), Belgian author. Born in Częstochowa, Poland, Scheinert was raised in Brussels, where he founded the *Revue juive de Belgique*. An aggressive style emphasized his sense of fellowship with the oppressed, whether Jews or non-Jews. Scheinert's works include the novels *L'apprentissage inutile* (1948), *Le coup d'état* (1950), and *Un silence provisoire* (1968); verse collections such as *Réquiem au genièvre* (1952), *Et la lumière chanta* (1954), and *Comme je respire* (1960); and literary essays, notably *Ecrivains belges devant la réalité* (1964).

SCHEINFELD, SOLOMON ISAAC (1860–1943), U.S. Orthodox rabbi, Hebraist, and author. Scheinfeld was born in Scaudvil, Lithuania. He was ordained by Rabbi Isaac Elhanan Spektor in 1890, immigrating to the United States the following year. After a year in Milwaukee (1892–93) and almost a decade in Louisville, Kentucky, Scheinfeld returned to Milwaukee's Beth Israel congregation in 1902, remaining there until his death. Acknowledged rabbinic head of Milwaukee's Orthodox community during his tenure, Scheinfeld exerted leadership in all areas – religious, educational, war relief, charity and welfare, and Zionism. His unorthodox views on the revision and reconstruction of the prayer book were expressed in *Ha-Shilo'aḥ* (1921).

His literary works include five volumes of moral and ethical reflections on Judaism: *Ha-Adam ba-Ma'aleh* ("The Superior Man," 1931); *Olam ha-Sheker* (1936); *Divrei Ḥakhamim* (1941); *Ẓiyyunim be-Derekh ha-Ḥayyim* ("Way-marks in the Path of Life," 2 vols., 1922–28). He also wrote articles in the Hebrew encyclopedia, *Oẓar Yisrael*.

BIBLIOGRAPHY: L.J. Swichkow and L.P. Gartner, *History of the Jews of Milwaukee* (1963), index; Even-Shayish, in: *Ha-Shilo'aḥ*, 25 (1911), 193–7.

[Louis J. Swichkow]

°SCHELER, MAX FERDINAND (1874–1928), German philosopher and sociologist. Scheler was born in Munich. His father came from an upper middle-class Protestant family and his mother from an Orthodox Jewish family that had lived in Franconia for centuries. Scheler himself converted to Roman Catholicism during World War I.

Scheler studied philosophy at the University of Jena; there his most prominent teacher was the idealist philosopher Rudolf Eucken, whose ideas overshadowed Scheler's early work. He also taught at Jena from 1902 to 1907, when he left to teach at the University of Munich. After moving to Munich Scheler turned to phenomenology, and his subsequent work reflected the influence of Edmund *Husserl and Franz Brentano. In 1910 Scheler went to live in Berlin as an academically unattached writer and formed close friendships with Werner *Sombart and Walther *Rathenau. During World War I he became a fervent nationalist and defended the "German war" with passionate intensity. In 1919 he accepted a chair at the University of Cologne, where he developed his views in the sociology of knowledge and also reconsidered his religious views. As a result of the latter, he left the Roman Catholic Church and elaborated his own doctrine, which asserted a vitalistic pantheism.

Scheler was an eclectic thinker who wove many disparate strands of ideas into the texture of his own work. Moreover, he was always open to new ideas and was not afraid to contradict his own earlier ones. His major theological work, in which he attempted to fuse phenomenological approaches with Catholic doctrine is *Vom Ewigen im Menschen* (1921; *On the Eternal in Man*, 1960). His work in social psychology began with *Ueber Ressentiment und moralisches Werturteil* (1912; *Ressentiment*, 1960) and was further extended in his *Zur Phaenomenologie der Sympathiegefuehle* (1913; *The Nature of Sympathy*, 1954). In his last work Scheler attempted detailed phenomenological descriptions of different feeling states emulating the Pascalian endeavor to outline a "logic of the heart." He opposed his holistic psychology to the scientific and analytic psychological approach that prevailed in his day.

Scheler's major philosophical work, *Der Formalismus in der Ethik und die materiale Wertethik* (2 vols., 1913–16, 1921^2), represents an attempt to build a new ethic on the basis of phenomenology in opposition to Kantian ethical formalism. His major contribution to the sociology of knowledge, *Die Wissensformen und die Gesellschaft* (1926), aims at a reconciliation of the Platonic doctrine of the immutability of the world of values with the relativist approach to values found in many modern doctrines. Scheler argues that, though men in different periods and different social strata elaborate widely different forms and standards of knowledge, this simply means that they all strive, each in historically and socially determined ways, to grasp particular aspects of the eternal and immutable sphere of value essences.

A restless spirit, Scheler had wide appeal, especially to the youth, in the hectic and unsettled days of the Weimar Republic. His work had a major influence on French existentialism and phenomenology after World War II. Only later did it become more widely known in England and America, where it attracted the attention not only of philosophers and sociologists but also of theologians. His writings were collected in *Gesammelte Werke* (10 vols., 1953–60).

BIBLIOGRAPHY: M.S. Frings, *Max Scheler. A Concise Introduction into the World of a Great Thinker* (1965); *Philosophy and Phenomenological Research* (March 1942); M. Dupuy, *Philosophie de Max Scheler*, 2 vols. (1959); J.R. Staude, *Max Scheler* (Eng., 1967).

[Lewis A. Coser]

°SCHELLENBERG, WALTER (1910–1952) Nazi official. Born in Saarbruck to minor German officials, Schellenberg studied medicine and law and graduated from the University of Bonn. He joined the Nazi Party in May 1933 and the home office of the SD in 1934. He worked on the consolidation of the SD and the security police, and became a trusted adviser of *Himmler and *Heydrich as deputy chief of the foreign intelligence service of the SD. In May 1941 he concluded an agreement with the German Army on the operation of the Einsatzgruppen (mobile killing units) in the Soviet Union. He was head of the united SS and Wehrmacht intelligence. As early as the summer of 1942, he foresaw the impending defeat of Germany and tried to persuade Himmler to seek a separate peace with the West, which necessitated saving certain Jewish lives as leverage for negotiations and even halting the "Final Solution" in order to gain some time. When the Abwehr was dismantled after the attempt in 1944 on Hitler's life, Schellenberg became the head of the combined intelligence services of the SS and the Wehrmacht. His power was only surpassed by Himmler's within the SS. He was tried in the American Zone trials at Nuremberg. He was acquitted on the crime of genocide but found guilty of complicity in the murder of Soviet POWs. Sentenced to six years, he was released in 1951 and moved to Switzerland, where he wrote his memoirs.

BIBLIOGRAPHY: G. Reitlinger, *SS: Alibi of a Nation 1922–1945* (1956), index; idem, *Final Solution* (1958^2), index; IMT, *Trial of the Major War Criminals*, 24 (1949), index.

[Yehuda Reshef / Michael Berenbaum (2nd ed.)]

°SCHELLING, FRIEDRICH WILHELM JOSEPH (1775–1854), German philosopher. Constantly moved by new insights beyond a position before having adequately stated it, Schelling is generally remembered only as a link between the philosophies of Johann Gottlieb *Fichte and Georg Wilhelm Friedrich *Hegel, a view doing justice neither to his profundity nor to his originality.

Schelling embraced absolute idealism (see *Philosophy, Jewish) before Hegel, and *existentialism before Søren Kierkegaard, who attended Schelling's 1841 lectures. His main periods of thought were: philosophy of nature (1797–99), aesthetic idealism (about 1800), absolute idealism (1801–04), philosophy of freedom (about 1809), "positive philosophy of revelation" (after 1815; N. Hartmann's periodization). Schelling believed that nature is an organism independent of experience. No lapse into pre-Kantian realism, this position drives Schelling beyond Fichte's ethical into an aesthetic idealism. Fichte's nature is non-self for the moral self; Schelling's is preself prior to and independent of self, an "unconscious artist" becoming self-conscious in art and philosophy.

Schelling believed that realistic philosophy of nature and aesthetic idealism are to be viewed as finite standpoints, to be united in absolute idealism as an absolute standpoint is attained. "The Absolute" becomes problematical, however, as freedom and evil, asserting themselves against it, fall outside it. Gradually the gulf widens between "essence" and "existence," and absolute idealism becomes a mere "negative" philosophy – an idealized system abstracted from existence – the preliminary to a new "positive" philosophy which leaps from the absolute to the existential standpoint, confronting existence and "narrating" the confrontations. Negative philosophy constructs the idea of God. Positive philosophy confronts God Himself in His historical revelations.

Although well-versed in Hebraic studies, Schelling had no room for or contact with Judaism prior to abandoning absolute idealism. This is partly due to his romanticism and pantheism (ways of thought out of sympathy with Judaism), largely because his absolute idealism, unlike Hegel's, tends to dissipate particularity in the Absolute, thus giving scant respect to history. Moreover, even when he deals with history, he divides it into pagan and Christian; Christ is "the peak and end of the world of the ancient gods," the Jewish God presumably included, and, "empiricism" being excluded from speculative theology, any "seed of Christianity… in Judaism" is denied (*Werke*, 1 (1856), 292, 296, 303). In line with his turn toward existentialism, however, Schelling's view of Judaism changed. Christian "neglect" of the Hebrew Bible is "almost indecent," for it is divinely revealed; e.g., the tetragrammaton – a name, not a concept – expresses the "divine substance" which is per se inexpressible, and as such referred to by *Elohim* (*Werke*, 2 (1856), 271–2). To the end Judaism remains, not "mythology," which expresses man's unredeemed condition, but the indispensable, revealed "ground" of the Christian revelation, Israel being its chosen bearer.

Jewish thinkers indebted to Schelling's earlier thought include Solomon *Formstecher who, however, subordinates the aesthetic to the ethical and also rejects absolute thought as "sublimated… gnosticism" (Guttmann). Franz *Rosenzweig's *Stern der Erloesung* (1921) reflects close affinity with Schelling's later thought, especially his *Ages of the World*.

BIBLIOGRAPHY: S. Formstecher, *Religion des Geistes* (1841); J. Guttmann, in: F.W.J. Schelling, *Of Human Freedom* (1936), introd. and notes; Guttmann, Philosophies, index.

[Emil Ludwig Fackenheim]

SCHENECTADY, a formerly industrial city situated on the Mohawk River in east central New York State. Of its 61,821 inhabitants (2000) about 5,200 Jews live in the city and suburbs. Jews first settled in Schenectady in the 1840s when Louis Jacobs sold clothing there, and in 1848 Alexander Susholtz settled with his family. Jonathan Levi, a peddler, settled next and would later become one of the major business leaders in the community. Within five years enough Jewish families had moved into the city to begin a congregation, which initially met in the homes of its members. On October 20, 1856, the congregation incorporated as Shaaray Shomayim (later Gates of Heaven). At the same time, Mordecai *Myers, a former State Assemblyman, relocated from Kinderhook in 1848 and was elected mayor in 1851 and 1854. The Jewish community bought land for a cemetery and the first burial took place in 1857. The first religious school was established in 1863. Between 1892 and 1907, Gates of Heaven moved from an Orthodox congregation to Reform. Meanwhile, in the 1870s, Jews from the Russian Empire arrived in Schenectady, and Hungarian Jews moved into the city after 1890, attracted by work available at General Electric. As late as the 1950s at least 30% of employed Jews found work at GE. Jonathan Levi played an instrumental role in attracting the Edison Co., that became GE, to the city. The Jewish community would later become split between permanent residents and professionals who worked at GE before being relocated. In the 19th century Jews worked as peddlers, small businessmen, grocers, tailors, laborers, and craftsmen.

Russian Jews did not want to join the predominantly German Gates of Heaven, and organized the Orthodox Congregation Agudas (later Agudat) Achim in 1890. By the 1920s, second-generation Russian Jews decided to modernize the synagogue, and it officially became Conservative in 1927. Until 1927 Agudas Achim emerged as the leading Orthodox congregation. Ethnic differences led Hungarian Jews to split from Agudas Achim and to found the Orthodox, but Hungarian, Ohab Zedek in 1893. Another split in Agudas Achim led followers of Rabbi Solomon Hinden to organize Adath Israel in 1914. New immigrants formed a separate congregation, Ohab Sholom in 1894. By 1916 the most Orthodox members of the community created a separate congregation, B'nai Abraham. Over time all the Orthodox synagogues merged into one congregation, with the last merger taking place in 1955 when Ohab Zedek merged with Ohab Sholom B'nai Abraham to form Beth Israel, the current Orthodox congregation in Schenectady. The Jewish community numbered 3,000 in 1913 and reached 5,000 in 1918. Later figures by Jewish organizations listed 3,800 in 1943, 2,800 in 1950, 4,200 in 1970, 5,700 in 1984 and 5,200 in the mid-1990s. Prior to 1945, the Jewish community lived primarily within the city limits, but the suburbanization of Jewish residents and institutions mean that the most recent figures suggest that at least half the community lives in suburban towns like Niskayuna.

The diversity of Jewish organizations reached its peak between 1910 and 1930. The first organization not affiliated with a synagogue was the Ladies Benevolent Society formed in 1883. Other charitable institutions included the United Hebrew Charities in 1897, Hebrew Sick and Benevolent Society in 1909, and the Hebrew Sheltering and Aid Society in 1913. Another philanthropic association, Montefiore Society, appeared in the 1880s and reached its peak of effectiveness in the 1890s. Women organized a chapter of the National Council of Jewish Women in March 1916. Jewish fraternal organizations included the Independent Order of Brith Abraham, started in 1900, Free Sons of Judah, 1905–16, Free Sons of Israel (around 1900), and B'nai B'rith, 1921. The first Zionist group, the Moriah Zionist Association began in 1913. By 1917 a chapter of the Socialist Labor Party (Po'alei Zion) was started and, by 1919, a chapter of the Zionist Organization of America. Hadassah started a chapter in 1921. During World War I, local Jews contributed to Jewish war victims in Europe and Palestine and to the Palestine Restoration Fund after the war. Congressman George Lunn of Schenectady, the former Socialist mayor, introduced a resolution in Congress in support of a Jewish homeland in Palestine. In the 1920s and 1930s support for Zionism waned in Schenectady, except for a small dedicated group of men and women. Reform Jewish leaders opposed the idea until after World War II. Between 1945 and 1948, some local Jews in Schenectady, Albany, and Troy helped smuggle bandages, ammunition, and arms to Palestine to defend Jewish settlements, and the community held a mass meeting in May 1948 to celebrate the independence of Israel. In 1967 and 1973, the local community rallied to the embattled Jewish homeland.

Other major Jewish associations were the Workmen's Circle branch, in 1912 and within a year the Jewish Socialist branch formed. A community *talmud torah* was founded in 1911 and chartered in 1912, which became the United Hebrew Community in 1923. Two young people's groups, the Apollo Club and Young Macabees, social and athletic groups, merged in 1916 to form the YMHA, followed by the YWHA a year later. The Ys incorporated in 1921 and merged with the United Hebrew Community to form the Jewish Community Center in 1929. Following the movement of the Jewish population, the JCC, the primary non-congregational organization of the Jewish community, relocated to Niskayuna. The first Jewish self-defense organization was the Jewish Citizens Committee, which began as a protest against Polish pogroms and the Ukrainian massacres, but, due to criticism from local Polish immigrants, the citizens' committee organized in June 1919 to represent all of Schenectady's Jews. Despite its intentions the committee did not last, and in 1938 local Jews, responding to activities of the German-American Bund and antisemitism in Germany, created the Jewish Community Council which was later incorporated in 1948. Both the Anti-Defamation committee of the local B'nai B'rith and the Jewish War Veterans, troubled by the rise in antisemitism, pushed for the creation of the Council. Before and after the war it helped resettle refugees and sent supplies to Jewish survivors in Europe and Palestine after World War II. By 2005, the local representational function had returned to the Jewish Community Center, while the Jewish Federation of Northeastern New York took over the responsibility for speaking for the Jewish communities of the Capital District, and pooling resources for activities that cut across local communities. As elsewhere in the country, synagogues and institutional buildings in downtown urban areas were sold as the Jewish residents moved to residential areas outside of the downtown area and to the suburbs. There is a Jewish Studies program at Union College in Schenectady that has added to the intellectual quality of the Jewish community.

BIBLIOGRAPHY: S. Weingarten, "The Biography of an American Jewish Community; Jewish Community of Schenectady, (Master's thesis, Siena College, 1952); P.W. Jacobs, "The Jewish Congregations of Schenectady," in: *Schenectady Union Star* (October 18, 1913); L. King and A. Mann, "Schenectady Jewry," in: *Tri-City Jewish Chronicle* (Dec. 1917), 17–23; N. Yetwin, "Soldier of Subsequent Fortune," in: *New York Alive* (Jan/Feb, 1989), 17–18.

[Harvey Strum (2nd ed.)]

SCHENIRER, SARAH (1883–1935), educational pioneer, founder of the *Beth Jacob school network. In Orthodox writings, Schenirer's life and work are described in the mythic, legendary terms usually reserved for renowned male rabbinic figures. Born to a ḥasidic family in Cracow, Schenirer received a formal education in Polish public schools until the age of 14, when she took up work as a seamstress to help support her family. In a short autobiographical sketch, she notes that from childhood she was drawn to Jewish learning and was of a pious temperament. As a young woman, she grew alarmed by the situation of her female contemporaries, exposed to the attractions of secular culture and with little Jewish knowledge to help preserve their identity. In Austrian-ruled Galicia, where Jews enjoyed equal rights from the late 1860s and compulsory public education existed, many rabbis and communal leaders had discussed the need for Jewish education for girls, but in the end it was the dedicated amateur, Sarah Schenirer, who made this a reality. By her own account, the impetus for her initiative came during her family's stay as refugees in Vienna after the outbreak of World War I. The evening lectures of Rabbi Dr. Flesch, a disciple of the Neo-Orthodox approach of Samson Raphael *Hirsch, inspired her to return to Poland and translate her ideas about education for girls into practice. Her first school, opened in Cracow in the fall of 1917, gave supplementary religion lessons to young girls after their studies in public school (this would be the nature of most of the later schools as well). By the time of Schenirer's death in 1935, the Beth Jacob school network in Poland had grown to 227 schools with over 27,000 pupils. Schenirer's disciples also would found schools in Austria, Czechoslovakia, Romania, Lithuania, Palestine, and the United States. Schenirer played a major role in the expansion of the network, traveling to dozens of towns throughout Poland and addressing meetings of parents and young girls, convincing them to set up local Beth Jacob schools. Schenirer was aided in her quest by the endorsement of leading rabbinic figures and by the adoption of Beth Jacob by the Agudat Israel movement. Agudah provided Beth Jacob with financial assistance, logistical guidance, and a literary forum, the Yiddish-language *Beys-Yankev Zhurnal*. Schenirer's personal dedication and charisma were supplemented by the organizational professionalism of Dr. Leo Deutschlander and by young, educated women he recruited from Germany to help staff summer training courses and, later on, the central teachers' seminary in Cracow founded by Schenirer. Schenirer cooperated with Deutschlander in the seminary's administration, and was instrumental in the founding of the Benot Agudat Yisrael youth movement for students and graduates of Beth Jacob. She composed curricular materials and wrote plays and articles on the holidays and moralistic themes. Her collected Yiddish writings (*Gezamelte Shriftn*) appeared in 1933 and later in Hebrew translation (see bibliography). Little is known about her personal life. Schenirer was evidently married for a very short time and divorced in her late twenties. Late in her short life she married Rabbi Yitzhak Landau, grandson of the Rebbe of Radomsk. She had no children of her own, but devoted her life to the hundreds of young women she taught and for whom she served as a model of feminine personal piety and learning.

BIBLIOGRAPHY: A. Atkin, "The Beth Jacob Movement in Poland (1917–1939)" (diss., Yeshiva University, 1959); P.Benisch, *Carry Me In Your Heart: The Life and Legacy of Sarah Schenirer, Founder and Visionary of the Bais Yaakov Movement* (2003); R. Manekin, "*Mashehu Ḥadash Legamrei: Hitpatteḥuto shel Ra'ayon ha-Ḥinukh* *ha-Dati le-Banot ba-Et ha-Ḥadashah*," in: *Masekhet*, 2 (2004), 63–85; Z. Scharfstein, *Gedolei Ḥinukh be-Ameinu* (1964), 226–43; S. Schenirer, *Em be-Yisrael: Kitvei Sarah Schenirer*, 3 vols. (1955); D. Weissman, "Bais Yaakov – A Women's Educational Movement in the Polish Jewish Community: A Case Study in Tradition and Modernity" (M.A. thesis, New York University, 1977); S. Pantel Zolty, *"And All Your Children Shall Be Learned": Women and the Study of Torah in Jewish Law and History* (1993).

[Gershon Bacon (2nd ed.)]

SCHENK, FAYE L. (1909–1981), U.S. Zionist leader. Faye Schenk was born in Des Moines, Iowa, daughter of Rabbi H.H. Zeichik, a noted talmudic scholar. In 1933 she married Rabbi Max Schenk, later spiritual leader of Congregation Shaare Zedek in Brooklyn, N.Y. From 1939 to 1949 the Schenks lived in Sydney, Australia, where Faye Schenk was a leader in the Women's International Zionist Organization. Settling in New York in 1949, she became active in *Hadassah, and after serving in numerous leadership capacities became national president in 1968. Mrs. Schenk remained national president of Hadassah until 1972 and in 1973 was elected president of the American Zionist Federation. She became a member of the Executive of the World Zionist Organization in 1977 and settled permanently in Israel. After serving for six months as chairman of the *Keren Hayesod, after the death of Ezra Shapiro, in 1978 she was appointed head of the organization department of the WZO.

[Gladys Rosen]

SCHENKER, HEINRICH (1868–1935), music theorist; the most important 20th century theorist of tonal music. Born in Wisniowczyki, Galicia. Schenker studied law as well as harmony with Bruckner in Vienna. After an early career as a composer, accompanist, editor, and critic (especially for the *Wiener Wochenblatt*), Schenker undertook more serious analytical and theoretical engagement. He developed new analytical procedures for the perception of musical structures. His most important achievements came to fruition in his last book, *Der freie Satz* (1935; *Free Composition*, 1979), the last book in the trilogy *Neue musikalische Theorien und Phantasien*. According to his theory, structural harmonies, which are ultimately derived from the background structure (*Ursatz*) of an upper descending voice (*Urlinie*) against bass arpeggiation of the tonic, are prolonged or composed out (*auskomponiert*) by techniques based on strict counterpoint, such as linear progressions and neighbor motion. Schenker appreciated and analyzed mainly the works of a few great composers from Bach to Brahms. Though originally based only on the works of the 18th and 19th centuries, Schenker's concepts have been applied to earlier and later music as well (cf. F. Salzer, *Structural Hearing*, 1952). Schenker's writings include the trilogy, the first two volumes being *Harmonielehre* (1906; *Harmony*, 1954) and *Kontrapunkt* (2 vols., 1910 and 1922; *Counterpoint*, 1987), and more analytical books, among them *Das Meisterwerk in der Musik* (3 vols., 1925, 1926, 1930; *The Masterwork in Music*, 1994, 1996, 1997) and *Der Tonwille* (1921–24).

Schenker wrote *Ḥasidic Dances*, ultimately published as *Syrian Dances*; his books and diaries include occasional reference to Jewish matters.

BIBLIOGRAPHY: O. Jonas, *Das Wesen des musikalischen Kunstwerks* (1934; trans. as *An Introduction to the Theory of Heinrich Schenker*, 1982)). **ADD. BIBLIOGRAPHY:** Grove online; H. Federhofer, *Heinrich Schenker nach Tagebuecher und Briefen* (1985); W. Pastille, *Ursatz: The Philosophical Background of Heinrich Schenker* (1986); C. Schachter, *Unfoldings: Essays in Schenkerian Theory and Analysis* (1999).

[Roger Kamien / Yossi Goldenberg (2nd ed.)]

SCHENKER, JOEL W. (1904–1985), U.S. theatrical producer and builder. Born in Manhattan, Schenker attended New York University and went into the real-estate business. But he also worked as an actor and co-wrote a play, *This Our House*, which folded after two performances on Broadway in 1935. He swore off the theater for years. In the construction field, he headed the Gregory-Roth-Schenker Construction Corporation and the Webb & Knapp Construction Corporation, building housing for veterans after World War II and then high-rise apartment houses and office buildings. He became prominent as a producer or co-producer of serious theater after he and Cheryl Crawford revived Sean O'Casey's *Shadow of a Gunman* in a widely hailed Actors Studio production. His first commercial hit on Broadway, *A Far Country* (1961), was Henry Denker's drama about Sigmund Freud. He then produced *Seidman and Son* (1963) with Sam Levene, and, in the same year, *A Case of Libel*, again by Denker and inspired by the book *My Life in Court* by Louis *Nizer. Schenker was a mainstay of the American Shakespeare Festival, serving as a trustee and executive producer. He also raised funds and served as an officer of the Jewish Theological Seminary of America and the building division of the United Jewish Appeal.

[Stewart Kampel (2nd ed.)]

SCHERESCHEWSKY, SAMUEL ISAAC JOSEPH (1831–1906), Episcopalian bishop of China. Born of Jewish parentage at Tauroggen (see *Taurage), Lithuania, Schereschewsky went to America in 1854, where he became a Christian in 1855. In 1859 he went to China as a missionary, first in Shanghai and then in Beijing (Peking), where he lived for 13 years (1862–75), and in 1877 was appointed Episcopalian bishop of China. Inspired by a visit of three *Kaifeng Jews to Beijing in March 1867, the missionaries induced Schereschewsky to visit the Kaifeng Jewish community in the middle of that year. He found some 200 or 300 Jewish families in Kaifeng, a fair proportion of them in good circumstances. They had entirely lost their religion, intermarried with the local population, and were scarcely distinguishable from them. After a stay of about 25 days he was driven out of the city by a mob. Schereschewsky spoke 13 languages, among them Hebrew and Chinese. While in Beijing, he began to translate the Pentateuch from Hebrew into Mandarin Chinese. In 1881 he had a stroke, which semi-paralyzed his hands. Using two fingers, he completed his work. His translation is still outstanding, and because of his physical handicap the work is known as the "Two Finger Bible."

BIBLIOGRAPHY: J.A. Muller, *Apostle of China. Samuel Isaac Joseph Schereschewsky, 1831–1906* (1937).

[Rudolf Loewenthal]

SCHERLAG, MARK (1878–1962), Austrian Zionist poet. Born in Chorostkow, Galicia, Scherlag studied law at the University of Vienna and supported himself as a bank clerk there. He joined the Zionist movement with the appearance of Theodor Herzl and developed personal ties with him. He contributed to the Zionist and general press and periodicals in German and Polish. Scherlag published lyric poems on Jewish subjects. He settled in Haifa in 1939, and, in the last years of his life, he recorded his memoirs of the early years of the Zionist movement.

His works include the following collections of poetry in German: *Einsamkeit* (1899), *Heimaterde. Judenlieder* (1922), *In der Fremde. Neue Judenlieder* (1919), and a selection of his poetry from 1900 to 1939 *Aus dem Leben* (n.d.).

BIBLIOGRAPHY: Tidhar, 5 (1952), 2245; M. Gelber, *Toledot ha-Tenu'ah ha-Ẓiyyonit be-Galiẓyah* (1958), 3–8.

[Getzel Kressel]

SCHERMAN, NOSSON (1935–), U.S. rabbi, publisher of *ArtScroll. Scherman was born in Newark, NJ, where his parents owned a mom-and-pop grocery store, and he was a product of its public school system, studying in the afternoon at a local *talmud torah*. At the age of 10 he entered Yeshivah Torah Vodaath, where he remained through Beit Midrash. In 1953, he was admitted to Beit Medrash Elyon, Torah Vodaath's postgraduate division in Monsey NY, where he studied for 11 years and was ordained. His primary teachers and influences throughout his adult life were Rabbi Yaakov *Kaminetsky and Rabbi Gedaliah Schorr, the roshei yeshivah of Torah Vodaath.

Scherman was a teacher and assistant Hebrew principal and general studies principal at Yeshivah Torah Temimah in Brooklyn for eight years, and then principal of Yeshivah Karlin-Stolin in Brooklyn for six. He was also head counselor of Camp Torah Vodaath from 1967 to 1969. From 1969 to 1990 he was editor of *Olomeinu/Our World*, the children's magazine of Torah Umesorah.

In 1976, Rabbi Meier *Zlotowitz of ArtScroll asked Scherman to edit and contribute an introduction to the Book of Esther. Like Zlotowitz, Scherman gave up his career to develop the ArtScroll Series and its parent company, Mesorah Publications, with Zlotowitz and Sheah Brander.

Early on, Scherman became general editor and was best known as the author of the Overviews, the introductory essays that present the background and perspective of dozens of books of Scripture and liturgy. In 1984, he published his first major work, the translation and commentary of the *siddur*, which was followed by the Rosh Hashanah and Yom Kippur *maḥzorim*. In 1993, he published the Stone Edition of the *Ḥumash*, with translation and commentary.

His "translation" of the *siddur* is not quite a translation – for example, the erotic Hebrew of the Song of Songs is not rendered into English. Instead, the allegory to God and Israel is treated as the *peshat*. The *siddur* appears in two versions. The Rabbinical Council of America, the Centrist Orthodox Rabbinical Movement, has its version with the prayer for the State of Israel and a slightly different introduction.

The success of the ArtScroll/Mesorah series is undeniable. ArtScroll is a fascinating combination of fervently Orthodox Judaism and an American aesthetic that wraps traditional Judaism in a visual idiom acceptable to the American sensibility. Zlotowitz's sense of the visual impact of a book is an indispensable ingredient in its success. Despite what outsiders may think, even the rejectionist Orthodox community that does not embrace modern culture has, perhaps inadvertently, acculturated itself to the offerings and packaging of the American marketplace.

ArtScroll publishes in English and in Hebrew and has brought its own unique styling to the Israeli and American marketplace. In the United States, it represents an important transition between Yiddish and English as the spoken language and the language of Jewish learning for fervently Orthodox Jews in America.

Modern Orthodox scholars have not been uncritical of ArtScroll's success. Its historical studies are wrapped, not in Western scholarship, but in hagiography; it seems as if every fervently Orthodox leader or rabbi is without blemish. Others on the right criticize it for enabling and empowering English rather than Yiddish or Hebrew to be the language of contemporary learning.

The Schottenstein Talmud has allowed many who would have otherwise lacked the skill and talmudic virtuosity to participate in *daf yomi* (studying a page of Talmud a day) programs. It has offered those learning in yeshivah the "English" experience of the Beit Midrash and has far outpaced the more sophisticated and erudite commentary of Adin *Steinsaltz in popularity and use.

Scherman's main project in 2006 was the Rubin edition of the Prophets, of which the Books of Joshua, Judges, and Samuel have been published and the Book of Kings was due to go to press.

For several years Scherman was a columnist for the *Forward* and the *Jewish Week*, and taught Mishnah and the Holocaust in a telephone lecture series.

[Michael Berenbaum (2nd ed.)]

SCHEUER, EDMUND (1847–1943), Canadian religious reformer and activist. Considered by many the "father of Reform Judaism in Canada," Scheuer was born in Bernkastel in the Prussian Rhineland and received his education there and across the river in Metz, in France. At the age of 17, he moved to Paris, attracted, according to some accounts, by the greater freedom accorded to Jews in France. There he entered the jewelry export business, acting as agent for a Hamilton, Ontario, firm owned by his brother-in-law, Herman Levy. In Paris, Scheuer was still a Sabbath observer, although he joined the Alliance Israélite Universelle, the organization founded for the purpose, inter alia, of spreading French culture among Jews outside France.

When the Franco-Prussian War interrupted his business, Scheuer emigrated to Canada and joined his brother-in-law's firm. Within months of his arrival in Hamilton in 1871, he was named treasurer of Anshe Sholom Synagogue, one of the very few synagogues in Canada where Jews of German origin predominated, and which was open to the Reform Movement which had swept over similar congregations in the United States. The next year Scheuer organized a Sabbath school, the first in Ontario, which he led until he moved to Toronto in 1886. From 1876 to 1886, he served as president of the congregation, which he nudged steadily in the direction of Reform. He also organized a chapter of the Alliance Israélite Universelle, the only one ever established in Canada. His activities in Hamilton illustrate two of Scheuer's interrelated passions with regard to Jewish life: Jewish education and the acculturation of immigrants.

In Toronto, Scheuer joined Holy Blossom, the still traditional synagogue of the established, acculturating Jews; there, too, he became the most forceful advocate of "American" Reform. And there, too, he organized a Sabbath school, perhaps the first "modern" Jewish school in the city. He served the synagogue in a variety of offices, including, in 1896, treasurer of the building committee for the new temple on Bond Street. In 1939, when the move to suburban Forest Hill was made, Scheuer, the only surviving member of the earlier campaign, was made honorary chair of the building committee.

But Scheuer's activities in Toronto ranged far beyond the temple's precincts. He was one of the organizers of the Federation of Jewish Philanthropies and served as its first president from 1917 to 1921. This, too, was an "Americanizing" move, following the lead of communities in the United States which were amalgamating and professionalizing their charitable efforts in these years. Scheuer also led the Zionist Free School for Girls, which met at an Orthodox synagogue, and worked to counter the influence of missionaries and socialists among Jewish young people.

In Toronto, Scheuer pursued the goal of acculturation in several ways. As school principal, he shaped the curriculum to emphasize ethics rather than Jewish particularity. For 40 years, he served as president of the Toronto chapter of the Anglo-Jewish Association, the British equivalent of the Alliance Israélite Universelle and a more suitable vehicle for Jewish acculturation in English Canada. For decades, he served as a justice of the peace, and he belonged to the Empire and Canadian clubs and the Toronto Board of Trade. In the 1930s, as fascist and Nazi sympathizers grew in numbers in Canada, Scheuer typically urged fellow Jews "to remain calm." Days before a violent riot in Toronto in 1933, he assured them that "Canadian laws – thank God – are just, our police excellent and well able to protect any class of citizens being molested by hoodlums." He was proved wrong, as the police stood by and allowed the violence to proceed.

The rising tide of antisemitism in Canada in the 1930s caused Scheuer to alter course somewhat. He became active in the Canadian Jewish Congress reorganized in 1933 to fight antisemitism and served as an honorary vice president from 1934 to 1939. He ceased writing letters to newspapers in defense of Jews and Judaism, once a civic task to which he devoted much time and energy. Now he preferred "background" meetings with editors and publishers as less likely to inflame.

Scheuer's life stretched almost a century from the liberal revolutions of 1848 through most of World War II, and it is no surprise that he had to adjust some of his early assumptions. But he remained to the end of his life both an advocate of modernization and acculturation in Jewish life and a dedicated and proud Jew. He could at the same time be "the father of Reform Judaism in Canada," at a time when Reform was not popular among Canadian Jews, and still the "grand old man of [all of] Toronto Jewry."

[Michael Brown (2nd ed.)]

SCHEUER, JAMES H. (1920–2005), a 13-term liberal U.S. congressman from New York, part of the post-World War II generation of political reformers. The son of a prosperous New York investor, he was born in Manhattan and received his bachelor's degree from Swarthmore College in 1942, a master's degree from Harvard Business School in 1943, and a law degree from Columbia Law School in 1948. He contracted polio on his honeymoon and spent a year recuperating in Warm Springs, Georgia, where Franklin Delano Roosevelt had also undergone rehabilitation from adult polio. For the rest of his life, Scheuer walked with a cane.

A multimillionaire real estate developer and lawyer, Scheuer was president of the Renewal and Development Corporation of New York City before seeking elected office. He sponsored urban renewal projects and middle-income housing developments in cities including Washington, Cleveland, St. Louis, Sacramento, and San Francisco.

Scheuer made political waves in the 1964 election when he and another reform Democrat, Jonathan B. Bingham, ousted incumbent congressmen who were part of the Bronx political machine, James C. Healey and Charles A. Buckley.

It seemed as if, with each decade's census and New York's diminished population, Scheuer was forced to run in another district and to serve another constituency. He lost re-election in 1972 after serving four terms in the 21st Congressional District, in the Bronx, when redistricting forced him to run against another incumbent congressman. He moved to the 11th district in Queens, where he won the 1974 election and three more, and then, in 1982, finally the redistricted 8th District, which covered part of Queens and Nassau County, where he served his final five terms. He announced his retirement after the 1990 census forced another redistricting. In each district, his agenda remained the same. He fought for the Environmental Protection Agency against Reagan administration attempts to dismantle it, and he fought the auto industry, which opposed his efforts to mandate safety belts and air bags. He was successful in both. Twice defeated for Congress, he kept coming back again and again. An urban and urbane man, he served as president of the National Alliance for Safer Cities (1972–73) and president of the National Housing Conference (1972–74).

An unapologetic, some would say an unrepentant, liberal, Scheuer believed in an activist role for government. His legislative agenda included Head Start for early education, environmental protection, and automotive safety.

He believed keenly in the right to privacy, which in American terms put him on the side of contraception and abortion, issues he believed were and should remain personal. In its obituary for Scheuer, the *New York Times* recalled that "He once had a hundred posters printed up that said, 'Someday the decision to have children will be between you, your spouse and your congressman.' The photograph showed a couple sitting in their bed with Mr. Scheuer, dressed in a suit, sandwiched between them."

After retirement from Congress he was appointed by President Clinton as United States director of the European Bank for Reconstruction and Development, founded to make loans to Eastern European and Asian countries and thus counter Communist influence. Together with his siblings and a family foundation established by his parents, he was deeply involved in support of Jewish philanthropies and development in Israel.

BIBLIOGRAPHY: *New York Times* (August 30, 2005); L.S. Maisels and I. Forman (eds.), *The Jew in American Politics* (2001).

[Michael Berenbaum (2nd ed.)]

SCHIBY, BARUCH (1906–ca. 1976), author and journalist of *Salonika. In 1927 Schiby founded the Zionist "Achdut" club in Salonika. When the Germans attacked Greece, he managed with friends to reach Athens in a small boat. As a student in Athens in World War II, he was involved in EAM resistance activities. In Athens, he received shelter from the Greek cabinet minister Prof. Niko Louvaris, whose contacts also helped him greatly in resistance activities. He was part of a special committee of Jews from this Communist political resistance movement who persuaded Rabbi Eli Barzilai of Athens not to hand over the community lists to the new German commander, Jorgen Stroop, and to flee the community for the mountains. He also wrote about the pro-German activities of Greek intellectuals for the Greek Academy, for which he received payment in order to survive during that difficult time. In late 1944, at the beginning of the Greek Civil War when England controlled the Greek government, he was arrested by the British and sent to the Al-Daba prison camp in *Egypt, and was chosen to represent the prisoners. He returned to Salonika and became director of the Jewish community.

Known mainly for his quarterly *Dhelfika tetradhia*, Schiby was a prominent literary figure and a leading Zionist. His *I fleghomeni vatos* ("The Burning Bush," 1968) discussed the origins of the Jews and various aspects of Judaism. His book *I Evrai* ("The Jews"), published in 1971, depicted ancient Jewish history for his Greek countrymen. He wrote several articles on the history of the Jews of Salonika and the Samaritan presence in Salonika from late antiquity. In the 1960s, he developed relations with the Spanish Academy in its renewed contact with Sephardi philology, language, history, and culture. He also edited a bilingual Greek-Ladino Haggadah for Pessah.

ADD. BIBLIOGRAPHY: Y. Kerem, "Rescue Attempts of Jews in Greece in the Second World War" (Heb.), in: *Pe'amim* 27 (1986), 77–109; B. Rivlin, "Athens," in: *Pinkas ha-Kehillot Yavan* (1999), 67–86.

[Rachel Dalven / Yitzchak Kerem (2nd ed.)]

SCHICK, ABRAHAM BEN ARYEH LOEB (19th century), Lithuanian rabbi and commentator on the Midrash. Schick lived in Slonim during the rabbinate of Isaac Shapira (called Eizel Ḥarif) but held no rabbinical post there. He devoted himself almost entirely to the study of Midrash and *aggadah* and published a number of commentaries on them.

These included *Zera Avraham* (1833), on the *Midrash Proverbs; Me'orei Esh* (1834), with a preface and extensive introduction, on the *Tanna de-Vei Eliyahu; MaḤazeh ha-Shir* (1840), on *Song of Songs Rabbah; Eshed ha-NeḤalim*, in five parts (1843–45), on the *Midrash Rabbah; Ein Avraham* (1848), on Ibn Ḥabib's *Ein Ya'akov*, and also dealing with the commentary to the *aggadot* of the Talmud by Samuel *Edels. Schick edited *Ohel Ya'akov*, the parables to Genesis and Exodus of Jacob Krantz (the Dubner Maggid).

BIBLIOGRAPHY: Fuenn, Keneset, 67; *Pinkas Slonim*, 1 (1962), 63.

[Itzhak Alfassi]

SCHICK, BARUCH BEN JACOB (also known as **Baruch Shklover**, from the name of his birthplace, Shklov; 1740?–after 1812), rabbi, physician, and one of the pioneers of *Haskalah of Eastern Europe. Schick was ordained as a rabbi in 1764 and subsequently served as *dayyan* in Minsk. In his youth he was already attracted to the Haskalah and general knowledge. His first scholarly work and his other works were lost in a conflagration. He traveled to London to study medicine and there joined the Freemasons. After qualifying as a doctor he moved to Berlin, where he became acquainted with the *maskilim* of the town, including Moses *Mendelssohn and Naphtali Herz *Wessely. In 1777 Schick published in Berlin Isaac *Israeli's astronomical work *Yesod Olam* from a defective manuscript in the possession of Hirschel b. Aryeh Lob *Levin, and that same year published his *Ammudei Shamayim*, a scientific commentary to Maimonides' *Hilkhot Kiddush ha-Ḥodesh*, adding to it his *Tiferet Adam*, a popular work on anatomy. In 1778, on his way back to Minsk, he visited Vilna and was in the group associated with Elijah b. Solomon (the Gaon of Vilna), in whose name he published a statement on the need for scientific knowledge for an understanding of the Torah. This strengthened Schick's standing in Jewish circles and influenced not only his contemporaries but also subsequent generations. He stated that the Gaon of Vilna advised him to translate scientific works into Hebrew in order to make their contents available to Jews. In the Hague in 1779, he published his *Derekh Yesharah*, on medicine and hygiene, and in 1780 he published from Latin a Hebrew translation of the first part of Euclid's geometry. In 1784 he was in Prague, where he published his *Keneh ha-Middah*, on geometry and trigonometry, which he translated from English (republished by him in Shklov in 1791, together with additional expositions to Maimonides' *Hilkhot Kiddush ha-Ḥodesh*). From Prague he returned to Minsk. After some time he settled in Shklov, and there he belonged to the *maskilim* whose needs were supplied by the wealthy Joshua *Zeitlin of Ustye near Shklov. Toward the end of his life he lived in Slutzk, where he served as *dayyan* and as court physician to Count Radziwill, and where he died. Among the manuscripts he left were a book of medical cures and the translation of the second part of Euclid. Schick devoted his energies to arousing his fellow Jews to the need for studying the arts and sciences. He regarded the neglect of the sciences as caused by the exile. He repeated the accusations of his predecessor, Israel Moses ha-Levi *Zamoscz, against the fanatical rabbis and leaders who persecuted and condemned the *maskilim*. To restore science to its former place of honor, he pleaded for a revival of Hebrew, in which scientific works intended for his people should be written.

BIBLIOGRAPHY: Zeitlin, Bibliotheca; Zinberg, *Sifrut*, 3 (1958), 325–8; Twersky, in: *He-Avar*, 4 (1956), 77–81; R. Mahler, *Divrei Yemei Yisrael*, 4 (1956), 53–56; B. Katz, *Rabbanut, Ḥasidut, Haskalah*, 2 (1958), 134–9; N. Schapira, in: *Harofe Haivri*, 34 (1961), 230–5; J. Katz, *Jews and Freemasons* (1970).

[Abraham David]

SCHICK, BELA (1877–1967), pediatrician. Born in Boglar, Hungary, Schick became an assistant at the Children's Clinic in Vienna and later associate professor of pediatrics at Vienna University. He left Austria for the U.S. and, in 1923, became pediatrician in chief at Mt. Sinai Hospital in New York, and in 1936 clinical professor of pediatrics at Columbia University. Schick was famous for his discovery of a skin test for determining susceptibility to diphtheria, known as the Schick test. This test enabled early diagnosis and treatment and thus made it possible to save thousands of lives. He also made important studies on scarlet fever, tuberculosis, and the nutrition of infants. He described a symptom for tuberculosis of the bronchial glands, known as the Schick sign. His publications include *The Serum Diseases* (with C. Pirquet, 1905), *Scarlet Fever* (with Th. Escherich, 1912), and *Diphtheria* (1931).

BIBLIOGRAPHY: S.R. Kagan, *Jewish Medicine* (1952), 367.

[Suessmann Muntner]

°**SCHICK, CONRAD** (1822–1901), German resident of Jerusalem, missionary, architect, surveyor, archaeologist, and model-builder. Born in Bitz (near Abingen, Württemberg) Schick was educated as a locksmith-apprentice in Kornthal (near Stuttgart), where he was exposed to the religious atmosphere of pietistic Wuerttemberg. In Basel, he joined Christian Friedrich Spittler's "Pilgrim's Mission" in St. Chrischona. In late summer of 1846 Schick arrived in Jerusalem as one of the first two missionaries sent by Spittler and established the "Bruederhaus" as their missionary center. He left Spittler in 1850 and joined the "London Society for Promoting Christianity among Jews" (London Jews' Society – LJS) as a carpentry teacher in the "House of Industry" educational institution in Jerusalem. In 1857 he became director of the school, serving until 1880. He was also responsible for all LJS assets in Jerusalem and its "house architect and builder." He lived in Jerusalem for 55 years, until his death.

Schick was undoubtedly the most significant and influential scholar among the residents of Jerusalem in the second half of the 19th century, a devoted lover of the city, gifted with a unique "talent for Jerusalem," which derived from his deep-rooted loyalty to the city, the Holy Land, and everything they represent to the devout Christian. In addition, he left his traces on the country's landscape: the monumental buildings he planned and constructed in Jerusalem. Schick engaged in a variety of topics. He is mentioned in most of the research on 19th-century Jerusalem, European and German colonization and settlement in Palestine, the history of Palestine's cartography and archaeology, 19th-century architecture in Jerusalem, and models and relief maps of the city and its monuments.

He took advantage of his ongoing presence, his familiarity with the city and the whole country, and his command of the local as well as European languages. He was involved in almost every study conducted in Jerusalem at the time. His importance reached its peak following the beginning of the organized study of Palestine, marked by the foundation of the PEF and, 12 years later, the German DPV. Schick was for both organizations the best "man in the field," the ideal "research agent." His reports and papers hold an unprecedented treasure of information concerning almost all periods in the history of Jerusalem as well as the present city. Modern researchers, in archaeology as well as history and historical geography, continue to make use of the data in Schick's studies.

He reached his scientific position through diligent work, boundless inquisitiveness, a long process of independent study, and a deep feeling for the country and the city, their history and religious traditions. Schick was an autodidact, combining the describer and reporter, the surveyor, researcher and discoverer. In four decades of scientific work, he published two books, a number of guides to various sites in Jerusalem, and hundreds of articles, reports, maps, and drawings. He participated, in one way or another, in almost all the research conducted in Jerusalem during the last third of the 19th century.

His works concerning the Herodium (Frankenberg), Solomon's Pools, the water aqueducts to Jerusalem, the Siloam inscription, and the subterranean cisterns of the Temple Mount are only some examples of his archaeological involvement and achievements. He was involved in the planning, and sometimes also in the building, of Talitha Kumi, both "Jesus-Hilfe" hospitals for lepers, the LJS sanatorium and the Diaconesses' hospital on Prophets Street, his own residence ("Tabor House") and the "Mahanaim House," the Jewish neighborhood Me'ah She'arim, the Ethiopian Church, and many other monumental buildings. In many of them, he cooperated with Theodor Sandel, an architect who belonged to the Temple Society.

Being one of the heads of the German community in Jerusalem, Schick participated in every local committee. He was a member of a long list of scientific societies. He was decorated by the Austrians and the Germans, and received the title of "royal building consultant" from the King of Württemberg and an honorary doctorate from the University of Tübingen.

BIBLIOGRAPHY: A. Carmel, "Wie es zu Conrad Schicks Sendung nach Jerusalem kam," in: ZDPV, 99 (1983), 204–18; H. Goren, G. Barkai, and E. Schiller (eds.), *Conrad Schick: For Jerusalem, Jerusalem* (Heb., 1998); H. Goren and R. Rubin, "Conrad Schick's Models of Jerusalem and its Monuments," in: PEQ, 128 (1996), 102–24; E. Kautzsch, "Zum Gedächtniss des koeniglich wuerttembergischen Bauraths Dr. Conrad Schick," in: *Mittheilungen und Nachrichten des Deutschen Palästina Vereins,* 8 (1902), 1–12; T. Sandel, "Der Koenigl. Wuerttemb. Baurat Dr. C. Schick," in: *Warte,* 58 (1902), 117–18; C. Schick, *Wie aus einem einfachen Mechaniker im Schwabenland ein koeniglicher Baurat in Jerusalem geworden ist,* ed. H. Grobe-Einsler (1966); C. Schlicht, "Baurat Dr. Conrad Schick," in: *Neueste Nachrichten aus dem Morgenlande,* 46 (1902), 3–8; A. Strobel, *Conrad Schick – Ein Leben fuer Jerusalem: Zeugnisse ueber einen erkannten Auftrag* (1988); S. Gibson, "Conrad Schick (1822–1901), The Palestine Exploration Fund and an 'Archaic Hebrew' Inscription from Jerusalem," in: PEQ, 132 (2000), 113–22; C.W. Wilson, "Obituary of Dr. Conrad Schick," in: PEFQS, 34 (1902), 139–42.

[Haim Goren (2nd ed.)]

SCHICK, MOSES BEN JOSEPH (1807–1879), Hungarian rabbi and *posek,* also known as "Maharam Schick." According to one tradition the name was chosen by the family following the law passed by the Austrian government making it obligatory for Jews to adopt surnames, and it was chosen as forming the initial letters of *Shem Yisrael Kadosh* ("the Jewish name is sacred"). Schick was born in Brezove in the Neutra (Nitra) district of Slovakia. He was orphaned when a child, and at the age of 11 went to study at the yeshivah of his uncle Isaac Frankel in Frauenkirchen. After three years he proceeded to the yeshivah of Moses *Sofer in Pressburg, where he remained for six years. Sofer recommended him as a suitable incumbent for the vacant post at Vergin near Pressburg, and he served there about 24 years. In 1861 he agreed to accept the rabbinate of Khust, where he established a yeshivah and remained until his death. Among his many pupils special mention may be made of Zussman Sofer of Paks, Zalman Spitzer of Vienna, and Wolf Sofer of Budapest, who are frequently mentioned in his responsa.

Schick fought against the Reform movement. Following the Braunschweig conference (1844) and the resolutions adopted there, he wrote in a responsum (YD 331) that the men assembled "are not rabbis but Karaites. They don the cloaks of rabbis in order to deceive and to act like the serpent. Some are not qualified in *halakhah* or as rabbis, but have become rabbis overnight." He protested especially against the resolution permitting mixed marriages. His call for a united front of Orthodox Jewry against the Reform movement was not accepted at that time. Following the publication in Hungary in 1867 of the law granting autonomy to the Jews and the demand of the Reformers to convene a congress to discuss the organization of the communities and education, Schick gave his full support to the plan to found an independent communal organization. In the Budapest congress of 1869, he fought for complete separation from the Reformers. In a lengthy responsum (OḤ 309) he details all the plans and proposals of the Reformers in order to justify his decision. Following the majority decision of the Austrian parliament in favor of the claims of the Orthodox community, the Landes-Organisations Statuten were formulated that were later confirmed in 1871. Schick, in a responsum of 1872, encouraged the acceptance of these statutes and opposed the principle of preserving the status quo (OḤ 307, 310). When the controversy broke out between Samson Raphael *Hirsch of Frankfurt and Seligmann Baer *Bamberger of Wuerzburg on whether to cooperate with the Reformers or form separatist congregations, Bamberger ruling that it was permitted to form one community with them, Schick protested in his responsum (OḤ 306), and under his influence Bamberger's view was rejected and Hirsch's opinion in favor of separation accepted.

Despite all his vigorous opposition to Reform, Schick took a moderate stand in certain matters. Thus he resisted the demand of the Orthodox rabbis for a prohibition against preaching in the vernacular, stating that "in the case of a God-fearing man, who we are certain is a talmudic scholar, and who preaches in the vernacular, and whose sole intention is to extend the border of our holy Torah … I find no reason to forbid him where the Congregation only wishes to listen in the vernacular, or if he does not do so they will appoint another who is unfit" (OḤ 70), and he refused to sign the *takkanah* of the rabbis which was adopted at the instigation of the extremist Hillel Lichtenstein, "that it is forbidden to preach or to listen to a sermon in a non-Jewish tongue." His love for the old *yishuv* in Ereẓ Israel is reflected in his polemic against Graetz's pamphlet *Mikhtav Zikkaron* ("Memorial Letter") which calumniated the organization of the old *yishuv* and protested especially against **ḥalukkah*, the lack of schools, and the paucity of secular knowledge.

Schick was a prolific respondent. Almost 1,000 of his responsa are extant: 345 on *Oraḥ Ḥayyim* (Munkacz, 1880), 410 on *Yoreh De'ah* (1881), 155 on *Even ha-Ezer* (Lemberg, 1884), and 62 on *Ḥoshen Mishpat* (*ibid.*). A new edition in two volumes was published in New York in 1961. He also published glosses to the *Mitzvot ha-Shem* (Pressburg, 1846) of Baruch b. Ẓevi Hirsch Heilprin and expositions and novellae on the 613 commandments, in two parts (Munkacz, 1895–98). The work on the 613 precepts was originally larger, but when Joseph *Babad's *Minḥat Ḥinnukh* (1869) was published first, Schick was distressed, saying that the latter had anticipated half his work, and as a result he abbreviated it. Also published were aggadic novellae on *Avot* (Paks, 1890); *Maharam Schick*, on the Pentateuch (Munkacz, 1905), and on *Ḥullin* (Satmar, undated); and *Derashot* (new edition 1968), including discourses given by him during the years 1839–72. His son, Joseph, published his father's works (OḤ 264) and wrote a short introduction to the *Yoreh De'ah* section of the responsa. Schick's son-in-law was Jacob Prager (OḤ 184; EH 99, 136), whose novellae are quoted at the beginning of Schick's responsa to *Yoreh De'ah*.

BIBLIOGRAPHY: S.Z. Schick, *Mi-Moshe ad Moshe* (1903), 23f.; P.Z. Schwarz, *Shem ha-Gedolim me-Ereẓ Hagar*, 2 (1914), 12a no. 180; 3 (1915), 44f., nos. 21–24; M.Z. Prager, *Maharam Schick al Avot* (1929), contains *Toledot Maharam Schick*: J.J. (L.) Greenwald (Grunwald), *Li-Felagot Yisrael be-Ungarya* (1929), 91–95; idem, *Le-Toledot ha-Reformaẓyon ha-Datit be-Germanya u-ve-Ungarya…* (1948); H.Y.T.L. Braun, *Darkhei Moshe he-Ḥadash* (1942); E.F. Feldmann (ed.), *She'elot u-Teshuvot Maharam Schick*, OH (1961), introd.; M.M. Pollak (ed.), *Derashot Maharam Schick* (1968), introd., 5–23.

[Yehoshua Horowitz]

°**SCHICKARD, WILHELM (Schickhard, Schickart, Guillielmus Schick(h)ardus**; 1592–1635), German *Hebraist, Orientalist, mathematician, and astronomer. Born in Herrenberg, Wuerttemberg, Schickard initially studied theology and became a Lutheran pastor; but he then began to devote his attention to Oriental languages and the sciences. In 1619 he was appointed professor of Hebrew at the University of Tuebingen, where he broadened his knowledge of Semitics and published several works displaying his profound erudition in Hebrew and rabbinic studies. In 1631 Schickard was appointed to the chair of astronomy at Tuebingen, after which he wrote many scientific treatises, but also continued to lecture on Hebrew until his death of the plague at the age of 43.

In the *Horologium Hebraeum* (Tuebingen, 1614), Schickard provided a highly intensified course in the Hebrew language, and the book was reprinted several times during the following decades. In another work, *BeḤinat ha-Perushim… hoc est examinis commentationum rabbinicarum in Mosen prodromus…* (*ibid.*, 1621), he condemned the practical Kabbalah, and went so far as to berate Johann *Reuchlin for taking it seriously. Schickard, who corresponded with Johannes Buxtorf II, also published *Mishpat ha-Melekh: Jus regium Hebraeorum* (1625); the quaintly entitled *Purim, sive Bacchanalia Judaeorum* (1633); and *Ecologae sacrae Veteris Testamenti Hebraeo-Latinae* (1633), in Latin and Hebrew, which contained extracts from the Bible, the Targum, and the Mishnah. His *Arbor Derivationis Hebraeae*, issued by his son, appeared posthumously in 1698 and his *Nova et plenior Grammatica Hebraica* in Tuebingen in 1731.

BIBLIOGRAPHY: Speidel, in: W. Schickard, *Horologium Hebraeum* (1731 ed.). introd.; Steinschneider, Cat Bod, 2564, no. 7130; ADB, 31 (1890), 174f.; F. Sécret, *Les Kabbalistes Chrétiens de la Renaissance* (1964), 330. **ADD. BIBLIOGRAPHY:** Ch.F. von Schnurrer, *Biographische und litterarische Nachrichten von ehemaligen Lehrern der hebraeischen Litteratur in Tübingen* (1792), 160–225; F. Seck (ed.), *Wilhelm Schickard…* (1978); idem (ed.), *Zum 400. Geburtstag von Wilhelm Schickard* (1995).

[Godfrey Edmond Silverman / Aya Elyada (2nd ed.)]

SCHIDLOWSKY, LEON (1931–), Israeli composer. Born in Santiago, Chile, Schidlowsky first studied piano and later harmony and composition at the National Conservatory of Music in Santiago. He continued his studies in Germany (1952–55). Returning to Chile, he was active in promoting contemporary music and in 1967 became professor of composition at the University of Chile. He immigrated to Israel in 1969 and was appointed professor of composition at the Rubin Academy of Music at Tel Aviv University. Schidlowsky was in charge of musical education at the Hebrew Institute in Santiago, and a number of his works dating from that time express the recent sufferings of the Jewish people – *Kristallnacht Symphony, Lamentation, Memento, Kaddish*, and others. In Israel he wrote *Babi Yar*, for piano, percussion, and strings (1970); *Serenata*, for chamber orchestra (1970); and *Rabbi Akiva*, for soloists, choir, and orchestra (1972). His work *Dadayamasong*, a dramatic scene for voice, clarinet, alto saxophone, cello, piano, and percussion, received a prize at the UNESCO International Composer's Rostrum (1976). He wrote in a variety of styles, from atonality to aleatory and graphic compositions, and was one of the most dedicated and consistent representatives of the innovative avant-garde in Israel.

ADD. BIBGLIOGRAPHY: NG²; A. Tischler, *A Descriptive Bibliography of Art Music by Israeli Composers* (1989), 203–18.

[Uri (Erich) Toeplitz and Yohanan Boehm / Jehoash Hirshberg (2nd ed.)]

SCHIFF, ADAM (1960–), U.S. lawyer, congressman. Schiff represents California's 29th Congressional District, including the communities of Alhambra, Altadena, Burbank, Glendale, Griffith Park, Monterey Park, Pasadena, San Gabriel, South Pasadena, and Temple City. Born in Framingham, Massachusetts, he is a graduate of Stanford (1982) and Harvard Law School (1985). Schiff served with the U.S. Attorney's Office in Los Angeles for six years (1987–93), most notably prosecuting the first FBI agent ever to be indicted for espionage. He ran for the State Assembly three times and lost to James Rogan twice. First elected to the State Senate in 1996, he was its youngest member. He chaired its Judiciary Committee and the Joint Committee on the Arts. He spearheaded legislative efforts to guarantee up-to-date textbooks in the classroom, overhaul child support, and pass a patient's bill of rights. He also taught political science at a local community college.

In 2000 he ran for Congress, defeating incumbent James Rogan, who had served on the House Judiciary Committee and pushed the impeachment of President Bill Clinton. Much of his initial support came from a backlash against Rogan. At the time, it was the most expensive race in history and one of the very few in which the impeachment was the issue. Hollywood mogul David *Geffen raised millions of dollars to defeat Rogan.

Schiff was a member of the House Judiciary Committee and the House International Relations Committee. He continued his interest in education. He was a self-described moderate and joined the "Blue Dog Democrats." He served on the Judiciary Subcommittee on Crime, Terrorism and Homeland Security and the Subcommittee on the Constitution. As congressman he introduced the Deadly Biological Agent Control Act to bolster the security at labs that stock agents such as anthrax, and the Sky Police Act to increase air security by training local police to serve as air marshals. He also introduced the Air Cargo Security Act to ensure that all air cargo on passenger planes be screened for explosives.

In March 2003, Schiff joined Reps. David Scott and Steve Israel in forming the Democratic Study Group on National Security in an effort to educate, inform, and develop policy on emerging national security issues. The group has hosted a wide range of speakers on topics such as international terrorism, defense, military transformation, shifting alliances, Iraq, homeland security, non-proliferation, Iran, Korea, the United Nations, and missile defense.

He also introduced the Rim of the Valley Corridor Study Act to enlist the National Park Service in protecting open space in Southern California. A member of the bipartisan House Education Caucus comprised of former educators, Congressman Schiff fought to expand opportunities for students. He introduced the Access to Higher Education Act to increase federal aid to students in public colleges, was instrumental in crafting legislation to create federal merit grants for students who excel in math and science, and cosponsored legislation to refocus national education policy on helping states and local school districts raise academic achievement levels. Schiff also supported federal assistance for class-size reduction, music and art education, and after-school programs.

BIBLIOGRAPHY: L.S. Maisel and I. Forman, *Jews in American Politics* (2001); M. Barone and R.E. Cohen, *The Almanac of American Politics* (2005).

[Michael Berenbaum (2nd ed.)]

SCHIFF, ANDRÁS (1953–), pianist. Born in Budapest, he started piano lessons with Elisabeth Vadasz and made his debut at the age of nine. He continued his musical studies at the Franz Liszt Academy, and later in London with George Malcolm. After winning prizes at the Tchaikovsky Competition in Moscow (1974) and at the Leeds International Competition (1975), Schiff embarked upon an international career. He gained recognition for his insightful and intellectual interpretations of the music of Bach. Recitals and special cycles of Bach, Haydn, Mozart, Beethoven, Schubert, Chopin, Schumann, and Bartók formed an important part of his activities, and he moved easily between solo recitals, concertos, ensemble playing, and the use of singers (notably Peter Schreier) and instrumentalists. He increasingly conducted performances of concertos from the keyboard. Schiff was the founder and the artistic director from 1989 to 1998 of the annual Musiktage Mondsee. In 1999 he created his own chamber orchestra, the Cappella Andrea Barca. His Haydn festival in the Wigmore Hall won the Royal Philharmonic Society/Charles Heidsieck Award for the best concert series of 1988–89, and in 1989 he was awarded the Wiener Flötenuhr, the Mozart Prize of the City of Vienna. He was also awarded the Bartók Prize (1991); the Claudio Arrau Memorial Medal from the Robert Schumann Society (1994); the Kossuth Prize, the highest Hungarian honor (1996); and the Musikfest-Preis Bremen (for outstanding international artistic achievement) in 2003. In 2001 he became a British citizen. Among his publications are "Schubert's Piano Sonatas: Thoughts about Interpretation and Performance," in *Schubert Studies* (1998), 191–208.

BIBLIOGRAPHY: Grove online; *Baker's Biographical Dictionary* (1997); C. Montparker. "The Insights and Intellect of Andras Schiff," in: *Clavier*, 34, no. 8 (1995), 6–11.

[Naama Ramot (2nd ed.)]

SCHIFF, DAVID TEVELE (d. 1792), rabbi of the Great Synagogue, London, from 1765 until his death. He was born in Frankfurt and served as *Maggid* ("preacher") in Vienna, head of the *bet ha-midrash* in Worms, and *dayyan* in Frankfurt. His rabbinate in London was marked by the continued growth of the Ashkenazi population (symbolized by the enlargement of the Great Synagogue in 1766), and by the progressive (though sometimes reluctant) recognition of the rabbi of the Great Synagogue as head of all English Ashkenazim. When the Hambro' Synagogue appointed Meshullam Zalman (Israel Solomon), grandson of Jacob *Emden, as their rabbi, most provincial Ashkenazim still recognized the authority of Schiff, but in *Portsmouth there was a bitter split on the issue. After Meshullam Zalman left London in 1780, Schiff acted for the Hambro' Synagogue also and the rift ended. Overworked and underpaid, he tried unsuccessfully to obtain appointments at Rotterdam and Wuerzburg. Schiff's responsa *Leshon Zahav* were published posthumously by his son (Offenbach, 1822). Several of his sermons are still extant, but his letters to Lord George *Gordon, refusing to receive him into the synagogue, have not been preserved.

BIBLIOGRAPHY: V.D. Lipman, *Social History of the Jews in England, 1850–1950* (1954), 38–39; C. Roth, *The Great Synagogue, London, 1690–1940* (1950), 29, 125ff.; C. Duschinsky, *Rabbinate of the Great Synagogue* (1921), index.

[Vivian David Lipman]

SCHIFF, DOROTHY (1903–1989), U.S. newspaper publisher. Born in New York City, she was daughter of Jacob *Schiff. Early interest in civic affairs led her to join the Ellis Island Investigating Commission and the Women's Trade Union League of New York. She became a director of the Henry Street Settlement and of Mount Sinai Hospital, and in 1937 was appointed by Mayor Fiorello LaGuardia to the New York City Board of Child Welfare. Her association with the liberal *New York Post* began in 1939. In 1942 she became president and publisher, and later editor in chief. She was the first woman newspaper publisher in New York. Under her direction, the paper grew in circulation and revenue. When, in the 1960s, many metropolitan newspapers in the U.S. were forced to suspend publication, the *New York Post* continued to thrive. Eventually it became the only evening newspaper in New York City. In 1976 she sold the *Post* to publisher Rupert Murdoch but remained a consultant to the paper until 1981. Schiff was married to publisher George Backer, newspaper editor Theodore O. Thackrey, and Zionist leader Rudolph *Sonneborn.

BIBLIOGRAPHY: *Current Biography*, 26 (Jan. 1965), 27–29. **ADD. BIBLIOGRAPHY:** J. Potter, *Men, Money and Magic: The Story of Dorothy Schiff* (1977).

[Lawrence H. Feigenbaum]

SCHIFF, HUGO (1834–1915), Italian organic chemist. Born in Frankfurt, Schiff was the brother of physiologist Moritz Schiff. He left Germany for political reasons. He was at University of Berne, Switzerland, and then joined his brother in Florence, where he was a professor at the Istituto di Studi Superiori (1863–66). He later worked in Pisa and the University of Turin (1876–79) and then returned to his professorship in Florence (1879). Compounds obtained from an aldehyde or a ketone and a primary amine are still known as "Schiff bases."

SCHIFF, JACOB HENRY (1847–1920), U.S. financier and philanthropist. Born in Frankfurt, Germany, he was the descendant of a distinguished rabbinical family (see *Schiff, Meir b. Jacob). He received a thorough secular and religious education at the local school of the Israelitische Religionsgesellschaft, then followed his father, Moses, who was associated with the Rothschild banking firm, into that occupation. At the age of 18 Schiff immigrated to the United States, entered a brokerage firm in New York, and became a partner in Budge, Schiff and Co. In 1875 he married the daughter of Solomon Loeb, head of the banking firm of Kuhn, Loeb and Co., and entered that firm. Schiff's remarkable financial abilities were recognized when he was named head of Kuhn, Loeb in 1885.

Schiff's firm soon became one of the two most powerful private investment banking houses in the United States, participating actively in fostering the rapid industrialization of the U.S. economy during the late 19th and early 20th century. Such firms as Westinghouse Electric, U.S. Rubber, Armour, and American Telephone and Telegraph were financed to some extent through Kuhn, Loeb's efforts. In addition, Schiff served as director or adviser of numerous banks, insurance companies, and other enterprises. His role in the consolidation and expansion of the American railroad network, the backbone of an industrialized society, was particularly influential. He gave his support to Edward H. Harriman in the reorganization of the Union Pacific Railroad and was a staunch associate of James J. Hill of the Great Northern Railway for many years. Huge sums were obtained by Kuhn, Loeb for the Pennsylvania, Baltimore and Ohio, and other railroad systems.

Schiff was prominently involved in floating loans to the government at home and to foreign nations, the most spectacular being a bond issue of $200,000,000 for Japan at the time of the Russo-Japanese War in 1904–05. Deeply angered by the antisemitic policies of the czarist regime in Russia, he was delighted to support the Japanese war effort. He consistently refused to participate in loans on behalf of Russia and used his influence to prevent other firms from underwriting Russian loans, while providing financial support for Russian Jewish *self-defense groups. Schiff carried this policy into World War I, relenting only after the fall of czarism in 1917. At that time, he undertook to support the Kerensky government with a substantial loan.

It was said of Schiff that "nothing Jewish was alien to his heart." Personally devout, proud of his family and religious heritage, Schiff used his immense personal wealth and influence on behalf of his coreligionists everywhere. His widespread philanthropic activities and communal interests brought him recognition as the foremost figure of his time in American Jewry. Although affiliated with Temple Emanu-El and the Reform movement in the United States, Schiff retained many of the Orthodox habits of his youth. He was especially active in the establishment and development of the Jewish Theological Seminary, viewing it as the fountainhead for a "reasonable Orthodoxy" attractive to the masses of newly arrived immigrants. Other institutions of Jewish learning, including Yeshivath Rabbi Isaac Elchanan (later Yeshiva College and University), as well as Hebrew Union College, received generous support from Schiff. Realizing the need for trained religious teachers, he provided funds for the establishment of Teachers' Institutes at the Jewish Theological Seminary and Hebrew Union College. When the New York Kehillah was organized, Schiff made substantial contributions to its Bureau of Jewish Education and supported the Uptown Talmud Torah in New York and similar schools.

Schiff had a deep interest in Jewish literature and contributed generously to the Jewish Publication Society. He provided funds for a new English translation of the Bible by Jewish scholars and established a fund for the translation and publication of a series of Hebrew classics. His donations aided the publication of the *Jewish Encyclopedia*; the acquisition by the Library of Congress and the Jewish Theological Seminary Library of major collections of rare books and manuscripts; and the establishment of the Jewish Division of the New York Public Library. His philanthropies were accompanied in many cases by intense personal participation. For example, not only was he a major contributor to the Montefiore Hospital in New York, of which he was president for 35 years, but he managed to visit there almost weekly. There were few Jewish institutions in New York or elsewhere. which did not benefit from Schiff's attention and funds. Such agencies as the Hebrew Free Loan Society, Educational Alliance, Home for Aged and Infirm Hebrews, YMHA, United Hebrew Charities, Jewish Protectory and Aid Society, and Hebrew Technical School, were among those receiving his aid. He was a large-scale contributor to the relief of victims of Russian pogroms (1903–05), to the American Jewish Relief Committee during World War I, and to postwar European Jewish relief. Schiff, who had access to American presidents, used his influence with them in urging U.S. support on behalf of Jews victimized in Eastern Europe. In 1906 he joined with other Jewish leaders in the formation of the American Jewish Committee and subsequently took a very active part in its efforts to protect the rights of Jews abroad and in the United States. Offended by Russia's refusal to honor passports held by American Jews, Schiff was prominent in the successful campaign to abrogate the Russo-American Treaty of 1832. During World War I, Schiff and the established American Jewish leadership came under increasing fire from newer, Zionist-oriented Jewish groups. He had strongly opposed the Zionist movement, rejecting it as a secular, nationalistic perversion of the Jewish faith, incompatible with American citizenship. On the other hand, he did aid agricultural projects and the Haifa Technical Institute in Palestine. Recognizing changing world conditions, Schiff announced in 1917 his support of a cultural homeland in Palestine for the Jewish people.

Proud of his Americanism, Schiff contributed generously in time and money to a multitude of civic activities and philanthropies. He donated $1,000,000 to Barnard College; contributed funds to establish the Semitic Museum at Harvard University as well as large sums to other universities; and supported the Henry Street Settlement, the American Red Cross, Tuskegee Institute, and countless others. He served on the New York City Board of Education, was vice president of the Chamber of Commerce, and participated in several special mayoral commissions. Although linked by family and cultural ties to Germany, Schiff patriotically supported the American war effort when the United States entered World War I.

BIBLIOGRAPHY: P. Arnsberg, *Jakob H. Schiff* (Ger., 1969), incl. bibl.; C. Adler, *Jacob H. Schiff: His Life and Letters*, 2 vols. (1928); DAB, 16 (1935), 430–2; H. Simonhoff, *Saga of American Jewry* (1959), 346–54; N.W. Cohen, in: JSOS, 25 (1963), 3–41; Z. Szajkowski, *ibid.*, 29 (1967), 3–26; 75–91; T. Levitan, *Jews in American Life* (1969), 152–5. **ADD. BIBLIOGRAPHY:** N. Cohen, *Jacob H. Schiff: A Study in American Jewish Leadership* (1999).

[Morton Rosenstock]

SCHIFF, MEIR BEN JACOB HA-KOHEN (known as the **MaHaRaM**; **M**orenu **Ha**-**R**av **M**eir Schiff; 1605–1641), talmudist and rabbinic author. Born in Frankfurt, where his father was a member of the *bet din* and a communal leader, Schiff was, in his early youth, considered a scholar of unusual ability. While still a boy, he turned to *Meir of Lublin with halakhic problems. At the age of 17, he was appointed rabbi of the important community of Fulda, where he also headed a notable yeshivah. He wrote down the essence of his lectures, novellae, and comments, which extend over the whole Talmud, but most of it was destroyed by fire in 1711. There exists a tradition that he was appointed rabbi of Prague in 1641. However, if the statement of his grandson is to be trusted, namely, that he lived only 36 years, he must have died immediately after his appointment. The novellae *Maharam Schiff* were published in Homburg-vor-der Hoehe (on Beẓah, Ket., Git., BM, and Ḥul., in 1737, and on Shab., BK, BB, Sanh., and Zev., in 1741). They were much sought after by students and were regarded as essential for the study of Talmud. Many editions were published, and they were also incorporated in the standard editions of the Talmud. A new annotated edition of his novellae on *Gittin* was published by S. Schlesinger in 1963.

Schiff avoids the casuistic manner that was prevalent in the yeshivot in his time and strives to arrive at an understanding of the text as its stands. For this reason, he also opposed suggestions that the traditional readings were faulty. In writing of *pilpul*, he complains of "the ink that has been spilled and the pens broken to give pilpulisitc interpretations to passages of the Talmud which I am able to explain according to this plain meaning." His books are distinguished by brevity and clarity of language. He takes special care to stress that he does not wish to give halakhic decisions, referring the reader on each occasion to the relevant halakhic literature. At the end of each tractate he gives an exposition connecting the tractate concluded with the one about to be studied at the yeshivah. In consequence, it is possible to determine the exact dates and order in which he taught. His novellae bear witness to his intellectual integrity. On more than one occasion he writes "I was mistaken," "There is no value in all I have written." He was acquainted with the works of his contemporaries, such as Solomon b. Jehiel *Luria, Samuel *Edels, and Meir of Lublin, and more than once disparages their views, belittling and scorning them with such phrases as "this is fit for children," "empty words," "he extends himself over a few futile difficulties." Because of the large interval between the writing and publication of his work, many errors crept in. Consequently many supercommentaries have been written, the most well known and the best being that of Mordecai Mardush of Poritsk, which is printed in the standard editions of the Talmud.

The many sermons appended to his books reveal that Schiff was a strong personality who did not hesitate to rebuke his community about those matters of which he disapproved. He accuses many of the communal leaders of desecrating the Sabbath, of not studying the Torah, of failing to support scholars, and of other offenses. His style in preaching does not differ from that of his contemporaries. Here he does permit himself the use of *pilpul*, although he eschewed it in the study of the Talmud. He also wrote on kabbalistic themes. The Schiff family of bankers are among his descendants.

BIBLIOGRAPHY: S.A. Horodezky, *Le-Korot ha-Rabbanut* (1910, repr. 1914), 191–200; J.J.(L.) Greenwald (Grunwald), *Lifnei Shetei Me'ot Shanah, o Toledot ha-Rav Eleazar Kallir u-Zemanno* (1952), 34; M. Horovitz, *Frankfurter Rabbinen*, 2 (1883), 35–40.

[Itzhak Alfassi]

SCHIFFMAN, LAWRENCE H. (1948–), U.S. Judaic scholar. Born in New York and educated at Brandeis University (B.A., M.A. 1970, Ph.D. 1974), Schiffman taught at the University of

Minnesota (1971–72), Hebrew Union College-Jewish Institute of Religion, New York (1975–79, 1983, and 1986), and from 1972 at New York University, where he was named Edelman Professor and chairman and director of undergraduate studies of the Skirball Department of Hebrew and Judaic Studies. He was a visiting professor at Yale, Ben-Gurion, Duke, Johns Hopkins, Toronto, and other universities, and lectured widely at universities and other public forums. Schiffman was the program director of NYU's excavations at Tel Dor, in conjunction with The Hebrew University and the Israel Exploration Society (1980–83), and was a fellow of the Institute for Advanced Studies at The Hebrew University of Jerusalem (1989–90). He served on the editorial board of the journal *Dead Sea Discoveries* from 1994. He was a fellow of the Association for Jewish Studies, the American Academy for Jewish Research, the Society for Biblical Literature (Qumran Section), and the Dead Sea Scrolls Foundation, among other scholarly and professional associations. He was a member of the editorial board for the Oxford Dead Sea Scrolls publication project *Discoveries in the Judean Desert* from 1991 until its completion in 2002 and co-edited the *Oxford Encyclopedia of the Dead Sea Scrolls* (with J.C. VanderKam, 2000). He was one of the organizers, and a director, of the Friedberg Genizah Project (1999–2002). He was the recipient of numerous grants for his work on the Dead Sea Scrolls and the Cairo Genizah texts.

Schiffman is a leading scholarly authority on early post-biblical Judaism, with a particular interest in the Dead Sea Scrolls. He is known not only to the scholarly community but to the general public, having been featured in several television documentaries on the Qumran discoveries. Schiffman's major work, *Reclaiming the Dead Sea Scrolls* (1994), argues that the Qumran community was founded by a schismatic Sadducean sect, rather than by a (proto-Christian) group of Essenes, and that not all the texts originated at Qumran. Among his other books are *The Halakhah at Qumran* (1975), *Sectarian Law in the Dead Sea Scrolls: Courts, Testimony, and the Penal Code* (1983), *Who Was a Jew? Rabbinic and Halakhic Perspectives on the Jewish-Christian Schism* (1985), *From Text to Tradition: A History of Judaism in Second Temple and Rabbinic Times* (with Michael Swartz, 1989), *The Eschatological Community of the Dead Sea Scrolls: A Study of the Rule of the Congregation* (1989), *Hebrew and Aramaic Incantation Texts from the Cairo Genizah* (1992), *Halakhah, Halikhah U-Meshiḥiyyut bi-Megillot Midbar Yehudah* (*Law, Custom, and Messianism in the Dead Sea Scrolls*, 1993), and *Texts and Traditions: A Source Reader for the Study of Second Temple and Rabbinic Judaism* (1998). He also edited a number of volumes of scholarly papers and essays and published many scholarly articles and reviews.

[Drew Silver (2nd ed.)]

SCHIFRIN, LALO (**Boris**; 1932–), composer, pianist, and conductor of Argentinian birth. He studied music, piano, and harmony in Buenos Aires and later in the Paris Conservatoire (1950), guided by Koechlin and Messiaen. Returning home, he established himself as a composer, arranger, conductor, and pianist who was equally at ease in popular, jazz, and art-music circles. He founded Argentina's first big band and later moved to New York (1958). There he played the piano in Dizzy Gillespie's jazz quintet (1960–62) and recorded with other known jazz artists. From 1962 to the early 1980s Schifrin concentrated on composition. He went to Hollywood (1964) and wrote numerous scores for both television and the cinema, including the memorable themes to *Mission Impossible* and *Dirty Harry*.

His works often involve jazz, funk, and disco elements, as well as a synthesis of contemporary art-music elements. Schifrin wrote many vocal and instrumental works in other fields, including concertos, suites, an oratorio (*The Rise and Fall of the Third Reich*, 1967), ballets and symphonic pieces. Among his later commissions was *Fantasy for Screenplay and Orchestra* (2002–3). Schifrin taught composition at UCLA (1968–71) but, from the 1980s onwards, concentrated on conducting, performing with leading orchestras such as the London Philharmonic and Symphony Orchestras, the Vienna SO, the Los Angeles Philharmonic, and the Israel Philharmonic. He conducted several concerts of the "Three Tenors" and was appointed music director of the Glendale SO (1989–1995). During his illustrious career, Schifrin received four Grammy Awards and six Oscar nominations. Among his other honors were BMI Lifetime Achievement Award (1988), Distinguished Artist Award (1998), and honorary doctorates. He was honored by the Israeli government for his "Contributions to World Understanding through Music" and by the SACEM and Cannes Film Festival in recognition of his significant contribution to music, film and culture.

BIBLIOGRAPHY: "Schifrin Wows Them in Israel with Music and Media Appearances (Tel Aviv Spring Festival)," in: *Variety*, 303 (May 20, 1981), 97; V. Sheff, "Lalo Schifrin – Profile," in: *BMI – Music World* (Winter 1989), 52–5; J. Burlingame, "Lalo Schifrin: An Appreciation," in *The Cue Sheet*, Jan. 2001, 17:1 (Jan. 2001), 3–20; Grove Online.

[Naama Ramot (2nd ed.)]

SCHILD, EDWIN (1920–), rabbi and community leader. Schild was born in Koeln-Muelheim (Cologne), Germany, and spent his teenage years under Nazi restrictions and persecution. In 1938, while he was attending the Jewish Teacher's Seminary in Wuerzburg, Schild survived *Kristallnacht*, only to be picked up by the Nazis and incarcerated in the Dachau concentration camp. He was released on condition that he emigrate. Early in 1939 Schild was able to arrange passage through the Netherlands to continue his studies at Yeshiva Torath Emeth in London, England, where he remained until May 1940. As the threat of a German invasion of the U.K. loomed and fears grew of covert Nazi agents, Schild was caught up in the mass internments of "enemy aliens." He was one of more than 2,200 mostly Jewish German and Austrian refugees transfered to Canada and incarcerated in detention camps. Although Canadian authorities were soon aware that most of the internees were legitimate refugees, anti-Jewish sentiment within the government kept the refugees locked behind barbed wire. Schild was interned from July 1940 to

February 1942. He was able to continue his studies within the camps and, when released, completed his academic and rabbinical studies in Toronto.

The senior rabbi of Toronto's Conservative Adath Israel Congregation from 1947 to 1989, Rabbi Schild, whose parents perished in the Shoah, devoted his career to promoting cross-cultural and interfaith relations. He chaired the Canadian Division of the Rabbinical Assembly of America and the Canada-Israel Committee, Ontario Region, and was an active board member of the Christian-Jewish Dialogue and honored with the Human Relations Award from the Canadian Council of Christians and Jews. In retirement he remained active as rabbi emeritus and embarked on yearly lecture tours of Germany, where he continued his interfaith efforts. In 2001 Rabbi Schild became a Member of the Order of Canada. He wrote *The Very Narrow Bridge. A Memoir of an Uncertain Passage* (2001).

[Paula Draper (2nd ed.)]

SCHILDER, PAUL FERDINAND (1886–1940), Austrian psychiatrist and psychoanalyst. Schilder was born in Vienna and studied medicine. His involvement with philosophic problems brought him to psychiatry; the year of his graduation he published three papers on neuropathological subjects. In 1914 his study of symbolism in schizophrenia intensified his earlier interest in Freud's work. Schilder combined concepts of the somatopsychic with Freud's idea of body ego and thus arrived at his own formulation of the body image. Along with his increasing interest in psychological and psychoanalytic problems, Schilder retained his deep interest in neuropathology, especially in early perception. The interrelation of the organic and psychological was to characterize Schilder's work for the rest of his life.

He published *Selbstbewusstsein und Persoenlichkeitsbewusstsein* (1914), in which he applied the principles of Edmund *Husserl's phenomenology to the psychiatric problem of depersonalization. After serving in World War I Schilder returned to Vienna to join the staff of Julius von Wagner-Jauregg's psychiatric clinic. He was invited to become a member of the Vienna Psychoanalytic Society, and in 1920 he delivered his first paper, "Identification," before the society. While at the clinic he wrote on the psychogenic aspects of organic conditions of the brain and published *Seele und Leben* (1923); *Medizinische Psychologie* (1923; *Medical Psychology*, 1953); and *Entwurf zu einer Psychiatrie auf psychoanalytischer Grundlage* (1925; *Introduction to a Psychoanalytic Psychiatry*, 1952).

In 1928 Schilder accepted the invitation of Adolf Meyer to go to the Johns Hopkins University Medical School. He was appointed clinical director of psychiatry at Bellevue Hospital and research professor of psychiatry at New York University College of Medicine in 1930. Schilder's later publications include *Brain and Personality* (1951) and *The Image and Appearance of the Human Body* (1935). He continued his teaching and research with various coworkers, especially with Lauretta Bender, whom he married in 1937. He pioneered psychoanalytic group therapy and finally became interested in child psychology, in which field he was critical of many aspects of Freud's conclusions.

BIBLIOGRAPHY: I. Ziferstein, in: F. Alexander et al. (eds.), *Psychoanalytic Pioneers* (1966), 457–68; O.F. Norton, *Psychoanalytic Theory of Neurosis* (1945), 650–2.

[Louis Miller]

SCHILDKRAUT, RUDOLPH (1862–1930), German actor; a star of the European and American theater. Born in Istanbul, Schildkraut grew up in Romania, and studied in Vienna. He subsequently acted in Vienna, Hamburg, and Berlin and won acclaim on the German stage with his portrayal of Shylock, which remained one of his great roles. Another of his notable characterizations was Jankel Shabshowitz in Sholem *Asch's *God of Vengeance* (1918). For five years he played at the Deutsches Schauspielhaus and then at Max *Reinhardt's theater. Going for a few years to America in 1911, he appeared for a season in the Yiddish theater, after which he resumed playing in German and English. The Yiddish plays in which he starred ranged from *Kreutzer Sonata*, based on Tolstoy, to *Shomer's *Eikele Mazik*. Back in Germany, he performed in movies such as *Der Shylock von Krakau* (1913), *Daemon und Mensch* (1915), and *Schlemihl* (1915), in which he acted alongside his son, Joseph, in the latter's debut. After the family immigrated to America, he appeared in films such as *His People* (1925), *The King of Kings* (1927), *A Ship Comes In* (1928), and *Christina* (1929).

His son, JOSEPH SCHILDKRAUT (1896–1964), grew up in Vienna, spent three years (1910–13) at the Academy of Dramatic Arts in New York during a tour his family made in America, but made his stage debut in Berlin under Max Reinhardt, in 1913. Returning to the United States he acted in *Liliom* (1921–23) and *Peer Gynt* (1923) for Theater Guild, then went to Hollywood and into a film career. He starred in many pictures and for a time managed the Hollywood Playhouse. Among his many roles, he appeared as Alfred Dreyfus in the movie *The Life of Emile Zola* (1937), for which he received the 1938 Academy Award for the Best Supporting Actor, and the heroine's father in *The Diary of Anne Frank* (1959). Schildkraut was an actor of vivid personality and wide range. His autobiography, *My Father and I*, appeared in 1950.

BIBLIOGRAPHY: *New York Times* (Jan. 23, 1964).

[Joseph Leftwich / Noam Zadoff (2nd ed.)]

SCHILLER, ARMAND (1857–?), French journalist. Born near Paris, Schiller worked in his father's printing house, studied law, and wrote for various papers. In 1879 he became general secretary of the editorial board of the daily *Le Temps* and held that position for many years. He was a professor at the Ecole du Journalisme, was made a member of the Legion of Honor in 1892, and elected syndic of the Association Professionelle des Journalistes in 1897.

°**SCHILLER, FRIEDRICH VON** (1759–1805), German poet, playwright, and philosopher, whose works influenced Hebrew literature and the *Haskalah. Schiller had only a few Jewish contacts, although he knew the writings of Moses *Mendelssohn and had a high regard for Solomon *Maimon. Schiller's stage adaptation of 1801 popularized *Lessing's *Nathan der Weise*. In his own writings there are only a few allusions to Jews. Perhaps the most intriguing of these is Moritz Spiegelberg, a character in his early drama *Die Raeuber* (1781). Though not explicitly presented as a Jew, Spiegelberg occasionally lapses into a Judeo-German idiom, speaks of Judaizing, and even refers to a project for the reestablishment of a Jewish state. In this portrayal Schiller may have had in mind the ideas diffused at the time in his native Wuerttemberg by followers of Jacob *Frank. Although Ludwig *Geiger and others denied that the character was a Jew, the Nazis inevitably presented him as one. During the 1920s, Erwin Piscator's Berlin production of *Die Raeuber* presented Spiegelberg in the guise of Leon *Trotsky.

There are echoes of biblical style in Schiller's poems, as in the ode to joy, "*An die Freude*," and in his dramas. While Schiller praised the "Hebrew nation" as important for "universal history" in his treatise *Ueber die Sendung Moses* (1790), he also adopted the hostile Bible interpretation quoted by *Voltaire, claiming that leprosy was the chief cause of the *Exodus from Egypt.

Translations and imitations of Schiller's poems and plays were published by *maskilim* in Galicia, and later in Russian Poland, notably by Abraham Ber *Gottlober, Micah Joseph *Lebensohn, Meir Halevi *Letteris, and Solomon Judah *Rapoport. Between 1817 and 1957 almost 60 Hebrew versions of works by Schiller by more than 80 translators were published. They include *Bialik's translation of the drama *Wilhelm Tell*. Yiddish parodies of Schiller's poems were extremely popular; Orthodox homes which banned other non-religious literature made an exception in the case of his works. German Jews, too, showed admiration for Schiller. *Heine, who parodied "*An die Freude*" in his "*Prinzessin Sabbat*," praised Schiller as the poet of freedom and internationalism. Ludwig August *Frankl and Leopold *Kompert showed their admiration for him in establishing a Schiller Stiftung to propagate his works, and rabbis, including Samson Raphael *Hirsch, eulogized him in their sermons. Jews stressed the poet's quest for a physical and spiritual freedom untrammeled by nationalist dogma, his belief in human equality influenced by *Rousseau, and his idealism. They identified Schiller with Germany and Germany with Europe, seeing in Schiller's writings the bridge to European culture.

BIBLIOGRAPHY: O. Frankl, *Friedrich Schiller in seinen Beziehungen zu den Juden und zum Judentum* (1905); L. Geiger, *Die Deutsche Literatur und die Juden* (1910), 125–60; S. Lachower, in: *Yad la-Koré*, 4 (1956/57), 59–75 (bibl. of Heb. trans.); P.F. Veit, in: *Germanic Review* (1969), 171–85; G. Scholem, in: *Commentary*, 11 (1966), 33–34; G. Rappaport, *Jewish Horizons* (1959, Heb. section), 17–22.

SCHILLER (formerly **Blankenstein**), **SOLOMON** (1879–1925), Hebrew educator and Zionist writer. Born near Bialystok, Schiller moved to Lvov to avoid conscription. His pamphlet in Polish on Jewish nationality and his articles dealt with the ideological basis for Zionism. He participated in the First Zionist Congress in Basle (1897) and laid the foundations for a nationalist Hebrew education in Galicia. In 1910 Schiller emigrated to Ereẓ Israel and settled in Jerusalem, where he was a teacher and later principal of the Jerusalem Reḥavyah Gymnasium. His published articles were collected and edited by Rabbi Binyamin in *Kitvei Shelomo Schiller* (1927).

BIBLIOGRAPHY: D. Sadan, *Goral ve-Hakhra'ah, Mishnato shel Shelomo Schiller* (1943), incl. bibl. p. 167–75.

[Getzel Kressel]

SCHILLER-SZINESSY, SOLOMON MAYER (1820–1890), rabbi and scholar. Born in Altofen (Budapest), Schiller received a traditional rabbinic education, attending Hungarian and other institutions, notably the Lutheran College at Eperjes (Presov); he graduated from the University of Jena in 1845. At Eperjes Schiller was given a faculty appointment for Hebrew and also became the local rabbi, and the atmosphere of tolerance in the college influenced him permanently. He succeeded markedly in child education, and through his eloquence in the pulpit, he fostered Hungarian patriotism. His rabbinical teachers, who included Aaron *Chorin, were moderates, but in 1845 he vigorously attacked in print the Reform resolutions of the Frankfurt Rabbinical Conference. During the Hungarian revolution, led by Kossuth (1848–49), Schiller added the Magyar "Szinessy" to his name and enlisted; he was wounded and captured but escaped from Temesvár via Trieste to England, where in 1851 he became rabbi of Manchester. While endeavoring to keep traditionalists and would-be reformers together, he became embroiled with the chief rabbi Nathan *Adler by attempting to extend his ecclesiastical jurisdiction over northern England; he was then persuaded by the reformers to join their new dissident synagogue, although his personal practice and outlook remained strongly traditional throughout his life. Schiller resigned his rabbinical post in 1860 and moved in 1863 to Cambridge. His bibliographical erudition earned him the appointment in 1866 as teacher (later reader) of talmudic and rabbinic literature at Cambridge University. He was the first professing Jew formally entrusted by Cambridge with the subject, and he taught and inspired a distinguished list of gentile rabbinical scholars, which included C. Taylor and W.H. Lowe. Schiller's principal scholarly achievement was his prolix *Catalogue of Hebrew Manuscripts Preserved in the Cambridge University Library*, a portion of which was published in 1876. He edited Book One of David *Kimḥi's commentary on the Psalms (1883) and *Romanelli's account of his Moroccan travels (*Massa ba-Arav*, 1885).

BIBLIOGRAPHY: R. Loewe, in: JHSET, 21 (1968), 148–89.

[Raphael Loewe]

SCHILLINGER, JOSEPH (1895–1943), music theorist and composer. Born in Kharkov, Schillinger studied conducting and composition with Nicolai Tcherepnin, among others, at the St. Petersburg Conservatory (1914–18). Until his emigration to New York in 1928, Schillinger pursued a career in the Ukraine as conductor and composer and helped organize the first jazz concert in Russia (1927). In New York, Schillinger continued to compose as well as teaching, but he is mainly remembered for his systematic theory of music composition, in which his mathematical training is evident. Schillinger believed in scientific methods as the basis of artistic creativity in all the arts (as described in *The Mathematical Basis of the Arts*, 1948). His most important book, *The Schillinger System of Musical Composition* (2 vols., 1941, 1946), attempts to explore all possible permutations of every musical parameter, showing them as geometrical forms. This modernist approach might be conceived as a predecessor of set theory, yet Schillinger's actual theory is limited to rather conventional constraints. For example, he presented rhythmic permutations in conventional meters only (see also *Encyclopedia of Rhythms* (1966)), and focused on unusual syncopations. Schillinger's private pupils include Jewish jazz composers George *Gershwin and Vernon Duke, as well as Oscar *Levant and Benny *Goodman, who were probably attracted by Schillinger's approach to rhythmic devices. Among his compositions are *First Airphonic Suite* (orchestra, 1929), *The People and the Prophet* (ballet, 1933), and many songs and piano pieces

BIBLIOGRAPHY: NG^2; F. Schillinger, *Joseph Schillinger: A Memoir* (1949); P. Nauert. "Theory and Practice in Porgy and Bess: The Gershwin-Schillinger Connection," in: *The Musical Quarterly* (1994).

[Yossi Goldenberg (2nd ed.)]

SCHINDLER, ALEXANDER M. (1925–2000), U.S. Reform rabbi, president of Union of American Hebrew Congregations. Alex Schindler was one of the best-known and most admired Jewish leaders in America in the last quarter of the 20th Century. He was born in Munich, Germany, in 1925, the son of a Yiddish poet and a feisty Jewish businesswoman. The family fled Hitlerism and made its way to New York City and then to Lakewood, New Jersey, where they made their living as chicken farmers. He enrolled at CCNY at the age of 16 and enlisted in the army in World War II, joining the ski troopers and winning a Purple Heart and a Bronze Star for bravery in the battles of Italy. After the war, he decided to become a rabbi, graduating from the Hebrew Union College and then serving seven years as assistant rabbi of Temple Emanuel of Worcester, Massachusetts.

He was known as a bold and successful leader of Reform Judaism but also as the preeminent spokesman of the entire Jewish Community in support of the cause of Israel. In the wider American community, Schindler was a well-known advocate of civil rights, economic justice, and improved interfaith relations. Known as a passionate spokesman of Reform Judaism, Schindler managed to gain the respect and affection of leaders of all denominations, bridging the gulfs of denominational and institutional rivalries. An assertive liberal in both religion and politics, he formed lasting friendships and alliances with traditional and conservative Jews in Israel and in America. He was a warm man, whose word could be trusted and thus even those who opposed him on ideological grounds never personalized those differences. He enjoyed a deep personal friendship with the long time leader of Agudath Israel in the United States Rabbi Moshe Sherer, though the two men could not have been further apart ideologically.

Reform Judaism is unique among American religious denominations in that the leader of the movement is the professional president of the congregational body rather than the head of a rabbinical school. As president of the Union of American Hebrew Congregations (now called Union for Reform Judaism), he significantly enlarged the membership of the Union and the scope of its program, lifting the Reform Jewish movement to the largest branch of American Judaism. As leader of the Union, he envisioned and brought into reality a Liberal Torah Commentary, the first such publication in America. He pioneered a revolutionary outreach program, in which congregations reach out to interfaith couples to make the non-Jewish partner comfortable and to encourage that partner to convert. He spearheaded a campaign of gender equality, transforming the American synagogue and the Reform rabbinate. He led a campaign for recognition of gay rights in the movement and in the rabbinate. He broke new and controversial ground – both within and outside the Reform movement – by championing the doctrine of patrilineal descent so that authentic Jewish identity would derive not only from a Jewish mother but equally from a Jewish father. Though differing with *halakhah*, the Reform position was in some ways more stringent than *halakhah* in that the identity was not automatic but had to be acknowledged and affirmed. He championed social justice, demanding economic justice for the weak and the poor even in the face of Reagan social cuts. He strengthened the work of the Religious Action Center in Washington and was a crucial part of efforts to establish a religious action center in Israel as well. He pushed for the creation of a Reform Zionism, leading to the creation of ARZA, the Reform Zionist association and a vital Reform Zionist movement. As an educator, he succeeded in gaining the approval of a pilot project for Reform Jewish day schools, which now includes seventeen full-time Reform day schools in the U.S. and Canada.

He became the best-known American Jewish leader of that era when he was elected chairman of the Presidents Conference of Major Jewish Organizations, the authoritative assembly of American Jewish leadership in support of Israel, during an especially tumultuous time. Becoming chairman in 1976, he was at his post when Menachem *Begin was elected prime minister of Israel. Shattering the long-established partnership between Israel's Labor governments and American Jewry, Begin's election was a shock to American Jewry. Schindler, a lifelong liberal and dove, publicly embraced Begin, a man with whose views he disagreed, as the elected prime minister of Israel's democracy, and demanded that the Jewish establishment give Begin a fair chance and not delegitimize him at the outset. This led to a deep personal friendship, in which Begin consulted with Schindler at many pivotal moments, including on the eve of Camp David and peace with Egypt, honored Schindler in Jerusalem, and brought him as his guest on official visits to Egypt and other countries. Despite this deep personal friendship, which endured until Begin's death, Schindler did not refrain from advocating a two-state partition, condemning Israel's invasion of Lebanon, and demanding equal respect for all branches of Judaism in Israeli life.

In all his life, Schindler prided himself on being, like his father before him, an *ohev yisrael*, a lover of the Jewish people. Although he lifted and strengthened the Reform Jewish movement, he took most pride in knitting together the fractious strands of Jewish life and Jewish unity.

[Albert Vorspan (2nd ed.)]

SCHINDLER, KURT (1882–1935), conductor, composer/arranger, and music editor. Born in Berlin, he studied at the piano conservatory with Friedrich Gernsheim and Carl Ansörge. He later studied musicology at the University of Berlin with Carl Stump and Max Friedländer. The latter introduced him to European folk music, while Gernsheim, in whose choral society he participated, instilled in him an interest in choral music. He made his official debut as composer at the Krefeld Music Festival (June 1902). As an opera conductor, he conducted the Stuttgart Opera (1902) and the Staatstheater in Wuerzburg (1903), and he was assistant to Felix Mottl and Hermann Zumpe at Munich and to Richard Strauss at the Berlin Opera (1904). Invited to join the conducting staff at the Metropolitan Opera, he immigrated to the United States in 1905. In 1909, he established the MacDowell Chorus, which, at Mahler's suggestion, evolved into the Schola Cantorum of New York. Until Schindler's resignation in 1926, the Schola ranked among the most outstanding choral societies in North America, whose programs combined master choral works, interspersed with novel arrangements of European folksongs, mainly Russian and Spanish. For two decades (1907–27), he served concurrently as music editor for the publishers G. Schirmer and Oliver Ditson. From 1912 to 1915 he served as choral director at Temple Emanuel. In 1926, at the point of physical and mental exhaustion, he sought refuge in Spain, where, from 1929 to 1933, he made three trips throughout northern Spain and Portugal which resulted in the posthumously published *Folk Music and Poetry of Spain and Portugal* (New York, 1941; Salamanca, 1991). In 1933, he established the first music department at Bennington College, Vermont, but resigned shortly thereafter due to failing health.

BIBLIOGRAPHY: NG² (includes a listing of his compositions and writings); *Diccionario de la Música Española e Hispanoamericana* (Madrid. 2002).

[Israel J. Katz (2nd ed.)]

°**SCHINDLER, OSKAR** (1908–1974), one of Israel's *Righteous Among the Nations, made famous by Thomas Keneally's novel and Steven *Spielberg's 1993 film *Schindler's List*. He was a Nazi and a war profiteer and yet essential to saving the lives of more than 1,000 Jews.

Schindler was born in Svitavy (Zwittau) in what after World War I became Czechoslovakia. In the mid-1930s Schindler joined Nazi Germany's military counterintelligence agency, the *Abwehr*, as a spy. He was arrested by the Czechs in 1938 for spying and after his release as part of the 1938 Munich Accord, helped with the invasion of the rest of Czechoslovakia and Poland in 1939. After World War II began, Schindler moved to Cracow, Poland, where he took over a former Jewish enamelware factory, Emalia, with the idea of making as much money as he could. At the instigation of his Jewish factory manager, Abraham Bankier, Schindler began to hire more and more Jews. Over time, he gained a reputation for treating his Jews well and in the fall of 1943 met with Jewish Agency representatives in Budapest, who convinced Schindler to act as a go-between for them in Cracow. Over time, his motivations changed and he became determined to save his Jews. By this time, Schindler had transformed Emalia into a subcamp of the nearby Plaszow camp, commanded by the monstrous Amon Goeth. When ordered by Goeth to close Emalia in the summer of 1944, Schindler instead got permission to move 1,000 Jews and the armaments wing of Emalia to Bruennlitz near his hometown. Though Schindler had nothing physically to do with the writing of the famed Schindler's List, there would have been no lists (one for men, one for women) without his Herculean efforts to transfer these Jewish workers. Between October 1944 and May 1945, another 98 Jews would be taken in by Schindler at Bruennlitz. During this period, he spent almost all of the money he had made in Cracow to save 1,098 Jews.

After the war, he and his wife, Emilie, who was with him at Bruennlitz, fled first to Bavaria and then to Argentina, the latter move with the help of a generous grant from the *American Jewish Joint Distribution Committee. Successful and innovative in wartime, Schindler was never able to duplicate that success or even a measure of it in his postwar life. Schindler returned to Germany in 1957 to apply for reparations for his lost factories from the West German government and never returned to Argentina and Emilie.

He was nominated to be in the first group of Righteous Among the Nations in 1962 though this nomination was withdrawn because of charges that he had stolen property and harmed several Jews during the war. Schindler became particularly close to the large community of Schindler Jews in Israel during this period and spent some of the happiest moments of his life in Israel. After his death in Hildesheim, West Germany, in the fall of 1974, his body was transferred to Israel, where he was buried in the Latin Cemetery on Mt. Zion. He and Emilie were named Righteous Among the Nations by Yad Vashem in 1993.

BIBLIOGRAPHY: E.J. Brecher, *Schindler's Legacy: True Stories of the List Survivors* (1994); D.M. Crowe, *Oskar Schindler: The Untold Account of his Life, Wartime Activities and the True Story Behind the List* (2004); T. Keneally, *Schindler's List* (1982).

[David Crowe (2nd ed.)]

SCHINDLER, RUDOLPH M. (1887–1953), U.S. architect. Born in Vienna, Schindler immigrated to America in 1913, and settled in Chicago. He worked in the office of Frank Lloyd Wright from 1916 to 1921. His Lovell House, Newport Beach (1926), represents a fusion of Wright's style with the international modern style as interpreted in Central Europe. After 1926 he worked with Richard *Neutra in Los Angeles. The buildings they produced were among the earliest examples of the international style in the U.S.

SCHINDLER, SOLOMON (1842–1915), U.S. Reform rabbi and social worker. Schindler, born in Neisser, Silesia, the son of an Orthodox rabbi, was sent to Breslau when he was 13 to train for the rabbinate. After two years he gave up his rabbinical studies, graduating from the gymnasium and eventually qualifying as a teacher. In 1868 he led a small congregation in Westphalia, but his views proved too liberal. A speech attacking Bismarck's conduct in relation to the Franco-Prussian War led to Schindler's departure from Germany, and he settled in the U.S. in 1871. At first he supported his family by peddling shoelaces, but after a short time became rabbi of the Adath Emuno Congregation, Hoboken, N.J. In 1874 Schindler was appointed rabbi of Congregation Adath Israel, Boston (Temple Israel). Until his time it had conformed to Orthodox practice, but under his leadership an organ, family pews, vernacular prayers, and eventually Sunday services were introduced. Schindler's sermons and lectures attracted wide attention in Boston. Influenced by Darwinism and Bible criticism, he adopted a radical and even assimilationist standpoint and was closely associated with Boston's advanced thinkers, particularly Minot J. Savage, a rebel against Christian Orthodoxy who eventually led the New York Community Church. From 1888 to 1894 Schindler was a member of the Boston School Board. Schindler's theological and political radicalism, and apparently his German background, proved unpalatable to his congregation, and he retired from the rabbinate in 1894, becoming superintendent first of the Federation of Jewish Charities and then of the Leopold Morse Home (1899). In a sermon entitled "Mistakes I Have Made" (1911) he withdrew from his earlier radicalism. Among Schindler's publications were *Messianic Expectations and Modern Judaism* (1886), and *Dissolving Views in the History of Judaism* (1888).

BIBLIOGRAPHY: A. Mann, *Growth and Achievement of Temple Israel; 1854–1954* (1954), 45–62; DAB, 16 (1935), 433–4; A. Mann, *Yankee Reformers of an Urban Age* (1954), 52–72 and passim.

[Sefton D. Temkin]

SCHIPER, IGNACY (**Yiẓḥak**; 1884–1943), historian and public worker. Schiper was born in Tarnow, Galicia. From his youth he was a member of the Po'alei Zion movement, and from 1922 of the General Zionists (*Al ha-Mishmar*), holding various public positions in the parties and acting as their emissary. During 1922–27 he was a deputy in the Polish Sejm. After the establishment of the Institute of Jewish Sciences in Warsaw in 1928, he lectured on the history of Jewish economy. Schiper died in a German concentration camp near Lublin.

Although his academic education was essentially a legal one, Schiper took an interest in historical research throughout his life. Within the group of Jewish historians which emerged in Galicia in the early 20th century (*Balaban, *Schorr), Schiper distinguished himself in the history of economics and of popular culture (in Yiddish). Whether this was due to his social outlook or to his limited Hebrew education, he thought that the study of the spiritual history of the nation and its leaders had been exhausted; "the Sabbath-Jew with his extra soul" was already well known, and there arose a need, he felt, to become acquainted with the secular aspect of the nation's life. Schiper's first work, in the sphere of Jewish economics, was his original research on the beginnings of capitalism among the Jews of the Western world (*Anfaenge des Kapitalismus bei den abendlaendischen Juden im frueheren Mittelalter*, 1907), which was also translated into Russian and Yiddish. Schiper then turned his attention to research into Jewish economy in Poland, at first during the Middle Ages and then during the modern era also.

His principal works in this sphere are *Studya nad stosunkami gospodarczymi Żydów w Polsce podczas średniowiecza* (1911, Yid. tr. 1926), and *Dzieje handlu żydowskiego na ziemiach polskich* (1937). Of his studies on the history of culture, two of his works are of note: *Kultur-Geshikhte fun di Yidn in Poyln beysn Mitlalter* (1926), which deals with the way of life of the Jews, and *Geshikhte fun der Yidisher Teater-Kunst un Drame: fun di Eltste Tsaytn bis 1750* (3 vols., 1927–28), which deals with theatrical art and drama. Schiper also occupied himself with other historical questions, such as Jewish autonomy in Poland, but he dealt mainly with Jewry's relationship to the external world, using primarily non-Jewish sources. A historian of great intuition and imagination, he promoted and enriched historical research on Polish Jewry, though he did not always trouble to establish his ideas on a firm historical footing.

BIBLIOGRAPHY: J. Hirschhaut, *Fun Noenter Over*, 1 (1955), 185–263 (incl. bibl.); R. Mahler, in YIVO *Bleter*, 25 (1945/46), 19–32; J. Shatzky, *ibid.*, 39 (1954/55), 352–4; Y. Gruenbaum, *Penei ha-Dor*, 1 (1958), 379–85; S. Eidelberg (ed.), *Yiẓḥak Shipper; Ketavim Nivḥarim ve-Divrei Ha'arakhah* (1967).

[Israel Halpern]

SCHIRMANN, JEFIM (**Ḥayyim**; 1904–1981), scholar of medieval Hebrew poetry. Born in Kiev, Schirmann received a doctorate in Berlin for his thesis *Die hebraeische Uebersetzung der Maqamen des Hariri* (Frankfurt 1930). He was one of the first to undertake research in medieval Hebrew poetry at the Schocken Institute for Research (first in Berlin, then in Jerusalem). In 1937 he began teaching medieval Hebrew poetry at the Hebrew University of Jerusalem, and subsequently was appointed to the chair in this subject. From 1954 to 1969 he edited **Tarbiz*, a quarterly for Jewish studies. He was a member of the Israel Academy of Sciences and Humanities and of the Academy of the Hebrew Language. In 1957 he was awarded the Israel Prize for Jewish Studies.

Schirmann's research spans the entire range of medieval Hebrew poetry. He began his activities by investigating the Hebrew poetry of Spain, both as an independent area of research and also with reference to its links with Arabic literature. At the same time he studied Italian Hebrew poetry. He compiled two large and unique anthologies of the most important existing texts of (1) Hebrew poetry written in Italy between the ninth and 20th centuries, *Mivḥar ha-Shirah ha-Ivrit be-Italyah* (Berlin, 1934); and (2) Hebrew poetry written in Spain and Provence from the 10th to the 15th centuries, *Ha-Shirah ha-Ivrit bi-Sefarad u-vi-Provence* (1961[3]). Schirmann laid the foundations for modern research and critical evaluation of secular and sacred Hebrew poetry, as well as of the rhymed tales composed by the Jews of Spain and Italy.

His many works in this field include "*Ha-Meshorerim Benei Doram shel Moshe ibn Ezra vi-Yhudah ha-Levi*" (in: YMḤSI, 3 pts., 2 (1936), 4 (1938), 6 (1945)); "*Ḥayyei Yehudah ha-Levi*" (in: *Tarbiz*, 9 (1938) and 11 (1939)); "*La métrique quantitative dans la poésie hébraïque du Moyen Age*" (in *Sefarad*, 8 (1948)); "Samuel Hannagid, the Man, the Soldier, the Politician" (in JSOS, 13 (1951)); "The Function of the Hebrew Poet in Medieval Spain" (ibid., 16 (1954)); "La poésie hébraïque du Moyen Age en Espagne" (in *Mélanges de philosophie et de littérature juives*, 3–5 (1962)), and "The Beginning of Hebrew Poetry in Italy" (in *The World History of the Jewish People*, Vol. 11: *The Dark Ages*, 1966).

Schirmann's later researches were devoted primarily to early medieval Hebrew poetry. Of particular note is the essay "Hebrew Liturgical Poetry and Christian Hymnology" (JQR 49, 1953, pp. 123–161), *Shirim Ḥadashim min ha-Genizah* ("New Poems from the *Genizah*," 1965), which contains, besides a large collection of unknown texts from different periods, a number of very important critical monographs on poets from various centers of Jewish life (Ereẓ Israel, Babylonia, North Africa, and Spain), and his collected articles in Hebrew, *Studies in the History of Hebrew Poetry and Drama* (1979). His critical edition of the secular poetry of Solomon ibn Gabirol (1974), completing the work initiated by H. Brody, can be seen as one of his most mature contributions to the history of medieval Hebrew poetry.

Several years after Schirmann's death, E. Fleischer published in two large volumes the important notes that he had left on the history of medieval Hebrew poetry with his own observations, updated bibliography, and commentaries: *The History of Hebrew Poetry in Muslim Spain* (1995) and *The History of Hebrew Poetry in Christian Spain and Southern France* (Heb., 1997).

Schirmann's numerous publications and long teaching career led to the creation of a new attitude toward research in medieval Hebrew culture. His approach to the Hebrew intellectual creativity of the Middle Ages was within the wider context of general contemporary culture, and he emphasized its connection with other cultures and literary creativities.

BIBLIOGRAPHY: S. Abramson and A. Mirsky (eds.), *Sefer Ḥayyim Schirmann* (1970); D. Pagis and E. Fleischer, ibid., 413–27, (bibl.). **ADD. BIBLIOGRAPHY:** D. Pagis, E. Fleischer, Y. David, *Kitvei Profesor Ḥayim Shirman (1904–1981): Reshimah Bibliyografit* (1983).

[Ezra Fleischer / Dan Pagis]

SCHISGAL, MURRAY (1926–), U.S. playwright. Schisgal was born in New York. His initial intention was to become a lawyer, and he did receive an LL.B. from Brooklyn Law School in 1953. Schisgal's first successful stage hit was the double bill *The Typists* and *The Tiger* (1963), which starred Eli Wallach and Anne Jackson. This was followed by his biggest hit comedy, *Luv* (1964), which was nominated for two Tony Awards – Best Play and Best Author. It was later made into a motion picture starring Jack Lemmon and Peter Falk (1967). Schisgal also wrote the play *Jimmy Shine* (1968), which starred Dustin Hoffman. Schisgal's other Broadway plays included *The Chinese and Dr. Fish* (1970), *An American Millionaire* (1974), *All over Town* (1975), and *Twice around the Park* (1983). He also wrote the plays *Ducks and Lovers* (1972), *Popkins* (1984), and *Oatmeal and Kisses* (1990).

With Larry *Gelbart he co-wrote the screenplay for *Tootsie* (1982), for which they received an Oscar nomination. He also produced the films *Boys and Girls* (2000) and *A Walk on the Moon* (1999).

Schisgal was nominated for an Emmy award for his TV productions *The Devil's Arithmetic* (1999) and *A Separate Peace* (2004). Schisgal's novel *Days and Nights of a French Horn Player* was published in 1980.

[Jonathan Licht / Ruth Beloff (2nd ed.)]

SCHLAMME, MARTHA HAFTEL (1922–1985), folk-art singer, pianist, and actress. Schlamme was born in Vienna, the only daughter of Meier and Gisa Braten Haftel, who were Orthodox Jews. She and her parents escaped the Nazis in 1938 through France to England, where her parents were interned by the English government on the Isle of Man. Martha chose to leave the Jewish school she attended and joined her parents there. At the camp she met Engel Lund, a singer from Iceland, who inspired her to become an international singer. Martha came to the U.S. in 1948, shortly after marrying Hans Schlamme.

Schlamme began her concert career in the Catskills, singing in Hebrew and Yiddish. Her venues soon included college campuses, concert halls, and nightclubs, as well as radio and television. By 1960, she had performed over a thousand concerts. A supreme interpreter of folk song, Schlamme concertized and recorded in 12 languages. She enthusiastically sang Jewish songs throughout her career. On the Vanguard, Folkways, Columbia, and MGM labels she produced 15 albums including *Martha Schlamme Sings Israeli Folk Songs* (1953); *Martha Schlamme Sings Folk Songs of Many Lands* (1958); and *Martha Schlamme Sings Jewish Folks Songs* (1957, and vol. 2, 1959).

Schlamme's early enthusiasm for Kurt *Weill brought her considerable attention and fame. She performed Weill's songs in Edinburgh at a venue called the Howff. This show grew and eventually came to New York, playing for months. For over 20 years she included Weill's music in her programs and produced the recordings *The World of Kurt Weill in Song* (1962), and *A Kurt Weill Cabaret* (1963). In 1965, she starred in a production of Weill's *Mahoganny* at the Stratford Festival in Ontario and two years later sang at Ravinia Music Festival in *A Kurt Weill Cabaret* with Alvin Epstein. In 1985, she appeared with Epstein at the Israel Festival in Jerusalem.

Schlamme sang on Broadway, playing the role of Golde in *Fiddler on the Roof* in 1968, and that same year appearing in *A Month of Sundays* and *Solitaire, Double Solitaire*. Schlamme became a teacher of song and acting at the Circle in the Square Theater School in New York and H.B. Studio. She was also close to activists in leftist politics, giving numerous benefit concerts. She recorded *German Folk Songs* on the Folkways label with Pete Seeger. In the 1960s, after an annulment of her first marriage, she married Mark Lane, a Democratic politician. Martha Schlamme suffered a stroke onstage at the Chautauqua Festival at age 60 in front of a large audience and died in nearby Jamestown, New York.

[Judith S. Pinnolis (2nd ed.)]

°SCHLEIERMACHER, FRIEDRICH (1766–1834), German theologian and preacher. The young Schleiermacher was an admirer of Henriette *Herz and frequented the salons of Berlin. He answered David *Friedlaender's audacious *Sendschreiben an Probst Teller* (1799) by advocating that Jews, as individuals, be granted complete emancipation in order to save the Church from contamination by insincere converts seeking equality. In his *Reden ueber die Religion* (1799; *On Religion*, 1955), he contended that Judaism was a dead religion, the essence of which lay in God and His chosen people. This historical dialogue, however, had ceased abruptly with the fall of the Jewish state; thus Judaism was not a true religion but rather a political body. Equating revelation with religious experience, he placed the Old Testament in a very subordinate position in relation to the New. On the other hand Schleiermacher, a powerful preacher, exerted a decisive influence on the style of L. *Zunz and other Jewish preachers of the era. Occasionally he attended the synagogue to listen to the young preachers, making comments to them afterward.

BIBLIOGRAPHY: F. Schleiermacher, *Briefe bei Gelegenheit der politisch-theologischen Aufgabe und des Sendschreibens juedischer Hausvaeter von einem Prediger ausserhalb Berlins* (1799); A. Altmann, in: YLBI, 6 (1961), 3–60; idem, in: *Studies in 19th Century Jewish Intellectual History* (1964), 72f.; W. Dilthey, *Leben Schleiermachers* (1966); H. Liebeschutz, *Das Judentum im deutschen Geschichtsbild von Hegel bis Max Weber* (1967), index. **ADD. BIBLIOGRAPHY:** F. Schleiermacher, *Kritische Gesamtausgabe* (1985–); M. Wolfes, in: *Aschkenas*, 14:2 (2004), 485–510.

[Andreas Kennecke (2nd ed.)]

SCHLESINGER, family of Austrian *Court Jews. MARX (MORDECAI) SCHLESINGER, son of Moses Margulies (*Margelioth), was active as military purveyor to the Austrian court before the 1670 expulsion of Vienna Jews, as well as financier to the court and supplier of precious metals for the royal mint. A leader of the Vienna community, he participated in the negotiations for the return of the expellees and was murdered in 1683 in Klosterneuburg. His son, BENJAMIN WOLF (d. 1727), settled in Eisenstadt in 1679 and was a large-scale military and coin supplier, particularly in Hungary, where he served the noble Esterhazy family. His business activity was conducted, however, from Vienna.

Another son, ISRAEL, was an ancestor of the renowned *Eger family. MARX (MARKUS) SCHLESINGER (d. 1754) figured prominently in the numerous wars of the period as a large-scale military purveyor, as well as financier to the Austrian court in millions of florins. In 1731 he was nominated imperial court purveyor (*Hoffaktor*) by Emperor Charles VI; he was already purveyor to the courts of electoral Palatinate, electoral Mainz, and ducal Brunswick, as well as court jeweler and purveyor to Charles Alexander of Wuerttemberg as of 1736. Although his forefathers had belonged to the *Oppenheimer and *Wertheimer circles, Marx was himself patron of Isaac *Leidesdorfer and L. *Gomperz. His far-flung activities eventually embroiled him in lawsuits with the government, and he died in extreme poverty, as did most of his children.

BIBLIOGRAPHY: M. Grunwald, *Samuel Oppenheimer und sein Kreis* (1913), index; *Magyar Zsidó Oklevéltár*, 3 (1937); 5 (1960); 9 (1966); 10 (1967); 12 (1969), index s.v.; A.F. Pribram, *Urkunden und Akten zur Geschichte der Juden in Wien* (1918), index; B. Wachstein, *Die Inschriften des alten Judenfriedhofes in Wien*, 1 (1912), index; S. Stern, *The Court Jew* (1950), index.

SCHLESINGER, family of music publishers. ADOLF MARTIN SCHLESINGER (1768–1848) was born in Berlin, where in 1810 he founded the firm Schlesinger'sche Buch und Musikalienhandlung, which was one of Beethoven's publishers. His greatest publication was Bach's *St. Matthew Passion* (1829). His two sons were HEINRICH SCHLESINGER (1807–1879) and MORITZ (MAURICE) ADOLF SCHLESINGER (1797–1871). Heinrich maintained the Berlin firm, while in 1834 Moritz established a firm in Paris which published works by Mozart, Chopin, Berlioz, *Meyerbeer, and Donizetti, and the *Gazette* (later *Revue) Musicale*. The German firm passed into other hands in 1864, and the French one in 1846.

SCHLESINGER, AKIVA JOSEPH (1837–1922), one of the first visionaries of modern Zionism. Born in Pressburg, Schlesinger was a graduate of Hungarian yeshivot and a student of Kabbalah. He was one of the spokesmen of the extreme religious elements of the Ḥatam Sofer (see Moses *Sofer) school of thought, which advocated complete separation from the "enlightened" and "neologic" elements. In his book *Lev Ivri* ("Hebrew Heart," 1865), he sharply attacked the "*meshannim*" and "*mitḥaddeshim*" ("innovators" and "reformers"). In 1870 Schlesinger went to Ereẓ Israel out of a conviction that the sole hope for religious Jewry lay in the establishment of a religious Jewish community in the Land of Israel. In 1873 he published the book *Ḥevrat Maḥzirei Atarah le-Yoshnah* or

Kolel ha-Ivrim ("The Society for the Restoration of Things to Their Former Glory" or "The Community of Hebraists"), in which he expounded his plan for the establishment of a worldwide association for the consolidation of religious Jewry. This association would set up a network of schools to educate the young generation in a religious spirit; its center would be in Jerusalem and its aim would be the establishment of a Jewish community living off the fruits of its own labor and in the spirit of the Torah. In his book Schlesinger expressed ideas similar to those which were later adapted by the Zionist movement (collection of contributions and tithes for the upbuilding of the country, renaissance of the Hebrew language, agricultural settlement, organization of self-defense, abolition of the barriers between communities and *kolelim* and their amalgamation into one – *Kolel ha-Ivrim*). Schlesinger was the leader of a group of Jerusalemites who tried to change the **ḥalukkah* system and divert the funds to agricultural settlement. The *ḥalukkah* trustees, who feared Schlesinger's ideas as a threat to their hegemony, boycotted and persecuted him, and he reponded with harsh polemic. In 1878 Schlesinger was one of the founders of Petaḥ Tikvah and, with the establishment of the new settlement, he called on religious Jewry to establish their own settlement movement to encompass truly religious Jews, without "heretical and outside elements."

BIBLIOGRAPHY: Minz and Kahane, in: L. Jung, *Men of the Spirit* (1963), 61–82; A.Y. Shaḥrai, *Rabbi Akiba Joseph Schlesinger* (Heb., 1942); Y. Trivaks and E. Steinman, *Sefer Me'ah Shanah* (1938), 387–98.

[Yehuda Slutsky]

SCHLESINGER, BENJAMIN (1876–1932), U.S. trade union leader and journalist. Born in Krakai, Lithuania, Schlesinger immigrated to Chicago in 1891, working in a sweatshop as a sewing-machine operator. At the end of the 1890s he moved to New York City. In 1903 Schlesinger was elected president of the infant International Ladies' Garment Workers' Union (ILGWU), but within a year a coalition of more conservative trade unionists defeated his bid for reelection. He then managed the New York Cloakmakers' Joint Board of the ILGWU but left in 1907 to become managing editor of New York's *Jewish Daily Forward.* During his seven years with the Yiddish daily, Schlesinger maintained his interest in the ILGWU, influenced union affairs, and prepared himself to return to union office at a more opportune time.

From 1910 to 1914, the radical socialist New York cloakmakers clashed with the more conservative and moderate leaders on the ILGWU's general executive board. The cloakmakers were defeated, but at the 1914 ILGWU convention they succeeded in removing the officeholders and elected Schlesinger president. Though committed to class warfare, he attempted to persuade socialists to abide by contractual agreements with employers. During the 1916 strike in the cloak trade, Schlesinger commanded the loyalty of both union radicals and conservatives, made himself acceptable to employers as a negotiator, and gained the support of local reformers and city officials. With the help of New York City's reform mayor, John Purroy Mitchell, he wrung from the cloak manufacturers an exceptionally favorable agreement, which relieved the union from resorting to independent arbitration and placed greater power in the hands of the trade unionists themselves.

From 1914 to 1923 Schlesinger guided the ILGWU with firmness and perception, until it became one of the largest and most progressive trade unions in the nation. But in 1923, worn down by years of poor health and depressed by the intra-union struggle between communists and anti-communists, Schlesinger resigned and returned to serve the *Forward.* In 1928, with the anti-communists in control, the ILGWU, its treasury depleted and its ranks decimated, turned to Schlesinger. He strove to revive internal unity, but the task, aggravated by the advent of the Depression, proved too much for him. He died shortly after his reelection in 1932.

[Melvyn Dubofsky]

SCHLESINGER, FRANK (1871–1943), U.S. astronomer and pioneer in stellar photography. Born in New York, Schlesinger obtained his doctorate with a thesis on a new type of measurement of a star cluster. He then began to develop his original methods for the determination of stellar parallaxes by means of celestial photography, revolutionizing the subject. In 1905 he was appointed director of the Allegheny Observatory, where he worked on the orbits of spectroscopic binary stars, devising simple methods of reducing spectrograms, and designing a new, sensitive measuring machine. In 1914 he started his ambitious plan of a large-scale parallax program. Within six years the first 365 star distances were determined, parallaxes with an average probable error of less than one hundredth of a second of arc. In 1920 he became director of the Yale University Observatory, and in 1925 he set up a South African station at Johannesburg with a 26-inch telescope of 36 feet focal length. The importance of these "trigonometric parallaxes" lies in the fact that they are the basis of the present distance scale of the universe. With their help, all spectroscopic and other distance determinations are eventually calibrated. In 1940 Schlesinger published his first "Bright Star Catalogue," giving all the essential data for all stars brighter than 6.5 visual magnitude. He did outstanding work on stellar proper motions and star positions obtained with wide-angle cameras, and a long series of these "Zone Catalogues" was published in the Yale Observatory Transactions. Schlesinger was a leading figure in the formation of the International Astronomical Union. He was its president from 1932 to 1935, and many other academic honors were awarded to him.

BIBLIOGRAPHY: *Bibliographical Memoirs of the National Academy of Science*, 24 (1947), 105–44; Spencer Jones, in: *Monthly Notices of the Royal Astronomical Society,* 104 (1944), 94–98.

[Arthur Beer]

SCHLESINGER, GEORG (1874–1949), German engineer. Born in Berlin, Schlesinger became professor of industrial science at Berlin's Technische Hochschule in 1904, one of the few Jews to hold such a position. A pioneer of industrial psychology, he created the department of psychotechnics. He wrote *Psychotechnik und Betriebswissenschaft* (1919) and edited the journal *Werkstatt-Technik*. He also designed modern factories, especially textile works. Dismissed from the Hochschule in 1933, Schlesinger went to Brussels University (1934–39), then to England, where he directed production engineering research at Loughborough College, Leicestershire.

SCHLESINGER, GUILLERMO (1903–1971), rabbi of the Congregación Israelita de la República Argentina. Born in St. Gallen, Switzerland, son and grandson of rabbis, he graduated from the Theological Seminary of Breslau (then Germany), in 1934 and received a Ph.D. in public economy from the University of Zurich in 1936. He immigrated to Argentina in 1937 and assumed the rabbinical chair of the Congregación Israelita in Buenos Aires. In 1939–1956 he was also the director of the Cursos Religiosos Israelitas (Jewish Religious Courses) of this congregation, which sustained a wide network of Jewish complementary schools, especially in the provinces and some in Buenos Aires. For many decades Rabbi Schlesinger was considered a semi-official chief rabbi of the community, especially among non-Jewish society, but not within Jewish society. In 1956 he participated in the establishment of the Latin American Fraternity of Synagogues. In 1961 Rabbi Schlesinger received an honorary doctorate from the Jewish Theological Seminary of America.

[Efraim Zadoff (2nd ed.)]

SCHLESINGER, ISIDORE WILLIAM (1877–1949), South African financier and entrepreneur. The son of an Austrian-Jewish immigrant in the United States, he went to South Africa in 1894. He built up an extensive financial and industrial empire in a relatively short time, beginning his career in Johannesburg as an insurance agent. In a few years he had established his own insurance and banking companies. In real estate he helped to develop a number of townships in Johannesburg and other cities. In 1914 he opened a chain of theaters and cinemas and for a long time held a virtual monopoly in those fields. He formed the first film production company in South Africa and, at his studios in Johannesburg, made the first regular South African newsreels and the earliest full-length films. He also established a broadcasting service, which was eventually taken over by the state to become the South African Broadcasting Corporation. His citrus-growing estate at Zebedelia (Transvaal) became one of the biggest in the world. He regarded this as his crowning achievement and, at his own wish, was buried there. His interests extended to Rhodesia, Portuguese East Africa, and Tanganyika, and he owned music halls in England. He played little part in public life but headed the Keren Hayesod campaign when Chaim *Weizmann visited South Africa in 1932.

He was succeeded as head of the Schlesinger Organization by his only son, JOHN SAMUEL SCHLESINGER (1923–).

BIBLIOGRAPHY: A.P. Cartwright, *South Africa's Hall of Fame* (1960).

[Louis Hotz]

SCHLESINGER, JOE (1928–), Canadian journalist, broadcaster. Schlesinger was born in Vienna and raised in Bratislava, Czechoslovakia. On June 30, 1939, only 11 years old, he and his younger brother, Ernie, escaped the Nazis, being among 664 children removed to England by young British stockbroker Nicholas Winton. Schlesinger spent the war years in a boarding school run by the Czech government-in-exile. At the end of the war, the brothers returned to Czechoslovakia in a futile search for their parents. Following a bout of tuberculosis, Schlesinger began work in Prague as a translator for the Associated Press but, escaping the Communist takeover of Czechoslovakia, in 1950 he made his way to Canada.

Schlesinger began his journalism career as editor of the campus newspaper while studying economics at the University of British Columbia. From 1955 to 1962 he was a reporter for the *Vancouver Province*, *Toronto Star*, and United Press International, and then for the *Herald Tribune* in Paris until 1966. He found reporting foreign news a calling, "… interpreting it, clarifying it, demystifying it, and making it interesting and relevant."

Schlesinger returned to Canada to begin a more than 40-year career in television at the Canadian Broadcasting Corporation (CBC). He held several key CBC posts, including executive producer of National News, head of TV News, chief political correspondent, and, notably, foreign correspondent. Schlesinger covered major events around the world, including the Arab-Israeli conflict, often from the heart of the action. Twice a refugee from Czechoslovakia, he returned to Prague to witness the Velvet Revolution that overthrew the Communist regime. "It was," Schlesinger recalled, "one of the great moments of my life. I was able to return, and watch that 'era,' that tyranny – the last of it – vanish. It was a kind of a personal vindication."

After retiring from the CBC news service in 1994, Schlesinger continued to produce and host documentaries, and he remains senior correspondent of CBC's flagship news program, CBC News: The National. His journalism was honored by three Gemini Awards and the John Drainie Award for distinguished contribution to broadcasting. He holds several honorary doctorates, and in 1995 he was named to the Order of Canada. He wrote *Time Zones: A Journalist in the World* (1990).

[Paula Draper (2nd ed.)]

SCHLESINGER, JOHN (1926–2003), English director. Schlesinger was born in London. Educated at Oxford, he toured in repertory until 1959 and then directed BBC-TV films. His first feature film was *A Kind of Loving* (1962), followed by *Billy Liar* (1963), *Darling* (Oscar nomination for Best Picture and Best Director, 1965), *Far from the Madding Crowd* (1967), *Midnight Cowboy* (Academy Award winner for Best Picture and Best Director, 1969), *Sunday, Bloody Sunday* (1971), *The*

Day of the Locust (1975), *Marathon Man* (1976), *Yanks* (1979), *The Falcon and the Snowman* (1985), *Madame Sousatzka* (1988), *The Innocent* (1993), and *Cold Comfort Farm* (1995). Schlesinger directed several plays, including *Timon of Athens* for the Royal Shakespeare Company. He was one of the most important British filmmakers of the post-1960 period.

[Jonathan Licht]

SCHLESINGER, KARL (1889–1938), Austrian financier and economist. He introduced methods of mathematical analysis and the calculation by probability of the movements of money and capital. Born in Budapest, Schlesinger lived in Vienna where he was a wealthy board member of many industrial and financial corporations. He was one of the few non-academic economists of reputation who were members of the Vienna Economic Society. Most of his views were expounded among friends during spirited sessions in Viennese coffeehouses. Schlesinger took his own life when the Germans entered Vienna in 1938.

His writings include *Theorie der Geld-und Kreditwirtschaft* (1914); *Veraenderungen des Geldwertes im Kriege* (1916); *Ueber die Produktionsgleichungen der oekonomischen Wertlehre* (1931).

[Joachim O. Ronall]

SCHLESWIG-HOLSTEIN, state of Germany. In the 17th century Danish kings, rulers of the dual duchies of Schleswig and Holstein, invited Sephardi merchants to settle there, and communities were founded in *Glueckstadt, Rendsburg, Friedrichstadt, and *Altona, which became the seat of the rabbinate and the leading community. While the other communities gradually declined economically, Altona prospered and attracted German Jews, who were permitted to settle in these cities and enjoyed special privileges despite the opposition of the Sephardim.

On March 29, 1814, the Jews in Denmark were granted emancipation, but this was abolished at the Congress of *Vienna by a decision which applied to the lands of the German Confederation. Jewish equality was championed by S.L. *Steinheim and Gabriel *Riesser. It was advocated in a series of petitions to the conservative provincial estates, and favored by King Christian VIII. Equality was temporarily obtained during the 1848–49 revolution, proclaimed by the parliament of the revolutionary duchies in which Jews participated; during the revolution Jews first settled in *Kiel. On July 14, 1863, a law granting complete emancipation was enacted. A year later the duchies were detached from Denmark and passed to Prussia in 1866. The Jewish population numbered 3,674 in 1835 (2,014 in Altona; 188 in Glueckstadt; 292 in Rendsburg; and 373 in Friedrichstadt, where they were 17% of the population). The figures were about 6,000 in 1925, with 5,000 in Altona, 600 in the new community of Kiel, and the remainder divided among the other dwindling communities; Altona was incorporated into Hamburg in 1937.

Rudolf Katz (d. 1961) was minister of justice of the state of Schleswig-Holstein in 1960, when there were 107 Jews in Kiel.

BIBLIOGRAPHY: W. Victor, *Die Emanzipation der Juden in Schleswig-Holstein* (1913); *Jahrbuch fuer die juedischen Gemeinden Schleswig-Holstein und der Hansestaedte* (1929–38); A. Linnvald, in: *Zeitschrift der Gesellschaft fuer Schleswig-Holsteinsche Geschichte*, 57 (1928), 299–364; H. Kellenbenz, *Sephardim an der unteren Elbe* (1958).

SCHLETTSTADT, SAMUEL BEN AARON (second half of the 14th century), Alsatian rabbi and *rosh yeshivah*. Samuel took his name from Schlettstadt, the town where he was apparently born. *Joseph (Joselmann) b. Gershom of Rosheim (in *Sefer ha-Mikneh*, written in 1546, publ. 1970) describes him as "a pious man, head of the exile," but biographical details about him are scant; however there is some information about a calumny in Strasbourg in which Schlettstadt was involved and which was the cause of his wandering to various countries. The affair is recounted in two sources: by Joseph of Rosheim (*ibid.*, 7f.), and in the documents of excommunication published by N. *Coronel in *Ḥamishah Kunteresim* (1864), 107b ff. Two Jews from Strasbourg were involved in a conspiracy with the knights of Andlau who were in the vicinity of the city. After Samuel issued an unheeded warning to the conspirators, the citizens approached him to pass judgment on them, and he sentenced them to death. The sentence was carried out on one of the informers, but his companion fled to the knights and apostasized. When the knights discovered that the informer had been put to death, they went to war against the men of Strasbourg, and Samuel was compelled to flee the city. He escaped, concealing himself in the fortress of Hohenlandsberg near Strasbourg, and lived there together with the students of his yeshivah for a number of years (1370–76). It seems likely that some of the members of the community had a hand in the incitement against Samuel, who waited in vain for the community leaders to take the steps that would enable him to return (it seems that it was necessary to appease the knights of Andlau with money).

In 1376 Samuel left his hiding place and traveled to the East. On his way he passed through several communities in Germany, where he received letters from various rabbis (including *Meir b. Baruch ha-Levi of Vienna) referring to him in complimentary terms and calling for action on his behalf. After 1381 he arrived in Babylonia, where he obtained a deed of excommunication from the *nesi'im* David (b. Hodaiah?) and Jedidiah (b. Jesse?), apparently directed against those individuals in Strasbourg who were involved in the affair. It laid upon the members of the community the duty of doing everything necessary to enable Samuel to return to Strasbourg and compensate him for his suffering and losses. From Babylonia he proceeded to Jerusalem, where he obtained two documents (published by Coronel) signed by various scholars (among them immigrants from Italy and Germany) supporting the excommunication by the *nesi'im*. As proved by H. Frankel (*Ha-Mikneh*, introd. 17), Joseph of Rosheim relied on this deed in his account of the incident, although there are certain variations between his description of the affair and that retailed in the deed. Equipped with these documents, Samuel made his way back and reached Regensburg. The people of Strasbourg made their peace with him. When he reached the Rhine, the students of the yeshivah came to meet him, accompanied by Samuel's son Abraham, whose boat capsized; he was drowned in the river before his father's eyes. There is a theory that Samuel met his death in the expulsion and massacre of the Jews of Strasbourg in the years 1380–88.

Samuel's best-known work is his *Ha-Mordekhai ha-Katan* (so called by Israel *Bruna in his responsa, Stettin 1860 ed., nos. 163, 170, 181a, 194 p. 72a, 207, 244), also referred to as *Ha-Mordekhai ha-Kaẓar* (Israel Isserlein, *Terumat ha-Deshen, pesakim* no. 192; Jacob Weil, responsa no.88), and *Kiẓẓur Mordekhai* (Azulai, Sh-G s.v.). As its title indicates, it is an abridgment of the *Mordekhai* by *Mordecai b. Hillel (in the Rhenish version). This work is mentioned by Jacob *Moelln (Responsa (Hanau 1610 ed.) nos. 87 and 174), and in *Minhagim, Hilkhot Sukkah* (Warsaw, 1874 ed., 52a) it is referred to as the "*Mordecai* [sic!] compiled by Samuel Schlettstade" and by Jacob *Landau in his *Agur*. From the extensive use made of it, it would appear that it had an independent value. The work has not yet been published, though many manuscripts of it are known. The work was compiled in 1376 (according to information in Ms. Parma, De Rossi no. 397, written in 1391), while Samuel was in the fortress of Hohenlandsberg. The date (1393) given in an Oxford manuscript (Neubauer, Cat., no. 672) is not, as Neubauer thought, the date of composition, but of the copying.

Samuel added notes containing rulings and additions from the work of various *posekim* to the *Mordekhai* which appear as an appendix in the printed editions (since the 1559 edition of Riva di Trento). These notes were written in the margins of the Rhenish version of the *Mordekhai* and included additions which are apparently extracts from the Austrian version (see Kohn, bibl.). Samuel's authorship of these notes, which was established by Zunz (HB, 9 (1869), 135), is clear from the notes to the *Mordekhai, Gittin* 456: "And I Samuel the unworthy," and *Yevamot* 111: "And see there in *Ha-Mordekhai ha-Katan* which I compiled"; it is possible, however, that not all the notes were compiled by him. The question of the author of the minor *halakhot* (*ẓiẓit, mezuzah, Sefer Torah*, and *tefillin*) in the *Mordekhai* is not yet clear. Ḥ.J.D. Azulai pointed out that Mordecai b. Hillel was not their author and that they did not occur in the *Mordekhai*. Zunz's conclusion that the author is Samuel because they are found in *Ha-Mordekhai ha-Katan* is not reliable, because, although it is certain that the minor *halakhot* found their way into the *Mordekhai* from it, it is not indisputable that Samuel was the author. An inscription in the Oxford manuscript (Neubauer, Cat, no. 672) of *Ha-Mordekhai ha-Katan* seems to indicate that Samuel was the author. It states: "The Alfasi and the *Mordekhai* did not compile works on the minor [tractates]. In consequence I, the unworthy, have done so …"; so too in the inscription on another such manuscript (Oxford 673). Nevertheless, the notes on the minor *halakhot* are certainly by Samuel and they contain allusions to his notes on the *Mordekhai* (no. 968) and vice versa (*Mordekhai Haggahah* Shab. 456, end of ch. 2). Jacob Weil (Responsa, 147) mentions a responsum written by Samuel.

Samuel's grandson, Abraham's son, compiled a work called *Shem ha-Gedolim*, containing biographical and bibliographical information (published by I. Benjacob in the collection *Devarim Attikim*, 2 (1846), 7–10).

BIBLIOGRAPHY: E. Carmoly, *La France Israélite* (1858), 138–44; Graetz-Rabbinowitz, 6 (1898), 14f.; Graetz, in: MGWJ, 24 (1875), 408–10; M.S. Kohn, *ibid.*, 26 (1877), 429–32, 477–80, 517–23 (= Sinai, 14 (1944), 38–45); Zunz, in: HB, 9 (1869), 135; Zunz, Ritus, 215; Neubauer, Cat, nos. 672, 673, 675, 676, 2444; N. Coronel, *Ḥamishah Kunteresim* (1864), 111b–2b; M. Wiener, in: *Achawa Vereins-Buch fuer 1867–5627*, 110–3; J. Freimann (ed.), Joseph b. Moses, *Leket Yosher*, 2 (1904), introd. 35 no. 73; H. Frankel-Goldschmidt (ed.), *Joseph of Rosheim, Sefer ha-Mikneh* (1970), 15–18 (introd.), 7–9, 24–29; Weiss, Dor, 5 (1904^4), 174f.

[Shlomoh Zalman Havlin]

SCHLIEFER, SOLOMON (1889–1957), rabbi of the Great Synagogue in Moscow. Schliefer was born in Aleksandrovka, Ukraine, where his father, Jeḥiel Mikhel Schliefer, officiated as rabbi. In the yeshivah of Lida he was a disciple of the founder of *Mizrachi, Rabbi Isaac Jacob *Reines, and, after being ordained as rabbi, he married Reines' granddaughter. After his father's death Schliefer became rabbi of Aleksandrovka, where his wife and son died of starvation during the civil war after the 1917 Revolution and his mother and brothers were murdered by Ukrainian nationalists. For a time during the early stages of the Soviet regime, Schliefer made his living as an accountant, but in 1922 he settled in Moscow and became secretary of the Great Synagogue congregation. Eventually he was appointed rabbi and chairman of the congregation and was very skillful in steering his way between the obligatory contacts with the Soviet authorities and his devotion to Judaism, to the congregation, and to the many Jewish refugees who fled to Moscow during World War II from various parts of the country.

Though careful not to serve as a tool of the official propaganda line on Jewish matters, Schliefer could not avoid signing a statement of several prominent Soviet Jews against the "aggression" of Israel during the Sinai Campaign, published in *Izvestiya* (Nov. 29, 1956). At that time he also received permission from the authorities to print – for the first time under the Soviet regime – a Jewish prayer book (3,000 copies). It consisted of photostated pages from pre-revolutionary prayer books, from which any reference to wars and victories (as, e.g., in the Ḥanukkah benedictions) were omitted. Schliefer called it *Siddur ha-Shalom* ("Peace Prayer Book," instead of the customary *Siddur ha-Shalem*, "complete prayer book"). He also printed for members of his congregation a Jewish calendar for the year 5717. Shortly before his death he opened and headed, with official authorization, the only legal yeshivah in the U.S.S.R., under the name Kol Ya'akov, which was located in the synagogue building. Under his successor, Rabbi Judah Leib *Lewin, a small number of ritual slaughterers were trained there, many of them from the Georgian Soviet republic. His son MOSES (by his second wife), who served as an officer in the Soviet army, was killed at the front in 1943.

SCHLOESSINGER, MAX (1877–1944), scholar and Zionist worker. Schloessinger, born in Heidelberg, was educated at the Universities of Berlin and Vienna, at the Israelitische Lehranstalt Vienna, and at the Berlin Hochschule fuer die Wissenschaft des Judentums. In 1903 he moved to New York as office editor of the *Jewish Encyclopaedia*. The following year he was appointed librarian and instructor at Hebrew Union College, Cincinnati, but resigned in 1907 following a dispute over Zionism. Returning to Germany, he began a successful import-export business. Shortly after the outbreak of World War I he moved to Holland for business reasons, and then settled in Palestine.

Schloessinger was active in Zionist work in Holland, serving as director of the Jewish National Fund. His friendship with J.L. *Magnes when both were students in Berlin led him to a close identification with the work of the Hebrew University. Schloessinger served as a member of the university's board of governors from its inception, and at various times acted as deputy to Magnes in the office of chancellor. In recognition of his contributions to the study of Islamic Jewish literature, Schloessinger was made a fellow of the University School of Oriental Studies. Owing to ill health, he moved to New York in 1939.

[Sefton D. Temkin]

SCHLOSSBERG, JOSEPH (1875–1971), U.S. trade union leader and journalist. Born in Koidanovo (now Dzerzhinsk), Belorussia, he went to the U.S. in the 1880s and worked in the sweatshops of the needle trade in New York City. The harsh and degrading working conditions among the immigrants in these places led him to join the radical left wing of the American socialist movement. He challenged Joseph *Barondess for leadership of the garment workers and broke with Morris *Hillquit, Meyer *London, and Abraham *Cahan over socialist policies and tactics. When Hillquit, London, and Cahan left the socialist labor party in 1898 and formed the more moderate socialist party, Schlossberg remained loyal to the revolutionary socialist labor party and edited the party's weekly *Der Arbeyter*. In 1913, during the strike of New York City men's tailors, Schlossberg supported the tailors against their parent organization, the United Garment Workers of America (UGWA), which opposed the strike. As a result of the conflict with the UGWA's national officials, the tailors formed their own local organization, the Brotherhood of Tailors, and elected Schlossberg secretary. In 1914 Schlossberg's supporters seceded from the UGWA convention and founded the Amalgamated Clothing Workers of America (ACWA). The new organization elected Sidney *Hillman president and Schlossberg secretary-treasurer, and for the next 25 years they proved an able and successful team. As secretary-treasurer he administered the organization's accounts, edited the union's journal *Advance* and its seven foreign-language journals, and wrote books and pamphlets on the programs of the ACWA, strenuously advocating social reform.

In 1940 Schlossberg resigned from office and devoted his time to community and Zionist affairs. Following the establishment of the State of Israel he worked for the *Histadrut, the Israel General Federation of Labor in the U.S., and became chairman of the American National Committee for Labor Israel. He believed that Israel's labor movement could achieve the socialist community that had eluded him in America.

BIBLIOGRAPHY: Rejzen, Leksikon, 4 (1929), 670–2.

[Melvyn Dubofsky]

SCHMELKES, GEDALIAH BEN MORDECAI (1857–1928), Polish talmudist. Schmelkes studied under his uncle Isaac *Schmelkes, rabbi of Lemberg. Although he was ordained rabbi in his youth and considered an outstanding talmudist, he at first refused to accept rabbinic office and engaged in business. When his business failed, however, he was appointed in 1893 rabbi of Przemysl, but the appointment was not officially recognized by the government. In 1898 he was appointed rabbi of Kolomyya, but his experiences there were difficult. In 1904 he returned to Przemysl and this time was recognized as chief rabbi. He was one of the few rabbis in Poland who officially joined the Zionist movement, and he played an active role in Zionist congresses. Schmelkes distinguished himself by his activities in the difficult period through which Galician Jewry passed during World War I. When he was expelled from Przemysl during the war, he refused to leave until the last Jews had departed. For a time he stayed in Vienna, returning to Przemysl in 1917. One of his sons, Moses, died in Siberia. Schmelkes had great influence both in ḥasidic circles and among the *maskilim*.

Most of his works in manuscript were lost, and only a small section of his novellae and sermons entitled *Imrei Regesh* (Piotrkow, 1931) was published. Supplements to them – *Masoret ha-Shas* (Talmud cross-references) – arranged by him were preserved; some of them were published by J.L. Maimon (see bibliography).

BIBLIOGRAPHY: A. Cahana, *Divrei Zikkaron* (1933); J.L. Maimon, *Middei Ḥodesh be-Ḥodsho*, 4 (1958), 137–8; *Sefer Przemysl*.

[Itzhak Alfassi.]

SCHMELKES, ISAAC JUDAH (1828–1906), talmudic scholar of Galicia. Schmelkes was born in Lemberg and was the son of Ḥayyim Samuel Schmelkes, claiming descent from Eleazar b. Samuel Schmelke *Rokeaḥ (see introduction to *Beit Yiẓḥak, Oraḥ Ḥayyim*, Przemysl, 1875). A pupil of Joseph Saul ha-Levi *Nathanson, head of the local *bet din*, he was hailed in his youth as a brilliant talmudic student. He served as head of the *bet din* in a number of towns before being appointed in Lemberg, where he remained until his death. His *Beit Yiẓḥak* (6 vols., 1875–1908), on the four parts of the Shulḥan Arukh, was widely acclaimed. His opinion on halakhic questions was sought by many prominent contemporary scholars.

[H.D. Modlinger]

SCHMELZ, USIEL OSCAR (1918–1995), demographer. Born in Vienna, Schmelz settled in Ereẓ Israel in 1939. From 1958 he headed the demographic and social divisions of the Central Bureau of Statistics, and from 1961 was Research Fellow in Jewish Demography at The Hebrew University of Jerusalem. Among his publications are *Jewish Demography and Statistics; 1920–1960* (1961), a bibliography, and *Criminal Statistics in Israel* (1962–64). He was co-editor of *Jewish Population Studies, 1961–1968* (1970), to which he contributed *A Guide to Jewish Population Studies*. He was *Encyclopaedia Judaica* departmental editor for demography of contemporary Jewry.

SCHMERLING, LOUIS (1912–1991), U.S. organic chemist, born in Milwaukee. Schmerling spent his working career with Universal Oil Products Company and did research in the field of hydrocarbon chemistry. He took out over 200 patents relating to catalysts, petroleum conversion, petrochemicals, insecticides, and flameproofing intermediates.

°SCHMID, ANTON VON (1765–1855), Christian publisher of Hebrew books in Vienna and patron of Hebrew literature. Apprenticed to the court printer Kurzbeck, Schmid was sent to the Oriental academy to study Hebrew. In accord with the policy of Joseph II to eliminate foreign competition in Hebrew publishing, he was sent to Lvov (Lemberg) to learn typesetting. Schmid showed efficiency and rapidly rose to be manager of the Hebrew department. Thereafter, he established himself as an independent printer of Hebrew books, greatly benefiting from an 1800 ordinance prohibiting the import of Hebrew books by Jews who were themselves excluded from the publishing business. His books, which gained a deservedly high reputation, were bought in the Jewish centers of Galicia and Hungary, as well as abroad. Schmid later began publishing books in other Oriental languages and in 1823 was ennobled. He published the standard works, the Babylonian Talmud and Shulḥan Arukh, as well as halakhic works and Jewish philosophy.

He employed Jewish typesetters and proofreaders, mainly from Galicia, who were granted special residence permits in Vienna. Among them were many luminaries of Haskalah literature: Salomon *Loewensohn, Samson *Bloch, Samuel *Romanelli, Judah Leib ben Ze'ev, Meir Obernik, and others. In 1820 Schmid encouraged Shalom ha-Cohen to publish the first volume of a yearbook, **Bikkurei ha-Ittim* ("First Fruit of the Times"), an important element in the development of the Haskalah movement in Austria. Schmid was also the first to print **Kerem Ḥemed*, the most important scholarly journal of the time. He donated a collection of all the Hebrew books he had published to the Vienna Jewish community (1814), which became the nucleus of the communal library. The firm was continued by his son Franz, who eventually sold it to the father of Isidor *Bush.

BIBLIOGRAPHY: M. Grunwald, *Vienna* (1936), index; Ḥ.D. Friedberg, *Toledot ha-Defus ha-Ivri* (1937), 94–101; K. von Wurzbach, *Biographisches Lexikon des Kaiserthums Oesterreich*, 30 (1875), 209–12; A. Yaari, *Diglei ha-Madpisim ha-Ivriyyim* (1944), 97, 174–5; A.F. Pribram, *Urkunden und Akten zur Geschichte der Juden in Wien*, 2 (1918), 380; B. Wachstein, in: *Die hebraeische Publizistik in Wien* (1930), xvff. (first pagin.); R.N.N. Rabinowitz, *Ma'amar al Hadpasat ha-Talmud*, ed. by A.M. Habermann (1952), 128–9, 133, 140. **ADD. BIBLIOGRAPHY:** R. Julius, in: *Jewish Book Annual*, 51 (1993–94), 195–202.

[Henry Wasserman]

SCHMIDT, JOSEPH (1904–1942), singer. Schmidt was born in Davideni, Bukovina. During World War I his family settled in Czernowitz, where he began singing in the synagogue choir and soon embarked on concert appearances. Parallel with these he became cantor in Czernowitz, and later at the Leopoldstadt Synagogue in Vienna and at the Adas Yisroel Synagogue in Berlin. Despite the extraordinary brilliance of his lyrical tenor voice, a stage career proved almost impossible, since Schmidt was only 4 feet 10 inches tall. His impresarios found the means of overcoming this difficulty by building his career on radio concerts, recordings, and operetta films in which his stature was raised by adroit camera work. Schmidt became one of the major European stars in the field of operetta and light music, and his recordings were bestsellers of the period. He also appeared successfully in England, the United States, France, and Belgium, and visited Palestine in 1934. In 1940 he was saved from arrest by gentile friends during the German invasion of Belgium and brought through France to Switzerland. Interned in a refugee camp ("Auffangs-Lager") in Gyrenbad, he contracted a serious throat ailment but was refused special treatment and admission into the regional hospital. He subsequently died in the camp. The quasi-autobiographical film *Ein Lied geht um die Welt*, in which he had starred, was reissued with scant success in 1952.

BIBLIOGRAPHY: Baker, Biog Dict, s.v.; C. Ritter, *Ein Lied geht um die Welt* (1955), a novel; K. and G. Ney-Nowotny, *Joseph Schmidt; das Leben und Sterben eines Unvergesslichen* (1963).

[Bathja Bayer]

SCHMIDT, SAMUEL MYER (1883–1965), newspaper editor, medical director, and representative of the Va'ad Hatzalah. Schmidt was born in Kovno, Russia (later Kaunas, Lithuania). His family came to Boston in 1896; Schmidt, one of six children, attended public school for a year, then worked at a variety of odd jobs to help him support the family. In 1899, he was offered a job in a rubber factory. There, he lost his right arm in a grinding accident but was determined not to be defeated by his disability. After trying a number of businesses, he prepared himself to enter MIT in 1907. He majored in biology and public health and graduated in 1911. While in school he volunteered in settlement houses in Boston, teaching Americanization classes to new immigrants. In 1913 Schmidt was appointed as an industrial health inspector and also director of the Boston Evening Center, carrying on his settlement work. Through an acquaintance with Boris *Bogen, (a national social work leader), he came to Cincinnati for one year to serve as superintendent of the Jewish Settlement. He returned to Boston, but the following year, joined the Joint Distribution Committee's (JDC) Zionist Medical Unit in Palestine, assigned especially to the problems of sanitation, cholera, and malaria. In 1919, he returned to the U.S., then accepted the call of the JDC and went to Poland as a member of the first relief unit. From 1921 to 1923, he served as medical director for Poland.

In 1926, he returned to Cincinnati to help organize the Wider Scope Program (later, Hillel). Schmidt published a manual on Jews and Jewish history for students. That same year he decided to establish a newspaper; the *Every Friday* was to serve as "a mirror of Jewish life in Cincinnati," reflecting the whole spectrum of Jewish life and opinion in the city. The paper underwent its vicissitudes with financial problems during the Depression, and competition with another Jewish paper which sought to undermine its circulation, but Schmidt persevered, and the paper continued weekly publication for almost 40 years.

In 1939 an editorial by Schmidt about the uprooting of Talmudic academies in Eastern Europe caught the attention of Rabbi Eliezer *Silver, head of the Union of Orthodox Rabbis and the Orthodox leader of the Cincinnati community. Silver prevailed on Schmidt to go to Lithuania as a representative of the Va'ad Hatzalah, to bring rescue and relief to the rabbis and students of the Eastern European yeshivot who had gathered in Vilna. So honored by this commission and impressed with the piety and purity of the rabbis he met, Schmidt determined to become a "whole Jew" and undertake a serious program of study and practice when he returned to Cincinnati.

When the war ended, Schmidt returned once more to Europe to give comfort and sustenance to the survivors of the Holocaust in the displaced persons camps. He described his reaction to these encounters in articles he sent home to the *Every Friday*. His readers back home were thus made intensely aware of the tragedy of the European Jews. On October 3, 1965, Samuel Schmidt collapsed and died in the presence of 500 friends and family members, at his own testimonial dinner in Cincinnati.

[Nancy Klein (2nd ed.)]

SCHMIEDL, ADOLF ABRAHAM (1821–1914), Austrian rabbi and scholar. Born at Prossnitz (Prostejov), Moravia, Schmiedl served as rabbi in Gewitsch, Moravia (1846–49); then as *Landesrabbiner* at Teschen, Silesia (to 1852) and later at Bielitz (Bielsko), Prosnitz, and Vienna.

Among his published works are *Studien ueber juedische, insbesondere juedisch-arabische Religionsphilosophie* (1869), *Saadia Alfajumi und die negativen Vorzuege seiner Religionsphilosophie* (1870), and *Die Lehre vom Kampf ums Recht im Verhaeltniss zum Judentum und dem aeltesten Christentum* (1875). He also published two volumes of homilies on the Pentateuch (*Sansinim*, 1859, 1885) and *Lekaḥ Tov* (Dutch translation, 1866).

SCHMOLKA, MARIE (1890–1940), Czech leader of the Jewish women's movement and social worker. Marie Schmolka (née Eisner), who was born in Prague, became associated with the Czech democratic movement and alienated herself from Judaism. After the death of her husband, a lawyer in Prague, she toured the Near East, and her visit to Palestine reawakened her attachment to Judaism. Upon her return to Prague, she joined the Zionist Organization, the WIZO, and the Jewish Party, of which she soon was one of the central figures. In the early 1930s she was the moving spirit in the establishment of the relief committee for the Jews of *Subcarpathian Ruthenia. In 1933 she was the initiator and director of the committee assisting Jewish refugees from Germany and later became the director of *HICEM. She subsequently took the central role in the relief campaign for Nazi victims, both Jews and non-Jews, and acted as the chairman of the coordinating committee of all the refugee organizations. She often attended the conferences of international committees in Geneva, Paris, London, and *Evian, as well as Jewish conferences dedicated to social and national causes. Her struggle on behalf of Jewish refugees who were stranded in no-man's-land (the narrow strip between the 1939 German and Czechoslovak borders) attracted worldwide attention. When Hannah *Steiner, the president of the Czech WIZO, was arrested on the day after the German occupation of Prague in March 1939, Marie Schmolka presented herself to the Gestapo and declared that she was responsible for all the activities of the relief committee. She was arrested and imprisoned for about two months in the notorious Pankrác prison. After her release, she resumed her work. In August 1939 she was authorized by the Nazi authorities to travel to Paris and London for negotiations to accelerate Jewish emigration from the Protectorate of Bohemia-Moravia. When World War II broke out, she established herself in London, where she was active on behalf of the Czechoslovak Jewish refugees and exiles. There she died suddenly, in March 1940, and was eulogized by Jan *Masaryk.

BIBLIOGRAPHY: Marie Schmolka Society of Women Zionists from Czechoslovakia, *In Memoriam…* (1944); WIZO, *Saga of a Movement; Wizo: 1920–1970* (1970), 236–8; C. Yachil, *Devarim al ha-Ẓiyyonut ha-Czekhoslovakit* (1967).

[Chaim Yahil]

SCHNABEL, ARTUR (1882–1951), pianist and teacher. A prodigy, born in Lipnik, Moravia, Schnabel studied in Vienna with Leschetitzky and from 1925 taught at the Hochschule fuer Musik in Berlin. He appeared as a soloist in the cities of Europe and on U.S. tours and also became widely known as a chamber-music player, especially with the violinist, Carl Flesch. When the Nazis came to power he settled in Switzerland and held, at Lake Como, master classes that acquired international fame. During World War II he lived in the U.S. Schnabel was a noted interpreter of Mozart, Schubert, and Brahms, and his readings of Beethoven were considered the most authoritative of his time. His playing was intellectual and contemplative rather than emotional. He was also a composer in a modernistic, atonal style, his compositions including a symphony, a piano concerto, orchestral and chamber music, and songs. He edited Beethoven's piano sonatas with an unprecedentedly detailed commentary, and also the Beethoven piano-violin sonatas jointly with Flesch. He wrote *Reflections on Music* (1933), *Music and the Line of Most Resistance* (1942), and *My Life and Music* (1961).

BIBLIOGRAPHY: C. Saerchinger, *Artur Schnabel, a Biography* (1957).

SCHNAITTACH, village in Bavaria, Germany. Although a Jew is first mentioned in 1498 at a trial in Schnaittach, some Jews presumably settled there long before that date. In 1505 an organized community is documented which by 1529 maintained a rabbi, a synagogue, and a cemetery (the oldest Jewish tombstone is from 1423). Six to 12 families resided there in the 16th century. During the Thirty Years' War (1618–48) Schnaittach suffered frequent pillage. A number of 18th-century *Court Jews came from Schnaittach, among them Seligman Loew and Anschel Levi. In 1747 there were 49 tax-paying families. A new cemetery was opened in 1833, and the ancient synagogue was restored in 1858 and again in 1932. The Orthodox community reached its peak in 1837, numbering 262 (17.6% of the population) and then declined to 175 in 1867; 53 in 1900; and only 42 in 1933. On Nov. 10, 1938, during Kristallnacht, the synagogue was desecrated (scrolls and other sacred objects were rescued by some SA men), but its historical value saved it from arson. By January 1939 the community no longer existed. The community has continued to maintain three cemeteries, although there were no Jews residing in the village in 1971. From 1985 to 1996 the building complex of the former synagogue, the ritual bath, and the rabbi's and cantor's house were restored. Since then, it has housed a remarkable exhibition on rural Jewish life in south Germany, presented by the Jewish Museum of Franconia (which has sites in Fuerth and Schnaittach).

BIBLIOGRAPHY: FJW, 283; PK Bavaria. **ADD. BIBLIOGRAPHY:** M. Hildesheimer, *The History of the Kehilat Schnaittach*, vol. 1–3 (1980); W. Tausendpfund and G. Wolf, *Die juedische Gemeinde von Schnaittach* (Mitteilungen. Altnuernberger Landschaft, vol. 30, 3) (1981) ; *Germania Judaica*, vol. 3 (1987), 1327–29; T. Harburger, *Die Inventarisierung juedischer Kunst- und Kulturdenkmaeler in Bayern*, vol. 3 (1998), 677–87; B. Purin, *Juedisches Leben in Schnaittach* (1999); idem, *Judaica aus der Medina Aschpah. Die Sammlung des Juedischen Museums Franken in Schnaittach* (2003). **WEBSITES**: www.alemannia-judaica.de; www.juedisches-museum.org/schnaittach.html.

[Larissa Daemmig (2nd ed.)]

SCHNAPPER, BER (1906–?), Yiddish poet. Born near Lemberg, the son of a poor cobbler, he was associated with the Galician Neo-Romantics whose center was Lemberg. His first book of lyrics *Opshoym* ("Scum," 1927) was influenced by his townsman, the poet M.L. *Halperin. In gray images and pessimistic tones, it depicted the small, decaying villages with their crooked streets and crumbling houses. In his last lyric collections, *Mayn Shtot* ("My City," 1932), *Mayse un Lid* ("Story and Poem," 1934), and *Bloe Verter* ("Blue Words," 1937), the mood was more nostalgic. "Lid tsu a Shtekn" ("Song to a Cane"), written on the eve of World War II, when Polish hooligans were attacking Jews with their canes, is an expression of the Jewish people's protest to heaven that a tree branch designed by God to blossom was being transformed by man into a club with which to split skulls. New poems continued to appear in journals into 1940. It is not clear when and where he died.

BIBLIOGRAPHY: M. Ravitch, *Mayn Leksikon* (1945), 264–6. **ADD. BIBLIOGRAPHY:** LNYL, 8 (1981), 748

[Melech Ravitch / Jerold C. Frakes (2nd ed.)]

SCHNEEBERGER, HENRY WILLIAM (1848–1916), U.S. rabbi. Born in New York City, Schneeberger obtained his B.A. and M.A. degrees from Columbia College. After receiving his rabbinical degree in 1871 from Rabbi Israel Hildesheimer in Berlin, he returned to New York in 1872 to become rabbi of Congregation Poel Zedek and one of the first native-born rabbis in the U.S. From 1876 until his death he served at Congregation Chizuk Amuno in Baltimore. He was active in local Hebrew education, the American Jewish Committee, and the Union of Orthodox Jewish Congregations of the United States and Canada. In addition he helped found the Jewish Theological Seminary in 1886 and translated the Book of Ezekiel for the Jewish Publication Society Bible translation (1917). He was the author of *The Life and Works of Rabbi Yehuda Hanasi* (1870) and contributed articles to the *Jewish Messenger* and the *American Hebrew*.

BIBLIOGRAPHY: Goldman, in: AJHSQ, 57 (1967), 153–90.

[Israel M. Goldman]

SCHNEERSOHN, family of ḥasidic leaders; descendants of the *ẓaddik* Shneur Zalman of Lyady, the founder of Chabad Ḥasidism (popularly known as *Lubavitch). (See Chart: Schneersohn Family). For details see *Shneur Zalman of Lyady.

SCHNEERSOHN, ISAAC (1879–1969), communal leader in Russia; founder of the *Centre de Documentation Juive Contemporaine (CDJC) in France. Born in Kamenets-Podolski, Russia, of the *Schneersohn ḥasidic family of Lubavitch rabbis, he completed his studies in 1905, and became **kazyonny ravvin*, first in Gorodnya and then in Chernigov. He was instrumental in the founding of several mutual aid organizations, cooperatives for Jewish artisans, and old-age homes. He also contributed to the improvement of the Jewish school system. In Russia, Schneersohn was a member of the moderate liberal Russian party, the Constitutional Democrats ("Cadets"). From 1916 to 1918 he was a member of the town council, later deputy mayor, of Ryazan. Schneersohn arrived in France in 1920 where he became an industrialist but pursued his Jewish social work as well. During World War II, as a refugee in southern France, he founded the Centre de Documentation Juive Contemporaine (CDJC) within the underground movement in Grenoble (1943). He became its founding chairman and presided over it until his death. After the liberation of France, the CDJC became a vital institute for the research of

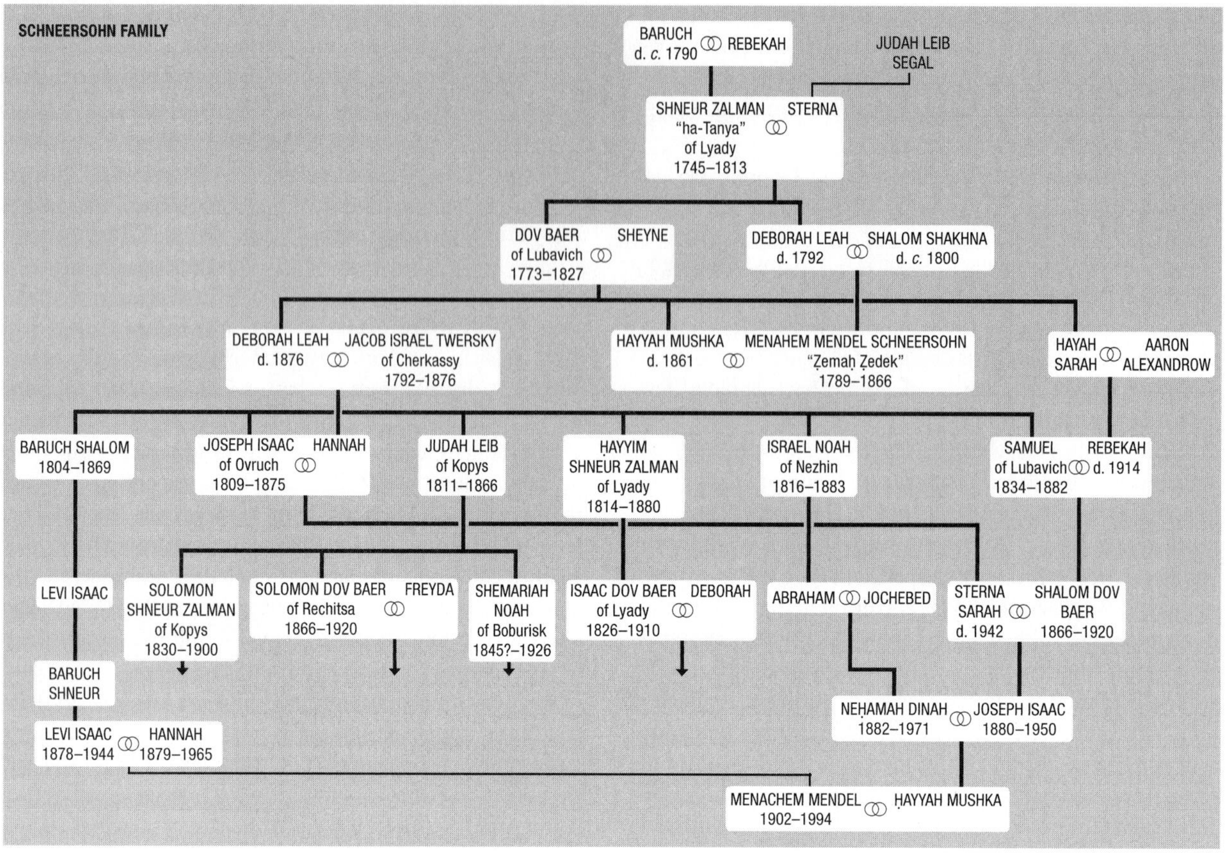

the Holocaust. By 1969, it had published 42 historical volumes, all of which are prefaced by Schneersohn. In 1952, Schneersohn launched the idea of a memorial to the unknown Jewish martyr. Despite many obstacles, this memorial was inaugurated in Paris on Oct. 30, 1956. Schneersohn's memoirs on the Russian period of his life were published in 1967 in Yiddish, under the title *Lebn un Kamf fun Yidn in Tsarishn Rusland 1905–1917, Zikhroynes*.

BIBLIOGRAPHY: *Le Monde Juif*, 25 no. 54 (1969), 1–11.

[Leon Czertok]

SCHNEERSOHN, MENACHEM MENDEL (1902–1994), ḥasidic rabbi, head of the Chabad-Lubavitch movement and a central figure in the world of Torah, Ḥasidism, and Kabbalah. Schneersohn was the seventh generation, in direct male descent of *Shneur Zalman of Lyady, the founder of the movement and the dynasty.

Schneersohn's main teacher in Jewish studies was his father, R. Levi Isaac Schneersohn, who was rabbi of Yekaterinoslav (now Dnepropetrovsk) in southern Russia, while his mother Hannah, the daughter of R. Meir Solomon Yanovsky, rabbi of Nikolaev, took care of his general education which included Russian, French, and mathematics. In 1924 he became engaged to his relative Ḥayyah Mushka, daughter of R. Joseph Isaac Schneersohn, then leader of Chabad.

Following the intervention of various governments, his future father-in-law was permitted to leave Soviet Russia in 1926, together with all the immediate members of his family, but Menachem Mendel was refused permission. As a result of strenuous efforts by his future father-in-law, however, he was enabled to come to Warsaw in 1929, where the marriage took place. It was already hinted at the wedding that R. Joseph Isaac, who had no sons, had designated Menachem Mendel as his successor, and after the marriage he began to instruct him for his future role, especially in the manuscripts of the previous Chabad leaders, only a few of which had been revealed to the followers of the movement.

Menachem Mendel also continued with his secular studies and in 1936 came to Paris, where he studied philosophy at the Sorbonne and graduated in electrical engineering, after which he returned to Warsaw. In 1940 R. Joseph Isaac succeeded in escaping from war-torn Warsaw, and after an adventurous journey arrived in New York. There he immediately took steps to rescue his son-in-law, who finally arrived in New York in 1941, where he obtained a position as an electrical engineer in the United States Navy.

In 1944 his father-in-law appointed him to head the Kehath Publishing House which began to publish the basic books of the Chabad doctrine. Menachem Mendel embellished the books with a wealth of quotations, explanations, and comments which revealed his comprehensive knowledge, particularly in the field of Kabbalah and Ḥasidism. In 1946 he was appointed head of the Merkos l'Inyonei Chinuch of the Ḥabad movement and, under his direction, there were established throughout the world yeshivot and schools, both for boys and girls, in the spirit of Chabad Ḥasidism.

Immediately after the death of his father-in-law (Jan. 28, 1950 – Shevat 10, 5710) R. Menachem Mendel was appointed his successor. From then on he devoted himself to the development of the Kabbalist philosophy of Chabad Ḥasidism and energetically applied himself to spreading Jewish knowledge throughout the world. From his small office at 770 Eastern Parkway, Brooklyn, he exercised control over hundreds of educational institutions, and to his headquarters there streamed pilgrimages of his admirers and those who sought answers to problems affecting the Jewish world, the State of Israel, or the world of religion as a whole, particularly in the sphere of religious mysticism. The "Rebbe," as he was universally known, laid down clear directives on all subjects.

R. Menachem Mendel displayed an ambivalent attitude towards the State of Israel; on the one hand he supported the doctrine of the right to the whole of the historic territory of the Land of Israel and forcefully objected to the surrender of any part of it, and on the other hand he vigorously criticized the way of life in Israel and negated the system of education prevailing there and even designated the State as part of the Diaspora (*galut*). Nor did he encourage his followers to go on *aliyah*. He waged a constant battle on the question "Who is a Jew?" forcefully insisting that only a person converted according to *halakhah* can be recognized as such. In the sphere of religious observance he demanded the wholehearted and meticulous observance of *halakhah* as well as of all customs sanctified by Jewish tradition. His followers are obliged to devote themselves to "spreading the fountains outside" by demonstrating both on the highways and public places in the large cities, as well as in small and neglected centers, in such details as the donning of phylacteries, the kindling of Sabbath lights, pronouncing the benediction over the *lulav*, the sounding of the *shofar*, the eating of *matẓah shemurah*, etc. These activities are organized as "military operations," with a fleet of vehicles which are known as "mitzvah tanks." From the Merkos l'Inyonei Chinuch there emerge streams of books, pamphlets and journals, designed for all age groups, in Hebrew, Yiddish, English, French, Russian, Arabic, German, and Turkish.

The "Rebbe" did not venture abroad and did not visit Israel. A modern, up-to-date communications center was installed at his headquarters, and from it all his talks were broadcast to over 30 communities throughout the world. R. Menachem Mendel vigorously denied the validity of scientific theories on the eternity of the world and published articles in which he denied that in fossils or even in archaeological artifacts there is any evidence to support it. He also adamantly opposed interfaith discussions or compromises in Jewish practice, but maintained that every Jew has to be attracted through love and affection towards observance of Judaism.

[Shmuel Avidor Hacohen]

Although never declaring himself to be the Messiah, the fact that the Rebbe was unequivocally of the opinion that these were messianic times led many in Lubavitch to imagine that the Rebbe himself was the Messiah. By 1990, a cult of personality swelled around the Rebbe. Sidewalk vendors sold postcards, ḥasidic tracts, and every conceivable souvenir imprinted with the Rebbe's face. Some Ḥasidim took the dollars the Rebbe was in the habit of handing out and laminated the Rebbe's face over George Washington's. The messianic excitement was strongest in Crown Heights and Kefar Ḥabad. By distinct contrast, the Rebbe's thousands of emissaries outside Crown Heights almost unanimously tried to distance themselves from the messianism and downplayed its significance.

In 1993, Schneersohn suffered a stroke that left him speechless and increasingly isolated from his Ḥasidim, with rare appearances limited to his wheelchair being perched on a balcony above the synagogue in 770 Eastern Parkway. When he was sighted, his Ḥasidim below the balcony would often erupt into messianic song, and imagined that the speechless Rebbe nodded his head in approval. There were occasional attempts by some Ḥasidim to get the Rebbe to "reveal himself." But one of the Rebbe's closest aides in his secretariat, Rabbi Yehuda Krinsky, always insisted that the Rebbe, while deeply committed to the messianic idea, never encouraged or wanted the speculation that he was the presumptive Messiah.

Schneersohn's death punctured the messianic balloon, though it is estimated that about a quarter of the hard-core believers in Crown Heights and Kefar Ḥabad continued to maintain that Schneersohn might yet be the Messiah, despite his death, a belief that became a lightning rod for criticism from the rest of the Jewish community, including fierce criticism from the Rebbe's emissaries as well.

After the Rebbe's death, the focal point for many of Schneersohn's followers became his grave in Queens, known as the "Ohel," where the Rebbe shared an open-roofed mausoleum in the Lubavitch plot in Old Montifiore Cemetery with his predecessor and father-in-law.

In an atmosphere that evokes the Western Wall, pilgrims to the grave come around the clock to recite Psalms, light candles, and bring letters requesting the Rebbe's intercession in Heaven. Chabad supporters purchased several private homes in the Cambria Heights section of Queens, just yards from Schneersohn's resting place, for a visitors center, a meditation area, study halls, and offices for support staff. Requests for the Rebbe's blessings continue to be sent every day by e-mails or faxes from around the world. On anniversaries special to Chabad, or on the eve of Jewish holidays, the visitors number well into the thousands.

[Jonathan Mark (2nd ed.)]

SCHNEIDER, ALAN (Abram Leopoldovich Schneider; 1917–1984), U.S. theatrical director. Born in Kharkov, Russia, Schneider taught drama at Catholic University, Washington, D.C. He staged Saroyan's *Jim Dandy* in 1941, and works by Shakespeare, Molière, Chekhov, and Wilder before becoming artistic director of the Arena Stage in Washington. He produced *Waiting for Godot* in 1956 and, after meeting Edward Albee in 1960, he directed all of Albee's plays, including *Who's Afraid of Virginia Woolf?* (1962), for which he won a Tony Award. He also directed plays by Harold Pinter.

Schneider was nominated for four other Tonys for Best Director: *The Ballad of a Sad Café* (1964); *Tiny Alice* (1965); *A Delicate Balance* (1967); and *You Know I Can't Hear You When the Water's Running* (1968).

Schneider wrote *Theatre Profiles* (1982) and *Entrances: An American Director's Journey*, which was published in 1986.

ADD. BIBLIOGRAPHY: H. Maurice, (ed.), *No Author Better Served: The Correspondence of Samuel Beckett and Alan Schneider* (1998).

SCHNEIDER, ALEXANDER (1908–1993), violinist. Born in Vilna, Schneider became leader of the Frankfurt Symphony Orchestra. Immigrating to the United States in 1933, he joined the Budapest Quartet as second violinist until 1944, and again from 1957, and formed several other chamber music ensembles. Together with the cellist Pablo Casals, he established the annual festivals held at Prades in the Pyrenees from 1950 onward and in Puerto Rico from 1957. He conducted at these festivals and also visited Israel for the summer music festivals.

SCHNEIDER, IRVING (1917–), U.S. real estate owner, philanthropist. Schneider graduated from the City College of New York in 1939 and spent all his professional career in real estate. For 50 years, Schneider was with Helmsley-Spear, rising to executive vice president and longtime partner of Harry Helmsley, the real estate magnate, in New York City. When Helmsley died in 1997, Schneider and Alvin Schwartz, who was married to Dorothy Spear, became co-chairman of the firm, which had its heyday in the 1960s and 1970s. But in the early years of the 21st century, the firm still managed 86 buildings, including the Empire State Building. Schneider, with Schwartz and Helmsley, owned a great deal of property in Manhattan's garment district and numerous office buildings. In May 1996 Helmsley-Spear was managing about 28 million square feet in 107 buildings in New York. After her husband's death, Leona Helmsley, who succeeded him, agreed to sell Helmsley-Spear to Schneider and Schwartz, ending a lawsuit they had brought against her, charging that she had tried to strip the company of assets, lowering its potential value to them. Helmsley-Spear's interests included stakes in the Helmsley Park Lane Hotel, the St. Moritz, the Starrett-Lehigh Building, and the Lincoln Building. Schneider and his wife were noted for their philanthropic support of two medical facilities for children, the Schneider Children's Medical Center of Israel in Petaḥ Tikvah, the most advanced pediatric hospital in the Middle East, and the Schneider Children's Hospital in New Hyde Park, N.Y. Schneider was vice chairman of the Association for a Better New York, vice president of the Realty Foundation of New York, an honorary trustee of the City College Fund, a life trustee of the UJA-Federation of New York, a member of the United Hospital Fund's President's Council and a board member of Tel Aviv University. He was a member of the board of governors of the Jewish Agency, a trustee of the Health Insurance Plan and vice chairman of National UJA. In 2004 Schneider gave $15 million to Brandeis University for its Heller School for Social Policy and Management to provide space for the Schneider Institute for Health Policy to expand its education and research agenda.

[Stewart Kampel (2nd ed.)]

SCHNEIDER, MATHIEU (1969–), U.S. hockey player, two-time NHL All-Star, U.S. Olympic team and Team U.S.A. member. Born in Manhattan and raised in New Jersey, Schneider was introduced to hockey at a young age by his father, who was an amateur hockey player and coach. A talented defender with solid offensive skills, Schneider was drafted by the Montreal Canadiens out of high school in the third round of the 1987 draft. After two seasons training in the Ontario Hockey League and being named an OHL First Team All-Star in both 1988 and 1989, Schneider was ready for service in the NHL, quickly becoming one of the Canadiens' top-scoring defensemen and a key component of their 1993 Stanley Cup team. Over the course of his 18-year career with six different teams through 2006, Schneider proved to be one of the most durable hockey players, and is only the eleventh American-born defenseman in NHL history to play in over 1,000 games. On November 26, 2005, Schneider registered a hat trick, becoming the first Detroit defenseman to accomplish the feat in 20 years. His skills on the ice have earned him a number of honors, including being named an All-Star in 1996 and 2003, a member of the U.S. Olympic team in 1998 and 2006, a member of Team U.S.A. in 1996 and 2004, and an alternate captain of the N.Y. Islanders in 1996 and the L.A. Kings in 2001–3.

[Robert B. Klein (2nd ed.)]

SCHNEIDER, MORDECAI BEZALEL (1865–1941), Hebrew grammarian. Schneider was born in Ligum close to Shavli, Lithuania, In addition to his comprehensive knowledge of Bible, Talmud, and Hebrew grammar, he also acquired a broad knowledge of classical literature and engaged in research in the Latin and Greek languages. His main occupation was in the sphere of Hebrew language. From an early age he maintained himself by teaching and from 1896 lived in Vilna, where for many decades he was a leading figure in Zionist activity and education. He began to publish from 1888 (in *Ha-Ẓefirah*) articles on educational topics, and in 1889 he published in Vilna an educational book, *Beit ha-Sefer*, which later appeared in several parts and numerous editions. As a result of this occupation he began linguistic research.

At first he published critical studies of many known grammar books in the periodicals *Ha-Shiloaḥ*, *Ha-Tekufah*, *Ha-Ẓefirah*, *Ha-Zeman*, *Tarbut*, *Haolam* and *Ha-Yom*, and then commenced to publish his magnum opus in which he summarized his life's work in research into the language – *Torat ha-Lashon ha-Ivrit be-Hitpatteḥutah ha-Historit me-*

Reshitah ad ha-Zeman ha-Aḥaron (vol. 1, pt. 1, historical section, 1923, 1928²; pt. 2, *Torat ha-Kol* (phonetics), 1924; pt. 3, *Torat ha-Tavnit* (morphology), first half 1924, second half 1925; vol. 2, *Torat Shimmush ha-Lashon* (syntax), pts. 1 and 2, 1939–40; pt. 3 was not published). He edited the periodicals *Li-She'elot ha-Yom* (1919), *Meḥkerei Lashon* 1920), and *Zeramim* (1932).

He continued working on his book in the ghetto of Vilna during World War II. He was killed in Punar.

BIBLIOGRAPHY: His autobiography, in: *Hadoar*, 21 (May 8, 1942); I. Klausner (ed.), *Sefer Yovel ha-Esrim shel ha-Gimnasyah ha-Ivrit... be-Vilna* (1936), 51–54. MEMOIRS: M. Dworzecki, *Yerushalayim de-Lita ba-Meri u-va-Sho'ah* (1951²), 29–30; S. Vardi, in: *Leshonenu*, 11 (1941–43), 305–6; Ẓ. Har-Zahav, *Dikduk ha-Lashon ha-Ivrit*, 1 (1951), 250–1.

[Getzel Kressel]

SCHNEIDERMAN, HARRY (1885–1975), U.S. editor and organization executive. Born in Saven, Poland, he was taken to the U.S. in 1890. From 1909 until his retirement in 1949 he was a member of the staff of the American Jewish Committee and functioned as its chief administrative officer from 1914 to 1928. He also undertook important editorial work, notably as editor of the *American Jewish Year Book* from 1920 to 1948.

In addition to editing numerous periodicals and reference works, he also compiled *The Jews in Nazi Germany* (1933, 1935²) and was coeditor of the *Contemporary Jewish Record* (1938–45), and chairman of the editorial board of *Who's Who in World Jewry* (1955, 1965²). Schneiderman was a founder and officer of the Jewish Book Council of America.

[Harry J. Alderman]

SCHNEIDERMAN, ROSE (1882–1972), U.S. labor union organizer and executive; sister of Harry Schneiderman. She was born in Saven, Poland, and taken to New York City in 1890. She soon went to work in a store, and later in a factory, and in 1903 she helped to organize the United Cloth, Hat, Cap and Millinery Workers Union. In 1904 she became its secretary and a member of its national executive board. She also helped organize the White Goods Workers Union and was in charge of its general strike in 1913. From 1914 to 1917 she was a general organizer of the International Ladies Garment Workers Union. Schneiderman was a delegate to the First National Working Women's Congress in Washington in 1918, to the Peace Conference in Paris in 1919, and to the International Congress in Vienna in 1923. Deeply involved in Farm Labor politics, she was that party's candidate for the U.S. Senate from New York in 1920. Schneiderman was president of the Women's Trade Union League from 1918 until her retirement in 1949, serving as labor adviser to several national labor and government agencies. She wrote (with Lucy Goldthwaite) *All for One* (1967), an account of her work in the labor movement.

SCHNIRER, MORITZ TOBIAS (1861–1941), physician and early Zionist. Born in Bucharest, from 1880 Schnirer lived in Vienna, where he qualified as a doctor in 1887. In 1882 he was among the founders of the *Kadimah society, the first nucleus of the Zionist movement in Austria. He joined *Herzl upon the latter's first appearance and assisted in preparations for the First Zionist Congress, the introduction of the *shekel, and the founding of the *Jewish National Fund. He was also the moving spirit behind the drawing up of the first constitution of the Zionist movement. Schnirer accompanied Herzl on his trip to Ereẓ Israel to meet Kaiser William II (1898) and was a member of the Zionist Executive until the Fourth Zionist Congress. The lecture he delivered at the First Congress formulated what was to remain the basic policy of political Zionism on settlement in Ereẓ Israel for many years, i.e., that settlement activities should not be continued until the Zionist movement received a charter for that purpose. Disagreement with Herzl and the demands of his medical practice prevented Schnirer from continuing to play an active role in the movement, although he remained in close contact with the Zionist Organization. He had a very large practice, and his medical textbooks (among others *Encyklopaedie der praktischen Medizin* (1906–09) and *Taschenbuch der Therapie...* (1925) ran into many editions. He also served as the editor of professional journals in German and French for several decades. He committed suicide together with his wife during World War II. Schnirer's reminiscences of his Kadimah days were published by N. Sokolow in Ḥibbat Ẓion (1935).

BIBLIOGRAPHY: L. Jaffe, *Sefer ha-Congress* (1950²), 359–60; N. Sokolow, *Ḥibbath Zion* (Eng., 1935), index; T. Herzl, *Complete Diaries*, ed., by R. Patai, 5 (1960), index.

[Getzel Kressel]

SCHNITTKE, ALFRED (1934–1998), composer. The son of a German Jewish father and a German mother, Schnittke was born in Soviet Russia. His first music studies between 1946 and 1948 were connected primarily with Vienna, where his father was working after World War II. He then absorbed the Austrian-German culture that marked him for the rest of his life. However, he was also educated in Russia. He studied in 1949–53 at the Choirmaster Department of the October Revolution Musical College, Moscow, now the Schnittke Institute; and in 1953–58 he studied composition at the Moscow Conservatory. After having taught instrumentation at the Moscow Conservatory (1962–72), he became a freelance composer and between 1962 and 1984 wrote 66 film scores as well as concert and theater works. His early compositions, like the oratorio *Nagasaki* (1958), were influenced by the Russian tradition of 19th century music. In the 1960s Schnittke himself studied the Western music of the 20th century that was formerly forbidden in the U.S.S.R. but at that time already tolerated. A great sensation of the 1970s was the 1974 premiere of his First Symphony, a polystylistic work following the traditions of Mahler and Berio in a highly individual way. The symphony was banned immediately after the first performance and remained so until Gorbachev came to power (1985). Being always uncommitted to the official Soviet ideology, Schnittke expressed his Christian religious beliefs in many of his works, including the Second Symphony (1979), which followed the Ordinary of the Roman Catholic Mass. In his Fourth Symphony (1983), Schnittke strove, in his own words, "to find the general in the dissimilar," while using melodic elements from Russian Orthodox, Gregorian, Protestant Lutheran, and synagogue chant and combining them in the final section of the work. From 1990 he lived in Hamburg (Germany), where he taught composition at the Hochschule fuer Musik und Theater. He was the recipient of several honors, including the Russian State Prize (twice, 1986 and 1995) and awards from Austria, Germany, and Japan.

BIBLIOGRAPHY: NG^2; A. Ivashkin, *Alfred Schnittke* (1996); A. Ivashkin (ed.), *Schnittke Reader* (1999).

[Yulia Kreinin (2nd ed.)]

SCHNITZER, ADOLF (1889–1989), Swiss jurist. Born and educated in Berlin, Schnitzer left Germany in 1933. After World War II he was a professor of German law at Geneva University and a consultant on international law. He was an authority on private international law and published numerous books and articles including *Handbuch des Internationalen Privatrechts* (1958^4).

SCHNITZER, SHMUEL (1918–1999), Israeli journalist. Born in The Hague, Schnitzer immigrated to Palestine in 1939. He entered journalism first at *Yedioth Aharonoth,* but left it for *Maariv* in 1948 in the so-called "putsch" led by Dr. Azriel *Carlebach. With their sharp analysis, his polemics attracted a loyal readership. He was appointed editor of *Maariv* in 1980, but his term was marked by a sharp, continuing drop in *Maariv*'s circulation, and in 1985 he was replaced as editor by Iddo Dissentchik but continued to write his column until the day he died. In 1997 the Israel Prize committee canceled its decision to award Schnitzer the prize for journalism after the Press Council ruled that a column Schnitzer had written in 1994 about Ethiopian Jews, which accused the Israeli government of permitting the *aliyah* of "thousands of apostates carrying dangerous diseases," was racist.

[Yoel Cohen (2nd ed.)]

SCHNITZLER, ARTHUR (1862–1931), Austrian playwright and author. Schnitzler's father, Professor Johann Schnitzler (1835–1593), was an eminent Viennese throat specialist. Since his patients included dramatic and operatic stars, young Schnitzler was in constant contact with theatrical life and began writing plays while still a youth. After qualifying as a physician at the University of Vienna, he edited the medical journal *Internationale klinische Rundschau* (1887–94). His own professional articles dealt mainly with psychotherapy, and his friend Sigmund *Freud later paid tribute to his poetic intuition.

In 1893 Schnitzler published a collection of seven short plays titled *Anatol* after the central character, an elegant philanderer. The book had a prologue in verse by Hugo von *Hofmannsthal. His first full-length play, *Das Maerchen* (1894), was a failure, but *Liebelei*, produced in 1895 at the Viennese Burgtheater, proved so successful that Schnitzler decided to devote himself almost entirely to writing. *Reigen* (1900), a series of interconnected dialogues satirizing conventional love affairs, gave rise to a lawsuit in Berlin. (Years later Max Ophuels produced *Liebelei* as a comedy and, after World War II, turned *Reigen* into the internationally successful film, *La Ronde*.)

As Schnitzler grew older, the inconstant bachelor and the single girl ceased to occupy the center of his attention, and he became increasingly interested in relations between husband and wife. In many of his works, especially in the full-length plays *Der einsame Weg* (1904), *Zwischenspiel* (1906), *Der Ruf des Lebens* (1906), and *Das weite Land* (1911), he explored with growing sensitivity the problems of married life. In groping for a satisfactory substitute for the traditional marital relationship and for a morality better adapted to 20th-century psychology, he pursued various, amoral bypaths, but ultimately came to reject all moral systems, old and new alike. In the years before World War I his plays were among those most often performed on the German and Austrian stage. He was also writing some of the novellas which were always a favorite genre and included *Lieutenant Gustl* (1901), *Casanovas Heimfahrt* (1918), and *Fraeulein Else* (1924).

In 1912 Schnitzler dramatized a problem of medical ethics in *Professor Bernhardi*. In this play a physician, who regards it as his duty to relieve the final hours of a dying man, prevents a Catholic priest from administering the last rites, fearing that this might subject his patient to unnecessary suffering. Since the physician is a Jew, he becomes a target for antisemitic attacks. Here, as in the novel *Der Weg ins Freie* (1908), Schnitzler expressed his views on the place of the Jew in modern life. He held that antisemitism was the natural outcome of the Jews' historical position as a minority group in every land, and that no amount of Jewish or Christian sentimentality would eradicate anti-Jewish prejudice. He had a positive outlook on the issue of Jewish survival and derided those Jews who hid their origin. He prophesied that, as the liberals and Pan-Germans had betrayed them, so would the politicians of the left. Schnitzler accepted neither Zionism nor assimilation as a solution, believing that each individual had to make his own adjustment. For himself, he preferred to continue the struggle against his enemies in Vienna, where he felt himself at home.

BIBLIOGRAPHY: R.H. Allen, *An Annotated Arthur Schnitzler Bibliography* (1966); J. Koerner, *Arthur Schnitzlers Gestalten und Probleme* (1921); R. Specht, *Arthur Schnitzler* (Ger., 1922); W. Mann, in: G. Krojanker (ed.), *Juden in der deutschen Literatur* (1926), 207–18; S. Liptzin, *Arthur Schnitzler* (Eng., 1932); H. Kohn, *Karl Kraus, Arthur Schnitzler, Otto Weininger; aus dem juedischen Wien der Jahrhundertwende* (1962), 13–29; O. Schnitzler, *Spiegelbild der Freundschaft* (1962); H.W. Reichert and H. Salinger (eds.), *Studies in Arthur Schnitzler: Centennial Commemorative Volume* (1963); H. Zohn, *Wiener Juden in der deutschen Literatur* (1964), 9–18; G. Baumann, *Arthur Schnitzler* (Ger., 1965); W.H. Rey, *Arthur Schnitzler; die spaete Prosa als Gipfel seines Schaffens* (1968); H. Kohn, in: YLBI, 6 (1961), 152–69.

[Sol Liptzin]

SCHOCKEN, family active in book publishing, Jewish culture, and newspaper publishing in Israel. The family dynasty was headed by Salman *Schocken (1877–1959), Zionist, art and book collector, and publisher. Born at Margonin, province of Posen (now in Poland), in 1901 Schocken, together with his brother Simon, founded the I. Schocken Soehne at Zwickau, which developed into a prosperous chain of 19 department stores. Passionately interested in Judaism, he used his fortune to collect rare books and manuscripts, and Jewish works of art. In 1929 he founded the Research Institute for Medieval Hebrew Poetry in Berlin, which edited hitherto unknown medieval Hebrew manuscripts that Schocken had acquired.

The Schocken Press

In 1931 Schocken Verlag was established, becoming an important avenue for the publication of Jewish literature in Germany, with the express aim of educating an assimilating community about its Jewish heritage. One of its first authors was S.Y. *Agnon, who was patronized by Salman Schocken from the first stages of his literary career. In 1934 Schocken himself moved from Berlin to Jerusalem, transferring both the Institute for Medieval Jewish Poetry and his library and art collections there. In addition to the works of S.Y. Agnon and Franz *Kafka, to which Schocken possessed the world rights, the press published more than 200 books in Germany, including the works of Martin *Buber, Franz *Rosenzweig, Baruch *Kurtzweill, Leo *Baeck, Hermann *Cohen, and Gershom *Scholem. Schocken was active in Zionist affairs first in Germany and later in Palestine, in the Jewish National Fund, and on The Hebrew University's Executive Council. In 1940 he moved to the United States, and years later moved to Switzerland, where he died. After his death, the Institute for Hebrew Poetry and his library and collections in Jerusalem became the *Schocken Institute for Jewish Research of the *Jewish Theological Seminary of America.

Following its closure by the Nazis in 1938, the Schocken Press was re-established in Tel Aviv. After Salman Schocken's departure for the United States with most of his children, the Schocken Press in Tel Aviv was managed by his son GERSHON "GUSTAV" (1912–1990) until 1970. Gershon, who had studied economics at Heidelberg University and the London School of Economics, continued the press's orientation toward high-quality Jewish and Hebrew literature, including the works of Nathan *Alterman, Saul *Tchernichowsky, and Uri Zevi *Greenberg. In 1962 Dan *Miron, a professor of literature (who was married to Yael, the daughter of Gershon's brother Gideon Schocken, himself an IDF army general), was appointed editor of the Schocken Press, and brought Yehuda *Amichai's works to the publishing house. But Gershon's involvement in the Schocken Press took second place to his main work as editor in chief of the **Haaretz* newspaper, and his seat in the Knesset in 1955–59 for the Progressive Party. In 1972 Gershon's daughter, RAHELI EDELMAN (1942–), a graduate in literature and economics, took over the press. The middle-sized publishing house became eclectic and financially sounder. Edelman branched out to include translations of foreign literature, selective non-fiction (including Shabbetai Teveth's biography of David Ben- Gurion), educational texts, and children's books. Contemporary Israeli literature was shunted aside. She was chairperson of the Book Publishers' Association of Israel in 1983–94.

In 1945, five years after his arrival in New York, Salman Schocken opened the Schocken Press in New York. It became a focus for German Jewish émigrés like Hannah *Arendt and Nahum *Glazer, who became the press's editor in chief. After Salman Schocken's death, his son THEODORE and son-in-law Herzl Rome took over the press with varying degrees of financial success. Among its Jewish authors were Nahum *Sarna, Cecil *Roth, Simon *Wiesenthal, Harold *Kushner, Lucy *Dawidowicz, and Aharon *Appelfeld. The press, which became structurally independent of the Tel Aviv-based Schocken Press, expanded from its focus on Jewish books into such fields as educational publishing, women's studies, history, literary criticism, and the Montessori books as well as cook books, particularly as mainstream U.S. publishers began to discover the Jewish book market. In 1987 the press was bought by Random House, but it remained as a separate imprint, structurally tied to Pantheon Books.

Haaretz

Gershon Schocken was most remembered as the publisher and editor for 51 years of the *Haaretz* newspaper which grew to become an independent quality daily. The financially ailing newspaper had been purchased by his father in 1935. Gershon continued the intellectual tradition which had characterized the paper under Moshe Gluecksohn's editorship. He succeeded in stabilizing the paper financially, ending Gluecksohn's practice of accepting financial support from Zionist institutions.

Notwithstanding the need for socio-economic justice in the young state, *Haaretz* under Schocken's editorship favored free enterprise, criticizing the excesses of collective socialism which characterized the first 30 years of statehood. After the 1967 war, concerned at the demographic threat which the annexation of the West Bank and Gaza posed to the Jewish character of the state, *Haaretz* advocated giving up most of the territories. In supporting the creation of the Jewish state, Gershon Schocken had sought to imbue it with the humanistic values that had influenced him in his youth in Germany. In the 1950s *Haaretz* questioned unlimited Jewish *aliyah* from North Africa, favoring a more selective policy. While cherishing Jewish culture, he opposed theocratic excesses, favoring a separation of state and religion, and Jewish pluralism.

Influenced by the European tradition of quality journalism, Gershon Schocken assiduously adhered to the separation of fact and comment, with the newspaper comprising two independent sections, news and opinion. However, this distinction was blurred somewhat later in the 1980s and 1990s, as *Haaretz*, like other newspapers, sought to carve out a place for itself in an age when television and radio had become the chief providers of breaking news, leaving the newspaper to concentrate on analysis and background. While the newspaper's editorial board reflected a spectrum of liberal and left-wing secular views, Schocken would use his veto as editor-in-chief to determine the line when there were differences of opinion. Socially reclusive, he also distanced himself from political leaders, with the noted exception of Chaim *Weizmann. In the 1940 and 1950s his relations with Ben-Gurion were tense. *Haaretz*, regarded by many as a maverick publication, championed the rule of law and human rights and the exposure of official corruption. Yet the paper was a member of the Editor's Committee – in effect a mechanism enabling Israeli officialdom to win the cooperation of the media on sensitive defense and diplomatic matters – and at times Schocken even served as its chairman. In 1991 Ariel *Sharon unsuccessfully sued the paper and its reporter Uzi Benziman after it accused him of deceiving Prime Minister Menachem *Begin during the 1982 Lebanon war when he was defense minister.

The arts and literature had a respected place in the newspaper, with a weekly Friday literature supplement from 1963, as well as another, more popular mid-week version introduced in 1995. Schocken himself wrote some poetic works under the pseudonym of Robert Pozen. He had attempted unsuccessfully between 1938 and 1942 and in 1948–49 to found evening newspapers – *Ha-Sha'ah* and *Yom-Yom*. *Haaretz* branched out to the local newspaper market with the creation of local newspapers in Jerusalem (*Kol ha-Ir*) and Tel Aviv (*Ha-Ir*) in 1979 and 1980, respectively, successfully tapping local advertising potential. Untypical of local journalism, which was inclined towards sensationalism, editorial content in the Schocken chain of 14 local newspapers was quality upmarket.

From the late 1980s, the newspaper's heavy style was spruced up with the arrival, as deputy editor (and after Gershon Schocken's death, editor), of Hanoch *Marmori, a graphic artist who introduced modern design and oversaw the expansion of the newspaper's size.

Gershon's son, AMOS SCHOCKEN (1944–), a graduate in economics from The Hebrew University and business management from Harvard University, had been appointed by his father as the *Haaretz* chain's managing director. He began a daily newspaper, *Ḥadashot*, in 1983, in an attempt to compete with the two major dailies, *Yedioth Aharonoth* and *Maariv*. Featuring many photos and headlines, the newspaper was decidedly anti-establishment. In 1984 the paper was closed briefly by the military censor, after it broke censorship regulations and printed a photo of an apprehended terrorist in the so-called No. 300 bus affair, who was later killed. *Hadashot* failed to carve out an audience for itself and, facing heavy losses, folded in 1992. With Gershon's death, Amos became *Haaretz* publisher. At the turn of the century, *Haaretz*'s editorial board was split over the Palestinian intifada, with Amos Schocken taking a decidedly left-wing position that justified the refusal of Israeli soldiers to serve in the territories for reasons of conscience. By contrast, Marmori as editor took a centrist position. With the demise of the party political press, *Haaretz* had become the country's only quality daily newspaper, with an important role in influencing the national agenda.

In 1997 Schocken established an English-language edition of *Haaretz*, including a translation of the Hebrew edition, and the local printing of the *International Herald Tribune*. He also began English-language and Hebrew-language internet newspaper websites drawing on *Haaretz*'s newsgathering resources. Both developments strengthened *Haaretz*'s standing, abroad and at home, beyond its narrow, elitist Hebrew audience. But he failed in his bid in the 1990s to branch out into the electronic media.

BIBLIOGRAPHY: H. Amior, "*Haaretz* Production: The Ideological Dispute Between the Owner and the Editor," in: *Ayin Shevi'it*, 47 (Nov. 2003) (Heb.); I. Elazar, "It's All About Money: *Haaretz* Changes Face," in: *Ayin Shevi'it*, 55 (March 2005) (Heb.); Katherine McNamara, "A Conversation About Schocken Books with Altie Karper," in: *Archipelago*, 5; H. Negid, "The Schocken Tribe," in: *Maariv* (March 29, 1991) (Heb.); A. Rubenstein, "A Man of the Twentieth Century," in: *Haaretz* (Jan. 18, 1991) (Heb.).

[Yoel Cohen (2nd ed.)]

SCHOCKEN, SALMAN (1877–1959), Zionist, art and book collector, and publisher. Born at Margonin, province of Posen (now in Poland), in 1901 Schocken, together with his brother Simon, founded the concern of I. Schocken Soehne at Zwickau, which developed into a prosperous chain of 19 department stores. Passionately interested in Judaism, as well as in all aspects of the mind, he used his fortune to collect rare books and manuscripts and became a Maecenas of general and Hebrew literature. He was patron and publisher of S.Y. *Agnon from the first stages of his literary activity. In 1929 he founded the Research Institute for Medieval Hebrew Poetry (under the direction of Ḥayyim *Brody) in Berlin, transferred to Jerusalem in 1934; it was concerned with editing hitherto unknown medieval Hebrew manuscripts which Schocken had acquired. In the early years of the Nazi rule Schocken Verlag, Berlin (1931–38), as a Jewish concern, was entitled to publish Jewish authors. Later Schocken established publishing houses in Tel Aviv (Hebrew) and New York (English). In 1934 Schocken moved from Berlin to Jerusalem and transferred his library and collections there, but went on to the United States in 1940.

From 1912 to 1945 he was very active in Zionist affairs. He was a director of the Jewish National Fund and a member of other public bodies. From 1934 to 1945 he was chairman of the Executive Council (administration) of The Hebrew University. After his death, the Institute for Hebrew Poetry and his library and collection in Jerusalem became the *Schocken Institute for Jewish Research of the *Jewish Theological Seminary of America. In 1952 a *Festschrift*, *Alei Ayin*, was published in his honor, containing contributions on biblical and post-biblical Hebrew literature and belles lettres by a circle of his friends, including Martin Buber, Gershom Scholem, and S.Y. Agnon.

His son, GERSHON (1912–1990; see previous entry), was the owner and chief editor of the leading morning daily *Haaretz* (from 1939). He was director of the family publishing house in Israel and was a Knesset member representing the Liberal party (1955–59).

BIBLIOGRAPHY: S. Moses, in: YLBI, 5 (1960), 73–104; G. Schocken, in: *Haaretz* (Oct. 18, 1967).

SCHOCKEN INSTITUTE, scholarly institute in Jerusalem which houses the Schocken Library and the Research Institute for Medieval Hebrew Poetry. The Schocken Library was started in Germany at the beginning of the 20th century by Salman *Schocken and grew into one of the largest and most important collections of early Hebraica in the world. In 1934 the library was moved to Jerusalem, to a building especially constructed for its purposes by Eric *Mendelsohn. The collection includes 60,000 volumes, among them several thousand first and early editions and incunabula (books printed before 1501; the incunabula are held at the Jewish National and University Library).

Starting in the early 1930s, the Research Institute for Hebrew Poetry collected photographs of poetic **Genizah* fragments from the major libraries of the world. Under the direction of Ḥ. *Brody, with A.M. *Habermann, J. *Schirmann and M. *Zulay, the Institute issued publications in the field of medieval Hebrew poetry, and seven volumes of studies (*Yedi'ot ha-Makhon le-Ḥeker ha-Shirah ha-Ivrit*, 1–7 (1933–58)). Of special note are M. Zulay's edition of the *piyyutim* of *Yannai (1938); Ḥ. Brody's edition of Moses *Ibn Ezra's *Diwan* (2 vols., 1935–42); A.M. Habermann's edition of the *piyyutim* of *Simeon b. Isaac (1938); and J. Schirmann's anthology of Italian Hebrew poetry, *Mivḥar ha-Shirah ha-Ivrit be-Italyah* (1934).

In 1961 the Schocken Institute became associated with the *Jewish Theological Seminary of America. In 1964 E.S. Rosenthal became research director of the Institute, and its activities were gradually enlarged. An institute for Talmud was added, which prepares critical editions of talmudic texts and their commentaries. The Institute published a yearbook, *Perakim*. Renewing its activities in the field of medieval poetry under the directorship of J. Schirmann, the Institute published M. Zulay's *Ha-Askolah ha-Payytanit shel Rav Sa'adyah Ga'on* (1964); Sh. Abramson's *Bi-Leshon Kodemim* (1965); and J. Schirmann's *Shemu'el Romanelli* (1969).

Later activities included the acquisition of the Rabbi Moses Nahum Yerushalimsky Collection, consisting of more than 25,000 archival items, including more than 6,000 letters and 4,000 postcards. The archive contains a wealth of raw material on public issues, Jewish education, Jewish law and customs, and numerous communal problems of Russian and Polish Jewry in the late 19th century. The library of Saul Liebermann, one of the leading Jewish scholars of our generation, was brought to Israel in the 1989. It consists of over 10,000 volumes of unique rabbinic and research reference material, including many first editions. Liebermann's notes and glosses are to be found among many of the book leaves.

BIBLIOGRAPHY: Ḥ. Brody, in: YMḤSI, 1 (1933), ix–xvi; 3 (1936), vii–xii.

[H. Jacob Katzenstein]

SCHOEFFER, NICOLAS (1912–1992), sculptor and painter. Schoeffer was born in Kalosca, Hungary, and after studying at the Academy of Fine Arts, Budapest, he continued at the Ecole des Beaux-Arts, Paris. From 1935 he lived permanently in Paris. He was one of the leading contemporary exponents of kinetic art. While his origins lie in sculpture, his earliest important influence was the abstract painting of Mondrian. Based on the theory of Cubism, Mondrian's work narrowed artistic expression and experience to the interplay of squares and right angles and the intensity of a few primary colors. Schoeffer concentrated entirely on the right angle, from which he developed a theory of "Spatiodynamism." In a lecture at the Sorbonne in 1954, he defined this theory as "the constructive and dynamic integration of space in a plastic work." In practice, the art objects based on this theory are metal constructions whose composition creates or suggests illusory movement. In due course Schoeffer incorporated transparent materials in his work, so that the interplay with solid metals, which in turn dissected space rather than encasing or occupying it, resulted in a greater lightness and diversity of rhythms. One of his most successful essays is the 52-meter-tall "luminodynamic" tower in Bouverie Park, Liège, which incorporates rectangular and highly polished rotating elements to reflect light as well as sound. This tower relates to further theories of "Luminodynamism" and "Chronodynamism"; the first involves polished reflective surfaces and the second synchronized sound effects. Schoeffer made a number of public tower-sculptures to illustrate these theories. Audiovisual experiments occupied him in later years, in particular the "Musiscope," whereby he "played" a keyboard which both makes sounds and projects color formations on a screen. He also produced a series of brilliant mobile sculptures, usually in transparent plastics, which rotate electrically and reflect light.

[Charles Samuel Spencer]

SCHOENBERG, ALEXANDER JULIUS WILHELM (1892–1985), German organic chemist. From 1927 to 1934 he was professor of organic chemistry at the Berlin-Charlottenburg Polytechnicum. Forced to leave Germany, he spent three years in the department of Medical Chemistry of the University of Edinburgh, Scotland, and then was professor of chemistry at the University of Cairo until 1957 and director of its chemical institute. Returning to Berlin, he was made professor emeritus at the Polytechnicum in 1958.

SCHOENBERG, ARNOLD (1874–1951), composer, teacher, and theorist; discoverer of the "method of composition with twelve tones related to one another" as he himself described it. Born to an Orthodox family in Vienna, Schoenberg became converted to Christianity in 1898 under the influence of Gustav *Mahler. He returned to Judaism, however, on July 24, 1933, at a formal religious ceremony in Paris, at which one of the witnesses was Marc *Chagall. Schoenberg was extremely active on behalf of German refugees during the Nazi period. He was a devoted Zionist and in 1951 accepted an invitation to head the Rubin Academy for Music established in Jerusalem, but his state of health prevented him from taking up the appointment.

In music he was self-taught, except for several months of instruction from his friend, the composer Alexander Zemlinsky (1872–1942), who eventually became his brother-in-law. The deepest creative influences in his early years were Brahms and Wagner, as can be seen in his early string quartet in D major (1897), his string sextet *Verklaerte Nacht* (1899), and his gigantic cantata *Gurrelieder* (1900–11).

Schoenberg became increasingly free in his treatment of dissonance until his work transcended tonality. His piano piece Opus 11, no. 1 (1909) is the first composition to dispense completely with "tonal" means of organization. There followed a series of compositions in which extreme emotionality was counterbalanced by extreme brevity. Sometimes, as in *Erwartung* (1909) and *Pierrot Lunaire* (1912), a text helps to provide that unity which "classical" tonal means could no longer furnish. Schoenberg was continually seeking new means of tonal organization. After much experimentation he told Josef Ruler in July 1921: "Today I have discovered something which will assure the supremacy of German music for the next hundred years." It was the method of composition with twelve tones ("dodecaphony"). In this method, a basic row containing the twelve notes of the chromatic scale, in an order predetermined by the composer, serves as the foundation for an entire composition. Schoenberg found this method invaluable for securing unity. He used it for the rest of his life, with occasional returns to tonality, as in the suite for strings in G major (1934).

It was many years before Schoenberg won full acceptance as a composer, but in 1925 he was appointed director of a master school for musical composition at the Prussian Academy of Arts in Berlin. This position was taken from him on "racial" grounds in September 1933, and he responded with a formal return to the Jewish faith, which he had abandoned in his youth. A month later he emigrated to America. After a year in Boston and New York, he taught for many years, first at the University of Southern California, then at the University of California in Los Angeles. In America Schoenberg completed some of his best works. These include his fourth string quartet (1936); *Kol Nidre* (1939); piano concerto (1942); and *A Survivor from Warsaw* (1947). During this period he also wrote four of his theoretical books: *Models for Beginners in Composition* (1943), *Structural Functions of Harmony* (1954), *Preliminary Exercises in Counterpoint* (1963), and *Fundamentals of Musical Composition* (1967). His *Style and Idea* appeared in 1950 and his *Letters*, edited by E. Stein, in 1964. His Jewish loyalties, the Holocaust, and the establishment of the State of Israel are strongly reflected in his musical works, in works such as *Der Biblische Weg*, and the cantatas *Dreimal Tausend Jahre* and *Israel Lives Again*. The texts of these works were written by Schoenberg himself, with the exception of that of *Dreimal Tausend Jahre*, which was written by Rabbi Dagobert Runes. Three of his great works with religious themes, the cantata *Die Jakobsleiter*, the opera *Moses and Aaron*, and the cycle of *Modern Psalms*, were unfinished at his death on July 13, 1951. *Moses and Aaron*, however, has been highly successful in its two-act form, and this dramatic confrontation of priest and prophet may well stand as Schoenberg's strongest work.

Schoenberg's influence on the music of the 20th century was immense. After World War II his technique of composition was studied intensively both in Europe and United States, after the ban on it during Nazi rule. At the same time, some of the postwar avant-garde composers who considered Schoenberg not consistent enough when using his own technique preferred to lean on the work of his famous pupil Webern, who was more strict in following the rules of dodecaphony. However, despite all the debates about Schoenberg's method, he is now considered a brilliant innovative mind and one of the classics of 20th century music.

BIBLIOGRAPHY: R. Leibowitz, *Schoenberg and His School* (1949); D. Newlin, *Bruckner – Mahler – Schoenberg* (Eng., 1947), 209–77; R. Leibowitz, *Schoenberg and His School* (1949); H.H. Stuckenschmidt, *Arnold Schoenberg* (Ger., 1951, Eng., 1959); J. Rufer, *The Works of Arnold Schoenberg* (1962); K.H. Woerner, *Schoenberg's Moses and Aaron* (1963); W. Reich, *Schoenberg; A Critical Biography* (1971); MGG; Riemann-Gurlitt; Grove Dict.: Baker, Biog Dict. **ADD. BIBLIOGRAPHY:** NG²; C. Rosen, *Arnold Schoenberg* (1975); E. Hilmar (ed.), *Arnold Schoenberg: Gedenkausstellung 1974* (1974); C. Dahlhaus, *Schoenberg and the New Music* (1987); A.L. Ringer, *Arnold Schoenberg: The Composer as Jew* (1990); J. Brand and C. Hailey (eds.), *Constructive Dissonance: Arnold Schoenberg and the Transformations of 20th-Century Culture* (1997); A.L. Ringer, *Arnold Schoenberg: Das Leben im Werk* (2002).

[Yulia Kreinin (2nd ed.)]

SCHOENE, LOTTE (née **Charlotte Bodenstein**, 1891–1977), soprano singer. Schoene was born in Vienna, where she studied, making her debut at the Volksoper there in 1912. In 1917 she was engaged at the Vienna Imperial Opera, and sang there until 1925, after which year she moved to Berlin. She also sang regularly at the Salzburg Festival from 1922 to 1934, her pure lyric soprano in Mozart roles winning great admiration. She settled in Paris in 1933, and made appearances at the Opéra and Opéra-Comique, but on the outbreak of World War II she went into hiding in the French Alps. In 1945, Schoene resumed her career as a concert singer, but retired in 1953 to teach singing in Paris.

[Max Loppert (2nd ed.)]

°**SCHOENERER, GEORG VON** (1842–1921), Austrian antisemitic politician. Schoenerer, the son of a railway entrepreneur and nobleman, was elected to parliament (Reichsrat) in 1873 after making a name for himself as an energetic estate owner who improved the economic and social lot of the peasants. There he joined the left-wing, radical-democrat nationalists and repeatedly shocked the house with his outspoken anticlericalism, anti-Hapsburg views, and demagoguery. In 1878 he began to air opinions about the allegedly harmful Jewish plutocracy and its domination of the press, but his opposition to the admission of Jewish refugees from Russian pogroms in 1882 was unsuccessful. He was supported by Heinrich *Friedjung and Victor *Adler, who helped him draft the popular 11-point Linz program (which combined Prussian-oriented nationalism, social reform, and semi-socialistic measures). Schoenerer added a twelfth point in 1885: "In order to realize these reforms, the removal of Jewish influence from all fields of public life is indispensable." Despite his continuing popularity, Schoenerer was never able to forge a stable party organization and was constantly causing rifts in his ranks. On March 8, 1888, after a drinking bout, he led an assault on the offices of the *Neues Wiener Tageblatt*, which he considered Jewish-owned, for prematurely announcing the decease of Emperor William I of Germany. Despite the support of K. *Lueger and others, he was stripped of his title, deprived of his seat for five years, and imprisoned. He returned to parliament in 1897 with five supporters, and in 1901 his party obtained 21 seats. However, his party soon distintegrated and Austrian antisemites came to prefer Lueger's clerical and pro-Hapsburg *Christian Social Party.

Schoenerer's ambitions were thwarted by his own intransigence, self-glorification, and despotic manner, which left him isolated politically. His long-term significance for the rise of Nazism was decisive. He turned to racism, acclaiming Karl Eugen *Duehring and other racists, and helped spread the "*Voelkische Weltanschauung*." Successful in enlisting the support of various and often conflicting social strata, he gained main adherents from the small-town lower-middle class and was extremely popular with the Burschenschaften (see *Students' Associations, German), who formed his bodyguard, uniting these elements with his vulgar slogan: What the Jew believes is irrelevant, the piggish mess lies in the race. ("*Was der Jude glaubt, ist einerlei, In der Rasse liegt die Schweinerei*").

He was much admired by the Nazis, who, immediately after the *Anschluss*, named a street in the Jewish section of Vienna for him; they also promoted Eduard Pichl's study on him and, in 1942, held a memorial exhibition in Vienna. Schoenerer has importance for historians because he was the first to exploit antisemitism in changing the direction of foreign policy and disrupting the internal structure of the state, techniques later closely copied by Nazism.

BIBLIOGRAPHY: F. Bilger, in: *Neue Oesterreischische Biographie*, (1938), 76–87 (incl. bibl.); O. Karbach, in: JSOS, 7 (1945), 3–30; D. van Arkel, "Anti-semitism in Austria" (unpublished Ph.D. thesis, Leiden University, 1966); C.E. Schorske, in: *The Journals of Modern History*, 39 (1967), 343ff. **ADD. BIBLIOGRAPHY:** A.G. Whiteside, *The Socialism of Fools. Georg Ritter von Schoenerer…* (1975), index; P. Pulzer, *The Rise of Political Anti-Semitism in Germany and Austria* (1988), index; M. Wladika, *Hitlers Vaetergeneration…* (2005).

[Henry Wasserman / Evelyn Adunka (2nd ed.)]

SCHOENFELD, JOSEPH (1884–1935), Hungarian Zionist and editor of Hungarian/Zionist periodicals. He was among the founders of Maccabea, the Zionist students' society in Budapest, which was founded on Herzl's initiative in 1903 and prepared Hungarian-speaking Zionist leaders for Hungary, Slovakia, Transylvania, and North Yugoslavia. From 1912 to 1914, and then from 1927 to 1935, he was the editor of the organ of the Hungarian Zionist Federation *Zsidó Szemle* ("Jewish Review"). His articles defended the Zionist movement against opposition, especially by the Jewish weekly *Egyenlöség* ("Equality"), which enjoyed the support of the Budapest Neolog community and advanced an assimilationist line.

Schoenfeld fought for the reunification of Hungarian Jewry, which had split into opposing groups – Orthodox and Neolog – in 1871. He was a gifted orator, employing humor and sarcasm in his speeches. He translated Herzl's *Der Judenstaat* into Hungarian in 1919, and published *Vissza a Gettóba* ("Return to the Ghetto," 1919) and *Harcban a Zsidóságért* ("In the Battle for Israel," 1928), both of which contain a selection of his articles on Jewish problems and Zionism in Hungary and in general.

BIBLIOGRAPHY: H.Z. Zehavi, *Me-ha-Ḥatam Sofer ve-ad Herzl* (1965), 325–6.

[Jekutiel-Zwi Zehawi]

SCHOENHACK, JOSEPH (1812–1870), Hebrew writer and lexicographer. Born in Tiktin, Poland, he wrote one of the first works on natural science in Hebrew – *Toledot ha-Areẓ*, in three volumes (*Toledot ha-Ḥayyim* (1841, with commendatory prefaces by rabbis and *maskilim*), *Toledot ha-Ẓemaḥim*, and *Toledot ha-Muẓakim* (both 1859), treating, respectively, zoology, botany, and mineralogy. The books were schematically presented – the names of the animals, plants, and minerals appeared in Hebrew with a German translation (in Hebrew letters); the text was augmented by many footnotes that examined the names of species mentioned in the Bible and in talmudic literature. He used a German name only when no Hebrew name was available. With the help of Schoenhack, Mendele Mokher Seforim determined the names of animals in his book *Toledot ha-Teva*.

Schoenhack also compiled a dictionary, *Ha-Mashbir he-Ḥadash*, for the language of the Targum, the Talmud, and the Midrash (1859) based on the *Arukh* by *Nathan of Rome, but he noted the origin of each word and translated it into German (in Hebrew letters). In 1869 he added to *Ha-Mashbir* a book called *Sefer ha-Millu'im*, in which he added words not printed in the *Arukh*.

BIBLIOGRAPHY: Klausner, Sifrut, 4 (1954), 133; *Ha-Maggid*, 49 (1870), 388.

[Yehuda Slutsky]

SCHOENHEIMER, RUDOLF (1898–1941), German biochemist. Born in Berlin, Schoenheimer worked in the Institutes of Pathology of the universities of Berlin (1922–23) and Leipzig (1923–25). He was a leader in the Blau-Weiss Zionist Youth Movement. In 1926 he became professor of pathological chemistry at the University of Freiburg. With the advent of the Nazi regime, he went to America, as professor of biological chemistry at Columbia University (1933–41). His career ended in suicide during World War II.

Using stable isotopes (particularly deuterium and nitrogen-15) as tracers, he followed the metabolism of cholesterol and of fats through the mammalian body, and his findings led to marked changes in the views then held on metabolism.

BIBLIOGRAPHY: Clarke in: *Science*, 94 (1941), 553; Quastel, in: *Nature*, 149 (1942), 15; J.C. Poggendorff, *Biographisch-literarisches Handwoerterbuch der exakten Naturwissenschaften*, 7a (1961), incl. bibl. of his works.

[Samuel Aaron Miller]

SCHOEPS, HANS JOACHIM (1909–1980), professor and scholar of religious history. Schoeps, who was born in Berlin, emigrated to Sweden in 1938, returning to Germany after World War II. In 1947 he began teaching religious and intellectual history at the University of Erlangen and was appointed professor in 1950. From 1947 he edited *Zeitschrift fuer Religions-und Geistesgeschichte*. While his interests have ranged over a wide field, his writings have dealt mainly with earliest Christianity. Schoeps' relationship to the Jewish community has been a clouded one. Beginning with his early publications in the 1930s, Schoeps, a prolific writer, adopted a radical dialectical Jewish theology which excluded all nomistic as well as national-cultural elements, bringing Judaism very close to Christianity but stopping short of baptism. His speculative theological position, influenced by the writings of the 19th-century Jewish philosopher Solomon Ludwig *Steinheim, was, he wrote, acceptable neither to liberals nor Orthodox. More significant, however, was his espousal of an extreme German nationalism, which led, in the decisive year of 1933, to the conviction that it was possible for the "German Jews," as distinguished from the Eastern European Jews then in Germany and the Zionists, to come to terms with the National Socialists.

Among his books are *Theologie und Geschichte des Judenchristentums* (1949); *Aus fruehchristlicher Zeit* (1950); and *Paul* (Ger. 1959; Eng., 1961). The *Jewish Christian Argument* (1965) is a useful description of the view of Christianity in the writings of Jewish authors. In 1956 he published his autobiography, *Die letzten dreissig Jahre*. In it he noted with regret his failure to recognize the true face of Nazism (his own parents died in concentration camps). Of Judaism itself he wrote of a hope for something completely new that in confrontation with the death of the six million might yet emerge.

BIBLIOGRAPHY: K. Toepfner (ed.), *Wider die Aechtung der Geschichte* (1969); G. Lindeskog, *ibid.*, 15–18.

[Lou H. Silberman]

SCHOLEM (Shalom), GERSHOM GERHARD (1898–1982), the most important scholar of Jewish mysticism and a towering figure in Jewish intellectual life. Born to an assimilated family in Berlin, he was attracted in his youth to Judaism and Zionism and studied major Hebrew Jewish texts and Kabbalah by himself. After completing a Ph.D. thesis in 1923 on *Sefer ha-Bahir*, he arrived in Israel, and taught at the Hebrew University, becoming the first professor to devote all his studies and teaching to the topic of Jewish mysticism. His achievement in surveying all the major stages and writings belonging to this topic is staggering. In the difficult times of the 1920s and 1930s, he traveled to all the major European libraries and systematically studied all the available manuscripts. In 1939 he delivered a series of lectures in New York, which became the first comprehensive analysis of the historical and phenomenological aspects of the entire range of Jewish mysticism: *Major Trends in Jewish Mysticism*, which is also his most influential and widely read book. One of the chapters of this book, dealing with the Heikhalot literature, was complemented by a collection of studies printed in New York, under the title *Jewish Gnosticism, Merkabah Mysticism, and the Talmudic Tradition*.

Building upon his perusal of manuscripts, he published from the mid-1920s a series of articles in Hebrew in which he identified many anonymous manuscripts, and from 1948, a series of analyses about the beginning of Kabbalah. In its most elaborated form, it appeared in English posthumously as *Origins of the Kabbalah*, translated by A. Arkush and edited by R.Z.J. Werblowsky (1987).

Alongside those studies he identified, published, and analyzed in detail the main documents pertinent to Shabbateanism, and in 1957, he published in Hebrew the most important synthesis of the historical and religious aspects of the Shabbatean movement in the lifetime of *Shabbetai Ẓevi. Sixteen years later, Princeton University Press produced an enlarged English version of this book, *Sabbatai Sevi, the Mystical Messiah*, translated by R.J.Z. Werblowsky.

From 1948, Scholem was a permanent participant in the Eranos encounters in Ascona, Switzerland, where he lectured and interacted with the major scholars of religion of his generation, such as Carl G. Jung, Mircea Eliade, and Henry Corbin. The lectures he delivered there in German were printed in the volumes of *Eranos Jahrbuch* and collected in two German volumes, translated into English by R. Manheim as *On the Kabbalah and Its Symbolism* (1969) and *On the Mystical Shape of the Godhead* (1991), and into Hebrew by Joseph ben Shlomo as *Pirkei Yesod be-Havanat ha-Kabbalah u-Semaleha* (1976). These studies represent the most important articulations of Scholem's phenomenology of Kabbalah, treating seminal matters in Jewish mysticism. In 1972 he formulated his last summary of his understanding of Kabbalah in the various entries he contributed to *Encyclopedia Judaica*, which were collected in the volume *Kabbalah* (1974).

The main themes that represent his thought are the emergence of Kabbalah in Europe in mid-12th century as the result of a synthesis between Gnostic and Neoplatonic elements; the rise of messianic interest among the kabbalists after the expulsion of the Jews from Spain; the reaction to the trauma of the expulsion in the theories of the Safed kabbalists, especially the Lurianic one; the spread of this type of messianic Kabbalah among wider audiences, which prepared the way for the emergence of the Shabbatean movement, and last but not least, the assumption that the wide influence of the Shabbatean movement had an impact on the emergence of three main religious developments since the 18th century: Ḥasidism, Enlightenment, and Reform. Scholem was especially interested in Messianism and dedicated much of his energy to writing seminal studies about the "messianic idea" in Judaism in all its forms: see especially *The Messianic Idea in Judaism* (New York, 1972). A leitmotif in his writing is the importance of antinomian, paradoxical, and dialectical forms of thought in Kabbalah on the one hand, and the absence of mystical union in Jewish mysticism, on the other.

His deep involvement in the intellectual life in Israel and in the Jewish world generated numerous articles, most of which have been collected in three Hebrew volumes edited by Abraham Shapira, and in some English ones.

Scholem established a school of scholars in Jerusalem which he described as historical-critical, and directed a series of doctoral theses by renowned scholars such as Isaiah Tishby, Efraim Gottlieb, Rivka Schatz-Uffenheimer, Meir Benayahu, Joseph ben Shlomo, Amos Perlmutter, Yehuda Liebes, and Amos Goldreich. His impact on a long line of Israeli and American scholars and intellectuals was tremendous. Among them we may enumerate Zalman Shazar, S.Y. Agnon, Isaac Baer, Nathan Rotenstreich, Chaim Wirszubski, and R.J.Z. Werblowsky; and in America, Harold Bloom, Robert Alter, and Cynthia Ozick.

Scholem was widely recognized as the leading scholar in Judaica in the 20th century and was accorded numerous prizes and honorary titles, among them the Israel Prize, the Bialik Prize, and the Rothschild Prize, and served as the head of the Israeli Academy of Science and Humanities.

He wrote an autobiography, *From Berlin to Jerusalem*, and corresponded with many persons, including Walter Benjamin. Several monographs have been dedicated to his life and thought: e.g., David Biale, *Gershom Scholem, Kabbalah and Counter-History* (Cambridge, MA, 1979), and Joseph Dan, *Gershom Scholem and the Mystical Dimension of Jewish History* (New York-London, 1988).

His rich library is indubitably the best one in the field of Jewish mysticism, and it became part of the Jewish National and University Library, serving as a major resource for studies in the field. A catalogue raisonné of his library has been printed in two volumes, edited by Joseph Dan and Esther Liebes, *The Library of Gershom Scholem on Jewish Mysticism* (Jerusalem, 1999).

[Moshe Idel (2nd ed.)]

SCHOLEM, WERNER (1895–1940), communist politician and lawyer. Scholem was the third son of the Berlin printer Arthur Scholem and his wife, Betty, and the elder brother of Gerhard (Gershom) *Scholem. After a short involvement with Zionism, Scholem became a member of the Socialist Party at the age of 18. Being attached to the leftist and pacifistic wing of the SPD, he refused to volunteer for service in World War I. In 1915 he was drafted and was wounded a year later. In 1917, while taking part in an anti-war demonstration in uniform, he was arrested and accused of high treason, yet was released after a few months. Scholem moved to Hannover and married a comrade from the workers' movement, Emmy Wiechelt. After the foundation of the USPD (Independent Social Democratic Party of Germany) he became editor of the Party's paper, *Volksblatt*, in Halle/Saale. In 1921 he became the youngest member of the *Preussischer Landtag* and was appointed to the editorial board of the *Rote Fahne*. He was elected to the *Reichstag* in 1924 and became a leading figure of the KPD (Communist Party of Germany). In 1926 he was expelled from the Communist Party as a prominent protagonist of the so-called "ultra-left" anti-Stalinist opposition. Scholem turned away from politics and resumed his law studies, which he finished in 1931. After the Nazis came to power, Werner and Emmy Scholem were immediately imprisoned, but soon released. In April they were arrested again, this time by the Gestapo, and accused of high treason. With the help of a friend, Emmy was released and managed to escape with the couple's two daughters to London in 1934. In 1935 Scholem was interned in the concentration camp Torgau, and was transferred to Dachau in 1937. On July 17, 1940, Werner Scholem was murdered in the Buchenwald concentration camp.

BIBLIOGRAPHY: I. Shedletzky (ed.),*Mutter und Sohn im Briefwechsel 1917–1946* (1989); M. Buckmiller and P. Nafe, in: M. Buckmiller, D. Heimann, and J. Perels (eds.), *Judentum und politische Existenz* (2000), 61–81. M.Triendl and N. Zadoff, in: *Freitag* 26 (June 18, 2004), 18.

[Mirjam Triendl (2nd ed.)]

SCHOLES, MYRON S. (1941–), economist, financier, and educator; joint winner of the 1997 Nobel Prize for economics. Born in Timmins, Ont., Scholes earned his B.A. in economics in 1962 at McMaster University in Hamilton, Ont., where he had lived since the age of 10. He completed his M.B.A. in 1964 and Ph.D. in 1969 at the University of Chicago. While working on his dissertation, he took a position in 1968 as assistant professor in finance at the Sloan School of Management at Massachusetts Institute of Technology (MIT). In 1973 Scholes returned to the University of Chicago as an associate professor (later promoted to professor) in the Graduate School of Business; a decade later, in 1983, he joined the finance and law faculty at Stanford University's Graduate School of Business and Law School and attained his current status of emeritus in 1996.

Scholes grew up surrounded by family who were involved in business; in particular, his mother directed him toward the field and even assisted him with his first investment account as a teenager. After his mother's death when he was 16, he remained mindful of her vision for his future throughout his academic years. During his graduate studies he developed a passion and dedication for research.

In his 30-plus years of teaching, Scholes wrote a vast collection of articles on economic and finance topics in various business periodicals. However, none were more revolutionary than his and Fischer Black's 1973 "The Pricing of Options and Corporate Liabilities" in the *Journal of Political Economy*, which introduced their equation on stock options pricing. Later that year Robert Merton's similar research culminated in his paper "The Theory of Rational Option Pricing" (in the *Bell Journal of Economics*), and the three collaborated to prove their theory in the live market with their 1976 mutual fund, Money Market/Options Investment, Inc. The successful results caused a dramatic eruption of "derivatives" markets, and its usage has not only endured but also led to Scholes and Merton's selection as co-recipients of the 1997 Nobel Prize in economics. (Black had passed away in 1995.)

Among Scholes' many professional affiliations were managing partner at Oak Hill Capital Management, chairman of Oak Hill Platinum Partners, and the American Finance Association's president in 1990, as well as serving on the board of directors of several corporations. In 1993 Scholes and Merton were two founders of the Greenwich, Conn.-based Long-Term Capital Management (LTCM), a hedge fund that he left not long after its downfall in 1998 (but prior to its liquidation in 2000). He holds honorary doctoral degrees from the University of Paris-Dauphine (1989), McMaster University (1990), and Belgium's Katholieke Universiteit Leuven (1998). In 1991 he co-wrote with Mark A. Wolfson the book *Taxes and Business Strategies: A Planning Approach* (updated second edition, 2001).

[Dawn Des Jardins (2nd ed.)]

SCHOMBERG, English family. MEYER LOEW SCHOMBERG (1690–1761), born in Fetzburg, Germany, was one of the first Jews to be accepted at a German university, receiving a degree in medicine from the University of Giessen (1710). He subsequently settled in London, and became a member of the Royal College of Physicians (1722) and a Fellow of the Royal Society (1726). Appointed physician to the Great Synagogue, he built up a fashionable clientele. He wrote *Emunat Omen* in 1746, criticizing the English Jewish community for its mean outlook and defending his own unorthodox way of life. His sons ceased to be identified with Judaism. ISAAC SCHOMBERG (1714–1780), the eldest, became (after some initial difficulties) censor of the College of Physicians. His twin, RAPHAEL or RALPH SCHOMBERG (1714–1792), was a notary public as well as a physician. He tried his hand at literature and published volumes of poetry and plays which were of poor quality. HENRY SCHOMBERG (c. 1715–1755) rose to the rank of lieutenant colonel in the army. Meyer's youngest son, SIR ALEXANDER SCHOMBERG (1720–1804), commanded the ship which covered Wolfe's landing at Quebec in 1759 during the British conquest of Canada. He served as the model for Hogarth's painting *A Naval Officer* and was knighted in 1777. He was the father of Admiral SIR ALEXANDER WILMOT SCHOMBERG (1774–1850), naval writer, and probably of ISAAC SCHOMBERG (1753–1813), commissioner and deputy comptroller of the navy (1808–13) and editor of *Naval Chronology* (1802). Members of the family continued to be prominent in British life, particularly in the navy and army, until recently. However, they had no Jewish associations. This family was unrelated to another family of British Schombergs, the Dukes of Schomberg and their descendants, who were gentiles from Germany. They were also prominent in British public life and military affairs in the 18th and 19th centuries.

BIBLIOGRAPHY: A. Rubens, *Anglo-Jewish Portraits* (1935), 109–11, 155; P. Emden, *Jews of Britain* (1943), 83–85; B.G. Sack, *History of the Jews in Canada*, 1 (1945), 44–45, 250; C. Roth, *History of the Great Synagogue London, 1690–1940* (1950); Samuel, in: JHSET, 20 (1964), 83–100; D.M. Little and G.M. Kahrl (eds.), *Letters of David Garrick*, 3 vols. (1963), index. **ADD. BIBLIOGRAPHY:** ODNB online; Katz, England, 232–33.

[Cecil Roth]

SCHON, FRANK, BARON (1912–1995), British industrialist. Schon was born in Vienna and educated at the universities of Prague and Vienna, where he studied law. After settling in England, he founded in West Cumberland the chemical manufacturing firm of Marchon Products in 1939 and Solway Chemicals in 1943; he was chairman and managing director of both until 1967. In 1956 Marchon Products became part of Albright and Wilson, of which Schon was a director from 1958 to 1972; he was a director of Blue Circle Industries (formerly Portland Cement) from 1967 to 1982. Schon took a prominent part in the public and cultural life of the north of England, serving on the council and court of Durham University and Newcastle University. He was chairman of the Cumberland Development Council from 1964 to 1968. From 1969 to 1979 he was chairman of the National Research Development Corporation, a public agency concerned with the promotion of inventions in the national interest. He was knighted in 1966 and created a life peer in 1976.

BIBLIOGRAPHY: H. Pollins, *Economic History of the Jews in England* (1982), 220–1

[Vivian David Lipman]

SCHONFELD, VICTOR (1880–1930), English rabbi and educator. Schonfeld was born in Hungary. He served as rabbi of the Montefiore Society in Vienna until 1909, when he went to the North London Beth Hamidrash, which became the Adath Yisrael Synagogue in 1911. In 1920 Schonfeld took up an invitation to become head of the Mizrachi schools in Ereẓ Israel; dissatisfied with conditions, he returned to his former post two years later. In 1927 he founded the Union of Orthodox Hebrew Congregations in England, and in 1929 he established the Jewish Secondary Schools Movement. Schonfeld was an outstanding preacher and teacher, wielding great influence beyond the confines of his congregation, partly through the youth society, Ben Zakkai, which he founded. Apart from publishing a number of textbooks for religious schools, a volume of his sermons and essays was published posthumously by his son Solomon (*Judaism as Life's Purpose*, 1930; a shorter edition *Life's Purpose*, 1956).

SOLOMON SCHONFELD (1912–1984) was born in London and succeeded his father in 1933 as rabbi of the Adath Yisrael Synagogue, resigning from this post after 25 years' service; he also took over as presiding rabbi of the Union of Orthodox Hebrew Congregations. Schonfeld became principal of the Jewish Secondary Schools Movement, which he successfully expanded after World War II. Together with his father-in-law, Chief Rabbi Joseph *Hertz, he set up the Chief

Rabbi's Emergency Council, which in 1938–39 brought rabbis and other religious personnel to England from Central Europe and provided them with positions. Through the same organization he saved, both before and after the war – from Poland in particular – many hundreds of children. He was critical of the methods of the Refugee Childrens' Movement in England, which in his opinion failed to assure their religious upbringing.

Among Schonfeld's publications are *Jewish Religious Education* (1943), a handbook with syllabi for teachers and parents; the *Universal Bible* (1955), pentateuchal texts with translation and notes; and *Message to Jewry* (1959), addresses and articles.

BIBLIOGRAPHY: JC (Jan. 3, 1930; Jan. 10, 1930); S. Schonfeld, in: V. Schonfeld, *Life's Purpose* (1956), 5–7; JC (Dec. 5, 1958), 11; *ibid.* (Dec. 12, 1958), 20.

SCHONFIELD, HUGH JOSEPH (1901–1988), British writer and New Testament scholar. Born in London, he entered publishing in 1932, when he produced *A New Hebrew Typography* in which he devised a lower case alphabet for the printing of Hebrew. He first made his name as a biographer with *Richard Burton: Explorer* (1936) and *Ferdinand de Lesseps* (1937). He also published various historical works such as *This Man Was Right: Woodrow Wilson Speaks Again* (1943) and *The Suez Canal in World Affairs* (1952; revised ed. 1969).

Schonfield, however, owed his main reputation to a long series of works, often controversial, in which he dealt with primitive Christianity, whose Jewish roots he first emphasized in *Besorat Mattai: An Old Hebrew Text of St. Matthew's Gospel* (1927) and *According to the Hebrews: A New Translation of the Toldoth Jeshu …* (1937). In his *History of Jewish Christianity from the First to the Twentieth Century* (1936), Schonfield endeavored to revive the cause of the first-century Ebionite or "Nazarene" Church of Jerusalem, long silenced by the triumphant Gentile Church, and proclaimed the establishment of a "Jewish Christian independent religious communion" of Jews who believed in the messiahship of Jesus but remained separate from any Church denomination. To varying extents, the same approach characterizes *Jesus: A Biography* (1939), *The Jew of Tarsus: An Unorthodox Portrait of Paul* (1946), *Saints Against Caesar: The Rise and Reactions of the First Christian Community* (1948), and *Those Incredible Christians: A New Look at the Early Church* (1968).

A noted lecturer and broadcaster, Schonfield continued his research in *The Authentic New Testament* (1955), an original translation from the Greek, together with an introduction and notes relating the text to rabbinic sources, which became a bestseller. In this, as in other of his later works – such as *Judaism and World Order* (1943); *The Song of Songs* (1960), translated from the Hebrew with notes and an introduction; and *A Popular Dictionary of Judaism* (1962) – Schonfield stressed his Jewish identity and apparently retreated from his earlier wholehearted advocacy of Judeo-Christianity. He also wrote *Secrets of the Dead Sea Scrolls* (1956); *A History of Biblical Literature* (1962); *The Passover Plot* (1965), a reappraisal of the messianic initiative of Jesus; and *The Politics of God* (1970). *The Pentecost Revolution* (1974), an account of the "Jesus Party" up to the outbreak of the Jewish War against the Romans in 66 C.E., is a sequel to *The Passover Plot*. Schonfield was one of the most popular and controversial writers on early Christianity in modern Britain.

[Gabriel Sivan]

SCHOOLMAN, BERTHA S. (1897–1974), U.S. Zionist leader. Bertha Schoolman, who was born in New York City, studied at Hunter College and at the Teachers Institute of the Jewish Theological Seminary. From 1919 to 1923 she taught at the Central Jewish Institute, and from 1922 to 1946 she was a director of children's summer camping. Her Zionist activity brought her appointments to the national board of Hadassah in 1935 and the World Zionist Actions Committee from 1937. During over 30 years of Hadassah work, Bertha Schoolman held national offices, including secretary (1940–41), vice president (1941–43), and national chairman of Youth Aliyah (1956–60).

Her husband, ALBERT SCHOOLMAN (1894–1980), educator, was born in Lithuania. He headed the Central Jewish Institute of New York, the first American Jewish community center with an educational focus. In 1919 Schoolman established the Cejwin Camps, the first system of Jewish educational camps in the United States, with which he remained actively associated. Schoolman was president of the National Council for Jewish Education and a founder of the American Association for Jewish Education. Schoolman's educational philosophy was rooted in the Reconstructionist view of Judaism.

[Leon H. Spotts]

SCHOR, ALEXANDER SENDER BEN EPHRAIM ZALMAN (d. 1737), talmudist. Schor, who was probably born in Lvov, married the daughter of Mordecai b. Leibush of Zolkiew, president of the *Council of Four Lands. For a time Schor was rabbi of Hovnov, Belz district, but in 1704 he resigned, not wishing to bear the responsibility of the rabbinate, and went to live in Zolkiew, where he remained for the rest of his life, earning his living as a distiller. In 1733 Schor published *Simlah Ḥadashah*, a digest of the laws of ritual slaughter – *sheḥitah* and *terefot* – with an extensive commentary entitled *Tevu'ot Shor*. An appendix named *Bekhor Shor* contains novellae on both the *halakhah* and *aggadah* to tractate *Ḥullin* and other tractates. The *Tevu'ot Shor* attained great popularity. It has been republished at least 17 times and came to be regarded as the authoritative work on the subject. Schor generally assumes a stringent interpretation of the relevant laws. In practice, a knowledge of *Tevu'ot Shor* was regarded as a prerequisite for a *shoḥet* before he was granted a *kabbalah*, a permit to practice *sheḥitah*. The name of the book became almost a concept: of an expert in the laws of *sheḥitah* it was said that "he is an expert in the *Tevu'ot Shor*."

Commentaries were written on it, the most important being *Levushei Serad* of D.S. Eybeschuetz (Moghilev, 1812) and the *Tikkunei ha-Zevaḥ* of Isaiah Borochowitz (1883).

BIBLIOGRAPHY: Ḥ.D. Friedberg, *Toledot Mishpaḥat Schor* (1901), 15–19; S. Buber, *Kiryah Nisgavah* (1903), 13–14; Ch. Tchernowitz, *Toledot ha-Posekim*, 3 (1947), 258–60.

[Itzhak Alfassi]

SCHOR, EPHRAIM SOLOMON (The Elder) BEN NAPHTALI HIRSCH (d. 1633), Polish rabbinical scholar. He was the son-in-law of Saul *Wahl, and legend has it that Saul Wahl married off his young daughter hurriedly to Schor despite the disparity in age to forestall the desire of the king to marry her (*Gedullat Sha'ul*, ed. by H. Edelmann (1854), 4a–b); there is no historical basis for the legend. Schor belonged to a Moravian family. From 1613 to 1624 he was rabbi of Grodno, then Szczebrzeszyn and Brest-Litovsk, and finally Lublin. In 1618 he was one of the rabbis who signed a *takkanah* of the *Council of Four Lands. The esteem in which he was held can be gauged from the fact that his *haskamah* ("approbation") to the *Ikkarim* of Joseph *Albo with the commentary *Eẓ Shatul* (Venice, 1618) appears before that of Meir of *Lublin. Schor's fame rests on his *Tevu'ot Shor* (Lublin, 1615–16), a digest of the *Beit Yosef* to the *Turim* in which he adds and comments upon the sources of the *Tur* of Jacob b. Asher, which are not given in *Beit Yosef* (Lublin, 1605/6). His responsa and decisions are frequently quoted by his contemporaries. In order to distinguish him from his relative, Alexander *Schor, who also wrote a work under the same title, he is occasionally referred to as "The Elder Tevu'ot Shor." His son JACOB, the author of *Beit Ya'akov* (Venice, 1693), novellae to *Sanhedrin*, was, like his father, rabbi of Brest-Litovsk.

BIBLIOGRAPHY: S. Feinstein, *Ir Tehillah* (1885), 24, 153; I.T. Eisenstadt and S. Wiener, *Da'at Kedoshim* (1897/98), 30 (2nd pagination); S.B. Nissenbaum, *Le-Korot ha-Yehudim be-Lublin* (1899), 35f.; H.D. Friedberg, *Toledot-Mishpaḥat Schor* (1901), 9f.; F.H. Wetstein, in: *Sefer ha-Yovel… N. Sokolow* (1904), 289f.; Halpern, Pinkas, 34f.

[Itzhak Alfassi]

SCHOR, ILYA (1904–1961), U.S. metalsmith, painter, and printmaker. Born in Zloczoq, Poland, Schor was the son of a Hasidic painter. Before attending the Academy of Fine Arts in Warsaw, he worked as an apprentice to an engraver and goldsmith. He continued his studies in Paris before coming to New York in 1941. Schor achieved a reputation as a worker in metal. His jewelry and ritual objects, such as *kiddush* cups and Torah crowns, are filled with delicate, detailed, and intricate design. He did a great deal of work for ritual use in synagogues, such as doors for the ark of Temple Beth-El, Great Neck, New York. With artists such as Percival Goodman, Seymour Lipton, Ben Shahn, and Milton Horn, Schor contributed work which reflected the post-World War II Jewish community's renewed interest in the synagogue as both a spiritual and cultural gathering place: original and handcrafted ritual objects, sculpture, painting, and windows emphasized the importance of the synagogue in Jewish community life. Schor's work was reminiscent of pre-Emancipation Jewish craftsmen. His oils and some of the books he illustrated with woodcuts depicted life in the small Jewish communities of his boyhood. His woodcut *Fiddler*, composed of simple, flat shapes with a minimum of detail, recalls a figure of the Eastern European shtetl. He illustrated *The Sabbath: Its Meaning for Modern Man by Abraham Heschel* (1951), *The Earth Is the Lord's': The Inner World of the Jew in Eastern Europe*, also by Heschel. Rather than working in the Abstract Expressionist style of his peers, Schor always remained a narrative, figurative artist who referred to traditional Jewish religious or cultural subject matter, making art in a manner which combined both folk and modernist sensibilities.

BIBLIOGRAPHY: G.C. Grossman, *Jewish Art* (1995); A. Kampf, *Jewish Experience in the Art of the Twentieth* Century (1984).

[Nancy Buchwald (2nd ed.)]

SCHORR, ABRAHAM ḤAYYIM BEN NAPHTALI ẒEVI HIRSCH (d. 1632), Galician rabbi. It has been assumed that Schorr was of German origin since his father signed himself "Hirsch of Alsace," and Moses *Isserles in a responsum (no. 95) wrote to him urging him to remain as a rabbi in Germany. Schorr himself, however, served as rabbi in Galicia, in Satanov, Belz, and possibly Kremenets. His main work was *Torat Ḥayyim*, novellae on *Bava Kamma, Bava Meẓia*, and *Bava Batra* (1624), and on *Eruvin, Sanhedrin, Shavu'ot, Avodah Zarah, Ḥullin*, and *Pesaḥim* (1634), both published together in Prague in 1692. The work was based on the courses which he gave in his yeshivah and was widely used. The main purpose of the work was to establish the *halakhah* between Rashi and the tosafists when they differed, but it also contains aggadic material.

His *Ẓon Kodashim* on the order *Kodashim*, which he wrote together with his friend R. Mordecai Asher of Brzezany, was published posthumously by Schorr's grandson, Ḥayyim b. Ozer of Hildesheim. He is mentioned in the responsa of Benjamin Aaron *Slonik (no. 88) and by Joseph Solomon *Delmedigo in his *Elim* (Odessa ed. 1864, 93–95). According to tradition, Schorr died in Belz and was buried in Lemberg.

BIBLIOGRAPHY: Fuenn, *Keneset*, 368; S. Buber, *Anshei Shem*, (1895), 2; H.D. Friedberg, *Toledot Mishpaḥat Schorr* (1901), 6–8; R. Margaliot, in: *Sinai*, 26 (1950), 119–20; Z. Horowitz, *Le-Korot ha-Kehillot be-Polanyah* (1969), 98; E.Z. Margolioth, *Ma'alot ha-Yuḥasin* (1900), 36, 38–40.

SCHORR, BARUCH (1823–1904), cantor and composer. Schorr was born in Lemberg to a ḥasidic family; his musical abilities were recognized early and he served as a *meshorer* ("singer") with well-known cantors. He officiated in various small communities before becoming cantor in Lemberg in 1859. A pious Jew, he was at the same time interested in European culture and musical techniques. He applied these techniques in his compositions, which, however, are firmly based on traditional motifs (especially in the *ahavah rabbah* *shtayger*). Thus his compositions are noteworthy for their ease of rendition and depth of feeling. Schorr composed an opera, *Samson*, which was performed in 1890 in Lemberg's Jewish theater. After the performance he was led onto the stage by the prima donna, in order to receive the audience's ovation. This behavior was considered unseemly by the synagogue authorities, who suspended Schorr from office for four Sabbaths. Offended, he left for the U.S., where he stayed for five years until a delegation was sent from Lemberg to recall him to his post. He remained there until his death, which occurred while he was officiating on the last day of Passover. Schorr also wrote commentaries on the Pentateuch and Ecclesiastes. All six of his sons became cantors, and one of them, Israel, published his father's compositions in *Neginot Baruch Schorr* (1906). Many of these melodies are actually the work of the younger Schorr, who also rearranged some of his father's harmonies. Another relative named ISRAEL SCHORR (1886–1935) was also a celebrated cantor in Europe and the U.S. He was the composer of *She-Yibbaneh Beit ha-Mikdash*, one of the best-loved cantorial compositions of modern times.

BIBLIOGRAPHY: S. Perlmutter, in: Jewish Ministers Cantors' Association of America, *Die Geshikhte fun Khazones* (1924), 89–91; Idelsohn, Music, 286, 290, 309–10; J. Grob, in: *Monatsschrift der juedischen Kantoren* (April–May, 1930), 4–5: H.H. Harris, *Toledot ha-Neginah ve-ha-ḥazzanut be-Yisrael* (1950), 416–8.

[David M.L. Olivestone]

SCHORR, DANIEL (1916–), U.S. journalist. Schorr was born in New York City, the son of Russian immigrants. He began his journalistic career at 12 when he came upon a woman who had jumped or fallen from the roof of his Bronx apartment building. After calling the police, Schorr phoned the *Bronx Home News* and was paid $5 for the tip. In a career of more than six decades, Schorr earned many awards for journalistic excellence, including three Emmys, and decorations from European heads of state. He was also honored by civil liberties groups and professional organizations for his defense of the First Amendment. After serving in Army Intelligence during World War II, Schorr began writing from Western Europe for *The Christian Science Monitor* and later the *New York Times*, witnessing postwar reconstruction, the Marshall Plan, and the creation of the NATO alliance. In 1953 his vivid coverage of a disastrous flood that broke the dikes of the Netherlands brought him to the attention of Edward R. Murrow of the Columbia Broadcasting System. Schorr joined CBS News as its diplomatic correspondent in Washington. In 1955, with the post-Stalin thaw in the Soviet Union, he received accreditation to open a CBS bureau in Moscow. His two-and-a-half-year assignment culminated in the first exclusive television interview with a Soviet leader, Nikita S. Khrushchev, filmed in his Kremlin office in 1957 for CBS's *Face the Nation*. Schorr's repeated defiance of Soviet censorship, however, eventually landed him in trouble with the KGB, the secret police, and, after a brief arrest on trumped-up charges, he was barred from the Soviet Union at the end of 1957. For the next two years, Schorr reported from Washington and the United Nations, covering Khrushchev's tumultuous tour of the United States in 1959, interviewing Fidel Castro in Cuba, and traveling with President Dwight D. Eisenhower to South America, Asia, and Europe. In 1960 Schorr was assigned to Bonn as CBS bureau chief for Germany and Eastern Europe and covered the Berlin crisis and the building of the Berlin Wall. In 1972, while being assigned to Washington, Schorr began a full-time assignment for CBS as its chief correspondent on the Watergate break-in story. Schorr's exclusive reports and on-the-scene coverage of the Senate Watergate hearings earned him three Emmys. He unexpectedly found himself a part of his own story when the hearings turned up a Nixon "enemies list" with his name on it and evidence that the president had ordered that the Federal Bureau of Investigation investigate him. This "abuse of a Federal agency" was one count in the Bill of Impeachment on which Nixon would have been tried had he not resigned in August 1974. That fall, Schorr again became part of his own story. When the House of Representatives voted to suppress the final report of its intelligence investigating committee, Schorr arranged for publication of the advance copy he had obtained. This led to his suspension by CBS and an investigation by the House Ethics Committee, in which Schorr was threatened with jail for contempt of Congress if he did not disclose his source. At a public hearing he refused on First Amendment grounds. The committee voted 6 to 5 against a contempt citation. Schorr resigned from CBS and wrote his account of his stormy experience in a book, *Clearing the Air*. In 1979 Schorr was hired by Ted Turner to help create the Cable News Network, and he served in Washington as senior correspondent until 1985. Subsequently Schorr worked primarily for National Public Radio as senior news analyst, working effectively as he approached 90. In 2002 Schorr was elected to the American Academy of Arts and Sciences. He was the author of *Stay Tuned: A Life in Journalism* (2001) and *Forgive Us Our Press Passes* (1998).

[Stewart Kampel (2nd ed.)]

SCHORR, FRIEDRICH (1888–1953), bass-baritone. Born in Nagyvarád, Hungary, Schorr sang at Graz, Prague, and Cologne, and at the Berlin State Opera (1923–31). In 1938 he emigrated to the United States and sang at the Metropolitan Opera. One of the foremost Wagnerian singers of his time, he excelled as an interpreter of the roles of Hans Sachs and Wotan and often appeared at the Wagner Festivals in Bayreuth.

SCHORR, JOSHUA HESCHEL (commonly known as **Osias Schorr**; 1818–1895), scholar, editor, and second-generation Galician Haskalah leader. Born in Brody, Galicia, to a prominent and affluent family, Schorr became a successful merchant, but devoted much of his time to Jewish scholarship. In his youth he was befriended (through correspondence) by Samuel David *Luzzatto and later financed the publication of a number of Luzzatto's works. In the 1850s Luzzatto broke with Schorr because of the latter's radicalism. Schorr's initial writings were translated from their original Hebrew and published in German Jewish periodicals. The earliest articles centered on social and literary themes and appeared in Ludwig *Philippson's *Die Allgemeine Zeitung des Judenthums*. His first major article appeared in *Jost's *Israelitische Annalen*, and constituted an early attempt to formulate a theoretical basis for reforming Jewish law without denying the principle of authority. In the early 1840s he frequently contributed to *Zion*, a Hebrew periodical which appeared in Germany. Schorr's major writings, however, were published in *He-Ḥalutz, a yearbook which he edited and which appeared intermittently between 1851 and 1887. Intended as the literary organ of a small group of radical *maskilim* who advocated social and religious reforms, *He-Ḥalutz* became devoted almost entirely to scholarly articles after publication of Volume 5 in 1860. Subsequent to the publication of Volume 6 in 1861, the periodical was written exclusively by Schorr. During the years 1879–84 Schorr again became involved in the struggle between Galician *maskilim* and adherents of Orthodoxy, against whom he published many satirical verses in *Ivri Anokhi*, a Hebrew periodical issued in Brody. He corresponded with the leading Jewish scholars of his day, including Abraham Geiger, Abraham Krochmal, Leopold Zunz, Marcus Jost, and Moritz Steinschneider, as well as Bernard Felsenthal, a prominent American Reform rabbi. Schorr's writings advocating religious and social reforms were of two kinds: first, satirical diatribes attacking the alleged ignorance and obscurantism of the Orthodox, and often influenced by the style of his friend, Isaac *Erter; and, second, scholarly polemics seeking to demonstrate that talmudic and rabbinical laws are products of a specific time and are, therefore, without absolute authority. In the polemical articles his technique was to point out errors and contradictions in talmudic and later halakhic literature, and he did not limit his critical approach to post-biblical texts. Schorr was one of the earliest Hebrew scholars to apply critical methods to the Bible, including the Torah itself, which aroused the wrath of his Orthodox opponents. To the Jewish masses of Eastern Europe he became the very symbol of heresy and, as such, appears as a quasi-fictional character in the works of S.Y. *Agnon. Influencing an entire generation of East European *maskilim* – Moses Leib *Lilienblum and Judah Leib *Gordon, for example, acknowledged their debt to him – Schorr also had some effect on a number of American Reform rabbis. Toward the end of the 19th century he became an eccentric recluse. He left his valuable library of manuscripts and early prints and a substantial estate to the Viennese Rabbinical Seminary.

BIBLIOGRAPHY: Klausner, Sifrut, 4 (1953), 58–77; E. Spicehandler, in: HUCA, 31 (1960), 181–222; 40–41 (1970), 503–28; idem, in: SBB, 2 (1955–56), 20–36 (bibl.).

[Ezra Spicehandler]

SCHORR, MOSES (Mojżesz; 1874–1941), Polish rabbi and scholar. Schorr, born in Przemysl, Galicia, studied at the Juedisch-theologische Lehranstalt and the University of Vienna. In 1899 he became lecturer in Jewish religious subjects at the Jewish Teachers' Seminary in Lemberg, where he also engaged in wider educational and social work. In 1904 he was appointed lecturer and in 1915 professor of Semitic languages and history of the ancient Orient at Lemberg University, a chair which he later held in Warsaw. He was called there in 1923 to succeed S. *Posnanski as preacher at the moderately Reform Tłomacka Street synagogue, in which capacity he was also a member of the Warsaw rabbinical council. Schorr was one of the founders in 1928 of the Institute for Jewish Studies, which was the rabbinical seminary of Poland; he served there as lecturer in Bible and Hebrew, and for some years as rector. A member of the Polish Academy of Sciences, from 1935 to 1938 he was a member of the Polish Senate, defending the precarious rights of Polish Jewry against mounting official and unofficial antisemitism. When Germany invaded Poland in September 1939, he fled eastward, but was arrested by the Russians, who moved on Poland from the east. Transported from prison to prison, he ended up in Uzbekistan, where he died.

Among Schorr's many scholarly works, the first treated Joseph *Nasi's correspondence with King Sigismund Augustus of Poland (in MGWJ, 41 (1897), 169–77, 228–37). In 1899 he published *Organizacja Żydów w Polsce… aż do r. 1772*, a history of Polish Jewry's legal status and inner organization from its beginnings to 1772, which became basic to all further research in this field. This was followed by *Żydzi w Przemyclu do końca XVII wieku* ("The Jews of Przemysl to the End of the 18th Century," 1903), and a critical edition (1909) of the privileges granted to the Jews of Cracow by King Stanislaus Augustus in 1765. From Jewish history in Poland Schorr turned to Semitic studies, in particular ancient Babylonian and Assyrian law, becoming one of the leading scholars in this field and making it accessible to legal scholars unfamiliar with cuneiform script. Between 1907 and 1910 he published 184 legal documents with their transcription, translation, and a commentary under the title *Altbabylonische Rechtsurkunden…* (3 vols.). His *Urkunden des altbabylonischen Zivil und Prozessrechts* (1913) has remained an important reference book. A jubilee volume in Hebrew and Polish was published in 1935, on the occasion of his 60th birthday, as well as a memorial volume in Hebrew, *Kovez Madda'i le-Zekher M. Schorr* (1945).

BIBLIOGRAPHY: M. Balaban, in: *Księga jubileuszowa ku czci… Mojżesza Schorra* (1935); M. David, *ibid.*; A. Weiss, in: *Kovez Madda'i le-Zekher Moshe Schorr* (1945), ix–xiii; Y. Gruenbaum (ed.), EG, 1 (1953), 303–4; J. Guzik, in: S.K. Mirsky (ed.), *Ishim u-Demuyyot be-Ḥokhmat Yisrael be-Eiropah ha-Mizraḥit Lifnei Sheki'atah* (1959), 207–22; bibl; 217–22.

SCHORR, NAPHTALI MENDEL (1807–1883), pioneer Galician Hebrew journalist and short-story writer; brother of Joshua Heschel *Schorr.

His publications include a periodical entitled *Ha-Ẓir* (1858), a collection of short stories *Har ha-Mor* (1855–77), a Hebrew translation of *Brahmanische Weisheit* ("Indian parables") under the title *Masat Nefesh* (1867), and a new edition of *Beḥinat ha-Olam* by *Jedaiah ha-Penini with his own commentary (1885). His contributions to newpapers and periodicals were usually signed I.L.R. (Heb. ילר), the last letters of his names.

BIBLIOGRAPHY: N.M. Gelber, in: *Arim ve-Immahot be-Yisrael*, 6 (1955), 218–9.

[Getzel Kressel]

SCHORSCH, GUSTAV (1918–1945), Czech actor and producer. One of the founders of the avant-garde theater "D 99" in Prague, he also worked at the Czech National Theater. After the German occupation in 1939 he was deported to the *Theresienstadt concentration camp. While there, he organized lectures and play readings, and in secret classes and rehearsals conducted at night, under the most difficult conditions, formed a group of actors who gave highly accomplished theatrical performances. Those of the group who survived played an important part in Czech postwar theater life. Schorsch's work came to an end in the autumn of 1944, when he was transferred to *Auschwitz. In January 1945 he was killed by the Nazis.

BIBLIOGRAPHY: Frýd, in: *Terezin* (Eng., 1965), 207ff.; Šedová, *ibid.*, 219ff.

[Avigdor Dagan]

SCHORSCH, ISMAR (1935–), Jewish historian and sixth chancellor of the *Jewish Theological Seminary. Born in Germany, Schorsch was three when his family came to the United States in December 1938, a month after *Kristallnacht*. He grew up in Pottstown, Pennsylvania, where his father, Rabbi Emil Schorsch, served as a congregational rabbi. Schorsch was educated at Ursinus College and later at JTS, where he was ordained in 1962. At Columbia University he studied under Salo W. *Baron and Fritz Stern and earned his doctorate in Jewish history in 1969. After serving as a U.S. Army chaplain, he joined the faculty of JTS, rose to the rank of provost during the tenure of his mentor, Gerson D.*Cohen, and was appointed chancellor upon Cohen's retirement in 1986. Schorsch has announced his intention to retire from that post in 2006 and to return to full-time teaching and scholarship.

As an historian, Schorsch has published many works on aspects of modern German-Jewish history. Stressing that Jews are historical actors, not merely victims of persecution, he analyzed the response of German Jewry to antisemitism in the pre-World War I period. The main focus of his scholarship was the intellectual history of modern Jews, especially the German-Jewish *Wissenschaft des Judentums movement. He studied the rise of historical thinking as a source of authority within modern Judaism and delineated both reformist and conservative tendencies within that new trend. Schorsch assumed the presidency of the Leo Baeck Institute, a research institute devoted to German-Jewish history, in 1985.

Having become chancellor of JTS in the midst of an epochal debate over the impact of feminism on Conservative Judaism, Schorsch identified himself as a "militant centrist." He quickly completed the process of opening JTS professional schools to qualified women candidates by bringing the Cantorial School into line with the Rabbinical School, which had begun admitting women late in Cohen's tenure. Under his leadership, JTS expanded its training program for Jewish educators into a Graduate School of Jewish Education. Schorsch also oversaw the growth of the seminary's Jerusalem campus. He has promoted collaborative initiatives with other institutions, notably the 1991 Project Judaica program, which has brought JTS-trained scholars to the Russian State University for the Humanities in Moscow to help revive Jewish learning in Russia. Near the end of his tenure in 2005, JTS had grown significantly, with an enrollment of 700 students in its various programs. With the percentage of American Jews self-identifying as Conservative dropping in recent years, Schorsch has acknowledged that strengthening the center of the Jewish religious spectrum remains a priority for his successor and his movement in the future.

As a spokesperson for Conservative Judaism, Schorsch addressed both his denominational constituency and a broader audience. In October 2005, he completed a twelve-year cycle of weekly Torah commentaries, through which he engaged Conservative Jewry more directly than any of his predecessors. He has been a frequent and outspoken critic of the Israeli Chief Rabbinate, charging it with intransigence and disregard of the broader Jewish community. In national affairs, he has brought Jewish perspectives to contemporary political debates over environmentalism, health care, welfare reform, and separation of church and state.

[Michael Panitz (2nd ed.)]

SCHOTTLAENDER, BENDET (**Benedict Schott**; 1763–1846), German educator and reformer. Schottlaender, who was orphaned at an early age, received a traditional education before coming under the influence of the ideas of the Enlightenment. He supported himself by tutoring until he met Israel *Jacobson, who appointed him teacher and subsequently principal of the *Seesen school. An able administrator and controversial reformer and innovator (concerning confirmation, use of German in the liturgy, music, etc.), he held this post for 33 years. He was also Jacobson's influential aide in the Jewish Consistory of *Westphalia and was partly responsible for its daring and unpopular reforms, which he tried to make acceptable by stressing education as the panacea for the ills of German Jewry. In this vein he contributed to *Ha-Me'assef* and *Sulamith*. In 1806 Schottlaender presented a memorandum on the necessity for improved education for Jews to the Paris *Assembly of Jewish Notables convened by Napoleon. In 1808 he published his pamphlet *Sendschreiben an meine Brueder die Israeliten in Westfalen, die Einrichtung eines juedischen Consistoriums betreffend.*

BIBLIOGRAPHY: J.R. Marcus, in: HUCA, 7 (1930), 537–77.

[Henry Wasserman / Noam Zadoff (2nd ed.)]

SCHOTTLAND, CHARLES IRWIN (1906–1995), U.S. social welfare expert. Born in Chicago, Schottland received a B.A. from UCLA in 1927; he received a social work certificate from the Graduate School of Social Work in the New York School of Social Work in 1929; and he graduated from the University of Southern California Law School in 1933. He was director of the California Relief Administration from 1933 to 1936. During his service as lieutenant-colonel in the U.S. army in World War II, he served as chief of section of the Displaced Persons Branch at Allied Supreme Headquarters, Paris (1944–45), and as the assistant director of the United Nations Relief and Rehabilitation Administration (UNRRA) for Germany (1945). After directing the New York Child Care Association (1946–48), he headed the California State Department of Social Welfare (1950–54). Appointed by President Eisenhower as commissioner of social security in the Department of Health, Education, and Welfare (1954–59), he directed the American social security system. In 1959 Schottland became professor and dean of the Graduate School for Advanced Studies in Social Welfare at Brandeis University, and was elected acting president of Brandeis University in 1970. Active in national and international organizations, he was president of the National Conference of Social Welfare, 1953, 1959–60; assistant treasurer-general and vice president of the International Conference of Social Welfare (1962–68); and president of the International Conference in 1968. He was also president of the National Association of Workers (1967–69). He was the principal adviser to the U.S. delegation at the United Nations Social Commission (1955 and 1957). He was chairman of the 1981 Arizona White House conference on aging. He also served as chairman of the Arizona Governor's Council on Aging; president of the National Senior Citizen Law Center; president of the American Society on Aging; and a board member of the Pima Counsel on Aging and the National Council on Aging.

In addition to many articles and papers published in journals and conference proceedings, he was the author of "Poverty and Income Maintenance for the Aged," in M. Gordon (ed.), *Poverty in America* (1965), *The Social Security Program in the United States* (1963), and *New Strategies for Social Development Role of Social Welfare* (1971). He edited *The Welfare State: Selected Essays* (1967).

[Joseph Neipris / Ruth Beloff (2nd ed.)]

SCHOTTLANDER, BERNARD (1924–1999), sculptor. Schottlander was born in Mainz, Germany, but emigrated to London in 1939. Initially trained as a metalworker, he first took up art studies in 1946, and continued to administer his own engineering works before devoting himself wholly to sculpture in 1963. The influence of this occupation is fully evident in his monumental, ambitious metal constructions, superbly fabricated and based on simple, near-geometrical forms. His gaunt abstract shapes suggest symbolic undertones, like huge Easter Island idols, but he represents them as forms without literary or religious programs. Schottlander has rapidly achieved considerable prominence both in England and abroad. He was invited to the 1967 Sculpture Symposium in Toronto, Canada, and to many other important international gatherings. He formerly exhibited regularly at the Anely Juda Gallery, London, but to solve the problem of displaying his enormous works, he took to exhibiting them in public spaces. He taught at the St. Martin's School of Art, London.

[Charles Samuel Spencer]

SCHOTZ, BENNO (1891–1984), British sculptor. Schotz was born in Estonia, the son of a watchmaker, and at the age of 20 joined his brother at Glasgow University. He became a naturalized British subject in 1930. In the 1920s he exhibited at the Royal Glasgow Institute of Fine Arts and other venues in Scotland and England. From 1938 to 1960 he was head of the Sculpture Department at Glasgow School of Art. Influenced by Epstein, Schotz established himself with a series of portraits of distinguished Scotsmen. He also made portraits of famous Jews: Herzl, Sholem Asch, Lord Samuel, and Ben-Gurion. Schotz's deep Jewish feelings are reflected in a series of more experimental works, such as *The Prophet* (1957). The Catholic Church in Scotland commissioned from him monumental decorations for new churches.

Schotz is regarded as one of the most important Scottish sculptors of the 20th century and is sometimes known as the "Scottish Epstein." He was buried in Jerusalem. Schotz wrote an autobiography, *Bronze In My Blood: The Memoirs of Benno Schotz* (1981).

ADD. BIBLIOGRAPHY: ODNB online.

[Charles Samuel Spencer]

SCHRADER, ABE (1900–2001), U.S. apparel manufacturer. Schrader came to the U.S. in 1921 practically penniless, after feeling the effects of bigotry as a member of the Polish Army, and became the quintessential garment industry success story, an iconic figure whose life spanned the entire 20th century.

His mother had hoped he would become a rabbi, but he joined his uncle's company as a shipping clerk for $10 a week. After learning to cut patterns, he opened his own factory and was a contractor from 1927 to 1952. During World War II, his business prospered when he was contracted to make uniforms for the Women's Auxiliary Army Corps. In the early 1950s, Schrader decided to leave the anonymity of contracting and put his own name on the clothes he made. He briefly went into business with Leonard Arkin but eventually opened his own company, Abe Schrader Corp., building a $70 million business known for tasteful dresses and separates. The company went public in 1969, and in 1984 he sold his business to Interco Inc. of St. Louis for almost $40 million, remaining as chairman. Four years later Interco began to sell off its apparel units and Schrader tried to buy his company back. He could not come to terms, however, and retired in February 1989.

In addition to being a leading dress manufacturer for almost 40 years, Schrader led a campaign to have New York City recognized as "the fashion capital of the world," helped open channels between the industry and the city's government, and led the fight to have part of Seventh Avenue – the heart of the city's garment district – renamed Fashion Avenue. Schrader was also active politically. After becoming a major fundraiser for the 1964 presidential campaign of Lyndon B. Johnson, a man he admired because of his stance on civil rights, Schrader was invited to the White House on numerous occasions. He also led campaigns to raise money for the Federation of Jewish Philanthropies and for Israel Bonds. Schrader was known for his wry wit and intelligence and could quote Sartre, Dostoyevsky, and the Talmud as easily as he could price a dress. Although Schrader was an activist on behalf of his fellow manufacturers, he believed in labor unions and was a long-time confidante of David *Dubinsky, president of the International Ladies Garment Workers Union.

For many of the years he had been in business, Schrader was joined by his son Mort, who became president of Abe Schrader Corp. in 1968. Another son, Steven, was with the company for a short time, but established his own career in publishing. In 1988, the Fashion Institute of Technology in New York named one of its apparel manufacturing labs the Abe Schrader Production Laboratory. Schrader marked his 100th birthday in October 2000 with a party for more than 200 guests at New York's Plaza Hotel. He spent part of the night dancing.

[Mort Sheinman (2nd ed.)]

SCHRAMECK, ABRAHAM (1867–1948), French politician. Schrameck was born in Saint Etienne into a family of Alsatian Jews. His grandfather was a soldier in Napoleon's army. He was made *chef de cabinet* to the Paris chief of police, following the government decision to order a retrial of *Dreyfus. He achieved a considerable reputation as an administrator in preventing serious disorders and was subsequently appointed secretary-general of the Bouches-du-Rhône department which included Marseilles, then harried by criminal gangs. Once more Schrameck carried out his task with distinction and was later made prefect of the Tarn-et-Garonne and Bouches-du-Rhône districts. In 1914 Schrameck was appointed governor general of Madagascar, where he suppressed German plots against the French administration and organized the supply of materials for the Allies from the island. He also introduced economic reforms which increased the loyalty of the natives to France. Schrameck returned to France in 1920 and sat until 1940 as a senator for the Bouches-du-Rhône department. He was twice minister of the interior and was also minister of justice and a member of several Senate committees. A professing Jew, he vigorously defended the Jewish cause.

[Shulamith Catane]

SCHRECKER, PAUL (1889–1963), historian of philosophy. Born in Vienna, he was appointed associate editor of the Prussian Academy of Sciences' project of publishing the complete critical edition of Leibniz's works. The project was suspended in 1933, under the Nazis. Schrecker lost his post and fled to Paris, where he worked in the Centre Nationale de la Recherche Scientifique on the history of philosophy and the history of science. With D. Roustan, he began a critical edition of Malebranche's writings. The first volume appeared in 1938, and the second was under way when the Germans took over Paris. He prepared an edition of some of Leibniz' Latin writings, which he translated into French also. An English translation of some works of Leibniz by Schrecker and his wife appeared posthumously. He immigrated to the United States and was professor at the New School of Social Research, 1941–45, and at Swarthmore, Haverford, and Bryn Mawr colleges near Philadelphia, and from 1950 to 1961 at the University of Pennsylvania. He wrote many articles on themes in the history of philosophy, history of science, and philosophy of history, and a book, *Work and History: An Essay on the Structure of Civilization* (1948).

[Richard H. Popkin]

SCHREINER, MARTIN (**Mordechai**; 1863–1926), scholar in the field of medieval Jewish and Islamic letters. Schreiner was born into a poor family in Nagyvarad, Hungary, and in his youth lost his father, a Hebrew teacher. During 1882–87 he studied at the Rabbinical Seminary and the University of Budapest, where he came under the influence of Ignaz *Goldziher. Schreiner served as rabbi in Csurgo in 1887–92, and during 1892–94 as instructor at the Jewish Teachers' Training Institute in Budapest. From 1894 to 1902 he was a professor at the Lehranstalt fuer die Wissenschaft des Judentums in Berlin. Becoming mentally ill in 1902, he spent the rest of his life, a quarter of a century, in a sanatorium.

Schreiner's contributions to learning appeared in 1884–1902 and were of an increasingly high order, marked by erudition and penetrating analysis of Islamic intellectual development, its impact on medieval Jewish thought, interfaith polemics, Jewish philosophy, and *Karaism. While his scholarly work was published in German or French, he wrote in a more popular vein in Hungarian. He was interested in current communal affairs and exercised a strong influence on his students. His last major publication was *Die juengsten Urteile ueber das Judenthum* ... (1902), directed against the academic Jew-baiting of de Lagarde, E.V. Hartmann, E. Meyer, and Houston Chamberlain.

Most of his studies appeared in MGWJ (vols. 34, 35, 40, 42, 43); ZAW (vol. 6); REJ (vols., 12, 29, 31); ZDMG (vols. 42, 45, 48, 52, 53); ZHB (vols. 1, 3); *Bericht der Lehranstalt fuer die Wissenschaft des Judentums*, 13 (1895); 18 (1900); the Acts of the VIII Orientalist Congress; and *Semitic Studies in Memory of G.A. Kohut* (1897), 495–513.

BIBLIOGRAPHY: K. Wilhelm, in: *Living Legacy, Essays in Honor of Hugo Hahn* (1963), index; B. Elsass, in: *Emlékkönyv* (of the Budapest Seminary), 2 (1927), 100–6; A. Scheiber, in: *Israelitisches Wochenblatt fuer die Schweiz* (Sept. 4, 1964).

[Moshe Perlmann]

SCHREKER, FRANZ (1878–1934), composer and conductor. Born in Monaco, after studying in Vienna Schreker became conductor of the Volksoper there (1907) and founded the Vienna Philharmonic Choir (1908). He became head of the State High School for Music, Berlin, and in 1932, professor of composition at the Prussian Academy of Arts. He was dismissed in 1933 when the Nazis rose to power. Schreker was known for his operas, which had rich Wagnerian orchestration, daring harmonies, and somewhat erotic libretti that were written by the composer. Among them were *Der ferne Klang* (1912), *Vom ewigen Leben* (1929), and *Christophorus* (1932).

SCHRENZEL, MOSES (1838–1912), ideologist of Jewish nationalism. Born in Lemberg, Schrenzel was a property owner and, as is apparent from his book on banking problems in Austria (1876), was well informed on economic matters. In 1881 he published a booklet entitled *Die Loesung der Judenfrage* ("The Solution of the Jewish Problem") and in the same year brought out a supplement. The booklets express the writer's disillusionment with Jewish emancipation in Europe, especially in light of the situation of the Jews in the most advanced country in Western Europe, Germany. He saw the only solution to the Jewish problem in the establishment of an independent Jewish state and Jewish engagement in agriculture there. The best locality for the Jewish state, he believed, was North America, since in Ereẓ Israel land was expensive, and once the rulers of Ereẓ Israel, the Turks, discovered Jewish activities there "not only will they expel us, they will also annihilate us." These two pamphlets aroused much opposition, both among those who believed in emancipation and those who favored the settlement of Ereẓ Israel. The similar ideas advanced by Leon *Pinsker in his *Autoemancipation*, which appeared after Schrenzel's pamphlets, lead to the assumption that he had read the pamphlets before publishing his book, besides being aware of the controversy they had aroused in the press. Several years later Schrenzel changed his opinion about Ereẓ Israel and founded a society called Kreuzer Verein ("Penny Society"), the contributions of whose members were intended for the purchase of land in Ereẓ Israel for the purpose of Jewish settlement. The society, whose regulations emphasized national ownership of the land to be purchased, never reached the stage of practical activity.

BIBLIOGRAPHY: D.B. Weinryb, in: *Davar*, Literary Supplement (Oct. 23, 1936), 2–3; *ibid.* (Oct. 30, 1936), 5–6 (Heb. trans. of the booklets with introduction).

[Getzel Kressel]

SCHRIRE, VELVA (1916–1972), South African cardiologist. Schrire was born in Kimberley, South Africa, and after completing his medical studies at the University of Cape Town proceeded to London, where he studied cardiology at the National Heart Hospital. Returning to South Africa, he founded the Cardiac Clinic at the Groote Schuur Hospital in Cape Town in 1951, and under his leadership the clinic achieved an international reputation, with Schrire playing a decisive part as a member of the team under Dr. Christiaan Barnard which performed the first heart transplant in history. In 1964 he was appointed associate professor of medicine at his university, and was promoted to full professor a few weeks before his death. Together with Barnard he published *The Surgery of Common Congenital Cardiac Malformations* (1966) and, in the same year, *Clinical Cardiology.*

SCHUB, MOSHE DAVID (1854–1938), Ereẓ Israel pioneer. Born in Moineşti, *Romania, Schub was a *shoḥet* in his home town. As early as the 1870s he was among the founders of an association for settlement in Ereẓ Israel, which sent him to buy land there in 1882. He acquired the abandoned settlement Ja'ūna near Safed. At the end of that year *Rosh Pinnah was established on this land, Schub was elected head of its committee and obtained permission from the Turkish authorities in *Damascus to build houses there. When the settlement came under the patronage of Baron *Rothschild, Schub refused to cooperate with Rothschild's officials, gave up his land, and became headmaster of the first Hebrew school in the settlement. In 1891 he under took the management of the new settlement *Mishmar ha-Yarden and was later manager of *Ein Zeitim. At the invitation of Ḥovevei Zion he went to Germany in 1896 to run the exhibition of Jewish settlements in the Holy Land held in *Berlin and Cologne. There he met Theodor *Herzl, became one of his ardent supporters, and accompanied him on his visit to Ereẓ Israel in 1898.

He wrote many articles in Hebrew, Yiddish, and German on the problems of Jewish agricultural settlement. His writings include a history of the settlement, *Yesud ha-Ma'alah* (1931), and his memoirs, *Zikhronot le-Veit David* (1937), which is also a valuable source on the early history of Jewish settlement in Ereẓ Israel.

BIBLIOGRAPHY: I. Klausner, *Ḥibbat Ẓiyyon be-Romanyah* (1951), index; idem, *Mi-Katoviẓ ad Basel* (1965), index.

[Yehuda Slutsky]

°**SCHUBERT, KURT** (1923–), Austrian scholar. Schubert, a Catholic, was born in Vienna. He was the founder and head of the Institute for Judaic Studies (Judasitik) at Vienna University and chairman of the Austrian Christian-Jewish Friendship League. Schubert initiated the establishment of the Austrian Jewish Museum in Eisenstadt and was appointed to eliminate antisemitic references in Catholic textbooks and passion plays. He edited the periodicals *Kairos* (1959–94/5) and *Studia Judaica Austriaca* (1974–92). Among Schubert's published works are *Die Religion des nachbiblischen Judentums* (1955); *Israel – Staat der Hoffnung* (1957); *Die Gemeinde vom Toten Meer* (1958; Eng. transl. *Dead Sea Community*, 1959); *Die Kultur der Juden* (2 vol., 1970, 1979); *Juedische Geschichte* (1995); and, together with his wife, Ursula, *Juedische Buchkunst* (2 vol., 1983, 1992).

BIBLIOGRAPHY: C. Thoma, in: C. Thoma, G. Stemberger, J. Maier (eds.): *Judentum* (1993) 9–21; [no author], in: *David*, 11 (1999), 25–29, 42.

[Mirjam Triendl-Zadoff (2nd ed.)]

SCHUBERT, LIA (1926–), dancer and choreographer. Schubert was born in Vienna and trained with the Russian ballerinas Preobrazhenska and Egoreva in Paris. During World War II, her family was deported but she escaped. After the war, she worked with Leonid Massine and, in 1950, was a dancer and the choreographer of the Malmö City Theater in Sweden. In 1953, she moved to Stockholm and, in 1957, founded the Ballet Academy at Stockholm University, which she directed until she left for Israel in 1968. In 1969, Schubert and Caj Lottman, known professionally as Caj Selling, the male star of the Royal

Swedish Ballet, founded the Institute for Dance in Haifa. The Institute comprised a children's dance school, a two-year training course for dance teachers, and, in 1971–74, a modern dance company called The Dancers Stage. In 1974, Schubert and Lottman established The Haifa Piccolo Ballet, which performed in the style of classical ballet. In 1976, Selling left the company to become the artistic director of the *Batsheva Dance Company. Although the Institute was highly esteemed, it accumulated debts and, in 1980, Schubert left Israel and returned to Sweden. Most dance teachers in Haifa and the north of Israel, as well as many dancers, were students at the Institute.

[Ruth Eshel (2nd ed.)]

SCHÜCK, JOHAN HENRIK EMIL (1855–1947), Swedish literary historian. Born in Stockholm, Schück was the child of a mixed marriage, his mother being a non-Jewess. From 1898 until 1920 he was professor of literature at the University of Uppsala, where he also served as rector (1905–18). His historical approach to literary research profoundly influenced later Swedish criticism and his gifted teaching produced several outstanding pupils, notably Oskar Ivar *Levertin and Martin *Lamm. In 1918, five years after his election to the Swedish Academy, Schück was honored with the post of president of the Nobel Foundation. After publishing an important study of Shakespeare (1883–84), he planned a large history of world literature, only two parts of which appeared: *Antiken* (1900) and *Den israelitiska litteraturen* (1906). Later, however, he produced a six-volume manual of general literature (1919–26); histories of the Swedish people (1913–15) and of the Swedish Academy (1935–39); and a history of the literatures and academies of antiquity (8 vols., 1932–44). His outstanding achievement was the monumental *Illustrerad svensk litteraturhistoria* (1895–97; 7 vols., 1926–33²), written in collaboration with Karl Johan *Warburg. Together with R.G. Berg and F. Böök he also published an immense anthology of Swedish literature from 1500 to 1900 (30 vols., 1921–22) and an anthology of world literature in Swedish translation (3 vols., 1932). As a critic, Schück always excelled in clear analysis of genres and literary periods.

°SCHUDT, JOHANN JAKOB (1664–1722), German Christian Hebraist, pedagogue, and Orientalist from Frankfurt am Main. The son of a Lutheran priest, Schudt studied theology in Wittenberg, and in 1684 went to Hamburg to study Oriental languages, including Hebrew. In 1689 he returned to Frankfurt, where he served in different positions in the local gymnasium, becoming its rector in 1717.

Schudt devoted himself especially to the fields of Hebrew and Jewish history and antiquities. He became interested in the Jews, their customs and history through his Oriental studies and meetings with Jews in Hamburg and Frankfurt. Another factor accounting for his interest was his desire to convert Jews to Christianity. The writing of what later became his most renowned work, *Juedische Merkwuerdigkeiten* ("Jewish Peculiarities," 1714–18), was motivated by the great fire of the Frankfurt ghetto on Jan. 14, 1711. The work consists of four volumes. The first volume is a detailed account of Jewish communities all over the world. In the second volume, which is devoted to an ethnographic depiction of the Jews of Frankfurt, Schudt provides detailed and mostly first-hand information about their history, ways of life, customs, professions, language, and clothing. The third volume contains Yiddish poems, such as the account of the Vincent *Fettmilch disturbances, a Purim play and comedy, and legislation concerning Frankfurt Jewry. The fourth volume contains supplements to the first three.

Although Schudt stated that his aim was to seek the truth and avoid all preconceived opinion, he drew upon doubtful sources which presented the Jews in an unfavorable light, and often referred to *Eisenmenger's *Entdecktes Judentum*. Thus he transmitted such contemporary prejudices as that Jews were predisposed to usury and cheating, deploring their supposed insolence and pride, and their *foetor Judaens* ("Jewish stench"). However, he was skeptical of the *blood libel and the alleged desecrating of the *Host. When Schudt presents actual reports, especially those dealing with the Jews of Frankfurt, his books are an important historical source for the life and culture of the German Jews in the 17th century. Among his many works one should also note *Compendium historiae judaicae* (1700), *Vita Jephtae* (1701), and *Juedisches Franckfurter und Prager Freuden-Fest* (1716).

ADD. BIBLIOGRAPHY: Y. Deutsch, "Johann Jacob Schudt – Der erste Ethnograph der juedischen Gemeinde in Frankfurt am Main," in: F. Backhaus et al. (eds.), *Die Frankfurter Judengasse* (2005), 57–65; C.J. Joecher, *Allgemeines Gelehrten Lexicon* (Leipzig 1751; repr. 1961), 368–9; H. Schreckenberg, *Die christlichen Adversus-Judaeos-Texte und ihr literarisches und historisches Umfeld (13.–20. Jh.)*. (1994), 704–5; B. Suchy, *Lexikographie und Juden im 18. Jahrhundert* (1979), 12–13.

[Reuven Michael / Aya Elyada (2nd ed.)]

SCHUECK, JENÖ (1895–1974), Hungarian rabbi. Schueck was born in Onod, north Hungary, where his father was rabbi. After World War II he was appointed rabbi to one of the districts of Budapest, where he founded and maintained a home for Orthodox Jewish children from the country districts. He was appointed chaplain to the Hungarian armed forces and later Senior Orthodox chaplain. In this capacity he was extremely active in finding solutions to the problems of *agunot*. During this period Schueck played a prominent part in the reconstruction of Orthodox Judaism in Hungary. In 1960 he was appointed rabbi of Miskolc and became president of the Hungarian Council of Orthodox Rabbis. At the request of the Hungarian authorities he joined the World Union of Hungarians, an organization centered in Budapest for the promotion of the Hungarian viewpoint throughout the world. He represented Hungarian Orthodox Jewry at the Conference of European Orthodox Rabbis held in London in 1965.

Among his publications in Hungarian are *As ortodoxia a felszabadulás után* ("Orthodox Judaism after the Liberation," Yearbook, Budapest, 1959); *A két Szofer dinasztia* ("Two Dynasties of the Sofer Family," Yearbook, Budapest, 1960/61); *A miskolci hitközség multijából* ("On the History of the Community of Miskolc," Yearbook, Budapest, 1971/72). He also published an annual *Luaḥ*.

BIBLIOGRAPHY: L. Saluó, in: *Uj Élet* (Sept. 1, 1974).

[Yehouda Marton]

°**SCHUERER, EMIL** (1844–1910), leading Protestant New Testament scholar. Born in Augsburg, Germany, the son of a merchant, Schürer studied theology at the universities of Erlangen, Berlin, and Heidelberg. In Heidelberg he was particularly influenced by Richard Rothe. He received his doctorate at Leipzig in 1868 and taught at the universities of Giessen (from 1878), Kiel (from 1890), and Göttingen (from 1895), where among his colleagues he counted Willamowitz-Möllendorf and Julius Wellhausen. Two achievements of his many-sided scholarship are especially noteworthy: his founding in Leipzig in 1876 of the *Theologische Literaturzeitung*, which he published for many years, thereby wielding an enduring influence on the critico-historical research of his time; and, even more important, his *Geschichte des juedischen Volkes im Zeitalter Jesu Christi* (Leipzig, 1901–09; index volume 1911). These were the third and fourth editions; the first appeared in 1874 under the title *Lehrbuch der neutestamentlichen Zeitgeschichte*, and the second (Leipzig, 1886–1900) also appeared in English under the title, *A History of the Jewish People in the Time of Jesus Christ* (1885–91). In 1888 a partial translation appeared in Dutch. Another partial translation is *A History of the Jewish People in the Time of Jesus*, edited with an introduction by Naḥum N. Glatzer (New York, 1961, 1963).

Schuerer's historiographic concept evolves from a thesis which he formulated in the introduction as follows: "There is not one detail in evangelic history, not one word in Jesus' message, which can be understood without a knowledge of Jewish history and of the Jewish people's world of ideas." An elucidation of New Testament history can therefore in particular be expected from research into post-biblical Judaism of this era. Schuerer's achievement thus differs from that of all his predecessors by excluding from his study the non-Jewish ancient world and, simultaneously, by aspiring to make critical use as comprehensively as possible of all available sources (literary texts, inscriptions, papyri, coins), together with almost all of the so-called secondary literature. That his historical review commenced not with the conquest of Jerusalem by Pompey, but with the Maccabean revolt – because it was here that he detected the origins of later developments in the Jewish people's internal history – also constituted a new approach. Schuerer's encyclopedic work, dry and without stylistic pretensions, does not attempt to put forward daring hypotheses or even historico-theological interpretations. Occasionally, he seems to show a cool reserve with regard to the material, which, in his presentation of the Jewish religion, leads to a conspicuous narrowing of his horizon, as he restricts himself to dealing only with the messianic expectation and with the external fulfillment of the Law. This reserve approaches unconcealed hostility in the chapter "Das Leben unter dem Gesetz" (II, 464–96) in which he deals with the legalistic side of Jewish piety, taking the point of view of the New Testament.

By the 1960s the need was felt for a thorough revision and updating of what was by then considered a minor classic. The new English edition was organized by the late Matthew Black (1908–1994) of the University of St. Andrews, and carried out by three Oxford scholars, Geza Vermes, Fergus Millar, and Martin Goodman, with the late Pamela Vermes as literary editor, under the title *The History of the Jewish People in the Age of Jesus Christ* in three volumes (1973, 1979, 1986/87). The editors resolved not to mark additions, corrections, and deletions in the text, but to revise it directly, introducing four types of change: (a) the removal of out-of-date items of bibliography and purely polemical material; (b) the revision of the bibliographies; (c) the correction and modernization of the references to, and quotation of, literary texts, papyri, inscriptions and coin legends in Greek, Latin, Hebrew and Aramaic; and (d) above all, the addition of relevant new archaeological, epigraphic, papyrological and numismatic material. This has meant the introduction not only of fresh data of a type already known to Schuerer, but also of wholly new areas of evidence, such as the Babylonian tablets relative to Seleucid chronology, the Dead Sea Scrolls, and the Bar Kokhba documents.

The revised work has preserved as much as possible of the original Schuerer and has offered a substantially updated compendium for research for the use of late 20th and early 21st-century historians of Judaism in the age of Jesus. The new English Schuerer has subsequently been translated into Spanish (*Historia del pueblo judio en tiempos de Jesus*, 1985) and into Italian (*Storia del popolo giudaico al tempo de Gesù Cristo*, 1985–99).

BIBLIOGRAPHY: A. Harnack, in: *Theologische Literaturzeitung*, 35 (1910), 289–92; A.B. Titius, *Realenzyklopaedie für protestantische Theologie und Kirche*. 24 (1913), 460–46 (with bibliography); G.F. Moore, in: HTR, 14 (1921), 237–41; E. Bammel, in: *Deutsches Pfarrerblatt*, 60 (1960), 225–26. **ADD. BIBLIOGRAPHY:** M. Hengel, "*Der alte und der neue Schuerer*," in: JSS, 35 (1990), 19–72; A. Oppenheimer (ed.), *Juedische Geschichte in hellenistisch-roemischer Zeit – Wege der Forschung: Vom alten zum neuen Schuerer* (1999).

[Heinz Schreckenberg / Geza Vermes (2nd ed.)]

SCHUHL, PIERRE-MAXIME (1902–1984), French philosopher. Born in Paris, he received his doctorate there in 1934. He taught at Montpellier and was appointed professor at Toulouse in 1938. In World War II Schuhl was a captain in a motorized division; he was captured and spent 1940–44 at the Colditz camp for officers of various Allied countries. After the war he became a professor at the Sorbonne, and chairman of its philosophy department in 1962. He was also editor of the *Revue philosophique* from 1952, and editor of the series *Bibliothèque de Philosophie contemporaine*. In addition, Schuhl was president of the Société des Etudes Juives (1949–52). His main interest was in Greek philosophy, especially that of Socrates and

Plato. He wrote on these subjects as well as on their influences on later thinkers, ancient and modern.

His books include *Platon et l'art de son temps* (1933, 1952^2); *Essai sur la formation de la pensée grecque* (1934, 1949^2; his thesis); *Machinisme et philosophie* (1938, 1947^2); *Etudes sur la fabulation platonicienne* (1947); *Pour connaître la pensée de Lord Bacon* (1949); he edited, *Trois essais de Montaigne* (1951); *L'Oeuvre de Platon* (1954); *Etudes platoniciennes* (1960), which includes an essay on contacts between Jewish and Greek thinkers; and *Le Dominateur et les possibles* (1960).

[Richard H. Popkin]

SCHULBERG, BUDD WILSON (1914–), U.S. author. Born in New York, Schulberg was for some time, like his father, a Hollywood screenwriter. His first and best-known novel, *What Makes Sammy Run?* (1941), is largely a description of a ruthless Jewish success-hunter in Hollywood during the 1930s, with a sentimental portrayal of Sammy's East Side family. From 1943 to 1946 he served in the U.S. Navy, in the Office of Strategic Services, and was decorated for collecting the photographic evidence used at the Nuremberg Trial (1945–46). Schulberg's subsequent works include *The Harder They Fall* (1947); *The Disenchanted* (1950); *Some Faces in the Crowd* (1953); and the script of the prize-winning film, *On the Waterfront* (1954), which Schulberg turned into a novel, *Waterfront* (1955). During the hearings of the House Un-American Activities, Schulberg was identified as a member of the Communist Party. In 1951, in a telegram to HUAC, as well as in subsequent testimony, Schulberg stated that he had a Communist affiliation from 1937 to 1940 but pointed out that his "opposition to communists and Soviet dictatorship is a matter of record." Among his later works are *From the Ashes: Voices of Watts*, edited by him and published in 1967, and *The Four Seasons of Success* (1972), his understanding of what several writers made of their success and/or failure. His autobiography, *Moving Pictures: Memories of a Hollywood Prince*, was published in 1981.

ADD. BIBLIOGRAPHY: N. Beck, *Budd Schulberg: A Bio-Bibliography* (2001); E. Bentley, *Thirty Years of Treason: Excerpts from Hearings before the House Committee on Un-American Activities, 1938–1968* (1971).

SCHULHOF, ISAAC (d. c. 1733), rabbi; chronicler of the siege of Buda (Ofen, see *Budapest) of 1686. Born in Prague, on his mother's side he was a descendent of *Judah Loew b. Bezalel. He married the daughter of Ephraim Cohen, a fugitive from the *Chmielnicki massacres. The family settled in Buda in 1666, where Ephraim was appointed rabbi; he died in a plague, before the siege. After the death of his father-in-law, Schulhof became the leading figure in one of the circles for prayer and study which devoted three nights a week to prayer. In his work *Megillat Ofen* ("Scroll of Ofen"), he describes the capture of the city from the Turks, the desperate defense they put up, and the extreme cruelty of the Austrians, who looted, massacred, and thirsted after Jewish blood. His wife Esther lost her life and his eight-year-old son was taken captive and carried off to Raab (*Györ) in northwestern Hungary, where he died as a result of the torments endured in captivity. Schulhof parted from the prisoners and after many hardships arrived in *Mikulov. He proceeded to Prague, where he was appointed *dayyan* in 1697, remarried, and lived to an old age.

His only work (published by S. *Kohn and D. *Kaufmann in 1895) is an important source not only for the events described therein but also for information on that period and contemporary Jews.

BIBLIOGRAPHY: D. Kaufmann, *Die Erstuermung Ofens...* (1895), introduction; idem, *Gesammelte Schriften...*, 2 (1908–10), 296–327; S. Kohn, *Héber kutforrások és adatok Magyarország történetéhez* (1881).

[Baruch Yaron]

SCHULHOF, MOSHE (1947–), *ḥazzan*. Schulhof was born in New York, and is the son of Rabbi Dov Ber Schulhof, former president of Agudat Israel in Budapest. As a boy he sang in the choir of Seymour Silbermintz. He studied in the Mir and Beth Joseph *yeshivot* in New York, and learned cantorial music with David *Koussevitzky, furthering his musical studies at the Brooklyn Conservatory. At the age of 18 he was appointed cantor to the Adath Jeshurun synagogue in the Bronx, and afterwards served as cantor at the Shaare Torah synagogue in Pittsburgh. He then moved to the Adath Jeshurun synagogue of Montreal in Canada, and later to Shaarei Tefila synagogue in Los Angeles. Subsequently he became cantor of the Aventura Turnberry Beth Jacob Jewish Center in North Miami Beach and a faculty member of the Academy of Jewish Religion in New York. Schulhof is also a recognized authority on *nusaḥ ha-tefillah* as well as a gifted teacher of *ḥazzanut*, having many students who are themselves professional cantors. During his career, Schulhof performed in concerts with the Israeli Philharmonic, was the featured artist at the international Cantors' Convention, and often performed on "Cantorial Cruises." Schulhoff has an extensive discography including *Greeting from Russia*, *Masterpieces of the Synagogue*, *Moshe Schulhof and the Johannesburg Jewish Male Chorus*, and *From Generation to Generation*.

[Akiva Zimmerman / Raymond Goldstein (2nd ed.)]

SCHULHOFF, JULIUS (1825–1898), piano virtuoso and composer. Born in Prague, Schulhoff made his debut in Dresden in 1842. He later moved to Paris and gained the patronage of Chopin, to whom he dedicated his first composition. After a series of recitals and concert tours he devoted himself to teaching in Dresden in 1870, and shortly before his death moved to Berlin. His compositions, all for the piano, include a sonata, études, and waltzes. His light, brilliant pieces such as his *Galop di Bravura* were particularly successful.

His great-grandnephew, ERWIN SCHULHOFF (1894–1942), was also a pianist and composer. He was born in Prague, taught at the Prague Conservatory and from 1935 worked for the Czech radio. He was active in the promotion of contemporary music in his many concert tours and especially at the

Festivals of the International Society for Contemporary Music. In 1942 he was seized by the Nazis and died in the Wuelzburg (Bavaria) concentration camp.

His compositions favor the grotesque and make use of atonal and polytonal devices, jazz-like idioms, and quartertone experiments. They include symphonies; works for voice and orchestra; a ballet, *La Somnambule* (1931); an opera, *Plameny* ("The Flames", 1932); and chamber music. His works with political themes are *Symphony of Freedom* (1941) and his oratorio *The Communist Manifesto*, performed posthumously in Prague in 1962.

BIBLIOGRAPHY: Grove, Dict; MGG, s.v. (incl. bibl.).

SCHULLER, GUNTHER (Alexander; 1925–), U.S. horn player and composer. Born in New York, Schuller studied and later taught at the Manhattan School of Music. He played the horn in the Cincinnati Symphony Orchestra and at the Metropolitan Opera, New York (1945–59). In 1957 he coined the term "Third Stream" for the combination of jazz improvisations with classical musical forms, and in 1962 directed the first international jazz festival in Washington. His interests as a composer ranged widely over both popular and classical traditions, and he made syntheses of diverse elements and techniques developed by 20th-century composers: Stravinsky's rhythm, Schoenberg's serialism, Webern's orchestration, and Babbitt's principles of "combinatoriality." His compositions include a *Symphony for Brass* (1950); a ballet, *Variants* (1960); a piano concerto (1962); a cello concerto (1945); two operas: *The Visitation* (Hamburg, 1966), which is based on Kafka's novel *The Trial*, and *The Fisherman and His Wife*, a chamber opera for children (Boston, 1970). A collection of his writings can be found in his book *Musings: The Musical Worlds of Gunther Schuller* (1986).

BIBLIOGRAPHY: Grove Music Online; L. Larsen: "A Study and Comparison of Samuel Barber's 'Vanessa,' Robert Ward's 'The Crucible,' and Gunther Schuller's 'The Visitation' (diss., U. of Indiana, 1971).

[Israela Stein (2nd ed.)]

SCHULMAN, KALMAN (1819–1899), Hebrew writer of the Haskalah era. Born in Stari Bichov, Belorussia, he studied in his youth in Lithuanian yeshivot but, attracted by the Haskalah, he studied Bible, grammar, and German independently. He settled in Vilna in 1843, where he tutored the sons of affluent families. He joined the circle of *maskilim* in the town and became a close friend of the poet M.J. *Lebensohn. From 1849 to 1861 he taught Hebrew language and literature in the high school attached to the state rabbinical school. After leaving this post he devoted himself to literary work, and was under contract with Romm publishers, who paid him a pittance that scarcely enabled him to support his family. His books, mostly translations, were intended to spread Haskalah among the Hebrew reading public and youth. Schulman was moderate and careful in expressing his ideas, and his books, many of which went through several editions, were also popular in Orthodox circles. His widely read abridged translation of *Mystères de Paris* (1857–60 and five more editions in the next half-century), an adventure novel by the French writer, Eugène Sue, was an innovative experiment in the translation of a contemporary novel into Hebrew; it triggered a dispute, for the conservative circles believed it was sacrilegious to use the Hebrew language for a description of the Paris underworld. This controversy probably deterred Schulman from translating more novels, and he devoted himself to translating and adapting scientific books. *Divrei Yemei Olam*, a history in nine volumes, based on Georg Weber and other German historians, was commissioned by Ḥevrat Mefiẓei Haskalah (*Society for the Promotion of Culture among the Jews of Russia; 1867–84). His translation of Josephus from German into Hebrew, focusing on the *Wars of the Jews* (1861–63), was the first rendition of the Jewish historian into Hebrew. His book on Bar Kokhba's heroism, *Harisot Beitar* (1858), was influential and popular. Schulman, a prolific contributor to the Hebrew press, published a series of books and compilations dealing with the history of Palestine and its environs, *Toledot Ḥakhmei Yisrael* (4 vols., 1873–78). Schulman used a florid biblical Hebrew, and was skillful in the presentation of new terms. His books have been forgotten, but in their time played an important role in developing the Hebrew reading public. Among his other works are *Safah Berurah* (1848) and the geographies, *Mosedei Ereẓ* (1871–77), and *Meḥkerei Ereẓ Rusyah* (1870).

BIBLIOGRAPHY: Klausner, Sifrut, 3 (1953), 361–88; A. Sha'anan, *Ha-Sifrut ha-Ivrit ha-Ḥadashah li-Zerameha* (1962), 219–22; Waxman, Literature, 3 (1960^2), 310–2; Kressel, Leksikon, 2 (1967), 890–2.

[Yehuda Slutsky]

SCHULMAN, SAMUEL (1864–1955), U.S. Reform rabbi. Schulman, born in Russia, was taken to the U.S. as a small child. By the age of 13 he had a significant knowledge of Hebrew and of the Talmud. He received his B.A. from the City College of New York in 1885 and then went to the Berlin Hochschule fuer die Wissenschaft des Judentums (1885–89), where he received his ordination. Returning to the U.S., he briefly served as rabbi in New York City and then in Helena, Montana, from 1890 to 1893 and in Kansas City from 1893 to 1899. In 1899 Schulman moved to Temple Beth El in New York City, remaining there until 1927 when it merged with New York's Temple Emanu-El, the wealthiest and most prestigious Reform congregation in the U.S. He retired in 1935. An eloquent orator, Schulman was also one of the most learned figures in Judaism in the U.S. Reform movement, on which he sought to exert a moderating influence. He was president of the Central Conference of American Rabbis from 1911 to 1913 and president of the Association of Reform Rabbis of New York from 1921 to 1926. He was president of the interdenominational Synagogue Council of America from 1934 to 1935 and director and vice president of the YMHA Association of New York. In addition, he served as one of the non-Zionist members chosen to sit on the executive committee of the Jewish Agency for Palestine in 1929. His main activity outside the rabbinate, however, was devoted to the Jewish Publication Society of America; he was a member of its publishing committee for many years and took part in the society's retranslation of the Bible into English that commenced in 1903 and was concluded in 1917. He argued for the greater incorporation of Jewish ritual into Reform Judaism and was a moderating force at the Columbus Platform of 1937, that repudiated the earlier *Pittsburgh Platform.

[Hillel Halkin]

SCHULMANN, ELIEZER (1837–1904), Hebrew writer; researcher into the history of Yiddish language and literature. He was born in Salant, Lithuania, and became treasurer of one of the large enterprises of the *Brodski family in Kiev. Financially independent, he spent his free time doing research and contributed to various Hebrew papers (*Ha-Shaḥar, Ha-Asif, Pardes, Ha-Shiloʾaḥ*, etc.). He made his name in Hebrew literature with his richly researched studies of Heine and Ludwig Boerne (*Mi-Mekor Yisrael*, 1877 and 1894), which illuminated these writers' characters, actions, and era. For many years Schulmann pursued research into the Yiddish language and its early literature.

Noteworthy among his essays on this subject is *Imkei ha-Safah* (*Ha-Shiloʾaḥ*, 4 (1898)), and a monograph, *Safah Yehudit-Ashkenazit ve-Sifrutah mi-Keẓ ha-Meʾah ha-Tet-Vav ad Keẓ Shenot ha-Meʾah ha-Yod-Ḥet* ("German-Yiddish and its Literature from the Late 15th Century to the Late 18th Century," 1913). His attitude to what he termed a "mixed language" was negative, but he saw in Yiddish "an integral part of us, in which the spirit of our nation is displayed just as in our primal literature, Hebrew." The book is important for its originality and the abundance of citations from manuscripts and old editions.

BIBLIOGRAPHY: Rejzen, Leksikon, 4 (1929), 548–52; Klausner, Sifrut, 5 (19572) 275–9; Waxman, Literature, index.

[Yehuda Slutsky]

SCHULSINGER, JOSEPH (d. 1943?), Belgian author. A religious Zionist active in Antwerp Jewish life, Schulsinger contributed to various Jewish periodicals. *La génuflexion d'Alénou* (1932), his historical drama about Jewish persecution in Ferrara, led to an interesting correspondence with the French poet and playwright Paul Claudel (*Cahiers de Paul Claudel*, vol. 7, 1968). He was deported by the Nazis.

°**SCHULTENS, ALBERT** (1686–1756), Dutch Orientalist. Schultens studied theology and Oriental languages in his native city Groningen, where in 1706 he defended his *Dissertatio theologica-philologica de utilitate linguae Arabicae in interpretanda sacra lingua*. In 1707 he studied in Utrecht with Adrian *Reland, whose emphasis on interpreting Hebrew with the help of, inter alia, Persian, strengthened Schultens' conviction of the importance of Oriental cognates for the retrieval of the *primitiva significatio* or *origines* of Hebrew. In 1713 Schultens was appointed ordinary professor in Franeker. In 1729 he left for Leiden, where he was entrusted with the supervision of the Oriental manuscripts. Within three years, he was appointed professor *linguarum orientalium*.

Schultens employed the inductive empirical method characteristic of Dutch enlightened science. His comparative methodology (known as the Dutch School) was based on the theory of the "sisterly relationship" between Hebrew and Arabic, and deeply influenced 18th-century study of Hebrew, both in the Netherlands and abroad.

Schultens published grammatical works, including *Institutiones* (Leiden, 1737) and *Vetus et Regia Via Hebraizandi* (Leiden, 1738), various dissertations on the comparative method (*Oratio de fontibus*, 1713, *Origines Hebraeae*, 1724, *Oratio de linguae Arabicae antiquissima origine*, 1729), and philological commentaries on Job (1737, also translated into English and German) and Proverbs (1748).

BIBLIOGRAPHY: BWN, 17:526–30; NNBW, 5:707–11; J. Nat, *De studie van de Oostersche talen in Nederland in de 18e en 19e eeuw* (1930); J.G. Gerretzen, *Schola Hemsterhusiana* (1940). J. Noordegraaf, in: *History and Rationality* (1995), 133–55; A.J. Klijnsmit, in: *Helmantica*, 154 (2000), 139–66.

[Irene E. Zwiep (2nd ed.)]

SCHULTZ, DUTCH (**Arthur Simon Flegenheimer**, "The Dutchman"; 1902–1935), U.S. gangster of the 1920s and 1930s, only boss of Murder Incorporated to be killed by Murder Inc. Born in Manhattan to Emma Neu and Herman, Austrian-German immigrants, Schultz was raised in the Bronx after his father abandoned the family when Schultz was young. Leaving school at 14 in order to support himself and his mother, Schultz worked for low-level mobsters at a neighborhood nightclub and robbed crap games before graduating to burglary. On December 12, 1919, he was caught breaking into an apartment in the Bronx and arrested and sentenced to jail, the first of 13 arrests but his only prison sentence. After serving 15 months, he took on the name "Dutch Schultz," the nickname of a notorious young gangster from the late 1800s. Schultz rode shotgun in trucks for mobster kingpin Arnold *Rothstein, and by 1928 was in business for himself working as a bootlegger and extortionist. With a quick temper and a reputation for brutality, Schultz muscled in for complete control in the Bronx of bootlegging, eliminating anyone who crossed him, like Legs Diamond and Vincent Coll, and, some say, Rothstein. With the end of Prohibition, he moved on to the numbers racket, and soon was named by the FBI as Public Enemy #1. On January 25, 1933, the state of New York indicted Schultz for tax evasion in the sum of $92,103.34. Schultz moved to Newark, New Jersey to evade arrest, but on November 28, 1934, he was surrendered in Albany on the tax indictment charges. The case in Syracuse ended in a hung jury on April 29, 1935, and he was acquitted in a second tax trial in Malone, N.Y., on August 2, 1935. Schultz wanted to have Special Prosecutor Thomas E. Dewey assassinated and presented a plan before the heads of the national Syndicate, including Lucky Luciano, Lepke *Buchalter, and Meyer *Lansky. But the Mob worried about the backlash of such a murder, and voted against the plan. Schultz left the meeting saying he would do it himself within 48 hours. As a result, hit men working for Buchalter's Murder, Inc. shot Schultz and three cohorts two days later on October 23, 1935, at the Palace Chop House, which served as Schultz's headquarters in Newark, N.J. The three bodyguards were shot dead, but Schultz was taken to Newark Hospital and held onto life for another day. As time passed, Schultz began talking incoherently and nonsensically, influenced by a high fever and large quantities of morphine. Police assigned a stenographer to write down everything he said right until he died at 8:35 P.M. on October 24, 1935. Schultz received last rites in his hospital room from a Roman Catholic priest at the request of Schultz's 21-year-old wife, Frances, after he had been baptized three months earlier while awaiting trial in Malone. At his funeral in a Catholic cemetery three days later, only his mother, sister, wife, and Father McInerney, who performed a Catholic service, were present. His mother had a Jewish *talit*, or prayer shawl, draped over the coffin.

Schultz's life, and specifically his death-bed confession, became legend, and were used by writers as the basis of numerous novels and feature films, including E.L. *Doctorow's *Billy Bathgate* (1989), which was made into the 1991 movie starring Dustin *Hoffman; William Burroughs' *The Last Words of Dutch Schultz* (1969); and the 1997 film *Hoodlum*. He was also the subject of Paul Sann's *Kill the Dutchman! The Story of Dutch Schultz* (1971).

[Elli Wohlgelernter (2nd ed.)]

SCHULTZ, HOWARD (1953–), U.S. entrepreneur. Born and reared in Brooklyn, N.Y., Schultz won a football scholarship to Northern Michigan University and graduated in 1975 with a major in communications. He had a variety of jobs and in 1981 traveled to Seattle to inspect a coffee bean store called Starbucks that had been buying many of the Hammarplast Swedish drip coffeemakers he was selling. After being hired by Starbucks, he became its director of marketing and operations in 1982. In Italy, Schultz discovered that coffee bars existed on practically every block and served as meeting places. The Starbucks owners resisted Schultz's plans to serve coffee in the stores, so Schultz quit and started his own coffee-bar business. It was an instant success, and a year later Schultz bought Starbucks for $3.8 million. The company began to expand rapidly in the 1990s, and Schultz introduced his customers to espresso drinks, café latte, and the frappuccino. Schultz did not pay his employees much, but he gave them comprehensive health coverage, including benefits for unmarried spouses. These moves increased loyalty. Starbucks went public in 1992 and grew at a rate of 25 to 35 percent a year. By the early 21st century the company had almost 4,000 stores in 25 countries, serving 15 million people a week. In 2000 Schultz bought the Seattle Supersonics professional basketball team, and he also owned the Seattle Storm in the women's professional league. He was also a significant stakeholder in Jamba Juice. Although he was a fervent supporter of Israel, Schultz did not have success with his Starbucks investment in Israel. All six coffeehouses in Tel Aviv closed in 2003.

[Stewart Kampel (2nd ed.)]

SCHULWEIS, HAROLD MAURICE (1925–), U.S. rabbi, theologian, community leader. Born in the Bronx, N.Y., Schulweis was educated at Yeshiva College, Jewish Theological Seminary of America, New York University, and the Pacific School of Religion in Berkeley, Calif. He taught philosophy at City College of New York before taking pulpits in Parkchester, N.Y., Oakland, Calif., and Encino, Calif.

Schulweis is widely regarded as the most successful and influential synagogue leader in his generation. His theology of the American synagogue extended the traditional role of the synagogue to encompass the full cultural life of a living Jewish community. Beginning in 1970, at Valley Beth Shalom in Encino, Schulweis introduced a series of synagogue innovations that spread widely among American congregations. These include: Synagogue-based "Havurot" – small groupings of families sharing learning and celebration in congregants' homes; "Response" – a support and educational organization welcoming gays and lesbians and their families into the synagogue; and "Keruv" – a vigorous outreach to unaffiliated Jews and "unchurched" Christians, offering classes and counseling toward conversion into Judaism.

As a theologian, Schulweis has reconsidered the classical concept of God. He locates God not above but *within* and *between* human beings, not a vertical relationship but communal and internal. The conception of "the God within and between" allows him to argue that revelation is both divine in origin and carried out by human powers of expression. Morality is the expression of conscience, which is a living nexus between the divine and the human in everyday life. Schulweis thought that by defining God as the source of history's dynamic, the conception of the personal God reduces the human being to passivity and subservience. Instead, Schulweis argues for a two-dimensioned conception: Elohim, the amoral God of nature; Adonai, the God of transformation, whose attributes of goodness – Godliness – we make real in bringing the world closer to perfection. Thus, the focus of religious experience and reflection for Schulweis is not God but "Godliness." This "predicate theology" concentrates upon God's attributes of goodness instead of arguing the existence of a personal, "Subject" God. In this way, Schulweis rescues belief from the problem of evil, and simultaneously restores the dignified place of the human being as God's Covenantal partner.

This conception runs aground if there is some circumstance wherein Adonai's attributes of Godliness are totally absent. The Holocaust would seem to present this scenario, prompting some to proclaim that the God of the Bible died at Auschwitz. In response, Schulweis notes that despite the overwhelming evil of the Holocaust, there remained "sparks" of Adonai even in that most benighted moment. In the late 1960s, Schulweis was introduced to a Jewish family rescued and hidden from the Nazis by German Christians. In response he founded The Jewish Foundation for the Righteous as a way of celebrating the heroic goodness of Christians who rescued Jews in German-occupied Europe.

In a similar way, Schulweis argued that action is demanded in all circumstances of moral darkness. He cofounded MAZON, as an answer to poverty in America, and established Jewish World Watch, a coalition of Jewish organizations dedicated to alleviating suffering and raising political awareness of on-going genocide around the world.

Rabbi Schulweis wrote many books, including: *Approaches to the Philosophy of Religion, Evil and the Morality of God, For Those Who Can't Believe, Finding Each Other in Judaism, In God's Mirror,* and two books of original religious poetry and meditation: *From Birth to Immortality* and *Passages in Poetry*.

[Edward Feinstein (2nd ed.)]

SCHULZ, BRUNO (1892–1942), Polish author and painter. Born in Drogobycz, Galicia, Schulz trained as an architect and during the years 1924–39 taught art in the high school of his home town. *Księga Bałwochwalcza*, a volume of his collected pictures, appeared in 1922–24. He first made his mark as a writer with reviews published in 1933 in *Wiadomości Literackie*. The two surviving works of fiction which Schulz produced were *Sklepy cynamonowe* (1934) and *Sanatorium pod klepsydrąá* (1937), both volumes of short stories. He set his tales in a small town, much like his own, though bereft of local color, combining authenticity with fantasy and myth. Like *Kafka, whose novel *The Trial* he translated into Polish (1936), Schulz was a literary pioneer of the magical and absurd and he mingled personal recollections with visionary fantasy. *Mesjasz* ("The Messiah"), a novel which he wrote shortly before World War II, remained unpublished and has been lost. In 1938 Schulz was awarded a prize by the Polish Academy of Literature for his two published works, which were accompanied by his own illustrations. Schultz' two collections were translated into English by Celina Wieniewska and published in the Penguin series "Writers from the Other Europe," edited by Philip Roth. The first collection to appear was *The Street of Crocodiles*, followed by *Sanatorium under the Sign of the Hourglass* (1979) consisting of 13 stories, partly re-creations of childhood memories. Isaac Bashevis Singer called them "the work of one of the most remarkable writers who ever lived." V.S. Pritchett called *The Street of Crocodiles* "a masterpiece of comic writing: grave yet demented, plain yet poetic, exultant and forgiving..." Cynthia Ozick's *Messiah of Stockholm* is an imaginative fable about the search for Schulz's lost manuscript. During the Nazi occupation Schultz was murdered by the S.S.

BIBLIOGRAPHY: J. Ficowski, *Regiony wielkiej herezji* (1967); I. Witz, in: *Nowa Kultura*, 39 (1962). **ADD. BIBLIOGRAPHY:** J. Ficowski, Introduction to *The Street of Crocodiles* (1977); idem, *Regions of the Great Heresy: Bruno Schulz – a Biographical Portrait* (2002); Cz. Z. Prokopczyk, *Bruno Schulz, New Documents and Interpretations* (1999); J. Updike, "Schulz's Charred Scraps," in: *Odd Jobs* (1991), 751–56; V.S. Pritchett, "Bruno Schulz: Comic Genius," in: *Lasting Impressions, Essays 1961–1987* (1990), 128–32.

[Stanislaw Wygodzki]

°**SCHUMACHER, GOTTLIEB** (1857–1924), architect, cartographer, and archaeologist. Born in Zanesville, Ohio, in his childhood he went to live in the German Templer colony in Haifa. Until 1918 he worked in Haifa as an architect and contractor, building roads, bridges, houses, and also some Jewish settlements. He traveled widely and surveyed the Jaulan (1885) and the Hauran and northern Ajlun (1886) for the Palestine Exploration Fund, and in 1891, the Hauran and Belqa for the Deutscher Palaestinaverein. Every year from 1894 to 1902 he visited parts of Transjordan. He was the first to excavate at Megiddo (1903–05) and worked as well at Baalbek (1903–04) and Samaria (1908).

In 1924 he published a map of Transjordan (*Karte des Ostjordanlandes*). He also published *Tell el-Mutesellim* (Ger., 1908), the report on his excavations at Megiddo; *Jaulân* (Eng., 1888); *Across the Jordan* (1886); and *Northern Ajlûn* (1890). The remainder of his notes on Ajlun were published by C. Steuernagel.

[Michael Avi-Yonah]

SCHUMAN, WILLIAM HOWARD (1910–1985), U.S. composer. Born in New York, Schuman studied at the Malkin conservatory there. After holding various teaching posts, he became director of publications for the music publishing firm of G. Schirmer, Inc. (1945–52). He was head of the Juilliard School of Music (1945–62) and in 1962–1969 became president of the Lincoln Center, New York. He wrote ballets, symphonies, choral works, chamber music, and songs. Among his best-known compositions are *Symphony for Strings* (no. 5; 1945) and the ballet *Undertow* (1945). The emotional intensity of his work and its vigorous rhythms and complexity of contrapuntal structure established him as one of the most prominent American composers of his generation.

BIBLIOGRAPHY: Grove, Dict; MGG; Reimann-Gurlitt; Baker, Biog Dict.

SCHUMANN, MAURICE (1911–1998), French politician and journalist. Born in Paris, Schumann worked for the French news agency, Havas, in London and Paris, and in 1939 became political editor of *L'Aube*. Following the fall of France, Schumann went to London and was head of the French radio service of the BBC from 1940 to 1944. He was a member of the provisional consultative assembly from 1944 to 1945 and was one of the founders of the Mouvement Républicain Populaire (MRP). From 1945 to 1958 Schumann represented the MRP in the Constituent Assembly and the National Assembly and later became head of the party. Subsequently he held office in several coalition cabinets as foreign minister (1951–54) and was a minister of state for scientific research (1967–68) and minister of social affairs (1968–69). In 1969, following the election of Georges Pompidou as president of France, Schumann was once more made minister of foreign affairs (serving until 1973), in which capacity he faithfully carried out his government's pro-Arab policy. In 1974 he was elected to the French Academy. Schumann converted to Christianity in his youth and took no part in Jewish affairs.

His writings include *Le Germanisme en Marche* (1938); *Honneur et patrie* (1945); *Le vrai malaise des intellectuels de gauche* (1957); and two novels, *Le Rendez-vous avec quelqu'un* (1962) and *La Voix du couvre-feu* (1964).

SCHUR, ISSAI (**Isaiah**; 1875–1941), mathematician. Schur was born in Mogilev, Ukraine. In 1920 he became professor of mathematics at the University of Berlin. He specialized in the theory of numbers, particularly with regard to finite groups and their representations. He is widely known as the author of "Schur's lemma," which states that the only operators that commute with a unitary irreducible representation are the scalar multiples of the identity operator. Schur is also credited with extending the finite group theory to compact groups and is noted for his work in the representation theory of the rotation group. With the rise of Nazism he emigrated to Ereẓ Israel, where he lived until his death.

[Aaron Lichtenstein]

SCHUR, ZEV WOLF (**William**; 1884–1910), pioneer Hebrew writer and journalist in the United States. Born in Lithuania, he settled in the United States in 1888 and spent most of his life in poverty. A friend of Abraham *Mapu, Schur devoted himself to Hebrew literature, traveled and taught in many countries, including the Far East, and wrote about his voyages in the periodicals *Ha-Meliẓ*, *Ha-Yom*, and *Ha-Shaḥar*. His travelogues were collected in two books: *Maḥazot ha-Ḥayyim* (1884) and *Masot Shelomo* (1886/7). He was an ardent pioneer of the Hebrew press in America and, later, of political Zionism, participating in the Fourth Zionist Congress. Under his editorship the periodical *Ha-Pisgah* (1889–99), in which *Tchernichowsky made his literary debut, attracted the best Hebrew writers in America and some Hebrew writers from abroad. After it ceased publication, it was continued as *Ha-Teḥiyyah* (1899–1900). Schur wrote several novels in Hebrew. His most important book is *Neẓaḥ Yisrael* (1897), a defense of Judaism against Christian attacks, against Reform Judaism, against socialism and anarchism. It affirms the twin axiom: the eternal existence of Jewry and the eternality of the Torah. Supporting nationalism, it was the first Hebrew work in America to react favorably to political Zionism.

BIBLIOGRAPHY: AJYB (1904–05), 183; J. Kabakoff, *Ḥalutzei ha-Sifrut ha-Ivrit ba-Amerikah* (1966), 131–210; Waxman, Literature, 4 (1960^2), 1266, 1299.

[Eisig Silberschlag]

SCHUSSHEIM, AARON LEIB (1879–1955), early member of *Po'alei Zion. Born in Radymno, Galicia, Schussheim became a basket weaver when a boy. In 1905 his search for work brought him to Cracow, where he joined the Po'alei Zion movement. After the publication of his first articles in Yiddish, he became the editor of the Po'alei Zion Yiddish newspaper *Der Yidisher Arbeter* in 1906. Schussheim continued to work at his trade at the same time. Years later the previous coeditor S. *Kaplansky said of him: "In the basket weaver of Cracow we found a born journalist," and the period of Schussheim's editorship was indeed the paper's finest era. He educated his readers in the principles of socialism and Judaism and also developed the paper's literary section. Schussheim served in the Austrian army during World War I and after his demobilization continued his journalistic career in Vienna and Galicia. In 1926 he emigrated to Argentina, and was a member of the editorial board of the Yiddish daily *Di Yidishe Tsaytung* in Buenos Aires until his death. He wrote hundreds of articles and essays for the paper, a few of which were published in his book *Fun Klayne un Groyse Zakhen* (1949). He also published a booklet on Menahem *Ussishkin (Yid., 1943).

[Mendel Singer]

SCHUSTER, English family of German origin. The founder of the Frankfurt mercantile family of Schuster was JUDEL JOSEPH SCHUSTER (d. 1782), who started a cotton-goods business in 1750. It was enlarged by his son, SAMUEL JUDAH, who in 1786 established the firm of Gebrueder Schuster. By the time Samuel Judah's eldest son, JOSEPH SAMUEL (1785–1858), became the head of the firm, it was doing a considerable amount of trade with England, and violated the restrictions imposed by Napoleon when he occupied Frankfurt. As a result of the penalties imposed, the Schusters decided to leave Germany. Two of Joseph Samuel's brothers, LEO and SAMUEL, emigrated to England in 1808, while the youngest brother HENRY moved to Brussels, although his son LOUIS followed his uncles to England. Joseph Samuel stayed behind to wind up the business and in the event remained in Frankfurt and carried on Gebrueder Schuster as a banking house. Joseph Samuel's son, FRANCIS JOSEPH SCHUSTER (1823–1906), was a citizen of considerable standing in Frankfurt, where among his activities was directorship of the Municipal Bank. In 1869, not wishing to become a Prussian citizen after the city's annexation, he too decided to emigrate to England. Like his uncles before him, he started his new life in Manchester and then moved to London, where he became a partner in the firm of Schuster, Son and Co., merchants and bankers. Francis Joseph's three sons were ERNEST JOSEPH SCHUSTER (1850–1924), Sir Arthur *Schuster (1851–1934), a noted mathematical physicist, and SIR FELIX SCHUSTER (1854–1936; see below). It is not known if they abandoned Judaism before leaving Germany, but none of them had any connection with the Jewish community in England. Ernest Joseph was a partner in the family firm for many years before becoming a member of the bar. He was an authority on international law and lectured for the Institute of Bankers and the London School of Economics. Felix Schuster, the youngest of Francis Schuster's three sons, became a leading figure in British banking and played an important part in the direction of the country's finances during World War I. He joined the family firm at the age of 19 and was a partner at 24. Part of the business was taken over in 1887 by the Union of London and Smith's Bank, of which he was governor from 1895 until, in 1918, it merged with the National Provincial Bank. Sir Felix – he had been created a baronet in 1906 – became a director and one of the two alternating chairmen of the great new concern. Among the many public offices he held was membership of the Council of India (1906–16). Another member of the family to achieve distinction was CLAUDE SCHUSTER, first BARON SCHUSTER (1869–1956), a grandson of Leo Schuster. A barrister educated at Winchester and Oxford, he was head of the legal branch of the Board of Education and several other governmental bodies, and from 1915 to 1944 was clerk of the crown in Chancery and permanent secretary to the Lord Chancellor. In 1944–47 he was head of the Allied Control Commission in Austria. He was knighted in 1913 and made a peer in 1944. Ernest Schuster's son SIR GEORGE ERNEST SCHUSTER (1881–1982), educated at Charterhouse and Oxford, was a major figure in the British administration in India, serving as finance minister in the Viceroy's Council in 1928–34. From 1938 to 1945 he was a Liberal National member of Parliament. In 1961 he was one of the founders of Voluntary Service Overseas and was later involved in the creation of Atlantic College. His autobiography, *Private Work and Public Causes* (1979), appeared when he was 98.

ADD. BIBLIOGRAPHY: ODNB online.

SCHUSTER, AARON (1907–), chief rabbi of Amsterdam. Born in Amsterdam to parents who had recently emigrated from Russia, he was trained at the Ashkenazi Rabbinical Seminary of Amsterdam and graduated in classics at Amsterdam University. On ordination in 1941 he was appointed one of the communal rabbis of Amsterdam. In 1943, he was deported with other Dutch rabbis and his wife to Bergen-Belsen, where he was the only Dutch rabbi to survive. In 1955, after the death of Chief Rabbi Justus Tal, he was appointed chief rabbi of Amsterdam, holding the position until the end of 1972, when he resigned in order to settle in Israel. The synagogue which he attended regularly was named in his honor.

Schuster was rector of the Ashkenazi Rabbinical and Teachers' Seminary in Amsterdam from 1948 to 1972, and a member, and later chairman, of the Chief Rabbinate of The Netherlands, a standing conference of all Orthodox rabbis in that country. In this capacity he took the initiative, in 1957, in the establishment of the conference of (Orthodox) European Rabbis. While strictly Orthodox and uncompromisingly opposed to Reform, which during the 1950s and 1960s became active in The Netherlands, he represented, within the Orthodox community, the more tolerant attitude of most prewar Amsterdam rabbis, in contrast to the more extreme one of some of his postwar colleagues. A modest *Liber Amicorum*, with contributions by several Orthodox chief rabbis abroad, was published in his honor in 1971.

[Henriette Boas]

SCHUSTER, SIR ARTHUR (1851–1934), British scientist. Schuster was born in Frankfurt. When in 1866, following the war with Austria, the free city passed to Prussia, his father decided to emigrate and to join the Manchester branch of the family's merchant-banking firm. In 1870, Arthur Schuster entered the business, but soon decided on an academic career. He studied physics and mathematics and did research on the spectrum of nitrogen (he coined the word spectroscopy). He worked in Heidelberg under Gustav Robert Kirchoff and Robert William Bunsen. In 1874 he returned to England, and at the age of 23 took charge of Sir Norman Lockyer's expedition to Siam to study the solar eclipse. There and elsewhere he obtained valuable visual observations and instructive photographs of solar corona. For several years Schuster worked and lectured at Owen's College, Manchester, and also at the Cavendish Laboratory, Cambridge, under James Clerk Maxwell and John William Strutt Rayleigh. From 1881 to 1907 he held a professorship at Manchester. There he became the friend and guide of Chaim *Weizmann.

Schuster is known for his work on the discharge of electricity through gases and in seismology. In addition to working intensively as a research scientist he was an active administrator, taking a leading part in the organization of three universities – Manchester, Liverpool and Leeds. In 1904 he drew up the program of the International Union for Solar Research in collaboration with Hale and Arrhenius. In 1915 he was president of the British Association, and in 1918 he participated in the formation of the International Research Council. He was foreign secretary of the Royal Society from 1920 to 1924.

BIBLIOGRAPHY: F.W. Dyson, *Monthly Notices of the Royal Astronomical Society*, 95 (1935), 326–30.

[Arthur Beer]

SCHUSTER, MAX LINCOLN (1897–1970), U.S. publisher. Born in Kalusz, Austria, Schuster founded with Richard L. Simon (1899–1962) the book-publishing firm of Simon and Schuster. Established in 1924, the firm attracted immediate attention through its advertising and promotion innovations. In their first year Simon and Schuster published crossword puzzle books, which proved to be very popular and very profitable. They then branched out into publishing literary nonfiction, humor, self-help, and fiction. In 1939 the partners, with Leon Shimkin and Robert F. de Graff, organized Pocket Books, Inc., which became the first mass paperback publisher in the United States. Three years later, Simon and Schuster established Little Golden Books, a successful series of colorful books for young children. In 1957 Simon ended his association with the firm, and in 1967 Schuster sold his interest in the firm to Leon Shimkin (1907–1988), who became president.

In 1988 Simon and Schuster were inducted posthumously into the Publishing Hall of Fame for "a lifelong commitment to book publishing."

Schuster edited the book *A Treasury of the World's Great Letters from Ancient Days to Our Own Time* (1940).

[Israel Soifer / Ruth Beloff (2nd ed.)]

SCHUSTERMAN, CHARLES (1935–2000) and **LYNN** (1939–). U.S. business persons and philanthropists, Charles Schusterman was born to Russian immigrants living in Tulsa, Oklahoma. A graduate of the University of Oklahoma with a degree in petroleum engineering, Schusterman became a successful entrepreneur and generous philanthropist, whose charitable efforts helped to revitalize Jewish life in America, the former Soviet Union and Israel.

Lynn Josey Schusterman was born in Kansas City, Missouri. She was raised in Oklahoma City, Oklahoma, and moved to Tulsa after she married Charles in 1962. Lynn served as president and CEO of their eponymous family foundation. Their daughter, Stacy Schusterman, served as a member of the foundation board.

In addition to co-founding and directing the Charles and Lynn Family Foundation (CLSFF), Lynn plays a leadership role in several national and international charitable organizations responsive to her philanthropic and religious goals. In 2006 her positions included president of BBYO, the largest, non-denominational Jewish youth group in North American; co-chair of the International Board of Governors of Hillel: The Foundation for Jewish Campus Life; and president of STAR (Synagogues: Transformation and Renewal), a philanthropic partnership conceived to promote Jewish renewal through the synagogue.

Charles ("Charlie") Schusterman founded Samson Resources Company in 1971. Over the next 30 years, Samson grew to rank among the largest independent energy exploration and production companies in the United States. In 1983, shortly before his 48th birthday, Charlie was diagnosed with chronic myelogenous leukemia (CML). He responded to this disease with characteristic vigor, but later developed a second illness, interstitial lung disease (ILD), from which doctors believe he ultimately died in 2000.

In 1987, during the most trying times of Charlie's battle with CML, he and Lynn established their foundation with an emphasis on education. While not overtly spiritual or religious, the couple also identified strongly with Judaism and their deep affiliation with the Jewish people permeated every aspect of their philanthropic agenda. "In a very short time," Rabbi Irving "Yitz" Greenberg remarked when Charlie died, "The Schustermans established themselves as world leaders on the frontier of philanthropy for Jewish renewal."

Their passion to work on behalf of Judaism and Jewish causes was fueled by their first visit to Israel together in 1977. It was during that experience that Lynn, in her own words, "fell in love with being Jewish." The Schustermans eventually purchased an apartment in Jerusalem and increased their funding of causes vital to the security and economic future of the Jewish state, as well as to organizations that supported the overall social well-being of its citizens, especially children and those most in need.

Since its creation, the CLSFF has pledged and contributed more than $110 million toward the two causes that form its mission: its hometown of Tulsa and Jewish people wherever they may reside. It is known for its tactical and hands-on approach to philanthropy and for challenging its recipients to strive for excellence both in programs and in administration. Experts in the field have described the CLSFF as a model of strategic private philanthropy widely recognized for its professionalism, its ability to act quickly, and its willingness to take risks. The CLSFF also has a reputation for taking the long view in its grant-making; many of the groups it supported in its earliest years continue to receive funding today.

Locally, the CLSFF supports Oklahoma-based, non-sectarian charitable groups that help people help themselves, especially organizations that focus on education, children, and community service. Among its grantees in the early 21st century were the University of Oklahoma-Tulsa, the Tulsa City County Library Commission, the Parent Child Center of Tulsa, and the Community Action Project of Tulsa County, an organization that helps families in economic need achieve self-sufficiency. The foundation also seeks to create links between the programs it funds in Oklahoma and projects with similar missions in Israel.

Nationally and internationally, the CLSFF supports organizations that bring greater vitality and relevance to Jewish life. Its pursues its mission – to help spread the joy of Jewish living, giving, and learning – in communities throughout the world, from Moscow to Minneapolis and from Montevideo to Modi'in. The CLSFF seeks to ensure that a community of proud and educated Jews thrives for generations to come, even as increasing numbers of Jews count themselves among the unaffiliated and the intermarried. The foundation's support for programs that make Judaism more accessible has produced positive results in all of the geographic areas upon which it has chosen to focus: United States, Israel, and the former Soviet Union.

In America, the CLSFF has funded a carefully selected array of programs and organizations including Birthright Israel, which has brought tens of thousands of college-age students to Israel to experience the same sense of connection that Charles and Lynn felt during their first family trip to Israel. The CLSFF also supports the American Israel Education Foundation, The Foundation for Jewish Camping, MyJewishLearning.com, and The Curriculum Initiative, a project designed to provide quality Jewish experiences for Jewish high school students attending boarding or other private schools.

The foundation also supports a diverse and growing number of Israel-based organizations, including the Beit Lynn network, a growing number of facilities designed to treat victims of child abuse and neglect, and the Meitarim network of schools, institutions that educate Jewish children in a religiously pluralistic environment. In the former Soviet Union, the CLSFF promotes Jewish renewal through its contributions and work with Hillel, the American Jewish Joint Distribution Committee, the Hebrew Union College, and the World Union of Progressive Judaism.

One of the hallmarks of the foundation's operating philosophy is to engage in coalition-building of philanthropic partnerships, in efforts such as Birthright Israel and the Partnership for Excellence in Jewish Education (PEJE). Such partnerships leverage resources for maximum effect, and reflect the foundation's continued adherence to the Schustermans' leadership model. In particular, the CLSFF encourages unity among Jewish organizations, and stresses that Jews from all denominations, backgrounds, and affiliations should work cooperatively on matters of mutual concern. The CLSFF also places a high priority on the professional development of those working on behalf of the Jewish people and sponsors several conferences each year to assist in that effort.

The CLSFF maintains offices in Tulsa, Washington, D.C., and Jerusalem.

[Alana Hughes (2nd ed.)]

SCHUTZBUND, REPUBLIKANISCHER, Austrian paramilitary organization. The organization was founded in 1922 at the initiative of the Social Democratic Party in opposition to the *Heimwehr, the right-wing paramilitary organization. Its leaders included Julius Deutsch, Rudolf Rafael Loew, Otto *Bauer, and Julius *Braunthal. At its height in the late 1920s it had approximately 40,000 members, including several hundred Jews, mainly in Vienna. It was disbanded by E. *Dollfuss in 1933 but continued to operate as an underground army until it was put down in the February uprising of 1934. Like the Social Democratic Party, the Schutzbund was careful not to be branded as a *Judenschutztruppe* ("Jew-protector troop"). The question whether it should protect Jewish gatherings in the second district of Vienna (Leopoldstadt) from Heimwehr and Nazi attacks often became the subject of intense controversy; Schutzbund units would protect Jewish assemblies, wearing their uniforms but not their badges or service-belts. The organizational forms of the Schutzbund and the related workers' sports movement influenced the *Hapoel and the *Haganah in Palestine. Rudolf Rafael Loew was a member of the Schutzbund's military leadership and its financial officer. He immigrated to Palestine in 1938, where he became a member of the Haganah's general staff and later director of the Israeli military archive.

BIBLIOGRAPHY: A. Ḥefeẓ (ed.), *Vinah ha-Adummah* (1964); O. Naderer, *Der bewaffnete Aufstand* (2004).

[Meir Lamed / Evelyn Adunka (2nd ed.)]

SCHUTZJUDEN (Ger. "protected Jews"), Jews who held letters of protection. In the Holy Roman Empire, from 1236 on, Jews were considered serfs of the chamber (**servi camerae regis*), a special class of the population protected and taxed by the emperor. Later the emperors transferred their rights over the Jews to the free cities and territorial princes, who issued letters of protection for a regular fee to the Jews living within their dominions, thereby making them their subjects. The letter of protection (*Schutzbrief*), either general (to a community) or personal, included articles on commercial privileges, religious rights, freedom of movement, and taxation, and had to be renewed regularly. In the 17th and 18th centuries, when impoverished Jews from Eastern Europe sought rights of trade and residence in the west, the number of protected Jews became restricted and any increase was resolutely opposed by Christian (and sometimes Jewish) merchants. Most of the immigrants were therefore granted only letters of safe-conduct (*Geleitbriefe*) and further entrance rights were restricted, but some managed to obtain the highly coveted status of *Schutzjuden*, while a growing number of Jews were *unvergleitet* ("without letters of safe-conduct") and thus without secure legal status. In the late 18th and early 19th century, through the influence of the Enlightenment, letters of protection were often drawn up containing educational and commercial conditions which the recipient had to fulfill. *Schutzjuden* continued to be a common feature of German Jewry until full emancipation was granted to the Jews.

BIBLIOGRAPHY: Kisch, Germany, s.v. *Jewry protection (Judenschutzrecht)*; H.H. Hasselmeier, *Die Stellung der Juden in Schaumburg-Lippe 1648–1848* (1967); I. Rivkind, *Yidishe Gelt* (1959), 264–6; R. Kestenberg-Gladstein, in: JJS, 5 (1954), 159ff.; D.A. Winter, *Geschichte der Juden in Moisling/Luebeck* (1968), 86–123.

SCHWAB, HERMANN (1879–1962), German journalist and historical writer. In his native Frankfurt Schwab joined the school of the Israelitische Religionsgesellschaft (see S.R. *Hirsch). He was employed from 1902 to 1927 in the metal enterprises of Aron Hirsch near Berlin and in Halberstadt. He also worked as a journalist for the *Frankfurter Zeitung*, the *Vossische Zeitung* and other newspapers, was editor of the Juedischer Volksschriftenverlag, and author of Orthodox children's books. A supporter of *Agudat Israel and its founder, Jacob *Rosenheim, Schwab organized its war orphans' fund during World War I, which established a number of orphanages in Poland. From 1927 he ran a press service in Berlin which he continued after emigrating to England in 1934. In London, he became president of the Golders Green Beth Hamidrash.

His main published works are: *Kindertraeume: Ein Maerchenbuch fuer juedische Kinder* (1911; *Dreams of Childhood*, 1945); *Orthodoxie und Zionismus…* (1919); *Aus der Schuetzenstrasse* (1923; *Memories of Frankfurt*, 1955); *A World in Ruins: History, Life and Work of German Jewry* (1946); *The History of Orthodox Jewry in Germany* (1950); *1933: Ein Tagebuch* (1953); *Jewish Rural Communities in Germany* (1956); and *Chachme Ashkenaz* (Eng., 1964).

BIBLIOGRAPHY: E.S. Schwab (ed.), *Hermann Schwab* (1963); A. Carlebach, "Hermann Schwab," in: LBI Yearbook (1962); P. Arnsberg, *Die Geschichte der Frankfurter Juden…* (1983), vol. 3, 477–79.

[Archiv Bibliographia Judaica]

SCHWAB, JOSEPH J. (1909–1988), U.S. educator, who emphasized the study of the philosophies of education and science in connection with the preparation of school curricula. Born in Columbus, Mississippi, Schwab began to teach at the University of Chicago in 1936 and was appointed professor of natural sciences in 1953. Although his interest was in general education, he was also concerned with Jewish education, as indicated by his paper *The Religiously Oriented School in the United States: Memorandum on Policy* (1964). He served as editor of the first experimental editions of the textbooks of the American Institute of Biological Sciences and as supervisor of its *Teachers' Handbook*. He was on the academic board of the Melton Research Center for Jewish education at the *Jewish Theological Seminary of America and the consulting editor of its Bible project textbooks. In 1938 and in 1965 he was awarded the University of Chicago's Quantrell Award for Excellence in Undergraduate Teaching.

His publications appeared in many professional journals. His books include *Eros and Education* (1958), *The Teaching of Science as Enquiry* (1962), *Education and the Structure of the Disciplines* (1961), *College Curriculum and Student Protest* (1969), and *Science, Curriculum, and Liberal Education: Selected Essays* (1978).

ADD. BIBLIOGRAPHY: L. Shulman, "Joseph Jackson Schwab," in: E. Shils (ed.), *Remembering the University of Chicago* (1991) 452–68; A. Block, *Talmud, Curriculum, and the Practical: Joseph Schwab and the Rabbis* (2004).

[Abraham J. Tannenbaum / Ruth Beloff (2nd ed.)]

SCHWAB, LÖW (1794–1857), chief rabbi of Pest, Hungary. Born in Kruknau, Moravia, he studied in Nikolsburg (*Mikulov) and Pressburg (*Bratislava) under Mordecai b. Abraham Naphtali *Banet and Moses *Sofer respectively. Having served first as rabbi of Prossnitz (*Prostejov), Schwab was invited to become chief rabbi of Pest in 1836. An outstanding talmudist and orator, Schwab also succeeded in creating an atmosphere of tolerance and conciliation in his congregation. The term of his rabbinate coincided with increasing Magyarization within Hungarian Jewry, which culminated in the struggle for full *emancipation. Schwab encouraged the members of his community to cultivate the use of the Hungarian language, and to engage in agriculture and other productive labor: he was one of the founders of the Society for the Promotion of Handicrafts and Agriculture among Hungarian Jews (MIKÉFE).

In 1844 he submitted a proposal to publish the main tenets and principles of the Jewish religion, in order to prove their compatibility with the requirements of a modern state, to refute slanders by the opponents of Jewish civil rights, and to allay their suspicions. His proposal was rejected by the rabbinic council of *Paks (1844), but in 1846 his own congregation of Pest entrusted him with preparing this publication. It was printed in both Hungarian and German as a compendium of religious instruction for secondary school graduates and went into seven editions.

During the 1848 revolution Schwab voiced his opinions on both religious and secular political matters. Although admitting the need for some moderate and cautious innovations in the religious sphere, Schwab strongly opposed the extreme reformist program of the congregation led by Ignaz *Einhorn. He supported, however, the Hungarian national liberation movement, including the declaration of independence from Hapsburg rule (1849). On the suppression of the revolutionary struggle, Schwab was arrested with his son-in-law, Leopold *Löw.

Schwab's published works include religious poems, in Hebrew and German, and some sermons.

BIBLIOGRAPHY: L. Loew, in: *Ben Chananja*, 1 (1858), 23–30; M. Ehrenteil, *Juedische Charaktetbilder* (1866), 42–57; S. Büchler, *A zsidók története Budapesten* (1901), 416–76; *Magyar Zsidó Lexikon* (1929), 776–7.

[Jeno Zsoldos]

SCHWAB, MOÏSE (1839–1918), French scholar. Schwab, born in Paris, attended the *Talmud Torah* of Strasbourg. He served as secretary to Solomon *Munk, the Orientalist, during 1857–66, later writing his biography: *Salomon Munk, sa vie et ses oeuvres* (1900). In 1869 Schwab began a 40-year career with the *Bibliothèque Nationale, first as an assistant and later as associate keeper. His scholarly interests were wide: he translated the Palestinian Talmud into French (*Talmud de Jérusalem*, 11 vols., 1871–90; repr. 1961), and he wrote *Abravanel et son époque* (1865); *Histoire des Israélites* (1866, 1895^2); and *Vocabulaire de l'Angélologie* (1896–99). Schwab also published *Les Incunables orientaux et les impressions orientales au commencement du XVI siécle* (1883). He described the Hebrew manuscripts and incunabula in the library of the Alliance Israélite (1904) and in other French and Swiss libraries.

Schwab contributed many articles to the *Revue des Etudes Juives*, the *Journal Asiatique*, and the bulletins of the Bibliothèque Nationale. Of particular importance is his *Répertoire*, a bibliography of articles published on Jewish subjects in learned journals between 1665 and 1900 (1899, 1914–23). The *Répertoire*, arranged alphabetically according to authors, lists 112 items by Schwab himself. His great erudition was not always matched by equal exactitude, and his work must therefore be checked thoroughly.

BIBLIOGRAPHY: D. Sidersky, *Moïse Schwab, sa vie et ses œuvres* (1919).

[Colette Sirat]

SCHWAB, SHIMON (1908–1995), German and American Orthodox rabbi. Born in Frankfurt am Main, Germany, Schwab was brought up in the Separatist Orthodox community founded by Samson Raphael *Hirsch. Unlike most German Orthodox rabbis, who received a seminary education, Schwab studied at the traditional Lithuanian yeshivas in Telz and Mir from 1926 to 1931 and received his ordination from three distinguished Lithuanian rabbis, among them Chaim Ozer Grodzinski. Despite his German background and devotion to the customs of German Jewry, Schwab remained under the influence of the Lithuanian yeshiva world for the rest of his life and tried to introduce its ethos into German Jewish life.

After an initial tenure as a rabbi in the large Bavarian rural community of Ichenhausen, Rabbi Schwab immigrated to the United States in about 1936 to serve as rabbi of Congregation Shearith Israel in Baltimore, one of the most strictly Orthodox congregations in the city at the time. In 1958 he accepted the post of assistant rabbi to the 76-year-old Rabbi Joseph *Breuer of Congregation K'hal Adath Jeshurun in Washington Heights (the heir to the Frankfurt Separatist Orthodox community at the northern end of Manhattan). He and Rabbi Breuer were co-rabbis of the congregation until the latter's death in 1980, after which Schwab served as the main rabbi of the congregation.

Rabbi Schwab helped to steer the already strictly Orthodox "Breuer community" to the right, by placing greater emphasis on traditional Torah learning and treating exclusive study of Torah as an equally valid approach to Samson Raphael

Hirsch's philosophy of "*Torah im derekh ereẓ*" (the integration of Torah and secular knowledge). He was a strong leader of his community, exerting his influence through his eloquent English language sermons, articles in the congregational newspaper, and active supervision of the community of some 1,000 families. He expanded the community's educational system to include an adult yeshivah and kollel and a women's teachers seminary, while continuing such other aspects of the community's institutional network as *kashrut* supervision, the ritual bath, and youth organizations. Schwab strongly encouraged his community to remain in Washington Heights despite the growing influx of a Hispanic population into the neighborhood. Under his leadership, the congregation spearheaded a neighborhood patrol and created a neighborhood Jewish communal council to represent the needs of all the Jews of the neighborhood. These efforts were able to slow the exodus of his congregants from the neighborhood.

Schwab was a leader of the Agudath Israel of America, a lifelong advocate of the Hirschian policy of Austritt [non-cooperation with non-Orthodox forms of Judaism], and a fierce anti-Zionist. Besides his commentaries on the Bible, essays on history and Jewish thought (*hashkafah*), Schwab was probably best known for two volumes *Heimkehr ins Judentum* (Frankfurt 1934), which called into question German Orthodoxy's compromises with modern culture and *Elu ve-Elu. These and Those* (New York, 1966) which gave equal weight to religious sources supporting and opposing secular studies.

[Steven Lowenstein (2nd ed.)]

SCHWABACHER, SIMEON ARYEH (1819–1888), rabbi and preacher. Born in Oberndorf, Wuerttemberg, Germany, Schwabacher served as rabbi and preacher in Prague, Hamburg, Landsberg, and Schwerin. Later he went to Lemberg (1856–60) to act as preacher of the "enlightened" congregation, and in 1860 he was invited by the *maskilim* of Odessa, with the support of the governor of the town, Count Stroganov, to act as **kazyonny ravvin*. His sermons in German made him well known; he published several works of homiletics, introduced new practices into the Great Synagogue of the town such as a choir, and concerned himself with the organization of modern relief activities for the poor. He also established the vocational school Trud, a mutual aid society of Jewish shop clerks, a soup kitchen, an orphanage, and an old-age home. His ignorance of Yiddish constituted a barrier between him and the masses and with the rise of a Russian-speaking class of *maskilim* his influence with the Jewish intellegentsia also declined. His opposition to Ḥibbat Zion also caused him to lose popularity within the community, and in 1887 Schwabacher was removed from his rabbinical office. During his 27 years as rabbi he made an important contribution to the shaping of the character of the Odessa community as the first modern community in Russia.

BIBLIOGRAPHY: M. Reichsberg, *Penei Aryeh* (1889), J. Hayot, *Misped Mar*, in: *Sefer Mazkeret Kodesh le-Sh. A. Schwabacher* (1902); *Nedelnaya Khronika Voskhoda*, 7 (1888), 1226, 1251–55.

[Yehuda Slutsky]

SCHWABE, MOSHE (**Max**; 1889–1956), classical scholar. Schwabe studied classical philology first in his native Halle, then in Berlin. His dissertation on Libanius, the fourth-century C.E. rhetorician of Antioch, presaged his interest in the Hellenistic East and in the Jewish history of that period. An ardent Zionist from his youth, Schwabe was among the founders of the first pioneer group (*ḥalutzim*) in Germany. After World War I he headed the department of schools in the Lithuanian Ministry of Jewish Affairs and was deeply involved in the Hebrew and Zionist movements of Lithuania. Settling in Jerusalem in 1925, Schwabe joined the Hebrew University faculty and established the department of classics. He served as dean of the faculty of humanities (1945–47), and later as rector (1950–52).

Schwabe's field of research was Greek-Jewish epigraphy in Ereẓ Israel, and he became the leading interpreter of Greek inscriptions, especially those found in *Bet Alfa, *Caesarea, and *Bet She'arim. His meticulous interpretations of Greco-Jewish inscriptions was an important contribution to the understanding of Ereẓ Israel history and of the Jewish role in the Hellenization of the East. Schwabe's research was published in leading Israeli and foreign periodicals.

He published reports on the excavations at Bet She'arim (together with N. Avigad); contributed to jubilee and memorial volumes, and to the *Sefer ha-Yishuv*; edited the Philo translation by J. Mann, with an introduction and notes (1931); and coedited the memorial volume for Y.H. Lewy (1949) and the Dinaburg (Dinur) jubilee volume (1949). He also edited the classics division of the *Encyclopaedia Hebraica*. The first volume of *Ereẓ Yisrael, Meḥkarim bi-Ydi'ot ha-Areẓ...* (1951) was dedicated to him, and includes a bibliography of his writings.

[Shalom Perlman]

SCHWADRON (Sharon), ABRAHAM (1878–1957), Israeli folklorist, collector, and Hebrew writer. Born in Zloczow (Zlochev), Galicia, into a well-known ḥasidic family, Schwadron grew up in a Zionist atmosphere. He studied with his uncle Shalom Mordecai Schwadron, the gaon of Berezhany, but also finished high school and studied chemistry at the University of Vienna. In 1927 Schwadron settled in Ereẓ Israel, where he devoted himself to publicist pursuits and to his unique collection of autographs and portraits of great Jews, which he began in his youth and bequeathed to the Jewish National and University Library, Jerusalem.

Schwadron's publications include "*De naturae saltibus*," on philosophy (in *Archiv fuer systematische Philosophie*, 19 no. 1 (1913), 50–64); stories such as *Die banalen Ansichten und der tragische Tod des Ziegenbocks Jaraz* (1924), and *Zikhronot me-Olam ha-Ḥatulim* (1914); translations into German, for example of Bialik's famous poem "*Be-Ir ha-Haregah*" (*Nach dem Pogrom*, 1920); and music, including tunes for the Passover *Haggadah* and for poetry by *Raḥel. However, he was mainly concerned with Zionist polemics and the basic principles of Zionism which he interpreted in the light of his particular point of view. His approach to Zionism, which he termed radical, "cruel," and maximalist, was based on the principle that the complete solution to the Jewish problem was through the settlement of millions of Jews in their homeland. Schwadron's campaign of incessant and aggressive admonition, reflected in *Mauschelpredigt eines Fanatikers* (1916), *Von der Schande eurer Namen* (1920), and *Aus der Zionisten-Predigt eines Fanatikers* (1925), was at first conducted in German and owed much of its style to the influence of Karl *Kraus, with whom he cooperated in *Die Fackel*.

After he had settled in Ereẓ Israel he continued in the same vein in Hebrew, acquiring a pungent polemical style in that language as well. He published hundreds of critical and admonitory articles in almost every Hebrew newspaper, making *Aḥad Ha-Am and his followers, such as those in the *Berit Shalom movement, his main target. He also published some pamphlets, including *Torat ha-Ẓiyyonut ha-Akhzarit* ("The Doctrine of Cruel Zionism," 1944), and began to publish his collected writings, *Mi-Shenei Evrei ha-Sha'ah* ("From Both Sides of the Hour," 1946).

BIBLIOGRAPHY: Schweizerischer Verband der Freunde der Hebraeischen Universitaet Jerusalem, *Zum Andenken an Josef Chasanowitsch und Awraham Scharon* (1960).

[Dov Sadan]

SCHWARTZ, ABRAHAM JUDAH HA-KOHEN (1824–1883), Hungarian rabbi. Schwartz was a pupil of Moses Sofer and of Benjamin Wolf Levi. From 1861 to 1881 he served as rabbi of Bergszasz and for a number of years in his native town of Mad. He was an active participant in the rabbinical gathering in Nagymihaly in 1866 and at the congress held in Budapest in 1869. Although his personality was molded by the atmosphere of Pressburg, which was opposed to Ḥasidism, after a visit which he made to the head of the ḥasidic dynasty of Nowy Sacz (Zanz), Ḥayyim Halberstam, he became deeply attached to him and to Ḥasidism. He spent the festival of Shavuot in Zanz for 26 successive years. He also had connections with Isaac Meir Alter, the head of the ḥasidic dynasty of Gur (Gora *Kalwaria). Although he left only one work, responsa *Kol Aryeh* (1904), its influence on the rabbis of Hungary was very great. One of his grandchildren, Dov Beer Spitzer, wrote his biography – *Toledot Kol Aryeh* (1940).

BIBLIOGRAPHY: N. Ben-Menahem, in: *Aresheth*, 4 (1966), 418–46; idem, *Be-Sha'arei Sefer* (1967), 107–15, 188–90.

[Naphtali Ben-Menahem]

SCHWARTZ, ABRAHAM SAMUEL (1876–1957), Hebrew poet. Born in Lithuania, he immigrated to the United States in 1900. He became a physician in New York City in 1906. Schwartz's poetry, written over a period of 50 years and collected in a posthumous volume in 1959, is conservative in form and predominantly lyrical and ethical in coloration. His long poem "Job" is an interesting and even daring conception: Job returns, after all his afflictions, to his original affluence, but he misses the great privilege of contending with God about the order of the world. Other biblical and post-biblical themes on which he wrote poems include Ruth, Jeremiah, R. Johanan b. Zakkai, and Rashi.

BIBLIOGRAPHY: M. Ribalow, *Ketavim u-Megillot* (1942), 180–3; A. Epstein, *Soferim Ivrim ba-Amerikah* (1952), 17–30; A.S. Schwartz, *Shirim* (1959), 7–18, 321–63 (evaluations by Zalman Shazar and S. Halkin), 19–32 (autobiographical sketch); Waxman, Literature, 4 (1960), 1071–72.

[Eisig Silberschlag]

SCHWARTZ, ANNA JACOBSON (1915–), leading U.S. economist and economic historian. Schwartz was born and educated in New York City, the daughter of Pauline Shainmark Jacobson and Hillel Jacobson, recent immigrants from Eastern Europe. Anna Jacobson received her B.A. from Barnard College in 1934 and her M.A. (1935) and Ph.D. (1964) from Columbia University. In 1935, she married Isaac Schwartz, a controller for an importing firm. She and her husband had four children.

After working briefly for the U.S. Department of Agriculture and the Columbia University Social Science Research Council, Schwartz became a research assistant in the National Bureau of Economic Research in 1941 and was promoted to senior research associate 20 years later. In 1981–82, Anna Schwartz served as staff director of the U.S. Gold Commission and was in charge of writing the Gold Commission Report. She held various part-time academic positions at Brooklyn (1952), Baruch (1959), and Hunter Colleges (1967–69) of the City University of New York as well as at New York University (1969–70), and was appointed adjunct professor of economics at the CUNY Graduate Center in 1986, soon after she became emerita research associate of the NBER.

Schwartz, known for her meticulous attention to detail, was a leading authority on economic statistics, economic history, international monetary systems, and monetary economics. She published numerous articles, reviews, and books, both on her own and in collaboration with other prominent economists such as Walt W. Rostow, Milton Friedman, and Michael D. Bordo. Among her most important publications coauthored with Milton Friedman are *A Monetary History of the United States, 1867–1960* (1963); *Monetary Statistics of the United States* (1970); and *Monetary Trends in the United States and the United Kingdom: Their Relations to Income, Prices, and Interest Rates, 1867–1975* (1982). In 1987–88, Schwartz served as president of the Western Economic Association. She received honorary degrees from the University of Florida (1987), Stonehill College (1989), and Iona College (1992). In 1989, *Money, History, and International Finance: Essays in Honor of Anna J. Schwartz*, edited by Michael D. Bordo, was published in her honor. In 1993, the American Economic Association recognized Schwartz as a Distinguished Fellow.

BIBLIOGRAPHY: R. Lipsey, "Schwartz, Anna Jacobson," in: *Jewish Women in America* 2: 1216–17; *American Economic Review*, 84, no. 4 (Sept. 1994).

[Harriet Pass Freidenreich (2nd ed.)]

SCHWARTZ, DAVID (1897–1985), U.S. apparel manufacturer. Schwartz, a native New Yorker, was raised in Harlem, then a neighborhood of Jewish and Italian immigrants. He went to work as a shipping clerk at 13, spent his life in the garment industry, and built his company, Jonathan Logan Inc., into the biggest independent dress business in the U.S. When Schwartz was 19, he and a friend named William Schwartz (no relation) started their own firm, TruSize Dress Co. They later formed Gladdy Dress Co. and created a new entity, Gladdy TruSize. They remained partners until 1937, when David Schwartz purchased Jonathan Logan Dress Co., then unknown, and began turning it into one of the garment industry's biggest success stories. He added numerous labels and categories to the core Logan line of popularly priced dresses, either through internal growth or acquisition. In 1960 Jonathan Logan Inc. made history by becoming he first company making only women's apparel to be listed on the New York Stock Exchange when it merged with Butte Copper & Zinc Co., a mining company, whose assets were then sold off to Anaconda Copper. Logan subsequently formed a division called Butte Knit, specializing in knitted apparel at a time that classification was just beginning to flourish. It became one of the company's most valuable units. In 1963, Logan recorded more than $100 million in annual sales, the first women's clothing business to reach that milestone. Schwartz guided Logan until 1964, when he appointed his son president and chief operating officer but remained as chairman. RICHARD J. SCHWARTZ was then 25 years old, the youngest president of any business on the New York Stock Exchange. He became chairman in 1977, when his father retired. In 1984, United Merchants & Manufacturers acquired Logan, which had diversified into sportswear and swimwear. Its divisions included Misty Harbor, The Villager, Rose Marie Reid, Modern Juniors, Etienne Aigner, R&K Originals and Alice Stuart. The Schwartz family owned more than 7 percent of the stock, gaining almost $45 million in the deal. Richard Schwartz left the apparel business in 1985, opened his own investment concern and operated the David Schwartz Foundation. In 1999 he was named chairman of the New York State Council on the Arts. David Schwartz was an active fundraiser for United Jewish Appeal, the Jewish Memorial Hospital, Brandeis University, the Albert Einstein College of Medicine at Yeshiva University, New York University Hospital, and Lincoln Center for the Performing Arts.

BIBLIOGRAPHY: *Women's Wear Daily* (Dec. 31, 1985).

[Mort Sheinman (2nd ed.)]

SCHWARTZ, DELMORE (1913–1966), U.S. poet, author, and critic. Born in Brooklyn, Schwartz was a member during the 1930s and 1940s of the literary-political group centered in the magazines *Partisan Review* (of which he was editor, 1943–55) and *Commentary*. In 1938 he won fame overnight with his first book, *In Dreams Begin Responsibilities*. This combined 35 lyric poems of "experiment and imitation" with other writings, including the short story which gave the book its title. His other works include two volumes of short stories, *The World is a Wedding* (1948) and *Successful Love and Other Stories* (1961); a verse-play, *Shenandoah* (1941); and a collection of lyrics, *Vaudeville for a Princess* (1950). Existence for Schwartz was fraught with terror, frustration, agony, and disappointment, and to him the Jew symbolized alienation. His deep vein of pessimism was expressed by a character in *The World is a Wedding*, who says, "You can't fool me, the world is a funeral." Schwartz found his most profound drama in the East European Jewish dream of America as the land of golden streets, freedom, and boundless opportunity. In his long, ambitious prose poem, *Genesis* (1943), which discussed the American Jew's self-preservation, as well as in various short stories, Schwartz described with biblical grandeur the immigrant's dream of the New World, his early struggles, his successes and failures, his marriages and children, the conflict between parents and children, the pressures of World War I, the ensuing boom, and the depression of the 1930s. During the years 1940–47, Schwartz taught at Harvard and Princeton universities.

Schwartz appears as the eponymous protagonist of Saul Bellow's *Humboldt's Gift* (1975).

ADD. BIBLIOGRAPHY: J. Atlas, *Delmore Schwartz: The Life of an American Poet* (1977); R. Phillips (ed.), *Letters of Delmore Schwartz: Selected and Edited* (1984); E. Pollet (ed.), *Portrait of Delmore: Journals and Notes of Delmore Schwartz, 1939–1959* (1986).

[Maurice Zolotow]

SCHWARTZ, FELICE NIERENBERG (1925–1996), pioneering U.S. advocate for the advancement of women in the workplace. Born in New York City, the daughter of Albert and Rose (Kaplan) Nierenberg, Schwartz was a graduate of Smith College. In 1945, she founded the National Scholarship Service and Fund for Negro Students (NSSFNS), an organization dedicated to increasing opportunities for African-American students in higher education. The wife of a physician and mother of three, Schwartz founded Catalyst in 1962, with the goal of enabling women to rejoin the workforce. Catalyst developed a nationwide network of 250 resource centers and counseled women who wished to combine family duties with part-time employment. Concentrating on placing women in the public sector, the organization pioneered several job-sharing pilot projects. Schwartz co-authored *How to Go to Work When Your Husband Is Against It, Your Children Aren't Old Enough*, and *There's Nothing You Can Do Anyhow* (1972) with colleagues, Margaret H. Schifter and Susan S. Gilotti.

In the 1970s and 1980s, when increasing numbers of women were forced to seek full-time work, Catalyst shifted its focus from the private to the public sector and from counseling to research and advocacy. Catalyst also began promoting the participation of women in corporations and their recruitment on corporate boards. During these years Schwartz became a widely respected expert on work and family issues, and Catalyst increasingly served in an advisory capacity to major companies and firms.

Schwartz's final years at Catalyst were colored by the national controversy ignited over her article "Management

Women and the New Facts of Life" (*Harvard Business Review* (January/February 1989)). A call to action to corporate leaders to remove the barriers to productivity and advancement still facing female managers, the article posited two ends of a spectrum along which corporate women fall: the "career primary" woman and the "career family" woman. As a result of her suggestion that creating policies to accommodate the "career family" woman was good business, she came to be known as the "mommy track author" and was the subject of hundreds of articles on the "mommy track controversy." Ironically, after 27 years dedicated to the advancement of women, the founder of Catalyst was accused of establishing barriers to women's advancement.

Schwartz retired as president of Catalyst in 1993. She died a month after completing her third book, *The Armchair Activist: Simple Yet Powerful Ways to Fight the Radical Right.*

BIBLIOGRAPHY: "Schwartz, Felice Nierenberg," Smith College Centennial Study. Oral History Project (1971); *Who's Who of American Women* (1992–93).

[Gail Twersky Reimer (2nd ed.)]

SCHWARTZ, FREDERIC (1951–), U.S. architect, founder of Frederic Schwartz Architects. Born in New York, Schwartz worked in the city for over 22 years, won many prizes, and lectured to university audiences all over the world. He earned his A.B. Architecture from the University of California at Berkeley in 1973 and his Master of Architecture from the Harvard School of Design in 1978. Among his many awards were the Rome Prize in Architecture (1995); Deutsch Inc. Decade of Design Competition; and a National Endowment for the Arts Design Fellowship in 1983. His drawings and designs were seen in over 50 exhibitions from the Paris Biennale des Beaux Arts in 1982 to the Venice Biennale in 1992 and were included in the Avery Library, Columbia University permanent collection. Schwartz Architects won the revised contract for the construction of the $315 million Whitehall Ferry Terminal building in New York. Opened in 2005, the terminal was designed to accommodate 70,000 people a day commuting from Staten Island. The plans called for a 200,000-square-foot glass and steel building with an open feeling so that people can feel they are already on the water, and also includes a roof deck for viewing Lower Manhattan, the upper harbor, and Governor's Island. Schwartz was the winner from among over 320 entrants in a competition to design the New Jersey memorial to those who died in the September 11, 2001, attack on the World Trade Center. Outside of New York, New Jersey lost more residents (674) than any other state. The memorial was slated to be erected in Liberty State Park on the banks of the Hudson River, affording a direct view of Lower Manhattan where the Trade Center stood. Named "Empty Sky," the title of a song by New Jersey rock star Bruce Springsteen, the design calls for a pair of brushed stainless steel walls 200 feet long and 30 feet high, the footprint of the vanished towers. The names of the victims are to be etched on the walls in random fashion. A paved bluestone path runs between the walls. Space for visitors to express their grief by leaving items at the base of the walls are meant to personalize sorrow in contrast to the cold steel. The area is to be surrounded by a grove of dogwood trees. Schwartz was a runner-up with architect Rafael Viñoly in the competition to design a master plan for rebuilding the World Trade Center site. As a keynote speaker at a conference on Business Geography and Human Conditions, Schwartz described his vision of the rebuilt World Trade Center as a world cultural center. The towers would be the tallest structures in the world, but not containing offices, with a spectacular outdoor amphitheater 20 floors up.

[Betty R. Rubenstein (2nd ed.)]

SCHWARTZ, GERALD (1940–), Canadian businessman and philanthropist. Schwartz was born in Winnipeg, Manitoba. He received his B.A. and LL.B. degrees from the University of Manitoba and an M.B.A. from Harvard University. In 1977 he co-founded CanWest Capital, which later became CanWest Global Communications, and in 1983 he founded Onex Corporation, a worldwide investment company of which he remains the president and CEO. Schwartz has been active with more than 70 firms, among them Celestica, IBM's former manufacturing arm, and others in such diverse areas as airline catering, electronics manufacturing services, and automotive components manufacturing. His holding company, whose firms include parts manufacturer Dura Automotive and the Loews Cineplex motion picture theater chain, had revenues of $23 billion in 2002.

Schwartz has been generous in support of the Canadian and Canadian Jewish communities. In 1999, for example, he made a multimillion dollar donation to St. Francis Xavier University in Antigonish, Nova Scotia, which was used to establish the Gerald Schwartz School of Business and Information Systems. A long-time Liberal Party supporter, Schwartz was also reportedly the top corporate fundraiser in Prime Minister Paul Martin's successful campaign to lead the Liberal Party of Canada.

Together with his wife, Heather *Reisman, chief executive of Indigo Books and Music, Schwarz founded the Gerald Schwartz/Heather Reisman Centre for Jewish Learning at Holy Blossom Temple in Toronto, where they live. The Centre is designed to engage the members of Holy Blossom more deeply in Judaism and in issues of Jewish responsibility. Schwartz and Reisman have also endowed a lecture series at Holy Blossom – free and open to the public – to which many of the world's major figures have been invited to speak. Schwarz was also deeply involved with the 2004 organization of the Canadian Council for Israel and Jewish Advocacy, which now oversees Canadian Jewish Congress and Canada Israel Committee activities.

In 2003 Gerald Schwartz and Heather Reisman were the first husband and wife team to be honored with the University of Manitoba's International Distinguished Entrepreneur Award.

[Mindy Avrich-Skapinker (2nd ed.)]

SCHWARTZ, ISRAEL JACOB (1885–1971), Yiddish poet and translator. Born in Petroshun, Lithuania, he began his literary career translating some of *Bialik's poems into Yiddish. In 1906 he emigrated to New York and, as soon as he had mastered English, translated poems by Shakespeare, Milton, and Walt Whitman. He participated in the publications of the literary movement Di *Yunge, but dissociated himself from its rebelliously militant members. In 1918 he settled in Lexington, Kentucky, where he found rich material which he incorporated in his verse epic, *Kentoki* ("Kentucky," 1925), translating it himself into Hebrew (1962). It is generally rated as one of the finest achievements of American Yiddish literature. The hero of this narrative is a Jewish peddler who rises from poverty to affluence in the course of decades of hard work and just dealings with his neighbors and becomes a respected, prosperous pillar of Kentucky society. Schwartz's verse autobiography, *Yunge Yorn* ("Young Years," 1952), wove a web of enchantment about his native Lithuanian town along the Nieman River and about the Kovno yeshivah where, together with traditional studies, he became familiar with Bialik's Hebrew, *Reisen's Yiddish, and Herzl's Zionist visions. *Yunge Yorn* ends with his departure from home for the New World. Because of Schwartz's lifelong preoccupation with translating contemporary Hebrew poets, his Yiddish style has a rich Hebraic flavor.

BIBLIOGRAPHY: Rejzen, Leksikon, 4 (1929), 511–14; J. Glatstein, *In Tokh Genumen* (1956), 261–6; F. Zolf, *Undzer Kultur Hemshekh* (1956), 195–221; M. Gross-Zimmerman, *Intimer Videranand* (1964), 295–301; Kressel, Leksikon, 2 (1967), 899; Waxman, Literature, 4 (1960), 1039–40; S. Liptzin, *Maturing of Yiddish Literature* (1970), 37–9. **ADD. BIBLIOGRAPHY:** Sh. Bikel, *Shrayber fun Mayn Dor,* 2 (1965), 37–40; Sh. Niger, *Yidishe Shrayber fun Tsvantsikstn Yorhundert,* 2 (1973), 131–45; LNYL, 8 (1981), 566–9; R. Wisse, *A Little Love in Big Manhattan* (1988), 14, 43–4, 52–4, 229.

[Sol Liptzin]

SCHWARTZ, JOSEPH HA-KOHEN (1877–1944), Hungarian rabbi and author. Born in Felsővisó, Hungary (now Viseul-de-Sus in Romania), Schwartz was the son of Naphtali ha-Kohen Schwartz and a pupil of Jacob *Tennenbaum. He edited the periodical *Va-Yelakket Yosef* for 20 years, from 1899 to 1918, in Bonyhad. In 1924 he moved to Grosswardein (Oradea), where he served as rabbi to the Maḥzikei Torah society and published several important books.

The most valuable are: *Ẓafenat Pa'ne'aḥ* (1909), notes on the *Yad Yiẓḥak* of Abraham Isaac Glueck; *Ginzei Yosef* (1930); and *Va-Yiẓbor Yosef* (1936), responsa. A detailed bibliography of his many publications published by Ben-Menahem in his *Mi-Sifrut Yisrael be-Ungaryah* (1958, 330–70), includes his testament, written a few months before his death in the Holocaust, together with a biography of him.

[Naphtali Ben-Menahem]

SCHWARTZ, JOSEPH J. (1899–1975), U.S. communal leader and Semitics scholar. Schwartz was born in Russia and taken to the United States in 1907. He studied at the Rabbi Isaac Elchanan Theological Seminary in New York (1915–21) and at Yale University (1926–28), and he taught at the American University, Cairo, Egypt (1928), and at Long Island University (1930–33). His first work in the community was as director of public information (1929–31) and executive director (1931–38) for the Federation of Jewish Charities in Brooklyn, New York. During World War II, with the approval of the U.S. War Refugee Board and through neutral representatives, he negotiated the rescue of thousands of Jews from Germany and the occupied countries. As chairman of the European executive council of the *American Joint Distribution Committee (JDC; 1940–49), Schwartz supervised relief and welfare programs in 30 countries, involving over one million people. After the war he directed the transfer of over 500,000 Jews to Israel from Europe, North Africa, and the Middle East. He also helped 100,000 Jewish refugees emigrate to the U.S., Canada, and Latin America. In 1945, at President Truman's request, he assisted Earl G. Harrison, the U.S. member of the Intergovernmental Committee on Refugees, in surveying and writing the first report to the U.S. people on the conditions of displaced persons in the camps in the U.S. zones of occupation.

He was director general of JDC (1950–51) and from 1951 to 1955 was vice chairman of the United Jewish Appeal; from 1955 to 1970 he was vice president of the State of Israel Bond Organization. From 1967 he served as president of the Encyclopaedia Judaica Research Foundation. Schwartz achieved general recognition as one of the foremost Jewish social workers. He was also known as one of the most effective and successful large-scale fund raisers. A former editor of *Scripta Mathematica*, he published articles and monographs on Semitics and Jewish affairs.

BIBLIOGRAPHY: Y. Bauer, *Flight and Rescue: Brichah* (1970), index.

SCHWARTZ, LAURENT (1915–2002), French mathematician. Born in Autouillet near Paris, Schwartz received his formative mathematical and political education at the Ecole Normale Supérieure. After military service he eventually completed his mathematical doctoral thesis in 1943 at the University of Clermont-Ferrand in Vichy France, temporarily conjoined with the University of Strasbourg. As a Jew with well-known left-wing political views, he was in increasing danger after the Germans occupied the whole of France in November 1942. He took refuge in St. Pierre-de-Paladru, a small hamlet near Grenoble, where his most influential mathematical ideas began to crystallize despite the constant problems of survival. After a one-year appointment at the University of Grenoble (1944), he became professor of mathematics at the University of Nancy (1945–52) before moving to the Sorbonne in 1952. In 1958 he became a professor at the Ecole Polytechnique (1953–83), where in 1966 he founded the Centre de Mathématique. His major work concerned the concept of distributions leading to the Fourier theory of distribution transforms. His work broadened the scope of calculus and brought Paul Dirac's ideas of "delta functions" in quantum mechanics within the scope of rigorous mathematics. For this work he was awarded the Fields Medal in 1950, the mathematicians' equivalent of the Nobel Prize. He was a brilliant teacher of mathematics for professional and lay audiences and in his sabbaticals did much to establish mathematics teaching in underdeveloped countries. His honors included membership in the Académie des Sciences. He was also an expert on butterflies.

Schwartz was a Trotskyist as a student, but he was eventually disillusioned with political affiliation. He became a passionate supporter of individual freedom and rights and an anticolonialist over French policy in Algeria and U.S. policy in the Vietnam war, even though his views provoked temporarily unfavorable reactions from the French and U.S. governments. He maintained that mathematical discovery is rigorous and subversive, principles to be followed in life in general. An atheist, he was nonetheless committed to Jewish rights and an early advocate of organized anti-Nazi Jewish military action.

[Michael Denman (2nd ed.)]

SCHWARTZ, MANFRED (1909–1970), U.S. painter, illustrator, and educator. Born in Lodz, Poland, he immigrated to New York in 1920 at the age of 11. In Paris, he attended the Sorbonne and the Académie de la Grande Chaumiere; in America, he was educated at the Art Students League, New York, the Cape Cod School of Art, and the National Academy of Design. Prodigiously talented, Schwartz exhibited at the inception of his career with such luminaries as Edward Hopper, Maurice Vlaminck, and Andrew Wyeth. His teachers included the Ashcan School artists John Sloan and Charles Hawthorne. He moved to Paris in 1929, where he studied both classicism and the art of his immediate predecessors, Vincent van Gogh, Paul Cezanne, and Picasso. Schwartz also became active in the School of Paris. He was known first, from the mid 1930s through the 1940s, for a liberated, colorful version of synthetic cubism applied to circus subjects, such as jugglers and acrobats. The oil painting *The Juggler* (1935) demonstrates this period in his art: depicting a figure balanced on her torso with arms upraised as she juggles several balls, the composition is executed in vibrant reds, violets, and black, which flatten the already simplified forms. By 1950, Schwartz had already had several solo shows at prestigious galleries, including the Lilienfeld and Durand-Ruel Galleries. At the urging of Henri Matisse, he traveled to the French town of Étretat on the Normandy Coast in 1950. Having already obtained a reputation among French artists, including Courbet, Monet, and Braque, as an area with unparalleled luminosity, Étretat captured Schwartz's eyes and imagination as well: observing the movement of radiance and shadow on the town's seafront, the artist made paintings and drawings which reflected his new, keener sense of the relationship between color and light. Schwartz returned to Étretat in 1960. Unlike other artists who had visited this Normandy town, Schwartz did not focus on representation of the cliffs, but rather the beach, which he infused with color and light in order to stress the flatness of the canvas or paper. By the 1960s, he gradually restricted his work to a form of pointillism, based on empirical observation, which he mobilized in order to represent light, rather than landscape. Thousands of his cool, graded dots converge or disperse to describe constellations, nebulae, pebbles, and sand. Schwartz also worked in Provincetown, Massachusetts. He was a member of the Federation of Modern Painters and Sculptors and the American Abstract Artists. He has had solo retrospectives at the Brooklyn Museum of Art, the Providence Museum of Art, and the Whitney Museum. His work has been exhibited at the Art Institute of Chicago, the Carnegie Institute, and the Metropolitan Museum of Art. His work is in the collections of the Brooklyn Museum, the Guggenheim Museum, and the Whitney Museum, among other institutions.

BIBLIOGRAPHY: *Manfred Schwartz: The Last Ten Years. Jan 17–Feb. 24, 1974, Museum of Art, Rhode Island School of Design.* Providence: Museum of Art, Rhode Island School of Design (1974); M. Schwartz, *Étretat: An Artist's Theme and Development* (1965).

[Nancy Buchwald (2nd ed.)]

SCHWARTZ, MAURICE (1890–1960), U.S. Yiddish actor. Schwartz was the last major figure in the Yiddish theater of New York. He flourished at a time when there were about 20 Yiddish shows on Second Avenue in New York City, and his Jewish Art Theater was among the last to close. He belonged to the older theatrical tradition; he had an impressive figure, he used wide gestures, and though he tended to be flamboyant, like many of his school, he achieved performances of great dignity.

In 1901, Schwartz reached New York with his parents from Sedikov in the Ukraine, and grew up on the Lower East Side. He made his debut with a Yiddish stock company in Baltimore in 1905 and seven years later was engaged by David Kessler for the opening of the Second Avenue Theater. Here he remained until launching the Jewish Art Theater in 1918. During the 40 years that followed, Schwartz became known in almost every corner of the Yiddish-speaking Diaspora. He toured North America, South America, Europe, Israel, and South Africa. His company had a repertoire of 150 plays from Shakespeare, Lope de Vega, Toller, and George Bernard Shaw to Shalom Aleichem. He was known especially for his playing of Reb Malech in Singer's *Yoshe Kalb*, Luka in Gorki's *The Lower Depths*, Oswald in Ibsen's *Ghosts*, Shylock in *The Merchant of Venice*, and the title role in *King Lear*. The Jewish Art Theater became an institution in New York, breeding talent for both the Yiddish and English-speaking stage. Schwartz's vital performances drew the Broadway critics, who found his theater vital and perceptive. The Jewish Art Theater lasted until 1950, when both audiences and companies had moved out of Second Avenue. An attempt to revive it in 1955 met with little success. Schwartz turned to motion pictures, but without success. In 1960 he went to Israel hoping to establish a Yiddish art center. He attracted a number of Israel players to his company and opened in *Yoshe Kalb* but two months later he died.

BIBLIOGRAPHY: Z. Zylbercweig, *Leksikon fun Yidishn Teater,* 3 (1959), 2327–68, incl. bibl.

[Richard F. Shepard]

SCHWARTZ, MELVIN (1932–2006), U.S. physicist and businessman, Nobel Prize winner. Born in New York City, Schwartz studied at Columbia University, from which he received his Ph.D. in 1958. He was an associate physicist at Brookhaven National Laboratory from 1956 to 1958 and on the faculty of Columbia University from 1958 to 1966, becoming a professor in 1963. From 1966 to 1983 he was a professor at Stanford University. He was also chief executive officer of Digital Pathways, Inc. in Mountain View, California. In 1991 he became associate director of high-energy and nuclear physics at Brookhaven National Laboratory.

A member of the American National Academy of Sciences and a fellow of the American Physics Society, he was also on the board of governors of the Weizmann Institute in Israel.

In 1962 he and two colleagues, Jack *Steinberger and Leon M. *Lederman, developed a means for utilizing neutrinos, subatomic particles, to aid in determining the structure of other basic particles. In 1988 they were the recipients of the Nobel Prize in physics in recognition of the greater understanding of elementary particles and forces resulting from their work.

SCHWARTZ, PHINEHAS (Pinḥas) SELIG HA-KOHEN (Sigmund; 1877–1944), Hungarian scholar. He was born in Felsővisó and died in the Holocaust. His most important work is *Shem ha-Gedolim me-Ereẓ Hagar* (3 vols., 1913, 1915), a series of biographies of Hungarian rabbis and a bibliographical list of their works. In 1935 and 1941 he published supplements in two pamphlets (all photocopied 1950). Despite its many errors, the book still serves as a biographical source for the rabbis of Hungary.

Between 1932 and 1935, Schwartz published a Torah periodical entitled *Or Torah* and several valuable works on specific topics, including: *Yizraḥ Or* (1925, photocopy 1952), the order of the blessing of the sun; *Givat Pinḥas* (1926), on the laws of the slaughter and examination of animals; *Ateret Paz* (1928), on the laws of the priestly blessing; *Minḥat Omer* (1931, photocopy 1969), on the laws of the counting of the Omer; *Temimei Derekh* (1935, 2nd ed. Szatmar, 1947, photocopy in German, no date), on the laws of the blessing and prayers on going on a journey; *Minḥah Ḥadashah* (1937, photocopy N.Y. 1969), topics connected with Shavuot; *Shulḥan Arukh Yoreh De'ah* (1938), on the laws of the redemption of a firstborn, together with his own novellae on that topic. A detailed list of his works was published by N. Ben-Menahem in *Aresheth*, 4 (1966), 427–35.

[Naphtali Ben-Menahem]

SCHWARTZ, STEPHEN (1948–), U.S. theater composer. Born in New York City, Schwartz studied piano and composition at the Juilliard School of Music while in high school and graduated from Carnegie Mellon University with a degree in drama. He returned to New York and soon began to work in the Broadway theater. His first major credit was the title song for the play *Butterflies Are Free*, which was also used in the movie version. In 1971 he wrote the music and new lyrics for *Godspell,* for which he won several awards including two Grammys. This was followed by the English texts, in collaboration with Leonard *Bernstein, for Bernstein's *Mass,* which was commissioned for the opening of the John F. Kennedy Center for the Performing Arts in Washington, D.C. The following year he wrote the music and lyrics for *Pippin* and two years later, *The Magic Show*. At one point all three shows were running on Broadway simultaneously. After stumbling with *The Baker's Wife,* in 1976, he wrote the musical version of Studs *Terkel's *Working,* which he adapted and directed, winning the Drama Desk Award as best director, and contributed four songs to the score. He also co-directed the television production. Next came songs for a one-act children's musical, *The Trip*, and a children's book, *The Perfect Peach.* His next major triumph was in collaboration with the composer Alan Menken on the score for the animated Disney feature *Pocahontas* (1995), for which he received two Academy Awards and another Grammy, and *The Hunchback of Notre Dame* (1996). He also provided songs for the first animated feature for DreamWorks, *The Prince of Egypt* (1998), for which Schwartz won another Academy Award for the song "When You Believe." In 2003 he returned to Broadway as composer and lyricist of *Wicked,* a prequel to *The Wizard of Oz*, which enjoyed a long run.

[Stewart Kampel (2nd ed.)]

SCHWARTZENBERG, ROGER-GERARD (1943–), French professor of law and politician. Born in Pau, France, Schwartzenberg, a brilliant student and scholar, was appointed professor at the law school of Orleans at the age of 25. While pursuing his university career, he joined the Mouvement des Radicaux de Gauche (MRG), a moderate leftist party traditionally pro-Israel, of which he was elected president in 1981. A long-time supporter of French President Mitterrand, Schwartzenberg was entrusted with the difficult university portfolio, as Secretary of State for University Affairs, in the Socialist government in 1983. His main task was to streamline the cumbersome structure of the French university system while retaining it most positive assets, richness and diversity; its democratic character; and above all, the fact that tuition is completely free. He continued to sit as a deputy in the National Assembly in the 1980s and 1990s, while also serving as mayor of Villeneuve-Saint-Georges (Val-de-Marne) in 1989–95. In 2000–2 he was minister of research.

Schwartzenberg wrote a number of textbooks and political pamphlets: *La campagne présidentielle de 1965* (1967); *La force juridique des décisions administratives* (1968); *Traité de sociologie politique* (1971); and *L'État Spectacle, essai sur et contre le star-system en politique* (1977).

[Gideon Kouts]

SCHWARTZMAN, SYLVAN DAVID (1913–1994) U.S. Reform rabbi, academician, administrator. Schwartzman was born in Baltimore and received his B.A. from the University of Cincinnati in 1936. In 1941, he was ordained at *Hebrew Union College, which awarded him an honorary D.D. in 1981. In addition, he earned a Ph.D. from Vanderbilt University in 1952 and an M.B.A. from the University of Cincinnati in 1970. After ordination, he became rabbi of Congregation Children of Israel in Augusta, Georgia (1941–47), following which he spent a year as director of Field Activities for the *Union of American Hebrew Congregations (1947–48) and two years as rabbi of the Temple in Nashville, Tennessee (1948–50).

In 1950, Schwartzman was appointed professor of Jewish Religious Education at HUC-JIR in Cincinnati, where he remained until his retirement in 1981. While on the faculty, Schwartzman served as chairman of the Academic Senate and as faculty representative to the board of governors. In 1975, he was named dean of the Cincinnati campus of HUC-JIR, but resigned after one year because of what he termed the lack of a "free hand to carry out my responsibilities." For the entire 30 years of his tenure at HUC-JIR, he also served on the Reform movement's Joint Commission on Jewish Education; and for many years he was on the executive committee of the National Association of Temple Educators. Upon his retirement, Schwartzman was elected finance chairman of the *Central Conference of American Rabbis, and in that capacity also served as chairman of the Committee on Budget and Finance and on the executive board of the CCAR (1981–83). He was also elected president of the National Association of Retired Reform Rabbis and was co-chairman of the group's Mitzvah Fund at the time of his death.

Schwartzman is the co-author of two critically acclaimed books, in two very different fields. His *Our Religion and Our Neighbors* (with Milton G. Miller, 1959, rev. 1963, rev. 1971), the first book ever published in Jewish religious education for the teaching of comparative religion, earned him the Emanuel *Gamoran Curriculum Award from the National Association of Temple Educators. His *Elements of Financial Analysis* (with R.E. Ball, 1977, rev. 1984) was selected for the "Investors Book Shelf of the Year" by *Business Week* magazine. He also wrote *Reform Judaism in the Making* (1955); *Rocket to Mars* (1953, rev. 1969); *Reform Judaism Then and Now* (1971); *The Story of Reform Judaism* (1949, rev. 1958); and *The Living Bible* (with J. Spiro, 1962).

BIBLIOGRAPHY: The Nearprint Files of the American Jewish Archives, Cincinnati.

[Bezalel Gordon (2nd ed.)]

SCHWARZ, ADOLF (Aryeh; 1846–1931), rabbi and scholar. Born in Hungary, Schwarz studied at the Breslau Juedisch-theologisches Seminar, where he was Z. *Frankel's favorite pupil and intimate friend. From 1875 he was rabbi in Karlsruhe, a post he accepted at Frankel's behest in spite of his misgivings about the use of the organ in the Karlsruhe synagogue. In 1893 he became head of the newly founded Israelitisch-theologische Lehranstalt in Vienna, where he trained several generations of modern rabbis and teachers as leaders of traditional Judaism. Schwarz enjoyed the respect and affection of his pupils and did much to raise the intellectual and moral standards of Viennese Jewry.

His scholarly work was a conscious effort to continue in the paths of his teacher Frankel and was devoted mainly to the understanding of the Talmud and its methodology. His prize-winning essay on the Jewish calendar (1872), written while a student at Breslau, was followed by his studies on the Tosefta (*Tosefta... Shabbat*, 1879; *Eruvin*, 1882, *Tosefta Zera'im*, 1890) in which he examined its relationship to the Mishnah. At the same time he published its text in the order of the Mishnah with a Hebrew commentary, *Hegyon Aryeh*. In later years Schwarz continued this work, issuing editions of the tractates *Ḥullin* (1901), *Bava Kamma* (1912), and *Horayot* (1929). His principal contribution to talmudic scholarship was his *Controversen der Schammaiten und Hilleliten* (1893) which was followed by six monographs on the *hermeneutic rules: *Die hermeneutische Analogie in der talmudischen Literatur* (1897), *Der hermeneutische Syllogismus in der talmudischen Literatur* (1901), *Die hermeneutische Induktion* (1909), *Die hermeneutische Antinomie in der talmudischen Literatur* (1913), *Quantitaetsrelation* (1916), and *Der hermeneutische Kontext* (1921). A summary of these appeared in 1923 (*Hauptergebnisse der wissenschaftlich-hermeneutischen Forschung*, 1923). Schwarz found that a main cause of the halakhic controversies between the schools of Shammai and Hillel, apart from the weakened power of the Sanhedrin and the consequent shift from practice to theory, was a disagreement on the use of the (seven) hermeneutical rules ascribed to Hillel. Schwarz's modern approach provoked some sharp polemics from Orthodox scholars (A. Friedmann, *Penei ha-Dor*, 894–6). He also devoted a major study to Maimonides' Code (*Der Mishneh Torah*, 1905), in which he examined the logical as well as the artistic structure of the *Mishneh Torah*. A great number of his lectures and sermons appeared in print, as well as many articles in periodicals and some polemics against R. *Kittel. On the occasion of his 70th birthday his friends and pupils published a *Festschrift* (1917, with bibliography) as did his pupils ten years later (*Minḥat Bikkurim*, 1926). A memorial volume (*Sefer Zikkaron...*, 1946) commemorated the centenary of his birth.

His son, ARTHUR ZECHARIAH SCHWARZ (1880–1939), was a scholar and bibliographer. Born in Karlsruhe, Schwarz followed his father in Jewish scholarship. Graduating from the Israelitisch-theologische Lehranstalt and the University of Vienna, he was appointed district rabbi and teacher of Jewish religion in that city, but devoted much of his time to scholarship. As a young man he was attracted, in contrast to his father, by Herzl and the Zionist movement and contributed regularly to their official organ, *Die Welt*. When the Nazis invaded and usurped power in Austria, Schwarz was arrested and tortured by the Gestapo. Broken in body and soul, he was able to leave for Ereẓ Israel where he died soon afterward.

His interest in Jewish bibliography and the study of Hebrew manuscripts owed much to the influence of A. Ratti, later Pope Pius *XI, whom he met on a visit to the Ambrosiana Library at Milan. As a model for his bibliographical work he took M. *Steinschneider. The first fruit of his studies was *Die hebraeischen Handschriften der k. und k. Hofbibliothek in Wien* (1914), in which he described those manuscripts not included in the previous and rather unsatisfactory catalogs of Goldenthal, Deutsch, and Kraft. The work was very favorably received and Schwarz was encouraged to publish a comprehensive catalog, which appeared in 1925 (*Die hebraeischen Handschriften der Nationalbibliotek in Wien*). His detailed scholarly description of the 212 manuscript collections and 160 fragments represented a new and exemplary standard of bibliographical scholarship. This was followed by *Die hebraeischen Handschriften in Oesterreich* (vol. 1, 1931), describing 283 manuscript collections, the greater part of which belonged to the Vienna Jewish community library (250), the rest to other Jewish public and private collections as well as to some monasteries. This catalog remained unfinished, though the author had prepared up to no. 302 for press.

Schwarz contributed numerous bibliographical articles and book reviews to learned periodicals. He also published a number of texts discovered in the course of his research, such as Jacob *Sasportas' letters to the Hamburg Jewish community (*Allim*, 2 (1935), 20–23), a letter by Abraham b. Ḥiyya ha-Nasi to Judah b. Barzilai (*Festschrift… A. Schwarz*, 1917), and a supplement to Yomtov b. Abraham Ishbili's (Ritva) *Sefer ha-Zikkaron* (*Ha-Ẓofeh le-Ḥokhmat Yisrael*, 7 (1923), 299–304). The latter was the result of his preparing a manuscript of Naḥmanides' Pentateuch commentary for publication: he had published a sermon by him in 1913. He also prepared Sasportas' anti-Shabbatean *Ẓiẓat Novel Ẓevi* for publication, Schwarz's manuscript serving as basis for Y. Tishbi's edition of 1964. His son BENJAMIN became professor of mathematics at the Technion in Haifa, and his daughter TAMAR married Teddy *Kollek, mayor of Jerusalem.

BIBLIOGRAPHY: F. Perles, *Adolf Schwarz zu seinem 70. Geburtstage* (1916); B.Z. Sicher, in: *Sefer ha-Zikkaron le-Veit ha-Midrash le-Rabbanim be-Vinah, Yoẓe la-Or li-Melot Me'ah Shanim le-Huledet R. Aryeh Schwarz* (1946), 17–24; M. Waxman, in S. Federbush (ed.), *Ḥokhmat Yisrael be-Ma'arav Eiropah*, 1 (1958), 482–90; D.S. Loewinger, *ibid.*, 257–64 (on A.Z. Schwarz).

SCHWARZ, DAVID (1845–1897), airship inventor. Schwarz, a fairly wealthy timber merchant in Zagreb who taught himself the principles of engineering and mechanics, decided that a rigid airship could be built by using aluminum. The industrial production of this metal had been greatly facilitated by the discovery in 1886 of an electrolytic process. Schwarz gave up his business and began to do research on the properties of aluminum; he showed that it could be soldered and hardened. After some years, he interested General Krieghammer, the Austrian minister of war, in an airship which he began constructing in 1890. However, government financing for actual flight experiments was not forthcoming. Schwarz then went from Vienna to Russia, where he made some successful flights. In 1892 he went to Germany and constructed an improved form of his airship. However, the German government procrastinated in its financing of flight tests until January 1897. When Schwarz received the telegram informing him of the German government's willingness to finance the flight tests, he died of shock. In November 1897 Schwarz's dirigible was flown from Tempelhof Field. It crashed and was destroyed after being flown for four hours. The pilot saved his life by jumping out of the dirigible. Count Zeppelin, who witnessed the flight, bought all Schwarz's plans and designs from his widow, and then rebuilt Schwarz's airship with his own modifications. This rebuilt airship was the famed "Zeppelin."

BIBLIOGRAPHY: E. Heppner, *Juden als Erfinder und Entdecker* (1913), 55–57.

[Samuel Aaron Miller]

SCHWARZ, HARRY HEINZ (1924–), South African politician, lawyer, and Jewish communal leader. Born in Cologne, Germany, Schwarz immigrated to South Africa in 1936 as a refugee from Nazism. He served as a navigator in the S.A. Air Force during World War II, after which he qualified as a lawyer at the University of the Witwatersrand. He practiced as both an advocate and an attorney, amongst other things serving on the defense team of Nelson Mandela and other anti-apartheid activists during the 1963–64 Rivonia Trial. Schwarz's political career commenced with his election to the Johannesburg City Council in 1951. As a member of the opposition United Party, he was leader of the Provincial Opposition from 1963 to 1974. He entered Parliament on the UP ticket in 1974 and was official Opposition spokesman on finance in 1974–75 and 1977–87. He was leader of the breakaway Reform Party in 1975–77, until it merged with other opposition groups to form the Progressive Federal Party. From 1990 to 1994, although still on the opposition benches, he served as South Africa's ambassador to the United States. Schwarz was an outspoken critic of the government's racial policies throughout his parliamentary career and frequently denounced antisemitism. He served on the management committee of the South African Jewish Board of Deputies from 1983 to 2000.

[David Saks (2nd ed.)]

SCHWARZ, LEO WALDER (1906–1967), U.S. author and editor. Born in New York, Schwarz was active in communal and educational work. During World War II he was awarded a battle commission in Normandy by General Patton and stayed in Germany until 1947 as the Joint Distribution Committee's director for displaced persons in Munich. This experience formed the basis of his book, *The Redeemers* (1953), which dealt with the return of Jewish concentration camp survivors to freedom. He was adviser to Jewish students in South African universities (1959–61) and professor of Judaic studies at the Iowa University's School of Religion (1960–62).

Among his publications are an anthology of Jewish memoirs and autobiography, *Memoirs of My People Through a Thou-*

sand Years (1943, 1963²); *The Root and the Bough* (1949); and several Jewish anthologies, among them *The Jewish Caravan* (1935, 1965²), *A Golden Treasury of Jewish Literature* (1937), *Feast of Leviathan* (1956), and *The Menorah Treasury* (1964). He also edited *Great Ages and Ideas of the Jewish People* (1956). Together with Louis Linn, Schwarz also wrote *Psychiatry and Religious Experience* (1958).

[Sol Liptzin]

SCHWARZ, RUDOLF (1905–1994), conductor. Born in Vienna, Schwarz joined the Düsseldorf Opera as répéptiteur at the age of 18 and conducted an opera there the following year (1924). From 1927 to 1933 he was at Karlsruhe under Josef Krips. When Hitler came to power, he was forced to resign, and in 1936 was appointed musical director of the *Juedische Kulturbund (Jewish Cultural Organization) in Nazi Germany. In 1941 he was sent to Bergen-Belsen, and after his release in 1945, he settled in England. He directed the city orchestras in Bournemouth (1947–50) and Birmingham (1951–57). From 1957 to 1962 he was chief conductor of the BBC Symphony Orchestra, and then became principal conductor of the Northern Sinfonia Orchestra, Newcastle (1967–1973). He furthered the performance of British music, including new works by Bliss, Gerhard, Hamilton, Rubbra and Tippett; and in 1958 he conducted the première of Britten's Nocturne. Schwarz was generally admired for his perceptive skill in a variety of classical and, especially, contemporary music. He was made a Commander of the Order of the British Empire in 1973.

BIBLIOGRAPHY: Grove Music Online.

[Israela Stein (2nd ed.)]

SCHWARZ, SAMUEL (1880–1953), discoverer of 20th century Crypto-Jews. Born in Poland, Schwarz was a mining engineer by profession. In 1915 he moved to Portugal and settled in Lisbon, but his work involved travel through the undeveloped stretches of the country. In 1917, on a surveying trip to remote *Belmonte, on the Spanish border, Schwarz met a group of persons who practiced certain Jewish rituals. They married only among themselves and observed in their own way the Sabbath and the major Jewish festivals. Schwarz identified them as Crypto-Jews or Cristãos-Novos, who were believed to have faded into extinction shortly after the Portuguese *Inquisition was abolished in 1821, but who instead continued to live as *New Christians. Their Jewish observance had suffered considerably from its underground nature and from a lack of formal education and leadership. Schwarz publicized his discovery in the Portuguese review *Arqueologia e história* (4 (1925) 5–115)) and subsequently in the book *Os cristãos-novos em Portugal no século XX* (1925). At about this time Artur Carlos de *Barros Basto, a descendant of New Christians who had achieved importance in Portuguese national life, openly espoused Judaism and vigorously began to organize his fellow New Christians in a return to the Jewish fold. These activities served to underscore the practical aspects of Schwarz's discovery, and considerable interest arose among British Jews toward educating the Portuguese descendants of Crypto-Jews into the mainstream of the faith. Schwarz and Barros Basto did not get along well and mutual antagonism and suspicion characterized their relations.

For a time Schwarz was president of Lisbon's Jewish community. In 1922 he took title to a 15th-century synagogue of *Tomar, opening it as a museum for Portuguese Hebrew inscriptions, called the Museu Luso-Hebráico de Tomar. Schwarz published a study of epitaphs and inscriptions of Portugal's early Jewish inhabitants, *Inscrições hebráicas em Portugal* (1923). He was a member of the Portuguese archaeological society, and a leader of the Portuguese association of Polish nationals.

A Hebrew version of his *Os cristãos-novos em Portugal no século XX* came out in Jerusalem in 2005. Stuczynski's introduction is the most extensive study of Samuel Schwarz' career.

BIBLIOGRAPHY: Roth, Marranos, 363–5; *Grande enciclopédia portuguesa e brasileira*, 27 (1945?), s.v. (includes complete list of Schwarz's writings). **ADD. BIBLIOGRAPHY:** I. Steinhardt, in: *Revista de estudos judaicos*, 7 (2004), 64–65; S. Schwarz, *The New Christians in Portugal in the 20th Century*, trans. into Hebrew with introduction by C.B. Stuczynski (2005), introduction and bibliography, 11–88. Schwarz's writings are listed on pp. 75, 86.

[Aaron Lichtenstein]

SCHWARZ, SOLOMON (1883–1973), Russian Social Democratic politician and historian. Born into an assimilated family in Vilna, Schwarz studied medicine, law, and economics at German and Russian universities. He was repeatedly arrested by the czarist authorities for his socialist and trade union activities. Following the outbreak of the Russian Revolution in February 1917, he was made head of the social insurance department of the Provisional Government's Ministry of Labor. After the Bolshevik seizure of power, Schwarz led the Menshevik opposition to the Bolsheviks until his arrest and imprisonment. He was allowed to leave Russia in 1922 and settled first in Germany, and after 1933, in France. While living in Germany and France he began his research on contemporary Russian history, much of which was published in *Sotsialisticheskiy Vestnik*. In 1940 Schwarz settled in the U.S., where he continued his research. He served as an adviser to the *American Jewish Committee, and the New School for Social Research, and was associated with the Russian Institute of Columbia University. In 1970 he settled in Jerusalem where he became an adviser on Soviet and Soviet-Jewish affairs at the Hebrew University. Schwarz was a recognized authority on social and economic conditions in the U.S.S.R. and the history of Soviet Jewry. He was one of the first to disclose that millions of Soviet citizens were subjected to forced labor in camps and prisons. After the death of Raphael *Abramowitz, Schwarz became the last editor of *Sotsialisticheskiy Vestnik*, but was compelled to cease publication because of a shortage of contributors and readers.

His writings include a number of works on general Russian affairs, among them *Management in Russian Industry and Agriculture* (with G. Bienstock and A. Yugow, 1944) and *Labor in the Soviet Union* (1951). His works on Jewish affairs include *The Jews in the Soviet Union* (1951) and *Yevrei v Sovetskom Soyuze s nachala Vtoroy mirovoy voyny, 1939–1965* ("The Jews in the Soviet Union since the Beginning of World War II," 1966), which became standard works; and *Sovetskiy Soyuz i arabo-izrailskaya voyna 1967 goda* ("The Soviet Union and the Arab-Israel War of 1967," 1969). He also wrote an important article on *Birobidzhan in *Russian Jewry 1917–1967* (ed. by J. Frumkin et al. (1968), 342–95).

SCHWARZ, YEHOSEPH (1804–1865), rabbi and early Ereẓ Israel geographer. Born in Floss, Bavaria, Schwarz studied at the University of Wuerzburg, devoting himself to the understanding of the Bible and the oral tradition. In 1829 he prepared a map of Ereẓ Israel in Hebrew and German that was published in three editions by 1832. He settled in Jerusalem (1833) and lived there until his death, being the first Jew, after *Estori ha-Parḥi, to devote himself to the study of historical topography of the Land of Israel. Schwarz registered the rising and setting of the sun 4,000 times and composed a calendar of the length of each day of the year in Jerusalem, which was published in 1860 by his son-in-law R. Azriel Aharon Yaffe. In 1845 he published *Tevu'ot ha-Areẓ* ("The Produce of the Land") in Jerusalem. It deals with the borders of Ereẓ Israel, its topography, the division of the country according to the Bible and the rabbinic tradition, the genealogy of the peoples (Gen. 10), geographical names in the Bible, Jerusalem, and the Temple Mount. It also includes chapters on the flora and fauna, climate, and the earthquakes of the country and a section devoted to the history of Ereẓ Israel from the destruction of the Second Temple. This book was translated into English by Isaac *Leeser under the title *A Descriptive Geography and Brief Historical Sketch of Palestine* and printed together with a map and illustrations in Philadelphia, Pennsylvania, in 1850 (reprint 1970), when Schwarz visited there on behalf of the scholars of Jerusalem. Two years later the book appeared in German, translated by Israel Schwarz, the author's nephew. It is less valuable than contemporary scientific works on the subject (e.g., Edward *Robinson's) because Schwarz ignored the achievements of Christian scholars. However, the book contains about a hundred correct identifications of places based on talmudic literature. Schwarz headed a "*yeshivah ketannah*," i.e., an elementary yeshivah for students before proceeding to an ordinary yeshivah, and published his work on *halakhot* and *aggadah* in *Sarei ha-Me'ah* (Jerusalem, 1861), and *Divrei Yosef* (*ibid.*, 1862).

BIBLIOGRAPHY: A.M. Luncz, in: *Lu'aḥ Ereẓ-Yisrael li-Shenat 5661* (1900).

[Abraham J. Brawer]

SCHWARZBARD, SHOLEM (**Samuel**; 1886–1938), Yiddish poet who assassinated *Petlyura. Born in Izmail (Bessarabia), Schwarzbard, who was active in the revolutionary movement of 1905 and organized Jewish *self-defense during the pogroms, had to escape from Russia in 1906. Ultimately he settled in Paris as a watchmaker. In World War I, he joined the Foreign Legion and was awarded the Croix de Guerre. In 1917 he returned to Russia. In Odessa he joined the Red Guard and fought against the Cossack followers of Simon Petlyura and his henchman Smessenko, who carried out pogroms of unprecedented ferocity in the Ukraine in the winter of 1919. Fifteen of Schwarzbard's own relatives were among the thousands of Jews massacred. In 1920 he published a book of poems in Yiddish (*Troymen un Virklikhkayt*, "Dreams and Reality") and returned to Paris. Petlyura himself settled there in 1921. Schwarzbard shot him dead in May 1926. In the trial which followed, Schwarzbard was acquitted after a moving address by his counsel, Henri Torrès (October 1927). His experiences are recorded in his autobiography *Inem Loyf fun Yoren* ("In the Course of Years," 1934). He died in Cape Town, South Africa.

BIBLIOGRAPHY: H. Torrès, *Le procès des pogromes* (1928); E. Tcherikover, *Di Ukrayner Pogromen in Yor 1919* (1965), passim. **ADD. BIBLIOGRAPHY:** M. Reyzn, *Groyse Yidn Vos Ikh Hob Gekent*, (1950), 213–20; LNYL, 8 (1981), 575–76.

SCHWARZ-BART, ANDRÉ (1928–), French novelist. Schwarz-Bart was born in Metz, the son of immigrants from Poland. His childhood and education were disrupted by World War II, and at the age of 15 he joined the Maquis. He was arrested by the Germans, but escaped and served in the French army after the Liberation. Returning home, he learned that his entire family had been murdered in Nazi camps. After several years of hardship he was able to complete his education at the Sorbonne. Schwarz-Bart's first novel, *Le Dernier des justes* (1959; *The Last of the Just*, 1961) sought to reinterpret the old Jewish legend of the **Lamed Vav Ẓaddikim* ("Thirty-Six Hidden Saints") in terms of the martyrdom of European Jewry, from the 12th-century massacre of *York to *Auschwitz. The author's comparative ignorance of Jewish history and culture – the legacy of his tragic boyhood – led him to distort the real tradition by making the *Ẓaddikim* (his "*Justes*") a hereditary clan, rather than three dozen hidden saints whose virtues preserve the Jews in each generation. Paradoxically, therefore, there is a distinctly Christian element in this tale of preordained self-sacrifice, whereby men's sins are atoned for by Schwarz-Bart's *lamedvovniks*. Despite this blemish, *The Last of the Just* remains a powerful indictment of Christendom from the era of until the death of the fictional Ernie Levy, the "last of the just," in the European Holocaust. A kind of Jewish passion play, Schwarz-Bart's novel was awarded the Prix Goncourt in 1959. Schwarz-Bart received the Jerusalem Prize in 1966. A dedicated champion of society's outcasts, Schwarz-Bart later turned to the problems of non-whites, whose emancipation and restoration to dignity he advocated no less than he had that of the Jews. In collaboration with his West Indian wife, Simone, he embarked on a seven-part epic, the first volume of which, *Un Plat de porc aux bananes vertes*, appeared in 1967.

In 1972, he published *La mulatresse Solitude* (*A Woman Named Solitude*, 1973), a novel about an episode of the 1802 revolt against the reinforcement of slavery in the French colonies of the Antilles. André and Simone Schwartz-Bart then published together, in 1989, a seven-volume encyclopedia of black women, *Hommage à la femme noire* (*In Praise of Black*

Women, 2001). The *Museum of Jewish Art and History in Paris organized a one-day symposium with André Schwartz Bart on the May 25, 2003.

BIBLIOGRAPHY: C. Lehrmann, *L'Element juif dans la littérature française*, 2 (1961), 185–91. **ADD. BIBLIOGRAPHY:** F. Kaufmann: *Pour relire Le dernier des Justes – réflexions sur la Shoah* (1961).

[Claude (André) Vigée / Philippe Boukara (2nd ed.)]

SCHWARZBART, ISAAC IGNACY (1888–1961), Zionist leader in Poland. Born in Chryzanow, Galicia, Schwarzbart completed his legal studies at the University of Cracow (1913). He was active in the academic Zionist society, Ha-Shaḥar, while still a student and was the chief editor of the Polish-language Zionist daily *Nowy Dziennik* (1921–24). He was the chairman of the Zionist Federation in west Galicia and Silesia and wrote its history in the *Cracow Book*. Schwarzbart was among the main founders of the World Movement of *General Zionists, of which he was chairman from its establishment in Cracow in 1931 until the split in 1935, after which he became the chairman of the General Zionists B. He became a member of the Zionist General Council in 1933. In 1938 he led the establishment of a committee to coordinate the activities of all the Zionist groups in western Galicia and Silesia. He was elected to the Polish Sejm in 1938. At the outbreak of World War II he fled to Romania and aided Polish refugees and Polish and Romanian Jews who were making their way to Palestine. He then became a member of the Polish government-in-exile in Paris and London (1940–45). From 1946 Schwarzbart lived in the U.S., where he directed the administrative department of the *World Jewish Congress. He published articles in Polish and Yiddish and also brought out a book on Jewish life in Cracow from 1919 to 1939 entitled *Tsvishn Beyde Velt Milkhomes* ("Between the Two World Wars," 1958), as well as booklets on the Warsaw Ghetto (1953).

[Getzel Kressel]

SCHWARZBERG, SAMUEL BENJAMIN (1865–1929), Hebrew publisher and editor in Poland and the U.S. Schwarzberg, who was born in Russia, published Hebrew books at the close of the 19th century in Warsaw, among them I.L. *Peretz' Hebrew poems, *Ha-Ugav* (1894). Arriving in the United States in 1897, he became editor of the Hebrew monthly *Ner ha-Ma'aravi* which appeared from 1895 to 1897. In 1898 he published a 33-page pamphlet *Tikkatev Zot le-Dor Aḥaron* ("This Shall be Written for the Final Generation"), a scathing attack on the attitude of the Jews toward the new Hebrew literature. He fought Yiddishism and its standard-bearer Chaim *Zhitlowsky. He also published a bibliography of the works of Senior *Sachs.

BIBLIOGRAPHY: Persky, in: *Hadoar*, 31 (1952), 398–400; 37 (1954), 694–6; Kressel, Leksikon, 2 (1967), 900; Waxman, Literature, 4 (1960²), 1049.

[Eisig Silberschlag]

SCHWARZFELD, Romanian family whose members were prominent in literary activity in the 19th and 20th centuries. Its first notable member, BENJAMIN SCHWARZFELD (1822–1897), was born in Galicia, and settled with his family in *Jassy when he was a boy. In his early years he wrote Hebrew poems and translated German poetry into Hebrew which were published in Hebrew periodicals. He also wrote articles on the contemporary situation of the Jews in Moldavia. He was among the pioneers of Haskalah in *Romania, and founded the first modern Jewish school in Jassy (1853–57). In 1860 he was appointed inspector of the Jewish schools in Moldavia. He was active on the board of the modern temple (founded in 1861), was a member of the community council, and of the governing board of the Jewish hospital in Jassy. He was also a banker and founded an insurance business.

Benjamin's sons, Elias, Wilhelm, and Moses (see below), were journalists and historians, and may be regarded as the founders of Jewish historiography in Romania. Benjamin's nephew was the poet Benjamin Fundoianu, known later in France under the name Benjamin *Fondane. The eldest son, ELIAS SCHWARZFELD (1855–1915), historian and novelist, founded *Revista Izraelită* in 1874 in which he published his first Jewish novel. He edited a political weekly, *Fraternitatea* from 1881 to 1885. In 1881 he graduated in law. His main achievement was in the field of history of the Jews in Romania. He published numerous historical studies, mostly in *Anuarul pentru Israeliți* ("Jewish Yearbook"), edited by his brother Moses. As vice president of the Fraternitatea Zion lodge he was instrumental in founding B'nai B'rith lodges in Romania. He was among the Romanian Jewish writers who were expelled in 1885 for attacking the official antisemitic policy. Settling in Paris, he became secretary of the Jewish Colonization *Association (ICA). There Schwarzfeld continued his historical activity, and was coeditor of the *Egalitatea* founded in 1890 in Bucharest by his brother Moses. He wrote *Les Juifs en Roumanie* (1901) combating the assertions of anti-Jewish Romanian historians. His two essays, "The Jews of Romania from the earliest time to the present day" and "The situation of the Jews in Romania since the Berlin Treaty" (1878), were published in the *American Jewish Year Book* for 5662 (1901–02); other essays on the history of the Jews in Romania appeared in *Jewish Quarterly Review* and *Revue des études juives*. In 1914 he published the history of the founding of the Jewish villages in Moldavia. Schwarzfeld also wrote several novels on Jewish themes.

His brother, the third son of Benjamin, MOSES SCHWARZFELD (MOISI, 1857–1943), was also a prolific writer on Jewish subjects. At the age of 20 he edited the first issue of *Anuarul pentru Israeliți* ("Jewish Yearbook"), a collection of studies in Jewish history and folklore which appeared for 19 years, to which the most noted Jewish writers in Romania contributed. His biography of the Romanian Jewish author, Moïse *Cilibi (1883; 1901²), attracted attention, and in 1887–90 he edited three volumes of the proceedings of the Julius *Barasch Historical Society, named after the noted Jewish physician and author (on whom he also wrote a monograph in 1919); he published several historical essays there. The weekly he founded in 1890, *Egalitatea*, dealt widely with Jewish affairs and was Zionist in tendency; it appeared for 45 years. Of no less importance was his work as a recorder of Jewish folklore. He collected more than 10,000 Jewish fables and proverbs.

The second son of Benjamin, WILHELM SCHWARZFELD (1856–1894), researched the tombstone inscriptions in the Jewish cemetery at Jassy, and investigated the history of Jews of Moldavia who had been converted to Christianity. He also took an active part in the development of the Julius Barasch Historical Society, and published a number of historical and philological essays.

BIBLIOGRAPHY: M. Schwarzfeld, in: *Anuarul pentru Israeliți*, 19 (1897–99), 177–87.

[Theodor Lavi]

SCHWARZMAN, ASHER (1890–1919), Yiddish poet. Born in Vilnia, Ukraine, Schwarzman grew up in a rural environment in Kiev province, and early came under the influence of *Bialik, who was a family friend. He composed youthful poems in Hebrew, Russian, Ukrainian, and Yiddish. From 1911 he served in the Russian cavalry. Although he was subjected to humiliations because of his Jewish origin, he was decorated for bravery during World War I and was wounded in action at the front. After the war, he lived in Kiev and participated in the publications of the Kiev Group of Yiddish Communist writers. He was closely connected with his cousin D. *Hofstein, who later edited his poems. After the Kiev pogrom of August 1919, Schwarzman enlisted to fight the counterrevolutionary bands and was killed in battle, leaving a legacy of hardly more than 60 poems, all of very high quality. His heroic death lent an aura to his personality and gave rise to lyric tributes by D. Hofstein, L. *Kvitko, I. *Fefer, A. *Vergelis, A. *Kushnirov, E. *Fininberg and M. Khashtshevatski, his biographer. His *Lider un Briv* ("Poems and Letters," 1935) includes a bibliography.

BIBLIOGRAPHY: Rejzen, Leksikon, 4, 529–31; S. Tenenbaum, *Shnit fun Mayn Feld* (1949), 439–43; N. Meisel, *Noente un Eygene* (1957), 208–23; Sh. Niger, *Yidishe Shrayber in Sovet-Rusland* (1958), 16–30; *Osher Shvartsman, Gevidmet dem 20 Yortog fun Zayn Heldishn Toyt* (1940). **ADD. BIBLIOGRAPHY:** Bal-Makhshoves, *Dos Dorem-Yidntum un di Yidishe Literatur in XIX Yorhundert* (1922), 54–57; M. Khashtshevatski, *Osher Shvartsman, Zayn Lebn un Shafn* (1940); LNYL, 8 (1981), 578–80.

[Sol Liptzin]

SCHWARZSCHILD, KARL (1873–1916), German astronomer and mathematician. Born in Frankfurt, Schwarzschild published his first paper, on celestial mechanics, at the age of 15, and worked at the Kuffner Observatory, Vienna, from 1897 to 1899. Schwarzschild taught at the University of Goettingen in 1901 and was elected a member of the Academy of Sciences in 1905. In 1909 he was appointed director of the Astrophysikalisches Observatorium in Potsdam, and in 1913, a member of the Berlin Academy and professor at the university. In 1914 he was involved in war work and contracted the rare infectious disease that was to kill him. His achievements were far ahead of his time; he probed deeply into the field of astronomy, celestial mechanics, stellar motions, the foundations of the new science of astrophysics, and into wide areas of theoretical physics, optics, electricity, and atomic theory. He achieved lasting results of fundamental importance. His great quality was the mathematical insight which enabled him to think about, and work simultaneously on, two or three problems which to other researchers appeared to belong to quite different areas. He was an eminently practical man, devising new instruments and advanced observational methods which remained valid often with only very small modifications. His lectures were prototypes of lucidity, and his success in transmitting the most difficult ideas was unrivaled. Several lectures have become classic, for instance "*Vom Universum*" (Frankfurt, 1908).

His son, MARTIN (1912–), was an astronomer and astrophysicist. Born in Potsdam, Germany, he became a research fellow at the Institute for Theoretical Astronomy in Oslo (1935–36) and then emigrated to the United States. He was appointed professor of astronomy at Princeton University in 1950. His contributions to astronomy cover a wide range, centered mainly around the complex problems of stellar structure and evolution. His publications include a monograph, *Structure and Evolution of the Stars* (1958). He was involved in astronomical space programs. He was awarded the Gold Medal of the Royal Astronomical Society in London in 1968.

BIBLIOGRAPHY: Born, in: *Vistas in Astronomy*, 1 (1955), 41–4; S. Oppenheim, in: *Vierteljahrsschrift der astronomischen Gesellschaft*, 58 (1923), 191–209; Sommerfeld, in: *Umschau*, 20 (1916), 941–6; L.G. Henyey, *Publications of the Astronomical Society of the Pacific*, 77 (1965), 233–6.

[Arthur Beer]

SCHWARZSCHILD, STEVEN SAMUEL (1924–1989), U.S. rabbi, editor, scholar, and professor of Judaic Studies. Born in Frankfurt, Germany, to a family long established there, Schwarzschild was raised in Berlin and escaped with his family to the U.S. in 1939. He was ordained at the (Reform) Hebrew Union College in Cincinnati. His most important teacher there was the talmudist Samuel Atlas. Schwarzschild's HUC doctoral dissertation was on the philosophy of history in Nachman Krochmal and Hermann Cohen. In 1948 he returned to Berlin to serve as rabbi of the reconstituted Jewish community. This was followed by rabbinical posts in North Dakota and near Boston (where he became close to the late Rabbi Joseph B. *Soloveitchik), and then an academic career at Washington University in St. Louis. A highly influential rabbi, Schwarzschild was editor of *Judaism – A Quarterly Journal* (1961–69); under his stewardship it was one of the few serious journals of scholarship and opinion in the North American Jewish world of that time. Ever-hard to classify, Steven Schwarzschild for a long time was the only rabbi to hold simultaneous membership in Reform and Conservative rabbinical associations, but saw as his rabbinic teacher the Orthodox Rabbi J.B. Soloveitchik and later found much to learn from the Ultra-Orthodox rabbis Isaac Hutner and Joel Teitelbaum (the Satmar Rebbe).

A democratic socialist, Schwarzschild was also a leading Jewish exponent of pacifism and vegetarianism. He followed Hermann Cohen in the latter's resistance to Zionism, although, out of Jewish solidarity, he was very circumspect in his public criticisms of Israel.

Schwarzschild placed *halakhah* at the center of his vision of Judaism, seeing it as an expression of a system of moral ideals making demands upon reality. Schwarzschild adopted Maimonides as an intellectual and Jewish standard, citing him over and over again in his writings, and using him as a hook on which to hang his interpretations of Judaism. For Schwarzschild, Maimonides anticipated the critical idealism of Immanuel Kant as explicated by Hermann Cohen. In Schwarzschild's eyes, both Maimonides and Kant (correctly) understood that much that other thinkers see in reified terms should be seen as regulative concepts.

The author of scores of philosophical, historical, and theological essays, Schwarzschild also edited some of the works of Hermann Cohen and introduced the English speaking world to the thought of Franz Rosenzweig in his *Franz Rosenzweig: A Guide to Reversioners* (London, 1960).

BIBLIOGRAPHY: M. Kellner (ed.), *The Pursuit of the Ideal: Jewish Writings of Steven Schwarzschild* (1990); K. Seeskin, "The Rational Theology of Steven S.Schwarzschild," in: *Modern Judaism*, 12 (1992), 277–86.

[Menachem Kellner (2nd ed.)]

SCHWEID, ELIEZER (1929–), Israeli philosopher, scholar of Jewish studies, and educator. Born in Jerusalem to socialist-Zionist parents who made aliyah to Palestine in 1924/5, he was educated in the "worker's-stream" school system established by the Zionist labor movement. He was active first in the Maḥanot ha-Olim youth movement and later in the Tenu'ah ha-Me'uḥedet. In 1947 Schweid joined his youth movement's *hakhsharah*, with which he enlisted in the Palmaḥ and fought in Israel's War of Independence. Upon release from military service in 1949 he became a founding member of kibbutz Ẓor'a.

In 1953, Schweid began his studies at the Hebrew University under such formidable figures as Gershom Scholem, Shlomo Pines, and Yitzhak Baer. He joined the faculty of the university in 1961 and subsequently redesigned the discipline of Jewish Thought as a course of study that includes all intellectual endeavor within Jewish civilization, from biblical literature to the present. His most important contribution to Jewish scholarship, in this regard, was the introduction of Jewish Thought in the modern period as a legitimate focus in both teaching and systematic research. Schweid's scholarly and philosophical works delve into the breadth and depth of modern Jewish Thought, though he also contributed to the research of medieval Jewish philosophy, as well as biblical thought.

Schweid always displayed a deep interest in Jewish education, including his role in establishing (1974) Kerem, the humanistically oriented teachers college in Jerusalem aimed at training teachers in Jewish studies for the non-religious Israeli public schools; his involvement in "the Shenhar Commission" (1995), which formulated a new approach to Jewish studies in the general educational system in Israel; and his teaching at the Schechter Institute of Jewish Studies in Jerusalem. He was awarded the Israel Prize in Jewish Thought in 1994.

As a philosopher of Judaism, Eliezer Schweid is best known for his focus on the concept of Judaism as culture. His particular understanding of Jewish existence may be seen as a combination of the attitude initially held by the eastern European *Haskalah of the 19th century, and that of the western European Liberal Judaism and the *Wissenschaft des Judentums which developed within its environment. The latter contributed to Schweid's interpretation of Judaism from a universal-humanistic perspective and religio-philosophical dimension. The thinkers whose writings had the biggest influence on him are Ḥayyim Naḥman *Bialik, Aharon David *Gordon, and Hermann *Cohen. Bialik's call for a renewal of Jewish culture and religiosity, combining modern secularism with a deep commitment to the continuity of Jewish tradition, reappears in Schweid's work as a call for the general public to take responsibility for Jewish culture in all its aspects (see: *The Jewish Experience of Time: Philosophical Dimensions of the Jewish Holy Days*, trans. by Amnon Hadary, (2000)). A.D. Gordon's philosophy of nature, on the other hand, serves as the basis for Schweid's particular interpretation of Zionism as an extension of Jewish life, and for his ethical-religious vision of a future Jewish society that may be described in terms of prophetic-socialism. In *Masot Gordoniyyot Ḥadashot – Humanism Globalizaẓya, Post-Modernism ve-ha-Am ha-Yehudi* (2005), Schweid uses various insights acquired through his studies of Gordon's writings to delineate the social, cultural, and moral challenges facing the Jewish people in the present period of globalization, and to show how these challenges may be met successfully. Finally, Schweid found in the thought of Hermann Cohen a basis for discussing the religio-ethical value of Judaism as a historical religion. From the beginning, Schweid's understanding of Judaism as culture was of a secularist orientation, in that for him culture is the result of human creativity. And yet, over time, he came to emphasize more and more the religious elements of Judaism as necessary to bring to fruition the social and ethical orientations already emphasized in the socialist-Zionist education he received as a youth.

As an educator and a philosophical observer of Jewish education in its social-cultural context, Schweid's approach may be seen as similar to that of the American Jewish philosopher, Mordecai *Kaplan. The Israeli equivalent to Kaplan's presentation of Judaism as a civilization is Schweid's demand that we understand Judaism as a broad culture in which non-religious Jews must be party to the continued existence of the Jewish heritage and contribute to its current development. Like Kaplan, Eliezer Schweid's philosophical reflection on the problems of Jewish existence is that of a man of faith who nevertheless is deeply rooted in the tenets of modern secularism.

A full bibliography of Schweid's works is in Yehoyada Amir (ed.), *Derekh ha-Ru'aḥ* (*Eliezer Schweid Jubilee Volume*), vol. 1 (Jerusalem, 2005), 451–97.

BIBLIOGRAPHY: Y. Amir, *Derekh ha-Ru'aḥ* (2005), 3–162 (studies of various aspects of his philosophy and scholarly works);

M. Oppenheim, "Eliezer Schweid," in: S. Katz (ed.), *Interpreters of Judaism in the Twentieth Century* (1993), 301–24; G. Greenberg, "Consoling Truth – Eliezer Schweid's 'Ben Hurban le'yeshua'," in: *Modern Judaism*, 17:3 (1997), 297–311.

[Joseph Turner and Yehoyada Amir (2nd ed.)]

SCHWEINFURT, city in Bavaria. A Jew is first mentioned there in 1212; the community dates from at least 1243. Jews acted as moneylenders to the local aristocracy in 1310. The community suffered during the *Rindfleisch persecutions in 1298 and the *Black Death massacres of 1349. Emperor Charles IV permitted Jews to return to the city in 1368. Both a synagogue and a cemetery are recorded in the 15th century; the oldest tombstone dates from 1432. A *Judengasse* is mentioned in 1437. There were 100 Jews in the city in 1553, but two years later they were expelled. No Jews returned to Schweinfurt until the mid-19th century. There were 27 Jews in the city in 1852, and a community was organized in 1864. Its numbers rose to 490 (3.9% of the total population) in 1880 but subsequently declined to 363 in 1933 and 120 in 1939. A cemetery was consecrated in 1874 and a synagogue in 1877. Schweinfurt was the headquarters of the Union of Orthodox Communities in Bavaria during R. Solomon Stein's tenure (1894–1934). On Nov. 10, 1938, most Jewish homes were ransacked, the synagogue was looted and desecrated, and the community buildings were destroyed. On April 24, 1942, there were 23 persons deported to *Izbica near Lublin, and 54 more were sent to *Theresienstadt on October 9. Three Jews lived in Schweinfurt in 1969. There are memorials at the site of the destroyed synagogue (consecrated in 1973) and at the Jewish cemetery.

BIBLIOGRAPHY: S. Stein, *Geschichte der Juden in Schweinfurt* (1899); idem, *Die israelitische Kultusgemeinde zu Schweinfurt a. Main seit ihrer Neubegruendung* (1914); FJW, 297; *Germania Judaica*, 1 (1963), 323–24; 2 (1968), 3 (1987), 756; 1353–60; PK Bavaryah. **ADD. BIBLIOGRAPHY:** B. Ophir and F. Wiesemann (eds.), *Die juedischen Gemeinden in Bayern 1918–1945* (1979), 398–401; *Dokumente juedischen Lebens in Schweinfurt* (Veroeffentlichungen des Stadtarchivs Schweinfurt, vol. 4) (1990); I. Schwierz, *Steinerne Zeugnisse juedischen Lebens in Bayern* (1992²), 111; T. Harburger, *Die Inventarisierung juedischer Kunst- und Kulturdenkmaeler in Bayern*, vol. 3 (1998), 703–5. **WEBSITE:** www.alemannia-judaica.de.

SCHWEITZER, EDUARD VON (1844–1920), Hungarian soldier. In the Austro-Prussian War of 1866, Schweitzer was decorated for gallantry and transferred to the officers' training school. He fought with distinction in the war against Turkey in 1878, receiving a second decoration. He was knighted in the following year and received permission to enter the staff officers' course. Because Schweitzer refused to convert to Christianity, he was refused admission to the general staff. However, he continued to advance as a result of the personal intervention of the emperor Franz Joseph. In 1898 he was given command of a crack infantry regiment. The emperor is reported to have told a minister, who hinted that a Jewish officer should not remain in such an exalted post, that Schweitzer was one of the best commanders in the army. In 1908 he was promoted to lieutenant field marshal. He retired in 1912. For many years Schweitzer was president of Jewish charities in Vienna.

[Mordechai Kaplan]

SCHWERIN-GOETZ, ELIAKIM HA-KOHEN (1760–1852), Hungarian rabbi. Schwerin-Goetz was born in Schwerin (Skwierzyna), Poland, and added the name of the town to his family name of Goetz. While still young he went to study in the yeshivot of Posen (Poznan) and later in Pressburg (now Bratislava). In 1782 he went to Prague, where, in addition to pursuing his talmudic studies, he devoted himself to secular studies, particularly mathematics. In 1796 he settled in Baja in southern Hungary and lived at first with his father-in-law. Already during this period students attracted by his reputation as a scholar gathered around him, and he founded a small yeshivah. He struck up a friendship with Meir *Eisenstadt, the young rabbi of the community. It was not until 1812, when he was 52 years of age, that he first took a position as rabbi of Szabadka in southern Hungary (now Subotica, Vojvodina). When Meir Eisenstadt left Baja, Schwerin-Goetz was appointed to succeed him in 1815. During his period of office the community made great spiritual progress and because of him became the center for all the communities of the region. In 1827 the convention of representatives of the communities of the region elected him district rabbi. In his method of learning he was opposed to *pilpul*. He was also opposed to Ḥasidism and to the study of Kabbalah. Though he criticized the attempts of Aaron *Chorin, rabbi of Arad, to introduce reforms in Judaism, he nevertheless took a decidedly liberal stand, especially in matters of personal status such as marriage and divorce. He participated in the convention of Hungarian rabbis in Paks in 1844 and there opposed the current of religious extremism. His relations with Moses *Sofer, the dominant figure of his time among Hungarian rabbis, were at first friendly but later became strained. In the great controversy concerning Jonathan Alexandersohn, rabbi of Hejöcsaba, which at this time occupied the rabbis of Central Europe, Schwerin-Goetz opposed the stand of Moses Sorer and actively supported the persecuted Alexandersohn, who was also a vehement opponent of Ḥasidism (see also Benjamin Ze'ev *Rapoport). The outcome of this controversy marked the victory of extreme Orthodoxy in Hungary over a more liberal approach. His grandson was Samuel *Kohn (1841–1920), Hungarian Jewish historian who wrote Schwerin-Goetz's biography.

BIBLIOGRAPHY: J. Alexandersohn, *Ehrenrettung...* (1847); H. Lemberger, in: *Carmel, Allgemeine Illustrierte Judenzeitung*, 1 (1860); S. Kohn, in: *Magyar Zsidó Szemle*, 15 (1898), 117–34, 209–37, 304–25; 16 (1899), 17–34, 135–62; P.Z. Schwartz, *Shem ha-Gedolim me-Ereẓ Hagar*, 1 (1913), 23a, no. 16.

[Yehouda Marton]

SCHWIEFERT, PETER (1917–1945), author; son of a Jewish mother and non-Jewish father, Fritz Schwiefert, a German dramatist.

Schwiefert left Germany in 1938 and went first to Portugal and then to Athens, where he lived in poverty. His mother, on the other hand, escaped to Bulgaria, where she married a Bulgarian, renounced Judaism, and converted to Christianity. Peter Schwiefert, who was greatly influenced by the Jewish atmosphere of his maternal grandparents' home, determined to live as a loyal Jew. Nevertheless, he remained passionately attached to his mother, and the separation from her, his acute loneliness, and the desire to probe her ways and make her face up to the issues, which she tried to avoid, while clarifying his own position, served as the basis of *L'Oiseau n'a plus d'ailes* ("The Bird No Longer Has Wings"; ed. Claude Lanzmann, 1974) consisting mostly of letters to his mother, and although written in German, they were posthumously published in a French translation. The title is taken from one of these letters – a long and poignant one – written in November 1944, filled with hopes for the future as well as with a thirst for retribution for the terrible German crime, and reached his mother six months after his death. The book constitutes not only a fine literary work but a moving document, a testimony of rare moral integrity. "The proclamation of my Jewish being," he writes, "is the most absolute thing I can imagine and feel for me and in me." Therefore he goes on to say that being Jewish is not, as his mother wanted to believe, a matter of choice or the result of a decision to enter upon a new path.

A sensitive, dreamy, meditative intellectual, Schwiefert chose the hard course of military service against Nazi barbarism. He fought in Syria, Africa, Italy, and France. During that period he came to regard Ereẓ Israel as his home, and though neither religious nor Zionist in the ordinary sense, he studied Torah and observed the Sabbath and festivals. He died in action at the beginning of 1945.

ADD. BIBLIOGRAPHY: P. Schwiefert, *L'oiseau n'a plus d'ailes... Les lettres de Peter Schwiefert*, ed. C. Lanzmann (1974); idem, *The Bird Has No Wings: Letters*, tr. Barbara Lucas, ed. C. Lanzmann (1976).

[Denise R. Goitein]

SCHWIMMER, DAVID (1966–), U.S. actor. Schwimmer was born in Queens, NY, but moved with his parents to Los Angeles as a child. Encouraged by a high school instructor to attend a summer program in acting at Northwestern University in Chicago, he later returned to Northwestern and earned a bachelor's degree in speech and theater. Along with seven other Northwestern graduates, he co-founded Chicago's Lookingglass Theater Company in 1988. Schwimmer tried out for a role in a television pilot, but lost out. The show was not produced, but it was reconceived as a show for singles and was sold to NBC as *Friends* in 1994. Schwimmer was the first of the four major actors to be cast. The show, with Schwimmer playing a perpetually kvetching, neurotic paleontologist named Ross Gellar, was an instant hit and was the cornerstone of the network's economic success for the ten years it ran on Thursday nights. Each of the stars was reportedly earning $750,000 an episode in 1994. By the end of its run, the actors were earning far more and stood to earn even more as the show went into syndicated reruns. Schwimmer directed many episodes of the comedy and earned an Emmy nomination in 1995 as best supporting actor in a comedy series. He branched out to film and later stage, and appeared in *The Pallbearer*, *Breast Men*, *Six Days Seven Nights*, and *Uprising*, a film about the Holocaust. He also appeared in the Steven Spielberg-Tom Hanks television production *Band of Brothers*. Schwimmer spoke out often about antisemitism, recounting incidents as a child, and noted more than once that the slain civil rights workers in Mississippi were two Jews and an African-American. "When it comes to certain prejudice and the hatred that still pervades this country," he said on national television, "I'm a Jew first and not a white person."

[Stewart Kampel (2nd ed.)]

SCHWIMMER, ROSIKA (1877–1948), feminist and world federalist. Rosika Schwimmer, who was born in Budapest, became one of the leaders of the feminist movement in Hungary in the early years of the 20th century. At the outbreak of World War I she went to the United States to urge President Wilson to mediate the conflict. Touring the country and writing numerous articles, she joined Jane Addams and others to form the Women's Peace Party, and was also active in Henry Ford's abortive efforts to bring the war to an end. During the last days of the conflict she returned to Hungary and joined the short-lived government of liberal Count Michael Karolyi. When Admiral Horthy's reactionary regime came to power, she was smuggled out of the country by friends and reentered the United States. Though denied U.S. citizenship because of her pacifist beliefs, a case she appealed to the Supreme Court and lost in 1929, she continued to campaign for world peace and the establishment of a federal world government. In this capacity she served as vice president of the International League for Peace and Freedom, and as president of the International Campaign for World Government, whose headquarters were located in her home in New York City.

BIBLIOGRAPHY: *New York Times* (Aug. 4, 1948), obituary; *Survey Geographic*, 37 (1948), 379ff.; American Civil Liberties Union, *The Case of Rosika Schwimmer* (1929); J. Addams, *Women of The Hague* (1915), passim; International Committee for World Peace, Prize, *Rosika Schwimmer, World Patriot* (1937).

[Judith S. Stein]

SCHWINGER, JULIAN SEYMOUR (1918–1994), U.S. physicist and educator; Nobel laureate. Schwinger, who was born in New York City, entered college at the age of 14 and when only 19 years old received his Ph.D. from Columbia University. He was subsequently research associate at the University of California (1940–41), instructor, then associate professor, at Purdue University (1941–43), staff member of the metallurgical laboratory at the University of Chicago (1943), and associate professor at Harvard (1945–47). In 1947 he was appointed a full professor at Harvard, one of the youngest in its history. Schwinger, Richard Phillips *Feynman, and Shinichiro Tomonaga were awarded the Nobel Prize for physics in 1965 for their work (conducted independently of one another) which laid the foundation for the field of quantum electrodynamics. Schwinger wrote *Particles and Sources* (with D. Saxon, 1969) and *Discontinuities in Wave Guides* (1969). He edited *Selected Papers on Quantum Electrodynamics* (1958).

From 1972 until his death Schwinger worked at the University of California. He was enormously respected, was a highly gifted lecturer, and supervised a succession of outstanding graduate students, 70 in all, of whom three received Nobel Prizes. He also received many honors, including the first Einstein Prize (1951), the National Medal of Science (1964), and the Nature of Light Award of the National Academy of Sciences of the U.S. (1949).

SCHWOB, MARCEL (1867–1905), French scholar, essayist, and biographer. Schwob was born in Chaville, near Paris. He began his career as a journalist, but spent much time on medieval and philological studies. His erudition is evident in all his writing, particularly his studies of François Villon, and most notably in *Spicilège* (1896). His writing is pure, rich, and varied. *Coeur double* (1891) and *Le Roi au masque d'or* (1893) are tales based on legend and history and *La Croisade des enfants* (1896) on medieval narrative. His outstanding *Vies imaginaires* (1896) is a collection of the lives of princesses, poets, pirates, and murderers, based on scholarly texts and bringing history dramatically to life. His philosophic and poetic impact is achieved sometimes by fantasy, sometimes by an ethereal, dreamlike atmosphere. Thus his novel *Le Livre de Monelle* (1894) is full of frail, unhappy little girls, reminiscent of Maeterlinck's *Pelléas et Mélisande* (1892). He was a friend of Oscar Wilde, who dedicated *Salome* to him.

Schwob's other works include *Etude sur l'argot français* (1889); *Mimes* (1894), a book of verse; *La Lampe de Psyché* (1903); and translations from Shakespeare and Defoe. For the last ten years of his life Schwob suffered from an incurable disease. His collected works appeared in ten volumes (1927–30).

BIBLIOGRAPHY: P. Champion, *Marcel Schwob et son temps* (1927); H. Clouard, *Histoire de la littérature française du symbolisme à nos jours*, 1 (1952), 139–40.

[Denise R. Goitein]

SCIAKI, JOSEPH (Pepo; 1917–1998), Greek lawyer and author. Sciaki wrote *Pikres alithies* ("Bitter Truths," 1952), a book of short stories, one of which deals with Jewish life in Athens. He wrote historical articles in *Chronika*, the historical periodical of the Greek Jewish Board of Communities in Athens. He also published a short study on the Athenian/Corfiote Jewish activist and journalist Mois Caimi as representing Greek Jewry; as well as a piece on the ancient history of Chalkidan Jewry. He was born to a Romaniot Greek-speaking family in Chalkis in the Evia Peninsula. He sat for years in the Gennadion Library, the Gennadion Newspaper Reading Room, and the National Library in Athens and recorded references to Greek Jewry throughout the ages. He had a keen interest in Hellenistic Jewry in the late classical period and the Jews in the Greek Peninsula in particular. Unfortunately, he published little and kept most of his knowledge to himself. After his death, his family established an archive of his papers in Athens.

[Rachel Dalven / Yitzchak Kerem (2nd ed.)]

SCIALOM, DAVID DARIO (1880–1966), physician in *Tunis. Scialom was a specialist in tropical diseases and was the personal medical attendant of the bey of Tunis and his court. A man of extraordinary simplicity, he was first and foremost the physician of the lower classes, being called "the ghetto doctor." He published articles on physical characteristics of the Tunisian population (1906); on the 1911 cholera epidemic in Tunisia; on influenza and tuberculosis among Tunisian Jews (1920, 1921); and on Mediterranean fever.

BIBLIOGRAPHY: J. Vehel, in: *L'Union Marocaine*, 4 (July 25, 1935).

[Robert Attal]

SCIENCE FICTION AND FANTASY, JEWISH. Fantasy is a genre of literature in which realistic narratives are disrupted by unnatural or unexplainable events. The term "Science Fiction" (SF) emerged during the 1930s as a catchall descriptor for a publishing category with roots traceable to 18th-century Gothic romance, 19th-century scientific romance, and early 20th century pulp fiction. A subset of the fantastic – forms of expression that are not generally realistic – SF focuses on the world as it might have been, may be, or could become, depending on the occurrence, advent, or continuation of a particular set of seemingly possible cultural, social, scientific, or technological developments. As such, it is more realistic in orientation than fantasy, and contains various thematic preoccupations and subgenres, including Space Opera, Time Travel, Utopia/Dystopia, Artificial Intelligence/Robotics, Alternate History, and some offshoots of Horror, or Dark Fantasy.

As a discrete brand of commercial fiction, SF was first discerned, and subsequently marketed, by Hugo Gernsback (1884–1967), a Belgian-Jewish immigrant to the U.S. sometimes referred to as the "Father of Science Fiction" (although Gernsback first referred to the genre as "Scientifiction"). In 1927, Gernsback launched *Amazing Stories*, the first magazine dedicated exclusively to SF. Often blamed (because of his emphasis on technological speculation at the expense of literary proficiency) for SF's literary ghettoization and for its formative reputation as sub-literate, Gernsback nevertheless became the namesake for the Hugo, the genre's premiere achievement award.

Traditional Jewish Attitudes toward the Fantastic

It would overstate matters to describe either fantasy or science fiction as necessarily Jewish, or even as bearing any great degree of Jewish specificity. Indeed, the word "imagination" only made its first appearance in the Hebrew language during the 12th century, in Maimonides' *Guide of the Perplexed*, where it was referred to as the literal *dimyon* or in terms of *ko'aḥ ha-medammeh* (the imaginative faculty). As scholar David Stern observes in *Rabbinic Fantasies: Imaginative Narratives from Classical Hebrew Literature*, normative Judaism regarded even its own non-didactic imaginative literature – "mere stories and profane matter" – with ambivalence or contempt. This is not to say that many of the seminal biblical and post-biblical Jewish texts (most of which embarked upon narrative embellishment either to fill in gaps in the original Torah narrative or to resolve contradictions) were not thoroughly permeated by what we would now call the fantastic. Imaginative works, which included Midrash (exegetic tales, such as the eighth-century *Pirkei de-Rabbi Eliezer* or the 16th-century *Sefer ha-Yashar*) *mashal* (parables and fables), *aggadah* (rabbinic legends, typically found in Talmud or Midrash), medieval apocalyptic literatures (such as *Sefer Zerubbabel*), sacred biographies (like the *Sefer Ḥasidim*), *maqama* (rhymed prose narrative typified by Abraham *Ibn Ezra's 12th-century *Ḥai ben Mekiẓ*, about a journey to the six planets of the medieval solar system and their imaginary inhabitants); Merkabah (mystical theories of creation), and the apocryphal and pseudepigraphical *Heikhalot* texts (describing heavenly journeys), were rarely regarded as inherently imaginative. Indeed, the more imaginative the narrative, the more emphatic the author or redactor's insistence on its veracity. Unabashedly imaginative tales were generally deemed far inferior to legal, philosophical, or even mystical texts elevated to canonical or near-canonical status.

Disdain for the purely imaginative persisted as a hallmark of Hebrew literature even after the 19th century; it remains partly responsible for a resistance to the fantastic that endures to this day among writers and readers of contemporary Hebrew-language fiction. However, Hebrew writers such as S.Y. *Agnon, Benjamin *Tammuz, Ḥayyim Naḥman *Bialik, M.J. *Berdyczewski, Ḥayyim *Hazaz, Yehudah Ya'ari, Yitzhak *Oren, M.Z. *Feierberg, Aharon *Appelfeld, Pinḥas *Sadeh, Yoram *Kaniuk, Yiẓḥak *Orpaz Averbuch, David *Shahar, David *Grossman and, A.B. *Yehoshua, and Yiddishists such as I.L. *Peretz, and I.B. *Singer, have variously embraced biblically and talmudically inspired folk tales, often reformulating the aggadist tradition for modern secular sensibilities.

Other renowned Jewish writers who incorporated strong fantastic elements into their work include Isaac *Babel, Saul *Bellow, Michael *Chabon, Paddy *Chayefsky, Matt Cohen, E.L. *Doctorow, Nathan Englander, Jonathan Safran Foer, Stephen Fry, William *Goldman, Mark Helprin, Joseph *Heller, Franz *Kafka, Arthur *Koestler, Jerzy *Kosinski, Doris *Lessing, Primo *Levi, Bernard *Malamud, Cynthia *Ozick, Ayn *Rand, Mordecai *Richler, Philip *Roth, Art *Spiegelman, *Franz Werfel, and Herman *Wouk.

A Universe of Jewish SF Writers

The contributions of unusually large numbers of Jewish writers, editors, and publishers to the development of American, Russian, and (to a lesser extent) British SF, and the incorporation of themes and devices inspired by biblical and post-biblical rabbinic sources, suggest that SF may, like talmudic Judaism, provide an ideal venue for consideration of the inherent mystical or mysterious. Literary theorist Eric Rabkin regards SF and fantasy in a manner akin to talmudic Judaism: a mode of truth-seeking and reality-testing in which normative concepts of reality can be understood as a collection of perspectives and expectations that we learn to abide by in our daily existence. In Judaism, these perspectives are made to accord with holy writ, whereas in SF and what Rabkin calls "Fabulism," they are arbitrarily and subjectively laid down by the author. Hence, perhaps, critic Leslie Fiedler's observation that, "even in its particulars, the universe of science fiction is Jewish."

Jewish writers and editors associated with the *fantastique* include Forrest J. Ackerman, Isaac *Asimov, Peter S. Beagle, Eluki Bes Shahar, Alfred Bester, Robert Bloch, David Brin, Carol Carr, Howard Chaykin, Jack Dann, Ellen Datlow, Avram Davidson, Corey Doctorow, George Alec Effinger, Max Ehrlich, Neil Gaiman, David Gerrold, Stephen Goldin, Louis Golding, Lisa Goldstein, Phyllis Gotlieb, Martin Harry Greenberg, Isidore Haiblum, Joe W. Haldeman, Russell Hoban, Guy Gavriel Kay, Cyril Kornbluth, Henry Kuttner, Stanislaw Lem, Jacqueline Lichtenberg, Richard Lupoff, Barry N. Malzberg, Judith Merril, Nicholas Meyer, Sam Moskowitz, Mike Resnick, Joanna Russ, Carl *Sagan, Pamela Sargent, Nat Schachner, Robert Sheckley, Robert Silverberg, Curt Siodmak, Norman Spinrad, Arkady and Boris Strugatski, William Tenn (Philip Klass), Sheri S. Tepper, Harry Turtledove, Joan D. Vinge, Stanley Grauman Weinbaum, Donald Wollheim, and Jane Yolen.

Origins in Jewish Myth

While some SF scholarship traces the genre as far back as the Babylonian *Epic of Gilgamesh*, through the subsequent speculations of Johannes Keppler, Jonathan Swift, Thomas More, Rabelais, and Cyrano de Bergerac, one can point to the apocryphal Books of *Enoch (excluded from the Hebrew Bible yet still a canonical text for Ethiopian Jewry) as an antecedent to SF tales – the most famous being British writer Olaf Stapledon's 1937 novel *Star Maker*, in which a human mind embarks through space and time on a quest to unlock the mysteries of creation. The Bible's most formative component – the so-called "J-source" – has been characterized by scholar Harold Bloom as a particularly ironic and deliberate work of fantasy. The Hebrew Bible certainly reconfigured or introduced myths that resonate through the contemporary *fantastique*, most notably Genesis, the Garden of Eden, the sons of God and the daughters of men, the Tower of Babel, the Flood, the decimation of Sodom and Gomorrah, the Abrahamic Covenant, the Exodus, the parting of the Red Sea, the giving of the Torah and, of course, the End Time, or Apocalypse.

"All mythology," observed Karen Armstrong, "speaks of another plane that exists alongside our own world, and that in some sense supports it." Not incidentally, science fiction has sometimes been described as a mythology for the contemporary world. (Some of the more simple-minded SF treatments of biblical myth, however, inspired British writer and SF historian Brian Aldiss to christen these tales "Shaggy God stories.")

While the purpose of science fiction has never been to prophesize so much as to comment on the present, the prophetic traditions of the Bible (many of them established in the

Book of Daniel) certainly accord with science fictional efforts to delineate the general topography of things to come. Yet post-biblical Jewish myths have also resonated, sometimes formatively, often profoundly, within contemporary fantasy and science fiction. One of the most ubiquitous, the *golem* (Hebrew for "shapeless form") was first referred to in Psalm 139. Renowned in various 20th-century novels and plays celebrating the kabbalistic skills of Rabbi *Judah Loew (1525–1609), the Maharal (Hebrew acronym for *Morenu ha-Rav Loew* ("Our Teacher Rabbi Loew") of Prague, this soulless homunculus was purportedly fashioned from clay and blessed with supernatural powers, but eventually defied its creator and ran amok. This oft-recounted folk tale is believed to have inspired Mary Shelley's *Frankenstein* (1818), consensually the first identifiable example of modern science fiction. It remains an influential precursor for myriad SF stories featuring robots and androids.

Tales involving dybbuks, wandering souls that attach themselves to living people, have made regular appearances in Jewish folklore since the 16th century, and were popularized on the Yiddish stage in the U.S. in 1920 by S.Y. An-Ski. Such tales helped inspire stories about spirit possession, a mainstay of religious fantasy and gothic horror, and, alternately, about another SF mainstay, rogue artificial intelligence (AI). Some scholars regard the dybbuk as a literary response to the psychological conflicts generated by Jewish emancipation.

The *Lilith myth, a midrashic invention dating back to 1000 C.E. and depicting Adam's second wife as a temptress night-demon who steals men's seed and bears them illegitimate children, has become an icon of the feminist movement and a staple of feminist science fiction. Lilith figures centrally in C.L. (Catherine Lucille) Moore's *Fruit of Knowledge* (1940), in Octavia E. Butler's *Dawn* (1987) and *Lilith's Brood* (2000), in Jack L. Chalker's *Lilith: A Snake in the Grass* (1981), in George Macdonald's *Lilith* (1981), and in *Lilith's Dream: A Tale of the Vampire Life* (2003) by Whitley Strieber.

Christological myths about Jews have also figured in contemporary SF. The *Wandering Jew, a 13th century English apparition that reappeared in 17th-century German pamphlets, fueled a number of best-selling novels in the mid-19th century. The archetype has reappeared in SF novels as disparate as Louis Golding's *This Wanderer* (1935), Wilson Tucker's *The Planet King* (1959), Walter M. Miller's *A Canticle for Leibowitz* (1960), and Dan Simmon's *Hyperion* (1990), and, somewhat more obliquely, as the titular character in David Brin's *The Postman* (1985). The *Left Behind* franchise series launched by Tim F. LaHaye and Jerry B. Jenkins in 1995, meanwhile, envisions the advent of a Revelations-inspired Rapture, which begins with a miraculously thwarted attack on Israel, but results in the mass conversion or decimation of world Jewry following the tumultuous seven-year "Tribulations" preceding the Last Days. Veteran SF editor and historian Brian Stableford published an anthology in 1991 called *Tales of the Wandering Jew*.

Thematic Anthologies and Collections

Jewish themes and characters have been explored in various modern science fiction and fantasy collections, most notably in two anthologies, *Wandering Stars* (1974) and *More Wandering Stars* (1984), both edited by Australia-based American writer Jack Dann, and both largely and sardonically focused on issues pertaining to intermarriage (with aliens, one of them a sentient, ambulatory vegetable), who (or what) is a Jew, and various near and far-future Jewish and Israeli Holocausts. A pair of short novels, *Can Androids Be Jewish?* by Joe Sampliner, and *Miriam's World* by Sol Weiss, appeared in 1996 in *The Stars of David: Jewish Science Fiction. Jewish Sci-Fi Stories for Kids* (1999), by Rivka Lisa Perel, contains stories by Stephanie Burgis, Eliot Fintushel, Yaacov Peterseil, Miriam Baskin, Dan Pearlman, and Mark Blackman.

Jews, the Universe, and Everything

L. Borodulin is reputed to have written the first Yiddish science fiction novel, *Af Yener Zayt Sambatyon* ("On the Other Side of Sambatyon River," 1929), about a journalist who encounters a mad scientist in the land of the Red Jews (referring not to Russia, but to lost tribesmen). Other offerings in Yiddish include A. Tanenboym's *Tsvishen himel un vaser: a visenshaftlikher roman* ("Between Sky and Water: A Scientific Romance," 1896), *Doktor und tsoyberer* (1899) and *Di shvartse kunst: a vissenshaftlikher roman* ("The Black Art: A Scientific Novel," 1899); Solomon Bogin's *Der Ferter Internatsyonal, Fantastishe Dertseylung* (The Fourth International," 1929); Leon Kussman's *Narnbund, Fantastishe Trilogye* ("Union of Fools," 1931); Y.L. Goldshtayn, *Tsuzamenbrukh oder iberboy: fantastisher roman in fir teyln* ("A Fantastic Tale in Four Parts," 1934); Velvl Tshernovetski's *Erev der Ferter Velt-Milkhome, Hines-di Kenign Fun Mars* ("On the Eve of World War IV: The Martian Queen," 1959); and Leybl Botvinik's *Di Geheyme Shlihes: Fantastishe Dertseylung* ("The Secret Mission," 1980).

For the most part, however – and despite serious offerings in French, Russian, and even Hebrew – English remains the lingua franca of contemporary SF, Jewish or otherwise. In Walter M. Miller's *A Canticle for Leibowitz* (1960), a post-nuclear holocaust Catholic Order grapples with the meaning of an obscure ancient document that belonged to a beatified Jewish physicist. A Jewish psychotherapist traveled back in time in Michael Moorcock's *Behold the Man* (1967), whence he replaced the historical Yeshua on the cross to ensure the Passion unfolds as described in Gospel. Curt Siodmak preserved the DNA-based memories of a Nazi scientist within a Jewish-American scientist's brain in *Hauser's Memory* (1968); Harry Harrison's *The Daleth Effect* (1970) concerned an Israeli scientist who discovers an anti-gravity device, and subsequently spirits it out to Denmark rather than see his invention used to fight the Cold War. Isidore Haiblum's *The Tsaddik of Seven Wonders* (1971) offered a Yiddish-inflected romp through alternate time tracks, considering, among other outcomes, a world in which the Hasmonean revolt against King Antiochus never occurred, and in which the defenders of Masada had defeated the besieging Romans. In *The Texas-Israeli War: 1999* (1974), Israel emerged from World War III unscathed and overpopulated, and Israeli mercenaries were called in to rescue the kidnapped American president from the renegade state of Texas. Leonard Harris' *The Masada Plan* (1976) involved a weakened Israel about to succumb to a combined Arab attack, and which secures a cease-fire through planetary nuclear blackmail. In Michael J. Halberstam's *The Wanting of Levine* (1978), America's first Jewish president forestalls civil war; Allan Topol's *The Fourth of July War* (1978) envisioned a joint American-Israeli takeover of Saudi oil fields. In *The Divine Invasion* (1980), SF virtuoso Philip K. Dick grappled with the dybbuk of a 14th-century rabbi; in his final novel, *The Transmigration of Timothy Archer* (1982), he retold, through an SF prism laden with kabbalistic speculation, the story of defrocked Episcopalian Bishop James Pike, who in fact died rather bizarrely in the Negev desert in 1969 while searching for pre-Christian artifacts. Phyllis Gotlieb considered the plight of the last Jew in the universe in *Tauf Aleph* (1984). David Brin and Gregory Benford's *Heart of the Comet* (1986) features an Israeli scientist and former kibbutznik in self-imposed exile from a theocratic Jewish state. In *The Devil's Arithmetic* (1988), Jane Yolen sent a 12-year-old American Jewish girl uninterested in her family's Holocaust experiences back to wartime Poland; in *Briar Rose* (1992), Yolen used the Jewish folktale to offer a somewhat different glimpse into the era's horrors. Joel Rosenberg wrote two novels, *Not for Glory* (1988) and *Hero* (1990), set on the Jewish planet of Metzada, which exports Israeli-style mercenaries. In Martin Amis's *Time's Arrow* (1991), an aging Nazi death camp doctor begins living his life backwards, re-experiencing his complicity in Auschwitz redemptively, as gassed Jews return to life and he heads back to the womb of creation. In *Snow Crash* (1992), Neal Stephenson analyzed the talmudic concept of "building a fence around the Torah" in an information-dense "Cyberpunk" (a cultural sub-genre of science fiction that emerged during the 1980s and is typically set in a not-so-distant, dystopian, over-industrialized society setting). In Harry Turtledove's *Worldwar* tetralogy, an alternate history/SF hybrid beginning with *In the Balance: An Alternate History of the Second World War* (1994), Jews, Nazis and other unlikely partners ally against an alien invasion that interrupts the Final Solution. Lisa Goldstein pits a kabbalistic magician against a mystic rabbi during the Holocaust in *The Red Magician* (1995). Mary Doria Russell, a Catholic convert to Judaism, sent a team of Jesuits and a Sephardi Jew in *The Sparrow (1996)* and its sequel, *Children of God* (1998), to a planet of enslaved sentient herbivores in dire need of exposure to liberation theology. Scientist Bart Kosko envisioned an all-out nuclear conflagration consuming Israel and its neighbors in *Nanotime* (1997). *In Days of Cain* (1997) by J.R. Dunn, a group of time travelers confront time guardians who try to prevent them from erasing Auschwitz from the timeline. In *Planet of the Jews* (1999), Philip Graubart explored the growth of a Star Wars-like publishing phenomenon, when a hack writer popularizes a far-fetched intergalactic saga involving remnants of the Jewish people and recounted by a young ḥasidic couple. In *The Cure* (1999) by Sonia Levitin, a non-conformist composer 300 years hence is sent back to France, circa 1348, where a stint as the son of a wealthy Jewish moneylender facing the spread of the Black Plague is intended to purge him of his subversive passion for music. In *Just like Beauty* (2002), Lisa Lerner chronicled the adventures of an adolescent Jewish girl trying to come to terms with her Jewish past in a corporatist future befuddled by mindless sex and violence. Similarly, in *Dante's Equation* (2003), Jane Jensen combined Kabalistic lore and theoretical physics to account for a ḥasidic rabbi who purportedly disappeared from Auschwitz in a flash of light. Robert Zubrin's satiric novel, *The Holy Land* (2003), postulates a race of aliens who stage an impromptu return to their ancestral homeland, located in a small section of the state of Washington. Peaceful and industrious refugees from a distant war, the aliens, obvious stand-ins for Zionists, attract the immediate ire of their fellow Washingtonians and the U.S. government.

A Glut of Golems

In the post-feminist fable, *He, She and It* (1991; U.K. 1992 as *Body of Glass*), Marge Piercy explored the *golem* myth while considering a dystopian future characterized by nuclear fallout and environmental catastrophe. The novel directly concerned the destruction of the Middle East, the emergence, within a Balkanized America, of the freebooting Jewish community of Tikva, and within the shattered former state of Israel, the birth of a Jewish-Palestinian feminist collective reliant on cloning for propagation. In *Kiln People* (2002), David Brin, the son of the late Los Angeles Jewish newspaper editor Herb Brin, used the *golem* myth to explore the prospects of immortality, as people regularly inject their consciousnesses into expendable clay doppelgangers. He also featured a sentient Jewish dolphin in his "Uplift" series. In *The Iron Council* (2004), British author China Miéville grafted weird fantasy with a Trotskyist sensibility to the archetypal western, casting "golem master" Judah Low as a gay rebel who makes a bid for personal and political freedom by absconding with a "perpetual train." Alexander C. Irvine's *The Narrows* (2005) opens in a Detroit factory in an alternate World War II, where workers work under a rabbi to manufacture golems tasked with fighting Hitler's minions.

Golems have cropped up in many other mainstream and genre offerings for at least 50 years, beginning with Roger Zelazny's *This Immortal* (1966) and providing the focus of numerous fanciful stories by Avram Davidson, Isaac Asimov, Ted Chiang, and others. The *golem* has appeared as well in poems by (non-Jewish) Argentinean "magical realist" Jorge Luis Borges; in Gregory Keyes' *A Calculus of Angels* (1999); in Michael Chabon's Pulitzer-winning novel, *The Amazing Adventures of Kavalier & Clay* (2000); in Frances Sherwood *The Book of Splendor* (2002); in Terry Pratchett's humorous *Discworld* novels *Feet of Clay* (1996) and *Going Postal* (2004); in the second book of Jonathan Stroud's Bartimaeus Trilogy, *The Golem's Eye* (2004); in an episode of television's *X-Files*; in several comic books (including DC's *Ragman* (1976) and *Monolith* (2004) as well as Marvel's *The Invaders* (2004), and, most recently, as a brilliant parody of the superhero comic book genre by Israeli artist Uri Fink.

Counterfactual Thought-Experimentation

The Holocaust remains a thematic and philosophical preoccupation for many contemporary Jewish writers. Fantasy, often denigrated as escapist, nevertheless offers an occasionally useful lens through which to consider a human event at once both singular and ineffable, and most often simply beyond the ability of realistic fiction to accurately represent. The challenge of representation becomes exponentially harder for writers who not only did not directly experience the event, but who were not even alive when it transpired. Some fantasists, SF writers, and children's authors outside of Israel have resorted to the familiar SF trope of time travel to confront and either undo, or wreak revenge for, the decimation of European Jewry. Others have adopted a more versatile and, thanks to recent developments in particle physics (which postulates the endless generation of parallel worlds), a more realistic SF device: alternate, or counterfactual, history.

Whether conducted by writers of fiction or historians, alternate histories are usually intended as classical thought experiments that posit different outcomes to historical events due to vital alterations – fictional tweaking of points of divergence – in the sequence of events during critical moments in human development. An offshoot of both conventional historical study and of contemporary science fiction, alternate history tries, whether in fiction, film or essay form, to imagine what the world might look like today, in the recent past, or in the near (and occasionally far) future, had some key variant in the historical timeline taken a pivotal turn toward a different direction. Initially disdained for its subjectivity, alternate history has come increasingly into vogue in recent years, becoming a recognizable, if not yet entirely commonplace, literary and cinematic commodity.

Of the myriad historical events available for imaginative inquiry (most notably a failure of the Protestant Reformation, a Southern victory in the American Civil War, a failed bid for American Independence), not a few have concerned themselves with the vagaries of Jewish history. The earliest known example of what we today would term alternate history is the apocryphal *Sefer Yehudit* (Book of Judith), which depicted a reversal of the Babylonian conquest and a return to Zion by Jewish exiles that never actually happened. Another example is Benjamin *Disraeli's *The Wondrous Tale of Alroy* (aka, *The Prince of the Captivity, A Wondrous Tale* (1833), dramatized in 1907 as a musical by P.P. Grunfeld), about a 12th-century Jewish false messiah who founds a global empire.

No event, however, surpasses the Nazi defeat in 1945 as a focal point for counterfactual speculation. Among devotees and practitioners of alternate history, this variant is known as "Hitler Victorious (HV)." Within this variant of alternate history, Hitler's war against the Jews becomes a central preoccupation, second only, perhaps, to questions about the extent and nature of possible domestic collaboration under a Nazi regime.

Scores of HV and other alternate history stories, novels, film, and TV adaptations and series have appeared in Great Britain, the U.S., and Germany since the 1930s, and in the early 21st century showed few signs of ceasing to enthrall writers, readers, and viewers. Noteworthy recent examples, including those considered outright science fiction, include Philip K. Dick's Hugo-winning novel, *The Man in the High Castle* (1962); *If Israel Lost The War* (1969), by Richard Z. Chesnoff, Edward Klein, and Robert Littell; Norman Spinrad's *The Iron Dream* (1974); Len Deighton's *SS-GB: Nazi-Occupied Britain, 1941* (1978); Robert Harris's *Fatherland* (1993); Harry Turtledove's *In the Presence of Mine Enemies* (2003); Philip Roth's *The Plot Against America* (2004); and Michael Chabon's *The Yiddish Policemen's Union* (2006).

Thematic anthologies include *Hitler Victorious: Eleven Stories of the German Victory in World War Two*, edited by Gregory Benford and Martin Harry Greenberg (1986); *Alternate Histories: Eleven Stories of the World as it Might Have Been*, edited by Charles G. Waugh and Martin Harry Greenberg (1986); *The Way it Wasn't: Great Science Fiction Stories of Alternate History*, edited by Martin Harry Greenberg (1996); *Virtual History: Alternatives and Counterfactuals*, edited by Niall Ferguson (1997); *Roads Not Taken: Tales of Alternate History*, edited by Gardner Dozois and Stanley Schmidt; and *The Best Alternate History Stories of the 20th Century*, edited by Harry Turtledove and Martin H. Greenberg (2001). Noteworthy non-fictional treatments include *What If?: The World's Foremost Military Historians Imagine What Might Have Been*, edited by Robert Cowley (1999), and *What If? 2: Eminent Historians Imagine What Might Have Been* (2001); *Third Reich Victorious: Alternate Decisions of World War II*, edited by Peter Tsouras (2002); *What Might Have Been: Imaginary History from Twelve Leading Historians*, edited by Andrew Roberts (2004); and *The World Hitler Never Made*, by Gavriel D. Rosenfeld (2005).

Antisemitic SF

Many SF writers of the late 19th and early 20th centuries were influenced by, and even propagated, the normative racism of their day, including antisemitism. Unflattering and even malevolent images of Jews (and blacks and Asians) occurred in the writing of Edgar Rice Burroughs, H.P. Lovecraft, M.P. Shiel, Clark Ashton Smith, Louis Tracy, King Wallace, H.G. Wells, and Jules Verne. Gernsback, though nominally Jewish, translated and published supremacist utopian fantasies by the German Otfried von Hanstein in *Amazing Stories*.

A number of writers subsequently found SF useful for disseminating antisemitic agendas. French poet Robert Brasillach published a poem in 1943 about a future visit to the V'mcennes Zoo, where mothers bring their children to attend the death of the world's last living Jew. In *The Turner Diaries* (1982), Andrew MacDonald concocted a thoroughly racist and antisemitic libertarian fantasy chronicling a white Christian insurrection against a Jewish and African-American-controlled U.S government. The book has become a canonical text for American white supremacists, and is believed to have inspired the bombing of the Federal Building in Oklahoma. Another anti-Jewish tract that resorted to apocalyptic SF-tinged scenarios was *Serpent's Walk* (1991), by Randolph D. Caverhall. The book chronicles the rise of a new American fuehrer and an Israeli-created plague that ultimately turns on its makers, decimating world Jewry and the various "mongrel" races Caverhall purports to despise. David Britton's *Lord Horror* (1986) provoked vigorous argument as to whether his novel was in fact antisemitic or a deliberate, if entirely over-the-top, parody of antisemitism. In 1993, a non-Jewish producer of the TV series *Star Trek: Deep Space 9* complained that his fellow producers – both of them Jewish – had peopled the series with thinly veiled antisemitic alien "Shylocks" whose holiest book, "The Rules of Acquisition," malevolently parodied the Talmud. A novel, *The Hand that Signed the Paper* (1995), generated controversy in Australia when it was discovered that its author, Helen Demidenko, was not the daughter of a Ukrainian father victimized by Jewish commissars, as she described herself, but a British immigrant, Helen Darville, who used her book to vent spleen upon Ukranian Jewry and justify Ukranian collaboration with the Nazis.

Israeli Science Fiction and Fantasy

The Jewish state, reconstituted in 1948 as the State of Israel, may be the only country in the world to have been at least partly inspired by a science fiction novel. The work in question was called *Altneuland* (1902; *Old-New Land*), and was written by the Austrian journalist Theodor (Binyamin Ze'ev) *Herzl on the heels of his Zionist manifesto *Der Judenstaat*, (1896; *The Jewish State*). The earlier pamphlet was a *cri de coeur* lamenting the deplorable condition of Jews throughout the European Diaspora and containing the blueprint for the modern Zionist movement that within a half century would achieve sovereignty in parts of the historic Jewish commonwealth in Palestine. The latter publication, a thinly plotted work of fiction, was an attempt to fire up the political imagination.

"If you will it," Herzl declared in an utterance that resounds with a science fiction sensibility, "it is no dream." Fearful lest his own dream be dismissed as a frivolous Romantic fancy, however, Herzl initially sought to dissociate Zionism from the utopian discourse that had returned to vogue during the 19th century with the publication, in 1888, of Edward Bellamy's *Looking Backward, 2000–1887*. At least one other such work, Theodor Hertzka's *Freiland: Ein Sociales Zukunftbild* ("Freeland: An Image of Future Society," 1890) is believed to have directly influenced Herzl's decision to craft *Altneuland* as a conventional utopian novel, quite possibly because of the many editions it had inspired as well as some of the real-world utopian passions it had tapped.

With his otherwise mundane story of a modern, liberal, technocratic, German-speaking Jewish commonwealth, where Jews (with Arab compliance) could engage in the kind of human engineering that would allow them to shed two millennia of disfiguring dispersion and subjugation, Herzl was actually one of literally dozens of Jewish thinkers indulging in the utopian literary and ideological speculation as to what a future Jewish state might look like. One of these, *Massa le-Ereẓ Yisrael bi-Shenat Tat be-Elef ha-Shishi* ("A Trip to the Land of Israel in the 800th Year of the Sixth Millennium"), published in 1892 by the Hebrew writer Elhanan Leib *Lewinsky and envisioning the flowering of Hebrew culture in Palestine, would have been recognizable as a scientific romance to H.G. Wells, who made his genre debut in 1895 with *The Time Machine*. Another such book was Max Austerberg-Verakoff's *Das Reich Judaea im Jahre 6000 (2241)*, published in 1893 and depicting a mass exodus of Jews from Europe, their settlement in Ereẓ Israel, and the founding there of a Jewish state with Hebrew as its official language. *Looking Ahead* (1899), by Henry Pereira Mendes, offered an American response to Herzl's *Der Judenstaat* (and a Zionist response to Bellamy's tome), describing a future Jewish state with Jerusalem as its capital. Isaac Fernhof described a future state called Israel in the aptly named *Shenei Dimyonot* ("Two Imaginings"). Hebrew-Yiddish writer Hillel Zeitlin published another such tract, *In der Medinas Yisroel in Yor 2000* ("In the State of Israel in the Year 2000"), in 1919, following Great Britain's proclamation of its Balfour Declaration. In Mandatory Palestine, Boris *Schatz wrote *Yerushalayim ha-Benuyah* ("Rebuilt Jerusalem"), published in 1924 and concerned with social and labor issues of the period. In 1921, Russian-based Hebrew author Shalom Ben Avram published *Komemiyut* ("Resurgence"), which contained an astute and accurate portrayal of future mass immigration and the challenges and benefits of *aliyah*.

Most of these writings failed to inspire great notice or enthusiasm. Two, however, attained something of *Altneuland's* stature as a constituting document – a text containing some of the basic myths of the new Hebrew society slated to arise in Palestine. These were Abraham *Mapu's *Ahavat Ẓiyyon* ("Love of Zion," 1853), a historical novel set in an idealized Kingdom of Judah during the reigns of Ahaz and Hezekiah, and Yosef Luidor's *Yoash* (1912/13), the *Akedah* (Binding of Isaac) as a Maccabean myth set against the struggle against the Arabs during the Second Aliyah.

Herzl strived mightily to avoid donning the mantle of utopian visionary even as he sought, in *Altneuland*, to use the genre's conventions to stir the imaginations of Jewish and Gentile readers in a manner that would provoke sympathy and support. But the term "utopian," even a half century before *Altneuland*, carried pejorative associations of impracticality, naiveté, and wish fulfillment. The Zionist movement –as well as the new Hebrew republic – would move mountains to avoid being stigmatized for what it was – a modern, unabashedly utopian, thoroughly realistic political movement driven, not by imaginative musings or imperialistic hubris but by desperate circumstances and diminishing options.

It has been argued that the contemporary State of Israel not only grew out of science fiction, but also has quite literally lived it every day of its unlikely existence. In their most desperately fanciful imaginings, neither Herzl nor his fellow

Zionist utopians would have entertained the possibility that a mere century after the first Zionist Congress in 1898, the world would include a Jewish democracy six-million strong with the most powerful economy in the region, a first-rate military able to project devastating force thousands of miles away, seven major research universities, its own satellites and astronaut in orbit, and pride of place as a world-class scientific and technological innovator.

Despite these achievements, and despite a breakneck pace of change that heralds fundamental and continual transformation at nearly every level of Israeli society, the fantastic, in most manifestations outside of the literal, fares almost as poorly now – and is as thoroughly stigmatized as *déclassé* – as during Herzl's heyday.

Reasons for the inordinately low premium still placed by Israeli readers and Israeli letters and arts on most forms of the literary *fantastique* since the founding of the state in 1948 are varied, complex, and contradictory. Despite their talent for hard-nosed realism, Israel's founding pioneers did not, in fact, forsake the strong utopian component of Zionist ideology. Nor did the founding generations restrict their imaginings and activities merely to bringing into being a new Jewish commonwealth. A homeland in and of itself would be insufficient – even unsustainable – unless in recreating theirs, Jews could reclaim their dignity and independence, shattered during 2,000 years of dispersion, through physical labor and martial self-sufficiency.

A human engineering project of such scope and ambition, however, required a clean break with a Jewish past and culture deemed moribund, shameful, or disfiguring. With roots in the Russian Pale, many of the pre-state Yishuv's writers and ideologues, already predisposed to the conventions of Russian literary realism, deliberately cut themselves off from the imaginative reservoir of the Jewish past. The task of the Israeli writer was to grapple with questions of religious, national and personal identity considered through the prism of the Zionist endeavor in the land of Israel. As Israeli literary theorist Ortsion Bartana has argued in his study of the work of Yoram *Kaniuk, Yitzhak *Orpaz Averbuch, and David *Shahar, Israeli writers are invariably bound up in these larger issues and simply cannot create characters who are not in some way involved in the redemptive communal effort or affected by it.

The so-called "Palmaḥ Generation" of the 1950s added social realism to their literary menu, but they, too, consigned centuries of Jewish myths, stories, motifs, images, tropes, commentaries, and super-commentaries to history and literature's dustbin. Some of Israel's leading contemporary writers, most notably David *Grossman, Meir *Shalev, Etgar Keret, and Orly *Castel-Bloom, have, in recent years, acquainted themselves with, and even incorporated, some of the trappings of magical realism. To the extent that they take up the tropes of fantasy, however, it is most often to cast their glance backward, to the formative years of the nation-building effort, and almost never ahead into the foreseeable or distant future. For these writers, as indeed for their predecessors, outright science fiction and fantasy remain, even with the advent of the new millennium and the *fantastique's* growing popularity and accumulating literary gravitas worldwide, at the far margins of Hebrew letters.

Israelis have yet to establish their own national borders. Any consideration of imaginary realms must therefore be seen as frivolous or escapist. With the proverbial day-after-tomorrow almost always fraught with peril, not a few Israelis prefer to avoid long-term speculation of any kind. Indeed, the culture seems almost to fetishize its fascination for the here-and-now. SF is considered a foreign import reflective of normative values far removed from Israel's, where the struggle to consolidate a nation and its territory is ongoing and all consuming.

Whereas most Israeli fiction (and indeed, most modern fiction) concerns itself with the individual's psychological response to the exigencies of a particularistic life, SF and fantasy, almost by definition, consider broader questions of society's place in a changing world and a boundless cosmos. In a country where even the ground under one's feet is not assured, such concerns are considered a luxury bound to distract and weaken. Israel has yet to contend fundamentally and directly with its relationship with its minority populations, and is only beginning to grapple with the exigencies of its relationship with the Palestinians in the West Bank and Gaza. Other issues that remain to be resolved include the rift between secular and religious, between Ashkenazim and Sephardim, and between haves and have-nots. Those Israelis oriented toward any future beyond one characterized by perennial strife and insecurity are therefore often dismissed as *astronautim*.

Also, many Israelis mistakenly consider fantasy and science fiction to be a form of children's entertainment. Despite the musings of Bruno Bettelheim and other devotees of the fairy tale, not a few continue to believe that fantasy and fairy tales stir up subconscious fears in children unavoidably saddled from an early age with various forms of existential angst. And indeed, Jewish literature lacks a mythic basis for the kinds of heroic or Arthurian fantasy that might generate a Jewish version of *The Lord of the Rings*, a *Narnia*, or a *Harry Potter*.

Hebrew, moreover, appears to be at a disadvantage compared to the richer, more agile Yiddish language in conveying what fans of SF and fantasy call "a sense of wonder." Indeed, the mere act of settling on a Hebrew term for science fiction initially inspired argument, with some arguing for *mada dimyoni* (imaginary science), with the majority finally favoring *mada bidyoni* (fabricated science).

Perhaps of greatest consequence for prospective and publishing writers, though, is the Israeli literary establishment's continuing disdain for commercial literature of almost any kind as inherently unserious, and its sense that science fiction and fantasy represent the lowest forms of commercial fiction. Israeli aficionados themselves regard indigenous forays into the genre as inherently substandard, and prefer imports or translations. And publishers must contend with the fact that Israel publishes so many books every year that most books – genre or non-genre – do well if they cover their expenses.

Tales of Zion's Fiction

A number of works construable as fantasy and science fiction nevertheless trickled into the Yishuv as early as 1931, when Reuven Grossman translated and published a Hebrew collection of stories by Edgar Allan Poe. Translations of stories and novels by Jules Verne and H.G. Wells soon followed; most were marketed as children's literature. Several immigrants to pre-state Palestine, including the Russian-Hebrew poet Zalman *Shneour, playwright Jacob Cohen, and Austrian novelist Leo *Perutz, indulged an occasional literary penchant for the fantastic. Cohen's *Beluz* (1939) concerned a hidden city of immortals at ideological loggerheads over whether to share their secret. Perutz (1882–1957) wrote a series of baroque phantasms, including *The Marquis de Bolibar*, in which the Wandering Jew defeats a German regiment under Napoleon, and novels such as *The Master of the Day of Judgment* (1929) and *The Virgin's Brand* (1934), in which aspects of human civilization are inspired by viruses, fungi, and other unseen conveyances.

The first identifiably SF novel to be published in Israel in the immediate post-Independence period was *Yisrael be-Shenat 2000* ("Israel in the Year 2000"), published by S. Goldfluss in 1951. The name is believed to have been a pseudonym, but the book proved oddly prescient, even alluding, in metaphoric terms, to the likelihood of future Arab uprisings. American science fiction writer Avram Davidson, an Orthodox Jew, lived in Israel from 1948 to 1953 and served in the Israel Defense Forces during Israel's War of Independence. Polish-born Mordecai Roshwald, who sojourned in Israel and taught at the Hebrew University before leaving for Great Britain, wrote two well-regarded post-nuclear holocaust novels, *Level 7* (1959) and *A Small Armageddon* (1962). Lionel *Davidson, a British-born immigrant, wrote *The Sun Chemist* (1976) about the rediscovery of a lost formula devised by British chemist (and Israel's first president) Chaim *Weizmann that uses sweet potatoes to tap solar energy. Davidson wrote two other genre novels, *The Rose of Tibet* (1962) – a lost world fantasy – and a children's fantasy adventure, *Under Plum Cake* (1980).

During Israel's first decade, local publishers began to publish as many as 30 Hebrew translations of science fiction standards a year, including novels by Robert Heinlein, Poul Anderson, and Frederic Brown as well as Verne, Wells, and Huxley. An early example of this kind of activity was provided by the publishing house Matzpen (Compass), which specialized in a line of translations edited by renowned Israeli SF pioneer and namesake of the nation's top SF prize, Amos Geffen. The early 1950s, however, were marked in Israel by economic hardship, with the country's limited resources earmarked for massive immigrant absorption and defense, and with little cash left for light reading. These publishing ventures failed, but some intrepid local fans proceeded to publish two different SF magazines, both launched in 1958. *Mada Dimyoni* (*Imaginary Science*) ran for 12 issues, *Kosmos: Sipurei Mada Dimyoni* (*Cosmos: Imaginary Science Stories*) folded after four.

At the start of the 1970s, buoyed by the economic gains following the 1967 War, Am Oved launched a series of translations of SF standards that, in fact, continues to this day. Another well-established publisher, Masada, followed suit with a new series of translations edited by Geffen. Their efforts proved successful enough to induce nearly every major commercial Israeli publishing house to launch an SF line of its own, under the respective banners of local SF mavens (and established academics) Adi Tzemach, Emanuel Lottem, and Dorit Landes.

The economy nosedived in the aftermath of the 1973 Yom Kippur War, during which time only one Israeli of literary consequence, poet David *Avidan, expressed any interest in the genre. A respected poet, Avidan was one of a very few writers who not only wrote science fiction but happily embraced the label and its conventions, going so far as to name his own publishing company The 30th Century. Avidan incorporated such standard SF themes as time travel, sentient computers, the destruction of humanity, and telepathic powers into both his poetry and his various stage productions. In 1979, Avidan wrote and directed a short SF film, *Sheder min ha-Atid* ("Broadcast from the Future"), based on one of his poems. Avidan belonged to the Israeli avant-garde, but he was not the only Hebrew poet to have addressed concerns usually the purview of science or science fiction. Others to have dipped their pens in this well included Romanian-born poet Dan *Pagis (1930–1986), scientist Zvi Atzmon (1948–), and writers Shlomo Shoval, Maya *Bejerano, (1949–), and Rahel Chalfi.

The election of the Likud in 1977 spurred growth in the consumer market, creating new demands for entertainment, including popular literature. In 1978, Tel Aviv University students Eli Teneh and Aharon Hauptman launched a glossy SF monthly, *Fantasia 2000*, which ran for 44 issues over four years and became the standard-bearer for local science fiction fandom. The magazine appealed mostly to adolescent males, some of whom emulated their counterparts in the U.S. and the U.K., starting clubs and publishing mimeographed pamphlets and newsletters, called fanzines. The magazine published dozens of stories culled mostly from the New York-based *Magazine of Fantasy and Science Fiction* (F&SF), running ample book and film review sections as well as popular science columns and covers by talented local artists, including Avi Katz, who in 2000 would be commissioned to design an issue of millennial Israeli stamps dedicated to "SF in Israel" and slated to coincide with a major conference in 2001. Another in-house artist was Victor Ostrovsky, who would achieve notoriety in 1991 as a Mossad renegade and best-selling writer of (largely fabricated) exposes.

Apart from being the country's longest-running SF magazine and the source of 400 stories, many now deemed canonical, *Fantasia* had the added distinction of publishing close to 100 original, hitherto unpublished Israeli Hebrew-language SF stories. While few of these proved exceptional, some were competent, and the mere existence of a venue for Hebrew SF spurred many young people to try their hand at writing.

Some of them went on to careers in letters. In this, *Fantasia* mimicked some of the American magazines of the 1930s and 1940s, which also functioned as greenhouses for up-and-coming writers and researchers. The late Israeli astronaut, Col. Ilan *Ramon, claimed to have read the magazine assiduously, saying that while he typically hid it from his peers in the Air Force, SF made him receptive to the possibility, one day, of an Israeli foothold in space.

Israel's forays into Lebanon, however, put a damper on both the economy and on activities deemed frivolous. *Fantasia* folded, and a major international science fiction convention that had been slated to commence in June 1982 in Jerusalem was canceled. Two other magazines that had emerged during the same period as *Fantasia* fell by the wayside as well: *Mada Bidyoni* (by now, the consensual term for Science Fiction), folded after a single issue; a second, a rechristened *Kosmos*, gave up the ghost after six, both victims not so much of the zeitgeist as of poor quality and inadequate resources. A number of fly-by-night publishers that had climbed on the SF bandwagon, some producing poor translations of marginal titles, quickly imploded as well. By 1984, Am Oved, with Dorit Landes at the helm of its SF line, had the genre to itself.

As Israel's Lebanon adventure bogged down, and as the political, religious, and cultural polarization of the Jewish state became more pronounced, various writers, many of them established in the Israeli mainstream, began to make forays into the fantastic, some of them producing undeniable science fiction, though they asserted, for reasons of commerce and prestige, that it was anything but. In fact, at least one Israeli author, I. Hayek, had come down with a bad case of the apocalyptic shudders as early as 1968, when his novel, *The Next War*, contemplated a 40-day-long doomsday battle between Israel and the rest of the world. The 1980s, however, produced what for Israel constituted a veritable deluge of nightmare visions of the imminent future, beginning with Amos *Kenan's *Shoah 2* ("Holocaust 2," 1975), and proceeding through David Yaron's *Ha-Patria* (1981), Moshe Ben David's *Ha-Beriḥah ha-Aḥaronah* ("The Final Escape," 1984), and David Melamed's *Ha-Ḥalom ha-Rivi'i* ("The Fourth Dream," 1986), each offering variations on Israel's impeding destruction.

In September 1982, nearly half a million Israelis gathered in Tel Aviv to demonstrate against the war in Lebanon. In February 1983, a right-wing heckler tossed a grenade at Peace Now protesters in Jerusalem, killing a 33-year-old kibbutznik and paratroop officer. Kach firebrand and Jewish Defense League founder Meir *Kahane, meanwhile, traveled throughout the country calling Arabs "dogs" and promising a day of reckoning. The prospect of destruction from without had always been an integral component of the collective Israeli psyche. But suddenly, internal dissension, which had rendered the erstwhile Jewish republic 2000 years earlier vulnerable to external forces, appeared even more likely to precipitate Israel's eventual undoing.

In 1984, Amos Kenan, a veteran of the War of Independence, responded to this cumulative angst with *Ha-Derekh le-En-Harod* ("The Road to En-Harod"), which postulated a right-wing military putsch and a concurrent attempt to change the distant past, and enhance Jewish fortunes, with a time travel device. The book, which was translated into French, English, and Arabic, won a literary prize from the PLO, and was adapted for film by Israeli director Doron Eran in 1989. In 1996, Kenan would complete his dystopian triptych with *Blok 23: Mikhtavim mi-Nes Ziyyonah* ("Block 23: Letters from Nes Ziyyonah"), depicting the utter destruction of the Jewish state.

Throughout, Kenan vehemently denied having ever written science fiction (except in an interview in *Fantasia 2000*, which of course none of his literary confreres would admit to having read). The stigma attached to the genre, however, did not dissuade other Israeli writers of note from indulging in the form. A favorite theme involved a fundamentalist takeover, à la Iran's Ayatollahs, by ultra-Orthodox Jewish zealots. Examples of sci-fi in *shtreimels* (festive fur hats worn by ḥasidic men) included Binyamin *Tammuz's *Pundako shel Yermiyahu* ("Jeremiah's Inn," 1984), Yitzhak *Ben Ner's *Malakhim Ba'im* ("Angels Are Coming,"1987), Motti Lerner's *Ḥevlei Moshi'aḥ* ("Messianic Pangs," 1988), and Assi *Dayan's *Tokhen ha-Inyanim* ("Table of Contents," 1989) and from a right-wing perspective, Ora Shem Or's *Ha-Karirist* ("The Careerist," 1990).

Variations on this theme ensued during the 1990s, culminating with Michal Peleg's *Ha-Ir ha-Penimit* ("The Inner City," 1998) and Hadi Ben Amar's *Be-Shem Shamayim* ("In the Name of Heaven," 1998). Ironically, a number of books that indulged in various SF trappings appeared during this time that were written for the sensibilities of Orthodox youngsters in Israel and in various enclaves in New York and Los Angeles. Their purpose was purely didactic.

While many of the books and stories appearing during the late 1970s and 1980s reflected the parochial political and social anxieties of the time, a number of Israeli authors turned to science fiction to explore more universal themes. Some of these stories and novels went so far as to feature protagonists with Anglo-Saxon names operating in nondescript or foreign settings. In 1973, A. Kalev published *Groteska* ("Grotesque"), a series of absurdist novellas weighing man's place in the universe. In 1980, David Melamed, a graduate of *Fantasia 2000*, published his first and only collection of SF stories, *Ẓavu'a be-Korundi* ("A Hyena in Corundi"). Though well received within the country's fledgling SF community, the book did not perform well in the marketplace, and after writing his aforementioned novel, *The Fourth Dream*, Melamed deserted the genre entirely.

In 1982, Israeli geneticist Ram Moav published a hard-SF tome, *Zerimat Ḥakhamim* ("A Flow of Wise Men"), and in 1985 followed up with *Luna: Gan Eden Geneti* ("Luna: Genetic Garden of Eden"). Both novels focused on the wider implications of genetic engineering for humanity in general and touched upon Israel more tangentially. Hillel Damron's *Milḥemet ha-Minim* ("War of the Sexes," 1982) left the exigencies of the Arab-Israeli struggle to the pundits, contemplating a future Jewish state riven by gender-based struggles. Israeli literary theorist Ortsion Bartana published two related titles, *Serifot* ("Burnings," 1985) and *Ha-Sha'ot ha-Tovot Hen Sha'ot ha-Laylah* ("The Best Hours Are the Hours of the Night," 1994). Bartana also wrote a related non-fiction treatise, *Ha-Fantaziyyah be-Sipporet Dor ha-Medinah* ("Fantasy in Israeli Literature in the Last Thirty Years," 1989). *Fantasia* veteran Yivsam Azgad published two SF titles, a juvenile, *Avodat Nemalim* ("Ant Work," 1992), and *Ma'of Kelulot* ("Cuticula," 1995), while fellow *Fantazionnaire* Shlomo Shoval published *Be-Medinot ha-Shamayim* ("In the Countries of Heaven") in 1998.

Bibliographer Lavie Tidhar, a former kibbutznik living in South Africa, has established a world-class reputation as a science fiction writer who favors Israeli settings and characters, and works with Jewish and Christological myth in a sub-genre he calls "Hebrewpunk." His novel *An Occupation of Angels* (2005) concerns the murder of archangels that first materialized over the Nazi death camps in 1945. He also published a play, *There Will Be A Time* (2005), that purportedly takes place at the cusp of a black hole. Tidhar won the 2003 Clarke Bradbury International Science Fiction Competition sponsored by the European Space Agency.

Ironically, as commercial fiction began to come into its own during the 1990s, with detective novels by Batya *Gur and political thrillers by Ram Oren regularly achieving best-seller status, those inclined to the *fantastique* in Israel began to express a greater interest in outright fantasy than in SF. Reflecting this shift in interest, a number of small publishing houses, including Mitzuv and Opus, began publishing extensive lines of fantasies, as well as role-playing games of the *Dungeons & Dragons* variety, with an occasional SF title thrown in to keep the wells primed.

One development that may bode well for the future of Israeli SF is the immigration, since the fall of the Soviet Union, of more than a million Russians, many of whom had established themselves as professional SF writers, editors, and publishers. Whether they can continue to pursue this interest in Israel, either within the Russian-speaking and -reading community, or once they achieve proficiency in Hebrew, remains to be seen.

Israeli publishing houses now issue some 40 genre-related titles yearly, some 15 percent of them indigenous efforts. *Ḥalomot be-Aspazia* ("Pipe Dreams"), a bimonthly fan magazine created by Ron Yaniv and edited by Geffen Award winner Vered Tochterman, began publishing original local SF stories on a bimonthly basis in 2003. The country boasts several clubs and an organization, including The Israeli Society for Science Fiction and Fantasy (http://www.sf-f.org.il), which organizes yearly lecture series and conventions, awards its annual literary prize – the Geffen Award, and publishes a glossy magazine featuring original stories, *Ha-Meimad ha-Asiri* ("The 10th Dimension"). Israeli *Star Trek* fans have their own society, and publish their own journal, *Starbase 972*.

Other Israels

Although still gun-shy of science fiction and fantasy, Israeli writers have generated dozens of counterfactuals – Alternate Histories – both as fiction and in essays. Notably, relatively few deal directly with the Holocaust, reflecting a deep-seated Israeli taboo against any kind of fanciful consideration of the event, most especially by those who did not experience it outright. Examples of allohistorical fiction include Dan *Almagor's *Ilu Rak* ("If Only," 1990), about Hitler's premature death; Shmuel Argaman's *Takala be-Ḥalal* ("Mishap in Space," 2000), in which the Soviet Union and the Cold War endure; David Avidan's *Et Tu, Brute* (1973), in which Caesar outwits his assassins; Uri *Avnery's *Ha-Telai ha-Shaḥor* ("The Black Patch," 1986), in which Nazi Germany develops along non-antisemitic lines; Eli Bar-Navi's *Suryah ha-Deromit asher le-Ḥofo shel ha-Yam ha-Tikhon* ("Southern Syria, on the Coast of the Mediterranean," 1998), in which Palestine became a part of postwar Syria; Israel Bartal's *Medinah Mizraḥit Ketanah le-Lo Tasbikh* ("A Small, Eastern Nation Without a Complex," 1998), in which the Jews never rebelled against Rome, and hence never went into exile; Dorit Ben-Tovim's *Nad Ned* ("See-Saw," 1997), postulating an Israeli defeat in 1960 and a Jewish Intifada against Palestinian police; Uri Fink and Shadmi Koren's *Profil 107* (1998), a graphic novel about Israeli superheroes emerging from World War II military experiments; Yanai Gose's *Be-Mehoza Yisadeti et Medinat ha-Yehudim.* ("At Mehoza I Founded the Jewish State," 1995), about a pro-Jewish Babylonian empire in 502 C.E. that supports a Yemenite Jewish state against Ethiopia; Yitzhak Laor's *Am, Ma'akhal Melakhim* ("The People, Food Fit for a King," 1993), in which Israeli soldiers refuse to fight in the Six-Day War; Isaac Oren's *Ha-Kongres* ("The Congress," 1968), in which historians use a device that demonstrates alternate historical outcomes; Amiram Pal's *Masa be-Merḥav ha-Zeman* ("Journey in the Dimension of Time," 1980), in which time travelers prevent the fall of Jerusalem in 700 B.C.E.; Doron Rosenblum's *Ha'im Yesh Mekhubad ba-Ulam?* ("Is There a Notable in the House?", 2000), in which Albert Einstein agrees to become Israel's first president in 1948; Arye Sivan's *Le-Olam Al Tomar Ilu* ("Never Say If," 2001), a poem imagining a French takeover of Palestine after World War I; Jacob Weinshall's *Ha-Yehudi ha-Aḥaron* ("The Last Jew," 1946), in which victorious Nazis working on a huge space project discover a Jew living in Madagascar; Ivor H. Yarden's *On the Death of Hitler's Assassin*, in which Hitler's murder in 1938 by a Jewish assassin leads to a massive pogrom, causing the assassin to be reviled by world Jewry after his release from prison four decades later; Ben-Dror Yemini's *Lo Matimim le-Ḥalom ha-Ẓiyyoni* ("Not Fit for the Zionist Dream," 1988), in which Sephardi Jews were barred from immigrating to Israel in 1949; and Oren Ziblin's *Ahalan Ḥaver* ("Howdy, Friend," 2000), in which Rabin is spared assassination, and peace with Syria results.

It is a testament to the vigor of Israeli literature that it can sustain itself on a literary tradition dating back less than one century. To be sure, the country is, in per capita terms, a publishing powerhouse and a voracious consumer of books, not a few of which are, and have been, identifiable as science fiction or fantasy. Literary scholar Alan Mintz has observed: "No culture, however thickly substantial, can forgo its past, especially when it extends so far back in time, without running the risk of desultory shallowness … around the margins there are [in Israel] signs of cultural insufficiency that may signal more serious problems if a deeper connection to the past is not made." To which many within the somewhat beleaguered universe of Israeli science fiction might well add, "or to the future."

BIBLIOGRAPHY: N. Barron (ed.), *Anatomy of Wonder: A Critical Guide to Science Fiction* (2004); M. Chaikin, *Angel Secrets: Stories Based on Jewish Legend* (2005); *The Cambridge Companion to Science Fiction* (2003); N. Ben Yehuda, *Deviance and Moral Boundaries: Witchcraft, the Occult, Science Fiction, Deviant Sciences and Scientists* (1987); J. Clute and J. Grant (eds.), *The Encyclopedia of Fantasy* (1999); J. Clute and P. Nicholls (eds.), *The Encyclopedia of Science Fiction* (1993); T. Todorov, *The Fantastic; a Structural Approach to a Literary Genre*, tr. from the French by R. Howard (1973); C. Fredericks, *The Future of Eternity: Mythologies in Science Fiction and Fantasy* (1982); J. Newman and M. Unswoth, *Future War Novels: An Annotated Bibliography of Works in English Published since 1946* (1984); M. Penn (ed.), *Ghosts and Golems: Haunting Tales of the Supernatural* (2001); J. Neugroschel, *Great Tales of Jewish Fantasy and the Occult: The Dybbuk and Thirty Other Classic Stories* (1997); O. Bartana, *Ha-Fantaziyyah be-Sifrut Dor Hamedinah* (1960–1989) (1989); H. Schwartz, *Lilith's Cave: Jewish Tales of the Supernatural* (1991); D. Suvin, *Metamorphoses of Science Fiction: On the Poetics and History of a Literary Genre* (1979); *Mi Tarzan Ve'ad Z'beng* (2002); J. Dann, *More Wandering Stars: An Anthology of Outstanding Stories of Jewish Fantasy and Science Fiction* (1984); D. Stern and M.J. Mirsky, *Rabbinic Fantasies: Imaginative Narratives From Classical Hebrew Literature* (1990); H. Schwartz, *Reimagining the Bible: The Storytelling of the Rabbis* (1998); I. Saggiv-Nakdimon, *Mada Bidioni be-Yisrael* (1999); N. Ben-Yehuda, "Sociological Reflections on the History of Science Fiction in Israel," in: *Science Fiction Studies*, 38, vol. 13, pt. 1 (1986); DLZ Media (ed.), *The Stars of David: Jewish Science Fiction: Volume One* (1996); S. Bayar, *Teaching Jewish Theology Through Science Fiction & Fantasy* (1997); W.W. Wagar, *Terminal Visions: The Literature of Last Things* (1982); R. Reilly, *The Transcendent Adventure: Studies of Religion in Science Fiction/Fantasy* (1985); J. Dann, *Wandering Stars: An Anthology of Jewish Fantasy and Science Fiction* (1974); G. Rosefeld, *The World Hitler Never Made* (2005); J. Neugroschel, tr. and compiler, *Yenne Velte: The Great Works of Jewish Fantasy and the Occult* (1976).

[Sheldon Teitelbaum and Eli Herstein (2nd ed.)]

SCLIAR, MOACYR (1937–), Brazilian author and physician. The city of his birth, Porto Alegre, is often the setting of his books. He established a career as one of Brazil's most important contemporary writers and as a successful medical doctor working in public health. Scliar is often compared to North American Jewish authors such as Philip Roth and Mordecai Richler. His novels and short stories are commonly characterized as a unique blend of Jewish humor, Yiddishkeit, and Latin American magical realism. He received some of the most prestigious literary awards of Brazil and Latin America, including the Casa de las Américas prize (1988). Most of his major works have been translated into English and many other languages. As a whole, Scliar's approximately 30 books provide a unique lens through which to view both Brazilian and Jewish culture.

The novel *The Centaur in the Garden* (1980) is one of his most representative and well known. It is the fantastic story of a centaur born to Russian parents who is raised as a Jew in rural Brazil. Guedali, the main character, serves as a metaphor for those who exist at the margins of dominant culture and as a symbol of the cultural hybridism of which he is a product. His life story is an allegory of the search for identity, self-discovery, and ultimately the multiplicity of human existence. The novel *The Strange Nation of Rafael Mendes* (1983) is a mix of fantasy and history; the story is revealed through a Brazilian businessman who discovers his Jewish roots as a descendant of Maimonides. The novel traces the history of the Jewish presence in Brazil and the title character learns he belongs to the "strange nation" of the Jewish people in addition to being Brazilian. In *O ciclo das águas* (1976) Scliar narrates the story of the Jewish white slave trade in Brazil through the voice of a prostitute who was deceived into emigrating from Poland to Brazil in the 1930s. In the novel *A mulher que escreveu a Bíblia* (1999) Scliar utilizes Harold Bloom's *The Book of J* as a point of departure to invent the story of a woman who lived in King Solomon's time and was responsible for writing the Bible. His complete short stories have been published in English as *The Collected Stories of Moacyr Scliar* (1999). Scliar is no doubt one of the most influential of Jewish writers from Latin America.

[Darrell B. Lockhart (2nd ed.)]

SCORPION (Heb. עַקְרָב, *akrav*; pl. *akrabbim*). The scorpion is mentioned once in the Bible as a dangerous creature of the wilderness (Deut. 8:15). The word *akrabbim* is also used for prickly thornbushes (I Kings 12:11; Ezek. 2:6), and Ascent of Akrabbim (*Ma'aleh Akrabbim) in the Negev (Num. 34:4) owes its name either to the scorpions or to the thorns found there. Ten species of scorpion are found in Israel, the most dangerous of which is *Buthus quinquestriatus*. This species is found mainly in deserts, but it occurs also in inhabited regions. When young, the scorpions are yellowish white, later becoming yellow, brown, or black. One of the minor miracles mentioned as occurring in the Second Temple period was that "no serpent or scorpion inflicted injury in Jerusalem" (Avot 5:5).

BIBLIOGRAPHY: Lewysohn, Zool, 298f., nos. 398, 399; J. Margolin, *Zoologyah*, 1 (1943), 116–9; J. Feliks, *Animal World of the Bible* (1962), 136. **ADD. BIBLIOGRAPHY:** Feliks, Ha-Tzome'aḥ, 263.

[Jehuda Feliks]

SCOTLAND, northern part of Britain. Although there are records of applications by individual Jews for rights of trade and residence in Edinburgh as early as 1691, and there is reason to believe that a short-lived congregation was established there in 1780, the first organized Jewish community in Scotland, that of Edinburgh, was not established until 1816. It was followed shortly by that of Glasgow. The mass immigration from Eastern Europe in the late 19th and early 20th centuries brought many Jewish settlers to Glasgow, but comparatively few to Edinburgh. Of the 15,000 Jews living in Scotland in 1971, all but some 220 resided in Glasgow (13,400) and Edinburgh (1,400). The remainder were distributed in Dundee (84), Ayr (68), Aberdeen (40), and Inverness (12). In the mid-1990s the Jewish population of Glasgow dropped to approximately 6,700 and that of Edinburgh to approximately 500. According to the 2001 British census, there were 4,224 declared Jews by religion in Glasgow, 763 in Edinburgh, 30 in Aberdeen, and 22 in Dundee. There is a Scottish Council of Jewish Communities, and a range of Jewish institutions, especially in Glasgow. Dr. Kenneth Collins has written widely on the history of Scottish Jewry in such works as *Aspects of Scottish Jewry* (1987), which he edited. Relations between Jews and non-Jews in Scotland have always been harmonious.

BIBLIOGRAPHY: A. Levy, *Origins of Scottish Jewry* (1959); C. Bermant, *Troubled Eden* (1969), 54–59.

°SCOTT, CHARLES PRESTWICH (generally known as **C.P. Scott**; 1846–1932), British editor and supporter of the Zionist cause. Born in Bath, Scott was first the editor and later the owner of the great liberal daily, the *Manchester Guardian*. From 1895 to 1906 he was a leading Liberal member of parliament. Scott met Chaim *Weizmann at a private party on Sept. 16, 1914, and became a staunch friend of Weizmann and of Zionism thereafter. He introduced Weizmann to D. *Lloyd George, Herbert *Samuel, and other British statesmen, and thus helped Weizmann and his colleagues in their dealings with the British government that led to the *Balfour Declaration. In a letter to Harry *Sacher he explained his Zionism in the following words: "To make the Jew a whole Jew… to clear him up in his own eyes and the eyes of the world – that seems to me sound, at least as an ideal, and there may be a chance now of moving a long way towards it." After Turkey's entrance into World War I, Scott stressed the importance of Palestine for British interests. Scott also revealed to Weizmann the details of the *Sykes-Picot treaty and thus contributed to its undoing. After Weizmann introduced Vladimir *Jabotinsky to Scott, the *Manchester Guardian* editorially supported the idea of the *Jewish Legion and contributed substantially to its realization. Scott remained a firm supporter of the Zionist movement and the *yishuv* in Palestine throughout his life. Ironically, after 1967 the *Guardian* newspaper (now published from London rather than Manchester) became a venomous critic of Israeli policy, one of the most important disseminators of left-wing anti-Zionism in the British mainstream.

BIBLIOGRAPHY: J.L. Hammond, *C.P. Scott, 1846–1932: The Making of the "Manchester Guardian"* (1946), 31–74; L. Stein, *The Balfour Declaration* (1961), 131–6; Ch. Weizmann, *Trial and Error* (1949), index; T. Wilson (ed.), *The Political Diary of C.P. Scott* (1970). **ADD. BIBLIOGRAPHY:** ODNB online.

[Benjamin Jaffe]

°SCOTT, SIR WALTER (1771–1832), Scottish poet and novelist. *Ivanhoe* (1819), one of his "Waverley Novels," set in 12th-century England, introduces Isaac of York and his daughter Rebecca. The juxtaposition of these two, as well as many incidental features of the book, recalls the story of Shylock and Jessica in *Shakespeare's *Merchant of Venice*. However, Scott's characters are, in their ethical intention, the opposite of their Shakespearean prototypes. Though a usurer, Isaac is a basically noble character, while Rebecca is the true heroine of the novel. She nurses the eponymous hero back to health and, when she falls into the hands of the villainous Knight Templar Bois-Gilbert, gives expression to the moral virtues of her race and fiercely condemns the false code of honor of medieval chivalry. Rebecca was apparently inspired by Rebecca *Gratz of Philadelphia, of whom Scott had heard from his friend, Washington Irving.

Toward the end of his life, Scott drew another set of Jewish characters in *The Surgeon's Daughter* (1827). These are far less sympathetic than the Jews in *Ivanhoe*. Richard Middlemas, the half-Jewish rogue, is ambitious, violent, and treacherous. The novel ends somewhat theatrically with his being crushed to death by an elephant in India.

BIBLIOGRAPHY: E.N. Calisch, *The Jew in English Literature* (1909), 117, 123–6, 141; D. Philipson, *Jew in English Fiction* (1911), 70–87; E. Rosenberg, *From Shylock to Svengali* (1960), 103–14, index. **ADD. BIBLIOGRAPHY:** ODNB for recent biographical references; A.A. Naman, *The Jew in the Victorian Novel* (1980).

[Harold Harel Fisch]

SCOUTING. The Jewish youth movements which emerged in the first half of the 20th century in central and eastern Europe (e.g., *Blau-Weiss) were influenced more by the German variety (mainly the Wandervögel) than by the British scouting movement founded by Baden-Powell. However, the Zionist youth organization Ha-Shomer (so called after the watchmen's organization in Ereẓ Israel bearing the same name; see *Ha-Shomer), which emerged in western Galicia (then under Austrian rule) before World War I, was a full-fledged scouting movement and employed its usual educational methods and techniques. During World War I (Vienna, 1916) this organization merged with other Zionist youth groups to form the large Zionist youth and pioneering movement *Ha-Shomer ha-Ẓa'ir, which preserved in its educational system, particularly for the younger age groups (from 11 to 17), a strong element of scouting (Heb. *ẓofiyyut*). Similar educational techniques were widely used between the two world wars in most other Zionist or Zionist-oriented youth movements in eastern Europe, such as Betar, Ha-Shomer ha-Le'ummi, and Ha-No'ar ha-Ẓiyyoni. In western European countries, particularly Great Britain (see below) and France, Jewish scout troops and similar youth formations emerged, often established for religious reasons or for the purpose of preventing total assimilation, but at first they did not adopt the Zionist program. In the case of France, they played a considerable role in the active resistance against the Nazi occupation (see below). In

Palestine a full-fledged Jewish scout movement was formed in 1919, shortly after the establishment of the British mandatory regime. Gradually it became an important factor in the pioneering settlement effort in the country. After the establishment of the State of Israel (in 1948) it also comprised non-Jewish (Druze and Arab) units (see below). The Israel Scout movement maintains fraternal contacts and exchanges with *Young Judea in the United States, which also incorporates certain scouting methods in its educational system.

In Great Britain

Since England was the original home of Baden-Powell's Boy Scout movement, Jewish youngsters were quickly attracted to scouting and, although no religious stipulations prevented their joining local troops, specifically Jewish groups were founded. This was especially the case in the major centers of Jewish population after World War I. During the 1920s and 1930s Jewish Boy Scout and Girl Guide troops were organized in London, Manchester, and Leeds, and others also flourished in cities such as Birmingham, Glasgow, and Liverpool. Increasing competition from the various Zionist youth movements – which also fostered scouting activities – and the disruption caused by the World War II era and the growth of the Jewish youth clubs combined to reduce the appeal of the Boy Scouts and Girl Guides after 1945. The movement nevertheless retained its popularity in certain areas and in 1970 there were several troops in London and others in Hove, Leeds, Manchester, Glasgow, and other towns. A synagogue at the Boy Scout Center in Gilwell Park, Essex, was consecrated in 1957.

A rival movement in Great Britain was the Jewish Lads' Brigade (JLB), founded in 1895 as a Jewish equivalent to the (Protestant) Boys' Brigade. The JLB, which trains its members "in loyalty, honor, discipline, and self-respect," with the emphasis on good citizenship, is organized on semi-military lines – with officers, NCOs, uniforms, and parades – and has had a fluctuating appeal. However, after a noticeable decline in the postwar years, it underwent a significant revival in the 1960s and by 1970 had about 20 branches in the Greater London area alone; there were also large groups in Glasgow and Liverpool (both of which included girls' sections), and in Birmingham and Manchester. The Glasgow JLB boasted the world's only Jewish bagpipe band. Both the Jewish scouts and the JLB appointed Jewish chaplains, and their members often formed guards of honor for visiting dignitaries at Jewish communal events and memorial services, in conjunction with adult organizations such as the Association of Jewish Ex-Servicemen and Women. It remained a thriving movement into the 21st century, with hundreds participating in summer camps and a full range of year-round programs, including a three-week Israel tour.

In France

The Jewish Scout Movement (Eclaireurs Israélites) was founded in France in 1923 by the electronic engineer Robert Gamzon (known as "Castor") with a dual purpose: to employ the methods of the scouts in order to imbue a Jewish consciousness into French Jewish children threatened by total assimilation, and to encourage the integration of recently arrived young Jewish immigrants within French society. The early development of the movement was slow. In 1935 there were 3,000 members in Paris (the largest group), as well as groups in Strasbourg, Mulhouse, Lyons, and Marseilles, and in Tunis, Algiers, Oran, and Casablanca in North Africa. When Hitler came to power, the arrival of German Jews in France, especially Leo Cohn (a brother of the Israel jurist Haim *Cohn), enabled the movement to intensify its attachment to Judaism; at the same time the Nazi threat brought it closer to Zionist ideology. Gamzon then elaborated the "pluralist" outlook of the movement: the scouts, who declared their adherence to Judaism, were authorized to identify themselves with one of the Zionist trends – Zionist, religious, or liberal – but a "common minimum" of religious observance (Sabbath and *kashrut*) was to prevail in all scouting activities.

From this period the movement was concerned with the problems of young refugees. In 1939 a training farm was established which welcomed young immigrants and older scouts; a carpentry workshop was also opened in Paris in the scout headquarters (the first community center).

During World War II the activities of the movement were modified in important respects and encompassed five spheres:

(1) The maintenance of normal scout groups and the establishment of new groups in all the towns of the Southern Zone (Vichy France), where there were many Jewish refugee families. There was also an enormous expansion in North Africa, where groups were established in more than 50 towns.

(2) The establishment of children's homes for non-French children separated from their parents. At the end of 1943 these homes were closed down for security reasons and the children were entrusted, under false names, to peasants or placed in non-Jewish boarding schools.

(3) The establishment of 13 rural groups throughout the Southern Zone for training in agricultural work and eventual *aliyah* to Palestine. A considerable number of this youth eventually settled in Israel.

(4) The creation of a social service for youth which hid young Jews who were in danger and provided adults with false French identity cards. Over 30,000 such documents were forged and distributed by social workers, who thus risked their lives. About 100 of them were arrested by the Gestapo.

(5) The establishment of an underground combat unit. In 1944, the boys of the rural unit of Lautrec decided to join the resistance movement (Maquis) and fight the Germans. This Jewish Maquis of 70 members was led by Gamzon and Gilbert Bloch and incorporated within the secret army of the Free French. Supplies were parachuted to it on many occasions. Its headquarters were attacked by the German army and seven boys, including Gilbert Bloch, lost their lives. On Aug. 22, 1944, this same group, in conjunction with two others, attacked an armored train between Mazamet and Castres

(Tarn) and put it out of action, thereby liberating these two towns and taking 3,000 prisoners.

After World War II the movement was reorganized on a more normal basis; groups were maintained or reconstituted in most towns, and the movement's total membership was 10,000. In 1946 Gamzon founded the Ecole Gilbert Bloch for training youth leaders for the movement and the Jewish organizations of France and North Africa. Rapidly developing into a center of advanced Jewish learning, the school was subsequently headed by Leon Askenazi (known as "Manitou") for many years. The two leaders of the movement, Shimon Hammel (known as "Chameau") and Gamzon, settled in Israel in 1947 and 1949, the latter at the head of a group of 50 former scouts which settled in Sedeh Eliyahu and then in Nir Eẓyon. In 1971 the movement had around 5,000 members in all the towns of France. Its general orientation was religious but not Orthodox. Its long-standing interest in Israel developed into a definite Zionist orientation in 1970, so that knowledge of Israel became one of its focal points, along with Judaism as such and art, music, and sports. In the early 2000s it had around 4,000 active members in 55 groups and organized 60 summer and winter camps in France and abroad (Israel, Peru, Madagascar, Canada, eastern Europe).

[Denise Gamzon]

In Israel

The first troop of scouts (*ẓofim*) in Palestine was started in 1919 at the *Herzlia gymnasium (high school) in Tel Aviv and, together with groups in Jerusalem and Haifa, founded Histadrut ha-Ẓofim be-Israel (the "Jewish Scouts' Federation"). The federation was dissolved after the secession of some sections in 1930 (see the State of *Israel: Youth Movements) and re-formed in 1936 under the aegis of the Education Department of the Va'ad Le'ummi. As the Jewish scout organization was coeducational, it was not admitted to the world movement and did not participate in international scout meetings during the Mandatory period. In 1938 the *ẓofim* started sending members for agricultural training, and in 1941 the federation adopted pioneering on the land as one of its aims. Its graduates founded *Ma'agan Mikha'el in 1949 and subsequently established 26 other kibbutzim.

In 1951 the federation was accepted into the world movement and in 1953 merged with Muslim, Christian, and Druze scouts in Israel to form Hitaḥadut ha-Ẓofim ve-ha-Ẓofot be-Israel (the Israel Boy and Girl Scout Federation). There is also a separate section for religious scouts (*ẓofim datiyyim*). In 1957 the Girl Scouts (*ẓofot*) were affiliated to the corresponding world movement. The *ẓofim* differ from most organizations of this kind elsewhere in having troops (*shevatim*, or "tribes") comprising all three age groups; 8–10 years, 11–14, and 15–19. In the first two there are separate units for boys and girls, each with its own program; the last comprises both. All the constituent sections, Jewish, Muslim, Christian, and Druze, participate on an equal basis in the jamborees held in Israel and send representatives to international scouting events.

Unlike other youth movements in Israel, the federation is not associated with any party or sectional organization; it operates within the framework of the schools and under the supervision of the Ministry of Education and Culture, which appoints half the members of its governing body. It lays stress on good citizenship and national service, including agricultural pioneering and service in *Naḥal outposts. In the early 2000s it had about 70,000 members: 45,000 in the Federation of Jewish Scouts; 13,000, mostly Muslim, in the Organization of Scouts from Arab Schools; 2,000 in the Muslim Arab Scouts and 2,000 in the Greek Orthodox Arab Scouts; 3,000 in the Organization of Catholic Scouts; and 5,000 in the Organization of Druze Scouts. The Arab movements have separate sections for boys and girls; the Druze scouts are all boys, in keeping with the community's religious traditions.

SCRANTON, city in N.E. Pennsylvania, U.S.; county seat of Lackawanna County. The earliest Jews, who came to Scranton before the Civil War, lived in Wilkes-Barre, where a synagogue existed, and came to Scranton to peddle their wares. Scranton grew because of the large coal fields located nearby. Many immigrants, just after the Civil War, were brought to the area just to become miners. The Jews came to open stores and businesses.

By 1860 there were enough Jews who had settled in the city so that they could form their own congregation, "Anshei Hesed." The synagogue was actually incorporated in 1862. Itinerant rabbis assisted them throughout the war. In 1866 a property was purchased on Linden Street. Just prior to Passover in 1867, on a Friday afternoon, the synagogue building was dedicated with great fanfare in the city. The guest speaker was Rabbi Isaac Meyer Wise, then a rabbi in Cincinnati. A few years later when he founded the Reform movement in America with a rabbinical school, HUC, and a congregational arm, UAHC, "Anshei Hesed" was one of the first congregations to affiliate.

Rabbis served two functions in Scranton – first as the spiritual leader and second as the Jewish educator. At times the rabbi even led a school in German and English, teaching both secular and religious subjects. In 1869 the Amos lodge of B'nai B'rith was founded with 18 members. The lodge still exists and holds two annual events of substance. One honors a local Jewish leader; the second has become most noteworthy as the Americanism Award Dinner. Over the 40 years of its existence until 2005, the award was given to leading citizens of the community, including Governor William Scranton, a Scranton native.

Even before the major Eastern European immigration started, Hungarian Jews began to find their way to Scranton as early as 1877. The first Orthodox synagogue was founded in 1886 by Hungarian Jews and was located in the "Flats," where the immigrant population of Jews, Irish, Italians, and Polish lived. The "Flats" became a major center of the Jewish community until the synagogues, butcher shops, and Hebrew schools were flooded out in 1956.

The second Orthodox synagogue formed was located in downtown Scranton and included Lithuanian and Russian Jews, who prayed differently than their Hungarian brethren. That synagogue was listed in the first volume of the *American Jewish Yearbook* as established in 1895. When the wealthier Reform Jews began to move to the Hill section, they built a new synagogue in that area and became "Temple Hesed." Their original building was sold to a new Orthodox group and was renamed the "Linden Street Synagogue." Several fascinating tales about the building are recorded in a book by A.B. Cohen.

In 1907 a young, brilliant yeshivah graduate got a job in Scranton at the local Montefiore School. His name was Harry Wolfson and he became a legend in America Jewish academia. Within a few months he completed grammar school. By the time he graduated Central High School in Scranton in 1910, he had earned the right to be the valedictorian and had also been awarded a four-year scholarship to Harvard College. Once Wolfson entered Harvard he never left, ultimately being given the Littauer Chair, the first Judaica chair in an American university. Wolfson had a soft spot in his heart for Scranton, maintaining ties with people whom he had met during his three years in the community.

The Jewish community of Scranton grew rapidly before World War I. One noted rabbi who served the "Linden Street Synagogue" was Wolf Gold. After moving to New York, Gold was very active in Mizrachi and became the head of America Mizrachi before making *aliyah* in the 1930s. When Israel became a state on May 14 1948, Gold was in Jerusalem because of the siege. He could not attend the signing of Israel's Declaration of Independence in Tel Aviv, but space was left for him and two others. He and Golda Meir are the only American signatories on that monumental document in Israel's history.

Shortly after World War I, led by M.L. Goodman, a Scranton news baron, a Conservative synagogue, Temple Israel, was founded in 1921. The synagogue benefited from the great interest of the leadership in Jewish education. In 1923 Louis Wolf was hired to be a teacher. The following year Dr. Max Arzt became the rabbi of Temple Israel. Between the two, Temple Israel created one of the most outstanding afternoon Hebrew schools complemented by a Junior Congregation, which became a model for Conservative synagogues throughout the U.S. At Temple Israel Arzt produced an outstanding weekly bulletin, gave excellent sermons on the topics of the day rooted in traditional sources, and made it quite clear what a synagogue-center could accomplish.

In the early 1930s, Scranton Jewry grew to 8,000 and then its numbers began to diminish. With clothing factories, needlework trade and other industrial plants, Scranton Jews made it possible for Scranton itself to have sufficient employment in 1935 for 135,000 people. Arzt left in 1939 to become the vice chancellor of the Jewish Theological Seminary. His students continue to remember him and his talented educator Louis Wolf.

Following World War II, during which 1,200 Scranton Jews served, Temple Israel grew dramatically, with a Hebrew school of 375 at its peak. The rabbi, Simon Shoop, who served from 1949 to 1990, led the congregation to become the most traditional Conservative synagogue in North America. Shoop, who had a doctorate, was one of the first to teach courses on the Holocaust, which he initiated at the University of Scranton and Marywood University, both Catholic schools. Among Shoop's students was Professor Michael Brown, a Jewish historian at York University in Canada, and Professor Mark Harris of the USC film school, who won three Oscars for documentary films, including *The Long Way Home* and *The Kindertransport*.

Another student of the Shoop era, Ralph Levy, has invented many toys including the talking "Furby."

A most fascinating personality arrived in Scranton from Baltimore in 1955. His name was Harry Weinberg, and he had bought all the bonds of the Scranton Transit Company, which had been on strike for over 300 days. Weinberg, without any formal education, was an entrepreneur in the most exciting way. During his decade in Scranton, he bought almost a quarter of million dollars of real estate in the city. His love was for transit companies. He bought the Dallas Transit company and other companies in the West. He also bought the Fifth Avenue Bus Company, even though the mayor of New York said that he would not let Weinberg run it. Within a week in the early 1960s, Weinberg made over a million dollars when he had to sell.

He was actually looking at Hawaii as a real center for financial growth. First, he purchased the Honolulu Transit Company. Once he saw the possibilities in that area, he moved to Hawaii. From 1966 until 1989, Harry Weinberg became the largest landholder in Hawaii. His fortune began to grow and his main interest was in creating a major foundation. By the time of his death in 1991 the Jeanette and Harry Weinberg Foundation was worth almost a billion dollars. Just before his death he promised the University of Scranton 6 million dollars for a new library building and for a Chair of Jewish Studies. The library was completed in 1992 and the Jesuits all call it the Weinberg library. Professor Marc Shapiro holds the Weinberg Judaica chair.

Since 1980 there has been a definite change in Scranton, as Temple Hesed and Temple Israel have grown smaller. The Orthodox community is led by the Lakewood Yeshiva branch in Scranton. Rabbi Moshe Fine, a rabbi in the community for 27 years, has built the Orthodox community through his teaching, his determined leadership, and his pastoral skills. There were about 3,000 Jews in Scranton in 2005; almost half were Orthodox Jews.

In 2002 Rabbi David Geffen of Temple Israel received agreement from Father McShane, president of the University of Scranton, for an exhibit on the history of the Jews of Scranton to be mounted at the university. The exhibit was held in the spring and summer of 2004, curated by Arnine Weiss, a noted educator. Scranton thus participated in the 350-year celebration of the Jews' arrival in New Amsterdam.

[David Geffen (2nd ed.)]

SCRIBE. The Hebrew term for "scribe" is *sofer*, a participle form of the root *spr*, meaning "to count." It is a Canaanite word, appearing in Ugarit (*rb spr*, "chief scribe") as well as a loanword in an Egyptian text – *sofer yodeʿa*, i.e., "wise scribe" (Papyrus Anastasi I; late 13th century B.C.E.). It may be a cognate to Akkadian *šāpiru*, "secretary, official." The first biblical reference to *sofer* is found in the Song of Deborah (Judg. 5:14). Another term used frequently in the Hexateuch is *shoṭer*, which probably meant "recorder." This functionary is associated with food rationing (Num. 11:16; Josh. 1:10; cf. Prov. 6:7), raising the levy (Ex. 5:6, et al.; Deut. 20:5; cf. II Chron. 26:11), and the law courts (Deut. 1:15; 16:18). The root of *shoṭer* is derived from the cognate Akkadian *šatāru*, "to write," and reappears in later Aramaic and Hebrew in *sheṭar*, "a written document" (see also Job 38:33). The common Akkadian word for scribe was *tupšarru* which appears as *ṭi/afsar* in Nahum's prophesy of the destruction of Nineveh (3:17) and Jeremiah's words on Babylon's doom (51:27). The change from *sh* to *s* probably reflects Assyrian pronunciation.

As in neighboring lands, the Israelite scribe learned his profession in family-like guilds (cf. "the families of scribes who inhabited Jabez," I Chron. 2:5). A 15th century B.C.E. text does indicate the existence of scribal schools in Canaan proper. It is a letter written by a teacher to a student's father living in Shechem asking for the long overdue tuition fee that could be paid in kind. The teacher describes his relationship to his students as that of a parent. (For a more detailed description of the scribe studies see *Education.)

W.F. Albright reads this important text:

> Unto Birashshena say:
> Thus Baniti – [Ashirat (?)]:
> From three years (ago) until now thou hast not caused me to be paid –
> is there no grain nor oil nor wine (?)
> which thou canst send?
> What is my offense that thou has not paid [me]?
> The children who are with me continue to learn–
> their father and their mother every [day] alike am I…
> Now [behold] whatever [there is] at the disposal of
> [my lord let him send] unto me, and let him inform me!

During the time of David, a certain Seraiah (II Sam. 8:17; Sheva, II Sam. 20:25; Shisha, I Kings 4:3; Shabsha, I Chron. 18:16) was appointed royal scribe. Both his sons Elihoreph and Ahijah followed him in Solomon's court. R. de Vaux has argued that this post, like most of David's cabinet, was adopted from Egyptian models. Furthermore, A. Cody maintains that the name Shisha etc. is a barbarism of the Egyptian term *ssh*, meaning "scribe." B. Mazar argues for a Canaanite origin for David's officials and derives all the above forms from an original Hurrian name *Šewe-šarri*. Among the returnees to Judah in early Persian times were "the sons of Hassophereth" – perhaps "members of the scribal office" – listed among the descendants of Solomon's servants (Ezra. 2:55 = Neh. 7:57). The Judean monarchy produced a prominent scribal family that influenced the political scene for several generations (II Kings 22:3, 12, 14; 25:22; Jer. 26:24; 36:11, 12):

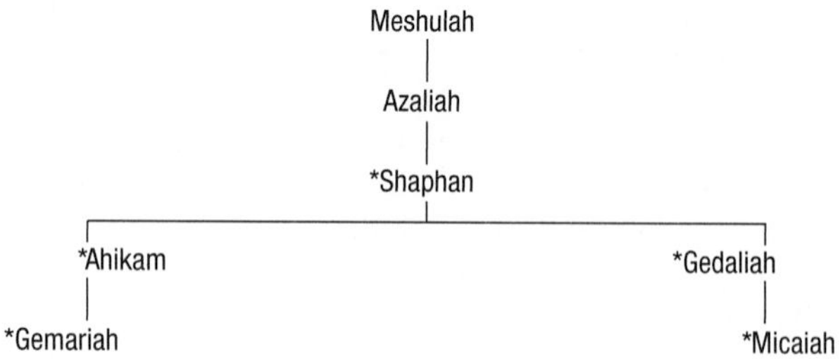

Scribes of various degrees of competence were attached to all government and temple offices. Apparently there were also independent scribes who either served the public or were in the employ of men of means. The highest scribal post was that of royal scribe. It is difficult to determine his exact position among the king's other ministers, even if it is assumed that the various biblical lists follow the principle of order of importance (see II Sam. 8:16–18 = I Chron. 18:15–17; II Sam. 20:23–26; I Kings 4:2–6). In the time of Hezekiah, the royal scribe seems to be of a lower rank than royal chamberlain (*aʾsher ʿal ha-bayit*) but higher than *mazkir* (Isa. 22:15–25; 36:3; II Kings 18:18, 37 and also II Chron. 34:8). Exactly what the duties of the royal scribe were is unknown. Besides fulfilling an advisory capacity (II Kings 18:18 ff.; 22:14.; cf. I Chron. 27:32), he seems to have been in charge of financial matters (II Kings 12:1lff.; 22:3 ff.). This function may underlie the original meaning of the title, which may have been "accountant." Quite likely, other ministries had their own scribal service. The priesthood definitely needed literati (I Chron. 24:6; II Chron. 34:13) and so did the chief of staff (II Chron. 26:11; II Kings 29:19 = Jer. 52:25). City governments, as well, required lists of prominent landowners for purposes of taxation and army service (Judg. 8:14). The public at large would also turn to a scribe to draw up documents of legal (Deut. 24:1; Isa. 50:1; Jer. 3:8; 32:11) or religious character (Deut. 6:9; 11:20). Wealthy gentry could afford a personal secretary for their business affairs (cf. the inscribed handles from Gibeon, late seventh century). Baruch son of Neriah served Jeremiah in this capacity, though the relationship may be better characterized as that of master and disciple (Jer. 32:12; 36:4, 18; 43:3; 45:1 ff.). Several inscribed seals from the Monarchy period bearing the title *sofer* have been discovered in and around Palestine: *ʾmẓ hspr* (אמץ הספר), *lkmshʿm/kmshʾl/hspr*, (לכמשעם כמשאל הספר), *lhwdw sprʾ* (להודו ספרא). They are all probably non-Israelite in origin. The Persian Empire, consisting of many peoples and languages, is noted for its efficient civil service and far-flung system of communication (Esth. 3:12; 8:9). Each governor was assisted by his own scribe (Ezra 4:8, 9, 17, 23). The contemporary Aramaic papyri from Elephantine shed much light on scribal practice of that time. One of the prominent Jewish personalities of the period was Ezra the Scribe (BK 82a; Sanh. 21b). H.H. Schaeder suggested that Ezra's title (Ezra 7:6, 12) probably testifies to his high position in the Persian court, perhaps "secretary for Jewish affairs." During the Second Temple Period the word *soferim* had a special connotation.

[Aaron Demsky]

In Judaism

Later the scribe was a professional expert in the writing of Torah scrolls, **tefillin*, **mezuzot*, and bills of *divorce. Scribes are, therefore, known as *sofer setam* סוֹפֵר סְתָ"ם; *setam* סְתָ"ם being composed of the Hebrew initials of *Sefer Torah, tefillin*, and *mezuzot*. These have to be written with a feather quill in indelible ink, in straight lines, and on specially prepared parchment. It is inferred from the Bible that every Jew should write for himself a Torah scroll (see Deut. 31:19; see Sanh. 21b). Expertness, however, being required in writing a Torah scroll, the commandment can only be fulfilled by ordering it from a scribe. The profession of scribe was indispensable to the Jewish community, and according to the Talmud (Sanh. 17b) a scholar should not dwell in a town where there is no scribe. In the talmudic period, scribes were poorly paid lest they become rich and desert their vocations, leaving the community without their services. The scribe writing a Torah scroll must devote utmost attention and care to the writing; he is forbidden to rely on his memory and has to write from a model copy (Meg. 18b). His guide is the professional compendium for scribes, *Tikkun Soferim*, which contains the traditional text of the Torah, the specific rules concerning the decorative flourishes (*tagin*, "crowns") on certain letters, the regulations as to the spacing of certain Torah sections ("open" or "closed" pericopes), and the rules for writing Torah scrolls in which each column begins with the Hebrew letter *vav* (*vavei ha-ammudim*). Only the Scroll of Esther may be adorned with artistic illustrations but not the Torah scroll, although Alexandrian scribes are said to have gilded the name and appellations of God (Sof. 1:9). When writing a Torah scroll a scribe must especially prepare himself so that he writes the names of the Lord with proper devotion and in ritual purity. It is, therefore, customary that he immerse himself in a ritual bath (*mikveh*) before beginning his work. (The rules for the writing of Torah scrolls and other ritual texts are laid down in Sof. 1–10; Maim. Yad, Tefillin, Mezuzah, 1–10; Sh. Ar., YD 270ff.) Scribes also acted as recording clerks and court secretaries of the *bet din* and were, therefore, also called *lavlar*, from the Latin *libellarius*. They wrote legal documents such as bills of divorce (*get*) and contracts. In *halakhah* there are established rules as to who pays the scribe's fee. The general principle is that the person who receives the greater benefit from a transaction has to pay the scribe, e.g., the buyer of property and the borrower of money. In modern times printed forms are used for most legal transactions and the only document that has to be written by an expert scribe is the bill of divorce.

BIBLIOGRAPHY: H.H. Schaeder, *Esra der Schreiber* (1930); R. de Vaux, in: RB, 48 (1939), 394–405; J. Begrich, in: ZAW, 58 (1940–41), 1–29; W.F. Albright, in: BASOR, 86 (1942), 28–31; B. Maisler (Mazar), in: BJPES, 13 (1947), 105–14; A.L. Oppenheim, *Ancient Mesopotamia* (1964), 235–49; idem, in: AS, 16 (1965), 254; A. Cody, in: RB, 72 (1965), 381–93; A.F. Rainey, in: EM, 5 (1968), 1010–17; idem, in: PIASH, vol. 3, no. 4 (1969); idem, in: JNES, 26 (1967), 58–60; Pritchard, Texts, 432ff., 476, 490. IN JUDAISM: Eisenstein, Dinim, 287.

SCROLL OF ANTIOCHUS (Heb. מְגִלַּת אַנְטִיוֹכוֹס) or Scroll of the Hasmoneans (Heb. מְגִלַּת בֵּית חַשְׁמוֹנַאי), popular account of the wars of the Hasmoneans and of the origin of the festival of *Ḥanukkah. The scroll has been handed down in several Aramaic versions, probably dating from the late talmudic period (its Aramaic language indicates the period between the second and fifth centuries C.E. in Palestine). It is first mentioned in the **Halakhot Gedolot* (ed. by A. Hildesheimer (1890), 615, cf. also the ed. princ. (Venice, 1548), 141d) which describes it as originating in "the oldest schools of Shammai and Hillel"; unlike the Scroll of Esther, it is not read on the holiday with which it is connected and will be elevated to this position only "when there arises a priest with Urim and Thummim."

Saadiah, in his *Sefer ha-Gallui*, deals more fully with the scroll. He calls it "The book of the Sons of the Hasmoneans" (כתאב בני חשמונאי) and quotes a sentence which, with minor variations, is also found in the existing version (v. 23 in ed. Filipowski and Gaster); the scroll which he knew was probably also already punctuated and divided into verses. Nissim of Kairouan assigns the scroll an important position in the literature of the Apocrypha; in the introduction to his *Sefer ha-Ma'asiyyot*, he promises to relate the entire history of the Jews, "with the exception of that contained in the Scroll of Esther, the Scroll of the Hasmoneans (presumably the Scroll of Antiochus) and the 24 books [of the Bible]." Isaiah di Trani reports on the custom of reading the scroll in synagogues on Ḥanukkah (cf. his *tosafot* to *Sukkah* 44b (Lemberg, 1868), 31b).

Contents of the Scroll

King Antiochus, who has already conquered many countries, decides in the 23rd year of his reign to destroy the Jewish people, because it adheres to another law and other customs and secretly dreams of dominating the world. He sends to Jerusalem his commander in chief Nicanor, who instigates a massacre there, sets up an idol in the Temple and defiles the entrance hall with pigs' blood. On the pretext of being willing to submit to Antiochus' commands, *Jonathan, a son of the high priest Mattathias, gains a secret audience with Nicanor, and kills him with a sword concealed under his robe; he then attacks Nicanor's army, which is now without a leader, and only a few of the soldiers succeed in escaping and returning by ship to Antiochus. In commemoration of the victory, Jonathan has a pillar erected in the town, bearing the inscription "The Maccabean has killed strong men." Antiochus then sends to Jerusalem a second commander, Bagris; he metes out a terrible revenge upon the town and upon those Jews who have returned to the faith (here the scroll includes the story related in I Macc. 5:37–40 and II Macc. 6:16 of the devout people in the cave who were killed on the Sabbath because they would not fight to defend themselves). Jonathan and his four brothers defeat Bagris, who escapes and returns to Antiochus. He is equipped with a new army and armored elephants and then makes an attack on Judea. Judah Maccabee now appears in the story for the first time; and Jonathan, the third son of Mattathias, henceforth remains in the background. At the news of Bagris' approach, Judah proclaims a fast and calls for prayers in Mizpah (cf. I Macc. 3:46ff.); the army then goes into battle and wins several victories, though it pays for them with the death of its leader. Now old Mattathias himself assumes command of the Jewish soldiers; the enemy is decisively defeated, and Bagris is taken prisoner and burned. When Antiochus is told the news, he boards a ship and tries to find refuge in some coastal town; but wherever he arrives he is greeted with the scornful cry: "See the runaway!" so that finally he becomes desperate and throws himself into the sea. At this same time, the Jews are reconsecrating their Temple; while searching for pure oil for the lamp, they find a vessel bearing the seal of the high priest and dating back to the time of the prophet Samuel. By a miracle the oil, which is sufficient in quantity for only one day, burns in the lamp for a full eight days; and this is why Ḥanukkah, the festival commemorating the reconsecration of the Temple, is celebrated for eight days.

Author of the Scroll

As can be seen from this summary, the author was totally ignorant of the historical circumstances at the time of the Maccabees and made no use of any reliable sources on the period. The following points must be emphasized in connection with the text:

(1) The statement at the end of the scroll that 206 years elapsed between the beginning of the Hasmonean dynasty and the fall of the Second Temple is entirely correct if the time is reckoned from the first year of John Hyrcanus (135 B.C.E.) until the destruction of Jerusalem. This method of dating from the first year of John's reign, which was still being used in the Hebrew business documents of the later talmudic period (RH 18b), was most probably the sole point of reference which made the author of the scroll give 135 B.C.E. as the first year of the Hasmoneans. This incorrect assumption also seems to have been the basis for the legend about the high priest Jonathan, who according to the scroll led the revolt of the Maccabees.

(2) In view of their form and content, the stories about Nicanor, set as they are in the spirit of a later period, are intended to provide information on the festival of Nicanor's Day (13th Adar) rather than to relate events that actually took place during the time of the Maccabees (Meg. Ta'an. 12; Ta'an. 18b).

(3) The story of the miracle of the oil, which is also found in talmudic writings (Meg. Ta'an. 9, Shab. 21b), could have originated only at a time when Ḥanukkah had already become a festival lasting eight days; and it serves as a reason for the practice of lighting the candles.

Thus the author of the scroll was aware of customs and recollections which the people of his time still cherished in memory of the Hasmonean victory, even though the historically reliable sources were unknown to him. Moreover, the tone of the whole story and the way in which the events of the period are represented are evidence that in his day there was no longer any interest in a political evaluation of the Hasmoneans; all that was important was to explain the origin of certain halakhic prescriptions concerning Ḥanukkah, and the origin of several later customs. Hence it is understandable that the author of the *Halakhot Gedolot*, as stated above, connects *Megillat Ta'anit with the Scroll of Antiochus and ascribes both works to the schools of Shammai and Hillel. In talmudic tradition (Shab. 13b), the editing of *Megillat Ta'anit* is attributed to scholars of earlier generations; discussions on questions of *halakhah* relating to Ḥanukkah are ascribed to the schools of Shammai and Hillel (Shab. 21b), and it was the statements on *halakhah* which were the main source of interest to talmudic scholars editing the two scrolls.

The Language of the Scroll

The language of the original scroll was Western Middle Aramaic. From the language it can be established that the scroll was composed in Ereẓ Israel and was possibly edited from a language point of view in Babylonia (as was the Targum Onkelos). The scroll is written in a historiographical style; it imitates ancient Jewish sources (i.e., biblical Aramaic, *Megillat Ta'anit*) and closely follows the historiographical style of the Bible in the Aramaic versions found in the Targums. The language of the scroll was not the spoken language of its author but rather a literary language; even if the author knew, as seems likely, the Palestinian dialect of Aramaic, he nonetheless uses an Aramaic which was very close to the Targum Onkelos.

Editions of the Scroll

The scroll was first edited by H. Filipowski from a manuscript in the British Museum (*Sefer Mivḥar ha-Peninim u-Megillat Antiochus* (1851), 73–100). Besides the Aramaic version, there is also a Hebrew one; but this is only a late translation of the Aramaic text (published by D. Slutzki, Warsaw, 1863, with an introduction and amendments). Jellinek published a second manuscript (*Beit ha-Midrash*, 6 (1932^2), 4–8), and J. Taprower a third (*Kevod ha-Levanon*, 10, pt. 4 (1874), 17–28). The most complete publication is that of M. Gaster, which is based on six manuscripts (*Transactions of the Ninth International Congress of Orientalists*, 2 (1893), 17–27); S.A. Wertheimer published another manuscript in *Leket Midrashim* (Jerusalem, 1903), 13b–18a; a facsimile edition of a European version by L. Nemoy, *The Scroll of Antiochus* (New Haven, 1952); a critical edition, based upon Yemenite texts provided by super-linear vocalization, by M.Z. Kadari, "The Aramaic Antiochus Scroll," *Bar-Ilan, Sefer ha-Shanah*, 1 (1963), 81–105, *Bar Ilan, Sefer ha-Shanah*, 11 (1964), 178–214; the princ. ed. re-edited by I. Joel, KS 37 (1961/62), 132–6. The version given by J.D. Eisenstein (in *Oẓar Midrashim* (1915), 185–9) is an unaltered reprint of the text by Slutzki. The scroll has been translated into Latin, German, Spanish, Arabic, and Persian.

BIBLIOGRAPHY: C. Josephson, *Die Sagen ueber die Kaempfe der Makkabaeer* (1889); A. Harkavy, *Zikkaron la-Rishonim ve-Gam* *la-Aḥaronim*, 5 (1891), 205–9; M. Gaster, in: *Transactions of the Ninth International Congress of Orientalists*, 2 (1893), 3–32 (= *Studies and Texts*, 1 (1925–28), 165–83; 3 (1925–28), 33–44); A. Neubauer, in: JQR, 6 (1893/94), 570–7; I. Abrahams, *ibid.*, 11 (1898/99), 291–9; F. Rosenthal, *ibid.*, 36 (n.s., 1945/46), 297–302; S. Krauss, in: REJ, 30 (1895), 214–9; I. Lévi, *ibid.*, 45 (1902), 172–5; Schuerer, Gesch, 1 (1901–3 ^{34}), 158f.; S.A. Wertheimer, in: *Leket Midrashim* (Jerusalem, 1903), 13b–18a; A. Jellinek, *Beit ha-Midrash*, 1 (1938^{2}), xxv, 142–6; 6 (1938^{2}), vii–ix, 4–8; S. Tedesche and S. Zeitlin, *The First Book of Maccabees* (1950), 60; L. Nemoy, *The Scroll of Antiochus* (1952); A. Shalit, in: *Tarbut ve-Sifrut* (Dec. 20, 1957); M.Z. Kadari, in: *Leshonenu*, 23 (1959), 129–45; idem, "The Aramaic Antiochus Scroll," in: *Bar Ilan, Sefer ha-Shanah*, 1 (1963), 81–105; 2 (1964), 178–214; I. Joel, in: KS, 37 (1961/62), 132–6.

[*Encyclopaedia Judaica* (Germany)]

SCROLL OF ESTHER (Heb. מְגִלַּת אֶסְתֵּר, *Megillat Ester*), the festal scroll of *Purim, the only one of the Five Scrolls to bear the title *megillah* as part of its traditional name (see *Scrolls, the Five). The Scroll of Esther tells the story of the salvation of the Jews of the Persian Empire.

Contents

The Persian king *Ahasuerus, in the third year of his reign, climaxes 180 days of banqueting for his officials with an additional feast of seven days for the entire populace of Shushan. On the seventh day of this party, the king, while drunk, orders Queen *Vashti to appear so that all may appreciate her beauty. When the queen refuses, the king, having consulted his advisers, removes Vashti from her position, and a decree is sent to all the husbands of the realm ordering them to dominate their own households (chapter 1).

A contest is held among all the beautiful maidens of the kingdom to find a successor to Vashti. One of the girls taken to the palace is *Esther, or Hadassah, the cousin of *Mordecai the Jew. Esther, concealing her origins, finds favor in the eyes of the king and is chosen to succeed Vashti. Mordecai, who is one of the officials who "sit in the King's Gate," learns of a plot against the king devised by two of his eunuchs. He reveals this to Esther, who in turn informs the king. The eunuchs are executed (chapter 2).

Ahasuerus elevates *Haman the Agagite, a descendant of Agag king of Amalek (1 Sam. 15), above his other courtiers, and all the king's courtiers bow to Haman in recognition of his distinguished rank. Mordecai refuses on the grounds that he is Jewish, presumably because there is a perpetual feud between Amalek and the Jews (Ex. 17: 14–16; Deut. 25:17–19). Angered by this snub, Haman resolves to exterminate Mordecai and the entire Jewish people and determines the appropriate day by lot. He then persuades the king that the Jews are a subversive people who should be eliminated, reinforcing this argument with an offer of 10,000 talents of silver. Ahasuerus authorizes Haman to deal with the Jews as he chooses. Haman writes to all the royal governors appointing the 13th of Adar for the slaughter of the Jews (chapter 3).

Learning of the decree, Mordecai appeals to Esther to intercede with the king. In spite of the mortal danger of appearing before the king without being specifically summoned, Esther agrees to spend three days fasting and then to go to the king (chapter 4). On the third day, Esther approaches the king and is spared. She requests that the king and Haman come to a banquet that night. At the banquet, Esther refuses to reveal her true wishes, but merely asks that Ahasuerus and Haman attend a second banquet she will give on the following night. Haman returns home proud of having been so honored. At the advice of his wife and supporters, he prepares a stake 50 cubits high upon which to hang Mordecai (chapter 5).

Since the king cannot sleep that night, he orders that the royal annals be read to him, and thereby discovers that Mordecai had never been properly rewarded for denouncing the two eunuchs. He asks Haman's advice concerning a means of honoring someone whom the king deems worthy of honor. Haman, thinking he is the chosen one, proposes a procession in royal garb upon a royal horse through the streets of the city, with a noble leading the horse and proclaiming: "This is what is done for the man whom the king desires to honor." The king then orders Haman to do this for Mordecai (chapter 6). At the second banquet, Esther denounces Haman as plotting the destruction of her people. When Haman appeals to Esther for mercy, the king, thinking he intends to ravish her, orders him to be hanged on the stake prepared for Mordecai (chapter 7).

Haman's place in the king's favor is taken over by Mordecai, but Haman's decree sealing the fate of the Jews poses a serious problem, since according to the Medo-Persian constitution a royal decree may not be revoked (both the idea of a Medo-Persian partnership and the attribution to it of this law are taken, with other features, from Dan. 6). Mordecai, however, writes to all the satraps, governors, and other important officials of the realm authorizing the Jews to defend themselves and to destroy anyone who may attack them (chapter 8). Mordecai's prestige is sufficient to insure that the royal officials favor the Jews on that fateful day. Instead of being exterminated on that day, the Jews seem to have suffered no casualties at all; instead, they themselves kill 500 of their enemies as well as the ten sons of Haman in Shushan, and 75,000 enemies in the provinces. At Esther's request, the Jews of the capital are also given the following day, the 14th of Adar, to avenge themselves on their foes. The Jews are so feared that many gentiles pretend to be Jews (this and not "are converted to Judaism," is the meaning of *mityahadim*, 8:17).

The days following the battles, the 14th of Adar in the provinces and the 15th in Shushan, are declared by Mordecai and Esther days of feasting and merrymaking forevermore, and they are designed "the days of Purim" in memory of the lots that Haman cast (chapters 9–10). As is pointed out by H.L. Ginsberg, Esther 9:30–31 obliquely justifies the innovation of a new festival with no basis in the Torah, by invoking the authority of the prophet Zechariah (who had flourished in the reign of Ahasuerus' predecessor Darius I) in that they call the ordinance of Mordecai and Esther "an ordinance of 'equity and honesty'" and state that its content was: "These days of Purim shall be observed at their proper time, as Mordecai the Jew – and now Queen Esther – has obligated them to do, and just as they have assumed for themselves and their descendants the obligation of the fast with their lamentations." The reference is to Zechariah 8:19: "Thus said the Lord of Hosts: The fasts of the fourth, fifth, seventh, and tenth months [corresponding to the modern 17th of Tammuz, Ninth of Av, Fast of Gedaliah, and Tenth of Tevet] shall be turned into joy and gladness and happy seasons for the House of Judah; just love honesty and equity." The reference to this verse implies the following midrashic interpretation of it: having adopted those fasts, the House of Judah is bound – as a matter of honesty and equity – to adopt new holidays as well.

Historicity

The Scroll of Esther claims to be a simple historical account of events that actually took place in the fortress of Shushan, or Susa. It is true that there was a Persian king named Ahasuerus; for Ahasuerus is merely a Hebrew form (the consonantal text of the Hebrew is quite close to the way the name is written in Aramaic documents; the vowel points added in medieval times made for distortion) of the Persian name which the Greeks heard as *Xerxes. Xerxes I (for it is he who is meant, since the reign of Xerxes II was ephemeral) reigned from 486 to 465, B.C.E. It is also true that the name Marduka (= Mordecai) is attested as a personal name in documents of the period and as a Jewish name in Ezra 2:2 and Nehemiah 7:7. Finally, the author of Esther is well acquainted with Persian customs and court practices, as is illustrated by Vashti's refusal to degrade herself and appear at the drinking party. A Persian wife left when the drinking began.

Nevertheless, accepting Esther as veritable history involves many chronological and historical difficulties. If Mordecai was exiled from Judea with Jehoiachin (589 B.C.E.), as Esther 2:6 suggests, he would have been over 100 years old at the time of Xerxes I. Herodotus reports that Xerxes' queen was neither Esther nor Vashti, but a Persian general's daughter named Amestris (Hist. 7:114). Herodotus also says that the Persian king could only choose a queen from among seven Persian noble families (3:84). In addition, the entire plot is full of improbabilities; for example, while Mordecai is well known as a royal Jewish courtier (3:4), his cousin and adopted daughter, whom he visits daily (2:11), can successfully conceal her nationality and religion. Finally, the story often seems mockingly serious and suspiciously areligious. Prayers are never addressed to God in the hours of danger and need, and no mention is made of thanksgivings to God after the salvation of the Jews. Indeed, the rabbis of the Talmud had to read references to God into the Scroll of Esther (Meg. 7a). The Greek translation (see below) and the Aramaic targums made the book much more pious. Assuming that Esther is not veritable history, there are innumerable possibilities for the book's origin, date of composition, historical context, meaning, and purpose.

Interpretations

One significant group of scholars considers Esther, much like Daniel, a pseudepigraph, in which the narrative set in Persia is merely a stage setting for the true meaning. Willrich, for example, suggests that Ahasuerus is really Ptolemy Euergetes II (170–164 B.C.E. and 145–117 B.C.E.); Esther, his queen, Cleopatra III, who was friendly to the Jews; and Haman, the anti-Jewish party at the Ptolemaic court. Haupt and Lewy have proposed solutions that understand Esther in relation to the periods of the Maccabees and Herodians, respectively. A detailed examination of one example of these "historical" interpretations of Esther will reveal the difficulties inherent in this approach. R.H. Pfeiffer argues that Esther was written during the Hasmonean era, specifically at the time of John Hyrcanus (135–104 B.C.E.). Haman, Pfeiffer proposes, looks like a caricature of Antiochus Epiphanes. He persecutes the Jews on the grounds that they are different from other peoples (3:8), just as Antiochus ordered that all peculiar national customs be discontinued (I Macc. 1:41). The Jews in Esther have taken matters into their own hands with great success, and, indeed, ultimately force the gentiles to convert to Judaism (8:17), just as they did under the Maccabees. The author of Esther, like that of Maccabees, is militantly nationalistic, more ardent in his patriotism than in his religious zeal. He outwardly conformed to religious practice, but "appears to have made no demands on God and to have expected that God would make none of him." The background of Esther, according to Pfeiffer, is therefore neither the Persian period nor the period of the persecution of Antiochus (168–165 B.C.E.) but rather the reign of John Hyrcanus. Hyrcanus, among his other achievements, forced the conquered Idumeans to accept Judaism by compulsory circumcision. Represented in our book by Mordecai and Esther, Hyrcanus was the author's ideal and hero. These parallels between the events described in Esther and those of the Maccabean period are, however, at best broad and general. Furthermore, the reign of Hyrcanus may not represent the low level of spiritual life essential to Pfeiffer's argument. Finally, if Esther is the product of intense nationalism, why does the author allow his heroine to hide her Jewish origin and enter the harem of a gentile king? Why must the Jews depend on successful intrigues at court and not revolt openly, as Hyrcanus' ancestors had done?

Another school of thought bases its interpretation on the fact that the names of Mordecai and Esther are derived from the names of the Babylonian deities *Marduk and Ishtar. This approach sees the story as an account of the conflicts of these gods or of their worshipers. The most extensive formulation of this approach is that of Lewy. Lewy's analysis of Esther begins with the fact that the Septuagint and II Maccabees preserve different features of the story than the Hebrew text. Thus, according to the Septuagint, the Persian king is Artaxerxes rather than Xerxes. Haman is called Bugaean and not the Agagite, and the name of the holiday is Phrouraia, or Phourdaia, and not Purim. Finally, the holiday is called the "Mardochaic day" in II Maccabees 15:36.

A proper understanding of these divergences, Lewy maintains, can solve the problem of the origin and purpose of Esther and of the feast of the 14th and 15th of Adar which it proclaims. The Phrouraia or Phourdaia suggests the Persian festival of Favardigan which was celebrated from the 11th to the 14th of Adar. The Jews adopted a Babylonianized version of this feast and also accepted the Babylonian legends connected with the festival. The name of the festival in II Maccabees 15:36, the "Mardochaic day," does not mean the day of Mordecai but the day of the Mardukians or worshipers of Marduk. Bugaean suggests a worshiper of Mithra. Combining this information with the clear fact that the name Esther is equivalent to Ishtar, Lewy proposes that it is now possible to reconstruct the Babylonian original behind the last eight chapters of Esther. These chapters recount the threat to the worshipers of Marduk which resulted when *Artaxerxes II (404–358) instituted the cult of Mithra, a threat from which they were saved by the goddess Ishtar. Another legend concerning Ishtar is behind the story in the first two chapters of the book. This legend tells of the elevation of Ishtar-Esther over the Elamite goddess Mashti-Vashti.

While Lewy's interpretation explains many features of Esther, it must be considered more as a hypothesis or conjecture rather than as proof. It seems far too complicated to be true, and accounts for the features of Esther only by disregarding the scientific canon of economy. The same canon of economy would account for the absence of God's name and of prayer and thanksgiving and of dietary and marital restrictions: Esther was produced in non-pious circles in which ethnicity mattered more than religion.

Recent Research

Research on the Scroll of Esther, in particular the contributions of E. Bickerman, has elucidated many aspects of this deceptively simple book. Bickerman has solved many of the problems left unsolved by the other commentators we have considered. He has clearly recognized the literary structure of the book and the fact that, while it may be ultimately based on actual events, Esther contains two originally independent plots derived from Oriental romance: one plot of harem intrigue of which Esther is the heroine, and another of court intrigue of which Mordecai is the hero. Mordecai's story is based on a type of Oriental romance. It is the story of the struggle between the vizier and the dashing new courtier who outwits the vizier and replaces him in the king's favor. Mordecai's refusal to bow to Haman (3:2), which puzzled the later Jewish commentators, is thus comprehensible as an attempt by Mordecai to demonstrate his equality with Haman. Haman is angry, consults his friends and prepares the stake. Meanwhile, the episode of the king's sleepless night occurs, and at its conclusion Haman must honor Mordecai. Finally, Haman is overthrown and Mordecai replaces him in the king's favor.

The second plot is that of the queen who brings about the downfall of the vizier. In Esther, the conflict between Haman and the queen is accidental, as he does not know that she is Jewish. This cannot have been the motive in the original story or stories. Yet the fact that Esther is not the "original story" explains one puzzling feature of the book – the non-Jewish, if not un-Jewish, character of the narrative. The heroes of the original story were not Jewish. These two plots were combined quite effectively. Having heard stories of the struggles of a Jewish courtier and of a Jewish queen against an evil vizier, the author combined them. However, traces of the independent stories can still be seen in several places in the book, as in the two separate epistles at the end (9:20–28 and 9:29–32) or in the unexplained presence of two where one would suffice – the delay being necessary for Mordecai's first triumph over Haman on the night of the king's insomnia. The Scroll of Esther presents Purim as a festival commemorating the victory of the Jews, but it is odd in that it occurs on the day following the victory, unlike other Jewish festivals celebrated on the anniversary of the event itself. It is therefore clear, Bickerman concludes, that the author of Esther invented his story to explain an already existent festival. Purim, Bickerman suggests, was originally a seasonal festival of mock ritual combat between "our side" and "their side" celebrated for two days in the capital and one day in the countryside, followed by a day of pleasure. Similar festivals are well known in the ancient world. On these days, stories such as those which eventually contributed to Esther were told for the pleasure of the celebrants.

This festival, originally a local feast of the Jews of Shushan and Persia (cf. Meg. 7a), received the name Purim after the story of Mordecai and Esther had been elaborated. The name Purim is based on the story of Esther and is properly explained by our author as being derived from the lots (Akkadian *pūrū*; not a Persian word) which Haman cast to determine the date for the annihilation of the Jews (3:7; 9:24).

This analysis of Esther makes it difficult to propose a specific date for its author, since most of the motifs occurring in the book are now explained as belonging to the long tradition of Oriental romance. Nevertheless, a few facts may be established. The author was definitely a Persian Jew, possibly from Shushan. He certainly wrote before 78/77 B.C.E., the date the Greek translation of Esther (see below) was brought to Egypt, and before the composition of II Maccabees 15:36, which mentions the 14th of Adar as the "Day of Mordecai."

Much recent research has been directed to the way in which Esther presents a picture of Persian life quite similar to that drawn by the Greeks (see Berlin, xxviii–xxxii); Persians love luxury and are constantly drinking. Persian emperors are controlled by women. Persians love making laws and finding ways of getting around them. Herodotus' portrayal of the bloodthirsty Amestris is refracted in Esther's request for additional killing (Est. 9:12–14). Another avenue focuses on the ways in which Esther borrows elements from earlier biblical books, which were already Scripture for the author. The virgin search in Esther 2:2 is borrowed from I Kings chapter one; In Esther 8:2 Ahasuerus gives Mordecai the ring off his finger just as Pharaoh does in Genesis 41:42. (Other parallels to the Joseph story were already pointed out over a century ago by Rosenthal.) More significant, the Book of Esther permits the Jews to right ancient sins of omission and commission. In I Samuel 15, Mordecai's ancestor Saul and his troops had disobeyed the divine will by sparing King Agag of Amalek, and by taking Amalek's possessions for themselves in violation of the laws of *ḥerem*. In Esther, the Jews kill Haman and all his sons (9:7–10) along with all their other enemies, but as we are informed three times (9:10, 15, 16), take no plunder for themselves although they had received royal permission to do so (8:11). Feminist scholarship has also been attracted to Esther, as has redaction criticism (see Moore in DBI).

Canonization and the Greek Version

One direct result of the non-Jewish atmosphere which pervades the Scroll of Esther was the refusal of some of the rabbis to admit Esther into the Jewish canon. The Talmud (Meg. 7a) preserves debates on whether Esther was written with the proper divine inspiration (*Ru'aḥ ha-Kodesh*) and whether it "defiles the hands" like other scriptural works. The major objection to including Esther in the canon seems to have been the lack of clear references to God, His providence, or His intervention in the events of our story. The stridently militant and anti-gentile tone of the concluding chapters added to the rabbis' objections. They seem to have been afraid that Esther might arouse the jealousy and hatred of non-Jews. Ultimately, of course, the book was admitted (Meg. 7a and Rashi ad loc.). The Christian reception of Esther was historically cool. The book is never quoted or alluded to in the New Testament. Martin Luther declared his hostility to II Maccabbees and Esther, and famously wished they did not exist "for they judaize too greatly and have much pagan impropriety."

Esther was translated into Greek by Lysimachus son of Ptolemy of Jerusalem. His translation was brought to Egypt in the "fourth year of the reign of Ptolemy and Cleopatra," according to the colophon at the end of the Greek version. Of the three Ptolemies associated with a Cleopatra in the fourth year of their reign, the most probable one in this case is Ptolemy XII Auletos and his sister and wife Cleopatra V. Documents about Ptolemy XII and Cleopatra V are the only ones which illustrate in the same royal style as the colophon. The translation was thus brought to Egypt in the year 78/77 B.C.E.

Lysimachus follows his original fairly closely, although he obviously felt free to adapt and alter the text for the sake of clarity or his own notions of probability. For example, he makes the slaughter of the opponents of the Jews occur on the same day as the festival rather than on the day before, so that Purim will be celebrated on the anniversary of the victory, as were Hellenic and Jewish festivals.

The Greek translation also contains six passages not found at all in the Hebrew text. These passages should not all be understood as entirely new compositions of Lysimachus. The representations of Esther on the walls of the synagogue at *Dura-Europos also contain scenes not in the Hebrew text. This suggests that the author of the Hebrew Esther only utilized part of a larger circle of stories concerning his heroes. Lysimachus' "additions" and the paintings at Dura-Europos may be other elements of this cycle.

The character and purpose of these additions have been much debated. Three purposes, at least, can be discerned. These passages add a religious element, specifically prayer, to the book to help explain how and why the Jews were saved. The additions also adapt the book to the tastes of contemporary readers by introducing documents, namely the decrees of Haman and Mordecai. Finally, a particular interpretation of the conflict between Haman and the Jews is emphasized. Haman's decree, according to the Greek version, charges the Jews with exclusiveness and disloyalty which endanger the state. The Jews, in Mordecai's decree, answer that their God is the ruler of the world who takes and gives away kingdoms. Sovereigns ought to recognize this, as Ahasuerus ultimately does, understanding that those who oppose the Jews are the real traitors who seek to deprive the kingdom of the support of the "chosen people" and of their God. This exchange of charges of disloyalty fits well into the reign of Alexander Yannai, and it may be conjectured that this is when Lysimachus translated the work.

[Albert I. Baumgarten / S. David Sperling (2nd ed.)]

In Art

Since the talmudic period it has been customary to write the Book of Esther on parchment in the form of a scroll, and the rules governing its production and writing are basically the same as those for a traditional Torah scroll. It is not known when and under what circumstances artistic embellishment of Esther scrolls began. The earliest extant illuminated Esther scrolls emanate from 16th-century Italy, commissioned by well-to-do Italian Jews. Cylindrical or polygonal cases were often made to house such scrolls, often provided with a crank handle to roll the parchment through a vertical slot. Cases were made of copper, tin, and wood, but fine silver and some ivory cases have survived as well.

The decoration and illustration of Esther scrolls, mostly by unknown Jewish artists, reached its height during the 17th and 18th centuries, in Italy and other countries in Europe, particularly Holland. The great demand for an illustrated *megillah* led the makers to produce engraved scrolls, printed from copper plates, while the text was still copied by hand, as required by Jewish law. Some of the best-known engraved Dutch *megillot* were produced by the Jewish engraver Shalom *Italia (1619–1664?), born and raised in Italy.

The decorative programs of Esther scrolls usually depict the Esther story in great detail, one episode after the other. The episodes usually refer directly to the text column in the center, but often include midrashic elements. The narrative scenes are often set in exquisite landscapes or contemporary buildings. Other forms of decoration include architectural elements, allegorical representations, nude putti, the signs of the zodiac and the twelve tribes, heavenly Jerusalem, and scenes that reveal the daily life of the Jews of the time, particularly scenes related to the celebration of the festival.

Outside Italy and Holland figurative representations in *megillot* appear among the Ashkenazi communities in Ger-

Figure 1. Illuminated Scroll of Esther from southern France, early 16th century. The illustration on the left shows the hanging of Haman's ten sons. Cecil Roth Collection.

Figure 2. Opening section of an engraved megillah *from Italy or Holland, 17th/18th century. Height 8 in. (20 cm.). Cecil Roth Collection. Photo Werner Braun, Jerusalem.*

man-speaking lands: Germany, Austria, Bohemia, and Moravia. Many of the attractive *megillot* from these lands were produced by the scribe-artists of the so-called "Moravia School" of Hebrew illumination (for example, Aaron Wolf Herlingen of Gewitch or Meshullam Zimmel of Polna). Noteworthy are also the fine silver cases from these lands, at times engraved with the Triumph of Mordecai or other central episodes in the Esther story. Some figurative scrolls are also known from Poland and France (Alsace).

Examples of decorated *megillot* are extant from Turkey, Greece and the Balkans, and Morocco, where they were mainly decorated with floral, architectural, or other decorative designs. *Megillot* from former centers of the Ottoman Empire were often housed in ornamental silver cases – *megillot* from Istanbul in exquisite gold-plated silver cases made in a delicate filigree technique. In other lands of Islam and the East, decorated *megillot* were not as common. Notable are the colorful *megillot* of Baghdad, which feature in large capitals along the upper border a long list with the genealogy of Mordecai (tracing him back to Abraham) and contain Haman's genealogy, upside down, going back to "wicked Esau."

The art of the illustrated scroll, which declined in the 19th century, was revived in the 20th by artists of the *Bezalel School, Ze'ev Raban (1890–1970) in particular, who created *megillot* with images showing the influence of Persian miniatures mixed with Western-Orientalist symbolic elements. Side by side with the new hand-illuminated *megillot*, graphic artists in the Land of Israel joined efforts in issuing colorfully decorated printed Esther scrolls, which were far less expensive and thus popular, especially in the early days of the young state. With the improvement of the conditions of life and renewed interest in Jewish tradition in the late 20th century, young artists, including women, revived the art of the hand-illuminated *megillah*.

[Shalom Sabar (2nd ed.)]

BIBLIOGRAPHY: H. Gunkel, *Esther* (Ger., 1916); J. Hoschander, *The Book of Esther in the Light of History* (1923); H.S. Gehmann, in: JBL, 43 (1924), 321–8; H. Lewy, in: HUCA, 14 (1939), 127–51; R.H. Pfeiffer, *Introduction to the Old Testament* (1941), 732–47; Kaufmann Y., Toledot, 4 (1960), 439–48; S. Talmon, in: VT, 13 (1963), 419–55; E. Würthwein, *Esther, Handbuch zum Alten Testament* (1964); E.J. Bickermann, *Four Strange Books of the Bible* (1967), 171–240; H.L. Ginsberg, *The Five Megilloth and Jonah* (1969), 82–88. **ADD. BIBLIOGRAPHY:** L. Rosenthal, in: ZAW, 15 (1895), 278–84; idem, in: ZAW, 17 (1897), 125–28; C. Moore, in: ABD, 2:632–42; idem, in: DBI, 1:349; M. Fox, *Character and Ideology in the Book of Esther*; J. Levenson, *Esther, A Commentary* (1997); A. Berlin, *The JPS Bible Commentary: Esther* (2001). C. Benjamin, "An Illustrated Venetian Esther Scroll and the Commedia dell'Arte," in: *The Israel Museum News*, 14 (1978), 50–59; idem, *The Stieglitz Collection: Masterpieces of Jewish Art* (1987), 259–83; E. Frojmovic, "The Perfect Scribe and an Early Engraved Esther Scroll," in: *British Library Journal*, 23:1 (1997), 68–80; J. Gutmann, "Estherrolle," in: *Reallexicon zur Deutschen Kunstgeschichte* (1969), vol. 6, cols. 88–103; S. Liberman Mintz, "A Persian Tale in Turkish Garb: Exotic Imagery in Eighteenth-Century Illustrated Esther Scroll," in: J. Gutmann (ed.), *For Every Thing A Season: Proceedings of the Symposium on Jewish Ritual Art* (2002), 76–101; M. Metzger, "The John Rylands Megillah and Some Other Illustrated Megilloth of the XVth to XVIIth Centuries," in: *Bulletin of the John Rylands Library*, 45 (1962), 148–84; idem, "A Study of Some Unknown Hand-Painted Megilloth of the Seventeenth and Eighteenth Centuries," in: *Bulletin of the John Rylands Library*, 46 (1963), 84–126; idem, "The Earliest Engraved Italian Megilloth," in: *Bulletin of the John Rylands Library*, 48 (1966), 381–432; idem, "La Meghillàh illustrata della Comunità israelitica di Padova," in: *Rassegna Mensile di Israel*, 32 (1963), 88–98; M. Narkiss, "The Œuvre of the Jewish Engraver Salom Italia (1619–55?)," in: *Tarbiz*, 25 (1956), 441–51; 26 (1956), 87–101 (Heb.), R. Wischnitzer, "The Esther Story in Art," in: P. Goodman (ed.), *The Purim Anthology* (1973), 222–49.

SCROLLS, THE FIVE (Heb. *ḥamesh megillot*), a designation for the five shortest books of the Hagiographa (Heb. *Ketuvim*): Song of *Songs, *Ruth, *Lamentations, *Ecclesiastes, and Esther. Although in modern printed Hebrew Bibles the Five Scrolls constitute a unit, this was not originally the case. Thus, in an ancient tradition, recorded in *Bava Batra* 14b, in which the order of the books of the Hagiographa are listed, the *megillot* are placed in chronological order among the other books of the *Hagiographa*. The order is given as follows: Ruth, Psalms, Job, Proverbs, Ecclesiastes, Song of Songs, Lamentations, Daniel, the Scroll of Esther, Ezra, and Chronicles (see *Bible, Canon). In manuscripts of the Hebrew Bible the *megillot* are grouped together. The Leningrad manuscript (1008), on which the *Biblia Hebraica* of Kittel, from the third edition onward, is based, groups the *megillot* together in chronological order. In other printed Hebrew Bibles the *megillot* are grouped according to the order of the festivals on which they are read by the Ashkenazim in the synagogue:

(1) The Song of Songs is read in the Ashkenazi ritual on the intermediate Sabbath of *Passover, or on the seventh day of that festival (eighth in the Diaspora), if the latter coincides with a Sabbath. It is read at the *Shaḥarit* service prior to the reading of the Torah. In the Sephardi ritual it is read before the *Minḥah* service on the afternoon of the seventh day of Passover (eighth day outside Israel). In certain communities, the Song of Songs is also read after concluding the Passover *Haggadah* on *seder* night. The association of the Song of Songs with Passover is thought to be due to the traditional rabbinic exegesis which interprets the Song as an allegory of the love between God and Israel; Passover is the springtime of this love (Song 2:11–13) and the "honeymoon" of God and Israel (Jer. 2:2). In many congregations the Song of Songs is also read on Friday evenings before the Kabbalat *Shabbat service, at which the "bride," the Sabbath, is welcomed.

(2) Ruth is read on *Shavuot, in most rites, at the *Shaḥarit* service prior to the reading of the Torah. In the Diaspora, it is read on the second day of Shavuot. In the Sephardi and Italian rituals, it is divided into two parts and recited on both mornings (or afternoons). The association with Shavuot is based on the seasonal reference to "the beginning of the barley harvest" (Ruth 1:22); on the traditional belief that King David – whose genealogy concludes the book (Ruth 4: 17–22) – was born and died on Shavuot (Tos. to Ḥag. 17a TJ, Beẓah 2:4, 61c); and on

the parallel drawn between Ruth's embracing the Jewish faith and Israel's accepting the Torah at Mount Sinai on Shavuot.

(3) Lamentations, a dirge over the destruction of Jerusalem and the Temple, is read on the Ninth of *Av as part of the synagogue service. It is recited in the evening and in the morning (see Tur, OḤ 559).

(4) Ecclesiastes is recited on the intermediary Sabbath of *Sukkot, or on the eighth day of the festival (Shemini Aẓeret), if the latter coincides with a Sabbath. It is read during the morning service before the reading of the Torah. In some Oriental rites, it is read in the *sukkah*. Ecclesiastes (11:2) has been interpreted by some commentators as an allusion to the duty to rejoice during the eight days of Sukkot (cf. Deut. 16:15). The warning (Eccles. 5:3–4) not to defer the fulfillment of vows (including donations to the poor and to the sanctuary) was also thought to be particularly appropriate at the last festival of the annual cycle. Others have suggested that the somber and pessimistic outlook of Ecclesiastes fits the atmosphere of autumn.

(5) Esther is read as the central rite in the *Purim festival in both the evening and morning services.

The custom of reading the Five Scrolls originated in various periods. The Scroll of Esther was read already in the Second Temple period; the reading of Lamentations is mentioned in *Ta'anit* 30a; and the post-talmudic tractate *Soferim* (14:18) records only the custom of reading Esther, the Song of Songs, and Ruth, although in an order different from the modern practice. The introductory blessing ("who has sanctified us by Thy commandments and commanded us to read…") is recited only before the reading of Esther. Likewise, only the Scroll of Esther must be written on parchment. In Jerusalem, however, the blessing is said prior to the reading of all the scrolls (with the exception of Lamentations), and all are read from a parchment scroll.

Musical Rendition

THE SONG OF SONGS, RUTH, AND ECCLESIASTES. Discussions about the sanctity of Song of Songs are already reflected in Mishnah Yadayim 3:5. In Sanhedrin 101, it is explicitly forbidden to "treat the Song of Songs *ke-min zemer*," i.e., as if it were a (secular) song. The choice and positioning of the masoretic accents in the text of the Song of Songs seem to imply that a definite convention in their musical execution, perhaps in the form of ornate psalmody, was present in the minds of the masoretes. It is difficult to use these data as evidence that the original folk-song tunes of the Song of Songs could still have survived in talmudic times, but it is at least clear that a folk-song tradition was still attached to it. The presently observable traditions, however, show that most of the melodic formulas for the rendition of the Song of Songs, Ruth, and Ecclesiastes are late developments, and that they are often indebted to previously existing melodic conventions connected with other books of the Bible or parts of the liturgy. Differences between the melodies or formulas are found not only as regards the various communities but also within many communities for the communal or solo singing of the text, as demonstrated especially in Yemen. The adaptation of secular tunes for the Song of Songs is mentioned as late as 1870 (*Mikra Kodesh* by R. Mordecai Abbadi of Aleppo). In many communities there are common melodies for several of the scrolls, such as one melody for Ecclesiastes and Ruth. In the Polish-Lithuanian tradition there is one melody for the Song of Songs, Ruth, and Ecclesiastes, and this melody shows the clear influence of the masoretic cantillation of the Pentateuch. In some Near Eastern communities such as Aleppo, the *maqāma* tradition of the surrounding area is also reflected clearly (Idelsohn, *Melodien* 4, no. 338 for Ruth and no. 339 for Ecclesiastes).

Esther

The traditional view that Esther should be read "like a letter" has greatly influenced its musical rendition. There is also the traditional practice of changing the motives or the tempo where especially gladdening or sad events come to be narrated. A.Z. *Idelsohn's analysis of the Babylonian melody for Esther showed that it is very near to that used for Ruth, with the addition of motives from the Song of Songs – the borrowing of motives in Ashkenazi tradition is especially developed (*talsha* and *munnaḥ-legarmi* from Lamentations, and *talsha gedolah* and *darga* from the reading of the "21 books," and *kadma veazla*, with certain changes, from the prayer mode of the High Holy Days (see *Cantillations). Idelsohn's division of the Esther melodies by style into two basic areas – Yemen, Persia, Syria, London Sephardi, and Carpentras, as against Iraq, Eastern Sephardi, and Morocco – needs further study. In addition to the melodic relationships between Song of Songs, Ruth, and Ecclesiastes, the following are also to be noted: Song of Songs and Esther (Morocco) and Ruth and Esther (Iraq).

Lamentations

As Idelsohn showed, the scale of the singing of Lamentations is peculiar, and it was his opinion that it had no parallel in the traditional Jewish repertoire. This scale is also found among the Syrian (Maronite and Jacobite) Christians and among the Copts in Egypt: in ascending order it progresses G-sharp, A, B-natural, C, D, E-flat; all the internal cadential movements end on A, and the final endings are on G sharp. In many Jewish traditions there are slight changes in the melody from chapter to chapter, and the last chapter especially has a melody of its own.

The masoretic accents of the scrolls do not always find expression in their melodies. Some readings resemble more the simplest forms of psalmody and do not take the accents into account at all. In others a psalmodic fundament is at least clearly discernible (cf. Song of Songs in Morocco, Idelsohn *Melodien* II, no. 173, p. 56). In Idelsohn's opinion the lyrical atmosphere of some of the scrolls, such as Ruth and Song of Songs, does not permit an emphatic rendition of the text. This would be the reason why the more melodic accents – such as *shalshelet* and *merkha kefulah* – do not appear in the scrolls, and that some others, such as *zarka*, are used very sparsely. Against this, it must be said that the choice of the accents was not dictated by the contents of the text but by its structure.

The Order of the *Megillot* after the Pentateuch

1.	2.	3.	4.	5.
mss. Nos. 1, 2, 3	mss. Nos. 4, 5 ,6	mss. Nos. 7, 8	mss. No. 9	Early Editions
Song of Songs	Esther	Ruth	Ruth	Song of Songs
Ruth	Song of Songs	Song of Songs	Song of Songs	Ruth
Lamentations	Ruth	Ecclesiastes	Lamentations	Lamentations
Ecclesiastes	Lamentations	Lamentations	Ecclesiastes	Ecclesiastes
Esther	Ecclesiastes	Esther	Esther	Esther

The nine mss. collated for this table are the following in the British Museum: (1) Add. 9400; (2) Add. 9403; (3) Add. 19776; (4) Harley 5706; (5) Add. 9404; (6) Orient. 2786; (7) Harley 5773; (8) Harley 15283; (9) Add. 15282.

The fifth column represents the order adopted in the first, second and third editions of the Hebrew Bible, as well as that of the second and third editions of Bomberg's *Quarto Bible* (Venice 1521, 1525), in all of which the five *Megillot* follow immediately after the Pentateuch

BIBLIOGRAPHY: J.L. Baruch and T. Lewinski, *Sefer ha-Mo'adim*, 2 (1952^2), 26; 3 (1953^2), 118–29; 4 (1952^2), 226–35; 6 (1955), 35–82; 7 (1957^2), 170–201; Idelsohn, Melodien, introd.; idem, Music, index; A. Herzog and A. Hajdu, in: *Yuval*, 1 (1968), 194–203.

[Avigdor Herzog]

SCULPTURE.

The Biblical and Talmudic Periods

Within the general context of the problem of representational art among the Jews in antiquity, sculpture, together with *medals and *seals, was in a special category. The Bible (Ex. 20:4) forbade the "graven image" in the most explicit fashion, more categorically and comprehensively than the mere likeness. Hence, while the representation of human or animal figures on a plane surface was condoned or permitted most of the time during the periods in question, greater difficulties were constantly raised with regard to three-dimensional representations on medals and seals, and four-dimensional sculptures in the round. Indeed, in some Orthodox circles, even making an impression with a seal bearing the human or animal form was considered religiously objectionable, since by doing so a man actually "made" a graven image, even though not for worship or veneration. From a very early period, however, this was qualified in practice. The *Cherubim of the Tabernacle and in the Temple of Solomon were representations in the round. A fourth century Jewish scholar states (TJ, Av. Zar, 3:1, 42c) that all manner of images (פרסופים, *parsufim*, mod. Heb. *parẓufim*; i.e., "visages," from the Greek πρόσωπον) were to be found in Jerusalem before its destruction in the year 70 C.E. Even if this information is not quite accurate, it is obvious that this scholar himself had no objection to graven images as such. R. *Gamaliel in the second century C.E. is said to have had a human head engraved on his seal. A statue of the ruling Parthian monarch stood as a patriotic symbol in the synagogue where *Abba Arikha and *Samuel worshiped in Nehardea (RH 24b). The talmudic statement (Av. Zar. 42b) that "all images are permissible except those of human beings" presumably refers to their retention when they were found rather than to their manufacture.

In the Middle Ages

The rabbis of northern France discussed and even permitted the representation of the human form in the round, provided that it was incomplete (Tos. to Av. Zar. 43a). Even *Maimonides (Yad, Avodat Kokhavim 3:10–11), while forbidding the human form in the round, apparently sanctioned three-dimensional animal figures. In the Renaissance period, carved lions flanked the steps leading up to the ark in the synagogue at Ascoli in Italy, although this eventually gave rise to objections. There are traces of Jewish sculptors in Spain in the Middle Ages, including the anonymous Jew who was said to have been responsible for the first recorded statue of Francis of Assisi (1214). There were also a number of metal workers whose work included the making of figures in gold and silver. Jaime Sanchez, the Aragonese court sculptor, was assisted in his work by a certain Samuel of Murcia, who is even designated as rabbi. Some scholars maintain that the eminent German sculptor Veit Stoss (Wit Stwosz, 1447–1542), creator of the altar of the church of St. Mary in the Polish city of Cracow, whose earlier life is wrapped in mystery, was in fact of Marrano birth, and even recorded the fact in Hebrew characters in one of his paintings.

The fashion of commissioning portrait medals was known among Italian Jews of the Renaissance period, such as Gracia *Nasi and members of the *Norsa and *Lattes families. The actual work was done by non-Jewish artists, but one Jew, Moses da *Castelazzo, was employed as a medalist at the court of Ferrara, though none of his productions can be identified. Biblical and other scenes in high relief appear on the tombstones in some of the cemeteries of the Sephardi communities of the Atlantic seaboard, especially Amsterdam. In the Jewish cemetery in Curaçao in the West Indies, the deathbed scene is sometimes shown on the tombstone with the likeness of the deceased in high relief. Nevertheless, there seems to have been some reluctance among the Jews to tolerate sculpture in the complete sense of the term. The earliest bust of a Jew is usually held to be that of Moses Mendelssohn by P.A. Tassaert (1727–88). The bust of Antonio Lopes *Suasso, Baron Avernas le Gras, attributed to Rombout Verhulst (1624–98), is, however, of an earlier date. But as late as the 20th century, there were Orthodox Jewish collectors in western Europe who refused to allow sculptured figures in their homes unless they were either defective or slightly mutilated. In the light of this attitude, Jewish medalists of some reputation came into evidence relatively early, while Jewish sculptors emerged only in the 19th century.

[Cecil Roth]

The 19th and 20th Centuries

Jews entered the field of sculpture about 1850, some years after the first Jewish painters appeared. Few of these 19th-century sculptors are remembered today, although some of their work survives on the facades or in the interior of public buildings, in the squares of large cities, in parks, or in the vaults of museums. Possibly the earliest to achieve a measure of fame was the Hungarian, Jacob *Guttmann, for whom Prince Metternich and Pope Pius IX sat, but whose name is not to be found in any history of modern art. Guttmann shares the fate of scores of non-Jewish sculptors of his time, who were famous in their day, obtained gold medals and held professorships, but fell into oblivion with the emergence of Auguste Rodin (1840–1917), who was to overturn the prevailing notions concerning the function and scope of sculpture.

These men were gifted enough to furnish Victorian society with statues of celebrated statesmen or generals, or with the knickknacks that adorned the tables and mantelpieces of upper-middle-class homes. Most of these pieces were conceived in a style that might be described as "sentimental naturalism." Often, tolerably good likenesses of individuals were created, yet they suffered largely from an excessive preoccupation with detail. Works on literary or religious themes were frequently burdened with an all too obvious and even trite "symbolism." Thus, of 19th-century Jewish sculptors, Samuel Friedrich *Beer is chiefly remembered for his association with Theodor Herzl and the Zionist movement rather than for his own work. Similarly, Boris *Schatz is revered today as the founder of the *Bezalel School of Art and the Bezalel Museum in Jerusalem, while his actual works are no longer held in high esteem.

After 1900, artists discarded the academic formula. Art is imitation of nature, and Jewish sculptors, like their non-Jewish confrères, stressed the emotional or expressionist element, abandoning mechanical accuracy or photographic likenesses. They were encouraged in this by the discovery and evaluation of aboriginal art from Africa and Oceania, which, nonnaturalistic in character, made a strong impact by its daring simplifications and exaggerations of forms. Among the authors of pioneering studies of African sculpture were Carl Einstein (1885–1940) and Paul Westheim (1886–1963). It is remarkable that almost all the Jewish sculptors whose careers began around 1910 came from east European communities, where the taboo against the making of three-dimensional objects was still strong. They included Enrico (Henoch) *Glicenstein; Elie *Nadelman; Chana *Orloff; Anton and Naum Nehemia *Pevsner (d. 1977) who were brothers; Ossip *Zadkine; and Moyse *Kogan. The best known of this group of sculptors is Jacques *Lipchitz, in whose work can be found figures and groups drawn from Jewish and biblical themes. Another well-known sculptor, Sir Jacob *Epstein, born in New York and living most of his life in England, was the son of Polish immigrants. The Italian painter Amadeo *Modigliani first worked as a sculptor and left more than 20 carvings as evidence of an unusual talent.

Although most of the modern sculpture belongs to the category of expressionism, Jews have also been pioneers in post-expressionist trends, among them Làszló Moholy-Nagy (1895–1946), and Naum Nehemia Pevsner. In the United States, two dentists who became sculptors, Herbert *Ferber and Seymour *Lipton, achieved wide acclaim, Ferber with lead and bronze pieces that, while abstract, were imbued with psychological or symbolic meaning, and Lipton with roughly textured metal works that, equally abstract, are vaguely reminiscent of plants or animals. The huge assemblages of scraps of wood of Louise Nevelson (1900–1988) create environments of their own. Of a later generation than these is George *Segal, whose white plaster figures are cast from living models and placed in pseudo-realistic settings such as shops or bedrooms. A naturalized Frenchman, Hungarian-born Nicolas Schoeffer (1912–1992), created complicated constructions making use of light, and even noise. In England, the pioneer of minimal sculpture was Anthony *Caro.

While the synagogue for a long time rejected any decoration in the round, in the 1950s and 1960s more and more Reform temples and, to a lesser degree, Conservative congregations, especially in the United States, commissioned the services of sculptors to fashion large *menorot* and other ritual objects, or to decorate walls with semi-abstract designs of such symbols as the Burning Bush or the Tablets of the Law.

[Alfred Werner]

Sculpture in Ereẓ Israel

In the same way as painting was continuous and intense in Palestine after 1906, sculpture also flourished as the result of the efforts of a few sculptors over a considerable period. Avraham Melnikoff (1892–1960) is known for his famous "Lion" at Tel Ḥai (1926), and Zeev *Ben Zvi, who taught sculpture at the Bezalel School from 1936, had a good knowledge of cubism and left some important works. It was the more academic school of sculpture, represented by Moshe Ziffer (1902–1989), Aharon Priver (1902–1979), and Batya Lishansky (1900–1990), which dominated the field prior to the establishment of the State of Israel. During this time there was hardly any open-air sculpture. In 1938, however, Yitzhak *Danziger executed his "Nimrod," which was in itself an attempt to create a synthesis between Middle Eastern sculpture and the modern concept of the human figure. Danziger's art underwent profound changes after World War II, and he became the leader of the younger generation of sculptors. His style rapidly became more abstract. Not only did he work in new materials, such as iron, but he attacked the double problem of open-air sculpture and its integration into its surroundings and its relation to town planning. Yeḥiel *Shemi, Dov *Feigin, Moshe Sternschus (1905–1992), Kosso Eloul (1920–1995), and David *Palombo followed Danziger in developing abstract styles of their own. They were in turn copied by younger sculptors, such as Ezra Orion (1934–), Menashe Kadishman (1932–), and Buky (Moshe) Schwartz (1932–). Two others who worked on monumental sculptures and integrated them into urban landscapes were Igael *Tumarkin and Shamai *Haber.

[Yona Fischer]

BIBLIOGRAPHY: Yidisher Kultur Farband, *One Hundred Contemporary American Jewish Painters and Sculptors* (1947); B. Satt, *A*

Jewish Town in Sculpture (1958); C.S. Spencer, in: *Ariel*, 18 (1967), 19–24; B. Kirschner, *Deutsche Spottmedaillen auf Juden* (1968), incl. bibl.

SEA, SONG OF THE (Heb. שִׁירַת הַיָּם), the name given to the exuberant hymn of triumph and gratitude (Ex. 15:1–18) sung by "Moses and the Children of Israel" after the crossing of the Red Sea. It relates the miracle of the parting of the Red Sea and the drowning of the Egyptians when "the waters returned and covered the chariots and the horsemen, even all the host of Pharaoh" (*ibid.* 14:28).

The Song falls into two natural halves: verses 1–13a, describing the actual destruction of the Egyptian hosts; and 13b to the end, a vivid imaginary picture of the pangs and terror which seized the inhabitants of Canaan and of the neighboring countries (including, anachronistically, Philistia). It concludes with the confident assurance (mentioned already in 13b) that the Children of Israel will enter the Land of Israel and build the sanctuary and with the triumphant declaration of the eternal sovereignty of God.

This division is substantially that given by F.M. Cross and D.N. Freedman. Other modern scholars however detect a more complicated structure. Cassuto sees it divided into three strophes:

(a) verses 1b–6,

(b) verses 7–11,

(c) verses 12–16, with verses 17–18 as an epilogue; whereas Rozelaar proposes four:

(a) verses 2–5,

(b) verses 6–10,

(c) verses 11–13

(d) verses 14–17, with a prologue (verse 1b) and an epilogue (verse 18).

Critical View

Many scholars have seen in the Song of the Sea references to Ancient Near Eastern myths of the war between the ruling deity (Marduk, Baal) and the sea-god with its helpers (Leviathan, Rahab). In the Song of the Sea, however, if there are any such vestiges of the myth, they are mere clichés or figures of speech; the sea is a passive tool of God's will. Some scholars (e.g., A. Bentzen) even regard the Song as part of a hypothetical enthronement festival celebrating YHWH's victory over His primordial enemy, the sea, though there is no cogent evidence whatsoever of the existence of such a festival. Dates suggested for the Song's composition range from the 12th century B.C.E. to the end of the First Temple period. F.M. Cross and D.N. Freedman date it on orthographic and linguistic grounds from the 12th to the 10th centuries B.C.E. Yet the mention of God's sanctuary is probably a reference to Solomon's Temple, and the declaration of God's rule means His rule in Zion. The poem is probably to be dated, therefore, at the end of the united monarchy (S.E. Loewenstamm). The Song of Miriam quoted in verse 21, which is identical with the opening of the Song of the Sea, is either the original kernel of the Song or a refrain from it, indicating that the whole song was sung. The Song of the Sea is basically independent of the JE and P narratives, but it may have served as the primary source of the P narrative, which took literally the phrases about the waters being heaped up like a wall (verse 8) and elaborated upon them. The Song is probably the oldest extant source for the story of the sea crossing, just as the Song of Deborah (Judg. 5) antedates the prose account of the Israelite victory over the Canaanites (Judg. 4).

[Michael V. Fox]

Liturgical Usages

The Song of the Sea has special regulations both in the manner in which it is written in the Torah Scroll, and the manner in which it was chanted. It is written in 30 lines, its outward form resembling "half bricks set over whole bricks" (Meg. 16b), thus:

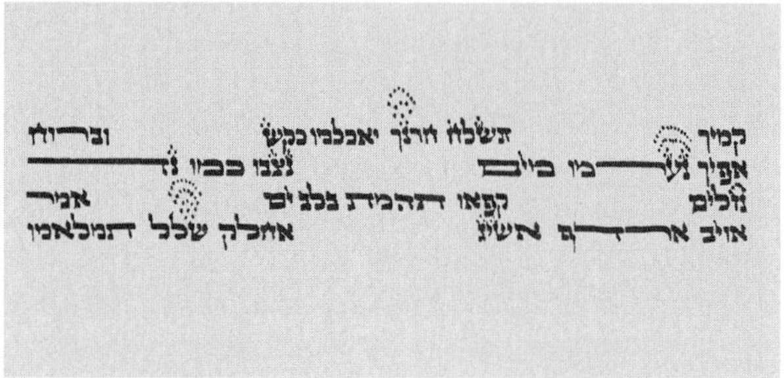

It was also chanted in a special fashion. In the Talmud (Sot. 30b) three different methods of rendering it are given, and each obviously reflects different local usages. R. Akiva declared that it was read in the same way as the *Hallel, i.e., the cantor declaimed it, and the congregation responded merely with "heads of chapters," i.e., they made the response "I will sing unto the Lord" after every verse. R. Eliezer the son of R. Yose the Galilean states that the congregation repeated the whole Song after him, while R. Nehemiah said that the cantor and congregation recited the verses alternately (so Elbogen; for a full discussion see his Gottesdienst).

The Song of the Sea occupies a prominent place in the liturgy. It is read in the Sabbath portion on which it occurs (*Be-Shallaḥ*) and that Sabbath is called *Shabbat Shirah*. It is the scriptural reading of the seventh day of Passover; the custom also developed among some ḥasidic sects of chanting it at a special ceremony at midnight of that evening. In Israel, large crowds assemble at the beach in Tel Aviv and Eilat on the seventh day of Passover, where it is ceremonially sung. It is included in the daily **Pesukei de-Zimra*, and in some congregations when the father of a child to be circumcised that day is in synagogue, it is read antiphonally by reader and congregation.

In Jewish Tradition

The fact that Miriam took out the women to sing the Song separately was taken as the authority for the segregation of the sexes in prayer in the synagogue (Mekh. Shirah 10, 44a, Midrash Lekaḥ Tov to Ex. 15:20).

In some communities the custom was observed to distribute food specially to birds, the traditional songsters, on *Shabbat Shirah*, but the custom was disapproved of by some authorities (Magen Avraham to OḤ, 324, 11, subsection 7).

[Louis Isaac Rabinowitz]

BIBLIOGRAPHY: M. Rozelaar, in: VT, 2 (1952), 221–8; A. Bentzen, *Introduction to the Old Testament*, 1 (1952²),163; F.M. Cross and D.N. Freedman, in: JNES, 14 (1955), 237–50; S.E. Loewenstamm, *Masoret Yeẓi'at Miẓrayim be-Hishtalshelutah* (1965), 112–20; U. Cassuto, *A Commentary on the Book of Exodus* (1967), 173–82; Elbogen, Gottesdienst, 541ff.; S.J. Zevin, *Le-Or ha-Halakhah* (1964³), 241–50; D. Litvin, *The Sanctity of the Synagogue* (1959), 173ff.

SEAL, SEALS.

In the Ancient Period

The seal was employed from the beginning of the historical era as a method of identifying property, as protection against theft, to mark the clay stoppers of oil and wine jars or the strip with which packaged goods were bound, and for other uses. Gradually seals became invested with magic powers. With the spread of writing in the early days of the Mesopotamian dynasties, seals were used as signatures on clay-tablet inscriptions. In Egypt, seals were used to sign papyrus scrolls. In various regions, including Palestine in the early Canaanite period, earthenware vessels were imprinted with seals before they were fired. Seals were made of a variety of stones which were usually semiprecious. The carving and relief were done by means of a simple drill, an auger, or a stylus. Cylinder seals were usually pierced through their length and threaded on a fastening pin, cord, thread, wire, chain, or – from the second millennium B.C.E. – on a ring. Ancient seals are of great value in the study of ancient art, religion, and mythology, as well as the legal and social structures of ancient societies. Seals found in archaeological excavations are important for chronology, and Hebrew seals are useful in the study of Hebrew paleography and the Hebrew onomasticon.

Four main types of seals, classified according to their shape and function, were used.

(1) Cylinder seals, pierced lengthwise, and between 1 and 2 in. (3 and 5 cm.) in length. They originated in Mesopotamia and spread over the entire Ancient Near East. They were engraved with symbols of worship and mythological and hunting scenes. When they were inscribed with writing, it was in the cuneiform of Western Asia. The cylinder when rolled over the soft clay imparted a long row of impressions. Clay vessels have been found in Palestine bearing impressions of cylinder seals from the early Bronze Age (third millennium B.C.E.), and from the second millennium B.C.E. Some of these seals were imported, from Mesopotamia, but most of them were made in Ereẓ Israel and in adjoining countries, particularly Syria. Syrian-Hittite, Mitanni, and mixed styles can be distinguished among them. Most of them are made of hematite.

(2) Scarab seals, which were small Egyptian seals, oval-shaped, approximately 7/10 × 4/10 in. (18 × 12 mm.), and generally made of amethyst, carnelian, or faience. They were generally slightly convex and were carved to resemble the sacred scarabaeus beetle of Egypt, often including legs around the perimeter. The base was level and engraved with hieroglyphs representing the names of kings, officials, and individuals; and titles, blessings, and incantations. It was also engraved with the figures of gods, men, animals, and birds; and floral and geometric designs which were imprinted by means of pressure. Many such scarabs were exported to all the countries of the region, but others were made in Palestine and other lands under Egyptian influence. Some unusually large scarab seals imported from Egypt have been found in Ereẓ Israel. Such seals have been discovered in most archaeological excavations of the second millennium B.C.E. They are particularly numerous in the Hyksos period (18th–17th century B.C.E.). During that period and after, Egyptian writing and words were carelessly copied, and the names of Egyptian monarchs – especially of Tuthmosis III and Ramses II – were engraved long after their deaths. Many of these seals were obviously not used functionally but rather as charms or jewelry.

(3) Scaraboid seals. These became widespread during the middle Israelite era (ninth to fifth centuries B.C.E.). They resemble the former category but are not carved with the beetle shape on their backs or legs along the perimeter. They were used mostly for signatures or to mark possessions and were common in Syria, Phoenicia, and Palestine. The base of these seals was generally engraved with an inscription in the Phoenician-Hebrew script, in Hebrew, Phoenician, or Aramaic, and they are commonly known as Hebrew seals. The inscriptions were sometimes combined with decorative designs in the mixed Phoenician style, with mythological subjects, flora and fauna, and geometrical patterns. It would appear that the mythological figures lost some of their religious significance and gradually became common decorative motifs throughout the region. These motifs include the figures of human beings, animals, and winged legendary creatures, such as the griffin or the sphinx, the winged beetle, winged serpent (uraeus), the winged sun, and so on. The chief function of the seal was vested in the name engraved upon it, which was often left undecorated. The name of the owner of the seal was frequently given together with that of his father, sometimes with the word "son" and sometimes without it (e.g., Shebna Ahab, Remaliah son of Neriah, etc.). There were also women's seals (Abigail wife of Asaiah, Aliah handmaiden of Hananel, etc.). While most of the seals were personal, a few contained the name of a "servant" (official) and his monarch (Shema servant of Jeroboam, etc.) or the official's name and title (Jaazaniah servant of the king, Gealiah son of the king, Gedaliah the steward of the palace, etc.). The importance of the seal and its usage in biblical days is evident in various texts, letters, or documents that were sealed with a seal (I Kings 21:8; Isa. 29: 11; Job 38: 14). The king's ring was synonymous with the king's seal, and it symbolized royal power (Esth. 8:8). Ordinary citizens also carried seals (Gen. 38: 18). As a figure of speech the seal represented something precious and cherished (Jer. 22:24; Hag-

gai 2:23; Song 8:6). Scaraboid seals were also used during the Persian era (fifth and sixth centuries B.C.E.).

(4) Conical seals. During the late Babylonian and Persian eras (seventh to fourth centuries B.C.E.), conical seals with round, or octagonal, somewhat convex, bases, usually made of clear chalcedony, were commonly used. They originated in Mesopotamia, and their bases are generally inscribed with ritual motifs. In later periods they also had decorative motifs engraved on their outer surface.

Archaeological excavations in Palestine have yielded many vessels of the second part of the middle Israelite era (eighth to sixth centuries B.C.E.) imprinted with their owners' seals. Some bear the name of a royal official (Elikam, Eliakam steward of Yaukin (= Jehoiakin)). A lump of clay with the seal imprint "Gedaliah steward of the palace," which was used to seal the cord around a papyrus scroll, has also been found. There has been a great deal of interest in vessels bearing upon their handles a royal stamp consisting of the inscription "of the king," together with one of the following names: Hebron, Soco (*swkh*), Ziph, and Mamshith (*mmsht*). The first three are names of towns; there is some dispute concerning the fourth. In any event, these vessels appear to have been used in collecting royal taxes. Similarly, vessels of the Persian and early Hellenic eras were also imprinted with official seals bearing one of the words: Judah, Jerusalem, or Moza. Among the *Yahud* (Judah) imprints, there are some which include the name of a person followed by the Aramaic word *peḥārā* (the potter). Two important Jewish impressions have been found from the late Second Temple period. They are little clay plaques between 1 and 2 in. (3 and 5 cm.) in length. One bears the name of the city of Gezer and the other the name of a type of wine, "tamad," and the name of the vintner, "Hoshea," engraved between the arms of a swastika. Both seals are in the square Hebrew script and were probably used to seal wine jars.

[Nachman Avigad]

Post-Biblical Period

Apart from the biblical חותם, rabbinical literature used the Aramaic words גושפנקא and עזקתא, עזקא (*ibid.*) and the Greek ספרגיס (σφραγίς) as synonyms for seals or signet rings. Seals could be made not only from gems but also from sandalwood and metal (Kel. 13:6; for iron see Ber. 6a). They were engraved with emblems and figures, except the human one, though a halakhic distinction is made between a figure in relief and one engraved (Tos. to Av. Zar. 5:2, 468 and parallels); emblems on the seals of some well-known rabbis are mentioned (Git. 36a). The use of seals was restricted for Jews in the event that the emblem was idolatrous (*ibid.*, cf. TJ, 4:4, 44a for an incident with Bar Kappara), and there are a number of instances in which seals are reported to have been used for magical purposes (Ber. 6a; Shab. 66b; Git. 68a). They were normally used for signing documents, however, though generally the signature of witnesses alone was sufficient. Vessels containing foodstuffs were sealed to assure the ritual fitness of the contents (Av. Zar. 31a). In addition, all sorts of objects, valuable or less valuable, were stamped to mark ownership (Tos. to Av. Zar. 5:1, 468 and parallels). The Mishnah speaks of seals for packing bags as distinct from letter seals (Shab. 8:5). While men may go out with a signet ring on their hand on the Sabbath, women may not as this is not adornment for them (Shab. 6:1; 3). While, by implication, women did not normally wear signet rings, the Talmud mentions the גזברות ("woman treasurer") as an exception (*ibid.* 62a). Seals were also worn hanging from one's neck or garment (Tos. Shab. 5:8, 116; TB, 58a). The Albertinum Museum in Dresden formerly had two seals dating from the second to the third centuries C.E., one of which was an amethyst with a *menorah emblem and the other a cornelian with a seven-branched *menorah* between two pillars. A small bronze seal ring in Isaac Einhorn's collection in Tel Aviv bears a similar seven-branch *menorah* on it. A seal in the Israel Museum (formerly in the Heinrich Feuchtwanger Collection no. 615) bearing the inscription כנשתא דפרג is probably from Babylonia dating from the fifth or sixth century.

After the Arab conquest of Babylonia, the caliph Omar (634–44) prohibited the use of seals by Jews (and Christians), except for the exilarchs, on whose seal a fly was engraved (*Bustanai b. Haninai). This privilege was no doubt granted to the exilarchs and the *geonim*. The *gaon* *Hai b. Sherira (d. 1038) had a seal with a lion as an emblem, signifying Davidic descent. With the revival of the exilarchate in the 12th century, the right to have an official seal was restored as well. Large wooden seals for meat, bread, or cheese are known from the East, mainly from Egypt from the Fatimid period, as for example, Berlin Staats-Museum, cf. Synagoga, Recklingshausen no. A. 32.

In Europe the use of seals spread among the Jews in imitation of the coats of *arms and other heraldic devices prevalent among kings and the nobility, the higher clergy and monasteries, and cities and guilds; later the custom spread to the rising class of burghers. Jewish businessmen and financiers needed seals for the purpose of signing business documents; in the 13th century the seal on a document was regarded as more important than the signature. Not only did individual Jews have their own seals but Jewish communities had them as well (e.g., Augsburg, Cologne, Metz, Regensburg, Ulm). The use of seals met with the opposition of some rabbis, who regarded it as imitating non-Jewish practices. Others, however, such as *Baruch b. Isaac of Regensburg and *Moses of Coucy, defended the use of seals, some even using them themselves, such as the tosafist *Samson b. Samson, Israel *Isserlein, and Jacob *Moellin (Maharil, 14th century), whose seals bore the emblem of a lion. *Meir b. Baruch of Rothenburg permitted the wearing of a signet ring on the Sabbath. In 1906 the gold ring of a certain Abba b. Abba was found in Breslau. Made and ornamented in the Gothic style, it had a seal and the inscription, "This is not in imitation of Amorite (non-Jewish) practices."

In several countries the authorities intervened in the use of seals by Jews. As early as 1206, Philippe II of France decreed that promissory notes should have the special Jews' seal attached to them – which was to remain, however, in the custody of two city notables – while his son Louis VIII prohibited the use of seals by Jews entirely. In Navarre they had to seal their documents with the royal seal. In Portugal, Jews' seals were already in use in the 12th century, and in the 15th, the chief rabbi (*Arraby Moor), as well as the seven provincial *dayyanim*, had their own seals by virtue of royal decree. Later in the century the chief rabbi was entitled to use the royal seal. The earliest Jewish seal mentioned in Central Europe is that of an Austrian official in 1257, while that of a Jewish banker of Regensburg is noted in 1297. In the 14th century reference is made to a decree of Duke William of Austria concerning promissory notes to be sealed by the Jews' judge, to be entered in the *Judenbuch* of the city of Pressburg (Bratislava), and to be signed with seals by a Christian and a Jew. Among the taxes levied on the Jews, "seal taxes" occupied an important place.

From the 13th century onward in Spain and Germany many seals of Jews, mainly of communities, have been preserved. That of Augsburg had the double eagle with the Jews' hat; the Regensburg one had a crescent with a star, an emblem that can be found on contemporary non-Jewish seals as well. Two Jewish seals from Spain are preserved in the British Museum, London, probably dating from the 14th century; one was the seal of the Seville community, the other of Todros b. Samuel ha-Levi. Many promissory notes of Jews, which were deposited with the Exchequer of the Jews in England, had Jews' seals affixed to them, some engraved with figures. A Jewish *sigillificus* (seal maker) is mentioned in Dijon, France, about 1363. The absence of errors in the Hebrew inscriptions is an indication of Jewish craftsmen having been employed, while the cock on the seal of Peter b. Moses of Regensburg (1391) points to a Christian seal maker.

Jewish seals were distinguished from others by their inscription in Hebrew and the absence of the human figure. Apart from Hebrew, some seals had Latin or vernacular inscriptions as well; double seals, in particular, had Hebrew on one side and the other language on the reverse. Such a seal was used by Saul *Wahl, the 16th-century Polish financier. Emblems in use included animals, flowers, cups, hats ("Jews' hat"), the crescent, and stars. Occasionally the figures reflect the name, so-called *armes parlentes* (but also Davidic descent), e.g., a lion for Judah, a bear for Issachar, a bull's head for Joseph – as in the seal of *Josel of Rosheim – a stag as on the seal of Herz (= Hirsch) Wertheimer of Padua (16th century), the rose bush of the Rosalis family in Hamburg, and Spinoza's thorny branch. Men of priestly descent had outspread hands on their seals, levites a water jar. Solomon *Molcho's seal had two mountains (the hills on which he had his vision) and that of *Shabbetai Ẓevi, a serpent (נחש being numerically equivalent to משיח – Messiah). David Portaleone, the physician, had a lion crouching on a gate as his seal in accordance with the family tradition. The handle of his seal, in the Einhorn Collection, depicts the sacrifice of Isaac. Certain families of Frankfurt and Worms used their house signs on their seals as well. Other emblems reflected the occupation of the owner, e.g., the anchor for merchants. The seal used by three brothers had three Jews' hats with their points meeting. Some of these symbols were set in an escutcheon and appeared on the background of a three-cornered shield, a pentagram, or David's shield, as in the seal of Jacob b. Nathaniel-Daniel, treasurer of the archbishop of Trier (1341–47). This was really the privilege of those "born to the shield and helmet," but Jews used the shield only (*écu français*). The name was usually engraved on the periphery of the generally round but also square and parabolic seals.

From the Middle Ages there are also seals of *kashrut*, mainly for meat. A metal seal in the collection of Cecil Roth has the word *kosher* inscribed on it.

From the 16th century the seals of the Jews of Poland were generally crudely made. In Hungary the use of seals by the leaders of the Jewish community was common from the end of the 15th century. These seals showed engraved human figures, animals, and Hebrew monograms in the Renaissance style. In the 16th–17th centuries the use of seals by the Jews in Germany and Austria became more widespread, mainly for business purposes. They reveal a tendency to reproduce the signs of the zodiac, due to a belief in astrology, as well as allegorical designs in the baroque style.

The Prague community, by privilege of Ferdinand II in 1627, had the Shield of David surrounding a Swedish hat; the inscription was *Sigillum Antiquae Communitatis Pragensis Judaeorum*, with the letters מגזדרד (Magistrat) in the corners. In Prague the Jewish butchers' and barbers' guilds also had their own seals, traditionally of great antiquity but certainly not later than the 17th century. The communities of Vienna (1655), Fuerth, and Kremsier (1690) also had the Shield of David on their money. Halberstadt (1661) had a dove with an olive branch over the Holy Ark with the inscription "Gute Hoffnung," and Ofen had the Ark as well. In the mid-18th century the chief rabbi of Swabia at Pfersee had an official seal. Somewhat later (1817) both the Sephardi and Ashkenazi congregations of Amsterdam were granted seals, as was the Sephardi congregation of Hamburg. The Paris *Sanhedrin of 1807 had a seal with the imperial eagle and the two Tablets of the Law; the *consistory of Westphalia bore the arms of the state on its seal, as did the Philanthropin school of Frankfurt. Moses *Mendelssohn's seal had his initials both in Hebrew and German. Seals – generally those of the authors themselves – on printed Hebrew books were intended to prevent forgery and theft; the first known seal of this type dates from 1598. A comparative study of medieval seals throws light on Jewish-Christian relations and on the influence of one community on the other. Much research is still required in this field, particularly relating to Jewish seals in Italy, Spain, and France, as well as in Germany from 1350 onward.

One of the largest Palestine seal collections of the last century in the Israel Museum is mostly from the former Heinrich Feuchtwanger Collection. To a large extent these are seals of institutions and individuals – as well as *kasher* seals – of 19th- and 20th-century Ereẓ Israel. The inscriptions are in Hebrew, Arabic, Latin, and Cyrillic letters, sometimes with dates, both Jewish and secular. The engravings are of the panoramas of the holy cities of Jerusalem, Hebron, Safed, or particular holy places in them such as the Western Wall, the Ḥurvah Synagogue, and the Cave of Machpelah. Other figures used are animals, trees, outspread hands in priestly blessing, etc. While most of these seals belong to the old *yishuv*, there is a seal of *Yesud ha-Ma'alah, one of the early new settlements (founded 1883). The collection also contains a series of 18th- and 19th-century seals of German, Austro-Hungarian, East European, Italian, Turkish, and even Yemenite origin, mostly of communities and their rabbinates, and *kasher* seals. Among them is that of S.J.L. Wormser, the Baal Shem of Michelstadt, and another belonging to a woman.

BIBLIOGRAPHY: P.E. Newberry, *Egyptian Antiquaries: Scarabs* (1906); Diringer, Iscr; A. Rowe, *Catalogue of Egyptian Scarabs, Scaraboids, Seals, and Amulets in the Palestine Archaeological Museum* (1936); H. Frankfort, *Cylinder Seals* (1939); S. Yeivin, *Toledot ha-Ketav ha-Ivri* (1939), 129ff.; idem, in: *Eretz Israel*, 6 (1961), 47–52; B. Parker, in: *Iraq*, 11 (1949), 1–43; A. Reifenberg, *Ancient Hebrew Seals* (1950); S. Moscati, *L'epigrafia ebraica antica* (1951). POST-BIBLICAL PERIOD: A. Wolf, in: JE, 11 (1925), 134–40 (important bibliography); Drauss, Tal Arch, 1 (1910), 200–2; C. Roth, in: JHSET, 17 (1953), 283–6; P.J. Diamant, in: EH, 17 (1965), 228–30 (bibliography); Z. Avneri, in: *Ha-Congress ha-Olami le-Madda'ei ha-Yahadut*, 2 (1969), 163–70 (also summary in French); M. Narkiss, in: BJPES, 12 (1946), 72–74; I. Shachar, *Osef Feuchtwanger, Masoret be-Ommanut Yehudit* (1971), nos. 541–662.

SEA OF THE TALMUD, a post-talmudic expression indicating the vastness of the Talmud, the innumerable subjects it deals with, and its all-embracing character. Although it is not found in the Talmud itself, the comparison between the vastness of knowledge and the sea is already found in the Bible: "The earth shall be full of the knowledge of the Lord, as the waters cover the sea" (Isa. 11:9); "Canst thou find out the deep things of God?… The measure thereof is longer than the earth and broader than the sea" (Job 11:9). The same image appears in the Apocrypha: "The first man knew her not perfectly, for her understanding is fuller than the sea, and her counsel is greater than the deep" (Ecclus. 24:28f.). In the Jerusalem Talmud there is a concept which, while not directly comparing the Talmud to the sea, does embody the simile; R. Simeon b. Lakish transmitted: "Just as there are little waves between the great waves of the sea, so are the slightest details, even to the specific teachings of its letters, found in the general laws of the Torah" (TJ, Sot. 8:3, 22d). One of the earliest passages where the expression occurs is in the preface to *Menorat ha-Ma'or* (c. 1300) by Isaac *Aboab: "The precious pearls that lie upon the bed of the sea of the Talmud, the aggadic passages so rich in beauty and sweetness."

[Harry Freedman]

SEASONGOOD, U.S. family prominent in Cincinnati, Ohio, during the second half of the 19th and the 20th centuries. LEWIS SEASONGOOD (1836–1914), who was born in Burgenstadt, Bavaria, immigrated to Cincinnati, Ohio, in 1851. He worked in the dry goods business and subsequently became a partner in the firm of Heidelbach, Seasongood & Co. Long prominent in city and state public life, Seasongood was a founder and treasurer (1872) of the Cincinnati Exposition, served as one of the four U.S. commissioners to the Vienna Exposition (1873), and was a Cincinnati sinking-fund commissioner (1875). He was appointed quartermaster general and commissary general of Ohio (1880). Seasongood was also active in Jewish communal affairs, and was a longtime executive board member of the Union of American Hebrew Congregations.

His brother ALFRED SEASONGOOD (1844–1909), who was also born in Burgenstadt, immigrated to the U.S. in 1860. He also worked in the dry goods firm of Heidelbach, Seasongood & Co. In 1868 he became a full partner in the firm of J. & L. Seasongood. Alfred, who became a staunch anti-slavery Republican soon after his arrival in Cincinnati, reputedly exercised great influence in that party, though he held neither elective nor appointive office.

Lewis' son MURRAY SEASONGOOD (1878–1983), who was born in Cincinnati, Ohio, was a lawyer and mayor of Cincinnati. Seasongood was admitted to the Ohio bar in 1903, and practiced law privately for several years. He was active in the political reform movement, which fought and finally destroyed the power of the Cox machine in Cincinnati and introduced the council-manager form of municipal government, elected by proportional representation, in 1924. Seasongood was elected mayor of Cincinnati by the nine-man council in 1926, serving two terms until 1930. He was a capable, well-respected mayor who expanded numerous services while reducing costs. During this period, he also headed the Cincinnati City Planning Commission. Seasongood's other public posts included chairman of the Ohio Commission for the Blind (1915–25); member of the U.S. Civil Service Commission's Loyalty Review Board (1947–53); and security counsel to the U.S. Atomic Energy Commission's Personnel Clearance Security Board (1954–59). From 1925 to 1959 he lectured in law at the University of Cincinnati. He established the Hamilton County Good Government League and served for many years as national president of the Legal Aid Society. President Herbert Hoover appointed him to a national commission to investigate housing conditions. In 1974 he was named one of the 100 Greatest Ohio Citizens. Seasongood, who lived to be 104, practiced law into his nineties at the law firm of Paxton & Seasongood.

Long active in Jewish affairs, Seasongood served as a member of the Hebrew Union College's board of governors (1913–42); board member of the Joint Distribution Committee; and executive committee member of the American Jewish Committee (1938–47).

His books include *Local Government in the United States, A Challenge and an Opportunity* (1933; 1934^2); *Cases on Municipal Corporations* (1934; third edition (1953) with C.J. Antieau); and *Selections from Speeches: 1900–1959 of Murray Seasongood* (1960).

SEATTLE, city and port in the state of Washington; located in the far N.W. of the United States; Jewish population estimated at 37,000 in the early 21st century. Euro-Americans settled Seattle in 1851. Attracted to Seattle's growing economic success, a temperate climate and abundance of natural resources such as lumber and coal, Jews began arriving in 1868. In 1897, when gold was discovered in Alaska's Klondike region and Seattle became an embarkation point for those going to the gold fields, many more followed to take advantage of the many business opportunities. By the early 1900s, Seattle, the state's largest and most dynamic city, had an active Jewish community made up of people from Central and Eastern Europe and the Mediterranean Basin (Turkey, Marmara, and the island of Rhodes).

B'nai B'rith, established in 1883 was the city's first Jewish organization. As the number of eastern European Jews increased, men formed new lodges, sorting out members by connection with synagogues. A women's auxiliary, Emma Lazarus, chartered in 1916, brought women into the organization. Other voluntary groups that provided money and a proper burial service for the poor quickly followed.

On a more social level, Jewish men in 1910 founded the Young Men's Hebrew Association (YMHA). During World War I, the YMHA provided soldiers on leave from Camp Lewis, an army camp near Tacoma, Washington, with a bed and a place to meet other Jews. Seattle's large Sephardi population formed the Young Men's Sephardic Association (YMSA). The restriction barring Jews from fraternities and sororities at the University of Washington inspired Jewish students to organize a local Menorah Society in 1913.

To help the growing Jewish community and increasingly large immigrant population, Jewish women established several organizations. The earliest, the Seattle Ladies' Hebrew Benevolent Society, began in 1892. Over the years it has evolved to become the Jewish Family Service (JFS), the largest Jewish social service organization in the state. The Seattle Section, National Council of Jewish Women, joined the ranks of Seattle Jewish organizations in 1900 and within a few years established a Settlement House for poor immigrants. The NCJW was followed, in 1913, by the Hebrew Ladies Free Loan, which made interest-free loans. The Caroline Kline Galland Home for Aged opened its doors in 1916 and is now a nationally recognized skilled nursing facility. There are also two retirement homes, Council House and the Summit at First Hill.

Swamped by the increasing arrival of Russian refugees, Washington Jewry in 1915 set up a branch of the Hebrew Immigrant Aid Society (HIAS) and established a shelter house for those who had no sponsors.

In the early 1920s, new groups such as Hadassah, the Jewish Consumptives Relief Society, Mizrachi, the Seattle Sephardic Brotherhood, and the Jewish Federation of Greater Seattle, joined the roster of philanthropic and social groups. The Federation is now the coordinating umbrella organization for local non-congregational Jewish groups. Most of the groups are still active and have been joined by a myriad of others, such as the American Jewish Committee, the Stroum Jewish Community Center of Greater Seattle, and the Holocaust Survivors Assistance Office.

To keep track of the social, organizational, and congregational events and to "enable the Jews of Seattle and the Northwest to become better acquainted with each other," Sol Krems, an active member of the Seattle Jewish community, published *The Jewish Voice* in 1915. After its demise, Herman Horowitz began *The Jewish Transcript* (JT News) in 1924. The newspaper focused on news, people, politics, religion, and education both locally as well as nationally and internationally.

In 1889 Seattle Jews planned their first congregation, Ohaveth Sholum, a quasi-Reform temple, and purchased land for a Jewish cemetery. It survived until 1896. Seattle's Orthodox Bikur Cholim Synagogue, the oldest surviving congregation in the state, began as a benefit and benevolent society in 1889, but within a decade became a religious congregation.

Reform-minded Jewish people organized Temple De Hirsch in 1899. In 1906, Herzl, an Orthodox synagogue attracted members interested in promoting Zionism. It would become Conservative in 1932. Seattle's Sephardi community, which by 1913 had the largest number outside of New York, launched their own religious institutions, Sephardic Bikur Holim, Ahavath Ahim, and Ezra Bessaroth congregations.

Because the Sephardi immigrants spoke Judeo-Spanish (Ladino) not Yiddish, were poor, and unskilled, and ate strange foods, the Ashkenazim at first questioned their Jewishness. Later, Ashkenazi Jews and the larger community grew to know and appreciate their customs and culture and realized that Seattle is fortunate in having such a large Sephardi community. This turn of events began in the 1940s with Rabbi Solomon Maimon, who grew up in Seattle and became the first Sephardi Jew in America to receive ordination. Today Sephardi Studies is a special area in the Jewish Studies Program at the University of Washington. The famed Benaroya Symphony Hall is named to honor the substantial gift of Jack and Rebecca Benaroya, a testament to the Sephardim's success. Although the 2001 demographic study of Jewish Seattle shows that their numbers have declined in proportion to the total number of Jews because new migrants are generally not Sephardi, this vibrant community's culture and resources remain important.

Except for Ohaveth Sholum and Ahavath Ahim, all the early religious institutions are still active. With growth in the Jewish population after World War II, new groups joined the list. In 2005, there were 18 active congregations in the greater Seattle area. Besides the traditional Conservative, Orthodox, and Reform, they embrace a meditation synagogue, a gay and lesbian congregation, a Jewish Renewal movement, and a Lubavitch center.

Before 1913, Seattle youth learned Hebrew in the area's congregational Hebrew schools. After 1913, the community began its support of a Hebrew School. Though Hebrew education floundered over the years, a *talmud torah* eventually opened and had its own school building. In 1945, Rabbi Solomon

Wohlgelernter of Bikur Cholim and Rabbi Solomon Maimon, of Sephardic Bikur Holim launched a Jewish day school (now the Seattle Hebrew Academy). Since that time, Jewish youth have the opportunity to study in several day schools, ranging from preschool to high school. In addition the area congregations have active mid-day and Sunday school programs.

Though Seattle never had an exclusively Jewish neighborhood, in 1910 some 85 percent of Seattle's Jews, both Ashkenazi and Sephardi, lived in Seattle's central area. In the early 21st century, 64% of Seattle's 37,000 Jews lived in the city and its nearby northern suburbs, 26% east of Lake Washington in the towns of Bellevue, Mercer Island, and Redmond, and the rest live in the outlying suburbs such as Kent and Renton. In the 2001 survey, 4 out of 10 Jewish respondents had moved to Seattle within the past 10 years. More than half the Seattle Jews are fourth generation. About one-in-five Jewish households belongs to a religious congregation and these are growing more ethnically diverse because of conversions, adoptions, and intermarriage.

Whether they moved to Seattle from the eastern United States or came from Europe, before World War II most Jewish families earned their living as merchants. With more and more Jews entering college, this changed as Jews entered the professions. Many men and women in Seattle joined the faculty of the University of Washington, opened a medical or legal office, became Boeing engineers, or developed software programs for Microsoft. When they worked in business, it was usually with a large firm and not a small neighborhood store. A few, such as Howard *Shultz, who launched Starbuck's, and Jeff Brotman, creator of Costco, established businesses with national reputations.

The increasing number of Jewish faculty at the University of Washington led to the establishment of a Jewish Studies Program in 1974. Now a part of the Henry M. Jackson School of International Studies, it is the premier institution in the academic study of Jewish history and culture. An annual lecture series established by Samuel and Althea Strom brings in persons with international reputations to the area. It has also led to fine publications. This and many other programs are open to the public and have contributed to an increased awareness of the richness of Jewish life in the United States and throughout the world.

The end of the 20th century and the beginning of the 21st have witnessed a flowering of Seattle's Jewish community. Jewish citizens are leaders in local secular charities and business enterprises. Examples are the Herb Bridge family, which includes a State Supreme Court justice, a physician, an attorney, business leader, and rabbi; and Althea and Samuel Strum, who have funded Jewish Studies programs at the University of Washington and contributed to every Jewish organization in the state.

BIBLIOGRAPHY: M. Cone, H. Droker, J. Williams, *Family of Strangers: Building a Jewish Community in Washington State* (2003).

[Jacqueline Williams (2nd ed.)]

SEBAG, surname widely used in North Africa, particularly in *Morocco. HANANIAH SEBAG (d. after 1570) was a wealthy merchant in *Fez; the problem of his inheritance preoccupied the *dayyanim* of both the *megorashim* and the *toshavim*. Their legal conclusions became law in the rabbinical tribunals of Morocco. The family subsequently settled in *Meknès, *Marrakesh, and in *Mogador (c. 1770). R. ISAAC BEN ABRAHAM SEBAG (d. after 1725), scholar, poet, and *dayyan* in Meknès, wrote *Shir Yedidut* ("Song of Friendship"), well-known *piyyutim* in Morocco. R. SOLOMON BEN SHALOM SEBAG (d. 1780), *dayyan* in Marrakesh, was well known as a talmudist and legal authority. A number of his decisions were published in the responsa of various Moroccan rabbis. SOLOMON SEBAG (d. before 1790), a leader of the Meknès community, was wealthy and one of the benefactors of his community. The poet David b. Hassine dedicated some of his poems, published in *Tehillah le-David* ("Praise of David," Amsterdam, 1807), to him. SOLOMON BEN MASʿUD BEN ABRAHAM SEBAG (fl. early 19th cent.), born in Mogador, was sent to *London in 1799 to manage the family's business. His success enabled him to publish several works in English and Hebrew by Moroccan authors, among them the above-mentioned *Tehillah le-David* and *An Historical Account of the Ten Tribes* (London, 1836) by Moses *Edrehi. He was also the official secretary to his uncle Meir *Macnin, the Moroccan ambassador. In 1813, Sebag married Sarah, the elder sister of Sir Moses *Montefiore. His son JOSEPH added Montefiore to his own name, thus founding the Sebag-Montefiore family. JUDAH BEN MASʿUD (1832–1923), born in *Lisbon, lived in *Brazil for many years and amassed a considerable fortune there. In about 1890 he settled in Mogador, the place of his family's origin, and became one of its most prominent leaders. He was politically active on behalf of his coreligionists, who benefited from his generosity.

BIBLIOGRAPHY: J. Toledano, *Ner ha-Ma'arav* (1911), 132, 146, 165, 190; J. Ben-Naim, *Malkhei Rabbanan* (1931), 74b, 76b, 114b, 117b.

[David Corcos]

SEBASTIAN, MIHAIL (originally **Josef Hechter**; 1907–1945), Romanian novelist, playwright, and critic. Sebastian, who was born in Brăila, practiced as a lawyer in Bucharest, but from the age of 20 devoted himself mainly to writing. He came to be widely recognized as the most versatile and significant Jewish figure in Romanian literature. Between 1927 and 1940 Sebastian contributed to, among others, *Cuvîntul, Urmia, Rampa, Viața Românească*, and *Revista Fundațiilor Regale*, on which he also worked as an editor; and from 1927 to 1929 he also wrote for the official Romanian Zionist paper, *Știri din lumea evreească*. Sebastian's humanity and courage as a critic won him great respect. At his death much of his work remained scattered in the archives of the journals in which it originally appeared.

Sebastian was greatly interested in Marcel *Proust, on whom he published an important study in *Corespondența lui Marcel Proust* (1939). He first achieved success with *Femei* ("Women", 1933), stories analyzing the psychology of seven different women. His sensitive descriptions of physical passion again appeared in his "novel of adolescence," *Orașul cu salcîmi* ("The Town with Acacia Trees," 1935), and *Accidentul* ("The Accident," 1940).

The most representative of Sebastian's novels was *De două mii de ani* ("For the Past 2,000 Years," 1934) which dealt with the problem of the Jew in an alien community. Written in the form of a diary, it portrays the spiritual torment of a Jewish intellectual unable to find a solution to his doubts in either Communism or Zionism. The novel contains a preface by Nae Ionescu who, under the influence of current antisemitism, suggested that the Jews were fated to suffer because they had not accepted Jesus, the Christian messiah. Attacked both by Romanian nationalists and by Zionists, Sebastian replied in a mordant and ironic book, *Cum am devenit huligan* ("How I Became a Hooligan," 1935), which accused Ionescu of moral and intellectual dishonesty, denouncing the preface as a monstrous act of injustice.

It was as a dramatist that Sebastian won fame even beyond Romania. Three of his best plays have for their theme the intellectual's flight from a reality to which he is unable to adjust himself. *Jocul de-a vacanța* ("Let's Play Holiday," 1936, staged 1938); *Steaua fără nume* ("The Nameless Star," 1943, and produced in 1944 under a fictitious name because of Nazi anti-Jewish laws); and *Ultima Oră* ("Last Hour," 1943–44, staged 1946) all show the hand of a master. Sebastian's plays have been translated and performed in many languages, including English, Hebrew, and Chinese. He was killed in a road accident after the liberation of Romania from the Nazis.

BIBLIOGRAPHY: G. Cálinescu, *Istoria Literaturii Române…* (1941), 876–8; idem, *Ulysse* (1967), 290; C. Petrescu, *Opinii si Atitudini* (1962), 206–14, 250; B. Elvin, *Teatrul lui M. Sebastian* (1955); D. Littman, in: *Studii si Cercetări de Istorie Literară și Folclor*, 5 no. 1–2 (1956), 213–42; P. Georgescu, in: *Viața Romînească*, no. 7 (1962).

[Dora Litani-Littman]

SEBBA, SHALOM (1897– 1975), Israel painter and designer. Born in Germany, he settled in Palestine in 1936. The strong influence of the theater world is seen in the simplicity of his designs and in his choice of materials. He designed for theaters in Germany, in Stockholm, and in Israel for the Habimah Theater.

SECONDHAND GOODS AND OLD CLOTHES, TRADE IN. In Western and Central Europe and Italy trade in secondhand goods and old clothes was an integral part of *moneylending against pledges, as the pawned and forfeited articles (jewelry, clothing, etc.) had to be sold. As many of the goods had to be refurbished or repaired, dyeing, tailoring, and mending became ancillary occupations. Later it became a separate trade which, until the spread of the industrial and technological revolutions, catered to the needs of large sectors of the population.

The trade in old clothes in Italy, known as *strazzaria* (from *straccio, strazzo*, "rag"), was conducted mainly through *peddling and eventually came to include trade in new garments and cloth as well. From the 16th to the 18th centuries it was the most important Jewish occupation after moneylending. The *strazzaiuoli* often dealt in imported wares, thereby angering the local textile and clothing manufacturers. A 1667 list of 112 Jewish households in Mantua (about one-half of the community) included eight traders in secondhand goods, five tailors, three renovators of clothes, two clothing shops, three scrap-iron traders, and 15 "general" merchants. Fifty years later there were 25 dealers in old clothes and secondhand goods, 19 textile and cloth merchants, and nine traders in scrap iron. *Strazzaria* was a major and characteristic occupation of Roman Jewry even before the issue of Pope *Paul IV's extremely restrictive and discriminatory bull of 1555, *Cum nimis absurdum*, which made it the sole trade permitted to them. In the mid-19th century the historian F. Gregorovius reported:

> If we now enter the streets of the ghetto itself we find Israel before its booths, buried in restless toil and distress. They sit in their doorways or outdoors on the street which affords scarcely more light than their damp and dismal rooms, and tend their ragged merchandise or industriously patch and sew… The daughters of Zion sit upon these rags and stitch anything that can be stitched. They have a reputation for great art in patching, darning, and piecing, and it is said that no rent in any sort of drapery or fabric can be so fearful that these Arachnes cannot make it invisible and untraceable… It was frequently with painful sympathy that I looked upon them, pale and exhausted and stooped, as they diligently plied their needles, men as well as women, girls, and children (*The Ghetto and the Jews of Rome* (1966), 66f.).

Their lot and vocation continued well into the 20th century, though many branched off into the antiques trade and the clothing industry. In 1940 the licenses of the street vendors of old and new clothes were revoked and in the subsequent persecutions they were particularly hard hit.

Elsewhere in Europe Jews frequently traded in old clothes, at first in association with moneylending and later, in conjunction with related crafts, peddling, and textile trading. In the Netherlands and England, as well as other countries with large numbers of Jewish immigrants, Jews were active in the trade in secondhand goods. In Amsterdam poor Ashkenazi Jews were officially designated as "repairers of old clothes." The mended clothes were exported in large quantities to various destinations. One of the richest merchants in Amsterdam was instructed by a Jew in Poland to pay a Polish Jew in Amsterdam a sum of 10,000 to 12,000 guilders for the sale of rags. These may have been utilized for paper production. In London the old clothes trade was situated in the "Rag Fair," in Rosemary Lane (Royal Mint Street), where there were about 500 to 600 Jewish old clothes dealers in 1850 (in 1800 there had been about 1,000). The "old clo" men, as they were called after their traditional call, brought their wares to two exchanges, Isaac's & Simmons and Levy, from where they were resold either to wholesale merchants or to retail dealers for a variety of purposes. The German and Dutch Jews who entered the secondhand-clothing and rag dealers' markets at Houndsditch in the East End in the 18th century, later dominated the trade and thereby fixed the area of future Jewish settlement in London. The rag trade became obsolete with the rise in the standard of living of the masses and the introduction of Isaac Singer's sewing machine and modern methods of mass production of ready-made clothing. In different countries and at various times when traditional Jewish occupations were attacked (as in Prussia in the 18th century) the trade in secondhand goods also came under pressure. In Paris in 1911 there were about 1,500 Jewish old clothes dealers (*brocanteurs*) and 400 ragpickers (*chiffonniers*); in 1941, 2,533 traders in secondhand goods were recorded. Their real number on both dates was probably larger; the majority were impecunious immigrants from Eastern Europe (M. Roblin, *Les Juifs de Paris* (1952), 108).

Both in England and the U.S. some Jews extended their activities from the secondhand goods trade to buying and selling waste products in general. A case study on Detroit by J.S. Fauman (in JSOS, 3 (1941), 41ff.) revealed that while there had been no Jewish dealers in waste products (such as paper and scrap metal) there until 1870, from 1880 Jews were predominant, and the location of the lots and junkyards moved in relation to the areas of Jewish residence. "The waste industry, low in status, poorly organized, requiring little capital and unattractive to other groups, was easily accessible to Jews." Enterprises of this kind attracted and held Jews because of resemblances to their traditional commercial activities, because of strong familial ties, and because the independence of this type of trade enabled them to close their businesses on the Sabbath and festivals. The Detroit pattern prevailed in many other cities. An economic survey made by *Fortune* magazine ("Jews in America" (1936), 43) estimated that 90% of the scrap-iron and steel industry (worth half a billion dollars in 1929) was Jewish-owned. Through trade in waste materials and particularly in ferrous and nonferrous metals many Jews entered the metal industry, especially in Germany (see *Metals and Mining).

BIBLIOGRAPHY: R. Glanz, *Jew in the Old American Folklore* (1961), 147–65; S. Simonsohn, *Toledot ha-Yehudim be-Dukkasut Mantovah* (1964), index s.v. *Mishar Seḥorot Meshummashot*; V.D. Lipman, *Social History of the Jews in England* (1954), 13, 31ff.; Roth, Italy, index s.v. *Ragpickers* and *Second-hand Dealers*; idem, in: HUCA, 5 (1928), 353ff.; idem, *History of the Jews in Venice* (1930), 173ff.; Z. Szajkowski, *Franco-Judaica* (1962), nos. 48, 191, 309, 1395–493; H. Heilig, in: JGGJC, 3 (1931), 307–448; H. Bloom, *Economic Activities of the Jews of Amsterdam* (1935), index s.v. *Old Clothes*; J. Rumney, in: JHSET, 13 (1932–35), 332ff.; L.P. Gartner, *Jewish Immigrants in England* (1960), 82–4; W.M. Glicksman, *In the Mirror of Literature* (1966), 195f.

[Henry Wasserman]

SECTS, MINOR. In addition to the main sects which existed during the period of the Second Temple and after, such as the *Pharisees, the *Sadducees, the *Essenes, the *Therapeutae and the *Dead Sea sects, the sources mention a number of others. As will be noted, some scholars identify some of these sects with those belonging to the above-mentioned categories.

Bana'im

The Bana'im were an Essene-like Jewish sect in Palestine in the second century. The name occurs only in *Mikva'ot* 9:6 where a passage referring to the question of dipping clothing for levitical purification records: "Garments belonging to the Bana'im may not have a mudstain even upon one side, because these people are very particular concerning the cleanliness of their clothing, and any such spot would prevent the purifying water from actually penetrating the garment as it is usually worn; but with a *bor* [an unlearned and uncultured man], it matters not if his clothing contain a red spot at the time of dipping, for such a one is not particular about cleanliness."

Considerable debate centers around the meaning of Bana'im and the activities of the sect in Palestine. Two separate theories have developed on the origin of the name. One group of scholars identifies it with *banah* ("to build") and explains them as "scholars who occupy themselves with the study of the world's construction." Frankel (see bibl.) understands the word *banai* to mean "building master" or "builder" and accordingly concludes that the Bana'im were an Essene order employed with the ax and shovel (cf. Jos., Wars, 2:178).

Other scholars, among them Sachs and Derenbourg, consider Bana'im to be derived from the Greek βάλάνέῖόν ("bath"), and suggests that it means "those who bathe." In this case, the meaning would make the sect similar to the *Tovelei Shaḥarit* or Hemerobaptists. A third suggests that they might be the followers of Bannus, who was apparently an Essene hermit, with an emphasis on the ritualistic pledge. It is more probable that the word means simply "bathers" and refers more to the clothing and its cleanliness at the bath than to a specific sect. If the word *bor* in the passages quoted from *Mikva'ot* is interpreted as "a well" rather than "an uncultured person" then the purity of the garment would be dependent on whether the mud was from a large or small pit, and again it is a question of the garment rather than the type of person.

Hypsistarians

The Hypsistarians were a semi-Jewish sect who worshiped God under the name θεός Ύψιστος Παντοκράτωρ ("The most High and Almighty One"). Its members lived on the Bosphorus in the first century C.E. and were found from time to time in Asia Minor until the fourth century. They were Jewish to the extent that they observed the Sabbath and some of the dietary laws, but they deviated from Judaism in that they entertained a certain pagan awe for fire and light, the earth and sun, although no indication is given that they practiced any idolatrous worship or prayer rites. They are probably related to, and may be identical with, either the Mossalians ("Meẓallin"), or the Euchomenoi, or the Euphemitai who are distinguished as "God-worshipers who also worshiped the Almighty God at the blaze of many lights." The Hypistarians may also be related to the *Yirei Shamayim* ("venerators" or "worshipers of heaven"), mentioned in *Codex Theodosianus*, xvi, 5:43 and 8:19. The general view is that they were undoubtedly a remnant of Jewish proselytes who retained a few pagan notions but were regarded as hostile to Christian doctrine.

Hemerobaptists

The Hemerobaptists (Heb. *Tovelei Shaḥarit*; "Morning Bathers") were part of the baptist group for which the baptismal rite of initiation is the single most important feature. Significant of the Hemerobaptists is that this baptismal rite was repeated each day, rather than once and for all. The Hemerobaptists were probably a division of the Essenes who placed particular emphasis on bathing as a ritualistic cleansing before the hour of prayer each morning in order to be able to pronounce the Name of God with a clean body (Tosef., Yad., end). Samson of Sens translates a section of this Tosefta which refers to this cleansing: "The morning bathers said to the Pharisees: 'We charge you with doing wrong in pronouncing the Name without having taken a ritual bath.' Whereupon the Pharisees said: 'We charge you with wrongdoing in pronouncing the Name with a body impure within.'" The sect is also mentioned in the Talmud (Ber. 22a). Hemerobaptist baptism differed from proselyte or synagogal ablutions in that this baptism was both symbol and sacrament.

John the *Baptist was probably a Hemerobaptist, as is suggested in *Clementine Homilies* (2:23). His followers were eventually absorbed into the Christian Church, although a part may have gone to the sect of Mandeans in lower Mesopotamia. A remnant of this group was still active in the third century C.E. Several early Christian authors make mention of the Hemerobaptists. Hegesippus (See Eusebius, *Hist. Eccl.*, iv, 22) refers to them as one of the Jewish sects or divisions opposed to Christians; Justin calls them "Baptizers." According to the Christian editor of the *Didascalia* ("Apostolic Constitutions," vi, 6), the Hemerobaptists do not make use of their beds, tables, and dishes until they have cleansed them. This is a misunderstanding of the true purpose of this sect, i.e., bodily cleansing. Another author, Epiphanius, asserts that the Hemerobaptists deny future salvation to persons who do not undergo daily baptism.

Maghāriya.

Maghāriya was a sect that appeared during the first century B.C.E. according to *Kirkisānī. The name is Arabic, meaning "men [people] of the caves" and refers to their practice of keeping their books and sacred writings in caves in the surrounding hills of Palestine. Doctrinal differences with the rest of the Jewish community pivoted around the Maghāriya's transcendental view that God is too sublime to mingle with matter. They therefore rejected the idea that the world was directly created by God, but rather held that an intermediary power, an angel, was responsible for that act and now represents God in the created world. The sect wrote its own peculiar commentaries on the Bible and attributed the Law, all communications, and all anthropomorphic references, not to God, but to this angel. Two writings of importance, the *Alexandrian* and a later work, *Sefer Yadu'a*, were kept; the rest were of little apparent significance.

Some scholars have identified the Maghāriya with the Essenes or the Therapeutae. Harkavy gives as his reasons for such identification:

(1) the name of the sect, which according to him, does not refer to its books but to its followers, who lived in caves or in the desert, this being known to have been the Essene mode of life;

(2) the coincidence in the date of its foundation with that of the Essenes;

(3) Maghāriya theory of the angel which is in keeping with the tenets of the Essenes;

(4) Kirkisānī's omission of the Essenes from his list of the Jewish sects, which would be unaccountable had he not considered the Maghāriya to be identical with the Essenes. Harkavy identifies the *Alexandrian* author with Philo, who underwent the training period for the Essenes, and suggests that the angel in Maghāriya doctrine might be identical with Philo's *Logos*. Harkavy's hypothesis has found wide acceptance. S. Baron states that they are clearly related to the Qumran community and thus distinguishes between the Qumran community and the Essenes. Baron also disagrees with Harkavy's identification of the "Alexandrian" with Philo since he considers it highly unlikely that Arabic or Hebrew translations of Philo's works were known in Kirkisānī's time. (For the modern period see *Subbotniki; *Somrei Sabat.)

BIBLIOGRAPHY: BANA'IM: Z. Frankel, in: *Zeitschrift fuer die religioesen Interessen*, 3 (1846), 455; M. Sachs, *Beitraege zur Sprachund Alterthumsforschung*, 2 (1854), 199; Derenbourg, Hist; J. Hamburger, *Real-Enzyklopaedie fuer Bibel und Talmud*, 2 (1873), 84; J. Levy, *Woerterbuch ueber die Talmudim und Midraschim*, 1 (1924^2), 241. HYPSISTARIANS: J. Bernays, *Gesammelte Schriften*, 1 (1885); F. Cumont, *Hypsistos* (1897); Schuerer, Gesch, 3 (19094), 18. HEMEROBAPTISTS: S. Krauss, in: JQR, 5 (1892–93), 127; Graetz, Gesch, 3 (1905^5), 92; W. Brandt, *Die juedischen Baptismen* (1910); M. Simon, *Jewish Sects at the Time of Jesus* (1967). MAGHĀRIYA: Graetz, Gesch, 6 (1870), 192; A.E. Harkavy, *Le-Korot ha-Kittot be-Yisrael* (1895); Jellinek, in: OLZ, 12 (1909), 410; Baron, Social^2, 5 (1957), 196; M. Simon, *Jewish Sects at the Time of Jesus* (1967).

[Menahem Mansoor]

SECUNDA, SHOLOM (1894–1974), composer. Secunda was born in Aleksandia (Kherson region), Ukraine. His family moved to Nikolayev in 1897 and immigrated to New York in 1908. As a child, Secunda had already been a *meshorer* and assistant *ḥazzan*. In New York he began studying music and in 1913 was engaged at the Oden Yiddish Theater as "chorister, composer, and errand-boy." His first musical play, *Yosher* ("Honesty"), written with Solomon Shmulevich, was produced there in 1914. Subsequently he became musical director and composer at most of the Yiddish theaters in New York, Philadelphia, St. Louis, etc. During that time he also continued his musical studies at the Juilliard School, Columbia University, and, for one year, with Ernest *Bloch. From 1950 to 1961 Secunda was musical director of the Brooklyn Jewish Center and from 1967 music lecturer at New York University and Hunter College.

Secunda's compositions include dozens of Yiddish musical plays and operettas; an opera called *Sulamith* (based on *Goldfaden's libretto); songs to texts of *Yehoash, *Reissen, *Frug, and others; various orchestral, chamber, and choral works; and musical liturgical works (two Sabbath services, and High Holy Days and festival services). Among his songs, three became especially popular: *"Dos Yidishe Lid," "Dona, Dona,"* and *"Bay Mir Bist Du Sheyn."*

BIBLIOGRAPHY: Z. Zylbercweig, *Leksikon fun Yidishn Teater*, 2 (1934), 1515–18.

[Bathja Bayer]

SEDAKA, NEIL (1939–), pop composer and performer whose songs appeared on the music charts from the 1950s through the early 21st century; member of the Songwriter's Hall of Fame. Born in Brighton Beach, Brooklyn, Sedaka is the son of Mac, a Turkish Jewish immigrant and cab driver, and Eleanor (Appel), a concert pianist of East European descent. Sedaka's parents bought him a piano before he was 10, and he attended Juilliard School of Music. At his bar mitzvah, his parents were approached to discuss training him to be a cantor. At 16, Arthur *Rubinstein named him one of the finest classical pianists in New York City high schools. Despite the classical training, Sedaka formed a pop music vocal group while at Brooklyn's Lincoln High School and began his recording career shortly after. From 1959 to 1963, songs co-written by Sedaka and Howard Greenfield sold more than 25 million records. The two were among creators of the "Brill Building Sound" in the late 1950s and early 1960s that was dominated by young, primarily Jewish songwriters, including Neil *Diamond, Carole *King, and Paul *Simon. Sedaka's best-known Billboard Hot 100 hits are: "Oh, Carol" (a reference to King, a onetime girlfriend) (#9), "Calendar Girl" (#4) and "Happy Birthday Sweet Sixteen" (#6) in 1961, "Breaking Up Is Hard to Do" (#1) (1962), "Laughter in the Rain" (#1, 1975), and "Bad Blood" (#1, also 1975). Sedaka re-released "Breaking Up Is Hard To Do" as a ballad in 1974 and made music history when it reached #1 on the charts, becoming the first song recorded in different versions by the same artist to reach the Top Ten. "Breaking Up" was later listed by recording industry group BMI as one of the 50 most performed songs of the 20th century. He and Greenfield wrote "Love Will Keep Us Together," a No. 1 hit for The Captain and Tennille and the bestselling record of 1975. In 1980, Sedaka had a Top Ten hit with "Should've Never Let You Go," which he recorded with his daughter, Dara; it was one of the few father-daughter songs ever to make the charts. He continued to reach the charts sporadically in coming years, becoming one of the only performers to reach the pop music charts in six decades, and recorded jazz and pop classical albums, as well. He also recorded an album of Yiddish songs in 2003, and released a Christmas album in 2005. Sedaka was inducted into the Songwriter's Hall of Fame in 2004, had a street named after him in Brooklyn, and was given a star on the Hollywood Walk of Fame. In 2005 he received the Sammy Cahn Lifetime Achievement Award from the National Academy of Popular Music/Songwriters Hall of Fame. The prolific Sedaka had written more than 1,000 songs by 2005. In 2005, a petition was circulated to have Sedaka named to the Rock and Roll Hall of Fame.

[Alan D. Abbey (2nd ed.)]

SEDEH BOKER (Heb. שְׂדֵה בּוֹקֵר; "Cattle Rancher's Field"), kibbutz in the central Negev hills of Israel, 11 mi. (19 km.) S. of Yeroḥam, affiliated with Iḥud ha-Kevuẓot ve-ha-Kibbutzim. Sedeh Boker, founded as a pioneer outpost in 1952, was initially an isolated "farming cooperative" in the middle of the desert, unaffiliated with any nationwide settlement association. The settlers were mostly veteran Israelis of different political affiliations. They began with horse breeding, but later introduced sheep flocks and orchards. They reclaimed the loess soil for farming from the desert by special methods. Irrigation depends on the rare flood waters in the rainy season and sewage water. Farming is based on the orchards as well as vineyards, organic citrus groves, and poultry. Sedeh Boker also operates a cellotape factory. From the end of 1953, David *Ben-Gurion and his wife made their home at the kibbutz. In the mid-1990s the population of Sedeh Boker was approximately 365 and at the end of 2002 it was 471.

[Efraim Orni / Shaked Gilboa (2nd ed.)]

In 1965 Midreshet Sedeh Boker was founded on the initiative of Ben-Gurion. It comprised a teachers' training seminary, a boarding high school whose students were mostly from Negev towns and settlements, and a school for field studies. The Midrashah, located 3 mi. (5 km.) south of the kibbutz, on the rim of the wild Zin Canyon, provides both general education and vocational training, with emphasis on the natural sciences. It defines itself as an interdisciplinary center for desert studies and hosts elementary schools, high schools, and field schools, offering advanced seminars. The Midrashah includes two academic research centers: the Institute for Desert Research and the Ben-Gurion Heritage Center.

[Yosef Shadur / Shaked Gilboa (2nd ed.)]

WEBSITE: www.boker.org.il

SEDEH ELIYAHU (Heb. שְׂדֵה אֱלִיָּהוּ), kibbutz in central Israel, in the Beth-Shean Valley, affiliated with Ha-Kibbutz ha-Dati. Sedeh Eliyahu was founded in 1939 by religious pioneers from Germany. In 1970 Sedeh Eliyahu had 375 inhabitants, increasing to 656 in 2002. Farming was intensive and fully irrigated, based on field crops, dates, vineyards, vegetables, organic farming, fish breeding, and dairy cattle. The kibbutz manufactured spices and biological pest control products (Bio-Bee). The name of the kibbutz commemorates Rabbi Elijah *Gutmacher.

WEBSITE: www.seliyahu.org.il.

[Efraim Orni / Shaked Gilboa (2nd ed.)]

SEDEH NAḤUM (Heb. שְׂדֵה נחום), kibbutz in northern Israel, on the border of the Harod and Beth-Shean valleys, affiliated with Ha-Kibbutz ha-Me'uḥad. Together with *Nir David, Sedeh Naḥum was the first *stockade and tower outpost in the valley. It was founded in 1937 by pioneers from Poland and Austria. In 1970, Sedeh Naḥum had 290 inhabitants, increasing to 335 in 2002. Farming was highly intensive and fully irrigated, including plantations and poultry. The kibbutz ran a plastic factory as well. Its name commemorates the Zionist leader Nahum *Sokolow.

WEBSITE: www.sde-nahum.org.il.

[Efraim Orni]

SEDEH NEḤEMYAH (Heb. שְׂדֵה נְחֶמְיָה), kibbutz in northern Israel, in the Ḥuleh Valley, affiliated with Iḥud ha-Kevuzot ve-ha-Kibbutzim. Sedeh Neḥemyah was founded in 1940 by pioneers from Holland and Czechoslovakia in the vicinity of the then-existing Ḥuleh Swamps. In 1970 Sedeh Neḥemyah had 304 inhabitants, rising to 383 in 2002. Farming was intensive and fully irrigated, based on field crops (in partnership with Kibbutz *Amir and Kibbutz *Shamir), fruit orchards, and citrus groves. The kibbutz also manufactured plastic products. Its name commemorates the Dutch Zionist Nehemiah de *Lieme.

[Efraim Orni / Shaked Gilboa (2nd ed.)]

SEDEH WARBURG (Heb. שְׂדֵה וַרְבּוּרְג), moshav in the southern Sharon, Israel, near Kefar Sava, affiliated with Ha-Iḥud ha-Ḥakla'i. Sedeh Warburg was founded in 1938 by middle-class immigrants and later joined by other newcomers, mainly from Poland. Farming was highly intensive and fully irrigated. In 1970 Sedeh Warburg had 380 inhabitants, increasing to about 500 in the mid-1990s and 956 in 2002. Its name commemorates the Zionist leader Otto *Warburg.

[Efraim Orni]

SEDEH YA'AKOV (Heb. שְׂדֵה יַעֲקֹב), moshav in northern Israel, southeast of Kiryat Tivon, affiliated with Ha-Po'el ha-Mizrachi Moshavim Association. Sedeh Ya'akov was founded in 1927 by immigrants from Poland, Lithuania, and Hungary. The moshav raised field and garden crops, citrus groves, fruit orchards, dairy cattle, and poultry. In 1970 the moshav, including the religious Youth Aliyah village, Neveh Ammi'el (named for Rabbi Moses A. *Amiel), numbered 500 inhabitants, rising to about 740 In the mid-1990s and 821 in 2002. The name of the moshav commemorates Rabbi I.J. *Reines.

[Efraim Orni]

SEDER (Heb. סֵדֶר; "order," "arrangement"). The word *seder* occurs only once in the Bible, in the plural (Job. 10:22), but it is extensively used in rabbinical literature. The best known of these uses are the following:

(1) The pericopes of the Bible according to the triennial cycle. These divisions are called *sedarim*, hence the Aramaic form *sidra*, popularly but wrongly used, particularly in Yiddish (*sedra*) for the weekly portion (instead of *parashah*).

(2) The six orders into which the Mishnah is divided. See *Shas.

(3) An order of prayers. Although the word usually employed is *siddur*, that of R. Amram is properly called the *seder* of R. Amram.

(4) An order of service and worship. This is the most extensive use of the word. Thus there is reference to the *seder* of the *benedictions (RH 4:5), of the sounding of the **shofar* (RH 4:9), and for fast days (Ta'an. 2:1), while the detailed description of the daily sacrifice concludes "thus was the *seder* of the daily offering in the service of the House of God" (Tam. 7:3). Similarly the service in the Temple is called the *seder *Avodah*. The most common use of the word in this sense is the *seder* of Passover, which, in the *piyyut* on the conclusion of the prose part of the **Haggadah* is called *siddur Pesaḥ* (for a full description see *Passover).

SEDER OLAM (Heb. סֵדֶר עוֹלָם; "The Order of the World"), name of two midrashic, chronological works called respectively *Seder Olam Rabbah* ("The Great *Seder Olam*") and *Seder Olam Zuta* ("The Small *Seder Olam*").

Seder Olam Rabbah

Seder Olam is mentioned in the Talmud (Shab. 88a; Yev. 82b; et al.) and is ascribed by the Palestinian *amora* R. Johanan (third century) to the second-century *tanna* Yose b. *Ḥalafta (Yev. 82b; Nid. 46b). The work is divided into three parts, each consisting of ten chapters. Part one enumerates the dates of major events from the creation of the world until the death of Moses and the crossing of the Jordan by the Israelites under Joshua; part two, from the crossing of the Jordan to the murder of Zechariah, king of Israel; part three, chapters 21–27, from the murder of Zechariah to the destruction of the Temple by Nebuchadnezzar; and chapter 28, from the destruction of the Temple to the conquest of Babylon by Cyrus. Chapter 29 and the first part of chapter 30 cover the Persian period, which is stated to be only 34 years. The larger part of chapter 30 contains a summary of events from the conquest of Persia by Alexander until the Bar Kokhba Revolt. This summary may be an epitome of a large section shortened by some later editor uninterested in post-biblical history. The book is written in a dry but clear Hebrew style. It is embellished with midrashic interpretations of biblical passages which are used as sources for the chronological calculations.

Yose b. Ḥalafta, the presumed author of *Seder Olam Rabbah*, probably had access to old traditions that also underlay the chronological computations of the Jewish Hellenistic chronographer *Demetrius (third century B.C.E.). The most significant confusion in Yose's calculation is the compression of the Persian period, from the rebuilding of the Temple by Zerubbabel in 516 B.C.E. to the conquest of Persia by Alexander, to no more than 34 years. Like other rabbinic scholars, he believed that Zerubbabel (sixth century B.C.E.), Malachi,

Ezra, Nehemiah (all fifth century B.C.E.), and Simeon the Just (third century) were all contemporaries. The work in its present form has gone through many hands. Some quotations from it in the Talmud are missing in the extant text (see bibl. Ratner, Mavo, 118ff.). On the other hand, the book contains many later additions (*ibid.*, 134ff.).

Seder Olam Rabbah was the first to establish the era "from the creation of the world" (*ab creatione mundi*, abbreviated A.M. for *anno mundi*). Utilizing the biblical chronology and reconstructing post-biblical history as well as he could, the author arrived at the conclusion that the world was created 3828 years before the destruction of the Second Temple by the Romans. According to this calculation the destruction took place in the year 68, which is in contradiction to the accepted chronology that it took place in the year 70 C.E. An attempt to harmonize the contradiction was made by E. Frank (see bibl.). It was a long time until the reckoning according to the *anno mundi* era took root in Jewish chronology. For many centuries the calculation of the *Seder Olam Rabbah* was of interest only to talmudic students who tried to satisfy their curiosity for historical reconstruction. The usual calculation accepted by Jews in talmudic and even post-talmudic times was that of the Seleucid era, beginning with the year 312 B.C.E., and usually referred to in Jewish literature as *minyan shetarot* ("dating of documents"). Only when the center of Jewish life moved from Babylonia to Europe and the calculation according to the Seleucid era became meaningless was it replaced by that of the *anno mundi* era of the *Seder Olam*.

The first mention of the *anno mundi* date is in the chronological book *Baraita di-Shemu'el* (eighth–ninth centuries; see A. Epstein, *Mi-Kadmoniyyot ha-Yehudim* (1957), 18, 193), on tombstones in Venosa, southern Italy (ninth century; see U.(M.D.) Cassuto, in: *Kedem*, 2 (1945), 99–120), and in the commentary of Shabbetai *Donnolo (tenth century, Italy) on the *Sefer Yeẓirah* (ed. by David Castelli (1880), 3). From the 11th century onward it became dominant in most of the Jewish communities in the world. In the 16th century, Azariah de *Rossi was the first Jewish scholar to doubt the antiquity of the usage of this era (see *Me'or Einayim*, ch. 25). Until the 12th century the book was known only as *Seder Olam*, but the word *rabbah* was then added in order to differentiate it from the chronicle *Seder Olam Zuta*. The first to use the name *Seder Olam Rabbah* was Abraham b. Nathan ha-Yarḥi (see *Sefer ha-Manhig*, 52ab).

The book has gone through many editions and was commented upon by many scholars, among them Jacob *Emden, *Elijah b. Solomon Zalman Gaon of Vilna, and B. Ratner, who devoted to the book a separate large introduction (*mavo*) containing valuable critical references. A Latin translation by G. Genebara of *Seder Olam Rabbah* and *Seder Olam Zuta* appeared in 1577, and another one appeared in 1692. An attempt at a critical edition of the book was made by Alexander Marx, who published the first ten chapters of it with a German translation in 1903.

Seder Olam Zuta

This is an anonymous early medieval chronicle. Written mostly in Hebrew and partly in Aramaic, it consists of ten chapters. The first six chapters deal with the chronology of 50 generations from Adam to Jehoiachin, king of Judah, who was exiled by Nebuchadnezzar to Babylon and according to this chronicle was the first of the Babylonian exilarchs. Chapters 7–10 deal with 39 generations from Jehoiachin until the end of the Babylonian exilarchate under the Sassanid dynasty. The object of the chronicle is presumably to show that the exilarchs were of Davidic descent and that the lineage of these exilarchs had died out in Babylon when Mar Zutra (II) left Babylonia for Ereẓ Israel in 520. A detailed account of Mar Zutra's adventures is given at the end of the book to substantiate this contention. This part, which enumerates the exilarchs of the fourth and fifth centuries, is historically important as it is the only source of information for this period. The Karaites also traced back the descent of their exilarchs through this record.

There is a difference of opinion concerning the time of composition of this chronicle. Many hold that it was written about 804, which corresponds to the date given in the De Rossi manuscript (Parma) published by Schechter (MGWJ, 39 (1895), 23–28). However, this may be a later addition. According to others it was written in the time of the *savoraim (sixth century), and others claim that it was written when there was considerable doubt about the authenticity of the genealogy of the Babylonian exilarchs (second half of the seventh century; see *Bustanai b. Ḥaninai). For the biblical period the author drew on the *Seder Olam Rabbah* and for the talmudic period, on the chronicles or chronological lists which were composed in the Babylonian academies (*Sifrei Zikhronot le-Veit David, Sifrei Beit David*; see *Iggeret Sherira Ga'on*, ed. Lewin, 96). Abraham Zacuto included the greater part of this chronicle in his *Sefer Yuḥasin* (see *Sefer Yuḥasin ha-Shalem*, ed. by H. Flipowski and A.Ḥ. Freimann, 91–93).

BIBLIOGRAPHY: SEDER OLAM RABBAH: B. Ratner, *Mavo le-Seder Olam Rabba* (1894); idem (ed.), *Seder Olam Rabba* (1897), reprint with introd. by S.K. Mirsky (1966); A. Marx (ed.), *Seder Olam* (1903); E. Frank, *Talmudic and Rabbinical Chronology* (1956), 11ff.; Baron, Social², 8 (1958), 204–10. SEDER OLAM ZUTA: F. Lazarus, in: *Bruell's Jahrbuecher*, 10 (1890), 157–70; M. Grossberg (ed.), *Seder Olam Zuta* (1910); Ḥ. Tykocinski, in: *Devir*, 1 (1923), 171ff.; A.D. Goode, in: JQR, 31 (1940/41), 149–69; M.J. Weinstock (ed.), *Seder Olam Zuta ha-Shalem* (1957); Dinur, Golah, 1 pt. 1 (1958²), 264f.

[Judah M. Rosenthal]

SEDEROT (Heb. שְׂדֵרוֹת), development town in the southern Coastal Plain of Israel 11 mi. (18 km.) S. of Ashkelon. Sederot's beginnings were in 1951, when immigrants from Kurdistan and Persia were housed in temporary huts near kibbutz *Nir Am and found occasional employment as hired laborers, mainly in farming, in the vicinity. In 1954 the place became *a ma'barah* (transitory immigrant camp), called Ma'barat Gevim-Dorot; it absorbed newcomers from North Africa. In 1956 it was declared a development town and permanent housing schemes were started. In the ensuing years, Sederot continued to suffer from unemployment caused by the lack of local industry, from an exorbitant burden of welfare cases, and consequently, from a large turnover of population. The situation improved in the 1960s when industries were set up in the town and the simultaneous industrialization of the region's kibbutzim provided additional places of work for Sederot residents. Projects were devised to attract skilled labor and professionals from among new immigrants and veteran Israelis, thus also attempting to diversify the town's population – 7,500 in 1970 – the majority of whom originated from North Africa, mainly Morocco. Local industry included enterprises in food packing (citrus, poultry, etc.), as well as metal and textile plants, cotton mills, etc. In the mid-1990s the population was approximately 14,600, rising to 19,400 in 2002 on an area of around 2 sq. mi. (5 sq. km.). In 1996 Sederot received city status. Unemployment reached the 12% mark in the early 2000s. Located barely half a mile (800 m.) from Beit Hanun in the northern Gaza Strip, Sederot came under Kassam rocket attack in the al-Aqsa Intifada, with nearly 100 hitting the town between 2001 and 2004 and four residents killed and dozens injured. Dozens more hit the town after Israel's disengagement from the Gaza Strip in 2005. Sederot is known for its native rock groups (such as Tipex). Since 2001 its cinemateque has hosted the Southern Film Festival in conjunction with nearby Sapir College. It also operates *ḥaredi* and *hesder* yeshivot.

[Efraim Orni / Shaked Gilboa (2nd ed.)]

SEDOT YAM (Heb. שְׂדוֹת יָם), kibbutz in central Israel on the site of ancient Caesarea, affiliated with Ha-Kibbutz ha-Me'uḥad. Sedot Yam was founded in 1940 by Israel-born youth of the Ha-No'ar ha-Oved movement and by Youth Aliyah graduates from Germany and Hungary (among them Hannah *Szenes). Initially, the kibbutz took on as its principal assignment pioneering in sea fishing, but abandoned this branch in the course of time and developed fruit orchards, irrigated field and fodder crops, etc. The kibbutz also produced quartz surfacing products (CaesarStone) and other surfacing materials (marble, granite, ceramics). It had a small museum containing ancient artifacts uncovered in the area. In 1970 Sedot Yam had 510 inhabitants, increasing to 634 in 2002.

WEBSITE: www.sdot-yam.org.il.

[Efraim Orni / Shaked Gilboa (2nd ed.)]

SEDRAN (Sedransky), BARNEY (1891–1969), U.S. basketball player. Born in New York, Sedran was considered too small for high school basketball but became a varsity player at the City College of New York (1909–11). He turned professional in 1911, and in 15 seasons his teams won a number of championships.

Only five feet four inches tall and weighing 118 pounds, the smallest regular professional player, he excelled nevertheless in all phases of the game, and in 1913 set an all-time scoring record of 34 points on 17 field goals without the benefit of a backboard. From 1932 to 1946, Sedran coached such teams as the Brooklyn Jewels, Kate Smith Celtics, Wilmington Bombers, and New York Gothams. In 1962 he was elected to the Basketball Hall of Fame.

BIBLIOGRAPHY: B. Postal et al. (eds.), *Encyclopedia of Jews in Sports* (1965), 92–93.

[Jesse Harold Silver]

SEDUVA (or **Sheduva**; Pol. **Szadów**; Rus. **Shadov**), city in N. central Lithuania. The Jewish community in Seduva dates from the 15th century. Seduva was the birthplace of R. Moses of *Kiev. In 1766 there were 508 Jews who paid the poll tax, and in 1897 the Jewish population numbered 2,695 (61% of the total population). During World War I Jews were deported to the interior of Russia, only some of them returning after the war, and in 1923 only 916 (28% of the total population) remained. Subsequent migration abroad and to the large cities reduced the number of Jews even further; in 1939 there were only 200 Jewish families in Seduva. Shortly after the German invasion the community was completely destroyed. The Russian-Jewish historian Pesaḥ (Piotr) *Marek was born in Seduva.

BIBLIOGRAPHY: *Yahadut Lita*, 3 (1967), 362.

[Yehuda Slutsky]

SÉE, family originally from Lorraine; the name is said to derive from the Seille River. Toward the end of the 16th century, most of the members of the family had settled in *Alsace and Lorraine (in Metz, Bergheim, Rappoltsweiler (Ribeauvillé), and Colmar), but later most of them lived in Paris. During the 19th and 20th centuries, its members included the politician CAMILLE SÉE (1847–1920), the playwright EDMOND *SÉE (1875–1959), the physician GERMAIN SÉE (1818–1896), the soldier Léopold *Sée (1822–1904), and the historian HENRI SÉE (1864–1936), whose works on economic history, *La vie économique et les classes sociales en France au XVIIIe siècle* (1924) and *Histoire économique de la France* (2 vols., 1939–42), are of lasting importance. He also contributed articles on French Jewish history to the *Revue d'études juives*.

BIBLIOGRAPHY: Kaufmann, in: REJ, 20 (1890), 309–11; Ginsburger, in: REJ, 50 (1905), 113; idem, in: *Souvenir et Science*, 2 (1931), nos. 2, 3; 3 (1932), no. 2; E. Sitzmann, *Dictionnaire de biographie des hommes célèbres de l' Alsace*, 2 (1910), 766.

SÉE, EDMOND (1875–1959), French playwright. Born in Bayonne, Sée forsook the law to write witty plays analyzing human emotions. Mainly comedies in the 18th-century French classical tradition, these include the highly successful *La brebis* (1896), *L'indiscret* (1903), *L'irrégulière* (1913), *La dépositaire* (1924), and *Charité* (1932). He also wrote two romantic novels, *Un cousin d'Alsace* (1918) and *Notre amour* (1920), and critical works such as *Le théâtre français contemporain* (1928).

SÉE, LÉOPOLD (1822–1904), French general. Born in Bergheim, Alsace, into a distinguished French family, Sée graduated from the military academy at St. Cyr and in 1850 was appointed to one of the famous Zouave regiments with the rank of captain. He was sent to Algeria to fight against insurgent tribes and in 1854 his regiment was transferred to Crimea on the outbreak of war against Russia. Sée fought in the bitter battles of Alma and Inkerman and at the siege of Sebastopol. Twice wounded, he was mentioned in dispatches and received the Legion of Honor. He led a Zouave battalion in the attack on Port Malakoff. By the end of the Crimean War, Sée was a very popular figure in France and was transferred to the Imperial Guard at Versailles. In 1859 he served in the Italian campaign. On the outbreak of the Franco-Prussian War in 1870, Sée commanded his regiment at the siege of Metz. He was wounded and taken prisoner, but was released because of the severity of his wounds. Sée became a lieutenant general in 1880 and commanded various army divisions until his retirement in 1887. Throughout his life, he was active in Jewish affairs and was a member of the French Jewish Consistory.

[Mordechai Kaplan]

SEEKERS AFTER SMOOTH THINGS, or "Givers of Smooth Interpretations" (Heb. דּוֹרְשֵׁי חֲלָקוֹת, *doreshei ḥalakot*), a designation given in the *Qumran texts to certain people who followed a different (and presumably less exacting) application of the law than that favored by the Qumran community. At the beginning of the Zadokite Admonition (CD 1:18) those who paid heed to the "man of scoffing," the "spouter of lies," are said to have "given smooth interpretations" (a phrase probably derived from Isa. 30:10, where the rebellious people say to the prophets, "speak unto us smooth things, prophesy delusions" – i.e., tell us what we like to hear). From samples of these "smooth interpretations" given later in the same work (CD 4:19ff.), with special reference to the marriage laws and the rules of purity, it seems most probable that the people referred to are the Pharisees.

In the *Thanksgiving Psalms the tension between the community and the "seekers after smooth things" finds repeated expression: the psalmist has become "a man of dispute for the interpreters of error… a spirit of jealousy to all who seek after smooth things," (1QH 2:14ff.) and he praises God for having "redeemed the soul of the poor man (*evyon*) from the seekers after smooth things" (1QH 2:32). Those who were formerly his friends and companions have become "interpreters of falsehood and seers of deceit," who (he says) "have devised plans of Belial against me, to make me exchange Thy law, which Thou hast engraved on my heart, for 'smooth things' to be given to Thy people" (1QH 4:10ff.). From this it appears that the Qumran community and the "seekers after smooth things" once belonged to the same group, but the parting of the ways came when the *Teacher of Righteousness received his special revelation and organized his *Yaḥad. The teacher may well be the psalmist whose voice is heard in these passages from the Thanksgiving Psalms. In the Nahum Commentary from Cave Four at Qumran, Demetrius, king of Greece, is said to have "attempted to enter Jerusalem by the counsel of the seekers after smooth things" but met with fearful retribution at the hands of the *Lion of Wrath, who "took vengeance on the seekers after smooth things in that he proceeded to hang them up alive." This is best interpreted as pertaining to the rebellion against Alexander *Yannai in 94–88 B.C.E., during which his insurgent subjects (among whom the Pharisees were prominent) tried to enlist the aid of Demetrius III (Eukairos) against him. When the rebellion was put down, he crucified 800 of their leaders. The commentator on Nahum plainly does not approve of the "seekers after smooth things" (otherwise he would not have used such a disapproving designation for them), but still less does he approve of the blasphemous atrocity perpetrated by the Lion of Wrath.

BIBLIOGRAPHY: A. Dupont-Sommer, *Essene Writings from Qumran* (1961), notes on passages cited above; C. Rabin, *Qumran Studies* (1957); Allegro, in: JBL, 75 (1956), 89ff.; Roth, in: *Revue de Qumran*, 2 (1960), 261ff.

[Frederick Fyvie Bruce]

SEELIGMANN, ISAC LEO (Arieh; 1907–1982), Bible scholar. Born in Amsterdam, he was the son of the bibliographer Sigmund *Seeligmann. Leo Seeligmann studied both at the Netherlands Israelite Seminary and at the Municipal University of Amsterdam (Latin and Greek). From 1936 onwards he taught at the Seminary. Despite deportation to Westerbork and Theresienstadt, he and his family survived World War II. In 1946 he became curator of the Bibliotheca Rosenthaliana, the Judaica and Hebraica Department of the Amsterdam University Library, and worked together with Leo Fuks, who would succeed him in 1950, to fill the gaps and to try to continue the pre-war history of the collection. He combined both his rabbinical training and his philological studies in his Ph.D. dissertation on *The Septuagint Version of Isaiah* (Leiden 1948, re-edited in *The Septuagint Version of Isaiah and Cognate Studies*, 2004). He aimed at understanding the Septuagint as a document of Jewish-Alexandrian theology. In 1950 he joined the Bible Department of the Hebrew University of Jerusalem, where he taught as a lecturer and as a professor for 25 years. Shortly before his death he was presented with a three-volume *Festschrift* as a measure of the esteem many scholars held for him.

In addition to his book on the Septuagint, Seeligmann's scholarly contribution was in his lectures at international congresses and his articles in periodicals and *Festschriften*. A selection of these, in German and English, was published in *Gesammelte Studien zur Hebräischen Bibel* (2004), including translations from Hebrew.

In his first lecture for the International Organization of Old Testament Scholars (later: for the Study of the Old Testament) in Copenhagen 1953, he drew attention to the flexibility of biblical stories and literary motives in "Voraussetzungen der Midraschexegese" and later, on the same theme, in "Anfänge der Midraschexegese in der Chronik" (1980).

He became fascinated by the theme of the different stages of writing history in the Hebrew Bible. Among the fruits of his research into biblical historiography are "Hebräische Erzählung und biblische Geschichtsschreibung" (1962), "Von historischer Wirklichkeit zu historiosophischer Konzeption in der Hebräischen Bibel" (1971), and his last congress lecture in Goettingen, "Die Auffassung von der Prophetie in der deuteronomistischen und chronistischen Geschichtsschreibung" (1977).

He demonstrated his interest in philological research in articles such as "Untersuchungen zur Textgeschichte der Hebräischen Bibel" (1956) and "Indications of Editorial Alteration and Adaptation in the Massoretic Text and the Septuagint" (1961). Among his other works are *Phasen uit de geschiedenis van het Joodsch historisch bewustzijn* (1947); *Profetie en profeten in Israel* (1927); and *Tekst-, Litteratuur- en godsdienstgeschiedenis van het Oude Testament* (1935).

His colleague Rudolf Smend (Goettingen) wrote an extensive biographical sketch which highlights the trends of Seeligmann's research.

BIBLIOGRAPHY: Isac Leo Seeligmann, The *Septuagint Version of Isaiah and Cognate Studies*, ed. by R. Hanhart and H. Spieckermann (2004); idem, *Gesammelte Studien zur Hebräischen Bibel.* Mit einem Beitrag von R. Smend, ed. by E. Blum (2004), including bibliog.; *Studia Rosenthaliana*, 38 (2005/6) includes an English translation of a long passage of Smend's biographical sketch.

[F.J. Hoogewoud (2nd ed.)]

SEELIGMANN, SIGMUND (1873–1940), bibliographer and historian. Born in Karlsruhe, Germany, Seeligmann came to Amsterdam in 1884, later studying at its rabbinical seminary. Maintaining worldwide contacts with Jewish scholars, he put his rich knowledge and important library at their disposal. Of his many articles and monographs on Jewish bibliography and the history of the Jews in the Netherlands, especially important are "Het geestelijk leven in de Hoogduitsche Joodsche Gemeente te's Gravenhage" ("The Spiritual Life of the Dutch Jewish Community in The Hague," in: D.S. van Zuiden, *De Hoogduitsche Joden in 's Gravenhage* (1913)); and *Bibliographie en Historie; bijdrage tot de geschiedenis der eerste Sephardim in Amsterdam* ("Bibliography and History; Contribution to the History of the First Sephardim in Amsterdam," 1927). Many of his writings are collected in his *Varia* (1935), nos. 1–36, in one volume. His original theories on the settlement of Conversos in The Dutch Republic and his emphasis on the special character of Dutch Jewry (Seeligmann coined the by now legendary phrase *species hollandia judaica*) greatly stimulated the study of this chapter of Jewish history. In 1919 he founded the Genootschap voor Joodsche Wetenschap in Nederland ("Society for the Science of Judaism in the Netherlands"). He was active in many Jewish institutions, including a term as president of the Dutch Zionist Organization.

[Frederik Jacob Hirsch / Irene E. Zwiep (2nd ed.)]

His son, Isac Leo *Seeligmann (Arieh; 1907–1982), biblical scholar, was born in Amsterdam, and served as lecturer in the Netherlands Israelite Seminary from 1936 to 1939. In 1946, after returning from a Nazi concentration camp, he was librarian at the University of Amsterdam. In 1950 he joined the department of Bible at the Hebrew University of Jerusalem, becoming professor in 1966.

BIBLIOGRAPHY: L. Hirschel, in: *Ha'Ischa*, 12 (1940); M.H. van Campen, *In Memoriam Sigmund Seeligmann* (1941).

SEESEN, town in Lower Saxony, Germany. Throughout its history the Jewish community of Seesen was small, its numbers never exceeding 200. In 1801 the financier and Court Jew Israel *Jacobson founded and richly endowed the Jacobson Schule in Seesen as a means of implementing his humanistic and reform ideals. Modern subjects and vocational instruction were emphasized. The school began to accept Christian pupils in 1805, and later in the 19th century lost its Jewish character. In 1810 the Seesen synagogue (the controversial Jacobsontempel), featuring for the first time in Germany an organ, choir, and sermons in German, was consecrated as an offshoot of the school. There were 54 Jews in Seesen in 1819; 178 in 1871; and 209 in 1895. In 1852 a nonsectarian orphanage was founded by Jacobson's son Mayer. It was closed in 1923 and reopened in 1929 as a Jewish youth sanatorium. Only 30 Jews lived in Seesen in 1933, when Jewish teachers and pupils were expelled from the school and its foundation funds confiscated. After World War II, a short-lived community of 60 was established, but by 1952 only nine remained. A liberal Jewish community was founded in 1997. It numbered 43 in 2005. All the members are immigrants from the former Soviet Union. They use a room in the original Jacobson school. The community is a member of the Union of Progressive Jews in Germany.

BIBLIOGRAPHY: M. Eliav, *Ha-Ḥinnukh ha-Yehudi be-Germanyah* (1960), index; M. Kreutzberger (ed.), *Bibliothek und Archiv*, 1 (1970), 255; FJW, 416; G. Ballin, in: *Genealogie* (1969). **ADD. BIBLIOGRAPHY:** G. Ballin, *Geschichte der Juden in Seesen* (1979); Z. Asaria, *Die Juden in Niedersachsen* (1979), 444–56; *Germania Judaica*, vol. 3 (1987), 1362; M. Berg, *Juedische Schulen in Niedersachsen* (*Beitraege zur historischen Bildungsforschung*, vol. 28) (2003).

[Larissa Daemmig (2nd ed.)]

°**SEETZEN, ULRICH JASPER** (1767–1811), German explorer. He studied medicine in Goettingen. During his extensive travels in the Near East, he visited Palestine (1802), Mecca and Medina (1810), and Yemen (1811), where he was poisoned. His diaries were edited posthumously by Kruse and Fleischer (1854–59). Seetzen was the first of the scientific explorers of the 19th century. His knowledge of Arabic and his courage enabled him to visit unexplored regions, such as the Dead Sea. He was the first European to note the ruins of Masada (Sabba), although he did not identify the site.

ADD. BIBLIOGRAPHY: J.P.J. Olivier, in: M. Weippert and S. Timm (eds.), *Meilenstein* (1995) 164–71; H. Weippert, in: *ibid.*, 324–32; J. Schienerl, *Der Weg in den Orient. Der Forscher Ulrich Jasper Seetzen*... (2000).

[Michael Avi-Yonah]

SEFER HA-ḤAYYIM, an anonymous Ashkenazi-ḥasidic treatise, unique in its combination of mystical esoteric theology with ethical teaching. Whereas all other works of *Ḥasidei Ashkenaz deal with either one area or the other, the author of *Sefer ha-Ḥayyim* attempts first to establish a theological basis – beginning with the essence of God, His holy Names, and His different powers, and concludes with the ethical problems of good and evil tendencies among men, suggesting ways to overcome them. Because some theories in this work closely resemble basic kabbalistic ideas, *Sefer ha-Ḥayyim* is important for the history of Jewish mysticism. R. Moses *Taku attributes the book to R. Abraham *ibn Ezra. There seems to be no basis for this, however, even though the author used Ibn Ezra's exegetical and theological works. In the introduction of *Sefer ha-Ḥayyim* the author numbers 15 chapters, briefly describing their contents; the text, however, does not follow that structure, and entire subjects mentioned in the introduction are either missing or appear in a different order.

BIBLIOGRAPHY: Y. Dan, *Torat ha-Sod shel Ḥasidut Ashkenaz* (1968), 143–56, 230–5; G. Scholem, *Ursprung und Anfaenge der Kabbala* (1962), 160f.

[Joseph Dan]

SEFER HA-MA'ASIM LI-VENEI EREẒ YISRAEL, halakhic work written in Ereẓ Israel. In 1930 B.M. *Lewin published two fragments from the *Genizah* collection in Oxford of the *Sefer ha-Ma'asim* with an introduction (*Tarbiz*, 1.1 (1930), 79–101). Since then various additional fragments have been published by J.N. *Epstein and J. *Mann. All these fragments together amount to only 15 pages, but in 1972, Z.M. Rabinowitz published the largest extract yet found, consisting of ten pages. This additional extract makes possible a fuller evaluation of the importance of this work. These fragments confirm the conclusion of Epstein that the work belongs to the end of the Byzantine and the beginning of Arab rule in Ereẓ Israel (end of the 7th century) and the *terminus ad quem* is provided by the fact that the far-reaching geonic enactment, permitting the **ketubbah* of a woman to be levied from movable goods of the orphaned children, enacted in 787 C.E., was unknown.

The word *Ma'asim* refers to the fact that the work consists of practical halakhic discussions, excluding laws which had no practical application. As such it affords interesting glimpses into aspects of the life of the Jews in Ereẓ Israel at the time. Thus it reveals that Jews engaged extensively in agriculture and cattle raising and that they rented land for this purpose from the Arabs.

The importance of the work lies in the fact that unlike other halakhic codes and commentaries which are based mainly upon the Babylonian Talmud, *Sefer ha-Ma'asim* is the first and earliest example of the codification of the *halakhah* according to the Jerusalem Talmud and the *halakhah* observed in Ereẓ Israel until the time of *Yehudai Gaon and his disciples (8th century).

The *Sefer ha-Ma'asim* contains some laws and customs for which there is no other source. Further extracts from the *Sefer ha-Ma'asim*, from the literary legacy of the late Prof. Mordecai Margaliot, have been published.

BIBLIOGRAPHY: Z.M. Rabinowitz, in: *Tarbiz* 41:3 (1972).

[Louis Isaac Rabinowitz]

SEFER HA-NEYAR, an anonymous book of halakhic decisions by one of the last French tosafists of the late 13th or early 14th century. Extremely strange and farfetched theories were put forward by Jewish bibliographers and chroniclers about this book, which was known to them only by hearsay. Only after its publication did it become possible to gain an idea of its true nature. The work contains about 40 chapters, embracing all the *halakhot* governing the day-to-day observance of the Jew. The book chiefly relies on the teachings of the great French and German scholars, the tosafists, down to *Isaac of Corbeil and *Perez b. Elijah of Corbeil who are, however, rarely mentioned by name. The author also made use of the works of the great Spanish *posekim*, such as Maimonides and Isaac Alfasi, and the **Halakhot Gedolot*. In its general character, sources, and aims, there is a strong resemblance between *Sefer ha-Neyar* and the **Kol Bo*, another anonymous work. The *Neyar*, however, appears to have been compiled before the *Kol Bo*, since it contains very few references to *Meir b. Baruch of Rothenburg and Pereẓ of Corbeil. The *Sefer ha-Neyar* describes the customs of France and Germany, and contains valuable halakhic, literary, and historical material, for which it is often the sole source. One of its main sources was the work of a certain Baruch Ḥayyim b. Menahem, a scholar not otherwise known. From the quotations themselves it is clear that Baruch was a pupil of *Samson of Sens and of his own father, who was also a pupil of Samson and of the brothers *Moses and *Samuel of Evreux. Anonymous *haggahot* ("glosses") have been added to the text of the book; although they resemble it in content and in use of sources, they seem to be by another scholar who lived a generation later than the author of the work, and may have been his pupil. There are also a number of anonymous *haggahot* of a different type, entitled *Nofekh*; the exact relationship between them and the book itself is not clear. Some consider that the name of the work (apparently not its original name) was derived from the French town Niort (and there are additional indications that the book originated there). Others connect it with the introduction into France of writing paper (*neyar*, "paper") at the end of the 13th century, it being one of the first books written on paper. The book enjoyed a wide circulation and manuscripts of it are extant. Later its popularity declined. The only halakhist to quote the work, in his responsa, was Joseph *Colon. The first part of *Sefer ha-Neyar* (25 chapters) was published in New York in 1960 by G. Appel.

BIBLIOGRAPHY: G. Appel (ed.), *Sefer ha-Neyar* (1960), introd.; idem, in: *Sura*, 2 (1955–56), 356–87 (Heb.); H. Gross, in: REJ, 7 (1883), 74–7.

[Israel Moses Ta-Shma]

SEFER HA-YASHAR (Heb. סֵפֶר הַיָּשָׁר; "The Book of Righteousness"), an anonymous work, probably written in the 13th century, one of the most popular ethical books in the Middle

Ages. The book was published for the first time in Venice, in 1544, and since then has been reprinted many times. It was frequently attributed to R. *Tam, the tosafist, who wrote a book by that name (*Sefer ha-Yashar le-Rabbenu Tam*, Vienna, 1811); his writing, however, is concerned only with halakhic problems. Some manuscripts attribute the book to Zerahiah ha-Yevani, but there is no evidence to bear out the authenticity of such an ascription. Some scholars have suggested that the author might have been R. *Jonah Gerondi, one of the foremost writers in the field of ethics in the 13th century; however, the difference between R. Jonah's known views and those expounded in *Sefer ha-Yashar* would suggest otherwise.

There is also some confusion regarding the nature of the book and the school of ethical concepts to which the author adhered. The style and language conform to contemporaneous philosophical ethical writings and ideas; the author especially made use of Aristotelian terms and concepts. The work, however, is also marked by a tendency to deviate from the central stream of philosophical conventional ethics. This is evidenced in some of the main ideas. The difference is so great that some scholars have concluded that the author might have been a kabbalist who did not want to reveal the full scope of his mystical beliefs. Some ideas in the work also bear great similarity to the ethical concepts of the Ashkenazi ḥasidic movement which reached its peak in the 13th century, and especially to **Sefer ha-Ḥayyim*, which was written by one of the *Ḥasidei Ashkenaz.

Most of the unusual ideas are found in the first part of the work which describes the creation and explains why the wicked were created together with the righteous. The rest of the work is concerned, in a rather conventional way, with the main themes of Jewish ethics: love and fear of God, repentance, prayer, and good deeds. In several editions there are variations in the arrangement of the chapters and even in the content. No critical edition of this work has been published, and until the correct text is ascertained, the problems concerning the authorship and the underlying philosophic thought cannot be solved satisfactorily.

BIBLIOGRAPHY: I. Tishby, *Mishnat ha-Zohar*, 2 (1961), 657–8 n. 12; J.M. Toledano, in: HḤY, 11 (1927), 239; G. Vajda, *L'Amour de Dieu dans la théologie juive du moyen âge* (1957), 181 n. 1; G. Scholem, *Ursprung und Anfaenge der Kabbala* (1962), 94–96.

[Joseph Dan]

SEFER ḤUKKEI HA-TORAH (Heb. סֵפֶר חֻקֵּי הַתּוֹרָה; "The Book of the Laws of the Torah"), one of the earliest and most detailed treatises in Hebrew in the fields of education and educational ethics. This short work, dealing with the problems of education at its various levels, describes the first level, *midrash katan*, a community school, and the later one, *midrash gadol*, a yeshivah, to which, according to the book, every community should send a quota of its children. In the *midrash gadol*, the students, who study and live with their teachers, somewhat monastically, are forbidden to marry or communicate with society until they conclude their studies. *Sefer Ḥukkei ha-Torah* is found in manuscript Bodleiana Neubauer, Cat, 1 (1886), 181, no. 873, 2b. It was first published in Guedemann's *Ha-Torah ve-ha-Ḥayyim* (see bibl.).

The date, provenance, and purpose of this work are not known. Nor is it known whether this system was practiced in any Jewish community, or whether it is simply a utopian suggestion. Any similarity which various scholars have attempted to uncover between practices described in *Sefer Ḥukkei ha-Torah* and those which existed in Babylonia, France, or England has not been satisfactorily proven.

BIBLIOGRAPHY: M. Guedemann, *Ha-Torah ve-ha-Ḥayyim*, 1 (1896), 73–80, 217–9; Ish-Shalom (Friedmann), in: *Beit Talmud*, 1 (1881), 61f., 91–4; Loeb, in: REJ, 1 (1881), 159f.; D. Kaufmann, in: *Goettinger gelehrte Anzeigen* (1881), 1640–64; reprinted in his *Gesammelte Schriften*, 2 (1910), 208–15; Assaf, Mekorot, 1 (1925), 6–12; J. Jacobs, *Jews of Angevin England* (1893), 243–51.

[Joseph Dan]

SEFER TORAH (Heb. סֵפֶר תּוֹרָה; pl. *Sifrei Torah*; scroll of the law), scroll containing the Five Books of Moses written on parchment according to strict rules and used mainly for reading at public worship (see *Torah Reading). The *Sefer Torah* is normally written by a specialist known as a *sofer* ("scribe").

The Writing of the Scroll

The tools and materials used by the scribe are parchment, quill, ink, stylus and ruler, and *tikkun* ("guide") – a book with the Torah text. The Torah is written on parchment manufactured from specified sections of the hide of a kosher animal. The hide consists of three layers, but only the flesh side of the inner layer and the outer side of the hairy layer may be used for Torah parchment (Shab. 79b). The method of cleaning and softening the hide, which must be of the best quality, has changed throughout the centuries. During talmudic times, salt and barley flour were sprinkled on the skins which were then soaked in the juice of gallnuts (Meg. 19a). There is, however, a reference to the use of dogs' dung for this purpose (Yal. Ex. 187). Nowadays the skins are softened by soaking them in clear water for two days, after which the hair is removed by soaking the hides in limewater for nine days. Finally, the skins are rinsed and dried and the creases ironed out with presses. The processor must make a verbal declaration when soaking the skins that his action is being performed for the holiness of the *Sefer Torah*. Whereas reeds were used as pens in the days of the Talmud, quills are used today, the quill of the turkey feather, which is sturdy and long lasting, being preferred. The *sofer* cuts the point of the feather to give it a flat surface, which is desirable for forming the square letters, and then slits it lengthwise.

The ink must be black, durable, but not indelible. During talmudic times a viscous ink was made by heating a vessel with the flame of olive oil, and the soot thus produced on the sides of the vessel was scraped off and mixed with oil, honey, and gallnuts (Shab. 23a). Ink is now made by boiling a mixture of gallnuts, gum arabic, and copper sulfate crystals. Some scribes also add vinegar and alcohol. To ensure that the letters will be straight and the lines equally spaced, 43 thin lines are drawn across the width of the parchment with a stylus and ruler. Two additional longitudinal lines are drawn at the end of the page to ensure that all the lines end equally. To enhance the appearance of the printing on the parchment a four inch margin is left at the bottom, a three inch margin at the top, and a two inch margin between the columns.

Although there is no law regulating the number of pages or columns a Torah must have, from the beginning of the 19th century a standard pattern of 248 columns of 42 lines each was established. Each column is about five inches wide since by tradition there must be space enough to write the word לְמִשְׁפְּחֹתֵיהֶם (Gen. 8:19), the longest occurring in the Torah, three times.

Before the *sofer* begins his daily work, he performs ritual ablution in a **mikveh*. To avoid mistakes, talmudic *soferim* copied from another scroll, and according to one tradition there was a copy of the Torah kept in the Temple which scribes used as the standard (Rashi to MK 3:4, TJ, Shek. 4:3, 48a). Before commencing, the scribe tests the feather and ink by writing the name "Amalek" and crossing it out (cf. Deut. 25:19). He then makes the declaration, "I am writing the Torah in the name of its sanctity and the name of God in its sanctity." The scribe then looks into the *tikkun*, reads the sentence aloud, and proceeds to write it. Before writing the name of God the *sofer* repeats, "I am writing the name of God for the holiness of His name."

The Torah is written in the square script known as *Ketav Ashuri*, of which there are two different types: the Ashkenazi, which resembles the script described in the Talmud (Shab. 104a), and the Sephardi, which is identical with the printed letters of the Hebrew alphabet currently used in sacred texts. The thickness of the letters vary and it is often necessary for the *sofer* to make several strokes to form a letter. The scribe holds the feather sideways to make thin lines, and flat, so that the entire point writes, to make thick lines. Particular care must be given to those letters that are similar in appearance (e.g., *dalet* and *resh*) so that they can be easily distinguished. Each letter must be complete, with the exception of the "split *vav*" in the word *shalom* in Numbers 25:12. Although Hebrew is read from right to left, each individual letter in the *Sefer Torah* is written from left to right. Six letters are written particularly small (e.g., the *alef* in the first word of Lev. 1:1) and 11 letters are written very large (e.g., the *bet* in the first word of Gen. 1:1). There must be a space between the letters, a greater space between the words, and a nine letter gap between the portions. A four line separation is made between each of the Five Books of Moses.

Seven of the 22 letters of the alphabet have special designs on the upper left hand corner of the letter called *tagin*. Shaped somewhat like the letter *zayin*, three such *tagin* are placed above the letter, touching it lightly. The center *tag* is slightly higher than the two on the ends. The Torah contains no vowels or punctuation marks. However, there are a number of dots over several words (e.g., Deut. 29:28; see *Tikkun Soferim). There are two *shirot* or songs in the Torah which are written in unique fashion. *Shirat ha-Yam* (Ex. 15:1–19) has a nine letter gap in the middle of each sentence, and these gaps are so spaced that they appear like "half bricks set over whole bricks" (Meg. 16b; Shab. 103b). *Shirat Ha'azinu* (Deut. 32:1–43) also contains a nine letter separation in the middle of each sentence, but these blank spaces form a single space down the center of the entire column.

After the copying of the Torah has been completed, the sheets of parchment are sewn together with *giddin*, a special thread made of tendon tissue taken from the foot muscles of a kosher animal. Every four pages are sewn together to form a section or *yeri'ah*. These sections of parchment are sewn on the outer side of the parchment, with one inch left unsewn both at the very top and bottom. To reinforce the *giddin*, thin strips of parchment are pasted on the top and bottom of the page. After connecting the sheets the ends are tied to wooden rollers, called *aẓei ḥayyim*, by inserting the *giddin* in holes in the rollers. The *eẓ ḥayyim* consists of a center pole, with handles of wood and flat circular rollers to support the rolled-up scroll. Besides serving as a means of rolling the scroll, the *aẓei ḥayyim* also prevent people from touching the holy parchment with their hands. In Oriental and some Sephardi communities, the flat rollers are not employed since the Torah scrolls are kept in an ornamental wooden or metal case (*tik*).

[Aaron Rothkoff]

Invalid and Disqualified Scrolls

Mistakes in the Torah scroll can generally be corrected, since the ink can be erased with a knife and pumice stone. However, a mistake in the writing of any of the names of God cannot be corrected since the name of God may not be erased, and such faulty parchments must be discarded. When a mistake is found in a *Sefer Torah*, the wimple is tied round the outside of its mantle as a sign that it should not be used until the mistake has been corrected. According to the Talmud, a *Sefer Torah* which has less than 85 correct letters is to be discarded (Yad. 3:5; Shab. 116a). This number is the number of letters in Numbers 10:35–36, which is sometimes regarded as a separate book (hence the references to seven instead of five books of the Torah: Gen. R. 64:8; Lev. R. 11:3). However, it was later laid down that too extensive corrections rendered the scroll unsightly and therefore invalid (for this and other details see **Haggahot*). If a scroll is beyond repair, it is placed in an earthenware urn and buried in the cemetery.

It was customary to bury such scrolls alongside the resting place of a prominent rabbi (Meg. 26b). The Mishnah (Git. 4:6) permits the purchase of a *Sefer Torah* from a non-Jew at its market value and the Talmud (*ibid.*, 45b) even records that Rabban Simeon b. Gamaliel permitted the purchase of those written by a non-Jew. Another tradition, however, laid it down that a scroll written by a non-Jew must be stored away, while one written by a heretic must be burned since it is feared that he may have maliciously altered the text (*ibid.*).

The Duty to Possess a Sefer Torah

It is regarded as a positive biblical commandment for every Jew to possess a *Sefer Torah*, the word "song" in Deuteronomy 31:19, "now therefore write ye this song for you," being interpreted to apply to the Torah as a whole. Even if he has inherited one from his father he is still obliged to have one of his own (Sanh. 21b). He may write it himself, or have it written on his behalf by a *sofer*, or purchase one, but "he who writes it himself is regarded as though it had been given to him on Mt. Sinai" (Men. 30a).

On the basis of the statement of the Talmud (*ibid.*) to the effect that he who corrects even one letter in a *Sefer Torah* is regarded as though he had himself written it, a custom has developed which both gives every Jew a portion in a *Sefer Torah* and symbolically regards him as having fulfilled the command of writing one. The *sofer* writes only the outlines of the words in the first and last passages of the *Sefer Torah* and they are completed at a ceremony known as *Siyyum ha-Torah* ("the completion of the Torah"). Those present are honored by each being invited to fill in one of the hollow letters, or formally authorize the *sofer* to do so.

Sanctity of the Sefer Torah

The *Sefer Torah* is the most sacred of all Jewish books. A valid *Sefer Torah* must be treated with special sanctity and great reverence (Yad, Sefer Torah 10:2). Its sanctity is higher than that of all other scrolls of the books of the Bible, and therefore, though one *Sefer Torah* may be placed on top of another, or on the scroll of another book, another scroll must not be placed on it (Meg. 27a).

It is obligatory to stand in the presence of a *Sefer Torah* (Mak. 22b; Kid. 33b) both when the ark is opened to reveal the scrolls and when it is being carried, and it is customary to bow reverently or kiss it when it passes. The bare parchment must not be touched with the hand. So insistent were the rabbis on this that they declared "He who touches a naked *Sefer Torah* will be buried naked," although the statement was modified to mean either "naked of good deeds" or "naked of the reward for good deeds" which he would otherwise have had from reading it (Shab. 14a). For this reason the *yad* ("pointer") is used for reading and the Sephardim cover the outside of the parchment with silk for the same reason.

It was forbidden to sell a *Sefer Torah* except to provide the means for marrying, studying (Meg. 27a), and for the *ransom of captives. Should a *Sefer Torah* accidentally fall to the ground, the whole congregation is obliged to fast for that day. It was permitted and even enjoined to disregard the Sabbath in order to save not only the *Sefer Torah* but even its case from destruction (Shab. 16:1), and should it be burnt one had to rend one's garment (MK 25a); if one saw it torn one had to rend the garment twice, "once for the writing and once for the parchment" (*ibid.* 26a, cf. the statement of Hananiah b. Teradyon when he was being burnt at the stake wrapped in a scroll, "I see the parchment burning but the letters soar aloft" (Av. Zar. 18a)). The *Sefer Torah* must not be carried about unless for religious purposes, and even for the purpose of reading from it at services held at a temporary place of worship, such as a **shivah*, it may not be taken there unless it is read on at least three occasions. When it is transferred to a permanent site it is usually done with full ceremonial. The *Sefer Torah* is carried through the streets under a canopy and the procession is accompanied by songs and dances.

Among the Sephardim before the reading of the law, and among the Ashkenazim at its conclusion, the *Sefer Torah* is ceremoniously held aloft (**Hagbahah*), its writing exposed to the congregation, who recite "and this is the Torah which Moses set before the children of Israel (Deut. 4:44), according to the commandment of the Lord by the hand of Moses." One must make every effort to acquire a beautiful *Sefer Torah* (Shab. 133b). Unless it is corrected, a text of the *Sefer Torah* that is in error may be kept only 30 days (Ket. 19b). When it is transferred to a permanent site it is usually done with full ceremonial. The *Sefer Torah* is carried through the streets under a canopy and the procession is accompanied by songs and dances.

Other Uses

In addition to its main use for reading the scriptural portions in synagogue (see Reading of the *Torah), the *Sefer Torah* is used on a large number of ceremonial occasions. According to the Mishnah (Sanh. 2:4) it accompanied the king in battle, and on the occasions of public fasts for drought the ark with the *Sifrei Torah* was taken out into the public square and the supplications and exhortations were recited in front of it (Ta'an. 2:1). It also played a central role in the ceremony of **Hakhel.*

During the Middle Ages the solemnity of taking an oath was enhanced by the vower making it while grasping a *Sefer Torah*. For the same reason three leading members of the congregation stand round the **ḥazzan* while he is reciting **Kol Nidrei* on the eve of the *Day of Atonement.

In modern times it is extensively used. Seven *Sifrei Torah* are taken out for the circuits with the *four species on *Hoshana Rabba, and on the next day (in the Diaspora two days later) the sevenfold circuit of the synagogue with all the *Sifrei Torah* is the central part of the ceremonial of *Simḥat Torah. The custom of the worshippers joyfully dancing with the *Sefer Torah* on this occasion is widespread.

BIBLIOGRAPHY: S. Ganzfried, *Keset ha-Sofer* (1835, 1902^2, repr. 1961); Eisenstein, Dinim, 298–302; L. Blau, in: *Soncino-Blaetter*, 1 (1925–26), 16–28; M. Higger (ed. and tr.), *Seven Minor Treatises* (1930), 9–19; Y.Z. Cahana, in: *Sinai*, 16 (1945), 49–61, 139–59; Y. Zimmer, *ibid.*, 68 (1971), 162–72; Israel Ministry of Religions, *Leket Dinim bi-Khetivat Se-Ta-M* (1960); S. Rubenstein, *The Sefer Torah* (1965).

[Louis Isaac Rabinowitz]

ṢEFIRAH, SAADIAH BEN JOSEPH (middle of the 19th century), Yemenite author of the work *Kesef Ẓaruf* (Jerusalem, 1896), novellae on the Torah. The work includes extracts from ancient and recent biblical commentators, especially from the *Ḥemdat Yamim*, which is attributed to *Shabbazi. A supplement containing *Ma'yan Gannim*, extracts and explanations on the Song of Songs, as well as funeral sermons, is attached to the work. The son of the author, JOSEPH ṢEFIRAH, immigrated to Ereẓ Israel in 1870 and settled in *Jerusalem; he copied his father's work and introduced his own novellae (Jerusalem, 1931).

BIBLIOGRAPHY: J. Saphir, *Massa le-Teiman*, ed. by A. Yaari (1951), 191.

[Yehuda Ratzaby]

SEFIROT (Heb. סְפִירוֹת; sing. סְפִירָה, a fundamental term of the *Kabbalah. It was coined by the author of the *Sefer Yeẓirah* who designated by it the ten primordial or ideal "numbers" (from the Hebrew root *safor*, to numerate). From the first sources of kabbalistic literature onward it was used in a much wider sense and denotes the ten stages of emanation that emerged from *Ein-Sof and form the realm of God's manifestation in His various attributes. Every single *Sefirah* points to an aspect of God in His capacity of Creator, forming at the same time a whole world of divine light in the chain of being. The whole of the ten *Sefirot*, forming the "*Sefirot* Tree," is conceived as a dynamic unity in which the activity of God reveals itself. The rhythm of the unfolding *Sefirot* is the fundamental rhythm of all creation and can be detected on each of its different levels. For details on the doctrine concerning the *Sefirot* see *Kabbalah.

[Gershom Scholem]

SEGAL, ARTHUR (1875–1944), German painter. Born at Jassy, Romania, he moved to Berlin in 1892 to study at the Academy of Art. In 1895 he continued his artistic training in Paris and Munich at the private school of Schmid-Reutte and Fehr. Segal began as an impressionist painter and started to create landscapes such as *The Meadow*, *The Field of Wheat*, or *German Landscape* in the period 1896–1903 (private collections) under the influence of the neo-impressionist Giovanni Segantini. In 1903 he married his cousin Ernestine Charas and returned to Berlin, where he exhibited various paintings at the Berliner Secession Gallery in 1907 and 1909, his style of painting now changed to Neo-Expressionism. In 1910 he and 27 other artists, among them Heckel, Tappert, Kirchner, Richter, and Schmidt-Rottluff, founded the organization Neue Sezession, a movement that revolted against German impressionism. Segal chose still life, landscapes or urban views as his motifs to express his new attitude to painting. From 1914 to 1920, deeply shocked and terrified of the brutality of World War I, he lived in Ascona, Switzerland with his family. Back to Berlin, his intellectual approach to painting then caused him to change his style again and to evolve an individual form of cubism, dividing many of his pictures into four equal parts. Most of these paintings stem from the period of 1922 to 1925 and show abstract compositions in cubistic forms with a prism-like scheme of intense colors. One of his most well-known paintings, is *Prismatische Konstruktion* (1923, Petit Palais, Geneva).

When Hitler came to power, he left Germany for the Spanish island of Mallorca and in 1936 settled in London, where he founded "Arthur Segal's Painting School" for professionals and non-professionals, which became a synonym for therapy with the help of the arts. He died during the London "Blitz" in 1944 of heart failure. His books include *The Objective Impersonal Laws of Painting* (1929).

ADDED BIBLIOGRAPHY: W. Herzogenrath, P. Liška, *Arthur Segal, 1875–1944* (1987; with catalogue raisonné).

[Jihan Radjai-Ordoubadi (2nd ed.)]

SEGAL, BERNARD (1907–1984), U.S. Conservative rabbi, administrator. Segal was born in Lipno, Poland, and immigrated to the United States in 1922. He received a B.S. from Columbia University in 1931 and was ordained at the *Jewish Theological Seminary in 1933, earning a D.H.L. there in 1950. He served briefly as rabbi of the Patchogue Jewish Center on Long Island, N.Y. (1933–34), before becoming rabbi of Queens Jewish Center (1934–40). He was the first Jewish chaplain in the United States to be called to active duty in World War II, serving as chairman of the Chaplaincy Availability Board (1943–46) and co-chairing the Conservative movement's Wartime Emergency Commission (1944–45). He was discharged in 1945 with the rank of lieutenant colonel, staying on in the Army reserves as founding president of the Association of Jewish Chaplains of the Army and Navy of the United States (1945–47).

Returning to civilian life, Segal assumed the first of a series of leadership positions in the Conservative movement, becoming the first executive director of the *Rabbinical Assembly (1945–7) as well as director of the Joint Placement Commission of the Rabbinical Assembly and the Jewish Theological Seminary. In 1947, Segal was appointed executive vice president of the Rabbinical Assembly, where he continued to oversee placement of rabbis during the post-war growth years. In 1949, he moved from the Rabbinical Assembly to JTS, first as assistant to the president (1949–51) and then as executive vice president (1951–53). Recognizing the need for Jewish educators, he encouraged graduates to pursue careers in Jewish education. He also directed the National Ramah Commission (1950–54).

In 1953, Segal was appointed executive director (executive vice president from 1970) of the United Synagogue of America, now the United Synagogue of Conservative Judaism, where he spent the next 23 years, until his retirement, supervising the expansion of the organization, creating new departments, and hiring more professionals. He emphasized education, creating programs for synagogue members of all ages, developing curricula for congregational schools, publishing educational materials, establishing Solomon *Shechter day schools in numerous communities, launching the Burning Bush press as the imprint of the National Academy of Adult Jewish Studies, and distributing the *El Am Talmud*. Striving always to foster unity in the Conservative movement, he led the United Synagogue into joining with the Rabbinical Assembly and the National Women's League in forming the Commission on Social Action (1954). In 1957, he was instrumental in founding the World Council of Synagogues and implementing uniform standards for synagogue practices. He also brought the United Synagogue into the membership fold of umbrella organizations of American and world Jewry, such as the *Conference of Presidents of the Major American Jewish organizations and the *World Zionist Organization.

Outside of the Conservative movement, Segal was a member of the Board of Directors of the Committee on Religion in American Life (1954–56), the New York City Mayor's Commission on Housing (1954–58) and the New York Association for Middle Income Housing (1960–68). Following his retirement in 1977, he moved to Jerusalem, Israel.

BIBLIOGRAPHY: P.S. Nadell, *Conservative Judaism in America: A Biographical Dictionary and Sourcebook* (1988).

[Bezalel Gordon (2nd ed.)]

SEGAL, BERNARD GERARD (1907–1997), U.S. attorney. Born in New York City, Segal grew up in Allentown and Philadelphia, Pennsylvania. After graduating from the University of Pennsylvania Law School, Segal served as deputy to the Pennsylvania attorney general from 1932 to 1935. At age 24, he was the youngest person to ever assume that position. He taught at the American Institute of Banking (1936–39) and at Franklin and Marshall College (1937–38), joining the law firm of Schnader, Harrison, Segal, and Lewis in 1936. A friend of the Kennedy family, Segal was appointed by Attorney General Robert Kennedy, in 1962, to help set up a commission that would dispatch Northern lawyers to handle civil rights cases in the South. He served on several American Bar Association committees from 1952 to 1968 and was the first Jew to be elected president of that organization (1969–70). Later, President Lyndon Johnson selected Segal to head the National Legal Service Program, which established legal services for the poor.

Besides holding many positions on government committees and in various foundations and legal institutes, Segal served as president of the Allied Jewish Appeal of Philadelphia; director of the American Jewish League for Israel; vice president and trustee of the Jewish Publication Society of America; honorary director of the Jewish Family Service; and trustee of the Hebrew University of Jerusalem, whose law library is named for him.

Regarded by many as one of the greatest lawyers in recent American history, Segal was known as "the conscience of the bar," who strived to promote individual rights and the rule of law. Among his many honors and awards, Segal received the American Bar Association's Gold Medal; the U.S. Attorney General's National Civil Rights Award; the National Conference of Christians and Jews' National Human Relations Award; the NAACP Legal Defense Fund's Judge William H. Hastie Award; and the World Peace through Law Award as the World's Greatest Lawyer.

Segal wrote *Pennsylvania Banking and Building and Loan Law* (1935).

SEGAL, ERICH (1937–), U.S. novelist. Born in Brooklyn, N.Y., the son of a rabbi, Erich Wolf Segal attended Harvard University, graduating as both the class poet and Latin salutatorian. He also obtained his master's and doctorate from Harvard. While a professor of comparative literature at Yale University in 1967, Segal wrote the screenplay for the Beatles' wildly successful animated feature film *Yellow Submarine*. He collaborated on other screenplays and tried to sell a romantic story he wrote about two students attending Harvard. It failed to sell, but his literary agent suggested he turn the script into a novel. The result was a literary and motion picture phenomenon, *Love Story* (1970), starring Ali McGraw and Ryan O'Neal. It tells the story of two college students: Oliver, the emotionally vacant son of rich parents, and the Italian-American Radcliffe girl he falls in love with, Jenny. The film is considered one of the most romantic of all time. Its catchphrase is "Love means never having to say you're sorry." Another famous quote is "What can you say about a 25-year-old girl who died? That she was beautiful and brilliant. That she loved Mozart and Bach. The Beatles. And me." The book was the leading seller of fiction for 1970 in the United States and was translated into more than 20 languages. The movie of the same name was the No. 1 box-office attraction of 1971 and won Academy Award nominations for best picture, best actor, actress, supporting actor, director, and original screenplay, by Segal. Ironically, its success virtually destroyed Segal's academic credibility with his colleagues. Segal went on to write more novels and screenplays, including a sequel to *Love Story*, called *Oliver's Story* (1977). He also published a number of scholarly works and taught at the college level. His books include *The Comedy of Plautus* (1968), *Doctors* (1988), *The Death of Comedy* (2001), and *Oxford Readings in Greek Tragedy* (2001).

[Stewart Kampel (2nd ed.)]

SEGAL, ESTHER (1895–1974). Yiddish poet; sister of J.I. *Segal. Segal was born in Solobkovits (now Solobkovtsy), Ukraine. Her father, a cantor, died when she was young. In 1910 the family emigrated to Canada to join her mother's siblings. Segal attended a religious school in Montreal, then worked in a factory while studying in the evening. She later attended the Jewish Teachers Seminary in New York. She married poet A. Sh. Shkolnikov.

Segal wrote from a young age, but did not publish any work until 1922, when her work appeared in the collection *Epokhe*, edited by her husband, her brother, and A. Almi. Following this debut her work appeared in many literary journals in Canada, the United States, Lithuania, and Poland. In 1928 her only book, *Lider*, was published by a Toronto branch of the Labor-Zionist Yidish-Natsyonaler Farband. She continued to write poetry for journal publication, including lyrics, children's poems, and poems on topics of social concern. Her husband died in 1962, and in 1965 she moved to a kibbutz in Israel, where she lived until her death.

BIBLIOGRAPHY: *LNYL*, 396; *100 Yor Yidishe un Hebreishe Literatur in Kanade*, 180.

[Faith Jones (2nd ed.)]

SEGAL, GEDALIAH BEN ELIEZER (18th century), preacher. He lived in Boskowitz (Boskowice), where his father, Eliezer, was the rabbi, and studied under Phineas of Boskowitz. Gedaliah wrote the ethical work *Ammudei Gavra* (Bruenn, 1756), based upon the statement in the Mishnah (Avot 1:2) that the world is based upon three things: Torah, divine service, and the practice of charity. Segal discusses the various types of charity – visiting the sick, hospitality to wayfarers, support of scholars, etc. The chapter *Ma'aser Ani* ("Poor Man's Tithe") deals with the laws of **terumot and ma'aserot*, making abundant use of talmudic, midrashic, and halakhic sources. The author, influenced by kabbalistic literature, borrows its terminology and quotes from the *Zohar. *Ammudei Gavra* contains three other works on halakhic themes: a work by David Skutsh, a relative of Gedaliah; the novellae of Gedaliah's son, Eliezer, who died aged 18; and the novellae of Abraham Katz Gibitsh, who also died young.

SEGAL, GEORGE (1924–2000), U.S. sculptor and painter. Best known for his stark, plaster sculptural figures placed in real environments, Segal was born in the Bronx to immigrant parents from Eastern Europe. He studied at various schools, including Cooper Union (1941–42); Rutgers University (1942–46; 1961–63); and New York University (1948–49), where Larry *Rivers was a classmate. Initially Segal painted the human form in a gestural, colorful fashion influenced by Abstract Expressionism, but by 1958 he discovered that sculpture was a more effective way for him to convey his interest in the psychology of the figure. Early experimentations were made from burlap, wire, and plaster and executed in a rough, expressive manner akin to his painterly work, but beginning in the summer of 1961 Segal was casting live models from medical bandages saturated with plaster to capture pose and mood. *Butcher Shop* (1965, Art Gallery of Ontario, Toronto), an homage to his father – a kosher butcher in the Bronx during the Great Depression who died six months before the conception of the piece – presents a plaster cast of Segal's mother slaughtering a plaster chicken behind a glass window labeled "Kosher Butcher" in Hebrew. Her impressionist rendering betrays the artist's touch, a technique especially vivid in work completed before 1971 when Segal kept his casts hollow. Indeed, in 1971 Segal began to reproduce negatives of the interior of casts rather than piecing together molds of his models' bodies, thereby creating more lifelike, smoothly rendered, and detailed sculptures.

Segal executed many public commissions, notably *In Memory of May 4, 1970: Kent State – Abraham and Isaac* (1978), cast in bronze as an allegory in commemoration of the four students killed by National Guardsmen at Kent State University when they were protesting the Vietnam War. After the controversial sculpture was rejected by Kent State it was subsequently erected at Princeton University in November 1978. *The Holocaust* (1983), commissioned by the city of San Francisco, overlooks Lincoln Park. The memorial shows several corpses lying on the ground with a lone living figure standing behind a barbed wire fence. The plaster model of the tableau is on display at New York's Jewish Museum.

BIBLIOGRAPHY: M. Friedman and G.W.J. Beal, *George Segal: Sculptures* (1978); J. van der Marck, *George Segal* (1979); P. Tuchman, *George Segal* (1983); S. Hunter and D. Hawthorne, *George Segal* (1989).

[Samantha Baskind (2nd ed.)]

SEGAL, GEORGE (1934–), U.S. actor. Born in New York, Segal graduated from Columbia University in 1955. He began his career on the off-Broadway stage. He moved on to television and Broadway, appearing in the plays *Gideon* (1961); *Rattle of a Simple Man* (1963); and *Art* (1998).

He made his film debut in 1961 in *The Young Doctors*. Segal's stardom was assured with two performances in successive films, *King Rat* (1965) and *Who's Afraid of Virginia Woolf?* (1966), the latter winning him an Oscar nomination for Best Supporting Actor. Segal has starred in more than 50 motion pictures, including *The Quiller Memorandum* (1966); *The St. Valentine's Day Massacre* (1967); *Bye Bye Braverman* (1968); *No Way to Treat a Lady* (1968); *Loving* (1970); *Where's Poppa?* (1970); *The Owl and the Pussycat* (1970); *Born to Win* (1971); *The Hot Rock* (1972); *A Touch of Class* (1973); *Blume in Love* (1973); *California Split* (1974); *The Black Bird* (1975); *Fun with Dick and Jane* (1977); *The Last Married Couple in America* (1980); *Look Who's Talking* (1989); *For the Boys* (1991); *Me, Myself and I* (1992); *Flirting with Disaster* (1996); *The Cable Guy* (1996); and *The Mirror Has Two Faces* (1996).

In addition to his roles in dozens of TV movies, Segal starred in the TV crime series *Murphy's Law* (1988–89) and the sitcom *Just Shoot Me* (1997–2003).

[Jonathan Licht / Ruth Beloff (2nd ed.)]

SEGAL, HUGH (1951–), Canadian author, political strategist, educator, and pundit. Segal was born in Montreal into a family of modest means. He attended Jewish parochial school but, unusual in the heavily Liberal Party-supporting English-speaking Jewish community of Montreal, Segal was early drawn to the Conservative Party of John Diefenbaker. In 1962, when Segal only 13, Diefenbaker, then Conservative prime minister, visited Segal's school and so impressed Segal that he campaigned on behalf of his local Conservative Party candidate in the 1962 federal election. The Conservative candidate lost the seat but Segal was hooked on politics and went on to become an influential Conservative Party insider.

In 1972 Segal graduated in history from the University of Ottawa, where, very active in the Young Conservatives, he was elected student union president. Also in 1972 and again in 1974 Segal unsuccessfully sought election in Ottawa for a seat in the House of Commons. While never elected to public office, as a high-profile Red Tory, fiscally conservative but socially liberal, Segal served on the staff of Robert Stanfield, leader of the Opposition, was a senior aide to Ontario premier William Davis, and a close advisor and, for a time, chief of staff to Prime Minister Brian Mulroney. In 1998 he ran unsuccessfully against Joe Clark to lead the Conservative Party of Canada. More recently, Segal unsuccessfully warned against the merger of the federal Conservative Party with the more socially conservative Alliance Party.

From 1999 Segal was president of the Institute on Research on Public Policy and taught in the School of Policy Studies at Queen's University in Kingston, Ontario. He was also a director of various public companies and active in a number of charitable, educational, and community organizations. He was often called upon by the media to comment on Canadian political issues. In 2003 he was honored with the Order of Canada. He wrote *No Surrender: Reflections of a Happy Warrior in the Tory Crusade* (1996) and *In Defence of Civility: Reflections of a Recovering Politician* (2000).

[Harold Troper (2nd ed.)]

SEGAL, JACOB ISAAC (**Yankev Yitshok**; 1896–1954), Yiddish poet. Segal was born in Solobkovtsy, Ukraine, the second youngest of seven children. For most of his childhood Segal lived in Korets, Ukraine, one of the original centers of Ḥasidism and a place idealized in many of his poems. He received a basic religious education in *ḥeder* and *talmud torah*. In 1911, when he was 15, he immigrated to Canada and settled in Montreal, near his sister Esther Segal, later a Yiddish poet in her own right. For a number of years he worked as a tailor in the garment industry and then taught at the Montreal Folks Shule, one of the first Yiddish-language day schools in Canada. Encouraged by Moshe Shmuelson, editor of the Yiddish daily the *Keneder Odler* ("Canadian Eagle"), he began to publish Yiddish poetry in 1915. His first volume of verse, *Fun Mayn Velt* ("From My World"), appeared in 1918. He was immediately recognized by Yiddish literary critics as a gifted poet, notable for strong feeling and natural, idiomatic diction.

Segal assumed a leadership role in the development of Yiddish culture in Canada. He helped to establish a number of journals: *Nyuansn* ("Nuances," 1921), *Epokhe* ("Epoch," 1922), and *Royerd* ("Untilled Soil," 1922–23) and as editor held them to a high literary standard. In 1923, after a short sojourn in Toronto, he and his wife and daughter moved to New York. There he enjoyed the companionship of the new generation of Yiddish poets: *Mani-Leib, Zisha *Landau, M.L. *Halpern, and Jacob *Glatstein. Segal returned to Montreal in 1928 after the death of his young daughter, Tsharnele, whom he often addresses in later poems.

Thereafter Segal continued to teach in Yiddish schools and to write and edit for the *Keneder Odler*. As an essayist, he wrote regularly on literary topics and on educational and cultural issues. From 1941 until his death he was coeditor of the literary pages along with Melech *Ravitch. In addition, he contributed to nearly all the Yiddish literary journals of his day and served as president of the Canadian Yiddish Writers Union. Segal was a prolific poet and the author of 12 volumes of poetry, among them, *Sefer Idish* ("The Book of Yiddish," 1950), the last collection published in his lifetime, and *Letste Lider* ("Last Poems," 1955), published posthumously.

Many of Segal's poems move from the pain and emptiness of the present to an idealized past, embodied in the ḥasidic masters and in shtetl figures. Segal also wrote on entirely different themes, with a different tone and emotional impact. He wrote poems of carefully observed cityscape and season and inward-looking poems, examining his moral worth and his purpose as a poet. He also wrote many times about Yiddish, the instrument and common bond of the culture he attempted to preserve.

Segal's diction is most often simple, but the flow of thought in his poems is complex. He continually plays with meaning, as in the use of religious terms in contexts that have to do with the Yiddish language or his role as a poet. His verse is musically sophisticated. He moves easily from the speaking to the singing voice and uses countable meter as a framework for more open poetic rhythms.

Some of Segal's work has been translated, in: I. Howe and E. Greenberg, *Treasury of Yiddish Poetry* (1969); I. Howe, R. Wisse, and K. Shmeruk, *The Penguin Book of Modern Yiddish Verse* (1987); A. Boyarsky and L. Sarna, *Canadian Yiddish Writings* (1976); and P. Anctil's translation of J. Segal, *Poèmes Yiddish* (Montréal, 1992).

After his death, the annual J.I. Segal Award for Yiddish Literature was established in his honor in Montreal.

BIBLIOGRAPHY: LNYL, 4 (1965), 397–403; J. Glatstein, *In Tokh Genumen* (1956), 183–97; A. Fuerstenberg, in: *Yiddish*, 4, no.3 (1981), 63–76; S. Friedman, in: *An Everyday Miracle* (1990), 115–28; H.M. Caiserman-Vital, *Yidishe Dikhter in Kanade* (1934), 9–10, 27–49.

[Seymour Levitan (2nd ed.)]

SEGAL, LOUIS (1894–1964), U.S. labor Zionist leader. Segal, who was born in Lowicz, Poland, and was taken to the United States in 1905, lived in Galveston, Texas, and then in St. Paul, Minnesota. While in his teens, he worked in a cap factory and helped found a Hat, Cap, and Millinery Union local in the city, rising to a vice presidency in that union. At the age of 32, he became general secretary of the Jewish National Workers Alliance (*Farband), which then had about 5,500 members. Under his lifelong leadership it grew to more than 40,000 members, expanding considerably its fraternal benefits. Segal also served on the executives of the World Zionist Organization and the Jewish Agency for Israel.

Some of his Yiddish writings are collected in *Apshetsungen vegn Khaver L. Segal in a Tsol Artiklen fun Khoson Yovel tsu der Gelegenheyt fun Finf un Tsvontsik Yor Fayershaft* (1951; "L. Segal, Review and Articles: Jubilee Volume on the Occasion of Twenty-five Years of Leadership").

SEGAL, MOSES HIRSCH (**Zevi**; 1876–1968), Bible scholar. Segal was born in Lithuania and educated at rabbinical academies and at London and Oxford universities, serving at the latter as tutor in biblical and Semitic studies (1906–09). He served congregations in Newcastle, Swansea, and Bristol. In 1926 he became lecturer in Bible and Semitic languages at the Hebrew University of Jerusalem (full professor: 1939). Segal was an expert in the Hebrew language, and his grammatical lexical studies, *A Grammar of Mishnaic Hebrew* (1927; Heb. ed., *Dikduk Leshon ha-Mishnah*, 1935) and his work on the principles of Hebrew phonetics (*Yesodei ha-Fonetikah ha-Ivrit*, 1928), have remained widely used. He also edited two volumes of E. Ben-Yehuda's *Millon ha-Lashon ha-Ivrit* (vol. 8 (1928); vol. 9 (1929)).

In his writings on the Pentateuch, Segal casts doubt on the validity of the Documentary Theory (see *Pentateuch). His explanation is essentially a modification of the traditional doctrine of Mosaic authorship. In a series of articles elaborated in his last published book, *The Pentateuch, its Composition and its Authorship...* (1967), he maintained that the post-Mosaic sections of the Torah were erroneously associated with Moses by later generations, just as numerous additions to the Oral Law are incorrectly attributed to Moses. The result of his biblical scholarship, reflected throughout his introduction to the Bible (*Mevo ha-Mikra*, 4 vols., 1946–50, 1967^7), is the reaffirmation of the Bible's literary and artistic excellence. His other works include critical studies on the Damascus Covenant and Ben Sira as well as many articles on various books of the Bible and medieval Jewish exegetes. He was awarded the Israel Prize for Jewish Studies in 1954.

His son, SAMUEL, LORD SEGAL (1902–1985), physician and politician, was a Labor member of parliament (1945–50), and was made a life peer in 1964. Another son, JUDAH BEN-ZION SEGAL (1912–2003), was professor of Semitic languages at the School of Oriental Studies, London University.

BIBLIOGRAPHY: J.M. Grintz and J. Liver (ed.), *Sefer M.Z. Segal* (1964), incl. a complete bibliography until 1964; M. Haran, in: *Molad*, 3 (1970), 97–106.

[Zev Garber]

SEGAL, SAMUEL, BARON (1902–1985), British politician and physician. Segal, the son of Prof. M.H. *Segal, was born in London. He qualified as a physician and served from 1939 to 1945 in the Royal Air Force medical service with the rank of squadron leader and subsequently (1951–62) as a regional medical officer of the Ministry of Health. After unsuccessfully contesting parliamentary elections for the Labour Party before World War II, he was elected Labour member of Parliament for Preston in 1945 and served in Parliament till 1950.

In 1964 he was created a life peer and took an active part in discussions in the House of Lords, serving on many parliamentary delegations, and becoming in 1973 a deputy speaker and deputy chairman of committees of the House of Lords (of which the Lord Chancellor is ex officio Speaker). His services to Anglo-Israeli relations were many and varied, including chairmanship of the Anglo-Israel Association and presidency of the Anglo-Israel Archaeological Association. With a home near Oxford, he was identified with the preservation of Oxford's amenities, received the honor of Honorary Fellowship of Jesus College, Oxford, and served as honorary president of the Oxford Jewish congregation. His medical interests were reflected in his chairmanship of the National Society for Mentally Handicapped Children and of the British Association for the Retarded. Though an active politician, his scholarly and courteous approach gained him a reputation as a statesmanlike expert of Middle Eastern and medical subjects.

BIBLIOGRAPHY: Who's Who (1978); *Jewish Year Book*.

[Vivian David Lipman]

SEGAL, URI (1944–), Israeli conductor. Born in *Jerusalem, Segal studied the violin and conducted at the Rubin Conservatory in Jerusalem, and then conducting at the Guildhall School of Music in London (1966–69). In 1969, he won first prize in the Dimitri Mitropoulos Conducting Competition in New York, which resulted in his becoming an assistant conductor to *Bernstein with the New York Philharmonic Orchestra. From 1970 he began touring in Europe and America, conducting many of the great orchestras such as the BBC Welsh Orchestra in Cardiff, the English Chamber Orchestra (1971), and the Chicago SO (1972). In 1973 he was appointed as a regular guest conductor with the South German Radio Orchestra in Stuttgart. He was musical director and principal conductor of the Philharmonica Hungarica in Germany (1981–85) and principal conductor of the Bournemouth Symphony Orchestra (1980–83). In 1982 he was appointed principal conductor of the Israel Chamber Orchestra and in 1989 principal conductor of the Osaka Orchestra, Japan. Among his recordings are works by Stravinsky, piano concertos by Mozart and Beethoven, and oboe concertos by Françaix, Honegger, and Ibert.

BIBLIOGRAPHY: Grove online, s.v.

[Israel Stein (2nd ed.)]

SEGALL, LASAR (1891–1957), Brazilian painter and sculptor. Born in Vilna, Lithuania, to a religious family, Segall studied at the Design Academy of Vilna in 1905 and moved the next year to Berlin, where he studied at the Imperial Superior Academy of Arts until 1910. Segall rebelled against the strict academic discipline and presented his works in an exposition of the "Freie Sezession," one of the precursor movements of expressionism. In 1910 he moved to Dresden, where he joined the Fine Arts Academy as Meisterschueller (student-instructor) with his own atelier and freedom of creation. After being accepted in the German Expressionist movement at the end of 1912, he traveled for the first time to Brazil, and his exhibitions in Campinas and São Paulo were among the first presentations of modern art in Brazil. After eight months he returned to Dresden. In 1919 Segall participated in the foundation of the "Dresdner Sezession, Grupe 1919," and in the next four years he participated in the German Expressionist movement, presenting exhibitions in The Hague, Frankfurt, and Leipzig and publishing two albums: *Bubu* (1921) and *Remembrance from Vilna* (1922).

In 1923 Segall settled in Brazil. He joined the modernist group and held his first exhibition in São Paulo. Afterwards he exhibited the first works of his Brazilian stage in Berlin and

Dresden. In 1927 Segall adopted Brazilian citizenship and in 1928 traveled to Paris for three years, where he began to sculpt. Back in Saõ Paulo (1932) he founded and led the Society for Modern Art. In 1938 he represented Brazil in the International Congress of Independent Artists in Paris. In this period he started to work with socio-political themes and produced a collection related to the experience of immigrants and the war. In the 1940s and the 1950s he presented his works in exhibitions in Brazil and the United States.

The Jewish perspective is present in some of Segall's works. In a number of paintings he included Hebrew letters and he signed a few in Hebrew. Other paintings were focused directly on Jewish themes: *Rabino con alunos* ("Rabbi with Students" – 1931), *Rolo de Tora* ("Torah Scroll" – 1922 and 1933), *Pogrom* (1937), *Navio de Emigrantes* ("Emigrants' Ship" –1939/1941), *Campo de Concentração* ("Concentration Camp" – 1945), *Êxodo* ("Exodus" – 1947), and others that were part of the collection *Visões de Guerra 1940–1943* ("Visions from War 1940–1943").

BIBLIOGRAPHY: *O Museu Lasar Segall* (1991).

[Efraim Zadoff (2nd ed.)]

SEGALOWITCH, ZUSMAN (1884–1949), Yiddish poet, novelist, and journalist. Born in Bialystok, Segalowitch was educated privately, worked in a factory, organized labor strikes, and was frequently arrested. In 1903 Segalowitch published his first poem in Russian, but a year later turned to Yiddish as his language of expression. In his first collection of lyrics, *Shtile Troymen* ("Quiet Dreams," 1909), his strong romantic penchant is clearly revealed, but it was "In Kazmerzh" (1912), a poem in which he describes a village where young men dreamed of freedom in a stifling traditional environment, that brought him early fame. The first poetic product of Segalowitch's Warsaw period was a cycle of love poems, *Tsaytike Troybn* ("Ripe Grapes," 1920); these were followed by popular ballads and sentimental poems. In the poetic drama *Di Vant* ("The Wall," 1915), Segalowitch combined militancy with sentimentalism and advocated Jewish resistance to wrongs inflicted upon them. His novels *Di Vilde Tsilke* ("Wild Tsilke," 1922); *Romantishe Yorn* ("Romantic Years," 1923), an autobiographical trilogy, and *Di Brider Nemzar* ("The Nemzar Brothers," 1929), were very popular and were translated into Polish. In Warsaw Segalowitch wrote lyrics that were put to music and sentimental stories for the dailies *Haynt* and *Moment*. He also presided over the Association of Yiddish Writers and Journalists. In his memoirs, *Tlomatske 13* (1946), he gave a moving though somewhat idealized account of the association, which served as a center of Yiddish culture between the world wars. The Holocaust and its aftermath radically altered every aspect of Segalowitch's writing. During the Nazi invasion of 1939 he escaped from Poland one step ahead of the Nazis, the terror and horror of which he vividly described in *Gebrente Trit* ("Burnt Steps," 1947). *Dortn* ("There," 1946), is a heartrending elegy which he dedicated to Samuel *Zygelbojm, the Bundist leader who committed suicide in London in 1943 to awaken the world's conscience to Jewish suffering. He wrote it upon his arrival in Tel Aviv, where visions of the less fortunate Jews trapped in Europe pursued him relentlessly. The poetic style of his works during this period became one of bitter accusation. In this final period of creativity, Segalowitch eulogized the devastated Polish-Jewish culture and his own destroyed generation.

BIBLIOGRAPHY: Rejzen, Leksikon, 2 (1967), 667–73; LNYL, 6 (1965), 481–9; *Segalovitsh-Bukh* (1933); M. Ravitch, *Mayn Leksikon* (1945), 150–2; J. Glatstein, *In Tokh Genumen*, 1 (1947), 9–17; 2 (1956), 128–35; L. Finkelstein, *Loshn Yidish un Yidisher Kiyem* (1954), 255–66; H. Leivick, *Eseyen un Redes* (1963), 254–7; S. Liptzin, *Maturing of Yiddish Literature* (1970), 175–80.

[Sol Liptzin]

SEGHERS, ANNA (pseudonym of **Netty Radvanyi**, née **Reiling**; 1900–1983), German novelist. Born in Mainz, she joined the German Communist Party in 1929. In 1933 she fled to Paris and visited Republican Madrid during the Spanish Civil War. In 1941 she moved to Mexico City, but in 1947 returned to Germany, settling in East Berlin. The novels of Anna Seghers combine a highly poetic form with a strong socialist element, describing the living conditions of the lower classes in many countries – fisherman, peasants, and miners. A convinced Communist and an outspoken anti-Fascist, she was active in the fight against Nazism. Her prizewinning first novel, *Der Aufstand der Fischer von Santa Barbara* (1928), was followed by *Die Gefaehrten* (1932); *Der Weg dutch den Februar* (1935), which deals with the uprising of the Viennese workers in 1934; and *Die Rettung* (1937). *Das siebte Kreuz* (1941), written in her Mexican exile, which became a best seller in America as *The Seventh Cross* (1942), was an expression of her faith in the innate decency of human beings. Other works by Anna Seghers were *Transit* (1941; Eng. trans. *Transit Visa*, 1945); *Die Toten bleiben jung* (1949); and *Die Entscheidung* (1959), hailed in East Germany as a masterpiece of Socialist Realism. She received many awards after World War II, including the International Lenin Peace Prize of the U.S.S.R. (1951). Her later works include *Ueber Tolstoi-Ueber Dostojewski* (1963); *Die Kraft der Schwachen* (1965); *Das wirkliche Blau* (1967), and *Das Vertrauen* (1968).

BIBLIOGRAPHY: R.C. Andrews, in: *German Life and Letters*, 8 (1954/55), 121–9; F. Lennartz, *Deutsche Dichter und Schriftsteller unserer Zeit* (1959[8]), 713–6; *Anna Seghers, Briefe ihrer Freunde* (1960).

[Rudolf Kayser]

SEGORBE, city in Valencia, E. *Spain. It appears that many Jews settled in Segorbe after the Christian conquest. In 1270 the taxes of the city were leased by Astruc Jacob Sisson, and in 1274 the community was combined with *Murviedro and Onda *Burriana to form a single district (*collecta*), paying 2,000 solidós in taxes. Several extant details on the community are known from the second half of the 14th century. The financial situation of the community during this period is reflected in a query (Responsum, 282) addressed to R. Isaac b.

Sheshet *Perfet (Ribash). The responsum indicates that the community borrowed money from Muslims in order to redeem a *Sefer Torah* crown which had previously been pledged. Some community leaders did not agree to stand surety for the debt, and the community therefore took it upon itself, under the strength of a ban, to repay the debt within one year. A number of members who had not been present at the proclamation of the ban demanded that it be abrogated because of debts already owed by the community for taxes to the crown. The ban was lifted and R. Isaac b. Sheshet ratified its abrogation. Although it is clear that the community of Segorbe was affected by the persecutions of 1391, the degree to which the community suffered is not known. In 1393 Juan I acquitted Jacob Hassan of Murviedro and his wife of having committed several "offenses," including the accusation that Jacob had given unleavened bread to a *Converso of Segorbe. There is no information on the community during the 15th century, and it is possible that none existed. At some unspecified time the small number of Jews living in Segorbe moved to neighboring Murviedro.

BIBLIOGRAPHY: Baer, Spain, 1 (1929), index; Neuman, Spain, 2 (1944), 233.

[Haim Beinart]

SEGOVIA, town in Old Castile, central Spain. The community of Segovia was one of the most important in Castile, and several of the nearby communities were under its jurisdiction. The Jewish quarter was located in the center of the town, on land belonging to the cathedral. The Jewish cemetery was at the place now called Cuesta de los Hoyos. There were many synagogues in Segovia, the biggest of which was confiscated in 1420. It was built in the Mudéjar style, like the Santa María la Blanca synagogue of *Toledo, and was probably erected at the same time (13th century). In 1572 the building became the property of the Franciscan nuns. It caught fire in 1899.

The community of Segovia achieved prosperity in the 13th century, together with other communities in Castile. The earliest sources on the Jews in Segovia are from this century. At the end of this century there were around 300 Jews in Segovia. It was an important center of Kabbalah.

The community was beset by difficulties in the war between Pedro the Cruel and Henry of Trastamara in 1366–69. In the introduction to his *Mekor Ḥayyim*, R. Samuel ibn Seneh *Zarza describes the plight of many communities in Castile. In Segovia itself the Jews were attacked and robbed of the securities and promissory bills which they had in their possession, and King Henry canceled the debts owed by Christians to Jews. In about 1390 there were about 50 Jewish homeowners in Segovia. There were 23 craftsmen in the community, among them weavers, saddlers, tailors, furriers, smiths, potters, and painters, as well as a few merchants, a physician, and a bullfighter. A center for the study of the *Kabbalah was founded in Segovia, which was the reputed burial place of the kabbalist Jacob Gikatilla.

When persecutions broke out in 1391, the king was in the town and from there he issued instructions to deal with the rioters in different cities. In Segovia itself, however, the authorities were unable to protect the Jews, and, as elsewhere, some of them converted to Christianity. The community subsequently recovered, though it never attained its former prosperity. In 1409 John II complied with the *kahal's* request and exempted it from the current *alcabala* tax on meat and wine. In 1412 he granted to the convent of Santa María de la Merced in Segovia the right to lease a synagogue with all its accessories. This was a compensation for lands taken from the convent, on which Jews had been settled due to the segregation enforced between Jews and recent *Conversos. In 1415 the Jews of Segovia were accused of a *Host desecration. According to Alfonso de Espina's work, *Fortalitium Fidei*, Don Meir *Alguades himself was involved, but the author's authority in this matter is unreliable. The community declined from the late 1430s. In the 1480s Segovia became a center of anti-Jewish and anti-Converso activity, inspired by Tomas de *Torquemada. In 1485 Abraham *Seneor – who had been made *alguacil* (an executive officer) of the community's tribunal for life, lodged a complaint with the court against Antonio de la Peña, who incited the masses to violent anti-Jewish feelings. Seneor also acted against the town's *alcalde*, who had vetoed the baking of unleavened bread, and against the apostate José Talavera, who informed against the community and was finally imprisoned. Anti-Jewish activity came to a head at the close of the 1480s, when the inquisitor Fernando de Santo Domingo appeared in Segovia. He wrote an introduction to a book published there against the Talmud. Another book on Jewish customs was published in Segovia at that time by Antonio de Avila, the "specialist" on Jewish affairs in the La *Guardia trial. The town council continued to restrict the Jews of Segovia in acquiring food and shelter, as in other cities of Castile. At the same time the community grew in size, due to the arrival of Jews expelled from Andalusia. Among the wealthy Jews of Segovia several were active as tax farmers, in and outside the town, during the decade of 1480–90, among them R. Meir *Melamed, son-in-law to Abraham Seneor, Don Isaac b. Joseph *Caro, and others. In 1488 two anti-Jewish polemical works were written in Segovia: *Libro de Alborayque* and *Censura contra el Talmud*. The decree of expulsion from Spain was issued in May 1492. Abraham Seneor and Isaac *Abrabanel arranged for Jewish property in Segovia to be sold to the Conversos who remained there. At that time the community of Segovia was the most important one in Castile. The exiles from Segovia probably left for Portugal; with them went the last rabbi of the town, Simeon *Maimi, who died a martyr in Portugal in 1498.

The Jewish quarter has been very well described by J.A. Ruiz Hernando. Until 1412 the Jews lived in the area of San Andrés, where they had two synagogues, and in San Miguel, where they had their Sinagoga Mayor, today the Corpus Cristi. From 1481, the Jewish quarter was enclosed. The Jewish quarter began in Corpus Cristi and continued through the *Judeía vieja* and in the streets beyond as far as the Gate of San Andrés. Until the beginning of the 15th century there were three synagogues in Segovia: Mayor, Vieja or Menor, and the sinagoga de los Burgos. At the time of the expulsion there were two other synagogues: the new Mayor (after the confiscation of the first, turned into Corpus Cristi) and the sinagoga del Campo. The new sinagoga Mayor, in the calle Barrionuevo, is today a girls' school which is run by the Jesuit monastery. Part of the Ark has been discovered. Abraham Seneor had a *bet midrash* in his house.

BIBLIOGRAPHY: Baer, Spain, index; F. Fita, in: *Boletin de la Real Academía de la Historia*, 9 (1886), 344–89; I. Loeb, in: REJ, 14 (1887), 254–62; A. Marx, *Studies in Jewish History and Booklore* (1944), 85, 91; A. Rodríguez Moñino, in: *Analecta Sacra Tarraconensia*, 18 (1945), 111–87; F. Cantera y Burgos, *Sinagogas españolas* (1955), 285–90; idem, in: *Sefarad*, 4 (1944), 305; Suárez Fernández, Documentos, index. **ADD. BIBLIOGRAPHY:** J.A. Ruiz Hernando, *El barrio de la aljama hebrea de la ciudad de Segovia* (1980); idem, *Historia del urbanismo en la ciudad de Segovia del siglo XII al XIX* (1982), 2 vols.; E. Gutwirth, in: *Proceedings of the 6th World Congress of Jewish Studies* (1982), vol. 2, 49–53; idem, in: Y. Kaplan (ed.), *Jews and Conversos; Studies in Society and the Inquisition* (1985), 83–102.

[Haim Beinart / Yom Tov Assis (2nd ed.)]

SEGRE (Segrè), family in northern Italy, possibly of Spanish origin. The following are among its most important members: JUDAH (14–15th centuries), author of *tosafot* on *Ḥullin* and *Eruvin*; his son NETHANEL (d. 1535), a scholar who lived in Lodi; JACOB BEN ISAAC (c. 1629), rabbi of Casale Monferrato, poet and liturgist, author of a *seliḥah* on the siege of Casale in 1629; ABRAHAM BEN ZERAH (d. 1641), *dayyan* in Alessandria; NETHANEL BEN AARON JACOB (d. 1691), born in Chieri, later of *Cento. A collection of his responsa, entitled *Ezer Ya'akov*, is extant in manuscript. ABRAHAM BEN JUDAH (17th–18th centuries), rabbi, poet, and book collector in Casale Monferrato; ḤAYYIM (17th century), lived in Padua. He was considered a supporter of *Shabbetai Ẓevi and was one of the three delegates sent from Italy to the East in 1666 to study the Shabbatean movement. His work *Binyan Av* on the regulations for blowing the *shofar* is unpublished. His son ELISHA lived in Vercelli and was the father of Joshua Benzion *Segrè (c. 1705–1797). BENJAMIN, grandson of Ḥayyim (18th–19th centuries), a scholar in Vercelli, was the father of Salvatore *Segre (1729–1809). ABRAHAM BEN JUDAH (d. 1772) was born in Turin. At the age of 25 he emigrated to Safed and later lived in Jerusalem. He studied under Israel Ashkenazi and wrote commentaries on the Mishnah and on Maimonides' *Mishneh Torah*, responsa, and sermons. Several times he traveled abroad as a rabbinical emissary. Other noted members of the family were Corrado *Segrè (1863–1924), mathematician; Gino *Segrè (1864–1942), jurist; Roberto *Segrè (1872–1936), general; Arturo *Segrè (1873–1928), historian, and Emilio Gino *Segrè (1905–1989), Italian-American nuclear physicist.

BIBLIOGRAPHY: Mortara, Indice, s.v.; S.D. Luzzatto, *Autobiografia* (1882), 48–50; Yaari, Sheluḥei, index; G. Bedarida, *Ebrei d'Italia* (1950), index.

[Elia Samuele Artom]

SEGRÈ, ARTURO (1873–1928), Italian historian. Segrè was professor of history in the Liceo d'Azeglio of Turin and also lecturer in the university. He specialized in the history of Piedmont and the House of Savoy, particularly in the 16th and 19th centuries. A founder of the series *Collana Storica Sabauda*, he contributed two biographies to it – *Vittorio Emanuele I* (1928) and *Emanuele Filiberto* (1928) – published posthumously. Among his other writings was *Storia del commercio* (2 vols.; 1923). He was also editor of *I diarii di Girolamo Priuli* (1912), one of the most important sources for the history of Venice, for the new edition of Muratori's *Rerum Italicarum Scriptores*.

[Donald Weinstein]

SEGRE, BENIAMINO (1903–1977), Italian mathematician. Segre was professor of mathematics at Bologna University until he was dismissed in 1938 under the Fascist anti-Jewish laws. He was then invited to England by the Society for the Protection of Science and Learning and spent the years until 1946 at the Universities of London, Cambridge, and Manchester. He returned to his chair at Bologna in 1946 and moved to Rome in 1950. He was elected president of the Accademia Nazionale dei Lincei in 1968. Segre made important contributions to geometry. His books include *Non-singular Cubic Surfaces* (1942) and *Arithmetical Questions on Algebraic Varieties* (1951).

SEGRÈ, CORRADO (1863–1924), Italian mathematician. Segrè was appointed professor of geometry at Turin in 1888. He was awarded the mathematical prize of the University of Turin in 1883 and shared the Royal Prize of the Accademia Nazionale dei Lincei with Volterra in 1898. Segrè's main work was in the projective geometry of higher dimensions and in projective differential geometry. He contributed the definitive article "Mehrdimensionale Raeume" to the *Encyklopaedie der mathematischen Wissenschaften* (vol. 3 (1912), 769–972).

BIBLIOGRAPHY: Baker, in: *London Mathematical Society Journal*, 1 (1926), 263; Loria, in: *Annali di matematica pura ed applicata*, 2 (1924–25).

[Barry Spain]

SEGRÈ, EMILIO GINO (1905–1989), nuclear physicist and Nobel Prize laureate. Segrè, who was born in Tivoli, Italy, studied at Rome University, where he later assisted Enrico Fermi in research on the use of neutrons as missiles to break up the uranium atom. He conceived the idea that an element having the atomic number 43, which theory had shown must exist, might be produced by neutron bombardment. The discovery of this element had been reported ten years earlier, but not confirmed. During a visit which he paid to the University of California in 1937, Segrè was given a sample of molybdenum (the element with atomic number 42) which had undergone a process shown by J.R. *Oppenheimer to be the equivalent of neutron bombardment. Segrè analyzed this sample when he returned to Italy. He traced what had become of the radioactivity it had already lost and thereby located small quantities of element 43, which he called "technetium." In 1938, when racial legislation was introduced in Italy, Segrè emigrated to the U.S. His work at the University of California led to the synthesis of astatine, another hitherto undiscovered element. After World War II, he participated in the search for an elementary particle known as the "antiproton," whose existence and nature were inferred from very advanced reasoning. In 1955 the team of Segrè and Owen Chamberlain reported on the formation of the antiproton. For this achievement, they shared the Nobel Prize for physics four years later (1959). The antiproton discovery was followed by studies of its properties and interactions, as well as those of the antineutron. He retired in 1972, but remained active, with traveling and writing taking up much of his time.

In the immediate postwar years Segrè edited an influential three-volume handbook on experimental nuclear physics. He served as chairman of the editorial board overseeing the publication of the collected papers of Enrico Fermi. In 1964 he authored a text on nuclei and particles and in 1970 a biography of Fermi. His lectures on the history of physics were made into two accessible books. His autobiography appeared posthumously in 1993. He also served for 20 years (1958–77) as editor of the *Annual Review of Nuclear Science.*

BIBLIOGRAPHY: T. Levitan, *Laureates: Jewish Winners of the Nobel Prize* (1960), 103–7; *Chemical and Engineering News*, 37 (1959), 86f., 104f.

[J. Edwin Holmstrom / Bracha Rager (2nd ed.)]

SEGRÈ, GINO (1864–1942), Italian jurist. Born in Bozzolo, Mantua, Segrè lectured at the universities of Camerino, Cagliari, Messina and at Parma before being appointed to the chair of Roman law at the University of Turin in 1916. He was a member of the Italian Academy of Sciences, of the Accademia dei Lincei, served on the commission for the reform of Italian civil law, and was the author of many monographs, mainly on Roman public and private law. A staunch liberal and a loyal Jew, Segrè suffered persecution by the Italian Fascists and many of his writings were banned and destroyed. In 1952 his disciple Professor G. Grosso edited Segrè's *Scritti varii di diritto Romano.*

In 1974 another book of his articles appeared, *Dalla radice pandettistica alla maturità romanistica. Scritti di Diritto Romano,* with a preface by his disciple G. Grosso, who also published an article on his work in his memory, "G. Segré a trent'anni dalla morte" (in: *Bullettino Ist. Dir. Rom.* 75 (1972), 1ff.).

BIBLIOGRAPHY: E. Betti, in: *Revista Italiana per le Scienze Giuridiche*, 18 (1942), 200–41, 302–19; G. Grosso, in: *Rivista di Diritto Commerciale*, 40 (1942), 338–40; A. Candian et al., in: *Temi* (1962); V. Arangio Ruiz, in: *Rendiconti dell'Accademia Nazionale dei Lincei*, 2 (1947), 607–12. **ADD. BIBLIOGRAPHY:** G. Grosso, S.G., *Novissimo Digesto Italiano*, 16 (1969), 891 f.

[Alfredo Mordechai Rabello / Mordechai-Alfredo Rabello (2nd ed.)]

SEGRÈ, JOSHUA BENZION (Salvador; c. 1705–c. 1797), Italian *dayyan* and rabbi. Born probably in Casale Monferrato, Segrè went to Scandiano in 1735 or 1736 as a children's tutor (*melammed tinokot*), but pretended to function as a fully fledged teacher (*moreh hora'ah*), claiming that he had graduated at the Mantua yeshivah. This claim caused him to quarrel with the rabbis of Reggio Emilia under whose jurisdiction he came. At the age of 23 he had already shown his taste for polemics by writing *Asham Talui* against Christianity in which, although not particularly well versed in Latin, he attempted mainly to prove that *Jerome had made many errors in his translation of the Old Testament. G.B. De *Rossi published a synopsis of the work, criticizing it severely.

Segrè also wrote a polemic against Guilio *Morosini's *Derekh ha-Emunah (La Via della Fede).* As well as writing commentaries on the Bible, Kabbalah, and *halakhah*, he was the author of a commentary on Psalms, *Ẓorer u-Moreh* (a summary of the laws of *terefah*), a booklet on Hebrew grammar, and an Italian translation of the principal prayers, partly in verse. The works were never published. His booklet *Kol Omerim Hodu* (Mantua, 1740) celebrates the inauguration of a reconstructed synagogue in Scandiano, financed by the *Almansi family (in whose house the synagogue was located).

BIBLIOGRAPHY: A. Marx, in: *Studies in Jewish Bibliography… in Memory of A.S. Freidus* (1929), 256 no. 32, 258 nos. 42–4, 275, 277f.; A. Balletti, *Gli ebrei e gli estensi* (1930²), 160–1; S. Krauss, in: ZHB, 8 (1904), 20–27; D. Simonsen, *ibid.*, 43–45; Neubauer, Cat, nos. 2406–7 and 1999; Margoliouth, Cat, nos. 561–2; L. Padoa, in: RMI, 33 (1967), 31–41, 442–56.

[Menachem E. Artom]

SEGRÈ, ROBERTO (1872–1939), Italian soldier. Son of an army colonel, Segrè was made an officer at the age of 18 and joined the artillery corps. He was transferred to the general staff in 1902. He served in the Italo-Turkish war (1911–12), and was decorated several times. During World War I Segrè commanded artillery formations in the battle of Gorizia (1916) and in 1917 was made chief of staff of the fifth army corps. After the war he was appointed head of the Italian-Austrian Armistice Commission. Segrè was eventually promoted to lieutenant general and corps commander. He served in this last capacity until the racial laws of 1938 forced him to resign his commission. An outstanding gunnery officer, Segrè was capable of using heavy artillery with devastating effect. He published numerous military studies and books on military history and politics and was awarded several decorations, including the Cross of Savoy.

BIBLIOGRAPHY: E. Caviglia, *The Three Battles of the Piave* (1924). **ADD. BIBLIOGRAPHY:** A. Rovighi, *I Militari di Origine Ebraica nel Primo Secolo di Vita dello Stato Italiano*, Roma (1999), 88.

[Massimo Longo Adorno]

SEGRE, SALVATORE (Joshua Benzion; 1729–1809), Italian rabbi. Segre was born in Vercelli, and was a wealthy property owner. One of the few Italian rabbis who inclined toward Reform, he served in the rabbinate and on the town council of

Vercelli after the occupation by the French revolutionary army. When Napoleon convened the Sanhedrin in Paris in 1806 (see French *Sanhedrin), Segre was one of the North Italian delegates. In a speech delivered in Paris on Aug. 15, 1806, he obsequiously praised the emperor and the following February he was chosen *av bet din* of the Sanhedrin. When the work of the Sanhedrin was finished Segre returned to his rabbinical position in Vercelli. In 1809 he went back to Paris and died during his visit.

BIBLIOGRAPHY: Graetz, Hist, 5 (1895), 488, 490, 495; Ghirondi-Neppi, 207; R. Anchel, *Napoléon et les Juifs* (1928), index.

[Menachem E. Artom]

SEIBER, MÁTYÁS GYÖRGY (1905–1960), composer. Seiber was born in Budapest and from 1919 to 1924 studied music at the academy there, mainly with Kodály. He was the most prominent of a group of young composers hailed by Kodály in an influential article as the new hope of Hungarian music. In 1926, after a period of traveling, he became a teacher at the Hoch conservatory in Frankfurt on the Main, where he stayed until 1933. Among his pedagogical innovations was the establishment, against strong objection, of a class for the study of jazz. From 1933 to 1935 he taught in Budapest and then settled in London. In 1960 he was killed in a car accident in South Africa. Kodály dedicated the choral work *Media vita in morte sumus* to his memory.

Seiber's early works rank among the most important of the Hungarian school, and his later ones, with their utilization of both pre-classic and 12-tone techniques, made contributions to the contemporary European musical achievement. They include several stage works, *Transylvanian Rhapsody* for orchestra (1941), three string quartets, songs, study works for jazz percussion and the accordion, incidental music for some 25 films and many plays (including Buechner's *Wozzeck*, and the music for the BBC's bicentenary production of Goethe's *Faust* in its entirety), works for solo instruments and orchestra, and choral works, including the cantata *Ulysses*, based on James Joyce's novel (1948).

BIBLIOGRAPHY: Grove, Dict; MGG, s.v.; Riemann-Gurlitt; Baker, Biog Dict.

[Bathja Bayer]

SEID, RUTH (1913–1995), U.S. novelist who wrote under the pen name **Jo Sinclair**. Born in Brooklyn, the fifth child of Ida (Kravetsky) and Nathan Seid, she grew up in Cleveland. Although family poverty precluded higher education, Seid was determined to be a writer and read voraciously in Cleveland public libraries. During the depression, she worked as a researcher, editor, and writer for the WPA and wrote fiction and plays in her spare time. In 1938, she befriended Helen Buchman, a married woman with a family, who invited Ruth to live in her home and supported her writing ambitions.

Seid took on her pseudonym in order to publish in magazines such as *Esquire*, which only accepted work written by men. This non-ethnic, androgynous pen name reflected Seid's ambiguous literary identity, which straddled religious, racial, and gender categories. Her first published story, "Noon Lynching," in *New Masses*, 20 (1936), is one of many she wrote that dealt with African American characters. Other early stories addressed poverty, self-hatred, sexuality, and Seid's own experiences in the work world. Critics have identified central Jewish themes in her novels as well as in such short stories as "Second Blood," The Medal," and "The Red Necktie." In 1946, Seid published her first novel, *Wasteland*, which won the prestigious $10,000 Harper Prize. In his *PM* review of the novel, Richard Wright praised its representation of Jewish family life and called it a "monumental psychological study." The novel centers on a self-hating photographer, Jacob Braunstein, who changes his name to John Brown to hide his Jewish identity. Urged by his lesbian sister Debby, Brown consults a psychiatrist to work out his neuroses. The novel is organized around references to Passover and the *seder*. The Holocaust also hovers in the background; at the conclusion of the novel, Jakes embraces his Jewish American identity by enlisting in the army to fight on behalf of America and European Jewry.

After *Wasteland*, Seid published *Sing At My Wake* (1951) and *The Changelings* (1955), a novel dealing with Jewish and Italian responses to African Americans moving into their neighborhood. The novel treats issues of sexuality, as well, and is considered a gay-lesbian classic. Seid's well-received fourth novel, *Anna Teller* (1960), about a Hungarian immigrant Jewish family, headed by a formidable matriarch, has strong Holocaust themes. With the rise of feminist, ethnic, and queer studies in the closing decades of the 20th century, interest in Seid/Sinclair's writing increased. Three of her novels were reissued and an abridged version of her memoir, *The Seasons: Death and Transfiguration* (1993), was published. Sinclair spent her last years in Jenkintown, Penn., with her partner Joan Sofer.

BIBLIOGRAPHY: "Jo Sinclair," in: *Current Biography* (1946), 557–59; G. Wilentz, "Jo Sinclair (Ruth Seid)," in: A. Shapiro et al. (eds.), *Jewish American Women Writers* (1994); S. Horowitz, "Jo Sinclair," in: P.E. Hyman and D.D. Moore (eds.), *Jewish Women in America*, vol. 2 (1997), 1087–9.

[Wendy Zierler (2nd ed.)]

SEIGEL, JOSHUA (1846–1910), rabbi. Born in Kitzburg, Poland, Seigel is perhaps best known for his controversial halakhic treatise, *Eruv ve-Hoẓa'ah*, an interpretation of Jewish law that allowed Jews to carry things on the East Side of Manhattan on the Sabbath. He believed that the island of Manhattan was surrounded by a natural **eruv*, a stance rejected by most of his rabbinic peers.

Seigel started out as a Talmud scholar under the direction of Rabbi Leibel Ḥarif of Plotsk and Rabbi Joshua of Kutna, who ordained him as a rabbi. Seigel received another ordination later on from Rabbi Joseph Kara of Vlatzlovak. He inherited his father's pulpit as rabbi of Sierpc, Poland, but not with unanimous consent from the community. Seigel was not a ḥasid, so many of the ḥasidic members of Sierpc resisted his leadership, despite the intervention of Rabbi Joshua of Kutna.

Later known as the "Sherpser Rav," Seigel left Europe in 1884 and immigrated to the United States. In New York, he became rabbi of a poor congregation of families divided between ḥasidic and non-ḥasidic traditions. His Polish ancestry set him apart from the Lithuanian rabbis who came to the United States in the late 19th century. Due to this tension, Seigel declined to join the Agudat Harabbonim, a union of mostly Lithuanian-educated rabbis formed in 1902.

Seigel negotiated a position as *mashgi'aḥ* for several New York slaughterhouses and butcher shops, a good way to earn supplementary income to his modest – inadequate – synagogue-pulpit salary. By 1890 almost 20 Galician congregations relied on Seigel for *kashrut* guidance, and many Galician butchers remained under his rabbinic supervision.

In 1908, Seigel went to Palestine in hopes of living in Jerusalem, but the harsh climate prevented him from taking up permanent residence there. A year later, he returned to New York. Seigel left a a posthumous work of responsa titled *Oznal Yehoshua*.

[Lynne Schreiber (2nd ed.)]

SEINFELD, JERRY (1954–), U.S. comedian and television star. Born in Brooklyn, New York, Seinfeld grew up in the Long Island town of Massapequa. He graduated from Queens College, New York, in 1976, with a double major in theater and communications. He worked at a variety of odd jobs while trying to break into the field of stand-up comedy.

His big break came when he was talent-spotted for Johnny Carson's *Tonight Show* in 1981. His first appearance was a success and the prelude to dozens more on the same program. He also became a regular on David Letterman's *Late Night* show after that program debuted in 1982. In 1987 he enjoyed his first solo television credit with "Jerry Seinfeld: Stand-Up Confidential," while in 1988 he earned an American Comedy Award as Funniest Male Stand-up Comic.

In 1988 Seinfeld and his friend Larry *David developed the idea for the *Seinfeld* show, based upon the daily life of a stand-up comedian and his group of friends. It premiered on NBC in July 1989 and maintained its status as one of the most popular and successful of American television sitcoms (1990–98). Proclaiming itself as being about nothing, the show follows the interactions and involvements of four neurotic and self-centered characters – Jerry Seinfeld as played by himself, Cosmo Kramer (Michael Richards), George Costanza (Jason *Alexander), and Elaine Benes (Julia *Louis-Dreyfus) – surrounded by a cast of no less quirky characters, as they sit around and talk themselves into impossibly complicated situations. The show spares no one, not even the handicapped, cruising along blithely and irreverently with its distinct brand of New York cynicism and its own brand of good-humored callousness.

Nominated nine times for an Emmy, *Seinfeld* – and Seinfeld – took home the award in 1993 for Outstanding Comedy Series. In 1992 and 1993 he won the American Comedy Award for Funniest Male Performer in a TV Series.

In 1998, he wrote and starred in a one-man benefit show entitled *Jerry Seinfeld: Live on Broadway*. Seinfeld wrote the books *Seinlanguage* (1994) and *Sein Off* (1998), and the children's book *Hallowe'en* (2002).

ADD. BIBLIOGRAPHY: J. Levine, *Jerry Seinfeld: Much Ado about Nothing* (1993); J. Oppenheimer, *Seinfeld: The Making of an American Icon* (2002).

[Rohan Saxena and Ruth Beloff (2nd ed.)]

SEINI (Hung. **Szinérváralja**), village in Transylvania, N.W. Romania; until the end of World War I and between 1940 and 1944 within Hungary. A geographical-historical description of Hungary published in 1799 mentions Jewish inhabitants among the Catholics and Protestants in Seini. There is also information that speaks about the attempt of Jews to establish themselves in the place during the previous century. A community headed by a rabbi probably existed by the close of the 18th century; from its inception the community was Orthodox. In 1885 the community became the official center for the Jews in the surrounding area. The Jewish population numbered 673 (13% of the total population) in 1930.

The Seini community was important in the history of Transylvanian Jewry because of the Hebrew printing press established there by Jacob Wieder. The first Hebrew work was printed in 1904 and the last in 1943. Between the two world wars the press was among the most important in Transylvania. It printed religious works, religious periodicals, and several works in Yiddish. A member of this family of printers, the son of the founder, Judah Wieder, settled in Haifa in 1932 and established a press there.

Between the two world wars, and especially during the Depression of the early 1930s, many local Jews left the area and moved to larger towns, where they hoped they would be able to support their families.

Holocaust and Contemporary Periods

During World War II, in the summer of 1944, at the time of the deportations of Jews from northern Transylvania, the Hungarian Fascist authorities sent all the Jews in Seini to the death camp at *Auschwitz via the Satu Mare ghetto.

The survivors formed a small community after World War II, numbering 150 in 1947, but after a while their numbers declined as a result of emigration to Israel and other countries. The community organization ceased to exist. The three Jewish families who still remained in Seini in 1971 took care of the large and ancient synagogue, which, though in a state of dilapidation, was still standing.

BIBLIOGRAPHY: J.J. Cohen, in: KS, 33 (1958), 388–403.

[Yehouda Marton / Paul Schveiger (2nd ed.)]

°SEIPEL, IGNAZ (1876–1932), Austrian statesman, Catholic prelate, and university professor; leader of the *Christian Social Party and five times chancellor of Austria

(1922–24; 1926–29). Although his party's program demanded the restraining of Jewish influence, he personally was of the opinion that "antisemitism was for the gutter," but he tolerated it in his party, particularly among student groups. While in office his attitude toward Jews was always unprejudiced and even benevolent in matters of religion and conscience. In his bitter struggle against the Social Democratic Party he was confronted by many leaders of Jewish origin, in particular their leader Otto *Bauer. Among his principal advisers were also persons of Jewish descent. His financial adviser was Gottfried Kunwald, his legal counsel Wilhelm Rosenberg, while in foreign affairs he was assisted by Dr. Gruenberger. Seipel came to reject parliamentary democracy and supported a constitution based on occupational estates in the sense of the papal encyclical "*Quadragesimo Anno*." Although not favoring Fascism and dictatorship, he furthered the Fascist *Heimwehr as a temporary counterweight to the Socialists.

BIBLIOGRAPHY: B. Birk, *Dr. Ignaz Seipel* (Ger., 1932); W. Thormann, *Ignaz Seipel. Der europaeische Staatsmann* (1932); *Festschrift… Union oesterreichischer Juden* (1937); J. Tsoebl, in: H. Hantsch, *Gestalter der Geschichte Oesterreichs* (1962), 589–609; V. Reimann, *Zu gross fuer Oesterreich* (1968). **ADD. BIBLIOGRAPHY:** K.V. Klemperer, *Ignaz Seipel: Christian Statesman in a Time of Crisis* (1972); F. Rennhofer, *Ignaz Seipel: Mensch und Staatsmann* (1978).

[Hugo Knoepfmacher]

SEIR, MOUNT (Heb. הַר שֵׂעִיר), biblical name for a number of regions, the appellation originally meaning "hairy," i.e., wooded.

(1) The area originally inhabited by the Horites (Gen. 14:6; Deut. 2:4) and later by the Edomites, the children of Esau (Gen. 32:4; 33:14, 16). An archaeological survey of the region south of the Zered River has shown that it was inhabited by an Early Bronze Age population until about the 20th century B.C.E. After a gap, the kingdom of Edom was established in the same area in about 1300 B.C.E. Seir is mentioned in Egyptian sources from the time of *Merneptah. The Israelites were ordered to leave the area in the possession of "their brethren, the children of Esau," who dwelt in Seir (Deut. 2:4, 5, 8; Josh. 24:4). Actually, they were unable to penetrate the strong defenses of the Edomites and were forced either to pass between them and the Moabites or go around Seir. Nevertheless, Balaam prophesied that the region would fall to Israel (Num. 24:18), as it did in the days of David. Part of Seir was later occupied by the Simeonites (I Chron. 4:42). Jehoshaphat and Amaziah, kings of Judah, fought against the people of Seir (II Chron. 20:22–23; 25:11). The prophets Isaiah and Ezekiel use the name as a synonym for Edom (Isa. 21:11; Ezek. 35). The area is now known as Jebel (Ar. al-Jibāl), a mountainous region (highest point: Jebel Hārūn, 1396 m.) which is well watered (up to 400 mm. annual rainfall) and wooded in parts. The name is attributed to parts of the Negev west of the Arabah in Deuteronomy 1:2 and 1:44 and some scholars place the theophany referred to in Deuteronomy 33:2 in this area.

(2) An area on the northern border of the territory of Judah, between Kiriath-Jearim and Chesalon (Josh. 15:10). Most of this mountainous region was evidently wooded until the period of the United Monarchy.

(3) An unidentified locality, the place to which Ehud escaped from Jericho after killing Eglon, the king of Moab (Judg. 3:26; as Seirah).

BIBLIOGRAPHY: Abel, Géog, 1 (1933), 389–91; Aharoni, Land, index.

[Michael Avi-Yonah]

SEIXAS, family of prominent U.S. communal leaders. GERSHOM MENDES SEIXAS (1746–1816) was the first nativeborn Jewish minister in the United States and one of the most noted of early American Jews. He was the grandson of ABRAHAM MENDES SEIXAS, a London broker, and the son of ISAAC MENDES SEIXAS (1709–1782), founder of the American branch of the Seixas family, who was at various times a merchant in New York, Connecticut, Rhode Island, and New Jersey. Isaac Seixas married Rachel Levy (1719–1797), daughter of Moses *Levy, in 1740, and Gershom Seixas was one of seven children. He studied with the *ḥazzan* Joseph Pinto and in 1768 was appointed *ḥazzan* of Congregation Shearith Israel in New York. During the turmoil of the American Revolution, Gershom and his family moved first to Connecticut in 1776 and then to Philadelphia in 1780, returning to New York in 1784. While in Philadelphia, Seixas served as minister to Congregation Mikveh Israel, which he helped to organize. Constantly troubled over questions of salary and housing, he served as the community expert on Jewish law and practice, attending to ritual matters concerning birth, marriage, and death, and considerations of synagogue service. He was instrumental in saving the Jewish cemetery at Chatham Square, in New York, from obliteration. In 1793 he organized a Hebrew school and in 1803 taught at the Polonies Talmud Torah School. A year before, he helped establish Hebra Hased Va-Amet and earlier in 1798 the Kalfe Sedeka Matten Besether, both charitable institutions. He was also a self-taught *mohel* and *shoḥet.*

Among Seixas' more noted sermons was one which he delivered in 1798 in a defense of French-American relations, despite bitter opposition in New York to the French Revolution. Other sermons called for relief funds for refugees of Indian attacks on the old northwest frontier (1799) and relief for those made homeless by the British during the war of 1812 (1814). Gershom was invited to President Washington's inauguration in 1789. He served as a trustee of the Humane Society and of Columbia College from 1784 to 1814. In 1784 he was elected by the New York State Legislature to the first Board of Regents of the State University.

Seixas' brothers were: ABRAHAM MENDES (1751–99), an officer in the revolutionary army who fought in the southern colonies; BENJAMIN MENDES (1748–1817), one of the founders of the New York Stock Exchange; and MOSES MENDES (1744–1809), one of the organizers and first cashier of the Bank of Rhode Island and in 1790 president of the Newport congregation. DAVID G. (1788–1865), one of Gershom Seixas' children, established the Deaf and Dumb Institute in Philadelphia. He was among the first to discover ways of burning anthracite coal, and helped to introduce daguerrotypes to the U.S. Seixas manufactured crockery in Philadelphia, and has been credited as the father of this art in the U.S.

BIBLIOGRAPHY: D. de Sola Pool, *Portraits Etched in Stone* (1952), index; J.J. Lyons, in: AJHSP, 27 (1920), 346–70.

[Leo Hershkowitz]

SEJM, the Polish parliament (from 1922 also the senate as an upper house) During the existence of the Polish republic between the two world wars, there were six terms which varied in length and electoral principles. The first or legislative term (1919–22) produced the 1921 constitution. It operated in a time of emergency, when the young state was being consolidated while at war with external enemies and undergoing an internal ferment caused by alien national groupings. Jewish representation, with 11 seats, was only 3% as against a proportion of 11% for the general population. The delegates elected from the Jewish lists constituted a parliamentary club called the "Free Union of the Delegates of Jewish Nationality in the Sejm," consisting of Zionists, Orthodox, *Folkspartei, and *Po'alei Zion, most of whom had a definite connection with the "National Jewish Council" which was under Zionist influence. The struggle for national and civil rights against the hostility of most of the Sejm required daring, a capacity for suffering, and perseverance. The small number of Jewish members prevented in the beginning a suitable representation in the parliamentary committees and thus limited their possibilities of political action.

The Second Sejm (and Senate) (1922–27) was of particular importance. It provided a background to considerable political changes in the stormy life of the country and in the means adopted by the Jewish representatives in their struggle, their number having reached 35 in the Sejm and 12 in the Senate as a result of their being organized during the election in the framework of the *Minority Bloc. This enabled them to overcome the obstacles in the perverse election regulations. In that situation of party divisions and social struggle in the Sejm and outside, there was an increase in the importance of the Jewish Club (Kolo Zydowskie) which had become consolidated. Its successive presidents were O. *Thon, Yiẓḥak *Gruenbaum, L. *Reich, and M.A. *Hartglas. The Jewish deputies were active in important committees, and in the plenum were outstanding through their speeches on specifically Jewish subjects and even on general questions. The leadership throughout that entire period was in the hands of the Zionist group, which was split by matters of principle into two schools of thought: the radical faction led by Gruenbaum, standing for greater links with the national minorities and a policy of fighting the government, and the Galician Zionists, headed by Reich and Thon, who had reservations about adhering too closely to the minorities alliance and attempted to achieve a rapprochement with the Polish government by means of an "agreement" (*Ugoda).

The last four Sejms marked a reduction in the importance of the legislature following the progressively stronger Fascist tendencies of the Polish government. These were expressed primarily in a sharp struggle between the "*Sanacja*" government and the parliamentary opposition, which began in 1935 as a result of the new constitution which attacked electoral freedom through selective candidature and appointment made by ruling circles. In an atmosphere of political pressure by the regime, the disintegration of the Minority Bloc, and the inclusion of Jewish candidates in the government list (BBWR), there began a most drastic process of contraction in Jewish representation in the Sejm and the Senate, as shown in these figures: Third Sejm (1928) – 22 Jewish seats; Fourth Sejm (1930) – 11 Jewish seats; Fifth Sejm (1935) – 6 Jewish seats; Sixth Sejm (1938) – 7 Jewish seats. Under these conditions of internal disruption among the Jewish representatives and intensified manifestations of antisemitism both among the extreme reactionary parties and in the government camp (*OZON), there was no chance of developing real political activity, apart from a defensive attitude of despair and expressions of protest against the injury to the Jewish population, which was caught up in a process of grave decline.

BIBLIOGRAPHY: I. Schiper (ed.), Żydzi w Polsce odrodzonej, 2 (1932), 286–359; L. Halpern, *Polityka żydowska w Sejmie i Senacie Rzeczypospolitej Polskiej 1919–1933* (1933); H.M. Rabinowicz, *Legacy of Polish Jewry* (1965), 45–63; I. Schwarzbart, *Tsvishn Beyde Milkhomes* (1958), 206–52. **ADD. BIBLIOGRAPHY:** A. Ajnenkiel, *Historia Sejmu polskiego* (1989); *Sprawozdania stenograficzne z posiedzen Sejmu RP 1919–1922, 1922–1939*; S. Netzer, *Ma'avak Yehudei Polin al Zekhuyoteihem ha-Ezraḥiyot ve-ha-Le'ummiyot 1918–1922* (1980).

[Moshe Landau]

SEKIRYANY (Rom. **Secureni**), village in Bessarabia, E. Chernovtsy oblast, Ukraine. Jews began to settle in Sekiryany at the invitation of the owner of the place, who wished to develop his estate after the Russian annexation of Bessarabia in 1812. As a result of Jewish immigration to Bessarabia which continued until the end of the 19th century, the community grew, numbering 5,042 Jews (56% of the total population) in 1897. Thus for all practical purposes, Sekiryany became an urban community even though it formally held the status of a village and it served as a commercial center for all the villages in the area. Jews marketed agricultural products and supplied farmers with their needs. They also were engaged in crafts and agriculture. After Bessarabia was annexed by Romania in 1918 the community developed an active public life. A network of educational institutions was established, including a kindergarten, elementary and high schools, all maintained by the Tarbut Organization, and a *talmud torah*. In 1920 a Jewish hospital was founded. Jews numbered 4,200 (72.6% of the total population) in 1930.

[Eliyahu Feldman]

Holocaust Period

Following the Nazi-Soviet pact of 1939, Bessarabia passed to the Soviet Union. On July 6, 1941, Sekiryany was captured by German-Romanian forces. These troops killed all the Jews they found in the villages on the way and in Sekiryany itself they killed 90 Jews in the first two days of the occupation. Many Jews committed suicide. The local peasants were incited to attack and rob the Jews, thus setting a three-day pogrom in motion. On the third day the Jews were driven to the cemetery and tortured by the troops. A few days later all the Jews were sent on a month-long death march. They were first led to *Brichany, where they spent eight days in the homes of the local Jewish families; then to Koslov where they were left in the open for three days, without food, water, or sanitary facilities. Whoever lifted his head was shot to death on the spot. The survivors were dispersed in the neighboring villages in groups of 200, to be reassembled a few days later and dispatched to Moghilev, *Transnistria (i.e., Mogilev, Ukraine). From there, still numbering a few thousand at this time, they were transferred to Skazinets, and some returned to their home town. Throughout these wanderings they subsisted on the grass and rotten beets collected along the road. Those unable to carry on were buried alive. The old and the sick were shot to death in a forest near Skazinets, and others succumbed to the cold, hunger, and epidemics. In the woods near Kosouty they underwent a brutal body search, during which a large number were killed. Their next stop was Obodovka, where they were locked in a pigsty and could not leave to bury their dead. The survivors were then taken to the kolkhoz Dubina, and to Bershad. By this time, only a few were still alive. After the expulsion of its native Jews, Sekiryany became a large concentration camp for 30,000 Jews from the entire district. The camp was disbanded on Oct. 3, 1941, and all its inmates deported to Transnistria.

[Jean Ancel]

BIBLIOGRAPHY: Z. Iggeret (ed.), *Sekuri'an (Bessarabyah) be-Vinyanah u-ve-Ḥurbanah* (1954), 89–120; Herz-Kahn, in: *Eynikayt* (Aug. 23, 1945); M. Carp, *Cartea neagră*, 3 (1947), index.

SELA, MICHAEL (1924–), Israeli biochemist and immunologist. Born in Poland, Sela was taken to Bucharest as a child and immigrated (1941) to Palestine. He graduated in chemistry from the Hebrew University of Jerusalem (M.Sc. 1947, Ph.D. 1954). He became active in the **Aliyah* movement from Italy and helped many Jewish displaced persons reach Ereẓ Israel. He then spent two years (1948–50) as commercial secretary to the Israel Legation in Prague.

Sela began his scientific career as a biophysicist under Ephraim *Katzir in Reḥovot, and developed a special interest in immunology. He headed the new unit in that science established in 1963, when he was made professor, and in the ensuing years did extensive research and teaching in the subject. He wrote many papers for scientific journals, edited several books, and lectured widely in Israel and at international forums. His work in elucidating the chemical basis of antigenicity won him the Rothschild Prize (1968). Nine years earlier he received the Israel Prize in natural sciences for work on synthetic polypeptides as protein models. In 1966 he undertook a survey of immunological research in Russia and Hungary for the WHO and between 1975 and 1979 served as council chairman of the European Molecular Biology Organisation (EMBO).

Among the posts he held at the Weizmann Institute of Science are dean of biology (1970–75), vice president (1970–71), and president (1975–85). In 1976, Sela was elected a foreign member of the U.S. Academy of Sciences, president of the International Union of Immunological Societies, and a member of the Pontifical Academy of Sciences (in the Vatican). He received several additional prizes, including the Baillet-Latour Prize in Belgium and the Wolf Prize in Israel. His name is linked with the drug against multiple sclerosis which he created at the Weizmann Institute and which was developed by Teva Pharmaceutical Industries under the name Copaxone. He is an institute professor and deputy chairman of the Board of Governors of the Weizmann Institute of Science.

[Julian Louis Meltzer]

SELBSTEMANZIPATION, the first Zionist newspaper in Western Europe, in German. The idea of the newspaper originated in the group centered on the first Zionist student group in Western Europe, *Kadimah, and its name reflected the admiration felt by members of the group for Leo *Pinsker and the influence exerted on them by his book of the same name. The paper first came out in 1885, in Vienna, under the editorship of Nathan *Birnbaum, and with the encouragement of Pinsker. It was the first newspaper in Western Europe to be entirely devoted to advocating the Zionist cause, from its editorials to the notes on local events. The word Zionism itself was used for the first time in its columns (by Birnbaum, in 1890). The moving spirit behind the paper was Birnbaum, whose articles on current affairs and ideological essays on the national character of the Jewish people polemicized both against assimilationism and socialist cosmopolitanism. The paper devoted much of its space to Ereẓ Israel and its resettlement, and became the central organ of the Zionist movement in the West. It experienced great financial difficulties and ceased publication in the middle of 1886 after one and a quarter years of existence. The *Esra society in Germany, then at the height of its activities for the settlement of Ereẓ Israel, renewed publication in September 1886, transferring the paper to Berlin and changing its name to *Serubabel*. Although Birnbaum continued to write for the paper, Willi *Bambus now became its moving spirit. Since Esra was mainly concerned with Ereẓ Israel, the paper devoted most of its space to this cause, as well as to research and information on Ereẓ Israel. The debate with those opposed to the Jewish national idea continued in its columns, and the first attempts were made to bring about a rapprochement between Eastern and Western Jewry. The paper again ceased publication because of financial difficulties (July 1888) and renewed publication on April 1, 1890, under its original name and editor. In its new form, *Selbstemanzipation* constituted a synthesis between its two previous forms. It opposed Baron de *Hirsch's proposed settlement program in Argentina. The paper also involved itself in the elections to the Austrian parliament, supporting I.S. Bloch, the candidate who was closest to the Zionist line. Two of the paper's main opponents in Vienna were the rabbis and scholars M. *Guedemann and A. *Jellinek.

With the arrival of the Hebrew writer Reuben *Brainin in Vienna (1891), ties with Eastern Jewry were further strengthened, and the paper began to devote much of its space to the new Hebrew literature. Birnbaum's Zionist articles continued to feature prominently in the paper (whose subtitle "Jewish National Organ" was replaced in May 1893 with "Zionist Organ") and it played an influential part in the establishment of the united Zionist Federation of Austria and Galicia in 1893. In 1894 the name of the paper was changed to *Juedische Volkszeitung* with the addition of "formerly *Selbstemanzipation*." The paper was transferred to Berlin, but the editorial board remained in Vienna. While there were no policy changes, the addition of a group of young men later to constitute *Herzl's immediate following (S.R. *Landau, M. *Ehrenpreis, O. *Thon, H. *Loewe, etc.) to the paper's contributors made it into the representative organ of the Zionist movement before Herzl. At the beginning of 1895, however, the paper ceased publication.

BIBLIOGRAPHY: Y. Meisel, in: A.E. Kaplan and M. Landau (eds.), *Vom Sinn des Judentums* (1925), 19–33; G. Kressel, in: *Shivat Ẓiyyon*, 4 (1956), 55–99.

[Getzel Kressel]

SELBSTWEHR ("Self-Defense"), Jewish weekly founded in Prague. It was first published in 1907 and appeared regularly until the fall of 1938. After amalgamation with the *Juedisches Volksblatt*, a weekly published in *Ostrava, it was the most widely read Jewish newspaper in Czechoslovakia. Editors of the paper included Siegfried Katznelson, later manager of the publishing house Juedischer Verlag, Berlin; Leo Herrman, later general secretary of the Keren Hayesod, Jerusalem; Felix *Weltsch; and Hans Lichtwitz (Uri Naor; d. 1988), later of the Israel Foreign Ministry, Jerusalem. Among regular contributors were Max *Brod and Martin *Buber. *Selbstwehr* was the official organ of the Czechoslovakian Zionist Movement and the German-language organ of the Juedische Partei, which represented the interests of the Jewish minority in Czechoslovak internal politics. After World War I *Selbstwehr* also published the annual "Jewish Almanac", edited by Felix Weltsch and Friedrich *Thieberger, which dealt mainly with cultural activities in Palestine. The regular monthly supplement, *Die Juedische Frau* ("The Jewish Woman"), edited by Hannah *Steiner, was the official organ of Czechoslovak WIZO. *Selbstwehr* had to cease publication after the Munich agreement.

[Uri Naor]

°**SELDEN, JOHN** (1584–1654), English parliamentarian, lawyer, and antiquarian. Selden was a prominent member of the Antiquarian Society – the important forum for research in the 17th century. He had an exceptional command of Oriental languages, notably of both biblical and rabbinical Hebrew.

His attitude toward Jews and Judaism was marked by contradictions. Thus, in his short *Treatise on the Jews in England* (1617), he gives credence to ritual murder, albeit as past history. On the other hand, in all his works on Jewish subjects he expresses boundless admiration for rabbinical scholarship, which sometimes borders on the grotesque (cf. Ehrman, in: *Papers from the Fourth World Congress of Jewish Studies* 1 (1967), 181–3 (Heb.), 267 (Eng. abstract)). In his famous *Table Talk* he also writes sympathetically about Jews. Selden's amazing familiarity with the intrinsic problems of rabbinical scholarship and his erudite exposition of rabbinical law, which runs into many volumes, form a unique contribution to scholarship. A list of the short titles of his rabbinical writings indicates the extensiveness of his work in this field: *History of Tithes* (1617), leading up to questions on the relations between church and state; *De Jure Naturali et Gentium* (1640), on international law (a work to which particular attention is drawn by Shabtai Rosenne in "The Influence of Judaism on the Development of International Law," *Netherlands International Law Review*, 5 (1958), 128–30); *De Anno Civili* (1644), a work which first refers to the doctrines and practices of the Karaites; *Uxor Ebraica* (1946), on Jewish marriage and divorce laws; *De Synhedriis* (1650), on the constitution of Jewish ecclesiastical courts, drawing attention to relevant parallels with the constitution of the Church as regards the division of authority between clergy and laymen; *De Successionibus* (1631), on Jewish laws of inheritance. In fact all his works, and not just his specific rabbinical writings, make frequent reference to rabbinical sources.

It was probably to explain or justify and also occasionally to protest against specific Christian institutions that Selden had recourse to rabbinical sources. Thus, for instance, when he was writing his *Uxor Ebraica*, his friends assumed that his aim was to throw further light on a topic of Christian interest. R. Cudworth wrote to him from Cambridge (Mss. Seld. 108, Arch. Seld. A, Bodleian Library, Oxford): "I hope in your Worke de Nuptys Hebrays you will bring something to light which the world is yet ignorant of, for the clearing of our Saviour's descent from David's line"; Cudworth then goes on in a scholarly fashion to point to an apparent contradiction between Abrabanel's commentary on Isaiah and an instance in the Talmud, touching as it were on the Christian viewpoint under discussion. As to Selden's treatment of the sources of Jewish law, it is certain that he did not rely merely on secondary sources (e.g., the works of Johannes *Buxtorf, I and II) but read the Talmud (both the Babylonian and the Jerusalem) at least to the extent of looking up references suggested to him in Jewish and non-Jewish post-talmudic works. His library was apparently crowded with different editions of the Talmud as well as the most varied works of the post-talmudic rabbinical literature (Selden Handlist, *Libri Bibl. Seld.*, Bodleian Library, Oxford). It is evident, however, that his main source was Maimonides' Code, which he preferred to the standard codes of

Arba'ah Turim and Shulḥan Arukh. Whatever the shortcomings of Selden's rabbinical writings may have been, the inaccuracies, obscurities, and digressions which were severely exposed by Herzog (in: *Journal of Comparative Legislation*, 13 (1931), 236–45), it is clear that by stimulating interest in rabbinics he greatly contributed to Christian scholarship as well as to modern Judaic studies.

BIBLIOGRAPHY: Margoliuth, in: *Macray's Annals*; Ehrman, in: *Christian News from Israel*, 13 no. 1 (1962), 22–25. **ADD. BIBLIOGRAPHY:** ODNB online.

[Arnost Zvi Ehrman]

SELDES, GEORGE (1890–1995), U.S. journalist and author. Born in Alliance, New Jersey, Seldes was a crusading pamphleteer who wrote exposés of many facets of American life. He started as a reporter, and was night editor of the *Pittsburgh Post* (1910–16). Going to New York, he became managing editor of *Pulitzer's Weekly* (1916). He was a war correspondent during World War I, in Syria 1926–27, and in Spain 1936–37. His candid reporting led to his expulsion from more than one country, such as Russia and Italy. He served as head of the Berlin and Rome bureaus of the *Chicago Tribune* until he resigned in 1928 and returned to New York. From 1940 to 1950 Seldes, as a media critic, published a weekly bulletin of "inside" news called *In Fact*, which attained a circulation of 175,000. In 1941 he began writing about the dangers of tobacco but few newspapers would carry the stories, as many of their advertisers were cigarette companies.

Seldes, who lived to 104, spent his life fighting for a free, fair, and responsible press. In his view, the best formula for the media was "the facts fairly and honestly presented; truth will take care of itself."

In *You Can't Print That* (1929), *The Truth Behind the News* (1929), and *Lords of the Press* (1938), Seldes assailed what he considered the venality of American journalism. *Sawdust Caesar* (1935) was a debunking biography of Mussolini. His other books include *Freedom of the Press* (1935), *Facts and Fascism* (1943), *Our Thousand Americans* (1947), *The People Don't Know* (1949), *Tell the Truth and Run* (1953), *The Great Quotations* (1960), *Never Tire of Protesting* (1968), *Even the Gods Can't Change History* (1976), *The Great Thoughts* (1985), and his autobiography, *Witness to a Century* (1987), which he completed at age 96.

Richard Goldsmith's film *Tell the Truth and Run: George Seldes and the American Press* (1996) was nominated for an Academy Award for Best Documentary.

ADD. BIBLIOGRAPHY: R. Holhut (ed.), *The George Seldes Reader* (1994).

[Lawrence H. Feigenbaum / Ruth Beloff (2nd ed.)]

SELDES, MARIAN (1928–), U.S. actress. Born in New York City to critic Gilbert and Alice (née Hall) Seldes, as a teenager Seldes studied with the American Ballet from 1941 to 1944, debuting on stage in *Petrouchka* (1942). In her late teens she changed her focus to acting and enrolled in the Neighborhood Playhouse School of the Theatre, making her stage acting debut with the Cambridge Summer Theater in 1945. After graduating at 19, Seldes made her Broadway debut in *Medea* (1947) in a small role as the attendant to the title character. After supporting roles in *Crime and Punishment* (1947), *That Lady* (1949), *The Tower Beyond Tragedy* (1950), and *The High Ground* (1951), Seldes made her silver-screen debut in *The Lonely Night* (1952). Seldes returned to Broadway for *Ondine* (1954) and *The Chalk Garden* (1955) before trying her hand in Hollywood again with the films *The True Story of Jesse James* (1957), *Crime and Punishment* (1959), and *Crime and Passion* (1959). In 1960, she returned to New York for the Broadway play *The Wall* (1960) and then went on to star in original Broadway productions, including Tennessee William's *The Milk Train Doesn't Stop Here Anymore* (1964) and Edward Albee's *Tiny Alice* (1965) and *A Delicate Balance* (1966), which earned her a Tony Award for best actress. In 1968, Seldes began teaching drama at the Julliard School, a position she held for 22 years. After her turn in *Equus* from 1974 to 1976, she starred as the murdered wife of a playwright in *Deathtrap*, a role that lasted from 1978 to 1982. In 1981, she wrote the novel *Time Together*. In 1990, Seldes married writer-director Garson *Kanin. After leaving Julliard, Seldes returned to Hollywood to portray Alice B Toklas in *Gertrude Stein and a Companion* and Charlotte Sandler, the mother to Terri Garr's character in the short-lived sitcom *Good and Evil*. Following more television work, Seldes returned to Broadway for *Ivanov* (1997), which included one-time Seldes student Kevin Kline. Less than two months after the March 13 death of Kanin, Seldes came to the aid of *Ring Round the Moon* (1999) after the actress portraying Madame Desmermor fell ill; the role earned her a Drama Desk and a Tony Award nomination. Other award-nominated turns followed in *The Butterfly Collection* (2001), *The Play about the Baby* (2001), and *Dinner at Eight* (2003).

BIBLIOGRAPHY: "Seldes, Marian," in: *Contemporary Authors* (2001). **Website:** http://ibdb.com/person.asp?ID=16116, Marian Seldes –Internet Broadway Database; Internet Movie Database.

[Adam Wills (2nd ed.)]

SELDIN, HARRY M. (1895–1975), U.S. oral surgeon. Born in Russia, Seldin was taken to the U.S. in 1905. From 1919 to 1924 he was an instructor in the dental department of New York University, and headed its department of general anesthesia from 1926–31. He was associate director of the dentistry division of the Department of Hospitals, New York City, from 1928 to 1930, and director from 1930 to 1934. In 1934 he was appointed consulting oral surgeon to the Harlem Hospital in New York and in 1942 to the Peekskill Hospital in Westchester County, New York. Seldin played a leading part in the establishment of the Hebrew University-Hadassah School of Dentistry in Jerusalem founded by the Alpha-Omega Fraternity. He was governor of the Hebrew University and of Tel Aviv University. In 1960 he founded the Harry M. Seldin Center of Oral-Maxillary Surgery at the Rambam Hospital in Haifa.

Seldin was the author of a textbook on oral surgery, and his achievements in this field earned him academic honors and the highest awards of his profession in the United States and abroad.

SELEKMAN, BENJAMIN MORRIS (1893–1962), U.S. labor relations expert. Born in Bethlehem, Pa., Selekman worked in the field of Jewish social work and labor relations. He was executive director of the Associated Jewish Philanthropies of Boston from 1929 to 1945, and was professor of labor relations at the Harvard University School of Business Administration from 1945 to 1962. Though impressed by the degree of goodwill shown by many employers in improving industrial relations and in particular by the efforts of John D. Rockefeller after the bitter Colorado Fuel and Iron Company's Ludlow, Colorado, strike, Selekman regarded social conflict in labor relations as virtually unavoidable. They were part of the process of economic development and the emergence of democratic social stability. Selekman's work leaned heavily upon the relevance of psychoanalytical insight. His numerous writings include *Labor Relations and Human Relations* (1947), *Power and Morality in a Business Society* (1956), and *A Moral Philosophy for Management* (1959).

BIBLIOGRAPHY: *New York Times* (April 8, 1962), obituary.

[Mark Perlman]

SÈLESTAT (Ger. **Schlettstadt**), town in the department of Bas-Rhin, Alsace, in eastern France. The presence of Jews in Sélestat is confirmed from at least the beginning of the 14th century. While town officials succeeded in protecting Jews from outside attacks, particularly from the *Armleder bands, a number of Selestat's inhabitants attacked them in 1347 and again in 1349, believing that they were responsible for spreading the *Black Death. As a result of these attacks, several Jews were murdered and others fled. Others accepted baptism, but they were soon accused, with the rest of the Jewish population, of spreading the Black Death. The synagogue was confiscated and converted into an indoor market; from the middle of the 16th century it was used as an arsenal. The Jews returned a short while later, but they were again expelled at the beginning of the 16th century. The street which was known at first as "Judenschuel" and later as the Rue des Juifs was inhabited by this second community. From that time onward, Jews visited Sélestat for trading purposes, but they were not allowed to settle there. During the 17th century Jews from neighboring localities acquired a plot of land for use as a cemetery, which still existed in 1971. A new Jewish community was not established in Sélestat until after the French Revolution. It was soon the third largest Jewish settlement in Alsace. The population continued to decline throughout the 19th and early 20th centuries, however. Between the two world wars, the community numbered approximately 250. The synagogue, which was erected in 1890 and sacked by the Germans during World War II, was later rebuilt. The community was reconstituted after the war, and in 1971 numbered 180 persons.

BIBLIOGRAPHY: Germ Jud, 2 (1968), 744–6; J. Geny, *Schlettstadter Stadtrechte* (1902), passim; I. Dukerley, in: *Archives Israélites*, 22 (1861), 631ff.; M. Ginsburger, *ibid.*, 96 (1935), 142f.

[Bernhard Blumenkranz]

SELEUCIA, name of two cities.

(1) City in Gaulanitis, S.E. of Lake Ḥuleh. Seleucia was among the numerous cities and fortresses captured by Alexander Yannai during his campaign in Transjordan. With the outbreak of the war against Rome (66 C.E.), Seleucia was fortified by Josephus, who describes the area as having very strong natural defenses. Early in the revolt, however, Seleucia was induced by Agrippa II to come to terms with the Romans (Jos., Wars, 1:105; 2:574; Life, 187, 398). See Schuerer, Hist, 89f., in connection with the cities of Gadara and Abila.

(2) City on the west bank of the Tigris (south of modern Baghdad), founded by Seleucus I Nicator (312–280 B.C.E.). During the Parthian period the city was inhabited mainly by Greeks and Syrians, and Pliny gives its population as 600,000 (*Natural History*, 6:122). Relations between the two elements were strained, and conditions were exacerbated when, in the first century C.E., a large number of Jews took refuge in Seleucia, after the defeat of the Jewish leader *Anilaeus (c. 35). At first the Jews joined with the Syrians but this alliance was successfully broken up by the Greek party. Subsequently there developed a common enmity toward the Jews, and in a sudden attack upon the community over 50,000 Jews were said to have been slain. The surviving Jews eventually fled to *Nehardea and *Nisibis, both beyond the Seleucid sphere of influence.

BIBLIOGRAPHY: Pauly-Wissowa, 2nd series, 3 (1921), 1177f., s.v. *Seleukeia (am Tigris)*; Neusner, Babylonia, index in every vol., s.v.

[Isaiah Gafni]

SELEUCID ERA, the basis for Jewish reckoning of years during the Second Temple period, and in certain Jewish communities down to the late medieval period and until comparatively modern times. This era, commonly referred to in Hebrew as *minyan shetarot* (see *Calendar), coincides with the founding of the Seleucid monarchy, but there are discrepancies regarding the precise beginning of the cycle. Whereas the return of Seleucus I Nicator to Babylon, following the battle of Gaza (autumn 312 B.C.E.), is officially regarded as the date of the founding of the empire, it appears that certain nations, including possibly the Jews, regarded the following year, 311 B.C.E., as the beginning of that era.

BIBLIOGRAPHY: Schuerer, Gesch, 1 (1901⁴), 32–40; E. Mahles, *Handbuch der juedischen chronologie* (1916), 402; W. Kubitschek, *Grundriss der antiken Zeitrechnung* (1928), 70ff.; E. Frank, *Talmudic and Rabbinical Chronology* (1956), 30–5; E.J. Bickerman, *Chronology of the Ancient World* (1968), 70–72.

[Isaiah Gafni]

°SELEUCUS IV PHILOPATOR, Seleucid monarch 187–176 B.C.E.), son of *Antiochus II the Great. Following the crushing defeat by the Romans at Magnesia (190), the Seleucid Empire found itself in extreme financial difficulties, and these were to have a direct effect in altering the friendly relations cultivated by Antiochus III with the Jews of Palestine. In an attempt to raise funds for the Seleucid treasury, Seleucus dispatched his minister *Heliodorus to Jerusalem. The mission whose purpose was to appropriate funds on deposit in the Temple treasury, was encouraged by Simeon, an official of the Temple. According to the description in II Maccabees (1:1ff.), Heliodorus was miraculously prevented from entering the treasury. Forced to return empty-handed to Seleucus, he was eventually responsible for the assassination of the king. Seleucus IV was succeeded by his younger brother *Antiochus IV Epiphanes.

BIBLIOGRAPHY: Schuerer, Gesch, 1 (1901[4]), 169; E.R. Bevan, *House of Seleucus*, 2 (1902), 120–5.

[Isaiah Gafni]

SELF-DEFENSE (in modern Jewish history). Jewish efforts against attacking mobs in Russia and in Austria-Hungary from the end of the 19th century until shortly after World War I. The nature of the pogroms in this period (especially in the years 1881–82, 1903–05, and 1917–20) taught Jews that they occurred with the compliance of the governing authorities and at times even at their instigation. The government, therefore, could be no guarantee of protection. A segment of the Jewish community gradually became aware of the necessity for Jews to come to their own defense and to concern themselves with the safety of their brethren and the protection of their property. They should not depend for their security on the forces of law and order of a hostile government, and on occasion they must even oppose those forces directly. This point of view gained strength in the wake of the revolutionary movement throughout Russia and the rise of modern Jewish nationalism (both its Zionist and its socialist-Diaspora manifestations) which reawakened the sense of national honor among Jews. In the *Pale of Settlement in Russia there was an overcrowded Jewish population, and in many of the cities and towns in this area Jews constituted the majority of the local population, or at least a very substantial minority. There was a steady increase in the number of Jewish artisans and workers who were physically fit and knew how to wield a knife or ax. Conscription into the Russian army created, especially among the lower strata of Jewish society, a pool of young men accustomed to military discipline and trained in defense tactics.

During the pogroms of 1881–82, self-defense was organized spontaneously in different places. Equipped mainly with light arms, the defenders relied on the numerical strength of the Jewish masses to try to prevent the rioting mobs from penetrating their streets (especially in *Berdichev and *Kirovograd (Yelizavetgrad), and *Warsaw). In *Balta, the teacher Eliezer Mashbir organized a self-defense unit largely made up of porters, coachmen, and apprentices, and even set up a form of communication through signaling with blasts of the *shofar*. The founders of the self-defense movement in Odessa were M. *Ben-Ammi and W.M. *Haffkine. They had to overcome the opposition of those Jewish revolutionaries who believed that pogroms merely expressed the anger of the awakening Russian proletariat and therefore Jews should not act with the police against the people, even when the people were in the wrong. The first such group of defenders, composed mostly of students and Hebrew teachers, turned to the synagogues and made a special effort "to attract the butchers and coachmen." The wealthy did not take part, nor did their synagogues participate. The equipment of these fighters consisted of "sticks, axes, and iron poles – pistols were rare." During actual pogroms their defense activity had very limited success in itself; it was effective mainly in the poorest quarters, even when the Jews had to stand up to the combined strength of the army and the police. More than 100 of the defenders were arrested, among them Haffkine, who had a revolver in his hand when he was seized. Although those who were captured were mainly simple men, they never revealed at their trial that students were the initiators of the movement. In the succeeding years the youth and workers continued in their efforts to form defense organizations. In the proceedings instituted against 14 Jews in 1897, it became clear that in Minsk that year a group of defenders which had been hastily assembled had been able to strike back with combat weapons against soldiers rioting in the marketplace.

The pogroms of 1903, especially that in *Kishinev, created renewed interest in self-defense. Although even in Kishinev there had been individual examples of courageous defenders, the slaughter there symbolized in the mind of the Jewish community the weakness and shame of their general defenselessness in the face of their attackers. The Russian government had announced its official opposition to organized defense. However, all active nationalist Jewish circles, the youth in particular, whether Zionists or socialists, concluded that their collective defense was a spiritual as well as a physical necessity. In April 1903, two weeks after the Kishinev pogroms, the *Aguddat Soferim Ivrim* ("Hebrew Writers League"), including *Aḥad Ha-Am, Ḥ.N. *Bialik, M. Ben-Ammi, S. *Dubnow, and Y.Ḥ. *Rawnitzki, issued an announcement, composed by Aḥad Ha-Am, stating that "it is degrading for five million people … to stretch out their necks to be slaughtered and to call for help without attempting to protect their property, dignity, and lives with their own hands." They demanded the establishment of a permanent organization to defend against and repel attackers "in all places where we live," and they urged that "a general gathering of the representatives of all major Jewish communities within our land" should be convened for this purpose. This same outlook also gradually became evident within leftist Jewish circles, although for them the decision to act against the masses of the Russian people was a bitter one. In its policy statement of 1903, the *Bund declared "violence must be answered with violence, wherever it comes from." A group of left-wing Zionist students called for "the same healthy, free response made by a man when a wild animal leaps upon him … acquire as many weapons as you possibly can!" This mood found its strongest poetic expression in Bialik's poem "The City of Slaughter," which sharply condemns the shame of the meek acquiescence of the "calves for the slaughter."

In Odessa, collective defense was set up at this time, with Vladimir *Jabotinsky as one of the active participants. They collected money, bought guns by the dozens, and prepared small arms. In proclamations in Yiddish and in Russian they urged the youth to arm itself. However, the various leftist organizations, which had been fairly active in the area of self-defense, did not join forces with Jabotinsky's group, and still less were they prepared to act jointly with bourgeois circles; the Bund in particular was strongly opposed to such cooperation. Between 1903 and 1905 collective defense units were set up in the cities and towns of Belorussia and the Ukraine. In Yekaterinoslav (*Dnepropetrovsk), for instance, the *Po'alei Zion were the organizers: they raised money, acquired guns, and "in the smithies special iron poles were fashioned, with iron spikes on them." To improve their marksmanship, they went out to deserted islands on the River Dnieper for target practice. Two hundred students in *Kiev formed a defensive unit, "each armed with a large stick, a Finnish knife, and pistol." The artisans in the group fashioned hand-combat weapons. The defenders were divided into groups of ten, and whenever the outbreak of a pogrom appeared imminent they took up their arms and mobilized for action in private homes with telephones. They also had spies among the potential attackers, and a number of non-Jewish teachers at the university aided the defenders. Similar organizations were established in *Shklov, *Vilna – where Michael *Helpern was one of the leaders – Warsaw, and *Rostov on the Don. The Minsk experience in setting up defensive units was used as a model for the entire area. The self-defense organization in *Gomel (Homel) developed from the nucleus known as Gibborei Ẓiyyon ("The Heroes of Zion"), the military unit of the Po'alei Zion, and "during the summer of 1903 the entire city was organized, blacksmiths ... butchers, and wagon drivers, each separately," and the rest of the citizens along occupational lines. (There was also a separate defense unit of the Bund.) When the army mounted an attack against them in 1903, many fell and numerous others were captured and brought to trial. Seeing that the army was on the point of attacking them, the defenders had tried to arouse the Jewish masses against the pogromists. Even the government-appointed rabbi of *Kremenchug, A.Y. Friedenberg, issued a proclamation in Russian in 1903 calling for collective defense and convening a conference of all the neighboring communities for the purpose of "consulting on the establishment of secret defensive units in various places." Ḥayyim Berlin, the rabbi of Moscow, took part in this convention.

In 1904 the self-defense movement was widespread throughout many cities and towns, but the splintering-off into factions and the growing revolutionary tide among the workers prevented real cooperation and unity. In many cities there were a number of parallel defense groups – affiliated with the Bund, Po'alei Zion, etc. Yet in the face of a pogrom they usually united, and even secured the help of the ordinary "unpolitically minded" Jews. The Bund defense group in Dvinsk (*Daugavpils) successfully repelled its attackers in 1904, and, when its leader, Mendel Daitch, was sentenced to death for an attack on a police officer during what was actually a general revolutionary action, *Meir Simḥah ha-Kohen, the rabbi of Dvinsk, proclaimed a fast and called for the recitation of psalms to mark his righteous act of defending his fellow Jews. Revolutionary circles began to take pride in this central and unifying activity for Jewish self-defense. V. Fabrikant, the left-wing Zionist, described how in 1904 "a defensive unit ... was set up. At its center was organized labor, and the rest of the elements both organized and unorganized were on the periphery." He also stated that "every Jew, even one of the higher echelons of the bourgeoisie, is entitled to be defended by us if he is in danger of injury solely because he is a Jew." Defining the goals of self-defense, he said it was a war "for our present ... for the possessions of the poor; for the lives of our brethren of Israel who are in distress; for the honor of our sisters; for our national honor ... for our future as a nation." He also recommended taking retaliatory action against individuals who stirred up pogroms and against those officials who were lax in their duty to protect Jewish citizens. Even Bundist circles recognized as desirable the continued existence of defense units and of their branching-out into other cities and towns. The Bund claimed the honor of setting up the committees for self-defense. At the initiative of Po'alei Zion, an all-Russian conference on self-defense programs was convened in Odessa on Jan. 6, 1905; Aḥad Ha-Am and S. Dubnow promised to speak there. However, since some letters dealing with conference plans were intercepted and several of the delegates were arrested, the full-scale meeting envisaged did not take place.

When the government turned "the wrath of the masses" against the Jews in 1905, an extensive self-defense movement existed in many Russian cities and towns. The nucleus of the movement came from the Jewish labor parties and their military units, and it had a widespread following among the rest of the people. Although anxious to form countrywide links among its units, the movement was weakened by party and class divisions and suspicion. Organized defense groups are known to have existed in 42 cities; 30 of these went into action, particularly in October of 1905. The most important were in Odessa, Akkerman (*Belgorod-Dnestrovski), *Zhitomir, *Starodub, Yelizavetgrad, Yekaterinoslav, *Chernigov, and Rostov on the Don. Some enlightened Russian non-Jews aided the cause of Jewish self-defense and in Odessa the university assisted the defenders. In the battles of 1905, 132 fighters fell, including four women and a number of Russians. Both the strength and the weakness of the self-defense endeavor were clearly embodied in its activity in Zhitomir, in which three organizations were involved: the Bund, Po'alei Zion, and the "non-labor Zionists." In clashes with rioters and security forces (May 6–7, 1905) all three groups worked together under the command of a young Bundist. The battle lasted for four hours and 13 of the defenders fell. From Berdichev and *Chudnov

Jewish defense groups came to the aid of the Jews of Zhitomir. However, this example of cooperation between cities ended in tragedy; when the Berdichev unit came up against a crowd of rioters at a railway station, the local Jews – fearful of the mob – refused to give them refuge. Ten of the Berdichev group were killed. The dangers inherent in the movement of the Jewish defense units throughout Russia were also revealed in many other incidents, as in October 1905, when 23 fighters belonging to the defenders' group from *Rechitsa perished in Odessa. Other cities also witnessed a wide range of defensive activities, including Poltava, where the head was Izhak *Ben-Zvi. In Yekaterinoslav the fighters succeeded in killing 47 of their attackers.

After 1905 the strength of the self-defense movement waned along with the lessening of revolutionary tensions within Russia. In 1909 the central ammunition storage dump of the Bund was liquidated. However, the circumstances of the civil war in 1917–20 brought new and stronger calls for self-defense and initiated new methods of setting it in motion. In those years pogroms were perpetrated not only by the rioting masses but also by bands of soldiers and even by regular units of the forces of the warring sides. In such conditions of social upheaval and the disintegration of the czarist army, the defense movement was obviously likely to gain greater support than previously through the aid of Jewish soldiers and because of the revolutionary excitement prevailing among the leftist factions. Nevertheless, it was also liable to rapid collapse, for it could not stand alone against attackers who were trained troops of regular or semi-regular armies. Those soldiers of the disintegrating army who had some nationalist consciousness made a great effort to set up a Jewish defense force which would concentrate on guarding the honor, lives, and property of their brethren. Drawing attention to the force of 400,000 Jewish soldiers in the Russian army, they pointed out that various other peoples were attempting to establish units of their own from the fragments of the czarist army. Especially active in the Ukraine in 1917 was the Iggud ha-Ẓeva'i ha-Yehudi ("Jewish Military League"), whose president was Isaac Gogol. In the beginning the leftist factions opposed the separatist goal of the defensive groups, but by the time they had come to the conclusion, in 1918, that Gogol was right, they had missed their opportunity. The Ukrainian army attacked the Iggud and murdered its president.

From then on self-defense became a local matter, at most the concern of a very limited area. Even then there were some Jewish soldiers among the defenders, but their success depended solely on local conditions and the qualities of the local defenders. In spite of these circumstances, there were defense units which enjoyed limited success. In *Golovanevsk, for instance, a township of 1,200 Jewish families, many of whom were artisans, a company of defenders which had repelled pogromists in 1905 was reformed in 1917 under the command of an ex-soldier. They set up a permanent guard of 25 men, who appeared as if they were "in charge of the place" and confiscated or bought arms from deserting soldiers and sailors. They also purchased a cannon and prepared bombs. Several times men of the defense force went to the outskirts of the town and fought in the fields – at times alongside the Red Army and at times on their own – to repel bands of approaching attackers. The defense organization was active there until its leader fell at the end of 1919. In *Bershad too the defenders rallied around a nucleus of soldiers who had just returned from the front. At their head was a capable leader, Moshe Dubrovensky. This defense unit waged bitter battles with roving armed bands and held its position of strength until 1919. On the eve of Purim 5679 (1919), some of the finest of their company, their leader among them, fell in action during a battle with a troop of Cossacks that stormed the city. Similar information has been preserved about defense fighters in other towns.

The value of Jewish self-defense in Russia was not limited to its own time and place alone. The goal which became clearly articulated in the movement – to protect the Jewish community independently of the state authorities – pointed the way for the Jews in Ereẓ Israel under Turkish rule and later in their struggle with the British Mandate authorities. From the ranks of these defenders came many of the methods and leaders of the *Haganah in Ereẓ Israel.

[Haim Hillel Ben-Sasson]

In Austria-Hungary

Jewish soldiers' committees were founded in some major garrisons of Austria-Hungary at the time of the dissolution of the empire (1918). Officers who were members of Zionist students' and youth organizations formed units of Jewish soldiers returning from the front, which were instrumental in protecting Jewish life and property. They wore cockades in the Zionist colors, utilized Hebrew text in their official seal, and were seen by some Jews as presaging the coming of the Messiah. They put themselves at the disposal of the Jewish national councils (see *Nationalrat) then established in Vienna and Prague. Besides Vienna and Prague (where the committee was under the command of Samuel Hugo *Bergman), soldiers' committees were set up in *Brno (Bruenn), *Olomouc (Olmuetz), Terezin (*Theresienstadt), and other towns. A Jewish company effectively protected the Jewish quarter of *Bratislava (Pressburg) while possession of the town was contested between Czechoslovakia and Hungary.

[Meir Lamed]

After World War I

After World War I and its aftermath, no self-defense units of a solidly organized and permanent character are known to have existed. In the 1930s in some universities of Central Europe, which by tradition were closed to the entrance of police, antisemitic and Nazi students sometimes attacked their Jewish colleagues, who then organized themselves for self-defense.

During World War II, under the conditions of the *Holocaust, the struggle of ghetto fighters and the *partisans, as well as the rebellion of some Jews in the extermination *camps themselves, formed a unique chapter of heroism and desperation exceeding the usual definition of self-defense.

After World War II, particularly in Latin American and Arab countries, members of Jewish sports organizations and Zionist youth groups organized self-defense units against antisemitic and neo-Nazi violence (as by the Tacuara in Argentina; see *Neo-Nazism) and aggressive Arab nationalists (in Iraq and in some North African countries).

Jewish Defense League

In 1968 a group under the name Jewish Defense League (JDL) was formed in several sections of Brooklyn, N.Y. At first the group, consisting mostly of Orthodox young people, served as a semi-vigilant unit to protect local Jews from physical attacks, mainly by delinquent blacks and Puerto Ricans. Later the group grew into a quasi-political movement, using the slogan "Never again" (with reference to the Holocaust and citing Vladimir *Jabotinsky extensively). In the contemporary style of "confrontation" and "direct action" engulfing certain sections of U.S. youth, it adopted the "defense" of Soviet Jewry, Israel, and Jews in Arab countries by forceful means in New York and other U.S. cities. Its declared aim was to disrupt commercial and cultural exchanges and tourism between the U.S. and U.S.S.R. The JDL achieved a high degree of publicity and also entered into sharp controversy with the organized Jewish community, to which it refused to adhere. Its leader, Rabbi Meir *Kahane, became a focus of polemics in the U.S. and other countries, as well as in the Jewish and general press (see, e.g., Michael T. Kaufman, "The Complex Past of Meir Kahane," in the *New York Times*, Jan. 24, 1971).

Kahane moved to Israel in 1971 and in 1976 founded *Kach, the Israeli branch of the Jewish Defense League. He was assassinated in New York in 1990. In the meantime the U.S. branch continued to operate (for a chronology of its activities in the ensuing decades see www.adl.org, the Anti-Defamation League website). In 2001, JDL chairman Irv Kugel was charged with conspiracy to commit acts of terrorism. In 2002, while in detention, he fell 18 feet to his death at the Federal Detention Center in Los Angeles. After his death the JDL split into rival factions.

BIBLIOGRAPHY: E. Heifez, *Pogrom Geshikhte 1919–1920*, 1 (1921), 200–12; N. Shtif, *Pogromen in Ukraine in Tsayt fun der Frayviliker Armey* (1923), 54–57; *Reshummot*, 3 (1923); E. Tcherikower, *In der Tkufe fun Revolutsie* (1924), 157–210 (= *Yehudim be-Ittot Mahpekhah* (1958), 341–557); A.D. Rosenthal, *Megillat ha-Tevaḥ*, 1–3 (1927–32); idem, *Ha-Haganah ha-Ivrit be-Ir Boguslav* (1944); S. Dubnow, in: *Ha-Tekufah*, 24 (1928), 416–20; Y. Midrashi, *Bershad ve-ha-Haganah Shellah* (1935); L. Motzkin, in: *Sefer Motzkin* (1939), 123–34; I. Halpern, *Sefer ha-Gevurah*, 3 (1950); *Die Judenpogrome in Russland*, 1–2 (1909); A.M. Rabinowicz, in: *The Jews of Czechoslovakia*, 1 (1968), 247 n. 43; R. Weltsch, in: *Der Jude* (1918); S. Ha-Kohen Weingarten, *Toledot Yehudei Bratislava* (1960), 129–33.

SELF-HATRED, JEWISH. The phenomenon of self-hatred arises among minority groups forced together by outside pressure and produces a negative attitude on the part of members toward their own group, but the very word is absent from important dictionaries of the English language, and it would appear to have been coined by Theodore Lessing (see below), since in his book dealing with it he gives it in quotation marks.

It was first diagnosed in Central European Jewish social theory and fiction. As expressed by Jews, it is both a group phenomenon and an individual trait. One Jewish group may take a hostile position toward another, e.g., German Jews against East European Jews in Europe; Orthodox Jews against Conservative and Reform Jews in the United States and the State of Israel; and *vice versa*. A Jew who expresses self-hatred, according to Kurt Lewin, "will dislike everything specifically Jewish, for he will see in it that which keeps him away from the majority for which he is longing. He will show dislike for those Jews who are outspokenly so, and will frequently indulge in self-hatred" (Lewin, *Resolving Social Conflicts*. p. 164).

With the decline of positive traits of Judaism and Jewish identification in Western Diaspora communities, both in Europe before World War II and in the United States afterward, self-hatred became endemic. The most important early analysis of the phenomenon among Jews appeared in Berlin, 1930, in Theodor *Lessing's *Juedischer Selbsthass* (Berlin, 1930). To the self-hating Jew, all misfortune derives from the fact that one is Jewish. The Jews, moreover, are held responsible for their own fate and are therefore "to blame for all their misfortunes." Clinical reports by Lessing include Jews who urge the Aryans to exterminate the Jews like vermin, and others who remained childless or even committed suicide so as "to remove the stain of Jewishness from mankind." Lessing therefore describes Jewish self-hatred as an acute pathology of psychosis.

In Western democracies, on the other hand, Jewish self-hatred appears as a chronic malady of neurosis. But, while in Central Europe the self-hating Jew removed himself as far as possible from Jewish associations, in the United States he found himself at the top of Jewish community life. Lewin diagnosed this phenomenon in 1941. "In a minority group, individual members who are economically successful… usually gain a higher degree of acceptance by the majority group. This places them culturally on the periphery of the underprivileged group and makes them more likely to be 'marginal' persons. They frequently have a negative balance and are particularly eager not to have their 'good connections' endangered by too close a contact with those sections of the underprivileged group which are not acceptable to the majority. Nevertheless, they are frequently called on for leadership by the underprivileged group because of their status and power. They themselves are usually eager to accept the leading role in the minority, partly as a substitute for gaining status in the majority, and partly because such leadership enables them to have and maintain additional contact with the majority." This type of person Lewin calls "the leader from the periphery." He uses his position to de-Judaize the Jewish community and remove those traits which make Jews Jewish.

With the renaissance of Jewish pride and self-respect consequent upon the establishment of the State of Israel and its positive impact upon Jewish and world public opinion of the 1950s and 1960s, Jewish self-hatred tended to decline. Indeed, the rise to public prominence of clearly identified Jewish personalities in the Western democracies and of the State of Israel served as a powerful antidote to both public and private self-hatred. Evidence of the development of Jewish self-respect is the dramatic shift in budgets of Jewish community federations and welfare funds, and of public opinion affecting those budgets in favor of positive evidences and programs of Jewish self-identification.

Lewin regarded Jewish self-hatred as a social-psychological phenomenon in that it occurs among entirely normal persons. He therefore concluded: "Jewish self-hatred will die out only when actual equality of status with the non-Jew is achieved. Only then will the enmity against one's own group decrease to the relatively insignificant proportions characteristic of the majority groups. Sound self-criticism will replace it." It is generally maintained, therefore, that through Jewish education feelings of inferiority and fear may be counteracted by positive identification with the Jewish people. For example, Zionism in the Germany of the 1930s was a powerful force in the face of Hitler for hope and Jewish affirmation (*"Jasagen zum Judentum"*). On this subject Lewin further commented: "… there is nothing so important as a clear and fully accepted belonging to a group whose fate has a positive meaning. A long-range view, which includes the past and the future of Jewish life, and links the solution of the minority problem with the problem of the welfare of all human beings, is one of these sources of strength. A strong feeling of being part and parcel of the group and having a positive attitude toward it is … sufficient condition for the avoidance of attitudes based on self-hatred." Since, as noted, Zionism before 1948, and the State of Israel thereafter, provided that locus of unity and long-range view of a past of courage and a future of hope which Jewish self-esteem demands, it is not to be wondered at that the growing impact of Zionist activity in the Western countries as well as among the Jews of the former U.S.S.R. materially limited the formerly commonplace and endemic expressions of this phenomena.

BIBLIOGRAPHY: K. Lewin, *Resolving Social Conflicts; Selected Papers on Group Dynamics* (1948), 159–68, 186–200; T. Lessing, *Der juedische Selbsthass* (1930); J. Neusner, in: *Midstream* 15 (1969), 34–53; idem, *American Judaism: Adventure in Modernity* (1972), 15–34, 61–116.

[Jacob Neusner]

SELIG, ALLAN H. (**"Bud"**; 1934–), U.S. baseball commissioner. Originally a highly successful auto dealer in his hometown of Milwaukee, Selig first became involved in professional baseball in 1963 as the largest stockholder of the publicly owned Milwaukee Braves. Two years later the Braves left for Atlanta, and the disappointed Selig formed an organization dedicated to bringing baseball back to Milwaukee. An exceptional opportunity arose when the expansion Seattle Pilots failed in their maiden 1969 season, and Selig led a consortium of investors in purchasing, and promptly moving, the Pilots to Milwaukee for the 1970 season and renaming them the Brewers. Over the next two decades, the Brewers organization would be given an award seven times for excellence in management. When in September 1992 Commissioner Fay Vincent resigned, fellow baseball owners turned to the now senior Selig to act as interim commissioner via his new role as chairman of the Executive Council. Six years later, Selig was elected by his peers to become the official ninth commissioner of Major League Baseball. During his 14 years as acting and official commissioner through 2005, Selig was involved in a number of turbulent episodes, including a 272-day strike in 1994 and 1995, which saw the cancellation of the 1994 World Series, the early termination of the 2002 extra-inning All-Star Game because of a lack of pitchers, and the steroids controversy which exploded in 2005. Among the major changes implemented by Selig during his tenure were interleague play, revenue sharing between big and small market clubs, the institution of the three-division format in each league, and the creation of wild card berths along with an extra tier of playoffs. In recognition of his efforts on behalf both of baseball and various causes, Selig was the recipient of a plethora of awards and honors, including the 2003 Jewish Foundation for the Righteous Recognition of Goodness Award, the 2001 Sports Torch of Learning Award from the American Friends of the Hebrew University, the 1994 Anti-Defamation League's World of Difference Award, the 1993 Ellis Island Medal of Honor, the 1989 August A. Busch Jr. Award (equivalent to the MVP award), the 1983 U.S. Olympic Committee Sportsman of the Year Award, and the 1981 International B'nai B'rith Sportsman of the Year Award. In July 2001, Selig created an endowment to establish the Allan H. and Suzanne L. Selig Merit Scholarship Fund at the Rothberg International School at the Hebrew University of Jerusalem.

[Robert B. Klein (2nd ed.)]

SELIG, PHINEAS (1856–1941), New Zealand journalist and newspaper proprietor. Born in Melbourne, Australia, Selig was the son of Rev. B.A. Selig (formerly of Penzance), reader and *shoḥet* to the Wellington community, who had emigrated there in 1862. After a career as a reporter and correspondent, he founded (with A.E. Bird) the *New Zealand Referee* (1884) and was manager of the *Christchurch Press* (1901–23). During the 1920s and 1930s he was the outstanding figure in the New Zealand press. For 20 years he was president of the New Zealand Newspaper Proprietors' Association and Canterbury Master Printers' Association. A leading administrator of athletics and boxing, he was president of the New Zealand Trotting Association for 25 years. He played an influential role in the Jewish community and was president of the Canterbury Hebrew Congregation in Christchurch from 1917 to 1941 and supported Jewish and Palestine appeals.

ADD. BIBLIOGRAPHY: R. Harvey, "Phineas Selig," in: *Dictionary of New Zealand Biography.*

[Maurice S. Pitt]

SELIGMAN, family of international bankers from Baiersdorf, Bavaria, where they are known from the early 18th century. JOSEPH SELIGMAN (1819–1880) was the oldest son of David, the village weaver and an itinerant trader in woolens. Joseph, after attending university, immigrated in 1837 to the United States, where he was first employed in a small Pennsylvanian mining town. Soon he sent for his brothers, and pooling their resources they peddled in Pennsylvania, then moved to Alabama and Missouri, and in 1846 made New York their headquarters as wholesale clothiers. They also ran a store at Watertown, New York, where they formed a friendship with the then Lieutenant Ulysses S. Grant, the future president of the United States. After the discovery of gold in California, the Seligmans installed themselves in San Francisco in the city's only brick building. The Seligmans benefited from a clothing monopoly and the gold they received was shipped to New York, where it established the firm's credit. Their family's business interests were ultimately concentrated in banking in New York City. After the outbreak of the Civil War Joseph placed more than $200 million of United States Government securities in Europe, mainly in Germany and Holland. In 1864 the present firm of J. & W. Seligman & Company was formed in New York, with branches in London, Paris, Frankfurt, New Orleans, and San Francisco. The London and Paris branches became independent, and were known respectively as Seligman Brothers Limited and Banque Seligman. The branch in Frankfurt operated under the name of Seligman & Stettheimer. The San Francisco office was the forerunner of the Anglo & London-Paris National Bank. During the 1870s the firm assisted the government in connection with the treasury's refunding of the national debt and the resumption of specie payment. The firm became prominent in railroad financing and headed the De Lesseps Panama Canal syndicate; it also entered international underwriting for railroad construction, public utilities, and a wide range of industrial enterprises including General Motors and Republic Iron and Steel. The firm served as fiscal agents of Puerto Rico and as financial advisers to foreign governments. During World War I the firm held major positions in all Allied loan syndicates and invested heavily in United States Government bonds. In recent times the company has operated as an international issuing and underwriting house, securities dealer, and foreign exchange trader, and provides most investors' services. It also heads one of the largest investment trusts in the United States, the Tri-Continental Corporation. Joseph Seligman, the firm's first senior partner, was followed by his brother JESSE (1827–1894) who in turn was succeeded by Joseph's son ISAAC NEWTON (1855–1917). Another of Joseph's sons was EDWIN ROBERT ANDERSON *SELIGMAN. By 1970 there were no more bearers of the name among the firm's partners. The family was prominent in New York's German-Jewish society and members were among the founders and members of the boards of Temple Emanu-El and the Ethical Culture Society and generously contributed to Jewish and general charities.

BIBLIOGRAPHY: *Family Register of the Descendants of David Seligman* (1913); L. Herz, *Die vierteltausendjaehrige Geschichte der Familie Seligman, 1680–1930* (1935), incl. bibl.; R.L. Muir and C.J. White, *Over the Long Term: the Story of J. and W. Seligman and Co. 1864–1964* (1964); L. Wells, *The Seligman Story* (Ms., 3 vols., 1931); S. Birmingham, *Our Crowd* (1967), index; G.T. Hellman, in: *New Yorker Magazine*, 30 (Oct. 30, 1954), 34–40.

[Joachim O. Ronall]

SELIGMAN, CHARLES GABRIEL (1873–1940), British physician and anthropologist. Born in London and educated at St. Paul's school, Seligman trained as a physician oriented to medical research. He became professionally interested in anthropology as a result of his participation as a medical researcher in the Cambridge Torres Straits Expedition. In 1903 he persuaded Major Cooke Daniels, a wealthy American, to finance an expedition to New Guinea. This research culminated in his work *The Melanesians of British New Guinea* (1910). Seligman served as lecturer and subsequently as professor, holding the first chair of anthropology established at the University of London. His wife, BRENDA ZARA SALAMAN SELIGMAN (1883–1965), became his professional collaborator and was also an important anthropologist. Together the Seligmans undertook a number of other expeditions, to Ceylon to study the Veddahs and to the Sudan. In between the field sorties, Seligman continued his research in pathology; he was elected a fellow of the Royal College of Physicians and a member of the Royal Society. During World War I he served as a medical officer and worked in a psychoneurotic hospital where he saw the clinical value of Freudian psychoanalysis, which he later applied to anthropology. In his fieldwork Seligman regarded himself as a natural historian of ethnology, studying living societies with scientific detachment. He rejected the extreme diffusionist theories and investigated carefully the diffusion and transmission of culture traits. Seligman's research prepared the way for Bronislaw Malinowski's fieldwork in Melanesia.

BIBLIOGRAPHY: E.E. Evans-Pritchard et al. (eds.), *Essays presented to C.G. Seligman* (1934), 381–5. **ADD. BIBLIOGRAPHY:** ODNB online.

[Ephraim Fischoff]

SELIGMAN, EDWIN ROBERT ANDERSON (1861–1939), U.S. economist. A member of the *Seligman banking family of New York, Seligman began teaching at Columbia in 1885 and held the post of professor of political economy and finance from 1888 to 1931, when he became professor emeritus in residence. His wide-ranging interests and his sense of social responsibility involved him in many academic, public, and civic organizations and institutions. He was instrumental in forming the American Economic Society and served as its president, 1902–04. He also served a term as president of the National Tax Association, and the American Association of University Professors, and chaired its committee which in 1915 published the fundamental report on academic freedom. In his special field, public finance, he was a consultant member of numerous public committees, at the city, state, and federal levels, as well as in international organizations. In 1932, while lecturing at Havana University, he undertook, at the request of President Gerardo Machado, the reorganization of Cuba's fiscal system. His writings on taxation were influential since many of the innovations he advocated were adopted, and the terminology he originated passed into common use.

He published 15 works on taxation and economics generally, including *The Economic Interpretation of History* (1902), a significant contribution to the development of the subject; *Principles of Economics* (1905); *The Economics of Farm Relief* (1929); and *Price Cutting and Price Maintenance* (1932). His wide range of interests enabled him to become the chief promoter and editor in chief of the *Encyclopaedia of the Social Sciences* (15 vols., 1930–35), to which he also contributed articles and biographies. He was also editor of the *Columbia Series in History, Economics, and Public Law*, and the *Political Science Quarterly*. A bibliography of his writings was published in 1931 by Columbia University; his correspondence was published by Joseph Dorfman in 1941, and a collection of memorial addresses in 1942.

BIBLIOGRAPHY: *Family Register of the Descendants of David Seligman* (1913); L. Herz, *Die vierteltausendjaehrige Geschichte der Familie Seligman, 1680–1930* (1935), includes bibliography; L. Wells, *The Seligman Story* (Ms., 3 vols., 1931); G.T. Hellman, in: *New Yorker Magazine*, 30 (Oct. 30, 1954), 34–40.

[Joachim O. Ronall]

SELIGMAN, HERBERT SPENCER (1872–1951), British army officer. Born in London, Seligman attended St. Paul's school and the Royal Military Academy. In 1892 he was commissioned in the Royal Artillery. He fought in the South African war, being awarded the Queen's Medal, and on the outbreak of World War I was sent as commander of a battery to the front in western France. Seligman was given command of an artillery brigade in 1915 and in the following year commanded the artillery of the Seventh Division. Subsequently he was made commanding officer of the Cavalry Corps artillery, and took part in the Allied assault on the German lines in the summer of 1918. Seligman was mentioned in dispatches six times and received numerous decorations. After the war he was promoted to honorary brigadier general and served in the Territorial Army until his retirement in 1935.

BIBLIOGRAPHY: J. Ben Hirsch, *Jewish General Officers* (1967), 88.

[Mordechai Kaplan]

SELIGMANN, CAESAR (1860–1950), leader of Liberal Judaism in Germany. Born in Landau, Seligmann was appointed preacher of the Liberal synagogue (Temple) in Hamburg in 1889, and from 1902 to 1939 he officiated as rabbi in Frankfurt. In 1910 he published for the Liberal synagogue (Western synagogue) a two-volume prayer book (*Israelitisches Gebetbuch*, 2nd ed. 1928) that was even more extreme than any proposed by the German Reform movement to that date. One of the founders of the *Vereinigung fuer das liberale Judentum in 1910, he edited its organ, *Liberales Judentum*, which appeared from 1910 to 1922. In cooperation with I. *Elbogen and H. *Vogelstein, in 1929 he published the "unified prayer book," restoring to the Liberal rite many traditional prayers which had been previously excluded. His other works include a collection of popular lectures, *Judentum und moderne Weltanschauung* (1905), and a history of the Reform movement, *Geschichte der juedischen Reformbewegung von Mendelssohn bis zur Gegenwart* (1922). When addressing the Liberal rabbis in Wiesbaden in 1937, on the occasion of the 100th anniversary of the rabbinical conference convened by A. *Geiger, Seligmann advised his colleagues to become reconciled with Zionism. In 1939 he moved to London, where he lived until his death. His autobiography, *Mein Leben. Erinnerungen eines Grossvaters*, was written in 1941 but only one chapter was published.

BIBLIOGRAPHY: *Juedisch-Liberale Zeitung, Festnummer* (Dec. 11, 1930); B. Italiener, in: *Synagogue Review*, 24 (1949–50), 277ff.; YLBI, 5 (1960), 346–50.

[Jacob Rothschild]

SELIGMANN, KURT (1900–1962), U.S. painter, illustrator, graphic artist, printmaker. Born in Basle, Switzerland, Seligmann studied at the Geneva Academy of Art. He lived in Paris from 1929 to 1938, where he joined the circle of the Surrealists. Seligmann and his wife relocated to the U.S. in 1939, and while living there played a crucial role, with the assistance of Alfred Barr, in facilitating the immigration of a large number of artists and writers fleeing the Nazis, including André Breton and his wife, André Masson, Paul Eluard, and Pierre Mabille. Breton and Eluard included his work in their *Dictionnaire abrégé du surréalisme,* published to accompany the International Exposition of Surrealism in Paris in 1938. Seligmann's imagery characteristically features anthropomorphic figures, sometimes ominous, intertwined in complex convolutions of drapery; he often adorned these heterogenous figures with feathers, helmets, heraldic insignia, and references to alchemy. He also fashioned objects like *Ultra-meuble.* Like many other Surrealist artists, Seligmann's art responded to the development of psychoanalysis and its revelations about the dark and irrational aspects of dreams and the unconscious, a preoccupation understandable during a lifetime which witnessed two world wars. His art also references a much earlier tradition of medieval and 16th century German and Swiss artists, including Albrecht Altdorfer, Hans Holbein, and Matthias Grunewald, artists whose works also possessed an engagement with violence and human suffering. Seligmann exhibited at the Nierendorf, Durlacher, and Ruth White Galleries, as well as designing sets and costumes for ballets choreographed by Hanya Holm and George Balanchine. He participated in the "Artists in Exile" show at the Pierre Matisse Gallery in 1942. In the 1940s, he was a regular contributor to the Surrealist periodicals *View* and VVV. He taught at Briarcliff Junior College and Brooklyn College. Towards the end of his life, he spent the preponderance of his time at his farm in Sugar Loaf, N.Y, located an hour away from New York City. In addition to his art, Seligmann's interests included the occult, mysticism and tarot; in fact, he wrote a treatise titled *The Mirror of Magic* (1948). He also developed a passion for Native American art. In addition to producing a large body of etchings, lithographs, and paintings, he illustrated many books. His work has been exhibited at numerous museums, including the Art Institute of Chicago, the Carnegie Institute, the Museum of Modern Art, and the Whitney Museum. His art has been collected by museums and galleries around the world, including the Bibliotheque Nationale, the Guggenheim Museum, the Metropolitan Museum of Art, the Whitney Museum, and the Yale University Art Gallery, among other places.

BIBLIOGRAPHY: S. Barron, *Exiles and Emigrés: The Flight of European Artists from Hitler* (1997); G. Durozoi, *History of the Surrealist Movement*, tr. by A. Anderson (2002); A. Kampf, *Jewish Experience in the Art of the Twentieth Century* (1984).

[Nancy Buchwald (2nd ed.)]

SELIGSBERG, ALICE LILLIE (1873–1940), U.S. Zionist and civic leader. Alice Seligsberg was born in New York City. Although her parents were founders of the Ethical Culture Society, she was to identify herself fully with the Jewish community. She became an active social worker, conducting girls' clubs and working with the Hebrew Sheltering Guardian Society Orphanage. To help place children leaving the orphanage, she founded Fellowship House, serving as president during 1913–18, and was also responsible for other programs to aid orphans. Alice Seligsberg's friendship with Henrietta *Szold led to her involvement with Zionist projects and Hadassah. In 1917 she helped organize the American Zionist Medical Unit and was in charge of its staff of 44 medical and administrative personnel when it embarked secretly for Palestine in June 1918. There Alice Seligsberg laid the foundations for Hadassah's comprehensive medical program in Palestine. In 1919 she became executive director of the Palestine Orphan Committee of the Joint Distribution Committee to help care for displaced and abandoned children. Upon her return to the United States, Alice Seligsberg helped organize Junior Hadassah to aid the war orphans. She served as national president of Hadassah (1920–21) and during 1924–40 was senior adviser to Junior Hadassah. In 1942 Hadassah established the Alice L. Seligsberg Vocational School for girls in Jerusalem in her memory.

[Gladys Rosen]

SELIGSON, ESTHER (1941–), Mexican author. Born in Mexico City, she studied French and Hispanic literature at the Universidad Nacional Autónoma. Seligson was an accomplished translator into Spanish of such authors as Edmond Jabés. Her writing covers a broad spectrum of genres that include poetry, essay, novel, short story, and literary criticism. Her creative work is characterized by a profound introspection, lyrical quality, and relationship to diverse literary traditions. Many of her early works – *Luz de dos* (1978), *Diálogos con el cuerpo* (1981), *Sed de mar* (1987), among others – have been collected in one volume titled *Toda la luz* (2002). Similarly, her novel *La morada en el tiempo* (1981) has been reissued (2004). It is her most well-known work and is a singular example of her style and contribution to Mexican letters. The novel is clearly influenced by the author's own spirituality as well as kabbalism. In general, her narrative fiction can be said to be lacking in traditional plot and character development. Seligson is much more interested in writing narrative that serves as a form of meditation, a way to unravel the mysteries of the human condition through poetics. This is clear from her first book, *Otros son los sueños* (1973), to her later *Simiente* (2004), which is a meditative collage on suicide and is based on a personal experience. As a literary critic Seligson examines the work of authors as diverse as Elena Garro, Virginia Woolf, Clarice Lispector, Marguerite Yourcenar, and Franz Kafka in her book *La fugacidad como método de escritura* (1988). In 2005 Seligson lived in Israel.

[Darrell B. Lockhart (2nd ed.)]

SELIḤOT (Heb. סְלִיחוֹת). The word *seliḥah* means "forgiveness," and in the singular is used to indicate a *piyyut* whose subject is a plea for forgiveness for sins. In the plural, the word is used for a special order of service consisting of non-statutory additional prayers which are recited on all fast days, on occasions of special intercession, and during the Penitential season which begins before *Rosh Ha-Shanah and concludes with the *Day of Atonement.

The Mishnah (Ta'an. 2:1–4) gives the order of service for public fasts, usually proclaimed during periods of drought. It provided, inter alia, for the addition of six blessings to the normal eighteen of the daily **Amidah*, and gives the concluding formula before the actual blessing for each:

> May He Who answered our father Abraham on Mt. Moriah answer you…, may He that answered our fathers at the Red Sea… Joshua in Gilgal… Samuel at Mizpah… Elijah in Carmel… Jonah in the belly of the whale… David and his son Solomon…

The first mention of a distinct order of *Seliḥot* occurs in *Tanna de-Vei Eliyahu Zuta* (23 end):

> David knew that the Temple was destined to be destroyed and that the sacrificial system would be abolished as a result of the iniquities of Israel, and David was distressed for Israel. With what would they effect atonement? And the Holy One blessed be He said, "When troubles come upon Israel because of their iniquities, let them stand together before Me as one band and confess their iniquities before Me and recite before Me the order of Seliḥot and I will answer them"… R. Johanan said, "The Holy One blessed be He revealed this in the verse 'and the Lord passed before him and proclaimed, the Lord, the Lord God, manifest and gracious etc.' (Ex. 34:6 which gives the thirteen divine attributes). This teaches that the Holy One blessed be He descended from the mist like a *sheli'aḥ ẓibbur,* enveloped in his *tallit* and stood before the ark and revealed to Moses the order of *Seliḥot*."

It was not until the ninth century that such an order of *Seliḥot* is found, in the *Seder* of R. Amram, and these two passages, the "May He Who answered" and the scriptural verse quoted

Ezra ha-Sofer, *as included in the* Seliḥot *in Yemen and sung to one of the two melodic patterns belonging to the traditional* Seliḥot *mode. From Idelsohn,* Melodien, *vol. 1, 1925, no. 80.*

above, together with a number of others, are the essential elements in it, as in all subsequent *Seliḥot*.

During the course of time, however, a considerable number of *piyyutim*, of which the *Seliḥah* is the most important, were added to this basic formula. There are a great number of different rites in many individual communities, as distinct from countries evolving their own order of *Seliḥot. Seliḥot* composed by great personalities such as Saadyah Gaon, Gershom b. Judah, Rashi, Solomon ibn Gabirol, etc. are included in orders of *Seliḥot*. The *Seliḥot* were at first inserted, as indicated by the Mishnah, after the appropriate sixth blessing of the *Amidah* (the prayer for forgiveness for sins), but the Palestinian custom of reciting them after the *Amidah* prevailed (Sh. Ar., OḤ 566:4) and became the almost universal custom. The Italian and Roman rites, however, retain the old custom. Originally *Seliḥot* were recited only on fast days, both statutory and special, proclaimed in times of trouble, their recitation being a form of *ẓidduk ha-din*, the justification of God. Since God was just, the calamities were the result of Israel's sins, and the evil could be averted by confession and praying for forgiveness for those sins. Their extension to what is at the present time the most widespread recital of *Seliḥot*, those of the Penitential days, derived from the custom of fasting on the six days before Rosh Ha-Shanah, when *Seliḥot* were said in connection with the fast, and the custom of saying *Seliḥot* was then extended over the *Ten Days of Penitence (including the Day of Atonement, but not Rosh Ha-Shanah; cf. *Mordekhai*, Yoma, beginning). The Sephardim follow the custom of reciting *Seliḥot* for the 40 days from Rosh Ḥodesh Elul to the Day of Atonement, but the Ashkenazi custom is to commence reciting them on the Sunday before Rosh Ha-Shanah or of the preceding week should Rosh Ha-Shanah fall on Monday or Tuesday. (Sh. Ar., OḤ 581 and Rema in loc.). The *Seliḥot* for the first day are usually recited at midnight and thereafter before the morning service.

In addition to the *Seliḥot* on statutory fast days and the Penitential season, *Seliḥot* have been composed for semiofficial voluntary fasts undertaken by pious individuals. They are "BaHaB" – fasts undertaken on the Monday, Thursday and Monday following the festivals of Passover and Sukkot (*ibid.* 492) and, during a leap year, on the Thursday before the eight Sabbaths during which the scriptural portions from *Shemot* to *Teẓavveh* (called from their initial letters **Shovavim Tat*) are read, and on Yom Kippur Katan. *Seliḥot* are also recited by the members of the *ḥevra kaddisha* at their annual service, and to avert plague affecting children.

A critical edition of the Ashkenazi *Seliḥot* with notes was published by D. Goldschmidt. An edited version of the *Seliḥot* service for the whole year, along with an English translation, was issued by Abraham Rosenfeld of London (1957). For the different kinds of *piyyutim* in the *Seliḥot* see **Tokheḥah*; **Akedah*; **Teḥinnah*; **Bakkashah*.

BIBLIOGRAPHY: Idelsohn, Liturgy, 251–3; A. Rosenfeld, *The Authorised Selichot for the Whole Year* (1957), ix–xvi.

[Louis Isaac Rabinowitz]

SELIKOVITCH, GEORGE (**Getsl Zelikovitsh**; 1855–1926), Yiddish and Hebrew writer and scholar. Born in Rietavas (Riteve), Lithuania (in 1855, as Z. Goldberg clarifies), he studied Semitics and Egyptology at the University of Paris. For a while he worked at the Bibliothèque Nationale in Paris and, in 1885, accompanied Lord Kitchener as a translator on his expedition to relieve General Gordon at Khartoum. In 1887, after traveling in Turkey, Greece, Italy, and North Africa, he reached the U.S., where he briefly lectured on Egyptology at the University of Pennsylvania and at the Franklin Institute of Philadelphia. He then settled in New York and became active as a Yiddish journalist. In 1890 he joined the Yiddish *Tageblat*, where be remained with short interruptions until his death, writing scholarly articles and serial fiction. His weekly column "*Literatur un Lomdes*" ("Literature and Learning") reviewed important works of Jewish scholarship. He contributed to the *Jewish Encyclopaedia* and to the Hebrew encyclopedia *Oẓar Yisrael* ("Treasure of Israel"). His most important contributions to Hebrew literature are his *Ẓiyyurey Massa* ("Travel Portraits," 1910), a description of his journey in Ethiopia, and *Torat Budha* ("Buddha's Teaching," 1922), a translation into biblical Hebrew of Buddha's sayings. He also translated into Hebrew part of the Egyptian *Book of the Dead*. Among his publications are *Literarishe Brif* ("Literary Letters," 1909); an Arabic-Yiddish textbook (1918); and *Geklibene Shriftn* ("Collected Writings," 1913), consisting of stories, sketches, poems, and critical essays. He was a pioneer feminist, a satiric feuilletonist, and an author of erotic and sensationalist fiction.

BIBLIOGRAPHY: Rejzen, Leksikon, 1 (1926), 1105–07; LNYL, 3 (1960), 667–70; E. Schulman, *Geshikhte fun der Yidisher Literatur in Amerike* (1943), 41–4; A. Almi, *Momentn fun a Lebn* (1948), 224–9. **ADD. BIBLIOGRAPHY:** Z. Goldberg, *"Getsl Zelikovitsh – Maskil ve-Ittonai Yehudi ba-Mifneh ha-Me'ot"* (Diss., 1995; Eng. abstract in *The Mendele Review*, 8:11 (2004)). **WEBSITE:** http://shakti.trincoll.edu/~mendele/tmrarc.htm).

[Elias Schulman / Leonard Prager (2nd ed.)]

°**SELIM I** (reigned 1512–20), Ottoman sultan. The son of Sultan *Bayazid II, Selim was the ninth Ottoman sultan. Demonstrating military prowess, he was favored by the army over his elder brother Ahmed to succeed his father. He succeeded within a short time to ward off the Safavid (Persian) menace and to destroy the *Mamluk Sultanate, annexing *Syria and *Egypt and the Muslim holy places in Mecca and *Medina to his domains. Through these conquests, the *Ottoman Empire became the leading Muslim power.

Jewish exiles from Spain and Portugal were welcomed by the Ottoman sultans. Joseph *Hamon (d. 1518) became Selim's physician. The sultan displayed a benevolent attitude towards the Jews and permitted the construction of new synagogues. Elijah Mizrachi was the chief *dayyan* of Constantinople and in Selim's time there existed the office of **kahya*, i.e., a liaison officer between the Jewish communities and the government, among whose functions was the collection of taxes.

BIBLIOGRAPHY: S. Shaw, *History of the Ottoman Empire and Modern Turkey*, vol.1 (1976), 79–86; M. Rosen, *A History of the Jewish Community in Istanbul*, 1: *The Formative Years, 1453–1566* (2002), index; H. Inalcik, *The Ottoman Empire the Classical Age 1300–1600* (1973), index.

[Butrus Abu-Manneh (2nd ed.)]

°**SELIM II** (reigned 1566–74), Ottoman sultan, the son of Sultan *Suleiman the Magnificent and his favorite wife, Hurrem Sultan (Roxelana). During his reign *Cyprus was conquered from *Venice (1570–71). In the ensuing naval battle of Lepanto (October 1571), a combined fleet of Venice, the Papacy, and *Spain defeated the Ottoman fleet and destroyed it. Prominent Sephardi families such as Dona Gracia and her nephew and son-in-law Don Joesph *Nasi were close to the court during his reign. Other families, such as *Hamon, De Segura, and Ibn Ya'ish, were also influential. Joseph Nasi acquired the leasing of the taxes of Naxos along with the title of Duke, and Dona Gracia that of *Tiberias and its surroundings.

BIBLIOGRAPHY: S. Shaw, *History of the Ottoman Empire and Modern Turkey*, vol. 1 (1976), 175–79; M. Rosen, *A History of the Jewish Community in Istanbul: I The Formative Years, 1453–1566* (2002), 210–1, index; H. Inalcik, *The Ottoman Empire the Classical Age 1300–1600* (1973), index.

[Butrus Abu-Manneh (2nd ed.)]

SELJUKS (Arab. *Saljūq*), dynasty of Turkic origin which ruled *Iran and the surrounding countries in the 11th and 12th centuries. The conquest of much of the Middle East by the Seljuks, who founded an empire extending from Central Asia to the Mediterranean, influenced *inter alia* the situation of its Jewish subjects.

The Seljuks adopted and developed various institutions of military and civil administration which became the basis of much of the government structure in many of the states which succeeded them, including the *Ayyubids, the *Mamluk Sultanate, and the *Ottoman Empire; among the most important of these institutions was the military land-tenure system known as *iqṭā'*, which some scholars mistakenly call "Oriental feudalism." No less important, they supported and helped restore the primacy of orthodox *Islam, known as Sunnism. From their crossing of the Oxus to *Khurasan in 1035 at the head of their Turcoman warriors, which resulted in the conquest of Persia (Iran), they saw themselves and projected an image as champions of orthodox Islam and "the friends of the caliph." The 200 years prior to their conquests had seen an increased influence of Shiʿite heretical sects and the establishment of Shiʿite dynasties, such as the *Fatimids in 969 in *Egypt and later in parts of *Syria (including Palestine), and the Buwayhids in *Iraq and western Persia. This latter dynasty even held sway over the *Abbasid caliphs, who had been reduced to virtual puppets. The Seljuks, therefore, had the sympathy of orthodox scholars and notables who facilitated their conquest in many places. In 1055 the Seljuk leader Tughril Bey entered *Baghdad and concluded a solemn treaty with the Abbasid caliph, who recognized him as "king of the East and the West," and granted him the title "sultan." This was the first time this title was officially used in the Islamic world for the *de facto* ruler of the caliph's realm, whose authority now was recognized as mainly *de jure*. Accordingly, the Seljuks made great efforts to stress the Islamic tendency of their policy and to strengthen the hold of orthodox Islam; in fact, in many ways they saw their main enemy as the extreme Shiʿite Fatimids, and not the non-Muslims. This being said, when Seljuk armies invaded Christian countries, there were often massacres of monks, churches were burnt, and nonconformist Muslim groups were required to adapt to orthodox Islam; some of these more extreme measures were apparently the initiative of local commanders or Turcoman tribesmen and did not necessarily always represent the policy of the central government. The Seljuks founded religious colleges (*madrasas*) to educate new generations of theologians in the spirit of orthodox Islam. Their graduates, rigidly orthodox, became the class of scholars from which government officials were recruited, as were the teachers of the new colleges. The result was a strong, loyal, and militant class of Sunni scholars, who in turn influenced the tone and policy of Seljuk rule. The Seljuk official *par excellence* was the wazir Niẓām al-Mulk, who served the sultans Alp Arslan (1063–72) and Malikshah (1072–92) until his assassination. Besides being responsible for the orderly running of the vast empire and the establishment of a network of *madrasas* (called the Niẓāmiyya after him), he wrote a work in the Mirror-for-Princes genre, known as the *Siyaset-Nameh*, which gives tremendous insight into the working of these bureaucrats-*cum*-scholars' minds.

The 1070s and 1080s also saw the conquest by Turcomans, more or less under Seljuk authority, of Syria and Palestine. There is ongoing discussion among scholars about the nature of this rule and the degree of violence which the local population, including the small Jewish communities, suffered. In any event, by the mid-1090s the Fatimids had regained control over Palestine. Seljuk victories in Anatolia and Syria, including the conquest of Jerusalem, had indirectly contributed to the initiative of the first Crusade, which led to the conquest of Jerusalem in 1099 by the Franks. Ironically, by the time the Crusaders arrived in Syria at the end of the 1090s, the Seljuk state had begun to fall apart in this area and even further east, and no concerted resistance to the invaders could be offered. On the other hand, Seljuk authority was maintained in central and east Iran (and in Anatolia under another branch of the family) until the mid-12th century.

The orthodox Seljuks and their client princes considered reenactment of the so-called Covenant of *Omar, i.e., the repressive laws designed to differentiate and humiliate non-Muslims, as an integral part of their policy. Shortly after the conquest of Persia (Iran) and Babylonia (Iraq), a series of decrees were issued, enforcing the old repressive laws on Christians and Jews, and manifestations of intolerance occurred. Ibn al-Jawzī and other chroniclers dwell on the efforts to implement the Covenant of Omar in Babylonia. In 1058 the non-Muslims of Baghdad were forced to wear signs on their dress. Similarly, there were attempts to dismiss them from government positions. In 1062 taverns were closed, depriving Jews and Christians of a major source of revenue. The measures taken in 1085 by the Abbasid caliph al-Muqtadī (1075–94) reinforced the Covenant of Omar in its entirety. (We should remember, however, that the caliph's power was limited, so the extent of these measures may not have extended far beyond Baghdad.) Non-Muslims were required to wear distinctive signs on their turbans; they could not raise their voices when praying, nor build houses higher than those of their Muslim neighbors. Again taverns were closed and wine was poured into the streets. In 1091 the caliph decreed that the **dhimmīs* wear yellow headgear and girdles of various colors, and a sign of lead around their necks as well. Women had to wear shoes of different colors, such as one red and the other black. The Arabic chronicler reports that the promulgation of these laws caused many non-Muslims to embrace Islam, in order to escape the humiliation. In 1105, however, the laws were abolished. In a diploma issued by Sanjar, the last Seljuk ruler of central and eastern Persia, to the *muḥtasib* (inspector of markets and public morals) of Mazandaran, among his many responsibilities, he is called upon to make sure that the *dhimmīs* wear distinguishing clothing to mark their inferiority. As can be seen, the Jews were not selected especially for restrictive measures under the Seljuks, but rather were swept up in general anti-*dhimmī* fervor, which also affected the more numerous Christians

The Arabic historians reveal that the measures of the caliphs and the Seljuks authorities *vis-à-vis* the *dhimmīs*, the aim of which was their humiliation, were not kept consistently. One outstanding example of the selective and far from consistent implementation of the Covenant of Omar was the Jewish tax-farmer Ibn ʿAllān, one of Niẓām al-Mulk's protégés, who was executed by some of the latter's opponents in 1079–80. On the other hand, the *jizya* (poll tax) taken from the non-Muslims was regularly collected, making an important contribution to the revenues of the empire (and representing a real burden to the *dhimmīs*, both as individuals and communities). Large Jewish communities existed in Baghdad and Nishapur, as well as other large cities of the Seljuk empire. *Benjamin of Tudela, writing several years after the end of Seljuk power in central and eastern Persia, notes Jewish communities in Hamadan, Isfahan, Nahavand, and Shiraz. These Jewish inhabitants were probably mostly involved in trade and commerce.

While not always enforced, Seljuk policy towards the *dhimmīs*, like many other Seljuk institutions, served as models for subsequent dynasties. Therefore its importance should not be underestimated.

BIBLIOGRAPHY: J.A. Boyle, *The Cambridge History of Iran*, vol. 5: *The Saljuq and Mongol Periods* (1968); C. Cahen, *Pre-Ottoman Turkey* (tr. J. Jones-Williams, 1968). M. Gil, *A History of Palestine, 634–1099* (tr. E. Broido, 1992), 409–29; D.O. Morgan, *Medieval Persia, 1000–1797* (1988), 25–50.

[Eliyahu Ashtor / Reuven Amitai (2nd ed.)]

SELLERS, PETER (Richard Henry; 1925–1980), British actor. Born in Portsmouth, the son of a non-Jewish pianist and a Jewish mother, Agnes *née* Marks, Peter Sellers was educated at a Catholic school to the age of 14 and was originally a jazz drummer. Joining the RAF in 1943, he discovered his talent for mimicry while entertaining the forces in India. After the war he worked in vaudeville and in 1952, with Spike Milligan and Harry Secombe, began *The Goon Show,* a radio comedy series that became a national favorite. Success took him into television and the London theater. After several small film roles, he appeared with Alec Guinness in *The Ladykillers* (1956). He first won wide notice in the U.S. with *The Mouse That Roared* (1959), in which he played several roles. Though most of his films were comedies, he won the British Film Academy Award for his serious portrayal of a union member in *I'm All Right, Jack*, a 1959 satire on trade unionism. His other films include *Dr. Strangelove* (1963), in which he played three roles; *What's New, Pussycat?* (1965); *The Return of the Pink Panther* (1975); *Murder by Death* (1976); *The Pink Panther Strikes Again* (1976); *Revenge of the Pink Panther* (1978); and *Being There* (1979). Sellers was one of the most famous and memorable British comic actors of his time.

BIBLIOGRAPHY: P. Evans, *Peter Sellers: The Mask Behind the Mask* (1968). **ADD. BIBLIOGRAPHY:** ODNB online; A. Walker, *Peter Sellers* (1981); M. Starr, *Peter Sellers* (1991); R. Lewis, *The Life and Death of Peter Sellers* (1994).

[Lee Healey / Jonathan Licht]

°SELLIN, ERNST (1876–1946), German Bible scholar and archaeologist. Sellin was professor of evangelical theology at various universities. In the field of Bible research, he published *Einleitung in das Alte Testament* (1900, 1950[8]) in which he emphasized the literary critical method. His book on the prophets, *Der aelteste Prophetismus* (1912), contains studies on the history of prophecy, the messianic age, and a comparison of the appearance of God in the Bible and the signs of divinity among pre-Hebrew peoples. He also wrote books on Job (1919), Moses (1922), and a commentary on the minor prophets – *Das Zwoelfprophetenbuch* (1922, 1929–302–[3]). In his introduction to this commentary (p. 8), he sharply attacked Bible criticism of the previous 50 years. Sellin claimed that whatever exponents of that school could not reconcile with their theory they rejected as meaningless additions and, therefore, their approach to the prophetic literature was basically unsound. He also edited a series of 13 volumes of Bible commentaries, *Kommentar zum Alten Testament*, the first of which appeared in 1913. He published studies of the religious background of the biblical period, *Beitraege zur israelitischen und juedischen Religionsgeschichte* (2 vols., 1896–97).

In a history of Israel in the biblical period (*Geschichte des israelitisch-juedischen Volkes*, 2 vols., 1924–32), Sellin points out the relation between Israel's geographic position and the history of its community life. He differentiated between legends and history and emphasized the importance of religion, which he regarded as a decisive fact in the development of Jewish history. Sellin also made important contributions to archaeology. He conducted excavations at Tell-Ta'annek, Jericho (1907–08), and Shechem (1913–14) and published reports of his work. Although his methods are outdated, his discoveries at these sites are of great value.

BIBLIOGRAPHY: KS, 1 (1924), 254–5; 35 (1960), 182; E. Sellin, *Einleitung in das Alte Testament*, ed. by L. Rost (19599), preface.

[Yehuda Komlosh]

SELTZER, LOUIS BENSON (1897–1980), U.S. newspaper editor. Born in Cleveland, Ohio, Seltzer was the son of Charles Alden Seltzer, who became a successful writer of western stories. Seltzer joined the *Cleveland Press* as a reporter in 1916. In 1928 he became its editor and made it the most widely read daily in Ohio. Using the power of the press to confront and condemn injustice, he tried to thwart it at every opportunity. Also dedicated to making the paper as relevant to the readers' lives as he could, he created departments to deal with almost every major and minor interest of readers as well as a public service bureau that oversaw a wide range of annual projects for the benefit or entertainment of readers. He believed that "If you don't get the flavor of the town into your paper, you've missed the boat." A dynamic personality, Seltzer became a force in American journalism, serving on many national editorial committees and on the Pulitzer Prize committee. He retired as editor in 1966.

Seltzer also served as the national director of the National Conference of Christians and Jews. However, not wanting to relegate himself to any single local group in Cleveland, he spread his time and energy among such diverse positions as a leader of the Boy Scout organization; head of the Welfare Federation; chairman of the United Community Defense Services; president of the Convention and Trade Show Bureau; and director of the YMCA. His autobiography, *The Years Were Good*, appeared in 1956. He also wrote *Six and God* (1966).

[Ruth Beloff (2nd ed.)]

SELVINSKI, ILYA LVOVICH (1899–1968), Soviet Russian poet. The son of a furrier, Selvinski was born in Simferopol. In 1933–34 he was a member of a Soviet polar expedition. Primarily known for his unconventional experimental verse, Selvinski was one of the foremost exponents of constructivism, an offshoot of futurism. Repeatedly attacked over the years for his inability or unwillingness to conform to the norms of orthodox Soviet writing, Selvinski continued to publish prolifically and preach assorted heresies. Thus, in 1947 he dared to propose that "Socialist symbolism" supplant Socialist realism as the official style of Soviet literature. Most of Selvinski's poetry is narrative. His longer works include *Ulyalayevshchina* (1927), a brisk, colorful account of the Civil War, which contains a tale of the exploits of heroic Red guerillas and their picturesque anarchistic adversaries. *Zapiski poeta* ("Notebooks of a Poet," 1928), which contains several effective parodies of Soviet poets, displays Selvinski's satirical gifts. *Pao-Pao* (1932) is a whimsical verse play about the transformation of an ape into a human being. Some of Selvinski's works describe his native Crimea. During World War II he wrote a number of moving poems dealing with the tragic fate of Russian Jewry and three big Russian historical tragedies in verse. After the war he received high decorations for his conduct as an officer and commissar. Shortly before his death Selvinski published *O yunost moya!* (1967), a fictionalized account of his youth which includes some portraits of non-Ashkenazi, Tatar-speaking Jews in the Crimea during the Civil War, and even some references to their Zionist sentiments. *Davayte pomechtayem o bessmertye* ("Let us Dream of Immortality") was published posthumously in 1969.

[Maurice Friedberg]

SELZ, OTTO (1881–1944?), German psychologist. Born in Munich, he first taught in Bonn until, in 1923, he was appointed professor at the Handelshochschule (a business college) at Mannheim. In 1933, when the Nazi regime came to power, he was dismissed and he emigrated to the Netherlands. During World War II he was deported and killed in a concentration camp, probably in 1944.

His work was concerned primarily with thought processes and foreshadowed the modern approach to the psychology of thinking. His theories grew out of the work of the Wuerzburg school, which rejected the notion that thinking could be analyzed by detailed self-observation. He also reacted against G.E. Mueller's constellation theory, which interpreted thinking along purely associative lines. In 1913 and again in 1922 Selz called for a psychology of thinking that dealt primarily with processes rather than content. His theory of productive and reproductive thinking (1924) marked a major turning point as the first attempt to deal with these two processes in a single theoretical framework. In its main elements, his theory anticipated modern theories of thinking and fits in well with some recent work on computer simulation of human problem solving. His major works include *Ueber die Gesetze des geordneten Denkverlaufs* (1913), *Zur Psychologie des produktiven Denkens und des Irrtums* (1922), and *Die Gesetze der produktiven und reproduktiven Geistestaetigkeit* (1924).

[Helmut E. Adler]

SELZNICK, U.S. family in the film industry. LEWIS B. SELZNICK (1872–1933), who was born in Kiev, emigrated to Pittsburgh and started a jewelry business there. Later he moved to New York. In 1910 he joined a film-making company and, becoming general manager, he persuaded the *Shubert brothers, the theatrical producers, to allow him to turn stage shows into films. He thereupon made *Trilby*, *The Boss*, and *Wildfire*, in which actors who later became famous played. Selznick also helped to start the star system. MYRON SELZNICK (1898–1944), his eldest son, born in Pittsburgh, worked with his father and they formed Select Pictures. During the 1920s the Selznicks controlled a multi-million-dollar business. The family fortune was, however, wiped out in the 1929 crash. Myron then became a press agent in Hollywood. DAVID OLIVER SELZNICK (1902–1965), Lewis' youngest son, also born in Pittsburgh, became a production assistant on Westerns at MGM studios and rapidly rose to the front rank of Hollywood's producers. He worked for Paramount and later RKO, making such films as *A Bill of Divorcement*, *The Animal Kingdom*, and *King Kong*. Returning to MGM as vice president, he produced major successes such as *Rebecca* (1940), *Dinner at Eight* (1933), *David Copperfield* (1935), *Anna Karenina* (1948), *Duel in the Sun* (1947), and *Gone with the Wind* (1939), then the most expensive and successful film yet made. David Selznick made or discovered many stars and at the height of his career was voted top producer by U.S. exhibitors for ten successive years. His exacting demands, however, led to many disputes with directors and actors, some of whom refused to work with him. Among his later films were *The Prisoner of Zenda* (1952), *A Star is Born* (1954), *A Tale of Two Cities* (1957), and *A Farewell to Arms* (1957).

BIBLIOGRAPHY: *Current Biography Yearbook 1965* (1965), 381.

[Ellis Nassour]

SEMAḤOT (Heb. שְׂמָחוֹת; also called *Evel*, divided into *Evel Rabbati* and *Evel Zuta*), the classic rabbinic text on death and mourning, one of the minor tractates generally appended to the Babylonian Talmud. Although it is not included in the Codex Munich, the only complete manuscript of the Babylonian Talmud, it does appear in its editio princeps (Venice, 1523) and in many of the later printed editions. The euphemistic title, *Semaḥot* ("Rejoicings"), which is usually applied to it, was already used by the Franco-German scholars in the 11th century. The Babylonian Talmud cites a work bearing the name *Evel Rabbati* as the source for three tannaitic rulings (MK 24a, 26b; Ket. 28a). In response to a query on the nature of this work, the *Gaon* Natronai (head of the academy at Sura 853–58) writes: "*Evel* is a tractate of Mishnah containing most of what is taught in *Ellu Megalleḥin* [the third chapter of MK]; there are two such tractates, one major, the other minor" (Z. Wolfensohn (ed.), *Ḥemdah Genuzah* (1863), 17a; on the identity of the minor tractate, see M. Higger (ed.), *Massekhet Semaḥot* (1931), 59–72, 211–29). Although modern scholars disagree as to whether the tractate on mourning mentioned in the Talmud and described by the *gaon* is to be identified with this text, the medieval commentators apparently took this identity for granted (D. Zlotnick (ed. and trans.), *The Tractate "Mourning,"* 1, n.). Most modern scholars favor a late date for this work, placing the time of final redaction at about the middle of the eighth century. There is nothing in the text, however, pointing clearly to a late date. The latest authorities cited are Judah *ha-Nasi and his contemporaries in the third century. It is written in the language of the Mishnah; its style and structure throughout is that of the *tannaim*. It therefore seems preferable to follow the ancients in suggesting an early date – the end of the third century (D. Zlotnick, *ibid.*, 4–7).

The text, which contains 14 chapters, begins with the legal status of the dying man, asserting that he must be considered the same as a living person in every respect. The second chapter discusses those people who did not die a natural death, e.g., suicides or executed criminals. Although funeral rites were withheld from them (Sem. 2:1, 6; D. Zlotnick, *ibid.*, 100, no. 1), they were never denied a burial. In later chapters, the behavior and activities of the mourners during the seven- and thirty-day mourning periods are treated in detail, and rules of conduct are set down for priests and for close and distant relatives of the deceased. Burial practices not considered elsewhere in rabbinic literature are also found here, such as the custom of inspecting the dead to make certain that death had actually occurred (8:1). Several rites, discontinued in the Diaspora lest the Jews become a cause for derision or be accused of sorcery, are also discussed: e.g., the requirement of the mourner to invert the bed, to cover his mouth and head in the manner of the Arabs, and to bare the arm and shoulder during the funeral procession (D. Zlotnick, *ibid.*, 12–13). What is, perhaps, the most complete martyrology to be found in tannaitic literature is included in this tractate (ch. 8), as is the classic eulogy of R. Akiva for his son (8:13).

The standard Hebrew commentary to this work, the *Naḥalat Ya'akov* by R. Jacob Naumburg, was written during the 18th century and is found in the regular editions of the Babylonian Talmud. A critical edition of the first four chapters with a German translation was published by M. Klotz (1890). The first critical edition of the entire text was published by M. Higger (1931). An English translation including an introduction and notes with an appended Hebrew text edited from manuscripts has been published by Dov Zlotnick (1966).

BIBLIOGRAPHY: Bruell, Jahrbuecher, 1 (1874), 1–57.

[Dov Zlotnick]

SEMAN, PHILIP LOUIS (1881–1957), U.S. educator and organization executive. Seman, who was born in Warsaw, Poland, went to the U.S. in 1892. After holding positions with Jewish organizations in New York and St. Louis and teaching at Washington University's School of Social Economy (1908–10), Seman became director of the Jewish People's Institute of Chicago in 1913. He held this post until 1945, during which time he turned the institute into a vitally important institution in Chicago Jewish life and became recognized as a national leader in Jewish social work. During his tenure in Chicago, he was co-founder of Hillel (1923); president of the National Conference of Jewish Social Service (1931); vice president of the National Conference on Social Work (1932); member of the executive commission of the White House Conference on Child Health and Protection; and chairman of the Chicago Recreation Commission (1934). After retiring from the institute Seman moved to Los Angeles, where he became a member of the board of the Bureau of Jewish Education (from 1947), and of the faculty and board of overseers of the University of Judaism (from 1949).

His works include *Jewish Community Life* (1924); *The Jewish Community Center* (1925); *Problems of the Leisure Hour* (1927); *Training for Leadership* (1928); *Social Orientation* (1930); and *Community Culture in an Era of Depression* (1932).

SEMIKHAH (Heb. סְמִיכָה; "laying," lit. "leaning" of the hands). The word is used in two senses.

Of Sacrifices

The act of *semikhah* constituted the dedication by the owner of animals sacrificed on the altar. The act, which was obligatory whenever sacrifices were offered by individuals (Men. 9:7; Maim. Yad, Ma'aseh ha-Korbanot 3:6), was carried out by the owner laying both his hands with all his might between the horns of the animal immediately before it was dispatched (Lev. 1:4ff.; Sifra 4; Maim. loc. cit. 3:13). The ceremony took place in the courtyard of the Temple, where the animal was slain (Men. 93a, b). It had to be performed with bare hands, so that nothing might interpose between them and the head of the beast (Maim. loc. cit.). It did not apply, with two exceptions, to communal sacrifices (Men. 9:7), nor to birds (Git. 28b). Another requirement was that the act had to be carried out by the owner in person and could not be performed by proxy (Men. 9:8; Maim. loc. cit. 3:8).

Of Judges, Elders, and Rabbis

All Jewish religious leaders had to be ordained before they were permitted to perform certain judicial functions and to decide practical questions in Jewish law. The Bible relates that Moses ordained Joshua by placing his hands on him, thereby transferring a portion of his spirit to Joshua (Num. 27:22, 23; Deut. 34:9). Moses also ordained the 70 elders who assisted him in governing the people (Num. 11:16–17, 24–25). The elders ordained by Moses ordained their successors, who in turn ordained others, so that there existed an unbroken chain of ordination from Moses down to the time of the Second Temple (Maim. Yad, Sanh. 4:2). For some centuries the tradition of ordaining by the laying of the hands was continued, but the rabbis later decided to ordain by merely conferring the title "rabbi" either orally or in writing (*ibid.*, 4:2).

Ordination was required both for membership in the Great Sanhedrin, and the smaller Sanhedrins and regular colleges of judges empowered to decide legal cases. Three rows of scholars always sat before the Sanhedrin, and whenever it became necessary to choose a new member, a scholar from the first row was chosen and ordained (Sanh. 4:4). During the time of Judah ha-Nasi it was decreed that any religio-legal decision, including decisions relating to purely ceremonial law, could only be given by those properly authorized (Sanh. 5b). While any qualified Jewish person could serve as a judge in civil cases, only Jews of pure descent were eligible to adjudicate in criminal matters involving capital punishment (Sanh. 4:2). Ordination was also required to judge in cases involving corporal punishment and fines, to intercalate months and years, to release the firstborn animals for profane use by reason of disqualifying blemishes, to annul vows, and to pass the ban of excommunication (*ḥerem*). Only a transfer of the Divine Spirit which originally rested on Moses empowered the ordained person to make decisions in these crucial areas. Ordination could be limited to only one or some of these various functions. The lowest degree of ordination entitled the rabbi to decide only religious questions, while the highest degree entitled him to inspect firstlings, in addition to deciding religious questions and judging criminal cases (Sanh. 5a; Maim. loc. cit. 4:8). The complete formula of ordination was "*Yoreh Yoreh Yaddin Yaddin. Yattir Yattir*" ("May he decide? He may decide. May he judge? He may judge. May he permit? He may permit"). Rav, the founder of the academy of Sura in Babylonia, was authorized to exercise only the first two of these three functions since it was feared that his excessive knowledge of blemishes might enable him to declare a blemish permanent and the animal thus be permitted for profane use, where to the bystanders it appeared transitory (Sanh. 5b). The privileges of ordination could also be limited to a specific period. R. Johanan only ordained R. Shaman for the duration of his Babylonian visit (*ibid.*).

The ordination itself, which required the presence of three elders, one of whom was himself ordained, was originally performed by every ordained teacher upon his pupils (Sanh. 1:3; TJ, Sanh. 1:3, 19a). Nevertheless, as the influence of the Babylonian exilarch increased, it became necessary for the ordinants to obtain his authorization before serving as judges in Babylonia (Sanh. 5a). In Ereẓ Israel it also became necessary for individual scholars to obtain the consent of the patriarch before ordaining their pupils. On account of the high regard entertained for the patriarchs of the house of Hillel, who were the recognized heads of the Jewish community of the Holy Land during the centuries subsequent to the demise of Rabban Johanan b. Zakkai, no ordination was considered valid without the patriarch's consent. The patriarch himself was at first permitted to confer it without consulting the Sanhedrin. Later the patriarch could only grant the degree in cooperation with the court (TJ, Sanh. 1:3, 19a). The term used in the Holy Land in the days of the Jerusalem Talmud for ordination was *minnui* (literally "appointment" to the office of judge). In Babylonia the designation of *semikhah* (*semikhuta* in Aramaic) was retained (*ibid.*). On the day of ordination, the candidate wore a special garment (Lev. R. 2:4). After the ceremony, the scholars present praised in rhythmic sentences the person ordained. At the ordination of R. Ze'ira it was sung: "No powder, no paint, no waving of the hair, and still a graceful gazelle"; at the ordinations of Ammi and Assi: "Such as these, such as these ordain unto us" (Ket. 17a). After the ceremony, it seems that the ordinand delivered a public discourse on a specific topic (cf. the case of the incompetent teacher, Sanh. 7b). *Semikhah* could only be granted by scholars residing in Ereẓ Israel to scholars present in the Holy Land at the time of their ordination. The ordinand did not have to be present at the ordination; it sufficed if the ordaining teachers sent a message to him, as long as they all were in Ereẓ Israel (Maim. Yad, Sanh. 4:6). It is related that Johanan was grieved because he could not ordain Ḥanina and Oshaya since they did not reside in Palestine (Sanh. 14a). It is also related that there were two sages, Jonathan b. Aknai and Simeon b. Ẓirud, one of whom was ordained because he was in Palestine while the other was not because he left. The appellation of "*rabbi*" is therefore never used for the Babylonian *amoraim* since they did not possess *semikhah*, and they have the title "*rav*." As a result, the Babylonian sages were dependent upon their Palestinian colleagues. "We submit to them" was the Babylonian attitude (Pes. 51a). Nevertheless, to expedite justice, the Babylonian scholars were empowered to adjudicate all monetary cases as the "agents of the judges in Israel" (BK 84b). Once ordained in Palestine, a scholar could exercise his full authority even outside its borders.

After the *Bar Kokhba Revolt (132–35 C.E.), the Roman emperor Hadrian attempted to end the spiritual authority still wielded by the Sanhedrin, which had been shorn of all government support, by forbidding the granting of *semikhah* to new scholars. It was declared that "whoever performed an ordination should be put to death, and whoever received ordination should be put to death, the city in which the ordination took place demolished, and the boundaries wherein it had been performed uprooted" (Sanh. 14a). R. *Judah b. Bava was executed for ordaining several of his pupils in a no-man's-land between Usha and Shefaram. It is not clear when the original *semikhah* with the powers described above was discontinued. Majority opinion favors the latter part of the fourth century during the time of Hillel II. According to Naḥmanides (cf. his notes on Maimonides, *Sefer ha-Mitzvot*, no. 153), this happened before the fixing of the permanent calendar by Hillel in 361 C.E. Some date it with the extinction of the patriarchate at the death of the last patriarch, *Gamaliel VI, in 425 C.E. Others set the time as late as 1062 with the death of Daniel b. Azariah, the *Gaon* of Palestine. Still others cite proof that this traditional ordination continued until the time of Maimonides.

[Aaron Rothkoff]

In Medieval and Modern Times

Due to the changing conditions of Jewish life, which transformed some of the functions of the rabbinate, *semikhah* acquired new connotations. In the geonic period the *rosh golah*, the *exilarch, conferred a license (*reshut*) only "to effect compromises among litigants, to investigate legal disputes, to act as arbitrator, and to execute legal documents." The *geonim* too were authorized to appoint scribes, leaders in public worship, judges (*dayyanim*), and teachers. In the tenth century *Sherira Gaon wrote: "The row [in the academy] takes the place of the Sanhedrin and its head takes the place of Moses our teacher," thus continuing to a certain extent the claim to a kind of sacred order among the academy scholars. The head referred to evidently is the *av bet din*. *Samuel b. Ali, *Gaon* of Baghdad in the 12th century, defined the functions and authority of the *av bet din* when writing of R. *Zerachiah b. Isaac ha-Levi: "We have ordained him *av bet din* of the academy and have empowered him to render decisions in money and ritual matters, to proclaim the firstborn permissible for profane use by reason of blemishes, to preach the Torah in public, to deliver lectures, and to appoint an interpreter." The 12th-century traveler *Benjamin of Tudela wrote that in his day the exilarch had the authority to appoint local clergymen in Persia and in many other countries and that they came to him to secure the right to deliver decisions. *Judah b. Barzilai of Barcelona (11th–12th century) distinguished between a *ketav minnui*, a certificate of appointment as *dayyan* or head of an academy, and a *ketav masmikh*, a certificate of ordination "whereby they ordain one of the students to be called rabbi or *ḥakham*. Cases involving fines are not adjudicated outside Ereẓ Israel and ordination is not effected by the laying on of hands on the head of the ordinand. They merely write a certificate of ordination."

These reformulations and transformations of the ancient *semikhah* tend to show that from the fifth century onward there was both a document of appointment to office and an act conferring powers, which was always of a sacral nature. This was particularly strong in the centralistic and aristocratic regime of the geonic leadership but the sacral element was never present to the same extent as that involved in ancient *semikhah*. Despite this continuity of many elements of the traditional *semikhah*, attempts at its complete restoration were made from time to time. As early as the days of *Elijah ha-Kohen Gaon of Palestine in 1083 such an attempt was made. From the very structure and logic of an autonomous pattern of national leadership and of a cultural scale of values in which learning and the scholar were supreme, it can be deduced that everywhere in Jewish communities – even after the 12th century – there was some formula for conferring judicial function and powers and for attesting to scholarly achievements. Of necessity this would be to some greater or lesser extent of a sacral nature. After the *Black Death, and under the influence of diplomas and titles conferred by Christian universities, the term *semikhah* reappeared in Ashkenaz (Franco-Germany), becoming transformed into a diploma conferred by a teacher on his pupil which affirmed his capacity and right to be judge and teacher. The first waves of the Spanish exiles tended to regard the Ashkenazi *semikhah* as evidence of an improper pride and imitation of Christian ways. Yet various factors – the messianic hopes entertained after the expulsion, the feeling that it was necessary to respond to exile and dispersion by the restoration of a central sacral authority, and the urge for an authority that could grant penance and absolution to people who labored under a sense of guilt for having lived for some time as **anusim* – combined to recall Maimonides' view that in principle *semikhah* could be restored (see above), and on the basis of this to advocate ordaining one man who would renew the sacral chain of ancient *semikhah*, thus later restoring the Sanhedrin and paving the way for repentance and the Messiah.

[Isaac Levitats]

Controversy on the Renewal of the Semikhah

Despite the continuity of the Jewish judiciary even after the loss of the traditional formal *semikhah*, there have been some attempts to reinstitute the original *semikhah*, Maimonides' viewpoint is focal to this concept of renewal for he ruled that "if all the Palestinian sages would unanimously agree to appoint and ordain judges, then these new ordinants would possess the full authority of the original ordained judges" (Yad, Sanh. 4:11). Based on this ruling, an attempt was made in 1538 by R. Jacob *Berab of Safed, at that time the largest community in Ereẓ Israel, to restore the practice of ordaining. At Berab's initiative, 25 rabbis convened, and they ordained Berab as their chief rabbi. Berab then ordained four other rabbis, including Joseph *Caro, the author of the Shulḥan Arukh, and Moses di *Trani. Caro ordained Moses *Alshekh, who later ordained Ḥayyim Vital, the leading disciple of R. Isaac *Luria. Berab hoped that he could thus unify the various Jewish communities by ultimately reestablishing a Sanhedrin. Cases involving fines could now be judged again, and flagellation, which was required by law to atone for the sins of the Conversos, could be ordered by the court. However, Berab had neglected to obtain the consent of the Jerusalem rabbis. The latter felt slighted and rejected Berab when he requested that they recognize his authority. They protested his innovation, and the head of the Jerusalem rabbinate, *Levi ibn Ḥabib, wrote an entire treatise to prove the illegality of Berab's actions (*Kunteres ha-Semikhah*). A caustic controversy arose between Ibn Ḥabib and Berab, and after the latter's death in 1541 the renewed institution of ordination gradually languished into obscurity. Modern scholars have approved Ibn Ḥabib's opposition; it was also felt that he feared that Berab's actions would arouse messianic speculations which could result in a false messianic movement (see B. Revel in bibl.). It may also be that Ibn Ḥabib held that it was not permitted to hasten the advent of the messianic era by reestablishing the Sanhedrin but to wait for Divine initiative (see J. Katz in bibl.).

With the establishment of the State of Israel in 1948, R. Judah Leib *Maimon, Israel's first minister of religious affairs, made a similar plea to restore the Sanhedrin. He was, however, opposed by the overwhelming majority of his colleagues of the non-Orthodox groups as well as by rabbis of the extreme right. Israel's then Ashkenazi chief rabbi, Isaac *Herzog, was also hesitant, and again the attempt came to naught.

"Neo-Semikhah" and Hattarat Hora'ah

The term *semikhah* has also been utilized for ordination other than the formal traditional *semikhah*. It has evolved from the term *hattarat hora'ah* which literally means "authorization to render decisions" in matters permitted or forbidden by Jewish religious law. The infinitive *lehorot*, in the sense of the authoritative interpretation of the law, occurs in connection with the duties of the descendants of Aaron, the priests, who also served as teachers and judges in Leviticus 10:11 (cf. Deut. 17:9 ff.). It was also understood in this sense in the Talmud (Ker. 13b). The *hattarat hora'ah* generally was a rabbinical diploma testifying to the fitness of the person to whom it had been issued. It also empowered the recipient to fulfill the functions of a rabbi, which were originally those of acting as a judge for the members of the community that engaged him. At first this document did not resemble the language of the original *semikhah*, it did not state *yoreh yoreh yaddin*, and had none of the far-reaching authority of the original *semikhah*. The earliest form of *hattarat hora'ah* was called *iggeret reshut* ("letter of permission") or *pitka de-dayyanuta* ("writ of jurisdiction"). Such a document, composed in Aramaic in the geonic period of the ninth century, reads:

We have appointed Peloni b. Peloni [i.e., N., son of N.] a justice in the town of… and have invested him with authority to administer the civil laws, and to supervise all matters relating to the Commandments and that which is prohibited and permitted and connected with the fear of God. He has the authority to do that which he thinks is proper to anyone not obeying his verdicts. The miscreant is likewise liable to [the punishment of] Heaven" (A. Harkavy (ed.), *Zikkaron la-Rishonim ve-Gam la-Aḥaronim*, 4 (1887), 80).

Originally, the title "rabbi" was restricted to religious authorities performing the functions of judges ordained with the formal tradition of *semikhah*. As stated, their counterparts in Babylonia were always referred to as "rav" (cf. Sanh. 136f. and BM 85bf). The title "rabbi" appears again in the Middle Ages. It was then bestowed on both Ashkenazi and Sephardi authorities in rabbinic law, although not in the same sense as its previous usage during the talmudic period when the original *semikhah* was still granted. By the 13th century, documents of "neo-*semikhah*" ordination began to resemble the format of the traditional *semikhah*. Recipients were empowered to be *yoreh yoreh* in matters of rituals, while the more advanced student was permitted to be *yaddin yaddin* in all areas of Jewish law. The Sephardim made more discriminate use of this rabbinical epithet than the Ashkenazim by calling the ordinary rabbinic scholar *ḥakham*, and reserving the more honorific designation of "rabbi" for men of outstanding learning (cf. David Messer Leon's *Kevod Ḥakhamim*, ed. by S. Bernfeld (1899), 63). During the second half of the 14th century the title *Morenu* ("our guide and teacher") was introduced as the designation for one who possessed "neo-*semikhah*" in Franco-Germany. Formulas for "neo-*semikhah*" were fixed, as well as the stipulation of well-defined qualifications and privileges for those possessing this degree. Formerly there was no need for all rabbis and scholars to carry a patent of *semikhah* with them since their authority rested on personal, rather than institutional grounds. This changed with the uprooting of yeshivot and communities in the 14th and 15th centuries in Franco-Germany. Formal *semikhah* became a necessity for safeguarding the academic standards of the rabbinate at a time when the dispersal and migration of scholars and yeshivot endangered the continuity of academic traditions. However, as soon as *semikhah* was formalized, a process of institutionalization set in, thus making it possible for lesser types of scholars to attain rabbinical authority and privilege. This was also hastened by the oncoming practice of local rulers to appoint "chief rabbis" for the purpose of tax administration. The social, personal, and academic problems involved in the "Ashkenazi *semikhah*" continued to form a subject for lively discussion among scholars well into the 17th century. It came under heavy attack from Sephardi rabbis after the expulsion from Spain.

Occasionally, *semikhah* became a source of income for rabbis and it was necessary for communities and general councils to promulgate *takkanot* regarding the privileges and qualifications connected with *semikhah*. By the end of the 16th century, the title of *Morenu* had ceased to be of a purely academic character and it was increasingly used as a symbol of social status in the communities (see Breuer in bibl.). The scholar equipped with this "neo-*semikhah*" was only able to exercise his authority with the consent of the community that elected him. His jurisdiction was limited to that community. R. Isaac b. Sheshet rendered a decision (1380) on this point in the case of the French community of Provence, which would not permit the interference of R. *Meir b. Baruch of Rothenburg in its affairs (*Teshuvot ha-Ribash*, nos. 268–73). Meir had ordained and appointed a new chief rabbi for Provence who he felt was worthier than the community's own choice. Nevertheless, his intervention was rejected. Because of his involvement in this type of dispute, some scholars erroneously thought that Meir had attempted to reintroduce the original formal *semikhah*. However, within the confines of his own community the scholar's jurisdiction was supreme. No other rabbi had the right to intervene without his consent (cf. Samuel Archivolti's *Palgei Mayim* (Salonika, 1608), 15a).

It was an established principle, dating from the time of the *tannaim*, that no pupil was to issue a decision in the presence of his teacher (Er. 63a). The age for receiving *semikhah* or the *hattarat hora'ah* was 18. Eleazar b. Azariah was appointed head of the academy at this age (Ber. 27b, 28a) as was Rabbah (Ber. 64a; cf. Yev. 105a) and Hai Gaon. David Messer Leon received his title at 18, at Naples (*Kevod Ḥakhamim*, 64). The question of what degree of learning entitles a scholar to receive the diploma from his teacher is fully discussed by Messer Leon. It is necessary for the student to master the original sources of Bible and Talmud and to possess logical reasoning power. In the 18th and 19th centuries it became customary for aspiring rabbinical students to receive ordination from leading rabbinical figures, in addition to the diplomas they received from their own teachers. They were orally tested by noted rabbis, and if found sufficiently learned and worthy, they were also granted certificates of ordination by these well-known scholars. The following is the text of such a diploma granted by R. Isaac Elhanan *Spektor of Kovno (d. 1896), from whom most Russian rabbis of the second half of the 19th century received their "neo-*semikhah*":

> קושט אמרי אמת ניתן לכתוב על האי גברא יקירא ברב ...יליד ...ופלפלתי עמו הרבה והוא מלא דבר ה׳ בש״ס ובפסוקים וגם הנהו דרשן מפואר נאה דורש ונאה מקיים: ובכן אמר יישר כוחו וחילו לאורייתא, ויורה יורה ידין ידין בד״מ ואו״ה וגו״ח וטוט״ה [בדיני ממונות ואיסור והיתר וגיטין וחליצה וטומאה וטהרה]: ויהא רעוא שישלח לו הרחמן מקום מכובד לפי כבודו כי ראוי והגון הרב הנ״ל לנהל צאן קדשים. ובאתי עה״ח יום...ימים לחדש... לפ״ק: נאם יצחק אלחנן החופ״ק קאוונע:
>
> Verily, these words of truth may be ascribed to that worthy man, rabbi…, a native of…, with whom I have fully discussed the Talmud and codes in which I find him to be filled with the Word of the Lord. He is also an excellent preacher, preaching what is moral and practicing what he preaches. Therefore I say: Let his power and might in the Torah be encouraged. Let him teach and decide in all matters of monetary, dietary, and ritual law, *get* and *ḥaliẓah*, and laws relating to cleanliness and uncleanliness. May it be the will of the Almighty to send him an hon-

orable position in accordance with his virtues. The said rabbi well deserves and is truly competent to guide a flock. Signed on this date… Isaac Elhanan, who dwells here in the holy congregation of Kovno.

Modern Practice of Ordaining Rabbis

During the 19th century, a drastic change took place with regard to the position, requirements, and training of rabbis. The change originated in Germany, which became the center for the development of Reform Judaism and for the scientific study of Jewish history and the Jewish religion. Knowledge solely of the Talmud and codes was no longer deemed sufficient, and many communities now demanded that their rabbis be versed in the vernacular, secular studies, and auxiliary Judaic subjects. The yeshivot and unsupervised instruction by individual rabbis were found to be increasingly unsatisfactory. The discontent with the traditional rabbinate was further intensified by the rapid spread of Reform Judaism. To meet these new conditions, rabbinical seminaries were organized in rapid succession. With the development of these schools, curricula were evolved which no longer placed the stress on Talmud and codes. The more the particular seminary moved away from Orthodoxy, the less its curriculum emphasized Talmud and related subjects. Bible, homiletics, Jewish history and philosophy, the grammar of Hebrew and of cognate languages, pastoral psychology, and synagogue administration gradually became integral required courses of study for rabbinical students. Many of these seminaries no longer granted the traditional rabbinical degree, but rather certified their graduates as "preachers and teachers in Israel." Some schools granted two different diplomas. Most graduates were simply awarded the "preacher and teacher" degree, while the more advanced students also received the traditional *yoreh yoreh yaddin yaddin* ordination after passing special examinations in Talmud and codes. Some schools continued to include the traditional formula of ordination in the format of its degree, but this formula was now being utilized in the ceremonial sense rather than as an indication of the graduate's knowledge of the codes.

In contemporary Israel, where there are solely traditional yeshivot which ordain rabbis, the traditional method and form of ordination is utilized. In the United States, the Rabbi Isaac Elchanan Theological Seminary of *Yeshiva University also ordains its graduates in the traditional fashion after they complete a course of study which stresses Talmud and codes. The Jewish Theological Seminary does not grant the traditional ordination to its students. The Hebrew Union College includes the traditional formula of *yoreh yoreh yaddin yaddin* in the Hebrew version of its certification, but this is purely in the formal sense. The title "*rabbi*" is therefore no longer an indication, as it was up to the last centuries, that its bearer is thoroughly acquainted with the Talmud and codes, but it is the commonly accepted title for the spiritual leaders of all Jewish denominations, Orthodox, Conservative, Reform, and Reconstructionist.

[Aaron Rothkoff]

Ordination of Women

Female rabbinical ordination began to be seriously pondered in the late 19th century in Germany and the United States as a natural, if uncomfortable, consequence of Reform Judaism's insistence on the equality of men and women. Ordaining women also emerged as part of a larger debate about women's rights and their access to the learned professions. If women wished to become doctors, lawyers, and ministers, professions which then largely excluded them, why should they not also aspire to the rabbinate? However, the ambivalence of Reform Jewish leaders, who struggled to balance their long-stated commitment to the religious emancipation of Jewish women with their own ingrained prejudices about women's proper sphere, and their perceptions of the receptivity of their congregations to female rabbis, delayed a positive commitment to women's ordination for nearly a century, despite a series of challengers. It took the collision of second-wave feminism with American Judaism to propel women into the rabbinate in a sustained and institutionalized way. By the first decade of the 21st century, the presence of hundreds of female rabbis had expanded traditional notions of religious leadership throughout the Jewish world.

The American debate over female rabbis first surfaced publicly in the 1890s as the press ordained the charismatic female Jewish preacher Ray *Frank "the girl rabbi of the golden west." In the decades that followed, a series of individuals challenged the established American rabbinical seminaries, each seeking unsuccessfully to become the first woman ever ordained and hoping to blaze a path for others to follow. These include Martha Neumark (1904–1981), whose request for a High Holiday pulpit, following three years of intensive study at Hebrew Union College, ultimately led to a 1923 vote by the lay board of governors supporting the policy of only ordaining men. The aspirations of other able women of this era were also disappointed, including those of Helen Hadassah Levinthal who was not ordained with her male classmates at the Jewish Institute of Religion in 1939, despite becoming the first American woman to complete a rabbinic curriculum. Apparently, none of these challengers were aware that in 1935, in Germany, Regina *Jonas (1902–1944) had already been privately ordained. She used her rabbinic position to offer solace to her persecuted co-religionists in Nazi Germany, but, because she shared their fate, the news of her breakthrough perished with her.

In the 1950s, the question of women's ordination received new attention when the story of Paula Herskovitz *Ackerman, a *rebbetzin* who succeeded her late husband in the pulpit was considered so newsworthy that her picture appeared in *Time* magazine. Publicity about the growing success of women in the Protestant ministry also prompted Reform rabbis, Jewish journalists, and leaders of the Reform National Federation of Temple Sisterhoods to return to the question of women rabbis. Concurrently, in the 1950s and 1960s, a small group of idealistic and able women students had come to HUC-JIR with hopes that their studies would lead to rabbinic ordination. The question of female ordination gained greater urgency in the 1960s. As many Americans and American Jews embraced a feminist commitment to egalitarianism, female ordination became an important symbol of Judaism's commitment to gender equity.

Sally Jane *Priesand (1946–), a talented and tenacious young woman, became the first woman rabbi in North America in 1972, ordained by the Hebrew Union College-Jewish Institute of Religion in Cincinnati, Ohio. The decision to ordain Priesand was never a foregone conclusion, but it seems likely that proclaiming a woman rabbi no longer appeared so revolutionary against the backdrop of the dramatic social and political upheavals in American life in this epoch. By acquiescing to women's ordination, Reform leaders were able to portray themselves as continuing their historic project of adapting Judaism to respond to modernity while simultaneously demonstrating Reform Judaism's commitment to women's equality. Two years later the Reconstructionist movement ordained its first female rabbinic student, Sandy Eisenberg *Sasso (1947–), and, in 1985, after a vociferous public debate that lasted slightly over a decade, the Conservative movement followed suit with the ordination of Amy *Eilberg (1955–). Even as the question of the permissibility of women's ordination closed in the liberal movements of American Judaism and the first women were ordained in Great Britain and in Israel, engaged Orthodox Jews began to ask if and when there would be female Orthodox rabbis. In the early 21st century, halakhically knowledgeable women served as rabbinic assistants in some Modern Orthodox congregations in North America, and as expert advocates on legal issues connected with women's status in Israel.

As the struggle for female ordination closed for many, the history of women in the rabbinate has opened. Women rabbinical students and rabbis have had a transformative impact on their seminaries, their congregants, and their male colleagues, and have faced numerous challenges in the effort to reconcile Judaism with women's voices and perspectives. The first generations of female rabbis learned to convince congregations to hire them, to establish their authority in a hitherto exclusively male profession, and to negotiate for benefits such as maternity leave. Moreover, female rabbis have confronted the marginalization of women's voices and views in the sacred texts and liturgy of Jewish tradition and have focused attention on models of female strength, intelligence, and leadership in the Jewish past. Many have joined with other contemporary Jewish women to create new rituals to recognize and sacralize moments of change, joy, and despair in women's lives. They have also extended their feminist critique to include the challenges that face gays and lesbians.

In every context in which they function, on pulpits and in classrooms, under the *ḥuppah* and at the circumcision table, women rabbis have enlightened their congregants, students, and male colleagues about the impact of gender in Judaism and for Jewish women. In doing so, they have reshaped modern Judaism in ways utterly unimaginable a short half century ago.

See also *Rabbis, Rabbinate; *Rabbinical Training, American; Rabbinical Seminaries.

[Pamela S. Nadell (2nd ed.)]

BIBLIOGRAPHY: W. Bacher, in: MGWJ, 38 (1894), 122–7; Judah ben Barzilai of Barcelona, *Sefer ha-Shetarot*, ed. by S.Ḥ. Halberstam (1898, repr. 1967); L. Ginzberg, *Geonica*, 1 (1909); Graetz, Hist, index, s.v. *Ordination*; Schuerer, Gesch, 2 (1907⁴), 237–67; H.J. Bornstein, *Mishpat ha-Semikhah ve-Koroteha* (1919); B. Revel, in: *Horeb*, 5 (1939), 1–26; Baron, Community, 2 (1942), 67–68, 79, see also index s.v. *Ordination*; Y.L. Maimon, *Ḥiddush ha-Sanhedrin bi-Medinatenu ha-Meḥuddeshet* (1951); J. Newman, *Semikhah (Ordination); a Study of its Origin, History and Function* (1950), incl. bibl., xiii–xiv; J. Katz, in: *Zion*, 16 (1951), 28–45 (second pagination, Eng. summary, iii); S.B. Hoenig, *The Great Sanhedrin* (1953); S. Zeitlin, *Religious and Secular Leadership* (1943); idem, in: JQR, 7 (1916/17), 499–517; 56 (1966), 240–1; 31 (1940/41), 1–58, 287–300; M. Benayahu, in: *Sefer Yovel… Baer* (1960), 248–69; H. Mantel, *Studies in the History of the Sanhedrin* (1961), index; J. Katz, *Sefer Zikkaron le-Binyamin de Vries* (1961), 281–94; H.Z. Dimitrovsky, in: *Sefunot*, 10 (1966), 113–92 (Eng. summary, 12–13); Z. Falk, in: *De'ot*, 30 (1966), 233–42 (also in: *Sinai*, 58 (1966), 239–49); Breuer, in: *Zion*, 33 (1968), 15–46; H.H. Ben-Sasson, *Toledot Am Yisrael*, 2 (1969), 264–7. **ADD. BIBLIOGRAPHY:** S. Greenberg (ed.), *The Ordination of Women as Rabbis: Studies and Responsa* (1988); E. Klapheck, *Fraeulein Rabbiner Jonas: The Story of the First Woman Rabbi* (2004); P.S. Nadell, *Women Who Would Be Rabbis: A History of Women's Ordination, 1889–1985* (1998); H. Ner-David. *Life on the Fringes: A Feminist Journey toward Traditional Rabbinic Ordination* (2000); S. Sheridan (ed.), *Hear Our Voice: Women Rabbis Tell Their Stories* (1994); *And the Gates Opened: Women in the Rabbinate* (film, 2005); R. Alpert, S. Levi Elwell, and S. Idelson (eds.), *Lesbian Rabbis: The First Generation* (2001).

SEMILIAN, SAVIN SOLOMON (1902–), Romanian journalist and historian of Romanian Jewry. Born in Brăila, Semilian edited the economic columns of various Bucharest papers and wrote for most Romanian literary magazines and Jewish journals until dismissed during the Nazi regime. After World War II he resumed work as economic editor of the daily *Cotidianul*, *Naţiunea*, and other papers. He also wrote the history of Braila Jewry and on Jewish elements in Romanian folklore. He became librarian of Bucharest's Jewish archives and edited *Revista Cultului Mozaic*, a cultural fortnightly published by the Federation of Jewish Communities.

SÉMINAIRE ISRAÉLITE DE FRANCE, institute of higher education of Jewish and secular learning; also known as École Rabbinique; founded in Metz in 1829 and transferred to Paris in 1859. The Séminaire Israélite de France has trained rabbis, *ḥazzanim*, and Hebrew teachers for France and French-speaking countries. It has followed the motto of *Torah im derekh ereẓ* ("Torah combined with general culture") to meet the needs of modern Judaism. During the German occupation the seminary went to Vichy, Chamallières, Lyons; officially suppressed in 1943, it maintained semi-secret activity until the end of the war. Its directors from 1919 were the chief rabbi J. Bauer (1919–32); M. Liber, the renowned scholar (1932–51); H. Schilli (1951–75); E. Gugenheim (1977); E. Chouchena (1977–91); M. Gugenheim (1992–). Basic studies include: Talmud; Bible, with the ancient rabbinical and more recent commentaries; philosophy; ancient and modern Hebrew literature and Jewish history; homiletics and liturgy. The program of general studies consists of philosophy and French literature. Students can, or are encouraged to, follow a general academic course at the same time. Studies are spread over a period of one to five years according to a student's previous qualifications. During their program of study, students are encouraged to attend a yeshivah in Israel for one year. They undergo various terms of probation, namely as *talmud torah* teachers, at the *bet din*, and in the communities. Formerly a preparatory section, which admitted younger pupils who had not yet obtained the baccalaureate and which was known as the *talmud torah*, had been affiliated with the institution. Another branch, the École de Pédagogie et de Liturgie, previously trained *ḥazzanim* and Hebrew teachers. The central consistory assumes the administrative and financial responsibility of the institute, with increasing financial difficulties moving into the 21st century. The chief rabbi of France is the legal president of the administrative commission, and the institute provides boarding facilities for an average of 15 to 20 students. The final examination includes the preparation of a memorandum ("mémoire") and a rabbinical degree is awarded. Three degrees, on an average, are awarded each year. As the oldest institution of the seminary-type in the world and the last one existing in Western Europe, the SIF has recruited more than 400 students, more than 300 of whom obtained the degree of rabbi, *ḥazzan* or teacher. In the early 21st century it faces the new, contradictory aspirations concerning the role of the rabbis and suffers from a lack of prestige and even from some suspicion among that part of religious Judaism whose references are in the "world of the yeshivot." Its library, with some 60,000 volumes, is unique in Paris despite losses in previous decades; in certain fields it is complementary to that of the *Alliance Israélite Universelle. The library was restored in 2004 and scholars have access to it; its manuscripts are on deposit in the Alliance library.

BIBLIOGRAPHY: J. Bauer, *L'École Rabbinique de France 1830–1930* (1930); R. Berg, *Histoire du Rabbinat français (16e–20e siècle)*, (1992). **WEBSITE:** www.viejuive.com/associations/sif.

[Henri Schilli / Jean-Pierre Rothschild (2nd ed.)]

SEMITES, a term originally referring to those peoples listed in the table of nations (Gen. 10) as descendants of Noah's son Shem (Sem in the LXX and the Vulgate). The derivative "Semitic" was coined as a linguistic term by A.L. Schloezer in 1781 (in J.G. Eichhorn (ed.), *Repertorium fuer biblische und morgen laendische Literatur*, 8 (1781), 161). Shem is given five sons who had 21 descendants, making a total of 26 peoples derived from him. These include the Elamites and the Assyrians, the Lydians (but note Gen. 10:13), the Arameans, and numerous Arab tribes (Gen. 10:21–31). They are spread from Lydia, eastward through Syria and Assyria, to Persia. Their northern boundary is Armenia, and their southern, the Red Sea and the Persian Gulf. Early in the development of modern ethnology it was realized that the list in Genesis combines peoples that sometimes have nothing in common but geographic propinquity. "Semite" was then defined by the supposed physical characteristics of the chief surviving representatives of the list, the Jews and the Arabs: dolichocephalic skulls; curly and abundant hair; slightly wavy or straight strong beard, predominantly black; prominent (straight or aquiline) nose; oval face (DB, s.v.).

The problematic nature and evil results of earlier racial theories have led to a restriction of the terms Semite and Semitic in careful modern usage to linguistic categories. Aside from the biblical referent, the linguistic is the only modern scholarly-scientific use of the term. The combination of peoples under the rubric Semites in Genesis 10 is not justified by the linguistic criterion. The common features of the languages of the Assyrians, Arameans, and Arabs, which suffice to mark them as members of one family, set them apart from the "Semite" Lydians (Lud) and Elamites, whose languages are totally unrelated. These common features comprise the identifying marks of the Semitic *languages, and in current usage the peoples speaking these languages are called Semitic – today mainly the Jews (Hebrew) and Arabs, but in ancient times the Akkadians, the Amorites, the Babylonians, the Phoenicians, and the Canaanites as well. A striking instance of divergence between modern and ancient classification is the case of the Canaanites and Phoenicians. Genesis 10:6 and verses 15–19 represent them as Hamites, perhaps owing to their close relationship with Hamitic Egypt over many centuries. However, the languages of Phoenicia and Canaan – the best known of which is Hebrew (Isa. 19:18) – are Semitic in the modern sense, as are the peoples who spoke them. (The "Hebrews" do not appear at all in the table of nations; however, it is generally supposed that Eber, a descendant of Shem (Gen. 10:21, 25), is their eponym.) For the modern ethnological classification of the "Semites" see the article Theory of *Race; for the political use of the term, see *Antisemitism.

[Moshe Greenberg]

SEMITIC LANGUAGES, the name given by A.L. Schloezer in 1781 to the language family to which Hebrew belongs because the languages then reckoned among this family (except Canaanite) were spoken by peoples included in Genesis 10:21–29 among the sons of Shem.

1. Wider Background

The Semitic family forms part of a wider grouping generally called Hamito-Semitic, but lately also known as Afroasiatic or Afrasian. This includes with certainty:

(a) Ancient Egyptian and its descendant, Coptic;

(b) the Cushitic languages, comprising a large number of mostly little-explored languages spoken in the northeast corner of Africa, the most important ones being Beja (on the Red Sea coast), Galla (in Ethiopia), and Somali;

(c) Berber, with numerous dialects, spread from the Siwa Oasis in Egypt to Morocco, and southward into the Sahara (Tuareg). Less well established is the status within this family of the Chadic languages of West Africa, the chief of which is

Hausa, and of the Central-Saharan group. Genetic relationship has often been claimed between the Semitic languages and the Indo-European family (to which English belongs as one of the Teutonic languages, as well as Latin and its descendants, Greek, Slavonic, Iranian, Sanskrit, Hittite, etc.). Though such a connection is intrinsically probable, no definite proof has been provided.

2. The Semitic Family

About 70 distinct forms of Semitic are known, ranging from important languages with large literatures to language forms used over a limited territory and either entirely unwritten or possessing but few preserved documents. It was usual, until a short time ago, to group all these into five great branches: Canaanite, Aramaic, Akkadian, Arabic, and Ethiopic, each with an important literary language at its center, and the other forms treated as dialects. This division can no longer be maintained because of the discovery of languages that do not fit into any of those branches, and the rise of doubts with regard to the genetic justification of the assumption of such branches as Canaanite, Aramaic, or Arabic. It is, however, still convenient to describe the languages and dialects roughly in the order of the above branches.

3a. Northwest Semitic

This is the grouping to which Hebrew belongs. Starting from the north, there is Ugaritic, on the seacoast in the northwest corner of Syria, documented in the 14th–13th centuries B.C.E. by poetry, mainly epic, and by administrative lists and letters. While quite distinct from Hebrew as a language, it closely resembles Hebrew in its poetical style, and its study has thrown much light on certain aspects of Hebrew literature. South of Ugaritic, along the coast as far as Haifa and even beyond, was the area of Phoenician. The oldest inscriptions have been variously dated to the 17th, 12th, or even ninth century B.C.E. In the Phoenician homeland, inscriptions appear down to the first century B.C.E. Inscriptions in this language are also known from Cyprus, from Cilicia (the inscription of Azatiwada of the eighth (?) century is the longest Phoenician inscription known), and from various places in the Mediterranean as far west as Spain, from Marseille, from Pyrgoi in Italy, etc. In Carthage, a Phoenician colony, the language developed a distinct form, called Punic, and in its latest stage, documented down to the first centuries C.E., Neo-Punic. In Punic there exists the only continuous text which shows what Phoenician sounded like, namely the Punic passages in Latin script inserted in the play *Poenulus* by Plautus (254–184). From these it is also learned that at least second-century Phoenician was more different from Hebrew than can be guessed from the unvocalized Semitic script of the inscriptions.

The earliest attestation of the language of Phoenicia, however, is not in documents written in that language, but is obtained through the mistakes made by scribes in that area in the Babylonian cuneiform text of the Tell el-Amarna *Letters (14th–13th centuries B.C.E.), as well as in a small number of local words used to gloss certain Babylonian words in those letters. These so-called Canaanisms show clearly that already at that time a language was spoken in the area which had typical features of later Phoenician. However, the senders of the Tell el-Amarna Letters were not only local rulers in what later became Phoenicia, but also in the inland of Syria and further south in Palestine. The Canaanisms in letters from all those areas are so similar that a single language was used in that entire region. That there should have been no marked differences of language in such a large, geographically broken-up and politically disunited area is rather strange, and in fact there is evidence of at least one difference, in the development of the sibilants, between Jerusalem and the areas further north, which appears in place names. Therefore the question may be asked whether the Canaanisms in the Tell el-Amarna Letters do not represent a common literary language rather than the actual spoken local forms. This problem, still unsolved, is of great importance to the history of Hebrew, in view of the large-scale Canaanite element in that language. The evidence, however, speaks in any case for the assumption that a language very close to Hebrew was spoken in Palestine in the period preceding the Israelite conquest. Unfortunately there exists no later literary document in the language of the non-Israelite Semitic population of Palestine. All views about the relation between Canaanite and Hebrew are based on extrapolations from what is known of Phoenician and of pre-Israelite Canaanite. Apart from the Tell el-Amarna Letters, there are two other sources of information about the Semitic languages spoken in Palestine. One source is the Semitic loanwords in Ancient Egyptian and the few words in Egyptian texts put into the mouths of Semites. This material is unmistakably Northwest Semitic, but cannot be further defined with any certainty, and there are many items the semantic identification of which is doubtful. Part of it is written in the so-called syllabic hieroglyphic spelling, and according to the reading of this system by W.F. Albright, the Semitic words show *u* in places where Semitic *ā* is represented in Canaanite by *ō*. The other source is a number of inscriptions in an early form of alphabetic writing, which has not yet been satisfactorily deciphered, and some in legible Canaanite script, of which a few may be non-Israelite.

To the south of Canaan a number of inscriptions have been found in the Sinai Peninsula, some superimposed upon datable Egyptian objects. The whole series is variously dated by scholars between 1900 and 1500 B.C.E. Their Semitic character has not been doubted, but the attempts at decipherment have not produced enough agreement even to identify their language with assurance as Northwest Semitic.

Proceeding inland, east of the coastal languages described, from south to north, there is in southern Transjordan evidence of three ancient peoples: the Edomites, the Ammonites, and the Moabites. The few Ammonite and Edomite inscriptions found are insufficient to allow conclusions as to the exact character of those languages. As for Edomite, quite a few scholars have sought evidence concerning the Edomite language in the deviations of the Book of Job from normal biblical Hebrew, some drawing the conclusion that it was a form of Arabic, others, especially N.H. Tur-Sinai, that it was Aramaic. King Mesha of Moab set up a lengthy inscription, of which now two copies are known. Unless the view of Segert is accepted that the inscription is in Hebrew, written by an Israelite, it must be concluded that eighth-century Moabite was very similar to biblical Hebrew, at least as far as its consonantal skeleton was concerned. A plaster text found at Tell Deir Alla (biblical Succoth?) revealed an unknown Northwest Semitic dialect, though some consider the language of the text to be Aramaic.

The linguistic situation in inland Syria is complicated. At Mari and in Mesopotamia, one finds in the second quarter of the second millennium large numbers of personal names of a Northwest Semitic character, and at Mari also a few common nouns apparently belonging to the same language. Historically, these names are connected with the nomad people called Amurrū. Although the bearers of these names ruled Mari and Babylonia, they did not, as far as is known, produce any documents in their own language, but used Akkadian, and the proper names are practically all there is to go on in reconstructing the language they spoke; it shows connections with Ugaritic and Canaanite. It is still a moot point whether the *Emōrī* mentioned in the Bible were Amurrū. Also the connection between the Amurrū and the central Syrian state of Amurru is not clear. Because of the position of the Amorites as a link between Mesopotamia and Syria and Palestine, it is possible – but cannot be proved at present – that the Amorite language had considerable influence upon the rest of Northwest Semitic.

At Zenjirli, in northern Syria, there are, for a short period in the eighth century B.C.E., inscriptions in the local language of a region called Sham'al or Ya'udi. This so-called Samalian stands about halfway between Phoenician and Aramaic. The existence of such an intermediate dialect is of importance for determining the origins of the most widely developed branch of Northwest Semitic, Aramaic. It is widely believed, following the researches of Moscati and Mazar, that Aramaic, used from the early ninth century onward in inscriptions from northern Syria to Damascus, did not come as a separate language with the Aramaic tribes from outside Syria, but rather spread from the region of Damascus as a result of the unification of large parts of Syria under the tenth-century kingdom of Damascus. The presence of certain "Aramaic" phonetic features in the Hebrew of the 11th-century Song of Deborah shows that Northern Hebrew shared these features with the Damascus dialect. As a result of political events, dialects in middle and northern Syria, which originally may have resembled Amorite and/or Ya'udic, became Aramaicized. (For the later fortunes of this language, see *Aramaic.) The great importance of the Aramaic language group for the study of Hebrew is due

(a) to its being the best-preserved member of the Northwest Semitic branch,

(b) to its persistent influence on Hebrew at almost all the stages of the latter's development, and

(c) to the existence of several specific Jewish-Aramaic dialects at various times, beginning with biblical Aramaic and ending with today's colloquials from Iraqi, Turkish, and Iranian Kurdistan.

3b. East Semitic

This is represented by the various branches of the Akkadian language and by Eblaitic. The former is divided into Old Akkadian (c. 2500–1950 B.C.E.), Babylonian (which also was used as a literary language in Assyria), and Assyrian. Akkadian was written in a script that expressed syllables, and hence also indicated the vowels, but on the other hand seems to have been in several respects phonetically imperfect, owing to its having been adapted originally from a non-Semitic language, Sumerian. Documents were written mainly with a stylus on clay tablets (cuneiform), and are thus practically imperishable. The huge number of private letters, contracts, public documents, and literary texts preserved makes Akkadian one of the principal sources for ancient Semitic. Various forms of Akkadian served in the second millennium B.C.E. for purposes of official correspondence in Syria and Palestine. The outstanding case of this is the Tell el-Amarna Letters. This use of Akkadian bears witness to what must have been extensive cultural influence. In its wake, hundreds of Akkadian words entered the Hebrew language, and this number was further increased during the political contacts in the ninth to sixth centuries and once more through indirect loans via Aramaic. It appears that by a gradual process, between the eighth and the sixth centuries, Akkadian died out as a spoken language, and was in its homeland replaced by Aramaic. Its written use, however, continued on a smaller scale after 539, and Akkadian documents so far discovered can be dated as late as 75 C.E. Eblaitic is the language of the Syrian city of Ebla and is attested from the 24th–23rd centuries B.C.E. It too is written in cuneiform, though many features of the language are obscured by the orthography and thus its classification is difficult. Some have argued that it is an early dialect of Akkadian.

3c. South Semitic

The earliest attestation of South Semitic speech are a number of names borne by leaders of the Aribi tribes whom Assurbanipal and Sennacherib fought in the Syrian Desert and in northern Arabia. Their language seems to have belonged to a group of dialects now called Proto-Arabic or Ancient North Arabian. The chief one is Thamudic, attested along the northern and southern edge of Arabia as well as in Transjordan. Others are Dedanite and Liḥyānic in biblical Midian, and Ṣafaitic in an area east of Damascus. The numerous inscriptions consist mainly of names, but give enough information about the language to show that it is related to Arabic. The time of these inscriptions extends from c. 500 B.C.E. to 500 C.E. The Nabatean inscriptions in Transjordan, southern Palestine, and Sinai (c. 150 B.C.E.–300 C.E.), and the Palmyrene inscriptions in the Syrian Desert (first–third centuries C.E.), though in Aramaic, were put up by speakers of Arabic dialects, and provide further information about the earlier history of that language. Later Arab philologists have preserved some data on dialects spoken in the peninsula closer to the seventh century, and there are also a few inscriptions. It is probable that Classical Arabic was formed as an intertribal *lingua franca* before 500 C.E. It is first attested by a fairly large number of poems of the sixth century and by the Koran in the early seventh century. Owing to the Muslim conquests, Arabic became the vehicle of a far-flung and lively culture, with uninterrupted literary use until the present day. From the beginning, much Arabic was written by people who did not speak it, and through the efforts of grammarians and schools it has maintained its grammar and syntax, and much of its vocabulary, almost unchanged. Since the Muslims conquered the entire territory occupied by Semitic languages in Asia, the speakers of such languages gradually gave up their own speech in favor of Arabic, and only small islands of Aramaic and of South Arabian persisted. On the other hand, Arabic absorbed many words from those languages.

A short time after the conquests there is evidence that spoken Arabic differed profoundly from the written form; in part it seems to have continued pre-Classical dialects. In the Middle Ages Christians and Jews often wrote an Arabic that showed influence of the spoken forms. Except for Maltese, no spoken Arabic colloquial achieved official status as a written language, but there was some popular literature in various dialects, and of course many have been recorded and described by mainly western linguists.

At the southern end of Arabia an entirely different group of languages exists. It is attested since about the middle of the first millennium B.C.E. by inscriptions in a number of Ancient South Arabian languages: Sabean, Minean, Ḥaḍramautic, etc. Minean inscriptions have also been found in biblical Midian, probably set up by a trading colony. Owing to the absence of vowels and the rigid style of the texts, these languages are only partly recoverable; but what is known shows some interesting similarities with Northwest Semitic. Ancient South Arabian speech died out probably before 1000 C.E.; inscriptions were set up until just prior to the Islamic period. What is probably a distinct branch of the same language group, spoken in an area outside that in which Ancient South Arabian culture flourished, is at present represented by Mahri (Mehri), Shaḥari (Shkhauri), Harsusi, and Botahari, spoken at the southern tip of the Sultanate of Muscat and Oman, and by Soqotri, spoken on the island of Socotra in the Indian Ocean. These very archaic and, for the comparative study of Semitic, highly interesting languages, are only rather sketchily recorded, mainly by a mission of Austrian scholars in the late 19th century. Eritrea and the adjoining Ethiopian region of Tigre, with its capital Aksum, appear to have been colonized by South Arabians. At first, in the beginning of the Christian Era, Sabean was used on monuments, but by the third century C.E. there are texts written in the local language, Ge'ez (Ethiopic), first in South Arabian characters, then in a special script, which in the fourth century was provided with regular vowel markings by adding short strokes or circles and other alterations in the shape of letters. Until the tenth century, Ge'ez literature consists entirely of translations of Christian religious texts; after the 12th century, when Ge'ez was no longer spoken, it served also for original writing. The present spoken languages of Semitic stock in Ethiopia are undoubtedly related to Ge'ez. Tigrinya, the language of Eritrea, and Tigre in northern Ethiopia and the Sudan, seem to be direct descendants of Ge'ez, while the exact connection with the southern group, consisting of Amharic, Gafat, Argobba, Harari, and Gurage, the latter a cluster of rather divergent dialects, is not clear. Amharic, written since the 14th century, is now the rapidly developing official language of Ethiopia.

4. The Divisions of Semitic

The most widely accepted view is that the first division which Semitic underwent, probably before 3000 B.C.E., was between East Semitic (Akkadian) and all the rest. At a later date, but before 2000 B.C.E., West Semitic divided into a northern and a southern branch. Northwest Semitic then divided into Canaanite and Aramaic; Southwest Semitic into Arabic and South Arabian plus Ethiopic. The units mentioned again broke up into the languages actually attested. Another version of this view associates the theory of the "family tree" with successive "waves" emerging from the original home of the Semites, by most assumed to have been the Arabian Peninsula: first the Akkadians, then the Canaanites, Aramaeans, Ethiopians, and finally the Arabs. The picture here presented has been questioned since the discovery of Ugaritic, Amorite, and Deir Alla, which do not fully fit into the accepted division of Northwest Semitic, and since the realization that Arabia could hardly have supported sufficient population for such large waves of emigration before the domestication of the camel not long before 1000 B.C.E. No alternative theory has yet been generally accepted, either with reference to the original homeland of the Semites – or of the Semitic language family – or to account for its subdivisions. Some scholars have questioned the existence of either a proto-Canaanite or a proto-Aramaic, and suggested that Northwest Semitic was in 2000 B.C.E. still undifferentiated, and the closer similarity of some languages to each other might be due to later influences of one upon the other. Recently many scholars have preferred a classification that divides West Semitic into a South Semitic branch that includes South Arabian and Ethiopian, and a Central Semitic branch consisting of Arabic and the Northwest Semitic languages.

5. Proto-Semitic

SOUNDS. Proto-Semitic probably had the sounds indicated in the following table.

Ordinary plosives:	p	b	t	d	k	g
Fricatives:			th	dh	kh	gh
Nasals:	m		n			
Emphatic sounds:		ṭ	ṣ	ẓ	ḍ	q
Sibilants:		s	z	sh	ś	s̱
Gutturals:		ʿ	ḥ	ʾ	h	
Other consonants:		l	r	w	y	
Vowels:	a	i	u	ā	ī	ū

Recent studies have reconstructed *ṭ*, *ṣ*, and *q* as originally glottalic or ejective; *s*, *ś*, and *sh* as *ᵗs*, *ḻ*, and *s* respectively; and *ḍ* as *ḻʾ*.

REMARKS ON GRAMMAR. Proto-Semitic nouns had at least three cases: nominative ending in *-u*, genitive in *-i*, and an adverbial accusative case in *-a*. The feminine nouns ended mainly in *-t*, but there were other suffixes. There was no definite article. The plural of nouns seems to have been expressed in a number of different ways. There was also a dual.

The most remarkable feature of the verb in Semitic and Hamitic is the possibility of varying the meaning of the verbal root by prefixes: *sh*, and perhaps also *ʾ*, to express causation (to make someone else do the action); *t* and *n* (also infixed *t* after the first root letter) for passive and reflexive. The middle or the last root letter could also be doubled or repeated, or part of the root repeated, to express various modifications, such as repetition or an elusive quality called emphasis. Internal vowel changes in the stem expressed intransitivity and the passive voice.

There were three tenses, fully preserved only in Akkadian: the perfect *yaqtul*, the imperfect *yaqattil*, and a form to express state rather than action, *qatil* or *qatala*. The first two were conjugated by a combination of prefixes and suffixes, the last by suffixes only. Moods and certain other variations were indicated by adding vowels or *n* to the first two tenses. These tenses were only partly for the expression of time; it is thought that their main function was aspect: *yaqtul* expressed an action that takes place once and was accomplished, while *yaqattil* indicated that an action goes on for some time. This aspect function is still clearly seen in the biblical Hebrew perfect and imperfect tenses.

The outstanding peculiarity in syntax is the nominal sentence, which corresponds roughly to English sentences containing "is" (though its use is much wider), but contains no words for "is." These sentences are timeless, and it seems that Proto-Semitic did not yet possess the possibility to express the perfect and imperfect moods by a verb meaning "to be", since the verbs for this purpose differ in the various languages. A special type of nominal clause enables the Semitic languages to take any element out of an ordinary verbal or nominal sentence and to place it in front of the sentence, making it the subject, and the rest of the sentence (with a pronoun to represent the word taken out) the predicate. For example, the sentence "The way of God is in storm" is transformed into "God (is) his way is in storm" (cf. Nahum 1:3).

All Semitic languages make use of the same root in different functions within the same sentence, mainly to express emphasis, such as "a killer killed" (= someone killed), "he killed a killing", "she pancaked pancakes" (II Sam. 13:6), "the boy (was) a boy" (I Sam. 1:24).

6. Relation of Hebrew to Other Semitic Languages

If the changes from the Proto-Semitic situation are taken as an index of the genetic relationship between languages it will be found that Hebrew shares important developments with different languages. Thus it shares with Phoenician, considered with Moabite to be closest to Hebrew, the development of original *ā* to *ō*. It appears that Phoenician, like Hebrew, lengthened short vowels under certain circumstances; it pronounced the lengthened *a* as *ō*, and in this agrees with the Ashkenazi and Yemenite, but not the Sephardi pronunciation of Hebrew. The changes of *dh* to *z*, *th* to *sh*, ẓ and ḍ to ṣ are common to Hebrew, Moabite, Phoenician, and Akkadian, while those of *gh* to ʿ and *kh* to ḥ appear in Hebrew, Moabite, Phoenician, and Aramaic only. Hebrew agrees with Aramaic in changing *ś* to *s* (probably late), while Phoenician and Akkadian changed it into *sh*, as did Ugaritic. Ugaritic changed ḍ to ṣ, but not ẓ. The only sound change that Ugaritic is known to have shared only with Phoenician, Moabite, and Hebrew, is that of initial *w* into *y*. Though the earlier development of the sounds of Aramaic was rather different from the Hebrew, Hebrew underwent two important changes which it shares with later Aramaic:

(a) the ordinary plosives *p, b, t, d, k, g* came to be pronounced as fricatives *f, v, th, dh, kh, gh* when preceded by a vowel, unless they were doubled;

(b) short vowels in unstressed open syllables (unless lengthened) were reduced to an indeterminate vowel *ĕ* (*šĕwa* mobile). This (as also the further reduction, called *šĕwa* medium) continues to turn plosives positioned after it into fricatives. Hebrew, Phoenician, and Aramaic lost at an early stage the ability to pronounce short vowels at the end of a word, and through this gave up the cases of nouns; in Arabic the same change occurred only after 600 C.E.

It should be noted that Ugaritic was almost as close to Proto-Semitic in its sound system as were Ancient South Arabian and Classical Arabic, and therefore quite unlike Hebrew. Neither did it resemble Hebrew closely in its grammar. The main feature common to Ugaritic, Phoenician, and biblical Hebrew was the *-m* ending for the masculine plural, as opposed to *-n* in Moabite, Aramaic, and Arabic, but also in mishnaic Hebrew. However, Ugaritic, like Tell el-Amarna Canaanite, still distinguished a nominative *-ūma* from genitive and accusative *-īma*, while Phoenician and Hebrew have *-īm* only. Hebrew early elided the *t* of the feminine ending *at(u)*, Phoenician only very late, Arabic first in the end of the sentence, and after 600 C.E. throughout (the *t* remains in the construct state). With Phoenician, Moabite, and Ancient North Arabian, Hebrew shares the article *ha-*; with Phoenician, Aramaic, and Classical Arabic the *ha-* or *hā-* before the demonstrative pronoun (Heb. *ha-zeh*).

Biblical Hebrew and Moabite stand alone in preserving the old perfect form *yaqtul* when preceded by *wa-* ("and"), while at the same time using the old stative form, *qatal*, as a perfect when not preceded by "and" (i.e., at the beginning of an utterance, or in the middle of a sentence). Phoenician, Ya'udic, Old Aramaic, and perhaps Ancient North Arabian abandoned the old perfect *yaqtul* altogether much earlier than Hebrew, which did so only during the Second Temple period. Classical Arabic still has some remnants of perfect *yaqtul*. Ancient South Arabian has very rare cases of perfective *wa-*

yaqtul, Ehiopic only perfective *qatala*. Ugaritic poetry usually employs perfective *yaqtul*, but the administrative prose only perfective *qatala*. Hebrew thus was more conservative than neighboring languages in carrying out a change characteristic of the whole of West Semitic.

Characteristic of Tell el-Amarna Canaanite, Hebrew, Moabite, and Phoenician (where it is only attested late) is the ending *-tī* of the first person singular of the perfect (elsewhere *-tu*). The first person singular pronoun *'nk* (Heb. *ānōkhī*), as opposed to *'n* (Heb. *ănī*), also in Akkadian, Ugaritic, Phoenician, Moabite, and Ya'udic, is an ancient form, found also in Egyptian, Somali (*aniga*), and Berber. It ended in *-i* also in Tell el-Amarna Canaanite and in Phoenician.

The Hebrew *hāyāh* ("to be"), from *hwy*, is also found in Aramaic, Ya'udic, rarely in Akkadian, and according to an ancient lexicon possibly also in Ugaritic, while the ordinary verb for "to be" in Ugaritic is *kwn*, as in Phoenician, Arabic, South Arabian, and Ethiopic. The use of *yesh* ("there is"), from *'yth*, is paralleled by Ugaritic, Aramaic, and Akkadian; in Arabic only in the negative. The Hebrew negative *ēyn* ("there is not") is found in Ugaritic, Late Phoenician, Moabite, and Babylonian. Phoenician and Akkadian have *sh-* as relative pronoun and mark of the genitive; this is found in very early Hebrew (the time of the Judges), in the Hebrew of the Second Temple period, and in mishnaic Hebrew. It is not clear what the relation is between this and the Classical Hebrew *ăsher* in the same sense. The Hebrew accusative sign *et* is also found in Moabite, Phoenician (*'yt*), Ya'udic (*wt*), and early Aramaic (*yāt*).

A survey of the first 100 Phoenician (not Punic) words in the dictionary shows that 82% have the same meaning in Hebrew. A comparison with Ugaritic on the basis of the basic word list of Morris Swadesh shows 79% with the same meaning as in Hebrew. Comparisons with other languages according to the same list indicate the following percentages of correspondence with Hebrew: 66% for Syriac, 53% for Akkadian, 50% for Arabic, and 47% for Ge'ez (Ethiopic). Calculation of these results according to Swadesh's lexicostatisical method suggests that these differences reflect not only the difference in the date at which these words were recorded, but also different degrees of relationship, corresponding to the accepted "family tree" grouping of the Semitic languages (cf. para. 4). The following examples will give some idea of the forms the same word takes in different Semitic and Hamaitic languages.

(1) "Water": Heb. *mayim*, Ug. *mym*, Syr. *mayyē*, Old Akk. *mū*, Ar. *mā'un*, Eth. *māy*, Egyptian *mw*, Somali *māh*, Berber *aman* (pl.), Chadic *am, yam*.

(2) "Name": Heb. *shēm*, Phoen. *shm*, Ug. *shm*, Syr. *shmā*, Akk. *shumu*, Ar. *ismun*, Ge'ez *sĕm*, Beja *sim*, Hausa *sūnā*.

(3) "Three": Heb. *shālōsh* (fem.), Late Punic *salus*, Ug. *thlth*, Syr. *tlāth*, Ar. *thalāthun*, Ge'ez *shalās*.

(4) "Fingernail, claw": Heb. *ṣippōren*, Syr. *ṭephrā*, Akk. *ṣupru*, Ar. *ẓufrun*, Soqotri *ṭifer*, Ge'ez *ṣĕfĕr*, Cushitic (Agau) *ch'iffer*, Berber (Tuareg) *atfer*.

7. The Origin of Hebrew

The thoroughly "Hebraic" character of Tell el-Amarna Canaanite, as far as it can be discerned from the glosses (cf. para. 3a), demands an answer to the question how the Israelites, who came from outside the country, arrived at speaking a language so closely similar to that which had been spoken in Palestine before the conquest. Since the outstanding similarities (*ō* for *ā*,*-tī* in the first person perfect, *ānōkhī* ("I") with *ī*) are restricted to a well-defined and comparatively small area, it is impossible to claim that they would have appeared already in the speech the patriarchs brought from their home in Mesopotamia. It is generally assumed that the Israelites, either in the patriarchal period or after the conquest, adopted the Canaanite speech. Hans Bauer, G.R. Driver, H. Birkeland, and other scholars, however, saw in Hebrew traces of an admixture of the former language spoken by the Israelites. This *Mischsprache* ("mixed language") theory has been employed to account for certain inconsistencies and doublets in Biblical Hebrew grammar and vocabulary, e.g., for the fact that *ā* did not always become *ō*, and for the coexistence of *wa-yaqtul* and *qātal* to express the perfect (and *wē-qātal* and *yiqtol* for the imperfect).

BIBLIOGRAPHY: SEMITIC AND HAMITO-SEMITIC: T.A. Sebeok (ed.), *Current Trends in Linguistics*, 6 (1970), 237–527; A. Meillet and M. Cohen (eds.), *Les langues du monde* ([2]1952), 82–181; I.M. Diakonoff, *Semito-Hamitic Languages* (1965); M. Cohen, *Essai comparatif sur le... Chamito-Sémitique* (1947); H. Fleisch, *Introduction à l'étude des langues sémitiques* (1947); G. Bergstraesser, *Einfuehrung in die semitischen Sprachen* (1928); W. Wright, *Lectures on the Comparative Grammar of the Semitic Languages* (1890); C. Brockelmann, *Grundriss der vergleichenden Grammatik der semitischen Sprachen*, 2 vols. (1908–13); S. Moscati (ed.), *An Introduction to the Comparative Grammar of the Semitic Languages* (1964); H.L. Ginsberg, in: *World History of the Jewish People*, ed. by Mazar, 2 (1970), 102–24; D. Cohen, *Dictionnaire des racines sémitiques* (1970-); E. Lipiński, *Semitic Languages: Outline of a Comparative Grammar* (1997); R. Hetzron (ed.), *The Semitic Languages* (1997); A. Dolgopolsky, *From Proto-Semitic to Hebrew: Phonology* (1999); B. Kienast, *Historische Semitische Sprachwissenschaft* (2001); M. Krebernik, "The Linguistic Classification of Eblaite," in: *The Study of the Ancient Near East in the 21st Century* (1996). GRAMMARS AND DICTIONARIES OF SEMITIC LANGUAGES (except Aramaic and Hebrew): C.H. Gordon, *Ugaritic Textbook* (1965); J. Huehnergard, *Ugaritic Vocabulary in Syllabic Transcription* (1987); D. Sivan, *A Grammar of the Ugaritic Language* (1997); J. Tropper, *Ugaritische Grammatik* (2000); Z.S. Harris, *A Grammar of the Phoenician Language* (1936); J. Friedrich, *Phoenizisch-Punische Grammatik* (1999[3]); A.v.d. Branden, *Grammaire phénicienne* (1969); Z.S. Harris, *Development of the Canaanite Dialects* (1939); W.R. Garr, *Dialect Geography of Syria-Palestine, 1000–586 B.C.E.* (1985); A.F. Rainey, *Canaanite in the Amarna Tablets* (1996); G. Garbini, *Il Semitico di nord-ovest* (1960); J. Hoftijzer-K. Jongeling, *Dictionary of the North-West Semitic Inscriptions* (1995); C.R. Krahmalkov, *Phoenician-Punic Dictionary* (2000); idem, *A Phoenician-Punic Grammar* (2001); M. Sznycer, *Les passages puniques... dans le "Poenulus" de Plaute* (1967); S. Segert, in: *Archiv Orientální*, 29 (1961), 197–267; W.F. Albright, *The Proto-Sinaitic Inscriptions and Their Decipherment* (1969[2]), H.B. Huffmon, *Amorite Personal Names in the Mari Texts* (1965); G. Buccellati, *The Amorites of the Ur III Period* (1966); I.J. Gelb, *Computer-Aided Analysis of Amorite* (1980); F. Groendahl, *Die Personennamen* *der Texte aus Ugarit* (1967); W.v. Soden, *Grundriss der Akkadischen Grammatik* (1995[3]); idem, *Akkadisches Handwoerterbuch* (1958ff.); *Chicago Assyrian Dictionary* (1956ff.); A. v. d. Branden, *Les inscriptions thamoudéennes* (1950); W. Caskel, *Lihyan und Lihyanisch* (1954); C. Rabin, *Ancient West-Arabian* (1951); EIS s.v. *Arabiyya*; J. Fueck, *Arabiya* (1950, Fr. tr. 1955); S. Hopkins, *Studies in the Grammar of Early Arabic* (1984); A.F.L. Beeston, *The Arabic Language To-Day* (1970); W. Wright, *A Grammar of the Arabic Language* (1896–98); E.W. Lane, *An Arabic-English Lexicon* (1863–93); J.G. Hava, *Arabic-English Dictionary for the Use of Students* (1899); J. Blau, *The Emergence and Linguistic Background of Judaeo-Arabic* (1999[3]); idem, *A Grammar of Medieval Judaeo-Arabic* (Heb., 1961); idem, *A Grammar of Christian Arabic* (1966–67); A.F.L. Beeston, *A Descriptive Grammar of Epigraphic South Arabian* (1962); idem et al., *Sabaic Dictionary* (1982); M. Hoefner, *Altsuedarabische Grammatik* (1943); K. Conti Rossini, *Chrestomathia arabica meridionalis epigraphica* (1931); J.C. Biella, *Dictionary of Old South Arabic: Sabaean Dialect* (1982); S.D. Ricks, *Lexicon of Inscriptional Qatabanian* (1989); A. Jahn, *Grammatik der Mehri-Sprache* (1905); idem, *Die Mehri-Sprache in Suedarabien* (1902); M. Bittner, *Studien zur Shkhauri-Sprache*, 4 vols. (1915–17); W. Leslau, *Lexique soqotri* (1938); B. Thomas, *Four Strange Tongues from South Arabia* (1937); T.M. Johnstone, *Harsusi Lexicon* (1977); idem, *Jibbali Lexicon* (1981); idem, *Mehri Lexicon* (1987); A. Dillmann, *Ethiopic Grammar* (1907); M.M. Chaine, *Grammaire éthiopienne* (1938); A. Dillmann, *Lexicon Linguae aethiopicae* (1865); W. Leslau, *Comparative Dictionary of Geez* (1987); idem, *Ethiopic and South Arabic Contributions to the Hebrew Lexicon* (1958); E. Ullendorff, *The Semitic Languages of Ethiopia* (1955); W. Leslau, *Bibliography of the Semitic Languages of Ethiopia* (1946). THE ORIGIN OF HEBREW: H. Bauer and P. Leander, *Historische Grammatik der hebraeischen Sprache*, 1 (1922), 1–25; G. Bergstraesser, in: OLZ, 26 (1923), 253–60, 477–81; H. Bauer, *Zur Frage der Sprachmischung im Hebraeischen: eine Erwiderung* (1924); G.R. Driver, *Problems of the Hebrew Verbal System* (1936); H. Birkeland, *Akzent und Vokalismus im Althebräeischen* (1940).

[Chaim M. Rabin]

SEMMEL, BERNARD (1928–), U.S. historian. Born in New York City, Semmel taught at Columbia University and at Park College and was appointed professor of history at the State University of New York at Stony Brook. He later became Distinguished Professor of History at the Graduate School, City University of New York

Semmel's historical studies were in modern British history and modern European intellectual history. His works include *Imperialism and Social Reform* (1960), *Jamaican Blood and Victorian Conscience* (1963), *The Rise of Free Trade Imperialism* (1970), *The Methodist Revolution* (1973), *John Stuart Mill and the Pursuit of Virtue* (1984), *The Liberal Ideal and the Demons of Empire* (1993), and *George Eliot and the Politics of National Inheritance* (1994). He edited the *Occasional Papers of T.R. Malthus* (1963).

[Ruth Beloff (2nd ed.)]

SEMON, SIR FELIX (1849–1921), British physician. Semon was born in Danzig, Germany, and settled in London in 1874, where he obtained a position as a clinical assistant at the Throat Hospital. From 1882 to 1897 he was physician for diseases of the throat at St. Thomas' Hospital and from 1894 to 1896 president of the Laryngological Society of London, which he helped to found. When he retired the Semon Lectureship was founded in his honor at the University of London.

Semon counted prominent English and overseas personalities among his patients and attended Queen Victoria and other members of the royal family as well as Gladstone. At the queen's recommendation he became confidential physician to Prince Edward, who made him physician extraordinary to the king after his accession to the throne. He was knighted in 1905.

Semon was vice president of the National Hospital for Epilepsy and Paralysis. His research into the progressive destructive lesion of the motor nerve supplying the laryngeal muscles brought him to the formulation of the Semon-Rosenbach Law. His published a number of works including an autobiography (ed. by H.C. Semon and T.A. McIntyre, 1926).

BIBLIOGRAPHY: P.H. Emden, *Jews of Britain* (1943); *Who was Who 1916–1928*.

SEMON, RICHARD WOLFGANG (1859–1918), German zoologist. Born in Berlin, he was educated at Jena, where in 1891 he was appointed professor extraordinary. In that year Semon undertook an extensive voyage of exploration to Australia and the Malay Archipelago to study the primitive reptile-like mammals and the Australian lungfish, both of which had great interest for students of evolution. The results of this expedition appeared in an extensive series of scientific publications, including Semon's classic monographs on the embryology of the lungfish. Semon wrote an account of his travels in a book *Im australischen Busch* (1896; *In the Australian Bush*, 1899). In 1897 Semon left his professorship at Jena and went to Munich. He then devoted himself to the theoretical problems of evolution.

Semon's theory, set forth in *Die Mneme* (1904; *The Mneme*, 1921), was an attempt to describe a mechanism for the inheritance of acquired characteristics. His thesis was that the organism is permanently affected by its reactions to external stimuli. These reactions produce impressions or "engramms," which modify the development of the progeny through "somatic inductions" that affect the germ cells. The power of the organism thus to accumulate a record or "memory" of past reactions to the environment Semon termed the "mneme." This theory, which was found mystical and lacking in a convincing experimental basis, was rather coldly received by most biologists, and is today of historical interest only.

BIBLIOGRAPHY: W. Gutmann, *Psychomechanik: Freud und Semon* (1922).

[Mordecai L. Gabriel]

SENAAH or **MIGDAL SENAAH** (Heb. סְנָאָה), a name which has been variously interpreted. The children of Senaah are listed after those of Jericho in the enumeration of Jews returning from the Babylonian Exile (Ezra 2:35; Neh. 7:38). In the Persian period, it may have been the second capital of the Jericho district. Eusebius mentions a Magdalsenna 8 mi. (c. 13 km.) north of Jericho (Onom. 154:16) and a watchtower (*migdal*, "tower") is shown in this location on the Madaba Map. It has been identified with Khirbat al-Bayūdāt.

[Michael Avi-Yonah]

SENATOR, DAVID WERNER (1896–1953), Zionist administrator. Born in Berlin, Senator was active in various social welfare bodies in Germany and was secretary-general of the European Office of the *American Jewish Joint Distribution Committee in Berlin from 1925 to 1930. He joined the Jerusalem Executive of the *Jewish Agency as a "non-Zionist" member from 1930 to 1935 and served as treasurer and later head of the Immigration Department and the Department of Settlement of German Jews. Senator then returned to Europe and directed the Central Committee for Aid and Reconstruction of the Reich Representation of German Jews (Zentralausschuss fuer Hilfe und Aufbau der Reichsvertretung). A moderate on the Jewish Agency Executive, he resigned in 1935 as a result of his opposition to the "activist" policy of the Jewish Agency. He became an administrator of the Hebrew University and was the executive vice president of the university from 1949 until his death. Senator supported a policy of Jewish-Arab rapprochement through his membership in *Berit Shalom. He died in Atlanta, Georgia, while on a tour of European and American universities.

BIBLIOGRAPHY: Tidhar, 7 (1956), 2909–10.

[Kurt Loewenstein]

SENATOR, HERMANN (1834–1911), German internist. Senator, who was born in Gnesen, province of Posen, became professor of internal medicine at the Augusta Hospital in Berlin. Later, he was appointed a director of the Charité Hospital and professor at the University of Berlin. Senator carried out research and wrote about the treatment of diabetes, on albuminuria and its significance in health and disease, on renal diseases and hemorrhagic disorders of the spleen, on polycythemia and plethora, and on peripharyngeal phlegmon.

BIBLIOGRAPHY: S.R. Kagan, *Jewish Medicine* (1952), 295.

[Suessmann Muntner]

°**SENDLER, IRENA** (1910–), head of the children's section of the Council for Aid to Jews (codenamed Zegota), a Polish underground organization created in the latter part of 1942 and which operated primarily in the Warsaw area; and Righteous Among the Nations. In the early days of the German occupation, Sendler worked to alleviate the suffering of many of her prewar Jewish friends and acquaintances. As a social worker for the Social Welfare Department of the Warsaw municipality, she carried a special permit allowing her to visit the ghetto area, ostensibly for the purpose of combating contagious diseases. This afforded her ample opportunity to learn of the terrible conditions inside the ghetto and try to alleviate the suffering of the people there with additional clothing, medicine, and money. In the summer of 1942, Irena Sendler was invited to join Zegota, which was then in the stages of formation. Readily consenting to this, she had already assembled a group of people dedicated to her charitable work, including her companion Irena Schulz, and she developed a widespread network of contacts inside and outside the ghetto. Under the codename Jolanta, with the help of her coworkers, she arranged for Jewish children to be smuggled out of the ghetto and for sheltering them in secure places either with non-Jewish families or in religious institutions. "I myself had eight or ten flats where Jews were hiding under my care," Irena proudly recalled. The sheltering families received financial support from Zegota for their additional expenses. In October 1943, she was betrayed and arrested by the Gestapo, taken to the infamous Pawiak prison, and brutally tortured. Failing to elicit information from her, her inquisitors condemned her to be shot. However, unbeknownst to her, the Jewish underground operating in the Warsaw region had managed to contact and bribe one of the Gestapo agents, and on the day of her execution she was freed, although she was officially listed among those executed. Forced to stay out of sight for the remainder of the German occupation, Irena carried out her humanitarian activities from her hiding place. Irena Sendler explained that the motivation for her humanitarian work came from lessons learned at home. Her father was a physician, and most of his patients were poor Jews. "I grew up among these people. All my life, I had Jewish friends." She then added, "My family taught me that what matters is whether people are honest or dishonest, not what religion they belong to." In 1965, Irena Sendler was awarded the title of Righteous Among the Nations by Yad Vashem.

BIBLIOGRAPHY: Yad Vashem Archives M31–153; J. Kermish, "The Activities of the Council of Aid to Jews," in: I. Gutman and E. Zuroff (eds.), *Rescue Attempts During the Holocaust* (1978), 367–98; I. Gutman, *Encyclopedia of the Righteous Among the Nations: Poland*, vol. 2 (2004), 702.

[Mordecai Paldiel (2nd ed.)]

SENDREY, ALFRED (**Szendrei, Aladar**; 1884–1976), musician and writer on music. Born in Budapest, Sendrey became an operatic conductor in Hungary. From 1911 to 1914 he conducted in Chicago and New York, and later in Berlin, Vienna, and Leipzig. He wrote on radio music and conducting, but his most important work was an extensive *Bibliography of Jewish Music* which, completed in 1943, was published in 1951 (reprinted 1969). It was the first work of its kind and became a standard book of reference. From 1945 to 1952 he taught at the Westlake College of Music, Los Angeles, and in 1962 became professor of Jewish music at the University of Judaism in Los Angeles. Sendrey published several works on the history of Jewish music, including *Music in Ancient Israel* (1969). His compositions include an opera, a ballet, and a number of orchestral and choral works.

BIBLIOGRAPHY: A.M. Rothmueller, *Music of the Jews* (1967^2), 283.

°**SENECA THE ELDER** (**Annaeus Seneca**; c. 55 B.C.E.–40 C.E.), Roman rhetorician. He was the father of Seneca the Younger, the philosopher, and the grandfather of the poet Lucan. He mentions a Sosius who had suppressed the Jews (*Suasoria* 2:21). There are grounds for believing that this was the Gaius Sosius who had supported Herod against *Antigonus.

[Jacob Petroff]

°SENECA THE YOUNGER (Lucius Annaeus Seneca; c. 5 B.C.E.–65 C.E.), Stoic philosopher and adviser to *Nero. He mentions the properties of the *Dead Sea (*Quaestiones Naturales* 3:25) and seems to allude to Jewish abstinence from certain foods (Epistulae, 108:22). He disapproves of the practice of lighting lamps for the Sabbath (Epistulae 95:47). The most extensive comments of Seneca on Jews are cited by Augustine. The Sabbath is blamed for encouraging indolence among the Jews, a criticism echoed by many subsequent Latin authors. Seneca gives evidence that at the time there was widespread sympathy for, and acceptance of, Jewish customs (an acceptance of which he heartily disapproves; *De Civitate Dei*, 6:10).

BIBLIOGRAPHY: Reinach, Textes, 262–4.

[Jacob Petroff]

SENED, ALEXANDER (1921–2004), Israeli writer. Born in Poland, Sened studied in a Hebrew secondary school and immigrated to Palestine together with his parents in 1934. A trainee of No'ar Oved ("Labor Youth"), he later became an instructor of pioneer training in Ginnosar and Tel Yosef. In Europe between 1945 and 1948, he helped organize "illegal immigration." In Poland, he met his wife, YONAT (1926–), and returned with her to kibbutz Revivim in the Negev at the outbreak of the War of Independence. His literary work, with his wife as coauthor, began with the publication of a diary (1946). The couple wrote *Adamah le-Lo Ẓel* ("Land Without Shade," 1951), about the conquest of the Negev, and *Bein ha-Metim u-vein ha-Ḥayyim* ("Between the Dead and the Living," 1964), the saga of young Polish Jews before the War who were committed to Zionism and Communism. The novel depicts the spirited youngsters who would later initiate the Jewish uprising in Poland or manage to come as pioneers to Israel. The uprising in the Warsaw Ghetto is also the theme of the novella *Nikra Lo Leon* ("Let's Call Him Leon," 1985). Kibbutz society and the gap between ideal and realization is depicted in *Kevar Ereẓ Noshevet* ("The Land is Already Inhabited," 1981). In other prose works the couple follows experimental narrative venues. Thus, *Tandu* (1974) tells about a couple undertaking a trip to the United States, yet the linear plot is layered with memories of past experiences and recollections of diverse places. The couple's last book, *Armonim, Tavasim u-Petakim mi-Shamayim* ("On Chestnuts, Peacocks and Tokens from Heaven") appeared just a week before Alexander Sened's death. A comic-philisophic picaresque novel, it unfolds the fate of Abrasha and his beloved sister-in-law, Bluma-Rosa, who in a way represents the Diaspora Jew, wandering from one place to another and failing to integrate into the kibbutz society. The couple received many literary awards, including the Brenner and Agnon Prizes. For translations see the ITHL website at www.ithl.org.il.

ADD. BIBLIOGRAPHY: I. Perlis, in: *Al ha-Mishmar* (March 27, 1981); Y. Golan, in: *Davar* (March 13, 1981); Y. Kaniuk, "*Kevar Ereẓ Noshevet*," in: *Maariv* (March 6, 1981); G. Shaked, *Ha-Sipporet ha-'Ivrit*, 4 (1993); M. Shaked, "*Yoman shel Zug Meohav*," in: *Alei Siaḥ*, 33 (1993), 93–8; S. Keshet, "Tracing Social Change," in: *Kibbutz Trends*, 22–3 (1996), 49–54; idem, "*Ha-Kelafim ha-Kozvim shel ha-Dor ha-Shelishi*," in: *Shorashim*, 10 (1997), 73–87.

[Getzel Kressel / Anat Feinberg (2nd ed.)]

SENEOR, ABRAHAM (c. 1412–c. 1493), one of the most prominent Jewish courtiers in Spain during the expulsion period. During the reign of King Henry IV (1454–74) he acted as chief tax farmer of Castile. In 1468, in appreciation of his numerous services, the king appointed him *albedin* of the Jewish community of *Segovia, where he lived. In 1474, when Spain was united under the Catholic Monarchs, they expressed their gratitude to Abraham Seneor for his numerous services and did not forget his favorable stand in their struggle for power. From 1476 he appears as the rabbi and supreme judge of the Jews of Castile and the assessor of the Jewish taxes throughout the kingdom. He enjoyed the special protection of the kings, who allocated him an income of 150,000 guilders for life (1475) and exempted him from the restrictions on dress which had been imposed on the Jews of Spain (1479). In 1488 he was appointed treasurer of the Hermandad, a military organization which was established to maintain order and security in the country. Since Jews were not admitted to this office, his involvements were registered in the name of one of the Christian courtiers.

Criticisms have been voiced against Abraham Seneor by Jewish scholars and authors of contemporary Hebrew chronicles, claiming that he was an unbeliever and that he had become rabbi of the Jews because of royal patronage without the consent of the Jews. During his period of office, however, he did much to assist the Jewish communities, and in a letter which the Jews of Castile sent to their coreligionists in Rome in 1487 they referred to him as the "exilarch over us." On many occasions he protected the Jews of Spain from violent incitements by monks and the cruel hands of the *Inquisition. After the conquest of *Malaga by *Ferdinand and Isabella in 1487, his efforts were directed toward the redemption of Jewish captives. The authors of Jewish chronicles describe his position and wealth at length: "He rode together with 30 mules," "he rode a mule and wore a golden necklace… all the dignitaries of the kingdom accompanied him."

Pressure by Ferdinand and Isabella that he should convert to Christianity finally prevailed and he decided to abandon Judaism, together with his son-in-law Meir *Melamed and the members of his family. At a public ceremony, which the sovereigns arranged in honor of the event, at *Guadalupe on June 15, 1942, they themselves served as godfathers for the baptism. Seneor then changed his name to Fernando Nuñez Coronel. A few days later he was appointed *regidor* of Segovia, a member of the royal council, and chief financial administrator of the crown prince.

BIBLIOGRAPHY: Baer, Urkunden, 2 (1936), index; Baer, Spain, 2 (1966), index s.v. *Abraham Seneor*; Suarez Fernández, Documentos, index. **ADD. BIBLIOGRAPHY:** E. Gutwirth, in: *Michael*, 11 (1989), 169–229.

[Joseph Kaplan]

SENIGALLIA, town on the Adriatic coast of Italy. Jewish loan bankers made their appearance there in the 14th century. As a result of Church pressure, the anti-Jewish decrees imposed in the second half of the 16th century were enforced in Senigallia also, when the town was under the rule of the Della Rovere family. In 1631 the town came under the direct rule of the popes with the rest of the duchy of Urbino; three years later a ghetto was instituted for the 40 families. During the next century and a half, the Jewish population trebled; many Jews also attended Senigallia's famous fair. In 1789 there were about 600 Jews living in the town. Taking advantage of the temporary withdrawal of the French occupying forces in 1799, the populace sacked the ghetto, killed 13 Jews and drove the rest into temporary exile. In 1870 around 300 Jews lived in Senigallia. In 1969 there were 30 Jews living in Senigallia, who were considered a part of the *Ancona community.

BIBLIOGRAPHY: Roth, in. HUCA, 10 (1935), 468–71; Milano, Bibliotheca, index.

[Ariel Toaff]

SENIOR, MAX (1862–1939), U.S. businessman and communal leader. Senior, who was born in Cincinnati, Ohio, became the president of Model Homes Company, one of the first companies to construct low-cost housing on a large scale. Active in Jewish affairs, Senior was a founder of the United Jewish Social Agencies, a forerunner of the contemporary community chest. In 1896 he was the prime founder of the United Jewish Charities of Cincinnati, one of the first American Jewish philanthropic federations, and later served as its president. He was elected the first president of the National Conference of Jewish Charities in 1899. During World War I Senior and Boris D. *Bogen, while serving as European representatives for the Joint Distribution Committee in Holland, established a network whereby relief funds and supplies from the U.S. could be funneled to the war-ravaged territories, particularly German-held Poland, through Dutch Jewish intermediaries. Senior was also active on behalf of the Cleveland Jewish Orphan Asylum, headed the Shoemaker Clinic for the Promotion of Negro Health and Welfare in Cincinnati, and served as a member of the Ohio State Tuberculosis Association.

SENIOR, SOLOMON (16th century), Marrano notable. Descended from Abraham *Seneor, the last crown rabbi of Castile, who converted to Christianity, Solomon Senior was born a Marrano under the name Juan Perez and is said to have become governor of Segovia. He later escaped to *Turkey, where he adopted Judaism and entered the service of Joseph *Nasi, duke of Naxos, becoming his principal adviser on political matters. Nasi so relied on his judgment that he was spoken of as the other's right eye. Solomon Senior was the father of Dr. Francisco Coronel (Coronello), who was ostensibly a Catholic; the latter administered the duchy of Naxos for Nasi and defended it when attacked by the Venetian fleet during the War of Cyprus (1571).

BIBLIOGRAPHY: C. Roth, *House of Nasi, Duke of Naxos* (1948), 87.

[Cecil Roth]

°**SENKO, YASUE** (1888–c. 1950), Japanese "specialist" on Jewish affairs. An army officer in 1927–1928, he traveled in Palestine and Europe to study Jewish problems. On his return, he published *Kakumei Undo wo Abaku* ("Revolutionary Movements Exposed," 1931) and soon became known as one of Japan's leading antisemites. In *Yudaya no Hitobito* ("The Jewish People," 1937) he continued his attacks on the Jews. In 1938 Senko, promoted to colonel, was dispatched to Manchuria to advise the Japanese army on policy toward the Jewish communities but his antisemitism abated in the following years and at times he tried to protect the Jews in *Manchuria and *Shanghai. In 1945 he was captured during the Soviet occupation of Manchuria, and after 1950 nothing further was heard of him.

[Hyman Kublin]

SENLIS, town in the Oise department, N. France. The presence of Jews in Senlis is confirmed from at least 1106, when *Odo of Cambrai stopped in Senlis on his way to Poitiers, and held a religious disputation with a Jew of the town named Léon. In 1208 at the latest, Jews lived in a special quarter, the *Judaria*, a sign of their numerical importance. Later most of them lived on two streets, the Grande Juiverie, which subsequently became the Rue de la Chancellerie, and the Petite Juiverie, which became the Impasse du Courtillet. However, from a comparison of the amounts which the Jews paid, at the close of the 13th century, toward the Jewish *badge tax and their share of the poll tax, it is clear that the financial resources of the community were more significant than its numbers. No renowned Jewish scholar seems to have lived in Senlis. There is no evidence that the Jews returned to Senlis after the expulsion in 1306.

BIBLIOGRAPHY: Gross, Gal Jud, 660f.; Bernard, in: *Compte-rendus et Mémoires de la Société d'Histoire et d'Archéologie de Senlis*, 6th series, 5 (1934–39), li–lv; E. Mueller, *Monographie des Rues, Places et Monuments de Senlis*, 1 (1880), 148ff.; L. Lazard, in: REJ, 15 (1887), 250, 254 (esp.).

[Bernhard Blumenkranz]

SENNABRIS, locality in Galilee, 30 furlongs (c. 3½ mi.; 5½ km.) from Tiberias, bordering on the Jordan Valley (Jos., Wars, 3:447; 4:455, as Ginnabris). Vespasian camped there on his way into Galilee in 68 C.E. In 351 C.E. the army of Ursicinus, the general of Gallus Caesar, reached Sennabris and oppressed the inhabitants. An *Umayyad palace of the caliphs located there was in use from the time of Muʿāwiya (661–680) up to the eighth century. The village and the bridge over the

Jordan continued to be of some importance in the Crusader and *Mamluk periods. The exact identification of Sennabris is still debated, with some identifying it with Kinneret near the issue of the Jordan from the Sea of Galilee, a location adjoining Bet Yeraḥ, in agreement with the Jerusalem Talmud (Meg. 1:1, 70a). Another proposed identification is with Senn en Nabra.

BIBLIOGRAPHY: A. Laarisalo, *The Boundaries of Issachar and Naphthali* (1927), 81–82; Albright, in: AASOR, 2/3 (1923), 36; Mayer, in: IEJ, 2 (1952), 183ff.; Bar-Adon, in: *Eretz Israel*, 4 (1956), 50ff. **ADD. BIBLIOGRAPHY:** Y. Tsafrir, L. Di Segni, and J. Green, *Tabula Imperii Romani. Iudaea – Palaestina. Maps and Gazetteer.* (1994), 226.

[Michael Avi-Yonah]

°**SENNACHERIB** (Akk. **Sin-aḫḫê-eriba**; Heb. **סַנְחֵרִב, סַנְחֵרִיב**), king of Assyria and Babylonia (705–681 B.C.E.), son of *Sargon II. During his reign the northern and eastern frontiers were relatively calm; however, he had to deal with rebellions in Babylonia and Syro-Palestine. In 702 Sennacherib defeated *Merodach-Baladan, who, upon his return from exile in Elam, had deposed the new Babylonian king. In 689 the Babylonians, supported by Elam, revolted again. Sennacherib met them at Hallulê, on the Tigris, and defeated them but not without heavy losses. To solve the Babylonian problem once and for all, he destroyed Babylon and let the Euphrates flow over it.

In 701 Sennacherib marched against the rebels of Syro-Palestine. He went from victory to victory: Sidon, Ammon, Moab, Edom, Ashkelon, Ekron, and Lachish fell before him. At Elteke he defeated a considerable Egyptian army, which had come to the rescue of Ekron. It was from Lachish that he sent a mission headed by the *Tartan, *Rab-Saris, and *Rab-Shakeh, to *Hezekiah in Jerusalem in order to convince him to surrender (II Kings 18:13–19:37; Isa. 36–37). According to his annals, Sennacherib took 46 fortified cities and "small cities without number" of Judah; he made 200,150 prisoners of war and exacted from Hezekiah a heavy tribute – 30 talents of gold and 800 (300 according to II Kings 18:14) talents of silver. Although he besieged Jerusalem, he was unable to take the city, for "that night the angel of the Lord went forth, and slew 185,000 in the camp of the Assyrians" (II Kings 19:35). Another version tells of a legion of rats that invaded the Assyrian encampment (Herodotus) and a third version tells of a pestilential sickness (Berosus). Whatever happened, the fact remains that Sennacherib was forced to abandon the siege and return to Assyria. Sennacherib is remembered as a great builder; he enlarged and embellished *Nineveh, built and restored various temples and public buildings all over Assyria, and undertook very important hydraulic works.

He was assassinated by one of his own sons in a temple of Nineveh. For further details see *Mesopotamia.

In the Aggadah

After having previously conquered the rest of the world (Meg. 11b), Sennacherib equipped a massive army against Hezekiah, consisting of 45,000 princes, each enthroned in a golden chariot and accompanied by his ladies and courtesans, 80,000 warriors in coat of mail, 60,000 swordsmen, and numerous cavalry (Sanh. 95b). With this vast army Sennacherib marched on Judea in accordance with the disclosures of his astrologers, who warned him that he would fail to capture Jerusalem if he arrived too late. He rested at Nob and from a raised platform observed the Judean capital, which appeared weak and small to him. When his warriors urged him to attack, he bade them rest for one night before storming the city the next day. This delay spared Jerusalem since Saul's sin against the priests at Nob was fully expiated on that very day (Sanh. 95a). That night, which was the eve of Passover, the entire army was annihilated when Hezekiah and the people began to recite the *Hallel* Psalms (Ex. R. 18:5). The death of the Assyrians occurred when the angels permitted them to hear the *ḥayyot* ("celestial beings") sing praises to God (Sanh. 95b). Their souls were burnt, although their garments remained intact (Ex. R. 18:5). Sennacherib and his two sons were among the few survivors. On his return to Assyria, Sennacherib found a plank which was part of Noah's ark and made it an object of worship. He vowed that if he prospered in his next ventures he would sacrifice his sons to it. His sons overheard this vow and put him to death (Sanh. 96a). They fled to Kardu where they released the many Jewish captives there. With them they marched to Jerusalem and became proselytes. The well-known scholars *Shemaiah and *Avtalyon were the descendants of these two sons of Sennacherib (Git. 57b; Targ., II Kings 19:35, 37).

BIBLIOGRAPHY: Ginzberg, Legends, 4 (1947[5]), 267–72; 5 (1946[3]), 361–6.

SENS, town in the Yonne department, N. central France. The mention of an expulsion of the Jews from Sens around 876 in an 11th-century chronicle is seemingly a confusion and probably refers to the expulsion, at the beginning of the 11th century, of Duke Raynaud of Sens, who "Judaized" and called himself the "king of the Jews." However, it is certain that in 1146 King Louis VII officially authorized the settlement of Jews in Sens. According to a local chronicler writing a short while later, he also allowed them to have synagogues and cemeteries. Soon after, Pope Alexander III intervened to protect the Jews of Sens from the Christians who attempted to baptize them by force and disturbed them at worship and during burial services. Even King Philip Augustus is said to have assisted the Jews at the beginning of his reign, despite the zeal of Archbishop Guy of Noyers. According to a local chronicler, it was this archbishop who was responsible for the massacre of the Jews of *Bray-sur-Seine in 1190. Having returned to Sens in 1198 (after their expulsion from the kingdom in 1182), the Jews erected a synagogue in 1208 which Pope Innocent III deemed to be too high. Archbishop Gauthier de Cornut adopted a favorable attitude toward the Jews both in local affairs and in a more general way, such as at the time of the disputation of Paris in 1240. After their expulsion in 1306, there was no further Jewish community in Sens during the Middle Ages. Although there was both a Grande and Petite Juiverie street, only the latter had been inhabited by the Jews. The synagogue, which is said to have contained paintings of religious ceremonies, was demolished about 1750. The most eminent of the scholars of Sens was *Samson b. Abraham, tosafist, legal authority, commentator, and liturgical poet. Other tosafists who lived in Sens were Eliezer (c. 1175), and Moses and Isaac ha-Levi (c. 1250). Nathan b. Joseph *Official and his son Joseph b. Nathan, author of *Yosef ha-Mekanne*, probably lived in Sens.

A small Jewish community existed in Sens before World War II and there were still about 50 Jews there in 1941. A new small community, consisting mainly of Jews from North Africa, was established in the 1960s. In 1970 there were 50 Jews living in the town.

BIBLIOGRAPHY: Gross, Gal Jud, 661f.; idem, in: REJ, 6 (1882), 167–86; 7 (1883), 40–77; H. Bouvier, *Histoire de l'Eglise et de l'Ancien Archidiocèse de Sens*, 3 vols. (1906–11), index; C. Porée, *Histoire des Rues et des Maisons de Sens* (1920), 286, 289ff.; B. Blumenkranz, *Juifs et Chrétiens dans le Monde Occidental, 430–1096* (1960), 63; idem, *Les Auteurs Chrétiens Latins du Moyen Age* (1963), 253.

[Bernhard Blumenkranz]

SENTA (Hung. **Zenta**), town on the Thissa River, Vojvodina province. Jews arrived there during the 18th century, mostly from Hungary and Moravia. They engaged in trade of cereals and textiles though quite a few were artisans. The first rabbi was Isaac Heilborn, followed by Solomon Klein and Moses Leibowitz. A *ḥevra kaddisha* was founded in 1858. In the wake of the great split that occurred in Hungarian Jewry in 1868/69, the local Jewry separated, too, into *Neolog (Reform) and Orthodox communities. A small group declared itself status quo, as did some of the communities in Hungary which did not join either of two rival groups. This phenomenon was unique as far as Yugoslavia was concerned. Consequently, there were three *kehillot* in Senta. The Orthodox renamed themselves inexplicably "Sephardim." This was probably in imitation of what occurred in the community of *Sighet in Romania, where a dissident group of Orthodox Jews eccentrically adopted the name, also without any Sephardi members. A Neolog synagogue was built in 1873, another in 1929.

A yeshivah was established, headed by Rabbi Eliezer Rausnitz. Michael *Fekete, mathematician and well-known professor at the Hebrew University, was born in Senta.

Among the Senta rabbis, Hermann-Zvi Schweiger was a prominent Hebraist. Neolog community leaders were Armin Graf, Nathan Kramick, and Solomon Ehrenfeld. Armin Fischer was the Zionist leader.

During the Holocaust all the Jews perished. The "Sephardi" rabbi, without a single Sephardi present, was Moses Teitelbaum; he was extricated from a concentration camp, eventually reaching the United States and joining the Satmar congregation in New York. The *kehillot* were not renewed. The great synagogue was demolished and a smaller one serves as a sports club.

BIBLIOGRAPHY: *Israel-Juedische Wochenschrift* No. 3 (1940); "*Yehudei Vojvodina be-Et ha-Ḥadashah*," in: *Yalkut*, no. 2 (ed. Z. Loker) (1994), 92–93 and 112.

[Zvi Loker (2nd ed.)]

SEPARATION OF POWERS, a fundamental principle of Public Law, which seeks to distinguish between the roles and powers of a number of different public authorities operating in tandem, such as the legislative, executive, and judicial authorities. On the one hand, this principle is meant to prevent too great a concentration of power in the hands of a single authority (such as a king in previous times, or a government or parliament, in our own day); on the other, this model is meant to fashion a system of controls, checks and balances, to ensure the proper and appropriate operation of a public authority. In modern times, this model was developed in the wake of ideas first presented as an appropriate democratic model by Montesquieu in his book, *The Spirit of Laws*. It goes without saying that this principle, as it exists today, did not exist in ancient legal systems such as Jewish Law, based on a central monarchic regime. Nevertheless, one can find more than a few principles in Jewish Law which are consistent with the model of separation of powers, even if not identical to it.

Separation of powers does not find formal expression in Jewish Law, but at times is expressed in the practical realm. Thus, for example, the prophets held prominent status in Biblical times but, being outside the institutionalized system, were free to, and indeed did, criticize the king, and were a balancing factor to his ruling power. In other cases, by contrast, we find the prophet involved in royal affairs, and even in the appointment of judges (I Sam. 8:1–3). Similarly, during the early Biblical period we find the model of "elders" and "princes" working concurrently, each with their own powers. Their concurrent functioning created the requisite balances for a suitable social system. A striking example of the separation between the two branches, the judicial and the executive, is found in the command, "You shall appoint *judges and officers* in all your gates which the Lord your God gives you, according to your tribes; and they shall judge the people with righteous judgment" (Deut. 16:18).

The structure of government during the monarchic period expresses a classic model of centralized authority, in which most of the power is concentrated in the hands of one ruler. Thus, for example, we find that the king of Israel was involved, not only in running his kingdom, but also in legislation (such as laws imposing tax payments). The king (such as Solomon) also served as judge. So strongly identified did these two tasks become that in biblical language the term "judge" (*shofet*) relates not only to court judges who must decide cases between litigants, but also to the king or ruler (see, for example, I Sam. 8:6: "give us a king to judge us").

Maimonides (Yad, Melakhim) also highlights the merging of sovereign functions in the position of the king. In addition to serving as the executive authority, the king functioned simultaneously as both legislator and judge (see, for example, Yad, Melakhim 4:10). In addition, in the Middle Ages members of the public authority (see *Public Authority) were involved on a regular basis in both legislative and judicial activities, such as judicial interpretation and sentencing. The responsa literature attests to hundreds of such cases (see

*Takkanot, *Takkanot ha-Kahal) by *tuvei ha-kahal,* the communal leadership, who were the central executive authority in the Jewish community. This blurring of roles, which clearly goes against contemporary principles of separation of powers, indeed aroused opposition among some of the scholars of Jewish Law, and a number of them regarded this blurring of roles as the reason for the opposition found in Scripture itself to the enthronement of a king over Israel, who would concentrate too much power in his own hands without proper and effective checks and balances (see Meir Ish-Shalom's commentary on Sifre, 105:1, n. 4).

Similarly, the *Sanhedrin, the Great Court of Seventy One, and the local courts in the Jewish communities of the Middle Ages (see *Bet Din) not only engaged in adjudication but, alongside their role as the supreme judicial authority, also dealt with legislation (regarding the passage of communal enactments, see *Takkanot and *Takkanot ha-Kahal) and with law enforcement functions (such as in punishing criminals; see *Punishment).

The Courts in the State of Israel

The model of separation or non-separation of powers, as expressed in the sources of Jewish Law, has been discussed in the Israeli courts on several occasions. In one instance, the Supreme Court (Justice Y. Cohen) highlighted the substantive difference between the modern legal system (which prevents a judge from engaging in execution of the law or in legislation) and Jewish Law, in which the judge is granted the authority to both rule and legislate (FH 39/75, *Israel Port Authority v. Ararat,* 31 (1) PD 545). In two other cases, the Supreme Court (Justice M. Elon) stressed that, unlike the model of the court under Jewish Law, which holds the power to mete out and administer punishment ("The court administers lashes and other punishments not prescribed by the Torah" – Yev. 90b), in modern law, which maintains separation of powers, it is accepted that changes in legislation are made by legislators and not by the courts (App. 22/83 *Kraus v. the State of Israel,* 37 (1) PD 369; Cr.A. 543/79 *Avishai Nagar v. the State of Israel,* PD 35(1) PD 163–170).

This issue of "Separation of Powers" was also discussed by the Supreme Court in connection with the question of whether or not a judge is entitled to deal with political issues. Relying on sources in Jewish Law, the Supreme Court (Justice Goldberg) noted the dual role of the rabbinic judge, who played a central role not only in Jewish judicial authority, but also in communal leadership. He stressed the difference between this approach and that prevalent in our day, in which there is separation of powers between the two roles (HC 732/84 *Tzaban v. the Minister of Religious Affairs,* 40 (4) PD 153). This issue occupied both the civil and rabbinical courts in Israel with respect to the communal status of the Chief Rabbinate of Israel and the ability of its members – both rabbis and *dayyanim* (judges in rabbinical courts) – to participate in activities obviously in the realm of the executive branch. In another case, the question arose of *dayyanim*'s involvement (as part of the judicial branch) in the functioning of the religious councils (being part of the executive branch). The District Court (Judge N. Hendel) relied on sources from Jewish Law to support his decision that it was inappropriate for one branch to impinge on the activities of another branch, and for *dayyanim* to be involved in activities associated with the executive authority (SSA (Beer-Sheba) 276/05 *Shana and Bros. v. Haziza and Bros.* (not published).

BIBLIOGRAPHY: M. Elon, *Ha-Mishpat ha-Ivri* (1988), 49–51; idem, *Jewish Law* (1994), 55–57; G. Alon, *"Eilein de-Mitmanin be-Kessef,"* in: *Meḥkarim be-Toledot Yisrael,* 2:23; A. Hacohen, *"Ha-Rabbanut ha-Rashit le-Yisrael: Hebbetim Mishpatiyyim,"* in: I. Warhaftig (ed.), *Ha-Rabbanut ha-Rashit le-Yisrael: Shivim Shana le-Yisuda,* (2000), 159–219; A. Hacohen, *Parshanut Takkanot ha-Kahal ba-Mishpat ha-Ivri* (2003), 40–56; Y. Engelard, *"Ma'amadah shel Mo'eẓet ha-Rabbanut ha-Rashit ve-Samkhut ha-Piku'aḥ shel Beit ha-Mishpat ha-Gavoha le-Ẓedek,"* in: *Ha-Praklit,* 24 (1966), 68; Y. Lior, *"Ofi ha-Malkhut be-Yisrael,"* in: *Iyyunim be-Sefer Shemuel,* vol. 1 (1992), 145; Sh. Yevin, *"Od le-Inyan Shofet Melekh,"* in: *Leshonenu,* 33 (1969), 3–6; E. Yinon and Y. David, *Ha-Rabbanut ha-Mamlakhtit: Beḥirah, Hafrada ve-Ḥofesh Bitui* (2000).

[Aviad Hacohen (2nd ed.)]

SEPHARAD (Heb. סְפָרַד), the site of a colony of exiles from Jerusalem, mentioned in Obadiah 20. It is predicted that the exiles in Sepharad would possess the cities of the south.

Sepharad was identified as *Sardis, the capital of Lydia in Asia Minor, after the publication by E. Littmann of a bilingual Aramaic-Greek inscription found in the excavations of Sardis in which Sepharad is equated with Sardis. This identification is supported by another bilingual inscription, in Lydian and Aramaic, found at Sardis, in which Sepharad is written in the date formula at the opening of the Aramaic part (see bibl. for Donner and Roelling; and Kent).

Targum Jonathan renders Sepharad as Ispamia or Spamia, and the Peshitta, as Ispania, i.e., Spain. From the end of the eighth century C.E., Sepharad became the usual Hebrew appellation for the Iberian Peninsula.

BIBLIOGRAPHY: E. Littmann, *Sardis,* 6, pt. 7 (1916), 23–28; C.C. Torrey, in: AJSLL, 34 (1918), 185–98; R.G. Kent, *Old Persian…* (1953^2), s.v. *Sparda (S'fard-)*; H. Donner and W. Roellig, *Kanaanaeische und aramaeische Inschriften,* 1 (1962), no. 260; 2 (1964), 306–7.

SEPHARDIM (Heb. סְפָרַדִּים, sing. סְפָרַדִּי, Sephardi), descendants of Jews who lived in Spain or Portugal before the expulsion of 1492. (The term Sephardim is often erroneously used for other Jews of non-Ashkenazi origin.) *Sepharad, mentioned in Obadiah 1:20, was connected fancifully or erroneously with Hispania, the Latin name for Spain.

Legend holds that there were Jews in *Spain as early as Solomon's time. In any case, the settlement is extremely old. Jews suffered persecution there during the period of the Visigoths, which ended when the Arabs conquered the country in 711 C.E. Thus politically and linguistically the Jews of Spain were put in touch with the center of Jewish life in Babylonia-Iraq and carried on the tradition of Babylonian Jewry. The Muslim era in Spain gave rise to the "Golden Age" of Spanish

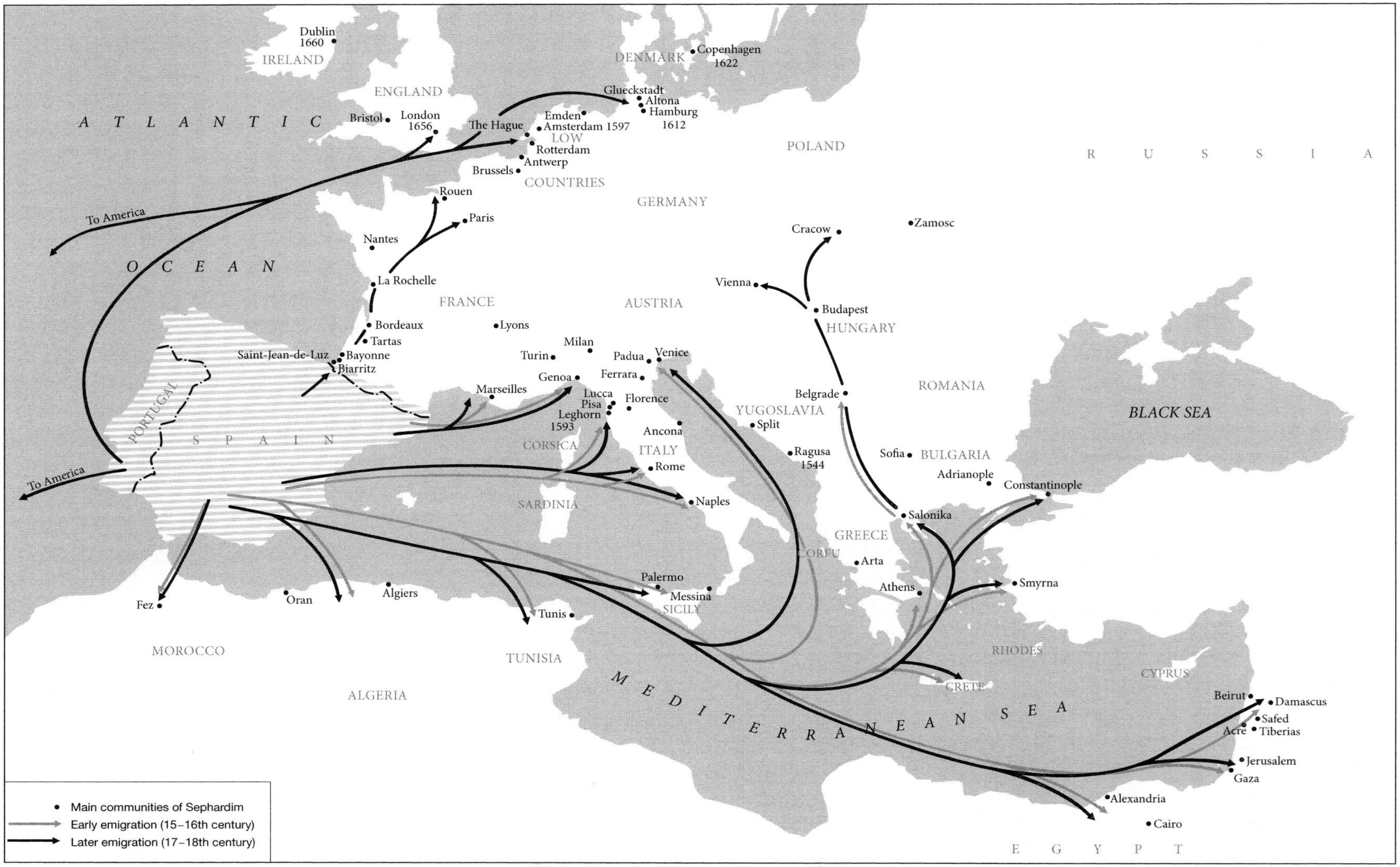

Waves of Sephardi emigration from Spain and Portugal after the expulsion of 1492, with dates of establishment of new communities where known. Based on a map drawn by H. Bainart.

Jewry, which produced such figures as the statesman *Ḥisdai ibn Shaprut, the statesman, poet, and halachist *Samuel ha-Nagid, the poet Moses *ibn Ezra, the poets and philosophers Solomon ibn *Gabirol and *Judah Halevi, and above all, the physician, philosopher, and halakhist Moses *Maimonides.

After the Almohad persecutions of 1148, Jewish life in Spain was concentrated in the Christian parts of the country, which, in the course of the *Reconquista*, gradually extended over the entire peninsula. The vigorous and creative Jewish community was disrupted in 1391 by an outbreak of persecutions that led to wholesale insincere conversions to Christianity, creating so-called "New *Christians," or Conversos, many of whom in fact only outwardly professed Christianity but practiced Judaism in secret and taught their children to do likewise. The Inquisition was established to extirpate the scandal of Christians relapsing to a previous "dead" faith, but its work was hampered by the presence of unconverted Jews over whom the Inquisition had no authority. Accordingly, in March 1492 a decree of expulsion was issued against all Jews who refused to accept Christianity, and this edict officially remained in force until 1968. Some accepted conversion; others, perhaps as many as 250,000, moved away to North Africa, Italy, and especially Turkey, where Sultan Bayazid II admitted them gladly. The seaport of *Salonika, in particular, became a great center of Sephardim, with all the important Spanish towns and districts being represented there by congregations that maintained their identity.

Thus was created the Sephardi Diaspora, a dispersion within a dispersion that not only looked back to Ereẓ Israel as its homeland, but had been indelibly impressed by a long sojourn in Spain. The exiles took with them the language and songs of Spain, which they preserved with fidelity; the foods of Spain, so that the Bulgarian or Serbian Jew would eat *pastel* or *pandeleon*; and children's games, so that in the Balkans a game with nuts called *el castillo* was played to the recitation of an old Spanish quatrain; while R. Joseph *Caro, the Sephardi author of the *Shulḥan Arukh (the standard code of Orthodox Judaism) draws on words like *panadas* (a kind of croquette with meat), *pala* (a baker's peel), or *limones* (lemons) to express domestic items for which he found no equivalent in the rabbinic Hebrew of his day. The Sephardim bore Spanish personal and family names, and their world view had been shaped by the customs and conduct of their Spanish neighbors.

A century later the formation of another branch of Sephardi Jewry began – the Marrano *Diaspora. Many *Crypto-Jews had moved to Portugal, where the danger of detection was less. From there they slipped away in increasing numbers to lands where they could cast off their Christian mask and reassume Judaism. The freedom which Holland achieved from Spain at about this time made *Amsterdam the great center of the Marrano Diaspora, which evolved into the Western Sephardi Diaspora or Portuguese *Nacion*. Portuguese Jews moved there in great numbers, especially during the 17th century, often totally ignorant of Jewish practice and the Hebrew language, but anxious to learn. A magnificent synagogue was built, and educational institutions were founded whose students are thus described in 1680 by the much traveled Shabbetai *Bass:

> In my eyes they were as giants on account of their expertise in the Bible text and Hebrew grammar. Moreover they can compose songs and poems, and speak Hebrew fluently... the teachers are paid from community funds according to their merits and do not need to flatter anyone...

Subsequent migrations of Sephardim took place to England and the Americas, as well as to centers of Western Europe such as *Bordeaux, *Bayonne, and *Hamburg. These Sephardim differed from the Sephardim of the East in that their day-to-day language was Portuguese, although they also knew Spanish, which they used for commerce and as a semi-sacred language for Bible translation. They remained in the mainstream of West European culture, frequently writing their vernacular in Roman rather than Hebrew script.

Language

The Spanish language, as it was preserved by the Sephardim, is called *Ladino, Judezmo, or Judeo-Spanish. It has a number of archaic characteristics (e.g., the preservation of original *j* and *sh* sounds, which standard Spanish has lost, as well as peculiar lexical and syntactic features, including loan words from Hebrew, Turkish, and other languages) and makes a quaint and pleasing impression on speakers of the standard language. According to the research of David Bunis, Judeo-Spanish came to contain a great many Hebrew and Aramaic loan words since the 16th century. It was greatly influenced by regional languages like Ottoman-Turkish, Turkish, Greek, Bulgarian, Serbian, and after the mid-19th century French and Italian. In Spanish Morocco, in the communities of Tangiers, Tetuan, Melilla, Ceuta, and elsewhere, the dialect of the language was called *Haketia*. Ladino was formerly written in the rabbinic cursive script called Solitreo (the modern, originally Ashkenazi, Hebrew cursive never having been in use among Sephardim), but with efforts at modernization in Turkey, the Roman alphabet was adapted to Ladino and is now generally used. Ladino is still spoken by Jews in Turkey, Greece, and adjacent countries, as well as by immigrants to Israel, the U.S., Latin America, and elsewhere. It seems probable, however, that the dialect will be extinct within a short time, and efforts are being made in Jerusalem and Madrid to record the language systematically. Portuguese survived as the language of the Marrano Diaspora until the early 19th century; it still survives in some centers in certain fossilized usages, for example in the prayer for the queen in Amsterdam and the announcement of congregational honors and elections in London.

Literature

The literature of the Sephardim may be divided into three categories:

(1) works written in Hebrew;

(2) works written in Spanish (including Ladino) and Portuguese;

(3) anonymous folk literature in Ladino.

The first category, consisting of Bible commentary, polemic literature, poetry, drama, legal texts, and kabbalistic works by such individuals as Isaac *Abrabanel, Joseph Caro, *Manasseh Ben Israel, and David Franco *Mendes, forms part of the mainstream of Hebrew literature of the period and will not be treated here.

The second category includes works written before the expulsion of the Jews. Notable are the *Proverbios Morales* of *Santob de Carrión (based on talmudic sources) and the Bible translation with glosses made by Moses *Arragel at the command of Don Luis de Guzman (1430). Writing subsequent to the expulsion tends to be derivative or polemical, directed mainly toward the edification of those deficient in Hebrew. In consequence, translations or adaptations from the Hebrew form a substantial part of this literature. The famous Ferrara Bible of 1553 was soon adapted to a Ladino version for the benefit of eastern Sephardim. Other parts of the Bible which appeared in Spanish were a Pentateuch paraphrase by Isaac *Aboab da Fonseca (Amsterdam, 1681), a paraphrase of the Psalms by Hamburg-born Leon *Templo, and paraphrases of the Song of Songs, based on the Targum, for liturgical use. The Mishnah was translated into Spanish, as were other monuments of Jewish literature such as Judah Halevi's *Kuzari*, translated by Jacob *Abendana (Amsterdam, 1663), Baḥya ibn Paquda's *Duties of the Heart* (Amsterdam, 1610), of which a Portuguese version by Samuel Abbas appeared in 1670, and later still a Ladino version. Even Ben Sira was translated into Ladino by a Serbian rabbi, Israel Ḥaim (1818).

Leading polemical works include Samuel *Usque's *Consolaçam as Tribulaçõens de Israel* (Ferrara, 1553), a set of dialogues in Portuguese relating Jewish history from earliest times and intended to confirm the Conversos in their faith and display the divine plan for Israel. Manasseh Ben Israel wrote his *Conciliador* ("The Conciliator", 1632), reconciling places in scripture which appear to contradict one another, and his *Experanza de Israel*, on the *Ten Lost Tribes, was translated into Latin, English, Dutch, Hebrew, and German during the 19th century. David *Nieto, rabbi of the London community, wrote the *Matteh Dan* (London, 1714) to demonstrate the authority of the Oral Law. Isaac *Cardozo, who was born in Portugal and reassumed Judaism in Italy, wrote *Las Excelencias y Calunias de los Hebreos* (Amsterdam, 1679), in which he describes at length the ten privileges of the Jewish people and the ten slanders brought against them.

Ethical and inspirational works included Moses *Almosnino's *Regimento de la Vida* (Salonika, 1564) and *Extremos y grandezas de Constantinople* (Madrid, 1638), and Abraham Israel Pereira's *La Certeza del Camino* (Amsterdam, 1666), a treatise on divine providence and the love of God. Preeminent is the *Me-Am Lo'ez, an elaborate commentary on the Bible based on talmudic and midrashic sources which was initiated by the Turkish scholar Jacob *Culi and continued after his death by others. This work rapidly became the vade mecum of the Ladino-speaking Sephardim and achieved the status of a sacred book. Its imaginative character, combined with its religious themes, made it a perfect vehicle of combined entertainment and edification. It derived from a circle of Jewish savants who deliberately aimed at raising the spiritual level of the Jews of the Ottoman Empire, among whom poverty, ignorance, and illiteracy were rife. Other members of this circle included Abraham de Toledo, who wrote *Complas de Yosef* (Constantinople, 1722); Isaac Magrizo; and Abraham Asa.

Original writers include Daniel Levi *Barrios, who was born in Spain, reassumed Judaism in Italy, and from there went to Amsterdam. He wrote sonnets, pastoral romances, and a panegyric on three martyrs burned alive in Cordoba in 1665 entitled *Contra la Verdad no hay Fuerça* (Amsterdam, 1666). Another poem of 550 lines celebrating a martyr burned alive in 1644 was written by Antonio Enríquez *Gómez. The *Poema de la Reyna Esther* (Rouen, 1637) by João Pinto *Delgado can be understood only in the light of its rabbinic background.

The folk literature of the Sephardim consists of an enormous corpus of ballads in Ladino, the *romancero*, which survives in manuscripts and, precariously, in the memories of the older generation of Ladino speakers. Menendez Pelayo published ten ballads he received from Salonika in 1885, and this was followed by Menéndez Pidal's *Catálogo del romancero judío-español* (in *El Romancero*, Madrid, 1927). The work of collection and publication goes on, chiefly in Israel and the U.S.

Religious Practice

While the Sephardim do not differ from the Ashkenazim in the basic tenets of Judaism, with both groups viewing the Babylonian Talmud as their ultimate authority in belief and practice, there are great differences in matters of detail and outlook. Once the trauma of persecution in Spain had worn off, many Sephardim settled in places where they enjoyed a life relatively free of external constraints in the practice of their religion, and they had a fair measure of security of life and property. This may be the reason why many of them displayed a more sympathetic attitude to outside culture, and were ready to see good outside the "four cubits of the law." Sephardim follow the codification of R. Joseph Caro (*Maran* "our master"), the Shulḥan Arukh, in matters of religious law without regard to the strictures of R. Moses b. Israel *Isserles, whom they call *Moram*, which may mean equivocally "our teacher and master R. Moses" or "their teacher" (i.e., of the Ashkenazim). The compilation by R. Joseph Caro represents a more liberal and permissive trend than that approved by the Ashkenazi authorities. For example, Sephardi authorities permit rice to be eaten on Passover, and allow whole eggs found inside a slaughtered chicken or vegetables cooked in a pot previously used for meat to be eaten with milk products. Ashkenazi authorities forbid all such practices, and instances could be multiplied.

Many differences, however, simply reflect a difference in custom or interpretation, with no implication of leniency. Thus, a blessing is recited on the head phylactery only if there has been an interruption after placing that for the hand, and the straps are wound outwards rather than inwards. The festive branch used on the festival of Sukkot is bound together without the holder used by the Ashkenazim and is often decorated with colored ribbons. At the Passover home service, lettuce, rather than horseradish, is used for bitter herbs.

The synagogue service differs considerably from that of the Ashkenazim. The Scroll of the Law is raised before its public reading, rather than after, and the script in which it is written is characteristically different. The synagogue itself has a somewhat different arrangement. The reading desk is at the west end, and all services are conducted from it, unlike Ashkenazi practice where certain prayers are read from the desk at the side of the ark. Their ark is frequently a triple structure, consisting of a large closet in the middle and a smaller one on either side. The text of the prayers differs in detail; the involved synagogue poetry of the *Kallir (sharply criticized by Abraham ibn Ezra in his commentary to Eccles. 5:1) is totally absent, being replaced by compositions of the Spanish poets Judah Halevi, Moses ibn Ezra, and Solomon ibn Gabirol. The synagogue chants are simpler and brighter than those of the Ashkenazim, who nevertheless find them monotonous and lacking in warmth. Sephardim tend to be especially punctilious in their rendition of the sacred scrolls. Sephardi pronunciation of Hebrew is particular to place the tonic accent on the syllable prescribed by grammar, predominantly the ultimate, and distinguishes two complementarily distributed colorations (*a* and *o*) of the vowel *qameṣ*.

Many religious technical terms (e.g., the names of the notes used in the cantillation of the scrolls) are different from those of the Ashkenazim, and these serve as a shibboleth which marks the Ashkenazi as soon as he uses one of his terms. (See Table: Sephardim: Common Terms.)

Sephardim tend to be very insistent on preserving these slight differences, probably because they are conscious of their minority status within the Jewish community, and tend to develop the same rigorous adherence to custom vis-à-vis the Ashkenazi community as the Orthodox Jewish community as a whole does to the outside world. It is not uncommon at the present time for a deep or even fanatical attachment to Sephardi tradition to be coupled with laxity in observance of Jewish law.

[Alan D. Corre]

Patterns of Secularization of the Western Sephardi Diaspora in the 17th Century in Jewish Law

Examined here is the secular direction of the processes of change which took place among the West European Sephardi Diaspora by referring to two separate historical and social meanings which the term "secularization" can have within Jewish society.

One meaning is that of departure or liberation from religious influence in areas of social and cultural activity which had previously been strictly in the domain of religion.

The second meaning is the transfer or translation of religious symbols and values to a secular context. The differentiation between these two meanings is of particular importance for analyzing the processes of change which took place among the Western Sephardi Diaspora in the 17th century in light of the possibility, already discernible, that the Jews would abandon the Torah and the commandments without taking this to be a withdrawal from the content of Jewish life or Jewish society. In order to gain some notion of the secular trend among the group under discussion, it is sufficient to refer to the social and historical significance of the concept *ummah* ("nation"; Spanish: nación; Portuguese: nação) and to the increasing emphasis among this Diaspora on communality of race and blood.

There is no doubt that the term *ummah* denotes first and foremost, in the social and historical context under discussion, communality of fate and social and cultural solidarity among the Marranos (who were forced to convert to Christianity), former Marranos, and at times also "New Christians" (who may or may not have been forced to convert) scattered throughout the "Terras de judesmo" (Lands of Judaism, i.e., where Judaism could be practiced freely) and "Terras de idolatria" (Lands of Idolatry, i.e., countries under the influence of Spain and Portugal), including the Lands of Forced Conversion (*arẓot ha-shemad*) in the Iberian peninsula. Communality of fate is of course problematic from the aspect of Jewish law (*halakhah*), when speaking of "New Christians," and when referring to actual Marranos, who had the opportunity to leave their countries of residence but did not do so. Yet even more important is the term *ummah* itself or the Western Sephardi self-identification as *benei ha-ummah* (members of the nation; Spanish: miembros de la nación; Portuguese: membros da nação). These terms appear frequently in the community registers of the Western Sephardi congregations and were often used by the rabbis of that period as a substitute for *Kehillah Kedoshah* (holy congregation) and as a general appellation for members of the Western Sephardi Diaspora as well as the general Sephardi Diaspora, both eastern and western. Moreover, even though the communality which the term *ummah* denotes was not initially intended to serve a religious value but rather a social, economic, and political one, and despite the fact that this term in the specific context of "trading nation" and in the broader context of "cittadini di un dato paese viventi in paese straniero" ("citizens of a given country living in a foreign country"), which does not refer especially to Jewish society,[6] we see that it becomes intertwined with the ritual sphere. Thus, for instance, rule 39 of the Book of Regulations (*Livro dos Acordos da Nação Ascamot*) of the Amsterdam congregation "Talmud Torah" admonishes against performing a circumcision upon anyone who is not included among *benei ummatenu*, "members of our nation." This is also the case regarding the blurring of the limits of the term "congreção" and the term "nação" as they appear in texts of excommunication (*ḥerem*) warnings as can be seen a number of times, for example, in the *Livro de Memorias* of that same community.

A blurring of the distinction between a situation which can be described as "natural" and between an existence with "holy" religious significance is distinctly noticeable also in the repeated use of the concept "*shimmur*" (Spanish: conservación; Portuguese: conservação) in the community books of the Western Sephardi congregations by its systematic combination precisely with the term *Kahal Kados* ("holy congregation"), and not to the concept of worshiping God. This is so much the case that at times it seems that the "holiness" of the Jewish people or the holiness of a certain community takes the place, as it were, of the "holiness" of the Torah, and that the true destiny of Jewish religion is to serve the needs of man or, alternatively, the needs of the society to which he belongs.

In the same vein is the emphasis placed on communality of blood and race by the former Marrano Isaac *Cardozo in his *Las Excelencias de los Hebreos*, as well as in statements by *Manasseh Ben Israel in his *Iggerert ha-Anavah* concerning nobility and the purity of blood of the Jewish people. This is also true for the former Marrano Isaac *Orobio de Castro, who expresses a skeptical opinion regarding those who join the nation as converts, since "they will never become Israel nor of the seed of Abraham," even "if they are beloved by God," because "Israel is not a spiritual entity, but a nation."

This stringency over lineage in the blood, the nobility in the race, and the biological connection to society, goes beyond the concepts of religious superiority demonstrated by the rabbis of that time, such as for example, Saul Levi *Morteira and Isaac *Aboab da Fonseca. It certainly does not mesh with the position of the majority of the sages of Israel, foremost among them being Moses *Maimonides who feels that this nation is from the beginning of its history a "nation of converts," and that the father of Israel is the father for anyone who follows in the way of Abraham. Yet it is clear that this stringency concerning race and blood reflects a certain development in thought, based on an awareness that Judaism has national content which is not dependent upon accepting the commandments.

A number of historians have noted these phenomena and claimed that this specific development on the issue of "Who is a Jew?" is to be found in the Spanish concepts of *honra* (honor) and *hidalguia* (pedigree) and in the ideological socio-cultural model of purity of blood (*limpieza de sangre) which already existed in Spain in the 15th century. Although this explanation is interesting and even daring in its humanistic perspective, it is not quite correct historically.

If we refer not only to terminology, then the biological belonging to "the seed of Abraham who loves Him," which serves as a barrier against converts in a certain historical context, is that which safeguards and encourages, in a different historical context, the continuation of the connection of the Marranos themselves to the Jewish nation. This can be understood from the testimonies of Profiat Duran of the 14th century, Isaac *Arama of the 15th century, and even from statements of Isaac *Abrabanel who was among the exiles leaving Spain in 1492. The difference between the version of Orobio di Castro and that of Duran, Arama, and Abrabanel is that the latter are not stringent over the purity of origin and blood of someone seeking to take upon himself the obligation of the commandments, but rather to the purity of the origin and blood of one who disengages himself from that obligation.

The skeptical declaration by Orobio di Castro that they who join the Jewish nation as converts, that is, who become observant Jews, "will never be part of Israel and not of the seed of Abraham," leads not only to the past of Di Castro as a Marrano, but also to the distinction in the Book of Numbers between the declaration of Moses, "and do all My commandments, and be holy unto your God" (Num. 15:40), and that of Korah, "seeing all the congregation are holy" (Num. 16:3).

In the dispute between Moses and Korah, Korah was punished for saying things unacceptable to Moses and apparently irritating to God. Yet the concept of "Holy Nation" (*goy kadosh*) in "essence" appears, albeit in a different, secondary status in Judaism, over and over again in traditional Jewish thought. For *Judah Halevi the convert can approach God but cannot become a prophet, because prophecy is the heritage only of descendants of Jacob. According to the Zohar, the soul of the convert is not on the same level as that of the Jew by birth despite the fact that this new soul descends upon him from heaven during the conversion process.

In *Orot Yisrael* by the 20th-century rabbi Abraham Isaac *Kook, the Patriarchs influence the natural side of the Jewish people while Moses influences the studious side (through the Torah, the spiritual base). "In the future," writes Rabbi Kook, "Moses will be completely linked with the Patriarchs and the Messiah will be revealed."

The national, primordial as it were, content of Judaism may be discernible in history and Jewish thought wherever it is not enough to contrast the Jewish people with other nations over the observance of commandments. This is so both whether against the background of deep divisions between societies and peoples, or the background of rapprochement between societies and nations, and the fear of the blurring of the boundaries of the minority society with the majority.

At least Jewish society was still in the process of building its "centers," to use the terminology proposed by the sociologist E. Shils, a society in which a large part of the members were taking their first steps in Judaism, when speaking of observing commandments.

In the same social and historical setting, Rabbi 'Moses Raphael D'*Aguillar stresses the hesitations and difficulties facing those Jews as Jews in the transfer from their places of residence (*neste captiveyro*) in Spain and Portugal to their new places of residence and observance of Judaism, including the objective difficulties of learning the "holy doctrine" (*sagrada doctrina*). Others also describe these problems, among them the former Marrano physician Elijah di Montalto, who lived in Paris, and Immanuel *Aboab.

In Western Sephardi society of the 17th century, the emphasis on the biological-racial foundations, as it were, of Judaism served a certain function, namely, a social need which was one of the expressions of "faith for the sake of the nation".

To be sure, when speaking of Mannaseh ben Israel, his address when he extols the special virtues of the Jewish people, i.e., its nobility and purity of blood, is the English society of the time of the Cromwell protectorate, and not Jewish society. However, neither Di Castro nor Isaac Cardozo discusses these virtues except as a barrier and fortress for Jewish existence in the face of Christianity.

When speaking in Jewish historiography about processes of secularization among the Western Sephardi Diaspora in the 17th century, it is usual to speak of "emancipation" or "emerging from" the influence of religion in the areas of social and cultural activity which had previously been controlled by religion. In the same context, emphasis is placed on the integration of Sephardi Jews into the world of intellectual creativity of Western Europe, their contribution to the European "crisis of conscience" of the 17th century, and their part in the development of capitalist economy in the new centers in northwest Europe, Hamburg, Amsterdam, and London.

However, a question which has not been asked but should be is: What is the social and historical significance of the process of "liberation" and "emancipation"? What was "liberated," and to which social models *within Jewish society* itself did this "emergence" lead in replacing old models?

This question was apparently not relevant in the generation of Rabbi Moses *Hagiz, who in his work *Sefat Emet* did not distinguish between the social aim of integration within the non-Jewish majority society and the goals of change directed toward the Jewish society of origin. He therefore calls both by the term *ḥolelim*, a term which was derived from the Hebrew root *ḥ, l, l*, which means contempt and derision of the holy by turning it into the profane. However, this question is relevant, because even if there is a historical link between the two aims, a differentiation must be made between one who goes from identifying with one religious national, social, cultural unit to identifying with another, and one who does not accept the authority of halakhic tradition, but stubbornly insists on his historical, ethnic, and social belonging.

This distinction is to be found even when speaking of the extreme heterodox such as Juan de *Prado, on the one hand, and *Spinoza, on the other. Both of them leaned towards Deism and to the rationalism of the early Enlightenment, but their attitude to the Jewish community and to the question of their belonging to that community was completely different. While Prado sought to have the excommunication placed on him repealed and to be readmitted to the Jewish community, Spinoza apparently accepted his banishment from the community without regret.

The fact that within the confines of Western Sephardi society the patterns of community organization and leadership were maintained in their traditional form throughout the 17th century and most of the 18th demands an explanation. A negative explanation, that during this period the historical conditions were not ripe for the development of an "ideology of change intended to lead to a change in the patterns of Jewish society," is inadequate. The weakness of this explanation is that it focuses mainly on the perspective of Jewish-Christian relations, in an attempt to latch onto a historical process at the final point of that historical process (Jewish integration into modern Western civilization) and in its understanding the concept of secularization as denoting the process of emancipation from the yoke of religion. This approach ignores the main characteristic of secularization in this society, that is, the transfer or translation of concepts, symbols, and beliefs from their transcendental-salvational origin to temporal uses, more specifically, to the sphere of society itself as an autonomous entity, distinct from Jewish religion.

To ignore this characteristic of secularization is also to ignore that for the public involved there was clearly a basic element of enjoyment in belonging to the congregation, and not only a feeling of subservience and sacrifice. This is also the case with the upper classes, the big businessmen, who enjoyed the relative freedom in which they could finally live as members of the elite, even when they were among their own people. The fact that during the 18th century there was a relative increase among Sephardi merchants who refused to take upon themselves any role in the community, or to contribute to it financially, is linked both to the process of leaving one world of collective being and joining another and to the gradual economic decline of this social class.

The question is not of the stability of the social system during this period of change, but rather the nature of that stability. What did the conformism to the social order of the *iehidim*, elected community leaders, represent?

Placing the stress on *iehidim* rather than institutions is important, since it has happened in Jewish history that communal organizations continued to exist even in order to serve the social and political needs of the non-Jewish majority society, needs which have nothing to do with religious tradition or even Jewish solidarity. The question is whether the stability of the social system represents the original historical effort at creating a sphere of religious "holiness," where whatever located outside of it becomes secular, or does it represent social needs linked to ensuring the maintenance of the society as a cultural, historical, ethnic unit, with no alternative framework for its existence?

One who succeeded in describing the basic features of the secularization of the society under discussion was Spinoza, who determined – albeit not precisely in relation to Jewish society – that "it is almost impossible to know what a person is, that is, whether he is a Christian, Turk, Jew, or pagan, except… by the fact that he visits this or that house of worship, or finally by the fact that he is devoted to this or that outlook and is accustomed to answering Amen to the words of his teacher."

Spinoza does indeed include among his statements on collective signs of recognition issues of manner and dress, but from the text cited we can see that even those signs of recognition were not important for him.

What would have been significant for him was apparently the fact that the Ma'amad of the congregations of Amsterdam,

Hamburg, or London could enact regulations and obligate the *iehidim* to obey them "Em nome del Dio Benditto" ("in the name of blessed God") and "para sevico… de Dio Benditto" (in service to blessed God), even when between this activity and the religious idea of the *kehillah* there was nothing more in common than the public itself and the structural significance of the religious notion.

If we use as an example the *Dotar* of Amsterdam, we find that this institution, which was called "Santa Companhia" (Hebrew: *ḥevrah kedoshah*, "holy society") maintained close connections with Marranos and even with "New Christians," who were still in conflict over their religious identification. The institution in any case considered itself their patron and assisted them.

Albeit as far as Spinoza was concerned, "the reason for this evil" (the devaluation which had taken place with regard to the esteem of religious "holiness") was that the Church "is becoming a mass movement in the guise of religion." Yet, with his aristocratic, overbearing attitude to the "masses," Spinoza ignores the fact that the church is changing not only because of an ostensible lowering of the value of religious "holiness," but also because the "Church" is the body which will take upon itself in situations of social or national crises, the role of the model society (the "good," "true" society) which is embedded in the base of all social organization.

From the point of view of religion itself, one of the indications of the decline of religion is its turning into the servant of society and the social order. An outstanding example of this trend can be taken from the statements of Leone *Modena in his *Magen ve-Ẓinnah* (in referring to D'Acosta's objections to Rabbinical Judaism) that "a basic element of the divine intention in the Torah is that we should all of us observe it and each detail in one manner, and not one this way and one another, for if not so Israel will not be one nation!"

In *Sefat Emet* by Moses Hagiz, the opposite trend emerges whereby "*ammudei ha-Torah*" ("pillars of the Torah") take precedence over the existence of the world and the existence of the Jewish people itself. "For this purpose (being tested and observing commandments)," says Hagiz, "He, God, made us one nation in our land."

One of the most striking institutional manifestations demonstrating that the territory of "religious" holiness (halakhic-institutional, in the term of Y. Leibowitz) was growing ever more restricted in this society, was the historical fact that the Western Sephardi congregations had problems in training rabbis from among themselves, not only in the difficult times of their establishment but also at the end of the 17th and beginning of the 18th centuries. The small number of people looking for a career for themselves as rabbis (most of the young "devote their time exclusively to commerce," according to the statement of Rabbi Judah Leib of Zelichev), while the prestige of the rabbi or of the *talmid ḥakham* was declining, as can be learnt from Rabbi Moses Hagiz or even Rabbi Judah Leib of Zelichev. There was also a significant decline in the power of the sages of the community who served alongside the *parnasim*, the sages who were also called by the title "Ḥaham da nação" ("sage of the nation").

Even the Amsterdam community, despite its central position in matters of *halakhah* among the Marrano Diaspora of Western Europe, already in the early 17th century had to seek the assistance of the Sephardi centers in the Ottoman Empire, North Africa, and Italy when looking for rabbis. This is also true of the Sha'ar Shomayim congregation in London and the Beth Israel community of Hamburg, which struggled fiercely over issues of the rabbinate. The decline in the status of the *talmid ḥakham* was also attributable to the increased importance of other "wisdom" (*ḥokhmah*) or "knowledge," representing a non-Torah sphere of learning.

It is to this type of knowledge to which Abraham Pereira is referring in his book *Espejo de la Vanidad del Mundo*, where he is careful to differentiate between that side of man's nature with which he searches for truth wherever it may be found and "conducts research," and another side of his character whereby he admires things "because they are new." The latter facet is considered by Pereira to be likely to lead to the disowning of tradition, because "What could be a greater new thing than to turn a sinner towards God?" But this distinction of Pereira's between knowledge and truth depends in effect upon the recognition that Jewish tradition does not ignore the realm of non-Torah knowledge, and does not even oppose it (on condition that it does not contradict the teaching of the Torah).

Maimonides himself mentions in his *Guide for the Perplexed*, "the Spaniards of our people" (i.e., of the 12th century) "who all accept the words of the philosophers and lean toward their interpretations as long as they do not contradict any fundament of the Torah." Long before Maimonides, Midrash Lamentations Rabbah (2:13) stated: "If someone should say to you that there is wisdom among the nations, believe [him]; there is Torah among the nations, do not believe [him]." This shows us that even when dealing with the confrontation of the individual Jew with a culture foreign to him, it does not necessarily follow that there is a conflict with the binding nature of tradition, or alternatively of "social deviation."

The prevailing error among historians on this point generally stems, as J. Katz has shown, "by analogy to the 19th century," to a period in which "the traditional society was no longer a total society, but one with peripheral members who have abandoned tradition," and despite this, or apparently because of this, it is ostensibly more "traditional" than in the traditional period in its own time.

The same is true in the economic sphere. There was nothing improper in the participation of the Jews in the stock exchange of Amsterdam or London, as long as they also reserved for themselves time for Torah study. Yet there was serious fault to be found in Jews going to the stock exchange as described by the Sephardi Jew Joseph Penso de la *Vega in his satirical work, *Confusion de Confusiones*, written in Amsterdam in 1688, because in that stock exchange "whoever steals more earns more." It is not accidental that the book includes no discussion of the halakhic or Jewish significance of dealing in the stock exchange despite the fact that it is directed to Sephardi Jews, not only because Jews like Joseph Penso de la Vega knew how to separate the "holy" from the "profane," but mainly because the book's intention is to "entertain" and "to paint with the brush of truth" the reality of the exchange itself. The statements quoted above with regard to the intellectual and economic spheres apply as well to the area of the arts. Here too *halakhah* recognizes various degrees of approaching the profane.

In terms of institutions, in the same way that the obligation of discipline binding on individuals of the congregation towards the leaders of the community was not derived in Western Sephardi society exclusively from a religious command to "pay heed to the voice of their elders, the makers of fences, and the protectors of the hedges," so the presence of the *iehidim* in the synagogue was not dependent exclusively upon observing the commandments and religious obligations. It is a fact that even the heretics, such as Spinoza, maintained a seat for themselves in the Great Portuguese synagogue in Amsterdam almost up to their excommunications. Perhaps, as J. Katz says – albeit in a different context – because "the most traditional, rooted sub-meaning of the adjective Jew is connected to religion." The regulations and prohibitions on business conversations in the synagogue and the need for emphasizing time and again the biblical commandment "Revere my sanctuaries" (Lev. 26:2) – as for example the emphasis of Pereira on the respect and awe which we are to bring to the Holy Temple" – lead to the assumption that there were mundane conversations during prayer services. Yet, although prayer must come from the heart and "with humility," we would not suggest that in this too one should not see excess criticism of the patterns of behavior of Sephardi Jews in the synagogue.

Regular conversations as well as those concerning livelihood were carried on in the synagogue and even were the subject of conflicts, almost through the entire history of this institution. It was not without reason that a distinction was made between the synagogue as a place of gathering for prayer and study and as a place in which all come together is already found in the Talmud (B. Shab. 32a), "R. Ishmael ben Eleazar said: Because of two sins *ammei ha-areẓ* die – because they call the holy ark (*aron kodesh*) *arana* (a plain cabinet) and because they call the *bet keneset* a meeting hall (*bet ha-am*)."

One should not assume that the *ammei ha-areẓ* about whom the *baraita* is speaking had committed such as grave sin as to deserve death (albeit, divine and not by a court) only because they were not fluent in the language of the sages (*lashon ha-kodesh*, i.e., Hebrew), since they were Aramaic speakers. They were guilty of having blurred the boundaries between the "holy" and the "profane."

At the same time, the threat of secularization does not draw its strength precisely from the secular concepts of the surrounding, non-Jewish society or culture, but from the contrastive parallel which socio-historical reality creates between the synagogue and the holy ark, on the one hand, and the meeting hall and the cabinet, on the other.

This is to be stressed not in order to show that tendencies towards secularization existed in traditional Jewish society many centuries before the meeting with pre-modern or modern secular society, which is an important fact in itself. We emphasize this issue in order to learn of the very possibility of blurring the borders between the "holy" and the "profane" within the boundaries of the synagogue or within the limits of the community itself.

[Ezer Kahanov]

Eclipse of Sephardi Jewry

After the middle of the 17th century a contraction in the importance of the Sephardi element in relation to the rest of the Jewish world took place. During the Middle Ages (from c. 1000 to 1492) the Jews of Spain formed a most numerous and active part of the Jewish people, perhaps at least one half of world Jewry. From the mid-17th century, however, their relative (though not absolute) importance dwindled. Shabbateanism, the movement of the false messiah Shabbetai Ẓevi, which was extremely popular in Salonika and Izmir from the 1650s until his messianic proclamation, arrest, and conversion to Islam in 1666, brought the Ottoman communities to spiritual and economic ruin. The reverberations of the movement were later felt in Amsterdam, Hamburg, Altona, and Poland in the early 17th century. Support and suspicion of Shabbateanism caused division between Sephardi communities in these areas of Northern Europe.

In modern times the Ashkenazi portion of the Jewish people has constituted approximately nine-tenths of the whole. Before the Holocaust, of the approximately 16,500,000 Jews in the world, about 15,000,000 were Ashkenazim and only 1,500,000 Sephardim and other non-Ashkenazi communities. The numerical decline was inevitably accompanied by a contraction in intellectual and cultural productivity, and the energetic Ashkenazi Jews took the lead. Eminent Sephardim in the modern period include Sir Moses *Montefiore and Adolphe *Crémieux; Benjamin *Disraeli also came from a Sephardi family. Among the fathers of the rebirth of the Jewish settlement in Ereẓ Israel were, besides Montefiore, the American Sephardi Judah *Touro, and the Bosnian rabbi Judah *Alkalai.

By the 19th century the celebrated old Sephardi communities in Western Europe and the U.S., established in the 16th and 17th centuries, had been numerically far outnumbered by the Ashkenazi element there. Although contributing less to Jewish culture, the Sephardim preserved their former homogeneity and pride in their historical heritage. The greatest center of this group was still Amsterdam, though the Spanish and Portuguese community in London had attained great significance. In the *Ottoman Empire the Sephardim still preserved their ancestral traditions, and their economic and political position was favorable. They had the same rights as other minorities in the Ottoman Empire (see *Capitulations). *Salonika continued to be the greatest center of Sephardi Jewry in the world. Its Sephardi Jews contributed greatly to the industrialization of the city, the Alliance Israélite Universelle had eight schools in the city, the community had numerous daily newspapers in Judeo-Spanish and French, and an active Judeo-Spanish theater existed from the latter quarter of the 19th century until the Holocaust. It had an elaborate philanthropic structure and an active Zionist movement. The ultra-secular and anti-Zionist Jewish socialist workers movement numbering some 6,000 Jewish Sephardi tobacco workers represented a fourth of the local Jewish community, and laid the foundations for the Greek Communist movement. *Izmir and *Sarajevo were also prolific Sephardi communities with yeshivot, numerous synagogues, and communal mutual aid societies. Izmir had an active Judeo-Spanish press and theater life. Sarajevo had a special rabbinical seminary and strong Sephardi youth and cultural movements. In North Africa the degree of Jewish well-being was proportionate to the extent of European influence. Westernization and the British penetration into Egypt brought considerable amelioration of the condition of the Jews there. In *Algiers the French had conferred full rights of French citizenship on the Jews, though this led to a local antisemitic movement, and an outbreak of anti-Jewish rioting in 1897. The French occupation of *Tunis was also beneficial to the Jews, but in most of *Morocco the old medieval maltreatment and code still prevailed.

After World War I

The hopes that western influences would gradually lead to a marked improvement in the position of the Jews in the Balkans and Middle East did not materialize. After World War I, when large stretches of the former Ottoman Empire passed to the various Balkan powers, large populations were transferred in order to lessen friction between Greece and Turkey by ensuring greater homogeneity. In Salonika, the Jewish population, formerly in the majority, was reduced to about one-fifth of the total, and the Greek authorities began to take steps to replace Jewish economic and cultural influence by Greek. In Turkey, now being reorganized on national lines, the former privileged position of ethnic minorities came to an end. Many Jews emigrated from both Greece and Turkey to Western Europe, America, and especially to Spanish America. Istanbul Jewry underwent Turkification after the founding of the modern Turkish Republic in 1924, became greatly secularized, and Judeo-Spanish was put aside at the expense of modern Turkish. Political Zionism was scorned. As all international movements were banned in Turkey, Zionist activities went underground and dwindled. The 1934 antisemitic riots in Eastern Thrace and in the region of the Dardanelles and Tekirdag, prompted by Armenian, far-right Turkish, and pro-Nazi nationalist elements, was the beginning of the end for the old Sephardi Jewish community of Edirne (Adrianople) and other Sephardic communities in European Turkey and the Dardanelles. Some 12,000 Jews became refugees and moved to Istanbul.

Holocaust

During World War II, the Nazis first tried to sow division by discriminating between Jews of various origins. In Holland, the Sephardim were left until last, but eventually almost all were "liquidated." The small communities came to an end, and the illustrious Spanish and Portuguese community of Amsterdam was reduced to one-tenth of its former number. In Italy, the old Sephardi communities of *Venice, *Ferrara, *Florence, and *Leghorn suffered appallingly. The victimization of the Jews in the Balkans was carried out on a far larger scale, and most were eventually sent to the death camps. In Bulgaria, which had a long tradition of just treatment of the Jews, the government was able to evade the enforcement of the German orders, but most males were sent to forced labor and more than half of the Jews of Sofia were moved to the periphery. That strongly Zionist community survived almost intact to find its way after the war en masse to Ereẓ Israel. The Bulgarian pro-German government deported the Jews of Yugoslavian Macedonia and Greek Thrace to their deaths in Treblinka, and the Bulgarians shot on the shore of the Danube River some 1,100 Jews from Cavalla and Cuomotini, Greece, who were sent by boat from Lom, Bulgaria. The local Croatian, Bosnian, and Serbian Fascists and their German masters in Yugoslavia almost wholly annihilated the Jewish population there. Most of the Jews of the vibrant Sephardi communities in Belgrade and Sarajevo were murdered on Yugoslavian soil in concentration camps and the Jasenovac death camp run by the Croatian Fascist Ustase movement. The traditional Sephardi communities of Monastir and Skopje were deported by the Bulgarian occupier to Treblinka, where all those deported were gassed upon arrival. Although the small Athens community suffered less owing to the aid of the Orthodox patriarch Damascenos, the number of those deported in the rest of Greece rose in some places to 99%, and almost the whole of the Salonika community perished.

The Jews of Turkey suffered from the Varlik Vergisi luxury tax in 1942. Many who could not pay the exorbitant sums were sent to forced labor in camps like Askale. In Izmir, the wealthy industrialist Rabenu Politi paid the equivalent of $46 million to ransom his community members from harsh labor. As a result of this wealth tax, most of Turkish Jewry moved to Israel in the late 1940s and early 1950s, leaving 20,000 Jews mainly in Istanbul and only 1,500 Jews in Izmir.

In Romania, 12,000 Sephardi Jews perished in the Holocaust. The Sephardi communities in Bucharest, Craiova, Braila, Turnu Severin, Timishoara, and elsewhere ceased to exist.

In Holland, 4,000 of the country's 5,000 Sephardim from Amsterdam and The Hague were deported by the Nazis to Sobibor, Auschwitz, and Theresienstadt. The majority of the Sephardim in Vienna and Hamburg were also murdered in the Holocaust.

After World War II

As antisemitism had spread in Europe, the attitudes toward Jews in the countries of North Africa and the Middle East changed for the worse. Ostensibly this was bound up with artificially stimulated opposition to Zionism in the Arab and

Muslim countries. After Israel's *War of Independence (1948), the position of the Jews in this region became increasingly precarious. A mass emigration began, in which many eventually arrived in Israel.

While Sephardi Jewry was almost annihilated in Europe and had largely moved from Asia (except Israel), a new Sephardi Diaspora came into being in circumstances very different from the old. In the interwar years emigrants from the eastern Mediterranean countries augmented the old Sephardi communities of *London, *Paris, and New York (see below). New Sephardi groupings were also founded, including congregations in *Salisbury (Rhodesia) and the Belgian *Congo by emigrants from *Rhodes (whose ancient community was almost annihilated by the Nazis during World War II). Large numbers of emigrants established themselves in Central and South America, where they found themselves linguistically more at home. The rapid growth of the new communities in *Latin America has been one of the most remarkable and significant events in Jewish history of the past generation. In Buenos Aires, the Damascan and Aleppoan Jews had their own synagogues and institutions. The Rhodian and Turkish Jews had their own synagogues in the Buenos Aires area, but they were more secular than the Syrian Jews. There also was a small Moroccan community in Buenos Aires. Since the 1990s, the Sephardim in Mexico City have been a majority of the general Jewish community. The Judeo-Spanish speaking community, and the separate Monte Sinai (Damascan) and Aleppoan communities with their synagogues, schools, and cultural and philanthropic organizations outnumber the Ashkenazim, and are a major part of the future communal trend.

Whereas the majority of Jews in Latin America and North America are of Ashkenazi origin, increasing numbers are speaking Spanish, and an important Jewish-Spanish cultural life is developing. Thus while the antecedents and synagogue rites of these communities are Ashkenazi, their cultural life links up with that of medieval Spain and cannot fail to be influenced by the Spanish intellectual and literary traditions.

[Cecil Roth / Yitzchak Kerem (2nd ed.)]

In the United States

In 1654, 23 Jews fleeing Portuguese reprisals in Brazil found refuge in the Dutch colony of New Amsterdam (see *New York), where they established the Shearith Israel Congregation, popularly known as the Spanish and Portuguese Synagogue of New York City. Other Sephardi congregations followed along the Atlantic coast. The contribution of the Sephardim was greater than their small numbers would suggest. They were prominent in the struggle for civil rights, and as craftsmen, merchants, ship owners, manufacturers, professionals, public servants, and writers they enriched the life of the general American community. They constituted about half of the estimated 2,000 Jews living in the American colonies. Many of the colonial Sephardim migrated to the British colonies from the Sephardi communities in the Caribbean, where there had been Jewish Portuguese settlement since the late 16th century under the British, Dutch, and Danish in *Jamaica, *Curacao, *Barbados, and later in Nevis, St. Eustatius, the *Dominican Republic, St. Croix, Trinidad, Tobago, *St. Thomas, and elsewhere. With the increase in English, German, and Polish Ashkenazim during the 19th century, the Sephardim played a correspondingly lesser role in the life of the U.S. Jewish community. However, the descendants of these "Founding Fathers" continue to hold a very respectable place in U.S. society. They often take the initiative in cultivating Sephardi religious and cultural activities, and take pride in their distinctive "Portuguese *minhag*," a hallmark in dignified Jewish worship. From 1900 onward, marked numbers of Oriental Sephardim immigrated to the U.S. from the Balkans, Asia Minor, and Syria. The exodus was precipitated by natural disasters, the rise of nationalism among the Balkan peoples, and the general economic and political deterioration in the Ottoman Empire. In the period from the Young Turk Revolution in 1908 to the fixing of U.S. immigration quotas in 1924–25, 50,000–60,000 Sephardim arrived in the U.S. After World War II, the U.S. Sephardi community was augmented by several thousands from Morocco, Egypt, Iraq, Syria, Iran, Israel, and some of those who left Cuba after 1959.

The 20th-century arrivals from the Levant were segregated from the mass of Yiddish-speaking East European Ashkenazim by linguistic, social, and cultural barriers, and they also felt estranged from the highborn indigenous Sephardim. Moreover, they further divided themselves into three language groupings: Judeo-Spanish, Greek, and Arabic. Dispersed through the efforts of the Industrial Removal Office, small Sephardi colonies were soon to be found in *Rochester, *Philadelphia, *Cincinnati, *Chicago, *Atlanta, *Montgomery, *Portland (Oregon), *Seattle, and *Los Angeles. More than 30,000 Sephardim, however, settled in New York City and provided the basis for organized Jewish communal life.

Following the pattern of their Ashkenazi brethren, they established mutual aid societies named after their native towns. Several attempts were made to unite the Sephardim. The first, encouraged by the *kehillah* of New York City, was the Federation of Oriental Jews, founded in 1912. All three language groups were represented, but it failed to receive the financial support of its constituent societies and disappeared within a few years. In 1924 the Spanish-speaking societies united to form the Sephardic Jewish Community of New York. The hub of its activities was its center in Harlem. With the decline of Sephardim in the area and the economic depression from 1929, the "Community" fell apart in 1933.

Between 1915 and 1952 mergers took place among the various mutual aid societies to form the most representative self-help organization, the Sephardic Jewish Brotherhood of America. It claims a membership of more than 3,000 families. The Central Sephardic Jewish Community of America, founded in 1941, tried to pattern itself after the old world Sephardi *kehillah* by appointing as its head a chief rabbi to coordinate the religious and educational activities of its constituent institutions. The CSJCA worked with Jewish national organizations in aiding victims of the Holocaust and supporting projects on behalf of Sephardi students in Israel and in Arab countries. One beneficiary was the Sephardic Home for the Aged. The home has a central concern for all Sephardim in the New York area. It served the needs of the Sephardi aged and also as a focus for community-wide functions. A singular loss to the Sephardi community was the discontinuance of the Ladino press. Two publications, *La America* (1910–23) and *La Vara* (1922–49), served as a strong unifying force, at least for those who knew the language. No English periodical emerged to fill the role formerly served by this press.

In 1971 there were some 33 Sephardi synagogues situated in 15 U.S. cities loosely affiliated with each other either through the Union of Sephardic Congregations and/or the World Sephardi Federation. The larger congregations maintain *talmud torahs*, where an attempt is made to transmit Sephardi traditions and the Sephardi *nusaḥ*. Two day schools were sponsored by "Syrian" communities in Brooklyn, the Magen David Yeshivah and Aḥi-Ezer. Sephardi children from Aleppo and Damascus received maximal Hebraic-religious education, which enabled them to pursue advanced Jewish studies. A concerted effort was made by Yeshiva University beginning in 1964 to train leadership through its Sephardic Studies Program. Future rabbis, teachers, and scholars were trained to meet the needs of the Sephardi community. Since the death of Ḥakham Solomon Gaon in 1994 and the resignation of Dr. Mitchel Serrels, the program has floundered and has little effect on the strengthening of Sephardi life in North America. The American Sephardi Federation was founded in 1976 by Prof. Daniel Elazar and strengthened in the 1980s and afterward by the New York-born philanthropist Leon Levy, who was of Turkish familial origin.

[Hyman Joseph Campeas / Yitzchak Kerem (2nd ed.)]

In Ereẓ Israel

The emigration of the Jews from Spain that took place in the 15th and 16th centuries coincided with a relatively liberal Ottoman regime which allowed the Jewish refugees to settle in all parts of the empire, including Ereẓ Israel. The Jewish population of the country consisted at the time of four distinct communities: the Ashkenazi, which then included other immigrants from European countries, e.g., from Italy; the Sephardi, i.e., refugees from Spain; the North African, known as the "Moghrabi"; the "Mustarabs" or "Moriscos," i.e., the autochthonous Jews who had never left the country. After the expulsion from Spain, the Sephardim quickly became the predominant element in the larger towns of the country, and from the 16th century they played a decisive role in transforming *Safed into the spiritual center of world Jewry, particularly by their leading scholars, religious poets, and mystics who settled there. They were able to produce their epoch-making works (e.g., Joseph Caro's Shulḥan Arukh, Solomon Alkabez's religious poetry, Moses Cordovero's and Ḥayyim Vital's mystic philosophy, etc.) while living and working in a relatively free and economically productive and self-supporting Jewish population, in contrast to Jerusalem and other towns in Ereẓ Israel and in most Diaspora countries. In the same period, Don Joseph *Nasi and Doña Gracia Mendes made their bold attempt at settling Jews in the reconstructed town of Tiberias and its neighborhood. The Sephardim also outgrew in numbers and influenced the other Jewish communities in Jerusalem, though the immigration of *Judah Ḥasid and the first waves of ḥasidic immigrants from Eastern Europe in the 18th century tended to change the balance. At first both primary communities, the Sephardi and the Ashkenazi, cooperated in sending emissaries to Diaspora countries for collecting funds and defending Jewish interests vis-à-vis the authorities. But with the introduction of the "*capitulations" for non-Ottoman residents in the 19th century, and the organization of the first separate *kolelim* which later merged into a "general committee" (*va'ad kelali*) of all Ashkenazi groups, the dividing line between Sephardim and Ashkenazim became greatly stressed, particularly when the Sephardi chief rabbi in Jerusalem, bearing the title *rishon le-Zion*, was, from 1842, recognized officially as the **ḥakham bashi*. This process, which culminated during the British Mandatory period in the establishment of a dual Ashkenazi-Sephardi chief rabbinate, caused all non-Ashkenazi "Oriental" communities to affiliate with the Sephardi rabbinical authorities, thus creating the semantic confusion around the term "Sephardim" in both Ereẓ Israel and the Diaspora. In appointing Jews as officials, the British administration in Palestine often preferred members of old Sephardi and other non-Ashkenazi families, born in the country and speaking Arabic as well as Hebrew, to the "newly arrived" Zionist Ashkenazim. However, it did not succeed by this and other methods in politically dividing the Jewish population along the "ethnic" community line, and many Sephardi Jews, born in the country, held important positions in the *Va'ad Le'ummi and all other *yishuv* bodies. The dual chief rabbinate, however, continued to exist under the State of Israel. Only in the Israel army did a quick process of unification of religious services, including a unified prayer book (*nusaḥ aḥid*), take place under the guidance of the army rabbinate. During the mass immigration to Israel of the 1950s and 1960s, the Oriental communities greatly increased, and through their high birthrate, tended to outnumber the Western, mostly Ashkenazi, element in the country. But only a minority of the new non-Ashkenazi immigrants – those from Bulgaria, Greece, Turkey, and some North Africans – are, strictly speaking, Sephardim, i.e., descendants of Spanish and Portuguese Jews whose vernacular was Ladino. Some attempts were made to exploit politically the fact that many of the Oriental Jews from Muslim and other Afro-Asian countries, like India, belong to the lower strata of society, often feel underprivileged, and can only gradually – with considerable difficulties – work their way up into the upper strata of Israel society. But on the whole these attempts failed, mainly because of the general trend of the "merger of exiles" fostered by the organized efforts of the state in the schools, the army, settlement projects, etc. However, in the framework of preserving the vanishing "ethnic" community culture, efforts were made by the Ben Zvi Institute as well as by specialists in the field, to record and publish Sephardi liturgy and songs, often under the auspices of commercial record companies like Hed Artzi and Adama in Israel, Tara in New York, Tecnosaga in Madrid, Spain, and The Jewish Music Research Center of the Hebrew University of Jerusalem at the National Library in Jerusalem. The performance of Sephardi folklore, such as the show *Bustan Sefaradi* by Yiẓḥak Navon (1971) and Sephardi *romanceros*, enjoy much popularity with the Israel public. Ladino radio broadcasting in Jerusalem began in the late 1970s with the musical composer Yitzhak Levy, and was continued by Moshe Shaul, who also edits the Judeo-Spanish Latin-letter Sephardi periodical *Aki Yerushalayim*, which places the emphasis on Judeo-Spanish revival. The Council of the Sephardi Community in Jerusalem in 1971 announced plans to establish a Center for the Study of Sephardi culture under the auspices of the Hebrew University, to be called Misgav Yerushalayim and to be located in the Old City. Since the 1980s, the institute has been housed on the Mount Scopus campus of the Hebrew University of Jerusalem. In the late 1990s, the Israeli government promulgated a law to establish national authorities for Yiddish and Ladino. The National Authority for Ladino Culture – established in Jerusalem and with branches in Tel Aviv, Beersheva, and Haifa – has a teacher training program, sponsors courses and scholarships for Ladino studies at Israeli universities, and organizes public seminars and weekend retreats. Ladino is available as an Israeli baccalaureate exam for those who wish to specialize in it, and it is taught at the high school level at the Amalia Religious Girls School in Jerusalem. In the 1990s, Avner Perez founded the Sefarad Institute for research into Ladino literature in Ma'aleh Adumim. Ladino language and literature university programs were started at Bar-Ilan University and Ben-Gurion University. Dr. Shmuel Refael started the discipline at Bar-Ilan University in the early 1990s, and the department was endowed by Naima and Yehoshua Salti of Istanbul. At Ben-Gurion University, Prof. Tamar Alexander chaired the Moshe David Gaon Department for Ladino Culture from 2003, assisted by the scholars Avner Perez and Eliezer Papo. Unfortunately, funding for the Eliashar Center for Sephardi Studies at the same university was cut severely in 2002 by the Israel Ministry of Education, and most of its courses were canceled.

1992: The Quincentennial Year of the Expulsion of the Jews from Spain

CELEBRATIONS, COMMEMORATION, REMEMBRANCE, AND PUBLIC AWARENESS. The 500th anniversary of the expulsion of the Jews from Spain was commemorated throughout the Sephardi world. In the United States, synagogues put Sephardi themes on their cultural agendas. The community of Indianapolis, for example, produced over 20 relevant events during 1992. Laurence Salzmann's exhibition on Turkish Jewry entitled "Anyos Munchos y Buenos" traveled to dozens of cities in the United States and also in Europe. Other traveling exhibitions included "Mosaic: Jewish Life in Florida"; the Beth Hatefutsoth (Diaspora Museum of Tel Aviv) exhibition "In the Footsteps of Columbus: Jews in America in 1654–1880"; "Turkish Jews: 500 Years of Harmony" organized by the Quincentennial Foundation of Istanbul (QFI); and the Anti-Defamation League's "Voyages to Freedom: 500 Years of Jewish Life in Latin America and the Caribbean." At the Yeshiva University Museum in New York, the exhibition "The Sephardic Journey: 1492–1992" was displayed throughout most of the year. The Judeo-Spanish singing groups "Voice of the Turtle" and "Voices of Sepharad" had busy concert schedules in the USA and in Europe.

In addition, various academic conferences were held in the U.S. Arizona and Mexico were centers for activities highlighting the recent revelation of numerous crypto-Jews of Spanish-speaking origin among their population. The University of Tucson has taken an active interest in Sephardi studies and promoted Sephardi scholarship and guest lectures.

In England, Rabbi Abraham Levy of the Spanish and Portuguese Lauderdale Road Synagogue produced and sponsored numerous publications, lectures, and other cultural events. The Jewish community of Brussels and its local "Sepharad '92" group were extremely active. In Thessaloniki, Greece, the Society for the Study of Greek Jewry and the local Jewish community organized numerous lectures. Large academic conferences were held in Istanbul and in Thessaloniki. Thessaloniki also hosted an international Judeo-Spanish song festival and an exhibition. France saw a memorial service at the Salonikan-founded Rue de St. Lazare synagogue and an academic conference, part of which was hosted in Geneva, Switzerland.

In Israel, the Shazar Center organized numerous international academic conferences and historical workshops on the Sephardi experience. The Sephardi Public Council of Jerusalem produced several cultural events, and the Committee of Sephardi and Oriental Communities in Jerusalem hosted several concerts. The Center for Spanish Jewish Studies of Lewinsky College in Ramat Aviv presented a lecture program, and the Museum of Tel Aviv University put on exhibits on the Jewish experience in Spain. Branches of the Turkish Immigrant Association organized evenings of Judeo-Spanish conversation and song.

Several Sephardi families in Israel organized reunions around the quincentennial year, including the Castel, Meyuhas, and Abravanel families. The Abravanel family sponsored a reunion and conference in New York City, while the Toledanos assembled in Spain.

The Public Council for the 500 Year Festivities was headed by former Israeli president Itzhak Navon, who hosted the Israeli Television series "Jerusalem in Spain."

In Spain, the March 31, 1992, ceremony, where King Juan Carlos annulled the expulsion decree, attracted the attention of world Jewry and the media. Spain hosted numerous academic conferences, and Spanish presses published hundreds of scholarly books on Spanish and Sephardi Jewry.

The only major foundation created for the 1992 festivities, which produced results, was the Quincentennial Foundation of Istanbul. It organized two major academic conferences and a gala banquet attended by Israeli President Herzog, Turkish President Ozal, and Turkish Prime Minister Demirel, began restoration of the Ochrid Synagogue, sponsored a photo exhibition, a film, concerts, and planned an educational kit.

In Latin America, major conferences were held in Buenos Aires, Argentina, and in Rio de Janeiro and São Paulo, Brazil. The Asociación Internacional de Escritores Judios En Lengua Hispana y Portuguese and NOAJ, *Revista Literaria* sponsored two monumental conferences; one in Jerusalem and another in Miami. In Mexico City, several cultural events were held and Sephardi books were published.

In England, a lengthy film was made on the liturgical music of the Sephardi Diaspora communities. In New York, the film *Ottoman Salonika* was finished and presented at the end of the year. Several of the films about Columbus' discovery of America mentioned the presence of a Jew in his crew, but none went into depth on this point or related to his alleged Jewish background, which in any case was disproved convincingly by two Mexican Jewish historians and the veteran historical biographer of Columbus, Taviani.

[Yitzhak Kerem]

BIBLIOGRAPHY: General: M. Molho, *Usos y costumbres de los Sefardíes de Salónica* (1950); M.J. Bernadete, *Hispanic Culture and Character of the Sephardic Jew* (1953); H.J. Zimmels, *Ashkenazim and Sephardim* (1958); J.M. Estrugo, *Los Sefardies* (1958); R. Renard, *Sepharad. Le Monde et la Langue judéo-espagnole des Sephardim* (1967); A.D. Corré, in: JSOS, 28 (1966), 99–107; *Sefarad* (Madrid, 1941). History: M. Levy, *Die Sephardim in Bosnien* (1911); A. Cassuto, *Gedenkschrift der portugiesisch-juedischen Gemeinde in Hamburg* (1927); J.S. da Silva Rosa, *Geschiedenis der Portugeesche Joden te Amsterdam 1593–1925* (1927); J. Nehama, *Histoire des Israélites de Salonique*, 5 vols. (1935–59); A. Galanté, *Histoire des Juifs d'Istanbul* (1941); A.M. Hyamson, *Sephardim of England* (1951); D. de Sola Pool, *An Old Faith in the New World* (1955); Roth, Marranos; idem, *World of the Sephardim* (1954); A.D. Corré and M.H. Stern, in: AJHSQ, 59 (1969), 23–82; S.B. Liebman, *The Jews in New Spain* (1970). LANGUAGE: M.L. Wagner, *Beitraege zur Kenntnis der Judenspanischen von Konstantinopel* (1914); idem, *Caracteres Generales de Judeo-Español de Oriente* (1930); C.M. Crews, *Récherches sur le judéo-espagnol dans les pays balkaniques* (1935); J. Subak, in: *Zeitschrift fuer Romanische Philologie*, 30 (1906), 129–85. LITERATURE: M. Gruenbaum, *Juedisch-spanische Chrestomathie* (1896); I. González Llubera, *Proverbios Morales* (1947); I.S. Revah, *João Pinto Delgado* (1954); M. Molho, *Literatura Sefardita de Oriente* (1960); D. Gonzalo Maeso, *Me-Am Lo'ez. El gran comentario biblico Sefardi* (1964); S. Usque, *Consolation for the Tribulations of Israel*, tr. by M.A. Cohen (1965); J.M. Millas Vallicrosa, *Literatura hebraico española* (1968^2); I.J. Lévy, *Prolegom to the Study of the Refranero Sefardi* (1969). THE ROMANCERO: I. González Llubera, *Coplas de Yoçef* (1935); M. Menéndez y Pelayo, *Antología de Poetas Liricos Castellanos*, 8 (1944); M. Attias, *Romancero Sefaradi* (1956); H.V. Besso, in: *Sefarad*, 21 (1961), 343–74; S. Armistead and J. Silverman, *Diez romances Hispánicos en un manuscrito sefardí de la isla de Rodas* (1962). Bibliographies: Kayserling, Bibl; J.S. da Silva Rosa, *Die spanischen und portugiesischen gedruckten Judaica in der Bibliothek… "Ets Ḥaïm" in Amsterdam* (1933); H.V. Besso, *Ladino Books in the Library of Congress* (1963). In the U.S.: A. Wiznitzer, *The Records of the Earliest Jewish Community in the New World* (1954); *The American Sephardi*; M. Behar, in: *Les Cahiers Sefardis* (Sept. 1947); A. Matarasso, *ibid.* (June, Sept. 1947); L.M. Friedman, *Rabbi Ḥayyim Isaac Carigal, his Newport Sermon and his Yale Portrait* (1940); M.A. Gutstein, *The Story of the Jews of Newport, 1658–1908* (1936); L. Hacker, in: *Jewish Social Service Quarterly* (Dec. 1926), 32–40. **ADD. BIBLIOGRAPHY:** B. Rivlin, Y. Kerem, and L. Bornstein Makovetsky, *Pinkas Hakehillot Yavan* (1999); E. Benbassa and A. Rodrigue, *Sephardi Jewry, A History of the Judeo-Spanish Community, 14th–20th Centuries* (2000); J. Gerber, *The Jews of Spain: A History of the Sephardic Experience* (1992); G. Nahon, *Métropoles et périphéries sefarades d'Occident* (1993); David M. Bunis, *A Lexicon of the Hebrew and Aramaic Elements in Modern Judezmo* (1993).

SEPHARVAIM (Heb. סְפַרְוָיִם, סְפַרְוַיִם), one of the cities from which the king of Assyria brought settlers to Samaria, after the conquest of the Kingdom of Israel (II Kings 17:24). Sepharvaim is also mentioned among the city-states which, as King Sennacherib of Assyria boasts, were unable to hold out against the king of Assyria (I Kings 18:34; 19:13 = Isa. 36:19; 37:38).

Two principal suggestions have been made for the identification of the city. Some identify it with Sippar, one of Babylonia's leading sacred cities, on the ground that it is mentioned together with Babylon and Cuthah (II Kings 17:24), and indeed the annals of Sennacherib tell of the deportation of inhabitants from both Sippar and Cuthah. The identification of Sippar with Sepharvaim is supported by the forms ספרים (I Kings 17:31) and ספריים ($1QIsa^a$ 36:19; 37:13), (Heb. ספרוים) being apparently a scribal error due to the similarity of the letters *vav* and *yod*. The name (Heb. ספרוים) appears to be the dual form, indicating a twin-city, and in fact Sippar consisted of *Si-ip-ar ša Šamaš* and *Si-ip-ar ša A-nu-ni-tum* ("Sippar of the god Shamash" and "Sippar of the goddess Anunitum"). Others identify Sepharvaim with Sibraim (Ezek. 47:16), situated in Syria between Damascus and Hamath. This identification is based on the fact that in II Kings 18:34 Sepharvaim is mentioned together with Hamath and Arpad, and that the Peshitta of Ezekiel 47:16 reads Sepharvaim instead of Sibraim. The gods of Sepharvaim, *Adrammelech and *Anammelech (II Kings 17:31), were worshiped, according to the proponents of the first identification, in Sippar in Babylonia, and according to the proponents of the second, in Sibraim in Syria. It is difficult to decide definitely in favor of one rather than the other identification. The suggestion that the biblical passages are to be explained as referring at times to Sippar and at times to Sibraim is not very probable, since in four of the passages (I Kings 18:34; 19:13; Isa. 36:10; 37:15) the three cities Hamath, Ivvah (Avva), and Sepharvaim are named together, showing that the same Sepharvaim is meant in all of them, and it is difficult to suppose that a different one is intended in I Kings 17:31.

BIBLIOGRAPHY: G.R. Driver, in: *Eretz Israel*, 5 (1959), 18–20 (Eng.). See commentaries to II King 17–18 and Isaiah 36–37.

[Isaac Avishur]

SEPHIHA, HAIM VIDAL (1923–), Judeo-Spanish linguist and activist. Sephiha was born in Brussels to a Sephardi family from Istanbul. During the German occupation of Belgium, he was arrested in 1943 and deported to Auschwitz in September. He survived the death camp, where his father perished. After liberation, he resumed his studies in natural sciences, graduating in 1948 and working as a chemical engineer; however, he eventually decided to study and defend the linguistic and cultural heritage of his community. As a student and assistant teacher of Hispanic linguistics at the Sorbonne in Paris, in 1967 he started to give lectures and workshops on Judeo-Spanish at the National Institute of Oriental Languages (INALCO). His understanding of the language is based on a clear distinction between its two fundamental modalities. Whereas he reserves the term "Ladino" for the old "liturgical language" in which the Sephardi Jews rendered sacred Hebrew texts into a "calqued" Judeo-Castilian, he describes the vernacular as a versatile "language of fusion" built up from different medieval Iberian dialects and integrating elements from Hebrew and the modern linguistic environment. In 1970, Sephiha presented his doctoral thesis, a comparative study of two 16th-century Ladino translations of Deuteronomy and, in 1979, he obtained a professor's degree for his theoretical analysis of the Ladino language. His chair at the University of Paris-VIII, which he has held since 1981, was transformed three years later into an INALCO chair in Judeo-Spanish studies, the first university chair ever dedicated to this subject. Sephiha, who retired in 1991, was instrumental in securing academic acceptance and public support for the "agonizing language" he spoke and taught. Besides his scientific and popular publications, from 1972 he launched several calls for revival of the language and in 1979 founded the "Association *Vidas Largas* for the Defense and Promotion of the Judeo-Spanish Language and Culture," which organizes educational work in Sephardi communities as well as the rescue of literary, musical, and architectural treasures. Judeo-Spanish has since been included among the recognized minority languages of France. In 2003, Sephiha inaugurated at the Auschwitz site a memorial in honor of the 160,000 Judeo-Spanish victims of the Holocaust.

Among his writings are *Le Ladino (judéo-espagnol calque): Deutéronome, versions de Constantinople (1547) et de Ferrare (1553)* (1973), *L'agonie des Judéo-Espagnols* (1977), *Le Ladino (judéo-espagnol calque): Structure et évolution d'une langue liturgique* (1982), and *Le judéo-espagnol* (1986).

BIBLIOGRAPHY: W. Busse and M.C. Varol (eds.), *Hommage à Haïm Vidal Sephiha* (1986); "The Instruction of Judeo-Spanish in Europe," in: *Shofar*, 19:4 (2001), 58–70.

[Carsten Wilke (2nd ed.)]

SEPPHORIS (Heb. *Ẓippori*), ancient city located in the heart of Lower Galilee (map ref. 176/239). The site is situated some 18 mi. (29 km.) from Tiberias to the east and the same distance from the Mediterranean to the west. It lies approximately 4 mi. (6 km.) to the northwest of Nazareth, rising ca. 1,000 ft. (300 m.) from the surrounding valleys: the Netofa Valley to the north and the Nazareth basin to the south. Arab residents of a village called Safuriyye occupied the site until the 1948 war and a moshav was founded there in 1949. The ancient city, consisting of a summit and lower city, underlies much of the medieval ruins, which were associated with the citadel on the summit, a museum of the National Parks Authority since 1995. The Citadel served as a small castle in Crusader times when the site was known as Le Sepphorie; it was renovated in the mid-18th century by the Bedouin governor of Galilee and again in 1889 by the Turkish sultan, who added a second story; it served as a school until 1948.

The first mention of Sepphoris in a literary source occurs in Josephus in connection with the Hasmonean king Alexander *Yannai, who successfully repulsed the attack of Ptolemy Lathyrus of Egypt (Ant., 13:338). The site subsequently became the administrative capital of the Galilee ca. 57 B.C.E. when Gabinius, Pompey's legate to Syria, made it one of his five *synedria*, or councils (Ant., 14:91; War, 1:170). The city was taken by *Herod the Great in 37 B.C.E. (Ant., 17:271) and presumably served as his northern command post for the remainder of his reign. At the death of Herod in 4 B.C.E. a rebellion broke out at the site, the so-called War of Varus, which sought to remove Sepphoris from Herodian rule (War, 2:68; Ant., 17:289). The rebellion was supposedly crushed and the city burned, and many of its inhabitants were taken as slaves. Recent archaeological work at the site has not substantiated Josephus' report on this event.

In the first century C.E., *Herod Antipas, who inherited the site as part of the tetrarchy of Galilee and Peraea (Transjordan), fortified the city and made it the "ornament of all Galilee, and called in Autocratoris" (Ant., 18:27). The precise nature of Antipas' fortification and building and renovation are still not adequately understood, even after considerable work at the site. The city enjoyed autonomous rule under Antipas and served as the capital of Galilee, before he moved it to Tiberias. The role of Sepphoris during the Great Revolt against Rome was pro-Roman, with many of the residents exhibiting "pacific sentiments" (War, 2:30–31); coins minted there under Emperor Nero (66–67 C.E.) refer to the city as Eirenopolis or "City of Peace." After the revolt the city experienced great growth as a result of the many newcomers from the south, and it became the foremost city in Galilee. At the beginning of the reign of Antoninus Pius (138–61) the city became known as Diocaesarea in honor of Zeus and Casear, precisely the time when members of the Sixth Legion were stationed at nearby Leggio. What happened at Sepphoris or nearby during the Second Revolt is unclear. Sepphoris reached its zenith as a Jewish seat of learning and cultural center during the reign of Caracalla (198–217), when the Sanhedrin was moved there and Rabbi *Judah the ha-Nasi lived in the city. Under Rabbi Judah's leadership, the Mishnah was edited and published there and Sepphoris remained a major seat of learning throughout the rabbinic period. Though it suffered greatly from the earthquake of 363 C.E., it was rebuilt soon after and by the sixth century a bishop was head of a major Christian community there. By the Umayyad period the city was identified as Saffuriyya in written sources.

The first major archaeological work was undertaken at Sepphoris in 1931 under the direction of Leroy Waterman of the University of Michigan. His team identified the theater and what they believed to be a church on the western summit along with numerous domestic installations. Eric Meyers and James Strange surveyed the site in the 1970s with the view of excavating there. Meyers subsequently codirected the Duke-Hebrew University Excavations there with Ehud Netzer and Carol Meyers from 1985 to 1989 and Strange directing the South Florida Excavations during that time and into the 1990s. Meyers' new team was reorganized in 1993 after the Hebrew University team went independent under the leadership of Zev Weiss. Another project headed by Z. Tsuk focused on the water system and was sponsored by Tel Aviv University and the National Parks Authority. Sepphoris became "Zippori National Park" in 1992. Major restoration work and numerous historic buildings and structures have since been incorporated into the National Park, including the Citadel Museum, the Dionysos Mansion, the Nile Mosaic Building, and the Synagogue with the zodiac mosaic.

Major discoveries that have illuminated the history of the city include the following: the theater, probably dated to the period after 70 C.E.; a series of private domiciles on the western summit that include more the 20 ritual baths that date to the Roman period; a fort on the western summit dated to the late Hellenistic period; the great Dionysos Villa or Mansion with peristyle courtyard and a mosaic with scenes from the life of Dionysos with Greek labels, dated to the third century C.E.; the lower city with its two great streets intersecting, the east-west *decumanus* and north-south *cardo*, dating from the early Roman period and lasting until the Byzantine period, flanked by colonnaded sidewalks and a series of shops and small houses; a Byzantine church in the lower city; the Nile mosaic building with exquisite mosaics dating to the Byzantine period; the Byzantine-period synagogue with a zodiac mosaic; and the incredible water system with aqueducts, dated to the end of the first century C.E. and operational until the Byzantine era. Lying outside the city and in the moshav Ẓippori are a series of tombs that have been accidentally discovered through the years and the great Crusader Church of St. Anne, which lies within the compound of the Franciscan property to the west of the Citadel.

The recovery of the material culture of Sepphoris from the Hellenistic to the medieval periods has led to an unprecedented reevaluation of the role of the city in the history of the Land of Israel and of Galilee in particular. Its rich heritage of mosaic art and building styles places it squarely in the mainstream of Greco-Roman culture and suggests that its incredible importance as a city of Jewish learning was not unrelated to the fact that by the time of Rabbi Judah's presence there Jewish life was completely at home in the world of Hellenistic culture.

BIBLIOGRAPHY: C.L. Meyers and E.M. Meyers, "Sepphoris," in: *The Oxford Encyclopedia of Archaeology in the Near East* (1997), 4:527–36; E.M. Meyers, "Aspects of Roman Sepphoris in the Light of Recent Archaeology," in: F. Manns and E. Alliata (eds.), *Early Christianity in Context* (1993), 29–36; E.M. Meyers, E. Netzer, and C.L Meyers, *Sepphoris* (1992); R.M. Nagy, C.L. Meyers, E.M. Meyers, and Z. Weiss (eds.), *Sepphoris in Galilee: Crosscurrents of Culture* (1996); E. Netzer and Z. Weiss, *Zippori* (1992); Z. Weiss, *The Sepphoris Synagogue* (2005); R. Talgam and Z. Weiss, "The Mosaics of the House of Dionysos at Sepphoris," in: *Qedem*, 44 (2004).

[Eric M. Meyers (2nd ed.)]

SEPTUAGINT, the oldest Greek translation of the Bible. The designation Septuagint, from the Latin *septuaginta*, "seventy," is based on the legend contained in the apocryphal Letter of *Aristeas, according to which 72 elders of Israel, six from each tribe, translated the Law into Greek, in Alexandria, during the reign of *Ptolemy II Philadelphus (285–246 B.C.E.). On the basis of this legend it can be inferred that the Pentateuch was translated into Greek in Alexandria during the first half of the third century B.C.E.

The designation Septuagint was extended to the rest of the Bible and the noncanonical books that were translated into Greek during the following two centuries. For full details, see *Bible, Translations.

SEPÚLVEDA, town in central Spain, N.E. of Segovia. The Jewish community of Sepúlveda belonged to the bishopric of *Segovia and became prosperous in the 13th century. In a *fuero* ("charter") given by Fernando IV to the town of Sepúlveda in 1305, the Jews there were granted different urban privileges. These included the liberty of trading in the local market and the right to call witnesses from both sides in trials involving Jews and Christians. The Jews were also allowed to have a cemetery within the town boundaries, in exchange for a special tax on pepper. But it was stated in the town's *fuero* that a Christian woman who nursed a Jewish (or Moorish) child should be flogged and driven out of the town. Jews were forbidden to buy meat for three days following Passover, Shavuot, and Christmas, with the exception of goat meat. In 1494, two years after the edict of expulsion from Spain, one Pedro Laínez returned to Sepúlveda, converted to Christianity, and consequently had his property restored.

BIBLIOGRAPHY: Baer, Spain, index; P. Marin Pérez et al., *Los Fueros de Sepúlveda* (1953); Suárez Fernández, Documentos, 71, 532f.

[Haim Beinart]

SEQUEYRA, JOHN DE (1712–1795), early American physician. Sequeyra was born in London, scion of a Sephardi family noted for its physicians. He received his medical degree at the University of Leyden, Holland, in 1739 and migrated to Virginia about 1745, spending almost his entire life in Williamsburg. Appointed the first visiting physician to the insane asylum in that town (1773), Sequeyra later was elected to the hospital's court of directors. In 1773 he was called in to treat

Governor Botetourt in his fatal illness. Sequeyra first introduced into Virginia the custom of eating the tomato as a vegetable, formerly considered to be poisonous. He wrote a number of medical essays, including "Diseases in Virginia."

BIBLIOGRAPHY: W.B. Blanton, *Medicine in Virginia in 18th Century* (1931), 320–1.

[Robert Shosteck]

SERAIAH (Heb. שְׂרָיָהוּ, שְׂרָיָה; "YHWH is prince").

(1) Son of Neriah, son of Mahseiah. Seraiah was from a family of high officials who served under *Zedekiah, king of Judah (596–586 B.C.E.). This family apparently had pro-Babylonian sympathies, and Seraiah acted as Zedekiah's emissary to Babylon (Jer. 51:59). At the same time he also served as Jeremiah's emissary, which indicates that he supported the prophet as did *Baruch, who was apparently his brother. His official title was "quartermaster" (Heb. *sar menuḥah*, Jer. 51:59), although the Septuagint and Theodotion describes him as "officer in charge of gifts" (Heb. *sar minḥah* or *sar menaḥot*). If the latter versions are correct, Seraiah son of Neriah is to be identified with the chief priest Seraiah who was exiled to Babylonia (Jer. 52:24).

(2) The chief priest in Jerusalem at the time of the fall of the city (II Kings 25:18 = Jer. 52:24), who was put to death at Riblah by Nebuchadnezzar. He was an ancestor of Ezra (Ezra 7:1; I Esd. 8:1).

(3) A captain of the Judean forces who joined Gedaliah at Mizpah (II Kings 25:23; Jer. 40:8), in the assurance that he would be treated well by the latter.

(4) An officer of King Jehoiakim who was sent by the king to arrest Jeremiah and Baruch (Jer. 36:26). The name Seraiah appears as the name of a woman in a papyrus from Elephantine (Cowley, Aramaic, 22:4, p. 67).

BIBLIOGRAPHY: S. Yeivin, in: *Tarbiz*, 12 (1941), 260.

SERAPH (Heb. שָׂרָף, *saraf*), the term seraph, whose etymology is obscure, appears in the Bible in two distinct contexts. It appears in the singular and plural as the name of a species of serpent (Num. 21:6; Deut. 8:15; Isa. 14:29; 30:6). In Numbers 21 the Lord sends "seraph-snakes" to punish the complaining Israelites (when the people complain the Lord tells Moses to make a "seraph" and place it on a standard, to serve as a homeopathic apotropaic device, whereupon Moses makes a copper *serpent (snake, 21:9)). In Isaiah 14:29 and 30:6, the word *saraf* is qualified by the word *me'ofef*, "flying," so that it appears that the seraph-snake is a purely legendary species.

Seraphim in Isaiah 6:2, 6 must be distinguished from the foregoing. These are depicted as composite semidivine beings with three pairs of wings; they stand, fly, and proclaim God's ineffable holiness before the divine throne. As guardians of a throne they recall the *cherubim in Ezekiel 1, although unlike the latter they do not serve as a divine chariot. Winged figures flank the throne depicted on the sarcophagus of Hiram of Tyre, and have been found on incense altars and ivories. A basalt relief from Tell Ḥalaf shows a composite deity with three pairs of wings, holding a snake in each hand. This figure resembles the seraphim of Isaiah 6, although it might be an apotropaic like the seraph/copper serpent in Numbers 21 and archaeological sources. The apotropaic intercessor function typologically connects the first and second cases of its appearance.

BIBLIOGRAPHY: G.B. Gray, *Numbers* (ICC, 1912), 277; idem, *Isaiah 1–27* (ICC, 1912), 104ff.

[Michael Fishbane]

SERBIN, HYMAN (1914–1995), U.S. aerodynamicist. From 1937 he did research at the Institute for Advanced Studies at Princeton. He was chief aerodynamics engineer of the Fairchild Engine and Aircraft Corporation from 1940 to 1947, when he became professor of aeronautical engineering at Purdue University, Indiana. In 1955 he returned to industry, first as an assistant to the director of scientific research in the Convair division of General Dynamics Corporation and later with the Rand Corporation and Hughes Aircraft Company.

[Samuel Aaron Miller]

SERBU, IERONIM, originally **Aron-Hertz Erich** (1911–1972), Romanian author. Although Serbu published a collection of stories and sketches in 1940, he only attracted attention in 1955 with his novella *Nunta în stepă* ("Wedding on the Steppe"), on life in a Transnistria concentration camp. This was notable for its characterization and documentary value. In other works, such as *Podul amintirilor* ("Bridge of Memories", 1963, 1967[2]), he dealt with Romania's postwar social metamorphosis.

SEREKH (Heb. סֶרֶךְ), word appearing in several places in the Talmud (Nid. 67b, passim), with the meaning "example," "habit," or "rule." It appears as almost a technical term in the *Qumran texts to denote the community's "rule" of life or some aspect of it, and is used practically as the title (or part of the title) of some of the community documents. Thus the Manual of *Discipline is "[the book of the ru]le of the community" (*[sefer ser]ekh ha-yaḥad*; 1QS 1:1), the rule of the congregation is "the rule for the whole congregation of Israel in the latter days" (*ha-serekh le-khol adat Yisrael be-aḥarit ha-yamim*; 1QSa 1:1), the *War Scroll is (probably) "[the book of the rule]of war" (*[sefer serekh]ha-milḥamah*). Both the noun and its cognate verb *sarakh* ("set in order") are particularly common in the War Scroll in the sense of military dispositions and the like. The officers are *anshei ha-serekh* (1QM 7:1; 13:1). The use of the term in other texts may be due to the members of the community regarding themselves as continually engaged in a holy war, against spiritual enemies if not against the mortal sons of darkness.

"This is the rule (*serekh*) for the men of the community" (1QS 5:1); "this is the rule (*serekh*) for all the hosts of the congregation" (1QSa 1:6); "this is the rule (*serekh*) for all the judges of the congregation" (CD 10:4); "this is the rule (*serekh*) for the session of the many" (1QS 6:8) – these are samples of the characteristic use of the word.

BIBLIOGRAPHY: Y. Yadin, *Scroll of the War of the Sons of Light Against the Sons of Darkness* (1962), 148ff. See also bibliography under *Discipline, Manual of; *War Scroll; *Yaḥad.

[Frederick Fyvie Bruce]

SERENI, ANGELO PIERO (1908–1967), Italian jurist. Born in Rome, Sereni became professor of international law at the universities of Ferrara and Bologna. After the promulgation of antisemitic legislation in 1938, he left Italy for the United States where he wrote his best known work, *The Italian Conception of International Law* (1943), which became a standard textbook. Sereni returned to Italy after World War II and resumed his chair at Ferrara.

He wrote extensively on international legal disputes and dedicated his major work, *Diritto Internazionale* (5 vols., 1956–65), to "the sacred memory of Angelo Sereni [Sereni's uncle], Teacher of Justice, and Enzo *Sereni, fallen for Freedom." A number of Sereni's important works touched upon matters of special Jewish interest. In "*La situazione giuridica di Gerusalemme*" (in *Foro Italiano*, 83 no. 11–12, 1950), he argued that Israel's sovereignty over West Jerusalem was indisputable since the United Nations resolutions to internationalize Jerusalem were only recommendations that had not been carried out and therefore did not negate Israel's jurisdiction. He also criticized a decision of the Italian Cassation Court in upholding the refusal of the Italian authorities to hand over a Nazi criminal for trial, maintaining that the decision was inconsistent with adherence to the Genocide Convention which recognizes genocide as a political crime.

[Alfredo Mordechai Rabello]

SERENI, ENZO ḤAYYIM (1905–1944), Italian pioneer in Palestine, labor leader, writer, and one of the *Haganah emissaries parachuted into Europe during World War II. Born in Rome, the descendant of the distinguished and assimilated *Sereni family, he "discovered" Zionism after attending the Thirteenth Zionist Congress in Carlsbad (1923). He was one of the first in Italy to promote settlement in Palestine as a social ideal. He was a socialist with religious aspirations, seeking spiritual perfection in the light of modern philosophy. After completing his university studies and being involved in a conflict with the authorities because of his anti-Fascist and pacifist activities, he settled in Palestine in 1927. He first worked in an orange grove in Reḥovot. Later he joined in founding kibbutz Givat *Brenner. He was also active in the *Histadrut, *Mapai, and Ha-Kibbutz ha-Me'uḥad movement. Sensing the approach of war, he went several times as an emissary to Germany and other European countries (1931–34) to train *ḥalutzim*. During the Arab riots in Palestine (1936–39), he stood out as a pacifist, and even in times of tension went unarmed to Arab villages. However, as soon as World War II broke out he joined the British Army, and edited newspapers and radio broadcasts in Italian. His military activities for the Allies in Iraq in 1941 were accompanied by clandestine Zionist educational work among Jewish youth, many of whom he transported across the desert to Palestine.

On his return to Palestine, Sereni devoted himself to the preparation of groups of parachutists to drop behind enemy lines to join partisans and help rescue Jewish survivors (see *Haganah). Despite strong opposition, he insisted on being dropped into that part of Italy which was still under Nazi control. For some unknown reason, he landed in the German lines. He was immediately captured and sent from camp to camp until he was finally shot in *Dachau on Nov. 18, 1944. In 1951 his book *Mekorot ha-Fashizm ha-Italki* ("Sources of Italian Fascism") was published. He also wrote *Arabs and Jews in Palestine* (1936) and *Ha-Aviv ha-Kadosh* ("The Holy Spring," 1947). Kibbutz Neẓer *Sereni was named after him, as was a cultural center in Givat Brenner.

His wife, ADA (b. 1905), shared most of his missions. In the process of searching for her husband, she became a central figure in the organization of "illegal" *immigration to Palestine through Italy. She succeeded in winning the cooperation of the postwar Italian authorities in the Jewish rescue operation in spite of strong British counterpressure. In the 1960s she organized and led the Associazione Italia-Israele in Rome. She subsequently settled in Jerusalem. Ada Sereni was awarded the Israel Prize in 1995. Her book *Sefinot le-lo Degel* ("Ships without a Flag," 1973) is about the "illegal" immigration to Palestine.

BIBLIOGRAPHY: C. Castelbolognesi, preface to E. Sereni, *Ha-Aviv ha-Kadosh* (1947); C. Urquhart and P.L. Brent, *A Hero of Our Times* (1967); A. Milano et al. (eds.), *Sefer Zikkaron le-Ḥayyim Enzo Sereni* (Heb. and It., 1970).

[Calev Castel]

SERERO, family of Spanish scholars who settled in *Fez after the Expulsion, bringing their considerable library with them. There is no available information on the first generation of the Serero family in Morocco. Saul ben David *Serero (1575–1655) was the most prominent *ḥakham* of Fez in his day. He was a signatory to the *takkanot* of 1602. His interest in history resulted in a chronology of the events of his period, *Divrei ha-Yamim* ("Chronicles"), fragments of which are extant. He wrote *Perek ha-Shi'urim* and legal decisions which were published in *Zekhut Avot* (Pisa, 1812), *Urim ve-Tummim*, an index on the Shulḥan Arukh, and sermons and a commentary on Proverbs, and a volume of sermons which reveals him as an original thinker and well versed in contemporary philosophy. Serero's nephew, EMMANUEL BEN MENAHEM (c. 1610–1680), was appointed *dayyan* during his uncle's lifetime. He corresponded with R. Jacob *Sasportas. A number of his responsa were published in the works of Moroccan rabbis. His nephew, MENAHEM BEN DAVID (1628–1701), a fiery preacher, was rabbi in Fez. An outstanding halakhic authority, he was the recipient of numerous queries concerning the *takkanot of the megorashim* (expellees) and their customs.

His son JOSHUA (1670–c. 1740) was a scribe, preacher, and poet. He left a journal of reminiscences on the scribes of the *bet din* of his time, and a number of his *piyyutim* were published in the collection *Yismaḥ Yisrael* (1931) and in *Shir Yedidut* (1927). His son EMANUEL (c. 1705–1775), rabbi, poet, and author, wrote a collection of *piyyutim*, a number of which were published in Sephardi *maḥzorim*, and a commentary on the *Haggadah*.

MATTATHIAS BEN MENAHEM (1718–c. 1788), grandson of Joshua, was one of the five members of the Fez *bet din*. Some of his legal decisions were published in *Zekhut Avot* and in the works of Moroccan *ḥakhamim*. He was survived by seven learned sons: (1) MENAHEM (1744–1780), talmudist and *dayyan*, who wrote *Lekaḥ Tov* when he was only 17. (2) SAUL (1746–1807), rabbi in Fez, was a member of the *bet din* of R. Elijah ha-Sarfati. During the reign of al-Yazid he fled with him to Sefrou, serving as *dayyan* there. A number of his legal decisions were published in the responsa *Avnei Shayish* (1934–35) of Saul Joshua Abitbol. (3) JOSHUA (1748–1819), rabbi and *dayyan*, was a pietist and ascetic. Several of his legal decisions were published in the works of Moroccan rabbis. (4) ḤAYYIM DAVID (1750–1826), rabbi and *dayyan* who wrote novellae on the tractate *Pesaḥim*, letters and proverbs, and legal decisions, some of which were published in the works of Moroccan rabbis. (5) JUDAH (1755–1835), rabbi and *dayyan*, was a talmudist. (6) JACOB (1770–1851), rabbi and *dayyan*, was a pietist and kabbalist. A number of his legal decisions were published in *Shufrei de-Ya'akov* (1910) of R. Jacob Berdugo. (7) NAḤMAN, rabbi and pietist.

JONATHAN BEN HAYYIM DAVID (1775–1833), was *dayyan* in Fez. A poet, some of his poems are recited in Morocco. A number of his legal decisions were published in the works of Moroccan rabbis. His brother MATTATHIAS (1806–1891), who was known as *Mattityah ha-Kadosh* ("the holy Mattathias"), was a rabbi and *dayyan* in Fez. His son JUDAH BENJAMIN (1834–1926), rabbi and *dayyan*, was a research scholar, copyist, grammarian, and expert in the linguistic style of Ibn Ezra. Some of his legal decisions were published in the works of his contemporaries. JOSEPH BEN RAPHAEL JOSHUA ZION (1843–1902), *dayyan*, was a pietist and kabbalist. When the Arabs conducted a pogrom in the mellah of Fez in 1912, they burned a number of houses, including his synagogue and its famous library, which was totally destroyed, together with his writings and legal decisions. His brother MATTATHIAS (d.c. 1935) was appointed head of the *bet din* of Fez in 1929. His son ḤAYYIM DAVID (d.c. 1968) was appointed *dayyan* in Mogador, going from there to Fez, where he was *dayyan* until his death.

BIBLIOGRAPHY: J.M. Toledano, *Ner ha-Ma'arav* (1911), index; J. Bon-Naim, *Malkhei Rabbanan* (1931), s.v.; G.Vajda, *Un Receuil de Textes Historiques Judéo-Marocains* (1951), index. s.v.

[Haim Bentov]

SERERO, SAUL (1566–1655), Moroccan rabbi. Serero was born in *Fez, where his family had taken up residence after the expulsion of the Jews from *Spain in 1492. In 1602 he was appointed a member of the *ma'amad* of Fez, and in 1621 succeeded Samuel *Abendanan as head of the local *bet din*. He was also head of a yeshivah, where he had in his possession many manuscript works of the rabbis of Spain, inherited from his parents and grandparents. His reputation as a halakhist spread throughout Morocco, and one of the rabbis of Algiers in a responsum refers to him as "unique in his generation, his word was accepted everywhere as law; no contemporary rabbi could be compared to him."

Most of Serero's works have remained in manuscript, including a homiletical work, a commentary on Proverbs, and kabbalistic works. His most important work is *Urim ve-Tummim*, a veritable juridical encyclopedia in two parts, the first an alphabetical index of halakhic themes, the second a kind of biographical-bibliographical dictionary, and including a short treatise on weights and measures (*Perek ha-Shi'urim ve-ha-Middot*).

Fragments of a history of Fez, covering the period 1603–1651, have been translated and published by G. Vajda, *Un recueil de textes historiques judéo-marocains* (1951).

BIBLIOGRAPHY: H. Zafrani, *Les Juifs du Maroc* (1972).

[Haim Zafrani]

SERGHI (Marcoff), CELLA (1907–1992), Romanian novelist. Serghi's works, which often ran to several editions, include *Pănza de păianjen* ("The Spider's Web," 1938), *Cîntecul Uzinei* ("Song of the Plant," 1951), and *Fetele lui Barotă* ("Barota's Daughter," 1958). *Cartea Mironei* (1965, 1967[2]), which deals with the wars and horrors of the years 1935–1945, contains a fine psychological study of a concentration camp survivor tormented by memories of his lost family.

SERI, DAN BENAYA (1935–), Hebrew writer. Seri was born in Jerusalem. He worked for many years as a civil servant for the Ministry of Agriculture. His first novel, *Ugiyot ha-Melaḥ shel Savta Sultana* ("Grandma Sultana's Salty Biscuits") appeared in 1980 (Italian translation 2004) and tells the story of a second marriage which is overshadowed by prejudices and omens, passions and heated dreams. Seri's prose depicts the world of Sephardi Jews in Jerusalem, drawing on folkloric sources. His second novel, *Mishael* (1993), set in a Bucharan-Jewish neighborhood in Jerusalem, recounts the mysterious pregnancy of middle-aged Mishael following the death of his barren wife. Old traditions and superstitions are interwoven in a prose-fabric full of fantasy and insight. Seri also published two collections of novellas. The first, *Ẓipporei Ẓel* ("Birds of Shade," 1987) includes the story *"Elef Neshotav shel Naftali Siman Tov,"* which has been adapted to the screen. The second, *Dagim Metim Be-Yafo* ("Dead Fish in Jaffa," 2003) tells, amongst others, of Aharon Polombo, a widowed tailor, who travels from Izmir in Turkey to Jaffa and on to Jerusalem in order to deliver some letters to a mysterious woman. The bizarre and the groteseque characterize this novella as well as the second story in the volume, *"Se'udah Tunisait."* Individual stories have been translated into various languages, and further information is available at the ITHL website at www.ithl.org.il.

BIBLIOGRAPHY: A. Feinberg, "Small Sins and Their Wages," in: *Modern Hebrew Literature*, 8:1–2 (1982–83), 78–81; H. Halperin, "*Ta'alumat Elef Neshotav shel Naftali Siman Tov*," in: *Iton 77*, 101 (1988), 20–21; H. Hever, *Sendvichim shel Mahapekhan: Tenu'ah bein Perspektivot eẓel D.B. Seri*," in: *Siman Keriah*, 20 (1990), 394–97; G. Shaked, *Ḥelkaim ve-Nidkaim*, in: *Efes Shetayim*, 2 (1993), 23–32; M. Bat-Moshe Hurvitz, "*Leshonot Shonot shel Amirah be-Siaḥ Sippuri*," in: *Am ve-Sefer*, 9 (1995), 30–52; Y. Ben-David, "*Ẓel ha-Mavet ve-ha-Geroteskah*," in: *Haaretz Sefarim* (October 29, 2003).

[Anat Feinberg (2nd ed.)]

°**SERING, MAX** (1857–1939), German agricultural economist. Sering, who was born in Barby, taught in Bonn and, after 1889, in Berlin. He cooperated with Walter *Rathenau in organizing Germany's essential materials policy in World War I. In drafting the German *Siedlungsgesetz* (farmers' settlement law) of 1919, his views prevailed over those of Franz *Oppenheimer, whose emphasis was on agricultural producers' cooperatives. Having opposed racial discrimination in German agricultural legislation after 1933, Sering was vilified by the **Stuermer* on account of his part-Jewish ancestry. One of the relatively few active German resisters of the Nazis, he transferred his research institute's comprehensive library to the International Conference for Agrarian Science, thus protecting it from confiscation. A member of Pastor Niemoeller's Confessional Church, he stood by his Jewish former students.

BIBLIOGRAPHY: Dietze, in: *Berichte ueber Landwirtschaft*, 168 (1957).

[Hanns G. Reissner]

SERKIN, PETER ADOLF (1947–), pianist. Serkin's rich musical heritage extends back several generations: his grandfather was violinist and composer Adolf Busch and his father was pianist Rudolf *Serkin. Peter Serkin was born in New York and studied with his father and with Lee Luvisi and Mieczyslaw Horszowski at the Curtis Institute of Music (1958–64). His other teachers included Karl Ulrich Schnabel and the flautist Marcel Moyse, who exerted vital musical influence on him. In 1959 Serkin made his Marlboro Music Festival and New York City debuts. From then his performances with symphony orchestras, recital appearances, chamber music collaborations, and recordings were acclaimed worldwide. Serkin was noted for his passion, keyboard virtuosity, and individualistic approach. He acquired a distinguished reputation in both traditional and contemporary scores, and from the early 1970s played rock, jazz, and improvisations. In 1973 he formed the Tashi group with the clarinetist Richard Stoltzman, violinist Ida Kavafian, and cellist Fred Sherry. After leaving the group in 1980, he renewed his appearances as recitalist and soloist. In 1983 he became the first pianist to win the prize for outstanding artistic achievement awarded by the Accademia Musicale Chigiana in Siena, and also joined the faculty of Mannes College. He later took up teaching posts at the Juilliard School and Curtis Institute of Music and taught regularly at the Tanglewood Music Center. Among the important world premieres he performed are Lieberson's First and Second Piano Concertos with the Boston Symphony Orchestra and works by Henze, Takemitsu, and Berio.

BIBLIOGRAPHY: Grove online; *Baker's Biographical Dictionary* (1997); S. Isacoff, "Peter Serkin: The Right Stuff," in: *Keyboard Classics*, 7:2 (1987), 4–6; C. Montparker, "Peter Serkin: A Pianist for All Seasons," in: *Clavier*, 28:9 (1989), 10–15.

[Naama Ramot (2nd ed.)]

SERKIN, RUDOLF (1903–1991), pianist. Born in Eger, Bohemia, Serkin made his first public appearance at the age of 12. He began his concert career in Berlin in 1920, and made his American debut in Washington in 1933 with the violinist Adolf Busch, whose daughter he married, and with whom he had already formed a famous duo in Europe. In 1939 he became head of the pianoforte faculty at the Curtis Institute, Philadelphia. Serkin toured Europe, the United States, and the Orient, and was recognized as one of the master performers of classical repertoire in his generation. His son Peter *Serkin (1947–) was also a concert pianist.

SERL BAS JACOB BEN WOLF KRANZ (18th century), author of *Tkhine imohos min Rosh Hodesh Elul* (*Tkhine* of the Matriarchs from the New Moon of Elul). Serl was the wife of the rabbi and apothecary Mordecai ha-Cohen Rappoport, head of the rabbinical court of Novy Oleksiniec and author of *Imrei Noam* (Oleksiniec: 1767 or 68). Since it is known that Rappoport was the son-in-law of the famed Maggid (Preacher) of Dubno, Jacob ben Wolf Kranz (1740?–1804), it seems likely that Serl's father, named on the title page of her *tkhine* as "the famous Rabbi, our teacher Jacob Segan Levi of Dubno," was the Maggid. The text of the first part of the *tkhine* also contains an authorial acrostic that reads: "Serl, daughter of the rabbi, the great luminary, his honor our teacher Rabbi Jacob."

Tkhine imohos min [or: *fun*] *Rosh Hodesh Elul* was published in several 18th century editions, in various recensions, and under slightly varying titles; among the earliest are Lvov, 1783/4, and Frankfurt-an-der-Oder, 1789/90 (under the title *Tefillas imohos*, an altered text but clearly a variant of the original). There are also numerous undated editions, and, as is usual for Eastern European *tkhines*, the bibliographical history is difficult to establish. The text contain four sections: a *tkhine* on the theme of repentance for sins to be recited every day of the month of Elul; a *tkhine* to be recited on Rosh Ha-Shanah when the Torah scrolls are taken from the ark and the Thirteen Attributes are recited; the "*tkhine* of the Matriarchs for the shofar"; and an addendum containing the prayers for *tashlikh* and *yizkor* with Yiddish translation and interpretation.

There are several notable aspects of this text. The first section of the *tkhine*, in addition to its alphabetical acrostic, alternates between short Hebrew sentences, some of them biblical verses, and paragraphs in Yiddish that expand on their themes, demonstrating Serl's knowledge of Hebrew. The material for the recitation of the Thirteen Attributes expands on the themes of the Torah and *haftarah* portions of Rosh Ha-Shanah. In addition, the Torah scrolls themselves are asked to advocate for the worshiper in her quest for forgiveness and long life, as well as on behalf of redemption for the people of Israel. Finally, and most distinctively, the "*tkhine* of the Matriarchs for the *shofar*" draws on biblical and midrashic themes to characterize the four biblical matriarchs. Moreover, each mother of Israel is requested to act as an intercessor for the worshiper in a manner appropriate to her own life. For example, Rebecca, who had to leave her parents at an early age, is asked to protect the life and health of the worshiper's parents.

BIBLIOGRAPHY: H. Liberman. *Ohel Raḥel* (1979 or 80), 432–54; C. Weissler, *Voices of the Matriarchs* (1998), 145–46, 177–78.

[Chava Weissler (2nd ed.)]

SERLING, ROD (1924–1975), U.S. writer and producer. Born Edward Rodman Serling in Syracuse, N.Y., he spent most of his childhood in Binghamton in upstate New York. After he graduated from high school in 1942, Serling enlisted with the U.S. Army's 11th Airborne Division paratroopers, serving three years in the South Pacific. In 1946, he studied at Antioch College in Ohio, where he was active in the college's radio station, writing, directing, and acting in several on-air productions. During his senior year at Antioch, Serling took second place in a CBS-sponsored script-writing contest. After graduating college in June 1950, Serling took a job as a script writer for WLW radio in Cincinnati, Ohio, and then one as a continuity writer for WKRC-TV. Before long Serling was selling freelance radio scripts, and in 1951 he sold a television script to *Lux Video Theatre*. By the beginning of 1955, he had sold 90 scripts to shows like *Kraft Television Theatre, Studio One,* and *General Electric Theater*, where his script for *Patterns* earned him an Emmy Award; NBC aired the production twice and United Artists adapted it for the screen. In April 1955, Serling signed a deal to write scripts for CBS, which featured the *Playhouse 90* premier *Requiem for a Heavyweight* (1956), which earned him a second Emmy. Disenchanted with censors, Serling conceived a novel way to address social issues: science fiction; he conceived and produced an anthology TV series he called *The Twilight Zone* (1959–64) that featured Serling as host. He wrote 90 of *Twilight Zone*'s 151 episodes, and the show would go on to land three more Emmys for Serling (Serling won more Emmys for writing drama in his lifetime than any other writer). On *The Twilight Zone*, Serling was able to address such issues as civil rights, the Holocaust, lynchings in the South, and the incipient Vietnam War. In 1965, Serling was elected to a two-year term as head of the National Academy of Television Arts and Sciences, the first writer to be so honored. After the end of the series, Serling wrote features, including *Seven Days in May,* and supplied the famous ending for *Planet of the Apes* (1968). In 1970 he co-created the horror anthology series *Night Gallery* (1969–73). He spent the remaining years of his life teaching writing at Ithaca College in New York. Serling, a heavy smoker, had a heart attack in May 1975. After undergoing open-heart surgery, he died one month later. In 2001, a remake of one of Serling's teleplays, *A Storm in Summer* (2000), won a Daytime Emmy for outstanding writing – Serling defeated the other contestants despite having been dead for more than 25 years.

[Adam Wills (2nd ed.)]

SERMONETA, JOSEPH BARUCH (1924–1992), historian. After a short stay in Palestine during World War II he pursued academic studies in humanities at the University of Rome. In 1953 Sermoneta settled in Jerusalem, where he directed the sections devoted to the history and philosophy of the Middle Ages and that of Italian literature in *Ha-Enẓiklopedyah ha-Ivrit* (1953–1963). He was the *Encyclopaedia Judaica* (first edition) departmental editor of Italian literature.

Appointed professor of Jewish Thought and of Italian–Jewish literature and languages (1962) at the Hebrew University, Sermoneta's main academic fields of interest were the close relationship between Christian scholastic philosophy and the writings of Jewish intellectuals such as R. Hillel Ben Samuel of Verona, Judah Romano, Jacob Anatoli, and Moses of Salerno between the 13th and the 15th centuries, and Italian Jewish vernacular language, including Italian-Jewish vernacular translations of the Bible and liturgical texts in the vernacular. In both fields Sermoneta's works were innovative and pathbreaking. He was co-editor with Robert Bonfil of *Italia*, dedicated to the history, literature and thought of Italian Jews.

BIBLIOGRAPHY: A. Melamed, "Sermoneta, Joseph Baruch," in: *Ha-Enẓiklopedyah ha-Ivrit*, vol. 3 (addenda), 739–40; VV.AA., *Ricordo di Joseph Baruch Sermoneta, Studi e interventi in memoria del Prof. Joseph Baruch Sermoneta Za"l nel trigesimo della sua scomparsa* (1994); H. Sermoneta, "*Joseph Baruch Sermoneta, Korot Ḥayyim u-Ketavim,*" in: A. Ravitzky (ed.), *Meromei Yerushalaim, Sefer Zikharon le Joseph Baruch Sermoneta* (1998; reprinted in *Italia*, vol.13–15 (2001), in memory of J.B. Sermoneta).

[Samuele Rocca (2nd ed.)]

SERMONS TO JEWS. While at all times zealous Christians sought the opportunity of personally propagating their faith among Jews, the first recorded instance of systematic conversionist sermons is apparently from France in the ninth century. Archbishop *Agobard of Lyons in his *Epistola de baptizandis Hebraeis*, written between 816 and 825, indicates that on his instructions the clergy of Lyons went every Saturday to preach in the synagogues, attendance on the part of the Jews presumably being compulsory. This was probably not a unique or localized happening. With the foundation of the *Dominican order (1216) the system was regularized. Conversionist sermons which the Jews had to attend are referred to in 1242 in a law of James I of Aragon, which received papal approval. After the Disputation of *Barcelona in 1263, the king himself actually delivered a conversionist harangue in the synagogue and later issued an order enjoining the Jews and Saracens to listen quietly to the addresses of the preaching friars who had come to convert them – though in 1268 he forbade the preachers to be escorted by more than ten persons. Pablo *Christiani (d. 1274), who was then a leading anti-Jewish propagandist, obtained permission to preach in the synagogues also from the king of France. It was however only in 1278 that the compulsory conversionist sermon received explicit papal authorization in the bull *Vineam soreth* of Pope *Nicholas III (and see papal *bulls); obedience to this was enjoined in England in the following year by Edward I. It was enforced only sporadically however, as for example in the intense anti-Jewish campaign conducted in Spain by the fiery Vicente *Ferrer in the early years of the 15th century. In Sicily, at that time under Aragonese rule, Fra Matteo di Girgenti was appointed *Lettore degli ebrei* ("Reader [i.e., Preacher] to the Jews") in 1428.

With the anti-Jewish reaction which accompanied the Counter-Reformation, the institution of conversionist sermons was placed on a new basis. In a bull, *Vices eius nos* of Sept. 1, 1577, Pope *Gregory XIII ordered the Jews of Rome and other places in the Papal States to send a certain quota of their number on specified occasions to one of the churches to hear a sermon which might open their eyes to the true faith. The same pope's bull, *Sancta mater ecclesia* of exactly seven years later, reverted to the subject and laid down more precise conditions. From then on, the institution was a regular abuse of Jewish life in the Papal States (including *Avignon and the *Comtat Venaissin in France) and in other parts of the Roman Catholic world as well. It was in Rome itself that the abuses were most extreme. Here 100 Jews and 50 Jewesses had to attend the designated church each week in order to listen to these addresses, generally delivered by an apostate from Judaism whose fee was paid by the Jewish community. Beadles armed with rods saw to it that they paid attention, and examined their ears to ensure that they were not plugged. Michel de Montaigne records that when he was in Rome in 1581 he heard a sermon delivered apparently by Andrea del Monte, who is known to have used language of such unmeasured violence that the Jews appealed to the papal Curia for protection. The sermons delivered in the Church of Santa Croce in Florence in 1583 by the apostate Vitale de' Medici (formerly Jehiel da Pesaro) were published. At Ferrara, a special entrance was made from the ghetto to the Church of St. Crispino, where the sermons were delivered, so that the Jews would not be subject to insult when they passed through the street.

In Venice, the authorities forbade the introduction of the conversionist sermon, but it was allowed in neighboring Padua. In 1630 the emperor Ferdinand II instituted conversionist sermons in Vienna, in the auditorium of the university, 200 Jews including at least 40 adolescents having to attend on each occasion. In Prague, the Jesuits initiated conversionist sermons in the same year. Though elsewhere there was some relaxation of the system in the 18th century (in Mantua, for example, where it was abolished in 1699), the institution of the conversionist sermon continued in the Papal States, both in Italy and in France, down to the period of the French Revolution. In Italy it was renewed after the fall of Napoleon and the restoration of papal rule, to be abolished by Pope Pius IX in 1846 during the liberal period at the beginning of his pontificate. The well-known poem by Robert *Browning, "Holy Cross Day," attempts to reflect the state of mind of the Jews on these occasions.

BIBLIOGRAPHY: Baron, Social², 9 (1965), 79ff., 274ff.; 14 (1970), 60–61, 238–9, 327, 392; S. Grayzel, *Church and the Jews in the XIIIth Century* (1966²), 15–16, 257ff., 281; A. Milano, *Il Ghetto di Roma* (1964), index; P. Browe, *Die Judenmission im Mittelalter und die Paepste* (1942).

[Cecil Roth]

SEROR, family of Algerian origin. R. SOLOMON (16th–17th century) was the author of the second part of *Ḥut ha-Meshullash* ("Triple Cord," in Responsa *Tashbaẓ*, Amsterdam, 1838). The brothers JOSEPH and TOBIAS, scholars and wealthy merchants, died in the epidemic which decimated the population of *Algiers in 1625. R. SOLOMON BEN TOBIAS (d. 1664) was chief rabbi of Algiers. R. RAPHAEL JEDIDIAH SOLOMON BEN JOSHUA BEN SOLOMON (1681–1737), the most important member of the family, was born in Algiers, where he was later chief rabbi. He was an expert on the history of the community of Algiers and wrote some highly esteemed religious poems. As a result of his herbal treatments, he became widely known as a skilled physician. His life was marked by misfortunes. He was overcome by sickness, lost several of his children, ruined himself in commercial transactions on land and sea, and finally died in poverty. Seror left many works, his responsa being published under the title *Peri Ẓaddik* ("Fruit of the Righteous," Leghorn, 1748). Among his disciples were R. Abraham Yafil, Joseph Seror, and R. Judah *Ayash, who wrote a poem in his honor and had it printed at the beginning of his work *Beit Yehudah* ("House of Judah"). R. JOSEPH (d. 1755) was a talmudic scholar and *dayyan* in Algiers. He left many responsa, which were published in *Divrei David* ("Words of David") of R. David Mendola of Leghorn and *Beit Yehudah* of R. Judah Ayash.

BIBLIOGRAPHY: I. Bloch. *Inscriptions tumulaires des anciens cimetières israélites d'Alger…* (1888), 21–3, 45–50, 57; Hirschberg, Afrikah, 2 (1965), 44ff., 116, 155ff.

[David Corcos]

SEROUSSI, ELÍAS (1896–1983), leader of the Jewish community in Uruguay. Born in Alexandria, Egypt, he immigrated with his family to Uruguay in 1926. He took part in the founding of the Comunidad Israelita Sefaradí (Jewish Sephardi Community) and was its president for many years from 1932. Elías Seroussi was also president of the umbrella organization of Uruguayan Jews, Comité Central Israelita, from 1941 to 1951. He was part of the leadership of B'nai B'rith, Círculo Social Sefaradí, and Comunidad Israelita del Uruguay. He immigrated to Israel in 1974.

His son RAFAEL SEROUSSI (born in Alexandria in 1923) was a Zionist leader in Uruguay and very active in public and social life in Israel. In Uruguay he was secretary of the founding commission of the Federación Juvenil Sionista (Zionist Youth Federation) established in 1944, and its second president (1946–47) and editor of its publication, *Aliá*. Rafael Seroussi immigrated to Israel in July 1948 and fought in the War of Independence. A chemist by profession, he participated in missions of PATWA (Professional and Technical Workers' Aliyah) to promote *aliyah* among professionals in Latin America (1953–55). He was secretary of the Organización de Latinoamericanos en Israel (Organization of Latin Americans *Olim* in Israel) for 15 years and served as its president from 1973 to 1975. Rafael Seroussi was very active in organizations of mutual relations with Latin America, such as the Israel–Costa Rica Friendship League and the Israel–Latin America Chamber of Commerce.

[Efraim Zadoff (2nd ed.)]

SEROV, VALENTIN (1856–1911), Russian painter. Born in Moscow, the son of the composer Alexandre Serov and a Jewish mother, Serov was virtually adopted as a child by the great art patron Sava Mamontov after the death of his father. At Mamontov's Abramtsevo art colony he met the leading artists of the day, including Repin and Mark *Antokolski. He was then sent to study at the St. Petersburg Academy (1880–1885), where a fellow-pupil, Mikhail Vrubel, became a close friend; in turn Serov introduced Vrubel to Mamontov, who encouraged young artists to design for his theater. At the Academy, Serov also befriended the young Léon *Bakst, encouraging his interest in stage design. Serov also became a colleague of Diaghilev and Alexander Benois, and one of the original members of the "World of Art" movement, from which emerged the Ballets Russes. He was a major influence on Diaghilev's "World of Art" movement, which heralded almost all important modern tendencies in Russian art and theater. After a period in Italy, Serov returned to Russia to establish himself as one of the leading Russian artists, painting most of the leading personalities of his time, and in 1897 was appointed official portrait-painter to the czar. His drawing of Pavlova was used for the first poster of the Ballets Russes in 1909; for the season he designed the decor for his father's opera *Judith* presented by Diaghilev in Paris, with costumes by Bakst, and in 1911 he painted a curtain for the ballet *Schéhérazade,* designed by his friend Bakst. Serov's work is mainly in the Russian Museum, Leningrad, and the Tretyakov Gallery, Moscow, including portraits of Mamontov, Ida *Rubinstein, the Jewish painter Isaac *Levitan, and his masterpiece *The Girl With Peaches* (1888), a study of Mamontov's daughter Vera.

[Charles Samuel Spencer]

SERRA, RICHARD (1939–), U.S. sculptor and draftsman. San Francisco-born Serra studied from 1957 to 1961 at the University of California at Berkeley and at Santa Barbara, after which he received a B.S. in English literature. At Yale University (1961–64), where he worked with Josef Albers, Serra earned a B.A., M.A., and M.F.A. His art of the late 1960s emphasized temporality, process, and site specificity, the latter of which has been a continuing value in Serra's art. For *Splashing* (1968), for example, Serra threw molten lead into the angle where the floor and wall meet in a room. The hardened, splattered result recalls paintings by Jackson Pollock, but unlike Pollock's canvases, Serra's work is ephemeral. During this time Serra also experimented with various industrial materials, such as rubber and fiberglass, in non-narrative works designed for interior spaces. Through the late 1960s, Serra explored the effects of gravity on heavy, temporarily installed, abstract sculpture, and on the viewer's confrontation with the weighty, unsecured piece. Two hundred tons of metal, stacked 20-feet high, loomed perilously over the viewer surveying *Stacked Steel Slabs* (*Skullcracker Series*) (1969, Fontana, California, destroyed). In the early 1970s, Serra began making canvas drawings of his sculptures after they had been conceived.

Several sculptures from the early 1980s are enormous, minimalist and geometric in form, and at times controversial. The public sculpture *Tilted Arc* (1981) was made on commission from the United States General Services Administration for New York City's Federal Plaza. Many viewed the 12-foot-tall, 120-foot-long curved, tilted plate of Cor-ten steel as threatening in conception, divisive of pedestrian space, and constrictive of the Plaza's view. After a federal court case during which Serra argued that moving the sculpture would be a violation of his contract and would destroy the site-specificity of the piece, the sculpture was removed in 1989.

From the 1980s Serra worked on several sculptures related to Holocaust remembrance. Installed next to the Berlin Philharmonic, *Berlin Junction* (1987) memorializes those who lost their lives at the hands of the Nazis. *Gravity* (1993), a 10-inch-thick, 10-foot-square standing slab of Cor-ten steel, was made on commission for the Hall of Witnesses at the United States Holocaust Memorial Museum.

In 1987 Serra installed an outdoor sculpture at the Israel Museum in Jerusalem. Serra was honored with his first American retrospective at the Museum of Modern Art in 1986.

BIBLIOGRAPHY: R.E. Krauss, *Richard Serra: Sculpture* (1986); E. Güse (ed.), *Richard Serra* (1988); R. Serra, *Writings, Interviews* (1994); H. Foster (ed.), *Richard Serra* (2000).

[Samantha Baskind (2nd ed.)]

SERRAI (**Serres**), town in Macedonia, Greece, E.N.E. of *Salonika. There was a Jewish community in Serrai in Byzantine times. There are scant references to Jews in Serres in the 12th and 14th centuries. After the Ottoman conquest of *Istanbul in 1453, Jews were forcefully transferred to the capital in the framework of the *sorgun*, and there they formed Kahal Serron. Jews settled in Serres after the expulsions from Spain (1391), from Bavaria (1470) and from Spain (1492). Italian Jews were also found in Serrai in the 15th century. Expulsees from Spain and Portugal came to Serres in the 16th century. Also former Portuguese *anusim* (Marranos) who had previously settled in Salonika relocated to Serrai for its lucrative commercial opportunities. The Judeo-Greek speaking Romaniots ruled the community at the beginning of the 16th century, but by the end of the century their presence was no longer felt. In the 16th century both a Sephardi and an Ashkenazi synagogue were in existence. The Jews lived in a special quarter in the old city. The community was strengthened in the 16th century by the presence of Rabbi Joseph Taitazak, and afterward by the elder Rabbi Joseph Firman and his son, Rabbi Solomon ha-Serroni. When Firman left in the 1560s to serve in Salonika and elsewhere in the Greek Peninsula, Serrai deteriorated as a Torah center. In the 18th and 19th centuries, several noted rabbinical scholars lived in the town, among them: Ḥayyim Abraham Strumza, the author of *Beit Avraham* and *Yerekh Avraham*; Ḥayyim Abraham b. David, author of *Tiferet Adam*; Mordecai Aseo, author of *Higgid Mordekhai*; and Nissim Muṣeiri, author of *Be'er Mayim Ḥayyim*. During the time of Rabbi Strumza (late 18th–early 19th century), the old synagogue was destroyed and replaced by a newly built synagogue called *Kahal Gadol*, with rooms for a yeshiva, library, and guests. The ground floor contained a small Talmud Torah, and the sanctuary had 2,000 seats for those that came to pray, including an *Ezrat Nashim*, a woman's section. On Yom Kippur during the Kol Nidre evening service, there was a tradition of an *azkara*, a memorial service, for all the communal leaders and rabbis since the 16th century. This tradition continued until the Bulgarians set the city ablaze in 1912.

Ereẓ Israel emissaries, like Rabbi Moshe Halevi (Harma"l) Nazir and Yosef Cohen, visited the Serrai Jewish community from 1668 to 1684. Local Jews from Serrai also went to Ereẓ Israel on pilgrimages. The messianic activities of David *Reuveni and Solomon *Molcho aroused much fervor in Serres. The members of the rabbinic Taitazak family supported the messianic movement and the study and dissemination of Kabbalah. Until the last third of the 19th century, the Hamon, Ovadia, and other families continued local traditions of forming special societies for encouraging the study of Kabbalah.

The Jews of Serrai dealt mostly in wholesale and retail trade: in tobacco, cotton, opium, wheat, barley, and manufactured goods. There were also artisans among them, such as blacksmiths and cobblers. In the 19th century, the Jews dealt mostly in banking and commerce.

The Jews who had moved to the suburbs of the city founded their own synagogue, called Midrash. This caused communal dissension, and Rabbi Raphael Asher Kovo of Salonika in 1873 decided that on the Sabbath and holidays the Jews could only pray at the old synagogue. Violence eventually erupted, and Joseph Salmona was murdered. Echoes of communal division remained for many years.

Until the mid-19th century, the youth of the community learned in a primitive traditional *meldar* (ḥeder). In 1866 a modern Talmud Torah was formed and French was taught. In 1873 a new school was established where Hebrew, Turkish, and French were taught, and Yaakov Azaria of Salonika came from Salonika to be principal. In the early 1880s the school had to close due to financial constraints. In 1895, with help from the Alliance Israélite Universelle and Baron Hirsch, a school was established. Mercado Kovo was the principal from 1895–1901. In 1901 a mixed (coed) Alliance Israélite Universelle school was established with 150 students (103 boys and 47 girls). In 1909–1910 a new modern school that cost 40,000 Francs was built, but it burned down in 1913.

At the end of the 19th century, with the advent of modern education, several educated Jewish personalities emerged in Serrai. The last chief rabbi of Serrai was Samuel Raphael ben Haviv (1813–1887), author of *Amar Shmuel*. He was an important *posek* (halakhic decisor), orator, and poet. Another rabbi, Avraham Strumza, died in 1889. After his death, the community deteriorated spiritually.

At the end of the 19th century, the economic situation took a turn for the worse. The Salonikan-Istanbul railroad did not stop at Serrai, and the city was not on the principal trade routes as it once had been. Jews began migrating to Salonika, Kavalla, Zanthi, and Drama, and the community became poor. At the beginning of the 20th century, the Jewish community consisted of 30–40 affluent families of bankers, merchants, moneylenders, and insurance agents; 100 middle-class families which engaged primarily in petty trade; and 50 poor families which were dependent on financial assistance from the affluent.

During the Balkan Wars (1912–13), the Jewish population numbered approximately 1,300; when the Bulgarian army invaded the town, it burned down the main synagogue, the Jewish school, and 115 of 140 houses. The Jews themselves were saved only upon the intervention of Jews serving with the Bulgarian forces. Some of the Jews took refuge in Bulgaria, while others moved to *Drama and *Kavalla. When the Greeks reoccupied the town after the summer of 1913, the Jewish community was reorganized. The Greeks ruled until early 1916, and were replaced by the Bulgarians for two years.

The Balkan Wars and World War I led to the deterioration of the Jewish community of Serrai, and many of the Jews migrated to other parts of Greece, like Salonika, Drama, and Cavalla, and to Bulgaria. Most of the Jews who left Serrai did not return to the city, but Jewish refugees migrated there from elsewhere. The Jewish community slowly recovered and rebuilt itself. Some of the Jewish houses destroyed by the Bulgarians were rebuilt with the financial assistance of the American Jewish Joint Distribution Committee. Most of the local Jews found employment in the workshops of the Austro-Greek Tobacco Company, whose vice president was a local Jew, Joseph Faraggi.

In 1929 there were 90 Jewish families in the city. In 1932 the community numbered 800, with half coming from Salonika, Drama, and Xanthi to work in the tobacco industry. The Jews suffered greatly from the economic depression in the early 1930s. A new Jewish school was built, and by 1932 it had 200 students, 40 of whom were not Jewish, but Greek-Orthodox. With the arrival from Asia Minor of Greek-Orthodox refugees from 1922 onward, relations between the Jews and the Greek-Orthodox deteriorated.

In 1940, the community had a membership of 600. The Bulgarians pressured the Jewish community to collaborate with them against the Greeks, and wanted the Jews to sign statements attesting to the advantages of Bulgarian rule and its preference over Greek rule, but the Jews refused. In February 1942, the Bulgarians issued anti-Jewish regulations forbidding

Jews to work in commerce, and compelling Jews to designate their homes and businesses as Jewish-owned. In 1942, Jews began fleeing the city. In March 1943, around 475 Jews were deported by the Bulgarians for the Nazis to Treblinka via the Gorn Djumaya internment camp in Bulgaria. Bulgarians and Greek-Orthodox collaborators occupied the Jewish homes, stores, and workshops. Valuables were sent away on trains, and the rest of the personal property of the Jews was sold in a public auction. All those deported were gassed in Treblinka. Only three Jews were left in 1948. There were no Jews in Serrai in the 1960s. The Jewish school was used as a Greek school, and Jewish tombs can be found in the old Jewish cemetery or in the municipal museum.

BIBLIOGRAPHY: M. Covo, *Aperçu historique sur la communauté israélite de Serrès* (1962). **ADD. BIBLIOGRAPHY:** B. Rivlin, "Serres," in *Pinkas Ha-Kehillot Yavan* (1999), 300–10.

[Simon Marcus / Yitzchak Kerem (2nd ed.)]

SERRES, village in the Hautes-Alpes department, S.E. France. The presence of Jews was confirmed there, as in the neighboring localities of Dauphiné (such as Aspres-sur-Buëch and Veynes), from at least 1315. The rapid growth of the community can be surmised from the increase in the taxes it paid: 100 gold sous in 1321, six livres in 1322, and 80 livres in 1324. Although 93 Jews of Veynes lost their lives in the *Black Death persecutions in 1348, those of Serres do not appear to have been molested. The epitaph of a certain R. Joseph, son of R. Nathan, was found to the west of the village, on a site where the ancient land registers place the Jewish cemetery. Jews were last mentioned in Serres toward the close of the 15th century.

BIBLIOGRAPHY: Elgy (= L. Jaques), in: *Bulletin de la Société d'Etudes Historiques, Scientifiques, Artistiques et Littéraires des Hautes-Alpes*, no. 50 (1958), 186–9; J. Imbert, *Histoire de Serres* (1966), 45–48; Gross, Gal Jud, 650.

[Bernhard Blumenkranz]

SERUSI, family of diplomats in Tripolitania (*Libya) in the 17th, 18th, and 19th centuries. In 1683 NISSIM negotiated between Tripolitania and France. In the second half of the 18th century MOSES was an agent and an interpreter for the French. ABRAHAM (I) was given temporary charge of the French consulate in Tripoli during *Napoleon's invasion of *Egypt in 1799 and later efficiently served Yusuf Pasha, the bey of *Tripoli. The Serusi family were also leaders of the Jewish community. ABRAHAM (II) and ḤAI were among the signatories of the tax requirement for producers of a certain type of silk in 1848. DAVID was vice consul of *Italy in *Mogador in about 1900.

BIBLIOGRAPHY: Hirschberg, Afrikah, 2 (1966), 194–9.

SERUYA, Moroccan family. The first known member was R. ISAAC ṢERUYA, a signatory in 1494 to the first *takkanah* of the Spanish expellees in *Fez. The Ṣeruyas, who engaged in maritime trade, were established in *Sale-Rabat. When the sultan Moulay Yazīd seized power in 1790 and persecuted the Jews, they settled in Gibraltar. SOLOMON was a wealthy merchant as well as a pious scholar who contributed to the publication of Hebrew works, including R. Pethahiah Berdugo's *Rosh Mashbir*; it was published in Leghorn in 1840 by Samuel *Levy-Yuly, a former *dayyan* of Gibraltar. JACOB, a wealthy merchant, established himself in Rabat in 1839, where he was appointed consular agent of Great Britain, Spain, the United States, and Portugal. He returned to Gibraltar in 1847 after he had some disputes with the Moroccan government. SOLOMON (1926–), was Gibraltar's minister of ports and tourism (1959–64) and minister of economic development (1965–69).

BIBLIOGRAPHY: J.M. Toledano, *Ner ha-Ma'arav* (1911), 78; Miège, Maroc, 2 (1961), 243, 251, 333.

[David Corcos]

SERVANT OF THE LORD (Heb. עֶבֶד ה'), the technical term used to designate the Servant mentioned explicitly or implicitly by Deutero-*Isaiah. In 1892 B. Duhm first published his commentary on Isaiah in which he separated four Servant songs from the rest of Deutero-Isaiah and contended that they were not the work of that prophet. From that time both Jewish and Christian exegetes have proposed many candidates to bear the title of the "Servant of the Lord." These interpretations may be divided into two basic categories: collective and individual. Collective interpretations have included collective Israel, ideal Israel, empirical Israel, pious remnant of Israel, prophets, priests, or a selective combination of the above. Individuals who have been suggested to have been the actual Servant or to have served as the prototype for the depiction of the Servant have ranged from Deutero-Isaiah, Trito-Isaiah, and Cyrus to Hezekiah, Jehoiachin, Josiah, Uzziah, Meshullam, Ezekiel, Sheshbazzar, Eleazar, Moses, Job, or an anonymous contemporary of Deutero-Isaiah. Most of these suggestions have no followers today. Other theories have suggested that the personality is corporate, messianic, or mythological. Christian tradition identified the Suffering Servant with Jesus. The pericopes of the Servant songs themselves, first identified as Isaiah 42:1–4; 49:1–6; 50:4–9; 52:13–53:12, are also subject to scholarly question, with many commentators adding verses to the first two sections and others including additional passages from Deutero-Isaiah as parts of songs. Particularly subject to debate are the questions whether the portrait of Servant is consistent throughout, whether or not the Servant described in chapter 53 died, and what was the actual mission or missions of the Servant.

BIBLIOGRAPHY: BIBLE: H.H. Rowley, *The Servant of the Lord....* (1965^2), 3–60; C.R. North, *The Suffering Servant in Deutero-Isaiah* (1956^2); H.M. Orlinsky, in: VTS, 14 (1967), 1–133; Y. Kaufmann, *The Babylonian Captivity and Deutero-Isaiah* (1970), 128–62. CLASSICAL JEWISH INTERPRETATIONS: A. Neubauer and S.R. Driver, *The Fifty-Third Chapter of Isaiah According to Jewish Interpreters*, 1–2 (1969).

[Shalom M. Paul]

SERVI, FLAMINIO (Ephraim; 1841–1904), Italian rabbi and publicist. Servi, born in Pitigliano, studied at the Collegio Rabbinico and the University of Padua, serving as rabbi in the northwestern communities of Monticelli, Mondovi, and from 1872 Casale Monferrato. In 1874 he founded the monthly *Il Vessilo Israelitico* as a successor to *Educatore Israelitica*; his son FERRUCCIO continued to edit it after his death until 1922. Servi favored the assimilation of Jews into Italian culture and society while remaining loyal to Jewish faith and observance. He was active in promoting a unified organization for Italian Jewry and in relief for the persecuted Jews of East Europe and North Africa. In addition to numerous articles in the Italian Jewish press dealing with the history of Italian Jewish communities and other subjects, he published *Gli Israeliti d'Europa nella civiltá* (1871).

BIBLIOGRAPHY: Milano, Bibliotheca, nos. 1417–30; Milano, Italia, 374; *Vessillo Israelitico*, 52 (1904), 49–58.

[Daniel Carpi]

SERVI CAMERAE REGIS (Lat. "servants of the royal chamber"), definition of the status of the Jews in Christian Europe in the Middle Ages, first used in the 13th century. The *Kammerknechtschaft*, as it was termed in German, was explained in the Holy Roman Empire (in effect Germany) as a consequence of the enslavement of the Jewish people to the Roman emperors Vespasian and Titus after their defeat in the war of 66–70 C.E.; other rulers inevitably claimed the same right. In fact, however, the term implied not only an inferiority of status but also royal and imperial protection. The status of the Jews was above that of the serfs, and theoretically they were subject only to royal authority. The ruler had the right to tax them for the benefit of his treasury (*camera regis*), but at the same time he had a duty to protect them when they were in danger from others. The so-called "Laws of Edward the Confessor" (England, 12th century) defined the status implied in the phrase in the clearest terms:

> All Jews, wherever in the realm they are, must be under the king's liege protection and guardianship, nor can any of them put himself under the protection of any powerful person without the king's license, because the Jews themselves and all their chattels are the king's. If, therefore, anyone detain them or their money, the king may claim them, if he so desire and if he is able, as his own.

The phrase *servi camerae regis* was not used after the Middle Ages, but the conception powerfully affected the status of the Jews down to modern times.

BIBLIOGRAPHY: Baron, Social², 9 (1965), 135–92, 308–31; idem, in: *Sefer Yovel le-Y. Baer* (1961), 102–24; Kisch, Germany, index, s.v. *Chamber Serfdom of Jews*; H.H. Ben-Sasson, *Toledot Am Yisrael*, 2 (1969), 99–102; S. Grayzel, *Church and the Jews in the xiiith Century* (1966²), index; 359–64.

[Cecil Roth]

SERVITUDES (Heb. שִׁעְבּוּדִים, *shi'budim*). Generally a person is prohibited from using his land in such manner as to cause an interference with his neighbor's quiet use or enjoyment of his own land. A man may therefore restrain his neighbor from such use and compel him to remove the cause of the disturbance. However, this right is not always available and the use of land in certain ways – even if disturbing to the neighbor – must sometimes be suffered by him (see *Nuisance). A person may agree with his neighbor to refrain from a particular use of his land, injurious to the latter, even if permitted by law; or to use his land in a manner injurious to his neighbor, even if such use is not permitted by law. In such event a proprietary right over the land is respectively granted to and extracted from the adjoining landowners. This right, called a *shi'bud* in the codes, is comparable to an "easement" in English law and serves to encumber land in favor of an adjacent owner, without the land being in the latter's possession.

Halakhic sources mention two categories of servitudes of this nature:

(1) use of land, which, without involving the use or employment of neighboring land, causes injury to the neighbor, such as the emanation of noise, smoke, noxious odors, moisture, and so on, to the adjacent land, or when the latter is made to vibrate, or when the crops thereon are damaged;

(2) an act which involves an encroachment on and the use or enjoyment of neighboring land, such as erecting projecting brackets on which chattels can be hung, affixing beams onto a neighboring wall, diverting the flow of rainwater onto a neighboring courtyard, or placing a ladder on neighboring premises in order to reach one's own roof (*Sma*, ḤM 153:16 and *Netivot ha-Mishpat, Mishpat ha-Kohanim, ibid.*). These servitudes are distinct in two ways; firstly the encumbered land is not in the possession of the rightholder, and secondly, they may be exploited only by the use of the adjoining land. Hence it may be said that the servitude is one of land to neighboring land. The right may be acquired for a specific period or for good.

The term *Shi'budim* also has a wider meaning including all rights in the property of another (*jura in re aliena*). These include rights which are not specifically tied to the use of or encroachment on neighboring land and which may extend to both movable and immovable property, whether or not the rightholder is in possession of the encumbered property. Such *Shi'budim* are rights to use and enjoyment of the property itself and are a kind of limited form of ownership in the encumbered property, being a kind of *kinyan perot* and not a servitude only (usufruct; see *Ownership). These property rights are governed by laws which are entirely different from those applicable to the above-mentioned servitudes (easements). Instances thereof are: the acquisition of "a tree for its fruit, a dwelling for its occupation, sheep for its wool, a dovecote for the doves that will hatch therein, a hive for the honey that will accumulate there, an animal for its young, a slave for his handwork" (Maim. Yad, Mekhirah, 22:14; 23:2). These rights are a form of *kinyan perot* (usufruct), i.e., acquisition of the right to enjoy the use of the property itself (Maim., *ibid.*, 23:1). After *kinyan perot*, the most important servitude of this class is the right of way over the servient land (BB 99b), whether a private path or public road. It is considered a propriety right in the land and not an encumbrance (see Resp. Rashba, cited in

Beit Yosef; ḤM 153, no. 8; cf. his Nov. BB 23a, 28b). The Talmud discusses the applicable laws in detail – including such matters as the measure of the width of private and public roads, the respective rights of the parties, the modes of acquisition, and the circumstances in which the landowner may change the route of a public road passing over his field.

Easements are acquired in the same way as other legal rights, i.e., by an act of *kinyan* (see Modes of *Acquisition). In the opinion of the *geonim* and the scholars of Spain (Nov. Ramban, BB 59a; ḤM 155:35), they may also be acquired in a tacit manner, by the adverse use of the servient land without protest from its owner, who is aware of such use; but other proprietary rights mentioned above can be acquired in express manner only, like the acquisition of ownership (Nov. Rashba, BB 23a, 28b). The scholars of France differ, holding that all servitudes must be expressly acquired (*Maggid Mishneh*, to Yad, Shekhenim, 11:4; Tur, ḤM 154). Consequently, a servitude exercised for three years, accompanied by the holder's plea that it was acquired from the neighbor, is evidence of title, as in the case of a plea of ownership to land. Other scholars are of the opinion that a servitude may be acquired by exercise of the right for a period of three years, without the need for any such plea (Tos. to BB 23a; s.v. והא; see also *Ḥazakah*). All the scholars agree that easements of a particularly onerous nature are not customarily agreed to in a tacit manner and therefore have to be expressly acquired by purchase or gift with an accompanying *kinyan*. Instances thereof are the encroachment of smoke, noxious odors, etc. onto neighboring land, even if existing for a number of years (Sh. Ar., ḤM 155:36). Some scholars are of the opinion that such servitudes, even when expressly consented to and assigned by way of sale or gift, cannot be validly acquired, and the assigner may withdraw his consent on a plea of mistaken *kinyan*, i.e., the mistaken belief that he would be able to bear the relevant harm (Tos. to BB 23a). Many of the *posekim* are of the opinion that insufferable harm in this context includes any interference with the neighbor's person, but not mere interference with his use of his property (Nov. Ramban, *ibid.* 59a). Easements are terminated in the same manner in which they are created. Thus the obligation may be extinguished if the servient owner repurchases the servitude, or if the dominant owner has ceased to exploit the servitude in a manner indicating his abandonment and waiver of its use, when it cannot be revived by renewed use (Resp. Rashba, vol. 1, no. 1133).

In the State of Israel, servitudes are governed by an original Israel law, the Land Law, 1969, which recognizes all kinds of *jura in re aliena*. Most of them can be acquired, in addition to the usual modes of acquisition, also by prescriptive use followed by registration in the Land Registry.

BIBLIOGRAPHY: M. Bloch, *Das mosaisch-talmudische Besitzrecht* (1897), 49–59; Gulak, Yesodei, 1 (1922), 134, 141f., 146–8; Herzog, Instit, 1 (1936), 365–70; ET, 7 (1956), 664–7; 10 (1961), 628–96; Z. Warhaftig, *Ha-Ḥazakah ba-Mishpat ha-Ivri* (1964), 241–60. **ADD. BIBLIOGRAPHY:** M. Elon and B. Lifshitz, *Mafte'aḥ ha-She'elot ve-ha-Teshuvot shel Ḥakhmei Sefarad u-Ẓefon Afrikah* (legal digest) (1986), 78; B. Lifshitz and E. Shohetman, *Mafte'aḥ ha-She'elot ve-ha-Teshuvot shel Ḥakhmei Ashkenaz, Ẓarefat ve-Italyah* (legal digest) (1997), 51.

[Shalom Albeck]

°SESSA, KARL BORROMAEUS ALEXANDER (1786–1813), Breslau physician and antisemitic author. His first dramatic effort, *Unser Verkehr*, a crude farce ridiculing post-emancipation Jewry, achieved instant and widespread success.

The play was first presented in 1813 and published in 1815 (Breslau). It portrays a shabby young Jewish peddler who entertains ambitions of developing his artistic talents and thus make his way into society. Through an error he finds brief acceptance by a ludicrous nouveau riche Jewish banking family. The play was widely performed in rural southern Germany (it was banned in Austria, Saxony, and Berlin) and inspired numerous imitations. Both the original work and its imitators expressed the resentment and opposition of the population to the emancipation and to the new breed of Jewish "upstarts," which was also the excuse for the *Hep! Hep! disturbances in 1819.

BIBLIOGRAPHY: L. Geiger, in: AZDJ, 67 (1903), 78–81; V. Eichstaedt, *Bibliographie zur Geschichte der Judenfrage* (1938), 57–9; E. Sterling, in: HJ, 12 (1950), 115; K. Goedeke, *Grundriss zur Geschichte der deutschen Dichtung*, 11 pt. 1 (1951), 435–8; E. Frenzel, *Judengestalten auf der deutschen Buehne* (1940), index.

SESSO, SALAMONE DA (c. 1465), Italian armorer, born at Sesso, northern Italy. He was baptized on entering the service of Ercole d'Este, duke of Ferrara, with whom he remained, and was thenceforth known as Ercole "dei Fideli." Da Sesso also worked for the marquess of Mantua and Pope Julius II. He specialized in the manufacture of elaborate swords and daggers adorned with pagan scenes, classical symbols, and nude figures. His most famous weapon was executed for Cesare Borgia and is known as the "Queen of Swords."

SETER, MORDECAI (Marc Starominsky; 1916–1994), Israeli composer. Seter was born in Novorossiysk (Russia) and immigrated to Ereẓ Israel in 1926. In 1932, he studied in Paris with Paul Dukas and Nadia Boulanger and graduated in 1937 from the Ecole Normale de Musique, returning to Ereẓ Israel the same year. In Tel Aviv he taught harmony, form, and counterpoint over the following five decades. In 1951, he joined the faculty of the Israel Conservatory (later renamed the Rubin Academy), Tel Aviv. In 1972 he became a full professor at Tel Aviv University and taught there until his retirement in 1985.

In 1937, composer Joachim *Stutschewsky lent him a volume of *Idelsohn's *Thesaurus* (*Hebräisch-orientalischer Melodienschatz* (Sephardi Jewish tunes), which inspired him and became a source of melodies for his first acclaimed composition *Sabbath Cantata* (choir and orchestra, 1940). Idelsohn's book and his own research into traditional Middle Eastern Jewish tunes, forming his collection *Niggunim*, served as a springboard to Seter's first period of composition in the 1940s, including *Motets* (1940) and *Festive Songs* (1943–49).

Seter's second period, in the 1950s, focused on chamber music. His *Ricercar* (for violin, viola, cello, and string orchestra; string quartet version, 1953–56, both a triple fugue and a variation form) won the International Rostrum of Composers Prize (UNESCO, Paris, 1961). *Ricercar* was also staged as a ballet by the Batsheva Dance Company, the American Ballet Theatre, and the Ballet Rambert. In his third period, which began in the late 1950s, Seter turned to orchestral music. His first orchestral works were *Sinfonietta* (1957) and *Variations* (1960, Israel Philharmonic Orchestra commission).

His signature work, *Midnight Vigil* (1957–61), was written first as a small ballet, commissioned by choreographer Sarah *Levi-Tanai for her Inbal Dance Theater. It was based partly on Yemenite tunes portraying a kabbalistic vision of redemption in Zion. Its fourth version, a 31-minute radiophonic oratorio, won him (with the librettist Mordechai Tabib) the Prix Italia; and the fifth and final version, a 43-minute oratorio for soloist, three choirs and orchestra, brought him the Israel Prize. All versions of *Tikkun Ḥaẓot*, as most of Seter's orchestral works, were premiered by conductor Gary *Bertini, who was one of Seter's composition pupils in the late 1940s. In the early 1960s, American choreographer Martha Graham commissioned Seter to write two ballets: *Judith* and *Part Real Part Dream* (*Fantasia Concertante*). A third ballet, *Jephtah's Daughter*, was commissioned for the Batsheva Dance Company. His last major symphonic-choral work was *Jerusalem* (1966).

Following the national and international successes of the 1960s, Seter surprisingly began refusing any more commissions, reduced his contact with performers, rejected institutional positions and began to write introverted and original chamber music, both in terms of style and technique. From 1970 until his last work in 1987, he wrote approximately half of his oeuvre – mostly unknown works today: 46 paradigmatic late-style compositions, roughly half for the piano and half for small chamber ensembles. Most of these works are based on his own modes (comparable to both Stravinsky's series for his late works and Messiaen's modes), ranging over 12–25 diatonic notes for each mode. His modes create unity and coherence in terms of melody, counterpoint, and harmony, but his notation, rhythms, and forms remain rather conservative. Among his late works are the set *Chamber Music 1970* (including *Intimo, Epigrams, Automn, Requiem*), *Concertante* (piano quartet no. 1, 1973–81), *Events* (1974), and four string quartets (1975–1977). Notable among his works of the 1980s are his *Piano Quartet No. 2* (1982), *Violin and Piano* (1985), and his piano works *Sonata* (1982), *Dialogues* (1983), *Opposites Unified* (1984), and *Presence* (1986), all premiered by Ora Rotem, who recorded two CDs of his piano works of the 1980s, issued before the composer's death.

Seter was perceived as a composer with a highly individual style. He considered renaissance and baroque forms, such as the toccata, motet, cantata, chaconne, and passacaglia, as optimal for the coveted East-West synthesis, believing that these forms could potentially be compatible with the Oriental concept of music. His techniques and style attracted composers to study his work, especially his peers Partos and Boskovich as well as composers of the second generation (*Sheriff, *Orgad, and *Braun). His special status among the founders of Israeli music was symbolically cemented during the Israel Philharmonic Orchestra's millennium concert, programming Seter's *Midnight Vigil* along with Bach's B Minor Mass and Beethoven's Ninth.

BIBLIOGRAPHY: NG and Grove Music Online; P. Landau, *Mordecai Seter* (1995), a 24-page booklet, including a short biography, work list, bibliography, and discography; R. Fleisher, *Twenty Israeli Composers* (1997), 108–19; R. Seter, "Yuvalim be-Israel: Nationalism in Jewish-Israeli Art Music, 1940–2000" (Ph.D. dissertation, Cornell University, 2004), 249–339.

[Ronit Seter (2nd ed.)]

SETH (Heb. שֵׁת), antediluvian patriarch, son of Adam and Eve. The Bible has preserved two different traditions regarding Seth. In one Seth is the third son of Adam and Eve, born to them after the murder of Abel (Gen. 4:25 (J)). His name is said to derive from the fact that God "provided" (*shat*) another son to replace Abel. In the genealogy of Adam, however, Cain and Abel are not mentioned, the implication being according to some exegetes that Seth was Adam's first son (5:3 (P); cf. I Chron. 1:1). This source also furnishes the information that Seth lived to the age of 912 years and that his eldest son was Enosh, who was born when Seth was 105 (Gen. 5:6–8).

In the Aggadah

Seth was born circumcised (ARN^2; Mid. Ps. 9:7), and he inherited the garments which God Himself had made for Adam (Num. R. 4:8). His nature is reflected in the fact that "the generations of man" end with Seth and his son, Enosh (Gen. 4:26). They were the last human beings to be created solely in the image of God; after their death centaurs began to appear (Gen. R. 23:6). Seth is also associated with the messianic era. The future generations of the righteous will be the descendants of Seth (PdRE 22), who will himself be one of the "seven shepherds" counseling the Messiah after the resurrection of the dead (cf. Micah 5:4; Suk. 52b).

In Islam

Seth (Arabic *Shith*) is not mentioned in the *Koran, but he does appear in post-Koranic literature, where the meaning of the name is given as "a present from Allah" (cf. Gen. 4:25). All the survivors of the Flood are his descendants and as a result all the Arab genealogists trace the descent of mankind from him.

BIBLIOGRAPHY: See Commentaries to Genesis, ch. 5. IN THE AGGADAH: Ginzberg, Legends, index; I. Ḥasida, *Ishei ha-Tanakh* (1964), 429–30.

[HaÏm Z' ew Hirschberg]

SETI I (**Menma ʿrē-Sety**; c. 1303–1290 B.C.E.), Egyptian pharaoh. The second ruler of his line, Seti may be regarded as the real founder of the Nineteenth Dynasty (c. 1304–1195 B.C.E.). Under his direction Egypt reasserted her control over Palestine, the Lebanon region, and southern Syria, which had been lost in the chaotic years of the later Amarna period. The new Egyptian Asiatic empire which he founded, unlike the earlier one (which in fact was no more than a "sphere of influence"), was based upon the permanent military occupation of these regions. In addition to his many monuments in the north of Egypt, a small temple which he built near Timna in the Arabah was discovered in 1969 at the site erroneously believed to have been King Solomon's Mines.

BIBLIOGRAPHY: R.O. Faulkner, in: *Journal of Egyptian Archaeology*, 33 (1947), 34–9; idem, in: CAH^2, vol. 2 (1966), 23:4–10; A.H. Gardiner, *Egypt of the Pharaohs* (1961), 247–55.

[Alan Richard Schulman]

SETTLEMENT HOUSES. Founded in Europe, North America, and Asia in response to the urban poverty that accompanied industrialization and immigration, the Settlement House movement originated with Toynbee Hall, in London's East End in 1884. Distressed by working class conditions in urban slums, a group of college-educated men and women "settled" into a house among the poor. They hoped to bridge the gap between classes as they gathered data on the impact of poverty and experimented with progressive social programs.

The American Settlement House movement was begun by Stanton Coit, an adherent of the *Ethical Culture Movement, who founded the Neighborhood Guild (later the University Settlement) on Manhattan's Lower East Side in 1886. Three years later, Jane Addams founded Hull House in Chicago. Addams drew other women into the movement, and they formed a strong political network of female reformers who became involved with local, national, and international campaigns for public health and welfare. By 1910, over 400 U.S. Settlement Houses, funded by philanthropists, and often drawing on the Protestant social gospel of good works, offered medical and social welfare programs as well as education and recreation. The majority of American Settlements were staffed by educated women whose efforts lead to social welfare legislation and the professionalization of social work.

The Settlement House movement coincided with the mass emigration of East European Jews and Jews took active roles in all aspects of the Settlement movement, as donors, administrators, resident staff members, and clients. Lillian *Wald one of the few Jews in the early American Settlement movement, directed the Henry Street Settlement in Manhattan from 1893 to 1933. Her funding came largely from Jewish philanthropists, principally Jacob H. *Schiff, and her clientele was largely Jewish immigrants. However, Wald was criticized over the lack of Jewish content in her institutional offerings. In response to this perceived weakness, as well as in reaction to occasional Christian missionary work among Jewish immigrants, middle-class Jews in cities throughout the U.S. and Europe founded specifically Jewish Settlement Houses. In the U.S., these Settlements often grew out of Jewish women's organizations, especially the *National Council for Jewish Women, which aimed to aid and "Americanize" working-class immigrant women and their children. Staff members set up playgrounds and kindergartens, offered classes in art and theater, and established domestic science training programs. Tensions based in differences in social class, political orientations, and religious practice often proved particularly poignant in these institutions, especially in debates between workers and clients on the use of Yiddish and support for Zionism.

The most prominent U.S. Jewish Settlement was the Educational Alliance, founded by Jewish philanthropists in Manhattan in 1889. The Alliance successfully addressed various social problems for those living in the tenements of Manhattan's Lower East Side. While all Settlement Houses tried to "make Americans" out of immigrants, adhering largely to an Anglo-Protestant model, the Alliance tried to "make" American Jews, in line with the tenets of assimilated Reform Judaism. As first-generation East European immigrants came of age in the 1920s, they took leadership positions and changed the culture of Settlement Houses to be more accepting of Yiddish and of Jewish particularisms generally. Countless memoirs attest to early 20th-century Settlements providing Jewish immigrants with their first exposure to a world beyond their immigrant and Orthodox Jewish enclaves. These immigrants chose from the offerings of Settlement Houses and integrated into the American mainstream on their own terms. Serving as Settlement administrators and staff members, hundreds of Jews, especially Jewish women, gained practical and professional training and experience. Many went on to lead social welfare policy initiatives in private and public agencies.

By the 1920s, Settlements overall were in decline. In America, this was due to the reduction in immigration and the targeting of progressive social workers during the Red Scare. In addition, Jewish Settlement Houses contended with changing urban populations, as Jews moved increasingly beyond initial areas of settlement. Some Settlements moved with these populations and became community centers; others, like the Alliance, stayed to offer programs to a new population of (largely non-Jewish) urban dwellers.

BIBLIOGRAPHY: M. Carson, *Settlement Folk: Social Thought and the American Settlement Movement, 1885–1930* (1990); M.N. Feld, "Lillian D. Wald and Mutuality in Twentieth-Century America" (Brandeis University Ph.D. dissertation, 2002); E. Rose, "From Sponge Cake to *Hamentashen*: Jewish Identity in a Jewish Settlement House, 1885–1952," in: *Journal of American Ethnic History*, 13 (1994), 3–23; A. Schwartz, "Americanization and Cultural Preservation in Seattle's Settlement House," in: *Journal of Sociology and Social Welfare*, 26 (1999), 25–45.

[Marjorie N. Feld (2nd ed.)]

SETUBAL, port in S. central Portugal; third largest city of continental Portugal. During the reign of John III (1521–57), Setubal became an important crypto-Jewish center as a result of the activities of the so-called Messiah of Setubal, Luis *Dias. Although poor and uneducated, Dias won the devotion of numerous *Marranos and even Christians. Unlike those of the remote districts, Setubal's Marrano community had become extinct by the 20th century (see *Portugal). A dozen Jewish families settled in Setubal after the liberal realignment of 1910.

BIBLIOGRAPHY: Roth, Marranos, 146–8 (bibl.); R. Southey, *Letters Written During a Short Residence in Spain and Portugal* (1799), 320–50; A. Mendes, *O Algarve e Setubal* (1916).

[Aaron Lichtenstein]

SE'UDAH (Heb. סְעוּדָה var. סְעֻדָה; "meal" or "banquet"; in Yiddish pronounced *sude*), a festive meal. Eating and drinking are considered as pious and sanctifying acts if their purpose is to keep physically fit and healthy and if the prescribed laws and customs are observed. Among these are the washing of hands before a meal at which bread is consumed (see *Ablution); pronouncing the appropriate benedictions over the different foods served at the meal; the recital of *Grace after Meals (Deut. 8:10) or of a shorter benediction (*berakhah aḥaronah*). The religious quality of a meal should be enhanced by being abstemious and avoiding gluttony, and especially by discoursing on the Torah at table. Persons engaging in discussion of Torah during the meal "are as though they had eaten of the table of God"; those who did not, "are as though they had eaten of sacrifices of the dead" (Avot 3:3). The Talmud describes in detail the various customs and good manners to be observed at meals, either when eating in private or in company. They include rules concerning the invitation and seating of guests, the mixing of the wine, the serving of the dishes, etc. (Ber. 7; TJ, Ber. 6:6, 10c–d; Tosef., Ber 4–7; DER 6–9, DEZ 5).

Etiquette demanded that a glass of beverage should not be drunk in one draught (Beẓah 25b); all food, especially *bread, be treated with reverence (Ber. 50b); a person refrain from talking while eating lest the food should go down the wrong way and cause him to suffocate (Ta'an. 5b). Proper chewing of food was advised for good health (Shab. 152a), and the custom of lengthening the dinner was regarded as leading to longevity (Ber. 54b). Eating was strictly to be done in the home, and a person eating in the street was compared to a dog (Kid. 40b).

Babylonian Jews followed the dining customs of the Persians, and wealthy Palestinian Jews those of the Romans. They, too, indulged in sumptuous and boisterous banquets (Philo, Cont. 5–7; Wisd. 2:7–9; et al.), causing rabbis in the Talmud to warn against gluttony (Ḥul. 84a; Avot 2:8, "more flesh, more worms"). They regarded the table as a substitute for the holy altar in the Temple (Ber. 54b–55a), and taught man that he could atone for his sins by inviting the poor to eat with him. As at the altar (Lev. 2:13), there must always be salt on the table (Isserles to Sh. Ar., OḤ 167:5). The master of the house, who himself served the guests, was lauded for imitating the Patriarch Abraham who had himself waited on the three angels (Gen. 18:7–9) and Moses who had waited on the elders of the people (Mekh., Amalek, 3–end). The Talmud discusses whether the master of the house is permitted to renounce the honor otherwise due to him by serving his guests personally. The *nasi* R. Gamaliel, at his son's wedding, served R. Joshua and R. Eliezer; the latter refused to be served by a *nasi* but R. Joshua, however, did not object, stating that R. Gamaliel followed in the footsteps of the Patriarch Abraham (Kid. 32b; Mekh. *ibid.*). According to the Talmud, breakfast should be eaten between the fourth and the sixth hour after sunrise (Pes. 12b). Two meals a day, one in the morning and one in the evening, were regarded as sufficient except on the Sabbath, when a third meal was eaten in honor of the day (see **Se'udah Shelishit*). The main meal was to include meat and should be eaten in the evening, as was counseled by Moses (Yoma 75b).

The Talmud distinguished between two categories of festive meals: (1) feasts of a nonreligious nature, *se'udah shel reshut*, at which students and scholars are advised not to participate (Pes. 49a); and (2) *se'udah shel mitzvah*, banquets held in connection with religious acts, such as weddings, circumcisions, etc., participation in which is regarded as a religious duty. To the latter category belong: (1) the three meals a person is obliged to eat every Sabbath (Shab. 117b) and at which it is customary to sing religious hymns (**zemirot*). The third, taking place on Sabbath afternoon, called *se'udah shelishit*, was invested with importance in *Kabbalism and *Ḥasidism (see Zohar, Ex. 88b); (2) *se'udat *melavveh malkah*, the meal held after the departure of the Sabbath; (3) meals on the holidays and festivals (Sh. Ar., OḤ 529:1); (4) the *Passover meal at the *seder* (Mishnah, Pes. 10); (5) the *Purim dinner (Esth. 9:18; Sh. Ar., OḤ 695:1–2); (6) *se'udah mafseket* (Ber. 8b; Sh. Ar., OḤ 604:1), the meal before the fast of the *Day of Atonement; (7) the Rosh Ḥodesh meal which originated in biblical times (I Sam. 20:24), and was later observed in commemoration of the banquet arranged by the *Sanhedrin after they proclaimed the New Moon (RH 2:5; Sof. 19:9). It was a widespread custom until modern times (Sh. Ar., OḤ 419); (8) the festive meal on *Simḥat Torah, arranged by the "Bridegroom of the Torah" (*ḥatan Torah*; Isserles to Sh. Ar., OḤ 669); (9) the festive banquet on the occasion of completing the study of a Talmud tractate; this occasion called **siyyum* originated in the times of the Babylonian talmudic academies (Shab. 118b–119a; Isserles to Sh. Ar., YD 246:26); (10) the *se'udat siyyum* of which the firstborn partakes on the morning of the eve of Passover. Participation at the *se'udah* supersedes the firstborn fast. The banquet is sometimes called *se'udat bekhorot*; (11) the festive banquet of the burial brotherhood (**ḥevra kaddisha*) on *Adar the Seventh (or in some places on Lag *ba-Omer).

The following banquets at joyous family events are also regarded as *se'udah shel mitzvah* and to participate at them is a meritorious act: (1) the *circumcision banquet (already mentioned in the Talmud (TJ, Ḥag, 2:1, 77b; also PdRE 29), and in the Shulḥan Arukh (YD 265:12) as well as the meals at the vigil ceremony after the birth of a boy and on Sabbath eve prior to his circumcision, called by different names; *shavu'a ha-ben, sholem zokher*, etc. (see *Childbirth Laws and Customs); (2) the meal at a *pidyon ha-ben*, the ceremony of the redemption of the firstborn (Isserles to Sh. Ar., YD 305:10); (3) the festive meal on the occasion of a *bar mitzvah (Gen. R. 53:10); (4) betrothal and wedding meals (*se'udat erusin* and *se'udat nissu'in* or *hillula*; Ket. 8a; Ber. 31a) which in ancient times lasted for seven days (Judg. 14:17) and for which a three-days' preparation was deemed necessary in the time of the Talmud (Ket. 2a); (5) the meal on the occasion of the consecration of a new home (*se'udat ḥanukkat ha-bayit*; Tanh. Bereshit, 2); (6) in many communities, it was also customary to arrange a meal on the occasion when a child started his first Bible lesson, called in Eastern Europe (in Yiddish) *khumesh mahl*; (7) *se'udat havra'ah*, "the meal of comfort" by which mourners are comforted and sustained right after the burial. This custom of consolation dates back to biblical times (II Sam. 3:35; Jer. 16:7) and became a religious duty in talmudic times (Ket. 8b; MK 26b–27b; Sof. 19:12. See also Maim. Yad., Evel, 13:8; Sh. Ar., YD 378).

Aggadic literature makes reference to the *se'udat livyatan*, the eschatological banquet at which God will entertain the righteous in the world-to-come, serving them the meat of the *Leviathan and wine stored since the creation of the world (*yayin ha-meshummar*; BB 74b–75a; see also: Jellinek, *Beit ha-Midrash*, 6 (1938²) 150–1).

BIBLIOGRAPHY: Eisenstein, Dinim, 294–5; Ḥ.N. Bialik and Y. Rawnitzki, *Sefer ha-Aggadah* (1952⁴), 460–4; Sh. Ar., OḤ, 157–212.

[Meir Ydit]

SE'UDAH SHELISHIT (Heb. סְעוּדָה שְׁלִישִׁית; "third meal"), name for the third meal eaten on the Sabbath. The eating of three meals on the Sabbath is considered by the rabbis as a positive commandment based on the repetition of the word "today" in Exodus 16:25: "Eat that [the manna] today, for today is a Sabbath unto the Lord; today ye shall not find it in the field" (Shab. 117b–118a). This commandment is also binding upon women (Sh. Ar., OḤ 291:6). The *se'udah shelishit* is the only Sabbath meal at which *Kiddush is not recited (Tur. OḤ 291), although two loaves are still placed on the table (Sh. Ar, *ibid.*). This meal, eaten in the afternoon of the Sabbath day, must not commence prior to the time for the beginning of the *Minḥah* prayer (Sh. Ar., OḤ 291:2). Ḥasidim especially developed the custom of spending hours at the table listening to their *rebbe*, singing special hymns and wordless melodies. It became customary to chant *zemirot* and Psalm 23 at this meal.

SEVARAH, the legal logic employed by halakhic scholars in their reasoning. This logic is founded on observation of the characteristics of human beings as they are disclosed in their social relations with one another and on a study of the practical realities of daily life. *Sevarah* may serve both as a historical source of law – a source which factually and indirectly leads to the creation of a particular legal rule – and as a legal source of law – a source recognized by the particular legal system as a direct means for the acceptance of a legal rule into that system. (On the different sources of law, see **Mishpat Ivri*.) Logic may also serve as a historical source in the functioning of the other legal sources of Jewish law. Thus, for instance, when a particular legal rule is created by means of the legal source of Midrash (see *Interpretation), the interpretative activity constitutes the direct creative source of that rule; however, the interpreter is guided along his interpretative path by logic and reasoning, which therefore form the historical-factual source of the rule. The same is true of rules created by means of legal sources of legislature, that is **takkanah*, **ma'aseh*, and **minhag*, where the rules are naturally created and fashioned as the outcome of certain needs as dictated by logic and practical exigencies. It is as a historical source in the aforementioned sense that *sevarah* is quoted as a basis for the study and understanding of the *halakhah* (see, e.g., Git. 6b; Shab. 63a; Suk. 29a, et al.). On the other hand, *sevarah* functions as a legal source whenever it serves as the direct source of a particular rule, that is whenever such rule is created by virtue of logic and reasoning alone, outside the framework of and without assistance from any other legal source such as *Midrash, minhag*, or *ma'aseh*.

An important place is assigned to *sevarah* as the creative source of halakhic norms in all fields of the *halakhah*, whether in relation to the precepts between man and his Maker or the laws pertaining to relations between man and his fellow man in matters of ritual law or civil law. The high regard in which *sevarah* was held also finds expression in the manner of the laws originating from this legal source. Thus a law having its creative source in *takkanah* or *minhag* is numbered among the category of laws known as *de-rabbanan* (see **Mishpat Ivri*), whereas a law having its direct source in *sevarah* is generally numbered among the category known as *de-oraita* (Chajes, in bibl., and see below). The honorable status thus lent a rule originating from *sevarah* is attributable to the fundamental principle which underlies the whole of the halakhic system, namely, that the Torah was given on the authority (*al da'at*) of the halakhic scholars (see *Authority, Rabbinical); hence every rule founded on the logical reasoning of the halakhic scholars originates, as it were, from the Torah itself, because the logic of the halakhic scholars corresponds with the logic embodied in the Torah.

Sevarah as the Creative Source of General Legal Principles

It is an important principle of Judaism that a person who is told to transgress or else suffer death should transgress rather than be killed (Sanh. 74a), since the laws of the Torah were given so that man should live by them and not die because of them (Yoma 85b; Yad, Yesodei ha-Torah 5:1). However, in three cases a person given the choice between transgression or death should choose the latter; idolatry, incest (including adultery), or murder (Sanh. 74a; Pes. 25a–b; et al.). As regards idolatry and incest the rule was established by way of biblical exegesis (Sanh. 74a), but with regard to murder the rule was derived logically, and not by way of exegesis, as follows: "The *sevarah* is… who shall say that your blood is redder? Perhaps the blood of the other is redder!" (Sanh. 74a); for "as far as the murderer is concerned, since in the end man is anyhow destined to die, why should it be permissible for him to transgress? Who knows that the Creator holds his life to be of greater worth than that of his fellow?" (*Rashi*, ad loc.). Thus the rule in regard to the shedding of blood a person should choose death rather than transgression has its legal source in *sevarah*.

There are a considerable number of general legal principles operating in the field of both ritual and civil law which similarly originate from the legal source of *sevarah*. The rule that the burden of proof is on the claimant is derived from logic on the reasoning that just as the person who has a pain seeks out a doctor and recites his symptoms (and it is not the doctor who runs around to find out who is ill), so too the person who has a claim against another must first bring proof to substantiate his claim, and the defendant need not first prove that he is not liable on such claim (BK 46b). So too a woman's statement that she was married and became divorced – there being no witnesses to the fact that she was married – is believed as regards her becoming divorced, in terms of the rule pertaining to the laws of evidence that "the mouth which has rendered prohibited is the mouth which has rendered permissible"; this rule is derived from the logical reasoning that since she prohibited her own self (to others) she may also permit her own self (Ket. 2:5; Ket. 22a; from this rule there was derived in amoraic times the rule of *miggo*; see *Pleas; *Evidence).

The two aforementioned rules are expressly stated as having their legal source in *sevarah*, and this also appears to be the case with reference to a number of further rules and principles, for instance as regards the principle of *ḥazakah* as a legal presumption – such as the presumption that a person is alive (Git. 3:3), the presumption of legal competence (*ḥezkat kashrut*; BB 31b), the presumption of bodily fitness (Ket. 7:8), and numerous other kinds of presumptions. Logic is also the source of the rule regarding reliance on the majority, even when the majority is not a factual one (such as a majority of the judges hearing a particular case), but is based on surmise alone [Ḥul. 11a; the biblical passages cited there with regard to several kinds of majority and *ḥazakah* are in the nature of **asmakhta* ("mere allusion") alone; see also *Interpretation]. These presumptions have validity in all fields of the *halakhah*, in matters of the civil law as well as matters of ritual prohibitions and permissions, and even in matters which are *de-oraita*: "For matters learned by way of *sevarah* are of the same value as the actual statements of the Torah itself… since the power of observation deriving from experience is of precisely the same value to them [the halakhic scholars] as a matter learned through application of the exegetical *middot*" (see *Interpretation; Chajes, in bibl., 118–30).

Sevarah in the Amoraic Period

A substantial proportion of the laws and principles deriving from *sevarah* are attributable to an early period of the *halakhah*. From talmudic sources it is also possible to conclude that the use of *sevarah* as a legal source of the *halakhah* was particularly resorted to during amoraic times – just as the *amoraim* laid down rational rules with regard to the use of other legal sources and the modes of studying the *halakhah* (see **Takkanot*; **Asmakhta*). Thus in regard to forbidden food and drink R. Johanan laid down that the taking of even half of the determined measure was also forbidden by the pentateuchal law – since one half-measure may combine with another half-measure to constitute a full measure, it follows that he will be eating that which is forbidden (Yoma 74a). The *amoraim* stated that in respect to various laws it may be said that they have their source either in a biblical passage or in *sevarah*, for instance as regards certain matters relating to the laws of evidence (Sanh. 30a), the laws of *ḥaliẓah* (Yev. 35b) and in other fields (see, e.g., Shevu. 22b and Tos. loc. cit.).

In other cases the *amoraim* searched for the legal source of a particular rule and came to the conclusion that such a rule had its origin in the legal source of *sevarah*. An interesting illustration of this is to be found in the discussions of the *amoraim* concerning the legal source of the rule that three years' possession of real property confers presumptive rights of ownership (i.e., upon a claim of lawful acquisition with subsequent loss of the title deed, but with possession for the said period without protest from the former owner; see **ḥazakah*). The *amoraim* confronted difficulties in attributing the source of the rule to Midrash (see *Interpretation) and to Kabbalah (see *Mishpat Ivri*) in turn, and then Rabba determined the legal source of the rule thus: "The first year a person guards his title deed and so he does the second and third years; thereafter he guards it no longer" (BB 28a–29a). That is to say, logic – which is founded on the observation of daily practical life – teaches that a person who purchases property takes care to guard his title deed for a period of three years as proof against any challenge to his right in such property; however, after three years have elapsed without any such challenge, he no longer sees need to guard the material evidence of his ownership since he is already sure that he is fully in possession of the property and does not contemplate the possibility that his right to it will any more be challenged. This *sevarah* was accepted as the legal source of the rule that three years' possession of property suffices to prove the possessor's acquisition thereof according to law, even when the latter cannot produce his title deed or any other proof (for additional substantiation of the rule, see *Ḥazakah).

Sevarah continued to be a creative legal source in the post-talmudic period. However, the halakhic literary sources of this period, unlike those of the talmudic period, do not generally specially emphasize the fact that certain rules have their source in *sevarah*, as is generally done in the case of *minhag*, *takkanah*, and other legal sources. Hence painstaking research is required in order to distinguish the post-talmudic halakhic literary principles which originate from *sevarah*.

BIBLIOGRAPHY: Weiss, Dor, 2 (1904[4]), 48f.; J.M. Guttmann, in: *Devir*, 2 (1924), 128–30; Ch. Tchernowitz, *Toledot ha-Halakhah*, 1 (1934), 151–63; Z.H. Chajes, *The Student's Guide Through the Talmud* (1960[2]), 29–31, 118–30; M. Elon, in: ILR, 2 (1967), 550. **ADD. BIBLIOGRAPHY:** M. Elon, *Ha-Mishpat ha-Ivri* (1988), 1:122ff., 805–28, index; idem, *Jewish Law* (1994), 1:137ff., 987–1014, index; idem, *Jewish Law (Cases and Materials)* (1999), 97–98; *Enẓiklopedyah Talmudit*, vol. 10, s.v. "*harḥakat nezikin*" 628, 644; index.

[Menachem Elon]

SEVASTOPOL, city in Crimea, Ukraine. Jews lived there in the Greek period when the city was called Khersones. Shortly after its foundation in 1784, Jews began to settle in Sevastopol, many of them from Galicia. They engaged in commerce and crafts and some acted as purveyors to the local garrison. The community was severely struck by a plague which broke out in the town in 1825. The development of the community was brought to a sudden halt as a result of the government's decision in 1829 to prohibit residence in the town, which had become the chief Russian naval base on the Black Sea, to all Jews, as constituting a danger to security, with the exception of those who served in the army. Jews already living there were ordered to leave the town within two years, and even temporary residence or visits were restricted. The order did not apply to the *Karaites. The local authorities unsuccessfully attempted to have the order rescinded, pointing out the harm which would be caused to the Jews themselves and to the town generally. The expulsion was halted for three years, after which Sevastopol was closed to Jews. In 1842, even a temporary stay by Jews in Sevastopol was limited to one month. During the Crimean War (1854–56) many Jews took part in the defense of Sevastopol and about 500 fell in battle. A monument was erected to their memory in the city in 1864. From 1859 various categories of Jews (merchants registered in the guilds, with their servants and clerks, and artisans) were authorized to live in Sevastopol; there was also some alleviation in the attitude toward visits and temporary residence of Jews in the town. Thus the Jewish settlement was renewed during the second half of the 19th century, and in 1880 numbered 400. In 1874 a "house of prayer for soldiers" was opened in Sevastopol, and in 1884 the construction of a synagogue was completed. Jews began to play an important role in the foreign trade which passed through the port, especially grain commerce. By 1897 3,910 Jews lived in Sevastopol (7.4% of the total population), including about 70 families of "Krimchaks" (Jews from Crimea itself). About 830 Karaites were also living in the city. In 1907 the authorities again began to expel Jews from various parts of Sevastopol, and by 1910 their numbers had decreased to 3,655. With the revolution of 1917 and abolition of all the anti-Jewish restrictions, many more Jews settled in Sevastopol. By 1926 their numbers reached 5,204 (7%). In 1939 they numbered 5,988 (5.5% of the total population).

Holocaust and Contemporary Periods

Sevastopol was occupied by the Germans on July 12, 1941. They soon collected 4,200 Jews who remained in the city and from its environs, and they murdered them in ditches outside the town and in gas vans. A small synagogue and Jewish cemetery were maintained in the late 1960s.

BIBLIOGRAPHY: M.I. Mysh, *Rukovodstvo k russkomu zakonodatelstvu o yevreyakh* (1890); D. Polonski, *Istoricheskiy ocherk sevastopolskoy yevreyskoy obshchiny* (1909).

[Yehuda Slutsky]

SEVENTY SHEPHERDS, VISION OF, the modern name of the treatise, also known as the "Dream-Visions," included in chapters 83–90 of the Ethiopic Book of *Enoch. Like the whole Book of Enoch, the treatise is extant in an Ethiopic translation from Greek, a fragment of which (Enoch 89:42–49) is preserved in a Vatican manuscript. The treatise dates from the beginnings of the Maccabean period and was known to the author of the Book of Jubilees (cf. 4:19). Chapters 83–84 contain Enoch's prophetic dream about the coming flood and form an introduction to a long dream-vision about the entire history of mankind from Adam to the eschatological salvation. This history appears to Enoch as an allegorical story, in which human actors are represented by animals. The allegory is mostly external and clumsy, but this is why its content can be easily revealed, making the treatise an important document in the Jewish conception of history and eschatology. The author hints at the common motif of the slaying of the prophets (89:51). At the end of the first commonwealth, because of its sins, God gave Israel into the hands of 70 shepherds, i.e., the angelic princes of the gentiles (the 70 nations); he told them how many of the sheep (Israel) they could allow to be destroyed, but they exceeded their orders and slew more than was required of them. This means that before the destruction of the First Temple, the Babylonian exile, and the loss of independence, God's people Israel, which had sinned, was handed over to the powers of the nations to live under the unrightful dominion of their guardian angels. In the last period of history, lambs are born to the white sheep (i.e., Israel) which are no longer blind as all the others before them had been; these are evidently the "Ḥasidim" of the Maccabean revolt. The sheep from which a great horn sprouts (Enoch 90:9) undoubtedly represents Judah Maccabee. The real history, known to the author, finishes with 90:13, and from there he describes what he thinks to be the imminent eschatological future. The great sword given to Israel for their last battle against the gentiles (90:19, 34) occurs also in the *Sibylline Oracles (III, 673, 780–2) and in an apparently Jewish apocalypse included in Lactantius' Institutions. After the final victory God will judge the fallen angels together with the guardian angels of the nations and apostates (90:20–27). The eschatological happy end begins with a prophecy about the New Jerusalem. The old one will be removed and laid in the south of the land. In its place God will bring the New Jerusalem. The idea of the New Jerusalem is not yet connected with the destruction of the one already existing. The dispersed Jews will return and the righteous gentiles convert. Only at the very end of the eschatological drama (90:37–38) do two messianic persons appear: the first is evidently the Davidic Messiah; the description of the second one seems to allude to Deuteronomy 33:17 (the blessing of Joseph). Thus the work is possibly the oldest evidence for the idea of the Messiah son of Joseph. As this treatise was evidently composed in the midst of the wars of Judah Maccabee (d. 160 B.C.E.), and written some years after the Book of Daniel, it is one of the oldest Jewish apocalypses.

BIBLIOGRAPHY: O. Gebhardt, in: *Archiv fuer wissenschaftliche Erforschung des Alten Testamentes*, 2 (1871), 163–246; D.S. Russel, *The Method and Message of Jewish Apocalyptic* (1964), 200–2; D. Flusser, in: IEJ, 9 (1959), 99–104.

[David Flusser]

SEVER (Zilberman), ALEXANDRU (1921–), Romanian novelist, author, and playwright. A publisher's editor during the years 1949–1958, he began writing plays such as *Boieri și țărani* ("Boyars and Peasants," 1955), but was best known as a prose writer. His novels include *Cezar Dragoman* (1957), *Uciderea pruncilor* ("The Massacre of the Innocents," 1966), and the technically original *Cercul* ("The Circle," 1968). Sever also published literary studies on Shakespeare and Melville (1964), Sinclair Lewis (1965), and Goethe and Eckermann (1966).

°**SEVERUS** (sometimes called **Serenus**), pseudo-messiah (or in some sources the Messiah's forerunner) in Babylonia about 720 C.E. The cataclysmic series of Muslim victories in the seventh century, culminating in the great Arab siege of Constantinople (717–8), provided the climate for an upsurge of messianic expectation among the Jews. In several Byzantine (both Greek and Syriac) chronicles Severus is described as a Syrian Christian who converted to Judaism. According to these sources, he attracted a large following, mainly of Jews but including some Christians, and gathered their money and assets, allegedly in order to bring them to the Promised Land. The Muslim authorities put him to death during the reign of Hisham (724–43). Severus introduced ritual innovations contrary to talmudic but not to biblical law, such as permission to work on the second days of holidays, modifications of *kashrut* laws, and the abolition of the prevalent marriage and divorce laws. After his death his followers, unlike those of such previous pseudo-messiahs as *Abu ʿIsā al-Iṣfahāni (c. 680s) and the Jew of Pallughta (Pumbedita?; 645), returned to the mainstream of Judaism, perhaps sending an inquiry to *Natronai Gaon (I). Severus was thought to have influenced Byzantine Jews and the risk of their affecting the loyalty of his other subjects may have been a reason for their persecution by Leo III. Because of the impression he made on Christians, Severus continued to be mentioned in Christian sources until the 14th century.

BIBLIOGRAPHY: J. Starr, in: REJ, 102 (1937), 81–92; Baron, Social², 5 (1957), 193ff., 380–2; A. Sharf, in: *Byzantinische Zeitschrift*, 59 (1966), 37–46; idem, *Byzantine Jewry* (1971), index.

[Andrew Sharf]

°**SEVERUS, ALEXANDER (Marcus Aurelius Alexander Severus**; 208), Roman emperor 222–35 C.E. Relations between the Severi and the Jews were notably favorable, and in this framework one "Severus, the son of Antoninus" mentioned in talmudic literature has been identified with Alexander Severus (Nid. 45a; Av. Zar. 10a; cf. S. Krauss, JE 1, 356). Although this identification is not altogether certain, it has also been suggested that the synagogue in Rome known as the "Synagogue of Severus" (כנשתא דאסוירס; cf. *Bereshit Rabbati*, ed. Albeck, p. 209; Frey, Corpus, 1 (1936), 501, and p. lxxxi) is named after Alexander Severus. These proposals are supported primarily by the biography of Alexander Severus in the *Scriptores Historiae Augustae*, which states that among those images in the private chapel of Severus was also one of Abraham. Although written in the middle of the fourth century, the general impression in this work of a continuation of good relations between the emperor and the Jews is probably a definite one.

BIBLIOGRAPHY: M. Avi-Yonah, *Bi-Ymei Roma u-Bizantiyyon* (1961³), 53; A.F.V. Jardé, *Etudes critiques sur la vie et la règne de Sévère Alexandre* (1925).

[Isaiah Gafni]

°**SEVERUS, SEPTIMIUS (Lucius Septimius Severus)**, Roman emperor, 193–211 C.E. Among the rival claimants for the Roman throne whom Severus defeated in the Civil War of 1937 was Pescennius Niger, who had been proclaimed emperor in Syria. In this struggle the Jews of Ereẓ Israel sided with Severus. That they liked him also can be seen from an inscription of the year 197, written in Greek, which was found in Safed. The Samaritans, however, ranged themselves against Severus, and continued to fight until 197. As a punishment, after his victory, the town of Neapolis (Shechem) was deprived of its *ius civitatis* (Spartianus, Severus, 9:5). In 202 the emperor forbade, under the threat of heavy penalties, conversion to both Judaism and Christianity (*ibid.*, 17:1; "*Judaeos fieri sub grave poena vetuit. Idem etiam de Christianis sanxit*"), but he was tolerant toward those who were Jewish by birth. The jurists Ulpian and Modestinus report that Jews could be appointed to high public offices, but would be exempt from those formalities (*Necessitates*) which were contrary to their monotheistic faith (*Corpus Iuris Civilis; Digesta* 50:2, 3; 27:1–15). Although according to J. Juster this exemption was in force even before the time of Severus, S. Lieberman (in: *Annuaire Université Libre de Bruxelles* 7) believed that both Christians and Samaritans could not have enjoyed such exemptions because of the oath that had to be taken on assuming public office. (S.W. Baron is more cautious in his conclusions.)

BIBLIOGRAPHY: Juster, Juifs, 1 (1914), 258, n. 4, 259, 267; M. Platnauer, *The Life and Reign of the Emperor Lucius Septimius Severus* (1918); Fluss, in: Pauly-Wissowa, pt. 2, 4 (1923), 1940–2002; A. Stein, *Der roemische Ritterstand* (1927); E. Manni, in: *Rivista di Filologia* (1947), 211f.; F.-M. Abel, *Histoire de la Palestine*, 2 (1952), 139–52; M. Avi-Yonah, *Bi-Ymei Roma u-Bizantiyyon* (1952²), 54ff.; Baron, Social², 2 (1952), index; V. Colorni, *Gli Ebrei nel sistema del Diritto Comune* (1956), 3–4 (see n. 10); Y.F. Baer, in: *Scripta Hierosolymitana*, 7 (1961), 77–149; M.A. Levi, *L'Impero Romano*, 2 (1967).

[Alfredo Mordechai Rabello]

SEVILLE (Sp. **Sevilla**), leading city of Andalusia, S.W. *Spain. According to a tradition, the Jewish settlement in Seville was of very ancient date; it is related that Jews arrived there at the time of the destruction of the First Temple, and among the families were descendants of the House of David, including the *Abrabanel family. However, it is difficult to adduce evidence for the presence of Jews in this locality during the 11th to 10th centuries B.C.E., unless Seville, or another place within direct proximity of it, is identified with the *Tarshish mentioned in the Bible. There is no doubt that a Jewish settlement existed during the period of Visigothic rule in the peninsula. During the seventh century C.E., *Isidore of Seville wrote anti-Jewish polemics there. When the city was conquered by the Muslims in 712 they formed a Jewish guard for its defense; these soldiers settled in the city and its surroundings.

Muslim Period

Under the *Umayyads, Seville prospered and became an important cultural center. The Jewish community of Seville was one of four major communities in Muslim Spain. *Saadiah b. Joseph Gaon addressed Seville Jewry in the mid-tenth century in his letter to the leading communities in Spain (Abraham ibn Daud, *Sefer ha-Qabbalah, Book of Tradition*, ed. by G. Cohen (1967), 79). The Jews engaged in commerce and medicine and had a virtual monopoly on the profession of *dyeing. Seville served as a refuge for Jews escaping from *Córdoba after the Berber conquest in 1013. Jewish opponents of *Samuel ha-Nagid in Granada fled to Seville, its major opponent. During the 11th century the Jewish population increased as a result of the anti-Jewish riots in *Granada, as well as a large influx of Jews from North Africa seeking economic improvement. Under the Abbasid dynasty (1023–91) prominent Jews served in various capacities at court. During the reign of al-Muʿtaḍid (1024–69) the wealthy scholar Isaac b. Baruch *Albalia served as court astrologer and head of the Jewish community. His son, the scholar Baruch b. Isaac Albalia, uncle of the historian Abraham *Ibn Daud, was born in Seville. Abraham b. Meir ibn Muhajir also served as vizier and head of the Jewish community under the Abbasid king. Important families included the Ibn al-Yatom, Ibn Kamneill, Ibn Mujahir, and the Abrabanel families. Under the Almoravids (11th century), Seville was a major cultural center. Abu Ayub Sulayman ibn Mu'allim of Seville served as court physician and Abu al-Hasan Abraham b. Meir ibn Kamneil as a diplomat under King Ali ibn Uūsuf (1106–43). The poets Abu Sulayman ibn Mujahir and Abul al-Fatḥ Eleazar ibn Azhar and the scholar Meir ibn Migash lived in Seville in the early 12th century. Seville Jewry suffered the same fate as the other Andalusian communities in the wake of the Almohad conquest and was entirely destroyed.

Location of the Jewish Quarter

Under Muslim rule the Jewish quarter was situated in the western part of the city, in the present parishes of Santa Magdalena and San Lorenzo, where the Cal and Cal Maior streets ("Community Street") are still to be found. This was probably the old Jewish quarter (*judería vieja*), which was then also the Moorish quarter. The al-Shawwār Gate, known as the Judería Gate during the Middle Ages and later as the Meat Gate (Puerta de la Carne), was situated within the boundaries of the quarter. The other Jewish quarter, established after the city was conquered by the Christians, extended from the Carmona Gate, through the San Esteban, Las Aguilas, and de Abades streets, to the Cathedral, the Oil Street, and the Alcazar to the city wall. Ballesteros (see bibliography) may, however, have been correct in stating that from the Alcazar the boundary of the quarter passed through Matías Gago Street, Soledad, to San Nicolas and from there to Madre de Dios Street, St. Bartholomé Square, and Vidrio Street to Tintes Street, through the "Rose" alley. The main street of the Jewish quarter was the one that started in the Puerta de la Judería (today de la Carne) and ended at the gate that used to be in front of San Nicolás, in other words the streets that nowadays are called Santa María la Blanca and San José. The busiest part of the quarter was the square that is today called plaza de Santa María la Blanca. Important localities and streets in the Jewish quarter were the Cruces street and the streets of the Levíes and Archeros, where the original doors of the synagogue (now Santa María la Blanca) were and are still preserved but not used. Santa María la Blanca had been a mosque before it was given by Alfonso X in 1252 to the Jews to use as synagogue together with other two mosques. In 1391 this synagogue was converted into the present church. In the Santa Cruz place there was a synagogue, also formerly a mosque, which was converted into a church in 1391. Before its destruction by the French in 1810, it occupied a large part of the Santa Cruz place. The third mosque that was turned into a synagogue used to be where San Bartolomé church stands. In Susona street, according to legend, lived Susona, who was connected with the plot of the Conversos against the Inquisition. At the time of the expulsion of the Jews of Andalusia in 1483 (see also below), the quarter was surrounded by a wall which ran as far as San Esteban. The inner wall had two gates. There were many synagogues in the quarter, including one erected by Samuel b. Meir ha-Levi *Abulafia of Toledo during the 14th century. The archdeacon of Ecija, Ferrant *Martínez (see also below), enumerated 23 synagogues in Seville during the second half of the 14th century, and related that he destroyed them. The origin of such a large number is unknown; he may have included the yeshivot in this number. Some of the synagogues were converted into churches: Santa María la Blanca is particularly well known. After the quarter ceased to exist, it was named "New Quarter" (*Barrionuevo*) but its remains may still be seen in the Santa Cruz quarter.

The Jewish cemetery of Seville was near the Puerta de la Carne, formerly de la Judería, in the Bujaira, where the Colegio de Potacoeli now stands. The Inquisition in Seville sat in Triana castle, after a brief period in the Dominican monastery of San Pablo.

[Haim Beinart / Yom Tov Assis (2nd ed.)]

After the Christian Reconquest

In 1248 Seville was captured by the armies of Ferdinand III (1217–52). The Jews of the city prepared a key for him on which was engraved in Hebrew: "the King of Kings will open, the King of the land shall come" (the key is preserved in the cathedral treasury). The Jewish quarter succeeded in obtaining the three mosques situated within its boundaries, which were converted into synagogues. In the distribution of properties which took place after the Christian conquest, and later during the reign of Alfonso X of Castile, many Jews obtained real estate in the form of houses, arable land, olive groves, and vineyards in the city and its outskirts. Those who received the properties were obliged to settle in Seville and a royal decree stipulated that owners of property in the city would not benefit from any rights unless they lived there permanently. Among these Jews were Don Todros b. Joseph ha-Levi *Abulafia and his son Joseph, who at the time of his death bequeathed many properties to the city (1273); they were confiscated and presented to the local church. Immediately after its capture the Christians succeeded in converting Seville into an international commercial center. Its trade extended to the ports of Spain, Portugal, and North Africa, and many Jews took part in this commerce.

In 1254 Alfonso x inaugurated two annual fairs in Seville. The Jews who attended them or participated in them were granted freedom of trade and an exemption from taxes. In 1256 Alfonso nevertheless ordered each of the elders of the community, its leaders, and the Jews of Seville to pay 30 denarii to the head of the Church, a payment which had also been made by the Jews of Toledo. The Jews of the city also paid tithe and firstfruit taxes to the archbishop of Seville (as also did the Moors there). The rights of the Jews of Seville stipulated, among other articles, that lawsuits between Jews and Christians should be brought before the judges of the town, with the exception of suits pertaining to tax farming. There were also community regulations against adultery and marital offenses. Despite this, there were Jewish women who lived in concubinage with Christians (*barraganas*) and enjoyed defined rights in the city. In Seville, Jewish women acted as mourners for Christians. In practice, the living conditions of the Jews of Seville did not differ from those of the other Jews of the kingdom, with the exception of rights granted to them on the strength of their residence in this border region.

The registers of the office of Sancho iv for 1293–94 show that the annual tax paid by the Jews of Seville amounted to 115,333 maravedis and five sólidos. The community of Seville appears to have numbered 200 families during that period, and it may be assumed that the overwhelming majority were wealthy. During the course of the 14th century, the community succeeded in consolidating itself and in attaining a fair cultural and economic level. The Jews of the community took part in the lease of municipal taxes in the city and the region under its jurisdiction, as well as in economic activities promoted by the government. During the 14th century Jewish physicians were employed as municipal officials – a situation not found, for instance, in Toledo. The physicians of the city were members of the Ibn Zimra family; they also engaged in various financial activities. In 1312 the community succeeded in obtaining the king's permission to hang an *informer then active in Seville; R. *Asher b. Jehiel commended the community for this action. In 1342 King Alfonso xi requested Pope Clement vi to release the synagogue built in Seville by Joseph de Ecija so it could be employed for the purpose for which it was built. In advocating the Jews' case the king stressed their economic and military utility in the war against the Muslims.

Activities of Ferrant Martinez

In 1378 the archdeacon of Ecija, Ferrant Martínez, began anti-Jewish agitation in Seville. He called for the destruction of the 23 beautiful synagogues of the Jews and the closure of their quarter so that they would not come into contact with the Christians. The Jews of the town complained about the hatred which he fomented and the prohibitions which he issued against the residence of Jews in the archbishopric of Seville. In 1382 John i ordered Martínez to cease his activities, but he pursued his campaign. The leaders of the community still complained to the crown about Martínez in 1388, while he claimed that he was acting with the approval of the archbishop of Seville to separate the Jews from the Christians. In 1390 Henry iii ordered the archbishop of Seville to act against Martínez with firmness and restore to the Jews the synagogues which had been confiscated; the head of the Church of Seville was to bear the responsibility if the order was not carried out. Activities such as these were frequent occurrences in Spain as in other countries, when young and fanatical clergymen acted arbitrarily and upon their own initiative against the Jews, and presenting the government and Church with their violence as a *fait accompli*.

Persecutions of 1391

On June 4, 1391, the anti-Jewish disorders which were later to sweep all the towns of the Crowns of Castile and Aragon broke out in Seville. The rioters in Seville, including soldiers and sailors who went by boat from one place to another inciting the population, teaching others from their experience. The community was almost totally destroyed: some of its members died as martyrs, a minority escaped; others converted and left the Jewish fold. The synagogues were turned into churches and the churches acquired substantial real estate in the form of land, charitable trusts, shops, workshops, and houses which had formerly belonged to Jews and the community. Henry iii granted houses to his chief mayordomo, Juan Hurtado de Mendoza, and the chief justice, Diego López de Estúñiga, which had been the property of the community, and the synagogues to the city of Seville.

Decline of the Community

The remaining Jews of Seville were unable to recover from the persecutions of 1391 and their rehabilitation was extremely slow. In 1437 a number of Jews appealed to John ii to regularize the matter of their residence in their quarters. In the Santa Cruz quarter the 75 houses in which Jews lived and worked were rented. In another quarter, near the Santa María la Blanca church (a former synagogue), there were 56 houses. A letter from Pope Nicholas v to the bishop-administrator of Seville records an exceptional action by the Jews of Seville in 1449 when a plague broke out there. After the example of the Christians, who organized a religious procession in the town, the Jews of Seville organized a procession during which they took out the Torah scrolls, scattered branches, and decorated the streets, thus imitating the custom and ritual of the Christians in their processions, as if to insinuate that God had not accepted the plea of the Christians.

Despite several expressions of sympathy on the part of Christian inhabitants, the situation of the community appears to have been serious. In 1474 the community paid an annual tax of only 2,500 maravedis, and this sum was reduced to 2,000 maravedis in 1482. On Dec. 8, 1476, the Jews were ordered to leave their quarter and move to two places; one of them was the Corral de Ferez, the other, the Alcázar Viejo. They were to cover the expenses of repairs to their new places of residence.

On Jan. 1, 1483, the crown acceded to the demand of the *Inquisition and an expulsion order was issued against all the Jews of Andalusia. A period of 30 days was given to the Jews to leave. The actual decree of expulsion is not extant but much information is available on the procedure of its execution. When the general decree of expulsion of the Jews from Spain was issued in March 1492, Seville was a port of embarkation for the exiles, most of whom left for North Africa.

At the beginning of the 20th century, Jewish settlement in Seville began again. Most of the Jewish settlers came from North Africa. In addition to these families, there were also refugees from Germany who arrived there during the early 1930s. The several dozen Jews in Seville were joined in the 1960s by Jewish arrivals from Morocco and Algeria.

Conversos in Seville

Little information is available on the history of the *Conversos in Seville during the first half of the 15th century. Until the expulsion and after it the Conversos in Seville were known for their adherence to Judaism and their loyalty to Jewish law. They maintained extremely close relations with their Jewish brothers, and anyone of whom it was said that he was a Converso of Seville, or that he had stayed there, was considered a Jew in every respect. After the attacks on the Conversos in Córdoba in 1473, many of them fled to Seville. The Conversos in Seville also gradually became aware of the danger which threatened them and large numbers left for North Africa and other places. Others organized guards in their quarter to protect their lives and even hired 300 equestrian knights and 5,000 infantrymen. When acts of hostility broke out against them they were unable to defend themselves, and with the Conversos of Córdoba they tried to establish themselves in *Gibraltar. During that period R. Judah ibn Verga conducted a campaign among them calling on them to return to Judaism and to leave the kingdom before it was too late.

When Ferdinand v and Queen Isabella visited Seville in 1477, the head of the San Pablo Dominican monastery in the city, Alonso de Hojeda, and others pointed out to the monarchs the religious situation in their city and requested the establishment of an Inquisition. The monarchs accepted their demand, and from there addressed themselves to Sixtus iv. In 1480, two years after the authorization was granted, Miguel de Murillo and Juan de San Martín were appointed inquisitors, but it was only on Jan. 1, 1481 that they began their merciless activities. As a first measure they ordered all the noblemen of the surroundings (among them some of the kingdom's highest ranking personalities such as Rodrigo Ponce de Leon) to deliver all fugitive Conversos to them. Documents of the Inquisition tribunal of Seville are not extant, but various state documents and chronicles of those days are filled with descriptions of the activities of the inquisitors and their proceedings against the Conversos. Large numbers of both wealthy and poor folk were arrested, imprisoned, tried, and burned at the stake. Among those tried were members of the Ibn Shoshan, Adoba, and Abulafia families. At first the Conversos sought to defend themselves and began to hoard weapons. A popular tradition relates that the daughter of Diego de Shoshan revealed the project to her Christian lover, who alerted the Inquisition, which struck a hard blow at the Conversos involved in this scheme. In August 1481, when a plague broke out in the city, many Conversos were authorized to leave it after they had deposited their money as a surety, but a large number of them did not redeem their surety and fled (among them the Hebrew printer Juan de Lucena) to North Africa, Portugal, and Italy. The Inquisition also followed the Conversos to the surrounding villages; wherever it arrived, numerous Conversos died as martyrs.

According to a cautious estimate, over 700 men and women were burned at the stake in Seville between 1481 and 1488, while over 5,000 were returned within the fold of the Church. At the end of 1484 a convention of the inquisitors of the kingdom was held in Seville in the presence of *Torquemada. It defined the procedure of the Inquisition and was thus the first conference for the study and improvement of working methods of the Inquisition. In Seville, the Conversos and travelers who arrived in the harbor were spied upon and the Inquisition searched every ship which entered or left. This situation continued until the abolition of the Inquisition during the 19th century.

[Haim Beinart]

BIBLIOGRAPHY: Baer, Spain, index; Baer, Urkunden, index; A. Ballesteros, *Sevilla en siglo XIII* (1913); J. González, *Repartimiento de Sevilla*, 2 vols. (1951); Cantera-Millás, Inscripciones, index; B. Eloy Ruano, in: *Hispania*, 85 (1962), 23–37; Suárez Fernández, Documentos, index; H.C. Lea, *A History of the Inquisition of Spain*, 1 (1906), 160ff.; 4 (1906), index; B. Llorca, in: *Sefarad*, 2 (1942), 118ff.; F. Cantera, *ibid.*, 4 (1944), 295–349; B. Llorca, *Bulario Pontificio de la Inquisición* (1949), 48–67. **ADD. BIBLIOGRAPHY:** J. de Mata Carriazo, in: *Homenaje a don Ramón Carande*, vol. 2 (1963), 95–112; J.V. Baruque, in: *Historia, Instituciones, Documentos*, 1 (1974), 221–38; A. Collantes de Terán Sánchez, in: *Historia, Instituciones, Documentos*, 3 (1976), 167–85; K. Wagner, *Regesto de documentos del Archivo de Protocolos de Sevilla referents a judíos y moros* (1978); A. Domínguez Ortíz, in: *Nueva revista de filología hispánica* 30 (1981), 609–16; A. Herrera García, in: *Sefarad*, 41 (1981), 95–110; I. Montes Romero-Camacho, in: *La sociedad medieval andaluza; grupos no privilegiados. Actas del III Coloquio de historia medieval andaluza* (1984), 57–75; idem, in: *La ciudad hispánica durante los sig;os XIII al XVI; Actas del coloquio*, 1 (1985–87), 343–65; idem, *Andalucía entre oriente y occidente (126–1492). Actas del V Coloquio internacional de historia medieval de Andalucía* (1988), 551–68; R. Sánchez Saus, in: *En la España medieval*, V, *Estudios en memoria del Profesor D. Claudio Sánchez-Albornoz*, 2 (1986), 1119–39; F. Fernández Gómez and A. de la Hoz Gándara, in: *I*

Congreso de Arqueología Medieval Española. Actas, 4 (1986), 49–72; J.A. Ollero Pina, in: *Hispania Sacra*, 40 (1988), 45–105; F.J. Lobera Serrano, in: *Cultura neolatina*, 49 (1989), 7–53.

SEVITZKY, FABIEN (1893–1967), conductor. Born in Vichny-Volotchok, Russia, Sevitzky adopted an abridged form of the family name so as not to seem to be imposing on the fame of his uncle, Serge *Koussevitzky. He was a double-bass player in Russian orchestras and toured Russia as a virtuoso. In 1922 he moved to Poland, and then to the United States. He played in the Philadelphia Orchestra and founded the Philadelphia String Sinfonietta in 1925. From 1935 to 1955 he was permanent conductor of the Indianapolis Symphony Orchestra which, under his direction, became one of the leading U.S. orchestras.

SEX. Neither biblical nor talmudic Hebrew possesses a specific term for sex. While classical Jewish literature is replete with references to it, the subject is never treated separately and systematically. The most intimate and frank discussions on sex are featured frequently in the Talmud and have always been a natural part of religious education, unmarred by self-consciousness. Nevertheless, laws concerning forbidden relations should not be expounded in public (Ḥag. 2:1 and 11b), since "there is no guardian against unchasteness" (Ket. 13b). The Jewish attitude to sex, then, shows a certain apparent ambivalence or, more correctly, a balance between extremes. It insists on a stern discipline of moral restraints and yet avoids excessive prudery or asceticism. On the one hand, Judaism regards moderation and self-control in sex as the essence of "holiness" (Lev. 19:2, and commentaries), condemning unchaste conduct as among the most heinous offences against God and society and branding as capital crimes such perversions as sodomy and pederasty (Lev. 20:13, 15–16) as well as adultery (*ibid.*, 10) and incest (*ibid.*, 11ff.). On the other hand, it rejects the notion of considering the sex instinct as intrinsically sinful or shameful. The sex drive should be sublimated rather than suppressed, for "were it not for the evil inclination, no man would build a home and marry" (Gen. R. 9:7). Indeed, to the rabbis, who frowned on *celibacy, it was this instinct which completed the creation of the world and caused God to pronounce His work as "very good" (Gen. R. *ibid.*).

Legislation on sex occupies considerable space in the codes of Jewish law, as do warnings against lewdness in thought, word, or deed in the moralist literature of Judaism. Building on the foundations of the pragmatic laws in the Torah and of the passionate denunciation of pagan licentiousness by the prophets, the rabbis erected a complex structure of regulations to govern every area of sex life. Particularly extensive are the rules of family *purity based on the prohibition of sexual relations with a menstruant woman (Lev. 20:18). Similarly elaborated are the laws on birth *control, *sterilization, and *abortion, as well as the ban on *prostitution (based on Deut. 23:18), and indeed on any sexual relations outside lawful wedlock (Maim., Yad, Ishut 1:1–4). To guard against illicit intimacies, any meetings in private between individuals of opposite sexes are also strictly prohibited (Sh. Ar., EH 22), just as the Bible forbids men or women to wear each other's clothes (Deut. 22:5) to prevent levity and promiscuity (see commentaries). Many additional rabbinic rules seek to curb lewd thought and immodest conduct, even among spouses (Sh. Ar., EH 21–25).

Though far removed from the Freudian concept of sex as the ultimate key to normal and abnormal behavior in childhood as in mature life, the rabbis often asserted the predominance of the sex urge and the effort needed to control it. "Who is mighty? He who subdues his lust" (Avot 4:1), and "for most people there is nothing harder in the entire Torah than to abstain from sex and forbidden relations" (Maim. Yad, Issurei Bi'ah, 22:18) are typical statements. Characteristic, too, is the interpretation given to the rite of *circumcision, the "covenant" between God and Israel and the first law enjoined upon the first Jew, as symbolizing the primacy of hallowing the sex act by an operation "to weaken the organ of generation as far as possible, and thus cause man to be moderate" (Maim., Guide, 3:49).

BIBLIOGRAPHY: L.M. Epstein, *Sex Laws and Custom in Judaism* (1948); J. Preuss, *Biblisch-talmudische Medizin* (1923[3]); P. Elman (ed.), *Jewish Marriage* (1967); Baron, Social[2], index.

[Immanuel Jakobovits]

°SEXTUS EMPIRICUS (late second century C.E.), Greek physician and philosophical writer in whose works on Skepticism (extant) the Jewish abhorrence of pig's flesh is mentioned (*Pyrrhonic Sketches* 3:223).

SEXUAL OFFENSES. Although the technical term for sexual offenses in general is *gillui arayot* (lit. "the uncovering of nakedness"), the term is usually (though not always: cf. Ex. 20:23; Isa. 47:3, et al.) employed to denote carnal knowledge (Lev. 18:6–19). In the present context, however, the term "sexual offenses" includes offenses committed by prohibited sexual intercourse, offenses of unlawful sexual conduct short of intercourse, and related offenses presumably motivated by the sexual urge.

As well as acts of *adultery and *incest, the Bible also prohibits sodomy and homosexuality (18:22), denouncing such acts as "abhorrent" and making them capital offenses (20:13); having carnal relations with any beast is also made a capital offense (18:23; 20:15–16). These offenses were punishable by stoning to death (Sanh. 7:4; Maim Yad, Issurei Bi'ah, 1:4), and the beast with which the offense had been committed was also destroyed (Lev. 20:15–16). A married girl (i.e., *me'orasah*, her legal status after *kiddushin*, but before *ḥuppah*; see *Marriage) who was found not to have been a virgin (though claiming to be one upon her *kiddushin*) is liable to be stoned to death, "for she did a shameful thing in Israel" (Deut. 22:20–21). Both she and her seducer are thus punished if they had intercourse with each other by mutual consent (Deut. 22:23–24); but where the girl did not consent her seducer alone is liable to execution (Deut. 22:25–27).

It is noteworthy that apart from this particular case and cases of adulterous or incestuous intercourse, rape as such is not a criminal offense in Jewish law: the rapist will merely be held liable to pay the girl's father 50 shekels of silver by way of bride-price, "and she shall be his wife, because he has humbled her; and he may not put her away all his days" (Deut. 22:28–29). Under talmudic law, the rapist must also compensate the girl for the physical and psychological damage she sustained (Ket. 42a–43b). But if the girl refuses to marry him, he is not compelled to marry her (Ket. 39b). If a girl was raped by several men, she is given the choice of the one who is to marry her (TJ, Ket. 3:6, 27d; for further details see *Rape).

It is an offense to have intercourse with a woman, including one's wife, "having her sickness," i.e., **niddah* during the period of her menstruation (Lev. 18:19 and 20:18). The penalty is *karet* (see *Divine Punishment): "both of them shall be cut off from among their people" (*ibid.*). If they were warned beforehand and witnesses are available, they are liable to be flogged (Mak. 3:1).

It is an offense, punishable by flogging, to have sexual intercourse with a non-Jew, by way of purported or intended marriage (*ibid.*, 12:1). For other sexual intercourse with a non-Jew (which is not criminal), flogging may be administered by way of rebuke and admonition (*makkat mardut*; *ibid.* 12:2). The biblical story of Phinehas (Num. 25:6–8) gave rise to the rule that where intercourse between Jew and an idolatress takes place in public, any person present may kill them (Sanh. 9:6; Yad, Issurei Bi'ah 12:4). Failing such summary execution, the offender is liable to divine punishment and to be flogged (*ibid.* 12:6).

Marrying a person born of an adulterous or incestuous union (see **Mamzer*) and having sexual intercourse with him or her is a criminal offense punishable by flogging (*ibid.* 15:2). Marrying a person whose testes are crushed or whose member is cut off (Deut. 23:2), and having (or attempting to have) sexual intercourse with him, is also punishable by flogging (Yad, Issurei Bi'ah 16:1) – although the offense was qualified so as to apply only where the infirmity had not existed from birth but was acquired later by human act or accident (*ibid.* 16:9; Yev. 75b). It is similarly an offense punishable by flogging to castrate a person by causing injury to his sexual organs (Shab. 110b) – an offense which was extended even to the castration of animals (Tosef., Mak. 5:6; Yad, Issurei Bi'ah 10); but does not apply to females (*ibid.*) nor to castrations that do not cause injury to sexual organs (*ibid.* 16:11).

Some particular offenses apply to *kohanim* (priests) only: e.g., a *Kohen* who marries a divorcee, a harlot (including a non-Jewess), or a woman born of a prohibited union with a priest (Lev. 21:7), and has sexual intercourse with her, is guilty of an offense and liable to be flogged (*ibid.* 17:2), and so is the woman partner (*ibid.* 17:5). The high priest who had sexual intercourse with a widow (Lev. 21:13–14) was also liable to be flogged (Yad, Issurei Bi'ah 17:3).

The only sexual offense short of intercourse is "approaching" (Lev. 18:6) any person with whom intercourse is prohibited under penalty of death (including divine punishment). Embracing and kissing such persons, and other such precoital activities, are offenses punishable by flogging (Yad, Issurei Bi'ah 21:1). But it is no offense – however reprehensible and "foolish" it may be in some cases – to embrace or kiss one's mother, daughter, sister, or aunt, or such other relatives who do not normally arouse the sexual urge (*ibid.* 21:6; see *Incest). The prohibition against "cult prostitution" (Deut. 23:18) was interpreted as creating the offense of sexual intercourse with a harlot (cf. Lev. 19:29), both she and the man being liable to be flogged (Maim. Yad, Na'arah Betulah, 2:17). But however much *prostitution may be condemned (cf. e.g., Jer. 3:1–3), it appears in biblical times to have been widespread (cf. Gen. 34:31; 38:15; Judg. 11:1; 16:1; Isa. 23:15–16; Prov. 7:9–22; et al.) and not punishable. In post-talmudic times, sexual licentiousness was punished as a matter of course (cf. e.g., *Halakhot Pesukot min ha-Ge'onim*, 94).

There are several prohibited acts which do not amount to punishable offenses, but which may render the perpetrator liable to flogging by way of admonition and rebuke: e.g., indecent gestures or suggestions to women with whom intercourse is prohibited (Yad, Issurei Bi'ah, 21:2); lesbian conduct among women (21:8); sexual intercourse with one's wife in public (21:14); being secluded with a woman with whom intercourse is prohibited – other than one's mother, daughter, or (menstruous) wife, and also except a woman married to another man (because, in the latter case, the flogging might bring her into disrepute; 22:3).

In the State of Israel, rape is punishable with up to 14 years' imprisonment; when committed in the presence of several accessories to the crime, the punishment is up to 20 years' imprisonment (Section 152, Criminal Code Ordinance, 1936, as amended in 1966). Constructive (statutory) rape (sexual intercourse with an infant girl) has been extended up to the girl's age of 17. Proven acts of sodomy (homosexuality), buggery (carnal knowledge *per anum*), and bestiality (carnal knowledge of animals) are felonies. The largest group of sexual offenses comes under the heading of "indecent acts" – for which the penalty may increase in gravity if they are committed by force, or upon children, or in public. The law relating to procuration for purposes of prostitution and the keeping of brothels was restated and made considerably more severe in the Penal Law Amendment (Prostitution Offenses) Law, 5722 – 1962.

[Haim Hermann Cohn]

In the State of Israel

As of 1977, the law regulating sexual offenses is the Penal Law, 5737 – 1977 (hereinafter: "the Law"). In 2005, the basic penalty for rape was 16 years imprisonment and, under aggravated circumstances – such as rape of a minor or rape accompanied by threat to use a weapon – the penalty was 20 years imprisonment (Article 345 of the law). The prohibition on homosexual relations which had previously existed in Article 351(3) of the law was repealed in 1988 (Penal Law (Amendment No. 22) 5748 – 1988, (S.H. 62).

RAPE IN MARITAL RELATIONS. Jewish law absolutely prohibits the wife's rape by her husband. The Supreme Court (CA 353/62, *El Fakir v. Attorney General*, 18(4) PD 200; Judge Binyamin Halevi) criticized the position of English law, which at the time permitted the husband to force his wife to have sexual relations with him: "This outlook is not commensurate with human dignity and the dignity of marriage… A woman who agrees upon marriage to have sexual relations with her husband does not thereby agree to the use of force or the threats of severe physical maiming of her body. A woman is not 'like a prisoner taken by the sword' with her husband, and is entitled to the freedom of her body just as her husband is" (page 219 of the decision).

In this statement Judge Halevi made reference to the Rambam's statement, according to which: "A woman who has prevented her husband from having sexual intercourse is called rebellious, and she is to be asked why she has rebelled. If she says I find him repulsive and cannot have intercourse with him willingly, he is compelled to divorce her, because she is not like a captive who must have intercourse with someone she detests" (Yad., Ishut 14.8; regarding *moredet*, see *Husband and Wife). It should be stressed that, in any case, according to Jewish law it is prohibited to have intercourse by coercion; even if the wife's refusal is not justified, the wife may not be compelled to do so, although in this case she is liable to be considered "rebellious" or to lose the rights conferred to her by the marriage.

In the *Cohen* case (CA 91/80 *Cohen v. the State of Israel*, 35 (3) PD 281; Justice Bechor) the Court discussed the position of Jewish law on this matter in some detail. At the focus of the Cohen affair was the term "unlawful" in Article 345 of the law (as formulated at the time of the Cohen affair), which defines the act of rape as one who "has *unlawful* sexual intercourse with a female, against her will…" The accused claimed – and there was no factual dispute that he had had intercourse with his wife against her will – that the element of "unlawful" required under Article 345 did not exist, because according to Jewish law he had the right, as her husband, to have sexual relations with his wife; therefore, similar to English law, a husband who coerced his wife to have sexual relations with him does not thereby commit an offense of rape under the law, because the coercion of intercourse was "lawful." Justice Bechor rejected the defendant's argument, stating that under Jewish law the husband is prohibited from forcing his wife to have intercourse. He stressed that, according to the Torah, it is the husband's duty toward his wife to have sexual relations with her ("her food, her raiment, and her conjugal rights, he shall not diminish"; Exod. 21:10), while there is no imperative in the Bible or Talmud imposing a parallel obligation on the wife. Her obligation, rather, stems from her commitment in the marital agreement, which imposes an obligation on her part to give herself to her husband (p. 288 of the verdict). Insofar as the source of the wife's commitment is her undertaking at the time of her marriage, it is obvious that the wife did not agree that her husband would have sexual relations with her by rape, and has no such obligation (see: M.Elon "*Ma'amad ha-ishah*" ('Status of Woman'), 218 *et seq.*; N. Rakover "*Yaḥasei Ishut bi-Khefiyyah*," 305). Justice Bechor further cited the statement in the Talmud: "Rabbi Bar Ḥama said in the name of Rav Assi: It is forbidden for a man to coerce his wife to a *devar mitzvah* [i.e., to have sexual relations]" (Eruvin 100b) as well as the statement of the Rabad of Posquières: "As it was stated in tractate *Eruvin* that a person who coerces his wife to a '*devar mitzvah*' is considered evil, because it has been said 'Also, that the soul be without knowledge is not good and he that hasteth with his feet sinneth.' (Prov. 19:2). Accordingly, rape is forbidden even with his wife; rather, if he needs to have that act [i.e., sexual intercourse] he should conciliate his wife and then have sexual relations with her" (Rabad, quoted in Tur, OḤ 240 and in Tur, EH 25; pp. 288–89 of the verdict). Summarizing his verdict, Justice Bechor said:

> The conclusion I have reached accords with the basic principle of the dignity of woman as a free person and not as a slave, who is subject to her owner's good will in such a sensitive and delicate matter – principles which have, regrettably, not been realized in the legislation and adjudication of enlightened and advanced countries in the world. And it is not difficult to imagine how sad the fate of a woman can be in those countries, particularly in light of the fact that, according to the laws of the country or religion concerned, it is not easy and at times difficult or even impossible to arrive at the solution of divorce. It may be that this feeling is what brought about a certain alleviation in England, when it was decided that the wife's duty to have sexual relations against her will and as a result of coercion does not apply if a situation of legal separation exists between the couple, even if they are not divorced. I might add that the Jewish people may be proud of the progressive and liberal approach of its heritage and *halakhah* with respect to such matters since ancient times (p. 291 of the Verdict; *Ma'amad ha-Iishah*, ibid).

RAPE THAT ENDS IN CONSENT. According to Jewish law, a married woman who has had sexual relations with a man who is not her husband is permanently forbidden to her husband; hence, her husband is obliged to divorce her. However, if the woman was raped by the other man, then the woman is not forbidden to her husband, unless he was a *kohen* (member of a hereditary priestly family; see *Marriage, Prohibited). In a case in which the man initially forced himself upon the woman, but during the course of the act she came to consent, it is ruled that the woman is nevertheless not forbidden to her husband: "Rabba stated: Any woman, the outrage against whom began under compulsion, even though it terminated with her consent; and even if she [the raped woman] said, 'Leave him be,' and even if she states that, had he not attacked her, she would have hired him [to have relations with her], is permitted [to her husband]. What is the reason? She came to be overwhelmed by her passion [i.e., that during the course of the act her passion was aroused, so that even this passion that overcame her against her will is considered as rape]" (Ket. 51b; Yad., Ishut 24.19).

The Supreme Court (Cr. A. 115/00, *Teib v. State of Israel* 54 (3) PD 289. 308, (per Justice Yitzhak Englard) ruled in a case in which the defendant charged with rape argued that he had misunderstood the woman's refusal to have sexual relations, because at the end of the act the woman had cooperated, and her physiological and sexual response to his acts had been positive. The Court determined that, similar to the case in Jewish law regarding "initial rape that ends in consent," the woman's response should not be regarded as constituting consent to sexual relations, and one could not say that in such a case the man could have formed the impression that the woman consented to his actions.

SEXUAL DEGRADATION. Section 348 of the law prohibits the perpetration of an indecent act, defined as "any act intended for sexual excitement arousal, gratification or degradation." The Supreme Court discussed a case in which a robber ordered women whom he had robbed to remove all their clothes. The District Court convicted the defendant, in addition to the crime of robbery, with that of performing an indecent act. In an appeal before the Supreme Court, the defendant argued that he ought not to be convicted of the offense of an indecent act, because the purpose of ordering the women to remove their clothes was not to sexually abase them, as required by this law, but in order to determine whether they were concealing money on their bodies; hence, it was incorrect to attribute criminal intent to him with respect to the offense of "sexual abasement." The Supreme Court (Cr. A. 3728/04 *Deviri v. The State of Israel*, per Justice Eliakim Rubinstein) rejected the defendant's argument and ruled that the defendant was well aware of the fact that the act of taking off their clothes would cause the women's sexual degradation. In the matter of coercing nudity on a person as sexual degradation, the court referred to the story about Queen Vashti, of whom we are told (Esther 1:11) that King Ahasuerus commanded that she be brought wearing the royal crown "to show the peoples and the princes her beauty; for she was fair to look on." The Midrash interpreted the command as a demand that she be brought to the banquet wearing only her royal crown, i.e., in the nude (See Megillah 12b, PdRE 48, Esther Rabbah 12). *Midrash Sifri de-Aggadata – Midrash Abba Guryon 1* interprets the words "'…with the royal crown' Rabbi Abba said: that she should be wearing nothing but the crown and she should be nude. Rabbi Shimon Bar Naḥmani said in the name of Rabbi Yonatan: Evil persons are not judged in Hell except in the nude, as has been said, 'O Lord, O Lord, when thou awakest, thou shalt despise *their image*' (Ps. 73:20)" – meaning that very fact of coercing a person to be nude is a degradation (cf. *Ma'amad ha-Ishah*, 223–28).

[Menachem Elon (2nd ed.)]

BIBLIOGRAPHY: Guttmann, Mafte'aḥ, 2 (1917), 122–8; S. Assaf, *Ha-Onshim Aḥarei Ḥatimat ha-Talmud* (1922), passim; ET, 1 (1951^3), 168–72, 5 (1953), 295–300; 12 (1967), 49–74; G. Melber, *Averat Innus va-Averot Miniyyot Aḥerot ba-Mishpat ha-Ivri u-va-Mishpat ha-Angli…* (Diss. Jerusalem 1960), summary in Eng.; EM, 2 (1965), 935–7. **ADD. BIBLIOGRAPHY:** M. Elon, *Ha-Mishpat ha-Ivri* (1988), 1:48, 72, 175, 185, 208, 248, 282ff., 287, 290ff., 297, 312, 318, 396, 414, 456ff, 654, 655, 670, 692ff., 697, 711, 722, 790ff.; 2:842, 1070; idem, *Jewish Law* (1994), 1:53, 80, 194, 208, 234, 289, 334, 339ff., 344ff., 354, 373, 380ff.; 2:483, 505, 556ff., 810, 827ff., 855, 860, 877ff., 891, 969ff.; 3:1030, 1291; M. Elon and B. Lifshitz, *Mafte'aḥ ha-She'elot ve-ha-Teshuvot shel Ḥakhmei Sefarad u-Ẓefon Afrikah* (legal digest) (1986), 3–5, 9–13, 173; B. Lifshitz and E. Shochetman, *Mafte'aḥ ha-She'elot ve-ha-Teshuvot shel Ḥakhmei Ashkenaz, Ẓarefat ve-Italyah* (legal digest) (1997), 4–5, 6–11; M. Elon, *Ma'amad ha-Ishah, Mishpat ve-Shipput, Masoret u-Temurah, Arakheyah shel Medinah Yehudit ve-Demokratit* (2005), 216–28; N. Rakover, "Coercive Marital Relations between a Man and his Wife," in: *Shenaton ha-Mishpat ha-Ivri* (1980), vol. 6–7, 295 (Heb.); N. Rakover, "*Hitgabberut ha-Yeẓer ke-Ta'anat Ones*," in: *Teḥumin*, 18 (1998), 197; Y. Zefira, "*Yaḥasei Ishut bi-Khefiyyah*," in: *Teḥumin*, 24 (2004), 222.

SEYMOUR, DAVID (**Chim**; 1911–1956), U.S. photographer. Chim was born in Warsaw, where his father was a pioneer Hebrew and Yiddish publisher. He studied photography and the graphic arts at the Leipzig Academy. In 1931 he moved to Paris, where he shared a studio with Robert *Capa and Henri Cartier-Bresson, and became a free-lance press photographer. At the outbreak of the Spanish Civil War he went to Spain and at the end of the war covered the journey of 1,000 Spanish loyalist refugees to Mexico. At the outbreak of World War II, Chim went to the United States, where he joined the air force and served as a photo intelligence officer. In Paris he rejoined Capa and Cartier-Bresson and together they founded Magnum Photos, one of the foremost international photographic agencies. His first peacetime assignment was a picture story of UNESCO for which he photographed his moving studies of homeless children in war-torn Europe. He befriended children everywhere, helped to support them, and where possible, settled them in private homes. Chim frequently visited Israel and was killed while covering the Sinai Campaign of 1956.

[Peter Pollack]

SEYMOUR, JANE (**Joyce Penelope Wilhelmina Frankenberg**; 1951–), actress. Born in Hayes, England, to a British father and a Dutch mother, she assumed the stage name of Jane Seymour at age 17, after King Henry VIII's third wife. Her film career began in 1969 with an uncredited role in *Oh! What a Lovely War*. Her first major film role was as Lillian Stein, a Jewish woman seeking shelter from the Nazis, in the 1970 war drama *The Only Way*. Other feature films include *Young Winston* (1972); the James Bond movie *Live and Let Die* (1973); *Sinbad and the Eye of the Tiger* (1977); *Somewhere in Time* (1980); *Lassiter* (1984); and *Wedding Crashers* (2005).

Seymour appeared in numerous TV movies and series, most notably as Dr. Michaela Quinn in the TV series and movie *Dr. Quinn, Medicine Woman* (1993–2001), a role that earned her three Emmy nominations. She won a Best Supporting Actress Emmy for her performance in the TV miniseries *Onassis* (1988) and was nominated for Best Actress Emmys for the miniseries *Captains and the Kings* (1976) and *War and Remembrance* (1988).

In 1999 Seymour was named an Officer of the Order of the British Empire (OBE) by Britain's Queen Elizabeth II. She has served as the official spokesperson for UNICEF and the international ambassador for Childhelp U.S.A. In 2005 she became a U.S. citizen.

Seymour was married to theater director Michael Attenborough (1971–73); after two other divorces, she married film director James Keach in 1993. She wrote several books, including *Remarkable Changes* (2003); *Two at a Time: Having Twins* (2001); and *Jane Seymour's Guide to Romantic Living* (1986).

[Ruth Beloff 2nd ed.)]

°SEYSS-INQUART, ARTHUR (1892–1946), Austrian Nazi lawyer who prior to the *Anschluss* was active in nationalist circles. He was appointed by the Austrian chancellor Kurt von Scnushnigg to the Council of State in the hope that he would mediate with the extreme Right. In 1938, because of German pressure on Austria, Seyss-Inquart was appointed minister of the interior in the Austrian cabinet, a function in which he executed the coup that led to the Austrian *Anschluss* to Germany that year. He then became chancellor of Austria, and later *Reichsstatthalter* (a high official whose task was to coordinate the activities of various ministries in occupied territories). In October 1939 he became deputy governor general of Poland, where he looked for territory for the Lublin Reservation. On May 19, 1940, he was appointed *Reichskommissar* for Holland, with the hope that he could copy his Austrian performance in Holland. He remained in this post until the German capitulation on May 5, 1945.

Seyss-Inquart was known for his devotion to *National-Socialism and his blind obedience to Hitler. His antisemitism was less extreme than that of many other Nazi leaders, but this did not prevent him from efficiently carrying out the persecution of the Jews in Holland. Only occasionally was he more moderate, probably for political reasons. Still he took an active role in the deportation of Jews in Holland. He wanted to be the initiator of operations and not have outside parties infringing on his area of responsibility. However, he never entered into conflict with Hitler on any policy, so that Hitler, as a token of his esteem, designated Seyss-Inquart foreign minister in his will. Sentenced to death at the Nuremberg trials, Seyss-Inquart was executed by hanging.

BIBLIOGRAPHY: E. Davidson, *Trial of the Germans* (1966), 446–82; G.M. Gilbert, *Nuremberg Diary* (1947), index; IMT, *Trial of the Major War Criminals*, 24 (1949), index; H.J. Neumann, *Arthur Seyss-Inquart* (Dutch, 1967).

[Jozeph Michman (Melkman) / Michael Berenbaum (2nd ed.)]

SFARD, DAVID (1905–1981), Yiddish writer and editor. Born in Trisk, Volhynia, he initially received a traditional Jewish education, then attended Hebrew-Polish schools (1919–26) and studied philosophy and participated in the literary circle of I.M. *Weissenberg in Warsaw (1926–28). His first poetic collection, *Shtaplen* ("Steps," 1929) appeared while he was studying in France (1928–31), where he wrote a doctoral dissertation on Hegel. In 1932 he returned to Warsaw and became actively involved in leftist Yiddish literary life, in 1933 becoming a member of the illegal Polish Communist Party. In 1939 he fled to Soviet-occupied territory. Repatriated to Poland in 1946, he occupied a prominent position in Jewish cultural life, especially as editor of the publishing venture Yidish-Bukh, which published more than 200 books. His own writings include the verse collections *Lider* ("Poems," 1957), and *Borvese Trit* ("Barefoot Steps," 1966), literary criticism, short stories, and translations. In 1969 he immigrated to Israel.

BIBLIOGRAPHY: LNYL, 6 (1965), 527–30. **ADD. BIBLIOGRAPHY:** D. Sfard, *Mit Zikh un mit Andere* (1984).

[Sol Liptzin / Gennady Estraikh (2nd ed.)]

SFORNO, OBADIAH BEN JACOB (c. 1470–c. 1550), Italian biblical commentator and physician. Born in Cesena, Sforno was especially attached to his brother Hananel, who for a time supported him financially. Nothing is known about his father. In Rome Obadiah studied philosophy, mathematics, philology, and, in particular, medicine, which profession he followed; there on Cardinal Grimani's recommendation he taught Hebrew from 1498 to 1500 to the Christian humanist Johannes *Reuchlin. He met David *Reuveni when the latter was in Rome (1524). After staying in various cities, he finally settled at Bologna, where he played an active role in resuscitating a Hebrew printing house and in organizing the community. He established a *bet-midrash* which he conducted until his death. His renown was such that Italian rabbis addressed *halakhic* questions to him, and his decisions were quoted in the responsa of Meir *Katzenelbogen, who referred to him in terms of great esteem (Resp. Maharam of Padua, nos. 48–49).

Obadiah's reputation rests chiefly on his commentary on the Pentateuch, Song of Songs, and Ecclesiastes, which first appeared in Venice in 1567; on Psalms (Venice, 1586), on Job (*Mishpat Ẓedek*, Venice, 1589) and on Jonah, Habakkuk and Zechariah which were published in the Rabbinic Bible, *Kehillot Moshe* (Amsterdam, 1724–28). While generally limiting himself to the literal exegesis of the biblical text and at times going beyond this to give an exposition in keeping with the contemporary scientific outlook (e.g., on the Creation), he avoids mystical and kabbalistic interpretations. He pays comparatively little regard to philology, being on the whole satisfied to elucidate the contents of a passage without entering into a philological analysis. He does not give historical explanations or identify places except in rare instances, availing himself, however, of his medical knowledge in his exegesis, e.g., Genesis 43:27, and in explaining the reasons for the commandments.

In his commentary on the Song of Songs and Ecclesiastes, as well as on the Pentateuch, he employs allegory, e.g., in expounding the reason for the injunction of the red *heifer. Instead of dealing separately with individual difficulties in a verse, he prefers to incorporate the solution in a brief running comment on the passage as a whole. He takes pains to emphasize the inner connection between different parts of a verse and to account for duplications in phraseology, e.g., Genesis 43:28. In many instances he deals with the motives that inspired acts of heroism. His explanation is at times extremely incisive, e.g., Genesis 39:19. While often quoting rabbinical statements in support of his views, he rarely makes use of historical *aggadot*.

He aimed at inculcating a love for mankind in general and not only for fellow Jews, the difference between them being quantitative and not qualitative (Ex. 19:5), and his commentaries contain frequent references to humanistic ideas. In line with this he quoted that "righteous gentiles are undoubtedly dear to Me" i.e., to God (loc. cit.), and "the whole of mankind is Thine own treasure" (Deut. 33:3). At times, however, he introduces his views in a somewhat artificial manner, e.g., Numbers 23:22–24.

His commentary on the Pentateuch is prefaced by an introduction entitled *Kavvanot ha-Torah* ("The inner meaning of the Torah"), in which he deals with the structure of the Pentateuch and the reasons for its precepts, in particular for the sacrifices, on which he dwells at some length. His wide learning is reflected in his other literary productions. Thus he wrote a philosophical work *Or Ammim* (Bologna, 1537), in which he sought to refute the views of Aristotle, which are in conflict with the principles of Judaism, by employing the basic elements of the Greek philosopher's own teachings. He translated the work into Latin, under the title *Lumen Gentium*, dedicating it to King Henry II of France (Bologna, 1548). He wrote a commentary on *Avot* (published in the *Roman Maḥzor*, Bologna, 1540–41), as well as other unpublished works: a translation of Euclid's eight books, a Hebrew grammar, some responsa, and smaller works on various subjects.

[Avie Goldberg]

His pentateuchal commentary was edited after his death by his brother HANANEL, an eminent talmudist. OBADIAH BEN ISRAEL SFORNO, Venetian talmudist, was the publisher of *Yemin Adonai Romemah* (Venice, c. 1600) by Menahem Azariah da *Fano. SOLOMON SHEMAIAH BEN NISSIM SFORNO (d. 1617), rabbi of Asti and then of Venice, was the author of various works, largely unpublished; these include responsa, some of which were included by Jacob *Heilbron in his *Naḥalat Ya'akov* (Padua, 1622), and commentaries to different biblical books. He edited Judah Halevi's *Kuzari* with Judah Moscato's commentary (Venice, 1594).

[Ariel Toaff]

BIBLIOGRAPHY: E. Finkel, *Obadja Sforno als Exeget* (1896); A.Z. Aescoly (ed.), *Sippur David ha-Re'uveni* (1940), 113–4 (first pagination); L.A. Wohlgemuth, in: *Scritti… Sally Mayer* (1956), 120–5 (Heb. section); J. Volk, in: *Sefer Niger* (1959), 277–302 (incl. bibl.); Laras, in: *Sinai*, 62 (1967), 262–7; Fuerst, Bibliotheca, 3 (1863), 319; Mortara, Indice, 61; Colorni, in: RMI, 28 (1962), 78–88; C. Roth, *Jews in the Renaissance* (1959), index.

SHAALBIM or **SHAALABBIN** (Heb. שַׁעַלְבִּין; שַׁעַלְבִים).

(1) Town in the territory of the tribe of Dan, together with Aijalon (Josh. 19:42). The place was inhabited by Amorites, who submitted to the tribe of Ephraim (Judg. 1:35). One of David's "mighty men," Eliahba the Shaalbonite, was born there (II Sam. 23:32; I Chron. 11:33). Shaalbim was included with Beth-Shemesh in Solomon's second administrative district (I Kings 4:9). Jerome mentions a village called Selebi to the north of Emmaus (PL, vol. 25, p. 488).

Shaalbim is identified with the village of Salbīt, northwest of the Aijalon Valley. This place was found deserted in the 19th century, but was later resettled by inhabitants of the nearby village of Beit (Bayt) Duqqū. In 1948 it was occupied by the Israel army whose soldiers discovered a mosaic-paved floor with an inscription in old Hebrew script. Excavations by the Hebrew University in 1949 revealed a Samaritan synagogue. The building is rectangular, approximately 50.5 × 26.4 ft. (15.40 × 8.05 m.) and oriented toward the northeast, in the direction of Mt. Gerizim. It contained the remains of two mosaic-paved floors, one above the other, approximately 5.9–11.5 in. (15–28 cm.) apart. The lower floor, the better preserved of the two, is decorated in black, red, and white and contains a rectangular panel 19.7 × 10.4 ft. (6 × 3.20 m.) with a rosette pattern in a crowstep border. In the center is a circle, 4.7 ft. (1.45 m.) in diameter, with a Greek inscription mentioning the *eukterion* (praying place). Below the inscription are two seven-branched candlesticks, and between them is an ornament which has been interpreted as a symbol of Mt. Gerizim. To the north of the panel and close to its border is an inscription in Samaritan script of Exodus 15:18; "The Lord will reign for ever and ever." Another fragmentary Samaritan inscription was found south of the panel. The synagogue apparently dates to the fourth century C.E.; it was probably destroyed in the fifth or sixth century.

[Michael Avi-Yonah]

(2) In 1951 a kibbutz was established at Shaalbim. In 1970 there were 270 inhabitants. Affiliated with Po'alei Agudat Israel, it was founded as a *Naḥal outpost by members of the Ezra movement together with Israel-born youth. Later, immigrants from English-speaking and other countries joined the settlement. Its population was 1,232 in 2004, including a *hesder* yeshivah and other educational facilities. Nearby was the religious rural settlement of Nof Ayalon with a population of 2,377.

[Efraim Orni]

BIBLIOGRAPHY: Abel, Geog, 2 (1938), 438; Sukenik, in: BRF, 1 (1949), 26ff.; *Enẓiklopedyah la-Ḥakirot Arkhe'ologiyyot be-Ereẓ Yisrael* (1970), 548–9. **ADD. BIBLIOGRAPHY:** Y. Tsafrir, L. Di Segni, and J. Green, *Tabula Imperii Romani. Iudaea – Palaestina. Maps and Gazetteer* (1994): 226, s.v. "Selebi."

SHAANAN, AVRAHAM (1919–1988), Hebrew writer and literary critic. Born in Galicia, Shaanan went to Palestine in 1935. Between 1953 and 1957 he was the London correspondent for the daily *Davar*, and subsequently edited its weekly literary supplement. He lectured in comparative literature at Tel Aviv University (1957–61) and was cultural attaché to the Israel Embassy in Paris from 1963 to 1966, and editor of the literary supplement of *Davar*. His stories and articles first appeared in *Gilyonot* and then in other literary journals in Israel and abroad.

His books include *Ha-Olam shel Mahar* ("The World of Tomorrow," 1952), stories; *Hillel Kawerin* (1955), a novel; *Iyyunim be-Sifrut ha-Haskalah* ("Studies in Haskalah Literature," 1952), dealing with the influence of French literature on Haskalah writers; *Millon ha-Sifrut ha-Ḥadash – ha-Ivrit ve-ha-Kelalit* ("A Dictionary of Modern Hebrew and World Literature," 1959; 1970; 1978) and a study of Shaul Tchernichowsky (1984). His major work is a history of modern Hebrew literature, *Ha-Sifrut ha-Ivrit ha-Ḥadashah li-Zrameha* ("Trends in Modern Hebrew Literature," 4 vols. 1962–67, incomplete). He also published an anthology, *Soferei Olam* ("World Authors," 1966), 21 works by world-famous authors translated into Hebrew, with introductions, biographies, and notes.

BIBLIOGRAPHY: Y. Friedlander, *Historiyografiyah shel ha-Sifrut*, in: *Yedioth Aharonoth* (March 31, 1978).

[Getzel Kressel]

SHA'AREI SHEVU'OT (Heb. שַׁעֲרֵי שְׁבוּעוֹת), work on the laws of oaths, consisting of 20 chapters. It is extensively quoted by the early *posekim* such as *Meir of Rothenburg, as well as in the *Ittur* of *Isaac b. Abba Mari and in the *Mordekhai* of *Mordecai b. Hillel. The authorship of this work has been a subject of dispute among scholars. It has been attributed erroneously to Isaac b. Reuben Alfasi. It now appears, however, that Isaac b. Reuben merely wrote an edited translation from the Arabic of David b. Saadiah's *Mishpetei Shevu'ot* and added a short rhymed introduction giving his own name in acrostic. As a result the work was wrongly ascribed to him. As the work is usually published together with the *halakhot* of Alfasi, it is often referred to as "the *She'arim* (lit. "gates," i.e., chapters) of R. Alfasi."

BIBLIOGRAPHY: Michael, Or, no. 1085; I. Friedlaender, in: MGWJ, 55 (1911), 502f.; L. Ginzberg, in: REJ, 67 (1914), 141–3; S. Assaf, in: KS, 3 (1926–27), 296f.

SHA'AREI TIKVAH (Heb. שַׁעֲרֵי תִּקְוָה), urban community in Samaria. The town is located in western Samaria, on the western slopes of the Samarian mountains, northeast of Petaḥ Tikvah. It was established in 1983 and the first settlers arrived in 1985. The founders sought to create an urban community with a mixed religious and secular population. In 1990 Sha'arei Tivkah received municipal council status. In 2002 its population was 3,650. In the town's vicinity are remains from the Second Temple period.

WEBSITES: www.shaarey-tikva.muni.il; www.moetzetyesha.co.il.

[Shaked Gilboa (2nd ed.)]

SHA'AR HA-AMAKIM (Heb. שַׁעַר הָעֲמָקִים; "Gateway of the Valleys"), kibbutz in northern Israel, on the ridge separating the Zebulun and Jezreel valleys, 1 mi. (2 km.) W. of Kiryat Tivon, affiliated with Kibbutz Arzi ha-Shomer ha-Ẓa'ir. Sha'ar ha-Amakim was founded in 1935 by pioneers from Yugoslavia. In the 1936–39 Arab riots the settlement came under frequent attack in an attempt to dislodge it from its strategic position. In 1970 the kibbutz had 580 inhabitants, maintaining a stable population into the 21st century. It developed intensive, fully irrigated farming based on field crops, plantations, fishery, and dairy cattle. The kibbutz owned Chromagen Solar Energy Systems, a leader in the field.

WEBSITE: www.sharmakim.org.il.

[Efraim Orni / Shaked Gilboa (2nd ed.)]

SHA'AR HA-GOLAN (Heb. שַׁעַר הַגּוֹלָן; "Gateway of the Golan"), kibbutz founded in 1937 on the northern bank of the Yarmuk river, central Jordan valley, Israel. Next to the kibbutz is an 8,000-year-old prehistoric settlement. It was first excavated by M. Stekelis in the years 1949–52. He uncovered remains of a previously unknown culture, which he named "Yarmukian Culture" after the nearby river. Pottery appears here for the first time in Israel, gives this cultural stage its name as Pottery Neolithic. In the years 1989–2004 Y. Garfinkel conducted large-scale excavations and uncovered ca. 3,000 sq.m.

The new excavations clarify that Sha'ar ha-Golan is of outstanding importance for a number of reasons. Surveys and excavations have shown that it is some 20 hectares in area, making it one of the largest settlements of its period in the world. The excavations uncovered three large courtyard houses, ranging between 250 and 700 sq.m. in area. Monumental construction on this scale is unknown elsewhere in this period. The houses consist of a central courtyard with several small rooms around it. This is an architectural concept that still exists in traditional Mediterranean societies. The courtyard house makes its first appearance at Sha'ar ha-Golan, giving the site a special importance in architectural history. The houses were separated by streets that constitute evidence of advanced community planning. Three passageways were uncovered, including a central street about 3 m. wide, paved with pebbles set in mud, and a narrow winding alley 1 m. wide. These are the earliest streets discovered in Israel, and among the earliest streets built by man. A well, 4.26 m. deep, was dug into the water table. It is indicative of advanced hydrological knowledge and technological engineering. Exotic objects discovered in the excavations include sea shells from the Mediterranean, polished stone vessels made from alabaster (or marble), and blades made from obsidian (volcanic glass) from Turkey. These point to trade connections extending over 700 km.

About 300 art objects were found at Sha'ar ha-Golan, making it the main center of prehistoric art in Israel and one of the most important in the world. Among the outstanding art objects are figurines in human form made of fired clay or carved on pebbles. The overwhelming majority are female images, interpreted as representing a goddess. The clay figurines are extravagant in their detail, giving them a surrealistic appearance, while the pebble figurines are minimalist and abstract in form. Because of the unique artistic quality of the figurines the Metropolitan Museum of New York and the Louvre Museum in Paris have mounted 10-year exhibits of selected objects. In Israel, figurines are exhibited at the Israel Museum in Jerusalem and in the local museum built in Kibbutz Sha'ar ha-Golan.

[Yosef Garfinkel (2nd ed.)]

The kibbutz is affiliated with Kibbutz Arẓi Ha-Shomer ha-Ẓa'ir. It was founded by pioneers from Czechoslovakia as a tower and stockade settlement and soon came under attack in the Arab riots. In the *War of Independence, the kibbutz lay exposed to attack and, on May 18, 1948, it became untenable as the invading Syrian Army, together with Iraqi and Jordanian contingents, took nearby Ẓemaḥ and advanced on Deganyah. The site was recaptured, however, together with the neighboring kibbutz Massadah, two days later. Both villages had been completely destroyed, and although they remained on the front line, the settlers immediately began reconstruction. In the following two decades, and particularly in the period preceding the *Six-Day War (June 1967), the nearby Syrian and Jordanian positions repeatedly harassed the kibbutz. Although the capture of the Golan Heights in June 1967 removed the danger from the Syrian side, the kibbutz, situated on the Jordanian border as well, continued to suffer from frequent shelling. In 1970 Sha'ar ha-Golan had 590 inhabitants, dropping to 503 in 2002. In spite of its security problems, the kibbutz developed a model economy based on subtropical irrigated field crops, bananas, avocados, dates, beehives, poultry, and dairy cattle. It also had a plastics factory, a few stores at the nearby Ẓemaḥ junction, and guest rooms.

[Efraim Orni / Shaked Gilboa (2nd ed.)]

BIBLIOGRAPHY: Stekelis, in: IEJ, 1 (1951), 1ff.; 2 (1952), 216–7; E. Anati, *Palestine before the Hebrews* (1963), 263ff. **WEBSITE:** www.shaar-hagolan.co.il.

SHA'AR ḤEFER-BEIT YIẒḤAK (Heb. שַׁעַר חֵפֶר; "Gateway to Ḥefer [plain]"), moshav in central Israel, E. of Netanyah, affiliated with Ha-Mo'eẓah ha-Ḥakla'it. The moshav consists of four separate settlements: Beit Yiẓḥak founded in 1939 by a group of settlers from Germany; Gan Ḥefer, inhabited by second-generation farmers, mostly from Netanyah, belonging to the *Benei Binyamin association founded in 1940; Sha'ar Ḥefer, established by immigrants from Czechoslovakia founded in 1940; and Nirah, established in 1941 by middle-class immigrants from Czechoslovakia. At the beginning, each settlement was independent, but soon after their establishment, it was proposed to unite them. First Gan Ḥefer was united with Sha'ar Ḥefer. Later on, in the 1950s, Sha'ar Ḥefer merged with the adjacent moshav Nirah. In 1970 the combined Sha'ar Ḥefer had 350 inhabitants. In 1972, Sha'ar Ḥefer and Beit Yitzhak were united as a single settlement, Sha'ar Ḥefer-Beit Yiẓḥak. The population of the united settlement was 1,560 inhabitants at the end of 2002, thanks to new housing and the absorption of newcomers. The moshav's economy was based on citrus groves, vegetables, milch cattle, and poultry. Beit Yiẓḥak was known for its natural confiture factory.

WEBSITE: www.beit-yitzhak.org.il

[Efraim Orni / Shaked Gilboa (2nd ed.)]

SHA'ATNEZ (Heb. שַׁעַטְנֵז; Gr. κίβδηλος, "counterfeit"), cloth combining wool and linen. Leviticus 19:19 and Deuteronomy 22:11 prohibit the wearing of *sha'atnez*, in the former passage explained as *beged kil'ayim*, "cloth made from a mixture of two kinds of material," in the latter passage explained as "wool and linen together." While the meaning of the term is therefore clear, its etymology is obscure, modern speculation ranging from unlikely Hebrew combinations (e.g., *sa'arat-a'nez* supposedly meaning "[sheep's] hair-[flax] stalk") to the no more likely Coptic (*saht*, "woven," *nudj*, "false" [cf. the LXX]), and vulgar Arabic (*shash*, "black gauze," *'atmuz*, "strong") derivations. The word looks foreign.

The clothing of the priests was notably exempt from the prohibition of *sha'atnez*. Exodus 28:6, 8, 15, and 39:29 prescribe that various pieces be made of linen and colored wool interwoven (cf. Kil. 9:1: "Priests wear only wool and linen [i.e. *sha'atnez*] when they serve in the temple"). This suggests that the general prohibition was grounded on the taboo character of such a mixture, pertaining exclusively to the realm of the sacred (cf. Maimonides' view, below).

The rabbis interpret the word *sha'atnez* as being a compound standing for *shu'a* (שׁוּעַ; each thread smoothed out by the process of carding); *tavui* (טָווּי; each strand spun); and *nuz* (נוּז; woven or twisted together). The Torah's prohibition against *sha'atnez* therefore only applies when a strand of wool and one of linen, each carded, spun, and twisted, have been joined together by weaving, sewing, or tying (Kil. 9:8). The rabbis, however, prohibited the wearing of wool and linen even when their threads are simply sewn, tied, or pasted together (Nid. 61b; Rashi to Hor. 11a). The prohibition was extended to include sitting on *sha'atnez* fabrics although the Torah originally only forbade the wearing of mixed garments (Ta'an. 27b). It is, however, permitted to utilize *sha'atnez* shrouds for a corpse (Nid. 61b).

In accordance with the general principle that a positive precept overrides a negative one, it is permitted to attach blue woolen ẓiẓit to a linen garment (Men. 40a). It was likewise permitted for priests to wear garments of mixed texture prescribed by the Torah when performing priestly service in the Sanctuary (Yoma 69a).

Although the prohibition is considered a prime example of a divine statute which has no rational explanation (חוֹק), Jewish thinkers throughout the ages have attempted to rationalize its intent. Maimonides explained that the wearing of mixed garments was forbidden since heathen priests wore such garments (*Guide of the Perplexed* 3:37). Naḥmanides suggested that the person mixing diverse kinds was guilty of displaying that he was improving upon the species created by God (Commentary to Lev. 19:19) while S.R. Hirsch saw in this commandment a reminder to man that he must guard his assigned purpose and place in the world just as the species must be distinctly preserved (Commentary to Lev. 19:19, tr. by I. Levy (1958), 534f.).

Elaborate chemical and microscopic tests have been developed to check for the presence of *sha'atnez* in clothing. In many cities with large Jewish populations, *sha'atnez* laboratories have been established to check for *sha'atnez* in garments.

BIBLIOGRAPHY: F. Brown, S.R. Driver, and C.A. Briggs, *A Hebrew and English Lexicon of the Old Testament* (1962), s.v. (etymology); Koehler-Baumgarten, s.v. (etymology); Ben-Yehuda, Millon, s.v. (etymology); D. Feldmann *Shimmushah shel Torah* (1951), 128–36; Eisenstein, Dinim, 429f.

[Aaron Rothkoff]

SHABAD (Szabad), ZEMAḤ (1864–1935), physician, communal leader, and publicist, one of the heads of the Vilna community, known for his cultural and political activities. Born in Vilna, in 1881 Shabad moved with his family to Moscow, where he completed his studies in the faculty of medicine at Moscow University (1884–89). In 1894 Shabad settled in Vilna, devoting himself to work in a hospital, where he became a director and a well-known internist. For many years he was chairman of *YEKOPO. Believing in the principle of "productivization" in Jewish occupations, he promoted the development of *ORT, serving as its chairman until 1925. Shabad was distinguished for his manifold activities in the field of public health, as founder of the Vilna branch of *OZE, which was affiliated to the national organization of *TOZ. In this framework he devoted himself to the central organ of TOZ, *Folksgezund*, in which he published articles dealing with medical research, and formulated many medical terms in Yiddish.

During World War I he worked to save the Jewish masses in the battle areas from epidemics and hunger. In 1919–20 he served as president of the democratically elected community council, and between 1919 and 1927 was a member of the Vilna municipal council. Politically he was close to the Folkist Party (*Folkspartei) in Poland; he cultivated ideological and personal relations with S. *Dubnow before the Russian Revolution and also later when Dubnow left Russia. Following a disagreement with Noah *Prylucki, a split occurred in the party in 1926. Later Shabad, as head of the dissidents whose center was in Vilna, made contact with the *Minority Bloc led by Y. *Gruenbaum, and in 1928 was elected a member of the Polish Senate. There he fought manifestations of antisemitism and discrimination by the government. At the end of his life he became close to the neo-Territorialist (see *Territorialism) movement. Supporting Jewish cultural and national autonomy (see *Autonomism), and as one of the active members of the Central Yiddish School Organization (CYSHO), he struggled for the rights of secular schools with Yiddish as their language of instruction. He was one of the founders of the *YIVO research institute which was established in Vilna.

BIBLIOGRAPHY: Z. Rejzen, *Vilne* (1935), 737, 744; Rejzen, Leksikon, 4 (1929), 429–34; M. Shalit (ed.), *Oyf di Khurves fun Milkhomes un Mehumes* (1931), 574–602, 903; *Dr. Zemah Shabad, der Visenschaftler un Publitsist* (1937).

[Moshe Landau]

SHABAZI, SHALEM (fl. 17th century), the greatest of Yemenite Jewish poets. Some 550 of his poems and hymns are extant, written in Hebrew, Aramaic, or Arabic. In all of them, his name appears in acrostic form either at the beginning of the stanzas or in the poem itself. No details are known regarding his life except what can be deduced from his poems. Living in a period of persecutions and messianic anticipations for Yemenite Jewry, Shabazi gave faithful poetic expression to the suffering and yearning of his generation, whose national poet he became. It seems that he wandered in poverty throughout *Yemen. Many legends describe him as a *ẓaddik* and miracle worker; his tomb in *Taiz was considered holy and became a shrine where both Jews and Muslims prayed for relief from sickness and misery. His poetry deals primarily with the religious themes of exile and redemption, the Jewish people and God, wisdom and ethics, Torah, and the life to come. Many of his poems deal with the glorious past of the Jews in their own land, from which the author draws faith and hope for renewed greatness in the future. He wrote poems dedicated to the Sabbath and festivals, marriage, and circumcision. His ethical poems are outstanding for their teaching and gentle moralizing. *Kabbalah and mysticism based on the works of the kabbalists who preceded R. Isaac *Luria play an important role in his poetry. Academic and medieval scientific themes are also a frequent feature. His rare secular poems deal with discussions between concrete and abstract objects. His poems are not confined to any one theme, but combine several subjects in one and the same work. Their style, comparable to that of rabbinical literature, is prosaic and easy, making his poetry readily accessible to the masses. About half the poems in the Yemenite *diwan*, published in many editions, are by him. R. Halevi's edition (1998) includes more than 200 liturgical poems attributed to Shabazi.

BIBLIOGRAPHY: W. Bacher, in: *Jahresbericht der Landes-Rabbinerschule in Budapest*, 33 (1909–10); Idelsohn, in: *Mizraḥ u-Ma'arav*, 1 (1929), 8–16, 128–40; A.Z. Idelsohn and H. Torczyner, *Shirei Teiman* (1930), 88–221; Ratzabi, in: *Sefunot*, 9 (1965), 135–66; idem, in: KS, 43 (1967–68), 140–59 (incl. bibl.). **ADD. BIBLIOGRAPHY:** Sh. Seri, *Shirim Ḥadashim le-Rabi Shalom Shabazi* (1976); Sh. Meḳinṭon, *Shirei Rabenu Shalem Shabazi* (c. 1979); R. Ahroni, in: *Hebrew Annual Review*, 9 (1985), 5–30; Sh. Rada'i and A. Ḳoraḥ, *Shirei ha-Rav ha-Ga'on Shalom Shabazi* (1986); E. Dori and M. Ben Ami, *Diẓan: Sefer ha-Shirim shel Shalom Shabazi* (c. 1993); R. Halevi, *Shirat Yisra'el be-Teman: Mi-Mivḥar ha-Shirah ha-Shabazit-Teimanit* (1998).

[Yehuda Ratzaby]

SHABBAT (Heb. שַׁבָּת), first tractate in the Mishnah, Tosefta, and the two Talmuds of the order *Mo'ed*, dealing in 24 chapters with the laws relating to Sabbath and its observance. The last four chapters are missing in the Jerusalem Talmud.

Chapter 1 deals with the problems of "domains" (*reshuyyot*, see *Reshut) and with questions concerning what may or may not be done on Friday before sunset. Chapter 2 deals with the kindling of the Sabbath lights. Chapters 3–4 are on keeping food warm or warming it up on the Sabbath. Chapter 5 concerns the injunction that one's domestic animals rest on the Sabbath. Chapter 6 discusses what one may carry as a part of one's apparel and includes an interesting discussion as to whether weapons are to be regarded as apparel. Chapter 7 is notable for its enumeration of the 39 principal categories of works forbidden on the Sabbath. It also discusses the sin-offering due for the inadvertent violation of the Sabbath and the minimal quantities which incur guilt. Chapter 8 continues the question of quantities, chapters 9–15 deal with the definitions of these various labors, and Chapter 16 discusses mainly the problems arising from conflagration. Chapters 17–18 deal with **mukẓeh*, chapter 19 with the problem of circumcision on the Sabbath, and chapters 20–24 with a great variety of questions relating to the Sabbath, such as bathing, casting lots, attending to the dead, and feeding cattle.

The following passages of the Babylonian *Gemara* deserve particular mention: the description of the origin of Ḥanukkah (21b); the discussion on whether the Books of Ezekiel, Ecclesiastes, and Proverbs should be considered canonical (13b, 30b); the humility and leniency of *Hillel in contrast to the stringency of *Shammai (29b–30a); differences in the attitude of the sages toward Rome and the story of Simeon b. *Yoḥai hiding in a cave for 12 years (33b); and on the ministering angels (*malakhei ha-sharet*) accompanying the Jew from the synagogue to his home on the Sabbath eve (119b). The Tosefta to this tractate is divided into 18 chapters. Chapters 6–7 refer to many interesting customs and superstitions, some of which are denounced as idolatrous.

The tractates *Shabbat* and *Eruvin* were originally one tractate. The last chapter of *Eruvin* belongs to *Shabbat* as does that of the Tosefta. The Mishnah of *Shabbat* derives from various sources and different layers can be detected. Most conspicuous is the combination of Mishnah collections. It contains some of the Mishnah of Meir, Judah, Yose, Simeon, and Eleazar. It contains matters that belong together but which are scattered in various places and also conflicting views both in different places and in one and the same Mishnah. Several of the *mishnayot* (1:11; 13:1–3, 6, 8; 14:3; et al.) are clearly of early date. Nevertheless the Mishnah of *Shabbat* in its present form is in the main from the version of Akiva's pupils. From the arrangement of the Tosefta it is clear that it had in front of it mishnaic sources different in arrangement and scope. The whole of the chapter dealing with "the customs of the Amorite" in the Tosefta chapters 6 and 7 (see above) is from the Mishnah of Yose. The talmudic tractate was translated into English by H. Freedman in the Soncino edition (1938).

BIBLIOGRAPHY: Epstein, Tanna'im, 282–99; Ḥ. Albeck, *Shishah Sidrei Mishnah*, 2 (1958), 9–15.

[Arnost Zvi Ehrman]

SHABBAT BERESHIT (Heb. שַׁבַּת בְּרֵאשִׁית, "the Sabbath of Genesis"), the first Sabbath after *Sukkot on which the new annual cycle of the Torah reading in synagogue begins (see also *Triennial Cycle), the previous cycle having been completed on *Simḥat Torah. Its name refers to the first word of the Bible "*Bereshit*" – "In the beginning." It is customary on this Sabbath to call to the Torah reading the person who acted on Simḥat Torah as *Ḥatan Bereshit* (see *Bridegrooms of the Law; *Torah, Reading of). The term "Shabbat Bereshit" in the above sense is fairly recent. In ancient sources this term refers to any Sabbath, as against other holidays which were also called "Sabbath." Similarly, the seventh year of *Shemittah* was called "*Shabbat.*"

SHABBAT HA-GADOL (Heb. שַׁבַּת הַגָּדוֹל; "the great Sabbath"), Sabbath preceding *Passover. The name *ha-Gadol* ("the great") derives, according to some opinions, from the declaration in the *haftarah* (Mal. 3:4,24) "Behold, I will send you Elijah the prophet before the coming of the great and terrible day of the Lord" (*ibid.*, 3:23). This *haftarah* was selected in accordance with the popular belief that the messianic redemption of Israel will occur in the same month as its deliverance from the Egyptian bondage (RH 11a). Another opinion on the institution of the "great Sabbath" before Passover is that it was influenced by the Christian concept of the Saturday before Easter. In some ancient rabbinic sources the Sabbaths preceding Passover, Shavuot and Sukkot were also called *Shabbat ha-Gadol* (Elbogen, Gottesdienst, 551). On this Sabbath it is customary to read the greater part of the Passover **Haggadah* during the afternoon service. In traditional synagogues, the rabbi delivers a sermon devoted almost exclusively to the rites and the *dietary laws pertaining to Passover.

BIBLIOGRAPHY: Eisenstein, Dinim, 401–2.

SHABBETAI BEN MEIR HA-KOHEN (1621–1662), Lithuanian rabbi, commentator on the Shulḥan Arukh, and *posek*. He was also known as the Sha-Kh from the initials of the title of his book, *Siftei Kohen*. Shabbetai was born in Amstivov near Vilkaviskis. In his youth he studied under his father and later under *Joshua Hoeschel b. Joseph in Tykocin, moving subsequently to the yeshivah of Cracow with his teacher. From there he proceeded to Lublin, where he studied also under *Naphtali b. Isaac ha-Kohen. While still young he returned to Vilna, where he married the daughter of the wealthy Samson Wolf, a grandson of Moses *Isserles. Shabbetai's father-in-law provided for all his material needs and he was able to devote himself wholly to study. His renown soon spread among scholars and he was appointed *dayyan* in the *bet din* of Moses *Lima in Vilna. In Cracow in 1646, Shabbetai published his first work, *Siftei Kohen*, on the Shulḥan Arukh, *Yoreh De'ah*. This work received the approbation of the greatest Polish and Lithuanian scholars and since 1674 has been published in most editions of the *Yoreh De'ah*. That same year also saw the publication of the commentary *Turei Zahav* to the *Yoreh De'ah* by *David b. Samuel ha-Levi, who was already renowned and accepted as a *posek*. Shabbetai thereupon wrote criticisms to *Turei Zahav* entitled *Nekuddot ha-Kesef*. Although it was only published after the death of both Shabbetai and David ha-Levi (Frankfurt on the Oder, 1677), many of the criticisms reached the ears of David ha-Levi during his lifetime and he replied to them. These were published at the end of the commentary *Turei Zahav* with the title *Daf Aḥaron* ("Last Page") and were read by Shabbetai, who replied in his *Kunteres Aḥaron* ("Last Addendum"), published at the end of *Nekuddot ha-Kesef*.

The halakhic dispute between the views of David ha-Levi and Shabbetai, even after their deaths, was continued by other scholars. In most cases the rabbis of Poland and Lithuania ruled in accordance with Shabbetai, while those of Germany accepted the view of David ha-Levi. In contrast to many of the Polish scholars who preceded him and who criticized the author of the Shulḥan Arukh, Joseph *Caro, Shabbetai attempted to justify him fully. In his commentary on the *Yoreh De'ah*, he attempts to explain and clarify Caro's statements and to decide between Caro and the criticisms made by Moses Isserles. Shabbetai also wrote a commentary on the *Ḥoshen Mishpat*, which was published after his death with the text of the Shulḥan Arukh (Amsterdam, 1663). In this work, too, he explains the rulings of Caro but does not refrain from criticizing them; nor did he hesitate to criticize his other predecessors where their ruling did not appeal to him, or where he thought they had erred in their halakhic decisions. His rulings are based not only upon the principles of the Talmud and *posekim* but also upon logic and reason, although he did not abstain from the use of *pilpul*. His work is a classic of its kind and has been accepted to the present day as an authoritative reference work for halakhic authorities.

During the persecutions suffered by Lithuanian Jewry in 1655 (a continuation of the massacres of 1648–49), Shabbetai was compelled to flee from Vilna to Lublin, but only three months later the rioters reached Lublin, and Shabbetai succeeded in escaping to Bohemia. He stayed first in Prague, and then for a time in Dresnitz, Moravia, after which he was appointed rabbi of Holesov, where he died. Shabbetai, who had a polished, elegant, and facile style of writing, also had a historical sense. He portrayed the Chmielnicki persecutions of 1648–49 in his *Megillat Eifah* (Amsterdam, 1651), in which he described the events and the sufferings through which the Jews of Poland passed during that era. This work is an important historical document and has been translated into German and Russian. He also composed *seliḥot* (publ. in Amsterdam, 1651), in which he poured out his bitter complaints. He charged his children and grandchildren always to observe the *takkanot* of the Councils of the Lands and to appoint the 20th of Sivan as a day of fast, on which they should recite the *kinot* he compiled.

During the period he was rabbi in Holesov he became friendly with a Christian scholar. In the library of the academy in Leipzig there is a holograph of a Hebrew letter dated Feb. 3, 1660, which Shabbetai wrote "to him whom I love as myself, the philosopher magister Valentino Wiedreich." Shabbetai informs him that he has sent him the book of Elijah Baḥur and asks him to keep in touch with him (*Bikkurei ha-Ittim*, 10 (1829), 43–44).

His other works are: *He-Arukh* (Berlin, 1767), a commentary on the *Arba'ah Turim, Yoreh De'ah* of Jacob b. Asher; *Tokfo Kohen* (Frankfurt on the Oder, 1677), on the laws of possession and undecided laws (*teiku*); *Gevurat Anashim* (Dessau, 1697), on chapter 154 of the Shulḥan Arukh, *Even ha-Ezer*, to which are appended ten responsa written by his father; and *Po'el Ẓedek* (Jesenice, 1720), on the 613 commandments as enumerated by Maimonides, divided for the seven days of the week.

BIBLIOGRAPHY: Davidson, Oẓar, 4 (1939), 466; C.B. Friedberg, *Keter Kehunnah* (1898); S.M. Chones, *Toledot ha-Posekim* (1910), 586–90; Halpern, Pinkas, 78f., 83f., 153, 182, 275; Ch. Tchernowitz, *Toledot ha-Posekim*, 3 (1947), 138–58; B. Katz, *Rabbanut, Ḥasidut, Haskalah* (1956), 108–11; idem, in: *Sefer Yovel le-Y. Baer* (1960), 335f.; S. Knoebil, *Toledot Gedolei Hora'ah* (1927), 87–95; D. Tamar, in: *Aresheth*, 3 (1961), 169 n. 13; Y. Yudlov, in: KS 45 (1970/71), 451.

[Shlomo Eidelberg]

SHABBETAI BEN ẒEVI HIRSCH OF RASZKOW (?–1757?), widely respected Lurianic kabbalist, a colleague of R. *Israel b. Eliezer Baal Shem Tov (Besht), who possessed expert knowledge of kabbalistic writings. He composed a *siddur* (prayerbook), with *kavvanot* (theurgic meditations) according to Isaac *Luria (completed mid-1750s; published in Korets, 1797 (3 vols.); Lemberg, 1866 (1 vol.), repr. Jerusalem 1980, 2005). This *siddur* also contains eight contemplative practices from the Besht. In addition, it has contemplative instructions of an ecstatic devotional nature not attested to in other East European Lurianic *siddurim*. One important theurgic variant in the *kavvanot* of the Silent Prayer (**Amidah*) found in no other Lurianic *Siddur*, except for those of the Jerusalem kabbalistic school of R. Shalom *Sharabi, may suggest contact between these two schools of Lurianic Kabbalah, perhaps through the agency of R. Gershon of Kutov, the brother-in-law of the Besht, who took up residence in Israel in 1746 and traveled back and forth in the mid-1750s. A manuscript of R. Shabbetai's *siddur* was consulted by R. Asher Margolius when he prepared the Lurianic *Kavvanot siddur* used by the *kloiz* of Brody (Lvov, 1788, repr. Jerusalem 1980, 2005, fol. 3a–b). The Lemberg edition of the Raszkower *siddur* contains glosses from two prominent 19th-century ḥasidic kabbalists: R. Israel of Kozhnitz and R. Ẓevi of Zhidachov. In 1995, a manuscript facsimile of vol. 1 of the Raszkower *siddur* was published. Completed in 1760 by R. Abraham Samson of Raszkow, son of R. *Jacob Joseph of Polonnoye, the primary recorder of the teachings of the Besht, it contained one of the eight aforementioned teachings. The Korets, 1784–5 edition of the classic theurgic Lurianic work, *Pri Eẓ Ḥayyim*, was published from a manuscript with R. Shabbetai's glosses. In addition, R. Shabbetai re-edited a Lurianic work entitled *Seder Kelalut Tikkun ve-Aliyyat ha-Olamot* (Lvov, 1788; previously published in *Sefer ha-Gilgulim*, ed. R. David Gruenhaut; Frankfurt, 1684). Also extant from his hand are five manuscripts of classic Lurianic works such as *Mevo ha-She'arim* and *Ez Ḥayyim*. He copied these between 1748 and 1756. The work copied in 1756 was incomplete and was finished by another scribe in 1759. Also, extant is an epistle discussing fine points of scribal law written by R. Gershon of Kutov, and copied in 1755 by R. Shabbetai at the behest of the Besht. It was later published in the rare Responsa, *Mishne Avraham* (Zhitomir, 1868).

BIBLIOGRAPHY: A.J. Heschel, "Rabbi Gershon Kutover: His Life and Immigration to the Land of Israel," in: S.H. Dresner (ed.), *The Circle of the Baal Shem Tov* (1985), 44–113, especially 83–89 and note 187, and 107–8); M. Kallus, "The Relation of the Baal Shem Tov to the Practice of Lurianic *Kavvanot* in Light of his Comments in the *Siddur Rashkov*," in: *Kabbalah: Journal for the Study of Jewish Mystical Texts*, vol. 2 (1997), 151–69; idem, "The Theurgy of Prayer in the Lurianic Kabbalah" (Ph.D. diss., Hebrew University of Jerusalem, 2002, 280–84.

SHABBETAI ẒEVI (1626–1676), the central figure of Shabbateanism, the messianic movement named after him.

Background of the Movement

Shabbateanism was the largest and most momentous *messianic movement in Jewish history subsequent to the destruction of the Temple and the *Bar Kokhba Revolt. The factors giving rise to its extraordinarily widespread and deep-seated appeal are twofold. On the one hand there was the general condition of the Jewish people in exile, and the hopes for political and spiritual redemption fostered by Jewish religious tradition and given great emphasis in Jewish thought, which at all times could provide fertile soil for the blossoming of messianic movements aimed at ushering in redemption. On the other hand there were the specific conditions contributing to the impetus of the movement that began in 1665. Politically and socially, the position of the Jews in the various countries of the Diaspora was still basically the same and, with few exceptions, they pursued their specific way of life apart from the surrounding Christian or Muslim society, facing humiliation and persecution at every turn of political events and in constant awareness of their insecurity. The great wave of anti-Jewish persecution in Poland and Russia which set in with the *Chmielnicki massacres in 1648 deeply affected Ashkenazi Jewry and had wide repercussions, especially through the large number of captives in many countries whose ransom led to lively agitation. Soon after this disaster came the Russian-Swedish War (1655) which also struck those areas of Polish Jewish settlement which had not been shattered by Chmielnicki's attacks. Important as these factors undoubtedly were to the upsurge of messianic hopes in Polish Jewry, they are not sufficient to explain what actually happened, and no doubt local conditions prevailing in various parts of the Diaspora contributed their share. But the political and social events are only one part of the story.

The central and unifying factor behind the Shabbatean movement was of a religious nature, connected with the profound metamorphosis in the religious world of Judaism caused by the spiritual renewal centered in Safed in the 16th century. Its decisive feature was the rise of the *Kabbalah to a dominant position in Jewish life and particularly in those circles which were receptive to new religious impulses and formed the most active sector of the Jewish communities. The new Kabbalah which went out from Safed, especially in its Lurianic forms, wedded striking concepts to messianic ideas. It could be characterized as messianism pervading mysticism, thus introducing a new element of tension into the older Kabbalah, which was of a much more contemplative nature. Lurianic Kabbalah proclaimed an intimate bond between the religious activity of the Jew as he performs the commandments of the law and *meditations for prayer and the messianic message. All being has been in exile since the very beginning of creation and the task of restoring everything to its proper place has been given to the Jewish people, whose historic fate and destiny symbolize the state of the universe at large. The sparks of Divinity are dispersed everywhere, as are the sparks of the original soul of *Adam; but they are held captive by the *kelippah*, the power of evil, and must be redeemed. This final redemption, however, cannot be achieved by one single messianic act, but will be effected through a long chain of activities that prepare the way. What the kabbalists called "restoration" (*tikkun*) implied both the process by which the shattered elements of the world would be restored to harmony – which is the essential task of the Jewish people – and the final result, the state of *redemption announced by the appearance of the *Messiah, who marks the last stage. Political liberation, and all that the national myth connected with it, were seen as no more than external symbols of a cosmic process which in fact takes place in the secret recesses of the universe. No conflict was foreseen between the traditional national and political content of the messianic idea and the new spiritual and mystical note which it acquired in Lurianic Kabbalah. Those susceptible to the kabbalistic theology of Judaism focused their activity on hastening the arrival of the "world of *tikkun*" by an ascetic life which, though in strict accordance with the demands of the law, was permeated with virtual messianism. This messianism, however, was not an abstract hope for a distant future: what made Lurianism a dynamic factor in Jewish history was its proclamation that almost the whole process of restoration had been completed and that the final redemption was just around the corner. Only the last stages had to be passed through and redemption would be at hand.

As they gained ascendancy and dominated religious life, ideas like these became a common catalyst for an acute precipitation of messianic fervor. In fact, Lurianic Kabbalah became a dominant factor only about 1630–40 and the ideology of the Shabbatean movement is closely connected with this development. That the movement had an overwhelming appeal to such different centers of the Diaspora as Yemen and Persia, Turkey and North Africa, Italy and the Ashkenazi communities can be explained only by the fact that the intense propaganda of Lurianism had created a climate favorable to the release of the messianic energies aroused by the victory of

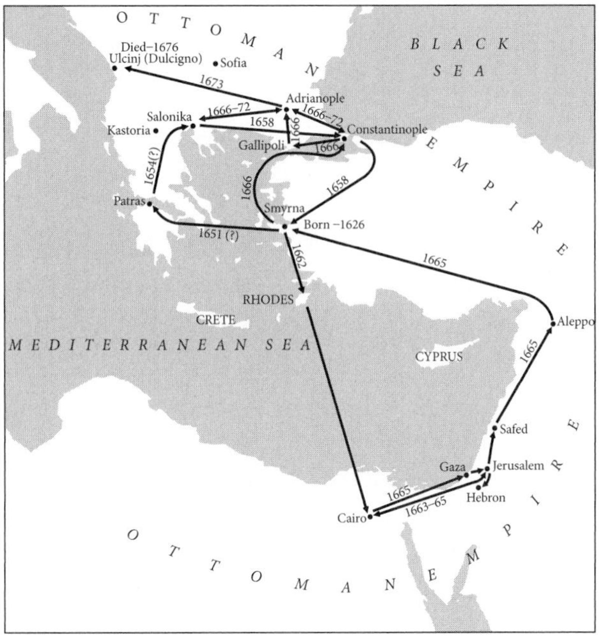

Journeys of Shabbetai Ẓevi.

the new Kabbalah. This is the reason why places like Amsterdam, Leghorn, and Salonika, where the Jews lived relatively free from oppression, nevertheless became crucibles of the movement and centers of Shabbatean activities.

Shabbetai Ẓevi's Early Years and Personality

The figure of the man who occupied the center of the movement is a most unexpected and surprising one. By now, his biography is one of the most completely documented of any Jew who played an important role in Jewish history. Shabbetai Ẓevi was born in Smyrna (Izmir) on the Ninth of Av, 1626 (unless the date was manipulated to conform with the tradition that the Messiah would be born on the anniversary of the destruction of the Temple). His father, Mordecai Ẓevi, came from the Peloponnesus (Patras?), probably from a family of Ashkenazi origin, and as a young man settled in Smyrna, where he first was a modest poultry merchant and later became an agent for Dutch and English traders. The great economic rise of Smyrna in those years made him wealthy and Shabbetai Ẓevi's brothers, Elijah and Joseph, were actually wealthy merchants. Shabbetai Ẓevi received a traditional education. His gifts being early recognized, he was destined by his family to become a *ḥakham*, a member of the rabbinic elite. He studied under Isaac de Alba and later under the most illustrious rabbi of Smyrna at that time, Joseph *Escapa, and seems to have been ordained as a *ḥakham* when he was about 18. He had a thorough talmudic training and even his bitterest detractors never accused him of being an ignoramus. According to one source, he left the yeshivah at the age of 15, beginning a life of abstinence and solitude and studying without the help of teachers. He was emotionally closely attached to his mother and at an early period developed an intense inner life. Starting out on the path of asceticism he was beset by sexual temptations, references to which have survived. In his adolescent years he also embarked on the study of Kabbalah, concentrating mainly on the *Zohar, *Sefer ha-*Kanah*, and *Sefer ha-Peli'ah*. Having acquired considerable proficiency in kabbalistic learning, he attracted other young contemporaries who studied with him.

Between 1642 and 1648 he lived in semi-seclusion. During this period he began to display a character that conforms largely to what handbooks of psychiatry describe as an extreme case of cyclothymia or manic-depressive psychosis. Periods of profound depression and melancholy alternated with spasms of maniacal exaltation and euphoria, separated by intervals of normality. These states, which are richly documented throughout his life, persisted until his death. Later they were described by his followers not in psychopathological but in theological terms as "illumination" and "fall" or "hiding of the face" (the state where God hides his face from him). His mental affliction brought to the fore an essential trait of his character: during his periods of illumination he felt impelled to commit acts which ran counter to religious law, later called *ma'asim zarim* ("strange or paradoxical actions"). Their content changed from time to time but a predilection for strange and bizarre rituals and sudden innovations pervaded them all. One thing was constant to these exalted states – his inclination to pronounce the Ineffable Name of God, the Tetragrammaton (see *God, Names of). In the periods of melancholy, which were of uneven length, he retired from human contact into solitude to wrestle with the demonic powers by which he felt attacked and partly overwhelmed. The exact moment that this illness broke out is not known, but at the latest it took place in 1648 when the news of the Chmielnicki massacres reached Smyrna. Starting to utter the Name of God in public, he possibly also proclaimed himself the Messiah for the first time. Since by then he was known to be mentally afflicted nobody took this seriously and his behavior caused no more than a temporary commotion. It seems that his extravagances aroused more compassion than antagonism. Between 1646 and 1650 he contracted two marriages in Smyrna which, since they were not consummated, ended in divorce. In his home town he was considered partly a lunatic and partly a fool, but since he had a very pleasant appearance and was highly musical, endowed with a particularly fine voice, he made friends, though not adherents of his kabbalistic speculations. In these years he began to speak of a particular "mystery of the Godhead" which had been revealed to him through his spiritual struggles. He used to speak of the "God of his faith" with whom he felt a particularly intimate and close relation. It is not clear whether by this he meant only the *Sefirah Tiferet* (see *Kabbalah), which he saw as the essential manifestation of God, or some supernal power which clothed itself in this *Sefirah*. At any rate, the term *Elohei Yisrael* ("the God of Israel") took on a special mystical meaning in his parlance. His compulsion to violate the law in his illuminated states, which were sometimes accompanied by imagining experiences of levitation, and his repeated claims to be the Messiah, finally led the rabbis, including his teacher Joseph Escapa, to intervene; around 1651–54 they banished him from Smyrna.

For several years Shabbetai Ẓevi wandered through Greece and Thrace, staying for a long time in Salonika, where he made many friends. But this stay also ended in disaster when, during one of his exalted states, he celebrated a ceremonial nuptial service under the canopy with the Torah, and committed other acts which were considered intolerable. Expelled by the rabbis, in 1658 he went to Constantinople, where he spent nine months. There he befriended the famous kabbalist David *Ḥabillo (d. 1661), an emissary of the Jerusalem community. During this period he made a first attempt to rid himself of his demonic obsessions by means of practical Kabbalah. On the other hand, during one of his ecstatic periods he not only celebrated the three festivals of Passover, Shavuot, and Sukkot all in one week, behavior which was bound to arouse hostility, but went so far as to declare the abolition of the commandments and to pronounce a blasphemous benediction to "Him, who allows the forbidden." Expelled once more he returned to Smyrna, where he stayed until 1662, keeping mostly to himself and going through a prolonged period of profound melancholy. In 1662 he decided to settle in Jerusalem and traveled there via Rhodes and Cairo, where he made many contacts. Throughout this period there is no trace of any messianic agitation around him, and his genial and dignified behavior during his normal state of mind and his rabbinic and kabbalistic scholarship made him a respected figure. By the end of 1662 he reached Jerusalem, staying there for about a year, wandering around the holy places and tombs of the saints of old. His parents died about this time (his mother perhaps even earlier). There seems to have been a great deal of talk about his strange character and attacks of offensive behavior, but this was counterbalanced by his ascetic tenor of life. In a sudden emergency, in the fall of 1663, he was sent to Egypt as an emissary for Jerusalem and performed his mission with some success. He stayed in Cairo until the spring of 1665, becoming closely connected with the circle around Raphael Joseph Chelebi, the head of Egyptian Jewry, who was in deep sympathy with ascetic and kabbalistic tendencies.

From time to time Shabbetai Ẓevi's messianic fancies returned and it is probable that in one of these fits of illumination he decided to marry Sarah, an Ashkenazi girl of doubtful reputation who either had arrived by herself from Italy or was brought over on his initiative when he heard rumors about her from Italian visitors. She was an orphan of the 1648 massacres in Podolia and used to tell curious stories about herself and her upbringing by a Polish nobleman. After some years in Amsterdam she had gone to Italy, where she served with families and Jewish institutions in Mantua. Rumors that she was a woman of easy virtue preceded her and were current even later in the intimate circle of Shabbetai Ẓevi's admirers. Possibly influenced by the example of the prophet Hosea who married a whore, Shabbetai Ẓevi married Sarah in Cairo on March 31, 1664. In the winter of 1664–65, however, being troubled about his violations of the law, he tried to exorcise his demons; thus (according to his own testimony in a reliable source) he asked God to take away from him all his abnormal states, and entered an extended period of stability.

The Beginning of the Shabbatean Movement

The peripeteia in Shabbetai Ẓevi's life came with the news that a man of God had appeared in Gaza who disclosed to everyone the secret root of his soul and could give each person the particular formula for the *tikkun* that his soul needed. When the story of *Nathan of Gaza's powers spread, Shabbetai Ẓevi "abandoned his mission and went to Gaza in order to find a *tikkun* and peace for his soul," in the words of the first report that has been preserved about the beginnings of the movement. Around mid-April 1665 he arrived in Gaza to visit the physician of the soul; by then the latter had had (in February 1665) an ecstatic vision of Shabbetai Ẓevi as the Messiah, springing no doubt from the tales about him he had heard in Jerusalem, where Nathan had studied in 1663 under Jacob *Ḥagiz. These tales and the figure of the man whom the 20-year-old Nathan had often seen in the Jewish quarter of Jerusalem had impressed themselves on his mind and crystallized in his new vision when he took up the study of Kabbalah in Gaza. Instead of curing Shabbetai Ẓevi of his malady, Nathan tried to convince him that he was indeed the true Messiah. At first refusing to pay any heed to his importunities, Shabbetai Ẓevi nevertheless accompanied Nathan on a pilgrimage to some of the holy places in Jerusalem and Hebron, during which they discussed their visions and their validity. Nathan, an outstanding young rabbi, was the first man to confirm independently Shabbetai Ẓevi's own messianic dreams and, moreover, to explain the peculiar rank and nature of the Messiah's soul in the kabbalistic scheme of creation. They returned to Gaza in the beginning of Sivan (mid-May). According to one story, they were celebrating the night of Shavuot in Nathan's house along with a group of rabbis, when Nathan fell into a trance and announced Shabbetai Ẓevi's high rank before the assembly; according to another version, this happened in the absence of Shabbetai Ẓevi, who had one of his attacks of melancholy and stayed away. About this time, Nathan produced an apocryphal text attributed to one Abraham he-Ḥasid, a contemporary of the famous Judah he-Ḥasid, who as it were prophesied the appearance of Shabbetai Ẓevi and foretold his early life in apocalyptic terms, proclaiming him the redeemer of Israel. When, some days after Shavuot, Shabbetai Ẓevi entered another period of illumination, he had absorbed all these new events and, now sure of himself and of Nathan's prophetic gifts, returned to his former messianic claims with renewed strength. On the 17th of Sivan (May 31, 1665), in Gaza, he proclaimed himself as the Messiah and swept with him the whole community, including its rabbi, Jacob *Najara, grandson of the celebrated poet, Israel *Najara. Some weeks of frenzied excitement followed. Riding around on horseback in majestic state Shabbetai Ẓevi summoned a group of his followers, appointing them as apostles or representatives of the Twelve Tribes of Israel.

The messianic news spread like wildfire to other communities in Palestine, but encountered strong opposition from some outstanding rabbis of Jerusalem, including Abraham *Amigo, Jacob *Ḥagiz, Nathan's teacher, Samuel *Garmison (Germizan), and Jacob *Ẓemaḥ, the famous kabbalist, who spoke out against Shabbetai Ẓevi. Having been denounced to the qadi of Jerusalem, he traveled to the city in a large company and succeeded in setting the mind of the qadi at rest. What exactly happened in Jerusalem in June 1665 is not clear. In kingly fashion Shabbetai Ẓevi circled Jerusalem seven times on horseback, winning over some of the rabbis like Samuel *Primo, Mattathias *Bloch, Israel *Benjamin, and Moses *Galante (the fact of the latter's adherence to Shabbetai Ẓevi was later suppressed). His conflict with the majority of the rabbis came to a head and they banished him from the town, but, after informing the rabbis of Constantinople of what happened, they apparently took no other active steps against the messianic propaganda, refraining from answering the many letters that were addressed to them about the events and maintaining an enigmatic silence throughout the following year.

Nathan, on the other hand, who now appeared as the prophet and standard-bearer of Shabbetai Ẓevi, and the group around him were very active. He proclaimed the need for a mass movement of repentance to facilitate the transition to the coming redemption, a step which was sure to win many hearts and could scarcely be opposed by the rabbinic authorities. People from the surrounding countries flocked to him to receive individual penance or wrote to him asking to reveal to them the root of their soul and tell them how to "restore it." Excessive fasts and other ascetic exercises became the order of the day, but Nathan proclaimed the abolition of the fast of the 17th of Tammuz which instead was celebrated as a day of joy in Gaza and Hebron. Letters went out, first to Egypt and the circle of Raphael Joseph, telling of the wondrous deeds of the prophet and the Messiah. One of the striking new features in these letters was the announcement that neither the prophet nor the Messiah was obliged to give proof of his mission by performing miracles, but that Israel should believe in Shabbetai Ẓevi's mission without any external proof. The actual history of the subsequent mass movement is characterized by the intrinsic contradiction between this demand for pure faith as a redeeming value and the overwhelming wave of legends and reports of miracles which swept the Diaspora. The first reports that reached Europe were, curiously enough, not about Shabbetai Ẓevi, but about the appearance of the lost Ten Tribes of Israel, who were said to be marching under the command of a prophetic and saintly man of God about whom all sorts of miraculous stories were told. According to some versions they were conquering Mecca, according to others assembling in the Sahara Desert, and in a third version marching into Persia. Rumors of this kind, coming from Morocco, reached Holland, England, and Germany in the summer of 1665, without giving any indication of what actually had happened in Gaza or naming Shabbetai Ẓevi or making any mention of the appearance of a Messiah. By contrast, there was a great deal of commotion in the Oriental Jewish communities, which had more direct communication with Palestine.

In September 1665, fortified by a new revelation, Nathan addressed a long letter to Raphael Joseph, announcing in the first part the changes which had taken place in the hidden worlds with the arrival of redemption and explaining what these changes entailed for the practice of kabbalistic devotions. The *kavvanot* ("meditations") of Isaac *Luria were no longer valid because the inner structure of the universe had changed and no holy sparks were left under the domination of the powers of evil, the *kelippot*. The time of redemption had come, and even though some might oppose it they could not prevent it and would do harm only to themselves. Shabbetai Ẓevi had the power to justify the greatest sinner, even Jesus, and "whoever entertains any doubts about him, though he may be the most righteous man in the world, he [Shabbetai Ẓevi] may punish him with great afflictions." In the second part of the letter Nathan predicts or rather outlines the course of events from the present moment until complete redemption is achieved. Shabbetai Ẓevi would take the crown from the Turkish king, without war, and make the sultan his servant. After four or five years he would proceed to the River Sambatyon to bring back the lost tribes and to marry Rebecca, the 13-year-old daughter of the resuscitated Moses. During this period he would put the Turkish sultan in charge, but the latter would rebel against him in his absence. This would be the period of the "birth pangs of redemption," a time of great tribulation from which only those dwelling in Gaza would be exempt. The whole tenor of this part of the letter is legendary and mythical. Between the present time and the start of the actual messianic events there would be an interval of one year and several months which should be used for doing penance all over the Jewish world. For this purpose Nathan composed liturgies, one set for the general public and another set for the initiate, comprising *kavvanot* and mystical prayers for the extended fasts prescribed by him. These were sent out to Europe and other places along with the first long announcements regarding the advent of the Messiah in the fall of 1665.

Shabbetai Ẓevi in Smyrna and Constantinople

The first reports about Shabbetai Ẓevi reached Europe early in October 1665, and in the following two months detailed accounts, deeply imbued with legendary material, arrived in Italy, Holland, Germany, and Poland. Why all the correspondents from Gaza, Jerusalem, and Egypt who became so eloquent from September 1665 onward kept silent during the three months after the events in Gaza is still unexplained. There is also a considerable gap between the events in Europe after the news finally came through and what happened in those months to Shabbetai Ẓevi himself. When he left Jerusalem under a cloud, probably before the fast of the 17th of Tammuz, he proceeded through Safed to Aleppo, where he arrived on the 8th of Av (July 20, 1665) and left on August 12. Although his fame had preceded him, he refused to appear publicly as the Messiah, but talked to several people in private, including Solomon *Laniado and other members of the rabbinic court who became his enthusiastic supporters. Similarly, when he arrived in Smyrna a short time before Rosh Ha-Shanah (beginning of September 1665) he kept to himself for a long time, staying with his brother Elijah. In the meantime, a great commotion flared up in Aleppo where, in October and November, the first phenomena of Shabbatean prophesying appeared. Not only unlettered people, men and women, were swept up in the excitement, but also rabbis and scholars, such as Moses Galante from Jerusalem who had come as an emissary and was caught up in the general turmoil, also following Shabbetai Ẓevi to Smyrna and Constantinople. From Aleppo there is the first testimony, outside Palestine, about a general revivalist atmosphere in which there were reports of appearances of the prophet Elijah and a common fund was set up to maintain the poor and those who would be affected by the widespread halt in commercial activities.

Although Shabbetai Ẓevi's arrival in Smyrna was preceded by all kinds of letters and rumors which were bound to have precipitated much tension and many expectations, nothing spectacular happened for almost three months. The rabbis of Smyrna had received a letter from the rabbinate of Constantinople about Shabbetai Ẓevi's excommunication in Jerusalem, yet no action was taken against him. It was only when his state of ecstasy returned, in early December, and he became feverishly active in his own way, starting a wild commotion and performing many of his "strange acts," that the rabbis made an attempt to stop him; but by then it was too late. The enthusiasm and excitement he engendered swept Smyrna Jewry off its feet. Within a period of three weeks, the community was thrown into an uproar and the intensity and public character of the proceedings assured them the widest possible echo. There were not only several thousands of Jews but also a considerable merchant colony of English, Dutch, and Italian traders whose reports to their European friends supplemented the news that now began to stream out of Smyrna from Jewish sources. Although Shabbetai Ẓevi was in continuous correspondence with Nathan, he now acted on his own. The stormy events that followed are fully documented in many sources.

Shabbetai Ẓevi used to recite the morning prayers in one of the synagogues "with a very agreeable voice that greatly pleased those who heard him"; he gave alms very liberally; rose at midnight to perform ritual immersions in the sea; and there was nothing bizarre about his ascetic behavior. But on one of the first days of Ḥanukkah he appeared "in royal apparel" in the synagogue and created a great sensation by his ecstatic singing. About the same time a delegation arrived from Aleppo – Moses Galante and Daniel Pinto and two laymen – who had first made a visit to the prophet in Gaza and now wished to greet him officially as the Messiah of Israel. During Ḥanukkah week, Shabbetai Ẓevi "began to do things that seemed strange: he pronounced the Ineffable Name, ate [forbidden] fats, and did other things against the Lord and His Law, even pressing others to do likewise," behavior characteristic of his states of illumination. The infectious presence of believers spurred him on to more radical manifestations. A deep cleft became evident between the majority of "believers" and a minority of "infidels," and *ma'aminim* and *koferim* became the fixed terms for those who adhered to faith in Shabbetai Ẓevi and those who opposed him. Nathan's epistle to Raphael Joseph was widely distributed and contributed to the growing dissension. To a large extent the common people joined the camp of the believers without inhibitions or theological misgivings; the glad tidings conquered their hearts, and the fascination of Shabbetai Ẓevi's personality, with its strange mixture of solemn dignity and unrestrained license, contributed its share. Hundreds of people, largely drawn from the poorer elements of the community, accompanied him wherever he went. But from the beginning many burghers, wealthy merchants, and brokers joined the movement, as well as rabbinic scholars, including some of his former fellow students.

The three members of the rabbinic court who were still opposed to Shabbetai Ẓevi deliberated the wisdom of opening proceedings against him. Proclaiming public prayers in reaction, Shabbetai Ẓevi once more indulged his taste for majestic pomp and behaved with great audacity. On Friday, December 11, the crowd tried to storm the house of Ḥayyim Peña, one of the leading "infidels," and on the following day matters came to a head. After beginning to recite the morning prayers in one of the synagogues, Shabbetai Ẓevi broke off and, accompanied by a large crowd, proceeded to the locked doors of the Portuguese congregation, the headquarters of his opponents. Taking up an ax, he started to smash the doors, whereupon his opponents opened them and let him in. An astonishing scene followed. Shabbetai Ẓevi read the portion of the Torah not from the customary scroll but from a printed copy; ignoring the priests and levites present, he called up to the reading of the Law his brothers and many other men and women, distributing kingdoms to them and demanding that all of them pronounce the Ineffable Name in their blessings. In a furious speech against the unbelieving rabbis, he compared them to the unclean animals mentioned in the Bible. He proclaimed that the Messiah b. Joseph, who according to aggadic tradition must precede the advent of the son of David, was a certain Abraham Zalman, who had died a martyr's death in 1648, and recited the prayer for the dead in his honor. Then he went up to the ark, took a holy scroll in his arms, and sang an ancient Castilian love song about "Meliselda, the emperor's daughter"; into this song, known as his favorite throughout his life, he read many kabbalistic mysteries. After explaining them to the congregation, he ceremonially proclaimed himself the "anointed of the God of Jacob," the redeemer of Israel, fixing the date of redemption for the 15th of Sivan 5426 (June 18, 1666). This was in conformity with a date announced by Nathan in one of his more optimistic moods, when he considered the possibility of an earlier advent than originally predicted. Shabbetai Ẓevi announced that in a short time he would seize the crown of "the great Turk." When Ḥayyim *Benveniste, one of the dissenting rabbis present, asked him for proof of his mission, he flew into a rage and excommunicated him, at the same time calling on some of those present to testify to their faith by uttering the Ineffable Name. The dramatic scene amounted to a public messianic announcement and the substitution of a messianic Judaism for the traditional and imperfect one. There is reliable testimony that, besides other innovations in the law, he promised the women that he would set them free from the curse of Eve. Immediately after this Sabbath he dispatched one of his rabbinical followers to Constantinople to make preparations for his arrival.

In the wave of excitement Benveniste's doubts were carried away and on the following day he joined the camp of the believers. A smoldering conflict between him and one of the other members of the court, Aaron *Lapapa, may have played some part in his conversion. At any rate, on the 5th of Tevet (December 23) Shabbetai Ẓevi engineered the expulsion of Lapapa from his office and the appointment of Benveniste as the sole chief rabbi of Smyrna. Summoned before the qadi once more to explain his behavior, Shabbetai Ẓevi again succeeded in reassuring him. In the next few days all the believers were asked to come and kiss the hand of the messianic king; most of the community did so, including some "infidels" who were afraid of the mounting terrorism of the believers. Immediately after this regal ceremony, Shabbetai Ẓevi decreed the abolition of the fast of the Tenth of Tevet. When this act aroused the opposition of some of the rabbis, the angry crowd wanted to attack them. Solomon *Algazi, a great scholar and famous kabbalist who persisted in his opposition, was forced to flee to Magnesia and his house was plundered. Lapapa hid in the house of one of his colleagues. On the following Sabbath the name of the Turkish sultan was struck out from the prayer for the ruler and a formal prayer for Shabbetai Ẓevi as the messianic king of Israel was instituted, a custom later followed by many communities throughout the Diaspora. Instead of his actual name, the practice began at this time of calling him by the appellation *amirah*, an abbreviation of *Adoneinu Malkenu yarum hodo* ("our Lord and King, may his majesty be exalted") and an allusion to the term emir. The new term was widely used in Shabbatean literature up to the beginning of the 19th century.

A festive atmosphere of joy and enthusiasm marked the succeeding days. Many people from other Turkish communities arrived and joined the movement, among them Abraham *Yakhini, a famous preacher and kabbalist in Constantinople, who had known Shabbetai Ẓevi since 1658 and now became one of his most active propagandists. In a fit of mass hysteria, people from all classes of society started to prophesy about Shabbetai Ẓevi. Men, women, and children fell into a trance, declaiming acknowledgments of Shabbetai Ẓevi as Messiah and biblical passages of a messianic nature. When their senses returned, they remembered nothing. About 150 "prophets" arose in Smyrna, among them Shabbetai Ẓevi's wife and the daughters of some of the "infidels." Some had visions of Shabbetai Ẓevi's crown or saw him sitting on the throne, but most of them produced a mere jumble of phrases and quotations from the Bible and the prayer book, repeated over and over again. Trade and commerce came to a standstill; dancing and festive processions alternated with the penitential exercises prescribed by Nathan. Psalm 21, which had been given a Shabbatean interpretation in Gaza, was recited at each of the three daily services, a custom which spread to many other communities. As well as distributing the kingdoms of the earth among the faithful, Shabbetai Ẓevi appointed counterparts of the ancient Israelite kings from David to Zerubbabel and several of these obtained handwritten patents from the Messiah. The appointees were his main supporters in Smyrna but included some of his devotees from Palestine, Egypt, Aleppo, Constantinople, and Bursa (Brussa). Many other messianic dignitaries were appointed. After this, his last activity in Smyrna, Shabbetai Ẓevi sailed to Constantinople on Dec. 30, 1665, accompanied by some of his "kings." His behavior during this period was as consistent as his unstable mind would allow: he was sure of his calling and believed that some supernatural intervention would bring his messianic mission to fruition. In the meantime the Turkish authorities in the capital had been aroused by the alarming reports. The news from Gaza and Smyrna had already divided the community and the waves of excitement rose high. Letters from places through which Shabbetai Ẓevi had passed combined factual reports with increasingly fanciful stories and raised the messianic fever to an even higher pitch. Even before his arrival a prophet arose in Constantinople, Moses Serviel or Suriel, a young rabbi from Bursa who, unlike the other "prophets," revealed Shabbatean mysteries in the language of the Zohar and was credited with a particular charisma. The Messiah's arrival was considerably delayed by extremely stormy weather and in the meantime the atmosphere in the capital became critical. Some of the heads of the community seem to have warned the government, which had already taken steps to arrest Shabbetai Ẓevi in Smyrna, where the order arrived too late, or on his arrival in Constantinople. The non-Jewish population was caught up in the excitement and satirical songs about the Messiah were sung in the streets, while the Jewish masses, certain that many miracles would take place immediately after his arrival, showed a marked pride before the gentiles.

The policy pursued by the grand vizier, Ahmed Köprülü (Kuprili), one of Turkey's ablest statesmen, is remarkable for its restraint. Revolts were frequent in Turkey and the rebels were generally speedily put to death. That this was not the immediate consequence of Shabbetai Ẓevi's arrest after interception by boat in the Sea of Marmara on Feb. 6, 1666, did much to strengthen the belief of the faithful. Amid great commotion, he was brought ashore in chains on Monday, February 8. By this time the disruption of normal life and commerce had reached a peak. One or two days after his arrest, Shabbetai Ẓevi was brought before the divan, presided over by Köprülü. Since the Turkish archives from this period were destroyed by fire, no official Turkish documents about the movement and the proceedings in this case have survived, and reports from Jewish and Christian sources in Constantinople are conflicting. It is true, however, that the vizier showed surprising leniency and patience, to which Shabbetai Ẓevi's undoubted charm and the fascination of his personality may have contributed. He may have wanted to avoid making a martyr of a Messiah who, after all, had not taken up arms against the sultan and had simply proclaimed an unrealistic mystical takeover of the crown. Shabbetai Ẓevi was put in prison, at first in a "dark dungeon" but later in fairly comfortable quarters, and the high official responsible for the police and the prison, possibly after accepting substantial bribes, permitted him to receive visits from his followers. It was said that he could have obtained his release by a very large bribe which his followers were prepared to pay, but that he refused, thereby greatly enhancing his reputation. He was still self-confident. During this period, he had returned to a normal state, led an ascetic life, preached repentance and claimed no special privileges. The rabbis of the capital who visited him in prison found a dignified scholar who bore his sufferings with an air of nobility, rather than a sinner who set himself above the Law and tradition. The rabbis were divided among themselves, some of the outstanding ones, among them Abraham Al-Nakawa, taking his side. A new set of miracles was reported in the letters written during those months from Constantinople, proving that the enthusiasm continued unabated. When the sultan and the vizier left for the war on Crete, the order was given to transfer Shabbetai Ẓevi to the fortress of Gallipoli, where important political prisoners were detained, on the European side of the Dardanelles. The transfer was made on April 19, the day before Passover. Once more in the grip of a state of illumination, Shabbetai Ẓevi sacrificed a Passover lamb and roasted it with its fat, inducing his companions to eat this forbidden food and blessing it with the now customary blessing of "He who permits the forbidden." By means of bribes, the believers soon converted his detention into honorable confinement, and the fortress became known as *Migdal Oz* ("tower of strength"), with reference to Proverbs 18:10.

The Movement in the Diaspora

The letters arriving in all parts of the Diaspora from Palestine, Egypt, and Aleppo in October and November 1665, and later from Smyrna and Constantinople, produced a tremendous excitement, and the similarity of the reactions everywhere indicates that the causes of the response went far beyond local factors. Messianic fervor took hold of communities that had no immediate experience of persecution and bloodshed as well as those which had. Social and religious factors were no doubt inextricably combined in the outbreak. Poverty and persecution bred Utopian hopes, but the situation of the Jewish people as a whole provided the relevant background. Although the Lurianic doctrine of *tikkun* and redemption expressed a social situation too, its real content was essentially religious. It is this interlocking of the various elements in the historical makeup of the Shabbatean movement which accounts for its dynamics and explosive content. Later the movement was presented in a different light in a strenuous attempt to minimize the part played by the upper strata of Jewish society and the spiritual leaders, and to ascribe the vehemence of the outbreak to the blind enthusiasm of the rabble and the poor, but this is not borne out by contemporary evidence. The response showed none of the uniformity based on class conditions. Many of the rich took a leading part in spreading the messianic propaganda, although there was no lack of those who, as the saying went at the time, "were more interested in great profits than in great prophets."

Five factors contributed to the overwhelming success of the messianic awakening:

(1) The messianic call came from the Holy Land, from the center that stood for pure spirituality at its most intense. A message from there would be received in Persia, Kurdistan, or Yemen with a respect which it could scarcely command had it arrived from Poland or Italy. The tremendous prestige of the new Kabbalah which emanated from Safed also played a part.

(2) The renewal of prophecy with the conspicuous figure of Nathan, the brilliant scholar and severe ascetic turned prophet, helped to obscure the more dubious facets of Shabbetai Ẓevi's personality which, indeed, played little or no role in the consciousness of the mass of the believers.

(3) The efficacy of traditional and popular apocalyptic beliefs, whose elements were not relinquished but reinterpreted, played its part. The old eschatological visions were retained but many new elements were absorbed. The conception of the future was, throughout 1666, thoroughly conservative. At the same time, however, the propaganda was also addressed to a widespread group of kabbalists, to whom it presented a system of ambiguous symbols. Nathan's symbolism satisfied his readers by its traditional terminology, and the apparent continuity enabled the new elements to exist, undetected, under cover of the older kabbalism.

(4) The prophet's call to repentance played a decisive role, appealing to the noblest longings in every Jewish heart. Who, even among the movement's opponents, could condemn the one demand which the prophet and the Messiah made in public?

(5) There was, as yet, no differentiation between the various elements taking part in the movement. Conservative minds, responding to their sense of unbroken continuity, saw in it the promise of fulfillment of traditional expectations. At the same time the message of redemption appealed to the utopianists who longed for a new age and would shed no tears for the passing of the old order. The national character of the movement obscured these contrasts in the emotional makeup of its participants.

Since the main mass outbreaks of the movement occurred in places far removed from the scene of Shabbetai Ẓevi's own activities, and Nathan the prophet never actually left Palestine, during the heyday of the events people were dependent on letters and other means of communication which presented a wild mixture of fact and fancy, the latter no less appealing to emotion and the imagination than the former.

To a large measure the movement developed out of its own momentum, adapting new features to older traditions and conceptions. There is nothing surprising in the similarity of the phenomena in places far distant; they correspond both to the basic similarity of the Jewish situation and the traditional response to it, and to the uniformity of the propaganda that came from the believers in Turkey. Of some importance in Europe were many reports from Christian sources, which of course depended mostly on Jewish informants but added exaggerations and distortions of their own. The many broadsheets and pamphlets that appeared during 1666 in English, Dutch, German, and Italian were avidly read by the Jews and often taken as independent sources confirming their own news. A secondary factor was the sympathy shown to the movement by millenarian circles in England, Holland, and Germany, since it seemed to confirm the belief widespread in these groups that Christ's second coming would occur in 1666. Peter Serrarius in Amsterdam, one of the leading millenarians, did much to spread Shabbatean propaganda to his many Christian correspondents. There are, however, no grounds for the assumption that the outbreak of the movement itself was due to the influence of Christian millenarian merchants on Shabbetai Ẓevi during his years in Smyrna.

While the majority of the people in those communities of which we have firsthand knowledge, and in those influenced by them, joined in the general enthusiasm, led everywhere by a group of devoted and determined believers, there were also many instances of bitter quarrels and differences with the "infidels." A mounting wave of messianic terrorism threatened those who spoke derisively of Shabbetai Ẓevi and refused to take part in the general excitement. A number of influential rabbis, who in their hearts were skeptical about the whole upheaval (like Samuel *Aboab in Venice), were careful not to antagonize their communities, and cases of open rabbinical opposition were somewhat rare. Such stubborn adversaries were Joseph ha-Levi, the preacher of the community at Leghorn, and Jacob *Sasportas, who had no official position at the time, and was staying in Hamburg as a refugee from the plague in London. A highly articulate and learned letter writer, he maintained a vivid correspondence with friends and acquaintances, and even with people unknown to him, to inquire about the truth of the events and to voice carefully worded opposition to the believers, though using words of strong condemnation to those who shared his opinion. Later (in 1669) he assembled (and heavily edited) large parts of this correspondence in *Ẓiẓat Novel Ẓevi*.

Repentance alternating with public manifestations of joy and enthusiasm was the order of the day, and detailed reports from many parts of the Diaspora describe the excessive lengths to which the penitents went. Fasts and repeated ritual baths, mortifications which were frequently of an extreme character, and lavish almsgiving were practiced everywhere. Many people fasted for the whole week; those who could not manage this fasted for two or three consecutive days every week and women and children at least every Monday and Thursday. "The ritual bath was so crowded that it was almost impossible to enter there." The daily devotions for day and night arranged by Nathan were recited, and many editions of them were published in Amsterdam, Frankfurt, Prague, Mantua, and Constantinople. At night people would lie down naked in the snow for half an hour and scourge themselves with thorns and nettles. Commerce came to a standstill everywhere. Many sold their houses and property to provide themselves with money for the journey to the Holy Land, while others made no such preparations, being convinced that they would be transported on clouds. More realistic wealthy believers made arrangements for renting ships to transport the poor to Palestine. Reports from small towns and hamlets in Germany prove that the messianic revival was not limited to the larger centers. From many places delegations left to visit Shabbetai Ẓevi, bearing parchments signed by the leaders of the community which acknowledged him as the Messiah and king of Israel. A new era was inaugurated: letters and even some published books were dated from "the first year of the renewal of the prophecy and the kingdom." Preachers exhorted the people to restore all ill-gotten gains, but no cases where this was actually done are on record. People waited avidly for letters from the Holy Land, Smyrna, and Constantinople which were often read in public, giving rise to great excitement and frequently to violent discussions. There were hardly any differences in the reactions of Ashkenazi, Sephardi, Italian, and Oriental Jewry, and in congregations composed largely of former Marranos – such as the "Portuguese" communities of Amsterdam, Hamburg, and Salonika – the messianic fervor was particularly strong. In North Africa, where the movement struck deep roots, a former Marrano, the physician Abraham Miguel *Cardozo in Tripoli, became one of the most active protagonists. Other active supporters were the rabbis of Morocco, many of whom were well acquainted with *Elisha Ḥayyim b. Jacob Ashkenazi, the father of Nathan the prophet, through his visits to their country as an emissary of Jerusalem. Poems in honor of Shabbetai Ẓevi and Nathan were composed in Yemen, Kurdistan, Constantinople, Salonika, Venice, Ancona, Amsterdam, and many other places, but at the same time one of the outstanding opponents of the movement in Italy, the poet Jacob *Frances in Mantua, with the help of his brother Immanuel, composed a passionate set of verses denouncing the movement, its heroes, and followers (*Ẓevi Muddaḥ*). But these were lone voices in the wilderness; that the Italian communities were generally enraptured is vividly revealed in the notebook of a Jew from Casale who traveled throughout northern Italy at the end of 1665 and the early months of 1666, reflecting in his spontaneous descriptions the atmosphere prevailing there (*Zion*, 10 (1945), 55–56). Moses *Zacuto, the most esteemed kabbalist of Italy, gave somewhat reluctant support to the movement. Some Jews who had settled in the Holy Land sent glowing reports about the awakening to their contemporaries in the Diaspora, but it can be said in general that everyone wrote to everyone else. Even the wife of a poor wretch from Hamburg who lay in prison in Oslo faithfully reported to him in Yiddish on the latest news received in Hamburg. At the other end of the scale Abraham Pereira, said to be the richest Jew in Amsterdam and certainly a deeply devout man, lent his enormous prestige to the cause and, after publishing a comprehensive book of morals for repentant sinners (*La Certeza del Camino*, 1666), left with his entourage for the Levant, although he was held up in Leghorn. In Poland and Russia boundless enthusiasm prevailed. Preachers encouraged the repentance movement, which acquired yet more extravagant modes of expression. No opposition from the rabbinical side is recorded. In public processions of joy the Jews carried portraits of Shabbetai Ẓevi taken from Christian broadsheets, provoking riots in many places such as Pinsk, Vilna, and Lublin, until in early May 1666 the Polish king forbade such demonstrations of Jewish pride. The living memory of the massacres from 1648 to 1655 gave the movement overwhelming popular appeal.

The news of Shabbetai Ẓevi's arrest in Gallipoli in no way diminished the enthusiasm; on the contrary, the fact that he was not executed and seemingly held in an honorable state only tended to confirm his mission. Samuel Primo, whom Shabbetai Ẓevi employed as his secretary (scribe), was a past master of the majestic and bombastic phrase and his letters conveyed an aura of imperial grandeur. Shabbetai Ẓevi signed these pronouncements as the "firstborn son of God," "your father Israel," "the bridegroom of the Torah," and other high-flown titles; even when he started signing some of his letters "I am the Lord your God Shabbetai Ẓevi" only a few of the believers seem to have been shocked. Moses Galante later claimed to have left him because of this. No reliable account of Shabbetai Ẓevi's conduct during the first period of his arrest in Gallipoli has been preserved, but there are indications that he had frequent periods of melancholy. When he entered an elevated state of illumination once more, people flocked to him in great numbers and the prison, with the help of bribes, was converted into a kind of royal court. The "king," who made no bones about his messianic claims, impressed his visitors deeply. An official letter from the rabbis of Constantinople to the rabbinate of Jerusalem, asking them to set up a commission of inquiry consisting of four representatives from Jerusalem, Safed, and Hebron, remained unanswered. When in March 1666 the rabbis of Venice asked for an opinion of the Constantinople rabbinate, they were given a positive answer disguised as a commercial communication about the quality of the goat skins "which Rabbi Israel of Jerusalem has bought." They wrote: "We looked into the matter and examined the merchandise of Rabbi Israel, for his goods are displayed here under our very eyes. We have come to the conclusion that they are very valuable… but we must wait until the day of the great fair comes." Hundreds of prophets arose in the capital and the excitement reached fever pitch. As the fasts of the 17th of Tammuz and the Ninth of Av approached, Shabbetai Ẓevi's euphoria mounted; he not only proclaimed the abolition of the fasts but instituted new festivals in their stead. The 17th of Tammuz became the "day of the revival of Shabbetai Ẓevi's spirit" and, indulging in prescribing in minute detail the liturgy to be recited on this occasion, he turned the Ninth of Av into the festival of his birthday. In Turkey, where the news was quickly spread, almost everybody followed his instructions and the day was celebrated as a high holiday. A delegation from Poland, among whose members were the son and son-in-law of R. David ha-Levi of Lvov, the greatest rabbinic authority of his country, visited him during the week following the 17th of Tammuz and found him in an ecstatic frame of mind. His dignity and majestic deportment conquered their hearts.

Many pilgrims believed the Messiah's imprisonment to be no more than a symbolic, outward show, a belief supported by a kabbalistic tract by Nathan, "A disquisition about the dragons," written during the summer of 1666. In it Shabbetai Ẓevi's particular psychology was explained in terms of a metaphysical biography of the Messiah's soul and its struggles with the demonic powers from the time of creation until his earthly incarnation. These struggles left their mark on him and explain the alternations between the times when he is held a prisoner by the *kelippot* and his periods of illumination, when the supernal light shines upon him. Even in faraway Yemen, where the excitement ran high, the details of Shabbetai Ẓevi's biography (based on a mixture of fact and legend) were expounded in a kabbalistic fashion by the anonymous author of an apocalypse, "The valley of vision," written late in 1666. As early as July the delegates from Poland were handed, under Shabbetai Ẓevi's signature, a kabbalistic tract explaining the events of his life as founded on deep mysteries. Even in Palestine and Egypt, where the letters abolishing the fast of the Ninth of Av could not have been received in time, the initiative for the abolition was taken by Nathan of Gaza and his followers, among whom Mattathias Bloch was very active in Egypt. Nathan himself planned more than once to meet Shabbetai Ẓevi but actually never left Gaza. There was a minority of "infidels" in Egypt too, including some outstanding Palestinian rabbis who had settled there, but in the face of the general enthusiasm they behaved very cautiously. In Algiers and Morocco the movement encountered no serious opposition on the part of the rabbis and leaders of the community.

Shabbetai Ẓevi's Apostasy

The movement reached its climax in July and August 1666 when everyone waited expectantly for great events to unfold. The turning point came in an unforeseen way. A Polish kabbalist, *Nehemiah ha-Kohen from Lvov or its vicinity, came to see Shabbetai Ẓevi, apparently on behalf of some Polish communities. Arriving on September 3 or 4, he spent two or three days with him. The reports about their meeting are conflicting and in part clearly legendary. According to one source, Nehemiah argued less on kabbalistic grounds than as a spokesman of popular apocalyptic tradition, which he interpreted in strictly literal fashion. He failed to see any correspondence between Shabbetai Ẓevi's activities and the predictions of older aggadic writings on the Messiah. Dissatisfied by kabbalistic reinterpretations, he stressed the absence of a visible Messiah b. Joseph who should have preceded Shabbetai Ẓevi. Other sources maintain that the argument was about Nehemiah's own role since he himself claimed to be the Messiah b. Joseph, an assertion rejected by his host. Whatever the fact, the acrimonious debate ended in disaster. Nehemiah suddenly declared, in the presence of the Turkish guards, his willingness to adopt Islam. He was taken to Adrianople, where he denounced Shabbetai Ẓevi for fomenting sedition. No doubt the Jewish masses blamed Nehemiah for subsequent events, and even after his later return to Judaism in Poland he was persecuted for the rest of his life for having surrendered the Messiah to the Turks. However, it is quite possible that Nehemiah's action was simply a pretext and that the Turkish authorities had by then become alarmed by the events taking place in their country. There are indications of several complaints about Shabbetai Ẓevi, including charges of immoral behavior. The bustle and exuberance at Gallipoli came to an end when, on September 12 or 13, messengers arrived from Adrianople, and took the prisoner there on September 15.

On the following day he was brought before the divan, in the presence of the sultan, who watched the proceedings from a latticed alcove. Once more, the accounts of what happened at the court are contradictory. The believers reported that he was in one of his low melancholic states, and, behaving with utter passivity, allowed events to take their course. They depicted his apostasy as an act imposed on him, in which he took no part at all. The facts were certainly different although he may well have been in one of his low states at the time. He was examined by the court or privy council and denied – as he had done before under similar circumstances – ever having made messianic claims. According to some he even made a long speech about this. Finally he was given the choice between being put to death immediately or converting to Islam. According to one source, Kasim Pasha, one of the highest officials and a little later the brother-in-law of the sultan, conducted the decisive talk, "so handling him that he was glad to turn Turk." But all other sources agree that this role was played by the sultan's physician, Mustapha Hayatizadé, an apostate Jew. He convinced Shabbetai Ẓevi to accept the court's offer, which apparently had been decided upon before he himself was brought in. The physician acted mainly as an interpreter, Shabbetai Ẓevi's Turkish being rather poor at the time. Sultan Mehmed IV, a deeply religious man, was likely to sympathize with the possibility that such an outstanding Jewish personality might induce many of his followers to take the same step, and the council's action was certainly also influenced by tactical considerations. Agreeing to apostatize and put on the turban, Shabbetai Ẓevi assumed the name Aziz Mehmed Effendi. Being considered an important convert, he was granted the honorary title of *Kapiči Bashi* ("keeper of the palace gates"). A royal pension of 150 piasters per day was added to the appointment. Several of the believers who had accompanied him followed him into apostasy, as did his wife when she was brought from Gallipoli some time later. The date of the conversion, Sept. 15, 1666, is confirmed by many sources. Shabbetai Ẓevi's state of mind after his apostasy was one of deep dejection, as evidenced by a letter written one week later to his brother Elijah.

After the Apostasy Until Shabbetai Ẓevi's Death

The apostasy produced a profound shock, paralyzing leaders and followers alike. In wide circles it was simply not believed and it took some time until the truth was accepted. The waves of excitement had been high, but deeper feelings were involved: for many believers the experience of the messianic revival had taken on the dimensions of a new spiritual reality. The tremendous upheaval of a whole year had led them to equate their emotional experience with an outward reality which seemed to confirm it. Now they were faced with a cruel dilemma: to admit that their belief had been wholly in vain and that their redeemer was an imposter, or to cling to their belief and inner experience in the face of outward hostile reality and look for an explanation and justification of what had happened. That many accepted the second alternative and refused to give in proves the depth of the movement. Because of this, the movement did not come to an abrupt end with the apostasy, an act which in all other circumstances would have terminated it automatically. Who could have dreamed of a Messiah who would forswear his allegiance to Judaism? On the other hand, the rabbis and communal leaders, particularly in Turkey, acted with great circumspection. Their policy was to hush up the whole affair, to calm the excitement by pretending that little had actually happened, and to restore Jewish life to the "normal" state of exile, for which the best method was to ignore the whole course of events and to let time and oblivion heal the wound. This policy was widely followed in other countries. If it were asked how a whole nation could have been allowed to nourish such high hopes only to be deceived at the end, no discussion of God's inscrutable counsels could be allowed. There was also the apprehension, particularly in Turkey, that the authorities might proceed against the Jewish leaders who had permitted the preparations for a messianic revolt, and it appears that the Turkish authorities desisted from taking such a step only after considerable vacillation. In Italy, the pages in the Jewish community records which bore witness to the events were removed and destroyed on the order of the rabbis. Official silence also descended on the literature published in Hebrew for many years. Only dim echoes of lawsuits connected with it and other hints at the movement of repentance appeared here and there.

The facts, however, were different. Again, Nathan of Gaza played a decisive role although it remains an open question whether the initiative for a "theological" explanation of the apostasy was taken by him or by Shabbetai Ẓevi after he had recovered from his stupor. When Nathan received the news from Shabbetai Ẓevi's circle in early November 1666 he immediately announced that it was all a deep mystery which would resolve itself in due time. He left Gaza with a large entourage in order to arrange a meeting with Shabbetai Ẓevi, who by then had received instruction in the religion of Islam. The rabbis of Constantinople, most of whom had given up their belief, took steps to prevent this. Traveling first to Smyrna, where a considerable group of believers persisted in their faith, Nathan stayed there during March and April; although very reserved in all his relations with outsiders, he began to defend the apostasy and Shabbetai Ẓevi's continued messianic mission to the believers. The central point of his argument was that the apostasy was in reality the fulfillment of a mission to lift up the holy sparks which were dispersed even among the gentiles and concentrated now in Islam. Whereas the task of the Jewish people had been to restore the sparks of their own souls in the process of *tikkun* according to the demands of the Torah, there were sparks which only the Messiah himself could redeem, and for this he had to go down into the realm of the *kelippah*, outwardly to submit to its domination but actually to perform the last and most difficult part of his mission by conquering the *kelippah* from within. In doing this he was acting like a spy sent into the enemy camp. Nathan linked this exposition with his earlier metaphysical explanation of the biography of Shabbetai Ẓevi as a struggle with the realm of evil, to which his "strange actions" bore witness even in his earthly life. The apostasy was nothing but the most extreme case of such strange actions. He had to take upon himself the shame of being called a traitor to his own people as the last step before revealing himself in all his glory on the historical scene. By placing the paradox of an apostate Messiah, a tragic but still legitimate redeemer, at the center of the new, developing Shabbatean theology, Nathan laid the foundation for the ideology of the believers for the next 100 years. He, and many others after him, searched the Bible, Talmud, Midrash, and kabbalistic literature for references to this basic paradox and came up with a rich harvest of daring, audacious, and often outright heretical reinterpretations of the older sacred texts. Once the basic paradox was admitted, everything seemed to fall in line. All the objectionable acts of the biblical heroes, strange tales of the *aggadah* (*aggadot shel dofi*), and enigmatic passages of the Zohar – everything seemed to point, in typological exegesis, to the scandalous behavior of the Messiah. With Shabbetai Ẓevi's acquiescence, these ideas were taken up by the heads of the believers and given wide circulation. The rabbis forbade discussion of these heretical ideas, which would be refuted by their very paradoxicality. In the meantime they simply ignored them.

During 1667–68 the excitement slowly ebbed. When Nathan tried to see Shabbetai Ẓevi in Adrianople, he was met in Ipsala by a delegation of rabbis who forced him to sign a promise that he would give up his design (May 31, 1667). In spite of this he visited Shabbetai Ẓevi and continued to visit him from time to time and to proclaim him as the true Messiah, announcing several dates for the expected final revelation. On Shabbetai Ẓevi's orders he went to Rome for the performance of a secret magic ritual destined to hasten the fall of the representative of Christendom. His appearance in Venice on Passover 1668 created a great sensation. The rabbis published a pamphlet summing up the interrogations in Ipsala and Venice, and claiming that Nathan had denounced his errors. Nathan repudiated all these declarations and was obviously supported by a considerable number of believers. He completed his mission in Rome and returned to the Balkans, where he spent the rest of his life, alternating between Adrianople, Sofia, Kastoria, and Salonika, all places with a strong Shabbatean following.

Shabbetai Ẓevi himself lived in Adrianople and sometimes in Constantinople until 1672, succeeding in being allowed to lead a double life, performing the duties of a Muslim but also observing large parts of Jewish ritual. The Turks expected him to act as a missionary, but the 200 heads of families whom he drew to Islam were all secret believers whom he admonished to remain together as a group of secret fighters against the *kelippah*. Periods of illumination and depression continued to alternate, and during the sometimes lengthy periods of illumination he acted in the same manner as before: he instituted new festivals, confirmed his mystical mission, and persuaded people to follow him into Islam, which by then was called "the Torah of grace," in contradistinction to Judaism, "the Torah of truth." Several reports about his libertinism during "illumination" seem well founded. In one of these periods, in April 1671, he divorced his wife, but took her back when the illumination left him although he had already made arrangements for another marriage. A Hebrew chronicle by one of his visitors describes in detail his extraordinary behavior. Revelations by celestial agents, of which some accounts have been preserved, were frequent in his circle. Primo, Yakhini, and Nathan frequently visited him but were never asked to embrace Islam, and they were accepted by the believers in Turkey as his legitimate spokesmen. Although they were still very strong in the Balkans and Asiatic Turkey, the Shabbateans were gradually driven underground but were not actually excommunicated. The borderline between the apostates and those who remained Jews sometimes became blurred although the latter were generally noted for their extremely pious and ascetic way of life. Shabbetai Ẓevi himself, who enjoyed the sultan's favor, formed connections with some Muslim mystics among the Dervish orders. Letters between his group and the believers in North Africa, Italy, and other places spread the new theology and helped to create an increasingly sectarian spirit. After a denunciation of his double-faced behavior and sexual license by some Jews and Muslims, supported by a large bribe, Shabbetai Ẓevi was arrested in Constantinople in August 1672. The grand vizier wavered between executing or deporting him, but finally decided to exile him, in January 1673, to Dulcigno in Albania, which the Shabbateans called Alkum after Proverbs 30:31. Although allowed relative freedom, he disappeared from public view, but some of his main supporters continued their pilgrimages, apparently disguised as Muslims. In 1674 his wife, Sarah, died and he married Esther (in other sources called Jochebed), the daughter of Joseph Filosof, a respected rabbi of Salonika and one of his chief supporters. From time to time during "illuminations," he still envisioned his return to his former state and considered that the final redemption was near.

During the last ten years of his life, especially in Adrianople, he used to reveal to the elect – frequently before he demanded their submission to "mystical apostasy" – his special version of the "mystery of the Godhead." According to this the "God of Israel" was not the first cause or *Ein-Sof*, but "a second cause, dwelling within the *Sefirah Tiferet*," that is to say manifesting itself through this *Sefirah* without being identical with it. The two main points of this doctrine, which was of crucial importance in the later development of Shabbateanism, were:

(1) The distinction between the first cause and the God of Israel, implying – and this thesis was upheld in different versions by the radicals in the movement – that the first cause has no providence over creation, which is exercised only by the God of Israel who came into being only after the act of *ẓimẓum*: this doctrine aroused particular revulsion in the Orthodox camp and was considered highly dangerous and heretical.

(2) The distinctly Gnostic character of the division, though with the difference that the religious evaluation of the two elements in this dualism is reversed: the second-century Gnostics thought of the hidden God as the true God, considering the "God of the Jews" as an inferior and even detestable being. Shabbetai Ẓevi, Nathan, and Cardozo, however, turned the order of values upside down: the God of Israel, although emanated from the first cause, was the true God of religion, whereas the first cause was essentially irrelevant from the religious point of view. Some time before his death Shabbetai Ẓevi dictated a longer version of this doctrine to one of his scholarly visitors, or at least induced him to write it down. This text, later known as *Raza di-Meheimanuta* ("The Mystery of the True Faith"), instituted a kind of kabbalistic trinity, called in zoharic terms the "three bonds of the faith." It consisted of The Ancient Holy One (*Attika kaddisha*), The Holy King (*Malka kaddisha*), also called The God of Israel, and his *Shekhinah*. No reference was made to the Messiah and his rank, or to his relation to these hypostases. This doctrine differed considerably from the system developed earlier by Nathan of Gaza in his *Sefer Beri'ah* ("Book of Creation"). Both texts had a profound influence on subsequent Shabbatean doctrine and their echoes are audible in the hymns sung by the later sectarians in Salonika which are extant.

A number of letters from Shabbetai Ẓevi's last years testify to his continuing belief in himself, at least during his periods of illumination. His last letter, written about six weeks before his death, asks his friends in the nearby Jewish community of Berat in Albania to send him a prayer book for the New Year and the Day of Atonement. He died quite suddenly two months after his 50th birthday, on the Day of Atonement, Sept. 17, 1676. Nathan propagated the idea that Shabbetai Ẓevi's death was merely an "occultation" and he had actually ascended to and been absorbed into the "supernal lights." Such a theory of apotheosis was in line with Nathan's earlier speculations on the gradual deification of the Messiah, but left open the question of who would then represent the Messiah on earth. Nathan himself died shortly after, on Jan. 11, 1680, in Skoplje in Macedonia. During the preceding year one of his disciples, Israel Ḥazzan of Kastoria, wrote long homilies on some psalms reflecting the state of mind of the circle closest to Shabbetai Ẓevi and the gradual construction of a heretical and sectarian doctrine.

The Shabbatean Kabbalah

As Shabbetai Ẓevi himself was not a systematic thinker and spoke mainly in hints and metaphors, Nathan of Gaza must be considered the main creator of a rather elaborate system which combined a new version of Lurianic Kabbalah with original ideas about the position of the Messiah in this new order. His ideas gained wide currency and their influence can be detected in many seemingly orthodox kabbalistic tracts in the next two generations.

Nathan accepts the Lurianic doctrine of *ẓimẓum* (see *Kabbalah) but adds a new, even deeper layer to his conception of the Godhead. From the beginning there are in *Ein-Sof* two kinds of light or aspects – which could even be called "attributes" in *Spinoza's sense – the "thoughtful light" and "the thoughtless light." The first comprises all that is focused on the purpose of creation. But in the infinite wealth of *Ein-Sof* there are forces or principles which are not aimed at creation and whose sole purpose is to remain what they are and stay where they are. They are "thoughtless" in the sense that they are devoid of any idea directed to creation. The act of *ẓimẓum*, which occurred in order to bring about a cosmos, took place only within the "thoughtful light." By this act the possibility was created for the thoughtful light to realize its thought, to project it into the primordial space, the *tehiru*, and there to erect the structures of creation. But when this light withdrew, there remained in the *tehiru* the thoughtless light, which had taken no part in creation and, by its very nature, resisted all creative change. In the dialectics of creation, it therefore became a positively hostile and destructive power. What is called the power of evil, the *kelippah*, is in the last resort rooted in this noncreative light in God himself. The duality of form and matter takes on a new aspect: both are grounded in *Ein-Sof*. The thoughtless light is not evil in itself but takes on this aspect because it is opposed to the existence of anything but *Ein-Sof* and therefore is set on destroying the structures produced by the thoughtful light. The *tehiru* which is filled with the thoughtless light, mingled with some residue of the thoughtful light which remained even after *ẓimẓum*, is called *golem*, the formless primordial matter. The whole process of creation proceeds therefore through a dialectic between the two lights; in other words, through a dialectic rooted in the very being of *Ein-Sof*.

When, after *ẓimẓum*, the thoughtful light was streaming back in a straight line (*kav ha-yosher*) into the *tehiru*, starting there processes which are very similar to those described in Lurianic Kabbalah, it penetrated only the upper half of the primordial space, as it were overwhelming the thoughtless light and transforming it, thereby building the world of its original thought. But it did not reach the lower half of the *tehiru*, described as "the deep of the great abyss." All the statements of Lurianic ontology and the doctrine of cosmic restoration or *tikkun* which Israel must achieve through the strength of the Torah relate to the upper part of the *tehiru* only. The lower part persists in its unreconstructed and formless condition until the advent of the Messiah, who alone can perfect it, bringing about its penetration and transformation by the thoughtful light. In fact, the thoughtless lights, too, build structures of their own – the demonic worlds of the *kelippot* whose sole intent is to destroy what the thoughtful light has wrought. These forces are called the "serpents dwelling in the great abyss." The satanic powers, called in the Zohar *sitra aḥra* ("the other side"), are none other than the other side of *Ein-Sof* itself insofar as, by its very resistance, it became involved in the process of creation itself. Nathan developed a novel theory about processes which took place in the *tehiru* even before the ray from *Ein-Sof* penetrated there, being brought about by the interaction between the residue of the thoughtful light and the forces of the *golem*. They produced modes of being connected with the first configurations of the letters which were to form the Torah and the cosmic script. Only at a later stage, after the straight line shone forth and penetrated the *tehiru*, were these first structures, called the work of primeval creation (*ma'aseh bereshit*), transformed into the more substantial structures (*ma'aseh merkavah*). All the Lurianic processes connected with the breaking of the vessels and the *tikkun* were now adapted to the dialectics of the two lights.

In this conception of creation the figure of the Messiah plays a central role from the outset. Since *ẓimẓum* the soul of the Messiah had been submerged in the lower half of the *tehiru*; that is, since the beginning of time it stayed in the realm of the *kelippot*, being one of those sparks of the thoughtful light that had remained in the *tehiru* or perhaps having been snatched in some way by the *kelippot*. This soul, invaded by the influx of the thoughtless light and in bondage to its domination, has been struggling since the beginning of the world amid indescribable suffering to free itself and set out on its great task: to open up the lower part of the *tehiru* to the penetration of the thoughtful light and to bring redemption and *tikkun* to the *kelippot*. With their final transformation a utopian equilibrium and unity would be produced between the two aspects of *Ein-Sof*. The "straight line" cannot go forth into the abyss before the Messiah has succeeded in escaping from the domination of the *kelippot*. He is essentially different from all those souls which play their part in the processes of *tikkun*. In fact, he was never under the authority of the Torah, which is the mystical instrument used by the power of the thoughtful light and the souls connected with it. He represents something utterly new, an authority which is not subject to the laws binding in the state of cosmic and historic exile. He cannot be measured by common concepts of good and evil and must act according to his own law, which may become the utopian law of a world redeemed. Both his prehistory and his special task explain his behavior after he had freed himself from the prison of the *kelippah*.

This doctrine enabled Nathan to defend each and every "strange act" of the Messiah, including his apostasy and his antinomian outbreaks. He is the mystical counterpart of the red heifer (Num. 19): he purifies the unclean but in the process becomes as it were impure himself. He is the "holy serpent" which subdues the serpents of the abyss, the numerical value of the Hebrew word *mashi'aḥ* being equal to that of *naḥash*. In a way, every soul is composed of the two lights and by its nature bound predominantly to the thoughtless light which aims at destruction, and the struggle between the two lights is repeated over and over again in every soul. But the holy souls are helped by the law of the Torah, whereas the Messiah is left completely to his own devices. These ideas were developed in the new heretic Kabbalah in great detail and in different versions, disclosing an uncanny sense for formulating paradoxical tenets of belief. They responded precisely to the particular situation of those who believed in the mission of an apostate Messiah, and the considerable dialectical force with which they were presented did not fail to impress susceptible minds. The combination of mythological images and dialectical argument added to the attraction exercised by Nathan's writings.

The Shabbatean Movement, 1680–1700

Outside the circles of the believers Shabbetai Ẓevi's death went unnoticed by the Jewish world. Among the believers it produced much soul-searching; some of his followers seem to have left the camp immediately after his death. Even his brother Elijah, who had joined him in Adrianople and had converted to Islam, returned to Smyrna and Judaism. The activities of the Shabbatean groups were mainly centered in three countries, Turkey, Italy, and Poland (particularly Lithuania), where vigorous leaders and various prophets and claimants to the succession to Shabbetai Ẓevi appeared. Though there were many believers in other parts of the Diaspora, such as Kurdistan and Morocco, these three centers were the most important. The largest groups in Turkey were in Salonika, Smyrna, and Constantinople but in most of the Balkan communities Shabbateanism survived and not infrequently members of the rabbinical courts were secret adherents. In Constantinople, their head was Abraham Yakhini, who died in 1682. A group of rabbis and kabbalists encouraged the more unlettered believers in Smyrna, although the Orthodox regained control there as in most places. From 1674 to 1680 Cardozo occupied the leading place among the Shabbateans in Smyrna after he had been forced to leave Tripoli around 1673, and later also Tunis and Leghorn. In Smyrna he found many followers, the most important of whom were the young rabbi *Elijah b. Solomon Abraham ha-Kohen Ittamari (d. 1727), who became one of the most prolific writers and moral preachers of the next two generations and never seems to have abandoned his basic convictions, and the cantor Daniel b. Israel

*Bonafoux, who claimed the powers of a medium, especially in his later years.

During these years Cardozo began a prolific literary output, composing numerous lesser and larger books and tracts in which he expounded his own brand of Shabbatean theology. Beginning with *Boker Avraham* (1672), he propagated the theory that there is a difference of principle between the first cause, which is the God of the philosophers and the pagans, and the God of Israel who revealed himself to the Patriarchs and to the people of Israel. The confusion between the two is Israel's main failure in the era of exile. The people were particularly misled by the philosophers of Judaism, *Saadiah Gaon, *Maimonides, and all the others. Only the teachers of the Talmud and the kabbalists had kept the flame of the true religion secretly burning. With the approach of redemption, a few elect souls would grasp the true meaning of Israel's belief, that is to say, revelation as against philosophy, and the Messiah (as prophesied by a midrashic saying) would reach the knowledge of the true God, Shabbetai Ẓevi's "mystery of the Godhead," by his own rational efforts. In the meantime, this paradoxical view could be supported by a true interpretation of traditional texts even though the blind rabbis thought it heresy. Cardozo made no use of the novel ideas of Nathan's Kabbalah but constructed a system of his own which had considerable dialectical power. In most of his writings he avoided the question of Shabbetai Ẓevi's mission, though he defended it in several epistles written at different periods of his life. For a considerable number of years, at least, he saw himself as the Messiah b. Joseph who, as revealer of the true faith and sufferer of persecution by the rabbis, must precede the final advent of Shabbetai Ẓevi, after which all the paradoxes of Shabbatean belief would be resolved. Between 1680 and 1697 Cardozo lived in Constantinople, Rodosto, and Adrianople, not only arousing much controversy by his teachings but also causing great unrest through his prophecies about the imminent messianic end, especially in 1682. He was finally forced to leave these parts and spent the last years of his life mainly in Candia (Crete), Chios, and, after vainly trying to settle in Jerusalem, in Egypt. The outstanding supporter of strict adherence to rabbinic tradition in practice as long as Shabbetai Ẓevi had not yet returned, he consistently battled against antinomian tendencies, although he too foresaw a complete change in the manifestation of the Torah and its practice in the time of redemption. Cardozo's influence was second only to Nathan's; his writings were copied in many countries and he maintained close relations with Shabbatean leaders everywhere. Many of his polemics were directed against Samuel Primo on the one hand, and the radical Shabbateans of Salonika on the other. Primo (d. 1708), who later became chief rabbi of Adrianople, opposed any outward Shabbatean activity and disclosed his steadfast belief and heretical ideas only in secret conclaves.

In Salonika the situation was different. The number of believers was still quite large and the family of Shabbetai Ẓevi's last wife, led by her father, Joseph Filosof, and her brother Jacob *Querido, displayed their convictions quite openly. Nathan had important followers among the rabbis, including some highly respected preachers and even halakhic authorities. The continuing state of turmoil, especially after Nathan's death, produced a fresh wave of excitement and new revelations. Visions of Shabbetai Ẓevi were very common in many circles of the believers but here, in 1683, they led to the mass apostasy of about 300 families who considered it their duty to follow in the Messiah's footsteps, in contradistinction to those Shabbateans who maintained, like Cardozo, that it was of the essence of the Messiah that his acts could not be imitated or followed by anyone else. Along with the first apostates among Shabbetai Ẓevi's contemporaries, the new group, led by Filosof and Solomon Florentin, formed the sect of the *Doenmeh, voluntary Marranos, who professed and practiced Islam in public but adhered to a mixture of traditional and heretical Judaism in secret. Marrying only among themselves, they were soon identified as a separate group by both Turks and Jews and developed along their own lines, forming three subsects. A certain amount of *antinomianism was common to all their groups, but this tendency was given preeminence by the subsect under the leadership of Baruchiah Russo (Osman Baba) who, in the first years of the 18th century, created another schism by teaching that the new spiritual or messianic Torah (*Torah de-Aẓilut*) entailed a complete reversal of values, symbolized by the change of the 36 prohibitions of the Torah called *keritot* (meaning punishable by uprooting the soul and annihilating it) into positive commands. This included all the prohibited sexual unions and incest. It seems that this group also developed the doctrine of the divinity of Shabbetai Ẓevi and later of Baruchiah himself, who died in 1721. This doctrine of incarnation was later wrongly ascribed to all Shabbateans and created much confusion in the reports about them. Baruchiah's group became the most radical wing of the Shabbatean underground. Most of the believers, however, did not follow the example of the Doenmeh and stayed within the Jewish fold, even in Salonika, where they disappeared only after a considerable time. Several well known rabbis of Salonika and Smyrna in the 18th century such as Joseph b. David, Abraham Miranda, and Meir *Bikayam, were still in secret sympathy with Shabbatean teachings and beliefs. Scholars who studied with Nathan or his pupils in Salonika, like Solomon *Ayllon and Elijah Mojajon, who later became rabbis of important communities such as Amsterdam, London, and Ancona, spread the teachings of the moderate wing of Shabbateanism which adhered to Judaism and even tended to excessive pietism. Between 1680 and 1740 a considerable number of the emissaries from Palestine, especially from Hebron and Safed, were "tainted" with Shabbateanism and apparently also served as links between the various groups of believers in the Diaspora.

The second center existed in Italy, first in Leghorn, where Moses *Pinheiro, Meir Rofe, Samuel de Paz, and Judah Sharaf (at the end of his life) were active, and later in Modena. Abraham *Rovigo in Modena was passionately devoted to Shabbateanism of a distinctly pietistic character and, being a widely reputed scholar and kabbalist as well as a member of a very rich family, became the man to whom all "believers" turned, particularly visitors passing through Italy from the Land of Israel, Poland, and the Balkans. His convictions were shared by his intimate friend *Benjamin b. Eliezer ha-Kohen, the rabbi of Reggio, Ḥayyim Segré of Vercelli, and others. They watched for every sign of a new impulse and reported to each other the news they received from their visitors and correspondents. Revelations of heavenly *maggidim*, who confirmed Shabbetai Ẓevi's supernal rank and the legitimacy of his mission and also added new interpretations of the Zohar and other kabbalistic matters, were then common. Rovigo's papers, many of which have survived, show the wide distribution of Shabbatean propaganda between 1680 and 1700. Benjamin Kohen – a rabbi who displayed a portrait of Shabbetai Ẓevi in his house! – even dared to publish a commentary on Lamentations which took up in detail Nathan's aphorism that in the messianic era this biblical book would be read as a collection of hymns of joy (*Allon Bakhut*, Venice, 1712). Baruch of Arezzo, one of Rovigo's group, composed in 1682–85, probably in Modena, a hagiography of Shabbetai Ẓevi, *Zikhron le-Veit Yisrael*, the oldest biography of this kind that has survived. Nathan's writings were copied and ardently studied in these circles, and illuminates who claimed heavenly inspiration such as Issachar Baer *Perlhefter and Mordecai (Mokhi'aḥ) *Eisenstadt from Prague (between 1677 and 1681), and later (1696–1701) Mordecai Ashkenazi from Zholkva (Zolkiev), were received with open arms and supported by Rovigo. When Rovigo realized his plan for settling in Jerusalem in 1701, the majority of the members of the yeshivah he founded there consisted of Shabbateans. Before leaving Europe, Rovigo went with his disciple Mordecai Ashkenazi to Fuerth, where he saw through press a voluminous folio, *Eshel Avraham*, written by the latter and based on the new reading of the Zohar he had received from heaven. Being devoted followers of rabbinic tradition, people of Rovigo's brand of Shabbateanism deviated from halakhic practice only by secretly celebrating the Ninth of Av as a festival. Even this practice was sometimes abandoned. In general, outside the rather small circle of the Doenmeh, the followers of Shabbetai Ẓevi did not differ from other Jews in their positive attitude to halakhic practice, and the differences between them and "orthodoxy" remained in the realm of theological speculation. The latter, of course, no doubt had far-reaching implications for the Jewish consciousness of the believers which cannot be underrated. The question of the position of the Torah in the messianic age, which was already the object of serious discussion in Shabbetai Ẓevi's own circle and in Cardozo's writings, especially in his *Magen Avraham* (1668), could not remain an abstract one. But there is no indication that before 1700 heretic practices, as opposed to ideas, were characteristic of Shabbateanism.

This also holds true of the movement in Ashkenazi Jewry. Almost immediately after Shabbetai Ẓevi's death it was speculated whether he may have been the suffering Messiah b. Joseph rather than the final redeemer. Taking this position in Prague in 1677 was Mordecai Eisenstadt, an ascetic preacher who attracted a large following during the next five years. Together with his brother, who was probably the later famous rabbi Meir Eisenstadt, he traveled through Bohemia, southern Germany, and northern Italy, exhorting the people not to lose faith in the forthcoming redemption. Learned rabbis like Baer Perlhefter supported his claims although Baer later left his camp and perhaps Shabbateanism altogether. Even where Shabbetai Ẓevi was revered as the true Messiah, as was the case in most groups, there was no lack of claimants for the role of the Messiah b. Joseph who would fill the interregnum between the "first manifestation" of Shabbetai Ẓevi and his second. Even during the latter's exile in Albania, such a claimant had already appeared in the person of Joseph ibn Ẓur in Meknès (Morocco), an ignoramus turned prophet who threw many communities into great agitation by proclaiming the final redemption for Passover 1675. His sudden death put an end to the upheaval, but not to the deep-rooted belief in Shabbetai Ẓevi in Morocco. More lasting was the impression created by another prophet of this type in Vilna, the former silversmith Joshua Heshel b. Joseph, generally called Heshel Ẓoref (1663–1700). Originally an unlettered craftsman, he became "reborn" during the great upheaval of 1666 and for many years was considered the outstanding prophet of the Shabbatean movement in Poland. Over a period of more than 30 years he composed the *Sefer ha-Ẓoref*, divided into five parts and said to represent something like the future Torah of the Messiah. In fact, its thousands of pages, based on mystical and numerological explanations of *Shema Yisrael*, proclaimed him as Messiah b. Joseph and Shabbetai Ẓevi as Messiah b. David. Its attitude toward rabbinical tradition remains completely conservative. Several parts of these revelations are preserved; some of them, curiously enough, came into the hands of *Israel b. Eliezer Ba'al Shem Tov and were held in high esteem by him and his circle. In his last years Heshel Ẓoref moved to Cracow and encouraged the new movement of the Shabbatean Ḥasidim.

Another prophet of this type, a former brandy distiller called Ẓadok, appeared in 1694–96 in Grodno. The stir such men created reverberated as far as Italy, and Rovigo and his friends carefully collected testimonies about these events from Polish visitors. One of these was the Polish Shabbatean Ḥayyim b. Solomon from Kalisz, known as Ḥayyim *Malakh, a very learned man and apparently a powerful personality. In 1691 he studied in Italy those of Nathan's writings which had not yet become available in Poland, and after his return propagated their teachings among the rabbis of Poland. Later he went to Adrianople and, under the influence of Primo, left the moderates and became a spokesman for a more radical branch of the movement. He joined forces with Judah Ḥasid from Shidlov, a famous preacher of repentance and a leader of the moderates. Between 1696 and 1700 they became the moving spirits of the "holy society of Rabbi Judah Ḥasid," a group composed of many hundreds of people, most of them probably Shabbateans, who indulged in extreme ascetism and prepared to emigrate to Palestine, there to await Shabbetai Ẓevi's second manifestation. Groups of them passed through many communities in Poland and Germany, arousing great enthusiasm. Although they never declared themselves openly as Shabbateans, little doubt remains on this score. Several rabbis in large communities who were aware of the true character of these Ḥasidim unsuccessfully tried to stop the propaganda. At the end of 1698, a council of the Shabbatean leaders of the Ḥasidim was held in Mikulov (Nikolsburg; Moravia) and was also attended by Heshel Ẓoref.

Shabbateanism in the 18th Century and Its Disintegration

The *aliyah* of the Ḥasidim to Jerusalem in 1700 represented a peak of Shabbatean activity and expectations, and in the great disappointment of its failure, as after the earlier failure of Shabbetai Ẓevi, several followers embraced Christianity or Islam. Judah Ḥasid died almost immediately after his arrival in Jerusalem in October 1700, and conditions in Jerusalem shattered the movement. Dissension broke out between the moderates, some of whom seem to have buried their Shabbatean convictions altogether, and the more radical elements led by Malakh. He and his faction were expelled but even the moderates could not maintain their foothold in the Holy Land and most of them returned to Germany, Austria, or Poland. One influential Shabbatean who remained was Jacob *Wilna, a kabbalist of great renown. Many believers had proclaimed 1706 as the year of Shabbetai Ẓevi's return and the disappointment weakened a movement that had lost its active drive. It was driven completely underground, a process hastened by the spreading rumors of the extremist antinomian and nihilist teachings of Baruchiah. Increasingly, although wrongly, Shabbateans were identified with this extreme wing whose followers were not satisfied with mystical theories and visionary experience, but drew consequences in their personal adherence to the Law. Malakh went to Salonika, then spread the gospel of secret antinomianism in Podolia, where he found fertile ground especially in the smaller communities. There is insufficient information regarding other parts of Europe to allow a clear differentiation between the various factions in the underground movement. It is obvious, however, that the antinomian slogan propagated by the radical wing that "the nullification of the Torah was its true fulfillment," and that, like the grain that dies in the earth, the deeds of man must become in some way "rotten" in order to bring forth the fruit of redemption, had a strong emotional appeal even to some talmudists and kabbalists, though, essentially, it represented an antirabbinic revolt in Judaism. That it alarmed the rabbinic authorities, who considered the children of these sectarians as bastards and therefore no longer admissible to the fold, was only logical. On the other hand, there is evidence that not a few of the most influential moral preachers and authors of moral literature of a radical ascetic bent were secret Shabbateans of the moderate and ḥasidic wing. Many of the most influential "*musar-books*" of this period belong to this category, such as *Shevet Musar* by Elijah Kohen Ittamari (1712), *Tohorat ha-Kodesh* by an anonymous author writing in the first decade of the century (1717), and *Shem Ya'akov* by Jacob Segal of Zlatova (1716). Some kabbalists who also wrote moral tracts in Yiddish belonged to this camp, such as Ẓevi Hirsch b. Jerahmeel *Chotsh, and Jehiel Michael *Epstein.

Shabbatean propaganda thus polarized around two different centers. The moderates who conformed to traditional practice and even overdid it could produce a literature which, avoiding an open declaration of their messianic faith, reached a wide public unaware of the convictions of the authors. Not a few homiletical, moral, kabbalistic, and liturgical books were published whose authors hinted in devious ways at their secret belief. The radicals, who became particularly active between 1715 and 1725 after Baruchiah had been proclaimed as "Santo Señor" and an incarnation of the Shabbatean version of the "God of Israel," had to be more careful. They worked through emissaries from Salonika and Podolia and circulated manuscripts and letters expounding their "new Kabbalah." The circles in Poland known as Ḥasidim before the advent of Israel Ba'al Shem Tov, which practiced extreme forms of ascetic piety, contained a strong element of Shabbateanism, especially in Podolia. In Moravia Judah b. Jacob, commonly called Loebele *Prossnitz, caused considerable upheaval after his "awakening" as a Shabbatean prophet, traveling through the communities of Moravia and Silesia and finding many followers, some of whom persisted even after his fraudulent "magical" practices were unmasked and he was put under a ban (1703–06). Meir Eisenstadt who, like a number of other outstanding rabbis, had been in sympathy with the movement and was then officiating at Prossnitz left him and turned against him; but Prossnitz remained the seat of a sizable Shabbatean group throughout the 18th century. A little later, 1708–25, another center of Shabbateanism crystallized in Mannheim, where some members of Judah Ḥasid's society, including his son-in-law *Isaiah Ḥasid from Zbarazh, found refuge in the newly established *bet ha-midrash*. About the same time Elijah Taragon, one of Cardozo's pupils, made an unsuccessful attempt to publish his master's *Boker Avraham* in Amsterdam (1712).

While all these developments took place mainly in a twilight atmosphere or underground and received little general attention, a great public scandal broke out when another Shabbatean illuminate, this time a very learned one, succeeded in publishing the only large text of Shabbatean theology printed in the 18th century. Nehemiah Ḥiyya *Ḥayon from Sarajevo had been educated in Jerusalem, served as a rabbi in his home town, and was in contact with the sectarians in Salonika and with Cardozo's circle before he returned to Ereẓ Israel. There he composed a highly elaborate double commentary on *Raza di-Meheimanuta*, Shabbetai Ẓevi's last exposition of the mystery of the Godhead, which Ḥayon now claimed to have received from an angel or, on other occasions, to have found in a copy of the Zohar. Forced to leave Ereẓ Israel because of his Shabbatean activities, he stayed for several years in Turkey, where he made enemies and friends alike and, about 1710, arrived in Venice, either on his own initiative or as an emissary. With the support of some secret sympathizers, but in general posing as an orthodox kabbalist, he succeeded in obtaining the approbation of rabbinical authorities to publish his three books: *Raza di-Yhuda* (Venice, 1711), *Oz le-Elohim* (Berlin, 1713) and *Divrei Neḥemyah (ibid.*, 1713). Of these *Oz le-Elohim* was the main work, containing his aforementioned commentaries on Shabbetai Ẓevi's text, whose title he changed to *Meheimanuta de-Kholla.* Amid polemics against Cardozo, he expounded his own version of the doctrine regarding the "three bonds of faith," the Shabbatean trinity of *Ein-Sof*, the God of Israel, and the *Shekhinah.* He carefully avoided linking this in any way with Shabbetai Ẓevi, whose name is never mentioned in any of these books, although *Divrei Neḥemyah* contains an extremely ambiguous homily attacking and at the same time defending those who apostatized for the sake of the God of Israel, that is the Doenmeh. It was only when he came to Amsterdam at the end of 1713, where he enjoyed the protection of Solomon Ayllon, himself a former secret adherent of Shabbateanism, that the heretical character of his books and especially of *Oz le-Elohim* was recognized by Ẓevi Hirsch *Ashkenazi, the rabbi of the Ashkenazi community in Amsterdam. In the ensuing violent quarrel between the Amsterdam Sephardi and Ashkenazi rabbis, which produced a lively polemical literature, Shabbatean theology was for the first time discussed in public, being attacked by rabbis like David *Nieto, Joseph *Ergas, and Moses *Ḥagiz, and a host of other participants in the fight against the heresy. Ḥayon vigorously defended his "kabbalistic" doctrine, stoutly but vainly denying its Shabbatean character. About 120 letters concerning this controversy were published in various sources. Several rabbis who were suspected of secret Shabbateanism refused to join in the bans pronounced against Ḥayon who, by the end of 1715, was forced to leave Europe. In his attempt at vindication by the rabbis of Turkey he received only halfhearted support.

When he returned to Europe in 1725, his arrival coincided with another Shabbatean scandal and brought his efforts to naught. This latter upheaval was connected with the increasing propaganda of the extremist followers of Baruchiah who had gained a strong foothold in Podolia, Moravia, and especially in the yeshivah of Prague, where the young and already famous Jonathan *Eybeschuetz was widely considered their most important supporter. From 1724 onward several manuscripts were circulated from Prague which contained kabbalistic explanations couched in ambiguous and obscure language but whose gist was a defense of the doctrine of the "God of Israel," his indwelling in *Tiferet*, and his intimate connection with the Messiah, without explicitly mentioning, however, his character as a divine incarnation. The testimony pointing to Eybeschuetz as the author, particularly of the kabbalistic but doubtless heretical manuscript *Va-Avo ha-Yom el ha-Ayin*, is overwhelming. When this and many other Shabbatean writings from Baruchiah's sect were discovered, in Frankfurt in 1725, among the luggage of Moses Meir of Kamenka (Kamionka), a Shabbatean emissary to Mannheim from Podolia, a great scandal ensued. A whole network of propaganda and connections between the several groups was uncovered, but Eybeschuetz' considerable reputation as a genius in rabbinic learning prevented action against him, particularly as he placed himself at the head of those who publicly condemned Shabbetai Ẓevi and its sectarians in a proclamation of excommunication dated Sept. 16, 1725. In many other Polish, German, and Austrian communities similar proclamations were published in print, also demanding that all who heard them should denounce secret Shabbateans to the rabbinical authorities. The atmosphere of persecution which then prevailed led the remaining Shabbateans to go completely underground for the next 30 years, especially in Poland.

After these events the figure of Jonathan Eybeschuetz remained in twilight, and indeed he poses a difficult psychological problem if (as may be evidenced through a study of the pertinent texts and documents) he must in fact be considered the author of the aforementioned manuscript. When, after his glorious career as a great teacher, preacher, and rabbinic authority in Prague, Metz, and Hamburg, it was discovered in 1751 that a considerable number of amulets he had given in Metz and Hamburg/Altona were in fact of a Shabbatean character, another great uproar followed, engulfing many people in Germany, Austria, and Poland in a heated controversy. His main opponent was Jacob *Emden, the son of Ḥayon's foe in Amsterdam and an indefatigable fighter against all surviving Shabbatean groups and personalities. His many polemical writings published between 1752 and 1769 often widely overshot their mark, as in the case of Moses Ḥayyim *Luzzatto, but they contain much valuable information about Shabbateanism in the 18th century. Eybeschuetz' defense of the amulets was particularly weak and largely self-defeating. He argued that the text of the amulets consisted only of mystical Holy Names which had their root in kabbalistic books and could not be deciphered as a continuous text. Comparison of the amulets, however, proves the contrary. The cryptograms used differed from one item to the other, but they always contained an assertion of the messianic mission of Shabbetai Ẓevi and a reference to Shabbatean views on the "God of Israel."

The secret Shabbateans in central Europe saw Eybeschuetz as their most prominent figure, whereas the orthodox were deeply shocked by the possibility that an outstanding representative of rabbinic and kabbalistic spirituality might have leanings toward heretical ideas. Many of them refused to entertain such a possibility and stood by him. The confusion even in the camp of orthodox kabbalists was considerable and they, too, were divided. The issue under discussion was greatly complicated by personal and irrelevant factors, but the conflict demonstrated how deeply rooted were apprehensions regarding the entrenchment of the Shabbateans in many communities. This is also borne out by numerous testimonies from many sources recorded between 1708 and 1750, even before the controversy between Eybeschuetz and Emden took place. Nathan of Gaza's writings were still studied not only in Turkey, but in Morocco, Italy, and among the

Ashkenazim. Several authors describe the method of Shabbatean propaganda among those who had only a modest talmudic learning or none at all but were drawn to the study of *aggadah* which the sectarians knew how to use and explain along their own lines. This method of attracting people and then slowly initiating them into the tenets of the sectarians was persistently used for over more than 80 years in Poland, Moravia, Bohemia, and Germany. Much ambiguity was permitted by the widespread heretical principle that the true believer must not appear to be what he really was and that dissimulation was legitimate in a period where redemption had taken place in the secret heart of the world but not yet in the realm of nature and history. People were allowed to deny their true belief in public in order to conceal their conservation of the "holy faith." This went so far that a work presenting a summary of Shabbatean theology, like Jacob Koppel Lifshitz' "Gates of Paradise," written in the early years of the 18th century in Volhynia, was preceded by a preface vehemently denouncing the Shabbatean heresy! This double-faced behavior came to be seen as a characteristic trait of the sectarians who, from the beginning of the 18th century, became known in Yiddish as *Shebsel* or *Shabsazviniks*, with the connotation of "hypocrites." There is full proof that a fair number of men of great talmudic learning, and even officiating rabbis, joined these groups and found it possible to live in a state of high tension between outward orthodoxy and inward antinomianism that perforce destroyed the unity of their Jewish identity. In places like Prague a number of highly respected families formed a nucleus of secret believers, and there is evidence that in some places influential Court Jews protected the sectarians or belonged to them. Many of the Moravian Shabbateans held positions of economic power. There is also evidence about the secret rituals performed in these groups, especially in Podolia, where the followers of Baruchiah were concentrated in places such as Buchach, Busk, Glinyany, Gorodenka, Zolkiew, Nadvornaya, Podgaitsy (Podhajce), Rogatin (Rohatyn), and Satanov. The eating of forbidden fat (*ḥelev*) or severe transgressions of sexual prohibitions were considered as initiation rites. Kabbalists and *Ba'alei Shem* (see *Ba'al Shem) from Podhajce who became known in Germany and England between 1748 and 1780, such as Samuel Jacob Ḥayyim *Falk, the "Ba'al Shem of London," and Moses David Podheizer, a close associate of Eybeschuetz in Hamburg, came from these circles.

The heated controversy about the revelations of Moses Ḥayyim Luzzatto in Padua, which began in 1727, and the messianic tendencies of his group engaged much attention in the following ten years. Although even in their secret writings Luzzatto, Moses David *Valle, and their companions repudiated the claims of Shabbetai Ẓevi and his followers, they were without doubt deeply influenced by some of the paradoxical teachings of Shabbatean Kabbalah, especially those concerning the metaphysical prehistory of the Messiah's soul in the realm of the *kelippot*. Luzzatto formulated these ideas in a manner which removed the obviously heretical elements but still reflected, even in his polemics against the Shabbateans, much of their spiritual universe. He even tried to find a place for Shabbetai Ẓevi, though not a messianic one, in his scheme of things. The idea of an apostate Messiah was utterly unacceptable to him as were the antinomian consequences drawn by the Doenmeh and their sympathizers, but his claims to heavenly inspiration and novel kabbalistic revelations, coming as they did immediately after the excommunication of the sectarians in 1725 and 1726, aroused grave apprehensions in Italy and some places in Germany that had special experiences with Shabbateanism. Similarly, a generation later the first antagonists of latter-day Polish Ḥasidism suspected it to be nothing but a new branch of Shabbateanism. In both cases the suspicions were wrong but they had some foundation in the teaching and behavior of the newcomers. More complicated is the case of the voluminous work *Ḥemdat Yamim*, first published in Smyrna in 1731 and later several times in Zolkiew and twice in Italy. This anonymous work described in detail Jewish life and ritual from the point of view of Lurianic Kabbalah but was permeated with the spirit of strictly ascetic Shabbateanism as it was promoted in Jerusalem and Smyrna by kabbalists like Jacob Wilna and Meir Bikayam. Adopting several Shabbatean innovations, it included even hymns written by Nathan of Gaza and a whole ritual for the eve of the new moon whose Shabbatean character is obvious. Though feigning an earlier origin, it was probably composed between 1710 and 1730, allegedly in Jerusalem but probably somewhere else. Its very attractive style and rich content secured it a wide public, and in Turkey it was accepted as a classic, a position it maintained. However, not long after its publication in Podolia in 1742, the work was denounced by Jacob Emden as composed by Nathan of Gaza (wrongly) and propagating Shabbatean views (rightly). This opposition notwithstanding, it was still frequently quoted but withdrawn from public circulation in Poland and Germany.

Independently of the Eybeschuetz affair, a momentous explosion of Shabbateanism in its last stage occurred in 1756 in Podolia with the appearance of Jacob Frank (1726–91) as the new leader of the extremist wing. Imbued with the main ideas of Baruchiah's sectarians in Salonika, he returned to his native milieu after spending many years mainly during his childhood and adolescence in Turkey. He was already then reputed as a new leader, prophet, and reincarnation of Shabbetai Ẓevi. (For details of the movement he instigated see *Jacob Frank and the Frankists.) In the stormy years between 1756 and 1760 a large part of Frank's followers converted to Catholicism, constituting a kind of Doenmeh in Poland, only in Catholic disguise. These events and especially the willingness of the Frankists to serve the interests of the Catholic clergy by publicly defending the blood libel in the disputation at Lvov (1759) deeply stirred and aroused the Jewish community in Poland and had wide repercussions even outside Poland. The majority of the Shabbateans, even of Frank's own sectarians, did not follow him into the Church and groups of Frankists remained within the Jewish fold in Poland, Hungary, Moravia, Bohemia, and Germany. Frank's main contribution was threefold.

(1) He divested Shabbateanism of its kabbalistic theology and the abstruse metaphysical speculations and terms in which it was clothed, substituting instead a much more popular and colorful version, couched in mythological images. The unknown and as yet inaccessible "Good God," the "Big Brother" (also called "He Who stands before God"), and the matron or virgin or plain "she" – an amalgam of the *Shekhinah* and the Virgin Mary – constitute the Frankist trinity. Frank saw Shabbetai Ẓevi, Baruchiah, and finally himself as emissaries and somehow incarnations of the "Big Brother," whose mission would be completed by the appearance of an incarnation of the feminine element of this trinity. Frank's tendency to throw away the "old books" contrasted sharply with the continuous predilection of his followers to study them, especially those who remained Jews.

(2) His version of Shabbateanism took on an unabashedly nihilistic character. Under the "burden of silence" the true believer, who has God in his secret heart, should go through all religions, rites, and established orders without accepting any and indeed annihilating all from within and thereby establishing true freedom. Organized religion is only a cloak to be put on and be thrown away on the way to the "sacred knowledge," the gnosis of the place where all traditional values are destroyed in the stream of "life."

(3) He propagated this nihilistic religion as the "way to Esau" or "Edom," encouraging assimilation without really believing in it, hoping for a miraculous revival of a messianic and nihilistic Judaism through the birth pangs of a universal upheaval. This conception opened the way to an amalgamation between this last stage of Shabbatean messianism and mysticism on the one hand and contemporary enlightenment and secular and anticlerical tendencies on the other. Freemasonry, liberalism, and even Jacobinism could be seen as equally valuable means to such final ends. It is small wonder that wherever such groups existed the Jewish communities fought them vehemently even though only rather vague rumors of Frank's secret teachings reached them.

Frankists in central Europe joined forces with the older Shabbatean groups, including the admirers of Eybeschuetz, and some of Eybeschuetz' own sons and grandchildren joined the Frankist camp. In the 1760s there was still active Shabbatean propaganda in the yeshivot of Altona and Pressburg. An emissary, Aaron b. Moses *Teomim from Gorodenka, propagated Shabbateanism in northern and southern Germany and, in 1767, tried to enlist the help of Christian sympathizers, claiming to have set out on his mission on behalf of the Polish prince Radziwill, a well-known protector of the Frankists. The Jewish and apostate Frankists remained in close touch, particularly through their meetings at Frank's "court" in Brno and later in Offenbach. Although they were deeply impressed by Frank's sayings and epistles, their own activities never equaled the ferocity of his subversive and nihilist visions. During the first decades of the 19th century Shabbateanism disintegrated even as a loosely organized sect and, apart from those who reverted to traditional Judaism, disappeared into the camp of Jewish liberalism and, in many cases, indifference. The sectarian groups of the Doenmeh in Turkey and the Catholic Frankists in Poland, especially in Warsaw, survived much longer. While those in Warsaw broke up probably after 1860, to this day there are some still extant in Turkey.

BIBLIOGRAPHY: SOURCES: J. Sasportas, *Ẓiẓat Novel Ẓevi*, ed. by Y. Tishby (1954); J. Emden, *Torat ha-Kena'ot* (1752); idem, *Sefer Hitabbekut* ISH (1762); J. Eybeschuetz, *Luḥot Edut* (Altona, 1775); N. Bruell (ed.), *Toledot Shabbetai Ẓevi* (1879); A. Freimann, *Inyenei Shabbetai Ẓevi* (1912); A.M. Habermann, *"Le-Toledot ha-Pulmus Neged ha-Shabbeta'ut"* in: *Kobez al Jad*, n.s. 3 pt. 2 (1940), 185–215; G. Scholem, *"Gei Ḥizzayon, Apokalipsah Shabbeta'it mi-Teiman," ibid.*, n.s. 4 (1946), 103–42; idem, *Be-Ikvot Mashi'aḥ* (1944; collected writings of Nathan); M. Attias and G. Scholem (eds.), *Shirot ve-Tishbaḥot shel ha-Shabbeta'im* (1948); *Sefunot*, 3–4 (1959–60; *Meḥkarim u-Mekorot le-Toledot ha-Tenu'ah ha-Shabbeta'it Mukdashim li-Shneur Zalman Shazar*); J. Frances, *Kol Shirei*..., ed. by P. Naveh (1969). STUDIES: SCHOLEMYADA (WORKS BY G. SCHOLEM): *Messianic Idea in Judaism and Other Essays* (1971); *Ḥalomotav shel ha-Shabbeta'i R. Mordekhai Ashkenazi* (1938); *Shabbetai Ẓevi ve-ha-Tenu'ah ha-shabbeta'it Bime Ḥayyav* (1957); revised and augmented, in English under the title, *Sabbatai Sevi, The Mystical Messiah* (1973); KS, 16 (1939–40), 320–38 (on the Emden-Eybeschuetz controversy); *Meḥkarim u-Mekorot le-Toledot ha-Tenu'ah ha-Shabbeta'it Mukdashim li-Shneur Zalman Shazar*; J. Frances, 84–88 (on Shabbateanism in missionary literature); 35 (1970), 126–80 (on Moses Dobruschka); *Sefer Dinaburg* (1948), 235–62 (on Mordekhai Eisenstadt); *Alexander Marx Jubilee Volume* (Heb., 1950), 451–70 (on Elijah Kohen Ittamari and Shabbateanism); *"Le mouvement sabbataïste en Pologne,"* in: RHR, 143–4 (1953–55), *Beḥinot*, 8 (1955), 79–95; 9 (1956), 80–84 (on the book *Ḥemdat Yamim*); *"Perush Mizmorei Tehillim me-Ḥugo shel Shabbetai Ẓevi be-Adrianopol,"* in: *Alei Ayin; Minḥat Devarim li-Shelomo Zalman Schocken* (1952), 157–211; *Eretz Israel*, 4 (1956), 188–94 (on two Mss. regarding Shabbateanism in the Adler collection); *"Iggeret Natan ha-Azzati al Shabbetai Ẓevi ve-Hamarato,"* in: *Koveẓ al Yad*, n.s. 6 (1966), 419–56; Graetz, Gesch, 7 (1896), 428–524; C. Anton, *Kurze Nachricht von dem falschen Messias Sabbathai Zebbi* (1752); *Nachlese zu seiner letztern Nachricht* (1753); A. Danon, *Essays* (1971); *Ḥalomotav shel ha-Shabbeta'i R. Mordekhai* (Istanbul, 1935); D. Kahana, *Toledot ha-Mekubbalim, ha-Shabbeta'im ve-ha-Ḥasidim* 2 vols. (1913–14); D. Kaufman, in MGWJ, 41 (1897), 700–8 (a letter of Benjamin Cohen, dated 1691); M. Freudenthal, *"R. Michel Chasid und die Sabbatianer," ibid.*, 76 (1932), 370–85; A. Epstein, *"Une lettre d'Abraham Ha-Yakhini à Nathan Gazati,"* in REJ, 26 (1893), 209–19; A. Amarillo, *"Te'udot Shabbeta'iyyot,"* in: *Sefunot* 5 (1961), 235–74; I. Sonne, *"Overim ve-Shavim be-Veito shel Avraham Rovigo," ibid.*, 5 (1961), 275–96; M. Friedman, *"Iggerot be-Farashat Pulmus Neḥemyah Ḥiyya Ḥayon," ibid.*, 10 (1966), 483–619; S.Z. Shazar, *Sofero shel Mashi'aḥ* (1970; repr. from *Ha-Shilo'aḥ*, 29 (1913)); idem, *"Ma'aseh Yosef Dela Reina ba-Masoret ha-Shabbeta'it,"* in: *Eder ha-Yakar, Sefer Yovel... S.A. Horodezky* (1947) 97–118; idem, *Ha-Tikvah li-Shenat Ha-Ta-K* (1970; on I.V. Cantarini); M. Benayahu, *"Yedi'ot me-Italyah u-me-Holland at Reshitah shel ha-Shabbeta'ut,"* in: *Eretz Israel*, 4 (1956), 194–205; idem, in: *Sinai*, 46 (1960), 33–52 (on responsa regarding Shabbatean movement); idem, *"Mafte'aḥ le-Havanat ha-Te'udot al ha-Tenu'ah ha-Shabbeta'it bi-Yrushalayim,"* in: *Studies in honor of G. Scholem* (1968), 35–45; I. Sonne, *"Le-Toledot ha-Shabbeta'ut be-Italyah,"* in: D. Frankel (ed.), *Sefer Yovel le-Alexander Marx* (1943), 89–103; H. Wirshubski, *"Ha-Te'ologyah ha-Shabbeta'it shel Natan ha-Azzati,"* in: *Keneset*, 8 (1944), 210–46; M. Perlmuter, *R. Yonatan Eybeschuetz ve-Yaḥaso el ha-Shabbeta'ut* (1947; incl. Eng. summary); A.Z. Aescoly, *"Itton*

Flandri al Odot Tenuat Shabbetai Ẓevi," in: *Sefer Dinaburg* (1950), 215–36; M. Wilensky, "*Arba'ah Kunteresim Angliyyim al ha-Tenu'ah ha-Shabbeta'it*," in: *Zion*, 17 (1952), 157–72; A. Yaari, *Ta'alumat Sefer* (1954; on *Ḥemdat Yamim*); idem, "*Mi Hayah ha-Navi ha-Shabbeta'i R. Mattityahu Bloch?*," in: KS, 36 (1961), 525–34; S. Hurwitz, "*Shabbatai Zwi*," in: *Studien zur Analytischen Psychologie* in: *C.G. Jungs*, 2 (1955), 239–63; R. Shatz, in: *Beḥinot*, 10 (1956), 50–66 (on Sassportas' *Ẓiẓat Novel Ẓevi*); S. Simonsohn, "A Christian Report from Constantinople Regarding Shabbetai Zebi," in: JJS, 12 (1961), 33–85; Y. Tishby, *Netivei Emunah u-Minut* (1964); A. Rubinstein, "*Bein Ḥasidut le-Shabbeta'ut*," in: *Bar-Ilan*, 4–5 (1965), 324–39; H.P. Salomon, "Midrash, Messianism and Heresy in Spanish-Jewish Hymns," in: *Studia Rosenthaliana*, 4 no. 2 (1970), 169–80. **ADD. BIBLIOGRAPHY:** J. Barnai, "Christian Messianism and the Portuguese Marranos: The Emergence of Sabbateanism in Smyrna," in: *Jewish History*, 7 (1993), 119–26; idem, "The Outbreak of Sabbateanism – The Eastern European Factor," in: *Journal for Jewish Thought and Philosophy*, 4 (1994), 171–83; idem, *Sabbateanism – Social Perspectives* (Heb., 2000), 20–29; S. Berti, "A World Apart? Gershom Scholem and Contemporary Readings of 17th century Christian Relations," in: *Jewish Studies Quarterly*, 3 (1996), 212–14; R. Elior (ed.), *The Sabbatean Movement and Its Aftermath: Messianism, Sabbateanism, Frankism*, 2 vols. (Heb., 2001); A. Elqayam, "Sabbatai Sevi's Manuscript Copy of the Zohar," in: *Kabbalah*, 3 (1998), 345–87 (Heb.); M. Goldish, *The Sabbatean Prophets* (2004); M. Idel, "Saturn and Sabbatai Tzevi: A New Approach to Sabbateanism," in: P. Schaefer and M. Cohen (eds.), *Toward the Millennium, Messianic Expectations from the Bible to Waco* (1998), 173–202; Y. Liebes, *On Sabbateanism and Its Kabbalah, Collected Essays* (Heb., 1995).

[Gershom Scholem]

SHABTAI, AHARON (1939–), Israeli poet and translator. Shabtai was born in Tel Aviv and studied ancient Greek literature at the Hebrew University. He taught at Tel Aviv University and was well known as a translator of Greek drama into Hebrew. Shabtai published his first collection of poems, *Ḥadar Morim* ("Teacher's Room") in 1966. More than a dozen collections followed, among them *Ha-Po'emah ha-Beitit* ("The Domestic Poem," 1976), *Sefer ha-Kelum* ("The Book of Nothing," 1981), *Begin* (1986), *Gerushin* ("Divorce," 1990), *Zivah* ("Ziva," 1990) and *Ḥodesh Mai ha-Nifla* ("The Beautiful Month of May," 1997) and *Shemesh, Shemesh* ("Sun, Sun," 2005). Shabtai addresses political issues while vehemently criticizing the Israeli Occupation and the corrosion of moral values. Other poems dramatize Shabtai's personal experiences, focusing on love and sexuality while deliberately offending good taste and decorum. Two collections have appeared in French translation (1987; 1990) and two volumes were published in English: *Love and Selected Poems* (1997; 1999) and *Selected Poems* (2003).

BIBLIOGRAPHY: O. Bernstein, "*Al ha-Po'emah ha-Beitit*," in: *Siman Keriah*, 7 (1977), 419–21; A. Sachs, "*Meshorerei ha-Anti Metaforah: A. Shabtai ve-Harold Schimmel*," in: *Ha-Kongres ha-Olami le-Mada'ei ha-Yahadut*, 6:3 (1977), 171–77; G. Levin, "What Different Things Link Up: Hellenism in Contemporary Hebrew Poetry," in: *Prooftexts*, 5:3 (1985), 221–43; A. Altaras, "*Lakaḥat be-Ḥeshbon: Al Ha-Po'emah ha-Beitit*," in: *Akhshav*, 50 (1985), 84–89; E. Mishori, "*Mi-Erotikah le-Pornografiyyah*," in: *Akhshav*, 57 (1992), 270–76; Sh. Sandbank, "*Shirah Lo Retuvah*," in: *Ḥadarim*, 11 (1994), 162–67; Sh. Beram, "*Al Aharon Shabtai ve-ha-Korpus ha-Po'emah ha-Beitit*," in: *Dappim le-Meḥkar be-Sifrut*, 12 (2000), 155–79; Y. Mazor, "*Lesalek et ha-Estetikah min ha-Salon*," in: *Moznyaim*, 75:7 (2000), 24–27.

[Anat Feinberg]

SHABTAI, YAAKOV (1934–1981), Israeli writer. Despite his untimely demise, Shabtai had established himself as a master of several genres: sketches, plays, poems, stories, and novels. Even though only one of his novels was completed, with another not finally edited, it is in the field of the Hebrew novel that Shabtai made his most significant contribution to Israeli literature. He combined a bleak, realistic outlook with a humor unusual on the Israeli literary landscape, bringing a touch of Yiddish irony and fluency to the archetypically local scene. From the outset, in his first volume of short stories, *Ha-Dod Peretz Mamri* (1972), he imprinted this scene with an elegiac tone, mourning the loss of a vanishing world embodied in the death of the narrator's grandmother. It is not just an individual who is passing, but a generation, and, with that generation, a way of life and an earlier, now departed civilization.

His most remarkable and permanent work is the completed novel, *Zikhron Devarim* (1977; *Past Continuous*, 1985). It is primarily a portrait of three individuals, three middle-aged Israeli men whose lives in Tel Aviv over a nine-month period, are presented in the context of two events in the "life" of one of them. The two events which frame the narrative are the death of Goldman's father, which sets the scene, with the tragic and hilarious funeral, and then Goldman's own demise, precisely nine months later. This time frame, as noted by one of the other characters, Caesar, precisely fits the period of gestation. And it remains as an ironic comment that the time required for the creation of a life is signaled here by two points of life's closure. The innovation, for the Hebrew novel, lies in the manner of its telling. The whole is presented as a single paragraph. Although the narrative is broken up into separate sentences, there is no separation into chapters. Its is a single sequence, as it were, to be read in one breath, clearly an impossible demand made upon the reader by a work of 280 pages. The English translation dispenses with this typological requirement.

This work is a *roman fleuve*, although in this particular rendering of the genre, all is compressed in one volume. Here the consciousness of the three heroes, presented through the objective, omniscient eye of a third person narrator, is passed from one to the other over the period described. But there is a seemingly seamless shift in place, time, and person that allows the reorientation of the narrative. Although we are presented with an ongoing narrative, that sequence also comprises flashbacks and memories, as well as projections forward. Thus there is a comprehensive portrait here of the human frame, albeit offered through a specific lens. The three characters also constitute a microcosm of attitudes, as well as a society in miniature. Goldman, through his father's and his own death, acts as an anchor. Clearly, he cannot comment on the latter event, so Caesar, who cannot believe that good things can come to an end, acts as a necessary foil. The third character, Yisrael, the youngest of the three, is a rather undefined figure, living in the shadow of the other two, and taking his posture from them. Caesar charges around, blustering, protesting, womanizing, gourmandizing. Goldman experiments with philosophies and interpretations of life. Yisrael, quietly and rather ill-naturedly, observes from the sidelines.

Here, there is no single hero. But there is a force that shapes their lives, as well as the pulse of the society that encases it. That force is the movement of time. In the second novel, which was later edited by the author's widow together with the critic Dan Miron and published posthumously under the title *Sof Davar* (1984; *Past Perfect*, 1987), a different stance and literary technique are adopted. The single paragraph technique is abandoned, and instead we have a narrative in four parts with a single hero. But each section adopts a different standpoint, culminating in the finale which explicitly surrenders any presumption of naturalism. An omniscient narrator comments on the central character, Meir, who is on the way to death, and beyond (*"sof davar,"* a quotation from Ecclesiastes, means "the end of the matter").

The prominent element in Shabtai's work is the tragic sense of life, and its impending end. However, this is presented with a vibrant and original brio. Shabtai's plays include: *The Life of Caligula* (1975); *The Chosen* (1976); *Don Juan and His Friend Shipel* (1978); *The Spotted Tiger* (1985); *Crowned Head and Other Plays* (1995); and *Eating* (1999).

BIBLIOGRAPHY: H. Herzig, *Ha-Shem ha-Perati* (1994); D. Miron: *Pinkas Patu'aḥ* (1979); L. Yudkin, *1948 and After: Aspects of Israeli Fiction* (1984); idem, *Beyond Sequence: Current Israeli Fiction and its Context* (1992).

[Leon I. Yudkin (2nd ed.)]

SHACHAR, ARIE (1935–2006), Israeli geographer specializing in urban geography and planning. Shachar was born in Haifa. He attended The Hebrew University of Jerusalem, receiving his Ph.D. in 1965 and joining the Department of Geography there (professor from 1979). He was visiting professor in the School of Architecture and Urban Planning of the University of California several times (1970, 1976, 1980, 1982, 1986, and 1988). In 1980–83 he was head of the department of geography at The Hebrew University and in 1982–97 he was chairman of the National Committee of Geography in the Israel Education Ministry. He also served as a planning consultant in Panama and Ecuador as well as to the UN and in, 1972–92 was chairman of the General Program Committee of Hebrew University in charge of planning the new Mt. Scopus Campus. Shachar was chief editor of the *City and Region* journal and chairman of the editorial board of *The Atlas of Israel* (1985–95), as well as a member of the international board of the *Progress in Planning* journal (1994–97). He also wrote dozens of articles and reports. In 1999 he was awarded the Israel Prize in geography.

[Shaked Gilboa (2nd ed.)]

SHADKHAN (Heb. שַׁדְּכָן), marriage broker or matchmaker. In return for a financial consideration, the *shadkhan* arranges and assists a union between two people, taking into consideration not only the compatibility of the couple but also the suitability of their families. Although the Bible does not describe in detail how marriages were arranged, Genesis 24:1–67 tells how Abraham's servant chose a wife, Rebekah, for Isaac. The story implies that the servant had the authority to use his discretion in making the choice. However, Isaac's son, Jacob, chose his own wife. During the talmudic period marriages were arranged by the heads of the two families, with no broker involved (Shab. 150a). Sometimes, however, marriages were arranged by the couples themselves (Kid. 13a). Arranged marriages were considered so essential that "Rav punished any man… who betrothed a woman without previous *shiddukhin*" since he regarded this as licentious behavior (Kid. 12b).

The term *shadkhan* in its present meaning first appears in rabbinic literature in the 13th century. *Mordecai (b. Hillel) discusses whether the broker should receive his fee even if the marriage does not take place (BK 172). In Austria the *shadkhan* was not paid until after the marriage had taken place, while in the Rhenish countries he was paid as soon as the parties reached an understanding (Responsa Meir of Rothenburg, ed. Prague no. 498; A. Berliner, *Aus dem Leben der deutschen Juden im Mittelalter* (1900, 43)).

The *shadkhan* was entitled to a higher fee than that awarded to the business *sarsur* or broker. The latter was only given one-half to one per cent of the business transactions he negotiated while the *shadkhan* received two per cent of the dowry involved. When the contracting parties lived more than ten miles apart, the marriage broker received three per cent of the dowry for his efforts (S. Buber, *Anshei Shem*, 1 (1895), 25).

The matchmaking profession was originally highly esteemed, and famous rabbis such as Jacob *Moellin and Jacob *Margolioth earned their livelihoods from this occupation. A 17th-century writer cautioned matchmakers, "When you are arranging a marriage between two parties, never exaggerate, and always tell the truth." He added that "in earlier times, none but scholars were *shadkhanim*" (idem, in: JQR, 3 (1891), 480). Rabbis and scholars were the natural go-betweens in the Middle Ages when fathers were anxious to obtain learned and pious sons-in-law.

In time, the traditional integrity of the marriage broker began to decline. A principal reason was the fact that men with unstable backgrounds and occupations were tempted into the profession's uncertain undertakings. The peculiar persuasive and social talents required for this profession stimulated the development of a unique type of personality. Generally, the *shadkhan* could be relied upon to be a perpetual chatterbox, lively, good-natured, and even impudent. Amid the raillery and guilelessness, however, an element of maliciousness could be detected. A classic type in Jewish folklore and fiction, the *shadkhan* is portrayed in all the bright plumage of his loquaciousness. His genius for euphemistically glossing over the physical and character defects of his clients is legend.

BIBLIOGRAPHY: I. Abrahams, *Jewish Life in the Middle Ages* (1932[2]), 186f.; P. and H. Goodman, *The Jewish Marriage Anthology* (1965), 103–5.

SHADMOT DEVORAH (Heb. שַׁדְמוֹת דְּבוֹרָה), moshav in northern Israel, northeast of Kefar Tavor, affiliated with Tenu'at ha-Moshavim. It was founded in May 1939, a few weeks after the publication of the anti-Zionist White Paper by the British government. The founders, originally from Germany, had first settled in a moshav shittuffi, *Moledet, but left to establish the moshav, Shadmot Devorah. In 1970 the moshav had 166 inhabitants; in 2002, 367. Its economy was based on field crops, fruit orchards, and dairy cattle. Devorat ha-Tavor, a silk- and honey-production visitors center is located in the moshav. Shadmot Devorah ("fields of Devorah") is named for Dorothy (d. 1988; Devorah), wife of James de *Rothschild.

[Efram Orni / Shaked Gilboa (2nd ed.)]

SHADRACH, MESHACH, ABED-NEGO (Heb. שַׁדְרַךְ, עֲבֵד נְגוֹ ,מֵישַׁךְ), three young men of aristocratic Judahite stock whose Hebrew names were respectively Hananiah ("The Lord was gracious"), Mishael (perhaps "Who is what God is?"), and Azariah ("The Lord helped"). Together with Daniel they were taken into the Babylonian court of *Nebuchadnezzar because of their handsome appearance, wisdom, and ability to learn. In accordance with known practice they were assigned Babylonian names and taught the language and literature of the Chaldeans (probably Akkadian). Refusing to be defiled by eating pagan food, the youths providentially throve on a diet of grains and greatly surpassed the wisdom of all the king's magicians (Dan. 1). They quickly rose in rank, Daniel attaining the position in the "King's Gate" and the other three being put in charge of the "administration" of the province of Babylon (Dan. 2:49). The three refused to worship the pagan image erected by Nebuchadnezzar, were cast into a fiery furnace, and miraculously emerged alive. Nebuchadnezzar acknowledged the greatness of their God and confirmed their rule in Babylonia (Dan. 3). "The Three Children" thus became a paradigm of faithfulness to God (cf. 1 Macc. 2:59).

[Bezalel Porton]

In the ancient Greek and Latin versions of Daniel there is an addition inserted between 3:23 and 3:24. This addition consists of 68 verses and may have been composed in either Hebrew or Aramaic. In the Apocrypha it appears as "The Prayer of Azariah and The Song of the Three Young Men." It is possible that Hananiah-Shadrach (Gr. Sedrach) is the Sedrach to whom the Christian *Apocalypse of Sedrach* was attributed (M.R. James, *Apocrypha Anecdota* (1893), 127–37).

The Hebrew names of the three companions are quite common in the period of the Second Temple and occur both in biblical and post-biblical sources. There is no certain etymology for the Babylonian names Shadrach and Meshach but it has been suggested that Abed-Nego is a variation of Abed-Nebo ("Servant of Nab").

[Michael E. Stone]

BIBLIOGRAPHY: W.H. Bennett, in: Charles, Apocrypha, 1 (1913), 625–37; Schuerer, Gesch, 3 (1909[4]), 452ff.; Klausner, Bayit Sheni, 1 (1951[2]), 80; O. Eissfeldt, *The Old Testament, an Introduction* (1965), 588–90 (incl. bibl.).

SHAFFER, SIR PETER (1926–), English playwright. Born in Liverpool, Shaffer was educated at Cambridge, where he edited the university magazine *Granta*. He became a music and theater critic and wrote several plays for broadcasting but made his name with the stage play *Five-Finger Exercise* (1958). On the surface a conventional domestic comedy, this study of a middle-class English family vying for the affections of a young German tutor dealt with relationships which other playwrights of the time either ignored or evaded. In 1962 Shaffer scored another success with *The Private Ear and the Public Eye*, two one-act studies of the gap between reality and appearance, in which the apparently conventional situation was again treated in psychological depth. His later plays are more ambitious: *The Royal Hunt of the Sun* (1964), a spectacular chronicle play, depicts the incursion of Cortez into the Peru of the Incas; *Black Comedy* (1965) attempted to extend the currently fashionable "sick joke" into a full-length theatrical performance.

[Philip D. Hobsbaum]

Shaffer achieved an outstanding success with his *Equus* which was first performed on Broadway in 1974. A psychological thriller about a boy who blinded six horses, based upon an actual incident which occurred in England in 1972, Shaffer worked on it for over two years. In it, he delves into the sexual and other motivations for this outrage which are revealed in long dialogues between the boy and a psychiatrist. His play *Amadeus* (1979), about the alleged murder of Mozart by Antonio Salieri, was made into a famous film (1984) which won the Academy Award for Best Picture. He was knighted in 2000. His twin brother, ANTHONY SHAFFER (1926–2001), was educated at Cambridge and became a barrister. He was also a noted playwright, especially of mysteries. He was the author of the long-running *Sleuth* (1970), made into a film in 1977, *Frenzy* (1973), one of Alfred Hitchcock's last films, and dramatizations of several of Agatha Christie's works. The two brothers sometimes collaborated, using the pseudonym "Peter Anthony."

ADD. BIBLIOGRAPHY: ODNB online for Anthony Shaffer; G.A. Plunka, *Peter Shaffer* (1988); M.K. MacMurraugh-Kavanagh, *Peter Shaffer: Theatre and Drama* (1998).

SHAG (Zwebner), ABRAHAM (1801–1876), Hungarian rabbi. Shag was born in Galgóc and studied under Moses Sofer. He first served as rabbi in the small town of Czeszté and then in Kobelsdorf, one of the "seven communities" in Hungary. He was distinguished both for his keen intellect and his firm and upright character. He was a member of the Jewish Congress of 1869. He left behind many works, but only his *Ohel Avraham* (1881) responsa, and his *Derashot ha-Rosh* (1904) have been published. Shag was one of the rabbis in Hungary who raised his voice against the communal schism and published a proclamation on the subject in *Ha-Maggid* (1868). His followers did not like it and it was largely ignored. In 1873 Shag immigrated to Ereẓ Israel, undoubtedly influenced by his teacher Moses Sofer. In 1846, when the *Toleranz* tax was abolished, he justified its original imposition on the grounds that unlike other settlers whose intention it was to become permanent citizens and enjoy citizens' rights, the Jew regards himself only as a temporary resident, since he is enjoined by his religion to await the coming of the Messiah, and hence should pay for his stay in the country. Moreover, the paying of the tax indicates the depth of his faith and his expectation of the imminent advent of the Messiah and it is fitting that he should pay for the right of residence.

BIBLIOGRAPHY: M. Stein (ed.), *Magyar rabbik*, 1 (1905), 36f.; S. Weingarten, *He-Ḥatam Sofer ve-Talmidav* (1945), 107–11; I.D. Shag, *Lappid Esh* (1954).

[Naphtali Ben-Menahem]

SHAHAL (Fatal), MOSHE (1934–), Israeli politician and attorney, member of the Seventh to Fourteenth Knessets. Born in Baghdad, Shahal grew up in a traditional middle class family and attended an English school. At the age of 12 he first read Karl Marx's *Capital*, which greatly influenced his way of thinking. In 1950 he immigrated to Israel with his family, which lived at first in transit camps (*ma'barot*) in Beit Lid and Ashkelon. He settled in Haifa in the late 1950s. As a member of the ruling *Mapai, Shahal was involved in efforts to quell the Wadi Salib riots, organized by militants of Oriental origin against the background of claims of discrimination that broke out in July 1959. Shahal was a member of the Haifa Labor Council in 1959–71, and a member of its secretariat in 1964–71. He was a member of the Haifa Municipal Council in 1965–69.

In 1964 he studied economics, sociology, and political science at Haifa University, and then continued his studies for a law degree at Tel Aviv University, which he received in 1969. In 1970 he became a partner in the Ben-Israel & Shahal law firm, in which he remained until 1983, then joining the Solomon & Lifshitz firm where he remained for a year.

Shahal entered the Seventh Knesset in 1971, and soon turned into an expert on the Knesset Rules of Procedure. He became a member of numerous Knesset Committees, but was especially active in the Constitution, Law and Justice Committee, and the Finance Committee. In 1974–76, during the term of the Eighth Knesset, he served as chairman of the Israeli Consumers Council, and was a member of the Knesset delegation to the Council of Europe. In the Ninth and Tenth Knessets he was chairman of the Alignment parliamentary group, and a member of the Knesset delegation to the Inter-Parliamentary Union. In the Tenth Knesset he served as deputy speaker.

Shahal was one of the chief negotiators of the coalition agreement between the *Israel Labor Party and the *Likud in 1984, which culminated in the establishment of a National Unity Government based on parity and with rotation in the premiership. He was then one of the initiators of the Arrangements Law that accompanied the Economic Stabilization Plan of 1985, which was designed to save the Israeli economy from a catastrophe. In the National Unity Governments of 1984–90 Shahal served as minister of energy and infrastructure, playing an active role in numerous ministerial committees, as he was to continue to do in future governments of which he was a member. In 1987 he met with the Iraqi ambassador in Washington in an effort to open a channel of communication with Iraq. In 1988–90 Shahal acted as liaison minister between the government and the Knesset. After Peres failed to form a government following Labor's departure from the National Unity Government in March 1990, he joined the Zadok, Stricks, Shahal & Co. law firm in Tel Aviv, but left the partnership after the Labor electoral victory in the elections to the Thirteenth Knesset. In the beginning of 1992, before the elections, Shahal considered contesting the Labor leadership, but finally decided not to participate in the contest that was won by Yitzhak *Rabin. In the government formed by Rabin after the elections, Shahal was first appointed minister of communications, but then returned to the ministry of energy and infrastructure, and also served as minister of police. In 1994 he once again became the liaison minister between the government and the Knesset. Shahal was a member of the ministerial teams that dealt both with the Palestinian and the Syrian issues. Though he was never considered a dove, he was known for his pragmatic approach. Already in 1995 he raised the idea that Israel should defend itself against Palestinian terrorist attacks by constructing a fence between itself and the territories handed over to the Palestinians. In the field of energy he supported cooperation with Israel's neighbors – especially Egypt and Jordan. In the government formed by Shimon*Peres after Rabin's assassination in November 1995 he was appointed minister of internal security.

In the course of the Fourteenth Knesset Shahal participated in a meeting with the Follow-Up Committee of Israeli Arabs, to discuss ways of saving the peace process following the Likud victory in the elections to the Fourteenth Knesset. He resigned from the Knesset in March 1998, and opened his own law firm in Tel Aviv but continued to play an active role in the Israel Labor Party. One of the subjects he continued to deal with in his professional capacity as an attorney was the Israeli energy market, which he had helped to reshape as minister of energy and infrastructure.

[Susan Hattis Rolef (2nd ed.)]

SHAHAM, GIL (1971–), Israeli violinist born in the U.S. In 1973 he moved with his parents to Israel, where at the age of seven he studied with Samuel Bernstein at the Rubin Academy. While studying with Haim Taub, he made his orchestral debut with the Jerusalem Symphony Orchestra (1981).The following year he played with the Israel Philharmonic under Mehta and begun his studies with Dorothy DeLay and Jens Ellerman at Aspen. In 1982, after taking first prize in Israel's Claremont Competition, Shaham became a scholarship student at Juilliard, where he worked with DeLay and Hyo Kang. In 1989 he began his studies at Columbia University, New York. His subsequent solo career brought him engagements with the New York Philharmonic Orchestra, the Philadelphia Orchestra, the Berlin Philharmonic Orchestra and the Frankfurt RSO, among others. In 1989 he caused a sensation when he replaced *Perlman playing the Bruch and Sibelius concertos at the Royal Festival Hall, London. In 1990 he made his London recital debut at Wigmore Hall. A further highlight in his career was his debut recital at Carnegie Hall, New York, in 1992. Shaham performs regularly with leading orchestras and conductors throughout Europe, Japan, and the U.S. as well as in recitals and ensemble appearances on the great concert stages and at the most prestigious festivals. He has appeared with the IPO in many concerts in Israel and abroad. He is noted for his mature musicianship, mesmerizing technique, and rich, colorful tone. He also has the intellect and dramatic flair to transcend routine interpretations. His wide repertoire includes recordings of works by Mendelssohn, Tchaikovsky, Korngold, Prokofiev Vivaldi, Bartok, and Arvo Pärt. Among his awards are the Avery Fisher Career Grant (1990) and Premio Internazionale of the Accademia Chigiana in Siena (1992).

BIBLIOGRAPHY: Grove Music Online; Baker's Biographical Dictionary (1997) E. Eisler. "Gil Shaham: Unspoiled by success," in: *Strings*, 14 (Nov.–Dec. 1999), 50–61.

[Naama Ramot (2nd ed.)]

SHAḤAM, NATHAN (1925–), Hebrew writer, son of Eliezer *Steinman and brother of writer David Shaḥam. Born in Tel Aviv, Shaḥam served in the *Palmaḥ and on the southern front during the *War of Independence and later joined kibbutz Bet Alfa. He began publishing in 1944 and wrote fiction, plays, and stories for children. Shaḥam served as Israel's cultural attaché in New York (1977–80) and was vice chairman of the Israel Broadcasting Authority and chief editor of Sifriat Po'alim Publishing House. Many of his works, written in a traditional realistic style, were fueled by an unmistakable ideological concern, dealing with crucial issues of Israeli life, such as war, kibbutz life, immigration and, not least, disillusionment. His early novel *Even al Pi ha-Be'er* (1956) presents the committed pioneer, Eliyahu Weisman. Young, engaged Palmaḥ members are depicted in *Dagan ve-Oferet* (1948), *Ha-Elim Aẓelim* (1949), and *Tamid Anaḥnu* (1952). *Shikkun Vatikim* (1958) deals with the norms and life-style of the kibbutz while *Ḥokhmat ha-Misken* (1960) describes the immigration of the Polish, previously Communist Jews to Palestine. The world of the German-Jewish immigrants, the so-called Yekkes, is depicted in *Guf Rishon Rabbim* (1968), whereas the charms of Europe prevail in *Halokh va-Shov* (1972). Other works include the plays *Hem Yaggi'u Maḥar* (1949); *Kera Li Siomka* (1950); and *Yoḥanan bar Ḥama* (1952), and novels such as *Eẓem el Aẓmo* (1981; *Bone to the Bone*, 1993), *Sidrah* (1992), and *Lev Tel Aviv* (1996). No doubt one of Shaḥam's finest works is the novel *Revi'iyat Rosendorf* (1987; *The Rosendorf Quartet*, 1991; German, 1990), the portrait of four members of a string quartet in pre-state Israel. Only one of them, Friedman, feels committed to the Zionist project and in fact suffers from guilt feelings for not being a good enough pioneer. The others feel alienated, strangers in a place supposed to be their home. Moreover, viola-player Eva von Staubenfeld hates the country, which, in her opinion, is nothing but a place of exile: She criticizes the ugliness of the place and the petit bourgeois mentality. The fifth figure in the novel, observer of and loyal listener to the quartet as well as the narrator of its story, is the German writer Egon Loewenthal, who reflects upon the difficulties of writing in a new language, so different from his mother-tongue, and provides the reader with a kind of "diary of exile." For Nathan Shaḥam, himself a viola player, music becomes a complex metaphor for a universal language which rejects nationalism and transcends the pettiness of mundane life. In a subsequent novel, *Ẓilo shel Rosendrof* (2001), Shaḥam sends his protagonist to Germany to find out what has happened to the musicians and to the narrator. *Pa'amon be-Kijongdzu* ("A Bell in Ch'ongiu," 2005) is Joseph Schneider's belated confrontation with his harrowing experiences as a passenger of a plane hijacked by Palestinian terrorists, in which Shaḥam reflects on moral and political issues. Shaḥam received the Bilaik Prize and the American National Jewish Book Award for Fiction. His story "Coming Home" is included in James A. Michener (ed.), *Firstfruits* (1973), "Speak to the Wind" in G. Abramson (ed.), *The Oxford Book of Hebrew Short Stories* (1996). For further information concering translations, see the ITHL website at www.ithl.org. il.

BIBLIOGRAPHY: P. Lander, in: *Moznayim*, 45 (1977), 53–9; E. Pinhus, "History in a Life: Shaham's 'Thin Partitions,'" in: *Modern Hebrew Literature:* 5:1–2 (1979), 78–80; N.H. Toker, "*Setavim Yerukim ve-Aforim be-Sippurei N. Shaham*," in: *Moznayim*, 50:3 (180), 215–9; M. Gilboa, "*Amerikah ke-Makom*," in: *Migvan* (1988), 113–26; A. Feinberg, "Exil und Heimatlosigkeit. Juedische Identitaet und Zugehoerigkeit bei juedischen und israelischen Autoren," in: *Hofgeismarer Protokolle*, 265 (1989), 155–67; G. Shaked, *Ha-Sipporet ha-Ivrit*, 4 (1993), 317–47; N. Sokoloff, "Israel and America: Imagining the Other," in: *The Other in Jewish Thought and History* (1994), 326–52; H. Hever, "*The 'Other' Will Arrive Tomorrow*," in: *Contemporary Theatre Review*, 3:2 (1995), 91–106; Z. Shavitsky, "Nathan Shaham's Rosendorf Quartet – A Microcosm of the German Jewish Experience," in: *Abr-Nahrain*, 35 (1998), 135–144; R. Domb, "'Ut Pictura Poesis.' Text, Image, Identity and Ideology in Shaham's 'Series,'" in: *Arabic and Middle Eastern Literatures*, 4:2 (2001), 179–187.

[Anat Feinberg (2nd ed.)]

SHAḤAR, DAVID (1926–1997), Hebrew writer. Shaḥar was born in Jerusalem, being the fifth generation of a Jerusalemite family. He studied at the Hebrew University and published his first book, a collection of stories *Al Ha-Ḥalomot* ("Concerning Dreams"), depicting a wide range of Jerusalemite characters, in 1955. This was followed by novels, stories, and books for children (*Sodo shel Riki*, 1961; rpt. 1988). Shaḥar's major work is *Heikhal ha-Kelim ha-Shevurim* ("The Palace of Shattered Vessels"), a work he wrote over 30 years, comprising eight volumes. Among these are *Kayiẓ bi-Reḥov ha-Neviim* (*Summer in the Street of the Prophets*, 1973), *Ha-Masa le-Ur Kasdim* (*A Voyage to Ur of the Chaldees*, 1978), *Yom* *ha-Rozenet* ("The Day of the Countess," French translation 1981), *Ningal* (French: 1985), *Yom ha-Refaim* ("The Day of the Ghosts," French: 1988) and *Ḥalom shel Tammuz* ("A Tammuz Night's Dream," French: 1989). This monumental work, one of the finest examples of the modern Hebrew picaresque, traces the changes in Israeli society and the transformations of the Zionist dream, focusing on a variety of figures living in Jerusalem, in the vicinity of Hanevi'im Street and the Geulah neighborhood, from the Ottoman period up to the 1970s. While the so-called Palmaḥ-Generation favored the realistic style and the writers of the 1960s advanced a symbolic-allegoric prose, Shaḥar deployed a narrative technique embracing satirical elements, dream-like scenes, comic episodes, reminiscences and kabbalistic allusions, creating an original poetic of mnemonics. Small wonder then that Shaḥar's work has been compared to Marcel Proust's *Remembrance of Things Past*. Indeed, Shaḥar's writings enjoyed tremendous success in France. He was awarded the French Prix Médicis Etranger and was appointed Commandeur dans L'Ordre des Arts et des Lettres by the French government. A former chairman of the Hebrew Writers Association, he was honored in Israel with various prizes, including the Bialik and Agnon prizes. The last work of Shaḥar, who died in France, is the fragment *El Har ha-Zeitim* ("To the Mount of Olives," 1998). Shaḥar's prose has been translated into many languages, and information about translations is available at the ITHL website at www.ithl.org.il.

BIBLIOGRAPHY: S. Katz, *Ha-Ani ve-Giborav be-Sippurei D. Shahar* (1975); M. Neige, "Jews, Muslims, and Christians in the Work of D. Shahar," in: *JeQ* (1978), 41–46; N. Bersohn, "D. Shahar's Trilogy 'The Palace of Shattered Vessels'. A Combination of Literary Genres," in: *Modern Hebrew Literature*, 6:1–2 (1980), 34–42; M. Puni, *Mekorot Yehudiyyim ki-Ysodot Me'aẓẓevim bi-Yẓirato shel D. Shahar* (1980); B. Keller, "La Jérusalem de D. Shahar," in: *Foi et Vie*, 89:1 (1990), 39–49; G. Shaked, *Ha-Sipporet ha-Ivrit*, 5 (1998), 119–33; S. Katz, "Un Palais plein d'éclats de lumière cachés," in: *Cahiers du Judaisme*, 4 (1999), 115–23; O. Baziz, *Ha-Kelim le-Olam Lo Yukhlu le-Hakhil et ha-Shefa: Ḥayyav vi-Yẓirato shel D. Shaḥar* (2003); J. Hassin, "*Bein Marcel Proust le-David Shaḥar*," in: *Ẓafon*, 7 (2004), 99–122; M. Ginsburg Peled, *Shattered Vessels: Memory, Identity and Creation in the Work of D. Shahar* (2004); Sh. Zeevi, in: *Mikarov*, 14 (2004), 56–71.

[Anat Feinberg (2nd ed.)]

SHAHAR, SHULAMIT (1928–), historian specializing in the Middle Ages. Shahar's work is considered groundbreaking. Her studies on women, children, and the aged – social groups that had not been studied before in the medieval period – became milestones in the study of social history. Shahar was born in Latvia and immigrated to Palestine in 1933. In 1965 she received her B.A. degree in history and English literature and in 1961 she received an M.A. degree in general and Jewish history from the Hebrew University of Jerusalem. In 1965 she received her Ph.D. from the Sorbonne. In 1967 she began to work in the history department of Tel Aviv University and in 1990 she was made professor. In 1986–89 she was head of the department. In 1990–93 she was head of general studies at Tel Aviv University. She was also a visiting professor at Cambridge and Oxford Universities. Shahar wrote many articles and books, including *The Fourth Estate* (1983), *Childhood in the Middle Ages* (1990), *Growing Old in the Middle Ages* (1997), and *Women in a Medieval Heretical Sect* (2000). In 2003 she was awarded the Israel Prize in history.

[Shaked Gilboa (2nd ed.)]

SHAḤARIT (Heb. שַׁחֲרִית; "dawn prayer"), the daily morning service and the most elaborate of the three prescribed daily prayers. Its institution is traditionally attributed to the patriarch Abraham (on the basis of Gen. 19:27), and the rabbis later made its recitation obligatory to replace the daily morning sacrifice (*Tamid*) performed in the Temple (Ber. 26b).

Shaḥarit consists of the following components: (1) *Morning Benedictions; (2) **Pesukei de-zimra*; (3) reading of the **Shema* and its benedictions; (4) **Amidah;* (5) **Taḥanun*, on days when it is recited; (6) *Torah reading, on mornings when it is required; (7) **Ashrei*, Psalm 20 and a collection of biblical quotations; (8) **Aleinu le-Shabbe'ah*. There are no basic variations in the text of the prayers recited each morning with the exception of the text of the *Amidah*, additions to the *pesukei de-zimra* on Sabbaths and festivals, and the addition of **Hallel* on festivals and the *New Moon. In some rites, **piyyutim* are also inserted during the morning prayers on certain Sabbaths and festivals. In most Israeli cities, the priestly blessing is recited each morning in the framework of the *Amidah*.

The time for the morning service is governed by the laws which determine the period for the recitation of the *Shema* and the *Amidah*. The start of the period in which the *Shema* should be recited begins with daybreak and concludes after a quarter of the day has passed (Ber. 1:2; Sh. Ar., OḤ 58:1). The time for reciting the *Amidah* begins with sunrise and ends after a third of the day has passed (Ber. 4:1; Sh. Ar., OḤ 89:1; and see *Day and Night). Extremely pious people (*vatikin*) were therefore careful to begin their prayers with daybreak so they could complete the recitation of the *Shema* by sunrise and recite the *Amidah* immediately afterward (Ber. 26a). If the morning prayers are delayed past their proper time for recitation, they may still be said until midday (Ber. 4:1; Sh. Ar., OḤ 89:1). If, by accident, the morning *Amidah* was not recited, an extra *Amidah* is added at the *Minḥah* service.

During daily morning services, the **tallit* and **tefillin* are worn for the duration of the prayers. On Sabbath and festivals, only the *tallit* is worn. On the Ninth of *Av, it is customary according to many rites to wear neither *tallit* nor *tefillin* for *Shaḥarit*, but to wear them for the **Minḥah* prayers. Once the blessing preceding the *pesukei de-zimra*, **Barukh she-Amar*, is recited, the supplicants are forbidden to speak or to interrupt the prayers until the conclusion of the *Amidah* (Sh. Ar., OḤ 51:4).

BIBLIOGRAPHY: Elbogen, Gottesdienst, 14ff.; Idelsohn, Liturgy, 73ff.; E. Levy, *Yesodot ha-Tefillah* (1952^2), 129ff.; E. Munk, *The World of Prayer*, 1 (1961), 17ff.

SHĀHIN, Judeo-Persian poet. Though a few short fragments of Judeo-Persian poems were found in the Cairo **Genizah*, Shāhin is regarded the first and greatest Judeo-Persian poet who flourished during the 14th century. Most probably Shāhin, meaning "falcon," is the pen name of the poet that appears in many places in his poetic productions; his real name and personal life are unknown. Scholars who briefly mentioned Shāhin's works claimed that he was from *Shiraz, but internal evidence shows beyond any doubt that he was not from Shiraz or any place in the southern or central parts of Iran. He may have belonged to the Greater *Khorāsān, probably the city of Merv. Shāhin is as great to the Persian Jews as the composer of Shāh-Nāmeh, Firdowsi, is to the Iranians.

Shāhin's first poetic work is a paraphrase of the four last books of the Pentateuch which has to do with the life and deeds of Moses and the children of Israel, hence it was named "Musā-Nāmeh" by Simon *Ḥakham of Bukhara and Wilhelm Bacher of Budapest (see bibl.) who showed interest in the works of Shāhin. The poet himself titled this work *Sharḥ-i Torah* ("Exegesis of the Torah"). It is indeed a rather free interpretation which makes use of Midrashim and even Muslim sources. Musā-Nāmeh, which contains about ten thousand verses, was completed in 1327 C.E.

Shāhin's second poetic work is *Tafsir Megillat Ester* ("Interpretation of the Book of Esther"), which is known to scholars by the name of *Ardashir-Nāmeh*. Ardashir (ruled 465–425 B.C.E.), according to Shahin, is Ahasuerus, though most scholars consider Xerxes (in Persian Khashāyār, ruled 486–465 B.C.E.) to be the king who married Esther. Ardashir-Nāmeh consists of three separate but interwoven stories: (1) that of the Book of Esther; (2) a love story related to the Shiruyeh, the son of Vashti, and a Chinese princess, Mahzād; (3) a brief narration of the life and deeds of Cyrus the Great, mostly based on the Book of Ezra, hence this part is sometimes known as Ezrā-Nāmeh. Here Shāhin talks about Cyrus the son of Esther the Queen, a belief held also by some Muslim historians such as Ṭabarī. The depiction of nature, hunting, and battle is superb. Ardashir-Nāmeh contains about six thousand verses and was completed in 1333 C.E.

Shāhin's third poetic work is a paraphrased versification of the first book of the Pentateuch, the Book of Genesis, which was named by the poet *Sharḥ-i Torah, Sefer Bereshit*, and by scholars *Bereshit-Nāmeh*. The major part of this work narrates the story of Joseph and Potiphar's wife, hence it is also known as "Yosef va Zolaikhā." *Bereshit-Nāmeh* makes extensive use of Midrashim and especially Muslim sources known as *Qiṣaṣ al-Anbiyā*ʾ (the stories of the prophets). As the poet's last work, it displays maturity of mind, great erudition, and profound knowledge of the Persian language with all its rhetorical devices. *Bereshit-Nāmeh*, which contains about ten thousand verses, was completed in 1359 C.E.

Simon Ḥakham published all of Shāhin's works in Jerusalem.

BIBLIOGRAPHY: J.P. Assmusen, "Judaeo-Persica I, Shāhin Shirāzis Ardashirnāma," in: *Acta Orientalia*, 28 (1964), 243–61; W. Bacher, *Zwei juedisch-persische Dichter Schahin und Imrani* (1908); D. Blieske, *Šāhin-e Širazis Ardaširs-Buch* (1966); Sh. Ḥakham, *Shāhin Torah* (1905); idem, *Sefer Sharḥ Shāhin al Megillat Ester* (1910); V.B. Moreen, "A Dialogue between God and Satan in Shāhin's *Bereshit-Nāmah*," in: Sh. Shaked and A. Netzer (eds.), *Irano-Judaica*, 3 (1994), 127–41; A. Netzer, "A Judeo-Persian Footnote: Shāhin and 'Emrāni," in: *Israel Oriental Studies*, 4 (1974), 258–64; idem, "Some Notes on the Characterization of Cyrus the Great in Jewish and Judeo-Persian Writings," in: *Acta Iranica*, 2 (1974), 35–52; idem, *Oẓar Kitvei-Yad shel Yehudei Paras be-Makhon Ben Zvi* (1985); idem, "The Story of the Prophet Shoʿayb in Shahin's Musānāmeh," in: *Acta Iranica*, 16 (1990), 152–67; idem, "Notes and Observations Concerning Shāhin's Birthplace," in: Sh. Shaked and A. Netzer (eds.) *Irano-Judaica*, 4 (1999), 187–202; E. Spicehandler, "Shāhin's Influence on Bābāi ben Lotf: The Abraham-Nimrod Legend," *ibid.*, 2 (1990), 158–65.

[Amnon Netzer (2nd ed.)]

SHAHN, BEN (1898–1969), U.S. painter and printmaker. Born in Kaunas (Kovno), Lithuania, he was taken to the United States at the age of eight. He studied lithography and for many years supported himself and his family by means of commercial lithography. A liberal in outlook, Shahn attracted attention through his gouache paintings on the Sacco-Vanzetti case and the case of labor leader Tom Mooney. The Mexican artist Diego Rivera, also a liberal, hired Shahn as his assistant in painting the fresco *Man at the Crossroads*, for the RCA Building in Rockefeller Center, New York. This controversial fresco was finally removed to Mexico City. During the Depression Shahn was commissioned by the government to paint several murals for public buildings. He helped form the Artists' Union and the American Artists' Congress. During World War II, Shahn designed posters for the Office of War Information. He taught at several universities and museum art schools, had many one-man shows, and was represented at international shows such as the biennial exhibitions at Venice and São Paulo. In the winter of 1956–57 he gave a series of lectures at Harvard University, published under the title *The Shape of Content* (1957). Shahn often dealt with Jewish subject matter. He made drawings for the production of a play, *The World of Sholom Aleichem* (1953), and designed windows for Temple Beth Zion in Buffalo, New York (1965). As a calligrapher, he repeatedly made use of the Hebrew alphabet, especially in the books *Alphabet of Creation* (1954) and *Love and Joy about Letters* (1963; for which he also wrote texts), and in a series of de luxe editions of the *Haggadah* (1965). Drawings of the *Haggadah* had been executed about 1930 and all but one of these were bought for the Jewish Museum, New York, and are now one of its most prized possessions. The Oriental touch in some of these drawings is due to Shahn's acquaintance with the Jews of *Djerba, where he spent almost a year. When he was seventy, several retrospective exhibitions of his works were held. Shahn raised the aesthetic level of graphic art in the United States. As a draftsman, he was often a commentator on the social scene, always outraged at injustice, but also amused by humanity's foibles and weakness.

BIBLIOGRAPHY: S. Rodman, *Portrait of the Artist as an American* (1951); J.T. Soby, *Ben Shahn*, 2 vols. (Eng., 1963).

[Alfred Werner]

SHAḤOR (Czerny, Schwartz), family of pioneers in Hebrew printing in Central Europe. ḤAYYIM joined the first printing group in *Prague (see *Kohen family) in or before 1514. After 1522, when the group disbanded, he joined Meir Michtam in issuing two works of prayer, in 1525 and 1526. During most of 1526 he evidently prepared almost all the woodcut illustrations for the Passover *Haggadah* of Gershom Kohen. Some have doubted that Shaḥor made almost all the woodcuts for the *Haggadah* as he is not mentioned in the colophon; however, four illustrations contain a small letter *shin* and it was the practice of non-Jewish woodcut artists to mark their work with their initials. Moreover, one of the four represents King David, and David was also his father's name. The *shin* similarly appears near a lion in the *Haggadah's* third full border (ornamenting the verse *shefokh ḥamatekha*); Shaḥor could have considered the lion a suitable "family crest," for it is a royal symbol, and his father's personal name was synonymous with royalty in ancient Israel and in Jewish tradition. Furthermore, in his Pentateuch of Augsburg (1533) the first page of every book is ornamented with two small figures: one, a crab, is probably a zodiacal sign of his birth month; the other, a lion, was evidently retained as a "family crest." To adorn the opening page of his Pentateuch of Ichenhausen (1544), he copied onto a new woodcut the complete third border of Gershom Kohen's *Haggadah* with the lion (Kohen retained and reused the original), and he used it again for the opening page of his *seder seliḥot* of Heddernheim, 1545. It might be noted, too, that in the 1518 Pentateuch of Prague's pioneer printers, Shaḥor is listed second (after Gershom Kohen) in the colophon to part 1 (end of Exodus), which part contains two full borders; in the colophon to part 2, which has no new woodcut ornamentation, he is listed last. This indicates that he made those two borders as well.

In April 1527 a royal privilege made Gershom Kohen the sole Hebrew printer in Bohemia and Shaḥor had to leave Prague. Taking with him a good amount of type and equipment, he became an itinerant printer, comparable only to Gershom *Soncino (although his output was much smaller). About 1529 he settled in Oels, Silesia (near Breslau), where he printed a Pentateuch with a partner. A storm destroyed the printing shop, however, and Shaḥor left Silesia. In 1531 he reached Augsburg, a center of humanism, where he apparently used the press of August Wind, a Christian printer who issued some Hebrew texts for the clergy. Until 1540 he produced nine works of quality (including a modest but handsome Passover *Haggadah* in 1534), evidently helped by his son ISAAC and son-in-law Joseph b. Yakar, who were listed in the colophon of their edition of Jacob b. Asher's *Turim* (1540). In this period (1531–40) Shaḥor traveled about, too, in an attempt to sell his stock. Conditions worsened, though, and in the final years in Augsburg the family could not issue its planned volumes. At his request the influential apostate Paulus Emilius went to Ferrara, Italy, in 1541–42 to explore possibilities for the Shaḥor family to settle there, but nothing came of it. In 1543 the family moved to Ichenhausen, Bavaria, where it issued a prayer book with Judeo-German translation as well as a Pentateuch. Political unrest and local war made them move on, however, to Heddernheim, near Frankfurt on the Main, where they resumed printing in 1545.

Evidently, though, the family finally concluded that there was little hope for a stable future in Germany, for it soon left for *Lublin, perhaps by 1547. An official permit for printing could not be obtained until 1550, by which time Shaḥor had died and his son-in-law Joseph b. Yakar had left to try his luck in Italy. With *Giustiniani he produced a Pentateuch in Venice (1548), but then rejoined the family. Until 1554 he and Ḥayyim's son Isaac Shaḥor ran the press jointly, producing a notable Polish *maḥzor* in 1550. By 1557 Shaḥor had died, leaving a small son; his brother-in-law might also have died, as his name no longer appears in the press's output. The family craft was carried on by Kalonymus b. Mordecai Jaffe, the husband of Ḥayyim Shaḥor's granddaughter (i.e., Joseph b. Yakar's son-in-law), together with two partners, one of whom may have been an elder son of Ḥayyim Shaḥor's son Isaac. The family's printing privilege of 1550 was renewed in 1559, and under Kalonymos and his sons the press continued in Lublin for many years.

BIBLIOGRAPHY: A.M. Habermann, in: KS, 31 (1955–56), 483–500 (with full bibliography); idem, *Ha-Sefer ha-Ivri* (1968), 127–8, 138, 196; C. Wengrov, *Haggadah and Woodcut* (1967), index.

[Charles Wengrov]

SHAKED, GERSHON (1929–2006), one of the most prominent scholars and the foremost historian of Modern Hebrew narrative fiction in the second half of the 20th century. His research and criticism have touched on nearly every author and literary phenomenon in modern Hebrew literature from the 1850s onward, in monographs on individual authors and studies of literary schools. Although he has devoted most of his work to Hebrew fiction, Shaked has also made significant contributions to the study of modern Hebrew drama and poetry and of Jewish literature by central European authors writing in German (Kafka, Joseph Roth, Stefan Zweig) and by American-Jewish authors (such as Saul Bellow and Philip Roth). Shaked's significant influence as a scholar of culture and literature can be discerned from concepts and terms he coined and which have become an integral part of Hebrew critical discourse, such as: "The New Wave" (the name he gave to the group of authors also known as "The State Generation": Amos *Oz, Aharon *Appelfeld, Yehuda *Amichai, A.B. *Yehoshua, Amalia *Kahana-Carmon); "Genre" and "Anti-Genre" (following Y.H. *Brenner's critical writing); the terms "naïve literature" and "ironic literature" (which he used to delineate two different directions in early 20th century literature, representing conflicting world views and poetics); "Homo-Economicus" (a characterization that marked Mendele's poetics); and "a literature against all odds" and " there is no other place" (phrases that stem from Brenner's oeuvre, reflecting Shaked's ideological stance which affirms Zionism despite its errors and flaws).

Shaked was born in Vienna as Gerhard Mandel. In 1939, following the "Anschluss" and the imprisonment and release of his father from Buchenwald, he was sent to Palestine, later to be joined by his parents. Shaked was educated at an Israeli boarding school and later graduated from the Herzliya Gymnasium. After his military service, he studied Hebrew literature, the Bible, and history at the Hebrew University. In 1964 he earned his Ph.D. with a thesis about Hebrew historical drama during the period of "Revival" (1880–1948).

He went on to study in Switzerland and in 1959 began teaching at the Hebrew University of Jerusalem, where he eventually became professor and chair of the department of Hebrew literature and taught until his retirement. Shaked was guest professor at various universities worldwide and was awarded the Bialik Prize (1986) and the Israel Prize (1993).

In the opening remarks to his early book *Bein Ẓeḥok le-Dema* (1965), Shaked questions the critical tradition that evaluated Mendele by the degree of accuracy of his description of reality. Shaked asks: "What has the account of reality got to do with the force of a creative literary heritage?" Later on, under the influence of the so-called "Reception Theory," he wrote social historical essays on Israeli culture. In *Sifrut Az, Ka'an ve-Akhshav* (1993), he focuses on the "relationships between the different social models and literature." In *Gal Ḥadash ba-Sifrut ha-Ivrit* he wrote: "The underlying assumption is that literature mirrors culture (note: culture – not reality!), and cultural self-awareness is one of the important contributions literary criticism can make." Shaked labored on the refinement of such self-awareness throughout his long career.

Shaked's early work was influenced by Anglo-American "New Criticism," but he never adopted its teachings completely. In his remarks to *Omanut ha-Sippur shel Agnon* (1976), Shaked admits: "I have tried to learn from different researchers; but I have not practiced theories and have not leaned on doctrines. The author and his work have stood at the center of my study (…). It is no secret that of all the various approaches the one closest to me is that which positions 'the craft of narrative fiction' itself at the center of the critical or interpretative discussion."

Shaked identified himself as a skeptical New Critic and structuralist, but in 1971 he moved in the opposite direction in his book *Im Tishkaḥ Ei Pa'am*. The book's title is a phrase borrowed from Bernard Malamud: "Nathan, she said, if you ever forgot you are a Jew, a Goy will remind you." In his study of Jewish American literature, Shaked's underlying assumption is that Jews writing in different languages and different literatures share a common ground. This inter-Jewish relation may be characterized through mentality, themes, and motifs.

Before embarking on his monumental five-volume history of Hebrew narrative prose, Shaked had already formed the conviction that sociology, ethnicity, and personal biography or identity must be an integral part of literary debate. Shaked's *Gal Ḥadash ba-Sipporet ha-Ivrit* (1970) turned out to be the book which canonized Yehoshua, Oz, Applefeld, and Kahana-Carmon. Years later, Shaked re-formulated his observation, as the assumptions which underlined his early study of *Gal Ḥadash* now seemed inaccurate to him: "The premises that the literature of the New Wave distanced itself from collective social questions and focused on individual issues was wrong. This generation was involved from the outset in collective questions, but expressed its concern for the collective in ways different from those of the previous generation."

Early in his brilliant career Shaked began to think about a monumental history of modern Hebrew narrative fiction. A retrospective scrutiny of his writings reveals the seeds Shaked had sown in preparation for this project and the ways in which he prepared himself for it.

The preliminary process included two slim volumes: *Al Arba'a Sippurim* (1963) and *Al Sheloshah Maḥazot* (1968). In these textbooks, Shaked introduced the tools of close readings of drama and fiction. These tools allowed Shaked to practice one of the convictions he adopted from his teacher Emile Stieger, a conviction he later tried to pass on to his own students: "you must grasp that which grabs us" about a literary text. Shaked established the historiosophical grounds for his work in two other early works: *Bein Ẓeḥok le-Dema* and *Ha-Maḥazeh ha-Ivri bi-Tekufat ha-Teḥiyyah*. With regard to the first, the question may arise, why did Shaked choose to focus on Mendele in his early scholarly work? One of the answers, according to Shaked's own testimony, is Mendele's central position in the Hebrew canon that compelled the young scholar to stage a "new internal debate" between previous generations of scholars and himself. That new internal debate, with Mendele acting as mediator, is a fundamental aspect of Shaked's historio-literary research. Shaked crowned Mendele (that is, Sholem Yankev *Abramovitsh, or "Mendele Mokher Seforim") the founder of modern Hebrew literature. His late book, *Mendele, Lefanav ve-Aḥarav* (2005), goes back to Mendele, recapitulating Mendele's revolutionary influence on Hebrew literature in a re-reading of *Sefer ha-Kabẓanim* and in relation to Smolenskin, Charles Dickens, Agnon, Bashevis Singer, and others.

According to Shaked, Mendele is the leading figure of a new position marked by the disillusionment and disappointment with the universalist premises of the *Haskalah* on the one hand and a recognition of the dramatic rise of a nationalist Jewish movement on the other hand.

In the first volume of *Ha-Sipporet ha-Ivrit*, Shaked notes that there are some who consider the pogroms of 1881 as the turning point in Hebrew literature. According to him, the social, thematic, and artistic changes in the "book and bookmakers market" took place only in the 1890s, with Mendele focusing primarily on Hebrew, instead of mostly Yiddish writing. This tradition paved the way for the dominance of the "literature of revival," or – in Shaked's terminology – "the Zionist master-plot" (also: "the Zionist master narrative").

The second principle emerging from Shaked's internal debate with previous scholars concerns the innovation he recognized in Mendele's conception of humankind. Prior to Mendele, *Haskalah* authors saw people first and foremost as idea-centered beings. A person was homo sapiens, or rather homo ideologicus. Other characteristics including primal needs such as sex, food, physical security, and emotional connection were ignored. Mendele reversed the order, as did Shaked. The conceptual human was of little interest to him. Instead, he considered the economical being, homo economicus, and the sexual being in their corporeal physical as well as psychological aspects.

The reciprocal ties between ideological, biological, physical, sociological, and psychological components in the balance that Mendele created are valuable to Shaked for mainly two reasons. First, because he is unwilling to ignore the ideological level yet prefers works which challenge it, armed with irony. Shaked has always praised authors who burst hot ideological balloons and ridicule ideological characters. Correspondingly, Shaked has been critical of authors who "conform," those who serve as a voice for dominant ideological stands. Second, Shaked has a distinct preference for the comical mode, according to Northrop Frye: the comical in its various shadings is consistently based – especially in Mendele's writing – on a "lowering" depiction and on observing people from their stomachs and below.

Bein Ẓeḥok le-Dema marks the point of departure for a great historical research. *Ha-Maḥazeh ha-Ivri ha-Histori bi-Tekufat ha-Teḥiyyah* heralds some of the compositional characteristics of Shaked's monumental project of Hebrew narrative prose. Like the five-volume *Ha-Sipporet ha-Ivrit (1880–1980)*, this book focuses on a genre or a master-genre. In the drama project the time frame is explicit: the period of "revival." In the book on narrative fiction the limits are not as clear cut, but rather implied. The fiction studied here frames one hundred years of Zionism. The most essential common denominator of these two projects is their teleological goal. In both, the author views the past in order to better understand it but also in order to understand the present. In his introduction to *Ha-Maḥazeh ha-Ivri*, Shaked distinguishes between an "archeological" method that does not import the past into the present and a "current events" method that touches the past as "material the playwright-interpreter interprets without reviving the material itself." It seems that already in this early work Shaked found his golden mean between the historical and the historiosophical. This path served him in many of his research projects and reached its peak in the history of modern Hebrew narrative fiction. The closer Shaked comes to his own time, the more he takes on the role of historical interpreter alongside that of a literary historian. His discussions of the Sinai war, the Lavon affair, and the Eichmann trial in the fifth volume illustrate this. Shaked's biography has developed into a crucial interpretative tool as well, as can be seen in the chapter on Ruth *Almog in the fifth volume.

There are distinct differences between the early *Ha-Maḥazeh ha-Ivri* and the late *Ha-Sipporet ha-Ivrit* which need to be mentioned. In the early book, Shaked studies the work of several dramatists without attempting to group his portraits into a comprehensive dramatic story. As he says in the introduction to the book, it "follows the history of topics, structures, characterization and dialogue, and attempts to paint a synoptic picture of different angles" – not an evolving developmental structure that would proceed as a plot of a story or a play might. In his comprehensive history of modern Hebrew narrative fiction on the other hand, Shaked created a compositional structure that is committed to analytical "objective" categories; at the same time it adheres to an internal plot and rationale. In other words, in this book Shaked appears as researcher and dramatist. Indeed, this monumental study is a vast performance that includes dozens of main characters and hundreds of marginal ones, attempting not only to delineate them as they were, but also as who they might have been. For this purpose Shaked constructs plots and counter-plots which are motivated by ideological, socio-historical, and psychological tensions, and by purely artistic tensions as well.

Literary research is the heart of Shaked's work, but he has not detached himself from contemporary literature. He has closely followed the literature written in the last fifty years, reviewing individual works and tracing wider literary trends and directions which he marked, named, characterized in great detail, and evaluated according to clear aesthetic and thematic criteria. In the 1950s he was a part of the "*Likrat*" group (together with Nathan *Zach, Benjamin *Harshav, Aryeh *Sivan, Moshe *Dor, and others), that introduced a poetics and cultural agenda.

Shaked stood by the cradle of the "New Wave" authors, read some of their works in manuscript, and encouraged the poetic direction their works took. In his numerous literary reviews he repeatedly demanded "literary realization" of the authors, that is, a full and detailed depiction of social and human situations.

In 2001 Shaked published his first novel, *Mehagerim*, a story of immigration based on his own experience. The book was translated into German (2006). His influence on Israeli fiction made its way into various fictionalized portraits that authors such as R. Almog and A.B. Yehoshua painted of him in their prose.

BIBLIOGRAPHY: A. Band, "A History of Modern Hebrew Fiction," in: *Prooftexts*, 1:1 (1981), 115–8; E. Fiedler, "Gershon Shaked y el facsinate mundo de la ficcion hebrea," in: *Coloquio*, 11 (1983), 51–55; A Mintz, "On Gershon Shaked's S.Y. Agnon: A Revolutionary Traditionalist," in: *Hebrew Studies*, 32 (1991), 61–6; W. Iser, "German Jewish Writers during the Decline of the Hapsburg Monarchy. Assessing the Assessment of G. Shaked," in: *Ideology and Jewish Identity in Israeli and American Literature* (2001), 259–73; Y. Pelleg, "The Critic as a Dialectical Zionist," in: *Prooftexts*, 23:3 (2003), 296–382;

[Yigal Schwartz (2nd ed.)]

°**SHAKESPEARE, WILLIAM** (1564–1616), English playwright and poet. *The Merchant of Venice* (1596) has been claimed as the play in which Shakespeare found himself "in the fullest sense." As with other major comedies of his so-called second period, the main emphasis was to have been on the romantic plot. It is, however, Shylock and the bond story, originally intended as a comic subplot, which has proved to be the actual focus of interest down to the present day. Bassanio requests that his friend Antonio, a merchant, provide him with money for his expedition to Belmont. In order to raise the necessary sum, Antonio takes a loan from the Jewish usurer, Shylock. The latter, instead of demanding interest, suggests a "merry bond," according to which, if Antonio should default, Shylock would be entitled to a pound of flesh nearest to Antonio's heart. Not only does Antonio default but, when the day of payment comes, Shylock's daughter Jessica is found to have eloped with Lorenzo, a friend of Antonio, taking with her a large part of her father's money. Embittered by this double blow – "My ducats and my daughter!" – Shylock demands the "penalty and forfeit" of the bond from Antonio. However, Portia, the Lady of Belmont, disguised as a lawyer, saves the situation, pointing out that the bond does not entitle Shylock to a single drop of blood. Antonio's life is saved, and Shylock himself becomes liable to the confiscation of his whole estate through having sought the life of a citizen of Venice. This penalty is "mercifully" reduced to half, but only on condition that he embraces Christianity.

The mainstream view is that Shylock is the type of the monstrous, bloodthirsty usurer of medieval legend. Gobbo, his comic servant, tells us that his master is "the very devil incarnation," and later, when Shylock appears, one of the characters remarks that the devil "comes in the likeness of a Jew." From time to time Shylock is "demythologized," especially in his famous speech, beginning "I am a Jew. Hath not a Jew eyes? Hath not a Jew hands, organs, dimensions, senses, affections, passions?" Many modern critics believe that Shakespeare's depiction of Shylock is much more ambiguous than was previously held, and must be contrasted with the two-dimensional portrayals of Jews in English drama up to that time. Shylock is seen as marking a stage in Shakespeare's evolution as a writer. *The Merchant of Venice* was probably written three or four years after *Richard III*, with its unquestionably evil protagonist, and paved the way for the more ambiguous depictions in Shakespeare's later works. Much about *The Merchant of Venice* poses as yet unanswerable questions: how and where did Shakespeare meet any Jews, since they were legally barred from living in England? Did he visit Venice, which the play describes with the apparent knowledge of an eyewitness? From what source did the name "Shylock," unknown in Jewish usage, derive?

It is generally believed that the trial and execution in 1594 of Queen Elizabeth's *Marrano physician, Rodrigo *Lopez, suggested some features of the Shylock story. This episode provoked a good deal of antisemitic feeling in England at the time.

In England, Edmund Kean's portrayal of Shylock in 1814 was notable for its tragic intensity, while Sir Henry Irving in 1879 acted the part in a radically idealized form, muting the evil qualities of Shylock. The play has often been translated into Hebrew and has been performed in Israel several times. *The Merchant of Venice*, and Shakespeare's views of Jews, have attracted a wide range of comment and analysis, which have certainly not diminished in recent years. Recent studies of these topics include Martin D. Yaffe, *Shylock and the Jewish Question* (1997), and James Shapiro, *Shakespeare and the Jews* (1997). For better or worse, Shylock probably remains the most famous depiction of a Jew in English literature.

[Harold Harel Fisch / William D. Rubinstein (2nd ed.)]

In Hebrew

Since there is as yet no great dramatic literature in Modern Hebrew literature, there can be no significant discussion of Shakespeare's impact upon it. Scattered traces of Shakespeare's influence, usually through German translations, can be found in the poetry of the Haskalah. Joseph *Ha-Efrati's play about King Saul, *Melukhath Sha'ul* (Vienna, 1794), shows, in structure and imagery, that its author must have read *Macbeth, Hamlet*, and *King Lear*. In *Meliẓat Yeshurun* (Vienna, 1816), an analysis of the forms of biblical poetry, Solomon Levisohn quotes some lines from *Henry IV, Part II*, in his own rich, though very inaccurate, prose rendering. The tone, and sometimes the same words, of Lady Macbeth's soliloquy ("Come you spirits that tend on mortal thoughts" etc.) are reproduced in Yael's monologue in Micah Joseph *Lebensohn's epic poem, *Ya'el ve-Sisera*, written about the middle of the 19th century.

The first translations of Shakespeare into Hebrew, *Othello* (1874) and *Romeo and Juliet* (1878), were by Isaac Edward *Salkinson, and remained unsurpassed for at least two generations. Salkinson's translations were done at the insistence of Perez *Smolenskin, the Hebrew novelist and essayist, then editor of the monthly *Ha-Shaḥar*, published in Vienna. In his foreword to Salkinson's translation of *Othello*, Smolenskin wrote: "Shakespeare's plays in the Holy Tongue! If all Israel had known and loved the language of their forefathers, and if all those who understand and love Hebrew could comprehend what great prize the translator of these plays has brought into the treasure-house of our language, then indeed would the day on which the first play by Shakespeare appeared in Hebrew become a victory celebration!" Salkinson rendered Shakespeare into strong, lucid, biblical Hebrew writing in free verse of 13 to 16–17 syllables) which did justice to the poetry and dramatic power of the original. Salkinson's isolated achievement appears the greater when set against the background of the florid, padded, imprecise Hebrew style prevailing in Hebrew letters at the time.

In his introduction to *Romeo and Juliet*, Salkinson identified the vulgar speech of the uneducated and the clever, facetious, sometimes multilingual, prattle of the well-born, as the major pitfalls which faced him as a translator. To this day, these remain among the major difficulties in translating Shakespeare into Hebrew. In the two decades that followed the publication of Salkinson's work, only three translations appeared: L. Barb's very weak rendering of *Macbeth* (1883), done from Schiller's free and at times distorted German translation; Z. Elkind's translation of *The Taming of the Shrew* (1893), and S.L. *Gordon's translation of *King Lear* (1899). A quarter of a century elapsed before David *Frischmann's translation of *Coriolanus* (1924) appeared. Frischmann, a most gifted translator, rendered the play entirely within the frame of biblical syntax and idiom. Following the same tradition is H.J. Bornstein's translation of *Hamlet* (1926), which first appeared in serial in the newspaper *Ha-Ẓefirah* in 1900. The use of biblical Hebrew in rendering Shakespeare reached perhaps its peak in Ḥ.N. *Bialik's translation of the first act of *Julius Caesar* (1929). Done from a Russian translation while containing most of the merits of that tradition, it falls short of an adequate rendering of the Shakespearean idiom. Marking the transition toward a freer idiom, where spoken Hebrew is reflected in a predominantly biblical syntax, are Simon *Halkin's translation of *The Merchant of Venice* (1929), the first Shakespeare translation by an American Hebrew poet, and Saul *Tchernichowsky's translation of *Twelfth Night*, which was in Habimah's repertoire when it came to Tel Aviv from Moscow in 1931. In the succeeding years, American Hebrew poets produced a number of translations: E. *Lisitzky translated *Julius Caesar* (1933) and *The Tempest* (1941); B.N. *Silkiner, *Macbeth* (1939); Israel Ephros, *Hamlet* (1944), *Timon of Athens* (1953), and *Coriolanus* (1959); Simon Halkin, *King John* (1947); and Hillel *Bavli, *Antony and Cleopatra* (1948). Translators with an American background who settled in Palestine included: R. *Avinoam (Grossman), who translated *King Lear* (1944), *Antony and Cleopatra* (1947), and *Romeo and Juliet* (1959); and Harry (Zvi) Davidovich, who translated *Hamlet* (1942), *A Midsummer Night's Dream* (1943), *The Winter's Tale* (1945), and *Macbeth* (1946). Although these men had a better knowledge of English than their predecessors (with the sole exception of Salkinson), most of them suffered from a lack of contact with the sound of spoken Hebrew, and from the fact that they wrote in the old penultimate syllable meter. A few of these translators scanned in accordance with the accent of spoken Hebrew, but most of their efforts were of inferior quality.

It became obvious that more accurate and idiomatic translations would be produced only by writers who were in contact with the Hebrew-speaking community in Ereẓ Israel, and who were responsive to the increasing demands of the Hebrew theater. Several translations done in the 1940s and 1950s, though highly flawed (some were done from Russian and German translations, or by writers with an incomplete knowledge of English), achieved considerable success in blending classical Hebrew diction with the sound of everyday speech. At their best, they combined the poetical, the idiomatic, and the vulgar without offending the historic character of the language. The pioneers in this endeavor were Abraham *Shlonsky, *Hamlet* (1945) and *King Lear* (1955), and Nathan *Alterman, *Merry Wives of Windsor* (1946), *Othello* (1950), *Julius Caesar* (1958), and *Anthony and Cleopatra* (1965). They were followed by Raphael Eliaz, *The Taming of the Shrew* (1954), *Romeo and Juliet* (1957), *Twelfth Night* (1960), *Richard the Third*, and *Henry the Fourth* (1961); Lea *Goldberg, *As You Like It* (1957); and T. Carmi, *A Midsummer Night's Dream* (1964). Ephraim *Broido's translation of *Macbeth* appeared in 1954, followed by translations of *The Tempest, Much Ado about Nothing, A Midsummer Night's Dream* (all in 1964), and *Comedy of Errors* (1965). In 1971 he completed his translation of Shakespeare's sonnets. The sonnets had been previously translated by Shin *Shalom in 1943. I.J. Schwarz had published ten of the sonnets in *Ha-Tekufah* (XVIII) in 1923.

[Ephraim Broido]

In Yiddish

The earliest attempt to render Shakespeare into Yiddish appears to be Bezalel Vishnepolsky's naive prose version of *Julius Caesar* (1886). In the 1890s, the American Yiddish theater, influenced by English-language Broadway productions of Shakespeare's great tragedies, staged a number of his plays in incompetent translations, generally from the German. It was Jacob *Gordin who, with his highly effective melodrama *Der Yidisher Kenig Lir* ("The Jewish King Lear," 1892), permanently linked the Yiddish repertoire to Shakespeare, thus initiating a stream of adaptations and borrowings from the great playwright's plots. Gordin's play, essentially very Jewish, is on the theme of generational conflict; similarly, child-parent conflict is the substance of Gordin's *Mirele Efros* (1898), whose original subtitle was "The Jewish Queen Lear." The Shakespearean element in these plays is slight, as is also the case with the Romeo and Juliet echoes in Gordin's *Di Litvishe Brider Lurye* ("The Lithuanian Luria Brothers," 1894), Isidor Zolotorevsky's *Der Yeshive Bokher oder Der Yidisher Martirer* ("The Seminarian or The Jewish Martyr," 1899) and Leon *Kobrin's *Der Blinder Muzikant oder Yidisher Otelo* ("The Blind Musician or Jewish Othello," first staged 1903). Maurice *Schwartz provided a Judaized version of *The Merchant of Venice* in his 1947 dramatization of Ari ibn Zahav's Hebrew novel, *Shaylok ha-Sokher mi-Venetsia* ("Shylock, the Merchant of Venice").

During the first two decades of the 20th century, Shakespeare's plays were frequently acted on the Yiddish stage in both Europe and the U.S. By and large the productions suffered from inept translations, bombastic delivery, and general artistic immaturity. With the development of the Yiddish art theater movement, this situation altered radically. In 1929, in the U.S., Maurice *Schwartz produced *Othello* in Mark Shweid's translation, and in the same year in Poland, Michael *Weichert directed an impressive *Merchant of Venice*, translated by the poet Israel Stern. In 1938 the Polish director L. Schiller staged *The Tempest* in Aaron *Zeitlin's translation, with the noted A. *Morewsky playing Prospero. The greatest of all Shakespeare productions in Yiddish was the Moscow Jewish State Theater's *King Lear* of 1935, with the translation by the poet Shmuel *Halkin. The leading role was played by Solomon *Mikhoels, and the fool's role by the great comic actor, Benjamin Zuskin.

Good translations made serious Yiddish productions of Shakespeare possible in the 1930s. The first "literary" translation of Shakespeare into Yiddish was the work of the young anarchist poet Joseph *Bovshover, whose *Merchant of Venice* (1899) marks an advance. The poet I.J. *Schwartz was more successful with his *Hamlet* and *Julius Caesar* (1918), and, in the Soviet Union, I. *Goldberg produced nine workmanlike translations (1933–38). Ber *Lapin's translation of the *Sonnets* (1953) also merits mention. It is in the theatrical rather than the literary realm that Shakespeare in Yiddish has enjoyed a full and varied life. Joel Berkowitz has shown that "[t]he ways in which Yiddish playwrights and actors in the United States re-imagined Shakespeare's plays had far-reaching implications for the American Yiddish theater." And that theater was important to immigrant American Jews.

The unlikely conjunction "Shakespeare" and "Yiddish" crops up in unsuspected places. Steve Suissa's film *Le Grand Role* (2004) gave central plot significance to a planned Yiddish adaptation of *The Merchant of Venice*. Concerning Michael Radford's film, *The Merchant of Venice* (2004), Sam Sokolove wrote: "Al Pacino… gives us a fully Yiddish Shylock" (*San Diego City Beat*, Apr. 27, 2005); Richard von Busack (*Metroactive Movies*, Jan. 12, 2005) also saw Pacino's Shylock as Yiddish-flavored. Anniversary occasions surrounding the almost legendary Solomon Mikhoels inevitably stimulate references to his famed *King Lear* production in the Moscow Yiddish Art Theater in 1935.

[Leonard Prager]

BIBLIOGRAPHY: L. Prager, in: *Shakespeare Quarterly*, 19:2 (Spring, 1968), 149–63, includes bibliography; Z. Zylbercweig, in: *Ikkuf Almanakh 1967*, ed. by N. Meisel (1967), 327–46; M.J. Landa, *The Jew in Drama* (1969²), 70–85, index; G. Friedlander, *Shakespeare and the Jew* (1921); J.L. Cardozo, *Contemporary Jew in the Elizabethan Drama* (1925), 207–53; T. Lelyveld, *Shylock on the Stage* (1961), index; S.A. Tannenbaum, *Shakspeare's The Merchant of Venice, a Concise Bibliography* (1941); M. Roston (ed.), *Ha-Olam ha-Shekspiri* (1965); M. Halevy, in: *Jewish Quarterly* (Spring, 1966), 3–7; (Winter, 1966), 10–16; J. Bloch, in: JBA, 14 (1956/57), 23–31. **ADD. BIBLIOGRAPHY:** J. Berkowitz, *Gained in Translation: Shakespeare on the American Yiddish Stage* (2002); D. Abend-David, *"Scorned My Nation," A Comparison of Translations of the Merchant of Venice into German, Hebrew and Yiddish* (2003); J. Gross, *Shylock: Four Hundred Years in the Life of a Legend* (1992); J.M. Landau, *Studies in the Arab Theater and Cinema* (1958), index.

SHAKI, ISAAC (1852–1940), Turkish rabbi. Born in a village near *Istanbul, he was a student of R. Solomon Kimḥi. Shaki first became a merchant, and it was not until middle age that he devoted himself to Torah study and research. He was *av bet din* and a member of the *bet din ha-gadol* in Istanbul, writing several books in Ladino in order to provide the masses of the people with religious literature in a language with which they were familiar.

His main work was *Historia Universal Judia* (1898–1927), a 16-volume survey of Jewish history. Other works by Shaki were *Millei de Avot* ("Words of the Fathers," in Ladino *Tresoro del Judaismo*) 3 pts. (1907–08), an extensive commentary on *Avot, and *Binah le-Ittim* (1897), dealing with the Jewish calendar. Some of his works are extant in manuscript.

BIBLIOGRAPHY: A. Galante, *Histoire des Juifs d'Istanbul*, 1 (1941), 148.

[Abraham Haim]

SHALEM (Heb. שָׁלֵם)

(1) A place whose king *Melchizedek was visited by Abraham (Gen. 14:18). It is generally agreed that the name refers to Jerusalem, especially in view of Psalms 76:3, in which Shalem is equated with Zion; this is also the view of Josephus (Ant., 1:180).

(2) A town in the Jordan Valley close to Aenon (Gk. for "many waters") where *John was reported to have been baptizing (John 3:23). Later Christian writers, such as Eusebius (Onom. 40:1) and Jerome in his Latin edition of the *Onomasticon (Liber de Situ et Nominibus* 266c; though he later changed his mind), identified it with a locality in the Jordan Valley 8 mi. (c. 13 km.) south of Scythopolis (Beth-Shean). Christian pilgrims, such as Egeria (c. 384 C.E.), visited the site, then called Sedima (Solyma?), near which was a spring or pool. The area is indicated by a row of greenish mosaics on the *Madaba Map (mid-6th century). It may be identical with the Salem mentioned in the Book of Judith (4:4), in which the villages were alerted at the approach of Holofernes, i.e. on the outskirts of the mountains of Samaria. A possible identification is with Tell al-Radgah (present-day Tell Shalem), c. 8 mi. (12 km.) south of Beth-Shean (Scythopolis). This location has numerous springs: 13 in an area of 4 × 4 kilometers; Ambrose in his writings (II, 1432) claimed there were 12 springs at "Ennon." On the north side is Tell Shalem. Since Egeria was told that Aenon was situated 200 yards (= 183 m) away, Aenon might very well be situated to the northwest of the ancient mound at ʿAin Ibrahim which has a sheikh's tomb.

(3) The Shalem Rabta ("Great Shalem") of Samaritan sources, called Sanim by Eusebius (Onom. 160:13), which is identified with the village of Sālim, approximately 4 mi. (6 km.) east of Nablus. According to Samaritan tradition, a synagogue was built there in the fourth century by their hero Bavah Rabbah.

BIBLIOGRAPHY: Hertzberg, in: JPOS, 8 (1928), 169ff.; Albright, in: BASOR, 19 (1925), 18; idem, in: AASOR, 6 (1926), 43–44; Tzori, in: *Bikat Beit Shean* (1962), 163–64; I. Ben-Zvi, *Sefer ha-Shomronim* (1935), 68. **ADD. BIBLIOGRAPHY:** For a discussion regarding the location of Salem and Aenon: S. Gibson, *The Cave of John the Baptist* (2004), 238–41; for an alternative view, see: J. Murphy O'Connor, "Sites Associated with John the Baptist," in: *Revue Biblique*, 112 (2005), 253–66.

[Michael Avi-Yonah / Shimon Gibson (2nd ed.)]

SHALEM, SAMUEL (d. 1760), scholar and emissary. Born in *Salonika, Shalem was a pupil of R. Abraham Gategno. In 1745 he went to Constantinople, emigrating from there to *Tiberias. During his time in Salonika he spoke with Ereẓ Israel emissaries, and in his writings he quoted several Torah novellae that he heard from Hebron and Safed emissaries. From 1755 he traveled for about five years as an emissary from Tiberias to *Turkey, *Italy, *France, and *Germany. The letter concerning his mission – written by the *ḥakhamim* of Tiberias and describing the troubles of Tiberias in the wake of the wars between the sons of the sheikh Ḍāhir el-Omar, ruler of Tiberias – is extant. The collection of his responsa includes many of his halakhic replies to problems raised in the communities of *Izmir, Turin, Avignon, Ferrara, Verona, Leghorn, Trier, Metz, Hamburg, etc. He died in Izmir on his return journey. His responsa and halakhic novellae were collected and published as *Melekh Shalem* (Salonika, 1769).

BIBLIOGRAPHY: Yaari, Sheluḥei, 511–4; S. Shalem, *Melekh Shalem* (1769).

[Avraham Yaari]

SHALEV, AVNER (1939–), chairman of Israel's *Yad Vashem directorate. Born in Jerusalem, Shalev served in the Israel Defense Forces between 1956 and 1980, reaching the rank of brigadier general. Shalev was wounded in action on the Egyptian front during the Six-Day War. Between 1972 and 1974 he served as bureau chief for chief of staff David *Elazar. Other army positions included head of the Information and Instruction Division of the General Staff; education officer at the IDF Officers School; chief education officer and head of the Education Corps, where he was editor-in-chief of the IDF Radio Station and the IDF weekly magazine; and senior lecturer at the IDF National Security College.

After retiring from military service, Shalev served as director general of the Culture Authority in the Ministry of Education and Culture and chairman of the National Culture and Art Council. He was also a member of the directorate for various national museums and cultural institutions in Israel. In these positions he was responsible for devising and directing national culture policy and encouraging, supporting, and overseeing the funding of all types of cultural and artistic activity in Israel. Shalev also introduced policies to raise the standards of Israel's leading cultural institutions and advanced and promoted new cultural programs, such as art and culture festivals throughout the country, in order to increase cultural awareness and involvement. Another achievement in this period was to transform the Antiquities Division of the Ministry of Education into a national authority. Shalev was also instrumental in enhancing educational opportunities in regional areas by promoting the accreditation of educational institutions there and enabling their students to obtain recognized degrees.

From 1993 Shalev served as chairman of the directorate of Yad Vashem, the Holocaust Martyrs' and Heroes' Remembrance Authority in Jerusalem, where he initiated a multi-year development plan aimed at equipping Yad Vashem with the necessary tools to address the challenges of Holocaust remembrance in the 21st century. As part of this plan Shalev placed education as a high priority at Yad Vashem and spearheaded the establishment of the International School for Holocaust Studies as well as a new Museum Complex, and served as the chief curator of the new Yad Vashem Holocaust History Museum, which opened in March 2005. During his tenure he also brought about the uploading of Yad Vashem's Database of Holocaust Victims' Names onto the Internet, harnessing modern technology in the service of Holocaust remembrance and education.

Shalev studied modern history of the Middle East and geography and graduated from the IDF Command and Staff College and National Security College. Among his publications are *To Bear Witness – Holocaust Remembrance at Yad Vashem* (2005).

SHALEV, MEIR (1948–), Hebrew writer. Shalev, son of poet Yitzhak *Shalev, was born in *Nahalal. He grew up in that much acclaimed agricultural cooperative and later in Jerusalem, and studied psychology at the Hebrew University. For many years he produced and hosted radio and television programs and is also known for his journalistic contribution to various newspapers. His first publications were books for children and the volume *Tanakh Akhshav* ("Bible Now," 1985), a personal, modern look at diverse biblical episodes. His first novel for adult readers *Roman Rusi* (1988; *The Blue Mountain*, 1991; 2001) was an outstanding success among Israeli readers and turned Shalev overnight into one of the most popular contemporary Hebrew prose-writers. The novel recounts the chronicle of pioneering settlers in the Jezreel valley. The narrative point of view is that of a grandson who is brought up on myths and legendary stories of days gone-by. *Esav* (1991; *Esau* 1993) unfolds the story of a baker's family against the backdrop of Jerusalem and the Galilee from the beginning of the 20th century up to the 1970s, highlighting the complex relations between fathers and sons and the pivotal role played by women and mothers. *Be-Veito ba-Midbar* (1998; "His House in the Desert," German, 2000) is the story of 52-year-old Rafael Meyer, whose development was shaped by four men and six women, including his grandmother, his aunts, and his ex-wife. Indeed, the power of women to mold and dictate the lives of men is a recurrent theme in Shalev's writing. Shalev interweaves in his rich and multi-layered narrative biblical associations with mythic materials and archetypal patterns, underscoring memory and sensual experience. Fantasy and humor are essential elements in his fiction. Other books include the novels *Ke-Yamim Aḥadim* (1994; *As a Few Days*, 1999) and *Fontanella* ("Fontanelle," 2002). Among Shalev's books for children are *Ha-Yeled Ḥayyim ve-ha-Miflezet* (1982; *Ḥayyim and the Monster of Jerusalem*, 1990), *Gumot ha-Ḥen shel Zohar* (*Zohar's Dimples*, 1987; German: 1995), *Aba Ose Bushot* (1988; *My Father Always Embarrasses Me*, 1990) and *Ha-Traktor be-Argaz ha-Ḥol* ("The Tractor in the Sandbox," German, 1999). His books have been translated into many languages, and information is available at the ITHL website at www.ithl.org.il.

BIBLIOGRAPHY: H. Halkin, "Bread and Circuses," in: *The Jerusalem Report* (November 7, 1991); S. Shiffman, "On the Possibilty of Impossible Worlds: Meir Shalev and the Fantastic in Israeli Literature," in: *Prooftexts*, 13:3 (1993), 253–67; R. Brenner Feldhay, "Mother's Curse or Cursed Mother (Shalev's *Esau*)," in: *Jewish Studies Quarterly*, 4:4 (1997), 380–400; W. Zierler, "On Meir Shalev's Esau," in: *Ariel*, 107–8 (1998), 183–84; A.Navot, in: *Maariv* (April 16, 1998); G. Shaked, "Die konservative Revolution der jungen israelischen Dichter: Tendenzen der achtziger and neunziger Jahre," in: *Judaica*, 54:1–2 (1998), 36–55; Y. Zerubavel, "Revisiting the Pioneer Past: Continuity and Change in Hebrew Settlement Narratives," in: *Hebrew Studies*,

41 (2000), 209–24; L. Garfinkel, "*Fontanella*," in: *Ma'agalei Keriah*, 29 (2002), 90–96; H. Halperin, "*Eleh Toledot Mishpaḥat Yofe: Ha-Mitos ha-Ereẓ Yisraeli shel 'Fontanella'*," in: *Moznayim*, 77:1 (2003), 25–28; E. Negev, *Close Encounters with Twenty Israeli Writers* (2003); Y. Oren, "Post-Zionism and Anti-Zionism in Israeli Literature," in: *Israel and the Post-Zionists* (2003), 188–203.

[Anat Feinberg (2nd ed.)]

SHALEV, YITZḤAK (1919–1992), Hebrew poet and novelist. Born in Tiberias, he became a teacher in Jerusalem. His first poems were published in *Moznayim* and *Davar*, and subsequently appeared in a large number of newspapers and literary journals.

Among his volumes of poetry are *Oḥezet Anaf ha-Shaked* (1951), *Kolot Enosh Ḥammim* (1954), *Kol Annot* (1955), *Elohei ha-Noshek Loḥamim* (1957), *Shirei Yerushalayim* (1968), and *Na'ar Shav min ha-Ẓava* (1970). He also wrote a novel about the Jewish defense activities during the riots in Palestine in 1936, *Parashat Gavri'el Tirosh*. In 1969 he wrote the novel *Dam va-Ru'aḥ*. He is the father of writer Meir *Shalev.

BIBLIOGRAPHY: Goell, Bibliography, 39; A. Cohen, *Soferim Ivriyyim Benei Zemannenu* (1964), 224–6; S. Kremer, *Ḥillufei Mishmarot be-Sifrutenu* (1959), 160–70; Waxman, Literature, 5 (1960^2), 16–18.

[Getzel Kressel]

SHALEV, ZERUYA (1959–), Hebrew writer. Shalev, born on Kibbutz Kinneret, studied Biblical Studies at the Hebrew University, and published a collection of poems in 1989. Six years later her first novel, *Rakadeti, Amadeti* ("Dancing, Standing Still," 1993) came out, the story of a woman whose marriage is disintegrating, confronting her with suppressed anxieties and dormant passions. It was, however, Shalev's second novel, *Ḥayyei Ahava* (1997; *Love Life*, 2000), which made the author famous worldwide. The novel, an outstanding bestseller in Israel, describes the stormy relationship between Ya'arah, a married woman who is trying to complete her dissertation on legends describing the destruction of the Temple, and the much older Aryeh, a married man, who, as it turns out, was once her mother's lover. The relationship between the two is characterized by obsessive intensity, sado-masochistic sexuality, infatuation, yearning, and revulsion. Shalev, one of the most successful contemporary Hebrew writers, was awarded the Book Publishers' Associations' Golden and Platinum Book Prizes for this novel as well as for her third novel, *Ba'al ve-Ishah* (2000; *Husband and Wife*, 2002). The latter focuses on the crisis in the marriage of Na'amah and Udi, after the husband has undergone a Kafkaesque metamorphosis and is unable to live a normal life. In 2005 Shalev published the third novel in her family-trilogy: *Tera* ("Late Family") is the story of 36-year-old archeologist Ella Miller, who sets out to explore the freedom and joys of a new love relationship, leaving behind her family. Shalev's language is rich and captivating, her descriptions bold and vivid. Love, sexuality and betrayal, motherhood, family life and commitment are the major themes in her prose. Shalev also wrote a book for children "Mama's Best Boy" (2000). Shalev won the German Corine Book Award (2001) and the French Amphi Award.

For translations of her prose, see the ITHL website at www.ithl.org.il.

BIBLIOGRAPHY: A. Wimer, "*Kamah Ḥomer be-Tezah Sheḥorah Aḥat: Al Ḥayyei Ahava*," in: *Dappim le-Meḥkar be-Sifrut*, 12 (2000), 317–31; S. Zur, "*Zu Yalduti ha-Sheniyyah: al Yaldut ve-Imahut be-Ba'al ve-Ishah shel Z. Shalev*," in: *Moznayim*, 74:9 (2000), 32–35; Y. Schwartz, "The Frigid Option: A Psychocultural Study of the Novel *Love Life* by Z. Shalev," in: *History and Literature* (2002), 479–88; T. Yaniv, "*Keriah Intertekstualit be-Aggadot ha-Ḥurban be- Ḥayyei Ahavah shel Z. Shalev*," in: *Dimui*, 22 (2003), 75–79.

[Anat Feinberg (2nd ed.)]

SHALISH (Heb. שָׁלִישׁ), one with whom an article or money is deposited and who has authority to dispose of it according to law or in accordance with stipulated conditions.

Types of Deposit

The deposit can be effected by a single person who deposits something with the *shalish* to give to another person or to buy some article, or by two people who have greater trust in a third party than in one another, as, for instance, where there is a difference of opinion between them and they deposit an object with the *shalish* until it is established who is entitled to it, or where a debtor has paid his creditor only part of the debt and they deposit the bill of debt with a *shalish* until the balance is paid (Ket. 5:8, 6:7; BB 10:5; Tosef., BM 1:10; cf. *Rema*, ḤM 56:2).

The conditions to which the *shalish* is subject may at times be affected by the defect of *asmakhta*, as in the following example: If a debtor repays part of his debt and gives his bond to a *shalish* saying: "If I do not give you [the balance] by such at date, give the creditor his bond, so that he can again claim that part of the debt is already paid" (BB 10:5); the *tannaim* disagree on whether the *shalish* must act in accordance with this condition, and the Talmud explains that the dispute stems from the argument that the condition is defective because of *asmakhta* (BB 168a). The *halakhah* established that the condition is void and the *shalish* need not return the bond to the creditor, unless the appropriate procedure has been followed, such as an act of *acquisition in the presence of an important (*ḥashuv*) *bet din* in order to rectify the defect of *asmakhta* (Sh. Ar., ḤM 55:1).

The status of *shalish* can arise without any specific act. For example, if a wife has been administering her husband's property, or an administrator has been appointed over a person's property in circumstances where the owner has given the administrator absolute authority over all his possessions and trusted him completely, and the owner then dies, the administrator has the credibility of a *shalish* (Sh. Ar., ḤM 56:7, and *Siftei Kohen* thereto, n. 34).

The Credibility of the Shalish

A *shalish* is, in general, accorded greater credibility than a single witness. "The admission of a litigant is as good as a hundred witnesses, but the *shalish* is believed more than both. If one [litigant] says one thing, the other [litigant] another, and the *shalish* something else, the *shalish* is believed" (Tosef., BM 1:10). The reason for this special credibility of the *shalish* is that the depositor has reposed confidence in him (Git. 64a; and see in detail PDR 1:294–5). For this reason it has been concluded that even a *shalish* who is a relative also merits credibility, despite the fact that a relative is disqualified from giving evidence (Sh. Ar., ḤM 56:1). The *shalish*, is believed in preference to the debtor or creditor. If two witnesses contradict him, however, he is not believed (Sh. Ar., ḤM 56:2, *Sma* and *Siftei Kohen* thereto).

If someone has in his possession another's property and claims that its owner handed it to him as a *shalish* and the owner denies this, one opinion is that the one possessing the property is believed (Sh. Ar., ḤM 56:1): "Even if the owner claims: You robbed me of it, and the other retorts: It is not so, but you appointed me a *shalish* between you and so and so, the other is believed" (*Sma*, ḤM 56:1 n. 7). On the other hand, some *posekim* argue that if this were so, anyone could seize his fellow's property and enter into a collusive agreement with another and say, I am a *shalish*. Accordingly, they hold that the *shalish* is not believed unless the depositor admits that the property was deposited with him as a *shalish* (*Siftei Kohen*, ḤM 56:1 n. 5).

The *shalish* is believed without an oath, since he is not a litigant and is backed by the presumption: "A man does not sin when he personally gains nothing by it" (Hai Gaon, in *Oẓar ha-Ge'onim*, ed. by B.M. Lewin, 10 (1941), 143, no. 352; Sh. Ar., ḤM 56:1). If the date fixed for the return of the deposit passes and the *shalish* has not returned it, he is still a *shalish* and is still believed (Sh. Ar. *ibid.*). The unique credibility of the *shalish* continues only as long as the deposit is still in his possession (Tosef., BM 1:10; Sh. Ar., ḤM 56:1; *Divrei Ge'onim*, 107:7). It is thus considered a sensible precaution to return the deposit in the presence of the *bet din* and clarify the facts in its presence, lest a dispute should arise between the parties, and, if the *shalish* has already parted with the deposit, he would not be believed (Sh. Ar., ḤM 56:3). One opinion is that it is possible to restore the deposit to the *shalish* so that he would again have credibility (*Siftei Kohen*, ḤM 56, no. 20; *Divrei Ge'onim*, 107, no. 6).

Liability of a Shalish

A *shalish* who acts contrary to the conditions made with him may become liable to compensate for any loss caused by his action. If he returns to the creditor a bond deposited with him, contrary to what was stipulated, he is subjected to a ban until he undertakes to compensate the debtor for any loss sustained as a result of the return of the bond. If the *shalish* does not undertake to compensate, and the creditor obtains payment unjustly by means of the bond returned to him, the *shalish* does not have to compensate the debtor, since this is only a case of damage caused indirectly by **gerama* and the rule is that there is no liability for damages caused by *gerama* (*Rema* ḤM 55:1; *Divrei Ge'onim*, 107, no. 10). If, on the other hand, contrary to the stipulation, the *shalish* returns the bond to the debtor, the *shalish* must compensate the creditor, for this is a case of *garmi* (as opposed to *gerama*), when the tort-feaser is liable to pay (*Siftei Kohen*, ḤM 56, no. 4; *Divrei Ge'onim* 107, nos. 11 and 12).

The *shalish* is at liberty to retract and restore the deposit to the parties. If the parties do not want to take it back, he can hand it over to the *bet din*. A *shalish* who is paid for his services, however, cannot retract (*Arukh ha-Shulḥan*, ḤM 56:17).

"The claimant pays the expenses of the *shalish* (*Rema*, ḤM 56:1), for it is always the one for whose benefit and advantage something is effected who has to pay the cost" (*Sma*, ḤM 56 n. 13; *Arukh ha-Shulḥan*, ḤM 56:23). It is customary to write a deed when something is deposited with a *shalish* (for the wording of such a deed, see *Sefer ha-Shetarot* no. 65, and see **Shomerim*).

BIBLIOGRAPHY: *Paḥad Yiẓḥak*, s.v. *Shalish, Shelishut*; I.S. Zuri, *Mishpat ha-Talmud*, 7 (1921), 53; Gulak, Yesodei, 2 (1922), 191f.; 4 (1922), 161; Elon, Mafte'aḥ, 387–90.

[Nahum Rakover]

SHALKOVICH, ABRAHAM LEIB (pen name **Ben-Avigdor**; 1867–1921), Russian Hebrew author and pioneer of modern Hebrew publishing. Born in Zheludok province of Grodno, Shalkovich settled in Warsaw in 1891. In 1889 he wrote a sharp criticism of the **ḥalukkah* system in *Ha-Meliz* (nos. 82–83), and his first story, "*Elyakim ha-Meshugga*" ("Eliakim the Insane"). In 1891 he began publishing the "*Sifrei Agorah*" series, offering Hebrew literature in an attractive and reasonably priced booklet form. The series served as the medium of the "new wave" which sought to revitalize Hebrew literature and to introduce the realism then current in Europe. The success of the "*Agorah*" books prompted Shalkovich to set up the Aḥi'asaf publishing house in Warsaw (1893), and he edited the first three volumes of the *Lu'aḥ Aḥi'asaf* annual (1894–96). He also contributed to *Ha-Pardes*, and to *Ha-Zeman*, published by Ezra *Goldin. In 1896 he left Aḥi'asaf and set up Tushiyyah, a new company which published translations from foreign languages. In 1901 Shalkovich founded a children's weekly called *Olam Katan*, and in 1904 renewed the publication of the daily *Ha-Zeman*.

His work as a publisher demanded his entire energy and curtailed his own writing. In 1913 he founded the Aḥisefer publishing house, which also issued the miscellany *Netivot* (1913) in the editing of which he had a share. In *Netivot* he published a long article, "*Aḥad Ha-Am u-Venei Moshe*" (pp. 238–90), on Aḥad Ha-Am whom he had previously supported and admired. Shalkovich died suddenly in Carlsbad, while attending the Twelfth Zionist Congress.

Shalkovich was among the first of the modern Hebrew writers to stress the problems of the individual Jew rather than those of the Jewish people. In his story "*Menaḥem ha-Sofer*" (1893) he called for a true portrayal of the Jewish scene in a simple realistic vein. But Shalkovich did not always remain loyal to his own views. The novel *Lifnei Arba Me'ot Shanah* (1892) was written in a florid and sentimental style. While Shalkovich's stories have little literary merit, he deserves respect as an innovator in Hebrew literature and a pioneer in modern Hebrew publishing.

BIBLIOGRAPHY: *Ben Avigdor Jubilee Volume* (1916); Fichmann, in: *Ha-Tekufah*, 12 (1921), 477–80 (reprinted in his *Ruḥot Menaggenot* (1952), 387–94); Lachower, Sifrut, 3 pt. 2 (1931), 14–21; Klausner, Sifrut, index, s.v. *Ben-Avigdor*; A. Cohen, in: *Hadoar*, 11 (1921), 19–21; Waxman, Literature, 4 (1960), 80–84; Goell, Bibliography, 1955–56.

[Gedalyah Elkoshi]

SHALLON, DAVID (1950–2000), Israeli conductor. Born in Tel Aviv, Shallon studied violin, viola, and French horn at the Tel Aviv Academy of Music. In 1974, after service in the Israel Army Band, he studied in Vienna and completed the conducting class with Hans Swarowsky. From 1974 to 1979 he was assistant to Leonard *Bernstein for Europe. From 1980, he conducted leading orchestras as the Berlin PO, the London SO, the Israel PO, and the San Francisco SO; he also appeared at many of the major European festivals and conducted at leading opera houses, including Vienna, Frankfurt, Duesseldorf, and the New Israeli Opera. He was musical director of the Duesseldorf SO (1987–93), the Jerusalem SO from 1992 to 2000, and the Luxembourg PO in 1997. Several Israeli composers, among them Noam *Sheriff, dedicated works to him. Among his recordings are viola concertos by Bartók, Hindemith, Schnittke, and Mark *Kopytman.

BIBLIOGRAPHY: Grove online, s.v.

[Israela Stein (2nd ed.)]

SHALLUM (Heb. שַׁלֻּם, שַׁלּוּם; probably a hypocorism of a name like שֶׁלֶמְיָהוּ – "Yahweh has preserved or requited"), son of Jabesh, one of the last kings of Israel. Shallum came to the throne in the 39th year of the reign of *Uzziah in Judah, after killing *Zechariah son of Jeroboam II and thus putting an end to the dynasty of Jeroboam (II Kings 15:10). Shallum ruled Israel from Samaria for one month (15:13), apparently between Elul and Tishri, 747 B.C.E. The throne was taken from him by *Menahem son of Gadi, who formed a conspiracy against him and killed him (15:14). Some scholars interpret the designation "son of Jabesh" as a reference to the city of *Jabesh (-Gilead) and take it as indicating that Shallum was from this city.

BIBLIOGRAPHY: Bright, Hist, 253; Tadmor, in: A. Malamat (ed.), *Bi-Ymei Bayit Rishon* (1962), 180ff.; J.A. Montgomery, *The Book of Kings* (ICC, 1951), 449; J. Gray, *I and II Kings, A Commentary* (1963), 562ff.

[Josef Segal]

°**SHALMANESER III** (**Shulmānu-asharid** ("Shulmanu is leader") III), ruler of Assyria 859–824 B.C.E. Shalmaneser inherited from his father, the cruel Ashurnasirpal II (883–859 B.C.E.), a well-equipped army and the desire to extend his rule over Syria and Phoenicia. Over a period of some 20 years (858–838 B.C.E.), he succeeded in subduing most of the small kingdoms from the Euphrates in the north to the Jordan in the south. He was the first Assyrian king to come into direct contact with an Israelite monarch and probably the first to traverse Israelite territory.

The main sources for the history of Shalmaneser's reign are the royal annals, which were "edited" some five times during his lifetime. The texts have been compiled and translated by E. Michel in *Die Welt des Orients* 1 (1947) and following volumes. In addition to these and other inscriptions, there are also many reliefs from the reigns of Ashurnasirpal and Shalmaneser which clearly indicate their military innovations as well as their contacts with foreign countries. Of particular interest is the Black Obelisk, one of whose registers depicts an Israelite delegation from King *Jehu presenting gifts to Shalmaneser (c. 841 B.C.E.).

Shalmaneser's western campaigns began in his first regnal year when he defeated the league of north Syrian states, including *Beth-Eden, *Carchemish, Kummukh (i.e.,*Commagene), Samal, Hattina, and *Cilicia. A direct result of this was the formation of an even stronger south-Syrian league which succeeded in holding off the Assyrian advance for over a decade.

In 853 B.C.E., Shalmaneser crossed the Euphrates for the second time and proceeded to the city of Pethor (see Numbers 22:5), where he received tribute from the north-Syrian kingdoms. He continued on to Halab, the center of the cult of Hadad, where he met the combined forces of 12 states in one of the great battles of antiquity. Opposing the Assyrians was the triumvirate of Hadadezer (*Ben-Hadad II) of Damascus, Irhuleni of Hamath, and *Ahab the Israelite: they were accompanied by smaller contingents from the Phoenician coast-Byblos (!), Arqanta, Arvad, Sianu (see Genesis 10:17–18), and Usanta in addition to troops from Egypt, the south Syrian Amanah (or perhaps the Ammorites), and an Arabian tribe. According to the Syrian text, this army totaled 3,940 chariots, 1,900 cavalry, over 62,000 infantry, and 1,000 camel riders. Judging from the fact that Shalmaneser did not press on beyond Karkar nor resume his successive campaigns against the league for another four years in 849, and then again in 848 and 845 B.C.E., it seems that at best the battle ended in a military deadlock, if not in an Assyrian defeat. Of note is the large force under Ahab's command, which may indicate, as Malamat suggests, a minor league including Ahab's vassals, Moab, and possibly Ammon, in addition to Jehoshaphat king of Judah with his vassals Edom and possibly Philistia (see I Kings 22:4; II Kings 3:4ff.). Certainly, this text sheds much light on Ahab's stature in the international theater, a fact only hinted at in the Bible (I Kings 18:10, see also Meg. lla).

It was only in Shalmaneser's 18th year (841 B.C.E.) that he succeeded in breaking through the south-Syrian front. To a great extent this was made possible by internal changes among the allies. *Hazael had usurped the throne after killing Ben Hadad II, probably to be identified with Hadadezer mentioned in the annals. While he continued the anti-Assyrian policy of his predecessors, Hazael renewed the border wars against

Israel with greater vigor (II Kings 8:12). This new source of tension was one of the factors that precipitated the overthrow of the dynasty of Omri by the military officer Jehu Ben Nimshi (II Kings 9:1ff.). The latter may have made overtures to Shalmaneser, thereby disengaging the Israelite army from the south-Syrian camp, which ultimately led to its dissolution.

Shalmaneser first met Hazael's troops in the mountain passes of the anti-Lebanon (Sirion). Hazael retreated to his capital *Damascus, where he withstood the siege. Shalmaneser, after burning the outskirts of Damascus, continued into the Hauran, "the bread basket" of Syria and Israel, probably destroying many settlements in his wake. Some scholars would see a later historic reference to this march in Hosea's mention of the spoiling of Beth Arbel in Transjordan by a certain Shalman (10:14). From there Shalmaneser crossed Israel to the mountains of Ba'li-ra'si, which is on the Mediterranean coast. There he received tribute from Jehu "the son of Omri" and from Baalimanzeri the king of Tyre. Quite plausibly, this mountain should be identified with Mount Carmel, which traditionally served as the boundary between Israel and Phoenicia.

Shalmaneser returned only once more, in 838 B.C.E., in a punitive expedition against Hazael, who subsequently became the dominant power in the area. During his later years, Shalmaneser was occupied with campaigns in northern Syria and with rebellion in Assyria proper against his heir Shamshi-Adad V.

[Aaron Demsky]

°**SHALMANESER V** (727–722 B.C.E.), son of *Tiglath-Pileser III. He reigned in Babylonia under the name of Ubulai. None of his royal inscriptions, if indeed he composed any, have survived, with the result that knowledge of the period is indirect. From the 7th century B.C.E. Aramean ostraca found at *Assur, it seems that he took captives from Beth-Eden. Josephus quoting Menander of Tyre (*Antiquities* 9:284) notes that Σέλαημψας had for several years unsuccessfully besieged Ussu, the older, mainland district of Tyre. This last campaign was related to a wide range of insurrections in the area. At this time, *Hoshea ben Elah conspired with the Egyptian king of Sais (!) in the delta. Shalmaneser took Hoshea captive and laid siege to *Samaria (II Kings 17:3ff.). The Babylonian Chronicle ascribes the destruction of Shamarain, i.e., Samaria (cf. the Aramaic pronunciation in Ezra 4:10) to Shalmaneser, though the final capture of the city was probably carried out by his famous successor *Sargon II in 722/21 B.C.E.

BIBLIOGRAPHY: Y. Aharoni, in: *The Western Galilee and Its Coast* (Heb., 1965), 56ff.; A. Malamat, in: J. Liver (ed.), *Historia Ẓeva'it shel Ereẓ Yisrael Bime ha-Mikra* (1964), 246ff; H. Tadmor, in: IEJ, 11 (1960), 143ff.; H. Tadmor, in: JCS, 12 (1958), 33–40.

[Aaron Demsky]

SHALOM, ABRAHAM (d. 1557?), rabbi, also known as **Ha-Rosh** (from the initials of R. Shalom). Abraham Shalom was born in Salonika to a family of rabbis, possibly the grandson of Abraham b. Isaac *Shalom (d. 1492). He studied with his friend Solomon ha-Levi *Alkabez under Joseph *Taitaẓak in Salonika, and later became a teacher there. In about 1530 he settled in Safed, where he became the disciple and colleague of *Jacob Berab I; he was one of the four scholars who received **semikhah* (rabbinical ordination) from Berab. Shalom, the colleague of Joseph *Caro and Moses of *Trani, served as *dayyan* and head of a yeshivah. His grandson Abraham b. Eliezer Shalom was one of the most important rabbis of Safed.

BIBLIOGRAPHY: Conforte, Kore, 36a, 49b; Neubauer, Chronicles, 1 (1887), 140; Rosanes, Togarmah, 2 (1938), 175; 3 (1938), 97, 426; Yaari, Sheluḥei, 243–4; Benayahu, in: *Sefer Yovel… Y. Baer* (1960), 249; Dimitrovsky, in: *Sefunot*, 6 (1962), 93, 111; 7 (1963), 49, 66.

[Abraham David]

SHALOM, ABRAHAM BEN ISAAC BEN JUDAH BEN SAMUEL (d. 1492), Catalonian (Spain) philosopher and translator of philosophical writings. Shalom is known to have translated two works from Latin into Hebrew: a compendium of the physical sciences by Albertus *Magnus, *Philosophia Pauperum*, under the title *Ha-Pilosofyah ha-Tivit* ("Natural Philosophy"), extant in manuscript form (Hamburg Ms. 266); and a discussion of certain problems in Aristotle's *Organon* by Marsilius of Inghen, under the title *She'elot u-Teshuvot* ("Questions and Answers," see S. Pinsker, *Likkutei Kadmoniyyot* (1860), 152, second page). Shalom's preface to the latter, in which he polemicizes against the opponents of secular-scientific studies, together with the index of the questions, was published by A. Jellinek under the title *Marsilius ab Inghen* (1859). Shalom's major work, *Neveh Shalom* (Constantinople, 1539; Venice, 1574), gives evidence of the author's thorough command of the fields of knowledge of his time, and is rich in quotations from Greek and Arabic philosophical literature. In its external form, *Neveh Shalom* is a series of homilies on various aggadic passages drawn from the talmudic tractate *Berakhot*. Into this framework Shalom weaves a number of philosophic discussions in which he undertakes to review the philosophic statements of his predecessors, to consider just those views which are in harmony with Scripture, to decide which among them is correct, and, especially, to prove that "Moses *Maimonides is true and his teaching is true" (see *Neveh Shalom*, author's introduction; see also 1:14, 21a). In other words, he undertakes to defend Maimonides' philosophy with its particular equilibrium between Greek philosophy and scriptural teachings. Shalom's defense is directed both against the more radical position of *Levi b. Gershom, who felt that Maimonides had compromised philosophy, and also against the more conservative position of Ḥasdai *Crescas, who felt that Maimonides had compromised scriptural religion. His assumption that Maimonides' authority is supreme in all questions sometimes led Shalom into difficulty in his attempts at harmonization of different authorities. There were, in fact, cases where he felt that religious considerations demanded a different position from that which Maimonides had apparently held. His solution to the dilemma consisted in showing that Maimonides' statements, in such cases, should not be taken in their obvious sense. Thus, he himself frequently leaned toward Crescas' views on religious questions, but, on the other hand, he refuted many of Crescas' criticisms of Maimonides by stating that Maimonides had really intended to say, or implied, just what Crescas criticized him for not saying.

Shalom's discussions reveal a careful study of Maimonides, Levi b. Gershom and Crescas, as well as other Jewish writers and non-Jewish philosophers, especially *Averroes. His own method does not display any great originality. He sometimes expounds, in different passages, inconsistent positions on the same question. This imprecision is due to the fact that Shalom did not attach importance to all the topics which he discussed. There are just a few subjects which were fundamentally significant for him because of their religious implications, and, when dealing with those he was careful to state a definitive and consistent position. However, the various technical philosophic problems upon which he touched concerned him less, and he did not always exercise the same care with them. In general, the philosophical sections of *Neveh Shalom* have a strong apologetic motif. They are designed less to discover new truths than to defend, first the doctrines of the Jewish religion, as Shalom understood them, and then, the philosophical positions of Maimonides. His methods of argumentation in these sections are appropriate to that end.

BIBLIOGRAPHY: H. Davidson, *The Philosophy of Abraham Shalom* (1964); H.A. Wolfson, *Crescas' Critique of Aristotle* (1929), index, 715, s.v. *Abraham Shalom*.

[Herbert Davidson]

SHALOM, ISAAC I. (1886–1968), U.S. businessman and philanthropist. Born in *Aleppo, *Syria, Shalom immigrated in 1910 to the United States, where he settled in New York City. There he started a small textile business, and in 1921 he established the handkerchief firm of I. Shalom & Co., which developed into one of the leading manufacturers in its field in the U.S. A lifelong supporter of Orthodox Jewish educational institutions, Shalom was instrumental in 1945 in founding *Oẓar Hatorah, an organization that provided Hebrew education for tens of thousands of Jewish children in the Arab countries of North Africa and the Middle East. Shalom was also an active Zionist who established many enterprises in Israel and was one of the leaders of the Sephardi and Syrian communities in New York City.

[Hillel Halkin]

SHALOM, SHIN (pseudonym of **Shalom Joseph Shapira**; 1904–1990), Hebrew poet and author. Born in Parczew, Poland, Shalom was a descendant of distinguished ḥasidic rabbis. He received a religious and secular education at his grandfather's "court," which moved to Vienna in the wake of World War I. Here he began to write poetry, at first in German and later solely in Hebrew. His grandfather, R. Ḥayyim Meir Jehiel Shapira, spent many years preparing the family for immigration to Palestine; in 1922 some 30 members of the family immigrated to Jerusalem, where Shalom attended a teachers' seminary. In 1926 he joined those rabbis in his family who founded Kefar Ḥasidim in the Valley of Jezreel, and taught Hebrew in this settlement. In 1928 he moved to Rosh Pinnah in the Galilee. Shalom described this period in his book *Yoman ba-Galil*. From 1930 to 1931 Shalom studied philosophy at the University of Erlangen (Germany). He returned in 1932 to teach in Jerusalem; later he moved to Reḥovot and finally settled in Haifa (1954). In 1968 Shalom was elected chairman of the Hebrew Writers' Association of Israel. His works won varied literary awards and his collected works were published in eight volumes (1966–68). The lyrical and dramatic tension in Shalom's poetry is created between the "I" of the universe (whom he sometimes calls "Him") and the personal "I." He envisages the life of man and of the world as a constant ascent, accompanied by falls, a Jacob's ladder touching the ground with its top rung in the sky; an ascent from the personal "I" to the infinite "I," from the life of the moment to eternal life. This journey from "I" to "I" finds its strongest expression in Shalom's two main books of poetry, *Panim el Panim* ("Face to Face," 1941) and *Sefer Ḥai Ro'i* (1963). In the former it is a magical journey within the inner soul; in the latter the journey is made real through living characters and plastic portrayal of sights and situations. Shalom's two novels – *Yoman be-Galil* ("Galilee Diary," 1932) and *Ha-Ner Lo Kavah* ("The Candle Was Not Extinguished," 1942) – are useful for deciphering his poetry. The former is a first-person narrative concerning the love of a Jewish teacher for an Arab girl. *Ha-Ner Lo Kavah* focuses upon the life of a poet whose private struggle to ensure that "the candle does not go out" corresponds with the nation's struggle for independence and strength. Shalom's verse dramas also depict the struggle and confrontation between the two "I"s, between time and eternity. The drama, *Shabbat ha-Olam* ("The World's Sabbath," 1945) is based on the tragic antinomy between the *tanna*, Elisha b. Avuyah, who abandoned religious practice and his disciple, R. Meir, who remained steadfast in his belief. Elisha's desecration of the Sabbath constitutes, in a way, a revolutionary call for the casting off of the yoke of the law and, on the other hand, the observance of the Sabbath by R. Meir and his wife, Beruryah, is aimed at preserving tradition. Only in the cave of the mystic Simeon b. Yoḥai is the secret of the affinity between the "Sabbath of the country" and the "Sabbath of the world" revealed. "The Cave of Josephus" was based on the life of Josephus. In connection with his poetical philosophy, Shalom also gave strong expression to the revival of Israel.

The close friendship between Shalom and Max *Brod prompted joint literary efforts, such as the historical play *Sha'ul Melekh Yisrael* ("Saul, King of Israel," 1944); Brod also wrote the libretto for the first Hebrew opera (music by Marc *Lavry) based on Shalom's play *Dan ha-Shomer* (1945) – a story inspired by the foundation of kibbutz *Ḥanitah – and composed several musical works on Shalom's poems, of which the most important is *Requiem Ivri* ("Hebrew Requiem") for solo voice and orchestra. Other Israeli composers, including

Paul Ben-Ḥaim, Zeira, and Nardi have also set poems by Shalom to music. A list of his works translated into English appears in Goell, Bibliography, index, s.v. *Shin Shalom*.

[Gideon Katznelson]

In 1971 Shin Shalom published the volume of poetry *Maḥteret ha-Shir*, the ninth volume of his collected works, and in 1972 *Kokhav ha-Tekumah*, an epic of the rebirth of Israel, in which he gives expression to his faith in the meaning of the world and the mission of a man, an affirmation which stands in opposition to the depiction of violence and the absurd which characterizes much of contemporary poetry.

In 1973 he was awarded the Israel Prize, and simultaneously there appeared a special volume comprising 48 reviews of his poems during his half-century of activity.

BIBLIOGRAPHY: M. Ribalow, *The Flowering of Modern Hebrew Literature* (1959), 207–36, including translation; Waxman, Literature, 5 (1960^2), 12–16; B. Kurzweil, *Bein Ḥazon le-Vein ha-Absurdi* (1966), 110–54; G. Katznelson, in: *Me'assef*, 5–6 (1966), 275–94; S. Shpan, *Massot u-Meḥkarim* (1964), 102–10: I. Rabinovich, *Be-Ḥevlei Doram* (1958), 62–100; R. Wallenrod, *The Literature of Modern Israel* (1956), index. **ADD. BIBLIOGRAPHY:** H. Barzel, *Meshorerim al Shirah* (1970); E. Zoref, *Beshulei Sipporet ve-Shirah: Masot al Agnon, Bialik ve-Shalom* (1971); H. Fisch, "On the Poetry of Sh. Shalom," in: JBA, 32 (1974–75), 7–14; R. Ben Yosef, "*Or ha-Ganuz*," in: *Ariel*, 43 (1977), 18–30; A. Lipsker, *Adam bein Tevel ve-Semel: Shalom – ha-Simbolizm be-Shirato* (1982); idem, *Temurot Poetiyyot be-Shirat Shin Shalom* (1984); S. Avneri, *Shirat Shin Shalom* (1984); Y. Akaviahu, *Noge'a be-Lev ha-Olam: Al Shirat Shin Shalom* (1992); A. Ahroni, "Shin Shalom's Highest Gift," in: *A Song to Life and World Peace* (1993), 37–43; Z. Luz, "*Meitav ha-Shir, le-Shin Shalom*," in: *Ẓafon*, 7 (2004), 245–47.

SHALOM, SILVAN (1958–), Israeli politician, member of the Knesset since the Thirteenth Knesset. Shalom was born in Gebs, Tunis, and was brought by his parents to Israel the following year. As a student at Ben-Gurion University, he served as chairman of the Students Association there on behalf of the Likud and as deputy chairman of the National Students Association. He graduated from Ben-Gurion University in economics and accounting in 1983, and worked for a period as a journalist. He received an M.A. in Public Administration in 1991 and a law degree in 1996, both from Tel Aviv University.

Shalom served as director general of the ministry of energy and infrastructure in 1989–90, when Moshe *Shaḥal of the Labor Party was minister, and as chairman of the board of directors of the Electricity Corporation in 1990–92.

Shalom was first elected to the Thirteenth Knesset on the Likud list in 1992, serving on numerous Knesset Committees. In the Fourteenth Knesset he served as chairman of the coalition in the Finance Committee, was chairman of the lobby for the advancement of soccer and of the lobby for encouraging industry in Samaria. From July 1997 to July 1998 he served as deputy minister of defense, under Yitzhak Mordechai. In July 1998 he was appointed by Prime Minister Binyamin *Netanyahu as minister of science and technology. In the government formed by Ariel *Sharon in 2001 Shalom was appointed deputy prime minister and minister of finance. When Sharon formed his second government after the elections to the Sixteenth Knesset in 2003, the Ministry of Finance was given to Binyamin Netanyahu and Shalom was appointed deputy prime minister and minister for foreign affairs. Shalom objected to Sharon's plan for disengagement from the Gaza Strip and Northern Samaria, but accepted the position of the majority, and supported it.

In December 2005 he ran for the chairmanship of the Likud after Sharon left it to form the Kadimah Party, and came in second to Netanyahu.

[Susan Hattis Rolef (2nd ed.)]

SHALOM ALEICHEM (**Sholem Aleykhem**; narrative persona and subsequent pseudonym of **Sholem Rabinovitsh (Rabinovitz)**; 1859–1916), Yiddish prose writer and humorist born on February 18, 1859 (old style; March 2, new style), in Pereyaslav (today: Pereyaslav-Khmelnitski) on the left bank of the Dnieper (Dnipro), downstream from Kiev, as the third child of Menakhem-Nokhem Rabinovitsh, a wealthy timber and grain merchant and Khave-Ester, née Zeldin. Together with Sholem Yankev *Abramovitsh (often misidentified as his fictional narrator, Mendele Moykher Sforim) and I.L. *Peretz, Shalom Aleichem is regarded as one of the three major classical writers of Yiddish literature. He rapidly achieved widespread popularity with the reading public, though it took him longer to achieve lasting critical acclaim. By canonizing Abramovitsh as the "grandfather" of Yiddish literature and castigating the facile and highly popular pulp-fiction of *Shomer, he brought aesthetic criteria to bear on Yiddish literature and became the first to see himself as occupying a position within a Yiddish literary tradition. In fact, he was barely 24 years younger than Abramovitsh, but this difference was crucial, since the political turmoil and the pogroms of the 1880s had discredited the *Haskalah or Jewish Enlightenment movement, making for an altogether more resigned, milder, and less didactic tone in Shalom Aleichem's work. He was distrustful of all ideology and could offer only aesthetic solutions to the problems of Jewish existence. It is true that he manifested considerable enthusiasm for the Zionist cause, but he does not seem to have been very sanguine about its chances of success. He promoted his vision of Yiddish writing capable of standing comparison with other literatures in the two volumes of his lavishly produced *Di Yidishe Folksbibliotek* ("The Jewish Popular Library," 1888–89) in which inter alia he published works by Abramovitsh, Peretz, and Isaac Joel *Linetsky as well as early versions of his own novels, *Stempenyu* (1889; *Stempenyu*, 1948) and *Yosele Solovey* (1890; "The Nightingale: Or the Saga of Yosele Solovey the Cantor," 1913). These novels are both restrained, tragic love stories in which self-fulfillment is sacrificed to traditional concepts of modesty; the author was not entirely successful in reconciling form and content. The *Folksbibliotek*-project was abandoned in 1890 when Shalom Aleichem lost his fortune on the stock exchange. However, his reputation owes less to his novels than to his epistolary satire, *Menakhem-Mendl* (begun in 1892; "Menakhem Mendel and Sheyne Sheyndl," 1948) and his loosely structured series of monologues, *Tevye der Milkhiker* (begun in 1895; *Tevye the Dairyman*, 1987). It was in these series that Shalom Aleichem found the style most suited to his genius, and he continued working on them almost up to the time of his death, creating personae whose voices enabled him to express his ironic view of a traditional society in crisis.

Most of his fiction, which also included the stories he wrote for Jewish holidays and his many children's stories, appeared in the first instance as feuilletons in various newspapers, being collected in book-form usually at a much later date. The ability that Shalom Aleichem had shown in these tales to capture scenes from a child's perspective found its most virtuoso expression in *Motl Peyse dem Khazns* (serialized between 1907 and 1916; *The Adventures of Mottel, the Cantor's Son*, 1953). In this cycle of stories he created a brilliantly ironic account of the misfortunes of a widow and her children and their later peregrinations from the Ukrainian market town to New York, as seen through the eyes of the youngest carefree son, Motl. Shalom Aleichem also wrote critical reviews and poems and tried writing for the stage, but without great success. In the theatre, it was dramatizations of his stories by other hands that achieved lasting fame, most notably the Tevye stories which eventually became the well-known musical drama, *Fiddler on the Roof* (1964). Shalom Aleichem was still at work on his lightly fictionalized autobiography, *Funem Yarid* (1916–17; *From the Fair: The Autobiography of Sholom Aleichem*, 1985) and the continuation of *Motl Peyse* at the time of his death. His multifarious oeuvre constitutes a Jewish *comédie humaine*, portraying the transition from the old order of traditional life to modern times. Through it runs the recurrent theme of unrealizable aspiration, followed by catastrophe and renewed hope, epitomizing courage in adversity and survival against all odds both in the Old World and the New. The tragic is constantly interwoven with the comic, while his characters and perspectives embody powers of regeneration in the face of adversity.

In 1861 his family had moved to Voronkov (Voronka), somewhat closer to Kiev, where he attended *ḥeder*. Voronkov was later to be satirized in his works as the archetypal *shtetl*, Kasrilevke. However, 10 years later Menakhem-Nokhem Rabinovitsh was defrauded and the family returned to Pereyaslav where the 12-year-old boy helped his father run a modest inn. The following year his mother died of cholera, and his father remarried. The death of his mother had a particularly traumatic effect on the young Rabinovitsh which is indirectly, almost unconsciously, reflected in a number of his works. In 1873–36, he attended the Russian secondary school (gymnasium) in Pereyaslav on a scholarship. It was during these years that he composed his first literary creation in the form of a glossary of his stepmother's curses (unpublished), thus early revealing his ability to face adversity with humor. He also began writing Hebrew biblical romances in the manner of Abraham *Mapu, his father's favorite author. After graduating with distinction from the gymnasium Rabinovitsh became a private tutor in Russian, Hebrew, and other subjects in and around Pereyaslav. The following year, as the result of a stroke of good fortune, he was offered the position of private tutor to the daughter of the wealthy merchant, Elimelech Loyev. Rabinovitsh and his teenage pupil, Olga/Hodl read Hebrew and European literature together and fell in love. Some two to three years later, becoming aware of the tender feelings between tutor and pupil, Loyev dismissed Rabinovitsh. It was at about this time that his earliest Hebrew pieces were published in the popular maskilic Warsaw newspaper, *Ha-Ẓefirah*.

Rabinovitsh now secured the office of *obshchestvenny ravvin* or government rabbi in Lubny. During the years in Lubny he contributed further pieces in Hebrew not only to *Ha-Ẓefirah* but also to *Ha-Meliẓ* on social and educational issues. In 1883 Olga came across an article by Rabinovitsh and was able to locate him through the publisher. On May 12 (old style; Lag ba-Omer) of the same year, their marriage took place in Kiev against her father's wishes. However, Loyev was soon reconciled, insisted that Rabinovitsh give up the post of *ravvin*, and invited him back to the estate at Sofiyevka, where he was able to pursue his literary activities free from financial worries.

With the appearance from 1881 onwards of Alexander *Zederbaum's (Tsederboym) St. Petersburg weekly *Dos Yidishe Folksblat*, at that time still the only Yiddish periodical, Rabinovitsh felt encouraged to pursue his enthusiasm for Yiddish literature and wrote his first Yiddish story, "*Tsvey Shteyner*" ("Two Stones," 1883) which was serialized in this periodical. This piece was dedicated to O[lga]-E[limelekhovna Loyeva]. The action is a tragic version of the romance between himself and Olga/Hodl in which the heroine commits suicide and the hero becomes deranged (thus anticipating the underlying themes of *Yosele Solovey*). Rabinovitsh later became dissatisfied with this story, hence its omission from collected volumes throughout his lifetime.

A further story, "*Di Vibores*" (1883; "The Election," 1994) was published in *Dos Yidishe Folksblat* and was signed for the first time "Shalom Aleichem." Rabinovitsh resorted to a pseudonym since this satire attacks the affluent leaders of a Jewish community, named in the story as *Fintsternish* ("darkness"), though clearly Lubny was meant. The *nom de plume*, initially intended as a temporary stratagem, became a narrative persona. Feeling that his talents lay primarily in the realm of Yiddish humor, he adopted the name permanently, and, indeed, it was eventually destined to become the appellation by which he was universally known. In *Funem Yarid* he also explains that the pseudonym was in part adopted for the sake of his family who shared the prejudices against Yiddish at that time prevalent in intellectual circles. Like "*Tsvey Shteyner*," this story was never reprinted in Shalom Aleichem's lifetime.

In November 1883 the young couple moved to Belaya Tserkov (Bila Tserkva), south of Kiev, where Shalom Aleichem at first worked as inspector of sugar estates for the Kiev Jewish millionaire, Israel *Brodsky, whose name together with that of *Rothschild was to become emblematic of fabulous wealth in Shalom Aleichem's fiction. After leaving Brodski's employ, Shalom Aleichem and Olga remained in Belaya Tserkov, financially supported by Loyev. In the early 1880s Shalom Aleichem published a number of further slight sketches, epistolary skits, and stories in *Dos Yidishe Folksblat.* Whereas in these years Shalom Aleichem's aspirations lay in the direction of the novel and he attached little importance to his feuilletonistic work, it was in these short pieces that he developed his abilities as a writer of monologues and epistolary sketches, and it was these skills that were later to avail him in the masterpieces, *Menakhem-Mendl, Tevye,* and *Motl Peyse.* As time went by, he further honed the feuilleton style which he learnt inter alia from Gogol and which became his real forte. It was precisely these monologues and sketches that earned him his popularity and in which he was able to give free rein to his ironic fantasies.

During these years in Belaya Tserkov, Shalom Aleichem and Olga began spending the summer months in a *dacha* in the village of Boyarka not far from Kiev, as they continued to do until he left Russia in 1905. This village later served as the model for the fictional village of Boyberik in the Tevye stories and other works. In 1884 their daughter Ernestine/Khaya-Ester was born, the first of six children (four daughters and two sons). In 1885 Loyev died. Shalom Aleichem inherited a very considerable fortune and ventured into business speculations in Kiev.

In 1886 the first of his stock exchange stories was published in *Dos Yidishe Folksblat* adumbrating the virtuosity of the *Menakhem-Mendl* letters. In this same year appeared *Di Veltrayze* ("Journey round the World," 1886), his first independent publication, while over the winter 1886–87 further feuilleton sketches were serialized in *Dos Yidishe Folksblat* anticipating the Kasrilevke stories.

A major landmark in Shalom Aleichem's literary career was the appearance in 1887 of "*Dos Meserl*" (1886; "The Pocket-Knife," 1920). This story attracted a particularly favorable review by Simon *Dubnow in the influential St. Petersburg Russian-Jewish journal *Voskhod,* which represented the beginning of critical acclaim for Shalom Aleichem, but it was not until considerably later that his genius was widely appreciated. The story relates the terror of a young boy unable to resist the temptation to steal a penknife from an amiable *maskil* or freethinker who lodges with his parents. The story concludes on an edifying note attributable to the waning influence of the Haskalah on Shalom Aleichem's early career. "*Dos Meserl*" epitomizes the style of Shalom Aleichem's many children's and holiday tales which revolve around minor domestic problems and their resolution seen through the eyes of child protagonists or deal with crises in the preparation for a Jewish festival that have a happy outcome. These stories were some of Shalom Aleichem's most popular works, appearing in the holiday issues of periodicals and widely enjoyed in the family circle, making Shalom Aleichem's name truly a household word. "*Dos Meserl*" and "*Tsvey Shteyner*" were translated into Russian and came to the favorable attention of Leo Tolstoy and Maxim Gorki.

That same year Shalom Aleichem wrote "*Legboymer*" ("Lag ba-Omer," 1887) in memory of that festival in 1883 when it fell on May 12, i.e., his wedding day. The story relates how a group of *kheyder* lads escape their *rebbe*'s birch for a day and sally forth into the countryside on Lag ba-Omer only to be assailed by a gang of Ukrainian youths and so badly beaten that their leader, Zyame, altogether eludes any further flogging by the *rebbe*, since after three weeks in bed he dies. This was also the year in which Shalom Aleichem moved with his family to Kiev, the model for his fictional Yehupets, to deal on the stock exchange.

In 1888 Shalom Aleichem began his life-long campaign for higher standards in Yiddish literature with two publications. *Shomers Mishpet* ("The Trial of Shomer," 1888) constituted a savage attack on pulp-fiction, especially that of Nokhem-Meyer Shaykevitsh, known as Shomer, at the time by far the most popular of Yiddish authors, a prolific writer of sentimental pulp fiction whose plots were usually lifted from the works of Charles Paul de Kock, Alexandre Dumas père, or their like. Shalom Aleichem accuses Shomer of corrupting the Jewish people with escapist and morally dubious fantasies which bear no relation to the realities of Jewish life. In "*Der Yidisher Dales in di Beste Verk fun Undzere Folks-Shriftshteler*" ("Jewish Poverty in the Best Works of Our National Writers," 1888) he distinguished between such trashy romantic *shund* and realistic works such as *Fishke der Krumer* (1869; *Fishke the Lame*, 1920) by Abramovitsh, whom he dubs the *zeyde* ("grandfather") of Yiddish literature. A number of other writers are similarly singled out for praise on account of the realism of their works including Isaac Meir *Dik, Linetsky, Abraham *Goldfaden, and Mordecai *Spector. It is Shalom Aleichem's view that events portrayed in serious literature must be realistic and plausible within the framework of Jewish society. His novel, published the same year, *Sender Blank un Zayn Gezindl* ("Sender Blank and His Household," 1887) with its flights into the world of pure fantasy is a parody of the *shund*-novel, but at the same time it is severely critical of the vulgar insensitivities of the Jewish plutocracy, thus anticipating a theme which was to reappear frequently in his works.

However, by far his most significant achievement at this time was his editing of *Di Yidishe Folksbibliotek*. The publication of this annual or anthology of the best of earlier and contemporary writing in Yiddish was made possible by the considerable financial resources which Shalom Aleichem had inherited from his father-in-law. Before its collapse, *Di Yidishe Folksbibliotek* appeared in two volumes published in Kiev in 1888–89. The first volume comprised items by authors such as Linetsky and Abramovitsh, as well as pseudonymous pieces by himself, including "*Lider funem Kheyder: Vinter*" (1888; "Song of the Kheyder," 1994), signed Shlumiel. "Grandfather" Mendele (Abramovitsh) was encouraged to return to writing in Yiddish and was represented by the revised and expanded prologue and first part of his "*Dos Vintshfingerl*" (1888; *The*

Wishing Ring, 2003). In addition, Shalom Aleichem had persuaded Peretz, who had previously published only in Hebrew and Polish, to contribute his extraordinary narrative poem "*Monish*" (1888; "Monish," 1939) for which Shalom Aleichem paid him the unprecedented fee of 300 rubles. It is interesting to observe that in the process of editing Peretz's text, Shalom Aleichem found it necessary to remove the author's frequent Polonisms in the interest of a wider readership. Peretz resented Shalom Aleichem's having done so without consultation, and for a number of years relations between the two men were soured. There were also contributions from David *Frishman and Simon Samuel *Frug, who had hitherto written exclusively in Hebrew and Russian respectively and who had both had their Yiddish literary debuts only a few months earlier in *Dos Yidishe Folksblat*. The first volume concludes with a short essay, "*Etlekhe Verter vegn Zhargon Oysleyg*" ("A Few Words concerning Yiddish Spelling," 1888) in which Shalom Aleichem calls for a standard orthography and a grammar of the Yiddish language, while advocating that homophones should be differentiated by their spelling and that the orthography of words from the Germanic component should be approximated to the German spelling. In the *baylage* ("supplement") appeared Shalom Aleichem's novel *Stempenyu*. Though in some ways resembling *Sender Blank*, this was Shalom Aleichem's first consciously Jewish romance, and it appeared with a prefatory letter to *zeyde* Mendele whose counsels had inspired it.

When his father died in that same year, Shalom Aleichem gave literary expression to his mourning in *A Bintl Blumen* ("A Bouquet of Flowers," 1888), a literary bouquet laid on his father's grave, subsequently shortened and revised as "*Blumen*" ("Flowers," 1903). This pamphlet comprised 18 stories, including "*Koysl Marovi*" ("The Western Wall"). His father had been a lover of Hebrew literature and had nurtured ambitions for his son in this direction. The death of his father did have the incidental effect of relieving Shalom Aleichem from the pretense of not being a Yiddish writer.

The second volume of *Di Yidishe Folksbibliotek* comprised Shalom Aleichem's comedy "*Di Asife*" ("The Assembly," 1889), signed Shulamis, whose protagonist is a *ravvin*, as until recently he had been himself, and "*A Briv tsu a Gutn Fraynd*" ("A Letter to a Good Friend," 1889) in which he replies to criticism that had been made of "*Stempenyu*": "It is necessary to observe," he writes, "that a young Jewish woman is unlike other women in the world." Gentile heroism may well consist in giving free reign to the passions; Jewish heroism consists in controlling one's feelings. Furthermore, fictional characters must be figures with whom the common people can identify. Formerly authors had protagonists who were either angels or demons, but modern readers demand characters whom are closer to psychological reality. This volume contains the second part of Abramovitsh's "*Dos Vintshfingerl*," further items by Peretz and Linetsky as well as contributions by Frug, Abraham Ber *Gottlober, Goldfaden, *Ben-Ami and Mikhl *Gordon.

In a supplement to the second volume of *Di Yidishe Folksbibliotek*, the novel *Yosele Solovey* appeared. As in the case of *Stempenyu*, this is a restrained, unconsummated Jewish love story in which self-fulfillment is sacrificed to customary concepts of modesty, and the traditional Jewish woman pines for her outsider hero, in this case a highly talented itinerant cantor. It ends with the death of the heroine and the madness of the hero. There are some thematic similarities with his "*Tsvey Shteyner*." At the same time a host of caricatured figures provide comic relief. The judicious fusion of comedy and pathos is in some ways reminiscent of Dickens. It is instructive to compare Shalom Aleichem's delicacy and apprehensions concerning the credibility of a Jewish love story with the uninhibited sexuality of the play *Yankl der Shmid* ("Yankl the Blacksmith," performed 1906) written less than 20 years later by David *Pinski.

The consistently high quality of the *Folksbibliotek* aroused considerable interest, and it was recognized by many as representing a turning point in the development of Yiddish literature. But the reactions were far from universally favorable. In 1889 Judah Leib *Gordon wrote in Russian to Shalom Aleichem, sharply censoring his intention to raise the status of *zhargon*-literature. At most, Gordon claimed, Yiddish might be tolerated as means of enlightening the ignorant masses, but otherwise he regarded it as the curse of the Diaspora.

In October of 1890 Shalom Aleichem was preparing to edit a third volume of *Di Yidishe Folksbibliotek* when the stock market crashed and he lost his entire fortune. He moved his family to Odessa and traveled to Czernowitz, Vienna, and Paris to escape his creditors, while his mother-in-law attempted to pay off his debts. In 1891 he returned to Russia and, with help from his mother-in-law, once again began trading on the stock exchange. The collapse of the *Folksbibliotek* in the same year as that in which *Dos Yidishe Folksblat* ceased publication deprived Shalom Aleichem of publishing outlets for Yiddish works, and in consequence he wrote nothing in Yiddish throughout 1891 and returned for a while to writing in Russian. It was during this period, inspired very largely by Nikolai Gogol's oral-style or *skaz*-monologues (as they are called by Bakhtin and the Russian Formalists), that Shalom Aleichem found the style most suited to his genius.

In 1892 Shalom Aleichem made further preparations for a third volume of the *Folksbibliotek* but lacked the financial means to bring this project to fruition. Instead he contented himself by putting everything he published in Yiddish that year into his *Kol Mevaser tsu der Yidisher Folksbibliotek* ("Advertiser for the Jewish Popular Library"), this time without contributions by others, though in a number of cases he again signed his own pieces with pseudonyms (such as Shulamis and Dr. Solomonis Rabinus). Here he published "*London*," an earlier version of "*London*" (1909), the first series of his Menakhem-Mendl letters, concerning the comic vicissitudes of an archetypal *luftmentsh* and unsuccessful speculator. Shalom Aleichem continued to extend his epistolary Menakhem-Mendl series until 1913. *Kol Mevaser*... also included the "folksong" "*Shlof, Mayn Kind*" ("Sleep My Child"), which soon became so popular that when in 1901 the major Yiddish song collection by Saul *Ginzburg and Pesach [Piotr] *Marek appeared in St. Petersburg, "*Shlof, Mayn Kind*" was listed as being anonymous.

The mid 1890s were a period of comparative literary inactivity. In May 1893 Shalom Aleichem and his family moved to Kiev, where he continued to speculate on the stock exchange and attempted to act as a commodity broker. Meanwhile he and his family continued to spend their summers in the *dacha* at Boyarka, and in the summer of 1894 a chance encounter with a vivacious dairyman delivering butter and cheese to families vacationing in the vicinity became a formative experience, since this figure would serve as the model for the series of Tevye stories which he soon began to write and on which he continued working sporadically for most of the rest of his life. Later that year he wrote *Yakneho"z, oder dos Groyse Berznshpil* ("Hocus-Pocus: Or the Great Stock-Exchange Gamble"). This was his first complete play, a satire in the style of Pushkin on the life of the speculators and nouveaux riches of Kiev in which he had been so deeply involved.

In August 1897 Shalom Aleichem attended the First Zionist Congress in Basel recording his impressions in *Der Yidisher Kongres in Bazl* (1897; "The Jewish Congress in Basel," 1984). In fact, Shalom Aleichem's interest in the Zionist cause had already begun in 1888 when he had joined the Ḥovevei Zion movement and the following year he had invited one of their most prominent leaders, Abraham Menahem Mendel *Ussishkin, to report on the welfare of the colonists in Palestine in the second volume of the *Folksbibliotek*. He turned these interests to literary account in "*Oyf Yishev Erts-Yisroel: Zelik Mekhanik*" (1890; "Selig Mechanic," 1984), a story with a propagandistic Zionist message. Immediately after attending the Basel conference, he wrote the essay "*Oyf Vos Badarfn Yidn a Land*" (1898; "Why Do the Jews Need a Land of Their Own?" 1984). It is a popular but cogently argued statement of the Zionist case: antisemitism will only be overcome when Jews have a state in Palestine. The same year, while living in Berdichev, he incorporated some of these ideas into *Meshiekhs Tsaytn: A Tsienistisher Roman* ("Messianic Times: A Zionist Novel," 1890).

In 1900 Shalom Aleichem wrote "*Der Zeyger*" (1900; "The Clock That Struck Thirteen," 1900), one of his "stories for Jewish children," a slight monologue told by an anonymous narrator and inhabitant of Kasrilevke about his grandfather's pendulum clock that had been in the family for generations and was his pride and joy. It served the whole town as its time-piece, despite the *maskil*'s hair-splitting attempts to prove it a minute or two fast, until, that is, the day it struck thirteen. More and more hopeless attempts are made to repair the clock, but finally, just in the middle of an exciting story, it collapses under the weight of the heavy objects that have been attached to the pendulum to try and keep it going. Everybody was understandably distressed, and the narrator, still a child, had nightmares about the clock. The prevailing atmosphere is one of melancholy recognition of the obsolescence of tradition. It has even been asserted that the story embodies a subliminal reference to the death of his mother when the young Rabinovitsh was still only 13.

That same year Shalom Aleichem wrote his famous satire *Der Farkishefter Shnayder* (1900; "The Haunted Tailor," 1979). This, the most Gogolian of Shalom Aleichem's stories is typical of his genre of fantastic tales. The narration is in the macaronic style of an old *pinkes* or chronicle and tells the story of a henpecked yet opinionated and self-important tailor, Shimen-Elye Shma Koleynu, who is persuaded by his wife to go to the neighboring *shtetl* to buy a goat so that his numerous hungry children may have an ample supply of milk. Halfway between the two villages he stops at an inn belonging to his cousin Dodi to whose lack of learning he tactlessly alludes. Returning with the goat he has purchased he spends the night at the inn. When he arrives home the next day, the goat is unmilkable. Yet, when he attempts to return the goat, the *melamed*'s wife, from whom he bought it, milks it in front of the rabbi's court. Back at home the story repeats itself and the tailor is taken ill, accepting the innkeeper's story that the goat is bewitched. It is left to the reader to draw the conclusion that the innkeeper took his revenge by switching the female goat with a male goat (and vice versa) each time the tailor passed through. The characterization is largely achieved through the formulaic words of the characters. In addition to the humor that arises from Shimen-Elye's solecisms and his conflations of Aramaic and Ukrainian, an element of irony is introduced in that the theme of duplicitous substitution is suggested to the mind of the reader by the references to Rachel and Laban.

In the early years of the new century Shalom Aleichem was already supporting himself and his large family almost entirely by writing, especially for the St. Petersburg and Warsaw daily papers. By 1903, in fact, he felt able to abandon business activities altogether. It was during this period that he wrote many of the stories in his Kasrilevke series, including among others "*Kasrilevker Tramvay*," "*Kasrilevker Hoteln*," "*Kasrilevker Restoranen*," "*Kasrilevker Vayn un Kasrilevker Shikirim*," "*Kasrilevker Teater*," "*Kasrilevker Sreyfes*," and "*Kasrilevker Banditn*" (1901; "Transportation," "Hotels," "Restaurants," "Liquor," "Theater," "Fires," "Bandits," collected in English as *A Guide to Kasrilevke*, 1973). Most of the Kasrilevke stories satirize *shetl* life in Voronkov and Berdichev. Over the years, while revising his works, Shalom Aleichem gradually brought more stories into this cycle by inserting the name Kasrilevke where previously he had written Berditshev, Mazepevke, or some other toponym. The ethos of these stories may be exemplified by "*Dreyfus in Kasrilevke*" (1902; "Dreyfus in Kasrilevke," 1979). Zeydl is the only person in Kasrilevke who subscribes to a newspaper, and it is through him that the inhabitants of Kasrilevke anxiously follow the second Dreyfus trial, which took place in 1899. When once more a guilty verdict is pronounced, they simply cannot believe it. "*Se kon nit zayn!*" ("It is impossible") shout the outraged inhabitants of Kasrilevke, and it is not the judges or false witnesses in Paris whom they blame but Zeydl. "Idiots," replies Zeydl and thrusts the newspaper into their faces, but they just refuse to understand. "Who was right?" asks the narrator in conclusion. The well-known story "*Ven Ikh Bin Roytshild*" (1902; "If I Were Rothschild," 1979) was also written in 1902 and also belongs to the same cycle. This is the monologue of a Kasrilevke *melamed* whose wife is pestering him for money for the coming Sabbath. If he were rich, he muses, not only would he make sure that his wife had enough so that he could pursue his teaching in peace, he would not only provide for the sick and the poor in Kasrilevke, but he would endow yeshivot and ensure that even the Gentiles had no need to go to war. In fact, he might even abolish money altogether which is surely the root of every evil inclination, but then how would he provide for the Sabbath right now? The story combines realistic observation of the crushing poverty of the *shtetl* with a touching portrayal of the unworldly aspirations of many of its inhabitants. A further Kasrilevke story written at this time was "*Oysgetreyselt*" (1902; "A Yom Kippur Scandal," 1979) which was subsequently included in the "*Kleyne Mentshelekh mit Kleyne Hasoges*" series. This famous tale takes the form of an anonymous narration of the scandal that was reported to have arisen when a Litvak visitor was apparently robbed of 1,800 rubles in the Kasrilevke synagogue during the Yom Kippur service. The rabbi immediately ordered the doors to be locked and for everyone's pockets to be turned out. All comply with the exception of Leyzer-Yosl, the much-lauded son-in-law of the local magnate, who makes all manner of excuses to avoid being searched. When finally his pockets are examined, gnawed chicken bones are found, to his own shame and to the mortification of the rabbi, but to the huge amusement of the townsfolk. "'Well,' we all asked with one voice, 'and what about the money?' – 'What money?' asked the man innocently, watching the smoke he had exhaled. – 'What do you mean – what money? The 1,800 rubles!' – 'Oh,' he drawled. 'The 1,800. They were gone.' – 'Gone?' – 'Gone for ever.'" There is masterly irony in the laconic pacing of this dénouement.

At this time Shalom Aleichem also revised four volumes of his works which the Folksbildung publishing house in Warsaw issued as *Ale Verk fun Shalom Aleichem* ("The Complete Works of Shalom Aleichem," 1903). This was the first of several collected works published during his lifetime and subsequently, and was an important milestone in his literary career. This title was, however, a misnomer. Neither this collected works edition nor any of its successors was ever even remotely comprehensive. Then in August 1904, Shalom Aleichem edited *Hilf: a Zaml-Bukh fir Literatur un Kunst* ("Help: An Anthology for Literature and Art") and himself translated three stories submitted by Tolstoy as well as contributions by other prominent Russian writers in aid of the victims of the Kishinev pogrom.

In 1904 Shalom Aleichem was still living with his family in Kiev in a degree of comfort and tranquility that he had seldom experienced before and was at work on feuilletons, monologues, Kasrilevke and Tevye stories for *Der Fraynd* (St. Petersburg), *Der Veg* (Warsaw) and other papers, but this comparative calm was soon to be shattered by political events. An adumbration of the turmoil to come is to be found in Shalom Aleichem's story "*Yoysef*" (1905; "Joseph," 2004) which appeared in *Der Veg*. This is the monologue of a conceited but not altogether despicable young fop who confesses "in confidence" to the writer how he is besotted by a girl who waits at table in her mother's restaurant. She, however, adores Yoysef, a Bundist conspirator, so the narrator ingratiates himself with the Bundists, talks about Karl Marx and August Bebel and attends a clandestine meeting in the forest at which Yoysef speaks. He observes that the earnest young men at the meeting are dressed in Gorki-style black blouses (a style that Shalom Aleichem himself affected from time to time). When the *dzhentlmen*, as the conspirators call him, finally asks Yoysef for his advice, he simply recommends speaking to the girl directly, since he has no time for such trifles. The conspiracy is discovered and Yoysef is arrested. Returning from a business trip the *dzhentlmen* finds that the restaurant has disappeared.

Literary reflections of political ferment were soon followed by all too real historical events. In October Shalom Aleichem and his family lived through the three days of the Kiev pogrom associated with the failed 1905 revolution. As angry mobs surged through the streets, the family sought refuge in the Hotel Imperial. After these experiences Shalom Aleichem resolved to leave and moved via Radziłłow and Brody to Lemberg (today: Lvov) in Austrian Galicia. Whereas others had lost faith in Russian liberalism two years earlier in the aftermath of the Kishinev pogrom, for Shalom Aleichem 1905 was the turning point. A further motive for leaving Russia may have been his apprehension that his political satires could have unpleasant consequences. What little financial security there had been in the Kiev years disappeared and, although he was by now the most famous of Yiddish writers, whose works were enjoyed by a vast readership, he was now cut off from his publishers. He began a reading tour that took him to many points in Galicia and Romania. Leaving his family in Geneva, where Abramovitsh was at the time, he continued his reading tour to Paris and London. From this time on Shalom Aleichem became increasingly dependent financially on enervating but hugely successful lecture tours, and it was only on such tours that he ever again returned to Russia.

In 1906 Shalom Aleichem made his first visit to the United States, arriving on October 20 in New York, where he was given an exhilarating welcome in both the Yiddish and English-language press. Two plays were commissioned from him, and the Hearst Press offered him a lucrative contract. Shalom Aleichem remained in the Bronx for some months and on February 8, 1907, a dramatization of *Stempenyu*, produced by Boris Tomashevski, was staged at the People's Theater, while on the same night "*Der Oysvorf: oder Shmuel Pasternak*" ("The Outcast: Or Shmuel Pasternak"), a version of *Yakneho"z* which Shalom Aleichem had specially adapted for Jacob Adler, was performed at the Grand Theater. Both plays were excessively sentimentalized for the New York theater audience, and both were box-office disasters. Meanwhile Hearst's *Jewish American* collapsed and Shalom Aleichem was unable to interest the Yiddish press in his *Motl*. In the early summer he returned to Geneva via The Hague, a disappointed man.

In August Shalom Aleichem attended the 8th Zionist Congress in The Hague as the delegate of New York Federation of American Zionists. It was here that he met Ḥayyim-Naḥman *Bialik for the first time and formed a close friendship with him. His impressions of this event are recorded in "*Ayndrukn fun Tsionistishn Kongres*" (1907; "Impressions from a Zionist Congress," 1984). In the early autumn he went on holiday in the Alps near Geneva and invited Bialik to visit him there. They were joined by Abramovitsh and Ben-Ami as well. It was at this time that the four of them posed in a photographer's studio for the famous comic portrait showing them in a boat with Shalom Aleichem standing behind holding an upright oar. He describes this meeting in "*Fir Zenen Mir Gezesn*" (1908; "Once There Were Four," 1979). It was at this time that Shalom Aleichem was diagnosed with tuberculosis.

Shalom Aleichem's continued preoccupation with the Kiev pogroms of 1905 and their aftermath were reflected in his novel *Der Mabl* ("The Flood") which was serialized 1907–8 in *Vorhayt*. In 1918 the novel appeared in book-form under the title *In Shturem* (*In the Storm*, 1984). This novel reflects the reactions of progressive Jewish youth to the pogroms to which Shalom Aleichem and his family had come all too close. Embodied in the lives of the protagonists, we see the tensions that existed between universal and national solutions to Jewish social problems. The original title implied that a "flood" would sweep away cruelty and violence. The change in title indicates a subsequently less sanguine view of social progress.

In 1908 Shalom Aleichem was once again compelled by financial constraints to undertake a reading tour in Russia. He had by now become famous for his recitations, and the tour went well until in early August in Baranovichi, some distance north of Pinsk, he suffered a severe recurrence of tuberculosis and was diagnosed as having open pulmonary tuberculosis. After two months of rest in Baranovichi itself, he moved to the resort of Nervi on the Ligurian coast for further recuperation. This setback was to some extent offset by the celebration of his 50th birthday and 25 years of literary creativity in 1909. A committee of authors secured the rights to his works and returned them to him, thus ensuring him a permanent income. During this period some of Shalom Aleichem's works began to appear in Russian translation and met with much critical acclaim.

In Nervi, perhaps realizing that his health prognosis was not very favorable, Shalom Aleichem made a first start on his autobiography *Funem Yarid*. However, he soon set it aside in order to work on other projects including his *Ayznban-Geshikhtn* (*Railroad Stories*, Engl. 1987), which were written and published over a period stretching from 1902 to 1911, although of the 20 stories that eventually constituted this series, as many as nine were written in various sanatoria during this period of convalescence in 1909. In these stories Shalom Aleichem skillfully exploits a situational framework of fleeting encounters, such as he must often have experienced when traveling between venues on his frequent and grueling reading tours and paints a picaresque composite picture of the precarious economic circumstances of Jews living in those western parts of the Russian Empire in which they were permitted to reside. Dan Miron shrewdly observes that it is a token of the increasing modernity of Shalom Aleichem's work that his narrators become progressively less severe in their critique of social reality. The traveling salesman is a "caricature of the maskilic 'watchman' or the Mendelean sarcastic commentator" [*Image*, p. 334].

Two of these *Railroad Stories*, both written in 1909, may serve to characterize this important cycle in Shalom Aleichem's oeuvre. "*Stantsye Baranovitsh*" (1909; "Station Baranovich," 1979) is named after the very station at which Shalom Aleichem himself had almost died the year before. The narrator heard the story from his father who had it from his own father. It happened in the days of Nikolai I. Kive, a Jew who had permitted himself a number of injudicious remarks, was condemned to run the gauntlet. Reb Nisl, the narrator's grandfather arranges a simulated funeral and then slips Kive over the border into Austrian Galicia. From then on Kive sends begging letters, threatening to return and confess. Finally he threatens to send Reb Nisl's letters to the police. At that point the train arrives in Baranovichi. The narrator hurriedly alights and the story is never finished. "May Station Baranovichi burn to the ground!" This is almost a shaggy-dog story in which much of the ironic humor lies in the ploys with which the narrator plays his audience much as Shalom Aleichem does his. What, after all, would the devoted readers of Shalom Aleichem's *Ayznban-Geshikhtn* have done had Shalom Aleichem really died? "*A Khasene on Klezmer*" (1909; "The Wedding That Came without Its Band," 1979) is a story told to the narrator one hot afternoon in a railway compartment by a merchant with a penchant for euphemistic irony who relates the humorous side of the 1905 pogroms. On this occasion the arrival of the drunken pogromists was delayed just long enough by the blessed inefficiency of the railway for the Cossacks summoned by the police superintendent to arrive and establish order. That salvation should take the form of a regiment of mounted Cossacks is in itself highly ironic.

Shalom Aleichem's unhappy experiences with the New York Yiddish theater found expression in the serialization between 1909 and 1911 of *Blondzhende Shtern* (*Wandering Star* (sic), 1952). The themes bear comparison with those of *Stempenyu* and *Yosele Solovey*, and the novel takes the form of a complex and picaresque story in which two Jewish artists make their way from the *shtetl* to Second Avenue. The hero is a brilliant star on the Yiddish stage who degenerates both as artist and human being in the New World, unlike the heroine, a singer, who ventures outside the narrowly Jewish world and preserves her integrity. The affinity with Charles Dickens, who was much admired by Shalom Aleichem, is particularly clear in the Whitechapel scenes.

Between 1909 and 1913 Shalom Aleichem and his family moved between health resorts in Nervi and the French Riviera, in the winter, and Switzerland and St. Blasien in the Black Forest, in the summer. Despite ill health and feverish literary activity, this was once more a relatively tranquil and secure interlude in Shalom Aleichem's life. This was also the period in which the "Jubilee" edition of his works in 16 volumes *Ale Verk: Yubileum Oysgabe* ("Complete Works, Jubilee Edition," 1909–15) was prepared for publication. This edition, which was interrupted owing to difficulties during World War I, did much to establish Shalom Aleichem's literary reputation which had earlier been belittled in some quarters.

The fourth volume of the *Yubileum Oysgabe* (1910) comprises *Menakhem-Mendl* (1910; *The Letters of Menakhem-Mendl and Sheyne-Sheyndl*, 2002). This is the so-called "canonized version" of the Menakhem-Mendl letters that were further, but somewhat unsatisfactorily, expanded as *Menakhem-Mendl: Nyu-York-Varshe-Vin-Yehupets* (1913; *The Further Adventures of Menachem-Mendl: New York – Warsaw – Vienna – Yehupetz*, 2001). Taken together these series of letters somewhat loosely constitute an epistolary novel, in part inspired by Abramovitsh's *Kitser Masoes Binyomin Hashlishi* (1878; *The Travels and Adventures of Benjamin the Third*, 1949). The textual history is somewhat complex, but the 1910 version is the most artistically cohesive. To some extent a self-portrait, though Shalom Aleichem sought to minimize this perception in his introduction to this second edition, Menakhem-Mendl travels from place to place naïvely confident in the imminence of prosperity, meanwhile corresponding with his down-to-earth and skeptical wife, Sheyne-Sheyndl. She urges him to forget his harebrained schemes and hurry home. Her attitude, which is initially somewhat credulous, becomes increasingly skeptical and eventually downright contemptuous, though in the revised versions her tone becomes less abrasive and her common sense is more sympathetically portrayed. Menakhem-Mendl is the quintessence of the *luftmentsh* trying his hand at all manner of activities, including the stock exchange and the commodity market. He acts as insurance agent, marriage broker, and journalist and eventually goes to New York, though this last episode was dropped in the final version. In the interaction between husband and wife, as Ruth Wisse has shrewdly observed, we see transferred into two characters Tevye's ironic alternation between optimism and tragic resignation. Miron refers to Menakhem-Mendl and Sheyne-Sheyndl as Don Quixote and Sancho Panza-like archetypes. Marxist critics such as Max Erik have sought to stress Shalom Aleichem's presentation of the hopelessness of Menakhem-Mendl's schemes as an implied critique of capitalism. It would be more accurate to say that Menakhem-Mendl's misfortunes are symptomatic of the arbitrary restrictions placed by the czarist regime on Jewish enterprise, but this is too narrow a perspective. Menakhem-Mendl's willingness to believe that at any moment he will make his fortune and finally free himself and his family from material worries is an ironic reflection of the theme of utopian and eschatological hope that runs through much of Jewish literature.

The fifth volume of the *Yubileum Oysgabe* comprises *Motl Peyse dem Khazns* (1911; *The Adventures of Mottel, the Cantor's Son*, 1953). Shalom Aleichem was at work on *Motl Peyse* from 1907 right up to a few days before his death. It is a fragmentary novel whose first-person narrator is initially almost nine years-old and may be about 11 by the end of the second part, though his putative age has been the subject of some controversy. After the death of his father and the forced sale of the family's household goods, Motl immigrates with his mother to the U.S. in what Seth Wolitz perceptively describes as a carnivalesque Exodus or secular burlesque of the *Haggadah*, with the flight from the slavery under the czar across the European wilderness and the Atlantic to the promised city. The critical irony results from the discrepancy between Motl's carefree perception of what are for him wonderful adventures and the perils endured by his mother and indeed the whole community of Russian Jews constantly threatened by pogroms. Meanwhile Motl, rather like Huckleberry Finn, is preoccupied with his blithe pranks or with helping his elder brother in comically vain efforts to make money by selling ink or *kvas*. The omission of chapters 5 and 16 from volume 5 was occasioned by the publisher's wish to promote the volume as being suitable for children. For the complete text see either vols. 18 & 19 of the Folksfond edition of *Ale Verk fun Shalom Aleichem* ("Complete Works of Shalom Aleichem," 1920) or Khone Shmeruk's exemplary edition which follows the 1913 Progres text.

The seventh volume of the *Yubileum Oysgabe* (1911) comprises the *Tevye der Milkhiker* cycle which by this point was almost complete. The full cycle consists of the following episodes: 1. "*Kotoynti*" (1903; "I Am Not Worthy," 1994), which had been included in 1895, is omitted from the *Yubileum Oysgabe* and was advisedly not reprinted until after the author's death. In this prefatory letter, the reader is introduced to the eponymous hero for the first time. Tevye is overawed by Shalom Aleichem's condescending to put him "in a book" and is ashamed of his supposed lack of learning. However, "*Kotoynti*" and "*Vakhalaklakoys*" (1918; "Tevye Reads the Psalms," 1969), far from adding anything, detract somewhat from the poignancy of the stories concerning Tevye's daughters; 2. "*Dos Groyse Gevins*" (1903; the revised version of the story originally entitled "*Tevye der Milkhiker*," 1895; "Tevye Strikes It Rich," 1979) and relates how Tevye, a country Jew, who struggles to improve his knowledge of scripture, became a dairyman as a result of the generosity of two Yehupets ladies to whom he had given a lift after they had lost their way in the forest; 3. The sequel is "*A Boydem*" (1899; "The Bubble Bursts," 1949) which relates how Tevye entrusts his savings to his distant relative, Menakhem-Mendl, who loses everything on the Yehupets stock-exchange; 4. In "*Hayntike Kinder*" (1899; "Modern Children," 1949) it is related how Tevye's eldest daughter, Tseytl, chooses to marry the sickly young tailor, Motl Kamzoyl, rather than the rich elderly butcher, Leyzer-Volf; 5. "*Hodl*" (1904; "Hodel," 1946) was written just one year before the outbreak of the 1905 revolution. Tevye is offered a financially attractive match for Hodl, his second daughter, but it transpires that she is secretly betrothed to Pertshik, a revolutionary whom Tevye had invited to tutor his daughters, an ironic allusion perhaps to Shalom Aleichem's own romance with Olga/Hodl some quarter of a century earlier. After a hasty wedding, Pertshik departs on a secret mission, is arrested and exiled. As Hodl leaves to join her husband in Siberia, Tevye, who prides himself on his manly stoicism, weeps bitter tears; 6. "*Khave*" (1906: "Chaveh," 1948) is the story of Tevye's third daughter who elopes with an autodidact Ukrainian clerk whom she regards as a "second Gorki." Tevye attempts to intervene with the village priest but is rebuffed. In accordance with halakhic requirement and despite the promptings of his heart, Tevye performs ritual mourning for his daughter as though she were dead and rejects her when she accosts him in the forest. There is considerable irony in the fact that the threat of assimilation is associated with the name of Gorki, a writer much admired by Shalom Aleichem; 7. "*Shprintse*" (1907; "Shprintze," 1995) relates how, after the political upheavals of 1905, many wealthy Jews fled from the cities to the countryside, and Tevye had good business delivering diary products to their *dachas*. The feckless son of a rich widow woos Shprintse, Tevye's fourth daughter. At first Tevye is apprehensive but gradually warms to the idea, beginning once again to dream of the acts of charity he would be able to perform as the father of a millionairess. Suddenly, however, Tevye is summoned by the widow's brother who treats Tevye as a wily schemer and offers him money as compensation for breach of promise. Tevye is so shocked that he simply turns on his heels. Shprintse drowns herself; 8. In "*Tevye Fort keyn Erts-Yisroel*" (1909; "Tevye Goes to Palestine," 1995), Shalom Aleichem meets a well-dressed Tevye traveling on a train. In the meantime his wife, Golde, has died and his youngest daughter, Beylke, in order to ease her father's misfortunes, has married the proverbially rich Pedahtsur, a parvenu who had made a fortune during the Russo-Japanese war. By now Tevye realizes that even Hodl had done better with her exiled revolutionary idealist. In Pedahtsur's ostentatious mansion, Tevye is a silent witness to his daughter's misery. Embarrassed by Tevye's humble profession, Pedahtsur is ready to pay for him to go to Palestine. Tevye, who has always dreamed of visiting Rachel's tomb and the Western Wall, accepts the offer, expecting never to see his children again. In 1911 Shalom Aleichem saw Tevye's departure for Palestine as the culmination of the cycle. However, three years later, he added one more story together with an epilogue; 9. In "*Lekh-Lekho*" (1914; "Get Thee Out," 1949) after an interval of many years Shalom Aleichem encounters Tevye once more. The planned journey to the Holy Land had been abandoned when Pedahtsur had gone bankrupt and Motl Kamzoyl had died leaving Tevye responsible for his daughter, Tseytl, and her children. In 1905 pogroms had begun in the large towns and became widespread. The peasants, with whom Tevye had lived in the village in peace for decades, come to his house explaining that, though they have nothing against him personally, they have no choice but at the very least to break a window or two. But this is nothing compared to what happens at the time of the trial of Menahem Nendel *Beilis, when he is driven out of his village. At the moment of departure, Khave returns to share her family's misfortunes. Tevye asks Shalom Aleichem whether he was right to be forgiving, but Tevye, whose grandchildren are waiting, has to leave before Shalom Aleichem has time to answer.

"*Vakhalaklakoys*" is the sequel to "*Lekh-Lekho*." It was first published posthumously at the time of the editing of the Folksfond edition. Shalom Aleichem once again meets Tevye on a train and Tevye takes the opportunity to elaborate further on how it was back in 1905, when the *hromada* or rural assembly had decreed that the Jews be made to feel the wrath of the general community. Tevye had quick-wittedly devised a test to determine whether God truly wanted him to suffer or not, in which the peasants had to attempt to repeat tongue-twisters such as "*vakhalaklakoys*" and "*memaymakim*." The choice of these words is, of course, not determined solely by their refractory phonetic qualities, but represents yet another level of Tevye's (and the author's) irony: "Let them be confounded and put to shame that seek after my soul: let them be turned back and brought to confusion that devise my hurt… Let their way be dark *and slippery*: and let the angel of the Lord persecute them" (Ps. 35:4–6); "*Out of the depths* have I cried unto thee, O Lord. Lord hear my voice: let thine ears be attentive to the voice of my supplications" (Ps.130:1–2). It is sometimes held that Tevye has a shaky grasp of scripture and that his supposedly clumsy misquotations are an element in Shalom Aleichem's humor. Roback for example speaks of "malapropisms" and much the same view is taken by Butwin. More accurate assessments are offered by Michael Stern, Hillel Halkin, and Joseph Sherman: the truth is that Tevye is always in control of his quotations, and whether he cites literally, in modified form or, as he occasionally does when addressing a Pedahtsur or a Leyzer-Volf, in deliberate doggerel, it is always to appropriate ironic effect. When considering Tevye and his quotations – which serve also to anchor the narrative within the context on Jewish literary tradition – it is well to bear in mind that they represent a kind of mythopoeia, a use of language to transcend an unsatisfactory environment, and as such Tevye is a correlative of Shalom Aleichem, and of the artist in general.

The peasants meanwhile not surprisingly fail Tevye's test and in recognition of the fact that Tevye has lived peaceably among them for so many decades and that he is "a Jew, certainly, but not a bad man," they allow him to break a couple of his own windows *pro forma*. Tevye concludes by bemoaning the insecurity of the Diaspora, but emphasizes by contrast the naturally superior intelligence of Jews which imposes upon them higher moral obligations. Tevye's final word is that should the Messiah not come in the meantime, then perhaps he and Shalom Aleichem may meet again in Yehupets, Odessa, Warsaw, or even America, but in the meantime Shalom Aleichem should give his greetings to the Jews he meets, tell them not to worry and say that "our ancient God lives." Although supposedly related, Menakhem-Mendl and Tevye are very different characters, but they have in common that each episode takes them to a new crisis or catastrophe from which they "bounce back," as Miron puts it, by the power of their fortitude.

The figure of Tevye was based in part on the real-life model encountered in Boyarka but was at the same time inspired by Abramovitsh's itinerant hero, Mendele, a fact to which Shalom Aleichem makes a veiled allusion, as Ken Frieden has noted, in "Hayntike Kinder." Tevye sees himself as a modern Job and alternates between restrained altercations with the inscrutable deity and total resignation. Though he loses his home, his wife, and his daughters, his outlook remains one of self-ironizing good humor. In the revised versions, the narration is entirely in Tevye's voice, enlivened by polyphonic embedding of the disparate voices that Tevye constantly cites. Indeed, it may be said that one of Shalom Aleichem's most characteristic strengths is his ear for distinctive, idiosyncratic discourse, as is also seen clearly in the monologues and the railroad stories.

Though Shalom Aleichem gently mocks would-be social reformers, social tensions nevertheless form an important part of the thematic structure of his Tevye-cycle and of his works in general. An important theme is the contrast between grinding rural penury and the affluence of Jewish urban bourgeoisie of Yehupets (i.e., Kiev). Inequalities of wealth, generational conflict and the contrast between the genders are seen as a microcosm of the strains in Jewish social life in late 19th-century Russia. The political disillusionment that sets in after the collapse of the 1905 revolution is echoed in the contrast between Hodl's idealism and Beylke's resigned pragmatism. Also much in evidence is the dichotomy between Tevye's frequently asserted faith that God will provide and the acerbic skepticism that he applies to the dilemmas of daily life.

The celebration of the beauty of nature in the Ukrainian landscape re-echoes similar passages in Abramovitsh, while the topic of animal welfare is reflected in the story "*Tsar-Balekhayim*" ("Pity for Living Creatures," 1968) and elsewhere.

In 1914 Shalom Aleichem wrote four film screenplays in Russian that were never produced or published, but which included an adaptation of *Tevye* which was utilized in part by Charles Davenport in 1919 when he directed his silent film *Khave*. In 1915 Shalom Aleichem also wrote a dramatized version of the Tevye stories "*Khave*" and "*Lekh-lekho*," entitled "*Tevye der Milkhiker: A Familyen-Bild in Fir Aktn*" ("Tevye the Dairyman: A Family Portrait in Four Acts," 1923), which the famous actor and director Maurice *Shwartz staged in Vienna in 1924. In 1939 Shwartz filmed *Tevye der Milkhiker* which became one of the most successful of all Yiddish movies. In 1925 *Menakhem-Mendl* was adapted for the cinema under the direction of Alexander *Granovsky as *Yidishe Glikn* ("Jewish Luck") with inter-titles by Isaak *Babel and with Solomon *Mikhoels in the role of Menakhem-Mendl. The most celebrated transformation of Shalom Aleichem's Tevye stories was the musical, *Fiddler on the Roof* (1964), with a score by Sheldon Harnick and Jerry Bock.

The 12th volume of the *Yubileum-Oysgabe* (1912) comprises "Marienbad" (1911; *Marienbad*, 1982), an epistolary novel. Shalom Aleichem returns here to social milieux comparable to those depicted in *Yakneho"z*, creating a comedy of manners in which the vain pretensions of the superficial nouveau-riche Jewish bourgeoisie of Warsaw is exposed to biting satire, tempered by Shalom Aleichem's compassionate understanding of the all-too-human folly which drives their actions. The work consists of a polyphony of epistolary voices exemplifying a wide range of Yiddish registers from the *Galitsyaner* to the *Litvak*, from the Russified speech of Odessa to the semi-illiterate writing of the lottery winner, or to the pretentious Hebrew of pompous fools. Equally interesting from the socio-linguistic point of view is the high status accorded to German, which various characters attempt to employ with varying degrees of accuracy. The complex plot of *Marienbad* involves numerous wealthy Jews and their wives mainly from Nalewki Street in Warsaw, but also from Kishinev, Bialystok, Odessa, etc., whose spouses are in Marienbad nominally in order to take the waters, but who are in reality more concerned with flirting, playing cards, or securing matches for their daughters. "The world has changed," as the main female protagonist, Beltshi Kurlender, writes to her husband in Warsaw, and these characters, whose ancestors had for centuries lived the traditional life of the *shtetl*, have seen their world transformed by wealth and are themselves often amazed at the changes their lives have undergone. Not so far, perhaps as to permit anything particularly reprehensible to occur, but through misunderstandings, gossip, and the malice born of blind jealousy, severe matrimonial strife and at least one divorce result. Bourgeois Jewish Warsaw and Tevye are, of course, worlds apart, but the Yamaytshikhe and Tevye have in common the problem of finding matches for numerous daughters. The action is datable to the summer of 1911 on account of the mention of the visit of the *shadkhn*, Svirski, to the 10th Zionist Conference, which Shalom Aleichem himself attended in Basel in August. Note also the irony with which Khayim Soroker, for example, laments his failings as a writer, while his wife, Ester, compares his letters to a feuilleton.

In 1911 Shalom Aleichem's works began to appear in the Hebrew translation of his son-in-law, the Yiddish and Hebrew writer Y.D. Berkovitz, *Kitvei Shalom-Aleikhem* ("Works of Shalom-Aleichem," 3 vols., Warsaw, 1911–13). In fact, Shalom Aleichem had been participating in the preparation of this edition from 1905 onwards. The relationship of Shalom Aleichem's Russian and Hebrew works to his Yiddish oeuvre has still to be adequately investigated, but it may be said that, in a manner which is similar to the gestation of many of Mendele's works and anticipates the relationship between the Yiddish and English versions of the works of Isaac *Bashevis Singer, Shalom Aleichem worked together with Berkovitsh and made changes to the text, especially the endings, during the process of translation, and these emendations were in turn adopted in subsequent Yiddish editions.

The 16th volume of the *Yubileum-Oysgabe* (1915) comprises an incomplete version of the novel *Blutiker Shpas* (the complete text is only to be found in the 1923 two-volume edition; *The Bloody Hoax*, 1991). This novel was later dramatized and popularized as *Shver tsu Zayn a Yid* ("It's Hard to Be a Jew," 1948). It explores the complexities of Jewish-gentile relations and narrates the romantic complications arising in the household of Dovid Shapiro as the result of the exchange of identities between the talented Jewish student, Hershl Shneyerson, who lacks a *pravozhitel'stvo* or residency permit and is unable to secure a university place, and his friend, Ivan Ivanov, the privileged son of a Russian general.

In 1913 Shalom Aleichem commenced work on a truly comprehensive edition of his works that was planned to comprise 40 volumes. In fact, only 28 volumes appeared posthumously (1917–23).

In the spring of 1914 he set out on a reading tour of Russia which was to take him to 20 cities including Warsaw, where he visited Peretz (see: "*A Vokh mit Y.L. Perets*" ("A Week with I.L. Peretz," 1915). At the beginning of World War I, Shalom Aleichem was taking a holiday on the Baltic coast of Germany following the conclusion of his Russian tour. As an "enemy alien" he was obliged to leave Germany and managed to reach Copenhagen, where he remained for several months in ill health and without financial support until he was able to embark for the U.S., where he arrived with his family (except for his eldest son, Misha) in December. In New York he was once again given an enthusiastic welcome and a reception was organized for him in Carnegie Hall, but serious support was not forthcoming. Cut off from his income in Europe, he was obliged to undertake further reading tours and wrote for the New York Yiddish press. He was diagnosed as having incipient diabetes, but was not in a financial position to spend the winter in the south as his doctors advised.

In 1915 Shalom Aleichem's autobiography, *Funem Yarid*, was serialized in *Der Tog*. In the past he had made several attempts to begin this work, but it was not until 1913, while living in Switzerland, that he began writing *Funem Yarid* in earnest. He lived to write two and a half of the projected 10 parts. In its incomplete form, the story covers the author's childhood and his romance with Olga Loyeva up to the moment at which they are about to be parted. It is noticeable that the cyclical structure of this work is comparable to that of *Tevye*, *Menakhem-Mendl* and other works with their ever recurring *peripeteiai* of the stroke of luck followed by catastrophe.

On September 19, 1915, while living in Lenox Avenue in Harlem, Shalom Aleichem was deeply shocked to hear of the death of Misha, from tuberculosis in a sanatorium in Copenhagen. On receiving this shattering news, Shalom Aleichem decided to rewrite his "*Tsavoe*" (1923; "The Last Will and Testament of Shalom Aleichem," 1994).

Despite failing health, financial difficulties compelled him to undertake yet another reading tour in 1916. One of his last stories, "*A Mayse mit a Grinhorn*" (1916; "Business with a Greenhorn," 2004), was published in *Di Vorhayt* in January. This monologue is told directly to the reader, without the need for Shalom Aleichem to act as addressee, in the voice of Mr. Baraban, a Jewish-American businessman, full of complacent contempt for the "greenhorn," potentiated by ugly sexual jealousy. This is a portrait of sheer meanness in the ruthless commercial atmosphere of New York City and is further evidence of Shalom Aleichem's growing disillusionment with the purported advantages of the New World. The story is so interlarded with Anglicisms that Berkovitz found it necessary to append a glossary, and it is evidence of Shalom Aleichem's uncannily accurate ear for language that after a comparatively brief acquaintance with the U.S. he was able to make virtuoso, satirical use of this register. In this context it is interesting to note that in a high proportion of the surviving portraits of Shalom Aleichem, he is depicted with his pocket notebook in his hand and it was undoubtedly to his habit of constantly noting down the turns of phrase that he heard around him that much of the accuracy of his narrative voices may be attributed.

On May 13, 1916, shortly after moving to Kelly Street in the Bronx and while still at work on the last unfinished chapter of *Motl Peyse dem Khazns*, Shalom Aleichem died of tuberculosis. Vast crowds attended his funeral, and he was mourned throughout the Jewish world. He was buried in the "Honor Row" of the Arbeter Ring section of the Mount Carmel Cemetery in Queens, New York.

After his death his popularity continued to increase not only with the Yiddish readership, but also in translation, especially in Russian, English, and Hebrew. In the 1920s and 1930s Shalom Aleichem's reputation grew steadily as the result of positive evaluation by such critics as *Baal-Makhshoves, M. *Wiener, Maks *Erik, Elye Spivak and I.J. *Trunk.

Works and Correspondence

The most complete edition of Shalom Aleichem's works to date is the *Folksfond* edition in 28 vols., 1917–25, reprinted several times. Valuable for its critical introductions is the 16-vol. edition of the *Oysgeveylte Verk* ("Selected Works," Moscow, 1935–41). In 1948 a critical edition of Shalom Aleichem's collected works was initiated in Moscow by N. Oyslender and A. Frumkin. Only the first three volumes (of a projected 20) appeared. These include the complete Yiddish belletristic writings of the years 1883–90, most of which are unavailable elsewhere. The editorial work of Oyslender and Frumkin together with Kh. Shmeruk's editing of *Dos Meserl* (1983) and *Motl Peyse* (1997) serve as models for a complete critical edition of Shalom Aleichem's works, which remains an as yet unrealized desideratum.

Much of Shalom Aleichem's correspondence remains unpublished. Selections are to be found in Y.D. Berkowitz (ed.), *Dos Shalom Aleichem Bukh* (1926, 1958); *Oysgeveylte Verk* 16 (1941); A. Lis (ed.), *Briv fun Shalom Aleichem, 1879–1916* (1995). For a list of published letters to individuals see U. Weinreich, in: *Field of Yiddish* (1954), 280–1.

Selective List of Works in English Translation

Stempenyu, tr. H. Berman (1913); *Inside Kasrilevke*, tr. I. Goldstick (1945, 1973); *The Old Country*, tr. J. & F. Butwin (1946, 1973); *Sholom Aleichem Panorama*, ed. M.W. Grafstein, 1948; *Tevye's Daughters*, tr. F. Butwin (1949, 1999); *Wandering Star*, tr. F. Butwin (1952); *The Adventures of Mottel, the Cantor's Son*, tr. T. Kahana (1953, 1999); *The Bewitched Tailor*, tr. B. Isaacs (1956, 1999); *Selected Stories*, ed. A. Kazin (1956); *Stories and Satires*, tr. C. Leviant (1959, 1999); *The Tevye Stories and Others*, tr. J. & F. Butwin (1965); *Old Country Tales*, tr. C. Leviant (1966, 1999); *Some Laughter, Some Tears*, tr. C. Leviant (1968, 1979); *The Adventures of Menahem Mendl*, tr. T. Kahana (1969, 1999); *Holiday Tales of Sholom Aleichem*, tr. A. Shevrin (1979, 1985); *The Best of Sholom Aleichem*, ed. I. Howe & R. Wisse (1979, 1982); *Marienbad*, tr. A. Shevrin (1982); *Why Do the Jews Need a Land of Their Own?* tr. J. Leftwich & M. Chertoff (1984); *In the Storm*, tr. A Shevrin (1984); *From the Fair: The Autobiography of Sholom Aleichem*, tr. C. Leviant (1985, 1986); *The Nightingale: Or the Saga of Yosele Solovey the Cantor*, tr. A Shevrin (1985, 1987); *Tevye the Dairyman and the Railroad Stories*, tr. H. Halkin (1987); *Tevye the Dairyman and Other Stories*, tr. M. Katz (1988); *The Jackpot*, tr. K. Weitzner & B. Zumoff (1989); *The Bloody Hoax*, tr. A. Shevrin (1991); *Selected Works of Shalom Aleichem*, ed. M.S. Zuckerman & M. Herbst (1995); *Song of Songs*, tr. Curt Leviant (1996); *A Treasury of Sholom Aleichem Children's Stories*, tr. A. Shevrin (1996); *Nineteen to the Dozen: Monologues and Bits and Bobs of Other Things*, tr. T. Gorelick (1998); *The Further Adventures of Menachem-Mendl*, tr. A. Shevrin (2001); *The Letters of Menakhem-Mendl & Sheyne-Sheyndl and Motl, the Cantor's Son*, tr. H. Halkin (2002). Many further translations have been published in anthologies, journals and collections including *Classic Yiddish Stories of S.Y. Abramovitsh, Sholem Aleichem, and I.L. Peretz*, ed. K. Frieden (2004).

Biography

No critical biography of Shalom Aleichem has yet been written, but there is a rich memoir literature: Y.D. Berkovitsh, *Ha-Rishonim ki-Vnei Adam: Sippurei Zikhronot al Shalom-Aleikhem uVnei-Doro* (1938–43, 1959, 1976[3]), tr. as *Undzere Rishoynim* (1966); Y.D. Berkovitsh, "Memories of Sholem Aleichem," tr. K. Frieden (from *Dos Shalom Aleichem Bukh*), in K. Frieden (ed.), *Classic Yiddish Stories* (2004), 207–40; V. Rabinovitsh, *Mayn Bruder, Shalom Aleichem: Zikhroynes* (1939); M. Waife-Goldberg, *My Father, Sholom Aleichem* (1968, 1971). Attempts at objective biography are to be found in U. Finkl, *Shalom Aleichem, 1859–1939* (1939); U. Finkl, *Shalom Aleichem: Monografye* (1959).

BIBLIOGRAPHY: B. Borokhov, "Di Bibliografye fun Shalom Aleichem," in: *Shprakhforshung un Literatur-Geshikhte* (1966), 218–67; L. Fridhandler, "Guide to English Translations of Sholom Aleichem," in: *Jewish Book Annual*, 45 (1987–88), 121–42; D.N. Miller, "Sholem-Aleichem in English: The Most Accessible Translations," in: *Yiddish*, 2/4 (1977), 61–70; U. Weinreich, "Principal Research Sources" and "Guide to English Translations of Sholom Aleichem," in: *The Field of Yiddish* (1954), 278–84, 285–91; Y. Yeshurin, in: *Tevye der Milkhiker* (1966), 256–84. RESEARCH: Many thousands of articles and reviews have been written on Shalom Aleichem's works. The following selection is of necessity very limited: Z. Rejzen, in: *Leksikon*, 4 (1929), 673–736; Z. Zilbercweig, in: *Leksikon fun Yidishn Teater*, 4 (1963), 3309–578; LNYL, 8 (1981), 677–720; A. Aharoni, *Shalom-Aleikhem be-Or Ḥadash* (2002); Bal-Makhshoves, "Shalom Aleichem," in: *Geklibene Shriftn*, 1 (1929), 91–100; Y. Dobrushin, "Shalom Aleichems Dramaturgye," in: *Tsaytshrift*, 2–3 (Minsk, 1928), 405–24; I. Druker, *Shalom Aleichem: Kritishe Shtudyen* (1939); M. Erik, "Oyf di Shpurn fun Menakhem-Mendlen," in: *Bikhervelt*, 1 (1928), 3–10; 2 (1928), 13–17; K. Frieden, "Sholem Aleichem: Monologues of Mastery," in: *Modern Language Studies*, 19 (1989), 25–37; *idem*, *Classic Yiddish Fiction, Abramovitsh, Sholem-Aleichem, and Peretz* (1995), 95–224; Y. Glatshteyn, "Menakhem-Mendl," in: *In Tokh Genumen* (1947), 469–84; J. Hadda, *Passionate Women, Passive Men* (1988), 43–55; H. Halkin, introductions to *Tevye the Dairyman and the Railroad Stories* (1987), ix–xli, and *The Letters of Menakhem-Mendl and Sheyne-Sheyndl and Motl, the Cantor's Son* (2002), vii–xxix; R. Keenoy, "Sholem Aleichem," in: *Jewish Writers of the Twentieth Century* (2003), 530–3; S. Liptzin, *The Flowering of Yiddish Literature* (1963), 88–97; C.A. Madison, *Yiddish Literature: Its Scope and Major Writers* (1971[2]), 61–98; D.B. Malkin, *Ha-Universali be-Shalom-Aleikhem* (1970); N. Mayzl, *Undzer Shalom Aleichem* (1959); D. Miron, *The Image of the Shtetl and Other Studies* (2000), 128–334; S. Niger, *Shalom Aleichem: Zayne Vikhtikste Verk, Zayn Humor un Zayn Ort in der Yidisher Literatur* (1928); A. Norich, "Portraits of the Artist in Three Novels by Sholem Aleichem," in: *Prooftexts*, 4:3 (1984), 237–51; N. Oyslender, "Der Yunger Shalom Aleichem un Zayn Roman *Stempenyu*," in: *Shriftn fun der Katedre*, 1 (1928), 5–72; L. Prager, "Shalom Aleichem's First Feuilleton Series," in: *Jewish Book Annual*, 44 (1986–7), 120–31; D.G. Roskies, *Against the Apocalypse* (1984), 163–95; D. Sadan, "*Sar ha-Humor*," in: *Avnei Miftan* 1, (1961), 26–56; M. Samuel, *The World of Sholom Aleichem* (1973); N. Sandrow, *Vagabond Stars: A World History of Yiddish Theater* (1996), 179–83; Kh. Shmeruk, *Ayarot u-Khrakhim: Perakim bi-Yẓirato shel Shalom-Aleikhem* (2000); E. Spivak, *Sholem Aleykhems Shprakh un Stil* (1940); Y.Y. Trunk, *Shalom Aleichem, Zayn Vezn un Zayne Verk* (1937); idem, *Tevye un Menakhem-Mendl in Yidishn Velt-Goyrl* (1944); S. Werses, "Shalom-Aleikhem: ha-Arakhot ve-Gilguleihen ba-Aspaklaryah shel Ḥamishim Shenot Bikoret," in: *Molad*, 133–34 (1959), 404–21; M. Viner, *Tsu der Geshikhte fun der Yidisher Literatur in 19tn Yorhundert*, 2 (1946[2]), 235–378; M. Waxman, *A History of Jewish Literature*, 4:1 (1960[2]), 507–21; J. Weitzner, *Sholem Aleichem in the Theatre* (1994); R.R. Wisse, *The Schlemiel As Modern Hero* (1971), 41–57; idem, *The Modern Jewish Canon* (2000), 31–64; idem, *Sholem Aleichem and the Art of Communication* (1980).

[Hugh Denman (2nd ed.)]

SHALOM ALEIKHEM (Heb. שָׁלוֹם עֲלֵיכֶם; "peace be upon you").

(1) A form of greeting common among Jews. The reply to the greeting is *aleikhem shalom* (Heb. עֲלֵיכֶם שָׁלוֹם; lit. "upon you be peace"). The greeting is mentioned, in the singular form in the Talmud: "A teacher should be greeted with 'Peace to thee, my master,' and should be answered (if he makes the first greeting) with, 'Peace be with thee, my master and teacher'" (Ber. 27b, and Rashi ad loc.; see also Sh. Ar., YD 242: 16). In modern Hebrew, the greeting is often shortened to *shalom* (see Form of *Greetings).

(2) Opening words of hymn welcoming Sabbath angels to the home. It is recited by the head of the family upon re-

turning from the synagogue on the Sabbath eve. The hymn, which is of late composition, is known only in the Ashkenazi rite. It is based on the talmudic statement (Shab. 119b) that on the Sabbath eve two ministering angels accompany every Jew from the synagogue to his home.

BIBLIOGRAPHY: Davidson, Oẓar, 3 (1930), 465 no. 1268.

SHALOM BEN YIZḤAK OF NEUSTADT (c. 1350–c. 1413), talmudist, teacher of Jacob *Moellin, in whose works there is much information on him. Shalom apparently lived for a time in Vienna and is therefore sometimes referred to as "Maharash of Vienna," but moved to Neustadt. His teachers were his father, whose interpretations of *halakhah*, kabbalah, and the Torah he quotes, Israel of Krems, and other Austrian rabbis. He established a yeshivah at Neustadt, later known as the yeshivah of Israel Isserlin, which was one of the most important in Austria.

His two sons – Yonah and Yudel – served as rabbis in Vienna and in Neustadt, respectively, and are mentioned several times in his book of sermons. Yonah died a martyr's death, following the edict of 1420 in Austria.

The responsa of Shalom are scattered throughout the rabbinical works of his contemporaries and of his disciples, and constitute reliable source material for the history of the Austrian Jews. S.Y. Spitzer has published *Hilkhot u-Minhagei R. Shalom (Derashot Maharash)* (1977), containing 546 items dealing with various laws of the Shulḥan Arukh, which is also valuable source material for the customs of Ashkenazic Jews of his time, the organizational and economic conditions of the Jewish communities, and the relations between Jews and non-Jews. His works reflect the harsh conditions under which the Jews of Central Europe lived at the end of the 14th century.

BIBLIOGRAPHY: S. Spitzer, *Halakhot u-Minhagei Rabbeinu Shalom mi-Neustadt (Decisions and Customs of R. Shalom of Neustadt)*, Introduction 10–24 (1977).

[Yehoshua Horowitz]

SHALOM SHAKHNA BEN JOSEPH (d. 1558), founder of talmudic scholarship in Poland. He came from an affluent family and was a pupil of Jacob *Pollak. At an early age he was appointed rabbi and *rosh yeshivah* in Lublin. His letter of appointment as chief rabbi of Lesser Poland by the government in 1541 is still in existence. It even included the right of capital punishment. His yeshivah soon became known as a great center of study to which students flocked from all over Europe, and his rabbinical court attained countrywide prominence. From that time on Lublin was a center for Talmud study and one of the important communities, where from time to time the *Council of Four Lands held its meetings. His mode of study closely adhered to the casuistic method of **pilpul*. None of his works is extant; our knowledge of him is derived from the statements of his son, Israel, and those of his distinguished disciples, such as Moses *Isserles, his son-in-law, who refers to him in terms of great esteem (responsa 41, 61), *Ḥayyim b. Bezalel, and Benjamin Aaron Solnik (cf. also the letter of his son Israel to Isserles, *ibid.* 25), David Gans, *Ẓemaḥ David*, 1 (1592), 314, and the preface of Ḥayyim Bezalel to his *Vikku'aḥ Mayim Ḥayyim* (1712). These statements, mostly in Isserles' responsa, reveal his logical and sound common sense, avoidance of dogmatism, and due consideration for contemporary circumstances and needs. As a result, he was reluctant to have his decisions be accepted as final, and for the same reason refused to write any halakhic work. Nevertheless, some of his written responsa have been found and printed. He showed considerable independence and firmness (responsa, Solomon *Luria (16); Meir of Lublin (138) and *Masat Binyamin* (16) of Benjamin Aaron Slonik).

BIBLIOGRAPHY: S.A. Horodezky, *Shelosh Me'ot Shanah shel Yahadut Polin* (1945), 15ff.; Ch. Tchernowitz, *Toledot ha-Posekim*, 3 (1947), 38ff.; Zinberg, Sifrut, 3 (1958), 171ff.; Fishman, in: *Sinai*, 4 (1939), 218–20; Assaf, *ibid.*, 532ff.

[Shlomo Eidelberg]

SHALON (Friedland), RAḤEL (1904–1988), Israeli engineer. Born in Poland, Raḥel Shalon went to Palestine in 1925. She served in the *Haganah (1925–48), and was a major in the Israel Defense Forces. She became professor of civil engineering at the Haifa Technion in 1952; dean of the School of Graduate Studies, 1958–62; and senior vice president in charge of research in 1963. She wrote "Cement and Concrete" (1939) and "Cementitious Materials" (1964), and edited the monthly *In the Field of Building* from 1952. Shalon was chairwoman of international research committees on building in hot climates.

SHALTIEL, DAVID (1903–1969), Israeli soldier and diplomat. Born in Hamburg of a Sephardi family, Shaltiel went to Palestine in 1923 and served in the French Foreign Legion from 1926 to 1931. In 1932 he returned to Palestine and joined the *Haganah, for which he became an arms purchasing agent in Europe. Arrested by the Nazis in 1936, he was freed through Haganah efforts in 1939. In 1940 he established Haganah counterintelligence and was chief of Haganah intelligence (1941–42, 1946–48). He was the commander of Jerusalem during the *War of Independence, and received the rank of *alluf*. In 1950 Shaltiel was appointed Israel military attaché in France, Benelux, and Italy. He was minister to Brazil and Venezuela (1952–56), minister (then ambassador) to Mexico and the Caribbean Islands (1956–59), and from 1963 to 1966 ambassador to Holland.

BIBLIOGRAPHY: Dinur, Haganah, 2 pt. 3 (1963), index.

[Netanel Lorch]

SHAMGAR (Heb. שַׁמְגַּר), son of Anath, deliverer of Israel who flourished in the period of the Judges. According to Judges 3:31, he saved Israel by slaying 600 Philistines with an oxgoad. The Song of Deborah describes the times in which Shamgar lived as so dangerous that the highways were unused, travelers preferring to walk through the safer byways (Judg. 5:6). The reports about Shamgar are unusual in that no information of a personal or family nature is given about his tribal affiliation, the exact time at which he lived, or the duration of his influence. It is not said that he judged Israel, nor are his death or burial recorded. It is only known that he lived after *Ehud and before *Deborah. The name Shamgar appears to be of Hurrian origin and may well be *Šimig-ar*(*i*), "[the god] Shimike gave." "Anath" was the name of a Canaanite goddess. It may have a mythological association or it may refer to the birthplace of the hero, a Canaanite town in Galilee. There is no certainty, therefore, that Shamgar was an Israelite. The connection between his exploits against the Philistines and the report of Judges 5:6 is also unclear. It is not likely that he attempted to clear the roads of marauding Philistine bands, since at the time of Deborah (c. 1125 B.C.E.) the Philistines did not yet constitute a threat to Israel. Some scholars believe that Shamgar was a foreign oppressor who, like Sisera later on, may have brought northern Palestine under his control and oppressed the Israelites. The author of the late reference in Judges 3:31 would thus have derived Shamgar, the Israelite judge, from the older Song of Deborah (5:6), a misappropriation which transformed a foreign oppressor into an Israelite judge. This view is also highly unlikely since the Song of Deborah parallels Shamgar with Jael, who is clearly pro-Israelite. It has been observed that Shamgar's adventure bears striking resemblance to those of *Samson, who also used the jawbone of an ass to slay the Philistines (Judg. 15:15–16). In fact, he may have belonged to the time of Samson.

BIBLIOGRAPHY: W.F. Albright, in: JPOS, 1 (1921), 55–62; Noth, Personennamen, 122–3; B. Mazar, in: *Palestine Exploration Fund* (1934), 192–4; J.T. Milik, in: BASOR, 143 (1956), 3–6; Bright, Hist, 157; Y. Kaufmann, *Sefer Shofetim* (1962), 112, 134; F. Ch. Fensham, in: JNES, 20 (1961), 197–8; C. Gordon, in: A. Altmann (ed.), *Biblical and Other Studies* (1963), 13.

[Nahum M. Sarna]

SHAMGAR, MEIR (1925–), Israel jurist. Born in Danzig, Shamgar arrived in Palestine in 1939. Arrested for underground activities in the Irgun Ẓevai Le'ummi, he was held under administrative detention by the Mandatory authorities from 1944 until 1948. Later, as a colonel of the Israel Defense Forces, he was Military Advocate-General from 1961 until 1968. Appointed Israel's attorney-general in 1968, he appeared for the government in the dramatic Shalit "Who is a Jew?" case and in the Sussman Inquiry Commission into the El Aksa fire. In 1971 he led an investigation into crime and from 1972 devoted most of his time to various economic offenses and gained a reputation for hard but fair investigating and prosecuting. As a member of Prime Minister Rabin's "think tank," he took an active part in the drafting of the legal formulation of the Israel-Egypt disengagement agreement after the Yom Kippur War. He was appointed to the Supreme Court in 1975 and in 1983 he became president of the Supreme Court, a position he held until 1995, when he retired. As a justice Shamgar was a staunch defender of freedom of expression, ruling in favor of the media when their democratic rights were challenged. As president of the Supreme Court, he worked to improve the administrative systems of the courts, introducing methods of supervision, reporting, and control. He also oversaw the move to the new Supreme Court building. In 1996 he headed the commission investigating Yiẓhak Rabin's assassination. In 2005 he received the Democracy Award for his contribution to Israeli democracy.

[Alexander Zvielli / Shaked Gilboa (2nd ed.)]

SHAMI, YITZḤAK (1888–1949), Hebrew writer. Born in Hebron, he taught in Ekron, Damascus, and Philippopolis (Plovdiv), Bulgaria. In 1919, he returned to Hebron where he served as a teacher and was active in the Jewish community. He moved to Tiberias in 1926, and finally settled in Haifa in 1930.

His first short story, "*Ha-Akarah*," set in the Sephardi community, was published in *Ha-Omer* (1907). Subsequently his stories dealing with the Sephardi and Arabic milieu of Palestine appeared in various literary journals in Palestine and abroad (including *Ha-Tekufah*, *Ha-Shilo'ah*). His collected stories, with an introduction by Asher Barash, were published posthumously (*Sippurei Yitzḥak Shami*, 1951). A new edition of *Nikmat ha-Avot* with an introduction by G. Shaked appeared in 1975. *Hebron Stories*, a collection in English translation with an introduction by Arnold J. Band, appeared in 2000. For English translations of his works, see Goell, Bibliography, p. 75.

BIBLIOGRAPHY: A.H. Elḥanani, *Siḥat Soferim* (1960), 195–202; B.I. Michali, *Le-Yad ha-Ovnayim* (1959), 133–45; I.R. Molho, *Nekuddot Ḥen me-ha-Olam ha-Sephardi ba-Dorot ha-Aḥaronim* (1958), 50–57. **ADD. BIBLIOGRAPHY:** Z. Ogen, *Y. Shami*, in: *Bikkoret u-Farshanut*, 21 (1986), 35–52; N.R. Bersohn, "Y. Shami's Stories: A Western Approach to a Near Eastern Milieu," in: *Modern Hebrew Literature*, 4:1 (1978), 3–9; G. Shaked, *Ha-Sipporet ha-Ivrit*, 2 (1983), 68–82; Y.H. Halevi, "*Minhagim ve-Halikhot bi-Yẓirato shel Y. Shami*," in: *Mehkarei Yerushalayim be-Folklor Yehudi*, 15 (2003), 97–116; H. Hever, in: *Tarbiz*, 71:1 (2003), 151–64.

[Getzel Kressel]

SHAMIR (Heb. שָׁמִיר), kibbutz in northern Israel on the Golan slope and the eastern rim of the Ḥuleh Valley, 8 mi. (12 km.) S.E. of Kiryat Shemonah, affiliated with Kibbutz Arẓi ha-Shomer ha-Ẓa'ir. Shamir was founded in 1944 by a group from Romania who previously maintained a temporary camp near Ramat Yoḥanan. Until the *Six-Day War (1967) the kibbutz was a border settlement, exposed to Syrian artillery. It struggled to reclaim for agriculture its hilly land, covered with basalt boulders. Shamir's economy improved when it was allocated land in the Ḥuleh Valley, particularly after the completion of the drainage project there. In 1968, Shamir had 430 inhabitants, increasing to 546 in 2002. It raised irrigated field crops (in partnership with Kibbutz *Amir and Kibbutz *Sedeh Neḥemya), deciduous fruit orchards, beehives, cattle, and poultry. The kibbutz specialized in honey production and operated optical and nonwoven fabric plants. The name Shamir, meaning "sharp stone" or "corundum," hints also at the Ha-Shomer ha-Ẓa'ir movement.

WEBSITE: www.shamir.org.il.

[Efraim Orni / Shaked Gilboa (2nd ed.)]

SHAMIR, MOSHE (1921–2004), Hebrew author. Shamir was born in Safed and raised in Tel Aviv. He was a member of the *Ha-Shomer ha-Ẓa'ir movement and held a position on its national board. From 1941 to 1947 he was a member of kibbutz Mishmar ha-Emek, and in 1944 joined the Palmaḥ. He founded and edited the literary magazines *Yalkut ha-Re'im, Daf Ḥadash*, and *Massa*, and edited *Ba-Maḥaneh*, the underground weekly of the *Haganah and later the official weekly of the Israel Defense Forces. From 1969 until 1971 he headed the Jewish Agency Aliyah Department in London.

In the initial stage of his career Shamir was interested predominantly in the human aspect of social, class, and national problems. In *Yalkut ha-Re'im* he published several stories which were highly critical of kibbutz life and were not included in later collections of his works. This attitude is reflected even in some of his stories for children. In his short stories for adults, the moral is less obvious, although he is still concerned with problems of class and social structure ("*Nashim Meḥakkot ba-Ḥuẓ*," "*Yihyeh Ḥam Yihyeh*"), human problems in the kibbutz ("*Ḥut ha-Zemer ha-Nizḥi*," "*Ad Or ha-Boker*"), and problems of immigration and the Holocaust ("*Em ha-Hardofim*").

Many of Shamir's articles and stories are devoted to Israel's struggle before and during the War of Independence, especially in the stories included in *Ad Eilat* (1950). These works are general emotional apotheoses of the goals and achievements of the *yishuv*. The native-born Israel hero who is committed to the ideals and goals of his country and whose life and personality are shaped by them attains its romantic crystallization in the novel *Hu Halakh ba-Sadot* (1947). The hero, Uri, the young Israeli, grows up amid family entanglements in his kibbutz home and reveals his traits of courage, ruggedness, hidden sensibility, cruelty, and honesty by his dedication to his family, to Mikah (his refugee girlfriend), to his comrades in the Palmaḥ, and in his military activities. Uri became the central figure in Shamir's works and appears in various guises in two main variations: first, as the born leader capable of stirring groups to action, exemplified by Alik in his stories for youth: "*Eḥad Efes le-Tovatenu*" (1951) and "*Alik ve-ha-Kallaniyyot*," whose early chapters resemble the above stories. Other evolutions of this central character are Ami in the play *Kilometer 56* (1949) and the slum children in "*Shekediyyot Yafot*" and "*Aggadot Lod*"(1958; in *Nashim Meḥakkot ba-Ḥuẓ*). A more complex and obscure variant appears as Moshe, first in *Taḥat ha-Shemesh* and in its sequel *Ki Eirom Attah* (1951).

Shamir's historical novels show a turning-point in his work. The central character did not change, but the author's attitude toward him underwent a severe crisis. The earlier unrestrained apotheosis disappeared, and instead the hero's motives were criticized. By placing him in a different historical context (Alexander Yannai of the Hasmonean era), Shamir reveals how the positive qualities of his hero – leadership and determination –lead in a dialectic manner to negative results. Alexander Yannai, himself a victor over oppression, evolves into a cruel tyrant until his brother Absalom, who had idolized him, revolts against him. Shamir also turns his attention to the psychological make-up of the ruler whose ends justify his means in the historical-biblical novel *Kivsat ha-Rash* (1956). Here, and in even a sharper manner in his play *Milḥemet Benei-Or* (1955), Shamir reaches an utter negation of hero worship, in the character of King David, who crushes Uriah in order to achieve his egotistical aims. In *Ki Eirom Attah*, a novel, his theme is the intellectual and erotic revolt of youth against the collectivist values Shamir once lauded. He sets the novel in the 1930s and takes up several problems which concerned Israel's intellectual world in the 1950s. The hero who rebels against the values of his movement reflects the Shamir of the 1950s, questioning the validity of the *sancta* of his youth.

Shamir's novel *Ha-Gevul* (1966) deals with the condition of Israeli society in the 1960s. One of the heroes of this society, Rafi Orlan, becomes tired of his style of life and finds his way into the no-man's land between Jewish and Arab Jerusalem. The novel attempts to describe the Israeli "decline" in the 1960s, the feeling of being under siege, the UN soldiers, the *nouveau riche*. Those who live on the border provide the background of the work.

Positive social themes likewise dominate Shamir's plays. Despite his questioning of the nationalist-pioneer values of his youth, in the end he reaffirms them (*Beit Hillel*, 1951; *Leil Sufah, Sof ha-Olam*, 1954; *Gam Zo le-Tovah*, 1958; *Shettei Shabbatot, Ad Or ha-Boker*). Only in two later plays, *Me-Aggadot Lod* and *Ha-Ramkol*, does he deviate from this position, both in his artistic presentation (atmospheric lyricism in lieu of naturalism) and in his ideological point of view. In two plays, *Ha-Layla la-Ish* and *Ha-Yoresh*, Shamir deals with social criticism, as he did in the novel *Ha-Gevul*.

Shamir is a romantic capable of writing on many subjects. His best works are those novels written in the naturalist genre. He depicts his stories against broad and rich backgrounds, has a keen sense of structure, and utilizes complex narrative techniques. Mythological motifs play a role in *Ki Eirom Attah*, and a vast architectural scope surrounds *Melekh Basar va-Dam* (1951). Likewise he tried his hand at epistolary technique in *Ha-Gevul*, a novel in which he also varies the narrative point of view.

Shamir began to write in a high literary style filled with pathos; his descriptions are elaborate and his dialogues contain a mixture of Arabisms and slang. *Sof ha-Olam* is also written in the dialect of Israel's various ethnic communities. In *Melekh Basar va-Dam*, he attempted to imitate the language of the Mishnah, but in *Kivsat ha-Rash* he decided against the attempt to imitate the biblical language. His dramatic abilities fall short of his narrative talents. Most of his plays are staged stories (see below) whose dramatic adaptations prevent an adequate characterization. In the two plays *Ha-Layla la-Ish* and *Ha-Yoresh* he tried to introduce modern techniques (flashbacks taken from the style of Arthur Miller and the epic sense of Berthold Brecht) without allowing these techniques to distort the subject of the drama. After the Six-Day War, Shamir turned to political endeavors through his identification with the "Greater Israel" movement. He served in the Ninth Knesset (1977–1981) as a representative of the Likud. His works, *Ḥayyai Im Ishma'el* (1968) and *Nes Lo Karah Lanu* (1968), are to be understood against this background. After the Camp David Agreement, Shamir left the Likud and was a founder of the nationalist Teḥiyyah party. In 1988 he was awarded the Israel Prize for Hebrew fiction.

His works comprise the following – Novels: *Hu Halakh ba-Sadot* (1947, appeared in four editions, and was later dramatized and performed), *Taḥat ha-Shemesh* (1950, revised edition 1956), *Bemo Yadav* (1951, five editions), *Melekh Basar va-Dam* (1954, ten editions; *The King of Flesh and Blood*, 1958), *Kivsat ha-Rash* (1957, four editions, translated into English), *Ki Eirom Attah* (1959), *Ha-Galgal ha-Ḥamishi* (1961; *The Fifth Wheel*, 1961), *Ha-Gevul* (1966); a saga of a pioneering Israel family entitled *Raḥok Mi-Peninim* – part one, *Yonah mi-Ḥazer Zarah* (1973), part two, *Hinomet ha-Kallah* (1984), part three, *Ad ha-Sof* (1991); plays: *Hu Halakh ba-Sadot* (1948, performed by the Cameri Theater), *Kilometer 56* (1949, performed by Orot Theater), *Beit Hillel* (1951, performed by Habimah Theater), *Sof ha-Olam* (1954, performed by Ohel Theater), *Milḥemet Benei Or* (1955, performed by the Cameri Theater), *Gam Zo le-Tovah* (1958, performed by Ohel Theater), *Ḥamishah Ma'arekhonim* (1959, performed by several groups), *Ha-Yoresh*; children's Stories: "*Yedidav ha-Gedolim shel Gadi*" (1947), "*Eḥad Efes le-Tovatenu*" (1951), "*Kullam be-Yaḥad*" (1959); miscellaneous: "*Poreẓei ha-Derekh li-Yrushalayim*" (1948), *Ad Eilat* (1950, short stories and sketches), *Nashim Meḥakkot ba-Ḥuẓ* (1952, stories), *Ha-Ḥut ha-Meshullash* (1956, stories, 3 editions), *Be-Kulmos Mahir* (1960, articles, essays, literary sketches). The 1990s saw the publication of Shamir's poems (*Kim'at Kol ha-Shirim*, 1991), collections of essays, such as *Protokol shel Mappolet* (1991), and the biography of Reuben Hecht (1994). Shamir's last work was the biographical novel titled *Yair* (2001), the life story of Avraham "Yair" Stern, the leading figure of the Leḥi underground movement, who in a way represented Shamir's historical and national world view. Translations into English include the story *Until Daybreak*, which is included in the anthology bearing this title (ed. by Amos Oz, 1984), and the play *He Walked through the Fields*, which is available also in Herbert S. Joseph (ed.), *Modern Israeli Drama* (1983).For other works in English see Goell, Bibliography, index as well as the ITHL website at www.ithl.org.il.

BIBLIOGRAPHY: D. Aran, in: *Massah*, 2 (1952); M. Tochner, in: *Beḥinot be-Vikkoret ha-Sifrut*, 3 (1953), 30–5; S. Zemach, *ibid.*, 2 (1952), 9–25; G. Shaked, *Gal Hadash ba-Sipporet ha-Ivrit* (1970), 13–6, 21f., 31–41; idem, in: *Bamah*, 3 (1959), 39–42; E. Schweid, *Shalosh Ashmorot* (1964), 185–201; D. Patterson, in: *Judaism*, 7 (1958), 337–44; I. Gour, in: *Bamah* (1971), no. 48–9, 21–64; D. Miron, *Arba'ah Panim ba-Sifrut ha-Ivrit Bat Yameinu* (1962), 343–75. **ADD. BIBLIOGRAPHY:** D. Patterson, "Moshe Shamir," in: *Israeli Writers Consider the "Outsider"* (1993), 100–1; N. Gertz, "The Book and the Film: He Walked through the Fields," in: *Modern Hebrew Literature*, 15 (1995), 22–6; S. Nash, "The Clash of Ideologies and Heroes in Shamir's Trilogy," in: *Between History and Literature* (1997), 65–80; E. Fuchs, "Public Men, Private Women: Women in Shamir's Novels," in: *Shofar*, 16:1 (1997), 74–84; N. Frenkel, *Ha-Terilogiyah Raḥok Mi-Peninim: Madrikh Iyyuni* (2000); L. Permuter, "'Le brebis du pauvre,' roman de Moshe Shamir," in: *Yod*, 8 (2002–2003), 97–111; Sh. Levi, "*M. Shamir, Maḥazai Yisraeli*," in: *Teatron*, 123 (October 2004).

[Gershon Shaked]

SHAMIR (Yazernitzki), YITZHAK (1915–), pre-state underground leader and Israeli prime minister, member of the Eighth to Thirteenth Knesset. Born in Ruzinoy, in Eastern Poland, Shamir studied at a Hebrew gymnasium in Bialystok, and was a member of the *Betar youth movement. He studied law in Warsaw, but immigrated to Palestine in 1935 before completing his studies and enrolled at the Hebrew University of Jerusalem. In 1937 he joined the Irgun Ẓva'i Le'ummi (IẒL), but in 1940 was one if the members who broke away from the IẒL and joined Loḥamei Ḥerut Yisrael (Leḥi), of which he was one of the founders. The following year he was arrested by the British, but managed to escape. Following the murder of the Leḥi commander, Ya'ir *Stern in 1942, Shamir became a member of the triumvirate that led the movement, and coordinated its organizational and operational activities. As one of the leaders of Leḥi, Shamir was believed to have been connected to the decision by the organization to assassinate the British Colonial Secretary, Lord Moyne, in Cairo in November 1944 – a decision executed by two members of the Leḥi. He was arrested by the British a second time in 1946, and was sent to Eritrea, but once again managed to escape, and was granted political asylum in France. He returned to Israel upon the establishment of the State, and until 1955 engaged in trade. In 1955 he was appointed to a senior post in the Mossad, in which he served until 1965, when he returned to engage in business, and played an active role in the struggle for Soviet Jewry. In 1970 Shamir joined the Ḥerut Movement, and was elected to its executive, running the party's Immigrants Department and later its Organizational Department. In 1975 he was elected chairman of the Ḥerut Executive.

Shamir was elected to the Eighth Knesset in December 1973, and was a member of the Foreign Affairs and Defense Committee and the State Control Committee. After the elections to the Ninth Knesset in May 1977, he was elected speaker of the Knesset – the first speaker from the Likud. After the resignation of Moshe *Dayan from the government in March 1980 Shamir was appointed minister for foreign affairs in his place. He continued to serve as minister for foreign affairs in Menaḥem *Begin's second government, in the Tenth Knesset, and following Begin's resignation at the end of August 1983 was chosen as the Likud's candidate to succeed him. Shamir became prime minister in October 1983, and continued to serve simultaneously as foreign minister until September 1984. Shamir led the Likud in the elections to the Eleventh Knesset in 1984, but the election results created a stalemate between the two main parties, and a National Unity Government was established with an agreement regarding a rotation in the premiership. Thus, Labor leader Shimon *Peres served as prime minister for the first two years, with Shamir serving as vice premier and foreign minister, and from 1986 to 1988 the two switched positions. In March 1987 Shamir was formally elected as leader of the Ḥerut Movement. In May, he initiated the rejection by the government of the London Agreement, concerning the calling of an international conference on peace in the Middle East, signed between Foreign Minister Peres and King Hussein of Jordan.

Shamir led the Likud in the 1988 elections to the Twelfth Knesset, and even though he had the option to establish a narrow right-wing–religious government, preferred to establish another National Unity Government. In May 1989 – a year and a half after the outbreak of the first Intifada, he joined Minister of Defense Yitzhak *Rabin in initiating a four-part plan that included a proposal to hold elections in the West Bank and Gaza Strip, for a local Palestinian leadership with which Israel could negotiate a settlement. However, when opposition to the plan within the Likud mounted, his position hardened, and in March 1990 the Labor Party left the government and initiated a vote on a motion of no-confidence in the government that resulted in his government falling. After Peres failed to form an alternative government, Shamir formed a narrow government in June 1990. In October 1991, Shamir participated in the Madrid Conference sponsored by the U.S. and Soviet governments. However, the Conference led to the disintegration of his government, and in the elections to the Thirteenth Knesset held in 1992 the Likud, once again led by Shamir, lost. Shamir did not resign from the Knesset, but in March 1993 Binyamin *Netanyahu was elected as chairman of the Likud. Shamir did not run in the elections to the Fourteenth Knesset, and became increasingly critical of Netanyhu's leadership and his having signed the Hebron and Wye River Agreements with the Palestinians.

BIBLIOGRAPHY: A. Na'or, *Ideologiyyah ve-Ivvutei Tefissah bi-Kevi'at Mediniyyut: Yizḥak Shamir ve-Emdat ha-Likkud be-Inyan Atid ha-Shetaḥim ha-Muḥzakim bi-Ydei Ẓahal* (1998).

[Susan Hattis Rolef (2nd ed.)]

SHAMMAH (Heb. שַׁמָּה; alternatively, שִׁמְעָה, שִׁמְעִי, שִׁמְעָא), the name of a number of biblical figures.

(1) An Edomite chief, the son of Reuel, and the grandson of Esau (Gen. 36:13, 17; I Chron. 1:37).

(2) The third son of Jesse (I Sam. 16:9; 17:13). He is referred to as Shimeah in II Samuel 13:3, where he is identified as the father of Jonadab, and as Shimei in II Samuel 21:21, where he is identified as the father of Jonathan, David's giant-killing warrior. I Chronicles 2:13 and 20:7 refer to him as Shimea. In the latter verse he is identified again as the father of Jonathan.

(3) The son of Agee, Hararite, one of the three mighty men of David who single-handedly defeated the Philistines when they attempted to invade a field of lentils (II Sam. 23:11–12). The parallel passage in I Chronicles 11:12–14 has "barley" for "lentils," and wrongly attributes the feat to Eleazar.

(4) A Harodite, one of the mighty men of David known as the "thirty" (II Sam. 23:25), who is probably identical with the son of Agee, mentioned above.

[Shlomo Balter]

SHAMMAI (**Ha-Zaken**, i.e., **The Elder**; c. 50 B.C.E.–c. 30 C.E.), one of the **Zugot*, the leaders of the Sanhedrin. Hillel's first colleague was *Menahem the Essene and Shammai was appointed to succeed him as **av bet din* when he retired. Nothing is known of the early life of Shammai except for the statement that he was a builder by occupation (Shab. 31a). Shammai was the founder of the great school which, called after him, was known as Bet Shammai. In general Bet Shammai took up a stringent attitude as compared with the lenient one of its counterpart *Bet Hillel. Shammai himself, however, did not always adopt a stringent line, and of some 20 *halakhot* transmitted in his name, he adopts a stringent view in about two-thirds of the cases, while in the other third he takes the lenient view.

Other Halakhot

On five topics, most of which deal with levitical cleanness and uncleanness, Shammai, adopting a more stringent approach, disagreed with both Bet Hillel and Bet Shammai (Eduy. 1, 7–8, 10–11), but in one detail of the *halakhot* of cleanness and uncleanness he took a lenient view contrary to the opinion of Bet Shammai and in accordance with that of Bet Hillel (Or. ii, 12). Against the view of the other sages, Shammai held that he who appoints an agent to kill a person is himself liable (Kid. 43a citing in the name of the prophet Haggai, a tradition based on Nathan holding David responsible for the death of Uriah). Shammai wished to insist on his minor son fasting on the Day of Atonement "but they ordered him to feed him with his own hand" (Tosef. Yoma 4 (5):2). He also acted against the view of the sages when, his daughter-in-law having on Sukkot given birth to a male child, "he broke away the roof plastering and put a sukkah-covering over the bed for the sake of the child" (Suk. 2:8). On the other hand he adopted a lenient view on two cases: in his opinion an offensive war and a siege begun three days before the Sabbath were not to be interrupted on that day, and though one was forbidden to set out on a long voyage in the Mediterranean Sea less than three days before the Sabbath, a short one could be undertaken even on the eve of the Sabbath. Shammai wanted to declare that a field improved during the Sabbatical Year was not to be sown in its eighth year, but he did not do so because "the times were not free" (or poor) and "only a *bet din* after him issued a decree about it" (Tosef. Shev. 3, 10). Many of Shammai's *halakhot* appear to be based on the literal interpretation of the biblical text, yet it is difficult to detect a consistent line in his *halakhot*, most of which deal with the laws of levitical cleanness and uncleanness. Despite his reputation for irascibility, Shammai's dictum was "Make your study of the Torah a matter of established regularity, say little and do much, and receive all men with a friendly countenance" (Avot, 1, 15).

BIBLIOGRAPHY: Weiss, Dor, 1 (1904^4), 145–76; L. Ginzberg, *On Jewish Law and Lore* (1955), 77–124; Derenbourg, Hist, 116–8, 149ff., 176–92, 463ff.; Schuerer, Gesch, index; Graetz, Gesch, 3 (1905^5) 212f.; G.F. Moore, *Judaism in the First Centuries of Christian Era, The Age of Tannaim*, 1 (1927), 72–82.

[Moshe David Herr]

SHAMMASH (Heb. שַׁמָּשׁ), salaried beadle or sexton in the community, the synagogue, rabbinical court, or a *ḥevrah*. A *shammash* performed a number of functions varying in accordance with the measure of autonomy or the nature of the religious institutions he served: tax collector, bailiff, process server, secretary, messenger, almoner, all-around handyman, grave digger, or notary. He sometimes acted as *shulklaper*, knocking on window shutters with a mallet to summon Jews to prayer, to announce the arrival of the Sabbath, or to waken people for pre-dawn penitential services. By signing the minutes of the *kahal* or of an association, he testified to their correctness. In Vilna he had to take an oath that he would strictly observe and enforce the communal statutes. He often acted as a diplomat or was sent as an envoy to another community. The *ḥevra kaddisha* of 19th-century Russian communities sometimes employed an *oylem shamash* to run errands. Along with the rabbi and cantor, the *shammash* was one of the three employees who received a regular salary and shared in the income from fees and largesse distributed at weddings or other festive occasions. He also supervised the local institutions, whether synagogue, **hekdesh*, or association. In larger towns there was a variety of specialized functionaries by that name. In the *ḥevra* the term *shammash* was used to denote the period of apprenticeship served by a new member.

BIBLIOGRAPHY: Baron, Community, 3 (1942), index s.v. *Shammash*; I. Levitats, *Jewish Community in Russia 1772–1844* (1943), index s.v. *Beadle*.

[Isaac Levitats]

SHAMOSH, YIZḤAK (1912–1968), Syrian author and translator. He practiced law in *Aleppo and *Damascus, edited *Le Commerce du Levant*, and contributed to literary periodicals in *Egypt and the Levant. After settling in Palestine in 1937, he taught Arabic at the Hebrew University and held high posts in Israel's Broadcasting Authority and Ministry of Justice. He was an expert on the modern Arabic short story and the literature of the Arabic diaspora in the U.S.

ADD. BIBLIOGRAPHY: J.M. Landau, "*Yizḥak Shamosh, Ha-Moreh, he-Ḥaver, ve-Ḥoker ha-Sifrut ha-Aravit ha-Ḥadashah*," in: *Ha-Mizraḥ He-Ḥadash*, 18, nos. 69–70 (1968), 162–63.

[Shmuel Moreh]

SHAMRI, ARIE (1907–1978), Yiddish poet. Born into a pious family in Kaluszyn, Poland, Shamri early came under the influence of the Zionist ideology of *Ha-Shomer ha-Ẓa'ir and immigrated to Palestine in 1929, joining kibbutz *Ein Shemer, from which he derived his new name. Beginning in 1936 his poetry appeared in the Warsaw weekly *Literarishe Bleter* and other Yiddish journals. His first book to be translated was the Hebrew translation (by A. *Shlonsky) of *Lamed-vav Shirim al Lezer Tsipres* ("36 Poems about Leyzer Tsipres," 1939). After the Holocaust Shamri's poetry, filled with love for nature, displays a renewed identification with the ḥasidic world of his Polish childhood. Among the collections of his poems are *In Toyer fun Teg* ("In the Gate of the Days," 1947), *A Shtern in Feld* ("A Star in the Field," 1957), and *Gezangen in Shayer* ("Songs in the Barn," 1970). In 1983 his essays were collected in the volume *Aynzamlung* ("Gathering"). From 1966 he headed the Tel Aviv publishing house Yisroel-Bukh and among others he edited and published there *Vortslen* ("Roots," 1966), an anthology of prose and verse by Israeli Yiddish writers.

BIBLIOGRAPHY: J. Glatstein, *In Tokh Genumen* (1956), 373–7; M. Ravitch, *Mayn Leksikon*, 3 (1958), 431–2; S. Bickel, *Shrayber fun Mayn Dor*, 2 (1965), 160–5; 3, (1970), 54–59. **ADD. BIBLIOGRAPHY:** LNYL, 8 (1981), 745–7; D. Sadan, *Heymishe Ksovim*, 1 (1972), 140–4.

[Sol Liptzin]

SHAMSKY, ARTHUR LOUIS (**Art**; 1941–), U.S. baseball player, member of the 1969 champion New York Mets. Born in St. Louis, Shamsky began his professional career in 1960 by hitting a home run in his first at-bat playing for Geneva in the New York Penn League. He made his Major League debut with Cincinnati on April 17, 1965. An outfielder with a sweet left-handed stroke, Shamsky hit 21 home runs in only 96 games the following season while platooning against right-handed pitchers, with four HRs coming in consecutive at-bats on August 12–14 to tie the record. His bat was sent to Cooperstown. After being traded to the Mets on November 8, 1967, Shamsky became a hero to New York's Jewish community when he hit .300 with 14 HRs and 47 RBIs as the cleanup-hitting fourth outfielder and left-handed pinch hitter for the 1969 championship team. Like other Jewish players before him, Shamsky refused to play in a Yom Kippur doubleheader that season. His seven hits in 13 at-bats led all batters in the NL Championship Series sweep against Atlanta. The following season, Shamsky hit.293 and registered career-highs in games (122), hits (118), runs (48), and RBIs (49). He remained with the Mets until 1972, when he played in a total of 22 games for the Chicago Cubs and Oakland A's before back problems forced his retirement. His lifetime numbers were .253 in 665 games, with 68 HRs, 194 runs, and 233 RBIs. After retiring Shamsky worked as a sports broadcaster on radio and television for eight years, and was a radio & television announcer for the New York Mets from 1979 to 1981. He is the author of *The Magnificent Seasons* (2004).

[Elli Wohlgelernter (2nd ed.)]

SHANDLING, GARRY (1949–), U.S. comedian-actor. Shandling was born in Chicago, Ill., and moved with his family to Tucson, Arizona, for the health of his older brother Barry, who later died from cystic fibrosis. Growing up, Shandling was a fan of comedy, often watching *The Tonight Show* and Woody Allen films. After graduating from Palo Verde High School, Shandling went on to study electrical engineering and then marketing at the University of Arizona. However, he was more interested in writing jokes than taking notes in class. After completing his bachelor's degree, he remained at his alma mater for postgraduate work in creative writing. After meeting George Carlin following a Tucson performance and getting positive feedback from some material he had written,

Shandling moved to Los Angeles in 1973. He wrote scripts for *Sanford and Son* (1972–77), *Welcome Back, Kotter* (1975–79) and *Three's Company* (1977–84). In 1977, a freak traffic accident left him with a crushed spleen and other serious injuries. As he recovered, he vowed to become a vegetarian, take up exercise, and try his hand at stand-up comedy. In 1978, he made his first stand-up appearance at a Comedy Store amateur night. He continued to work on his stand-up routine, which featured self-deprecating humor about his appearance and his inadequacies with women. On March 18, 1981, he made his first appearance on Johnny Carson's *Tonight Show*, a major break that aided his stand-up career. In 1984, Shandling wrote and starred in *Garry Shandling Alone in Vegas* for Showtime. Two years later, he had parlayed multiple appearances on *The Tonight Show* into a permanent guest host spot, but later turned it down to focus on his Showtime sitcom spoof, *It's Garry Shandling's Show* (1986–90), which was later rebroadcast on the FOX network. Like his sitcom lampoon, his next series, HBO's popular *The Larry Sanders Show* (1992–98), ridiculed television talk shows. In 1993, Shandling turned down a $5 million offer from NBC to take over *Late Night* from David Letterman, who had moved to CBS. Shandling made his first feature film appearance with a cameo in *The Night We Never Met* (1993), which he followed with a supporting role in *Love Affair* (1994) and a dramatic part as a Hollywood producer in *Hurlyburly* (1998). He co-wrote and starred in the feature comedy *What Planet Are You From?* (2000), and in 2004 he hosted the Primetime Emmy Awards. In 2006, he joined an all-star cast to voice the animated film *Over the Hedge*.

BIBLIOGRAPHY: "Shandling, Garry," in: *Newsmakers*, Issue 4 (1995); "Shandling, Garry," in: *Contemporary Authors* (2003); "What Planet Is Garry Shandling From?" in: *Jewish Journal* (March 3, 2000).

[Adam Wills (2nd ed.)]

SHANGHAI, port in Kiangsu province, E. China. It was opened to foreign trade in 1843. A flourishing foreign community developed there, including Jews of various nationalities. They were mostly Sephardim from Baghdad, Bombay, and Cairo, including such well-known families as *Sassoon, *Kadoorie, Hardoon, *Ezra, Shamoon, and Baroukh. There were three synagogues in Shanghai, and between 1904 and 1939, 12 Jewish magazines in English, German, and Russian were founded there. The leading one was *Israel's Messenger*, a Zionist monthly established in 1904 by N.E.B. Ezra and published until his death in 1936. Before World War I the Jewish population numbered around 700, with 400 Sephardim of Baghdad origin, 250 Europeans, and 50 Americans. Most of them were engaged in commerce, while a few were in the diplomatic service and in medicine or teaching. Their number was substantially increased to around 25,000, first by Jews from Russia fleeing from the 1917 Revolution, then between 1932 and 1940 by refugees from Nazism in Germany and German occupied countries who found out that they could enter the free port of Shanghai without visas. The Japanese closed Shanghai to further immigration and after the outbreak of the Pacific war in December 1941 they deported to Shanghai most of the Jews living in Japan or in transit to other countries. Substantial aid was given locally, especially by Sir Victor Sassoon, Horace Kadoorie, and Paul Komor. Additional funds came from abroad. With the outbreak of the Pacific war, the position of all Jews became desperate. Most of them were kept in semi-internment under miserable conditions in the *Hongkew district, subject to the whim of the Japanese occupation forces. They had great difficulty in finding employment, and most of their property was confiscated under one pretext or another. Almost all of them left Shanghai after World War II, largely with American help, for Israel, the United States, or other parts of the world. A few elderly people remained to live out their days under the Chinese Communists.

Hebrew Printing

Apart from J.J. Sulaiman's *Kunteres Seder ha-Dorot* (1921), the main period of Hebrew printing in Shanghai was during World War II and immediately after (1940–46), when remnants of Lithuanian yeshivot (Mir, Slobodka), as well as Lubavitch Ḥasidim, found refuge in Shanghai and printed – mostly photostatically – rabbinic, ethical, and ḥasidic works in limited editions for their own use. To the 80 items enumerated by Z. Harkavy (in *Ha-Sefer*, no. 9, 1961, 52–3; *Hashlamot le-Mafte'aḥ ha-Maftehot* (by S. Shunami, 1966), 3–4) have to be added – at least – the above work by J.J. Sulaiman and S. Elberg's *Akedat Treblinka* (Yid., 1946). Hebrew newspapers were printed in Shanghai as early as 1904.

BIBLIOGRAPHY: A. Ginsbourg, *Jewish Refugees in Shanghai* (Shanghai, 1940); A. Sopher, *Chinese Jews* (Shanghai, 1926); H. Dicker, *Wanderers and Settlers in the Far East* (1962), index; YIVO, *Catalogue of the Exhibition "Jewish Life in Shanghai"* (1948); A. Mars, in: JSOS, 31 (1969), 286–91.

[Rudolf Loewenthal]

SHANKER, ALBERT (1928–1997), U.S. labor leader. Shanker, who was born in New York City, taught in the New York City public school system from 1952 to 1959, when he resigned to become a trade union organizer for the city's teachers. Elected president of the 55,000-member United Federation of Teachers (UFT) in 1964, Shanker, as the teachers' legal bargaining agent, led the UFT in winning considerable improvements for teachers and assurances of more effective teaching methods in slum schools.

His most serious problem as UFT head resulted from the partial implementation of a school decentralization plan, which would have placed teachers under the control of 30 elected local school boards. The attempt by the administrator of one black and Puerto Rican "demonstration district" to remove union teachers – all of whom were Jews – from his district precipitated three city-wide school strikes which virtually closed New York City public schools in September and October 1968; the large majority of the teachers in the city system were Jewish. Charges and countercharges of racism and antisemitism and violent tactics by black militants in some areas profoundly disturbed New York City Jews and exacerbated race relations (see *Black-Jewish Relations in the U.S.). The strike settlement was a clear victory for the union, addressing its main points.

From 1974 until his death Shanker served as president of the American Federation of Teachers, and retained his presidency of the UFT until 1986. He was vice president of the AFL-CIO Central Labor Council of New York City, and the Jewish Labor Committee. From 1970 to 1997 he had a column in the *New York Times* entitled "Where We Stand," which dealt with topics relating to education, labor, and current events.

The Albert Shanker Institute in Washington, D.C., established in 1998 in his honor, is a nonprofit organization dedicated to generating ideas and promoting policy proposals relating to children's education; unions as advocates for quality; and freedom of association in the public life of democracies.

ADD. BIBLIOGRAPHY: D. Mungazi, *Where He Stands: Albert Shanker of the American Federation of Teachers* (1995); AFT's *American Teacher* (April 1997).

SHANKMAN, JACOB K. (1904–1986), U.S. Reform rabbi. Born in Chelsea, Massachusetts, Shankman, a boy prodigy, entered Harvard University at the age of 14 and graduated by 1923. He received his M.A. in 1925 at the age of 21. He was ordained at Hebrew Union College in 1930. He was then appointed to the Third Street Temple, Troy, New York, and in 1937 to Temple Israel, New Rochelle, where he was awarded life tenure and remained as rabbi until 1974 and then as rabbi emeritus. During 1943–46 he served as a chaplain with the U.S. Navy. Under his leadership the temple flourished and drew many Jews, moved to Westchester County, and became the preeminent Reform Congregation of the county. A new building was erected in the early 1960s. Not content with local leadership alone, Shankman served on the Hebrew Union College board of governors (1952–59) and was president of its alumni association (1958–59). Apart from rabbinic and civic bodies in the New York area, Shankman's principal public activity was with the World Union for Progressive Judaism. He was its American director from 1957 to 1964; chairman of the World Executive Committee from 1959; and president of the organization in 1964–1970

[Sefton D. Temkin / Michael Berenbaum (2nd ed.)]

SHANKS, HERSHEL (1930–), U.S. lawyer, author, and editor, particularly of archaeological materials. Shanks was born in Sharon, Pennsylvania, a small town on the Ohio border. He graduated from Haverford College (B.A. in English), Columbia University (M.A. in sociology), and Harvard Law School (LL.B.). He then joined the U.S. Justice Department, where he handled cases in the United States Courts of Appeal and the Supreme Court. Thereafter he practiced law privately in Washington for more than 25 years, often establishing important precedents in the law. He wrote widely in legal journals and published a book on a great American jurist, entitled *The Art and Craft of Judging: The Opinions of Judge Learned Hand*. Although he had never formally studied the Bible or archaeology, he published his first book related to these subjects, *The City of David – A Guide to Biblical Jerusalem*, during a sojourn in Jerusalem in 1972–73. On his return to the United States, while continuing to practice law, Shanks founded *Biblical Archaeology Review* (BAR), which began as a 16-page pamphlet written entirely by himself; in the early 2000s the magazine had over a quarter of a million readers. Almost all major scholars in Bible and archaeology have published articles in BAR, in which they often explore fresh perspectives for a non-scholarly audience. BAR is known especially for exploring controversies in the world of biblical archaeology, with the editor often taking his own strong stand. Shanks founded two other magazines, *Bible Review* in 1985 and *Archaeology Odyssey* in 2000. For over 15 years, beginning in 1987, he also served as editor of *Moment*, a Jewish magazine founded by Elie Wiesel and Leonard Fein, and edited by Fein for 12 years before Shanks became editor.

Shanks is the author of a number of books including *Judaism in Stone – The Story of Ancient Synagogues* (1979), *Jerusalem – An Archaeological Biography* (1995), *The Mystery and Meaning of the Dead Sea Scrolls* (1998), *The Brother of Jesus* (with Ben Witherington III, 2003), and *Solomon's Temple – Myth or Reality? A History of Jerusalem's Temple Mount* (2006). His articles and reviews have appeared in scholarly journals such as the *Israel Exploration Journal*, the *Jewish Quarterly Review*, and the *Harvard Law Review*. Literally hundreds of his articles have appeared in the magazines he has edited. He is also the editor of two widely used textbooks: *Ancient Israel – From Abraham to the Roman Destruction of the Temple* (rev. ed. 1999) and *Christianity and Rabbinic Judaism* (1988). His many newspaper and magazine articles have appeared in the *New York Times*, the *Washington Post*, the *Wall Street Journal*, *Commentary* and *The American Scholar*.

[Shimon Gibson (2nd ed.)]

SHAPERO, HAROLD (**Samuel**; 1920–), U.S. composer and pianist. Born in Lynn, Massachusetts, Shapero studied the piano with Eleanor Kerr and composition with Sergey Slonimsky (1936–37), Ernst Krenek (1937), Walter Piston (1938–41), Paul Hindemith (1940–41), and Nadia Boulanger (1942–3). During the 1940s Shapero had associations with Arthur *Berger, Irving Fine, and Leonard *Bernstein, who conducted the première of his symphony in 1948 and recorded it in 1954. Together with them, he formed Brandeis University's first music department, where Shapero taught for over 30 years, eventually appointed professor of music in 1952 and founding and directing its electronic music studio. Among his students were Joel Spiegelman, Richard *Wernick, David Epstein, and Sheila Silver. Shapero wrote orchestral works, piano, and chamber music, in which traditional forms are combined with dodecaphonic techniques. His works earned a series of awards, including the Prix de Rome (1941) and a Naumburg Fellowship (1942). His compositions include *Symphony for Classical Orchestra* (1948); *Credo* for orchestra (1955); a Hebrew cantata *Until Day and Night Shall Cease* (1954), commissioned by the American Jewish Tercentenary Committee;

and *Three Hebrew Songs* for tenor, piano and string orchestra (1988): *They Who Sow at Night* (S. Shalom), *Eagle! Eagle Over Your Mountains* (S. Tchernikowsky), *Will There Yet Come Days of Forgiveness* (L. Goldberg). As a pianist, he gave the premières of his keyboard and chamber works, also recording a number of them.

BIBLIOGRAPHY: Grove Music Online.

[Israela Stein (2nd ed.)]

SHAPERO, NATE S. (1892–1990), U.S. business executive. Shapero's business career in his native Detroit made him one of the leading men in the pharmaceutical industry and a director of the National Bank of Detroit. Shapero served in the U.S. Navy during World War I and as a dollar-a-year-man in the U.S. Treasury Department during World War II. Actively participating in many civic and charitable undertakings in his hometown, he was also intensely interested in Jewish institutions, including Israel's Weizmann Institute, Brandeis University, Sinai Hospital, and Temple Beth El of Detroit. He was president and honorary chairman of the board of Cunningham Drug Stores; chairman of the board of Marshall Drug Company and Broward Drug Company; president of the Michigan Association of Chain Drug Stores and of the Michigan Welfare Commission. He and his wife, Ruth, donated funds to endow the museum at Temple Beth El and the nursing school of Sinai Hospital, which later became a part of Wayne State University.

SHAPHAN (Heb. שָׁפָן; "rock badger, hyrax, coney"), son of Azaliah, Josiah's scribe and the head of one of the most influential and pro-Babylonian families in the last days of Judah (II Kings 22:3). Shaphan was one of the messengers sent by the king to the prophetess Huldah concerning the finding of the new book in the Temple (II Kings 22:14; see *Deuteronomy). Later, his sons were supporters of the prophet Jeremiah. One of them, *Ahikam, used his influence to save *Jeremiah from death when the latter prophesied the destruction of Jerusalem (Jer. 26:24). A second son, *Elasah, one of the men sent to Babylon by Zedekiah, took Jeremiah's letter to the elders in exile (Jer. 29:3). Mention is made of two or more sons of Shaphan, *Jaazaniah and *Gemariah. Jaazaniah is only mentioned among the elders in Jerusalem seen by Ezekiel in a vision in Ezekiel 8:11. The information about Gemariah is more definite. It was in his chamber at the Temple gate that the scribe Baruch read Jeremiah's scroll "to the people" in the reign of Jehoiakim (Jer. 36:10ff.). Shaphan's son Micaiah was present, but he himself was sitting with other officials in conference. Apprised by Micaiah, they warned Baruch to go into hiding with Jeremiah, and they later pleaded with the king not to burn the scroll. The family's sympathy with the prophet was further evidenced by the fact that Jeremiah was put under the guardianship of Shaphan's grandson, Ahikam's son *Gedaliah, who was appointed governor of Judah by the Neo-Babylonian captors of Jerusalem (Jer. 39:14; 40:5).

BIBLIOGRAPHY: S. Yeivin, in: *Tarbiz*, 12 (1941), 255ff.

[Yuval Kamrat]

SHAPIRA (Spira), ḥasidic family known as the Munkacs dynasty; named after the town of Munkacs (Mukachevo), the seat of the dynasty. Its founder, SOLOMON SHAPIRA (1832–1893), was born in Ribatic near Peremyshlyany, Galicia, the son of Eliezer Shapira of Lancut and grandson of Zevi Elimelech *Dynow. A disciple of Ḥayyim *Halberstam of Zanz, he also visited the ḥasidic rabbis of Ropczyce (Ropshits), Rymanow, Ruzhyn, and Belz. He held rabbinical posts at Sasov, Stryzow, Lancut, and Tarnogrod, and in 1881 was appointed rabbi of Munkacs. He was succeeded by his son ẒEVI HIRSCH (1850–1913), who was born at Stryzow and with his father settled in Munkacs. He was a disciple of Ḥayyim Halberstam of Zanz and of Ezekiel of Sieniawa. Until 1893 he headed the *bet din* in Munkacs; from that year, when his father died, he became rabbi of the town. Like his predecessors, he was also a ḥasidic *ẓaddik*. Under him Munkacs became an important center of Ḥasidism. He was an active member of the committee of Orthodox rabbis of Hungary. Toward the end of his life, he opposed the efforts of the German Orthodox sector to associate the Hungarian Orthodox in founding *Agudat Israel, through whose influence the leaders of German Orthodoxy sought to strengthen the religious elements in Germany. Ẓevi Shapira, however, feared that a close collaboration would result in a weakening of Orthodoxy in Hungary. Although he appreciated the efforts of the German Orthodox to strengthen their ranks, he did not wish to see what he regarded as their liberal way of life penetrate to Hungary. He was active in strengthening traditional education and objected to the compulsory attendance by Jewish children in the general schools. He also opposed the special schools which had been established in several communities so that Jewish youth should not have to attend school on Sabbath, and called upon his Ḥasidim not to send their children to them. Ẓevi Hirsch was an authority in both the *halakhah* and mystic spheres.

His most important works are *Darkhei Teshuvah* on the Shulḥan Arukh, *Yoreh De'ah* (1893), *Ẓevi Tiferet* (1912), responsa, and *Be'er Laḥai Ro'i* (1903–21), on the *Tikkunei Zohar*, one of the most noteworthy commentaries on this difficult work. The author attempts to present "the simple meaning of the secrets." Ẓevi Hirsch regarded it as his most notable work, even though his *Darkhei Teshuvah* was acclaimed by the leading rabbinical authorities.

Ẓevi Hirsch was succeeded by his son ḤAYYIM ELEAZAR SHAPIRA (1872–1937), rabbi of Munkacs from 1913 and ḥasidic *ẓaddik*. He succeeded in combining talmudic dialectics with the ability to reach halakhic decisions and a wide knowledge of Kabbalah and ḥasidic learning. He had many admirers and many opponents, and exercised great influence over the rabbis of Hungary even after Munkacs (Mukachevo) had passed to Czechoslovakia. Of lively temperament, he intervened in communal affairs beyond his community, and was even more adamant than his ancestors in opposing all innovation. An extremist opponent of Zionism, *Mizrachi, and *Agudat Israel, he regarded every organization engaged in the colonization of

Ereẓ Israel to be inspired by heresy and atheism. Redemption was to be a miraculous phenomenon, and any natural activity – political or colonizing – was liable to lead to a holocaust. He opposed the *Balfour Declaration. On the other hand, he supported the "old *yishuv*" and was the president of the *Kolel* Munkacs in Jerusalem. In 1930 he visited Palestine, where he met and encouraged the anti-Zionist elements. His Ḥasidim viewed this journey as an apocalyptical act.

After the example of his father, he called for the maintenance of traditional education and for its financial support. He opposed the Hebrew schools which were established in eastern Czechoslovakia between the two world wars, and condemned the Hebrew secondary school of his town. His struggles were not only ideological, and he occasionally became involved in local disputes with rival *ẓaddikim*, waging a campaign of many years with the *ẓaddik* of *Belz, Issachar Dov Roke'aḥ, who lived in Mukachevo from 1918 to 1921. His works include *Minḥat Elazar*, responsa (1–4, 1902–30); *Divrei Kodesh*, sermons (1933); *Ḥamishah Ma'amarot* (1922); and *Sefer Mashmi'a Yeshu'ah* (1919, 1956). Ḥayyim Eleazar's son-in-law JOSHUA JERAHMEEL RABINOWICZ (1913–), son of Rabbi Nathan David of Parczew, became rabbi of Ḥolon in Israel.

BIBLIOGRAPHY: D. Gelb, *Sefer Beit Shelomo* (1928, 1962²); M. Goldstein, *Sefer Massa'ot Yerushalayim* (1931); I.M. Gold, *Sefer Darkhei Ḥayyim ve-Shalom* (1940); S. Weingarten Ha-Kohen, in: *Arim ve-Immahot be-Yisrael*, 1 (1946), 359–66.

[Efraim Gottlieb]

SHAPIRA, ABRAHAM (1870–1965), one of the first Jewish *Shomerim* ("Watchmen") in Ereẓ Israel. Born in Novaya Mikhailovka, southern Russia, Shapira was taken to Ereẓ Israel at the age of ten; his family lived first in Jerusalem and later in *Petaḥ Tikvah. From his youth he displayed outstanding courage and was held in awe by the local Arabs. In 1890 he was appointed head of the *Shomerim* in Petaḥ Tikvah and enlisted the aid of the local Bedouin and the young Jewish settlers. As part of the general arrests made after the Turkish discovery of *Nili during World War I, Shapira was deported to Damascus to stand military trial, but he was acquitted and drafted into the Turkish army in Istanbul. Afterward, he took part in the defense of Petaḥ Tikvah against Arab attack in May 1921 and was among the initiators of the peace ceremony between the settlement and its Arab neighbors. Shapira often served in the role of negotiator in the quarrels between Jews and their *Shomerim* and served as honorary president of the Association of Jewish *Shomerim*. Shapira, a colorful, romantic figure, was beloved by all who knew him. Chaim Weizmann wrote about him in *Trial and Error*:

> He was a primitive person, spoke better Arabic than Hebrew, and seemed so much a part of the rocks and stony hillsides of the country that it was difficult to believe that he had been born in Russia. Here was a man who in his own lifetime had bridged a gap of thousands of years; who, once in Palestine, had shed his Galuth environment like an old coat….

BIBLIOGRAPHY: Y. Edelstein, *Avraham Shapira* (Heb. 2 vols., 1939); Y. Ya'ari-Poleskin, *Ḥolemim ve-Loḥamim* (1964³), 331–6; idem, *Sefer Ha-Yovel le-Petaḥ Tikvah* (1929), 372–81; Dinur, Haganah, index.

[Yehuda Slutsky]

SHAPIRA, AVRAHAM ELKANA KAHANA (1917–), Israeli religious leader and former chief rabbi. Shapira was born in Jerusalem, where he studied at Yeshivat Eẓ Ḥayyim and then at Hevron Yeshivah under Rabbi Moses Mordechai Epstein and Rabbi Ezekiel Sarna. After his marriage, Shapira was invited to teach at the Merkaz ha-Rav Yeshivah, where he remained for over 50 years. In his youth, he was friendly with Avraham Yeshayahu Karelitz (the Ḥazon Ish), Ẓevi Pesaḥ Frank, Isaac Zev Soloveitchik, and Isser Zalman Meltzer. In 1956, he was appointed to the Rabbinic *Bet Din* in Jerusalem. In 1974, he joined the High Rabbinic Court, joining the Rabbinic Council of the Chief Rabbinate in 1980. Three years later he was elected Ashkenazi chief rabbi, serving until the end of his term in 1993.

In 1982, after the death of Rabbi Ẓevi Judah Kook, son of the founder of Merkaz ha-Rav, the venerated Rabbi Abraham Isaac ha-Kohen Kook, a power struggle ensued over the post of *rosh yeshivah*. In the end, Shapira was named the *rosh yeshivah* at Merkaz ha-Rav, as opposed to Rav Ẓevi Tau. The tension between them continued with the appointment of Shapira's son as the executive director of the yeshivah and was further exacerbated by Shapira's emphasis on teaching more Talmud and less Bible and Jewish thought at the yeshivah. The bubble finally burst in 1997, when Shapira decided to allow Merkaz ha-Rav students to attend courses at the yeshivah leading to a teaching certificate. Tau, along with a number of other teachers and a good number of students, broke away from Merkaz ha-Rav and formed his own yeshivah, Har ha-Mor.

During his term as chief rabbi and afterwards as well, Shapira, together with his colleague, Chief Rabbi Mordechai *Eliyahu, became the spiritual leader of the religious Zionist camp in Israel. Thus, for over 20 years, he spoke out on political and social issues of concern to religious Zionism. During the events leading up to the Israeli government's disengagement from Gaza in 2005, Shapira was a vocal opponent of the removal of the Jews from their homes and the uprooting of Jewish communities in Gaza. Shapira even issued a halakhic decision forbidding IDF soldiers from obeying commands to participate in the actual disengagement. Of the hundreds of religious soldiers that participated in the removal of the Jews, fewer than 40 refused to obey their officers' commands.

Shapira's first published work was *Zekher Yiẓḥak*, an edition of the responsa of Isaac Jacob Rabinowitz of Ponevezh (1948). In 1989, his collected lectures on the Talmud, *Shi'urei Maran ha-Gaon Rav Avraham Shapira*, appeared in six volumes. From 1990 to 2003, three volumes of Shapira's essays were published, titled *Minḥat Avraham*. *Morashah*, a further collection of essays, appeared in 2005.

BIBLIOGRAPHY: http://he.wikipedia.org/wiki.

[David Derovan (2nd ed.)]

SHAPIRA, ELIJAH BEN BENJAMIN WOLF (1660–1712), rabbi, preacher, and halakhist. Elijah studied under his grandfather, Aaron Simeon Shapira, and Abraham Abele *Gombiner. He was the brother-in-law of Jacob *Reischer and of David *Oppenheim. He served as rabbi in Kolin, Bohemia, and from 1702 in Tiktin, resigning this post when he was appointed head of the yeshivah and preacher in his native Prague (though according to some he continued to act as rabbi of Tiktin while in Prague).

Elijah gained renown through his works: *Eliyahu Zuta*, a short commentary on the *Levush* of Mordecai b. Abraham *Jaffe, published with the text (Prague, 1689); *Eliyahu Rabbah*, a more extensive and profound commentary to the same work, published with the Shulḥan Arukh, *Oraḥ Ḥayyim* (Sulzbach, 1757), to which it served as a kind of supplement; *Shishah Shitot me-Ḥiddushei Eliyyah Rabbah* on the tractates *Ketubbot, Kiddushin, Gittin, Bava Kamma. Bava Batra, and Ḥullin*, published in Zurich in 1768. Many of his other works – sermons, novellae, and responsa which had remained in manuscript – were destroyed in the great fire of Prague in 1754.

Shapira died in Prague; his sons were Aryeh Leib, rabbi of Leipen, and Samuel, head of the Prague *bet din*.

BIBLIOGRAPHY: Ch. Tchernowitz, *Toledot ha-Posekim*, 3 (1947), 185–6; M. Bar-Yuda and Z. Ben-Nachum (eds.), *Sefer Tiktin* (1959), 74–5.

[Itzhak Alfassi]

SHAPIRA, ḤAYYIM MOSHE (1902–1970), Israeli politician; leader of the National Religious Party. Born in Grodno, Belorussia, Shapira from his youth was imbued with a religious Zionist spirit. He was active in organizing the Ẓe'irei ha-Mizrachi movement and did much for the *aliyah* of religious *ḥalutzim* to Ereẓ Israel. After moving to Warsaw he became one of the leaders of the organization. Afterward he went to Berlin and studied at the Hildesheimer Rabbinical Seminary. In Berlin Shapira also became the leader of Ẓe'irei ha-Miẓrachi and was sent as a delegate to the 14th *Zionist Congress (1925). From that time on he attended all Zionist Congresses and was also elected to the Zionist General Council as a representative of *Ha-Po'el ha-Mizrachi. Shapira settled in Palestine in 1925 and became a central figure in his movement and in Mizrachi. In 1935 he was elected as an alternate member and then a full member of the Zionist Executive and served on it until the establishment of the State of Israel as head of the Immigration (*aliyah*) Department.

Shapira made several visits to Jewish centers around the world and in 1938, after the Anschluss of Austria, he went to Vienna on a mission to organize the rescue of Jews and facilitate their migration to Ereẓ Israel. In the 1940s, during the struggle against British policy in Palestine, Shapira played an important role in preventing fratricidal conflicts between the *Haganah and *Irgun Ẓeva'i Le'ummi. In 1948, he was appointed a member of the People's Council (Mo'eẓet ha-Am) and of the Provisional Government of the State of Israel as minister of immigration and of health, in which capacity he organized the mass immigration that began during the *War of Independence. On the eve of the elections to the first *Knesset (1949), Shapira was among the initiators of the "United Religious Front" and was elected on its behalf as a member of the first cabinet. In 1957, when a grenade was thrown in the Knesset, Shapira was seriously wounded. His life was in danger, and he was then given the additional name of Ḥayyim (in accordance with traditional Jewish custom). He served in almost all governments – as minister of immigration, health (1948–49 and 1961–65), the interior (1949–52 and 1959–70), and religious affairs and social welfare (1952–58). On the eve of the *Six-Day War (1967), he played an important role in establishing the government of national unity. At the 21st world conference of the Mizrachi and Ha-Po'el ha-Mizrachi in 1968, Shapira was elected president of its world center.

BIBLIOGRAPHY: D. Lazar, *Rashim be-Yisrael*, 2 (1955), 33–38.

[Itzhak Goldshlag]

SHAPIRA, ḤAYYIM NACHMAN (1895–1943), critic of Hebrew literature. Born in Minsk, Russia, he was a lecturer in Semitic languages at the University of Kovno from 1925 to 1940 and was also an active Zionist. During the Nazi occupation, he furthered cultural activity in the Kovno ghetto, and was killed along with his wife, his mother, and his only child. A student of the German school of aesthetics of the 1920s, he sought to introduce this discipline into the analytical study of Hebrew literature. Shapira published stories and articles, especially in *Gilyonot, Haolam*, and *Moznayim*. During the last years of his life, he worked on his magnum opus, *Toledot ha-Sifrut ha-Ivrit ha-Ḥadashah* ("A History of Modern Hebrew Literature"), which was to consist of 12 volumes. Only one volume was published dealing with the Haskalah in central Germany (1784–1829). In it, he stresses the ideological direction of the beginnings of modern Hebrew literature, viewing it as a product of the secular "this-worldly" attitude of the enlightened. At the same time, he places Hebrew literature within the context of the aesthetic theory of the Enlightenment, offering some fine insights into its artistic aspects. A reprint of this volume appeared in 1967, with the addition of a biographical essay by Benzion Benshalom. The manuscript of the second volume, which dealt with Hebrew literature in Galicia and Lithuania, was destroyed in the ghetto.

BIBLIOGRAPHY: Kressel, Leksikon, 2 (1967), 968–9.

[Getzel Kressel]

SHAPIRA, JOSHUA ISAAC BEN JEHIEL (d. 1873), rabbi and talmudist. Known as Eizel Ḥarif ("sharp") because he was one of the keenest intellects and most outstanding pilpulists of his day, he was *av bet din* successively at Kalvarija, Kutno, Tiktin, and, finally, Slonim.

Shapira was the author of (1) *Emek Yehoshua* (1942), in two parts: part 1 – 24 responsa on the Shulḥan Arukh; part 2 – 16 occasional homilies; (2) *Naḥalat Yehoshu'a* (1851), in two parts: part 1 – responsa on several *halakhot* and various subjects in the Babylonian and Jerusalem Talmuds; part 2 – Sabbath and festival homilies, and, at the end, a eulogy on his father; (3) *No'am Yerushalmi*, commentary and glosses on the Jerusalem Talmud – on *Zera'im* (1863), *Mo'ed* (1866), *Nashim* (1868), *Nezikin* (1869); (4) *Ibbei ha-Naḥal* (1855?), homilies; (5) *Sefat ha-Naḥal* (1859), homilies and comments on *aggadot* in the Babylonian and Jerusalem Talmuds; (6) *Aẓat Yehoshu'a* (1868), commentary on the questions asked by the "sages of Athens" (Bek. 8b); (7) *Marbeh Eẓah* (1870), commentary on the aggadic statements of Rabbah bar Ḥana; (8) *Marbeh Tevunah* (1872), on the basic principles of the Babylonian and Jerusalem Talmuds. Shapira was one of the few scholars in his generation who attached as much value to the Jerusalem Talmud as to the Babylonian, a fact amply reflected in his commentaries.

BIBLIOGRAPHY: S.M. Chones, *Toledot ha-Posekim* (1910), 481.

[Samuel Abba Horodezky]

SHAPIRA, KALONYMOUS KALMAN (1889–1943), ḥasidic rebbe of the Warsaw Ghetto. Born in Grodzisk, Shapira was a descendant of the seer of Lublin (*Jacob Isaac ha-Ḥozeh mi-Lublin) and the maggid of Kozienice (Israel ben Shabbetai Hapstein *Kozience). After his father died when he was three, a family member took charge of his education. Married at 15, at the age of 20 he became a rebbe and then the rabbi in Piaseczno, near Warsaw. In 1923 he founded a yeshivah, Daas Moshe, which became an important ḥasidic institute in prewar Poland. His educational goals were ambitious. He wanted nothing less than to create, in the words of his biographer, Nehemia Polen, a "core group" of students of "sublime stature" to revitalize the ḥasidic movement. The goal of education as he envisioned it was that a child must experience the inner life of Torah. He outlined his goals in his first book, *Ḥovat ha-Talmidim* ("The Student's Responsibility") published in 1932, the only work to be published while he was alive. He emphasized joy and renewed vitality for the yeshivah world.

Polen describes him as physically imposing, "handsome and well groomed, distinguished and elegant." An account of his early war experience was published in the *Forward* on March 30, 1940. Refusing to abandon his flock in Warsaw, he saw his son, daughter-in-law, and sister-in-law killed in the first days of the German bombings, and a few weeks later his mother died.

Shapira tended to the religious needs of the community, including its *mikva'ot*, and worked with relief kitchens that served 1,500 people a day assisted by the *American Jewish Joint Distribution Committee. He also continued to teach Torah week in and week out, composing impassioned *derashot* on the weekly portion that related not only to the words of the Torah but to the conditions of ghetto life. They were preserved and published under the name *Esh Kodesh* ("The Holy Fire," 1960).

His one remaining daughter was deported during the great *Aktion* of the summer of 1942. She was murdered in Treblinka. The rebbe remained in the ghetto and lived through the Ghetto Uprising, where he was captured and incarcerated. He died in Trawniki. Of *Esh Kodesh*, Polen concludes: "It is testimony to faith in learning, teaching, human communication, language, and – most of all the redemptive power of compassion."

BIBLIOGRAPHY: N. Polen, *The Holy Fire: The Teachings of Rabbi Kalonymus Kalman Shapira, The Rebbe of the Warsaw Ghetto* (1994); K.K. Shapira, *Sacred Fire: Torah from the Years of Fury 1939–1942*, ed. D. Miller, trans. J.H. Worsch (2000).

[Michael Berenbaum (2nd ed.)]

SHAPIRA, MEIR (1887–1934), Polish rabbi, *rosh yeshivah*, educationalist, and communal leader. Shapira received ordination when he was only 15 years old from Isaac *Shmelkes, Meir Arikh, and his teacher, his maternal grandfather, Samuel Isaac Schor. Shapira manifested his future interest in Jewish education as early as 1910, when in his first position as communal rabbi of Gliniany, he founded his first yeshivah in his own home, later transferring it to his next post in Sanok. He rapidly gained a reputation among Polish Jewry, and was elected to the chair of the education committee of Polish *Agudat Israel in 1919 and to the leadership of the whole organization in 1922. Shapira also became a Jewish spokesman in Polish government circles in 1923. He was elected to the Polish Sejm, where he was noted for his forceful speeches and outspoken criticism of antisemitism. Within two years, however, Shapira decided to devote the whole of his life and energy to Jewish education. He thereupon resigned from the Sejm in 1924, accepted the post of rabbi in Piotrkow, and worked for the development of the two enterprises which remain his greatest contribution to Jewish education.

The first enterprise was a program of studies (still in existence) which has passed into Jewish nomenclature as the *daf yomi* ("daily page"). At the 1923 congress of Agudat Israel, Shapira proposed that every Jew undertake to study each day one identical page of the Talmud. The plan envisaged a communal completion of the study of the Talmud every seven years. Shapira himself participated in the completion of the first cycle in 1931. Shapira's second achievement was the establishment of Yeshivat Ḥakhmei Lublin. He first conceived of the idea of this yeshivah in 1922, and two years later, after a highly strenuous fund-raising tour of Europe and North America, laid the foundation stone in the presence of leading Jewish rabbis and dignitaries. This institution was unique in conception, character, and even architecture. Shapira was vigorously opposed to the poor amenities, unattractive surroundings, and penurious atmosphere characteristic of the traditional yeshivot. He set a precedent, now universally followed, by equipping his establishment at Lublin with an excellent library (much of it his own), with spacious living and dining quarters, and with appropriate lecture halls. The academic standards themselves were maintained by a rigorous selection of applicants, including a growing number of ḥasidic youth. Shapira frequently lectured to the students and participated in their daily studies, activities, and even meals.

In 1933 Shapira accepted an invitation to become rabbi of Lodz, on condition that the community honor the yeshivah's debts. The condition was accepted, but Shapira died before assuming the post. Shapira was an enigmatic and colorful personality, in whom a deep understanding of rabbinic lore was combined with a nimble wit and love of life. The former is indicated in his responsa *Or ha-Me'ir* (1926), and in various collections of essays published by his pupils. The latter was revealed in the songs and melodies he composed while dancing with his students. Many of his witty aphorisms are still quoted. The manner of his death was characteristic of his life. Realizing that his end was near, he requested his students to dance in song around his bed; while they were so engaged, he breathed his last breath.

BIBLIOGRAPHY: S. Nadler (ed.), *Sefer ha-Yovel... Me'ir Shapira* (1930); M.W. Niestępower, *Ha-Yoẓer vi-Yẓirato* (1937); B. Mintz, *Me'ir be-Ahavah* (1943); I. Frenkel, *Men of Distinction*, 2 (1967), 31–39; A. Sorski (ed.), *Rabbi Me'ir Shapira be-Mishnah, be-Omer u-ve-Ma'as*, 2 vols. (1964–67).

[Mordechai Hacohen]

SHAPIRA, YESHAYAHU (1891–1945), ḥasidic Ereẓ Israel pioneer and leader of religious labor Zionism. Shapira was born in Grodzisk, Poland, the youngest son of the ḥasidic rabbi Elimelech of Grodzisk, and was educated by his maternal grandfather in a deeply ḥasidic spirit, which included singing and playing the violin as a form of religious service. His education was also permeated with an ardent love of Ereẓ Israel, so much so that as a youngster Shapira took an extraordinary decision for his environment and joined the Zionist movement. In 1914 he even went to Ereẓ Israel, but hastened back to his family because of the outbreak of World War I. In Poland he participated in the foundation of *Mizrachi (1917), and in his Hebrew address at the founding conference he called on all Orthodox Jews to liquidate their businesses in the Diaspora and settle in Ereẓ Israel. Shapira settled in Palestine in 1920 and became the head of the Immigration and Labor Department of the Mizrachi center in Jerusalem. He organized a group of 120 religious workers to build the Rosh-Pinnah–Tabgha road and another of 50 workers, including himself, to clean Solomon's Pool near Jerusalem. He was one of the founders and leaders of Ha-Po'el ha-Mizrachi, the first group of which was formed in his home in Jerusalem. In 1924 he went to Poland as an emissary and influenced young ḥasidic rabbis, such as Yeḥezkel Taub and Israel Eliezer Hofstein, to settle together with their disciples on the land in Palestine. These groups founded the settlements of Naḥlat Ya'akov and Avodat Yisrael, which later merged into *Kefar Ḥasidim, and some of them founded Kefar Ata.

In 1933 Shapira became the manager of the central cooperative bank Zerubavel in Tel Aviv, but ten years later he decided to return to farming by settling in *Kefar Pines, and his house there became a spiritual center for members of Ha-Po'el ha-Mizrachi. He wrote many essays and articles, particularly on economic problems of settlement and cooperation, and was beloved for his devotion and modesty. He died in Jerusalem.

BIBLIOGRAPHY: Tidhar, 3 (1958), 1328–30.

SHAPIRA FRAGMENTS, portions of a manuscript of Deuteronomy, claimed to be of exceptionally early date, which were offered for sale in Berlin and London by Moses William Shapira (c. 1830–84), a Jewish-born Christian antiquarian from Jerusalem. The fragments consisted of 15 leather strips, brought to Europe in July, 1883. Shapira's story was that they had been found by Arabs some years previously in the Wadi Mujib in Transjordan, and that he had bought them from one of the finders. In 1878 he sent copies to Konstantin Schlottmann of Halle, who pronounced them fabrications. Shapira then placed them in a bank in Jerusalem, but on receiving new encouragement he took them to Leipzig in July, 1883, and submitted them to Hermann Guthe. Guthe in his turn concluded that they were forgeries, and in September of that year published a detailed study of them, entitled *Fragmente einer Lederhandschrift, enthaltend Moses letzte Rede an die Kinder Israel*, in which the complete text of the fragments was compared with the Masoretic Text. From Leipzig Shapira went to Berlin (July 10) and offered the fragments to the Royal Library. An expert committee was convened to examine them, consisting of A. Dillmann, E. Sachau, A. Ermann, and M. Steinschneider, who unanimously (apparently without knowing of Guthe's investigation) concluded that they were forgeries.

From Berlin Shapira went to London (arriving there on July 26) and offered his fragments to the British Museum for £1,000,000. The script on the fragments was closely similar to that on the Moabite Stone (c. 850 B.C.E.), and Shapira and many members of the British public, who were greatly excited by the fragments, were willing to ascribe a Mosaic date to them. Such a date would inflict a mortal blow, they thought, to critical theories of the composition of the Pentateuch; and insofar as these theories were founded on the distribution of divine names in the Pentateuch, it was noteworthy that the fragments, by exhibiting the reading *Elohim* where the Masoretic Text had YHWH, showed the precarious nature of this foundation. The British Museum appointed C.D. Ginsburg to report on the fragments. He too found them to be forgeries. His conclusions were that they were strips cut from the margins of old scrolls, treated with oil to give the impression of antiquity, and incribed with letters imitating those on the Moabite Stone by a northern European Jew in whose pronunciation of Hebrew there was no distinction between *ḥet* and undageshed *kaf*, or between *tet* and *taf*. (Oral tradition in the British Museum adds that the writing had been done with a steel pen.)

This adverse finding was the more bitter for Shapira because it was confirmed by C.S. Clermont-Ganneau, who saw some of the fragments in the museum; it was he in particular who first affirmed that they had been cut from old synagogue scrolls. Clermont-Ganneau, eleven years before, had exposed as fakes pieces of "Moabite" pottery which Shapira had sold to Germany. Suspicions of prejudice on his part can, however, be set aside in view of the unanimity with which other scholars decided against the authenticity of the fragments. Humiliated and discredited, Shapira committed suicide in a Rotterdam hotel on March 9, 1884.

More recently the question of the character of his fragments has been reopened in the light of the Qumran discoveries, particularly by M. Mansoor (see bibliography). It has been suggested that they might be comparable to biblical fragments in the Paleo-Hebrew script found in the caves, and that the textual deviations could be evidence of a paraphrase (such as the "Sayings of Moses" from Qumran Cave 1) rather than a transcript of the biblical text. The detailed internal evidence marshaled by Ginsburg seems conclusive enough, but doubts will probably not be silenced unless it is possible to secure and examine the Shapira fragments themselves, most of which appear to have been bought in 1885 by the bookseller Bernard Quaritch but have not been subsequently located.

BIBLIOGRAPHY: J.M. Allegro, *Shapira Affair* (1965); Rabinowicz, in: JQR, 47 (1956/57), 170ff.; Mansoor, in: *Transactions of the Wisconsin Academy of Sciences, Arts and Letters*, 47 (1959), 183–229; M. Harry, *La petite fille de Jerusalem* (1914), a fictionalized account by Shapira's daughter.

[Frederick Fyvie Bruce]

SHAPIRO, ABBA CONSTANTIN (1839–1900), Hebrew poet. Born in Grodno, Shapiro studied photography, then lived in Vienna and St. Petersburg, where he married a Christian woman and was baptized. His apostasy haunted him throughout his life and is a hidden undercurrent in much of his poetry. He gained fame and fortune in St. Petersburg as an art photographer: he was the personal photographer of prominent Russian officials and of L.N. Tolstoy. From 1877 his poems appeared in most of the Russian and Hebrew literary periodicals. Shapiro's poetry, replete with Jewish and occasionally Zionist themes, was collected by J. *Fichmann in one volume, *Shirim Nivḥarim* (1911). Shapiro also published *Sedom* (1900), a poem on Dreyfus, cast in a biblical setting, and a critical essay on Turgenev's story "The Jew," "*Turgenev ve-Sippuro 'Ha-Yehudi,'*" in *Ha-Meliẓ*, 19 (1883).

BIBLIOGRAPHY: Toren, in: *Moznayim*, 17 (1944), 41–54, 143–51 (includes bibliography); J.S. Raisin, *Haskalah Movement in Russia* (1913), 98; Waxman, Literature, 4 (1960^2), 210.

[Getzel Kressel]

SHAPIRO, ALEXANDER M. (1929–1992), U.S. Conservative rabbi. Shapiro was born in Brooklyn, N.Y., and received a B.A. from Brooklyn College as well as a B.H.L. from the *Jewish Theological Seminary, in 1950. He was ordained at JTS in 1955 and earned a Ph.D. from Dropsie University in 1970. From 1955 to 1957, he served as a chaplain in the United States Army. He was director of United Synagogue Youth activities in Philadelphia (1957–59) before becoming rabbi of Temple Beth Tikvah in the Philadelphia suburb of Erdenheim (1957–68). Under his leadership, the congregation won two Solomon Schechter Awards, for its school and library. In the summers, he served as director of *Camp Ramah in the Poconos and then director of Leaders' Training Fellowship at the Ramah camps in Wisconsin, California, and Canada.

Shapiro is credited with organizing and leading – over the objections of the United Synagogue – the first protest by a Jewish group in front of the Soviet embassy in Washington, D.C., on October 6, 1964. His activism ushered in a new era of Jewish picketing and vigils on behalf of Soviet Jewry.

In 1968, Shapiro turned to academia, joining the faculty of Temple University, where he taught in the Department of Religion (1969–70) – although he also served as co-rabbi of Philadelphia's Germantown Jewish Center (1968–69). In 1970, Shapiro moved to Israel, where he lectured at Beersheba's Ben-Gurion University and the David Yellin Teachers' Seminary in Jerusalem as well as for the Overseas Student Programs at Hebrew University. He returned to the United States in 1972 to assume the pulpit of Congregation Oheb Shalom in South Orange, N.J., a synagogue that had been headed previously by two leaders of Conservative Judaism and former presidents of the *Rabbinical Assembly, Charles *Hoffman and Louis *Levitzky. He served on the boards of the Jewish Federation of Metropolitan New Jersey (1972–76), the Solomon Schechter School (1973–81), and Jewish Family Services (1973–76), and was elected president of the New Jersey Region of the Rabbinical Assembly, where he initiated a study of the effects of congregational demands on rabbis and their families.

Shapiro emerged as a national leader of the Rabbinical Assembly when he was elected treasurer of the organization (1980–82), then vice president (1982–84) and ultimately president (1984–86). During his tenure in office, and following years of his lobbying for equal rights for women in the pulpit, the RA voted to amend its constitution and admitted its first women members, JTS graduate Amy *Eilberg, and Beverly Magidson and Jan Kaufman, who had been ordained elsewhere. This step reopened concerns of the more traditional members of the Conservative movement, prompting Shapiro to join with JTS chancellor Gerson *Cohen in establishing a committee to articulate Conservative ideology. As president, Shapiro also participated in a delegation of Jews and Catholics who met in the Vatican to discuss the implementation of *Nostra aetate* with Pope John Paul II.

Shapiro also sought to engage in interdenominational dialogue, becoming the first Conservative rabbi to address the annual convention of the Orthodox *Rabbinical Council of America and taking that opportunity to revive the proposal that a national **bet din* be established to deal with matters of personal status, such as marriage, divorce and conversion. His RCA counterpart, Rabbi Louis *Bernstein, returned the visit and appeared before the RA that year – the first and last time such an exchange took place. While president, he also had the distinction of being arrested during a 1985 demonstration in front of the Soviet consulate in New York City – an act of civil disobedience and courage reminiscent of his participation in a civil rights march in Birmingham, Alabama, with Martin

Luther King, Jr., in 1963: the presence of Shapiro and 18 rabbinical colleagues in *kippot* electrified and inspired a large assembly of southern African-Americans; the hotel in which he stayed was bombed shortly after his departure.

A scholar in the area of medieval responsa, Shapiro contributed articles and essays to numerous academic journals and reference books. He was also the co-editor (with Burton Cohen) of *Studies in Jewish Education and Judaica in Honor of Louis Newman* (1984).

BIBLIOGRAPHY: P.S. Nadell, *Conservative Judaism in America: A Biographical Dictionary and Sourcebook*, 1988.

[Bezalel Gordon (2nd ed.)]

SHAPIRO, ARYEH LEIB BEN ISAAC (1701–1761), scholar and grammarian. Raised in Vilna, Shapiro married a daughter of Mordecai b. Azriel, one of the city's most respected residents. As a young man, he maintained a correspondence with the Karaite scholar Solomon of Troki, the author of *Appiryon*. Shapiro ranged beyond the boundaries of traditional learning, for in addition to his vast knowledge of the Talmud he studied logic and mathematics, and wrote a work on Hebrew grammar, *Kevuẓat Kesef* (Zolkiew, 1741). His other works include a two-part commentary on *Massekhet Soferim* entitled *Naḥalat Ari'el* and *Me'on Arayot*, which were published together with the tractate at Dyhernfurth in 1732. Also extant is a responsum dated 1754, which appears in *Teshuvat Shemu'el* (Vilna, 1859) by R. Samuel of Indura. Shapiro, in his later years, served as a *dayyan* and scribe of the Vilna community.

BIBLIOGRAPHY: S.J. Fuenn, *Kiryah Ne'emanah* (1860), 111f.; Fuerst, Bibliotheca, 3 (1860), 371; Benjacob, Oẓar, 516.

SHAPIRO, ASCHER HERMAN (1916–2004), U.S. mechanical engineer. Born in Brooklyn, Shapiro taught at the Massachusetts Institute of Technology, where he became professor of engineering (1962), head of the department of mechanical engineering (1965), and an Institute Professor (1975). He was associated with the National Advisory Committee on Aeronautics and the U.S. Atomic Energy Commission. He did research on the aerodynamics of high-speed flight and turbomachinery, on propulsion systems, and on biofluid dynamics of the cardiovascular, pulmonary, and urinary systems. He took out patents on fluid-metering apparatuses, combustion chambers, propulsion systems, turbomolecular vacuum pumps, and industrial centrifuges. Shapiro wrote *Dynamics and Thermodynamics of Compressible Fluid Flow* (2 vols., 1953–54) and *Shape and Flow; the Fluid Dynamics of Drag* (1961).

[Samuel Aaron Miller]

SHAPIRO, BENJAMIN (1913–), Israeli biochemist. Shapiro was born in Germany and immigrated to Ereẓ Israel in 1926. He received his doctorate in science from the Hebrew University in 1940 and was appointed associate professor in 1953 and full professor in 1958. He was awarded the Israel Prize for medicine in 1955.

SHAPIRO, BERNARD (1935–), Canadian educator, administrator, public servant. Bernard Shapiro was born in Montreal. In 1954 he graduated from McGill University with a B.A., after which he and his twin brother, Harold, took over for several years the management of the family's popular restaurant in Montreal, Ruby Foo's. He and his brother left Montreal to pursue higher degrees. Bernard earned a doctorate in education from Harvard in 1967 and was hired by the University of Boston. He was appointed an associate dean at Boston before returning to Canada as dean of education at the University of Western Ontario and later vice president academic and provost. From 1980 to 1986 he was director of the Ontario Institute for Studies in Education in Toronto. In 1985 he headed a provincial Commission on Private Schools in Ontario which, among its recommendations, called for partial provincial funding of Jewish and other religious schools. This recommendation was never implemented.

In 1986 Shapiro was appointed Ontario's deputy minister of education and held several other major deputy minister posts before he retired from the Ontario public service in 1992 to become a professor of education and public policy at the University of Toronto. Shapiro returned to Montreal as principal of McGill University in 1994, a position he held until 2002. He also oversaw the American National Jewish Population Survey (NJPS) review process before its release by the United Jewish Communities. In 2004 Shapiro began a five-year term as ethics commissioner of Canada, responsible for the administration of the code of conduct for members of the House of Commons as well as the prime minister's ethical guidelines for cabinet ministers and other public office holders.

Active in the Montreal Jewish and non-Jewish communities, in 2004 Shapiro and his wife, Phyllis, a professor of education at McGill University, were Montreal's Negev Dinner honorees. In 1999 he was appointed an Officer of the Order of Canada.

[Harold Troper (2nd ed.)]

SHAPIRO, DAVID S. (1909–1989), U.S. Bible scholar and rabbi. Born in Philadelphia, Shapiro studied at the Hebrew Theological College of Chicago and the Illinois Institute of Technology. He served as the rabbi of Orthodox congregations in Savannah, Georgia (1936–38); Erie, Pennsylvania (1938–41); Indianapolis, Indiana (1941–48); and Milwaukee, Wisconsin (1948–1989). Shapiro also taught at the University of Wisconsin and the Graduate School of the Hebrew Theological College.

In 1936 he published *Yesodei ha-Dat ha-Universalit*, an attempt to establish the theory of a universal religion on the basis of rabbinic sources. Shapiro issued *Midrash David* in 1952, consisting of essays on the festivals and halakhic discourses. In 1961, his *Torat Moshe ve-ha-Nevi'im* appeared. It includes biblical studies which attempted to prove the dependence of the prophets on the Mosaic law.

SHAPIRO, ESTHER JUNE (1934–), U.S. producer and screenwriter. A Brooklyn native, Shapiro began her entertainment career writing for television. One of her first jobs was writing a 1966 episode of *The Iron Horse*. She also wrote for *Love of Life* (1969–70) and was executive story consultant for *Love Story* in 1973–74. Shapiro married Richard Shapiro, also a producer and screenwriter, in 1960. In 1975, the pair wrote the screenplay for the NBC movie *Sarah T.: Portrait of a Teenage Alcoholic*. Two years later, they produced and wrote the ABC movie *Intimate Strangers* (1977). The same year, they wrote for the CBS television movie *Minstrel Man*. In 1981, the two collaborated as the creators of *Dynasty*, a prime time soap opera, which the couple also wrote for until 1989. In 1983–84, the Shapiros worked as cocreators and executive producers of *Emerald Point*. Shapiro also wrote for the show. In 1985, the pair created *Dynasty II: The Colbys*, a spin-off of the original series, for which Shapiro also wrote. Shapiro was an executive producer for the ABC television movies *The Three Kings* and *Cracked Up* in 1987. The next year, she became executive producer of the television show *HeartBeat* (1988), which she also wrote. The following year, the couple wrote and were executive producers for the NBC television series *When We Were Young*. In 1991 the pair returned as writers for the television movie *Dynasty: The Reunion*. Other television movies the couple worked on are *Blood Ties* (1991), *The Colony* (1996), *Living the Life* (2000), and *The Motel* (2005).

[Susannah Howland (2nd ed.)]

SHAPIRO, EZRA Z. (1903–1977), Zionist and communal leader. Shapiro, born in Volozhin, Russia, was brought by his family to Cleveland, Ohio, in 1906. Early in his life Shapiro became active in advancing Jewish education and in the Zionist Movement, two causes which he served vigorously on the local, national, and international levels. He became president of the Zionist District of Cleveland in 1924 and ten years later was elected chairman of the national executive committee of the Zionist Organization of America. As president of the Cleveland Hebrew Schools (1939–43) and the Cleveland Bureau of Jewish Education (1953–56), he helped create the system of communal education there. At the 1951 Zionist Congress, Shapiro, as chairman of its committee on fundamental problems, was instrumental in drafting the Jerusalem program redefining Zionist goals for the post-State era. He was a leader of the World Confederation of General Zionists and the American Jewish League for Israel which he helped found in 1957. He was vice president of the American Association for Jewish Education, 1959–66. Other areas of Cleveland public life in which Shapiro was active include his post as city law director (1933–35); member of the Cleveland Community Relations Board from 1963 and vice chairman from 1966; trustee of the Jewish Community Federation from 1934; and president of the Jewish Community Council (1942–45). In 1971 he settled in Jerusalem and became director of the Keren Hayesod-United Israel Appeal.

[Judah Rubinstein]

SHAPIRO, HAROLD (1935–), U.S. scholar and administrator. Born in Montreal, Shapiro held dual American and Canadian citizenship. He earned his bachelor's degree from McGill University in 1956 and his Ph.D. in economics from Princeton in 1964. Shapiro joined the faculty of the University of Ann Arbor in 1964 as an assistant professor, becoming an associate professor in 1967. In 1970 he was named a full professor of economics and became chair of the department of economics in 1977. He served as a research scientist at the Institute of Labor and Industrial Relations and at the Institute of Public Policy Studies. His fields of interest included econometrics, mathematical economics, science policy, the evolution of higher education, and money and banking. Shapiro published numerous articles in academic journals, including the *International Economic Review* and *Journal of Comparative Economics*, and he wrote and edited several books, including *Tradition and Change: Perspectives on Education and Public Policy* (1987).

Shapiro was named vice president for academic affairs of the University of Michigan at Ann Arbor in 1977, and he also served as chairman of the executive board of the University of Michigan hospitals. In 1980 he was elected president of the university and chairman of its board of regents. In 1988 he was named Princeton University's 18th president, the first Jew to serve in that office and he served in that capacity until his retirement in 2001. He also held a faculty appointment as professor of economics and public affairs; he became professor emeritus.

Shapiro served as a member of the Bretton Woods Committee, the American Philosophical Society, the Institute of Medicine of the National Academy of Sciences, and the Government-University-Industry-Research Roundtable of the National Academy of Sciences. He was a member of the presidential Council of Advisors on Science and Technology from 1990 to 1992, and he chaired the Institute of Medicine's Committee on Employer-Based Health Benefits. In 1996 he was appointed by President Bill Clinton to chair the National Bioethics Advisory Commission, which issued the report *Cloning Human Beings* in June 1997.

Shapiro served as a trustee of the Alfred P. Sloan Foundation, the Universities Research Association, the Educational Testing Service, and the University of Pennsylvania Medical Center. He also served on the board of directors of the Dow Chemical Company and the American Council on Education. He was a fellow of the American Academy of Arts and Sciences.

[Dorothy Bauhoff (2nd ed.)]

SHAPIRO, HARRY LIONEL (1902–1990), U.S. anthropologist. Born in Boston, Massachusetts, Shapiro graduated from Harvard University in 1923. The following year, he travelled to Norfolk Island in New Zealand to study the Pitcairn Islanders, who were the descendants of the mutiny that had taken place in 1789 aboard the British naval vessel *Bounty* in the South Pacific. After receiving his Ph.D. from Harvard in 1926, Shapiro served as assistant curator in physical anthropology at the American Museum of Natural History, and rose to become curator and chairman of the department in 1942, in which capacity he remained until he retired in 1970. At the same time, he was also a professor of anthropology at Columbia University (1942–73). An officer of various professional organizations and lecturer at various institutions, he was a founding member of the American Association of Physical Anthropologists (1930) and served as secretary (1935–39) and vice president (1941–42). He served for many years as a member and in 1953–54 as chairman of the division of anthropology and psychiatry of the National Research Council. His expertise was primarily in physical anthropology, human biology, race, and population.

Among his many honors and awards, Shapiro received the Theodore Roosevelt Distinguished Service Medal (1964); a Distinguished Award for Contributions in Science from the New York Academy of Sciences (1977); and the T. Dale Stewart Award for Distinguished Service from the American Academy of Forensic Sciences (1983).

Among his books are *The Heritage of the Bounty* (1936), *Migration and Environment* (1939), *Race Mixture* (1953), *Aspects of Culture* (1956), *The Jewish People: A Biological History* (1960), and *Peking Man* (1974). He also edited *Man, Culture, and Society* (1956).

[Ephraim Fischoff / Ruth Beloff (2nd ed.)]

SHAPIRO, IRVING SAUL (1916–2001), U.S. business executive. Born in Minneapolis, the son of immigrants from Lithuania, Shapiro rose to become chairman of the giant DuPont Company and corporate America's lead liaison with Washington in the 1970s. A lawyer trained in litigation – he graduated from the University of Minnesota with a bachelor of law degree in 1941 – he joined DuPont in 1951 as a specialist in antitrust after working in the Office of Price Administration and the Justice Department in Washington. His rise at DuPont was punctuated by high-profile legal landmarks. He became closely acquainted with the company during a lengthy antitrust case that in 1962 led to DuPont's relinquishing its 37 percent stake in General Motors. Winning the trust of the DuPont family, he rose steadily at the company until he was named chairman and chief executive in 1974, the first lawyer to hold that title. Although he had little formal education in business or science, Shapiro said he developed a deep-seated understanding of business and a flair for dealing with customers from his father, who ran a dry-cleaning business in Minneapolis.

Shapiro took charge of DuPont in trying times. There was an energy crisis in the United States, and the costs of raw materials and fuel were soaring for the company, a petrochemical maker, as the economy was sliding into recession. Shapiro pulled DuPont out of numerous unprofitable businesses and put money into the others. He set up DuPont's first energy department, which created conservation programs and partnerships with oil companies and other manufacturers to develop synthetic substitutes for oil and gas. Many of the management and business models he instituted remained in place for decades. At the time, in the 1970s, antibusiness sentiment was running high. Shapiro defended American business, asserting that too much regulation was hampering America's ability to compete with Europe and Japan. Numerous products, including DuPont's Freon, were being accused of contributing to the depletion of the earth's ozone layers, while others were being labeled carcinogens. Many new regulations and restrictions were promulgated, many of which Shapiro believed stemmed from hysteria, not science.

In 1976 Shapiro was elected chairman of the Business Roundtable, an influential group of business executives. He made regulatory reform a cornerstone of his two-year tenure. He also became a personal adviser to President Jimmy Carter, and was intimately involved in drafting the response to the 1977 boycott some Arab countries placed on companies doing business with Israel. Shapiro was active in Jewish community affairs in Wilmington, Del., and at one time headed its Jewish Federation.

[Stewart Kampel (2nd ed.)]

SHAPIRO, KARL JAY (1913–2000), U.S. poet and critic. Born in Baltimore, during World War II Shapiro was a soldier in the Pacific campaign. From 1950 to 1955 he edited the Chicago periodical *Poetry*, and from 1956 he was professor of English at the State University of Nebraska. He wrote forcefully on many kinds of experience and showed a preoccupation with his own attitude toward Judaism. In such early poems as "The Synagogue" and "The Jew" (both 1943), he affirmed that his religion was flexible and easily diluted, and that he tried to write freely, "one day as a Christian, the next as a Jew." In his *Poems of a Jew* (1958), which he called "documents of an obsession," Shapiro asserted that "man is for the world, not for the afterworld"; yet, while rejecting any special Jewish commitment, he declared that mere abandonment of the Jewish religion did not negate Jewish identity, and he even admitted a measure of pride (in the poem "Israel") in the Jewish state's restoration of dignity to the Jewish name. In an interview published in 1981, he said: "In my case, the tradition was the Jew, not Judaism, not the religion, but the existence of the Jew as a person, as a creature, even as a kind of mystical presence."

He believed that Walt Whitman was America's greatest poet. He was also appreciative of Dylan Thomas as well as of William Carlos Williams. He said that "it wasn't until some of the contemporary English poets like Auden and Spender began to publish …[that] I really saw the possibilities of using contemporary English … contemporary twentieth-century English…."

His critical works include an *Essay on Rime* (1945), a critique of poetry in verse; *Beyond Criticism*, lectures (1953), reprinted as *Primer for Poets* (1965); *In Defense of Ignorance* (1960); and *The Bourgeois Poet* (1964), on the poet in society. He also wrote the Pulitzer Prize-winning *V-Letter and Other Poems* (1944); *Trial of a Poet …* (1947); *Poems, 1940–1953* (1953); an anthology *Selected Poems* (1968); *To Abolish Children, and Other Essays* (1968); and *White-haired Lover* (1968), a collection of love poems. His novel *Edsel* appeared in 1971; *Poet: An Autobiography in Three Parts*, in 1988; *The Wild Card: Selected Poems, Early and Late*, edited by Kunitz and Ignatow, in 1998; and *Creative Glut: Selected Essays of Karl Shapiro*, edited by Robert Phillips, in 2004.

BIBLIOGRAPHY: L. Bartlett, *Karl Shapiro, A Descriptive Bibliography: 1933–1977* (1979); P. Gerber, "Trying to Present America: A Conversation with Karl Shapiro," in: *Southern Humanities Review* (Summer 1981), 193–208; J. Reino, *Karl Shapiro* (1981)

SHAPIRO, (Levi Joshua) LAMED (1878–1948), Yiddish writer. Born in Rzhishchev (near Kiev), Shapiro, his early writings in hand, went to "conquer Warsaw" in 1896, but returned home two years later and supported himself by tutoring. In 1903, again in Warsaw, he published several short stories in local Yiddish periodicals and then began a period of wandering which continued to the very end of his life: to America in 1905, where he contributed stories to *Di Tsukunft* and reported briefly for the *Forverts*; in Warsaw again in 1909, he joined the staff of the daily, *Der Fraynt*, and translated from European literature. In 1910 he published his first collection, *Noveln* ("Stories"). In spite of financial and geographic instability, the decade 1908–18 was the most prolific of his career: he published his most notorious pogrom story, "*Der Tseylem*" ("The Cross"), and a number of other works which were later collected in *Di Yidishe Melukhe* ("The Jewish State," 1919). He began to drink heavily, however, suffered frequent depressions, and wrote ever more sporadically. Hopes of perfecting an invention of color cinematography took Shapiro to Los Angeles in 1921, but he returned to New York after his beloved wife Freydl's death in 1927. In 1931 he published a new story collection, *Nyu-yorkish*, focusing on the confusing life of immigrant Jewish men. A series of further literary projects, including the attempt to edit his magazine, *Studio* (1933), were unsuccessful. After a brief period of working for the Federal Writers Project of the WPA in 1937–38, Shapiro returned for the last time to Los Angeles. In 1945 he published a series of essays on literary themes entitled *Der Shrayber Geyt in Kheyder* ("The Writer Goes to School"). In 1948 he died from the effects of alchoholism. Shapiro's chaotic, restless life stands in sharpest contrast to his carefully controlled, tightly structured, and polished stories. Although many of his works explore violence and human conflict, particularly the wild frenzy of pogroms, the highly visual form of his narration and compression of detail produce a static or classical effect. Shapiro is often called "The master craftsman of the Yiddish short story."

BIBLIOGRAPHY: L. Shapiro, *Ksovim* (1949), 19–33 (biographical notes by Sh. Miller); Rejzen, Leksikon, 4 (1929), 465–9; J. Glatstein, *In Tokh Genumen* (1956), 82–91. **ADD. BIBLIOGRAPHY:** L. Garrett (ed. and trans.), *The Cross and Other Jewish Stories by Lamed Shapiro* (2006).

[Ruth Wisse / Leah Garrett (2nd ed.)]

SHAPIRO, RAMI (1951–), U.S. rabbi. Shapiro was born in 1951 in Springfield, Mass. He received a bachelor's degree from the University of Massachusetts, a master's degree in religious studies from McMaster University, and rabbinic ordination from Hebrew Union College-Jewish Institute of Religion in 1981. He received a Ph.D. in contemporary Judaism from Union Institute in Cincinnati, and took advanced training in counseling.

Shapiro served as rabbi of Temple Beth Or in Miami from 1981 to 2000, a congregation that affiliated with Reconstructionist Judaism. During this time he led the congregation to explore new and participatory forms of Judaism and spiritual growth, transforming conventional American synagogue patterns. He developed creative interpretations of liturgy, encouraged adult study and daily spiritual practice, and initiated an ethics and spiritual curriculum for teenagers called "What Would a Mentsch Do?"

Rabbi Shapiro took an active role in the Reconstructionist Rabbinical Association and Ohalah, the Jewish Renewal rabbinic network, as well as the Reform movement. From 2000 to 2002 he was rabbi of the Metivta Center for Contemplative Judaism in Los Angeles. From 1994 to 2004 he directed an Internet site for Jewish study and spiritual growth, Virtual Yeshiva (later called SimplyJewish.com.). From 2002 he headed the One River Foundation, an interfaith institute sharing the spiritual insights of Judaism, Christianity, Islam, and other religions, and continued to write and to teach widely.

Shapiro developed guides to death and mourning for non-Orthodox Jews. His creative translations of liturgy were used in many congregations. Shapiro developed an extensive approach to Jewish ritual and spiritual life, challenging liberal Jews to do more. His book *Minyan* (1997) was built around the theme of ten key principles of Jewish life, derived from but not always identical with areas of tradition. He advocated ethical consumption (based on *kashrut*), balancing work and play (Shabbat), and daily acts of kindness (*gemilut ḥasadim*) as well as urging daily spiritual practices such as silence and chanting God's names. Among his writings are creative reinterpretations of a number of classic Jewish texts, including selections from the Bible, *Pirkei Avot*, and ḥasidic tales. He wrote *Wisdom of the Jewish Sages: A Modern Reading of Pirke Avot* (1993); *Minyan: Ten Principles For Living a Life of Integrity* (1997); *The Way of Solomon: Finding Joy and Contentment in the Wisdom of Ecclesiastes* (2000); *Proverbs: The Wisdom of Solomon* (2001); *Hasidic Tales: Annotated and Explained* (2003); *The Prophets: Annotated and Explained* (2004).

[Robert Tabak (2nd ed.)]

SHAPIRO, ROBERT (1942–), U.S. lawyer. Shapiro, who was born in Plainfield, N.J., received his undergraduate education at the University of California at Los Angeles and his law degree from Loyola of Los Angeles. He was admitted to the bar in 1969 and served as a deputy district attorney in Los Angeles from 1969 to 1972. For the next 15 years he was a solo practitioner. Beginning in 1995 he was a partner in Christensen, Miller, Fink, Jacobs, Glaser, Weil & Shapiro, a firm with 120 lawyers and a major litigation practice, as well as corporate, transactions and real-estate practice. Throughout the course of his career, Shapiro defended a number of well-known clients. But none of them, who included the pornographic movie star Linda Lovelace, the television personality Johnny Carson, and the son of the actor Marlon Brando, achieved the notoriety of the case involving O.J. Simpson, who stood trial in 1994 for the murder of his wife and her friend. Shapiro, by then a well-known criminal defense attorney, replaced Simpson's original lawyer on the case, but he was forced to play a secondary role behind others on the defense "dream team" group of lawyers, headed by F. Lee Bailey and Johnnie Cochran. Shapiro bristled at his co-counselors and, when Cochran took over, he often criticized them. Simpson was cleared of the murders in a startling verdict. After the trial, Shapiro told reporters that he viewed with disgust some of the tactics employed by the defense team. "Not only did we play the race card," he said on national television, referring to the defendant, who was black, "we dealt it from the bottom of the deck." He was the author of *The Search for Justice, A Defense Attorney's Brief on the O.J. Simpson* Case (1996).

[Stewart Kampel (2nd ed.)]

SHAPIRO, SAMUEL HARVEY (1907–1987), lawyer, legislator, and governor. Shapiro, who was born in Estonia and grew up in Kankakee, Illinois, became city attorney there in 1933. Elected district attorney of Kankakee County in 1936 on the Democratic ticket, he resigned in 1941 to enlist in the U.S. Navy, in which he served for four years. In 1946 Shapiro was elected to the Illinois House of Representatives, and served 14 years. He became known for his sponsorship of mental health legislation and his exposure of corrupt officials in the state hospital system. In 1960 Shapiro was elected lieutenant governor of Illinois, and was reelected in 1964. During 1967–68 he served as acting governor, and when Governor Otto Kerner resigned in May 1968, Shapiro succeeded him. He was defeated for reelection in 1968. Shapiro was a president of Kankakee's Temple Israel, a founder and president of the Kankakee B'nai B'rith, and a member of the Anti-Defamation League. Shapiro wrote *Messages to the General Assembly of Illinois* (1968).

[Bernard Postal]

SHAPIRO, SAUL BEN DOV (1797–1859), Lithuanian rabbi. Shapiro was brought up in Krakinov by his uncle R. Moses Luria until 1811, after which he went to study in Ponevezh. Eventually he became a teacher under Isaac ha-Levi, the rabbi of Ponovezh, succeeding him in 1839. In 1853 he was appointed rabbi in Seduva, where he died.

Of his many novellae on the Talmud, *Midrash Rabbah, Sifrei, Yalkut Shimoni*, and Maimonides, and his responsa, sermons, and eulogies, only one book has been published: *Ḥemdat Sha'ul*, responsa on the Shulḥan Arukh, *Oraḥ Ḥayyim* and *Yoreh De'ah*, which was published by his son Moses (1903). However, his novellae are included in Moses b. Uriah Rappoport's commentary *Toledot Moshe* (1889), and also as an appendix to Moses Rappoport's *Imrei Moshe on Megillat Esther* (1889).

BIBLIOGRAPHY: *Yahadut Lita*, 3 (1967), 102.

[Anthony Lincoln Lavine]

SHAPIRO, YA'AKOV SHIMSHON (1902–1993), Israeli lawyer and politician. Shapiro was born in Russia and studied at the Medical School of Kharkov University. He came to Ereẓ Israel in 1924 and was one of the founders of the kibbutz Givat ha-Sheloshah. Later, Shapiro studied at the Jerusalem Law School and practiced as a lawyer. In 1948–49 he was Israel's first attorney-general. He was a member of the Second Knesset (1951), the Third (1955) and the Seventh (1969). In 1965 he was appointed minister of justice, retaining the office in Golda Meir's cabinet in 1969. In June 1972, however, following a storm over the acquittal of Mordecai Friedman, manager of the Netivei Neft oil company, on charges of irregularity, Shapiro submitted his resignation and it was cited as a rare example of a minister accepting responsibility for the mistakes of his department. On August 30, however, he rejoined the cabinet. In October 1973 he again submitted his resignation, following a controversy over criticism he made of the conduct of the Yom Kippur War by Moshe Dayan, the minister of defense, and the resignation took effect 48 hours later.

SHAPP, MILTON JERROLD (Shapiro; 1912–1994), U.S. industrialist and governor of Pennsylvania. Born in Cleveland, Ohio, Shapp moved to Philadelphia in 1935 and worked in the sale of electronic products. To avoid antisemitic sentiment, he changed his name from Shapiro to Shapp but continued to practice Judaism openly. In 1946 he founded Jerrold Electronics Corporation, which pioneered in the development of cable television access. It became a major force in the television industry, making Shapp a multimillionaire. An equal opportunity employer, Shapp hired African-Americans, Hispanics, and other minority groups; and he was one of the first executives to promote women to top management positions. In 1963 the Pennsylvania AFL-CIO named him Man of the Year, the first time a business executive was selected for that honor. In 1967 he sold his interest in the company to the General Instrument Company so that he could concentrate on politics.

In 1960, at the request of President-elect Kennedy, Shapp served as chairman of the New Growth-New Jobs conference in Philadelphia and submitted a report suggesting programs for improving job opportunities in Philadelphia. During the Kennedy administration, he served as consultant to the Peace Corps and to the U.S. Department of Commerce on Area Development problems, and was vice chairman of the National Public Advisory Committee on Area Development. Shapp first ran for the Pennsylvania governorship in 1966 but was defeated.

In 1968 he served as chairman of the Committee for Pennsylvania State Constitutional Revision. In that year he backed Eugene Mc-Carthy for president, losing the support of some labor leaders who had backed him in 1966. As a liberal, and an opponent of the Vietnam War, Shapp had the endorsement of Americans for Democratic Action and of the New Democratic Coalition. He supported state legislation attempting to prevent the sending of Pennsylvania citizens into undeclared wars. Shapp also supported abortion reform. He was elected governor of Pennsylvania in 1970 by a wide margin, becoming the first Jew to hold that office. In 1974 he won a second term by a large margin as well, serving until 1979. He was the first Pennsylvania governor to succeed himself in the 20th century. As governor, he established the Pennsylvania State Lottery, administered by the Department of Aging which his administration created. The lottery was just one of Shapp's successful attempts to restore the state to stable financial footing.

In 1976 he ran for the Democratic nomination for president but did not make it into the primaries.

Shapp served Jewish organizations in many capacities, especially the American Jewish Congress; the Allied Jewish Appeal of Philadelphia; and the Federation of Jewish Agencies of Greater Philadelphia.

He wrote *My Impressions ... Israel at Age 25* (1973).

SHAPSHAL (Szapszał) SERAYA BEN MORDECHAI (1873–1961), leader of East European Karaites, Russian Turkologist and diplomat. Born in Bakhchesaray (Crimea), he studied in the Karaite school of Simferopol where his teacher was Samuel *Pigit, but he did not graduate. In 1899 he graduated from the Oriental Department of St. Petersburg University and served as translator at the Russian Foreign Office. In 1901 he was appointed as a personal tutor of the Iranian Crown Prince Mohammad Ali Shah and, after the coronation of the latter, Shapshal became his court minister and adviser and ennobled as "khan." In Iran he acquired the nickname "bloody Shapshal," because he urged the Shah to crush the Iranian Constitutional Movement. Following the revolution in Iran, he was expelled from the country in 1908 as a Russian spy and returned to the Russian Foreign Office, teaching at the same time Turkish and Azeri in St. Petersburg University. Despite his lack of religious education and traditional way of life, in 1911 Shapshal was elected as *ḥakham* of West Russian Karaites, but he declined this office. After the demise of the *ḥakham* S. Pampulov, this office was offered to Shapshal, but he encountered strong opposition among Crimean Karaites, who did not want "bloody Shapshal" as a leader. He again declined this office and was elected only in 1915 as *ḥakham*. He began with religious reforms, which were aimed at severing Karaite religion and tradition from its Hebrew and Jewish roots, and shaping the new Turkic-Khazar identity. One of his innovations was the complete exclusion of Hebrew language and literature from the curriculum of Karaite schools. In this period he established a Karaite library-museum, "Karai Bitiqligi," which included the books and archive of the Karaite Spiritual Council from Crimea and Odessa. This library contained tens of thousands of printed editions and manuscripts in the Hebrew, Arabic, and Karaite languages. Shapshal also established a periodical "The News (Izvestiya) of the Karaite Spiritual Council" in Russia under his own editorship and published nine numbers (1917–19).

In 1919, after the Bolshevik occupation of the Crimea, which caused the deaths of masses of local population, Shapshal escaped to Istanbul and worked there at a Georgian bank. Later he was appointed as a librarian to catalogue the manuscripts in Abdul Hamid II library. In 1928 Shapshal was appointed as *ḥakham* of the Karaites in Poland and Lithuania and changed the name of this title to "gahan" (khan), to obliterate the Hebrew term and to demonstrate the Turkic background of the Karaites. From this period until the end of his life he resided in Troki. After the partition of Poland and Soviet occupation in 1939, Shapshal lost this office and became a Soviet scholar of Orientalism. After the Nazi invasion of Lithuania in 1941, he occupied the office again. He met with German authorities and convinced them of the non-Jewish racial background of the Karaites. The Nazi officials in Vilna arranged the "scientific debate" between Shapshal and the Jewish historian Zelig Kalmanovich (who was in the Vilna Ghetto and was killed by the Nazis) about the origins of the Karaites.

After World War II, following the return of Soviet occupation, Shapshal again lost his office and enrolled in the Karaite kolkhoz at Troki. Later, until the end of his life, he was a senior researcher in the Institute for History and Law of the Academy of Sciences of Soviet Lithuania.

While a student Shapshal published two booklets in Russian about Crimean Karaites: *Karaimy I Chufut Qaleh* (1896) and *Karaimy, zapiski krymskago gornago kluba* (1897). Later he published several books and articles on Turkology.

Shapshal was a spiritual leader of the Karaites, who was not accepted by the majority of the community but whose ideology led to a great extent to the de-Judaization and assimilation of East European Karaites. According to his theories, they originated from Khazars and Polovtsi. Shapshal claimed that Karaism was very close to early Christianity, and that Anan ben David recognized Jesus and Muhammad as prophets, who were sent to the Gentiles but influenced Karaism. As to East European Karaites, he claimed that they had adopted the Mosaic religion secretly keeping Turkic pagan cults, beliefs, and customs, which had a central role in the Karaite legacy.

BIBLIOGRAPHY: B. Elyashevich, *Materialy k serii narody i kultury XIV*, no. 2 (1993), 214–17; M. Kizilov. "New Materials on the biography of S.M. Szapszal (1928–1939)," in: *Materialy Deviatoy Mezhdunarodnoy Konferentsii po Iudaike*, (2002), 255–273; M. Polliack (ed.), *Karaite Judaism: A Guide to Its History and Literary Sources*, (2003), index; D. Shapira, in *Proceedings of the 14th Congress of the Turk Tarih Kurumu* (2006).

[Golda Akhiezer (2nd ed.)]

°**SHAPUR (Shahpuhr)**, the name of three Persian kings of the Sassanid dynasty. The first reigned from 241 to 272 C.E., the second from 309 to 379, and the third and last from 383/4 to 388/9. In rabbinic literature apparently only the first two are mentioned.

SHAPUR I. Samuel, the head of the academy at Nehardea, discussed with Shapur I, with whom he was on friendly terms, religious topics (Sanh. 98a; Suk. 53a), the tense political relations between Persia and Rome (Ber. 56a), and also other subjects. Although aggadic in their extant form, the conversations, in view of their subject matter and contents, are historical. The Jewish community in Babylonia, a large ethnic-religious group recognized by the authorities, was a political and economic factor of considerable importance, and Jewish representatives met the king or other representatives of local authorities to discuss matters of common concern. In the days of Samuel, as during the third century generally, Persia, which included Babylonia, was the scene of a particularly animated religious ferment. There were the sect of Mani and the fanatical priest Kartir who was actively hostile to all non-Mazdean religious minorities. His boast of his ill-treatment of the followers of various religions, the first to be mentioned being the Jews, was found in an inscription. Under such circumstances the Jews appealed to the authorities for protection, these contacts providing an occasion for discussions on religious topics. In any event, talmudic literature records no complaint against Shapur I (see Samuel's reaction in MK 26a).

SHAPUR II. Many statements refer to the contacts and ties between Shapur II, and particularly between his mother Ifra Hormizd, and the Babylonian *amoraim*. While still a baby, Shapur II succeeded to the throne and until his majority the regency consisted of several members of the aristocracy and the queen mother. In his lengthy reign two periods may be distinguished. The first concluded in 363 C.E. with the defeat of the emperor Julian in his campaign against the Persian empire, ushering in the second period during which the political position of the Jews of Persia improved in recognition of their unexpected loyalty to the empire. It had been feared that they would revolt against Shapur II and assist Julian, who had promised the Jews of Ereẓ Israel that he would rebuild the Temple in Jerusalem on his return from the Persian War. While Shapur II, at the instigation of the Mazdean priests, persecuted the Christians in the Persian empire, he did not intentionally harm the Jews, a distinction resulting from Christian hopes of a victory for Christian Byzantium, his mortal enemy, with which they were believed to be in contact. To finance his protracted wars against Rome, Shapur II demanded considerable sums of money from the Jews, of which Rava complained in the '30s and '40s of the fourth century C.E. (Ḥag. 5b). Because of these wars, the Jews, like the rest of the population, were compelled to billet soldiers in their homes (Pes. 5b; Ḥul. 94b), and as a result there were cases of rape (Ket. 3b). Isolated instances of premeditated attacks on the Jews may also have occurred (SOZ, ed. Neubauer, 72), but the evidence is inconclusive, and may refer to Shapur I. A conversation took place between Shapur II and R. Ḥama on a halakhic subject, that of the burial of the dead (Sanh. 46b), for contrary to the *halakhah* the Persians interred a corpse only when all its flesh, which they believed defiled the earth, had been consumed by wild beasts or birds of prey. Aggadic in character but indicative of the good relations that existed between Ifra Hormizd, the queen mother, and the Jews are the talmudic statements that she sent money for charitable purposes to R. Joseph (BB 8a) and also to Rava (BB 10b), and a sacrifice to the latter to be offered in honor of Heaven (Zev. 116b); that she protected Rava from the king's anger (Ta'an. 24b); and that she submitted to him a halakhic problem (Nid. 20b).

BIBLIOGRAPHY: T. Noeldeke, *Gesehichte der Perser und Araber. des Tabari* (1879), 25–42, 52–68; idem, *Aufsaetze zur persischen Geschichte* (1887), 97ff.; S. Funk, *Die Juden in Babylonien*, 1 (1902), 71f.; 2 (1908), 4, 5, 13; idem, in: MGWJ, 49 (1905), 534–56; M. Sprengling, *Third Century Iran* (1953); Widengren, in: *Iranica Antiqua*, 1 (1961), 132 (Eng.).

[Moshe Beer]

SHAR'AB, geographic region between Ibb and Tai'zz in southwest *Yemen, most of it a plain plateau, and on its east side the main *San'a-Dhamār-*Yarīm route. There were scores of Jewish communities in the region. Their method of study consisted of the memorization of texts by continued repetition. The main subjects of study were *aggadah* and Midrash on the one hand, and Kabbalah, particularly the Zohar, on the other. The great Yemenite poets of the Mashtā family, Joseph b. Israel and Shalom *Shabazī, were from Shar'ab, as was R. Shalom *Sharabi, the kabbalist. Shabazī has been the most popular personality of Yemenite Jewry throughout all its long existence. There were many religious and kabbalist scholars among them who tended to deal with miraculous deeds. They preserved the correct emphatic pronunciation of the *qof* and had two other linguistic peculiarities: (a) the complete identification of *ṣeri* and *ḥolam*, as was common to the Jews of Babylon and the Jewish communities in the vicinity, but reflecting the ancient Hebrew pronunciation in the land of biblical Judea; (b) the pronunciation of *gimmel* with a *dagesh* as *g*, unlike all other Yemenite Jews who pronounce it *j* (and in Arabic as well). Most of them were weavers, silversmiths, tailors, and shoemakers, but some were also landowners and coffee planters, whose fields were cultivated by Arabs. Their immigration to the Land of Israel commenced in 1911–12, following Sh. Yavne'eli's mission to Yemen. At first they were settled near the Kinneret, but they later moved to Kefar Marmorek. Many of them became residents of the Ha-Tikvah Quarter in Tel Aviv. In the moshavot they worked in agriculture and in the cities as manual laborers.

BIBLIOGRAPHY: S. Ḥozeh, *Sefer Toledot ha-Rav Shalom Shabazi u-Minhagei Yahadut Shar'ab be-Teiman* (1973); Y. Tobi, in: *Ḥozeh* (1973), 19–21; idem, "*Ṣeri ve-Ḥolam be-Mivta Yehudei Teiman*," in: Y. Raztaby (1967), 52–57.

[Yosef Tobi (2nd ed.)]

SHARABI, SHALOM (1720–1777), Jerusalem kabbalist. Sharabi was born in *Sana in *Yemen, where the study of *Kabbalah and mysticism was widespread. in his youth, he emigrated to Ereẓ Israel via *Damascus. In Damascus he was involved in a controversy with the local rabbis concerning the meaning of the minimum quantity ("the size of an olive") prescribed for the eating of *matzah* on Passover night. When he arrived in *Jerusalem, he prayed and studied at the kabbalistic yeshivah Bet El, which had been founded in 1737 by the kabbalist Gedaliah Ḥayon. There the prayers were held in accordance with the mystical meditations of Isaac *Luria. Like the Jerusalem kabbalists, he studied only the Lurianic Kabbalah, as transmitted through the works of Ḥayyim *Vital, Luria's outstanding pupil. Soon he became widely known as a man of outstanding piety and as a kabbalist. Sharabi succeeded Gedaliah Ḥayon as head of the yeshivah after the latter's death (1751). During his leadership, he did much for the yeshivah, initiated important regulations, and arranged the order of prayer. He became known as one of the greatest rabbis in Jerusalem and his signature appears on several documents preserved from this period. In 1754 and 1758, he and other rabbis of Jerusalem signed the note binding the association of kabbalists, *Ahavat Shalom*. In 1774 he signed next to the leaders of the community of Jerusalem on a letter for emissaries to Western Europe.

Sharabi's life was embellished by legends even from his youth, and in Ereẓ Israel he was famous as a saint and miracle worker. Popular tradition links his departure from Yemen with a miracle that occurred after a rich Muslim woman tried to seduce him. In Bet El he worked as a servant and hid his learning from others; only miraculously was his deep knowledge of Kabbalah discovered and he became a member of the kabbalistic circle. According to legend, the prophet Elijah appeared to him, and he was an incarnation of Luria. After his death, his name became greatly revered among the Jews of Jerusalem and among the kabbalists of Bet El. His grandson, Solomon Moses Ḥai Gagin, wrote a poem of praise on his expertise in *Eẓ Ḥayyim* and in *Shemonah She'arim* of Ḥayyim Vital. The members of Bet El used to prostrate themselves on his grave on the Mount of Olives on the commemoration of his death. His signature was Shalom Mizraḥi di-Ydi'a Sharabi and his titles Ha-Reshash or Ha-Shemesh (both are Hebrew acronyms of Shalom Mizraḥi Sharabi).

Sharabi's books are on Lurianic Kabbalah. Particularly famous is his prayer book *Nehar Shalom* (Salonika, 1806), which includes in detail the secrets and mystical meditations on prayers and on *mitzvot* for the entire year according to Luria's Kabbalah. It became popular in Ereẓ Israel and North Africa after his death. His contemporary, Ḥ.J.D. *Azulai, attested that Sharabi studied the Lurianic teachings in depth and presented the mystical meditations of Luria clearly and correctly. He annotated corruptions in the texts and elucidated lacunae and contradictions. His glosses and explanations of Luria's writings are an important source for their understanding.

The missing part of the work was published later in an edition of *Eẓ Ḥayyim* (1866–67; 1910). It was published in Jerusalem in two editions (1911–12; 1916). Parts of the prayer book were published under different titles and in many editions from 1911. He also wrote *Reḥovot ha-Nahar*, a commentary on Luria's principles (Salonika, 1806); and *Emet ve-Shalom*, glosses to Ḥayyim Vital's *Eẓ Ḥayyim* (Salonika, 1806), later published in *Eẓ Ḥayyim* (Salonika, 1842; Jerusalem, 1866–67).

BIBLIOGRAPHY: Azulai, 1 (1958), 174; Ashor b. Israel, in: *Lu'aḥ Ereẓ Yisrael* (ed. Luncz), 19 (1914), 69–78; Abraham Nadaf, *Seridei Teiman* (1928), 5; A.L. Frumkin, *Toledot Ḥakhmei Yerushalayim* (1929), 116–9; Ariel ben Zion, *Sar Shalom Sharabi* (1930).

[Yehuda Ratzaby]

SHARANSKY (Shcharansky), NATAN (Anatoly; 1948–), Jewish dissident in the Soviet Union and Israeli politician, member of the Fourteenth and Fifteenth Knessets. Born in Donetsk, in Ukraine, Sharansky started studying mathematics and computer sciences in 1966, obtaining his degree from the mathematics and physics institute in Moscow. After the Soviet invasion of Prague in August 1968, he decided to join the struggle for human rights in the Soviet Union. In 1973 he first applied for an exit permit in order to immigrate to Israel, but his request was denied. He proceeded to become an articulate spokesman for Jewish emigration from the Soviet Union to Israel, but refused to cooperate with Israel's efforts vis-à-vis Jews who left the Soviet Union for other destinations. Following the signing of the Helsinki Agreement for Security and Cooperation in Europe in 1975, he joined the Helsinki group in the Soviet Union headed by Andrei Sakharov, and was its contact man with Western journalists reporting on the dissident movement in the Soviet Union. Sharansky convinced Yuri Orlov to lead a small group of Jewish and non-Jewish dissidents to refuse exit visas that the Soviet Union was willing to offer them in order to get rid of them, so that they could continue to monitor the Soviet failure to comply with the Helsinki Accords. Accused in a March 1977 *Izvestia* article of working for the CIA, Sharansky was arrested shortly thereafter on charges of treason and espionage, and sentenced to 13 years imprisonment. Having gained some fame as a dissident before his imprisonment, there was a good deal of international activity to get him released. His wife Avital, whom he had married in 1974 and who had managed to leave for Israel, stood at the head of the campaign for his release. Sharansky was finally released as part of an exchange of prisoners between the United States and the Soviet Union on February 11, 1986, and received a hero's welcome in Israel. Sharansky continued to be active on behalf of Soviet Jewry, and in 1988 was elected head of the Zionist Forum – an umbrella organization engaged in helping in the absorption of immigrants from the former Soviet Union. Following the Declaration of Principles in 1993, he established an organization called "Mabat Lashalom" to follow the agreements between Israel and the Palestinians. In 1996, prior to the elections to the Fourteenth Knesset, he formed a new immigrants' party called Yisrael ba-Aliyah. The new party, which was considered moderately right-wing, gained seven seats and joined the government formed by Binyamin *Netanyahu. Sharansky was appointed minister of industry and trade. In the late 1990s he was accused by former prisoner of Zion Yuli Nudelman of having collaborated with the KGB, but the accusations were never substantiated. In the elections to the Fifteenth Knesset Yisrael ba-Aliyah gained six seats, and joined the government formed by Ehud *Barak. Sharansky was appointed minister of the interior – a ministry that was important for the new immigrants – after the Ministry had been in the hands of *Shas for most of the previous fifteen years. However, Sharansky and his party left the government over Barak's peace policy in July 2000. Sharansky then joined the government established by Ariel *Sharon in 2001, and was appointed deputy prime minister and minister of construction and housing. In the elections to the Sixteenth Knesset Yisrael be-Aliyah gained only two seats, and Sharansky decided to resign his Knesset seat. The two Yisrael be-Aliyah MKs then joined the Likud. In Sharon's new government Sharansky, no longer a member of the Knesset, was appointed minister without portfolio in charge of Jerusalem. In the controversy within the Likud concerning Sharon's disengagement plan Sharansky joined the "rebels," who objected to the plan, and after all the parliamentary efforts to foil the plans failed, resigned from the government in May 2005. His 2004 book, *The Case for Democracy: The Power of Freedom to Overcome Tyranny and Terror*, was warmly praised by U.S. President Bush. Among his other writings are (Anatoly and Avital Shcharansky) *The Journey Home* (1986) and *Fear No Evil* (1988).

BIBLIOGRAPHY: A. Shcharansky, *Habayta: Sippuro Shel Anatoly Shcharansky* (1980); M. Gilbert, *Shcharansky: Hero of Our Time* (1986); A. Silberman, *Freedom in Slavery: The Story of Natan Sharansky* (1990); Y. Nudelman, *Sharansky Beli Masekhah* (1999).

[Susan Hattis Rolef (2nd ed.)]

SHARETT (Shertok), MOSHE (1894–1965). Zionist leader, and prime minister of Israel 1954–55. Member of the First to Fifth Knessets. Sharett was born in Kherson in Ukraine. His parents, who were members of the *Bilu movement, settled in Ereẓ Israel in the early 1880s but returned to Russia. As a child Sharett went to a modern *heder*, and attended a Russian gymnasium in Kherson. At the same time grew up in a Zionist atmosphere and studied Hebrew. In 1906 his family resettled in Palestine, first in the Arab village of ʿAyn Sīniya in Samaria, where Sharett learned Arabic and gained a close insight into the life and customs of the Arab villagers. This experience accompanied him in later life, making him more sensitive to Arab feelings and sensitivities. In 1908 the family moved to Jaffa and Sharett's father, Jacob, was one of the founders of the Aḥuzat Bayit quarter, from which Tel Aviv grew. In the years 1908–13 Sharett attended the Herzliya gymnasium in Tel Aviv. When his father died, he helped support the family by giving private lessons in Hebrew, Turkish, and Arabic. With his classmates Eliyahu *Golomb and Dov *Hos (both of whom married sisters of Sharett's), David *Hacohen, and others, he established close ties with pioneers of the Second Aliyah. After graduating from high school, he went to Constantinople to study law. Upon the outbreak of World War I he volunteered for the Turkish army, and received the rank of officer. He served in Macedonia and in Aleppo, inter alia as an interpreter of the commander of the German Army operating in Turkey.

At the end of the war Shertok returned to Palestine, and in 1919 was among the founders of *Ahdut ha-Avodah, in which he became a close associate of Berl *Katznelson. In 1920 Sharett went to England to study at the London School of Economics, where one of his professors was Harold *Laski. In London he became active in the British Po'alei Zion movement. He returned to Palestine in 1925 and was nominated by Katznelson as deputy editor of the newly founded Histadrut-owned daily *Davar*. Upon the recommendation of Chaim *Arlosoroff in 1931 he was appointed Secretary of the Jewish Agency's Political Department. Following Arlosoroff's assassination in 1933, Shertok was elected by the Eighteenth Zionist Congress as his successor as head of the Political Department, a post he held until the establishment of the State of Israel in 1948. Sharett was responsible for day-to-day contacts with the British Mandatory authorities, the preparation of the Jewish case for presentation to the various British commissions of inquiry on the situation in Palestine, and a wide range of activities in the field of information and public relations. In 1937, and again in 1947, Sharett supported partition, if that would lead to the establishment of a Jewish state. It was on his initiative that the Jewish Supernumerary Police were established in the course of the Arab Revolt of 1936–39. At the outbreak of World War II he was one of the leaders of the recruitment of Jews from Palestine to the British army, playing an important role in the establishment of the *Jewish Brigade. On June 29, 1946 – "Black Saturday" – he was one of the Jewish leaders arrested by the British, and was detained for four months at the Latrun detention camp. In 1947 he played a major role in the diplomatic battle to get the UNSCOP partition plan approved (see *Palestine, Inquiry Commissions, and *Palestine, Partition) by the UN General Assembly. Upon the establishment of the State of Israel he was appointed as its first foreign minister, which is when he officially changed his name from Shertok to Sharett. Sharett was responsible for establishing Israel's highly professional foreign service and opening diplomatic delegations in dozens of countries around the world, paying special attention to Latin America. He was among those who supported contacts with West Germany, and signed the Luxembourg Agreement with Konrad *Adenauer over the issue of *restitution payments to Israel in 1952. Though in later years he was to be criticized for allegedly opting for a totally Western orientation and accused of neglecting Asia, he had in fact made efforts to establish contacts within the framework of the Asian socialist movement, but enjoyed only limited success. While he favored nonalignment, within the objective constraints, including the major role played by Egypt and other Muslim states within the nonaligned bloc, such an option did not exist for Israel. When David *Ben-Gurion temporarily retired to Sedeh Boker in January 1954, Sharett succeeded him as prime minister, retaining the Foreign Affairs portfolio and handing the Defense portfolio to Pinḥas *Lavon. It was in the course of his premiership that the "*esek bish*" (later named the *Lavon Affair) took place, though he himself was not implicated. When Ben-Gurion resumed the post of prime minister in November 1955, Sharett continued to serve as foreign minister, but due to growing differences of opinion between the two men over Ben-Gurion's activism, he resigned in June 1956. He was critical of the *Sinai Campaign, which took place four months after his resignation, viewing it as rash. In 1960 he was elected chairman of the Zionist Organization and Jewish Agency Executive. He continued to support strong links between the State of Israel and the Zionist Organization, and devoted his last years to Zionist endeavors among the Jewish communities abroad. He also continued to be active within Mapai. In the Lavon Affair controversy that continued to bedevil Mapai, Sharett was one of Ben-Gurion's principal opponents. The Affair finally led to the breakup of Mapai in 1965 – the year of his death. In these years Sharett, who was a master of the Hebrew language and engaged in the translation of poetry in foreign languages into Hebrew, also served as chairman of the Am Oved publishing house. He passed away in Jerusalem and was buried in the Old Cemetery in Tel Aviv.

Throughout his political career Sharett was well served by his capacity for clear and systematic thinking, his analytical power, his thoroughness and diligence, and his unusual linguistic talents (he was proficient in eight languages). He never relied on intuition, but examined every question in detail, took pains to acquire a thorough knowledge of the material, and studied the arguments of the other side. In speech and in writing he was a perfectionist in regard to both form and content.

Several educational institutions, a fund for the encouragement of young artists, as well as several neighborhoods and numerous streets throughout Israel bear his name.

Among his writings are *Texts of Addresses Presenting the Position of the Government of Israel on the Future of Jerusalem, During the Fourth Session of the General Assembly of the United Nations, 1949* (1950); *The Challenge of the Land* (1960); and a "political diary," *Yoman Medini* (1968–76).

BIBLIOGRAPHY: S. Lachower, *Kitvei Moshe Sharett: Bibliographyah 1920–1965* (1920–65); W. Eytan, *Moshe Sharett, 1894–1965* (1966); M.Z. Rosensaft, *Moshe Sharett: Statesman of Israel* (1966); A. Saviv, *Moshe Sharett: Pioneer and Statesman* (1967); U. Bialer, *David Ben-Gurion u-Moshe Sharett: Tadmiyyot ve-Haḥlatot Erev Hakamat ha-Medinah* (1971); R. Yanai-Strassman, *Hashpa'at Ma'arekhet ha-Emunot ve-ha-Tefissot shel Manhig Politi al Iẓuv Mediniyyut ha-Ḥuẓ: "Ha-Kod ha-Operativi" shel Moshe Sharett* (1981); S. Farhah, *Yaḥaso shel Moshe Sharett la-She'elah ha-Aravit bein ha-Shanim 1918–1939* (1988); G. Sheffer, *Moshe Sharett: Biography of a Political Moderate* (1996).

[Susan Hattis Rolef (2nd ed.)]

SHARETT (Shertok), YEHUDAH (1901–1979), Israeli composer; brother of Moshe *Sharett. Born in Kherson, Yehudah Sharett was brought to Ereẓ Israel at the age of five and shared in the family's adventurous settlement in the Arab village of ʿAyn Sīniya. After their move to Jaffa he studied violin and music at the institution directed by Shulamith Ruppin (later the "Shulamit Conservatory"). In 1922 he joined kibbutz *En-Harod; there he founded the "Emek Quartet" whose members gave many concerts in agricultural settlements and at the same time continued to fulfill their daily stint of manual labor. In 1926 he joined kibbutz *Yagur. In 1929 he went to Germany to study with the noted music educator Fritz Joede. Upon his return he began to compose intensively for the needs of his kibbutz, from simple children's songs to his crowning achievement – the *Yagur Passover Seder Service*. Between 1937 and 1939 Sharett published eight song collections called *Anot* which principally contained his own songs and compositions. They were the first music publications of the workers' movement and the first of their kind in the country.

No. 2, for *Omer and Passover, already contained the nucleus of the *seder*; no. 4, "for the days of siege and bloodshed" served for ceremonies during the Arab riots; no. 8 included choral works by 16th- and 17th-century European composers, with words adapted by Sharett. Of Sharett's songs and choral pieces, the following became especially popular: *Kumu To'ei Midbar* (words by Bialik; choral setting, edited by Josef *Tal); *Ha-Bonim ba-Ḥomah*; a group of songs by the poet Raḥel, including *Ve-Ulai, Hen Damah be-Dami Zorem; Lo Sharti Lakh Arẓi* (early 1930s); *El Al be-Eyal* (D. Shimoni); and *Ha-Geshem Ḥalaf Halakh Lo* (Song of Songs). The Passover *seder* service (*Seder Pesaḥ Nusaḥ Yagur*, 1951) evolved with the collaboration of the members of Yagur. Its basic text is the "Spring" and "Exodus" passages from the Song of Songs and the Book of Exodus, together with a considerable part of the traditional *Haggadah*. Participation is distributed between the celebrants, an adult's choir, a children's choir (with a small percussion ensemble), adult and child soloists, adult and child speakers, and an "ad hoc" ensemble of available instruments. Almost all nonreligious kibbutzim in Israel adapted Sharett's *seder*, or many parts of it. A few of the melodies (such as Sh. *Postolsky's *Ha Laḥma Anya*) were taken from other composers, but the *seder*, as a whole, is Sharett's creation.

In 1953 Sharett left Yagur and settled in *Neveh Yam. From that time he also worked on the creation of "kibbutz liturgies" for the High Holidays.

BIBLIOGRAPHY: *Enziklopedyah le-Musikah. Ishei ha-Musikah ha-Yisre'elit ve-ha-Kelalit* (1959), 779–84; P.E. Gradenwitz, *Music and Musicians in Israel* (1959), 122; *Who Is Who in ACUM* (1965); B. Bayer, in: *Dukhan*, 8 (1966), 89–98.

[Bathja Bayer]

SHAREZER (Heb. שַׂרְאֶצֶר), an abbreviated Babylonian name meaning "… [name of deity] protect the king" (cf. Nergal-Sharezer; Jer. 39:3, 13).

1. According to II Kings 19:37 (= Isa. 37:38; cf. II. Chron. 32:21), Sharezer and *Adrammelech murdered their father, King Sennacherib, in the Temple of Nisroch and fled to Ararat.

2. The name in Zechariah 7:2, sometimes read Sharezer, should most likely be combined with the preceding word and read Bethel-Sharezer (see *Regem-Melech).

BIBLIOGRAPHY: J.P. Hyatt, in: JBL, 56 (1937), 387ff.; J.A. Montgomery, *The Book of Kings* (ICC, 1951), 498–9.

[Bezalel Porten]

SHARFMAN, ISAIAH LEO (1886–1969), U.S. economist. Born in the Ukraine, Sharfman was brought to the United States in 1894, and in 1910 began his teaching career at the Imperial Pei-Yang University in Tientsin (China). Returning to the United States in 1912, he became a member of the faculty of the University of Michigan, and was later professor. From 1927 until his retirement in 1955 he served as chairman of the economics department. He was a member of many federal boards and commissions. In 1955 he became a trustee of Brandeis University and was deeply involved in all of its affairs. Sharfman's magnum opus was *The Interstate Commerce Commission* (5 vols., 1931–37).

His other publications dealt mainly with public control of economic activity, especially federal regulation of transportation. His analysis of regulatory problems reflected profound legal knowledge and a sense of social justice. He considered the regulatory process as a means for a democratic society to bring its economic affairs under rational and orderly control.

[Joachim O. Ronall]

SHARGOROD (Pol. **Szarogród**; in Jewish sources **Sharigrad**), town in Vinnitsa district, Ukraine; until 1793 within Poland. An organized Jewish community existed there from the latter half of the 17th century. Both Jewish and gentile inhabitants of Shargorod suffered from continued assaults by the Cossacks. In this period the community erected a magnificent fortified synagogue. When the town was conquered by the Turks toward the end of the 17th century, the building was used as a mosque. During the 18th century the Jews of Shargorod played an important role in the trade with Turkey. In 1765 the community numbered 2,210, and was then the largest in Podolia. At the end of the 17th and the first half of the 18th centuries Shargorod was a center of Shabbateanism. The ḥasidic leaders Naphtali Herz of Shargorod and *Jacob Joseph of Polonnoye were active in the town, the latter holding rabbinical office until 1748. In the 19th century the Jews engaged in the trade of agricultural products, the manufacture and sale of alcoholic beverages, owned most of the 125 town shops, peddling in the villages of the region, and crafts. In 1881–82 the community suffered from pogroms. The Jewish population numbered 3,570 in 1847 and 3,859 (73% of the total) in 1897. By the beginning of the 20th century there existed a Jewish state school for girls and two private schools, apart from *ḥadarim*. In 1926 the community numbered 2,697 (55.9%), and by 1939 the number had dropped to 1,664 (74.6% of the total population). Between the wars there existed a Jewish town council and a Yiddish school. Most of the Jews worked in cooperatives and kolkhozes. Shargorod was occupied by the Germans on July 22, 1941, and annexed by the Romanians to Transnistria in September. A ghetto and a Jewish police were established. In October–November the Romanians added about 5,000 Jews – mainly from Bukovina, but also from Bessarabia – to the 1,800 Jews of the town and its environs. The crowding in the ghetto caused epidemics, and by June 1942 some 1,449 had died of typhus. The Judenrat fought the epidemics by opening a hospital, a pharmacy, and a sanitation station. With the help of the Aid Commitee from Bucharest it organized shops where food, medicine, clothes, and other essentials were produced. An orphanage and school for 186 children was opened. About 1,000 Jews were dispersed on June 30 into 10 nearby villages, and in May 1943 some 175 were sent to a labor camp in Trikhaty (near Nikolayev), where they perished. In September 1943 there were still 2,731 Jews from Bukovina and 240 from Bessarabia in the Shargorod ghetto. In 1979, 800 Jews (23% of the total population) lived there, but there was no synagogue. Most of the Jews left in the 1990s.

BIBLIOGRAPHY: I. Schiper, *Szieje handlu żidowskiego na ziemiach polskich* (1937), 259f.; G. Loukomsky, *Jewish Art in European Synagogues* (1947), index; S.A. Horodezky, *Le-Korot ha-Ḥasidut* (1904), 7–11, 17–28; M. Teich, in: *Yad Vashem Studies*, 2 (1958), 219–54.

[Shimshon Leib Kirshenboim / Shmuel Spector (2nd ed.)]

SHARLIN, WILLIAM (1920–), U.S. cantor. Born in Brooklyn, he attended the Yeshiva of Harlem and then a yeshivah in the Bronx before attending the Talmudical Academy of Yeshiva University and the Bet Midrash le-Morim at Yeshiva. His parents moved to Jerusalem, Palestine in 1935, where he studied at the Jerusalem Conservatory of Music and the Bet Midrah le-Morim run by Mizrachi. His returned with his parents to New York in 1939 and attended high school at night and then Manhattan School of Music, receiving both his B.A. and M.A. in 1949. His studies were interrupted by war service and he was in the U.S. army between 1942 and 1945. Thus, he was both a learned Jew and a classically trained musician, at home in the synagogue and at home in all facets of music, classic and contemporary.

In 1949 Sharlin entered the School of Sacred Music at HJUC-JIR and then entered its cantorial program while pursuing graduate work at the Cincinnati Conservatory of Music.

He moved to Los Angeles in 1954, combining a part-time position at the newly formed Leo Baeck Temple and teaching at the Hebrew Union College's Los Angeles Campus. He remained at Leo Baeck until his retirement in 1988, introducing many of his compositions in different services and for special education. He had a firm grasp of the seriousness of liturgical movement and was a cantor at a time when many Reform congregations had soloists and choirs. He brought to the synagogue, in the words of its Rabbi Leonard Beerman, a sense of musical vitality and the musically possible. Although a formally trained musician, he was one of the first to introduce the guitar to synagogue service, bringing the liveliness and informality of the camp experience back into the synagogue.

At Hebrew Union College, he was chairman of the Department of Sacred Music. Among the programs he established was a program for cantorial certification and one for synagogue organists. He also continued a long tradition of

Ḥanukkah lamp made from stone, 6th century En-Gedi.
Photo: Z. Radovan, Jerusalem.

The production of ceremonial objects was a major venue through which Jews expressed their artistic abilities, despite the partial prohibition against sculpture. The focus centered on items related to the synagogue and prayers, festivals, and home rituals. Materials and styles for the same function varied among the dispersed Jewish communities, lending a rich texture to the overarching Jewish civilization.

CEREMONIAL OBJECTS

(opposite page):
Tiered *seder* set, Poland, 18th–19th century. Cast, cut-out, and engraved brass; painted and stained wood; ink on paper; embroidered silk; linen; and cotton. 13-3/4" x 14" (35 x 35.5 cm). *Gift of the Danzig Jewish Community. The Jewish Museum, New York.*

(this page):
A Torah shrine wall painting in Dura Europos, one of the earliest known synagogues, c. 245 C.E. *Photo: Z. Radovan, Jerusalem.*

Decorative paper cutting hung in the *sukkah* to indicate the direction of prayer, eastern Germany, 19th century. *Photo: Z. Radovan, Jerusalem.*

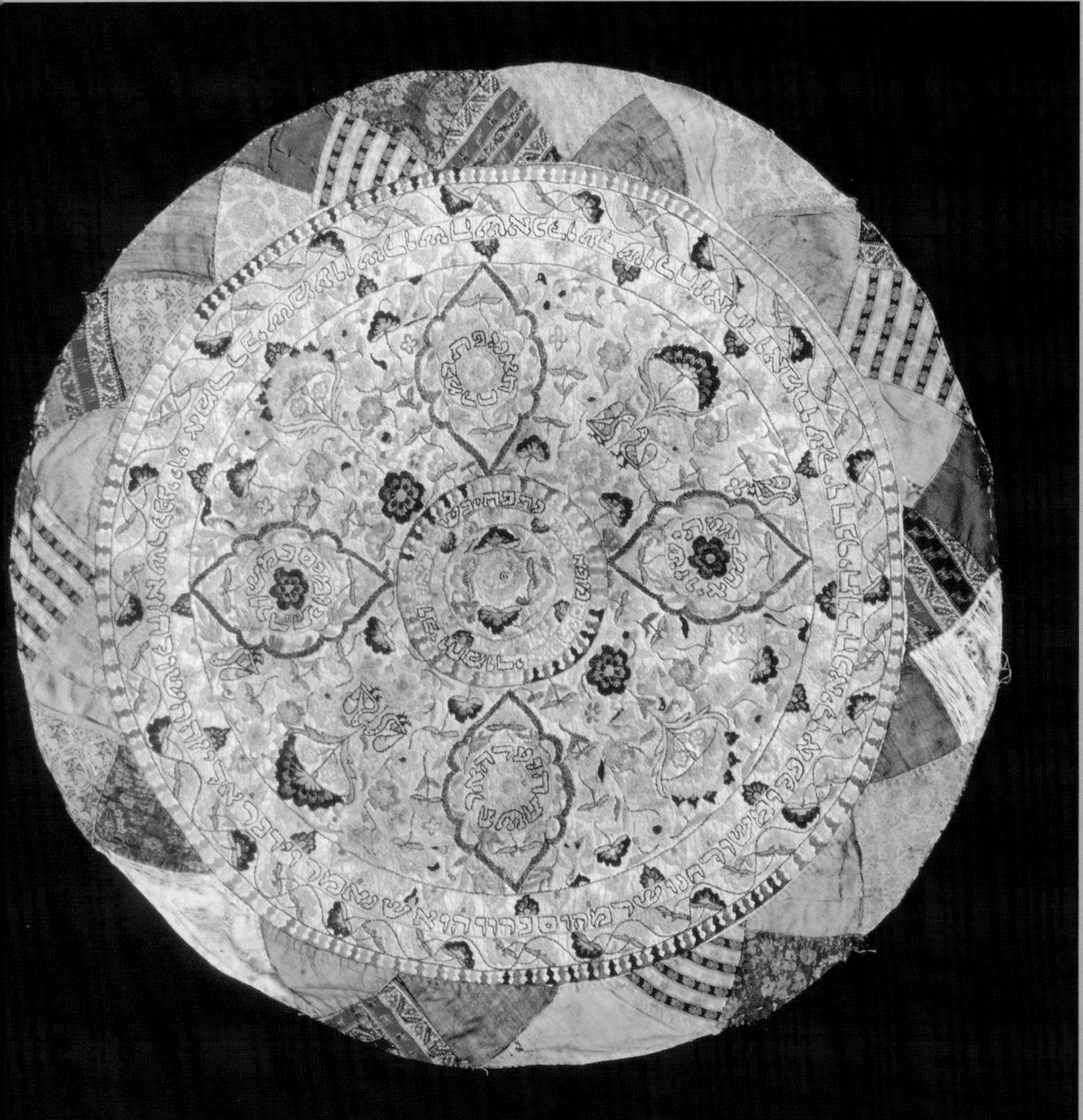

Cover for the Sabbath table. Kurdistan, early 19th Century. Cotton: embroidered with polychrome silk; polychrome silk and wool border, 88 cm, F 6033. *Gift of Dr. Harry G. Friedman. The Jewish Museum, New York.*

(opposite page):
Tallit **(prayer shawl),** ***tallit*** **bag, and** ***tefillin*** **(phylacteries) bag, Shanghai, 1904. Silk, embroidered with silk thread.** *Gift of Mr. and Mrs. Revan Komaroff. From the Collection of the Hebrew Union College Skirball Museum, Los Angeles.*

(this page):
Torah scroll in its decorated silver case, Iraq, c. 19th century. *Photo: Z. Radovan, Jerusalem.*

Torah case, Kaifeng, China, possibly 18th century. Wood, lacquered, and gilt; bronze; and iron. *From the Collection of the Hebrew Union College Skirball Museum, Los Angeles.*

RIGHT: Torah case and finial, Afghanistan, 18th century. Wood, silver, and cotton. *Collection, The Israel Museum, Jerusalem. Photo: Z. Radovan, Jerusalem.*

working with individuals and training them in a mentoring program as cantors. He continued that well into the age of retirement. He was a composer and arranger as well as a cantor. Among his more important works was the service that he composed for the inauguration of Alfred Gottschalk, his former colleague in Los Angeles, as president of Hebrew Union College-Jewish Institute of Religion in 1971. His collected works have been published.

BIBLIOGRAPHY: J.E. Cohen, "The Life and Music of Cantor William Sharlin" (M.A. thesis, HUC-JIR, 1990); K.M. Olitzsky, L.J. Sussman, and M.H. Stern, *Reform Judaism in America: A Biographical Dictionary and Sourcebook* (1993).

[Michael Berenbaum (2nd ed.)]

SHARM EL-SHEIKH, TIRĀN ISLAND, AND TIRĀN STRAITS. Sharm el-Sheikh and Sharm al-Mā (Sharm el-Moye) are two small bays on the southeastern coast of the Sinai Peninsula, opening out to the Red Sea. They are situated 10 mi. (16 km.) north of Ra's Muhammad, the southern tip of Sinai, and 15 mi. (24 km.) southwest of the Tirān Straits and the southern end of the Eilat Gulf. The two bays are separated from each other by a narrow headland. The Arabic name of the first is related to the tomb of a Bedouin sheikh on its shore; in 1956, it was given the Hebrew name Mifraẓ \Shelomo ("Solomon's Bay"). Sharm al-Mā means "Water Bay." The local climate is arid-tropical, with summer temperatures in the 95–104° F (35–40° C) range, and precipitation remaining well below the 1 in. (25 mm.) annual average. The shore beyond the bays is hemmed in by coral reefs and mangrove thickets.

Tirān Island, at the southern issue of the Eilat Gulf, is composed of a northern and southern part, with a bay thrusting deeply into its eastern coast. Measuring 23 sq. mi. (59 sq. km.), it is over 7 mi. (12 km.) long and 6.5 mi. (11 km.) wide. Although mostly flat, a mountain 500 meters high rises at its southern end. The island is today uninhabited and has no fresh water supply. East of it lies the smaller Sināfir (Senappir) island (surface 9 sq. mi., 24 sq. km.), which belongs to Saudi Arabia. Between Tiran and the Ra's Nuṣrānī Cape on the Sinai Coast, a 4 mi. (7 km.) wide strait connects the Eilat Gulf with the Red Sea; coral reef isles, however, reduce its width to 2.5 mi. (4 km.), and the width where the water depth permits a secure passage to ocean-going vessels does not exceed 200–300 meters.

In the late Roman and early Byzantine periods, when Jewish centers of Arabia and Ethiopia developed trade with the Red Sea, a community of Jewish merchants was founded on Tiran in the fifth century, which named itself "Yotvat." It was destroyed by Emperor Justinian in 535 C.E. On the Sharm el-Sheikh shore, Bedouin occasionally camped. Paul *Friedmann, who planned to found a Jewish state in Midian to absorb Jewish refugees from czarist Russia, set up a temporary camp in Sharm al-Ma'. The Turks sent a unit of soldiers to Midian to prevent the group's landing there. The episode contributed to exacerbate the Turko-British quarrel over Sinai, and a decade later proved to have a negative influence on Theodor *Herzl's el-Arish project.

After Israel's War of Independence (1948), the Egyptians built camps and fortifications at Sharm el-Sheikh and Ra's Nuṣrānī, with the intention of blocking the Tirān Straits to Israel shipping. To give them a foothold for the purpose, Saudi Arabia ceded Tirān Island to Egypt in 1949. Egypt thus repudiated the international law requiring that such waterways remain open to the shipping of all nations, even when both their sides are under the same political authority. The blockade was broken in the *Sinai Campaign, when Israel forces reached the Sharm el-Sheikh and Tirān area overland on Nov. 3, 1956, blowing up the huge guns at Ra's Nuṣrānī which had dominated the straits. On the basis of the maritime powers' undertaking in the United Nations that free shipping through the Tirān Straits would be guaranteed, Israel evacuated all of Sinai. A UN force was stationed at Sharm el-Sheikh and Ra's Nuṣrānī, guarding the straits and thereby permitting the development of Eilat as Israel's Red Sea port. In May 1967, Egypt demanded the withdrawal of the UN troops from the Sharm el-Sheikh area, a request immediately complied with. Nasser declared the Tirān Straits closed to Israel shipping. This became a principal factor in triggering the *Six-Day War, in which the Sharm el-Sheikh area once again came under Israel's control on June 7, 1967. Subsequently, it was Israel's declared policy that in any peace agreement Sharm el-Sheikh and the Tiran Straits had to remain under Israel control, together with a strip of land to connect it with Eilat. In 1968 the first bathing facilities were installed at Sharm el-Sheikh, and in 1971 a project was announced to build a town there. Early in 1971, the 150 mi. (250 km.) long highway between Sharm el-Sheikh and Eilat was completed. Following the peace treaty between Israel and Egypt, Sharm el-Sheikh was returned to Egypt, but many Israelis (and others) continued to take their vacations there.

[Shlomo Hasson / Efraim Orni]

SHARON (Scheinerman), ARIEL (Arik; 1928–), Israeli soldier and politician, member of the Knesset from the Eighth Knesset. Sharon was born in Kefar Malal and went to highschool in Tel Aviv. He joined the Haganah in 1945, and in 1947 served in the supernumerary police of the Jewish settlements. In the War of Independence he served as a platoon commander in the Alexandroni brigade and was severely wounded in the battle for Latrun. At the beginning of 1949 he was appointed company commander, and in 1951 an intelligence officer in the Central Command. In 1952–53 he studied history and Eastern studies at the Hebrew University of Jerusalem, and was then appointed commander of the 101 commando unit, established to carry out reprisal operations against Arab marauder attacks. In 1954 the unit was merged with a paratroop regiment, headed by Sharon, and continued its unconventional activities behind enemy lines. The unit's level of performance was considered high, but it was occasionally criticized for its lack of restraint, such as during the operation in Qibyah, in which women and children were also killed. In the Sinai Campaign of 1956 Sharon fought as commander of a paratroop brigade. However, as a result of the large number of casualties in a battle that took place in the Mitleh Pass, which many viewed as being superfluous, he fell out with Chief of Staff Moshe *Dayan. In 1957 he was sent to the Camberley Staff College in Great Britain, and after his return his advancement in the IDF was frozen by Chiefs of Staff Ḥayyim *Laskov and Ẓevi Ẓur. In 1958–62 he commanded an infantry brigade and the Infantry School, simultaneously attending the Law School at Tel Aviv University.

It was only after the appointment of Yitzhak *Rabin as chief of staff in 1964 that Sharon's military career once again started to advance. Rabin appointed Sharon head of the Northern Command Staff, and in 1966, after he received the rank of major general, as head of the IDF Training Division. In the *Six-Day War he led an armored brigade which broke through Egyptian fortified positions in Um-Kattaf and Abu 'Ageila. After the War he returned to his previous position as head of the Training Division, in which capacity he moved several training bases to the West Bank. In 1969 he was appointed commander of the Southern Command, in which capacity he fortified the Bar-Lev Line and played an active role in the War of Attrition. In this period he was highly critical of Chief of Staff Haim *Bar-Lev. In 1971 he concentrated most of his efforts into fighting against terrorist cells in Gaza and removing the Bedouins from Northern Sinai. The latter activity was criticized by the chief of staff. In this period, though he was still in uniform, Sharon made some proposals of a political nature. In September 1970, in the course of "Black September" in Jordan, he argued (in closed military circles) that Israel should not have helped save King Hussein's skin in his battle against the PLO, but rather aligned itself with the PLO against the king. The background to this idea was Sharon's objection to any Israeli withdrawal from Judea and Samaria, and his belief that an alternative solution would have to be offered the Palestinians. Regarding the Sinai, he proposed that Egypt be allowed to maintain a civil administration there, while the IDF would continue to hold it for a period of 15 years. In the meantime trust would be established between the two sides, to be followed by negotiations toward a settlement. However, his ideas were not taken seriously by the government of Golda *Meir.

In June 1973, after Sharon reached the conclusion that he was unlikely to be appointed chief of staff, he resigned from the IDF and entered the political arena, joining the *Israel Liberal Party. He immediately launched a campaign for the expansion of *Gaḥal through the inclusion of additional parties and groups and played a leading role in the establishment of the Likud. Upon the outbreak of the *Yom Kippur War, however, he returned to active service as commander of an armored division and led his men across the Suez Canal into Egypt proper. Despite the brilliant success of this operation, he was once again severely criticized for disobeying orders and showing disrespect for his superiors.

After demobilization, Sharon ran in the elections to the Eighth Knesset on the Likud list and was elected to the Knesset.

However, feeling ineffective as an ordinary Member of the Knesset in opposition, he resigned from the Knesset in December 1974 and accepted an emergency appointment in the IDF. Half a year later he was appointed by Prime Minister Rabin as his special advisor. A year later he resigned as advisor and formed a new political party, Shlomzion, which gained two seats in the elections to the Ninth Knesset in 1977. After the victory of the Likud in the elections, Shlomzion merged with it, and Sharon was appointed by Menaḥem *Begin as minister of agriculture in his government, and chairman of the Ministerial Committee on Settlement, in which capacities he encouraged the establishment of new settlements in the territories occupied during the Six-Day War. In this period he was considered the patron of *Gush Emunim. After the resignation of Ezer *Weizman from the post of minister of defense in May 1980, Begin refused to appoint Sharon to the post. However, after the elections to the Tenth Knesset in 1981, Begin finally gave way, and Sharon was appointed minister of defense. Not long after his appointment, Sharon started planning a major operation in Lebanon to stop the launching of Katyushas on Northern Israel and to oust the PLO from Beirut and southern Lebanon. He also sought to remove the Syrians from Beirut and install a government in Lebanon that would be willing to sign a peace treaty with Israel. After an attempted assassination of the Israeli ambassador to London, Shlomo Argov, Sharon decided, in June 1982, to embark on Operation Peace for Galilee. However, two months before this, he implemented the very sensitive operation of withdrawal from the Rafa Salient and the removal of the settlers from Yamit and other Jewish settlements in the area.

Regarding Lebanon, the government approved a limited operation, at a depth of 40 kilometers from the border with Israel. Yet Sharon continued the operation into Beirut, while, according to Menaḥem Begin's son Ze'ev Binyamin *Begin, keeping vital information from the prime minister and misleading him. Sharon personally approved the entry of the Christian Phalange troops into the refugee camps of Sabra and Shatilla the day after Lebanon's president-elect, Bashir Jemayel, was assassinated. Following the massacre that occurred in the camps, Sharon was found by the Kahane Committee of Inquiry set up by the Israeli government – after massive popular pressure to investigate the event – to be responsible for not preventing the massacre, and he was forced to resign from the Ministry of Defense, remaining in the government as minister without portfolio. Despite opposition in the *Israel Labor Party, Sharon was appointed minister of industry and trade in the National Unity Government formed in 1984. Soon after entering his new position Sharon traveled to the U.S. to appear in a libel suit that he had brought against *Time* magazine, which had published an article stating that the Kahane Committee Report included a secret appendix, according to which Sharon had encouraged the Jemayel family to take revenge against the Palestinians for Bashir's assassination. Sharon won the suit on the facts but failed to prove malice. Sharon remained in the Ministry of Industry and Trade until February 1990 and continued to support Jewish settlement in the territories, proposing that the Palestinians be given 11 autonomous areas.

Following the government's decision on May 15, 1989, to hold elections in the territories, Sharon headed a group in the Likud, that also included David *Levy and Yitzhak *Modai, which tried to undermine the plan, and went so far as to leave the government in February 1990, after a stormy meeting of the Likud Central Committee. However, after the Labor Party brought the National Unity Government down in March, he rejoined the narrow government formed by Yitzhak *Shamir as minister of construction and housing. In this position Sharon assisted private associations that were engaged in purchasing property in the Old City of Jerusalem and in East Jerusalem for Jewish settlement, and was involved in purchasing tens of thousands of caravans to house the wave of new immigrants from the former Soviet Union that started pouring into Israel after 1989. Sharon opposed Israel's participation in the Madrid Conference in October 1991. In February 1992 he contended for the Likud leadership, but came in third after Shamir and Levy. He did not contend for the Likud leadership in 1993 opposite Binyamin *Netanyahu, after the Likud's electoral defeat in the elections to the Thirteenth Knesset in 1992.

In the government formed by Netanyahu after the elections to the Fourteenth Knesset in 1996, a new Ministry of National Infrastructures was tailor-made for Sharon. Following Netanyahu's defeat in the direct election for prime minister held in 1999, and Netanyahu's decision to leave politics temporarily, Sharon finally assumed the leadership of the Likud. It was Sharon's decision at the end of September 2000 to pay a well-publicized visit the Temple Mount that triggered the outbreak of the second Intifada and led to the final breakdown of Barak's efforts to work out a permanent settlement with the Palestinians.

In the elections for prime minister held in February 2001 Sharon defeated Ehud *Barak. Following the elections, he set up a national unity government. Soon after his victory he cancelled the system of direct election of the prime minister. With the full cooperation of Minister of Defense Binyamin *Ben-Eliezer, who briefly served as chairman of the Labor Party, Sharon used massive force to try to crush the increasingly violent Intifada and, in the end of March 2002, launched Operation Defensive Shield, involving wide-scale incursions into the Palestinian towns in the West Bank, and preventing Yasser *Arafat from leaving his residence in the Mukata'a compound in Ramallah. In November 2002, the Labor Party decided to leave the government, and new elections were held two months later.

In the elections to the Sixteenth Knesset the Likud, under Sharon's leadership, won an impressive victory. Sharon sought to establish another national unity government, but Labor refused, and he established a coalition with Shinui, the NRP, and the National Union. After the elections, Sharon approved the construction of a defensive fence to separate Israel from the West Bank and make it difficult for terrorists to enter Israel, arguing that the location of the fence did not imply the delineation of Israel's future borders. At the beginning of 2004 he introduced a unilateral disengagement plan, involving the dismantlement of all the Jewish settlements in the Gaza Strip, and several in Northern Samaria, as well as full Israeli withdrawal from these areas. This move led to a serious rift within the Likud and the breakup of his coalition. The disengagement took place in August 2005 (see *Gush Katif). In January 2005 he established an alternative coalition with the Labor Party and the Ashkenazi *ḥaredi* parties, and with the help of several opposition parties managed to get the Knesset to approve the implementation of the disengagement plan and the 2005 budget on March 30, 2005. At this point Sharon never specified what his plans were following the disengagement. Despite the very difficult political, military, and economic situation, and serious allegations of financial irregularities raised against him and his two sons, Omri and Gilad, Sharon's popularity soared.

In November 2005, with the Likud Central Committee threatening to depose him as party chairman over his political policies and Likud MKs and cabinet ministers also opposing him, Sharon left the Likud and founded the Kadimah Party, taking with him leading Likud figures, such as Ehud *Olmert, Tzipi *Livni, and Meir *Sheetrit, and joined by disaffected Labor Party leaders such as Shimon *Peres. On January 4, 2006, Sharon suffered a massive stroke which left him incapacitated. Ehud Olmert of Kadimah became acting prime minister and led the party to an election victory in March 2006.

Sharon's eldest son, Omri, was elected to the Sixteenth Knesset on the Likud list.

With David Chanoff, Sharon published *Warrior: the Autobiography of Ariel Sharon* (1989).

BIBLIOGRAPHY: M. Shavit, *On the Wings of Eagles: The Story of Arik Sharon, Commander of the Israel Paratroopers* (1972); U. Even, *Arik: Darko Shel Lohem* (1974); U. Dan, *Sharon's Bridgehead* (1975); Z. Schiff and Ehud Ya'ari, *Milḥemet Sholal* (1984); U. Benziman, *Sharon, an Israeli Caesar* (1985); D. Aharavi, *General Sharon's War Against Time Magazine: His Trial and Vindication* (1985); U. Dan, *Blood Libel: the Inside Story of General Ariel Sharon's History-Making Suit Against Time Magazine* (1987); A. Adiv and M. Schwartz, *Sharon's Star Wars: Israel's Seven Star Settlement Plan* (1992); U. Dan, *Ariel Sharon ba-Milḥamah la-Shalom 1948–2001* (2001); Y. Kotler, *Ha-Zarzir ve-ha-Orev: Ariel Sharon ve-Shimon Peres kemot she-Hem* (2002).

[Susan Hattis Rolef (2nd ed.)]

SHARON, ARYEH (1900–1984), Israeli architect, among the most influential architects in Israel specializing in public buildings. Born in Poland, he went to Palestine in 1920 and joined kibbutz Gan Shemuel, working as a mason. Between 1926 and 1930, he studied architecture at the Bauhaus in Dessau, Germany, and then worked for two years in Berlin. He returned to Ereẓ Israel in 1932 and planned and built many cooperative housing projects in Tel Aviv. He grasped the connection between the social and political views of the Bauhaus to the Zionist ideology of the Yishuv. He also planned the new Beilinson Hospital, the old and new Agricultural Center, the Bet Brenner building in Tel Aviv, the Ichilov Hospital, Tel Aviv, various buildings of the Weizmann Institute in Reḥovot, and of The Hebrew University, Jerusalem. His architecture was known for the relationship between his buildings and their natural surroundings and corresponded to the development of modern architecture over the years. It can be characterized as international and pragmatic. From 1948 to 1953 Sharon was head of the Israel Government Planning Department and as such was responsible for the design of many of the new settlements.

BIBLIOGRAPHY: A. Elhanani, *The Struggle for Independence. The Israeli Architecture in the Twentieth Century* (1998).

[Abraham Erlik / Shaked Gilboa (2nd ed.)]

SHARON, NATHAN (1925–), Israeli biochemist. Sharon was born in Brisk, Poland, and immigrated to Palestine in 1934. He was educated at Tel Aviv High School and earned his M.Sc. (1950) and Ph.D. (1953) in biochemistry from the Hebrew University of Jerusalem. He was a research assistant at the Agricultural Research Station, Reḥovot (1949–53), before joining the staff of the department of biophysics at the Weizmann Institute (1954), where he was appointed professor (1968) and head of department (1973–83 and 1987–90). He was dean of the faculty of biophysics and bioengineering for three periods between 1976 and 1986. He was professor emeritus after 1995. He also carried out postdoctoral research at Harvard Medical School and Massachusetts General Hospital, Boston, and at Brookhaven National Laboratory, Upton, New York (1956–58). Sharon's research initially concerned lectins, the proteins found in plants, microbes, and mammalian cells that combine with carbohydrate-containing proteins, and later extended to the broader field of sugar-containing proteins called glycoproteins and the associated field of glycobiology. These proteins have important roles in the growth and differentiation of normal cells and the changed behavior of cancer cells. Sharon has a particular interest in cell surface molecules in the family called adhesins and their role in permitting invading microbes to attach to and infect cells. He has used his discoveries to suggest simple forms of treatment, such as cranberry juice to prevent urinary tract infections, and to develop longer-term strategies for blocking microbial adherence to host cells. Sharon's achievements have been internationally recognized by many distinguished honors and awards. These include election to the Israel Academy of Sciences and Humanities (1992), the Israel Prize in biochemistry and medicine (1994), and foreign membership in the Academia Europaea (1999), the Polish Academy of Sciences (2000), and the American Society for Microbiology (2001). He served as a visiting professor at many leading universities in North America and Europe. Even after attaining emeritus status he continued to contribute original and frequently cited scientific papers and to write authoritative reviews. His books on lectins and complex carbohydrates are highly regarded. His interest in scientific education includes three books of popular science and chairmanship of influential Israeli committees concerned with the advancement of science.

[Michael Denman (2nd ed.)]

SHARONAH (Heb. שָׁרוֹנָה), moshav in northern Israel, in Lower Galilee, 3 mi. (5 km.) W. of Yavne'el, affiliated with Tenu'at ha-Moshavim. The village's land was acquired in 1913 by American Jews and a year later, in World War I, the ground was abandoned. After the land passed over to the Jewish National Fund, moshav Sharonah was founded (1938) by a Gordonia pioneer group from Eastern Europe, as part of an endeavor to reinforce the "settlement bridge" between the Jezreel and Kinnarot valleys. In 1970 Sharonah had 178 inhabitants, increasing to 441 in 2002. Its farming was based on field crops, fruit orchards, and cattle. The name is mentioned by Eusebius (Onom. 162:4, 5).

[Efraim Orni]

SHARP, ISADORE NATANIEL (**Issy**; 1931–), Canadian hotel executive and philanthropist. Founder, chairman, and chief executive officer of Four Seasons Hotel Inc., Sharp was born in Toronto, Ontario. He graduated as an architect from Toronto's Ryerson Institute in 1952 and began in the construction business with his father, Max Sharp. On his first trip to Europe in the late 1950s, Sharp became interested in building luxury hotels and in 1961 opened the Four Seasons Motor Hotel in Toronto. From that first hotel he created a worldwide chain that has set the industry standard for fine travel accommodation. In 2005, Four Seasons Hotels and Resorts had 66 hotels in 29 countries and more than 20 properties under development. In addition to numerous corporate directorships, Issy Sharp also applied his leadership skills to charitable and community causes. He initiated the corporate sponsorship program supporting the Terry Fox Marathon of Hope and is the founder of the annual Terry Fox Run Program, the largest single-day fundraising event for cancer research worldwide. In 1983, in recognition of his work on behalf of the Canadian Cancer Society, Sharp was the first recipient of the Ruth Hartman Frankel Humanitarian Award. He continued to serve as a director of the National Terry Fox Run and the Terry Fox Humanitarian Award Program, as well as a governor of the Canadian Council of Christians and Jews. In 1985 he served as co-chairman of the United Jewish Appeal and in 1989 was named the Negev Dinner honouree by the Jewish National Fund of Canada. Among numerous other business and community honors and awards, Sharp was appointed an Officer of the Order of Canada in 1993.

[Andrea Knight (2nd ed.)]

SHARUHEN (Heb. שָׁרוּחֶן), city in the territory of the tribe of Simeon (Josh. 19:6); in the Septuagint, the name is translated as "their fields" (*sedoteihem*). The parallel passage in Joshua

15:32 has Shilhim, and that in I Chronicles 4:31 has Shaaraim. Opinions are divided between these being variations of the same name or different places. In Egyptian sources, Sharuhen appears as a Hyksos stronghold besieged for three years by the army of Ahmose I after the expulsion of the Hyksos from Egypt. It remained an Egyptian fortress under Thutmosis III. It was evidently the starting point of Shishak's Negev campaign (no. 125 in his list of Canaanite cities). These data have led Albright to identify Sharuhen with Tell al-Fāriʿa (present-day Tel Sharuhen), an ancient mound on the Besor River, about 18½ mi. (30 km.) west of Beer-Sheba. Between 1927–1929 it was excavated by *Petrie, who identified it with Beth-Pelet. Remains include a Hyksos fortification; strata of the Philistine, Israelite, and Persian periods; Hyksos and Philistine tombs; Jewish coins; and a Roman fort.

BIBLIOGRAPHY: F. Petrie, *Beth Pelet* (1930); Albright, in: BASOR, 33 (1929), 7; Alt, in: JPOS, 15 (1935), 310ff.; Abel, Geog, 2 (1938), 451; Aharoni, Land, index.

[Michael Avi-Yonah]

SHAS (Heb. ש״ס), an abbreviation consisting of the initials of *Shishah Sedarim* (Heb. שִׁשָּׁה סְדָרִים), or *Shita Sidra* (Aram. שִׁיתָּא סִידְרָא), the "six orders" into which the Mishnah is divided. The full Aramaic term is found in *Bava Meẓia* 85b, the full Hebrew in *Esther Rabbah* 1:12. The abbreviation does not appear in the manuscripts of the early editions of the Talmud and was first used in the Basle edition (1578–81) because of the objection of the censor to the term Talmud. It appears in *Ḥagigah* 10a and *Shabbat* 63a. In both of these passages the Munich manuscript reads תַּלְמוּדָא (*talmuda*). *Tosafot* to *Sanhedrin* 24a quotes *Avodah Zarah* 19b שְׁלִישׁ בַּשַּׁ״ס (*shelish ba-Shas*; "A third of one's time should be devoted to *Shas*") where the printed editions read בַּתַּלְמוּד (*ba-Talmud*).

BIBLIOGRAPHY: R.N.N. Rabbinovicz, *Ma'amar al Hadpasat ha-Talmud*, ed. by A.M. Habermann (1952), 76f. esp. n. 7.

[Harry Freedman]

SHAS (Sephardi Torah Guardians), Israeli political party. Shas was established in 1984 before the elections to the Eleventh Knesset, in protest over the small representation of Sephardim in the *ḥaredi* *Agudat Israel, and with the support of Rabbi Eliezer Menaḥem *Shach. Shas' spiritual leader from the very start was former Chief Sephardi Rabbi Ovadiah *Yosef, who established a seven-member Council of Torah Sages. At first the party's political leader was Rabbi Yitzhak Ḥayyim Peretz. True to its slogan of "restoring the pristine splendor" (*Haḥzarat Atarah le-Yoshnah*) Shas established an independent education system called El ha-Ma'ayan, and started to actively engage in bringing members of the Sephardi community back to religion. In the elections to the Eleventh Knesset Shas won four seats, compared to Agudat Israel's two, receiving not only the support of *ḥaredi* voters, but also of many traditional voters. While Shas followed an extreme policy on issues of religion and state, at first it followed a moderate policy on the peace issue, after Yosef had declared that lives were more important than territories.

Shas joined the National Unity Government formed in 1984, and Peretz was appointed minister of the interior. He resigned in January 1987 over the Shoshana (Susan) Miller affair, after the High Court of Justice ruled that Ms. Miller be registered in her ID card as Jewish, even though she has been converted to Judaism by a Reform rabbi. The Ministry of the Interior was now run by the director general of the ministry, Aryeh *Deri. Peretz later returned to the government as minister without portfolio.

In the elections to the Twelfth Knesset in 1988, Shas won six seats, and once again joined the National Unity Government, in which Deri, now officially recognized as the political leader of Shas, was appointed minister of the interior. It was Deri, in collusion with Haim *Ramon of the *Israel Labor Party, who helped Shimon *Peres bring down the government in March 1990, when five of Shas' MKs were absent during a vote on a motion of no-confidence in the government. But after Peres failed to establish a new government, Shas joined the new right-wing–religious government established by Yitzhak *Shamir.

In the elections to the Thirteenth Knesset in 1992 Shas retained its six seats, and despite allegations of mismanagement of funds by the party's educational institutions and charges of corruption against several of its Knesset members, Prime Minister Yitzhak *Rabin included Shas as the only religious party in his government, offering Shas many of the power positions previously held by the *National Religious Party. After a prolonged struggle, Shas managed to bring about the removal of Shulamit *Aloni from the Ministry of Education and Culture. However, external pressures and criminal charges brought against Deri that resulted in demands by the attorney general that he resign, led to its resignation from the government in August 1993, one month before the signing of the Declaration of Principles with the PLO in Washington. Efforts to bring Shas back into the government failed. Nevertheless, it joined Ramon's new list in the *Histadrut elections in May 1994, and was thus a partner to the revolutionary changes in the Histadrut that followed.

In the elections to the Fourteenth Knesset in 1996, Shas, still under Deri's political leadership, but now less dovish than before, garnered 10 Knesset seats and joined the government formed by Binyamin *Netanyahu, even though Deri himself was not given a ministerial post. Deri was, nevertheless, allegedly involved in the attempts to get Ronnie Bar-On appointed attorney general. In the elections to the Fifteenth Knesset in 1999, Shas, now under the political leadership of Rabbi Eliahu (Eli) Yishai, received a record 17 seats. Shas joined the government formed by Ehud *Barak, but left over Barak's willingness to make far-reaching concessions to the Palestinian Authority. It then joined the government formed by Ariel *Sharon after he won in the elections for prime minister held in 2001. In the elections to the Sixteenth Knesset held in 2003, Shas lost six of its seats to the Likud. This was due to the departure of Deri from the political scene, divisions in the Sephardi *ḥaredi* camp, a deterioration in Shas' financial situation, and some embarrassing statements by Rabbi Yosef in the course of his weekly lessons. Shas remained outside the new government formed by Sharon, and despite talks held with the Likud at the end of 2004 and the beginning of 2005 about a possible entry of Shas into the government after the departure of the National Union, the NRP, and Shinui, Shas, believing that early elections lay ahead, chose to remain outside. In the course of the Sixteenth Knesset Shas opposed the government both over Netanyahu's economic policy that greatly reduced social transfer payments, and especially child support benefits, and over Sharon's disengagement policy. In the March 2006 elections to the Seventeenth Knesset, Shas received 12 seats and rejoined the government with four cabinet posts, including Yishai as minister of industry, trade and labor.

BIBLIOGRAPHY: M. Friedman, *Ha-Ḥevrah ha-Ḥaredit* (1991); H. Nir'el, *Tenu'at ha-Sephardim Shomrei ha-Torah – Shas: Hithavvuto shel Shesa'a Ada'ati Dati ba-Migzar ha-Ḥaredi* (1992); M. Rahat, *Shas – Ha-Ru'ah ve-ha-Ko'aḥ: Eikh Nizḥah Shas et ha-Politikah ha-Yisra'elit* (1998); A. Dayan, *Ha-Ma'ayan ha-Mitgaber: Sippurah shel Tenu'at Shas* (1999); Y. Peled, *Shas: Etgar ha-Yisra'eliyyut* (2001); R. Tesler, *Beshem ha-Shem: Shas ve-ha-Mahapekhah ha-Datit* (2003); Y. Lupo, *Ha-Im Taḥzir Shas Atarah le-Yoshnah* (2004).

SHASHU, SALIM (1926–), Iraqi poet and journalist. A Baghdad lawyer and teacher, Shashu immigrated to Israel in 1951 and edited the Arabic weekly *al-Manār*, also working for the Arabic section of the Israel Broadcasting Authority. He hailed Israel's military achievements in his nationalist poems. His verse collection *Fī 'Ālam al-Nūr* ("In the World of Light," 1959) was dedicated to President Ben-Zvi.

[Shmuel Moreh]

SHATNER, WILLIAM (1931–), Canadian actor-writer. Shatner was born in Montreal. His paternal grandfather, Wolf Shattner, had changed the family name after emigrating from the Ukraine. Even before his teen years, Shatner was working professionally for the Canadian Broadcasting Company. He studied business at McGill University and in 1951 acted in the Canadian feature *The Butler's Night Off*. He had planned to go into the clothing business with his father after graduating with a bachelor's degree in 1952, but instead joined the Canadian Repertory Theatre (1952–54) in Ottawa and then the Stratford Shakespeare Festival (1954–56) in Stratford, Ontario. He played Ranger Bob on the children's television series *Howdy Doody* in 1954 and starred in a live adaptation of Herman Melville's *Billy Budd* (1955). In 1956 Shatner made his Broadway debut with *Tamburlaine the Great*. In 1958, he made his U.S. feature film debut in *The Brothers Karamazov* and starred in the Broadway production of *The World of Suzie Wong*, which took the 1959 Theatre World Award. Shatner appeared in the feature *Judgment at Nuremberg* (1961) while working in television programs like *Playhouse 90* and *Studio One*, and then in the Broadway production of *A Shot in the Dark*. In 1962, he starred in the acclaimed film *The Intruder*, which he followed with appearances on *The Twilight Zone* and *77 Sunset Strip*, and a starring role in the short-lived television series *For the People* (1965). In 1966, Shatner was cast as Captain Kirk in *Star Trek*, a part he played until NBC canceled the series on Sept. 2, 1969. After a divorce wiped out his finances he continued to act on television, including an adaptation of the book *Go Ask Alice* (1973), but the role of Kirk had typecast Shatner and he found himself mostly relegated to bit parts in action films. Shatner rejoined the *Star Trek* cast and provided the voice for Kirk in an animated series (1973–75). This was followed by a failed attempt to relaunch a syndicated live *Star Trek* series, which evolved to become a series of films that featured Shatner's Kirk from 1979 to 1994. Shatner found himself back on television as a cop in the series *T.J. Hooker* (1982–86) and then as host of the reality television series *Rescue 911* (1989–95). In 1989, Shatner began publishing his long-running *TekWar* series of science-fiction novels and helped adapt them to television. After serving as a spokesperson for Priceline.com from 1998, he returned to acting in 2003 with guest appearances as Denny Crane on David E. Kelley's *The Practice*, which earned him an Emmy for best guest actor. In 2004, he joined the spin-off series, *Boston Legal*, reprising his role as Crane and earning a Golden Globe and another Emmy. Shatner was a longtime breeder of American quarter horses, and raised money for various charities, including Ahead With Horses and Children's Museum of Los Angeles.

BIBLIOGRAPHY: "Shatner, William," in: Contemporary Authors Online (Thomson Gale, 2005); "William Shatner," at: http://en.wikipedia.org.

[Adam Wills (2nd ed.)]

SHATZKES, MOSES (1881–1958), *rosh yeshivah*. Born in Vilna, Shatzkes was raised by his stepfather, Isaac *Blaser, a foremost exponent of the *Musar movement. Shatzkes studied at the *Telz yeshivah where he became a leading disciple of its *rosh yeshivah*, Eliezer Gordon. In 1909 Shatzkes was appointed rabbi of Lipnishki, and in 1915 of Ivo, both in the province of Vilna. After World War I, he was active in guiding Vilna's Jewish relief organization and the Va'ad ha-Yeshivot. In 1930 he was elected to the important position of the rabbi of Lomza, and in this capacity served as one of the leaders of Polish-Lithuanian Jewry until the war forced him to flee to Vilna in 1939. There he was appointed the head of the Grodno yeshivah after the death of its previous *rosh yeshivah*, Rabbi Simeon *Shkop. He immigrated to the United States in 1941, and became a senior member of the faculty of the Rabbi Isaac Elhanan Theological Seminary of the Yeshiva University. Shatzkes' annotations to Blaser's works were published under the title *Anaf Peri* as an appendix to the second volume of the latter's *Peri Yizḥak* (Jerusalem, 1913).

BIBLIOGRAPHY: O.Z. Rand, *Toledot Anshei Shem* (1950), 132.

[Aaron Rothkoff]

SHATZKES, MOSES AARON (1825–1899), Hebrew writer. Born in Karlin, Belorussia, he studied in Lithuanian yeshivot, and then joined the *Haskalah movement. He gained a literary reputation through his book *Ha-Mafte'aḥ* ("The Key," 1869). The book analyzes talmudic legends, starting from the premise that they are merely ethical allegories, not to be taken literally. This theory, acceptable to the moderates of the Haskalah movement, was anathema to Orthodox Jews, who tried to prevent publication of the book, and in some towns even burned copies. Shatzkes wrote articles in the same vein (*Ha-Asif*, 2 (1885), 241–61; *Ha-Sifrut*, 3 (1889/90), 103–18; and others). In Yiddish he published anonymously *Der Yudisher for Pesakh* ("Preparations for Passover," 1881) in which he attacked superstitions associated with the Passover festival. Toward the end of his life, he moved to Kiev, where he became a leading figure in the Haskalah circle, noted for his pungently witty conversation.

BIBLIOGRAPHY: Rejzen, Leksikon, 4 (1929), 494–500; Kressel, Leksikon, 2 (1962), 975–6.

[Yehuda Slutsky]

SHATZKY, JACOB (1893–1956), historian. Born in Warsaw, Shatzky received his doctorate in 1922 for a dissertation on 19th-century Polish-Jewish history. During World War I he served as an officer in the Polish Legion. From 1913 on he wrote Polish articles and reviews on Jewish literary and historical subjects. He came to write mainly in Yiddish after 1922, the year he settled in the U.S., where he was one of the founders of the U.S. section of *YIVO. From 1929 until his death he was librarian of the New York State Psychiatric Institute.

Shatzky's range was extraordinarily wide: Spinoza, psychiatry, theater, music, folklore, literature, language, and other areas. His principal field, however, was Eastern European Jewish history, and his major work was his history of Warsaw Jewry. He was an indefatigable and often querulous reviewer of scholarly works. The quality and accuracy of his own historical scholarship has often been questioned.

BIBLIOGRAPHY: M. Kosover and M. Unger, in: *Annual of the Yiddish Scientific Institute*, 2 (1939), 249–329 (Yid.), list of works 1913–39; Malachi, in: *Shatsky Bukh* (1958), 325–68, list of works 1940–56; Rejzen, Leksikon, 4 (1929), 489–94.

[Leonard Prager]

SHAUL (Shaool), ANWAR (1904–1984), Iraqi poet and journalist. Born in *Baghdad, Shaul was editor (1924–25) of the Arabic-language Iraqi Zionist journal, *al-Miṣbāḥ*. At that time he also wrote poems expressing his Jewish national convictions. He was secretary of the Baghdad Jewish community for three years, but then became estranged from the Jewish community. In 1937 he went so far as to sign an anti-Zionist declaration.

Shaul was the first Iraqi to deal with the life of the masses and to demand the abolition of the veil and an improvement in the status of women. His first stories were published in the anthology *al-Ḥiṣād al-Awwal* ("The First Crop," 1930). He compiled an anthology of translated short stories titled *Qiṣaṣ min al-Gharb* ("Stories from the West," 1937). His other books are *Fī Ziḥām al-Madīna* ("In the Tumult of the City," 1955) and a volume of poems, *Hamasāt al-Zamān* ("Whispers of Time," 1956). Like his colleague Meir Baṣri (1912–), he considered himself an Iraqi Jew, a member of the Arab Iraqi nation; he did not immigrate to Israel with the great majority of Iraqi Jewry in 1951. However he left Iraq in 1971. He was a prolific writer and published in literary periodicals in the Arab world.

BIBLIOGRAPHY: E. Marmorstein, in: JJSO (Dec. 1959), 187–200.

[Hayyim J. Cohen]

SHAVEI ZION (Heb. שָׁבֵי צִיּוֹן; "Those who Return to Zion"), moshav shittufi in northern Israel, in the Acre Plain, 2 mi. (3 km.) S. of Nahariyyah, affiliated with Ha-Iḥud ha-Ḥakla'i. Shavei Zion was founded in 1938 by a group of German-Jewish immigrants who were descended from generations of farmers and cattle merchants in the village of Rexingen, Wuerttemberg. Shavei Zion was one of the first villages to adopt the moshav shittufi form of settlement. Although not strictly Orthodox, the settlers preserve traditional Judaism as part of their social organization. In 1970 the village had 312 inhabitants, rising to 619 in 2002. The moshav economy was based on industry, farming, and tourism, including a plastics factory and a resort and beach.

[Efram Orni / Shaked Gilboa (2nd ed.)]

SHAVELSON, CLARA LEMLICH (1886–1982), U.S. labor organizer, suffragist, communist, and consumer activist. Born to religiously observant parents in Gorodok, Ukraine, Lemlich was already a committed revolutionary when her family came to the United States in 1903. At 17, she supported her family by working in a Lower East Side shirtwaist (blouse) manufacturing shop.

In 1905, Lemlich began organizing waistmakers into the nascent *International Ladies Garment Workers Union and was a co-founder of ILGWU Local 25. At a time when most of the union consisted of skilled male workers, Lemlich's recruits were largely young immigrant women. She emerged as a leader of a strike at the Leiserson shop in the fall of 1909. Company guards and policemen singled Lemlich out on the picket line, breaking six of her ribs and arresting her 17 times. In November, 1909, Lemlich interrupted a mass meeting called by the ILGWU. Wresting the podium from a roster of speakers that did not include any working women, she called for a general strike. Her oration in Yiddish ignited what became known as the "Uprising of the Twenty Thousand." In subsequent weeks, 30 to 40 thousand garment workers, mostly young Jewish women, walked out of their workplaces.

Following the strike settlement, garment shops in New York would not hire Lemlich. After working part time as a union organizer, she accepted a full time job as a suffrage advocate. Her relationship with the middle-class women who hired her quickly soured, and she was fired within the year. Soon after, Lemlich married Joe Shavelson and moved to Brooklyn. Now a housewife with children, she began mobilizing other women in her own position, insisting that housewives, as the prime consumers for working class families, were as important to the class struggle as wage-earners.

Under the rubric of the Communist Party, which she joined in 1926, Shavelson co-founded the United Council of Working Women. Initially supporting striking workers with food and childcare, the group expanded its scope by leading food boycotts, rent strikes, and demonstrations. In 1935, the group changed its name to the Progressive Women's Councils and continued its consumer protests with other New York women's organizations. Their alliance started the successful meat boycott of 1935 which spread from New York to major urban areas across the nation and reduced the price of meat in hundreds of American cities.

Shavelson remained politically active until the end of her life. Through the 1950s, despite FBI monitoring, she protested the nuclear arms race and the Rosenberg executions. She continued her political work through the 1960s and 1970s, where, at the Jewish Home for the Aged in Los Angeles, she helped the orderlies organize a union.

BIBLIOGRAPHY: A. Orleck, *Common Sense and a Little Fire: Women and Working Class Politics in the United States, 1900–1965* (1995); idem, "Shavelson, Clara Lemlich," P.E. Hyman and D.D. Moore (ed.), in: *Jewish Women in America* (1998), 2:1238–41; M. Tax, *The Rising of the Women: Feminist Solidarity and Class Conflict, 1880–1917* (1980).

[Rachel Kranson (2nd ed.)]

SHAVUOT (Heb. שָׁבוּעוֹת; "weeks," Pentecost, "the 50th day"), the festival celebrated on the sixth of Sivan (and also on the seventh outside Israel). The biblical names for the festival are: "Ḥag Shavuot" ("Feast of Weeks," Ex. 34:22; Deut. 16:10); "Yom ha-Bikkurim" ("The Day of the First-fruits," Num. 28:26), and "Ḥag ha-Kaẓir" ("The Harvest Feast," Ex. 23:16). The rabbinic name is "Aẓeret" (RH 1, 2; Ḥag. 2, 4). This word, of uncertain meaning but generally translated as "solemn assembly," occurs also in connection with the day following the Festival of Sukkot (Lev. 23:36; Num. 29:35). This would seem to suggest that, for the rabbis, Shavuot is an additional one day feast to Passover just as there is an additional one day feast to Tabernacles (see Targ. Onk. to Num. 28:26 and PdRK 192a–93a).

History

This feast, one of the three *pilgrim festivals (Deut. 16:16), marked the end of the barley and the beginning of the wheat harvest. According to the critical view, it was probably a midsummer festival in origin and taken over from the Canaanites. It is stated in Leviticus: "From the day after the Sabbath, the day that you bring the sheaf of wave-offering you shall count (until) seven full weeks have elapsed: you shall count fifty days, until the day after the seventh week; then you shall bring an offering of new grain to the Lord" (Lev. 23:15–16 and to 21). Leviticus 23:11 states that the sheaf was waved on the day after the Sabbath on the festival of Passover. Thus Shavuot falls 50 days after this day. The *Sadducees (and later the *Karaites) understood the term "Sabbath" in these verses literally; hence, for them Shavuot always falls on a Sunday. The *Pharisees, however, interpreted "Sabbath" as the first day of Passover (which was a *Sabbath*, "day of rest") so that for them Shavuot always falls on the 51st day from the first day of Passover (Sifra Emor Perek 12; Men. 65a–66a). The *Beta Israel (Falashas) interpreted "the day after Sabbath" as meaning the day after Passover so that for them Shavuot falls on the 12th of Sivan. The community of *Qumran apparently interpreted "Sabbath" as the Sabbath after the end of the Passover festival, and as they had a fixed solar calendar, this "Sabbath" always fell on the 26th of Nisan so that Shavuot always came out on Sunday the 15th of Sivan.

On this festival in Temple times two loaves (*shetei ha-leḥem*) were "waved before the Lord" (Lev. 23:17–20). These had to be offered only from the finest wheat, from produce grown that year in Ereẓ Israel (Men. 8:1). Shavuot was associated with the bringing of the **bikkurim*, "the first ripe fruits," to the Sanctuary (Ex. 23:19; Deut. 26:1–11). The Mishnah (Bik. 1, 6) states that the period for bringing them was any time from Shavuot to Sukkot. The villagers would first assemble in the large town of the district and would go up together with their first ripe fruits to the Temple, where they would be welcomed with song by the levites (Bik. 3:2–4). In rabbinic times a remarkable transformation of the festival took place. Based on the verse: "In the third month after the children of Israel were gone forth out of the land of Egypt, the same day came they into the wilderness of Sinai" (Ex. 19:1), the festival became the anniversary of the giving of the Torah at Sinai. The description of the feast in the liturgy is "*zeman mattan toratenu*" ("the time of the giving of our Torah"). The transformation was in accord with a process to be observed in the Bible in which the ancient agricultural feasts were transformed into festivals marking the anniversaries of significant historical events in the life of the people. Both Passover and Sukkot are connected with the Exodus; it was natural to link Shavuot with this event.

It is possible that the Pharisees insisted that Shavuot be observed on a fixed day because they wished to affirm that the festival commemorated the Sinaitic theophany which occurred on the 50th day after the Exodus (following the general Pharisaic belief in an oral Torah reaching back to Moses which the Sadducees denied), and because a purely agricultural festival had little meaning for the town dwellers who made up the Pharisaic party (L. Finkelstein, *Pharisees* (1962³), 115–8, 641–54). If this is correct, the transformation into a historical feast took place before the present era. However, neither Josephus nor Philo refers to Shavuot as "the time of the giving of our Torah," and none of the references in the rabbinic literature to the Torah being given on this day (e.g., Shab. 86b) is earlier than the second century C.E., though there may well have been a tradition far earlier than this. The earliest clear references to Shavuot as the anniversary of the giving of the Torah are from the third century, e.g., the saying of R. Eleazar that all authorities agree that it is necessary to rejoice with good food and wine on Aẓeret because it is the day on which the Torah was given (Pes. 68b).

In some medieval communities it was customary to introduce children to the Hebrew school on Shavuot, the season of the giving of the Torah. At this initiation ceremony the child, at the age of five or thereabouts, was placed on the reading desk in the synagogue and from there was taken to the school where he began to make his first attempts at reading the Hebrew alphabet. He was then given cakes, honey, and sweets "that the Torah might be sweet on his lips." In many modern synagogues, particularly Reform, the confirmation of older children takes place on Shavuot (see *Bar Mitzvah).

The Laws and Customs of Shavuot

Unlike Passover and Sukkot, Shavuot has few special rituals, and those it does have are late. This is entirely explicable in view of the development of the festival mentioned above. The harvest associations no longer had much meaning once the Temple was destroyed, and there are no biblical ceremonies connected with the giving of the Torah since this motif is post-biblical. In modern Israel attempts have been made to revive some of the harvest ceremonies (see *Kibbutz Festivals). In the synagogue it is customary to read the Book of Ruth on Shavuot. Among the reasons given are that the events recorded in Ruth took place at harvest time (Ruth 2:23); that Ruth was the ancestor of David (Ruth 4:17) who, traditionally, died on Shavuot; that Ruth's "conversion" to Judaism is appropriate reading for the festival which commemorates the giving of the Torah; and that Ruth's loyalty is symbolic of Israel's loyalty to the Torah. The portion of the Torah read in the synagogue on the first day is the account of the theophany at Sinai (Ex. 19:1–20:26). In the Ashkenazi rite it is prefaced by chanting the Aramaic **Akdamut* hymn composed by Meir b. Isaac Nehorai of Orleans (11th century) in praise of Israel's faithfulness to the Torah. The *haftarah* for the first day is the vision of Ezekiel (Ezek. 1–2) because of its parallel to the vision of the whole people at Sinai. The *haftarah* for the second day is Habakkuk's prayer (Hab. 3) because it similarly describes a theophany. This, too, is prefaced by an Aramaic hymn in praise of the Torah, "**Yeẓiv Pitgam*," composed by Jacob b. Meir of Troyes (1100–1171). Under the influence of the Kabbalah it became customary to spend the whole of the first night as a vigil in which selected passages from all the Jewish religious classics are read (*tikkun leil Shavuot*). A less observed custom is to recite the whole of the Book of Psalms on the second night because of the association of the festival with David.

The Torah reading for the first day (Ex. 19–20) includes the *Ten Commandments. Although the Mishnah (Tam. 5:1) states that the Ten Commandments were recited each day in the Temple, the rabbis discouraged their recitation outside the Temple to refute the claims of the "sectarians" that only these, and not the whole Torah, were given to Moses at Sinai (Ber. 12a). During the Middle Ages there were some protests against the practice of standing while the Ten Commandments were read on Shavuot. However the custom for the whole congregation to stand is still followed on the grounds that the talmudic objection to any special significance being attached to the Decalogue cannot apply to congregational reading from the Scroll, since the whole of the Torah is written in the Scroll. The account of the revelation on Mount Sinai is usually sung to a specially solemn tune.

It is customary to adorn the synagogue with plants and flowers on Shavuot because, tradition has it, Sinai was a green mountain; and with trees, because Shavuot is judgment day for the fruit of the tree (RH 1:2). Some authorities disapproved of the custom because of its similarity to certain church rites (see **Ḥukkat ha-Goi*). It is a home custom to eat dairy products on Shavuot because the Torah is compared to milk (Song 4:11) and because the law of the first fruits is placed in juxtaposition to a law concerning milk (Ex. 23:19). In some communities it is customary to eat triangular pancakes stuffed with meat or cheese because the Torah is of three parts (Pentateuch, Prophets, and Hagiographa) and was given to a people of three parts (priests, levites, and Israelites) on the third month through Moses who was the third child of his parents.

BIBLIOGRAPHY: S. Zevin: *Ha-Mo'adim ba-Halakhah* (1949²); C. Pearl, *Guide to Shavuoth* (1959); Y.T. Lewinsky, *Sefer ha-Mo'adim*, 3 (1953²); H. Schauss, *Guide to Jewish Holy Days* (1966⁴), 86–95.

[Louis Jacobs]

SHAW, ARTIE (**Arthur Arshawsky**; 1910–2004), jazz clarinetist, bandleader, composer, and arranger. Born in New York, Shaw joined Johnny Cavallaro's dance band in 1925 as an alto saxophonist. From 1926 to 1929 he worked in Cleveland as musical director and arranger for an orchestra led by Austin Wylie. He then toured as a tenor saxophonist with Irving Aaronson's band. From 1931 to 1934 he worked as a freelance studio musician and in 1937 formed a conventional swing band. This group, which included Billie Holiday, marked his breakthrough to public fame and established him as a rival to Benny *Goodman. In the 1940s Shaw formed several bands, among them the Gramercy Five, which became one of the leading exponents of the swing style at that time. He put together his last Gramercy Five in October 1953, then in 1954 went into retirement. Shaw was a public figure whose handsome looks and eight marriages (among others to the film actresses Lana Turner and Ava Gardner) made him a darling of gossip columnists. Among his biggest hits were Cole Porter's "Begin the Beguine" (1938), "Summit Ridge Drive" (1940), "Frenesi," and "Little Jazz" (1945). He published an autobiographical novel, *The Trouble with Cinderella*, in 1952.

BIBLIOGRAPHY: Grove online, s.v.; E.L. Blandford, *Artie Shaw* (1974), biodiscography.

[Israela Stein (2nd ed.)]

SHAW, BENJAMIN (1898–1988), U.S. financier. Shaw, who spent virtually his whole life in the garment business, began as a dress manufacturer but became known as "Mr. Seventh Avenue" because of his skill as a financial backer and advisor to a series of highly successful designers. Those in whom he invested included Oscar de la Renta, Halston, Norman Norell, Jane Derby, Donald Brooks, Geoffrey Beene, Giorgio San'

Angelo, and Stephen Burrows. In addition, he introduced at least two Paris designers to the U.S. and helped make Gloria Vanderbilt an iconic jeans label. Shaw backed his designers with his production expertise, his network of retail contacts, and his money.

Born in Kiev as Benjamin Schwartz, he was brought to New York City at the age of three. As a child, he got his first taste of the garment business when he was sent to find buttons and zippers for his mother, Rose, a dressmaker on the Lower East Side. His formal education ended early and he went to work as a messenger. After learning the rudiments of sales and production and changing his name to Shaw because "there were too many Schwartzes in the Manhattan telephone directory," he became a partner in Wieman, Wilkes & Shaw in 1925. Four years later, the stock market collapsed and so did his company. In 1935, Shaw launched a dress house called Elfreda and ran it until 1954, when he retired. Six months later, he was back in business, first importing the apparel collections of French designers Nina Ricci and Pierre Balmain for an American customer. In 1956 he bought into the Jane Derby dress firm, where Oscar de la Renta subsequently became the designer. In 1969, a few years after Derby's death, the company – then named for de la Renta – was sold to publicly owned Richton International. Shaw, his son Gerald, and de la Renta bought it back in 1974. In the interim, Shaw invested in Halston, one of the most popular U.S. designers of the 1970s and early 1980s. When the Halston business was sold in 1973, Shaw said, he "made millions." Other associations with designers followed. Gerald Shaw, who became president of Oscar de la Renta Ltd., said of his father, "He couldn't make a pattern, but he could tell whether a dress worked. He had a talent for spotting talent."

[Mort Sheinman (2nd ed.)]

SHAW, IRWIN (1913–1984), U.S. novelist, playwright, and scriptwriter. Born in Brooklyn, Shaw gained overnight fame with his one-act antiwar drama *Bury the Dead* (1936), dealing with a group of dead soldiers who refuse to be buried. *The Gentle People* (1939), about a group of Brooklyn folk who turn upon a gangster, demonstrated Shaw's gift for seeing a fable in everyday life and was regarded as an anti-Fascist parable. His World War II experiences in the U.S. army inspired a book of short stories, *Act of Faith* (1946), and his first novel, *The Young Lions* (1948). One of the outstanding novels of the war, *The Young Lions* dealt with the problem of antisemitism in the army and dramatically portrayed the careers of one German and two American soldiers and their fateful encounter toward the end of World War II. Shaw's other novels include *The Troubled Air* (1951), about the treatment of actors suspected of being Communists; *Lucy Crown* (1956); *In the Company of Dolphins* (1964); and *Voices of a Summer Day* (1965). As a writer, Shaw was noted for his liberal outlook and masterly technique, evident in short-story collections such as *Sailor off the Bremen* (1939), *Welcome to the City* (1942), *Mixed Company* (1950), and *Tip on a Dead Jockey* (1957, 1959^2). His plays include *Sons and Soldiers* (1944), *Assassin* (1946), and the comedy *Children from Their Games* (a play in two acts, 1963), but in this genre Shaw was generally less successful, although he was prominent as a writer of screen and radio plays. Shaw wrote the text for *Report on Israel* (1950), an album of photographs by Robert *Capa. He also provided the text for Paris/Magnum Photographs, 1935–1981 (1981). Among his later works are *Rich Man, Poor Man* (1970); *Evening in Byzantium* (1973), and *Paris! Paris!* (illustrated by Ronald Searle, 1977). His *Short Stories, Five Decades* appeared in 1978.

BIBLIOGRAPHY: J.R. Giles, *Irwin Shaw: A Study of the Short Fiction* (1983); M. Shaynerson, *Irwin Shaw: A Biography* (1989).

[Joseph Mersand]

SHAWN, DICK (1923–1987), U.S. actor. Originally from Buffalo, NY, Shawn (né Richard Schulefand) began his comedy career during World War II while serving with the Army. He moved to New York City after winning a University of Miami talent show and appearing on the television show *Arthur Godfrey Talent Scouts*. By 1955 Shawn was performing at New York's Palace Theater, had made guest appearances on *The Ed Sullivan Show*, and was performing at Las Vegas nightclubs. He made his film debut in the 1956 movie *The Opposite Sex*. In 1960, he signed on with 20th Century Fox and starred in their film *The Wizard of Baghdad*. In this satire on the Arabian Nights, Shawn played a laidback genie. The same year, he acted with fellow comedian Ernie Kovacs in *Wake Me When It's Over*. Three years later, he had a role in the all-star comedy *It's a Mad, Mad, Mad, Mad World* (1963). Shawn's most famous role was that of a hippie actor named Lorenzo St. DuBois (L.S.D.) who is cast as a singing Adolf Hitler in Mel Brooks' 1968 comedy *The Producers*. In one scene, Shawn is credited for inventing the "high five" when, instead of putting out his hand for fellow actor David Patch to "give him five," he held it up and Patch slapped it. Other Shawn movies include *Way … Way Out* (1966), *Penelope* (1966), *Looking Up* (1977), *Beer* (1985), and *Maid to Order* (1987). Shawn was also highly regarded for his one-man stage show *The Second Greatest Entertainer in the Whole Wide World*, during which he lay motionless on stage during the entire intermission (1985). Shawn's final movie, *Rented Lips* (1988), came out after his death.

[Susannah Howland (2nd ed.)]

SHAYEVITSH, SIMKHA-BUNIM (1907–1944), Yiddish poet and novelist. Born in 1907 in Lenczyce, Poland and interned from 1940 in the Lodz ghetto, Shayevitsh responded to the mass deportations in late 1941 with "*Lekh-Lekho*" ("Go"), a long poem evoking the traditional Jewish past in contrast with the tragic historical present. A second poem on expulsion followed in "*Friling 1942*" ("Spring 1942"), contrasting the promise of spring's arrival with the horrors of ghetto life. In the ghetto he met Chava Rosenfarb, became her mentor, and read more of his poetry to her, all of which has been lost. On August 28, 1944, Shayevitsh was deported to Auschwitz, where he was among the last sent to the gas chamber. The two poems (found in the ghetto's ruins) and two letters were published by the Jewish Historical Commission (1946). His subsequent influence on Yiddish writers was considerable, despite the meagerness of his surviving output.

BIBLIOGRAPHY: Kh. L. Fuchs. *Lodzsh shel Mayle: dos Yidishe Gaystige un Derhoybene Lodzsh* (1972); B. Mark, *Di Umgekumene Shrayber fun di Getos un Lagern un Zeyere Verk* (1954); C. Rosenfarb, in: *Di Goldene Keyt*, 81 (1973), 127–41; D. Roskies, *Against the Apocalypse* (1984).

[Goldie Morgentaler (2nd ed.)]

SHAZAR (Rubashov), SHNEUR ZALMAN (1889–1974), third president of the State of Israel, scholar and writer, member of the First to Third Knessets. Shazar (acronym for Shneur Zalman Rubashov) was born in the Belorussian town of Mir in the province of Minsk. In 1892, after a disastrous fire in Mir, the family moved to the nearby townlet of Stolbtsy, where Shazar received a *ḥeder* education under the influence of *Chabad, in addition to being influenced by his parents' Zionism. The influence of his Hebrew teacher and the writings of Ber *Borochov brought him to the *Po'alei Zion Movement, and during the 1905 revolution he was active in propagating the movement's ideas and organizing Jewish *self-defense units in Belorussia and the Ukraine. Attending the clandestine Po'alei Zion conference in Minsk in July 1906, he became acquainted with Izhak Ben-Zvi and started to participate in the editorial and publishing activities of the movement. In 1907 he moved to Vilna, where he first met and worked with Borochov, Jacob *Zerubavel, and Raḥel Yanait (see Raḥel *Ben-Zvi), and translated Russian articles written by Borochov and Ben-Zvi into Yiddish for the movement's journal, *Der Proletarisher Gedank*. Arrested along with the other leading members of the movement in the summer of 1907, he was jailed for two months. After his release, he enrolled as a student at the "Academy of Jewish Studies," then newly established in St. Petersburg by Baron David *Guenzburg. The historian Simon *Dubnow and the Hebrew writer and scholar J.L. *Katzenelson ("Buki ben Yogli") were two distinguished faculty members, who particularly influenced the young Shazar. To support himself he edited *Der Yidisher Emigrant*, organ of the *Jewish Colonization Association (ICA), and also wrote for Yiddish papers *Der Fray* in Russia, and *Dos Naye Lebn* in the United States.

In 1911 Shazar spent the summer in Ereẓ Israel working in the *kevuẓah* in Merhavyah, and met Berl *Katznelson and the poetess *Raḥel. He left Russia the following year and attended the universities of Freiburg-im-Breisgau and Strasbourg. While confined to Berlin as an enemy alien during World War I, he continued his studies at the University of Berlin, attending courses with historian Friedrich Meinecke. Shazar's fields of specialization were East European Jewish history, the Shabbatean movement, and biblical criticism. Shazar was also involved in Zionist activity, contributing regularly to the *Juedische Rundschau*. In 1916 he was one of the founders of the Labor Zionist movement, and in 1917 of the *He-Ḥalutz Movement in Germany. At the Po'alei Zion conference held in Stockholm in 1919, he was appointed, along with Nachman *Syrkin, Naḥum *Nir, and Ḥayyim *Fineman, to survey conditions in Palestine and work out a program for cooperative economic development. He helped edit the report prepared in Yiddish by the mission in 1920, and wrote the chapters on Jewish labor and on the *kevuẓot*. In 1920 he married Rachel *Katznelson, whom he had first met in St. Petersburg, in Jerusalem. Shazar participated in the Po'alei Zion Conference in Vienna in 1920, where the movement split on the issue of how to relate to Communism. Shazar emerged as one of the spokesmen of the group that objected to Communism. He opened the founding assembly of the World He-Ḥalutz Organization in 1921, and from 1922 to 1924 lectured on history at the Jewish Pedagogic Institute in Vienna.

Settling in Palestine in 1924, Shazar became a member of the Secretariat of the *Histadrut and joined the editorial staff of its daily *Davar*, becoming the paper's editor-in-chief and head of the Histadrut publishing house, Am Oved, in 1944. He served in these capacities until 1949. All along he carried out numerous missions abroad on behalf of the Histadrut, the World Po'alei Zion, *Mapai, and the Zionist movement. Shazar was a member of the Jewish Agency delegation to the United Nations General Assembly in November 1947, and at that time established contact with the Lubavitcher rebbe Menachem Mendel *Schneersohn, convincing him to establish Kefar Ḥabad in Israel. Ever since his boyhood Shazar had been emotionally and intellectually involved with the Chabad Movement. In later years he regularly visited Kefar Ḥabad. During his two visits to the United States as president, in 1966 and 1971, he called on Schneersohn in Brooklyn.

Shazar was elected to the First Knesset on the Mapai list and served as minister of education and culture from 1949 to 1951, and in this capacity was responsible for passing the Compulsory Education Law of 1949. He served as a member of the Knesset until October 1956, when he resigned. Following the Soviet government's refusal to accept him as Israeli ambassador to Moscow, he became a member of the Jewish Agency Executive in 1952, and headed the Department of Information. In 1954 he was appointed head of the Department of Education and Culture in the Diaspora. From 1956 to 1960 he was acting chairman of the Agency's Jerusalem Executive.

On May 21, 1963, the Knesset elected Shazar as the third president of the State of Israel, and on March 26, 1968, he was reelected for a second five-year term. During his presidency he represented Israel in numerous state visits abroad. During the 1964 visit of Pope *Paul VI, the pope was received on his arrival at Megiddo by President Shazar, who also took leave of him in Jerusalem.

Like his predecessor, Izhak Ben-Zvi, Shazar made his residence a center for Israeli and Jewish scholars, writers, and artists. The Bible Study Group, first established by David *Ben-Gurion, met there regularly, as did the circle for Study of Diaspora Jewry conducted in cooperation with the Hebrew University's Institute of Contemporary Jewry. A year after completing his two terms as president, Shazar passed away.

Shazar's writings span 70 years. His literary work took many forms, from poetry and autobiographical fiction, to scholarly treatises and journalistic articles. He wrote freely in both Yiddish and Hebrew, and was noted for his unique style, that applied both lyricism and biblical influences to contemporary issues. He first produced a "magazine" at the age of ten, and a piece he wrote appeared in *Ha-Meliẓ* of March 17, 1903. His first Yiddish article, a plea for the unification of the Socialist Zionist parties, appeared in America in 1910, and his first Hebrew article – an impression of his visit to the Western Wall – in Jerusalem in 1911.His career as Labor Zionist editor began after World War I in the German *Po'alei Zion's Oyf der Shvel* (1918) and the Viennese *Das Arbeitende Eretz Yisrael* (1921–23). After the Po'alei Zion split of 1920, Shazar sharply attacked the left's decision not to participate in the Zionist Congress. Writing for Aḥdut ha-Avodah's weekly, *Kunteres*, during his participation in the Labor Zionist research mission, he gave notable expression to the reaction evoked by the Arab attacks in Jerusalem in 1920: "Is Jerusalem to be another Kishinev?" From the first issue of *Davar* until the 1970s, he contributed not only hundreds of unsigned editorials, but, under his own name and pseudonyms, essays on numerous topics. From 1930 to 1932, he edited the monthly *Aḥdut ha-Avodah* with Chaim *Arlosoroff, and from 1953 the yearbooks of *Davar.*

As early as his student days, Shazar had been drawn to the study of the Shabbatean movement and to biblical criticism. In the former he was attracted by the passion for national redemption which he sensed as central within the mystic yearning of European Jewry in the dark days of the 17th century. He wrote his first article on the subject in *Ha-Shilo'aḥ* in 1913. His work on the subject of Jewish mysticism was published in the Russian Jewish Encyclopedia and numerous studies. His contribution to the field was acclaimed by Gershom *Scholem.

Shazar played a pioneering role in introducing modern Bible criticism in the Hebrew language. He had himself studied under Professor Novak at Strasbourg, and in 1914 he translated from Russian into Hebrew essays on the subject by Max Soloveichik (*Solieli). Shazar's contribution to Yiddish philology grew out of his study under Dubnow of responsa literature as a source for East European Jewish history of the 15th to the 17th centuries. Coming upon numerous Yiddish phrases in the testimony of witnesses, he collected and analyzed the linguistic material. In his preface to an edition of Eduard Gans's speeches of 1821–23, Shazar cast light on the inner world of early 19th-century German-Jewish assimilationists, and founders of Jewish scholarship. His essays on Marx and Lassalle expressed his interest in the Jewish role in socialism, while his essays on Borochov, Ben-Zvi, Syrkin, and Berl Katznelson illuminate the beginnings of the Socialist Jewish Labor movement. The wide scope of Shazar's cultural knowledge and interests added depth to the many contacts and meetings involved in his activity as president of the state.

His autobiographical sketches, collected in *Kokhevei Boker* (1950; *Morning Stars*, 1967) and reprinted many times, appeared in English, French, Yiddish, and Spanish translations. His biographical evaluations of leaders in Zionism and Jewish culture were assembled in *Or Ishim* (1963). A bibliography of the writings of Shazar from 1903 to 1973, a new edition of *Or Ishim* in three volumes, and an album on Shazar were all published in 1973. Shazar's verse, including much translation, appeared in many journals; his Yiddish translation of a selection of Raḥel's lyrics appeared in 1932. Correspondence between Raḥel and Shazar was published in *Ha-Ḥofim Ha-Shanim: Mikhtavim 1909–1963, Raḥel ve-Zalman Shazar* (1999).

BIBLIOGRAPHY: A. Manor, *Zalman Shazar: Yiḥudo ve-Yeẓirato* (1961); idem, *Nesi Yisrael, Zalman Shazar* (1970); *Zalman Shazar: Nasi ve-Sofer* (1969); Leksikon Kressel, *Al Po'alo ha-Mada'i shel Zalman Shazar* (1969); S. Kraus, *Nasi ve-Ḥasid: Masekhet ha-Kesharim she-Nirkemah bein ha-Rabbi mi-Lubavitch ve-Ḥasido R' Shne'or Zalman Robashov-Shazar* (1999).

[Susan Hattis Rolef (2nd ed.)]

SHCHEDRIN, town in Polesie district, Belarus. In 1841 Ḥayyim Golodetz, a timber dealer, established a Jewish colony on the estate of Shchedrin. By the end of the 19th century some of the settlers engaged in general agriculture and some in the timber business of the Golodetz family. In 1897 there were 4,022 Jews in Shchedrin (95% of the total population of the town), about 40% of them engaging in agriculture. A decline in the timber trade in the area and the subsequent departure of the Golodetz family resulted in a general emigration from the town. In 1926 there were 1,759 Jews (91 percent of the population) in Shchedrin. The Soviet government attempted to develop agriculture and in 1930 over half of the 380 remaining Jewish families were engaged in that occupation, about half of them living on the kolkhoz Sotsialistishe Veg. About 30 percent were engaged in crafts. A local Jewish council operated until the 1930s, as did two Yiddish schools, one for the kolkhoz children. The Germans arrived in July 1941, and in March 1942 they murdered the 1,500 Jews living there.

BIBLIOGRAPHY: Y. Hershnboim, *Shchedrin* (Yid., 1931); J. Slutsky (ed.), *Sefer Bobruisk*, 2 (Heb. and Yid., 1967), 806–24; L. Golodetz, *History of the Family Golodetz* (1954).

[Yehuda Slutsky / Shmuel Spector (2nd ed.)]

SHEALTIEL (Heb. שְׁאַלְתִּיאֵל (Haggai 1:1); abridged שַׁלְתִּיאֵל (Haggai 1:12, 14; 2:2)), biblical name meaning "I asked of God," referring either to the request for a son (cf. I Sam. 1:17, 20, 27) or some other personal benefit (cf. Ps. 27:4 – request to reside permanently in the Temple). The name is unique and its bearer was either the first or the second son of King Jehoiachin (I Chron. 3:17), who was exiled from Judah at the age of 18 in 597 B.C.E. (II Kings 24:8). A Babylonian ration tablet of 592 B.C.E. lists Jehoiachin and five sons, so that Shealtiel may have been born prior to his father's exile. His son (nephew according to I Chron. 3:17ff.), given the Babylonian name *Zerubbabel, served as governor of Judah under Darius (Haggai 1:1; cf. Ezra 3:2; Neh. 12:1).

BIBLIOGRAPHY: W.F. Albright, in: BA, 5 (1942), 49ff.

[Bezalel Porten]

SHEAN, AL (**Schonberg**; 1868–1949), vaudeville actor. Born in Dornum, Germany, and brought up in New York, Shean became well known with the Comedy Four, which he led for 15 years. He then teamed with Ed Gallagher for a time, but subsequently appeared in plays, taking roles like Stonewall Moskewitz in *Betsy* (1926), Father Malachy in *Father Malachy's Miracle* (1937), Von Barwig in *The Music Master* (1941), and Manny Siegelmann in *Meet a Body* (1944). His sister was the mother of the *Marx Brothers.

SHEAR, MURRAY JACOB (1899–1983), U.S. biochemist. Shear was born in New York. After doing research in several hospitals, he worked at the National Cancer Institute, Maryland, becoming chief of Chemical Pharmacology Laboratory from 1947. His research focused on the mechanism of deposition of bone salts, the genesis of tumors by chemical agents, and the chemotherapy and immunology of cancer. He served as chairman on several cancer research societies and was active in Jewish communal affairs.

SHEARER, NORMA (1902–1983), U.S. actress. Born Edith Norma Shearer in Westmount, Quebec, Canada, to lumber/construction company president Andrew Shearer and Edith Mary Fisher, Shearer was schooled in the family's middle-class home until 1912, when she enrolled in the Montreal High School for Girls. In 1914, she transferred to Westmont High School. She had been a child model, and at 14 won a beauty contest. A fan of silent film actress Pearl White, Shearer dreamed of becoming an actress herself. When the family business began to decline and her parents were forced to sell their home in 1919, Shearer quit school and went to work plugging sheet music. Her mother left her father in 1920, taking Shearer and her sister Athole to New York. Florenz Ziegfeld rejected Shearer for his Follies, but she was able to find extra work with her mother and sister in the films *The Flapper* (1920), *Way Down East* (1920), and *The Restless Sex* (1920). During this time Shearer also worked as an art model to help bring in money. After securing Edward Small as an agent, Shearer got roles in *The Stealers* (1920), *The Sign on the Door* (1921), and *The Leather Pushers* (1922). Universal Studios manager Irving *Thalberg tried to sign Shearer, but the studio was unwilling to pay for moving expenses. Thalberg soon quit Universal and went over to the Mayer Company, where he was able to secure a six-month contract and moving expenses for Shearer and her family. Her first films for Mayer were *The Wanters* (1923) and *Pleasure Mad* (1923). After Mayer merged with Metro and Goldwyn to become MGM, Shearer's first film for the new studio was *He Who Gets Slapped* (1924). Following her engagement to Thalberg, Shearer converted to Judaism with the help of Wilshire Boulevard Temple's Rabbi Edgar Magnin. The rising star of such films as *His Secretary* (1925) and *After Midnight* (1927) married Thalberg on Sept. 29, 1927. After her return from a European honeymoon, Shearer starred in MGM's second talkie, *The Trial of Mary Dugan* (1929). In 1930, she won the best actress Oscar for *The Divorcee* and gave birth to her son, Irving Grant Thalberg Jr. In 1932, Shearer became a U.S. citizen. One of the highest-paid actresses of the Depression era, she was dubbed by others in the industry as Queen Norma or Queen of the Lot. In 1935, she gave birth to her daughter, Katherine. Shearer returned to film after a yearlong absence with *Romeo and Juliet* (1936), but three weeks after the film's Aug. 20 New York premier, Thalberg died from a congenital heart defect. After the devastating loss of her husband and fighting off a severe case of pneumonia, Shearer intended to retire but ended up signing a final six-picture contract with MGM, which included *Marie Antoinette* (1938) and *The Women* (1939). She finally retired in 1942. Shearer remained active in Hollywood, presenting the first Irving G. Thalberg Memorial Award in 1945 and helping to establish the careers of Janet Leigh and Robert Evans in the 1950s, but she mostly focused on her family. Her health began failing in the 1970s, and by the 1980s she was moved to the Motion Picture and Television Fund's hospital in Woodland Hills, California, where she died. She is buried next to Thalberg at Forest Lawn in Glendale, California.

BIBLIOGRAPHY: "Shearer, Norma," in: *The Scribner Encyclopedia of American Lives* (1998).

[Adam Wills (2nd ed.)]

SHE'AR YASHUV (Heb. שְׁאָר יָשׁוּב), moshav in the Ḥuleh Valley, affiliated with Ha-Oved ha-Ẓiyyoni. She'ar Yashuv was founded in 1940 by pioneers from Eastern Europe, as the third of the "Ussishkin Fortresses" near the country's northeastern corner. It made little headway and was uninhabited after the War of Independence. In 1949, the village was settled anew by immigrants from Hungary and had 153 inhabitants by 1968, growing to 245 in the mid-1990s and 327 in 2002. Only a small group was still engaged in farming at the turn of the century. In 1997 the moshav was the site of a collision between two IDF helicopters, taking the lives of 73 soldiers. A monument in memory of the dead is located in there. The name, "A Remnant Shall Return," is taken from Isaiah 10:20–22.

[Efram Orni / Shaked Gilboa (2nd ed.)]

SHEBA (**Schieber** or **Schiber**), **CHAIM** (1908–1971), Israeli physician and medical educator. Born into a ḥasidic family in a small village in Bukovina, Sheba went to Palestine in 1933. He worked as a sick fund physician until 1936, and then joined the staff of the Beilinson Hospital in Petaḥ Tikvah. After service with the Royal Army Medical Corps in World War II, he became chief medical officer of the *Haganah in 1947, and on the establishment of the state was appointed chief medical officer of the Israel Defense Forces. In 1951 Sheba became director-general of the Ministry of Health, but resigned two years later to take over the direction of Tel Ha-Shomer Hospital, Ramat-Gan, which under his guidance developed into one of the country's leading medical institutions. In addition to being head of this hospital's department of internal medicine he became, in 1965, an associate clinical professor at the Hebrew University-Hadassah Medical School in Jerusalem. In 1966 he was appointed a vice president of Tel Aviv University. Sheba did fieldwork in parasitology with Saul *Adler in the 1930s, and his many scientific publications cover a wide variety of subjects, ranging from amebiasis to population genetics, and from relapsing fever to hemolysis due to enzyme deficiencies. He was awarded the Israel Prize in 1968. After Sheba's death in 1971, the Tel Ha-Shomer Hospital was renamed after him.

[Shabbetai Ginton]

SHEBA BEN BICHRI, a member of the tribe of Benjamin. Sheba ben Bichri belonged to the clan of Becher, whose eponymous ancestor was the second son of Benjamin (Gen. 46:21; I Chron. 7:6).

Playing on the jealousy which was aroused among the tribes of Israel by David's apparent favoritism in arranging to have Judah welcome him back first at the Jordan after the crushing of the revolt of *Absalom in Transjordan, Sheba blew a horn with the cry, "We have no share in David, neither have we any portion in the son of Jesse; every man to his tents, O Israel" (II Sam. 19:41–44; 20:1); and instead of escorting David to Jerusalem, the men of Israel marched ahead after Sheba to their homeland. Had David not taken successful steps to assert his authority over Israel, Sheba would presumably have tried to induce Israel to make him king. But David did assert his authority. David, who in order to woo Judah had sent, while still in Transjordan, a promise to *Amasa to make him army commander in place of *Joab (II Sam. 19:14), assigned to Amasa and the men of Judah the task of pursuing and liquidating Sheba. He gave Amasa three days in which to raise the levies of Judah, but because Amasa was delayed, the king sent out *Abishai with his men and Joab with the rest of the professional fighting units. When Amasa arrived tardily at the rallying point, Joab treacherously, but understandably, murdered his rival. Then he and Abishai marched through Israel all the way to Abel of Beth-Maacah in the north. Though the last five words of II Samuel 20:14 are unclear, it seems that the population of the districts through which Joab's men marched actually joined them. Evidently, whatever knowledge they may have had of the incident at the Jordan did not make them sufficiently anxious to secede from David and to make them want to risk clashing with the troops that had so decisively crushed the rebellion of Absalom. When Joab attacked Abel of Beth-Maacah, "a wise woman" of the town (probably with the approval of the townspeople) stepped onto the wall and asked for a parley with him; on receiving his assurance that he would not hurt the town or any of its inhabitants provided they surrendered Sheba, she went and got the people of the town to toss Sheba's head over the wall to the besiegers.

On the consequences of the rebellion for David's kingdom, army, and chief officers, see *David; *Amasai; *Joab.

[Harold Louis Ginsberg]

In the Aggadah:
The immediate cause of Sheba's rebellion against David was the fact that he saw portents that the kingdom should be divided. His error was that he falsely and vaingloriously interpreted these signs to refer to his own elevation and to the throne (Sanh. 101b). He is also condemned as an idolator (Tanḥ. B. Va-Yera, 12).

BIBLIOGRAPHY: H.P. Smith, *Book of Samuel* (ICC, 1912), 366–71; M.Z. Segal, *Sefer Shemu'el* (1956), 356–72; Bright, Hist, 188. IN THE AGGADAH: Ginzberg, Legends, index; I. Ḥasida, *Ishei ha-Tanakh* (1964), 397.

SHEBNAH (Heb. שֶׁבְנָה, שֶׁבְנָא).

(1) The scribe of King Hezekiah, mentioned in connection with the episode which took place during the siege of Jerusalem by Sennacherib king of Assyria (701 B.C.E.; II Kings 18:17–19:37, and in the parallel passage in Isa. 36–37). He was one of the delegation of Hezekiah's three senior officials dispatched to negotiate with the Assyrians. However, their mission having proved of no avail in the face of the Assyrians' demand for complete surrender, they were sent to the prophet Isaiah to seek the advice of God (II Kings 19:1ff. and the parallel passage in Isa. 37).

(2) Shebnah, who bore the titles "steward" and "who is over the household," was the object of Isaiah's rebuke (Isa. 22:15–25). In this passage, which has the character of a personal admonition, Isaiah prophesies that Shebnah will be removed from his position, exiled to "a large country," and replaced by Eliakim (*ibid.* 22:19–23).

The identification of this Shebnah with the one mentioned in II Kings 18–19 is not definite. The main difficulties are:

(a) the difference in the titles; and

(b) in Isaiah's rebuke reference is made to Shebnah's downfall and exile and not to his being reduced to a lower position, and hence his status in II Kings as second in rank to Eliakim, who is there described as "over the household," cannot be interpreted as the fulfillment of Isaiah's prophecy. Those who assume that the reference is to the same person explain these difficulties, as well as the reason for the prophet's sharp rebuke of Shebnah, against the background of Isaiah's advocacy of a policy of nonintervention, and of Shebnah apparently being the leader of the opposing, pro-Egyptian group which called for an uprising against Assyria. According to this view, the rebuke in Isaiah 22 refers to an earlier period than that reflected in II Kings 18–19: in the former, Shebnah still occupied the eminent position of being "over the household," while in the latter, which describes events during Sennacherib's siege, the prophecy had already been fulfilled, Shebnah having been degraded from his exalted station and appointed to the less important position of "scribe." Some ascribe these administrative changes not to politics arising from Judah's policy but to the deplorable personality of Shebnah, who exploited his position to advance his personal interests, as is evident from the literal meaning of the passage in Isaiah: "What have you to do here and whom have you here... you who hew a tomb on the height and carve a habitation for yourself in the rock? [22:16]... and there shall be your splendid chariots" (verse 18b). It is conjectured, on the basis of the first part of verse 16, that the reference here is to a foreigner. On the basis of this verse, as also on paleographical, archaeological, and chronological grounds, it is contended that the sepulcher discovered by Ch. Clermont-Ganneau in the village of Siloam belonged to Shebnah. On its facade is an inscription of three lines ascribing the sepulcher to יהו אשר על הבית..., "...*Yahu* over the household" the name being reconstructed as [שבנ]יהו

BIBLIOGRAPHY: W.F. Albright, in: JBL, 51 (1932), 77ff.; H.G. May, in: AJSLL, 56 (1939), 146–8; N. Avigad, in: *Eretz Israel*, 3 (1954), 69ff.

[Nili Schupak]

SHECHEM (Heb. שְׁכֶם), ancient Canaanite and Israelite city situated between Mt. Ebal and Mt. Gerizim in a fertile and well-watered valley in the heart of the central hill country of Ereẓ Israel. Shechem has been identified with the ancient mound known as Tell al-Balāṭa, 1 mi. (2 km.) east of modern *Nablus, also called Shechem in modern Hebrew parlance. The site has been excavated by an Austrian expedition (1913–14), German expeditions (1926–32), and an American expedition from 1957 onward. In the Bible, Shechem is first mentioned in connection with Abraham's arrival in Canaan; he sanctified the place and built an altar there at "Elon [the terebinth] of Moreh" (Gen. 12:6). After leaving Succoth Jacob returned to Shechem, where he bought land and his sons Simeon and Levi destroyed the city following the rape of their sister Dinah (*ibid.*, 33:18ff.). Joseph was later buried in the plot of land purchased by Jacob (Josh. 24:32). Excavations at Shechem have revealed that the town already existed in the Middle Bronze Age II (Patriarchal period). Remains uncovered from this period include a defensive wall, a large beaten-earth platform, and a cylinder seal impression from the time of the Egyptian 12th Dynasty. The first mention of the town in Egyptian documents (in the tomb inscription of Khu-Sebek from the time of Sesostris III, 1878–1843 B.C.E., and in the later Execration Texts) belongs to the same period. The town flourished in the Hyksos period (c. 1750–1650 B.C.E.), when it was strongly fortified by a double defensive wall; another wall enclosed the acropolis and a large building, 66 × 98 ft. (20 × 30 m.), probably a temple, was also built. In the late Hyksos period (1650–1550 B.C.E.) a great temple was erected, 108 × 92 ft. (33 × 28 m.), with massive walls 18 ft. (5½ m.) thick. It contained a beaten-earth altar and an entrance flanked by a pair of *maṣṣevot* ("pillars"). The city gates were of the triple type, made of pairs of parallel limestone blocks. After the Egyptian conquest of Canaan (18th Dynasty), Shechem suffered a decline; the temple was reconstructed on a lesser scale with much weaker walls; a huge *maṣṣevah* stood in front of its entrance. Shechem at this time, however, was still politically important; it was ruled by Labayu, known from the Tell el-Amarna letters as an ally of the Ḥabiru and a rebel against Pharaoh. Shechem is not mentioned among the cities conquered by the Israelites under Joshua but it was the scene of the great covenant for which Joshua assembled the tribes (Josh. 24), and it has thus been suggested that Shechem was

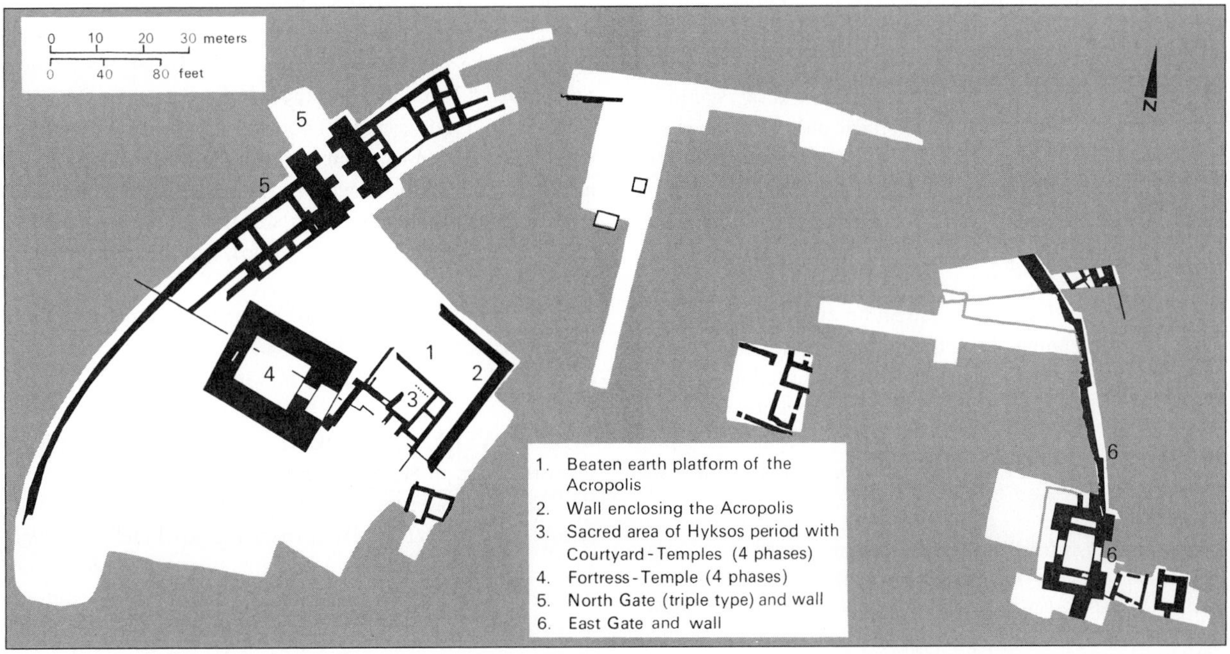

Plan of Tell al-Balāta, identified with Shechem, showing main features and digging areas. Based on G.E. Wright, Shechem, the Biography of a Biblical City, *1965.*

peacefully absorbed by the invading tribes. The archaeological evidence furnishes no proof of a violent destruction of the city as noted at other Canaanite sites, and its transition from the Late Bronze to the Early Iron period was apparently peaceful. In the period of the Judges, Shechem was the center of the kingdom of Abimelech son of Gideon (Jerubbaal) who was "made king by the terebinth of the pillar that was in Shechem," after being supplied with money from the "house of Baal-Berith" ("Lord of the Covenant," Judg. 9). Later, however, the people of Shechem rebelled against Abimelech, who conquered the city and razed its walls. The various localities in the city mentioned in this narrative have been tentatively identified by the excavators: the "Beth-Millo" ("house of Millo") with the above-mentioned Hyksos temple built on a platform (Judg. 9:20); the "terebinth of the pillar" is taken to refer to a sacred tree near the *maṣṣevah* of the Late Bronze Age temple (*ibid.*, 9:6); the city gate with the East Gate, the only one in use from the Late Bronze Age onward (*ibid.*, 9:35, 40, 44). The filling of pits beneath the temple with charcoal and early 12th century B.C.E. pottery may represent evidence of Abimelech's destruction of Shechem. After Solomon's death, his son Rehoboam was repudiated as king by the ten tribes at Shechem (I Kings 12). Jeroboam, crowned king in his place, established his first capital at Shechem (*ibid.*, 12:25). Some archaeological evidence was found for his rebuilding of the East Gate (c. 922 B.C.E.). In the period of the Divided Monarchy, Shechem comprised some well-built quarters, with two-storied houses, and poor sections; its other buildings include large granaries, which recall the role of Shechem reflected in the Samaria ostraca as a center for the collection of taxes in kind. In about 724 B.C.E. the richer quarters of the city were apparently destroyed by the Assyrians. These houses were rebuilt and the new stratum contains a quantity of Assyrian pottery. Further destructions of the city seem to have been connected with Assyrian punitive expeditions in 673 and about 640 B.C.E. Shechem was resettled as a poor town, and this settlement disappeared in the fifth century B.C.E. In the Hellenistic period the town revived as an extensive and powerful city. Its resettlement has been connected with the expulsion of the *Samaritans from Samaria itself after their revolt against Alexander the Great; they established their settlement near Mt. Gerizim, on which their sanctuary stood. The Hellenistic city was destroyed in 129 B.C.E. by John Hyrcanus; great amounts of earth were spread over the remains and the mound was leveled off. The site later contained an insignificant village. Eusebius (Onom. 150:1ff.) and the author of the *Madaba Map still distinguish between the site of Shechem and the city of Nablus (Neapolis) established in 72 B.C.E., but most later writers erroneously equate the two.

BIBLIOGRAPHY: F.M.T. Boehl, *De opgraving van Sichem* (1927); E. Sellin, in: ZDPV, 49 (1926), 229–36, 304–27; 50 (1927), 265–74; H. Steckeweh, *ibid.*, 64 (1941), 1–20; G.E. Wright, in: BASOR, 144 (1956), 9–20; 148 (1957), 11–28, 161 (1961), 11–54; 167 (1962), 5–13; E.F. Campbell and J.F. Ross, in: BA, 26 (1963), 2–27; G.E. Wright, *Shechem; The Biography of a Biblical City* (1965); idem, in: D.W. Thomas (ed.), *Archaeology and Old Testament Study* (1967), 355ff.; H. Raviv, in: *Tarbiz*, 33 (1963/64), 1–7; *Enẓiklopedyah la-Ḥafirot Arkheologiyyot be-Ereẓ Yisrael*, 2 (1970), 539–49. **ADD. BIBLIOGRAPHY:** B. Bagatti, *Ancient Christian Villages of Samaria* (2002), 61–69; Y. Tsafrir, L. Di Segni, and J. Green, *Tabula Imperii Romani. Iudaea – Palaestina. Maps and Gazetteer.* (1994), 194–95; G.S.P. Grenville, R.L. Chapman, and J.E. Taylor, *Palestine in the Fourth Century. The Onomasticon by Eusebius of Caesarea* (2003), 147–48; Y. Magen, *Flavia Neapolis*, Judea and Samaria Publications Series (2005).

[Michael Avi-Yonah]

SHECHTMAN, DAN (1941–), Israeli materials scientist and crystallographer. He was born in Tel Aviv and graduated from the Technion, Haifa, where he received his B.Sc. in mechanical engineering (1966), M.Sc. (1968), and Ph.D. in materials engineering (1972). After obtaining his Ph.D. he was an NRC fellow at the Aerospace Research Laboratories, Ohio, where he studied the microstructure and physical metallurgy of titanium aluminides. In 1975 he joined the Department of Material Engineering at the Technion, where he became a distinguished professor. In the years 1981–83, he spent a sabbatical at the Johns Hopkins University and NBS where, while studying rapidly solidified aluminum transition metal alloys, he made the discovery of the Icosahedral Phase, which had a profound influence on the course of materials and crystallography research and opened the new field of quasiperiodic crystals. The unexpected paradigm-breaking discovery which initially startled the scientific community has become an established one and is known as the science of quasi-crystals. Following the discovery, the International Union of Crystallography adopted a new definition of a crystal. Shechtman's discovery of the quasi-periodic crystals has revolutionized several sciences and brought the quasiperiodic atomic order to the forefront of physics, chemistry, crystallography, and material sciences, and opened new avenues for novel practical use. Shechtman was elected to the Israel Academy of Sciences and Humanities in 1996, to the American National Academy of Engineering in 2000, and to the European Academy of Sciences in 2004. He is a recipient of many prizes and awards, including the Israel Prize in physics (1998), Wolf Prize in physics (1999), the Gregori Aminoff Prize of the Royal Swedish Academy of Sciences (2000), and the EMET Prize in chemistry (2002).

Shechtman was very actively involved in science education in the school system in Israel.

[Bracha Rager (2nd ed.)]

SHEDLOVSKY, THEODORE (1898–1976), U.S. physical chemist. Born in St. Petersburg, Russia, Shedlovsky went to the U.S. in 1908. From 1927 he worked at the Rockefeller Institute for Medical Research (now the Rockefeller University), and became professor there in 1957. He wrote mainly on the electrochemistry of solutions and of biological fluids and was the author of *Electrochemistry in Biology and Medicine* (1955). He became a member of the U.S. National Academy of Sciences.

SHEEP. In the Bible the term *ẓon* indicates both sheep and *goats (Lev. 1:10; 3:6; et al.); only once does it refer to sheep alone, as distinct from *izzim* ("goats"; I Sam. 25:2). In the Mishnah both are referred to as *behemah dakkah* ("small cattle"). The most common strain of sheep in Israel is the broad-tailed sheep *Ovis vignei platyura*, derived from the desert sheep *Ovis vignei (orientalis)*, domesticated during the Middle Stone Age. The bodily construction and way of life of this strain is adapted to the conditions of existence in dry regions such as Ereẓ Israel and its vicinity. The wool, particularly of the lambs, is usually white (Ps. 147:16; Isa. 1:18). The body of most of the sheep native to Ereẓ Israel is white; only the head and feet are brown. Some of the sheep, however, also have brown spots on other parts of the body. These can be born also to parents with white fleeces, and Jacob, when tending Laban's sheep, asked to receive as wages "all the dark ones among the sheep" born from white parents; a modest-seeming request to which Laban agreed (Gen. 30:32–37; see *Biology). In the local breed some are raised for meat and others for wool (cf. II Kings 3:4). The ewe has no horns, while the ram has curved ones (cf. Gen. 22:13). This shape of horn also appears on ancient drawings. From it was fashioned the *shofar of "rounded ram's horns" (RH 3:4). As stated above, the Israel sheep is distinguished by its broad and heavy tail (in the male it can reach a weight of 20 pounds, and is mentioned several times in the Bible (Ex. 29:22; Lev. 3:9; et al.)). The tail fat serves as stock when there is a shortage of pasture, particularly in summer.

The sheep was a main source of meat, hence the expression "sheep for slaughter" often found in the Bible (Isa. 53:7; et al.). Its milk was also of importance (Deut. 32:14), while the wool was a basic necessity of life (Hos. 2:7). Its skin was valuable, being used for shoes, clothing, and hangings (Ex. 25:5). The fertility of the sheep is mentioned as a blessing (Ps. 144:13). The ewes normally gave birth to one lamb, but under favorable conditions they had twins – the "paired" of Song of Songs 6:6. The season of conception depends upon the state of the pasture. With the early ones, the primiparous, it begins in Adar; others conceive later. The early ones are the *mekushrot* ("stronger") of Scripture and the later ones the *atufim* ("feebler," cf. Gen. 30:41–42). The period of gestation of five months is mentioned in the Talmud (RH 8a). The weak and innocent sheep, the potential victims of beasts of prey, symbolize in prophetic parable and allegory the Israelite nation and its fate (Jer. 23:2–3; Ezek. 34:6–22; et al.).

Many terms for sheep occur in the Bible. A male in its first year is called *keves* (Lev. 12:6), the female, *kavsah* (Lev. 14:10), *kivsah* (II Sam. 12:3), or *kisbah* (Lev. 5:6). The adult male is *ayil*, in Aramaic *dekhar* ("male"; Ezra 6:9). *Ayil meshullash* is one three years old (Gen. 15:9). The mature female is *raḥel* (Isa. 53:7; et al.). *Taleh* is used for the young of both sheep and goats (Isa. 40:11); the fully grown sheep is the *seh* (Gen. 30:32; Ex. 12:5). A prime species of sheep for meat was called *karim*. These came chiefly from the unpopulated border regions: Bashan (Deut. 32:14), Kedar (Ezek. 27:21), Moab (II Kings 3:4), Edom (Isa. 34:6), and Amalek (I Sam. 15:9). With the growth of the Jewish population of Israel from the beginning of the period of the kings, the pasture areas gradually diminished, being crowded out by agriculture. During the time of the Mishnah, when agriculture in Israel reached its peak of development, a regulation was enacted that small cattle were not to be reared in the populated part of the country, but only in desert areas and in Syria (BK 7:7), as well as in its forests (BK 81a). During that era the shepherd who was suspected of penetrating into agricultural areas to pasture his flock was treated with contempt (Sanh. 26b). At the close of the talmudic period, after the destruction of Israel's agriculture, the land was once more converted into extensive grazing areas.

BIBLIOGRAPHY: G. Dalman, *Arbeit*, 6 (1939, repr. 1964), 170 ff.; S. Bodenheimer, *Ha-Ḥai be-Arẓot ha-Mikra*, 2 vols. (1949–56), index, s.v. *Keves*; J. Feliks, *Animal World of the Bible* (1962), 17; idem, *Ha-Ḥakla'ut be-Ereẓ Yisrael bi-Tekufat ha-Mishnah ve-ha-Talmud* (1963), 112–5; idem, in: *Teva va-Areẓ*, 7 (1964/65), 330–7. **ADD. BIBLIOGRAPHY:** Feliks, Ha-Ẓome'aḥ, 296.

[Jehuda Feliks]

SHE'ERIT HA-ḤAZZAN (12th century), *paytan* and poet in Egypt. There are several *piyyutim* in manuscript signed "She'erit," which does not necessarily mean that all belong to the same author. A *paytan* named She'erit ha-Levi is known, and another named She'erit ha-Ḥazzan the Blind, the son of Japhet. The *paytan* in question here is probably "She'erit ha-Ḥazzan," the Splendor of Ḥazzanim, b. Shemariah, the Glory of Ḥazzanim, who, in 1160, lived near Fostat. This can be deduced from a *Genizah piyyut*, published by *Schirmann (see bibl.). From the style of the *piyyutim*, it appears that he was considerably influenced by the Spanish school. In addition to the *piyyut "Shilḥah ve-Have Ẓori le-Ẓirai"* ("Send and bring balm to my pangs"), Schirmann also attributes to him the *seliḥah "Shivtei Yeshurun Lekha be-Shir No'amim"* ("The tribes of Yeshurun address themselves to Thee in song"), which is signed only "She'erit."

BIBLIOGRAPHY: Mann, Egypt, 2 (1922), 293; H. Schirmann, *Shirim Ḥadashim min ha-Genizah* (1965), 103–5, 463 no. 228.

SHEETRIT, MEIR (1948–), Israeli politician, member of the Tenth and Eleventh Knesset, and then again from the Thirteenth Knesset. Sheetrit was born in Ksar a-Suk, Morocco, to a family of rabbis. He immigrated to Israel with his family in 1957. At first the family settled in the development town of Netivot, but later moved to Yavneh. He studied at the Givat Washington High School and in Kefar Batyah. He enlisted in the army in 1968, and was discharged from the medical corps with the rank of captain in 1973. Sheetrit had started studying microbiology and biochemistry at Bar-Ilan University in 1964, before his military service. He received his master's degree in public administration from the same university. He joined the Likud and ran on its ticket in the elections for mayor of Yavneh in 1974, after being rejected by the Labor Party. At the age of 25 he was elected as mayor of Yavneh, serving in this position until 1987. In 1986 he received the prestigious Local Government Prize, the Education Prize, and the Quality of

Life Prize from the president of the State. He was first elected to the Tenth Knesset on the Likud list in 1981, serving in a variety of Knesset committees, including the Finance Committee. He was elected treasurer of the Jewish Agency and Zionist Organization, in which capacity he served in 1988–92. In the course of his service as treasurer he was accused of fraud and breach of trust and put on trial, but was completely exonerated. Sheetrit did not serve in the Twelfth Knesset but ran once again in the elections to the Thirteenth Knesset, and after the Likud's bitter defeat in these elections, considered contesting the Likud leadership. However, due to the fatal illness of his daughter he decided to withdraw from the contest. In the Thirteenth Knesset, in addition to chairing the sub-committee for Higher Education in the Education and Culture Committee, he served as chairman of the Knesset computerization committee. In the Fourteenth Knesset he served as chairman of the Likud parliamentary group and chairman of the coalition, and as deputy speaker, until being appointed minister of finance in February 1999, after the resignation of Ya'akov Ne'eman from the post, and three months before the elections to the Fifteenth Knesset. In the Fifteenth Knesset, he was appointed minister of justice in the government formed by Ariel *Sharon in March 2001, even though he had hoped to receive the Education and Culture portfolio. In the government formed by Sharon after the elections to the Sixteenth Knesset he served as minister in the Ministry of Finance, under Binyamin *Netanyahu, and after the resignation of Avigdor Lieberman of the National Union in July 2004, started serving as minister of transportation. In September he was appointed as the liaison minister between the government and the Knesset. He was one of the proponents within the Likud for bringing the *Israel Labor Party into the government, and was a supporter of the disengagement plan. In late 2005 he followed Sharon out of the Likud to form the new Kadimah Party.

He was a member of the board of trustees of the University of Ben-Gurion in Beersheba, and of the Open University, and a member of the Executive of Bar-Ilan University.

SHEFARAM (Heb. שְׁפַרְעָם; Ar. Shefā ʿAmr), town in western Galilee. The earliest mention of Shefaram occurs in talmudic sources (RH 31a–b; Sanh. 13b, 14a; Av. Zar. 8b), which describe it after Usha as a seat of the newly reconstituted Sanhedrin, following the War of Bar-Kokhba and the persecutions of Hadrian. From Shefaram the Jewish authorities moved to Bet She'arim. In the crusader period it was known as Le Safran, a possession of the Templars; churches of St. James and St. John were located there. It was the headquarters of Saladin in 1191, when it was renowned for the woods and vines growing in the vicinity. In 1761 Ẓāḥir al-ʿAmr, the Bedouin ruler of Galilee, established his capital there, building a fortified castle and naming the place in Arabic after himself, Shefā ʿAmr. An attempt to settle Jews there in the 16th century had failed, but at the invitation of Zahir al-ʿAmr the Jews successfully renewed their efforts to settle in Shefaram. In 1813, Jews from Safed, fleeing an epidemic, settled in Shefaram. Later, in 1850, Jewish families from North Africa settled there. The community, most of whose members were farmers, maintained itself through the 19th century, although in dwindling numbers: 60 persons in 1856; 13 families in 1895; four families in 1900. The last Jew left the place in 1920, leaving behind a synagogue and a large cemetery. Shefaram's total population in 1881 was 2,500 according to Palestine Exploration Fund data; in the 1922 census it was 2,288; and in 1931 it was 2,824.

When the town was occupied by the Israeli army in June 1948, a number of Muslim inhabitants fled, while other villagers from the vicinity moved in. The population grew from 3,412 in 1948 to 7,225 in 1961 and to 10,000 inhabitants (Christians, Druze and Muslims) in 1968. In 1987 Shefaram received municipal status. The city's area is 8.5 sq. mi. (22 sq. km.). By 2002 the population of Shefaram had increased to 30,300 inhabitants. Among them, 57% are Muslims, 27.5% Christians, and 14.5% Druze. Until modern times the town's built-up area remained within its narrow, ancient nucleus, but when expansion began, the inner quarter remained inhabited by Christians, while Druze inhabited a northwestern quarter and Muslims a northeastern part. After the founding of the state, new suburbs with a mixed population were built, including a housing area for Israeli war veterans from minority groups. Shefaram's position, midway between Haifa and the Christian center of Nazareth, attracted Galilean villagers, as well as non-Jews from other towns of the region, who were seeking relatively cheap housing. Bedouin who have given up nomadic life have also settled at Shefaram. The town supplied administrative and commercial services to non-Jewish villages in the region, among them Sakhnīn, I'billin, and Tamra, and holds a weekly market. Health, welfare, and employment services are also extended to the Bedouin tribes in the vicinity. Approximately 12% of the people work in agriculture, 44% in local commerce and services, and the rest commute to work in Haifa and its industrial zones.

[Michael Avi-Yonah / Shlomo Hasson]

SHEFAYIM (Heb. שְׁפָיִים), kibbutz in central Israel, 2½ mi. (4 km.) N. of Herzliyyah, affiliated with Ha-Kibbutz ha-Me'uḥad. Shefayim was founded in 1931 by pioneers from Poland. Initially the kibbutz members earned a livelihood mostly as hired laborers. In the late 1930s and in the 1940s, Shefayim served as a clandestine landing for *"illegal" immigration. In 1945 it was subjected to severe searches by British forces. In 1970 the kibbutz numbered 550 inhabitants, increasing to 780 in the mid-1990s and 883 in 2002. Farming is highly intensive and fully irrigated. The kibbutz also ran a 168-room hotel and water park. Another mainstay of its economy was a big shopping center kept open on the Sabbath and holidays and attracting people from all over the center of the country. The name is taken from Isaiah 41:18.

[Efraim Orni / Shaked Gilboa (2nd ed.)]

SHEFFER, HENRY M. (1883–1964), U.S. logician. Born in the Ukraine, Sheffer was taken to the U.S. at the age of 10. After teaching in various institutions, he was appointed to Harvard in 1916 and became a professor there in 1938.

Though Sheffer wrote little, he had many seminal ideas which exerted their influence on the development of symbolic logic through the outstanding logicians whom he trained, including William Van Orman Quine and Susanne K. Langer. His method of working was through a critical exposure of fallacies and then a demonstration of how they could have been avoided. He also stressed the importance of the way the basic postulates of a system are set out, an idea which proved fruitful as much in general philosophy as in logic itself.

In 1913, Sheffer published a paper showing that all Boolean functions could be expressed in one primitive term, the Shefferstroke function. (C.S. Pierce had discovered this but never published it.) Though most of his ideas were only suggested, Bertrand Russell and Alfred North Whitehead were impressed by Sheffer's originality, and in 1925 said his work "would demand a complete rewriting of their *Principia Mathematica*." A volume of essays, *Structure, Method, and Meaning* (New York, 1951) was published in his honor.

BIBLIOGRAPHY: F. Frankfurter, in: P. Henle et al. (eds.), *Structure, Method and Meaning* (1951), xv–xvi.

[Richard H. Popkin]

SHEFFIELD, steel manufacturing city in N.E. England. Some Jews may have settled in Sheffield in the 18th century, but the first family of note was the Bright family, many of whose descendants, however, later married non-Jews. There was an incipient community in 1827 centered around the Jacobs family, who maintained a synagogue in their own home and employed a *shoḥet*. A permanent congregation was organized in 1838 and in 1851 was able to buy the premises used as a synagogue and advertise for a minister. During the mass immigration of 1881 to 1914, a number of Russo-Polish refugees settled in Sheffield; by the beginning of the 20th century the Jewish population was 800. However, it was more difficult for Jews to enter steel industries than clothing industries and consequently Sheffield attracted proportionately fewer Jews than many other manufacturing cities in northern England. In 1953 the two synagogues were amalgamated; there were a number of communal and Zionist organizations in the city, as well as a University Jewish Society and Hillel House. In 1969 Sheffield had a Jewish population of 1,600 (out of a total of 490,000). In the mid-1990s the Jewish population dropped to approximately 800. In 2001, the British census found 763 declared Jews in Sheffield. The city has an Orthodox and a Reform synagogue. Armin Krausz's *Sheffield Jewry* (1980) is a sociological study of the community.

BIBLIOGRAPHY: C. Roth, *The Rise of Provincial Jewry* (1950), 99; Lipson, in: *Transactions of the Hunter Archeological Society*, 6 no. 3, 117–25; JYB; V.D. Lipman, *Social History of the Jews in England, 1850–1950* (1954), 24, 102, 138, 171.

[Vivian David Lipman]

SHEFTALL, U.S. family among the original (1733) Jewish settlers of *Savannah, Georgia. BENJAMIN SHEFTALL (1692–1765), who was born in Prussia, was active in the establishment in 1735 of Congregation Mikveh Israel, which he seems to have served as *shammash* and *shohet*. He had two sons, Mordecai (by his first wife Perla) and Levi (by his second wife Hannah Solomons). Benjamin kept the congregation's vital records, which were continued by his son Levi. Benjamin served as interpreter and supplier to a Georgia community of Lutherans from Salzburg. In 1748 he sent to England for *tefillin* and prayer books for Mordecai's bar mitzvah, the first recorded observance of this rite in America. Two years later, Benjamin was naturalized at Charleston, South Carolina. That same year, he joined a group of Christians in creating Georgia's first philanthropic organization, the St. George (later Union) Society, to assist widows and orphans. Benjamin was a modest landowner and small-time merchant when he died.

MORDECAI SHEFTALL (1735–1797) enlarged his father's mercantile enterprises and land holdings. He aided in the reorganization of Mikveh Israel in 1774 and functioned as a *mohel*. Supporting the American revolutionary cause, he became chairman of his parish committee, which seized British imports and records. He subsequently served as a colonel in the Georgia brigade and as commissary general of purchases and issues to the state militia. He and his son Sheftall were captured, paroled, recaptured, shipped to Antigua, and paroled again, whereupon they made their way to Philadelphia. Mordecai took an active role in the building of that city's synagogue in 1782. He tried privateering, purchasing a ship with the small amounts Congress paid on its indebtedness to him. The end of the war brought him to Savannah, where he remained. One of his sons, SHEFTALL (1762–1847), became an attorney in Savannah, while another, MOSES (1769–1835), was a Savannah physician trained by Benjamin Rush.

LEVI SHEFTALL (1739–1809), second son of Benjamin, became a butcher. He joined his brother Mordecai in the revolutionary cause but was accused of Tory sympathies for carrying on trade in British-occupied Savannah. After living for several years in Charleston, he returned to Savannah and helped reestablish Mikveh Israel. He was its president by 1789, when he wrote a congratulatory letter to George *Washington. He served as U.S. agent, and agent for fortifications, at Savannah until his death.

BIBLIOGRAPHY: M.H. Stern, in: AJHSQ, 52 (1962/63), 169–99; 54 (1964/65), 243–77; J.R. Marcus, *Early American Jewry*, 2 (1953), passim.

[Malcolm H. Stern]

SHEFTEL, MIKHAIL (1858–1922), jurist and communal leader in Russia. Born in Zhitomir, Sheftel became one of the most noted lawyers in Russia. After the pogroms in *Kishinev, he took part in the judicial inquiries aimed at clarifying the circumstances surrounding the pogroms and exposing their political nature to the Russian public. He was a member of the central committee of the League for the Attainment of Equal Rights for the Jewish People in Russia. In 1906 he was elected to the Russian parliament (*Duma) as deputy from Yekaterinoslav (Dnepropetrovsk) and joined the Kadet (Liberal) faction. When the Duma was dissolved, Sheftel was among the signatories to the "Vyborg Manifesto" and in consequence was sentenced to three months' imprisonment. He was active in Jewish communal and scientific associations in Russia and contributed to the *Yevreyskaya Entsiklopediya* and to the Russian-Jewish press. He also took part in the activities of the Jewish Society for War Victims (*YEKOPO), which gave assistance between 1915 and 1919 to Jewish refugees and expellees from areas near the front in Western Russia.

BIBLIOGRAPHY: *Yevreyskiy Vestnik*, no. 4 (1922).

[Yehuda Slutsky]

SHEḤITAH (Heb. שְׁחִיטָה), the Jewish method of slaughtering permitted animals or birds for food. The underlying principle of the procedure is to kill the animal in the swiftest and most painless way possible by cutting horizontally across the throat, severing the trachea (windpipe), the esophagus, the jugular veins, and the carotid arteries. The knife (see below) is drawn across the throat of the animal in one or more swift, uninterrupted movements. In the case of animals most of the trachea and esophagus must be severed, while with birds it is sufficient to sever the largest part of either one. In the first instance, however, both are severed even in birds. "Then thou shalt kill of thy herd and of thy flock which the Lord hath given thee, as I have commanded thee" (Deut. 12:21) is the Pentateuchal basis of *sheḥitah*. Maimonides lists *sheḥitah* among the 613 commandments (*Sefer ha-Mitzvot*, 146) and rabbinic authorities state (Ḥul. 28a): "Moses was instructed concerning the rules of *sheḥitah*."

The Shoḥet

In early times there were no "professional" *shoḥatim* (sing. **shoḥet*). Any adult versed in the *halakhah* was allowed to perform the act of *sheḥitah*. In medieval times it was resolved that would-be *shoḥatim* in order to obtain a license (*kabbalah*) had to pass an examination (conducted by a rabbi) on the theory and practice of *sheḥitah*. A synod convened in Germany around 1220 resolved that no man could act as a *shoḥet* without such a license.

A *kabbalah* certificate is nowadays issued to an applicant who has successfully passed an oral examination on the laws of *sheḥitah* and *terefah* (see *Dietary Laws) and has correctly performed ritual slaughter, at least three times, in the presence of experts. Only meat of animals slaughtered by a *shoḥet* who possesses a *kabbalah* certificate is fit for consumption according to religious law (i.e., *kasher*, cf. Sh. Ar., YD 1). *Kabbalah* certificates are not issued to minors, women, or to mentally or physically handicapped persons (e.g., a deaf-mute or an idiot), although, if they perform the *sheḥitah* properly, their slaughter is ritually valid (*ibid.*, 1:2, and Ḥul. 1:1). In Yemen there were women ritual slaughterers and it is even recorded that on Jan. 13, 1556, R. Isaac Immanuel de Lattes of Mantua gave a *kabbalah* to a woman.

A rabbi should not issue a *kabbalah* certificate to a person who is his close relative, or irresponsible, or to someone who is lax in the fulfillment of religious duties. Excluded also are persons inclined to drunkenness or those whose "hands are unsteady." In order to retain his status, the *shoḥet* is obliged to rehearse the rules of ritual slaughter every day during the first 30 days of receiving the *kabbalah* certificate, then once a month during the first year, and after that at least once in three months. He is also obliged to inspect, from time to time, the sharpness of his knife (or knives) or to have them inspected, upon request, by rabbinic authorities.

The Knife

In the *sheḥitah* procedure, the knife (known as *ḥalaf*) has to be spotlessly clean and smooth, without a single notch or dent, and it has to be examined before and after *sheḥitah*. The examination is performed by passing the edge of the knife gently back and forth against the tip of the finger and the fingernail; any imperfection in the blade can thus be discovered. The knife must be at least twice as long as the width of the animal's throat and must not be pointed. Usually very high grade steel is used in order to avoid notches. One of the important stages in the training of a *shoḥet* is to learn how to set the knife to exquisite sharpness.

The Act

The act of *sheḥitah* is preceded by a benediction. One authority has ruled that the absence of the benediction renders the meat non-kosher, but the general opinion is that although a benediction should be recited, its omission, *post facto*, does not affect the validity of the act. *Sheḥitah* may not be performed on the Sabbath but, *post facto*, it is valid if so performed. Any one of the following five movements can disqualify the *sheḥitah*: *shehiyyah* – if the slightest pause or interruption occurs during the *sheḥitah* act; *derasah* – if the knife is pressed into the neck instead of moving firmly back and forth; *ḥaladah* – if the knife gets stuck behind the food pipe; *hagramah* – if the cut is not made in the prescribed section; *ikkur* – if the tissues are torn out rather than cut.

For birds and undomesticated animals (*ḥayyot*) the blood must be covered after the *sheḥitah*. This is done by placing sand or soil underneath, slaughtering, and then spreading more soil over the split blood, at which time a special benediction is pronounced. One of the reasons given for this procedure is that these animals owe nothing to man (as opposed to domesticated animals) and thus their slaughter is more shameful.

Reasons Given for Shehitah

Underlying these minute regulations is the concept of *ẓa'ar ba'alei ḥayyim*, the deep concern not to inflict pain on any living creature. The *sheḥitah* procedure was thus devised to make animal slaughter instantaneous and painless (see *Animals, Cruelty to). Maimonides writes in a similar vein: "The commandment concerning the killing of animals is necessary because the natural food of man consists of vegetables and the meat of animals; the best meat is that of animals permitted to be used as food. No doctor has any doubts about this. Since, therefore, the desire to procure good food necessitates the slaying of animals, the law enjoins that the death of the animal should be as easy and painless as possible" (*Guide of the Perplexed*, pt. 3, 48).

Anti-Shehitah Movements

Though the concept of *sheḥitah* is rooted in humane aspects and the laws are directed to perform the act as swiftly as possible and render the animal insensitive to pain almost instantly, from time to time there have been attempts in the non-Jewish world to ban *sheḥitah*. While some of these were motivated by humanitarian concern, in many cases the agitation was a manifestation of antisemitism.

An anti-*sheḥitah* movement was started in Germany in the middle of the 19th century. The first country to ban *sheḥitah* was *Switzerland, which outlawed it by plebiscite (178,844 votes to 115,931) on Aug. 20, 1893. Later *sheḥitah* was forbidden in Norway (Jan. 1, 1930), Bavaria (May 17, 1930), Nazi Germany (April 21, 1933), Sweden (1937), Fascist Italy (1938). Severe restrictions were imposed on the Jews of Poland in 1936. During World War II *sheḥitah* was banned in the countries under Nazi hegemony.

In the United States, *sheḥitah* is protected in a number of states (in 1915 a law was passed in New York according to which it is an offence to sell as kosher an article that is prohibited for Jewish consumption). Similarly, the Act of Parliament of August 13, 1928, which provides for the humane slaughter of animals in Scotland, makes a special provision for *sheḥitah* (Article 8). Subsequently, an act passed on July 28, 1933, which provides for the humane and scientific slaughter of animals, and the Slaughter of Animals (Consolidation) Act (1958) further safeguarded *sheḥitah* in Britain. They require that in abattoirs cattle and sheep be instantaneously slaughtered or be rendered insensible by stunning until death supervenes, but food intended for Jews and Muslims is exempt from the foregoing provision (a private member's bill to forbid *sheḥitah*, introduced in the British Parliament, was defeated in 1968). There are similar legal safeguards in Finland, the Republic of South Africa, and Ireland. Many slaughterhouses have special large padded casting pens and other similar devices to get the animal into the required position swiftly and painlessly.

In recent years, the anti-*sheḥitah* movement has been revived in a number of countries. Medical and veterinary authorities such as Lister, Virchov, and Vogt and more than 450 of the most eminent physiologists, pathologists, and heads of veterinary colleges in Great Britain have become convinced that the Jewish method is absolutely humane. The British physician Lord Horder stated in 1940: "Careful and critical scrutinising of this method of slaughtering leaves me in no doubt whatever that it is fraught with less risk of pain to the animal than any other method at present practised." Similar sentiments were expressed by Sir William Bayliss, professor of general physiology at the University College of London: "The Jewish use of the knife is a humane method of slaughter which compares favourably with any other process. The result of the cut made by the Jewish expert is to produce immediate insensibility, from which the animal does not recover. The pain, if any, is momentary, and at the worst is but slight."

Stunning

Many of the opponents of *sheḥitah* have advocated electrical stunning before the act which would render the animal unconscious and thus insensitive to pain. The *halakhah* strongly opposes such stunning prior to *sheḥitah*. Stunning often causes a strong jerk of the muscles, which could impair the act of *sheḥitah*. It may also injure the brain and lungs, rendering the animal forbidden. The stunning furthermore causes extravasation of blood so that small blood clots form in the meat, hemorrhages, and severe congestion of muscles.

The laws of *sheḥitah* are codified in Sh. Ar. YD, ch. 1–28.

[Harry Rabinowicz]

Communal Aspects

In many regions and during many periods *sheḥitah* provided a major source of income for the communal leadership. The first signs of organized communal control over *sheḥitah* appeared at the end of the tenth century in Ramleh, Ereẓ Israel, and in Egypt. The old profession of *tabbaḥ*, combining slaughterer and meat seller, was divided into two, when the *kaẓẓav*, the butcher, ceased to act as slaughterer, a function which was acquired by the specialist *shoḥet*. This became the rule, albeit with some exceptions, in the kingdoms of Christian Spain and in the Sephardi Diaspora after 1492. The *shoḥet* was also expected to act as *bodek*, to examine the animal lungs for *kashrut*. Usually the *shoḥet* was granted **ḥazakah* or perpetual tenure; he did not have to stand for reelection and could be dismissed only for transgression. This right was often transmitted to his heirs and sometimes remained in the same family for many generations. In Venice he was called the *sagatino*. In order to pay the *shoḥet's* salary, the community arranged to collect fees for his services. Periodically the *shoḥet's* work in the abattoir was inspected by the local rabbi or *dayyanim*; many communities hired two *shoḥatim*. In smaller settlements the *shoḥet* often combined his work with the office of cantor, teacher, or other paid communal functions. As the *shoḥet* was responsible for many minutiae in the proper exercise of his function, his character and piety were as important to the community as his technical expertise. Some kabbalists, chief among them the anonymous 14th-century Spanish author of *Sefer ha-Kaneh* and *Sefer ha Peli'ah*, attacked the whole conception of meat-eating and cattle-slaughtering as a part of the general life-style. On the other hand, the development of the concept of metempsychosis made *sheḥitah* and the *shoḥet* participants in the right way of liberating the soul from its material environment if both the action and the man were pious and proper (see also *Sacrifices in Kabbalah).

The method of *sheḥitah* and attitude to it of Ashkenazi Jewry developed largely on the same lines. In Ḥasidism the mystical appreciation of *sheḥitah* became an ideological and social mark of the movement. Tales told about *Israel b. Eliezer Ba'al Shem Tov express a deep concern with the personality of the *shoḥet*; miraculously the Ba'al Shem Tov was able to know and disclose the sins of the *shoḥet* in various places. Ḥasidism introduced a different technique for the fine sharpening of the *shoḥet's* knife. As the circle around *Elijah b. Solomon Zalman, the Gaon of Vilna, objected to the introduction of highly polished knives, contending that such instruments were prone to denting, the ḥasidic *sheḥitah* became both a divisive factor in the community and a unifying element among the Ḥasidim. In 1772 a *ḥerem* was proclaimed against the ḥasidic *sheḥitah*, its knives, and its *shoḥatim*, which "are of a certainty blemished with the taint of heresy. Meat [or cattle] slaughtered by these burnished knives is not *kasher*." As Ḥasidism spread, the close tie between the rabbi and the *shoḥet* made the introduction of ḥasidic *sheḥitah* a tangible sign that the Ḥasidim had taken over the community and the rabbinate.

The *kahal* acquired monopolistic control over all *sheḥitah* and sale of *kasher* meat. Soon the income from *sheḥitah* was employed not merely to defray expenses but also to underwrite educational, charitable, and other communal endeavors. As early as the 12th century in Castile there are references to such a meat tax. Throughout the Sephardi world it was known as *gabela* and in Morocco in modern times it was called *hakdish*. In Poland from the 17th century and in Russia it was called *korobka*. In Berlin the *sheḥitah* tax is first documented in 1723, but it probably existed long before that. Often these taxes became the mainstay of communal income. In modern times various states – often on the initiative of the *maskilim* – used the meat tax as a method of financing their own enterprises, educational and otherwise, among the Jews. As East European Jewry migrated to Western Europe and the New World they instituted the *sheḥitah* tax there too. In New York the *shoḥet* was at first a functionary of the synagogue rather than of the community as a whole. In the 20th century, with the development of canned meat and canning factories and the concentration of great numbers of Jews in a few communities, *sheḥitah* underwent many changes. The *kasher* butchers were supervised by a *mashgi'aḥ* ("supervisor") or as he was called in London a *shomer* ("watchman"). Each properly slaughtered animal or fowl was identified by a *plombe*, a lead disc stamped *kasher* and showing the date of slaughtering. Every can of meat had to be similarly marked. Attempts were made to ensure central supervision over *kashrut* in order to check the many abuses that had appeared. In Palestine the Mandatory government adopted regulations which provided that in each city *sheḥitah* must be under the control of a single board representing the various groupings in the community. In Israel *sheḥitah* has remained under the general supervision of the Mo'aẓot Datiyyot ("religious councils") and the rabbinate.

[Isaac Levitats]

Women and Sheḥitah

Women are tacitly included when the Mishnah states that everybody slaughters, that their slaughtering is acceptable, and that they are not included among those whose slaughtering is unacceptable (Ḥul. 1:1). According to Zevaḥim 3:1, slaughtering, even of the most holy things (*kodshei kodashim*), by women, slaves, and the impure, is acceptable. On the one hand, this statement seems to put women in the category of those who do not usually slaughter while, on the other, it affirms that women could slaughter sacrifices. The only condition is that those who are impure should not come into contact with the meat. According to Zevaḥim 31b, "everybody slaughters" means that women have the authority to do so in the first instance (based on Lev. 1:5, where the commandment to slaughter was not limited to priests); that their slaughtering is "acceptable" means after the fact (Ḥul. 2b). The Jewish traveler *Eldad (ben Mahli) ha-Dani (c. 880) left behind a small code of law, *Hilkhot Ereẓ Yisrael* ("Laws of the Land of Israel"). Beginning with the Tosafists, medieval rabbis rebut arguments purportedly found in *Hikhot Ereẓ Yisrael* against women's slaughtering; these include claims that women are feebleminded, physically weak, and prone to fainting. Instead, they affirm that women may slaughter on their own (e.g. Tos. Ḥul. 2a, d.h. *hakol*; Zev. 31b, kol; Kid. 36a, d.h. Hakabalot; 76b, d.h. *ein bodekin;* Er. 59b, d.h. *ve-tehumin*; MT Sheḥitah 4:4; Commentary on the Mishnah Ḥullin 1:1; Commentary on the Mishnah Zevaḥim 3:1; Meir of Rothenberg, Shut Maharam 4 (Prague), no. 193; Jacob ben Asher, Tur YD 1). *Orḥot Ḥayyim* and *Kolbo* of the 13th–14th centuries deem it acceptable for women to slaughter for themselves, *le-atzman*, but not for others, *lo le-aḥerim* (OḤ Hil. Sheḥitah, no. 3; Kolbo, no. 107). Jacob ben Judah *Landau, 15th century author of *Sefer ha-Agur*, represents a major turning point in the development of rabbinic discourse on the subject. He states that while it is obvious that a woman may slaughter, "It is a custom in all the Jewish diaspora that they do not slaughter and I have never seen the practice of doing so. Therefore, there is no reason to allow them to slaughter because custom cancels, and the custom of our fathers is Torah" (*Sefer ha-Agur*, Hil. Sheḥitah, no. 1062). Joseph *Caro contests Jacob ben Judah Landau's view that the custom is that women do not slaughter; he also asserts that women's slaughtering for themselves means slaughtering by themselves, that is alone (*levadan*) without anybody supervising them (BY YD 1; Kesef Mishnah, Hil. Sheḥitah 4:4). Limitations on women's slaughtering were accepted by Moses *Isserles of Cracow and by Solomon ben Jehiel *Luria of Poznan (Rama, SA YD 1; *Yam shel Shelomo*, Ḥul. 1:1). Luria raised the possibility that fear of their husbands will lead women to hide mistakes; he ruled that because of the many stringencies recently added to the process of slaughtering and of the greater concern that they will faint, women are not allowed to slaughter for others or at all (*Yam shel Shelomo*, Ḥul. 1:2). One relatively late attempt to limit women's slaughtering in Italy reveals what may have been a new or a previously understated argument. In 1728, in an exchange with Abraham Yaḥyah of Modena, Shabbetai Elhanan ben Elisha *del Vecchio accepted all the traditional arguments for women's slaughtering, even for sacrifices, but expressed concern that a women in a state of impurity might touch the animal.

In contrast with efforts by rabbis elsewhere in Christian Europe to limit women's rights to slaughter, licenses appear in early modern Italy for specific women not only to slaughter but also to porge (*nikkur* or *treibern*) animals. Porging, removal of fat, veins, nerves, and sinews after the animal has been ritually slaughtered, is a complex process. The involvement of women in kosher slaughtering and porging has been construed by some as proof of an improvement in the condition of women among Italian Jews. Others have argued that the reason women were allowed to slaughter was not emancipation but so that they could provide food for their families in isolated locations, such as summer houses in the mountains, or in distressed circumstances. Italian Jewish women who demonstrated under supervision that they had sufficient knowledge and expertise to slaughter, to examine, and to porge received permission to slaughter both fowl and cattle unsupervised (*beinah levein atzmah*) for all Jews (*lekhol yisrael*).

[Howard Tzvi Adelman (2nd ed.)]

BIBLIOGRAPHY: J.J. Weinberg, *Teshuvah be-Inyan Himmum ha-Behemot* (1934); J.J. Berman, *Shehitah: A Study in the Cultural and Social Life of the Jewish People* (1941); I. Lewin et el., *Religious Freedom: the Right to Practice Shehitah* (1946); S.D. Sassoon, *A Critical Study of Electric Stunning and the Jewish Method of Slaughter (Shechitah)* (1956); Y.J. Grunwald, *Ha-Shoḥet ve-ha-Sheḥitah ba-Sifrut ha-Rabbanit* (1956); S.E. Freedman, *Book of Kashruth* (1970), 28–46; Shunami, Bibl, 1051–52, 2482; Baron, Community, 3 (1942), index, s.v. *Slaughtering and Slaughterers;* I. Levitats, *Jewish Community in Russia, 1772–1844* (1943), index s.v. Korobka; Ch. Shmeruk, in: *Zion*, 20 (1955), 47–72; B. Homa, *Shehita* (1967); Cohen, Lord, of Birkenhead, Hansard, House of Lords, 3rd Dec. 1962; I.M. Levinger, *Untersuchung zum Schaechtproblem* (1961); B. Homa, *Shehita, The Jewish Method of Slaughtering Animals for Food* (1961). **ADD. BIBLIOGRAPHY:** WOMEN AND SHEḤITAH: H. Tz. Adelman, "Religious Practice among Italian Jewish Women," in: L. Fine (ed.), *Judaism in Practice: From the Middle Ages through the Early Modern Period* (2001), 204–8; idem, "Rabbis and Reality: Public Activities of Jewish Women in Italy during the Renaissance and Catholic Restoration," in: *Jewish History*, 5 (1989), 32–34, 39.

SHEIKH, ABRAHAM BEN SHALOM HA-LEVI AL- (c. 1749–1829), community leader, liturgical innovator. Al-Sheikh was born and lived in *San'a. He was the grandson of the **nagid* R. Yiḥye ha-Levi, who headed the Jewish community of San'a after the return from the Exile of *Mawza', when he founded the Al-Sheikh synagogue, the first to be built in the new Jewish walled-off neighborhood (*qā' al-yahūd*). After the fall of the Iraqi family, he was appointed by the imam as supervisor of his mint and as president of the Jews of Yemen. As a wealthy man, he donated much money to the poor and helped orphans marry, built *mikva'ot* and a boys' school for the community from his own funds, and improved his family synagogue, already known for its beautiful traditions and valuable collection of books. He instituted a mixed rite of customs and prayers in the synagogues by introducing several changes and reforms based on Sephardi prayer books and the opinion of R. Joseph Caro (*shāmī*). This provoked the criticism of conservative (*baladī*) scholars. Al-Sheikh wrote a work on the *masorah and the musical notes of the Scriptures, *Ḥelkat Meḥokek* (in manuscript).

BIBLIOGRAPHY: A. Qoraḥ, *Sa'arat Teman* (1954), 24–25.

[Yehuda Ratzaby / Yosef Tobi (2nd ed.)]

SHEINDLIN, JUDITH (1942–), U.S. judge. Judith Blum Sheindlin was born in Brooklyn, N.Y., and educated at American University in Washington, D.C., and New York Law School. Beginning in 1972, Sheindlin prosecuted juvenile delinquency cases for ten years, until she was appointed a judge of Family Court in Manhattan. She retired from the bench in 1996 and began a television career as Judge Judy, an irrepressibly outspoken judge constantly admonishing plaintiffs and defendants. For more than ten years, Sheindlin rendered opinions sharply and quickly in a widely syndicated and extremely popular half-hour series. Her husband, GERALD, who graduated from Long Island University and Brooklyn Law School, became a judge in the Bronx and then an acting justice of the State Supreme Court. He retired at 65 to begin a television career as Judge Jerry of *The People's Court*. He had presided over 86 murder trials and published 65 opinions, but his show, frequently aired back to back with his wife's, was not as successful as hers. Nevertheless, the couple's television earnings far eclipsed their salaries on the bench. Judge Judy was the author of several books, including *Don't Pee on My Leg and Tell Me It's Raining* and *Beauty Fades, Dumb Is Forever: The Making of a Happy Woman* (1999).

[Stewart Kampel (2nd ed.)]

SHEINKIN, MENAHEM (1871–1924), Zionist leader in Russia and Ereẓ Israel. Born in Ulla (near Vitebsk), the son of an ḥasidic rabbinical family, Sheinkin studied to become a rabbi. He became attracted to the *Haskalah movement, however, and enrolled at Odessa University. An early Zionist, he was a delegate to the Second Zionist Congress in 1898. In 1900 he visited Ereẓ Israel for the first time and from there went to London as a delegate to the Fourth Zionist Congress. A year later he became the **kazyonny ravvin* in Balta, Podolia. He was a member of the *Democratic Fraction of the Zionist Movement; took part in the activities of the Ẓiyyonei Zion, who opposed the *Uganda scheme at the Seventh Congress (1905); and was then elected a member of the Zionist General Council. He was forced to resign from his post as an officially appointed rabbi when he refused to give up his Zionist activities. In 1906 he went to Ereẓ Israel, where he directed Ḥovevei Zion's information and immigration office in Jaffa and was one of the founders of Tel Aviv (1909). When World War I broke out, he was exiled by the Turks from Ereẓ Israel and went to the United States, where he was among the founders of the Zion Commonwealth Company and organized groups for settlement in Palestine. He returned to Palestine in 1919 and became director of the Zionist Commission's immigration office. In 1924 he went to the United States on behalf of the Zion Commonwealth Company and was killed in a road accident in Chicago. A central street in Tel Aviv and one of the city's suburbs are named after him. His writings were published posthumously as *Ketavim* (1935).

BIBLIOGRAPHY: A. Ḥermoni, in: *Ketavim* (1935), first pagination, 11–16; D. Smilansky, *Im Benei Dori* (1942), 133–45; Tidhar, 4 (1950), 1608–10.

[Yehuda Slutsky]

SHEINKMAN, JACOB (1926–2004), labor leader and Jewish communal leader. Sheinkman was born in New York City. After serving in the Navy in World War II, he attended Cornell University and was one of the first graduates of the School of Labor and Industrial Relations. He then became an organizer for the International Pulp, Sulphite and Paper Mill Workers. He joined the Amalgamated Clothing Workers of America as a lawyer in 1953. In 1958 he became general counsel of the Amalgamated Clothing Workers of America, AFL-CIO; in 1968 he became a vice president, and in 1973 secretary-treasurer. In 1974 he was elected president of the Jewish Labor Committee, where he served three terms and lobbied for strong U.S.-Israeli ties. He also served as vice president of the AFL-CIO Industrial Union Department, as a member of the executive committee of the American ORT, and as a member of the board of trustees of Cornell University. During the 1980s, as a strong opponent of U.S. policy in Central America, he founded and co-chaired a national committee on labor rights in Central America, which served as an organizing base for union activists opposing U.S. military intervention in El Salvador and Nicaragua. From 1987 to 1995 Sheinkman was president of the Amalgamated Clothing and Textile Workers Union. After negotiating the union's merger with the International Ladies' Garment Workers' Union, he retired to form the Union of Needletrades, Industrial and Textile Employees (UNITE).

[Milton Ridvas Konvitz / Ruth Beloff (2nd ed.)]

SHEKALIM (Heb. שְׁקָלִים), fourth tractate in the order of *Mo'ed, which deals, in eight chapters, with the annual half-shekel tax collected for the maintenance of the Temple and its services and with allied subjects. There is no *Gemara* in the Babylonian Talmud but there is in the Jerusalem Talmud, and this *Gemara* is usually included in the printed editions of the Babylonian Talmud. There is Tosefta, divided into three chapters. The reason for placing this tractate in the order of *Mo'ed*, dealing with festivals, is somewhat problematic. Since *Shekalim* deals principally with matters connected with the Temple, its expected place might have been in the order *Kodashim* ("Holy Things") together with the tractates *Middot* and *Tamid*. It is probable, however, that its inclusion in *Mo'ed* is connected with the opening paragraph of *Shekalim*, which says: "on the first of Adar, announcement is made concerning *shekalim*… on the 15th, the *Megillah* is read in the walled cities…" This formulation associates *shekalim* with the idea of an "appointed time," which is the basic meaning of *mo'ed*. Moreover, the first paragraph of chapter 3 significantly links the periodical allocations from the shekel funds with the festivals of Passover, Shavuot, and Sukkot.

It is also remarkable that the various printed editions and manuscripts of the Mishnah, Tosefta, and the Babylonian and Jerusalem Talmuds differ widely as to the place of *Shekalim* in the sequence of tractates within the order *Mo'ed*. There are a few instances of its being placed ninth, 11th, or 12th, but it is most frequently found as either fourth or fifth. Following the rule that tractates with a higher number of chapters take precedence, *Shabbat* (24), *Pesaḥim* (10), and *Eruvin* (10) took the first three places, while *Shekalim* and *Yoma*, each with eight chapters, vied for the fourth place. But there is evidence, coming from geonic times, that *Shekalim* used to be studied before *Yoma*, and eventually the placing of *Shekalim* as the fourth tractate of *Mo'ed* prevailed.

As to biblical provisions concerning the half-shekel tax, Exodus 30:11–16 sees it as a onetime measure for the purpose of a popular census. But in II Kings 12:5–17, 22:3–7, II Chronicles 24:5–14, 34:8–14, and in Nehemiah 10:33–34 it appears as a permanent institution. It is remarkable that the last mentioned source speaks of a "third part of a shekel," having in mind Persian currency.

The contents of the eight chapters of this tractate are as follows: chapters 1–2 deal with the time and manner of levying this tax. Chapters 3–4 deal with the allocations of the shekel fund, when they were made, and how they were to be used. Chapter 5 lists the various chief officers of the Temple and speaks, in particular, about the administration of the funds. Chapter 6 says first that there were in the Temple 13 "chests" for money donated, two of which were marked for shekel contributions. It then goes on to list other things of which there were 13 in the Temple. Chapter 7 first discusses the use to which lost money found on the Temple premises should be put, and goes on to consider similar questions, e.g., that of meat or cattle picked up in the sanctuary or elsewhere in Jerusalem or in the provinces. Various other questions are also touched upon, e.g., a burnt-offering sent by a heathen from abroad. Chapter 8 discusses a variety of questions which have nothing to do with the subject matter of this tractate, except for the incidental statement that the law of *shekalim* became obsolete with the destruction of the Temple. The following aggadic passages from the Jerusalem Talmud to the tractate are well known: "No monuments need to be put up for the righteous, their deeds are their memorial" (2:7, 47a), and "Whoever settles in Israel, speaks Hebrew, eats his fruit in ritual purity, and reads the *Shema* morning and evening is assured of the world to come" (3:4, 47c).

The tractate *Shekalim* for the most part consists of early material, and there are sections and chapters which have come down in their original form. All the officials mentioned in chapter 5 lived between the time of *Agrippa I and the destruction of the Temple (41–70 C.E.), and some of them are mentioned by name in Josephus, while three others are mentioned also in the Mishnah of **Middot* and **Tamid*, which were arranged at the end of the Temple era. Yose b. Ḥanan played a considerable part in its arrangements, and one may assume with certainty that chapters 3, 5, and 6 are actually by him. The Tosefta contains many variations of and additions to the Mishnah, chiefly in the names of the officials. Hence it is evident that the Tosefta utilized the Mishnah of a different *tanna*. Despite this it is clear that the source of the Tosefta is not later than that on which the Mishnah is based. *Judah I (ha-Nasi) also made use of the *mishnayot* of later *tannaim* who taught this tractate, among whom should be noted Judah b. Ilai, from whom apparently comes the whole of chapter 1; Simeon (ch. 2:1–4 and ch. 7); and Yose, chapter 4 being apparently wholly from him. There is much information about the shekel offering, both in Ereẓ Israel and the Diaspora. The New Testament refers to the "collectors" of the half-shekel in *Capernaum (Kefar Nahum) to whom Peter gave a *sela on his own behalf and on behalf of Jesus (Matt. 17:24–27). Josephus (Ant. 18:311f.) describes the methods whereby the Jews of Nehardea and Nisibis sent their half-shekel, and *shekalim* from Egypt are already referred to in the *Elephantine papyri and by Philo. The Mishnah was translated into English by H. Danby in 1933.

BIBLIOGRAPHY: Epstein, Tanna'im 25–27, 338–45; Ḥ. Albeck, *Shishah Sidrei Mishnah*, 2 (1958), 183–6.

[Arnost Zvi Ehrman]

SHEKANZIB, town in Babylonia situated on the Tigris River between the settlements of Sikara and Humaniya. The first known reference to the existence of a Jewish settlement in Shekanzib is in the second half of the third century C.E. *Sherira Gaon relates that one of his ancestors, *Rabbah b. Avuha, settled there after the partial destruction of Nehardea by Papa b. Nazer in 259 C.E. (*Iggeret Rav Sherira Ga'on*, ed. by B.M. Lewin (1921), 82). Naḥman of Nehardea paid occasional visits to Shekanzib (Yoma 18b). Concerning the character of the Jews of Shekanzib the Talmud relates: Our holy teacher commanded his children four things (one of which was): Do not live in Shekanzib because its people are frivolous and will affect you with their frivolity (Pes. 112b). "Our holy teacher" usually refers to Judah I ha-Nasi, who died in the year 219 C.E., and if the reading is correct it would show that the inhabitants of Shekanzib already had a bad reputation at the beginning of the third century even in Ereẓ Israel. Some, however, read simply "our teacher" (see Kohut, Arukh, 8 (1926^2), 73 s.v. *Shekanzib*), and the reference may be to Rav or to Rava, who described the funeral customs of Shekanzib (MK 28b).

BIBLIOGRAPHY: Neubauer, Geogr, 363; J. Obermeyer, *Die Landschaft Babylonien* (1929), 190–2; A. Berliner, *Beitraege zur Geographie und Ethnographie Babyloniens* (1884), 64f. **ADD. BIBLIOGRAPHY:** B. Eshel, *Jewish Settlements in Babylonia during Talmudic Times* (1979), 241.

[Moshe Beer]

SHEKEL, coin minted in Ereẓ Israel.

Shekel

Originally the shekel was a unit of weight for means of payment in gold and silver. In the third millennium B.C.E. one already finds this unit of weight in Babylonia, weighing there 8.4 grams; it was divided into 24 giru (Heb. *gerah*). 60 Babylonian shekels were a mina (Heb. *maneh*) and 60 mina a biltu (Heb. *kikkar*). This system was introduced in Canaan with some alteration, as the *maneh* generally consisted of 50 shekels only. As the *kikkar* was equivalent to 60 *maneh*, it amounted to 3,000 shekels in Canaan, instead of 3,600 in the Babylonian system. The shekel as a unit of weight for gold is mentioned in Genesis 24:22 and Joshua 7:21 (for the shekel as a unit of weight for silver, see Gen. 23:16; II Sam. 14:26; II Kings 15:20; Zech. 11:12–13).

There were two standards of shekel weights, namely the Babylonian and the Phoenician. Both standards had a heavy and light system: Babylonian – heavy, 22.0–23.0 grs.; light, 11.0–11.5 grs; Phoenician – heavy, 14.5–15.3 grs.; light, 7.3–7.7 grs.

The shekel weight during the First Temple period relates to the light Babylonian system. In the fourth century B.C.E. Phoenician silver coins, such as the Sidonian double shekel and Tyrian stater, circulated in Ereẓ Israel. The former, whose average weight was 26.43 grams, relates to the Phoenician heavy weight, though being somewhat lighter. It may be compared with the Tyrian staters of that period, which are of an average weight of 12.9 grams, two of which would approximate the Sidonian double shekel.

Ptolemy II (285–246 B.C.E.) reformed this coinage by reducing the weight of the tetradrachm from the Attic standard (17.46 g.) to the Phoenician standard (14.30 g.). Thus, the tradition of the Phoenician shekel was kept alive and adopted later by the city of Tyre, which issued shekels from 126 B.C.E. until about 56 C.E. These had an average weight of 14.2 grams and were of good silver. They were therefore recommended by the sages for payment of the Temple tax (Shek. 1:7). During the Jewish War (66–70 C.E.), due partly to a shortage of Tyrian shekels, which had not been issued by then for about ten years, the Jewish authorities issued silver shekels of their own, with the legends *Shekel Yisrael, Ḥaẓi ha-Shekel* ("half-shekel") and *Reva ha-Shekel* ("quarter shekel").

Perutah

The only Jewish coin denomination mentioned in the Mishnah, Talmud, and Midrash besides the shekel is the perutah. Numismatists identify this denomination with the Hasmonean and early Herodian coinage, that of the Roman procurators, and the smaller coins of the Jewish War. The Hasmoneans undoubtedly adjusted their coinage to the Seleucid standard. Their perutah had an average weight of 2 grams and an average size of about 15 mm.; it may be compared to the Seleucid dilepton. The Hasmoneans also had a lepton, or half-perutah, and a trilepton, or 1½ perutah. The perutah of that weight and size was retained until about 30 C.E. From the time of Agrippa I (42 C.E.) onward, the perutah increased in weight and size to an average of 2.55 grams and 17 mm.; this brought it close to the weight and size of the Roman quadrans, which under Nero weighed 3.21 grams and was 17–18 mm. The relation of the perutah to the silver coinage is mentioned in the Talmud (Kid. 2a, 12a) in two variations:

(a) 192 perutah in a dinar, which corresponds to the Seleucid system and therefore refers to the Hasmonean period, and

(b) 144 perutah in a dinar, which reflects the situation after 30 C.E. when the weight and size of the perutah were increased and Ereẓ Israel was under Roman control.

Ḥezi and Revi'a

The only bronze Jewish coins that bear an indication of their denomination are those of the fourth year of the Jewish War (70 C.E.). Ḥezi ("half") appeared on the large bronzes and *revi'a* ("quarter") on the smaller sized coins, but it is not known of what denomination these coins were halves and quarter. All suggestions to solve this problem remain hypothetical.

Other Denominations

The Herodian tetrarchs Antipas and Philip II, as well as the kings Agrippa I and II, adjusted their coin denominations to the city coin system prevailing in Ereẓ Israel and therefore have no Jewish character. The same also applies to the coinage of the Bar Kokhba War (132–35 C.E.), which is overstruck on the money then in circulation, i.e., the Roman silver coinage, both imperial and provincial, and the Ereẓ Israel city coins. The silver tetradrachm, however, was called *sela* by the Jews and the silver denarius *zuz*. The various denominations mentioned in the Mishnah, Talmud, and Midrash refer mainly to Roman coinage (see *Coins, In Talmudic Literature).

[Arie Kindler]

In the Zionist Movement

The biblical name shekel was given by the First Zionist Congress (1897) to the fee and card of Zionist membership. Its price was fixed at 1 franc, 1 mark, 1 Austrian crown, 2 shillings, half a dollar, 40 kopeks, etc. The shekel also served as a voting certificate for elections to the Zionist Congress, and until the 25th Congress (1960) the number of delegates allocated to a certain election area (country) was calculated on the basis of the total of shekels sold there. Ereẓ Israel had the privilege of the "double shekel," being entitled to twice the number of delegates that any other country received for the same number of shekels. The reverse side of the shekel bore the text of the Zionist program and for 25 years, after the 18th Congress (1933), also the "discipline clause," meaning that the discipline of the World Zionist body takes precedence over that of any other Zionist body.

The growth of the World Zionist Organization is reflected in the number of shekel holders: 164,333 in 1907; 584,765 in 1923; 1,042,054 in 1939; 2,159,840 in 1946; and 2,148,029 in 1960. The new constitution of the World Zionist Organization (1960) retained the shekel as a token of Zionist allegiance and voting card, fixing its cost at between 15 and 50 cents or their equivalent, but making the size of congress representation independent of the shekel sales. The 27th Congress (1968), by resolving that each country may itself determine the system of congress elections to be held there, abolished the shekel as an obligatory institution and left it to the countries to decide whether to retain the shekel as a certificate of membership and voting card for the members of the local Zionist Organization concerned.

In 1970 a decision was taken by the Israel Knesset to call the unit of Israel currency "shekel," renamed "new shekel" in 1985 and equal to 1,000 old shekels in the face of runaway inflation.

[Aharon Zwergbaum]

BIBLIOGRAPHY: F.W. Madden, *History of Jewish Coinage and of Money in Old and New Testament* (1864, repr. 1967 with Prolegomena by M. Avi-Yonah), incl. bibl.; idem, *Coins of the Jews* (1881); T. Reinach, *Les Monnaies Juives* (1887); A. Reifenberg, *Ancient Jewish Coins* (1947²); idem, *Israel's History in Coins* (1953); S. Yeivin, *Milḥemet Bar Kokhva* (1957²), 80f.; Ben David, in PEQ, 100 (1968), 145ff.; 80f.; J. Fraenkel, *History of the Shekel* (1956²).

SHEKHINAH (Heb. שְׁכִינָה; lit. "dwelling," "resting"), or Divine Presence, refers most often in rabbinic literature to the numinous immanence of God in the world. The *Shekhinah* is God viewed in spatio-temporal terms as a presence, particularly in a this-worldly context: when He sanctifies a place, an object, an individual, or a whole people – a revelation of the holy in the midst of the profane. Sometimes, however, it is used simply as an alternative way of referring to God himself, such as "The Holy One Blessed be He," or "The Merciful One." For example, on the verse, "After the Lord your God shall ye walk… "(Deut. 13:5), the Talmud comments: "And is it possible for a man to walk after the *Shekhinah?*… Rather this means that one should follow [emulate] the virtues of the Holy One, Blessed be He" (Sot. 14a). The term, though seemingly hypostatized in certain passages, must be viewed purely figuratively and not as representing a separable aspect of God or as being in any sense a part of the Godhead. The latter notion is totally alien to the strict monotheism of rabbinic Judaism for which the unity of the divine Essence is a basic premise. The references to *Shekhinah* which are open to misinterpretation, e.g., those which talk of God placing His *Shekhinah* in the midst of Israel (cf. Sif. Num. 94), or where the *Shekhinah* is pictured as talking to God (Mid. Prov. to 22:28), are the product of homiletic license. The rabbis themselves were not unaware of the dangers of misinterpretation, and occasionally preface their remarks with *kivyakhol*, "as if it were possible" (Mekh. Pisḥa 12; see also S. Schechter, *Some Aspects of Rabbinic Theology* (1909), 40, n. 1; E.E. Urbach, *Ḥazal* (1969), 33, n. 15; 50).

One of the more prominent images associated with the *Shekhinah* is that of light. Thus, on the verse, "… the earth did shine with His glory" (Ezek. 43:2), the rabbis remark, "This is the face of the *Shekhinah*" (ARN¹ 2, 13a; see also Ḥul. 59b–60a). Both the angels in heaven and the righteous in *olam ha-ba* ("the world to come") are sustained by the radiance of the *Shekhinah* (Ex. R. 32:4; Ber. 17a; cf. Ex. 34:29–35). This association with light has led to the view that the *Shekhinah* is some kind of luminous material, a being of light created by God. This view is found among certain medieval Jewish philosophers, and was even propounded by a rabbinic scholar in comparatively recent times (J. Abelson, *The Immanence of God in Rabbinical Literature* (1912). For criticism of his views see Urbach, *ibid.*, 32, 35). Nevertheless, the imagery of light, shining glory, radiance, etc., is commonly associated with the numinous in religio-mystical language in general, and does not necessarily have the literalistic connotations of a separate luminous entity. In the case of the *Shekhinah* this is further borne out by a consideration of the ways in which the term is used in the literature.

In the Targums

The term *Shekhinah*, in its Aramaic forms, is frequently found in the Targums, particularly in Targum Onkelos. It is employed together with other "intermediary" terms such as *memra yakara* ("noble word"), to paraphrase certain references to God, thus avoiding the overtly anthropomorphic implications of various biblical expressions. For instance, the verse "the Lord is not in your midst" (Num. 14:42), Onkelos translates "the *Shekhinah* of God is not in your midst" (see also Targum on Num. 14:14, and note the double paraphrasis). The verse "you cannot see My face, for man shall not see Me and live" (Ex. 33:20) is rendered, "You cannot see the face of My *Shekhinah*" (see also Ex. 33:14–15). And "to put His name there" (Deut. 12:5) becomes "to rest His *Shekhinah* there" (see also 12:11).

In Talmud and Midrash

The talmudic and midrashic usage of *Shekhinah* does not have quite the same apologetic overtones which are apparent in the Targums; on the whole it is wider in extension and in texts of different dates it varies considerably in nuance. In origin *Shekhinah* was used to refer to a divine manifestation, particularly to indicate God's presence at a given place. This did not imply a limitation of God's omnipresence, however, since it is said that the *Shekhinah* is in all places (BB 25a), and that just as the sun radiates throughout the world so does the *Shekhinah* (Sanh. 39a). Even those special places and objects which God imbues with an extra holiness by His presence – such as the thorn bush in which He revealed Himself to Moses, or Mount Sinai, or the Tabernacle in the wilderness – in connection with which the term *Shekhinah* is most often used, teach us that no place is devoid of His presence: neither the lowliest of trees, nor the barest of mountains, nor a wooden sanctuary (Shab. 67a; Sot. 5a; Ex. R. 34:1). Though the presence of God is everywhere, the *Shekhinah* rests preeminently on Israel rather than on the gentiles (Ber. 7a; Shab. 22b; Num. R. 7:8), for Israel is a people chosen and sanctified by God to be carriers of His will to the world. Israel's sins led to the destruction of the Temple, where the *Shekhinah* was always present (this is true at least of the First Temple; the Second was thought to have been devoid of the Divine Presence; cf. Yoma 9b). According to one view, the destruction of the Temple caused the departure of the *Shekhinah* to heaven (Shab. 33a; Ex. R. 2:2). In opposition to this, however, we find it said that even while Israel are unclean the *Shekhinah* is with them (Yoma 56b); when they are exiled it goes into exile with them, and when they come to be redeemed the *Shekhinah* will be redeemed too (Meg. 29a).

The *Shekhinah* does not only rest on the people of Israel as a whole, but a wide variety of subgroups are said to influence the *Shekhinah* for good or for ill. On the one hand where ten are gathered for prayer, or even one sits and learns Torah, there the *Shekhinah* is (Ber. 6a). It watches over the sick (Shab. 12b); rests between man and wife if they are worthy (Sot. 17a); he who gives charity is fit to receive it (BB 10a); as is he who is particular in fulfilling the *mitzvah* of *ẓiẓit* (Men. 43b). On the other hand, he who walks with an upright posture (i.e., is proud), as it were, pushes against the feet of the *Shekhinah* (Ber. 43b); so does he who sins in secret (Hag. 16a); it does not rest on those who are sad, lazy, playful, light-headed, or engage in idle conversation, but only on those who perform a *mitzvah* in joy (Shab. 30b); scoffers, flatterers, liars, and slanderers will never be recipients of the *Shekhinah* (Sot. 42a). A righteous judge causes the *Shekhinah* to rest on Israel, but an unrighteous one drives it away (Sanh. 7a). The term also figures in such expressions as "under the wings [i.e., patronage] of the *Shekhinah*." Proselytes are said to be taken in "under the wings of the *Shekhinah*" (Shab. 31a; SER 6:29; see also Tosef., Hor. 2:7, though Zuckermandel has "under the wings of heaven." Moses was taken to his burial place wrapped in the "wings of the *Shekhinah*" (Sot. 13b).

The *Shekhinah* is commonly associated with the charismatic personality and is thought to rest on specific outstanding individuals. "The *Shekhinah* only rests on a wise, rich, and valiant man who is tall of stature" (Shab. 92a; cf. Ned. 38a). Several of the talmudic rabbis were considered to deserve that the Divine Presence rest on them, except that their generation was unworthy (Sot. 48b; Suk. 28a; see also MK 25a). This charismatic association seems to be connected with the idea that certain individuals possess *Ru'aḥ ha-Kodesh*, the Holy Spirit (for a discussion of the interrelationship of *Shekhinah* and the Holy Spirit, see *Ru'aḥ ha-Kodesh*). The use of the term *Shekhinah* would thus seem to range from the numinous revelation of God, as in the theophany at Sinai or the awe-inspiring presence speaking to Moses from the Tabernacle, to the more mundane idea that a religious act, or *mitzvah*, draws man nearer to God. Sometimes the term is simply an alternative for "God," while at others it has overtones of something separate from the Godhead; it may be used in a personalized or depersonalized way. From the point of view of Jewish theology it would be a mistake to overemphasize any given use to the exclusion of the others, and it is important to view it in the perspective of the Jewish monotheistic background as a whole. It is also possible to take a somewhat demythologized view of the rabbinic conception of the *Shekhinah*, for such a view is even expressed in the talmudic literature itself, albeit as the opinion of a single individual: "R: Yose said, 'The *Shekhinah* never came down to the world below, nor did Moses… ascend on high'" (Suk. 5a).

[Alan Unterman]

In Jewish Philosophy

Unlike the rabbinic sages, who generally identified *Shekhinah* with the Presence of God, or even with God Himself, the medieval Jewish philosophers were concerned with avoiding any possible anthropomorphic interpretations of this concept, and therefore went to great lengths to point out that *Shekhinah* refers not to God Himself, nor to any part of His Essence, but rather to an independent entity, created by God. According to Saadiah Gaon, the *Shekhinah* is identical with *kevod ha-Shem* ("the glory of God"), which served as an intermediary between God and man during the prophetic experience. He suggests that the "glory of God" is the biblical term, and *Shekhinah* the talmudic term for the created splendor of light which acts as an intermediary between God and man, and which sometimes takes on human form. Thus, when Moses asked to see the glory of God, he was shown the *Shekhinah*, and when the prophets in their visions saw God in human likeness, what they actually saw was not God Himself but the *Shekhinah* (see Saadiah's interpretation of Ezek. 1:26, I Kings 22:19, and Dan. 7:9, in *Book of Beliefs and Opinions*, 2:10). By emphasizing that the *Shekhinah* is a created being which is separate from God, Saadiah avoids any possible compromising of the divine unity and any hint of anthropomorphism. Judah Halevi follows Saadiah in interpreting the *Shekhinah* as an intermediary between God and man, maintaining that it is the *Shekhinah*, and not God Himself, which appears to prophets in their visions. Unlike Saadiah, however, Judah Halevi does not speak of the *Shekhinah* as being a created light. It seems that he identifies the *Shekhinah* with the Divine Influence (*ha-Inyan ha-Elohi*), about whose meaning there is much disagreement among scholars. According to Judah Halevi, the *Shekhinah* dwelt first in the Tabernacle, then in the Temple. With the destruction of the Temple and the cessation of prophecy, the *Shekhinah* ceased to appear, but will return with the coming of the Messiah (*Kuzari*, 2:20, 23; 3:23). Judah Halevi distinguishes between the visible *Shekhinah* which dwelt in the Temple and was seen by the prophets in their visions and which disappeared with the destruction of the Temple, and the invisible spiritual *Shekhinah* which has not disappeared but is "with every born Israelite of virtuous life, pure heart, and upright mind" (*ibid.*, 5:23).

Maimonides accepts Saadiah's view that the *Shekhinah* is a created light, identified with glory. He too associates the *Shekhinah* with prophecy, explaining that it is the *Shekhinah* which appears to the prophet in his vision (*Guide of the Perplexed*, 1:21). Explaining prophecy as an overflow from God through the intermediation of the active intellect (*ibid.*, 2:36), Maimonides writes that man apprehends God by means of that light which He causes to overflow toward him, as it is written, "in Thy light do we see light." Some interpreters of Maimonides believe that the *Shekhinah* corresponds to the active intellect itself, which is the lowest of the ten intellects (see Intellect), and which communes with the prophets (Yad, Yesodei ha-Torah, 7:1). However, there are also passages in which Maimonides identifies the *Shekhinah* with God Himself rather than with some other being. For example, in his exegesis of Exodus 24:10 (*Guide*, 1:28), Maimonides interprets the "feet" of God as the throne of God on which sat the *Shekhinah* (i.e., God). In the 19th century Nachman Krochmal interpreted *Shekhinah* as pure spiritual power. Krochmal's philosophy of history, which is based on Hegel, asserts that every nation has a spiritual power, and that the Jewish people has the spiritual power in its purest form, which is directly rooted in the Absolute Spirit. This spiritual power of the Jews is called *Shekhinah* (*Moreh Nevukhei ha-Zeman*, ch. 7), and this notion explains the rabbinic sayings that wherever the Jews wandered the *Shekhinah* wandered. In the 20th century Hermann Cohen, following Maimonides in holding that *Shekhinah* must be understood metaphorically, defines it as "absolute rest which is the eternal ground for motion" (*Religion der Vernunft* (1929), 53).

The concept of *Shekhinah* played a very important role in kabbalistic and ḥasidic literature, while its role in Jewish philosophy is relatively minor. However, two modern philosophers, Martin Buber and Franz Rosenzweig, who were influenced to some extent by the kabbalistic tenor, make use of this concept and do not oppose anthropomorphism as did the earlier Jewish philosophers. Buber speaks of God as both immanent and transcendent, employing the kabbalistic terminology of "shells" and "sparks" of God (*On Judaism* (1967), 6, 27). *Shekhinah* is a theophany of the Exile that symbolizes the fact that the Jewish people was never abandoned despite the shame and degradation it suffered. Rosenzweig is much more explicit. He believes that the *Shekhinah* is the bridge between the "God of our fathers" and the "remnant of Israel" (*Der Stern der Erloesung* (1954³), 192–4). The descent of the *Shekhinah* upon man and its dwelling among man is conceived by Rosenzweig as a separation which occurs in God Himself. God descends and suffers with His people, wandering with them in exile. At the end, it is God who suffers the most, and the remnant of Israel who bears His sorrow. Most important is Rosenzweig's notion that the purpose of the *mitzvot* is to unify God and His *Shekhinah*.

[Rivka G. Horwitz]

In Kabbalah

The basic elements of the kabbalistic concept of the *Shekhinah* are found in the earliest kabbalistic work, *Sefer ha-Bahir*, where the *Shekhinah*, or *Malkhut*, is described as the daughter, the princess, the feminine principle in the world of the divine *Sefirot*. These motifs were developed in kabbalistic circles in the late 12th and 13th centuries and were mingled with philosophical ideas in the works of the Gerona circles and in the writings of Abraham Abulafia; many nuances were added in the works of Isaac the Blind, the Iyyun circle (see Kabbalah), and in the writings of Jacob and Isaac, the sons of Jacob ha-Kohen. Most of these motifs were drawn together by the author of the Zohar and his circle, especially Joseph Gikatilla. From this period, the end of the 13th century, the basic concept of the *Shekhinah* remained constant up to the time of Isaac Luria and his disciples in Safed and persisted into Hasidism, although certain modifications can be found in the works of every single kabbalist. This article deals with the basic elements of the concept common to all.

The *Shekhinah*, or *Malkhut*, is the tenth and last in the hierarchy of the *Sefirot*. In the divine world it represents the feminine principle, while *Tiferet* (the sixth *Sefirah*) and *Yesod* (the ninth) represent the masculine principle. All the elements and characteristics of the other *Sefirot* are represented within the *Shekhinah*. Like the moon, she has no light of her own, but receives the divine light from the other *Sefirot*. The main goal of the realm of the *Sefirot* (and of religious life as a whole) is to restore the true unity of God, the union of the masculine principle (mainly *Tiferet*) and the *Shekhinah*, which was originally constant and undisturbed but was broken by the sins of Israel, by the machinations of the evil power (the *sitra aḥra*), and by the exile. The restoration of the original harmony can be effected by the religious acts of the people of Israel through adhering to the Torah, keeping the commandments, and prayer.

The symbolism describing the *Shekhinah* is the most developed in kabbalistic literature. Most of the many and varied symbols refer to aspects of the *Shekhinah*'s relationship with the other *Sefirot* above her – such as her acceptance of the divine light from them, her relationship to them as a lower aspect of themselves which is nearer to the created world, and her coming close to the masculine element or moving further away from it. In another group of symbols the *Shekhinah* is the battleground between the divine powers of good and evil; because of her femininity and closeness to the created world she is the first and the main target of the satanic power. If the evil powers could fill the *Shekhinah* with their own evil essence, unity of the divine powers would be broken, constituting an enormous victory for the powers of evil. It is therefore the duty of man and the *Sefirot* to protect the *Shekhinah* from the designs of the *sitra aḥra*.

The *Shekhinah* is the divine power closest to the created world, of which it is the source and the sustaining power; the divine light which maintains the created world passes through the *Shekhinah*. The angels and the world of the Merkabah are all her servants. In kabbalistic theology the *Shekhinah* is the divine principle of the people of Israel. Everything that happens to Israel in the earthly world is therefore reflected upon the *Shekhinah* who waxes and wanes with every good deed and every sin of each individual Jew and the people as a whole; on the other hand, everything that happens to the *Shekhinah*, her relationship with *Tiferet* and other *Sefirot* and her battle against the evil powers, is reflected in the status of Israel in the earthly world. Study of the Torah and prayer bring a Jew near the *Shekhinah*, for she is symbolized as the Oral Law. The *Shekhinah* is the divine power usually revealed to the prophets, though sometimes higher divine powers may take part in such a revelation. She is also the first goal of the mystic who tries to achieve *devekut*, communion with the divine powers; though a mystic may reach higher divine powers through *devekut*, the *Shekhinah* is the first and the closest for mystical contact. The idea of the exile of the *Shekhinah*, resulting from the initial cosmic disaster and from Adam's fall, became of great importance in Lurianic Kabbalah. To fulfill every commandment for the purpose of delivering the *Shekhinah* from her lowly state and reuniting her with the Holy One, blessed be He, became the supreme goal. The notion of redeeming the *Shekhinah* from exile acquired new eschatological content.

[Joseph Dan]

Shekhinah as Female Symbol

The myth of the feminine Shekhinah evolved out of biblical wisdom literature, rabbinic texts, and early mystical ideas. Proverbs 8 portrays wisdom as God's daughter who serves Him as "a confidante and source of delight in every way" (8:30). Building on the second century B.C.E. Wisdom of *Ben Sira, the rabbis replaced the female hypostatic personified wisdom of Proverbs with the Torah, making the Pentateuch God's firstborn and the archetype for creation (Gen. R. 1:1). This is not to say that feminine imagery is absent in rabbinic literature. Drawing from biblical motifs, the rabbis metaphorically represent Zion, the community of Israel (*Keneset Yisrael*), Torah, and the Sabbath in female terms as God's spouse, daughter, sister, or mother. The *Shekhinah*, however, although grammatically feminine, remains male or at the very least androgynous in early rabbinic literature.

There are allusions to sexual activity in the divine realm in early Jewish mystical ideas recorded in *Heikhalot* writings (*Synopse* 183ff). This literature was mainly preserved by the German pietists of the 12th and 13th centuries, whose theology was strongly influenced by it. The sexual imagery nascent in *Heikhalot* literature was given further expression in a work entitled "Secret of the Nut," in which a student of *Eleazar of Worms describes a bi-sexual Godhead.

The mythic possibilities implicit in the female imagery of the rabbis and the sexual allusions of early Jewish mystics are actualized in the kabbalistic myth of the *Shekhinah*, the female aspect of the male God. The *Shekhinah* is the final *Sefirah*, mediating between heaven and earth and serving as the passive eye or door through which a mystic can achieve divine vision. The popularity of the *Shekhinah* in Kabbalah corresponds to and may have been influenced by the popularity of the cult of the Virgin Mary among contemporaneous Christians. The need for nurturing female images may be a response to similar theological needs and cultural stimuli.

Medieval kabbalists constructed the *Shekhinah* with female physiology and gender specific roles to express both divine processes and human mystical experiences. As mother, the *Shekhinah* may become pregnant and lactate, showering the earth with divine light. As menstruant, she comes under the sway of excessive judgment or the demonic powers (*sitra aḥra*) and metes out judgment to transgressors. As bride and wife, she engages in sexual relations with the male *Sefirot*, *Tiferet* and *Yesod*, and fosters unity in the cosmos. Because medieval kabbalists believed all liturgical and ritual acts affect both the terrestrial and heavenly realms, halakhically sanctioned physical intercourse between a male mystic and his wife on earth could foster both divine and mystical union, for the act enables both *Tiferet* and the male mystic to unite with the *Shekhinah*. Wives thus became a conduit through which their husbands could attain divine union. Drawing from talmudic tradition, medieval kabbalists deemed Friday night to be the most auspicious time to engage in sexual intercourse.

Sixteenth-century kabbalists in Safed made this myth the foundation of the newly instituted *Kabbalat Shabbat* ceremony and Solomon *Alkabez's *Lekha Dodi*, remains the liturgical manifestation of this kabbalistic ritual. Isaac *Luria further enlarged upon the importance of sexual union with the *Shekhinah* (also known in Lurianic Kabbalah as the *nukba de-zeir*), making the act not only a means to attain *devekut* (divine union), or a way to effect unity in the heaven, but also defining it as a way to repair the world (*tikkun olam*). Moreover, Lurianic kabbalists, who believed that intention was as important as the physical performance of the commandments, meditated upon uniting *Tiferet* with his *Shekhinah* before and during the performance of commandments in their *kavvanot* (lit. intentions)

The symbol of the *Shekhinah* has long been seen as one of the few examples of gender equality in Judaism. However, the inferior position of women in medieval society informed many kabbalistic conceptions of the *Shekhinah*. The *Zohar* describes the *Shekhinah* as a passive vessel lacking any distinct personality (see, inter alia, *Zohar* 1:181a). Consequently, the *Shekhinah* is like a revolving sword with the potential for both good and evil (*Zohar* 1:53b, 221b, 242a; 2:27b; 3:19b). When she is described in positive terms, she is often gendered male, as *Malkhut* or David; when she is under the sway of excessive judgment or the demonic "other side" she remains female.

Recently, some Jewish feminists have reclaimed the symbol of the *Shekhinah* as a means of supplementing what they perceive to be the patriarchal bias of Jewish theology. Judith Plaskow urges that the "long suppressed femaleness of God, acknowledged in the mystical tradition, but even here shaped and articulated by men, must be re-explored and reintegrated into Israel." Toward that goal, some feminist liturgists have reinterpreted mystical themes and emphasize the symbol of the feminine *Shekhinah* in innovative prayer rituals (Gottlieb).

[Sharon Faye Koren (2nd ed.)]

BIBLIOGRAPHY: S. Schechter, *Some Aspects of Rabbinic Theology* (1909); J. Abelson, *Immanence of God in Rabbinical Literature* (1912); A. Marmorstein, *Old Rabbinic Doctrine of God*, 1 (1927); G.F. Moore, *Judaism*, 3 vols. (1927–30), index; idem, in: HTR, 15 (1922), 41ff.; E.E. Urbach, *Hazal* (1969), index. IN KABBALAH: G. Scholem, *Von der mystischen Gestalt der Gottheit* (1962), 135–91 and passim; idem, *Ursprung und Anfaenge der Kabbala* (1962), passim; Scholem, Mysticism, passim; I. Tishby, *Mishnat ha-Zohar*, 1 (1949), 219ff. and passim. **ADD. BIBLIOGRAPHY:** D. Abrams. *Sexual Symbolism and Merkavah Speculation in Medieval Germany* (1997); L. Gottlieb, *She Who Dwells Within: A Feminist Vision of a Renewed Judaism* (1995); A. Green, "Bride, Spouse, Daughter: Images of the Feminine in Classical Jewish Sources," in: S. Heschel (ed.), *On Being a Jewish Feminist* (1983); M. Idel, "Sexual Metaphors and Praxis in the Kabbalah," in: D. Kraemer (ed.), *The Jewish Family* (1989); S. Koren "Kabbalistic Physiology: Isaac the Blind, Nahmanides, and Moses de Leon on Menstruation," in: *AJS Review* 28, 2 (2004), 317–39; Y. Liebes, *Studies in Kabbalistic Myth and Messianism* (1993); J. Plaskow, "The Right Question is Theological," in: S. Heschel (ed.), *On Being a Jewish Feminist* (1983); P. Schäfer., *Mirror of His Beauty: Feminine Images of God from the Bible to the Early Kabbalah* (2002); G. Scholem, "Shekhinah: The Feminine Element in Divinity," in: J. Chipman (ed.), *On the Mystical Shape of the Godhead* (1991); E. Wolfson, *Through a Speculum That Shines* (1994).

SHEKHTMAN, ELYE (**Eli Shechtman**; 1908–1996), Yiddish writer. Born in Vaskovichi (Polesie), he had a traditional education, including a year in the Zhitomir yeshivah (1921), studied literature at the Jewish Pedagogical Institute in Odessa (1929–33), and then lived in Kharkov (1933–36) and Kiev (1936–41) until his service as an officer in the Red Army in World War II, during which he was wounded in combat. He was subsequently arrested, imprisoned, and released after Stalin's death. Thereafter he lived in Kiev until his immigration to Israel in 1972. His first stories appeared in 1928. His major work was his epic novel depicting Jewish life in Russia from the early 20th century into the 1970s, *Erev* ("On the Eve"), published first in a censored version (Moscow, 1965), then later in a complete version (Tel Aviv, vols. 1–4, 1974; vols. 5–6, 1979; vol. 7, 1983). Among his other books are *Oyfn Sheydveg* ("At the Crossroads," 1930; stories about post-revolutionary life), *Farakerte Mezhes* ("Plowed-under Borderlands," 1932–36; novel), *Polyeser Velder* ("Polesian Forests," 1940; stories), *Baym Shkie-Aker* ("At the Sunset-Field," 1974); *Ringen oyf der Neshome* ("Links on the Soul," 4 vols. 1981–88), and *Tristia* ("Sadness," 1996). He was the recipient of the Itsik Manger Prize, the Chaim Zhitlowsky Prize, the Fernando Jeno Award (Mexico), and the Congress for Jewish Culture Award. His works have been translated into French, English, and Hebrew.

BIBLIOGRAPHY: I.Y. Druker, in: *Shtern* (Minsk), 7–8 (1937) 116–31; G. Mayzel, in: *Di Goldene Keyt*, 55 (1966), 243–8; Sh. Bickel, *Shraber fun Mayn Dor*, 3 (1970), 287–94; D. Sfard, in: *Bay Zikh*, 5 (1975), 124–7; LNYL, 8 (1981), 767–9; Sh. Luria, in: *Di Goldene Keyt*, 125 (1988), 25–37; *Yidishe Kultur*, 58:1–2 (1996), 3–48 (Shechtman issue).

[Jerold C. Frakes (2nd ed.)]

SHELA (first half of the third century C.E.), Babylonian *amora* and *resh sidra* ("head of the academy") in Nehardea (*Iggeret R. Sherira Ga'on*, ed. by B.M. Lewin (1921), 78). For a while Shela was the most celebrated religious authority in Babylon, but gradually his importance was overshadowed by *Samuel and later by *Rav, when the latter returned to Babylon. This transition is indicated in the sources. Thus it is related that Rav once came to Shela's academy incognito and was appointed the **amora* (the expounder to the students) of Shela. While Shela was expounding, Rav commented that in the presence of R. *Ḥiyya he had explained a certain detail differently. Shela immediately realized that his *amora* was the distinguished Rav and refused to continue to employ him in a subservient capacity (Yoma 20b; TJ, Shek. 5:2, 48d). Rav's position became of such authority that after listening to an exposition of Shela with which he disagreed, he waited until Shela left and then appointed an *amora* to explain the topic as he understood it. In another case Shela permitted a woman to remarry under questionable circumstances, with the result that Rav considered excommunicating him. Samuel, however, persuaded Rav to consult first with Shela, who later admitted his mistake (Yev. 121a). Shela and Rav disagreed on other occasions (Sanh. 44a).

This change in Shela's status is also illustrated by the following episode. Shela and his disciples were always the first to pay honor to the exilarch, but Shela later granted this privilege to Samuel. When Rav arrived in Babylon, Samuel transferred this honor to him. When Shela's disciples objected to their master thus being the third to be received, Samuel changed places with Shela (TJ, Ta'an. 4:2, 68a). R. Ḥisda referred to Shela as a great authority (Ket. 75a). Shela's learning was studied by the rabbis of Caesarea (TJ, Mak. 2:7, 31d). It seems that the school of Shela continued after his death, since his school and that of Rav are mentioned as disagreeing on a number of halakhic issues (Git. 52b; Kid. 43a; Sot. 42b; RH 23a).

BIBLIOGRAPHY: Hyman, Toledot, 1112f.; Ḥ. Albeck, *Mavo la-Talmudim* (1969), 177f.; Halevy, Dorot, 2 (1923), 223–6; Neusner, Babylonia, 2 (1966), index.

SHELAH, SAHARON (1945–), Israeli mathematician. Born in Jerusalem, Shelah received his Ph.D. in mathematics from the Hebrew University of Jerusalem (1969). He was simultaneously professor of mathematics at the Hebrew University and Rutgers University, New Jersey. Shelah's main research interests are in the sphere of mathematical logic, and especially model theory and set theory. His classification theory and the idea of proper forcing have applications of fundamental importance to cardinal arithmetic. He also solved many famous and previously intractable problems in algebra and topology. He was a prolific writer of original papers and influential books. His 1994 book, *Cardinal Numbers,* won the Bolyai Prize for the year 2000 of the Hungarian Academy of Sciences for the best mathematical monograph on original research, nominally awarded every five years but the first in modern times. His honors include the Wolf Prize (2001) for his work on mathematical logic and set theory.

[Michael Denman (2nd ed.)]

SHELDON, SIDNEY (1917–), U.S. author. Born in Chicago, Sheldon went to Hollywood at 17 to be a screenwriter. He got a job as a script reader for Universal Studios at $17 a week. In his spare time, Sheldon and a collaborator worked on their own scripts, eventually writing a number of "B" pictures for Republic Studios. He joined the Air Force during World War II and earned pilot's wings. Upon his discharge, he began to write for Broadway. At age 25 he had three musical hits simultaneously on Broadway: *Merry Widow, Jackpot,* and *Dream With Music*. Next came *Alice in Arms*, starring Kirk *Douglas in his first Broadway appearance, and, later, *Redhead* with Gwen Verdon, for which Sheldon won a Tony Award. Returning to Hollywood, Sheldon won an Academy Award for *The Bachelor and the Bobby Soxer,* starring Cary Grant, and wrote a number of memorable and commercially successful films, including *Easter Parade* with Judy Garland and Fred Astaire, *Annie Get Your Gun, Jumbo,* and *Anything Goes*, with Bing Crosby. After leaving Hollywood as a writer/director/producer, he became involved in television when ABC asked him to create a show for a young actress named Patty Duke. Over two years, Sheldon wrote 78 scripts for *The Patty Duke Show*. He then created, wrote, and produced the hit series *I Dream of Jeannie,* which brought Sheldon an Emmy nomination. The show ran for five years. He also created the popular detective series *Hart to Hart*. He wrote his first novel, *The Naked Face* (1970), and it earned the Edgar Allan Poe Award from the Mystery Writers of America for best first novel. Three years later, he produced *The Other Side of Midnight,* which firmly established him as a bestselling author. Each of his successive novels, *A Stranger in the Mirror* (1976), *Bloodline* (1977), and *Rage of Angels* (1980) through *The Sky Is Falling* (2001) and *Are You Afraid of the Dark?* (2004) dominated the bestseller lists. All told, Sheldon wrote over 200 television scripts, 25 major motion pictures, six Broadway plays, 18 novels, which sold more than 300 million copies, and a memoir, *The Other Side of Me.*

[Stewart Kampel (2nd ed.)]

SHELEM (Weiner), MATTITYAHU (1904–1975), Israeli composer. Born in Zamoscz, Poland, Shelem went to Palestine in 1922, worked in agriculture and road building and in 1927 joined kibbutz Bet Alfa. For a time he was a shepherd, and the shepherds' and shearing festival songs which he composed at that time were his first popular works. In 1940 Shelem joined kibbutz *Ramat Yoḥanan. From 1944 onward Shelem was chiefly active as a teacher and *Youth Aliyah instructor in his kibbutz. In 1958 he founded an archive there (Makhon le-Havai u-le-Mo'ed) to collect the documentation on the development of the forms of festival and holiday celebration in the kibbutzim (see *Kibbutz Festivals).

Shelem's songs, to which he always wrote the words, were created for the immediate needs of kibbutz life – from kindergarten to communal celebrations. The following list contains Shelem's best-known songs in approximate chronological order.

BET ALFA PERIOD: *"Hoi At Ereẓ ha-Kaddaḥat," "Bi-Meẓiltayim u-ve-Tuppim," "Ha-Koremim, ha-Yogevim," "Seh u-Gedi," "Sisu ve-Simḥu bi-Yhudah," "Simhu Na u-Firku ha-Ol," "Hinneh Geshem, Geshem Ba," "Na'alẓah ve-Nismeḥah," "Shir la-Sadnah," "Yoḥanan ve-Gavri'el."* RAMAT YOHANAN PERIOD: *"Adarim," "Shime'u, Shime'u," "Rav Berakhot," "Natu Ẓelalim (Shabbat ba-Kefar)," "Ez va-Keves Kevar Nigzazu,"* Omer ceremony pageant (1943, see below), *"Ve-David Yefeh Einayim"* (the third part of the melody added by Eliyahu Gamliel), *"Ro'eh ve-Ro'ah," "Shiru ha-Shir," "Havu Lanu Yayin, Yayin," "Hen Yeronan"* (c. 1953, addition to the Omer).

Shelem's *Omer, celebrated in Ramat Yoḥanan from 1945 onward and adopted in many other kibbutzim, is one of the two central "new ceremonies" developed by the secular kibbutz movement (the other being Yehudah *Sharett's *seder*). It is a reconstruction of the ancient ceremony, based mainly on the Mishnah, and is made up of recitations, solo and small choir songs, songs for the participating public, dances (created by Lea Bergstein), and the symbolic actions of harvesting and presentation of the first sheaves. Many of the songs have entered the Israel folk repertoire, such as "*Bi-Yhudah u-va-Galil*," "*Shibbolet ba-Sadeh*," and "*Panah ha-Geshem*."

BIBLIOGRAPHY: M. Weiner (= Shelem), *Hava'at ha-Omer; Massekhet Ḥag ve-Shirah* (1947); M. Shelem, in: *Taẓlil*, 3 (1963), 205; 7 (1967), 179–81; 10 (1970), 99; I. Shalita, *Enẓiklopedyah le-Musikah – Ishei ha-Musikah ha-Yisre'elit ve-ha-Kelalit* (1959), 776–9.

[Bathja Bayer]

SHELI'AḤ ẒIBBUR (Heb. שְׁלִיחַ צִבּוּר; "envoy or messenger of the community"), designation of a person who in public synagogue worship officiates as reader and cantor (see also **Ḥazzan*). The main function of the *sheli'aḥ ẓibbur* is to lead the congregants in communal worship by repeating aloud the benedictions of certain parts of the prayers or the introductions to them, certain doxologies (e.g., **Barekhu*), and the **Amidah*; by reciting the intermediary **Kaddish* prayers; and by leading the congregants in the recital of responsive readings and hymns. The Shulḥan Arukh (OḤ 53:4–9) lists the qualifications required of a *sheli'aḥ ẓibbur*: (1) humility, (2) acceptability to the congregation, (3) knowledge of the rules of prayer and the proper pronunciation of the Hebrew text, (4) an agreeable voice, (5) proper dress, (6) a beard. The requirement of a beard is, however, waived except for the High Holy Days (*Magen Avraham* to Sh. Ar., OḤ 53:6). Except for the recital of hymns and psalms (e.g., **Pesukei de-Zimra*) only a male after *bar mitzvah age may officiate.

BIBLIOGRAPHY: Elbogen, Gottesdienst, 488–502.

SHELOMI (Heb. שְׁלֹמִי), town in northern Israel. Shelomi is located on the slopes of Western Galilee, 8 mi. (12 km.) east of Nahariyyah. The town's area is 2.3 sq. mi. (6 sq. km.). It received municipal council status in 1960. In 2002 the population numbered 4,930, among them 22% new immigrants. The town's industry was based on metal and medical equipment plants. The name derives from the biblical figure Achihud ben Shelomi, who lived in the land of Asher.

WEBSITE: www.cityindex.co.il

[Shaked Gilboa (2nd ed.)]

SHELOSHET YEMEI HAGBALAH (Heb. שְׁלֹשֶׁת יְמֵי הַגְבָּלָה; "the three days of limitation"), the name given to the three days immediately preceding the festival of Shavuot. The scriptural sources for distinguishing these days are found in Exodus 19:12, where God commands Moses, "And thou shalt set bounds unto the people," and Exodus 19:15, where Moses orders the children of Israel, "Be ready against the third day." (See also the discussion in *Shabbat* 87a as to how many days of "limitation" were ordered by God and how many by Moses.) The original limitations were against touching Mount Sinai (Ex. 19:12) and against having sexual intercourse (*ibid.* 19:15). The people were also commanded to sanctify themselves during these days (ibid. 19:10 and 14). According to the *halakhah*, marriage celebrations and haircuts, otherwise prohibited during most of the period between Passover and Shavuot, are permitted during these three days (Sh. Ar., OḤ 493:3 and *Mishnah Berurah*, ad loc.).

SHELOSHIM (Heb. שְׁלֹשִׁים; "thirty"), designation of 30 days of mourning after the death of close relatives (parents, child, brother, sister, husband, wife) counted from the time of the burial. According to *halakhah*, the bereaved has to observe the following *mourning rites during this period: (1) not to wear new clothes (or even festive clothes on Sabbaths and festivals); (2) not to shave or have a haircut; (3) not to participate at festivities, including weddings, circumcision, and *pidyon ha-ben* (see Redemption of *Firstborn) meals except if it is the birth of his own child; (4) not to marry; (5) to abstain from going to entertainments. It is also customary to change one's permanent seat in the synagogue during the *sheloshim* period. If the 30th day falls on a Sabbath, the mourning period terminates before the entrance of the Sabbath; shaving and haircutting, however, may not be performed until Sunday.

The three *pilgrim festivals and Rosh Ha-Shanah cause the *sheloshim* period to be shortened in the following way: If the mourner observes the mourning rites of **shivah* for at least one hour prior to the commencement of Passover or Shavuot, the *shivah* is waived and the observance of *sheloshim* is reduced to 15 days after the festival. In the case of *Sukkot, the mourner has to observe the *sheloshim* for only eight days after the festival. If the mourner observes at least one hour of *shivah* before the commencement of Rosh Ha-Shanah, the *shivah* is waived and the Day of Atonement annuls the *sheloshim*; if he observes one hour's mourning before the Day of Atonement, *shivah* is waived and the subsequent Sukkot festival annuls the *sheloshim*. The minor festivals of Ḥanukkah and Purim do not shorten the *sheloshim*. Should a person learn of the passing of one of his close relatives within 30 days of his death (*shemu'ah kerovah*), he has to observe the complete mourning rites of *shivah* and *sheloshim*. If, however, the news reaches him more than 30 days after the death (*shemu'ah reḥokah*), the mourning rites of *shivah* and *sheloshim* are observed for only one hour.

BIBLIOGRAPHY: D. Zlotnick, *The Tractate Mourning* (1966), index s.v. *30 days*; H. Rabinowicz, *A Guide to Life* (1964), 92–99; Maim., Yad, Evel 6–7; Sh. Ar., YD 389–403; J.M. Tukazinsky, *Gesher ha-Ḥayyim*, 1 (1960), 247–49.

SHELUḤEI EREẒ ISRAEL (Heb. "emissaries of Ereẓ Israel"), the name for messengers from Ereẓ Israel sent abroad as emissaries to raise funds. During the patriarchate after the destruction of the Second Temple, emissaries were sent in groups (TJ,

Hor. 3:7, Pes. 4:8); sometimes a father and a son were sent together. The senders of these emissaries were usually the heads of the Ereẓ Israel religious administration, or its communities. During Roman rule the sender was the patriarch. With the cessation of the patriarchate in 429 C.E. the sending of emissaries ceased, but was renewed after the Arab conquest of Ereẓ Israel in the 630s, when the emissaries were sent by the *geonim* and the heads of the academies. In general, emissaries did not act on behalf of two towns at the same time, an exception being Shabbetai Baer, who was sent (1674) from *Jerusalem, *Hebron, and *Safed. Usually a single emissary was dispatched on a mission, but at times two were sent, as in the case of Joseph b. Moses of Trani and Abraham Shalom III who went to Istanbul in 1599, while occasionally two emissaries, an Ashkenazi and a Sephardi, were sent. The *Azulai, *Israel, Navon, and Meyuḥas families perennially provided emissaries.

There were several kinds of deeds and letters that the emissary needed on his journey:

(1) *Iggeret kelalit* ("general letter"), the most important of the emissary's letters, was a lengthy and detailed document written on parchment, mainly in ornate style. It contained a request for financial support with a detailed description of the town's troubles as well as its virtues. The letter was signed by the rabbi, the *dayyanim*, and the other important members of the community. The letter was always written in Hebrew, but from the 18th century some emissaries translated it, or its most important points, into the language of the locality to which they were sent, sometimes even printing it.

(2) *Iggeret li-nedivim* ("letter to philanthropists"), directed to individual philanthropists, being merely an abridgment of the general letter.

(3) *Shetar ko'aḥ harsha'ah mishpati* ("power of attorney"), a widespread custom was that the emissary received power of attorney from his senders, giving legal force to his demands as an accredited agent to collect the contributions.

(4) *Shetar tena'ei ha-sheliḥut* ("deed of terms of the mission"), deed to confirm the conditions stipulated between the emissary and his principals concerning the former's salary and expenses to be deducted from the funds raised. On his return the emissary was required to present an account of the income and expenditures of his mission. From the 17th century it was customary to give the emissary one-third of his income, and in exceptional cases only one-quarter.

(5) *Shetar pitturin* ("bill of nonliability"), deed freeing the emissary from every liability imposed upon him by his senders, with the aim of giving confidence to future emissaries.

(6) *Pinkas ha-sheliḥut* ("account book of the mission"), account book of the mission which every emissary took with him. The heads of the donor communities, as well as individuals, noted in the *pinkas* the amounts they gave. On the one hand the account book served as the emissary's evidence of the contributions he collected in each place, and on the other as propaganda in the places to which he was going. In most cases the communities' leaders briefly repeated the contents of the emissary's letter of appointment in their notes, sometimes stressing that the amount given was the result of a special effort because of their love for Ereẓ Israel. The emissary entered his expenses in the *pinkas*, and on returning home he delivered it to the community which sent him, doing this to attest the veracity of his accounts. The *pinkas* also served as a guide for future emissaries, to help them in arranging matters at the time of their mission. Ereẓ Israel emissaries frequently reached remote communities, despite the numerous dangers surrounding them. Many of the emissaries left written impressions of their missions, only some of which are extant. The *pinkasim* and descriptions of the missions, providing information on the number, occupation, habits, etc. of the members of the communities, are of considerable historical importance, particularly in the case of remote communities where no other records are extant. The most important of such works include Ḥ.J.D. *Azulai's *Ma'gal Tov ha-Shalem* (1934), the diary of his travels during two missions (1753 and 1773) for Hebron, and Jacob *Saphir's *Even Sappir* (1866), on his mission from Jerusalem to Egypt, Yemen, and the Far East in the late 1850s.

From the *Mamluk period until the Turkish conquest in 1517, a few emissaries were sent on behalf of the yeshivot of Ereẓ Israel. From the second half of the 16th century missions were executed in the name of the town or the community, and by the first half of the 17th century a gradual consolidation of a permanent system of missions from the three holy cities, Jerusalem, Hebron, and Safed (referred to as YaḤaẒ), began to take place. Each of the three cities regularly sent its own emissary once every few years to each of the mission regions. The emissary was called *sheli'aḥ kolel*, or *sheli'aḥ kolelot*, the latter designation serving as an indication that he was sent on behalf of the entire population of the town. From 1740 Tiberias – after being rebuilt – also joined this group. At first the heads of the Diaspora communities insisted that emissaries not be sent separately for each Ereẓ Israel community, an exception being made in the case of the Ashkenazi and Italian communities of Safed and the Ashkenazi community of Jerusalem, which were allowed to send their own emissaries to their countries of origin. Special dispensation was given to these communities in order to encourage immigration from their countries of origin. From 1777, authority was given to one Jerusalem institution, the kabbalist yeshivah Bet El, also called the yeshivah or community of the Ḥasidim (the pious), to send emissaries regularly. At times, temporary permission was granted an institution or yeshivah whose economic plight was serious to send its own special emissary. One Jerusalem rabbi, Yom Tov *Algazi, authorized Jerusalem emissaries to collect special contributions in the course of their mission for a personal need, namely, to redeem a child from captivity. Missions of a temporary nature were also common in localities other than the four towns. From the beginning of the 19th century the communities began to act separately, each sending its own emissary to maintain its institutions. This phenomenon eventually brought an end to the missions (see below).

The Karaite community of Jerusalem also sent emissaries to the members of its community in the Diaspora. The first such emissary (from the middle of the 17th century) known by name was David b. Joshua ha-Ḥazzan.

From time to time private emissaries, due to personal poverty and severe economic plight, left Ereẓ Israel to collect contributions. They were provided with letters of recommendation signed by the heads of the *yishuv*, being similar in form, and at times also in content, to those borne by the emissaries, but in them the emissary's troubles were stressed. From the 18th century such individuals who obtained these letters were called *sheliḥim le-aẓmam* ("emissaries on their own behalf"). At first the emissary was sent to a particular country or a group of adjacent countries, but the region of the mission was not restricted; sometimes the emissary was permitted during the course of his journey to determine the extent of the region of his mission, being guided by his desire and the prevailing conditions.

Gradually more precise regions of activity were determined. In the 17th century there were already four mission regions: Turkey, including Syria, the Balkans, and the Mediterranean islands; Frankia, including Italy, France, Germany, and later also Poland and Lithuania; Maghreb, North Africa; and Arbistan, including Persia, Iraq, Kurdistan, Afghanistan, and Bukhara. Emissaries were also sent to Egypt, the Yemen, and India. The duration of the emissary's stay in the locality of his mission was not fixed. In general he used his own discretion, and its length depended upon the needs, possibilities, and prospects of collecting the maximum amount of money. Sometimes its duration was determined by his health, or whether or not he was able to adapt himself to harsh and unpleasant conditions in the country of his mission. In general the mission did not last longer than three or four years, but there were occasional emissaries who stayed ten years and more. Sometimes an emissary was sent two or three times to the same country. During their travels emissaries were exposed to all kinds of hardships that at times endangered their lives. Some died during their mission or in consequence of it. Some were robbed by highwaymen, taken captive, or imprisoned on the charge that they were spies. Of the 850 known emissaries, 85 died during their journey or in the locality of their mission. The ability and greatness of the emissary did not necessarily stem from his own personality but chiefly from his principals, i.e., as a consequence of the authority in Ereẓ Israel in whose name he spoke. The heads of a number of communities were accustomed to receive the emissary with royal splendor, song, and praise. In Oriental countries he stayed in most cases at the home of one of the wealthy members of the community, while in European lands the community hired accommodation for him. Sometimes the heads of the community compiled poems in his honor, as Moses *Zacuto was accustomed to do.

Emissaries who died during their mission received the honor that was their due; they were eulogized fittingly by the rabbis of the communities and *kinot* were recited for them. In Oriental countries it was customary to exaggerate in praise of the emissaries and ascribe miraculous deeds to them. There were messengers who pretended to be emissaries of Ereẓ Israel, particularly in Ashkenazi countries where they did not know the customs of Ereẓ Israel and did not recognize the florid signatures of its scholars. When such deceit was revealed, it gave rise to doubt regarding the motives of many emissaries. An additional occurrence that caused a decline in the honor accorded the emissaries, though indeed unusual, was the rivalry between the emissaries of different towns when they met in one place. At times there were serious frictions between them. Some emissaries, who were not treated with honor because of this, demanded that they be treated properly not for their own sake but for the honor of Ereẓ Israel. As a result there were instances of emissaries who scolded communities where they were not treated in a dignified manner. If they found no other way to gain their ends, they made use of the power of *ḥerem*, which was proclaimed in Jerusalem in front of the Western Wall. *Megillat Ahima'aẓ* (ed. by B. Klar (1944), 18–19) mentions a story from the tenth century about a Jerusalem emissary in Venosa, in southern Italy, where one of the worthies of the community, the well-known *paytan* *Silano, scoffed at the emissary. The latter related the incident to his principals in Jerusalem and they excommunicated Silano.

Historical Survey

After the destruction of the Second Temple Vespasian substituted a fiscal tax for the half-shekel paid by the Jews for Temple sacrifices, which was called **fiscus Judaicus*. In the anarchy of the third century this tax ceased to be collected and world Jewry was prepared to give toward the maintenance of the courts of the patriarch (**nasi*) in Ereẓ Israel. The patriarchs also used these funds to maintain the academies and needy students. Like the half-shekels in former times, these contributions, later called *aurum coronarium*, were collected annually. To collect them the patriarchs on occasion dispatched distinguished emissaries. Equipped with a letter of authorization (*igra di-ykar*; Aramaic, "letter of honor") from the patriarch Judah (c. 230–286), Ḥiyya b. Abba (late third century) visited the communities in Syria and Rome. He was the first recorded professional Jewish fund raiser; his letter read: "We are sending you our emissary, a great man who is to be treated as ourselves" (TJ, Ḥag. 1:8, 76d, Ned. 10:10, 42b). In describing the emissary Joseph of Tiberias, who converted to Christianity, a detailed description of the rank of the emissary and his functions is transmitted by Epiphanius (one of the Church Fathers in the fourth century): "This Joseph is regarded by them as one of the notables, for those who are called emissaries take their places after the patriarch. They sit together with the patriarch and can frequently discuss matters with him both by day and night in order to inquire and obtain counsel from him, and they put before him halakhic words from the Torah … [The patriarch] sent him with letters to Cilicia, and when he arrived there he collected from every town in Cilicia all the tithes and contributions of the Jews of the province … Since he was an emissary, for this office is so called by them, he was very severe … he expelled and removed from their offices many of the members of the synagogue: laymen, priests, elders and readers…" In talmudic sources the collection of money by emissaries is called *migbat ḥakhamim* ("collection of scholars"; TJ, Hor. 3:7). From the second half of the fourth century the Roman emperors became envious of the money of the emissaries, which at times reached enormous sums, and when the office of patriarch was abolished in 429, the sending of emissaries was explicitly prohibited by the emperors Theodosius II and Valentinian. The sending of emissaries was later renewed, and in the eighth century two emissaries of Ereẓ Israel are known to have been active in Venosa in the south of Italy; it is not certain whether they were sent from Jerusalem or Tiberias. The tombstone on a Roman grave found in this city states that the dead maiden was the only child of a distinguished family and that she was eulogized by two emissaries and two rabbis. In the second half of the ninth century an emissary is known to have come to this city from Jerusalem and preached there every Sabbath (*Megillat Aḥima'aẓ*, ed. by B. Klar (1944), 18–19).

In the second half of the tenth century a Jerusalem emissary named R. Jonah ha-Zaken b. R. Judah ha-Sefaradi is mentioned as having been sent to distant lands. He is the first emissary referred to by name after the close of the Talmud. His letter as emissary for 977 or 987 is also extant, and it contains all the components of the letters of the 16th-century emissaries and their successors. In the first half of the 11th century the two sons of the *Gaon* *Solomon b. Judah traveled as emissaries of the Ereẓ Israel yeshivah. During this period emissaries went with two aims: to maintain the central Torah foundation, i.e., the yeshivah and its scholars, and to ease the heavy burden of taxation imposed upon the Jewish community in the country. These funds were not however intended to maintain the poor, who were supported by the local charity of Ereẓ Israel. On the other hand, the emissaries of Tiberias were sent out to raise funds to maintain the poor flowing into the town, who called themselves *meyasserim* ("sufferers"), since a not inconsiderable number of the poor were among the sick who came to bathe in its healing waters.

The first known emissary from the Mamluk period was Jacob, who was sent by the yeshivah in Acre of *Jehiel b. Joseph of Paris in the second half of the 13th century. He took a list of the graves of the *ẓaddikim* (righteous men) in Ereẓ Israel with him as propaganda. There are no other emissaries from the 13th and 14th centuries who are known by name. *Isaac b. Sheshet Perfet (the Ribash) alludes to a Jerusalem emissary to Spain in about 1390 (Responsa, no. 508). In the 15th century the Jewish population in Jerusalem grew through immigration from Italy, Franco-Germany, and Oriental countries, many of whom were poor, and there was need to collect donations on their behalf outside Ereẓ Israel.

From the beginning of the Ottoman period (1517), the sending of emissaries continued to increase and take on a permanent character (more or less along the lines mentioned above). Among the Ereẓ Israel emissaries of this period were those who are generally considered its most distinguished scholars: Bezalel *Ashkenazi, Moses *Alshekh, Joseph of *Trani, Yom Tov *Ẓahalon, Nathan *Spira, *Hezekiah da Silva, and Ḥayyim Joseph David Azulai. At times immigrant scholars, whose influence on the communities of their native countries was great, were sent. A number of scholars are also known to have feared to immigrate to Ereẓ Israel lest they be required to return to their country of origin as emissaries, e.g., *Benjamin ha-Kohen of Reggio. Suitable persons from among the scholars could not always be found to carry out missions, and then men of inferior standard were used. Sometimes this resulted in the choice of unworthy persons who embezzled the funds collected. In 1629 opposition to the emissaries was heard for the first time from the heads of the Italian community of the island of Corfu. In their letter to the heads of the Jerusalem community they informed them that they no longer wanted emissaries to visit as the great expense involved in this swallowed up most of the money; they assured the leaders that they themselves would take care to transmit the contributions to their agent in Venice.

The leaders of the Jews of Amsterdam succeeded in 1824 in abolishing the sending of emissaries not only to their own town but also to all the communities of Western Europe. They further resolved that there should be a permanent center in Amsterdam for the Ereẓ Israel contributions from all the communities in the West. The institution that centralized the contributions was called Ḥevrat Terumat Kodesh ("Society for Holy Contributions"); however, this name was quickly forgotten and it became known as Pekidei u-Mashgiḥei ve-Amarkelei Ereẓ Israel ("Officers, Overseers, and Treasurers of Ereẓ Israel"). Ẓevi Hirsch Lehren was the head of the central fund for many years. Following its establishment, a similar one was founded in New York in 1832, Ḥevrat Terumat ha-Kodesh. The leaders of the Ereẓ Israel *yishuv* accepted this arrangement with pleasure, even though their spiritual independence was restricted as many matters were dictated to them by the Amsterdam center. From time to time an emissary was sent in spite of their express commitment to refrain from doing so. Lehren firmly prevented these emissaries from operating in Western Europe. The Venetian community also followed the lead of Amsterdam, but its center did not succeed in collecting a reasonable sum of money, and in 1863 a pamphlet was printed in Trieste containing letters from the heads of the four holy towns with a request that the new regulation be reexamined and rescinded. The scholars gave assurances that the sending of emissaries would be conducted in an orderly and honorable manner. Thus, the organization of emissaries retained its special character only in Amsterdam.

Activities in the Diaspora

The function of the emissary in the later centuries may be defined as (1) activities for Ereẓ Israel, and (2) for the communities of the Diaspora.

ACTIVITIES FOR EREẒ ISRAEL. *The Collection of the Contributions.* The emissary strove to obtain the maximum contribution from the communal fund. He then turned to the philanthropic members of the community, although not every community permitted him to turn to its members. In some communities, however, the rabbis encouraged individuals to make a separate contribution as distinct from the other contributions of the community. In some communities in Italy and in Amsterdam the rabbis placed at the disposal of the emissary one or two patrons who guided and counseled him, and taught him how to carry out the collection, as well as to whom to turn with requests for separate contributions. In many communities it was customary to collect donations on certain days of the year or on special celebrations. Sometimes this took place during the calling up to the reading of the *Torah. The funds were centralized in the hands of a treasurer called the *gabbai Ereẓ Yisrael* ("Ereẓ Israel collector"), or *pekid Ereẓ Yisrael* ("Ereẓ Israel officer"), from whom the emissary received the money. Every important community had some religious trust (*hekdesh*) on behalf of Ereẓ Israel. In some communities it was customary to impose fines on transgressors for the benefit of Ereẓ Israel. In the important communities there were special funds called *Kuppot* ("Funds") or *Ma'ot* ("Monies") *Ereẓ Yisrael.*

Over the years special funds were added for each of the four holy towns, and even for their different institutions. The Karaites also had funds in their communities, which were called *Im Eshkaḥekh* ("Lest I Forget Thee") or *Zikkaron Im Eshkaḥekh* ("A Reminder Lest I Forget Thee"). The division of the contributions in Ereẓ Israel was made in accordance with a definite system fixed by mutual agreement, as each of the four towns sent emissaries abroad. At the end of the 16th and the beginning of the 17th centuries they divided the funds into 24 parts: Jerusalem took seven, Safed ten, Hebron three, with the other four going to others. At that time Tiberias was in ruins. With the growth of the populations of Jerusalem and Hebron and the decline of Safed's, the share of the former in the division was larger. Thus, in 1670 Jerusalem took 12 parts, Safed eight, and Hebron four. This division lasted until 1740, when Tiberias was resettled and its part in the division was fixed once more. At the beginning of the 19th century the funds were divided into 28 parts: Jerusalem took 11 parts, Safed seven, Hebron six, and Tiberias four. At times, when the situation in Ereẓ Israel was bad and they could not manage with the contributions, the heads of the Diaspora communities put a special tax on their members for the benefit of Ereẓ Israel – in Venice in 1601, in Istanbul in 1727. Similarly, indirect taxes were placed on certain goods in Istanbul in 1763. The half-shekels donated on Purim were also devoted to Ereẓ Israel.

A special collector was appointed in each community whose duty was to supervise the donations. In Oriental countries the supervisors were generally appointed by the emissaries or the heads of the Ereẓ Israel communities. When the mission was completed, the head of the community confirmed in writing the sum of money given to the emissary. The emissary also left proof (in the communal *pinkas*) in the hands of the head of the community that he had received this amount (see below). At times some emissaries also accepted donations from Christians, as did the kabbalist Nathan Spira of Jerusalem in 1656–60, but there were scholars who held that according to the Torah it was forbidden to accept funds from Christians. When asked about this, Moses *Ḥagiz declared it permissible, and a number of emissaries in the 19th century are known to have taken money from Christians. Some of the contributions were transmitted to Ereẓ Israel by way of local centers. From the 17th century such centers existed in Venice, Leghorn, Istanbul, Amsterdam and Lvov (Lemberg). At the beginning of the 19th century one was also established in Vilna. Venice was the center of the funds of Italy in Europe; Leghorn chiefly those of North Africa, but also of Europe; and Amsterdam chiefly those of Western Europe. The funds from Poland which were contributed at the *Council of the Four Lands were centralized in Lvov and transmitted from there by way of Istanbul, which was the most important center as it was the one nearest to Ereẓ Israel and the capital of the Ottoman government. Donations from the Turkish communities and the Balkans, as well as those from Eastern Europe (see above), were transferred to Istanbul. There were also smaller centers in Vienna, Prague, and Frankfurt on the Main.

Propaganda Methods. The emissaries used the general letter (see above) to help raise donations. There were also special letters to philanthropists and homilies in praise of Ereẓ Israel generally, as well as of the town assigned the emissary. The emissary was accustomed to preach on the first Sabbath of his arrival in the community and in practice his work commenced with this. Sometimes he brought with him some soil from the holy land for the communal worthies, drawings of the holy places and the graves of the *ẓaddikim* (pious men), or scrolls of Esther and amulets from Ereẓ Israel. An important medium utilized for publicity was the printing of various books about Ereẓ Israel, whether compiled by themselves or others, in order to awaken the readers' love for Ereẓ Israel and interest in its affairs. The books included descriptions and illustrations of holy places and the graves of *ẓaddikim* in Ereẓ Israel, descriptions of travels to Ereẓ Israel, geographical descriptions of the country, maps, etc. Sometimes the emissaries printed books describing the immediate events which had given rise to their mission, among them *Ḥorvot Yerushalayim* (Venice, 1636), by anonymous authors, describing the difficult conditions of *Jerusalem in 1625; *Zimrat ha-Areẓ* (Mantua, 1745) by Jacob *Berab (III), describing the resettlement of Jews in Tiberias in 1740; and *Korot ha-Ittim* (Vilna, 1840), a detailed description of the riots against the Jews of Safed during the revolt of the fellahin against Ibrahim Pasha in 1834, and of the Safed earthquake in 1837. Similarly, many propaganda books were published describing the virtues and the praise of Ereẓ Israel. Additional propaganda media were poems and *piyyutim* in praise of Ereẓ Israel which the emissaries circularized in the localities of their activities.

ACTIVITIES FOR THE COMMUNITIES OF THE DIASPORA. The emissary's mission to the Diaspora had another side. It also aimed at bringing the Jews of the Diaspora nearer to the affairs of Ereẓ Israel. This found expression in the spiritual influence of the emissaries, who regarded themselves as bound to teach and guide the exiles in spiritual matters. Sometimes the emissaries were asked by the exiles to make decisions in matters of *minhagim* and *halakhah* that they could not decide themselves. The emissaries had already begun to make improvements in the communities and to give halakhic decisions during the era of the patriarchate, when the messengers of the patriarch were accustomed to appoint the heads of communities and the supervisors of communal arrangements. This trend in affairs continued in effect until the missions came to an end. The emissary drew this power not simply from his personality but by virtue of the authority of Ereẓ Israel and of the great Torah scholars who were the signatories of his letter of appointment. For this reason, care was taken in general to dispatch men of stature. As a result the exiles looked upon rabbinical ordination by the Ereẓ Israel rabbis as something grand and superior. Thus, many rabbis of communities were accustomed to request confirmation of ordination for their pupils. Similarly, authors among the exiles who wanted to raise the public stature of their works attempted to win commendations for them from the emissaries. The Torah novellae (*ḥiddushei Torah*) and sermons of the emissaries found attentive listeners, and works by Diaspora scholars include novellae and homilies heard from the emissaries.

Ereẓ Israel Emissaries and Spiritual Movements

From the 15th century Ereẓ Israel emissaries played an important role in Jewish spiritual movements. Their influence in the outbreak of the spiritual storms flowed from their very personalities but their main influence stemmed from their authority as Ereẓ Israel emissaries. The Kabbalah, which developed and was consolidated in Safed in the 16th century, was spread throughout the Diaspora by kabbalist emissaries who circulated and published during their missions their own works and those of others. Thus, for example, Gedaliah *Cordovero, son of the well-known kabbalist Moses *Cordovero, organized the distribution of his father's writings, whose two works were published during Gedaliah's mission to Italy in 1582. Similarly, Abraham *Almosnino, the Jerusalem emissary to Frankfurt on the Main, brought *tikkunim* and *sodot* there in 1592 which he had copied from the manuscript of one of the pupils of R. Isaac *Luria. To a large degree it was the Ereẓ Israel emissaries who circulated reports of the existence of the ten tribes and thereby aroused waves of redemption yearnings and the will to immigrate to Ereẓ Israel. In 1527, the well-known Jerusalem kabbalist Abraham b. Eleazar ha-Levi transmitted information about the ten tribes and about indications of redemption and return in the wars of the *Beta Israel (Falashas) in Ethiopia. Similarly, the 17th-century letter of Baruch Gad concerning the Benei Moshe (sons of Moses) is remarkably like the story of *Eldad ha-Dani (and hence may be regarded as a forgery). The Benei Moshe complain about their bad conditions and desire with all their might to immigrate to Ereẓ Israel. The letter made a great impression on the Jerusalem inhabitants, who wished to restore the city to its former glory, as well as upon the Jews of Eastern Europe, who were severely agitated after the massacres of 1648–49 and were in need of consolation, hope, and salvation. Gad's letter was distributed by Ereẓ Israel emissaries throughout the Diaspora for a period of 250 years and was republished 15 times. A number of the emissaries attempted during their travels to discover traces of the ten tribes, some acting on behalf of their principals and others on their own behalf, e.g., *David D'Beth Hillel, one of the pupils of Elijah Gaon of Vilna.

The Shabbatean movement, which agitated most communities of Europe from the beginning of the second half of the 17th century, was also bound up with the emissaries, who played a decisive role in it. The pseudo-messiah *Shabbetai Ẓevi was sent as an emissary from Jerusalem to Egypt in 1664. *Nathan of Gaza was the son of the emissary Elisha Ḥayyim b. Jacob Ashkenazi. There is no doubt that the latter in the course of his work as an emissary – after Shabbetai Ẓevi had revealed himself – helped to spread the teaching of his son. Moreover, the scribe of Shabbetai Ẓevi, Samuel of Primo, went abroad in 1662 as a Jerusalem emissary. Later, he undoubtedly made use of his contacts with the communities of Turkey in order to spread his belief in Shabbetai Ẓevi. There were also emissaries who opposed Shabbateanism. When Ḥiyya b. Joseph Dayyan was in Italy in 1673 as an emissary, he censured Shabbateanism. Shabbetai Baer acted in a similar manner when he was on a mission in 1674.

The Ereẓ Israel emissaries also took an active part in the Nehemiah Ḥiyya *Ḥayon polemic at the beginning of the 18th century. Solomon *Ayllon, rabbi of Amsterdam who was a Safed emissary, was among his chief supporters, while Moses Ḥagiz, when an emissary of Jerusalem in Europe, was one of his most vigorous opponents. The Ereẓ Israel emissaries also played an important role in the polemic which was stirred up in 1729 around the personality and writings of Moses Ḥayyim *Luzzatto and continued for a number of years, giving rise to a controversy in the Jewish world. The Ereẓ Israel emissaries intervened in the dispute which centered around Jacob *Emden and Jonathan *Eybeschuetz. Abraham Israel, Jerusalem emissary in 1752, defended Eybeschuetz, and the document the latter received from him carried great weight and strengthened his stand. Emden was enraged by the Ereẓ Israel emissaries in particular and by its inhabitants in general, accusing them of Shabbatean tendencies.

The emissaries also played an important part in the Reform polemic which commenced in 1796. It started when in the same year a false report was published in one of the French newspapers that the Jews of Italy were preparing to introduce religious reforms. This grew from a rumor that a large convention of Italian rabbis in Florence had resolved to abrogate various prohibitions. Several Italian communities were stirred that same year to deny this report, and they published a special pamphlet. The moving spirit in all these activities was provided by several Ereẓ Israel emissaries who were then in Italy; among the signatories were Ḥayyim Baruch Saporta, the Safed emissary, and the Hebron emissaries Ephraim *Navon, Judah Leon, and Ḥayyim J.D. Azulai, and others. This pamphlet was also published the same year in Hamburg in German translation. In the Reform controversy only two emissaries, Ḥayyim Judah Ayash and Judah Aaron Takli, sided with the reformers when an organ was introduced into a Hamburg synagogue in 1817. Abraham b. Eleazar ha-Levi, the Jerusalem emissary in 1819, Nathan *Amram in 1842, and Israel Moses *Ḥazzan in 1845 came out against the religious reforms.

The emissaries helped in no small degree in the spread and revival of the Hebrew language, preaching mainly in Hebrew during their missions. In many of the communities the leaders thought of appointing the emissaries as rabbis or *dayyanim*, and many agreed to the proposals, accepting the appointment on completion of their mission. In times of need they used their influence to assist the communities in material matters, generally in isolated communities in the East. In 1750 in Nikopol, Bulgaria, the Safed emissary Ezra Malki helped mobilize financial support from Polish Jews to rebuild the synagogue named after Joseph Caro, which was in ruins. Cruel treatment of the Jews of Irbil, Kurdistan, in 1867 moved the emissaries to approach the Alliance Israélite Universelle to intervene on the community's behalf. In 1871, after the riots of their rebellious Kurdish neighbors, the Jerusalem emissary in Kurdistan, Raḥamim de la Rosa, and the heads of the community signed the emissary's letter requesting financial help. Ereẓ Israel emissaries also helped greatly in freeing the "black" Jews in *Cochin, India, who were regarded by their white brethren as slaves.

Emissaries' Activities on Their Own Behalf

As there was no printing press in Ereẓ Israel from the end of the 16th to the 19th centuries, the emissaries utilized their missions to the Diaspora as Ereẓ Israel emissaries to publish their own works. During their missions they succeeded in distributing their works, thus bringing greater honor upon themselves. In practice, most of the works of Ereẓ Israel scholars were published by their authors during their missions, or during the mission of another emissary. A number of the emissaries compiled their works during their travels, e.g., H.J.D. Azulai compiled his *Shem ha-Gedolim*. Usually the emissary referred to his adventures in the introduction. The distribution of the emissary's works at the time of his mission undoubtedly brought him financial profit, and there were even cases in which the emissary on his return was requested to divide his profits with his principals, as the publication of his works and their distribution was made possible primarily as a result of the mission. While on their missions, some emissaries made frequent visits to libraries to examine expensive and rare books and manuscripts. Some Ereẓ Israel emissaries regarded their missions simply as a means of livelihood and were sent numerous times to various countries.

Historical Importance of the Emissaries

The sending of emissaries played an exceptionally important part in Jewish history in general, and in the history of Jewish settlement in Ereẓ Israel, in particular. It constituted one of the most important chapters in the history of Ereẓ Israel between the destruction of the Second Temple and the birth of Zionism, and in the history of the relations between the inhabitants of Ereẓ Israel and the Jews of the Diaspora. The letters of the emissaries and documents about them are important sources for understanding the events that occurred in their times and the causes that gave rise to their missions. Their importance is also considerable for the histories of the communal institutions in Ereẓ Israel. On the other hand, the account books of the emissaries constitute an important source of the history of the communities in which they worked and of the relations between the communities and Ereẓ Israel. The modern scholar Abraham *Yaari compiled with great diligence and extraordinary erudition everything known (and not known until his research) on this subject in his monumental work *Sheluḥei Ereẓ Israel* (1951).

BIBLIOGRAPHY: Yaari, Sheluḥei; idem, in: *Sinai*, 29 (1951), 345–58; idem, in: *Sura*, 3 (1958) 235–54; 4 (1964) 223–49; idem, in: *Sefer ha-Ḥida*, ed. by M. Benayahu (1959), 105–40; idem, in: I. Ratzaby and I. Shavtiel (eds.), *Harel, Koveẓ Zikkaron… R. Alshekh* (1962), 218–25; idem, in: *Maḥanayim*, 93–4 (1964), 158–167; M. Benayahu, in: *Sinai*, 32 (1953), 300–19; 35 (1954), 64–66, 317–40; idem, in: KS, 28 (1952/53), 16–35; idem, in: *Sura*, 2 (1956), 208–26; 3 (1958), 217–34; idem, in: *Sefunot*, 2 (1958), 137–89; 6 (1962), 35–40; idem, in: *Oẓar Yehudei Sefarad*, 2 (1959), 77–81, 5 (1962) 101–8; idem (ed.), in: *Sefer ha-Ḥida* (1959), 35–36, 38–42; idem, *Rabbi Ḥayyim Yosef David Azulai* (1959), index s.v. *Sheluḥei Ereẓ Yisrael* and *Sheliḥut Ereẓ Yisrael*; idem, in: *Miscellanea di studi in memoria di D. Disegni* (1969), 5–21 (Heb. part); A. Ben Jacob, in: *Yerushalayim*, 5 (1955), 257–86; I. Ben-Zvi, in: *Scritti in onore di R. Bachi* (1950), 116–20; idem, in: *Sinai*, 30 (1952), 80–86; idem, in: *Reshumot*, 5 (1953), 51–62; idem, in: *Sinai, Sefer ha-Yovel* (1958), 13–26; idem, in: *Oẓar Yehudei Sefarad*, 5 (1962), 7–10; 7 (1964), 77–86; idem, in: *Sefunot*, 6 (1962), 355–97; idem, *Meḥkarim u-Mekorot* (1966), 179–280; D. Brilling, in: *Yerushalayim*, 4 (1953), 220–31; idem, in: *Sinai*, 42 (1958), 30–42; idem, in: *Sefer ha-Ḥida*, ed. by M. Benayahu (1959), 141–77; idem, in: *Sura*, 4 (1964), 250–75; idem, in: BLBI, 18 (1965), 315–25; idem, in: *Festschrift… J.E. Lichtigfeld* (1964), 20–49; M. Eliav, in: *Sinai*, 62 (1968), 172–88; I.S. Emmanuel, in: *Sefunot*, 6 (1962), 399–424; A.M. Habermann, *ibid.*, 7 (1963), 255–66; Y. Kafaḥ, in: *Yerushalayim*, 5 (1955), 287–306; A.I. Katsh, in: *Sefunot*, 7 (1963), 229–54; 8 (1964), 321–35; J. Katz, in: *Beḥinot*, 2 (1952), 69–73; S. Marcus, in: *Yerushalayim*, 4 (1953), 232–42; 5 (1955), 229–32; E. Mayer, in: BLBI, 9 (1966), 101–118; I. Ratzaby, in: *Sinai*, 65 (1969), 141–9, 333–4; B.A. Rivlin, in: *Yad Yiẓḥak Rivlin* (1964), 108–50; S. Simonsohn, in: *Sefunot*, 6 (1962), 327–54; idem, *Toledot ha-Yehudim be-Dukkasut Mantovah*, 2 vols. (1962–64), index s.v. *Sheluḥim u-Sheliḥut*; I. Sonne, in: *Sefunot*, 5 (1961), 275–95; J.M. Toledano, in: *Yerushalayim*, 4 (1953), 215–8; idem, in: *Oẓar Genazim* (1960), passim.

[Abraham David]

SHELUḤOT (Heb. שְׁלוּחוֹת; "shoots," "sprouts"), kibbutz in northern Israel at the foot of Mt. Gilboa, 3 mi. (5 km.) S.W. of *Beth-Shean, affiliated with Ha-Kibbutz ha-Dati. Sheluḥot was founded at the time of the capture of Beth-Shean in the War of

Independence (May 10, 1948) by immigrants from Germany and Hungary. In 1970 Sheluḥot had 340 inhabitants; in 2002, 414. Its farming was based on irrigated field and fodder crops, palm orchards, dairy cattle, poultry, turkeys, and carp ponds. It operated electrical and metal factories and guest rooms.

[Efraim Orni]

SHEM (Heb. שֵׁם), eldest son of Noah, father of the "Semitic" peoples, including the Hebrew people. The meaning of the name is uncertain. It is possibly to be explained as Hebrew, meaning "fame," "name," "appellation." The Akkadian *šumu*, which is the same word, means not only name but also "son." As the eldest son, Shem always appears first in the list of Noah's three sons (Gen. 5:32; 9:18; 10:10; et al.). Together with his brothers and their wives, Shem and his wife accompanied Noah into the ark at the time of the Flood (7:7), and was also present with them during the covenant made with God afterward (9:8). As an individual personality, he appears only in Genesis 9:20–27 in the episode of Noah's drunkenness when the sensitive and modest behavior of Shem and his brother *Japheth contrasts sharply with that of *Ham. For this deed Noah blessed Shem and Japheth, "Blessed be the Lord, the God of Shem; let *Canaan be a slave to them" (verses 26–27). This passage clearly foreshadows the subjection of the Canaanites and implicitly identifies Shem with the future people of Israel. It is of interest that YHWH is here called the "God of Shem" and is not cited in connection with the other two brothers. In the list of nations in Genesis 10, Shem is the father of five sons who had 21 descendants, making a total of 26 peoples derived from him. Few of these had any known connection with Israelite history and the principle of their grouping cannot be determined with any degree of certainty (10:21–31). The genealogy of Shem appears last in the table of nations because of its great importance, the order being climactic. It serves to connect the list with the birth of Abraham by drawing attention to the fact that Shem was the "ancestor of all the descendants of Eber" (verse 21). The detailed genealogy of Shem through the line of Eber is resumed in chapter 11 (verses 10–26) where it concludes with the birth of Abraham, the father of the Hebrew nation. Shem is not again referred to in the Bible other than in the Chronicler's repetition of the Genesis genealogies (I Chron. 1:4, 17, 24).

[Nahum M. Sarna]

In the *Aggadah*

Shem's importance in the *aggadah* is due entirely to his being Israel's ancestor. Noah's blessing of Shem (Gen. 9:26 ff.) is accordingly interpreted as a blessing of Israel. Noah's execration of Canaan condemning him to be a slave to his brothers (*ibid.*) was used to justify Israel's conquest of the land of Canaan, for "whatever a slave possesses belongs to his master" (Sanh. 91a). Ever since the time of Hyrcanus I's victorious campaigns in Samaria and Idumea (Jos., Ant. 13:254 ff.; Wars, 1:62 ff.) the apologetic tendency to defend such conquests against the charges that they were aggressive acts made its appearance; and it was for the same reason that Noah was said to have distributed the world between his three sons in such a manner that Shem received the middle of the earth, including in particular the Land of Israel (Sanh. *ibid.*; Gen. R. 1:2; PdRE 24; Mid. Ḥag. to Gen. 9:27; cf. Jubilees 8:10 ff.). Although he is listed as the oldest of the three sons of Noah (Gen. 5:32; 6:10; 10:21), Shem is considered by the rabbis to have been the youngest, but yet the wisest, most important, and most righteous (Sanh. 69b; Gen. R. 26:3; 37:7 et al.). Since the primacy of younger brothers is an established motif in biblical historiography, Shem, too, had to be younger in years, but superior in every other respect. Thus, he was born circumcised (ARN^2, 2, p. 12; Gen. R. 26:3) – a distinction shared with some of the greatest biblical personalities (*ibid.*, Tanḥ. B., Gen. 32; Mid. Ps. 9, 7, ed. Buber, pp. 84 f.); and it was he who took the initiative to cover his father's nakedness (cf. Gen. 9:23), for which he was blessed that his (Israelite) descendants should cover themselves with the fringed *tallit* and that the Divine Presence should rest only in Jerusalem (Yoma 10a; Gen. R. 26:3; 36:6, 8; Tanḥ. B., Gen. 49).

Shem was also privileged to have God's name associated with his (Gen. R. 26:3; cf. Gen. 9:26). He was, moreover, endowed with the gift of prophecy, and for 400 years he prophesied to the nations of the world, but to no avail (SER, 141 f.). Finally, he was identified with Melchizedek, king of Salem, who served there as high priest in Abraham's time (cf. Gen. 14:18 ff.) but was deprived of this privilege in favor of Abraham because he had blessed Abraham before God (Gen. 14:19 ff.; Ned. 32b; Gen. R. 26:3; 43:6; Lev. R. 25:6; Num. R. 4:8; ARN op. cit). The real reason, however, was the role played by Melchizedek in Christian literature, where he became a prototype of Jesus (cf. Heb. 5:6 f.; 7:15–17; cf. also Ginzberg, Legends, vol. 5, 225 f., n. 102). In line with the rabbinic concept of the pre-existence of the Torah and its institutions prior to the revelation at Sinai, Shem's "tents" (Gen. 9:27) were accordingly identified as a *bet midrash* – an academy with which Eber, Shem's great-grandson, subsequently became associated, and which also served as a *bet din* (Mak. 23b; Gen. R. 36:8; 85:12; Targ. Ps.-Jon. to Gen. 9:27 and 25:22). It is said that Israel's Patriarchs studied at the academy of Shem and Eber (Targ. Ps. Jon, to Gen. 24:62 and 25:27; Gen. R. 63:10), and that students of the Law will be privileged to study in the world to come at the heavenly academy of Shem, Eber and other heroes of Israel (Song R. 6:2 no. 6; Eccles. R. 5:11 no. 5).

[Moses Aberbach]

BIBLIOGRAPHY: A.H. Sayce, *Races of the Old Testament* (1891), 38–66; L. Rost, in: *Festschrift A. Alt* (1953), 169–78; S. Simons, in: OTS, 10 (1954), 155–84; U. Cassuto, *A Commentary on the Book of Genesis* (1964), 216–24; A. Reubeni, *Ammei Kedem* (1970). IN THE AGGADAH: Ginzberg, Legends, 1 (1942^2), 161–74, 274, 332; 5 (1947^6), 181–2, 187, 192 ff.; 7 (1946), 434.

SHEMA, READING OF, the twice daily recitation of the declaration of God's unity, called the *Shema* ("Hear") after the first word in Deuteronomy 6:4; also called *Keri'at Shema* ("the reading of the *Shema*"). As it had developed by at least as early as the second century C.E., the *Shema* consisted of three portions of the Pentateuch – Deuteronomy 6:4–9; Deuteronomy 11:13–21; and Numbers 15:37–41, in this order – together with the benedictions of the *Shema*, two to be recited before the *Shema* and one after in the morning, and two before and two after in the evening (Ber. 1:1–5, 2:2). The morning benedictions before the *Shema* are: "Who formest light and createst darkness…" (*Yoẓer Or*, Hertz, Prayer, 108–14) and "With abounding love…" (**Ahavah Rabbah, ibid.*, 114–6), and "True and firm…" (*Emet Ve-Yaẓiv, ibid.*, 126–8), after it (see *Shaḥarit). The evening benedictions before the *Shema* are "Who at Thy word bringest on the evening twilight…" (*Ma'ariv Aravim, ibid.*, 304), and "With everlasting love…" (**Ahavat Olam, ibid.*, 306), and "True and trustworthy…" (*Emet ve-Emunah, ibid.*, 310–2), and "Cause us to lie down in peace…" (**Hashkivenu, ibid.*, 312), after the *Shema* (see *Arvit).

Development of the Practice

It is difficult to determine the stages through which this development took place. At a very early period the Deuteronomic injunction "And these words which I command thee this day … and thou shalt talk of them" (6:6–7 and 11:19) were understood as a commandment to read the *Shema*, perhaps in response to the challenge of Zoroastrian dualism, though as late as the third century C.E. some held the view that the duty of reciting the *Shema* is rabbinic and the verses refer not specifically to the *Shema* but to the "words of Torah" in general (Ber. 21a). The *Nash papyrus, dating from the Hasmonean period, contains the Ten Commandments and the first portion of the *Shema*. The Mishnah (Tam. 5:1) records that in the Temple all three portions of the *Shema* were recited together with the Ten Commandments, and explicit reference is made here to the benediction after the *Shema, Emet ve-Yaẓiv*, and to another benediction before the *Shema*, which is identified at a later period (Ber. 11b) with *Ahavah Rabbah*. At a later period, too, there are indications that special significance was attached to the first verse of the *Shema* (Ber. 13b; Suk. 42a). It is not implausible, therefore, to see the successive stages as (1) the reading of the first verse; (2) the reading of the first portion; (3) the reading of all three portions, together with *Emet ve-Yaẓiv* and *Ahavah Rabbah*; (4) the addition of the other benedictions.

In any event, it was a long established practice at the beginning of the present era to read the *Shema* in the evening and morning as can be seen from the fact that the schools of Hillel and Shammai (see *Bet Hillel and Bet Shammai) debated as to how it should be read. The school of Shammai took the words "when you lie down and when you get up" literally, and ruled that the evening *Shema* should be recited while reclining and the morning *Shema* while standing upright. The school of Hillel ruled that "when you lie down…" refers to the times of reading, i.e., in the evening and in the morning, but that no special posture is required. The ruling followed is that of the school of Hillel (Ber. 1:3).

There was much debate in the tannaitic period as to the times of reciting the *Shema*. The eventual ruling is that the evening *Shema* can be recited from nightfall until dawn, though ideally it should be recited before midnight; the morning *Shema* can be recited from the first traces of the dawn until a quarter of the day (Ber. 1:1–2; Ber. 2a–3a, 9b).

INCLUSION OF THE BARUKH SHEM. After the first verse of the *Shema* it has been customary from rabbinic times to recite under the breath the doxology, uttered as a response in the Temple, "Blessed be the name of His glorious Kingdom for ever and ever" (*Barukh Shem*). The midrashic explanation is that this was recited by the patriarch Jacob on his deathbed when his sons declared their loyalty by reciting the *Shema*. Since Jacob said it, we too repeat it, but since Moses did not say it, we recite it *sotto voce* (Pes. 56a). Another midrashic explanation is that when Moses went up on high, he heard the ministering angels saying *Barukh Shem*, and he brought it down for Israel to use. Since it was stolen from the angels, Israel recites it silently, but on the *Day of Atonement, when Israel is pure as the angels, it is recited in a loud voice (Deut. R. 2:36).

Various suggestions have been made to account historically for the insertion of *Barukh Shem*. Thus it may have been introduced by the Pharisaic opponents of Herod and the Sadducean priesthood in order to emphasize the belief in the sole sovereignty of God as against the aristocratic tendency to admit the sovereignty of the caesars (see Abrahams, Companion, iii); or as a response at a time when the *Shema* was read verse by verse led by the reader (Elbogen, Gottesdienst, 26); or as a substitute for the Temple response after the destruction of the Temple (Ḥ. Albeck (ed.), *Shishah Sidrei Mishnah, Zera'im* (1958), 328), which might explain why the later custom is to recite *Barukh Shem* in a loud voice on the Day of Atonement, since this was the day on which it was especially recited in Temple times (Yoma 3:8, 4:1, 6:2).

RECITATION OF SHEMA BEFORE RETIRING. In addition to the twice daily reading of the *Shema* as part of the morning and evening prayers the practice was introduced in the amoraic period of reciting the first section before retiring (*Keri'at Shema al ha-Mittah*). The source in the Talmud (Ber. 4b) is the saying of R. Joshua b. Levi: "Though a man has recited the *Shema* in the synagogue, it is meritorious to recite it again on his bed." The proof text was given as: "Tremble and sin not; commune with your own heart upon your bed, and be still. Selah" (Ps. 4:5). Later on in the same passage (Ber. 5a) the practice is connected with the fear of demons, whom it is said to drive away, but it is uncertain whether this was the true origin of the custom. Maimonides (Yad, Tefillah, 7:2), as usual in such circumstances, makes no mention of the demon motif but simply records the duty of reciting the first paragraph of the *Shema*, and he takes "on the bed" literally.

OTHER RITUAL USES OF THE SHEMA. The first verse of the *Shema* is also recited in the early morning (Hertz, Prayer, 30); when the Torah scroll is taken from the ark on Sabbaths and festivals (*ibid.*, 480); during the *Kedushah* in the *Musaf* on Sabbaths and festivals (*ibid.*, 530, 816, etc.); and on the deathbed (*ibid.*, 1064). The first verse of the *Shema* is recited once, and *Barukh Shem*, three times, at the conclusion of the services on the Day of Atonement. The portions of the *Shema* from Deuteronomy 6:4–9; 11:13–21 are included in the parchments enclosed in the **mezuzah* and **tefillin*. The remains of *tefillin* for the head found in Qumran (XQ Phyl. 1–4) were acquired by Y. Yadin in 1969 and proved to contain, among additional biblical texts, Deuteronomy 6:4–9. It is presumed that the original fourth scroll from these remains, which is now lost, contained Deuteronomy 11:13–21.

The Laws of the Shema

The *Shema* should be recited with full concentration on the meaning of the words; if, however, it was recited without concentration, it is unnecessary to repeat it, provided the first verse was recited with concentration. If the *Shema* is recited while walking, it is necessary to stand still for the recitation of the first verse. It is customary to place the right hand over the eyes while reciting the first verse as an aid to concentration, and, for the same reason, the first verse should be recited in a loud voice. One should not wink or gesticulate while reading the *Shema* but should recite it in fear and trembling. The *Shema* should be recited sufficiently loudly for it to be heard by the ear, since it is said: "Hear, O Israel." Care must be taken to enunciate the words clearly, and this applies especially to two consecutive words, the first of which ends and the second of which begins with the same letter. The *Shema* can be recited in any language, but with the same clarity of enunciation one is expected to use for the Hebrew. If one is in doubt as to whether he has recited the *Shema*, it is necessary to recite it in order to make sure. It is forbidden to interrupt the recitation of the *Shema*. It is forbidden to recite the *Shema* in a place that is not scrupulously clean, or in front of the naked body. Women (who are exempt from carrying out precepts dependent on a given time) and little children have no obligation to recite the *Shema* but may do so if they wish. It is customary for women, nonetheless, to recite the *Shema*.

The total of the words of the *Shema* together with *Barukh Shem* is 245. It is customary for the reader to repeat the last two words of the *Shema* and the first word of the following benediction, thus bringing the total up to 248, corresponding to the limbs of the body and the number of positive precepts. When the *Shema* is recited in private, the total is made up by reciting before the *Shema* the three words *el melekh ne'eman* ("God, faithful King!"). The usual translation of the first verse of the *Shema* is "Hear, O Israel: The Lord our God, the Lord is one." Other translations are "The Lord our God is one Lord" (AV); "The Eternal, the Eternal alone, is our God" (Moffatt); "The Lord is our God, the Lord alone" (new Jewish translation, JPSA (1962), following Ibn Ezra).

The Shema in Jewish Thought

The *Shema* is in Jewish thought the supreme affirmation of the unity of God and is frequently called "the acceptance of the yoke of the Kingdom of Heaven." The original meaning of the first verse may have been that, unlike the pagan gods who have different guises and localities, God is one. At first the main emphasis in the *Shema* was seen to be in opposition to polytheism; there is only one God, not many gods. R. *Akiva is reported to have recited the *Shema* just before his execution by the Romans (Ber. 61b), and generally Jewish martyrs recited it as they went to their deaths. Perhaps from earliest times (see S.R. Driver, *Deuteronony*, ICC (1902), 89–91), but certainly from later, the word *eḥad* ("one") was understood also to mean "unique." God is not only one and not many, but He is totally other than what paganism means by gods. Seen in this light, the *Shema* is not only an affirmation that there are no other gods, but that God is the Supreme Being. God is different from anything in the universe He has created. This was the general view of the medieval Jewish philosophers and kabbalists (see, e.g., Baḥya ibn Paquda, *Ḥovot ha-Levavot*, 1:9–10). In ḥasidic thought, the further idea is read into the *Shema* that there is only God, the whole universe existing in Him, as it were, and only enjoying an independent existence from the human standpoint (panentheism; see Menahem Mendel of Lubavitch, *Derekh Mitzvotekha* (1953[5]), 118–24). This doctrine was treated as heresy by opponents of Ḥasidism.

VARIOUS INTERPRETATIONS OF THE FIRST VERSE. Christian exegesis in the Middle Ages interpreted the three divine names in the first verse of the *Shema* as referring to the Trinity (see JE, 12 (1905), 261 and J. Katz, *Exclusiveness and Tolerance* (1961), 19). Jewish commentators were naturally at pains to contradict this, and a current interpretation was that, in fact, the *Shema* asserts the opposite, that there is only one God and no three persons in the Godhead (see, e.g., *Da'at Zekenim* and Baḥa ibn Asher to Deut. 6:4 and Leon de Modena, *Magen va-Ḥerev* (ed. S. Simonsohn (1960), 31–32)). Very curious are the references in the Zohar to the three divine names in the first verse of the *Shema*. These represent the unity of three powers in the Godhead, which are the *Sefirot* of Lovingkindness, Judgment, and Beauty (*Ḥesed, Gevurah, Tiferet*), symbolized by the colors white, red, and green, or the *Sefirot* of Wisdom, Understanding, and Beauty (*Hokhmah, Binah, Tiferet*; Zohar 1:18b; 3:263a). The Zohar is strongly anti-Christian in intent and repeatedly stresses that all the Ten *Sefirot* are a unity with *Ein Sof*, so that it is absurd to read the Christian doctrine into it, as some of the Christian kabbalists have done. The possibility, however, that the formal zoharic interpretation was influenced by Christian exegesis of this verse cannot be ruled out (see I. Tishby, *Mishnat ha-Zohar*, 2 (1961), 278–80).

The word "Israel" (in "Hear, O Israel") is understood by the Midrash as referring to the patriarch Jacob (Deut. R. 2:35). The devout Jew addresses himself to his ancestor to declare that he has kept the faith. Abudraham understands it to mean that each Jew addresses his fellow. In ḥasidic thought (Dov Baer of Lubavitch, *Kunteres ha-Hitpa'alut*, in *Likkutei Be'urim* (1868), 54a), the idea is put forward that each Jew addresses the "Israel" part of his soul, speaking to the highest within him. Abudraham also remarks that the letter *ayin* of the word *Shema* and the letter *dalet* of the *eḥad* are traditionally written larger than the other letters in the Torah scroll so as to form the word *ed* ("witness"): the Jew testifies to God's unity when he recites the *Shema*.

Jewish devotional manuals sometimes advise the worshiper to have in mind while reciting the *Shema* that if he is called upon to suffer martyrdom for the sanctification of God's name, he will do so willingly and with joy (see, e.g., Alexander Suskind of Grodno, *Yesod ve-Shoresh ha-Avodah* (1965^2), 97–99). This author also advises the worshiper after he has recited the first verse of the *Shema* to have in mind the following:

> I believe with perfect faith, pure and true, that Thou art one and unique and that Thou has created all worlds, upper and lower, without end, and Thou art in past, present and future. I make Thee King over each of my limbs that it might keep and perform the precepts of Thy holy Torah and I make Thee King over my children and children's children to the end of time. I will, therefore, command my children and grandchildren to accept the yoke of Thy Kingdom, Divinity, and Lordship upon themselves, and I will command them to command their children, in turn, up to the last generation to accept, all of them, the yoke of Thy Kingdom, Divinity, and Lordship.

BIBLIOGRAPHY: Maim., Yad, Keri'at Shema; Sh. Ar. OḤ, 59–88; Abrahams, Companion, i–liv; Blau, in: REJ, 31 (1895), 179–201; Elbogen, Gottesdienst, 16–26; J.H. Hertz, *Pentateuch and Haftorahs*, 5 (1936), 100–11; E. Munk, *The World of Prayer*, 1 (1954), 88–119; L.J. Liebreich, in: REJ, 125 (1966), 151–65; Yadin, in: *Ereẓ Yisrael Meḥkarim bi-Ydi'at ha-Areẓ va-Attikoteha*, 9 (1969), 60–83.

[Louis Jacobs]

SHEMAIAH (Heb. שְׁמַעְיָהוּ, שְׁמַעְיָה), a prophet in the days of Solomon's son, Rehoboam king of Judah (I Kings 12:22–24 and the parallel passage in II Chron. 11:2–4; 12:5–8, 15). Shemaiah is associated with two events, one at the beginning of, the other during Rehoboam's reign. In I Kings and in the parallel account in II Chronicles it is related that Shemaiah cautioned Rehoboam not to embark on a war against the tribes of Israel that had rebelled against his authority, and warned him that "this thing is from Me [i.e., God]" (I Kings 12:24; II Chron. 11:4). According to II Chronicles 12:5–8, Shemaiah rebuked Rehoboam and his princes, and blamed them for the invasion of Judah by *Shishak king of Egypt. After Rehoboam and his princes had humbled themselves before the Lord "the word of the Lord came to Shemaiah: 'They have humbled themselves; I will not destroy them, but I will grant them some deliverance, and My wrath shall not be poured out upon Jerusalem by the hand of Shishak'" (II Chron. 12:7). The Chronicler attributes to Shemaiah "the Chronicles of Shemaiah the Prophet and of Iddo the Seer" (*ibid.*, verse 15), which probably means simply the part of the Book of Kings referring to Shemaiah's generation.

BIBLIOGRAPHY: J.A. Montgomery, *Kings* (ICC, 1951), 251.

[Nili Schupak]

SHEMAIAH (late first century B.C.E.), the colleague of *Avtalyon (see *Zugot*). In talmudic sources they are usually mentioned together. They are described as having taught in the same *bet midrash* (Yoma 35b), cooperating in an exemplary fashion. Like Avtalyon, Shemaiah was said to have been a convert to Judaism, descended from Sennacherib (Git. 57b; cf. TJ, Mak. 3:1, 81d). Those who identify Avtalyon with Pollio mentioned by Josephus, identify Shemaiah with Samaias, as one of the Pharisee leaders in the time of Herod. Shemaiah's dictum (Avot 1:10), "Love work, hate lordship, and seek no intimacy with the ruling power," probably reflects his attitude to the government of his time, and accords with Josephus' statement about Pollio (see *Avtalyon). Shemaiah and Avtalyon administered the *soṭah* rite, presumably within the framework of the Temple ritual (Eduyot 5:6). In an early discussion of faith and belief in rabbinic literature, Avtalyon expresses the view "that the faith in God of the children of Israel in Egypt sufficed for the Red Sea to be divided for them," while Shemaiah holds that this merit stemmed from Abraham's faith in God (Mekh. 2, 3). The late report that Shemaiah and Avtalyon were *darshanim gedolim* (masters of homiletical exposition) would seem to be anachronistic (Friedman, *Netiot le-David*, 234).

BIBLIOGRAPHY: A. Buechler, *Das Synhedrion in Jerusalem*, 178–81 (1902); S. Zeitlin, in: *Journal of Jewish Lore and Philosophy*, 1 (1919), 63–67; Klausner, Bayit Sheni, 3 (1950^2), 228f., 253–5; E.E. Urbach, in: *Tarbiz*, 27 (1957/58), 175. **ADD. BIBLIOGRAPHY:** S. Friedman, in: *Netiot le-David, Festschrift in Honor of David Weiss Halivni* (2004).

[Bialik Myron Lerner / Stephen G. Wald (2nd ed.)]

SHEMAIAH OF TROYES (11th century), French scholar. Shemaiah was one of *Rashi's closest pupils and appears to have been the father-in-law of Rashi's grandson, *Samuel b. Meir. Shemaiah helped Rashi edit his responsa and afterward collected and assembled them from the notes of his master. He also wrote up for him some of his halakhic decisions. He also assisted Rashi in editing his commentaries to the Talmud and in particular his commentary to the Bible, which Rashi read with him, correcting as he went along. Traces of Shemaiah's activities are detectable in Rashi's works. Occasionally short additions and notes made by Rashi orally have been added with Shemaiah's signature. Very often the additions have been merged with the text and are identifiable as additions only by comparison with manuscripts. Shemaiah himself, under the direction of Rashi, wrote commentaries to a number of tractates, but only those to *Middot* and *Tamid* have been preserved in two versions, one of which appears in all large editions of the Talmud since the Venice edition of 1522, and another in a work published by A. Berliner from a manuscript (in *Sefer Rashi*, see bibl.). Numerous *rishonim*, however, quote from his commentaries to many other tractates, and there are rulings of his which are known to have been handed to Rashi for his approval and signature. Shemaiah's *Seder Leil Pesaḥ* was published at the end of the *Dikdukei Soferim* to *Pesaḥim* (1874), and there remain in manuscript remnants of his commentaries on *piyyutim*. It is possible that this Shemaiah is identical with Shemaiah ha-Shoshanni, author of the Midrash to the weekly portion *Terumah*, who is known to have written commentaries to the *maḥzor*. Shemaiah served as the main source for knowledge of Rashi's teaching, and his collections were the basis of most of the extant anonymous books of the "school of Rashi," among them *Sefer ha-Pardes*, *Maḥzor Vitry*, *Siddur Rashi*, and others. The son of Shemaiah, Moses, was the editor of the halakhic work *Ha-Orah*, which contained much valuable material after the tradition of Rashi, and which was apparently the basis of the extant *Sefer ha-Orah* (1905).

BIBLIOGRAPHY: Epstein, in: MGWJ, 41 (1897), 257–63, 296–312; *Kitvei Abraham Epstein*, 1 (1950), 271–95; Berliner, in: MGWJ, 13 (1864), 224–31; idem, in: *Sefer Rashi* (1956), 141–8, 157–62; Poznański, in: *Perush al-Yeḥezkel u-Terei Asar le-Rabbi Eliezer mi-Belganẓi* (1913), xii–xiii (introd.); A. Aptowitzer, *Mavo le-Sefer Ravyah* (1938), 414–6; Urbach, Tosafot, index.

[Israel Moses Ta-Shma]

SHEMARIAH BEN ELHANAN (d. 1011), scholar in *Egypt. According to the legend of Abraham ibn Daud (G.D. Cohen (ed.), *The Book of Tradition* (1967), 64), Shemariah was one of *Four Captives who were taken prisoner in c. 970 while on a journey to collect contributions for the Babylonian academies, each of whom later established a school in a different country. Documents found in the Cairo **Genizah*, apparently originating from Babylon, state that he studied during the gaonate of *Sherira, with whom and with whose son and successor, *Hai Gaon, he corresponded, after he himself had become the head of the yeshivah at El Fostat. He was head of the local *bet din* and was famous as a preacher. He is referred to as "the *av bet din* of all Israel," possibly the title accorded the highest religious authority in the country. Shemariah wrote a commentary on the Song of Songs, which he dedicated to Judah b. Joseph Alluf of *Kairouan. He was in contact with the prominent rabbis of his day, such as Ḥushi'el of Kairouan and *Dunash ibn Labrat, in *Spain, who composed a laudatory poem in his honor. His son-in-law was *Sahlan b. Abraham, head of the Babylonian community at the beginning of the 11th century.

BIBLIOGRAPHY: Mann, Egypt, 1 (1920), 26–28, and index s.v.; Mann, Texts, 1 (1931), 86–89, 111 n. 5, 199–200 and index s.v.; S. Schechter, *Saadyana* (1903), 121–7; idem, in: JQR, 11 (1898/99), 643–50; Goitein, in: *Tarbiz*, 32 (1962/63), 266–72; Abramson, Merkazim, 156–73; idem, in: *Tarbiz*, 31 (1961/62), 195f.

[Eliyahu Ashtor]

SHEMARIAH BEN ELIJAH BEN JACOB (Ikriti; 1275–1355), philosopher and biblical commentator. Though probably born in Rome, he is known as Ikriti ("the Cretan") because, when he was still a child, his family moved to Crete, where his father had been called as a rabbi; he is also known as *ha-Yevani* ("the Greek"). Shemariah knew Greek, Italian, and Latin, and is noted for being the first medieval Jew to translate Greek literature directly from the original and not from Arabic or Hebrew translations, as had been done previously. Until the age of 30, the only Hebrew literature he knew was the Bible; only later did he study Talmud and philosophy. Invited to the court of Robert, king of Naples, he engaged in biblical studies and wrote philosophical commentaries (until 1328). His manner of interpretation satisfied even the Karaites, and, in the hope of reconciling them with the Rabbanites, he went to Spain in 1352. There, however, certain accusations were leveled against him, including the charge that he regarded himself as a messiah. He died in prison.

In *Ha-Mora* (1346), Shemariah attacked the opinions on creation of the philosophers; in his book *Amazyahu* he also attacked philosophy. Other works include *Elef ha-Magen* (a commentary on the tales and legends contained in the tractate *Megillah*, S.M. Schiller-Szenesy, Catalogue Cambridge Ms. 33/2), books on logic and grammar, biblical commentaries, and liturgical and secular poems, some of which were written in honor of David b. Joshua, a descendant of Maimonides.

BIBLIOGRAPHY: Geiger, in: *He-Ḥalutz*, 2 (1853), 25f., 158–60; idem, in: *Oẓar Neḥmad*, 2 (1857), 90–94; Zunz, Lit Poesie, 366f.; Steinschneider, *Uebersetzungen* 1 (1893), 499; Vogelstein-Rieger, 1 (1896), 446–50; Davidson, Oẓar, 4 (1933), 488; A.Z. Aescoly, *Ha-Tenu'ot ha-Meshiḥiyyot be-Yisrael*, 1 (1956), 220ff.; C. Roth, *Jews in the Renaissance* (1959), 71; Baer, Spain, 1 (1961), 359, 447.

[Zvi Avneri]

SHEMER, NAOMI (Saphir; 1930–2004), composer, song writer, and performer. Born at kevuẓat Kinneret, she studied at the Tel Aviv and Jerusalem Academies of Music. Among her teachers were Frank *Peleg, Ilona Vinze-Kraus, Joseph *Tal, and Abel *Ehrlich. She returned to kevuẓat Kinneret as a music teacher and there she composed her first songs especially for children. In 1956 she moved to Tel Aviv. Her songs, to most of which she composed both lyrics and music, became very popular and are considered as part of the Israeli song canon. In 1967, after being commissioned by the Israel Broadcasting Authority to write a song for the annual song festival, she wrote *Yerushalayim shel Zahav*, which immediately became popular. It became the theme song of the Six-Day War and achieved international fame. In many Reform movement services and among both Ashkenazi and Sephardi congregations in Israel and the Diaspora, the song was introduced into the liturgy for special occasions, such as Friday evening, the last *hakkafah* on Simhat *Torah, and the synagogue service on Israeli Independence Day. Considered to perfectly express the love of the nation for Jerusalem, the song was proposed in the Knesset as a new Israeli national anthem. By the mid-1980s there was not an Israeli singer or ensemble that had not performed one of Shemer's songs. Nicknamed the "national songwriter," she demonstrated a unique ability to express the national mood. Although her first works were published in the 1950s, her first book of songs, *Kol ha-Shirim* ("Complete Songs"), did not appear until 1967. Later publications included four additional song books (1975, 1982, 1995, 2003), as well as various collections for children. As a singer, she recorded a selection of her own songs. Her honors included the Israel Prize for Israeli song (1982), Jerusalem Prize (1983), and honorary doctorates from the universities of Jerusalem (1994) and Beersheba (1999).

BIBLIOGRAPHY: Grove Music Online.

[Gila Flam (2nd ed.)]

SHEMI (Schmidt), MENAHEM (1897–1951), Israeli painter. Shemi was born in Russia and immigrated to Palestine in 1913. In World War II, he served in the British army in Egypt, North Africa, and Italy. Shemi was one of the founders of the artists' colony in Safed (1949). Shemi was principally a landscapist. His palette, originally somber, became bright in his later years; his mystic, dreamlike canvases of Safed are considered his best works.

BIBLIOGRAPHY: M. Bassock (ed.), *Menaḥem Shemi* (Heb., 1958).

[Yona Fischer]

SHEMI, YEHI'EL (1922–2003), Israeli sculptor. Shemi was born to Esther and Moshe Stizberg, who immigrated to Ereẓ Israel in 1923 and settled in Haifa. Until the age of 13 Shemi was educated in a religious manner at home, as well as at the Neẓaḥ Israel school. After he was no longer observant, Shemi studied at the Reali High School and joined the Maḥanot ha-Olim youth organization. Shemi was an autodidact. All his artistic education was limited to a few painting classes under the instruction of Prof. Paul Konrad Hoenich of the Technion.

From 1939 on Shemi lived and worked in kibbutz Kabri. Through the art seminars that he organized in the kibbutz during the 1950s, he came in contact with many Israeli artists. He was one of the members of the New Horizons group, and his first steel sculptures were exhibited there. For a short while Shemi went abroad for a stay in the United States and in Paris. His meetings with world-famous sculptors influenced his own evolution. In 1986 Shemi was awarded the Israel Prize for art. Shemi's artistic style changed over time from figurative to abstract. The sculptures he created in the 1940s were carved in stone; some of them were lost when kibbutz Beit ha-Aravah was abandoned in May 1948. The works usually described human figures, usually monumentally and with rough texture (for example, *Father and Son*, 1954, kibbutz Ḥukkuk).

In the 1950s Shemi turned to working with iron. This transformation was not simply technical but also an open expression of a change in his point of view. The significance deriving from the change was Shemi's entrance into the modern world of sculpture. The impulse to work with additional techniques can be attributed to the modernist spirit in art that expressed swiftness, spontaneity, and an untraditional attitude. Soon afterward his technique changed and Shemi turned to the abstract, which is another modernist characteristic. His first large public assignment was created in this style, namely, the sculpture he erected for the Tenth Anniversary Exhibition in Jerusalem (1958, still standing in front of Binyanei ha-Ummah, Jerusalem). Later Shemi received many invitations from all over the country to create public sculptures, some of them as monuments.

Shemi worked with other types of materials, such as wood, torn iron, and concrete. One of his unique creations integrating art with architecture was his work at the Jerusalem Theater (1971). The geometric forms of the sculpture, as well as the bare concrete, were part of Shemi's art language. The huge size of this project and the fact that it was displayed as sculpture and not as a monument was significant for the artist.

BIBLIOGRAPHY: A. Baruch, *Yehiel Shemi: Secular Sculpture* (1988); M. Sgan-Cohen (ed.), *Yehiel Shemi* (1997).

[Ronit Steinberg (2nd ed.)]

SHEMONEH ESREH (Heb. שְׁמוֹנֶה עֶשְׂרֵה; lit. "eighteen"), popular name for the *Amidah prayer. The name stems from the fact that the weekday *Amidah* originally contained 18 benedictions (although today none of the various *Amidot* recited on different occasions consists of exactly 18 benedictions).

SHEM-TOV, VICTOR (1915–), Israeli politician, member of the Fifth, Sixth, Tenth, and Eleventh Knessets. Shem-Tov was born in the town of Samokov, Bulgaria. As a youth he was a member of the Maccabi ha-Ẓa'ir youth movement. He attended high school in Sofia, and in 1939, before immigrating to Palestine, joined the Socialist League. In 1946 he was elected, on behalf of Ha-Shomer ha-Ẓa'ir, to the Jerusalem Workers Council. In 1948–49 he was in charge of *Histadrut absorption programs during the years of mass immigration. In 1949–50 he served as chairman of the Bulgarian Immigrants' Association in Jerusalem, and as a member of *Mapam's Central Committee. He was elected to the Fifth Knesset in 1961, and represented Mapam in the Knesset Finance Committee. In 1961 he also became a member of the Histadrut Executive. In 1969, even though he was not elected to the Seventh Knesset, Shem-Tov became the first Mapam minister that was not a kibbutz member, being appointed as minister without portfolio in the government formed by Golda *Meir after the elections. In July 1970, after the *Likud left the coalition, he was appointed minister of health, in which position he introduced a National Health Insurance Bill that failed to pass. He continued to serve as minister of health in the Eighth Knesset, even though once again he was not an MK. In 1974, together with Minister of Transportation Aharon Yariv, Shem-Tov presented to Golda Meir's government a document containing what came to be known as the Yariv–Shem-Tov formula, that defined the Arab negotiating partners with whom Israel would be willing to negotiate a peace agreement. The document was published by Shem-Tov during a visit to Washington. It stated that the State of Israel would conduct peace negotiations with Jordan and with any Palestinian body that would recognize Israel's right to exist, would be willing to live in peace with it, and would refrain from committing acts of terror. The formula was once again presented in the government of Yitzhak *Rabin but was not brought to the vote, because it was supported by only five ministers. However, the formula was not rejected. In 1979–85 he served as secretary general of Mapam.

Shem-Tov was elected to the Tenth Knesset in 1981 and the Eleventh in 1984, and supported Mapam's decision to leave the Alignment with the *Israel Labor Party after Labor decided to enter a National Unity Government with the Likud.

[Susan Hattis Rolef (2nd ed.)]

SHENHAR (Shenberg), YITZHAK (1902–1957), Hebrew author. He was born in Voltshisk, a small town on the border of Galicia and the Ukraine. During World War I his family moved to Proskurov. An active member of the He-Ḥalutz movement, he started agricultural training before completing his studies. On his arrival in Ereẓ Israel in 1921 he joined the pioneers of the Third *Aliyah and worked as a building laborer, wagoner, railman, and farmer. From his youth he had written Hebrew poetry, and his literary activity, mainly in verse and drama, gained impetus on his arrival in Ereẓ Israel, where he published his first poem in 1924. Shenhar studied European literatures and languages for many years becoming well versed in some of them. From 1931 he devoted himself exclusively to literary activities, becoming a professional writer, a literary adviser to publishing firms, an editor, and a translator. As personal secretary to Salman *Schocken during the 1930s, he accompanied him on his travels in Europe and established connections with the Schocken Publishing House, which from the beginning of the mid-1940s published most of his books and translations. Shenhar worked for the United Jewish Appeal in South America in the early 1950s.

While Shenhar's creativity embraced a wide variety of works including fiction, poetry, plays, travel notes, and children's literature, his position in Hebrew literature and Israel cultural life was established mainly through his fiction and translations. Most of Shenhar's fictional writing comprises short stories and novelettes. It was only toward the end of his life that he ventured on a novel, which he did not complete. He was a master of the lyrical short story characterized by atmosphere and psychological nuances rather than by dramatic tension and plot development. Shenhar's works are within well-defined literary traditions, especially the late 19th-century tradition of the Russian psychological school, as exemplified by the short stories of Chekhov, and the Hebrew psychological novelette of the early 20th century. His style aspired toward an artistic balance and harmony, carefully striving for an equipoise between descriptions of social situations and landscape on the one hand and individual psychological portrayals on the other. He sought to give his subtle descriptions of atmosphere the firm base of a classic Hebrew style, drawing liberally on the ancient sources, especially the Mishnah and Midrash. Shenhar thus evolved a synthesis of style which is in the spirit of the Hebrew literature written by the followers of S.Y. Abramovitsh (Mendele Mokher Seforim). He may be described as a writer who tried to combine the descriptive "plastic" style of Mendele with the lyrical-psychological novella tradition of M.J. *Berdyczewski and U.N. *Gnessin.

Shenhar's stories may be classified according to their socio-historical background: stories about the Ukrainian small town and village against the backdrop of revolution and civil war (mainly in his first collection of stories, *Basar va-Dam*, 1941) to which also belongs the uncompleted novel published posthumously; stories about the tribulations of *ḥalutzim* and the trials of their acclimatization (mainly in *Me-Ereẓ el Ereẓ* 1943); stories on village and city life under the British mandate (in *Yamim Yedabberu*, 1945) and after Israel's independence. In the latter, Shenhar does not confine himself only to the mentality and problems of Russian Jewry and especially of the Russian-born *ḥalutzim* (as he did in his earlier collections). His canvas extends from the German immigrant to the Oriental Jew, and to different parts of the country, in an attempt to give a panoramic view of the multi-faceted new Jewish society. After the establishment of the State of Israel, Shenhar was among the first to turn to the new immigrants from Arab countries as a literary subject. He also wrote several biblical stories (*Me-Az u-mi-Kedem*, 1947) and symbolistic-surrealistic stories which have no socio-historical setting but are suspended in time and place.

Despite the variegated social background of Shenhar's stories he created one world, whose unifying element is a basic paradox: a world of frenzied and at times volatile activity and movement, revolutions, destruction, pioneering efforts and the struggle for national revival which is viewed through the eyes of the outsider who is alienated, passive, and static. The most typical characters of Shenhar's panorama are the pioneers whose fervor has cooled and who now live on the periphery of society. His anti-heroes, out of touch with their milieu, are in the literary trend of the "detached" or alienated heroes of M.J. Berdyczewski, Ḥ. J. *Brenner, U.N. Gnessin, G. *Schofman, and Y.D. *Berkowitz. Central to this trend is the theme of the young intellectual at odds with the traditional Jewish society of Eastern Europe which some of these writers (mainly Brenner) transposed to the ḥalutzic background of Ereẓ Israel. Shenhar's vivid, poignant and penetrating portrayal of the schism between the sensitive individual and the pioneering society makes him one of the main exponents of this trend. Nevertheless he departed from the traditional patterns: (1) his characters' alienation is not rooted in an exaggerated intellectualism (on the contrary, they are mostly non-intellectuals, some of whom are unable to express themselves articulately); (2) his stories are not mainly psychological portrayals of the heroes but fuse the psychological with broad social landscapes; (3) the rootlessness of most of his heroes is not as extreme as that of Gnessin's heroes. Though Shenhar's protagonists are incapable of identifying with the rhythm and intensity of the reality that surrounds them, their relation to it is not negative, even when they openly reject its coarseness and cruelty, or are skeptical about its blatant self-assurance. The hope for compromise or fusion is never absent from his stories. Thus Shenhar's works form one of the main links between the great fiction writers of the beginning of the century, such as Brenner and Gnessin, and some younger Israel-born writers, like S. Yizhar, who also describe the alienated, sensitive hero in the new pioneering society in a more optimistic vein than Brenner for instance.

Aside from his surrealistic writings and some biblical stories, few of Shenhar's narratives ring of despair; yet in most of his works there is a note of melancholy mingled with gentle irony. In this lies the very essence of Shenhar's importance as an Israel writer, i.e., his importance as an artist and intellectual simultaneously involved in the tempo and drive of Zionism yet sufficiently detached to see it objectively. Shenhar's work reflects all of Israel life from an original and individual point of view, throwing light not only on the successes in the revival of the Jewish nation in Israel but also on those who became its victims, on its weaknesses, and on the destruction that it sometimes wrought upon the beautiful, the noble, and the sensitive. While Shenhar always tended toward artistic descriptions, he helped to develop an independent consciousness among the intelligentsia of Ereẓ Israel and consequently to extend its capacity for self-criticism.

Shenhar was the foremost Hebrew translator of belletristic prose in his generation. He also translated poetry – Rilke, François Villon, and Chinese verse – but was most successful in his translations of great Russian literary works of the 19th century (Tolstoy's *Anna Karenina; Dead Souls* and other works by Gogol; works by N. Leskov and A. Chekhov, etc.). His translations were in the classic Hebrew style of his original writings which he used with skill, especially in those works that required linguistic virtuosity and an adherence to stylized archaisms. Shenhar was among those who set the principal norms for the translation of belletristic prose (he translated over 30 books). *Be-Shivah Derakhim* (1954) is a compilation of his travel notes; his collected stories were published posthumously (3 vols., 1960). His sister, Rivka Rochel-Shenhar, recorded her memories in *Beit Yiẓḥak Shenhar* (1986).

BIBLIOGRAPHY: A. Ukhmani, in: *Le-Ever ha-Adam* (1953), 176–83; Z. Luz, *Meẓi'ut ve-Adam ba-Sifrut ha-Ereẓ-Yisre'elit* (1970), 12–28; A. Lifschitz, in: *Me'assef Aggudat ha-Soferim*, 1 (1960), 497–506; D. Sadan, *Bein Din le-Ḥeshbon* (1963), 255–67; B. Kurzweil, *Bein Ḥazon le-Vein ha-Absurdi* (1966), 319–39; Y. Keshet, *Havdalot* (1962), 348–64; M. Gil, *Ketavim Nivḥarim* (1970), 174–86. **ADD. BIBLIOGRAPHY:** H. Weiss (ed.), *Yiẓḥak Shenhar, Mivḥar Ma'amrei Bikoret* (1976); R. Friedman, "*Mekomo u-Mashma'uto shel ha-Parodi be-Omanut ha-Sippur shel Y. Shenhar*," in: *Biẓaron*, 2:7–8 (1981), 16–24; G. Shaked, "*Ẓabarim, Olim, Pelitim, Al Yeẓirato shel Y. Shenhar*," in: *Meḥkarei Yerushalayim ba-Sifrut*, 3 (1983), 7–27; D. Nir, "*Tefisat ha-Midbar ba-Sifrut ha-Ivrit ha-Ḥadashah (Agnon, Shenhar ve-Yizhar)*," in: *Lashon ve-Ivrit*, 6 (1990), 15–20; A. Holtzman, "*Bein Shamayim ve-Areẓ*," in: *Sifrut ve-Ḥevrah ba-Tarbut ha-Ivrit ha-Ḥadashah* (2000), 228–42; N. Govrin, "*Galut be-Ereẓ Yisrael – Olei Germanyah bi-Yẓirato shel Y. Shenhar*," in: *Moznayim*, 78:5 (2004), 13–18.

[David Maisel]

SHENKAR, ARIE (1877–1959), pioneer of Ereẓ Israel industry. Born in Spitzinitz, Kiev district, Shenkar moved to Moscow in 1898, worked in a textile factory, and was active in the Russian Zionist movement. He was a member of the board of a Zionist group called Kadimah and was sent on its behalf to Berlin to purchase land in Ereẓ Israel through the *Hilfsverein der deutschen Juden. His house was a center of Zionist activity in Moscow, even during the early Soviet period. Shenkar went to Palestine in 1924 and bought the Lodzia textile factory, making it into a profitable enterprise. He devoted his efforts to the young local industry and was for many years the president of the Manufacturers' Association of Palestine. He interested foreign investors in Ereẓ Israel industry, founded the Palestine Industrial Bank, Ltd., and was its president. Shenkar also participated in many economic enterprises and contributed to educational institutions.

His estate was used to construct the first buildings for the physics and chemistry departments at Tel Aviv University, dormitories at the Hebrew University, Jerusalem, and for a scholarship fund. His house in Tel Aviv has been turned into the history museum of the city. The industrial center Kiryat Aryeh, which covers an area in Petaḥ Tikvah and Bene-Berak, is named in his honor, as is a vocational school for textiles in Ramat Gan. After his death, *Be-Emunah u-ve-Ma'as* (1963) was published, including his biography, his speeches, and his articles, as well as appreciations of him.

BIBLIOGRAPHY: D. Smilansky, *Im Benei Arẓi ve-Iri* (1958), 298–300; Tidhar, 2 (1947), 807–10; Hitaḥadut Ba'alei ha-Ta'asiyyah be-Yisrael, *Arie Shenkar, Ḥazono u-Fo'olo* (1959^2).

[Abraham Aharoni]

SHEPETOVKA, city in Khmelnitsky district, Ukraine. Its Jewish settlement was founded in the late 17th or early 18th century. In 1765 there were 317 Jewish poll-tax payers in the city. In the late 16th century it was a ḥasidic center, especially in the time of R. Pinhas of Koretz (1726–1791). In 1847, the Jewish population numbered 1,042, increasing to 3,880 (48.5% of the total population) in 1897. In 1926 the Jews numbered 3,916 (26.7%), and in 1939, 4,844 (20% of the total population). A Yiddish school with 300 pupils existed there. The Germans entered Shepetovka on July 5, 1941, and in July–August murdered 4,000 Jews from the town and its environs. In early 1942 a ghetto was established, and in fall 1942 it was liquidated and thousands of it inhabitants were murdered. In the late 1960s there was a Jewish population of about 2,500. Their last synagogue was closed down by the authorities in the early 1960s; most Jews left in the 1990s.

[Yehuda Slutsky / Shmuel Spector (2nd ed.)]

SHEPHATIAH BEN AMITTAI (d. 886 C.E.), *paytan* and spiritual leader. Shephatiah lived in Oria in southern Italy. When *Abu Aaron came to Italy in the mid-ninth century, he passed on to Shephatiah secrets of practical Kabbalah which the latter was to use in performing legendary deeds, as related in the *Chronicle of* *Ahimaaz. In about 856, when the Saracens attacked Oria, Shephatiah was sent to try and buy them off. About 873 Shephatiah traveled to Constantinople to plead for the annulment of anti-Jewish decrees issued by the Byzantine emperor Basil I. At the court he "delivered one of the princesses from the power of a demon" and as a reward Oria and four other communities are said to have been exempted from the edict. Of Shephatiah's many poems, only the *piyyut Yisrael Nosha* is known today. It is included in the *Ne'ilah* service on the Day of Atonement in the Ashkenazi liturgy.

BIBLIOGRAPHY: Roth, Dark Ages, index; Schirmann, in: YMḤSI, 1 (1933), 97–147.

[Yonah David]

SHEPHELAH (Heb. שְׁפֵלָה), biblical geographical term derived from *shfl* ("low"). The Shephelah is one of the component parts of the Promised Land, together with the mountain, the valley (Arabah), and the Negev (Deut. 1:7; Josh. 9:1; 12:8; and is so referred to in Jer. 17:26; 32:44; 33:13; Zech. 7:7). It refers to an area of hills and valleys, which separates the highlands from the coastal plain. In this sense, the Shephelah can only be regarded as a "lowland" from the point of view of those holding the higher parts of the country, i.e., the Israelites, as against the Canaanites of the plain or the Philistines. In particular, the term refers to the western fringe of the Judean mountains. In this region Joshua smote the Canaanite kings after the battle of Aijalon, defeating them from Jarmuth to Eglon (Josh. 10:40). Later, the tribe of Judah fought against the Canaanites in the Shephelah (Judg. 1:9). A still more precise definition is given in II Chronicles 28:18, which enumerates the cities of the Shephelah occupied by the Philistines in the time of Ahaz: they include Beth-Shemesh, Aijalon, Gederoth, Socoh, Timnah, and Gimzo. The struggle between the inhabitants of the Shephelah and the Philistines on the coast for possession of the region is reflected in Obadiah v. 19. The detailed description of the region in Joshua 15:33ff. reflects the division of Judah in the time of the divided monarchy, under Jehoshaphat or later, when the districts of Socoh, Lachish, and Mareshah (the second to the fourth districts) comprised the area of the Judean Shephelah.

The sycamore tree was characteristic of the region. Solomon made cedars as abundant in Jerusalem as sycamores were in the Shephelah (I Kings 10:27; I Chron. 1:15; 9:27). A special officer of the king was appointed to guard these trees (I Chron. 27:28).

The term is sometimes extended to other similar regions in the country. The Shephelah of Israel (Josh. 11:16) possibly refers to the hills and valleys bordering the mountains of Ephraim on the west. This definition, however, is somewhat artificial, for the western border of the mountains of Ephraim presents no such network of valleys and hills as is found in western Judah. The term appears as well in connection with the battle against Jabin, king of Hazor (Josh. 11:2); the location of this area between Kinneret and Dor suggests that here the term refers to the hilly region in southern Naphtali.

In the Hellenistic period, the area covered by the term Shephelah was extended westward, reaching from Bet Guvrin to Jaffa (I Macc. 12:38; Eusebius, Onom. 162:8). Talmudic sources (in particular Shev. 9:2; Tosef., Shev. 7:10; TJ, Shev. 9:2, 38d; Sif. Deut. 6) generalize the term and apply it to each of the three main districts of the country. In Galilee it refers to the area of Lower Galilee, below Kefar Ḥananyah, where sycamores grow; in Judea the Shephelah of Lydda is included in that of the south; in Transjordan it includes Heshbon, Dibon, Bamoth-Baal, and Beth-Maon. The area of the Judean Shephelah was resettled by Jews from 1882 onward and contains many agricultural settlements.

BIBLIOGRAPHY: Press, Ereẓ, 4 (1955), 918f.; G.A. Smith, *The Historical Geography of the Holy Land* (1931), 197ff.; Abel, Geog, 1 (1933), 416ff.; D. Baby, *The Geography of the Bible* (1957), 142ff.; Aharoni, Land, index.

[Michael Avi-Yonah]

SHER, SIR ANTHONY (1949–), actor, writer, and artist. Born in Cape Town, South Africa, Sher was educated at the Webber-Douglas Academy of Dramatic Art, London. He established his reputation on the London stage during the 1980s with a number of virtuoso performances. Unheroic in stature but with an intense, vivid personality, he brought enormous dynamism and panache to every part (rehearsals were always accompanied by body-training). His extensive repertoire ranged from appearances in Molière's *Tartuffe* and the most discussed *Richard III* since Laurence Olivier's, to *The Merchant of Venice* and *Singer* for the Royal Shakespeare Company. His roles for the National Theater have included Arturo Ui and Mark Gertler, while his playing of Arnold in *Torch Song Trilogy* was outstanding. He received the Olivier and Evening Standard Awards for best actor in 1985.

Apart from a consuming acting career, Sher was an accomplished artist who exhibited both at London's Barbican and the National Theater and a highly successful author whose novels *Middlepost* and *The Indoor Boy* both received highly enthusiastic reviews. One of the best-known contemporary British actors, Sher received many awards and three honorary degrees. He was knighted in 2000.

[Sally Whyte]

SHER, NEAL (1947–), U.S. lobbyist and government official. Sher joined the U.S. Department of Justice's *Office of Special Investigations (OSI) in 1979, becoming its director from 1983 to 1994. Established in 1979, OSI investigates, denaturalizes, and deports persons who took part in Nazi-sponsored acts of persecution, and excludes from entry into the United States any person listed on its "watch list" of suspected Nazi and Axis persecutors. Under Sher's directorship, 98 individuals who entered the United States under false pretenses by hiding their Nazi past were denaturalized, and many were deported.

Sher spearheaded several high-profile cases, including placing former Austrian president and United Nations Secretary General Kurt Waldheim on the "watch list," based on Waldheim's service in the Wehrmacht while in the Balkans and Greece as Jews were being deported and murdered there. Sher successfully prosecuted Arthur Rudolph, the former project director of NASA's Saturn V moon rocket program, who voluntarily left the country in 1984 when OSI proved he served from 1943 to 1945 as director of the Mittelwerk slave labor V-2 rocket factory. Sher also led the case against Karl Linnas, stripped of his citizenship in 1981 when OSI shed light on his past as commander of the Tartu concentration camp and his personal involvement in the killing of thousands of Jews.

One case under Sher's directorship was particularly controversial, that of John Demjanjuk, a retired Cleveland, Ohio, auto worker. In news attracting international attention, OSI accused Demjanjuk of being "Ivan the Terrible," a notorious Ukrainian guard at Treblinka. In 1982, Demjanjuk was stripped of American citizenship and deported to Israel and convicted of murder, though his conviction was overturned by the Israeli Supreme Court in 1993 for lack of evidence. A U.S. appeals court subsequently ruled that OSI had "acted with a reckless disregard for the truth." Demjanjuk was eventually stripped of his citizenship for his activities in several concentration camps.

From 1994 to 1996, Sher was executive director of the *American Israel Public Affairs Committee (AIPAC), the pro-Israel lobby based in Washington, D.C. He lobbied Congress to increase foreign aid to Israel, to pass anti-terrorism legislation, and to urge the move of the American embassy from Tel Aviv to Jerusalem. Following AIPAC, Sher consulted with the World Jewish Congress and joined a Washington, D.C.-based law firm.

In 1998, Sher became chief of staff of the International Commission on Holocaust Era Insurance Claims (ICHEIC), established to evaluate claims against several European insurance companies and to distribute proceeds from those claims to Holocaust survivors and victims' heirs. Sher's career at ICHEIC was cut short in 2002 when he admitted to improper use of agency funds and improprieties with respect to travel. Sher fully reimbursed ICHEIC but was subsequently disbarred from the D.C. bar. Ambassador Stuart Eizenstat, the senior government official who led efforts on Holocaust-era asset restitution in the Clinton administration, stated "I can only say it's a real tragedy ... and an exception to the decades of [Sher's] service to the country and to the Jewish community."

[Ralph Grunewald (2nd ed.)]

SHERF, ZE'EV (1906–1984). Israeli civil servant and politician, member of the Sixth and Seventh Knessets. Born in Izbor, Bukovina, which at the time was part of the Austro-Hungarian Empire, Sherf studied in *ḥadarim* and in a primary school, and later studied to be a goldsmith. In his youth he was active in Young *Po'aeli Zion and served as a member of its executive. He was also a member of the executive of the Social Democratic Youth in Romania. He settled in Palestine in 1925, and worked for three years as a clerk in the Fund of the Workers of Ereẓ Israel established by Po'alei Zion, which had joined the Histadrut in 1925. He joined kibbutz Shefayim of which he was a member for two years, and then spent five years on a mission abroad. In the years 1935–40 Sherf was secretary of the Histadrut sports association Hapoel, on behalf of Po'alei Zion. In 1940–44 he served in the administration of the *Haganah. In 1945 he was appointed secretary of the *Jewish Agency Political Department, serving in that capacity until 1947, under Moshe *Sharett. In 1948 he was appointed secretary of the Emergency Committee and the People's Administration, which directed the preparations for the establishment of the Jewish State and its civil service. As the final task of the People's Administration upon the termination of the British Mandate in Palestine, he drafted a proposal for the structure of the administration in the Jewish State – including the ministries and their budgets. Sherf served as the secretary of the Israeli government in 1948–57, and laid down the foundations for the government administration and the civil service. Later he became director of state revenues in the Ministry of Finance, and implemented a reform in the tax system. In the years 1961–63 he served as administrative director of the Weizmann Institute of Science, and in 1964–65 as advisor to Prime Minister Levi *Eshkol. In 1965 he was elected to the Sixth Knesset on behalf of Mapai on the Alignment list, and was appointed minister of commerce and industry, in which capacity he served until 1969. In 1968 he was also appointed minister of finance, after the resignation of Pinhas *Sapir. Sherf was reelected to the Seventh Knesset in 1969, and in the government formed by Golda *Meir after the elections was appointed minister of housing, in which capacity he served until 1974.

He wrote about the immediate days prior to the establishment of the State of Israel, *Sheloshah Yamim, 12–14.5.48*, and *ha-Shelavim ha-Aḥaronim be-Hakamat ha-Medinah* (1959).

[Susan Hattis Rolef (2nd ed.)]

SHERIFF, NOAM (1935–), composer, conductor. Born in Tel Aviv, he studied conducting and piano with Ze'ev Priel, horn with Horst Salomon, and composition (1949–57) with Paul *Ben-Haim. In 1955–59 he studied philosophy at the Hebrew University, Jerusalem. Sheriff pursued his musical training at a conducting course with Igor Markevitch in Salzburg (1955), and studied composition with Boris Blacher at the Berlin Musikhochschule (1959–62). He was music director of the Kibbutz Chamber Orchestra (1972–82), the Israel Symphony Orchestra Rishon le-Zion (1989–95), and the Israel Chamber Orchestra (2002–04) and, from 2004, the Haifa Symphony Orchestra. He taught at the Cologne Musikhochschule (1983–86), at the Rubin Academy of Music in Jerusalem (1986–89) and in Tel Aviv (1990–2000), and as the latter's director (1998–2000). He also served as music advisor to the Israel Festival (1985–88).

In 1957, on the occasion of the inauguration of the Mann Auditorium in Tel Aviv, his work *Festival Preludes* (*Akdamot le-Mo'ed*), which won the Sol Hurok prize, was performed by the Israel Philharmonic Orchestra conducted by Leonard *Bernstein.

Over the years Sheriff wrote many works which refer to specific national subjects and events. His music often displays linkage to various Jewish cultural sources and musical traditions. By fusing Eastern and Western, new and old (sometimes, ancient) musical elements in contexts rooted in the Jewish cultural heritage and openly based upon fundamental compositional models of Western music, Sheriff created a special musical idiom characterized by multiple historical sentimentality.

Sheriff's list of works includes *Israel Suite* for orchestra (1967); *Song of Songs* for flute and orchestra (1981); *Nocturnes*, Six Songs for voice and piano (1982); *Prayers* for string orchestra (1983); *La Folia Variations* for orchestra (1984); *Dodecalogue* (*Trei Assar*) for twelve celli (1984); *Meḥayyei ha-Metim* (*Revival of the Dead*), Symphony for tenor, baritone, boys' choir, men's choir and orchestra (1985); *A Vision of David* for orchestra (1986); *Violin Concerto* (*Dibrot*) (1986); *Cello Concerto* (1987/96); *A Sephardic Passion* for alto, tenor, mixed choir and orchestra (1992); *Scarlattiana*, Concerto for piano and orchestra (1994); *Psalms of Jerusalem* for tenor, bass, four mixed choirs and orchestra (1995); *String Quartet No.2* ("*Rosendorf*") (1996); *Akedah* (*The Sacrifice of Isaac*) for orchestra (1997); and *Bereshit* (*Genesis*) for soloists, children's choir and orchestra (1998).

Sheriff's awards include the first prize of the Israel Philharmonic Orchestra Conducting Competition (1959); the ACUM Prize for his life's work (1995); and the EMET Prize, sponsored by the AMN Foundation for the Advancement of Science, Art and Culture in Israel, under the auspices of the prime minister of Israel (2003).

[Yuval Shaked (2nd ed.)]

SHERIRA BEN ḤANINA GAON (c. 906–1006), *gaon* of Pumbedita from 968–1006. Sherira belonged to the family of the exilarchs, who claimed descent from David. His teachers were his father R. Ḥanina and his grandfather R. Judah, both of whom he mentions frequently in his responsa and who preceded him as *geonim* in Pumbedita. On the death of Nehemiah Gaon, who had been his opponent, Sherira was appointed to succeed him. This was a critical period for the two academies of Sura and Pumbedita. Financial contributions and the addressing of queries to the academies had practically ceased and the number of students was small. Sherira renewed the academy's ties with the communities, whose leadership he strongly rebuked for their indifference. Sherira's personality and fame as a scholar turned the tide for a while. Despite the great expansion of rabbinic learning in Kairouan in North Africa, in Spain, and in Franco-Germany, students came to Sherira from near and far. Although Sura declined, the leadership of Pumbedita not only regained its former prestige, but claimed supreme authority, and Sherira played a key role in making the Babylonian Talmud the supreme source of authority in the Jewish world.

Sherira was among the most prolific writers of responsa. One inquiry addressed to him by *Jacob b. Nissim b. Shahin in the name of the community of Kairouan led to the writing in 987 of his famous epistle, *Iggeret Rav Sherira Ga'on*, a classic of Jewish historiography. Jacob sought information as to when and how the Mishnah, the Tosefta, the *beraitot*, and the Talmud had been compiled. He inquired "whether the men of the Great Synagogue had really begun the writing of the Mishnah, and the Sages of each generation had written [more] parts of it until Rabbi [Judah] ha-Nasi came and compiled it." Sherira deals with the question in a scholarly manner, revealing himself a practical and accurate historian (with the possible reservation that his opinions on the exilarchs, descended from *Bustanai, from whom he claimed descent, may be colored). He discusses the activity of the *savoraim* in revising and compiling the Talmud, and continues the sequence of tradition to the geonic authorities. Under Sherirah and his son *Hai, the volume of geonic correspondence swelled to unprecedented proportions. Nearly half of the geonic responsa are attributed to them. Through their writings (in large part composed jointly), they greatly influenced the exegetical and judicial work of later ages. They frequently formulate rules which are of the highest importance for the interpretation of the Talmud. The majority of the responsa deal with questions of religious practice but some contain expositions and comments on passages of the Talmud and the Mishnah. Passages from a Bible commentary by Sherira are quoted by Jonah *Ibn Janaḥ and David *Kimḥi. It is unknown whether these encompassed all the books of the Bible. In addition to a glossary on the first and last orders of the Mishnah, Sherira wrote a commentary on several talmudic tractates, including *Berakhot, Shabbat*, and *Bava Batra*. Only a fragment of the last, apparently written in 972, has come to light (in: *Ginzei Kedem*, 5 (1934), 17–23). Sherira was less interested than his son Hai in Arabic literature, though he wrote in Arabic to communities in Muslim countries. Generally, he preferred to use Hebrew or Aramaic. In his decisions Sherira endeavored to decide in strict conformity with the law.

Sherira, who was interested in Kabbalah, believed that the mystical works *Shi'ur Komah* and *Heikhalot* contained ancient traditions, and that the anthropomorphic elements of the former work were to be interpreted symbolically as representations of profound mysteries. He seems to have explained the *aggadah*, however, in a non-mystical manner. Sherira wrote a work, *Megillat Setarim*, which apparently discusses the importance of the *aggadah*, but that part of the work is not extant. Two years before his death, Sherira appointed his son Hai as *Gaon*. He died at the age of 100 (*Sefer ha-Kabbalah* by Abraham Ibn Daud), and on the Sabbath following his death, a special scriptural passage, "Let the Lord, the God of the spirits of all flesh, appoint a man over the congregation" (Num. 27:16) was read, and in the prophetic reading (1 Kings 2:1–12) the last verse was changed to: "and Hai sat on the seat of Sherira, his father, and his kingdom was established greatly."

BIBLIOGRAPHY: A. Harkavy (ed.), *Teshuvot ha-Ge'onim* (1887), 188, no. 373; J. Mueller, *Mafte'aḥ li-Teshuvot ha-Ge'onim* (1891), 178–201; Mann, Texts, 1 (1931), 109 n.2; Baron, Social2, 6 (1958), 340–1, no. 46; H. Tykoczynski, *Takkanot ha-Ge'onim* (1959), passim; M. Havazelet, *Ha-Rambam ve-ha-Ge'onim* (1967), passim; Abramson, *Merkazim*, 46–57.

[Meir Havazelet]

SHERMAN, ALEXANDER ("**Allie**"; 1923–), U.S. football player and coach, twice named NFL Coach of the Year. Sherman began his career at his hometown school of Brooklyn

College playing quarterback, where he was named team captain in 1941. After graduating in 1943, Sherman was drafted by the Philadelphia Eagles, though in his first season they were the "Steagles" (Steelers + Eagles). Sherman retired from the NFL in 1947, having appeared in 51 games as a reserve quarterback. In 1949, he was named backfield coach for the Giants and was on their staff throughout the 1950s except for 1953–56, when he served as head coach in the Canadian Football League. Sherman was named head coach of the Giants in 1961 and responded by leading the 1961 Giants, who were bolstered by the addition of future Hall of Fame quarterback Y.A. Tittle, to a 10–3-1 record and a first place finish in the Eastern League. In recognition of the turn-around, Sherman was voted NFL Coach of the Year. For the 1962 season, Sherman was given an added gun with the return of receiver Frank Gifford to the lineup. Sherman, now working with three future Hall of Famers – Tittle, Gifford, and veteran linebacker Sam Huff – guided the Giants to a 12–2 record and another first place finish in the Eastern League. Again, Sherman was named NFL Coach of the Year, the first time a coach had won in two consecutive years. The Giants had another banner season in 1963, finishing atop the Eastern League for a third straight time with an 11–3 record. Giant's management rewarded Sherman with a 10-year contract. However, trades, retirements, and injuries took their toll, as the Giants would go 24–43–3 over the next five seasons, and Sherman was released. He would make one more appearance as a head coach, leading the North to a 27–16 victory over the South in the 1969 collegiate Senior Bowl. In later years, Sherman worked as an executive for Time-Warner, and, by appointment of Mayor Rudolph Giuliani, served for two years as the president of the New York City OTB Corporation.

[Robert B. Klein (2nd ed.)]

SHERMAN, ALLAN (1924–1973), U.S. singer, television producer, and writer. Born Allan Copelon in Chicago, Illinois, his parents were divorced when he was six. He never saw his father again, and in time took his mother's maiden name. His grandfather took him to see Yiddish plays, which inspired his love for theater. After he graduated high school, Sherman enrolled in the University of Illinois, where he wrote "The Compus Scout," a humor and gossip column for the school's daily newspaper. He enlisted in the army in December 1942 but was discharged five months later due to asthma. Sherman moved to New York and secured a job in May 1945 writing gags for radio comedian Lew Parker. He wrote jokes for *Cavalcade of Stars* and *The 54th Street Revue*, but his big break came with his co-creation of the game show *I've Got a Secret* (1952–67). The executive producers fired Sherman in 1958, saying that his focus was on too many outside projects. He continued to produce other programs until 1960, when he developed the game show *Your Surprise Package* for CBS and moved to Hollywood. While the program was canceled in 1962, Sherman's parodies had caught the attention of Hollywood's comedy luminaries. Using his connections, Sherman put out his first album on Warner Bros. Records, *My Son, The Folk Singer* (1962), which was followed by *My Son, the Celebrity* (1962), both of which were eventually certified gold. Even President Kennedy could be heard singing Sherman's songs. In 1963, Sherman released *My Son, the Nut*, which included the hit single *Hello Muddah, Hello Faddah*, a summer camp parody sung to Ponchielli's *Dance of the Hours*. Two weeks after the single's release, he served as guest host of *The Tonight Show* for one week, introducing Bill Cosby in his first television appearance. In 1965, he released his autobiography *A Gift of Laughter*, but a failed television special and disappointing sales from five subsequent albums led Warner Bros. to drop Sherman in 1966. Sherman continued working on projects, including providing the voice of Dr. Seuss' Cat in the Hat in *The Cat in the Hat* (1971) and *Dr. Seuss on the Loose* (1973), before his death from emphysema.

BIBLIOGRAPHY: "Sherman, Allan, in: *Dictionary of American Biography*, Supplement 9 (1994); "Sherman, Allan," in: Contemporary Authors Online (Gale, 2002).

[Adam Wills (2nd ed.)]

SHERMAN, ARCHIE (1911–), British property developer and philanthropist. Sherman was born and educated in Cardiff, S. Wales. In 1939 he moved to London, where he earned a reputation as an expert on shop properties and, after a successful career in real-estate, was invited to join the City Centre Public Property Company as a co-director with Charles Clore and Jack Cotton.

His overriding interest, however, was in supporting worthy causes, and though his Charity Foundation promoted the advancement of medical science at four of Britain's leading teaching hospitals (Guy's, St. Mary's, Barths, and Stoke Manderville) as well as a number of Jewish and general domestic charities.

He took up residence in Tel Aviv and eventually became a citizen of Israel. Over the years, he sponsored some 40 major projects across the expanse of Israel, from hospitals and homes for immigrants, sports centers and schools, university faculties and centers of Torah learning to day centers and kindergartens, several synagogues and *mikva'ot.*

He is only philanthropist to be accorded the distinction of a "double-first", as the First Worthy (*Neeman*) of Jerusalem and the First *Neeman* of Tel Aviv-Jaffa for his contributions to the upbuilding of Israel.

[Morris Unterman]

SHERMAN, JASON (1962–), Canadian playwright. Sherman was born in Montreal, raised in Toronto, and graduated from York University's Creative Writing Program in 1985. He successfully forged a mainstream playwriting career despite his recurring Judaic themes. Many of Sherman's characters wrestle with their Jewish identity, often rejecting religious faith in the face of contemporary society and politics. His plays also ask tough questions about world-changing events like the Holocaust and the Arab-Israeli conflict. The Winnipeg Jewish Theatre commissioned Sherman to write *None Is Too Many*

(1997), a docudrama adaptation of the socio/political text of the same name written by professors Irving Abella and Harold Troper. This text explores the racist Canadian immigration policies set for Jewish refugees before, during, and after World War II. Sherman's latest play *Remnants (A Fable)* (2003) once again takes up this shameful history, but this time he frames it within the biblical story of Joseph, son of Jacob.

Sherman also turned his critical attention to Zionism and its place in Jewish Canadian identities. In *League of Nathans* (1992), a trio of childhood friends endures a contentious reunion. Nathan Abramowitz, the play's protagonist, is confused about his Jewish Canadian heritage while Nathan Glass sees it as his duty to settle in Israel and make the land able to sustain a Jewish presence. In *Reading Hebron* (1996), the same Nathan Abramowitz questions his role in the oppression of Palestinians.

Sherman worked with professional companies across Canada and his plays have been produced at the Vancouver Playhouse, Toronto's Tarragon Theatre, and the National Arts Centre in Ottawa. He is an accomplished journalist with articles and essays appearing in *The Globe and Mail*, *Canadian Theatre Review* and *What*, a literary magazine he co-founded and edited between 1985 and 1990.

Sherman received the Governor General's Award in 1995 for *Three in the Back, Two in the Head*, was nominated for two others, and received the Chalmers Canadian Play Award for *League of Nathans* in 1993. Sherman's fluid dramaturgical structure, his high theatricality, and his ability to handle serious material with humor make him a driving force in Canadian theatre.

[Amanda Lockitch (2nd ed.)]

SHERRY, LAWRENCE (**Larry**; 1935–) and **NORMAN BURT** (**Norm**; 1931–), U.S. baseball-playing brothers. A native of Los Angeles, Larry Sherry was born with club feet and underwent operations at the age of six months to correct the deformity, having to wear braces to walk properly until the age of 12. At Fairfax High School, he was converted from an infielder to a pitcher because of his lack of speed. A right-handed pitcher, Larry Sherry made his Major League debut on April 17, 1958, and played for the Los Angeles Dodgers (1958–63), Detroit Tigers (1964–67), Houston Astros (1967), and California Angels (1968). In his 1959 rookie season, Sherry was called up on July 4 and went 7–2 with a 2.19 ERA as a started and reliever – including an almost unbelievable 0.74 ERA in 36.1 innings of relief pitching – to help lead the Los Angeles Dodgers to the World Series. He won the first game of the NL playoff against the Milwaukee Braves, yielding four hits and striking out four in 7.2 innings. In the World Series against the Chicago White Sox, Sherry relieved in all four Dodger wins, recording saves in Games 2 and 3 and wins in Games 4 and 6, while allowing only one run, eight hits, and a 0.71 ERA in 12.2 innings. He was named the World Series MVP, the first relief pitcher ever to win it. The rest of Sherry's career was anticlimactic, though in 1960 he went 14–10 with a 3.79 ERA, and led the NL with 13 relief wins, and in 1966 he registered a career high 20 saves (3rd in the league) for the Tigers. He was released on July 7, 1968, by the Angels with a career record of 53–44, a 3.67 ERA, and 82 saves. He is 6th on the all-time ERA list for Jewish pitchers, 7th in strikeouts, 8th in wins, and 4th in games. Sherry returned to the majors as a pitching coach with the Pittsburgh Pirates in 1977–78 and the California Angels in 1979–80.

Norm, Larry's older brother, was born in New York. A catcher, he made his debut on April 12, 1959, and played for the Los Angeles Dodgers (1959–62) and the New York Mets (1963). In 194 games, he batted .215 with 45 runs and 69 RBIs. Sherry managed the California Angels from July 23, 1976, to July 11, 1977. He is credited with helping Koufax's struggling career by advising him during spring training in 1961 to "just try to throw easier, throw more changeups, just get the ball over." On May 7, 1960, August 30, 1961, and June 28, 1962, Larry and Norm were battery mates, the 13th and last brother battery in MLB history, and the only Jewish brother battery in history. Norm's homer in the 11th inning won the 1960 game for Larry.

[Elli Wohlgelernter (2nd ed.)]

SHESHBAZZAR (Heb. שֵׁשְׁבַּצַּר, שֶׁשְׁבַּצַּר), the prince (*nasi*) of Judah at the beginning of the return to Zion of the Babylonian Exile (538 B.C.E.). According to the Book of Ezra (1:8–11), King Cyrus of Persia delivered the Temple vessels, taken by Nebuchadnezzar from Jerusalem, to Sheshbazzar, the prince of the Jews, who brought them to Jerusalem during the return from Babylon. This is also mentioned in Ezra 5:14, where Sheshbazzar is called governor. Opinions differ on the origin, rank, and role of Sheshbazzar during the return to Zion. Some assumed him to have been a gentile, Persian or Babylonian, governor in the service of the king of Persia; others thought that he was a Jewish officer, not from the House of David, who was appointed over Judah for a short while at the beginning of the return to Zion; and some even held that his role in connection with the return to Zion was to restore the Temple vessels to Jerusalem. However, the title "prince" by which the prophet Ezekiel designates the Davidic ruler (Ezek. 37:25), supports the supposition that Sheshbazzar was the leader of the people of Davidic origin, and was appointed ruler of Judah by the king of Persia. There were also those who attempted to identify Sheshbazzar with *Zerubbabel on the assumption that this was Zerubbabel's Babylonian name. This hypothesis is, however, unlikely if only because both Sheshbazzar and Zerubbabel are Babylonian names. Many scholars have accepted the more probable view, which identifies Sheshbazzar with Shenazzar, son of Jehoiachin, the uncle of Zerubbabel, who is mentioned in I Chronicles 3:18. An examination of the Septuagint transliterations of these two names supports the view of W.F. Albright that both revert to a basic form, Sin-ab-uṣur, a name common in the cuneiform documents of this era and found in an Aramaic document in the form of Shenabazar. If Sheshbazzar is Shenazzar, the uncle of Zerubbabel, then he quite naturally stood at the head of the returnees, and since he was born close to the time of the exile of Jehoiachin (c. 595 B.C.E.; see *Jehoiachin), he would have been about 60 years old at the time of the return to Zion, and apparently did not live long. Because he apparently stood at the head of the returnees for only a short time, the image of Zerubbabel overshadowed him in the narratives of subsequent generations, and thus Sheshbazzar is mentioned in the Book of Ezra only in connection with the return of the Temple vessels.

BIBLIOGRAPHY: E. Meyer, *Die Entstehung des Judenthums* (1896), 75ff.; S. Jampel, in: MGWJ, 46 (1902), 318ff.; J.W. Rothstein, *Die Genealogie des Koenigs Jojachin* (1902), 25ff.; W.F. Albright, in: JBL, 40 (1921), 108ff.; J. Gabriel, *Zorobabel* (1927), 48ff.; Alt, Kl Schr, 2 (1953), 333–4; Klausner, Bayit Sheni, 1 (1951), 150–3; J. Liver, *Toledot Beit David* (1959), 9–11, 79–87.

[Jacob Liver]

SHESHET (late third century and the first half of the fourth century C.E.), Babylonian *amora*. Sheshet's main teacher is not definitely known. He attended *Huna's lectures (Yev. 64b; Ket. 69a) and quotes statements in the name of *Jeremiah b. Abba (Eruv. 12a) and *Rav (Yev. 24b). He taught in Nehardea (Meg. 29a) and Maḥoza (Ned. 78a), and later founded an academy at Shilḥe on the Tigris (Letter of Sherira Gaon, ed. by B.M. Lewin (1921), 82). His most constant colleagues were *Naḥman b. Jacob and *Ḥisda. Sheshet suffered from both physical frailty (Pes. 108a) and blindness (Ber. 58a). However, although requiring the aid of a reader (Sanh. 86a), he overcame these difficulties by his great determination (Men. 95b) and an extremely retentive memory (Shev. 41b). It is recorded that Ḥisda's lips trembled in admiration when he saw the ease with which Sheshet quoted *beraitot* (Eruv. 67a).

The distinctive feature of his teaching was his insistence on the authority of precedent. He usually justified a decision by saying, "We have learnt it in the Mishnah or in a *baraita*" (BM 90a; Yoma 48b; Yev. 11b). His favorite question to his pupils was, "What is my source for this?" and his answer would be "For we have learned it in a *baraita*" (Kid. 68a; compare Yev. 35a, 58a; Shab. 123b). He was a keen scholar (Ber. 8a) and used to recapitulate his studies every 30 days (Pes. 68b). It was once said of him, "It is good when one possesses a keen understanding in addition to the inheritance of tradition" (Bek. 52b and Rashi ad loc., see Eccles. 7:11). He was, however, averse to the casuistry of Pumbedita. He once answered one of Amram's quibbling objections with the remark, "Are you not from Pumbedita, where they draw an elephant through the eye of a needle?" (BM 38b). *Naḥman testified that Sheshet taught *halakhot*, **Sifra*, **Sifrei*, *Tosefta, and all of the Talmud (Shevu. 41b). Sheshet himself admitted, however, that in matters of *aggadah*, "I cannot dispute with Huna" (Suk. 52b and Rashi ad loc.). He explained Proverbs 3:16, "Length of days is in her right hand, and in her left hand riches and honor," to mean that whoever studies the Torah with due respect receives as his reward length of days as well as riches and honor. He who does not do so, receives riches and honor, but is denied length of days (Shab. 63a). He was also the author of the maxim, "A borrower is the slave of the lender" (Git. 14a).

The Talmud illustrates his piety by recording that he never took more than four paces without wearing his *tefillin* (Shab. 118b and Rashi ad loc.). It is also related that a sectarian once taunted Sheshet that because of his blindness, he would not be able to know when the king, whom a large crowd was waiting to see, would pass by. Despite the efforts of the sectarian to mislead him, Sheshet nevertheless managed to identify the exact moment of the king's passage. In reply to the enquiry as to how he knew, he replied, "The earthly kingdom is like unto the heavenly, and (in I Kings 19:12–13) God's appearance is announced by a deep silence" (Ber. 58a).

BIBLIOGRAPHY: Bacher, Bab Amor; Hyman, Toledot, 1231–35; Ḥ. Albeck, *Mavo la-Talmudim* (1969), 312–4.

SHESTAPOL, WOLF ("**Velvele Khersoner**"; c. 1832–1872), *ḥazzan*. Shestapol was born in Odessa and as a youth sang with his father Samuel and with Bezalel *Shulsinger (Odesser). After his appointment as *ḥazzan* in Kherson he studied for some time with Solomon *Sulzer in Vienna. Shestapol derived his inspiration from those aspects of European art music which had become accessible to him in Odessa and Vienna. In his case, the dependence on Italian and French opera was extremely pronounced. His compositions, of a soft and lyrical character, became very popular and some of them were taken over into the Yiddish theater by *Goldfaden and others. They include *Omnam Ken, Musaf-Kaddish* for the Penitential holidays, *Ve-al ha-Medinot*, and *Adonai Zekharanu*.

BIBLIOGRAPHY: Idelsohn, Music, 308–9; Hyman H. Harris, *Toledot ha-Neginah ve-ba-Ḥazzanut be-Yisrael* (1950), 419–20; P. Minkowsky, in: *Reshumot*, 2 (1927), 129–30.

[Bathja Bayer]

SHESTOV, LEV (pseud. of **Lev Issakovich Schwarzmann**; 1866–1938), religious philosopher and man of letters, born in Kiev. His father was a wealthy textile manufacturer, and Shestov absorbed an interest in Yiddish and Hebrew literature. Much of his later work is at least congruent with his ḥasidic roots. He is known for his elegant and witty, aphoristic style, the range of his erudition and interests, and the trenchancy of his critique of rational speculation and systematic philosophy as modes of truth. His most outstanding gift as a writer was his ability to characterize thought and style by conveying a sense of the human experience that produced it, and he called his essays "pilgrimages through souls." Although he left no direct disciples, Albert Camus, Nicholas Berdayev, and D.H. Lawrence, among others, testified to his impact. He was close to, and appreciative of, even the philosophers whose efforts at system he set himself most strongly to oppose – Edmund Husserl and Karl Jaspers. His essays on Chekhov, Ibsen, Dostoevsky, and Tolstoy are famous.

Like the Ḥasidim, Shestov cultivated a respect for mystery and paradox that survived the most intensive rationalist training. He cared too much for inwardness, for inner experience as an access to salvation, to rest within what was orthodox in Judaism. At the same time he was too dismayed with the Logos of the Fourth Gospel, too smitten with love for the Old Testament God, with all his arbitrary caprice, to have other than short shrift for conventional or churchly Christianity. Yet Shestov was both a Jew and a Christian; and for him the fundamental antinomies were not between the Old and New Testament, or even between religion and atheism, but rather, as the titles of his last two books clearly state, between, *Speculation and Revelation*, and *Athens and Jerusalem* (1938). Well trained in logic and philosophy, Shestov was against rational speculation only insofar as he felt it attempted to limit human possibilities. He was against what he felt was Husserl's project of turning philosophy into a science, and believed that philosophy should concern itself primarily with questions that could not be answered by reason, but only by the "cries of Job" – i.e., by direct human experience. He believed that rational speculation ("Athens") had infected religion as well as philosophy. Against Philo and St. Thomas, Shestov cited Tertullian, who believed it was absurd; Luther, who grasped that the essence of action and therefore of "good works" was limitation, hence mediocrity, and that salvation could come by faith alone; and those biblical heroes of faith, Abraham and Job.

Trained as a lawyer at Kiev University, Shestov never practiced. Although early committed to radical politics, he never entertained illusions about the Bolshevik Revolution, and emigrated shortly after it occurred. In 1922 he became professor of Russian philosophy at the University of Paris.

BIBLIOGRAPHY: J. Suys, *Leo Sjestow's protest tegen de rede* (1931), incl. bibl.; B. Martin, in: CCARY, 77 (1967), 3–27; V.V. Zenkovsky, *A History of Russian Philosophy* (1953), 780–91; *Encyclopedia of Philosophy*, 7 (1967), 432–3; F.L. Vieira de Almeida, *La Tranchée de Chestov* (1926); B. Fondane, in: *Revue Philosophique*, 126 (1938), 13–50; B. de Schloezer, in: *Mercure de France*, 159 (1922), 82–115.

[Sidney Monas]

SHETAR (Heb. שְׁטָר), formal legal document, or deed, derived from the Akkadian *šatāru*, meaning writing.

Early Examples

The term *shetar* is not found in the Bible, where the term *sefer* is used to denote a legal document, such as *sefer keritut* in Deuteronomy 24:1 for bill of divorce, or *sefer ha-miknah* in Jeremiah 32:11 for bill of sale. In tannaitic literature the terms *iggeret*, *get*, and *shetar* are commonly used to designate various types of legal documents. Subsequently, the word *get* acquired a more limited meaning, restricted to a document expressing legal separation such as divorce or manumission of a slave. In geonic times, the term *ketav* was frequently used to designate a legal document. The only legal document whose execution is elaborately described in the Bible is the one referred to in Jeremiah, which seems to have been written in duplicate, and was subscribed to by witnesses. One copy was sealed; a second copy was left unsealed for ready access. The sealed document is the antecedent of the "tied deed" known as a *Doppelurkunde*. Such documents were in wide use in the Near East during the period of the First and Second Temples.

The earliest known and extant collection of legal documents of Jewish origin is one from the Jewish garrison in Yeb of the fifth century B.C.E., written in Aramaic, known as the *Elephantine Papyri. It is a collection of 33 complete legal documents of various kinds, including a *ketubbah*. They resemble the basic forms of Jewish documents as used in talmudic and post-talmudic times. In the Book of Tobit (probably composed in the second century B.C.E.) 5:3 there is a reference to a deed of deposit as well as to a marriage document. There is sufficient evidence to conclude that forms of legal documents were already standardized during the last two centuries of the Second Temple. Recently there have been discovered, among the *Dead Sea Scrolls, legal documents dating from the first century C.E., which conform to the standards referred to in tannaitic literature. It is noteworthy that despite the large number of references to legal documents in tannaitic and amoraic literature, no complete form of legal contract or bill of indebtedness is recorded in the Talmud. There are, however, references to individual clauses and expressions, and their legal effects. It is evident that formalities were strictly adhered to, and that formularies, i.e., prototype standard forms, were available to the scribes, who would either copy the forms or merely fill in the particular information (Git. 3:2). These formularies related to every area of human relationship. Professional scribes were generally employed, and during the period of the Second Temple bonds of indebtedness were deposited in special archives for safekeeping (Jos., Wars, 2:427).

From the geonic period there is preserved a collection of 28 formularies attributed to Hai Gaon, who died in 1038 C.E. (see bibl.). Many later collections are extant containing different types of forms, some including additional provisions to meet the demands of new exigencies. Asher Gulak edited a thesaurus of such formularies (*Oẓar ha-Shetarot*, 1926), containing 403 different forms, each representing a particular type of deed. Among these forms are private documents, such as family and commercial agreements, as well as judicial and communal *shetarot*.

One of the earliest forms of documents was the "tied deed," *get mekushar*, which is described in the Mishnah (BB 10:2) and Tosefta (BB 11:1). It was a formal legal document wherein the agreement was written on one side and the document was then folded. The parchment was cut at the top in strips which were tied together, and three witnesses then signed between the knots on the reverse side. Such documents have been found among the Dead Sea Scrolls. The Talmud relates that this type of document was instituted by the rabbis to make it more time-consuming and more difficult for priests, who might on impulse divorce their wives and are prohibited from remarrying even their former spouses (*Yad Ramah* to BB 160b; see *Divorce; *Marriage, Prohibited). In contradistinction to the *get mekushar* is the *get pashut*, ("plain deed"), which is not folded and tied and requires only two witnesses. This is the form in use today.

Format of the Shetar

Every *shetar*, as a formal document, requires the signatures of witnesses. It does not require the signature of the obligor. Credence is given, however, to documents either signed or written by the obligor, but unwitnessed, and which otherwise do not comply with the formalities of a *shetar*. Such a document is called *ketav yad* ("his own handwriting"; equivalent to a memorandum), and has the status of an oral understanding with all its legal consequences and without creating a lien on reality (Tur, 69; see *Lien; *Obligations, Law of). The *shetar* is somewhat different from modern western forms of contract which recite the facts of an agreement. The *shetar* records the testimony of the witnesses who state that on a given day the named obligors appeared before them and said such and such. For many centuries documents written in Israel and the countries of the Middle East and Africa would usually refer to the date according to the Seleucid calendar ("Era of the Documents"). Documents written in Europe usually referred to the year since creation ("Era of the Creation").

For the purpose of analysis, a *shetar* may be divided into two parts. The first part is the *tofes* (*typos*, "frame"), which is the general section of the instrument. A stereotyped copy may be used, not prepared specifically for the contract being undertaken. It contains the standard words of the preamble and the close of the document, as well as the words of obligation and additional clauses which protect the obligee in every conceivable way permitted. The *toref* contains the names of the parties, the date, the nature and amount of the obligation. During the centuries in which Jewish civil law governed the internal economic relations between Jews, there developed additional clauses and provisions, which were inserted into *shetarot* mainly for the protection of the obligee. These clauses include the following:

(1) A credence clause (*ne'emanut*) in which the obligor under the agreement asserts that he relieves the claimant of any oath which may be necessary, and that he considers the claimant's testimony that he has not been repaid sufficient to preclude the obligor from raising such a defense. The basis for this clause is to be found in *Shevu'ot* 42a. There are, of course, variants in the wording of such clauses which may strengthen the position of the claimant (Tur, ḤM 61).

(2) The right to collect from the best of the obligor's property (*shefer ereg nekhasin*). Though according to the Talmud a creditor can recover first from the average quality real estate of the debtor, and a woman for her **ketubbah* first from the least desirable land of her husband (see *Execution), this clause, which is found in the usual *ketubbah* and bill of indebtedness, improved the claimant's position, so as to recover from best quality realty.

(3) A clause allowing the claimant to recover costs of litigation (see *Execution).

(4) The obligor must sell his property to pay his obligation, rather than await a court sale (see *Execution).

(5) In some isolated cases there were even incorporated undertakings by the obligor of personal servitude or imprisonment in case of his default (see *Execution; *Imprisonment for Debt).

(6) A common clause allowing the claimant to render the document effective through the use of a non-Jewish court, and in some cases by personal force (see **Mishpat Ivri*). The end of the *shetar* usually included the statement that it was not a mere form but an actual document, and concluded with the words, *sharir ve-kayyam* ("firm and established"). Any provisions added after this phrase (other than corrections) are of no effect.

A legal instrument may not be written on a material which is susceptible to forgery. In the event of a correction, a mark must be made next to the corrected word or clause, and a reference to it must be added at the foot of the document, which must be witnessed (Tur, ḤM 42; see *Forgery).

To enforce a claim based on a *shetar*, the claimant must submit the document to a court of at least three persons to establish the authenticity of the witnesses' signatures. This may be accomplished either by the witnesses themselves identifying their own signatures, or by others testifying that they are familiar with the signatures of the witnesses, or by a handwriting analysis. Once the signatures are authenticated, the court appends a validation certificate, *henpek* (or *hanpek*) or *asharta*, which precludes any future challenge to the validity of the document. This proceeding before the court may take place without the obligor being present and even over his objection. Such certification is referred to in the Talmud (BM 7b) and appears among the Elephantine documents of the fifth century B.C.E.

The language of a document does not affect its validity. Indeed, in addition to Aramaic or Hebrew, legal instruments were written in Persian, Arabic, Latin, Greek, English, Spanish, and all other languages used by Jews. Bills of divorce, however, were subject to special rules.

Shetarot Written before Gentile Courts

The general rule, as stated in the Mishnah, is that all legal instruments written by non-Jewish courts and witnessed by non-Jews are valid, except for bills of divorce and manumissions of slaves (Git. 1:5). Although there existed differences of interpretation and application between various rabbinic authorities on this point, it was generally agreed that, where there was a basis for holding that the non-Jewish court was not totally corrupt, credence would be given to legal instruments such as contracts, deeds, and bills of indebtedness. A distinction is made between documents which evidence a business transaction, or at least state consideration, and which under the rule of **dina de-malkhuta dina* ("the law of the land is the law") required recognition, and deeds of gift which take on different legal incidents (Maim. Yad, Malveh ve-Loveh, 27:1). The medieval rabbis distinguished between deeds written in gentile courts and those written before notaries outside the court. Maimonides ruled the latter invalid, while Naḥmanides upheld their validity.

Types of Document

A review of the various types of documents assembled in Gulak's *Oẓar ha-Shetarot* is sufficient to indicate the wide scope of relationships covered by such documents. These may be divided into the following five categories:

(1) *Family Documents*: These include *betrothal agreements, *marriage contracts (see **ketubbah*), antenuptial agreements, releases between *husband and wife, *divorce documents, *ḥaliẓah* and *yibbum*, (see *Levirate Marriage), wills, deeds of trust (see **Shalish*; *Consecration and Endowment) and guardianship (see *Apotropos), and support contracts. It is evident that these documents cover the entire range of family relationships and evidence a sophisticated legal development. One of the more interesting documents is the *shetar shiddukhin* (see *Betrothal), a contract between two sets of parents in which both parties undertake to betroth their children to each other, and promise to contribute whatever dowry is involved. The difference between this and a *shetar erusin* ("contract of betrothal") is that the latter document deals with promises made to and by the prospective couple, while the *shetar shiddukhin* involves promises exchanged by their parents or guardians. The *get* ("divorce") contains specific formulas which are dealt with elsewhere (see *Divorce).

(2) *Business Documents*: These documents relate to economic relations between Jews and include bills of sale, gifts, leases, partnerships, *Iska* (see *Partnership), mortgages (see *Lien), bonds, receipts, *assignments, letters of *attorney, employment contracts (see *Labor Law), and escrow agreements. Each of these deeds had its own historical development. Thus, there exist many copies of partnership agreements in the Cairo *Genizah* which represent the frequent use of partnership, even on an international scale, during the period between the middle of the tenth to the middle of the 13th century.

(a) *Shetar Ḥov*, bond, bill of indebtedness. This is probably the most frequently used private legal document besides the *ketubbah*. In fact, when the term *shetar* is used without modification it refers to a *shetar ḥov*. It should be noted that a *shetar ḥov* may result from any type of credit or obligation transaction and need not be the result of a loan of money (see *Loans; *Obligations, Law of). A unique and important feature of the *shetar ḥov* (as well as of the *ketubbah*) is the fact that the *shetar ḥov* itself creates a lien on the debtor's real property, *aḥarayut nekhasim* or *shi'bud nekhasim*, which is an effective claim against that property even when it is sold to a third party. In other words, the *shetar ḥov* creates a mortgage on all the real property owned by the debtor on the date of the execution of the document. This provision was inserted into the *ketubbah* by Simeon b. Shetaḥ (Tosef., Ket. 12:1) in the first quarter of the second century B.C.E. The Talmud records a difference of opinion as to whether we do or do not imply the existence of such a lien when the phrase stating it is omitted. The final decision is that we attribute its omission to a scribal error, and assume the intention to create the lien. As a result of the creation of this lien, predated bonds are invalid because they prejudice the rights of other creditors, while postdated bonds are valid. During the geonic period the lien was extended by appropriate clauses in the document to movable property, and even to property to be acquired later than the time of the contract. The rabbinic courts, however, would not enforce the claim of a creditor against the movables sold by a defaulting debtor.

The Torah prohibits the taking of interest for a loan (Ex. 22:24; Lev. 25:36–38; Deut. 23:20–21), and indeed a document which states that interest is to be paid is invalid (see *Usury). The Elephantine documents do, however, contain penalty clauses which become operative if the debt is not repaid when due. Such a clause is prohibited by the majority of rabbinic opinion, but was widely used with approval in medieval England (during the 12th and 13th centuries), when a certain formal clause was included which stated that, on default of repayment, the loan was reloaned to the debtor via a gentile intermediary. This legal fiction permitted the acceptance of the interest. A *shetar ḥov* which does not state when the debt is due is repayable not earlier than 30 days from the date of the loan.

During the Second Temple period assignment of debts by the obligee was permitted. In fact the innovation of *prosbul was predicated on this assumption. In amoraic times, restrictions were placed on this right of assignment by permitting the assigner to forgive the debt after assignment (Kid. 48a). The Talmud also refers to bonds made out to the order of the holder. This type of document would be considered by modern standards as a bearer paper. The question as to whether or not an assignee could claim under such a document is left unresolved in the Talmud. In post-talmudic times, however, it was the custom to insert a phrase in the bond allowing the named creditor or his agent to claim on the bond. Subsequently, there developed a document which named no creditor, but merely evidenced indebtedness to holder *mukaz* (מוכ״ז; *moẓi ketav zeh*). In order to assign a debt from a named creditor to another, it was necessary to write a deed of transfer which, together with the original bond, had to be physically conveyed to the assignee. This procedure is called *ketivah u-mesirah* (see *Acquisition, Modes of). There is some question as to whether this would be effective as against the debtor. Another method employed was to write a letter of attorney, *harsha'ah*, which provided for the transfer of four ells of land together with the indebtedness. From the tenth century on these four ells were the ones theoretically owned by every Jew in Israel (see *Agency, Law of).

(b) *Shetar Iska*, a type of limited partnership agreement wherein the active partner borrows from a passive partner. Half the money is considered loan and half is investment in the business. This enables the active partner to pay a return to the passive partner, usually one third, without its being considered as usury. This type of agreement, which is referred to in the Talmud (BM 104b), was also called *shetar kis* and became very popular in the Middle Ages, when the Jews were very active in the moneylending business and would borrow additional loan capital from fellow Jews. Originally, the passive partner bore part of the risk of loss. Later amendments to the standard text of such a document included undertakings by the active partner which amounted to a guarantee to the passive partner against any loss (see Gulak, Oẓar, nos. 234 and 235). The *shetar iska* resembles the medieval Latin document known as *commenda* (see *Partnership; *Usury).

(c) *Suftaja* or *Diokne*, bills of exchange. This type of document was in use during the geonic period in the countries involved in the Mediterranean trade centering on Egypt. As a rule these documents were drawn on well-known banks in another city or country, which charged a fee for their issue. In this way they facilitated international trade and functioned very much like the modern bill of exchange or check. These documents did not conform to Jewish law, but were, nevertheless, enforceable in rabbinic courts, where the law merchant was applied to protect the businessmen who relied on these documents (A. Harkavy (ed.), *Zikhron Kammah Ge'onim* (1887), no. 232; see *Minhag*).

(d) *Mimram*, also *mimrane*, a note of indebtedness which was widely used among Jews in eastern Europe between the 16th and 19th centuries. The form of the document consisted of the signature of the debtor on one side of the note, and on the reverse side, exactly opposite the signature, a statement as to the amount owed, the terms of payment (date due), and sometimes the place of payment (*Siftei Kohen*, ḤM 48). The origin of the term is not clear. It is probably derived from the Latin, *membrana* ("parchment"). Some suggest that it is a derivative from the document of remembrance referred to in the responsa of *Asher b. Jehiel (Rosh, resp. no. 68:3) and corresponds to the Latin, *in memoriam*. The significant innovation of this document is the omission of the name of the creditor, which results in its being completely negotiable without any further requirements. The Jewish community councils of Poland passed special regulations protecting the holder of such notes, and implying, as a matter of law, waiver of defenses which the defendant may interpose. In fact, the *shetar mimram* does not conform to halakhic principle; nevertheless, it was granted rabbinic sanction as a result of its wide use (Baḥ Yeshanot, resp. no. 351). During the trade fairs in Poland there also developed the practice of having these notes signed in blank. Afterward the sum and terms of payment would be completed. This obviously involved the element of trust on the part of the purchaser (debtor) and a close relationship between the merchants. The use of *mimranot* was so widespread in 17th- and 18th-century Poland that a very substantial trade existed in the discounting and sale of such documents.

(3) *Court Documents*. Each stage of the rabbinic judicial process was recorded, and appropriate legal documents were issued by the court. These included summons (*hazmanah le-din*), decision (*pesak din*), appraisal of the debtor's property (*shuma*), writ of execution against the property (*shetar adrakhta*), and writ of execution against transferred realty (*shetar tirfa*).

(4) *Communal Documents*. From the time of the destruction of the Second Temple to modern times the Jewish community was self-governed as to its internal affairs. Thus it had its own system of taxation and means of enforcing compliance in accordance with the decisions of the rabbinic court and community councils. The decree of **ḥerem* ("excommunication") was its most powerful weapon. Other examples of community documents are ordination (**semikhah*), letters of appointment of rabbis, community loan bonds, right of settlement, and *ḥazakah*.

(5) *Miscellaneous Documents*. There are many other documents extant which cannot be classified under any of the above categories. Some of these are of historical interest. Among them are deeds of manumission of *slaves and bills of sale for slaves. One interesting document recorded by Gulak (*Oẓar* no. 399) is an order for anyone who had a claim against the overlord of Vienna in 1387 to come forward with his claim within 30 days or be forever barred.

[Abraham M. Fuss]

Contemporary Research into Legal Documents 1975–2005

The period 1975–2005 witnessed increased interest in the study of legal documents, and more in-depth study of those documents previously noted.

Y. Muffs, *Studies in Aramaic Legal Papyri from Elphantine*, was reissued with a long Prolegomenon by Baruch Levine (Leiden 2003). The work of Bezalel Porton and Ada Yardeni, *Textbook of Aramaic Documents from Ancient Egypt* (1989), newly copied and translated have expanded the scope of the studies,

Legal documents from the Dead Sea-Qumran discoveries have been published and are the subject of a number of studies which provide insights into the business activities and social lives of people living in the first centuries of the common era. In this category are Hannah M. Cotton and Ada Yardeni, *Aramaic, Hebrew, and Greek Documentary Texts from Nahal Hever and Other Sites* (1997; Discoveries in the Judean desert, vol. 27), and Klaus Beyer, *Die aramaischen Texte vom Toten Meer* (Gutenberg 1984), which has a section dealing with private documents, including both formal and informal legal documents from the Dead Sea area, see pages 304–27.

Gulak's *Das Urkundenwesen im Talmud*, published in 1935, has been translated into Hebrew with supplemental notes by Ranon Katzoff, *Legal Documents in the Talmud, In Light of Greek Papyri and Greek and Roman Law* (Jerusalem 1994).

The first collection of rabbinic formularies is that of *Saadiah Gaon (b. 882). M. Ben Sasson published substantial fragments from Saadiah's *Sefer ha-Edut ve ha-Shetarot* in *Shenaton ha-Mishpat ha-Ivri*, vols. 11–12 (1984–85), pp. 135–278. This is also the best scholarly edition of the early formularies.

The study of the Cairo *Genizah* documents was greatly stimulated by the work of S.D. Goitein and his classic *A Mediterranean Society*. Volume 1, published in 1967, dealt with economic matters. The fifth volume, the last, was published in 1988 shortly after his death. Goitein describes legal instruments, such as partnership contracts and other documents used in business and court proceedings, which have not been published as of 2005. For the legal historian it is necessary to have access to the texts of the documents to determine the nuances in the wording of documents which allow us to learn what problems those nuances are intended to solve. An example of such study is J. Rivlin's *Bills & Contracts From Lucena*, (1020–1025) (Heb., Bar-Ilan University Press, 1994), which consists of 45 original documents emanating from the Cairo *Genizah* which come from southern Spain and were written in Hebrew; the work provides commentary and reference to specific emendations. See also Rivlin's *Inheritance and Wills in Jewish Law* (Heb.; Bar-Ilan University Press, 1999), pp. 307–411, on which appear the texts of wills and gifts in contemplation of death from the Cairo *Genizah*, and his article in HUCA (Hebrew Section), vol. 73, p. 79ff.

There are stills thousands of documents unpublished from the *Genizah*. The Cambridge Taylor-Schechter collection, which is the largest depository of *Genizah* documents, has commenced a program of digitizing documents and putting them on the Internet. Hopefully it will be possible to study the legal documents directly within a few years.

Various collections of medieval *shetarot* which were required to be registered in government archives are still extant. Some of these are now being published. Thus, Elka Klein, *Hebrew Deeds of Catalan Jews – 1171–1316* (Barcelona-Girona 2004), is a welcome addition. The Hebrew documents are also translated into Spanish. Another work of this kind is Ignacio Ferrando, *23 Contratos Comerciales Escritos por Los Judios de Toledo en Los Siglos XIII Y XIV: Edicion Completa y Estudio Linguistico de los Datos Judeo-arabes y Andalusies* (University of Zaragosa 1994). The previously published collections of *shetarot* are listed in M. Elon, *Jewish Law: History, Sources, Principles*, vol. 3, pp. 1529–40; in N. Rakover, *Oẓar ha-Mishpat* (Tel Aviv 1990) and in *The Multi-Language Bibliography of Jewish Law* (Jerusalem 1990), p. 701.

Examples of studies which deal with particular historical aspects of *shetarot* are Edward Fran, *Ideals Face Reality, Jewish Law & Life in Poland 1550–1655* (Cincinnati 1997); A Fuss, *Mishpat Avraham*, (Heb., Jerusalem 2004).

[Abraham M. Fuss (2nd ed.)]

BIBLIOGRAPHY: L. Auerbach, *Das juedische Obligationenrecht* (1870), 199–505; Ph. Bloch, in: *Festschrift… A. Berliner* (1903), 50–64; L. Fischer, in: JJLG, 9 (1911), 45–197; V. Aptowitzer, in: JQR, 4 (1913/14), 23–51; I.S. Zuri, *Mishpat ha-Talmud*, 5 (1921), 43–59; Gulak, Yesodei, passim; Gulak, Oẓar (incl. bibl.); idem, in: *Etudes de papyrologie*, 1 (1932), 97–104 (Ger.); idem, *Das Urkundenwesen im Talmud…* (1935); Hai Gaon, *Sefer ha-Shetarot*, ed. by S. Assaf, in: *Musaf ha-Tarbiz*, 1 (1930), 5–77; I. Abrahams (ed.), *Starrs and Jewish Charters…* 3 vols. (1930–32); Z. Karl, in: *Ha-Mishpat ha-Ivri*, 5 (1936/37), 105–87; Herzog, Instit, 2 (1939), 314 (index), s.v.; H. Albeck, in: *Kovez Madda'i le-Zekher Moshe Schorr* (1944), 12–24; ET, 1 (1951^3), 218–20; 5 (1953), 717–42; J.J. Rabinowitz, *Jewish Law* (1956), passim; C. Roth, in: *Oxoniensia*, 22 (1957), 63–77; N. Golb, in: *Jewish Social Studies*, 20 (1958), 17–46; R. Yaron, *Introduction to the Law of the Aramaic Papyri* (1961); E. Koffmahn, *Die Doppelurkunden aus der Wueste Juda* (1968); M. Elon, Mafte'aḥ ha-She'lot ve-ha-Teshuvot, She'lot u-Teshuvot ha-Rosh (1965), 341–75; A.M. Fuss, *Dinei Yisrael* (4) (1973); H. Soloveitchik, *Tarbiz*, 41 (1972), 313; E. Strauss-Astor, *History of the Jews in Egypt and Syria*, vol.3 (1970); S. Assaf, in: R.J.L. Fishman (ed.), *Rav Saadya Gaon* (1943), p. 65ff; Y.Baer, *Die Juden Im Christlichen Spanien*, vol.1 (1929), 1044; M.D. Davis, *Hebrew Deeds of English Jews Before 1920* (1888, repr. 1969); **ADD. BIBLIOGRAPHY:** M. Elon, *Ha-Mishpat ha-Ivri* (1988), 1:501f, 773f; 2:1221f., 1282–1316, and index; ibid, *Jewish Law* (1994), 2:610f., 951f.; 3:1463, 1530–72; M. Elon and B. Lifshitz, *Mafte'aḥ ha-She'elot ve-ha-Teshuvot shel Ḥakhmei Sefarad u-Ẓefon Afrikah* (legal digest) (1986), 2:502–21; B. Lifshitz and E. Shochetman, *Mafte'aḥ ha-She'elot ve-ha-Teshuvot shel Ḥakhmei Ashkenaz, Ẓarefat ve-Italyah* (legal digest) (1997), 340–45.

SHETZER, SIMON (1900–1947), U.S. attorney, merchant, and Zionist leader. Shetzer was born in Detroit, Michigan, and after some years practicing law, he joined his family's wholesale dry goods distribution firm. In the 1930s Shetzer was a leader in Detroit Jewish life, organizing the Detroit Jewish Community Council and serving as its president (1937–41), among other activities. Long active in Zionist affairs, he served the Zionist Organization of America as president of the Michigan and then of the Midwest region. In 1941 he became national executive director of the ZOA, serving until 1943.

SHEVAT (Heb. שְׁבָט), the post-Exilic name of the 11th month of the Jewish year. Occurring in Assyrian and other early Semitic inscriptions, in biblical and apocryphal records (Zech. 1:7; I Macc. 16:14), and frequent in rabbinic literature (e.g., *Megillat Ta'anit*), the name is held to be etymologically connected with the root *sbt* from which terms are derived for instruments used in "beating" and "striking" in Semitic and in some Indo-European languages. The zodiacal sign of Shevat is *Aquarius*. In the present fixed Jewish calendar it invariably consists of 30 days, the 1st of Shevat never falling on Sunday or Friday (see *Calendar). In the 20th century, Shevat in its earliest occurrence extended from January 1st to 30th and in its latest from January 31st to March 1st. Historic days in Shevat are feasts; (1) Second of Shevat, the anniversary of the death of *Alexander Yannai (Meg. Ta'an. 11); (2) 15th of Shevat, the New Year for trees (see *Tu bi-Shevat; RH 1:1); (3) 22nd of Shevat, the anniversary of the assassination of the emperor *Caligula and the abolition of his blasphemous decree to erect his statue in the Temple in Jerusalem (Meg. Ta'an. 11; January 24th, 41 C.E.); (4) 28th of Shevat, the anniversary of the death of *Antiochus IV Epiphanes (Meg. Ta'an., *ibid.*); fasts: 5th (or 8th) and 23rd of Shevat, once observed in memory of the death of righteous men in the generation of Joshua the son of Nun (*ibid.*, 13; Jud. 2:10), and of Israel's battle against Benjamin and the idol of Micah (*ibid.*, 17–21).

[Ephraim Jehudah Wiesenberg]

SHEVELOVE, BURT (1915–1982), U.S. theater writer. Born in Newark, N.J., Shevelove graduated from Brown University and earned a master's degree in theater from Yale. After serving as a volunteer ambulance driver in World War II, he started his theatrical career in 1948 when he co-produced, directed, and wrote material for the revue *Small Wonder*. He directed a revival of *Kiss Me Kate* in 1956, then *Bil and Cora Baird's Marionette Theater*, and later *Hallelujah, Baby!*, which won a Tony Award as best musical in 1967. But as co-author with Larry *Gelbart of *A Funny Thing Happened on the Way to the Forum*, Shevelove scored his biggest triumph. The zany musical, with Zero *Mostel in the starring role, won six Tony awards, including best musical and best book. Based on the works of Plautus, *Funny Thing* had its origins in Shevelove's research on the plots of Plautus when he was a graduate student. In 1971, Shevelove directed a revival of *No, No, Nanette*, which brought Ruby Keeler, the film and stage star, out of retirement to win new fame. Shevelove, who worked with Stephen *Sondheim on *Funny Thing*, collaborated with him again in 1974 on an adaptation of Aristophanes's *The Frogs*, which he directed at Yale. The memorably unconventional production was performed in and around the Yale pool. In theater circles, Shevelove was well known as a play doctor, helping musicals that were in difficulty to reach Broadway. He also produced, directed, and wrote many television shows, for which he won Emmy and Peabody Awards.

[Stewart Kampel (2nd ed.)]

SHEVI'IT (Heb. שְׁבִיעִית; "Seventh Year"), fifth tractate in the Mishnah order **Zera'im*, dealing with the problems of the sabbatical or *shemittah* year. There is *Gemara* in the Jerusalem Talmud but not in the Babylonian.

The contents of the ten chapters of the mishnaic tractate are briefly as follows: Chapters 1–2 deal with the problems of *tosefet shevi'it*, certain agricultural works which had to be stopped, by rabbinical command, already in the sixth year, on the "eve of the seventh." Chapters 3–4 speak of works allowed during the sabbatical year. Chapter 5 deals with the special regulations concerning certain specific products and discusses the attitude toward people suspected of not observing the *shemittah*. Chapter 6 speaks of the differences between the various areas of the Holy Land as to *shemittah* observance. Chapters 7–9 define the plants and products subject to the law of *shemittah*, and discuss the ways and the circumstances in which use may be made of the products grown during the *shemittah* year. Chapter 10 speaks of the release of debts and discusses the institution of *prosbul.

The closing sentence of the tractate affords a good example of equity in Jewish law. Having mentioned that the sages are pleased with him who repays a debt despite the sabbatical year, it concludes that equally praiseworthy is he who keeps an agreement though it is not legally binding. Noteworthy in the same context is the concluding sentence of the tractate in the Jerusalem Talmud, which relates that as a matter of piety (*middat ḥasidut*) *Rav enjoined his household that if they promised a present to somebody they should not retract, even if the promise was not legally binding; he said this despite his known halakhic ruling that a withdrawal from an agreement not legally binding does not involve a formal breach of faith (*meḥussar amana, fidei laesio*: see BM 49a). Attention may be drawn also to the story of Abba b. Zevina, whom a gentile once threatened to kill if he did not eat the forbidden food he offered him; when the rabbi remained steadfast, the gentile declared that, in fact, he had wanted only to test his loyalty to Judaism, and, on the contrary, he would have killed him had he eaten it (TJ, 4:2, 35a–b).

The Tosefta to this tractate is divided into eight chapters. Interesting is the account of how the produce of the *shemittah* year used to be stored in communal granaries, and allocations made to the members of the community, each according to his needs, every Friday (8:1). The Mishnah was translated into English by H. Danby (1933).

For bibliography see the main articles on *Mishnah, *Talmud, and *Tosefta.

[Arnost Zvi Ehrman]

SHEVU'OT (Heb. שְׁבוּעוֹת; "Oaths"), sixth tractate of the order *Nezikin* in the Mishnah, Tosefta, and the Babylonian and Jerusalem Talmuds. It deals with oaths of various kinds but also with some aspects of ritual impurity. A link between these apparently diverse subjects is indicated in Leviticus 5:1–13. The fact that *Shevu'ot*, with eight chapters, follows *Makkot*, with three, seems to contradict the rule that the sequence of tractates within a given order is in the descending order of the number of chapters. However, it is clear from the Talmud (see Shevu. 2b, bottom; also Rashi in loc.) that *Makkot* was once joined to *Sanhedrin*, giving it a total of 14 chapters (see H.L. Strack, *Introduction to the Talmud* (1931), pp.27, 51; Ḥ. Albeck, *Mishnah, Seder Nezikin* (1952–9), p. 3).

The contents of the Mishnah in brief are as follows: chapter 1 opens with the terse statement: "Oaths are two, which are four," i.e., to the two kinds of oath referred to in Leviticus 5:3, called *shevu'ot bittui* ("oaths of utterance"), the Oral Law added two similar ones. Examples of these oaths are given at the beginning of chapter 3, and with them the discussion on oaths actually begins: "(I swear that) I will eat"; "I will not eat"; "I have eaten"; and "I have not eaten." This differentiation helps to establish whether, and what, sacrifices are due in case of their violations. The phrase, "two, which are four," characteristic of the oldest stratum of the Mishnah, is used also with regard to ritual uncleanness and introduces chapter 2. In fact, most of the rest of the first chapter deals with this subject, which is continued in chapter 3. Chapter 3 distinguishes between *shevu'at bittui* and *shevu'at shav* ("vain" or "false oath"). The latter applies when one asserts by oath something contrary to accepted knowledge, or impossible, e.g., swearing that a man is a woman or that one saw a flying camel. Swearing that one will violate a religious precept also belongs to this category. The following four chapters deal with judicial oaths. In fact it is because of the legal significance of the oath that *Shevu'ot* was placed in the order *Nezikin*, which deals predominantly with matters of law and judicial procedure. Chapter 4 deals with *shevu'at edut* ("oath of evidence"); chapter 5 with the *shevu'at ha-pikkadon* ("oath relating to bailments"), in accordance with Leviticus 5:21ff.; chapter 6 with the *shevu'at ha-dayyanim*, i.e., oaths imposed under certain circumstances by the court on the defendant; and chapter 7, having noted that according to Torah law the plaintiff has the privilege of being allowed to take an oath and consequently of receiving judgment in his favor, goes on to discuss instances when by rabbinical enactment the defendant also has the right to take an oath. Chapter 8 deals with the oaths of the four bailees (**shomerim*) in accordance with Exodus 22:6–16.

The Tosefta to this tractate is divided into six chapters. Chapter 1:5–7 and chapter 3 are of a halakhic Midrash (a *Mekhilta*) to Leviticus, which does not fit in with the work and has been inserted in the Tosefta. The terminology and the names of the *tannaim* mentioned in it make it clear that this fragment comes from the school of Ishmael. Tosefta 3:6 sees all crime as a rebellion against God, e.g., if one bears false witness, one commits an injustice not only against one's neighbor, but one also "denies Him who commanded: 'Thou shalt not bear false witness.'" Tosefta 3:7 gives expressions found in magical texts which served as incantations and, having found their way into Israelite folklore, were employed as oath formulas (Lieberman, Greek Hellenism, p. 91).

The *Gemara* of the Babylonian Talmud on this tractate includes a good deal of aggadic material. One discussion lists *mitzvot* which, if fulfilled as a reward, cause one to have male offspring (18b). Another cites a series of courtroom laws which assure fair trial (30b–31a). Thus, if a rabbinical scholar and an uneducated person *(am ha-areẓ)* come to be sentenced, both of them have the privilege of being seated. There is an interesting discussion of the names of God in 35a and b. The Babylonian Talmud (26a, cf. Tosef. 1:7) also gives the statement that Ishmael, a disciple of Neḥunya b. ha-Kanah who interpreted the whole Torah according to the hermeneutical rule of *kelal* and *perat*, followed the same principle, while Akiva, a disciple of Nahum of Gimzu who interpreted in accordance with *ribbui* and *mi'ut* ("extension and limitation"), construed the Torah like his master (see *Hermeneutics). The Jerusalem Talmud contains very little aggadic material. The major aggadic section discusses various types of atonements (1:9; 33b–c). It also quotes the first verse of the prayer for rain in Greek (3:10, 34d), as it was obviously recited by the common people on occasions of drought (Liebermann, *ibid.*, 8–20). *Shevu'ot* was translated into English in the Soncino edition by A.E. Silverstone (1935). For bibliography see the main articles on *Talmud, *Mishnah, *Tosefta.

[Arnost Zvi Ehrman]

SHEWBREAD or **SHOWBREAD** (Heb. לֶחֶם פָּנִים / הַפָּנִים; JPS, "bread of display"), the bread laid out in the Temple on the golden table (Ex. 25:30; I Sam. 21:7; I Kings 7:48; II Chron. 4:19) which is called "the table of Shewbread" in Numbers 4:7. The shewbread is also referred to as לֶחֶם הַתָּמִיד ("the regular bread"). On the other hand the Hagiographa use the terms לֶחֶם הַמַּעֲרֶכֶת (Neh. 10:34; I Chron. 9:32; 23:29), מַעֲרֶכֶת לֶחֶם (II Chron. 13:11), מַעֲרֶכֶת תָּמִיד (II Chron. 2:3), or simply מַעֲרֶכֶת (I Chron. 28:16; II Chron. 29:18, on the basis of Lev. 24:6–7). It is also called עֵרֶךְ לֶחֶם ("a row of bread": Ex. 40:23; cf. verse 4).

The manner in which the shewbread was prepared is described in Leviticus 24:5–9. Like most meal-offerings, it also was made of semolina. Consisting of 12 loaves, apparently corresponding in number to the tribes of Israel, the shewbread was arranged on the table in two rows of six loaves. Each loaf was made of two-tenths of an ephah, twice the quantity of the usual meal-offering (Num. 15:4, et al.), resembling in this respect only the two waveloaves of the Feast of Weeks (Lev. 23:17). Frankincense was placed on the shewbread (Lev. 24:7), but unlike the prescriptions for other meal-offerings it is here explicitly stated that the frankincense had to be pure, and furthermore that the token (portion אַזְכָּרָה) contained only the frankincense (in contrast to the token portion of a usual meal-offering, which contained some oil and fine flour in addition to the frankincense; Lev. 2:2). Thus no part of this bread was put on the altar, since only the token portion was burned. The talmudic *halakhah* prescribes that these loaves were to be of unleavened bread (Men. 5a; cf. Jos., Ant., 3:255), although this is not explicitly mentioned in the text, which likewise makes no reference to their being seasoned with salt, as was done with other meal-offerings (Lev. 2:13). However, the Septuagint (Lev. 24:7) adds Καῖ "αλας ("and salt"), and according to the *halakhah* the frankincense was to be salted before being burned on the altar (Men. 20a). The loaves were changed every Sabbath. On the basis of the relevant passages it may be presumed that the priest did not have to go into the Holy of Holies especially for this purpose, but would change the loaves when he came there on the Sabbath at the appointed times, that is, either in the morning or at dusk, to attend to the lamps or the incense altar. As in the case of most meal-offerings, the shewbread was eaten by males among the priests in a sacred place.

The evidence concerning the shewbread in the Sanctuary of Nob (I Sam. 21:1–7) does not substantially contradict the instructions contained in Leviticus; there is only a difference in presentation, like that between Priestly Code of laws and historical writings. Here, too, it can be seen that the shewbread consisted not of one but of several loaves (as shown by the plural הַמּוּסָרִים in verse 7); their number is not given, this detail being unnecessary for the narrative. The shewbread is here called לֶחֶם קֹדֶשׁ ("holy bread," verse 5). That given by the priest Ahimelech to David was presumably from the old loaves previously "removed from before the Lord" (verse 7) and as yet uneaten; it was not removed on that day by Ahimelech from the table especially for David and his men. The only point that conflicts with what is stated in Leviticus is the view expressed here that the old loaves could be eaten by non-priests in a state of purity, not specifically by priests in a holy place. This is, however, a general feature of the non-Priestly sources of the Bible, that sometimes permit to non-priests "sanctified" by purity what the Priestly sources (i.e., P and Ezek. 40–48) permit only to males among the priests.

The custom of placing loaves of bread on a table in a sanctuary before the god, coupled with other ritual acts, was prevalent in various places and times. Clear parallels of this custom existed in Babylonia, although not a few differences distinguish these from the specific crystallization in the Israelite style. Some have sought to find in Akkadian sources the special term *akāl pānu*, which corresponds to the biblical shewbread, but the reading has been found to be erroneous.

BIBLIOGRAPHY: P. Haupt, in: JBL, 19 (1900), 59; E. Meyer, *Die Israeliten und ihre Nachbarstaemme* (1906), 172–3; D. Hoffmann, *Das Buch Leviticus*, 2 (1906), 309–11; F. Thureau-Dangin, *Die sumerischen und akkadischen Koenigsinschriften* (1907), 50–51; idem, *Rituels accadiens* (1921), 62 ff.; G.A. Barton, in: JBL, 46 (1927), 88; F. Blome, *Die Opfermaterie in Babylonien und Israel*, 1 (1934), 248–9; Pritchard, Texts, 343 ff.; G.R. Driver, in: VTS, 4 (1957), 4; M. Haran, in: *Scripta Hierosolymitana*, 8 (1961), 278–9.

[Menahem Haran]

SHIBĀM, situated at the foot of the mountain below the stronghold of Kawkabān, 30 km northwest of *Sanʿa, *Yemen; once the capital of a small independent highland state. Ancient Ḥimyari inscriptions can be found on the stones of the city gate and in other old buildings of the town. It is located on the main route of commerce. It is called Shibām al-Kawkabān (or Shibām al-Ghirās) to distinguish it from the other, more famous Shibām in Ḥaḍramawt. The Jews lived in the neighboring village of Dhafrān; in about 1930 there were approximately 1,000 Jews. Jacob *Saphir stayed there in 1858 and left a vivid description of the Jewish community. Qāʿal-Yahūd (the Jewish Quarter), in which about 60 families lived, was part of the town, but was surrounded by a wall which severely crowded the inhabitants. There was almost no room for courtyards, since the houses and the streets were very narrow. The gates of the town were closed from evening until morning. The community of Shibām, with its three synagogues, was the spiritual center of the neighboring villages and also catered to their religious needs. The Jews were businessmen, silversmiths, ironsmiths, and tanners.

BIBLIOGRAPHY: J. Saphir, *Even Sappir* (1864), 77–78; C. Rathjens, *Jewish Domestic Architecture in Ṣanʿā, Yemen* (1957), 64–67.

[Yosef Tobi (2nd ed.)]

SHI'BUDA DE-RABBI NATHAN (Aram. "Rabbi Nathan's Lien"), a rule of law attributed to R. Nathan, a *tanna* of the second century, and cited in the Babylonian Talmud as follows: "Whence is the rule derived that if one man [A] claims a *maneh* [100 *zuz*] from his neighbor [B], and his neighbor [B] [claims a like sum] from another neighbor [C], that we collect from the one [C] and give it to the other [A]? From the verse, '… and he shall give it unto him to whom he is indebted'" (Num. 5:7 – Pes. 31a). The Bible does not state, "unto him who lent him the money" [B], but rather "unto him to whom he is indebted," i.e., to whom the principal rightfully belongs now [A] (Rashi, ad loc.).

The Substantive Law

In the Shulḥan Arukh the rule reads as follows: Reuben claims 100 from Simeon, and Simeon from Levi; we collect from Levi and give it to Reuben. No distinction is made as to whether Levi was already obligated to Simeon when the latter borrowed from Reuben or whether Levi had become obligated thereafter. Nor is any distinction made between a loan (see *Loans) having documentary attestation and one having only oral attestation (about these definitions see *Obligation, Law of). As long as both debtors acknowledge indebtedness, each to his respective creditor, we collect from Levi and give it to Reuben. This holds true for every type of obligation which Levi incurs toward Simeon, whether it be through loan, *sale, *lease, or hiring (see *Lease and Hire; ḤM 86:1). Indeed, the liabilities may have arisen from *torts, *damages, bailments (see **Shomerim*), and larceny (see *Theft and Robbery) as well. Nor need the two debts, i.e., of Simeon and Levi, have been of the same kind. For example, Simeon's indebtedness to Reuben may have arisen as the result of a loan, whereas Levi's indebtedness to Simeon may have been incurred through purchase. Similarly, Simeon's liability may be according to biblical law and Levi's according to rabbinic law (*Siftei Kohen*, ḤM 86:1). Reuben's ability to collect from Levi is limited to the circumstance that Simeon is insolvent (Sh. Ar., ḤM 86:2), although a dissenting opinion, which considers Levi virtually a debtor of Reuben, would extend the said liability even to those cases where Simeon was solvent (*Siftei Kohen*, ḤM 86:2).

According to most commentators, *Shi'buda de-Rabbi Nathan* differs from an ordinary *lien in being essentially a procedural device for the collection of debts rather than a substantive incumbrance on the property of the debtor. Thus, an ordinary lien attaches only to those properties of the debtor which were in his possession at the time he incurred the debt. Moreover, the indebtedness created through an ordinary lien may be discharged by the payment of money even in the case where the indebtedness arose through the delivery of a deposit or a pledge. R. Nathan's Lien, however, attaches to those properties the debtor acquired after he had incurred the debt as well, and the debtor could be compelled to deliver the object itself to his creditor's creditor. Yet, in the case where a debtor subsequent to his loan sold his property, Rabbi Nathan's Lien is ineffectual, for inasmuch as the debtor himself has no claim against the purchaser, his creditor also may have no claim against the purchaser. Under such circumstances, however, an ordinary lien is effective, and in the case of nonpayment the creditor may seize the property from the purchaser for the satisfaction of his (earlier) claim (*Keẓot ha-Ḥoshen*, ḤM 86).

Legal Analysis

Privity of contract is expressed in talmudic literature in the form of the refusal of a debtor to enter into litigation with his opponent on the ground that *lav baʿal devarim didi at* ("You have no claim against me," or "You are not my plaintiff"). *Shi'buda de-Rabbi Nathan* is a method of *assignment which Jewish law makes available in order to overcome, when necessary, the limitations created by the principle of privity. Rabbi Nathan's Lien differs from the other methods of assigning rights, such as: *maʿamad sheloshtan* (see *Assignment; *Obligation, Law of), which is a kind of assignment by substitution and requires the physical presence of the debtor, the assignor, and the assignee; *mesirat shetarot* (see *Acquisition), which effectuates assignment through the delivery of the bonds or notes of indebtedness to the assignee accompanied by a deed of assignment; and *harsha'ah* (see *Agency, Law of), which creates a power of attorney under the form of assignment. These three methods of assignment depend upon the initiative and consent of the assignor, whereas *Shi'buda de-Rabbi Nathan* creates what is essentially an automatically transferred obligation. In contrast with the other methods, however, *Shi'buda de-Rabbi Nathan* is limited to circumstances in which the assignee is a creditor of or claimant against the assignor. *Shi'buda de-Rabbi Nathan* finds its closest parallel in the statutory proceeding of garnishment in American law (see Herzog, Instit, 2 (1939), 214, n. 2).

Historical Development

Asher Gulak (*Ha-Ḥiyyuv ve-Shi'budav*, bibl.) maintains that *Shi'buda de-Rabbi Nathan* underwent a series of developments in talmudic times whereby it received a progressively wider application. The original statement of R. Nathan is to be found in Sifrei Numbers 3, and merely provides for the right of a creditor to collect his debt from monies which have been awarded to the debtor in court but which the latter has as yet not collected. The text of R. Nathan's statement as it appears in the Babylonian Talmud (e.g., Pes. 31a) represents, according to Gulak, a further development whereby debts owed to the debtor are construed as property of the latter and subject to collection on behalf of his creditor even before they have been awarded to the debtor in court. Thus, at this point the assignment of rights has been created without any reference, however, to lien. The final development of R. Nathan's statement is to be seen in the construction placed upon it by the Babylonian Talmud, namely, that there is a lien that the creditor has on all the properties of his debtor's debtors. This construction is part of the general tendency which Gulak discerns in the Babylonian Talmud, i.e., to incorporate lien into the very concept of obligation.

BIBLIOGRAPHY: N.A. Nobel, in: *Sefer… le-David Ẓevi… Hoffmann* (1914), 98–105; Gulak, Yesodei, 2 (1922), 101–3; 4 (1922), 193f.; Herzog, Instit, 1 (1936), 201–12; 2 (1939), 209–14; A. Gulak, *Toledot ha-Mishpat be-Yisrael bi-Tekufat ha-Talmud*, 1 (*Ha-Ḥiyyuv ve-Shi'budav*, 1939), 150f.; Elon, Mafte'aḥ, 396f. **ADD. BIBLIOGRAPHY:** M. Elon and B. Lifshitz, *Mafte'aḥ ha-She'elot ve-ha-Teshuvot shel Ḥakhmei Sefarad u-Ẓefon Afrikah* (legal digest) (1986), 533–34; B. Lifshitz and E. Shochetman, *Mafte'aḥ ha-She'elot ve-ha-Teshuvot shel Ḥakhmei Ashkenaz, Ẓarefat ve-Italyah* (legal digest) (1997), 358.

[Aaron Kirschenbaum]

SHIFRAH OF BRODY (fl. 1770s), author of a Yiddish *tkhine* (supplicatory prayer) for women. According to the opening page of *Tkhine Imrei Shifre* (*Tkhine* of the Words of Shifrah), she was the daughter of the learned Rabbi Joseph and wife of Rabbi Ephraim Segal, a *dayyan* in *Brody. Quite exceptionally for a Yiddish work by a female author, her work contains something close to a rabbinic approbation (*haskamah*): an unsigned paragraph in Hebrew labeled "*haqdamah*" ["Introduction"] describes Shifrah as a "prominent, learned, and wealthy woman" who is planning to travel to the Holy Land with her husband. This introduction asserts that "several rabbis and sages agree [*maskimim*] that she should publish this *tkhine.*" Residents of Brody were well represented among the approximately 300 Jews who accompanied several ḥasidic leaders to settle in Safed in 1777. Further, Brody, the home of the famed *kloyz* or study-house of mystical pietists, was rich in religious ferment and conflict, some of which is reflected in Shifrah's text.

Like most Eastern European *tkhines* published before 1835, *Tkhine Imrei Shifre* makes no reference to place or date of publication; internal evidence, however, places the text some time after 1770. In the first section Shifrah described the difficult contemporary conditions in the region of Brody. In the other parts of the book, she utilized kabbalistic, pietistic, and possibly Shabbatean/Frankist material to emphasize the significance of women's religious acts. The title of the *tkhine* alludes to the common book title *Imrei Shefer* (from Gen. 49:21, where it probably means "lovely fawn"), usually taken to mean "words of Torah." The four sections of the *tkhine* include a long *tkhine* on exile, repentance, and redemption; a daily *tkhine*, asking for assistance against distractions in prayer, help with livelihood, and protection for women in pregnancy and childbirth; a Sabbath *tkhine* which includes a kabbalistic interpretation of the women's *mitzvah* of candle-lighting; and a "Moral Reproof for the Sabbath," consisting almost entirely of material originating in the Zohar, which addresses proper Sabbath observance. The text is exceptional for its use of kabbalistic concepts, such as the divine *shefa'* (supernal abundance), its reference to the problem of devoted prayer, and its mention of the *Shekhinah* as an object of women's devotion.

BIBLIOGRAPHY: C. Weissler, *Voices of the Matriarchs* (1998), 89–103.

[Chava Weissler (2nd ed.)]

SHIFTAN, ZE'EV (**Ludwig**; 1920–1990), prominent Israeli geologist-hydrologist. Born in Görlitz, Germany, he grew up in Erfurt where his father Max (Moshe) was rabbi of that city's community. Having received a thorough general and Jewish schooling, Shiftan began studies in 1938 at the Breslau Rabbinical Seminary. Following *Kristallnacht he was taken on Nov. 10, 1938, to Buchenwald concentration camp. Freed when a Palestine immigration certificate was obtained for him, he emigrated to Palestine in Feb. 1939 and soon joined the Haganah. Leaning to the natural sciences, he found his way to geology, becoming a student, then assistant, of Professor Leo Picard. He lectured at the Hebrew University and the Haifa Technion. Concentrating on groundwater exploration and exploitation, he worked in the field and wrote papers and books. In 1966 he joined Tahal as consultant to its Hydrological Department and was for a time its head, working in Israel and other countries. The United Nations asked for his service and appointed him consultant in South America and elsewhere. Besides his scientific work he was active in social and cultural matters; he represented Israel in the B'nai B'rith world council and in January 1990 was elected president of its David Yellin Lodge of Jerusalem. On Feb. 4, 1990, he was among the nine killed in the terrorist attack on Israeli tourists in Egypt in which his wife, Yehudit, was also wounded.

[Efraim Orni]

SHIḤIN (Heb. שִׁיחִין) or **ASOCHIS**, Galilean city. The first mention of it is made by Josephus (Ant. 13:337; Wars 1:86), who describes its capture by Ptolemy Lathyrus on a Sabbath in approximately 103 B.C.E. It was obviously a large Jewish city at that time, for 10,000 inhabitants were taken captive. Josephus locates the city in a plain of the same name (plain of Asochis; Life, 207, 233, 384). Situated in the center of Galilee, it served as his headquarters for some time. The city survived the First Jewish War. It is referred to as Shiḥin or Kefar Shiḥin several times in talmudic literature. There it is described as a place where mustard was grown and as the site of a pottery industry, which used the black soil of the area. A fire in one of the kilns drew help from Castra at Sepphoris, from where Shiḥin was visible. The priestly family of Jeshebab (Huzpith) lived them after the war of Bar Kokhba. The identification of Shiḥin with Tell al-Badawiyya (see *Hannaton) is confirmed by the Roman pottery and ruins found on the site.

BIBLIOGRAPHY: Saarisalo, in: JPOS, 9 (1929), 35; Albright, in: BASOR, 11 (1923), 11.

[Michael Avi-Yonah]

SHIHOR, SHIHOR-LIBNATH (Heb. שִׁיחוֹר, שִׁיחוֹר-לִבְנָת).

(1) Geographical term used in the Bible and derived from the Egyptian *si-hor* ("lake of Horus") which originally referred to the lake in the eastern Delta near the Pelusiac branch of the Nile. It has been identified with the Egyptian Pa-she-Hor, "the Waters of Horus," which are mentioned in a 19th-Dynasty Egyptian text, Papyrus Anastasi III, 2:11–12 (Pritchard, Texts, 471). It marked the westernmost limit of Palestine in the south, extending to the Egyptian border (Josh. 13:3; I Chron. 13:5). The prophets occasionally identify it with the waters of Egypt (Isa. 23:3; Jer. 3:18).

(2) Shihor, with the addition of Libnath ("of the white willows") is used in Joshua 19:26 to indicate the southern boundary of Asher; it is mentioned with Mt. Carmel. Scholars are divided between its identification with the outlet of the Kishon River north of the Carmel and with the Naḥal Tanninim south of the Carmel (Ar. Nahr al-Zarqā or Miyāh al-Tamāsiḥ, "the waters of the crocodiles"), which may explain the associations of the name Shihor with Egypt; cf. the Crocodilopolis of Strabo.

BIBLIOGRAPHY: R. Dussaud, *Topographie historique de la Syrie…* (1928), 15; Abel, Geog, 1 (1933), 470; A.H. Gardiner, *Ancient Egyptian Onomastica*, 2 (1947), 201; R.A. Caminos, *Late Egyptian Miscellanies* (1954), 79; Aharoni, and, index.

[Michael Avi-Yonah]

SHILA OF KEFAR TAMARTA (c. second and third centuries C.E.), Palestinian *amora*. The name of his Judean home is always added to his personal name to distinguish him from an older Babylonian *amora* of the same name, and from Shila of Naveh, a contemporary. He was a student of R. Johanan, whose teachings he transmits (TJ, RH 2:9, 58b; TJ, Ḥag. 3:8, 79d). Although he seems to have engaged in *halakhah* (Nid. 26a), Shila is known mainly as an aggadist, and only aggadic statements of his are quoted. That he delivered his aggadic discourses publicly is evidenced by the introductory formula "R. Shila expounded" (*darash*; cf. Meg. 16a–b).

BIBLIOGRAPHY: Hyman, Toledot, s.v.

SHILL, LOUIS (1930–), South African businessman and politician. Born in Witbank, South Africa, he qualified as a chartered accountant through Witwatersrand and Stamford universities. One of the founders of Liberty Life in the late 1950s, he was founder and chief executive of Sage Fund in 1965, which introduced the concept of unit trusts in South Africa. He established Sage Group Limited in 1969. On 1 June 1993, he was appointed minister for national housing and public works, a post he held until May 1994.

[David Saks (2nd ed.)]

SHILOAH, AMNON (1928–), Israeli musicologist of the history and theory of Arabic music. Born in Argentina to Syrian parents, Shiloah settled in Palestine in 1941. He studied Arabic language and literature at the Hebrew University and musicology at the Sorbonne, where he obtained his doctorate in 1963. Shiloah was appointed senior lecturer at the Hebrew University musicology department in 1969 and was its chairman in the years 1971–74. He became full professor in 1978. He served as a board member of the International Musicological Society (1977–81), and won the Jerusalem Prize for research achievements in the study of Oriental Jewish music (1986). Shiloah was provost of the Rothberg School for overseas students (1992–95), and an honorary member for life at the European Seminar in Ethnomusicology (1995). He won the Grand prix de l'Académie Charles Cros: Litterature musicale for the French translation of his book *Music in the World of Islam*. Shiloah is one of the most prolific scholars of both Jewish and Arab traditional music.

Shiloah began his career as a musicologist of Israeli art music in the early 1950s, when he published interviews with 13 founding Israeli composers about national identity in their music (published in *Massa*, 1953). His *Massa* interviews have often been cited as a pioneer work, and his contribution to *Israel Music Institute News* (1990) was an influential contribution to the study of Orientalism in Israeli art music. Shiloah's magnum opus, *The Theory of Music in Arabic Writings (c. 900–1900)* (*Répertoire international des sources musicales*, Henle Verlag, Munich, series B/X, 1979 – a catalogue of manuscripts in libraries of Europe and the U.S.), was the culmination of years of work in European archives. The latter volume of this seminal text (RISM, series B/XA, 2003, describing manuscripts in Israel, Egypt, Morocco, Tunisia, Russia, and Uzbekistan) was similarly a result of another decade of research. His work was published in *Encyclopedia Britannica* (1974), *Die Musik in Geschichte und Gegenwart* (1976, 1994), the *Journal of the American Musicological Society* (1981), and *The New Oxford History of Music* (2001) – to cite a few among many publications (e.g., in *Cahiers de civilisation medievale, Ethnomusicology, Ariel, Acta Musicologica, Pe'amim*, and *Yuval*). His scholarship on Jewish music was summarized in his *Jewish Musical Traditions* (1992). Shiloah's work on Arab music culminated also in his *Music in the World of Islam: A Socio-Cultural Study* (1995; the book also appeared in French, Hebrew, and Arabic).

In the field of ethnomusicology, he established himself as both a pioneer scholar and a leading authority of Arab music and of Jewish traditional music. Shiloah's comprehensive list of publications encompasses over 240 items in four languages (English, French, Hebrew, and Arabic), including 15 books, edited works, records, and articles – a result of 50 years of work in the field of Arabic music, its ethnomusicology, the history of its theory, and its social-cultural history. Shiloah also advanced the fields of Jewish ethnomusicology, especially the study of Jewish-Arab and Sephardi traditions in their countries of origin from Morocco to Iraq, and in Israel. Finally, he has contributed significant writings to the study of Israeli art music.

[Ronit Seter (2nd ed.)]

SHILOAḤ (Zaslani), REUBEN (1909–1959), Zionist political officer and Israel diplomat. Born in Jerusalem, Shiloah possessed expertise on Arab affairs, combined with political imagination and a talent for analysis of international affairs. He was one of the *yishuv's* first emissaries to the Jews in Middle East countries (1931), and upon his return from Baghdad and Kurdistan he was at first active in the political field for the *Histadrut, later transferring to the *Jewish Agency's Political Department (1936). During World War II, he coordinated the *yishuv's* war effort with that of the Allies; he organized the parachuting of members of the *Haganah into enemy territory, initiated intelligence operations against the Axis powers, and was active in rescue missions to save the remnants of European Jewry.

Upon the establishment of the State of Israel (1948), Shiloah formed its political intelligence service and coordinated it with military and security intelligence. In his role as adviser on special affairs to the foreign minister, he established secret contacts with Arab statesmen in an effort to achieve mutual understanding and peace. Shiloah led the Israel delegation that held negotiations over the cease-fire with Transjordan (1949).

After a term of service as minister at the Israel embassy in Washington (1953–57), Shiloah was appointed political adviser to the minister of foreign affairs with ambassadorial rank. His later years were spent in quiet diplomacy for achieving closer ties between Israel and the non-Arab countries of the Middle East and Africa.

BIBLIOGRAPHY: A.I. Zaslansky, *Yeḥi Re'uven* (1960); D. Lazar, *Rashim be-Yisrael*, 1 (1953), 197–202.

[Katriel Katz]

SHILOAH, SILOAM (Heb. שִׁלֹחַ, שֶׁלַח), name applied to the waters of the Gihon spring in Isaiah 8:6; it is probably derived from the root שלח (*shlḥ*; "to send forth"), which occurs in Psalms 104:10 in connection with springs. The "pool of Shelah" mentioned in Nehemiah 3:15 as "lying by the king's garden" refers to the pool formed by the overflow of water in Hezekiah's tunnel, which led from the Gihon spring into the city. Archaeological researches have shown that this pool actually antedated Hezekiah's tunnel. An older open channel, constructed during the Middle Bronze Age, carried water from the Gihon along the eastern slope of the city of David in order to irrigate the "king's garden" in the "king's valleys," i.e., the Kidron. The overflow was led into the "pool of Shiloah." In later times the name Gihon was forgotten and the name Shiloah included the orifice of the spring itself. As such, it serves as a landmark in Josephus' descriptions of Jerusalem during the siege of Titus, and marked the boundary between the sections defended by John of Gischala and Simeon Bar-Giora (Wars, 5:140, 252).

According to Josephus, the "Old" or "First" Wall, which surrounded the Upper and Lower Cities, passed near the spring and the pool (erroneously called the "pool of Solomon," which in Greek is similar to "pool of Siloam"; Wars 5:145). This pool is already mentioned as a pool adjacent to the city fortifications in Nehemiah (3:15), but the Gospel of John (9:7, 11) clearly indicates its function as a place for ritual immersion in the story of the miracle of the blind man regaining his sight: "…And [Jesus] said unto him [the blind man], Go wash in the Pool of Siloam. He went his way therefore, and washed, and came seeing." In response to the questioning of his querulous neighbors, the blind man repeats his story: "A man that is called Jesus made clay and anointed my eyes, and said unto me, Go to the Pool of Siloam, and wash: and I went and washed, and received sight." In addition, the Mishnah tells us of the practice of filling stone cups (clearly the so-called "measuring cups") with water let down into the Siloam Pool (Par. 3:2). One should also mention an interesting text from Oxyrhynchus in Egypt – a fragment of an uncanonical gospel – which refers to a *mikveh*-like pool close to the Temple area with separate stairs for going in and out. The text refers to Jesus being challenged by a priest about the state of his purity: "He [Jesus] saith unto him, I am clean; for I washed in the Pool of David [probably the Pool of Siloam, i.e., as a reference to the "City of David"], and having descended down one staircase I ascended by another, and I put on white and clean garments, and then I came and looked upon these holy vessels [of the Temple]." Elsewhere, it is said that the Pool of David had "running waters," a reference to the flowing "living" waters that entered the Siloam Pool from the spring of Siloam. The concern for purity in Jerusalem and the use of these two pools is further clarified in the Mishnah in relation to the subject of the *zavim*, men with bodily emissions (semen). The rabbis advocated that following an emission of semen the man "conveys uncleanness to what he lies upon or sits upon, and [therefore] he must bathe in running water" (Zav. 1:1; cf. Mik. 1:8). Later we hear that a man is a *zav* if he has had three emissions during the time it takes to go the distance from "Gad-Yavan [which is perhaps an alternative name for the Bethesda Pool] to [the pool of] Siloam (which is time enough for two immersions and two dryings) …" (Zav. 1:5).

Excavations in 2004 at the junction of the Tyropoeon and Kidron Valleys by Reich and Shukrun brought to light the Siloam Pool of Second Temple times; it was apparently trapezoidal in shape (estimated to be 40–60 × 70 meters) with built steps and landings along at least three of its sides; the fourth (west) side is unexcavated. Their findings indicate that the pool was most likely built in its present form during the Second Temple period, with two stages of construction of which the earliest of these is dated to the late first century B.C.E. or first century C.E based on the plaster type and other features. The pool was fed with water which was channeled directly from the Siloam spring without any holding basin needed, but the excavators have suggested the pool might also have been fed with runoff rainwater from other directions.

The spring failed in 70 C.E. during the siege and the water was sold by the amphora (5:410). The name "ravine of Siloam" was applied to the Kidron; it was overhung by the rock of the Dovecotes (5:505). After the siege the ravine served as a refuge for the rebels (6:401). Talmudic sources refer several times to the Shiloah, particularly to the narrowness of its issue, which was not larger than an Italian issar (Tosef. Ar. 2:6). From the Middle Ages onward, the name Shiloah referred to the village on the eastern slope of the Kidron Valley (Ar. Silwān). The village was a suburb of Jerusalem, and the inhabitants worked the fields on the hill of Ophel. In 1884 Jews from Yemen established themselves in part of the village; in 1936 they were forced to abandon their houses. In 1967, after the *Six-Day War, it was incorporated into the Jerusalem municipal area.

BIBLIOGRAPHY: G. Dalman, *Jerusalem und sein Gelaende* (1930), 167ff.; Hecker, in: *Sefer Yerushalayim*, ed. by M. Avi-Yonah (1956), 191ff.; K. Kenyon, *Jerusalem…* (1967), 30–31, 77. **ADD. BIBLIOGRAPHY:** C.W. Wilson, "Siloam," in: J. Hastings (ed.), *A Dictionary of the Bible*, vol. 4 (1902), 515–16; R. Reich and E. Shukrun, "The Siloam Pool in the Wake of Recent Discoveries," in: *New Studies on Jerusalem*, 10 (2004), 137–39.

[Michael Avi-Yonah/ Shimon Gibson (2nd ed.)]

SHILOH (Heb. שִׁלֹה, שִׁלוֹ, שִׁילֹה), the amphictyonic capital of Israel in the time of the Judges, situated north of Beth-El, east of the Beth-El-Shechem highway and south of Lebonah (Judg. 21:19), in the mountains of the territory of Ephraim. Under Joshua, the tabernacle was erected at Shiloh (Josh. 18:1). Here lots were cast for the various tribal areas (Josh. 18) and for the levitical cities (Josh. 21:2) and here Israel assembled to settle its dispute with the tribes beyond the Jordan (Josh. 22:9, 12). Shiloh was the center of Israelite worship. During one religious celebration, the daughters of the city danced in the vineyards, an occasion used by the Benjamites, who could not get wives in any way except by abducting them (Judg. 21). Elkanah and his wife Hannah came there to worship and Hannah vowed her child Samuel to the Lord, whom he served as a servant of the sanctuary at Shiloh (I Sam. 1–2). In this sanctuary, the sons of Eli the priest sinned and the Lord revealed Himself to Samuel (I Sam. 3). When the Ark was taken from the city on its fateful journey to Eben-Ezer, never to return to Shiloh, a Benjamite brought news of the disaster to Eli, causing his death there (I Sam. 4). The destruction of Shiloh is alluded to in Jeremiah (7:12, 14; 26:6, 9; cf. Ps. 78:60). However, its priestly family retained its importance for some time after moving to Nob (I Sam. 21:1–9). Ahijah the son of Ahitub, a priest from Shiloh, appeared with the ephod in the camp of Saul before the battle of Michmas (I Sam. 14:3). The priestly family of the city was finally deposed by Solomon (I Kings 2:27). Ahijah the Shilonite prophesied the future kingship of Jeroboam the son of Nebat (I Kings 11:29–31; 12:15; 15:29; II Chron. 9:29). It was apparently in Shiloh that Jeroboam's wife consulted the prophet and heard the doom of the dynasty (I Kings 14:2–16). Jeremiah refers several times to the destruction of the city as a warning (7:12, 14; Ps. 78:60); his comparison of the fate of Shiloh with that foreseen for the Temple led to his being accused of blasphemy (Jer. 26:6–9). After the destruction of the Temple, the people of Shiloh were among those Ephraimites who came to sacrifice at Jerusalem (Jer. 41:5).

Shiloh is identified with Tell Seilun, 30 mi. (48 km.) north of Jerusalem, south of the ascent of Lebonah. The identification of biblical Shiloh with Saylūn was established by E. *Robinson and is generally accepted; the topographical position, the remains on the mound, and the name all support this identification. However, the position of the sanctuary within the ancient site is still a subject of dispute. Conder and Kitchener in the *Survey of Western Palestine* (1881–83) suggested the terrace north of the mound, a position unsupported by other evidence. The area south of the mound, with its ancient road leading to Turmus Aiya, the sanctuaries of Wali Yetim and Wali Sittīn, was seen by some scholars to be a much more likely spot for an open-air sanctuary around a tabernacle; a pre-Christian sanctuary can be assumed to have been located in a valley in which there are now a number of Muslim holy places and which, in Byzantine times, contained several churches. Nonetheless, it is quite possible that the sanctuary stood inside the city proper (see below). Archaeological excavations there were undertaken by a Danish expedition directed by H. Kjaer (1926, 1929), A. Schmidt (1932), and S. Holm-Neilson and B. Otzen (1963). New excavations were conducted at the site by I. Finkelstein between 1981 and 1984. These excavations exposed eight strata, ranging from MB II–Middle Ages. The MB III city was heavily fortified (the MB II village was unwalled), with a massive wall (3–5.5 m. wide), with remains standing to a height of up to 8 m. Supporting this wall on the precipitous eastern slope was an extensive glacis (25 m. wide), which incorporated a supporting wall (3.2 m. tall) in its structure. Among the remains of the city from this period were storage rooms and cultic vessels, indicating the presence of a shrine. This level was destroyed. The LB I remains consisted primarily of vessels with remains of animals, cast over the wall of the city and then buried. These remains are likely the remnant of cultic offerings. Given that there were no architectural remains discovered at this level, the site may have existed solely as a shrine. Given that the top of the tell has exposed bedrock, the presence of shrines here is based almost entirely on circumstantial evidence.

Iron I remains were attested throughout the site. More than 20 silos were discovered (including one that had carbonized wheat). Pillared public buildings were unearthed in one section of the tell, adjacent to the MB wall. These buildings had two levels, divided by a terrace wall. One building had a paved courtyard. More than 20 collared rim jars were discovered in a number of buildings. It is likely that these buildings were part of the shrine complex. The Iron I structures were destroyed in a conflagration, possibly the work of the Philistines. A village reappears in Iron II. More extensive villages are attested in Roman and Byzantine times (see below).

The evidence for sacred continuity at the site from MB III–Iron I is instructive for the history of Israel. Surveys done by Finkelstein in the region of the central hills established that Shiloh was indeed in the heart of a settlement landscape that had greatly expanded in Iron I. The area surrounding Shiloh was perhaps three times as densely populated as any other region in the hills. Given that the top of the tell was long ago exposed, the nature of the shrine constructed by the Israelites is not ascertainable, whether it was a permanent building (cf. I Sam. 3:15) or a portable shrine (cf. II Sam. 7:6f).

A Roman villa with a bath and a city wall were uncovered in the earlier excavations at the site. In the fifth century (the Byzantine period), a mosaic-paved basilica, measuring 25 × 12 m., was erected south of the tell; further north was a smaller chapel. Shiloh is also known from later sources. Eusebius places it in the toparchy of Acraba, which in his time belonged to Neapolis (Onom. 156:28ff.). Jerome found an altar there (Epistula 108; PG, vol. 25, p. 1953). On the Madaba Map, it appears west of Gilgal, following the tradition recorded by Josephus (Ant., 5:68), with the addition of a historical note: "there once the Ark." The site of Shiloh was well known to talmudic sages; R. Yose b. Karḥa recorded the saying of an elder who visited the place and still inhaled the odor of incense between its walls (Sanh. 103b). Jews continued to visit Shiloh to pray at the Masjad al-Sukayma, the Mā'ida ("Stone of the Table") and the tomb of Eli until the 14th century, as is recorded by Eshtori ha-Parḥi. At the wali ("Marabout") known as al-Sittīn or al-Arab'īn, a lintel, perhaps of a synagogue, is still extant and shows an amphora between two rosettes flanked by two jars. In the last century an ancient sarcophagus, supposedly that of Eli the priest, was being shown there.

BIBLIOGRAPHY: Albright, in: BASOR, 9 (1923), 10–11; Kjau, in: PEFQS, 60 (1927), 202–13; 64 (1931), 71–88; Eissfeldt, in: VT *Supplement*, 4 (1957), 138ff.; Aharoni, Land, index; M. Buhl and S. Holm-Nielsen, *Shiloh: the Pre-Hellenistic Remains* (1969). **ADD. BIBLIOGRAPHY:** Y. Tsafrir, L. Di Segni, and J. Green, *Tabula Imperii Romani. Iudaea – Palaestina. Maps and Gazetteer* (1994), 232, s.v. "Silo"; I. Finkelstein (ed.), *Shiloh: The Archaeology of a Biblical Site* (1993).

[Michael Avi-Yonah / Shimon Gibson (2nd ed.)]

SHILOH, YIGAL (1937–1987), Israeli archaeologist, expert on Iron Age town-planning and architecture in the Land of Israel. Born in Haifa, he was educated at the Hebrew University of Jerusalem, eventually joining the faculty in 1974. Shiloh received his Ph.D. in 1977, and a revised version of his dissertation was published in 1979 as *The Proto-Aeolic Capital and Israelite Ashlar Masonry*. From 1983 to 1986 Shiloh headed the Institute of Archaeology at the Hebrew University and was a visiting professor abroad.

As a student Shiloh participated in numerous excavations in Israel, notably in the Survey of the Judean Desert Caves, Masada, Tell Nagila, Ramat Raḥel, Arad, Megiddo, and Hazor. In addition to these digs, he also participated in an expedition working on a prehistoric site in northern Italy. From 1978 to 1987 Shiloh undertook major archaeological excavations in the area of the "City of David" in Jerusalem. He was the author of numerous articles and research papers. He was also the recipient of the prestigious Jerusalem Prize only one week before he succumbed to cancer at the young age of 50.

BIBLIOGRAPHY: J.M. Cahill and A. de Groot, "Obituary: Professor Yigal Shiloh, 1937–1987," in: *Bulletin of the Anglo-Israel Archaeological Society*, 8 (1988–89), 77; W.G. Dever, "In Memoriam – Yigal Shiloh, in: BASOR, 274 (1989), 1–2; T. Shiloh, "Shiloh, Yigal," in: *The Oxford Encyclopedia of Archaeology in the Near East*, vol. 5 (1997), 29–30.

[Shimon Gibson (2nd ed.)]

SHILS, EDWARD ALBERT (1910–1995), U.S. sociologist. Shils was born in Springfield, Massachusetts, to Russian Jewish immigrant parents. His father was a cigar maker in Springfield and then in Philadelphia, Pennsylvania. Shils attended Simon Gratz High School. At 17, he began studying the work of German sociologist Max Weber. Shils went on to study foreign languages at the University of Pennsylvania, graduating with a bachelor's degree in 1931. In the midst of the Great Depression, Shils was a supporter of the New Deal and went to work as a social worker. Fascinated with the makeup of societies, Shils' passion led him to take a position as a research assistant in sociology with the University of Chicago in 1934 and then a teaching position in 1938. Shils' early exposure to and translation of the works of European sociologists, such as Karl Mannheim and Weber, enabled him to serve as a bridge between American and European sociological research. During World War II, Shils served with the Office of Strategic Services, a progenitor to the CIA, interviewing captured German soldiers for the British government. In 1945, he collaborated with scientists from the University of Chicago who worked on the Manhattan Project to found the publication *The Bulletin of the Atomic Scientists*, to alert governments to the dangers posed by nuclear weapons and other weapons of mass destruction. From 1946 to 1950, Shils taught sociology at the London School of Economics; he was named an honorary fellow of the college in 1972. He returned to the University of Chicago, where he became an associate professor in 1947 and then a full professor in the Committee on Social Thought in 1950. In 1949, Harvard sociologist Talcott Parsons invited Shils to co-author a paper, titled *Toward a General Theory of Action* (1951), which sought to understand the interconnectedness of groups and individuals within society in a universal context. In 1952, Shils served as a lecturer at the University of Manchester. He returned to Chicago in 1953 as a professor both on the Committee on Social Thought and the school's sociology department. Shils spent time traveling through India from 1955 to 1956, and each year through to 1967, studying the country's intelligentsia. The growing conservatism of 1950s America and its attack on intellectuals inspired Shils' public challenge to McCarthyism with the publication of his book *Torment of Secrecy* (1956). In 1961, he received his master's degree from Cambridge University and published *The Intellectual Between Tradition and Modernity: The Indian Situation*. In 1962, he founded the quarterly journal *Minerva: A Review of Science, Learning and Policy*, which explores the link between scientific work at universities and public policy. In addition to his work with the University of Chicago, Shils served as a fellow of King's College, Cambridge from 1961 to 1970; a fellow of Peterhouse, Cambridge, from 1970 to 1978; an honorary professor from 1971 to 1977 at the University of London; and a professor at the University of Leiden from 1976 to 1977. Shils delivered the Jefferson Lectures in 1979 and was awarded the Balzan prize in 1983. He taught his last class in Chicago at the age of 84. He died of cancer in Chicago.

BIBLIOGRAPHY: "Shils, Edward Albert," in: *Encyclopedia of World Biography* (1998[2]); "Shils, Edward Albert," in: *The Scribner Encyclopedia of American Lives*, vol 4 (1994–1996); "Prof. Edward Shils, 84, Is Dead; Researcher on Intellectuals' Role," in: *The New York Times* (Jan. 26, 1995, Section D; Page 21; Column 1); "Obituary: Edward Shils, Committee on Social Thought, Sociology," in; *The University of Chicago Chronicle* (Feb. 2, 1995), chronicle.uchicago.edu/950202/shils.shtml.

[Adam Wills (2nd ed.)]

SHIMEI (Heb. שִׁמְעִי), son of Gera, a Benjamite and a relative of Saul, who insulted David as the latter fled during the rebellion of Absalom. The road from Jerusalem to the Jordan Valley led past Bahurim, in Benjamin, where Shimei resided. As David and his party marched by, Shimei came toward them, threw stones and earth at them, and called to David, "Filth! Filth! Murderer! Blackguard!" He gloated over David's predicament, saying that it was divine retribution for the blood of the house of Saul that David had shed. *Abishai wanted to kill Shimei on the spot but David restrained him, enduring this humiliation as a form of self-mortification whereby men seek to appease God in times of affliction (II Sam. 16:5–13). When David returned in triumph after Absalom's defeat, Shimei and a thousand Benjamites whom he had persuaded to join him arrived at the Jordan – before any other group of the House of David – and together with the Judahites welcomed him back and begged for clemency (II Sam. 19:17ff.). Clemency was granted, either because David considered Shimei's change of heart a sign of renewed divine favor (Rashi, II Sam. 19:23) or because he believed that a vindictive policy against those who had rebelled would prevent firm reestablishment of his reign (*Meẓudat David*, II Sam. 19:23). Any oath made by David was not binding on his son Solomon. Before his death David instructed Solomon to watch for an opportunity to do away with Shimei (I Kings 2:8–9). Solomon placed Shimei under close observation, and made him promise under pain of death to restrict his movements to within Jerusalem. When Shimei broke his vow in order to recover two runaway slaves, Solomon had him put to death (I Kings 2:36–46).

[Gershon Bacon]

In the Aggadah

Shimei, although a Benjamite (II Sam. 19:17), is called "the first of the house of Joseph" (*ibid.*, 19:21), in order to elaborate his plea for forgiveness from the king. It suggested that David should emulate the example of Joseph, who forgave his brothers (Mid. Ps. 3:3). Another opinion, however, is that "Joseph" is a euphemism for "the house of Israel" (cf. Amos 5:15). It thus paraphrases his plea: "All Israel has dealt ill with thee, and I more so than anyone else. Now all Israel sits waiting for whatever mercy you may show me. If you accept my apology, then all Israel will come forward and make peace with you" (Mid. Ps., *ibid.*). He failed, however, to persuade David to forgive him. The word *Nimreẓet* is used by David to describe Shimei's curse (I Kings 2:8). It is said to be a mnemonic to illustrate that Shimei was an adulterer (*no'ef*); a Moabite (*Mo'avi*); a murderer (*roẓe'aḥ*); and an abomination (*to'evah*; Shab. 105a). Shimei is deprived of any of the credit for having been an ancestor of Mordecai (cf. Esth. 2:5; Meg. 13a). The credit belongs to his wife, who save two righteous men (Jonathan and Ahimaaz) from Absalom (Mid. Sam. 32:4). Shimei's one recorded virtue is that, as long as he lived, Solomon did not marry the daughter of Pharaoh, but took Jewish wives (Ber. 8a). His eventual death was commensurate with his crime. Because he had sinned by word of mouth, Solomon slew him by pronouncing the name of God on him (Zohar, Exodus, 108a).

BIBLIOGRAPHY: R. Kittel, *Geschichte des Volkes Israel*, 2 (19257), 143–6; Noth, Hist Isr, 204; T.M. Mauch, in: IDB, 4 (1962), 331; G. Buccellati, *Cities and Nations of Ancient Syria* (1967), 198–9. IN THE AGGADAH: Ginzberg, Legends, index; I. Ḥasida, *Ishei ha-Tanakh* (1964), 422.

SHIM'ON, JOSEPH BEN JUDAH IBN (12th–13th centuries), physician, poet, and philosopher, contemporary of *Maimonides. Born in *Morocco, he was taught by Muslim teachers, and also received a traditional Jewish education, despite the fact that at that time the Jews of Morocco had to live as *anusim* ("forced converts"). He states in his *Ma'amar* *bi-Meḥuyyav Meẓi'ut* (see below) that he studied philosophy with a Muslim teacher. As a young man, he already achieved fame both as a Hebrew poet and as an expert in mathematics and medicine.

He escaped from Morocco to *Egypt, where be could profess his Judaism openly. He lived first in *Alexandria, from where he sent letters and *maqāmāt* to Maimonides, and later in Fostat, where he studied astronomy and philosophy with Maimonides (see his letter in *Iggerot ha-Rambam*, ed. by D.Z. Baneth, (1946), 7ff.). Around 1185 he went to *Syria and settled in *Aleppo, where he engaged in commerce (*ibid.*, 68) and became wealthy through commercial travels which took him as far as Babylon and India. Afterward, he became the court physician of the son of Saladin, Az-Zāhir-Ghāzī, king of Aleppo. He maintained a constant correspondence with Maimonides, and it was the latter's desire to complete the education of his "beloved disciple" that led him to write his *Guide* and to dedicate it to Ibn Shim'on. When he was in *Baghdad, he attempted to mediate between Maimonides and his opponent, *Samuel b. Ali, head of the Baghdad Academy (*ibid.*, 31ff.), and when the Babylonian scholar, *Daniel b. Saadiah, began to attack the doctrines of Maimonides, Ibn Shim'on demanded his excommunication. He wrote a theological-philosophical treatise on the creation of the world (Heb. trans. by M. Loewy, *Ma'amar bi-Meḥuyyav ha-Meẓi'ut in Drei Abhandlungen von Josef b. Jehuda*, 1879; *A Treatise as to Necessary Existence*, ed. and trans. by J.L. Magnes, 1904). Steinschneider mentions one medical work, presumably written by Ibn Shim'on (see bibliography). Medieval historians of science regard Ibn Shim'on as an eminent physician of his time. The identification of Ibn Shim'on with Joseph b. Judah ibn Aknīn has been proven to be incorrect.

BIBLIOGRAPHY: S. Munk, in: *Journal Asiatique*, 14 (1842), 5–70; M. Steinschneider, in: MB, 11 (1871), 119; A. Neubauer, in: MGWJ, 19 (1870), 348–55, 395–401, 445–8; A.Ḥ. Freimann, in: *Sefer ha-Yovel ... B.M. Lewin* (1939), 27–41; A.J. Heschel, in: *Sefer ha-Yovel ... L. Ginzburg* (1946), 164–70; D.Z. Baneth, in: *Sefer ha-Yovel li-Khevod G. Shalom* (1958), 108–22 (= *Tarbiz*, 27 (1958), 234–48); idem, in: *Oẓar Yehudei Sefarad*, 7 (1964), 11–20.

[Eliyahu Ashtor]

SHIMONI (originally **Shimonovitz**), **DAVID** (1886–1956), Hebrew poet. He was born in Bobruisk, district of Minsk, Russia, the son of a learned *maskil*. Shimoni studied with private tutors and read avidly, especially in the impressive library belonging to the father of his childhood friend, Berl *Katznelson. He soon began to write, publishing his first poem, a free translation from the Russian of Simon *Frug, in *Gan Sha'ashu'im*. His first original poem, "*Siḥat Resisim*" (1902), appeared in the children's paper *Olam Katan*, but his career is considered to have begun with the poem "*Bein ha-Shemashot*" (1902), published with *Bialik's encouragement in *Lu'aḥ Aḥi'asaf* (no. 12, 1904). His early lyric poems appeared in the best Hebrew journals such as *Ha-Zeman, Ha-Ẓefirah, Ha-Shilo'aḥ*, and *Ha-Me'orer*. For a short period he was employed in drawing revolutionary posters in Russian (1906), and from that year he also published poems in Yiddish. Because of government restrictions placed on the admission of Jews, he was not admitted to the university, so in 1909 he immigrated to Ereẓ Israel, where he stayed about a year. He worked in orange groves and as a watchman in Reḥovot and Petaḥ Tikvah, becoming particularly friendly with A.D. *Gordon and J.Ḥ. *Brenner. He also spent two months touring the country, and for the rest of his life drew on his impressions of that trip. He first wrote of these travels in *Ha-Zeman*, and later in his poetry. From 1911 to 1914 he studied Oriental philology and philosophy at various German universities. In 1911 his first collection of poems, *Yeshimon*, followed in 1912 by his second, *Sa'ar u-Demamah*, were published in Warsaw. He then began publishing his first idylls ("*Yardenit*" in *Ha-Shilo'aḥ*, "*Ba-Ya'ar be-Ḥaderah*" in *Ha-Po'el ha-Ẓa'ir*, "*Milḥemet Yehudah ve-ha-Galil*" in *Moledet*) and initiated in *Ha-Po'el ha-Ẓa'ir* the series "*Ba-Ḥashai*," which combined poetry, prose, and reflections. On the outbreak of World War I he returned to Russia, and spent the war in his native town and in St. Petersburg. At the beginning of the Revolution he moved to Moscow, where he became secretary to the editorial board of the newspaper *Ha-Am*. He also had original works and translations published by the *Stybel press. Cycles of his poems and his translations of Tolstoy, Lermontov, Pushkin, and Heine appeared in the first volumes of *Ha-Tekufah*.

After numerous attempts he left Russia and returned to Ereẓ Israel in 1921, where he produced *Mi-Midbar le-Midbar*, echoes of his wanderings at the end of the war and during the revolution, the idylls *Yovel ha-Eglonim, Ba-Derekh, Leket, Ha-Yoreh, Me-Aggadot Ẓefat*, and the poems *Eshet Iyyov* and *Be-Veit ha-Neḥashim*. In 1925 he settled in Tel Aviv and taught Bible and Hebrew literature at the Herzliyyah secondary school until the end of his life. He continued to write idylls (*Maẓẓevah, Si'onah*), dramatic poems, lyrics, chapters of *Ba-Ḥashai*, and introduced a type of satire and fable which mainly served as vehicles for his reaction to the events of the day. In addition to his literary work he plunged into public activity, becoming a member and eventually chairman of the *Academy of the Hebrew Language; the Writers' Association, Genazim, and the Israel Chapter of Friends of the Hebrew University.

Shimoni's poetry expresses Second Aliyah ideals and describes pioneer life in Ereẓ Israel. He belonged to the circle of leading Hebrew poets who were under the influence of Bialik and were the chief spokesmen of Hebrew literature for more than a generation. These poets shared the heritage of life in the Jewish towns of Europe, which had been shattered by history, and the attempts at rebuilding a new national life in Ereẓ Israel. Shimoni is known primarily through his idylls, which were avidly read by two generations of pioneers and are still an integral part of the Israel school curriculum. The pioneers, who sought in literature a confirmation and reaffirmation of their life, found in Shimoni's heroes an expression of the finest achievements of the *ḥalutzim*. For this reason the idylls overshadowed Shimoni's other work. The latter is characterized by two features: lyricism, poetry of the ego, of trouble and sadness; and didacticism, poetry which propagates ideas and educates through reproof and satire. Shimoni's early poetry was lyric – sad, gloomy, and severe. In later poems, although strong lyrical and elegiac elements are retained, the poet concerns himself more with public issues, contemporary problems, and the needs of the people.

Shimoni's lyricism revealed from his early youth a complex personality – serious, skeptical, and reflective – always wandering and seeking and meditating on the fundamental questions of existence and the tragic history of his people. The older he grew the more severe and uncompromising became his attitude toward life. As his sense of duty increased, it pushed the demands of his ego aside, and, together with his honesty and moral strictness, impelled him to abandon individualism for the nationalist idea. Shimoni expressed a feeling of alienation, a division between the real world – strange and hostile – and the imaginary region he craved for – between the "northern land" and the "eastern land." His youthful wanderings and the horrors of World War I explain something of Shimoni's tendency to see the dark side of life, but this tendency was reinforced by trends in Russian literature, especially the Byronism in Lermontov's and Pushkin's works, which he translated into Hebrew. Shimoni's writings also bear the influence of the *fin-de-siècle*.

In his first creative period, Shimoni sees life as a false vision, with sorrow and death as reality. His poems are full of shadows, twilight glimmerings, the sadness of falling leaves, the howling of winds, and lowering storms. They frequently contain expressions of ruined hopes, loss of youth, the paleness of shrouds, the death throes of eras, as if to say that while the whole world is feasting and bathed in light, the poet stands like a stranger at the roadside. They also communicate the sentiments of a young Jew longing to get into the great world which has never accepted him. Shimoni's poetry has nothing of the jubilation of youth, and even love is not able to disperse the clouds of his grief. He wrote a few love poems in his first creative period which occasionally reflect a moment of forgetfulness or a longing for oblivion and repose, but rarely the intoxication and exultation of happiness. Generally it is the girl who looks for love, while the grave youth sings to his beloved the song of "twilight."

Shimoni and Nature

Shimoni's strong affection for nature is revealed in his memoirs, where he stresses that from his youth he had a tendency to seclude himself in nature and attempt to penetrate the secrets of existence. When he was unable to wander and enjoy "the wide open spaces" he would soar in his imagination to lands where he could find solace from the real world. In fact, he makes use of nature mainly for giving utterance to his innermost thoughts; yet he wrote only a few epic nature poems. Almost everywhere his lively sense of scenery and his clear vision are engulfed in lyrical sentimentality. Shimoni turns mostly to nature's dark, sad side, recognizing that everything is ephemeral.

It was only some years after Shimoni's first visit to Ereẓ Israel that his impressions of the country began to dominate his spirit and his poetry. When he went back to Europe he wrote yearning poems about the landscape of Ereẓ Israel. When he returned to Ereẓ Israel, he experienced the difficulty of liberating himself from the landscape of his childhood and acquiring an intimate knowledge of a new one. In a poem written in 1924 he expresses his weariness of the overabundant and brilliant light in the country, and his longing for Russia's foggy days.

The Romantic Character of His Poetry

In his first creative period, the poet is remote from contemporary social and national problems and for the most part renounces the outer world. Only occasionally does he mention the wretched and dismal existence of the Jews, the horror of World War I, or react indirectly to various events of his time and place. He aspires to what is not of this world, and there, in the imaginary distances of time and place, he hopes to find his lost destiny. A long series of similes and images also gives expression to his yearning for that "somewhere" (including Zion) and his strong attraction to the unknown region of his heart's desire. Now and then one hears in Shimoni's poems the voice of revolt, which is hardly related to a real and clear-cut struggle, but is romantically vague.

From Regret to the Reality of Life

Although Shimoni's lyric poetry is melancholy, it should not be regarded as poetry of destruction and despair. In his somber meditation there are occasional flashes of humor, the play of opposites, in which some inner vitality courses.

In this very period of *Weltschmerz* and depression one can discern in his work the seeds from which his idylls grew. Among his numerous poems of sorrow there are some which look on the bright side of life and discover the source of joy. Slowly the poet achieves the will to live and contentment with that which exists. Shimoni, like many of his generation, was captivated by the romanticism of *Ḥibbat Zion and Zionism. Doubtless there was also a romantic influence, but immigration to Ereẓ Israel was much more than a matter of romanticism. When Shimoni settled permanently in the country, he abandoned most of the motifs of his lyrics. Influenced by Brenner, Shimoni, in the middle of his writing career, turned increasingly to topical poetry. Written in a militant and aggressive spirit, this poetry deliberately encouraged national service. Shimoni, ruled by a sense of national and public duty, was to write more and more poems in response to the events of the times, warning against weaknesses and dangers with the lashing tongue of the preacher, the bitterness of the satirist, beginning with *Al Sefod* (1921), continuing with *Ereẓ Yisrael* (1929), *Lo! Et Damenu Lo Nafkir* (1936), *Hithakhi Ahvat Yisrael…* (1939), and ending with a great number of poems of protest from the days of war, destruction, and ghettos.

Displaying neither surprising values nor new forms, Shimoni's poems did not receive great attention when they appeared. His style was generally that of the "classical" Hebrew poetry of his time, but he was one of the last to adopt it, when the style had already begun to decline and was exhibiting signs of weakness. Other young poets had embraced new methods. Although aware of these techniques, Shimoni kept to regular rhymes, a definite meter, and a symmetrical construction. Even when the poem is full of grief and stormy protest, the lines and rhymes are clear, considered, and subdued. The seriousness and severity of the poems is somewhat softened by a simple lucid style, whose elements and phrases are casual and ordinary. Shimoni was known as "an abstainer from form" because of his lack of original patterns, embellishments or surprising phrases. The numerous repetitions of the same motifs, the occasionally excessive length, the many allegorical features and general feeling of weariness sometimes lend the poems a gray, monotonous character. As against this, the reader is taken by the purity and veracity of the descriptions, the sincerity of feeling and the warm spirituality. It was to this that Bialik referred when he said of Shimoni: "His clothes are simple but he himself is festive."

Like other Hebrew poets, Shimoni changed from the Ashkenazi to the Sephardi accentuation at a fairly late stage. From 1932 onward his poems rhyme and scan according to the Sephardi accentuation, whereas all his earlier poems (i.e., the majority of his lyrics) must be read with the Ashkenazi penultimate meter stress and tonal emphasis if they are to be fully enjoyed. Shimoni's work is collected in (1) *Ketavim*, 4 vols. (1925–32); *Mivḥar Ketavim*, 2 vols. (1960), continued in 1965 by Dvir Publishing House (not completed). For translations of Shimoni's works into English see Goell, bibliography, index.

BIBLIOGRAPHY: J. Klausner, *David Shimoni, ha-Meshorer ve-Hogeh ha-De'ot* (1948) (incl. bibl. by B. Shohetman); *ibid.*, introd. to D. Shimoni, *Idylls* (Eng. 1957); A. Kariv, *Iyyunim* (1950), 318–20; Y. Keshet, *Be-Dor Oleh* (1950), 135–71; M. Ribalow, *Im ha-Kad el ha-Mabbu'a* (1950), 84–120; D. Sadan, *Avnei Boḥan* (1951), 96–102; idem, *Bein Din le-Ḥeshbon* (1963), 59–65; A. Barash, *Ketavim*, 3 (1952), 26f., 146f.; F. Lachower, *Shirah u-Mahashavah* (1953), 61–66; D. Kimḥi, *Soferim* (1953), 93–97; D. Zakkai, *Keẓarot* (1954), 394; Z. Shazar, *Or Ishim* (1955), 191–9; H. Bavli, *Ruḥot Nifgashot* (1958), 68–78; J. Fichmann, *Be-Terem Aviv* (1959), 126–56; S. Kremer, *Ḥillufei Mishmarot* (1959), 93–100; I. Lichtenbaum, *Soferei Yisrael* (1959), 119–22; I. Kohen, *Sha'ar ha-Te'amim* (1962) 185–8; idem, *Sha'ar ha-Soferim* (1962), 182–97; S.Y. Penueli, *Sifrut ki-Feshutah* (1963), 173–83; D.A. Friedman, *Iyyunei Shirah* (1964), 262–87; A. Blum (ed.), *Tenu'at ha-Avodah ba-Ḥinnukh u-va-Hora'ah* (1965); R. Katznelson-Shazar, *Al Admat ha-Ivrit* (1966), 139–43; M. Reicher, *Ha-Telem ha-Arokh* (1966), 111–4; E. Schweid, *Shalosh Ashmurot ba-Sifrut ha-Ivrit* (1967), 122–9; I. Hanani, in: *Ha-Po'el ha-Ẓa'ir* (1967); Waxman, Literature, 4 (1960), 312–7. **ADD. BIBLIOGRAPHY:** S. Weisblit, "*Ḥaluẓiyut ve-Ḥaluẓim ba-Idiliyot shel Shimoni*," in: *Haumah*, 55 (1978), 395–9; D. Laor, "*D. Shimoni – Y.H. Brenner, Sippurah shel Yedidut*," in: *Sefer Yizḥak Bakon* (1992), 157–201; Y.H. Halevi, "*Pe'amei Mashiah: Ha-Yehudi mi-Teiman ve-Torat Ereẓ Yisrael 'al pi D. Shimoni*," in: *Mahut*, 12 (1994), 78–98; Y. Oren, "*Lo Shirah Nishkaḥat!*" in: *M'aof u-Ma'aseh*, 6 (2000), 1–12.

SHIMONI, YOUVAL (1955–), Hebrew novelist. Shimoni was born in Jerusalem. He studied cinema at Tel Aviv University and published two novels which were hailed as major literary events by Israeli critics. *Me'of ha-Yonah* ("The Flight of the Dove"; German, 1994; French, 2001) is a postmodern prose narrative made up of two parallel stories, printed on the opposite pages of the book. The second novel, *Ḥeder* ("A Room"; French, 2004), is yet again a highly sophisticated prose work composed of three independent parts that weld into a single entity, oscillating between an army base and Paris, fusing cinematic techniques and reflecting on the substance of life and art. "This book reaches heights of heart-felt longing and grace," wrote Amos Oz.

BIBLIOGRAPHY: M. Ron, "*Le-Ever ha-Perurim*," in: *Siman Keriah*, 21 (1990), 189–201; A. Balaban, "*Ha-Alilah ha-Nosefet*," in: *Alei Siaḥ*, 31–2 (1992), 79–91; O. Bartana, "*Eikh Lehamit Modernizm*," in: *Dimui*, 5–6 (1993), 54–59; H. Herzig, "*Dialogim 'im ha-Modernizm ba-Sipporet ha-Ivrit*," in: *Alei Siaḥ*, 39 (1997), 39–45; H. Hever, "*Sifrut Yisra'elit bi-Zman Kibbush*," in: *Alpayim*, 25 (2003), 155–69; A. Feldman, "*Ha-Mediyum ha-Kolno'i ke-Metaforah shel Meẓi'ut post Modernit*," in: *Alpayim*, 25 (2003), 170–85; N. Ezer, "*Alegoriah ve-Simulkarah be-'Omanut ha-Milḥamah' le-Y. Shimoni*," in: *Iton 77*, 288 (2004), 18–21.

[Anat Feinberg (2nd ed.)]

SHIMRON (Heb. שִׁמְרוֹן), Canaanite city, first mentioned in the Egyptian Execration Texts (19th–18th centuries B.C.E.; E 55), where it appears as Šmw'nw; it appears as Šm'n in the list of conquered cities of Thutmosis III (15th century B.C.E.; No. 35). In the el-Amarna letters, Šamu-Adda, king of Šamhuna, is mentioned as an ally of the king of Acre (Letters 8:13; 224; 225:4). All these texts indicate a name like Šim'on for the city; in the Bible, however, it occurs as Shimron, with the Septuagint variant Συμοων. A king of Shimron took part in the coalition led by Jabin of Hazor and is listed among the kings defeated by Joshua (Josh. 11:1; 12:20; the name Shimron-Meron is explained in several manuscripts of the Septuagint as referring to two kings, one of Shimron and one of Meron). In Joshua 19:15, Shimron is listed among the cities of Zebulun, together with Nahalal and Beth-Lehem of Galilee. It appears in later periods as Simonias, a village on the frontier of Galilee, 60 stades (c. 7½ mi., 12 km.) from Gaba (Jos., Life, 115). It is mentioned as Sim'oniya in talmudic sources (Tosef. Shev. 7:13; TJ, Meg. 1:1, 70a). However, various scholars doubt the identification of biblical Shimron with Shim'on-Simonias. Shimron is identified with the present-day Khirbat Sīmūniyya, a prominent tell with springs in the vicinity; pottery on the surface includes types of the Early to Middle Bronze Ages, and remains of a synagogue have been identified there.

BIBLIOGRAPHY: Maisler, in: BJPES, 1 (4), 1ff.; idem, in: *Eretz Israel*, 3 (1954), 28; Abel, Geog, 2 (1938), 464; Aharoni, Land, index.

[Michael Avi-Yonah]

SHIN (Heb. שִׁין ;ש), the twenty-first letter of the Hebrew alphabet; its numerical value is 300. In the early Proto-Canaanite script the *shin* was drawn as a pictograph of a composite bow . Then in the Phoenician, Aramaic, and Hebrew scripts it was written 𐤔. While the Hebrew script preserved this form (cf. the Samaritan ࠔ), the Phoenician *shin* developed into 𐤔 → 𐤔 → 𐤔, and the Aramaic *shin* into 𐡔 → 𐡔 → 𐡔 which is the basic form of the Jewish *shin* שׁ. From the Nabataean 𐢗 → 𐢗. the Arabic evolved, which was used both for the *sin* (س) and *shin* (ش). Presumably, the later Proto-Canaanite or the early Phoenician *shin* was the model from which the Greek *sigma* Σ, ϟ – the ancestor of the Latin "S" – developed. See*Alphabet, Hebrew.

[Joseph Naveh]

SHINAH, SELMAN (1898–?), Iraqi lawyer, politician, and Hebrew writer. An officer in the Turkish army in World War I, Shinah was captured and exiled to *India until 1919. He was elected the Jewish representative in the Iraqi parliament in 1947 and 1949. He founded the Hebrew Writers' Union in 1920 and published a Zionist weekly in Arabic, *Al-Miṣbāḥ* ("The Menorah"), which lasted until 1929. He settled in Israel in 1951. His autobiography, *Mi-Bavel le-Ẓiyyon* ("From Babylon to Zion"), appeared in 1955.

SHINAR (Heb. שִׁנְעָר), place-name referring to *Mesopotamia, the area once termed Sumer and Akkad. In Genesis 10:10 the name Shinar as a geographical name appears alongside the names of such ancient Mesopotamian sites as Babel (Akk. Bāb-ili), Erech (Akk. Uruk), and Akkad. So, too, the Septuagint transcription of the name (i.e., Σεννααρ) is replaced by the rendering "Babylonia" in, e.g., Isaiah 11:11 and Zechariah 5:11. Various attempts have been made to determine the etymology of Shinar, relating it, in some way, to the name Sumer (see *Sumer). Whatever its ultimate etymology, the designation Shinar for Mesopotamia is paralleled in the el-Amarna letters (EA 35:49), where it appears as šanḫar, as well as in Egyptian records, where it is written *sngr.*

BIBLIOGRAPHY: J.A. Knudtzon, *Die El-Amarna Tafeln* (1964), 1080.

[Murray Lichtenstein]

SHINDOOKH, MOSES BEN MORDECAI, *nasi* of the *Baghdad community in the first half of the 18th century. He was also **ṣarrāf-bashi* ("chief banker") to the governor of the city. A man of generous disposition, he gave his support especially to religious scholars. In 1743 he was reported to Ahmed Pasha, the city governor, and sentenced to death. After Baghdad Jews paid a large sum to the pasha and Shindookh wrote off a debt the pasha owed him, the sentence was quashed and Shindookh was reinstated in office.

His grandson SASON BEN MORDECAI SHINDOOKH (1747–1830) was born in Baghdad, and became well known as a rabbi and kabbalist, a poet and preacher, and especially as the author of many works in the field of traditional and mystical Jewish studies. The poems that he composed were both of a religious and secular nature and some are didactic. They were written in the rhyme of Spanish-Hebrew poetry. Some of his *piyyutim* were included in *siddurim* and in books of *piyyutim* in the Babylonian rite. He also served as the permanent *ḥazzan* of the Great Synagogue in Baghdad. He was a practicing kabbalist, and became the subject of legends.

His published works include *Imrei Sason* (Baghdad, 1891); *Devar Beito* (2 parts, Leghorn, 1862, 1864); *Mizmor le-Asaf* (Leghorn, 1864); *Kol Sason* (Leghorn, 1859); *Sadeh Lavan* (Jerusalem, 1904); and *Tehillah le-David* (Baghdad, 1892). He also wrote many works which are extant in manuscript.

BIBLIOGRAPHY: A. Ben-Yaacob, *Yehudei Bavel* (1965), index.

[Abraham Ben-Yaacob]

SHINUI, Israeli center-liberal party that underwent several transformations after it was founded in July 1974, following the Yom Kippur War, by Amnon *Rubinstein, Mordechai Wirshubski, and others. The new party was the outgrowth of several protest movements that had emerged against the background of the *meḥdal* ("failure") which had led to the 1973 War. The founders of the party believed that deep political, economic, and social defects in Israeli society threatened the state's security, moral steadfastness, and ability to function properly, and that these could not be repaired by means of public protest alone, or by means of activity within the existing parties.

The ideological platform of Shinui was drafted in the form of eight principles, which included willingness to negotiate with Israel's neighbors on the basis of territorial compromise; amendment of the electoral system to ensure the responsibility of the representatives to their voters as well as the democratization of the parties and legally sanctioned state supervision of their proper operation; securing basic civil rights, guaranteed in a written constitution; avoidance of government intervention in the economy to advance sectorial interests, and intervention only for national requirements, and for the existence of the welfare state; basing the state public administration on the principle of personal responsibility, and the appointment and promotion of employees only on the basis of merit; organization of the education system with the goal of equal opportunities for everyone and ensuring a proper education for everyone, suitable for a democratic society with developed technological and scientific standards; closing the social gaps through an appropriate improvement of the taxation system, the salary policy, demographic planning and the organization of state welfare services; a fundamental change in the standards of public life and the services granted the citizens, by means of education, the upholding of the law, and suitable legislation.

In 1975, Shinui considered uniting with the Civil Rights Movement (CRM-Ratz), but the following year joined – on an individual basis – the new *Democratic Movement for Change (Dash), that received an impressive 15 seats in the elections to the Ninth Knesset in 1977. The DMC joined the government formed by Menaḥem *Begin despite Shinui's objection. Two days before the signing of the Camp David Accords in September 1978, the DMC disintegrated, and seven of its members established a parliamentary group by the name of Ha-Tenu'ah le-Shinui ve-Yozmah (the Movement for Change and Initiative). By July 1980 five members were left in the group, which changed its name to Shinui – The Center Party. In the elections to the Tenth Knesset in 1981 Shinui gained two seats, and in the elections to the Eleventh Knesset in 1984 – three seats. Shinui joined the National Unity Government formed in 1984, and Rubinstein was appointed minister of communications. In the course of the Eleventh Knesset Wirshubski left Shinui and joined the CRM, while Rubinstein resigned from the government in May 1987, because he felt that the government was not doing enough to advance peace, and because of the return of a member of Shas to the government. Shinui was then involved in an attempt at the establishment of a new Center movement with the Independent Liberal Party and the Liberal Center, but this attempt failed. Shinui received two seats in the Twelfth Knesset, and remained in opposition. Prior to the elections to the Thirteenth Knesset in 1992 it created a single parliamentary group and election list with the CRM and *Mapam, called *Meretz. Meretz won 12 seats in the elections, of which Shinui received two. Meretz joined the government formed by Yitzhak *Rabin, and Rubinstein was at first appointed minister of energy and infrastructures, and then, in June 1993, minister of education, culture and sports in place of Shulamit *Aloni. In the elections to the Fourteenth Knesset, Shinui once again received two seats of the 10 won by Meretz. After Meretz registered as a party, one of the two members of Shinui – Avraham Poraz – chose to remain outside the new party, and in March 1999 formed an independent parliamentary group together with Eliezer Sandberg, who had broken off from *Tzomet, which assumed the name of Shinui. In 1999, before the elections to the Fifteenth Knesset, Prof. Shalom Reichman, a staunch advocate of a constitution for Israel and founder and president of the Interdisciplinary Center in Herzliyyah, who was head of the Shinui presidium but was not interested in running for the Knesset, managed to convince journalist Yosef (Tomi) *Lapid to assume the political leadership of the party. Shinui, in its new incarnation, was now identified with efforts to reduce the flow of public funds to the religious parties and to enlist religious youths for military service. Shinui gained 6 seats in the Fifteenth Knesset, and chose to remain in opposition. In the elections to the Sixteenth Knesset, it won an impressive 15 seats. Most of its 15 members were new faces in the Knesset, who came from the professions and academia. Its declared goal after the elections was to convince the *Likud, under the leadership of Ariel *Sharon, to form a secular government with Shinui and the *Israel Labor Party. But when Labor leader Amram Mitzna resisted entering such a government, Shinui entered the new government in a coalition that also included the *National Religious Party and the National Union, with Lapid serving as minister of justice, Poraz as minister of the interior, Joseph Paritzky as minister of national infrastructures, and Yehudit Na'ot as minister of the environment. However, in December 2004, not long after Paritzky was replaced after being involved in a political scandal and Na'ot resigned after becoming fatally ill, Shinui left the coalition. The reason for its decision to leave the government was its objection to the decision to add more funding to the religious parties in the 2005 budget. Paritzky finally received the status of a parliamentary group in May 2005, and Shinui remained in opposition with 14 seats.

Intraparty strife in January 2006 following the party primary in which Lapid, though winning, faced a challenge to his leadership and Avraham Poraz was ousted from the number two position, led to Lapid and Poraz leaving the party. The ensuing split created two factions and Shinui's status was seriously undermined. The party won no seats in the Knesset election of March 2006.

[Susan Hattis Rolef (2nd ed.)]

SHINWELL, EMANUEL, BARON (1884–1986), British Labour politician. Born in London, the son of a small clothing manufacturer, Shinwell was brought up in South Shields and in Glasgow, where he lived for many years. He joined the British Labour Party at the age of 19 and was active in trade union work, often as a militant, becoming a member of the Glasgow Trades Council in 1906. During World War I he worked as an official of the Seamen's Union. He denied that he was a conscientious objector, claiming that his job was a reserved occupation. Nevertheless he supported J. Ramsay MacDonald's campaign in 1917 for a negotiated peace. In the immediate post-1918 period Shinwell was seen as an extreme leftist, one of the so-called "Red Clydesiders." This impression proved inaccurate: he was a consistent Labour moderate who became even less extreme over most issues as the years passed.

Shinwell entered Parliament in 1922 and was minister for mines in the short-lived Labour government of 1924. He lost his seat at the general election of that year, but returned to Parliament in 1928, and was a junior member of the Labour government of 1929 to 1931. Shinwell refused to follow Ramsay MacDonald into the 1931 national coalition and defeated MacDonald in his constituency of Seaham Harbour in 1935. Following the Labour election victory of 1945, Shinwell became minister of fuel and power with a seat in the cabinet. He was widely criticized for his apparent complacency during the severe winter of 1947–48 and was demoted to a post outside the cabinet in 1948, as minister for war. In 1950–51 he reentered the cabinet as minister for defense. From 1964 to 1967 he was chairman of the Parliamentary Labour Party. "Manny" Shinwell was for several years a veteran member of the House of Commons where he was a popular figure. In 1970, on his retirement, he was created a life peer. In his later years Shinwell vehemently opposed British entry into the European Economic Community. His writings include *The Britain I Want* (1943), *When the Men Come Home* (1944), *Conflict Without Malice* (1955), and *The Labour Story* (1963).

Though never officially associated with Jewish or Zionist organizations, Shinwell always prided himself on his Jewish origin. In 1938 he was involved in an incident in the House of Commons when a member uttered an antisemitic threat. He crossed the floor and delivered a resounding smack to the member in front of the whole House. In 1948, when Britain surrendered the mandate for Palestine and withdrew her forces, Shinwell, as minister for war, took measures so that Jews would not be discriminated against in the disposal of surplus military supplies. In later years he enthusiastically supported Israel's cause and took pride in her ability to defend herself. He wrote two volumes of autobiography, *I've Lived Through It All* (1973) and *Lead With the Left: My First Ninety-Six Years* (1981). A respected elder statesman, Shinwell died at the age of 101.

BIBLIOGRAPHY: *Current Biography* (Jan. 1943), 44–46. **ADD. BIBLIOGRAPHY:** ODNB online.

[Vivian David Lipman]

SHION (Heb. שִׁיאֹן), town belonging to the tribe of Issachar, together with Hapharaim and Anaharath (Josh. 19:19). Eusebius places a village of this name near Mt. Tabor (Onom. 158:13). The suggested identification with the springs called ʿUyūn al-Shaʿīn near Dabbūriyya is doubtful. Some scholars have identified this site with the Sigoph of Soen (according to some Mss.) fortified by Josephus (Wars, 2:573; Life, 188); as, however, nearby Mt. Tabor was certainly included in this fortified line, a fortress at ʿUyūn al-Shaʿīn would have been superfluous and it is preferable to read the names of the fortified place as Sogane (Jos., Life, 265; see *Sogane-Sikhnin).

BIBLIOGRAPHY: P. Thomsen, *Loca Sancta* (Ger., 1907), s.v. *Sigof*; Abel, Geog, 2 (1938), 464; Avi-Yonah, in: IEJ, 3 (1953), 95, n.4.

[Michael Avi-Yonah]

SHIPHRAH AND PUAH (Heb. שִׁפְרָה, פּוּעָה), two Hebrew women who served as midwives for the Israelites in Egypt (Ex. 1:15ff.). Ordered by Pharaoh to kill all male children at birth, Shiphrah and Puah, being God-fearing, disobeyed him, under the pretext that the vigorous Hebrew women were able to dispense with the services of a midwife. In reward for their heroic and virtuous behavior, God "established households" for Shiphrah and Puah (*ibid.*, 5:21), which probably means that they became the matriarchs of enduring families in Israel.

The name Shiphrah, which also appears in an Egyptian list of slaves in the form *Š-p-ra*, probably means "fair one." Puah may be related to the Ugaritic *pġt*, meaning "girl."

Shiphrah is identified with Jochebed, the mother of Moses (Sot. 11b). The name refers to the fact that as a midwife, she beautified (*meshapperet*, מְשַׁפֶּרֶת) the children which she delivered; and Israel multiplied exceedingly (*she-paru*, שֶׁפָּרוּ) as a result of her actions; and that she performed deeds which were pleasing (*shafru*, שָׁפְרוּ) to God (Ex. R. 1:13).

BIBLIOGRAPHY: Albright, in: JAOS, 74 (1954), 229 and note 50; Ginzberg, Legends, index; I. Ḥasida, *Ishei ha-Tanakh* (1964), 424.

SHIPLACOFF, ABRAHAM ISAAC (1877–1934), U.S. labor and Socialist leader. Shiplacoff, who was born in Chernigov, Russia, immigrated to the United States in 1891. He worked under sweatshop conditions as a sewing-machine operator for seven years, and then taught at Brooklyn Public School 84. During this period he founded the William Morris Educational Club, in Brownsville, Brooklyn, later part of the Socialist Party. He was a clerk in the customs service for a time.

An "old Socialist" devoted to the union movement, Shiplacoff held several union posts and served on the national executive committee of the Socialist Party, but due to his lack of skill as a tactician he did not establish himself in any one labor organization. He served as secretary to United Hebrew Trades for some years after 1910. As manager of the New York Joint Board of the Amalgamated Clothing Workers, he organized the tailors' general strike in 1920–21. He was president of the International Leather Goods Workers Union from 1927 to 1930. A magnetic speaker and a political aspirant who remained close to his community's feelings and needs, Shiplacoff was the first Socialist elected to the New York State Assembly. He represented his Brownsville (Brooklyn) district in Albany for two terms, 1915–18; in his second term he served as party leader. He was one of the Socialist leaders indicted for sedition under the Espionage Act in 1919, but the indictment against him was dismissed. Shiplacoff represented the 49th Aldermanic District in Brooklyn on the New York Board of Aldermen from 1919 to 1921. In 1929 he campaigned unsuccessfully for the post of Brooklyn Borough president. A park and playground in Brownsville were named for him in 1938.

BIBLIOGRAPHY: M. Epstein, *Jewish Labor in the U.S.A.*, 2 (1953), index; A.F. Landesman, *Brownsville: The Birth, Development and Passing of a Jewish Community in New York* (1969), 114–5, 119.

SHIPS AND SAILING.

Biblical Period

The first sailing vessel mentioned in the Bible is Noah's Ark (see *Ark of Noah).

The Phoenicians first developed marine navigation for purposes of commerce and communication along the sheltered part of the east Mediterranean coast, from the Gulf of Acre to Tyre and Sidon. Since, however, this area is rich in wood and natural inlets, the development of a fleet of larger ships, which could be used for commerce and communication between Asia and Africa via the Mediterranean Sea, naturally followed. Phoenician ships traveled the Mediterranean Sea parallel to the coasts, in a course which permitted them to stop and get provisions in ports established for this purpose in the natural inlets along the shore of the Mediterranean. The Phoenician fleet was a source of pride and wealth to the Tyrians and a target for attack by the prophet Ezekiel (Ezek. 27). In order to provide convenient terminals for ships sailing along the coasts, ports were established at the mouths of rivers. At first only anchorages for boats and small ships, they were gradually developed, by the hewing out of the harbor rocks and the building of suitable quays, into ports capable of affording ships the services required, such as those found in Dor, south of Haifa, in Caesarea, in Jaffa, in Gaza, and elsewhere. Along with the establishment of commercial fleets for interstate trade, there was construction of warships designed to guard the merchant fleet from pirates. These warships were light and strong and constructed in such a way that they could attain great maneuverability and high speed. Both the merchant ships and warships were propelled by sails as well as oars, and were equipped with large crews of oarsmen. The sail was set on the top of a central mast, and the oarsmen were arranged in one, two, or even three rows along the length of the boards of the ship.

Other nations whose history is connected with seagoing transportation are the "Sea Peoples" who penetrated the Near East in the 13th–12th centuries B.C.E. An impressive portrayal of their ships appears on the relief of Medinet Habu, which represents the sea battle between them and Ramses III. The development of seafaring vessels along the length of the unsheltered coast of Palestine was late, taking place only in the days of Solomon. During the period in which his kingdom expanded and extended to the Mediterranean Sea and the Gulf of Ezion-Geber (ʿAqaba), Solomon completed the construction of a large merchant fleet. The fleet was built with the assistance of Tyrian experts sent to him by Hiram, and was based in the port of Ezion-Geber, in order to develop trade with the distant countries of Africa, and so as not to compete with the Phoenician fleet which plied the coasts of the Mediterranean Sea (I Kings 9:26–28; 10:22; II Chron. 8:17–18). King Jehoshaphat's later attempt to build a merchant fleet similar to that of Solomon failed, the ships being wrecked at Ezion-Geber (I Kings 22:48; II Chron. 20:35ff.). In spite of the fact that the Israelites were not a seafaring nation, the Bible attributes close connections with marine transportation to two tribes of Israel: Zebulun and Dan. Of Zebulun it is written: "Zebulun shall dwell by the seashore; he shall be a haven of ships, and his flank shall rest on Sidon" (Gen. 49:13) and "for they [Zebulun] draw from the riches of the sea and the hidden hoards of the sand" (Deut. 33:18–19); of Dan: "and why did he [Dan] abide with the ships" (Judg. 5:17).

In the Bible there are many terms connected with sea traffic: pilots (*hovelim*, Ezek. 27:27), and mariners (*mallahim*, Ezek. 27:27, 29; Jonah 1:5); and rowers (Ezek. 27:29; cf. Jonah 1:13). There are references to a number of types of sailing vessels: *oʾni shayit*, a ship with oars (Isa. 33:21); *oʾni tarshish* ("ships of Tarshish"), large and heavy merchant ships (I Kings 10:22); *kelei gome*, apparently ships made from bundles of papyrus tied together (Isa. 18:2); *sefinah*, from the Akkadian *sapīnatu*, sailing vessel with a deck (Jonah 1:5), and others. In addition, details of parts of sailing vessels occur in common usage in the language of the Bible, such as *luhotayim* ("planks"; Ezek. 27:5); *toren* ("mast"; Isa. 33:23; Ezek. 27:5); *meshotim* ("oars"; cf. Ezek. 27:6); *nes* ("sail(s)"; cf. Isa. 33:23, Ezek. 27:7); *yarketei ha-sefinah* ("the hold of the ship"; Jonah 1:5); *rosh ḥibbel* ("the top of a mast"; Prov. 23:34); and *keresh* ("deck"; Ezek. 27:6). There is a vivid description of a storm overtaking a merchant fleet in the Mediterranean and the subsequent calm in Psalms 107:23–32. (See *Commerce, *Trade)

[Zeʾev Yeivin]

Post-Biblical Period

After its capture by Simeon the *Hasmonean, Jaffa became the main port of Judah; Pompey successfully suppressed the Jewish pirates' base there. *Herod developed the harbor of *Caesarea and built many ships. During the Jewish War, Jewish merchant ships engaged in piracy and inflicted losses on the Romans. Resistance to the Romans was particularly bitter on the Sea of Galilee (Jos., Wars 3, 462ff.).

Among the spoils displayed by Vespasian in his triumphal procession in Rome were "many ships" (Tacitus 7, 3–6). Coins commemorating the Roman victory also bore the legend *Victoria Navalis*. In the second rebellion (115–117), which took place mainly in *Egypt, North Africa, and *Cyprus, this form of warfare was widespread. Various maritime occupations were fairly common among Jews in mishnaic and talmudic times, upon the rivers of Babylon and on the seas. The Babylonian Talmud contains more than 200 technical-nautical terms as well as regulations for ordering river traffic; sailing was considered an honorable profession. The wealth of talmudic references have been the basis for a major study by D. Sperber. For centuries, well into the Christian era, *Alexandria had its own society of Jewish *navicularii* ("shipowners"), as well as seamen of all professions. During the anti-Jewish riots of 39 C.E., cargoes of Jewish ships were carried off and burned. Augustine and Jerome both recorded encounters with Jewish mariners; their contemporary, Bishop Synesius, wrote a satirical account of his experiences aboard a ship with a Jewish crew sailing from Alexandria to Corynna: when a storm rose on Friday afternoon the ship was left to dance freely upon the waves by the God-fearing mariners, to the extreme agitation of the passengers.

Ship representations from the Hasmonean and Early Roman periods have been found at Maresha and in the "Tomb of Jason," Jerusalem. An intact lower hull of a boat dated to the first century C.E. was excavated on the shores of the Sea of Galilee. Drawings of ships – merchantmen and galleys – are known from the Late Roman and Byzantine periods (e.g., at Nessana, Beth Shearim), as well as in mosaic floors (e.g., recently at Lod), X Legion bricks, and coins. A drawing of a merchantman, together with a Latin inscription, "Domine Ivimus," was uncovered in the Church of the Holy Sepulcher. Some authorities date it to the Byzantine period, while others suggest dating it to the Roman period.

[Henry Wasserman / Shimon Gibson (2nd ed.)]

As long as the Mediterranean remained open to the European West, Jewish traders were prominent in maritime contacts between the Mediterranean coast and the southern shores of the sea up to the ninth century. Gregory of Tours (sixth century) tells of a ship manned by Jews plying the coast of Provence and Liguria. Norman ships sighted in Carolingian times were thought to be either Jewish, African, or British. During the Muslim domination of the Mediterranean there is evidence in contracts, responsa, and descriptions of partnerships of Jews "in ships," i.e., in cargoes; Jewish ownership of "a third of a ship" is mentioned. Maimonides distinguishes between various legal forms of this financing of maritime trade. In the main, such Jewish merchants conducted their manifold and widespread trade in ships owned by gentiles. There were, however, notable exceptions: *Benjamin of Tudela observed that the Jews in *Tyre were shipowners. In southern France, particularly in *Marseilles, Jewish shipowners, who were barely differentiated from their Christian competitors, were active from the Byzantine era until well into the Middle Ages. Evidence of some Jewish shipping activities may be found in Aragon, Barcelona, Portugal, and the Balearic Islands in the late Middle Ages. Most Mediterranean ports contained Jewish merchants, brokers, and insurers, engaged in various aspects of shipping.

Jewish scholars may have helped spread the knowledge of early nautical aids like the compass, quadrant (predecessor of the sextant), astrolabe, and astronomical tables, from the Arab East to the Christian West. *Levi b. Gershom (1288–1344) devised an improved quadrant which continued in use for four centuries and was known as "Jacob's staff"; his invention was itself a refinement of the "Quadrans Judaicus" of Judah b. Machir. The famous "Alfonsine Tables" were translated into Spanish and amended by two Jewish physicians at the court of Aragon in the late 13th century. *Majorca was known for its nautical instruments, produced by Jewish craftsmen, and for its Jewish mapmakers, the most renowned of whom were Abraham *Cresques (d. 1387) and his son Judah, who completed his father's lifework, a map of the world. Apostatizing after the massacres of 1391, Judah Cresques entered the service of Prince Henry the Navigator and became director of his nautical academy at Sagres. Abraham *Zacuto constructed the first metal astrolabe, compiled astronomical tables, and was consulted by *Columbus, Vasco de Gama, and other leading navigators of the Age of Discovery. Some Jews participated in the great European voyages of discovery (see Gaspar da *Gama and Pedro *Teixera). Jewish merchants on the Barbary Coast and other Muslim Mediterranean coasts sometimes engaged in privateering and piracy (see also *Palache family).

The *Marrano Diaspora in the Mediterranean world, Northern Europe (Amsterdam, Hamburg, London), and the New World was active in international maritime commerce, mainly as entrepreneurs, merchants, brokers, and insurers. In *Altona and later in Copenhagen Portuguese Jews participated in the shipbuilding industry, developed the trade with Greenland, and pioneered in whaling; the authorities of *Glueckstadt attracted Portuguese Jews by offering them the right to engage in shipbuilding, from which they were excluded in all Hanseatic cities. In England a Marrano, Simon Fernandez, was chief pilot of Sir Walter Raleigh (see also Antonio Fernandez *Carvajal). In his "Humble Address on behalf of the Jewish Nation," *Manasseh Ben Israel emphasized the services the Jews could render to English shipping. Members of the *Schomberg family achieved distinction in the royal navy and merchant marines. Joseph d'Aguilar Samuda (1813–1885), a pioneer in the building of iron steamships, helped found the Institute of Naval Architects. Gustav Wilhelm Wolff, joint founder of the Harland and Wolff shipyards of Belfast, one of the world's largest, joined the Church of England at an advanced age. Sephardi Jews played an important role in colonial trade. The *Furtado and *Gradis families (who pioneered the Canada trade) were prominent among the shipping merchants of *Bordeaux. Marrano shipowners and shipbuilders were active in *Leghorn. In Antwerp the Mendes-Nasi family were prominent shippers in the spice trade and even had their own ships built.

Jews sailed the Indian Ocean, mainly in non-Jewish ships, playing a not inconsiderable role in shipping in the 11th–12th centuries and once more in the 16th–18th centuries. They were also active in shipping in Constantinople and worked as boatmen or porters in the ports of Constantinople (where the Jewish boatmen were known as *kaikjes*) and Salonika. In the British and Dutch colonies of North America, Jews were engaged in the oceanic colonial trade as well as in trade between the various colonies and in fishing enterprises (see Aaron *Lopez and *Touro family). Michael and Bernard Gratz, shippers of New York, outfitted privateers in the War of Independence. Captain John Ordronalux (1778–1841) was a highly successful privateer captain in the 1812–14 war between the United States and Great Britain. In South Africa the *De Pass brothers were the largest shipowners for many years in the 19th century; they were connected mainly with developing the whaling and fishing industries.

In modern times, Jewish participation in shipbuilding – as in other heavy industries – was not common. However, there were exceptions. When Alexander Moses of Koenigsberg began building a ship in 1781, the German builders protested; Frederick II allowed him to finish this one but not to build another. Albert *Ballin raised the standard of the Hamburg-Amerika Line and brought it international repute by introducing modern passenger services and winter pleasure cruises. Jens and Lucie Borchardt (1878–1969) developed tugboat shipping in Hamburg harbor; after the Nazi rise to power they continued their activity in Great Britain. In 1870 W. Kuntsmann (1844–1934) of Stettin founded the largest shipping firm on the eastern coast of Prussia. In Russia, Jews helped develop the internal river traffic: David S. Margolin organized a firm which owned 62 river steamboats on the Dnieper and in the 1880s G. Polyak built a fleet of petroleum tankers that sailed from the Caspian Sea up the Volga. Austrian Lloyd was organized by Italian Jews from *Trieste, as was the Navigazione Generale Italiana. Jacob *Hecht formed the Rhenania Rheinschiffahrts group in 1908 and the Neptun company in 1920 for river shipping.

For shipping in Israel see *Israel, State of: Economic Affairs; *Zim.

[Henry Wasserman]

BIBLIOGRAPHY: BIBLICAL PERIOD: C. Torr, *Ancient Ships* (1895); Cowley, Aramaic, 89–90; A. Koester, *Das antike Seewesen* (1923); idem, *Schiffahrt und Handelsverkehr des oestlichen Mittel-*

meeres (1924); S. Glanville, in: *Zeitschrift fuer aegyptische Sprache und Altertumskunde*, 66 (1931), 105–21; 68 (1932), 7–41; Sp. Marinatos, in: *Bulletin de Correspondence Hellénique*, 57 (1933), 170–235; R. Patai, *Ha-Sappanut ha-Ivrit* (1938); A. Salonen, *Die Wasserfarzeuge in Babylonien* (1939); idem, *Nautica Babylonica* (1942); J. Hornell, in: *Antiquity*, 15 (1941), 242–6; W. Saeve-Soederbergh, *The Navy of the XVIIIth Dynasty* (1946); J.G. Février, in: *La Nouvelle Clio*, 1 (1949) 128–43; A. Parrot, *Déluge et Arche Noé* (1953), 43–55; R.D. Barnett, in: *Archaeology*, 9 (1956), 91; idem, in: *Antiquity*, 32 (1958), 220–30; L. Casson, *The Ancient Mariners* (1959); S. Yeivin, in: JQR, 50 (1959/60), 193–228; J. Braslavi, in: *Elath* (Heb., 1963); Y. Yadin, *The Art of Warfare in Biblical Lands* (1963); L.Y. Radmani, in: Atiqot, 14 (1964), 710; G. Garbini, *Bibliae Oriente*, 7 (1965), 13ff.; J.M. Sasson, in: JAOS, 86 (1965), 126–38; R. North, in: *The Fourth World Congress of Jewish Studies* (1967), 197–202. POST-BIBLICAL PERIOD: S. Tolkowsky, *They Took to the Sea* (1964; incl. bibl.); R. Patai, *Ha-Sappanut ha-Ivrit* (1938; incl. bibl.); idem, in: JQR, 32 (1941/42), 1–26; C. Roth, *Venice* (1930), 175–80; H.I. Bloom, *Economic Activities of the Jews of Amsterdam* (1937), index; A.L. Lebeson, in: HJ, 10 (1948), 155–74; Tcherikover, Corpus, 1 (1957), 105; Baron, Social², 4 (1957), 183f.; 12 (1967), 46, 100f., 104ff.; E. Rosenbaum, in: YLBI, 3 (1958), 257–99; H. Kellenbenz, *Sephardim an der unteren Elbe* (1958); J. Frumkin et al. (eds.), *Russian Jewry* (1966), 139–40; S.D. Goitein, *A Mediterranean Society*, 1 (1967), passim; M. Grunwald, *Juden als Reeder und Seefahrer* (1902); idem, in: *Mitteilungen fuer juedische Volkskunde* (1904), no. 14, 82–84; H.J. Fischel, in: A.A. Neumann and S. Zeitlin (eds.), *The Seventy-Fifth Anniversary Volume of the Jewish Quarterly Review* (1967), 192–210; idem, in: JQR, 47 (1956/57), 37–57; M.A. Gutstein, *The Story of the Jews of Newport* (1936); D. Corcos, in: *Zion*, 25 (1960), 122–33. **ADD. BIBLIOGRAPHY:** Brindley, "The Sailing Ship at Bet-Shearim," in: *Sefunim (Bulletin)*, 1 (1966), 25–27; S. Gibson, "The Tell Sandahannah Ship Grafitto Reconsidered," in: PEQ, 124 (1992), 26–30; S. Gibson and J.E. Taylor, *Beneath the Church of the Holy Sepulchre, Jerusalem* (1994), 25ff.; S. Gibson, "A Brief Note on a Visit Made to El-'Auja…," in: D. Urman (ed.), *Nessana* I (2004), 246*; D. Haldane, "Anchors of Antiquity," in: *Biblical Archaeologist*, 53 (1990), 19–24. L. Casson, "Ships on Coins," in: A.L. Ben-Eli (ed.), *Ships and Parts of Ships on Ancient Coins*, vol. 1 (1975); L.Y. Rachmani, "Jason's Tomb," in: IEJ, 37 (1970), 61–100, Fig. 5a; S. Wachsmann et al., *An Ancient Boat Discovered in the Sea of Galilee* (1988); D. Sperber, *Nautica Talmudica* (1986).

SHIRAZ, capital of the former province of Fars, S. *Iran. The existence of a Jewish community in Shiraz is attested by Persian and Arab geographers from the tenth century. The funeral of a great Sufi leader in Shiraz (981) was attended by Muslims, Christians, and Jews. Muqaddasī (tenth century) states that there was a smaller number of Jews than Christians in the province. *Benjamin of Tudela (c. 1162) described Shiraz as a large city, with a Jewish population of about 10,000. With the rise in 1288 of *Saʿd al-Dawla, the Jewish physician and vizier of Arghūn Khān, the Jews of Shiraz shared in the considerable freedom enjoyed by all the communities in *Persia, and likewise were affected by the persecution which swept over Mesopotamian and Persian Jewry after the death of Arghūn Khān. The persecutions of the Jews in Shiraz under the Safavids are detailed in the Judeo-Persian chronicles of *Babai ibn Luṭf and Babai ibn Farḥad. Coja Jacob Aaron, a Jewish banker and broker of the English East India Company of Basra, went to Shiraz during the Persian occupation of *Basra in 1777. According to David d'Beth Hillel, there lived in Shiraz 700 Jewish families (about 3,500 people) in 1827. And according to the account of Benjamin II, 2,500 out of 3,000 Jews in Shiraz were forced to embrace *Islam in the middle of the 19th century. Later, most of the Jews returned to Judaism. In 1892, 1897, and 1910 there were severe pogroms in the Jewish quarter; many were killed and injured. During the 19th century, Christian missionary activities and the Bahai movement made inroads into the Jewish community which were countered by the establishment of an *Alliance Israélite Universelle school in 1909 (which closed in the 1960s). Toward the end of the 19th century, many Jews from Shiraz emigrated to Ereẓ Israel, including the families of Raḥamim Reuven *Melamed and Raphael Ḥayyim *Ha-cohen.

Approximately 12,000–15,000 Jews lived in Shiraz in 1948. According to the 1956 Iranian census, 8,304 Jews remained in Shiraz, which was then the second largest Jewish community in Iran. Approximately 2,000 Jews left for Israel between 1956 and 1968. Most were artisans and peddlers, but there were also merchants and moneylenders. About half the Jews received financial assistance until they left the city. Those who remained belonged to the middle classes, but in the 1960s Jews began to leave their ghetto. A yeshivah with 18 pupils, a teacher's seminary with 20 pupils, and schools were run by Oẓar ha-Torah and by ORT. The former had 1,100 pupils in 1949 and 2,020 in 1961. In 1960 about 1,000 Jewish children attended government schools. The town had a branch of the Iranian Jewish Women's Association and the Young Peoples' Association, Kanun Javanan. In 1967 the community numbered 7,000 Jews. In the year 2000, 13 Jews were arrested and brought to the revolutionary court in Shiraz on false charges of spying for Israel. They were sentenced to from one to 12 years in prison. Eventually all of them were released at the beginning of 2003. There remained in Shiraz about 3,000 Jews in 2005.

See *Iran.

BIBLIOGRAPHY: I. Ben-Zvi, *Meḥkarim u-Mekorot* (1966), index. **ADD BIBLIOGRAPHY:** L.D. Loeb, *Outcast: Jewish Life in Southern Iran* (1977); A. Netzer, "Jews of Shiraz," in: *Shofar* (July 2001) 22ff. (in Persian); idem, "Jews of Shiraz," in: *Padyavand: Judeo-Iranian and Jewish Studies* (1997), 203–304 (in Persian).

[Walter Joseph Fischel and Hayyim J. Cohen / Amnon Netzer (2nd ed.)]

SHIR HA-MA'ALOT (Heb. שִׁיר הַמַּעֲלוֹת; "Song of Ascent"), superscription of Psalms 120–134 (see *Psalms). (The superscription of Psalm 121, however, is *Shir la-Ma'-alot*.) These psalms are now generally understood to have been sung by the pilgrims as they went up to Jerusalem to celebrate the three *Pilgrim Festivals. Those carrying the firstfruits chanted Psalm 122 as they approached Jerusalem (TJ Bik. 3:2, 65c). In the Ashkenazi rite, these psalms are recited together with Psalm 104 on Sabbath afternoons during the winter season and also on *Tu bi-Shevat. Psalm 126 is sung in the home before *Grace after Meals on Sabbaths and festivals.

SHIR HA-YIḤUD (Heb. שִׁיר הַיִּחוּד; "Hymn of Unity"), a lengthy medieval liturgical poem divided into seven parts, one for each day of the week, praising God, extolling His uniqueness, and emphasizing the smallness of His creatures. Poetic beauty and sublimity of religious thought have placed the poem among the foremost liturgical compositions. Each line is divided into rhymed couplets, with four beats in each couplet. From the fourth line on, each verse throughout the remainder of the poem contains 16 syllables. The first three lines serve as an introduction, a free translation of which reads:

> I will sing to my God as long as I live,
> The God who has sustained me all through my life,
> To this day Thou hast taken me by the hand,
> Life and loving kindness hast Thou given me.
> Blessed be the Lord, blessed be His glorious name,
> For His wondrous kindness shown to His servant.

(trans. P. Birnbaum, *High Holiday Prayer Book* (1951), 101).

The identity of the author is uncertain and no trace of his name is to be found in any acrostical combination in the poem. *Heidenheim (*Ha-Piyyutim ve-ha-Paytanim*, s.v. Judah b. Samuel b. R. Kalonymus, in: Introd. to his *Shemini Aẓeret Maḥzor*) ascribes its authorship to *Samuel b. Kalonymus he-Ḥasid, the father of *Judah he-Ḥasid of Regensburg. A. Epstein (in *Ha-Goren*, 4 (1903), 96–98) has sought to identify Samuel b. Kalonymus Ḥazzan as the author.

Originally, the appropriate portion of the *Shir ha-Yiḥud* was recited in many congregations after the conclusion of the daily service. Some congregations only recited it on the Sabbath. The most prevalent contemporary custom is to recite the entire poem at the conclusion of the service on the eve of the *Day of Atonement, and to chant the appropriate daily section at the start of the morning service on *Rosh Ha-Shanah and the Day of Atonement. Its elimination from the daily and Sabbath services was probably due to the desire not to lengthen the service unduly, though some authorities also quoted the talmudic dictum that no mortal is capable of properly praising the Almighty (A. Lewisohn, *Mekorei Minhagim* (1846), no. 32). "It is as if an earthly king had a million denarii of gold, and someone praised him as possessing silver ones. Would it not be an insult to him?" (Ber. 33b).

BIBLIOGRAPHY: Reifmann, in: *Oẓar Tov*, 8 (1885), 20–5: A. Berliner, in: *Jahresbericht des Rabbiner-Seminars zu Berlin fuer 1908–1909* (1910) (= *Ketavim Nivḥarim*, 1 (1945), 145–70); A.M. Habermann (ed.), *Shirei ha-Yiḥud ve-ha-Kavod* (1948), 11–60; Elbogen, Gottesdienst, 81.

[Aaron Rothkoff]

SHISHAK (Heb. שִׁישַׁק), biblical name for Sheshonq (935–914 B.C.E.), founder of the 22nd (Bubastite) Dynasty of Egypt, and one of the last kings in Egyptian history to invade Palestine. His Tanite predecessors had markedly restrained themselves in this direction; Siamun captured Gezer in approximately 960 B.C.E., but immediately allied himself to *Solomon through a diplomatic marriage (I Kings 3:1; 9:16) and tried to restrain his Edomite protégé Hadad from revenge on Solomon (I Kings 11:14–22, 25). Shishak's campaign took place in the fifth year of *Rehoboam's reign (918/7 B.C.E.) and is recorded in I Kings 14:25–28, II Chronicles 12:2–12, and in a relief at Karnak listing the 165 conquered cities. The motive for the campaign may have been ingratitude on the part of *Jeroboam, who earlier had found protection at Shishak's court (I Kings 11:40). Rehoboam was distracted by a task force dispatched to the Negev that penetrated as far as Edom, and he was made to pay a ransom from the Temple treasury; Jerusalem and Judah remained untouched. His southern fortifications (II Chron. 11:5–12) may have been erected on this occasion. Shishak's main energies were directed against the north. He made a circuit of the area, bringing destruction on Gezer, Gibeon, cities in the Jordan valley, Shechem, Megiddo (where part of a stele bearing his name was found), and cities in the region of the Yarkon. Due to the destruction of Shechem, Jeroboam's residence was temporarily removed to Penuel (I Kings 12:25), which then also fell at the hands of Shishak's troops (it is not mentioned again in biblical sources).

[Irene Grumach]

In the Aggadah

Shishak's real name was *Zevuv* ("fly"), but he was so called because he longed (from the root *Ḥa-SHa-K*; "to desire") for the death of Solomon, whom he feared to attack (SOR 20). The treasures which he plundered from Jerusalem (cf. I Kings 14:25ff.) were those which the children of Israel had taken from Egypt at the time of the Exodus (Ex. 12:36; Pes. 119a).

BIBLIOGRAPHY: W.F. Albright, in: BASOR, 130 (1953), 4–11; B. Mazar, in: VTS, 4 (1957), 57–66; J. Gray, *I and II Kings. A Commentary* (1963), 114–6, 265, 313; G.E. Wright, *Shechem* (1965), 145. IN THE AGGADAH: Ginzberg, Legends, index; I. Ḥasida, *Ishei ha-Tanakh* (1964), 398.

SHITRIT, BEḤOR SHALOM (1895–1967), Israeli Sephardi leader. In his youth he came in contact with Second Aliyah pioneers near Tiberias. After the British occupation of Palestine he was one of the organizers of the police force in his native Tiberias and was appointed commander of the police in Lower Galilee. After training in the Police Officers' School, he worked in the department of criminal investigation in several towns. In 1933 he investigated the case of Chaim *Arlosoroff's murder. From 1935 until 1948 he served as magistrate in several towns. With the establishment of the State of Israel (1948), Shitrit became a member of the government, first as representative of the Sephardi and Oriental communities, holding the post of minister of police and minorities. Later he became a member of the Knesset for *Mapai and served as minister of police almost until his death. In organizing and developing the Israel police, he benefited from his broad experience in the police force and in court, as well as from his thorough knowledge of all the ethnic groups in Israel, their languages, and their customs.

BIBLIOGRAPHY: Tidhar, 1 (1947), 525–6; 13 (1963), 436.

[Yehuda Slutsky]

SHI'UR KOMAH (lit. "the measure of the body," namely the body of God), Hebrew term for an esoteric doctrine concerning the appearance of God in a quasi-bodily form. This doctrine developed in the tannaitic period as the most secret part of *Merkabah mysticism. When the mystic attained the vision of the supernal world and found himself standing before the throne, he was vouchsafed a vision of the *Shi'ur Komah* as the "figure in the form of man" which Ezekiel had seen on the throne in his first vision of the Merkabah (Ezek. 1:26). Not only was this doctrine consistent with the obviously anthropomorphic descriptions of God in many biblical passages, it was also reinforced by the interpretation of the Song of Songs as relating to God and Israel. The figure of the beloved as described there (Songs 5:11–16) served to legitimize the *Shi'ur Komah* doctrine, which was further embellished by the details given about the *ḥaluk*, the robe of glory with which this mystical body of God is clothed. Fragments of this doctrine have been preserved in several texts bearing the title *Shi'ur Komah* and in many allusions to it in midrashic literature. The fragments consist of a detailed description of the limbs of God in the figure of a man and this apparently deliberate and excessive indulgence in anthropomorphism proved shocking to later and more rationalistic Jewish thought. On the other hand, the kabbalists hailed it as a profound, symbolic expression of their own purely spiritual world. The fragments also contain an enumeration of the secret names of these limbs, but in the manuscripts preserved these names are already largely corrupted beyond recognition. The measures given for the several limbs may have contained some sort of numerical symbolism which can no longer be reconstructed. The height of the Creator is given as 236,000 parasangs, based on a numerological interpretation of Psalm 147:5 as "the height of our Lord is 236." The details, however, transcend any possibility of visualization and cannot really have been intended to indicate any concrete measurements. In the fragments preserved these obviously over-drawn anthropomorphisms are explicitly defined as describing not the substance of God but His "hidden glory," or the "body of the *Shekhinah*," *guf ha-Shekhinah*.

In the second half of the second century a Hellenized version of this speculation is to be found in the Gnostic Markos' description of the"body of truth." There also exist a number of Gnostic gems which, like the Hebrew fragments of *Shi'ur Komah*, bear the figure of a man whose limbs are inscribed with magical combinations of letters, obviously corresponding to their secret names (cf. C. Bonner, *Hesperia*, 23 (1954), 151). A clear reference to this doctrine is found as early as the Slavonic Book of Enoch (13:8): "I have seen the measure of the height of the Lord, without dimension and without shape, which has no end." At least two versions of this doctrine were current in later talmudic and post-talmudic times, one in the name of R. *Akiva and one in the name of R. *Ishmael (both published in the collection *Merkavah Shelemah* (Jerusalem, 1922), fol. 32–43). Two manuscripts from the 10th or 11th centuries (Oxford Hebr. c. 65, and Sasson 522) contain the oldest available texts, but even these are in different stages of corruption. According to the testimony of Origen (third century), it was not permitted to study Song of Songs in Jewish circles before the age of full maturity, obviously because of esoteric teachings like the *Shi'ur Komah* doctrine which were connected with it. The Midrashim on the Song of Songs reflect such esoteric understanding in many passages. The fragments of *Shi'ur Komah* were known in the sixth century, if not earlier, to the poet Eleazar ha-*Kallir. When the *Karaites attacked the anthropomorphic leanings of the rabbinic *aggadah*, *Shi'ur Komah* was among their main targets. *Maimonides considered it an invention of Byzantine aggadists and clearly inauthentic, but scholars like *Saadiah b. Joseph Gaon, *Judah Halevi, Abraham *Ibn Ezra, and Simeon b. Ẓemah *Duran tried to defend it as an allegory for sublime teachings. Duran explained it as pointing to pantheism (*Magen Avot* (Leghorn, 1784), fol. 21b). *Moses b. Joshua of Narbonne devoted a long "Epistle on *Shi'ur Komah*" to its philosophical interpretation on the lines of *Averroes' notion of "one single order and act in which all beings participate in common." Interpretations of *Shi'ur Komah* according to the traditions of the *Ḥasidei Ashkenaz in the 13th century are to be found in the *Sefer ha-Navon* published by Joseph Dan. The Spanish kabbalists did not try to comment on its details, but the author of the *Zohar imitated its general tenor in his descriptions of the divine configurations (*parẓufim*) in the *Idra Rabba* and *Idra Zuta*, which he evidently considered as the summit of his kabbalistical revelations, ascribed to R. *Simeon bar Yoḥai. Many kabbalists (*Jacob b. Jacob ha-Kohen, *Isaac b. Samuel of Acre, Judah *Ḥayyat) saw it as a description of *Metatron, or of the primeval Adam (*Adam Kadmon*).

BIBLIOGRAPHY: A. Schmiedl, *Studien ueber juedische… Religions-philosophie* (1869), 237–58; Salmon ben Yeruḥim, *Milḥamot ha-Shem*, ed. by I. Davidson (1934), 114–24; M. Gaster, in: MGWJ, 37 (1893), 179–85, 213–30; reprinted in his: *Studies and Texts*, 2 (1925–28), 1330–52; L. Nemoy, in: HUCA, 7 (1930), 364; G. Scholem, Mysticism, 63–67; idem, *Von der mystischen Gestalt der Gottheit* (1962), 7–47; idem, *Jewish Gnosticism, Merkabah Mysticism, and Talmudic Tradition* (1965), 36–42, 56–64, 129–31, and an appendix by S. Liebermann, *ibid.*, 118–26; A. Barb, in: *Journal of the Warburg and Courtauld Institutes*, 27 (1964), 5–6; J. Dan (ed.), *Sefer ha-Navon*, in: *Koveẓ al Yad*, 6, pt. 1 (1966), 199–223; A. Altmann (ed.), *Moses Narboni's Epistle on Shi'ur Komah*. in: *Jewish Medieval and Renaissance Studies*, ed. by Altmann (1967), 225–88.

[Gershom Scholem]

SHIVTAH (Heb. שִׁבְטָה) or **SOBATA**, former town in the Negev, 35 mi. (56 km.) southwest of Beersheba, near the Nessana highway. It was founded in the first century B.C.E. by the *Nabateans (only pottery and an inscription mentioning Dushara are known), but it expanded considerably under Christian rule during the course of the Byzantine period (4th to 7th centuries) and thrived until the Abbasid period (c. 800 C.E.), at which point it was finally abandoned. The original Nabatean name for the site may have been Shubitu. The town is mentioned in the later story of St. Nilus and in the Nessana papyri. The settlement (covering an area of about 22 acres) is unwalled and comprises many sumptuous residences, stables, various public buildings, three churches, public squares, and winding streets. Three types of stones of varying quality were used for building houses: a very hard limestone for the foundations and the walls of the lower stories; a yellowish medium-hard stone for the middle parts of the walls and the voussoirs of the arches; and a soft chalk for the upper stories and the cover-stones of the roofs. Wood was hardly used in private houses, except for shelves in built-in cupboards. The roofing of the private houses was based on a system of arches and cover-stones, and only in the churches were large quantities of wood used. The southern and older part of Shivtah is centered on two large pools. The nearby southern church was built after the other buildings. The northern part, covering 40 dunams (10 acres) with 340 rooms, contained a church with a tower, perhaps a public building, at its southern end and a large church dedicated to St. George at its northern extremity. This church consists of an open court, a narthex, a mosaic-paved side chapel, and a baptistry; the main church (66 × 37 ft.) has a nave and two aisles separated by six columns. It has three apses and its walls were once covered with white marble. Near the church was a large square surrounded by 36 shops and workshops (for potters, dyers, etc.).

The Byzantine-period inhabitants of Shivtah cultivated an extensive area in the Lavan Valley, amounting to 4,945 dunams (over 1,270 acres); rainwater from a drainage area of 77 sq. mi. (197½ sq. km.) was carried by means of a series of complicated channels into their fields. An excavation of farm buildings and a columbarium was made by C. Baly at the time of the Colt expedition, but remains unpublished. All the valleys, large and small, were traversed by dams, and an elaborate system of channels collected the rainwater from afar, in a ratio of 1:20 or 1:30 of catchment area per unit of arable field. Experiments in ancient methods of farming and water use are being carried out by M. Evenari of the Hebrew University on a reconstructed farm at Sobata. The presence of a number of wine-presses (described by the excavators as baths of a very economical type) indicates that grapes were probably one of the main crops. In the city itself, water was based on rainwater collected in cisterns and the cleaning of the reservoirs was a duty to be performed by every inhabitant; each house was also provided with one or two cisterns. In the 8th–9th centuries C.E. a small Muslim community lived at Sobata and built a small mosque near the South Church.

The first European scholar to visit Sobata was E.H. Palmer (1869), who suggested identifying it with Zepath, which Simeon conquered, changing its name to Hormah (Judg. 1:17). This identification has not been accepted. The site was later visited by A. Musil (1902); A. Jaussen, R. Savignac and H. Vincent (1905), who found the first Nabatean and Greek-Byzantine inscriptions; C.L. Woolley and T.E. Lawrence (1914); and T. Wiegand, who visited Sobata at the head of the Committee for the Preservation of Ancient Monuments attached to the Turco-German Headquarters (1916) and thus had the opportunity to correct some of the mistakes made by earlier scholars. In the years 1934–38 an expedition of New York University and the British School of Archaeology in Jerusalem, under the direction of H.D. Colt, made large-scale excavations at Sobata, the results of which have not been published. In the years 1958–59 the Israel National Parks Authority, under the guidance of M. Avi-Yonah, carried out some clearance and restoration of the ancient buildings. The North Church was studied by R. Rosenthal in the 1970s and later excavations were conducted by S. Margalit. An architectural appreciation of the site was also made by A. Segal. In 1981 A. Negev fully published the 30 or more inscriptions found at Shivtah (see L. Di Segni 1997). In 2000, Y. Hirschfeld prepared a new map of the site and made a detailed study of the architecture of the settlement. T. Tsuk also made a study of its water systems.

BIBLIOGRAPHY: C.L. Woolley and T.E. Lawrence, *The Wilderness of Zin* (1915), 72ff.; C. Baly, "Shivta," PEFQS, 68 (1935), 171–181; QDAP 8 (1939): 159; H.C. Youtie, "Ostraca from Sbeita," in: AJA, 40 (1936), 452–59; Y. Kedar, "Ancient Agriculture at Shivtah in the Negev," in: IEJ, 57 (1957), 178–89. **ADD. BIBLIOGRAPHY:** B. Brimer, "Shivta – An Aerial Photographic Interpretation," in: IEJ, 31 (1981), 227; A. Segal, "Shivta – A Byzantine Town in the Negev Desert," in: *Journal of the Society of Architectural Historians*, 4 (1985), 317–28; idem, *Architectural Decoration in Byzantine Shivta, Negev Desert, Israel* (1988); S. Margalit, "The North Church of Shivta: The Discovery of the First Church," in: PEQ, 119 (1987), 106–21; L. Di Segni, "Dated Greek Inscriptions from Palestine from the Roman and Byzantine Periods" (doct. diss., Hebrew University (1997), 813ff.; Y. Hirschfeld, "Man and Society in Byzantine Shivta," in: *Qadmoniot*, 36 (2003), 2–17; T. Tsuk, "Water Supply in Byzantine Shivta," in: *Qadmoniot*, 36 (2003), 18–24.

[Michael Avi-Yonah /Shimon Gibson (2nd ed.)]

SHIVVITI (Heb. שִׁוִּיתִי), the opening word, in Hebrew, of the verse: "I have set the Lord always before me" (Ps. 16:8). As a part of the daily prayer, the word became a cliché for Jewish devotion and common language. During the 18th and 19th centuries, and up to the present a votive tablet called "*Shivviti*," principally containing the above verse, was put up in front of those praying in the synagogue. These synagogue plaques contain other verses, concerning the Law and the Torah. Most of them were profusely decorated in shapes and colors. The most common motifs of decoration were the seven-branched *menorah* of the Temple, and symbolic buildings representing different "Holy Places" in Ereẓ Israel, such as Jerusalem or the tombs of sages and righteous men. Some are decorated with animals or mythical beasts and persons. Others serve as amulets, containing magical symbols, such as the Magen David, and magical verses. Most of the *Shivviti* plaques derive from Eastern Europe in the 19th century. There are, however, some plaques which come from North Africa, mainly from Morocco.

[Bezalel Narkiss]

SHKLOV (Pol. **Szklów**), city in Mogilev district, Belarus; within Poland until 1772. Jews apparently first settled in Shklov during the 16th century. By the end of the 17th century the traveler Korb wrote (*Regesty i nadpisi*, 2) that the Jews formed the "wealthiest and most influential class of the town," which was then a commercial center at the junction of trade routes between Russia and Western Europe. In 1746 the Shklov community broke away from the council of the "province of Reissen" (or "Russia," one of the provinces within the framework of the *Councils of the Lands) and became independent. There were 1,367 Jews in Shklov and its surroundings who paid the poll tax in 1766. When Shklov passed to Russia in the first partition of Poland in 1772, it was handed over to General Zorich. The Jews complained to the central government, which then restricted the authority of the master of the city. During the first 50 years of Russian rule Shklov became a commercial center of prime importance. Two large fairs were held there annually and the merchants attending it traveled from Central Asia and Moscow to the commercial towns of Central Europe. Shklov was also a center of Jewish culture. The disciples of *Elijah b. Solomon, the Gaon of Vilna, were influential there. Between 1783 and 1835 several printing presses operated in Shklov, and about 200 books were published. It was in Shklov that *Haskalah first actively emerged in the *Pale of Settlement. Baruch *Schick, Nathan (Note) *Notkin, and Joshua *Zeitlin were active there. The Hebrew version of *Kol Shavat Bat Yehudah* (1804) by Y.L. *Nevakhovich, which called on the Russian government to grant Jews equal rights, was published in Shklov. After the construction of new roads and railroads bypassing Shklov, the city began to decline. The community numbered 9,677 in 1847, 5,422 (77% of the total population) in 1897, and 3,119 (37.6%) in 1926. P. *Smolenskin describes Shklov in its decline in his stories *Ha-To'eh be-Darkhei Ḥayyim and Kevurat Ḥamor.* Zalman *Shneur, a native of Shklov, immortalized the community life and folklore in *Anshei Shklov*, and *No'ah Pandre.* After the Communist Revolution of 1917, communal life was liquidated. In the 1930s, 50 Jewish families earned their livelihood from working in three kolkhozes, one of them was a Jewish one with 30 families. In 1939 the Jewish population declined again to 2,132 (26% of the total population). The Germans arrived there in July 1941. They created two ghettoes for the local Jews and from the environs, one in town, housing 3,200, and the second in the neighboring town of Ryzhkovichi with 2,700 Jews. Young Jews were executed from time to time from both ghettoes. In early October 1941 both ghettoes were liquidated, and the inhabitants were murdered.

BIBLIOGRAPHY: *Prestupleniya nemetsko-fashistskikh okkupantov v Belorussii* (1963), 154–5.

[Yehuda Slutsky]

SHKLOVSKI, ISAAC VLADIMIROVICH (pseud. **Dioneo**; 1865–1935), Russian writer. Born in Yelizavetgrad (now Kirovograd), he started his literary career at the age of 16, contributing short stories, essays, and reviews for publications in south Russia. He was deported for his political activity to Sredne-Kolymsk, northern Siberia, from 1886 to 1892. There he became intimate with the life of the native population, about which he wrote in his Siberian notes, *Na kraynem severo-vostoke Sibiri* (1895; *In Far North-East Siberia*, 1916). In 1896 he moved to London, where he served as correspondent of *Russkiye Vedomosti* and other Russian journals, thus acquainting the Russian reader with life in England. His articles appeared later as books under such titles as *Ocherki sovremennoy Anglii* ("Notes on Contemporary England," 1903); *Angliyskiye siluety* ("English Silhouettes," 1905); and *Angliya posle voyny* ("Post-War England," 1924).

BIBLIOGRAPHY: J. Frumkin et al. (eds.), *Russian Jewry 1860–1917* (1967), 271.

SHKOP, SIMEON JUDAH (1860–1940), Lithuanian talmudist and *rosh yeshivah*. At the age of 12, Shkop was accepted as a student at Mir Yeshivah, and later proceeded to Volozhin. He married a niece of Eliezer *Gordon and in 1885 was appointed to the Telz Yeshivah, where he remained for 18 years. In 1903, he was appointed rabbi of Maltash, and in 1907 of Bransk. During World War I, the communal leaders urged him to leave before the Germans arrived, but he refused and stayed with his community. In 1920, at the request of Ḥayyim Ozer *Grodzinski, he was appointed head of the Sha'arei Torah Yeshivah in Grodno. Shkop developed a system of talmudic study which combined the logical analysis and penetrating insights of Ḥayyim *Soloveichik with the simplicity and clarity of Naphtali Ẓevi Judah *Berlin and which became known as the "Telz way of learning." Many of his students attained distinction, among them Elhanan *Wasserman, M.A. *Amiel, and I.J. *Unterman. Alive to the problems of the day, Shkop had a winning personality. He was an active member of the Mo'ezet Gedolei Torah of the Agudat Israel. Of his many works there have been published *Sha'arei Yosher* (2 vols., 1928); *Ma'arekhet ha-Kinyanim* (1936); novellae on *Bava Kamma, Bava Meẓiah*, and *Bava Batra* (1947; with a preface by his son), on *Nedarim, Gittin*, and *Kiddushin* (1952), and on *Yevamot* and *Ketuvot* (1957). His novellae have also appeared in *Ha-Posek* (1941–2) and *Ha-Ne'eman* (1951). As the Germans were about to enter Grodno during World War II, he ordered his students to flee to Vilna and he himself died two days later.

BIBLIOGRAPHY: *Sefer ha-Yovel ... Shimon Yehudah ha-Kohen Shkop* (1936), 9–80; Y.L. Fishman, *Anashim shel Ẓurah* (1947), 199–204; O.Z. Rand (ed.), *Toledot Anshei Shem* (1950), 143–4; *Elleh Ezkerah*, 2 (1957), 300–9; O. Feuchtwanger, *Righteous Lives* (1965), 110–4; A. Sourasky, *R. Shimon ve-Torato* (1972).

[Mordechai Hacohen]

SHLOM THE MINTMASTER (d. 1195), the first Jew mentioned by name in Austrian records. In charge of the mint and other property of Duke Leopold V, Shlom was entitled to acquire real estate and to employ Christian servants. He owned four plots of land near the synagogue in Vienna. (The assumption that he founded the first Jewish community there cannot be proved.) Although he lost a lawsuit in 1195 trying to reclaim a vineyard given by a burgher to a monastery, he was nevertheless granted some compensation. After a former servant of his had stolen some money from him and left to join the Crusades, Shlom had the man seized and imprisoned. Incited by the wife of the imprisoned man, the crusaders murdered Shlom and 15 others. Duke Leopold executed two of the murderers.

BIBLIOGRAPHY: Aronius, Regesten, nos. 336, 339, 363; H. Gold, *Geschichte der Juden in Wien* (1966), 1; Germ Jud, 1 (1963), 260, 397–9.

[Meir Lamed]

SHLONSKY, ABRAHAM (1900–1973), Hebrew poet, editor, and translator. Shlonsky holds a central position in the development of modern Hebrew poetry and modern Israel poetry in particular. His work marks the transition from the rhetorical, didactic, naturalist type of poetry of the European period to the modernist, symbolic, and individualistic poetry of the Palestinian and Israel periods. Modernism entered European and Russian poetry in the late 19th and early 20th centuries, but reached Hebrew literature somewhat later. Although symbolism and expressionism had some influence on Hebrew literature before Shlonsky's day, the subsequent shift to these types of poetry is primarily due to him. His contribution to the development of modern Hebrew literature goes beyond his achievements in poetry. By his manifold literary activities as editor, translator, polemicist, popular lyricist, editor for the theater, and author of children's literature, he set the literary tone for an entire generation.

Shlonsky was born in Karyokov, Ukraine. He always stressed the fact that he was born at the beginning of the 20th century, which qualified him as a 20th-century poet. The family were *Ḥabad Ḥasidim, deeply attached to Judaism and to *Aḥad Ha-Am's cultural Zionist ideology. His father was interested in folk music and composed the popular melody to Saul Tchernichowsky's poem *"Saḥaki, Saḥaki."* In her youth, Shlonsky's mother was active in the socialistic revolutionary movement in Russia. At the age of 13, Shlonsky was sent to Ereẓ Israel to study at the Herzlia High School. He returned to Russia shortly before the outbreak of World War I and continued his studies in the Jewish secular high school in Yekaterinoslav. He began writing poetry in his youth, and his poem *"Bi-Demei Ye'ush"* appeared in **Ha-Shilo'aḥ* in 1919.

In 1921, after wandering through Russia and Poland, Shlonsky returned with a group of *ḥalutzim* to Ereẓ Israel, where he worked on road building and construction, spending some time in kibbutz *En-Harod. Much of the atmosphere of that period is found in Shlonsky's cycles of poems: *Gilbo'a, Amal, Be-Ikvei ha-Ẓon*, and *Yizre'el*. Shlonsky dubbed himself "the road-paving poet of Israel." He did not confine himself to poetry out of conviction of the need to contribute to other literary fields and is to be counted among the writers of dialogue of the young Hebrew art theater, the lyrics of the Hebrew satiric theater, the famous limericks of the Purim balls of "Little Tel Aviv," and even the jingles for advertising Israel products. However, his major contribution was in the development of linguistic tools and devices for the writing of modern Hebrew poetry and his poetry itself.

In 1922, Shlonsky's first Ereẓ Israel poem appeared in the weekly periodical *Ha-Po'el ha-Ẓa'ir*, and in the same year he moved to Tel Aviv. Asher *Barash and Jacob Rabinowitz, publishers of the literary miscellany *Hedim*, drew him into their circle, considering him an outstanding representative of the younger generation of Ereẓ Israel poets, along with Uri Ẓevi *Greenberg and Yiẓḥak *Lamdan. In 1924 Shlonsky went to Paris to study. When the newspaper *Davar* was founded in 1925, its editor-founder, B. *Katzenelson, invited him to become a regular member of its editorial staff. Shlonsky took over the literary section of the newspaper, but this proved to be too narrow a framework for him and he joined the weekly literary magazine *Ketuvim*, which he edited jointly with E. *Steinman. This soon became the organ of authors who opposed the Writers' Union and the literary establishment. Despite its high caliber, *Ketuvim* was not financially solvent enough to support its editor and writers. In 1928 Shlonsky joined the staff of *Haaretz*, with which he remained until 1943, when he joined the editorial staff of *Mishmar* (founded in 1943). Upon the demise of *Ketuvim*, Shlonsky, who was one of the leading authors of the literary group Yaḥdav, founded the weekly *Turim* (first series 1933; second series 1938). He edited *Dappim le-Sifrut*, a literary supplement of the *Ha-Shomer ha-Ẓa'ir* weekly, and was the first editor of the literary page of the daily *Al ha-Mishmar*, and the quarterly *Orlogin*, which appeared from 1950 to 1957. Linked to the Mapam party, he was one of Israel's leading intellectuals participating in the left-wing world peace movement and heading Israel's delegations to world conferences of the movement. In addition he maintained personal contact with Soviet writers. From the late 1950s he became more outspoken in his criticism of the Soviet attitude to Israel and to Jewish culture in the Soviet Union. He was the initiator of the publication of the Hebrew translation of Boris Gaponov's Georgian epic *Oteh Or ha-Namer*.

Shlonsky's Poetry

Shlonsky's poetry was molded out of the world in which he lived. Scenes of horror of World War I, riots against Ukrainian Jews, the inherent contradictions of the Russian revolution (messianic yearnings on the one hand and chaos accompanied by outbursts of cruelty on the other) are themes in his poetry. He set out to avenge the *"Elef Yegonot"* ("Thousand Griefs") which he witnessed *"Be-Misholei Eloha"* ("In the Paths of the Almighty"). His poem *"Devai"* ("Sorrow") contains the lepers' song of protest, giving expression to their bitter condemnation of the world order, their rebellion, and their yearning for "spring." The poems in *Ba-Galgal* (1927) are bitter cries, and in *Be-Elleh ha-Yamim* (1930) Shlonsky reacts to the terror of the riots in Palestine at the end of the 1920s. With *Avnei Bohu* (1934), the product of his encounter with the Western European city, his poetry takes on a new meditative, existentialist dimension. The poems evoke the loneliness and anguish of modern man in the industrialized city. Shlonsky feels that it is his task to cry out and awake the world's sleeping conscience. Revolutions do not come about only by the sword; poetry also has great value in "preparing the hearts." He refuses to reconcile himself to the image of a generation full of deceit and illusions that does not revolt against the folly of mankind before its demise. Above all, he is appalled at the apathy of man toward a child's tears, death, suffering, and the impending catastrophe.

The horrors of the approaching Holocaust are expressed in *Shirei ha-Mappolet ve-ha-Piyyus* (1938). Another visit to some European capitals reproduced with greater force the feeling of alienation, orphanhood, and fear: "From a village fence, my eyes are pierced/by the four fangs of the swastika." Childhood fears, scenes of horror, and pogroms again float into the poet's consciousness, "Still today, even today, when they knock upon a door,/I fear to open, lest the night will enter." "The poems of the squared fear" take up the central motif of man's perverseness and his strange restricted and frightened world. The image "squared fear" developed out of Shlonsky's urbanistic poetry, whose foundations were laid in previous books, especially in *Avnei Bohu*. Here the European city, which Shlonsky likens to Sodom, is a frightening vertigo which forebodes evil and is haunted by the mad frenzy of passion and the shadow of the gallows. At the edge of night, however, the poet seeks the light of "*bereshit ḥadashah*" ("a new genesis"). He rediscovers the simple, sensual joys of life and the exultation of nature's wonders, which form the reconciliation motif of the poetry.

Al Millet (1947) is a direct continuation of *Shirei ha-Mappolet ve-ha-Piyyus*. Shlonsky begins the book with "*Bereshit Ḥadashah*," the same poem which concluded the previous book. The poems which follow sing of reconciliation with the world, the renewal of the love covenant with simple things, and the return to childhood, to the security of nature, and to the goodness of fertility. *Shirei ha-Leḥem ve-ha-Mayim*, which take up similar themes, conclude this phase in Shlonsky's writing.

The period of the Holocaust which followed is filled with fear and confusion. Shlonsky kept his silence – "It is a silence of a face against a gate covered by night." The poems in *Mi-Maḥashakim* ("From Darkness"), published a few years after they were written, express his helplessness and bewilderment during those terrible days. After the Holocaust, Shlonsky regained his art (*Ki Tashuv*). The poet's skill returned, enabling him to sing of the world's delights. The poet who believed that he was part of a generation which lived without fairy tales now rediscovered what he was unable to see in the days of darkness, but he did not return to love the world by ignoring or denying what had occurred. He affirms the world in spite of the horror, and consequently his love for it will be firmer and more secure. The poems in *Paris ha-Aḥeret* ("The Other Paris") tell of the new confrontation with the city that had once enchanted the poet.

In Shlonsky's collected works, a number of poems entitled *Mi-Sefer ha-Yoreh* are placed after the poems of *Al Millet*. These poems are related to those of *Sefer ha-Anakh* but the unanticipated occurred: *Sefer ha-Anakh* does not continue. Once more the foundations and certainties crumbled and confusion and amazement befell the poet. The familiar symbols are the tortured comparisons of the "capriciousness of the sword," storm, distractions, the hidden, the cloudy, and mute evil in *Shirei ha-Mappolet*.

Avnei Gevil (1960) contains Shlonsky's "mature poetry," although distinct elements already present in his early poetry survive. He does not return to motifs used in his early poetry, but transforms these motifs in keeping with the climate of a different period. This sense of time gives a contemporary quality to the book in that it breathes the atmosphere of the 1950s and its fear of a cosmic holocaust. The "fear of death" poems are permeated with a chilling silence ("*Shirei ha-Meruẓah ha-Ra'ah*") and the poet believes that there is wisdom in stating facts without an outcry and receiving judgment without a protest. The resignation to fate is not fatalism but a higher wisdom which recognizes the futility of protest. The prose-like lines in some of the poetry ("*Ne'um Peloni al Shekhunato*") are written under the influence of the new literature and are an indirect result of Shlonsky's perception of the times, which unintentionally brings about such forms of expression. Similarly the break in rhythm and the abandonment of rhyme and melodies spring from the poet's literary strength – not from his weakness. The revival of the poet's creative power does not come about only from the changes which take place within the poet, but reflect those which occur in the objective reality. It is not easy for a poet of Shlonsky's caliber to free himself from the memory of his past experiences, yet he cannot sustain his creative ability without constant contact with the present. Therefore, the blend of various elements, always the mark of great poetry, is found in *Avnei Gevil*. These elements are the synthesis of old and new, of the poetry of personal experience with that of creative wisdom, of excitement and reckoning, and of emotion and significance.

Mi-Shirei ha-Perozedor ha-Arokh ("From Poems of the Long Corridor," 1968), a book of meditative and emotional poetry, contains poems of reflections on life and death. "The long corridor" is the symbol of a hidden world, a world of secrecy and surprises, a "Kafkaesque" world. Man passes along a corridor with doors on each side; behind him the doors are open, in front of him they are closed. The poems, raising more questions than they answer, containing more doubts than certainty, are a statement of yearning rather than accomplishment, of protest rather than reconciliation. It seems that Shlonsky wished to contradict his previous works, not to lean on his past great achievement, but to struggle in an indirect way with the "questions of the day."

Like all innovators in literature, Shlonsky never favored complete disassociation with literary tradition. He advocated the blending of tradition and new values with the cultural heritage of the nation. He refused to cast off all the remnants of the past and begin from the beginning. A true innovator, he drew upon the best existing literature, yet built his original creative world. His innovations stem from his contempt for the worn and worthless clichés which had replaced vivid diction. He rejects forms of expression which no longer describe reality because deep changes have occurred in the life of society.

In the 1930s Shlonsky wrote many articles explaining his demand for a poetic renewal. He sarcastically attacked the low standard of literary achievements which pretended to give expression to the Ereẓ Israel way of life. He claimed that in an eventful era, poetry cannot exist only on "still waters," but that the literature of an uprooted generation should be as stormy and bewildering as the generation itself. It should be as full of contradictions and fears as the period in which it was created. "Man has turned his manner of life on its head… destroying the heritage of his past," wrote Shlonsky, "no father-mother; no *tallit* and *tefillin*; none of the old relationships between male and female; hardly anything of the conceptual system of the past exists, yet he insists on seeking his self-expression in the old workshop." The poet who rejects the current "poetry of the present experience" strives to create a poetry which is nurtured on the wellsprings of the experience of the generation.

This attitude was already found in Shlonsky's early poems. "*Hitgallut*" ("Revelation"), opening his collected poems, is the young poet's "platform" as he begins his odyssey. He knows that he must fulfill the mission of bringing the message of the "new thing" to the world. The young poet, standing on the threshold of the new world, sees the old world's slow destruction. He does not rejoice at this calamity. Torn between two worlds, he understands up to what point reality forces the culmination of the old, yet he cannot blind himself to the sorrow of its decline. Shlonsky writes of the new life using new forms. Hebrew poetry was not accustomed to the rhythm, the inner structure of the poem, and the modern tonality, yet his system of imagery is based on traditional concepts. He compares the roads to the straps of the *tefillin*; the country, "her skin like parchment, a parchment for the Torah," "is wrapped in light like a *tallit*," and houses stand like phylacteries. The poem "*Yafim Leilot Kena'an*" ("Canaan Nights are Beautiful"), he says, will be sung like Sabbath hymns. The symbol of the **Akedah* recurs several times.

Shlonsky found a most fitting new tone in the Sephardi pronunciation, in a rhyme which suits daily speech, and in new phonetics and new accentuation. In this field he was a pioneer.

Shlonsky's last volume of poems, *Sefer ha-Sulamot*, was sent for publication on the day of his death in 1973 and appeared posthumously the same year.

In 1977 *The Correspondence of Abraham Shlonsky* by Aryeh Aharoni was published. It consists of letters in Hebrew which Shlonsky sent during the last decade of his life to Jews in the U.S.S.R. who sought to establish contact with the cultural life in Israel and renew their ties with Hebrew literature. They were brought back to Israel by immigrants from Russia. The letters reveal the great lengths to which Shlonsky went to accede to their requests and deal mainly with Hebrew literature and poetry. In one of them he refers to the miracle of the revival of Hebrew in the U.S.S.R.

Every book of poetry Shlonsky published was a significant literary event. His works are *Devai* (1924), *Ba-Gilgal* (1927), *Le-Abba-Imma* (1927), *Be-Elleh ha-Yamim* (1930), *Avnei Bohu* (1934), *Shirei ha-Mappolet ve-ha-Piyyus* (1938), *Al Millet* (1947), *Avnei Gevil* (1960), and *Mi-Shirei ha-Perozedor ha-Arokh* (1968). All except the last two works were later published in two large volumes. Other works are the collection *Shirei ha-Yamim* (1946, mostly translated poems, some original), the three children's books *Alilot Miki Mahu* (1947), *Ani ve-Tali* (1957), *Uẓ Li Guẓ Li* (1966), and many translations from the best in world literature. The latter include translations of Shakespeare's dramas *King Lear* (1956) and *Hamlet* (1946), four of Chekhov's most important plays, Pushkin's poems "*Eugene Onegin*," and "*Boris Gudonov*" (1956), Gogol's *Revizor* (1935) and *The Marriage* (1945), Charles Da Coster's "*Till Ollenspiegel*" (1949), Romain Rolland's "*Colas Breugnon*" (1950), Michael Sholokhov's *And Quiet Flows the Don*, Isaac Babel's stories, and many more. He also translated much of world poetry, mainly from modern Russian lyric poetry. The correspondence between Shlonsky and Zila Shamir was published in 1997 as *Mikhtavim le-Meshoreret Ẓe'irah*.

For Shlonsky's works in English translation, see: Goell, bibliography, index, and the ITHL website at www.ithl.org.il.

BIBLIOGRAPHY: A.B. Yoffe, *Ha-Meshorer u-Zemanno* (1966); I. Levin, *Bein Gedi ve-Sa'ar* (1960); J. Fichmann, in: *Moznayim*, 15 (1952); D. Kena'ani, *Beinam le-Vein Zemannam* (1955); I. Cohen, *Sha'ar ha-Soferim* (1962), 323–31: S. Lachower, *Avraham Shlonsky*; bibl. [1922–1950] (1951). **ADD. BIBLIOGRAPHY:** A. Weiss (ed.), *Avraham Shlonsky: Mivḥar Ma'amrei Bikkoret al Yeẓirato* (1975); idem, *Ha-She'ifah el ha-Merkaz be-Shirat Shlonsky* (1980); Y. Goral, *Shirat Shlonsky* (1981); I. Levin (ed.), *Sefer Shlonsky* (1981); A. Hagorni-Grin, *Shlonsky ba-Avutot Bialik* (1985); H. Halperin, *Me-Agvaniyah ad Sinfonyah: Ha-Shirah ha-Kalah shel Avraham Shlonsky* (1997); R. Shoham, *Poetry and Prophecy: The Image of the Poet as a "Prophet," a Hero and an Artist in Modern Hebrew Poetry* (2003).

[Abraham B. Yoffe]

SHLONSKY, VERDINA (1905–1990), Israeli composer and pianist, born in Dniepropetrovsk, Ukraine. Her family immigrated to Palestine in the early 1920s. She studied piano at the Berlin Hochschule fuer Musik with Arthur *Schnabel and Egon Petri. In the late 1920s she moved to Paris, where she studied composition with Nadia Boulanger, Max Deutsch, and Edgar Varèse and changed her vocation from performance to composition. In 1934, Verdina returned to Palestine, where she remained until 1937. During these years she composed music for poems of Lea *Goldberg, Shin *Shalom, Raphael Eliaz, and her brother Abraham *Shlonsky, music for children and for the theater; symphonic, chamber, and piano music. She also began writing essays on musical topics for the Hebrew press. Verdina spent most of World War II in Paris and London. Despite the material and mental hardships of staying in Europe at that period, she managed to compose a few pieces. In 1944, she returned for good to Palestine. She continued to compose songs until the end of the 1950s, when she began focusing solely on compositions for piano, chamber, and orchestral music. Among her major works are *Images Palestiniènnes* for voice and piano; Symphony no 1; *Cinq Melodies sur le Poéme de Guillaume Apollinaire* for voice and piano; Concerto for Piano and Orchestra; String Quartet; *Hodaya* – Thanksgiving Cantata for Choir and Orchestra; Two Sonatas for Violin and Piano; *Silhouettes for Voice and Percussion*, and more. In her essays, published in the Israeli press, she portrayed musical life and the life of musicians in both Israel and Europe, and dealt with the lively ideological struggle between the supporters of avant-garde music and its opponents. These were also the topics of her prolific correspondence with leading musicians worldwide. Verdina, who was also a competent drawer, gave private piano lessons for her rather modest living, and taught during the late 1960s and early 1970s at the Tel Aviv Academy of Music. Her awards include First Prize of the French Government Competition for Women Composers for her *Poéme Hebraique* for voice and piano (1931); Bartok Prize for a string quartet (1948); prizes from ACUM for a string quartet (1973), and for life's work in music (1984).

Both professionally and socially, Verdina did not receive the recognition she deserved. Her archive, including a great many articles, letters, and musical compositions, is located in the Music Department of the National Library, Jerusalem.

BIBLIOGRAPHY: A. Tischler, *A Descriptive Bibliography of Art Music by Israeli Composers* (1988); Y. Wagman, "Verdina Shlonsky – In Memoriam," in: *IMI News* 90/1, Tel Aviv: Israel Music Information Centre Press, 1990.

[J. Aouizerate-Levin (2nd ed.)]

SHMERUK, CHONE (1921–1997), Yiddish scholar. Born in Warsaw, Shmeruk studied history at the university there. During World War II he was in the U.S.S.R., where he met many Soviet Yiddish writers. He returned to Warsaw in 1946 and then immigrated, via Stuttgart, to Israel in 1949. When the Yiddish department was opened at the Hebrew University of Jerusalem in 1950, he was one of Dov *Sadan's first students, also studying history with Israel *Halpern, Ben-Zion *Dinur, and Yitzhak *Baer. He taught Yiddish literature and culture at the Hebrew University from 1957 (professor, 1961, later chair of the Yiddish department). A member of the Israel Academy of Sciences and Humanities (1986), he received the Israel Prize in 1996.

Shmeruk studied many aspects of Ashkenazi cultural history and Yiddish literature, analyzing the relations between history, society, culture, language, and literature, and writing articles and books on a wide range of subjects, showing the role and functions of Yiddish in the Ashkenazi world, defined as a polysystem of languages and cultural trends. Shmeruk did not view Yiddish literature as an autonomous cultural entity, but demonstrated the complex links between Yiddish creativity and traditional sources, modern Hebrew, and the surrounding non-Jewish Polish, Russian, German, Italian, and American cultures. He wrote on all periods of Yiddish literature, from the earliest Yiddish text (1272) to his own contemporaries. Among his major books are *Sifrut Yidish, Perakim le-Toldoteihah* ("Yiddish Literature: Aspects of its History," 1978, rev. Yiddish trans., 1988), *Maḥazot Mikra'im be-Yidish 1697–1750* ("Yiddish Biblical Plays 1697–1750," 1979), *Sifrut Yidish be-Polin* ("Yiddish Literature in Poland," 1981), and *Ha-Keri'ah le-Navi* ("The Call for a Prophet," 1999). One of his fields of specialization was Jews in Soviet Russia and Poland and their Yiddish literature, on which his publications include *Ha-Kibbutz ha-Yehudi ve-ha-Hityashevut be-Belorusyah ha-Sovyetit (1918–23)* ("Jewish Settlement and Colonization in Soviet Belorussia (1918–23)," 1961); *Pirsumim Yehudiyyim bi-Verit ha-Moaẓot 1917–60* ("Jewish Publications in the Soviet Union 1917–60," 1961); a bibliography of Yiddish authors in the U.S.S.R., co-edited with I.J. Cohn, M. Pietzash, *et al.*; *A Shpigl oyf a Shteyn* ("A Mirror on a Stone"), co-edited with A. Suzkever, *et al.* (1964), an anthology of poetry and prose by 12 Yiddish writers in the U.S.S.R.; *The Esterke Story in Yiddish and Polish Literature* (1985); *Di Yidishe Literatur in Nayntsetn Yorhundert* ("Yiddish Literature in the Nineteenth Century," 1993); and *The Jews in Poland Between Two World Wars* (co-edited 1989). He also published on *shund* ("pulp literature") and children's literature, Jewish folklore, press, theater, education, Haskalah, Ḥasidism, the history of publishing, and illustrations of Yiddish books. He edited classical works of Jewish writers, such as Joseph *Perl's manuscript *Ma'asiyyot ve-Iggerot mi-Ẓaddikim Amittiyyim u-me-Anshei Shelomenu* (with Sh. Werses, 1969); *Der Nister (1963); S.J. *Abramovitsh, *Bialik and *Rawnitski's Letters (1966); *Sholem *Aleichem (1976); I.L. *Peretz, *Bay Nakht oyfn Altn Mark* (1971); Itzik *Manger, *Midresh Itsik* (1969, 1984); Isaac Bashevis *Singer, *Der Shpigl* (1975); Uri Zevi *Greenberg (1979); Israel *Rabon, *Di Gas* (1986); the middle Yiddish **Pariz un Viene* (1996); *The Penguin Book of Modern Yiddish Verse* (co-edited, 1987). He compiled with Sh. Werses a bibliography of S.J. Abramovitsh's writings and letters (1965) and was director of the series *Yidishe Literatur* (Hebrew University) and of a massive documentation of early Yiddish texts on microfiche. He served as consulting editor to the first edition of the *Encyclopaedia Judaica*. The encyclopedic range of his research, his international teaching, and decades-long mentoring quite literarily (re)constructed the field of Yiddish literary studies after the Holocaust and will continue to influence the course of research for decades to come.

[Jean Baumgarten (2nd ed.)]

SHMUEL-BUKH (*Sefer Shemuel*), 16th-century Yiddish epic. Considered the masterpiece of Old Yiddish midrashic epic, the narrative expertly reworks the biblical book of Samuel by means of an intimate knowledge of both post-biblical Jewish traditions (particularly those concerning the primary heroic characters Samuel, Saul, and David) and the conventions of the medieval German "minstrel epic," recasting the whole as an heroic epic. The text comprises 1,792 four-line stanzas of two rhyming couplets (AABB) (plus a colophon), each line divided rhythmically into two half-lines of three primary accents each (derived from the stanza characteristic of the Middle

High German *Nibelungenlied*). The melody to which the poem was performed became famous and was used for many other Yiddish poems of the period. While the issue of the author's identity has not been definitively resolved, Moses Esrim ve-Arba ("of the twenty-four books," i.e. a biblical scholar) named as author at the end of one early manuscript is now generally identified with an emissary from Jerusalem to Turkey in 1487, which accords with the conventional scholarly dating of the text (based on language use and topical references) to the late 15th century. The text is preserved in a complex tradition of 16th- and 17th-century manuscripts and printed editions (editio princeps, Augsburg, 1544) that precludes the construction of a critical edition.

BIBLIOGRAPHY: M. Weinreich, *Bilder fun der Yidisher Literatur-Geshikhte* (1928), 68–111; F. Falk and L. Fuks (eds.), *Das Schmuelbuch des Mosche Esrim Wearba*, 2 vols. (1961; facsimile of Augsburg, 1544]; Ch. Shmeruk, *Prokim fun der Yidisher Literatur-Geshikhte*, 182–99, J.C. Frakes (ed.), *Early Yiddish Texts: 1100–1750* (2004), 218–46; J. Baumgarten, *Introduction to Old Yiddish Literatur* (2005), 140–52.

[Jerold Frakes (2nd ed.)]

SHMUELI, EPHRAIM (1908–), educator, author, and historian. Born in Lodz, Poland, Shmueli immigrated to Ereẓ Israel in 1933. He taught at several U.S. institutions of Jewish learning, and in 1969 was professor of philosophy and religion at Cleveland State University.

Most of Shmueli's literary and journalistic efforts – all in Hebrew – were devoted to education, sociology, history, and philosophy. His works include *Demuyyot u-Me'ora'ot be-Toledot Ammenu* (1940), an account of important personages and events in Jewish history; *Masoret u-Mahapekhah* (1942), monographs on tradition and revolution in Jewish history; *Me-Az ad Attah* (1943), historical miniatures; *Toledot ha-Ẓiyyonut* (2 vols., 1947–50), a history of Zionism; *Be'ayot ha-Am ha-Yehudi ba-Zeman ha-Zeh* (1960), on the problems of contemporary Jewry; *Bein Emunah li-Khefirah* (1961), on the problems of faith and heresy in Jewish history; *Don Yiẓḥak Abravanel* (1963); and *Beit Yisrael u-Medinat Yisrael* (1966), on the main currents in U.S. Jewish life. Together with Max Mordechai *Solieli, he co-authored *Bi-Netiv ha-Dorot* (1944), a study on the destiny of Jewry. Shmueli published two textbooks of Jewish history, *Toledot Ammenu ba-Zeman he-Ḥadash* (7 vols., 1941–58) and *Korot Ammenu* (1968). In addition, he wrote a number of studies on non-Jewish themes, among them a monograph on Miguel de Cervantes (1952), and a work on Baruch *Spinoza (1963). His *Sheva Tarbuyyot Yisrael* (1980) appeared in English translation as *Seven Jewish Cultures: A Reinterpretation of Jewish History and Thought,* in 1990.

BIBLIOGRAPHY: A. Shaanan, *Millon ha-Sifrut ha-Ḥadashah* (1959), 847–8; Kressel, Leksikon, 2 (1967), 946.

[Eisig Silberschlag]

SHMUELI, HERZL (1920–2001), Israeli musicologist. Shmueli was born in Istanbul to parents of Russian descent. He began studying violin at 7 and piano at 10. In 1933 the family immigrated to Israel, where he studied with P. Ginzburg (until 1934) and later attended the Tel Aviv conservatory (1944–48), where he studied theory and composition with *Boscovitch. During 1950–53, he studied musicology in Zurich with Cherbuliez, composition and history with Hindemith at the university, and acoustics in the Zurich Eidgenuesische Technische Hochschule für Music. Receiving a Ph.D. for his thesis, on Jehudah Arjeh Moscato (1953, published in 1954), he returned to Tel Aviv and began teaching at the Israeli Academy of Music and at the Music Teachers' Seminary, of which he subsequently became director (1955–66). In 1966 Shmueli was one of the founders of the Musicology Department of Tel Aviv University, where he subsequently became the head of the department (1971–74, 1987–89) and professor. Shmueli established the Archive for Israeli Music there and served as dean of the Faculty of Visual and Performing Arts (1983–86) and chairman of the Israeli Musicological Society (1969–71). Shumeli was one of the pioneers in the research of Israeli music. His research centered on the Israeli song and art music, music education, and European music in the 18th–19th centuries. He emphasized the connections between music and other disciplines and established a methodology for analysis of the Israeli song. He directed a series of programs on music for Israeli Instructional TV and was consultant for the music department in the educational television division from 1969 to 1972. He edited several periodicals, among them music periodicals for youth (1957–66). Shmueli published books in Hebrew including *Ommanut ha-Musikah* ("Musical Theory," 1954), *Toledot ha-Makhelah* ("History of the Choir," 1963), and books about the Israeli song (1971), and Alexander Boscovitch, the latter with Jehoash Hirshberg (1995). Among his articles are "Stilelemente in Israeli-Lied 1925–1950," in *Festschrift Hans Conradin zum 70. Geburtstag* (1983), 249–60, and "Adolf Bernhard Marx (1795–1866): Deutscher Musiker, Judische Herkunft – Eine Dokumentation," in *Essays in Honor of Hanoch Avenary (1990–1991),* 216–28. He received the Israel Prize for musical research in 2001.

BIBLIOGRAPHY: *Baker's Biographical Dictionary of Musicians* (1997).

[Uri (Erich) Toeplitz / Naama Ramot (2nd ed.)]

SHMUSHKEVICH, YAACOV (1902–1941), Soviet air force commander. Born in Rokiškis, Lithuania, Shmushkevich fought in the Red Army during the Russian Civil War of 1918–20. In 1922 he was transferred to the air force, finishing flight school as a pilot in 1931. He rapidly gained promotion and was sent to Spain in 1936 to reorganize the Republican Air Force. In 1937 he commanded Madrid's air defense. On his return to the Soviet Union in the following year he was made a Hero of the Soviet Union. Subsequently Shmushkevich was made commander of the Soviet air force in the Far East, and took part in 1939 in the war with the Japanese in Khalkin-Khol. From November 1939 he was head of the Red Army Air Force, from May 1940 chief inspector of the Air Force, and from December 1940 aide to the chief of staff in air force matters. For his work in establishing the Soviet air defense he was made Hero of the Soviet Union for a second time, one of the few soldiers ever to have been accorded the honor twice. On June 4, 1940 he received the rank of colonel-general but shortly before the Nazi invasion of the Soviet Union, he was dismissed from his post. He was arrested in 1941, tried for treason, and executed on October 28, 1941 in Kuybishev. At the 20th Communist Party Congress in 1954, Shmushkevich was one of several executed Soviet figures to be posthumously rehabilitated. In 1967 the Soviet Army published a special work in his memory.

BIBLIOGRAPHY: F. Sverdlov: *Yevrei – Generaly, vooruzhonnykh cil U.S.S.R.* (1993).

[Mordechai Kaplan]

SHNEOUR (Shneur), ZALMAN (Zalkind; 1887–1959), Hebrew and Yiddish poet and novelist who, together with *Bialik and *Tchernichowsky, is considered to be one of the three great figures in Hebrew poetry of his generation. Shneour was born in Shklov, Belorussia; his father, Isaac-Eisik Shneour, was a descendant of *Shneur Zalman of Lyady. At the age of 13 he left for *Odessa, which was the great literary and Zionist center of the time. Young Shneour was particularly attracted to Bialik, who usually befriended young writers.

Warsaw and Vilna

As Hebrew projects were expanding in Warsaw, Shneour moved there in 1902, and on Bialik's recommendation was employed at Tushiyyah, a large publishing house, founded by the author and publisher Ben-Avigdor (A.L. *Shalkovich). At the same time he published his first poems in the children's newspaper *Olam Katan*. Shneour also published poems and short articles in the prestigious monthly *Ha-Shilo'aḥ*, and in the weekly *Ha-Dor*. His first Yiddish poems appeared in the weekly *Yidishe Folktsaytung* (Warsaw, 1902–03).

In 1904, Shneour moved to Vilna, where he found work on the editorial staff of the Hebrew daily *Ha-Zeman*. The paper included on its staff several young authors who later achieved renown in Hebrew literature. Vilna proved important to Shneour's Hebrew and Yiddish literary development. There he published his first collection of poetry, *Im Sheki'at ha-Ḥammah* (2 vols., Warsaw, 1906–07), his first novel, *Mavet*, and a collection of stories. Shneour's poems achieved great success and ran through several editions. He published poetry and prose in Vilna's Jewish periodicals. Whereas the Warsaw period had been one of the most difficult in his life (both because of his economic deprivation and feelings of foreignness), Shneour became acclimatized to life in Vilna. Shneour subsequently expressed his affection and reverence for the city in his poem *Vilnah* (first printed in the monthly *Miklat*, New York, 1920), and later in a special book with illustrations by Hermann *Struck (1923). Here he reached the peak of his talent and achieved facility of expression in Hebrew.

First Poems

Shneour's first book of verse, *Im Sheki'at ha-Ḥammah*, was enthusiastically received both by critics and readers. Bialik warmly praised the author in his essay *"Shiratenu ha-Ẓe'irah"* (*Ha-Shilo'aḥ*, 1908), calling Shneour "a young Samson whose seven locks have all grown overnight." Bialik also attributed to Shneour the qualities of the heroic man who "tears the young lion which roared against him as one tears a kid" (Judg. 14:5–6). The trenchant comparison with the "young Samson" was to be repeated by others. Long the idol of the young, Shneour was the poet of heroism and non-surrender, the symbol of revolt against the conventions and long-established customs of the ghetto.

When *Ha-Zeman* ceased publication at the end of 1905, Shneour left for Switzerland. There, inspired by the country's natural beauty, he began to write the long lyric poem *Be-Harim* ("In the Mountains," 1908). The major thrust of the poem is its contrast of nature – genuine, fresh, and strong – with the artifices and inauthenticities of civilization. Sections of the poem were eventually translated into some European languages including Russian (S. *Marshak in *Yevreyskaya antologiya*, edited by L. Jaffe and V. Khodasevich, Moscow, 1918).

In 1907 Shneour moved to Paris, where he continued his literary work while studying literature, philosophy, and natural sciences at the Sorbonne. From 1908 to 1913 he traveled throughout Europe and also visited North Africa. In this period he wrote the cycle of poems *Im Ẓelilei ha-Mandolinah* ("To the Strains of the Mandolin," 1912) in which the poet showers words of affection on a "lovely sunburnt Italian girl," whom he asks to play the mandolin. Although completely captivated by her charms, the poet does not forget that her ancient forefathers destroyed the Temple and caused the Diaspora. His ambivalence toward the girl involves the entire relationship between Jew and gentile. In one of the poem's most remarkable sections, *"Manginot Yisrael"* ("Melodies of Israel," 1912), Shneour describes the Jews' "revenge on the gentiles." The revenge, restricted to the realm of the spirit, entailed bequeathing to the gentile conquerors a conception of God that required them to abandon their beautiful and sensuous pagan deities. In 1913, at the time of the *Beilis trial, he wrote *Yemei ha-Beinayim Mitkarevim* ("The Middle Ages are Returning"), a prediction of European civilization's descent into the maelstrom of war and Jew-hatred. Shneour sensed the return of medieval antisemitism, which in the 20th century would be implemented in the name of patriotism rather than religion, and liberalism's faint-hearted response to this threat to civilized life.

At the beginning of World War I Shneour was in Germany, where he was interned along with all Russian subjects in that country. During the war years he studied medicine at the University of Berlin and worked in a hospital. In 1919, he visited the U.S. to contact various Yiddish newspapers with the object of becoming a regular contributor. However, he returned to Berlin, where, after the war and the Russian Revolution, authors and publishers fleeing from the Bolsheviks created a great literary center.

In Germany, Shneour resumed his literary activity and founded with Solomon Salzmann the *Hasefer* publishing house, whose publications included works by David Frischmann and Shneour (*Gesharim*, 1922[3], and *Vilna*, 1923). Because of his literary and publishing activity, Shneour did not continue his medical studies. In the early 1920s the group of Hebrew literary men in Germany dispersed. Shneour settled in Paris in 1923 and lived there until Hitler's troops invaded France in 1940, when he succeeded in escaping via Spain to the U.S. He lived in New York from 1941 until his immigration to Israel in 1951.

Yiddish Prose

The political and economic crises which afflicted Europe after World War I caused the market for Hebrew books to shrink to the point where authors were compelled to seek different livelihoods. Those years mark an interval during which Schneour paused in his writing of Hebrew prose, devoting himself rather to writing in Yiddish for the American Yiddish press. In his Yiddish articles and fiction Shneour tapped his childhood memories of "the old home," sketched Jewish life in Eastern Europe which had been disrupted or destroyed by war and revolution, described his encounters with prominent people, and searched the past for forgotten or obscure episodes in Jewish history. He became one of the most widely read Yiddish authors. His novels, some of which were first published serially in newspapers, have been translated into many languages, and have been widely acclaimed. They were also rendered into Hebrew by Schneour himself.

Sources of Inspiration

Shklov, on the River Dnieper, where Shneour spent his childhood, had been a place of Jewish settlement from the 17th century. In *Anshei Shklov* (1944), Shneour depicts with great artistry and fresh and lively humor the human types that populated the Jewish community in the city. Shklov, where Jews lived their peculiar inner life, was not exceptional among Jewish towns in the Russian *Pale of Settlement, but it achieved fame as a result of Shneour's memorable descriptions and has come to serve as a symbol of the *shtetl*. A new edition of the novel, with an introduction by Dan Miron, was published in 1999. *Ha-Dod Zyame*, the sequel to *Anshei Shklov*, delineates the character of Noah Pandre, a new Jewish type, powerful and unafraid, which began to emerge in the last century. Noah Pandre did not study in the *bet ha-midrash*; he was not a Torah scholar, but neither was he a bundle of nerves fearing every "driven leaf." A Jew by race and heredity, he was strong and fearless, his hands "the hands of Esau." A series of surprising episodes reveal the potent forces latent within Noah Pandre, who is reminiscent of ancient Jewish heroes. His deeds of bravery and strength earn him the respect even of gentiles for whom the Jew had been synonymous with a coward and one afflicted by God. The heroic character of Noah Pandre influenced Shneour's *Shir Mizmor le-Ammei ha-Araẓot* – a song of praise to the new type of Jew. *Ha-Dod Zyame* was translated into most European languages.

Shneour provided a kind of rehabilitation for the *ammei ha-areẓ*. Despite their ignorance of Jewish learning, Shneour observed that these people were endowed with other valuable qualities, the opposite of resignation, passivity, and fatalism. In appearance, too, the *am ha-areẓ* was not afflicted with the pallor and bent back of the scholar.

Later Poetry

In his poem cycle *Luḥot Genuzim* ("Hidden Tablets," 1948), Shneour imagined that in the archaeological excavations being carried out in Israel there might yet be found works written by the opponents of tradition – works like the Apocrypha, fortuitously preserved in other languages and later translated into Hebrew. According to the sages, such books as the Song of Songs and Ecclesiastes were to be prohibited from publication, but were miraculously saved from suppression and were ultimately included in the Bible.

The publication of *Luḥot Genuzim* aroused much controversy. The poem, written in biblical style, relates Israel's early history in a way that conflicts with the Bible. Schneour's critics accused the poet of identifying with the "authors" of the *Luḥot*, who held views offensive to Jewish tradition. Shneour defended himself with the claim that the work was a product of his imagination and that he had no intention of substituting the ideas of the *Luḥot* for those of the scriptural version (his admiration for which he had stressed in many of his poems, such as *Manginot Yisrael*). He merely presented the suppressed opinions of the "opposition," who were to be found in every era (Korah and his band, the "false prophets," the Sadducees, etc.). Literary critics also felt that artistically the work was a failure.

Shneour in Israel

Before formally settling in Israel, in 1951, Shneour had visited the country five times. For many years he had lived the life of the country, past and present, from afar deriving his poetic inspiration from it. He sang of its rebuilding by Jewish pioneers in his *Mi-Shirei Ereẓ Israel*. In Israel he adapted his story *Pandrei ha-Gibbor* as a play, which was staged by *Habimah. He also wrote for several daily papers such as *Davar* and *Ha-Boker*, publishing in the latter installments of his great epic, *Ba'al ha-Parvah*. He also revised his Hebrew poetry and prose, which were printed in various formats.

In the 1950s, as prolific as ever, Shneour engaged in collating his enormous output, and was planning new works, when he died in New York. His remains were transferred to Israel and reinterred in a grave next to those of Bialik and Tchernichowsky.

BIBLIOGRAPHY: J. Klausner, *Z. Shneour* (1947, autobiographical writings of Z. Shneour himself, which are collected in Klausner's book); J. Fichmann, in: *Kitvei Zalman Shneour* (1960), introd.; S. Zemach, *Eruvin* (1964), 51–62; Z. Shneour, *Bialik u-Venei Doro* (1953), passim (autobiographical items throughout the book); H. Bavli et al., in: *Hadoar*, 21 (1959); Rejzen, Leksikon, 4 (1929), 808–20; Waxmann, Literature, 4 (1960[2]), 281–98; Goell, Bibliography, index. **ADD. BIBLIOGRAPHY:** M. Mikam, "*Ha-Ḥavayah ha-Elohit be-Shirat Shneour*," in: *Sefer Shilo* (1960), 207–16; M. Tabenkin, *Shirat Zalman Sheour* (1965); G. Katzenelson, "*Be-Ikvot u-ve-Nigud la-Ikvot: Al Shirei ha-Ne'urim shel Shneour*," in: *Moznayim*, 28 (1969), 275–83;

D. Radavsky, "*Ha-Nose ha-Yehudi be-Shirat Shenour*," in: *Moreshet*, 9 (1973), 110–21; M. Delusznovski, "*Itzig Manger ve-Z. Shneour be-Paris*," in: *Moznayim*, 38 (1974), 164–68; A. Barkai, *Mishka'im Bialikiyyim be-Shirat Meshorerim Ivriyyim* (1976); U. Shavit, "*Ha-Omnam Ritmus Tanakhi?*" in: *Ha-Sifrut*, 30–31 (1981), 101–8; U. Ofek, "*Z. Schneour u-Terumato le-Sifrut ha-Yeladim Shellanu*," in: *Meḥkarim be-Sifrut Yeladim* (1985), 148–54.

[Aharon Zeev Ben-Yishai]

SHNEUR ZALMAN OF (Liozna-) LYADY (1745–1813), founder of *Chabad Ḥasidism. According to family traditions he was born in Liozna, Belorussia, on the 18th of Elul. After his marriage in 1760 he devoted himself to Torah study. Concluding that he knew "a little about learning, but nothing about prayer," in 1764 he decided to learn about Ḥasidism from *Dov Baer the Maggid of Mezhirech, leader of the ḥasidic movement. In Mezhirech he became one of the inner circle of the Maggid's pupils. He also studied as a friend and pupil with *Abraham b. Dov Baer. Although Shneur Zalman was one of the youngest pupils, the Maggid had a high opinion of him and in 1770 delegated to him the task of composing a new and up-to-date Shulḥan Arukh. Shneur Zalman worked on this book for many years but published only small parts of it. About one-third was printed posthumously (the rest had been destroyed by fire) and is known as the "Shulḥan Arukh of the Rav" (1814). Though not a ḥasidic work, it represents – as the Maggid had intended – a great halakhic achievement. It evidences Shneur Zalman's superb Hebrew style and his ability to provide lucid explanation and profundity without complexity. It became an authoritative halakhic source among the Ḥasidim of *Lubavitch.

In 1774, during the early period of the opposition to Ḥasidism by traditional Jewry, Shneur Zalman and *Menaḥem Mendel of Vitebsk went to Vilna in an attempt to meet with *Elijah b. Solomon, the Gaon of Vilna, and reach some kind of understanding between the Ḥasidim and *Mitnaggedim*, but the Gaon did not agree to meet them. After Menaḥem Mendel went to Ereẓ Israel with many of his followers, Shneur Zalman was left with two others as a deputy leader in Rydzyna (Reisen, Belorussia and adjoining areas). In 1788 Menaḥem Mendel formally appointed Shneur Zalman as ḥasidic leader of Reisen: this was really only a post facto appointment, as he already had many devoted personal pupils. It had become apparent that Shneur Zalman had created a distinct type of Ḥasidism, to become known as Chabad (see Chabad system, below). In 1797 he published (anonymously) his *Likkutei Amarim* ("collected sayings"), which became known as the *Tanya*. A masterly and systematic exposition of Ḥasidism, it was accepted as the principal source of Chabad Ḥasidism, "the written law of Ḥabad."

By then the influence of Shneur Zalman was already penetrating the strongholds of the *Mitnaggedim*, who made a last effort to check the spread of Ḥasidism by informing on its followers to the Russian government. *Avigdor b. Joseph Ḥayyim, the rabbi of Pinsk, formally accused Shneur Zalman of personal acts of treason against the state (his sending of money to Ereẓ Israel was interpreted as "helping the Turkish sultan") and of creating a new religious sect (all sectaries being forbidden in Russia). In 1798 Shneur Zalman was arrested and brought for trial to St. Petersburg. No exact details of this trial are known, though many legends have been related about it. He later received a full acquittal and was released on the 19th of Kislev that year. The day is celebrated among Chabad Ḥasidim as the "Holiday of Deliverance." Shneur Zalman was again arrested in 1801 under the same accusations but was released later in the year when Alexander I succeeded to the throne. From St. Petersburg, Shneur Zalman settled in the town of Lyady and became known as the "Rav of Lyady."

Subsequently there developed a marked difference in his exposition of Ḥasidism, a deepening of the scholarly element and new ways of expression. This change was among the reasons for a resurgence of inter-ḥasidic rivalry, which also had many personal sources. The opposing faction was headed by *Abraham (Katz) of Kalisk (then in Ereẓ Israel) and *Baruch of Medzhibezh, the grandson of *Israel b. Eliezer Ba'al Shem Tov. The strife caused Shneur Zalman much pain but did not weaken his influence. When the Franco-Russian war began, Shneur Zalman was among those who thought that a victory by the revolutionary French would be injurious to Judaism. He therefore brought all his influence in favor of the Russian side and fled with the defeated Russian armies. He became ill during the flight, died in Piena (Kursk district) and was buried in Hadich (Poltava district).

Shneur Zalman was one of the great Jewish personalities of his age, as great a scholar in talmudic studies as in *Kabbalah. He had a wide knowledge of science and mathematics, and his powers as a systematizer were enhanced by a fine style. Yet he was also a mystic and deeply emotional; he composed ḥasidic melodies and was a charismatic leader. All these qualities blended in a strangely harmonious way. His work is masterly on every subject, an almost unique combination of mysticism and common sense. His other important works are *Likkutei Torah* (Zhitomir, 1848), *Torah Or* (1836), and *Ma'amarei Admor ha-Zaken* (1958–60).

Schneersohn Family

Chabad Ḥasidism continued to be led by the descendants of Shneur Zalman of Lyady: DOV BAER (1773–1827), the eldest son of Shneur Zalman, became after his father's death in 1813 the leader of the majority of his father's Ḥasidim. He settled in the little town of Lubavitch, which became the center of Chabad. Under Dov Baer's leadership, the Chabad approach was strengthened and deepened. His blend of intellect and mysticism is expressed in his clear and profound commentaries on his father's works. He was a prolific writer and wrote many works, the majority being explanations of diverse subjects, among them *Kunteres ha-Hitpa'alut* (1876; *Tractate on Ecstasy*, 1963), according to his systematized Chabad Ḥasidism. At the same time he supported the idea of productivization in the Jewish economy and encouraged his Ḥasidim to take up manual occupations. He also persuaded all the Chabad

Ḥasidim in Ereẓ Israel to settle in Hebron (1820), which became the Chabad center there. Dov Baer was imprisoned for a time because of accusations against him by an informer but was released on the 10th of Kislev, which is celebrated as a minor holiday among Chabad Ḥasidim. He died in *Nezhin in Ukraine.

MENAḤEM MENDEL (1789–1866), grandson of Shneur Zalman (son of his daughter) and son-in-law of Dov Baer, became the leader of Chabad after his father-in-law's death. Orphaned while young, he was educated chiefly by his grandfather and from a very early age began to write on *halakhah* and Ḥasidism. He wrote numerous books and sermons, most of which remained in manuscript. He was generally acknowledged as one of the greatest Torah scholars of his day. His responsa *Ẓemaḥ Ẓedek* (1870–74, in honor of which he is referred to as the "Ẓemaḥ Ẓedek") is a highly esteemed halakhic work. Menaḥem Mendel greatly assisted the Chabad settlers in Hebron. The Russian government accorded him the hereditary title of an honored citizen, and he was acknowledged as one of the leaders of Russian Jewry. He fought the assimilationist policy of the government and the adherents of *Haskalah who gave it their support. The year before his death, no longer able to fulfill his manifold duties, he assigned them to his sons.

After Menaḥem Mendel's death the Ḥasidim could not reach an agreement on a leader, and most of his sons became leaders of different branches of Chabad Ḥasidim. As the basis for the division was mainly personal, they reunited after a time.

JUDAH LEIB founded the Kopys branch of Chabad (see below). Another son of Menaḥem Mendel, ḤAYYIM SHNEUR ZALMAN (1814–1880), became leader in Lyady, noted for his special way of worship. Collections of his sermons have been made (remaining in manuscript). His successor, ISAAC DOV BAER (1826–1910), published a commentary on the prayer book entitled *Siddur Maharid*. His many other writings remain in manuscript. He was the last leader of this branch, and after his death his followers returned to the main Chabad group.

Another branch of Chabad was headed by ISRAEL NOAH (1816–1883), rabbi and ḥasidic leader in Nezhin and the most notable scholar among Menaḥem Mendel's sons. These also included JOSEPH ISAAC, who became (in his father's lifetime) a ḥasidic leader in Ovruch in the Ukraine, but his circle was not a branch of Chabad Ḥasidism.

SAMUEL (1834–1882), youngest son of Menahem Mendel, was his successor in Lubavitch. Like his father, he was active on behalf of Jewry. Only a few of his works have been published. His son SHALOM DOV BAER (1866–1920) succeeded him in the leadership of Chabad. A dynamic personality, his most important achievement was the founding of the first ḥasidic yeshivah "Tomekhei Temimim" (1897), which led the way to a more organized and effective religious education in the Chabad movement and elsewhere. His literary work is closely connected with his educational work. In 1916 he began to establish a network of Chabad yeshivot in Georgia and was the first ḥasidic leader to spread Ḥasidism among non-Ashkenazi Jewry.

His son JOSEPH ISAAC (1880–1950) assumed the leadership of Chabad during the period of the civil war in Russia which followed the 1917 Revolution. An outstanding organizer, he began to reconstruct Jewish life and became the foremost religious leader of Russian Jewry. He fought courageously to resume religious activities under the Communist regime. Under his leadership the Chabad movement became the core of a strong Jewish spiritual revival. Although his activities were at first permitted, he was arrested in 1927, and only after powerful pressure within Russia and from abroad was freed on 12th–13th of Tammuz of that year, days commemorated by Chabad Ḥasidim as a holiday of deliverance. He left Russia and went to Riga (Latvia), where he organized new Chabad centers, and founded Chabad organizations throughout the world. In 1934 he settled in Poland and organized a network of Chabad yeshivot. After the outbreak of World War II and the German occupation of Poland, he was rescued and went to the United States. With undaunted energy he stimulated, from his headquarters in Brooklyn, a renaissance of Orthodoxy in the United States. Joseph Isaac founded modern organizations of Chabad, a network of schools and yeshivot, newspapers for adults and children, a flourishing publishing house, and numerous welfare organizations. In 1948 he founded *Kefar Ḥabad in Israel. He wrote a notable history of Chabad, and published many of his sermons and talks.

MENAḤEM MENDEL (1902–1994), the son and pupil of Levi Isaac Schneersohn of Yekaterinoslav and son-in-law of Joseph Isaac, also studied mathematics and science at the Sorbonne in Paris. After the death of his father-in-law in 1950, he became the seventh successive leader of Lubavitch Ḥasidism. Under his direction, its institutions expanded, new ones were founded, and the number of adherents throughout the world increased to over 25,000. He encouraged hundreds of young men to go out to Jewish communities everywhere to establish contact with the Jewish masses and bring them back to Orthodoxy. The Lubavitch Youth Organization, which he founded in 1955, has continued to play a vital role among Jewish college students. Regional offices were established around the globe, and Kefar Chabad served as the Lubavitcher headquarters in Israel. Under Schneersohn's direction the influence of Lubavitch spread far beyond the ḥasidic community and penetrated the mainstream of Jewish life in many parts of the world. Schneersohn, while not belonging to any formal rabbinical or political organization, was frequently consulted on Jewish problems and issues.

KOPYL BRANCH. This Chabad branch was founded by JUDAH LEIB (1811–1866), a son of Menaḥem Mendel of Lubavitch (see above). After his father's death in 1866, following a quarrel over the leadership, Joseph Leib settled in the town of Kopys where many of the Ḥasidim became his followers. He died, however, in the same year. He was succeeded by his son SOLOMON (SHNEUR) ZALMAN (1830–1900), under whose leadership his followers became a most important and active branch of Chabad Ḥasidism. A selection of Solomon's ḥasidic sermons was published in one of the important Chabad books, *Magen Avot* (1902); other sermons were published in *Derushim Yekarim* (ed. G.A. Yankelzon, 1903). Another son of Judah Leib, SHALOM DOV BAER (1840?–1908), a pupil of his elder brother, Solomon, was also a rabbi. He later assumed ḥasidic leadership in Rechitsa (now Belarus), which became a secondary center of Chabad Ḥasidism. After his brother's death, Shalom became the moving force of this branch. A third brother, SHEMARIAH NOAH (1845?–1926), a rabbi and later a ḥasidic leader in Bobruisk (central Belarus), was the last leader of this branch. He built one of the first ḥasidic yeshivot (1901) and wrote a book of sermons, entitled *Shemen La-Ma'or* (1864). Upon his death his followers joined the Lubavitch branch of the movement.

The Chabad System

After Shneur Zalman became recognized as an independent ḥasidic leader, the new trend in Ḥasidism became known as Ḥa-Ba-D, an acrostic of the kabbalistic term *ḥokhmah, binah, da'at* ("germinal, developmental, and conclusive" knowledge). Shneur Zalman's methodical approach, and the need to formulate Ḥasidism in order to transmit its study, gave rise to methodological changes in the approach to Ḥasidism, which also became to a certain extent changes in essence. Although some ḥasidic ideas had received definition before the advent of Shneur Zalman, it was based on no system which could be studied by regular methods. The conversion to an organized theory which could be studied (as in the *ḥadarim* founded by Shneur Zalman) necessitated an intellectual approach. Although Shneur Zalman did not reject the "intuitive" approach to Ḥasidism in principle, he emphasized that this "all embracing way" in practice held many dangers: it could encourage self-deception and especially could lead to the severance of the vital link between simple faith and emotion, and daily practical life. Shneur Zalman stressed the necessity of regular study and unceasing spiritual exercise as indispensable for achieving lasting results. From this he derived a new ethical concept of the "*beinoni*" ("the average man"). He defined the *ẓaddik* as an exceptional human type, whose characteristics are inborn and who directs all his spiritual life to attaining the transition to the divine. However, this person is extremely rare, and there exists a disconnect between him and the average man which is almost impossible to bridge. The practical Jewish ideal is a different figure, that of the *beinoni*.

The *beinoni* that "every man should aspire to become" is the person who does not manage in the unconscious depths of his soul to achieve complete spiritual identity with the Divine, yet in his practical life and in his emotions and intellect, he strives toward perfection. This is given additional importance by Shneur Zalman through emphasizing that the *beinoni* ranks parallel to the *ẓaddik*, but the degree of the latter can only be attained by exceptional individuals who are chosen from birth, whereas that of the *beinoni* is the ideal which may be achieved in practice and is required of every Jew. The *beinoni* is not required "to change darkness into light or bitter into sweet," nor can he induce evil to change to good: this task, which kindles heresies and their consequences, is the sole province of the *ẓaddik*. The *beinoni* is required to resist evil throughout his life, to reject it by virtue of his inner decision and the subjection of evil to good (control of the evil impulse). To achieve this aim, man is required to utilize his spiritual powers. Instinctive reverence, like "the hidden love that is in the heart of every Jew from birth," forms the primary basis from which every *beinoni* may advance to higher degrees of perfection. The *beinoni's* struggle against the evil impulse within him is sustained by knowing that "the brain rules the heart from birth" and by persevering in the use of *meditation (*hitbonenut*). Meditation on the greatness of the Creator and on love and reverence for Him results in the elevation of the primitive feelings in the sacred soul to a higher degree of "love and rational reverence." This does not necessarily imply an intellectual or rationalist approach to adherence to God but is essentially the propulsion of the hidden emotional life to a degree of full awareness. Similarly, strict attention is required to be paid to the accepted Jewish ethical behavior – such as punctiliousness in the performance of the precepts, additional stress on Torah study, and the worship of God in joyousness while repressing melancholy. In placing additional significance on the role of meditation as a primary means of achieving elevation in the ḥasidic progression, Shneur Zalman regarded study of Kabbalah not as a theoretical study but essentially as a means of strengthening faith in the Creator and of arousing the heart.

In consequence of its teachings and discourses, Ḥasidism develops into an independent study encompassing a variety of subjects which promote meditation. However, while Shneur Zalman did not diverge from the approach of his ḥasidic mentors in the abstract spheres of speculation, he systematized their teachings by the use of special methods of exposition. In particular he broadened and developed the exposition of Kabbalah (which had already begun during the lifetime of the Ba'al Shem Tov) by employing parables and examples from spiritual life. The symbols and principles of Kabbalah were understood as operating also in psychological problems. In his work *Sha'ar ha-Yiḥud ve-ha-Emunah*, Shneur Zalman summarizes his general theological concept, the basic problem being the reciprocal connection between God and the world. Although he accepts the view that the existence of the world has its origin in the hidden and concealed aspect of the divine nature, this does not lead him to deny the basic reality of the world as an illusion of the senses. He draws considerably upon the deductive methods of *Judah Loew, the Maharal of Prague, explaining that even the concealed and hidden aspects are revelations of other facets of the divine nature.

As a corollary to this explanation there arises the paradox of which Shneur Zalman makes regular use, that the physical world, precisely because it conceals the divine manifestation, is an expression of the highest degree of the divinity ("material creation derives from the divine substance"). This explanation also postulates conclusions concerning the conduct of man: fulfillment of the practical precepts just because they are materialistic and study of the Torah just because it is linked with material factors in the world are higher degrees than theoretical spiritual adhesion to God. The link with the apparent concealed divine presence in this world is the ascent which follows the descent of the soul into the body. Observance of the precepts, like Torah study, forms a link of real adhesion to God (and in fact the only link). It follows that love of God and reverence for Him, and even the feeling of adhesion to Him, are only a means of arousing the soul toward the true adhesion – through Torah study and observance of the precepts.

By emphasizing the unbridgeable chasm between the divine essence and any attempt at understanding and identification with it, it follows that the only bridge is through the channel of revelation – the Torah and its precepts – while in the life of the soul the most praiseworthy quality is the negation of selfhood. This negation is not expressed through self-mortification but is basically a "negation of existence," subjection of the individual wish; and "negation of reality" is the wish of the individual to identify with the divine will. Surrender of the soul, as one of the main forms of such negation, serves simultaneously as the basis for the path to worship of God in both the life of feeling and of action.

This interpretation of Ḥasidism, predicated on observance of the precepts out of a wish to identify with God, in study and meditation, is clearly an individualist process. Every Ḥasid is responsible for pursuing, and is obligated to pursue, independent worship activity, while the assistance of the ḥasidic congregation, and even of the *ẓaddik* himself, is not integral to divine worship. Hence Shneur Zalman does not dwell extensively on the status and nature of the *ẓaddik*. In his view the *admor* is a spiritual leader and guide who assists his Ḥasidim to find their individual way to God, while the ḥasidic group, or the isolated Ḥasid, can and are required to pursue their way by virtue of their independent powers and responsibility.

Shneur Zalman did not intend to present a complete theosophical system, like the kabbalists, nor did he engage in theological speculations for their own sake. Rather, he was a guide to the path leading to the true service of God. From his position as *ẓaddik*, Shneur Zalman sought to demonstrate that by following his advice the ḥasid would be realizing the verse, "the thing is very close to you, in your mouth and in your heart to observe it" (Deut. 30:14). He constructed a psychological system based on kabbalistic principles, distinguished by subtle analyses and penetrating to the depths of the human soul. His treatment of theology is arrived at incidentally through psychology, and hence his system may be regarded as Kabbalah in ḥasidic dress.

In his theology, Shneur Zalman presented a conception of theistic transcendence even of a somewhat pantheist nature. In this respect he is closer to the conception of Moses *Cordovero than to Isaac *Luria. On the one hand there is no limit to the greatness of God, and "the intellect cannot grasp it"; on the other, the term "infinite" (*Ein Sof) in its adverbial form is understood as "there is no object to the light emanating from Him," i.e., in terms manifested outside of Him. Shneur Zalman explains this by the use of the terms "surrounds all the worlds" and "fills all the worlds," i.e., on His own terms God is infinite (*Ein-Sof*), surrounding and encompassing everything. His greatness lies in that the only luminance revealed outside Him is infinitesimal, though this luminance supports and establishes all existence in the many worlds. Hence the concept of Shneur Zalman cannot be defined as total acosmism, as held by several scholars.

Shneur Zalman explains the concept of *ẓimẓum* ("contraction," see *Kabbalah) as being allegorical only, reflecting some inner compulsion. The abundance of the upper world would flow unimpeded in the act of creation, but *ẓimẓum* is constituted to conceal this light before the limited creatures.

Shneur Zalman emphasizes the importance of "germinal, elemental, and conclusive knowledge" (*ḥokhmah, binah, da'at*), i.e., those powers of the soul which are employed in intellectual activities, whose object is the immensity of *Ein-Sof*. However not the intellect alone, but attributes such as love and reverence and the like ought to be directed toward the Creator. Evil is not bad on its own terms and is constituted to serve as a challenge to man. Whoever manages to subject it (the *beinoni*), and even to convert it to good (the *ẓaddik*), augments holiness in the world and brings the Divine Presence to a complete harmony and the soul to great joy.

The Tanya

This is the first and primary work of the Chabad system, first published anonymously in 1796. Shneur Zalman himself calls the book *Likkutei Amarim* ("Collected Sayings"), but on the title page of the second edition it is designated "*Tanya*," and it has continued to be widely known by this name ever since. It has been translated into English (including pt. 5; 1964–66). The book consists of five parts:

(1) *Sefer shel Beinonim* ("The Book of the Average Man").

(2) *Sha'ar ha-Yiḥud ve-ha-Emunah* ("The Gateway of Unity and Belief"), called in the first edition *ḥinukh katan* ("brief instruction").

(3) *Iggeret Teshuvah* ("Letter of Repentance"); this exists in two editions: the first, and briefest, was published in Shklov in 1799, while the second edition, the longer version, was published in Shklov in 1806 and has been the most frequently republished. It is also called "*Tanya Katan*" ("Brief Tanya").

(4) *Iggeret ha-Kodesh* ("Letter of Holiness"), published in Shklov in 1814 soon after the author's death. Not all the letters have been published in their entirety, and their supplements are scattered in various texts.

(5) *Kunteres Aḥaron* ("Last Thesis"; Shklov 1814).

The 1814 Shklov edition of the *Tanya* includes all five parts, and this form has since been retained. Various abridgments and explanations have been written to the *Tanya*. The

Chabad Ḥasidim refer to it as the "written law of Ḥabad" and designate it for daily study.

Apart from the letters included in the "*Iggeret ha-Kodesh*" and "*Kunteres Aḥaron*," the rest of the parts of the book present a complete and consistent system, which develops out of the determination not to "fail" in precision of terminology and logic. This gives rise to complicated syntax and lengthy sentences, which make the subject difficult to comprehend. However, the *Tanya* is one of the few works of Ḥasidism which is not a collection of discourses but a complete systematic exposition and was developed by the originator of the system himself. When the book appeared, it was criticized adversely by both *maskilim* and *Mitnaggedim*, and even by the Ḥasid, Abraham of Kalish. But it eventually was greatly appreciated for the profundity of its thought and organized structure. However, commentators have not always succeeded in penetrating its inner meaning. Contradictions exist between Shneur Zalman's other books of discourses and the *Tanya*.

Successors to the Chabad System

Those continuing the system advanced by Shneur Zalman of Lyady merely explain and expand what he laid down. The principal contribution of his own descendants to the Chabad system was their selection of various subjects out of the total of those treated by him. Shneur Zalman's ramified work was given direction and definition principally by his son and successor Dov Baer. He placed even greater emphasis on the element of meditation and also expanded it. He strengthened the intellectual aspect of Chabad, designating the study of Ḥasidism not only as a means to an end but also an end in itself. By this he brought an additional distance between the Ḥasidism practiced by Chabad and the rest of the branches of Ḥasidism (see Aaron of *Starosielce).

Menaḥem Mendel, author of *Ẓemaḥ Ẓedek*, added halakhic works and also introduced a new category of ḥasidic writings. In *Derekh Mitzvotekha* (1911–12), on a part of the Torah precepts, Mendel employed a form which combined halakhah, kabbalah, and Ḥasidism; and in *Sefer ha-Ḥakirah*, he brought together concepts and terms from Jewish philosophical literature and the systems of Kabbalah and Ḥasidism. However, subsequently Chabad returned to the framework established by Dov Baer – ḥasidic sayings, mainly arranged according to the portions of the Law, which explain religious and theoretical problems (intellectual) or ethical-practical concerns (worship) according to Shneur Zalman's system. The works which expand the sphere of ideas (of the Kopys dynasty) or the kabbalistic context (those of Shalom Baer) still do not go beyond this general framework, hence the special status acquired by the *admorim* of Chabad as the sole authoritative exponents of the system. In contrast, a different, more personal type of literary work developed in the form of talks, in which guidance is the principal motif. They are not constructed in an organized form. In them the Chabad *admorim* of the last few generations express themselves freely, each in his own manner, through ethical tales or general explanations of contemporary problems.

BIBLIOGRAPHY: M. Teitelbaum, *Ha-Rav mi-Ladi u-Mifleget Ḥabad* (1913); D.Z. Hilman, *Iggerot Ba'al ha-Tanya u-Venei Doro* (1953); H.M. Heilman, *Beit Rabbi* (1965); Dubnow, Ḥasidut, index; M.L. Rodkinson, *Toledot Ammudei Ḥabad* (1876); R. Schatz-Uffenheimer, in: *Molad* (1963), 171–2; A.M. Habermann, in: *Alei Ayin* (1953), 293–370; M. Buber, *Tales of the Hasidim*, 1 (1968⁴), 265–71; J.I. Schneersohn, *The Tzemach Tzedek and the Haskala Movement* (1962); idem, *On the Teaching of Chassidies* (1959); idem, *Some Aspects of Chabad Chasidism* (1957); idem, *Lubavitcher Rabbi's Memoirs* (1966); M.M. Schneersohn, *Mafte'ah* (1968); idem, *Sefer ha-Toledot* (1947); N. Mindel, *Rabbi Schneur Zalman* (1969); idem, *R. Joseph Isaac Schneersohn* (1947); A.H. Glicenstein, *Rabbenu ha-Ẓemaḥ Ẓedek* (1967); idem, *Ha-Admor ha-Emẓa'i* (1950); idem, *Sefer ha-Toledot* (1967); H. Bunin, in: *Ha-Shilo'ah*, 28–31 (1913–15); L. Jung (ed.), *Jewish Leaders* (1953), 51–75.

[Avrum Stroll]

SHOCHAT, ISRAEL (1886–1961), founder and leader of the *Ha-Shomer organization. Shochat was born in Liskova in the province of Grodno (Belorussia) into a family of Jewish landowners. In his youth he joined the Po'alei Zion party and in 1904 went to settle in Ereẓ Israel. When he became acquainted with the Jewish settlements whose life was based on Arab labor and protected by Arab, Circassian, North African, and other non-Jewish watchmen, Shochat decided to establish a clandestine order whose objective would be to introduce Jewish workers and watchmen into the villages. In 1907 he attended the Eighth Zionist Congress and played a role in the establishment of the World Union of Po'alei Zion. In 1907 Shochat gathered about ten of his friends in Jaffa and founded the secret society, Bar-Giora. At the head of a group of friends, Shochat set out for Sejera (now *Ilaniyyah) in Lower Galilee and there convinced the surrounding settlements to entrust Jewish watchmen with guard duties. In 1909, at a meeting of the members of Bar-Giora, it was decided to establish the Ha-Shomer organization. Shochat was elected chairman of the Ha-Shomer committee, and within a few years this organization became an important factor in the life of the new *yishuv*. In 1910 Shochat attempted to set up a "labor legion" in order to introduce Jewish labor into the settlements based on communal life and discipline. The "legion" was short-lived because of a lack of members and the opposition of the Jewish labor parties to its methods. At the end of 1912, Shochat left for Constantinople with Izhak *Ben-Zvi and David *Ben-Gurion to study law.

With the outbreak of World War I, Shochat was among the initiators of a project for the establishment of a Jewish militia that would assist in maintaining order in the country. The Turkish authorities rejected this project, arrested Shochat and his wife, Mania Wilbushewitch *Shochat, and deported them to Brusa, Anatolia. In 1917 Shochat was allowed to attend the Po'alei Zion Conference in Stockholm, and with the end of World War I he returned to Palestine. Together with his comrades of Ha-Shomer, he joined *Aḥdut ha-Avodah and was among the founders of Haganah, the *Gedud ha-Avodah

(Labor Legion), and the Histadrut. His controversy with the leaders of Aḥdut ha-Avodah regarding the organizational system of the Haganah led to his resignation from the Haganah command. He attempted to pursue his own defense activities within the framework of Gedud ha-Avodah through a closed underground that established an arms depot in Kefar Giladi and sent members to Europe for military training. In 1925 he left for Moscow, where he held secret negotiations with high Soviet officials on the possibility of a collaboration between his group and the Soviet secret service, but these negotiations proved completely fruitless. Shochat and his colleagues were called before an internal body of the Histadrut to answer for their separatist political and defense activities. With the disintegration of Gedud ha-Avodah, Shochat was removed from all central public activities. During the 1930s he was active in the Ha-Po'el sports organization and the establishment of the first flying clubs in the country. As a lawyer he took up the defense of Haganah prisoners, and on the establishment of the State of Israel (1948) he acted as legal adviser to the minister of police. His memoirs were published in *Kovez ha-Shomer* (1937) and in *Sefer ha-Shomer* (1957). He was a brother of Eliezer *Shoḥat.

BIBLIOGRAPHY: Dinur, Haganah, 45; 2 (1959), 4–6, 8–10, 15; S. Sheva, *Shevet ha-No'azim* (1969).

[Yehuda Slutsky]

SHOCHAT, MANIA WILBUSHEWITCH (1880–1961), one of the leaders of the *Ha-Shomer organization. Born on the estate of Lososna, near Grodno, Belorussia, she left her father's house in her youth and went to work in her brother's factory in Minsk in order to become acquainted with the living conditions of the workers and assist them. There she became associated with revolutionary circles (*Gershuni and others) and was arrested during the summer of 1899. In prison she met the chief of the secret police of Moscow, Zubatov, who advanced the idea of establishing a workers' movement that would be loyal to the czar and supported by him ("police socialism," or "Zubatovshchina"). Zubatov convinced her that the establishment of a Jewish workers' party under the aegis of the authorities, concerning itself solely with professional and economic interests and abstaining from political activities against the regime, would be a blessing to the Jewish masses and would lead to an extension of Jewish civic rights. Under his influence she undertook to establish such a movement, and in the summer of 1901 she participated in the establishment of the Jewish Independent Labor Party. The workers organized within this party and the strikes they declared were successful because agents of the secret police supported them. They were stubbornly opposed by the Bund and the other Jewish Socialist groups, however. Mania Wilbushewitz played a central role in the party, and even discussed its affairs with the minister of the interior, *Plehve (May 1902).

With the change of the government's policy toward Zubatov's projects and under the impact of the Kishinev pogrom, the party reached an impasse and in the summer of 1903 announced its own dissolution. Mania Wilbushewitch subsequently underwent a period of grave crisis. She unsuccessfully attempted to assume a role in revolutionary activities. At the beginning of 1904, her brother Naḥum Wilbushewitch invited her to visit Erez Israel, and for a year she traveled through the country studying the conditions of settlement and came to the conclusion that only through collective agricultural settlement could a wide class of Jewish workers emerge – an essential condition for the development of Erez Israel into a Jewish country. In 1907 she undertook a journey to Europe and the United States in order to study various communist settlements. Upon her return, she sought out a group of men who would cooperate in the realization of her project and thus became associated with the members of the Bar-Giora group led by Israel Shochat. Under her influence its members settled on a farm near Sejera (Ilaniyah) and in 1907–08 undertook to farm it on a collective basis, thus inaugurating the first experiment of collective settlement in Erez Israel.

In 1908 she married Israel Shochat and with him was among the founders of Ha-Shomer (1909). She became a central figure in Ha-Shomer, where her spiritual influence prevailed. When World War I broke out, the Turkish authorities banished Mania and Israel Shochat to Bursa, Anatolia. It was not until the spring of 1919 (after they had traveled to Stockholm to attend the Po'alei Zion convention) that both returned to Palestine and joined the Aḥdut Avodah party. In 1921 Mania was a member of the first Histadrut delegation to visit the United States. Her presence aroused bitter polemics when the Bundists and the Communists recalled her collaboration with Zubatov and accused her of denouncing revolutionaries to the secret police. She then published her memoirs in the newspaper *Di Tsayt*. During the following years she devoted herself to the activities of *Gedud ha-Avodah, and after its dissolution she was active in Kefar Giladi. In 1930 she was among the founders of the League for Jewish-Arab Friendship. In 1948, she joined the Mapam party and settled in Tel Aviv, where she devoted herself to social work. She published memoirs in *Divrei Po'alot* (1930), *Kovez ha-Shomer* (1937), and *Sefer ha-Shomer* (1957).

BIBLIOGRAPHY: Dinur, Haganah, vols. 1–2 (1954), indexes; S. Sheva, *Shevet ha-No'azim* (1969); M. Mishkinsky, in: *Zion*, 25:3–4 (1959/60), 238–49.

[Yehuda Slutsky]

SHOFAR (Heb. שׁוֹפָר), an animal's horn prepared for use as a musical instrument. Together with the reed, it is one of the earliest musical instruments known to man which is still in use. Etymologically the word is connected with *šapparu*, meaning wild sheep (Koehler-Baumgartner, s.v. *shofar*). It is mentioned 69 times in the Bible and frequently in talmudic and post-talmudic literature.

History and Description

The *shofar* is first mentioned in Exodus 19:16 at the theophany on Sinai. It was used to proclaim the Jubilee Year and the proclamation of "freedom throughout the land" (Lev. 25:9–10); this verse is engraved upon the Liberty Bell in Philadelphia, Pennsylvania. It was to be sounded on *Rosh Ha-Shanah, which is designated as "*yom teru'ah*" ("A day of blowing"; Num. 29:1). It was also used as an accompaniment to other musical instruments (Ps. 98:6), in processionals (Josh. 6:4ff.), as a signal (Josh. 6:12ff., II Sam. 15:10), as a clarion call to war (Judg. 3:27), and in order to induce fear (Amos 3:6).

When used in the Temple, the *shofar* was usually sounded in conjunction with the trumpet (*ḥaẓoẓrah*). The Talmud (RH 27a) states that the trumpet was made of silver, while the processed horn of one of the five species of animal – sheep, goat, mountain goat, antelope, and gazelle – was used to fulfill the ritual commandment of the sounding of the *shofar*. It further declares (*ibid.* 26b) that the *shofar* should preferably be made of a ram's or wild goat's horn, because they are curved. Rabbi Judah states: "the *shofar* of Rosh Ha-Shanah must be of the horn of a ram, to indicate submission." Traditionally a ram's horn is sounded on those days because of its connection with the sacrifice of Isaac (the *Akedah*), the story of which is the Torah reading for the second day of the festival. Conversely, a cow's horn may not be used because of the incident of the golden calf (RH 3:2). The *shofar* may not be painted, though it can be gilded or carved with artistic designs, so long as the mouthpiece remains natural. A *shofar* with a hole is deemed halakhically unfit, though it may be used if no other is available (Sh. Ar., OḤ 586).

Sounds of the Shofar

The Bible refers to two kinds of trumpet sounds: *teki'ah* and *teru'ah* (Num. 10:5–8). The Mishnah (RH 4:9) describes the *teki'ah* as a long blast and the *teru'ah* as three *yevavot*, a wavering crying blast. It prescribes three sets of *shofar* sounds since the word *teru'ah* is mentioned in the Bible three times (Lev. 23:24, 25:9 and Num. 29:1), each set to consist of a *teki'ah*, a *teru'ah* and *teki'ah* thrice repeated (RH 33bf.).

In the talmudic period, doubt arose as to the exact nature of the *teru'ah*. Some held that it was a moaning sound (*genuḥei genah*) and others that it was an outcry (*yelulei yelal*). According to the first opinion, the sound was *shevarim* (broken sounds), while in the second view it was *teru'ah* – a tremolo of nine staccato notes. Rabbi Abbahu reconciled the difference by deciding that the first set of sounds should include both *shevarim* and *teru'ah*, i.e., *teki'ah, shevarim–teru'ah, teki'ah*, while the other two sets were to be composed as follows: *teki'ah, shevarim, teki'ah*; and *teki'ah, teru'ah, teki'ah* (*ibid.*). The *teki'ah* (blowing) is a glissando which begins on a lower note and swells into a higher. The *teru'ah* (alarm) is a series of staccato blasts upon the lower note. The *shevarim* (tremolo) is an alternation of higher and lower notes. The concluding note of each of the two series is a *teki'ah gedolah* (great blast); this is a long drawn-out note explained as a sign of the removal of the Divine Presence, hermeneutically deduced from Exodus 19:13: "When the ram's horn soundeth long, they shall come up to the mount."

Use on the Holy Days

During the month of Elul, the *shofar* is blown from the second day of the new month to usher in the penitential season (Rema, Sh. Ar., OḤ 581:1). There is a tradition that Moses ascended Mount Sinai for the second time on Rosh Ḥodesh Elul and that the *shofar* was sounded so that the children of Israel might not be misled. Thus, originally it was blown only on the first day of Rosh Ḥodesh Elul. Today it is sounded daily, except for the last day, throughout the month at morning service until Rosh Ha-Shanah is over, and once more on the Day of Atonement at the conclusion of the final service (*Ne'ilah*). This last, though, is a late custom.

On Rosh Ha-Shanah, Psalm 47 is recited seven times before the sounding of the *shofar*. This is symbolic of the seven circuits that the Israelites made around Jericho before the wall fell down at the blasts of the *shofar*, and of the seven heavens through which prayers must penetrate in order to reach the throne of God. There are two series of blasts: for the first, which is sounded before the *Musaf*, the congregation may sit before they rise to hear it, and hence it is called *teki'ot meyushav* ("sitting *teki'ot*"; to distinguish it from the second series, which is heard during the *Musaf Amidah*, for which the congregation has been standing all the time). This first series is preceded by two benedictions: (1) "Blessed be Thou O Lord our God King of the universe, who has sanctified us by Thy commandments and has instructed us to hear the call of the *shofar*"; (2) "Blessed be Thou … who has kept us in life, has sustained us and privileged us to reach this season of the year." The second series, the *teki'ot me'ummad* ("standing *teki'ot*") is heard three times during the reader's repetition of the *Musaf* (in the Sephardi rite also in the silent Amidah) at the conclusion of each one of its major sections (*Malkhuyyot* – the kingship of God; *Zikhronot* – the remembrance of the merit of our ancestors; and *Shofarot* – hope for the coming of the Messianic Era to be ushered in by the sound of the *shofar*). In some communities it is also customary to sound up to a total of one hundred sounds at the conclusion of the service

The *shofar* may be sounded only in the daytime. Women and children are exempt from the commandment to listen to it, but such is its place in the Rosh Ha-Shanah ritual that nearly all do. When Rosh Ha-Shanah occurs on the Sabbath, the *shofar* is not blown, the traditional reason being "lest he carry it (the *shofar*) from one domain to another (in violation of the Sabbath)" (RH 29b). When the Temple was in existence, it was sounded there even on the Sabbath, but not elsewhere. After the destruction of the Temple Johanan b. Zakkai permitted its use on the Sabbath in a town where an ordained *bet din* sat (RH 4:1). This, however, is not the normal practice in our times. The congregant sounding the *shofar* is called a *ba'al teki'ah* and anyone capable of doing so is permitted to blow it. The prompter, or caller, is the *makri*.

Other Uses

In about 400 C.E. in Babylonia, the *shofar* was sounded to announce a death (MK 27b). During the Middle Ages also, it was also blown on fasts (see Ta'an. 1:6), at excommunications (see Sanh. 76 and MK 16a), and at funerals. On Friday afternoon, six blasts were sounded at various intervals. At the first *teki'ah*, the laborers in the fields ceased their work. At the second, shops were closed and city laborers ceased to work. The third signaled that it was time to kindle the Sabbath lights. And the fourth, fifth, and sixth were a *teki'ah, teru'ah* and *teki'ah* formally ushering in the Sabbath (Shab. 35b). In modern times the *shofar* is used at the inauguration of a new president of Israel. During the Six-Day War in June 1967, the chief rabbi of the Israeli army blew it at the Western Wall after its liberation by the Israel Defense Forces, using the same *shofar* which he had sounded on Mt. Sinai in 1956. More and more in modern Israel the *shofar* has been used to mark various solemn occasions, especially by the Oriental communities.

Reasons for Sounding the Shofar

Anthropologists offer the theory that since many powers are ascribed to a horn, for example, frightening away demons, it was blown to produce magical results. The *shofar,* thus, is to scare off Satan and evil spirits (cf. RH 16b); and so it is fitting that it be used on Rosh Ha-Shanah to frighten away the "prosecuting attorney."

Most Jewish philosophers attempted to explain the significance of the *shofar.* Saadiah Gaon offered ten reasons for sounding it: (1) to proclaim the sovereignty of God, since it was the custom to sound the *shofar* at a coronation; (2) to herald the beginning of the ten days of repentance; (3) as a reminder to be faithful to the teachings of the Torah, since the *shofar* was heard at the giving of the Torah; (4) as a reminder of the prophets, the teachers of righteousness, who raised their voices like the *shofar* to touch our consciences; (5) to the sound of trumpets the Temple fell, and to the sound of trumpets it will be restored; (6) as a reminder of the *Akedah*, since the ram which was substituted for Isaac was caught in the thicket by its horns; (7) to inspire awe ("Shall the *shofar* be blown in the city and the people not be afraid?"); (8) as a summons to the Heavenly Court on the Day of Judgment to be judged; (9) as a reminder that the *shofar* will call together Israel's scattered remnants to return to the Holy Land; and (10) as a reminder of the day of resurrection, the return to life (quoted by Abudarham (Jerusalem, 1959 ed.), 269f.).

Maimonides gives a moving interpretation of the sounding of the *shofar*: "Awake O sleepers from your sleep, O slumberers arouse ye from your slumbers, and examine your deeds, return in repentance and remember your Creator" (Yad, Teshuvah 3:4).

BIBLIOGRAPHY: S.J. Zevin, *Ha-Mo'adim ba-Halakhah* (1963[10]), 40–54; J.L. Baruch (ed.), *Sefer ha-Mo'adim*, 1 (1947), 52–75, 172–75; S.Y. Agnon, *Days of Awe* (1965), 65–81.

[Albert L. Lewis]

SHOFAROT (Heb. שׁוֹפָרוֹת; "shofar verses"), last of the three central benedictions of the *Musaf* *Amidah* on *Rosh Ha-Shanah. The benediction is comprised of ten biblical verses which mention the **shofar* and which voice the hope for the messianic redemption of Israel and mankind, to be heralded by the sound of the "great *shofar*" (Isa. 18:3; Zech. 9:14). Joseph *Albo interpreted the benediction as being a statement of religious dogma (*Ikkarim* 1:4). In the Ashkenazi ritual, the *shofar* is sounded at the end of the *Shofarot* benediction during the repetition of the *Musaf Amidah*; in the Sephardi and Oriental rites it is also sounded during the silent *Musaf Amidah.* The recital of the *Shofarot* verses was ordained in the Talmud (RH 4:6; RH 32a–b). In the *Conservative and *Reform liturgies, the recital of the *Shofarot* verses is preceded by appropriate introductory and/or supplementary explanatory readings in the vernacular.

BIBLIOGRAPHY: Elbogen, Gottesdienst, 141–44; M. Silverman (ed.), *High Holiday Prayerbook* (1939), 157, 167–70 (Conservative); *Union Prayer Book*, 2 (1923), 82–84 (Reform); P. Birnbaum (ed.), *High Holiday Prayer Book* (1951), 389–94 (Orthodox).

SHOFMAN (Schoffmann), GERSHON (1880–1972), Hebrew writer, distinguished for his miniature short stories, his meditative and didactic sketches, and his epigrammatic essays on literature and life. Born in Orsha, Belorussia, Shofman received a traditional religious education; but as a result of diligent reading, first of Hebrew and then of Russian literature, he became acquainted with European culture and with the new trends in Hebrew literature developed under the influence of S.Y. *Abramovitsh (Mendele Mokher Seforim) and his disciples. Shofman's talent for short-story writing was revealed in his very first collection of stories, published in Warsaw in 1902. In that same year, he enlisted in the Russian army and served for almost three years. In 1904, during the Russo-Japanese War, he fled to Galicia, remaining there until 1913, when he left for Vienna. He then settled in an Austrian village, and lived there until he immigrated to Ereẓ Israel in 1938, where he eventually settled in Haifa.

Shofman published his stories and articles in various periodicals in Russia, Poland, Germany, Austria, England, and Israel. He also edited several literary journals. His collected writings first appeared in four volumes in 1927–35, and subsequently in a revised edition of four volumes (1946–52), to which a fifth was added in 1960. Shofman was awarded the Israel Prize for literature in 1957.

Shofman's writing is characterized by its conciseness and precision. His sentences are free of all literary embellishment and make no attempt at being dramatic; Jacob *Fichmann commented that "in their utter lucidity and strict precision they resemble scientific definitions." Even Shofman's metaphors are generally confined to an adverb or an adjective of not more than one or two words. Consequently, his narrative thrust depends on subtle innuendo and symbolic implications.

Shofman's stories have no plot in the ordinary sense. There is no real sequence of events; the stories consist rather of a succession of hurried utterances and episodic actions with no apparent close connection between them. Only as the narrative unfolds does it become evident that the actions and utterances related by the author are more than episodic. Events are governed by the iron laws of destiny; they are a necessary outcome of past action, as well as an omen for what may come to pass in the future.

Shofman's own history of wanderings comes out clearly in his stories and articles. But at the same time he writes in a somewhat depersonalized fashion, and consequently his works seem to encompass the many turning points in Jewish life in the 20th century: the collapse of Jewish tradition in Russia during the pre-World War I period, and the conceptual vacuum, rootlessness, and depression which overcame the Jews as a result; the counterwave of faith in the socialist revolution which initially swept away a part of Jewish youth, but which after the 1905 pogroms ended largely in despair; the further moral and spiritual decline which came about in the wake of World War I and increasing antisemitism during the interwar period and World War II; and the Jewish immigration to Ereẓ Israel, the State of Israel, and the life of the Jew as he attempted to free himself of the marks of degeneration and moral collapse.

The sociocultural nature of Shofman's themes constitutes the implicit rather than the explicit element in his writings. As seen from an external viewpoint, Shofman's hero is generally a total individualist ruled by desires on the one hand, and on the other hand by hidden forces which are apparently imperceptible to the human intellect. At times he struggles against these forces and at times he surrenders to them. At times he is passive and at times active. However, his existence, living as he does a gloomy and commonplace life, is almost always a marginal one. Depression, illness, degradation, the fear both of life and of death seem to thrust the hero into the position of being activated rather than acting; and in consequence of his experience he normally thinks of and cares for no one but himself. On the rare occasions when he does act for the benefit of society, even when he dies for it, he is in actual fact impelled by some hidden force, the significance of which he does not understand.

Shofman developed his own particular view of aesthetics in both his narrative and his meditative writings, and he demanded the same standards from others. His articles on literature and literary criticism, some of which were published in the series *Sirtutei Peḥam* ("Charcoal Drawings") and *Shetayim Shalosh Shurot* ("Two or Three Lines"), set out his convictions, often in a strongly polemical tone. On the other hand, when a work under review appeared to conform to his own standards, Shofman was generous with his praise.

For English translations of his works see Goell, Bibliography, 1505, 2465–85.

BIBLIOGRAPHY: J. Fichmann, *Benei Dor* (1952), 104–22; J. Klausner, *Yoẓerim u-Vonim*, 2 (1929), 208–22; S. Zemach, *Massah u-Vikkoret* (1954), 53–71; M. Ribalow, *Sefer ha-Massot* (1928), 105–29; I. Rabinovitz, *Ha-Sipporet ha-Ivrit Meḥappeset Gibbor* (1967), 91–100; Waxman, Literature, 4 (1960), 105–8; G. Katznelson, in: *Moznayim*, 33 (1960), 246–55; M. Gil, *ibid.*, 261–67. **ADD. BIBLIOGRAPHY:** N. Govrin, "*Zikkat Yeẓirato shel Shofman la-Mikra*," in: *Karmelit*, 16 (1970), 61–84; S. Ben-David, "*Idialism ve-Realizm bi-Yẓirat G. Shofman*," in: *Gazit*, 26:9–12 (1970), 7–9; M. Ovadyahu, "*G. Shofman, Aman ha-Sippur ha-Kaẓar*," in: *Bitzaron*, 63 (1972), 285–88; G. Shaked, *Ha-Sipporet ha-Ivrit*, 1 (1977), 385–403; S. Schmidt, *Demuyyot ha-Nashim be-Sippurei Berdyczewski ve-Shofman* (1978); N. Govrin, *Me-Ofek el Ofek: Gershon Shofman – Ḥayyav vi-Yeẓirato* (1983); Y. Even, *Ha-Prozah ha-Ivrit be-Dor Bialik* (1984); H. Barzel, *Ḥazon ve-Ḥizzayon* (1988); H. Herzig, *Ha-Sippur ha-Ivri be-Reshit ha-Me'ah ha-Esrim* (1992); A. Holtzman, "*Madu'a He'edimu Penei ha-Nahar?*" in: *Ẓafon*, 7 (2004), 51–59.

[Gideon Katznelson]

SHOHAM (Heb. שֹׁהַם, "Onyx"), town in central Israel. The town is located near Ben-Gurion Airport, halfway between Jerusalem and Tel Aviv. It was founded in 1993 and is under constant expansion, with an area of 5.2 sq. mi (13.5 sq. km.) and a 2002 population of 15,600. Its growth rate is one of the highest in Israel – 7% a year. The development of the town has been characterized by emphasis on environmental issues. It has around 60 acres of parkland utilizing a special water-saving system for watering. Every year Shoham hosts an Arts Festival during Sukkot and an International Mountain Bike Race in memory of Yitzhak *Rabin, late prime minister of Israel.

WEBSITE: www.shoham.muni.il.

[Shaked Gilboa (2nd ed.)]

SHOHAM (Polakevich), MATTITYAHU MOSHE (1893–1937), Hebrew poet and playwright. Born in Warsaw, and orphaned at an early age, Shoham was educated by his grandfather and uncle. He studied foreign languages and secular literature largely on his own. In 1930 he went to Palestine, but being unable to earn a livelihood, returned to Poland two years later. He served for three years as chairman of the Hebrew Authors' Association of Poland, and helped to edit its biweekly publication *Ammudim*; he also lectured at the Institute of Jewish Studies in Warsaw. Most of Shoham's poems, plays, and essays were published in *Ha-Tekufah, Moznayim, Gilyonot*, and *Ketuvim*. Only two of his works appeared in book form during his lifetime – *Ẓor vi-Yrushalayim* (1933) and *Elohei Barzel Lo Ta'aseh Lekha* (1937). His other works were published in collected form in 1965.

Lyric Poems

Shoham began his literary career by writing lyric and dramatic poems, his main themes being love and the biblical past. His vocabulary and style are archaic, and he frequently employs exotic figures of speech and highly dramatic symbolism. The power of Shoham's poems lies in their densely packed lines and in the depth of their mythic conception. This is apparent even in his early lyric cycles, such as "*Shulamit*" (*Ha-Tekufah*, 4, 1919), "*Negohot*" (*ibid.*, 7, 1920), "*Kaẓir*" (*ibid.*, 9, 1921), and "*Peret*" (*ibid.*, 19, 1923). The pervasive theme in these poems is sensual, primitive love, which is invariably linked to the recurrent cycle of time. A broad mythical conception of love and human life also dominates the poems "*Ahavah*" (*Ha-Tekufah*, 22, 1924) and "*Gadish*" (*Moznayim*, 3, 1931), and the prose poems *"El ha-Malkah"* (*Ha-Tekufah*, 6, 1920) and *"Nedudim"* (*ibid.*, 8, 1921).

Most of Shoham's longer poems are based largely upon a mythical conception of Jewish history. In *"Kedem"* (*Ha-Tekufah*, 14–15, 1922) and *"Ur Kasdim"* (*ibid.*, 26–27, 1930), the dramatic tension springs from the polarity between East and West. Shoham's view is that the salvation of Western man in general, and of the Jew in particular, depends upon his return to the Orient and the renewal of the supremacy of the Orient. In the war between light and darkness (Ormazd and Ahriman), light will ultimately triumph (*"Kedem"*) and Nimrod will regain his place in the world (*"Ur Kasdim"*). In *"Ereẓ Yisrael"* (*Ha-Tekufah*, 27, 29, 1935, 1936), the tension arises from the poet's confrontation with the myth-strewn landscape of Palestine. Exceptionally interesting are his poetic essays *To Scatter and to Winnow* dealing mainly with historiosophic problems of Jewish existence and aspects of poetry.

Dramatic Poems

Shoham is regarded as one of the major dramatists in Hebrew literature. His four verse plays deal with biblical themes against the background of eternal Jewish problems; and they are all characterized by the author's predilection for making the protagonists embrace opposing views of historical destiny. Shoham's first play, *Yeriḥo* ("Jericho," *Ha-Tekufah*, 20, 1924), is a dramatization of the fall of Jericho. The chief characters, Achan, a Hebrew, and Rahab of Jericho, are drawn to one another. Their love, perhaps, is a symbol of the attraction between the decadent culture of Jericho and the vigorous, vital Hebrew culture of the desert. Achan is the hero of the play, while Phinehas the priest, who condemns him to death because of his love for a foreign woman, is its villain. Shoham suggests that the salvation of the young nation depends upon the merging of the two cultures. At the close of the play, Eldad and Medad, the spiritual heirs of Moses, proclaim that the nation's message is not narrow and chauvinistic, like that of Phinehas, but universal, promising redemption for all.

In *Bilam* ("Balaam," *Ha-Tekufah*, 23–25, 1928, 1929), Shoham presents in a favorable light the liaison between Zimri the Hebrew and Kozbi the Midianite woman, a relationship forbidden by the priest. Phinehas, who opposes the union, is rebuffed by Moses who approves the love of the young people. Subsequently, however, the couple is murdered by the fanatical priest. But the basic theme of the play is found in its subplot – the conflict between Balaam, the prophet of darkness, and Moses, the prophet of light, and Balaam's final "regeneration out of sin." Balaam had grown up together with Moses, and had become estranged from him out of envy; but before Balaam's death he is redeemed from his darkness and accepts the teachings of his friend. Balaam's blessing is interpreted as the triumph of the inner light in his heart over the darkness which had engulfed him. The structure of the play, with its two plots, is complex. The action centers on the main plot (Kozbi – Zimri), which is largely a drama of intrigue, while the subplot is unfolded in Balaam's long discursive soliloquies. These soliloquies tend to weaken the dramatic effect of the play, but they undoubtedly add to its poetry.

Zor vi-Yrushalayim ("Tyre and Jerusalem," 1933; new edition 1992) was written during the author's stay in Ereẓ Israel – an experience which appears to have considerably altered his views on the relations between Jews and gentiles. In the earlier plays, these had been presented as relations of attraction, but they are now regarded as relations of dissociation. There can be no bond between Elijah the prophet and Jezebel, for she belongs to a foreign culture; and Elisha, who had initially courted Jezebel, dissociates himself from her when he receives the tidings of redemption. Ahikar, the prophet of Tyre, predicts that the culture of Tyre will not prevail over the culture of Israel until there is a "marriage" between El and Astarte; but the central theme of the play is the uniqueness of the Hebrew nation. No longer is the emphasis upon the tragic attachment which overpowers the heroes despite the taboos of society; it has shifted to the dramatic self-denial of Elisha, who conquers his impulses and rejects the temptations of Jezebel in favor of his spiritual ideal. The play also marks a considerable technical advance: there are fewer discursive elements, the dialogue is much more alive, and there is an increase in the use of dramatic techniques such as mime, crowd scenes, and shifts in the dramatic viewpoint.

Elohei Barzel Lo Ta'aseh Lekha ("Thou shalt not make to thyself molten gods," 1937) represents a remarkable change in Shoham's methods and outlook. The allegorical elements hinted at in *Bilam* now take precedence over the symbolic elements characteristic of the previous plays. Alongside the mythical characters, who represent concepts of nation and race, stand the two protagonists, Abraham and Gog, personifying two historical ideas – Abraham, the prophetic ideal of social salvation, and Gog, the racist concept that all breeds must be subjugated to the northern race. Echoes of the doctrine of Aryanism and Nazism are clearly discernible in the course of their struggle; this topicality leads to the appearance of numerous anachronisms, as for example a cannon. The common man (represented by Lot), who is crushed between the two opposing forces, feels that he must give up all hope of redemption in the distant future, for to struggle for it in this life can be disastrous. Here Shoham shows his preference for the insignificant, unimaginative Western man, rather than for the promulgators of lofty ideas, the implementation of which can lead to catastrophe. Technically, the latter is the most complex of his works, combining a plot of love and intrigue, involving Sarah, Hagar, and Lot's daughters, played out under the allegorical superstructure of the relentless struggle between Abraham and Gog.

Shoham's work is a mixture of primitive archaism and ideological expressionism. His archaic language and long reflective passages render his plays totally unsuitable for the stage; but his ideological passion, linked to a profoundly imaginative conception of historical situations, his original style, and his complex outlook have secured him a central place in the history of Hebrew drama and poetry. Although most of his characters are symbolic, the ideological and emotional tension between them generates a powerful dramatic atmosphere which does not depend on theatrical success alone.

BIBLIOGRAPHY: I. Cohen, in: M. Shoham, *Ketavim*, 1 (1964), 7–178; G. Shaked, *The Hebrew Historical Drama in the Twentieth Century* (1970); idem, in: *Scripta Hierosolymitana*, 19 (1967), 16–38; R. Kartun-Blum, *From Tyre to Jerusalem, the Literary World of Mattityahu Shoham* (1969); J. Oren, *Iyyunim be-"Ẓor vi-Yrushalayim" le-M. Shoham* (1967), incl. Bibliography. **ADD. BIBLIOGRAPHY:** G. Shaked, *Al Sheloshah Maḥazot* (1968); R. Kartun-Blum, *"Mahut ha-Shirah be-Maḥshavto shel Shoham,"* in: *Moznayim*, 28 (1969), 43–47; H. Barzel, *"Yeẓarim ve-Ideot be-Maḥazotav shel Shoham,"* in: *Bamah*, 48–49 (1971), 35–45; E. Wolfin, *"Ḥidushei Milim be Maḥazotav shel Shoham,"* in: *Ha-Ivrit ve-Aḥyoteha*, 2–3 (2003), 191–204.

[Gershon Shaked]

SHOHAM, SHLOMO-GIORA (1929–), Israeli criminologist. Shoham was one of first scholars to study criminal youth, the effectiveness of laws against crimes, drug abuse, and the personality traits of traffic offenders. He was born in Lithuania and moved to Israel with his parents in 1935. In 1953 he received an LL.M. and in 1960 an LL.D. from the Hebrew University of Jerusalem, School of Law, in law and criminology. He studied for a doctorate at Cambridge in 1958–59. In 1961 he began to teach at Bar-Ilan University and in 1965 served as associate professor at both Bar-Ilan and Tel Aviv universities. In 1969 he became head of the Institute of Criminology and Criminal Justice at Tel Aviv University and a year later became full professor. He also taught at Harvard, the Sorbonne, and Oxford universities. In addition to his academic work, Shoham was assistant district attorney in Jerusalem, assistant to the state attorney, and criminological advisor to the Israeli Ministries of Justice and Internal Security. In 1973 he lost his son, Giora, in the Yom Kippur War, and from that time appended his son's name to his own. Among his many books are *Rebellion, Creativity and Revelation* (1985); *Valhalla, Calvary and Auschwitz*, in German (1987); *The Bridge to Nothingness: Gnosis, Kabbala and Existentialism* (1988); *God as the Shadow of Man* (2000); and *Art, Crime and Madness* (2002). Shoham was awarded the Israel Prize in 2003 for criminology.

[Shaked Gilboa (2nd ed.)]

SHOHAT, AVRAHAM BEIGA (1936–), Israeli politician, member of the Knesset since the Eleventh Knesset. Born in Tel Aviv, he served in the IDF as a paratrooper in 1956–57. He was a member of kibbuz Naḥal Oz. In 1957–61 he studied construction engineering at the Technion in Haifa, serving as chairman of the Students Council there. In 1961–63 Shohat was a member of a team headed by Arie Lova *Eliav that planned the town of Arad in the Negev. In 1963–67 he was the regional director of Solel-Boneh in Arad and the Dead Sea area, and in 1967–89 he was head of the Arad Local Council. For part of this period he served as deputy chairman of the Local Government Center and as chairman of its Development Town Committee.

In 1985 Shohat ran the *Israel Labor Party census. He entered the Eleventh Knesset in May 1988, instead of MK Aharon Harel, who resigned. He was chosen to head the Labor Party election staff in the elections to the Twelfth Knesset later that year. In the Twelfth Knesset he served first as chairman of the Economics Committee and then as the chairman of the Finance Committee until February 1991. He then drew up the Labor Party economic platform for the elections to the Thirteenth Knesset, which defined those areas in which the government should be involved in the economy. In this platform the Labor Party for the first time accepted the need to privatize a portion of the government-owned corporations.

In the primaries for the Labor Party leadership held in February 1992, Shohat supported Yitzhak *Rabin, and in the government formed by Rabin after the elections, he was appointed minister of finance. In the period that he served as minister of finance, the rate of growth of the economy accelerated and unemployment fell. This was largely due to progress in the peace process, an end to most aspects of the Arab boycott, the establishment of diplomatic relations with both China and India, and the reestablishment of diplomatic relations with many states that had broken off relations after the Six-Day War or Yom Kippur War. However, there was a serious deterioration in Israel's trade deficit, and the rate of inflation started to rise in 1995. At the end of 1994, Shohat planned to introduce a tax on stock-market earnings, but owing to pressure from business circles, he withdrew the plan.

In the Fourteenth Knesset, when Labor returned to opposition, Shohat served as the Labor coordinator in the Finance Committee. After the election of Ehud *Barak as prime minister and after election to the Fifteenth Knesset in 1999, Shohat was once again appointed minister of finance. Following Shas's resignation from the government, Shohat also served as minister of national infrastructures. In his dual capacity as minister of finance and national infrastructures, Shohat managed to gain support against staunch opposition from senior Finance Ministry officials for the idea of resolving Israel's chronic water shortages by starting to plan desalination plants along the Mediterranean. Shohat was not chosen to serve as one of Labor's ministers in the government formed by Ariel *Sharon in 2001, nor was he chosen to serve as a minister when Labor joined Sharon's second Government in 2005.

In the Sixteenth Knesset he served as chairman of the Joint Committee for the Defense Budget.

[Susan Hattis Rolef (2nd ed.)]

SHOḤAT, ELIEZER (1874–1971), Second Aliyah pioneer, a founder of *Ha-Po'el ha-Ẓa'ir. Born in Liskova, Belorussia, Shoḥat settled in Ereẓ Israel in 1904. He began work in Petaḥ Tikvah as one the first laborers of the Second Aliyah and founded Ha-Po'el ha-Ẓa'ir along with eight other pioneers (1905). He was one of the first Jewish laborers to enter Galilee (1906), became a founding member (1907) of Ha-Ḥoresh (the first Jewish laborers' association in Galilee), a worker at Umm Juni (Deganyah) in 1910, a founder of the Galilee labor federation (1911), a member of the labor group at Merḥavyah in 1911 (which resulted in his imprisonment at Acre), and a founder of the first moshav ovedim, Nahalal (1921). He was a member of the Asefat ha-Nivḥarim. Shoḥat elaborated the labor movement ideology based on Jewish national and moral values. He compiled and edited labor movement literature, notably *Pirkei Ha-Po'el ha-Ẓa'ir* (13 vols., coedited with Ḥayyim Shurer), and edited the writings of labor leaders, including three volumes of the writings of A.D. *Gordon (coedited with S.H. *Bergman). His articles, speeches, and letters were published in *Bi-Netivei Avodah* (1967^2). He was a brother of Israel *Shochat.

BIBLIOGRAPHY: S. Sheva, *Shevet ha-No'azim* (1969).

[Yosef Shapiro]

SHOHETMAN, BARUCH (1890–1956), Hebrew bibliographer. Born in Podolia, Shohetman emigrated to Palestine at the end of 1925. From 1927, he worked in the National Library of Jerusalem, especially with the bibliographical quarterly *Kirjath Sepher*, and published essays and articles on historical, literary, and bibliographical subjects. A great part of his work was devoted to the history of Russian Jewry over the last generations, a field in which he was one of the leading experts. He published, with explanatory notes, hundreds of letters of various authors (including those of Aḥad Ha-Am, M. Ussishkin and S. Dubnow). He also published many bibliographical notes (most of them anonymously) in *Kirjath Sepher* as well as bibliographies to the works of Herzl, V.A. Tcherikover, B. Dinur, D. Shimoni, Ḥ.N. Bialik, N.H. Tur-Sinai (Torczyner), Tchernichowsky, and S.H. Bergman. For a detailed listing of his bibliographical work, see Shunami, Bibl. Shohetman was killed when Jordanian soldiers opened fire at a group of archaeologists visiting the settlement of Ramat Raḥel.

[Getzel Kressel]

SHOLAL (Sulal), ISAAC (d. 1524), last Egyptian **nagid*. Although of Spanish ancestry, by the early 15th century and perhaps even earlier Sholal's direct forebears were residing in Tlemcen, *Algeria. During the latter half of the 15th century Sholal himself resided in *Egypt, where he actively engaged in the grain trade and other pursuits. In 1502 he inherited the office of *nagid* from his uncle/brother-in-law Jonathan (Nathan) *Sholal, serving in this capacity until the Ottoman conquest in 1517, which saw the termination of the negidate. Various sources indicate that Isaac Sholal was intensely involved in the affairs of the *Jerusalem and *Safed communities as well as the Syrian communities on several levels. During his tenure as *nagid* he made a significant contribution to intellectual life in Jerusalem in the form of massive material support for two yeshivot. One reopened at his initiative, and he founded the other. Sholal also supported the Sephardi yeshivah in Safed. In addition, by promulgating regulations through the agency of his court, Sholal took steps aimed at legislating social issues in the Jerusalem community. In early 1517 Sholal came to Eretz Israel and settled in Jerusalem, but he was then an impoverished man, no longer able to contribute financially to the upkeep of the yeshivot. Nonetheless, in Jerusalem Sholal continued to exercise spiritual influence. He belonged to a circle of individuals who engaged in pietistic practices aimed at hastening redemption. He himself prescribed vigils "to pray and undergo privation for the sake of all our brethren in the Diaspora." Ever attuned to the incipient signs of the Messiah's approach, Sholal evinced particular interest in individuals who claimed descent from the Ten Tribes. Sources from the early 1520s indicate that he hosted individuals claiming such ancestry in Jerusalem and earlier in Egypt as well. Sholal's scholastic achievements and status among the Jerusalem halakhists are reflected in several of the halakhic decisions extant in *Kuntres Ḥiddushei Dinim* and in his correspondence with his contemporaries in Egypt and Jerusalem.

BIBLIOGRAPHY: A. David, "*Le-Toledot Benei Mishpaḥat Sholal be-Miẓrayim ve-Eretz Israel be-Sof ha-Tekufah ha-Mamlukit ve-Reshit ha-Tekufah ha-Ottomanit, Le-Or Mismakhim Ḥadashim min ha-Genizah*," in: A. Mirsky, A. Grossman, and Y. Kaplan (eds.), *Galut aḥar Golah; Meḥkarim be-Toledot Am Yisrael Mugashim le-Professor H. Beinart* (1988), 374–414; idem, "*Me'oravutam shel Aḥeronei ha-Negidim be-Mitzrayim be-Inyanah shel ha-Kehilah ha-Yehudit be-Eretz Israel*," in: *Te'udah*, 15 (1999), 293–332; idem, *Sha'alu Shelom Yerushalayim* (2003), 171–79, 188–97.

[Abraham David (2nd ed.)]

SHOLAL, NATHAN (Jonathan) HA-KOHEN (1437–1502), one of the last *negidim* in Egypt. Sholal was born in Tlemcen (Algeria) to a family of Talmud scholars. He emigrated to Italy and from there to Ereẓ Israel, settling in *Jerusalem before 1471 (or slightly earlier). Heavy taxation and the high-handed attitude of its leaders, the elders (*zekenim*), oppressed the Jewish community in Jerusalem and many left, including Nathan Sholal (not before 1481), and went to Egypt. In about 1484 he was appointed **nagid*, a post he held until his death. He rendered great assistance to Obadiah of *Bertinoro when the latter immigrated to Ereẓ Israel in 1488. According to various sources, he was a man well-versed in rabbinic law and with an aristocratic bearing. In his capacity as Egyptian *nagid*, he also had the Jewish communities in Ereẓ Israel (especially in Jerusalem) under his hegemony. He fulfilled the task of judge but owned property which he had acquired through trade. He was succeeded as *nagid* by his nephew and brother-in-law Isaac *Sholal.

BIBLIOGRAPHY: A. David, "*Le-Toledot Benei Mishpaḥat Sholal be-Mitzrayim ve-Ereẓ Israel be-Sof ha-Tekufah ha-Mamlukit ve-Reshit ha-Tekufah ha-Ottemanit, le-Or Mismakhim Ḥadashim min ha-Genizah*," in: A. Mirsky, A. Grossman, and Y. Kaplan (eds.), *Galut ahar Golah; Meḥkarim be-Toledot Am Yisrael Mugashim le-Professor H. Beinart* (1988), 374–76, 383–89, 395, 397–407; idem, "*Me'oravutam shel Aḥeronei ha-Negidim be-Mitzrayim be-Inyanah shel ha-Kehilah ha-Yehudit be-Eretz Israel*," in: *Te'udah*, 15 (1999), 296–97, 303–11; idem, *Sha'alu Shelom Yerushalayim* (2003), 171–79, 188–97.

[Eliyahu Ashtor / Abraham David (2nd ed.)]

SHOLEM ZOKHOR (Heb. שָׁלוֹם זָכָר; *shalom zakhar*; "peace to the male child"), name of a traditional home ceremony held on the first Friday evening after the birth of a boy. In some communities it is held on the eve of *circumcision. Besides *Sholem Zokhor* it is also called *Vigil* or *Vakhnakht* (Isserles to Sh. Ar., YD 265:12). For the *Sholem Zokhor,* relatives and friends gather at the home of the child's parents in order to congratulate them. After reciting the *Shema, the blessing from Genesis 48:16 and diverse psalms, as well as appropriate prayers, are said for the welfare of the mother and the newborn boy. The guests are served drinks, cakes, and fruits; in some places also lentils and chick-peas. Lentils, due to their round shape, symbolize the ever-recurring cycle of birth and decay. They are meant to be a consolation. The moments of sadness of the occasion are steeped in folklore which holds that the child has forgotten the holy Torah which he was taught in heaven before his birth. In Oriental communities, this ceremony is also called *Shasha* or *Blada* and includes the recital of special prayers and aggadic readings (from such books as *Berit Olam* (1948) or *Berit Yiẓḥak* (Amsterdam, 1719) in honor of the prophet *Elijah, the patron of the child at circumcision. The origin of the *Sholem Zokhor* ceremony, the participation in which is considered a *mitzvah*, is to be found in the Talmud where joy is expressed at the birth of a male child ("if a boy is born, peace comes to the world" (Nid. 31b)). In some communities, this ceremony is also called *Yeshu'at ha-Ben*, or *Shevu'at ha-Ben*, or simply *Ben Zokhor* (see Sanh. 32b, BK 80a, and Tos. *ibid.*, s.v. *le-vei*).

See *Birth.

BIBLIOGRAPHY: Eisenstein, Dinim, 417–18; H. Schauss, *The Lifetime of a Jew* (1950), 42, 56.

SHOMER (pseudonym of **Nahum Meyer Shaikevich**; 1849–1905), Yiddish novelist, dramatist. Born in Nesvizh, Russia, Shomer settled in Pinsk. He began his literary career in the 1870s with Hebrew translations from German in *Ha-Meliẓ*. Under the influence of Abraham Mapu and Kalman Schulman, he wrote many Hebrew short stories and about 200 Hebrew lyrics, which he later incorporated into his Yiddish tales. When he moved to Vilna, he was advised to write in Yiddish and soon became known for his popular novels, with which he achieved a mass appeal hitherto unprecedented in Yiddish letters. Before his literary career began, however, Shaikevich worked as a military contractor whose work took him to Bucharest, where he met Abraham *Goldfaden. Impressed by Goldfaden's Yiddish theater, Shaikevich began to write plays and organized his own theatrical troupe. When Yiddish performances were forbidden in Russia, he returned to Vilna and concentrated on fiction, sometimes making use of borrowed plots, in order to meet the demand of his ever-increasing audience. At the request of another theater troupe, Shaikevich moved to New York in 1889, where his plays were well received by both the audience and the Yiddish press. Artistic differences prompted Shaikevich to leave the theater and begin publishing his own literary journals. Meant to serve both as edification and as entertainment for an unsophisticated readership, Shaikevich's stories are filled with sentimental elements and fantastic themes, but also a sympathetic representation of the Jewish masses and a happy ending. The enormous popularity of Shaikevich's work spawned numerous imitators, although his style was reviled by his contemporary intellectuals. Led by *Sholem Aleichem (Sholem Rabinovitsh), detractors dubbed his potboiler fiction "Shomerism." Attacks on "Shomerism" culminated famously in Sholem Aleichem's 1888 pamphlet entitled *Shomers Mishpet* ("The Shomer Verdict"). Shaikevich answered that devastating critique in the introductions to many of his novels; he was convinced that his books performed the valuable function of bringing ethical education to the Jewish masses whose general education had been neglected. Later, his work was more positively received; Soviet critics emphasized the educational service performed by his narratives in the struggle to improve the lot of Jewish victims of poverty and oppression. He is also credited with creating a new Yiddish readership. According to his supporters, he developed the Yiddish audience later enjoyed by Sholem Aleichem, I.L. *Peretz, and others. Among his works are *Di Ungliklikhe Libe* ("Unhappy Love," 1882); *Der Oytser oder der Kalter Gazlen* ("The Treasure or the Cold Thief," 1884); *Eyn Ungerikhter Glik* ("Unexpected Luck," 1885); and *Der Yid un di Grefin* ("The Jew and the Countess," 1892).

BIBLIOGRAPHY: S. Niger, *Geklibene shriftn: Sholem Aleykhem* 3 (1928), 20–6; Reyzen, Leksikon, 4 (1929), 758–808; A. Veviorka, *Revizye* (1931); S. Niger, *Dertseyler un romanistn* (1946), 84–95; R. Shomer-Bachelis, *Unzer Foter Shomer* (1950), incl. bibl.; Z. Zylbercweig, *Leksikon fun Yidishn Teater*, 3 (1959), 2077–104; Waxman, *Literature* (1960), 485–86; S. Liptzin, *Flowering of Yiddish Literature* (1963), 83–86; C. Madison, *Yiddish Literature* (1968), 25, 29–30. **ADD. BIBLIOGRAPHY:** S. Liptzin, *A History of Yiddish Literature* (1972), 53–54; J. Glatstein, *Prost un Poshet* (1978), 130–35; LNYL 8 (1981), 731–45; D. Miron, *A Traveler Disguised* (1996), 28–30, 253–55; E. Shulman, in: *Yiddish*, 13 (2003), 56–64.

[Sarah B. Felsen and Jordan Finkin (2nd ed.)]

SHOMERIM (Heb. שׁוֹמְרִים; "bailees").

Biblical Classification

The law relating to a bailee (i.e., one who is entrusted with the money or chattels of another) is first given in the Torah (Ex. 22:6–14) in several statements of principle from which have been deduced the three categories of bailee, known as the *shomer ḥinnam*, the *shomer sakhar*, and the *sho'el*.

THE SHOMER ḤINNAM. The *shomer ḥinnam* (שׁוֹמֵר חִנָּם; lit. "an unpaid bailee") is based on the first case cited in the Torah of one who is given "money or stuff" to look after (Ex. 22:6–8). Such a bailee is not liable to the owner in the event of the goods being stolen (and the thief not apprehended), provided that he confirms on oath before the court that he had not embezzled or otherwise converted the goods to his own use (*lo shalaḥ yado*, lit. "not put forth his hand"). In fact, his duty of care is minimal and his liability is limited only to cases where loss resulted from his own negligence (cf. BM 3:10; Sh. Ar., ḤM 291:1). Thus, in the absence of proven negligence and subject to his taking the prescribed judicial oath, he would also not be liable for loss caused by inevitable accident or unforeseeable damage (i.e., *ones; Yad, Sekhirut, 1:2 and 3:1ff.; Sh. Ar., ḤM 291:6 and 9). It was such leniency which led to this particular portion of the text being construed as relating to the *shomer ḥinnam* (Yad. loc cit. 1:2) compared with the higher duty of care imposed on the *shomer sakhar* (cf. Laws of Hammurapi, 125, 263–7). On the other hand, any bailee, even a *shomer ḥinnam*, who meddles with the deposited article without the owner's authority is considered guilty of theft (i.e., larceny by conversion; see *Theft and Robbery) and is consequently liable for any subsequent loss. Indeed, according to Bet Shammai, the mere formulation of his intent to "put forth his hand," without his necessarily committing an actual act of conversion, suffices to render the bailee liable, but Bet Hillel does not extend the principle so far (BM 3:12; Yad, Gezelah, 3:11; Sh. Ar., ḤM 292).

THE SHOMER SAKHAR. The *shomer sakhar* (שׁוֹמֵר שָׂכָר; lit. "a paid bailee") is derived from the second case in the Torah of one who is entrusted with "an ass, or an ox, or a sheep, or any beast, to keep, and it be hurt, or driven away…" (Ex. 22:9–12). The fact that this case refers only to animals, whereas the previous case mentions "money or stuff," has been interpreted as drawing a distinction, not between the types of property deposited (cf. Philo, Spec. 4:35; *Rashbam*, Ex. 22:6), but between the types of bailment, since "the safekeeping of money or vessels is generally undertaken without payment [i.e., *shomer ḥinnam*], whereas that of animals is undertaken for reward [i.e., *shomer sakhar*]" (Naḥmanides to Ex. 22:6). In this case the bailee is liable in the event of the goods being stolen or lost (which is further authority for the conclusion that Scripture is here referring to a *shomer sakhar*), and he cannot be absolved even by taking the judicial oath, except in certain specific instances where accident was a contributory factor. However, liability could be avoided, on his taking the judicial oath, if loss resulted from the animal dying or being driven away (BM 7:8; Yad, Gezelah, 1:2; Sh. Ar., ḤM 303:1–2). The term "*sakhar*" has been given a wide interpretation, so as to include the receipt by the bailee of any benefit whatsoever from the article deposited. Accordingly, an artisan who is entrusted with an article on which he is to exercise his craft for remuneration is deemed a *shomer sakhar* (BM 6:6; cf. BM 43a; *Shitah Mekubbeẓet* BM 94a; *Sefer ha-Ḥinnukh* no. 59). However, during the talmudic period a rabbinical enactment specifically exempted a carrier from liability arising through his transportation of barrels "even though imposed on him in strict law… lest no person be willing to transport his neighbors' barrel" (Yad, Sekhirut, 3:2).

THE SHO'EL. The *sho'el* (שׁוֹאֵל, "borrower") is explicitly mentioned as the third type of bailee (Ex. 22:13–14), and on him is imposed the highest duty of care toward the owner of the article, since the bailee has borrowed it for his own benefit. He is therefore liable to make restitution in all cases of "damage or death," even though they are caused by inevitable accident or other unforeseeable circumstances, as well as in cases of theft or loss. Exceptionally, however, the *sho'el* may be able to avoid liability "if the owner of the article was with it at the time" – this being interpreted by the *tannaim* as referring to the case where the owner is borrowed or hired along with his animal or chattel (BM 8:1). The scope of this *halakhah* was extended to make it applicable in circumstances where the owner was with his property at the time the bailment was accepted, though not necessarily when the loss or damage later occurred, and also in circumstances where the owner was hired by the *sho'el* for purposes quite unconnected with the hiring of his property. Its application has even been extended to the other types of bailees (BM 95b; Yad, Sekhirut, 1:3 and She'elah, 2; Sh. Ar., ḤM 291:28). This exemption of the *sho'el* has been justified on the grounds that, in the circumstances mentioned, the owner would presumably take care to guard his own property (*Sefer ha-Ḥinnukh* no. 56; see also supplement to *Torah Shelemah*, 18 (1958), 187f.).

The cited text of the Torah concludes with the following statement: "If it be a hireling, he loseth his hire" (Ex. 22:14). This has been construed as a continuation of the provisions relating to the *sho'el*. However, the view of some scholars is that this phrase creates another category of bailee, distinguishable from the unpaying borrower, which is called the *sokher* ("hirer"; *Midrash ha-Gadol* to Ex. 22:14 and Rashi thereto; see also Ḥ. Albeck, in: *Sinai*, 50 (1961/62), 103f.). However, the laws of the *sokher* do not appear to be elucidated in Scripture (cf. Laws of Hammurapi, 249) and the *tannaim* disputed the question whether such a bailee is to be treated as a *shomer ḥinnam* or a *shomer sakhar* (BM 93a). Hence, "their laws [i.e., of bailees]… are three" (BM 93a; Yad, Sekhirut, 1:1). The *halakhah* was decided on the basis that the law of the *sokher* is that of the *shomer sakhar* (Yad, Sekhirut, 1:2; Sh. Ar., ḤM 307:1).

Measure of Damages

Generally, the degree of a bailee's liability in damages is proportionate to the degree of benefit he received from the bailment. Thus the *sho'el*, who enjoys full use of the article borrowed, is fully liable; the *shomer sakhar* (and the *sokher*), who derives partial or indirect benefit, may take the judicial oath for a part and compensate for a part; and the *shomer ḥinnam*, who receives no benefit, may simply take the judicial oath and escape all liability (TJ, Shevu. 8:1; Tos. to Ket. 56a–b).

The Torah lays down that a thief must compensate his victim by repaying either twice or four or five times the value of the stolen article (Ex. 22:3–8 and see *Theft and Robbery). If a bailee chooses to compensate the owner for an article stolen during its bailment, rather than take the judicial oath, the thief, if later apprehended, must pay the stipulated double, four-or five-fold penalty directly to the bailee and not to the owner (BM 3:1; Yad, She'elah, 8:1; Sh. Ar., ḤM 295:2). This ruling is based variously on scriptural authority (see Mekh. Sb-Y to 22:6; TJ, BM 3:1), on the principle of an assignment of rights by the owner to the bailee, and also on a rabbinical enactment (BM 34a: *Sefer Keritut*, 5:3, 165; Ritba, Nov. BM 34a).

The fact that certain types of property are referred to specifically in the text (e.g., money, stuff, animals) led the sages to conclude that the laws of bailment are not intended to apply to slaves, deeds, immovable property, consecrated property (*hekdesh*), and the property of idolaters (BM 4:9; BM 57b, 58a; Yad, Sekhirut, 2:1; Sh. Ar., ḤM 301:1), although the rabbis especially provided for the bailee's judicial oath to be taken in respect of consecrated property, lest such property "be treated lightly" (Yad, Sekhirut, 2:2). Nevertheless, the laws of bailment may be rendered applicable to the above-mentioned classes of property by way of a special undertaking to that effect (BM 58a; Yad, loc. cit.; Sh. Ar., ḤM 301:4).

Principles of Liability

The **posekim* are divided on the question of whether a bailee's obligations, and thus his consequent liability to the owner, commence immediately when the agreement between the two parties is concluded, or only after a *meshikhah* (legal act of acquisition; see *Acquisition, Modes of) of the bailment (Sh. Ar., ḤM 291:5). A general rule, which is based on logical deduction, is that a bailee is not liable for damage caused to the bailment while it is being used for the purpose for which it was received, e.g., a cow borrowed as a beast of burden that dies of its labors (*metah meḥamat melakhah*; BM 96b; Yad, She'elah, 1:1; Sh. Ar., ḤM 340:1).

A bailee who is able to safeguard his bailment with the help of others and fails to do so is considered negligent – a distinction being drawn between the respective duties of care owed by a *shomer ḥinnam* and a *shomer sakhar* (Yad, Sekhirut, 3:6; Sh. Ar., ḤM 303:8). Any necessary expenses involved in safeguarding a bailment are recoverable even by the *shomer ḥinnam* from the owner, as there is no obligation to incur such expense.

The laws of bailment may be expressly varied or excluded by agreement between the parties (BM 7:10); this view is even held by R. Meir, who considers it inapplicable in other legal contexts (BM 94a). The freedom of the parties to vary or exclude the general principles of the law is recognized even though the result may be to impose more stringent obligations on the bailee (Yad, loc. cit. 2:9; Sh. Ar., ḤM 291:27, 296:6, and 305:4).

Rights and Duties of a Bailee

One bailee may not entrust his bailment to another (Tosef. BM 3:1). If he does so and the bailment is lost or damaged, Rav held that the first bailee can only escape liability to the same extent as he would have been able to do had he retained the bailment, but R. Johanan held that he is liable even in the case of force majeure (BM 36a and Rashi thereto). Subsequently, this dispute was interpreted by Abbaye to mean that according to Rav there would be no liability even though a *shomer sakhar* entrusted his bailment to a *shomer ḥinnam*, whereas according to R. Johanan liability would arise even though a *shomer ḥinnam* entrusted his bailment to a *shomer sakhar*. Rava ruled finally that the *halakhah* should be in accordance with the opinion of R. Johanan – as explained by Abbaye – on the grounds that, as no privity of contract existed between the owner and the second bailee, the former was not obliged to accept the latter's judicial oath (BM 36a–b). Furthermore, the first bailee can avoid liability only if "inevitable accident" can be proved by independent witnesses (Yad, Sekhirut, 1:4; Sh. Ar., ḤM 291:26).

If a bailment deteriorates while it is in the care of the bailee, he has a duty to inform the owner immediately, if the latter is available (Hai Gaon, *Sefer ha-Mikkaḥ ve-ha-Mimkar*, ch. 6; Sh. Ar., ḤM 292:15). There is a dispute in the Mishnah over the bailee's obligations when the owner is not available, some *tannaim* taking the view that "fruit, even if wasting, must not be touched," while Simeon b. Gamaliel states that the "fruit" must be sold and its value thus preserved, but only at the direction of the court, i.e., not on the bailee's own initiative (BM 3:6). In talmudic times this dispute was regarded as referring to a case where the rate of deterioration was normal for the type of article involved, but in a case where the rate of deterioration was excessive, all scholars agreed that the bailee had a duty to sell the bailment (BM 38a; Yad, She'elah, 7:1; Sh. Ar., loc, cit.). Any such sale had to be to a third party and not by the bailee to himself, so as to avoid suspicion (Tosef., BM 3:8; Pes. 13a; Yad, She'elah, 7:5; Sh. Ar., ḤM 292:19).

A bailee may be relieved of his responsibility if the owner refuses to accept the return of his property. A statement in the Mishnah, that an artisan is a *shomer sakhar* who becomes a *shomer ḥinnam* upon his offering to return the article against payment, was later interpreted to mean that an artisan who expressly indicates to the owner that he wishes to be relieved of all responsibility for the article is thereafter exempted from any liability, even that imposed on a *shomer ḥinnam* (*Rema*, ḤM 306:1 and *Sma*, *ibid.*, n. 4). In the event of the owner being abroad, the bailee may be relieved of his obligations by depositing the article with the court, who will then appoint a trustee for it until the owner's return (Yad, She'elah, 7:12; Sh. Ar., ḤM 293:3).

A bailee from whom a deposited article is stolen must take three judicial oaths, affirming: that he was not negligent as regards his bailment; that he did not "put forth his hand" to it (see above); and that it is no longer in his possession (BM 6a and Rashi; Yad, She'elah, 4:1; Sh. Ar., ḤM 295:2). However, it was prescribed that a bailee who is prepared to pay compensation must nevertheless take the third of these oaths, "lest he has set his eyes on the bailment" (BM 34b), although Maimonides limited the application of this ruling only to cases where the article was not normally available in the open market (Yad, loc. cit. 6:1; Sh. Ar., ḤM 305:1).

A bailee who denies the existence of a bailment and commits perjury concerning it, but later admits to the truth, is obliged to compensate the owner to the extent of the article's capital value plus a fifth, and must also bring a guilt offering (Lev. 5:20–26; Shevu. 5 and 8:3; and see *Oath).

Modern Israel Law

In the State of Israel the law of bailments is governed by the Bailees Law, 5727 – 1967, which closely follows the principles of Jewish law as described above (see *Divrei ha-Keneset*, 49 (1967), 2148f.). Thus, the three categories of bailee are similarly defined (sec. 1), each attracting a different (and increasing) degree of liability, determined by the degree of benefit received by the bailee (sec. 2, and see explanatory remarks in: *Haẓa'ot Ḥok*, no. 676 (1965/66), p. 54). Also, the bailee is exempted from liability for damage or loss sustained while the article was being ordinarily used in accordance with the terms of the bailment (sec. 4). Yet further, the bailee is held liable if he knowingly fails to inform the owner that his property is likely to suffer damage (sec. 2(d)), and he is impliedly authorized to take such urgent steps as may be reasonably necessary to prevent such damage (sec. 6). The Bailees Law also deals with the question of a bailee who entrusts his bailment to another (sec. 3, 7), and makes detailed provision with regard to one who refuses to accept the return of his property from a bailee (sec. 11). Still following the principles of Jewish law, the freedom to contract out of the act is specifically allowed, namely: "The provisions of the act shall apply… where no different intention appears from the agreement between the parties" (sec. 14).

[Nahum Rakover]

During the Knesset debates on the Bailees Law, both the minister of justice, in his opening statement and especially during his reply, and other Knesset members from the various political parties, stressed that the bill was based on Jewish law, and much of the discussion was devoted to examining the relevant Jewish legal sources (see the remarks of Minister of Justice Joseph, and MKs Raphael, Abramov, and Hausner, 44 DK 215–218 (1966)).

The Bailees Law contains 16 sections, the great majority of which are based on Jewish legal principles. An interesting question with regard to the title of the statute arose at the second and third readings of the bill. The title originally proposed was the "Safekeeping of Property Law" (*Ḥok Shemirat Nekhasim*), a term unknown to Jewish law, whereas the term "bailees" (*shomerim*) is well known in Jewish law, which speaks of four types of bailees (*arba'ah shomerim*). The proposal to call the statute the "Bailees Law" was rejected in the Legislative Committee on the ground, among others, that statutory titles generally state the nature of the activity or transaction rather than that of the persons involved – e.g., the "Sale Law," rather than the "Sellers Law" (see the remarks of MK Azanyah, 49 DK 2149 (1967), and also those of MK Aloni, quoted *infra*). However, when the bill was presented for its second and third readings, the title was changed to the Bailees Law, 1967. Some of the reasons for the proposed change merit quotation (Remarks of MK Aloni, 49 DK 2148 (1967).

> When we began to deal in the committee with this law, which in effect transforms or translates the *Mejelle* and other legal rules into an Israeli code based on Jewish law, I did not understand what was meant by "safekeeping of property" until I saw the text of the various sections. Then I realized that we were concerned with the law of bailees (*shomerim*), as I had learned at school from the Bible and the Talmud; and, understandably, that was the primary association when I went over the material. In all innocence, I then asked why the statute is not entitled the "Bailees Law" rather than the "Safekeeping of Property Law," and I was told that this indeed had been the original intention, but that the word *shomerim* [bailees, which also means "watchmen" or "guards"] evoked in many people an association with the Ha-Shomer (the "watchmen") in the Galilee, with *Ha-Shomer ha-Ẓa'ir, a political youth movement, and with other such worthy organizations.
>
> It seems to me that… we are dealing with Jewish legislation governing the bailment of property that is entirely structured according to the four types of bailees in Scripture, and yet this statute fails to declare its connection with those [Scriptural] rules concerning bailees. This being the case, serious doubts arise as to whether the Knesset has acted properly up to this point – and we have very many years ahead of us – by cutting out associative words, symbols, concepts, and linkages which could promote attachment to our heritage, our history, and our cultural values, particularly in a field of which we are so proud. For it is our people who laid the foundation for social legislation in western thought.
>
> I was a teacher for a number of years, and I regretted that the Wage Protection Law was not called the "Wage Delay Prohibition Law," so that when teaching the Scriptural verse "The wages of a laborer shall not remain with you…" a teacher could drive the point home by telling his pupils that this law of the Torah still applies today That is the significance of continuity. Thus is fashioned the associative link that is educationally so important. This is perhaps the best kind of continuity, because it unites us all without religious or national compulsion, in that this ethical and legal basis serves as a general foundation for modern legal thought, and there is no need to be embarrassed or to hide the fact that its source rests on the foundation laid down by the Jewish people when the Torah came into being. It similarly pained me when we adopted the Severance Pay Law, the source of which is the verse "Do not let him go empty-handed: you shall furnish him (*ha'aneik ta'anik lo*) [out of the flock, threshing floor, and vat]," that the word *ma'anak* ("grant") is not a part of the title. It is a pity that a school teacher cannot point out the association between that law and the Scriptural verse. Not only in grade school, but even in the university, many do not realize the connection between the two. I want my children to know when they study this subject that this is not a legally unenforceable Biblical precept; it is intimately connected with daily life in Israel.

See also *ibid.*, for MK Azanyah's reply, admitting that the bill included many legal concepts of Jewish law but claiming that the Hebrew term *shomer*, "bailee," was not sufficiently indicative of the contents of the law):

This is not the place for a detailed review of the Bailees Law and how its provisions rest on principles of Jewish law. The first two sections of the statute are sufficient to illustrate the point we wish to make here.

After initially defining a "bailment" as "lawful possession not by virtue of ownership," Section 1 provides:

(b) A bailee of property who derives no benefit for himself from the bailment is an unpaid bailee (*shomer ḥinam*).

(c) A bailee of property who receives payment or derives

some other benefit for himself from the bailment, and is not a borrower, is a paid bailee (*shomer sakhar*).

(d) A bailee of property for the purpose of using or benefiting from it without paying consideration is a borrower (*sho'el*).

The names given here in Hebrew to these three types of bailees (the four types of bailees in Jewish law, so far as the applicable legal rules are concerned, are actually three; see Maimonides, Yad, Sekhirut, ch. 1), as well as their definitions, are based on Jewish law; anyone who has ever studied the passages on bailees in the Torah or in the Talmud will immediately note the close connection between these definitions and those sources.

Principles of Jewish law in regard to the categories of bailees and their respective levels of liability and duty of care were relied upon in court decisions particularly in view of the close connection between the Bailees Law, 5727 – 1967, and halakhic principles. CA 34/80 *Ali v. Sasson,* PD 36 (3) 281, was an appeal regarding an alleged lottery win where the relevant slip given to the lottery agent was not traced. The appeal was heard by Justice E. Scheinbaum who referred to the explanatory comments of the bill that emphasize the principles of Jewish law underlying the new legislation. The Supreme Court held that the lottery slip was an object that could be a subject of bailment and that the lottery agent did not keep it in a suitable way, and was thus negligent. The Court reviewed the categories of bailees in Jewish law and their respective liability, in particular that of the unpaid bailee, who is only liable for negligence (*peshi'ah;* Sh. Ar., ḤM. 291:1, 13, 14; cf. Maim, Yad, Sekhirut 1:2), defined as "failing to guard [the property] in the manner of bailees…" (Mishnah, BM 3.10). In finding the bailee negligent, the Court held that the lottery agent, as a paid bailee, could be found liable, being exempt from liability only if the loss or damage is caused by *ones* – i.e., *force majeure*, his liability being more extensive than that of the unpaid bailee, who is liable only for *peshi'ah* – negligence. However, as in this case the appellant's claim was based solely upon his testimony, the alleged damage was not proven and the appeal was dismissed.

In CA. 1129/01, *Atiah v. Ḥen Shaḥar etc.*, the Beersheba District Court ruled that the paid bailee was not liable for damage caused to an object in his care (a tractor, stipulated by the parties to be transported with its engine running, was damaged by fire as a result), though it was contended that regular use or use according to the conditions of the bailment cannot exempt the bailee from negligence. In finding the bailee not liable, the District Court held, in keeping with Jewish law, that since the parties may stipulate between themselves in regard to liability and the duty of care, and such stipulation need not conform to fixed halakhic principles (Maim., Yad, Sekhirut 2:9), the question was determined by the conditions of the bailment; consequently, in this case, the paid bailee was not liable for the damage caused.

An additional case also adjudicated in the Beersheba District Court, in which the Court ruled in accordance with the Jewish law on bailees, was the Ayalon case (CA 1260/01 *Ayalon Insurance Company v. Makhon Lev* (unpublished), given 17/6/03). In that case, a garage owner, who had received a car for repairs, notified its owner that he had completed the work, and that he could come to take his car. The owner requested the garage owner to leave it in the garage overnight, telling him that he would only take delivery of the car the next day. The garage owner agreed, but during the night the garage was burgled and the car stolen.

Under section 6 (b) of the Contract for Services Law 5734 – 1974, the contractor's responsibility for property is that of a paid bailee for the purposes of the Bailees Law. Section 6 (a) of the Law stipulates that when the work on the property in the contractor's possession has been completed, the customer must take delivery of the property at the time agreed upon or, in the absence of agreement, within a reasonable period of time after the contractor notifies him that he has completed the work. The trial court ruled that since the car owner did not come to take the car upon being notified by the garage owner that he could take it, the continued guarding of the car in the garage could be regarded as a favor. As such, the garage owner was an unpaid bailee, and was under no obligation to indemnify the owner for the theft. In the appeal court, the District Court judge J. Elon) interpreted the term "reasonable time" in the law in accordance with the Jewish law on bailees (after substantiating the connection between the Bailees Law and Jewish Law).

The judgment states that, indeed, under Jewish Law, from the moment of informing the customer that he should come and take his property, the artisan's status changes from that of a paid bailee to that of an unpaid bailee: "All artisans are regarded as paid bailees; but if they declare, 'take your property and then bring us money,' they rank as unpaid bailees" (Mishnah, BK 6:6). But in the talmudic passage discussing this provision in the Mishnah, a distinction is made between the artisan's notification as formulated above, and the case of the artisan who notifies the customer: "Bring money and then take your property" (BM 81b). In the latter case, together with his notification of completion of the work, the artisan makes its return to the customer conditional on the *payment of his fee*. This is the artisan's right of lien, by virtue of which he is a paid bailee (*Maggid Mishneh*, Rabbi Vidal de Tolosa (14th-century Spain); on Yad, Sekhirut 10:3).

The talmudic passage (*ibid.* 80a) offers two explanations regarding the nature of the "benefit," which confers him the status of a paid bailee even after having completed his work. The first, "as a result of benefit received due to the fact that the customer ignored all the other artisans and specifically chose him," means, in other words, that the artisan has an interest in *maintaining his reputation*, which will attract clients who know that they can rely on his responsibility and his safeguarding of property given to him to repair. The second, "for the benefit occasioned by his ability to withhold the property as against his fee, and that he is not required to make efforts to collect his fee," means, in other words, that the artisan's *right of lien* per se, which he has on the property given to him, is a "benefit" which converts him into a paid bailee of the property, even after completion of his work.

The Court stated that "in both cases, the Talmud's point of departure was that the actual payment of the artisan's work fee constitutes a *'benefit'* that gives him the status of a paid bailee for as long as his work is not completed. However, even after completion of his work and prior to the customer having regained his property, the contractor may still derive various benefits from his possession of the property, and it is by *virtue of these benefits that he retains* the status of a paid bailee for this additional period."

This was the background for the Court's construction of the term "reasonable time" in section 6 (a) of the Contract for Services Law as including the *benefits* that the artisan was likely to derive. Consequently, as opposed to, and in overturning the ruling of the trial court, the Appeal Court ruled that the time period of one night, during which the car remained in the garage, fell within the ambit of "reasonable time," that the garage owner was subject to the law governing the paid bailee, and therefore responsible.

[Menachem Elon (2nd ed.)]

BIBLIOGRAPHY: N. Hurewitsch, in: *Zeitschrift fuer vergleichende Rechtswissenschaft*, 27 (1912), 425–39; I.S. Zuri, *Mishpat ha-Talmud*, 5 (1921), 105–17; Gulak, Yesodei, 2 (1922), 65–68, 190–2; Z. Karl, in: *Tarbiz*, 7 (1935/36), 258–82; Herzog, Instit, 2 (1939), 175–96; Ḥ. Albeck, *Shishah Sidrei Mishnah*, introd. to BM; suppl. thereto, 3:1; Elon, Mafte'ah, 229–33, 308f., 376–9; U. Cassuto, *Commentary on the Book of Exodus* (1967), 285–8; N. Rakover, in: *Ha-Peraklit*, 24 (1968), 208–25; M. Elon, in: ILR, 4 (1969), 91–94. **ADD. BIBLIOGRAPHY:** M. Elon, *Ha-Mishpat ha-Ivri* (1988), I:112 n.139, 177, 276f., 293, 334, 505, 517f., 713, 785f.; 2:993, 1111, 1420–24; idem, *Jewish Law* (1994), I:125 n. 139, 196, 325, 349, 405f.; 3:615, 629, 881, 964f.; 3:1200, 1692–96; M. Elon and B. Lifshitz, *Mafte'aḥ ha-She'elot ve-ha-Teshuvot shel Ḥakhmei Sefarad u-Ẓefon Afrikah* (legal digest) (1986), 2:459–61; H. Albeck, *Shishah Sidrei Mishnah*, intro. to BM, supplement to BM 3:1; B. Cahanne, *Shomerim* (1998); U. Cassuto, *Commentary on the Book of Exodus* (1967), 285–88; J. Gulak, *Yesodei*, 2 (1922), 65–68, 190–92; 425–39; M. Corinaldi, *"Shomer she-Masar la-Shomer ba-Mishpat ha-Ivri u-ve-Ḥok ha-Shomerim,"* in: *Shenaton ha-Mishpat ha-Ivri* 2 (1975), 383; B. Lifshitz and E. Shochetman, *Mafte'aḥ ha-She'elot ve-ha-Teshuvot shel Ḥakhmei Ashkenaz, Ẓarefat ve-Italyah* (legal digest) (1997), 308–9; N. Rakover, in: *Ha-Peraklit*, 24 (1968), 208–25. 105–17; Z. Karl, in *Tarbiz*, 7 (1935/36), 258–82.

SHOMER ISRAEL (Heb. שׁוֹמֵר יִשְׂרָאֵל; "Guardian of Israel"), faction of the assimilationist movement (see *Assimilation) in Galicia during the second half of the 19th century, favoring German cultural orientation. Shomer Israel was organized in 1869 as an expression of the intensified political activity among the Jews following the Austrian constitution of 1867 and the prospects of *emancipation. Its founders included Filip Mansch, Rubin Bierer, and Joseph Kohn. They published a weekly, *Der Israelit*, aimed to spread education among the Jewish masses and make them aware of their civic and social obligations. It appeared for 35 years, first edited by Mansch. Its political outlook was centralist and pro-Austrian with a tendency toward German liberalism. On the initiative of *Der Israelit*, a Jewish-Ruthenian bloc was created in 1873 for the elections to parliament in Vienna; the bloc succeeded in obtaining three Jewish seats.

The German cultural and Austrian orientation of Shomer Israel was however unable to withstand the new tendencies which gradually emerged within Jewish intellectual circles sympathetic to Polish culture and loyal to the ideas of Galician autonomy. The Jewish youth who studied in Polish schools became imbued with a patriotic spirit, which was expressed by Bernard *Goldman, who arrived in Lemberg in 1870 and laid the foundations of a rival organization named Doreshei Shalom, and a newspaper **Ugoda*, which called for Polish assimilation. A new assimilationist organization *Aguddat Aḥim was also established and was active during the 1880s, when it challenged the views of Shomer Israel. Another opponent of Shomer Israel was the Orthodox sector led by Simeon *Sofer (Schreiber) who headed the *Maḥzikei Hadas society. When Sofer was elected to the Austrian parliament in 1879, he joined the "Polish Club," there; the Orthodox were particularly opposed to the conference of communities convened in Lemberg on the initiative of Shomer Israel in 1878, with the aim of reorganizing the communities. The leaders of Orthodoxy, rabbis Simeon Sofer of Cracow and Joshua Rokeaḥ of *Belz, called for a boycott of the conference because of its objectives to modernize Jewish life and its project to establish a rabbinical seminary.

BIBLIOGRAPHY: N.M. Gelber (ed.), EG, 4 (1956), 309–11; I. Schipper et al. (eds.), *Żydzi w Polsce odrodzonej*, 1 (1932), 393; J. Tenenbaum, *Galitsye, Mayn Alte Heym* (1952), 31–83.

[Moshe Landau]

SHOMRAT (Heb. שָׁמְרַת), kibbutz in northern Israel, 2 mi. (3 km.) N.E. of Acre, affiliated with Kibbutz Arẓi ha-Shomer ha-Ẓa'ir. Shomrat was founded as the first new settlement in the State of Israel on May 29, 1948, immediately after the capture of Acre in the *War of Independence. The settlers were pioneers from Hungary, Czechoslovakia, and Romania. In 1970 Shomrat had 324 inhabitants; in 2002, 358. Its farming included irrigated field and fodder crops, avocado plantations, dairy cattle and poultry. For many years the kibbutz had a furniture factory and was a partner in Ha-Shomer ha-Ẓa'ir industrial enterprises in the Haifa Bay area. It also operated guest rooms. The kibbutz achieved notoriety when a local girl was raped by a gang of kibbutz youngsters in 1988. Their initial acquittal caused a great public outcry and the act itself severely tarnished the kibbutz image. Four of the assailants were later convicted on appeal. The name Shomrat is derived from *shomer* ("guardsman"), and also evokes the Ha-Shomer ha-Ẓa'ir movement.

WEBSITE: www.at-shomrat.com.

[Efram Orni / Shaked Gilboa (2nd ed.)]

SHOMRON, DAN (1937–). Israeli soldier, thirteenth chief of staff of the Israel Defense Forces. Shomron was born in kibbutz Ashdot Ya'akov in the Jordan Valley. His military career began in 1956 when he was a paratrooper. During the Six-Day War of 1967 he commanded an armored division in Sinai, and later served as commander of the southern front. The *Entebbe raid in 1976, later renamed "Operation Yonatan," in which hostages from an Air France flight hijacked en route from Tel Aviv to Paris were rescued from Entebbe Airport near Kampala, Uganda, was under the command of Shomron, then a brigadier general, who also planned the operation. After occupying various staff positions, he became deputy chief of staff. In early 1987 he was named chief of staff, taking up the position in April of that year and serving until 1991. During his years as chief of staff he had to deal with the first *intifada*, which began in late 1987, and with the first Gulf War in 1991. After his retirement he served as chairman of Israel's Military Industries and then went into private business.

SHONFIELD, SIR ANDREW (**Schonfeld**; 1917–1981), British economist. Born in London, the son of Rabbi Victor Schonfeld, he was educated at St. Paul's and Oxford and served as a writer on the *Financial Times* (1947–57) and economics editor of the *Observer* (1958–61). Later he held such positions as chairman of the Social Sciences Research Council (1967–71) and director of the Royal Institute of Economic Affairs (1972–77). Shonfield is best known for his many writings on the mixed economy and modern economic developments, such as *British Economic Policy Since the War* (1958), *The Attack on World Poverty* (1960), and *Modern Capitalism* (1965). He delivered the 1972 Reith Lectures on European integration, and was knighted in 1978.

BIBLIOGRAPHY: ODNB online.

[William D. Rubinstein (2nd ed.)]

SHORE, DINAH (**Francis Rose Shore**; 1917–1994), U.S. singer. Born in Winchester, Tennessee, Shore graduated from Vanderbilt University in 1938. She started working on radio in 1938 and in 1940 starred in NBC's *Chamber Music Society of Lower Basin Street*. She appeared on Eddie Cantor's radio show, 1940–43. Her sentimental style suited the wartime and postwar periods, and her record "Yes, My Darling Daughter" sold a million copies. She sang in several films (*Up in Arms; Follow the Boys*, both 1944). The first female star to have her own prime-time TV variety show, her easy-going manner was successful on television when *The Dinah Shore Show* ran from 1951 to 1961. Her two subsequent TV variety shows were *Dinah's Place* (1970–74) and *Dinah!* (1974–80). Shore won eight Emmy Awards for her television programs and for her vocal performances (Best Female Singer). She was married to actor George Montgomery from 1943 to 1963.

Shore wrote and/or compiled six cookbooks, among them *Someone's in the Kitchen with Dinah* (1971); *Dining in Los Angeles* (with L. Grad, 1979); and *The Dinah Shore American Kitchen* (1990).

BIBLIOGRAPHY: B. Cassiday, *Dinah!: A Biography* (1979).

[Ruth Beloff (2nd ed.)]

SHORESH (Heb. שֹׁרֶשׁ), moshav shittufi in the Judean Hills, 12 mi. (20 km.) W. of Jerusalem, affiliated with Ha-Oved ha-Ẓiyyoni federation. In the Israel *War of Independence, the occupation of Sārīs (April 1948) was a decisive step and Shoresh was among the first villages established to secure the Jerusalem Corridor. It was founded in 1948 by settlers from Romania and Czechoslovakia. The soil underwent heavy reclamation work. Deciduous fruit orchards and vineyards were prominent farm branches; the moshav also grew field crops on the Coastal Plain. Its economy was supplemented by a resort village and public swimming pool. In 1970 the moshav numbered 190 inhabitants, rising to 374 in 2002. It lies in the midst of one of the country's largest afforested areas, notably the Martyrs' Forest. The name, "Root," was adapted from the Arabic Sārīs and is presumably derived from an ancient Hebrew name.

SHORT, RENEE (1916–2003), British politician. The daughter of a Jewish engineer from Eastern Europe, Short was educated at Manchester University and worked as a journalist and stage designer before entering politics. She served as a Labour member of Parliament from 1964 to 1987. In the early part of her political career she was one of the most left-wing of national politicians, a constant critic of the United States and a supporter of the Soviet Union, and chairman of the British-German Democratic Republic parliamentary group. She was also a strong feminist. In the 1970s, she moved to the center-left and was actively opposed by the "hard left" in the Labour Party. By the end of her career she had attracted considerable opprobrium from her former allies for attacking large-scale non-white immigration into Britain. Her left-wing stance meant that she never held a ministerial position, but she served as chairman of the influential House of Commons Select Committee on the Social Services from 1979 to 1987.

[William D. Rubinstein (2nd ed.)]

SHOSTAK, ELIEZER (1911–2001), Israeli politician. Shostak was born in Poland and immigrated to Ereẓ Israel in 1935. He was one of the founders of the *Ḥerut Party and was appointed secretary-general of the National (Revisionist) Labor Federation. A member of the Knesset representing Ḥerut, he resigned from the party in 1966 to form, together with Samuel Tamir, the Free Center, whose representatives they were in the Seventh Knesset, but he subsequently left it to join La'am.

Shostak was a member of every Knesset from the Second to the eleventh and was appointed minister of health in 1977 and again in 1981.

SHOVAL (Heb. שׁוֹבָל), kibbutz in southern Israel, in the northern Negev, 16 mi. (25 km.) N.W. of Beersheba, affiliated with Kibbutz Arzi ha-Shomer ha-Ẓa'ir. Shoval was founded on Oct. 6, 1946, as one of the 11 outpost settlements established in the same night in the South and Negev. The founders were pioneers from South Africa and Israel-born youth. They were later joined by immigrants from Romania, English-speaking countries, and other countries. In 1970 the kibbutz had

440 inhabitants. In 2002 the population was 505. Shoval pioneered in contour-plowing methods on its loess soils to prevent sheet erosion. It formed friendly ties with the al-Huzayyil Bedouin tribe camping in the vicinity. Near Shoval one of the first experimental, flash-flood reservoirs in the country was installed. With water for irrigation from the National Water Carrier, Shoval raised grain and field crops. It also maintained a large dairy herd and poultry and had three industries: chip processing, silk printing, and metal. Shoval is supposed to be the name of a biblical place in this area, preserved on the *Madaba Map in the form of Sobila (Σωβιλα) and in Arabic, as Bīr Zaballa. The name Shobal (Shoval) appears as a private name in I Chronicles 1:38, 40 and is connected with Bīr Zaballa preserved by the Arabs.

[Efram Orni / Shaked Gilboa (2nd ed.)]

SHOVAVIM TAT (Heb. שׁוֹבְבִים תַּ"ת), an acrostic composed of the initial letters of the names of the first eight weekly *sidrot* ("Torah portions") of the Book of Exodus which are read in the winter months between *Ḥanukkah and *Purim. Since diseases were prevalent, especially among infants, during the long and hard winter season, it was the custom to recite penitential prayers (*seliḥot*) on Thursdays of the weeks in which these portions were read in order to avert disastrous epidemics. These penitential prayers are recited in the morning service in the Ashkenazi ritual, or at the afternoon service only (Italian rite). In many European communities, it was customary to fast on these Thursdays; in others (North Africa) on the Mondays and the Thursdays of the *Shovavim Tat* period. Penitential prayers and fasting do not take place on Thursdays that coincide with a *Rosh Ḥodesh. Kabbalists (Isaac *Luria, Isaiah ha-Levi *Horowitz), attributed mystical concepts to the observance of *Shovavim Tat*.

BIBLIOGRAPHY: Eisenstein, Dinim, 403–4.

SHPIGLBLAT, ALEKSANDER (Spiegelblatt; 1927–), Yiddish poet and essayist. Born in Kimfolung (Campulung), Bukovina, Romania, he was interred with his family in work camps in Transnistria in 1941–43. After the war he studied at Bucharest University and in 1954–8 lectured there on Russian literature. In 1964 he settled in Israel and was editorial-staff secretary of *Di *Goldene Keyt* from 1972 until its closure in 1995. He first published in the Bucharest *Ikuf-Bleter* (Ikuf = Jewish Culture Association) in 1950 and there issued a volume of verse entitled *Heymland* ("Homeland," 1952). In Israel he published five volumes of verse: *Umruike Oysyes* ("Restless Letters," 1969); *Papirene Zeglen* ("Paper Sails," 1973); *Volknbremen* ("Cloudy Brows," 1979; *Neshome-Likht* ("Soul Light," 1997); *In Geln Tsvishn-Likht fun Erev Regn* ("In the Yellow Twilight before the Rain," 1998). The last volume includes poems written in Romania up to 1964, published in his other volumes and in *Di Goldene Keyt*, and translations into and from Yiddish in several languages. In 2000 he published a moving personal memoir of the Transnistria nightmare of Romanian Jewry: *Durkhn Shpaktiv fun a Zeyger-Makher* ("Through the Lens of a Watchmaker," 2000). He also authored an informal study of fellow Romanian Itsik Manger: *Bloe Vinklen: Itsik Manger, Lebn, Lid un Balade* ("Blue Corners: Itsik Manger, Life, Song and Ballad," 2002); a collection of three stories, *Shotns Klapn in Shoyb* ("Shadows Knock on the Window," 2003); and a novel, *Krimeve; an Altfrenkishe Mayse* ("Krimeve; An Old-fashioned Tale," 2005). His prose has a winning simplicity, clarity and directness; his verse is concision itself.

BIBLIOGRAPHY: LNYL, 8 (1981), 784–5.

[Leonard Prager (2nd ed.)]

SHPOLA, townlet in S. Kiev district, Ukraine. *Aryeh Leib (*Shpoler Zeyde*), a disciple of *Israel b. Eliezer the Ba'al Shem Tov, lived in Shpola during the late 18th and early 19th centuries. In the late 18th century there were 231 Jews. In 1847 the community numbered 1,516 Jews and in 1863, there were 2,534. The Kiev-Odessa railroad which passed near the town helped it to develop and become a center of the grain and sugar industry. In 1897 there were 5,388 Jews (45.3% of the total population) in Shpola. The Jews lived in the town proper, while the remainder of the inhabitants, mostly peasants, lived in the suburbs. The community suffered during the Civil War, and in 1919 both the soldiers of *hetman* Grigoryev (in May) and the armies of General *Denikin carried out pogroms. Under Soviet rule a Jewish city council existed, 95 families founded a Kolkhoz on the town outskirts, and 134 Jews worked in a furniture factory. Most of the Jewish children studied in a Yiddish school. There were 5,379 Jews (35%) in Shpola in 1926, the number dropping to 2,397 in 1939 (16.2% of the total population). The Germans occupied Shpola on July 30, 1941. On September 9 160 Jewish professionals were executed. In late September a ghetto was established where, owing to the very crowded living conditions, each day some 10 to 12 people died. On April 15, 1942, groups of able-bodied Jewswere sent to work camps where they perished. On May 15, 1942, 760 women, children, and elderly were murdered; 225 able-bodied workers were sent to Brodetsk camp, where they were killed in December 1942. Another 105 were murdered in Shostkiv camp, and the last Jews were murdered in the beginning of 1943. In 1959 there were about 600 Jews in Shpola again, but most left in the 1990s.

BIBLIOGRAPHY: D. Cohen, *Shpola* (Heb., 1965).

[Yehuda Slutsky]

SHRAGAI (Fajwlowicz), SHLOMO ZALMAN (1899–1995), religious Zionist leader. Born in Gorzkowice, Poland, his father was one of the Radzyń Ḥasidim and a member of Ḥovevei Ẓion and of Mizrachi. While still a youth, Shragai founded Ẓe'irei Mizrachi in his native city and published a religious Zionist newspaper entitled *Teḥiyyah*. He also directed *Mizrachi schools in various places. From 1920 until 1924, he lived in Czestochowa, was a member of the governing board of Mizrachi, and was a founder of He-Ḥalutz ha-Mizrachi and its training farm. He was also a leader of Ẓe'irei Mizrachi in Poland. He settled in Palestine in 1924 and in the following year was delegate to the divided conference of Ha-Po'el ha-Mizrachi in Palestine, the majority of whose delegates decided to join with the *Histadrut. Shragai belonged to the minority and, together with his friends, continued to maintain the independent framework of Ha-Po'el ha-Mizrachi and was elected to its executive. He was chosen as a delegate to Zionist Congresses and as a member of the Zionist General Council and the world center of Mizrachi. In 1929 he was elected to the Va'ad Le'ummi directorate and was head of its department of press and information. In 1946 Shragai was chosen as a member of the *Jewish Agency Executive in London. With the establishment of the State of Israel, he returned to the country and served as a member of the Jewish Agency Executive without portfolio. In 1950 he was elected mayor of Jerusalem and remained at this post until 1952. Two years later he was again elected to the Jewish Agency Executive as head of the Immigration Department and served in this position until 1968.

He was a contributor to the dailies *Ha-Ẓofeh* and *Letste Nayes* in Israel, as well as Hebrew and Yiddish papers abroad. He published books and pamphlets on the concept of religious Zionism and the thought behind the Torah va-Avodah movement. Among his works are *Teḥumim* (1952), *Ḥazon ve-Hagshamah* (1956), *Tahalikhei ha-Ge'ullah ve-ha-Temurah* (1959), *Sha'ah va-Neẓaḥ* (1960), *Pa'amei Ge'ullah* (1963), and *Zemanim* (1969).

BIBLIOGRAPHY: D. Lazar, *Rashim be-Yisrael*, 2 (1955), 182–5.

[Itzhak Goldshlag]

SHRAYBMAN, YEKHIEL (1913–), Yiddish writer. Born in Vadrashkov (Bessarabia) in the Russian Pale of Settlement, he recreated his birthplace as Rashkov, a symbolic landscape where he set most of his (semi-)autobiographical short novels, novellas, and poetic miniatures. His study at the Czernowitz pedagogical seminary (1930–32) ended with his dismissal for anti-Romanian political activity. He struggled for survival during the next seven years of hiding in Bucharest, during which he also worked as a prompter in a Jewish theater, which experience is reflected in his best-known novel *Zibn Yor mit Zibn Khadoshim* ("Seven Years and Seven Months," 1988). In 1940 he moved to the Soviet Union where he quickly became part of the literary establishment as a regular contributor to and member of the editorial board of the journal *Sovetish Heymland*. His works are a testimony to the history of Jews in the region, his self-reflective style encapsulating the fragmented and disappearing Jewish world. His books include *Dray Zumers* ("Three Summers," 1946), *Yorn un Reges* ("Years and Moments," 1973), *Shtendik* ("Always," 1977), *In Yenem Zumer* ("In that Summer," 1981), *Vayter …* ("Further …," 1984), *Yitsire un Libe* ("Creation and Love," 2000). His honors include the Meritul Civic Medal of the Republic of Moldova (1996), Ruzhi Fishman-Shnaydman (1997), and Zalman Rejzen (1999) awards.

BIBLIOGRAPHY: M. Hazin and I. Lahman, in: *Forverts* (Jan. 10, 1997), 12, 19; G. Remenik, *Portrety evreĭskikh pisatelei* (1982), 320–8; I. Chobanu, in: *Nistru*, 3 (1963), 155–7.

[Elena Katz (2nd ed.)]

SHREIER, FEIWEL (1819–1898), rabbi and one of the leaders of the Zionist movement in Galicia. Both in Bohorodczany, Galicia, Schreier studied under leading Galician rabbis and in 1861 became the rabbi of Bohorodczany. He was the oldest Galician rabbi and one of the most renowned for halakhic knowledge, to join the Zionist movement upon the appearance of Theodor *Herzl. Despite his advanced age, he was ready to travel to any community that requested a speaker on Zionism. He was the honorary president of the Galician Ahavat Zion society for the settlement of Ereẓ Israel, which founded the moshavah Maḥanayim. He published a number of books on *halakhah*, including a book by his teacher, Avraham David of Buczacz (*Da'at Kedoshim*). At the Third Zionist Congress (1899) he was eulogized by Herzl, to whom he was very close.

BIBLIOGRAPHY: M. Leiter, in: *Sinai*, 66 (1969/70), 158–63; N.M. Gelber, *Toledot ha-Tenu'ah ha-Ẓiyyonit be-Galiẓyah* (1958), index.

[Getzel Kressel]

SHRODER, WILLIAM J. (1876–1952), U.S. lawyer and civic leader. Shroder, who was born in Cincinnati, Ohio, engaged in private law practice in Cincinnati for 20 years, also serving as a special assistant U.S. attorney general in 1907 for drug-trust cases. In 1921 Shroder retired from law practice to devote himself fully to voluntary social and civic affairs.

He was president of Cincinnati's United Jewish Social Agencies during 1923–26; helped found the National Council of Jewish Federations and Welfare Funds in 1932, serving as its first president; and was vice chairman of the Jewish Distribution Committee from 1931 to 1939. Shroder held various civic offices; he was a member of the Cincinnati Board of Education from 1927 to 1934, serving the last four years as chairman. During his tenure in office he instituted equal pay for all teachers, regardless of sex or grade taught, and raised professional standards. The annual Shroder Award was given by the Council of Jewish Federations and Welfare Funds to a community institution with exceptional innovative programs.

[Kenneth D. Roseman]

SHTADLAN, a representative of the Jewish community with access to high dignitaries and legislative bodies. The name is derived from the Aramaic root שדל which in its reflexive form has the meaning "to make an effort" or "to intercede on behalf of." The *shtadlan* had to combine the roles and abilities of diplomat, advocate, and intercessor. The functions of the *shtadlanim* depended on the situation of the Jews in various countries through the ages. Their role diminished and ceased in Western Europe after the French Revolution but continued to be of great importance in Eastern Europe and especially in Russia until the second half of the 19th century. Most of the leaders of Jewish society in the Diaspora who came into contact with state or Church authorities carried out the functions of the *shtadlan*. The role and status of such influential Jews, deriving from their connections both with the court and with other Jewish leaders, is delineated by *Saadiah Gaon, writing from Baghdad to Egyptian Jewry in the tenth century: "Relate any wish or problem that you have in relation to the state [*ha-malkhut*] to us, for then we will order the honorable community members [*ba' alei battim ḥashuvim*] of Baghdad and they will bring you the royal resolve, in so far as the Lord our strength will enable them" (in: *Ginzei Kedem*, 2 (1923), 35). *Samuel ha-Nagid saw his mission as the defense of the Jews in the principality of which he was vizier and commander of the Muslim state and army. *Eliezer b. Joel ha-Levi of Bonn in 13th-century Germany considered that those who on weekdays interceded for the Jews with alien rulers should have the honor of being the prayer leaders of the community on the High Holidays. The name itself appears first in the 13th–14th centuries in Spain, where the term *mishtadlim* was used at first.

The Jewish policy in *shtadlanut* is explicitly defined in the resolutions of the conference of the communities of Catalonia and Valencia which met in *Barcelona in December 1354. Appealing to the king of Aragon and reminding him of the tradition of royal protection, they asked him to intercede for them to prevent mob violence and libels. They asked the pontiff "to bring to naught the evil designs of the populace who, should troubled days come… would in their foolish way torment the unhappy Jews. And let the pope command them that if, Heaven forbid, God should look forth from His Heaven and send down an evil judgment, they are not, in defiance of His will, to add another vile deed to their sins, but to strengthen themselves to walk in His ways, wherein he has commanded them to cherish us as the apple of their eye, because upon their faith we rest." Courageously they asked the pope to "explain that the Inquisition into heresy shall not pertain to Jews," since such is the Jewish religious entity that "even if a Jew strengthens the hands of a Christian who is a heretic to his faith, the stain of heresy cannot spread to the Jew, for it is impossible to ascribe to a Jew under the definition of heresy something which is right according to his faith" (Baer, Spain, 2 (1966), 26f.). The appeal is to reason, to tolerance, and to keeping faith with those who of necessity trust the ruling Christian powers.

Their actions and appeals throughout the Middle Ages prove that *shtadlanim* adopted an unequivocal stand on the question of Jewish rights. In a memorandum submitted in 1518 (a year before their expulsion), the Jews of *Regensburg answered the accusations brought against them point by point, observing in summing up: "If they want and need to keep Jews then they have to keep them humanely… and to fulfill what has been promised to them. That they have to keep Jews in Regensburg… and treat them humanely… our charters… show… We declare that we are Jews, and are no better than Jews" (R. Straus, *Urkunden und Aktenstuecke zur Geschichte der Juden in Regensburg…* (1960), no. 988. pp. 355–61). The explicit attitude of the Jews to humiliating legislation is revealed in the answer given by Johanan Luria in Alsace at the end of the 15th century in relation to the Jewish *badge: "It is [imposed] by the ruler's command. And if he should order me to carry a stone of two pounds' weight, I would have to do it. Verily this law is like other laws that you impose on us without reason" (H.H. Ben-Sasson, in: HTR, 59 (1966), 372ff.). The great *shtadlan* of the 16th century, *Joseph b. Gershon of Rosheim, constantly based his arguments on the concept of the natural equality of men (*ibid.*, p. 387). In his arguments against Martin *Luther, he appealed to the obligation "to comply with an undertaking and to preserve the peace of the land," averring that the refusal to meet such obligations would lead "Christian opponents of Luther to… fare even worse than the Jews" (idem, *The Reformation in Contemporary Jewish Eyes* (1970), 290). By the 16th century, many individual communities and also the *Councils of the Lands employed professional, salaried *shtadlanim* who had to litigate for individual Jews as well as for the whole body politic of the Jews. In the *Landesjudenschaft the *Court Jew or a relative of his was *shtadlan*, an office which carried considerable authority. In the phrasing of most charters for Jews, echoes can be heard through the Latin of the demands, formulations, and achievements of the *shtadlan*. His intervention was most frequently occasioned by *taxation, the *blood libel, and the *Host desecration accusations.

From the late 19th century the terms *shtadlan* and *shtadlanut* acquired a pejorative undertone; they were used derisively to decry Jewish representatives who failed to stand up with pride and courage against persecuting governments and came to denote those who showed weakness and an eagerness for compromise.

BIBLIOGRAPHY: S. Stern, *Court Jew* (1950); idem, *Josel of Rosheim* (1965); Baron, Community, 3 (1942), index s.v. *Shtadlanim*; Carstein, in: YLBI, 2 (1958), 140–56; J. Katz, *Tradition and Crisis* (1961), index s.v. *Court Jews*; F. Baer, *Protokollbuch der Landjudenschaft der Herzogtums Kleve* (1922); H.H. Ben-Sasson, *Toledot Am-Yisrael*, 2 (1969), index; S. Dubnow, *Pinkas Medinat Lita* (1925); S. Zitron, *Shtadlonim* (Yid., 1926); I. Levitats, *Jewish Community in Russia* (1943); Halpern, Pinkas; idem, *Takkanot Medinat Mehrin* (1952).

SHTAYGER (Yid. "mode", "manner"), term designating the musical modes of a traditional Ashkenazi synagogue song, characterized by an order of intervals which is unusual in European music. The *shtayger* are named after the initial words of certain prayers sung to them, with some differences in nomenclature between East and West Ashkenazi communities. The number of these synagogue modes is difficult to determine if all their variants and tonal shades are taken into account. Investigators usually restrict themselves to the more frequent and important ones and number three (J. *Singer, 1886) or four (I. *Schwarz, 1894) principal *shtayger*. These were imagined as the Jewish parallel of the medieval European Church modes and are accordingly described in terms of octave scales. Later the increased knowledge of non-European modal structures, such as the *maqāma* or *raga*, gave the clue for understanding the true nature of the *shtayger*. First, their "scales" need not be an octave repeating itself through the whole gamut; their tonal range may extend over less or more than eight notes, and the intervals may be altered in different octave pitches or in ascending and descending order. Another characteristic is given by the specific location of the keynotes, which serve as resting points of the intermediary and final cadences. Furthermore, certain *shtayger* are characterized by a stock of motives of their own. Thus, singing according to a *shtayger* comes very close to Oriental concepts of modality.

Two *shtayger* are by far the most important in both the West and East Ashkenazi traditions: the "*Ahavah Rabbah*" and the "*Adoshem Malakh*" *shtayger*. The "*Ahavah Rabbah*," featuring an augmented second, is rather frequent in synagogue music as well as in folksong and ḥasidic melodies; it has also been used for the musical characterization of the Jewish nation by Mussorgsky, Anton *Rubinstein, and other composers. The "*Adoshem Malakh*" *shtayger* (named after Ps. 93:1) always appears in connection with its 10 to 12 standard motives, which are combined in various ways and variants. Less frequent are the "*Magen Avot*," which resembles natural minor, and the "*Av ha-Raḥamim*" *shtayger*, with its two augmented seconds (sometimes mistaken, by superficial observers, for the so-called Gipsy Scale).

The circle of traditional *shtayger* is not a closed system but extends to many variant forms, which are only occasionally or even rarely used. The *Az be-Kol* (*Ra'ash*)" *shtayger*, in former times also called by the hitherto unexplained name "*Klavaner*," may serve as an example of these secondary modes. In the free compositions of individual cantors, modulation from one *shtayger* to the other frequently occurs and contributes much to the expressive power of the East Ashkenazi singing style.

The use of *shtayger* melodies in art music raises some problems, especially when their harmonization is attempted. Some convincing solutions have been found, as when the solo tune is allowed to display itself before a background of sustained chords (e.g., L. *Lewandowski's "*Ki ke-Shimkho*" for cantor and choir).

BIBLIOGRAPHY: H. Avenary, *Yuval*, 2 (1971), E. Werner, in: *New Oxford History of Music*, 1 (1957), 320–4; Z.Z. Idelsohn, in: HUCA, 14 (1939), 559–74; idem, in: A. Friedmann (ed.), *Dem Andenken Eduard Birnbaums* (1922), 62–69; J. Singer, *Die Tonarten des traditionellen Synagogengesanges; Steiger…* (1886; abstracted in A. Friedmann (ed.), op. cit., 90–100); E. Birnbaum, in: A. Friedmann (ed.), op. cit., 16f.; I. Schwarz, ibid., 198–206; P. Minkowski, in: Eisenstein, Yisrael, 4 (1907–13), 263; A. Friedmann, *Der synagogale Gesang* (1908²), 87ff.

[Hanoch Avenary]

SHTERN, Canadian family consisting of a father and four sons, all of whom have made their mark in Jewish literature. The most important of them, however, Ya'akov adopted the name *Zipper. All were born in Tyszowce, Poland.

ABRAHAM DAVID SHTERN (1878–1955) became a *dayyan* and *shoḥet* in his native town. In 1938, he immigrated to Canada and was appointed rabbi of the Zeirei Dat Vadaat Congregation of Montreal. He published three volumes of essays on biblical and ḥasidic themes, in a mixture of Hebrew and Yiddish: *Edut be-Yisrael* (1943); *Kevuẓat Kitvei Aggadah* (1947); *Ḥutim ha-Meshulashim* (1953), which are of considerable value from the point of view of both scholarship and folklore. SHOLEM SHTERN (1907–), a Yiddish poet and literary writer, immigrated to Canada in 1927. He was associated with the radical movement for many years, contributing to its Yiddish press, mostly on literary subjects. This association ceased, however, when the fate of Jewish writers and intellectuals under Stalin became known. His collections of poetry include *Nuntkejt* (Toronto, 1929) and *In der Fri* (Montreal, 1945). His two-volume novel in Yiddish verse *In Canada* (Montreal, 1960–63), is an unusual literary record of the Canadian scene. Another book, *Das Vayse Hoyz* (New York, 1967), was translated into Hebrew by Shimshon *Meltzer, under the title *Ha-Bayit ha-Lavan be-Harim* (Tel Aviv, 1972). Sholem Shtern's poetry and criticism of Yiddish writing have been widely published in important journals in Poland, the Argentine, Australia, Romania, South Africa, France, and Israel, as well as in Canada and the United States. He is represented in various anthologies and on recordings. YEHIEL SHTERN (1903–), educator and author, graduated from the Jewish Teachers' Seminary of Vilna, and taught in Poland before immigrating to Canada in 1936. There he became associated with the Peretz schools in Winnipeg, Calgary, Edmonton, and Montreal successively. His *Kheder un Bes Medresh* (New York, YIVO, 1950) won the Lamed Prize. ISRAEL HIRSCH SHTERN (1914–), poet and mathematician, graduated from the Vilna ORT school. After settling in Canada in 1937, he received his doctorate in mathematics from McGill University, where he was appointed associate professor of mathematics (1961–66); he also taught at Loyola College, Montreal (1966–69). Israel Shtern has written poetry in Yiddish and English, much of it under the pseudonym Ish Ya'ir. His collection entitled *Fables* appeared in England in 1967, and his *Out of the Burning Bush* in 1968. Much of his Yiddish work has been published in the United States, but he has also written English verse published in the smaller journals of England, Italy, India, Switzerland, the Philippines, Brazil, and Greece.

[David Rome]

SHTERN, ISRAEL (1894–1942), Yiddish poet, essayist, and literary critic. Shtern was born in the small Russian-Polish town of Ostrolenka and educated in the *musar* yeshivot of Lomzshe (Lomza) and Slovodka. In 1914 he moved to Vienna and spent three years in Austrian internment as an enemy alien. Here he became familiar with the newest currents of literature in the Hapsburg realm. In 1917 he settled in Warsaw. His first poems appeared in 1919 in *Vokhn Blat* and *Dos Folk*. Later on he continued to publish poems in the major Yiddish periodicals in Warsaw. His book reviews appeared regularly in the dailies *Haynt* and *Moment*. His basic theme is that God mirrors Himself in the poor, the suffering, the brokenhearted, the victims of social injustice. Shtern always stood on the periphery of Warsaw's literary circles. He spent most of his days among the Ḥasidim or poring over the Talmud. He remained poor and embittered both before World War II and during his years in the Warsaw ghetto. According to one report, he starved to death in the ghetto but, according to another report, he perished in the gas chambers of Treblinka. After his death, when his only published volume appeared, *Lider un Eseyen* ("Poems and Essays," 1955), edited by H. *Leivick, he became recognized as one of the most important Yiddish poets between the two world wars.

BIBLIOGRAPHY: Rejzen, Leksikon, 4 (1929), 626ff.; S. Bickel, *Shrayber fun Mayn Dor* (1958), 52–8. **ADD. BIBLIOGRAPHY:** I. Howe and E. Greenberg (eds.), *A Treasury of Yiddish Poetry* (1969) 225–6; G. Pomerantz, *Geshtaltn fun Mayn Dor* (1971); Y. Kahan, *Oyfn Tsesheydung* (1971), 231–45; Y. Goldenkorn, *Heymishe un Fremde* (1973), 33–9; Y. Turkov, in: *Di Goldene Keyt* (1973), 79–80; LNYL, 8 (1981), 645–8.

[Shlomo Bickel / Itay Zutra (2nd ed.)]

SHTETL (pl. **shtetlakh**; Russ. **mestechko**; Pol. **miasteczko**; Heb. עֲיָרָה), Yiddish diminutive for *shtot* meaning "town" or "city," to imply a relatively small community; in Eastern Europe a unique socio-cultural communal pattern. The real criteria for the size of a shtetl were vague and ill-defined, as the actual size could vary from much less than 1,000 inhabitants to 20,000 or more. When the community was very small it would be called a *klaynshtetl* or even a *shtetele*; however both terms could also carry the connotation of a parochial lack of sophistication or, at times, a feeling of warmth or nostalgia.

The shtetl pattern first took shape within Poland-Lithuania before the partitions of the kingdom. Jews had been invited to settle in the private towns owned by the Polish nobility that developed from the 16th century, on relatively very favorable conditions. In many of such private towns Jews soon formed the preponderant majority of the population. Their occupation in *arenda* led many Jews to settle in the villages around these towns, while many who settled in them were also engaged in *arenda* as well as having other business in the villages. Hence both the economy as well as the style of living in such towns had close links with the villages, in addition to assuming the all-pervading character of a "Jewish town." Originally dependent on the highly structured and powerful communities in the larger cities from which the settlers first came, these small communities increasingly acquired importance, since their development was unhampered by the established rights and inimical anti-Jewish traditions of the Christian townspeople, as the communities in the old "royal towns" had been. Thus the movement of Jews to smaller towns where they were needed, and therefore protected, by the greater and lesser Polish nobility, continued. The community of the private town often constituted the town itself for all intents and purposes, and therefore could strengthen and consolidate a homogeneous pattern of values, attitudes, and mores.

With the partitions of Poland-Lithuania the final crystallization of the socio-cultural pattern of the began amid the process of geopolitical differentiation of the communities on the territories divided between Poland's neighbors. In Russia, the shtetl developed in the Pale of Settlement. In 1815, Congress Poland was incorporated into the Pale, which continued to exist until the October Revolution of 1917. Within Austria-Hungary, the shtetl communities were scattered in Galicia, Bohemia, Sub-Carpathian Ruthenia, Bukovina, and Hungary. In the area under Prussia the shtetl pattern did not develop to the same extent. Despite the basic cultural homogeneity which had consolidated in the past few centuries, the communities in the partitioned regions developed specific social traits in each of the states in which they were situated. This was the result on the one hand of the varying cultures of their host societies and on the other hand of the differing social and economic policies and trends which developed in the host society under the Hapsburg emperors or Russian czars.

During the 19th century, the anti-Jewish persecutions, economic restrictions, and outbreaks of violence pressed increasingly on the socioeconomic foundations of the Jews, in czarist Russia in particular, while political and ideological revolutionary trends and movements began to undermine the strength of the life style of the shtetl, which became more and more unsatisfactory to younger generations. Thus weakened in its foundations, the shtetl entered the last phase of its existence. The liberal revolution of 1917 liquidated the Pale of Settlement, while the Communist revolution that followed liquidated the traditional shtetl life. Between the two world wars, independent Poland became the greatest Jewish center in Eastern Europe.

Life in the Shtetl

Yidishkeyt ("Jewishness") and *menshlikhkeyt* ("humanness") were the two major values of the community around which life centered. Both the sacred and the profane were integrated in this way of life. The traditional ideals of piety, learning and scholarship, communal justice, and charity, were fused in the warm and intimate lifestyle of the shtetl. Thus the *Yidishkeyt* and the *menshlikhkeyt* of the shtetl were expressed in innumerable activities, all of which were geared toward the goal of living the life of a "good Jew" and were manifested in the synagogue and at home, in the holiness of Sabbath and the humdrum existence of the market, in the structure of the community and in the organization of the family.

The Synagogue

The life of the Jew oscillated between synagogue, home, and market. In the synagogue he served God, studied His Law and participated in social activities created in response to the needs of the community and its individual members. The synagogue, whether a *shul*, a Ukrainian *kloyz*, or a Polish *shtibl*, was the house of prayer, the house of study, and the house of assembly combined. The seating arrangement in the synagogue reflected the social structure of the community: along the eastern wall, where the Ark was located, were ranged the most honored members of the community, the rabbi and the *sheyne Yidn* (the dignified Jews), the men of learning, of substance, and of status, i.e., men with *yihus* – symbol of distinction acquired through family position in the community or individual achievement in learning, business, or community participation. The seats facing the eastern wall were occupied by the *balebatim* or burghers, and behind them were placed the *proste Yidn* or common Jews – the humble folk, usually assumed to be ignorant, poor, and uneducated. The value of the seats decreased with their distance from the eastern wall, until at the western wall were found the beggars and needy strangers. These were cared for by various community institutions as well as special associations (see *ḥevrah*).

The Home

The home of the individual was the basic unit in the culture and life style of the shtetl; it was founded on a patriarchal and closely knit structure on traditional lines. His home was the place where the shtetl Jew enjoyed his *Yidishkeyt* in the serenity and peace of Sabbath, in the rituals of the Passover *seder*, or in the dignity and holiness of the High Holidays. It was where he derived the *nakhes* – the proud pleasure – from the achievement of his children, the son, or the son-in-law. There he fed the stranger on Friday, and provided meals to the poor student in the yeshivah. However the home was also part of the community, and hardly any important activity at home was separable from the synagogue or the total community. Birth and death, bar mitzvahs and weddings, illness and recovery, were family events which tied the home to the synagogue, and by extension to the community. No family event was a private event, for life in the shtetl was life with people, and therefore part of the total community life. Family joys, as well as family sorrows, were shared by the community, which had the right and duty to express its approval or disapproval about the conduct and behavior of the family as a whole or of each of its members. Thus community control over the life of its individual members became one of the major regulating forces in the shtetl society, which succeeded in surviving for centuries without a police force to maintain its internal law and order.

The Market

The market and marketplace were the source of livelihood and the meeting place with non-Jewish neighbors. The shtetl Jews served as middlemen between the big city and village economy. They brought urban products to the Polish, Ukrainian, or Romanian peasant who visited the market, or as peddlers bought from him the agricultural produce of the villages which they sold in the city. The financial scale of these transactions was limited. Only a few Jews in the shtetl engaged in enterprises on a larger scale involving substantial capital. The majority of the shtetl population lived in poverty, where the major problem was to earn enough during the week in order to be able to buy a chicken or a fish for Sabbath, or to save up enough money for Passover *matzot*. To make a living the shtetl Jew tried his hand at anything and often at a number of things. Trades and occupations could vary with the season, as well as with a special opportunity encountered at the marketplace. Men and women, old and young, were daily involved in the difficult task of *parnose* ("livelihood"). Often women and children remained in charge of the stall or the store, while men traveled in the area looking for bargains or peddling city wares.

The market was the area where the shtetl came in direct contact with the *goyim*, whose life patterns were alien and often hostile to the shtetl mores. The emphasis was considered by Jews to be on intellect, on a sense of moderation, on cultivation of peace, and on goal-directed activities within the framework of a tightly knit family and community. Among the *goyim*, the shtetl Jew saw the emphasis on the body, excess, blind instinct, sexual life, and physical force. For the Jews human power was in the mind and in the word, while for the *goyim* it appeared expressed in muscles and violence. The underlying feeling of the shtetl Jew in all transactions with the *goyim* was the conviction that no matter how friendly and neighborly the interaction might be, he was never sure that it would not end in bloodshed and death. The feeling was amply supported by experiences of riots, pogroms, and massacres, which often began at the marketplace and spread to homes and synagogues.

Dissolution of the Shtetl

The social, political, and economic forces in the 19th and 20th centuries eroded the patterns of life which had evolved in the shtel. Pogroms and persecutions, economic depressions and political revolutions caused mass migrations of Jews to larger cities in Europe and across the ocean to the United States. Eventually Hitler and the "final solution" brought death to millions of Jews in Eastern and Western Europe. The physical existence of the shtetl ended in the gas chambers and concentration camps of the Third Reich. However, despite the violent end of the shtetl community and of its life style, much of its influence has survived in Israel and in the Americas (e.g., U.S., Canada, Mexico, and Argentina). The children of the shtetl parents – immigrants and survivors of ghettos and concentration camps – became carriers of values shaped in the shtetl, to be reflected in behavior patterns and social attitudes as well as in the art and literature of Israel and of American Jews. The shtetl values are reflected in the novels of American Jewish writers such as Bernard Malamud, as much as in the classic portrayals of shtetl life by Shalom Aleichem or the paintings of Marc Chagall.

[Mark Zborowski]

Lives and Roles of Women

Gender hierarchies in the shtetl ascribed the mundane affairs of the world to women and lofty spiritual and religious pursuits to men. These expectations, perhaps more ideal than real, shaped women's spirituality, family life, economic activities, education, and political choices.

In response to the exclusion of women from arenas of public worship and study, "female variants" of Judaism emerged. Instead of the obligatory Hebrew prayers in the synagogue, women recited Yiddish prayers (**tkhines*) at home, which addressed everyday concerns. They also observed the three women's commandments: namely, **ḥallah*, **niddah*, and *candle lighting on the eve of the Sabbath and holidays. At social gatherings or in private, women read homilies (*Tsenerene*) or ethical books (*Lev Tov*, "A Good Heart," and *Brantshpigl*, "Burning Mirror") and pious tales (*Mayse Bukh*). Their models of piety were the biblical matriarchs, whom women invoked to intercede on their behalf. They also resorted to female leaders in the community for guidance and assistance; these might include the **rebbetzin* (rabbi's wife), *zogerke* (reader of prayers in their section of the synagogue), *gabete* (pious woman who oversaw public charity), and *klogerns* (women hired to wail at burials). Women's spirituality, though different from men's, remained strictly within male-determined religious norms.

The division of roles also reflected the value of the spiritual over the material. An inverted structure of work developed in the shtetl, which allocated the task of breadwinning to women in order to allow their husbands to study. While most couples shared economic responsibility, the cultural ideal dictated that a greater proportion of the burden fell on women. Wives of rabbinic scholars who studied at a distant yeshivah or ḥasidic women whose husbands spent their time in a *shtibl* or rebbe's home, often assumed the entire load. The primary site of female economic activity was the marketplace, where women ran small shops, peddled food products and household goods, and engaged in petty trade. In addition, women were active in the tobacco and alcohol trades. With the advent of industrialization in Russia in the late 19th century, women joined the workforce in handicrafts and small manufacturing. Notably, women in the general population were also highly active in the shtetl economy; hence, female work was not a unique feature of Jewish life.

Women's dominant role in the household economy extended to family relations. In many households, a matriarchal structure prevailed. The *Haskalah (Jewish enlightenment) movement in Eastern Europe attacked this gender role reversal (that is, a subservient husband and dominant wife) and blamed the inverse work structure for this phenomenon. Satires like *The Brief Travels of Benjamin the Third* (1878) by S.Y. *Abramovich (Mendele Mokher Seforim) focused on the degrading feminization of men and moral decline of "masculine women." In this particular novel, an emasculated husband runs away from his wife, "who wears the pants in the house," in search of the ten lost tribes. D. Biale suggested that the *maskilim*'s rebellion against matriarchal power may have stemmed from an animosity toward their mothers-in-law, who dominated their adolescent marriages (*Eros and the Jews*, 1992).

Jewish women also played a defining role in the socialization of their children, particularly daughters who remained in their care until they married. Given the high birthrate in Eastern Europe, Jewish women were pregnant during most of their childbearing years. Prolonged breastfeeding reduced fertility to some extent but birth control was fairly primitive and inaccessible. Births usually took place at home with the assistance of a midwife. Women hung amulets on the wall and recited prayers to protect newborn infants from evil spirits. Images of strong mothers and grandmothers who supported their families and arranged matches for all the children are common in the memoir literature.

Despite their power in the domestic sphere, women were vulnerable and became increasingly powerless in matters of divorce. This was due in part to Jewish law, which empowered men to dissolve marriages unilaterally. In the Czarist empire, where Jewish divorce rates were extraordinarily high, the childless woman, *moredet* (rebellious wife), and other "undesirable" wives were especially prone to divorce against their will. Moreover, a decline in rabbinic authority meant that women who sought to secure a divorce from a recalcitrant husband for wife beating or other reasons were usually unsuccessful. In desperation, some women turned to state courts to enforce a rabbi's verdict or to overturn an unjust ruling.

A gendered system of education was another product of shtetl life. I. Parush argues that because rabbinic authorities devoted all their energies to male religious learning, they neglected the education of women. During the 19th century, this "benefit of marginality" allowed women to acquire secular culture with greater ease. While some women remained illiterate, a large segment of Jewish women learned to read in Yiddish; this group was the first to read popular literature (often simplistic, sentimental chapbooks) at their own leisure. Upper-class daughters of Orthodox families even studied foreign languages and literature with governesses and private tutors. "Reading women," who experienced greater exposure to modern values, in turn served as agents of acculturation at home. Starting in the 1860s, Jewish girls flocked to the new state and private schools throughout the Russian empire; some even pursued higher education as *kursistki* (auditors). Similar trends took place in the Austro-Hungarian Empire, where secular education had been introduced even earlier.

"Seductive secularization" gradually led to ruptures within traditional society well into the first three decades of the 20th century. The most extreme form of rejection was conversion to Christianity and marriage with Christian partners; not surprisingly, women constituted a disproportionate number of Jewish converts in the late 19th century. Another venue of rebellion was to join a revolutionary movement. Women participated actively in the Bund, various branches of the Zionist movement, as well as general Russian and Polish socialist groups.

On the eve of World War II, women in the shtetl remained the most traditional constituency of European Jewry, despite the onslaught of modernity and change; this was due in part to the migration of more acculturated families to urban centers or abroad, in part to the resilience of old customs and communal values.

[ChaeRan Freeze (2nd ed.)]

BIBLIOGRAPHY: M. Zborowski and E. Herzog, *Life is with People* (1955); Dubnow, Hist Russ; L. Finkelstein (ed.), *The Jews: Their History, Culture and Religion*, 2 vols. (1949); Central Yiddish Culture Organizations, *The Jewish People, Past and Present*, 2 vols. (1946–48); A.J. Heschel, *The Earth is the Lord's: The Inner World of the Jew in East Europe* (1950); I. Abrahams, *Jewish Life in the Middle Ages* (1932); I. Levitats, *The Jewish Community in Russia, 1772–1844* (1943); M.

Samuel, *The World of Sholom Aleichem* (1943); U. Weinreich, *College Yiddish: An Introduction to the Yiddish Language and to Jewish Life and Culture* (1949); M. Zborowski, in: *Harvard Educational Review*, 19 (1949), 97–109; idem, in: *Social Forces*, 29 (1951), 351–64; idem and R. Landes, in: *Psychiatry*, 23 (1950), 447–64; A. Ain, in: *YIVO Annual of Jewish Social Science*, 4 (1949), 86–114; J. Lestschinsky, *Oyfn Rand fun Opgrunt* (1947). **ADD. BIBLIOGRAPHY:** C. Freeze, *Jewish Marriage and Divorce in Imperial Russia* (2002); P.E. Hyman, *Gender and Assimilation in Modern Jewish History* (1995), 50–92; I. Parush; *Reading Jewish Women* (2004); S.S.Weinberg, *The World of Our Mothers* (1988); C. Weissler, *Voices of the Matriarchs* (1998).

SHTIF, NOKHEM (pseudonym **Bal-Dimyen**; 1879–1933), Yiddish linguist, literary historian, author, and political leader. Born in Rovno, Volhynia, Shtif early became active in Jewish affairs: as a Zionist, member of the Jewish self-defense organization *Zelbshuts* during the pogroms in 1903, founder of a transitional Jewish socialist group (*Vozrozhdenie*, "Renaissance"), founder of the Sejmist Party (1906, part of the Socialist Territorialist movement), and founder of the revived *Folkspartey* (Jewish Democratic Party) in 1917. He became immersed in the study of older Yiddish literature as well as literary criticism. After settling in Berlin (1922), he was the main initiator and (together with M. *Weinreich, Z. *Rejzen, E. *Tcherikover, and others) a founder in 1925 of the Yiddish Scientific Institute, *YIVO, and published the first booklet on the aims of YIVO, *Vegn a Yidishn Akademishn Institut* ("On a Yiddish Academic Institute," 1924).

From 1926, after returning to Kiev where he had studied at the Polytechnic University (1899–1903), Shtif directed the linguistic section of the Institute for Yiddish Proletarian Culture and edited its periodical *Di Yidishe Shprakh* ("The Yiddish Language"), where his article "*Di sotsyale diferentsiatsye in yidish*" ("The Social Differentiation of Yiddish," 1929) appeared. He argued that many words and forms derived from Hebrew and Aramaic had become redundant in the Soviet environment and should therefore be discarded and, to the extent possible, excluded from the process of lexical innovation.

Among the numerous books and studies which he authored on Yiddish stylistic, orthographical, grammatical, dialectal, historical, and literary topics, are his pioneering *Yidishe Stilistik* ("Yiddish Stylistics," 1930) and his Yiddish translations of works by *Dubnow and *Guedemann. His autobiography appeared in *YIVO Bleter* (5 (1933), 195–225).

BIBLIOGRAPHY: J. Anilowicz, in: *YIVO Bleter*, 5 (1933), 226–46, bibl.; D. Nusinov, in: *Oyfn Shprakhfront, Zamlung*, 2 (1934), 91–96, bibl.; Rejzen, Leksikon, 1 (1926), 331–9; M. Weinreich, in: *Tsukunft* (June 1933), 358. **ADD BIBLIOGRAPHY:** G. Estraikh, *Soviet Yiddish: Language Planning and Linguistic Development* (1999); I.N. Gottesman, *Defining the Yiddish Nation: The Jewish Folklorists of Poland* (2003); D. Shneer, *Yiddish and the Creation of Soviet Jewish Culture* (2004).

[Mordkhe Schaechter / Gennady Estraikh (2nd ed.)]

SHUA, ANA MARÍA (1951–), Argentinean author. Born in Buenos Aires, she received a degree in education, with a specialty in literature, from the Universidad de Buenos Aires. She has worked as a journalist, publicist, and scriptwriter. In 1967, at the age of 16, she published a volume of poetry titled *El sol y yo*. This first book earned her two of the most prestigious literary awards in Argentina and initiated her lifetime career as a writer. She continued to receive numerous awards for her nearly 30 books, including a Guggenheim Fellowship, which she received to write her novel *El libro de los recuerdos* (1994). One of her most successful books, translated into English as *The Book of Memories* (1998), relates the story of her family's history of immigration and process of assimilation into Argentinean society. Her work covers a broad spectrum of topics and genres, from children's literature to science fiction. The novel *La muerte como efecto secundario* (1997) is an excellent example of the latter. Her work has begun to garner a significant amount of criticism, and she is now considered to be one of the foremost of contemporary women writers in Argentina and Latin America. She was often invited to lecture at universities in the United States.

Jewish topics are not central to Shua's work, though they do appear frequently. The aforementioned *The Book of Memories* is her most careful examination of Jewish identity and issues. Common in many of her books is her use of humor as a mode of expression. This may be seen in her short stories, novels, or even in the popular *Risas y emociones de la comida judía* (1993), a humorous cookbook that contains recipes as well as comical anecdotes on Jewish culture and tradition. Her wit is also evident in the book *El marido argentino promedio* (1991), a compilation of essays that examines Jewish and Argentinean eccentricities in relation to gender; mainly how men and women view life in often radically different ways.

Shua is most widely recognized for the way in which she is able to create interesting and entertaining narratives that also contain social criticism, feminist issues, and a constant questioning of tradition, history, memory, and values.

[Darrell B. Lockhart (2nd ed.)]

SHUB, DAVID (1887–1973), journalist and sovietologist. Shub was born in Fastov, in the Kiev oblast, to religious parents who, however, sent him to a Russian school instead of the traditional *ḥeder*. At the age of 16, he became acquainted with the activities of the Jewish Labor *Bund. In the same year (1903), he moved to the United States, but two years later returned to Russia via Switzerland, where he met Lenin, who invited him to join the Bolshevik fraction. Shub declined, but in Russia was arrested for participating in revolutionary activities and sentenced to forced military service in Siberia. He escaped from Irkutsk in 1907 and made his way to the United States, where he remained for the rest of his life.

Shub devoted himself to journalism, writing mostly in Yiddish, but also in Russian and English, concentrating on Russian politics and literature and scarcely dealing with Jewish subjects, apart from his interest in the Bund. He became a leading sovietologist. He was a member of the staff of the **Jewish Daily Forward* from 1924, contributing to it until 1972. He was also a regular contributor to the Yiddish political monthly

Der Veker, of which he was editor during the years 1922–27. He joined the Mensheviks in 1903 and remained a right-wing Menshevik all his life, continuing his fight against Bolshevism to the end of his life, in the firm belief that Russia would finally abandon it and emerge as a Social Democratic republic.

Shub wrote one of the first biographies of Lenin (Yiddish, 1928; English, revised and enlarged edition, *Lenin, a Biography*, 1948). Among his other works are *Helden un Martirer* ("Heroes and Martyrs," Yiddish, 1939), on Russian martyrs in the struggle against Czarism; *Sotsyale Denker un Kemfer* ("Social Thinkers and Fighters," Yiddish, 1968); and *Politicheskiye Deyateli Rossii*, 1850–1928 ("Political Figures: Russia, 1850–1928," Russian, 1969) based on the former work and on the radio scripts which he broadcast for Radio Liberty to the U.S.S.R. Shub's memoirs, *Fum di Amolike Yoren* ("From Bygone Days"), were published in 1970.

[Elias Schulman]

SHUBERT, family of U.S. theater proprietors and producers. SAM (1875–1905), LEE (1876–1953), and JACOB J. (1877–1963) became Broadway's most powerful theatrical dynasty. They were born in Syracuse, New York, sons of a peddler. Their rise to theatrical prominence began early in life. They first took over the Grand Opera House in Syracuse, and then acquired touring companies and theaters in upstate New York. In 1900 the Shuberts produced "*Quo Vadis?*" at the Herald Square Theater, New York, and from then until the 1920s they engaged in fierce competition with Klaw and Erlanger, the major theatrical syndicate prior to the Shuberts' arrival. Sam died in a railroad disaster, but the other brothers continued to build their theatrical empire. By 1956, the family enterprise owned or controlled about half the legitimate theaters in the nation, including 17 on Broadway. Faced with a government anti-trust suit, the brothers agreed to sell twelve theaters, and sever their connection with theatrical booking business. The Shuberts produced more than 500 plays. Jacob was one of the early backers of Florenz *Ziegfeld, and among the stars the Shuberts introduced to American audiences were Al *Jolson, Eddie *Cantor, Marilyn Miller, Fanny Brice, Ray Bolger, and Bert Lahr. They had a reputation as aggressive businessmen, but also displayed a sentimental feeling for the theater. Speaking on the decline of the legitimate stage, Jacob once said late in his career: "When they tear down a theater it's like someone in the family dying."

BIBLIOGRAPHY: H. Taubman, *The Making of the American Theatre* (1965), index, s.v.; J. Stagg, *Brothers Shubert* (1969); A. Greene and J. Laurie, *Show Biz From Vaude to Video* (1951), index, s.v.

[Raphael Rothstein]

SHUBOW, JOSEPH SHALOM (1899–1969), U.S. rabbi. A Conservative rabbi who was both a leader of the American Zionist movement and the Boston Jewish community, Shubow tended to the needs of Jewish soldiers and displaced persons in war-torn Europe.

Shubow was born in Olita, Lithuania, and came to the United States with his family. He attended Boston Latin High School before heading to Harvard, where he received an A.B. (1920), A.M. (1921), and Ph.D. (1959). In 1925, while a student there, he and Max Rhoade founded Avukah, the national student Zionist organization.

From 1923 to 1935 Shubow served as the literary editor for the *Boston Jewish Advocate* and from 1924 to 1931 was a correspondent and features writer for the *Jewish Telegraphic Agency*. Following in the footsteps of his younger brother, Rabbi Leo Shubow, he entered the Jewish Institute of Religion to study under Rabbi Stephen S. *Wise. Upon his ordination in 1933, he was installed as the first rabbi of Temple B'nai Moshe in Brighton, Massachusetts. Under his spiritual leadership, which lasted until his death (excepting his wartime service), it became one of the most thriving congregations of Greater Boston.

A gifted orator, Shubow was outspoken in his ardor for Zionism and in his concern for world Jewry. In June 1934, at a Harvard alumni reunion, Shubow publicly confronted Ernst Hafstaengel, a German Nazi and close friend of Adolf Hitler's, who had been invited as a guest of honor. Shubow questioned Hafstaengel as to what he had meant by his statement that the Jewish problem would soon be restored to normal, asking, "Did you mean by extermination?" Shubow would again display his boldness when in the 1950s he famously confronted the antisemitic Jesuit priest Father Leonard Feeney on the Boston Common.

In 1943, Shubow, then in his early forties, voluntarily enlisted in the U.S. Army. He served as a chaplain in Europe with the Ninth Army through 1946, and traveled with a portable ark that could be strapped to a jeep. In March 1945, having accompanied the troops who had just crossed the Rhine into Germany, he led a Passover *seder* in Goebbels's castle – an event that was front-page news around the world. After the war, in both displaced-persons camps and Berlin, he played a major role in reuniting Jewish families as well as in rekindling the spark of life in the liberated prisoners. For his compassionate efforts he was awarded a Bronze Star.

The American Jewish community highly respected Shubow, and he rose to a number of influential positions, including the presidency of the New England Division of the American Jewish Congress (1941–1943), the presidency of the Greater Boston Rabbinical Association (1950–1953), and the vice presidency of the Zionist Organization of America (1961–1969). He also was a delegate to the 1936 World Jewish Congress in Geneva.

In addition to being a pulpit rabbi and an activist, Shubow, who knew at least seven languages, was also a scholar of Judaism who studied with Harry Austryn *Wolfson throughout his life. Though a Conservative rabbi, he was highly esteemed for his personal virtues by the modern Orthodox Rabbi Joseph B. *Soloveitchik and by the ḥasidic Bostoner Rebbe Levi Yitzchak *Horowitz. Shubow and Soloveitchik were very good friends, but despite their mutual admiration, in 1954 the Rav refused to take part in a testimonial dinner in Shubow's honor since the event would also be celebrating the dedication of a new temple-building that would have mixed seating. Similarly, although Soloveitchik delivered a moving eulogy at Shubow's funeral, he would not enter the temple building.

BIBLIOGRAPHY: S. Farber. "Reproach, Recognition and Respect: Rabbi Joseph B. Soloveitchik and Orthodoxy's Mid-Century Attitude Toward non-Orthodox Denominations," in: *American Jewish History*, 89:2 (June 2001), 193–214.

[Justin Shubow (2nd ed.)]

SHUCHAT, WILFRED G. (1920–), Canadian rabbi. Shuchat was born in Montreal, Canada, and received his B.A. from McGill University in 1941. In 1945, he was ordained at the *Jewish Theological Seminary, which awarded him an honorary D.D. in 1971. After serving as rabbi of Congregation Sons of Israel in Albany, New York (1944–45) and Temple Beth El in Buffalo, New York (1945–46), he was appointed assistant rabbi of Congregation Shaar Hashomayim in Montreal, becoming rabbi in 1948. In 1993, he retired and was elevated to emeritus. Under his leadership, the synagogue instituted such pioneering programs as home study groups and the Shaar Israel–Shabbat Yachad Project, which connected congregants to Israel through a series of family weekends featuring religious and educational programming, as well as dialogue with Reform and Orthodox invitees. At Shuchat's initiative, Shaar Hashomayim also became the founder and co-owner of Camp *Ramah in Utterson, Ontario.

In the larger Jewish community, Shuchat co-founded in 1947 the Board of Jewish Ministers of Greater Montreal (now the Board of Rabbis), comprising the city's English-speaking rabbis, and was instrumental in creating its chaplaincy committee. He also served as chairman of the Religious Welfare Committee of the Canadian Jewish Congress, where he headed a committee on marriage and family that established the Jewish Introduction Service for singles. In 1960, he set up the *De Sola Club, a kosher dining club in Montreal. He also taught Judaism at the School of Nursing at the Jewish General Hospital. In 1967, he was the creator and program chairman of the Pavilion of Judaism at Expo 67, which attracted three million visitors – the most popular exhibition of its kind.

In the Conservative movement, Shuchat served on the Committee on Law and Standards of the *Rabbinical Assembly, but he is better known for being one of the original founders of the Union for Traditional Judaism (UTJ), an organization that promotes traditional Jewish observance within the framework of Conservative Judaism. UTJ sponsors a rabbinical college; a speakers' bureau; a preparatory program for lay men and women who would like to spend a year in intense Torah study; and a Masters in Public Administration, which offers in-depth training to Jewish leaders of the future. Among the books Shuchat wrote are *The Gate of Heaven: The Story of Congregation Shaar Hashomayim in Montreal* (2000) and *The Creation According to Midrash Rabbah* (2002).

[Bezalel Gordon (2nd ed.)]

SHULAMMITE, THE (Heb. הַשּׁוּלַמִּית), a feminine name or title occurring only in Song of *Songs 7:1 [6:13]. The phonetic similarity of Shulammite to Shunammite led to the identification of the dancer of Song of Songs with *Abishag, "the maiden from *Shunem," who was brought to King David in his old age (I Kings 1:1–4). The word is most plausibly explained as being indeed equivalent to הַשּׁוּנַמִּית," the Shunammite woman" (I Kings 1:3; II Kings 4:25), used (on account of the aforementioned Abishag) as synonymous with "beautiful woman."

[Keith N. Schoville]

SHULḤAN ARUKH (Heb. שֻׁלְחָן עָרוּךְ; "the prepared table"), name of a code written by Joseph *Caro, similar in form to the *Arba'ah Turim* of *Jacob b. Asher, but more concise and without stating any sources. The book is in fact a halakhic synopsis of Caro's previous commentary on the *Turim*, the *Beit Yosef*. It is divided into the same four major sections as the former: *Oraḥ Ḥayyim*, concerning the daily commandments, Sabbaths, and the festivals; *Yoreh De'ah*, dealing with various subjects, such as dietary laws, interest, purity, and mourning; *Even ha-Ezer*, on marriage, divorce, and related topics; and *Ḥoshen Mishpat*, dealing with civil and criminal law. In his decisions Caro relied on Isaac *Alfasi, *Maimonides, and *Asher b. Jehiel, generally following any two in cases of disagreement. The book was first printed in Venice in 1565 and notwithstanding serious objections to the work, ultimately became accepted as the code of Jewish law par excellence after amendments had been added by Moses *Isserles and other commentaries of later halakhic authorities had been written on it.

Isserles' Commentary

The admiration of Isserles for Joseph Caro was unbounded, and he refers to him in the most glowing terms. He found, however, one serious drawback in the Shulḥan Arukh as an authoritative code. Caro had completely ignored the halakhic decisions and *minhagim* of Ashkenazi Jewry which had grown up in Germany and Poland since Asher b. Jehiel, who was one of Caro's major authorities. As a note on the aim of the *Darkhei Moshe* (see below) states: "Its purpose is to include the new laws which are found in the *Or Zaru'a*, the *Aguddah*, the *Sha'arei Dura*, the *Issur ve-Hetter*, the responsa of Israel *Bruna, of the *Maharal and R. Meir of Padua, and the regulations for divorce and *ḥaliẓah* of *Benjamin Ze'ev, as well as many other collections whose innovations are innumerable … as well as the decisive law according to the *minhag*, originally from France, which we follow."

ADJUSTMENT OF HALAKHAH FOR ASHKENAZIM. It was the combination of this profound respect for the author and the realization of this serious defect which dictated the approach of Isserles to the Shulḥan Arukh of Caro. He does not criticize or attack; he explains and supplements. At first he wrote his *Darkhei Moshe* to the *Beit Yosef*, for the purpose of adjusting the *halakhah* there to that prevalent in Ashkenazi Jewry; only then did he add to the "table" (*shulḥan*) his additions to which he gave the apt name *Mappah*, "the Tablecloth." Both these elements are prominent in the remarkably succinct addition to Caro's work. His clarification of the original work is as important as his amendments and additions, and helped considerably toward its acceptance. Where the *halakhah* of Caro differs from that accepted by the Ashkenazi Jews, Isserles gives the law or the custom as was prevalent in those communities, adding "our *minhag* is," or "thus is the *minhag*."

As a result of the *Mappah*, the Shulḥan Arukh, as supplemented by Isserles, reflected the *halakhah* and norms of religious practice as they had developed in Germany and Poland and was thus acceptable to the Ashkenazim, while the text of Caro was equally acceptable to the Sephardim. Between its acceptability and its complete acceptance, however, there was a long and complicated road.

Opposition to Acceptance of Shulḥan Arukh

The most strenuous opposition to the acceptance of the Shulḥan Arukh as the authoritative code of Jewish law was based on grounds of principle. Its most powerful opponent was Solomon *Luria. In his *Yam shel Shelomo* he expressed his vigorous opposition to all codes which laid down the law. Every code gives rise to commentaries and supercommentaries which have just the opposite effect intended by the authors of the original code. The only source for the determination of *halakhah* was the Talmud. A similar attitude was taken by *Ḥayyim b. Bezalel.

The acceptance of the Shulḥan Arukh was also threatened by another work, the masterly *Levush* of Mordecai *Jaffe. Based upon both the *Beit Yosef* and the Shulḥan Arukh, it aimed at combining both of them into one work, giving some of the arguments of the former and bringing into the latter, as had Isserles, the Ashkenazi *halakhah* and *minhag*.

Final Acceptance of Shulḥan Arukh

The final acceptance of the Shulḥan Arukh as the authoritative code accepted by world Jewry was due mainly to two 17th-century commentaries which have become standard, the *Turei Zahav* ("*Taz*") of *David b. Samuel ha-Levi on the whole of Shulḥan Arukh, and the *Siftei Kohen* ("*Shakh*") of *Shabbetai b. Meir ha-Kohen on *Ḥoshen Mishpat* and *Yoreh De'ah*. David ha-Levi gave his commentary to *Oraḥ Ḥayyim* the title *Magen David*. The place of the *Siftei Kohen* on *Oraḥ Ḥayyim* was taken by the *Magen Avraham* of Abraham Abele *Gombiner, and the combined name *Meginnei Ereẓ* was given to both commentaries. Of David ha-Levi's commentaries, only those to *Oraḥ Ḥayyim, Yoreh De'ah*, and *Even ha-Ezer*, however, had the good fortune to be printed together with the text, the commentary *Me'irot Einayim* of Joshua *Falk being printed with *Ḥoshen Mishpat*.

It was not only the comprehensive nature of these commentaries and the fact that in them they effectively answered all the criticisms which had been leveled against the Shulḥan Arukh which finally established Caro's code as the authoritative code. These commentaries were the first to regard the Shulḥan Arukh as a separate halakhic work, independent of the *Tur* or the *Beit Yosef*, and as a result of their eminence, the Shulḥan Arukh became the final authority to which one turned for the definitive *halakhah*. It was they who were mainly responsible for the preference given to the Shulḥan Arukh over the *Levush*, and the *halakhah* was accepted to be "in accordance with the Shulḥan Arukh."

Shulḥan Arukh in the Development of Halakhah

However, the Shulḥan Arukh in this sense can be said almost to bear the same relationship to the text of Caro and Isserles as does the Talmud to the Mishnah. The text marks a stage, albeit a decisive one, in the continuous development of the *halakhah*. The text of Caro, even with the additions of Isserles, has been subject to a continuous process of commentary and supercommentary which has continually modified its decisions and brought in all new halakhic problems which have subsequently arisen. An important addition to *Oraḥ Ḥayyim* was the *Sha'arei Teshuvah* of Ḥayyim Mordecai Margolis and his brother Ephraim Zalman, and to the other three sections, the *Pitḥei Teshuvah* of Ẓevi Hirsch Eisenstadt, incorporating the new decisions given in the responsa literature from the time of Caro to that of the authors. The extent of this adjustment can be seen in the *Oẓar ha-Posekim*, still in process of publication. For example the third volume which treats of the first 17 paragraphs of the 17th chapter of *Even ha-Ezer* has no less than 167 folio pages of commentary which give a digest of all the various commentaries and modifications, mainly from the responsa, to the original text of Caro. H.J. Chajes has estimated that in one way or another, from Isserles to his own time, early in the 20th century, 60 percent of the original text of Caro has been subject to some adjustment.

Only parts of the Shulḥan Arukh have been translated into English, e.g., some sections of *Ḥoshen Mishpat* and *Yoreh De'ah* by C.N. Denburg, 2 vols. (1954–55).

BIBLIOGRAPHY: Ch. Tchernowitz, *Toledot ha-Posekim*, 3 (1967); J. Rothschild and I. Ta-Shema (eds.), *Arba Me'ot Shanah Shulḥan Arukh-Catalog* (1965), incl. bibl.; *Maḥanayim*, 96 (1965), ed. by M. Ha-Kohen, issue devoted to Shulḥan Arukh.

[Louis Isaac Rabinowitz]

SHULIM, JOSEPH ISIDORE (1912–2005), U.S. historian. Born in New Haven, Connecticut, Shulim graduated from Brooklyn College in 1933 and received his Ph.D. from Columbia University. While doing his graduate work, he began teaching at Brooklyn College, where he remained throughout his career until his retirement in 1973, serving for a time as deputy chairman of the Department of History. He was later named professor emeritus of history. His field was the French Revolution and its impact upon the North Atlantic community. He also was a member of the CUNY Graduate School faculty and a founding member of CUNY's Retirees Chapter, serving for many years on the executive committee and as vice president. Shulim was also active in collegiate Jewish affairs.

His major publications were *The Old Dominion and Napoleon Bonaparte* (1952), *John Daly Burk: Irish Revolutionist and American Patriot* (1964), and *Liberty, Equality, and Fraternity: Studies on the Era of the French Revolution and Napoleon* (1990).

[Ruth Beloff (2nd ed.)]

SHULKLAPPER (Yid. "the knocker who calls to the synagogue"), in Ashkenazi countries one of the sextons of the synagogue. Although the office is found from the High Middle Ages, its development is best known from Eastern Europe, where the sexton awakened the people with hammer knocks for the morning prayers, saying: "Jews, this morning arise for the service of the Creator." The *shulklapper* also announced the beginning of the Sabbath and holidays. In the last week before Rosh Ha-Shanah and also during the Ten Days of Penitence between Rosh Ha-Shanah and the Day of Atonement, the *shulklapper* announced the *Seliḥot* service. The number of knocks and their order differed according to the occasion and local custom. Other tasks of the *shulklapper* were to summon people for communal meetings, banquets, and funerals.

[Natan Efrati]

SHULMAN, CHARLES E. (1901–1968), U.S. Reform rabbi. Shulman, born in Berdichev, Russia, was taken to the United States in 1910. He received rabbinic ordination at Hebrew Union College in 1927. After serving congregations in Wheeling, West Virginia (1927–31), and Glencoe, Illinois (1931–41), Shulman led a Riverdale, New York congregation (1947–68). From 1943 to 1946 he was a chaplain in the U.S. Navy. Shulman was an active Zionist and interested himself in the Urban League and other public causes.

A prolific writer, his books include *Problems of the Jews in the Contemporary World* (1934), *Europe's Conscience in Decline* (1939), and *What it Means to be a Jew* (1960). All are preoccupied with the regression of morality in the 20th century, as evidenced by Nazism and the spread of antisemitism, and by the emphasis in international relations on political expediency rather than considerations of morality.

[Sefton D. Temkin]

SHULMAN, HARRY (1903–1955), U.S. lawyer and dean of Yale Law School. Shulman was born in Krugloye, Russia, and taken to the U.S. in 1912. From 1929 to 1930 he served as law clerk to Justice *Brandeis. He was special counsel to the U.S. Railroad Retirement Board during 1934–36. Shulman became professor of law at Yale in 1940, and shortly before his death was named dean of the Yale Law School. Along with his academic career, Shulman was reporter for the American Law Institute's Restatement of the Law of Torts (1937–39), and a member of the U.S. Attorney General's Committee on Administrative Procedure (1941–42), actively contributing to the modernization and reform of the administrative process in the U.S. Shulman's most important professional accomplishment was his pioneering work as a labor arbitrator, and particularly his significant years of service (1943–55) as the umpire charged with the final interpretation of the labor contract between the Ford Motor Co. and the United Automobile Workers, C.I.O. In this role he established innovative processes for peaceful and legal solutions to labor-management conflicts and collective bargaining. Shulman believed that the labor arbitrator should not merely take an objective position in the construction of the terms of a labor contract but rather had to become an integral part of the collective bargaining process. His Holmes Lecture at Harvard Law School (1955), "Reason, Contract and Law in Labor Relations," was evaluated as a major contribution to the institutional development of collective bargaining. Shulman was a specialist in torts, federal jurisdiction, administrative law, and trade regulations, as well as in labor law. He wrote, with F. Frankfurter, *Cases on Federal Jurisdiction and Procedure* (1937); with F. James, Jr., *Cases on Torts* (1942); and with N.W. Chamberlain, *Cases on Labor Relations* (1949).

BIBLIOGRAPHY: F. Frankfurter, *Of Law and Men* (1956), 253–6.

[Julius J. Marcke]

SHULMAN, MAX (1919–1988), U.S. author and humorist. Shulman was known for his bright style and witty situations, and for his Dobie Gillis character. He was especially popular among college students in the 1950s and early 1960s. He also wrote for motion pictures. Among his works were *Barefoot Boy With Cheek* (1943), *Sleep Till Noon* (1949), and *Rally Round the Flag, Boys* (1957).

SHULMAN, MILTON (1913–2004), British drama critic. Born in Toronto, Canada, Milton Shulman became a lawyer and served as an officer in World War II. After the war he became drama critic of the London *Evening Standard*, keeping the position for 38 years (1953–91), longer than virtually anyone else in Fleet Street history, and was one of Britain's most influential theater critics. He was also the paper's literary editor. Shulman stated that he had attended 5,000 premieres in the course of his career but had never seen a truly great play, and described John Osborne's *Look Back in Anger* as "self-pitying snivel." He wrote the well-known *Defeat in the West: The Story of the German Defeat in World War Two* (1947) and an autobiography, *Marilyn, Hitler and Me* (1999). His daughter ALEXANDRA SHULMAN was editor of London *Vogue* from 1992.

[William D. Rubinstein (2nd ed.)]

SHULMAN, VICTOR (pseudonym of **Israel Ḥayyim Shadovsky**; 1876–1951), organizer and journalist of the *Bund. Born near Kovno, Lithuania, Shulman became in his youth a member of a mixed Zionist and Socialist youth circle in Kovno, of which *Weiter (Devenishsky), and Shemuel *Tchernowitz were also members. In 1899 he joined the Bund and became active in Gomel, helping to affiliate the local social-democratic organization with the Bund. In Gomel he published the periodical *Kamf*, to which J.H. *Brenner was a contributor. Between 1901 and 1905 he was imprisoned and sent to Siberia. He helped organize the escape of exiled revolutionaries, among them *Trotsky and Dzerzhinski. Between 1905 and 1909 he was alternately active in Vilna and Warsaw, attended the seventh convention of the Bund (Lemberg, 1906), wrote for the press, and was once more imprisoned and exiled. At the end of 1909 he escaped to Switzerland, where he participated in Bund activities. From 1914 he lived in Warsaw, headed the trade unions which had begun to function legally, and acted as secretary of the weekly *Lebns Fragen*. In independent Poland and throughout the early period of the Nazi occupation, he worked on the Bund daily *Folkstsaytung*. In 1941 he reached New York via Lithuania with a group of Bund activists. There he engaged in writing and editing, mainly a history of the Jewish press, particularly the Bundist. His works include: *Bletlekh Geshikhte fun der Yidisher Arbeiter Bavegung* (1929); and, on Jews in Poland during World War I, *Yidn in Poyln* (1946), 733–890.

BIBLIOGRAPHY: Rejzen, Leksikon, 4 (1929), s.v.; I.S. Hertz (ed.), *Doyres Bundistn*, 1 (1956), 283–97.

[Moshe Mishkinsky]

SHULNER, DORA (Schulner, née **Feldman**; 1889–1962), Yiddish writer. Born in 1889 in Radomyshl, Kiev province, she immigrated to the U.S. in 1924. Her first stories appeared in the *Frayhayt* in 1940, and her work continued to appear in the *Chicago Jewish Courier*, *Undzer Veg*, *Kalifornye Yidishe Shtime*, and periodicals published in Toronto, Winnipeg, and Mexico. Her first book, *Azoy Hot es Pasirt* ("Thus It Happened") was published in Chicago in 1942, followed by *Miltshin un Andere Dertseylungen* ("Miltshin and Other Stories," 1946), *Esther* (1949), and *Geshtaltn* ("Figures," 1956). Most important is her frank portrayal of Jewish women in the Russian Pale of Settlement immediately before, during, and after the Russian Revolution and Civil War.

BIBLIOGRAPHY: LNYL 8 (1981), 595; F. Forman et al. (eds.), *Found Treasures* (1994), 91, 123, 364; P. Hyman and D. Ofer (eds.), *Jewish Women: A Comprehensive Historical Encyclopedia* (CD-ROM, 2005).

[Vivian Felsen (2nd ed.)]

SHULSINGER, BEZALEL (Bezalel Odesser; c. 1779–c. 1873), *ḥazzan*. Born in Uman, Russia, Shulsinger received no formal musical education. Nothing is known about him before 1826 when he was already a renowned *ḥazzan* and held a post in Odessa. From 1860 he lived in Jerusalem. Shulsinger's compositions, characterized by their lyrical simplicity and easy-moving grace, were taken down by members of his choir, many of whom later became famous *ḥazzanim*. Thus Shulsinger's influence on synagogue music was far-reaching, and many of his compositions achieved widespread popularity. One of them is "*Attah Noten Yad*," which he is supposed to have sung to his pupils upon his departure for the Holy Land.

BIBLIOGRAPHY: Idelsohn, Music, 267, 298; idem, *Thesaurus of Hebrew Oriental Melodies*, 8 (1923), xix–xx, and nos. 237–9; H. Harris, *Toledot ha-Neginah ve-ha-Ḥazzanut be-Yisrael* (1950), 396–9.

[David M.L. Olivestone]

SHULTZ, SAMUEL (1865–1917), Canadian jurist. Born in Victoria, British Columbia (B.C.), Shultz was the grandson of Judah P. Davies, one of the city's most important Jewish pioneers. He received a B.A. from the University of Toronto in 1888 and went on to earn a law degree. Returning to British Columbia in 1893, Shultz established a legal practice in Victoria and was for a time the vice president of Temple Emanuel. An avid sportsman, journalist, and musician, he was also a charter member of the Native Sons of B.C. and the Connaught Masonic Order. Shultz relocated to Vancouver in 1902, where he married in 1904, and in 1909–10 served a term as an alderman for North Vancouver and three terms as the president of the North Vancouver Conservative Association. In 1914 he was named to the Vancouver County Court, becoming the first Jewish judge in Canada and earning a high reputation for fairness and knowledge of the law. As an outspoken advocate of Jewish rights and a frequent contributor to discussions of public affairs and religious understanding, Shultz was also the founding president of the Vancouver B'nai B'rith lodge and the Vancouver Jewish community's first delegate to the national Zionist convention in 1917, where he was named to the board. He died suddenly several months later at the age of 52.

[Barbara Schober (2nd ed.)]

SHULVASS (Szulwas), MOSES AVIGDOR (1909–1988), scholar and educator. Born in Plonsk, Poland, Shulvass studied in Berlin. He lived in Ereẓ Israel from 1938 to 1948 and then immigrated to the United States, where he eventually became professor of Jewish history at Spertus College of Jewish Studies in Chicago.

His publications in many languages include historical studies on Italian Jewry. Of special interest are his books *Roma ve-Yerushalayim* ("Rome and Jerusalem," 1945); *Ḥayyei ha-Yehudim be-Italyah bi-Tekufat ha-Renaissance* ("Jewish Life in Renaissance Italy," 1955); and his biographical sketch of Samuel David *Luzzatto with documentary supporting material, *Pirkei Ḥayyim* (1951). He also published two volumes of essays on various aspects of Jewish history, *Bi-Ẓevat ha-Dorot* ("In the Grip of Generations," 1960) and *Between the Rhine and Bosphorus* (1964) as well as *Die Juden in Wuerzburg waehrend des Mittelalters* (1934). He also wrote *From East to West* (1971), *Jewish Culture in Eastern Europe* (1975), and *The History of the Jewish People* (1982).

BIBLIOGRAPHY: Kressel, Leksikon, 2 (1967), 889–90.

[Eisig Silberschlag]

SHUM, an abbreviation used in Jewish sources for the closely allied Rhine communities of *Speyer, *Worms, and *Mainz, based on the initial letters of the Hebrew names of the cities (שפירא, וורמש, מגנצא). Although there are legendary accounts of Jewish communities in the three cities in Roman times, it is probable that the first organized community of the three was founded in Mainz in the early tenth century. Settled communities followed soon after in Worms and later in Speyer; by the end of the 11th century each was well established. The municipal authorities were well disposed to the Jews, granting them economic rights and a high degree of autonomy. With the exception of a temporary expulsion from Mainz in 1012 and another disturbance there in 1084, Jews and gentiles lived largely at peace with one another. The Jews fulfilled a valuable role as traders and entrepreneurs, and maintained a high standard of living. Jewish cultural and religious life flowered first in Mainz, which soon became a leading Torah center. The existence of many small principalities combined with the absence of a central authority (unlike Babylonian influence on Spain) stimulated the growth of localism and jealous independence among the Rhine communities. R. Gershom b. Judah Me'or ha-Golah actively worked toward standardization and federation; his civil *takkanot* in particular are considered by L. Finkelstein to be of a constitutional nature. Scholars disagree about the source of some *takkanot* traditionally ascribed to R. Gershom and raise doubts as to whether he did indeed preside over gatherings of Jewish leaders; nevertheless, he undoubtedly laid the foundation for unified action among the three communities as well as other German communities associated with them.

In the generation that followed, the leadership of the Rhine communities passed to France, most specifically to *Rashi. However, while Rashi's influence was great in the Rhine cities where he had once studied, there is no evidence to support the view that he was the initiator of synodal legislation. During the course of the First Crusade (1096) there was coordinated action among the communities, in cooperation with their coreligionists in France, that sought in vain to avert the catastrophe. All of the Rhine communities suffered terribly at the hands of the crusaders but Mainz and Worms were particularly hard hit. The rebuilding period that followed reestablished both the economic prosperity of the communities and their standing as centers of learning. Effective joint action largely prevented further destruction in Germany during the Second Crusade (1146). In a *synod summoned in *Troyes in 1150 by Jacob b. Meir *Tam in order to consider the effects of the Second Crusade, the Rhine communities were ably represented by *Eliezer b. Nathan of Mainz and *Eliezer b. Samson of Cologne. The large number of participants at the conference attest the degree that the Rhine communities and those of France were prepared to coordinate their efforts, a development hastened, no doubt, by the tragedy and the challenge of the Crusades. Though the one ordinance that has been preserved refers to Jewish appeals to gentile courts and gentile officials (both problems of long standing), it is possible that other ordinances, now lost, were of more far-reaching practical importance. Another synod of a less representative nature was held in Troyes around 1160 without German representation. It is probable that the German communities held similar local conferences although there are few references to them in the sources. However, with the death of Jacob Tam and the deterioration of French Jewry at the end of the 12th and the beginning of the 13th century, leadership increasingly passed to Germany and particularly to Speyer, Worms, and Mainz. As early as 1196, in the wake of the Third Crusade, a synod was convoked at one of the *Shum* cities under the presidency of David b. Kalonymus. One of the vexing problems that Jewish law had long struggled with was the question of *yibbum* and *ḥaliẓah* (see *Levirate Marriage); the compromise that was reached was known thereafter in Jewish law as "*Takkanot Shum* in regard to *ḥaliẓah*." A new generation of creative scholars had arisen, including *Eleazar b. Judah of Worms (d. c. 1230), author of *Sefer Roke'aḥ*, Eliezer b. Joel ha-Levi, and *Simḥah b. Samuel of Speyer. They were to play a critical role in the three synods that followed at the beginning of the 13th century in which the allied *Shum* cities established their leadership positions within Ashkenazi Jewry; the decisions that were reached were to have a far-reaching effect on Jewish *autonomy during the centuries that followed.

The first of the synods, held some time before 1220, enacted a series of communal regulations known as *Takkanot Shum*. Among many other stipulations these provided that: Any Jew unjustly compelled to contribute to the treasury of a king or noble shall be aided by the rest of the community; no one shall divorce his wife without the consent of the three communities; books left in trust may not be seized by the community for taxes; and no Jew may accept religious office from gentile authorities. Because of their scope, the enactments had a major effect on the functioning of the Jewish community. A second synod held in Mainz in 1220 reenacted certain provisions and passed over others. Finally a third synod that took place in Speyer in 1223 synthesized the work of the prior two. Some years later another gathering in Speyer in 1250 provided that neither rabbi nor community could pronounce a *ḥerem* without the consent of the other. The pivotal role played by the *Shum* cities continued into the 14th century, and in fact a synodal conference was held in Mainz in 1306 to mobilize resources for the expelled French Jews, and another headed some time later by Ḥayyim b. Isaac Or *Zaru'a. However, the deteriorating position of the Jews in the *Shum* cities, particularly in the wake of the *Black Death persecutions of 1348/49, meant that the three together could no longer undertake the crucial responsibilities for western Jewry they had previously fulfilled. Nevertheless, each of the cities continued to make its unique contribution to Jewish life up to the period of the Holocaust.

See also the individual cities.

BIBLIOGRAPHY: E. Carlebach, *Die rechtlichen und sozialen Verhaeltnisse der juedischen Gemeinden Speyer, Worms und Mainz… bis zur Mitte des 14. Jahrhunderts* (1901); L. Rothschild, *Die Judengemeinden zu Mainz, Speyer und Worms von 1349–1438* (1904); F. Rosenthal, in: MGWJ, 46 (1902), 239–61; Aronius, Regesten, index; Baron, Community, index; Finkelstein, Middle Ages; *Monumenta Judaica, Handbuch* (1963), index; E. Roth, in: *Festschrift I.E. Lichtigfeld* (1964), 179–235; Germ Jud, 1 (1963); 2 (1968), index. **ADD. BIBLIOGRAPHY:** R. Barzen, in: *The Jews of Europe in the Middle Ages* (2004), 233–43.

[Alexander Shapiro and B. Mordechai Ansbacher]

SHUMIATCHER-HIRSCHBEIN, ESTHER (1899–1985), Yiddish poet. Born in Gomel, Belorussia, and emigrating with her family to Calgary, Canada, in 1911, she married Peretz *Hirschbein. Her poetry and two children's plays in verse reflect her many travels as well as political, natural, erotic, and (following the birth of her son, Omus, in 1934) maternal themes. After her husband's death she wrote poems of grief and mourning. Her poetry appeared in major Yiddish periodicals; her books were *In Tol* ("In the Valley," 1920); *Pasn Likht* ("Streaks of Light," 1925); *In Shoen fun Libshaft* ("In the Hours of Love," 1930); *Ale Tog* ("Every Day," 1939); *Lider* ("Poems," 1956). Although she continued to lecture and write, she published little from 1956 until her death, and was largely dependent on her family for support. Her works of 1934 and later were more highly regarded than her earlier writings.

BIBLIOGRAPHY: F. Jones, in: *Canadian Jewish Studies* 11 (2003), 15f; LNYL 8, 598; *100 Yor Yidishe un Hebreishe Literatur in Kanade*, 297f; LYLPF 4, 556f; B. Brennan, in: *Calgary Herald* (March 8–10, 1997).

[Faith Jones (2nd ed.)]

SHUNEM (Heb. שׁוּנֵם), city in the Jezreel Valley, at the base of the hill of Moreh. The first mention of it occurs in the list of cities conquered by Thutmosis III (no. 38; 15th century B.C.E.). In the Tell el-Amarna period (14th century B.C.E.), the city was destroyed by Labaia, the king of Shechem, and its fields were cultivated by the king of Meggido, using forced labor (el-Amarna Letter 248a, 250). In the Bible, it is described as a city in the territory of Issachar, together with Jezreel and Chesulloth (Josh. 19:18). The Philistines camped there before going to battle against Saul in Gilboa (I Sam. 28:4). Shunem was the birthplace of Abishag, David's companion in his old age (I Kings 1:3, 15; cf. Song 7:1). In 925 B.C.E. Shishak overran the city and it is mentioned in his list of conquered cities between Beth-Shean and Taanach (no. 28).

In the time of Eusebius, who places Shunem 5 mi. (8 km.) S. of Mt. Tabor (Onom. 158:11), the "house of Elisha" was shown to pilgrims there. In Crusader times, it was a benefice of the abbey of Mt. Tabor. The Jerusalem Talmud mentions R. Justa of Shunem, who lived in c. 400 C.E. (Shek. 1:1, 46a). The biblical site of Shunem is identified with the Muslim Arab village of Sūlim at the foot of the hill of Moreh, 3 mi. (5 km.) southeast of Afulah. Surface pottery on the ancient mound, situated northeast of the village, dates from the Middle Bronze Age to the Arab period. In 1968 the village had 725 inhabitants, increasing to 2,240 in 2002. Field crops and fruit orchards have been the main branches of farming.

BIBLIOGRAPHY: B. Mazar, *Toledot Ereẓ Yisrael* (1938), 144–45; Alt, in: PJB, 21 (1925), 35ff.; Abel, Geog, 2 (1938), 470–71; Aharoni, Land, index.

[Michael Avi-Yonah]

SHURER, HAIM (1895–1968), Hebrew journalist and editor. Born in Podolia, Shurer immigrated to Palestine in 1913. He worked in Galilee and Judea and was also a member of *Nahalal. From 1922 he was on the editorial board of *Ha-Po'el ha-Ẓa'ir and then became a member of the secretariat of the movement. Joining the editorial board of *Davar* in 1936, Shurer was editor in chief of the newspaper (1953–66), and his articles appeared in the press over several decades.

His books include: *Yosef Aharonowitz* (1938, 1962[2]); *Ha-Ḥayyal* (1946); *Im Nesi Yisrael* (1951); *Ba-Aliyyah ha-Sheniyyah* (1952); and *Kal va-Ḥomer* (1952). He edited: *Besarabyah* (1941); *Ha-Pogrom be-Kishinev* (with D. Vinitzki, 1963); and with E. Shoḥat, *Pirkei ha-Po'el ha-Ẓa'ir* (1935–39).

[Getzel Kressel]

SHUSHAN (Heb. שׁוּשַׁן or הַבִּירָה שׁוּשַׁן, Susa; "Palace of Shushan"; Akk. Šu-ša-an, Šu-(ú)-ši; Elamitic, Šu-šu-un; Gr. Σοῦσα), capital of *Elam and one of the capitals of the Persian Empire, present-day Qal' a-e-Shush, Iran, on the Shaur River (Elamitic, Ulai; Gr. Eululaios). The mound of Shushan contains an acropolis (450 × 250 m., 38 m. high), and a "royal city" with a keep (375–500 acres). Excavations on the site were begun by W.K. Loftus and W.F. Williams in 1851–52, continued by M. Dieulafoy (1884–86), and resumed in 1897 by J. de Morgan, followed by R. de Mecquenem and R. Ghirshman, on behalf of the French "mission" to Persia. The earliest remains belong to the Neolithic period of the fourth millennium; eight pottery styles were found there, the finest being Susa A., characterized by representations of stylized animals (Susa beaker, Louvre). About 3000 B.C.E., Shushan became the capital of Elam. Situated on the fringe of Mesopotamia, it was conquered by the Akkadians (when Puzur-Inshushinak was governor of Elam under Narâm-Sin, 2270–2234 B.C.E.) and then by Ur III (2106–2016 B.C.E.). Later the rulers of Elam captured Ur and exiled the last king Ibbi-Sin. In the Old Babylonian period the "grand regents" of Shushan paved the way to Elamite political power; in this period the Old Babylonian dialect of Shushan developed which influenced the Akkadian language. Legal documents of this period from Shushan illustrate the importance of Elamite-Akkadian legal institutions.

From 1350 to 1150 B.C.E. Shushan was the capital of a powerful Elamite kingdom; its kings plundered the cities of Mesopotamia and carried off the monuments of their kings (obelisk and statue of Manishtusu, victory stele of Narâm-Sin, dioritic head of Hammurapi, stele bearing the code of Hammurapi, boundary stones (*kudurru*) of the Kassite kings, etc. (all objects found in the excavations are in the Louvre)). Elamite art flourished during this period under the kings Untash-GAL (1234–1227), Shutruk-nahhunte (1207–1171), and Shilak-Inshushinak (1165–1151). The temples of the god Inshushinak and the goddess Ninhursag were decorated with reliefs and statues of lions of glazed clay. The bronze statue of Queen Napir-Asu, the wife of Untash-Huban (1234–1227 B.C.E.), is a masterpiece of Elamite art. The Elamites carried off the statue of Marduk from Babylon, a sacrilege avenged by Nebuchadnezzar I (1146–1123), who defeated them. Shushan was destroyed in 645 B.C.E. by the Assyrian king Ashurbanipal; the capture is represented on a relief at Nineveh. The city is shown walled, standing among palm groves and farms, with a fort on the banks of the adjoining river.

Shushan was captured by Cyrus of Persia, and was selected by Darius I as his winter residence and the starting point of the "royal road" to *Sardis. A building inscription of Darius lists the materials from which his palace in Shushan was built, including cedars from the Lebanon, and of the workmen, who included Ionians and Sardians. Darius' palace was built on the part of the mound facing the acropolis; it was destroyed by fire under Artaxerxes I (464–425 B.C.E.) and rebuilt by Artaxerxes II Mnemon (404–359 B.C.E.). The ruins of this palace include a dwelling house with three courts and an elaborate gate, as well as a throne hall (*apadāna*) with six rows of six columns. From these ruins the excavators removed the double bull capitals and the "Frieze of the Archers" in glazed brick, representing the Persian and Medean bodyguard of Darius. The biblical references (Dan. 8:2; cf. 11:45 where the *apadāna* is mentioned; Neh. 1:1 and above all the Scroll of *Esther) refer to Shushan as the residence of the kings of Persia.

The city was conquered by *Alexander in 330 B.C.E.; in 324 he arranged in Shushan a mass marriage of Macedonians with Asiatic women, to symbolize the concord of the peoples. Under the Seleucids and the Parthians, Shushan was a Greek polis (Seleukeia on the Eululaios), complete with archon, boule, and demos. Greek inscriptions and poems to Apollo and the goddess Nanaia extend back to the first century C.E. Shapur II (309–379 C.E.), the Sassanid king, destroyed Shushan because of a (Christian?) revolt and rebuilt it as Ērānshr-Shāpur. According to an old Pahlavi chronicle, Susa, like *Shushtar, was reestablished by the Jewish wife of the Sassanid ruler Yezdegerd I (399–420).

The city resisted the Arabs in 638 for a long time. It became deserted under Arab rule, although some people continued to live around the Nabi Danyal ("[Tomb of the] Prophet Daniel"), below the mound. This tomb, which was on the left side of the river where the Jewish quarter was situated, had caused so much jealousy among the Muslim inhabitants that in the time of the Seljuk sultan Sanjar (12th century), it was arranged, according to a Muslim source, that the coffin of Daniel be suspended from the bridge.

*Benjamin of Tudela (c. 1167) estimated the Jewish population at about 7,000 and mentioned 14 synagogues in the vicinity of the sepulcher of Daniel. The Jewish traveler *Pethahiah of Regensburg, however, found there about 10 years later only two Jews, a dyer and a weaver. In the early 19th century several thousand Jews lived in the vicinity. The city of Shushan was depicted on the east gate of the Jerusalem Temple, the so-called "Shushan Gate" (Mid. 1:3). The city is mentioned in Daniel 8:2. According to the Talmud, the eastern gate of the Holy Temple in Jerusalem was called Shusan (Meg. 2; see also Kel. 17:9; Mid. 1:3).

BIBLIOGRAPHY: Excavation reports published in 40 volumes of the *Mémoires de la Délégation en Perse* from 1900 onwards; V. Christian, in: Pauly-Wissowa's supplement 7 (1946), 1251–74; L. de Breton, in: *Iraq*, 19 (1957), 79–123; L.V. Berge, in: *Archéologie de l'Iran ancien* (1959), 71–83; R. Ghirshman, in: *Iranica antiqua*, 3 (1963), 145–53; idem, *Cinq campagnes de fouilles à Suse* (1952); IDB.

[Michael Avi-Yonah]

SHUSHTAR, also called **Sustar**, and by the Arabs **Tustar**, town situated in the southwest of Iran in the province of *Khuzistān near the river Kārun. There is a reference to Shushtari in the Babylonian Talmud (Sanh. 94a), which clearly differentiates it from another city called Shush, the latter being situated to the northwest of Shushtar. The Talmud says "Shush-Tar" means "more than Shush." Neubauer claims that it is possible that the talmudic reference is to Shushan. Obermeyer thinks that Shush, meaning "beautiful," is short for Shushan, and Shushtar means "more beautiful." However, Shush was the ancient capital of the Elamites, and later one of the four capitals of the Achaemenians which most probably was populated by Jews. The city was later destroyed and afterwards rebuilt near its ruins. According to local tradition, the coffin of the prophet Daniel was found in Shushtar and later on was brought to Shush. It should be said that the common name "Shushan ha-Birah" in Jewish sources is Shush (Susa in Greek sources) and not *Hamadan, as wrongly interpreted.

Shushtar entered Jewish history because of a very important and rich *Karaite family known as Tustaries. The head of the family, Esrail ben Ya'qub, and his three sons, Abul-Fazl, Yosef, and Sa'id, known as the Sahl family, became famous in Islamic history. Some members of the Tustari family founded important trade centers of textile in *Baghdad and in *Egypt. They most probably immigrated to *Cairo around 1020, where they became close political figures in the court of the *Fatimid Sultans. The Muslim geographers of the 14th century write about the beauty and the prosperity of the city, but no one mentions the existence of the Jewish community there. The city is not mentioned in the Chronicle of *Bābāi ben Lutf (17th century) nor in other known Jewish travelogues as a dwelling place of the Jews. But a 17th-century Armenian chronicler, Arakel, claims that Jews lived in Shushtar. Neumark reports that Jews had ceased to live in Shushtar some 30–40 years before his time (1884), which means about the middle of the 19th century. However, it is possible that some time before the 18th century, Shushtar was no longer a dwelling place for Jews, mainly because of persecutions. Curzon and Sykes both describe the character of the Shushtaris as "disagreeable and fanatical."

BIBLIOGRAPHY: Arakel of Tabriz, *Livre d'Histoires: Collection d'Historiens Arméniens*, transl. and ed. by M.I. Brosset, 1 (1874–76); G.N. Curzon, *Persia and the Persian Question* (1892), 2:363ff.; M. Gil, *Tustaries, Family and Sect* (1981); G. Le Strange, *The Lands of the Eastern Caliphates* (1905); A. Neubauer, *La Géographie du Talmud* (1888); J. Obermeyer, *Die Landschaft Babylonien in Zeitalter des Talmud und des Gaonats* (1929); E. Neumark, *Massa be-Ereẓ ha-Kedem*, ed. by Ya'ari (1947); P.M. Sykes, *Ten Thousand Miles in Persia* (1902), 252ff.

[Amnon Netzer (2nd ed.)]

SHUSTER, JOE (1914–1992), U.S. cartoonist. Joseph Shuster was born in Toronto, Ontario, Canada, the son of Jewish immigrants from Rotterdam and Kiev. As a boy, he worked at the *Toronto Star* but liked to sketch as a hobby. The fantasy world of the newspaper's color comics had a strong impact on him. The family moved to Cleveland, Ohio, when he was 10, and at 18 he met Jerry *Siegel, with whom he was to create Superman, the most famous and fabulous fictional superhero of the 20th century. When Superman first appeared, in 1938, its hero, mild-mannered Clark Kent, worked for *The Daily Star*, named by Shuster after his old employer in Toronto. When the comic strip received international distribution, the company permanently changed the newspaper's name to *The Daily Planet*. Superman's popularity helped establish comic books as a format and spawned a genre of costumed superheroes, from Spiderman to Wonder Woman to Captain Marvel. Superman became an industry unto himself. Faster than a speeding bullet, as he was described on the radio, the Man of Steel appeared in newspaper comics, animated cartoons, movie-theater serials, a television series, a Broadway musical, a novel, feature films, and a stream of franchised goods from lunch boxes and toys to bubble gum. In the 1970s alone, Superman sales exceeded $1 billion. Superman was reared as a normal American boy and grew up to become Clark Kent, but when danger loomed, he became the crusader for "Truth, Justice, and the American Way." He doffed his glasses, stripped to a blue bodysuit and red cape, and flew off, using X-ray vision and other powers to thwart the latest evil menace or global disaster. But Siegel and Shuster did not share in the money machine, having signed away their rights in 1938 for $130. After a series of bitter legal battles, both creators became destitute and even sold their old comic books as collectors' items worth thousands of dollars apiece. Shuster, partly blind and unemployed, lived in a very modest apartment in Queens, N.Y. Finally, Siegel and Shuster were granted $35,000 a year from the publisher of Superman, DC Comics, for the rest of their lives and were guaranteed that all comics, TV episodes, films, and other Superman references would state that the character was "created by Jerome Siegel and Joseph Shuster."

[Stewart Kampel (2nd ed.)]

SHUVAL, JUDITH (née **Tannenbaum**; 1926–), sociologist. Shuval was born in New York. She graduated from Hunter College, New York, where she was elected to Phi Beta Kappa, and received her doctorate in sociology from Harvard University in 1955. She also received the degree of Bachelor of Hebrew Letters from the Seminary College of Jewish Studies of the Jewish Theological Seminary, New York, in 1947. Emigrating to Israel in 1949, she was appointed project director and senior research associate at the Israel Institute of Applied Social Research, where she directed studies in the fields of housing, immigrant adjustment, medical sociology, ethnic relations, occupational sociology, urban settlement, and sociology of nursing. From 1955 to 1956 she was UNESCO advisor in social research at the Institute, on immigrant adjustment. From 1955 she was a member of the Department of Sociology at the Hebrew University of Jerusalem. In 1972 she was appointed associate professor in sociology at the Hebrew University and in 1979 professor of medical sociology. In 1991 she was appointed the Louis and Pearl Rose Chair in Medical Sociology at the Hebrew University. Subsequently she became the director of the medical sociology program. She was a fellow of the American Sociological Association and treasurer of the Israel Sociological Society, in which she served as a chairwoman. She contributed extensively to scientific journals. Her major fields of interest were health and migration, ethnic relations, and sociology of health.

Among her major works are *Immigrants on the Threshold* (1963), a sociological study of immigration to Israel during the first years of the state, *Social Functions of Medical Practice* (with A. Antonovsky and A.M. Davies, 1970), *The Dynamics of Transition: Entering Medicine* (1980), *Newcomers and Colleagues* (1983), *Social Dimensions of Health: The Israeli Experience* (1992), *Immigrant Physicians: Former Soviet Doctors in Israel, Canada and the United States* (with J.H. Bernstein, 1997), *Immigration to Israel: Sociological Perspectives* (edited with E. Leshem, 1998), and *Social Structure and Health in Israel* (with O. Anson, 2000). She was awarded the Israel Prize for social sciences in 1965. In 1981 she was awarded the Israel Gerontological Society prize for research in social gerontology.

[Shaked Gilboa (2nd ed.)]

SHVADRON, SHALOM MORDECAI BEN MOSES (1835–1911), Galician rabbi. He was born in Zolochev. Assiduous in his studies and possessing a phenomenal memory, he was, at the age of 16, familiar with the whole Talmud. He was ordained by J.S. *Nathanson and Moses Kluger, who did not usually ordain rabbis. After his marriage, he engaged in business, mainly in the timber trade, but in 1866 lost his fortune. Although offered important positions, he steadfastly refused to accept them, contenting himself with the rabbinate of small communities. The first was Potok, but finally he became rabbi of Brezen and was henceforth known as the "Rabbi of Brezen" or the "Maharsham" (the initials of **M**orenu **ha**-**R**av **Sh**alom **M**ordecai) from the title of his volume of responsa. His fame was much greater than the positions he held. He exercised firm control and the civil authorities used to transfer to him cases in which Jews were involved. He was a modest and friendly man. Consulted by some of the greatest scholars, he always used to answer his questioners without delay. Shvadron is best known for his responsa, four volumes of which appeared during his lifetime and three posthumously. These were accepted as authoritative and as essential for dealing with the practical problems of the time. They are distinguished by the painstaking care and clarity with which he analyzed the problem and quoted all the talmudic sources and commentaries, finally reaching a definite decision, by the simplicity of his style, by his anxiety to adduce every consideration that would enable him to reach a lenient decision while keeping strictly to the *halakhah*, and by his readiness to accept responsibility for his decisions.

Among his other works are *Gillui Da'at* on the Shulḥan Arukh, *Yoreh De'ah* (2 vols., 1913–26), and *Oraḥ Ḥayyim* (1920); *Da'at Torah* (1891) on the laws of *sheḥitah; Darkhei Shalom* (1929), a methodology of the Talmud and *posekim; Haggahot Maharsham* (1932) on the Talmud; *Mishpat Shalom* (1871) on the Shulḥan Arukh *Ḥoshen Mishpat*; and *Tekhelet Mordekhai* on the Pentateuch (1913).

BIBLIOGRAPHY: Bromberg, in: *Sinai*, 32 (1952/53), 295–9; O. Feuchtwanger, *Righteous Lives* (1965), 94–97.

[Mordechai Hacohen]

SHWED, GIL (1968–), founder, chairman, and CEO of Check Point Software Technologies. Shwed is considered the prodigy of Israeli high-tech. He began his programming career at the age of 12 in a company that dealt with artificial intelligence. Later he took courses at the Hebrew University of Jerusalem while still in high school. In the army he served in an Intelligence unit responsible for electronic data gathering. In 1993, at the age of 25, he developed, together with Check Point's two co-founders, the first firewall, the company's well-known security software product. In the following years, he led Check Point to global leadership in both the firewall and VPN markets, making Check Point a giant in the Internet security industry. Shwed has received numerous prizes and honors for his individual achievements and industrial contributions, including the Academy of Achievement's Golden Plate Award for his innovative contribution to business and technology in 2002; the World Economic Forum's Global Leader for Tomorrow Award for his commitment to public affairs and leadership in areas beyond immediate professional interests in 2003; and an honorary doctor of science from Israel's Technion in 2004.

WEBSITE: www.checkpoint.com.

[Shaked Gilboa (2nd ed.)

SIAULIAI (Ger. **Schaulen**; Rus. **Shavli**; Yid. **Shavl**), city in N. Lithuania. The Jewish settlement dates from the 17th century; in 1701 Jews received authorization to erect a synagogue. Trade with Germany and the establishment of a railway line fostered growth and economic prosperity, and by 1847 there were 2,565 Jews in the town. They built large factories, among them the tannery of Ḥayyim Frenkl (1879). In 1902 Jews numbered 9,847 (75% of the population); by 1914 this number had increased to 12,000. In 1915 the majority of Jews were, however, exiled to the interior of Russia. In independent Lithuania, Siauliai was the second largest city, and its Jewish community, numbering 8,000 in 1939, the second largest in the country. The economic and social influence of the Jews was widespread; they formed the majority of manufacturers of leather products – the shoe factory, Batas, was Jewish-owned – and were involved in the iron and chemical industries, as well as forming a large part of the force of clerks, laborers, and craftsmen of the town. The position of vice mayor of the town was held by a Jew. The Jewish community was outstanding for its organizational achievements and for its cultural and social institutions. The community supported a religious secondary school (Yavneh), a Hebrew secondary school, an elementary school, and a kindergarten, as well as several Yiddish schools. There were 15 synagogues, a yeshivah, and two libraries. Prominent scholars officiated there, among them Isaac Eisik Ḥaver (*Wildmann) and Joseph Zechariah *Stern. The kabbalist Solomon b. Ḥayyim *Eliashov was a resident of Siauliai. Before the arrival of the Germans in World War II, several hundred Jews had fled to Russia. Of those who chose to remain, several thousand were massacred by Lithuanians as well as Germans (mainly in the forests of Kuzhi) during the war. About 5,000 Jews (including 1,500 from surrounding areas) were interned in a ghetto. There were frequent *Aktionen* until July 1944, when the retreating Germans transferred those remaining alive to the concentration camps of Stutthof and Dachau, in Germany. Of the total number of Jews interned only a few hundred managed by various means to escape death. The remaining synagogue was closed by the authorities in 1960; the Jewish cemetery was destroyed and Jews were allowed to remove the bones of the deceased to the Vilna cemetery. In the late 1960s the Jewish population was estimated at about 4,000; in the 1990s Siauliai had a small Jewish community.

BIBLIOGRAPHY: A. Yerushalmi, *Pinkas Shavli* (1958); *Lite*, 1 (1951), 942–70, 1767–831.

[Dov Levin]

SIBERIA (Rus. **Sibir**), Asiatic part of the Russian Federation, extending from the Urals in the west to the Pacific in the east. The first Jews went to Siberia from Lithuanian towns captured by the Russians in the Russo-Polish war (1632–34); they were exiled there together with other prisoners. In 1659 a number of Jewish residents in the "German quarter" of Moscow were exiled to Siberia. At the beginning of the 19th century Jews were among the convicts sent to Siberia for settlement or hard labor. The latter founded the first Jewish communities there, e.g., in *Omsk, *Tomsk, Tobolsk, Kuibyshev (Kainsk) in western Siberia, and Kansk and Nizhneudinsk in eastern Siberia.

Since Siberia was outside the *Pale of Settlement, convicts continued to constitute the main Jewish element settling there throughout the 19th century. Due to the scarcity of Jewish women in Siberia at the beginning of the 19th century, Jews were allowed in 1817 to buy Kalmyk women, to make proselytes of them and marry them. In 1826 Jews were forbidden to settle in the border district of Siberia between the area of Russian settlement and that of the natives; in 1827 the husbands of Jewish women exiled to Siberia were forbidden to join them; and in 1836 Jewish women joining their exiled husbands were forbidden to take their male children with them. In 1834 Jews whose sentences had expired, as well as members of their families, were obliged to apply for special permission from the minister of finance to join local merchant guilds, in order to prevent "an undue multiplication of

Jews among the merchant class, and consequent damage to the native population."

In 1836 the Russian government, within the framework of its program to increase the number of Jews engaged in agricultural work, set aside 15,154 desyatins (409,138 acres) of land in western Siberia for Jewish agricultural settlement. In January 1837 *Nicholas I ordered the curtailment of Jewish settlement in Siberia: by this time, however, several hundred Jews had already arrived to participate in the project. On May 15, 1837, ordinances were issued "to prevent the immigration of Jews to Siberia, and to decrease the number of Jews settled there"; these decrees specified, inter alia, that only Jewish convicts aged 40 and over could be exiled to Siberia, and that even such settlers should be allowed in the outlying districts of the country only (in the Yakutsk district and on the further side of the Baikal). The ordinances further required that the sons of exiles (i.e., those under 18) be handed over as *Cantonists, as well as sons of exiles who had completed their terms of sentence; their descendants were also to be handed over as Cantonists, or to be removed to the Pale of Settlement before reaching the age of 16.

In 1857, under Czar Alexander II, Jews in Siberia were permitted to join merchant guilds on the basis of the existing general instructions regarding this matter, and in 1860 the Siberian Jewish children were permitted to remain with their parents. The same proclamation, however, forbade them to settle within 100 versts of the borders with neighboring countries. When after 1859 certain classes of Russian Jews were permitted to settle outside the Pale of Settlement, some of them found their way to Siberia. During this period the Jewish communities of Siberia consolidated and the characteristics of the typical "Siberian Jew" emerged: similar in dress and language to his Russian neighbor, ignorant in Jewish learning, and negligent of the *mitzvot*; he nevertheless possessed warm Jewish sentiments and was attached to the Jewish people and religion. The last quarter of the 19th century saw the emergence of an intelligentsia among Siberian Jewry, a few of whose members were political exiles. Some of the latter devoted themselves to investigating the customs and languages of the indigenous peoples, e.g., V.G. *Bogoraz, V. *Jochelson, L. Sternberg, M. Krol, S. Chudnovsky, N. Geker, and I. *Shklovski.

Jews of Siberia played a prominent role in the economic development of the area, especially in the fur trade. Some Jews, like the *Guenzburg family of St. Petersburg, participated in the development of Siberian gold mining. In 1897 there were 34,477 Jews in Siberia (0.6% of the total population): 8,239 in the region of *Irkutsk, 7,696 in the region of Tomsk, 7,550 in the Trans-Baikal region, 5,730 in the Yenisei region, and 2,453 in the region of Tobolsk. Some 2,689 Siberian Jews (8.25%) were then engaged in agriculture, 9,161 (28.10%) in crafts and industry, 12,362 (37.92%) in trade, 1,906 (5.85%) in transport, and 1,051 (3.22%) in private and public clerical work and the liberal professions. In the 1890s the entry of Jews into Siberia and the rights of the Jews living there were further restricted. The revised edition of the passport rules published in 1890 proclaimed a total ban on Jewish immigration to Siberia, save for those who were sentenced to exile or hard labor there. This ban became the fundamental rule regarding Jewish entry into Siberia and served as a basis for further prohibitions. In 1891 it was interpreted as including also those Jews who had the right to settle outside the Pale, and this interpretation was finally authorized in 1899; at the same time, however, it was established that the prohibition did not extend to Jews who were already living in Siberia.

From this time Siberia was closed to all Jews, except those sentenced to hard labor or exile. In 1897 the same ban served as a basis for a new law prohibiting Siberian Jews (except for the descendants of soldiers who had served in the army during the reign of Nicholas I) from residing in any other place but that of their registration as permanent residents. This order spelled deportation for thousands of Jewish families who were not living in the place where they were registered; the practical difficulties involved in the transfer of thousands of families from place to place prevented its being carried out. Thousands of Siberian Jews, however, were then left completely at the mercy of the markedly hostile local administration, with the threat of deportation constantly hanging over their heads.

On the other hand, the attitude of the Christian population in general toward the Jews was sympathetic, as may be gauged, among other things, from the election of the Jewish exile Avigdor (Victor) *Mandelberg to the second *Duma (1907). During World War I thousands of Jewish refugees from the front lines reached Siberia and exercised a considerable influence on Jewish community life there: The number of Jewish educational institutions grew, and political parties (e.g., the *Bund, *Zionist Socialists, *Po'alei Zion) were established. After the 1917 Revolution a congress of Jewish community representatives from all Siberia and the Urals was held in Irkutsk (January 1919) and a national council of Siberian Jews was elected. Representatives of the Zionist movement, which had spread widely in Siberia in the first years of the 20th century and greatly intensified its activities after the revolution, exercised a decisive influence at the congress. Thus, the congress resolved, inter alia, "that the work of building Ereẓ Israel will be included among the activities of the Jewish communities in Siberia and the Urals." The national council was headed by M. *Novomeyski, then officiating as the chairman of the Zionist Federation.

Soviet Rule

With the establishment of Soviet rule in Siberia, however, Jewish communal, cultural, and national institutions were gradually destroyed. Many wealthy and middle-class Jews left, most of them for China and a few for Palestine. The majority of the Jewish refugees living in Siberia returned to their homes in Poland and Lithuania. In 1926 there were only 32,750 Jews: 9,083 in the region of Irkutsk, 5,505 in the region of Tomsk, 4,389 in the region of Omsk, 3,040 in the region of Krasnoyarsk, and 2,301 in the region of Novosibirsk. Some 28,972 Siberian Jews lived in towns and 3,778 in rural districts. In 1939 the number of Jews rose to 63,844 persons, most of them in Khabarovsk Krai (district) – 22,473, including 13,291 of the Jewish Autonomic region – Birobidzhan; Novosibirsk district (11,191); and Irkutsk district (8,504). Except in the Jewish Autonomous Region where the Jews constituted 18.57% of the population, the Jews were a small percentage of the total population, only 0.6% and 2%. Most Jews lived in the capitals of the districts. The Soviet rulers exiled thousands of Zionists from European Russia to the most outlying parts of Siberia. Among the exiles was the poet Ḥayyim *Lenski, who described life in the concentration camps and the scenery of Siberia in his poetry. In 1928 the Soviet government assigned an area in eastern Siberia to Jewish settlement, and in 1934 it was declared an Autonomous Jewish Region (see *Birobidzhan). During World War II large numbers of Jewish refugees from the areas occupied by the Germans reached Siberia, and some of them remained there after the war ended. According to the 1959 census there were 12,429 Jews in the Novosibirsk oblast, 9,458 in the Omsk oblast, 10,313 in the Irkutsk oblast, 2,691 in the Buryat-Mongol republic, 8,494 in the territory of Khabarovsk, and 14,269 in Birobidzhan. The census, which did not cover the whole of Siberia, registered a total of 57,654 Jews (i.e., those declaring themselves as Jews). Some 53,266 (92.4%) lived in towns; 9,970 (17.3%) declared Yiddish as their mother tongue (excluding Birobidzhan – only 4,373, or 10%). In Novosibirsk, which became the capital of Siberia, the Jewish population (with a synagogue and an old Jewish cemetery) numbered in the late 1960s about 25–30,000, consisting of a small nucleus of Siberian Jews who had been there from czarist times – and their descendants – and mostly of Jews who had been evacuated from the western Soviet Union during World War II. In 2002, 3,330 Jews remained in the Novosibirsk oblast and 14,579 in the entire Siberian district.

BIBLIOGRAPHY: M.A. Novomeysky, *My Siberian Life* (1956); Ben-Ami (A.L. Eliav), *Between Hammer and Sickle* (1965); A. Druyanow (ed.), in: *Reshummot*, 3 (1923), 549–51; Ẓ. Shimshi, *Zikhronot* (1938), 92–102; A. Mandelberg, *Me-Ḥayyai* (1942), 21–25, 45–82; A. Zenziper (Rafaeli), *Pa'amei ha Ge'ullah* (1951), 143; idem, *Be-Ma'avak li-Ge'ullah* (1956), 57–60, 189–98, 213–8; S. Kushnir, *Sadot va-Lev* (1962), 47–71; M. Elkin, *Kaybaler stepes* (1934); M. Mysh, in: *Voskhod*, 9:7 (1889), 1–18; 9:8 (1889), 1–21; idem, *Rukovodstvo k russkomu zakonodatelstvu o yevreyakh* (1890), 243–51; Halpern, in: *Voskhod*, 20:3 (1900), 3–17; M.A. Lozina-Lozinski, *Sistematicheskiy sbornik razyasneniy pravitelstvuyushchogo senata po delam o zhitelstve yevreyev* (1902), 545–78; G. Belkovski, *Russkoye zakonodatelstvo o yevreyakh v Sibiri* (1905); B.D. Brutzkus, *Professionalny sostav yevreyskago naseleniya Rossii* (1908), table no. 8; Yu. Ostrovski, *Sibirskiye yevrei* (1911); V. Voytinski and A. Gornstein, *Yevrei v Irkutske* (1915); N.N. (I. Syrkin), in: *Yevreyskaya Starina*, 8 (1915), 85–99; Neiman, *ibid.*, 381–5; Kleinman, in: *Yevreyskaya Letopis*, 3 (1924), 124–34; Kirzhnitz, in: *Sibirskaya Sovetskaya Entsiklopediya*, 1 (1929), 869–73.

[Yehuda Slutsky]

SIBIU (Hung. **Nagyszeben**; Ger. **Hermannstadt**), capital of Sibiu province, Transylvania, Romania; until the end of World War I part of Hungary. By the end of the 15th century some Jews had commercial or other connections with Sibiu. Permanent Jewish settlement began there after the restrictions in Hungary on Jewish residence were abolished in 1848; however, there is also information about Jews trying to establish themselves in Sibiu from the middle of the 17th century. There were 478 Jews living in Sibiu (about 3% of the total population) in 1850. A permanent *minyan* was organized in 1860, and organization of community institutions began in 1876. In 1868 the community declared itself Orthodox. The first synagogue was built in 1878; a second large, handsome synagogue was opened in 1890. In 1881 there was a case of blood *libel in Sibiu. The Jewish population numbered 1,307 (4% of the total) in 1890, and 1,310 in 1920. The Orthodox Ármin Horowitz (1869–1934) was the rabbi of the community from 1890. A Sephardi community was organized in 1923. Zionist activity in Sibiu commenced immediately after the first Zionist Congress and grew rapidly in the period between the two world wars. A Jewish school was founded in 1919. The community also supported a Hebrew nursery school. The community numbered 1,361 (1.2%) in 1941, and 2,020 in 1947. The majority of the Sibiu Jews were speakers of German, and only some of them learned Hungarian and Romanian (the latter mostly after World War I). During World War II the community's institutions were liquidated, and under Romanian-Fascist rule the Jews in Sibiu were persecuted and their communal property was confiscated. Early in the war the city served as a district mobilization center for forced labor among Jews and, from August 23, 1944, as a refugee center. There were about 125 Jews living in Sibiu in 1970. Friday night and holiday prayers were still held in the great synagogue.

BIBLIOGRAPHY: A. Horowitz, *Denkschrift der autonomen orthodoxen israelitischen Kultusgemeinde zu Sibiu* (1928); S. Yiẓḥaki, *Battei Sefer Yehudiyyim bi-Transilvania bein Shetei Milḥamot Olam* (1970), 172.

[Yehouda Marton / Paul Schveiger (2nd ed.)]

SIBONI (al-Sab'uni), family of rabbis in Salé, Morocco. The most prominent member, AARON, was rabbi in Salé in the mid-17th century. He edited Moses Albaz's kabbalistic prayer book *Heikhal ha-Kodesh* (Amsterdam, 1653) and, with Jacob *Sasportas, condemned and wrote against the Shabbateans, particularly for not observing fast days. Aaron spent some time in Amsterdam as an international merchant. One of his letters to Sasportas describes the expulsion of Jews from Oran by the Spanish on Passover 1669 and the subsequent transformation of the synagogue into a church. His sons JOSHUA and DAVID were rabbis in Salé in the late 17th century and wrote homilies, most of which are extant in manuscript. SHALOM, rabbi in Salé in about 1853, composed dirges (*kinot*) and prayers, which are also extant in manuscript.

BIBLIOGRAPHY: Y. Benaim, *Malkhei Rabbanan* (1931), 25, 79, 86, 105; Hirschberg, Afrikah, 2 (1966), 105, 112, 253–4.

SIBYL AND SIBYLLINE ORACLES. The sibyl was a Greek prophetess-figure, apparently of Oriental origin. The sibyl utters her predictions not on being consulted, like established oracles, but spontaneously, in ecstatic exclamations. She is believed to dwell in grottos, to wander through many countries and to live for 1,000 years. Originally conceived of as a single person, various sibyls are found later in different countries, some bearing individual names. From *Alexander Polyhistor (first century B.C.E.) comes the earliest mention of a sibyl named Sambethe or Sabbe, described as Babylonian or Hebrew. Sibylline oracles, in hexametric verses, circulated in Athens in the fifth century B.C.E.; from Alexander the Great's time, these sided with the oppressed peoples and predicted doom to the wicked rulers. A standard figure in these oracles was the hoped for Mighty King from the East, who would liberate the conquered, punish the oppressors, and inaugurate a period of welfare and peace. A combination of Babylonian astrology and Persian millenarian speculations was the basis for a firm belief in a predestined future. In Rome, Sibylline Books, deposited in the temple of Jupiter Capitolinus, were consulted at moments when the senate had to make critical decisions. However, when the Roman Empire came to rule over Asia, Oriental sibylline literature evolved into virulent anti-Roman propaganda. Doubtless the strong note of hope for final redemption induced the Jews to adapt the popular pattern of sibylline poetry to the needs of their national-religious propaganda (see below). Christians regarded the sibyl as a heathen prophetess predicting the coming of Jesus and integrated the Jewish sibylline poetry in a larger corpus of Christian oracles. The pagan sibyls and the prophets of Israel, as two kinds of messengers of Jesus advent, stand side by side in Michelangelo's paintings on the ceiling of the Sistine Chapel in Rome.

Books of Sibylline Oracles

Christian libraries have preserved two different collections of Sibylline Oracles, counted as books 1–8 and 11–14 respectively. The first of these collections was compiled by Christians about 500 C.E. and contains definitely Christian passages (e.g., 8:217–50), but it was composed much earlier and the oldest stratum is Jewish, with only occasional Christian additions. Scholars differ about the extent of this Jewish stratum, but it certainly includes books 3, 4 and most of 5. There are also considerable Jewish elements in the second, much later and inferior, collection; thus in 13:81 the Emperor Decius, persecutor of the Christians, figures as one of the good emperors – a fact that excludes Christian authorship.

The oldest and most interesting of the Jewish parts is book 3, in which the sibyl is presented as Noah's daughter-in-law, coming from Babylonia. This agrees with the tradition about the sibyl Sambethe. Indeed, the account of the oldest generations of mankind, though following the biblical narrative, is combined with motifs known from parallel Babylonian myths whose previous polytheistic character is sometimes still discernible. Even a piece of rationalized Greek mythology that, following a prevalent Hellenistic theory, makes Kronos and his brothers into kings of olden times, seems to have come down to the author via Babylonia.

It may seem strange that Church Fathers, in their ample quotations from the book, ascribe it to the oldest Greek sibyl. This may be due to the fact that the author incorporated in the work a rich collection of older Greek oracles, referring to many places throughout the Hellenistic world which were threatened with various natural or political catastrophes. But there is a marked difference between these stereotyped predictions of calamities and the Jewish sibyl's own oracles of disasters, which were always motivated by moral or religious considerations, in keeping with Israel's prophetic tradition. This genuine prophetic vein reaches its climax in the passage where the sibyl addresses the Greek nation (3:520ff.). Although the fictitious form of predicting a distant future is maintained here, it is clear that the sibylline poet is referring to the great disaster that befell Hellas in his own time, i.e., the middle of the second century B.C.E., when Greece was ravaged by the Roman legions. Here the poetry, too, reaches its highest standard. The Homeric assonances give the verses an evocative power, and the poet's sympathetic feeling for humiliated Hellas echoes in the repeated use of the designation "barbarian" for the cruel enemy. The same strong emotion also elicits biblical allusions; the words "one man chases a hundred warriors" evokes Deuteronomy 32:30, and "five a whole company," Leviticus 26:8. It is thus evident that the calamity has both a Greek and a Jewish significance for the poet. The latter becomes clear where the sibyl reproaches the Greeks for their cardinal sin, apostasy from the true God in favor of meaningless idolatry, introduced by haughty kings in olden times. The poet hopes that in their present agony the Greeks will find the only way of salvation, back to God Whom they once had known, presenting them with an ideal image of Israel, the people of "pious men" sitting around the sanctuary of the One God.

The sibyl's glorification of Israel is centered around three points: monotheism, sexual purity, and social justice: (1) strict Jewish adherence to the One God implies rejection of magic, astrology, and foretelling the future. In stressing this point, the poet may be opposing a Samaritan tendency, known from a fragment of Pseudo-Eupolemos who depicts Abraham as a wise astrologer; (2) sexual purity of the pious people is sharply contrasted with the vices of the gentile world, the most horrible of which is homosexual prostitution; (3) the stress laid on social justice as a Jewish characteristic is especially interesting. The author represents details of biblical law not as commands but as actual facts; thus he can say that the Jews use just weights and measures, do not remove their neighbor's landmark, and help the widows and the poor, "for God in heaven has given the earth to all men in common." The unique political situation of a sovereign Judea under Hasmonean kings confronting an enslaved Hellas lends specific shades to the picture of messianic times. The forthcoming last great onslaught of the heathen armies against God's sanctuary, repelled by divine miraculous intervention, is depicted on Jewish apocalyptical lines, but tinged by the sibylline tradition of the redeeming "Mighty King" from the East. The final life of bliss contains some individual elements unparalleled in messianic literature: "A great peace will spread all over the world. Kings will be friends with one another till the end of time.

Immortal God will place in the starry sky a law, common to all mankind" (755–9).

Outbursts of hatred against Rome cannot belong to the original text of book 3, which was composed at a time when Judea was on excellent terms with Rome. Indeed, close analysis has shown that they result from a very late recast of the text. A completely different situation, however, prevails in books 4 and 5 which are imbued with an uncompromising hatred for Rome. The reason is obvious: they were written after the destruction of the Temple by Titus. Book 4 regards the eruption of Vesuvius (79 C.E.) as a divine punishment for this crime. It can therefore be assumed with certainty that the book was written fairly soon after this eruption. Book 5 has a surprisingly favorable opinion of the emperor Hadrian, indicating that it was written before the outbreak of the Bar Kokhba War (132 C.E.). In these two books messianic hopes are not directed at an immediate future, but they keep their specific sibyllistic, internationally minded vein. When the author of book 5 dreams of a rebuilt Jerusalem, connected by a long wall with the coastal town of Jaffa, he must have had in mind the image of Athens in her time of glory, when the famous "long walls" connected her with her seaport.

BIBLIOGRAPHY: J. Geffecken (ed.), *Die Oracula Sibyllina* (1902), best complete critical edition of the Greek original; M.S. Terry, *The Sibylline Oracles* (1890); S.A. Hirsch, *Book of Essays* (1905), 219–59; Charles, Apocrypha, 2 (1913), 368–406; H.N. Bate, *The Sibylline Oracles* (1918); A. Peretti, *La Sibilla babilonese* (1943); A. Kurfess, *Sibyllinische Weissagungen* (1951), incl. bibl.; S.K. Eddy, *The King is Dead* (1961), index.

[Yehoshua Amir (Neumark)]

SICARII, name, of Latin origin, used by *Josephus for Jewish patriots who maintained active resistance against the Roman government of Judea, and Jewish collaborators with it, during the period 6–73 C.E. The name derived from the Latin word *sica*, "curved dagger"; in Roman usage, *sicarii*, i.e., those armed with such weapons, was a synonym for bandits. According to Josephus, the Jewish Sicarii used short daggers, μικρά Ξιφίδια (*mikra ziphidia*), concealed in their clothing, to murder their victims, usually at religious festivals (Wars, 2:254–5, 425; Ant., 20:186–7). The fact that Josephus employs the Latin *sicarii*, transliterated into Greek as σικαριοι (*sikarioi*) suggests that he adopted a term used by the Roman occupation forces; his own (Greek) word for "bandit," which he more generally uses to describe the Jewish resistance fighters, is λῃσταί (*lestai*). For a full description of their activities, see *Zealots and Sicarii.

[Samuel G.F. Brandon]

SICHAR, Samaritan city described in the New Testament as situated near Jacob's well (John 4:5). According to the Mishnah, crops ripened earlier in its plain than elsewhere (Men. 10:2; cf. also 64b; Sot. 49b; TJ, Shek. 5:1, 48d). Jacob's well and the village of Sichar are shown separately on the Madaba Map, contrary to Eusebius' description of them as one unit (Onom. 164:1ff.). Other writers to mention the city are the fourth-century Bordeaux pilgrim (20:6ff.) and Jerome (*Peregrinatio Paulae*, 16). In the Middle Ages Samaritans settled there. It is identified with the Arab village ʿAskar, east southeast of Nablus and 595 ft. (183 m.) above sea level, with a plentiful spring.

BIBLIOGRAPHY: G.A. Smith, *Historical Geography of the Holy Land* (1896[4]), 305ff.; I. Ben-Zvi, *Sefer ha-Shomeronim* (1935), 63–67; O. Callaghan, in: DBI (1953), s.v. *Madaba*; Avi-Yonah, *Madaba Mosaic Map* (1954), no. 33.

[Michael Avi-Yonah]

SICHER, GUSTAV (Benjamin Ze'ev; 1880–1960), Czech rabbi. Sicher abandoned his early activities in the medical profession to become a rabbi. His first rabbinical post was in the Jewish community of the Bohemian town of Nachod. After World War I he was appointed rabbi of the largest Jewish congregation in Prague, Praha Vinohrady, and in the early 1930s became chief rabbi of Prague. After the German occupation of Czechoslovakia in 1939, Sicher immigrated to Ereẓ Israel, where he founded in Jerusalem a prayerhouse for Czech Jews and acted as rabbi for the patients of Hadassah Hospital. In 1947 he was recalled to Prague to the chief rabbinate of Bohemia. In this capacity he organized religious life in 51 communities reconstituted after the Holocaust. He also devoted himself to the enlargement of the Jewish Museum in Prague. Sicher's main literary work was the translation of the Pentateuch into Czech. In 1950, when religious marriages were legally invalidated in Czechoslovakia, Sicher was sworn by the prime minister, A. Zápotocký, to observe this law. In honor of his 75th birthday the Council of Jewish Religious Communities in Prague published a collection of "Jewish Studies" containing special essays and an appreciation of Sicher's literary work.

BIBLIOGRAPHY: *Věstnik židovských náboženských obcí*, 22 (1960), 23 (1961); *Židovska ročenka* (1960/61–1962/63) *Jewish Studies; Essays in Honor of… Gustav Sicher* (1955); P. Meyer et al., *Jews in the Soviet Satellites* (1953), index; R. Iltis (ed.), *Die aussaeen in Traenen…* (1959), passim.

[Erich Kulka]

SICHROVSKY, HEINRICH VON (1794–1866), Austrian railroad entrepreneur. While on a world tour, Sichrovsky was greatly impressed with the new railroads being built in England. Upon his return to Austria he made a thorough study of the subject; subsequently, together with Leopold von Wertheimstein, he interested Solomon *Rothschild in helping finance the first Austrian railroad, the Nordbahn, of which Sichrovsky served as general secretary till his death. For his services he was posthumously awarded the title of nobility, but he had no male descendants. His daughter, Elise, married Theodor *Gomperz, and his brother, Joseph, was also prominent in developing railroads. Sichrovsky was also active in Jewish communal affairs, particularly in the *ḥevra kaddisha* of Vienna (as of 1819) and as member of the community council (*Vorstand*; 1844–58). He was a noted member of the pre-1848 Viennese literary society known as the Ludlamshoehle.

BIBLIOGRAPHY: *Quellen und Forschungen zur Geschichte der Juden in Oesterreich*, 11 (1936), index; *Wurzbach Biographisches Lexikon*, 34 (1877), 213–5. **ADD. BIBLIOGRAPHY:** H. Sichrovsky, *Mein Urahn, der Bahnbrecher: Heinrich von Sichrovsky und seine Zeit* (1988).

SICILY, largest island in the Mediterranean, S.W. of the Italian peninsula.

History

There were probably Jews living in Sicily in the period of the Second Temple; the great Jewish rhetorician *Caecilius of Calacte moved from Sicily to Rome about 50 C.E., and the epigraphic records start in the third century. Even later than this, records are scarce. In 590 Pope *Gregory the Great ordered the ecclesiastical authorities to reimburse the Jews of *Palermo for the damage suffered by the expropriation of their synagogue. Following the conquest of *Syracuse, the Arabs, in 878, took many Jewish captives to Palermo. In a privilege granted after the Norman conquest by Roger I in 1094, Jews are mentioned as residents of Naso. In subsequent records Jews are mentioned in Syracuse, *Messina, and *Catania. *Benjamin of Tudela (c. 1171) mentions the existence of Jewish communities in Palermo and Messina. *Frederick II protected the Jews from persecution during the Crusades and entrusted them with some state monopolies, such as silk weaving and dyeing; he also freed them from ecclesiastical jurisdiction. An edict of 1310 issued by Frederick II of Aragon (1296–1337) prohibited Jews from practicing as physicians and holding public office; they were also forbidden to have Christian servants. A decree of Frederick III (November 1375) limited the jurisdiction of the *Inquisition over the Jews of Syracuse and stipulated that Jews could not be tried by that tribunal unless a secular judge was present. If a Jew was sentenced, he could not be detained in the prisons of the Inquisition but only in a state prison.

Although King Martin V of Aragon, who ruled Sicily from 1392 to 1410, was well disposed toward the Jews and restrained any outrage against them, he could not prevent the forced conversion of the Jews of Monte San Giuliano in 1392, when some of them were massacred; however, he punished those responsible. Jews in Sicily were frequently blamed for fictitious crimes and had to make amends by paying large sums of money, as happened in Catania in 1406. During the reign of Alfonso V (1416–58) the Sicilian Jews prospered. The restrictive regulations confining Jewish residence to ghettos and forced conversions were repealed by the sovereign, who also allowed Jewish physicians to practice their profession among Christians, confirmed the right of Jews to own real estate, and forbade the preaching of compulsory conversionist sermons to the Jews. In 1474 360 Jews, including men, women, and children, perished in a bloody massacre at Modica. Another massacre took place in Noto, where 500 Jews are said to have lost their lives. Subsequently acts of violence against the Jews alternated with measures to protect the communities.

Juridical Status

Under the Saracens the Jews lived in conditions of semi-liberty and were subject to the payment of special taxes, the *kharāj* and *jizya*. Under Norman rule (from the second half of the 11th century) they enjoyed judicial autonomy and could settle their disputes in accordance with Jewish law; they were permitted to own property (with the exception of Christian slaves); at times the sovereign ceded his rights to the bishops.

Although the Jews of Sicily enjoyed civil rights, they were formally considered **servi camerae regis* ("servants of the royal chamber") under Frederick II Hohenstaufen, and they enjoyed royal protection. In 1395, under King Martin, Jewish jurisdiction, with limited competence, was extended to the whole of Sicily by the appointment of a Jewish chief judge (**dienchelele*). The first two chief judges were members of the Syracuse community: Joseph *Abenafia and Rais of Syracuse. Following repeated protests by the Jewish communities on the island, who vigilantly guarded their juridical independence, this office was abolished in 1447, and judicial functions were finally conferred on the heads of the Jewish communities. The Jews of Sicily were obliged to pay taxes as citizens, apart from those which they paid as Jews. The communities were held responsible for the payment of the collective taxes. Limitation of civil rights or the imposition of taxes was varied at times by privileges granted to individuals or to communities.

Community Organization

In general, 12 notables or *proti* acted as leaders of the community, assisted by councillors who were in charge of administration. The latter could take action against those who were slow in paying taxes and could impound their possessions; they authorized weddings and divorces, ritual slaughterers, and the holding of offices in synagogue. In conjunction with the rabbi and the almoners of the community, the *proti* supervised all communal religious and administrative services and guarded against transgression of the directives contained in the regulations of the individual communities. Relations between the community and the government were a matter for the civic authorities, the representatives, and the special envoys.

Cultural Life

Occasional references in documents and manuscripts make it certain that Jewish learning flourished in Sicily, particularly in the Middle Ages. The first known European Jewish writer was the Sicilian Caecilius of Calacte (see above) who wrote rhetorical, historical, and critical works in Greek, of which only a few fragments have been preserved. The *dayyan* Maẓli'aḥ b. Elijah ibn *Al-Bazak was probably the teacher of the celebrated talmudist *Nathan b. Jehiel of Rome. Learned Sicilian Jews knew Hebrew, Italian, Greek, and Arabic, and some of them also Latin. Hence they could take part in the important task of translating scientific works, particularly from Arabic, into Hebrew or Latin. *Faraj (Ferragut) b. Solomon of Agrigento wrote a commentary to Maimonides' *Guide of the Perplexed* and translated for King Charles of Anjou the great medical treatise of Rhazes, known under the title *Liber Continens.* *Moses of Palermo translated important veterinary works from Arabic. There was a notable circle of poets in Sicily in the 12th century, including Samuel b. Nafusi of Palermo, Samuel of Messina, Moses el-Ḥazzan, and *Ahitub b. Isaac, who translated Maimonides' treatises on Logic from Arabic. Another Sicilian scholar who distinguished himself was the *dayyan* *Anatoli b. Joseph, who submitted a legal problem to Maimonides on behalf of the Jews of Syracuse. In the field of science, Jeremiah Kohen of Palermo wrote a commentary in Hebrew on *De sphaera* by Menelaus of Alexandria; Isaac b. Solomon *Alḥadib wrote works on astronomy and Elijah Kohen was author of a treatise giving astronomical tables for the latitude of Syracuse. In the sphere of biblical exegesis, Samuel *Masnut, who later immigrated to Spain, was a poet and writer of aggadic commentaries on books of the Bible, and Jacob *Sikili wrote a homiletical commentary on the Pentateuch. A representative figure of Jewish intellectual life in Sicily was Aaron *Abulrabi of Catania (c. 1400), who wrote a work (subsequently lost) in defense of Judaism and a supercommentary to Rashi's commentary on the Pentateuch. At the end of the 13th century the Spanish kabbalist Abraham b. Samuel *Abulafia also lived in Sicily. In 1466 King John II of Aragon authorized the Jews of the realm to open a *studium generale*, or university, with the right to appoint lecturers, to arrange courses, and award diplomas. The text of Naḥmanides' commentary to the Pentateuch (Naples, 1490) was revised and corrected by scholars of Messina.

The last Jewish scholar to come from Sicily was Joseph Saragossi, kabbalist and talmudist, who founded the neo-mystic school of Safed; he probably was not a native of Saragossa in Spain, but of Syracuse in Sicily. The records of Jewish culture in Sicily – now dispersed in libraries the world over – are contained mainly in manuscripts written in the 14th and 15th centuries in Sciacca, Palermo, Noto, Polizzi Generosa, and Syracuse.

The Expulsion

On May 31, 1492, a decree was issued ordering the expulsion of the Jews from Sicily, similar to that promulgated in Spain shortly before; this decree was given final effect within the month of January 1493. It is estimated that 37,000 Jews had to leave Sicily.

In 1695, again in 1702, and again determinedly in 1740–46, attempts were made by the government of the kingdom to attract Jewish settlement to Sicily again, but without success. In the period between the two world wars a small number of Jews settled in Palermo. There were about 50 Jews living in Sicily in 1965.

BIBLIOGRAPHY: G. di Giovanni, *L'Ebraismo della Sicilia* (1748); Zunz, Gesch (1845), 484–534; G. and B. Lagumina, *Codice Diplomatico dei Giudei di Sicilia* (1884–95); Ch. Senigaglia, in: *Rivista Italiana di Scienze giuridiche*, 41 (1906), 75–102; S.M. Stern, in: JJS, 5 (1954), 60–78, 110–3; A. Milano, in: RMI, 20 (1954), 16–24; C. Roth, in: JQR, 47 (1956/57), 317–53.

[Sergio Joseph Sierra]

SICK, PRAYER FOR. Among the earliest prayers recorded are those for the sick. Moses prayed for his leprous sister, Miriam: "Heal her now, O God, I beseech Thee" (Num. 12:13). When Hezekiah was gravely ill, he "turned his face to the wall and prayed unto the Lord" (Isa. 38:2). A benediction for the healing of the sick was incorporated as the eighth blessing in the daily *Amidah.* Those who visit the sick pray for their recovery (*Rema* to Sh. Ar., YD 335:4). In the Middle Ages the custom arose of invoking a blessing for the sick, known as the **Mi she-Berakh*, during the reading of the Torah. The person requesting the recitation of the prayer for a relative or friend usually pledges charity. On the Sabbath the prayer concludes as follows: "It is the Sabbath, when one must not cry out, and recovery will soon come" (Shab. 12a). The name of a gravely ill person is often changed during this prayer in accordance with the statement of the rabbis that a change of name cancels one's doom (RH 16b; *Sefer Ḥasidim*, ed. by R. Margalioth (1957), 213, nos. 244, 245, ed. by Wistinetzki, par. 365; see *Name, Change of).

Psalms are also read for a gravely ill person in the following order (according to one tradition): 90–108, 20, 38, 41, 86, 118. Those verses in Psalm 119 which begin with the letters of the sick person's name are then read. The recitation is concluded with the verses in the same psalm whose initial letters spell קְרַ"ע שָׂטָן (*kera Satan*; "Destroy Satan").

BIBLIOGRAPHY: H.M. Rabinowicz, *A Guide to Life* (1964), 12f.; J.M. Tukacinsky, *Gesher ha-Ḥayyim*, 1 (1960^{2}), 30ff.

SICK, VISITING THE (Heb. בִּקּוּר חוֹלִים; *bikkur ḥolim*). Visiting the sick in order to cheer, aid, and relieve their suffering is one of the many social obligations which Judaism has clothed with religious significance. God Himself is said to have observed this *mitzvah* when He visited Abraham who was recovering from his circumcision (Gen. 18:1; Sot. 14a). Man is enjoined to follow this divine example; the rabbis classified *bikkur ḥolim* as one of the precepts for which a man enjoys the fruits in this world while the principal remains for him in the world to come (Shab. 127a). The sick of the non-Jews are also to be visited along with the sick of Israel in the interests of peace (Git. 61a).

The visitor is encouraged to be considerate of the patient's welfare. He is not to visit too early in the morning or too late at night (Ned. 40a). Eliezer b. Isaac of Worms counseled: "Do not fatigue him by staying too long for his malady is heavy enough already. Enter cheerfully, for his heart and his eyes are on those who come in" (I. Abrahams (ed.), *Hebrew Ethical Wills*, 1 (1926), 40). The 12th-century moralist, Judah he-Ḥasid, declared: "Even the great should visit the humble. If a poor man and a rich man fall ill at the same time, and many go to the rich man to pay him honor, go thou to the poor man, even if the rich man is a scholar" (*Sefer Ḥasidim*, ed. by R. Margalioth (1957), 367, no. 361; cf. Ned. 39b). Relatives and close friends were advised to visit the sick person as soon as he became ill. Others visited after the first three days of his illness (TJ, Pe'ah 3:9, 17d). Rava requested that his illness not be announced on the first day since he might yet quickly recover (Ned. 40a; Rashi ad loc.). Whoever visits the sick "removes one sixtieth of his malady," while he who does not visit hastens the death of the ailing person (Ned. 39b–40a).

Merely visiting was not necessarily envisaged by the rabbis as the true fulfillment of this *mitzvah*. The sick person was also to be aided and his material needs satisfied. R. Eliezer advised, "When you visit a sick man who is without means, be quick to offer refreshments to him and he will esteem it as though you did uphold and restore his soul" (Abrahams, op. cit., 44). The visitor was also expected to comfort the patient by giving practical expression to his sympathy. It was important for the sick person to know that he is not left to suffer alone in his hours of pain and weakness (cf. Ber. 5b). The most important aspect of the visit was the prayer which the visitor had to recite for the sick person (see Prayer for *Sick). In the presence of the sick any language could be employed for this prayer (Shab. 12b; Sh. Ar., YD 335:5).

Bet Shammai did not permit the visiting of the sick on the Sabbath when sadness was to be avoided. The *halakhah*, however, is in accordance with the viewpoint of Bet Hillel, who did permit such visits (Shab. 12a). During the Middle Ages it was customary for the congregants to visit the sick when they left the synagogue on Sabbath mornings (I. Abrahams, *Jewish Life in the Middle Ages* (1932^2), 348ff.). A sick person should not be given bad news, nor should he be told of the death of a relative lest his own recovery be retarded (MK 26b).

It is meritorious to visit the sick many times as long as the frequent visits are not burdensome for the patient (Ned. 39b; Maim., Avel, 14:4). Those suffering from stomach trouble may not be visited since they will be embarrassed to be seen in such a state. Likewise, those for whom speech is injurious may not be visited (Ned. 41a). In these instances, one should stay in the anteroom and ascertain whether any assistance is necessary (Sh. Ar., YD 335:8). An entire chapter of the Shulḥan Arukh, *Yoreh De'ah*, is devoted to this precept (335).

BIBLIOGRAPHY: H. Rabinowicz, *A Guide to Life* (1964), 11–13; J.M. Tukacinsky, *Gesher ha-Ḥayyim*, 1 (1960^2), 27ff.

[Aaron Rothkoff]

SICK CARE, COMMUNAL. As a religious duty and social service the Jewish community, like the city, took care of its sick. Many communities engaged communal physicians as well as making other necessary arrangements. Many ordinances, prayers, and descriptions of treatment tell the story of the special care organized during times of plague and epidemics. Later, special *ḥavarot* ("associations"; see *Ḥevrah) were organized for sick care but the communal board continued to supervise and control them. There is no record of such associations until 14th-century Spain. In Saragossa a shoemakers' guild provided for sick care in 1336. There was a specialized *bikkur ḥolim* ("visiting the sick") society in Perpignan in 1380. These associations multiplied in the 15th century under such names as *confratrio visitandi infirmos* or *bicurolim*. No such societies existed in the rest of Europe until the 16th century. The Spanish exiles introduced them in Italy and from northern Italy they spread to Prague, and then to Central and Eastern Europe. In the 17th century Germany had only a few such associations, but by the 18th century they had become widespread there. Whereas the religious-educational associations and the craft guilds cared primarily for their own members, there were *bikkur ḥolim* societies specially for the poor. A *ḥevrah* of this type paid for a physician, druggists, barber-surgeons, hospital attendants, midwives, and others. Care was provided not merely for the poor; all communal members and well-to-do visiting merchants or scholars could depend on the association for help. Thus Jewish merchants from the Polish cities of Lissa and Krotoszyn who did business for part of the year in Breslau paid an annual fee entitling them to free medical and hospital care. Through the provision of voluntary visitors special care was taken to ensure that no sick person, rich or poor, should be left alone.

The legislation relating to the Jews in Galicia at the end of the 18th century, and in Russia in the first half of the 19th century, provided the organizations with legal status, and their regulations were published. A candidate for the association was usually required to pay an entrance fee, and to attend the association meeting regularly. The association obtained means for its activities from various sources. Apart from membership dues, generally collected on Fridays, which amounted to less only than those paid to the *ḥevra kaddisha*, the *bikkur ḥolim* association often administered legacies, investing the bequest in real estate, and apportioning the income to other charities and the legatees. The association also received a certain percentage of communal dues (e.g., those levied on meat or new clothing). Sometimes the *bikkur ḥolim* might levy a special tax of its own. The *bikkur ḥolim* association sometimes exercised a powerful influence in the community, since it might provide free loans and subsidize various charitable undertakings. It often also undertook provision of tickets for board and lodging to needy transients, the sponsorship, outlay, and celebration of circumcision, medical care in childbirth, and related necessities. It safeguarded the rights of the local physicians, who were exempted from communal taxes in lieu of the services they rendered to the poor. The leadership of the *bikkur ḥolim* was chosen by the members by the same method as adopted for electing the community leadership. The association aimed to obtain funds for its expenses from the wealthy members, and to free the needy from payments and material worry during illness. The articles of the *bikkur ḥolim* association defined the financial assistance to be afforded to those in need, stipulated the number of visits to the sick, enjoined members to submit regular reports on the condition of patients in the community, and designated night care in serious cases. Fraternal feasts were generally held during the three festivals of Passover, Shavuot, and Sukkot, for which the permissible outlay was regulated.

Societies of women, usually called *nashim ẓadkaniyyot* ("pious women"), were formed in the 18th century to act as nurses, to visit women who were sick or in confinement, to provide medical attention, offer prayers, sew shrouds, and ritually prepare the female dead. Middle-class sick persons were generally cared for at home, while the poor were placed in the *hekdesh. By the end of the 18th century first-rate modern Jewish *hospitals were opened in Breslau, Vienna, and Amsterdam. At first only transient merchants, travelers, and local servants used the new institutions, and it was not until well into the 19th century that local residents gained confidence in these modern hospitals.

BIBLIOGRAPHY: Baron, Community, index; I. Levitats, *Jewish Community in Russia, 1772–1844* (1943), index s.v. *sick visiting*; J.R. Marcus, *Communal Sick-Care in the German Ghetto* (1947); J. Katz, *Masoret u-Mashber* (1958), 187.

[Isaac Levitats / Natan Efrati]

SICKNESS.

HEALTH STATUS

Introduction

There are several available yardsticks for measuring intergroup differences in health status:

(1) lifetime longevity, i.e., average expectation of life in years (calculated at birth or other selected points in the age cycle);

(2) annual overall mortality rate, i.e., number of deaths during the year per 1,000 population (the obverse can alternatively be stated in positive terms as the group's annual overall survival rate);

(3) annual mortality rate from a specific disease;

(4) annual morbidity rate from a specific disease, e.g., number of new polio cases during the year per 1,000 population, irrespective of their life or death outcomes in that year. Within all the Jewish populations studied, longevity and annual survival rates are consistently higher for females than for males. In New York City (1949–51) the average annual death rate for Jewish males was 22% higher than for Jewish females.

Lifetime Longevity

Research according to the yardstick of lifetime longevity in the 1960s showed that Jewish women outlived Jewish men in three countries as follows: Israel (1965) – males, 70.7, females, 73.5; Canada (1961) – males, 68.4, females, 72.2; United States (the three cities Detroit, Milwaukee, and Providence, 1963), males, 67.0, females, 71.9.

This pattern is repeated almost universally in the non-Jewish world, despite enormous international contrasts in economic, political, and cultural levels and styles of life. Differences by sex are also visible across almost the entire age spectrum from the first year of life onward, most sharply of all above the age of 45. Also noteworthy is that among both sexes longevity is highest in Israel and lowest in U.S. Jewry. The longevity of Israel male Jews is one of the highest among the nations of the world, exceeded in 1968 by the male life expectancies only of Sweden (71.6), the Netherlands (71.1), Norway (71.0), and Iceland (70.8). On almost all other yardsticks of health status, the latter four Western countries also lead the world. Perhaps the most interesting finding of all emerges upon finer examination of age-specific mortality rates. In all available Canadian and U.S. studies, the Jewish age progression of mortality for both sexes deviates significantly from that of their non-Jewish neighbors. The divergence is most clearly evident in the four stages of the age cycle discernible in a Canadian study conducted in 1940–42 (Spiegelman, 1948).

Stage I. The first year of life. Here, among both sexes, the all-Canadian death rate was 2.5 times greater than for Jewish children. Infant mortality rates are, of course, influenced by differentials in SES (socioeconomic status).

Stage II. Ages 1 through 34. Here, compared to their all-Canadian peers at every age level, the Jewish death rates for each sex separately are consistently about 50% lower.

Stage III. Ages 35 through 54. The Jewish survival advantage continues in each sex, but by steadily shrinking margins with increasing age.

Stage IV. Age 55 and beyond. At age 55 for the first time Jews appear with higher mortality rates than their Christian fellow countrymen. Thereafter, the unfavorable Jewish margin in mortality rates widens progressively with advancing age.

The higher Jewish survivorship rates of U.S. and Canadian Jews from birth to the middle period of life can be explained by the tradition of being health-minded and health-active people, derived largely from their religious practices. The frequent use of medical resources is clearly an advantage for survival below the age of 45–55. It presumably must also operate beyond that point, with the result that the higher rate of Jewish mortality would have been higher still were it not for their greater use of medical resources. Two further facts should be taken into account:

(1) comparing the U.S. and Canadian studies of the 1960s with those of earlier decades, the Jewish tendency to outclimb non-Jewish mortality rates beyond the middle years was seen to become more pronounced;

(2) mortality rates of Israeli males and females in older age were significantly lower than Jews of the same age and sex in the U.S. and Canada. In fact, Israeli life expectancies at age 65 matched those of Swedish females (15.7 and 15.8 years for Israel and Swedish women, respectively) and exceeded those of Swedish males (14.4 and 13.9 years for Israel and Swedish men, respectively).

In subsequent decades, the life expectancy of Jews in advanced countries has been growing by about one year of life every five calendar years, and around the year 2000 it reached 80 years for women and 75 years for men. Although only little different from that of the general population in the corresponding countries or cities, a tendency for infant mortality to be lower among Jews persisted. On the other hand, crude mortality rates of Jews considerably exceed those of the respective general populations, mainly due to the overaged composition of the respective Jewish groups.

[Leo Srole]

MORBIDITY

Any comparison of morbidity between Jews and gentiles must take into account the wide variability of disease patterns among the Jews themselves. This variability stems from the heterogeneous composition of dispersed Jewish communities and the outside influence due to both marriage and conversion. Due to deficient health registration patterns, very little is known about the health status of Jewish or non-Jewish communities in Middle Eastern and North African countries. The information, therefore, can be based only on studies conducted in Israel and on limited studies in the U.S. and in a few European countries.

GENETIC DISORDERS. There are no genetic disorders with either a higher or a lower incidence in all Jews as a group. However, certain diseases are more prevalent among specific Jewish ethnic subgroups as compared to other subgroups and/or gentiles.

Hundreds of years of isolation of relatively small Jewish communities, both from their neighbors and from other Jewish communities, with consequently relatively frequent consanguineous marriages, have contributed to a higher frequency of several genetic disorders within certain Jewish subgroups. These are briefly summarized below:

Ashkenazi Jews. At least six rare metabolic disorders tend to appear more frequently among Jews of eastern European origin than among any other ethnic group in the world. Tay-Sachs disease (infantile amaurotic idiocy), a congenital lethal metabolic disorder with accumulation of lipids in the neurons of both the central and peripheral nervous systems, and manifested by arrest of development, progressive visual loss, and slowly occurring dementia, occurs in 1:6,000 Jewish births in the U.S. as compared to 1:500,000 among non-Jews; Neiman-Pick's disease, a similar condition, manifested by poor mental and motor development, is also more prevalent among Ashkenazi Jews. Gaucher's disease, a rare disorder of lipid metabolism, characterized by splenomegaly, skin pigmentation, bone lesions, and occasionally by hemorrhage and neurological symptoms, is found in about 1:2,500 Ashkenazi Jews; familial disautonomia (Riley-Day's disease), a rare congenital disorder, manifested by poor motor coordination, emotional instability, indifference to pain, inadequate sense of taste, tearless crying, excessive sweating, skin blotching, and frequent upper respiratory infections, has been described almost exclusively in Ashkenazi Jews, with a frequency of about 1:10–20,000. Pentosuria, a harmless, rare anomaly, characterized by an excessive excretion of L-xylulose in the urine, which is usually discovered on routine urinalysis and often mistakenly diagnosed as diabetes, occurs among Ashkenazi Jews in a frequency of 1:2,500–5,000 as compared to 1:40–50,000 among U.S. gentiles. Also, approximately one half of the observed cases of Bloom's syndrome, a rare childhood condition characterized by a marked sensitivity to sunlight, a small stature, and association with chromosomal abnormalities and leukemia, have been described in Ashkenazi Jews.

The first four of these inborn errors of metabolism have been traced back to a circumscribed area in Poland around the city of Bialystok.

Non-Ashkenazi Jews. Several other inborn errors of metabolism are prevalent among non-Ashkenazi Jews. The most prominent of these is a specific variety of hemolytic anemia (increased destruction of red blood cells), particularly upon contact with drugs or ingestion of fava beans. This disorder is based on a deficiency in the enzyme glucose-6-phosphate-dehydrogenase (G6PD), which is required for normal carbohydrate metabolism. The enzyme deficiency reaches a frequency of 58% in Jews coming from Kurdistan, 25% in the rest of Iraqi Jews and slightly lower frequencies in other eastern communities, in contrast with 0.5% in European Jews. Thalassemia, a chronic progressive anemia due to the presence of an abnormal hemoglobin which commences early in life, is also found primarily in Kurdistani Jews. The neighboring community of Iranian Jews has one of the highest world frequencies of the rare liver disorder, Dubin-Johnson's disease, which is characterized by a defect in bile excretion and accumulation of dark pigment granules in the liver. This disorder has recently been traced to Isfahan. Phenylketonuria, a congenital defect in the metabolism of phenylalanine, characterized by the excretion of phenyl-pyruvic acid in the urine, and which leads to severe mental retardation unless treated early, occurs primarily in Jews originating from Yemen and is practically nonexistent in Ashkenazi Jews. Familial Mediterranean fever (FMF), a disease manifested by repetitive inflammatory attacks of abdominal, pleural and joint pains, as well as by amyloidosis, is prevalent primarily among North African Jews, notably those coming from Libya.

As mentioned above, the presence of closed Jewish communities with frequent consanguineous marriage has enabled the conservation and perpetuation of the abnormal genes for the above conditions. The increase in frequency of inter-ethnic marriage, coupled with a decrease in consanguineous marriage and disappearance of ethnic barriers in Israel and elsewhere, should lead to a dilution of the gene pools and a decline in the overt frequency of these deleterious conditions.

See also *Genetic Diseases in Jew.

ACQUIRED DISEASES. (1) *Infectious.* It is impossible to valuate innate susceptibility to infectious diseases in any group, since their prevalence is mainly determined by environmental conditions. These include personal habits, public hygienic facilities, and sources of infective agents. In the past, better personal hygiene and adherence to strict rabbinical laws kept trichinosis (a disease transmitted through pork meat), and venereal diseases to an infinitesimal rate in most Jewish communities.

An interesting environmental situation arose in Israel, where each immigrating group brought with it diseases prevalent in its area of origin. Of special concern were schistosomiasis (bilharzia) in Yemenite and Iraqi Jews and filariasis (elephantiasis) in Cochin Jews, because these are debilitating diseases which spread easily under suitable conditions. Trachoma, a severe eye condition, and ringworm infection of the scalp were also of major importance among non-European immigrants. At present Israel resembles western countries with its low profile of infectious disease and with a health pattern similar to the one found in well-developed western countries.

(2) *Chronic.* Several studies conducted in the U.S. suggested a higher susceptibility of Jewish residents to coronary heart disease. Most probably, this is only partly related to the fact that, in general, Jews in this country belong to a higher socioeconomic stratum. Thus, Epstein et al. observed that the prevalence of the disease among Jewish clothing workers in New York City was twice that among Italians. A more recent study carried out by the Health Insurance Plan in New York City revealed the disease incidence among Jews almost 50% higher than among Catholics and 30% higher than among Protestants. These observations are in contrast with findings among other minority groups in the U.S., such as blacks, who have a relatively lower rate of this disease. It is difficult to assess which of the several known risk factors for coronary heart disease, i.e., diet, lack of physical activity, or stress, is responsible for the increased incidence among Jews. One cannot completely rule out a genetic background as a contributory factor, especially in view of studies indicating a higher susceptibility to the disease among people with certain specific blood groups.

In Israel, coronary heart disease has been constantly on the rise in all population groups. The increase followed the rise in standard of living, continuous stress, and decrease of physical activity. However, the process of assimilation has not yet abolished differences between various ethnic groups within the country. Early studies by Dreyfus, and Toor et al., suggested that Yemenites, and particularly newly arrived Yemenites, have a lower risk of acquiring the disease as compared to European-born Israelis, while veteran Yemenites as well as other non-Ashkenazi Jews in Israel have an intermediate range. These findings are compatible with differences in cholesterol levels between the groups, but again, differences in other life habits such as stress, physical activity, smoking, etc., could contribute to the observed difference in risk.

No definite data with regard to other cardiovascular diseases are available. Buerger's disease, a peripheral vascular disorder affecting primarily young males and manifested by inflammatory and occlusive changes in both arteries and veins, is apparently more prevalent among Jews of eastern European origin, both in Israel and elsewhere. There are some indications that diabetes may be more common among Jews in the U.S., but the data are inconclusive. Cohen suggested that Yemenite Jews have a lower rate of diabetes than other Jewish subgroups, while others observed a higher risk of diabetes among North African-born Jews. Since this is a disease with a certain genetic background, an interaction between heredity and environment could lead to diverse manifestations. It has also been suggested that hypertension and mortality from cerebro-vascular accidents are slightly higher among the North African-born Israelis. This could be related at least in part to a higher incidence of chronic renal disease in this ethnic group, particularly among the females. Regional enteritis and ulcerative colitis, two inflammatory conditions of the bowel, have also been found to be relatively more common among Jews in the U.S. than among gentiles. Jews have always been noted for a lower frequency of drinking. Consequently, both alcoholism and liver cirrhosis are considerably lower among Jews as a group, both in Israel and abroad.

CANCER. There is ample evidence today that several malignant neoplasms occur more frequently in Jews, while others are relatively rare. Furthermore, there is a marked variability in the risk for certain cancer sites within the main Jewish ethnic subgroups. Major cancer sites with a higher risk among Jews are cancer of the colon, breast, and ovary, which have been strongly correlated with higher socioeconomic status, as well as cancer of the pancreas and of the kidney, brain tumors, lymphoma, leukemia, and, among females, cancer of the lung and of the stomach. The higher rate of brain tumors noted among U.S. Jews is consistent with the finding that the incidence of these tumors is higher in Israel than anywhere else in the world.

In contrast, cancer sites occurring less frequently among Jews are the upper respiratory tract, i.e., pharynx, buccal, and the lung (males only), as well as cancer of the bladder, the esophagus (males only) and, to a certain extent, cancer of the prostate. The reason for the varying pattern between the two sexes in lung cancer is probably due to the fact that the most prevalent histological form in this neoplasm differs between the two sexes (odenocarcinoma in females, versus squamous cell carcinoma in males), so that, actually, the lower incidence of lung cancer among Jews is limited to the latter histological form only. The reason for the varying pattern in esophageal cancer is unclear. The one category that has drawn most attention as being rare in Jews is cancer of the uterine cervix. This apparent rarity had been construed as indicating a protective role of circumcision among Jews. More recently, it has been demonstrated that the rarity is limited to Jews of European origin, while in other Jewish communities, notably those originating in Morocco, the incidence may be even higher than that among gentiles in several European countries. The "protective" role of circumcision has also been challenged on the basis of controlled studies in England and the U.S., and by the fact that the disease is not rare in circumcised non-Jewish populations such as in Iran and Turkey. Thus, the low risk of cervical cancer among Jews in the U.S. and Europe as compared to their gentile neighbors is now considered to be related to better personal hygiene and differences in factors associated with sexual behavior, such as age at first intercourse and number of sexual partners. The recent hypothesis of a viral role in the etiology of cervical cancer is also consistent with the pattern of a closed community, and a lower rate of extramarital relationships among Jews until the recent time period. The relatively lower cervical cancer rate among European-born residents in Israel, as compared to the African- and Asian-born, is also consistent with these explanations. On the other hand, the long-term observation of the rarity of cancer of the penis among Jews as a group has not yet been refuted, and there is a strong probability that in this case circumcision may actually play a preventive role.

Community-wide studies of cancer incidence in Israel have demonstrated some parallelism with findings in the U.S. Two facts stand out:

(1) In general the cancer sites that occur more frequently among Jews in the U.S., as compared to gentiles, are more prevalent among the European-born Israelis, while those that occur more rarely among Jews in the U.S. are relatively more prevalent among non-European-born residents in Israel;

(2) The relative incidence of various malignant disorders in European – in contrast to Asian – and African-born groups in Israel shows a striking parallelism to the one of white versus nonwhite groups in the U.S. Since there is no common genetic background for the Israeli and American subgroups, it would seem that the similarities observed may be associated with inter-ethnic differences in socioeconomic status. These findings corroborate previously made observations regarding the role of environmental factors in carcinogenesis. To be more specific, cancer sites occurring more frequently among European-born Israeli residents are colon, breast, ovary, uterine corpus, brain tumors, gallbladder (females only), as well as leukemia and lymphoma in older age. Cancer of the stomach and lung are also higher among the European-born, contrary to the expected pattern of a lower risk of these tumors in higher socioeconomic groups, while cancer of the uterine cervix occurs more frequently among the North African-and to a certain extent, among the Asian-born. Cancer of the esophagus is more prevalent among Jews coming from Iran and Yemen, hepatic cancer among Yemenites, and bladder cancer among North African-born males, while residents coming from the Balkan countries (Bulgaria, Greece, and Turkey) have a considerably higher rate of cancer of the larynx. The two leading sites of cancer in Israel (excluding skin cancer) are lung and stomach in males and breast and stomach in females. This is true for all ethnic categories except for the North African-born females, where cancer of the uterine cervix assumes second place.

The effect of length of residence in Israel, namely the role of change in daily life habits on cancer incidence, has only partly been studied so far, due to lack of sufficient data. However, preliminary observations indicate that in all ethnic groups stomach cancer is lowest among the Israeli-born, intermediate in veteran Israelis, and highest in recent immigrants. There are also some indications that leukemia, at least among children, shows a similar gradient, with highest rate among immigrants, intermediate in first-generation Israelis, and lowest in second-generation Israelis. This is consistent with well-documented data elsewhere that cancer among migrants tends to assume an intermediate position between the range in the country of origin and their host country.

The Israel Ministry of Health has released the following figures for recent years:

Patients	Year		
	1990	1995	2001
Newly diagnosed with cancer during given calendar year	12,952	17,263	22,290
Cumulative no. of cancer patients (old and new cases) at end of given calendar year	33,000	48,231	66,129
No. of patients with newly diagnosed cancer of the trachea, bronchus, or lungs in the given calendar year	960	1,211	1,487
Females with newly diagnosed cancer of the breast during the given calendar year	2,046	2,550	3,222
No. of patients with newly diagnosed cancer of the cervix uteri during the given calendar year	127	157	202

[Baruch Modan]

BIBLIOGRAPHY: HEALTH STATUS: O.W. Anderson, in: E. Gartly Jaco (ed.), *Patients, Physicians and Illness* (1958), 10–24; A. Antonovsky, in: *Journal of Chronic Diseases*, 21 (1968), 65–106; S.J. Fauman and A.J. Mayer, in: *Human Biology*, 41 no. 3 (Sept. 1969), 416–26; M. Fishberg, *The Jews* (1911), 225–67 (age reversal in mortality); S. Graham, in: H. Freeman et al., *Handbook of Medical Sociology* (1963), 65–98; R.U. Marks, in: MMFQ, 45 (April, 1967), pt. 2, 51–108; D. Mechanic, "Religion, Religiosity and Illness Behavior: the special case of the Jews," in: *Human Organization*, 22, 202–8; H. Seidman, L. Garfinkel, and L. Craig, in: JJSO (Dec. 4, 1962), 254–73. MORBIDITY: A.M. Cohen, in: *Metabolism*, 10 (1961), 50; F.H. Epstein, E.P. Boas, and R. Simpson, in: *Journal of Chronic Diseases*, 5 (1957), 300; E. Goldschmidt and T. Cohen, in: *Cold Spring Harbor Symposia on Quantitative Biology*, 29 (1964), 115; R.M. Goodman (ed.), *Genetic Disorders of Man* (1970); W. Haenszel, in: *Journal of the National Cancer Institute*, 26 (1961), 37; B. Mac-Mahon, in: *ACTA, Unio Internationalis Contra Cancrum*, 16 (1960), 1716; C.E. Martin, in: *American Journal of Public Health*, 57 (1967), 803; V.A. McKusick et al., in: *Israel Journal of Medical Sciences*, 3 (1967), 372; J.H. Medalie et al., *ibid.*, 4 (1968), 775; B. Modan et al., in: *Pathology and Microbiology*, 35 (1970), 192; idem, in: *Proceedings of the Xth International Cancer Congress* (1970); V.A. Newill, in: *Journal of the National Cancer Institute*, 26 (1961), 405; H. Seidman, in: *Environmental Research*, 3 (1970), 234; S. Shapiro, in: *American Journal of Public Health (Supplement)*, 59 (1969), 1; Ch. Sheba, *ibid.*, 52 (1962), 1101; idem, in: *Lancet*, 1 (1970), 1230; R. Steinitz, *5-Years Morbidity from Neoplasms in Israel's Population Groups (1960–64)* (1967); M. Toor et al., in: *Circulation*, 22 (1960), 265. **WEBSITE:** www.health.gov.il.

SID (Sidilyo; Sirilyo), SAMUEL IBN (c. 1530), rabbi in *Egypt. Samuel studied under Isaac de *Leon in his native Toledo where he married the daughter of Isaac *Aboab. After the Expulsion from *Spain in 1492 Samuel arrived in Egypt, where he was a member of the *bet din* of Isaac Shulal. Before 1509 he signed, together with the other members of the *bet din*, a legal decision concerning the exemption of scholars from the payment of taxes (*Keter Torah* of R. Samuel de *Avila, Amsterdam, 1725, p. 1b). He was referred to as *Ba'al Nes* ("miracle worker"); according to local tradition, when the Egyptian governor, Aḥmed Pasha, rebelled against the Turkish sultan and persecuted the Jews in 1524, Samuel offered up prayers in his synagogue which resulted in the downfall of the governor. In memory of this event it became known after him as the Sidilyo Synagogue.

Samuel became famous for his small and important work *Kelalei Shemu'el*, which was written in 1522 and published in the book *Tummat Yesharim* (Venice, 1622). This was a handbook for the study of the Talmud, wherein the "rules" of the Talmud are presented in alphabetical order. In this work Samuel also describes the method of study used in the Spanish yeshivot. Parts of Samuel's commentary on *Avot* were published in the *Midrash Shemu'el* of Samuel b. Isaac *Uceda.

BIBLIOGRAPHY: E. Capsali, *Likkutim Shonim mi-Sefer de-Vei Eliyahu*, ed. by M. Lattes (1869), 106–7; Neubauer, Chronicles, 1 (1887), 140, 145, 152, 159, 161f.; Ashtor, Toledot, 2 (1951), 477–81; Dimitrovsky, in: *Sefunot*, 7 (1963), 43, 84–88, 90, 92, 95; Hirschberg, in: *Bar Ilan Sefer ha-Shanah*, 4–5 (1967), 445–6.

[Abraham David]

SIDNEY, SYLVIA (Sophia Kosow; 1910–1999), U.S. actress. Born in New York, Sidney first appeared there in 1927 and became internationally known after her part in the film *Street Scene* (1931). She played for the Guild Theater in *To Quito and Back* (1937) and for the Group Theater in *The Gentle People*, (1939). She acted in summer theaters, played in *The Four-Poster* on Broadway (1951), and toured in *Auntie Mame* (1958). Later Broadway stints included *Enter Laughing* (1963), *Barefoot in the Park* (1963), and *Vieux Carré* (1977).

Her films include *Through Different Eyes* (1929), *Madame Butterfly* (1932), *Jennie Gerhardt* (1933), *Sabotage* (1936), *Fury* (1936), *Dead End* (1937), *You Only Live Once* (1937), *You and Me* (1938), *The Searching Wind* (1946), *Love from a Stranger* (1947), *Les Miserables* (1952), *Violent Saturday* (1955), *Behind the High Wall* (1956), *Summer Wishes, Winter Dreams* (Oscar nomination for Best Supporting Actress, 1973), *I Never Promised You a Rose Garden* (1977), *Damien: Omen II* (1978), *Hammett* (1982), *Beetlejuice* (1988), and *Used People* (1992).

She performed in many television shows and TV movies, among them the TV series *Ryan's Hope* (1975) and *Fantasy Island* (1998), and the TV movies *Raid on Entebbe* (1977), *Siege* (1978), *The Shadow Box* (1980), *Come Along with Me* (1982), *Finnegan Begin Again* (1985), *An Early Frost* (Emmy nomination for Best Supporting Actress, 1985), *Pals* (1987), and *Andre's Mother* (1999).

Sidney was married to publisher Bennet Cerf (from 1935 to 1936) and actor/teacher Luther Adler (from 1938 to 1946).

She wrote *Sylvia Sidney Needlepoint Book* (with A. Lewis, 1968) and *Question and Answer Book on Needlepoint* (1974).

[Jonathan Licht / Ruth Beloff (2nd ed.)]

SIDON (also **Zidon**; Heb. צִידוֹן, צִידֹן), Phoenician port, N. of Tyre in Lebanon. The name (Phoen. צדן; Akkad. Ṣiddunnu) comes from the root *ṣwd* ("to hunt, fish"). Justin says that Sidon means "fish town" (*"piscem Phoenices sidon vocant,"* 18:13, passim), but W.R. Smith (bibl.) shows that *ṣwd* was used as part of a divine name (e.g., Ṣ-d-Tannith, Ṣ-d-Melkarth) and was probably a Baal of Lebanon, a food god. Sidon's wealth came from the resources of the sea (commerce, fish, purple dye from mollusks, and later, glass from the sand). Already by the 15th/14th century B.C.E. Sidon was famous as a religious site. The Ugaritic myth of Keret, king of Sidonians, mentions his visit to the shrines of *b'elt Ṣdynm* ("goddess of Sidon"; Keret, 4:197–202; 6:279). In later times Sidonian gods (especially Ashtoreth) were very popular with the Children of Israel (Judg. 9:6; I Kings 11:5, 33; II Kings 23:13). From early times Sidon, as the rest of Phoenicia, was under Egyptian control, but by the 13th century Sidon began to assert its independence and the Tell el-Amarna Letters testify to the secret intrigues of Zimridda, king of Sidon, with Abdi-Airta and his sons, the kings of the Amorites, although Zimridda ostensibly still professed loyalty to Pharaoh (S.A.B. Mercer, *The Tell Amarna Tablets* (1939), nos. 144, 145; cf. 83:26, 103:18, etc.).

It was its natural resources that made Sidon the leading port of the Phoenician coast by the 11th century B.C.E. It was mentioned in the Egyptian story, *The Journey of Wen Amon to Phoenicia* (Pritchard, Texts, 25–29), as having 50 ships in commercial contact with Egypt (11th century B.C.E.). About this time Tiglath-Pileser I (1115–1077 B.C.E.) of Assyria invaded Phoenicia, and received tribute from Sidon. By Homer's time (tenth/ninth century) Sidon's craftsmanship in metalwork was well known and highly prized; Menelaus gave Telemachus a present of a beautiful Sidonian gold cup (*Odyssey* 4:613–9); Sidon was termed "Sidon abounding in bronze" (Σιδῶνος πολυχάλκου) and was said to excel in gold and electrum (*ibid.* 15:425, 460), as well as dyed clothes (as quoted from Homer in Herodotus, *Histories*, 12:116). On account of this wealth Sidon was subject to frequent raids from the Greek islands of this period (*Odyssey* 15:427). Up to this time Sidon held the dominating position in riches, trade, and crafts on the Phoenician littoral, which entitled it to be called "Great Sidon" (Josh. 11:8; 19:28), and "the firstborn of Canaan" (Gen. 10:15), and lent the name Sidonian as a general term for Phoenician (I Kings 16:31). On the invasion of the Twelve Tribes, the Sidonians were living as far south as the hill country of Ereẓ Israel but they were driven back and Asher inherited their land (Josh. 11:8; 13:6; Judg. 1:31). Later they oppressed Israel together with the Amalekites but were beaten (Judg. 10:12).

In the Bible the Sidonians had great fame as carpenters and lumberers. David, Solomon, and the returning Exiles hired Sidonian carpenters to cut wood for the Temple (I Chron. 22:4; Zech. 9:2; Ezra 3:7). Sidon probably founded her colonies about the ninth century in Cyprus (cf. Cook, bibl. no. 11), Hippo, and Kition; and the eighth-century citizens of Sidon, Tyre, and Aradus (Arvad) founded Tripoli in Lebanon (Strabo, *Geography*, 15:2:15). From the late tenth century on Tyre gradually overtook Sidon in the hegemony of Phoenicia. Shalmaneser III (858–824) took tribute from Jehu of Israel and Sidon (Pritchard, Texts, 278). Sennacherib (705–681) drove out the rebel Elu-Eli, king of Tyre, who had conquered a large part of Phoenicia, and replaced him with the pro-Assyrian Ethbaal, king of Sidon, who had already submitted to Sennacherib in 701. In 677, Sidon rose against the rule of Sennacherib's son, Esarhaddon, who subsequently cast down the walls of Sidon and destroyed it, beheading her king, Abd-Melkarth. Esarhaddon then built a fort, "*Kar*," close to Sidon to overawe it, and gave its territory to Tyre. Shortly after 605, Jeremiah prophesied against Sidon, warning it to accept the yoke of Nebuchadnezzar (Jer. 25:22; 27:3; cf. Ezek. 28:22; Joel 4:4). The new Sidon remained subjugated to the Assyrians and then to the Babylonians, and when *Hophra of Egypt (588–568) organized the anti-Babylonian league with Judah and Ammon, he attacked Sidon for not joining their conspiracy (Herodotus, *Histories*, 2:161). Under Persian rule Sidon, together with Aradus, Byblos, and Tyre were granted internal autonomy, and later – in the fourth century – they federated, choosing Tripoli as the federal capital (Strabo, *Histories*, 16:2:22).

The maritime reputation of the Sidonians was so great that Darius especially sent to Sidon for ships and crews before invading Greece in 490 (Herodotus, *Histories*, 3:136). Under the rule of Artaxerxes III (359–338), the other cities of the federation (mentioned above) cunningly enticed Sidon into rebelling against Persia, promising support, but in effect not helping her at all. In 351, Artaxerxes set out for Sidon with 300,000 infantry and 30,000 cavalry. Tennes, king of Sidon, immediately fled, but the people of the city courageously refused to surrender and burned their ships in the harbor. When the Persians set the city on fire, the inhabitants locked themselves in their houses; more than 40,000 perished and the survivors were transported to Babylonia (Diodorus Siculus, *History*, 16:41–45). In this episode, Tyre and the other cities acted with deliberate calculation in order to destroy the commercial rivalry of Sidon forever.

With the conquest of Phoenicia by Alexander the Great in 333, Sidon, which was just beginning to recover, immediately surrendered and assisted him at the siege of her ancient enemy, Tyre. Alexander restored Sidon's constitution, returned to her the territories given to Tyre, and appointed Abdalonymus as king in place of Straton II (342–333), who had assisted the Persians (Justin, 11:10; Arrian, *Anabasis*, 2:20:1; Curtius, 4:1:16).

Ashtoreth was the supreme deity of Sidon (cf. "Ashtoreth, the god of Sidon," I Kings 11:33; II Kings 23:13) and was goddess of fertility and generation (cf. Herodotus, *Histories* 1:105). It was the charge of the kings to build "a house for the gods of Sidonians in Sidon, land of the sea, a house to Baal of Sidon [cf. I Kings 16:31 "Baal of the Sidonians"] and a house to Ashtart" (cf. I Sam. 31:10; Cook, bibl. no. 4). It seems that at this period the "Lord of Kings" (Ptolemy II) granted Sidon the territories of "the fields of Sharon" (cf. Deut. 3:9), "Dor and Jaffa" (loc. cit.). Shortly after 250 B.C.E., Sidon became a republic ruled by suffetes (Heb. *shofet*, annually elected magistrates). Josephus identifies the ruling bodies with the Greek Βουλή (Heb. הַזְּקֵנִים) and the δῆμος (Heb. הָעָם; Jos., Ant., 14:190). In 218, Antiochus III seized Tyre and Ptolemais from Ptolemy IV, but Sidon was strong enough to resist him and became a center of Ptolemy's operations (Polybius, 5:61, 69). In 200, Scopas (Ptolemy V's general) was defeated at Panion and after being besieged at Sidon surrendered the city to Antiochus, who thereby gained the whole of Coele-Syria by 198 (Jerome, commentary to Daniel, 11:15; Polybius, 10, frag. 7).

At the beginning of the Maccabean wars, Sidon (with Ptolemais and Tyre) persecuted the Jews of Galilee to whose rescue Simon Maccabee went in 163 (I Macc. 5:15). In 111, Sidon gained autonomy from the Seleucids, and this year was the beginning of a new era for Sidon. Pompey recognized her independence in 64 B.C.E. and ceded her territory up to Iturea (Mt. Hermon). Bronze copies of the edicts of Julius Caesar addressed to the council and people of Sidon in 47–44 B.C.E. in favor of John Hyrcanus and the Jews (recorded in Josephus). were set up in Sidon (Ant., 14:190–210). This period proved to be one of the richest periods financially in Sidonian history. Glassblowing was discovered at this time (probably in Sidon; cf. Pliny, 5:76, *Sidon artifex vitri*). Strabo describes Sidon's two harbors and expounds on her reputation for astronomy, mathematics, and navigation. After some major disturbances, Sidon and Tyre were placed under Roman jurisdiction by Augustus in 20 B.C.E. Sidon soon advanced to the foreground among Hellenistic cities and was beautified by Herod (Jos., Wars, 1:422; cf. Acts 12:20).

By this time, a large number of Jews resided in Sidon, as is testified by the pagano-Jewish inscriptions from Sidon; and a Jewish inscription ending with hopes for the resurrection (Frey, 2, nos. 875–7). The Jewish population also seems to have established for itself some notoriety (Matt. 11:22; Luke 10:14) and Jesus especially went to preach in its vicinity (Matt. 15:21; Mark 7:24). By the first century, Jews were so numerous in Sidon that the Sidonians were afraid of attacking them in 66 C.E., when the Jews of Syria were massacred in other Greek towns (Jos., Wars, 2:479). By Byzantine times, Sidon had lost most of its wealth (the cedars had been cut down, the purple dye was no longer a monopoly, and other places had superseded Sidon in glassblowing). Antoninus Placentius (570) wrote that Sidon was partly in ruins.

Sidon was described by numerous scholars and travelers in the 19th century, including E. Robinson, C. Volney, and others. The famous Sarcophagus of Eshmunazar, King of Sidon, was discovered in 1855 to the southeast of the city. The first excavation in the city was made by E.Renan in 1861. In 1912 G. Contenau excavated a graveyard containing sarcophagi, including one depicting a Roman merchant ship, as well as graves dating back to the 16th century B.C.E. and other finds. Contenau also discovered, next to the Crusader castle of St. Louis, a place where the purple dye was extracted from Murex shells. M. Dunand unearthed a temple dedicated to Mithra in 1924. Elsewhere he excavated the Temple of Eshmun and between 1963 and 1968 expanded the excavations around the sanctuary. Tombs dating from the end of the Middle Bronze Age to the beginning of the Late Bronze Age were unearthed in 1937 by P.E. Guigues. More tombs were cleared by M. Chehab in 1940, dating from the period between the 18th and 14th centuries B.C.E. The harbor installations were investigated by A. Poidebard between 1946 and 1950. From 1966 to 1969 Roger Saidah, of the Lebanese Department of Antiquities, excavated a Late Chalcolithic settlement of oval houses, superimposed by a cemetery with tombs ranging in date from the 14th century through the Early Roman period.

Although it was never large, a Jewish community existed in this ancient Phoenician city throughout the Muslim era. Benjamin of Tudela, the 12th-century traveler, reported that there were "twenty Jews" (families or taxpayers) in Sidon. The *Mamluks destroyed the citadel there after capturing the city from the crusaders; as an open city it began to decline during the latter part of the Middle Ages; its Jewish community did not increase. At the end of the 15th century there was a small community. R. Moshe Basola recounts that during his travels in Syria in the year 1521 there were no more than 20 families of Arabized Jews in Sidon. Under *Ottoman rule Sidon grew again, and the Jewish community also increased. Rabbinical writings of the period show that Jews in Sidon were active in commerce and some were tax collectors (Mabit, Resp. vol. 2, pt. 2, no. 62). R. Joseph Sofer of *Safed wrote that in 1762 there had been six *minyanim* (60 adult male Jews) in Sidon, but that most of them had died during the plague and barely one *minyan* survived. R. Mordecai, of the same period, mentions the Jews of Sidon (Resp. no. 16) saying that they did not have a rabbi at the time. David d'Beth Hillel recounts that Sidon had approximately 20 Jewish families in 1824, all Arabic-speaking and native-born; they were similar in customs to the Jews of Ereẓ Israel, and most of them were tradesmen. Most of the travelers mention the tomb of Zebulun, the son of Jacob, located south of Sidon, a place the Arabs called Sheikh Ṣadyā, that was venerated by Jews and Muslims alike. The traditional tombs of Oholiab the son of Ahisamakh, Bezalel, R. Eleazar Bartukha, and the prophet Zephaniah also were not far from Sidon.

[Eliyahu Ashtor / Shimon Gibson (2nd ed.)]

The Jewish community in Sidon remained traditional and its members observed the religious rituals. During the latter stages of the 1948 War, when the Israeli army occupied parts of South Lebanon, the homes of several members of the small Jewish community in Sidon, numbering 200 persons, were confiscated, and Palestinian refugees were installed in them. But the Lebanese government ordered the police to protect the Jews in the city and enabled them to return to their homes and property. In 1962, the Alliance school in Sidon was closed down, and in 1968 there were about 150–160 Jews in the city. In 1972, the *shoḥet* of the community left.

By 1975, most of the Jews in Sidon had left the city and only one family remained. Its head, Yosef Levy, worked as a tailor and made uniforms for the Lebanese army, and it maintained good relations with its non-Jewish neighbors. On June 5, 1982, when the Israeli army occupied Sidon, the Levys were permitted to stay in their home. When the Israeli army withdrew from the city, the remaining members of the family left with it and settled in Israel.

[Oren Barak (2nd ed.)]

BIBLIOGRAPHY: G.A. Cook, *North Semitic Inscriptions* (1903), indexes, appendix; P.K. Hitti, *History of Syria* (1951), index; *Oxford Classical Dictionary* (1950), s.v. *Sidon*; W. Robertson Smith, *The Religion of the Semites* (1927), 578; J.B. Bury, *History of Greece* (1952), 763–70; G. Roux, *Ancient Iraq* (1966), index; Pauly-Wissowa, s.v. *Sidon*; Frey, Corpus 2, no. 875–7; A. Yaari, *Iggerot Ereẓ Yisrael* (1943), index; J. Braslawsky (Braslavi), in: *Edoth*, 2 (1946/47), 193–201; idem, *Le-Ḥeker Arẓenu* (1954), 319–22. **ADD. BIBLIOGRAPHY:** N. Jidejian, *Sidon Through the Ages* (1971); K.E. Schulze, *The Jews of Lebanon: Between Coexistence and Conflict* (2001).

SIDON, KAROL EFRAIM (1942–), Czech writer, screenwriter, and playwright. Sidon was born in Prague. His father, a Jew, was executed in Theresienstadt in the Small Fortress after his deportation in 1944. In 1965–67, Sidon studied dramaturgy and screenwriting at the Film Academy of Music Arts in Prague. He worked as a screenwriter of animated films and as an editor at the journal *Literární listy*. After the Soviet occupation of Czechoslovakia, he lost his jobs. After signing Charter 77, he left for Germany in 1983, converted to Judaism, and took Judaic studies in Heidelberg and Jerusalem (rabbinical training). In 1990 he returned to the Czech Republic and became its chief rabbi as well as that of Prague.

All of Sidon's work is connected with Jewishness and is often based on the painful experiences of his childhood and adolescence. His fiction started with *Sen o mém otci* (1968, "Dream about My Father"), an emotive portrait of his late father, his mother, and stepfather. The author's adulthood and marriage are reflected in *Sen o mně* (1970, "Dream about Myself"). After these works, all others appeared in *samizdat* between 1970 and 1989: a philosophical-contemplative essay *Evangelium podle Josefa Flavia* ("The Gospel According to Josephus Flavius," 1974; 1990); the novel *Boží osten* ("The Sting of God," 1976; 1991), containing the short story *Polské uši* ("Polish Ears") which appeared together with *Brány mrazu* ("Gates of Frost, " 1977) in *Dvě povídky o utopencích* ("Two Stories about the Drowned People," 1988, in exile), both of which project the author's personal experiences, anxieties, and emotions onto his heroes, some of whom are Jewish. In the essay *Návrat Abrahamův* ("The Return of Abraham," 1986) Sidon interprets biblical history; in the collection of interviews *Když umřít, tak v Jeruzalémě* ("If One Must Die, Let It at Least Be in Jerusalem," 1977) and *Sedm slov* ("Seven Words," 2004), the author discusses philosophical and moral questions concerning Judaism. Of his plays, the best known are *Latriny* ("The Latrines," 1971); *Labyrint* ("Labyrinth," 1972); and *Shapira* ("Shapira," 1972). Sidon also wrote radio plays and screenplays. He translated many parts of the Old Testament and numerous prayers for Jews in the Czech Republic.

BIBLIOGRAPHY: J. Čulík, *Knihy za ohradou. Česká literatura v exilových nakladatelstvích 1971–1989* (s.d.); P. Kubíková and P. Kotyk, *Čeští spisovatelé – Czech Writers* (1999); A. Mikulášek et al., *Literatura s hvězdou Davidovou*, vol. 1 (1998), vol. 2 (2002); *Slovník českých spisovatelů* (1982).

[Milos Pojar (2nd ed.)]

SIDON, SIMEON (1815–1892), Hungarian rabbi. Sidon, who was born in Nádas, was a pupil of Moses *Sofer. His first rabbinate was in the small town of Cifer. In 1855 he was appointed rabbi of Tyrnau (Trnava). During his rabbinate the schism (1869) in Hungarian Jewry (see *Hungary) took place, and his community joined neither the Union of Orthodox Jews nor the *Neologist group but remained a *status quo community. When the Orthodox rabbis disqualified the halakhic rulings of the rabbis of those communities, about 40 families founded a separate Orthodox community. Sidon vigorously complained about this ruling, asserting that many of the status quo rabbis were outstanding and God-fearing talmudists. They had no power to force their congregants to join the Orthodox group. "Are they to leave their communities and become recipients of charity?" he protested. He remained with his community until his death. Sidon was himself an outstanding talmudic scholar and a gifted preacher.

He was the author of *Ot Berit* (1850), on the laws of circumcision and the redemption of the firstborn; *Shevet Shimon* (1884–88), responsa and halakhic novellae (on marriage and mourning); homilies on *Avot* (some of which were published in the *Even ha-Me'ir* (appended to Z. Horowitz, *Kitvei ha-Ge'onim* (1957) of Meir Stein); and *Beit Menuḥah* (1879) on Maimonides' *Mishneh Torah*.

BIBLIOGRAPHY: S. Sidon, *Shevet Shimon*, 3 (1888), introd.; P.Z. Schwartz, *Shem ha-Gedolim me-Ereẓ Hagar*, 2 (1914), 43a no. 110; *Magyar Zsidó Lexikon* (1929), s.v.

[Samuel Weingarten-Hakohen]

SIDRAH (Heb. סִדְרָה; "order," "arrangement"), popular term for the sections of the Pentateuch, read publicly in the synagogue on the Sabbath (see *Torah, Reading of). The term is found in talmudic literature to mean both "weekly portions" (Shab. 116b; Yoma 87a; TJ, Ta'an. 1:6, 64c), and schools in which sections of the Scriptures are read and interpreted (TJ, Ber. 3:1, 6b; TJ, Beẓah 1:6, 60c). In its Aramaic form (סִדְרָא, *sidra*) it can also refer to each of the six sections into which the Mishnah is divided.

SIEBERT, MURIEL (1932–), U.S. stockbroker. Siebert, who was born in Cleveland, Ohio, was the best-known woman on Wall Street in the second half of the 20th century. In 1967, she became the first woman to buy a seat on the New York Stock Exchange, and several years later she became the first woman to own and operate her own brokerage firm. In between she served five years, beginning in 1977, as New York State's first female superintendent of banking. A dropout from Case Western Reserve University, she lied about having a college degree to get her first job, as a $65-a-week researcher at Bache & Company, in 1954. By 1967 she was a partner in a tiny brokerage firm and an authority on aeronautics stocks; she earned $250,000 a year but felt she could do better. Because no major firm would hire her, she said, she bought a seat on the exchange for $445,000, joining 1,365 male members of the exchange. She transformed her firm into a discount brokerage house in 1975, on the first day that firms were permitted to negotiate commissions. She continued running the brokerage well into her 70s. She set up several charitable foundations, beginning in 1990 with the Siebert Entrepreneurial Philanthropic Program, which distributes half of the firm's net commission revenue on new issue corporate underwritings to a charity, usually chosen by the issuer or purchaser. In 1999, while president of the New York Women's Agenda, a coalition of more than 100 women's organizations, she developed a Personal Finance Program to improve the financial skills of young people. The program was initially designed to teach how to manage a checkbook and to understand the use and abuse of credit cards. The program was part of the economics curriculum of New York City high schools and was expanded to include such topics as the basics of money, banking, credit, budgeting, taxes, insurance, and investing. Siebert was also involved with many nonprofit, civic, and women's organizations, including the Economic Club of New York, the Council on Foreign Relations, and the New York Women's Forum, of which she was a founder and former president.

[Stewart Kampel (2nd ed.)]

SIEDLCE, city in E. Poland. Jews lived there from the middle of the 16th century, occupied as innkeepers, and later also as craftsmen and merchants. In 1794 a Jewish school and the house of the rabbi were built there; the Jewish cemetery was enlarged in 1798. In the 18th century there was a small Jewish hospital; a larger one was erected in 1890. The most noted rabbis of Siedlce in the middle of the 18th century were R. Meir, author of *Netiv Meir* (1931^2), and Israel Meisels (officiated 1858–67) son of Dov Berush *Meisels. In the second part of the 18th century the rabbis of Siedlce visited Warsaw where they carried out religious functions for Jews living there illegally. A group for the study of the Torah and Talmud was founded in Siedlce in 1839, and at the end of the 19th century a Bikkur Ḥolim society was established. During World War I a Jewish high school was opened. Yiddish periodicals published in Siedlce included the *Shedletser Vokhnblat*, which Abraham Gilbert began to produce in 1911. Jacob Tenenboim, who between the two world wars edited the weekly *Dos Shedletser Lebn* with Joshua Goldberg, also collaborated with Gilbert.

The lawyer Maximilian Appolinary *Hartglas contributed to this weekly.

The *Bund started activities in Siedlce around 1900. At first the Polish Socialist Party also had a great influence among the Jews in Siedlce, but Zionism won the greatest adherence, though all shades of Jewish political parties were active.

In 1906 the czarist Okhrana (secret police) organized a pogrom against the Jews of Siedlce in which 26 Jews were killed and many injured. In 1920 Siedlce was occupied by the Red Army, and after its recapture by the Poles antisemitic excesses occurred. The Jewish population numbered 3,727 (71.5% of the total) in 1839; 4,359 (65%) in 1841; 5,153 (67.5%) in 1858:8,156 (64%) in 1878; and 14,685 (47.9%) in 1921.

[Jacob Goldberg]

Holocaust Period

Before the outbreak of World War II there were 15,000 Jews living in Siedlce. The German army entered the town on Sept. 11, 1939, and began to take measures against the Jews. In November 1939 the Jewish population was forced to pay a "contribution" (fine) of 100,000 zlotys. On Dec. 24, 1939, the synagogue was burned down. During 1940 about 1,000 Jews from Lodz, Kalisz, and Pabianice (cities incorporated into the Third Reich) were forced to move to Siedlce. In March 1941 German soldiers organized a three-day *Aktion* in which many Jews were killed. The following August a ghetto was set up; it was closed off on October 1. The plight of the Jews in Siedlce then drastically deteriorated. In January 1942 another fine of 100,000 zlotys was imposed. On Aug. 22, 1942, about 10,000 Jews were deported to *Treblinka death camp where they were murdered. Only 500 Jews were allowed to remain in the diminished ghetto, though a further 1,500 stayed there illegally. On Nov. 25, 1942, the so-called small ghetto was liquidated and its 2,000 Jewish inmates deported to Gesiborki. The Germans concentrated all the survivors from Siedlce province in the town. Hundreds of them were shot on the way there or murdered in Gesiborki. All the others were deported within a few days to Treblinka and murdered. A few hundred remained in a forced labor camp near Siedlce until April 14, 1943, when they were executed.

During the deportations hundreds of Jews succeeded in escaping to the forests. They formed small groups which tried to bring in arms and resist the German units searching the woods. The majority of them were killed during the winter of 1942–43. In January 1943 the Germans reported the capture and execution of 150 Jews in different parts of Siedlce province. Some Jewish groups continued to offer armed resistance until the fall of 1943.

The Jewish community in Siedlce was not reconstituted after the war. Organizations of former Jewish residents of Siedlce were established in Israel, the United States, France, Belgium, and Argentina.

[Stefan Krakowski]

BIBLIOGRAPHY: *Sefer Yizkor li-Kehillat Siedlce li-Shenat Arba Esreh le-Ḥurbanah* (Yid., 1956).

SIEFF, ISRAEL MOSES, BARON (1889–1972), British industrialist and Zionist. He was born in Manchester, where his father, a migrant from Lithuania, founded a prosperous business. He and his brothers-in-law, Simon *Marks and Harry *Sacher, were closely associated in their devotion to Zionism, as well as in their commercial career. Sieff's wife, Rebecca *Sieff, was among the founders of WIZO and continued her active participation in that organization. It was in 1913 that Sieff, along with Marks, came to know Chaim *Weizmann, who was at that time a lecturer in Manchester University. From then on until Weizmann's death, the three brothers-in-law were among his closest friends and collaborators, notably in the critical labors which led up to the issue of the *Balfour Declaration. Under their leadership Manchester became arguably the major center of British Zionism. Sieff was one of the founders of and a regular contributor to the fortnightly review *Palestine*, which played its part in educating public opinion in England in favor of Zionism. In 1918, when the Zionist Commission headed by Weizmann went to Palestine to prepare the ground for the implementation of the Declaration, Sieff acted as its secretary. He joined Marks when the main offices of their firm, Marks and Spencer Limited, were transferred to London, and played a notable part in its development. He was the vice chairman and joint managing director of the company and in 1967 became its president. Not restricting his activities to Zionist matters, Sieff was the founder of Political and Economic Planning (PEP), an organization of internationally recognized authority, and was its chairman (1931–39), vice chairman (1939–64), and president from 1966. He was also a vice chairman of the Royal Anthropological Institute. A noted philanthropist, Sieff, together with other members of the family, founded the Daniel Sieff Research Institute at Reḥovot, from which the *Weizmann Institute of Science developed. His Zionist and Jewish activities were marked by his honorary presidency of the Zionist Federation of Great Britain and Ireland and of that body's Educational Trust, his chairmanship and vice presidency of the Joint Palestine Appeal, and his chairmanship of Carmel College. He was made a life peer in 1966. In 1970 his memoirs were published, *The Memoirs of Israel Sieff*. His younger son MARCUS JOSEPH SIEFF, BARON SIEFF OF BRIMPTON (1913–2001), who was educated at Manchester Grammar School and Cambridge, joined the family firm in 1945, became a director in 1954, and, after 1967, was managing director and chairman. He expanded the range of Marks & Spencer to include the sale of food. Like other members of his family he was a notable contributor to Jewish and Zionist causes. Sieff wrote an autobiography, *Don't Ask the Price* (1986). After his retirement the firm experienced increasing difficulties, and ceased to be a family or, indeed, a "Jewish" firm. Sieff was knighted in 1971 and received a life peerage in 1980.

ADD. BIBLIOGRAPHY: ODNB online; DBB; G. Rees, *St. Michael: A History of Marks & Spencer* (1973).

[Harry Sacher / William D. Rubinstein (2nd ed.)]

SIEFF, REBECCA (1890–1966), first president of *WIZO. The eldest daughter of Michael Marks, founder of Marks and Spencer, she was born in Leeds and educated in Manchester. Her husband, Israel *Sieff, and brother, Simon *Marks, were close friends and associates of Chaim *Weizmann, and she was instinctively drawn into their Zionist activity by her strong sense of tradition and historic continuity. She worked with the British Palestine Committee, which prepared the ground for the *Balfour Declaration, and was a founding member and first president of the Federation of Women Zionists of Great Britain and Ireland in 1918. In 1924 she was elected president of WIZO, which was founded in July 1920, holding this position until her death. She was especially active in the 1940s as a campaigner against British rule in Palestine and on behalf of Holocaust survivors. Rebecca Sieff was an excellent speaker with a brilliant mind and a forceful personality. She traveled extensively, speaking on behalf of WIZO and organizing its branches all over the world. She lived mainly at her home in Tel Mond, Israel, where she is buried.

BIBLIOGRAPHY: *The Memoirs of Israel Sieff* (1970). **ADD. BIBLIOGRAPHY:** ODNB online; R. Gassman-Sherr, *The Story of the Federation of Women Zionists of Great Britain and Ireland, 1918–1968* (1968).

[Rosa Ginossar]

SIEGEL, BENJAMIN "BUGSY" (1906–1947), U.S. mobster. Born Benjamin Hymen Siegelbaum in Brooklyn, New York, to Russian-born Jewish immigrant parents, Siegel, one of five children, grew up in Hell's Kitchen, where he joined a street gang on Lafayette Street. He started out as a thief, but soon resorted to extorting "protection" money from street vendors by pouring kerosene on their merchandise and setting it ablaze. Fellow gang members took notice of Siegel's quick, sociopathic temper, naming him Bugsy after the expression "crazy as a bedbug"; Siegel preferred to be called Ben and would attack anyone that used the nickname in his presence. At 14, Siegel merged his gang with Meyer *Lansky's. Known as the Bugs-Meyer Mob, the gang was based in Manhattan's Lower East Side and evolved to include gambling, car theft, bank robbery, and murder for hire. In 1930, the gang joined forces with Charles Luciano in an otherwise unheard of union at the time between Jews and Italians. As they began buying protection from police and local politicians, mobster Arnold *Rothstein took notice and turned to Luciano and the Bugs-Meyer Mob for help with bootlegging. Before long the gang was folded into the Syndicate, a collection of mobsters from around the nation, where Siegel would have a hand in creating Murder, Inc. A high-profile gang hit forced Siegel underground. The Syndicate sent Siegel, who was tired of being second to Lansky, to California in 1937 to establish a gambling presence. Siegel moved to Beverly Hills, hired Mickey Cohen as his lieutenant, and looked up an old friend from the neighborhood, actor George Raft. Together with local gang leader Jack Dragna, Siegel established a wire service to aid in bookmaking, illegal gambling operations, drug smuggling, and union racketeering. Siegel threw lavish parties at his mansion, rubbing elbows with some of Hollywood's biggest names. In Siegel's absence, Lansky became head of the Syndicate. In 1945, Siegel and Lansky set down plans for a gambling hotel in Las Vegas, The Flamingo. The projected cost of the hotel was $1.2 million, but the construction firms took advantage of Siegel's poor business acumen, driving costs up to $6 million. Siegel's girlfriend, Virginia Hill, took multiple trips to Zurich at the time, which led mob investors to suspect that Siegel was funneling money to Swiss bank accounts. Angry mob bosses discussed the possibility of a hit on Siegel during a December 1946 meeting in Havana, Cuba. The unfinished resort enjoyed a gala opening on December 26, 1946, but was closed soon after to finish construction. The Flamingo reopened again in March 1947 and by May was finally turning a profit. But it was too late. Mob patience had worn thin, and Siegel was gunned down in the living room of his Beverly Hills mansion one month later.

BIBLIOGRAPHY: "Siegel, Benjamin," in: *Outlaws, Mobsters and Crooks: From the Old West to the Internet* (1998); "Siegel, Benjamin," in: *Encyclopedia of World Biography* (1998^2); "An American Experience: Las Vegas – An Unconventional History." Benjamin Siegel Biography. PBS, at: www.pbs.org

[Adam Wills (2nd ed.)]

SIEGEL, IDA LEWIS (1895–1982), community worker, feminist, public official. Ida Lewis Siegel was born in Pittsburgh, Pennsylvania, shortly after her parents and two older brothers arrived from Lithuania. In 1893 her family moved again, this time to Toronto. Yiddish-speaking Ida devoted much of her life to bettering the lot of immigrants in Toronto, especially Jewish immigrants targeted by Christian missionaries in Toronto. In order to help immigrants both integrate and retain pride in their cultural and religious heritage, Ida organized, while still a teenager, programs to assist immigrant women learn mothercraft, English, and modern hygiene. It was the beginning of an almost 80-year career of pubic service.

Ida married Isidore Siegel, a traveling salesman and later shopkeeper, and they had six children. With her husband's support, and uncharacteristic of her times, Ida juggled home and community as she immersed herself in an array of community-based activities benefiting Jews and non-Jews alike. An ardent Zionist, she founded the Daughters of Zion, the first Zionist women's group in Canada, and in 1916 was a key organizer of Canadian Hadassah. She was also an early supporter of *Youth Aliyah. A lifelong pacifist, she opposed Canadian participation in World War I and, committed to public education, she helped organize the Home and School Association and was an activist on behalf of children's playgrounds and child welfare. She helped organize the local YM-YWHA, a Jewish medical dispensary – a preliminary step in the founding of the Mount Sinai Hospital in Toronto – and a Zionist Sunday school. A committed suffragette, she campaigned for the women's vote and, once achieved, pressed women both to exercise their ballot and run for public office. Living by example, in 1930 she was elected to the Toronto Board of Education in a largely Jewish neighborhood. She served until 1936 when she unsuccessfully ran for a seat on Toronto's city council, defeated, some argue, by voter uneasiness about electing a woman and a lack of support from Jewish political insiders, who felt a seasoned lawyer would more effectively represent Jewish interests. Undaunted, Ida Siegel went on to become the first woman vice president of the Zionist Organization of Canada and a member of the executive of the Canadian Jewish Congress. She was widely honored in both the Jewish and larger community.

BIBLIOGRAPHY: L.G. Pennacchio, in: *Canadian Jewish Historical Society Journal*, 9 (1985), 41–60; G. Labovitz, in: *Canadian Woman Studies*, 16 (Fall 1996), 95–98.

[Harold Troper (2nd ed.)]

SIEGEL, JERRY (1914–1996), U.S. cartoonist. Siegel, the co-creator of Superman, the first of the great comic book superheroes and one of the most recognizable fictional characters of the 20th century, was born in Cleveland, Ohio, the son of Jewish immigrants from Lithuania. A fan of movies, comic strips, and science fiction pulp magazines, Siegel corresponded with other science-fiction fans before publishing, in 1929, what may have been the first science fiction fan magazine, *Cosmic Stories*. In high school, Siegel befriended his later collaborator, Joe *Shuster. They created Superman (Siegel imagined Superman from his birth on the doomed planet Krypton and his rocket arrival on Earth to his superhuman powers and his mild-mannered alter ego, Clark Kent; Shuster gave Superman his skintight costume and accompanying cape). They were inspired by several fictional characters, including Tarzan and Popeye, and used Superman in short stories and a 1933 comic strip proposal. In 1938, after the idea had languished among other proposals, Superman was chosen as a cover feature for *Action Comics #1*, published by the future DC Comics. They signed away the rights to Superman for $130. In 1946, Siegel and Shuster, nearing the end of their 10-year contract to produce Superman stories, sued DC over rights to the characters they created. After a two-year fight, they relinquished their claim in return for about $100,000 and severed their relationship with DC. Siegel's later work appeared elsewhere but in 1975, nearly destitute, he launched a public-relations campaign to protest DC Comics' treatment of him and Shuster, who, partly blind and unemployed, lived in a threadbare apartment in Queens, N.Y. In 1978, after the first Superman movie made more than $80 million, DC, which over the years had received more than $250 million of the more than $1 billion that Superman generated from movies, television and a variety of commercial products, bowed to public opinion. Ultimately, Siegel and Shuster were granted $35,000 a year each for the rest of their lives and were guaranteed that all comics, TV episodes, films, and other Superman ephemera would be required to state that the character was "created by Jerome Siegel and Joseph Shuster."

[Stewart Kampel (2nd ed.)]

SIEGEL, MARK (1946–), Democratic Party activist and White House official. Born in Brooklyn and a product of its public schools, Siegel is a graduate of Brooklyn College (1967). He holds a master's degree (1968) and doctorate in political science (1972) from Northwestern University, where he specialized in American political behavior, elections, and the U.S. Congress. His dissertation was on the delegate selection process within the Democratic Party: "Toward a More Responsible Two Party System: The Politics of Reform." He was on the adjunct political science faculties of American University and George Washington University's Graduate School of Political Management, where he also directed the University's Semester in Washington program.

Siegel served as legislative assistant for domestic policy to Senator Hubert H. Humphrey (1971–72). He was executive director of the Democratic National Committee under the chairmanship of Robert S. Strauss, the first Jewish chairman of a major American political party (1973–77). Siegel became deputy assistant to President Jimmy Carter in January 1977, where he served as the liaison to the American Jewish community. During that tenure he was the first to propose a national memorial to the Holocaust that led to the creation of the President's Commission on the Holocaust, and the Holocaust Memorial Museum 15 years later on the Mall in Washington.

In 1978 Siegel became the first – and to date the only – Jewish White House official to resign from the inner circle of the president in protest over the Carter Administration's plan to sell F15 jet fighters to Saudi Arabia. Later that year in Jerusalem, Prime Minister Begin presented Siegel with the Jonathan Netanyahu award for civil courage.

For more than 20 years after leaving the White House, Siegel served as president of Mark A. Siegel and Associates, Inc., and International Public Strategies, Inc., lobbying firms dealing with domestic and international representation. After the September 11, 2001 terrorist attacks, he re-entered government as chief of staff to Congressman Steve Israel of New York, a member of the Arms Services Committee of the House of Representatives.

He has served as speechwriter to a long list of public officials including senators Humphrey, Bill Bradley, and Ted Kennedy, Prime Minister Benazir Bhutto of Pakistan, Prime Minister Henny Eman of Aruba, President Nursultan Nazarbaev of Kazakhstan, President Jimmy Carter, Vice President Walter Mondale, and Vice President Al Gore. Siegel served on the Board of the National Democratic Institute of International Affairs for 15 years, where he oversaw the Institute's party development and election monitoring in Asia. In 2000, Siegel served as the on-air consultant on the electoral college to the *Today* show during the presidential recount crisis.

He served as the vice president for government affairs of New Century Financial Corporation. Siegel is married to Judith Siegel, deputy assistant secretary of state for public diplomacy.

[Michael Berenbaum (2nd ed.)]

SIEGEL, MORTON K. (1924–), Jewish educator. Born in New York, he graduated from the Teachers Institute of Yeshiva University (1943) and received his B.A. from Yeshiva College and his Ph.D. from Columbia University (1952).

He began his career as educational director of Laurelton Jewish Center (1945–53) and then joined the staff of United Synagogue first as placement director of the Department of Education, and then as director for the Department of Youth Activities, where he led the dramatic growth of United Synagogue youth from 500 to 24,000 members. He initiated USY on Wheels, a tour of the United States for teenagers, and also the Israel Pilgrimage. Both programs have been in existence for more than four decades. He also launched ATID, the college-age program of United Synagogue. USY became the entry point into Jewish life for an entire generation of Conservative Jews, who went on to Camp Ramah – Siegel directed Camp Ramah in Connecticut for a time – and then into the rabbinate and Jewish professional or academic careers. As the Conservative movement was expanding into the suburbs, its youth programming was the most significant teenage programming in the American Jewish community and enabled the Conservative movement to attract and nurture its own leadership. In 1964 Siegel became director of the Department of Education when Walter Ackerman became dean of the University of Judaism's Teachers Institute.

The Department of Education set standards for the United Synagogue religious schools and newly emerging Solomon Schechter (Jewish Day) Schools as well as congregation nurseries and high schools. Curricular material was published and the department supervised the regional educational commission.

Siegel was a founder and first secretary of the Jewish Educators Assembly and taught at New York University during the 1970s. As he aged, he created new ways of Jewish learning including *Ḥazak*, which is nicknamed "USY for Mature Adults."

Taking the cue from the ongoing successes of the Kadima and USY youth groups, *Ḥazak* offers membership in an organization that provides camaraderie, social interaction, intellectual stimulation, religious guidance, and fun.

He is the author of a manual for the congregational school board member, with text prepared by Morton Siegel and Pesach Schindler and a syllabus on Zionism.

[Michael Berenbaum (2nd ed.)]

SIEGEL, SEYMOUR (1927–1988), U.S. rabbi, educator, and ethicist. Born in Chicago, Siegel was ordained at the Jewish Theological Seminary (JTS) in 1951 and earned a Doctor of Hebrew Letters from JTS in 1958. During a long career at JTS as Ralph Simon Professor of Jewish Ethics and Theology he developed through books, monographs, articles, courses, and lectures a theory and literature concerning Jewish ethics, theology and political life. He was instrumental in consolidating the relationship between the JTS in New York and the new rabbinical seminary of Latin America, the Seminario Rabinico Latinoamericano in Buenos Aires, by spending summers teaching there (1962–64) and worked tirelessly on social ethics in American life and ecumenical issues. Siegel's unique view of Jewish ethics, theology, political philosophy, and politics helped shape American Judaism (but especially Conservative Judaism) during a critical period in the 1960s–80s and has left an important legacy followed by a number of Jewish legal and ethical researchers. As chairman of the Rabbinical Assembly's Committee on Jewish Law and Standards (1973–80) he served in a period of activism in the movement's formulation of policies regarding the status of women, conversion, *kashrut*, biomedical ethics, abortion, birth control, artificial insemination, fetal and human experimentation, genetic engineering, war, and death and dying.

His idea of "ethical realism," or the need to formulate ethical decision-making on the basis of real circumstances (and only indirectly from idealized ethical principles), is basic to Siegel's Jewish ethics and view of politics. One of the most profound influences upon Siegel's formulation of ethical realism was Reinhold Niebuhr who taught at the Union Theological Seminary across the street from JTS. Many of Niebuhr's life experiences and views are paralleled in Rabbi Siegel's experiences and views. Siegel's "epiphany" came as a result of political and social unrest in the late 1960s and early 1970s. Siegel became politically more conservative in the 1970s and 1980s and became an advisor to three American presidents, Nixon, Ford and Reagan. President Reagan appointed him to be executive director of the U.S. Holocaust Memorial Council (1982–85) that was charged with constructing the national Holocaust Museum.

Siegel was also influenced by Abraham Joshua Heschel (d. 1972) on a number of spiritual and philosophical issues, particularly Heschel's conviction that the Jews had a vision of society which could and should influence general society as much as the general society influenced Judaism. Siegel marched alongside Heschel in the civil rights marches of the early 1960s and this translated into his work with the President's Commission for the Study of Ethical Problems in Medicine and Bio-Medical Research (1982). His concept of "A Bias for Life" that he drew from Jewish sources and that summarizes his view of medical ethics was incorporated into some final statements of House of Representatives reports and of the President's Commission on Bio-Medical Research.

After his death, St. Lawrence University purchased his library and personal archives and has established the Rabbi Dr. Seymour Siegel Memorial Library Collection and Archives and the Seymour Siegel Memorial Lecture on Judaism to benefit Jews and non-Jews who wish to explore Jewish ethics, general ethics and politics.

[Richard Freund (2nd ed.)]

SIEGMEISTER, ELIE (1909–1991), U.S. composer and writer. He was born in New York and studied at Columbia University and at the Juilliard School of Music, New York, as well as in Paris under Nadia Boulanger. In 1946 he formed the

American Ballad Singers, and later taught at Hofstra University.

Siegmeister's interest in American folk music was reflected in many of his own compositions, such as *A Walt Whitman Overture* (1940), *Ozark Set* (1944), and *Prairie Legend* (1947). He composed symphonies, operas (including *The Plow and the Stars*, 1963), orchestral works, chamber music, works for piano, choral works, and songs. His publications include *Songs of Early America* (1943), *Invitation to Music* (1961), *A Treasury of American Song* (1940, 1943²), and a manual, *Harmony and Melody* (1965).

BIBLIOGRAPHY: Baker, Biog Dict; Grove, Dict; MGG; Riemann-Einstein; Riemann-Gurlitt.

SIEMIATYCKI, CHAIM (**Semyatitski**; pseudonyms: **Khaym Tiktiner**; **Khayml**; 1908–1943), Yiddish poet. Born in Tykocin (Tiktin), Poland, of a rabbinical family, the yeshivah-trained Siemiatycki, who lost his father at a young age, went to Warsaw in 1929 to work at odd jobs and to write rather than enter the rabbinate. Encouraged in his poetry from his yeshivah days by Hillel *Zeitlin, he contributed poems as well as critical notices on new Yiddish poets to the Warsaw dailies *Moment* and *Haynt*, and to other periodicals. He was soon recognized as one of the leading young Polish-Yiddish poets. In 1935 he published his first modest collection of verse, *Oysgeshtrekte Hent* ("Outstretched Hands," 1935), followed by another quite slender volume, *Tropns Toy* ("Dew Drops," 1938). During the Nazi occupation of Warsaw, Siemiatycki found refuge in Soviet-occupied Bialystok. In 1941 he moved to Vilna, suffered in its ghetto, following the liquidation of which he was shot in a labor camp. Despite his modest literary output, Siemiatycki's remarkably simple and highly individual lyrics mark him as one of the most authentic of modern Yiddish religious poets. An excited sense of wonder at God's creation characterizes his poetry.

ADD. BIBLIOGRAPHY: LNYL, 6 (1965), 494–5; Sh. Belis, in *Di Goldene Keyt*, 114 (1984), 119–24; A. Bik, in *Shragai*, B (1985), 167–8.

[Leonard Prager / Eliezer Niborski (2nd ed.)]

SIEMIATYCZE, town in Bialystok province, E. Poland. Up to the 19th century Siemiatycze was the private property of Polish nobles; from 1807 until 1915 it was ruled by Russia. Jews are first mentioned as customs and tax farmers in Siemiatycze in a document of 1582. In 1700 R. Gedaliah of Siemiatycze and his brother Moses joined the movement of *Judah Ḥasid ha-Levi advocating the return of the Jews to Ereẓ Israel. Their journey was described by R. Gedaliah in a pamphlet entitled *Sha'alu Shelom Yerushalayim* (published in *Reshummot*, 2 (1922), with a foreword by Zalman Rubashov Shazar). Siemiatycze, one of the most prominent communities in the Council of the Four Lands, grew and developed economically in the first half of the 18th century becoming independent of the Tykocin (Tiktin) community in matters of taxation. When the ruling duchess, Anna Jablonowska (1728–1800), built a road through the Jewish cemetery, which was very close to her palace, the community protested; this long caused resentment, and she sought to pacify the Jews by building a beautiful synagogue (1755; still standing in 1971) near the former site. At the end of the 18th century a copper mill was founded under Jewish direction. There were 1,015 Jews in Siemiatycze in 1765; 3,382 in 1847; 4,638 (75.4% of the total population) in 1897; and 3,718 (65.3%) in 1921. Some earned their livelihood in crafts and industry, but the majority engaged in trade, particularly in forest products and grain. At the end of the 18th century, Jewish merchants from Siemiatycze traded as far as Leipzig and Frankfurt. From the 1860s Jewish merchants and contractors developed the local weaving industry. Between the two world wars Jewish industrialists set up a factory producing glazed brick tiles which employed a work force that was 50% Jewish. Jewish craftsmen worked in clothing, leather, lumber, metal, building, glazing, and coach-building. The Jewish economy was also supplemented by vegetable growing in the period of economic depression between the two world wars. It was also assisted by the Jewish Cooperative Peoples' Bank and by *Gemilut Ḥasadim* societies in the city.

In 1905 czarist police attacked Jewish youngsters strolling in the forest on Rosh Ha-Shanah, wounding ten of them and killing one. The next day young Jewish revolutionaries organized themselves into "fighting units," disarmed the police, and controlled the town for three weeks. Jewish *self-defense units were set up in Siemiatycze. They also showed their strength when Siemiatycze reverted to Poland after World War I and they prevented attacks by pogromists. At the beginning of the 20th century the revolutionary movements, with the *Bund in the forefront, won support among the Jewish workers' and craftsmen's unions. Between the two world wars undercover Communist groups were also influential in the town. A Zionist society, *Ẓe'irei Zion, was founded in 1902 and opened a library. The various Zionist parties were all active there in the interwar period. Between the two world wars there were in the town a primary yeshivah and later a Beit Yosef yeshivah; a Yiddish elementary school (up to 1924); a Hebrew *Tarbut and a Yavneh school. The last rabbi of Siemiatycze was Ḥayyim Baruch Gerstein, a leader of the Mizrachi movement in Poland who perished in the Holocaust.

[Dov Rabin]

Holocaust Period

In 1939 there were over 7,000 Jews in Siemiatycze, 2,000 of them refugees from western Poland. The Soviet authorities, who controlled the city from 1939 to 1941, forced Jewish merchants and manufacturers to move to nearby towns on the pretext that they were security risks to the city, which lay in a border area. In the summer of 1940 most of the refugees were exiled to the Soviet interior. On June 23, 1941, German forces entered. They immediately organized a Polish police force which set about attacking the Jews. The Germans set up a *Judenrat*, headed by J. Rosenzweig, and a ghetto in the area "across the bridge" (Aug. 1, 1941). About 6,000 Jews were imprisoned within the ghetto, including Jews from Drohiczyn,

Mielnik, and other towns. In deportations carried out on Nov. 2–9, 1942, the Jews were dispatched to *Treblinka. A second chairman was appointed for the *Judenrat*, Meir Shereshevski. Following the first deportation, the ghetto inmates met to discuss self-defense and planned to set the ghetto on fire should the Germans initiate another *Aktion* to liquidate the inhabitants. Shamai Plotnicki was sent to outlying villages to acquire arms. The resistance plan could not be carried out because the dates of deportations were moved forward to November 1942, when all the inhabitants were sent to their death. Some of the ghetto inmates tried to escape deportation by breaking through the walls; 150 of them were shot in the attempt. Of the 200 persons who managed to reach the forest, a number of them were forced back for lack of food and shelter. During this period groups of Jewish partisans were organized, one of which was headed by Hershl Shabbes. Clashes broke out between the Jewish partisans in the Brzezinski forests and the Polish underground AK (*Armia Krajowa*). When Siemiatycze was retaken by Soviet forces in May 1944, only about 80 Jews were left, but the Polish AK units continued to attack Jews. After the war the Jewish community of Siemiatycze was not reconstituted, but a society of former Jewish residents of Siemiatycze was formed and functioned in Israel and the U.S.

[Aharon Weiss]

BIBLIOGRAPHY: Halpern, Pinkas, index; R. Mahler, *Yidn in Amolikn Poyln in Likht fun Tsifern* (1958), index; J. Berger, *Księżna Pani na Kocku i Siemiatyczach* (1936), passim; E. Ringelblum, *Projekty przewarstwowienia Żydów w epoce stanisławowskiej* (1935), 55; Z. Auerbach, in: *Yevreyskaya Starina*, 4 (1911), 563; B. Wasiutyński, *Ludność żydowska w Polsce w wiekach XIX i XX* (1930), 83; *Kehillat Semiatich* (Heb. and Yid., 1965).

SIENA, city in Tuscany, central Italy. There is documentary evidence that a well-established Jewish settlement existed in Siena in 1229. It consisted mainly of moneylenders, who found conditions there favorable for their business. Although attacked in sermons by the most implacable Franciscan friars – Bernardino da *Siena at the beginning of the 15th century and Bernardino da *Feltre at its close – the Jews maintained their position. Between 1543 and the end of the 16th century at least 11 Jews graduated as physicians from the University of Siena. In 1571 Duke Cosimo I, anxious to receive the title of grand duke, gave in to the pressure of the Church and introduced ghettos in *Tuscany; Siena was one of the two places selected for the purpose. Conditions in the Siena ghetto in the 17th century, its quarrels and personalities, are strikingly illustrated in the diary of an uneducated Jewish peddler of low social and moral standing. In 1786 a new synagogue was built: the elaborate music sung on the occasion has been rediscovered and published. In March 1799, French troops occupied the town and the Jews were given full emancipation, but in the following June gangs of reactionaries from nearby *Arezzo descended on Siena, stormed the ghetto, and massacred 13 Jews, some of them inside the synagogue where the ark still bears the traces of the violence. According to Mussolini's special census of Jews in 1938, there were 219 Jews in Siena and the surrounding area. When the Germans occupied the area, most of these people disappeared into the Tuscan countryside to avoid roundups, but 17 Jews were deported from Siena and died at Auschwitz. In the years after World War II, the community had great difficulties in rebuilding itself. In the early 2000s the Jewish Community of Siena was composed of no more than 50 Jews. The synagogue, one of the most beautiful in Italy, is situated in via delle Scotte.

BIBLIOGRAPHY: N. Pavoncello, in: *Nova Historia*, 7, pt. 5–6 (1955), 31–51; idem, in: *Israel* (Rome, July 22, 1954; Aug. 11, 1955); Milano, Italia, index; Zolekauer, in: *Archivio giuridico*, 5 (1900), 259–70; *Bollettino senese di storia patria*, 14 (1907), 174–83; C. Roth, *Personalities and Events* (1953), 305–13; idem, in: HUCA, 5 (1928), 353–402; Cianetti, in: *Il nuovo giornale* (April 19, 1919); Zoller, in: RI, 10 (1913/15), 60–66; 100–10; L. Schwarz, *Memoirs of my People* (1943), 95–102; Adler, Prat Mus, 1 (1966), 132–54. **ADD BIBLIOGRAPHY:** R. Salvadori, *Breve storia degli ebrei toscani, IX–XX secolo* (1995).

[Ariel Toaff / Massimo Longo Adorno (2nd ed.)]

SIERADZ (Rus. **Seradz**), town in the province of Lodz, central Poland. Jews settled in the town around the middle of the 15th century and in 1446 there was a Jewish street. In the second half of the 16th century the struggle between the Jewish community and the townsmen was intensified as a result of the latter's complaint about competition from Jewish merchants. In 1569 King Sigismund II Augustus prohibited Jews from entering the town. They resettled in Sieradz during the 17th century, but their residence was forbidden once more in 1725. In 1765 there were only 17 Jews in Sieradz. Under Prussian rule (1793–1806) Jewish merchants and craftsmen again settled in Sieradz. The Jewish population of Sieradz rose from 177 (10% of the total population) in 1808 to 595 (19%) in 1827; 1,782 in 1857; 2,357 (35%) in 1897; and 2,835 (31%) in 1921. They earned their livelihood from trade in cereals, shopkeeping, tailoring, weaving, carpentry, and haulage. From 1829 to 1862 the authorities of Congress Poland restricted the Jews to a special quarter of the town where not more than one family could reside in a room and the houses were to be built of brick and covered by tiles. A number of Sieradz Jews joined the Polish rebels in 1863. After the retreat of the Russian army (1915), Jewish cultural institutions were established in Sieradz and the Zionists subsequently acquired considerable influence. Between the two world wars, various Jewish social and political organizations were active.

[Arthur Cygielman]

Holocaust Period

In 1939, 5,000 (about 40%) of the inhabitants of Sieradz were Jewish. The town was occupied by German forces on the third day of the war (Sept. 3, 1939), and looting of Jewish stores immediately spread. A number of Jewish hostages were taken and some were sent to Germany. In retaliation for alleged cases of shooting in the direction of German soldiers, all Jewish males were assembled and beaten, and some were killed. The ghetto was established on March 1, 1940, but no fence erected around it. During 1940–41 (before and after the establishment of the ghetto) the Jewish population of Sieradz decreased to about 25% of its prewar figure, as a result of deportations and flights to other towns of the Warthegau or to the territory of the General Government. In 1941 there were also sporadic transports of able-bodied Jews to the work camps near Poznan. By the beginning of 1942 only about 1,200 Jews remained and these were ordered to appear at a roll call twice daily. During their absence from their homes the remains of their property were looted. At the end of August 1942 the remainder of the Jewish population was sent to *Chelmno death camp with the exception of a few selected for forced labor in the *Lodz ghetto.

[Danuta Dombrowska]

BIBLIOGRAPHY: B. Wasiutyński, *Ludność żydowska w Polsce w wiekach XIX i XX* (1930), 10, 12, 27, 50, 71; M. Baliński and T. Lipiński, *Starożytna Polska*, 1 (1845), index; A. Eisenbach et al. (eds.), *Żydzi a powstanie styczniowe, materiały i dokumenty* (1963), index; I. Schiper, *Studya nad stosunkami gospodarczymi Żydów w Polsce podczas średniowiecza* (1911), index; idem, *Dzieje handlu żydowskiego na ziemiach polskich* (1937), index; R. Mahler, *Yidn in Amolikn Poyln in Likht fun Tsifern* (1958), index; D. Dabrowska, in: BŻIH, 13–14 (1955); T. Berenstein, *ibid.*, 38–39 (1961).

SIERPC (Rus. **Serpec**; Yid. **Sheps**), town in Warszawa province, N. central Poland; passed to Prussia in 1795 and was within Russia from 1815 to World War I, after which it reverted to independent Poland. A Jewish settlement in Sierpc is mentioned in documents in 1739 and 1766. In 1830 a government commission directed that Jews living in houses owned or leased by them were to be permitted to stay in Sierpc, while the rest were to be expelled. The community numbered 649 (67% of the total population) in 1800; 2,604 (56%) in 1856; 2,861 (42%) in 1921; and 3,077 (about 30%) in 1939. Jews earned their livelihood from the retail trade and crafts, generally on a small scale with inadequate earnings. They particularly suffered from the economic *boycott instigated by antisemites from 1912. Many Jews in Sierpc were dependent on outside relief, being helped by former residents of Sierpc in the United States who established a special "rescue fund" to aid them. Prominent rabbis of the town included Meir Devash (officiated 1790–1812); Moses Leib Benjamin Zilberberg (1830–40; d. Jerusalem, 1865); Mordecai b. Joshua Greenboim (1841–58); and Yeḥiel Mikhal b. Abraham Goldshlak (1865–1918), a disciple of the *ẓaddik* of Przysucha.

[Shimshon Leib Kirshenboim]

Holocaust and Postwar Period

In World War II, during the German occupation, Sierpc belonged to Bezirk Zichenau, established and incorporated into East Prussia by order of Hitler on Oct. 26, 1939. When the Germans entered on Sept. 8, 1939, German soldiers, *Volksdeutsche*, and Poles immediately began to loot Jewish shops. Frequent street and house raids to seize Jews for forced labor were made, and Jews were beaten up. During the Sukkot holiday the Germans set fire to the main synagogue. A young boy who entered the burning building to save the Torah scrolls was shot, and the following day, the Germans, on the pretext that the boy had been the incendiary, fined the Jewish community 50,000 zlotys.

On Nov. 8, 1939, deportation of the Jews from Sierpc began. The Jews were then driven out of the town where they were loaded on to wagons and taken some distance. They were subsequently forced to continue on foot in the darkness to Nowy Dwor, many being beaten on the way. The following day the police marched about 1,800 of them to Warsaw, while the rest managed to hide in Nowy Dwor. A few craftsmen whom the Germans wished to exploit remained in Sierpc interned in a special quarter. In addition a small number of the deportees returned to Sierpc, increasing the number in the ghetto to about 500.

The ghetto was liquidated on Feb. 6, 1942. Jews were loaded onto trucks sent to the ghetto in Mlawa district. On the way many were murdered.

Few Jews from Sierpc survived the war. Twenty-four survived internment in *Auschwitz. A few individuals saved their lives by hiding on the "Aryan side." Two of their number, who had escaped from the ghetto in Strzegów, were members of a partisan detachment in the vicinity of Plock, but after the war was over were murdered by Polish partisans.

In 1948 eight Jewish families, formerly resident in Sierpc, were living there. The societies of former residents of Sierpc influenced the municipal authorities to return the tombstones taken from the Jewish cemetery to pave the streets. The stones were used to erect a monument in memory of the Jews from Sierpc who perished in the Holocaust.

[Danuta Dombrowska]

BIBLIOGRAPHY: *Kehillat Sherpẓ; Sefer Zikkaron* (Heb., Yid., 1959).

SIERRA, SERGIO JOSEPH (1923–), Italian rabbi and publicist. Sierra was born in Rome, where he received a rabbinical and university education. As chief rabbi of Bologna (1948–59), he brought new life to the Jewish community after the disasters of World War II. From 1960 he was chief rabbi of Turin, and director of the Istituto Superiore di Studi Ebraici-Scuola Rabbinica "S.H. Margulies-Disegni." He was a member of the Consulta Rabbinica Italiana and professor of Hebrew literature at Turin University (1969).

Sierra published several essays on Jewish history and literature, particularly from the period of the Middle Ages (RMI, JQR) and a review of *Gli Studi Italiani di Ebraico Postbiblico* (1971). Among his books is *Il Valore etico delle Mizvoth* (1957), and a scientific edition of Bonafoux Bonfil Astruc's Hebrew translation (1423) of Boethius *De Consolatione Philosophiae* (1967).

[Alfredo Mordechai Rabello]

In 1979–80 he was one of the founders of the Associazione Italiana per lo Studio del Giudaismo (AISG); he was professor of Hebrew and Comparative Semitic Languages, University of Genoa (1984–93), president of the Assemblea dei Rabbini d'Italia (1987–92), and member of the scientific committee and the editing committee of the *Rassegna Mensile di Israel*. In 1979 the second edition of his *Il Valore etico delle Mizvoth* was published. Among his publications are Italian translations of classical Hebrew works: in 1983 he published his translation *I doveri dei cuori* of *Ḥovot ha-Levavot* by Baḥya ibn Paquda; in 1988 there appeared his translation of Rashi's Commentary to *Shemot, Esodo*; in 1990 *La corona regale, Keter Malkhut* by Solomon ibn *Gabirol. In 1996 he was co-translator of the *Tehilim Yerushalayim* and in 1998 co-translator of the *maḥzor: Seder Tefillot le-Ḥol, le-Shabbat u-li-Yamim Tovim*). He edited *La lettura ebraica delle Scritture* and *Scritti sull'Ebraismo in memoria di M.E. Artom*. In 1998 there appeared in his honor *Hebraica. Miscellanea di Studi in onore di S.J.S. per il suo 75 compleanno*, edited by F. Israel, A.M. Rabello, and A.M Somekh, with a bibliography and a list of publications. In 1992 he made *aliyah* to Jerusalem.

[Alfredo Mordechai Rabello (2nd ed.)]

SIESBY, GOTTLIEB ISASCHAR (1803–1884), Danish author and editor. A shoemaker turned journalist, Siesby endeavored to further his liberal political views in various publications. He finally became co-editor of the conservative daily *Flyveposten*, which he acquired together with J. Davidsen in 1852, but after some initial success the paper had to close down in 1870. Siesby published *Lyriske Forsøg* (1825), poems; two volumes of comic verse; and *Robinson* (1934), a play staged in Copenhagen.

°**SIEVERS, EDUARD** (1850–1932), Germanist, linguist, and student of classical Hebrew poetry. Sievers taught at Jena (1871), Tuebingen (1883), Halle (1887), and Leipzig (1892). In addition to his many important works in the field of Germanic studies, Sievers published contributions to New Testament studies. His main research in the area of Hebraica was on the interpretation of the metrical structure of biblical Hebrew poetry; the results of these efforts were published as *Metrische Studien* (4 vols., 1901–19). In this important work, he helped pioneer the proper understanding of Hebrew accentuation and elegiac verse, and was the first to introduce the anapaest as a metrical principle in understanding Hebrew rhythm.

[Zev Garber]

SIFRA (Aram. סִפְרָא), is a *midrash halakhah* from the school of R. Akiva on the Book of Leviticus. The Aramaic word *sifra* means "book" or "The Book." This name was commonly used in Babylonia, and most likely attests to the centrality and importance of this Midrash. In the Land of Israel this Midrash was called *Torat Kohanim*, corresponding to the name given to the Pentateuchal book. According to most scholars, *Sifra* from the school of R. Akiva contains Midrashim on Lev. 1:1–7:38; 10:8–18:6; 18:19; 18:24–20:5; 20:22–27:34 (the attribution of the Midrashim in *Beḥukotai* (Lev. 26:3 ff.) is doubtful). Several textual versions contain additional expositions from the school of R. Ishmael on Lev. 8:1–10:7; 18:1–7; 18:18; 18:28; 20:6–22 (see below).

As is indicated by the statement of the *tanna* R. Simeon, the son of R. Judah ha-Nasi, to Bar Kappara (TB Kiddushin 33a), and by the testimony of *geonim* and *rishonim*, *Sifra* was originally divided into nine sections. However, in the extant textual versions, the original portion of *Sifra*, which derives from the school of R. Akiva, is divided into eleven or twelve "*megillot*" or "*dibburim*": "*Nedavah*" or "*Vayikra*" (Lev. 1:1–3:17); "*Hovah*" or "*Nefesh*" (4:1–5:26); "*Ẓav*" (6:1–7:38); "*Sheraẓim*" (10:8–12:8); "*Nega'im*" (13:1–59); "*Meẓorah*" (14:1–57); "*Ẓavim*" (15:1–33); "*Aḥarei Mot*" (16:1–18:30, with omissions); "*Kedoshim*" (19:1–20:27, with omissions); "*Emor*" (21:1–24:23); "*Sinai*" (25:1–26:2); "*Be-Ḥukotai*" (26:3–27:34, with omissions). The introduction of a secondary division, corresponding to the weekly Torah portions according to the Babylonian custom, is probably responsible for the increase in the number of units in *Sifra*. Several proposed reconstructions of the original nine parts of *Sifra* were put forth in the past, but this question was satisfactorily resolved only recently, by S. Naeh, who based his precise definition of the boundaries of the nine sections on the division that is at the shared foundation of the manuscripts, and which is accurately preserved in MS. Parma. He also showed that the key to the division is not dependent on the content of the smaller units, but rather is determined by the more or less equal size of these nine units known as "*megillot*" (literally, scrolls). This, along with the name of the work as a whole: "*Sifra*," attests to its relatively early commitment to writing in a book. Each *megillah* or *dibbur* is divided into "*parashot*," that are further split into "*perakim*" (chapters), and these, into "*halakhot*," with a numerical total at the end of each unit of the *parashot*, *perakim*, and *halakhot* that it contains.

Sifra is quoted at the present in accordance with the edition of I.H. Weiss, that was published some one hundred and forty years ago (1862) in Vienna. The Weiss edition is based on the Venice printing and corrections in accordance with *Yalkut Shimoni*, along with a section of references to the parallels and short interpretive notes. In the absence of a complete scientific edition of *Sifra*, great weight must also be given to two photocopy editions of *Sifra* manuscripts: the photocopy of MS. Vatican 66, published with an introduction by Finkelstein, and the photocopy of MS. Vatican 31, published by Makor (Jerusalem, 1972).

A commentary on *Sifra*, almost to the end of *dibbura de-Nedavah*, was published in Breslau in 1915, from the posthumous legacy of R. Meir Friedmann (Ish Shalom), who drew upon several manuscripts. In 1983–1990 L. Finkelstein published a four-volume scientific edition of the first two *dibburim* of *Sifra* (*Nedavah* and *Hovah*), consisting of an introductory volume, the text volume that included references to the parallels and a concise interpretation, a volume of textual variants, and a volume with a lengthy commentary. A fifth volume, that was sent to press close to Finkelstein's death in 1992, contains indexes to the four preceding volumes, along with a collection of Finkelstein's scholarly articles on halakhic Midrash.

The text of Finkelstein's critical edition is based on MS. Vatican 66, unquestionably the best text of *Sifra*, and, in fact, the most accurate extant *midrash halakhah* codex. This manuscript is of Eastern origin, most likely Babylonia, and is dated to the tenth or ninth centuries. It preserves many remnants of pure Tannaitic language, original terminology, traces indicative of the incorporation of the foreign units from the school of R. Ishmael, and mainly, an abundance of good textual readings. The manuscript has "Babylonian" vocalization above the letters written by another scribe, who in many instances also corrected the writing of the initial scribe, to adapt its tradition and textual version to his method. In the textual variants volume Finkelstein listed the changes in all the manuscripts of *Sifra*: MS. Breslau 108 (currently in the Jewish Theological Seminary library in New York: JTS Rab. 2171), that is relatively close to MS. Vatican 66; the Constantinople 1523(?) printed edition, that comprises most of the portion of *Vayikra*, and that apparently also reflects an Eastern textual tradition; the Italian MSS. Vatican 31 and Parma 139; the Venice printed edition; the Franco-German MS. Oxford 151 and MS. London 341, that present the Franco-German textual tradition; pages from a Yemenite ms. possessed by Rabbi J.Y. Kafiḥ; many *Genizah* pages (photo reproductions of which appear at the beginning of the Introduction volume); and the versions of the major indirect textual witnesses in the *Yalkutim* and medieval commentaries and Midrashim. To complement this edition, attention should also be paid to a considerable number of *Genizah* fragments and other *Sifra* pages, mainly from Eastern Europe, that were identified after the publication of the edition.

Three commentaries on *Sifra* by *rishonim* have been published: the commentary of R. Abraham ben David of Posquieres, that of Rabbenu Hillel, and the commentary attributed to R. Samson of Sens; and a relatively large number of commentaries by *Aḥaronim*. To these we should add commentaries on *Sifra* still in manuscript form, several of which are being published in the Shoshana edition, and many testimonies of nonextant *Sifra* commentaries. All in all, we have evidence of fifty copies of *Sifra* and more than 40 commentaries on the Midrash. These figures, that greatly exceed the number of copies and commentaries for the other *midrash halakhah*, reflect the premier standing during the medieval period of this *midrash*, that was very commonly studied in the past, and was an unparalleled tool for the comprehension of difficult topics relating to sacred objects and the purity laws. The fate of the scientific publication of *Sifra*, on the other hand, has not been as positive, and it is to be hoped that this failing will be remedied in the not too distant future.

Sifra is singular in the paucity of aggadic material it contains, the lengthy deliberations characteristic of many of its midrashic expositions, the extensive use made of the extant Mishnah, and in the great proximity of its expositions to their parallels in the BT, that apparently possessed a Midrash very similar to the extant *Sifra*. According to Finkelstein, the redactors of the extant *Sifra* made use of an early Midrash on Leviticus, that had been used by the Torah scholars who instructed the priests in the work of the Temple and the sacrifices. Based on this assumption, Finkelstein attempted to resolve a long line of difficult expositions, in which the redactors cited the early Midrash verbatim, and added to it a later stratum, so that it would conform to their approach. This view suits Finkelstein's general stance in *midrash halakhah* research, but it seems that many of his proofs can be refuted. Brown, on the other hand, asserts that along with the ancient Midrashim, *Sifra* also contains exegeses reflective of a version later than their parallels in the two Talmuds, but his proofs are unconvincing.

The core midrash of *Sifra* is from the school of R. Akiva, but in a later period it was augmented by several lengthy passages from the school of R. Ishmael, that apparently came from another halakhic midrash from the latter school that has not survived:

(1) the *baraita* of thirteen exegetical methods by which the Torah is expounded, at the beginning of *Sifra*. This *baraita* appears in all the textual versions, and there is evidence that it was already in this opening position in the geonic period. The positioning of this *baraita* at the beginning of *Sifra* might possibly reflect the ancient practice of beginning the study of the Pentateuch with the Book of Leviticus. The *baraita* is composed of several sources: (a) the count of the thirteen hermeneutical methods, according to R. Ishmael; (b) the exemplification of these rules in the *Scholion* that does not always correspond to the original meaning of these principles in the initial *baraita*; (c) the seven hermeneutical methods of Hillel that were inserted in the middle of the rule of *shenei ketuvim*.

(2) *Mekhilta de-Milu'im*, that includes exegeses regarding the narrative of the dedication of the Tabernacle at the end of the portion of *Ẓav* and the beginning of *Shemini* (Lev. 8:1–10:7). Several textual versions of *Sifra* lack this *Mekhilta*, or include only a portion of it. The inner division signs of the *Mekhilta de-Milu'im* in the reliable manuscripts vary from the main body of *Sifra*, and the *Mekhilta* contains several terms from the school of R. Ishmael, and several matters whose content is characteristic of this school. The full version of *Mekhilta de-Milu'im* comprises two cycles of interpretations on Lev. 9:1 ("On the eighth day"), and two such cycles on Lev. 9:22–10:7. Several manuscripts, however, lack the first cycle of expositions on 9:22–10:7, and the beginning of the second cycle does not appear in one manuscript. The second cycle of exegeses on Lev. 9:22 ff. is markedly associated with the school of R. Ishmael, while the first set of exegeses on these verses lacks any clear indicators of its origin.

(3) *Mekhilta de-Arayot*. The original *Sifra*, from the school of R. Akiva, does not expound the prohibitions of incestuous and other forbidden sexual relations in *Aḥarei Mot* (Lev. 18:7–18, 20–23) and in *Kedoshim* (Lev. 20:10–21). This omission is understandable in light of R. Akiva's opposition to publicly expounding the passage containing these prohibitions. Several textual versions of *Sifra* add a second set of interpretations of Lev. 18:1–7, from *Aḥarei Mot*, and interpreta-

tions of the sexual prohibitions in Lev. 20:6–22 in *Kedoshim*. In the conclusion of this unit is an exposition of Lev. 18:18 and 28, not in the order in which they appear in Scripture. These hermeneutical units obviously did not originally belong to *Sifra* of the school of R. Akiva, as is attested by their absence from most of the textual versions, and from their inclusion, not in their proper place, in other textual versions. The usual division markers of *Sifra* are missing from these sections in MSS. Vatican 66 and Oxford. The hermeneutical method, the names of the rabbis, and the midrashic terms in these two units patently teach of their origin in the second Midrash on Leviticus, from the school of R. Ishmael, that apparently adopted R. Ishmael's permissive stance regarding the public exposition of the sexual prohibitions.

Along with these large units, *Sifra* also incorporates several short Midrashim from the school of R. Ishmael. All these remains indicate the past existence of a tannaitic Midrash from the school of R. Ishmael. This conclusion is also supported by a lengthy series of halakhic Midrashim from the school of R. Ishmael that are preserved in the Talmuds, and the *paytan* Yannai probably possessed such a midrashic work. At the present time, unfortunately, no direct remnant of this lost Midrash has been found.

Translations

English: J. Neusner, *Sifra: An Analytical Translation*, Atlanta 1988. German: J. Winter, *Sifra Halachischer Midrasch zu Leviticus*, Breslau 1938.

BIBLIOGRAPHY: Ch. Albeck, *Introduction to the Talmuds* (Heb., 1969), 113–123; idem, *Untersuchungen ueber die Halakhischen Midraschim* (1927), 97–105; R. Brown, "A Literary Analysis of Selected Sections of Sifra," in: *Proceedings of the Tenth World Congress of Jewish Studies*, (1990), 3, vol. 1, 39–46 (Heb.); J.N. Epstein, *Introduction to the Mishnaic Text* (Heb., 1948), 729–31; idem, *Prolegomena ad Litteras Tannaiticas* (Heb., 1957), 634–702; idem, in: E.Z. Melamed (ed.), *Studies in Talmudic Literature and Semitic languages*, vol. 2 (Heb., 1988), 108–24; L. Finkelstein, "The Core of the Sifra: A Temple Textbook for Priests," in: JQR, 80 (1989), 15–34; idem, *Sifra According to Codex Assemai LXVI* (1957); idem, *Sifra on Leviticus*, vols. 1–5 (Heb., 1983–1992); S.D. Fraade, "Scripture, Targum and Talmud as Instruction: A Complex Textual Story from the Sifra," in: J. Magness and S. Gitin (eds.), *Hesed ve-Emet: Studies in Honor of Ernst S. Frerichs* (1998), 109–21; M. Friedmann, *Sifra der alteste Midrasch zu Levitikus* (Heb., 1915); A. Geiger, *Kevuẓat Ma'amarim* (Heb., 1885), 165–72; A. Goldberg, "The Dual Exegeses in *Mekhilta de-Milu'im*," in: *Sinai*, 89 (1981), 115–18 (Heb.); G. Haneman, "On the Linguistic Tradition of the Written Text in the Sifra Ms. (Rome, Codex Assemani 66)," in: E.Y. Kutscher, S. Lieberman, and M.Z. Kaddari (eds.), *Henoch Yalon Memorial Volume* (1974), 84–98 (Heb.); Kahana, "The Development of the Hermeneutical Principle of *Kelal u-Ferat* in the Tannaitic Period," in: *Studies in Talmudic and Midrash Literature in Memory of Tirza Lifshitz* (2005), 173–216 (Heb.); idem, "Halakhic Midrash Collections," in: *The Literature of the Sages*, vol. 3b (2006); idem, *Manuscripts of the Halakhic Midrashim: An Annotated Catalogue* (Heb., 1995), 22–26, 60–88; S. Lieberman, "*Ḥazanut Yannai*," in: *Sinai*, 4 (1939), 221–50 (Heb.); E.Z. Melamed, *The Relationship Between the Halakhic Midrashim and the Mishnah & Tosefta* (Heb., 1967), 9–78; S. Naeh, "Did the Tannaim Interpret the Script of the Torah Differently from the Authorized Reading?," in: *Tarbiz*, 61 (1992), 401–48 (Heb.); idem, "Notes to Tannaitic Hebrew Based on Codex Vat. 66 of the Sifra," in: M. Bar-Asher (ed.), *Language Studies*, 4 (1990), 271–95 (Heb.); idem, "The Structure and the Division of Torat Kohanim, A: Scrolls," in: *Tarbiz*, 66 (1997), 483–515 (Heb.); idem, "The Structure and the Division of Torat Kohanim, B: Parashot, Perakim, Halakhot," in: *Tarbiz*, 69 (2000), 59–104 (Heb.); idem, "The Tannaitic Hebrew in the Sifra according to Codex Vatican 66" (Heb., Ph.D. diss., Hebrew University, Jerusalem, 1989); J. Neusner, "Sifra and the Problem of the Mishnah," in: *Henoch*, 11 (1989), 17–40; idem, "Sifra's Critique of Mishnaic Logic," in: *Hebrew Studies*, 29 (1988), 49–65; A. Shoshana, *Sifra on Leviticus*, vols. 1–3 (1981–1988); G. Stemberger, "Sifra-Tosefta-Yerushalmi: Zur Redaktion und fruhen Rezeption von Sifra," in: JSJ, 30 (1999), 271–311; idem, "Zu Eigenart und Redaktion von Sifra Behukotai," in: *Frankfurter Judaistische Beiträge*, 31 (2004), 1–19; E. Wajsberg, "The Difference Between the Midrashic Terms 'Talmud' and 'Talmud Lomar,'" in: *Leshonenu*, 39 (1975), 147–52 (Heb.).

[Menahem I. Kahana (2nd ed.)]

SIFREI (Aram. סִפְרֵי; Heb. סְפָרִים; "books") on Deuteronomy (SD), primarily a *midrash halakhah* of the school of R. Akiva, encompasses six sections from Deuteronomy: 1:1–30; 3:23–29; 6:4–9; 11:10–26:15; 31:14; 32:1–34:12 (the end of Deuteronomy). Each of these six units opens with the initial verse of a weekly Torah portion according to the custom of the Land of Israel, but the principle that guided the redactors of SD for the inclusion of Midrashim for these specific sections is unclear.

The *editio princeps* divides SD into *piska'ot* (סליק פיסקא – "the conclusion of the *piska*"), like the division of the printed edition of SN. Most of the manuscripts contain a division into verses (סליק פסוקא – "the conclusion of the verse"). In a number of places, there is an alternative division into chapters (סליק פירקא – "the conclusion of the chapter"), and in a relatively large number of locations, the unclear abbreviation פ' appears. In most of the complete manuscripts, however, the division is not regular, as it is in SN, and no division markers are preserved in several remnants from *Genizah* codices; some of the added notations of *piska'ot* in the relatively complete division of the printed edition disrupt the continuity of the expositions. At the same time, SD preserves several remnants of another, presumably earlier, division into "baraitot" and a later division into the Babylonian weekly Torah portions.

Most scholars regard the central unit of SD, that uninterruptedly expounds the halakhic passages in Deut. 12:1–26:15 (= *piska'ot* 59–303) as belonging to the school of R. Akiva. It is also accepted that the midrashim on the passages "Hear, O Israel" (Deut. 6:4–9) and "If, then, you obey" (Deut. 11:13–21) (= *piska'ot* 31–36; 41–47) contain clear signs pointing to an association with the school of R. Ishmael. The affiliation, however, of the aggadic sections in the first and last parts of SD is the subject of disagreement. Hoffmann initially thought that the entire first part of the midrash (*piska'ot* 1–58) is from the school of R. Ishmael, while the last part (*piska'ot* 304–357) belongs to that of R. Akiva. He later changed his opinion and also attributed the last aggadic section, beginning with *piska* 304, to the school of R. Ishmael. This view was fundamentally also held by Epstein, but he considered the aggadic section from the school of R. Ishmael at the beginning of SD as encompassing only *piska'ot* 1–54. Epstein placed the changeover point from the school of R. Ishmael to that of R. Akiva at the end of *piska* 54, under the influence of a *Geniza* fragment of *Mekhilta* on Deuteronomy, from the school of R. Ishmael that was discovered by Schechter and resembles SD, *piska* 54, but completely diverges from the latter beginning with *piska* 55. Goldberg reexamined this question and concluded that the aggadic sections at the beginning of SD (*piska'ot* 1–54, excluding the passages of "Hear, O Israel" and "If, then, you obey") and at its end are from the school of R. Akiva, in accordance with his general view that all the lengthy aggadic sections in ḤM belong to this school. It has been noted, however (see *Midrashei Halakhah*, (3) The Aggadic Material), concerning the aggadic material in ḤM, that most of the outstanding characteristics of the two schools do not find expression in the aggadic material and that there is in fact a high degree of similarity between the aggadic material contained in the parallel midrashim deriving from the two schools of tannaitic midrash. This similarity is quite noticeable in the aggadic material common to SD and *Mekhilta Deuteronomy*. In light of this, the "seam" at the beginning of *piska* 55 is to be viewed as a transition from the aggadic material that does not belong to either of the schools to the halakhic material from the school of R. Akiva.

L. Finkelstein published the scientific edition of SD, completed in Berlin in 1939, a month after the outbreak of World War II. Finkelstein based his edition mainly on five almost complete direct textual versions that include both SN and SD – the *editio princeps* and four manuscripts, six short *Genizah* fragments, *Midrash Ḥakhamim*, *Yalkut Shimoni*, and additional indirect textual versions. As regards the text, Finkelstein writes in his introduction: "For the most part, I chose the versions of MS. Rome, and I rejected it only where it was clear that another version was better and superior to it." In regard to the spelling in his edition, Finkelstein explained in his introduction that "the textual version of *Sifre* was redacted in the Land of Israel, and was obviously written in the Land of Israel spelling, or to be more precise, in the Galilean spelling. Many times a *yod* or a *vav* was added as an aid to vocalization, and the plural is usually marked with a *nun*, in place of a *mem*. For the convenience of the reader, I did not pay attention to these fine points and seemingly superfluous letters. In the main, I printed words in their usual spelling, although from the aspect of, and for the study of, Hebrew spelling, as well as for pronunciation, [not even] the crowns of letters nor the 'point of a *yod*' should be waived." To aid the reader, the textual variant section also lists textual versions that support Finkelstein's text, and not only the versions that differ from it. In the section of commentary and references to parallels, Finkelstein also made use of Horovitz's literary estate, citing him verbatim within brackets.

The first booklets of this edition were printed individually and were reviewed by Epstein and then Lieberman. Epstein harshly criticized Finkelstein's eclectic method of determining the text, in which he also incorporated, without any clear marker in the text itself, the versions of *Midrash ha-Gadol* that were taken from the second Midrash (MD) and other parallels, and also the emendations that the editor added on his own, and opposed to all the textual versions. Epstein similarly faulted the method of spelling adopted by Finkelstein in his edition, which frequently diverges from all the manuscripts. In addition to the methodological objections, Epstein also discussed a large number of topics, versions, and interpretations that were set forth in the edition. In conclusion, Epstein stressed that, despite all its drawbacks, "at long last we have the foundation of the text of *Sifrei* on which we can build, and the content and the builder are to be congratulated." Lieberman's criticism is more sympathetic. He, too, complained that Finkelstein emended the text in opposition to the manuscripts, but he emphasized the important contribution made by Finkelstein and the advantages of the edition in diverse areas, primarily the small number of corruptions it contains in relation to the size of the book, the stress placed on the mutual relations between the manuscripts that it presents, the large number of quotations from the literature of the *Rishonim*, the numerous references to talmudic and extra-talmudic parallels, and the up-to-date references to the scholarly literature.

A photocopy edition of Finkelstein's work was published in New York in 1969. In his introduction to this edition, Finkelstein notes, with refreshing candor, "I would still like to correct the mistakes that arose during the copying of the changes; and also the textual version, where I was so audacious as to emend the text in opposition to all the accepted versions, which should not be done, but I was childish at the time." He also directed the reader to quotations from SD in *Yalkut Talmud Torah* and Pseudo-*Rabad* that became available to him during the conclusion of his work and afterwards, and that should be taken into account.

All this compels the reader of Finkelstein's edition to check the textual variants and commentary sections constantly and thoroughly, in order, with their aid, to reconstruct the manuscript versions and to examine the editor's considerations in his determination of the text. Most of the direct and indirect textual versions of SD, as well as its commentaries, also include *Sifrei Numbers*, as is the case for MS. Vatican 32, the best textual version of *Sifrei Numbers* and SD. Although Finkelstein wrote that he had preferred its versions, in practice he digressed from it many times, and, in general, did not determine the text in accordance with this manuscript in most of the problematic passages, where he definitely should have remained faithful to its versions. Additionally, new texts of SD have since been discovered, in addition to the list of addenda that Finkelstein included at the beginning of his second edition, the most important of which are: some 45 leaves from the Cairo *Genizah*, Yehudah Nachum collection, and the archives of Modena and Nonantola, 13 leaves in MS. JTS Rab. 2392, and copious citations from SD in the Yemenite midrash in MS. Cincinnati 2026.

Dozens of expositions from the corresponding Midrash (*Mekhilta Deuteronomy*) were added to the central section of

SD (belonging the school of R. Akiva) in several manuscripts of the latter. These irregular expositions can be identified by their clear exhibition of characteristics of the school of R. Ishmael and especially by their presence in only a few textual versions, at times in a different place in each manuscript, as they interrupt the continuity of the original exegeses of SD. Some are explicitly labeled as "*tosefta*" (addition) in the commentaries of Rabbenu Hillel and other *Rishonim*. Finkelstein published these additions in his edition in small print, and Epstein also devoted a special discussion to them, in which he disagreed with several of Finkelstein's hypotheses regarding the origin of a number of expositions in SD as unoriginal marginal annotations. Now, with the discovery of additional *Genizah* fragments and Yemenite manuscripts, we see that these additions made their way from the marginal annotations only to the Western manuscripts of SD, while the Eastern textual versions of this Midrash lack these additions.

Regarding the unique nature of SD, Finkelstein observed that it still contains a significant number of early *halakhot* that follow the view of Beit Shammai and earlier remains from the Second Temple period, possibly even from the period of the prophets. An exacting study of Finkelstein's proofs teaches that many do not withstand the test of critical examination and that SD does not contain more early *halakhot* than the other ḤM. For a summary of the opinions concerning the redactors of SD, see the study by Epstein; for his commentaries on the Midrash, see the description of *Sifrei Numbers*.

Translations

English: R. Hammer, *Sifre: A Tannaitic Commentary on the Book of Deuteronomy (*New Haven-London, 1986); J. Neusner, *Sifre to Deuteronomy: An Analytical Translation* (Atlanta, 1987). German: H. Bietenhard, and H. Ljungman, *Der tannaitische Midrasch Sifre Deuteronomium* (Bern, 1984). Spanish: T. Martines, *Sifre Deuteronomio: comentario al libre de Deuteronomio*, vols. 1–2 (Catalonia, 1989–1997).

BIBLIOGRAPHY: Ch. Albeck, *Introduction to the Talmuds* (Heb., 1969), 127–29; idem, *Untersuchungen ueber die Halakhischen Midraschim* (1927), 84, 107–11; H.W. Basser, *Midrashic Interpretations of the Song of Moses* (1984); idem, *Pseudo-Rabad Commentary to Sifre Deuteronomy* (1994); J.N. Epstein, "Finkelstein L., Siphre zu Deuteronomium," in: *Tarbiz*, 8 (1937), 375–92 (Heb.); idem, *Introduction to the Mishnaic Text* (Heb., 1948), 731–33; idem, "Mechilta and Sifre in the Works of Maimonides," in: *Tarbiz*, 6 (1935), 343–82 (Heb.); idem, *Prolegomena ad Litteras Tannaiticas* (Heb., 1957), 625–30, 703–24; L. Finkelstein, *Sifra on Leviticus*, vol. 5 (1992), 40–88, 53*–101*; L. Finkelstein (ed.), *Sifre on Deuteronomy* (Heb., 1939); S.D. Fraade, *From Tradition to Commentary: Torah and Its Interpretation in the Midrash Sifre to Deuteronomy* (1991); idem, "Sifre Deuteronomy 26 (ad Deut. 3.23): How Conscious the Composition?" in: HUCA, 54 (1983), 254–301; idem, "The Turn to Commentary in Ancient Judaism: The Case of Sifre Deuteronomy," in: P. Ochs (ed.), *The Return to Scripture in Judaism and Christianity* (1993), 142–71; A. Goldberg, "The School of Rabbi Akiva and the School of Rabbi Ishmael in Sifre Deuteronomy, Pericopes 1–54," in: *Te'uda*, 3 (1983), 9–16 (Heb.); I.B. Gottlieb, "Language Understanding in Sifre Deuteronomy" (Ph. D. diss., New York University, 1972); idem, "Midrash as Philology," in; JQR, 75 (1984), 132–161; M. Kahana, "The Commentary of Rabbenu Hillel to the Sifre," in: *Kiryath Sepher*, 63 (1990), 271–80 (Heb.); idem, *The Genizah Fragments of the Halakhic Midrashim* (Heb.), 1 (2005), 227–337; idem, "Halakhic Midrash Collections," in: *The Literature of the Sages*, vol. 3b (2006); idem, Manuscripts of the Halakhic Midrashim: An Annotated Catalogue (Heb.; 1995), 97–107; S. Lieberman, "Siphre zu Deuteromium ed. L. Finkelstein," in: *Kiryath Sepher*, 14 (1938), 323–36 (Heb.); E.Z. Melamed, *The Relationship between the Halakhic Midrashim and the Mishnah & Tosefta* (Heb., 1967), 79–93, 142–45.

[Menahem I. Kahana (2nd ed.)]

SIFREI HA-MINIM (Heb. סִפְרֵי הַמִּינִים; lit. "books of the sectarians"). In Tosefta *Shabbat* 13:5, et al., it is stated that *gilyonim* (lit. "sheets of parchment") and *sifrei ha-minim*, may not be saved from fire on the Sabbath, but should be left to burn even if they contain Divine Names. On a weekday, however, according to Yose ha-Gelili, these Names should be cut out and the rest burned. For, according to R. Tarfon, unlike ordinary idolators who do not know God and therefore do not deny Him, **minim* ("sectarians") are those who recognize God but nonetheless deny Him. R. Ishmael adds that these books bring enmity between Israel and their Father in Heaven, presumably because they cause them to stray from the true path; *minim* should therefore be shunned (referring to Ps. 139:21–22). By *gilyonim* is meant Gospel texts, as is explicitly stated in the uncensored version of *Shabbat* 116a by Meir (second century) and Johanan (third century), who, satirically punning on the term *Evangelion*, call it *aven gillayon* (*gilyon*; "scroll of falsehood") and *avon gillayon* (*gilyon*; "scroll of sin") respectively (see Rabinovitz, Dik. Sof., 260, n. 60). For this reason, despite biblical citations and Names of God contained in these Gospel texts, they are left to be burned.

The term *sifrei ha-minim* is, however, somewhat more problematic. Bacher (in REJ, 38 (1899) 38–46), followed by Buechler and others, interprets it as meaning Torah scrolls written by *minim* (cf. Sif. Num. 16; see A. Buechler, *Studies in Jewish History* (1956), 272). But the term as found in *Ḥagigah* 15b (see Dik. Sof., 59, n. 3) and in *Sanhedrin* 100b (Dik. Sof., 303, n. 10) clearly cannot bear this meaning, but means heretical writings. Moore (Judaism, 1 (1946), 86f., 243f.), S. Lieberman (*Tosefta ki-Feshutah*, 3 (1962), 206f.), and others, suggest that *sifrei ha-minim* refers to Christian writings which abound in (reinterpreted) biblical citations. A new interpretation has been suggested by M. Margalioth, who published a newly recovered "book of magic from the talmudic period" (*Sefer ha-Razim*, 1966). It is a strange Hebrew treatise of Judeo-heathen character and is dated by the editor to the third or fourth centuries C.E. (p. 23–28). Margalioth concludes that when the Talmud speaks of *sifrei ha-minim* or *sifrei kosemin* ("books of diviners"; Tosef., Ḥul. 2:20, etc.), it refers to such a class of syncretist magical literature. However, his early dating of this text is still somewhat uncertain, and his explanation, though attractive, remains doubtful.

The *sifrei ha-minim* in Tosefta, *Yadayim* 2:13, mentioned there together with books of the Apocrypha, have no sanctity and therefore "do not render the hands that touch them ritually unclean." A comparison of this passage with that of *Yadayim* 4:6 and other related texts demonstrates conclusively, however, that the correct reading is *sefer hamiras*, meaning Homeric literature (see S. Lieberman, *Hellenism in Jewish Palestine* (1950), 105–14, especially 106 n. 39). However, this ruling remains true of *sifrei haminim* too.

BIBLIOGRAPHY: S. Hahn, in: *Emlékkönyv Dr. Mahler* (1937), 427–35.

[Daniel Sperber]

SIFREI (Aram. סִפְרֵי) **NUMBERS** (SN) is a *midrash halakhah* of the school of R. *Ishmael. The Aramaic word *sifrei* means "books," and this name was also given to a halakhic Midrash on Deuteronomy. In the past a halakhic Midrash on Exodus was also similarly named. SN consists of Midrashim on 11 biblical units: Num. 5:1–7:19, 7:84–8:4, 8:23–29:14, 10:1–10, 10:29–12:16, 15:1–41, 18:1–19:22, 25:1–14, 26:52–56, 27:1–31:24, and 35:9–34. A comparison of the material that is expounded with what is not teaches that most of the halakhic passages are the subject of exegesis, while a majority of the literary sections were disregarded by the Midrash. This criterion is not absolute, since several narrative sections, such as the complaint by the people in the wilderness or the act of Phinehas at Shittim, were expounded, while several halakhic topics lack any exegesis, such as the commandment to dispossess the inhabitants of the land and the destruction of the cult places (*bamot*).

SN was formerly divided into two books, each named after their beginning. The first was called "*Sefer va-Yedabber*," after the initial word of the first verse that is expounded in Num. 5:1: "The Lord spoke [*va-yedabber*] to Moses, saying," and the second apparently was named "*Sefer Zot*," because it opened with the words "This is [*zot*] the statute of the Torah" (Num. 19:2). Each of these two books is divided into secondary topics, and each topic is further divided into "*baraitot*." The numerical sum of the *baraitot* is listed at the end of each subject, in the interim division of each of the two books, and at the conclusion of each of the two books themselves. Another division of SN is by verses ("סליק פסוקא" – "the completion of the verse"), but this would seem to be a later apportionment. The division according to the Babylonian Torah portions in several second-rate textual versions is not original.

The scientific edition of SN, the editing of which was the result of thorough consideration, was published by H. Saul *Horovitz in Leipzig in 1917. The body of the edition is generally based on the *editio princeps* published in Venice 1546, with corrections and additions following two manuscripts – Vatican 32 and London 341 – and numerous citations from SN in *Yalkut Shimoni*, *Midrash Ḥakhamim*, the commentary on SN by Rabbenu Hillel, and in several medieval Midrashim. The text itself is accompanied by an apparatus listing textual variants and another consisting of a concise commentary that also contains references to the parallels. The edition begins with a lengthy introduction that includes, inter alia, a characterization of the hermeneutical method of SN. This is the first critical edition of any work from the tannaitic literature, and Horovitz began the preparation of his editions of *Mekhilta of R. Ishmael* and *Sifrei Deuteronomy* only following its completion.

When all is said and done, however, this initial edition suffers from several limitations. Additional direct textual versions of SN were discovered after the publication of Horovitz's edition, most importantly MS. Oxford 151, MS. Berlin Tubingen 1594.33, eight leaves of MS. Firkovich II A 269, *Yalkut Talmud Torah* by R. Jacob ben Hananel Sikili, which quotes extensive portions of SN, several commentaries on SN by *Rishonim*, Midrashim by *Rishonim* who made use of SN, and more. In determining the text of SN, Horovitz relied heavily upon the reworked and emended text of *Midrash Ḥakhamim*, which he considered to be the best textual version of SN; while MS. Vatican, the oldest manuscript of SN, was regarded by him to be a manuscript of lesser quality. Horovitz's erroneous appraisal of the manuscripts reflects a confusion between the textual versions of SN, on the one hand, and its parallels, on the other, and from an unawareness of several basic principles of talmudic philology that were developed only after the publication of his edition. Note should also be taken of his partial listing of textual variants and the tendency to harmonization that is evident in many of his interpretations.

As was mentioned above, the best manuscript of SN is Vatican 32, whose superiority to the other textual versions is expressed in various ways, such as: traces of the early division of SN, remnants of tannaitic language, rare or difficult words that were emended in other textual versions, original terminology, the style of the exegeses, the Mishnah of SN that other textual versions frequently emended in accordance with the extant Mishnah, *baraitot* that were not reworked in accordance with their parallels in TB, occasionally surviving remnants of early *halakhot*, a version of the Bible different from the masoretic text, and "foreign" texts whose exceptional nature is more clearly evident in this version. Along with its original formulations, MS. Vatican also contains many *homoiteleuton*, interchanged letters, and even a small number of emendations and adaptations. Obviously, other textual versions must be employed as well, both in order to reconstruct the original versions of SN and to study their evolution in the medieval period.

A number of *Rishonim* composed commentaries on SN, most of which also interpret *Sifrei Deuteronomy*. The most important of these works are the commentaries of Rabbenu Hillel, the commentary attributed to Rabad, the commentary in MS. Mantua 36, and that by R. Soliman Ohana. The especially outstanding commentaries on SN by **Aḥaronim* include those by R. David *Pardo, R. Meir *Friedmann (Ish Shalom), and R. Naphtali Zvi Judah *Berlin.

An exceptional feature of SN is the relatively large number of "foreign" texts that it incorporates, some of which are inserted in the middle of expositions, interrupting their continuity; while the placement of others does not follow the order of the Pentateuch. Some of these foreign texts are cited in SN in the name of R. *Judah ha-Nasi or were attributed to him in other talmudic parallels. Most of Judah ha-Nasi's other dicta in SN, which harmonize with the course of the expositions, were included as a last opinion presented in the conclusion of the exegesis. This fact leads us to believe that the initial redaction of SN was followed by the insertion of another stratum from "the school of Rabbi." Attention should also be paid to the fact that SN hardly contains expositions in the name of *tannaim* from the generation after R. Judah ha-Nasi, which is possibly indicative of the relatively early redaction of this halakhic midrash. The brevity of the exegeses in SN, in comparison with the other halakhic midrashim, and the relative paucity of associative expansions in this midrash would seem to support this suggestion.

Translations

English: J. Neusner, *Sifre to Numbers: An Analytical Translation* (1986), *piska'ot* 1–115. German: D. Borner-Klein, *Der Midrasch Sifre zu Numeri* (1997), 1–385; K.G. Kuhn, *Sifre zu Numeri* (1934; 1959). Spanish: M.P. Fernandes, *Midras Sifre Numeros* (1989).

BIBLIOGRAPHY: Ch. Albeck, *Introduction to the Talmuds* (Heb., 1969), 123–27; idem, *Untersuchungen ueber die Halakhischen Midraschim* (1927), 105–7; M. Bar-Asher, "A Preliminary Study of Mishnaic Hebrew as Reflected in Codex Vatican 32 of Sifre-Bamidbar," in: *Te'uda*, 3 (1983), 139–65 (Heb.); H.W. Basser, *Pseudo-Rabad Commentary to Sifre Numbers* (1998); D. Borner-Klein, *Der Midrasch Sifre zu Numeri* (1997), 389–777; J.N. Epstein, *Introduction to the Mishnaic Text* (Heb., 1948), 733–35, 747–51; idem, *Prolegomena ad Litteras Tannaiticas* (Heb., 1957), 588–624; M. Hirshman, "Rabbinic Universalism in the Second and Third Centuries," in: HRT, 93 (2000), 101–15; M. Kahana, "The Biblical Text as Reflected in MS Vatican 32 of the Sifre," in: Y. Sussmann-D. Rosenthal (eds.), *Talmudic Studies*, 1 (Heb., 1990), 1–10; idem, "The Commentary of Rabbenu Hillel to the Sifre," in: *Kiryath Sepher*, 63 (1990), 271–80 (Heb.); idem, *The Genizah Fragments of the Halakhic Midrashim*, 1 (Heb., 2005), 187–213; idem, "Halakhic Midrash Collections," in: *The Literature of the Sages*, vol. 3b (2006); idem, "Manuscripts Commentaries on the Sifre," in: *Studies in Memory of the Rishon Le-Zion R. Yitzhak Nissim*, vol. 2, 95–118 (Heb.); idem, *Manuscripts of the Halakhic Midrashim: An Annotated Catalogue* (Heb., 1995), 89–94; idem, "Marginal Annotations of the School of Rabbi Judah the Prince in Halakhic Midrashim," in: S. Jafet (ed.), *Studies in Bible and Talmud* (Heb., 1987), 69–85; idem, *Prolegomena to a New Edition of the Sifre on Numbers* (Heb., 1982); idem, "To Whom Was the Land Divided," in: *Gedenkschrift for Mordechai Wiser* (1981), 249–73 (Heb.); E.Z. Melamed, *The Relationship between the Halakhic Midrashim and the Mishnah & Tosefta* (Heb., 1967), 123–41; Y.M. Ta-Shema, "An Unpublished Franco-German Commentary on Bereshit and Vayikra Rabba, Mekhilta and Sifre," in: *Tarbiz*, 55 (1986), 61–75 (Heb.).

[Menahem I. Kahana (2nd ed.)]

SIFRE ZUTA DEUTERONOMY (SZD) is a *midrash halakhah* of the school of R. *Akiva. No direct manuscripts of SZD have been found, and the main source for the reconstruction of the Midrash is citations in the commentary of the Karaite sage Jeshua ben Judah on Deuteronomy, who quotes passages from it with relative accuracy. Other citations, of a more paraphrastic nature, are included in *Sefer Pitron Torah*, which was published by Urbach, and possibly also in *Midrash Ḥadash*, published by Mann. The name "*Sifre Zuta Deuteronomy*" is not documented in the literature of the *Rishonim* and was proposed in light of its high degree of similarity to *Sifre Zuta Numbers*. The close relation between these two works is clearly demonstrated by their common terminology and shared quotations and is also reflected in their vocabulary, names of rabbis, their Mishnah, which consistently differs from the extant Mishnah, and their unique *halakhot*.

About 130 short citations from SZD that expound verses from the portions of *Devarim*, *Va-Etḥanan*, *Ekev*, *Re'eh*, *Ki Teẓe*, and *Ki Tavo* have been found to date. The aggadic quotations from the portion of *Devarim*, chap. 1, fundamentally resemble their parallels in *Sifrei Deuteronomy* and *Mekhilta Deuteronomy*, albeit with a distinct and independent style and with several terms and expressions that are characteristic specifically of the school of *Sifrei Zuta*. The other expositions, which are concerned with halakhic issues, employ terms and hermeneutical methods of the school of R. Akiva, following the midrashic subschool of *Sifrei Zuta*.

BIBLIOGRAPHY: I.M. Kahana, *Sifre Zuta on Deuteronomy* (Heb., 2002).

[Menahem I. Kahana (2nd ed.)]

SIFRE ZUTA NUMBERS (SZN) is a midrash halakhah of the school of R. Akiva. The Aramaic word "*zuta*" means "small," paralleling the name "*Sifre Rabbati* [the large *Sifre*]" given to *Sifrei Numbers* (SN) by several of the *Rishonim*. The *Genizah* remains of SZN, however, do not attest to the limited scope of this midrash as compared to SN, and this name may possibly attest to its rarity. Other names for this midrash are "*Sifre*," *Zute*," *Sifre Yerushalmi*," "*Sifrei shel Panim Aḥerot*," *Mekhilta*," "*Makhalah*," and others. The exact extent of SZN has not been determined, but, like SN, it clearly opened with the exposition of the first *halakhah* in Num. 5:2 (as is demonstrated from the list of books discovered in a Cambridge *Genizah* fragment), skipped the expositions of the verses in Num. 31:25–35:8 (as in the *Genizah* fragment) just like SN, and as a general rule included midrashim on the same verses that are expounded in SN. In any event, no conclusions can be drawn, based on the chance non-preservation of relevant quotations, that certain passages or Torah portions were not the subject of exposition in SZN. This midrash was originally divided into several large subunits, each of which encompassed several topics. The large units, whose scope and names are not known to us, were divided into numbered "*parashot*."

Zunz was the first scholar to collect material about the Rishonim who brought citations from SZN and about the different names of this midrash, and following him, Brüll and other scholars thoroughly discussed the midrash. Schechter successfully identified and published a *Genizah* fragment consisting of two leaves from SZN, on the Torah portions of *Matot* and *Mas'ai*. At the same time B. Koenigsberger began to reconstruct the midrash in orderly fashion, but he was able to publish only two booklets, from the portion of *Bamidbar* to that of *Beha'alotekha*. The first reconstruction of SZN as a whole was made by Horovitz, initially with notes in German, and afterwards in Hebrew, with an independent apparatus of textual variants and an extensive commentary, that included references to the parallels. The second edition, published in Leipzig in 1917 together with Horovitz's edition of SN, also includes an introduction that describes the unique nature of the midrash.

Horovitz based his reconstruction primarily on the explicit quotations of "*Zute*" in *Yalkut Shimoni*, the passages in *Midrash ha-Gadol* that he asserted were copied from SZN, a *Genizah* fragment published by Schechter, quotations that were incorporated in *Num. Rabbah* on *Naso*, and other citations in the literature of the *rishonim*. After the appearance of the Horovitz edition, Epstein published a fragment of five leaves from SZN on the passage of the red heifer that he identified in material that had been sent to him from St. Petersburg. Also published were a small number of new citations from SZN found in the literature of the *Rishonim*, to which we may add several new quotations. The Horovitz edition may also be emended in accordance with MS. Oxford 2637 of *Yalkut Shimoni*, the manuscripts of *Midrash ha-Gadol* on Numbers, and the manuscripts and the *editio princeps* of *Num. Rabbah*. On the other hand, one should eliminate from the Horovitz edition a relatively large number of passages that were included on the basis of *Midrash ha-Gadol*, but that did not, in fact, originate in SZN, rather in other books, including SN, MS, the Mishnah, *Avot de-Rabbi Natan*, the two Talmuds, *Tanhuma*, *Mishnat R. Eliezer*, *Pirkei de-Rabbi Eliezer*, the *Mishneh Torah* of Maimonides, and the original additions made by the author of *Midrash ha-Gadol* himself.

SZN is the subject of two traditional commentaries (Jaskowicz and Garbus) and of modern studies written by three major scholars, Epstein, Albeck, and Lieberman, who devoted an entire book to this midrash. Although SZN is a Midrash from the school of R. Akiva, it is distinguished from the classic Midrashim of this school in a number of ways. It makes use of a relatively large number of unique terms, mentions the names of several Tannaim who do not appear elsewhere, possesses a style that is at times absent from the other sources, and uses rhetorical and poetical language, includes a large quantity of *halakhot* undocumented in other sources and otherwise unknown disagreements of Beit Hillel and Beit Shammai, and consistently quotes a mishnaic source that does not correspond to the extant Mishnah. The scholars have also noted that Rabbi's name is absent from this work. Lieberman drew this distinction into sharper focus by noting that the *halakhot* of R. Judah ha-Nasi and those of R. Nathan appear in SZN, but without attribution. Lieberman additionally indicated "clear allusions" against the Patriarchate in the expositions of SZN. In light of all the above, Lieberman concluded that the redactor of SZN was in conflict with the Patriarchate of R. Judah ha-Nasi, did not acknowledge the superior authority of the latter's Mishnah, and intentionally refrained from mentioning his name and that of R. Nathan, who was the son of the Exilarch, and thus "fined" both leaders, the **nasi* in the land of Israel, and the exilarch in Babylonia. It should be noted that the allusions against the court of the *nasi* found by Lieberman are not unambiguous. Nor is the omission of R. Nathan from SZN unique to this midrash; on the contrary, this feature is characteristic of all the midrashim of the school of R. Akiva.

It is also noteworthy that the material in the lengthy aggadic sections of SZN fundamentally resembles the parallel material in SN, albeit usually with slightly more detail. On rare occasions the aggadic material contains traces of the singular terms and central rabbis characteristic of the halakhic portion of this midrash, and the consistent approach of the aggadic material in a number of topics in SZN noticeably differs from the approach set forth in the parallel material in SN.

The exceptional character of SZN has challenged scholars to determine the identity of its final redactor. Epstein was the first to conclude that R. Hiyya redacted SZN in Sepphoris, to which Albeck objected, leading Epstein to change his view, albeit for other reasons, and to attribute the final ordering of SZN in Sepphoris to Bar Kappara. Lieberman discussed this at length, once again, and, based on other considerations, determined that although Bar Kappara redacted SZN, he did so in Lydda, and not in Sepphoris. But then after all this scholarly activity, a basalt lintel was uncovered in Dabura in the Golan, bearing the inscription: "This is the *beit midrash* of Rabbi Eliezer ha-Kappar." The entire issue accordingly requires re-examination, and it seems that only the discovery of new passages from this midrash, and from other midrashim that were redacted by this school, will likely advance the study of such issues.

Translation

D. Borner-Klein, *Der Midrasch Sifre Zuta* (Stuttgart 2002).

BIBLIOGRAPHY: Ch. Albeck, *Untersuchungen ueber die Halakischen Midraschim* (1927), 148–51; idem. "Zu den neueren Ausgaben halachischer Midraschim," in: MGWS, 75 (1931), 404–10; D. Borner-Klein, *Der Midrasch Sifre Zuta* (2002); N. Brull, "Der kleine Sifre," in: *Jubelschrift zum siebzigsten geburstage des Prof. Dr. H. Graetz* (1887), 179–93; J.N. Epstein, *Introduction to the Mishnahic Text* (Heb., 1948), 739–46; idem, "Mechilta and Sifre in the Works of Maimonides," in: *Tarbiz*, 6 (1935), 343–82 (Heb.); idem, *Prolegomena ad Litteras Tannaiticas* (Heb., 1957), 741–46; idem, "A Rejoinder," in: *Tarbiz*, 3 (1932), 232–36 (Hebr.); idem, "*Sifrei Zutta Parshat Parah*," in: *Tarbiz*, 1 (1930), 46–78 (Heb.); E.Z. Garbus, *Sifre Zuta al Bamidbar … in Perush Sapire Efrayim* (Heb., 1949); H.S. Horovitz (ed.), *Siphre zutta* (Heb., 1917); idem, *Der Sifre Zutta* (1910); J.Z. Jaskowicz, *Sifre Zuta al Sefer Bamidbar* (Heb., 1929); M. Kahana, *The Genizah Fragments of the Halakhic Midrashim*, I (Heb., 2005), 214–26; idem, "Halakhic Midrash Collections," in: *The Literature of the Sages*, 3b, Amsterdam 2006; idem, *Manuscripts of the Halakhic Midrashim: An Annotated Catalogue* (Heb., 1995), 95–96; idem, M.I. Kahana, *Sifre Zuta on Deuteronomy* (Heb., 2002), 38, 42–68; B. Koenigsberger, *Sifre Zuta*, vol. 1 (1984); 2 (1907); S. Lieberman, *Siphre Zutta: The Midrash of Lydda* (Heb., 1968); D. Orman, "Jewish Inscriptions from Dabura in the Golan," in: *Tarbiz*, 40 (1971), 399–408 (Heb.); S. Schechter, "Fragment of Sifre Zuta," in: JQR, 6 (1894), 656–63; L. Zunz, *Die gottesdientlichen Vorträge der Juden historisch entwickelt* (1892; Heb. ed. Ch. Albeck, 1974^3), 267.

[Menahem I. Kahana (2nd ed.)]

SIGHET (Hung. **Máramarossziget**), town in Crisana-Maramures, N.W. Romania, between 1940 and 1944, part of Hungary. Jews had already settled there by the 17th century and were taxed from 1728. Community life in Sighet was traditional and also influenced by religious trends, including *Ḥasidism. The Frankists (see Jacob *Frank) too found adherents there. Ten Jewish families (39 persons) lived in the town in 1746; there were 142 Jews in 1785–87, and 431 in 1831. An organized community already existed during the second half of the 18th century, when the rabbi was Ẓevi b. Moses Abraham (d. 1771) from Galicia, a determined opponent of the Frankist movement. Other rabbis included Judah ha-Kohen *Heller, who served there until his death in 1819; and Hananiah Yom Tov Lipa *Teitelbaum (1883–1904) of the ḥasidic family of *ẓaddikim*. The Sighet community had joined the organization of Hungarian Orthodox communities in 1883, but the liberal elements, amid considerable dispute, later founded their "Sephardi community." From 1906 its rabbi was Samuel Danzig (b. 1878), who perished in the Holocaust. The last rabbi of the Orthodox community was Jekuthiel Judah *Teitelbaum, who also died in the Holocaust. Sighet had yeshivot, Jewish schools, Zionist organizations, and Hebrew presses and libraries, including the Israel Weiss Library. Attempts were made to publish periodicals in Hebrew, Yiddish, and Hungarian. The majority of Jews in the district were impoverished. The Jewish population increased rapidly during the second half of the 19th century. There were 4,960 Jews in the town (about 30% of the total population) in 1891; 7,981 (34%) in 1910; 10,609 (about 38%) in 1930; and 10,144 (39%) in 1941, the highest proportion of Jews in any Hungarian town. Natives of Sighet included the Yiddish author Herzl Apsán (1886–1944); the humorist, editor, and author, Hirsch Leib *Gottlieb; the rabbi and historian Judah Jekuthiel *Greenwald; the Hebrew and Yiddish poet J. Holder (1893–1944); the author Elie *Wiesel; the violinist J. *Szigeti; the Yiddish author J. Ring; and the pianist Géza Frid. Between the two world wars the local Jews suffered from the Romanian Iron Guard, which tried to make it impossible for them to maintain any kind of Jewish life there.

During World War II, after the annexation of northern Transylvania by Hungary in 1940, the authorities began to curtail the economic activity of the Jews in Sighet. Men of military age were conscripted for forced labor in 1942, and in the summer of 1944 Hungarian and German Nazi authorities set up a ghetto, from which 12,000 Jews were deported to death camps.

In 1947 a Jewish community of about 2,300 was formed by returning survivors and Jews from other places. Only about 250 Jews remained in 1970. In 1959 the organization of Sighet Jews in Ereẓ Israel began publication of *Máramarossziget*, a periodical in Hebrew, Yiddish, and Hungarian on the history of the Jews in Sighet and the Marmures district. After 1989 there were several Jewish and official Romanian attempts to commemorate local Jewish life. Elie Wiesel's repeated visits contributed to a better knowledge of their history and heritage. In Israel there is a Sighet Organization which also aims to perpetuate the memory of those who died there.

BIBLIOGRAPHY: *Magyar Zsidó Lexikon*, s.v. *Máramarossziget*; MHJ, 3 (1937), 5 pt. 1 (1959), 5 pt. 2 (1960); 7 (1963); 8 (1965), index locorum in all volumes, s.v. *Máramaros vármegye, Máramarossziget, Sziget*; D. Schön, *Istenkeresök a Kárpátok alatt* (1964²); J.J.(L.) Greenwald (Grunwald), *Zikkaron la-Rishonim* (1969²); idem, *Maẓẓevet Kodesh... Siget u-Felekh Marmaros* (1952); N. Ben-Menahem, *Sifreihem shel Rabbanei Siget* (1949); idem, *Mi-Sifrut Yisrael be-Hungaryah* (1948), 330–86.

[Yehouda Marton / Paul Schveiger (2nd ed.)]

SIGMAN, MORRIS (1880–1931), U.S. labor leader. Born near Akkerman, S. Bessarabia, Sigman left Russia for England in 1901 and settled in New York two years later. He worked as a cloak presser in the needle trades and joined the Jewish labor movement, leading a cloak pressers' revolt against the International Ladies Garment Workers' Union (ILGWU). The cloak pressers formed an independent union affiliated to the Socialist Trade and Labor Alliance and later to the radical labor organization, Industrial Workers of the World (IWW). However, the IWW had little appeal to the Jewish workers of New York and in 1907 Sigman's union rejoined the ILGWU. Sigman devoted his energies to the creation of effective and stable trade unions in the needle trades. He organized the successful shirtwaist workers' strike (1909–10) and managed the picket committee during the cloakmakers' strike (1910). He was elected secretary-treasurer of the ILGWU in 1914 only to resign a year later, but after managing the New York Joint Cloak Board (1917–20), he was elected a vice president of the ILGWU in 1920. He retired in the following year but was recalled from retirement in 1923 to serve as ILGWU president in the face of an impending union split under pressure from the Communist Trade Union Education League. Sigman succeeded in defeating the communist challenge during his five years of office but on his resignation in 1928 he left the union a smaller and impoverished organization.

[Melvyn Dubofsky]

SIGNORET (Kaminker), SIMONE (1921–1985), French film actress. Born in Wiesbaden, Germany, the daughter of a French Army officer, Signoret (her mother's name) was brought up in Paris. A femme fatale role in *Macadam* (1946) started her rise to stardom in French films. In several productions she appeared with the singer and actor Yves Montand, whom she married in 1951. She achieved international stardom and an Oscar for her role in the British film *Room at the Top* (1959) and subsequently acted in other British, Italian, French, and American films, including *L'Aveu* (1970), *La Vie devant soi (Madame Rosa;* 1977), *L'Adolescente* (1979), and *Chère inconnue* (1980).

[Jonathan Licht]

SIGNS AND SYMBOLS. A sign, in biblical Hebrew *ʾot*, is a mark, an object, or an event conveying some particular meaning. A sign is called *mofet* ("portent") when it is portentous or marvelous in character. Symbols constitute a special category of signs. They are visible objects generally acknowledged to represent, by way of association or analogy, something that is invisible. Symbols are not to be confused with *myths, metaphors, or poetic comparisons. The symbolic acts of the prophets, reported in the Bible, are in fact symbols that are acted out. Ancient Hebrew does not possess a special term that corresponds exactly to modern understanding of a symbol, but words such as *ʾot* ("sign, token"), *mofet* ("portent"), *demut* ("likeness, shape"), *ẓelem* ("image, statue"), or *temunah* ("form") are sometimes used in a similar sense.

The direct or indirect author of an *ʾot* in the Bible is almost always God. According to C.A. Keller, this indicates that the term originally belonged to the religious sphere. In the oldest biblical texts, *ʾot* means an oracle or an omen by which God guaranteed that He entrusted someone with a special mission (Ex. 3:12; cf. 4:8–9, 17, 28, 30; Judg. 6:17; I Sam. 10:7, 9), or that His might will participate in an undertaking (I Sam. 14:10), or that a prophetic statement announcing future events is true (I Sam. 2:34; II Kings 19:29; 20:8, 9; Isa. 7:11, 14; 37:30; 38:7–8, 22; Jer. 44:29). The word *mofet* is also employed in this sense in I Kings 13:3, 5. *ʾot* designates also heathen omens (Isa. 44:25), especially astronomical ones (Jer. 10:2), and sometimes denotes a token of good faith (Josh. 2:12) or kindness (Ps. 86:17), evidence (Job 21:29), an example (Ezek. 14:8; cf. Ps. 71:7), or a distinguishing mark, e.g., the sign of Cain (Gen. 4:15), the blood mark on the Israelite houses in Egypt (Ex. 12:13), or the emblems of the tribes in the wilderness of Sinai (Num. 2:2; see *Banners).

God's miraculous interventions, principally in Egypt, are often considered "signs" which provided evidence of His supernatural power and of His election of the people of Israel (Ex. 7:3; 8:19; 10:1–2; Num. 14:11–12; Deut. 4:34; 6:22; 7:19; 11:3; 26:8; 29:2; 34:11; Josh. 24:17; Jer. 32:20, 21; Ps. 78:43; 105:27; 135:9; Neh. 9:10; cf. Isa. 55:13; cf. Ps. 74:9). In these texts, the word *oʾt* is practically synonymous with "wonder" or "miracle," and it is often employed as a parallelism for *mofet* (Ex. 7:3; Deut. 4:34; 6:22; 7:19; 26:8; 29:2; 34:11; Jer. 32:20, 21; Ps. 78:43; 105:27; 135:9; Neh. 9:10), which is also used in that sense in Exodus 4:21; 7:9; 11:9, 10; Joel 3:3; Psalms 105:5; I Chronicles 16:12; and II Chronicles 32:24, 31. Certain cultic institutions or sacred objects came to be regarded as "signs" commemorating divine actions in the past and containing a lesson for successive generations. Among these "signs" are the unleavened bread (Ex. 13:9), the dedication of the firstborn male (Ex. 13:16), the Sabbath (Ex. 31:13, 17; Ezek. 20:12, 20), the teaching of the *Shemaʿ* (Deut. 6:8; cf. 11:18), the originally ritual maledictions, characterized also as "portents," which are referred to in Deuteronomy 28:46, the censers that were converted into an overlaying of the altar (Num. 17:3), Aaron's rod (Num. 17:25), the twelve stones in the Jordan (Josh. 4:6), and the sanctuaries of the Lord in Egypt (Isa. 19:20; cf. 66:19), such as that of Elephantine, which were probably inspired by the Israelite places of worship. In the Priestly tradition of the Pentateuch, the rainbow (Gen. 9:12, 13, 17) and circumcision (Gen. 17:11) are called "signs of the covenant," *ʾot berit*, because they are guarantees of a covenant. The sun, moon, and stars are considered divine "signs both for festivals and for seasons and years" (Gen. 1:14; cf. Ps. 65:9).

In the prophetic books a "sign" (Isa. 8:18; 20:3, Ezek. 4:3) or "portent" (Ezek. 12:6, 11:24, 27; cf. Zech. 3:8) can also refer to a symbolic act or symbolic behavior. A number of such "symbolic acts," described or actually performed by the prophets, are recorded in the Bible. For instance, Hosea symbolized Israel's relation to the Lord in an unhappy marriage to an unfaithful wife (Hos. 1–3; but see *Hosea), and he named his children Lo-Ruhamah ("Not-Loved") and Lo-Ammi ("Not-My-People") to express the fate of the people (Hos. 1:6–9, cf. 2:3, 25). Isaiah used the same method and called his children by names such as Shear-Jashub ("A remnant shall return"; Isa. 7:3) and Maher-shalal-hash-baz ("Speed-Spoil-Hasten-Plunder"; Isa. 8:1–4). Thus he could say: "the sons whom the Lord has given me are signs and portents in Israel" (Isa. 8:18). He himself went "naked and barefoot… as a sign and a portent to Egypt and Cush" (Isa. 20:3). Other acts of this type are Ahijah the Shilonite's tearing his garment into 12 pieces and giving ten to Jeroboam to symbolize the partition of Solomon's kingdom (I Kings 11:29–31), and Zedekiah son of Chenaanah's butting with horns to show that the king of Israel would gore the Syrians with horns of iron (I Kings 22:11). Such symbolic actions are particularly common in Jeremiah and Ezekiel. For instance, Jeremiah shattered an earthen vessel in front of the people (Jer. 9:10–11) in order to symbolize in a concrete manner the destruction of Jerusalem. On another occasion, he carried a yoke to show that the yoke of Babylon would be placed upon Judah and its allies (*ibid.* 27–28). Ezekiel acted out the siege of Jerusalem (Ezek. 4:1–3) and the deportation (*ibid.* 12:1–16), thus becoming himself a "sign" (*ibid.* 4:3) and a "portent" (*ibid.* 12:6, 11) for the Israelites. And when the prophet lost his wife, the Lord forbade him to observe the rituals of mourning (*ibid.* 24:15–24) in order to serve as a sign for the people (24:24, 27). As noted by Naḥmanides in the 13th century (commentary on Gen. 12:6) and stressed by moderns like G. Fohrer, such actions symbolizing future developments are quasi-magical and serve to bring these events about.

The "symbolic acts" of the prophets are only one particular form of symbolism found in the Bible. Many of the Israelite symbols are similar to those of other Near Eastern peoples. In fact, the origins of army, civil, and religious forms which expressed themselves in symbols are the same throughout the Near East. For instance, the impressive symbolic ceremony connected with contracting a covenant is found in Mesopotamia, Syria, and Israel: An animal was killed and dismembered, and the partners in the covenant walked between the pieces to show that they invoked a similar doom of destruction upon themselves if they proved unfaithful to their oath (Gen. 15; Jer. 34:18–19). The verbal agreement was thus accompanied by a symbolic act which produced a profound and lasting impression on the mind, and indicated to both parties the fate they would deserve in case they violated the agreement. A similar symbolic gesture is found in Deuteronomy 21:4: The calf's neck was broken to call for the same fate upon the unknown murderer, while the elders of the city, by washing their hands (Deut. 21:6; cf. Ps. 26:6; 73:13), indicated symbolically that the city was free of guilt. It was believed that these symbolic actions were being executed in the presence of the deity who served as a witness and a guarantor of their permanent value. Therefore, lifting up the hand toward heaven and calling upon the authority of the deity was also a symbol used in taking an oath (Gen. 14:22; Deut. 32:40; cf. Ex. 6:8; Num. 14:30; Neh. 9:15, et al.).

In the realm of profane symbols, the giving of the hand showed that a relationship was established between two persons (II Kings 10:15; Ezek. 17:18). By having a person sit at one's right hand one showed a willingness to share authority with him (I Kings 2:19; Ps. 110:1), while by laying one's hand on a person, one symbolized the transference of power from one party to another (Num. 27:15–23). Similarly, blessing is conveyed, and sin transferred, by laying on of hands (Gen. 48:14; Lev. 16:21). Burial and mourning customs involved numerous symbolic actions. The mourner, for instance, demonstrated his sorrow by lacerating his body and cutting his hair (Jer. 7:29; 16:6; 41:5; 48:37–38; Ezek. 27:31; Amos 8:10; cf. Lev. 19:27–28; Deut. 14:1), by rending his clothes (I Sam. 4:12: II Sam. 1:11–12; 3:31) and girding himself with sackcloth (II Sam. 3:31), by placing ashes upon his head (I Sam. 4:12; Ezek. 27:30), and sitting on the ground (Gen. 23:2–3; Ezek. 26:16; Lam. 2:10). There were also funeral meals (Jer. 16:7; Hos. 9:4), originally conceived as a kind of communion with the dead which consoled the survivors. The enthronement of the king and the exercise of his authority, marriage ceremonies, and birth customs also involved different symbolic acts and the use of various symbols. However, it was mainly in the domain of the cult that symbols were employed. The worshiper, for instance, spread out his hands in prayer toward the deity, who was supposed to dwell in heaven or the Temple, to show that he desired to obtain divine mercy and help (Ex. 9:29, 33: I Kings 8:22, 38, 54; Isa. 1:15; Ps. 28:2; 44:21; 63:5; 141:2; Job 11:13; Lam. 2:19; Ezra 9:5; II Chron. 6:12, 13, 29). Of course, the most important religious symbols were the representations of the gods, called *ʾot* ("sign"; Ps. 74:4), *ẓelem* ("image, statue"; Num. 33:52; II Kings 11:18 = II Chron. 23:17; Ezek. 7:20; 16:17; 23:14; Amos 5:26), or *temunah* ("form"; Ex. 20:4; Num. 12:8; Deut. 4:12, 15, 16, 23, 25; Ps. 17:15; Job 4:16). In fact, the image was not merely a symbol of the god whom it represented. Rather, the god was supposed to be present within the image or to be identical with its essential nature. It is true, of course, that the official cult of the 12 tribes and the later Israelite cult in the Temple of Jerusalem were aniconic. However, the ark of the covenant symbolized God's presence among His people and Judges 17–18 refers to the Danite idol. A frequent appellative for the Lord is *ʾabbir Yaʿaqov/Yisrael* ("Bull of Jacob/Israel"; Gen. 49:24; Isa. 1:24;49:26; 60:16; Ps. 132:2, 5) or *ʿegel* ("Young Bull"; Ex. 32:4, 8; I Kings 12:28; Neh. 9:18). There is little doubt that the ancient Israelites borrowed their bull symbolism from the Canaanites. There is not, of course, a perfect equation between the Canaanite and ancient Israelite uses of this symbolism. For the Israelites, the bull signified power, whereas for the Canaanites it was primarily a symbol of sexual potency. It should be noted, moreover, that for the Israelites the "young bull" symbolized the platform upon which the unseen God stood, rather than God himself.

The lion was regarded as a symbol of strength and sovereignty. As an emblem of power, it became, most probably in the times of David and Solomon, the symbol of the tribe of Judah (Gen. 49:9). The figure of the lion is among the few which are found on glyptics. There is a carved figure of a roaring lion on the seal of "Shema', the servant of Jeroboam" (Pritchard, Pictures, 276). Lions also appear, together with oxen and cherubim, on the bases of the brass sea in the Temple (I Kings 7:29). The two pillars of Jachin and Boaz (I Kings 7:15–22; II Chron. 3:15–17) were probably borrowed from the two pillars of the temple of Melkart at Tyre. But, in general, the various images, cult objects, sacred garments, or rites performed in the Temple symbolized, at least originally, some specific religious conception. Even the cultic *Tabernacle erected for the ark and the Temple of Jerusalem, which were to the Israelites the visible dwelling places of God, were intended to symbolize His invisible abode.

For Talmudic period see *Divination.

BIBLIOGRAPHY: M. Farbridge, *Studies in Biblical and Semitic Symbolism* (1923, 1970); H.W. Robinson, *Old Testament Essays* (1927), 1–17; idem, in: JTS, 43 (1942), 129–39; C.A. Keller, *Das Wort* OTH *als "Offenbarungszeichen Gottes"*... (1946); G. Fohrer, in: ZAW, 64 (1952), 101–20; 78 (1966), 25–47; idem, *Die symbolischen Handlungen der Propheten* (1968²); K.-H. Bernhardt, *Gott und Bild*... (1956); E.L. Erlich, *Kultsymbolik im Alten Testament und im nachbiblischen Judentum* (1959); Z.W. Falk, in: VT, 10 (1960), 72–74 (Eng.); W. Kornfeld, in: ZAW, 74 (1962), 50–57; K.H. Bengstorf, in: G. Friedrich (ed.), *Theologisches Woerterbuch zum Neuen Testament*, 7 (1964), 199–268; CH Gordon, in: A. Altmann (ed.), *Biblical Motifs* (1966), 1–9; J. Ouelette, in: RB, 74 (1967), 504–16.

[Edward Lipinski]

SIGÜENZA, town in the province of Guadalajara, Castile, Central Spain. A Jewish community appears to have already existed there during the 11th century. In 1124 King *Alfonso VII granted to the bishop of Sigüenza the right of jurisdiction over the local Jews. Sigüenza was among the towns which prospered in old Castile in the 13th century. In 1280 a Jew named Abraham reached an agreement with the bishop of Sigüenza on the digging of salt mines there. The articles of the agreement indicate the equal rights of Jew and bishop. The mines were to become the property of the bishop after four years. This method of leasing, in which the bishop provided the tools and financed the digging, was also practiced during the 14th century. The Jewish quarter is mentioned in 1343 as being situated in San Vincente Street. Remnants of the synagogue have been preserved. The decline of the Castilian communities also overtook Sigüenza during the 15th century. The tax paid by the community in 1439 amounted to only 300 maravedis in the old currency, but, in 1491, the annual tax of the community amounted to 14,974 maravedis. In 1490 the community of Sigüenza was called upon to contribute 206,464 maravedis toward the redemption of the Jews taken captive in Málaga. At the time of the Expulsion of the Jews from Spain in 1492, a number of houses which had been owned by Jews since 1449 were sold to Christians because of the debts still owed by Jews. In 1493 the crown reacted in favor of the Conversos in the townlet and prohibited the use of derogatory names against them. In 1496 it was decided to sell the synagogue and the property attached to it. From that year the notary of the Inquisition tribunal lived there.

BIBLIOGRAPHY: Baer, Spain, index; Baer, Urkunden, 2 (1936), index; H. Rashdall, *Universities of Europe in the Middle Ages* (1936^2), 104–5; F. Cantera, *Sinagogas españolas* (1955), 304–8; Suárez Fernández, Documentos, index.

[Haim Beinart]

SIHON (Heb. סִיחוֹן, סִיחֹן), Amorite king of *Heshbon, which was a city N.N.E. of Mt. Nebo. According to biblical tradition Sihon conquered the territory of Moab, as far as the Arnon (Num. 21:26). When the Israelites, on their way from the wilderness to the Promised Land, asked his permission to pass through his territory, Sihon refused to grant it, and tried to bar their way. A battle took place, with the result that Sihon was defeated, his land conquered, and Heshbon destroyed (Num. 21:21–25; Deut. 2:26–37). An echo of this conquest was preserved in the poem of the "ballad singers" (Num. 21:27–30). Scholars differ as to the extent of Sihon's territory. M. Noth (see bibl.) thinks that he controlled only an area surrounding Heshbon, and that the boundaries given in Judges 11:22, for example, reflect the history of the subsequent Israelite occupation of the region. Others maintain that Sihon exercised his power over various Amorite and Midianite princedoms in the southern part of Gilead, from Arnon in the south to Jabbok in the north, and from the desert to the Jordan (cf. S. Ahitub, in bibl.; Num. 21:21–30; Deut. 2:26–37; Josh. 12:2; 13:21, 25–27; Judg. 11:21–22).

BIBLIOGRAPHY: Maisler, Untersuchungen, 39–42; M. Noth, in: ZAW, 58 (1940–41), 162–70; 60 (1944), 37–41; M. Diman (Haran), in: *Yedi'ot*, 13 (1947), 13–15; S. Yeivin, in: JNES, 9 (1950), 102; R. de Vaux, *Bible et Orient* (1967), 118–27; S. Ahitub, in: EM, 5 (1968), 1017–18.

SIJILL is an Arabic word which goes back to a Latin origin, and appears in a Koranic verse (XXI, 104) where it means "a scroll" of documents. In classical Arabic it was used for a document that contained the decisions of the kadi, then for a collection of such documents, and it hardly changed over the ages. As early as the second century of the Hijra a kadi was dismissed for failure to keep the Sijill records of his court properly. The keeping of such records became a regular judicial procedure, and the need for the correct formulation of such documents brought about the emergence of a distinct branch of legal literature from the eighth century. In a document from the middle of the 13th century in Jerusalem, the kadi points out the formal duty of the court scribe to count all the pages of the court proceedings and be their custodian (Jerusalem Sijill, Volume 237, page 98).

Scant references in the contemporary literature, as well as an impressive collection of several hundred pages from *Mamluk times recently discovered in Jerusalem, attest to the ongoing practice of registering court decisions by the kadi. However, it was under the Ottomans that this became systematically prevalent throughout the empire; hence, vast collections of court registers have survived to these days. Major towns like *Cairo, *Damascus, *Aleppo, Hamat, and smaller ones like Jerusalem, *Jaffa and Nablus, hold depositories of long series of bound volumes covering chronologically the cases adjudicated by the kadi.

The sijill of the Shar'i court of Jerusalem consists of more than 500 volumes (averaging 500 pages of 28 by 21 cm. mostly) of proceedings covering 400 years of Ottoman rule, up until the World War I. It stretches over a wide spectrum of topics: Civil and criminal litigations, economic and social matters, inheritances and personal status cases, endowments and religious practices, demography and topography, architecture and buildings, coins and prices, Sultanic decrees and taxation orders. Most cases concern the Muslim majority of the population, however, as Christians and Jews, too, came regularly to the court, this source is a trove of information on the realities of these communities. These registers, which are actually the drafts of the court decisions, mirror the precise chronological order in which they were given; hence, the thousands of cases concerning the Jews who resided in Jerusalem or visited it are inextricably mingled with the rest. They may, however, be grouped under the following categories: communal organization and institutions (leadership, *Karaites and other internal divisions, synagogues, ritual baths, cemeteries, communal debts and real estate, pilgrimage, taxation); relations with their neighbors (conversion to Islam, dress code, moral and physical offenses, wine production, thefts and losses, death); economic activities (professions, guild membership, real estate transactions, leasing and renting, financial transactions, loans and debts, waqf religious endowments); legal status (women and the family, guardianship, legacies, slaves and maids). The sijill thus reveals a totally new perspective for our understanding of Jewish life within the Ottoman society: the formal limitations they were subjected to and the occasional molestations they suffered notwithstanding, they enjoyed religious and administrative autonomy and were a constructive element of the local society and economy.

BIBLIOGRAPHY: de Blois, Little and Faroqhi, "Sidjill," in: EIS^2, 9 (1997); R.Y. Ebied and J.L. Young, *Some Arabic Legal Documents of the Ottoman Period* (1976); D. Little, *A Catalogue of the Islamic Documents from al-Haram al-Sharif in Jerusalem* (1984); A. Cohen, *A World Within – Jewish Life as Reflected in Muslim Court Documents from the Sijill of Jerusalem (Jewish Quarterly Review Supplement,* 1994); idem, *Jewish Life under Islam* (1984); A. Cohen and B. Lewis, *Population and Revenue in Towns of Palestine in the Sixteenth Century* (1978); A. Cohen, *The Guilds of Ottoman Jerusalem* (2001).

[Amnon Cohen (2nd ed.)]

SIJILMASSA (Sidjelmessa), town in S.W. *Morocco. Since the late Middle Ages the region has been called Tafilalet. Sijilmassa was founded in 757 by the Zenata *Berbers. An important Jewish community existed there from its inception, whose members controlled the gold trade and also carried on an extensive commerce as far as *Egypt and *India. In the region ancient Jewish tombstones from before the Second Temple period survived. The *Fatimid mahdi ʿUbayd-Allah was imprisoned in Sijilmassa in 909 after he had been denounced by a Jew. Once he regained his freedom, he seized the throne of Ifrīqiyā (present-day *Tunisia) and had the wealthy Jews of Sijilmassa murdered. The Jews who survived, however, rapidly rose to their former economic and social importance. The chronicler Abraham Ibn Daud writes that when Sijilmassa passed to the Cordoba *Umayyads, its community, like all the Jews in the caliphate, was placed under the authority of Jacob ibn Jau. Sijilmassa is repeatedly mentioned in traders' letters found in the Cairo *Genizah*. The town was a desert port and terminal for the caravans going south to the Sudan and east via *Kairouan to *Cairo. S.D. *Goitein analyzed *Genizah* documents which illustrated the operation of a Jewish network, based on kinship and religious ties, between partners in Almeria, *Fez, and Sijilmassa along the route to *Cairo.

During the 11th century the Jewish scholars of Sijilmassa established contact with the *geonim* of *Iraq and Ereẓ Israel. There are responsa sent by *geonim* to Sijilmassa. One of them was written by Hai Gaon. There is also one responsa collection which was sent by a Babylon *gaon* to Rabbi Joseph ben Amran, the *dayyan* of Sijilmassa. During this period new rulers, the Zenātes, remigrated to the region which, in addition to Sijilmassa, consisted of such distant towns with a Jewish majority as *Sefrou and Qalʿat Mahdī ben Tawala in the Fazāz (Middle Atlas) region. In 1054 the *Almoravides occupied Sijilmassa and ravaged all its territories. The Jews shared in the suffering, but once their rule was well established the Almoravides ameliorated the Jews' situation. A detailed report of events in Sijilmassa as recorded from eyewitness refugees was found in a letter written in 1148 by Shelomo ha-Kohen of Fustat to his father, a native of Sijilmassa who was then in *Aden. Students from Sijilmassa traveled to study Torah in the academy of Rabbi Joseph Ibn Migash (d. 1141) in the Andalusian city of Lucena.

In 1145 Sijilmassa allied itself with the *Almohads. A short while later, a new governor appointed by this dynasty presented the Jews of the town with the alternative of conversion to *Islam or death. Some 150 Jews preferred to die, while the others – led by the *dayyan* Joseph b. Amram who later returned to Judaism – converted. One of the town's scholars, R. Judah b. Farḥon, succeeded in escaping; he subsequently returned and became *dayyan* of the town. He maintained a correspondence with *Maimonides. Other scholars of Sijilmassa include: R. Saadiah b. Isaac, Abu-Yusef b. Mar Yusef who was the son of the chief *dayyan* Rabbi Joseph b. Amram, and R. Solomon b. Nathan, a great sage, who edited a prayer book in 1203. Another scholar, R. Judah b. Joseph Sijilmassi, lived in Sijilmassa at the close of the 14th century. Toward the end of their rule the fanaticism of the Almohads was mitigated, and Jews held senior positions in the Marinid economy, for in 1243/4 the treasurer of Sijilmassa was a Jew by the name of Ibn Shalukha. In 1247 King James I of Aragon gave a safe-conduct to a Jew, a resident of Sijilmassa, inviting him to move together with his family "and all the Jews and Jewesses" of Sijilmassa to Majorca and Catalonia. After the Merinid occupation Sijilmassa's trade developed considerably. The Jews extended their activities to Catalonia, Sicily, and other countries, to which large numbers of them also emigrated. The economic life of the Jews of Sijilmassa flourished and the Jewish tinsmiths were named by the Muslims "Filali," after the city name of Tafilalet, and were named "Moroccan" by the European traders. They were also manufacturers of carpets, wool blankets and also developed the indigo trade. Sijilmassa was destroyed after 1393 and all traces of the community disappeared. In the surrounding Tafilalet area many Jewish settlements continued, generally living in peace by paying tribute either to the *Berber rulers or to the Arab nomads. The Jewish community in the region flourished until the massacre in 1492. The expellees from *Spain after 1492 did not have any real influence in the region of Tafilalet, and the Jewish population did not adopt any Spanish or *Fez regulations. Rabbi Ḥayyim Gagin tells in his book *Ez Ḥayyim* that in 1526 the Muslim residents of one village in Tafilalet region plundered the Jewish residents and raped Jewish women. In 1623 Jewish women were captured in Tafilalet and sold to Muslims (Ibn Denan, *Divrei ha-Yamim shel Fez*, p. 42). At the beginning of the 18th century Rabbi Shelomo Adhan moved from Tafilalet to *Tetuan.

The capital of the region at that time was Erfūd. In the last years of the 19th century the English missionary Robert Kerr treated a few Jewish patients in Tafilalet. The emissary Raphael Makhluf Abraham Khayat visited the Tafilalet region in 1836. The Tiberian emissary to Morocco in 1890, Rabbi Elijah Iluz, was born in Mizgida by Tafilalet in 1860, but grew up in Tiberias. Many Jews who escaped from the Jewish quarter in Tafilalet settled in 1919 in Erfūd, while numerous others settled in the Bodinev community and in Algeria. They established their synagogue in Erfūd. The name Erfūd was written in Jewish contracts only from 1950. Many Jews continued to write the name of Sijilmassa in their contracts. The Abihaẓira family cooperated with the French government of the region and helped the French in occupying the area in the second decade of the 20th century. The Muslim residents took revenge and murdered David Abihaẓira. In 1942 the local French ruler in the little town Gurama, located in the Tafilalet region, degraded the Jews and behaved toward them with contempt. He obliged them to pay very heavy taxes, to wear only simple clothes with black hats and black shoes, forbade them to ride horses and forced them to fulfill other *Omar covenant restrictions. He also beat Jews who wore a tarbush. In 1947 the community of Erfūd numbered between 1,000 to 2,000. The immense Tafilalet area, which had only 6,500 Jews (2,898 men and 3,608 women) in 1947, was the source of considerable migration to northern Morocco and *Algeria. After 1948 most of the Jews left the Jewish quarter of Tafilalet and immigrated to Israel. According to Professor H.Z. Hirschberg who visited Tafilalet in the mid-1950s, the community of Tafilalet consisted then of the Abihaẓira academy and the O'Haley Yosef Yizhak Talmud Tora (of Chabad). More than 1,000 Jews lived there, many of whom were merchants. The shops were closed on Sabbath. In Risani, built on the ruins of Sijilmassa, c. 625 Jews lived in that time. The family Abihaẓira settled in Tafilalet for a few generations. In the responsa of Rabbi Jacob Abihaẓira, who lived in Risani (d. 1880), there are relevant historical materials about the local Jewish community. This rabbi was the religious leader of the Tafilalet region. His synagogue was destroyed by a French bomb in 1933. Rabbi Israel Abihaẓira immigrated to Israel only in the last wave of *aliyah* from Tafilalet in 1964. The wedding *minhagim* in the Erfūd community were identified with those of Tafilalet until the mid-1950s and based upon them. The marriage, divorce and mourning *minhagim* of Tafilalet were written by Shalom Abihaẓira in his book *Meliẓ Tov* (1973). In the community, marriage contracts according to the Sijilmassa version have survived. In the communities of Erfūd and Tafilalet there was a special annual ceremony called *Ḥuppat Ne'urim* (youth wedding) which was conducted in Tafilalet by Rabbi Jacob Abihaẓira. In Tafilalet a special version of the *Sharḥ* (the translation of the Bible in Morocco) was written. The local sages wrote the words which entered the *Sharḥ* in Hebrew characters according to rules insufficiently crystallized. The community of Erfūd existed from 1917 to 1975. The Jewish cemetery in Erfūd is sandy but otherwise well-preserved. The Jewish cemetery in the town of Risani is unwalled, facing the walls of the town.

BIBLIOGRAPHY: J.M. Toledano, *Ner ha-Ma'arav* (1911), index; Yaari, *Shlukhei*, 660, 724; D. Corcos, in: JQR, 54 (1963/64), 275; 55 (1964/65), 68ff.; idem, in: *Sefunot*, 10 (1966), 75ff.; Hirschberg, Afrikah, index; C.E. Dufourcq, *L'Espagne Catalane et le Maghreb aux xiiie et xive siècles* (1966), index; S.D. Goitein, *A Mediterranean Society*, vols. 1–6, index. **ADD BIBLIOGRAPHY:** H.Z. Hirschberg, *Me-Ereẓ Mevo ha-Shemesh* (1957), 117–27; A.N. Chouraqui, *Between East and West, A History of the Jews of North Africa* (1973), 51, 197–98; D. Corcos, in: S. Bar-Asher (ed.), *Ha-Yehudim be-Maroko ha-Sherifit* (1977), 98–102; E. Bashan, *Sheviyya u-Pedut ba-Ḥevrah ha-Yehudit be-Arẓot ha-Yam ha-Tikhon (1391–1830)* (1980), index; M.A. Friedman, *Jewish Marriage in Palestine, A Cairo Geniza Study*, 2 (1981), 114–29; 350–55; J. Heath and M. Bar-Asher, in: *Zeitschrift fuer Arabische Linguistik*, 9 (1982), 32–78; Y. Tobi, in: M. Abitbol (ed.), *Communautés juives des marges sahariennes du Maghreb* (1982), 407–25; N. Levtzion, in: *ibid.*, 253–68; Y. Tobi, in: Z. Malachi (ed.), *Yad le-Heiman, Koveẓ Meḥkarim le-Zekher A.M. Habermann* (1984), 345–60; M. Bar-Asher, in: *Massorot*, 2 (1986), 1–14; idem, in: *Leshonenu*, 48–49 (1985), 227–52; M. Amar, *Eẓ Hayyim le-Rabbi Ḥayyim Gagin* (1987), 75, 94; A. Stahl, in: S. Shitrit (ed.), *Ḥalutzim be-Dim'ah, Pirkei Iyyun al Yahadut Ẓefon Afrikah* (1991), 30–40; S. Bar-Asher (ed.), *Sefer ha-Takkanot, Sidrei ha-Ḥevrah ha-Yehudit be-Fes, Mishpaḥah, Hanhagah ve-Kalkalah* (1991), 38, 288; M. Ben-Sasson, *Ẓemiḥat ha-Kehillah ha-Yehudit be-Arẓot ha-Islam, Qayrawan 800–1057* (1996), index; E. Bashan, *Ha-Yehudim be-Maroko ba-Me'ah ha-Tesha Esre ve-ha-Misyon ha-Anglikani* (1999), 132; E. Bashan, *Yahadut Maroko, Avarah ve-Tarbutah* (2000), index; Y. Tsur, *Kehillah Keru'ah, Yehudei Maroko ve-ha-Le'ummiut 1943–1954* (2001), index; M. Nizri, in: *Mikedem u-mi-Yam*, 8 (2003), 352–92; M. Nizri, in: *Mahut*, 28 (2004), 59–110; M. Gil, *Jews in Islamic Countries in the Middle Ages* (2004), index.

[David Corcos / Leah Bornstein-Makovetsky (2nd ed.)]

SIKARIKON, a term in tannaitic literature, referring to property, particularly land and slaves, expropriated from Jews by the Roman authorities. Most of the relevant laws deal with the legal status of such land which has been acquired or which one wishes to acquire from the government. The origin of the word itself is obscure. Graetz suggests that it is connected with the *Sicarii and that the origin of the term is the *ius sikarikon*, so called because the Sicarii not only robbed their opponents but expropriated their lands, the name being later transferred to the Romans who confiscated the lands of the Jews after the destruction of the Temple. There is, however, no evidence at all to connect the Sicarii with the expropriation of land, and furthermore, in the course of time, the rabbis gradually came to recognize the right of the governments to expropriate, which was not the case with the Sicarii. Safrai also connects it with the *ius sikarikon*, but he takes the Sicarii to be those who defied Hadrian's decree against circumcision and were punished by having their property confiscated. In fact, Hadrian's prohibition of circumcision was based upon the statute *lex Cornelia de sicarius et veneficis*. The term *sikarikon* is used both for the law which annuls the ownership by the acquirer and for the concept itself, i.e., the expropriation of land by the authorities. According to this view the term *sikarikon* was coined during the years preceding the Bar Kokhba War, when the edict was decreed. It is possible that the word was extended during the early days to cover all political crimes against the government.

The development of the *halakhah* in the law of *sikarikon* may be noted particularly from the Mishnah. "There was no *sikarikon* in Judea for those killed in the war. From the period of those killed in the war there has been *sikarikon* there. How does this law apply? If a man buys a field from the *sikarikon*, and then buys it again from the original owner, his purchase is void, but if he buys it first from the original owner and then from the *sikarikon* it is valid.... This was the ruling of the early Mishnah. A later *bet din* laid down, however, that if a man buys property from the *sikarikon* he must pay a quarter to the original owner. This, however, is only the case when the original owner is not in a position to buy it himself, but if he is, he has the right of preemption. Rabbi *Judah ha-Nasi set up a *bet din*, and they decided by vote that, if the property had been in the hands of the *sikarikon* 12 months, whoever purchased it acquired the title, but he had to give a quarter of the price to the original owner" (Git. 5:6). Upon the identification of "the war" referred to in the first part of this Mishnah depends the difference of opinion referred to above as to the meaning of the term, *sikarikon*. Graetz (and Gulak) refer it to the Roman War, and Safrai to the Bar Kokhba War. The Mishnah notes that the law of *sikarikon* was cancelled in Judea in the time of the war, purchase from the gentile of the confiscated land being permitted. The reason for this law is explained in the parallel passage in the Tosefta: "The rule of *sikarikon* does not apply to Judea, that the country may be populated" (Tosef., Git. 5:1), i.e., the motive was to prevent the alienation of land in Judea from Jewish ownership. One should note that the distinction between Judea and Galilee (which is particularly stressed in the Jerusalem Talmud: "The rule of *sikarikon* always applies in Galilee" (TJ, Git. 5:6, 47b)) accords more with the period of the Bar Kokhba War than with the Roman War.

Three successive stages are noted in the development of the laws of *sikarikon*, making it progressively more lenient. The last stage in the days of Judah ha-Nasi provides that after 12 months the owner's right to his confiscated property lapses, the only obligation of the purchaser being to pay a quarter of the purchase price to him. One may perceive in these stages the results of two processes which had their effect either independently or together: first, the desire to normalize the economic conditions, and second, the gradual but progressive acknowledgment of Roman authority and its laws, as well as the good relations subsisting between the Roman government and the Jewish population at the end of the second century.

BIBLIOGRAPHY: H. Graetz, *Das Sikarikon-Gesetz* (1892); Rosenthal, in: MGWJ, 37 (1893), 1–6, 57–63, 105–10; Halevy, Dorot, 5 pt 1; Elbogen, in: MGWJ, 69 (1925), 249–57; Feist, ibid., 71 (1927), 138–41; Gulak, in: *Tarbiz*, 5 (1933/34), 23–27; Safrai, in: Zion, 17 (1952), 56–64; Alon, Toledot, 2 (1961^2), 56, 122f., 155f; Rokeaḥ, in: *Tarbiz*, 35 (1965/66), 122–31.

[A'hron Oppenheimer]

SIKHNIN or **SOGANE** (Heb. סִיכְנִין), town in Galilee, 20 stadia (3 mi.; c. 5 km.) from Arabah (Jos., Life, 265). It was one of the places fortified by Josephus during his command in Galilee in 66 C.E. (Wars, 2:573; Life, 188). Talmudic sources praise the fertility of the valley in which it was situated (Bikat Sikhnin; Mid. Tan. 26:9). Several scholars, including R. Judah, R. Ḥanina b. Teradyon, and R. Joshua, are mentioned either as residents of or as visitors in Sikhnin. A local synagogue is referred to in the Jerusalem Talmud (Meg. 4:5, 75b). In crusader times it was a fief known as Zachanin, for which the Teutonic order and the Barlais family contended. Remains on the site include Roman, Byzantine, and Arab pottery, as well as two tombs of venerated Muslims (*maqām*). It is the present-day Sakhnīn, an Arab village in Israel, numbering about 7,400 inhabitants in 1968 and 22,600 in 2002, 94% of them Muslims. In 1995 Sikhnin received municipal status. Its area extends to 3.7 sq. mi. (9.7 sq. km.). In 2004, the local soccer team, Iḥud Beni Sikhnin, became the first Arab soccer team to win Israel's State Cup.

BIBLIOGRAPHY: S. Klein (ed.), *Sefer ha-Yishuv* (1939), s.v.; Avi-Yonah, Geog, 136.

[Michael Avi-Yonah]

SIKILI, JACOB BEN HANANEL (13th–14th centuries), rabbi and author. His surname indicates that the family originated in the island of Sicily. In his youth he traveled widely, seeking out every available book dealing with the homiletic interpretation of the Bible. He finally settled in Cordoba in Spain. There he began to write the midrashic anthology *Talmud Torah*, on the basis of the mass of material culled from the 234 books he acquired during his wanderings. At that time there was a movement among the Jews of Spain to emigrate to Ereẓ Israel. Sikili, too, thought it preferable "to be a beggar in the Land of Israel having no fixed home, than to live permanently in the lands of wicked gentiles, the habitations of Edom and Ishmael" (*Minḥat Bikkurim, Parashat Pekudei*). In order to fulfill this wish he joined his friend R. Hezekiah. On the 20th of Ḥeshvan of 1317, both took a solemn vow to go to Ereẓ Israel within not more than two years. They also took an oath that they would live jointly for seven years from the moment they left Cordova. At the end of two years, after they had sold all their possessions and bought provisions for the journey, Sikili was prevented from fulfilling his vow as a result of a report that Portuguese warships were sailing the seas on the instructions of the pope, "to plunder and rob any Jew or Mohammedan they met on the sea."

Within a few years troubles beset him. Four of his five children died, and he attributed his sufferings to the nonfulfillment of his vow. He turned to *Asher b. Jehiel, then rabbi of Toledo, for permission to travel alone without waiting for Hezekiah. Asher wrote giving him the necessary permission and he immediately acted upon it. He was in Damascus in 1324, where in that same year he completed the *Talmud Torah* on the Book of Numbers, and on Deuteronomy in 1337. In Damascus, Sikili was one of the most honored members of the community, being recognized as a halakhic authority and biblical exegete. On the pressing request of the community he agreed to expound the meaning of the weekly portion every Sabbath afternoon (*Minḥah*; Introduction to *Torat ha-Minḥah*, Vienna Ms. 138). He collected these sermons and published them under the title *Torat ha-Minḥah*. Sikili paid frequent visits to Ereẓ Israel, traversing it from end to end. The literary fruits of these visits were incorporated in his *Sefer ha-Yaḥas* in which he mentions "every town and village of Israel and the persons buried there."

The complete manuscript of *Torat ha-Minḥah* is extant, though scattered among various libraries. Extracts from it were published in *Berakhah Meshulleshet* by Abraham Bik (1890), and with the *Talmud Torah* is extensively quoted in the *Torah Shelemah* of M.M. Kasher (1938^2–). There is a great similarity between it and the book of sermons of David b. Abraham ha-Nagid (*Midrash R. David ha-Nagid*, vol. 1, 1964, vol. 2, 1968). Similarly the whole of Sikili's *Talmud Torah* is extant in manuscript, but only extracts of it have been published (see bibl.). An excerpt only from the *Sefer ha-Yaḥas*, copied from an incomplete manuscript by Abraham Zacuto, is in Cambridge. Sikili mentions two other books which he wrote, *Gullat ha-Koteret* and *Yayin ha-Meshummar*.

BIBLIOGRAPHY: S. Poznański, in: HḤY, 3 (1913), 1–22, 97f., idem, in: *Festschrift S. Maybaum* (1914), 191–208: S.A. Wertheimer,

Oẓar Midrashim, Kitvei Yad (1913), 64–84 (= *Battei Midrashot*, 1 (1950²), 139–61); J. Mann, *The Bible as Preached and Read in the Synagogue*, 1 (1960), 270–346; 2 (1966), 130–66 (Heb. pt.); E. Straus (Ashtor), *Toledot ha-Yehudim be-Miẓrayim u-ve-Suryah*, 2 (1951), 364–5; S.H. Kook, *Iyyunim u-Meḥkarim*, 2 (1963), 273–91; Hurwitz, in: *Sinai*, 59 (1966), 29–38; Kupfer, in: *Kovez al Yad*, 17 (1968), 101ff.

[Ephraim Kupfer]

SIKKUTH AND CHIUN (Heb. סִכּוּת, כִּיּוּן), deities mentioned in Amos 5:26 in a warning sermon delivered to the people of the Kingdom of Israel, perhaps in Beth-El. Although the vocalization is modeled after *shikkuẓ* (*shiqquẓ*, "abomination"), the consonantal base suggests a pair of Mesopotamian astral deities, as was recognized by E. Shraeder (see bibl.) and others.

Sikkuth is identified with *Sag/k.kud/t* (transliterated in a Mesopotamian god list as Sa-ak-ku-ut!), an astral deity known also from the "An" god list found at Ugarit (originally from Nippurian and other Mesopotamian sources, see Weidner, in bibl.), where it appears as [d]*sag/k.k[ud]/t* = [ᵈ]*s[a]g/k.kud/t* (*Ugaritica*, 5 (1969), 214, line 44). (In other "non-Western" lists of gods and stars, Sikkuth has recently been identified with Ninurta, one of the chief Mesopotamian deities (known also in the "West" and sometimes identified with *Horon*). Sikkuth in Amos is a perfect transliteration of this star deity. Its appellation, *melekh* (Akk. *šarru*, "king"), alludes to the high rank of this deity, a (translated) classification device known from Ugaritic and other sources. This means that in the ritual to which Amos alludes Sikkuth is the most important figure. Chiun is identified with the Akkadian *Kajamānu* (in Akkadian intervocalic *m* comes to be pronounced like *w*, and so *m* was often written even for original *w*), "the steady one" (sometimes SAG. *US*), the appellation of the star god Saturn (hence Aramaic *Kewan*, Ar. *Kaiwan*). This pair of deities appears in astrological lists (of celestial observations) and also in the "release" (*lipṭur*) passage of the expiatory prayer and ritual known as *Šurpu* (2:180), among other gods of the night and stars: "… SAG. KUD. SAG. *UŠ* ᵈ*Immerija* [= *ilu-wer*, mentioned in the inscription of Zakir king of *Hamath] release!" This may be translated as "may Sakkut, Kajamānu release [from sin]." The appellation *ẓalmekhem* in Amos denotes the Akkadian star-idol *Ṣalmu*, usually the second participant in the ritual of celestial and expiatory prayers (see Speiser, in bibl.). Amos warns his listeners to exchange the sacrificial cult with the accompanying sacred music for justice, or they will be exiled, along with the images of those deities beyond *Damascus. He thus mentions them only in passing, and nothing is learned about the details of their cult in Israel.

BIBLIOGRAPHY: E. Schraeder, *Die Keilinschriften und das Alte Testament* (1883²), 443; A. Deimel, *Pantheon Babylonicum* (1914), 231; E.F. Weidner, in: AFO, 2 (1924–25), 1–18; 4 (1927), 78; E.A. Speiser, in: BASOR, 108 (1947), 5; E. Reinor, in: AFO *Beiheft*, 11 (1958).

[Pinchas Artzi]

SILANO (ninth century), one of the first Jewish liturgical poets in Italy. Silano is said by *Ahimaaz, in his *Sefer Yuḥasin* (= *Megillat Aḥima'aẓ*), to have been one of the scholars of Venosa in southern Italy. Once an emissary of the Jerusalem yeshivah arrived in Venosa, and, as was the custom there, he was invited to preach on the Sabbath. Silano translated the sermon into the vernacular from a written copy prepared by the emissary. On reading the translation the emissary was greatly distressed by Silano's introduction into the text of facetious remarks about the townspeople. After the emissary returned to Ereẓ Israel and related what had happened, the scholars of the Jerusalem yeshivah excommunicated Silano. When the aged Ahimaaz went to Jerusalem he was invited by the scholars of the yeshivah to act as reader during the Ten Days of Penitence. Among the *seliḥot* he read was one composed by Silano, "*Aloh ve-khaḥesh u-reẓo'ah ve-naḥesh* ("Cursing and lying and murder and sorcery"), in which the heretics (i.e., the Karaites), who had begun to increase in number during the ninth century, were vigorously attacked. This *seliḥah* made a strong impression on the scholars, who, when they learned the author's identity, decided to revoke the excommunication immediately. Another of Silano's *seliḥot*, one for the eve of Rosh Ha-Shanah, beginning *Enkat mesalledekha ta'al lifnei khisse khevodekha* ("The cry of those who praise Thee, to Thy throne shall rise"), was published in Lithuanian books of *seliḥot*. The German *maḥzor* inserted the first stanza of this *seliḥah* (*Enkat mesalledekha*…), together with fragments of other *piyyutim*, into the *Ne'ilah* prayer for the Day of Atonement. Silano's compositions confirm the assumption that the *paytanim* of Italy were influenced by those of Ereẓ Israel, since his style closely resembles that of Eleazar *Kallir, one of the early *paytanim* of Ereẓ Israel.

BIBLIOGRAPHY: Davidson, Oẓar, 4 (1933), 455; J. Marcus, in: PAAJR, 5 (1934), 85–93; Mann, Texts, 2 (1935), 117; B. Klar (ed.), *Megillat Aḥima'az* (1944), 18f., 67, 153, 161; S. Abramson, in: *Sinai*, 56 (1965), 238f.

[Abraham David]

SILAS.

(1) Jewish commander of the fortress of Lysias, in the region of Lebanon. The fortress was destroyed by Pompey during his campaign in Syria (63 B.C.E.; Jos. Ant., 14:40).

(2) A close friend of *Agrippa I during the latter's early hardships and imprisonment at Rome under Tiberius. When Agrippa became king (41 C.E.) Silas was appointed commander of the entire Judean army. His intimate relations with the king, however, eventually brought about his dismissal from office, since his tendency to overemphasize his loyalty to Agrippa in the early years was resented in the royal court. Silas was relieved of his command and imprisoned. Agrippa eventually regretted this harsh treatment and wished to release him, but the prisoner, by now obsessed with his grievance, declined the offer. After Agrippa's death (44) Silas was murdered by order of *Herod, king of Chalcis, and Helcias, commander of the Judean army (Jos. Ant., 18:204; 19:299, 317–25, 353).

(3) A Babylonian soldier in the Jewish ranks at the outset of the war against Rome (66 C.E.). Silas, who had deserted to the Jewish forces from the army of *Agrippa II, later led an

unsuccessful Jewish attack upon the city of Ashkelon, where he was slain (Jos., Wars, 2:520; 3:11, 19).

(4) Commander of Tiberias appointed by *Josephus. When *John of Giscala arrived in the city and appealed to the citizens to abandon their allegiance to Josephus, Silas informed the latter of the impending danger. Josephus thereupon marched to Tiberias with a force of 200 men and averted the danger (Jos., Wars, 2:616; Life, 89, 90, 272).

BIBLIOGRAPHY: Schuerer, Hist. 220, 334, n. 11; Klausner, Bayit Sheni, 3 (1950^2), 220; 4 (1950^2), 293f.; 5 (1951^2), 160, 181; A. Schalit, *Koenig Herodes* (1969), 9 n. 29.

[Isaiah Gafni]

SILBER, SAUL (1881–1946), Orthodox rabbi. Born in Alexandronsky, a small Lithuanian village, Silber grew to become a leader in American Zionist Orthodoxy. He attended *ḥeder* until he was 10, then moved with his family to Dvinsk in Latvia, where he studied Talmud under Rabbi Yom Tov Lipman and Rabbi Nachum Fefferman. At age 16, Silber joined a study group in Lida under Rabbi Isaac Jacob Reines. Reines was unique in his belief of the importance of studying secular subjects and mastering Jewish history and thought alongside Talmud study. He was hugely influential over Silber, who became a lifelong Zionist dedicated to yeshivah study that included secular subjects. Reines was an early founder of the Mizrachi religious Zionist movement, which was established in 1902.

In 1900, at the age of 19, Silber immigrated to America. Four years later, he married and started leading congregations in Youngstown and Columbus, Ohio. In 1910, Silber accepted a pulpit position at one of Chicago's most prestigious synagogues, Congregation Anshe Shalom. He may have received ordination earlier, but he definitively was granted rabbinic ordination by Rabbi Judah L. Gordan in 1921.

For 35 years, Silber was a role model for Orthodox Jewish life in Chicago and across the country. Trained in Lithuanian yeshivot, he differed from his peers in his fluent English, being well-versed in American history, literature and culture, and advocating a synthesis of secular and Talmud study. He also worked closely with non-Orthodox rabbis on communal matters.

Silber spoke in English and Yiddish from his pulpit, which he used as a vehicle for discussing contemporary issues. He mixed Torah references with secular literature in his talks. Silber was actively involved in the Central Relief Committee for the Joint Distribution Committee, American Jewish Congress, Mt. Sinai hospital in Chicago and orphanages and senior citizens' homes. He embodied a – then – new type of Orthodox rabbi that influenced the shape and direction of American Orthodoxy.

In his later years, Silber was a prominent member of Mizrachi, attending several World Zionist Congresses abroad. In 1926, he immigrated to Palestine in hopes of establishing a business there in the sale of oranges. Unfortunately, economic instability sent him back to Chicago a year later.

Silber helped found the Beth Midrash l'Torah yeshivah in Chicago, later named the Hebrew Theological College. He assumed its presidency in 1921, working closely with Rabbis Nissan Jablonski and Chaim Isaac Korb, its *roshei yeshiva*.

[Lynne Schreiber (2nd ed.)]

SILBERBERG, MENDEL (1886–1965), U.S. attorney and community leader. Silberberg, who was born in Los Angeles, practiced law there from 1908. A veteran of World War I, he founded the first American Legion Post in California. He was also active in the Jewish War Veterans, which named a post after him. He was president of the Jewish Community Council (1953), and the Los Angeles Lodge of B'nai B'rith. Silberberg was regarded as an astute and knowledgeable leader in political, community, and interfaith matters. He was chairman of the Community Relations Committee of the Jewish Federation Council for 30 years. He was influential in Republican Party circles.

[Max Vorspan]

SILBERBUSCH, DAVID ISAIAH (1854–1936), Hebrew and Yiddish editor and short-story writer. Born in Zaleszczyki, Galicia, his first work appeared in P. Smolenskin's weekly *Ha-Mabbit* in 1878. Together with Ẓevi Eleazar Teller, he published a Hebrew monthly *Ha-Or* in 1882 in Botoşani (Romania), where he lived until he moved to Vienna after World War I. In 1934 he settled in Palestine.

One of his stories, *Dimat Ashukim* ("The Tear of the Oppressed," 1887), deals with the persecution of Romanian Jews in the 1880s. It was one of the first stories in modern Hebrew literature to depict the poverty, disgrace, and degeneracy of Eastern European life and to suggest that Ereẓ Israel was the only solution. His memoirs appeared in *Mi-Pinkas Zikhronotai* (1936) and *Mentshen und Geshe'enishn* (1931). He wrote numerous short stories. Only one volume of his *Ketavim Nivḥarim* ("Selected Works," 1920) appeared.

BIBLIOGRAPHY: D. Sadan, *Avnei Boḥan* (1951), 23–28; Waxman, Literature, 4 (1960^2), 150.

[Gedalyah Elkoshi]

SILBERFARB, MOSES (1876–1934), political leader and writer in Russia. Silberfarb was born in Rovno, and studied law. He was one of the founders of the *Vozrozhdeniye group and *Jewish Socialist Workers' Party in Russia (1906), and helped to formulate their autonomistic program (see *Autonomism). He was imprisoned several times for political activities. After the 1917 Revolution Silberfarb became a leader of the *United Jewish Socialist Workers' Party. He headed the Ministry for Jewish Affairs of the Ukrainian Central *Rada* ("council, government"), and drew up a bill on national-personal autonomy. Between 1918 and 1920 he headed the Jewish People's University and Cultural League in Kiev. In 1921 he left for Warsaw where he continued to be active in Jewish affairs, becoming chairman of *ORT and active in JEAS (Jewish Emigrant Aid Society) and CYSHO (see *Education). In political outlook he moved closer to the ideology of the *Bund. Silberfarb wrote articles and books in Yiddish, Russian, and German, including *Dos Yidishe Ministerium un di Yidishe Natsionale Avtonomye in Ukrayne* (1919). His collected works were published posthumously (2 vols., 1935–37).

BIBLIOGRAPHY: LNYL, 3 (1960), 616–20; O.I. Janowsky, *Jews and Minority Rights (1898–1919)* (1933), 69f., 230–40.

[Max Wurmbrand]

SILBERG, MOSHE (1900–1975), Israeli judge and jurist. Silberg, born in Skaudvile, Lithuania, studied at the yeshivot of Kelm, Mir, Slobodka, and Novogrudok. He continued his studies at the University of Marburg and took up law at Frankfurt University. In 1929 Silberg settled in Palestine and taught in Tel Aviv; during this period he also gave public lectures on Talmud in Tel Aviv. In 1948 he was appointed judge of the district court of Tel Aviv and from 1950 to 1970 he was on the bench of the Supreme Court of Israel, of which he was deputy president from 1965 to 1975. From 1954 to 1969 he taught law of personal status at the Hebrew University in Jerusalem.

As a member of the Supreme Court, Silberg delivered several important decisions on matters of personal status, including controversial questions involving the definition of the term "*Jew." His rulings on other matters cover every aspect of law – civil and criminal, public and private – and substantially contributed to the development of Israeli case law.

Silberg also wrote extensively on talmudic law and personal status. He wrote *Ha-Ma'amad ha-Ishi be-Yisrael* ("Personal Status in Israel," 1957, 1961, supplement 1967); *Dienstvertrag und Werkvertrag im Talmudischen Rechte* ("Hiring and Contracting in Talmudic Law," 1927); *Ḥok u-Musar ba-Mishpat ha-Ivri* ("Law and Ethics in the Jewish Legal System" 1952); and *Kakh Darko shel Talmud* (*Principia Talmudica*) (1961). The latter appeared in an English translation under the title *Talmudic Law and the Modern State* (1973). In 1964 he was awarded the Israel Prize.

BIBLIOGRAPHY: Tidhar, 2 (1947), 1027–28, 14 (1965), 4575; Kressel, Leksikon, 1 (1965), 735.

[Chaim Ivor Goldwater]

SILBERMANN, ABRAHAM MORITZ (1889–1939), publisher, lexicographer, and translator. Born in Hungary, Silbermann was ordained as a rabbi at Berlin Rabbinical Seminary, but engaged in publishing and bookselling. In Berlin he issued the Horeb (photographic) editions of Talmudim and Midrashim, while at the same time preparing a Hebrew-German, German-Hebrew dictionary (with S. *Gruenberg, 1922[2]), as well as the Hebrew-English-German *Talmudic Dictionary* (with B. Krupnik-Karou, 2 vols., 1927). Silbermann later settled in England where, as publishing director of Shapiro, Vallentine and Co., he produced a translation of Rashi's Pentateuch commentary (with M. Rosenbaum, 5 vols., 1929–34), which did much to familiarize English-speaking Jews with this classic. Also popular was his *Children's Haggadah* (with A.S. Super; 1933, 1954[4]). His last work was the one-volume *Vallentine's Jewish Encyclopedia*, which he edited in collaboration with A.M. *Hyamson (1938).

SILBERMANN, ALPHONS (1909–2000), German lawyer, sociologist, and musicologist. Born in Cologne, Silbermann was music critic of the *Nieuwe Rotterdamsche Courant* from 1933. He escaped the Nazi regime, fleeing through Holland and France and reaching Australia in 1937. Silbermann became a lecturer at the State Conservatory of Music in Sydney. From 1952 he was director of socio-musical research at the French broadcasting service in Paris. In 1959 Silbermann returned to Germany as professor at the University of Cologne. His numerous publications dealing with sociology, music education, and music therapy (among other topics), include *Introduction à une sociologie de la musique* (1955); *Wovon lebt die Musik?* (1957, translated into several languages); *Das imaginaere Tagebuch des Herrn Jacques Offenbach* (1960, 1991); "Zur Neubelebung der Soziologie der Kunste," in *Hamburger-Jahrbuch-fuer-Musikwissenschaft* (9 (1986), 67–85); "Zum Einfluss deutschsprachiger Emigranten auf das Musikleben Australiens," in *Zu den Antipoden vertrieben: Das Australien-Exil deutschsprachiger Musiker.* (2000), 112–117. He also participated in several publications on Judaism, including *Deutsche Juden heute. Mit Beiträgen von Robert Neumann, Alphons Silbermann, Ludwig Marcuse, Hermann Kesten* (1975). In 1989 a special publication was dedicated to him: *Kunst- Kommunikation-Kultur: Festschrift zum 80. Geburtstag von Alphons Silbermann.*

His autobiography *Verwandlungen* (1989) is written with the wit and candor that made him admired and honored by his students and colleagues.

BIBLIOGRAPHY: G. Chase, "American Musicology and the Social Sciences," in: *Perspectives in Musicology* (1972), 202–20; E.K. Scheuch, "In Memoriam Alphons Silbermann (1909–2000)," in: *Communications*, 25:2 (2000), 210–224.

[Naama Ramot (2nd ed.)]

SILBERNER, EDMUND (1910–1985), Israeli economist and historian. Silberner was born in Borislav, Poland. He taught at Geneva University during 1939–41. After teaching in the U.S. at Princeton University from 1946 to 1950, Silberner immigrated to Israel and joined the faculty of the Hebrew University (1951), where he was appointed professor of economics in 1956. Silberner's main work was an analysis of the relationship between European socialism and the Jewish people, with a special interest in Moses *Hess, the Jewish socialist who turned proto-Zionist.

Silberner published a bibliography on Hess (1958); edited his correspondence (1959); and wrote the comprehensive *Moses Hess; Geschichte seines Lebens* (1966). Of particular importance among Silberner's other works is *Ha-Sozyalism ha-Ma'aravi u-She'elat ha-Yehudim* ("Western European Socialism and the Jewish Problem"; 1955).

[Michael A. Meyer]

SILBERSCHLAG, EISIG (1903–1988), Hebrew poet and critic. He grew up in a ḥasidic home in Metri, Galicia, migrated to the U.S., studied at the University of Vienna, and returned to the U.S. He was professor in Hebrew literature at the Hebrew Teachers College in Boston, and was its dean from 1948 to 1968. He published poems in *Hadoar, Ha-Tekufah*, and other Hebrew journals. The life-loving quality of his verse – mainly influenced by Tchernichovsky and Rilke – is evident in *Ha-Raz ha-Ḥasidi* and *Yerushat Beit Abba*. Silberschlag also wrote critical prose in Hebrew and English, and translated several comedies by Aristophanes. His poems were collected in *Bi-Shevilim Bodedim* (1931) and *Aleh Olam be-Shir* (1946).

His book *Saul Tschernichowsky – Poet of Revolt* was published in 1969. Other works include: *Mi-Pi Kushim, Sheva Panim le-Ḥavvah*, and *Tehiyyah u-Teḥiyyah ba-Shirah* (1938), a book of essays; *Yehudah Halevi* (1925), an epic poem; *Bi-Ymei Isabella* (1941), a collection of plays; *Sefer Turov*, edited with Y. Twersky; and *Ha-Tekufah* (vols. 30–31, 32–33), edited with A. Zeitlin. He translated the love songs of Paulus Silentiarius (1945, 1962²) and *Berenica* by Karl de Haas (1945).

BIBLIOGRAPHY: A. Epstein, *Soferim Ivrim ba-Amerikah* (1953), 209–28; M. Ribalow, *Ketavim u-Megillot* (1942), 224–9; Waxman, Literature, 4 (1960), 1255ff.; 5 (1960), 194ff.

[Jerucham Tolkes]

SILBERSTEIN, DAVID JUDAH LEIB (d. 1884), Hungarian rabbi. Silberstein was born in Bonyhad and studied under Meir Ash in Ungvar (Uzhorod). He served in several communities: Ujhely (Satoraljaujhely), Senta (Vojvodina), and Vacz near Budapest. He also lived in Jerusalem for eight years between 1859 and 1867. He was the author of the *Shevilei David* (1863), on the Pentateuch, and four volumes with the same name (1862–1880) on the four sections of the Shulḥan Arukh. He was in communication with the outstanding contemporary Hungarian scholars, among others, Moses Schick, Abraham Judah ha-Kohen Schwartz, Menahem Mendel Baneth, and Amram Blum. He died in Vacz. His son ISAIAH (1857–1930) was two years old when his father went to Jerusalem, and he returned with him to Hungary. At first he was a cloth merchant but in 1884 became rabbi of Vacz. He was the author of *Ma'asai le-Melekh* (2 vols., 1913–30), on the *Mishneh Torah* of Maimonides. He was a critic for the literary periodical *Tel-Talpiyyot* issued in Vacz under the editorship of David Ẓevi Katzburg, in which, in 1904, he expressed his opposition to Zionism and the Mizrachi, although at the same time he supported the old *yishuv* in Jerusalem.

BIBLIOGRAPHY: ON DAVID JUDAH LEIB: P.Z. Schwartz, *Shem ha-Gedolim me-Erez Hagar*, 1 (1913), 26a:50; A. Stern, *Melizei Esh al Ḥodesh Sivan* (1962²), 147:185; *Magyar Rabbik*, 3 (1906), 6f. ON ISAIAH: N. Ben-Menahem, *Mi-Sifrut Yisrael be-Ungaryah* (1958), 65f.; *Turei Yeshurun*, 3:14 (1971).

[Naphtali Ben-Menahem]

SILBERSTEIN, SOLOMON JOSEPH (1845–?), Russian poet and philosopher. Silberstein was born in Kovno. At the age of 19 he received rabbinical authorization from a number of rabbis in the provinces of Kovno and Vilna. He practiced as a rabbi in Dershunisok, Kovno, in 1867–68, and later emigrated to the U.S. He developed a system of natural theology based on the Mosaic, and the rabbinic and talmudic law as natural theology.

Silberstein wrote the following works: *Gelui Einayim* (1881), poems; *Ha-Dat ve-ha Torah* (1887); *Meẓi'ut Yehovah ve-ha-Olam* (1893); *The Universe and its Evolution* (1891); *General Laws of Nature* (1894); *The Disclosures of the Universal Mysteries* (1896); and *The Jewish Problem and Theology in General* (1904).

BIBLIOGRAPHY: AJYB, 6 (1904), 187–8.

SILBERSTEIN-ÖTVÖS, ADOLF (1845–99), Hungarian editor and author. Born in Budapest, from 1870 Silberstein-Ötvös was editor, for a short period, of the German-language newspaper *Temesvárer Zeitung*, and later worked for the *Pester Journal, Pester Lloyd*, and *Ungarischer Lloyd*. He translated the novels of Jókai and Mikszáth into German, and wrote studies of Aristotle and Gottschall. Much of his own best writing appeared in feuilleton form. His books include *Philosophische Briefe an eine Frau* (1878) and *Im Strome der Zeit* (4 vols.; 1894–1905). In Hungarian he wrote *Egy pesti Don Juan* ("A Don Juan of Budapest," 1885).

SILESIA (Czech **Slezsko**; Ger. **Schlesien**; Pol. **Śląsk**), region in E. central Europe. The earliest documentary evidence for the presence of Jews in Silesia dates from the 12th century. The first settlers whose names are known owned land near *Breslau; among those who arrived in this period were refugees from the *Crusades. Intensive economic development of the region and its consequent need for money brought about a Jewish monopoly in moneylending. Jewish immigration from Germany throughout the 13th and 14th centuries significantly increased the population and numbers of Jewish communities. Though synodal legislation in Breslau in 1267 sought to limit their contacts with Christians, a privilege of Duke Henry IV in 1270 granted them a measure of autonomy as well as physical protection. Over the course of five centuries, more than 50 Jewish communities were established in Silesia, the largest in Breslau, Brieg (*Brzeg), Glatz, *Glogau, Goerlitz, *Liegnitz, and *Schweidnitz. Their economic activities were productive for the region but nonetheless they helped generate hatred of Jews within the Christian community. A series of fires in Breslau in 1349 and 1360 were blamed on the Jews, and they suffered accordingly. Persecution similarly afflicted Jews during 1362 in Brieg (Brzeg), Guhrau (Gora), Laehn (Wlen), Loewenberg (Lwowek Slaski), and Neisse. In the mid-14th century, jurisdiction over the Jews had shifted to the municipalities, a development that stimulated persecution and frequent expulsions. The community produced a number of significant scholars in the period, among them R. Jacob b. Judah *Weil and R. David of Schweidnitz. Both the *Hussite Wars and the preaching of John *Capistrano took their toll of Jewish communities; as a result of the latter's preaching, the expulsion of the Jews of Breslau, as well as those of Liegnitz and Schweidnitz, took place in 1453 in connection with a trial for desecrating the *Host. By the end of the 15th century there were no Jews in nearly all of Middle and Lower Silesia. In accord with a royal edict of 1582, Jews were also forced to leave Upper Silesia. Only Jews in Glogau (Lower Silesia) and in *Zuelz (Upper Silesia) survived the expulsion, and later on formed the nucleus of the reconstituted Jewish communities of Silesia. Among the significant scholars of the 16th century was R. Benjamin of Silesia, a student of Solomon *Luria and author of *Masat Binyamin*.

In the 17th century, Jews began to arrive in Silesia once more. After the Thirty Years' War (1618–48) and following the *Chmielnicki massacres in Poland (1648), many Jews fled westward; some settled in Silesia where, in the main, they were proprietors of country taverns. By 1700 there were approximately 200 Jewish families in Silesia, the greater part of whom lived in Glogau and Zuelz (Bialb), while the rest were on the land; some families lived in Breslau and its suburbs, despite extreme opposition from the local citizens. In 1713 the Austrian government introduced a *Toleranzsteuer* ("tolerance tax") for Silesian Jews. In 1737 there were about 800 such taxpayers in Silesia, in addition to those who, like the Jews of Glogau and Zuelz, were exempt from this tax. After the annexation of Silesia by Prussia (1742) there were 1,100 Jewish families in 1751, who were organized in four communities – the Glogau community, the Zuelz community, the Silesian **Landesjudenschaft*, and the Breslau community, founded in 1744. While the Glogauer and Zuelz communities were led by rabbis, the rabbinate of Breslau was united with the *Landesjudenschaft*. Notable among the *Landesrabbiner* of this period were Baruch b. Reuben *Gomperz (1733–54) and Joseph Jonas Fraenkel (1754–93). From the end of the 17th century a Jewish printing press operated in *Dyhernfurth, where the Talmud was published.

Economically, Silesian Jewry consisted of three groups: the "*Landjuden*," who earned their living as lessees and *peddlers; the traders and merchants of Breslau, Glogau and Zuelz; and the privileged class, the wealthiest and most respected group who by their participation in supplying war materials and in the development of manufacture and industry obtained great wealth and at the same time earned the respect of the authorities. This group was also culturally the most advanced. Due to their wealth and influence, despite being a small minority, they occupied leading positions within Silesian Jewry long before the emancipation period. From their ranks came the pioneers of emancipation. In the midst of the internal struggle between traditionalists and proponents of enlightenment, the Prussian edict of March 11, 1812 gave Silesian Jews freedom on the economic and personal level. This law helped Jews even though (as in the rest of Prussia) they found difficulty in following crafts because of the opposition by the guilds. Appointment as a government official was difficult because of the unofficial religious barrier, which allowed only baptized Jews to be given such positions. A census of occupations in 1852 showed that for about 50% the major source of income was commerce, while 10% were to be found in skilled trades, and another 10% in the managing of inns. This division remained fairly unchanged even when Jews could participate in the newly established Silesian industries. On the other hand, the legal position of the Jewish communities, which in 1812 had lost their hegemony, changed. On the basis of the Prussian laws of July 23, 1847, 55 synagogal communities or synagogal districts were created: ten in the administrative area of Breslau, seven in the area of Liegnitz, and 38 in the district of Oppeln (*Opole). In 1888 the Jewish communities of Upper Silesia combined, while the synagogal communities of Lower Silesia, which included the districts of Breslau and Liegnitz, combined in 1897.

With the economic development of the area, the Silesian Jewish population also increased, from 11,500 in 1803 to 52,682 in 1880, which also brought about territorial changes. The community of Zuelz was displaced by the Upper Silesian communities, and Glogau was surpassed by Liegnitz. However, the community of Breslau became by far the most important in Silesia. Silesian Jewry made important contributions to Jewish as well as to German cultural life. Apart from famous rabbis and talmudists, there were also Hebrew writers and *maskilim*. For German Jewry the Breslau *Juedisch-Theologisches Seminar, founded in 1854, formed a center of Jewish culture and learning, as well as a training school for Jewish theologians.

After emancipation Silesian Jewry played an active part in the intellectual, cultural, and political life around them. One of the first Jewish poets in the German language was Ephraim Moses *Kuh (1731–1820) of Breslau, while one of the first Jewish poetesses in the German language was Esther Gad-Bernard (1770–1820), who was born in Breslau and was a granddaughter of Hamburg's chief rabbi, Jonathan *Eybeschuetz. Among the best-known modern writers from Silesia are Alfred *Kerr, Max *Tau, and Arnold *Zweig. In Silesia's scholarly life, people of Jewish descent played a prominent role. At the University of Breslau there were numerous lecturers of Jewish descent, but Jewish professors were very few in number until the Weimar Republic. Among these were the historian Jacob Caro and the botanist Ferdinand J. *Cohn. In the political parties Jews were especially active in the liberal movements. They were also prominent in political journalism. One of the first leaders of the German trade union movement, Ferdinand *Lassalle, was from Breslau. Among the more famous Silesian Jews or Silesians of Jewish descent were the Jewish historian Heinrich *Graetz, the medical researcher Paul *Ehrlich, the chemist Fritz *Haber, and the explorer Emin *Pasha (Eduard Schnitzer).

In the 20th century the Silesian Jewish community declined, numbers falling from 44,000 in 1920 to 34,000 in 1933. Under the Geneva convention, Jews were included in the minority rights guarantees for Upper Silesia. After the rise of Nazism, the Jewish community appealed to the League of Nations for aid; as a result their situation was better than that of Jewish communities in the rest of Germany. Even so, after 1933 increased emigration took place (see *Bernheim petition). In 1939 the number of remaining Jews was only 15,480, most of whom became the victims of the Nazi regime. Immediately after World War II, with the incorporation of the whole of Silesia into Poland, the surviving Jewish partners of mixed marriages also left Silesia, and no native Jews remained. In their stead came Jews from Poland and Russia, numbering about 52,000, of whom around 10,000 settled in Breslau (now called Wroclaw). This newly constituted community made use of the Storch synagogue, which had not been destroyed during the war. A Yiddish paper also appeared. Jews also settled in other Silesian cities, among them Liegnitz (Legnica), Reichenbach (Dzierzoniow), and Waldenburg (Walbrzych). With the establishment of the State of Israel, many emigrated there. After the Six-Day War (1967) the majority of Jews left Silesia.

BIBLIOGRAPHY: M. Brann, *Geschichte der Juden in Schlesien* (1896–1917); idem, *Die schlesische Judenheit…* (1913), I. Rabin, *Vom Rechtskampf der Juden in Schlesien (1582–1713)* (1927); idem, *Beitraege zur Rechts-und Wirtschaftsgeschichte der Juden in Schlesien im 18. Jahrhundert* (1932); M. Krentzberger, *Bibliothek und Archiv* (1970), 247–51; Theokratia, *Jahrbuch des Institutum Judaicum Delitzschianum* (1970), Bibliographie Bernhard Brilling: 191–220; P. Rosenthal, *Bleter far Geshikhte* (1961), 3–26; J. Stone, *Regional Guarantees of Minority Rights* (1933), 35–36, 220–1, 227–33; B. Brilling, in: *Zeitschrift fuer Ostforschung*, 15 (1966), 60–67; idem, in: MB, 11:6 (1947); 13:32 (1949); M. Rożkowicz, in: *Zydowskiego Instytutu Historycznego*, 50 (1964), 91–99; F. Rosenthal, *ibid.*, 34 (1960), 3–27; S. Bronszytejn, *ibid.*, 47–48 (1963), 59–78.

[Bernhard Brilling]

°SILIUS ITALICUS, TIBERIUS CATIUS ASCONIUS (26–101), Roman epic poet and public official. He flatters Vespasian and Titus in referring to their subjugation of Judea, which he, like Statius, calls Idumea (*Punica* 3:599f.).

[Jacob Petroff]

SILK (Heb. מֶשִׁי, *meshi*). Silk is mentioned once in the Bible by Ezekiel (16:10, 13) in his description of the splendid garments of the Israelite woman. The commentators identify this *meshi* with silk, and there may be an etymological connection between *meshi* and *si*, the Chinese word for silk, which may also be the origin of *shira, shira'in*, the word for silk in rabbinical literature. There is no doubt that Chinese silk was already known in Ereẓ Israel during the time of the Mishnah and Talmud and it is thought to have been brought to the Near East after the expeditions of Alexander the Great. In the Talmud silk is referred to under various names: *paranda, kallakh, mitakhsa, gushkera*, and *sirkin* (Gr. σηρικόν; Latin, *sericum*). It is possible that these names were connected with the methods of weaving the silk, as explained by *Nathan b. Jehiel in his *Arukh*: "*Kallakh, gushkera, mitakhsa shira'in*, and *sirikin* are all species of *shira paranda* (i.e., silk, see Shab. 20b) but their texture differs, some being woven fine and some thick." They may, however, have distinguished between Chinese silk and silk spun by the worms of local moths; a number of species are found in Israel, the largest being the *Pachypasa otus* moth whose worm spins a large cocoon of white threads. The silk of this moth was already used by the early Greeks, who wove clothes from it. Possibly this is the *meshi* of Ezekiel, and it is apparently the *kallakh* mentioned in the Mishnah (Shab. 2:1) among the materials which were not to be used for making the wick for the Sabbath lamp. In ancient times Chinese silk was very expensive and only wealthy people could afford garments made from it. Even Roman nobles could not afford *holoserikon*, i.e., a garment wholly woven from pure silk, and in the main wore *hemiserikon*, which was half wool or linen. The Midrash (Eccl. R. 1:7, no. 9) states that the reward of those that love God will be "one day *semisirikon* garments and on the morrow *holosirikon*," i.e., that their prosperity will increase. The cocoons were imported from China and woven in Ereẓ Israel, and the *mitakhsa* is probably this raw cocoon. According to the *aggadah*, R. Joshua b. Hananiah, in order to prove that Israel lacked nothing, "brought *mitakhsa* from Gush Ḥalav" (Eccl. R. 2:8, no. 2). In Ereẓ Israel cultivating the Chinese silkworm *Bombyx mori* began only in the Middle Ages, after the introduction of the white *mulberry. The earliest archaeological finds of silk found in Israel are from the Byzantine period, with fragments of mixed linen and silk found at Nessana; one fragment of pure silk must have been imported. Late Byzantine and Early Islamic examples of silk are known from Avdat and Naḥal Omer. Silk fragments from these periods are also known from excavations in Jordan and Syria. Medieval examples of silk are known from Qarantal Cave 38 (9th–13th centuries C.E.), and according to the researcher Orit Shamir they were made by different techniques (double-faced tabbies, weft-faced compound twills, and lampas weaves), and some of these required very sophisticated looms.

BIBLIOGRAPHY: Lewysohn, Zool, 358–9, no. 509; Krauss, Tal Arch, 1 (1910), 140–1; F.S. Bodenheimer, *Animal and Man in Bible Lands* (1960), 79–80; 137; J. Feliks, *Animal World of the Bible* (1962), 128.

[Jehuda Feliks / Shimon Gibson (2nd ed.)]

SILKIN, JON (1930–1997), English poet. Born in London, the son of a solicitor, Jon Silkin was a nephew of the British socialist politician Lewis *Silkin. He was educated at Jewish schools, in Wales, and at Dulwich College. At the age of 32, in 1962, he took a first-class degree at Leeds University. Silkin spent some years as a laborer before turning to the writing of poetry. In 1958, he was appointed Fellow in Poetry at Leeds University, but spent much of his time editing *Stand*, an avant-garde literary magazine which he had founded in 1957. Silkin's own early books of verse were *The Peaceable Kingdom* (1954), and *The Two Freedoms* (1958). In *The Reordering of the Stones* (1961) he experimented with a new and extreme terseness of language and he began to explore fresh terrain with his sequence of *Flower Poems*, republished in *Nature with Man* (1965), which reinterpreted familiar plants and flowers in political or social terms. His *Poems, New and Selected* appeared in 1966. His most celebrated poem is "Death of a Son," dedicated to a one-year-old child who died in a mental hospital. A highly individual critic, he was particularly interested in the poetry of World War I, and was an authority on Isaac *Rosenberg. He wrote an interesting book on World War I poets, *Out of Battle* (1972), and edited the anthology *The Penguin Book of First World War Poetry* (1979). Silkin lived much of his life in Newcastle-upon-Tyne. He visited Israel several times and wrote poetry on his Jewish background, which was collected in *Testament Without Breath* (1998).

BIBLIOGRAPHY: Abse, in: *Jewish Quarterly*, 13 no.3 (Autumn 1965), 10–11. **ADD. BIBLIOGRAPHY:** ODNB online.

[Philip D. Hobsbaum]

SILKIN, LEWIS, FIRST BARON (1889–1972), British lawyer and politician. Born in London, the son of a Hebrew teacher and wholesale grocer who had migrated from Lithuania, Silkin became a solicitor and then a prominent figure in London local government. He entered Parliament as a Labour member in 1936 and from 1945 to 1950 was minister of town and country planning in the Labour government of Clement *Attlee. In this capacity he piloted major planning legislation through Parliament, and was one of the progenitors of Britain's "New Towns" as well as of its national parks system. In 1950 Silkin was given a peerage with the title Baron Silkin, and from 1955 to 1964 was deputy leader of the opposition in the House of Lords. He was also active in Jewish affairs as president of the Trades Advisory Council, a body protecting Jewish commercial interests from discrimination, and of the British *Technion Committee.

Two of Silkin's sons also became prominent in law and politics. SAMUEL SILKIN, BARON SILKIN OF DULWICH (1918–1988), a barrister educated at Dulwich College and Cambridge, was elected a Labour member of Parliament in 1964 and in 1966 became recorder (i.e., judge) of Bedford. Silkin was appointed attorney general in the Labour government after the elections in February 1974, serving until 1976, but refused the knighthood which usually goes with the office. He retired from the House of Commons in 1983 and was given a life peerage. His brother John SILKIN (1923–1987), who was also educated at Dulwich College and Cambridge, and became a solicitor, was elected a Labour member of Parliament in 1963 and appointed parliamentary secretary to the Treasury and government chief whip in 1966. From 1969 to 1970 he was minister of building. Silkin was appointed minister for planning and local government in the Labour government after the elections in February 1974, with a seat in the cabinet, and minister of agriculture, fisheries and food in September 1976, serving until 1979. Generally on the left of the party, he was often a strong nationalist and opposed British entry into the European Community. In 1979–80 he served as the opposition spokesman on industry and during 1980 he became the shadow leader of the House of Commons. In November 1980 Silkin stood for the leadership of the Labour Party but received only limited support, and was also defeated for the deputy leadership in 1981.

ADD. BIBLIOGRAPHY: ODNB online.

[Vivian David Lipman / William D. Rubinstein (2nd ed.)]

SILKINER, BENJAMIN NAHUM (1882–1933), U.S. Hebrew poet. Born in Vilkija, Lithuania, Silkiner arrived in 1904 in the United States, where he taught Hebrew at a Hebrew elementary school and Bible at the Teachers Institute of the Jewish Theological Seminary in New York, until his death. He published several texts for Hebrew schools and, together with Israel *Efros and Judah *Even Shemuel (Kaufmann), an English-Hebrew dictionary (1929). His translation of *Macbeth* appeared in Warsaw in 1939. In 1913–14 he was also one of the editors of the Hebrew periodical *Ha-Toren*. Silkiner's main contribution to Hebrew literature is his emphasis on American themes. In his first book *Mul Ohel Timmurah* (1910), which is an epic poem of the struggles of the American Indian against the Spanish conquistadors, he draws his material from Indian lore and Spanish colonial history. The poem is included in *Shirim* (1927), a collection of his lyrics and narrative poems.

BIBLIOGRAPHY: *B.N. Silkiner Jubilee Volume* (1934), incl. bibl.; A. Epstein, *Soferim Ivrim ba-Amerikah*, 1 (1952), 31–38; H. Bavli, *Ruḥot Nifgashot* (1958), 86–120; E. Silberschlag, in: JBA, 18 (1960/61), 66–68.

[Eisig Silberschlag]

SILLS, BEVERLY (née **Belle Silverman**; 1929–), U.S. soprano singer. Born in New York City, Sills made her first public appearance as "Bubbles," becoming a child radio star at the age of three; at six she was singing coloratura soprano arias on "Major Bowes' Capital Family Hour." Giving up radio at the age of 12, she began piano lessons with Paolo Gallico and studied singing with Estelle Liebling (the teacher of Galli-Curci). She made her début in opera in 1947 with the Philadelphia Civic Opera (Micaëla in *Carmen*). After joining the New York City Opera Company in 1955, she first sang the part of Rosalinda in *Die Fledermaus*; among many other parts, she created the title role in Carlisle Floyd's *The Ballad of Baby Doe* (1956). In 1961, she retired to care for her deaf child, but in 1965 was persuaded by Julius *Rudel, director of the company, to return to the stage in Offenbach's *Tales of Hoffmann* in which she sang all three soprano roles. In 1966, during the opening season at the Company's new Lincoln Center opera house, she was a much-praised Cleopatra in Handel's *Giulio Cesare*; and her playing the title role in Massenet's *Manon* in 1968 led several critics to hail her performance, as well as the entire production, as the best in New York since World War II. Sills appeared at most of the major American and world opera houses, including the Vienna State Opera (1967); the Teatro alla Scala, Milan, in Rossini's seldom performed *L'Assedio di Corinto* (1969); the Royal Opera House, Covent Garden, in *Lucia di Lammermoor* (1970); and the Teatro la Fenice, Venice, as Violetta in *La Traviata* (1972). In all these roles, audiences admired her coloratura technique if not always a perfect steadiness or sweetness of voice, and she was an excellent actress with a warm stage personality. Sills announced that she would retire from opera on attaining the age of 50, and after fulfilling an assignment to sing at the world premiere of Menotti's *Juana La Loca* in San Diego in May 1978, she was appointed general director of the New York City Opera (1979–89). In June 1980 she was awarded the Freedom Medal by President Carter and in October that year gave her farewell performance. Sills published an autobiography (1987) and became chairperson of Lincoln Center for the Performing Arts (1993).

ADD. BIBLIOGRAPHY: NG^2.

[Max Loppert / Amnon Shiloah (2nd ed.)]

SILMAN, KADISH YEHUDA LEIB (1880–1937), Hebrew writer and satirist. Born near Vilna, Silman taught in Vilna's first Hebrew school in which Hebrew was the language of instruction, and later directed a "modern *ḥeder*" in Gomel. In 1907 he immigrated to Palestine and devoted his life to teaching, mostly in Jerusalem. He was one of the founders of Tel Aviv and of the neighborhood of Bet ha-Kerem in Jerusalem.

His literary poems, stories, and articles from Palestine (his series of newsletters to *Haolam* under the general title of "*Mikhtavim el Aḥ*") became famous. His contribution to the fields of popular ballads, poetry, satire, and humor was also of importance. His books for children include *Shirim la-Am* (1910); *Zimrei Am* (folk songs, 1927); *Lekhu Nerannenah* (70 folk songs with musical notes, 1928); *Mordekhai ve-Haman* (a play for children, 1934); and *Shimon Sevivon* (a story, 1937). In the field of humor, parody and satire, he published *Massekhet Bava Tekhnikah* (c. 1910) and *Shas Ereẓ Yisre'eli Katan* (a parody dealing with the language conflict, c. 1913). He also published satiric newspapers for several decades: *La-Yehudim* (irregularly between 1909 and 1927) and *Aspaklaryah* (1920).

[Getzel Kressel]

SILOAM (or **Shiloah**) **INSCRIPTION**, an inscription found in 1880 in the village of Siloam (Arab. Silwān) in Jerusalem. It contains six lines engraved on the rock wall of a tunnel known as the "Siloam tunnel" which, running through the spur of a hill, conveys water from the spring of Gihon to the east of the spur into the pool of Siloam to the west. In biblical times, the wall of Jerusalem made a southward loop, and the pool of Siloam lay within it. The language of the inscription is biblical Hebrew and its script is Paleo-Hebraic. It is about 32 cm. (12 in.) high and 72 cm. (28 in.) long and tells the story of the digging of the tunnel, a very respectable engineering feat for its day. The purpose of the inscription was apparently to commemorate the completion of the excavation by two groups of diggers who began working at the same time from the two ends of the tunnel until they met. The inscription and the tunnel date back to the days of King *Hezekiah of Judah, who sealed the springs outside the walls of Jerusalem in order to prevent the water from being used by a besieging army. In order to secure the supply of water for the city during the time of siege, he diverted the waters of the Gihon spring through the tunnel into the city (II Kings 20:20; II Chron. 32:3–4, 30; cf. Isa. 22:11). The project was terminated almost certainly before 701 B.C.E., the year of Sennacherib's campaign against Judah. In the 19th century, the inscription was cut out of the tunnel wall and removed to the Museum of Istanbul (then Constantinople).

BIBLIOGRAPHY: Pritchard, Texts, 321; Pritchard, Pictures, 275, 744; J. Simons, *Jerusalem in the Old Testament* (1952), 175–92; Burrows, in: ZAW, 70 (1958), 221–7 (Eng.); Stoebe, in: ZDPV, 71 (1955), 124–40; Amiran, in: *Qadmoniot*, 1 (1968), 13–18; Hecker, in: M. Avi-Yonah (ed.), *Sefer Yerushalayim* (1957), 191–218.

[Bustanay Oded]

SILVA, ANTÔNIO JOSÉ DA (known as "o Judeu"; 1705–1739), Portuguese playwright and martyr. Born in Rio de Janeiro, Brazil, Da Silva was of Converso origin and his family secretly remained loyal to Judaism. His father, João Mendes da Silva (1656–1736), was a prominent poet and lawyer who, until his death, managed to maintain the appearance of a faithful Catholic; his mother, Lourença Coutinho, was less compromising and it was as a result of her deportation to Portugal, when she was imprisoned on a Judaizing charge in 1713, that Da Silva and his father moved to Lisbon. While a law student at the University of Coimbra, he wrote a satire which provided the authorities with a pretext for arresting him, and he too was charged with Judaizing. Partly crippled by torture, Da Silva was eventually penanced and released. He practiced law but turned increasingly to writing and swiftly built up a reputation as the outstanding Portuguese dramatist of the era.

A prolific and versatile writer, Antônio da Silva created a series of stage satires criticizing the evils of contemporary society. These "comedies," which range from burlesque and parody to puppet show and comic opera and mingle prose dialogue with song, include *Vida do grande Don Quixote de la Mancha…* (1733), *Esopaida* (1734), *Encantos de Medeia* (1735), *O Anfitrião* (1736), *Variedades de Proteo* (1737), and *O Precipício de Faetonte* (1738). They were popularly known as the works of "The Jew" and were performed frequently during and after the 1730s. Da Silva's collected works (2 vols., 1744–46) were published anonymously until the end of the 18th century under the title *Theatro comico portuguez.*

In 1737 the playwright, together with his mother and newly married wife, was again arrested by the Inquisition. The women were released, but Judaizing charges were pressed against Da Silva, whose plays had made him many enemies. He had, it transpired, undergone circumcision, later joining the Franciscan order to divert suspicion from his heretical activities. Evidence of Sabbath observance and unorthodox fasting was provided by a colored slave girl. Prolonged torture failed to break his will and, when a secret court finally condemned him, not even the king himself could secure a reprieve. In October 1739 Da Silva was garroted and burnt at a Lisbon auto-da-fé. His wife, who witnessed his death, did not long survive him. Da Silva's tragic story has inspired several modern writers, including the Portuguese Camilo Castelo Branco (author of the novel *O Judeu*, 1906[3]), who was himself of Marrano origin.

BIBLIOGRAPHY: F. Wolf, *Don Antonio José de Silva* (Germ., 1860); Kayserling, Bibl, 101; T. Braga, *O Martyr da Inquisição portuguesa Antonio José da Silva, O Judeu* (1904); G.A. Kohut, *Jewish Martyrs of the Inquisition in South America* (1895), 35–50, 74–87; Roth, Marranos, 165–7.

[Godfrey Edmond Silverman]

°**SILVA, FLAVIUS**, Roman commander, conqueror of *Masada. Upon the death of Lucilius *Bassus he was sent to suppress the remaining rebels in the Judean desert. With a large army he undertook the siege of Masada, despite the enormous difficulties which he had to overcome in providing for his army, which included many non-combatants. After a siege lasting several months the fortress was taken. The rebels under *Eleazar b. Jair chose to die by their own hands rather than fall into the hands of the Romans. Silva returned with his army to Caesarea and later became consul in Rome.

BIBLIOGRAPHY: Jos., Wars 7:252, 275–9, 304–15, 407; Pauly-Wissowa, 12 (1909), 2617; Klausner, Bayit Sheni, 5 (1951[2]), 287ff.; Schuerer, Gesch, 1 (1901[4]), 638; Schuerer, Hist, 274, 277.

[Lea Roth]

SILVA, JOSHUA DA (d. 1679), English rabbi. Da Silva, who was born and trained in Amsterdam, was appointed haham of the Sephardi synagogue in London in 1670, serving also as *ḥazzan* and teacher. His sermons, *Discursos Predycaveys* (Amsterdam, 1688), published by his widow, contain valuable material for the social history of the Jews in London.

BIBLIOGRAPHY: Roth, Mag Bibl, 322; L.D. Barnett (tr.), *Libro de los Acuerdos* (Eng., 1931), index; A.M. Hyamson, *Sephardim of England* (1950), 41, 59.

[Cecil Roth]

SILVA, RODRIGO MENDEZ (Jacob) DA (1606–c. 1676), Marrano historian and genealogist. Mendez was born in Colorico, Portugal, and later settled in Madrid where he published numerous books on various aspects of Spanish history and genealogy. The most important was the widely read *Catalogo real de España*. These works led to his appointment as royal chronicler (*cronista general*) at the Spanish court. In 1659 he was arrested by the *Inquisition on a charge of Judaizing and after prolonged torture was admitted to penance. Later he managed to leave the country and take up residence in the *ghetto at Venice. There he adopted the name Jacob and was circumcised. As a Jew, he is said to have acted inconsistently in his beliefs and religious practices.

BIBLIOGRAPHY: J. Caro Baroja, Los judíos en la España moderna y contemporánea (1962), index; C. Roth, in: REJ, 89 (1930), 222–3.

[Cecil Roth]

SILVA, SAMUEL DA (16th–17th century), Marrano physician. He was born in *Oporto, Portugal, and later went to Hamburg, where he returned to Judaism. His translation into Spanish of the section on repentance (*Hilkhot Teshuvah*) from the *Mishneh Torah* of *Maimonides appeared in Amsterdam in 1613 under the title *Tratado de la Tesuvah o Contrición*. Subsequently, having read in manuscript a work by Uriel da *Costa critical of the Jewish tradition, da Silva wrote a polemic in reply entitled *Tratado da Immortalidade da Alma* ("Treatise on the Immortality of the Soul", Amsterdam, 1623), couched in strong language. Da Costa's *Examen das tradicoens Phariseas*, published in Amsterdam in 1624, was actually a second version of the manuscript that Da Silva had seen. In it Da Costa replied to the attack and referred to his critic as his "lying slanderer" in the subtitle.

BIBLIOGRAPHY: S. da Silva, *Tratado da Immortalidade del Alma*, ed. by De Jong (1935); Kayserling, Bibl, 40, 102; Brugmans-Frank, 517; M. Dos Remedios, *Os Judeus Portugueses em Amsterdam* (1911), 128–33; H. Kellenbenz, *Sephardim an der unteren Elbe* (1958), index; Melkman, in: *Studia Rosenthaliana*, 1:2 (1967), 24–26 (Eng.).

SILVER, ABBA (Abraham) HILLEL (1893–1963), U.S. Reform rabbi, Zionist leader. Silver was born in Lithuania and immigrated to the United States with his family in 1902. While studying at Yeshivat Etz Chaim (later, the Rabbi Yitzhak Elchanan Theological Seminary; see *Yeshiva University), he founded the Dr. Herzl Zion Club, a Hebrew-speaking group which evolved into *Young Judaea, the first Zionist youth organization in the U.S. He received a B.A. from the University of Cincinnati in 1915 and was ordained the same year at *Hebrew Union College, where he earned a D.D. in 1925. He was awarded an honorary L.D. by (Case) Western Reserve University, an honorary D.H.L. by Hebrew Union College, and an honorary D.H. by the University of Tampa.

Following ordination, Silver became rabbi of Congregation Leshem Shomayim in Wheeling, West Virginia (1915–17). In 1917, at the age of 24, and in spite of his outspoken Zionism, he became rabbi of The Temple (Congregation Tifereth Israel) in Cleveland, Ohio, arguably the largest Reform congregation in the country. Committed to the maintenance of basic Jewish tradition, he installed a **Sefer Torah* in the sanctuary's empty ark and moved the temple's weekly Sabbath worship service from Sunday to Saturday. He was instrumental in laying the groundwork for replacing the Reform movement's Pittsburgh platform with the 1937 Columbus platform. Infused with the spirit of the prophets of Israel, he denounced segregation and supported the right of labor to organize. He resigned from the Cleveland Chamber of Commerce over its anti-union policies and was a member of the special state labor commission that drafted Ohio's first unemployment insurance law. A self-appointed defender of the Jewish people, Silver was the founder (with Samuel Untermayer, and over the objections of some Jewish leaders) of the Non-sectarian Anti-Nazi League to Champion Human Rights, which organized a boycott of German goods in the 1930s.

Active in more than 30 local and national organizations, Silver was the founding president of the Cleveland Bureau of

Jewish Education (1924–32); president of the Cleveland Jewish Federation (1935–41); national chairman of the board of governors of the State of Israel Bonds; national chairman of the United Palestine Appeal (1938), and national co-chairman of the United Jewish Appeal; president of the *Central Conference of American Rabbis (1945–47); member of the board of governors of *Hebrew University; president of the alumni association of Hebrew Union College (1936–37), and chairman of its board of alumni overseers (1952); and president (1957–58) and honorary chairman (1945–46) of the *Zionist Organization of America.

A brilliant orator, Silver had the greatest impact and made his most important contributions as a founding chairman of the American Zionist Emergency Council (1943–45), and later as chairman of the American section of the Jewish Agency (1946–49). With the outbreak of World War II, he saw the opportunity to achieve the goal of a Jewish state. Perceiving that the postwar influence of the United States would be decisive, and winning the support of its people and government crucial, he (together with Stephen S. *Wise, although the two frequently clashed) succeeded beyond expectations in mobilizing public opinion, both Jewish and non-Jewish, on behalf of the Zionist cause. His public and private eloquence resulted in the passage of Congressional resolutions favoring the establishment of a Jewish Commonwealth, as well as in commitments of support enunciated in the Republican and Democratic Party platforms. The high point of his Zionist leadership came on May 8, 1947, when he presented the case for an independent Jewish state before the General Assembly of the United Nations, which passed the Partition Resolution on November 29 of that year, establishing the legal basis for the creation of the state of Israel. He returned again to the United Nations in May 1948 to announce that Israel had declared itself an independent state. It has been speculated that, had Chaim Weizmann not become the first president of Israel, Silver – widely considered one of the architects of modern Israel – might have been selected for that position. In 1950, a poll conducted by the *National Jewish Post* named him the leading figure of American Jewry. In 1952, he gave the benediction at the inauguration of President Dwight D. Eisenhower.

Although internal rivalries led Silver to leave his official posts in Zionist organizations, he constantly responded to appeals for his service in fundraising or for the use of his enormous prestige on behalf of Israel. Back in Ohio, he opposed a 1958 "right-to-work" amendment to the state's constitution. He was the recipient of many awards, including the Medal of Merit from the Jewish War Veterans (1951), the National Human Relations Award of the National Conference of Christians and Jews, and the Louis Brandeis Award of the American Zionist Council. The village Kefar Silver in Israel was named after him.

Silver's major books are *A History of Messianic Speculation in Israel* (1927), *The Democratic Impulse in Jewish History* (1928), *Religion in a Changing World* (1931), *Vision and Victory* (1949), *Where Judaism Differed* (1956), *Moses and the Original Torah* (1961), and *Therefore Choose Life* (1967), a selection of his sermons, addresses and writings (edited by H. Weiner). Silver died in his 45th year as rabbi of The Temple and was succeeded by his son, Daniel Jeremy *Silver.

BIBLIOGRAPHY: R.W. Zweig, J.D. Sarna, and M.A. Rader, *Abba Hillel Silver and American Zionism* (1977); M.L. Raphael, *Abba Hillel Silver: A Profile in American Judaism* (1989).

[Bezalel Gordon (2nd ed.)]

SILVER, DANIEL JEREMY (1928–1989), U.S. Reform rabbi. Daniel Jeremy Silver was the son of Abba Hillel *Silver (1893–1963). Born in Cleveland, Ohio, he was educated at Harvard University, received his rabbinical ordination from Hebrew Union College, and a doctoral degree at the University of Chicago. His first pulpit was Congregation Beth Torah in Chicago. In 1956 he became the associate rabbi at The Temple-Tifereth Israel in Cleveland, Ohio, where his father had been in service since 1917. Upon his father's death in 1963, Silver became the senior rabbi, where he remained until his own death in 1989.

Silver was an active participant in local Jewish and secular affairs. He was appointed to chair a committee of the Mayor's Commission on the Crisis in Welfare and served as vice president of the Cleveland Museum of Art; he taught Judaism at Cleveland State University and Case Western Reserve University, chaired the Congregational Plenum, and was active in the Jewish Community Federation of Cleveland. Nationally, he held leadership roles in the Reform movement's Central Conference of American Rabbis and edited the movement's journal for ten years. He was the president of the National Foundation for Jewish Culture and chaired its Academic Advisory Council. He wrote *Maimonidean Criticism and Maimonidean Controversy, 1180–1240* (1965); *A History of Judaism:* Volume I, *From Abraham to Maimonides* (1974); *Images of Moses* (1982); and *The Story of Scripture*, published posthumously in 1990.

BIBLIOGRAPHY: MS. 4850 Daniel Jeremy Silver Papers, Western Reserve Historical Society, Cleveland, Ohio.; "Daniel J. Silver, 61, Rabbi and an Author," in: *New York Times* (December 21, 1989), p. 20.

[Bezalel Gordon (2nd ed.)]

SILVER, EDWARD S. (1898–1974), U.S. lawyer. Born in New York, Silver served as secretary to Felix *Frankfurter when the latter was a professor at Harvard. He began his career of public service in 1929, when he joined the staff of the U.S. Attorney in New York. He served as Commissioner of the Alien Enemy Hearing Board, and in 1946 became District Attorney of Kings County, a position he held for ten years. In 1964 he was elected Kings County Surrogate, and from 1969 until the time of his death he was a member of the State Commission of Investigation. He was widely known for his work against crime and for prosecution of criminals and racketeers. Silver was active in many Jewish organizations, among them the Israel Bonds Drive, of which he was chairman of the New York campaign, and was president of the National Council of Young Israel.

[Milton Ridvas Konvitz (2nd ed.)]

SILVER, ELIEZER (1882–1968), rabbi and Orthodox Jewish leader. Born in Abel, Kovno province, Lithuania, Silver early achieved recognition for his unusual scholarly abilities. He studied under *Meir Simḥah ha-Kohen and Joseph *Rozin of Dvinsk, Ḥayyim Ozer *Grodzinski of Vilna, and Ḥayyim *Soloveichik of Brest-Litovsk. Silver immigrated to the United States in 1907 and became the rabbi of united Orthodox congregations in Harrisburg, Pennsylvania; Springfield, Massachusetts (1925); and Cincinnati, Ohio (1931), where he remained until his death. Silver was a leading spokesman for Orthodoxy on the American scene. In 1923 he was elected president of the *Union of Orthodox Rabbis, and he remained a member of its presidium until his death. He founded the U.S. branch of *Agudat Israel in 1939 and served as its first president. When the refugee yeshivah pupils reached Vilna in 1939–40 following the Nazi invasion of Poland, he founded the Va'ad Haẓẓalah, and during the ensuing years he applied the same body to rescuing European rabbis, scholars, and students. In 1946 Silver visited Europe and Ereẓ Israel as an official representative of the United States government to assist the war refugees. He continued to aid the many centers of rabbinic learning which were reestablished in Ereẓ Israel in cooperation with the Israeli Va'ad ha-Yeshivot.

In appearance and erudition an Orthodox rabbi of the old school, Silver possessed a scintillating and non-conformist personality and a remarkable sense of humor. His dedication and selflessness were highly regarded, and he was often called upon to mediate in disputes in communities throughout the United States. Silver was a constant contributor to talmudic and halakhic periodicals. He edited part of his talmudic novellae and they were published in two volumes entitled *Anfei Ereẓ* (1960–62). A biography entitled *Ish ha-Halakhah ve-ha-Ma'aseh*, edited by Menahem Glickman-Porush of Jerusalem, appeared in 1947.

BIBLIOGRAPHY: A. Rakeffet-Rothkoff, *The Silver Era in American Jewish Orthodoxy: Rabbi Eliezer Silver and his Generation* (1981); H. Karlinsky, in: *Shanah be-Shanah 5729* (1968), 366–71.

[Aaron Rothkoff]

SILVER, HAROLD M. (1900–), U.S. social worker and social welfare administrator. Silver was born in Russia and was educated in the United States. He served as director of the Detroit Jewish Family and Children's Service from 1933 to 1963, taught social work at Wayne University (1934–53), served on the executive committee (1940–50) and as president (1945–46) of the National Conference of Jewish Communal Service, and was active in Po'alei Zion. One of the founders of the National Association of Social Workers (1955), Silver was chairman of the association's commission on personnel standards (1955–58) and helped create the code of ethics and a set of adjudication procedures for professionals. He was also a charter member of the Academy of Certified Social Workers for experienced and especially qualified professionals. Silver immigrated to Israel in 1963 and was a consultant at the Israel Ministry of Social Welfare from 1963 to 1966 and then a member of the faculty of the Hebrew University from 1966.

SILVER, JOAN MICKLIN (1935–), U.S. film director. Born in Omaha, Nebr., to lumber dealer Maurice and Doris (née Shoshone) Micklin, both Russian immigrants, she studied at Sarah Lawrence College, graduating in 1956. After her marriage she moved to New York, where she worked on films for the Learning Corporation of American and wrote for the alternative newsweekly *The Village Voice* in the 1960s. She received a writing credit for one of the first films to address Vietnam veterans, *Limbo* (1972), and her first turn at directing was a documentary short *The Immigrant Experience: The Long Long Journey* (1972). While researching *Immigrant* she came across *Yekl*, a story about young Jewish newlyweds. The tale would serve as the basis for her first feature film, *Hester Street* (1975), which was created outside the Hollywood mainstream for $370,000 with her husband through their company, Midwest Films. *Hester Street* went on to gross $7 million, drawing resounding critical acclaim for its intimate historical portrayal of Jewish life in New York's Lower East Side, an Oscar nod for star Carol *Kane, and a Writer's Guild nomination for best screenplay. Her next feature film, *Between the Lines* (1977), drew on her time at *The Village Voice* but moved the action to Boston. In 1988, Silver put a modern twist on *Hester Street* with the release of *Crossing Delancy.* Silver followed this with the films *Lover Boy* (1989), *Big Girls Don't Cry ... They Get Even* (1992), and *A Fish in the Bathtub* (1999). Silver increasingly focused on directing intimate made-for-TV films, including the abortion-themed *A Private Matter* (1992) and the Warsaw ghetto tale *In the Presence of Mine Enemies* (1997). Silver has also directed plays and musicals for theater, including the Randy Newman-inspired *Maybe I'm Doing It Wrong* (1982) and *A ... My Name Is Alice* (1992). In 1995, she paired with Leonard *Nimoy to direct the radio series *Great Jewish Stories from Eastern Europe and Beyond* for National Public Radio.

[Adam Wills (2nd ed.)]

SILVER, RON (1946–), U.S. actor. Born Ronald Zimelman in New York City, Silver graduated from Stuyvesant High School, a specialized school in New York for mathematics, science, and technology. He studied Spanish and Chinese at the State University of New York at Buffalo. After graduating in 1967, he considered a career in intelligence before going on to graduate studies in Spain and Taiwan in 1968. After returning to the United States, he received his master's degree in Chinese history from St. John's University in Queens in 1970. Silver struggled to find a job that appealed to him, from social work to teaching Spanish at Roosevelt High School, a Jewish boarding school in Connecticut. Silver had taken some acting classes in college, and turned to study at the Herbert Berghof Studio and then Lee Strasberg's Actors Studio. He made his stage debut in *Kaspar* and *Public Insult* at the City Center Theater in 1971. In 1972, he was a cast member in the off-Broadway farce *El Grande De Coca-Cola*. In 1976, Silver was cast as nebbishy neighbor Gary Levy in the sitcom *Rhoda* (1974–78). He made his feature film debut in *Tunnelvision* (1976), which he followed with an appearance in the film *Semi-Tough* (1977). Silver was on the short-lived series *Dear Detective* in 1979. He starred in his own television series, *Baker's Dozen* (1982), but the show was canceled despite being nominated for an Emmy. Silver continued to act in films, including *Best Friends* (1982), *Lovesick* (1983) and *Silkwood* (1983). Silver then turned his attention to Broadway with two Mike Nichols-directed plays, *Hurlyburly* (1984) and *Social Security* (1986). In 1988, he was cast in the Broadway production of David Mamet's *Speed-the-Plow*, which earned him a Tony Award and a Drama Desk Award. Silver's turn as attorney Alan Dershowitz in the film *Reversal of Fortune* (1990) earned him critical acclaim. From 1996 to 1997, he had a recurring role as Tommy Wilmette on *Chicago Hope* (1996–2000). He returned to television for the 1998–99 season of *Veronica's Closet* and then starred in the Muhammad Ali biopic *Ali* (2001). He served as president of Actors' Equity Association from 1991 to 2000, and became an outspoken supporter of President George W. Bush after the Sept. 11, 2001, terrorist attacks. He has been an outspoken supporter of Israel as well.

BIBLIOGRAPHY: "Silver, Ron," in: *Contemporary Theater, Film and Television*, Volume 37 (Gale Group, 2002); "Silver, Ron," in: *Almanac of Famous People* (Gale Group, 2003[8]).

[Adam Wills (2nd ed.)]

SILVERMAN, ALEXANDER (1881–), U.S. glass chemist. Silverman was born in Pittsburgh. He worked for MacBeth-Evans Glass Company (1902–04). In 1918 he became professor of chemistry at the University of Pittsburgh. He invented illuminators for microscopes, and several varieties of colored glasses. Silverman was a member of the National Research Council (1938–41, 1947–50).

SILVERMAN, IRA (1945–1991), U.S. Jewish leader. Before his untimely death at the age of 46 from a parasite that he contracted when he visited China, Ira Silverman held some of the most important posts in American Jewish leadership. A native of Rockville Centre, New York, he was a graduate of Harvard University (B.A. 1966) with an M.A. in International Affairs from Princeton University (1968).

Among the positions that Silverman held was the presidency of the Reconstructionist Rabbinical College (1981–86). He was the first non-rabbi and as of 2006 the last to head the Seminary. He succeeded Ira Eisenstein, who had been the founding president and was to bring the institution from the generation of Mordecai Kaplan and his disciples to a new and younger generation. He was succeeded by Arthur Green, a distinguished scholar of Ḥasidism.

From the RRC he went on to become the director of the 92nd Street Y (1986–88), the crown jewel of the Y system, which was seeking to reinvigorate the Judaic contact of its many programs. He then returned to the American Jewish Committee where he had previously served as national program director, this time as its executive vice president (1988–90), where he was expected to bring sought after stability to it leadership in the post-Burt Gold era of the Committee. Illness beset him after a visit to China and in 1990 it became clear that he could not carry on the demands of his office. He remained at the AJC and director of the Institute on Human Relations until his death. Earlier in his career he was the director of federal government relations of the Association of American Universities, a Washington correspondent for *The Jerusalem Post* and *Yedioth Aharonoth*, a Tel Aviv newspaper. He was also the first director of the Institute for Jewish Policy Planning and Research, which was founded by the Synagogue Council of America. To each of these positions Silverman brought a deep Jewish commitment, which expressed itself in a commitment to social justice and human rights, which was at the core of his Judaism and shaped by its values.

[Michael Berenbaum (2nd ed.)]

SILVERMAN, JOSEPH (1860–1930), U.S. rabbi. Born in Cincinnati, he attended the University of Cincinnati, where he earned his B.A. in 1883. A year later he was ordained as the class valedictorian and received his D.D. from Hebrew Union College in 1887. He was a rabbi in Dallas, Texas, at Temple Emanu-El (1884–85), in Galveston at Temple Bnai Israel (1885–88), and at Temple Emanu-El, New York City (1888–1922), where he began as assistant rabbi and then served as rabbi after 1897. He was the first American-born rabbi to serve in New York. He was president (1900–03) of the Central Conference of American Rabbis and was founder and president of the Emanu-El Brotherhood. He wrote *A Catechism on Judaism* (1885), made numerous contributions to periodicals, and was active in Zionist work.

Among his other contributions, he was a consulting editor of the *Jewish Encyclopedia*. He was president of the New York Board of Ministers and founder and first president of the Association of Reform Rabbis of New York and Vicinity. An early opponent of Zionism, he became an active Zionist. Despite Emanu-El's undeserved reputation as an anti-Zionist congregation he was honorary vice president of the Palestine Foundation Fund and a member of the executive committee of the Masonic Foundation Fund. He was active in the Federation of Jewish Philanthropies, the organization to which his congregation traditionally gave leadership. He visited Palestine in 1923 and then traveled the U.S. encouraging philanthropic work in Palestine. He was more reluctant to advance political Zionism. He was a member of the Committee for Religious Congress of the Chicago World's Fair in 1893 and twice delivered the invocation at the House of Representatives. He wrote for the major Jewish periodicals of his day and was influential in the adoption of the Union Hymnal. He also wrote *The Renaissance of Judaism* (1918). He was active in ecumenical affairs, often the lone Jew represented among Christian clergy.

He opposed anti-Jewish portrayals in the theater and brought suit against Sholem Asch's *God of Vengeance*, which helped kill the play (during the Holocaust years Asch would not allow it to be performed lest the portrayal of Jews offer solace to antisemites; in recent years the play has enjoyed a revival in summer stock theater).

BIBLIOGRAPHY: *Universal Jewish Encyclopedia* (1943), 9:538; K.M. Olitzsky, L.J. Sussman, and M.H. Stern, *Reform Judaism in America: A Biographical Dictionary and Sourcebook* (1993); E. Nahshon, "The Pulpit and the Stage," in: *American Judaism* (March 2003).

[Michael Berenbaum (2nd ed.)]

SILVERMAN, LESLIE (1914–1966), U.S. engineer. Born in Chicago, Silverman was a member of the Department of Industrial Hygiene at Harvard University in 1937 where he was professor from 1958 and department head from 1961. This department pioneered studies in industrial hygiene and occupational medicine in the U.S. Silverman's research interests mainly concerned the analysis of airborne dust. During World War II he was responsible for the engineering aspects of programs which developed oxygen provision during high altitude flight and protective gas masks. His engineering and supervisory work after the war included radiological safety, solid waste management, and controlling air pollution. He was a consultant to the Atomic Energy Commission. His books *Industrial Air Sampling and Analysis* (1947) and *Handbook on Aircleaning* (1952) were standard texts.

[Michael Denman (2nd ed.)]

SILVERMAN, MORRIS (1894–1972), U.S. rabbi, scholar, and liturgist. Born in Newburgh, N.Y., Silverman was ordained rabbi at the Jewish Theological Seminary in 1922.

From 1923 to 1961 he served as rabbi of the Emanuel Synagogue in Hartford, Conn., and was a leader in virtually every aspect of Jewish life, prominently active in civic affairs, civil rights, interfaith activities, and Zionist work. He built the synagogue into one of the dominant congregations of New England and served with Hartford colleagues who also enjoyed long and distinguished tenures in the rabbinate.

His greatest influence on North American Jewry was through his role as a liturgical innovator and editor. Silverman began creating preliminary and experimental editions of various prayer books and booklets in the early 1930s. He eventually produced nationally distributed editions of twelve liturgical works, most published by the Prayer Book Press, which was established in Hartford to encourage dissemination of his work.

His *High Holiday Prayer Book* (1939 and 1953) combined the traditional Hebrew liturgy with new readings and notes, and introduced interpretive translations in "responsive reading" formats, which sought to encourage participation by worshipers of diverse backgrounds. It was eventually adopted by more than one thousand institutions, and was still in active distribution in 2005.

Silverman's *Sabbath and Festival Prayer Book* (1946) produced under the auspices of the Rabbinical Assembly, was adopted by most Conservative congregations; and, like his *Maḥzor*, has influenced subsequent publications in various sectors of Jewish life. For four decades it was synonymous with the liturgy of a Conservative Congregation.

His *Prayers of Consolation* (1953) introduced a new genre of worship texts for special occasions, combining traditional worship with selections from classical texts and 20th-century sources. Silverman's *Passover Haggadah* (1959) featured explanatory notes and interpretive readings, and pioneered the inclusion of commemorative material on both the Holocaust and the recently-created State of Israel, within the *seder* liturgy.

Between 1933 and 1961 Silverman also edited and coedited liturgical and instructional texts for young people. His son Hillel also became a rabbi and his grandson Jonathan is a prominent American actor.

[Walter Stern (2nd ed.)]

SILVERMAN, SIDNEY (**Samuel**; 1895–1968), British politician. Born in Liverpool, the son of a draper, Silverman was imprisoned in World War I as a conscientious objector, and, during the early 1920s, was employed as an English lecturer at Helsinki University. He then returned to London, becoming a solicitor. Silverman was elected to Parliament as a Labour member in 1935, retaining his seat until his death, and immediately established a reputation for independence and forthrightness. This led to numerous clashes with his colleagues in the Labour Party, of whose left wing he was a prominent member. During World War II he was one of the first persons in Britain to campaign on behalf of Jews being killed in the Holocaust, and raised the plight of the Jews in Parliament. In the immediate postwar period he was vocal in opposing Labour's policies in Palestine. On two occasions, in 1954, when he opposed German rearmament, and in 1961, when he voted against a party decision on service estimates, he was suspended from the Parliamentary Labour Party. His great achievement, the result of 30 years of campaigning, was the abolition of capital punishment in 1965.

Silverman was an expert on procedure. He came to be regarded as one of the most accomplished debaters in the House of Commons, and his parliamentary skill and his courage won him the affection of members of all parties. A dedicated Zionist, he spoke passionately and knowledgeably on Jewish causes in Parliament and consistently opposed the Palestine policies of Ernest *Bevin, foreign secretary in the 1945–50 Labour Government. He was chairman of the British section of the World Jewish Congress (1940–50) and later member of the World Executive Council (1950–60) and vice president of the Zionist Federation of Great Britain (1947–50).

BIBLIOGRAPHY: S.J. Goldsmith, *Twenty 20th-Century Jews* (1962), 115–9; E. Hughes, *Sydney Silverman: Rebel in Parliament* (1969). **ADD. BIBLIOGRAPHY:** ODNB online.

[Vivian David Lipman]

SILVERMAN, SIME (1872–1933), U.S. theatrical journalist. Born in Cortland, New York, Silverman wrote theatrical commentary for the New York *Morning Telegraph* (1896–1905) until he offended advertisers and lost his job. In 1905, on $1,500 borrowed money, he started *Variety*, a weekly trade magazine devoted exclusively to show-business content. He was the editor and publisher until shortly before his death. It took him 24 years to make the paper pay, but he turned it into an influential weekly noted for its robust style and authoritative insight. In his latter years he launched a Hollywood edition of the publication. *Variety* covered vaudeville at first but then expanded to encompass film, radio, television, and music. A rich source of trend-setting phrasing, the paper popularized such terms as "high-hat," "pushover," and "belly laugh."

BIBLIOGRAPHY: D. Stoddart, *Lord Broadway* (1941).

[Ruth Beloff (2nd ed.)]

SILVERS, PHIL (**Philip Silversmith**; 1911–1985), U.S. comedian. Born in Brooklyn, New York, Silvers started in vaudeville and toured for five years with the Minsky Burlesque Troupe. He began film work in 1940 and appeared on Broadway in 1947–49 in *High Button Shoes*. Other Broadway appearances include *Yokel Boy* (1939), *High Kickers* (1941), *Top Banana* (Best Actor/Musical Tony, 1952), *Do Re Mi* (Tony nomination, 1961), *How the Other Half Loves* (1971), and *A Funny Thing Happened on the Way to the Forum* (Best Actor/Musical Tony, 1972).

In 1955 he launched a long-running television comedy series, *The Phil Silvers Show* (1955–59), in which he played inveterate con artist Sergeant Ernie Bilko. Silvers won a Best Actor Emmy for the role in 1956.

His films include *You're in the Army Now* (1941), *Roxie Hart* (1942), *Just Off Broadway* (1942), *Cover Girl* (1944), *Four Jills in a Jeep* (1944), *Something for the Boys* (1944), *A Thousand and One Nights* (1945), *Summer Stock* (1950), *Top Banana* (1954), *Lucky Me* (1954), *It's a Mad Mad Mad Mad World* (1963), *A Funny Thing Happened on the Way to the Forum* (1966), *Follow That Camel* (1967), *Buona Sera, Mrs. Campbell* (1968), *The Boatniks* (1970), *The Strongest Man in the World* (1975), *Won Ton Ton, the Dog Who Saved Hollywood* (1976), *The Chicken Chronicles* (1977), *The Cheap Detective* (1978), and *There Goes the Bride* (1980).

Silvers' two books, which he co-wrote with Robert Saffron, were published in 1973: *This Laugh Is on Me: The Phil Silvers Story* and *The Man Who Was Bilko: The Autobiography of Phil Silvers*.

[Ruth Beloff (2nd ed.)]

SILVERSTEIN, ABE (1908–2001), U.S. aeronautical engineer. Born in Terre Haute, Indiana, Silverstein worked as an aerodynamic research engineer for the National Advisory Committee on Aeronautics from 1929 to 1940, concentrating on problems concerning full-scale wind tunnels. From 1945 to 1949 he was chief of both this division and the flight research division. Silverstein was chief of research (1949–52) and then assistant director (1952–58). He was director of space flight programs for the National Aeronautics and Space Administration from 1958 until 1961, when he became director of the NASA Lewis Research Center. After his retirement in 1969 he was the director of Environmental Planning at the Republic Steel Corporation in Cleveland, Ohio. He also served as a technical adviser for the Lake Erie International Jetport Task Force.

[Samuel Aaron Miller]

SILVERSTEIN, ALAN (1948–), U.S. rabbi. Silverstein was born in Philadelphia, Pennsylvania, and received a B.A. from Cornell University in 1970 and an M.A. from Columbia University in 1973. In 1975, he was ordained at the *Jewish Theological Seminary, where he earned a Ph.D. in 1990. He served as rabbi of Congregation Tifereth Israel in Cornwells Heights, Pennsylvania (1974–79), before becoming rabbi of Congregation Agudath Israel in Caldwell, New Jersey (1979–). In New Jersey, he was president of the New Jersey Region of the *Rabbinic Assembly (1984–86), of the Metrowest Board of Rabbis (1986–88), of the West Essex Clergy Association, and of the statewide New Jersey Coalition of Religious Leaders [of all faiths] (2003–05). He was also a member of the National Rabbinic Cabinet of the United Jewish Appeal.

In 1992, he was elected vice president of the Rabbinical Assembly, becoming president in 1994 (to 1996). As president, Silverstein worked to implement the three-fold approach of Conservative Judaism toward interfaith marriage: ideally promoting marriage within the faith; after the fact of intermarriage, facilitating the creation of Jewish households via conversion; finally, if no conversion is in the offing, advocating *keruv* – bringing the intermarried couple closer to Judaism and assisting them in selecting Judaism for their children and raising them unambiguously as Jews. Following his term of office, Silverstein served as vice president of the American Zionist arm of Conservative Judaism, Mercaz USA (1996–2004). In 1997, he became a member of the Founding Executive Committee of the National Council of Synagogues, until 2000, when he was elected president of the World Council of Conservative/Masorti Synagogues (2000–05). In this capacity, he established a central office in Jerusalem and hired the organization's first full-time executive vice president and other professionals. He also created a formal partnership between the council, whose name he changed to Masorti Olami, and Mercaz Olami, Conservative Judaism's global Zionist arm. Under Silverstein's leadership, the number of *kehillot* affiliated with Masorti Olami grew from 70 to 120, while its international youth movement, Noam, and young adult leadership network, Marom, grew concomitantly. In addition, 15 rabbis were placed in new congregational positions, and Chayl Masorti (the Masorti Peace Corps) was launched.

Silverstein has written numerous articles on intermarriage, conversion, and the Arab-Israeli conflict. He is the author of three books: *Alternatives to Assimilation: The Response of Reform Judaism to American Culture, 1840–1930* (1994); *It All Begins With A Date: Jewish Concerns About Intermarriage* (1995); and *Preserving Judaism in Your Family After Intermarriage Has Occurred* (1995).

[Bezalel Gordon (2nd ed.)]

SILVERSTEIN, LARRY (1931–), U.S. builder. Silverstein, who was born in New York, graduated from New York University. His father, Harry, a Russian immigrant, was a classical pianist who taught himself to be a broker of loft spaces in the Garment District. Larry went to work for his father to put himself through school and returned full-time after graduation. He built his career by becoming an expert in buying and flipping properties in Manhattan. He bought 11 West 42nd Street, near Bryant Park before its renaissance. He built on the far West Side, at 42nd west of 11th Avenue, and in lower Manhattan at 120 Broadway. The latter property was a 1.8-million square-foot giant occupying a full square block, steps from Wall Street. By the 1980s, Silverstein controlled more than 10 million square feet of Manhattan residential and commercial space. He set his sights on the last undeveloped parcel of the World Trade Center, at the northern tip of the site, and in 1980 he won the bid to build the original 7 World Trade. He constructed the 47-story tower and then set his sights on the Twin Towers of the Center. In 2001, backed by a number of investors, Silverstein signed a 99-year lease for the World Trade Center complex just seven weeks before the Twin Towers were destroyed. Silverstein was awarded an insurance payment of more than $3.5 billion dollars to settle his policy. In addition, the Silverstein group sued the insurers liable for the World Trade Center for another $3.5 billion, claiming that the two planes constituted two separate terrorist attacks. He won. Although Silverstein originally had only $14 million of his own money in equity in the place (a consortium of partners put up more than $100 million), the lease gave him the right to rebuild all 10 million lost square feet of office space, regardless of the wishes of victims' families, neighbors, or the governors of New York and New Jersey, whose Port Authority owns the land. It also gave Silverstein the authority to force through much of his own architect's design for the Freedom Tower, the 1,776-foot building that replaced 7 World Trade. (Daniel *Libeskind's original design for that building was cast aside.) The plan calls for Silverstein to construct five office towers that he has to rent. He also has to pay $120 million in rent a year, escalating to over $200 million by 2020, to the Port Authority. Silverstein was chairman of the Real Estate Board in New York, transforming it from a social club into a lobbying group. He enhanced his reputation early in his career with his philanthropic work for the United Jewish Appeal and his sponsorship of the New York University Real Estate Institute, where he taught an annual course.

[Stewart Kampel (2nd ed.)]

SILVERSTONE, GEDALYAH (1871/2–1944), U.S. rabbi. Silverstone (originally Zilbershtein) was born in 1871 or 1872 in Sakot (Saukotas), Lithuania, where his father, Isaiah Meir, was rabbi. In the 1880s Gedalyah studied at the Rasien and Telz yeshivot. In 1891 the Silverstones relocated to Liverpool, England, where Gedalyah's father accepted a rabbinical position. In 1901 Gedalyah was chosen as rabbi in Belfast, Ireland, where he served for five years. In late 1905 or early 1906 he immigrated to America and in late 1907 he settled with his family in Washington, D.C., and shortly thereafter was appointed as rabbi of three local congregations: Ohev Shalom, Adat Israel, and Talmud Torah. In the mid-1920s he was invited by congregation Tiferet Israel to serve as its rabbi, and in the following years Silverstone acted as chief rabbi of the Orthodox congregations of Washington. Silverstone was active in local Jewish institutions: He was one of the founders of a Jewish old age home, founded the first *Talmud Torah* in town, and was a member of B'nai B'rith and George Washington Lodge. On the national Orthodox level, Silverstone served as president of the Union of Orthodox Rabbis of the United States and Canada. Finally, following the prohibition laws (January 1920), he and his son Aaron were involved in various problematic aspects of selling wine for religious purposes.

Silverstone was a strong supporter of Zionism and the Jewish settlement in Palestine. He served as a delegate to the Sixth Zionist Congress, which convened in Basel in August 1903. In addition, he visited Palestine several times in 1922 and 1924 in order to examine the possibility of settling there, but this did not materialize, even though he testifies that he purchased land in Jerusalem and Jaffa. In 1936 and 1938 he visited Palestine again.

Silverstone was considered a locally popular and respected preacher and published at least 31 small books of sermons, each of which consists of 30–40 pages.

BIBLIOGRAPHY: K. Caplan, *Ortodoksiyah ba-Olam ha-Ḥadash: Rabanim ve-Darshanut be-Amerikah (1881–1924)* (2002), 339–41; H. Marrans, *Jews in Greater Washington: A Panoramic History of Washington Jewry for the Years 1785–1960* (1961), 70–72, 89; The Historical Records Survey, *Directory of Churches and Religious Organizations, Washington D.C.* (1939), 60–63.

[Kimmy Caplan (2nd ed.)]

SILVEYRA, MIGUEL DE (c. 1578–1638), Portuguese *Marrano poet, physician, and mathematician. Silveyra, who was a relative of the great classical scholar Thomas de Pinedo, began his professional career in Madrid, where he was royal mathematician and, later, physician to the House of Castile. In 1634 he was denounced to the Inquisition and fled to Naples, where he spent the remaining few years of his life. His masterpiece, *El Macabeo* ("The Maccabee"), a baroque heroic poem written in Castilian, was published in Naples at the royal expense in 1638. The 20 books of this epic relate the exploits of Judah Maccabee culminating in the restoration of the Temple. Although modern critics have considered *El Macabeo* excessively bombastic, the poem enjoyed great esteem throughout the 17th century. It was reprinted in Madrid (1731) and published in an Italian verse translation (Naples, 1810). Silveyra's other works include *El sol vencido* (Naples, 1639).

BIBLIOGRAPHY: J. Amador de los Ríos, *Estudios históricos, políticos y literarios sobre los judíos de España* (1848), 534–46; F.M. de Sousa Viterbo, *Poesias avulsas do Dr. Miguel de Silveira* (1906); E. Toda y Güell, *Bibliografía espanyola d'Italia…* (1927–31), no. 4700; A. Rubens, *Jewish Iconography* (1954), 112; J. Caro Baroja, *La Sociedad Criptojudía en la Corte de Felipe IV* (1963), 93–101.

[Kenneth R. Scholberg]

SILVIU, GEORGE (originally **Silviu Goliger**; 1899–), Romanian poet and journalist. Silviu's verse collections include *Flori şi fluturi* ("Flowers and Butterflies," 1922) and *Infrângeri* ("Defeats," 1934). He also wrote children's plays such as *Motanul incălţat* ("Puss-in-Boots," 1923), a work of literary importance produced in collaboration, and *Intîmplări cu tîlc* ("Meaningful Incidents," 1957), a volume of classical and ultramodern fables.

°**SIMA, HORIA** (1908–), leader of the Romanian *Iron Guard. A secondary school teacher in Transylvania, Sima was among the first to join the Iron Guard of *Codreanu and after Codreanu's death (1938) became its leader. In 1939 he fled to Germany but, after temporary conciliation with King Carol, accepted a portfolio in the Romanian government (summer 1940). Following King Carol's abdication (Sept. 5, 1940), he was vice president under *Antonescu at the head of the "National Legionnaire State." Sima then visited several cities to administer personally the expropriation of property belonging to Jewish businessmen. In January 1941 he led the abortive legionnaire rebellion against Antonescu, during which 120 Jews were killed in *Bucharest. Afterwards Sima fled to Germany, where he was interned. In a letter to *Himmler he blamed the Jews for his defeat and accused Antonescu of being manipulated by the Jews. In August 1944, following the anti-Nazi coup in *Romania, he became head of the Iron Guard government in exile in Vienna. After the end of the war, he organized the migration of factions of the Iron Guard who had fallen out with the Romanian authority, and was active in the neofascist movement. In his *Destinée du nationalisme* (1951) he professed a type of nationalism diverging from national socialism and fascism. He was subsequently reported living in Spain.

BIBLIOGRAPHY: P. Pavel, *Why Rumania Failed* (1944), index.

[Bela Adalbert Vago]

SIMA, MIRON (1902–1999), Israeli artist. Born in Proskurow, Ukraine, Sima grew up in a secular home with an excellent library that offered him an opportunity to learn about the Russian epic, as well as about European literature and art. Being Jews in Ukraine, Sima's family suffered from the pogroms, and in 1921 they moved to Poland. This tragic existence had a major influence on Sima's future artworks. In 1924 Sima moved to Dresden, where he studied at the Academy of Fine Arts until 1930. As a student Sima was granted three prestigious prizes and three honorable mentions. In 1932 Sima was awarded the prize of the City of Dresden for his painting *The Tool-Sharpener* (this painting was lost). In May 1933 Sima was ordered to leave Germany and, with the money he earned by selling some of his pictures, he immigrated to his family in Tel Aviv.

As soon as Sima arrived in Tel Aviv, he began to create and to exhibit, but the French-oriented art style of that city was not compatible with his approach as an artist. In Jerusalem Sima found German-born artists to whom he could articulate his feelings, and he moved there in 1938.

From his early days as an artist Sima was attracted to melancholic subjects. As a person with social sensibility, he turned to painting scenes of poverty and suffering. In Dresden he had made a woodcut portfolio called, *The Scream* (1924, Museum of Art, Ein Harod). The tragic images visible on those sheets of paper describe, in very expressive black and white, contrasts symbolizing death and mourning. They were seen as a reflection of his childhood experience. Later in his life Sima continued to deal with tragic subjects in his art. Although he found it unsuited to the atmosphere of renewal of the state of Israel during its first years, he managed to integrate the shady subjects with the colorful composition that expressed the light of the locale.

Sima used to work repeatedly on his subjects. In addition to his stage designs for the Ohel Theater, Sima created a lithographs album of portraits of the famous Israeli actress Hanna *Rovina (1937). Thanks to his visual sensitivity, the actres was described in dramatic, vivid gestures. One of his late woodcuts of Rovina as Medea (1957) hung in her house until she passed away.

Another album by Sima was dedicated to the German poet Else *Lasker-Schueler (the drawings were created in the 1940s, the album was first published in Germany in 1978, and later in Hebrew in 1983). With just a few lines, Sima captured her image, wandering around the streets of Jerusalem bent and lonely.

The melancholic atmosphere in Sima's art and the serious expression of his self-portrait can be misleading, since Sima was actually a very cheerful and vital person. He used to say that only owing to his sensitivity to the beauty of life was he sensible to its tragic aspect as well.

BIBLIOGRAPHY: G. Bar Or, *Miron Sima – From Dresden to Jerusalem* (1997).

[Ronit Steinberg (2nd ed.)]

SIMCHONI (Simchowitz), JACOB NAFTALI HERTZ (1884–1926), scholar, historian, and translator. Simchoni was born in Slutzk. He taught at the Hebrew High School in Lodz, Poland, from 1917 to 1924. In 1925 he joined the editorial board of the *Encyclopedia Judaica* (published by "Eshkol" in German and Hebrew), contributing many articles to both editions.

Simchoni's scholarly interests extended over a wide area, including history, archaeology, linguistics, and philosophy. He published essays in Hebrew periodicals (*Ha-Ivri he-Ḥadash, He-Atid, Ha-Ẓefirah, Ha-Tekufah*, and others) on Judah Halevi, Solomon ibn Gabirol, Gershom Me'or ha-Golah, Joshua Falk, as well as on more recent scholars and writers such as S.D. Luzzatto, Ḥ.N. Bialik and Hermann Cohen. Simchoni wrote a textbook of Jewish history (*Divrei Yemei Yisrael*, 2 vols. 1922–23) and an introduction to S. Tchernichowsky's Hebrew translation of the Gilgamesh epic (1924), and translated into Hebrew Josephus' *Wars* (1923, repr. several times) and *Against Apion* (1928). He defended the integrity of Josephus both as a man and as a historian and maintained that his actions, including his defection to Rome, were dictated by moral considerations and that his books were written with passionate love for his people and deep concern for truth. A memorial volume for Simchoni (*Ẓiyyunim*) was published in 1928.

BIBLIOGRAPHY: S. Bernfeld, I. Davidson, N. Goldmann, in: *Ẓiyyunim* (1928), 10ff.; G.R. Malachi, *ibid.*, 15–18 (bibl.); J.K. Mikliszanski, in: *Ishim u-Demuyyot be-Ḥokhmat Yisrael*, ed. S.K. Mirsky (1959), 187ff.

[Jacques K. Mikliszanski]

SIMEON (Heb. שִׁמְעוֹן), the second son of Jacob and Leah (Gen. 29:33) and the eponymous ancestor of the tribe of Simeon. The name is formed from the verb *shʿm* (שמע) with the addition of the suffix *on* (וֹן), and was given by Leah to her son because "the Lord heard" that she was unloved (*ibid.*).

Simeon the individual is mentioned in connection with the journey to Egypt in time of famine, when Joseph imprisoned him as a guarantee that Benjamin, the youngest brother, would be brought before him (42:24, 36; 43:23). In Genesis 34 he is referred to as, together with Levi, attacking the city of Shechem, killing its inhabitants in retaliation for the rape of their sister Dinah by Shechem, son of Hamor the Hivite, a prince of the land (cf. 49:5–6). However, many scholars see in this story echoes of the sojourn of the tribes of Simeon and Levi in central Palestine and a clash between them and the host population, even before the Israelites conquered the land. Such a supposition might explain why the Book of Joshua lacks any description of the conquest of Shechem and the mountains of Ephraim (but cf. Josh. 12). Shechem, it is presumed, was already in the hands of Simeon and Levi even prior to Joshua's invasion of Canaan. It was to Shechem that Joshua later gathered all the tribes of Israel and where they entered into a covenant to worship the Lord (Josh. 24). Some also find an allusion to Simeon's connection with the district of Shechem in the ceremony described in Deuteronomy 27:12, in which the Simeonites head the group delivering the blessing on Mt. Gerizim. Simeon is also cited together with Ephraim and Manasseh in II Chronicles 15:9. According to Judges 1:3, the Simeonites fought alongside the tribe of Judah at Bezek within Manasseh's district north of Shechem even before they turned southward to conquer the hill country of Judah (cf. Judg. 1:3).

In contrast to this meager evidence showing Simeon to be located in the center of the land, there exists a large body of tradition concerning the settlement of the tribe in the southern region of Canaan. According to the Book of Joshua, Simeon settled in the Negev (cf. I Chron. 4:28–33) "in the midst of the inheritance of the tribe of Judah" (Josh. 19:1). The passage does not trace the boundaries of Simeon's settlement, but lists its towns, including the principal town of Beer-Sheba. Simeon's settlement is also included in the description of Judah's territory in Joshua 15. It lay in the Negev district, since the Simeonites inherited part of Judah's allotment (Josh. 19:8). Moreover, the listings of the levitical towns include Simeon's along with Judah's (Josh. 21:9ff.; I Chron. 6:40–44). For these reasons Simeon's territory is also called

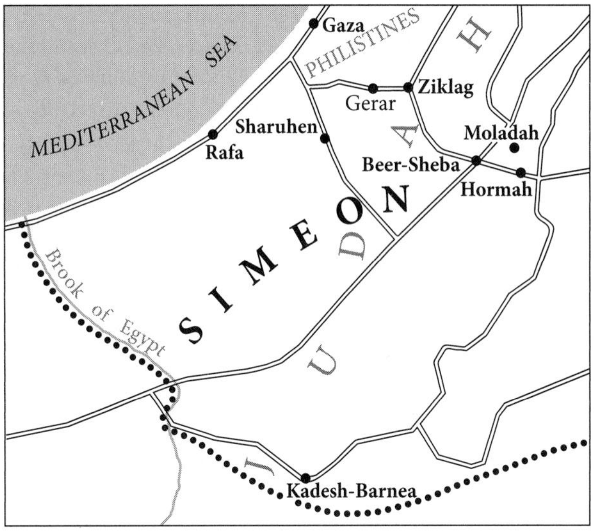

Territory of the tribe of Simeon. After Y. Aharoni, Lexicon Biblicum, *Tel Aviv, 1965.*

the "Negev of Judah," to distinguish it from other parts of the Negev which were named after different ethnic groups (I Sam. 27:10; 30:14; II Sam. 24:7). There is no unanimity about the dating of the lists of Simeonite cities (Josh. 19:1–8; I Chron. 4:28–33; cf. Josh. 15:20–32), some regarding them as early as the period of conquest of the land and the time of the Judges, others assigning them to the time of David and Solomon, or even as late as Josiah.

Many of the names of locations within Simeon's area are composed of the element "*ḥazar*," denoting small settlements lacking walls (Lev. 25:31; Neh. 12:29). These served groups of shepherds and semi-nomads who had not attained the level of urban culture (cf. Gen. 25:16; Isa. 42:11; Jer. 49:33). This fits the situation of the tribe of Simeon, which continued its pastoral life, ranging through the wide spaces of the Negev to pasture its livestock. Although Simeon's area of settlement is included in the Judahite region, which perhaps explains the omission of Simeon in Moses' blessing (Deut. 33), the Simeonites managed to preserve their tribal unity and traditions. This is proved by the existence of genealogies of Simeonite families from as late as the days of Hezekiah, king of Judah (I Chron. 4:24–43).

The grazing of livestock in the southern part of the land, throughout the Negev, involved constant struggles between the Simeonites and the desert and border tribes, an echo of which may appear in Jacob's blessing (Gen. 49:5–7) and in the report about families from the tribe of Simeon who in Hezekiah's time fought against the Meunites and Amalekites in the area of Gerar, spreading with their livestock over the Negev of Judah as far as Mt. Seir (I Chron. 4:38–43).

The genealogies of the Simeonites testify to familial ties between them and other Israelite tribes as well as non-Israelite elements. Shaul son of Simeon is the "son of a Canaanite woman" (Gen. 46:10; Ex. 6:15); Mibsam and Mishma, sons of Simeon (I Chron. 4:25), also appear among the sons of Ishmael (Gen. 25:13–14; I Chron. 1:29–30); Jamin (Gen. 46:10; Ex. 6:15; I Chron. 4:24) is also listed as a descendant of Ram, the firstborn of Jerahmeel (I Chron. 2:27); Zerah as Simeon's son (I Chron. 4:24) suggests familial ties between the tribe and the family of Zerah, son of Judah (Gen. 38:30), or possibly with an Edomite family descended from Esau (Gen. 36:17; I Chron. 1:37). It is also possible to find traces of familial ties between the tribe of Simeon and the Midianites in the association of Zimri son of Salu, a chieftain of the Simeonites, with Cozbi, daughter of Zur, the Midianite (Num. 25:6–19).

Although Simeon is considered Jacob's second son, the Simeonites enjoyed no outstanding position in the tribal organization of Israel either before or after the conquest and occupation of Canaan. There were no judges appointed from that tribe, and Deborah does not mention Simeon at all. During the period of the monarchy, the Simeonites and their territory formed an inextricable part of the Kingdom of Judah, the fate of its population being tied to that of the kingdom generally.

[Bustanay Oded]

In the *Aggadah*

The rabbinic attitude to Simeon was determined largely by his violent role in the Dinah affair (Gen. 34:25ff.); the need to explain his detention by Joseph (Gen. 42:24); Jacob's harsh criticism of Simeon and Levi (34:30; 49:5ff.) though the latter, being a priestly tribe, fared much better later on; the total omission of Simeon in Moses' blessing (Deut. 33); and the virtual disappearance of the tribe during the period of the Judges or the early monarchy. Simeon and Levi were only thirteen years of age when they massacred the Shechemites, and they did so independently and without consulting one another (Gen. R. 80:10). The purpose of this manifest exaggeration was no doubt to emphasize the great physical strength of Israel's ancestors. It was Simeon who devised the circumcision stratagem to weaken the Shechemites (*Sefer ha-Yashar, Va-Yishlaḥ* on Gen., p. 115); and it was his implacable hostility to Joseph which began the chain of events leading to Joseph's sale into slavery. Simeon proposed to have Joseph put to death (*ibid., Va-Yeshev* on Gen., p. 147; Tanḥ. B. Gen. p. 183 *et al.*), and it was he who threw him into the pit (Gen. R. 91:6; Tanḥ. *Va-Yiggash* 4) and ordered large stones to be cast on him to kill him (Tanḥ. B. Gen. 184). Joseph thus had good reason to arrest Simeon in Egypt (cf. Gen. 42:24); but he also wanted to separate him from Levi to avoid another massacre (Gen. R. 91:6). Simeon, who was endowed with extraordinary strength as well as a powerful voice which frightened all his enemies (Test. Patr., Sim. 2:3; Tanḥ. *Va-Yiggash* 4 *et al.*), refused to submit to detention, easily overcoming some seventy Egyptian warriors; but eventually he was overpowered by Joseph's son Manasseh (Tanḥ. *ibid.*). This account is in line with the general idealization of Israel's progenitors, most of whom were considered to have wielded supernatural powers. According to a more realistic view, however, Simeon was included in a list of the five weakest sons of Jacob (Gen. R. 95:4).

The tribe of Simeon, which was early absorbed by Judah, plays a relatively minor role in rabbinic literature. Along with the tribes of Reuben and Levi, the Simeonites are said to have refrained from idolatry and intermarriage with the Egyptians during the period of the Egyptian bondage (Song R. 4:7). This may be regarded as an apologetic compensation for Jacob's criticism of the ancestors of these three tribes (cf. Gen. 49:3ff.) with a view to removing any taint from Israel, which must be "all fair" and "flawless" (Song R. 4:7; cf. Shab. 55b–56a). It was, nevertheless, conceded that a large proportion of the Simeonites became seriously involved in the Baal-Peor affair (cf. Num. 25:1ff.), opposing the severe punishments ordered by Moses, and causing their chieftain Zimri to enter upon a confrontation with Moses and get involved in a fatal liaison with the Midianite woman (Sanh. 82a–b). In view of the enormous population loss suffered by the tribe of Simeon – from 59,300 in the first census (Num. 1:23) to 22,200 in the second (*ibid.* 26:14) – it was assumed that all 24,000 who had died in the plague following the sin at Baal-Peor (*ibid.* 25:9) were Simeonites (Gen. R. 99:7; Num. R. 21:8 *et al*). The relatively low esteem in which the tribe of Simeon was held is indicated by the humble role attributed to it in later Jewish history. Most or all poor people, beggars, and the notoriously poverty-stricken schoolteachers were supposed to be descended from Simeon (Gen. R. 98:5; 99:7; Yal. Gen. 158).

[Moses Aberbach]

BIBLIOGRAPHY: W.F. Albright, in: JPOS, 4 (1924), 149–61; Olmstead, Hist, 200; H.H. Rowley, *From Joseph to Joshua* (1950), 43–44; D. Allon, in: *Mi-Bifnim.* 17 (1953), 100–16 (Heb.); Alt, Kl Schr 2 (1953), 276–88; F.M. Cross and G.E. Wright, in: JBL, 75 (1956), 202–26; Y. Aharoni, in: IEJ, 8 (1958), 26–38; S. Talmon, *ibid.*, 15 (1965), 235ff.; Z. Kallai-Kleinman, in: VT, 8 (1958), 134–60. IN THE AGGADAH: Ginsberg, Legends, 1 (1942[2]), 395–404; 2 (19466), 11–16, 86–87, 142, 191–4; 5 (19476), 328–9, 348, 367; 6 (1946[3]), 137–8.

SIMEON BAR ISAAC (b. c. 950), one of the earliest German *paytanim*. Born in Mainz, where his grandfather *Abun had settled after leaving Le Mans in France, Simeon was a great scholar and the elder colleague of Rabbenu *Gershom b. Judah, "the Light of the Exile"; it is related that "they studied Torah together." His contemporaries and also later scholars claimed that Simeon was descended from the dynasty of King David and "experienced in miracles." In praise of him it was said "that he exerted himself for the communities and brought light to the exiles with his learning," and of his appearance that "he had the countenance of an angel of the Lord of Hosts." Because of his importance, he was called "Rabbana Simeon," and also "Ha-Gadol" ("the Great").

Simeon was an expert on prayers and *piyyutim*, and on customs in general. It is almost certain that he knew the *piyyutim* of *Yannai; he was undoubtedly influenced by those of Eleazar *Kallir, Solomon ha-Bavli, and *Moses b. Kalonymus, and it is probable that being a cantor he himself recited his *piyyutim*. He composed **yozerot*, **kerovot*, *seliḥot*, hymns, and *Rashuyyot le-Ḥatanim* (*piyyutim* sung in honor of bridegrooms before they went up to read the law on the Sabbath preceding their marriage and on that following it). His compositions bear clear traces of the language of the early *piyyutim*; they are suffused with pain at the persecutions and the tribulations which the Jews suffered during his lifetime. But his words are not specific, and there is no way of telling to which particular persecutions he is referring. Similarly, when he speaks in his *seliḥah "Elohim, Kamu Alai Zedim"* of those that reject the yoke of the Law, who "desecrate and despise the covenant of the patriarchs," for "the holy Sabbath has been willfully desecrated," it is impossible to know which sect he had in mind.

Simeon's *piyyutim* are to be found in *maḥzorim* of the French and German rites, and are recited to this day. Some of them mention the names Isaac and Elhanan; and it has been conjectured that these were his sons, and that their father wished to perpetuate their names in his poems. A legend relates that Elhanan was forcibly baptized, and rose to high office in the Church until he finally became pope. Upon the promulgation of a new anti-Jewish edict, Simeon was sent by the community to Rome in order to plead with the pope on behalf of his people. The pope, his son Elhanan, recognized Simeon; and then Simeon recognized his son. Elḥanan returned to Judaism, and his father perpetuated his name in a *kerovah* for Rosh Ha-Shanah. There would appear to be a grain of historical truth in the legend of a Jewish pope; and tradition has attached the story to the son of Simeon.

BIBLIOGRAPHY: Zunz, Lit Poesie, 111–5, 235–8; Germ Jud, 1 (1963), 189; Davidson, Oẓar, 4 (1933), 487; A.M. Habermann (ed.), *Piyyutei Rabbi Shimon bar Yizḥak* (1938); J. Prinz, *Popes from the Ghetto* (1966), 17–20.

[Abraham Meir Habermann]

SIMEON BAR YOḤAI (mid-second century C.E.), *tanna*. Simeon was one of the most important pupils of *Akiva. In the Mishnah, the Tosefta, and those *midrashei halakhah* belonging to the school of R. Akiva, he is almost universally called R. Simeon without any patronymic, whereas in the *midrashei halakhah* belonging to the school of R. Ishmael he is consistently called by his full name, R. Simeon ben Yoḥai. Because of his close association with the teachings of his master, tradition states that: "every anonymous statement in the *Sifrei* is by Simeon in accordance with the views of Akiva" (Sanh. 86a). Similarly, the Talmud reports the following statement: "Simeon said to his pupils: My sons, learn my rules, since my rules are refined from those refined by Akiva" (Git. 67a). The *aggadah* tells that Simeon and *Ḥanina b. Ḥakhinai studied under Akiva in Bene-Berak for 13 years (Lev. R. 21:8), and that when Akiva was imprisoned for teaching Torah in public, Simeon continued to study under him and attended on him (Pes. 112a). According to another tradition, Akiva once said to him, "It is sufficient for you that I and your Creator recognize your power" (TJ, Sanh. 1:3, 19a), and in this context it is stated that Simeon was also ordained by Akiva. Simeon was among the small group of Akiva's closest pupils who survived the failure of the Bar Kokhba revolt and "revived the Torah at that time" (Yev. 62b; cf. Gen. R. 61:3), establishing new centers of study in the Galilee. According to another tradition, Simeon was one of the five (or six) sages ordained later by *Judah b. Bava at the cost of the latter's life (Sanh. 14a). The historical authenticity of this tradition, however, has been seriously questioned, both because of the alternative tradition concerning the circumstances of Judah b. Bava's death (Tosef. BK 8:13), and also because of the alternative tradition concerning the ordination of Meir and Simeon by Akiva himself (cf. TY Sanh. 1:3, 19a; see Oppenheimer, 78–79).

In one tannaitic source, Simeon is quoted as saying, "Even the best of gentiles should be killed" (Mekh. *Be-Shallaḥ* 2), and it is reasonable to understand this statement against the background of the harsh decrees and religious persecutions of the Hadrianic era and the cruel martyrdom of Simeon's teachers. According to certain talmudic traditions preserved in Palestinian sources, Simeon spent an extended period of time in hiding, apparently in fear of the gentile authorities (Gen. R. 9:6, Eccles. R. 10:8, PRK 11:16, TY Shev. 9:1, 38d). In the Babylonian Talmud, these traditions are combined with other earlier aggadic sources to form an extended and continuous legend concerning the causes and circumstances of Simeon's flight from the Roman authorities, as well as the events surrounding his eventual triumphant emergence from the cave. According to this legend, "Simeon b. Yoḥai said (during a discussion with his companions): 'All that (the Romans) have accomplished is in their own interests. They have built market places to set harlots in them; baths to rejuvenate themselves; bridges to levy tolls.' Judah b. Gerim went and repeated this conversation, which reached the ears of the government. They decreed … 'Simeon, who uttered censure, is to be executed'" (Shab. 33b). To save their lives, Simeon and his son Eleazar were compelled to flee. They concealed themselves in a cave for 12 years and were preserved by miracle (*ibid.*). This solitary life and concentration on the study of Torah led to an uncompromising devotion to the study of Torah, almost to the exclusion of any other value or concern. This attitude is reflected in a number of other aggadic dicta associated with the name of R. Simeon. "Simeon b. Yoḥai says: 'Is that possible? If a man plows in the plowing season, and sows in the sowing season, and reaps in the reaping season… what is to become of the Torah? But, when Israel performs the will of God, their work is performed by others'" (Ber. 35b); "He who is walking by the way and reviewing what he has learnt, and breaks off and says, 'How fine is that tree, how fine is that field,' Scripture regards him as if he had endangered his soul" (Avot 3:7). Other dicta ascribed to R. Simeon include: "If Israel were to keep two Sabbaths according to the laws they would be immediately redeemed" (Shab. 118b); "It is better for a man to cast himself into a fiery furnace than put his fellow to shame in public" (Ber. 43b). Among four categories of people whom Simeon disliked was "one who enters his own house suddenly – much more so, his neighbor's house" (Lev. R. 21:8). He is also quoted as expressing an ardent love for the land of Israel, as "one of the three precious gifts given by God to the people of Israel" (Ber. 5a), and only it was found fit to be given to them (Lev. R. 13:2). The land of Israel is unique in the world, wanting for nothing (Sif. Deut. 37), and Simeon regarded departure from the land of Israel as a serious offense (Ex. R. 52:3). According to one tradition Simeon did not participate in the activities of the Sanhedrin in *Usha (of. Ber. 63b), but according to another tradition, however, Simeon did participate in Usha (Song R. 2:5). He also participated in the intercalation of the month in the valley of Rimmon (TJ, Ḥag. 3:1, 78c). In any case, he is portrayed as an active leader of the people, serving as an emissary of the Sanhedrin to Rome to plead for the abolition of the decrees against the observance of the commandments (Me'il. 17a–b).

He is mentioned as living in various places: in Sidon (Nid. 52b), in Bet Pagi (Tosef., Me'il. 1:5), and in Galilee (*ibid.*), but he established his yeshivah in the town of Tekoa, southeast of Jerusalem. The sages detected many typical principles in his methods, such as the establishing of general rules (Hor. 9a; Zev. 119b; et al.), the use of numbers (Kid. 16b; Ḥul. 127b), "definitions" (Tosef., Neg. 5:3), and interpreting the reason for the biblical law in order to establish thereby the *halakhah* (BM 115a). R. Simeon was chosen by the author of the *Zohar as the leading figure of this classic medieval kabbalistic work, and as a result this work was for centuries ascribed to the 2nd century *tanna*. For Simeon's death and place of burial, see *Meron, *Lag ba-Omer.

BIBLIOGRAPHY: Hyman, Toledot, 1178–89; I. Konowitz, *Rabbi Shimon b. Yoḥai* (1966); Frankel, Mishnah (1923), 177–82; Bacher, Tann; J.N. Epstein (ed.), *Mekhilta de-R. Shimon b. Yoḥai* (1955), 13–58; idem, Tannaim, 148–58; Z. Vilnay, *Maẓẓevot Kodesh be-Ereẓ Yisrael* (1963²), 324–43; E.E. Urbach, *Ḥazal, Pirkei Emunot ve-De'ot* (1969), index. **ADD. BIBLIOGRAPHY:** A. Oppenheimer, in: Z. Baras, S. Safrai, M. Stern. Y. Tsafrir (eds.), *Eretz Israel from the Destruction of the Second Temple to the Moslem Conquest* (Heb., 1982), 78–80.

[Israel Burgansky / Stephen G. Wald (2nd ed.)]

SIMEON BEN ABBA (third century), Babylonian-born *amora*. A pupil and kinsman of *Samuel, Simeon was a priest, the descendant of distinguished ancestors who were compared by *Johanan to the patriarch Abraham (TJ, Bik. 3:3, 65d). When Simeon went to Ereẓ Israel, he studied under the great *amoraim* of the first generation such as *Ḥanina and *Joshua b. Levi, and he transmitted their dicta. His main teacher however was Johanan, whom he served as a disciple serves his teacher, learning from him not only formally but practically through his behavior. Simeon transmits many of the customs of Johanan. He was a poor man, and Johanan applied to him the verse (Eccles. 9:11): "Neither is there bread to the wise." Nevertheless he would not accept gifts, and it is stated that Johanan would scatter coins when out walking so that Simeon could acquire them as finder (Ruth R. 5:7). Johanan was distressed that he was not able to ordain Simeon, who was consequently unable to receive the high office that was his due. Abbahu received the appointment but acknowledged that it should have gone to Simeon (TJ, Bik. 3:3, 65d). Since he could not establish himself in Ereẓ Israel he wished to leave and asked Ḥanina for a reference, but the latter refused, saying that in the world to come Simeon's ancestors would say, "We had one choice plant in Israel, yet you permitted it to depart from there" (TJ, MK 3:1).

Simeon also suffered in his family life. On the advice of Ḥanina he married his kinswoman, a daughter of Samuel who had been taken captive and taken to Ereẓ Israel by her captors. She did not live long; after her death he married her sister, who also died during his lifetime. Simeon bore his sufferings with courage and accepted them with equanimity. He expressed his submission to divine judgement in his homily (Gen. R. 9:11): "'Behold it was very good' (Gen. 1:31) refers to the attribute of retribution."

BIBLIOGRAPHY: Bacher, Pal Amor; Hyman, Toledot, 1152–55; Ḥ. Albeck, *Mavo la-Talmudim* (1969), 268.

[Israel Burgansky]

SIMEON BEN BOETHUS (surnamed **Cantheras**), high priest, appointed by Agrippa I in succession to Theophilus b. Anan. According to Josephus, Simeon's two brothers were also high priests, as was his father, Boethus, who because of his daughter Miriam (Mariamne) was nominated to the high priesthood by Herod (Jos., Ant. 19:297). This account, however, differs from another statement (*ibid.* 15:319–322) by Josephus to the effect that Herod married the daughter of Simeon b. Boethus, whom he appointed high priest and whose two brothers (according to another suggestion, his sons), Joezer and Eleazar, were also high priests. Of these two versions, the former is to be preferred, namely, that Boethus was appointed to the high priesthood by Herod, and his son Simeon by Agrippa I. Simeon Cantheras was not high priest for long, being deposed by Agrippa in favor of Matthias b. Anan (*ibid.* 19:313–6), who was likewise removed by Agrippa after a short while and replaced by Elyehoenai (Elionaeus) b. Cantheras (*ibid.* 19:342). A high priest of this name is mentioned in the Mishnah (Par. 3:5) as the son, not of Cantheras, but of Ha-Kayyaf (Caiaphas). Since the name Elyehoenai occurs nowhere else, it would appear that both the Mishnah and Josephus refer to the same high priest. Talmudic sources (Pes. 57a; Tosef., Men. 13:21) mention the house of Katros, and despite its similarity to Cantheras the two are not identical, since the Talmud explicitly distinguishes between the house of Boethus and that of Katros: Woe is me because of the house of Boethus, woe is me because of their staves ... Woe is me because of the house of Katros, woe is me because of their pens; according to Josephus, however, Cantheras and Boethus refer to the same family.

BIBLIOGRAPHY: Derenbourg, Hist, 215 n.2, 232f; Graetz, in: MGWJ, 30 (1881), 97ff.; Schuerer, Gesch, 2 (1907⁴), 271, esp. n. 14.

[Lea Roth]

SIMEON BEN ELEAZAR (second century), *tanna*; a contemporary of *Judah ha-Nasi. He was probably the son of *Eleazar of Bartota. Simeon dwelt in Tiberias and Johanan remembered him from his youth there (TJ, Ma'as. 1:2; cf. Gen. R. 9:5). Simeon was one of the pupils of *Meir and reported many *halakhot* in his name. He also served his teacher (Shab. 134a) and as a result learned many *halakhot* not known in the *bet ha-midrash* and ruled accordingly (TJ, MK 3:1). Accompanying Meir on his travels, he testified about his rulings under special conditions.

Only a few of his *halakhot* are found in the Mishnah, most of them being cited in the *beraitot*. Many of his *halakhot* are formulated as general statements; an excellent example is the formulation of the four domains to which the different laws of torts apply (BK 14a). He is frequently quoted in the *aggadah*. Among his most famous statements are the following: "Have you ever seen a beast or a bird with a craft? Yet they are sustained without trouble. But they were created only to serve me, while I was created to serve my Master. Surely then I should make a living without anxiety! But because I have acted evilly I have thus affected my livelihood" (Kid. 4:14, Tosef, Kid. 5:15–16, and see: Flusser). Also the following two dicta: "Impulse, a child, and a woman should be discouraged with the left hand and encouraged with the right" (Sot. 47a); "Pacify not thy fellow in the hour of his anger … nor strive to see him in the hour of his disgrace" (Avot 4:18). The following dictum reflects the generation after the Hadrianic persecution: "Every precept for which Israel submitted to death at the time of the royal decree, such as idolatry and circumcision, is still held firmly by them; while every precept for which Israel did not submit to death at the time of the royal decree, such as *tefillin*, is now somewhat neglected" (Shab. 130a). Because of an unfortunate incident in which he was involved, grossly insulting an ugly man, Simeon b. Eleazar coined the well-known aphorism: "A man should always be as gentle as the reed and not unyielding as the cedar." (Ta'an. 20a).

BIBLIOGRAPHY: Hyman, Toledot, s.v.; D. Flusser, *Judaism of the Second Temple Period – Sages and Literature* (Heb.; 2002), 326–36.

[Israel Burgansky]

SIMEON BEN GAMALIEL I (first century C.E.), *nasi* of the Sanhedrin in the generation of the destruction of the Temple. Josephus (Life, 191f.), of whom Simeon was a bitter opponent, praises Simeon as: "A man highly gifted with intelligence and judgment; he could by sheer genius retrieve an unfortunate situation in affairs of state." Simeon's words in *Avot* (1:17), "All my days I have grown up among the wise, and I have found nothing of better service than silence; not learning but doing is the chief thing; and he who is profuse of words causes sin," probably reflect the attitude he adopted during the stormy period of the conflict of opinions and sects, against the background of the dangers inherent in the revolt and the war. Some assert that Simeon was killed by the extremists who were opposed to his moderate leadership, but the view in the sources (Sem. 8; et al.) that he met a martyr's death at the hands of the Romans seems more probable, and he is thus traditionally included among the *Ten Martyrs. The Simeon b. Gamaliel mentioned without qualification in the Mishnah and in *beraitot* is usually Simeon b. Gamaliel II. However, the practical *halakhot* and **takkanot* connected with the Temple, such as the energetic action to keep down the price of birds for women to sacrifice after childbirth (Ker. 1:7), must apply to Simeon b. Gamaliel I. Especially striking is the description of him at the time of the Simḥat Bet ha-Sho'evah ("Festival of *Water-drawing"): "He used to juggle with eight burning torches and not one of them fell to the ground, and when he prostrated himself he placed his finger upon the pavement, bowed, kissed the ground, and immediately stood upright" (Suk. 53a). One halakhic ruling by him is quoted in *Eruvin* (6:2).

BIBLIOGRAPHY: Hyman, Toledot, s.v.

[Israel Burgansky]

SIMEON BEN GAMALIEL II (of Jabneh), *nasi* (first half of second century C.E.), the son of Rabban *Gamaliel of Jabneh and the father of *Judah ha-Nasi. Simeon was one of the few survivors after the Romans destroyed the house of the **nasi* in revenge for the Bar Kokhba revolt (Sot. 49b), and he was compelled to conceal himself during the whole period of the persecutions that followed the destruction of Bethar (Ta'an. 29a. on the assumption that the reference is to Simeon b. Gamaliel and not to his father). Even after the death of *Hadrian, Simeon could not appear in public, and for this reason apparently was absent from the meeting of the scholars that took place in order to renew the intercalation of the calendar in the valley of Rimmon, after the revolt (TJ, Ḥag. 3:1, 78c.). Similarly, he is not mentioned as having been present at the first session of the scholars in *Usha. When the persecution abated and the danger to his life passed, he was appointed *nasi* of the Sanhedrin at the second meeting of the sages in Usha, as the son of the *nasi* Gamaliel and a link in the chain of the *nesi'im* descended from Hillel. It is probable that the lengthy period when the Sanhedrin functioned without a *nasi* rendered Simeon's task a difficult one and he had to win his place with flexibility and understanding. According to the Babylonian Talmud (Hor. 13bf.), Simeon shared authority with the *av bet din*, Nathan the Babylonian, and with a third figure, the *ḥakham* (apparently the head of and the deciding factor in the yeshivah), Meir. It has, however, been argued that this threefold division of authority is an invention of the later aggadic tradition and was not in effect during the rule of Simeon, if ever (Goodblatt).

The fact that the scholars of Usha – Meir, Judah, Simeon b. Yoḥai and others – were recognized as the tradents of the heritage of the Oral Law as it began to crystallize in the period of Jabneh (see Sanh. 86a) made it difficult for Simeon to command the authority and status enjoyed by his father. As a result there was greater cooperation between Simeon b. Gamaliel and the members of the Sanhedrin than in the previous generation. He himself transmitted *halakhot* in the names of many members of the Sanhedrin and even accepted their rulings in practical *halakhah*: "Simeon b. Gamaliel said:

'It happened that my eyes were paining me in Caesarea, and Yose bei Rabbi permitted me and my servant to sleep outside the *sukkah*'" (Tosef., Suk. 2:2); and on another occasion, it is stated: "Simeon b. Gamaliel sent to the sages, and they said: 'That is a blemish'" (Bek. 6:9). In addition he was known for his humility and his son Judah described his virtue in superlative terms (BM 84f.).

According to the aggadic tradition of the Babylonian Talmud, Simeon b. Gamaliel took concrete steps to strengthen the status of the office of the *nasi* within the Sanhedrin and made specific decrees with this end in view: "When the *nasi* enters, all the people shall rise… when the *av bet din* enters, one row rises on one side and one row on the other… when the *ḥakham* enters, everyone rises (as he passes) and (then) sits down, until he has sat down in his place." According to this tradition Meir and Nathan took this decree as a personal affront, and decided to attempt to discredit Simeon b. Gamaliel and to remove him from office. Their plan was foiled and Simeon in turn attempted, unsuccessfully, to have them removed from the *bet ha-midrash*. Nevertheless, as a punishment for their opposition to the *nasi*, it was decreed that all subsequent statements made by Meir and Nathan should be introduced anonymously, the former being quoted merely as "others say," and the latter as "some say." (Hor. 13b–14a). While some scholars have held that this story accurately reflects the forms of communal leadership practiced during the late tannaitic period and have also accepted it as evidence of a power struggle between these well-known historical figures, Goodblatt has shown quite convincingly that this story is in fact a late Babylonian elaboration and embellishment of certain earlier Palestinian traditions (cf. TJ MK 3:1, 81c), and has little or no historical value.

Another tradition which relates to the need to strengthen the status of his office concerns the restoration of the dependence of Babylon upon Ereẓ Israel, particularly in regard to intercalating the month. Here too he encountered opposition from the Babylonian scholars (cf. TJ, Ned. 6:1; Ber. 63a). Readiness for, and predisposition toward cooperation with his colleagues, on the one hand, and a firm stand on the authority of the *nasi*, on the other, enabled Simeon to consolidate and further the status of the highest national institution.

There are some hundred *halakhot* in his name in the Mishnah and still more in the *beraitot* and the Tosefta. His authority is reflected in the well-known rule of R. Johanan: "Wherever Simeon b. Gamaliel taught in our Mishnah the *halakhah* follows him" (except in three cases, Ket. 77a). The Jerusalem Talmud (BB 10:14, 17d) gives the reason: "Because he gave fixed *halakhot* according to his *bet din*." Many aggadic statements are also ascribed to him on a variety of topics. Traces of the devastation and religious persecution of his time are easily discernible in them, such as: "Whoever eats and drinks on the Ninth of Av is as if eating and drinking on the Day of Atonement" (Ta'an. 30b); "Since the Temple was destroyed we ought not to eat meat or drink wine… he used to say, since they decree upon us not to study Torah, we ought to decree upon Israel not to marry… but do not interfere with Israel [by enacting such laws specifically] – better [if they transgress] that they act inadvertently rather than willfully" (Tosef., Sot. 15:10). In speaking of the value of remembering troubles and inscribing them in a book, in connection with the *Megillat Ta'anit, he said: "We too cherish the memory of troubles, but what are we to do, for they are so numerous that if we came to write them down we would not be able to do so." (Shab. 13b.). He gives a number of reminiscences of Jerusalem in previous ages and of the customs of its inhabitants (Ta'an. 4:8; BB 93b; Tosef., Ar. 1:13, and 2:6).

Some of his well known aggadic dicta are: "All my life I attended my father, yet I did not do for him a hundredth part of what Esau did for his father" (Gen. R. 65:16); "The ancients, because they could avail themselves of the Holy Spirit, ascribed their names to the event, but we… ascribe them to our ancestors" (*ibid.* 37:7); the reference is doubtless to the continuity of the dynasty of the *nasi*. He frequently preached in praise of peace: "By three things is the world preserved: by judgment, by truth, and by peace" (Avot 1:18); "Whoever makes peace in his own house is as if he makes peace in Israel" (ARN1 28, 85); "Great is peace, for even the ancestors of the tribes resorted to a fabrication in order to make peace" (Gen. R. 100:8). He also spoke in praise of God's manner of conducting the world: "How different are God's ways from man's! Man heals the bitter with the sweet, but the Holy One heals the bitter with bitter. How so? He puts something harmful [bitter wood] into something that has been harmed [the bitter waters] in order to perform a miracle" (Mekh., Va-Yassa 1). Especially does he give expression to his love for the people of Israel: "Come and see how beloved Israel is before the Omnipresent… in the past bread sprang up from the ground and dew came down from heaven… but now the reverse occurred, bread began to come down from heaven and dew to ascend from the ground" (Mekh., Va-Yassa 3).

BIBLIOGRAPHY: Hyman, Toledot, 1163–71; I. Konovitz, *Ma'arekhet Tanna'im* 4 (1969), 159–228; Frankel, Mishnah (1923), 188–95; Bacher, Tann; A. Buechler, *Studies in Jewish History* (1956), 160–78 (= REJ, 28 (1894), 60–74); Epstein, Tannaim, 163–8; Alon, Toledot, 2 (1961²), 69–78; Neusner, Babylonia, 1 (1965), 73–80 and index s.v. **ADD. BIBLIOGRAPHY:** A. Oppenheimer, in: Z. Baras, S. Safrai, M. Stern. Y. Tsafrir (eds.), *Eretz Israel from the Destruction of the Second Temple to the Moslem Conquest* (Heb., 1982); D. Goodblatt, in: *Zion*, 49 (1984), 349–74 (Heb.).

[Israel Burgansky / Stephen G. Wald (2nd ed.)]

SIMEON BEN ḤALAFTA (end of the second century C.E.), *tanna* in the transition period between the *tannaim* and the *amoraim*. Nothing is recorded concerning him in the Mishnah or the Tosefta, except for the one dictum: "The Holy One found no vessel that could contain Israel's blessing save that of peace" (Uk. 3:12), which was appended to the tractate *Ukẓin* and is thus the concluding statement of the whole Mishnah.

Simeon lived in Ein-Te'enah, between Sepphoris and Tiberias (TJ, Ta'an. 4:2). He studied under Meir, and his colleagues Ḥiyya and Simeon b. Rabbi (Judah ha-Nasi) were the outstanding scholars of the transition period. He frequented the home of Judah ha-Nasi (MK 9b), who also supported him financially in such a way as to cause him no embarrassment (Ruth R. 5:7). Most of his statements belong to the sphere of *aggadah* and he is in fact called "a *tanna* of the *aggadah*." Many remarkable stories are related about him (Eccles. R. 3:4), and about his sustenance which came in a miraculous manner, such as (Ruth. R. 3:4) when "a hand came down to him from heaven," or when he was attacked by hungry lions and two pieces of flesh came down from heaven, one of which satisfied its hunger, and the other was declared apparently suitable for his own consumption (Sanh. 59b). He supported himself by means of a field that he leased from Ḥiyya (Ruth R. 5:12). He apparently was accustomed to examine independently the veracity of traditional statements regarding flora and fauna. Thus he investigated the truth of the verse in Proverbs (6:6–7) on the wisdom of the ant in order to arrive at its meaning (Ḥul. 57b). Similarly concerning the laws of **terefah* in birds, he sought to prove that defects which according to other scholars rendered the bird *terefah* because their injuries were fatal could in fact be cured. He is also found exaggerating about unusual phenomena in the plant world: "I had a single pepper stalk in my property and climbed it as if climbing to the top of a fig tree" (TJ, Pe'ah 7:3). His inclination toward independent "empirical" investigation is also reflected in the story that he went out to listen to the vernacular employed by the common people in order to learn from it the meaning of difficult biblical words (Gen. R. 79:7). His wife bore their poverty with courage and even prevented him from using the gift he received miraculously from heaven (v. supra) in order not to diminish the reward preserved in the hereafter (Ruth R. 3:4).

[Israel Burgansky]

SIMEON BEN JEHOZADAK (first half of the third century), Palestinian *amora*. Simeon, who came of a family of priests, was the teacher of *Johanan, who transmitted *halakhah* and *aggadah* in his name (Yoma 22b, et al.). His name may also be mentioned in a *baraita* in *Sukkah* 11b (see Tos. *ibid.*; but see also the reading on 33a there). He died in Lydda and *Yannai and Johanan were among those who attended his funeral (TJ, Naz. 7:1, 56a). Among his aggadic dicta are "Any scholar who does not avenge himself and retains anger like a serpent is no scholar" (Yoma 22b) and "A man should not appoint an administrator over the community unless he has a basket of reptiles suspended on his back, so that if he becomes arrogant, he can say to him: Turn around!" (*ibid.*). The Talmud (Sanh. 26a) relates that he once went with Ḥiyya b. Zarnuki to intercalate the year at Asia (Ezion-Geber on the bank of the Red Sea – see Klein (ed.), *Sefer ha-Yishuv* (1939), s.v.). On their way they saw men working their fields in the sabbatical year. *Simeon b. Lakish, who accompanied them, criticized these men, but Simeon b. Jehozadak justified their action. It is possible, however, that the reference is to another *amora* of the same name.

BIBLIOGRAPHY: Hyman, Toledot, s.v.; Ḥ. Albeck, *Mavo la-Talmudim* (1969), 161.

[Yitzhak Dov Gilat]

SIMEON BEN JUDAH HA-NASI (first half of the third century C.E.), the younger son of *Judah ha-Nasi. The Talmud tells that Simeon transmitted traditions to such outstanding contemporary scholars as *Ḥiyya, *Levi, *Bar Kappara, although they apparently did not regard themselves as his pupils (Kid. 33a–b). Similarly, it tells that Judah I, on his deathbed, transmitted to Simeon "The orders of wisdom," when appointing him *ḥakham* of the yeshivah (Ket. 103b, but see TY Kil. 9:3, 32a, Ket. 12:3, 34d, Gen. R. 101 (100)). The view widely held is that Simeon served in the office of **ḥakham* during the whole period that his brother Gamaliel was *nasi*, as well as in the time of *Judah II (Nesiah I). Speaking of the great reward of those performing precepts, he said "If a person is rewarded for refraining from partaking of blood (Deut. 12:33), which is repugnant to man, how much more so will he and his future generations be deemed meritorious for refraining from robbery and incest to which men are attracted!" (Mak. 3:15).

BIBLIOGRAPHY: Epstein, Mishnah, 18–30; idem, Tanna'im, 227–9.

[Israel Burgansky]

SIMEON BEN LAKISH (third century C.E.), Palestinian *amora*. Simeon b. Lakish or Resh Lakish, as he is more concisely and commonly referred to in the Babylonian Talmud, was active in the communal and religious spheres mainly in Tiberias, where he may have been born as may be inferred from a conversation with a guard of the *bet ha-midrash* (Eccles. R. 3:9). Nothing is known of his origins except that his father's name was Lakish. He apparently studied under several sages (TJ, Kil. 9:4, 32b, end) among whom were Bar Kappara and Oshaiah of southern Ereẓ Israel, but it is not known who was his principal teacher. In his youth he sold himself to men who hired participants in gladiatorial contests – a common practice in Ereẓ Israel at the time (see TJ, Git. 4:9, 46a–b) – presumably because he had no other means of earning a livelihood; he made reference in his old age to this period of his life (TJ, Ter. 8:5, 45d). For a time he also worked as a plantation guard (TJ, MK 3:1, 81d). According to the *aggadah*, R. Johanan prevailed on him to study the Torah and gave him his sister in marriage (BM 84a). They had a son who was a scholar (Ta'an. 9a). Resh Lakish devoted himself with great diligence to the study of the Torah, systematically repeating his studies 40 times before having a lesson with Johanan (Ta'an 8a), and in time became one of the most esteemed sages in the Tiberias academy headed by Johanan. His halakhic argumentation was grounded both on keen logical deduction and on a knowledge of the traditions (Sanh. 24a; TJ, Git. 3:1, 44d), and when he died Johanan himself stated that a void had been created (BM 84a).

Resh Lakish showed partiality to no one in whatever concerned a halakhic decision and the actions of a *bet din*. He often argued against and disagreed with the views of Johanan, who on such occasions would say, "What can I do when one of equal authority differs from me?" (Ket. 54b, 84b). Neither did he defer to his contemporary Judah ha-Nasi II in any halakhic matter (TJ, Sanh. 2:1, 19d) and even reminded him of his duty to provide schools for children (Shab. 119b). Resh Lakish's interpreter, Judah b. Nahamani, on one occasion also condemned Judah ha-Nasi II's household for having appointed incompetent judges (Sanh. 7b). Whenever he saw or met Babylonian Jews in Ereẓ Israel, Resh Lakish criticized them in the harshest and most biting terms for not having returned to the country (in the days of Ezra and Nehemiah) and thus having been a contributory cause to the destruction of Ereẓ Israel (Yoma 9b). In this he expressed the general feeling current among people in Ereẓ Israel (Kid. 39b; TJ, Ber. 2:5c; et al.). Resh Lakish would assemble the sages of the academy and review with them Johanan's discourses so as to explain to them what they had been unable to grasp by themselves (BK 117a, and see Rashi ad loc., s.v. *mesayyem*). He was highly esteemed by the pupils of the academy and also by the people for his personal integrity, which was so great that it was said that if he was seen talking in public with anyone, that person would be lent money without any witnesses (Yoma 9b). He was always ready to help others even if it involved danger, risking his life to save Rav Assi (TJ, Ter. 8:10, 46b).

In his addresses, both to the academy pupils and to the wider public, he emphasized the importance of the *mitzvah* of studying the Torah, the great reward of its students and of supporting the poor ones among them. He admonished students to be diligent in their studies, for otherwise "if you forsake me [the Torah] for one day, I shall forsake you for two days" (TJ, Ber. 9:8, 14d; and in a clearer version in *Midrash Shir ha-Shirim*, ed. by E. Gruenhut (1897), 5:12, 40a–b). To him the study of the Torah was a divine task which was not to be neglected. Hence he held that a disciple of the sages was forbidden to afflict himself by fasting (Ta'an. 11b). He also said that "the words of the Torah abide only with one who kills himself for them" (Git. 57b); that one was not to accept services from a scholar (Meg. 28b); and that the sages were to be exempted from paying taxes for the city wall (BB 7b). He did indeed hold that "sometimes the neglect of [the study of] the Torah is its fulfillment" (Men. 99a–b, and see Rashi ad loc., s.v. *she-bittulah*), when such neglect is in order to observe certain *mitzvot*. He enjoined scholars to be amiable and to respect one another in their halakhic discussions (Shab. 63a); he deprecated undesirable traits: "If a sage becomes angry, his wisdom departs from him; if a prophet, his prophecy departs from him" (Pes. 66b), and "whoever scoffs will fall into Gehenna" (Av. Zar. 18b); and he warned against the evil inclination in one's heart: "Every day a man's evil inclination threatens to master him, and seeks to kill him" (Suk. 52b), "a man should always incite his good inclination against his evil inclination" (Ber. 5a), and "a person does not commit a transgression unless a spirit of folly enters into him" (Sot. 3a).

His love for the Jewish people was as great as his love for the Torah. Once when he and Abbahu went to Caesarea, which was inhabited by large numbers of non-Jews and hellenized Jews, and Abbahu denounced its inhabitants, Resh Lakish stopped him by saying, "God does not want evil spoken of Israel" (Eccles. R. 1:6). The difficult political and economic situation of the Jewish population in Ereẓ Israel in the third century C.E., a period of appalling military anarchy, forms the background of many of Resh Lakish's homilies in which he spoke of God's love for His people even when their fortunes had "declined to the lowest ebb" (TJ, Ber. 9:1, 13b; PR 140b). These conditions are also reflected in Resh Lakish's appraisal of the Roman government and its actions (Sot. 41b; Gen. R. 9:13; Lev. R. 13:5). Later generations referred to Resh Lakish and Johanan as the "two renowned authorities" (TJ, Ber. 8:7, 12c). According to the *aggadah*, Resh Lakish died from grief after Johanan, in a halakhic discussion between them, referred to the former's past as a gladiator by saying "A robber knows his trade." Deeply regretting this slip of his tongue, Johanan was so stricken with remorse that he died from mental anguish (BM 84a).

BIBLIOGRAPHY: Bacher, Pal Amor; Hyman, Toledot, 1193–1202; Frankel, Mevo, 129b; Ḥ. Albeck, *Mavo la-Talmudim* (1969), 190f.

[Moshe Beer]

SIMEON BEN MEGAS HA-KOHEN (sixth century?), Palestinian *paytan*. Though the precise period of Simeon's literary activity cannot be ascertained, certain structural elements in his *piyyutim* indicate that he preceded Eleazar b. *Kallir, but not *Yannai. Fragments of his work, which was evidently copious, are known only from *Genizah* finds. All the extant *piyyutim* belong to the category of *kerovot*. He probably composed a cycle of *kedushta'ot* (liturgical poems) for all the weekly portions of the Torah, in accordance with the triennial reading customs (see *Triennial Cycle) of Palestinian Jewry. Fragments of 30 such *kedushta'ot* are preserved in the manuscripts of the *Genizah*; several of his *kedushta'ot* for festivals have also survived. While the style and manner of his *piyyutim* are generally close to those of Yannai, Simeon's *kedushta'ot* excel in a number of unique structural details.

BIBLIOGRAPHY: Zulay, in: YMḤSI, 2 (1936), 221–31; J. Schirmann, *Shirim Ḥadashim min ha-Genizah* (1966), 3–8.

[Ezra Fleischer]

SIMEON BEN MENASYA (second–third century C.E.), *tanna*; a contemporary of *Judah ha-Nasi. Simeon's statements both in *halakhah* and *aggadah* are found mainly in *beraitot*. At times he disagrees with the Mishnah and at times supplements it. Only one of his statements is mentioned in the Mishnah (Ḥag. 1:7): "Who is it 'that is crooked and cannot be made straight' [Eccles. 1:15]? He that has incestuous relations with a woman and begets by her a **mamzer*," but the whole passage is taken from the Tosefta. He is also mentioned once in the sixth chapter of *Avot* (6:8) which is, however, a later addition to the Mishnah. He was a pupil of *Meir in whose name he transmits several *halakhot*. In a dispute with Judah ha-Nasi he fixed the *halakhah* according to the stricter view in a dispute of *tannaim* of an earlier generation (Beẓah 26a). It is possible that there is here a hint of his method of deciding the *halakhah*. He himself said of Judah: "These seven qualifications which the sages enumerated as becoming to the righteous, were all realized in Judah ha-Nasi and in his sons" (Avot 6:8). Judah used to quote him in matters of piety and abstinence (Eccles. R. 9:9). He and his colleague *Yose b. Meshullam were called "holy brotherhood" (TJ, Ma'as. Sh. 2:4; in TB, Beẓah 14b "holy community of Jerusalem" – see *Holy Congregation in Jerusalem). It seems that they were the heads of a movement which followed Pharisaic practices of a special stringency. The essence of their attempt to "combine Torah with a wordly occupation" (cf. Ber. 35b) is reflected in the following Midrash:

> Judah ha-Nasi said in the name of the holy brotherhood: 'Acquire a craft for yourself together with Torah…' and why does he call them 'holy brotherhood'? Because it included Yose b. Meshullam and Simeon b. Menasya who used to divide the day into three parts – a third for Torah, a third for prayer, and a third for work. Others say that they labored in the Torah throughout the winter and in their work throughout the summer (Eccles. R. 9:9, no. 1).

More widely known is his homily that also testifies to a similar outlook on life, regarding the law that the saving of life overrides the Sabbath: "'And the children of Israel shall keep the Sabbath' [Ex. 31:16] – the Torah said, profane for his sake one Sabbath, so that he may keep many Sabbaths" (Yoma 85b). He also laid great emphasis upon the education of children in the study of Torah: "Even God is filled with love for him who has a son toiling in Torah…" (Gen. R. 63:1).

BIBLIOGRAPHY: Epstein, Tanna'im, 182–3; S. Safrai, in: *Zion*, 22 (1957), 183–93.

[Israel Moses Ta-Shma]

SIMEON BEN NANAS (first half of the second century C.E.), *tanna*; contemporary and colleague of R. *Akiva, Simeon is usually referred to simply as "Ben Nanas." According to Maimonides (Yad., Zera'im, introd.) he was one of the five scholars referred to in the expression, "Those who argue before the Sages" (Sanh. 17b) whom the Talmud calls Simeon, Simeon, Simeon, Hanan, and Hananiah, but Rashi is not of the same opinion (cf. TJ, Ma'as. Shen. 2:9, 53d, and see: Friedman, *Netiot Le-David*, 250). The fact that Simeon is called simply "Ben Nanas" might indicate that the *halakhot* transmitted in his name were taught before he was ordained (cf. Ta'an. 3a), or that he was never ordained. His statements are found only in the *halakhah* and he frequently disputes in the Mishnah with Akiva. He specialized in civil law and was praised for this by Ishmael who said: "He who would become wise should engage in the study of civil law … and he who would engage in the study of civil law let him wait upon Simeon b. Nanas" (BB 10:8).

BIBLIOGRAPHY: Hyman, Toledot, s.v.; S. Friedman, in: *Netiot LeDavid, Festschrift in Honor of David Weiss Halivni* (2004).

[Israel Burgansky]

SIMEON BEN NETHANEL (second half of the first century C.E.), *tanna*. One of the five outstanding disciples of Johanan b. *Zakkai who called him "sin-fearing" (Avot 2:8), Simeon was a priest and married the daughter of *Gamaliel I (the Elder; Tosef., Av. Zar. 3:19). Very few of his sayings have been preserved. His saying in *Avot* (2:13) is: "Be careful in reading the *Shema* and the *Amidah*; and when thou prayest, regard not thy prayer as a fixed mechanical task, but as an appeal for mercy and grace before the All-present…; and be not wicked in thine own esteem." His reply to the question of his master as to "the good way to which a man should cleave" was "foreseeing the consequences" of all acts. "The evil way which man should shun" is "borrowing and not repaying, whether from man or from God," i.e., ingratitude (Avot 2:9). He plays a role in the later development of the mystic traditions surrounding the vision of the *merkavah* (TJ, Ḥag. 2:1; cf. TB 14b), but his role in these stories in all likelihood has no historical foundation (Wald).

BIBLIOGRAPHY: Hyman, Toledot, s.v. **ADD. BIBLIOGRAPHY:** S. Wald, "The *Derashah Ba-merkavah* of R. Eleazar ben Arakh" (Hebrew), in: JSIJ.

[Israel Burgansky / Stephen G. Wald (2nd ed.)]

SIMEON BEN PAZZI (second half of the third century C.E.), Palestinian *amora*. According to the *tosafot* (BB 149a) Pazzi was his mother's name, but according to Frankel (Mevo 121a) it was that of his father (Dik. Sof., Meg. 13a). Although Simeon was considered a halakhic authority, very few of his decisions are mentioned in the Talmud. He instructed those who fixed the calendar to draw it up so that neither Rosh Ha-Shanah nor the seventh day of Tabernacles (*Hoshana Rabba) should fall on the Sabbath, but when it became necessary for one of them to fall on the Sabbath the latter should be chosen. Simeon was essentially an aggadist. He handed down a large number of biblical interpretations by his teacher Joshua b. Levi, of whose *aggadot* he is the principal transmitter. His own *aggadot* contain exegetic and homiletic interpretations and comments, including parables, sentences, and maxims on God, the world, prayer, and the study of the Torah. He interprets the double *yod* in וייצר in Genesis 2:7 as emphasizing the inner struggle within man between the sensual (*yeẓir*) and the divine (*yoẓer*), and comments: "Woe to me because of my impulses; woe to me because of my Creator" (Ber. 61a). "When the patriarch Jacob was about to reveal the messianic time to his children (Gen. 49:1) the presence of God departed from him, whereupon he said 'Has an unworthy child sprung from me as Ishmael sprang from my grandfather Abraham and Esau from my father Jacob?' In answer his sons exclaimed '"Hear O Israel, the Lord our God the Lord is one" (Deut. 6:4) as only one God is in your heart so only one is in ours.' Jacob then said 'Praised be the name of the glory of His kingdom for ever and ever'" (Pes. 56a). In other texts this passage is ascribed to Resh Lakish. His statement in *Sotah* 41b that one may be obsequious to evil people in this world is a reflection of social conditions in his time.

BIBLIOGRAPHY: Bacher, Pal Amor; Frankel, Mevo, 118a; Hyman, Toledot, s.v.; Ḥ. Albeck, *Mavo la-Talmudim* (1969), 258–61.

[Elliott Hillel Medlov]

SIMEON BEN SAMUEL OF JOINVILLE (12th–13th century), French scholar. Simeon's father was a contemporary of Jacob *Tam, who on one occasion relied upon him for a halakhic ruling. Simeon was a pupil of *Isaac b. Samuel of Dampierre, with whom he was on particularly intimate terms. He is very frequently mentioned in the standard *tosafot* and his commentary on various tractates of the Talmud is cited in the works of *rishonim*. A few of his responsa have survived.

BIBLIOGRAPHY: Gross, Gal Jud, 255; Urbach, Tosafot, 280–1, 504, 522.

[Israel Moses Ta-Shma]

SIMEON BEN SHETAḤ (first century B.C.E.), one of the most prominent of the scholars of the Second Temple period. He was active during the reign of Alexander *Yannai and Queen *Salome Alexandra (Sifra, Beḥukotai, ch. 1), who according to certain late aggadic traditions was Simeon's sister (Ber. 48a, cf. Gen R. 91, Eccles. R. 7). In the train of tradition he, together with Judah b. Tabbai, constitute one of the **zugot*, succeeding *Joshua b. Peraḥyah and Nittai of Arbela (Avot 1:8; see Ḥag. 1:2). According to a tradition of R. Meir, Simeon was *av bet din* but the view of R. Judah (or the anonymous sages) is that he was *nasi* (Tosef., Ḥag. 2:8). According to one tradition (Tosef. Sanh. 6:6) Simeon b. Shetaḥ once criticized a halakhic decision of Judah b. Tabbai, who thereafter accepted upon himself "never to make a halakhic ruling without Simeon b. Shetaḥ's consent." The attempt in the Babylonian Talmud (Ḥag. 16b) to use this tradition to determine which of them was *nasi* and which *av bet din* was inconclusive. Moreover, in the parallel version of this story (Mekh. Nezikin, 20), the roles of Judah b. Tabbai, and Simeon b. Shetaḥ are reversed, and S. Friedman and others have shown that the version in the *Mekhilta* is the more original.

Tannaitic sources mention Simeon in a number of different contexts. In the *Sifra* (Beḥukotai, ch. 1, cf. TB Ta'an. 23a) "the days of Simeon ben Shetaḥ and Shlomẓu the Queen" are remembered as a time of extraordinary blessedness, when the rains were so plentiful that the "wheat was a large as kidneys, the barley as large as olives, and the lentils as large as gold *dinari*." The wheat of these legendary days was referred to in later times simply as "the wheat of Simeon ben Shetaḥ" (Ḥul. 119b). Similarly, Simeon ben Shetaḥ plays a role in the tannaitic aggadah concerning the wonder-working rainmaker, *Ḥoni ha-Me'aggel (Ta'an. 3:8, TB Ta'an. 23a). In this context Simeon threatens Ḥoni with excommunication, and in one place (Ber. 19a) the Bavli ascribes to Simeon a similar threat with regard to Todos of Rome, though it is clear from the parallel sources (Tosef. Beẓ. 2:15, TY Pes. 7:1, 34a, Beẓ. 2:7, 61c, MK 3:1 81d, TB Pes. 53a, Beẓ. 23a) that the association of Simeon ben Shetaḥ with the case of Todos is a late literary embellishment of an early tannaitic tradition. Both the Mishnah (Sanh. 6:4) and a tannaitic midrash (Sifre Deut. 221) mention a tradition according to which Simeon ben Shetaḥ "hanged 80 women in Ascalon on a single day," "because of the pressing need to make an example of them to others" (Sifre). No further information is reported in the tannaitic sources regarding this remarkable event, but the later aggadic tradition has woven around this tradition a number of fascinating legends concerning Simeon ben Shetaḥ and "the witches of Ascalon," involving spells and counter-spells, intrigues and counter-intrigues, false witnesses and revenge (TY Ḥag. 2:2, 77d–78a, TY Sanh. 6:6, 23c, Midrash Ten Commandments, end; cf. TY Sanh. 6:3 23b). Though not brought in the Babylonian Talmud itself, Rashi quotes this legend at length in his commentary to Sanh. 44b (cf. Rashi to Sanh. 45b). According to a Palestinian amoraic aggadic tradition (TY Ber. 7:2. 11b, Naz. 5:3, 54b, Gen. R. 91, Ecc. R. 7), Simeon ben Shetaḥ once came into conflict with King Alexander Yannai regarding a certain financial obligation which Simeon accepted upon himself, and which Yannai was led to believe that Simeon had failed to live up to. Simeon, fearing the king's anger, went into hiding, until a number of foreign dignitaries who were visiting Yannai requested Simeon's presence at court, in order to hear from him the words of wisdom for which he was famous. Simeon was then asked to lead the blessing over the meal, despite the fact that he had not himself partaken of the bread. In the version of this tradition found in the Babylonian Talmud (Ber. 48a–b), this minor incident is portrayed as all-out warfare between King Yannai and the Pharisees, of whom Simeon ben Shetaḥ was the leader. According to this tradition, Simeon ben Shetaḥ was summoned to court because Yannai "had killed all the sages, and there was no one left who knew how to perform the blessing after the meal." In a number of other places in the Babylonian Talmud, Simeon ben Shetaḥ is portrayed as playing a role in an ongoing, and frequently violent, conflict between the king and the sages (Sot. 47a, cf. TY Ḥag. 2:2, 77d, and Sanh. 6:6, 23c; Kid. 66a, cf. Meg. Ta'an., concerning the 28th of Tevet; Sanh. 19a–b), though there is little or no evidence for such a conflict in the earlier Palestinian talmudic tradition.

Tradition ascribes to Simeon b. Shetaḥ a number of *takkanot* in the spheres of domestic life and education. According to a tannaitic tradition, he introduced the stipulation that all the husband's property is pledged for the payment of the *ketubbah* (Tosef., Ket. 12:1 and parallels). He is credited with having pioneered education for the young by introducing school attendance for children (TJ, Ket. 8:11, 32c), hitherto the education of children being regarded as the responsibility of the parents alone. According to another tradition, Simeon established schools in Jerusalem and in the district towns and obliged parents to send their children to them (cf. BB 21a). He is also credited with a decree concerning the ritual impurity of metal vessels (TJ, Shab. 1:4, 3d, TB Shab. 14b).

BIBLIOGRAPHY: H. Mantel, *Studies in the History of the Sanhedrin* (1962), index; S. Zeitlin, *Rise and Fall of the Judaean State* (1962), index; L. Finkelstein, *The Pharisees* (1962), index; Weiss, Dor, 1 (1904⁴), 127 ff.; Hyman, Toledot, 1212–16. **ADD. BIBLIOGRAPHY:** S.

Friedman, "If They Have Not Slain They Are Slain; but If They Have Slain They Are Not Slain," in: *Sidra*, 20 (2005).

[Yitzhak Dov Gilat / Stephen G. Wald (2nd ed.)]

SIMEON HA-PAKULI (late first and early second century C.E.), one of the scholars of Jabneh in the time of *Gamaliel II. He is mentioned only once in the sources: "Simeon ha-Pakuli arranged the 18 benedictions in order before Rabban Gamaliel [II] in Jabneh" (Ber. 28b). It is assumed that this activity included a number of elements: the determination of the number of blessings, their subject matter, and their order (see **Amidah*). According to Rashi his name refers to his occupation as a seller of cotton tufts (*pakuli*).

BIBLIOGRAPHY: Hyman, Toledot, s.v.

[Israel Burgansky]

SIMEON THE HASMONEAN (called **Thassis**; d. 134 B.C.E.), the second son of *Mattathias. The origin of the name Thassis is obscure, and many conjectures have been put forward. Some think it is to be connected with the Hebrew *toses* (תּוֹסֵס, "vigorous") or *tashush* (תָּשׁוּשׁ, "weakling"), while others regard it as a variant of the Hebrew name Assi or the Syrian Tarsi.

On his deathbed, Mattathias recommended Simeon as counselor for Judah, who was military commander against the Syrians. Under Judah he played an independent role as commander of the expedition that went to the aid of the Jews of Galilee. According to II Maccabees (14:17) he attacked *Nicanor and was defeated by him. When Judah died, Simeon and his brother Jonathan buried him in the family sepulcher in *Modi'in. Simeon was Jonathan's right-hand man in the wars with the hellenizers and the Syrians. He distinguished himself, among other things, by relieving the city of Bathbasi which had been besieged by *Bacchides. He also took part with Jonathan in the war against Apollonius. At the time of Tryphon's rule in Syria, with Jonathan's rule at its zenith (145–143 B.C.E.), Simeon was appointed military governor of the whole coastal region of Israel from the Ladder of Tyre to the Egyptian border. During Jonathan's campaigns in Galilee, Simeon remained in authority in Judea, during which time he conquered Beth-Zur and fortified Adittha. On Jonathan's treacherous capture by Tryphon in 143 B.C.E., the leadership passed inevitably to Simeon, now the sole survivor of the Hasmonean brothers. He fortified Jerusalem, strengthened his hold on Jaffa, and prepared to face Tryphon, all the time endeavoring, but in vain, to ransom his brother from him. Tryphon's efforts to penetrate Judea were repelled by Simeon and he was forced to withdraw, but put Jonathan to death. Simeon buried Jonathan at Modi'in, where he erected a splendid monument in his memory. In the dispute over the throne in Syria Simeon supported *Demetrius II, who recognized his rule and waived his claim to tribute. The year 142 B.C.E. was regarded as the beginning of Judean independence and the years of Simeon's rule were reckoned from that date. Simeon also conquered Gazara (Gezer) and Judaized it, driving out the Syrian garrison from the citadel.

For a while after this Judea enjoyed a period of peace. The ties with Sparta and Rome were renewed. In the year 140, Simeon's position was confirmed by the nation. He and his children after him were appointed by a public assembly to the position of high priest, ethnarch, and commander of the army, thus establishing the Hasmonean dynasty. A copy of the resolution was engraved upon tablets which were set up in the Temple court. During the latter half of Simeon's rule the danger to Judean independence was renewed. Antiochus VII Sidetes became ruler of Syria, and endeavored to revive the shattered Seleucid Empire. Syrian relations with Simeon deteriorated and Cendebaeus was sent against Judea, but Simeon's sons defeated him. Soon after, during a tour of the country, Simeon was murdered in Jericho by his son-in-law *Ptolemy b. Abubus, who may have conspired with the Syrians. Simeon was succeeded by his son John *Hyrcanus.

BIBLIOGRAPHY: Schuerer, Hist, index s.v. *Simeon the Maccabee*; Meyer, Ursp, 2 (1921), 260–7; Klausner, Bayit Sheni, index s.v. *Shimon b. Matityahu*.

[Uriel Rappaport]

SIMEON HA-TIMNI (second century C.E.), *tanna*, a member of the Sanhedrin in the era of *Jabneh. His name derives from the town of Timnat near Beth-Shemesh (Judg. 15:6; cf. Rashi to Beẓah 21a) and has no connection with Yemen (Heb. *Teiman*). According to R. Naḥman b. Isaac the sages referred to in the anonymous formula: "It was discussed before the sages," are five well-known *tannaim*, of whom Simeon ha-Timni is one (Sanh. 17b). These rabbis apparently enjoyed the intermediate status of scholars of the *bet ha-midrash* who had graduated from that of "pupils" but had not yet been ordained. In point of fact none of these five scholars had the title "rabbi." Two of them are generally mentioned by their patronymics – Ben Azzai and Ben Zoma – and the phrase "Those who discussed before the sages" is sometimes used instead of the authors of the statement (Eduy. 1:10). To Simeon ha-Timni was applied a special attribute – the knowledge of "70 languages" – denoting exceptional members of the Sanhedrin, although its exact nature is not clear (Sanh. 17b). He is mentioned in the Mishnah and Tosefta as disputing with the greatest scholars of the generation, Akiva and Joshua, and especially noteworthy is his stand in the great dispute which agitated the scholars of that generation, on the halakhic definition of the **mamzer*. Simeon's ruling was already accepted as the *halakhah* in practice close to his time (Yev. 4:13).

Also preserved are some of his aggadic statements that were also made in the course of a discussion with several of his colleagues on the meaning of the words of his teacher, Akiva (Tosef., Ber. 4:16). Another dictum by him, preserved in the *aggadah*, is also connected with a question to which many answers were propounded by the *tannaim*: by what merit was the Red Sea parted for the children of Israel? Simeon's view was: "By the merit of circumcision" (Mekh. Be-Shallaḥ 4). References to his beneficent activities on behalf of the community have also been preserved (Tosef., Beẓah (Yom Tov) 2:6). Another dictum which some of the sources attribute to Simeon ha-Timni (Sif. Num. 103) may perhaps indicate his connection with mystic lore; he supports the view of Akiva, and even adds that the angels and "holy *ḥayyot*" do not see the Divine Presence.

BIBLIOGRAPHY: Hyman, Toledot, 1225f.; Bacher, Tann.

[Israel Burgansky]

SIMEON THE JUST, high priest in the time of Alexander the Great who was surnamed the Just both because of his piety toward God and his benevolence to his countrymen (see also Jos., Ant. 12:157). According to Josephus (Ant. 12:43), he is identical with *Simeon I, the son of Onias I and the grandson of Jaddua. Simeon the Just is also referred to in rabbinical literature. In *Avot* (1:2) he is mentioned as one of the survivors of the Great Assembly, and he is the author of the saying, "Upon three things the world is based: upon the Torah, upon divine service, and upon the practice of *gemilut ḥasadim* [charity]." In the same source he is indicated as the first in a chain of scholars descending to Hillel and Shammai. According to the Talmuds (TJ, Yoma 6:3, 43c–d; Men. 109b), he was the father of the *Onias who built a temple in Egypt. If this is so, then Josephus erred in identifying Simeon the Just with Simeon I and he is to be identified with Simeon II, the father of Onias III, who lived about 200 B.C.E. The chronology in *Avot* also supports the latter view. To the praise of Simeon the high priest given by Josephus and the rabbis (TJ, loc. cit.; Yoma 39a–b) may be added the words of Ben Sira referring to Simeon II (50:1–6): "Great among his brethren and the glory of his people was Simeon, the son of Johanan the high priest, in whose time the House was renovated, and in whose days the Temple was fortified. How glorious was he when he came out from the sanctuary! Like a morning star from between the clouds and like the fall moon on the feast days." Ben Sira praises his communal activities after the conquest of Judea by Antiochus III and his repair of the Temple (cf. Jos., Ant. 12:141). The great importance and honor given by Ben Sira to Simeon II also supports the view that it was he who was Simeon the Just, and that Josephus erred. Simeon the Just is also mentioned as the high priest who went forth to welcome Alexander (Yoma 69a; Meg. Ta an. 9), but chronologically it can apply to neither of the Simeons. In general the historical value of this story is very doubtful. However the suggestion that the origin of the story is to be found in a meeting that took place between Simeon (II) the Just and Antiochus III, who was his contemporary and ally, may be correct. Some scholars prefer the testimony of Josephus. Azariah dei Rossi (*Me'or Einayim*, Imrei Binah, ch. 22) makes the suggestion that perhaps Simeon the Hasmonean is meant.

BIBLIOGRAPHY: R. Marcus (ed.), *Josephus* (Loeb Classical Library), 7 (1943), 732–6 (incl. bibl.); Moore, in: *Jewish Studies… I. Abrahams* (1927), 348–64; Ḥ. Albeck, *Mavo la-Mishnah* (1959), 24f.

[Uriel Rappaport]

SIMEON OF MIZPAH (mid-first century C.E.), *tanna* at the close of the Second Temple era. As his name suggests he came from the town of Mizpah in Judah. It is related of him: "It once happened that R. Simeon of Mizpah sowed his field before Rabban Gamaliel, and they went up to the Chamber of Hewn Stone and put a question. Nahum the Scrivener said: 'I have a tradition from R. Measha who received it from his father, who had it from the *zugot, who had it from the prophets as a *halakhah* given to Moses at Sinai …'" (Pe'ah 2:6). The Gamaliel referred to is Rabban Gamaliel the Elder, and at that time Simeon must have been still a young man. The incident vividly portrays the custom of clarifying *halakhah* in the Chamber of Hewn Stone when the local scholars were unable to decide. R. Johanan states that Simeon was the *tanna* who taught the Mishnah *Tamid (TJ, Yoma 2:2). According to another opinion in the Babylonian Talmud (Yoma 14b), the intention of the tradition is to attribute to Simeon those *mishnayot* dealing with the daily sacrifice in the Mishnah *Yoma* which parallel those in *Tamid*. The tractate *Tamid* is written in a descriptive, lively, and flowing style, which has led some scholars to conjecture that Simeon presented an eyewitness account of the order of the Temple service.

BIBLIOGRAPHY: Epstein, Tanna'im, 27–31; Hyman,Toledot, s.v.

[Israel Burgansky]

SIMEON SON OF ONIAS I (first half of the third century B.C.E.), high priest. He was the grandson of *Jaddua, high priest in the time of Alexander the Great. According to the genealogical list given by Josephus, Simeon's son, *Onias II, was a minor when his father died, and in consequence Eleazar, the brother of Simeon, and Manasseh, his uncle, filled the office after Simeon. Only subsequently did Onias II become high priest. Josephus relates in two places that Simeon was called the Just because of his fear of heaven and love of his fellow-Jews (Ant. 12:43, 157). On the trustworthiness of this description see *Simeon the Just.

BIBLIOGRAPHY: Schuerer, Gesch, 2 (1907[4]), 419f.; 3 (1909[4]), 217; Klausner, Bayit Sheni, 2 (1951[2]), 163ff.

[Uriel Rappaport]

SIMFEROPOL, city in the Crimea, now in Ukraine. Simferopol was founded in 1784 and until the 1917 Revolution it was the chief town of the province of Tavriya (Taurida), Crimean peninsula. Krimchaks (Crimean Jews) from other localities in the Crimea and Ashkenazi Jews from the regions of the Pale of Settlement began to settle there soon after its foundation. The number of Jews registered as taxpayers in 1803 was 471. During the 19th century the Jewish settlement increased considerably as a result of intensified emigration from other regions of the Pale of Settlement to the Crimean peninsula. In 1897 the Jews numbered 8,951 (18.3% of the total population), about 500 of whom belonged to the Krimchak community. Some 1,000 Karaites also lived in Simferopol at that time. About a quarter of the Jews were small merchants and craftsmen. Some Jews were working in tobacco factories and printing houses, many of which belonged to Jews. There was a community hospital, two *talmudei torah*, 2 private schools, a vocational school for girls, and a public library. In October 1905 pogroms broke out in the city and 42 Jews were killed. During World War I and the Civil War years many Jews who fled or were expelled from the battle regions or who otherwise escaped the riotous bands found refuge in Simferopol. The city became an important Zionist center for helping Russian emigrants to Palestine via Constantinople. In 1926 there were 17,364 Jews (19.6% of the population) in Simferopol, with their number growing to 22,791 in 1939 (16% of the total population). In the 1920s Simferopol was a place from where the Jewish farm settlers dispersed over Crimea. Nine Jewish settlements with 324 families were organized in the environs of the city, concentrated in two Jewish rural councils. A Jewish vocational school and several Yiddish elementary schools operated in the city. The Germans captured Simferopol on November 1, 1941. According to them they found 12,000–14,000 Jews. Sonderkommando 11b who settled in the city started with executions and by December 13, 1941, had murdered more than 10,000 Jews and about 2,500 *Krimchaks. In 1959 according to the census there were again about 11,200 Jews in Simferopol. One synagogue was closed down in 1959, but as of 1968 another was still functioning and *matzot* were officially permitted to be baked there. Outside the city there is a mass grave of 14,000 Jews murdered by the Nazis. No monument has been erected in their memory. Several kolkhozes housed about 50% of the Jews of the area. Most of the city's Jews emigrated in the 1990s.

BIBLIOGRAPHY: *Die Judenpogrome in Russland*, 2 (1909), 163–8.

[Yehuda Slutsky / Shmuel Spector (2nd ed.)]

SIMḤAH BEN JOSHUA OF ZALOZHTSY (1711–1768), Polish author and Torah scribe. A preacher in the town of Zalozhtsy, near Brody, Poland, he was one of a group of ascetic Ḥasidim who had gathered around R. Naḥman of Kossov, many of whose teachings he cites. He composed two works containing moral preaching in homiletic style and principles of conduct according to the kabbalist Isaac *Luria: *Lev Simḥah* (Zolkiew, 1757) and *Neti'ah shel Simḥah* (ibid., 1763). Several times in his books, he implies that the redemption will take place in 1768. He left Zalozhtsy in May 1764, later encountering R. Naḥman of Horodenka and R. Mendel of Peremyshlyany, pupils of Israel b. *Eliezer Ba'al Shem Tov, who were also traveling to Ereẓ Israel. Sailing from Constantinople on September 15, they reached Jaffa on September 26 (the eve of Rosh Ha-Shanah). Simḥah and the ḥasidic leaders continued their journey by ship to Acre. Arriving in Safed, they found only 40–50 Sephardi families there. Unable to earn a living as a scribe, Simḥah returned after seven months to Europe. Arriving in Leghorn, Italy, he found a generous Jew, who welcomed him into his home. At his request, Simḥah wrote a book containing the full story of his journey. *Sippurei Ereẓ ha-Galil* ("Tales of Galilee") is a firsthand account of his experiences. Returning to Poland, Simḥah became a preacher in Brailow, where he remained until his death. A copy of his book was published by his son-in-law, Solomon *Dubno (Grodno, 1790), under the title *Ahavat Ẓiyyon* ("Love of Zion"). Solomon Dubno added extracts from the writings of other travelers, notably chapters on Jerusalem, Hebron, Nablus, and Egypt, which he took from the narrative of the Karaite *Samuel b. David (1641–42). He also added excerpts from various non-Jewish works. The book was republished under the title *Doresh Ẓiyyon* (1887) by Ḥayyim Eliezer Hausdorf. It was first published in its original form by A. Yaari.

BIBLIOGRAPHY: Luncz, in: *Yerushalayim*, 4 (1892), 137–52; J.D. Eisenstein, *Oẓar ha-Massa'ot* (1926), 237–51; A. Yaari, *Masot Ereẓ Yisrael* (1946), 382–423, 773–5; Scholem, in: *Tarbiz*, 25 (1955/56), 429–40; Yaari, *ibid.*, 26 (1956/57), 110–2; Tishbi, in: *Zion*, 32 (1967), 4–8.

[Avraham Yaari]

SIMḤAH BEN SAMUEL OF SPEYER (second half of the 12th and the beginning of the 13th century), German scholar. He may have been a descendant of Judah ha-Kohen, author of the *Sefer ha-Dinim* (see Aptowitzer). Simḥah was one of the rabbis and *dayyanim* of the Speyer *bet din* together with his kinsman (cousin?) Judah b. Kalonymus, who was also one of his teachers, and with Nathan b. Simeon (*Or Zaru'a*, BK no. 460 and *Beit ha-Keneset* no. 388). He studied – together with his colleagues Eleazar b. Judah (of Worms), author of the *Roke'aḥ*, and *Eliezer b. Joel ha-Levi (Ravyah) – under *Eliezer b. Samuel of Metz (Maharshal, resp. no. 29), Moses b. Solomon ha-Kohen of Mainz (*Ravyah* no. 1,024), and *Isaac b. Asher ha-Levi. There were ties of close intimacy between Simḥah and Eliezer b. Joel ha-Levi, and they corresponded on numerous halakhic problems, exchanging responsa (see Aptowitzer's list, pp. 200–5, 222f.).

Some of the responsa he addressed to various other scholars are extant (see *Germania Judaica*, 1 (1934), 344ff.). Among those who addressed problems to him was the renowned Italian scholar, Isaiah di Trani, who, though generally one of the severest critics of the scholars of Germany and France, expressed great esteem for Simḥah. Other quotations from his teachings are in the work of his distinguished pupil Isaac b. Moses of Vienna (Or Zaru'a), and Abraham b. Azriel in his *Arugat ha-Bosem* copies whole pages from Simḥah (Urbach, 344 n. 29). There are quotations in the books of French, German, and Italian authors. Urbach (p. 346) conjectures that most of the quotations, with the exception of the responsa and oral traditions, are from his large work, *Seder Olam*, which is no longer extant although there are many indications that such a work did exist (Zunz, Lit Poesie, 621). From quoted fragments it may be concluded that the work encompassed many fields. They reveal that it was his custom to enlarge on the details of the subject under discussion, and it can therefore be assumed that it was this, combined with the widespread habit of compilers to include quotations and abridgments of it in their compilations, that caused the disappearance of the work. There is mention of his commentary to the *Sifra* (*Or*

Zaru'a, Mikva'ot, no. 333, 336), and to the tractate *Horayot* (Tos. to Hor. 4a–b). There is no evidence that he wrote *tosafot* to tractates of the Talmud or a commentary to the *Mekhilta*, as some scholars thought (see Urbach, pp. 346f.). Ten of his *seliḥot* have been listed by Zunz (Lit Poesie, 311). Among his distinguished pupils was also Avigdor Katz of Vienna, who wrote down his teacher's words in his presence. Samuel b. Baruch of Bamberg also appears to have been one of his pupils and addressed queries to him (Urbach, 354).

BIBLIOGRAPHY: Zunz, Lit Poesie, 284, 309–11; H. Gross, in: MGWJ, 34 (1885), 309 n. 12, 558; B. Ratner, *Mavo le-Seder Olam Rabbah* (1894), 143; V. Aptowitzer, *Mavo le-Sefer Ravyah* (1938), 200–5, 222f., 412–4; Urbach, Tosafot, 341–7 and index.

[Shlomoh Zalman Havlin]

SIMḤAH BUNEM OF PRZYSUCHA (Pshiskha; 1765–1827), ḥasidic *ẓaddik* in Poland. He was born in Wodzislaw, Poland. His father, R. Ẓevi, was an itinerant preacher (*maggid*) in Poland and central Europe. R. Simḥah Bunem traveled to central Europe to learn from R. Jeremiah of Mattersdorf, and then to Nikolsburg (Mikulov) to learn from R. Mordeḥai Benet.

Upon returning to Poland he married Rivka, who faithfully accompanied him all of his life. It was then that he was drawn to Ḥasidism by R. Moshe Leib of Sasov and R. Israel of Kozienice. He worked for the Bergson family, which was close to ḥasidic circles, as a supervisor in their timber firm. R. Simḥah Bunem traveled to Leipzig and Danzig for business and took part in their cultural and social life, visiting the theater, playing cards, and socializing with the local *maskilim*. Later he learned pharmacology in Danzig and opened a pharmacy in Pshiskha. He knew German, Polish, and Latin, and dressed in modern style. At the same time he became close to R. David of Lelov, who convinced him to travel to R. *Jacob Isaac Horovitz (ha-Ḥozeh) of Lublin. Jacob Isaac recognized his qualities, but R. Simḥah Bunem, though deeply impressed, did not come under his influence. Afterward he met R. Jacob Isaac (ha-Yehudi ha-Kadosh) of Przysucha and became his disciple.

After the death of R. Jacob Isaac of Przysucha (1814), his eminent disciples accepted R. Simḥah Bunem as their rebbe. Under his leadership the character of Pshiskha Ḥasidism was crystallized, drawing many prominent disciples as well as bitter criticism. At a wedding known as "the big wedding in Ostila," where many rebbes gathered, there was an attempt to convince R. Abraham Joshua of Apta to excommunicate R. Simḥah Bunem and his followers. However, a delegation led by R. Isaac Meir Alter successfully defended him.

He was involved in Poland's political life as a member of the Jewish council, established by the authorities of Congress Poland. In his testimony to the government he said that the government's role is not to interfere with internal Jewish matters, but rather to improve the material condition of the Jews who suffer poverty, expressing a modern concept of the duties of the state.

In his last years he became blind. As he was dying he told his wife: "Why are you crying, all of my life I learned how to die."

His Religious Path

Already in Lublin R. Simḥah Bunem was known as "the wise," a quality that well describes his character and portrays his leadership. Like Jacob Isaac of Przysucha, he set the search for truth as the focal point of his religiosity. He exposed people's self-deception, pretensions, and shallowness in order to purify their intentions. Like his teacher, he recognized humility as the quality of a sincere person who does not deceive himself. In his time, the critical attitude toward social and religious order, typical to Pshsikha, became more extreme. Pshsikha Ḥasidim, who left their families behind to live in poverty in a group intensively searching for self-improvement, ridiculed religious conventions and conventionalism, and used to mock people who were full of self-importance, including unworthy *rebbes*.

However, unlike Jacob Isaac of Przysucha, the innocent, mystical devotee, the core of R. Simḥah Bunem's religious life was his insightful view of the world, holding a positive attitude toward the world and the human role in it. A stranger to his teacher's ecstatic life, he was involved with worldly life. He taught that one's duty is to delve into the essence of this Godly world, which leads to a higher degree of religious knowledge. This knowledge involves happiness and brings a person to *dvekut*, different in its nature from that of Jacob Isaac of Przysucha. Accordingly, the literature that influenced his religious path was found less in the Kabbalah and more in the works of Maimonides, R. Judah Halevi's *Kuzari*, and the Maharal. But, above all, he was a talmudic scholar, and praying, though still important, became less central.

Among R. Simḥah Bunem's disciples were R. Menaḥem Mendel of Kotsk, R. Isaac of Warka, R. Isaac Meir Alter of Gur, R. Mordecai Joseph Leiner of Izbica, and R. Ḥanokh of Aleksandrow.

R. Simḥah Bunem did not write a book. His teachings and biographical stories about him were first published more then 30 years after his death, among them *Kol Simḥah* (1859, 1903 revised); *Ramatayim Ẓofim* (1881); *Simḥat Yisrael* (1910); and *Si'aḥ Sarfei Kodesh* (1913–1932).

BIBLIOGRAPHY: A. Marcus, *Ha-Ḥasidut* (1980), index; Z.M. Rabinowitz, *R. Simḥah Bunem mi-Pshikhah* (1945); A.Z. Eshcoly, *Ha-Ḥasidut be-Polin* (2000), 73–89; R. Mahler, *Ha-Ḥasidut ve-ha-Haskalah* (1961), index; M. Buber, *Or ha-Ganuz* (1965), 54–6, 404–27; A. Brill, in: *Ḥazon Naḥum* (1998), 419–48.

[Yehuda ben Dor (2nd ed.)]

SIMḤAT TORAH (Heb. שִׂמְחַת תּוֹרָה; lit. "rejoicing of the Torah"), the last day of the holy days begun by *Sukkot. In the Diaspora Simḥat Torah falls on the 23rd of Tishri, the second day of Shemini Aẓeret, the festival which concludes Sukkot. In Israel, it coincides with Shemini Aẓeret (22nd of Tishri; see *Festivals). On this festival, the annual reading of the Torah scroll is completed and immediately begun again. Simḥat

Torah, as a separate festival, was not known during the talmudic period. In designating the *haftarah* for this day, the Talmud refers to it simply as the second day of Shemini Aẓeret (Meg. 31a). Similarly it is termed Shemini Aẓeret in the prayers and the *Kiddush* recited on this day. Its unique celebrations began to develop during the geonic period, when the one-year cycle for the reading of the Torah (as opposed to the *triennial cycle) gained wide acceptance.

The Talmud already specified the conclusion of the Torah as the portion for this day (i.e., Deut. 33–34; see Meg. 31a). The assignment of a new *haftarah*, Joshua, is mentioned in a ninth-century prayer book (*Seder Rav Amram*, 1 (Warsaw, 1865), 52a, but see Tos. to Meg. 31a). Later it also became customary to begin to read the Book of Genesis again on Simḥat Torah. This was done in order "to refute Satan" who might otherwise have claimed that the Jews were happy only to have finished the Torah, but were unwilling to begin anew (Tur, OH 669; cf. Sif. Deut. 33).

During the celebrations, as they continue to be observed by Orthodox and Conservative congregations, all the Torah scrolls are removed from the Ark and the *bimah* ("pulpit") is circled seven times (**hakkafot*). All the men present are called to the Torah reading (*aliyyot*); for this purpose, Deuteronomy 33:1–29 is repeated as many times as necessary. All the children under the age of bar mitzvah are called for the concluding portion of the chapter; this *aliyah* is referred to as *kol ha-ne'arim* ("all the youngsters"). A *tallit* is spread above the heads of the youngsters, and the congregation blesses them with Jacob's benediction to Ephraim and Manasseh (Gen. 48:16). Those who are honored with the *aliyyot* which conclude and start the Torah readings are popularly designated as the *ḥatan Torah* and *ḥatan Bereshit*; they often pledge contributions to the synagogue and sponsor banquets for their acquaintances in honor of the event (see *Bridegrooms of the Law). In many communities similar ceremonies are held on Simḥat Torah eve: all the scrolls are removed from the Ark and the *bimah* is circled seven times. Some communities even read from the concluding portion of Deuteronomy during the evening service, the only time during the year when the Torah scroll is read at night (Sh. Ar., OH 669:1).

The Simḥat Torah festivities are accompanied by the recitation of special liturgical compositions, some of which were written in the late geonic period. The *ḥatan Torah* is called up by the prayer *Me-Reshut ha-El ha-Gadol*, and the *ḥatan Bereshit* by *Me-Reshut Meromam*. The return of the Torah scrolls to the Ark is accompanied by the joyful hymns "*Sisu ve-Simḥu be-Simḥat Torah*" and "*Hitkabbeẓu Malakhim Zeh el Zeh*." A central role in the festivities is allotted to children. In addition to the *aliyah* to the Torah, the children also participate in the Torah processions: they carry flags adorned with apples in which burning candles are placed. There have even been communities where children dismantled *sukkot* on Simḥat Torah and burned them (*Darkhei Moshe* to OH 669 n. 3 quoting Maharil).

Ḥasidim also hold Torah processions on Shemini Aẓeret eve. Reform synagogues observe these customs, in a modified form, on Shemini Aẓeret, which is observed as the final festival day. In Israel, where the second day of the festival is not celebrated, the liturgy and celebration of both days are combined. It has also become customary there for public *hakkafot* to be held on the night following Simḥat Torah, which coincides with its celebration in the Diaspora: in many cities, communities, and army bases, seven *hakkafot* are held with religious, military, and political personnel being honored with the carrying of the Torah scrolls.

[Aaron Rothkoff]

In the U.S.S.R.

Among Soviet Jewish youth seeking forms of expressing their Jewish identification, Simḥat Torah gradually became, during the 1960s, the occasion of mass gatherings in and around the synagogues, mainly in the great cities Moscow, Leningrad, Riga, and others. At these gatherings large groups of Jewish youth, many of them students, sang Hebrew and Yiddish songs, danced the *hora*, congregated and discussed the latest events in Israel, etc. In the beginning, the Soviet authorities tried to disperse these "unauthorized meetings," but when Jewish and western public opinion began to follow them, and press correspondents as well as observers from various foreign embassies began attending them, the authorities largely reverted their attitude and even instructed the militia to cordon off the synagogue areas and redirect traffic, so as not to cause clashes with the Jewish youngsters, whose numbers swelled rapidly in Moscow into the tens of thousands. In many cities in the West, notably in Israel, England, the United States, and Canada, Simḥat Torah was declared by Jewish youth as the day of "solidarity with Soviet Jewish youth," and mass demonstrations were staged voicing demands to the Soviet authorities for freedom of Jewish life and the right of migration to Israel.

The Simḥat Torah Flag

Among the customs of Simḥat Torah, the object associated most with the holiday, at least in the world of children, is undoubtedly the ornamental flag known in Hebrew as *degel Simḥat Torah*, made of paper or cardboard, printed with rich and colorful pictures reflecting the meaning of the holiday. Until some years ago flags were customarily attached to coarse wooden sticks topped by apples, hollowed out and filled with a burning candle.

While it is not known when and where this custom originated, it is certainly an Ashkenazi *minhag*, especially popular in eastern Europe. The earliest known source mentioning such a flag is found in the enactments (*Takkanot*) issued in 1672 by Polish Jews who settled in Amsterdam. From this document it is evident that the custom originated earlier. The German Hebraist Johann *Bodenschatz describes the custom in his book *Kirchliche Verfassung der heutigen Juden* (Erlang, 1748): "They [the children] hold onto their flags upon which is inscribed 'standard of the camp' and the names of the tribes. They march as if they were soldiers."

Extant Torah flags from 19th-century eastern Europe are decorated by representations of Ḥasidim dancing with Torah scrolls, *sukkah* building, and biblical scenes and figures, and the deer and lion with the saying, "Be swift as a deer and strong as a lion" (Pirkei Avot 5:20). Later, the images included Zionist heroes and slogans. The custom has continued to the present day, adopting new symbols and heroes associated with the State of Israel but keeping the more traditional designs as well.

[Shalom Sabar (2nd ed.)]

BIBLIOGRAPHY: AA. Yaari, *Toledot Hag Simḥat Torah* (1964); S. Zevin, *Ha-Mo'adim ba-Halakhah* (1959[7]), 135–41; E. Wiesel, *The Jews of Silence* (1966). **ADD. BIBLIOGRAPHY:** R. Arbel (ed.), *Blue and White in Color: Visual Images of Zionism, 1897–1947* (1997); P. Goodman (ed.), *The Simhat Torah Anthology* (1973), 127–28; A. Kanof, *Jewish Ceremonial Art and Religious Observance* (1969?), 156–57; A. Ya'ari, *Toledot Ḥag Simḥat Torah: Hishtalshelut Minhagav bi-Tefuẓot Yisrael le-Dorotehen* (1964); R. Wischnitzer-Bernstein, *Gestalten und Symbole der jüdischen Kunst* (1935), 112.

SIMḤONI, ASSAF (1922–1956), Israeli military officer. Born in Nahalal, Simḥoni was descended from a pioneering family which moved to Ereẓ Israel from the Jewish agricultural settlements of south Russia and settled in various kibbutzim. His uncle, ZERUBAVEL YEVZERICHIN, was a leading member of the legal faction of the He-Ḥalutz movement in the U.S.S.R. who was arrested in 1926 for his Zionist activities and died in a Soviet labor camp. Assaf's mother, YEHUDIT SIMḤONI, settled in Geva and became a leading figure in the Israeli labor movement. Simḥoni joined the Haganah during the Arab riots of 1936–39 and in 1941 joined the Palmaḥ. During the War of Independence (1948) he participated in the battle for Mishmar ha-Emek and was the commander of the Palmaḥ batallion that broke through to kibbutz Negbah. He continued to serve in the Israel Defense Forces (IDF) and in 1951 was promoted to brigade commander with the rank of colonel. At the beginning of 1956 he went to England for an advanced military course but was recalled in the autumn of the same year and appointed commander of the southern command. On October 29 he commanded the IDF in the *Sinai Campaign and received the surrender of the Egyptian governor of the Gaza Strip. Simḥoni died shortly after the Sinai Campaign when his plane crashed inside Jordan. His body was returned to Israel, and he was posthumously promoted to major general.

[Yehuda Slutsky]

SIMLAI (second half of the third century C.E.), *amora*. Simlai was born in Nehardea, in Babylonia, (TJ, Pes. 5:3, 52a), but spent most of his life at Lydda, in Ereẓ Israel (Av. Zar. 36a). He also lived for some time in Galilee, where he ministered to Yannai the Great (BB 111a), and was the associate of young Judah III (Bek. 36b). He seems to have been a prominent member of Judah II's entourage (Av. Zar. 37a), and when the latter made a particularly controversial decision (TJ, Shab. 1:4, 3d), Simlai was sent to *Nisibis, in Babylon, in order to transmit it to the local authorities (Av. Zar. 36a). His ruling at Antioch, in Syria, is also recorded (TJ, Kid. 3:15, 66d). He transmitted sayings in the name of Eliezer b. Simeon (Sanh. 98a) and Samuel (PdRK 54b), and, despite Jonathan's initial scruples (Pes. 6:25), studied *aggadah* under him (TJ, Pes. 5:3, 32a). Simlai was a renowned authority in *aggadah* (Ber. 32a–b). One of his teachings is that in the time to come God will take a scroll of law in his embrace and proclaim, "Let whoever has occupied himself herewith, come and take his reward!" All the nations of the world will rush to testify for themselves, but, ultimately, God will Himself testify on behalf of Israel (Av. Zar. 2b–3a). He also explained that Moses' desire to enter Ereẓ Israel was based not on a wish to taste its fruit or enjoy its goodness, but on his eagerness to fulfill all the Torah (Sot. 14a). Simlai is the author of the statement (Mak. 23b) that the Torah contains 613 *commandments – 365 negative corresponding to the number of days in the solar year and 248 positive, corresponding to the number of organs in the human body (cf. Oho. 1:8). These he reduced successively to 11 (based on Ps. 15), to six (Isa. 33:15–16), to three (Micah 6:8), and to two (Isa., 56:1) fundamental principles, and finally to the single credo expressed by Habbakuk (2:4), "the righteous shall live by his faith" (Mak. 23b–24a). He also taught that "the Torah begins and ends with the practice of lovingkindness" (Sot. 14a).

BIBLIOGRAPHY: Bachir, Pal Amor; Hyman, Toledot, in: Ḥ. Albeck, *Mavo la-Talmudim* (1969), 190.

SIMLEUL-SILVANIEI (Hung. **Szilágysomlyó**; referred to in Jewish sources שאמלויא), town in Transylvania, N.W. Romania; until the end of World War I, and between 1940 and 1944, within Hungary. Jews began to settle there during the 18th century. An organized community was established in 1841; from its inception, the community was Orthodox. A synagogue was erected in 1850. In 1885 the community became the official center for the Jews in the surrounding area. Many local Jews fought in World War I in the Austro-Hungarian army. The influence of Ḥasidism was felt, particularly between the two world wars. The Jewish population numbered 838 (18.4% of the total) in 1891; 1,586 (21%) in 1930; and 1,496 (16.4%) in 1941. Between the two world wars Zionist activity was curtailed. The community's institutions included an elementary school for boys, opened in 1894, and one for girls (1921). The rabbi of the community from 1898 was the extreme Orthodox Samuel Ehrenreich (b. 1863), who was deported in the summer of 1944 with the members of his community to *Auschwitz.

Holocaust and Contemporary Periods

During World War II Jews from the vicinity, as well as from outlying regions, were interned in the ghetto which was established in Simleul-Silvaniei. Jews from other towns were also concentrated there before their deportation to Auschwitz. About 8,000 Jews passed through this ghetto on their way to the death camps.

Of those who survived after World War II, about 440 Jews gathered in Simleul-Silvaniei in 1947; they rehabilitated the community and maintained the synagogue, still standing in 1971. A rabbi headed the community for a while. The number of Jews subsequently declined as a result of emigration to Israel and other countries. In 1971 there were 40 Jews. Between the two world wars there was also a small Hebrew press in Simleul-Silvaniei. A Hebrew book was printed there in 1960.

BIBLIOGRAPHY: *Magyar Zsidó Lexikon* (1929), s.v. *Ehrenreich, Sziláysomlyó*; S.Z. Ehrenreich, *Even Shelomo* (1963).

[Yehouda Marton]

SIMMEL, GEORG (1858–1918), German philosopher and sociologist. Born in Berlin of converted parents, in 1885 Simmel became a lecturer at Berlin, but his appointment as professor (extracurricular) at Strasbourg was delayed until 1911 because of his Jewish origin and because he followed no religion. In 1914 he finally became full professor. In his early work *Ueber soziale Differenzierung* (1890) Simmel sees the essence of the modern development in the dissolution of the substance of society in a sum of interrelationships of participating individuals. Another early book, *Einleitung in die Moralwissenschaft* (1892), which he later rejected, sought to construct a system of morals describing man's moral life psychologically without evaluating it. *Die Probleme der Geschichtsphilosophie* (also 1892), greatly altered by Simmel in later editions, had considerable influence. In this work Simmel postulates that events must be distinguished from history. The philosophy of history seeks out those a priori assumptions of historical consciousness, the foundations on which "the historical world is built." Simmel pursued this idea in "*Das Problem der historischen Zeit*" ("The Problem of Historical Time") and "*Vom Wesen des historischen Verstehens*" ("The Essence of Historical Comprehension"), which are included in the collection *Bruecke und Tuer* (1957). He suggests there is no road to objective reality itself, only diverse subjective worlds, dependent on their categorical assumptions.

Simmel's relativism reached its peak in *Philosophie des Geldes* (1900), in which he tried to discover the relation of money to all spheres of our life – its influences on all branches of culture – and expose the spiritual, moral, and religious assumptions of historical materialism in order to overcome it. He especially emphasized the intellectual character of monetary economy. Simmel published his research on Kant in his book *Kant* (1904). Besides Kant's expression of intellectuality, others, no less true, are possible, as Simmel indicated in *Schopenhauer und Nietzsche* (1907), *Goethe* (1913), and *Rembrandt* (1916). Influenced by the antipsychological views of the neo-Kantians and Husserl, Simmel saw culture as a process itself, an objective view through which the contents moved from the soul into an objective framework having its own laws. Cultural values have autonomous validity separated from their creator's spiritual source. The soul's or life's essence is to produce the objective contents of culture from itself. "Life is more than life." Thus objective culture becomes the soul's path back to itself.

His studies on art, religion, and philosophy tried to show that each is a world in itself, not a derivative of another, because it depends on special subjective functions of life. In his books *Soziologie* (1908) and *Grundfragen der Soziologie* (1917), as well as in numerous essays, Simmel analyzes all processes of association and dissociation as psychic phenomena, but he also constitutes the science of sociology by separating the forms of association from their content in such a way that purely formal concepts of relationships become generalizable and thereby scientific in character. They remain constant in a multitude of concrete events. In this sense, Simmel has analyzed the formal nature and significance of numbers ("The Dyad and the Triad"), space, conflict, poverty, fashion, adornment, secret societies, and a host of other formal relationships, always recognizing the dialectical interplay of the individual and the group as the essence of all relationships. But he has not arrived at a systematic ordering of these relationships. Buber, in turn stimulated by Simmel, described Jewish existence as manifesting itself not so much in substance but in relationships, that is, as essentially social in character. In this fashion, Simmel's approach to sociology has become a cornerstone of the sociology of the Jews.

BIBLIOGRAPHY: H. Liebeschuetz, *Von G. Simmel zu F. Rosenzweig* (1970); L. Coser, *Georg Simmel* (Eng., 1965), incl. list of his works; R.H. Weingartner, *Experience and Culture: the Philosophy of Georg Simmel* (1962), incl. bibl.; K.H. Wolf (ed.), *Georg Simmel, 1858–1918: A Collection of Essays with Translations and a Bibliography* (1959); M. Susman, *Die geistige Gestalt G. Simmels* (1959); K. Gassen and M. Landmann (ed.), *Buch des Dankes an Georg Simmel* (1958).

[Samuel Hugo Bergman and Werner J. Cahnman]

SIMMONS, GENE (Chaim Witz; 1949–), bass guitarist for veteran U.S. rock band KISS, which he formed in 1973 with Paul Stanley (Stanley Harvey Eisen). Born in Haifa, the only child to Hungarian Holocaust survivors Flora and Feri, Simmons immigrated to New York with his mother in 1958, after his parents divorced. Adopting the family name Klein, his mother's maiden name, Simmons also changed his name to Gene, and in the late 1960s changed his name again, dropping Klein in favor of Simmons. As a boy Simmons was educated at a yeshivah in Williamsburg, Brooklyn. After graduating from Sullivan County Community College in South Fallsburg, NY, and Richmond College in Staten Island, Simmons taught sixth grade in Harlem in New York City. After putting together KISS and after several false starts, the band finally hit the big time in 1975 with the release of *Dressed to Kill*, the studio album that spawned "Rock and Roll All Nite" and "C'mon and Love Me," the band's first radio hits. A string of platinum albums followed, but the band remained most acclaimed for its live performances, which featured Simmons – under his stage persona of Demon – spitting "blood" (primarily yogurt and food coloring) and "breathing fire." The shows were accompanied by ostentatious pyrotechnics throughout. Simmons did little to play down his hell-raising image, and often encouraged it: In his autobiography *Kiss and Make-Up* (2001), he claims to have had sex with 4,600 partners. Simmons was also a movie and record producer, and appeared in a number of movies, including Michael Crichton's sci-fi movie *Runaway*. In 2004, Simmons sparked controversy during a KISS tour of Australia when he claimed that Islam was a "vile culture" that treated women worse than dogs.

[Simon Spungin (2nd ed.)]

SIMON, family of British printers and typographers. OLIVER SIMON (1895–1956) was born in Sale, Cheshire, the son of a cotton merchant. His mother was the sister of Sir William *Rothenstein. Simon was educated at Charterhouse and in Germany, served as an officer in the British army in World War I, and fought in the Palestine campaign. He trained as a printer in London and joined the Curwen Press of which he later became chairman and managing director. In 1923 he was a founder and editor of *The Fleuron*, a typography journal. He was also a founder of the typographers' Double Crown Club of which he was president in 1929. Simon was a director of the Soncino Press. As a typographer Simon had an enormous influence on the improvement of printing, typography, and type design. He edited with J. Rodenberg, *Printing of Today* (1928) and the *Curwen Press Miscellany* (1931), and was the author of *Introduction to Typography* (1945) and an autobiography, *Printer and Playground* (1956). Simon had a notable interest in Palestine, founding the Paladin Club, an influential discussion group whose members included Chaim *Weizmann.

His brother, HERBERT SIMON (1898–1974), was also a founding member of the Double Crown Club. He succeeded Oliver as chairman of the Curwen Press in 1956.

ADD. BIBLIOGRAPHY: ODNB online.

[John M. Shaftesley]

SIMON, family of U.S. entrepreneurs. MELVIN SIMON (1926–) and his brother, HERBERT (1934–), the sons of a tailor, were born in Brooklyn, N.Y., and raised in the Bronx. Mel earned an accounting degree from the City College of New York and later a master's degree there. He went into the Army, winding up in 1953 at Fort Benjamin Harrison in Indianapolis. He decided to stay in the city. After working as a leasing agent, he studied real estate in college and thought there was great potential. In 1959 he formed his own real-estate investment company, Melvin Simon & Associates, with Herb, who had also worked in real estate. The business was incorporated in 1960, with Mel owning two-thirds of the business and Herb, who was also educated at the City College of New York, the rest. Another brother, Fred, worked for the company but left in 1963. Their parents moved from New York to Indianapolis in 1961. Melvin Simon & Associates began by developing strip shopping centers anchored by groceries and drug stores. Their first shopping center was Southgate Plaza in Bloomington, Ind. Within five years the Simons were developing enclosed malls. By 1967 the company owned and operated more than 3 million square feet of retail property. It continued to expand throughout the country, adding one million square feet of property every year. By the 1980s the company opened three enclosed malls every year. In the 1970s Mel tried his hand at moviemaking. His production company lost millions. In 1983, the brothers bought the professional basketball team the Indiana Pacers. In 1990, DAVID (1961–), Mel's oldest son, a graduate of the University of Indiana and with a master's from Columbia, joined the company as chief financial officer. He became chief executive officer in 1995. The company went public in 1993, folding most of its properties into Simon Property Group and raising nearly $1 billion, at the time the largest real estate stock offering ever. Following a $3 billion merger with DeBartolo Realty Corporation in 1996, the company became Simon DeBartolo Group, the nation's dominant shopping center owner. In 1998 the company reverted to Simon Property Group, becoming the No. 1 mall owner in the United States. Also in 1998, Simon bought the Fashion Mall at Keystone at the Crossing, taking control of six of the seven regional shopping malls in Indianapolis. The company's projects include the Mall of America, outside Minneapolis, completed in 1992, and Circle Center Mall in Indianapolis, which opened in 1995. Overall, the Simons owned or operated about 350 properties in North America, Japan, and Europe. The Simons were known for their philanthropy. The family contributed $9 million toward construction of a research and teaching facility at the University of Indiana. They also served in Indianapolis on the boards of United Cerebral Palsy, the Muscular Dystrophy Association, and the Jewish Welfare Foundation.

[Stewart Kampel (2nd ed.)]

SIMON, ABRAM (1872–1938), U.S. Reform rabbi. Born in Nashville, Tennessee, he was educated at the University of Cincinnati where he earned his B.A. in 1894, the same year he was ordained by Hebrew Union College. In 1917, long after he had become rabbi of Washington Hebrew Congregation, Simon earned a Ph.D. from George Washington University, writing on the "The Constructive Character and Function of Religious Progress."

Upon ordination he served as rabbi of B'nai Israel Congregation in Sacramento and then as rabbi of Temple Israel in Omaha, Nebraska (1899–1904). Under his leadership the temple began to prosper financially, owing to an increase in pew rent. He earned a national reputation for innovation in Jewish education and was elected as the first rabbi of Washington Hebrew Congregation in Washington, D.C., in 1903. His predecessor had been *ḥazzan*. Gracefully and reluctantly, Temple Israel released him from his contract.

The history of Washington Hebrew Congregation records that "Rabbi Abram Simon came to the Congregation in 1904 and dedicated his life to scholarship and community activity. The photograph of his first Confirmation class in 1905 hangs in Ades Hall and begins a long series of pictures of every Confirmation class since. Rabbi Simon was a member of the Red Cross during World War I, broadcast radio lectures, and was president of both the Board of Education in Washington as well as the Conference of Christians and Jews. After his death, the Abram Simon School, a public elementary school, served as an ongoing recognition of his contributions."

In Washington, Simon became a communal leader. In addition to the Board of Education he was a trustee and later president of the Columbia Hospital for Women and also president of the Public Library of Washington. On the national level he was president of the Central Conference of American Rabbi from 1923 to 1925, a founder and later president of the Synagogue Council of America.

He was a founding member of the Reform movement's Committee on Jewish Education. His wife, Carrie Obendorfer *Simon, whom he married in 1896, founded the National Federation of Temple Sisterhoods, which eventually reached 100,000 women in 585 chapters during her lifetime. Pam Nadell, a distinguished American Jewish historian, said: "They pledged dues to help pay down the mortgage and recessed to polish the door knobs… They were extending their roles as homemakers to the synagogue."

As the federation's founding president until 1919, Simon launched the National Committee on Religion, which boosted synagogue attendance and set up Hebrew schools. She also pushed for more women on congregation boards and temple inclusion of interfaith families. She also worked for the Jewish Baille Institute. Her husband was an early enthusiast of women's participation. Fay Sonnenreich recalled that in the 1920, with the permission of Rabbi Abram Simon, she and another young girl sat in the pulpit, held the Torah and read from it.

"I still remember the shocked expressions on the faces of the congregation," she recalled many years later. "Dr. Simon told us afterwards that the board of trustees was angry with him for permitting girls to participate in what traditionally belonged to the men. But he believed in developing the potential of each individual, and his encouragement made a lasting impact upon our lives."

Rabbi Simon wrote *A Child's Ritual* (1909); *A History of Jewish Education* (1916); and *The Principle of Jewish Education in the Past* (1909).

BIBLIOGRAPHY: K.M. Olitzsky, L.J. Sussman, and M.H. Stern, *Reform Judaism in America: A Biographical Dictionary and Sourcebook* (1993).

[Michael Berenbaum (2nd ed.)]

SIMON, AKIBA ERNST (1899–1988), educator, religious thinker, and writer. Born in Berlin, he became an active Zionist in 1918, and co-edited *Der *Jude* with Martin *Buber, who had a decisive influence on his concept of Jewish nationalism and whom he joined in his relentless struggle for Arab-Jewish understanding. In his positive attitude to Jewish tradition he followed Franz *Rosenzweig. With a broad humanistic outlook, based on his historical and literary erudition and scholarship, he began his work as an educator in Germany and continued it, after settling in Palestine in 1928, as a teacher and co-director of secondary schools and seminaries. In 1934 he accepted Buber's call to join him in teachers' training and adult education programs for German Jewry under Nazi rule.

In 1935 Simon joined the staff of the Hebrew University, where he became professor of philosophy and history of education and, finally, director of the School of Education. He participated in Jewish education programs in various parts of the Jewish world and was a co-editor of the *Enẓiklopedyah Ḥinnukhit* ("Educational Encyclopedia"; 5 vols. 1961–66). Simon was a co-founder and board member of the Leo Baeck Institute and a contributor to its scholarly publications. He has served as a coeditor of Rosenzweig's letters and Buber's correspondence. In his religious conception Simon identified himself with the *Conservative Movement.

Simon defined his philosophy in numerous articles as a religious humanism. In his view our world is neither theocentric nor anthropocentric. It is to be looked upon not as a circle but as an elipse with two foci; God and man, bound to each other by that mutuality of correlation and tension that is meant by the concept of the Covenant. Certainly the human partner is the weaker one, but he is not nil. God has not created a perfect world, but rather has left it to man to work on its growing perfection. This activity takes on mainly two forms: politics and education, the former representing the problems in their full tragical rigor and the latter offering a modest chance of finding a way out.

In Judaism, the Covenant is realized by the Law of the Torah that forms the main link between God and His people. The *halakhah*, as a continuous dialogue between the written and oral tradition on one side and the changing reality of Israel and the world on the other side, is the classical way of translating prophetic ideas into human, individual, social, national, and international relations.

Simon was an active member of virtually every group advocating a binational state in Palestine. He was early a member of *Berit Shalom and later of the League for Jewish Arab Rapprochement. He held that the Jews must give the Arabs equal economic rights and accept Arab nationalism as valid as well as acknowledge the reality of the Arab fear of Jews.

Among Simon's writings may be mentioned *Ranke und Hegel* (1928); *Das Werturteil im Geschichtsunterricht* (1931); *Chajjim Nachman Bialik* (1935); *Aufbau im Untergang* (1934); *Mishnato shel Pestalozzi* (1962); *Bruecken* (1965); *Are We Still Jews?* (1982); *The Right to Educate, the Obligation to Educate* (1983); *Chapters in My Life* (1986); "Goethe and Religious Humanism," in: A. Bergstraesser (ed.), *Goethe and the Modern Age* (1949), 304–25; "Siegmund Freud the Jew," in YLBI, 2 (1957), 270–305; "Martin Buber and German Jewry," *ibid.*, 3 (1958), 3–39; "M. Buber the Educator," in: P.A. Schilpp and M. Friedman (eds.), *Buber* (1967), 543–76; "The Way of Law" in: A. Jospe (ed.), *Tradition and Contemporary Experience* (1970), 221–38.

BIBLIOGRAPHY: M.L. Diamond, *Martin Buber, Jewish Existentialist* (1960), 165–70; A.A. Cohen, *Arguments and Doctrines* (1970),

367–71; S.L. Hattis, *The Bi-National Idea in Palestine during Mandatory Times* (1970), index; YLBI, 15 (1970), 264.

[Yehoshua Amir (Neumark)]

SIMON, ARYEH (1913–), Israeli educator. Simon was born in Mainz, Germany and studied classical languages and philosophy at Heidelberg. Immigrating to Israel in 1935, he studied education and began to teach at the *Ben Shemen youth village in 1937. He served in the Jewish Brigade of the British Army in World War II and as an officer in the Israel Defense Forces in the War of Independence. After the war he devoted himself to education and was appointed director of Ben Shemen in 1964. In 1975 he was awarded the Israel Prize for education.

SIMON, CARLY ELISABETH (1945–), New York City-born folk and pop songwriter and singer who achieved the greatest part of her success in the 1970s, when several of her songs scored high on the pop music charts. Simon is one of four children of New York publishing magnate Richard L. Simon, co-founder in 1924 of the publishing house Simon & Schuster, and non-Jewish mother Andrea. Her father was an accomplished pianist who often hosted musicians, including Richard *Rodgers, Oscar *Hammerstein, and George *Gershwin, at the family home. Simon spent two years at Sarah Lawrence College before dropping out and forming a folk duo with her sister, Lucy, singing in 1960s coffeehouses as the Simon Sisters. They recorded the children's tune "Wynken, Blinken' and Nod," presaging her later work on children's music. Her early solo career met with little success. Her first manager, Albert Grossman, asked Bob *Dylan to rewrite the song "Baby Let Me Follow You Down" for Simon, but the recording was never released. Simon's second album in 1971 resulted in a Best New Artist Grammy Award and the Top 10 hit "That's The Way I've Always Heard It Should Be." She next reached #13 on the charts with "Anticipation" (later used in a famous ketchup commercial) in 1972. The song reputedly was about her love interest at the time, singer-songwriter Cat Stevens, later Yusuf Islam. She continued to write about her celebrity lovers, who included actors Warren Beatty and Jack Nicholson, and singers Mick Jagger and Kris Kristofferson, in her biggest hit, "You're So Vain," (#1, Adult Contemporary, 1973). The subject of the song has never been publicly revealed, although Dick Ebersol, president of NBC Sports, paid $50,000 to find out the name in a charity auction in 2003. Other 1970s chart hits included, "Mockingbird," with her husband James Taylor (#5, 1974) and "Nobody Does It Better," the theme from the James Bond film *The Spy Who Loved Me* (#2, 1977), presaging her later work on film scores. Her work failed to make major dents in the pop charts in the 1980s and 1990s, but her song "Let the River Run" won the Academy Award for Best Song in 1988 for the film *Working Girl*. As her mass appeal waned, Simon turned to recording albums of pop standards and Christmas tunes, as well as continuing her confessional, folk-tinged records, but returned to regular concert tours in 2005. Her children from her marriage to Taylor, Ben and Sally, continued the family tradition as folk music singer-songwriters. Simon was ranked 28th on TV music channel VH1's 100 Greatest Women of Rock and Roll, and by 2005 had released 29 albums and had 18 Top-20 singles on the U.S. and U.K. charts. Simon, who was inducted into the Songwriters Hall of Fame in 1994, wrote five children's books: *Amy the Dancing Bear* (1989), *The Boy of the Bells* (1990), *The Fisherman's Song* (1991), *The Nighttime Chauffeur* (1993), and *Midnight Farm* (1997).

[Alan D. Abbey (2nd ed.)]

SIMON, CARRIE OBENDORFER (1872–1961), founding president of the *National Federation of Temple Sisterhoods. Born in Uniontown, Alabama, Obendorfer moved with her family to Cincinnati, Ohio, where her mother began a chapter of the *National Council of Jewish Women (NCJW) in 1895. Carrie, a graduate of the Cincinnati Conservatory of Music, served as section secretary and became familiar with new possibilities for women's public identities as Jews. After her marriage in 1896 to Hebrew Union College graduate Rabbi Abram Simon, Carrie Simon encountered many settings where she would push these possibilities in new directions.

Simon continued to advance NCJW work while living in Sacramento, where her husband took his first pulpit in 1896, and then in Omaha and Washington, D.C., where they moved in 1899 and 1904, respectively. As NCJW struggled to reconcile the differing religious approaches of its diverse membership, Simon turned her attention to local congregational work. Synagogue sisterhood organizations devoted to congregational aid first emerged in the 1890s. Simon's husband is credited with the 1903 founding of a sisterhood at Omaha's Temple Israel. Carrie Simon established the Ladies Auxiliary Society of Washington Hebrew Congregation in 1905 for the purpose of "congregational work, pure and simple, and to endeavor to establish a more congenial and social congregational spirit."

In 1913 the Union of American Hebrew Congregations (UAHC), the synagogue federation of Reform Judaism, issued a call "to all ladies' organizations connected with congregations" to send delegates to Cincinnati "for the purpose of organizing a Federation of Temple Sisterhoods." Simon's work in organizing the meeting, attended by 156 delegates from 52 congregations (mainly the wives of delegates to the concurrent UAHC convention), was recognized in her election as president of the newly formed National Federation of Temple Sisterhoods (NFTS).

The new organization galvanized women in hundreds of Reform congregations. New sisterhoods were formed and many existing groups were revolutionized. The Ladies Auxiliary at Simon's own congregation renamed itself a Sisterhood and moved from holding occasional synagogue fundraisers to transforming the synagogue into a true social center. Simon's new role turned her into a speaker in demand across the country. She insisted that "there was no militancy" involved when she filled a pulpit; it simply represented "recognition accorded to the sisterhood."

NFTS grew quickly under her leadership, introducing thousands of women to unaccustomed public roles within the Jewish community. Simon was often one of a very few women representatives in national and international gatherings of Jewish leaders. She retired as NFTS president in 1919, but remained active in the organization as honorary president for the rest of her life.

BIBLIOGRAPHY: M.I. Greenberg, "Carrie Obendorfer Simon," in: P.E. Hyman and D.D. Moore (eds.), *Jewish Women in America*, vol. 2 (1997), 1260–61; P.S. Nadell and R.J. Simon, "Ladies of the Sisterhood," in: M. Sacks (ed.), *Active Voices* (1995).

[Karla Goldman (2nd ed.)]

SIMON, ERNST (1902–1973), Israeli biochemist. Simon was born in Berlin and received his education at the universities of Munich, Jena, and Berlin. In 1925, he was appointed research assistant at the Kaiser Wilhelm Institute of Biochemistry in Berlin, where he remained until Hitler's rise to power in 1933, when he moved to Paris and joined the Institute of Biological Physicochemistry there. He immigrated to Ereẓ Israel in 1935, joining the Daniel Sieff Research Institute, the forerunner of the Weizmann Institute of Science, a few months after its foundation, and remained at the Weizmann Institute until his death. He spent his early years there working closely with Weizmann on problems of fermentation, but was best known in later years for his pioneering studies on the mechanism of diabetes, carried out in the department of biodynamics.

SIMON, SIR FRANCIS EUGENE (1893–1956), physicist. Simon, who was born in Berlin, served through World War I and was awarded the Iron Cross for distinguished service. After the war he continued at Berlin University and became research assistant to the German chemist Walter Herman Nernst (1864–1941), as well as a lecturer on low-temperature physics. In 1931 he became professor and director of the laboratory for physical chemistry at the Technische Hochschule in Breslau. In 1933 Simon was invited to the Clarendon Laboratory in Oxford, where he built up one of the foremost low-temperature laboratories in the world. In 1935 Simon was appointed university reader (later to occupy a chair specially created in 1946) in thermodynamics. During World War II, he was responsible for some key research on an aspect of the manufacture of the atom bomb, although he was classified as an "enemy alien." In 1941 he was elected a Fellow of the Royal Society.

Simon was a vigorous campaigner for the proper use of science, the avoidance of waste, and the utilization of scientists in public affairs. From 1948 to 1951 he was scientific correspondent of the *Financial Times*. He was knighted in 1955.

BIBLIOGRAPHY: N. Arms, *A Prophet in Two Countries* (1966); N. Kurti, in: *Biographical Memoirs of Fellows of the Royal Society*, 4 (1958), 225–56.

[J. Edwin Holmstrom]

SIMON, HEINRICH (1880–1941), German journalist and editor. Simon was the eldest son of Felix Simon, owner of *Koenigsberger Allgemeine Zeitung*, and Therese, whose father, Leopold Sonnemann, had founded the *Frankfurter Zeitung*. The family ran both papers. Baptized as a child, Simon later left the Church but never formally returned to Judaism. He studied philosophy, art history, and economics in Berlin, Freiburg/Breisgau, and Erlangen. In 1905 he earned his doctorate with a work on Novalis. Simon joined the *Frankfurter Zeitung* in 1906 and eventually controlled its liberal editorial policy. In 1931 he wrote Sonnemann's biography. Forced to resign from his post, Simon immigrated to Palestine via Paris in 1934. He was a friend of *Huberman and first manager in 1936 of the Palestine Symphony Orchestra. In 1939 he retired and went to the U.S. His murder in Washington, in 1941, remains an unsolved mystery.

BIBLIOGRAPHY: *Frankfurter Zeitung und Handelsblatt* 76, No. 805–7 (1931); E. Kahn, in: LBIYB, 2 (1957), 228–35; E. Feder, *Heute sprach ich mit...* (1971), index; BHDE, 1 (1980), 700; B. von der Luehe, *Die Musik war unsere Rettung* (1998), index; NDB 22 (2005), 719*.

[Johannes Valentin Schwarz (2nd ed.)]

SIMON, HERBERT ALEXANDER (1916–2001), U.S. political scientist; authority on public administration, Nobel laureate. Born in Milwaukee, Wisconsin, Simon received his Ph.D. in political science from the University of Chicago (1943). In 1949 he was appointed professor of computer science and psychology at Carnegie-Mellon University in Pittsburgh, where he founded the Department of Computer Science. He remained at the university for his entire career. In his principal treatise on public administration, *Administrative Behavior* (1947), Simon discussed the position of the individual in the administration process and the psychological mechanisms that influence and condition his behavior. He laid down principles for the scientific study of public administration in a technological society and rejected the preexisting principles of public administration as mere "proverbs" or summaries of crude homely wisdom. In 1978 Simon was awarded the Nobel Prize for economics, for his pioneering research into the decision-making process within economic organizations. He is also considered a pioneer in the development of computer artificial intelligence.

Simon's other works include *Organizations* (1958), of which he was co-author; *The New Science of Management Decision* (1960); *The Shape of Automation for Men and Management* (1965); *Representation and Meaning* (1972); *The Sciences of the Artificial* (1981); *Scientific Discovery* (1987); *Models of Thought* (1989); and *Models of My Life* (1992).

ADD. BIBLIOGRAPHY: P. Earl (ed.), *The Legacy of Herbert Simon in Economic Analysis* (2001); J. March (ed.), *Models of a Man: Essays in Memory of Herbert A. Simon* (2004); H. Crowther-Heyck, *Herbert A. Simon: The Bounds of Reason in Modern America* (2005).

[Nimrod Raphaeli / Ruth Beloff (2nd ed.)]

SIMON, JAMES (1851–1932), German commercial magnate and philanthropist. After completing high school Simon joined his family's flourishing textile firm, Gebrueder Simon, which under his management became one of the largest firms in the world – boasting 40 to 50 million marks profits annually before World War I. Simon became an art collector and patron on a large scale, his largest donation being one of 350 items of Renaissance and Gothic art to the Neues Deutsches Museum in 1920. Ironically, his firm was at the same time in serious economic difficulties caused by the postwar crisis. These difficulties, compounded by his business integrity in a time of economic inflation, eventually caused the decline and bankruptcy (1931) of his firm. With his friend Paul *Nathan, Simon helped found the *Hilfsverein der deutschen Juden (1901), whose chairman he remained until his death. He helped to finance many of its activities, in particular by a 100,000 mark donation for the Haifa *Technion and support of vocational and manual training programs for East European Jews. Another of his achievements was helping to found the Deutsche Orientgesellschaft, which established the reputation of German Orientalists and archaeologists. Simon personally largely financed the excavations of Jericho and Tell el-Amarna.

BIBLIOGRAPHY: E. Feder, in: YLBI, 10 (1965), 3–23; U. Steinmann, *ibid.*, 13 (1968), 277–82.

[Reuven Michael]

SIMON, JEAN HENRI (1752–1834), engraver. Born in Brussels, the son of a seal engraver, Jacob Simon, Simon worked as early as 1767 as a gem engraver for Prince Charles of Lorraine. Moving to Paris, he became an engraver to Louis XVI. He held this position until 1792, when he joined the forces of the French Republic and became a lieutenant colonel in the Republican army. Falsely accused of treason, he fled France and worked as an engraver to the court of Spain. Simon returned with the advent of Napoleon and, after being twice wounded when a colonel in a regiment of lancers, he left the army and was appointed an engraver to the cabinet of Napoleon and engraver of title seals to the empress Josephine. He returned to Brussels after the fall of Napoleon and became engraver to King William I of the Netherlands. The medal production of Simon, though not as well known as his gem engraving, is also extraordinary. The Hague Museum has a fine collection of some two dozen of his medals. Simon engraved a series of 100 medals of illustrious men of the Low Countries. His two brothers, MAYER SIMON (1764–1821), better known as Simon de Paris, and SAMUEL SIMON (b. 1760) had distinguished careers as engravers, as did JEAN MARIE AMABLE SIMON, his son.

BIBLIOGRAPHY: D.M. Friedenberg, in: *The Numismatist* (July 1969), 896–7.

[Daniel M. Friedenberg]

SIMON, SIR JOHN (1818–1897), English lawyer and politician. Simon was the first Jew to practice at the common law bar and exercise the functions of a judge. Born in Jamaica, the son of a merchant, Simon went to England in 1833, graduated from London University in 1841, and was called to the bar a year later. After practicing in Jamaica for two years he returned to England, where he quickly won distinction in the courts. In 1858 he was junior counsel in the state trial following the Orsini conspiracy, a cause célèbre surrounding the attempted assassination of Napoleon III, and in the same year became an assistant to the judges of the county courts. He was later appointed president of the City of London court and became a sergeant-at-law in 1864 and a queen's counsel in January 1868. From 1868 until 1888 Simon was Liberal member of Parliament for Dewsbury. In the House of Commons he availed himself of every opportunity to champion the cause of oppressed Jewry throughout the world, and his efforts to arouse public opinion against the Russian pogroms led the lord mayor of London to convene a public meeting at Guildhall to register British indignation at the czarist persecution of Jews. His devotion to the Jewish cause in parliament led him to be known as "the member for Jewry." Simon was a founder of the Anglo-Jewish Association and a member of the Reform Synagogue. He was not related to either of the other prominent non-Jewish men with the same name as his, the Victorian surgeon and officer of health (1816–1904) or the barrister and cabinet minister (1873–1954), with whom he is sometimes confused. His son OSWALD JOHN SIMON (1855–1932) followed in his father's footsteps and continued to draw the attention of the British public to the plight of East European Jewry.

ADD. BIBLIOGRAPHY: ODNB online.

SIMON, JOSEPH (c. 1712–1804), pioneer U.S. merchant and land speculator. Simon, whose birthplace is unknown, lived in Lancaster, Pennsylvania, in 1732 and opened a general store. His business prospered, and he began to trade with Indians, accepting land in payment for his goods. In addition, the colony of Virginia granted Simon large tracts of land in the area which is now Kentucky. As his holdings were valueless while they remained vacant, Simon encouraged settlement by establishing a network of traders to supply the inhabitants of the backcountry with the goods they required. During the French and Indian War, Simon supplied General Braddock's army, and during the Revolution he performed the same service for General Washington.

BIBLIOGRAPHY: Rosenbloom, Biogr Dict, 159.

[Neil Ovadia]

SIMON, JOSEPH (1844–1915), Hungarian lawyer, secretary of the national council of Hungarian Jews. Born in Kapocs, he became a member and secretary of the Hungarian Jewish Congress of 1868–69, and from 1871 directed the National Council of Hungarian Jews (the *Neologist trend), a position he held through 25 years of stormy conflict. Simon first launched the struggle for opening a rabbinical seminary in 1877. He took up the defense for the accused during the *Tiszaeszlar blood libel case in 1882, and played an active role in the struggle for official recognition of the Jewish religion. Simon initiated a scholarship fund for needy Jewish students in institutions of higher learning, and organized a pension and relief scheme for families of the communal employees. He was among the founders of the Hungarian scholarly periodical **Magyar Zsidó Szemle* and the Jewish literary society Israelita Magyar Irodalmi Társulat (IMIT).

BIBLIOGRAPHY: M. Eisler, in: IMIT (1916), 226–37; L. Venetianer, *A Magyar Zsidóság története* (1922), 304–6; S.K. Endrei, in: *Magyar Zsidó Szemle*, 44 (1927), 230–4; L. Blau, *ibid.*, 50 (1933), 186–7.

[Jeno Zsoldos]

SIMON, JULIUS (1875–1969), Zionist leader and economist. Simon was born in Mannheim, Germany but was an American citizen because his father had participated in the American Civil War. At the height of his economic activities in Germany, particularly in banking, Simon became associated with the Zionist movement, especially after the "practical" Zionist trend began to prevail (1911). During World War I he engaged in banking in Switzerland and Alsace and became associated with the management of the *Jewish National Fund and its director, Nehemia de *Lieme, with whom he worked on its behalf in The Hague. After World War I he was invited by Chaim Weizmann to direct the economic activities of the Zionist Organization and devise economic plans for the period following the Balfour Declaration. It was then that he began to identify with the economic ideas expounded by the U.S. Zionists under the leadership of Louis D. *Brandeis. At the Zionist Conference in London, in July 1920, this group succeeded in appointing him to the Zionist Executive. Together with de Lieme and Robert Szold, he was sent to Palestine (November–December 1920) for the purpose of reorganizing the activities of the Zionist Organization. The report published by this committee (1921), with its scathing criticism of the work of the Zionist Organization and the Zionist Commission, aroused the opposition of Weizmann and the labor sector, as well as that of European Zionists. Its conclusions were not endorsed by the 12th Congress (1921), and Simon and the Brandeis group resigned from their posts in the Zionist Organization. They continued, however, to engage in economic activities in Palestine.

Between the two world wars Simon lived for a time in Jerusalem and later in the United States. He headed the *Palestine Economic Corporation, which played a prominent role in various economic projects in Palestine and remained active in economics until his death. His writings included *Die Juden und die Gebildeten unserer Tage* ("The Jews and the Educated of Our Days," 1916) and *Preparatory Steps for the Jewish Colonization of Palestine* (n.d.).

BIBLIOGRAPHY: R. Weltsch, in: MB (Sept. 7, 1945).

[Getzel Kressel]

SIMON, KATE (1912–1990), U.S. memoirist and travel writer. Born in Warsaw as Kaila Grobsmith to David and Lonia (Babicz) Grobsmith, Simon immigrated to New York City at the age of four with her mother and brother, joining her father, a cobbler, who had arrived three years earlier. Married twice, Simon wrote under the name of her second husband, Robert Simon, from whom she was divorced in 1960.

Simon received a B.A. from Hunter College and held various editorial positions. Her first book, *New York Places and Pleasures* (1959), written in a lively style and filled with little-known facts and unusual destinations, remains a classic guide to New York City. Simon wrote similar highly popular travel guides to Italy, London, Mexico, and Paris in the *Places and Pleasures* series between 1963 and 1978.

Simon's three memoirs, *Bronx Primitive: Portraits in a Childhood* (1982), *A Wider World: Portraits of an Adolescence* (1986), and *Etchings in an Hourglass* (1990), describe her childhood, youth, and adulthood, recounting her intellectual and social journey from the confines of a poor, ethnically mixed neighborhood to a cosmopolitan life of adventuresome travel. Simon's autobiographical writings bring a strong and unsentimental feminist focus to the Jewish immigrant experience. They are unusual in their frank depictions of such topics as sexuality and its ramifications, including child molestation and the lack of reliable birth control methods; familial discord; abandonment of religious tradition; her involvement in left wing politics; and the personal tragedies Simon experienced, including the deaths of her first husband, her daughter, and her sister from brain tumors, and the failure of her second marriage in the late 1950s.

BIBLIOGRAPHY: "Simon, Kate," in: *Encyclopedia Britannica*; M. Galchinsky. "Simon, Kate," in: P.E. Hyman and D.D. Moore (eds.), *Jewish Women in America*, vol. 2 (1997), 1261–62.

[Judith R. Baskin (2nd ed.)]

SIMON, SIR LEON (1881–1965), English Zionist leader, Hebrew writer, and British civil servant. Born in Southampton and educated at Manchester Grammar School and Oxford, in 1904 Simon entered the service of the General Post Office, becoming director of telegraphs and telephones (1931–35) and director of the savings bank (1935–44). For his services, he was knighted in 1944. Simon received a Jewish and Hebrew education from his father, a Manchester rabbi. He was particularly influenced by *Aḥad Ha-Am, who settled in London in 1907. He was also a member of the group of Zionists who were influenced by Chaim *Weizmann and supported his political efforts during World War I that led to the *Balfour Declaration (the Hebrew version of the Declaration was written by Simon). Simon was a member of the *Zionist Commission that visited Palestine in 1918 and took part in laying the cornerstone of the Hebrew University in Jerusalem. Later he served as chairman of the university's Executive Council (1946–49) and Board of Governors (1950–53). In 1945–46 he was a member of the Commission of Inquiry into Jewish Education in Palestine, on behalf of the British government. The only Jew on the commission, Simon objected to the conclusion that English should be the language of instruction in higher education. He lived in Jerusalem from 1946 to 1953; during that period he also worked in the Israeli Ministry of Posts, laying the plans for the post office bank (1950–53). After his return to England, he continued his association with several cultural projects in Israel.

Simon was a brilliant writer in both English and Hebrew. He published essays and articles in English on Zionism and Hebrew culture and literature. Some of his essays were collected in *Studies in Jewish Nationalism* (1920). He edited the anthology *Aspects of The Hebrew Genius: Essays on Jewish Literature and Thought* (1910) and wrote *The Case of the Anti-Zionists: A Reply* (1917) and *Zionism and the Jewish Problem* (1918). Together with Leonard Stein, he edited *Awakening Palestine* (1923). Simon's main work in English is his translation of Aḥad Ha-Am's writings, which were first published in journals and later in books (a list of translations and their editions is to be found in Goell, Bibliography, 83–84). In collaboration with J. Heller, Simon wrote a book entitled *Aḥad Ha-Am: Asher Ginzburg* (Heb., 1955; Eng., 1960), and together with I. Pograbinski he edited the second edition of Aḥad Ha-Am's letters (6 vols., 1956–60).

From 1910 Simon began to publish a series of essays in Hebrew on Greek literature (the first of their kind in Hebrew) in *Ha-Shiloʾaḥ*. They were later collected (1951) in his book *Perakim be-Sifrut Yavan ha-Attikah* ("Chapters on Ancient Greek Literature," 1951). He also translated into Hebrew seven of Plato's *Dialogues*, the *Memoirs* of Xenophon, and *On Liberty* by John Stuart Mill. On his 80th birthday, an anthology, *Eshkolot*, dedicated to the study of classical culture and including a bibliography by Ḥaim Toren (4th vol., 1960), was published in his honor.

[Getzel Kressel]

His brother, MAURICE SIMON (1874–1955), a Hebraist and translator, was born in Manchester. Because of a breakdown in health, Simon lived in South Africa for a while. Later he became associated with the work of the Soncino Press, founded in London by his relative J. Davidson, and was cotranslator (into English) of the *Zohar* (1931–34) and *Midrash Rabbah* (1939). He also cooperated in the Soncino translation of the Talmud (1935–52) and its Minor Tractates (1965). Simon edited the *Speeches, Articles and Letters of Israel Zangwill* (1937) and was coeditor of the *Essays and Addresses, by Samuel Daiches* (1955). He also wrote *Jewish Religious Conflicts* (1950) and numerous short studies in periodicals and reviews.

[Ruth P. Lehmann]

BIBLIOGRAPHY: Kressel, Leksikon, 2 (1967), 497f.

SIMON, NEIL (1927–), U.S. playwright. After working for television, Simon wrote his first successful comedy, *Come Blow Your Horn* (1961), which was followed by the book for the musical *Little Me* (1962), *Barefoot in the Park* (1963), *The Odd Couple* (1965), *Sweet Charity* (1966), and *Plaza Suite* (1968). Some of these were successfully adapted for the screen.

Simon's play, *God's Favorite* (1975), based on the Book of Job, in which a "messenger from God" announces to a successful cardboard box manufacturer that his faith in God is to be put to test, was widely acclaimed.

Very often, Simon bases his plays on autobiographical experiences and observations. Three plays from the 1980s, sometimes referred to as the "Eugene Trilogy," parallel the growth of Simon from teenager to successful writer. *Brighton Beach Memoirs* (1984) centers on Eugene Jerome, a Jewish adolescent growing up in 1930s Brooklyn. The characters, particularly Eugene's family, are taken from Simon's own childhood memories; Stanley, the brother whom Eugene idolizes, is based on Simon's brother Danny. *Biloxi Blues* (1986) follows Eugene's experience in army basic training during World War II. Away from his family and his Brooklyn neighborhood, he is confronted with fellow trainees from a variety of locales and backgrounds. Eugene also finds time to fall in love, lose his virginity, and confront an apparently psychotic drill instructor. In short, he grows up in this play. *Broadway Bound* (1987) relates Eugene and Stanley's attempt to break into comedy writing. The dissolution of their parents' marriage becomes fodder for their comedy sketches. At the end of the play, Eugene leaves home when his writing career takes flight, the boy at last becoming a man.

He wrote more comedies, among them *The Prisoner of Second Avenue* (1972), *The Sunshine Boys* (1973), *The Good Doctor* (1974), *Rumors* (1990), *Jake's Women* (1993), and *Laughter on the 23rd Floor* (1995), a play based on his time as one of Sid Caesar's television comedy writers. His *Plaza Suite* (1971) and *Chapter Two* (1979) were made into films, as were *The Prisoner of Second Avenue* (1975) and *The Sunshine Boys* (1975). He wrote the screenplay for *The Odd Couple II* (1998), a sequel to his play. His other writing includes the memoirs *Rewrites* (1996) and *The Play Goes On* (1999).

BIBLIOGRAPHY: R.K. Johnson, *Neil Simon* (1983); S. Fehrenbacher Koprince, *Understanding Neil Simon* (2002); E.M. McGovern, *Neil Simon: A Critical Study* (1979).

[Robert L. DelBane (2nd ed.)]

SIMON, NORTON (1907–1993), U.S. industrialist. Simon was born in Portland, Oregon. His business career began in 1932 when he bought a small food-packing plant. He developed his company into Hunt Foods Inc., which by 1943 had become one of the largest food-processing businesses on the West Coast. From this modest start, he developed a rapidly expanding diversified industrial complex, the holding company Norton Simon Inc., which included food processing and packaging, container manufacturing, soft drink industries, printing, and publishing, such as McCalls Publishing, *The Saturday Review of Literature*, Max Factor, Canada Dry, and Avis Car Rental. In 1969 Simon resigned as director and finance committee member of the holding company to concentrate on his cultural and educational interests through several foundations, mainly established to acquire and display works of art, to provide scholarships, and to support various charities. One major program of the foundations was the loan of art to public museums and universities. The *Duveen collection is centered on the Old Masters; other collections include paintings, drawings, and sculpture of the 19th and 20th centuries.

In 1974, seeking a permanent home for his collection, he was approached by the Pasadena Museum of Modern Art, of which he ultimately assumed control and the naming rights. Today, the Norton Simon Museum of Art in Pasadena has an extensive permanent collection of Western and Asian art, and promotes art education through special exhibitions, tours, and lectures.

Simon was married to actress Jennifer Jones from 1971.

BIBLIOGRAPHY: D. Mahoney, *Growth and Social Responsibility: The Story of Norton Simon Inc.* (1973).

[Joachim O. Ronall / Ruth Beloff (2nd ed.)]

SIMON, PAUL FREDERIC (1941–), U.S. pop and folk music songwriter known both for his collaboration with childhood friend Arthur ("Art") *Garfunkel and for three decades of solo albums; member of the Rock and Roll Hall of Fame. Simon was born in Newark, N.J., to Belle and Louis, a professional bassist who performed in television orchestras. The family relocated to Queens, New York, when Simon was in grade school, where he met Garfunkel. In 1957, Simon and Garfunkel were performing together as "Tom and Jerry," concerned that their real names sounded too Jewish, and recorded a minor hit song, "Hey Schoolgirl." Simon attended Queens College, where he earned a degree in English literature but spent a great deal of time on the fringes of New York's Brill Building songwriting scene. In 1964 Simon left for London to escape the insular New York folk music scene, which was dominated by Bob *Dylan. Simon maintained an antipathy to Dylan for decades, only resolving it with a joint tour in 1999. Simon and Garfunkel reunited in 1964 and helped create the wave of "folk rock" music. A version of "The Sound of Silence" from their first album, *Wednesday Morning 3 A.M.*, with electric guitar, bass, and drums, hit No. 1 on the pop charts. They followed up with a string of albums and songs that heralded the era of politically influenced, confessional singers, including *Parsley, Sage, Rosemary & Thyme* (1966), and the soundtrack of the 1967 film *The Graduate* (starring Dustin *Hoffman and Anne Bancroft), with the multiple Grammy-winning song, "Mrs. Robinson." *Bridge Over Troubled Water* (1970), Simon and Garfunkel's final album together, was their biggest hit. The gospel-influenced title song presaged the 1970s' search for spiritual tranquility following the turbulent 1960s, and spent six weeks at #1. The album included three other Top-20 hits: "El Condor Pasa" (#18), "Cecilia" (#4), and "The Boxer" (#7), and won eight Grammy Awards. The duo split after that, but periodically returned to tour together, including a 2004 concert at Rome's Colosseum that drew 600,000. Simon recorded successful solo albums in the 1970s, peaking with *Still Crazy After All These Years* (1975), which topped the charts, won the Grammy for Album of the Year, and included his only solo No. 1 single, "50 Ways to Leave Your Lover." In 1986 Simon released *Graceland*, which brought African music into the mainstream and paid homage to rock pioneer and early influence Elvis Presley in the title track about Presley's home, Graceland. It featured South African artists and rhythms and presaged the fall of that country's apartheid regime, but was criticized for abetting the white-led government. *Graceland* became Simon's biggest-selling solo album, and was named the Album of the Year. By 2005, Simon had released 41 albums including reissues, and placed nine solo tunes in the Top 20. Simon and Garfunkel had placed seven songs in the Top 10, including three No. 1 hits. Like many American Jewish songwriters, Simon rarely made overt reference to his religion or background. In his 1983 album *Hearts and Bones*, which chronicles the breakup of his marriage to half-Jewish actress Carrie *Fisher, Simon referred to "one and one half wandering Jews." He and Garfunkel were named to the Rock and Roll Hall of Fame in 1991, and Simon went in on his own in 2000. He received Kennedy Center Honors in 2002. Simon appeared in the 1977 Woody *Allen film *Annie Hall.*

[Alan D. Abbey (2nd ed.)]

SIMON, PIERRE (1925–), French physician and politician. Simon was born to a typical Jewish family from Alsace-Lorraine in which rationalism and tradition were combined. After World War II, he engaged in the two domains of gynecology and endocrinology in which the status and representation of women and life are implied. In 1953, he brought to France from the U.S.S.R. new obstetrical methods of painless childbirth, violently criticized at the times both by the church and the right-wing medical establishment. Despite the fact that in the France of the 1950s regulating birth was still a religious question, Simon introduced contraceptive methods, and notably the intra-uterine device which he named "stérilet." In 1956, he was active in the foundation of French Family Planning, which was aimed at educating medical staff in scientific innovations and progressive ideas regarding childbirth. Gaining the support at first of teachers and Protestants, Family Planning had to overcome the strong opposition of the Communist Party and of the right wing and Church representatives. The fight for contraceptive methods was then linked to political commitment, since the French law of July 1920 criminalized abortion as well as birth control promotion. In 1951, Simon created the Jacobin Club with Ch. Hernu, of the Radical Party, and conducted a public debate at the Commissariat au Plan. Taking into account the fact that French society was not yet ready to accept the idea of birth control, his first struggle was to dissociate the notions of abortion and birth control. In this regard, his *Contrôle des Naissances, Histoire, philosophie, morale* (1966) was a success, since it led to the passing, in 1967, of the so-called Neuwirth Law, legalizing contraceptive methods in France. He gained support from the Freemasons, in which he was active, and served as a member of several government cabinets. Author of the *Simon Report* about the French attitudes toward sexuality, known as the "French Kinsey" (1971), Simon was the first to conjoin sociological approaches and political thought in order to rethink sexuality. The legalization of abortion, by the so-called "Veil Law" (see Simone *Veil) enacted in 1975 was the realization of his efforts. As a Grand Master of the Grand Lodge of France (1969–71; 1973–75), Simon initiated a dialogue between the Catholic Church and Masonry – which had previously been anathematized by the Church. During the 1980s he pursued the fight for his ideals and was active in favor of the methods of artificial reproduction, simultaneously involving himself in the rethinking of the period of the end of life in the movement for the "right to die with dignity."

Among other books, he wrote *Rapport sur le comportement sexuel des Français* (1971), *De la vie avant toute chose* (1979), and *La Franc-Maçonnerie* (1997).

[Perrine Simon-Nahum (2nd ed.)]

SIMON, RALPH (1906–1996), U.S. Conservative rabbi. Simon was born in Newark, New Jersey, and received his B.A. from New York's City College in 1927. In 1931, he was ordained at the *Jewish Theological Seminary, and served as rabbi of Congregation Rodef Shalom in Johnstown, Pennsylvania (1931–36), and the Jewish Center of Jackson Heights in Queens, New York (1937–43). He was appointed rabbi of Congregation Rodfei Zedek in Hyde Park, Illinois (1943–1996; emeritus in 1987). Under Simon's leadership, Rodfei Zedek became one of the leading Conservative synagogues in metropolitan Chicago, boasting a Hebrew high school and model adult education institute. Simon served as president of the Chicago Board of Rabbis (1952–54), on the Board of Directors of the Jewish Federation of Metropolitan Chicago (1954–66), and as general chairman of Metropolitan Chicago's Israel Bonds Organization (1965–66). He was also vice chairman of the Illinois Board of Mental Health Commissioners (1955–62) and a member of the Chicago Commission on Human Resources (1958–71) and the Chicago Youth Welfare Commission (1956–63).

Simon is credited with one of the greatest initiatives of Conservative Judaism: the establishment of the first Camp *Ramah, in Wisconsin in 1947, the progenitor of a series of Hebrew-speaking, religiously oriented summer camps operating under the auspices of the Conservative movement. In 1968, he was elected president of the *Rabbinical Assembly (1968–70), where he worked to strengthen the Masorati movement in Israel and launched a program for the conversion of non-Jewish spouses of intermarried couples. He also brought his ecumenical activism as former president of the multi-racial Hyde Park–Kenwood Interfaith Council to the national post, inviting the still-controversial Martin Luther King to address the RA. In 1974, he was nominated to the Board of Directors of the *World Council of Synagogues.

Simon wrote *The Talmud for Every Jew* (1942) for the National Academy of Adult Jewish Studies and *Challenges and Responses,* a collection of his sermons (1985). His son Matthew was also a Conservative rabbi of B'nai Israel in Rockville, Maryland.

[Bezalel Gordon (2nd ed.)]

°**SIMON, RICHARD** (1638–1721), Catholic priest of the Oratorians Order. Simon first became interested in the Jews of his day while studying Hebrew at the Sorbonne. In order to further his studies, particularly in rabbinic literature, he established a friendship with an Italian Jew, a tobacco merchant named Jonah Salvador, even planning to cooperate with him in translating the Talmud. When Salvador informed him about the persecution of the Jews of *Metz resulting from the blood libel raised against Raphael Lévi, Simon came to their defense in his *Factum servant de réponse au Livre intitulé: Abrégé procès fait aux Juifs de Metz* (1670), a work which was widely circulated. Refuting the libel, the author recalled that Christians too had been the victims of similar accusations and that the popes themselves had come to the defense of the Jews on this account. On one occasion he demonstrated his solidarity with persecuted Jews of his day by signing a questionnaire for the Oratory as R. Simeon b. Joachim. Later, in his introduction to *Cérémonies et coûtumes qui s'observent aujourd'hui parmi les juifs* (Paris, 1674), his translation of Leone *Modena's *Historia dei riti ebraici*, Simon declared that it is impossible to understand the Christian religion without some instruction in that of the Jews, on which it was patterned. He published a supplement to this work in 1681, entitled *Comparaison des cérémonies des juifs et de la discipline de l'Eglise*. Between these two books he published his major work, *Histoire critique du Vieux Testament* (Paris, 1678), which gave rise to a storm of controversy. Simon was expelled from the Oratory and virtually the whole edition of *Histoire critique* was destroyed. In this book he relied to a great extent on the orientalist Gaulmin, one of the leading Christian scholars of talmudic and rabbinic literature in his day, although subsequently, and unjustly, almost completely forgotten. Simon was even more severe than Gaulmin in his strictures on Jewish writers, and in his later work, *Histoire critique des principaux commentateurs du Nouveau Testament* (Rotterdam, 1692), he was equally harsh in his attacks on hallowed Church doctrines. Simon s other works bear further witness to his scholarship, his insight into biblical criticism, and his fearlessness of controversial topics.

BIBLIOGRAPHY: F. Stummer, *Bedeutung Richard Simons fuer die Pentateuchkritik* (1912); J. Steinmann, *Richard Simon* (Fr., 1960), 33ff. and passim; G.H. Box, in: E.R. Bevan and C. Singer (eds.), *Legacy of Israel* (1927), 363–4; R. Anchel, *Juifs de France* (1946), 130, 139; F. Secret, *Kabbalistes chrétiens de la Renaissance* (1964), index.

[Bernhard Blumenkranz]

SIMON, SHLOME (1895–1970), Yiddish educator and children's author. Born in Kalinkovichi (Belorussia), Simon had a traditional education and worked as a village *melammed* before immigrating to the U.S. in 1913. After working in various jobs and serving in the army during World War I, he taught in Hebrew schools and became a dentist. Extensively active in Jewish education, for 15 years he was president of the Sholem Aleichem Folk Institute, edited the Yiddish children's magazine *Kinder-Zhurnal*, published extensively on Yiddish folklore, the Bible, and Jewish problems in Yiddish periodicals throughout Europe and North America, and wrote numerous children's books in Yiddish (some translated into English by his son, David), among them *Vortslen* (*My Jewish Roots*, 1956), *Tsvaygn* (*In the Thicket*, 1960), *Di Heldn fun Khelm* (*The Wise Men of Chelm*, 1942), and *Kluge Hent* ("Clever Hands," 1973)

BIBLIOGRAPHY: LNYL, 6 (1961), 413–5.

[Sol Liptzin / Jerold C. Frakes (2nd ed.)]

SIMON, SIDNEY (1917–1997), U.S. painter, sculptor, educator. Born in Pittsburgh, Pennsylvania, Simon studied at the Art Students League, the Pennsylvania Academy of Fine Art, and the Carnegie Institute. During the Depression, Simon executed murals for the Federal Arts Project. While a second lieutenant in World War II, he served as an official war artist, observing and depicting action in the Southwest Pacific theater, including New Guinea and the Phillippines. He was one of three artists appointed to the headquarters of Gen. Douglas MacArthur. His composition *USS Missouri* depicts an assembly of troops on the surface of an aircraft carrier, in the midst of combat. Simon underscores the moment's tension and energy by accelerating the viewer's gaze through the composition along two strong diagonal axes, one formed by the protruding gun turrets. After the war, Simon developed a successful career as a painter and sculptor. In 1960 he turned completely to sculpture; his work from this period demonstrates a range of styles, from classical realism to pop assemblage. The artist's 1961 assemblage *Kiosk* shows Simon appropriating motifs from his contemporaries Jasper Johns and Robert Rauschenberg, specifically in the introduction of letters in addition to reference to the human figure; in this wood construction, Simon situates a figure made of maplewood typeset (which never coheres into any words) behind a structure recalling a newspaper stand. The figure is framed by rectangular objects hanging diagonally (also fashioned of type), as magazines might be displayed. Simon executed many commissions including the entrance sculpture to the 747 Building (1972), New York, the West Point Jewish Chapel (1985), and the Graham Building, Philadelphia (1986). He obtained numerous prizes throughout his career, including the Greer Prize (1983), the National Academy of Design Award, the Adna Silver Medal, and the National Arts Club Award (1982). With artists Henry Varnum Poor, Charles Cutler, and Willard Cummings, he founded the Skowhegan School of Painting and Sculpture. His work has been exhibited at the Corcoran Gallery, the Museum of Modern Art, the National Gallery of Art, and the Whitney Museum, among other venues. The Corcoran Gallery, the Metropolitan Museum of Art, New York University, and the United States Air Force all own examples of his work.

BIBLIOGRAPHY: P.H. Falls, *Who Was Who in American Art* (1985); W.C. Seitz, *The Art of Assemblage* (1961).

[Nancy Buchwald (2nd ed.)]

SIMON, TAMÁS (1935–1956), Hungarian poet and playwright. His poetic novel *Don Juan* interpreted the famous story in a Jewish setting. After great suffering, he committed suicide.

SIMONA (sixth century), Babylonian *savora*. Simona was the head of the Pumbedita academy during the second savoraic generation. He was a contemporary of R. Eina, the head of Sura Academy (*Iggeret R. Sherira* ed. by Lewin p. 99). The two rabbis were responsible for additional notes to the Talmud (*ibid.*, 71). *Seder Tanna'im ve-Amora'im* gives the name of Simona's colleague as R. Giza and states: "They (Giza and Simona) did not add to or expand anything, but introduced paragraphing into everything taught." In addition, they divided the discussions in the Talmud according to the individual *mishnayot* and inserted opening phrases from the Mishnah in the talmudic discussions – a device which is lacking in the Jerusalem Talmud. *Seder Tana'im ve-Amora'im* praises the two rabbis very highly, saying that "by their merit heaven and earth were created," and with them the activity of the **savoraim* ended.

[Arie Strikovsky]

SIMONE, ANDRÉ (**Otto Katz**; 1895–1952), Czech journalist and Communist activist. Born into a bourgeois German family, he became a Communist in his youth, contributing regularly to the Communist press in Czechoslovakia and later in Germany. He joined the KPD in 1922, when he moved to Berlin to work for the publishing house of Leopold Schwarzschild. Siding with L. *Trotsky, he left the party in 1926. Beginning in 1927, he worked for the German theater director Erwin Piscator and, starting in 1929, in close cooperation with Willi Muenzenberg (1889–1940), for the Universum library of the Internationale Arbeiterhilfe (IAH). In 1930 Katz escaped a tax trial, leaving for Moscow, where he managed the Mežrabpom film company. When Hitler came to power in 1933, Katz was called to Paris to support Muenzenberg in his anti-Fascist work. From 1936 to 1939, Katz was involved in the Spanish Civil War, leading the Republican press agency "Agence d'Espagne" in Paris under his assumed name André Simone. In 1938, he joined the editorial staff of *L'Ordre*. After the outbreak of World War II he escaped to the United States and, in the summer of 1940, went on to Mexico. There he was among the founders of the Mexican branch of the KPD, the journal *Freies Deutschland*, and the publishing house El Libro Libre. In 1942, however, he worked as an advisor for the Latin American trade union, and in 1944 became an editorial staff member of the pro-Zionist *Tribuna Israelitica*. Returning to Prague in 1946, he was readmitted to the Communist party and was appointed foreign affairs editor of the party organ *Rudé Právo* and editor of the political review *Svetové rozhledy* ("World Views"). In the *Slánský trial in 1952, he was among those accused of "Trotskyite-Titoist-Zionist" activities, sentenced to death, and executed. In 1963, Simone was fully rehabilitated and in 1968 was posthumously awarded the Order of the Czech Republic. Among his works are *Neun Männer im Eis* (1929), *Das Braune Netz* (1935), *Spione und Verschwörer in Spanien* (1936), *J'accuse. The men who betrayed France* (1940), *Men of Europe* (1941), and *La batalla de Rusia* (1943).

BIBLIOGRAPHY: W. Sternfeld / E. Tiedemann (eds.), *Deutsche Exil-Literatur 1933–1945* (21970), 257; BHdE 1 (1980), 352–3; *Handbuch österreichischer Autorinnen und Autoren jüdischer Herkunft 18. bis 20. Jahrhundert* 1 (2002), No. 5004.

[Avigdor Dagan / Johannes Valentin Schwarz (2nd ed.)]

SIMONS, JAMES H. (1938–), U.S. mathematician, hedge-fund owner. A graduate of the Massachusetts Institute of Technology, Jim Simons earned a doctorate in mathematics from the University of California at Berkeley. From 1961 to 1964 he taught mathematics at MIT and Harvard University. In 1968 he became chairman of the math department at the State University of New York at Stony Brook. Simons was also a crypt analyst, or code breaker, and did important work in mathematics that helped lay the foundation for string theory. In the late 1970s he left academia to run a fund that traded in commodities and financial instruments on a discretionary basis. Over the next quarter of a century, his company, Renaissance Technologies, which uses computer-based models to predict price changes in easily traded financial instruments, was at the forefront of research in mathematics and economic analysis. Renaissance's models were based on analyzing as much data as can be gathered, then looking for nonrandom movements to make predictions. In 2006, Renaissance managed over $5 billion of hedge fund assets on which, over the previous 10 years, the compounded return was approximately 40 percent. Renaissance Technologies' Hedge Fund, the Medallion Fund, was perhaps the most successful large hedge fund ever. It was closed to new investors after 1991. In 2006 Simons was launching the Renaissance Institutional Equities Fund, designed to handle upwards of $100 billion, one that would become the industry's largest. The minimum investment was set at $20 million.

[Stewart Kampel (2nd ed.)]

SIMONSEN, DAVID JACOB (1853–1932), Danish rabbi, scholar, and bibliophile. Born in Copenhagen, Simonsen was the son of Jacob Simonsen, a banker and leader of the Jewish community. He studied Oriental languages at the University of Copenhagen and in 1874 was admitted to the Jewish theological seminary in Breslau where he was ordained as rabbi. He then returned to Copenhagen to assist the aged chief rabbi, Abraham Alexander *Wolff. When Wolff died in 1891 Simonsen was chosen to succeed him but he resigned his office in 1902. During a vacancy in the Copenhagen rabbinate from 1918 to 1920 he again functioned as rabbi.

When the Jews from Eastern Europe reached Denmark about 1904 after the *Kishinev pogroms, he helped them to integrate in their new home. During World War I, he led activities on behalf of war victims, taking special interest in the Jewish community in Palestine. An enthusiastic book collector, Simonsen had a library of about 40,000 volumes covering every field in Judaism, which he presented to the Royal Library of Copenhagen in the last year of his life; it now constitutes the principal part of the Judaica department, called "Bibliotheca judaica Simonseniana" in his honor.

Simonsen had an extensive Jewish knowledge but his literary output was confined mainly to scholarly articles. In addition, he contributed to the *Dansk biografisk leksikon*, the *Jewish Encyclopaedia*, *Juedisches Lexikon*, the German *Encyclopaedia Judaica*, and the Danish *Tidsskrift for jodisk historie og literatur.* Simonsen published a descriptive catalog in Danish and French of sculptures and inscriptions from Palmyra in the Glypothek in Copenhagen (1889), a treatise on the history of Hebrew printing (1901), and a translation into Danish of Jewish tales and legends (1928). About 100 of his articles are listed in the festschrift dedicated to him on the occasion of his 70th birthday (*Festskrift… David Simonsen*, Hebrew title *Nir David*, 1923).

BIBLIOGRAPHY: *Israeliter* (March 17, 1923); JC (June 24, 1932); Montzen, in: *American Hebrew* (Sept. 2, 1932); R. Edelmann, in: *Hokhmat Yisrael be-Ma'arav Eiropah*, 1 (1958), 361–8; *Feskrift i Anledning of Professor David Simonsens 70 Aaars Føselsdag* (1923).

[Julius Margolinsky]

SIMONSOHN, SHLOMO (1923–), Israeli historian. Simonsohn was born in Breslau, but immigrated to Ereẓ Israel as a child in 1933 and studied at the Hebrew University. From 1942 until 1947 he was a member of the *Haganah. He received his doctorate from London University. In 1957, he was appointed head of the department of Jewish history at Tel Aviv University, a position he held until 1988. From 1961 until 1964 he served as the director of the central library. He became a full professor in 1968. From 1969 to 1971 he was the dean of the Jewish Studies School, and from 1969 to 1992 the director of the Diaspora Research Institute. In 1970 he was one of the founders of the Bet Berl Teachers Training College. In the same year he was also one of the founders of the Diaspora Museum, serving on its board. Simonsohn served as rector of the University in 1971–77, while in the years 1973–74 he was also the chairman of the President's and Rector's Committee. He retired in 1993 and became chairman of the Diaspora Research Institute council. Simonsohn devoted himself mainly to the history of the Jews in Italy, on which he has published *Leon de Modena* (1953); *Magen va-Ḥerev* (1960), on Leone *Modena's anti-Christian tract; and *Toledot ha-Yehudim be-Dukkasut Mantovah* (2 vols., 1962–64). He was one of the founders and leaders of "Shurat ha-Mitnadvim," a voluntary public movement that was active in Israel in the 1950s with the aim of raising the standards of public life. Simonsohn was awarded the Ben Zvi Award in 1964 and the Shazar Award in 1996.

[Shaked Gilboa (2nd ed.)]

SIMON WIESENTHAL CENTER, Los Angeles international human rights organization originally aimed at Holocaust remembrance. Founded in 1977 by Rabbi Marvin *Hier, as The Simon Wiesenthal Center for Holocaust Studies the center opened its doors in Los Angeles two years later.

Named for Holocaust survivor and Nazi hunter Simon *Wiesenthal, the center's initial mission was to promote remembrance of the Holocaust, its victims and its perpetrators.

With widening interest in other fields, the name was shortened to Simon Wiesenthal Center; it defined its status as an international human rights organization, with a membership of more than 400,000 families. It continues its emphasis on Holocaust remembrance "by fostering tolerance and understanding through education, outreach and social action," and the prosecution of Nazi war criminals. It membership was gained by the skillful use of direct mail, just as the science of direct mail was beginning to flourish and was becoming an integral part of American political life. Thus, unlike B'nai B'rith, which has lodges, or the ADL, which has individual chapters and boards, and Hadassah, which is shaped by local and regional chapters, Simon Wiesenthal's membership is its base of contributors.

In expanding its original mission, the Center confronts contemporary issues, including racism, antisemitism, terrorism, and genocide. It monitors and acts on developments in Israel and the Middle East, extremist groups, neo-Nazism, and hate on the Internet.

The first major American Jewish institution to establish its headquarters in Los Angeles and on the West Coast, the center maintains offices in New York, Toronto, Miami, Jerusalem, Paris, and Buenos Aires, and is accredited as a nongovernmental organization (NGO) to the United Nations and UNESCO. Its Jerusalem office, headed by Efraim *Zuroff, is the one arm of the center that is actively engaged in hunting Nazi war criminals; it was instrumental in engaging post-communist East European countries in focusing of their war-time record of collaboration and cooperation with allied or occupying German forces in implementing the final solution. Its Paris office, headed by Shimon Samuels, organizes its efforts with the NGO and has been active in the fight against antisemitism in early 21st century Europe.

In 1993, the center opened the Museum of Tolerance, adjoining its Los Angeles headquarters, as a high-tech, hands-on experiential museum, which uses interactive exhibits to involve visitors in two major themes: the dynamics of racism and prejudice in America and the history of the Holocaust. The museum is called Beit Hashoah in Hebrew and the Museum of Tolerance in English, thus giving differently shaded emphasis to its double mission. The Holocaust part of the exhibition is portrayed not through artifacts but through innovative dramatization of key themes, which, by the use of sound, light, and action, pulses the visitor through each exhibition at a set pace.

During the first decade of its existence, the Museum of Tolerance received some four million visitors. An additional 110,000 public school students annually tour the exhibits as part of their studies.

The museum's Tools for Tolerance program conducts courses for American and foreign law enforcement officers, educators, judges, and other professionals, while many more people are reached through Internet programs, documentaries, teaching guides, conferences, and collaborative projects with ethnic community groups.

Using its own in-house production facilities, the Wiesenthal Center's Moriah Films division won Academy Awards for two of its feature documentaries, *Genocide*, narrated by Elizabeth Taylor and Orson Welles, in 1981, and *The Long Way Home* in 1997. These accomplishments forged close ties with glamorous Hollywood stars, who grace the center's banquets and public events.

In two major expansion moves in 2005, the Wiesenthal Center opened its New York Tolerance Center and broke ground in Jerusalem for the Center for Human Dignity–Museum of Tolerance, scheduled to open in 2009. When completed, the new complex, designed by Los Angeles architect Frank O. Gehry, will consist of seven buildings, including a museum, theater complex, international conference center, education center, and library. The idea of the Jerusalem center was met with considerable opposition by many Israelis and by Yad Vashem, the state's official Holocaust memorial authority.

Partially in response to such objections, the Wiesenthal Center pledged that its new project would not deal with the Holocaust, but stress tolerance among the different ethnic and religious groups within Israel, and between Jews and adherents of other faiths.

The New York Center in Manhattan functions mainly as a multimedia training facility, which has adapted the Tools for Tolerance program in courses for police, teachers, and others.

From its very beginning, under the leadership of Hier and his closest associate, Rabbi Abraham Cooper, the center's modus operandi has been characterized by bold, aggressive actions in response to perceived antisemitism or neo-Nazism anywhere in the world. Barely opened, the center in 1979 launched a successful national campaign to pressure the German chancellor and administration into rescinding the statute of limitations on the prosecution of Nazi war criminals. It played a highly public role in advancing the Office of Special Investigation of the Department of Justice, which was the arm of the American government that was responsible for the prosecution of Nazi war criminals. Martin Mendelsohn and Zuroff, who formerly served on the OSI staff, now work with the Wiesenthal Center.

The campaign's success put the center on the front page of the *New York Times* and on the map of Jewish organizational life. The center has never joined the Conference of Presidents of Major American Jewish Organizations, is perceived as a lone actor, and has often used this outsider status to its own advantage.

In other well-reported interventions, the center brought wider recognition to the World War II rescue efforts of Swedish diplomat Raoul Wallenberg, prodded Chile and other South American countries to extradite resident Nazi fugitives, offered a $1 million reward for information leading to the capture of Auschwitz doctor Josef Mengele, and sent a mission to the Soviet Union to investigate the plight of Jewish refuseniks.

In 1985, the center was part of the international protest against President Reagan's visit to a German military cemetery in Bitburg. Two years later, the center gathered 250,000 signatures on a petition to the Vatican to establish full diplomatic relations with Israel.

Following a fact-finding mission to Japan, the center drew attention to the proliferation of antisemitic works in Tokyo bookstores.

In the late 1980s and early 1990s, Hier helped organize an international conference on Jewish solidarity with Israel and engaged in a correspondence with Chancellor Helmut Kohl on the obligations facing a reunified Germany. Hier himself personifies the more aggressive and often more militant attitude of contemporary American Orthodoxy, though on the issue of tolerance, his is a strongly moderating influence in the Orthodox community.

Other campaigns have targeted anti-Israel actress Vanessa Redgrave, Holocaust deniers, Russian skinheads, Swiss banks, and black extremist Louis Farrakhan.

Exhibits have dramatized, among other topics, genocides of Armenians and Rwandans, the civil rights movement, and immigrants in the United States. In the early 21st century, the center was accused of diminishing its consideration of the Armenians in order not to gain the disfavor of the Turkish government, an important moderate, democratic Muslim ally of the United States and Israel.

The Center's high profile has drawn the attention of numerous critics from the very beginning. A Los Angeles group of survivors, which had been planning its own Holocaust museum for many years under the auspices of the Jewish Federation Council, the communal umbrella organization, was deeply resentful when the quick-acting Hier preempted their plans and secured the endorsement of Simon Wiesenthal.

In subsequent years, the Wiesenthal Center and its leaders have been criticized for a variety of reasons.

Hier's dual role as head of the center, as well as "dean" of Yeshiva University of Los Angeles, has come under fire, especially in light of some $50 million appropriated by the State of California for the Wiesenthal Center up to 2005, which critics contend violates the separation of church and state.

An early criticism, which has somewhat lessened with time, centers on the high-tech, interactive approach of the Museum of Tolerance exhibits, which, some complain, has given Holocaust remembrance a touch of Disneyland.

However, the popular success of the Museum of Tolerance has spawned some imitations and appears to endorse its 21st century multimedia approach.

The Wiesenthal Center has also earned the dislike of older established defense and communal organizations for allegedly encroaching on their "turf," assuming the role of spokesman for the entire Jewish people, and purposely exaggerating the dangers of antisemitism. Regarded as alarmist by some, its scholarly resources and achievements have also been challenged by critics.

[Tom Tugend (2nd ed.)]

SIMSON, early American New York family. SOLOMON (1738–1801) was born in New York City. A prominent merchant, he and his family were active throughout their lives in the Spanish-Portuguese Congregation Shearith Israel. He and his brother Sampson (see below) were active in founding the Chamber of Commerce of New York. Simson espoused the U.S. cause during the American Revolution, moving to Connecticut during the British occupation of New York City. After the war he returned to New York City. As head of Congregation Shearith Israel, he was active in having his congregation and those of Philadelphia, Richmond, Virginia and Charleston, South Carolina, jointly send a congratulatory letter to President George Washington in 1790. In 1795 he and Alexander Hirsch of New York City addressed a Hebrew letter to the Chinese Jews of Kai Feng Fu in Honan province, China. Active in New York politics, Simson was one of the founders of the Democratic-Republican Party of New York, serving as a vice president of the party and becoming its president in 1797.

Simson's brother, SAMPSON (the elder; c. 1725–1773), was also born in New York and was a prominent merchant there. Some time before the American Revolution he loaned a biblical Hebrew manuscript to Benjamin Kennicott of England for use in the latter's *Vetus Testamentum Hebraicum*.

Solomon Simson's son, SAMSON (the younger; 1781–1857), who was born in Danbury, Connecticut, was a lawyer and an Orthodox Jew, and was active in Congregation Shearith Israel as well as in philanthropic endeavors. At the Columbia College commencement exercises in 1800, he delivered a Hebrew oration of the "Historical Traits of the Jews from Their First Settlement in North America," which was the first sketch of U.S. Jewish history by a U.S. citizen. He studied law under Aaron Burr and was admitted to the bar in 1802, one of the first Jewish lawyers in New York City. For reasons of health, he gave up the practice of law after a few years, and lived quietly in Yonkers, New York, as a bachelor country gentleman. Simson was interested in prison reform, in Westchester County politics, and in religious and charitable movements in Yonkers, New York City, and Palestine. He aided in the founding of a number of institutions, serving as president of some. He corresponded with Isaac *Leeser and Warder *Cresson on matters concerning Palestine.

Among the agencies he helped establish were the North American Relief Society for the Indigent Jews in Palestine (1853), the Jews Orphan and Indigent Asylum (1852), the Jewish Theological Seminary and Scientific Institution (1852), and the Jews' Hospital of New York (the present Mount Sinai Hospital). He enabled the Russian Jewish congregation Beth Hamedrash Hagadol of New York to acquire a synagogue building. Simson made a cash bequest to Columbia College, the first of its kind.

BIBLIOGRAPHY: I.J. Benjamin, *Drei Jahre in America*, 1 (1862), 27–29; idem, *Three Years in America, 1859–1862*, 1 (1956), 61–64; Hershkowitz, in: AJHSQ, 56 (1966), 115–8; 200–2; Isaacs, in: AJHSP, 10 (1902), 109–17; J.J. Lyons and A. de Sola, *A Jewish Calendar for Fifty Years from A.M. 5614 to A.M. 5664* (1854), 167; B. Kennicott, *Ten An-*

nual Accounts of the Collation of the Old Testament Begun in 1760 and Completed in 1769 (1770), 161; J.R. Marcus, *Studies in American Jewish History* (1969), 54–107; Meyer, in: AJHSP, 37 (1947), 430–3; 46 (1956), 51–58; Perlman, *ibid.*, 37 (1947) 434; D. de S. Pool, *Portraits Etched in Stone, 1682–1831* (1952), passim; T. de S. Pool and D. de S. Pool, *An Old Faith in the New World, 1654–1954* (1955), passim; M.U. Schappes, *A Documentary History of the Jews in the United States 1654–1875* (1950), 82–83; Sokobin, in: AJHSP, 49 (1959), 39–52; A.F. Young, *Democratic Republicans of New York, 1763–1797* (1967), 186, 248, 394, 404.

[Isidore S. Meyer]

SIMSON, BERNHARD VON (1840–1915), German historian. Born in Koenigsberg, the son of Martin Eduard von *Simson, Bernhard von Simson was appointed lecturer at the University of Jena in 1863. He published two volumes of documents connected with the reign of the elector Frederick William of Brandenburg. He then entered the Prussian civil service as a recorder at the archives of Duesseldorf, but returned to teaching in 1874 as professor at the University of Freiburg im Breisgau. In 1887 he was elected to the Bavarian Academy of Sciences. Retiring in 1905 he returned to Berlin and was named a member of the general directorate of the *Monumenta Germaniae Historica* in 1907.

Among his most important works were: *Jahrbuecher des fraenkischen Reichs unter Ludwig dem Frommen* (2 vols., 1874–76); and *Jahrbuecher des Fraenkischen Reiches unter Karl dem Grossen 789 bis 814* (1883), which completed the work on Charlemagne begun by George Abel. Perhaps von Simson's most significant work was the revelation of the pseudo-Isidorian Le Mans forgeries which he described in *Die Entstehung der Pseudoisidorischen Faelschungen in Le Mans* (1886). He also wrote the sixth volume of Giesebrecht's *Geschichte der deutschen Kaiserzeit* (1895) and edited his father's memoirs, *Erinnerungen aus seinem Leben* (1900).

BIBLIOGRAPHY: A. Dove, *Ausgewaehlte Aufsaetze und Briefe*, 1 (1925), 310–2.

[Howard L. Adelson]

SIMSON, MARTIN EDUARD VON (1810–1899), German lawyer and politician. He was born in Koenigsberg into a distinguished Jewish family which converted to Christianity and he was baptized at the age of 13. In 1831 Simson was appointed lecturer in Roman law at the University of Koenigsberg and in 1836 was made professor. An active member of the Frankfurt National Liberal movement, he was also a member of the Frankfurt National Assembly in 1848–49 and its chairman from December 1848. In 1849 he led the delegation from the National Assembly which offered the crown of the German Empire to the king of Prussia, Frederick William IV. Von Simson was elected a member of the North German Parliament and subsequently of the Reichstag in which he sat as a National Liberal and became known as a brilliant orator. In 1870 he was leader of the parliamentary delegation which asked the king of Prussia to accept the crown offered by the princes as William I. Von Simson was president of the German High Court which sat in Leipzig and in 1888 he was ennobled. A distinguished and highly cultured personality, he was a founder and first president of the Goethe society.

BIBLIOGRAPHY: B. von Simson, *Eduard von Simson* (1900); Wininger, Biog, 5 (1930), 535f.

SIMSON, PAUL (1869–1917), German historian. Born in Elbing, East Prussia, Simson accepted a teaching post at the municipal college of Danzig. In 1906 he was appointed professor. During the interim he developed an interest in the city of Danzig and its history. His four-volume *Geschichte der Stadt Danzig* (1903–16) won him prominence as the author of the first scholarly history of Danzig. He was also active in Danzig's civic affairs, and became a member of the city council, where he was considered politically liberal. He started a civic group for conserving all architecture of significance in Danzig. Over the years, Simson maintained his stature as a scholar by publishing studies on East Prussia, Pomerania, Poland, and on the political and cultural history of Danzig.

SIN. In biblical Hebrew there are about 20 different words which denote "sin." It may be inferred, therefore, that the ancient Israelites had more concepts expressing various nuances of sin than Western thought and theology. A study of the biblical concept of sin, therefore, cannot disregard the diversity of words denoting sin. These words must be examined in their context, i.e., in the formulas and literary units in which they occur. An analytic study of the three most commonly used terms – *ḥeṭ*ʾ, *pesha*ʿ and *avon* (*ʿawon*) – has been undertaken by R. Knierim. As these are often found together (Ex. 34:7; Lev. 16:21; Num. 14:18; Isa. 59:12; Jer. 33:8; Ezek. 21:29; Micah 7:18–19; Ps. 32:1, 5; 51:3–7; 59:4–5; Job 7:20–21; 13:23; Dan. 9:24; cf. Isa. 1:2, 4; Ezek. 33:10, 12), even in poetic parallelism, there cannot be an appreciable difference of meaning among them, yet they are not simply synonymous.

The root *ḥṭ*ʾ occurs in the Bible 459 times. The original meaning of the verb *ḥaṭa*ʾ is "to miss" something, "to fail," as can be seen from Genesis 31:39; Leviticus 5:15–16; Numbers 14:40; Judges 20:16; Psalms 25:8; Proverbs 8:36; 19:2; and Job 5:24, which indicates that sin as denoted by *ḥṭ*ʾ was originally viewed as a failure, a lack of perfection in carrying out a duty. The root *ḥṭ*ʾ signifies a failure of mutual relations and corresponds, then, to the modern idea of "offense" rather than to that of "sin," which is a theological concept. One who fulfills the claims of a relation or an agreement is righteous, *ẓaddik* (*ẓaddiq*); one who does not, offends (*ḥṭ*ʾ *l-*) his partner. "What is my offense that you have so hotly pursued after me?" Jacob asks Laban (Gen. 31:36). David puts a similar question to Jonathan in connection with his relation to Saul (I Sam. 20:1). This relation was of such a nature that it required of David that he devote all his abilities to the service of Saul, and of Saul that he treat David as his loyal subject. The obligation was mutual as long as it was upheld by both parties. When Saul and David were in the same cave, and David was content to cut off the skirt of Saul's robe, he called out to Saul that it was now clear that he had not "offended" him (I Sam. 24:12). Then Saul acknowledged that David was righteous and that he himself was the offender (cf. I Sam. 26:21), since he had not fulfilled his obligations. All lack of obedience toward superiors is "offense," because in the relations between subordinates and superiors the former are expected to obey the latter. The Egyptian baker and cupbearer who were in prison with Joseph had been sent there because they had "failed" to obey the orders of Pharaoh (Gen. 40:1; 41:9). The people of Pharaoh were accused of "failing" (*ḥṭ*ʾ) in their duty, when they did not give any straw to the Israelites so that they might make bricks (Ex. 5:16). The same applies to every deed that is in conflict with, or causes the dissolution of, a community. So Reuben acknowledged that his brothers "sinned" against their brother Joseph (Gen. 42:22). When the king of the Ammonites attacked Israel, Jephthah sent him word explaining that there had always been a relation of peace between the two peoples, and he addressed to him the following reproach: "I have not 'sinned' against you, but you do me wrong to war against me" (Judg. 11:27). The "sin" is here a breach of the covenant relation between the peoples. When Sennacherib threatened Judah in 701, King Hezekiah sent a messenger to him, saying: "I have 'sinned'" (II Kings 18:14). The "sin" of Hezekiah consisted in a violation of his vassal duties. A "sinful" act, i.e., one of dereliction of duty, is thus a matter between two parties. The one who does not fulfill his obligations in relation to the other is a sinner with regard to the latter; he "sins against him," i.e., "he fails him," and so gives the other a claim upon him.

According to I Samuel 2:25, failure in carrying out one's duty can concern the relations between men or between God and man: "If a man offends against (*ḥṭ*ʾ) a man, God will mediate, but if a man offends against (*ḥṭ*ʾ) God, who shall act as mediator?" This passage indicates that the "sin" against God was conceived as an "offense," as a failure to fulfill one's obligation toward God. Since the root *ḥṭ*ʾ denotes an action, that failure is neither an abstraction nor a permanent disqualification but a concrete act with its consequences. This act is defined as a "failure," an "offense," when it is contrary to a norm regulating the relations between God and man. So, for instance, the infringement of the law of ban (*ḥerem*) appears in Joshua 7:11, 20 and I Samuel 15:3–19 as an "offense" or "sin" against God in view of the traditions partially recorded in Deuteronomy 20:10–18. That adultery is a "sin" against the Lord (Gen. 20:6, 9; 39:9; II Sam. 12:13) results from a law such as Exodus 20:14. Social mischiefs stigmatized as "sins" by the prophets (Isa. 58:1ff.; 59:2ff.; Jer. 2:35; 5:25; Ezek. 14:13; 16:51; 33:14; Hos. 12:9; Amos 5:12; Micah 3:8; 6:13) are, in fact, contrary to commandments of the divine law such as Exodus 20:16 (13); 23:1–9; Deuteronomy 27:17–19. The concept of *ḥṭ*ʾ extends not only to juridical, moral, and social matters, but also to cultic obligations, and even to involuntary infringements of ritual prescriptions (Lev. 4–5) or of occasional divine premonitions (Num. 22:34).

The root *psh*ʿ occurs in the Bible 136 times, and it too is found in early texts as Genesis 31:36; 50:17; Exodus 22:8; I Samuel 24:11; II Kings 8:20, 22; Amos 1–2; Micah 3:8; and Proverbs 28:24. Its basic meaning is that of "breach." In terms of international law, the breach of a covenant is thus called *pesha*ʿ (I Kings 12:19; II Kings 1:1; 3:5, 7; 8:20, 22; Hos. 8:1). In the realm of criminal law, *pesha*ʿ is the delict which dissolves the community or breaks the peaceful relation between two parties (e.g., Gen. 31:36; Ex. 22:8; Prov. 28:24). This is also the meaning of *psh*ʿ when used to express the sinful behavior of man toward God (e.g., I Kings 8:50; Ps. 25:7; 51:3). The verb *ʿawah*, found in the Bible 17 times, basically expresses the idea of crookedness, and thus means "to wrong" (Lam. 3:9), and in the passive form (*nifʿal*), "to become bent" (Ps. 38:7). The noun *ʿawon*, from the same root, is found 227 (229) times, and designates "crookedness." The use of these words in a figurative sense to denote the transgression, the guilt incurred by it, or the punishment, is of popular origin. The metaphor does not belong to the juridical terminology, but was assumed by the theological language. Isaiah 59:2, for example, says that the *ʿawonot* set up a wall between the Lord and the sinner.

The nouns *ḥeṭ*ʾ, *ḥaṭaʾah* or *ḥaṭṭaʾt*, *peshaʿ*, and *ʿawon*, and also the corresponding verbs, denote a "sin" in the theological sense of the word when they characterize a human deed as a "failure," a "breach," or a "crooked" action with reference to prescriptions that proceed finally from the stipulations of the Covenant. It is not the external nature of the act that makes it sinful. In biblical thought, the relation that creates the right to God's protection also creates the sin. There would be no sin if there were no covenantal law. The sinner is one who has failed in his relation to God, insofar as he has not fulfilled his obligation to God. In other words, it is a "sin" to violate, or to break, the Covenant (cf. Jer. 14:20–21). The biblical doctrine of sin is thus described in Jeremiah 16:10–12 in the following way: "When you tell this people all this, and they say to you: 'Why has the Lord threatened us with such terrible misfortune? What is our crime? What is the offense (*ḥṭ*ʾ) we have committed against the Lord our God?' – then answer them: 'It is because your fathers forsook Me. They followed other gods, worshiping them and doing obeisance to them, and forsook Me and did not keep My law. And you have done even worse than they did, each following his own stubbornly wicked inclinations and refusing to listen to Me.'" Even the sin of Adam and Eve, although not described as such in the Bible, was an act that destroyed a special relation between God and man (Gen. 3). The original sin does not appear in the Bible as an innate depravity common to all human beings in consequence of the fall of the first parents. Rather, the biblical tradition knows that "there is no man who does not sin" (I Kings 8:46; cf. Eccles. 7:20). The hyperbolic language in which the psalmist describes his own sinfulness, "I was even born in iniquity, my mother conceived me in sin" (Ps. 51:7; cf. Gen. 8:21), only stresses the ineluctable character of sin. Nobody can escape from it, as the sin can also be involuntary (Lev. 4–5) or proceed from ignorance (Gen. 20:6; Num. 22:34). A man is responsible for all his actions. Therefore sick people may conclude that their illness is a punishment for having offended God (Ps. 38:4, 19; 41:5). This does not mean, however, that the ancient Israelites did not make a distinction between an inadvertent sin and one that is committed willfully. This distinction clearly emerges in Numbers 15:27 and 30. The psychological sentiment of guilt is also expressed in various texts (Ps. 51; 78:17, 32; Prov. 21:4; 24:9; Job 31:30; cf. Gen. 4:7; Deut. 15:9; 22:26). The subjective aspect of a deed is even taken into account by the law, especially in Exodus 21:13–14 and Deuteronomy 19:4–5.

The idea of "deadly" or "mortal" sin originates in biblical expressions connecting *ḥṭ*ʾ with *mwt* ("to die," "death"; Num. 18:22; 27:3; Deut. 21:22; 22:26; 24:16; II Kings 14:6; Ezek. 3:20; 18:4, 20; Amos 9:10; II Chron. 25:4). The oldest text connecting the two is probably Amos 9:10, dating from the eighth century B.C.E.: "All the sinners of my people shall die by the sword." The connection of the formula expressing the death sentence with such an indefinite word as "sin" or "offense" cannot be original. It must be regarded as a generalization proceeding from theological reflection. Its original "setting in life" (*sitz im leben*) is still visible in Deuteronomy 21:22 and 22:16, which refer to the proceedings of the civil tribunal. Numbers 18:22 and 27:3, both of which belong to the Priestly tradition, reflect instead the sphere of sacral law. The remaining passages use the concept of "mortal sin" in a context of "prophetic" preaching.

In a certain sense, every sin may be regarded as "deadly"; for, if all people die, it is because all have sinned, and not in consequence of "the original sin." That the sinner must die is stated or assumed by many texts (Ex. 32:33; Lev. 20:20; 22:9; 24:15–17; Num. 9:13; 16:26; 17:3; 18:22, 32; I Sam. 15:18; I Kings 13:34; 14:11–18; 15:29–30; 16:12–13, 18–19; Isa. 13:9; 38:17; 43:27–28; 64:4–5; Jer. 8:14; Ezek. 3:20; 18:24; Amos 9:8, 10; Ps. 104:34). Stereotyped formulas say even that "each man shall die because of his sin" (*ḥṭ*ʾ: Num. 27:3; Deut. 24:16; II Kings 14:6) or "because of his transgression" (*ʿawon*: Josh. 22:20; Ezek. 4:17; 7:13, 16; 18:17, 20; 33:6, 8, 9; cf. Gen. 19:15). The sinner must indeed "bear (*ns*ʾ) his sin." The expression means practically "to take the blame upon oneself," and it normally refers to the sinner himself (Gen. 4:13; Ex. 28:43; Lev. 5:1, 17; 7:18; 19:8, 17; 20:17, 19, 20; 22:9; 24:15; Num. 5:31; 9:13; 14:34; 18:22, 23, 32; Ezek. 14:10; 44:10, 12). The law of retaliation demands, in fact, that the offender should be punished according to his sin. However, the same expression also occurs in early pleas for forgiveness (Gen. 50:17; Ex. 10:17; 32:32; I Sam. 15:25; Hos. 14:3; Ps. 25:18), in doxological formulas (Ex. 34:7; Num. 14:18; Micah 7:18; Ps. 32:1; 85:3), in a thanksgiving psalm (32:5), in a predication (Josh. 24:19), and in a Song of the Suffering Servant in Deutero-Isaiah (Isa. 53:12). In these texts, the one who takes the blame upon himself is God, the offended person, or a substitute of the sinner (cf. II Sam. 12:13–14). There are still other cases when one's *ʿawon* is borne by another person: by the priests (Num. 18:1), by Aaron (Ex. 28:38), by the husband (Num. 30:16), by the prophet Ezekiel (Ezek. 4:4–6), by the community (Lev. 22:16), by the scapegoat (Lev. 16:22), or even by a sacrificed goat (Lev. 10:17). It means that there was a possibility that the sin might not work its consequences upon the sinner. Accordingly, there was sense to the prayer for the forgiveness of sin (cf. I Kings 8:30, 34, 36, 50; Ps. 51:4; 79:9) or the intercession of a prophet (Gen. 20:7; Ex. 9:27–29; 10:17; 32:30–33; Num. 21:7; Deut. 9:18–20; I Sam. 7:5; 12:19; Jer. 14:11; 15:1). The ancient remedy, the sin-offering (*ḥaṭṭaʾt*), also worked both for the purification of the person and to obtain the forgiveness of the Lord. It is probable that the killed animal was originally regarded as a substitute for the sinner (cf. Lev. 10:17). The confession of sins was another means of winning forgiveness. In this way the sinner expels the sin from his heart; he shows at the same time that he does not intend to conceal his sin and to deceive the Lord.

The formula of the individual's confession of sins, expressed by the verb *ḥaṭaʾti* ("I have sinned"), is found in the Bible 30 times. It has beyond any doubt a ritual character, even if it is used twice in a rather colloquial way (I Kings 18:9; Neh. 6:13). In the other instances, it is employed with reference to sacral judicial proceedings, as shown by the juridical terminology of the context. It is used not only when someone has sinned against God (Gen. 39:9; Ex. 9:27; 10:16; Num. 22:34; Josh. 7:20; I Sam. 15:24, 30; II Sam. 12:13; 24:10, 17; Jer. 2:35; Micah 7:9; Ps. 41:5; 51:6; I Chron. 21:8, 17; cf. Job 7:20; 10:14; 33:27) but also against man (Gen. 20:9; 43:9; 44:32; Judg. 11:27; I Sam. 24:11; 26:21; II Sam. 19:21; II Kings 18:14; Jer. 37:18). More than half the occurrences are in ancient texts. The oldest form of the proceedings is most likely the one in Joshua 7:13–23, on the occasion of *Achan's sin at Jericho; it seems to be presupposed in Leviticus 5:5 and also Psalms 32:5. After the sinner was designated by the sacred lots, Urim and *Thummim, he had to present a public confession of his sin, which was confirmed by an inquiry. The sin could be forgiven or not, it could be expiated by a sacrifice or by putting the sinner to death. On the other hand, in I Samuel 15:24 and II Samuel 12:13 (cf. II Sam. 24:10–19), the casting of lots and public confession are dispensed with, the sin being confessed before the cultic prophet who accused the sinner in God's name. This procedure was probably characteristic of the early monarchical period. The individual confession of sins is also expressed by the words *peshaʿai* (Ps. 25:7; 32:5; 39:9; 51:3, 5) and *ʿawonotai* (Ps. 38:5; 40:13), by the singular *pishʿi* (Micah 6:7; Job 7:21; 14:17) and *ʿawoni* (Gen. 4:13; Ps. 32:5; 38:19), or else by various locutions using one of these words (Gen. 44:16; I Sam. 25:24; II Sam. 14:9). These confessions occur in many different contexts: prayer, praise, interrogation, etc.; the confession of sins is thus often indirect.

The formula of the national confession of sins is expressed by the verb *ḥaṭaʾnu* ("we have sinned"). This verbal form occurs in the Bible 24 times, but only twice in texts that are definitely ancient – Numbers 12:11 and 14:40, which seem to belong to the Elohistic tradition of the Pentateuch. However, the first of these two passages does not actually contain a national confession of sins, since the sinners are Miriam and Aaron; thus an individual confession of sins is applied to two persons at once. None of the remaining 22 attestations of the form can safely be dated before the late seventh century

B.C.E. (Num. 21:7; Deut. 1:41; Judg. 10:10, 15; I Kings 8:47; Isa. 42:24; Jer. 3:25; 8:14; 14:7, 20; 16:10; Ps. 106:6; Lam. 5:16; Dan. 9:5, 8, 11, 15; Neh. 1:6 (twice); II Chron. 6:37). All these texts have a cultic or sacral character. Other formulas of national confession of sins, expressed by the word *pesha'enu* ("our sins") can be found in Isaiah 53:5; 59:12; Ezekiel 33:10; Psalms 65:4; 103:12; and Lamentations 1:14, 22. As far as these texts can be dated, they were all composed in the sixth century B.C.E. The term *'awonenu*, or *'awonotenu*, also occurs with that meaning, namely, in Isaiah 53:5–6; 64:5; Psalms 90:8; Daniel 9:13; and Ezra 9:6, 13 – texts which are all Exilic or post-Exilic. It seems, therefore, that, contrary to the individual confession, the national one is a relatively late innovation in Israel's penitential liturgy (cf. E. Lipinski, *La liturgie pénitentielle dans la Bible* (1969), 35–41).

When God "forgives" one's sin, He "covers" or "hides" it (Micah 7:18; Ps. 32:1, 5; 85:3; Prov. 10:12; 17:9; 19:11; 28:13; Job 31:33), He "does not remember [i.e., that He overlooks]" it (Isa. 64:8; Ps. 25:7), He "bears" it Himself (Ex. 32:32; 34:7; Num. 14:18; Josh. 24:19; Hos. 14:3; Micah 7:18; Ps. 25:18; 32:1, 5; 85:3). Though it is merely said that the sin is forgotten, covered, not imputed to the sinner, God's forgiveness of sins is identical with the curing of the man and with the regeneration of his strength. It means, indeed, that God will not take him away "in the middle of his days" (Jer. 17:11; Ps. 55:24; 102:25), but will permit him to spend on earth the full span of human life, i.e., "70 years" (Isa. 23:15; Ps. 90:10). Then He will cut him off by death, for "there is no righteous man on earth who does good and never sins" (Eccles. 7:20).

[Edward Lipinski]

Rabbinic Views

The usual rabbinic term for sin is *averah*, from the root *avar* ("to pass over"; i.e., sin is a rejection of God's will). The rabbis rarely speak of sin in the abstract but usually of specific sins. There are sins of commission and omission – in the rabbinic terminology, the transgression of negative precepts and the failure to perform positive precepts (Yoma 8:8). Sins of commission are more serious than those of omission (Yoma 85:86a), and the term *averah* generally refers to the former. In one respect, however, the latter are more severe. If positive precepts have to be carried out at a certain time and that time has passed, the omission cannot be rectified, e.g., the failure to recite the *Shema* on a particular day. To this is applied the verse (Eccles. 1:15): "That which is crooked cannot be made straight, and that which is wanting cannot be numbered" (Ber. 26a). Sins involving the transgression of negative precepts are of two kinds – offenses against God and offenses against one's neighbor. The Day of Atonement brings forgiveness for sins committed against God, i.e., for purely religious offenses. It only brings forgiveness for offenses against other human beings if the wrong done to the victim has first been put right (Yoma 8:9). The intention to sin is not reckoned as sin except in the case of idolatry (Kid. 39b).

Sins are also divided into light and severe sins. The three most serious sins for the rabbis are murder, idolatry, and adultery and incest. It was eventually ruled that rather than commit these, a man must forfeit his life (Sanh. 74a). The light sins are those which "a man treads underfoot" (Tanḥ. B. Deut. 8b). A marked tendency to be observed in rabbinic homiletics is to encourage people to take the lighter sins more seriously by treating them as if they were far weightier offenses. Thus, whoever leaves the Holy Land to reside outside it is as if he had worshiped idols (Sifra, Be-Har 6); whoever bears evil tales is as if he denies the root principle of faith (Ar. 15b); whoever shames his neighbor in public is as if he had shed blood (BM 58b).

Those who cause others to sin were severely castigated by the rabbis. One who causes another to sin is worse than one who slays him, because the murderer only excludes his victim from this life, while the one who causes another to sin excludes him from the life of the world to come (Sif. Deut. 252). Jeroboam is the prototype of the one who leads others to sin (Avot 5:18).

Sin is caused by the evil *inclination (*yeẓer ha-ra*), the force in man which drives him to gratify his instincts and ambitions. Although called the "evil inclination" because it can easily lead man to wrongdoing, it is essential to life in that it provides life with its driving power. Were it not for the *yeẓer ha-ra*, remarks a rabbinic Midrash (Gen. R. 9:7), a man would not build a house, or marry, or have children, or engage in commerce. In similar vein is the curious legend (Yoma 69b) that the men of the Great Synagogue wanted to kill the *yeẓer ha-ra*, who warned them that if they were successful the "world would go down," i.e., would come to an end. They therefore imprisoned him for three days and then searched all the land for a new-laid egg without finding one. Passages such as these, however, must not be construed as suggesting any rabbinic acceptance of the inevitability of sin or of its condonation. The strongest expressions are used of the heinousness of sin and surrender to the *yeẓer ha-ra*. R. Simeon b. Lakish said "Satan, the *yeẓer ha-ra*, and the angel of death are one and the same" (BB 16a). The *yeẓer ha-ra* entices man to sin in this world and bears witness against him in the future world (Suk. 52b). The *yeẓer ha-ra* assaults man every day, endeavoring to kill him, and if God would not support him, man could not resist him; as it is said (Ps. 37:32): "The wicked watcheth the righteous and seeketh to slay him. The Lord will not leave him in his hand" (*ibid.*). Unless severe control is exercised man becomes the prey of sin. Commenting on II Samuel 12:4, it is said that the *yeẓer ha-ra* is at first called a "passerby," then a "guest," and finally "one who occupies the house" (*ibid.*). When a man sins and repeats the sin, it no longer seems to him as forbidden (Yoma 86b).

The much discussed question of whether there are any parallels to the Christian doctrine of original sin in rabbinic literature can be disposed of simply by noting that there are no such parallels. The passages which state that "four died through the serpent's machinations" (Shab. 55b) and that "the serpent copulated with Eve and infected her with his filth" (Shab. 146a), quoted in this connection, expressly exclude

Israel from the effects of the serpent's machinations and his filth, and in all probability are an intentional polemic against the doctrine of original sin. Nevertheless, while the rabbis do not see sin as hereditary – that man is bound to sin because of Adam's sin – their views are far removed from "liberal" optimism regarding man's inherent goodness, as the doctrine of the *yeẓer ha-ra* clearly demonstrates. It is recorded that the rival schools of Hillel and Shammai debated for two and a half years whether it were better for man not to have been created (i.e., because of his propensity to sin); it was finally decided that it would have been better if he had not been created, but since he has been let him investigate his deeds (Eruv. 13b).

Counsels are given to man as to how he can rise above sin. He should know that above him there is a seeing eye and a hearing ear and that all his deeds are recorded in a book (Avot 2:1). He should reflect that he comes from a putrid drop, that he goes to a place of dust, worms, and maggots, and that he is destined to give an account and a reckoning before the King of kings (Avot 3:1). But the study of the Torah and the practice of the precepts are the best method of avoiding sin (Sot. 21a). God says: "My children! I created the evil inclination, but I created the Torah as its antidote; if you occupy yourselves with the Torah you will not be delivered into [the inclination's] hand" (Kid. 30b). The school of R. Ishmael taught: "My son, if this repulsive wretch [the *yeẓer ha-ra*] attacks you, lead him to the house of learning: if he is stone, he will dissolve; if iron, he will shiver into fragments" (Kid. 30b).

[Louis Jacobs]

BIBLIOGRAPHY: L. Koehler, *Old Testament Theology* (1957), ch. 51; E. Jacob, *Theology of the Old Testament* (1958), pt. 3, ch. 1; J. Scharbert, in BZ, 2 (1958), 14–26, 190–213; L.F. Hartmann, in: CBQ, 20 (1958), 26–40; D. Daube, in: JJS, 10 (1959), 1–13; idem, *Sin, Ignorance and Forgiveness in the Bible* (1960); R. Knierim, *Die Hauptbegriffe fuer Suende im Alten Testament* (1965); idem, in: VT, 16 (1966), 366–85; K. Koch, in: *Evangelische Theologie*, 26 (1966), 169–90; W. Eichrodt, *Theology of the Old Testament*, 2 (1967), 380–483. RABBINIC VIEWS: S. Schechter, *Aspects of Rabbinic Theology* (1909), 219–343; G.F. Moore, *Judaism* (1958), 445–552; A. Buechler, *Studies in Sin and Atonement* (1928); C.M. Montefiore and H. Loewe, *Rabbinic Anthology* (1938), index; A. Cohen, *Everyman's Talmud* (1949), 95–103; E.E. Urbach, *Ḥazal* (1970), 371–392.

SIN, WILDERNESS OF (Heb. סִין).

(1) An area between Elim and Sinai, traversed by the children of Israel in their exodus from Egypt (Ex. 16:1); it is defined more specifically in Exodus 17:1 as the area before Rephidim. In the recapitulation of the wanderings through the desert in Numbers 33:11–12, the order is: Elim-Red Sea-Wilderness of Sin-Dophkah. The location of Sin naturally depends on the view taken of the route of the Exodus (see *Exodus). Accepting the traditional southern route, the desert of Sin would be identical to the plain of al-Marḥa (or al-Markha), between Wadi Baʿbʿa and Wadi Sidrī on the west coast of the Sinai peninsula; its position would then be between Elim (Wadi Gharandal?) and Dophkah (Ṣarābīṭ al-Khādim (?), the turquoise mines exploited in ancient times).

(2) Sin is mentioned in connection with the "stronghold of Egypt" in Ezekiel 30:15–16. It is probably identical with Syene (Aswān; Ezek. 29:10; 30:6), the southern boundary fortress of Egypt.

BIBLIOGRAPHY: Abel, Geog, 2 (1938), 212–3.

[Michael Avi-Yonah]

SINAI (Heb. סִינַי), peninsula situated between the two northern gulfs of the Red Sea, the Gulf of Eilat on the east and the Gulf of Suez on the west. It forms a triangle, each side of which measures about 200 mi. (320 km.). The peninsula consists of three main regions, each different in its geographical aspects. In the north is a sandy coastal plateau, partly traversed by dunes 20 mi. (32 km.) deep, which reach a height of 60–90 ft. (c. 18–27 m.), but which are passable in a northeast-southeast direction. A few wells of brackish water and palm groves in oases make the passage of this region easier. The sandy areas are narrow on the east, but expand into the desert of al-Jifār (the desert of Shur) on the west. The second zone is a limestone plateau intersected by valleys and ridges and known as Badivat al-Tīh. Its northern limit is formed by a series of mountains, including, from west to east, Jebel al-Jiddī (2,058 ft.), Jebel Yaʿallaq (3,200 ft.) and Jebel Halāl (or Ḥalāl; 2,714 ft.). South of these mountains, whitish limestone cliffs rise in a line of sheer precipices from the gravel-strewn surface of the ground. The Tīh desert extends eastward into the area around Kadesh, and westward up to the Suez region. Its sandy and rocky ground contains few watering points. The southernmost region of the Sinai Peninsula consists of a group of granite mountains intersected by deep wadis and their tributaries, between which rise rocky massifs with high pinnacles and deep gorges. The outstanding peaks in this area are Jebel Katerina (8,652 ft.), Jebel Mūsā, the traditional Mt. Sinai (7,486 ft.) and Jebel Sirbāl (6,791 ft.). The waters flowing from these snow-clad peaks in the winter have created several oases, the most important one being the central oasis of Fīrān (Paran). The mountain range of the south extends northward along the west coast; this part is rich in copper and turquoise, the greatest concentration of which exists at Sarābīṭ al-Khādim. West of it, the plain of al-Marḥa (Markha; see *Sin, Wilderness of) follows the west coast.

Situated between the Nile Valley and the land of Israel, Sinai was from earliest times traversed by a series of roads running from west to east, of which the three most important are a) the coastal road, known in the Bible as the "way of the land of the Philistines," which runs from the vicinity of Pelusium to Gaza, passing from one well to another; it is the shortest and most frequented route; b) the road which crosses the Tīh desert from Ismailia on the Suez Canal by way of Biʾr Jafjafa (or Gafgafa) and Biʾr al-Ḥamma to Abu Aweigila and to Niẓẓanah (ʾAwjā al-Ḥafīr); c) the Darb al-Ḥajj ("route of the pilgrimage" to Mecca from Egypt), which crosses the southern part of the Tīh desert by way of Qalʿat al-Nakhl and Biʾr al-Thamad, and by way of al-Kuntilla descends the Raʾs al-Naqb to Eilat. The less important north-south routes are, in the east, the road

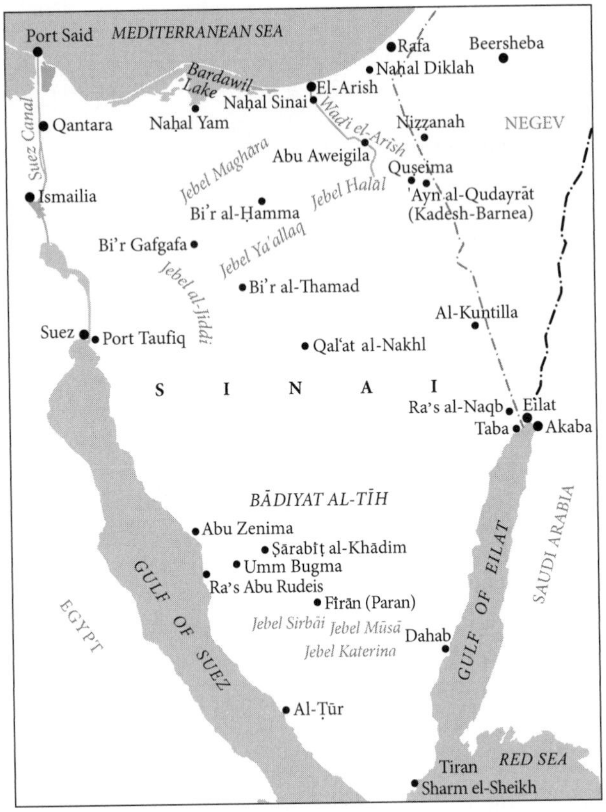

The Sinai Peninsula.

along the Wadi el-Arish (Brook of Egypt) by way of Kadesh-Barnea (ʿAyn al-Qudayrāt) and al-Qusei'ma to Kuntilla and, in the west, a road which follows the west coast to al-Ṭūr and Sharm el-Sheikh on the southern tip of the peninsula. Side roads lead from the latter road to the copper mines at Ṣarābīṭ al-Khādim and to Jebel Mūsā by way of Wadi Fīrān.

Pre-Biblical Period

Historically, the importance of the Sinai Peninsula has always been a result of its character as an area of transit from Asia to Africa and vice-versa. Evidence of settlement in this area begins with the Paleolithic Age, at which time Sinai was not yet a desert. In the Chalcolithic period it apparently served as a link between pre-dynastic Egypt and the settlements around Beersheba in Canaan. In the time of the early dynastic period in Egypt, expeditions were sent from the Nile Valley to exploit the copper mines, as Egypt itself had no metals; the presence of a *serekh* (hieroglyph) of Pharaoh Narmer at Tel Erani and a walled city, perhaps a symbol of Canaan, represented on the Narmer palette (from Hierankonopolis), show that the pharaonic armies were already traversing the peninsula at the beginning of the First Dynasty. In the Middle Bronze Age, the period of the Patriarchs, Sinai was relatively more densely settled than at later stages in its history; it was crossed by Abraham and Jacob on their way to Egypt. Later, it was traversed by the Hyksos invaders of Egypt. In their wake, the desert was occupied by nomadic tribes, related to Ishmael in the Bible (Gen. 25:17–18); the Egyptians referred to them collectively as *Shasu*. After the expulsion of the Hyksos (16th century B.C.E.), the pharaohs took steps to secure their kingdom by building a wall (*shur*) across the western end of the peninsula and by establishing a chain of forts along the coastal road to secure the watering points.

Biblical Period

It was during the New Kingdom that Sinai acquired its biblical fame. In the Bible, the desert of Sinai is situated between Rephidim and Mt. Sinai, with the wilderness of Sin between it and Elim (Ex. 16:1; 19:1–2). According to Numbers 33:15–16, it lay between Rephidim and Kibroth-Hattaavah and in Numbers 10:12, the wilderness of Paran is situated to the east of it. Mt. Sinai eclipsed the desert of Sinai in later literature as the identification of the place where the Law was given to Israel (Deut. 33:2; Judg. 5:5; Ps. 68:8, 18; Neh. 9:13). The identification of Mt. Sinai, and by implication that of the desert of Sinai, depends on the view taken of the route of the Exodus (see *Exodus); the traditional theory places Mt. Sinai at Jebel Mūsā, while others place it at Jebel Halāl (or Ḥalāl), or even in the Arabian Peninsula. The last identification is supported by the assumed connection between Sinai and the moon god, Sin. During the period of the Exodus, the desert was occupied by the Amalekites, who disputed the passage of the Israelites at Rephidim. The Egyptians left the desert nomads alone, while keeping control of the coastal road and the copper and turquoise mines at Ṣarābīṭ al-Khādim (Dophkah?). The beginnings of an alphabetic Semitic script, the so-called proto-Sinaitic alphabet, are evident in the inscriptions written by slaves who worked in the mines. In the period of the monarchy, Saul and David fought the Amalekites (1 Sam. 15:7, 27:8) and controlled northwest Sinai. The nomads of the region helped in Esarhaddon's campaign against Egypt, although some served as mercenaries in the Egyptian army. Later, they brought water to the army of Cambyses of Persia during his invasion of the Nile Valley; in return, the Persians allowed the kings of Kedar (the predecessors of the Nabateans) to maintain harbors on the coast of Sinai, between the Serbonic Lake and Ienysos, south of Gaza.

See also *Sinai, Mount.

Post-Biblical Period

In Hellenistic and Roman times, the interior of Sinai was left to the Nabateans as part of Arabia Petrea; only the coastal road was controlled by the Ptolemies and later by the Romans. After annexation of Nabatea by the Romans, it was regarded as part of Provincia Arabia, and after Diocletian, as part of Palestina Tertia (Salutaris). In the Byzantine period, the biblical associations with the region led to an increase in trade and pilgrimages across the desert. Justinian built a fortified monastery near Jebel Mūsā (Mount Sinai) and a bishopric was established at Paran. A chapel was constructed on the top of Jebel Mūsā. Ephrem the Syrian in one of his hymns (CSCO 323, 71–73) compares Mount Sinai to the Old Testament and the church on the mountain's summit to the New Testament, indicating that he viewed the church as a symbol of the ascendancy of Christianity over Judaism. Sinai was largely left to the Bedouin in Islamic and medieval times, until the excavation of the Suez Canal on the west increased its importance.

[Michael Avi-Yonah / Shimon Gibson (2nd ed.)]

Modern Period

A Zionist plan, in *Herzl's time (1902), to settle the El-Arish area (then under British administration as part of the British protectorate of Egypt), as a prelude to Jewish settlement in Ereẓ Israel (see *El-Arish Project), proved abortive. A border dispute between Britain and Turkey led, in 1906, to the final demarcation of a border line between the British protectorate and the *Ottoman Empire running from Rafa to Taba south of Akaba. This line was crossed during World War I by Turkish forces, which attacked the Suez Canal, and then by the British army, which conquered Palestine. The same line became the international boundary of Egypt and Mandatory Palestine. For several years after the war, Sinai formed a separate British administrative unit under Major C.S. Jarvis.

During Israel's *War of Independence (1948–49), the Israeli army, in pursuit of the retreating Egyptian forces, crossed the line and occupied eastern Sinai but was forced to withdraw unconditionally under political pressure from the United States and threats of British military intervention. In the *Sinai Campaign in 1956, the Egyptian army was routed by the Israeli army, which occupied the entire peninsula except for a strip along the Suez Canal. In 1957, Israel was again forced, mainly by the United States and the Soviet Union, to withdraw behind the armistice lines of 1949 without achieving a peace treaty with Egypt. The rapid aggressive buildup of huge Egyptian forces in Sinai in May 1967 was a major factor leading to the Six-Day War, when the whole of Sinai, up to the Suez Canal, was occupied by Israel. At the end of 1967 a census was conducted in northern Sinai and 33,800 Arabs and Bedouin were registered, 30,000 in El-Arish alone. After the Six-Day War the Israel military administration carried out a series of economic development projects, e.g., helping to erect factories in El-Arish; introducing better medical and educational services for the local population, including the Bedouin; and paving a modern highway from Eilat along the western coast of the gulf to Sharm el-Sheikh. Extensive geological and archeological surveys of the entire peninsula were carried out by Israeli scientists and experts. In the wake of the Yom Kippur War, Israel withdrew inland from the Suez Canal following the 1974 disengagement agreement and the 1975 interim agreement, returning the Abu Rudeis oil fields to Egypt and allowing it to reopen the Suez Canal.

In the meanwhile Jewish settlement activity had commenced in the Rafa Salient (Pitḥat Rafi'aḥ) in the northeast corner of Sinai, including the town of *Yammit, which had grown to 2,000 inhabitants by 1977, with another 2,000 in the surrounding settlements. These were abandoned in stages in accordance with the peace treaty signed with Egypt in 1979, in which Israel agreed to withdraw from all of Sinai by 1982, including the Yammit Region, whose settlements were razed.

BIBLIOGRAPHY: R. Weil, *La Presqu'île de Sinaï* (1908); W.M.F. Petrie, *Researches in Sinai* (1906); J. Ball, *The Geography and Geology of West-Central Sinai* (1916); C.S. Jarvis, *Yesterday and Today in Sinai* (1933); L. Prévost, *Le Sinai* (1937); H. Bar-Deroma, *Zeh Sinai*, (1967); E.H. Palmer, *The Desert of the Exodus*, 2 vols. (1871); Y. Aharoni and M. Avi-Yonah, in: *Antiquity and Survival*, 2 (1957), 287ff.; M. Harel; B. Rothenberg, et al., *Tagliyyot Sinai* (1967). **ADD. BIBLIOGRAPHY:** H.S. Palmer, *Sinai. From the Fourth Egyptian Dynasty to the Present Day* (1878); *The Sinai Journeys: The Route of the Exodus in the Light of the Historical Geography of the Sinai Peninsula* (1973); Z. Meshel and I. Finkelstein (eds.), *Sinai in Antiquity: Researches in the History and Archaeology of the Peninsula* (1980); U. Dahari, *Monastic Settlements in South Sinai in the Byzantine Period: The Archaeological Remains* (2000).

SINAI, MOUNT.

The Biblical Narrative

The mountain of God is first mentioned when God revealed Himself to Moses in the burning bush. God told Moses "when you have freed the people from Egypt, you shall worship God at this mountain" (Ex. 3:12), but in this tradition the mountain is called Horeb (E and D prefer "Horeb" to the "Sinai" of J and P). Elsewhere in the Torah we read that the People of Israel encamped at the foot of the mountain called Sinai, from the third month after the Exodus until the 20th of the second month of the second year (Ex. 19:1–Num. 10:11). While the people prepared themselves during three days for the theophany (divine manifestation; according to later Jewish tradition this was seven weeks after the Exodus), Moses set up a boundary line beyond which approach was prohibited under penalty of death, and himself ascended the mountain. On the third day God descended upon the mountain and uttered the Ten Commandments (Ex. 20; Deut. 5). He also gave Moses many more laws and ordinances for the people. Moses built an altar at the foot of the mountain and set up 12 stones representing the 12 tribes of Israel (Ex. 24). Moses, *Aaron, *Nadab, *Abihu, and 70 of the *elders of Israel then went up the mountain, where they saw the God of Israel. Mt. Sinai was then enveloped in a cloud for six days, while fire burnt on its summit. On the seventh day Moses ascended the mountain to receive the Tablets of the Law, remaining there for 40 days and nights. During his absence the people, led by Aaron, erected the *golden calf (Ex. 32). Moses returned, accompanied by his servant *Joshua, and angrily broke the stone tablets. Later he returned to the mountain and received the second tablets, as well as many other laws concerning different aspects of life, and the instructions for the erection of the *Tabernacle (Ex. 35ff.).

Mt. Sinai is regarded in biblical theology as the place of divine revelation and is often mentioned in the poetical passages describing theophany (Deut. 33:2; Judg. 5:5; Ps. 68:9, 18); when *Elijah sought God he went to the Mount of God, Horeb (I Kings 19:8). No other narrative of pilgrimage to this mountain is found in the Bible. Noth suggested that Numbers 33 is actually a "pilgrims' itinerary to Mt. Sinai in reverse." Since the mountain was called "The Mount of God" even before God's revelation to Moses, scholars have assumed that it was a place of worship even before the Hebrews came to it.

In its present context in the Pentateuch the tradition of Mt. Sinai is closely interwoven with that of the Exodus. Since the study of G. von Rad (1938), scholars tend to agree that this pericope originally formed a separate element in what Christian scholars call *Heilsgeschichte*, "History of Salvation." According to biblical scholars, the description of the events at Mt. Sinai does not reflect a historical occurrence; in fact it is a miracle tale adjudged by some to be a liturgical narrative (*Festlegende*) belonging to an ancient Festival of the *Covenant (*berit*). In Judges 5:5, the Hebrew god is called "Yahweh-of-Sinai" (Cross) unconnected to either covenant or revelation of the law. The same holds for the ancient poem Deut. 33:2–5, 26–28 (the remaining verses are later; see Seeligmann).

Location

There is no Jewish tradition of the geographical location of Mt. Sinai; it seems that its exact location was obscure already in the time of the monarchy (B. Mazar, and see below). Rabbinical literature was always more concerned with the contents and ideas of the Torah than with the question of where it was given. The Christian hermits and monks, mostly from Egypt, who settled in southern Sinai from the second century C.E. on, made repeated efforts to identify the localities of the Exodus with actual places to which the believers could make their way as pilgrims. The identification of Mt. Sinai either with Jebel Sirbāl near the oasis of Fīrān (Paran; Nilus, Cosmas Indicopleustes), or with Jebel Mūsā, can be traced back as far as the fourth century C.E. At the foot of Jebel Mūsā, the location of Mt. Sinai which came to prevail, the monks built a church and tower (Etheria) on the spot which they believed to be the place of the burning bush. In the sixth century C.E. Justinian added a fortress/monastery which, from the tenth century on has been connected with the legend and relics of St. Catherine of Alexandria. In spite of the gap between the biblical period and the rise of these traditions, they were accepted by many scholars, such as E. Robinson and E.H. Palmer.

In the 19th century an opinion arose that the description of the theophany on Mt. Sinai reflects a volcanic eruption. Since no volcanoes were active in historical times in the Sinai Peninsula, scholars removed the location of Mt. Sinai to the Arabian Peninsula. This seemed to fit in well with other data about the wanderings, such as the identification of Elim Elath, and the close connection of the Midianites who inhabited Arabia's west coast, with the story of the Exodus (Gal. 4:25 "For this Hagar Sina is a mountain in Arabia"). Although most modern scholars reject the theory that most of the wanderings took place in Arabia, it was maintained that Mt. Sinai is in Arabia by some (M. Noth, O. Eissfeldt, J. Koenig, H. Gese). Comparisons of the descriptions of theophanies in Ancient Near Eastern literature show that the appearance of the divinity on a mountain top with thunder and fire is a common element. Therefore there is no need to connect the theophany on Mt. Sinai with an actual volcanic eruption

If the location of Mt. Sinai is inseparable from the route of the Exodus, all that remains to be done is to find a prominent mountain along one of the three main routes alternatively proposed for the Exodus. Those who hold that the route passed through the northern part of the Sinai Peninsula identify Mt. Sinai with Jebel Halāl (or Ḥalāl), Jebel Ya'allaq, or Jebel Maghāra. Advocates of the route through the central region of Sinai suggest Jebel Sinn Bishr. The hypothesis of a southern route proposes the identification of Mt. Sinai with one of the many lofty peaks in the southern mountain range, such as Jebel Sirbāl, Jebel Mūsā, Jebel Katherina, Jebel Um Shomar, etc. If, however, the historic-traditional conclusion that the account of the Exodus and the tradition of Mt. Sinai were originally independent is accepted, there is no necessity to bring Mt. Sinai in geographical relation with the route of the Exodus. The Torah is shaped by the ideology that a unified nation of Israel entered the promised land with a complete set of laws that it received in the "land that no human passed through" (Jer. 2:6), taking nothing of the "practice of the land of Egypt … and the practice of the land of Canaan" (Lev. 18:3).

There are very few data by which one could locate the holy mountain. Even if Yahweh was originally associated with a specific southern mountain or mountains, as indicated in the ancient traditions of Deut 33, Judges 5, and Habakkuk 3, the multiple traditions surviving in the Pentateuch make an identification impossible (see above). The distance of a three-day journey from Egypt (Ex. 5:3) is not a criterion, not only because Moses might have understated his real objective, but mainly because this would mean deriving an actual geographical distance from a literary formula, the three days being a typological number. The same applies to the distance of 40 days from Beer-Sheba (1 Kings 19:8). The only indication of distance seems to be Deuteronomy 1:2: "Eleven days from Horeb to Kadesh-Barnea by the Mount Seir route"; but this itself is not enough to make even a plausible suggestion.

[Ora Lipschitz / S. David Sperling]

In recent years E. Anati has attempted to identify Mount Sinai at Har Karkom in the Negev Desert on the modern border between Egypt and Israel; his identification has not won many supporters, even though he has unearthed unusual finds at the site.

[Shimon Gibson (2nd ed.)]

In the Aggadah

The world is firmly established by virtue of two holy mountains, Moriah and Sinai (Mid. Ps. to 87:1). Had Israel not stood before Mount Sinai, the world would long have collapsed and been reduced to chaos (Ruth R. Proem 1). This mountain had five names: the mountain of God, Bashan, Gavnunim, Horeb, and Sinai (Ex. R. 2:4). Others say that it had three names: the mountain of God, because there God made known His Divinity; Sinai, because there He rejected (*sana*, שנא; lit. "hated") the celestials (He did not give them the Torah) and showed His love for the terrestrials (men, by giving them the Torah); Horeb, because the Torah, called *ḥerev* ("sword," Ps. 149:6) was given there (Ex. R. 51:8). Another interpretation given of the name is that from there "*sinah* ["hatred," i.e., for the Jewish people] descended to the world" (Shab. 89a).

The mountains quarreled for the honor of having the Torah given on them, but God declared: "Sinai is the only mountain on which no idolatry has been practiced; therefore it alone is fit for the honor" (Gen. R. 99:1). Another reason is that Sinai alone modestly assumed that it was too low to expect the honor; therefore God chose it (Num. R. 13:3). He therefore brought down the upper and the lower heavens and spread them over Sinai, like a bedspread over a bed (Mekh. to Ex. 19:20), and He came from Sinai to welcome Israel like a bridegroom goes out to welcome his bride (*ibid.*, *Yitro* 19:17).

God caused Sinai to tower menacingly over the children of Israel and said to them: "If you accept the Torah, it will be well with you; if not, here will be your burial" (Shab. 88a). When they accepted it, the lasciviousness with which the primeval serpent had infected mankind left them (*ibid.*, 146a), and when they proclaimed at Sinai, "'We will do and we will listen' (Ex. 24:7), they were vouchsafed the luster of the heavenly *Shekhinah*" (PR 21:101a). Further, there were no unclean persons or lepers, no lame, blind, deaf or dumb, imbeciles or fools, and there was no dissension among them (Song R. 4:7 No. 1). Every day a *bat kol* ("heavenly voice") proclaims from Mount Horeb: "Woe to men for slighting the Torah" (Avot 6:2).

[Harry Freedman]

BIBLIOGRAPHY: C.T. Beke, *Mt. Sinai a Volcano* (1873); idem, *Sinai in Arabia and of Midian* (1878); H. Gressmann, *Mose und seine Zeit* (1913), 409–19; W.J. Phythian Adams, in: PEFQS (1930), 135–49, 192–209; idem, in: JPOS, 12 (1932), 86–104; M. Noth, in: PJB, 36 (1940), 5–28; G. Hoelscher, in: *Festschrift… R. Bultman* (1949), 127–32; J. Koenig, in: RHPR, 43 (1963), 2–31; 44 (1964) 200–35; idem, in: RHR, 167 (1965), 129–55; W. Beyerlin, *Origins and History of the Oldest Sinaitic Traditions* (1965); G. von Rad, in: *Problem of the Hexateuch and Other Essays* (1966), 11–78; H. Gese, in: BZAW, 105 (1967), 81–94. **ADD. BIBLIOGRAPHY:** F. Cross, *Canaanite Myth and Hebrew Epic* (1973), 147–94; I.L. Seeligmann, *Studies in Biblical Literature* (1992), 189–204; G. Davies, in: ABD, 6:47–49; A. Rainey and R. Notley, *The Sacred Bridge* (2006), 120; M. Har-El, *The Sinai Journeys: The Route of the Exodus in the Light of the Historical Geography of the Sinai Peninsula* (1973); E. Anati, *Har Karkom: The Mountain of God* (1986); U. Dahari, "The Monastic Center Around Mount Sinai," in: *Monastic Settlements in South Sinai in the Byzantine Period: The Archeological Remains* (2000), 25ff. (with comprehensive bibliography on Mount Sinai in later sources). IN THE AGGADAH: Ginzberg, Legends, index.

SINAI CAMPAIGN (also known as Operation Kadesh), the short war (Oct. 29–Nov. 5, 1956) between Egypt and Israel, partly coinciding with the Anglo-French Suez Campaign, launched by Israel in the wake of mounting aggression by Egyptian fedayeen ("suicide") squads.

Causes of the Campaign

Israel's *War of Independence (1948–49) was terminated by *Armistice Agreements, not peace treaties, between the State of Israel and the neighboring Arab states. The vague conditions of the agreements (especially the provisions for demilitarized zones), the refusal of the Arabs to enter into negotiations for peace, and the absence of progress towards the solution of basic problems inevitably led to the aggravation of relations between Israel and her neighbors. Between 1949 and the Sinai Campaign in 1956, Arab acts of hostility caused approximately 1,300 Israel civilian casualties. In August 1955 Egypt launched the fedayeen squads for murder and sabotage inside Israel, and Israel, in turn, conducted reprisals on an ever-increasing scale.

At the end of September 1955, Egypt and Czechoslovakia, with Soviet blessings, concluded an arms deal for the provision of large quantities of Russian arms to Egypt. This confirmed Israel's suspicions of Egypt's aggressive intentions and, since it changed the balance of armament in the Middle East, provoked a new arms race. On Oct. 24, 1956, two weeks after an Israel reprisal raid on Qalqīliya, a joint Arab military command was established, including Egypt, Jordan, and Syria, with the Egyptian chief of staff at its head. At the same time, Egypt fortified the Straits of Tiran and placed heavy guns at Ra's Nuṣrānī, thus blocking the Red Sea route to Eilat. The passage of Israel shipping through the Suez Canal was already blocked. Operation Kadesh (the code name of the Sinai Campaign) was a preemptive offensive to catch the Egyptians off balance before their hostile preparations were completed. The timing of the campaign gave Israel apparent advantages. The Egyptian leadership had dissipated its efforts between several uncoordinated political and military objectives. After the nationalization of the Suez Canal, Egypt's expectation of military intervention by the Western Powers (particularly Great Britain and France) compelled her to move armored forces back from Sinai to the canal zone. Nevertheless, she continued to convert the Sinai peninsula into a military base for the invasion of Israel and, simultaneously, continued to provoke Israel with large-scale fedayeen raids. As a result of the arms deal, the Egyptian army was expanding, and engaged in absorbing new Soviet weapons – hitherto, it had been equipped primarily with British arms and its organization had been based on British patterns. The wholesale transition to Soviet weapons necessitated remodeling the army and its operational doctrine. At such a critical time it was a grave blunder to provoke the Western Powers by nationalizing the Suez Canal and to provoke Israel by intensifying fedayeen activities. The reasons for, and objectives of, the Anglo-French attack on Egypt were quite different from those of Israel. Nevertheless, the timing of both campaigns, which was termed by many outside observers as a "collusion" between Israel and the West European powers, had a direct tactical impact on Operation *Kadesh*. The objectives of Israel's operations, as defined in the order given to the Israel Defense Forces (IDF), were: destruction of the fedayeen bases in the Gaza Strip and on the Sinai border; prevention,

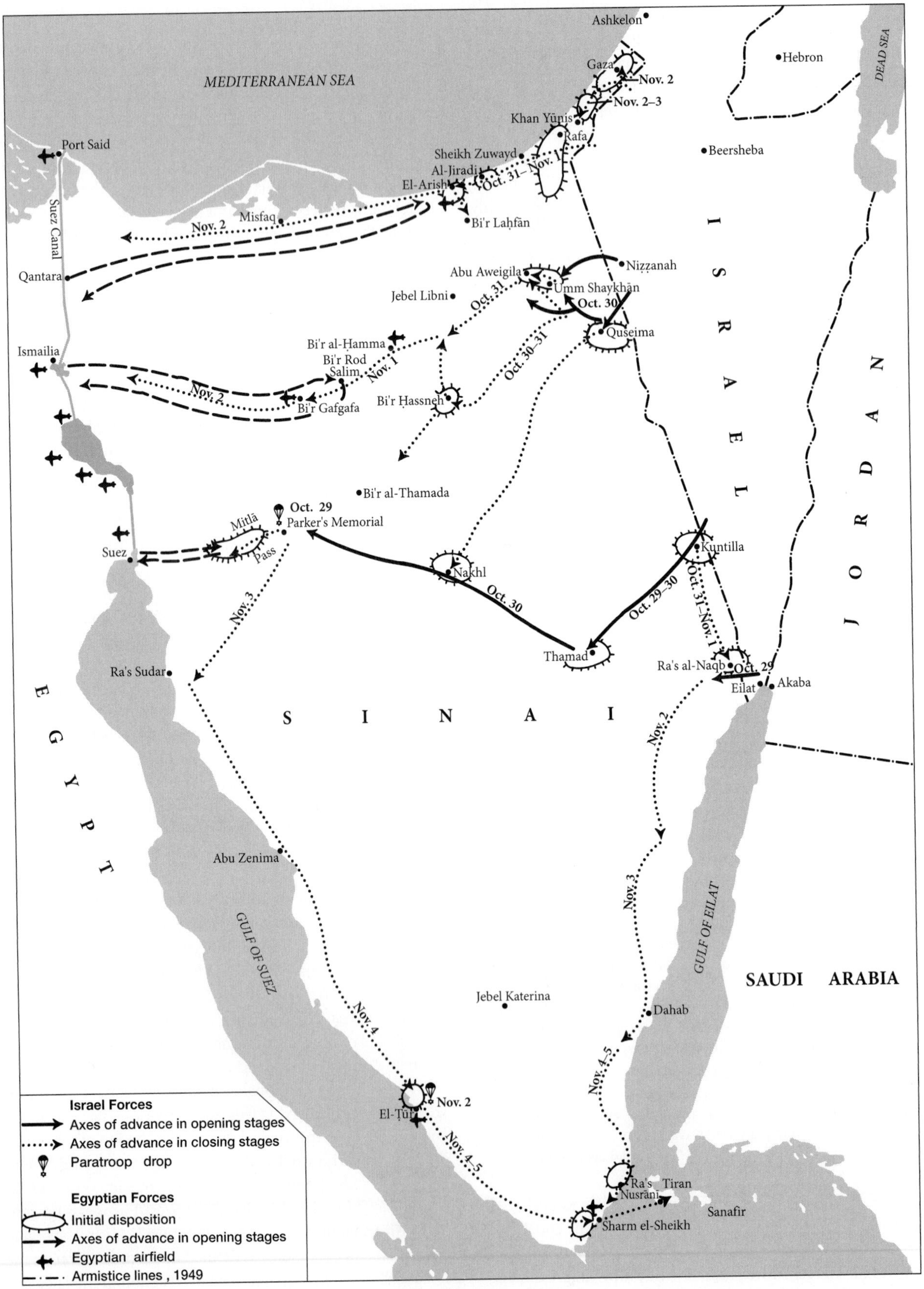

The Sinai Campaign, October 29–November 5, 1956. Based on Atlas of Israel, *Jerusalem, 1970.*

for however short a time, of an Egyptian attack on Israel by destroying Egypt's logistic establishment and the airfields in Sinai; and opening the Gulf of Eilat to undisturbed Israeli shipping. All these objectives were achieved.

The IDF had undergone many changes since the War of Independence: methods had been organized for the rapid mobilization of reserve units and of civilian vehicles and heavy mechanical equipment; weapons had been standardized and the forces trained in their use, especially in the air force and the armored corps; and a new system of tactics had been formulated and inculcated.

The Campaign

Though the Sinai Campaign lasted only eight days – from Oct. 29 to Nov. 5, 1956 – it may be divided into three phases: the opening phase on October 29–30; decision, October 31–November 1; exploitation, November 2–5.

PHASE 1: OCTOBER 29–30. In the late afternoon of October 29, an airborne battalion was dropped near Colonel Parker's Memorial in the west central area of the Sinai peninsula. Other units of the same airborne brigade moved as a mechanized column toward the same point, capturing al-Kuntilla, Thamad, and Nakhl, and reaching their destination on the night of October 30/31. With this opening move, all the Egyptian positions in northeast Sinai were outflanked, and the Suez Canal directly threatened.

In the early hours of October 30, the vital road junction of al-Quseima was captured, affording an additional gateway into Sinai from the east. This directly exposed the southern flank of the Third Egyptian Division in the northeast corner of Sinai. The seizure of the road junction enabled further Israel forces to outflank the Third Division and, at the same time, provided a second link-up with the paratroopers near Parker's Memorial. The most important achievement of this phase was the gaining of air superiority by the Israel Air Force long before the Anglo-French air forces attacked airfields in Egypt.

PHASE 2: OCTOBER 30–NOVEMBER 1. On the afternoon of October 30, a reconnaissance company ascertained that the Ḍayqa Pass was free of enemy forces. This enabled the armored brigade of the central task force to avoid a frontal clash with Egyptian forces, to get to the rear of the Abu Aweigila positions, and, in the most spectacular armored battles of the campaign, to seize the Abu Aweigila road junction and the enemy positions at the Rawāfa Dam. These victories blocked the escape route of the Egyptian brigade at Umm Qataf and Umm Shaykhān, between the frontier and Abu Aweigila. On the same afternoon, Israeli forces captured the enemy positions at ʿAwja Maṣrī near the frontier, along the Niẓẓanah-Ismailiya road. By the early evening the positions at Tarat Umm Basīs, seven kilometers from the border, had been occupied.

During the night, an infantry force, supported by artillery, took up positions on both sides of the road at Umm Ṭurfa, halfway between Umm Basīs and Umm Qataf, encircling the positions at Umm Qataf and Umm Shaykhān. In spite of transport difficulties caused by an Egyptian attempt to block the road through Umm Shaykhān, fuel and ammunition reached the Israeli armored brigade in the rear of the enemy positions. Head-on IDF attacks on these positions had failed, because they had been based on incorrect information and errors of judgment; but during the night of November 1/2, Egyptian troops withdrew from the positions, leaving their heavy equipment. During the next few days, these soldiers roamed aimlessly in the area between El-Arish, Abu Aweigila and the canal, until they were rounded up and taken prisoner.

At the same time, one armored force advanced westward. It had been reported that an Egyptian armored force was moving from the canal zone eastward, and the Israeli force laid an ambush at the Jebel Libni road junction. However, the Egyptian armored force never reached this point, for on the morning of October 31, pilots of the Israel Air Force sighted it on the road between Biʾr Gafgafa and Biʾr Ḥamma and proceeded to immobilize 90 of the vehicles. The remaining vehicles withdrew, and the Israeli armored force continued its advance westward, meeting stiff resistance from armor and artillery intended to delay the Israeli advance and allow the main body of Egyptian troops to withdraw across the Suez Canal. Orderly, organized retreat however, had already become impossible.

During the night of October 31–November 1, the IDF northern task force attacked in the northern sector and the fortified positions at Rafah were stormed, thus opening the way to the Suez Canal for an armored brigade. By the evening of November 1, armored forces had reached El-Arish, fighting all the way. At the same time there was a bloody clash in the southern sector, where the airborne brigade advancing westward from Parker's Memorial ran into an enemy ambush positioned in the caves of the Mitlā Pass. Only after fierce fighting were the paratroopers able to overpower the enemy. The general retreat from Sinai, ordered by the Egyptian high command on November 1, soon turned into a rout, with attacks by the Israel Air Force increasing the turmoil. Many Egyptian officers abandoned their men in order to save their own lives. During this phase the Egyptian destroyer *Ibrahim al-Awwal* was captured off Haifa by a combined operation of the Israel Navy and Air Force.

PHASE 3: NOVEMBER 2–5. In compliance with the Anglo-French ultimatum, the armored spearheads of the IDF halted at points ten miles from the canal on November 2, near Ismailiya on the central axis, and on November 3, in the vicinity of Qantara on the northern axis. There still remained two objectives: the capture of the Gaza Strip and the seizure of the Egyptian strongpoints at Raʾs Nuṣrānī and Sharm el-Sheikh on the Straits of Tiran. After the capture of Rafah, the Gaza Strip was cut off, and there remained only the troublesome task of mopping up scores of fortified positions and taking over the townships of Gaza, Khan Yunis, and Beit Ḥānūn. This action began on November 2 and was completed the following day.

The capture of Ra's Nuṣrānī and Sharm el-Sheikh was allotted to a reserve infantry brigade moving as a mobile column down the western shore of the Gulf of Eilat. On October 31 this column reached el-Kuntilla and, on the following day, Ra's al-Naqb, which had been seized two days earlier by other IDF troops. Since the Israel Air Force was fully occupied on the central axis, the mobile column waited until November 2 before continuing its advance. As bad road conditions and sporadic clashes with the enemy caused further delay, the general staff ordered the parachute brigade to move from Parker's Memorial toward the southern tip of the Sinai peninsula along the eastern shore of the Red Sea as far as the oil fields of Ra's Sudar. Simultaneously, paratroopers were dropped on the airfield at el-Tur. A pincer movement now threatened the last remaining Egyptian positions in Sinai. Ra's Nuṣrānī was evacuated by its garrison and, as the final act of the Sinai Campaign, Sharm el-Sheikh was stormed by the reservists on November 5.

IDF losses in the campaign were 171 dead, several hundred wounded, and four Israelis taken prisoner. Egyptian losses were estimated at several thousand dead and wounded, while 6,000 prisoners were taken. Immense quantities of armored vehicles, trucks, guns, and other military equipment were seized.

The Aftermath

As the result of a prolonged political struggle, in which both the United States and the Soviet Union opposed Israel, the IDF was compelled to evacuate the Sinai peninsula and the Gaza Strip. Troops of the United Nations Emergency Force (UNEF) were posted on the Egyptian side of the frontier and at Sharm el-Sheikh to guarantee free passage of Israeli shipping through the Straits of Tiran. Israel made it clear that any deviation from these arrangements would constitute a *casus belli*. The straits remained open until May 23, 1967, when Egypt ordered the evacuation of UNEF and closed the entrance to the Gulf of Eilat, thus precipitating the *Six-Day War.

BIBLIOGRAPHY: M. Dayan, *Diary of the Sinai Campaign* (1966); R. Henriques, *One Hundred Hours to Suez* (1957); S.L. Marshall, *Sinai Victory* (1958); E. O'Ballance, *The Sinai Campaign, 1956* (1959); T. Robertson, *Conspiracy* (1965) includes bibliography; A. Eden, *The Memoirs of Rt. Hon. Sir Anthony Eden; Full Circle* (1960), 419–584; H. Finer, *Dulles Over Suez…* (1964), includes bibliography; A. Nutting, *No End of a Lesson, The Story of Suez* (1967); H. Thomas, *The Suez Affair* (1967); L.M. Bloomfield, *Israel and the Gulf of Aqaba in International Law* (1957); A. Baufre, *L'expedition de Suez* (1967); E. Stock, *Israel on the Road to Sinai 1949–56* (1967); D. Ben-Gurion, *Israel – Years of Challenge* (1963).

[Jehuda Wallach]

SINCLAIR, CLIVE (1948–), British writer and critic. Sinclair was born in London. In 1973 he published his first novel *Bibliosexuality*. His short stories were published in two volumes, *Hearts of Gold* (1979) and *Bedbugs* (1982), collections which established him as a major talent among Anglo-Jewish writers. A feature of his stories is the strong focus on Jewish and Israeli themes, imagery, and idioms. He wrote a critical-biographical study of Isaac Bashevis *Singer and Israel Joshua *Singer, *The Brothers Singer* (1982). In 1983–87 Sinclair served as literary editor of the London *Jewish Chronicle*. Later novels include *Blood Libels* (1987) and *Augustus Rex* (1993), and an account of Israel, *Diaspora Blues* (1987).

[Susan Strul]

SINDABAR (or **Sindbad**, **Sindabot**), Indian sage who is the hero of an ancient book, *Mishlei Sindabar* (Parables of Sindbad) or *Sippurei Sindabar* (Tales of Sindbad), a collection of short stories of Buddhist origin. These belong to the type of stories dealing with the life of Asoka, "defender of the faith of Buddha," but in the course of time foreign motifs were blended into them. After many transmutations this book reached world literature, including Hebrew literature, by way of Arabic. In almost every language the names became distorted and the form of the stories underwent changes. The medieval translations were generally adaptations, every translator introducing changes in the original text, leaving out some things and adding others, and finally changing the stories round as he saw fit. Because of all these adaptations it is at times impossible to discern the original text on which the collection rested.

The Hebrew book called *Mishlei Sindbad* exists in various MSS, having first been printed in Constantinople in 1516 and appearing in five subsequent editions. Neither the translator nor his source is known. The Hebrew text is therefore an important source in investigating the history of the work. The framework of the stories is simple:

An Indian king has a son in his old age. When the latter is seven years old the king entrusts him to Sindabar, "the chief sage of India," to teach him wisdom and knowledge. The son grows up to become the wisest man in the realm. Just as the prince is about to return to his father, he and Sindabar see in the stars that if upon reaching home the prince does not preserve complete silence for the first seven days, but speaks like other men, he will be killed. The prince returns and the king is greatly troubled by his silence, for which he does not know the reason. The king has 80 wives, one of whom loves the prince. She tries to entice him to kill his father and rule in his stead. Shocked by what she says, the prince is silent. Fearing that he will expose her behavior to his father, the woman tells the king that the prince has tried to rape her and begs that he be condemned to death. When this becomes known to the king's seven advisers they go to him one by one to try and persuade him not to kill the prince. They tell him moving stories to influence him. The woman then comes to contradict the advisers, telling suitable stories of her own. When the seven days of silence are over the prince tells his father the truth. The king wishes to kill his wife, but the prince is sorry for her and begs his father to pardon her. The king recognizes the wisdom of his son, the pupil of Sindabar.

This book is also known in another Hebrew version, based on an Italian translation called *Parables of Erasto* by Isaac Uziel (15–16th centuries), published in Jerusalem in 1945.

The Hebrew version has been translated into Yiddish, German, and English (*Tales of Sendebar* (1967), tr. by M. Epstein).

See *Fiction, The Romance in Hebrew Literature.

BIBLIOGRAPHY: P. Kassel (ed.), *Mishlei Sindbad* (1888); A.M. Habermann (ed.), *Mishlei Sindbad* (1946); M. Epstein (ed. and tr.) *Tales of Sendebar* (1967).

[Abraham Meir Habermann]

SINGAPORE, republic; major entrepôt of S.E. Asia, formerly a British crown colony. The first Jews to settle there were of Baghdadi origin, mainly from India, who migrated to Singapore in 1840 when the *Sassoon family established business interests. Prayers were first held in a house in the street still known as "Synagogue Street." The Maghain Aboth synagogue was opened in 1878; it possessed a number of Torah scrolls in beaten silver cases brought from Baghdad. Another synagogue, Chased El, was built in 1904 by Sir Manasseh Meyer, reputed to be the richest Jew in the Far East. He also endowed a *talmud torah*. Local custom sanctioned conveyance to synagogue by rickshaw on Sabbath. The community remained largely Sephardi, but Ashkenazi immigrants from England, the Netherlands, China, Russia, and Germany also settled there. Most engaged in business and the professions. The community continued to be highly prosperous and important out of all proportion to its size. The 1931 census records that the 832 Jews and larger number of Arab residents were the largest house property owners in the city. There were over 1,500 Jewish inhabitants by 1939. Many were interned by the Japanese during World War II, and a number subsequently immigrated to Australia, England, the United States, and Israel. Apart from their contribution to commerce, Jews have taken a considerable part in political life and in 1955 David S. *Marshall became the first chief minister of the republic. The community is represented by the Jewish Welfare Board which publishes a monthly bulletin. There exist two synagogues with one officiating rabbi; social activities center in the Menorah Club. The community numbered approximately 450 in 1968. In the early 21st century the community numbered 300, many of them expatriate Israelis and American and British Jews. There was a rabbi and Sabbath services were held at the Waterloo Road and Maghain Aboth synagogues (Sephardi). The expatriates founded the United Hebrew Congregation. Sunday school classes were held for children and the community had a quarterly publication, *Shalom*. The community center was a focus of Jewish life and there was also an old age home.

[Percy S. Gourgey / Tudor Parfitt (2nd ed.)]

Relations with Israel

From the beginning of the 1960s, trade relations began to develop between Singapore and Israel. Israeli experts extended technical aid to Singapore, while a number of mutual visits were made by ministers, public figures, and senior officials. In 1968 a trade agreement was signed by the two countries and an Israeli trade mission opened in Singapore. In May 1969 diplomatic relations were established, and in July the Israeli ambassador presented his credentials. Technical cooperation included the dispatch of Israeli advisers to the Singapore army. In 1970 the two countries signed an aviation agreement. The Singapore-Israel Industrial R&D Foundation (SIIRD) was established in 1997 to promote, facilitate, and support joint industrial R&D projects between Singaporean and Israeli high-tech companies. The Economic Development Board (EDB) of Singapore and the Office of the Chief Scientist (OCS), of the Ministry of Industry and Trade of Israel are the two cooperating government agencies responsible for the research and development support fund.

BIBLIOGRAPHY: I. Cohen, *Journal of a Jewish Traveller* (1925), index. **ADD. BIBLIOGRAPHY:** E. Nathan, *The History of Jews in Singapore 1830–1945* (1986); T. Parfitt, *The Thirteenth Gate* (1987).

SINGER, ABRAHAM (1849–1914), Hungarian rabbi and scholar. He served as rabbi at Varpalota and wrote studies on the history of Hungarian Jewry and his community in particular. Among his publications is a work on the development of the Reform movement in the 19th century, *Paris, Braunschweig, Arad* (1899), as well as *Deutsch-ungarisches Handbuch der Matrikelfuehrung* (1884). His son LEO SINGER (d. 1944) also served as rabbi in Varpalota and wrote on Hungarian Jewish history.

He translated a number of Hebrew texts into Hungarian: Psalms (Zsoltárok, 1962²); the Passover *Haggadah* (1929); parts of Baḥya ibn Paquda's *Ḥovot ha-Levavot* (1907); and S. Ganzfried's *Kiẓẓur Shulḥan Arukh* (3 vols., 1934–39; repr. 1962). He also wrote belletristic works, among them Asmodáj (1922), a drama, and *Eszter királyné* (1928, 1940). In 1944 he was murdered by the Nazis.

BIBLIOGRAPHY: *Magyar Zsidó Lexikon* (1929), 790.

SINGER, BRYAN (1965–), U.S. writer, director, producer. Singer was born in New York, N.Y., and raised in Princeton Junction and Lawrenceville, N.J., by father Norbert (businessman) and mother Grace Sinden (environmental activist). Introverted as a child, Singer played piano from an early age, loved movies and the TV show *Star Trek*, and at 12, became fascinated with still photography. By his early teens, he was shooting 8-mm and Super-8 films in his backyard, with friend Ethan Hawke and schoolmate Christopher McQuarrie (who wrote the Oscar-winning screenplay for Singer's *The Usual Suspects*). He graduated high school in 1984, attended the School of Visual Arts in New York, then transferred to the University of Southern California. He was only 23 when his first major release, *Public Access*, garnered the prestigious Sundance Grand Jury Prize. Two years later, Singer directed the hit *The Usual Suspects* (1995). He directed and produced *Apt Pupil* (1997), adapted from a Stephen King short story which involved a neighbor with a Nazi past. He followed this by directing *X-Men* (2000), a $75-million reworking of the famed Marvel comic book for the big screen. This tale of reluctant superheroes piqued his interest, he said, because it is "about a gang of outsiders. They're mutants. The films I've made so far are about characters who hide something below the surface, some secret they don't reveal." The character Magnito is a Holocaust survivor. Singer directed and executive-produced the sequel X-2 (2003). Singer also produced the acclaimed TV series *House, M.D.* (2004).

[Amy Handelsman (2nd ed.)]

SINGER, CHARLES JOSEPH (1876–1960), British historian of science and medicine. The son of R. Simeon*Singer, Charles Singer spent several years as a physician before his interests turned to the history of medicine. He taught the subject at Oxford from 1914 to 1920, when he transferred to University College, London. He was promoted to a professorship in 1930. Singer served as president of the International Union of the History of Science (1947–1949), and in 1956 he and his wife Dorothea were joint recipients of that organization's highest award, the Sarton Medal. Singer's contributions to scholarship were prodigious. He produced over 400 books, translations, articles, and reviews. He published *The Evolution of Anatomy* (1925); *A Short History of Medicine* (1928, 1962²); and *A Short History of Biology* (1931). He translated many great anatomical works, including *Vesalius on the Human Brain* (1952) and *Galen on Anatomical Procedures* (1956). Among his extensive writings on the history of magic and its relationship to medicine and science was his *From Magic to Science* (1928). On the history of technology, he published a study of alum manufacture, *The Earliest Chemical Industry* (1948), and he helped to edit a five-volume *History of Technology* (1954–58). Throughout his career Singer maintained an active interest in Jewish history and affairs. In 1927 he collaborated with Edwyn R. Bevan in editing *The Legacy of Israel*, contributing jointly with his wife an essay on "The Jewish Factor in Medieval Thought." During the 1930s and 1940s, in response to the rise of Nazism, he wrote several articles and pamphlets on contemporary Christian attitudes toward Jews. He was also active in the rescue and protection of victims of Nazi oppression. His wife, DOROTHEA WALEY SINGER (1882–1964), social worker and scholar, was chairman of the bibliographical commission of the International Academy for Historical Science from 1947 to 1950, and vice president from 1950 to 1953.

BIBLIOGRAPHY: A.R. Hall, in: *Isis*, 51 (1960), 558–60 (Eng.); E.A. Underwood (ed.), *Science, Medicine and History Essays ... Charles Singer*, 2 vols. (1953), incl. bibl.

[Theodore M. Brown]

SINGER, GEORGE (1908–1980), conductor, composer and pianist. Born in Prague, Singer studied piano and composition at the Music Academy (1924–26) and won a piano competition (1925). He made his début as an opera conductor in the Neues Deutsches Theater (1926–30). Thereafter, Singer went to Hamburg to conduct the Staatsoper. In 1934 he returned to Prague, where he gave the first radio performance of the concert version of Dvořák's first opera, *Alfred*. When the Nazis invaded Czechoslovakia, he went to Palestine in 1939 on the "illegal" immigrant ship *Tiger Hill*. He was among the founders and conductor of the Palestine Opera, serving until 1945. On the establishment of the Israel Opera in 1947, he became its permanent guest conductor. Singer often conducted the Israel Philharmonic Orchestra, the Israeli Broadcasting Orchestra, the Israel Chamber Orchestra, the Haifa Symphony Orchestra, and the Rubinstein Festival. From 1947 he also toured widely conducting orchestras and operas in Europe, the United States, and Russia (1956), giving especially noteworthy performances of the works of Czechoslovakian and Israeli composers. Among the opera premières he conducted were Darius *Milhaud's *King David* (1954); *Avidom's *Alexandra the Hasmonean* (1959), and Karel *Salamon's *Vows*. He gave the premières of several Israeli orchestral works, such as *Avidom's Symphony no. 4; Ben Haim's *To the Chief Musician* for orchestra, Symphony No. 2 and *The Sweet Psalmist of Israel*; *Boskovich's Oboe Concerto; and *Gelbrun's Rilke Songs. He was known for his phenomenal facility in sight-reading and conducting every nuance of an orchestral score. Among his compositions are Sinfonietta for orchestra (1950), two suites for orchestra (1957, 1960), a piano concertino (1965) and vocal and piano music.

BIBLIOGRAPHY: Grove Music Online.

[Naama Ramot (2nd ed.)]

SINGER, HOWARD (1922–), author. A Conservative rabbi, he published a best-selling first novel, *Wake Me When It's Over* (1959), which was followed by *The Devil and Henry Raftin* (1967). *Bring Forth the Mighty Men: On Violence and the Jewish Character* (1969), a study of the Israeli fighting character, bitterly attacked the U.S. Jewish establishment for alleged reticence over the defense of the Jew.

SINGER, ISAAC BASHEVIS (1904–1991), Yiddish novelist, critic, and journalist. The younger brother of the novelists Ester Kraytman and I.J. *Singer, Isaac was born into a rabbinical family in Leoncin, Poland. He grew up in Warsaw, where he made his career until his emigration to America in 1935, though in 1917 he left the city with his mother and younger brother and lived for a few years in his mother's hometown of Bilgoraj, where his grandfather was rabbi. His education was traditional. He taught himself German and Polish. In Warsaw his home was on the poor and teeming Krochmalna Street, where his father held a *bet din*. The old-world tradition and way of life and his father's rich library inspired in him an interest in philosophy in general and in the Kabbalah in particular. His brother's example as a secular Yiddish writer was also of the greatest importance to Singer's artistic and moral development.

Singer's Pseudonyms

Prolific and versatile, Singer's multiple talents group themselves behind his various pseudonyms. He made his debut in the literary world with "*Oyf der Elter*" (in *Literarishe Bleter*, no. 60, 1925) which he signed "*Tse*" (צ׳). In the same journal that year (no. 80), his story "*Vayber*" was published under the pseudonym "Isaac Bashevis" (a derivative of his mother's first name, Bas-Sheva (Yid. for Bath-Sheba)), which he used only for his serious literary creations. Its adoption was prompted by the desire to avoid confusion with his famous brother, Israel Joshua Singer. For his more or less serious journalism Bashevis adopted the name Y. Varshavski, and for his feuilletons and lighter pieces, that of D. Segal. However, his pseudonyms are not inflexible: with shaping and reordering, Varshavski's memoirs became Singer's *Mayn Tatn's Beys-Din Shtub.*

Imagistic Portrayals of Inner Forces

Singer was recognized early in his literary career. His first major fictional work, *Sotn in Goray* (1935; *Satan in Goray*, 1955), had been preceded by short stories in such respected journals as *Varshever Shriftn* (1926–27) and the Warsaw *Globus* (1932–34), where *Sotn in Goray* and its antecedent "*Der Yid fun Bovl*" first appeared. The kabbalist protagonist of the latter, after life-long traffic with the occult, is finally claimed by the satanic host, despite his conscious will to resist. Here we see the implacable workings of dark inner forces which Singer projects in images derived from folklore. The typical Singer hero is virtually helpless before his passion: he is "possessed." The town of Goray in *Sotn in Goray* is "possessed" by the false messianism which in 17th-century Poland wrought havoc on Jewish life. "Let none attempt to force the Lord" is the moral of this parable for all times. This "anti-Prometheanism" (a term used by Shlomo *Bickel in his criticism on Bashevis) is a dominant note in Singer's work.

U.S. Publications in English Translation

In the United States, Singer's stories and serialized novels became a regular feature of the New York Yiddish daily *Forward*, and in the 1950s his stories began to appear in translation in serious magazines. His first *Forward* serial, *Di Familye Mushkat* (1950; *The Family Moskat*, 1950), is a realistic epical novel of pre-World War II Warsaw. *Satan in Goray* initiated the U.S. acclaim of Singer as the artist of the grotesque and demoniac who generated more interest than the realistic chronicler of the more recent Polish Jewish past. Of the volumes that Bashevis published in English from 1955, only three appeared in book form in Yiddish; two of these, five to six years after their English translation. Singer was thus in the curious position of writing for two very distinct audiences: the sophisticated public that read him in translation in *Commentary* and in the *New Yorker*, and the *Jewish Daily Forward* Yiddish readership, less sophisticated, but with wider Jewish knowledge. Singer declared that "nothing can spoil a writer more than writing for the translator" (*Commentary*, vol. 36, no. 5, 1963); yet the suspicion that he himself did persists.

Motifs and Styles of His Works

Singer was above all a marvelous and interesting storyteller, no matter where he might be leading his expectant, and often puzzled, reader. If his demons, imps, and spirits are regarded as a shorthand ("a kind of spiritual stenography" Singer called it) for complex human behavior, then one need not be distressed by the author's professed belief in their substantive reality. Singer's fictional writings include a variety of narrators and protagonists living on the margins of Jewish society, such as the mentally disturbed, criminals, prostitutes, and various other extraordinary individuals (e.g., the *Magican of Lublin*, 1960). Many of his fictional writings tend to center around the sexual and the sacred, especially their interrelationship: "In my stories it is just one step from the study house to sexuality and back again. Both phases of human existence have continued to interest me" (*In My Father's Court*, p. 175). Though eroticism has been present in Yiddish literature for over half a century, many Yiddish readers, preferring a "balanced view" of Jewish life and of man in general, find the sexual motif in Singer overworked and exaggerated.

Singer's serious fiction falls into three groups: his realistic novels, his short romances or novellas, and his short stories. To these may be added his memoirs (like *Mayn Tatn's Beys-Din Shtub*, 1950; *In My Father's Court*, 1966, a work which is both art and documentary; *Gloybn un Tsveyfl*, 1974, 1976, 1978; *A Little Boy in Search of God*, 1976; *A Young Man in Search of Love*, 1978; *Lost in America*, 1981; and others which only appeared in the *Forverts*), and also his autobiographical novels (like *Der Sertificat*, 1967; *The Certificate*, 1992; *Neshome Ekspeditsyes*, 1974; *Shosha*, 1978: and others). Singer is at home in a variety of styles, modes, and subjects; he moves freely from the medieval to the contemporary, from the naturalistic to the fantastic, from psychological illumination to parapsychological mystification. His typical pose is one of ironic detachment.

Realistic Novels

The Manor (1967; written in 1953–55), first serialized in the *Forward* under the title *Der Hoyf* of which it constitutes part 1, is a realistic family chronicle of late 19th-century Polish Jewish life. Similar in style to *The Family Moskat*, it suffers from the same loose structure but is largely redeemed by the same vividness. A continuation was called *The Estate* (1970).

Set in 19th-century Poland, *The Magician of Lublin* (1960) has for its protagonist a Jewish magician-acrobat Don Juan whose Faustian striving eventually leads to penitential self-incarceration. *The Slave* (1962; Yid., *Der Knekht*, 1967), a universalistic parable set in 17th-century Poland after the *Chmielnicki massacres, portrays an enslaved Jew who falls in love with the daughter of his peasant master; the gulf between them is bridged by the unifying and transcendent power of love. The miracle at the end of *The Slave* disturbs readers who look amiss at interference, whether authorial or supernatural.

Shadows on the Hudson (1998) is another realistic novel which introduces a large variety of New York Jews from different backgrounds and describes the complex interactions between them.

Shorter Fictional Works

It is in the shorter forms of fiction that Singer excels, and some of his stories (e.g., "Gimpel the Fool") are among the finest in any language. *Gimpel the Fool and Other Stories* (1957; Yid., *Gimpl Tam un Andere Dertseylungen*, 1963), *The Spinoza of*

Market Street (1961), and *Short Friday* (1964) are quite varied collections of short stories written over a period of many years. Their typical setting is the *shtetl*, often visited by Satan's emissaries. The demoniac tales, rich in grotesquerie and often narrated by devils and imps, range from studies in pathology to parables of the arbitrariness of the evil in life. Typically, it is through the weakness of the flesh that Satan conquers.

Free of demons and asserting the freedom to behave irrationally, *The Spinoza of Market Street* concerns an ineffectual philosopher who achieves salvation through the flesh. The irrational expresses itself in a context of "normalcy," where soup and sympathy come to acquire magical properties. "Gimpel the Fool" is in the great divine-fool tradition and recalls *Peretz's "Bontshe Shvayg." Its theme is the ambiguous nature of sublunary truth and reality: "No doubt," says Gimpel, "the world is entirely an imaginary world, but it is only once removed from the true world.… Whatever may be there, it will be real, without complication, without ridicule, without deception. God be praised: there even Gimpel cannot be deceived."

Singer's Place in Yiddish and World Literature

The leading exponent of Yiddish imaginative prose, Singer is also an important figure in contemporary world literature. Enjoying a somewhat ambiguous place among Yiddish writers, he is nonetheless firmly rooted in Jewish tradition. Like Yiddish literature itself, Singer's art is a unique amalgam of the indigenous and the naturalized, of specifically Jewish and general world culture. In recognition of his literary work he was awarded the Nobel Prize for literature in 1978, the first awarded for Yiddish literature.

BIBLIOGRAPHY: I.H. Buchen, *I.B. Singer and the Eternal Past* (1968); M. Allentuck (ed.), *The Achievements of Isaac Bashevis Singer* (1969); Fixler, in: *Kenyon Review* (Spring 1964), 371–86; I. Howe, in: *Commentary*, 30 (1960), 350–3; 36 (1963), 364–72; Dan Jacobson, *ibid.*, 39 (1966), 48–52; I.B. Singer, *Selected Stories* (1966), v–xxiv; S.E. Hyman, in: *The New Leader* (July 28, 1962); Eisenberg, in: *Judaism*, 11 (1962), 345–56; S. Bickel, *Shrayber fun Mayn Dor*, 1 (1958), 358–65; Gross-Zimmermann, in: *Goldene Keyt*, 60 (1967), 190–4; Y.Y. Trunk, *Di Yidishe Proze in Poyln* (1949), 136–49. **ADD. BIBLIOGRAPHY:** D.N. Miller, *Bibliography of Isaac Bashevis Singer 1924–1949* (1983); C. Shmeruk, "Polish-Jewish Relations in the Historical Fiction of Isaac Bashevis Singer," in: *The Polish Review*, 32 (1978), 401–13; idem, "The Perils of Translation: Isaac Bashevis Singer in English and Hebrew," in: E. Mendelsohn (ed.), *Literary Strategies – Jewish Texts and Contexts* (1996), 228–33; idem, "Between Autobiography and Fiction," Introduction to Isaac Bashevis Singer, *My Father's Court* (1996), V–XVII; J. Hadda, *Isaac Bashevis Singer – A Life* (1997); S.L. Wolitz (ed.), *The Hidden Isaac Bashevis Singer* (2001); H. Denman (ed.), *Isaac Bashevis Singer: His Work and His World* (2002).

[Leonard Prager / Nathan Cohen (2nd ed.)]

SINGER, ISIDORE (1859–1939), writer and editor. Singer, born in Weisskirchen, Moravia, edited the *Oesterreichische Literaturzeitung* in 1884–85 and then became literary secretary to the French ambassador in Vienna. In 1887 he moved to Paris where he was employed by the press bureau of the French foreign office. Active in the defense of Alfred Dreyfus, he founded and edited *La Vraie Parole* (1893–94), which was intended to counteract *Drumont's *La Libre Parole*. Singer was a man of vision; among the plans which he cherished was one for an "encyclopedia of the history and mental evolution of the Jewish race." An article in the *American Hebrew* convinced him that this purpose could only be accomplished in the U.S. and on reading it he traveled to New York (1895) where he set about enlisting support for his project. After many difficulties, *The Jewish *Encyclopedia* appeared in 12 volumes (1901–09), with Singer as managing editor. He was also managing editor of the *International Insurance Encyclopedia* (7 vols., 1910) and coeditor of *German Classics of the 19th and 20th Centuries*, in 20 volumes. From 1882 onward he wrote a steady stream of books in German, French, and English. He was the editor of a memorial volume for the victims of the Kishinev pogrom, *Russia at the Bar of the American People* (1904), and in 1922 he founded the American League for the Rights of Man.

BIBLIOGRAPHY: AJYB, 6 (1904/05), 188–9.

[Sefton D. Temkin]

SINGER, ISRAEL (1942–), chairman of the *World Jewish Congress and of the Conference on Jewish Material Claims Against Germany (the Claims Conference). Raised in Brooklyn, Singer was the child of refugees from Vienna who sought refuge in Switzerland, Germany, and France, eventually landing in a detention camp in France. They came to the United States in 1942. His father had a doctorate in economics and went into the costume jewelry business. His background was a mixture of right-wing religious views and Zionism. He went to Brooklyn College despite the fact that this was not permitted in the yeshivah in which he studied. He attended college at night, in a clandestine manner, where those few people who were also earning their rabbinical ordination were not deprecated. Jewish education and secular education were separate domains of learning and were considered in conflict with one another. He was ordained a rabbi in 1964 at Yeshiva Torah vo'Daath, and taught political science and Middle Eastern Studies at the City University of New York and, from 1969 to 1971, political theory in the department of politics at Bar-Ilan University in Israel. He made two brief departures from the academic world, to serve in the office of the mayor of New York during the Lindsay Administration and, later, to assist President Ford's administration during his reelection campaign.

Singer became an adjunct professor of political science at Brooklyn College in the late 1960s, where he led a sit-in to show Jewish students how to get the Judaic Studies department they wanted. He was a catalyst for one of the most active Jewish student bodies in America, and largely because of his actions, Brooklyn College eventually developed an excellent Judaic Studies Department that, among other things, pioneered Holocaust Studies.

Singer met Nahum *Goldmann, then the president of the World Jewish Congress, in Israel in 1969, when Goldmann was trying to make contact with the Russians in order to promote peace after the 1967 war. Singer, who was an activist on behalf of Soviet Jewry, introduced him to Ambassador Anatoly Dobrynin. Singer became a WJC expert on East-West relations. He became their operative, then their major activist. That was about the time that Edgar *Bronfman arrived, at the behest of his father Samuel, who wanted him to get involved.

Together Bronfman and Singer took an organization with an impressive title but not much of a constituency and transformed it into an effective arm of the Jewish community, raising its profile and leading many causes, including pressing the Kurt *Waldheim Affair to make the Austrians come to terms with his record as a German solider during World War II and the Swiss Banking issue, forcing the Swiss to confront their record of expropriation of survivors' bank accounts and their refusal to turn these account over to rightful heirs. In each of these cases, critics accused them of provoking antisemitism, but despite the accusations they persevered and were ultimately vindicated. Singer conducted the negotiations with the German government regarding the settlement of outstanding claims. His conduct was described even by critics as brilliant and indefatigable. As a result, after the death of Israel Miller, he also became chairman of the *Conference on Jewish Material Claims Against Germany. Critics of their work at the WJC accuse Bronfman and Singer of being too dovish and too critical of the Israeli government.

As chairman of the World Jewish Restitution Organization, Singer carried out negotiations to benefit Holocaust survivors and heirs of Holocaust victims around the world.

In early 2006, pursuant to an agreement between the World Jewish Congress and the attorney general of the State of New York, Singer, while not charged with any criminal violation, was removed from all fiduciary responsibility for the World Jewish Congress and was named to head a policy advisory group.

[Jeanette Friedman and Michael Berenbaum (2nd ed.)]

SINGER, ISRAEL JOSHUA (1893–1944), Yiddish novelist, playwright, and journalist. Born in Bilgoraj, Poland, the son and grandson of rabbis, Singer was the second child of a family of Yiddish writers that included his elder sister, Esther Singer *Kreitman, and younger brother, Isaac Bashevis *Singer. He received a traditional Jewish education and was influenced by the opposing strains of Jewish thought represented by his misnagdic mother and his ḥasidic father. When he was 14, the family moved to the ḥasidic court at Radzimin and then to Warsaw, where Singer worked as an unskilled laborer and proofreader. He studied painting and hid in an artists' atelier to avoid military service. By 1918, when he traveled to the Soviet Union, he had already begun publishing his earliest stories. Returning to Warsaw in late 1921, he was associated with the small, fluid group of writers called Di Khalyastre ("the Gang"), who opposed both social realism and romanticized depictions of Jewish life. Their journal, *Khalyastre*, included illustrations by Marc *Chagall and poems, stories, and essays by Peretz *Markish, Melekh *Ravitch, Uri Zvi *Greenberg, Y. *Opatoshu, Oser *Warszawski, David *Hofshtein, and Singer. When Singer published his most ambitious work up to that time, a short story entitled "Perl" ("Pearls," in *Ringen*, 1921), he attracted the attention of Abraham *Cahan, the editor of the New York daily *Forverts*. Singer served as a correspondent for the newspaper, reporting on his travels throughout Poland, the Soviet Union, and, in 1932, the U.S., where he finally settled in 1934. His travelogue, *Nay Rusland* ("New Russia," 1928), like his subsequent work, appeared first in *Forverts*. He wrote fiction under his own name and journalistic essays primarily under G. Kuper, his wife's maiden name.

His early works included *Erd-Vey* ("Earth Pangs," 1922), a symbolist drama which was effectively staged in 1923 by the New York Yiddish Art Theater; the short-story collections *Perl un Andere Dertseylungen* ("Pearls and Other Stories," 1922); and *Oyf Fremder Erd* ("On Foreign Ground," 1925). His first novel, *Shtol un Ayzn* (1927; *Blood Harvest*, 1935, and *Steel and Iron*, 1969), generated considerable controversy about the place of politics in fiction. Accused of not understanding politics and convinced that his critics were merely political hacks, Singer publicly renounced Yiddish literature, turning to journalism instead. But only four years later he published his second and most successful novel, *Yoshe Kalb* (1932; *The Sinner*, 1933, and *Yoshe Kalb*, 1965), a psychologically astute novel about a man who adopts two personalities and remains, until the end, an enigmatic figure. *Savinkov: Drame in 12 Bilder* ("Savinkov: a Play in 12 Scenes") appeared in *Globus* in 1933, before Singer's departure from Poland. He published three more novels after his arrival in the U.S.: *Di Brider Ashkenazi* (1936; *The Brothers Ashkenazi*, 1936, 1980); *Khaver Nakhmen* (1938; *East of Eden*, 1939); *Di Mishpokhe Karnovski* (1943; *The Family Carnovsky*, 1969). Adapted for the stage, *Yoshe Kalb* was performed in New York in 1932 and became one of the most successful plays ever produced in the Yiddish theater; less successful adaptations of his other novels followed: *Di Brider Ashkenazi* in 1938, *Khaver Nakhmen* in 1939, and *Di Mishpokhe Karnovski* in 1943. In addition, a collection of stories, *Friling* ("Spring," 1937) appeared in Warsaw and two more posthumous works appeared in New York: his autobiographical memoir, *Fun a Velt Vos iz Nishto Mer* (1946; *Of A World That Is No More*, 1970), and *Dertseylungen* ("Stories," 1949).

Singer was a successful and admired literary figure, most of whose works were translated into English during his lifetime. His family sagas, *The Brothers Ashkenazi* and *The Family Carnovsky*, written after the rise of Nazism, present a view of Jewish history as inexorably cyclical, repeating itself in every generation, even when the rest of the world moves on. His epic novel, *The Brothers Ashkenazi* traces the history of twin brothers and of the industrial city of Lodz. Written in the first years of Nazi rule, it ends with World War I, the Russian Revolution, and the establishment of an independent Poland. The fates of the religious and the Marxist, the assimilated and the traditional Jew are all identical. By the time Singer wrote *The Family Carnovsky*, he was explicitly coming to terms with the early years of what was already being called in Yiddish *khurbn* ("Holocaust"). The novel traces three generations through half a century, following the family from a Polish *shtetl* to Berlin to New York and ending almost at the moment of publication. At the end of the novel, Singer leaves his characters' fates uncertain, a sign of the difficulty of conceiving of a coherent conclusion to the conflicts of the novel and current history. Singer's energies were no doubt elsewhere. His correspondence during the period is full of increasing concern about his family's fate under the Nazis (he could not maintain contact with his mother and youngest brother, caught in the war's upheaval; neither survived the war, though Singer died still uncertain of their fates).

Singer's fiction examines the political and cultural upheavals in Jewish life between the two world wars and on two continents. They portray a seemingly endless series of wars, class conflicts, pogroms, shifts in borders, and messianic ideologies, critiquing every one of the many choices available to Jews of the period: traditional religious life, secularism, Yiddish culturalism, Zionism, socialism, even individualism. His primary theme is the ultimately destructive nature of any messianic belief in religious, social, or historical resolutions for the problems that beset the individual and the Jews. His fictions offer no resolutions to the tensions in which his characters find themselves, telling instead of the modern Jewish writer's responsibility to articulate these dilemmas and analyze them.

BIBLIOGRAPHY: I. Howe, in: *Commentary*, 41:3 (1966), 76–82; C. Madison, *Yiddish Literature* (1968), 452–78; I.B. Singer, *Mayn Tatn's Beys-Din Shtub* (1950), passim; *Yoshe Kalb* (1965), v–x (introduction by I.B. Singer); M. Ravitch, in: JBA, 26 (1968), 121–3; Sh. Bickel, in: *Zamlbikher*, 6 (1945), 444–8; idem, *Shrayber fun Mayn Dor*, 1 (1958), 317–27; LNYL, 3 (1960), 640–6; N. Mayzel, *Noente un Vayte*, 2 (1926), 233–9; idem, *Forgeyer un Mittsaytler* (1946), 372–93; B. Rivkin, *Undzere Prozaiker* (1951), 264–73; A. Zeitlin, in: I.J. Singer, *Fun a Velt Vos iz Nishto Mer* (1946), 5–12. **ADD. BIBLIOGRAPHY:** C. Sinclair, *The Brothers Singer* (1983); A. Norich, *The Homeless Imagination in the Fiction of I.J. Singer* (1991).

[Anita Norich (2nd ed.)]

SINGER, JOSEF (1841–1911), *ḥazzan*. Josef Singer was born in Hlinik, Hungary, where his father, Israel Singer (1806–1897), who had been a *meshorer* with Dovid'l Brod (Strelisker), was *ḥazzan*. From 1866 to 1874 Josef Singer was cantor in Beuthen (Upper Silesia) and from 1874 to 1880 chief cantor in Nuremberg. In 1881 he was called to Vienna to replace Solomon Sulzer upon the latter's retirement as chief cantor of the Viennese community in the Seitenstettengasse synagogue. He also taught singing at the Jewish Institute for the Blind and fostered the establishment of a cantors' school. He published a considerable number of studies on various aspects of *ḥazzanut*, chiefly in *Der juedische Kantor* and *Oesterreich-Ungarische Kantorenzeitung*, and the cantor's manual *Amidat Sheli'aḥ Ẓibbur* (1906). His most influential publication was the booklet *Die Tonarten des traditionellen Synagogengesanges (Steiger) – ihr Verhaeltnis zu den Kirchentonarten und den Tonarten der vorchristlichen Musikperiode* (1886; reprinted, with abbreviations, in Aron Friedman (ed.), *Dem Andenken Eduard Birnbaums*, 1 (1922): 90–100). There he attempted to systematize the *shtayger* patterns of Ashkenazi *ḥazzanut* by comparing their scale structure with ancient European and Greek scales and arriving at certain hypotheses as to their antiquity and "Jewishness." The undertaking was one of the earliest attempts of its kind, and unlike similar previous and later attempts, was based both on the author's profound knowledge of the tradition and on a serious attempt to utilize the resources of historical musicology as far as they were available at that time. Its basic weaknesses were only understood much later, and for a long time Singer's theses were taken up by many writers on Jewish music.

Singer's daughter Clara married the composer Oscar *Straus. His son SIMON (1870–1931) became a baritone singer at the Pressburg and Hamburg operas, but from 1900 onward made a career as a cantor, officiating first at Katowice and, after World War I, at Halle. He was also a composer and writer on music.

BIBLIOGRAPHY: Sendrey, Music, index; Friedmann, Lebensbilder, 1 (1918), 170; 2 (1921), 49–52; 3 (1927), 64–66; E. Birnbaum, in: *Juedisches Literaturblatt*, 15 (1886), fasc. 24–25 (repr. with remarks by L. Kornitzer, in: *Der juedische Kantor*, 6 (1932), 5:1–3); Wininger, Biog. s.v.

[Bathja Bayer]

SINGER, JOSEF (1923–), Israel aeronautical engineer. Born in Vienna, Singer went to Palestine in 1933. He served in the RAF (1943–46) and the Israel Defense Forces (1949–55), where he rose to the rank of major and was chief testing and development engineer. From 1965 he was professor of aeronautical engineering at the Technion in Haifa. He was also president of the Technion in 1982–86 and chairman of the board of Israel Aircraft Industries 1986–87. Singer did research work on aircraft structural analysis and shell theory. In 2000 he was awarded the Israel Prize.

[Samuel Aaron Miller]

SINGER, JOSEPH (1797–1871), Austro-Hungarian soldier. Born in Lemberg, Galicia, he was one of the first Jewish career officers in the Austro-Hungarian Army and fought against Napoleon in Italy. In 1832 as captain he was attached to the general staff of Field Marshal Radetzky. He fought in the Italian campaign of 1847/48. When Field Marshal Hess succeeded Radetzky in command of the Austrian army in Italy, Singer was appointed his chief of staff. He was promoted to field marshal-lieutenant in 1859. Throughout his life, Singer remained a Jew, and did not succumb to pressure to convert. On his death he received a state funeral.

[Mordechai Kapla]

SINGER, KURT (1885–1944), musicologist. Born in Berent in German Poland, Singer was music critic for the socialist newspaper *Vorwaerts*. In 1935 he became musical director of the Juedischer *Kulturbund. He moved to Holland in 1939 but was arrested during the German occupation and taken to the *Theresienstadt concentration camp, where he died. Singer wrote *Richard Wagner* (1913), *Bruckners Chormusik* (1924), *Berufskrankheiten des Musikers* (1927), *Diseases of the Musical Profession* (1932), and *Heilwirkung der Musik* (1927).

SINGER, LUDVIK (1876–1931), Czech political leader. Born in Kolin, Singer established himself as a lawyer first in his native town and afterward in Prague. In 1907 he joined the Zionist movement and soon became the leading personality among Czech-speaking Zionists. In 1916, his proposal to establish a Zionist newspaper led to the creation of the Czech *Židovské Zpravy* and the German *Selbstwehr.*

In 1917, during World War I, Singer advanced the idea of recognizing Jewish nationality in his country. It was quite natural for him to put forth the idea of founding the Jewish National Council (Židovská Národna Rada) in October 1918, following the example of the Czechoslovak National Council in Prague, which took power in the new state on October 28, 1918. He understood the necessity of reaching an understanding with the Czech National Council. On October 28 he led a delegation to discuss the future situation and the status of Jews. His initiative met with understanding. As chairman of the Jewish National Council, Singer participated in the Paris Peace Conference and achieved recognition for Jewish nationality in the Czechoslovak constitution of 1920, the first recognition accorded Jewish nationality in Europe. On January 4–6, 1919, the first Czechoslovak Jewish National Congress convened. The republic's Zionist leaders who participated in the Congress elected Singer president of the temporary Zionist Central Committee on January 5, 1919. Thus Singer became the head of two key political bodies of Czechoslovak Jewry, and its spokesman. He was also active in the regional leadership of Czech Jewry. On June 15, 1919, he was elected to the City Council of Prague, the first Jew to hold such a position. In 1930, when the Zionists defeated the Czecho-Jews (Čechú-židú) in the Prague elections of the Jewish community, Singer replaced the former president, August Stein.

Various tasks called for Singer's intervention. In 1918–19, when the Jews of Slovakia were regularly attacked and robbed and the national authorities discriminated against them, Singer met with Czech president Thomas Garrigue *Masaryk on June 24, 1919, to protest. The president intervened on behalf of the Jews in Slovakia. Similarly, when authorities in Slovakia and Carpatho-Rus discriminated against Jewish businesses on the Sabbath and Sunday and tried to force them to regulate their opening hours according to the Christian calendar, Singer intervened on behalf of the Jews.

BIBLIOGRAPHY: *Jews of Czechoslovakia*, 1 (1968), index; F. Weltsch, in: *Prag vi-Yrushalayim* (1954), 73–74: idem, in: *Selbstwehr*, 20 (1926), no. 7, 1–2; no. 8, 2–3.

[Milos Pojar (2nd ed.)]

SINGER, MILTON B. (1912–1994), U.S. anthropologist. Born in Warsaw, Poland, Singer was brought to the United States as a child and grew up in Detroit, Michigan. He received his B.A. (1934) and M.A. (1936) from the University of Texas, and his Ph.D. in philosophy from the University of Chicago. In 1940 Singer was appointed professor of social science at the University of Chicago, where previously he had served in other capacities. His primary interests were Indian civilization, theory of culture and culture change, and philosophical anthropology. In 1948 he received the Quantrell Award of Excellence in Undergraduate Teaching. He became a professor in the anthropology department in 1954 and continued to teach until his retirement in 1979, and was then named professor emeritus. Singer did considerable fieldwork in India. He helped organize and lead the Committee on Southern Asian Studies at the U of C (1955–70) and was instrumental in developing South Asia Studies at the university. He then expanded his work to include an anthropological approach to the study of American culture. In 1984 Singer received the Distinguished Scholar Award of the Association for Asian Studies.

Singer edited *Traditional India: Structure and Change* (1958) and *Krishna: Myths, Rites, and Attitudes* (1968). He wrote *Shame and Guilt: A Psychoanalytic and a Cultural Study* (with G. Piers, 1953), *Passage to More than India* (1967), *When a Great Tradition Modernizes* (1972), *Man's Glassy Essence* (1984), *Nuclear Policy, Culture, and History* (1988), and *Semiotics of Cities, Selves, and Cultures* (1991).

[Ephraim Fischoff / Ruth Beloff (2nd ed.)]

SINGER, PAUL (1844–1911), German socialist leader. Born in Berlin, Singer and his brother founded a successful ladies' clothing factory. At first a member of the German Liberal Party, he joined the Social Democrats in 1878 in protest against the passing of anti-socialist legislation and was elected to the Reichstag in 1884. His exposure of the spy system operated by the Berlin police led to his expulsion in 1886, but he was allowed to return in the following year, when he was made a member of the party executive and its chairman in 1890. Singer took part in several congresses of the Socialist International and gave financial assistance to the Berlin socialist daily the *Volksblatt*, forerunner of the central organ of the German Social Democratic Party, *Vorwaerts*. Singer was known for his strong sense of justice and his charitable contributions, being one of the founders of a refuge for the homeless in Berlin. He took no part in Jewish affairs.

BIBLIOGRAPHY: H. Gemkow, *Paul Singer, ein bedeutender Fuehrer der deutschen Arbeiterbewegung* (1957). **ADD. BIBLIOGRAPHY:** A. Herzig, in: JIDG, vol. 6 (1984), 123–149; U. Reuter, *Paul Singer* (2004).

SINGER, PESAḤ (1816–1898), Hungarian rabbi. Born in Ungarisch-Brod (Uhersky Brod), Singer studied at the yeshivah of Moses Sofer in Pressburg. For a number of years he was director of education of the Papa community. In 1846 he was appointed rabbi of Varpalota and in 1871 of Kirchdorf (Szepesujfalu). He was renowned as a talmudist, and A.B.S. Sofer, author of the *Ketav Sofer*, said wittily of him "there is no 'Second Pesaḥ' in our times." He was an assiduous student all his life and used to study standing, garbed in *tallit* and *tefillin*.

BIBLIOGRAPHY: A. Stern, *Meliẓei Esh al Ḥodshei Nisan … Tammuz* (1962²), 67; P.Z. Schwartz, *Shem ha-Gedolim me-Ereẓ Hagar* (1914), 29b no. 36/2.

[Samuel Weingarten-Hakohen]

SINGER, PETER (1946–), Australian-American philosopher of ethics. Born in Melbourne and educated there and at Oxford, Singer was one of the more controversial of recent philosphers. He was especially noted for pioneering the philosophy of "animal rights" in such books as *Animal Liberation* (1976) and for his controversial views on handicapped infants, described in *Should the Baby Live? The Problem of Handicapped Infants* (with Hega Kuhse, 1985). Because of his apparent reluctance to see a total divide between animals and humans, his views have aroused fierce debate. Singer taught at Monash University in Melbourne, Australia, before becoming professor of philosophy at Princeton in 1999.

[William D. Rubinstein (2nd ed.)]

SINGER, SIMEON (1848–1906), English rabbi. After serving as headmaster of Jews' College School, he was appointed minister of the Borough New Synagogue in London and from 1879 until his death of the fashionable New East End Synagogue. He edited and translated into English the *Authorised Daily Prayer Book*, first published in 1890 and known since as "Singer's Prayer Book," of which 522,000 copies in 27 editions had been distributed by 1970. Although minister of an Orthodox congregation, he was progressive in his religious views. He was not a Zionist but it was nevertheless in his home that Herzl first explained to Anglo-Jewry his idea for a Jewish state. He helped Sir Samuel *Montagu (later Lord Swaythling) to draw up in 1892 a petition to the sultan in the name of the Ḥovevei Zion for the cession of lands in Transjordan for Jewish settlement. His literary remains, including some historical studies, were published in three volumes by his son-in-law Israel *Abrahams (1908).

BIBLIOGRAPHY: I. Abrahams (ed.), *Literary Remains of the Rev. Simeon Singer*, 1 (1908), v–xliii; JC (Aug. 24, 31, Sept. 7, 1906); R. Patai (ed.), *The Complete Diaries of Theodor Herzl* (1960), index.

[Vivian David Lipman]

SINGER, YVONNE (1944–), Canadian artist. Singer was born in Budapest, when Hungary's Jews were most threatened and subject to extermination. Her father worked with Raoul *Wallenberg, the Swedish diplomat who rescued many Hungarian Jews, and as hospitals were closed to Jews, Yvonne was born in Wallenberg's flat, with Wallenberg as her godfather. After brief sojourns in postwar Holland and Switzerland, the family settled in Montreal in 1950. Scarred by the Holocaust, the family, like many other survivor-immigrants, left their Jewishness behind. Singer was unaware of her Jewish identity until an adult. Small wonder Yvonne Singer's art bespeaks recurrent themes of identity, subjectivity, gender and the body, history and memory.

With a B.A. in English and French literature from McGill University, the artist studied at the Ontario College of Art and received an M.F.A. with honors from York University, where she became associate professor of visual arts.

Singer works in sculpture, mixed media installation, and video art. Drawing on childhood experience and family life, her art explores immigrant uncertainties, the negotiations of intimacy, and the ineradicable anxieties of the Holocaust. *The Veiled Room* (1998) drapes the gallery with gauzy veils, one layer printed with texts from Sigmund Freud and the other with the names of influential German philosophers, politicians, writers, and artists. The fabric panels complicate the interior space, making a labyrinth of semi-translucent passages, and rendering the assertions of the printed texts vaporous and uncertain. In the video installation *The Trouble with Translation* (2004), two confronted monitors play off the languages and demeanors of family members. Mother, husband, and daughter tell their stories in regal Hungarian, sputtering and explosive Yiddish, and gracefully performed sign language. Each figure seems to counter the others with varying degrees of warmth, elegance, humor, and hauteur.

Singer's later works – bronze castings of the artist's hands and feet – turn to traditional sculpture media. Each piece captures the minutiae of skin, bone, and sinew in its surface, and in doing so conveys the tensions underlying ordinary poses and gestures. At the same time, the works offer much wider allusions, for they evoke fragments of ancient sculpture – the pinnacles of a classical past – as well as the broken bodies and dark history of Jewish catastrophe.

[Carol Zemel (2nd ed.)]

SINGERMAN, BERTA (1901–1998), Argentine actress and poetry recitalist. Born in Minsk, Belarus, Berta Singerman immigrated to Buenos Aires as a child and made her professional debut with the Compañia Nacional (National Theater Company). After a recital in Montevideo in 1913, she became the most celebrated reader of poetry in Latin America and toured throughout the continent. She became well known for her recitations of Federico García Lorca, Pablo Neruda, Juan Ramón Jiménez, and many other Spanish and Latin American poets. In 1946 she returned to the theater and acted for two years with an Argentine company in Buenos Aires and in Chile and Uruguay. One of her outstanding performances was in the title role in Ibsen's *The Lady from the Sea*. She was also well known in Brazil. In addition, she was also a cinema actress. Her first film, *La vendedora de Harrod's* (1921), was also her first step to celebrity. After two more films – *Nada más que una mujer* (1934) and *Ceniza al viento* (1942) – she dedicated herself exclusively to the theater but returned to the screen in the early 1980s. Her last film was *Estigma* (1982).

Berta Singerman also took part in Jewish and Zionist causes. In her career she donated proceeds from many performances all over Latin America to the Jewish National Fund and other Jewish campaigns. Her last performance was in 1990 in the opera theater of Buenos Aires – Teatro Colón.

Her younger sister, PAULINA (1911–1984), born in Buenos Aires, was also a well-known actress. She performed on the stage, in 12 movies – the first *La rubia del camino* (1938) and among others *Hay que casar a Paulina* (1944) – and on television. She had her own theater company and played in many countries of Latin America, in the United States, and in Spain.

[Efraim Zadoff (2nd ed.)]

SINIGAGLIA, Italian family originating from *Senigallia, a town in central Italy, on the Adriatic. Among its members may be mentioned: SOLOMON JEDIDIAH, rabbi of Scandiano in 1639. He later moved to Modena. His son ABRAHAM VITA, rabbi in Modena in the first half of the 18th century, left many works in manuscript including a commonplace book (Ms. Kaufmann nos. 464–66) covering the years 1722–33. His grandson, also called ABRAHAM VITA, was rabbi in Modena in the 18th and beginning of the 19th centuries. He wrote unpublished novellae on the Mishnah. JACOB SAMSON SHABBETAI (d. 1840) of Ancona was the author of various collections of ritual responsa and novellae on the Talmud: *Shabbat shel Mi* (Leghorn, 1807) and *Mattan ha-Sefer* (Leghorn, 1843). SOLOMON JEDIDIAH was rabbi of Modena in the 18th century. Some of his religious poems were published in the *Tikkun Ḥaẓot* (Leghorn, 1800). His son, MOSES ELIJAH (1763–1849), also rabbi of Modena, wrote sermons, ritual responses, and novellae. LEONE (1868–1944), of Turin, a musician, composed a number of works based on Piedmontese folklore.

BIBLIOGRAPHY: Mortara, Indice, 62; G. Bedarida, *Ebrei d'Italia* (1950), 142, 144; Ghirondi-Neppi, 158, 228–30.

[Ariel Toaff]

SINIGAGLIA, LEONE (1868–1944), composer. Born in Turin, Sinigaglia studied in Vienna, and in Prague with Dvořák, who interested him in folk music. His most important works are *Danze Piemontese*, for orchestra (first conducted by Toscanini, 1905) and the overture to Goldoni's play, *Le baruffe chiozzotte* (1907). He incorporated many of the tunes of his native Piedmont in his work and also published them in a collection, *Vecchie canzoni popolari del Piemonte* (6 fasc.), which appeared posthumously in 1957. Sinigaglia and his sister Alina both died of strokes on May 16, 1944, in the Ospedale Mauriziano in Turin, where they had fled from Fascist police who were rounding up Jews for deportation.

ŠINKO, ERVIN (**Franjo Spitzer**; 1898–1967), Yugoslav author and literary Communist from his youth. He published his first Hungarian verse collection, *Éjszakák és hajnalok* ("Nights and Dawns"), in 1916. He later wrote fiction and drama which appeared in both Croatian and Hungarian, and became a prominent editor and critic of Hungarian literature. Having played a part in Béla *Kun's abortive revolution and Soviet regime (1919), Šinko subsequently fled to Paris, where he wrote his most realistic novel, *Optimisti* ("The Optimists") in 1934. Although the book – which describes the revolution, its Jewish heroes, and its overthrow – gained the enthusiastic commendation of Romain Rolland, it was first published 20 years later in Yugoslavia (1953–54). Šinko's vain attempt to have his novel published in Moscow at the time of the Great Purges (1935–37) is depicted in his diary, *Roman jednog romana* ("A Novel about a Novel," 1955). After his return to Yugoslavia in 1939, Šinko fought with Tito's partisans and gained official recognition for his skillful polemics against the Soviet line following the split in the Cominform (1948). He wrote other novels, short stories, essays, and literary studies, and some of his works appeared in German and Russian periodicals. Šinko displayed a positive attitude toward his Jewish origin and cultural background in his literary and autobiographical writings. *Aronova ljubav* ("The Love of Aaron," 1951), a lyric story, with ḥasidic motifs interwoven in the central character, tells of a Jewish revolutionary who fights in the Spanish Civil War and later perishes in the Holocaust. In 1959, Šinko was appointed professor of Hungarian language and literature at the University of Novi Sad. As a Croatian author, he was also elected to full membership of the Yugoslav Academy of Arts and Sciences in Zagreb.

[Cecil Roth]

SINZHEIM, JOSEPH DAVID BEN ISAAC (1745–1812), first chief rabbi of France. Born in Trier, he married the sister of the wealthy communal leader H. *Cerfberr, and headed the yeshivah founded by his brother-in-law in Bischheim (1786), later transferred to *Strasbourg (1792). The persecutions during the Reign of Terror under Robespierre compelled Sinzheim to escape (1793). On his return, he acted as rabbi of Strasbourg (together with his nephew Abraham *Auerbach). In 1806 he was appointed to the *Assembly of Jewish Notables convened by Napoleon in Paris. His erudition and sagacity impressed many of the delegates from Italy and the German provinces, who accepted him as the leading authority on halakhic problems. Sinzheim was therefore entrusted with formulating the replies to the 12 questions put to the assembly by the government to test if Jewish precepts allowed the Jews to live on equitable terms with their French neighbors. He succeeded in satisfying the emperor that the Jews would accept the authority of the state and fulfill their obligations as citizens without giving up the principles of their faith and their traditions. The sermons that Sinzheim delivered in the synagogue (in Judeo-German) in honor of Napoleon also evidenced his loyalty to the state. Sinzheim was appointed president of the Great French *Sanhedrin in 1807 and became chief rabbi of the Central French *Consistory on its establishment in 1808. He was also chief rabbi of the Strasbourg consistory, although represented in office by R. Jacob Meyer, formerly one of the delegates for Alsace (Lower Rhine) at the assembly. While Sinzheim adopted flexibility in drafting the replies of the assembly, he adamantly opposed any change in the fundamental principles of Jewish tradition and religion as he interpreted them. Sinzheim was buried in the Père Lachaise cemetery in Paris, but his burial was not recorded, or the record was lost. In 1974 Mrs. Renée Neher-Bernheim located the grave.

[Moshe Catane]

He wrote the responsa *Yad David* (only one part published, Offenbach, 1799) on tractate *Berakhot* and the order *Mo'ed*, his avowed purpose being to complete the work of Ḥayyim *Benveniste's *Keneset ha-Gedolah* and Aaron *Alfandari's *Yad Aharon* by giving additional source references and comments scattered in other works. He claims to have added comments from no less than 300 works. *Yad David* also gives valuable autobiographical details. Sinzheim eschews the method of *pilpul, maintaining that his father had thus instructed him. At the beginning of the work there are comments by his nephew Abraham Auerbach, whom he also quotes frequently in the body of the book, and it also contains novellae by his brother-in-law Selig Auerbach. A booklet on the permissibility of the sale of the synagogue of Griessheim (Basle, 1804) includes a responsum of Sinzheim, written in Strasbourg, in which he permits the sale of synagogues and cemeteries, adding that this was a frequent occurrence in his days (p. 21). In 1810 he wrote an interesting responsum to a query by Jehiel Ḥayyim Viterbo of Ancona on the question whether Jewish girls are permitted to benefit from a government lottery to provide dowries for poor brides. The Jewish authorities were reluctant to accept it, but Sinzheim decided in favor. The responsum reflects the attitude he adopted at the Assembly of Notables. He pointed out that despite the talmudic prohibition against accepting gifts from idolaters, to accept this one was in the interest of good public relations; that in any case Christians are not regarded as idolaters; and that "at the present time it is our duty to pray for the welfare of the king and the royal family, as indeed we do every Sabbath."

[Yehoshua Horowitz]

BIBLIOGRAPHY: Ben Ammi [= M. Liber], in: *Univers Israelite*, 63, pt. 1 (1907), 645–51; J. Katz, *Exclusiveness and Tolerance* (1961), index; A.N. Roth, in: *Hagut Ivrit be-Eiropah* (1969), 361–4; Dubnow, Divrei, vol. 8, pp. 73–79.

SIPONTO, coastal town in Apulia, S. Italy. By the ninth century there was a Jewish settlement in Siponto, which became a considerable center of rabbinic learning. Young scholars from there went to study under *Hai Gaon in Pumbedita, becoming outstanding scholars; they included Leon b. Elhanan, Menahem ha-Kohen, and R. Judah, who spread Jewish learning in Italy. Another important scholar of Siponto was *Isaac b. Melchizedek, author of a commentary on the Mishnah, whose son Judah was encountered by *Benjamin of Tudela in Salerno. Among the liturgical poets of Siponto was Anan b. Marinus ha-Kohen, also a noted rabbinical scholar. Between the years 1256 and 1258 Siponto was deserted by its inhabitants because of an outbreak of malaria. Since then, there are no further records of Jews in the town.

BIBLIOGRAPHY: Ferorelli, *Ebrei nell' Italia meridionale* (1915); A. Schechter, *Studies in Jewish Liturgy* (1930), 115–7; Schirmann, Italyah, 68; Michael, Or, 508; Roth, Dark Ages, 258. **ADD. BIBLIOGRAPHY:** D. Abulafia, "Il mezzogiorno peninsulare dai bizantini all'espulsione," in: *Storia d'Italia. Annali 11, Gli ebrei in Italia. Dall'alto Medioevo all'età dei ghetti*, ed. Corrao Vivanti (1996), 5–44.

[Ariel Toaff]

SIPRUTINI, EMANUEL (18th century), cellist. The son of a Dutch Jew, Siprutini is known to have traveled in Italy and Spain. Leopold Mozart, father of the great composer, met him in London in 1764 and mentioned him as a great virtuoso on the cello. He also tried to convert him to Catholicism, but although Siprutini had by this time abandoned Jewish observances there is no evidence that he ever left Judaism. He dedicated his *Six Solos for a Violoncello* (1775?) to the English Jewish communal leader, Moses Franks (1719–89). At a later date Siprutini lived in Belgium as a wine-merchant.

BIBLIOGRAPHY: R. Eitner, *Quellen Lexikon*, 9 (reprint 1959), 183–4; 11 (1960), 171; W.A. Bauer and O.E. Deutsch (eds.), *Mozart, Briefe und Aufzeichnungen*, 1 (1962), 164–5; *British Union Catalogue of Early Music*, 2 (1957).

[Cecil Roth]

SIRAT, RENE SAMUEL (1930–), rabbi and scholar, former chief rabbi of France. Sirat was born in Bone, Algeria, and received his rabbinical ordination from the *Seminaire Israelite de France in 1952. In the same year he was appointed rabbi of Toulouse, remaining there until 1955, when he was appointed to be in charge of youth activities of the Consistoire Central of France. From 1965 to 1970 and again in 1977 he was professor at the seminary.

He received his doctorate from the University of Strasbourg in 1965, when he was appointed professor of Modern Hebrew at the National Institute of Oriental Languages and Civilization at the Sorbonne. From 1970 to 1973, he was director of the department for overseas students at the Hebrew University. In 1973, he published a new edition of *Omer ha-Shikheḥah*, written in the 16th century by the Algerian rabbi Abraham ben Jacob Gabichon, first published in Leghorn in 1748. In 1973 he created the General Inspection in charge of the teaching of Modern Hebrew in French public schools and headed it until 1981.

In 1980, following the decision of Rabbi Max Warschawski, chief rabbi of Strasbourg, to withdraw his candidature, Sirat was unanimously elected chief rabbi of France succeeding Rabbi Jacob *Kaplan. During his term as chief rabbi, which ended in 1988, he focused his activity on the promotion of Jewish education, particularly in the academic field, and on interreligious dialogue, including the controversary surrounding the Carmelite monstery at Auschwitz, which provoked a crisis between the Catholic Church and the Jewish world in 1986.

In 1988 he became chief rabbi of the Consistoire Central. He published an autobiography in 1990, *La joie austère*. He was the chairman of the Conference of European Rabbis and a founder and co-president, in 2002, of the European Council of Religious Leaders, an affiliate of the World Conference on Religion and Peace. Particularly notable were his participation, on January 24, 2002, in the Day of Prayer for Peace in Assisi (Italy), and his presence in front of the cathedral of Lyon when Cardinal Decourtray, a close friend of the Jewish community, was to be buried. He published articles on Judaism and a volume of a conversation with the historian Martine Lemalet, *La tendresse de Dieu* (1996).

[Philippe Boukara (2nd ed.)]

SIRET (Ger. **Sereth**) town in Bukovina, N. Romania, one of the oldest urban settlements; capital of Moldavia between 1363 and 1376. Situated at the crossroad of European routes linking the cities of Cernăuţi and Suceava, Siret was an important customs city and trade center (cereal, cattle, horses, swine, raw hides, etc.). A census of 1774 mentions eight Jewish families with a total 43 persons. Their number must have been higher if we are to consider the funeral stelae prior to 1775 and the fact that, after only seven years (1782), the Austrians evicted 61 Jews from the town. For the year 1787 we know the names of 36 house and distillery owners there. Representatives of the Siret Jews were among those who signed a memorandum to the authorities during this period, in which they requested permission to trade in wine and alcohol. Their request was rejected, and they were authorized to maintain one inn in the town and were restricted to serving Jews in transit through Siret to other places in Bukovina.

During the period when Bukovina and Galicia were united (1786–1849), the number of Jews in Siret grew substantially, so that in 1880 the Jewish population numbered 3,122 (37.1% of the total). Jews played an important role in Siret's economic development and were also active in general public life, owing to their position in trade, crafts, banking, the food and textile industries, and the professions. Between 1912 and 1918, there was a Jewish mayor, and other Jews were elected to the municipal council. The communities were led by a guildmaster (*staroste*), a well-known type of organization in Moldova. The epitaphs mention people with the function of *aluf, more hora'ah, dayyan*, illustrating a complex community life. The cemeteries contain graves dating from the beginning of the 18th century, with impressive funeral stelae presenting a diversity of adornments; several epitaphs constitute the traces of a community which stood out by virtue of its organization, accomplishments, and personalities. The community expanded and during the 18th century already had a rabbi. At first it was affiliated to the community of Suceava but gradually became independent. The regulations of the independent community were ratified in 1887. At the beginning of the 19th century, in addition to the central synagogue, there were four *battei midrash* and four houses of prayer. Their activity in the community sphere (social assistance, education, religion) is well-known. Before Bukovina was incorporated into Romania after World War I, the Jewish youth studied at the local German high school. There was also a yeshivah with a large number of students. The Vishnitz trend of Ḥasidism was dominant in the community. Cultural activity deeply rooted in Judaism and initiated by the elites unified the Jews from all social layers. Their interest was directed towards the vigorous cultural and political life of the metropolis of Bukovina. During World War I, Siret and its Jewish inhabitants suffered severely, particularly under Russian occupation. After the war, there were about 3,000 Jews living there.

After its reunification with Romania, there were many integration problems, owing to the loss of some important positions in economic, political, and social life, in administration, education, and adjustment to the new official language. Community life improved, its rehabilitation aided by the American Jewish Joint Distribution Commitee.

There is information on Zionist organizations of different social statuses operating there, and from the Siret community there arose leaders of the Zionist movement in Romania and then of the development of Israel (among others, Yitzhak *Artzi and Iehuda Shaari).

The antisemitic movements intensified, and the anti-Jewish laws, especially after 1938, marked the beginning of successive exclusion from socio-political life, which led to the annihilation of the economic base and to poverty. In July 1941 evictions occurred in Calafat, and in October 1941 many Jews were deported to Transnistria, where cold, famine, and typhus claimed 700 victims from among the members of the Siret community. During the post-war period, the population of the re-established community gradually decreased from 500 to 100 (1980) and completely disappeared by 2000.

BIBLIOGRAPHY: H. Gold, *Geschichte der Juden in der Bukowina*, 2 (1962), 105–7; I. Popescu Sireteanu, *Siretul – vatră de istorie şi cultură românească*, Iaşi, 1994; S. Sanie, *Dăinuire prin piatră. Monumentele cimitirului medieval evreiesc de la Siret* (2000); T. Weggemann a.s.o., *Die sprechenden Steine von Siret* (2001).

[Yehouda Marton / Silviu Sanie (2nd ed.)]

SIRILLO, SOLOMON BEN JOSEPH (d. c. 1558), rabbi, *posek*, and commentator on the Jerusalem Talmud. Sirillo was born in *Spain, and with the expulsion of 1492 proceeded to *Adrianople and *Salonika. In a work written in Adrianople he makes mention of his teacher *Elijah b. Benjamin ha-Levi, one of the most important scholars in Constantinople at the time. From Salonika he proceeded to Ereẓ Israel, settling in *Safed. Apparently after the death of Levi ibn Ḥabib in 1544 Sirillo moved to *Jerusalem and was appointed to succeed him. His rulings are occasionally mentioned in the responsa of his great contemporaries, such as *David b. Solomon ibn Abi Zimra (Radbaz), Joseph *Caro, Moses b. Joseph di *Trani, Samuel b. Moses *Medina, and others.

Sirillo's fame rests upon his commentary to the Jerusalem Talmud which covered the whole order *Zera'im* and tractate *Shekalim*, which he compiled in at least two editions. He began to compile the first edition while he was still in Salonika and the second, improved edition, in Ereẓ Israel. In the second edition he already used, in addition to manuscripts, the printed edition of *Venice in about 1522. Sirillo's interest in the Jerusalem Talmud arose from a practical consideration of *halakhah*, which resulted from his settling in Ereẓ Israel, where the agricultural laws applied to a much greater extent than in the Diaspora. These laws are contained in the order *Zera'im* which (apart from *Berakhot* which does not deal with agricultural laws) have no *Gemara* in the Babylonian Talmud but only in the Jerusalem Talmud. Since little attention had been paid to the Jerusalem Talmud, he found that many passages were obscure and the texts corrupt. "Unable to find in my generation a scholar well versed in the Jerusalem Talmud" and urged on by his colleagues, he devoted himself to writing a commentary to the 12 relevant tractates. It is one of the best commentaries to the Jerusalem Talmud, despite the fact that his readings are not the most exact, although he had before himself accurate manuscripts. The part on *Berakhot* was first published in 1875 by M. Lehmann, who also added notes in the margin, and that to the whole of *Zera'im*, in Jerusalem from 1934 to 1967. The commentary to *Shekalim* was published in 1958. Sirillo also compiled a commentary in the form of a *Gemara* to the Mishnah *Eduyyot*, which has not yet been published.

BIBLIOGRAPHY: Frumkin-Rivlin, 1 (1929), 64–67; S. Assaf, in: *Sinai*, 6 (1940), 517ff.; idem, *Mekorot u-Meḥkarim* (1946), 257; S. Lieberman, in: *A. Marx Jubilee Volume* (1950), Heb. pt. 301f.

[Abraham David]

SIRKES, JOEL (known as **BaḤ**, an abbreviation of *Bayit Ḥadash*; 1561–1640), one of the greatest talmudic scholars of Poland. Sirkes was born in Lublin and was rabbi in a number of communities, including Belz, Brest-Litovsk, and Cracow, where he was appointed *av bet din* and head of the yeshivah in 1619. Many of his students became leading rabbis in Poland, the most famous being his son-in-law, *David b. Samuel ha-Levi (the TaZ). Sirkes' chief work was the *Bayit Ḥadash* (Cracow, 1631–39), a critical and comprehensive commentary on the *Arba'ah Turim* of *Jacob b. Asher, in which he traced each law to its talmudic source and followed its subsequent development through successive generations of interpretation. He viewed with alarm the constriction of the law through codification and the growing dependence of his contemporaries on the Shulḥan Arukh. His major authorities were the Talmud, the *geonim*, the tosafists, *Alfasi, *Asher b. Jehiel, and Maimonides.

Sirkes, a scholar of independent judgment, rendered many controversial decisions. He allowed the acceptance of emoluments and special privileges by rabbis in return for their services. He extended the permission to sell leavened food to a non-Jew before Passover to include the sale of the room in which such food was found. Sirkes performed a marriage on the Sabbath when an orphan's future was at stake. He permitted the reading of secular, non-Hebrew books on the Sabbath and liberalized certain laws to allow for the greater enjoyment of the festivals. He saw no valid reason for the prohibition against listening to a woman's voice in song and permitted church melodies in the synagogue if they were universal in appeal. He was, however, very strict in issues of *issur ve-hetter*. Though opposed to philosophy and an adherent of Kabbalah, he rejected kabbalistic practices that were contrary to the *halakhah*.

Sirkes' literary legacy includes two volumes of responsa published posthumously, *She'elot u-Teshuvot Bayit Ḥadash* (Frankfurt, 1697) and *She'elot u-Teshuvot Bayit Ḥadash ha-Ḥadashot* (Koretz, 1785). In the *She'elot u-Teshuvot ha-Ge'onim Batri* (Turka, 1760) there are 22 responsa either by Sirkes himself or dealing with responsa which he had written.

BIBLIOGRAPHY: E.J. Schochet, *Bach, Rabbi Joel Sirkes. His Life, Works and Times* (1971); Mirsky, in: *Horeb*, 6 (1942), 41–75; Kossover, in: *Bitzaron*, 14 (1946), 23–31.

[Max Jonah Routtenberg]

SIROTA, GERSHON (1874–1943), *ḥazzan*. Born in Podolia, Sirota took his first position as *ḥazzan* in Odessa when he was 21. He officiated in Vilna for eight years, and in about 1908 became *ḥazzan* of the Tłómacka Street Synagogue in Warsaw. Sirota was regarded as one of the most accomplished tenors of his generation and was one of the most gifted *ḥazzan* virtuosos of all time. He possessed a dramatic tenor voice of great beauty and power, with a brilliant coloratura and climactic top notes, and a perfect voice control in all registers which enabled him to produce trills of exceptional length. His listeners were often deeply moved by the emotional intensity of his rendering of the liturgy, and he could also sing with a delicate sweetness. Sirota was a master of improvisation and recitative in the East European tradition, always remaining faithful to the appropriate **shtayger*, but he himself never composed. In partnership with his choral directors, notably Leo Low and David Eisenstadt, he made famous many outstanding ḥazzanic compositions including Isaac Schlossberg's *Reẓeh* and A.M. *Bernstein's *Adonai, Adonai*.

Sirota undertook numerous concert tours throughout Europe and the U.S. and was often compared to the leading operatic tenors of his generation. During his years at Vilna he sang annually for Czar Nicholas II and in 1903 became the first *ḥazzan* to make recordings. After leaving the Tłomacka Street Synagogue in 1927, Sirota devoted his time entirely to concert tours, but in 1935 took up the post of *ḥazzan* at Warsaw's Norzyk Synagogue. He was the only one of the great *ḥazzanim* of the time not to accept a position in the U.S. He and his family perished in the Warsaw ghetto. A monument was erected on his grave in the Gesia cemetery in 1961.

BIBLIOGRAPHY: H.H. Harris, *Toledot ha-Neginah ve-ha-Musikah be-Yisrael* (1950), 461–6; I. Fater, *Yidishe Muzik in Poyln* (1970), 164–71, incl. bibl.; idem, in: *Journal of Synagogue Music* (Nov. 1969), 16–21; P. Szerman, in: *Di Khazonim Velt* (June 1934), 21–22; M.S. Geshuri, in: EG, 1 (1953), 311ff.; A.E. Knight, in: *Record Collector* (Jan. 1955), 192.

[David M.L. Olivestone]

°**SISEBUT**, Visigoth king of Spain (612–621). He succeeded King Gundamar, and within three years his forces put down a revolt in Asturias and defeated the Byzantines twice. Better known, however, for his literary talent and personal piety, Sisebut was a likely continuator of anti-Jewish religious policies of *Reccared which had been abandoned by the latter's successors. Soon after ascending the throne, Sisebut ordered the Jews of his kingdom either to convert to Christianity or leave Spain. He further decreed that Jews who converted Christians to Judaism were to be executed and their property was to go to the royal treasury. In addition, Christian slaves owned by Jews were either to be sold to Christians or set free. Sisebut's policy of forced conversion found little support and was condemned at the time by Spain's foremost theologian, *Isidore, bishop of Seville. The king's general anti-Jewish religious policies were not popular in the realm, and his successor, Suinthila, reversed them, permitting Jews who had accepted baptism under duress to return to Judaism without penalty and encouraging those who had fled from Spain to return. The legislation forbidding Jews to own Christian slaves remained largely unenforced.

BIBLIOGRAPHY: S. Katz, *Jews in the Visigothic and Frankish Kingdoms of Spain and Gaul* (1937), index; B. Blumenkranz, *Juifs et Chrétiens dans le monde occidental, 430–1096* (1960), index; E.A. Thompson, *The Goths in Spain* (1969).

[Bernard Bachrach]

SISERA (Heb. סִיסְרָא), the leader of the coalition opposing Israel "by the waters of Megiddo" in the days of *Deborah (Judg. 4–5). Sisera is the object of extreme scorn in the poetic sequel, the archaic Song of *Deborah, which celebrates Israel's victory. No evidence exists concerning the involvement of the city of *Megiddo itself in this episode, and so the event is roughly dated at 1150–1125 B.C.E., before Megiddo's revival and following the destruction of the early 12th-century city. Sisera's name is entirely uncharacteristic of the Semitic context; the best linguistic affinities are found in Illyrian names with the element-*ero*. In the prose narrative, Sisera, "who dwelt in Harosheth-Goiim," is represented as field commander for "*Jabin king of Canaan, who reigned at *Hazor" (Judg. 4:2). The tradition is an old one and was long effective, as known from I Samuel 12:9 where the events surrounding Sisera stand as an example of God's judgment and deliverance. (It is believed that Bedan, in I Samuel 12:11, is miswritten for Barak.) On the other hand, in the bitterness which evoked Psalms 83:10, only the victory over Jabin and Sisera is important.

A location for Harosheth-Goiim has been suggested in the vicinity of Hazor. However, with the evidence for the historicity of Judges 4, the site of Tell-ʿAmr, at the southern edge of the Esdraelon plain near the mouth of the pass into the plain of Acre, remains the most probable location of Sisera's town. The tradition that calls it Harosheth "of the Gentiles," plus Sisera's non-Semitic name, combines with the fact that Tell-ʿAmr was founded in the early Iron Age to suggest that it belonged to one of the recently arrived Sea Peoples. (For another view see *Deborah.)

The implication of the narrator is that Sisera and his force fled the battlefield in opposite directions, the troops being overtaken and overwhelmed at Harosheth. Sisera escaped alone as far as Elon-Bezaanannim, whose location is uncertain, but is generally sought in Naphtali. It was a place to which certain *Kenites had migrated in an earlier period and where they had settled after contracting a treaty with Jabin, king of Hazor. The connection between the Kenites and Jabin is clear in the shift from standard narrative tenses to the use of a sentence having no verb at the point at which the Kenites and Jabin are mentioned together ("there (was) a peace treaty between Jabin… and the house of Heber the Kenite," Judg. 4:17). Thus, the final irony of both the prose and the poem is that Sisera, desperately seeking the relative safety of the borders in the far north, was killed by one whose clan had broken away from the Mosaic alliance, and by a woman at that. A glimpse of the later vicissitudes of Sisera's people is provided in the mention of "sons of Sisera" in the lists of Nethinim (Ezra 2:53; Neh. 7:55). Most of the Nethinim families were descended from prisoners of war (see Gibeonites and *Nethinim).

BIBLIOGRAPHY: P. Haupt, in: BZAW, 27 (1914), 197; Kittel, Gesch, 2 (1917), 82ff.; Noth, Personennamen, 64; W.F. Albright, in: BASOR, 62 (1936), 26–31; J. Simons, *Handbook for the Study of Egyptian Topographical Lists…* (1937), 158–69; A. Alt, in: ZAW, 60 (1944), 67ff; Noth, Hist Isr, 149–52, 162–3; Bright, Hist, 138; W.F. Albright, *The Biblical Period from Abraham to Ezra* (1963), 39–40; A. Malamat, in: H.H. Ben-Sasson (ed.), *Toledot Am Yisrael bi-Ymei Kedem* (1969), 72.

[Robert G. Boling]

SISKIND, AARON (1903–1991), U.S. photographer and teacher. Born in New York City, he attended City College of New York, where he graduated with a degree in literature in 1926. Siskind then taught English in New York public schools, only taking up photography as a pastime. In 1930, he joined the Photo League, a group of photographers who confirmed their solidarity with the political far left by creating documentary photos with social content. Under their auspices, Siskind produced photos of Harlem and of Bucks County, Pennsylvania, among other subjects. As the head of the Feature Group of the League, Siskind and others created the *Harlem Document* (1937–40), recording the overcrowded African-American New York neighborhood in a push for social justice. During the 1940s, Siskind's work reflected a growing interest in photographing natural objects from a close perspective, which lent his images an abstract quality only hinted at in his earlier documentary photographs. Organic material, such as leaves, or social detritus, such as defaced walls, muddied papers, weathered woods, and rusted metals, occupied Siskind's pictoral interest in their flatness and reservoir of rich indexical detail, like shadows, smudges, and graffiti. Between 1947 and 1951, he exhibited frequently at the Charles Egan Gallery, where many of the Abstract Expressionists exhibited. Siskind himself is considered one of the only Abstract Expressionists working in photography. He taught at Black Mountain College in 1951, and then at the Illinois Institute of Technology in

Chicago between 1951 and 1971, where he became director of the department of photography. In 1959, he published his first book *Aaron Siskind: Photographs*. Between 1971 and 1976, he taught at the Rhode Island School of Design. He was a founder and member of the Society for Photographic Education and the Visual Studies Workshop, Rochester, New York. He received many prestigious awards, including a grant from the National Endowment for the Arts, the Guggenheim Foundation, and the Governor's Prize for the Arts, Rhode Island. His work is in the collections of numerous institutions, including the Eastman House Museum, Getty Museum, the National Gallery of Art, and the Smithsonian American Art Museum. His work has been exhibited at many museums and galleries, including the Art Institute of Chicago, the Jewish Museum, New York, the Museum of Contemporary Art, Los Angeles, and the Museum of Modern Art.

BIBLIOGRAPHY: *Aaron Siskind, Photographer* (1965), incl. bibl.; D. Anfram, *Abstract Expressionism* (1990); M. Kozloff, *New York: Capital of Photography* (2002).

[Nancy Buchwald (2nd ed.)]

SISTERON, town in the Basses-Alpes department, S.E. France. After *Marseilles, *Arles, and *Tarascon, Sisteron was the fourth place in Provence where Jews settled. At the beginning of the 13th century there was a popular uprising in which 80 Jews were among the victims. According to Solomon *Ibn Verga's *Shevet Yehudah*, these events occurred in 1204 and 1205, but local sources date them around 1235. (The latter are more reliable because they are confirmed by an order of Charles I, count of Provence, who in 1257 was still penalizing those who had destroyed the castle of Sisteron and massacred Jews.) At the beginning of the 14th century Jews were also mentioned as living in at least five small localities of the bailiwick of Sisteron, namely, Bayons, Mison, Vaumeil, La-Motte-du-Caire, and Barles. Jews were last recorded in Sisteron in 1452. During World War II an internment camp situated in the town held many Jewish prisoners.

BIBLIOGRAPHY: E. de Laplane, *Histoire de Sisteron*, 1 (1843), 96, 461; idem, *Essai sur l'Histoire Municipale de la Ville de Sisteron* (1840), 111f., 84; Gross, Gal Jud, 665f.; B. Blumenkranz, in: *Bulletin Philologique et Historique* (1965), 612; Z. Szajkowski, *Analytical Franco-Jewish Gazetteer, 1939–1945* (1966), 155.

[Bernhard Blumenkranz]

SITBON, prominent family of wealthy merchants, rabbis, and community leaders in 18th-century *Tunis. ABRAHAM SITBON, who lived for many years in Bizerta, was an official and tax collector, who bore the title of *qaid*. As a leader of the Jewish community he entertained Ḥ.J.D. *Azulai on his visit to Tunis in 1773–74 and is mentioned in the latter's writings. SAMUEL and JUDAH were merchants and shippers; the latter traveled to Leghorn. JOSEPH (late 18th century) was a rabbi and kabbalist in Tunis. His kabbalistic treatise, *Ahavat Adonai*, a commentary on the *Idra Zuta*, was written in 1778 and published in Leghorn in 1871.

BIBLIOGRAPHY: Hirschberg, Afrikah, 2 (1965), 131, 137–9; D. Cazès, *Notes bibliographiques…* (1893), 302–4.

SITRUK, JOSEPH (1945–), chief rabbi of France. Sitruk was born in Tunisia, but raised from early childhood on in Nice. His brilliant high school record seemed to indicate a career in science, but his extracurricular activities, such as those in the French Jewish scouting movement, led him to choose a career in the rabbinate instead.

After completing his studies at the Seminaire Rabbinique of France, he began in 1970 to serve as the rabbi of Strasbourg. In 1975 Rabbi Jacob Kaplan, chief rabbi of France, put him in charge of the Marseilles community, the second largest in France. Within a few years Sitruk had succeeded in reorganizing this rather disparate community made up of various successive waves of immigration. In ever-increasing numbers Jews began to attend synagogue and return to religious practices.

On June 14, 1987, Joseph Sitruk was elected chief rabbi of France; he assumed office in January 1988. As successor to Chief Rabbi René *Sirat, he was the second Sephardi chief rabbi of France. His election confirms the role that Sephardi Jews now play in the leadership of French Jewry following the large immigration of North African Jews to France.

[Doris Bensimon-Donath]

SITTEON (Sutton) DABBAH, SHAUL DAVID (1850–1930), rabbi of the Aleppan community in Buenos Aires. Born in *Aleppo, Syria, in 1877 he was appointed a member of the *bet din* (rabbinic tribunal) there, and four years later became the rabbi of the city of Ain Tab. After ten years (1881–91), he returned to Aleppo and founded a yeshivah. In 1912 he went to visit his sons who had immigrated to Buenos Aires and was appointed rabbi of the Aleppan community in that city. Critical of the religious laxity that reigned in Buenos Aires, he started to impose strict halakhic rules on the immigrants from his home town who were used to a strong rabbinical authority. He founded the congregation Yesod Hadat, which controlled the *sheḥitah* and sale of kosher meat, and opened a *talmud torah* where studies were conducted in Arabic. His traditional approach was manifested in his resistance to the establishment of a modern system of learning "Hebrew in Hebrew." He was also active in the foundation of the burial society – Hesed Shel Emet Sefaradit de Aleppo – that later became the main communal framework of the Aleppan community (AISA – Asociación Israelita Sefaradí Argentina). Sitteon became famous with the ban against conversions in Argentina that was published in his book of Responsa *Dibber Shaul* (Jerusalem, 1928). The ban, which is still valid in several Sephardi communities in Latin America, was issued under the influence of Rabbi Aharon Goldman of Moisesville and received the *haskamot* of the chief rabbis of Ereẓ Israel. It decreed that no conversion would be accepted in Argentina, but permitted the acceptance of conversions by rabbinic tribunals in Jerusalem. Sitteon rarely participated in Zionist activities and was the representative of Agudat Israel for the Sephardi sector.

[Margalit Bejarano (2nd ed.)]

SIVAN (Heb. סִיוָן), the post-Exilic name of the third month of the Jewish year. Occurring in the Bible and in the Apocrypha (Esth. 8:9; I Bar. 1:8) and frequently in rabbinic literature (as in *Megillat Ta'anit*), the name is held to be etymologically connected with *samu* or *asamu* ("to mark" or "to appoint" in Assyrian, akin to *sim* in Hebrew). The zodiacal sign for this month is *Gemini*. In the present fixed Jewish calendar, it invariably consists of 30 days, the First of Sivan never falling on Monday, Thursday, or the Sabbath (see *Calendar). In the 20th century Sivan in its earliest occurrence extends from May 11th to June 9th and in its latest from June 9th to July 8th.

Historical anniversaries in Sivan comprise: 1. Third–Fifth of Sivan, the "Three Days of the Bounds" commemorating the three-days' preparation for the revelation on Mount Sinai (Ex. 19:10–16); 2. Sixth of Sivan (in the Diaspora also Seventh of Sivan), *Shavuot (the festival of Weeks); 3. Seventh, fifteenth, and sixteenth of Sivan, anniversaries of Hasmonean victories (Meg. Ta'an. 3); 4. Twenty-fifth of Sivan, Israel's defeat of Ishmael, Canaan, and Egypt in a contest adjudicated by Alexander the Great (ibid.); (7, 8, 9) Twenty-third, twenty-fifth, and twenty-seventh of Sivan, once observed as fasts (ibid., 13; Tur and Sh. Ar. OḤ 580) commemorating Jeroboam I's suspension of pilgrimages to Jerusalem and the martyrdom of the *tannaim*, *Simeon b. Gamaliel I, *Ishmael b. Elisha, *Hananiah Segan ha-Kohanim, and *Hananiah b. Teradyon.

[Ephraim Jehudah Wiesenberg]

SIVAN, ARYEH (1929–), Hebrew poet. Born in Tel Aviv, Sivan was a member of an elite unit in the Palmaḥ and took part in Israel's War of Independence. He studied Hebrew language and literature at the Hebrew University, worked as a high school teacher, and published his first collection of poems, *Shirei Shiryon* ("Poems of Armor"), in 1963. This was followed by a dozen collections, including *Liḥyot be-Ereẓ Yisrael* ("To Live in Ereẓ Israel," 1984), *Kaf ha-Kela* ("Hollow of the Sling," 1989), and *Ḥozer Ḥalilah* ("Recurrence," 2004). "Selected Poems 1957–1997" appeared in 2001. A member of the literary group *Likrat* ("Towards") in the 1950s, which sought to imbue Hebrew poetry with a refreshing poetic diction, Sivan's idiom avoids hyperbole and pathos, appealing in its directness and simplicity and yet retaining a clear melodious cadence. Many of the poems address the landscape and nature of Israel, recollect moments of childhood in the city of Tel Aviv, or contemplate the changes in the socio-political climate of Israel. Sivan wrote one novel, *Adonis* (1992; German translation: 1994), an enjoyable detective story, set in Tel Aviv during the Gulf War, which takes the reader back to the 1930s, depicting the political life and love affairs of the city's literati. Individual poems have been translated into diverse languages, and information about translation is available at the ITHL website at www.ithl.org.il.

BIBLIOGRAPHY: E. Cameron, "*A. Sivan's Ratifications*," in: *Modern Hebrew Literature:* 8:1–2 (1982/83), 82–86; Y. Bachur, "*Teva, Ḥayyim, Historiyyah ve-Ḥidotehem: He'arot la-Poetikah shel A. Sivan*," in: *Moznayim*, 62:4 (1988), 26–29; R. Litvin, "*Eḥad ba-Shayarah*," in: *Moznayim*, 64:5 (1990), 27–29; Y. Ben-David, "*Arba'im Shanah ba-Derekh – El Ahavato*," in: *Ahavah mi-Mabat Sheni* (1997), 159–62; R. Wichert, "*Ribui Panav shel Dayar Lo Mugan*," in: *Iton 77*, 228 (1999), 18–21; I. Ziv'oni, "*Ha-Balash ha-Perati bi-Sheliḥut Sizifit*," in: *Iton 77*, 240 (2000), 15–19; Y. Peles, *Madu'a Kimat lo Shom'im al Aryeh Sivan*," in: *Haaretz* (January 21, 2005); A. Kinstler, in: *Carmel*, 10 (2005), 109–13.

[Anat Feinberg (2nd ed.)]

SIVITZ, MOSHE (1855–1936), U.S. rabbi. Born in Zhitovian in the Kovno District of Lithuania, he went to study at Rabbi Isaac Horowitz's Yeshiva before returning to Zhitovian and studying with Rabbi Solomon Horowitz, after which he studied in Telz. He was ordained by Rabbi Eliezer Gordon of Telz and by Rabbi Isaac Elhanan Spektor. He continued his studies in Kovno and became a rabbi at about the age of 30, in Pikelen, Lithuania. He immigrated to the United States a year later and then accepted an offer to become rabbi of the Russian Shul in Baltimore. Within two years he moved to Pittsburgh to serve as rabbi of Bnai Israel and later of Kahal Yereim. He became a major figure in Pittsburgh Jewry, working with the larger community to build a community Jewish hospital, Montefiore. He opened the Crawford Street Talmud Torah, a school that was available to all members of the community.

His attitude toward America was negative. He was a staunch opponent of Reform Judaism, which had but recently proclaimed its Pittsburgh Platform. He regarded the focus on money and success prevalent in the United States as compromising the integrity of Judaism, as he felt that spirituality could flourish amidst poverty and found material success threatening. He was against preaching in English and continued to sermonize in Yiddish.

One of the speakers at the funeral of Rabbi Jacob Joseph, he admonished the crowd for their mistreatment of the chief rabbi. He struggled for a living, as did many Orthodox rabbis of his generation, when rabbis were paid less than cantors, and sought to maintain economic independence in order to limit the power of his congregants, whom he did not regard as being of the stature in learning and piety of the European laymen he had left behind. He felt that the economic condition of the American rabbi – essentially a hired employee of his congregants – compromised his authority.

Kimmy Kaplan, who wrote on his preaching, stressed that Sivitz regarded leaving Eastern Europe as exchanging spiritual values for corporeality. The *goldene medina* was a land of spiritual dryness; a land of ignorance and impiety. In the United States the values of the country were the main problem for Judaism. Thus, he was firmly in the camp of the rejectionist Orthodox, who refused to embrace the American vision. He helped form and was a vice president of *Agudat Harabbonim.

He wrote a number of books: *Ḥikrei Da'at* (2 volumes, 1898 and 1902), sermons based on the weekly Torah portion; *Sefer Beit Paga* (1904); *Peri Yehezkel* (1908); and *Matteh Aharon* (1914), material for sermons. He also authored a commentary on the Jerusalem Talmud entitled *Masbiah al Yerushalmi* (2 volumes, 1913, 1918) as well as *Ẓemaḥ ha-Sadeh* (1935). He also contributed to Judah Eisenstein's *Oẓar Yisrael* (1907–1913).

BIBLIOGRAPHY: K. Caplan, "The Concerns of an Immigrant Rabbi: The Life and Sermons of Rabbi Moshe Shimon Sivitz," in: *Polin* (1998); M.D. Sherman, *Orthodox Judaism in America: A Biographical Dictionary and Sourcebook* (1996).

[Michael Berenbaum (2nd ed.)]

SIX-DAY WAR, the war between Israel and *Egypt, *Jordan, *Syria, and *Iraq that lasted from June 5 to June 10, 1967, and in the course of which Israel routed the threatening Arab armies and occupied the Sinai Peninsula, the "West Bank" (Judea and Samaria), and the Golan Heights.

Background to the Conflict

The diplomatic negotiations following Israel's occupation of the *Sinai Peninsula in Operation "Kadesh" in October–November 1956 (see *Sinai Campaign) and, in particular, joint United States and Soviet pressure on Israel brought about a withdrawal of Israel forces from the Sinai Peninsula and the *Gaza Strip early in 1957. They handed over their positions to the newly formed United Nations Emergency Force (UNEF), which took up positions on the Straits of *Tiran and along the Israel border with Sinai and with the Gaza Strip. Israel's action followed the receipt of assurances from the great powers, particularly concerning the freedom of passage for shipping to and from Israel passing through the Straits of Tiran.

The Arab world was racked by upheavals. On July 14, 1958, King Feisal of Iraq was deposed and killed, and the regime, headed many times by General Nuri Sa'id, was overthrown by General Kassem. His unstable regime enabled the Soviet Union to achieve its first foothold in oil-rich Iraq and make its first moves in establishing a position in the Persian Gulf. A general reaction of unrest fomented by Nasserist elements throughout the area developed in Lebanon and Jordan. Civil war broke out in Lebanon, and at the urgent invitation of President Chamoun the United States Sixth Fleet landed a force of Marines to stabilize the situation, while the British Army flew forces to Amman to bolster King *Hussein's regime.

In February of the same year, following the rise to power of the Ba'ath party in Syria, Egypt and Syria had combined to establish the shortlived United Arab Republic. Syria became the northern center for the development of *Nasser's activities against Israel, hampered as he was in this respect along the Israel-Egyptian frontier by the presence of UN troops. From Syria he also developed his efforts to bring about the downfall of King Hussein. In September 1960 his agents succeeded in killing the Jordanian prime minister, Majali, who had taken a strong stand against Nasser's attempts to undermine the Hashemite regime in Jordan. King Hussein concentrated his forces along the Syrian border with the intention of invading, but was dissuaded at the last moment by British and U.S. pressure. In October 1961 Syria revolted against what had in fact become an Egyptian occupation and regained her independence.

While Israel's border with Egypt remained comparatively quiet, due partly to the presence of the UN forces, the center of Arab activity against Israel developed along the Syrian, and later along the Jordanian, border. The Syrians shelled Israel settlements from their advantageous positions on the *Golan Heights, laid mines, and developed a minor war of attrition along the frontier. On Feb. 1, 1960, after a long pause since 1956, the Israel Defense Forces carried out a reprisal raid against Syrian posts in Khirbat Tawfiq, on Lake *Kinneret. But the Syrians continued to attack fishing boats on the lake, shell villages in the *Ḥuleh Valley, and fire on agricultural workers in the demilitarized zones along the frontier.

In 1964 an Arab Summit Conference in Cairo, attended by the heads of state, decided to proceed actively with the diversion of the waters of the *Jordan River and to recognize a Palestinian entity. At this conference and at the Casablanca Conference which followed it, some £400 million were allocated for the purpose of implementing these decisions. In recognizing the Palestinian entity the Arab states gave official standing to Ahmed Shukeiri, head of the *Palestine Liberation Organization, and following the decisions of the conference he proceeded with the establishment of a Palestinian army.

The work on the diversion of the Jordan waters proceeded apace both in Lebanon and in Syria, where a canal was dug to divert the waters of the Ḥaẓbani in Lebanon and the *Banias in Syria into the *Yarmuk River in Jordan and thus deprive Israel of most of the Jordan waters. Israel had on many occasions declared that either the closing of the Straits of Tiran or the diversion of the Jordan waters would be considered a *casus belli*. Israel reacted to the diversion operations in a controlled but very firm manner, and in a series of engagements, involving artillery and tank fire, obstructed the diversion operations from time to time. In November 1964 Israeli planes were in action against parts of the diversion works out of artillery range. The Arab states were unwilling to be drawn into an all-out war as a result of this Syrian initiative. Indeed, Israel's activities brought the work to an end, for it became clear to the Arab leadership that pursuit of the diversion meant war with Israel.

The internal upheavals in Syria brought to the fore extreme segments of the Ba'ath party and the Syrians continued to send saboteurs to Israel through Jordan and Lebanon. King Hussein was at times unable or unwilling to control his own borders and prevent the incursions against Israel. In November 1966 the Israel Defense Forces struck at the village of al-Samʿu in the Hebron hills, a center of terrorist attacks; this was their first reprisal raid carried out in daylight together with armored and air elements. Following this attack King Husse-

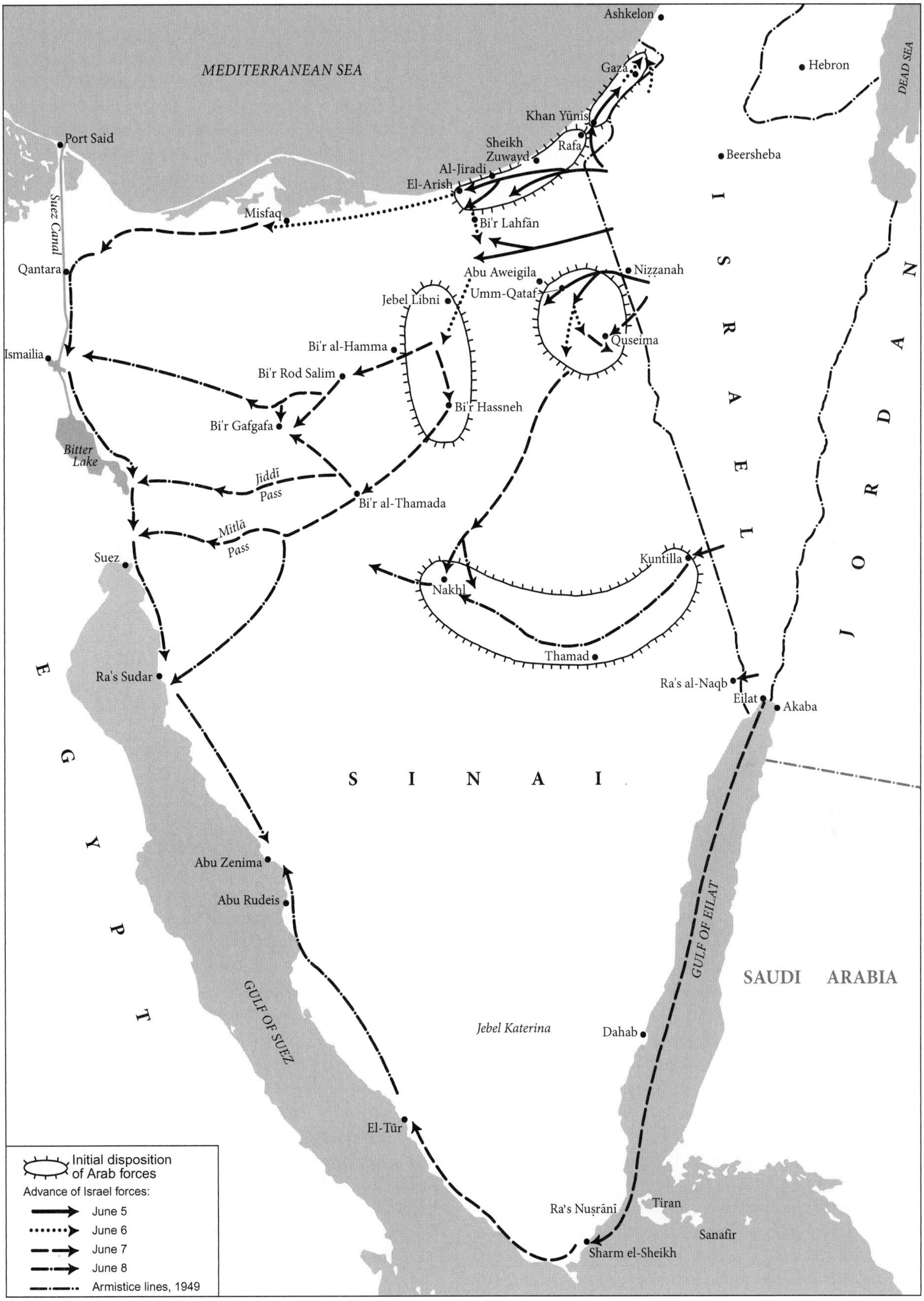

Map 1. The Six-Day War: Egyptian front.

in's regime appeared to be tottering and was bolstered by additional military aid from the United States.

Meanwhile Syrian provocations along the northern frontier continued, and infiltration into Israel from Syrian-based camps, via Jordan and Lebanon, continued. In April 1967 their interference with farming operations in the demilitarized zones on Lake Kinneret were stepped up, with increased shelling of Israeli border villages. On April 7, 1967, unusually heavy fire was directed by long-range guns against Israeli villages, and Israeli aircraft were sent into action against them. An air battle developed in which Syria lost six planes. Fearful of Israel's reaction to their provocations, the Syrians tried to impress on the Egyptians their apprehension of an impending Israel attack.

The Arab Threat

Early in May 1967 Nasser was at one of the lowest ebbs in his career. For five years his forces had been involved in the civil war in the Yemen without success against ill-armed tribesmen. He was in conflict with King Hussein, whom he described on May 1 as an "agent and slave of the imperialists." His relations with Saudi Arabia were near breaking point, and he could make no headway in the struggle against Israel. Against this background came the urgent request for assistance from Syria, strengthened by the appearance in Cairo on May 13 of a Soviet parliamentary delegation, which informed the Egyptians that Israel had massed some 11 brigades along the Syrian frontier. The Soviets, with an embassy in Tel Aviv, were obviously aware that this information was untrue, but they were interested in pressing Syria's case for political reasons of their own. The U.S.S.R. was particularly interested in strengthening the regime in Syria, which had afforded the Soviet Union her first major foothold in the Middle East, and, by influencing Egypt to threaten Israel from the south, gambled on strengthening Syria's security and hence the regime in Damascus.

In a well-publicized mass demonstration, Nasser proceeded to move large forces through Cairo en route to Sinai. Within a few days, by May 20, some 100,000 troops, organized in seven divisions of which two were armored (with over 1,000 tanks), had been concentrated in Sinai along Israel's border. A mass hysteria enveloped the Arab world. Nasser was again at the peak of his popularity, as one Arab government after the other volunteered support and was caught up in the enthusiasm of the impending strike against Israel. On May 17 Nasser had demanded the withdrawal of the UN Emergency Force, and the secretary-general of the United Nations, U Thant, acceded to the request without demur.

Once again, after ten years, Israel directly faced Egyptian forces along the frontier, and on May 22 Nasser declared the Straits of Tiran closed to Israeli shipping and to shipping bound to and from Israel. That such an act would be a declaration of war had been made clear by Israel. The major powers attempted to establish a naval force in order to implement the assurances made to Israel in 1957, but no force or action emerged. On May 26 Nasser told the Arab Trade Unions Congress that this time it was their intention to destroy Israel. On May 30 King Hussein flew to Cairo and signed a pact with Egypt placing his forces under the command of General Riad of Egypt; Iraq followed suit and signed a similar agreement. Contingents arrived from other Arab countries, such as Kuwait and Algeria. Israel was ringed by an Arab force of some 250,000 troops, over 2,000 tanks, and some 700 frontline fighter planes and bombers. The world looked on at what was believed by many to be the impending destruction of Israel, but no action was taken, and every effort was made by the Soviet and Arab delegates to the UN to minimize the seriousness of the situation and to permit developments to take their course. The Israeli government, headed by Levi *Eshkol, made urgent efforts to solve the crisis by diplomatic means, dispatching Foreign Minister Abba Eban to the heads of government of the Western great powers. The mission was in vain. A sudden change in French policy emerged and the traditional sympathy of the French government for Israel disappeared, against the background of a new French bid for Arab support.

The Israeli government was enlarged by the cooption of representatives of the opposition factions Gaḥal (M. Begin and Y. Sapir as ministers without portfolio) and Rafi (M. Dayan as minister of defense) and constituted an emergency government of national unity. World Jewry rallied behind Israel, and a total identification with Israel, such as had never been known before, was evinced by the Jews. Massive financial support was mobilized, and thousands of volunteers besieged Israel's embassies and consulates.

Israel Strikes Back: the Southern Front

The morning of June 5, 1967, found the Israeli armed forces, which under the command of Major General Yiẓḥak *Rabin had been mobilized since May 20, facing the massed Arab armies around Israel's frontiers. Israel's citizen army had been quietly and efficiently mobilized to defend the country against the impending Arab attack, which every Arab medium of mass communication announced was imminent. That morning the Israel Air Force commanded by Brigadier General Mordekhai Hod undertook a preemptive attack designed to destroy the Arab air forces and their airfields. Flying in low, under the Arab radar screens, Israeli planes destroyed the air forces of Egypt, Jordan, and Syria and planes of the Iraqi air force. In less than three hours 391 planes were destroyed on the ground and an additional 60 Arab planes were destroyed in air combat, compared to Israel's loss of 19 planes, some of whose pilots were taken prisoner. This brilliant air operation accorded Israel complete superiority in the air, and thereafter the Israel Air Force was free to give close combat support in the ground operations which ensued.

At 8 A.M. on June 5, while the Israel Air Force was pounding Arab strength, Israel's Southern Command, under Brigadier General Yeshayahu Gavish, moved its forces against the massed Egyptian armies in Sinai. (See Map: Six-Day War:

Egyptian Front). The command, facing seven Egyptian brigades including some 1,000 tanks, was composed of three divisional task forces commanded by Brigadier General Israel Tal on the northern sector of the front, Brigadier General Abraham Yoffe in the central sector, and Brigadier General Ariel Sharon in the southern sector.

The breakthrough was achieved in the general area of Khan Yunis-Rafa by Tal's forces. The brunt of the fighting was borne by S brigade, which exploited the breakthrough by overcoming very heavily defended positions at Sheikh Zuwayd and al-Jiradi and reaching El-Arish on the evening of June 5. The other main breach of the Egyptian front was effected jointly by the divisional task forces of Yoffe and Sharon. Yoffe's group moved across a trackless desert area and introduced itself in depth into a position north of the line Niẓẓanah-Abu Aweigila in the rear of the Egyptian defensive positions. The morning of June 6 found this force firmly positioned in the area of Bi'r Laḥfān and straddling the Abu Aweigila-Bi'r Laḥfān road, in the rear of the main Egyptian positions. Meanwhile Sharon's division carried out a perfectly executed night attack on the main Egyptian positions at Umm-Qataf covering the crossroads at Abu Aweigila. An infantry brigade marched across the dunes and attacked the positions from the north, while at the same time a parachute brigade landed by helicopter in the gun lines of the Egyptian force concentrated at Umm-Qataf and Abu Aweigila and destroyed them. By morning an armored brigade had passed through these positions, destroyed the armored elements in the area, and proceeded to break through in the direction of Jebel Libni. Meanwhile Israeli forces, following through the breakthrough at Khan Yūnis, fanned northward and were engaged in bitter fighting with the Egyptian and Palestinian forces in the Gaza Strip. Following the capture of Deir al-Balaḥ, parachute and infantry forces, after a fierce struggle, finally captured the Ali Muntar Hill dominating the town of Gaza.

Jerusalem and the Jordanian Front – the First Day

On the morning of June 5 a message was sent by the government of Israel through General Odd Bull of the UN Truce Supervision Organization advising King Hussein that Israel had no designs on Jordan and that, granted quiet on the Israel-Jordanian border, no harm would befall his country. On the same morning, however, King Hussein decided to honor his pact with Nasser, and his forces opened up a heavy barrage along the armistice lines, shelling Israeli villages and towns, including the outskirts of Tel Aviv, and bombing a number of inhabited areas sporadically. (See Map: Six-Day War: Jordanian Front).

The major brunt of the Jordanian shelling was felt in Jerusalem. Heavy indiscriminate shelling caused many casualties in the city. At approximately 11 A.M. the Jordanian forces moved against Government House in a demilitarized area on the Hill of Evil Counsel in Jerusalem, used as UN Headquarters. Israel's Jerusalem Brigade counterattacked and drove the Arab Legion out of this position. The Israeli forces maintained

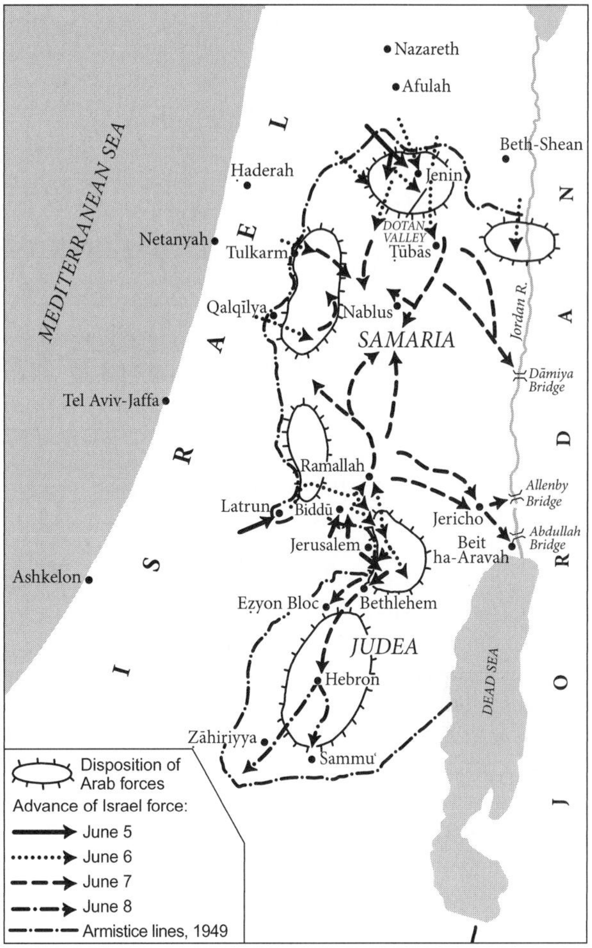

Map 2. The Six-Day War: Jordanian front.

the impetus of their attack, taking a number of positions, including the village of Ṣūr Bāhir on the road to Bethlehem. In the meantime a reserve armored brigade broke into the Jordanian positions on the north of the Jerusalem Corridor, the heavily fortified "radar" positions near Ma'aleh ha-Ḥamishah and positions of Sheikh ʿAbdal-ʿAzīz. A further breakthrough was effected at Beit Iksāʿ. These forces fanned out on the high ground north of the Jerusalem Corridor, taking the Jordanian positions at Biddū and Nabī Samwīl, and reaching the main road from the north to Jerusalem at Tell al-Fūl south of Ramallah.

On the night of June 5–6 an infantry brigade attacked the *Latrun enclave, captured the village and the police post, and advanced into the Judean Hills eastward along the Beit Horon road in order to join forces with the armored brigade at the gates of Ramallah. The Central Command, under Brigadier General Uzi Narkiss, was thus committed in Jerusalem, developing its counterattack toward the south of the city and an armored brigade followed by an infantry brigade from the coast taking the commanding features to the north of the corridor and moving eastward to cut the link of the Jordanian forces in Jerusalem with the north.

At this stage a reserve paratroop brigade under Colonel Mordekhai Gur, rushed to Central Command, was thrown into the battle on the night of June 5–6 without time for adequate preparation against the most heavily fortified Jordanian positions, which covered the northeast of Jerusalem and were manned by some two brigades. The fiercest fighting took place at the Police School and Ammunition Hill. The brigade suffered very heavy casualties before a breakthrough was achieved. It enabled the paratroopers to take the district of Sheikh Jarrāḥ, the American Colony, and the Rockefeller Museum area, and to reestablish a direct link with the Israeli enclave of Mount Scopus, which had been isolated from Israel by Jordanian forces for the past 20 years.

Meanwhile Israel's Northern Command, under Brigadier General David Elazar, attacked from the north with an armored brigade supported by infantry and broke into Jordanian-held territory on the West Bank along two axes of advance in the general area of Jenin. A heavy armored battle took place in this area, with the Jordanians reinforcing their armored forces from the Jordan Valley area. An Israeli counterattack finally smashed the Jordanian opposition. Israel's forces of the Northern and Central Command were, after 24 hours of fighting, converging from the south, the east, and the north of the West Bank triangle in the face of very obstinate Jordanian opposition. In the meantime Israel's naval forces under the overall command of Rear Admiral Shlomo Erel were operating on the approaches to Alexandria and a number of frogmen, who were later taken prisoner, succeeded in penetrating the defenses of that port and attacking a number of ships.

The Second Day's Fighting

The second day saw the forces of Tal in the northern sector of the Sinai front fanning out from El-Arish, one force continuing along the coastal road westward toward the Suez Canal and another force, which moved southward after a tank battle to take the El-Arish air field, attacking the heavily fortified Egyptian positions at Bi'r Laḥfān, already outflanked by Yoffe's intrusion across the desert. From this point the forces under Tal and Yoffe continued with a coordinated attack, Tal's task force advancing westward along the central road to the Suez and Yoffe's moving southward. Sharon's force continued to mop up in the general area of Umm-Qataf-Abu Aweigila and southward toward Quseima. At the same time a reserve infantry brigade, strengthened by armored forces and paratroopers, launched an attack on the city of Gaza, which was taken after very heavy fighting. The Gaza Strip was now in Israel's hands. Brigadier General Moshe Goren was appointed military governor of the Gaza Strip.

Meanwhile the historic battle for Jerusalem was being waged with all its ferocity. To the north of Jerusalem the reserve armored brigade continued the battle to clear the area between Jerusalem and Ramallah, a vital crossroads for the development of operations in the West Bank of the Jordan Kingdom. Tell-al-Fūl was captured after an armored battle. Part of the brigade moved southward, taking Shuaʿfāṭ to the north of Jerusalem and the general area of Givat ha-Mivtar, which fell after a second attack was launched against it. The hilly ground north of the Jerusalem Corridor was now safely in the hands of the Israel Defense Forces, thus enabling them to develop their push northward. The town of Ramallah surrendered. Meanwhile the forces of the Northern Command maintained their pressure southward toward the center of the West Bank. An infantry force attacked from the west, taking Qalqīlya and reaching al-ʿAzzūn. Jenin was finally taken by an armored force at noontime on June 6, and the armored brigade which captured the city proceeded southward, engaging in a major armored battle at the Qabāṭiyya crossroads. An additional Israeli armored force reached the Ṭūbās-Nablus road and was engaged by Jordanian armor. At midnight the Israeli forces renewed their attack, taking Ṭūbās and moving toward the Dāmiya bridge on the Jordan River, thus sealing off the northern part of the West Bank from possible reinforcement from eastern Jordan. The Israel Air Force was by now free to give close ground support to the forces on all fronts, which it proceeded to do with considerable effect.

The Third Day – the Capture of the Old City

June 7 was to be one of the most historic days in the history of Jewish arms. That morning Gur issued his orders for the capture of the Old City of Jerusalem, which had by now been completely surrounded by Israeli forces occupying all the heights around the historic city. The Lions' Gate, otherwise known as St. Stephen's Gate, was chosen as the break-in point. A sharp battle took place there, the paratroopers, supported by a small armored force, breaking in at the gate. Despite the fact that Israeli forces had avoided attacking the holy places, the Arabs used the al-Aqṣā Mosque as a sniping post and the entire area of the Temple Mount as an ammunition dump – despite pleas to the contrary from the Jordanian governor of Jerusalem and the Muslim religious authorities. The area was rapidly cleared with a minimum of damage to the holy places; at 10:15 A.M. the Israeli flag was raised over the Temple Mount and Jewry's holiest site, the *Western ("Wailing") Wall, was once again in Jewish hands.

Meanwhile the armored forces which had taken Ramallah continued toward Jericho, while the unit advancing from the direction of Nablus met with those coming from Ramallah and fanned down toward the Jordan River. At the same time the Jerusalem Brigade continued southward, taking Bethlehem and Hebron, which surrendered without a shot being fired, and also retaking the area of the Eẓyon Bloc, a group of Jewish settlements which had fallen to the Arab Legion in 1948. The entire West Bank was in Israel hands. Brigadier General Chaim Herzog was appointed military governor of the West Bank.

In the south Israeli naval forces sailing in the Gulf of Akaba took *Sharm el-Sheikh and opened the Straits of Tiran. Once again shipping was free to move through the straits to and from Israel. Meanwhile the race across the sands of Sinai was coming to its close as the three Israel divisional task forces pushed forward in an attempt to seal off Egyptian armored forces in the center of Sinai and prevent their withdrawal to the Suez Canal. Tal's forces captured the Egyptian military base of Bi'r Gifgafa and there withstood the last heavy armored counterattack on the part of the Egyptians. Yoffe's forces captured Bi'r Hassneh and rushed for the Mitla Pass in order to seal it off in the face of the retreating Egyptian armored forces. A huge trap for Egyptian armor was now being created. The Egyptian defenses in the area of Quseima, Abu Aweigila, and Kuntilla collapsed before the advance toward Nakhl of Sharon's forces, which proceeded systematically to destroy the Egyptian forces attempting to withdraw.

The Fourth Day – Israel's Forces Reach the Suez

On the fourth day of fighting, Tal's forces reached Qantara in the north and Ismailiya in the center and linked up along the bank of the Suez Canal, Yoffe's forces advanced in a two-pronged attack toward the city of Suez and in the direction of the Bitter Lake, while another section of his forces moved south toward Res Sudar on the Gulf of Suez. Israeli forces fanned southward along the Gulf of Suez toward Abu Zenima where they linked up with parachute forces that had landed at Sharm el-Sheikh and were moving northward. Desperate Egyptian attempts to break out were broken by the armored forces and above all by the Israel Air Force, and the Mitla Pass was converted into one huge Egyptian military graveyard. In this area one of the largest battles in the history of armored warfare, with approximately 1,000 tanks participating, had resulted in a decisive Israeli victory. The Israeli flag was raised along the Suez Canal, the Straits of Tiran were open, and the Egyptian forces, which only four days before had been poised to destroy Israel, were in disarrayed retreat, having lost most of their air force and leaving behind vast quantities of equipment, including some 800 tanks. Meanwhile in the north the Syrian forces had been continuously shelling the Israel villages along the border and a number of infantry and armored attacks against Israel villages were beaten off.

The Fifth and Sixth Days – the Golan Heights Taken

The Syrian attacks increased in intensity and covered a large number of Israeli towns and villages. The Israel Air Force, now freed from other fronts and having already destroyed the Syrian air force, brought the gun positions under attack. On Friday June 9 at noon, the Israel Defense Forces attacked the Syrian army on the Golan Heights. (See Map: Six-Day War: Syrian Front). The main break-in point was chosen in the northern sector of the Syrian front in the area of Tell ʿAzāziyāt. An infantry brigade and a reserve armored brigade bore the brunt of the attack against heavily fortified positions sited in tactically advantageous places, and the infantry forces dealt with one position after another in close hand-to-hand fighting, particularly fierce fighting taking place at Tell Fakhr. Losses were heavy on both sides. The armored force finally broke

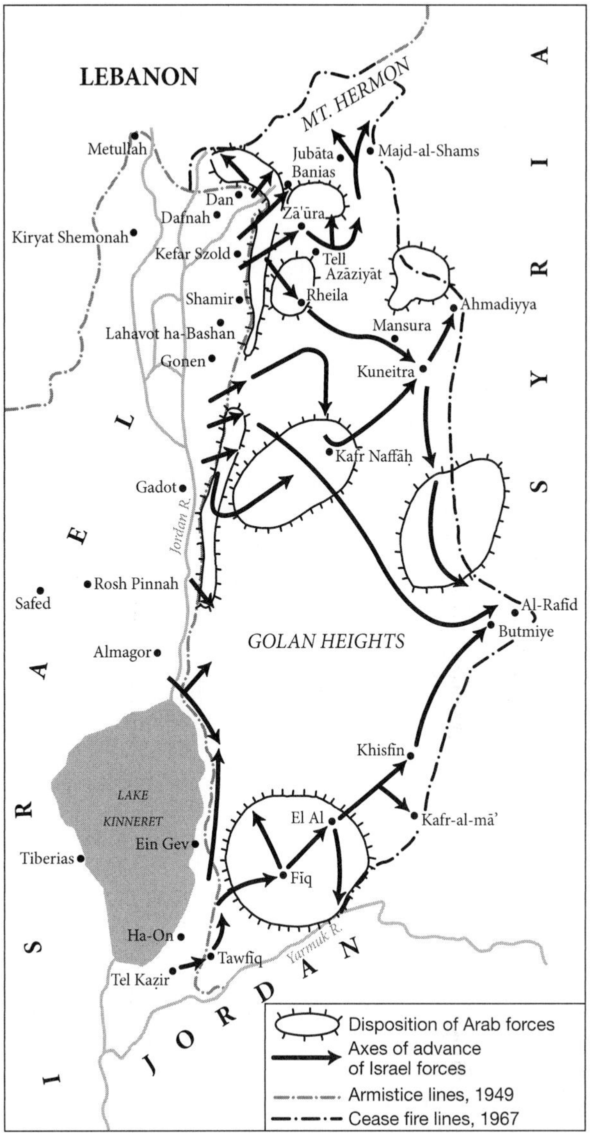

Map 3. The Six-Day War: Syrian front.

through the first line of defense, reaching the objective with two tanks in operation out of an entire battalion.

An additional armored force advanced and captured Banias, and while the breakthrough force now advanced rapidly toward Mansura and Kuneitra, a force under Brigadier General Elad Peled, which had previously been in operation on the West Bank, attacked in the area of Tawfiq; paratroopers were landed from helicopters in depth behind the enemy lines; an additional armored force moved up through Darbashiyya; and at 2:30 P.M. on Saturday, June 10, 24 hours after the commencement of hostilities, the town of Kuneitra was in the hands of the Israel Defense Forces, which were now firmly established on the Golan Heights. The danger of Syrian shelling had been removed from the Israeli villages. General Elazar's Northern Command forces ceased operation, following a UN-sponsored cease-fire, and established themselves along the lines reached by the advancing forces. The Israel Defense Forces were now established on the main highway leading to Damascus.

In six days the military force of the Arabs had been destroyed, their air forces were in ruins, hundreds of tanks were destroyed or captured, over 15,000 casualties had been inflicted on them, and almost 6,000 prisoners were in Israeli hands. Israel's military losses were 777 killed, 2,586 wounded, and a handful of prisoners, primarily pilots, all of whom were subsequently exchanged in return for the thousands of Arab prisoners. The Egyptian and the Syrian governments accepted a cease-fire agreement and UN observers were posted along the Suez Canal front and on the Golan Heights. Sporadic shooting took place, particularly along the neck leading from Qantara northward to Port Said, but by and large a period of comparative military quiet descended on the area. Nasser announced his resignation in a broadcast to the Egyptian people on June 9, but withdrew in the face of mass demonstrations calling for his return. In his resignation speech he made clear the part played by the Soviets in bringing on the war.

After the Six-Day War

Israel proceeded rapidly with the administration of the occupied areas and in a very short time had gained full control and had reestablished all essential services for the population. During the fighting approximately 100,000 Arabs fled from the West Bank to the East Bank, and following the occupation tens of thousands left voluntarily in order to join their families. The Israeli military policy was to allow the Arabs to govern themselves up to and including the municipal level as far as possible. The city of Jerusalem was reunited and the barriers of wire, mines, and hate fell as the people of two nations which had been divided for 19 years mingled once again, meeting and trading with each other. Gradually the governments's open-bridges policy, as enunciated by the minister of defense, General Moshe Dayan, evolved, Arabs from the West Bank moving freely to and fro across the Jordan River and trade developing between the occupied territories and the Arab world, particularly in the field of agricultural supplies. A liberal military administration ruled in the areas. The scene was set for some form of accommodation between the Arab world and Israel: King Hussein visited the capitals of the world, and it appeared that there was a preparedness to discuss some form of peace or coexistence with Israel; but all decisions were postponed pending the convening of the Arab Summit Conference at Khartoum in August 1967.

Before this conference, however, President Podgorny of the Soviet Union and Marshal Zakharov, the Soviet chief of staff, visited Cairo and committed themselves to the resuscitation of the Egyptian armed forces. President Podgorny later visited Damascus and made similar commitments, and a vast Soviet airlift began to replace almost two billion dollars' worth of equipment lost to the Israelis. Against this background, and doubtless influenced by it, the Khartoum Conference took place and the Arab policy of the "three noes" – no recognition of Israel, no negotiations with Israel, and no peace with Israel – was enunciated. Following this the prospects for a peaceful settlement waned in the face of Arab intransigence. The Palestine Liberation Organization was reorganized and Yaḥya Ḥammuda was named acting chairman of the Palestine Liberation Organization in place of Ahmed Shukeiri. All the Palestine terrorists and guerrilla organizations joined this new federation, apart from the Popular Front for the Liberation of Palestine, an extreme left-wing organization that engaged in terrorist activities against civilian aircraft and Israeli institutions abroad.

A concentrated attempt was made to mount terrorist and resistance operations in the occupied areas and in Israel. These took two forms: indiscriminate terrorist activity, such as bombs in the Tel Aviv bus station, the Hebrew University cafeteria, or on the grounds of the American consulate in Jerusalem, in which innocent civilians and passersby were killed and wounded; and a guerrilla war to be mounted from bases mainly on the east bank of the Jordan River. Gradually the Israeli security services developed a counteroffensive and, although terrorist activities were perpetrated from time to time, the situation was kept well in hand, and after three years most of the terrorist rings involved, both in the occupied areas and in Israel, had been rounded up.

The Israel Defense Forces took special action against the terrorists based in Jordan and in March 1968 destroyed their main base in Karama, near the east bank of the Jordan, in a major attack. Following this attack the Palestinian guerrillas withdrew their main bases from the area near the border and adapted their training and mode of operation accordingly. From time to time the Israel Air Force attacked their bases and concentrations, but the main battles took place in the darkness of the nights along the Jordan River, very heavy casualties being inflicted on the infiltrators. By mid-1969 Yasser Arafat admitted to over 700 killed, in addition to over 3,000 guerrillas held as prisoners by Israel. By the introduction of improved operational methods and new technological devices, the Jordan River was closed off to the guerrillas, and once again the Israel Defense Forces scored a resounding victory. The guerrillas, thwarted in their attempts to penetrate into Israel-held territory, devoted more and more energy to inter-Arab affairs and gradually became a source of considerable danger to the established regimes, particularly in Jordan and Lebanon. Their activity led to a number of serious clashes between the authorities and their forces in both Jordan and Lebanon, resulting in an unstable political situation.

The main military effort against Israel after the war was mounted by Egypt. From time to time Egyptian forces violated the cease-fire arrangement along the Suez Canal. In October 1967, an Israel destroyer, the "Eilat," was sunk while on patrol off the coast of Sinai by missiles fired by an Egyptian missile boat from the shelter of Port Said harbor. In retaliation Israel shelled the Egyptian oil refineries at Suez. Nasser announced a policy based on three phases: defensive, retaliatory, and offensive. In September–October 1968 he declared the opening of the retaliatory phase with heavy artillery bombardments along the canal, inflicting heavy casualties on the Israeli forces. Israel retaliated both along the canal and by deep commando penetrations into Egypt, in the Nile Valley and along the coasts. At the same time Israeli forces developed the construction of "the Bar-Lev Line," a series of fortifications along the length of the entire canal.

In March 1969 Nasser announced the opening of the offensive phase, declaring that the cease-fire no longer existed. The war of attrition that he waged against Israel escalated, and Israel's casualties along the canal rose, reaching a peak of 30 killed and over 70 wounded in July 1969. Israel's forces under the command of Lieutenant General Chaim Bar-Lev went over to the counterattack, choosing air power as its means of counteracting Egyptian superiority in artillery along the canal. Heavy air battles took place in the summer and autumn of 1969, when heavy casualties were inflicted on the Egyptian air force and control of the air was firmly established by the Israel Air Force. Between the end of the Six-Day War and the end of March 1970, 85 Egyptian planes had been shot down by Israel, and Egyptian losses were averaging eight planes to every one of Israel's. In September 1969 an armored Israeli force crossed the Gulf of Suez and sojourned over 20 hours on the Egyptian side, clearing a stretch of Egyptian military installations, including radar posts, some 31 mi. (50 km.) long. Following this action the Israel Air Force proceeded systematically to destroy Egypt's radar-warning system and anti-aircraft defenses, including SA-2 missiles supplied by the Soviets. This battle continued until, in November 1969, Egyptian missile bases along the canal had been destroyed for the third time, and Israel continued to counterattack the Egyptian forces along the canal. In January 1970 Israeli planes began to attack similar missile sites and other military installations deep in Egypt, including the Cairo area. At the same time commando raids designed to keep the Egyptian forces off balance, such as that involving the temporary occupation of Shadwan Island in the Red Sea, took place. Israeli planes continued to attack positions in Egypt and particularly along the canal with comparative freedom, and Israel gained the upper hand in the war of attrition.

At this stage, in March 1970, it was announced that Egypt had been supplied with SA-3 ground-to-air missiles manned by Soviet personnel. The Soviet penetration, which had been going on for years in Egypt and in Syria and which had brought thousands of advisers and technicians to these two countries, now intensified. This policy was part of a general build-up of a Soviet presence in the Mediterranean that had been going on for a number of years and in which the Soviet fleet played a major part, attaining a strength of over 60 vessels, including two helicopter carriers, the *Moskva* and the *Leningrad*. Israel's defense of the cease-fire lines and of her borders continued to be maintained. The administration of the occupied territories developed, and the first moves were made by Israel toward solving the Arab-refugee problem. Trade from the occupied territories to the Arab world reached IL 70,000,000 in exports in 1969, and imports from the Arab world to them topped IL 25,000,000. The Arab guerrilla forces had been fought to a standstill by Israel but had become an increasingly serious internal factor in the Arab countries. The Arab world was racked by revolution and unrest. Since the Six-Day War there have been revolutions or attempts at revolution in the Middle East in Iraq, South Yemen, Somalia, Sudan, Libya, and Saudi Arabia. Arab has fought Arab on the South Yemen-Saudi border, in Jordan, and in Lebanon, and Arab intransigence has continued to postpone any approach of peace.

In June 1970 the U.S. secretary of state William Rogers proposed that discussions be held between Israel, Egypt, and Jordan under the auspices of Ambassador Gunnar Jarring (as UN representative). On August 4 Israel accepted the Rogers proposal in order to achieve "an agreed and binding contractual peace agreement." This agreement also initated a cease-fire with Egypt, from August 7, for a period of three months, even though Israel regarded the original Security Council cease-fire resolution as still binding. Israel charged that Egypt with Soviet connivance had violated the cease-fire agreement by moving up missile sites into the Canal zone. The cease-fire was renewed by Egypt for a further period of three months on Nov. 5, 1970, and again for one month on Feb. 5, 1971. On March 7, 1971, President Sadat announced Egypt's refusal formally to extend the cease-fire but did not resume fighting.

BIBLIOGRAPHY: R.S. and W.S. Churchill, *The Six Day War* (1967); D. Kimche and D. Bawly, *The Sandstorm: The Arab-Israeli War of 1967* (1968); W.Z. Laqueur, *The Road to Jerusalem: The Origins of the Arab-Israeli Conflict 1967* (1968); A. Lall, *The UN and the Middle East Crisis* (1968); R. Bondy et al. (eds.), *Mission Survival…* (1968); R.J. Donovan, *Israel's Fight for Survival* (1967); T. Draper, *Israel and War Politics: Roots of the Third Arab-Israel War* (1968), incl. bibl.; P. Young, *The Israeli Campaign* (1967); J. Chance, *Conflict in the Middle East* (1965); M.M. Barnet, *The Time of the Burning Sun* (1968); Associated Press, *Lightning Out of Israel* (1967); Life, *Israel's Swift Victory* (1967); S.L.A. Marshall, *Swift Sword* (1967); S. Teveth, *The Tanks of Tammuz* (1969); *The Seventh Day: Soldiers Talk About the Six-Day War* (1970; *Middle East Record 1967* (1971). **ADD. BIBLIOGRAPHY:** C. Herzog, *The Arab-Israel Wars* (1982); M. Oren, *Six Days of War* (2002); J. Bowen, *Six Days: How the 1967 War Shaped the Middle East* (2003).

[Chaim Herzog]

°**SIXTUS IV** (b. **Francesco della Rovere**; 1414–1484), pope from 1471 to 1484. In Italy the reign of Sixtus IV marks a high point of tolerance. The pope used Jewish physicians, and perhaps employed Jews for the collection, copying, and translation of Hebrew works. He refused to canonize Simon of *Trent, allegedly a victim of Jewish ritual murder. It is clear, however, that the pope's tolerance was offset, outside his own domains, by local hostility. A generous bull of 1479 concerning the Jews of *Avignon was questioned and subsequently withdrawn. In November 1478 the pope issued a bull investing *Ferdinand and Isabella with extraordinary powers to appoint inquisitors in all parts of Castile. In January 1482 he condemned the excessive harshness with which they were carrying out their task, in a letter to the king and queen. Six chief inquisitors were appointed, including the notorious Tomás de

*Torquemada (Feb. 11, 1482), and invested with discretionary powers (April 17, 1482). The next year, yielding to pressure from King Ferdinand, the pope placed Torquemada at the head of the *Inquisition in Castile and Aragon.

BIBLIOGRAPHY: E.A. Synan, *Popes and Jews in the Middle Ages* (1965), 140ff.; P. Lamberti, in: REJ, 10 (1885), 170ff.; L. Bardinet, *ibid.*, 6 (1883), 9, 18f.

[Nicholas de Lange]

SIXTUS OF SIENA (1520–1569), Italian convert and anti-Jewish polemist. Sixtus was born in Siena. Shortly after his conversion he entered the Franciscan order and devoted himself to the study of the Bible. After a short while, he was charged with heresy and sentenced to die at the stake. Pope Pius *V saved him and transferred him to the Dominican order. In the Papal States Sixtus and another convert, Filippo Moro, preached the conversion of the Jews and incited the rabble against them. In 1559 he was instrumental in the burning of the Talmud in Cremona. On the other hand, he saved the Zohar from destruction, in the hope that mysticism and Kabbalah would turn the Jews to Christianity. His most important work was *Bibliotheca Sancta ex praecipuis Catholicae Ecclesiae auctoribus collecta* (Venice, 1566), an introduction to the Bible which includes an alphabetical list of Jewish commentators.

BIBLIOGRAPHY: *Bollettino senese di storia patria*, 14 (1907), 174–83; F. Secret, *Les Kabbalistes Chrétiens de La Renaissance* (1964), index; Roth, Italy, 302, 303f.

[Menachem E. Artom]

SIYYUM (Heb. סִיּוּם; "conclusion"), designation for celebrations held on certain occasions.

(1) *Siyyum *Sefer Torah* is a consecration ceremony held at the conclusion of the writing of a new Torah Scroll. The last, and sometimes the first, verses of the Torah are written by members of the congregation (each congregant filling in one letter); the scroll is then solemnly sanctified with special prayers and songs. The celebration is based on R. *Eliezer's interpretation of I Kings 3:15 (Song R. 1:1 no. 9).

(2) *Siyyum Massekhet* or *Siyyum ha-Shas* is the celebration held at the conclusion of the study of a Talmud tractate or of the whole Talmud. On this occasion the members of the study group recite special formulas of appreciation called הַדְרָן (*hadran*), in which they give thanks for having had the privilege of studying Torah; they petition for the opportunity to be able "to return again" to the study of this tractate. The *hadran* is chosen from rabbinic sources in the Talmud (Ber. 16b–17b) and is usually printed at the end of each tractate. On the occasion, a festive banquet is held (see **Se'udah*) at which the lecturer delivers a discourse on his novellae to the Talmud tractate that has just been completed (also commonly known as *hadran*). The custom of the festive banquet dates back to talmudic times (Shab. 118b–119a), and it is a *mitzvah* to participate. Study groups often plan, if possible, to complete a Talmud tractate on the day before Passover to allow the firstborn male to dispense with fasting on this day; partaking of the *siyyum* meal overrides the fast. (See *Fasting and Fast Days.)

(3) In North African Jewish communities, especially in Algeria, a *siyyum*, called *Ḥag Siyyum* or *Se'udat Yitro u-Moshe*, was yearly celebrated on the Thursday before the Sabbath on which the Torah portion *Yitro* (Ex. 18–20) was read in the synagogue. At the celebration (based on Ex. 18:12) the *Ten Commandments were solemnly read to the congregation and a festive banquet held at which chicken was served.

BIBLIOGRAPHY: Eisenstein, Dinim, 288–9.

SKALAT (Pol. **Skałat**), town in *Tarnopol district, Ukraine. Formerly within Poland, Skalat passed to Austria in 1772, reverting to Poland between the two world wars. There was a Jewish settlement in the town during the 16th century, and 686 Jews lived there in 1765. The Jewish population increased during the 19th century and numbered 3,256 (55% of the total) in 1890 and 2,791 (49%) in 1900. During the 19th century Ḥasidism had considerable influence in the community, but the Jews in Skalat had to contribute toward the maintenance of the German school, headed by Joseph *Perl, in Tarnopol. As a result of Skalat's proximity to the Russian border, economic life came to a standstill following World War I and many Jews were compelled to leave. In 1921 there were 2,919 Jews (49.1%) living in the town. Between the two world wars they engaged in commerce, retail trade, and crafts. The influence of the national movement and Zionism increased.

[Shimshon Leib Kirshenboim]

Holocaust Period

By 1939 there were 4,800 Jews in Skalat. When the town passed to Soviet rule (1939–41), all independent political activity was suppressed, and as private enterprise was stifled, Jews sought employment in government service and cooperatives. When the Soviet-German war broke out on June 22, 1941, about 200 Jews in Skalat fled with the retreating Soviet army. The town fell to the Germans on July 5, and that day 20 Jews were murdered by German troops. On July 6 Ukrainian nationalists killed 560 Jews. A Judenrat was set up, headed by Meir Nierler. He was accused of collaboration with the Germans in rounding up Jews for deportation. In the autumn of 1941, 200 young Jews were sent to a slave labor camp in Velikiye Borki. A group of Jewish women were sent for forced labor to Jagielnica. Early in 1942, 600 sick and elderly persons were rounded up and assembled in the synagogue, and from there taken to *Belzec death camp. In an *Aktion* on Oct. 21, 1942, 3,000 victims were sent to Belzec, while 153 Jews were shot in Skalat itself. On November 9, in a second raid, 1,100 were rounded up and sent to the death camp. On April 7, 1943, about 750 persons were murdered and buried in mass graves near the town. Following this *Aktion* a resistance group was organized, headed by Michael Glanz. The young members collected arms, but the Germans, aware of the existence of the group, advanced the date of the next *Aktion*, for which the group was still unprepared. In this *Aktion*, carried out on May 9, 1943, 660 persons were killed. The city was then declared *Judenrein*. Only 400 Jews survived in the local labor camp. A resistance group was formed in the camp as well, and when the partisan units under General Kowpak began operating in the vicinity, 30 Jews escaped and joined their ranks. All but seven fell in fighting against the Germans. On July 28, 1943, the last of the Jews in the Skalat camp were murdered. About 300 Jews had found temporary refuge in the forests in the vicinity, but they were attacked by the Ukrainian bands led by Bandera, and only 200 survived the war.

There are three monuments to the Jewish community of Skalat: the Holocaust memorial to the memory of what was done to the Jews of the town; The cemetery memorial for the community that lived before the Holocaust; and the Skalat Holocaust memorial in the Holon cemetery, erected by the surviving families of the people of Skalat.

[Aharon Weiss]

BIBLIOGRAPHY: Halpern, Pinkas, index; B. Wasiutyński, *Ludność źdowska w Polsce w wiekach XIX i XX* (1930), 121, 130, 147; M. Balaban, *Dzieje Zydł w Galicyi i w Rzeczypospolitej Krakowskiej, 1772–1868* (1914), index; A. Weissbrod, *Es Shtarbt a Shtetl: Megiles Skalat* (1948).

°**SKARGA, PIOTR** (**Piotr Powecki**; 1536–1612), Polish Jesuit preacher and antisemite. Skarga was one of the leaders of the Uniate Church in Brest (*Brest-Litovsk), which recognized papal authority. He supported the candidacy of King Sigismund III Vasa (1587–1632) for the Polish throne and upon the latter's selection was appointed preacher in his court, a position which gave him great political influence. His opposition to any form of accommodation or compromise with Protestants was a factor in the abolition of laws of religious tolerance in 1606. His hatred of Jews found expression in his works *Żywoty swiętych* ("Lives of the Saints," 1579) and *Kazania na niedzielę i Swięta* ("Sermons for Sundays and Festivals," 1597). Both books attempted to prove that Jews made sacramental use of Christian blood. Skarga's venom and his closeness to the king were responsible for outbreaks against the Jews of Cracow more than once in the 1690s and encouraged the authorities to conduct *blood libel and *Host desecration trials. His hatred of Jews was particularly apparent in the plan of the Jesuits of Lemberg to seize the *Nachmanovich family synagogue and in litigations on this matter conducted in the presence of the king during the years 1603–08.

BIBLIOGRAPHY: M. Balaban, *Żydzi lwowsey na przełomie XVI i XVII wieku* (1906), index; idem, *Historja Żydów w Krakowie i na Kazimierzu*, 1 (1931), 165–86.

[Arthur Cygielman]

SKARZYSKO-KAMIENNA (until 1928 Kamienna), town in Kielce province, E. central Poland. A mine workers' quarter in the 19th century, the locality received municipal rights in 1923. Jews settled in Kamienna in the 1890s with the development of industrial enterprises for steel production and tanning. A Jewish community was organized on the eve of World War I. In 1921 1,590 Jews constituted 20% of the total population. In addition to shopkeeping, they engaged in hide processing, shoemaking, mechanics, and dyeing.

Holocaust Period

Before World War II, 2,200 Jews lived in Skarzysko-Kamienna. The German army entered on Sept. 7, 1939, and immediately initiated anti-Jewish terror. On May 5, 1941, the ghetto was established. In October 1942 an *Aktion* took place in which the town's entire Jewish population was deported to the *Treblinka death camp and exterminated. After the liquidation of the ghetto a massive *Julag* (*Judenlager*), a slave labor camp, was set up in the town. In January 1944 the camp officially became a concentration camp. It existed until August 1944, when all its inmates were deported to other concentration camps, mainly *Buchenwald in Germany and the *Czestochowa- "HASAG" camp in western Poland. Altogether, about 15,000 Jewish prisoners passed through this camp, but over 10,000 of them perished there. Many prisoners died of hunger and disease due to the subhuman conditions prevailing in the camp. Others were murdered by the SS men on the camp's staff. A resistance organization active in the camp smuggled out a small number of prisoners for guerrilla activities, but preparations for a general armed revolt failed. After the war the Jewish community in Skarzysko-Kamienna was not reconstituted.

BIBLIOGRAPHY: B. Wasiutyński, *Ludność żydowska w Polsce w wiekach XIX i XX* (1930), 32; BŻIH, no. 15–16 (1955).

[Stefan Krakowski]

SKEPTICS AND SKEPTICISM. Skepticism in philosophy refers to the principle that all knowledge, whether sensory or conceptual, is subject to the limitations of the human mind and, thus, unreliable. No certain or absolute knowledge can be attained by man. This position was advanced by such Greek schools as the Sophists and the Pyrrhonists. They did not, however, consider revelation. In religious philosophy some thinkers, while accepting the skeptical view concerning knowledge acquired by natural means, have held that certain knowledge can be attained through the supernatural act of revelation. But others, while denying the skeptics' claim about natural knowledge, have found the claim of certain supernatural knowledge open to unresolvable doubt, requiring either rejection or suspension of judgment regarding its validity.

Although medieval Jewish thinkers offered varied interpretations of Judaism, none subscribed to extreme skepticism about man's ability to acquire certain knowledge naturally, though the historical forms of this skepticism were known to them (cf. Saadiah Gaon, *Emunot ve-De'ot*, ch. 4). All affirmed the existence of positive knowledge upon which the truths of Judaism, however understood, could be based. Joseph *Albo epitomized this viewpoint in his specific rejection of philosophic skepticism. Moreover, unlike such medieval Christian mystics as Peter Damian (1007–1072) and Bernard of Clairvaux (1091–1153), who minimized the possibilities of natural against supernatural knowledge, most Jewish philosophers were confident of the validity of human sensation and thought. This confidence generally exceeded even that of such Christian scholastics as Thomas Aquinas, who affirmed natural knowledge but still denied man's capacity to apprehend fully theological truth. *Saadiah Gaon expressed the general Jewish viewpoint in his discussion of the sources of knowledge in *Emunot ve-De'ot* (Introduction: 5). Of the four sources Saadiah enumerates, three are natural: sense perception, self-evident rational knowledge, and inference based on logical necessity; the fourth is reliable tradition. Saadiah further asserts that the theological truths of natural knowledge and revelation are fundamentally the same.

*Judah Halevi and Ḥasdai *Crescas came closest among Jewish thinkers to skepticism about naturally acquired knowledge. But natural knowledge to medievals consisted of neoplatonic Aristotelian metaphysics and physics, and Judah Halevi and Crescas denied the adequacy of these theories as ultimate theological truths. However, in their refutations of neoplatonic Aristotelianism, Judah Halevi and Crescas relied on reason and assumed the validity of empirical knowledge.

The question whether any medieval Jewish thinkers were skeptical of revelations as a source of knowledge cannot be unequivocally determined. This issue arises particularly in the thought of *Maimonides and *Levi b. Gershom. Maimonides specifically rejected the opinion that non-Mosaic prophecy arose supernaturally, but his view of Mosaic prophecy was deliberately obscure. From a number of veiled remarks, Maimonides' view appears to be that Moses' prophecy arose naturally as well. Levi b. Gershom's position seems, in the main, similar to that of Maimonides.

BIBLIOGRAPHY: Guttmann, Philosophies, 67, 122, 226; Husik, Philosophy, 152–3, 389; A.J. Reines, in: HUCA, 40–41 (1969–70), 325–61; H.A. Wolfson, in: *Hebrew Union College Jubilee Volume* (1925), 263–315; idem, in: HTR, 28 (1935), 69–133; S. Horowitz, in: *Judaica, Festschrift zu Hermann Cohens 70. Geburtstag* (1912), 235–52.

[Alvin J. Reines]

SKIDEL, town in Grodno oblast, Belarus; in Poland-Lithuania until 1785, and from 1807 incorporated into Russia. Jews settled in Skidel in the mid-18th century and later became the majority in the town. In 1765 there were 463 Jews in Skidel and nearby settlements. The number had grown to 1,080 in 1847; 2,222 (80% of the total population) in 1897; 2,231 (76.7%) in 1921; and about 2,800 (c. 80%) in 1931. Jews earned their livelihood by trading in grain and timber, in the retail trade, crafts, and tanning, especially from the end of the 19th century. Jewish craft guilds were established in Skidel as early as the beginning of the 19th century and political and trade unions (Bund, Po'alei Zion, etc.) at the beginning of the 20th. A Zionist movement was established in 1898. In the fighting in the area during the retreat of the Russian armies, much Jewish property was destroyed. At the end of World War I, when the Germans left in fall 1918, a town council and committee of organized Jewish workers functioned independently for a time.

During the interwar period, under Polish rule, all the Jewish parties were active in Skidel. In the municipal elections of 1927, eight Jewish representatives gained seats, two-thirds of the municipal council. A Jew was elected mayor. Jewish institutions included schools of *Tarbut and of the Central Yiddish School organization (CYSHO). The community came to an end in the Holocaust.

After World War II Skidel became a part of Russia again, and all traces of its past as a Jewish shtetl rapidly disappeared. The town center, which had featured yeshivas, synagogues, factories, hospitals, and homes, was never rebuilt. The remaining townspeople dismantled the Jewish cemetery and used the stones to build their homes. Skidel became the region's "Red City," or regional Communist Party headquarters. In the early 2000s, it had a train station, a rebuilt Catholic Church, a sugar refinery, a poultry factory, and an agricultural commune.

BIBLIOGRAPHY: M. Wischnitzer, in: *Lite*, 1 (1951), 975; H. Lapin, in: *Grodner Opklangen*, 5–6 (1951), 56.

[Dov Rubin / Ruth Beloff (2nd Ed)]

SKIERNIEWICE, town in Lodz province, central Poland. Jews settled there at the end of the 18th century. M. Balaban mistakenly attributed a charge of *Host desecration in 1562 as occurring in Skierniewice (in his *Historja Zydów w Krakowie i na Kazimierzu*, 1 (1931), 156). There were 73 Jews residing in Skierniewice (7% of the total population) in 1808, and 216 (11%) in 1827. At first, up to about 1850, the Jews there buried their dead in the Jewish cemetery at *Lowicz. Between 1827 and 1863 most of the Jews were allowed to reside only within the limits of a special quarter. An organized community was established in 1850, and some years later a large synagogue was erected (in 1970 the building was in use as a municipal club). Jews engaged in small trade and crafts, such as weaving, shoemaking, and tailoring, in transportation, horse dealing, and services to the local Russian army garrisons. In the second half of the 19th century the influence of *Ḥasidism, mainly of Gur (see *Gora Kalwaria) and *Aleksandrow, grew among the Jews of Skierniewice. In 1886 the *admor* of *Worky (Warka), Simon Kalish, moved his "court" to Skierniewice. At the end of the 19th century the rabbi of the town was Meir Jehiel ha-Levi *Holzstock, later *admor* of *Ostrowiec. The Jewish population numbered 766 (29% of the total) in 1857; 2,898 (36%) in 1897; and 4,333 (33%) in 1921. At the beginning of World War I, in 1914, most of the Jews were expelled from Skierniewice by the retreating Russian army, and the refugees did not begin to return to their homes until 1916. After the end of the war branches of the Zionist parties, the *Bund, and *Agudat Israel were organized in the town.

[Arthur Cygielman]

Holocaust Period

On the outbreak of World War II there were about 4,300 Jews in Skierniewice. The German army entered the town on Sept. 8, 1939, and persecution of the Jewish population began. In 1940 over 2,000 Jews from Lodz and the towns in its vicinity were forced to settle in Skierniewice, whose Jewish population grew to about 6,500. In December 1940 a ghetto was established, but after two months all the Jews were ordered to leave and settle in the *Warsaw ghetto. By the beginning of April 1941 there were no Jews left in Skierniewice. They shared the fate of Warsaw Jewry.

[Stefan Krakowski]

BIBLIOGRAPHY: P. Mojecki, *Żydowskie okrucieństwa i zabobony* (1598), 18; B. Wasiutyński, *Ludność żydowska w Polsce wiekach XIX i XX* (1930), 9, 21; I. Schiper, *Dzieje handlu żydowskiego na ziemiach polskich* (1937), index; I. Perlov (ed.), *Sefer Skierniewice* (Yid. 1955).

SKINK (Heb. חֹמֶט, *ḥomet*), a reptile of the family Scincidae, of which six genera are found in Israel. These differ greatly in their bodily structure, some lacking legs entirely and resembling snakes, while others have atrophied feet or resemble the lizard. The *ḥomet* is included among the reptiles that are forbidden as food and render unclean men and articles which come into contact with their carcasses (Lev. 11:30). The identification of the *ḥomet* with the skink is based on the rendering of the Targum as well as on its description in rabbinical literature. Some commentators identify the *ḥomet* with the snail, but it is highly improbable. The *ḥomet* is enumerated among other species of reptile, and in addition it is difficult to accept that the stringent laws of ritual uncleanness would apply to snails, which abound in Israel, and some of which are so small that it is difficult to avoid contact with them.

BIBLIOGRAPHY: Lewysohn, Zool, 279f., nr. 362; I. Aharoni, *Zikhronot Zo'olog Ivri*, 2 (1946), 233, 244; J. Feliks, *Animal World of the Bible* (1962), 98. **ADD. BIBLIOGRAPHY:** Feliks, Ha-Tzome'aḥ, 233.

[Jehuda Feliks]

SKIRBALL CULTURAL CENTER. The Skirball Cultural Center was established in Los Angeles in 1996 to promote Jewish heritage and American democratic ideals. Originally conceived in the 1980s as an offshoot of the Reform movement's Hebrew Union College – Jewish Institute of Religion, the center was founded by Rabbi Uri D. Herscher (1941–), then the College-Institute's executive vice president and dean of faculty, who was elected president and chief executive of the center upon its separate incorporation in 1995. Named for one of its early donors, noted philanthropist Jack H. Skirball, the center was designed by Israeli-Canadian architect Moshe Safdie. The campus includes a museum, a performing arts center, conference halls, classrooms, libraries, courtyards, gardens, and a café. In its first decade, the center attracted nearly five million visitors, becoming one of the world's major Jewish cultural institutions.

When Herscher transferred his administrative office to the Los Angeles branch of the College-Institute in 1979, the city was emerging as the second largest Jewish community in the United States and third largest in the world. Yet surveys showed that only one in five Jews belonged to a synagogue or any Jewish organization. The trend toward assimilation was so pervasive that rates of Jewish observance were barely higher among affiliated Jews than among the unaffiliated. Herscher immediately sought to raise the profile of the College-Institute. In 1981, he persuaded its board of governors "to explore the concept of establishing a cultural center to celebrate American Jewish life." The celebratory aspect of the project was crucial to Herscher's concept: American Jewry, the most populous, powerful, and prosperous of all Diaspora communities, had yet to appreciate its own accomplishments and promise; nor had it fully acknowledged its debt of gratitude to the nation whose hospitality and goodwill knew no precedent in Jewish history. While insisting that remembrance of the Holocaust and solidarity with the State of Israel were essential – Herscher himself was born in Tel Aviv, to parents whose families were decimated by the Nazis – he argued that Jewish life in America, if it were to survive, required its own foundation: a renewed acquaintance with ancestral Jewish values and an inclusive vision of American society. He came to envisage the center as a new institutional paradigm distinct from the synagogue or the Jewish community center: a "tent" where Jews and non-Jews alike would be welcome. In Los Angeles, "the Ellis Island of the twenty-first century," he saw the ideal home for such a venture. Inspired by his own formative experience as a 13-year-old immigrant, when the United States accepted him and his family with open arms, he conceived of the center as a way to "return that embrace."

Herscher's project found an early champion in Jack Skirball, a Reform rabbi whose later success as a film producer and real estate investor earned him a considerable fortune. A generous contributor to Hebrew Union College, Skirball underwrote the relocation of its museum collection from Cincinnati to Los Angeles in 1972. Skirball believed that the museum's Judaica artifacts could function as "storytellers," visual objects that could engage an audience less attuned to purely textual learning. Herscher's vision of a cultural center and Skirball's hopes for the museum coalesced in the notion of a core exhibition in which the artifacts would tell the story of the Jews from their biblical origins to their integration into present-day American life. The center would also present an array of cultural programs: changing exhibitions, concerts, lectures, theater, dance, literary readings, symposia, film, and educational activities for adults and children. This multivalent approach, Herscher and Skirball believed, would have the best hope of attracting those who had abandoned existing Jewish institutions.

Skirball was also instrumental in opening doors to the wider community, introducing Herscher to corporation executive Franklin D. Murphy, a former chancellor of UCLA. Murphy viewed the prospect of a Jewish cultural center as a salutary expression of American democracy: a "stitch in the fabric" of pluralism, strengthening society as a whole. With Murphy's endorsement, Herscher succeeded in garnering major pledges from the Ahmanson, Kress, and Times Mirror Foundations, the Getty Trust, and others. Remarkably for an avowedly Jewish project, nearly one-third of the center's capital funds derived from non-Jewish sources. Another key source of support was Robert D. Haas, then president of the Levi Strauss corporation and a personal friend of Herscher's from their college days at UC Berkeley. The Levi Strauss family and its many branches were renowned for their philanthropy in San Francisco, where Jewish and American civic virtue had long been seen as fully compatible. With Haas leading the way, San Francisco Jewry's leading families responded generously to Herscher's appeals for support.

Although the College-Institute's board of governors finally approved the project, it was on the daunting condition that Herscher raise the funds independently. Through singular gifts of persuasion and unremitting efforts over 15 years, he succeeded. A 15-acre site, adjoining a major freeway and linking the two centers of Jewish population in West Los Angeles and the San Fernando Valley, was acquired in 1983, and Safdie was engaged as architect the following year. Morris Bergreen, a prominent New York attorney, carried forward the leadership of Jack Skirball, who died in 1985, succeeding him as chairman of the Skirball Foundation. Construction began in 1990, and the center opened six years later. Its board of trustees, consisting of both Jews and non-Jews, was chaired by renowned Los Angeles attorney Howard I. Friedman, a former international president of the American Jewish Committee. It also included Bergreen and Audrey Skirball-Kenis, Skirball's widow.

The core exhibition, titled "Visions and Values: Jewish Life from Antiquity to America," incorporated the museum's artifacts, artworks, documents, photographs, and sound recordings in a sequence of gallery displays and multimedia installations. Predicated on the concept of a journey through history, the exhibition described how Jews adapted to different civilizations, periodically reimagining themselves while retaining their age-old ethics and beliefs. Special emphasis was laid on the consonance of those ethics and beliefs with American democratic principles: Hanukkah and Passover were associated with constitutional commitments to religious liberty and political freedom; Purim with the assertion of minority rights; Sukkot with Thanksgiving; the Hebrew prophets with the founding fathers; the decalogue with the Declaration of Independence. The emblem of the exhibition was a Hanukkah lamp, each of its branches surmounted by a miniature Statue of Liberty.

In its array of public programs, the center sought the same alloy of visions and values, reflected by the institutional collaborations that produced two of its changing exhibitions: "Freud: Conflict and Culture" (2000), organized in conjunction with the Library of Congress and the Getty Trust; and "Einstein" (2004–05), presented jointly by the American Museum of Natural History, the Hebrew University, and the Skirball Cultural Center. Complementing its schedule of exhibitions, the center presented a diverse range of performing arts, lifelong learning classes, and an active program of outreach education to local youth. Designed to acknowledge and engage the multiplicity of cultures represented in Los Angeles, the program grew to accommodate some 50,000 students annually, the vast majority from the public school system.

In the early decades of the 20th century, Horace Kallen suggested that Jewish culture, properly appreciated, constituted a crucial aspect of America's national history and character, with unique potential to revitalize the nation's democratic possibility. His contemporary Mordecai Kaplan argued that in the open society of the United States, the humane values of Jewish civilization were more likely to prevail than the narrow credal and theological claims of past generations. Nearly a century later, the Skirball Cultural Center effectively revived, or perhaps recast, these hopes for an American-Jewish synthesis. Under Herscher's leadership, the center's facilities, programs, and endowment grew rapidly. It broadened its vision as well: in 2000 its mission statement was expanded to address "people of every ethnic and cultural identity." Citing the example of Jonah at Nineveh, Herscher contended that the prophetic ideals of Judaism applied both within and beyond the Jewish community. The center's ultimate goal, he said, was "to take the walls down completely."

[Robert Kirschner (2nd ed.)]

SKLARE, MARSHALL (1921–1992), U.S. sociologist. Born in Chicago, Sklare received his M.A. from the University of Chicago (1948) and his Ph.D. from Columbia University (1953). Sklare was a study director in the Division of Scientific Research of the American Jewish Committee (1953–66), and from 1966 until 1970 he was professor of sociology at Yeshiva University.

Sklare directed numerous research projects under the auspices of the American Jewish Committee, chiefly using the techniques of survey research. From 1970 to 1990 he was professor of sociology at Brandeis University, where he founded the Cohen Center for Modern Jewish Studies, the first research center devoted to social scientific study of contemporary American Jewry. Sklare also served as president of the Association for the Social Scientific Study of Jewry (1973–75). In his memory, the association established the annual Marshall Sklare Award for outstanding scholarship in that field.

Sklare was a leading expert in the field of sociology of U.S. Jewry; his work is widely quoted, especially *Conservative Judaism: An American Religious Movement* (1955) and an edited volume, *The Jews: Social Patterns of an American Group* (1958). *Riverton Study: How Jews Look at Themselves and Their Neighbors* (1957, with M. Vosk) analyzes Jewish attitudes in a community setting; *Jewish Identity on the Suburban Frontier: A Study of Group Survival in the Open Society* (1967) is a study of the attitudes of suburban Jews toward themselves. He also wrote *America's Jews* (1971). *Observing America's Jews* (1993) is a collection of previously published essays, mostly from the 1970s. He edited *The Jew in American Society* (1974); *The Jewish Community in America* (1974); *Understanding American Jewry* (1982); and *American Jews: A Reader* (1996).

[Werner J. Cahnman / Ruth Beloff (2nd ed.)]

SKLAREW, MYRA (1934–), U.S. poet, essayist, short fiction writer, and educator. A Maryland native, Sklarew was a professor of literature at American University, where she also co-directed its MFA in Creative Writing. Her published writing focuses on Jewish themes, including her maternal grandmother's family's experiences in small villages in Lithuania, the Holocaust, and the relationship between the neuroscience of memory and Holocaust testimony. She is the recipient of numerous awards for poetry and fiction and was the president of the artist community Yaddo. Her work has been recorded for the Library of Congress's Contemporary Poets' Archive.

Sklarew trained as a biologist at Tufts University and worked in genetics research and neurophysiology at Cold Spring Harbor Laboratory and Yale University School of Medicine. Poetry courses and seminars encouraged her longtime interest in writing and the murder of family members who had remained in Lithuania infused her life as well as her work. Her frequent journeys to Lithuania to interview bystanders, witnesses, and survivors are reflected in her poems in *Lithuania* (1995) and *The Witness Trees* (2000). Widely published in a diverse group of journals, Sklarew's eight books also include *In the Basket of the Blind* (1975), *From the Backyard of Diaspora* (1976), *Blessed Art Thou, No-One* (1982), *The Science of Goodbyes* (1982), *The Travels of the Itinerant Freda Aharon* (1985), *Altamira* (1987), *Like a Field Riddled by Ants* (1988), *Eating the White Earth* (1994), and *Over the Rooftops of Time* (2003).

BIBLIOGRAPHY: S. Gubar, *Poetry After Auschwitz* (2003), 118–20.

[Myrna Goldenberg (2nd ed.)]

SKOLE, city in Lvov district, Ukraine; formerly within Poland, passed to Austria in 1772, and reverted to independent Poland between 1919 and 1939. A Jewish community existed in Skole from the 18th century. There were 1,063 Jews in the city and surrounding villages who paid the poll tax in 1765. In the second half of the 18th century Jews in Skole imported wine from Hungary. In the second half of the 19th century many Jews in Skole earned their livelihood in the timber trade, wood processing, manufacture of building materials, commerce in agricultural produce, and transportation. Jewish workers were employed in the local match factory. When Skole became a summer mountain resort toward the end of the 19th century, the Jews there also derived a livelihood in occupations connected with the holiday season. A summer camp for Jewish children of Lvov was situated there. The community numbered 1,338 (65% of the total population) in 1880; 2,095 (61%) in 1900; 3,099 (48%) in 1910; and 2,410 (40.2%) in 1921. In the period of independent Poland, after World War I, the Jews in Skole were impoverished, and received support from Jewish relief funds. There was an active communal and cultural life. The Zionist movement gained many adherents among the youth.

In the 1930s antisemitism grew rampant in the area. In 1938 there were 2,670 Jews in Skole. Commercial and community life were brought to an end in September 1939 when Skole was annexed to the Soviet Union. The Hungarian army arrived in July 1941; in August, the Germans took over and set up a Judenrat. In September 1942 most of the Jews were sent to labor camps. The Jews of Skole were ultimately executed in June and August of 1943.

BIBLIOGRAPHY: Halpern, Pinkas, index; David Mi-Boekhov, *Zikhronot* (1922), 50–51; B. Wasiutyński, *Ludność żdowska w Polsce w wiekach XIX i XXI* (1930), 100, 108, 123, 148; I. Schiper, *Dzieje handlu zydowskiego na ziemiach polskich* (1937), index. **ADD. BIBLIOGRAPHY:** Spector, Jewish Life.

[Shimshon Leib Kirshonboim / Ruth Beloff (2nd ed.)]

SKOPLJE (Macedonian **Skopje**; Turkish **Üsküb**; Heb. איסקופיא in Mss.), capital city of the Former Yugoslav Republic of Macedonia. In view of its favorable trade situation and the fact of Jewish settlement at nearby *Monastir, it is likely that Jews already lived in Skoplje during Roman times. Documentary mention of Jews there occurs during the time of the medieval Serbian empire. The first synagogue known to exist dates to 1366. A charter (*povelja*) of Czar Stephan Dushan speaks of lands leased to Jews, and another one refers to Jews as "possessions of the Empire," granted to a monastery. In the 16th century, Jews expelled from Spain arrived and settled, and were joined in the 17th century by numerous Marranos from Holland and elsewhere. There was possibly a Jewish cemetery in the 15th century, but one is definitely known of in the 16th century, when a *cortijo* ("communal yard") existed in 1548. In reality it was a small Jewish quarter consisting of two-story houses built around the *kortiz* (court-patio in local Judeo-Spanish). The private courtyards contained workshops of tanners and smiths and storage rooms for wool which was exported to Ioannina, Greece, and Venice, as well as home-produced goods.

By the end of the 17th century Skoplje had two distinct synagogues: *di abasho* (downtown), known as Beth Aron, and *di ariva* (uptown), known as Beth Yaacov. The town and its Jews suffered from many fires, epidemics, and foreign occupations. In 1689 Skoplje had 60,000 inhabitants, 3,000 of them Jews. In the 18th century Jews were cheese manufacturers, miners, spinners, pumpers, dealers in cotton, wax, guts, etc. During the 19th century there was a great influx of Serbians, who pushed the Jews, Walachians, and Armenians out of the commercial trade. The Jewish community stagnated and its members reverted mainly to money lending and changing, brokerage, and sub-proletarian occupations such as fruit-mongering, street peddling, etc. The Yugoslav regime did not bring any notable change in the economic and social situation of Jews, which was rather backward and pitiful, their number reaching 4,000 by 1940. The pre-Holocaust Skoplje *kehillah* was a traditionalist Sephardi community, with Judeo-Spanish as the common language – which was even used in some prayers – and a lively Judeo-Spanish folklore.

During the Ottoman and earlier Serbian rules, Jews had to pay a special tax, in addition to the *haratch* (poll tax). Jewish sources mention a *mas ha-begadim* (clothes tax for the army), and the *gabelle* was an internal Jewish duty, an impost (excise) paid to the community for *kasher* meat. The first of the relatively few known rabbis was Aaron Peraḥyah ha-Kohen. R.

Joseph b. Leb of Salonika complained in a responsum of 1560 about the ignorance of Skoplje Jews, sending them a teacher, R. Aaron Avuya, who founded a *talmud torah*. Later rabbis were Ḥayyim Baruch, Ḥayyim Shabbetai, and Samuel Jacob Kalderon. The kabbalist Nehemiah Ḥiyya Ḥayon, author of *Moda'ah Rabbah*, taught in Skoplje in 1689. According to some sources, there was a Karaite group in the city for a while, but it disappeared rapidly.

Holocaust Period

In April 1941 Skoplje, and the whole of Yugoslav Macedonia, was occupied by the Germans, who later put their Bulgarian satellites in control. Jews were immediately subjected to humiliations, plundering, and individual murders by German and Bulgarian troops, and Jewish businesses were quickly liquidated. Jewish refugees from Serbia – after the capitulation of Yugoslavia – were sent back north and murdered at Jajinci, near Belgrade. Persecutions and expropriations went on throughout 1942. Following an agreement reached between Danecker and Delev (see *Bulgaria), mass arrests were begun. Jews from Skoplje, together with their brethren gathered in from all over Macedonia – 7,215 in all – were brought to the ill-famed tobacco factory. They were left there without food or sanitary arrangements for four days and between March 22 and March 29 transported to Treblinka. None of them survived. A few Skoplje Jews escaped, spending the war years as prisoners of war in Germany. Some of them, like Zionist leader Joseph Bekhar, reached Israel after the Holocaust. After the war a small Jewish community was reconstructed, almost none of whose members belonged to the prewar *kehillah*.

In the early years of the 21st century around 40 Jewish families were living in the city, with a prayer house installed in the community's former offices. The cemetery was restored.

BIBLIOGRAPHY: Rosanes, Togarmah, 1 (1930^2), 151; 3 (1938^2), 74, 124–5; 4 (1935), 33, 149, 264–7; 5 (1938), 47; A. Hananel and E. Eškenazi, *Fontes hebraici … terrarum balcanicarum*, 2 vols. (1958–60), indexes; D. Ginsberg, in: *Omanut*, 5 (Zagreb, Jan.–Feb. 1941); Caballero, in: *Revista de Occidente*, 8 (1930), 365f.; Savez Jevrejskih Opština u Jugoslaviji, *"Zločini fašističkih okupatora"* (1952), 189–95 and 1957 (with English text, pp. 1–43). **ADD. BIBLIOGRAPHY:** Ž. Lebl, *Ge'ut va-Shever* (1986); idem, *Plima I slom* (1990.

[Zvi Loker]

SKOSS, SOLOMON LEON (**Zalman Leib**; 1884–1953), Arabic scholar. Skoss, born in Chusovoi, Siberia, studied at the yeshivah of Dubrovno and then served in the Russian army. He emigrated to the U.S. in 1907 and began a prolonged period of unrewarding employment, including a position as a beekeeper. One result of this work was his first essay, on beekeeping in the Talmud (repr. in his *Portrait of a Jewish Scholar*). By chance he took up the study of Arabic at the University of Pennsylvania and at Dropsie College, where his teacher was Benzion *Halper. After the latter's death in 1924 Skoss succeeded him, specializing in Judeo-Arabic philology. He was an outstanding scholar in his field, enormously industrious and productive, painstakingly accurate, inspiring to his pupils, and generously helpful to his colleagues.

Skoss edited and published *The Arabic Commentary of Ali ibn Suleiman the Karaite on the Book of Genesis* (1928) and *The Hebrew-Arabic Dictionary of the Bible* by David ben Abraham al-Fasi (2 vols., 1936–45). The posthumous result of his work on the hitherto unidentified and unpublished fragments of *Saadiah's Arabic work on Hebrew grammar was *Saadiah Gaon, the Earliest Hebrew Grammarian* (1955). His smaller essays (with a biography by S. Grayzel) appeared under the title *Portrait of a Jewish Scholar, Essays and Addresses* (1957). Skoss also contributed numerous articles to learned periodicals.

BIBLIOGRAPHY: S.L. Skoss, *Portrait of a Jewish Scholar, Essays and Addresses* (1957), introductory articles.

[Leon Nemoy]

SKULNIK, MENASHA (1892–1970), U.S. comedian. Born in Warsaw, Skulnik went to the U.S. in 1913, and toured with Yiddish stock companies in the U.S., South America, and Europe. From 1918 he acted in Yiddish musical shows in the theaters on New York's Second Avenue, becoming known for his portrayal of the little guy against the world. He played Uncle David in the radio serial *Rise of the Goldbergs* (1931–50) and subsequently starred in his own television program, *Menasha the Magnificent*. From 1953 he appeared in a number of plays on Broadway.

SKUODAS, city in N.W. Lithuania. In the 17th century the community of Skuodas was subject to that of Kedainiai and belonged to "the state of Zamut." Occasionally the state commission assembled in Skuodas, and in 1766 576 Jews paid the poll tax there. In 1847 the number of Jews in the city was 1,872; in 1897 there were 2,292 (60% of the total population). A synagogue existed from the early 18th century, housing an elaborate wooden ark. When an independent Lithuania was established in 1918, the Skuodas community also had a Hebrew-school system, including a secondary school. The cutting off of the sources of trade in Luebeck and Memel, however, contributed to the decline of the community and to a move to the larger cities. In 1921 there were 385 Jews in Skuodas; in 1939 there were approximately 250, all of whom were killed by the Nazi occupation forces.

BIBLIOGRAPHY: *Yahadut Lita*, 3 (1967), 367–8.

[Yehuda Slutsky]

SKVIRA, city in Kiev oblast, Ukraine. Skvira was an ancient town which was completely destroyed at the end of the 16th century. In 1736 it was mentioned as a village leased by a Jewish lessee. In 1789 there were 37 Jewish houses out of a total of 197 houses counted that year. In 1847 Jews registered in Skvira numbered 2,184. During the 1840s the *ẓaddik* R. Isaac Twersky (of the Chernobyl dynasty) settled in Skvira. The Jewish community was primarily engaged in the trade of grain and other agricultural products. In 1897 there were 8,910 Jews (49.5% of the population) in Skvira. During the Civil War, Jews suffered severely from belligerent armies and during the pogroms which frequently occurred, several hundred Jews were killed. The number of Jews decreased considerably after World War I and in 1926 there were only 4,681 Jews (33.6% of the population) remaining. Under the Soviet regime the religious and communal life of the Jews of Skvira was dissolved. The Germans entered the town in September 1941. Almost 1,000 Jews who did not succeed in escaping were murdered. The Jewish population was estimated in the late 1960s at about 500. The *Twersky ḥasidic line emanating from Skvira eventually settled in the U.S. where they founded their own township called New Square (Skvira) in Rockland County, New York.

BIBLIOGRAPHY: *Reshummot*, 3 (1923), 214–21; Y. Ereẓ (ed.), *Sefer Z.S.* (1963), 108–10.

[Yehuda Slutsky]

SLANDER. The only instance of defamation in biblical law for which a penalty is prescribed is that of the virgin (Deut. 22:19) – and that defamation is in the nature of a matrimonial stratagem (cf. Deut. 22:16–17) rather than of a specifically defamatory offense. Still, in order to invest the prohibition of defamation with the greatest possible weight, talmudic jurists interpreted the biblical injunction, "Thou shalt surely rebuke thy neighbor, and not bear sin because of him" (Lev. 19:17), as meaning that you may reprove your neighbor so long as you do not insult him; but if you make him blush or turn pale from shame or fury, then you have incurred guilt because of him (Sifra, Kedoshim 4:8; Ar. 16b). Other biblical exhortations – like "Thou shalt not go up and down as a tale bearer" (Lev. 19:16), or "Thou shalt not utter a false report" (Ex. 23:1), or "Thou shalt not hate thy brother in thy heart" (Lev. 19:17), or "Thou shalt not take vengeance, nor bear any grudge" (*ibid.*, 18), and "Love thy neighbor as thyself" (*ibid.*) – have all been summoned to help invest the prohibition of slander with biblical authority (Israel Meir ha-Kohen of Radin, *Ḥafez Ḥayyim, Petiḥah*). Particular prohibitions of insult, such as "Thou shalt not curse the deaf" (Lev. 19:14), or "Thou shalt not put a curse upon a ruler of thy people" (Ex. 22:27), were interpreted as particular instances of a general prohibition against insulting (Sifra, Kedoshim 2:13; Mekh., Mishpatim 19; Shev. 36a).

Though regarded as the violation of express biblical negative injunctions, slander is not punishable even by *flogging, because mere talk does not amount to an overt act, and only such acts are punishable (Yad, Sanhedrin 18:2). More severe are the moral and religious admonitions against slanderers: "even though the slanderer is not flogged, his sin is very great indeed, and the sages have said that he who makes another's face turn pale in public, has no share in the world to come" (Avot 3:12). "Therefore everybody must be very careful not to abase another man in public, not to call him a name which puts him to shame, nor to say anything that might embarrass him" (Yad, De'ot 6:8). Some scholars went so far as to put the slanderer on the same footing as a murderer, because both "shed blood" (BM 58b); and all slanderers are characterized as wicked and stupid (Yad, Ḥovel u-Mazzik 3:7).

It would appear that mere moral exhortations were found insufficient to curb the mischief. A later source provides specific sanctions as follows: A person calling another a slave, shall be placed under a ban (*niddui*; see **ḥerem*); a person calling another a bastard (**mamzer*) shall be liable to 40 stripes; and if a person calls another wicked, the other may interfere with his livelihood (Kid. 28a). Attempts were made to interpret these particular sanctions as talionic (cf. Tos. and *Beit ha-Beḥirah*, Kid. 28a); but it is not impossible that they simply reflect decisions taken in cases which had actually occurred. The sanction of *niddui* for calling a man a slave has been codified (Yad, Talmud Torah 6:14: Sh. Ar., YD 334:43); and as for the administration of disciplinary floggings (*makkat mardut*), the rule was eventually held to be subject to local customs: where customary local regulations provided for different sanctions for slander, the customary rule prevailed (Rosh, resp. 101:1; *Rema*, ḤM 420:41). In fact, disciplinary floggings appear to have remained in most places the most common punishment, at least for graver cases of slander (see e.g., Maharshal, resp. nos. 11, 28, and 59; *Yam shel Shelomo BK* 8:34, 48, and 49). In other places, and in lighter cases, fines were imposed – and we often find fines substituted for *niddui* or for floggings at the option of the insulted person who had first to be appeased (Tur, ḤM 420:33 and *Beit Yosef* thereto).

A particular instance of punishable slander is insulting a scholar. A person convicted of having insulted a scholar is liable to *niddui* as well as to a fine of one litra of gold awarded to the aggrieved scholar (Yad, Talmud Torah 6:12). This preferential treatment of scholars left its traces also in the civil law: while a person is not liable in damages for mischief done by word of mouth only (BK 91a; Yad, Ḥovel 3:5; ḤM 420:39), where a scholar was put to shame, he is awarded 35 gold dinars by way of fine (TJ, BK 8:6; Yad, Ḥovel 3:5; Rashba, resp., vol. 1 no. 475; Ribash, resp., nos. 27, 216, and 220). The civil and criminal remedies are, of course, overlapping and identical. The insulted scholar may always forgo the fine (Yad, Ḥovel 3:6). The remedy allowed to "scholars" was soon extended to all pious people (Rosh, resp. 15:10; Tur, ḤM 420:32), and eventually became obsolete when remedies for slanders were no longer confined to particular classes of persons.

Another particular instance of slander is that of widows and orphans. "Mistreating" widows and orphans means, literally, causing them distress; if you cause them distress by insulting them, God will heed their outcry as soon as they cry out to Him; His anger will blaze forth and He will put you to the sword, and your wives shall become widows and your children orphans (Ex. 22:21–23). This is a typical instance of *Divine punishment: for though the court will not impose flogging for this offense (see above), still the punishment therefore is expressly prescribed in the Torah: "and a covenant was concluded between them and the Creator of the World, that whenever they cry, He hears them and acts" (Yad, De'ot 6:10). Slandering the dead is also regarded as a great sin, to be expiated by fasting and prayers; and the court may punish it by fine (*Mordekhai*, BK 81–82; *Rema*, ḤM 420:38). While there are dicta to the effect that speaking the truth cannot constitute slander (*Rema*, HM 420:38), the better view seems to be that it is irrelevant whether the slanderous words were true or not (Israel Meir ha-Kohen of Radin, *Ḥafeẓ Ḥayyim* 1:1). In the State of Israel, the Knesset enacted "The Prohibition of Defamation Law 5725 – 1965" (as amended in 1967).

About Jewish legal principles in this law, see Elon, in bibl.

[Haim Hermann Cohn]

Even inanimate objects should not be disparaged, and the Talmud uses the biblical account of the ten spies who, upon their return from their mission, slandered the Holy Land (Num. 12–14) to emphasize the gravity of this sin. In fact, rabbinic tradition considers slander a violation of moral and spiritual obligations, and assigns to it a weight that is almost equal to the cardinal sins of idolatry, adultery, and murder combined (TJ, Pe'ah 1:1).

The most vicious form of slander is false accusations of calumnies made to a ruling authority (*malshinut*) with the intent of endangering a man's livelihood and even his life. *Informers, through slanderous accusations, sometimes jeopardized entire Jewish communities. They were, therefore, regarded as particularly vicious. They were placed in the category of those who commit assault with intent to kill, and putting them to death was authorized. If their intention to slander was clear, death was sanctioned even before the crime was committed. The extent to which Jewish communities were harassed by slander is indicated by the inclusion, in the daily *Amidah* service, of the prayer, "And for slanderers, let there be no hope."

[Sol Roth]

Israeli Law and Jewish Law

The halakhic principles of the laws of slander provided inspiration for legislation of the Defamation Law, 5725 – 1965, in its general approach if not in its details. For example, Section 14 of the Law grants protection in cases where "the matter published was true and the publication was in the public interest" while, according to the *halakhah*, as stated, the truth of the matter would apparently not constitute a defense. Acceptance of the overall approach of Jewish law in this matter, without necessarily adopting all of its numerous and specific details, seems the proper approach in this matter. It does not seem appropriate to turn the details of the *halakhah* into legal prohibitions, but they should be left, rather, as religious prohibitions alone. Furthermore, the various situations in which it is permitted by law to publish slander also originate in the need to balance between the individual's right to a good name, on the one hand, and freedom of expression and the freedom of public criticism, on the other. Decisive importance is accorded in Jewish tradition to the latter as well, as noted by the Supreme Court in the Neiman Affair (EA 2, 3/84, 2 *Neiman et al. v. Chairman, Central Elections Committee*, PD 39 (2) 225, 294–296; per Justice Menachem Elon. "The multiplicity of opinions is not a negative phenomenon or fault, but is substantive to the world of *halakhah*. 'There is no lack or peculiarity to say that the Torah is thereby made into two Torahs, Heaven forbid; to the contrary – such is the way of the Torah, for both are the words of the Living God" (*ibid.* p.295). (See also *Rights, Human: Freedom of Speech.) It may be noted that permission to utter slander, such as "beneficial defamation," also appears in certain cases in Jewish law: for example, under certain conditions it is permitted to recount slander about litigants, if it will lead to the resolution of the dispute (See Cr.A Jerusalem) 113/96 *Biton v. Kopf*; Justice Elyakim Rubinstein). By virtue of these, attempts are made to sustain a democratic system notwithstanding the numerous halakhic, although not necessarily legal, restrictions involved in the prohibition of defamation regarding such subjects as the publication of corrupt acts of public officials in the media or management of an election system (see bibliography, Ariel).

INTERPRETATION OF THE LAW IN ISRAEL IN LIGHT OF THE PRINCIPLES OF JEWISH LAW. The Supreme Court ruled that Jewish Law is an important source for construing the Defamation Law, in reliance on the explanatory notes to the original and amended draft bills, as well as in reliance on the Knesset debates conducted during passage of its legislation, which included extensive reference to the prohibition of defamation in Jewish Law, the scope of the prohibition and the sanctions found therein (LCA 531/88 *Avneri et al. v. Shapira*, PD 42 (4) 20; Justice Menachem Elon). In the *Avneri* case, the District Court had issued a temporary injunction against the publication of a book which, according to the plaintiff, defamed him. The Supreme Court decided not to intervene in the District court's decision, relying extensively on the principles of Jewish Law in the matter of prohibition of slander, on the one hand, and freedom of public criticism, on the other. In another case, the Jerusalem Magistrates Court utilized the halakhic principles regarding "beneficial defamation," as specified in the book *Ḥafetz Ḥayyim* (*Hilkhot Lashon ha-Ra*, sec. 10; *Hilkhot Issurei Rekhilut*, sec. 9) in its interpretation of the requirement of "public interest" in the aforementioned Section 14 of the Defamation Law:

> There is a need for credibility … nothing should be added or detracted. A first time publication is not the same as the publication of something already generally known. The wording must be fair, providing an exact description of the events as they occurred. Information that is dubious should be presented as such, and [should be published – ME] only if the chances of benefit deriving from the publication reasonably outweigh the chances of damage being caused. The publisher's intention should be thoroughly examined, for if he was motivated… by alien considerations, there is suspicion as to the credibility of the matter in general and the manner of its presentation in particular. Defamatory material should not be published for its own sake. Proportionality and sincerity are required. It should be recalled and mentioned that "life and death are in the hands of the tongue" (TA 374/02 *Cohen v. Olmert*; Judge Noam Solberg. See also 6122/01 *Segev v. Eyal*; Judge Noam Solberg).

There is a special prohibition against reminding a sinner of his previous offenses, which is part of "the Enactment for the

Encouragement of Penitents" (*takkanat ha-shavim*), and this prohibition, together with the other rules of Jewish Law, inspired legislation of the Crime Register and Rehabilitation of Offenders Law, 5741 – 1981 (see also *Punishment; and see ALA 18/84 *Adv. Anon, Adv. v. The State Prosecutor*, 44 (1) PD 353, per Justice Menachem Elon. CF (Jerusalem) *Anon v. Anon*, PM 54 (2) 397; Justice Zvi Tal).

What is the law when a person claims that a publication stating that he acted lawfully constitutes defamation exclusively because the society in which he lives regards actions in accordance with the law as negative and scandalous on the part of those engaged in them? In the *Dardarian* case (CA 466/83 *Ajiman v. Dardarian*, 39 (4) PD 734), the injured party was a Jordanian citizen who served as Archbishop of the Armenian Church in Jerusalem. He claimed that a publication stating that he cooperated with Israeli authorities and supported their actions and policy in Judea and Samaria constituted defamation because, in the society in which he lived, this fact could make him an object of hatred. The Supreme Court ruled that the claim should be rejected. Justice Elon's ruling was based on an analogy from Jewish Law concerning an illegal contract, invoking the Foundations of Justice Law, 5740 – 1980 (see *Mishpat Ivri). Under Jewish Law, the court will not deal with a contract whose purpose is the commission of an illegal act. On the other hand, where the very making of the agreement involves a transgression of a religious prohibition, it does not nullify the validity of the agreement, and the court will have recourse to it (see *Contract). This position was adopted in part by Israeli law, in Sections 30 and 31 of the Contracts (General Part) Law, 5733 – 1973, according to which a contract "the making, contents or object of which are illegal, immoral or contrary to public policy is void" (Section 30). At the same time, the court may, if it deems it just to do so, exempt a party from reimbursement of monies paid under a contract and, if one of the parties fulfilled his obligation under the contract, may require the other party to fulfill the corresponding obligation (Section 31). Justice Elon ruled that, similarly, the court may provide a remedy to a person claiming that he was defamed by a publication that stated that he behaved lawfully, if that publication defamed him in the society in which he lives. On the other hand, there are cases in which the State's interest "not to support to actions and opinions which would undermine the rule of law and State sovereignty" (p. 754) may prevail, and in those cases the court will not provide the claimant with a remedy. Justice Elon ruled that the instant case fell into the latter category. The view that cooperation with the Israeli authorities in the maintenance of law and order in Judea and Samaria is undesirable is "so heinous and serious … from the perspective of the foundations of the legal system of the State of Israel as a state governed by law, and from the perspective of the maintenance of Israel's security against its enemies, and is so opposed to the basic concepts of law and order, that it [the rejection of that view] overrides the right of the appellant not to be harmed in the eyes of members of his circle who hold this perverse view." As such the court was not prepared to award the plaintiff damages by reason of damages caused to him by that publication, which defamed him in the society in which he lived (*ibid.*).

[Menachem Elon (2nd ed.)]

BIBLIOGRAPHY: D. Daube, in: *Essays in Honor of J.H. Hertz* (1942), 111–29: ET, 1 (1951З), 160f.; 3 (1951), 49f.; 9 (1959), 207–14; N. Rakover, in: *Sinai*, 51 (1962), 197–209, 326–45; T.D. Rosenthal, *ibid.*, 53 (1963), 59–66; M. Elon, in: ILR, 4 (1969), 100–2. **ADD. BIBLIOGRAPHY:** M. Elon, *Ha-Mishpat ha-Ivri* (1988), 3:1378–80, 1434–36, 1555–57; idem, *Jewish Law* (1994), 4:1642–46, 1707–9, 1847–50; idem, *Jewish Law: Cases and Materials*, (1999), 524; M. Elon and B. Lifschitz, *Mafte'aḥ ha-She'elot ve-ha-Teshuvot shel Ḥakhmei Sefarad u-Ẓefon Afrikah* (legal digest) (1986), (2), 337–38; B. Lifshitz and E. Shochetman, *Mafte'aḥ ha-She'elot ve-ha-Teshuvot shel Ḥakhmei Ashkenaz, Ẓarefat ve-Italyah* (legal digest) (1997), 233; A. Ariel, "*Lashon ha-Ra be-Ma'arekhet Ẓibburit Demokratit*," in: *Ẓohar*, 6–7 (1981), 37, 41.

SLÁNSKÝ TRIAL, the first of a series of antisemitic show trials held in Czechoslovakia in the early 1950s whose prime victim was Rudolf Slánský (1901–1952), secretary-general of the Czechoslovak Communist Party after World War II. Of the 14 leading party members prosecuted for conspiracy against the state, 11 were Jews. Eight of these defendants – Ludvík Frejka, head of the economic department of the President's Office; Bedřich Geminder, head of the party's international department; Bedřich Reicin, deputy defense minister; Rudolf Margolius, deputy minister of foreign trade; Otto Fischl, deputy finance minister; Otto Sling, first secretary of the party in Brno; and André (Katz) *Simone, a leading Communist journalist, in addition to Slánský himself – were executed. The remaining three Jewish defendants – deputy foreign ministers Arthur *London and Vavro Hajdu and deputy minister of foreign trade Evžen Loebl – were sentenced to life imprisonment. Show trials aimed at eradicating the Titoist "heresy" from the leadership of the Soviet satellites were held shortly before in other East European countries (e.g., the Kostov trial in Bulgaria and the Rajk trial in Hungary), but the Slánský trial evolved a distinct anti-Jewish character. Foreign Minister Vlado Clementis, one of the three non-Jewish defendants sentenced to death (the other two being Slánský's deputy, Josef Frank, and deputy security minister Karel Šváb) was accused of Slovak "bourgeois nationalism" and Titoism, and an attempt was made to present him as "the Czechoslovak Rajk." But the main orientation of the prosecution was "anti-Zionist," anti-Israel, and openly antisemitic. The Slánksý Trial thus formed a direct link with the *Doctors plot and the wave of antisemitism in the Soviet Union in the last years of Stalin's regime (see *Antisemitism: the Soviet Bloc). In these trials, for the first time in the history of Communism, the antisemitic accusation of a worldwide Jewish conspiracy was openly proclaimed by an authoritative Communist forum (it was linked by the prosecution with the activities of the American Jewish *Joint Distribution Committee). The Jewish origin of the accused was repeatedly stressed, and their alleged crimes were traced to this prime cause. The prosecution stigmatized the accused as Zionists, although they had never had any connection with the Zionist movement and had, in fact, opposed Zionism all their lives.

The trials were part of an effort to consolidate power inside the Czechoslovak Communist Party in the hands of a group of leaders approved and manipulated from Moscow. The fact that Jews held many key posts in the party and state machinery – although Slánský was the only Jew in the Politbureau at the time – prompted an increase of latent popular antisemitism. This circumstance was utilized to strengthen the position of the inner circle of the Communist leadership and to put the blame for the rapidly worsening economic situation on prominent Jewish Communists. The trials were conducted under the direction and supervision of secret agents from Moscow and were also intended to help explain the change of Communist policy toward the State of Israel. The Israel legation in Prague was depicted as a center of espionage and anti-Czechoslovak subversion. Accusations were directed mainly against the first Israeli minister in Prague, Ehud *Avriel, and his successor, Aryeh *Kubovy, who was declared *persona non grata*. Two Israel citizens, Mordekhai Oren and Shimon Orenstein, were arrested, used as prosecution witnesses to prove Slánský's alleged contacts with "Zionist conspirators," and were later sentenced in a separate trial to long prison terms. The trials were a signal for a wave of anti-Jewish persecution. Hundreds of Czechoslovak Jews were thrown into prison or sent, often without trial, to forced labor camps. The situation gradually became less frenzied after Stalin's death; but only at the end of the 1950s, and in some cases even later, were victims of the Slánský Trial rehabilitated. The accusations against the Zionist movement and Israel, however, were not revoked, and relations between Czechoslovakia and Israel remained tense and unfriendly.

BIBLIOGRAPHY: R.L. Braham (ed.), *Jews in the Communist World: A Bibliography* (1961), 20–22; American Zionist Council, *Public Opinion on the Prague Trial* (1953); K. Kaplan, *Thoughts About The Political Trials* (1968); M. Oren, *Reshimot Asir Prag* (1958); S. Orenstein, *Alilah be-Prag* (1968); idem, *Lefi Pekuddah mi-Moskva* (1969); E. Loebl, *Die Revolution rehabilitiert ihre Kinder* (1968); idem, *Sentenced and Tried* (1969); *Proces s vedením protistátního spikleneckého centra v čele s Rudolfem Slánským* (1953); A. London, *The Confession* (1970); J. Slánska, *Report on My Husband* (1969).

[Avigdor Dagan]

SLATER, OSCAR (1872–1948), British underworld figure wrongly convicted of murder in Scotland. Born Oscar Leschziner in Oppeln, Germany, the son of a baker, Slater immigrated to England, working as a bookmaker and using many aliases. He was twice acquitted on charges of assault. From 1899 he lived in Edinburgh, apparently working as a professional gambler, pimp, and receiver, again under a variety of aliases. In 1908 a rich elderly woman was beaten to death in her Edinburgh apartment. Slater came under suspicion for trying to sell a pawn ticket for a stolen brooch and for immediately fleeing to America, giving false information as to his travels. He was arrested in New York and tried in Edinburgh. His defense was badly handled and he was convicted on a majority vote of the jury. His death sentence was commuted by the Scottish secretary to life imprisonment. Almost immediately a vocal campaign began which argued that he was wrongfully convicted, spearheaded by such notables as Sir Arthur Conan Doyle. In 1927 Slater was released and given £6000 compensation. There seems no doubt that he was innocent, and the Slater Case became a cause celebre of the miscarriage of justice. Slater died in obscurity in Ayr, Scotland, in 1948. Although Slater liked to describe himself as the "Scottish Dreyfus," historians have debated what role, if any, his Jewish background played in his conviction.

BIBLIOGRAPHY: ODNB online; T. Toughill, *Oscar Slater: The Mystery Solved* (1893); W.D. Rubinstein, *Jews in Great Britain*, index; B. Braber, "The Trial of Oscar Slater (1909) and Anti-Jewish Prejudice in Edwardian Glasgow," in: *History*, 88 (2003), 262–79.

[William D. Rubinstein (2nd ed.)]

SLATKIN, LEONARD (1944–), U.S. conductor. Born in Los Angeles into a distinguished musical family, he studied violin, viola, piano, and composition. He took conducting lessons at Indiana University (1962) and Los Angeles City College (1963), continuing his training with *Susskind at Aspen (1964) and with Morel at the Juilliard School of Music (1964–68). Slatkin made his Carnegie Hall debut at age 22. He was associated with the Saint Louis SO (1968–96) and became its music director in 1979. Under his direction the orchestra became a leading American ensemble. He was appointed musical director of the New Orleans Philharmonic SO (1977–79) and music director of the BBC SO (2000–4). In 1996 he became music director of the National SO of Washington. He has been guest conductor with major U.S. and European orchestras, festivals, and opera companies, making numerous recordings and appearances in radio and television programs. Slatkin combines the roles of internationally celebrated conductor, staunch advocate for music education, and champion of American music. He is known for his sure command of form and superb performances, for his adventurous programming, and for his interpretations of 20th-century American music as well as of the standard classical repertory. He worked with student orchestras and became in 2000 the director of the National Conducting Institute, a school that trains young music directors. Among his honors are Grammy awards, the National Medal of the Arts, and honorary doctorates as well as honors for his artistic contributions and for his work in the community.

BIBLIOGRAPHY: Grove Music Online; G. Crankshaw, "Leonard Slatkin: American Champion of English Music," in: *Musical Opinion*, 114 (Nov. 1991), 398–99.

[Naama Ramot (2nd ed.)]

SLATKINE, MENAHEM MENDEL (1875–1965), bibliographer. Born in Rostov on the Don, Russia, Slatkine studied at the yeshivah in Volozhin. He evinced an early interest in Hebrew bibliography and in 1903 published in the Hebrew daily *Ha-Meliẓ* (no. 241) an article, "*Pinnah Nishkaḥat*" ("A Forgotten Corner"), in which he drew attention to the need for an updated bibliography of Hebrew literature. In 1905 he settled in Switzerland where he engaged in the sale of old Hebrew books. He died in Geneva.

Slatkine was the author of *Shemot ha-Sefarim ha-Ivrim* (2 vols., 1950–54), on the titles of Hebrew books; *Reshit Bikkurei ha-Bibliografyah ba-Safrut ha-Ivrit* (1958), about Shabbetai *Bass and his *Siftei Yeshenim*, the first Hebrew bibliographical work; and *Oẓar ha-Sefarim, Ḥelek Sheni* (1965), which contains notes, corrections, additions, and an author index of Isaac Ben Jacob's *Oẓar ha-Sefarim*. Slatkine also wrote *Mi-Sefer ha-Zikhronot shel Rav Litai*. The book, which was published in Paris in the years following World War II, describes Jewish life in the 18th century in the form of "selected chapters" from the "memoirs" of the Lithuanian rabbis of the time.

BIBLIOGRAPHY: G. Kressel, in: *Moznayim*, 20 (1964–65), 420–1; S. Herman in: *Aresheth*, 4 (1966), 558.

[Tovia Preschel]

SLAVERY.

BIBLICAL LAW

The Hebrew term for slave, *'eved* (pl. *'avadim*), is a direct derivation from the verb 'bd, "to work"; thus, the "slave" is only a worker or servant. The *eved* differs from the hired worker (*sakhir*) in three respects: he receives no wages for his work; he is a member of his master's household (cf. Gen. 24:2; Lev. 22:11; and see below); and his master exercises *patria potestas* over him; for example, the master may choose a wife for the slave and retains ownership of her (Ex. 21:4) and he has proprietary rights in him (see below).

Classification

The following classes of *'avadim* are to be distinguished:

HEBREW SLAVES. A Hebrew could not become a slave unless by order of the court (for which see under Criminals, below) or by giving himself voluntarily into bondage (for which see under Paupers, etc., below; Yad, Avadim 1:1). Other slaves were always recruited from outside the nation. It has been opined that the epithet "*'eved 'ivri*," and the laws relating to Hebrew slaves (Ex. 21:2–6) would apply also to such non-Jewish slaves as were born into the household as the offspring of alien slaves (see, for instance, Saalschuetz, *Das Mosaische Recht* (1853), ch. 101).

ALIEN SLAVES. "Of the nations that are round about you, of them shall ye buy bondmen and bondwomen. Moreover of the children of the strangers that do sojourn among you, of them may ye buy and of their families that are with you which they have begotten in your land; and they may be your possession" (Lev. 25:44–45).

PAUPERS AND DEBTORS. A debtor who is unable to pay his debts may give himself in bondage to his creditor (cf. Lev. 25:39; Prov. 22:7; see also II Kings 4:1; Isa. 50:1; Amos 2:6, 8:6; Neh. 5:5). According to other opinions, the verse in Leviticus 25:39 deals with an ordinary pauper who sold himself and the debtor's bondage was against strict law, although it happened from time to time in practice (see Elon, *Ḥerut ha-Perat*, 1–10, and n. 9; *Execution (Civil)).

CRIMINALS. A thief who is unable to make restitution is "sold for his theft" (Ex. 22:2).

PRISONERS OF WAR. It would appear from Numbers 31:26–27 and Deuteronomy 20:10–11 that prisoners of war could be, and were, taken into bondage, but it has been contended that no prisoners of war were ever taken into private slavery (Kaufmann, Y., Toledot 1 (1937), 651).

FEMALE SLAVES. A father may sell his daughter into slavery (Ex. 21:7), usually apparently for household duties and eventual marriage (Ex. 21:7–11).

CHILDREN OF SLAVES. The Bible mentions "the son of thy handmaid" (Ex. 23:12), "he that is born in the house" (Gen. 17:12, 13; Lev. 22:11), indicating that the status of slaves devolved upon their children.

Termination of Bondage

HEBREW SLAVES. Hebrew slaves serve six years only and must be freed in the seventh (Ex. 21:2; Deut. 15:12). "And when thou lettest him go free from thee, thou shalt not let him go empty; thou shalt furnish him liberally out of thy flock, and out of thy threshing floor, and out of thy wine-press; of that wherewith the Lord thy God hath blessed thee" (Deut. 15:13–14; and see *Ha'anakah*). This short period of bondage conditioned the price of slaves: there is some indication of their market value in the provision that if an ox killed a slave, the owner of the ox must pay 30 shekels of silver to the master of the slave (Ex. 21:32). Whatever the master may have paid for the slave, "It shall not seem hard unto thee, when thou lettest him go free from thee; for to the double of the hire of a hireling hath he served thee six years" (Deut. 15:18). If the slave refuses to go free and wishes to stay on in his master's service, then the master pierces his ear with an awl and in this way the slave is bonded to him forever (Ex. 21:5–6; Deut. 15:16–17). If a Hebrew slave has been sold to an alien, he must be redeemed at once; he then enters into the redeemer's service, which terminates with the jubilee year (Lev. 25:47–54).

ALIEN SLAVES. Alien slaves serve in perpetuity: "Ye may make them an inheritance for your children after you, to hold for a possession, of them ye may take your bondmen forever" (Lev. 25:46). The same rule would appear to apply to prisoners of war.

DEBTORS. Whatever the amount of debt for which the debtor sold himself he must be freed on the first ensuing jubilee year (Lev. 25:40). The same is true of a pauper. In that year he regains his lands and holdings (Lev. 25:10, 13) and can go back to his family and ancestral home (Lev. 25:41).

FEMALE SLAVES. Female slaves sold into bondage by their fathers go free if their master's sons deny them their matrimonial rights (Ex. 21:11).

Slaves must be released for grievous bodily injury caused

to them: the master must let the slave go free "for his eye's sake" or "for his tooth's sake" (Ex. 21:26–27), if either be gouged out or knocked out by him.

Status of Slaves

Slaves are members of the master's household, and as such enjoy the benefit and are liable to the duty of keeping the Sabbath (Ex. 20:10, 23:12; Deut. 5:14–15) and holidays (Deut. 16:11–14, 12:18). They must be circumcised (Gen. 17:12–13); partake of Passover sacrifices when circumcised (Ex. 12:44), as distinguished from resident hirelings (Ex. 12:45); and may inherit the master's estate where there is no direct issue (Gen. 15:3) or perhaps even where there is (Prov. 17:2). Although slaves are the master's property (Lev. 22:11, etc.), they may acquire and hold property of their own; a slave who "prospers," i.e., can afford it, may redeem himself (Lev. 25:29; instances of property held by slaves are to be found in II Sam. 9:10; 16:4; 19:18, 30; cf. I Sam. 9:8). The killing of a slave is punishable in the same way as that of any freeman, even if the act is committed by the master (Ex. 21:20).

Treatment of Slaves

In the case of a pauper who sells himself into slavery or a man who is redeemed from bondage to a stranger, no distinction may be made between a slave and a hired laborer (Lev. 25:40, 53). A master may not rule ruthlessly over these slaves (Lev. 25:43, 46, 53) nor ill-treat them (Deut. 23:17); Ben Sira adds: "If thou treat him ill and he proceeds to run away, in what way shalt thou find him?" (Ecclus. 33:31). A master may chastise his slave to a reasonable extent (Ecclus. 33:26) but not wound him (Ex. 21:26–27). The workload of a slave should never exceed his physical strength (Ecclus. 33:28–29). A fugitive slave must not be turned over to his master but given refuge (Deut. 23:16). There was no similar rule prevailing in neighboring countries (cf. I Kings 2:39–40). The *abduction of a person for sale into bondage is a capital offense (Ex. 21:16; Deut. 24:7). In general, "thou shalt remember that thou wast a bondman in the land of Egypt" (Deut. 15:15), and that you are now the slaves of God Who redeemed you from Egypt (Lev. 25:55).

Implementation of Slavery Laws

From a report in Jeremiah (34:8–16) it would appear that the laws relating to the release of Hebrew slaves after six years' service were not implemented in practice: King Zedekiah had to make a "covenant" with the people that every man should let his slaves go free "at the end of seven years"; but hardly had the people released their slaves than they turned round and brought them back into subjection. In retribution for the failure to grant liberty to slaves, God would proclaim liberty "unto the sword, unto the pestilence, and unto the famine"; "and I will make you a horror unto all the kingdoms of the earth" (Jer. 34:17). According to Ezra (2:64–65) and Nehemiah (7:67), it would appear that in addition to the 42,360 people returning from Babylonia there were 7,337 slaves, male and female, and another 245 (or 200) musicians.

TALMUDIC LAW

Opinions are divided among modern scholars whether and to what extent slavery was practiced in post-biblical times. There is repeated mention of Tebi, the slave of Rabban Gamaliel (Ber. 2:7; Pes. 7:2; Suk. 2:1), and a freed slave formerly belonging to Tobiah the physician (RH 1:7) is also mentioned. In amoraic sources there are reports of cases of men selling themselves into slavery as gladiators (Git. 46b–47a), apparently from dire necessity (TJ, Git. 4:9). There is a strong talmudic tradition to the effect that all bondage of Hebrew slaves had ceased with the cessation of jubilee years (Git. 65a; Kid. 69a; Ar. 29a; Maim. Yad, Avadim 2:10), which would mean that from the period of the Second Temple the practice of slavery was at any rate confined to non-Hebrew slaves.

Classification

HEBREW SLAVES. The term *eved Ivri* is reserved for, and identified with, a thief unable to make restitution who is sold for his theft or a pauper who sold himself into bondage (Kid. 14b; Yad, Avadim 1:1). This implies that a Hebrew slave may not be resold. The earlier Mishnah provides that a Hebrew slave may be acquired by the payment of money or the delivery of a deed of sale (Kid. 1:2).

FEMALE HEBREW SLAVES. Many provisions applying to slaves in general do not apply to female slaves. Thus, a woman may not sell herself into slavery (Mekh. Nezikin 3; Yad, Avadim 1:2), nor is a woman thief sold into slavery, even though she cannot make restitution (Sot. 3:8; Yad, Genevah 3:12). Contrary to an express scriptural provision (Deut. 15:17), a female slave's ear may not be pierced (Sif. Deut. 122; Kid. 17b; Yad, Avadim 3:13). The female Hebrew slave can only be a minor below the age of 12 years whom her father (not her mother: Sot. 3:8; Sot. 23b) has sold into bondage (Ex. 21:7; Ket. 3:8; Yad, Avadim 4:1); he may do so only when he has no other means of subsistence left (Tosef. Ar. 5:7; Mekh. Sb-Y 21:7; Yad, Avadim 4:2) and must redeem her as soon as he has the means (Kid. 18a; Yad, loc. cit.).

NON-HEBREW SLAVES. Non-Hebrew slaves (*eved Kena'ani*) may be acquired by the payment of money, the delivery of a deed of sale, or three years' undisturbed possession (Kid. 1:3; BB 3:1) – to which were later added barter or exchange, and the physical taking into possession (Kid. 22b; Yad, Avadim 5:1; Sh. Ar., YD 267:25).

Terminations of Bondage

HEBREW SLAVES. As well as release after six years' service or the beginning of the jubilee year, five more possibilities were added. The slave may redeem himself by paying his master part of the purchase price proportionate to the period served; for example, if he had been bought for 60 dinars and had served four years, he could redeem himself by paying 20 dinars, the whole period of service being six years. The redemption money is paid by a third person, either to the slave or to the master, on condition that it is used only for the redemption (Kid. 1:2; Yad, Avadim 2:8). A slave may be released by a deed of release delivered by his master (Kid. 16a; Yad, Avadim 2:12). He is released on the death of his master, provided the master left no male descendants (Kid. 17b; Yad, loc. cit.). Where the slave has had his ear pierced, he is released on the death of his master, irrespective of the master's surviving issue (Kid. 1:2; Kid. 17b; Yad, Avadim 3:7). Where the master is a non-Jew or a *ger, the slave is released on his death (Kid. 17b; Yad, loc. cit.).

FEMALE HEBREW SLAVES. The provisions relating to release after six years' service, in the jubilee year, by payment, or by deed, also apply to female slaves. In addition, their bondage is terminated when the slave comes of age, i.e., shows "signs" of puberty (*simanim*: Kid. 1:2; Yad, Avadim 4:5; also see Legal Capacity), and by the death of the master, irrespective of the issue he left (Kid. 17b; Yad, Avadim 4:6).

ALIEN SLAVES. For alien slaves the bondage is terminated in various fashions. Release may be by payment of money, the price demanded by the master being paid to him by a third party, either directly or through the slave (Kid. 1:3; Yad, Avadim 5:2). A deed of release may be delivered by the master (Kid. 1:3; Yad, Avadim 5:3). A verbal release, or a promise of release, is not sufficient in itself, but the court may enforce it by compelling the master to deliver a deed (Sh. Ar., YD 267:73–74). The slave is freed if the master causes him grievous bodily injury: the two biblical instances of gouging out the eye and knocking out the tooth are multiplied, and a long list of eligible injuries has been laid down (Kid. 24b–25a; Yad, Avadim 5:4–14; Sh. Ar., YD 267:27–39). While the list in the codes was intended to be exhaustive, the better rule seems to be that all injuries leaving any permanent disfigurement are included (Kid. 24a). The rule is confined to non-Hebrew slaves only (Mekh. Nezikin 9); injuries inflicted on Hebrew slaves, male or female, are dealt with as injuries to freemen (BK 8:3; Yad, Ḥovel 4:13 and Avadim 4:6). A slave may also be released if his master bequeaths him all his property (Pe'ah 3:8; Git. 8b–9a; Yad, Avadim 7:9; YD 267:57). By marriage to a freewoman, or by his de facto recognition, in the presence of his master, as a free Jew (e.g., using phylacteries and reading the Torah in public; Git. 39b–40a; Yad, Avadim 8:17; YD 267:70) a slave obtained his freedom. Marriage to the master's daughter seems to have been a not infrequent means to emancipation (Pes. 113a).

Status of Slaves

Discussions went on for centuries whether slaves, *qua* property, are to be regarded as belonging to the category of movables or immovables; Gulak (Yesodei 1 (1922), 92) held that originally they were likened to land and only much later to personal property. In effect, they were likened to land as regards modes of *acquisition (money, deed, possession: Kid. 1:3), and in that they could not be the subject of *theft or **ona'ah* or bailment (see **Shomerim*; Sifra Be-Har 7:3; BM 4:9), but in other respects were treated as movables (cf. Tos. to BB 150a s.v. *avda; Rashbam* BB 68a s.v. *ella*; and see Herzog Institute, 1 (1936), 92–95. For the discussions on this question, see BK 12a; BB 68a, 150a; Yev. 99a; Git. 39a; TJ, Kid. 1:3; etc.). Slaves may be mortgaged (Git. 4:4; BK 11b; ḤM 117:5; YD 267:68; and see *Pledge). Slaves could be authorized to act as *agents for their masters, and for certain purposes were so authorized by law or custom (Tosef. BK 11:2–7; BK 119a; BM 96a, 99a; BM 8:3; Tosef. Pes. 7:4; Er. 7:6; TJ, Er. 7:6; Ma'as. Sh. 4:4; etc.). Slaves could not act as agents for *divorce (Git. 23b). Slaves could hold property of their own (Tosef. Ar. 1:2; Shek. 1:5; Pes. 8:2, 88b; Yev. 66a; TJ, Yev. 7:1; Tosef. BK 11:1; BB 51b–52a; Sanh. 91a, 105a; Ket. 28a; Meg. 16a; etc.), but they could not dispose of their property by *will (*Rashi* and Tos. to Nazir 61b). A slave must be circumcised (Shab. 135b; Yad, Milah 1:3; YD 267:1).

A slave is not answerable for his *torts, but when he comes into property after his release he may be held liable in damages for torts committed during bondage (BK 8:4). A slave has the right to stay in the Land of Israel, and may not be sold for export (Git. 4:6). If he is with his master abroad, he may compel him to take him to the land of Israel (Ket. 110b; Yad, Avadim 8:9; YD 267:84), and he may flee with impunity to the Land of Israel, the prohibition on extradition (Deut. 23:16) being applicable to him (Git. 45a; Yad, Avadim 8:10; YD 267:85).

A slave may not be sold to a non-Jew: such sale is tantamount to the slave's release, and the vendor may be ordered by the court to repay the buyer not only the price he received but as much as tenfold of the price as a fine. When the slave is redeemed in this way, he does not return to the vendor but goes free (Git. 4:6; Git. 44a–45a; Yad, Avadim 8:1; YD 267:80). Any slave – except a pauper who sold himself in bondage – can be married by his master to a non-Jewish female slave (Kid. 14b; Ker. 11a; Yad, Avadim 3:12). A bastard (**mamzer*) can legitimize his issue by marrying a female slave: her son would be a slave by birth and would become a pure freeman on his release (Kid. 3:13). A slave who has been jointly owned by two masters and is released by one becomes half-slave half-freeman; the remaining master may also be compelled by the court to release him (Git. 4:5; Yad, Avadim 7:7; YD 267:62–63).

Treatment of Slaves

The biblical "for to the double of the hire of a hireling hath he served thee six years" (Deut. 15:18) was interpreted as allowing slaves to be given double the work of hired laborers: while the latter work only during daytime, slaves may be required to work also at night (Sif. Deut. 123). The Talmud (Kid. 15a) states that this merely gives the master the right to give the slave a bondwoman in order to beget children. There is some early authority to the effect that a slave has no right to maintenance which can be enforced in law, notwithstanding his obligation to work (Git. 1:6; Git. 12a), the biblical "he fareth well with thee" (Deut. 15:16) being attributed to Hebrew slaves only (Kid. 22a). However, the predominant view, as expressed by Maimonides, is: "It is permissible to work the slave hard; but while this is the law, the ways of ethics and prudence are that the master should be just and merciful, not make the yoke too heavy on his slave, and not press him too hard; and that he should give him of all food and drink. And thus the early sages used to do – they gave their slaves of everything they ate and drank themselves, and had food served to their slaves even before partaking of it themselves… Slaves may not be maltreated or offended – the law destined them for service, not for humiliation. Do not shout at them or be angry with them, but hear them out, as it is written [Job 31:13–14]: 'If I did despise the cause of my man-servant or maid-servant when they contended with me, what then shall I do when God riseth up? and when He remembereth what shall I answer?'" (Yad, Avadim 9:8; and cf. YD 267:17). In another context, Maimonides says of the laws relating to slavery that they are all "mercy, compassion, and forbearance": "You are in duty bound to see that your slave makes progress; you must benefit him and must not hurt him with words. He ought to rise and advance with you, be with you in the place you chose for yourself, and when fortune is good to you, do not grudge him his portion" (*Guide* 3:39).

POST-TALMUDIC LAW

Slavery became practically extinct in the Diaspora, and was prohibited except insofar as the secular laws allowed it, for instance, where rulers sold tax defaulters into bondage or offered prisoners of war for sale into slavery (Yad, Avadim 9:4; Tur and Sh. Ar., YD 267:18). However, it was laid down that even these "slaves" ought not to be treated as such, except if they did not conduct themselves properly (Yad, Avadim 1:8; YD 267:16). An incident related in the Talmud (BM 73b) was relied on as a precedent for the proposition that bondage may be imposed as punishment for misconduct (YD 267:15).

BIBLIOGRAPHY: Z. Kahn, *L'Esclavage selon la Bible et le Talmud* (1867; Ger. tr., 1888, Heb. tr., 1892); M. Olitzki, in: MWJ, 16 (1889), 73–83; M. Mielziener, *The Institution of Slavery Among the Ancient Hebrews* (1894); D. Farbstein, *Das Recht der unfreien und der freien Arbeiter nach juedisch-talmudischem Recht* (1896); S. Rubin, in: *Festschrift… Schwarz* (1917), 211–29; idem, *Das talmudische Recht auf den verschiedenen Stufen seiner Entwicklung mit dem roemischen verglichen und dargestellt*, 1 (*Die Slaverei*, 1920); J.L. Zuri, *Mishpat ha-Talmud*, 1 (1921), 29–31; 5 (1921), 122–33; Gulak, Yesodei, 1 (1922), 35, 38, 92; 3 (1922), 67; M. Lurje, *Studien zur Geschichte der wirtschaftlichen und sozialen Verhaeltnisse im israelitisch-juedischen Reiche* (1927), 49–55; A. Gulak, in: *Tarbiz*, 1 (1930), 20–26; 2 (1930–31), 246; Herzog Instit, 1 (1936), 414 (index), s.v.; 2 (1939), 314 (index), s.v.; S. Assaf, *Be-Oholei Ya'akov* (1943), 223–56; J. Mendelsohn, *Slavery in the Ancient Near East* (1949); ET, 1 (1951^3), 74f., 77, 333f.; 2 (1949), 29–33, 320–2; 5 (1953), 727–42; 12 (1967), 720f., 738; M. Higger, in: *Mazkeret… Herzog* (1962), 520–3; S. Zeitlin, in: JQR, 53 (1962/63), 185–218; E.E. Urbach, *The Laws Regarding Slavery as a Source for the Social History of the Period of the Second Temple, the Mishnah and Talmud* (1964); M. Elon, *Ḥerut ha-Perat be-Darkhei Geviyyat Ḥov ba-Mishpat ha-Ivri* (1964), 1–17; B. Cohen, *Jewish and Roman Law*, 1 (1966), 159–278; 2 (1966), 772–7; K.E.R. Pickard, *The Kidnapped and the Ransomed* (1970). **ADD. BIBLIOGRAPHY:** M. Elon, *Ha-Mishpat ha-Ivri* (1988), 1:179f., 264, 272, 277, 286, 299, 315, 326, 345, 390, 412, 433f., 468, 483–84, 489, 535, 604, 749f., 813; 2:845, 885, 992f., 1108f.; 3:1367f.; idem, *Jewish Law* (1994), 1:200f., 309, 320, 326, 339, 357, 376, 415, 473, 2:504, 528f., 571, 588f., 596, 651, 748, 924f., 996; 3:1033, 1079, 1200f., 1333; 4:1631; M. Elon and B. Lifshitz, *Mafte'aḥ ha-She'elot ve-ha-Teshuvot shel Ḥakhmei Sefarad u-Ẓefon Afrikah* (legal digest) (1986), 2:317–19.

[Haim Hermann Cohn]

SLAVE TRADE. Jews engaged in the slave trade – although they never played a prominent role in it – from the early Middle Ages to the early modern period. While it was not proscribed to pagans, none of the three monotheistic religions either prohibited slavery or trade in slaves except insofar as converts to a particular religion were concerned. It was as if three circles were drawn, each opposing only the enslavement of its own members by a member of one of the other two. Thus the only legitimate objects of slavery and the slave trade were pagans and Jews, Christians, and Muslims captured in war by victors of either of the other religions. In Europe, aside from the Nordic countries, in the early Middle Ages there remained pagans in the Slav countries only (and their generic name, or variations thereof, became the appellation for the slave throughout Western Europe). Slaves were needed for agriculture, domestic service, and as eunuchs in Muslim harems. They were one of the few "commodities" that Europe could export to the Byzantine and later Muslim Mediterranean, from which it imported so much, thus restoring to some extent the balance of payments. The Jewish slave owner, however, was expected by the Church to release his slave the moment the latter converted to Christianity, sometimes by inducement. Jews also used slaves in their vineyards, and a forced conversion of a slave was a loss to them. As each slave owner in all religions considered himself responsible for the soul and behavior of his slaves, he felt in duty bound to convert them to his faith; in the case of the Jews, who were in a minority everywhere, this caused friction and problems for the Jewish owners. Thus tension colored the attitude to Jewish ownership of slaves and participation in the slave trade in Christian countries.

Under the Muslim rule in Spain, where there was a slave market in Baena in the ninth century, Jews owned slaves without hindrance as long as the slaves were not Muslims. However, there is no evidence of a slave trade carried on by Jews in Christian Spain (Baer, Spain, 1 (1961), 417). Slaves were employed primarily for domestic and agricultural service in the households of the Jewish upper classes, and this situation persisted for some time under Christian rule, especially in *Majorca, where Jews owned large estates and many slaves; in the middle of the 13th century James I put obstacles in the path of Jewish ownership of Moorish slaves in Majorca, who wished to be baptized and thereby freed. In late Roman Spain and Frankish Gaul, Church opposition to Jewish ownership of slaves was much in evidence. *Church councils repeatedly denounced Jewish ownership of Christian slaves and of those slaves who wished to convert to Christianity; but these denunciations remained ineffectual. Pope George the Great (sixth century) inveighed against a Jewish merchant, because his import of slaves from Gaul into Italy included some Christians. The Muslim conquest of Spain created a nearby market for slaves, to which Jews were accused of catering. Emperor Louis I the Pious granted a number of Jews (c. 825–8) the right to import foreign slaves and sell them within the confines of the empire. Archbishop *Agobard of Lyons claimed that royal officials in Lyons accepted the Jewish traders' view that heathen slaves who requested baptism should be considered as doing this solely in order to gain their freedom, and that this should not be granted unless the owner was paid the sum he demanded. Agobard denounced this view, claiming in the course of his arguments that in some cases Jews even sold people born Christian into slavery. Jewish slave traders (among others) are recorded in 906 in the custom dues rolls of Raffelstetten on the Danube, a major interregional market in the early Middle Ages. The Arab geographer Ibn-Khurdadbah (c. 870–92) includes slaves (eunuchs) among the many articles sold by the *Radhanites, said to have traveled from Franconia to China by sea or land. *Ibrahim ibn Yaʿqub, the Jewish traveler, recorded the presence of Jewish slave traders in Prague around 970 (alongside Muslims and Turks), and Bishop Adalbert of Prague resigned in 988 after failing to buy the freedom of a group of slaves bought by a Jewish trader. The Jews of that period regarded the Slavic east as the land of slaves par excellence – "Canaan" (see Gen. 9:25 and Midrashim to this verse). Jewish slave traders appear in the *Koblenz custom rolls of 1004; they are mentioned in 1009, when the margrave of Meissen was accused of selling slaves to Jews, and in 1085, when a Polish princess in Silesia was praised for buying up Christian slaves from Jews and freeing them. With the Christianization of most of the Slavs, this trade ceased as far as Jews in Christian Europe were concerned.

While responsa and deeds of manumission indicate the frequency of slaves, mainly women employed as housemaids and occasionally men who were business agents, in personal service in Jewish households in Muslim lands, a thorough study of conditions in Egypt in the 11–13th centuries reveals that "during the classical *Genizah* period the Jews had no share in the slave trade" (S.D. Goitein, *A Mediterranean Society* (1967), 140), in particular after Maimonides' time. Slave ownership in Muslim lands raised the problem of responsibility for the slaves' conversion to Judaism and, frequently, that of sexual relations between the owner and his female slave. *Ketubbot* quoted in Maimonides' responsa include the condition that the husband promise not to buy a female slave without his wife's consent, parallel to his promise not to take a second wife against his first wife's will. He also referred to the question of castration (forbidden in Jewish law) and the sale of eunuchs.

In the Ottoman Empire slavery flourished through the wars of expansion. Most wealthy Jewish families owned one or more slaves for domestic purposes. The Marrano Diaspora in the New World (particularly in the Carribean) became both customer for, and trader in, African and Indian slaves. Slave-owning Marranos settling in Protestant countries created serious legal difficulties (as in London and Hamburg); a Portuguese relative of Albertus *Denis was forced to leave Danzig because of public indignation at his treatment and ownership of slaves. The Ottoman authorities opposed Jewish participation in the slave trade, but one exception occurred during the 1571 war against *Cyprus when Jewish slave traders were required to pay a special state tax. Toward the end of the 16th century the sultan decreed also that a special tax be paid by Jews who owned slaves. Subsequently, slaves and slavery gradually disappeared from Jewish life. Modern European and U.S. historians up to the mid-1950s (including Jewish historians) confused the ownership of slaves by Jews with their part in the slave trade. The role of the Jews in the slave trade was also vastly exaggerated. This was done either to overemphasize the importance of Jews in early medieval trade or to put the odium of this trade onto the Jews (according to modern views – in disregard of the acceptability of slavery during the period of Jewish participation in it). This tendency was reinforced by antisemitic prejudices.

[Toni Oelsner and Henry Wasserman]

In the Americas

Until 1730 the Dutch West India Company maintained a monopoly on the importation of slaves into all the Dutch colonies in the Americas, but Jews appear to have been among the major retailers of slaves in Dutch Brazil (1630–54), because Jews possessed ready money and were willing to trade slaves for sugar. The bylaws of the Recife and Mauricia congregations (1648) included an *imposta* (Jewish tax) of 5 soldos for each slave which a Brazilian Jew purchased from the West Indies Company. In Curaçao, the Dutch occasionally gave permission to a merchant to conduct independent transactions in slaves; two such Jewish entrepreneurs were the brothers David and Jacob Senior, who came to the island from Amsterdam about 1685. Another Curaçao Jew, Manuel Alvares Correa (1650–1717), who was active in the local slave trade for many years, served in 1699 as an intermediary between the Dutch and Portuguese West Indies companies for the transfer of a shipment of slaves from Africa to Mexico via Curaçao.

In all of the American colonies, whether Dutch, French, or British, almost every merchant or trader had dealings in slaves: when he acted as auctioneer or agent for the sale of an estate, when he served his planter clients in the sale or purchase of slaves or in the pursuit of runaways. In the Barbados, until 1706, Jews were limited by law in the number of slaves they themselves could own, but in Jamaica there was no such restriction. Among the Jamaican Jewish merchants who seem to have specialized in the slave trade were David Henriques, Hyman *Levy, and especially Alexander Lindo (1753–1812), who was a major importer of slaves during the period 1782–92. During an investigation of slave mortality conducted in Jamaica in 1789, Lindo testifies that 150 slaves on a ship "consigned to" him had died in the Middle Passage and that another 20 perished after their arrival in Jamaica, but it is unclear whether he owned this slave shipment or any of the others in which he was involved. Members of the well-known *Gradis family of Bordeaux were active in the shipment of slaves from West Africa to such French colonies as Santo-Domingo (Dominican Republic).

On the North American mainland, a number of Jews were active participants in the infamous triangular trade, which brought slaves from Africa to the West Indies, where they were exchanged for molasses, which was in turn taken to New England and converted into rum for sale in Africa. David *Franks of Philadelphia was in this business during the early 1760s; Aaron *Lopez and Jacob Rodriguez *Rivera of Newport, Rhode Island, had at least one slaver on the high seas each year after 1764, and in 1772 and 1773 had a total of eight such ships under sail. Isaac Da *Costa of Charleston was another large-scale importer of slaves. In Louisiana, under both French and Spanish rule, the Monsanto brothers made frequent transactions in slaves; during 1787 they purchased 44 blacks.

Although Jews in Philadelphia and New York City were active in the early abolition movement, Jewish merchants, auctioneers, and commission agents in the Southern states continued to buy and sell slaves until the end of the Civil War. The fact that Jacob Levin of Columbia, South Carolina, and Israel I. Jones of Mobile, Alabama, two merchants who often dealt in slaves, were leaders of their Jewish communities in the 1850s is evidence that at no time did Southern Jews feel tainted by the slave trade. Levy Jacobs was an active trader in slaves both in New Orleans and in Mobile during the 1820s; Ansley, Benjamin, George, and Solomon Davis of Richmond and Petersburg, Virginia, went on the road to sell gangs of slaves in the states of the lower South beginning about 1838; B. Mordecai of Charleston had large slave pens alongside his warehouses and purchased $12,000 worth of slaves at one sale in 1859. But the total business activity of all the Southern Jews who dealt in slaves in any way probably did not equal the turnover of the largest single non-Jewish firm which specialized in slaves, Franklin and Armfield.

[Bertram Wallace Korn]

BIBLIOGRAPHY: S.D. Goitein, *A Mediterranean Society*, 1 (1967), index; T. Oelsner, in: YIVOA, 12 (1958/59), 184f.; idem, in: YLBI 8 (1962), 188f.; Baron, Social², 3 (1956), 30f., 243f.; 4 (1956), 187–96; 332–8; idem, in: *Essays on Maimonides* (1941), 229–47; Roth, *Dark Ages*, 27f., 306–10, 386, 410; S. Assaf, *Be-Oholei Ya'akov* (1943), 223–56; idem, in: *Zion*, 4 (1939), 5 (1940); M.S. Goodblatt, *Jewish Life in Turkey* (1952), 125ff.; A.S. Diamond, in: JHSET, 21 (1962–67); J. Starr, *Jews in the Byzantine Empire* (1939), index; D.B. Davis, *Problem of Slavery in Western Culture* (1966), 98ff.; S. Grayzel, *Church and the Jews in the 13th Century* (1966²), index; J. Parkes, *Church and Synagogue* (1934), index; M. Hoffman, *Der Geldhandel der deutschen Juden waehrend des Mittelalters* (1910), 15ff.; Baer, Spain, index; B.Z. Wacholder, in: HJ, 18 (1956), 89–106; I.A. Agus, *Urban Civilization in Pre-Crusade Europe* (1965), index; A. Hertzberg, *The French Enlightenment and the Jews* (1968), index; E. Taeubler, in: *M. Philippson Festschrift* (1916), 381–92; B. Blumenkranz, *Juifs et Chrétiens dans le Monde Occidental 430–1096* (1960), 18–55, 107, 190f., 337; C. Haase, in: *Die Staedte Mitteleuropas im 12. und 13. Jahrhundert*, ed. by W. Rauch (1963), 133 and n. 50; C. Cahen, in: REJ, 123 (1964), 499–504. IN THE AMERICAS: F. Bancroft, *Slave Trading in the Old South* (1931); Chyet, in: AJHSQ, 52 (1962/63), 295–300; I.S. Emmanuel, *Precious Stones of the Jews of Curaçao* (1957), 304; idem, *History of the Jews of the Netherlands Antilles* (1970), index; Friedenwald, in: AJHSP, 5 (1897), 60–97; B.W. Korn, *Early Jews of New Orleans* (1969); idem, *Jews and Slavery in the Old South* (1961); *Report, Resolution and Remonstrance of the Honourable the Council and Assembly of Jamaica at a Joint Committee on the Subject of the Slave Trade* (London, 1790); A. Wiznitzer, *Jews in Colonial Brazil* (1960), 72–73; idem, *Records of the Earliest Jewish Community in the New World* (1954), 28, 74; *Jamaica Royal Gazette* (March 30, 1782; Apr. 12, 1806); *Kingston Journal* (July 28, 1787; Nov 10, 1787); H.M. Alvares Correa, *Alvares Correa Families of Curaçao and Brazil* (1965), 10–11.

SLAVSON, SAMUEL RICHARD (1891–1981), U.S. group psychotherapy expert. Born in the Ukraine, Slavson arrived in New York with his family after escaping the pogroms in Russia. Working by day, he attended evening school at the Cooper Union, where he received a B.S. in engineering. He became a member of the Socialist Party in 1904, which led to his involvement with the labor movement. He was a key figure in the formation of the *International Ladies Garment Workers Union. Slavson was departmental director of New York's progressive Walter School from 1918 to 1921 and from 1921 to 1927 he was educational consultant of the Pioneer Youth of America. In 1927 he became director of research in child psychology at Malting House, Cambridge, England. In 1929 he returned to the United States and was consultant to a number of agencies dealing with problem children. In 1934 he became director of group psychotherapy at the Board of Jewish Guardians in New York, where he introduced group treatment for emotionally disturbed children. A pivotal figure in modern psychology and psychoanalysis, Slavson retired from that position in 1956. His *Introduction to Group Therapy* (1943) describes his principles, processes, and methods, as well as his criteria for accepting disturbed children for group therapy. Slavson was president of the American Group Psychotherapy Association (1943–45), and editor-in-chief of the journal *Group Psychotherapy*. From 1956 on, he continued to work and formulate new theories regarding the treatment of delinquent adolescents and institutionalized psychotics. He also wrote and lectured extensively.

His books include *Science in the New Education* (with Robert K. Speer, 1934), *Creative Group Education* (1937), *Recreation of the Total Personality* (1946), *The Practice of Group Therapy* (1947), *Analytic Group Psychotherapy* (1950), *Child-Centered Group Guidance of Parents* (1958), *A Textbook in Analytic Group Psychotherapy* (1964), and *Reclaiming the Delinquent by Para-analytic Group Psychotherapy and the Inversion Technique* (1965).

SLAVUTA, city in N. Kamenets-Podolski district, Ukraine. Slavuta was annexed by Russia after the second partition of Poland (1793) and was in the province of Volhynia until the 1917 Revolution. In 1765 the poll tax was paid by 246 Jews registered in Slavuta. During the late 18th and first half of the 19th century, the community became known for its printing press, founded in 1791 by R. Moses Shapira, son of the *zaddik* R. Phinehas b. Abraham of *Korets. Later Moses' two sons, Samuel Abba and Phinehas, took over the administration of the press. Three editions of the Babylonian Talmud, an edition of the Bible (with commentaries), the Zohar, and many other religious works, especially ḥasidic literature, were all produced handsomely and with great care by the press. In 1835 the press was closed down when the owners were arrested for the alleged murder of a worker who had supposedly denounced them for printing books without permission from the censor. There were 1,658 Jews registered in the community in 1847 and 4,891 in 1897 (57% of the total population). Under Soviet rule the community's institutions were destroyed. The Jewish population numbered 4,701 in 1926 (44.9%). During the German occupation of the city during World War II, those Jews who did not manage to escape were murdered. A mass grave marks the place where Jews were massacred by the Nazis in the vicinity of the town, with a monument erected to the memory of the dead and with inscriptions in both Russian and Yiddish. In the late 1960s the Jewish population was estimated at about 3,000. There was one synagogue administered by a rabbi. Most left in the 1900s.

BIBLIOGRAPHY: Ḥ.D. Friedberg, *Toledot ha-Defus ha-Ivri be-Polanyah* (1950), 104–9.

[Yehuda Slutsky]

°SLAWOJ-SKLADKOWSKI, FELICJAN (1885–1962), Polish politician. From May 15, 1936, to September 1939 he was Poland's prime minister and minister of interior. The period of Slawoj-Skladkowski's premiership was marked by political and social unrest. His government endorsed the antisemitic program of the *OZON to distract the Polish masses from the real problems of the prewar crisis. His declaration "nobody in Poland should be injured. An honest host does not allow anybody to be harmed in his home" reflected his policy toward the Jews. Nevertheless, sources of livelihood were taken away from Jews; Saturday was made a market day, markets were held far from town, many butcher shops were closed because of the **sheḥitah* law (January 1937), commercial licenses for Jews were restricted, as were bank credits for Jewish businessmen and craftsmen, excessive taxes were imposed, etc. The anti-Jewish economic boycott had official government support. The *numerus clausus was imposed against Jewish students who were placed on ghetto benches at the universities, and the number of Jews in the free professions (physicians, lawyers, etc.) was considerably reduced. Riots against students and the picketing of Jewish shops were considered a "natural instinct of cultural self-defense and tendency for economic self-sufficience." When riots and pogroms broke out in Radom, Czestochowa, Brest-Litovsk, Vilna, and Lvov, Jewish property valued at over 3 million zlotys was destroyed. The Slawoj-Skladkowski government encouraged rioters, intervening only against Jewish self-defense groups.

BIBLIOGRAPHY: S. Segal, *The New Poland and the Jews* (1938), 64–86, 143; R.L. Buell, *Poland: Key to Europe* (1939), 299–306; I. Gruenbaum, in: EG, 1 (1953), 113–6; J. Rothschild, *Pilsudski's Coup d'Etat* (1966), 398–9.

SLAWSON, JOHN (1896–1989), U.S. communal executive and social worker. Slawson, who was born in Poltava, Ukraine, was taken to the U.S. in 1904. From 1920 to 1924 Slawson was an investigator and psychologist for the New York State Department of Welfare. He was subsequently head of the Jewish welfare federations of Cleveland and Detroit (1924–32) and executive director of the Jewish Board of Guardians (1932–43). From 1943 to 1967 Slawson served as executive vice president of the *American Jewish Committee (AJC), where he directed a comprehensive program of scientific research on prejudice and the methods of combating group hostility. During his tenure, the committee grew into an international organization with more than 40,000 members and offices in 20 U.S. localities, as well as in Europe, Israel, and Latin America. In 1957 Slawson and an AJC delegation met with Pope Pius XII, the first audience ever accorded a Jewish organization by the Vatican.

He wrote *The Delinquent Boy* (1926), a basic treatise on juvenile delinquency; *The Role of Science in Intergroup Relations* (1962); and *Unequal Americans* (1979).

[Geraldine Rosenfield (2nd ed.)]

SLEPIAN, JOSEPH (1891–1969), U.S. electrical engineer. Slepian was born in Boston, Mass., receiving his B.Sc. degree in 1911, M.Sc. in 1912, and Ph.D. in mathematics in 1913 from Harvard. After postdoctoral work at the University of Gottingen in Germany, the Sorbonne in Paris, and Cornell University, he joined the Westinghouse Company in 1916, where he held research posts of increasing seniority at the company's Forest Hills research facility until he retired in 1956. His mathematical knowledge and engineering skills led to many inventions in the electrical supply industry. His research on lightning arresters disclosed the need for surge protection. His studies of ionized gases led to his invention of the deion circuit breaker and the ignitron for initiating and controlling electrical arcs. Late in his working career and after his retirement he worked on plasma methods for isotope separation. He was associated with the Manhattan Project in World War II. He found the atmosphere of a commercial laboratory highly conducive to his work, where he also organized teaching courses in basic and applied physics. His honors included the prestigious Edison Medal (1947).

[Michael Denman (2nd ed.)]

SLIOZBERG, HENRY (1863–1937), Russian jurist and communal worker. Born in Mir, Belorussia, Sliozberg was taken to Poltava, eastern Ukraine, by his family. Although he was an honors student in law at the university of St. Petersburg, Sliozberg was not accepted as a teacher there because he was a Jew. He became a successful private advocate but resigned to accept the (unofficial) position of legal counsel for the Russian Ministry of the Interior. In 1889 he became legal counsel on

Jewish affairs to Baron H. *Guenzburg. The baron entrusted Sliozberg with various important tasks, including drafting memoranda to the authorities and defending Jews before the supreme judicial institutions in St. Petersburg. Sliozberg then devoted himself to Jewish communal work, adopting a stand somewhere between the old intercession methods and that of the modern public campaign introduced and employed by Jewish intelligentsia at the beginning of the 20th century. In his struggles with his opponents and in his attempts to influence the ruling circles, Sliozberg bolstered traditional intercession tactics with legal argumentation. He joined the "defense bureau" founded by the Jewish intellectuals of St. Petersburg, an office set up to defend the rights of the Jews through organized legal action. He was among the founders of both the *Society for Equal Rights for the Jews in Russia (1905) and the "Jewish People's Group" (1907) into which groups the delegates of the non-Zionist, Russian-Jewish intelligentsia – most of whom were connected with the Cadet (Liberal) Party – had united. Sliozberg also participated in the work of the "Political Bureau Assigned to the Jewish Representatives of the State Duma," whose task it was to guide Jewish representatives at the *Duma on behalf of their fellow Jews. Sliozberg also worked with the legal defense organization which dealt with *blood libels, notably with the *Beilis case (1912). During World War I he was one of the leaders of the committee of assistance to Jewish war refugees (*YEKOPO). He also acted as chairman of the Jewish community of St. Petersburg. During the revolution, Sliozberg was imprisoned briefly and his property was confiscated. In 1920 he left Russia for France where he participated in the communal life of Russian and Russian-Jewish immigrants and also became head of the Russian-Jewish community in Paris. In 1934 he testified as witness for the prosecution at the trial regarding the Protocols of the *Elders of Zion in Berne. His memoirs, *Dela minuvshikh dney* ("Bygone Days," 3 vols., 1933), are an important historical account of the Jewish communal life in Russia of the generation preceding the revolution.

BIBLIOGRAPHY: V. Jabotinsky, in: G. Sliozberg, *Dela minuvshikh dney*, 1 (1933), ix–xiv (introd.); Kulisher, in: *Yevreyskiy Mir*, 2 (1941), 419–21; Kucherov, in: *Kniga o russkom yevreystve* (1960), 421–4; J. Frumkin et al. (ed.), *Russian Jewry 1860–1917*, 1 (1966), 226, 233–7, and index.

[Yehuda Slutsky]

SLOBODKA YESHIVAH, a leading European yeshivah which was dedicated to the ideals of the *Musar movement. In 1882 the yeshivah was founded in Slobodka, a suburb of Kouro, Lithuania, by R. Nathan Ẓevi *Finkel as an advanced school for the graduates of the local elementary yeshivah which had previously been established by R. Ẓevi Levitan. The new school made rapid strides after the leading yeshivah of this era, the *Volozhin yeshivah, was closed by the czarist government on Jan. 22, 1892. Many former Volozhin students enrolled at Slobodka, and in 1893 R. Finkel appointed two brothers-in-law, both brilliant Volozhin graduates, R. Isser Zalman *Meltzer and R. Moses Mordecai *Epstein, to be the heads of the Slobodka yeshivah. R. Meltzer left in 1896 to organize the Slutzker yeshivah, but R. Epstein remained associated with the school until his death in 1933. R. Finkel remained the yeshivah's dominant personality and fashioned its unique *musar* environment. He instituted a daily half-hour period devoted solely to the study of *musar* texts, and on Saturday nights he delivered *musar* lectures to the assembled students. In 1896 the yeshivah was caught up in a public controversy with those students and rabbis who had long opposed the innovations of the Musar movement. The yeshivah split in 1897 and those loyal to the ideals of R. Finkel and R. Epstein renamed their school Yeshivah Keneset Israel, in memory of the founder of the Musar movement, R. Israel *Lipkin (Salanter). The other students organized a new school which they called Keneset Bet Yiẓḥak, in memory of R. Isaac Elhanan *Spektor of Kovno. It was later headed by R. Baruch Ber Leibowitz and following World War I relocated in Kamenetz, Poland.

R. Finkel's yeshivah continued to expand; by 1899 it had an enrollment of over 300 students and a new building was constructed for the school. The yeshivah's position was further strengthened with the 1910 selection of R. Epstein to serve as the chief rabbi of Slobodka. Additional heads of the yeshivah were appointed, including R. Finkel's son, R. Moses Finkel, and son-in-law R. Isaac Sher. With the outbreak of World War I, the school was compelled to move from Slobodka to Minsk, and afterward to *Kremenchug, where it remained for the duration of the war. After its return to Slobodka, the yeshivah continued expanding rapidly during the 1920s. The student body increased to over 500, including scores of foreign students from Germany and the English-speaking countries. R. Finkel organized new divisions of the yeshivah to complement its educational program, including an elementary school named Even Israel and a secondary school called Or Israel. The culmination of these schools was the Slobodka *kolel*, which was established in 1921.

In 1924, following the Lithuanian government's decision to discontinue its previous practice of exempting all yeshivah students from military service, it was decided to open a branch of the school in Palestine, and Hebron was chosen for its location. R. Finkel joined the new school in 1925, and it soon attracted over 150 students. Following the Arab massacre of 1929 in which 25 yeshivah students were murdered, the school relocated in Jerusalem, where it continued to function under the name of the Hebron yeshivah. The original Slobodka yeshivah, under the leadership of R. Isaac Sher, continued its activities until June 23, 1941, when the Nazi invasion was imminent. Although most of the faculty and students perished during the Holocaust, the Slobodka yeshivah was reopened in *Bene-Berak following the conclusion of the war.

BIBLIOGRAPHY: E. Oshry, in: *Mosedot Torah be-Eiropah*, ed. by S.K. Mirsky (1956), 133–68; D. Katz, *Tenu'at ha-Musar*, 3 (n.d.); A. Rothkoff, in: *Jewish Life* (Feb.–March, 1969), 47–53; (Nov.–Dec. 1970), 34–42.

[Aaron Rothkoff]

SLOMAN, HENRY (**Solomon**; 1793–1873), British actor. Born in Rochester, Sloman was a popular comedian at the Coburg Theatre in London (later the Old Vic) and became a celebrity in the pantomimes and melodramas staged by Joseph Glossop. After Glossop's death in 1835, he went into partnership with his brother, CHARLES SLOMAN (1808–1870), in running the Rochester Theatre. Both were comic singers, and in addition Charles composed a number of songs, among them *Daughter of Israel and Maid of Judah.*

SLOMOVITZ, PHILIP (1896– 1993), U.S. journalist. Born in Minsk, Russia, Slomovitz worked on Jewish papers in Detroit, Mich., and became editor of the *Detroit Jewish News*, the first Jewish periodical in the country to be sponsored by a community, when it was founded in 1942. His syndicated articles appeared in both Jewish and non-Jewish journals. Slomovitz was active in Zionist and other American Jewish organizations. In 1943 he founded the American Association of English-Jewish Newspapers, of which he remained president until 1953.

SLONIK (Solnik), BENJAMIN AARON BEN ABRAHAM (c. 1550–c. 1619), Polish rabbi. Slonik was probably born in Grodno. He studied there in his youth under Nathan Nata Spiro. He was rabbi in Silesia (Joseph Katz, *She'erit Yosef* (Cracow, 1590), no. 47) and Podhajce (Meir of Lublin, *Responsa*, no. 110). He claims to have been in "Russia" as a youth (*Masat Binyamin*, no. 62), probably referring to southeastern Poland, which included the Ukraine and the Podolia region. He lived in Cracow for a period of time before and after the death of Moses *Isserles (*ibid.*, no. 80), but since no questions in his responsa were addressed to him from Cracow or its environs, it is not likely that he served there as rabbi.

"Benjamin Aaron, *ḥarif* of Tykocin," appears as one of 30 signatories of the 1590 decree of the *Council of the Lands which reenacted the prohibition against offering a bribe in order to acquire a rabbinic post (Harkavy, Perles). This probably refers to Grodno since Tykocin bordered it. The two communities disputed sovereignty over a large territory, and if Slonik was born in that area he could have been considered to have come from either community, which explains why his name does not appear in the records of Tykocin. Slonik studied under Solomon *Luria (Maharshal), Moses Isserles, and Solomon b. Leibesh of Lublin whom he calls the "second Maharshal." Luria had the greatest influence on his work. From him he learned lucidity, expositional skill, stylistic and grammatical precision, and a scientific approach to Jewish law. Isserles' influence is apparent in Slonik's use of the responsum as a vehicle for a thoroughgoing discussion of the legal background and principles which pertain to the question under discussion. Solomon b. Leibesh and Nathan Spiro were themselves influenced by Kabbalah, and inspired Slonik's interest in that subject, expressed in chance statements (no. 7, 99) and in his giving unusual weight to the opinion of the Zohar (no. 62).

His Works

Slonik was the author of the following works:

(1) *Masat Binyamin* (Cracow, 1633; often republished), containing 112 responsa, for the most part arranged chronologically, and several pages of the author's novellae on the Shulḥan Arukh:

(2) *Seder Mitzvot Nashim, Eyn schoen Frauenbuechlein*, a very popular Yiddish book printed three times during the author's lifetime and translated into Italian, dealing with the three principle duties of women, but also giving moral teachings on the conduct of women in every phase of family life (Cracow, 1577, 1585; Basle, 1602; and often reprinted; first translated into Italian by Jacob b. Elhanan Heilbronn in 1614, published in Padua, 1625);

(3) *Sefer ha-Ebronot*, a treatise on the leap year in the Hebrew calendar;

(4) *Seder Ḥaliẓah*, on release from the requirements of the levirate marriage. The latter two books are not extant.

In his response he included questions and comments by his two sons, Abraham and Jakel. He also mentioned his grandson Faivel (no. 95), and his two daughters, one of whom died during her father's lifetime. Abraham, who was rabbi of Brest-Litovsk, wrote several notes to his father's responsa, and edited them. He showed high regard for his relation by marriage, Moses b. Abraham of Przemysl, author of *Sefer Matteh Moshe* and *Sefer Ho'il Moshe*, who was a signatory, together with Slonik, on the 1603 proclamation of the Jaroslaw synod of the Council of Four Lands authorizing the printing of new books.

His Decisions

Slonik had an independent mind and, unafraid of controversy, frequently disagreed with his teachers and colleagues. He opposed the decisions of his colleagues in Podhajce even as a newcomer to the area (no. 21). He issued decisions on controversial questions which colleagues had hesitated to answer (no. 7). Some of his decisions are based on entirely novel principles. Thus, he uses the scientific observation that quick freezing preserves a body for long periods of time to validate testimony identifying a victim long after the three-day limit after death would ordinarily apply (no. 104). He accepted no source without having seen it himself (nos. 11, 26, 37, 47, 75, 76, 109). He disparaged the method and the judgment of R. Mordecai *Jaffe, accusing him of eclecticism (no. 32). His attitude in questions dealing with cases of deserted wives (*agunot*) is in opposition to the strict interpretation of Ashkenazi rabbis. Although an Ashkenazi himself, he accepted the more lenient ruling of the Sephardi rabbi Elijah Mizraḥi, in order to help these unfortunate women (nos. 105, 109), for times had become troubled and there were many Jews who lost their lives in the wars which raged along their trade routes through Walachia to Constantinople (nos. 29, 44, 45, 63, 65, 98, 105, 109).

He decided some cases purely on the basis of logic (nos. 72, 90, 109), historical evidence (nos. 38 and 57), empirical observation (nos. 69 and 108), medical knowledge, and anatomical research (no. 49). He rejected R. Shalom Shakna's method of *pilpul* in deciding Jewish law (no. 16). He permitted the calling of blind or illiterate men to the "reading" of the Torah, and pleaded for understanding and tolerance for the feelings of estranged Jews and sensitive women, so that they may be brought closer to Judaism (no. 62). His responsa include an analysis of the grammatical differences between the two versions of the Decalogue and he castigates cantors for improperly preparing the Torah reading, as well as for introducing into the synagogue service melodies borrowed from secular songs and the theater (no. 6). He dealt with community disputes, taxation, elections, sale of synagogues, divorce given under duress, murder, and manslaughter. Several of his decisions were aimed at resolving famous controversies of the day (nos. 22, 76, 77).

His decisions remained an authoritative source, not only for his contemporaries, but also for Polish and German rabbis for many years to come. They are often quoted and usually considered definitive by noted commentators to the Shulḥan Arukh, such as *Shabbetai b. Meir ha-Kohen and Abraham Abele *Gombiner.

BIBLIOGRAPHY: J. Perles, in: MGWJ, 16 (1867), 223; J.M. Zunz, *Ir ha-Ẓedek* (1874), ix, 12; M. Steinschneider, in: HB, 19 (1879), 82–83; Ḥ.N. Dembitzer, *Kelilat Yofi*, 1 (1888), 21aff.; A. Harkavy, *Ḥadashim gam Yeshanim*, 2:3 (1899); B. Katz, *Le-Korot ha-Yehudim be-Rusyah, Polin ve-Lita* (1899), 33, 34, 56; S.B. Nissenbaum, *Le-Korot ha-Yehudim be-Lublin* (1900), 21; M. Brann, *Geschichte der Juden in Schlesien*, 5 (1909), 191–201; Halpern, Pinkas, 15, 27, 29, 453; I. Lewin, in: *Hadorom*, 22 (1965), 5–18; H.H. Ben-Sasson, *Hagut ve-Hanhagah* (1958), 140–1; N. Shulman, "The Responsa Masat Binyamin" (Diss. Yeshiva University, 1970).

[Nisson E. Shulman]

SLONIM, city in Grodno district, Belarus; passed to Russia in 1795 and reverted to Poland between the two world wars. Slonim is mentioned in 1583 as one of the communities which were declared exempt from the special tax called "*srebshzizna*." Jewish merchants from Slonim traded with Lublin and Posen. By decision of the Lithuanian Council (see *Councils of the Lands) in 1623, the Jews of Slonim were placed under the jurisdiction of the *Brest community. From 1631 Slonim appears in the accounts of the *pinkas* of the Council of Lithuanian Jews as an independent community. A magnificent stone synagogue was erected there in 1642. In 1660 the Jews suffered persecutions by the armies of Stephan *Czarniecki. In the latter part of the 17th century the Jews of Slonim traded in wheat and timber with *Koenigsberg; later on wealthy merchants traveled to the *Leipzig fairs. Others earned their livelihood in contracting, manufacturing alcoholic beverages, and crafts. In 1764, after danger to the community from the advancing Russian armies had been averted, the day of deliverance, the 26th of Sivan, was subsequently commemorated in the community. The Jewish population numbered 1,154 in Slonim and its surroundings in 1766; 5,700 in 1847; 11,435 (78% of the total population) in 1897; 6,917 Jews (71.7%) in 1921; and 8,605 (52.95%) in 1931.

During the 19th century Jews engaged in wholesale trading in timber, furs, and hides, in transport and supplying the army, iron foundries, agricultural machinery, matches, tanneries, sawmills, and brick kilns. Jews also operated steam mills. The first textile factory in Slonim was founded in 1826 by a Jew, employing 35 workers, of whom 20 were Jewish. In the late 19th and early 20th century Jews engaged in the manufacture of woolen scarves, curtains, yeast, matches, agricultural machinery, and Jewish ritual articles.

Many Jewish homes were burned as a result of anti-Jewish hooliganism in 1881. Due to expulsions from nearby villages in 1882 the Jewish population in Slonim increased. In 1897 Jewish workers in Slonim began to organize in trade unions, and between 1902 and 1906 the *Bund, *Po'alei Zion and the *Zionist Socialist Workers' Party (SS) were influential. They established *self-defense groups to protect Jews against attacks, especially in the stormy period after the *Bialystok pogrom of 1906. In 1913 Jewish workers staged a strike to protest against the *Beilis case.

Traditional spiritual leaders of Slonim included Moses b. Isaac Judah *Lima, author of *Ḥelkat Meḥokek*, who served the community in the 1660s; Simeon b. Mordecai (officiated 1735–69); and Joshua Isaac b. Jehiel *Shapira, author of *Naḥalat Yehoshu'a* (1851), in the 1830s. In the mid-19th century Abraham b. Isaac Weinberg (1804–1884) founded a new branch of Ḥasidism and became the first of the *Slonim dynasty. The Slonim yeshivah, one of the oldest and most honored Lithuanian yeshivot, came under the influence of this ḥasidic trend.

All Jewish parties were active in Slonim between the two world wars, in independent Poland, including a *hakhsharah* farm of the He-Ḥalutz movement. The community had schools of the *Tarbut, CYSHO, and Taḥkemoni. A Yiddish quarterly, *Unzer Zhurnal*, was published from 1921 to 1925, and the weekly *Slonimer Vort* from 1926–1939.

[Dov Rabin]

Holocaust and Contemporary Periods

Immediately after the outbreak of World War II (Sept. 1, 1939), Slonim was inundated by thousands of Jewish refugees escaping from the advancing German army. Under the Soviet-German agreement the city passed to Soviet rule. In 1939–41, all Jewish community life was repressed, though Zionist groups attempted to function underground. Young people sought ways to reach Vilna, then under Lithuanian control, in an effort to reach Palestine from there. On April 12, 1940, about 1,000 Jewish refugees were exiled to Russia, among them Yiẓḥak Efrat, head of the community and the Zionist federation before the war.

On June 25, 1941, after war broke out between Germany and the Soviet Union, Slonim fell to German troops, who began to attack the Jews. On July 17, they carried out an **Aktion* in which 1,200 Jewish men were rounded up and murdered on the outskirts of the city. The German authorities exacted a fine of 2,000,000 rubles from the Jewish community, and set up a *Judenrat, first headed by Wolf Berman, but its members were murdered when they showed resistance to Nazi demands. The second chairman of the Judenrat was Gershon Kwint. At the end of August 1941 a "Jewish quarter" was allocated, but not sealed off immediately. On Nov. 14, 1941, in a second *Aktion*, Germans, Lithuanians, and Belorussians murdered 9,000 Jews in nearby Czepielow. A very few managed to escape from the death pits, returned to the ghetto, and received aid in its hospital. When the Germans found out, they were seized and murdered at the pits. Following this *Aktion* the ghetto, which now contained about 15,000 Jews, including refugees from the vicinity, was closed off. In the ghetto the Jews began to build hideouts in expectation of another raid. On June 29, 1942, the Germans and their collaborators surrounded the ghetto and set it on fire. In this *Aktion*, which continued up to July 15, many Jews perished in the flames; those who escaped and were caught were murdered in the fields of Pietralewicze. The Germans met with armed resistance from some of the youth who managed to wrest their arms from them and escaped to the forests. Only 800 Jews remained alive at the end of the attack, most of whom fled to the forests. About 300 of the remaining Jews were murdered in December 1942. Those who survived in the forests joined partisan activities. A group of Jews from Slonim became active members of the Schorr's partisan unit. In the struggle against the Germans they reached the swamps of the Pinsk area. On July 10, 1944, when the city was taken by Soviet forces, only 80 Jews were found there. Former Jewish partisans joined the Soviet army to continue the fighting against the Germans until the end of the war. In 1946 there were about 30 Jews living in Slonim.

BIBLIOGRAPHY: *Regesty i nadpisi*, 1 (1899), 203, 473; Halpern, Pinkas, index; S. Dubnow (ed.), *Pinkas ha-Medinah* (1922), index; *Pinkas Slonim*, 2 vols. (Heb. and Yid., 1962); I. Schiper, *Dzieje handlu żydowskiego na ziemiach polskich* (1937), index; H. Korobkov, in: *Yevreyskaya Starina* (1910), 23–24; A.S. Kamenetski, in: *Perezhitoye*, 4 (1913), 311; B. Wasiutyński, *Ludność żydowska w Polsce w wiekach XIX i XX* (1930), 80, 82, 84, 91, 202; J.S. Hertz, *Geshikhte fun Bund*, 2 (1962), 129; *Haynt* (July 25, 1939); M.A. Shulwass, in: *Beit Yisrael be-Polin*, 2 (1953), 13–35; *Yahadut Lita*, 3 (1967), index.

[Aharon Weiss]

SLONIM, ḥasidic dynasty. The founder of the dynasty was R. ABRAHAM BEN ISAAC MATTATHIAS WEINBERG (1804–1883) who, after heading the yeshivah in Slonim, became a Ḥasid. His teachers in Ḥasidism were the *ẓaddikim* Noah of Lachowicze (*Lyakhovichi) and Moses of *Kobrin. When Moses died, Abraham assumed the role of *ẓaddik* and became one of the leading rabbis of his time. His influence extended mainly throughout the northwestern part of the province of Polesie, Poland-Lithuania, between the cities of Slonim and Brest-Litovsk and between Kobrin and Baranovichi. Abraham's writings include *Ḥesed le-Avraham* (1886) and *Yesod ha-Avodah* (1892). His works, which include principles of his ḥasidic teachings, attest great scholarship. He advocated the study of Torah for its own sake, prayer with devotion (*devekut*), love and fear of the Creator, humility and confidence. He saw asceticism and mourning as ways of repentance. He also wrote a homiletic commentary on *Mekhilta*, entitled *Be'er Avraham* (1927). During Abraham's lifetime, his grandson NOAH (d. 1927) emigrated to Ereẓ Israel and settled in Tiberias, where Slonim Ḥasidim found a special place in the history of Ḥasidism in Ereẓ Israel from the late 19th century. The letters of the rabbis of Slonim to their fellow Ḥasidim in Ereẓ Israel were included in their writings. Abraham's disciple Menahem Nahum Epstein established his own dynasty of *ẓaddikim* in Bialystok. Another grandson, SAMUEL (d. 1916), succeeded Abraham as rabbi and excelled in strengthening religious life and institutions as well as in collecting funds for the Jewish community in Ereẓ Israel. Under Samuel, the Slonim dynasty became famous beyond its own circles for its special ḥasidic melodies. Samuel's teachings were incorporated in the works of his Ḥasidim, *Kunteres Kitvei Kodesh* (1948), *Kunteres Beit Avraham* (5 vols., 1950–54), and *Beit Avraham* (1958). After Samuel's death, a split occurred among the Slonim Ḥasidim. The majority chose as their leader Samuel's younger son, ABRAHAM (II; d. 1933), who lived in Bialystok and later in Baranovichi. In 1918 Abraham II established a major yeshivah in Baranovichi called Torat Ḥesed, where Lithuanian-Jewish scholarship and Ḥasidism were combined. Abraham made journeys to Palestine to visit his ḥasidic following there (1929, 1933). His teachings on the weekly portion of the Torah were published by his Ḥasidim in the *Beit Avraham*, mentioned above. His successor in Baranovichi was his son SOLOMON, who perished in the Holocaust in 1943 with many of his fellow Ḥasidim. His teachings and letters were published in the *Zikhron Kadosh* (1967). Meanwhile, in Slonim itself, Samuel's eldest son, ISSACHAR ARYEH (d. 1928), inherited his father's position. On Issachar's death his son ABRAHAM succeeded him and emigrated to Palestine in 1935, but did not serve as *admor*. In 1942, the Slonim Ḥasidim in Jerusalem established Yeshivat Slonim Beit Avraham. In 1955 the Slonim Ḥasidim elected ABRAHAM (III), the son of Noah (mentioned above), who had immigrated to Ereẓ Israel in his youth, as their *admor*.

BIBLIOGRAPHY: K. Lichtenstein, in: *Pinkas Slonim*, 1 (1921), 48, 58–61, 87, 124, 128–9, 159–60, 178, 217, 231, 243; W.Z. Rabinowitsch, *Lithuanian Ḥasidism* (1970).

[Wolf Zeev Rabinowitsch]

SLONIM, MARC (Marc Lvovich; 1894–1976), literary scholar. A member of the 1917 Russian Constituent Assembly, Slonim later moved to Prague, where he edited an émigré periodical (1922–32), and settled in the U.S. in 1941. He taught at Sarah Lawrence College, Bronxville, from 1943 onward, becoming the director of foreign studies there in 1962 and European consultant for foreign studies in 1968. His works include *The Epic of Russian Literature…* (1950), *Modern Russian Literature from Chekhov to the Present* (1953), and *Soviet Literature* (1964, 1967).

SLONIM, REUBEN (1914–2000), Canadian rabbi and journalist. Slonim was born in Winnipeg. After his immigrant father suffered a stroke, Slonim's mother was left to tend to her husband and three children. She and her children boarded at Jewish Orphanage and Children's Aid of Western Canada, where she was the cook. In his memoir *Grand to Be an Orphan* (1983), Slonim recalled that while the Orphanage offered educational opportunities, some of the staff also dished out beatings. With Orphanage support, Slonim studied at a yeshivah in Chicago and attended the Illinois Institute of Technology, where he received his B.S.A.S. in 1933. He then attended the Jewish Theological Seminary, where he was ordained and earned an M.H.L. in 1937. He also attended the Albany Law School, New York, between 1935 and 1937. In 1937 he became rabbi at Toronto's McCaul Street Synagogue, one of the first Canadian-born rabbis to serve a Conservative congregation, and he remained there for three years. For the next seven years he occupied pulpits in Cleveland and Troy (N.Y.) before returning to Toronto in 1947 to serve the McCaul Street Synagogue until its 1955 merger with the University Avenue Synagogue. He was not named to the senior position in the newly established Beth Tzedec Congregation.

Slonim held a variety of community positions, including president of the Toronto Zionist Council (1947–52) and chair of the Synagogue Council State of Israel Bonds (1955–60). Slonim grew angry, however, over the policies of the State of Israel and what he perceived as the uncritical support of Israel within the Jewish community. And to the horror of the Jewish community, he had a vehicle in which to express his views. In 1955 *The Toronto Telegram* hired Slonim as associate editor on the Middle East. Until the newspaper's demise in 1971 and later in the *Jewish Standard*, Slonim often attacked Orthodox influence on Israeli politics and Israel's treatment of Palestinians. He also championed Israeli withdrawal from occupied territories and strongly opposed the 1982 Lebanon war.

In 1971, Slonim was hired by a small and unaffiliated liberal Toronto congregation, Congregation Habonim, established in the spirit of German Liberal Judaism, by central European Holocaust survivors. Slonim attracted younger, Canadian-born congregants but, to the consternation of some, he also used his pulpit to condemn Israeli policy. After the war in Lebanon, he was dismissed. He described his time as a pulpit rabbi in *To Kill a Rabbi* (1987). He subsequently co-founded the Association for the Living Jewish Spirit, which until 1999 met on High Holidays.

Towards the end of his life, Slonim received belated recognition from the Jewish community. Rabbi Gunther *Plaut, who had often been at loggerheads with Slonim, later admitted that Slonim was unjustly ostracized by the Jewish community and regretted his own part in the process. In 1998, the Jewish Theological Seminary honored Slonim for his years of service.

In addition to his two memoirs, Slonim published *In the Steps of Pope Paul* (1965), an account of Pope Paul's visit to the Middle East; *Both Sides Now* (1972) summarizing his career at the *Toronto Telegram*, and *Family Quarrel: The United Church and the Jews* (1977) chronicling disputes over Israel between the Jewish community and the United Church.

BIBLIOGRAPHY: *Who's Who in Canadian Jewry* (1965), 411; L. Levendel, *A Century of the Canadian Jewish Press, 1880s–1980s* (1989); G. Plaut, Obituary, in: *Globe and Mail* (April 13, 2000); H. Genizi, *The Holocaust, Israel and the Canadian Protestant Churches* (2002).

[Richard Menkis (2nd ed.)]

SLONIMSKI, ANTONI (1895–1976), Polish poet, author, and critic. The son of a converted Warsaw physician and grandson of the Hebrew writer Ḥayyim Selig *Slonimski, Slonimski began his literary career during World War I, publishing his early *Sonety* and founding the "Pikador" group of poets in 1918. From the early 1920s he rose rapidly to become the leading personality in Poland's literary and cultural life, a master of the verse form and a keen and versatile drama critic. In 1920 he was the cofounder with Julian *Tuwim of the futurist "Skamander" group, and during the years 1924–39 wrote the leading theater reviews for the weekly *Wiadomości Literackie*, also contributing a regular satirical column from 1927. Slonimski published more than 40 books, including verse collections. He became a major focus of Polish intellectual interest in the 1930s, and also translated many foreign classics (Rimbaud, Mark Twain, Itzik *Manger). In 1939 he fled to England by way of Paris and during the years 1947–48 was head of UNESCO's literary section, subsequently directing the Polish Cultural Institute in London (1949–51). His verse that appeared during the war years included *Alarm* (1940) and *Popiół i wiatr* ("Ashes and Wind," 1942).

In the prewar Poland of Marshal Pilsudski, Slonimski trenchantly satirized bourgeois ignorance and stupidity and spurious racial and social theories. Though rehabilitated as chairman of the Polish Writers' Union (1956–59), he remained a nonconformist in postwar Communist Poland, preferring silence to any compromise with a totalitarian regime. His works and his personal stand exemplified the intellectual's independence and freedom of thought. Though raised as a Christian, Slonimski had a profound emotional regard for the Jewish people, which may be detected in poems such as his *Pieśń o Januszu Korczaku* ("Song about Janusz Korczak"), *Ahaswer* (on the Wandering Jew), and *Elegja miasteczek zydowskich* ("Elegy of the Shtetlakh"). Israel's War of Independence had wide repercussions in his poetry, and in 1967 Slonimski condemned those calling for Israel's destruction during the period preceding the Six-Day War.

BIBLIOGRAPHY: A. Kowalczykowa, *Linyki Słonimskiego 1918–1935* (1967); J. Slawiński, in: Twórczośí, 13:8 (1957), 79–105; A. Sandauer, *Poeci trzech pokoleń* (1962²); J. Kwiatkowski, *Szkice de portretów* (1960); *Wielka Encyklopedia Powszechna*, 10 (1967), 590.

[Stanislaw Wygodzki and Moshe Altbauer]

SLONIMSKI, ḤAYYIM SELIG (1810–1904), Hebrew popular science writer and editor. He also used the pseudonym Ḥazas (the Hebrew initials of his name). Born in Bialystok, he wrote popular science articles during the Haskalah period. His initial acquaintance with science was derived from old Hebrew books, but later he also read scientific literature in German. In 1834, he published the first part of his mathematics textbook entitled *Mosedei Ḥokhmah* ("Bases of Wisdom"). Halley's Comet appeared in the following year, and Slonimski wrote a popular work on astronomy, *Kokhva de-Shavit* ("Comet," 1835, 1857^2). He wrote another book on the same subject entitled *Toledot ha-Shamayim* ("The History of the Skies," 1838, 1866^2), which caused great controversy, because it demonstrated errors in the Hebrew calendar. Slonimski also explained his views on the Hebrew calendar in *Yesodei ha-Ibbur* ("Basic Intercalation," 1852, one part only; completed in 1853, 1883^3). His later works include *Meẓi'ut ha-Nefesh ve-Kiyyumah Ḥuẓ la-Guf* ("The Existence of the Soul and its Life Outside the Body," 1852), and *Yesodei Ḥokhmat ha-Shi'ur* ("Foundations of the Science of Calculation," 1865, 1899^2). Slonimski coined new Hebrew terminology where necessary. Some of his mathematical and astronomical interpretations of obscure passages in the Mishnah found their way into editions of the Mishnah printed in Zhitomir.

Slonimski was also an inventor. Among his inventions was a calculating machine, for which he was awarded a prize by the Russian Academy of Sciences (1844). In 1862, Slonimski founded **Ha-Ẓefirah*, a Hebrew newspaper devoted mainly to popular science articles written by himself and a team of collaborators, adherents of the Haskalah. The paper ceased publication after only a few months, upon Slonimski's appointment as inspector of the Government Rabbinical Seminary in Zhitomir and Hebrew censor for South Russia. In 1874, when the Seminary was closed down, he renewed publication of *Ha-Ẓefirah*, first in Berlin and, from 1875, in Warsaw. The periodical was edited in the moderate spirit of the Haskalah, avoiding conflicts with the Orthodox by presenting scientific innovations in a manner acceptable to them.

In 1884, Slonimski's disciples and admirers celebrated the 50th anniversary of his literary career, and two collections of his articles appeared under the title *Ma'amarei Ḥokhmah* ("Essays of Wisdom," 1891–94). In 1886, when *Ha-Ẓefirah* began appearing daily, Nahum *Sokolow joined the editorial board and, in effect, took over the editorship, though Slonimski continued to contribute articles. A list of his articles appeared in *Ha-Ẓefirah*, 14:91 (1887), 5–6. Slonimski's son Leonid *Slonimski converted to Christianity. Many of his grandchildren achieved distinction. Antoni *Slonimski, son of Stanislaw, was a well-known Polish poet; Alexander, a literary critic, Mikhail *Slonimski, a writer, Nicolas, a composer, and Henry *Slonimsky, a scholar.

BIBLIOGRAPHY: Klausner, Sifrut, 4 (1953), 123–5, 130–1; Akavia, in: *Davar Yearbook* (Heb., 1955), 387–96; Kressel, Leksikon, 2 (1967), 504–7; *Kol Kitvei Frishman*, 2 (1920), 21–27; N. Sokolow, *Ishim* (1958), 135–52; Waxman, Literature, 3 (1960), 331, 345; 4 (1960), 437.

[Yehuda Slutsky]

SLONIMSKI, LEONID ZINOVYEVICH (1850–1918), lawyer and publicist; son of Ḥayyim Selig *Slonimski, he was born in Zhitomir and graduated from the faculty of law of Kiev University in 1872. He settled in St. Petersburg and converted to the Greek Orthodox religion. He was a regular contributor of legal and sociological articles to Russian and international periodicals. From 1882 he was member of the editorial board of the liberal journal *Vestnik Yevropy*. Slonimski wrote on the juridical situation of Jews in Russia and abroad (*Yevreyskaya Biblioteka*, vol. 6, 1877), and dealt with the Jewish problem in many of his general articles. In 1906 he published a text of the Russian constitution, with a preface which caused its official suppression. Slonimski criticized the teachings of Karl Marx in his work *Ekonomicheskoye ucheniye Karla Marksa* (1898). His son ALEXANDER SLONIMSKI (1881–?) was a critic and novelist. He edited the authoritative editions of Pushkin's work. His son NICOLAS *SLONIMSKY was an American musicologist, conductor, and composer. Another son, Mikhail *Slonimski, was a distinguished Russian-Soviet writer.

BIBLIOGRAPHY: Ginzburg, *Historishe Verk*, 2 (1937), 266.

SLONIMSKI, MIKHAIL LEONIDOVICH (1897–1972), Soviet Russian author and critic. Born in Pavlovsk, of a prominent, highly assimilated family, Slonimski was the son of Leonid *Slonimski, nephew of the literary historian Semyon Vengerov, and a cousin of the famous Polish poet Antoni *Slonimski. He was one of the founders of the Serapion Brothers, a loose association of writers that came into being in 1921 for the purpose of protecting the autonomy of a literature already threatened by political pressures.

Slonimski's best work was written early in his career. In addition to some investigations of literary theory, this includes *Shestoy strelkovy* ("The Sixth Rifles," 1922), a collection of tales about the senseless horror of war and the Revolution; the autobiographical novel *Lavrovy* ("The Lavrovs," 1927), which portrays a young man who breaks with his petty, ineffectual, and selfish family to join the Revolutionary cause; and its less successful sequel, *Foma Kleshnyov* (1930). In 1949, at the height of the Stalinist terror, Slonimski published *Pervye gody* ("First Years"), a revised and more militantly Communist version of Lavrovy.

[Maurice Friedberg]

SLONIMSKY, HENRY (1884–1970), philosopher and writer, who was born in Russia, and was taken to the United States in 1890. He studied under Hermann *Cohen and earned his Ph.D. in 1912 with a dissertation published as "*Heraklit und Parmenides*" (in: *Philosophische Arbeiten*, 7 (1913), ed. by H. Cohen and P. Natorp). From 1914 to 1924 he taught philosophy at various U.S. universities. In 1924, Stephen S. *Wise appointed him professor of ethics and philosophy of religion at the Jewish Institute of Religion in New York. In 1926 he became dean of the school, retiring in 1952. As an inspiring teacher, who shared his intellectual and human problems with his students, he profoundly influenced many American rabbis. His studies in Jewish philosophy were published as *Essays* (1967). Despite Slonimsky's lifelong emphasis on "oral teaching," it is possible to see the thrust of his thinking from his sparse writings. On the face of it, his concern with human needs and emotions would seem to separate him from his great teacher H. Cohen, the rationalist par excellence, but on closer consideration the latter's decisive and pervasive influence becomes clear. The importance Slonimsky attaches to the Platonic tradition in the history of human thinking, his wariness of the "bourgeois" dangers to the Jewish truth, and his reinterpretations of episodes in general and Jewish philosophy exemplify the spirit of the "Marburg School." His single most important doctrine, that of the "humanized," finite, growing (i.e., anthropomorphic) God, had three constituent considerations: (1) the idea of a "limited God" explains the dysteleology of human suffering; (2) man's ethical responsibilities are greatly enhanced when they are needed for the "growth of God" (cf. Cohen's "correlation"); (3) the Jewish formulation of Kant's "asymptotic" concept of the ideal is echoed in Slonimsky's commitment to messianism, God and "religion of the future."

[Steven S. Schwarzschild]

SLONIMSKY, NICOLAS (1894–1995), musicologist, lexicographer, composer, and conductor. Born in St. Petersburg, Slonimsky was the son of Leonid *Slonimski and grandson of Ḥayyim Zelig *Slonimski. He studied at the St. Petersburg Conservatory (piano with Vengerova, his aunt, and composition with Kalafaty and Shteinberg). He went to the United States in 1923 and worked as opera coach at the Eastman School of Music in Rochester, New York (1923–25), and as secretary to Serge *Koussevitzky (1925–27). He founded and conducted the Chamber Orchestra of Boston from 1927 to 1934; he also conducted the Harvard University Orchestra (1927–30). Slonimsky was a lecturer at Colorado College (1940, 1947–49), Peabody Conservatory (1956–57), and UCLA (1964–67). He became a champion of modern American music, which he presented on lecture and performance tours. He edited the 4th to 7th editions of *Thompson's International Cyclopedia of Music and Musicians* (1946, 1949, 1952, 1956) and the 5th edition of *Baker's Biographical Dictionary of Musicians* (1958, re-issued with supplements in 1964 and in 1971). His writings include *Music since 1900* (1937), *Music of Latin America* (1945), *Thesaurus of Scales and Melodic Patterns* (1947), and *A Lexicon of Musical Invective* (1953) as well as a number of scholarly articles. He composed a number of works, some of them frankly tongue-in-cheek, such as *Moebius Strip Tease* (1965).

BIBLIOGRAPHY: NG²; R. Kostelanetz, "Conversation with Nicolas Slonimsky about his Composing," in: *Music Quarterly*, 74 (1990), 458–72; R. Stevenson: "Nicolas Slonimsky: Centenarian Lexicographer and Musicologist," in: *Inter-American Music Review*, 14 (1994), 149–55.

[Marina Rizarev (2nd ed.)]

SLONIMSKY, SERGEI MIKHAILOVICH (1932–), Russian composer, pianist, and musicologist, son of the writer Mikhail *Slonimski and nephew of Nicolas *Slonimsky. Slonimsky was born in St. Petersburg and studied composition (at the age of 11) with Shebalin (in Moscow from 1943 to 1945) and later with Volfenson, Evlakhov, and Arapov in St. Petersburg, as well as piano with Nilsen. He graduated from the St. Petersburg Conservatory in 1956, where he taught composition and became professor in 1976. The music of Mussorgsky and Prokofiev influenced Slominsky, yet he developed his own idiom based on Russian folklore, which he articulated in his works in a variety of compositional techniques.

Among his works are the operas *Virinea* (1967), *The Master and Margarita* (1972), *Maria Stuart* (1983), *Hamlet* (1990), and *Ivan the Terrible* (1998), the ballet *Icarus* (1970), ten symphonies (1958–92), instrumental concertos, symphonic chamber works, vocal and choral pieces in many genres, and music for the theater and cinema. As a musicologist, he wrote *Simfonii Prokofieva* (1964, based on his Ph.D. thesis) and essays on Mahler, Stravinsky, Shostakovich, Balakirev, and Russian folklore. A volume of his reviews and memoirs, *Burleski, elegii, difiramby v presrennoy prose* ("Burlesques, Elegies, Dithyrambs in Contemptible Prose"), was published in 2000. He also devoted his energies to the revival of music by forgotten composers of previous generations. His creative work inspired unusually rich musicological research.

BIBLIOGRAPHY: A. Milka: *Sergey Slonimsky* (1976); M. Rytsareva (Ritzarev): *Kompozitor Sergey Slonimsky* (1991); L. Gavrilova: *"Ivan Grozny" Sergeya Slonimskogo* (2000); M. Ritzarev: "Sergei Slonimsky and Russian 'Unofficial Nationalism' of the 1960–80s," in: *Schostakovitsch und die Folgen: Russische Music zwischen Anpassung und Protest* (E. Kuhn, J. Nemtsov, and A. Wehrmeyer, eds.) (2003), 187–210.

[Marina Rizarev (2nd ed.)]

SLOSS, MARCUS CAUFFMAN (1869–1958), U.S. lawyer and jurist. Sloss, who was born in New York City, practiced law in San Francisco. He was elected superior court judge for San Francisco city and county in 1900. In 1906 Sloss was appointed to fill a vacancy on the California Supreme Court and was then elected presiding judge of that court in the same year. Reelected in 1910 and 1918, he resigned the judgeship in 1919 to return to private law practice.

Extremely active in Jewish affairs, Sloss served as president of the Jewish National Welfare Fund of San Francisco and the Pacific Hebrew Orphan Asylum and Home Society, was associated with the Joint Distribution Committee, and was active in the American Jewish Committee. In other public affairs, Sloss was a member of the California Board of Bar Examiners, a trustee of Stanford University, and a board member of the San Francisco Public Library.

SLOTKI, ISRAEL WOLF (1884–1973), scholar and educator. He was born in Jerusalem and went to England in 1906, living first in London and later in Manchester. There he served as principal of the Talmud Torah school (1911–50) and later as director of Jewish education for Manchester (1946–50). He organized the first conference of religious Zionists in England (1918) and was secretary of the Mizrachi Center of the United Kingdom (1926–28). His publications include studies of ancient Hebrew poetry, annotated translations of 16 tractates of the Talmud (Soncino Press), commentaries and introductions to three books of the Bible, books on local Jewish history, and many contributions to scholarly periodicals. His son, JUDAH JACOB SLOTKI (1903–1988), also born in Jerusalem, arrived in England as a boy. He was superintendent of Jewish education in Manchester (1942–46), director of Jewish education in Leeds (1946–55), and from 1955 director of the Central Board of Hebrew Education in Manchester. In 1956 he established the S.H. Steinhart Training College for Hebrew teachers. From 1959 he was a vice president of the British Mizrachi Federation. He published translations of part of the *Midrash Rabbah* (Soncino Press) and of five books of the Bible, works for Jewish children, and a biography of Manasseh Ben Israel. His edited edition of *The Babylonian Talmud* was published in 1990.

[Godfrey Edmond Silverman]

SLOUSCHZ, NAHUM (1871–1966), scholar and writer, archaeologist and historian, traveler and translator. Born in Smorgan near Vilna, son of David Solomon Slouschz, rabbi, *maskil*, and early Zionist, Slouschz was taken as a child to Odessa. Odessa became the center of the Ḥovevei Zion movement and of the Hebrew renascence, and Slouschz took an active part in those political and cultural activities. He sided with Aḥad Ha-Am's critics and early became a political as well as a practical Zionist. He wrote on a variety of subjects for the Hebrew press both in Russia and in Ereẓ Israel, and for a time edited a Russian-Jewish paper, *Odesskaya Gazeta* (1897).

He visited Ereẓ Israel for a year in 1891 on behalf of the Odessa Palestine committee with a view to establishing a new settlement, then returned for a year in 1896. Slouschz then went to Geneva, where he studied classical and French literature. Here too he was active as a Zionist and was among the founders of the Swiss Zionist Federation. He was an early follower of Herzl, but in the wake of the *Uganda affair he joined for a time the Jewish Territorial Organization (see *Territorialism), investigating the possibilities of Jewish settlement in *Tripoli-Cyrenaica, which he visited (see his confidential report, translated by P.H. Magnus, 1907).

From Geneva Slouschz proceeded to Paris to study Semitics at the Ecole des Hautes Etudes and French literature at the Sorbonne. He published *Renaissance de la littérature hébraïque, 1743–1885* (1902), which was translated into English by H. *Szold (1909); *Poésie lyrique hébraïque contemporaine* (1911); *David Frischmann – poète* (1914); and *Poésies hébraïques de Don Jehouda Abrabanel* (1928).

In 1904 Slouschz was appointed to a newly founded chair of Hebrew language and literature at the Sorbonne. He also taught (1903–18) at the Ecole Normale Orientale of the Alliance Israélite Universelle. Between 1906 and 1914 he undertook a series of exploratory journeys on behalf of the Académie des Inscriptions et Belles Lettres to North Africa, where he studied Phoenician and Greek inscriptions, and also the life and history of the Jewish communities of the region.

The results were published under the following titles: *Etude sur l'histoire des Juifs et du Judaïsme au Maroc* (2 vols., 1906), *Hebréo-Phéniciens et Judéo-Berbères* (1908), *Hebréo-Phéniciens…* (1909), *Judéo-Hellènes et Judéo-Berbères* (1909), *Tefuẓot Yisrael be-Afrikah ha-Ẓefonit* ("Jewish Dispersion in North Africa," 1947), *Oẓar ha-Ketovot ha-Finikiyyot* ("Thesaurus of Phoenician Inscriptions," 1942). Slouschz also co-edited the *Corpus Inscriptionum Semiticarum* (1881–1935) and *La Revue du Monde Musulman*. He described his travels in a number of books: *Massa be-Miẓrayim* (1907), *Voyages d'études juives en Afrique* (1909), *Be-Iyyei ha-Yam* (1919), *Travels in North Africa* (1927; also as *Jews of North Africa*, 1944), and *Sefer ha-Massa'ot* (2 vols., 1942–43). He wrote, too, on the Jews of *Djerba (*Ha-I Palya*, 1957; *Ha-Kohanim Asher be-Jerba*, 1924); on an ancient Jewish queen in the Atlas Mountains (*Dahiyah al-Kahina*, 1934, 1953); and on the Marranos of Portugal (*Ha-Anusim be-Portugal*, 1932).

During World War I Slouschz was involved in activities to influence the French government in agreeing to the *Balfour Declaration, and he visited the United States in the same cause. While in New York he contributed to the Hebrew and Yiddish press, and acted as editor of the *Jewish Morning Journal*. In 1919 Slouschz settled in Ereẓ Israel, where he revived the Palestine Exploration Society and edited its publications. He conducted excavations at Tiberias, where he discovered the ancient second-century synagogue of Ḥammath (mentioned in the Talmud), including a beautiful stone *menorah* (*Ha-Ḥafirot be-Ḥammat shel Teveryah*, 1921). He also excavated at Absalom's Tomb in Jerusalem and began to excavate in Transjordan (*Ever ha-Yarden*, 2 vols., 1933).

In his early years Slouschz translated works by the Italian writer Paulo Montegazza, and during his years in Paris, a number of French writers, into Hebrew: Emile Zola (stories, and also a biography, 1899); Guy de Maupassant (with biography, 7 vols., 1903–04); and *Salammbô* by Flaubert (1922). A collection of his writings appeared under the title *Ketavim Nivḥarim* (2 vols., 1938–43).

BIBLIOGRAPHY: A.R. Malachi, in: JBA, 2 (1943), Hebrew section, 30–33; *Sifriyyat Rishonim*, ed by J. Churgin, 2:5 (1947), incl. bibl.; Kressel, Leksikon, 2 (1967), 510–2, incl. bibl.; P. Azai, in: *Haaretz* (Dec. 7, 1966).

SLOVAKIA (Slov. **Slovensko**; Ger. **Slowakei**; Hung. **Szlovákia**), Central European republic; 1918–1993, part of *Czechoslovakia; formerly a part of *Hungary. Since Slovakia was part of Hungary for almost 1,000 years, the annals of the Jews of this region were submerged in the history of the Jews of Greater Hungary. The Jews of Slovakia (termed "Upper Hungary," "Northern Hungary," or "Highland") were commonly called "Highland Jews" (*Oberlaender*).

Jews appeared for the first time on the territory of contemporary Slovakia in the Roman fortification of the first century C.E. (limes) in the southwest, along the Danube River. This was several hundred years before the appearance of the Slavonic tribes in the region. These Jews might have been slaves, tradesmen, or soldiers serving in the Roman Legions. In archaeological excavations of the fortifications, Jewish artifacts were discovered. The next possible appearance of Jews in the region might have been in the seventh century C.E. when a Frank tradesman named Samo (Samuel?) unified the Slavonic tribes against the Mongol Avars in 623–624. In the ninth century C.E., the first political bodies of the western Slavs were established. It seems that Jews had settled in municipal locations of the so-called Great Moravian Empire. These Jews might have been related to Jewish-Arabic tradesmen who wandered between Mesopotamia and Eastern Europe. The next significant Jewish appearance took place in the 10th century, when Jewish Khazar tribes accompanied the Magyar tribes that conquered the region. There is written evidence as well as that of names of localities along the Nitra River.

Jewish settlements, in both urban and rural locations, continued to appear in southwestern and western upper Hungary. A further influx of Jewish settlers, who came along the trade routes from Germany and perhaps the Balkans, established themselves in Greater Hungary. Papal and Magyar royal legislation testified to Jewish existence in ancient Hungary. In the territory of upper Hungary, they lived along the lower Hron, Vag, and Nitra rivers, as well as the Danube. By the end of the 11th century, they experienced severe persecutions, particularly during the First Crusade, which crossed the region. Most hard hit were the Jews of Bratislava (former Slovak name Presporok; Pressburg in German; Pozsony in Hungarian).

Sporadic references to the existence of Jews in the region are found from the mid-13th century. Official contemporary documents and rabbinical literature record a number of flourishing Jewish communities in Pressburg, Senica (Szenice), Trnva (Tyrnauo, in German; Nagyszombat in Hungarian); Nitra (Nyitra in Hungarian); Pezinok (Hung. Bazin); and Trencin (Trenteschin in German; Trencsén in Hungarian.) In the Pressburg (Bratislava) community alone in the 14th century there were 800 Jews, forming an autonomous political unit headed by a communal leader. Some of the Jews of this region engaged in agriculture and owned and cultivated vineyards, but the majority engaged in commerce and moneylending.

After the Tartar (Mongol) invasion of 1241, which left behind a devastated land, the ruling dynasty invited foreign settlers, including Jews, to rebuild the country. Again Jewish communities established themselves, frequently at the same location as the earlier ones. But their life was not tranquil, and in 1360 the Jews of Kosice (Kaschau in German; Kassa in Hungarian) were expelled from the city in 1494. Several Jews of Trnava were burnt at the stake because of a blood libel; the same happened in Pezinok in 1529. Local incidents occurred from time to time. A rigorous wave of persecution followed the defeat at Mohacs in 1526, where the Ottomans annihilated the army of the Magyar kingdom. Jews were expelled from towns and could live only in villages and places where they were admitted by the local nobles. In time, the nobles' willingness to accept Jews increased. Aware of the Jews' contribution to the economy, they would settle them on their estates and granted land for synagogues and cemeteries. They granted certain privileges in exchange for hefty taxes and the promotion of trade and industry. Jewish life began to flourish again in western and southern upper Hungary, where Jews expelled from Austria and Germany settled, augmented by Czech and Moravian Jewish settlers. There were large numbers of Jews in the northern part of upper Hungary which, in the 17th and 18th centuries, was known as "Magyar Israel." Many of these Jews were refugees from the atrocities of the Ukrainian Hetman Bogdan *Chmielnicki and the outrages of the *Haidamaks in Poland.

According to the 1785 census, the Pressburg community was the largest in Hungary, second to Nové Mesto nad Váhom (Waagneustadtl in German; Vágúhely in Hungarian). Trade routes, and in particular the movement of wine merchants from Hungary to Poland, helped promote Jewish life in eastern upper Hungary and Carpatho-Rus. From the 17th century, there was in increase in the influx of Moravian Jews seeking a haven from the Kurutz riots (1683), the residence restrictions, and the Familiants Law (1726). The majority of the newcomers settled in the western districts, bordering on Moravia, in places like Holic, Senica, Myjava, Nové Mesto nad Vahom, Tarencin, and Nitra. For many decades they preserved their old traditions, maintaining close spiritual and commercial ties with their kinsmen beyond the border. They even continued for some time to pay taxes to their former Moravian communities and to bury their dead there. Their synagogues were built on the models of those in Moravia, and services were conducted according to the Moravian rites. Youngsters from upper Hungary flocked to the Nikulov (Nikolsburg), Prostejov, and Boskovice *talmud torah* schools, and those from Moravia frequented the famous Pressburg and Vrbova yeshivot. Eventually, they started to establish their own centers of learning, such as Brezova pod Bradlom and Puchov. These were later replaced by wealthier communities or those with local importance. The Huncovce (Unsforf in German; Hunfalva in Hungarian) yeshivah served the Jews of north and east upper Hungary, the Dunajska Streda (Dunaszerdahely in Hungarian) and Galanta yeshivot served the center and southern Jewish population. Those three, along with the leading yeshivah of Pressburg, became the four leading yeshivot of upper Hungary. The leader was the yeshivah of Pressburg, which had been in existence since 1700, and was subsequently recognized by the government as an institution for the education of rabbis. It became particularly prominent through the influence of R. Moses Schreiber-*Sofer, whose descendants officiated for generations as rabbis of Pressburg and other towns. The yeshivah drew students from all over Europe.

The landlords of those regions – the Hungarian counts Palffy, Eszterhazy, Pongracz, etc. – welcomed Moravian Jews, most of whom were industrious merchants and craftsmen who helped to develop their estates and foster trade with neighboring countries. They granted them protection and, in some cases, even erected synagogues and contributed land for cemeteries. But the Jews were only slowly incorporated into the life of the region. In 1831 a cholera epidemic resulted in anti-Jewish riots in eastern Slovakia. The Jews were accused of having poisoned wells and causing the plague. During the Spring of Nations (1848–49), riots took place in many locations in western and central Slovakia. Many Jews enlisted to defend the Magyar Revolution by serving in the army. Some Jews joined the Slovak forces, defending Slovak national interests. During the Tisza Eszlar outrages, there were pogroms in upper Hungary (1882, 1883) as well. They were repeated when the Reception Law was accepted by the Hungarian parliament in 1896.

From the mid-18th century, a schism developed among Hungarian Jewry. While the Orthodox asked to preserve their centuries-long religious traditions, others promoted reforms (in local parlance, *Neologs). The schism led to the convocation of the Hungarian General Jewish Congress (1868–69) (see *Hungary), after which the communities split into three main congregations: Orthodox, Neolog, and Status Quo Ante.

With the establishment of the dual monarchy of Austria-Hungary in 1867, the Hungarian parliament passed the Emancipation Law the same year. The main aim of Hungarian domestic policy was assimilation of the minorities. To this end, Magyar became the official language of instruction and public administration. This "Magyarization" brought about a considerable amount of assimilation, especially among well-to-do middle-class Jews, who began to gravitate politically and culturally toward Budapest instead of Vienna. The liberal Hungarian authorities encouraged Jewish cooperation in the development of local industry, commerce, and finance. Jews began to be prominent in the free professions, such as education and journalism. The political economist Eduard (Ede) Horn of Nové Mesto nad Váhom became undersecretary at the Ministry of Commerce, the first Jew to rise to such a position in Hungary. While being a member of the Hungarian Parliament, Horn defended the interests of the Slovaks, thus promoting Jewish-Slovak understanding.

But the Slovak-Jewish understanding was a difficult affair, as the Magyars encouraged assimilation of the Jews into Magyar culture and policies, and encouraged their participation in the Magyarization drive of the authorities. Many Jews, in particular inhabitants of larger cities, the well-to-do, and those affiliated with Neology, actively supported Magyar nationalist interests. Thus they clashed with the Slovak nationalists. During the second half of the 19th century, Slovak nationalism increased. Attempts of some Slovak leaders to foster an understanding with Jews living in the territory were unsuccessful. This was exacerbated by the fact that several Slovak leaders, beginning with Ludovit Stur (1815–56), took a severe anti-Jewish stand, and the national poet Svetozar Hurban-Vajansky (1847–1916) was a racist. Many of these leaders were Lutherans, who represented the young but developing bourgeoisie. The nationalistic feelings of members of a religious minority merged with clashing economic interests. The Lutherans, sensing the pressure of the Catholic Church, wanted to cement their position in Slovak society. Thus the Slovak literati, many of them Lutherans, promoted Judeophobia in the land, which naturally added to the hostility toward the Magyarization. Soon the Lutherans were joined by the Catholics. Here the clergy, partially Magyarized, waved the first banners of Judeophobia. With the expansion of nationalism within the Catholic public, it took a leaf from the Protestant books and combined nationalism with antisemitism. Significantly, Jews from nationalistic cities, particularly the rural countryside, were less affected by Magyarization, and there were cases of Jewish-Slovak understanding. Immigrants from Galicia who flocked in particular to eastern Slovakia after the annexation of part of Polagdon by the Habsburg Monarchy (1771), not familiar with local conditions and needing to establish themselves economically, contributed much toward the hatred of Jews. An open campaign was conducted in the Hungarian parliament (see *Istóczy affair), and anti-Jewish riots took place in a number of towns (1882, 1883). The Reception Law (1896), which placed the Jewish religion on an equal standing with the Christian religion, gave rise to the foundation of the Slovak Clerical People's Party, whose basic tenets were anti-Liberalism and the struggle against Jewish influence, and became a major factor in spreading antisemitism among the devout Catholic population. The rise of Slovak nationalism at the end of the 19th century coincided with the beginning of Zionism; of the 13 local Zionist groups established in Hungary subsequent to the First Zionist Congress, eight were in Slovakia (Bratislava, Nitra, *Presov, *Kosice, Kezmarok, *Dolni Kubin and *Banska Bystrica). Moreover, Bratislava was the site of the first Hungarian Zionist Convention, held in 1903, as well as of the first World *Mizrachi Congress (1904). However, Zionist activity came to a standstill during World War I, only to reemerge with new impetus after the establishment of the Czechoslovak Republic (1918).

The end of the war (1918) was accompanied by a wave of political and social disturbances and outright robbery with no ideological basis. Dozens of Jews were killed, executed, and injured. The Bolshevik revolution in Hungary in 1919 spilled over into Slovakia. As many Jews were involved in leading the revolution, the situation of Jews in Slovakia was affected as well. Only when the Prague authorities took over the management of the country did the situation quiet down. During the disturbances, Jews escaped from the villages or were expelled. Occasionally Jews would defend themselves with weapons. Poverty among the Jewish population, one of the results of the disturbances, was slightly ameliorated by the Joint Distribution Committee.

The newly created democratic state brought about radical changes in the political status of Jews: for the first time, the Jews had the right to declare themselves members of the Jewish nation. The new framework also permitted collaboration among the Czech, Slovak, and Subcarpathian Jewish leaders. The first official contact was made with the participation of the delegation from Slovakia at the Congress of the Jewish National Council, which convened in Prague (Jan. 3–6, 1919). At this congress the foundation was laid for the formation of the Jewish Party (*Židovská strana). Upon the return of the delegates, the National Federation of Slovak Jews (Svaz Židov na Slovensku) was established at *Piestany on the model of the *Prague and *Brno National Jewish Council. It was to play an important role in the consolidation of the life of the Jewish population after the hardships of war and the revolutionary transition period (1918–19). Another factor that contributed significantly to the improvement of the situation of the Jewish masses was the work of the American *Joint Distribution Committee, which established credit cooperatives and granted individual loans. The organ of the Federation of Slovak Jews, *Juedische Volkszeitung* ("Jewish People's Paper"), launched in Bratislava on Aug. 2, 1919, came to play an important role in the struggle for the rights of the Jewish minority of Czechoslovakia. According to the first Czechoslovak population census (Feb. 15, 1921), 135,918 persons in Slovakia (4.5% of the total population) declared themselves Jewish by religion; 70,522 of them declared themselves Jewish by nationality; of them 34.62% were gainfully employed, and the rest were dependent family members. The majority of the Jewish population was engaged in commerce and finance, followed by industry, handicrafts, and agriculture. In the free professions, lawyers and physicians were predominant. Of the 217 existing congregations, 165 were Orthodox, governed by the Bratislava Autonomous Center; the remaining 52 were organized in the Congress (Neology) and Status Quo Ante associations, which later unified under the name "Jeshurun." The political chasm dividing the different congregations became manifest during the parliamentary elections, and factions such as the Conservative Jewish Party and the Jewish Economic Party attracted votes from the Jewish Party, which was struggling for the rights of the Jewish minority. Individual Jews were also members in the Social Democratic Party, the Magyar National Party, and the Communist Party. In the first two elections (1920, 1925), the Jewish Party was unable to muster 20% of the vote in one constituency and failed to enter the parliament of Prague; it was only during the third elections (1929) that it achieved representation through Ludvik *Singer (succeeded by Angelo *Goldstein) and Julius Reisz of Bratislava. The latter was also a delegate to the Provincial Assembly, created in Slovakia in 1927; his place in parliament was taken after the fourth elections, in 1935, by Ḥayyim *Kugel.

The years of stability in the late 1920s brought prosperity to a wide stratum of the Jewish population and a general upheaval in social and cultural life, centering mainly around the Zionist organizations, the newly founded youth movements, and *WIZO, all of which were instrumental in disseminating Jewish culture and the Hebrew language and fostering relations with Ereẓ Israel.

A new generation, for the most part socialist in outlook, was educated at Bratislava and Prague universities. The German and Hungarian language tradition still prevailed among the older generation, and Jewish writers and journalists continued to write in either of these languages. Blaming them for the process of Magyarization and claiming that they owned two-thirds of the nation's property, the spokesmen of the rightist Slovak People's Party openly incited the people against the Jews. In the late 1930s, anti-Jewish demonstrations in Slovakia were led by the Nationalist Youth Movement (Om ladina) and the Volksdeutsche students. In 1937 the delegate of the People's Party even proposed in the parliament of Prague that the Jews of Slovakia and Subcarpathian Ruthenia be transferred to *Birobidzhan because of their high birthrate and since anyhow they were Communists.

The situation of the Jews deteriorated greatly in the autumn of 1938. After the Munich conference, the Prague government was compelled to grant autonomy to Slovakia, and the Slovak People's Party seized power at the *Zilina conference (Oct. 6, 1938) and established a quasi-Fascist and antisemitic regime.

For Holocaust and contemporary periods, see *Czechoslovakia; *Czech Republic and Slovakia.

BIBLIOGRAPHY: MHJ; P. Ujvári, *Magyar Zsidó Lexikon* (1929); M. Lányi and H. Békeffi-Propper, *Szlovenszkói zsido hitközségek tortenete* (1930); R.J. Kerner (ed.), *Czechoslovakia, Twenty Years of Independence* (1940); D. Gross, in: *Juedisches Jahrbuch fuer die Slowakei* (1940); J. Lettrich, *A History of Modern Slovakia* (1956); L. Rothkirchen, in: *The Jews of Czechoslovakia*, 1 (1968). **ADD. BIBLIOGRAPHY:** Y.A. Jelinek, *Zidovská nabozenská obce na Slovensku v 19. a 20. storoci a ich spolocenská postaventie* (2002).

[Livia Rothkirchen / Yeshayahu Jelinek (2nd ed.)]

SLOVO, JOE (1926–1995), South African politician. Slovo was born in Lithuania and taken to South Africa when he was eight. After war service, he graduated in law at Witwatersrand University. In 1942 he joined the Communist Party, but after it was outlawed he was arrested and detained on several occasions in the 1950s and 1960s. He was one of the accused in the 1956–61 Treason Trial, which ended with charges being dropped or acquittal for all 156 defendants. He was one of the drafters of the Freedom Charter, the African National Congress's non-racist manifesto of 1955, and helped to organize the Congress's guerrilla wing, serving as its chief of staff. He worked from countries neighboring South Africa. Slovo was the first white appointed to the Congress's national executive (1985). In 1986 he became secretary general of the South African Communist Party. After 27 years of exile he returned to South Africa in 1990 and played a leading role in the negotiations leading to the transition from white minority rule to multiracial democracy in April 1994. He was appointed as the first minister of housing in the post-apartheid South African government under Nelson Mandela, a position he held for six months before dying of cancer early in 1995. His autobiography, *Slovo – The Unfinished Autobiography*, appeared posthumously later that same year.

[David Saks (2nd ed.)]

SLUCKI, ABRAHAM JACOB (1861–1918), Hebrew writer. Born in Novogorod Severski, Slucki began publishing articles in *Ha-Meliẓ* in 1884 and became assistant editor of the periodical during the editorship of the poet Judah Leib *Gordon (1887–88). The continued publication of his articles, even after the termination of his editorial activities, helped make *Ha-Meliẓ* into a paper of a strong Jewish nationalist character. He was particularly instrumental in disseminating the ideas of Ḥibbat Zion among the Orthodox. His anthology *Shivat Ẓiyyon* (1–2, 1891, and a few subsequent editions), which was a collection of the writings of the greatest rabbis of the generation favorable to the Jewish national idea, was very influential among these groups. He was among the originators of the idea of *Mizrachi and, together with Isaac *Reines, helped to establish the movement; he even gave it its name. Slucki was murdered in a pogrom in the town of his birth.

BIBLIOGRAPHY: Kressel, Leksikon 2 (1967), 507–8.

[Yehuda Slutsky]

SLUTSK (Pol. **Słuck**), town in Minsk district, Belarus; from the end of the 13th century under Lithuania; from 1793 under Russia and a district town in the province of Minsk until the Revolution. Jews are known to have lived in Slutsk, one of the oldest Jewish communities in Belorussia, from 1583. The community developed under the protection of the owners of the town, the princes Radziwill. Within the structure of the Councils of the *Lands Slutsk was at first subject to the community of Brisk (Brest-Litovsk), but it became independent from 1691 and was granted jurisdiction over the surrounding villages. From that date until 1764 Slutsk was one of the five leading Lithuanian communities which sent delegates to the Council of Lithuania, and the last session of this council was held there in 1761. Slutsk declined in the 19th century, becoming a township whose principal income came from retail trade, craftsmanship, and vegetable- and fruit-growing, the latter being renowned throughout Russia. From 1,577 in 1766 the number of Jews increased to 5,897 in 1847 and 10,264 (77% of the population) in 1897.

At the end of the 18th century Slutsk was one of the centers of the struggle against Ḥasidism, remaining a stronghold of the *Mitnaggedim*. The rabbis who held office in the community included Joseph Peimer (1829–64) and Joseph Baer *Soloveichik (1865–74). In 1897 Isser Zalman *Meltzer founded a yeshivah which attracted students from throughout the Pale of *Settlement. Several Hebrew writers and scholars came from Slutsk (Y. *Cahan, Y.D. *Berkowitz, J.N. *Simchoni, and E.E. *Lisitsky), as did the promoters of Haskalah and Ḥibbat Zion (Z. *Dainow and Ẓ.H. *Masliansky). Under the Soviet regime the Slutsk community shared the fate of Russian Jewry. Government schools in which the language of instruction was Yiddish were opened and remained in existence until the late 1930s. Yehezkel *Abramsky was rabbi of the community. In 1926 there were 8,358 Jews (53.3% of the total population) in Slutsk. When the town was occupied by the Germans in 1941, local Jews were massacred; those who remained alive were confined to a ghetto. On Nov. 11, 1942, the ghetto was liquidated. Ghetto prisoners were burned alive in their homes, and those who tried to run away were shot to death. Only several persons managed to survive these events. Three months later the remaining "useful" Jews were exterminated. Only a very few Jews lived in Slutsk in 1970 and there was no semblance of Jewish life.

In 2005, the general population of Slutsk numbered 63,439. Members of the Jewish community raised money to construct a Holocaust memorial in the center of the town, on the site where the Slutsk ghetto was located during World War II. The project was spearheaded by the Falevich brothers, Boris and Friedrich, who were two of the few survivors.

BIBLIOGRAPHY: S. Dubnow, *Pinkas ha-Medinah* (1925), index; Z. Gluskin, *Zikhronot* (1946), 17–19; E.E. Lisitsky, *Elleh Toledot Adam* (1951), 12–59; *Pinkas Slutsk u-Venoteha* (1962).

[Yehuda Slutsky / Ruth Beloff (2nd ed.)]

SLUTSKAYA, IRINA ("**Ira**," "**Slute**"; 1979–), Russian figure skater, Olympic silver medalist, two-time world champion, six-time European champion. Coached solely by Zhanna Gromova from the age of six, the Muscovite Slutskaya, whose father is Jewish, won her first senior international figure skating competition at the age of 14. By 2005, Slutskaya had garnered a total of 59 medals in senior internationals, including 30 gold medals and 18 silver medals, making her one of the top figure skaters in the world. Among her most impressive victories were two World Championships (2002 and 2005), six European Championships (1996, 1997, 2000, 2001, 2003, 2005), four ISU Grand Prix titles (2000, 2001, 2002, 2005), and six Cup of Russia titles (1996, 1997, 1999, 2000, 2001, 2004). She has also won the Russian nationals four times, while placing second twice, and third on three occasions. Slutskaya earned a silver medal at the 2002 Winter Olympics in Nagano, Japan.

[Robert B. Klein (2nd ed.)]

SLUTSKI, BORIS ABRAMOVICH (1919–), Soviet Russian poet. Though one of the most talented Soviet lyric poets of the middle generation, Slutski was believed to have been silenced for a number of years because of the often defiantly Jewish tone of his verse. His first efforts appeared as early as 1941, but it was not until well after Stalin's death that he was discovered by Ilya *Ehrenburg and the first anthology of his verse was allowed to appear (*Pamyat*, 1957). Slutski thereafter became firmly identified with the liberals in Soviet literature, sounding the alarm over the increasingly technocratic character of Soviet civilization that threatened destruction to the country's humanistic cultural heritage in *Fiziki i liriki* ("Physicists and Lyricists," 1959). Slutski's World War II army service brought him to the devastated Jewish settlements of western Russia, and the Holocaust inspired some of his most eloquent verse, much of it published only after Stalin's death. Following the sensation created by Yevgeni *Yevtushenko's poem "*Babi Yar" in 1961, and particularly after the vitriolic attacks on the non-Jewish poet for singling out the martyrdom of the Jewish victims of Nazism, an embittered and impassioned anonymous poem about the tragic fate of Russia's Jews was widely circulated in the U.S.S.R. Its author was said to be Slutski, but this was neither confirmed nor denied by

Slutski himself. In 1963 a Moscow publishing house brought out *Poety Izrailya*, the first collection of Israel poetry ever published in the U.S.S.R. in which many of the poets represented were either Communist Party members or sympathizers, and some of the texts were mutilated by Soviet censors. Slutski was listed as the editor of the collection, but he did not write the introduction which, in the U.S.S.R., was invariably entrusted to the editor.

BIBLIOGRAPHY: *Prominent Personalities in the U.S.S.R.* (1968), 585.

[Maurice Friedberg]

SLUTZKI, DAVID (d. 1889), publisher and businessman in his native Warsaw. Slutzki spent some time in St. Petersburg, where he befriended J.L. *Gordon, and moved to Hamburg, living there in great poverty. He was familiar with Jewish literature of all periods, particularly philosophic and meditative literature, and sought to publish new editions for the masses in a modern format with biographical introductions and notes. Accordingly, he published a proclamation at the beginning of the 1860s calling for a comprehensive edition of all the works of the Oral Law and the literature of the Middle Ages.

From 1863 to 1871 he published the following works in Warsaw: *Ḥokhmat Yisrael*, a series of works containing comprehensive introductions, prefaces, biographies of the authors, etc., as well as Jedaiah ha-Penini's *Beḥinat Olam* (1864); Solomon ibn Gabirol's *Mivḥar ha-Peninim* (1864); Maimonides' *Shemonah Perakim* (1864) and *Be'ur Millot ha-Higgayon* (1865); Saadiah Gaon's *Emunot ve-De'ot* (1864); Judah ibn Tibbon's *Ru'aḥ Ḥen* (1865); Judah Halevi's *Kuzari* (1866); and Baḥya ibn Paquda's *Ḥovot ha-Levavot* (1870). In addition, he published new editions of Manasseh of Ilya's *Sefer Alfei Menasheh* (Warsaw, 1860), *Megillat Antiyyokhus* (1863), and S. Pappenheim's *Arba Kosot* (1863).

BIBLIOGRAPHY: *Ha-Meliẓ* (1889), no. 256; *Ha-Ẓefirah* (1889), no. 265; A. Yaari, in: *Moznayim*, 3:27 (1932).

[Getzel Kressel]

SMELA (Smiela) city in Kiev district, Ukraine. By 1765 there were 927 Jews in Smela. During the 18th century Smela was subjected to many attacks by *Haidamacks, and was particularly affected by that of 1768. In 1847 the Jews numbered 1,270, and by 1897 the number increased to 7,475 (50% of the total population). During a pogrom perpetrated in Smela by the bands of Grigoryev in May 1919, over 80 Jews were killed and hundreds of Jewish houses, stores, and workshops were destroyed. The number of Jews in Smela was 5,867 (25.7% of the population) in 1923. Under German occupation during World War II the entire Jewish community was exterminated. In 1959 there were again approximately 1,800 Jews in Smela (4% of the total population). Most left in the 1900s. Within the Jewish community in Smela there is a Jewish community center, a Sunday school, a youth club, and a children's choir called Hatikva.

SMELSER, NELL JOSEPH (1930–), U.S. sociologist. Born in Kahoka, Missouri, Smelser received bachelor's degrees from Harvard University (1952) and Magdalen College, Oxford (1954) and a Ph.D. from Harvard in 1958. That year, he became a faculty member of the department of sociology at the University of California at Berkeley. After retiring from teaching, he became professor emeritus of sociology at Berkeley.

Smelser is one of the major representatives of a trend in American sociological theory that aims at the construction of systematic models as a guide to and determinant of concrete research. This provides the common denominator for many of Smelser's published works.

Smelser was elected to the American Academy of Arts and Sciences (1968), the American Philosophical Society (1976), and the National Academy of Sciences (1993). In 1994 he was elected director of the Center for Advanced Study in the Behavioral Sciences, an independent institution located on the campus of Stanford University. He had served on its board of trustees (1981 to 1993) and was chairman of the board (1985–86). He was also chairman of the center's Advisory Committee on Special Projects. In 1997 he was elected president of the American Sociological Association.

Smelser's books include *Theory of Collective Behavior* (1962), *Economy and Society* (with T. Parsons, 1956), *Comparative Methods in the Social Sciences* (1976), *Social Paralysis and Social Change* (1991), *The Social Edges of Psychoanalysis* (1999), and *Discouraging Terrorism* (2002). He edited the *American Sociological Review* (1962–1965), *Social Structure and Mobility in Economic Development* (with S.M. Lipset, 1966), *Personality and Social Systems* (with his brother, T. Smelser, 1963), *Essays in Sociological Explanation* (1968), *Behavioral and Social Science* (with Dean Gerstein, 1986), *The Social Importance of Self-Esteem* (with A. Mecca and J. Vasconcellos, 1989), *The Handbook of Economic Sociology* (with R. Swedberg, 1994), and *The International Encyclopedia of Social and Behavioral Sciences* (with P. Baltes, 2001).

BIBLIOGRAPHY: J. Alexander, G. Marx and C. Williams (eds.), *Self, Social Structure, and Beliefs* (2004).

[Werner J. Cahnman / Ruth Beloff (2nd ed.)]

°**SMEND, RUDOLPH** (1851–1913), German Bible critic. Smend taught at the Halle (1875), at Basle (1881), and Goettingen (1889). His major works dealt with source criticism of the Bible. His *Die Erzaehlung des Hexateuch auf ihre Quellen untersucht* (1912) defined J^1, J^2, E, and P as the four major strands of the Hexateuch and influenced O. *Eissfeldt's *Hexateuch-Synopse* (1922) and the pentateuchal criticism of H. Holzinger, J. Meinhold, and W. Eichrodt among others. In *Lehrbuch der alttestamentlichen Religionsgeschichte* (1893; 1899^2) he advanced the theory that Isaiah became a nationalist only in light of Assyrian domination, and with W. Nowack and A. Lods, who followed J. *Wellhausen's lead, he maintained that Hosea opposed in principle the institution of the monarchy. His study of the "I" references of the Psalter, in which he maintains that they refer to the congregation and not to the individual, provoked a vigorous reaction by opponents of this view. He wrote a detailed exegesis on the Wisdom of Ben Sira; a study of the Mesha stele (1886, with A. Socin); on the influence of the sayings of *Ahikar on the Greek Aesop fables (1898); and a commentary on Ezekiel (1880).

[Zev Garber]

SMILANSKY, MEIR (pseudonym, **M. Secco**; 1876–1949), Hebrew writer. Born in Kiev district, the brother of Moshe *Smilansky, Meir went to Ereẓ Israel in 1891, and joined his family at Ḥaderah, which had just been founded. In 1892 he returned to Russia where he was employed in his father's business enterprises. He went blind in 1915, and subsequently endured the pogroms in the Ukraine. In 1921 he finally returned to Ereẓ Israel, after several years of wandering, and, with the help of his relatives, rehabilitated himself.

Encouraged in his writing by N. *Sokolow, he published stories in *Ha-Ẓefirah*, in *Lu'aḥ Aḥi'asaf*, and especially in *Ha-Shilo'aḥ*, edited by *Bialik, who also helped Smilansky improve his style. These earlier works dealt with the Ukrainian village and its Jewish inhabitants. His later stories dealing with the pogroms against Ukrainian Jewry were collected in the volume *Even Tizak* (1940).

BIBLIOGRAPHY: Kressel, Leksikon, 2 (1967), 525.

[Getzel Kressel]

SMILANSKY, MOSHE (literary pseudonyms, **Ḥeruti**; **Ḥawaja Mussa**; 1874–1953), Hebrew writer and agricultural pioneer in Ereẓ Israel. Born in Telepino, a village in the province of Kiev, into a family of Jewish tenant farmers, he went to Ereẓ Israel in 1890 and was one of the founders of Ḥaderah. In 1893 he settled in Reḥovot where he was the owner of orange groves and vineyards.

An active Zionist, much of Smilansky's literary career, which he began in 1898, was devoted to publicistic writings. He contributed prolifically to the Jewish press in Russia (*Ha-Ẓefirah, Ha-Meliẓ, Ha-Ẓofeh, Lu'aḥ Aḥi'asaf, Ha-Shilo'aḥ*, and *Ha-Olam*), and to Hebrew periodicals in Ereẓ Israel and other countries, and was one of the co-founders of the literary journal *Ha-Omer*. Smilansky saw himself as a disciple of *Aḥad Ha-Am, and was one of the first contributors (writing under the pen name "Ḥeruti") to *Ha-Po'el ha-Ẓa'ir*. Deeply concerned with Arab-Jewish labor problems Smilansky opposed the demand by the Second Aliyah for exclusively Jewish labor in the colonies for economic and political reasons. After World War I he was active in organizations for the reclamation and acquisition of land. He was one of the founders of the Hitaḥadut ha-Moshavot in Judea, whose chairman he became during World War I, and of Hitaḥadut ha-Ikkarim (*Farmers' Federation), which he headed during its early years and whose periodical, *Bustanai* (1929–39), he edited. In 1918 he volunteered for the *Jewish Legion. Smilansky participated in unofficial and unpublicized talks with Arab leaders in 1936. After World War I he was a faithful supporter of Chaim *Weizmann's views, which are reflected in many of his articles in the Hebrew press (particularly *Haaretz*), and in the 1940s he opposed the struggle of the *yishuv* against the British regime in Palestine.

Much of Smilansky's literary activity was devoted to the history of Jewish agricultural settlement in Ereẓ Israel. Among his many works in the field are *Ḥaderah* (1930), *Reḥovot* (1950), and *Perakim be-Toledot ha-Yishuv* (6 vols. (1959) which ran into several editions). *Mishpaḥat ha-Adamah* (4 vols., 1943–53), a book of memoir sketches and first-hand impressions of the pioneers of the First and Second Aliyyot, is one of his finest works. During the last years of his life he wrote a sequence of autobiographical novels: *Bi-Sedot Ukraina* (1944), *Ba-Aravah* (1947), *Bein Karmei Yehudah* (1948), *Be-Ẓel ha-Pardesim* (1951), *Tekumah ve-Sho'ah* (1953), and *Ḥevlei Leidah* (1954).

Smilansky's fiction contains in particular stories on Arab life (under the pseudonym "Ḥawaja Mussa") which he began in 1906. These stories (collected in *Benei Arav*, 1964), written in a vivid descriptive style, are the first of their kind in Jewish literature. Smilansky reveals to the Jewish reader a new world – exotic, colorful, throbbing with its own rich humanity. Though in many of the stories Arab life is romanticized, the author's direct knowledge of the Arab ambience and way of life is documentarily valuable and the stories are of literary merit. Composed before World War I, the stories convey an amicable relationship between Arab and Jew. Other works by Smilansky include *Hadassah*, a novel depicting the beginning of the Second Aliyah; *Toledot Ahavah Aḥat* (1911), a short novel; *Sippurei Sava* (1946); *Ba-Har u-va-Gai* (1949); *Shemesh Aviv*; and *Im Peridah* (revised edition 1955). There are several collections of his works including *Kitvei Moshe Smilansky* (1924–1945), but none is complete.

BIBLIOGRAPHY: D. Smilansky, *Im Benei Dori* (1942), 212–16; J. Fichmann, *Be-Terem Aviv* (1959), 102–25; A. Cohen, *Israel and the Arab World* (1969), index. **ADD. BIBLIOGRAPHY:** M. Ungerfeld, "*M. Smilanski*," in: *Hadoar*, 53 (1974), 121; E. Reizin, *Reshit Darko ha-Ẓibburit shel Moshe Smilansky* (1982); G. Shaked, *Ha-Sipporet ha-Ivrit*, 2 (1983), 44–54; H. Hoffman, "*Bein Teimanim le-Ashkenazim be-Shishah Sippurei Ahavah*," in: *Pe'amim*, 21 (1985), 113–33; R. Domb, "*Demut ha-Aravi*," in: *Iton 77*, 84 (1987), 95–97; I. Basok, "*Psikhoanalizah be-Heksher Tarbuti ve-Politi, Diyyun ve-Hadgamah be-Sippurei 'Benei Arav'*," in: *Bikkoret u-Parshanut*, 29 (1993), 75–96; Y. Berlovitz, "*'Benei Arav' le-M. Smilanski*," in: *Iyyunim bi-Tekumat Yisra'el*, 4 (1994), 400–421; A. Zinger, *Ha-Shivah la-Karka* (1995); I. Basok, *Be-Ẓel ha-Pardesim, al Adamah Meẓora'at* (1996); A. Givoli, *Gishatto shel Moshe Smilansky la-Sikhsukh ha-Aravi Yehudi bi-Shenot ha-Sheloshim* (2003).

[Yehuda Slutsky]

°**SMITH, SIR GEORGE ADAM** (1856–1942), Scottish scholar of the Bible and geography of Palestine. Smith was ordained as a minister in the United Free Church of Scotland, became professor of Hebrew and Old Testament studies at Church College, Glasgow (1892), and was principal of Aberdeen University (1909–35). His main work was the *Historical Geography of the Holy Land* (1894, followed by 25 editions), which proved immensely popular as the best-written and most scholarly account of the subject. He had a profound understanding of the permanent geographical factors and their influence on history.

He also prepared an *Atlas of the Historical Geography of the Holy Land* (1915, 1936) and wrote *Jerusalem: The Topography, Economics, and History from the Earliest Times to A.D. 70* (2 vols., 1907–8). In the field of biblical research he wrote commentaries on Deuteronomy (1918), Jeremiah (1929^4), and the Twelve Prophets (1928^2).

[Michael Avi-Yonah]

°**SMITH, JOHN MERLIN POWIS** (1866–1932), U.S. Protestant biblical scholar. Smith taught Semitic languages and literatures at the University of Chicago, where he became full professor in 1915. He developed a longstanding attachment to biblical translations which culminated in *The Complete Bible: An American Translation* (co-edited by E.J. Goodspeed, 1941).

Smith was also a member of the American Standard Bible Committee responsible for the revision of the American Standard Version. To the *International Critical Commentary* he contributed the commentaries on Micah, Zephaniah, Nahum (1912; 1943^3), and Malachi (1912; 1937^2). In 1903 he helped to establish the Oriental Exploration Fund. In his writings, Smith advanced the theory that the Hebrew religion was a product of Israel's social experience reacting to alien cultures (*The Origin and History of Hebrew Law*, 1931, 1960^2; *The Religion of the Psalms*, 1922). In *The Moral Life of the Hebrews* (1923) he maintained that the uniqueness of the Hebrew religion was its ethical consciousness. Smith also contributed commentaries on Amos, Hosea, and Micah to the *Bible for Home and School* series (1914).

BIBLIOGRAPHY: W.G. Williams, in: AJSLL, 49 (1932/33), 169–71 (list of Smith's publications); J.H. Breasted, *ibid.*, 73–79; I.M. Price, *ibid.*, 80–86; E.J. Goodspeed, *ibid.*, 87–96.

[Zev Garber]

SMITH, JONATHAN Z. (1938–), scholar of religious studies. A native of New York City, Smith received his bachelor's degree from Haverford College in Pennsylvania and his Ph.D. from Yale's newly established Department of Religion in 1962. He taught in the department of religious studies at the University of California, Santa Barbara; then, in 1968, he joined the faculty of the University of Chicago, where he became the Robert O. Anderson Distinguished Service Professor of the Humanities. He also serves on the university's Committee on the Ancient Mediterranean World and on the Committee on the History of Culture, and he is an associate faculty member at the Divinity School.

Considered one of the most influential scholars of religion, Smith is best known for his analyses of religious studies and the problem of comparative work. Much of his research focuses on the religions of antiquity, including ancient Judaism and early Christianity, but he is renowned for his wide range of study and comparison of different historical periods and cultures. Calling religion "the creation of the scholar's study," Smith emphasizes the role of analytic purpose and choice in the academic study of religion. His work, in particular his examination of the implications of choice and his insistence on a relentless scrutiny of scholastic selection and viewpoint, is considered to have influenced the field's move toward an emphasis on theory and an inclusion of the study of politics.

Smith's works include *Map Is Not Territory: Studies in the History of Religions* (1978); *Imagining Religion: From Babylon to Jonestown* (1982); and *To Take Place: Toward Theory in Ritual* (1987), which stresses the importance of constructed ritual environments. His *Drudgery Divine: On the Comparison of Early Christianities and the Religions of Late Antiquity* (1990) examines four centuries of scholarship, discussing the mytheme of the "dying and rising god." In Smith's acclaimed 2004 work, *Relating Religion: Essays in the Study of Religion*, he provides an overview of his theoretical approach, connecting his theory to general education, and he outlines the methods of comparative study, including procedures of generalization and redescription, that he deems so essential to religious scholarship.

[Dorothy Bauhoff (2nd ed.)]

°**SMITH, MORTON** (1915–1991), U.S. scholar, educator, and historian of the ancient world. Smith, who was born in Philadelphia, served on the faculties of Brown, Drew, and Columbia universities, becoming professor of ancient history at the last. Smith made contributions to a number of fields, ranging from biblical studies to the history of magic.

In 1958 at Mar Saba, a Greek Orthodox monastery near Bethlehem in Israel, Smith found a copy of a letter ascribed to *Clement of Alexandria, the second-century director of the catechetical school of Alexandria. It contained excerpts of a *Secret Gospel of Mark*, which Smith subsequently translated. The letter remains a subject of great controversy.

Smith was particularly interested in the history of Judaism during the Second Temple period. Part of his comprehensive study of this topic was published as *Judaism in Palestine*; vol. 1, *To the Reign of Antiochus Epiphanes* (1971). He treated the latter part of the period in his "Palestinian Judaism in the First Century" (in: M. Davis (ed.), *Israel: Its Role in Civilization*, 1965). In this essay he assessed the actual role and influence of the Pharisees as simply one among several Jewish sects. Also relevant to this period is his *Makbilot bein ha-Besorot le-Sifrut ha-Tanna'im* (1945; *Tannaitic Parallels to the Gospels*, 1951; revised form of diss. in Heb.).

His other publications include *The Ancient Greeks* (1960), *Heroes and Gods* (with M. Hadas, 1965), *Palestinian Parties and Politics That Shaped the Old Testament* (1971), *The Secret Gospel* (1973), and *Jesus the Magician* (1981). He edited *Hope and History* (with R. Anshen, 1980) and *What the Bible Really Says* (with R. Hoffmann, 1993). A two-volume set of his collected essays, titled *Religions in the Graeco-Roman World*, was published in 1995.

BIBLIOGRAPHY: J. Neusner, *Christianity, Judaism and other Greco-Roman Cults: Studies for Morton Smith at Sixty* (1975); idem, *Are There Really Tannaitic Parallels to the Gospels?* (1993); S. Brown, *Mark's Other Gospel: Rethinking Morton Smith's Controversial Discovery* (2005).

[David Flusser / Ruth Beloff (2nd ed.)]

°SMITH, WILLIAM ROBERTSON (1846–1894), Scottish theologian and Semitist; born at New Farm, Aberdeenshire. His appointment as professor of Oriental languages and Bible exegesis in the Free Church College at Aberdeen in 1870 was ended in 1881 due to his radical views in regard to biblical revelation which he expounded in a series of articles for the *Encyclopaedia Britannica*. At that time at Edinburgh and Glasgow he delivered a series of lectures which were published as *The Old Testament in the Jewish Church* (1881, 1892^2) and *The Prophets of Israel* (1882). His stay in the Near East in the winter of 1879–80 and the following year influenced his views in regard to the religious institutions of the Semites, their religio-cultural beliefs, and the historical influence of their religion on biblical Judaism and early Christianity. He resumed his academic career in 1883 when he was appointed professor of Arabic at Cambridge. Poor health prevented him from publishing more than the first series of *Lectures on the Religion of the Semites* (1889, 1894^2; ed. by S.A. Cook with introd. and notes, 1927), a major scholarly endeavor which applied anthropological principles to biblical research.

Smith is remembered principally as an investigator of the nature of early Semitic religion. His study of primitive Arab life, as recorded in literature and as observed in the contemporary setting, led him to believe that it was identical in all its fundamentals with the early Semites as a whole. In his *Kinship and Marriage in Early Arabia* (1885) he expounded the theory that the most primitive social organization was matriarchal, with exogamous polyandry and a totemistic cult system. His assumed parallels among the Hebrews are unfounded and lack a critical scientific base. In his *Lectures on the Religion of the Semites* Smith maintained that the nature and significance of the earliest religious expression were best understood through a study of ritual practices exhibited within the social cult. He thus thoroughly investigated the ritual of sacrifice and its corollaries, communion and atonement, and championed the theory that these were the primary conceptions in primitive Semitic religion. His interpretation posited the common anthropological belief that religion was an integral part of society which cannot be separated from the social and political institutions of a group. He further stated that certain concepts labeled Priestly and post-Exilic by the K.H. *Graf-J. *Wellhausen school had an early date since rituals tended to remain unchanged from their beginnings down through recorded history. Successive periods of ritual practices reflected advances in religious psychology, but essentially the original ideas remain. Smith's root theory that the phenomena of Semitic religion are derived from a single source and are coordinated into a fixed system appears untenable. Yet his description of Israel's origins remains refreshing for a period dominated by the evolutionary approach of the school of biblical criticism.

BIBLIOGRAPHY: J.S. Black and G. Crystal, *The Life of W. Robertson Smith* (1912); H.F. Hahn, *The Old Testament in Modern Research* (1956), 47–54.

[Zev Garber]

SMOIRA, MOSHE (1888–1961), Israeli jurist, the first president of the Supreme Court of Israel. He was born in Koenigsberg, Prussia, into a Russian-ḥasidic family which had settled in Germany. He was enlisted into the German army during World War I. Between 1919 and 1922 he headed the first Hebrew school in Germany. He settled in Palestine in 1922. Between 1923 and 1948, he lectured on civil procedure at the Mandate law school. He became an expert on labor problems and participated in the drafting of the Workmen's Compensation Ordinance and in determining the legal status of the kibbutzim. Smoira was president of the Jewish Bar Association, as well as president of the honorary court of the World Zionist Organization. Upon the establishment of the State of Israel in 1948, he was appointed the first president of the Supreme Court in Jerusalem and held this position until 1954. Smoira was active in various institutions, including the board of governors of the Hebrew University.

[Benjamin Jaffe]

SMOIRA-COHN, MICHAL (1926–), Israeli musical administrator, educator, musicologist. Born in Tel Aviv, daughter of Moshe *Smoira (Israel's first Supreme Court president). She studied piano with Joseph Tal, graduated from the Palestine Academy of Music in piano and music history (1947), and became a teacher at the Israel Conservatoire in Jerusalem (1952). She was appointed director of the Haifa Orchestra. In 1956, she went to Sweden. After graduating from Uppsala University in 1958, she returned to Tel Aviv, where she was editor of *Bat Kol* and lecturer at the Music Teachers' Training Seminary and the Thelma Yellin School of Arts (1959). She wrote musical criticism in *Haaretz* (1963–66) and was lecturer on music aesthetics at the musicology department of Tel Aviv University (1965–67), and on music history and literature at the Rubin Academy of Music in Jerusalem (1966–73). In 1968, she became director of the music department of the Israel Broadcasting Authority, Jerusalem, and directed the Rubin Academy of Music in Jerusalem from 1979 to 1984. Active in Israel's cultural life and education, she chaired the Pedagogic Section of the education and culture department (1983), and served as chair and member of the jury of the "Arthur Rubinstein" and of the "Voice of Music Young Artists" competitions. Smoira-Cohn was a political and public activist for decades and one of the driving forces of the volunteer and non-profit sector in Israel and an advocate for women's causes. She was chair of Israel's Women's Organization; she became a member of the city council of Jerusalem and also created the Sovlanut (Tolerance) movement in 1982 (serving as the movement's chair for ten years). She received the Jerusalem Foundation Marthe Prize for Tolerance and Democratic Values in Jerusalem, for the year 2001. Among her Hebrew writings are *Ha-Musikah, Mavo Histori* (1966); *Folk Song in Israel* (1963); *On Eastern and Western Foundations in the Music of Israel* (1968); *On Meanings in Music* (1982); an autobiography, *A Personal Repertoire* (1997), and several articles. She also edited publications on the activity of the Jerusalem Rubin Academy of Music and Dance (in Hebrew, 1997/2003), and participated in the writing of the autobiography of her husband, Judge Haim *Cohn (1911–2002), published in 2005.

[Uri (Erich) Toeplitz and Yohanan Boehm / Naama Ramot (2nd ed.)]

SMOL (Samuel) of Derenburg (14th century), *Court Jew to four archbishops at *Magdeburg, Germany; one of the earliest of the Court Jews. First mentioned in 1347, Smol was a member of a commission arbitrating a dispute between the archbishop and the city of Hollefin in 1365. He was also referred to as representative of the prelate, and in 1366 he was one of four warrantors of a sum promised to the archbishop. In 1370 Smol was among those who participated in the decision in a dispute over the archbishop's inheritance. He was closest to the last archbishop, Peter, who called him "our Jew" and granted him and his children protection in 1372. Peter was, however, given warning about this relationship when the pope, Gregory XI, cautioned him that he would take strong measures if it were indeed true that he had permitted Smol to turn a church into a synagogue. On another occasion Gregory complained to the bishop of Naumburg about the latter's favoring a certain Jew "Marquand" who in all probability was Smol's brother, objecting to the bishop's extending friendship to the Jew and giving him jurisdiction over Christians.

BIBLIOGRAPHY: Lewinsky, in: MGWJ, 48 (1904), 457–60; H. Schnee, *Die Hoffinanz und der moderne Staat*, 1 (1953), 19–23; Germ Jud, 2 (1968), 160.

SMOLAR, HERSH (1905–1993), leader of the Jewish community in Poland after World War II. Born in Zambrow near Bialystok, Smolar became active in the Communist Party in his early youth and from 1920 to 1928 he lived in the Soviet Union. He studied in Moscow at the Yiddish Department of the Communist University of the Peoples of the West and edited and wrote for Yiddish youth publications. In 1928 he was sent to Poland as a Comintern agent. Arrested for these activities, he spent four years in prison. In 1939 he escaped from prison and arrived in Soviet-occupied Bialystok, where he became secretary of the short-lived Yiddish newspaper, *Bialystoker Shtern*. When the Germans occupied Bialystok in 1941, he was active in the underground in the *Minsk ghetto. Later, he fought with the partisans in the Naliboki forest, helped to organize many partisan units, and was editor of the party press. In 1946 he arrived in Warsaw and became head of the cultural department of the Jewish Central Committee in Poland, and then editor of the Yiddish newspaper *Folks-shtime* and chairman of the Jewish Cultural Alliance. His *Folks-shtime* editorial (Apr. 4, 1956), reprinted or cited by many periodicals all over the world, became the first semi-official source of information about the liquidation, in 1948–52, of Soviet Yiddish cultural institutions and their leading personalities. During the anti-Jewish campaign of 1967–69 he was expelled from the Polish United Workers Party and from his editorial position. In 1971 Smolar immigrated to Israel. His works include *Fun Minsker Geto* ("From the Minsk Ghetto," 1946); *Yidn on Gele Lates* ("Jews without Yellow Patches," 1948); and *A Posheter Zelner* ("An Ordinary Soldier," 1952), a drama. His Yiddish memoirs *Vu Bistu Khaver Sidorov?* ("Where Are You, Comrade Sidorov?" 1975), *Fun Ineveynik* ("From Inside," 1978), and *Oyf der Letster Pozitsye mit der Letster Hofenung* ("On The Last Position with the Last Hope," 1982) describe political and cultural activities in the Soviet Union and Poland relative to the Jews.

[David Sfard / Gennady Estraikh (2nd ed.)]

SMOLENSK, city in western Russia. From 1404 to 1514 Smolensk was a Lithuanian possession and from 1611 to 1654 it came under Polish rule. Jews are first mentioned in Smolensk at the end of the 15th century; in 1489 there were three Jewish tax farmers in the city. Although King Sigismund II prohibited Jews from residing in Smolensk when the city passed to Poland, Jews nevertheless continued to live there. According to the "Old Responsa" of the Bah (R. Joel Sirkes), about 80 Jews resided in Smolensk in 1616. When Smolensk was reconquered by the Russians (1654), Jews were compelled to convert and those who did not do so were either put to death or taken captive and deported to the Russian interior. Jewish merchants from Lithuania, however, continued to visit Smolensk or pass through the city on their way to Moscow even after the Russian conquest. At the beginning of the 18th century Lithuanian Jews again began to settle in Smolensk and its vicinity. They engaged in commerce and the lease of various utilities. This activity aroused the jealousy of their Christian rivals, and in 1722 two Christian townsmen of Smolensk appealed to the Synod for Jews to be expelled from the region on the claim that the Jews derided Christianity. One Jew, Baruch b. Leib (who was also accused a few years later of having converted a Russian officer, Alexander *Voznitsin, to Judaism) had erected a synagogue in his home village of Zverovich, near Smolensk. In 1727, on the basis of Christian complaints, instructions were given for Baruch and his coreligionists to be expelled from the region of Smolensk. During the same year Czarina Anna ordered the expulsion of all the Jews of Russia, but by 1731 Jewish merchants were authorized to visit Smolensk for business purposes. For all practical purposes Jews continued to live in Smolensk on a permanent basis. When the *Pale of Settlement was established in 1791 the region of Smolensk was not included in it, and until the abolition of the Pale in 1917, Jews were officially prohibited from living in the Smolensk region. Even so, some Jews who fell into the categories of those authorized to live outside the Pale settled in Smolensk during the 19th century, where they continued to play an especially active role in the timber trade of the region. In 1897 the number of Jews in Smolensk was 4,651, forming 10%

of the total population. In the whole of the region there were 11,185 Jews. The number of Jews in Smolensk increased considerably after the 1917 Revolution; in 1926 there were 12,887 Jews (16.2% of the population) in the city. In 1922 the Great Synagogue was confiscated by Soviet authorities. In 1929 the Jewish Teachers' Seminary, founded by the *Yevsektsiya, was transferred to Smolensk from Gomel. The Germans occupied the city in August 1941 and almost immediately established a ghetto for the Jews of Smolensk in Sadki. In June–July 1942 about 2,000 Jews were murdered. In the late 1960s there was a Jewish population of about 5,000. There was no synagogue. In the early 2000s, after the emigration of the 1990s, there were bearly 1,000 Jews in the entire Smolensk district. The city had a synagogue, a Jewish community center, a newspaper called *Yachad*, a youth club, a Sunday school, a drama club, a group of performers called Menora, and a social service that distributes food packages.

BIBLIOGRAPHY: B. Katz, *Le-Korot ha-Yehudim be-Rusyah, Polin ve-Lita* (1898), 56; S. Ginsburg, *Historishe Verk*, 3 (1937), 142–3; R. Brainin, *Fun Mayn Lebns Bukh* (1946), 111–47; M. Osherowitch, *Shtet un Shtetlekh in Ukraine*, 2 (1948), 213–25; Kh.D. Rivkin, *Yevrei v Smolenske* (1910).

[Yehuda Slutsky]

SMOLENSKIN, PEREZ (1840 or 1842–1885), Hebrew novelist, editor, and publicist. A leading exponent of the *Haskalah in Eastern Europe and an early advocate of Jewish nationalism, Smolenskin is best known for the important Hebrew monthly *Ha-Shaḥar* which he founded in 1868, and edited – 12 volumes in all – until his death.

Early Life

Born in Monastyrshchina, in the province of Mogilev, White Russia, into a life of privation, hardship, and sickness, he witnessed at the age of five the press-ganging of his eldest brother, himself a mere child, into the army of Czar Nicholas I. The lad was never heard of again, and Smolenskin included a description of the terrifying experience in the second part of his largest and best-known novel, *Ha-To'eh be-Darkhei ha-Ḥayyim*. His father, who had earlier been a fugitive for more than two years because of false accusations, died when Perez was barely 11. A year later Smolenskin left home to join his elder brother at the yeshivah of Shklov, where he remained for nearly five years, maintaining himself by "eating days," i.e., his material needs being provided for by a different member of the community every day – in the manner of poor yeshivah students. Introduced to the ideas of Haskalah by his brother, he began to read secular books and to learn Russian. For these practices he was so persecuted that he fled to ḥasidic centers, first to Lubavich and then to Vitebsk, where he spent the years 1858–60/1. The portrait of Ḥasidism later reflected in his novels is highly critical. After a year of wandering through southern Russia and the Crimea, supporting himself by singing in choirs and preaching in synagogues, he reached Odessa in 1862. There he remained for five years, studying music and languages, and earning his living as a Hebrew teacher.

Early Literary Career

It was in Odessa that Smolenskin also embarked upon his literary career when he published a number of articles in the Hebrew journal *Ha-Meliẓ*. His first story, "*Ha-Gemul*," describing the ingratitude of the Poles toward the Jews who sided with them in the revolt against Russia (1861–63), appeared in Odessa in 1867. Simultaneously, he had composed his first novel *Simḥat Ḥanef* ("The Joy of the Godless"), which couches a series of lengthy expositions tracing the dependence of certain aspects of Shakespeare's *Hamlet* and Goethe's *Faust* on the singular Hebrew spirit informing the Books of Job and Ecclesiastes within the framework of a story depicting the shallow and frivolous attitudes of many of the ostensibly enlightened Jewish teachers in Odessa.

Founder and Manager of Ha-Shahar

Leaving Odessa in 1867, Smolenskin traveled through Romania – acquiring Turkish nationality en route – Germany, and Bohemia, before finally settling in Vienna in 1868, where he worked first as a proofreader and Hebrew teacher. Realizing that his plan to study at the university was quite impracticable, he abandoned hope of obtaining a systematic secular education and founded *Ha-Shaḥar*, which he henceforth published, edited, and managed, while serving simultaneously as proofreader, distributor, and one of its principal contributors. The journal became the most effective Hebrew literary platform for the Haskalah (Enlightenment) movement in its later period, and for the nationalist movement in its early stages. For almost 17 years Smolenskin devoted himself, body and soul, to the production of his cherished monthly, which consumed both his energies and his financial resources. From the outset Smolenskin conceived the journal as an instrument to make the Jewish people increasingly aware of its terrible plight and strengthen its internal resources, fostering at the same time the spread of a genuine enlightenment and a broad culture. Simultaneously, the monthly was to serve as a powerful weapon against any sham or hypocritical aspects of Orthodox Judaism or Ḥasidism which Smolenskin considered inimical to the public interest. It was equally committed to waging war on the exponents of a false enlightenment, whose assimilationist tendencies were undermining the national unity and eroding the distinctive life based on adherence to Torah and the later traditional literature. Above all, the journal epitomized Smolenskin's passionate loyalty to the Hebrew language and Hebrew literature, which he regarded as the real foundations of Jewish nationalism and a substitute for national territory as long as the nation lacked a state. To despise the language, therefore, was tantamount to an act of treachery toward Judaism and the Jewish people. As the fame of his journal spread, Smolenskin's contribution to the development of modern Hebrew literature became increasingly important. In the field of Jewish research, the monthly facilitated the publication of many weighty articles and even whole books by major scholars. It also served as a forum for the propagation of ideas and the discussion of a wide range of contemporary issues. In addition, it provided a hospitable framework for the publication of belles lettres, literary criticism, and book reviews. Primarily, however, it enabled its indefatigable editor to publish his own arresting articles, stories, and novels.

Financial Difficulties

In spite of all the effort required to produce *Ha-Shaḥar*, Smolenskin's literary activities yielded no financial reward; he was thus compelled to embark upon two long and tiring journeys – the first to Western Europe in 1870, and the second to Russia in 1881 – to seek support for his journal. To meet the additional obligations arising from his marriage in 1875, he undertook the management of a printing house, while in 1878 he launched a new magazine which, however, did not survive for more than nine months. The first eight numbers appeared fortnightly, under the title *Ha-Mabbit*. The remaining 18 issues appeared on alternate weeks under the titles *Ha-Mabbit* and *Ha-Mabbit le-Yisrael*. In addition to his manifold literary activities, Smolenskin also devoted much time and energy to public affairs. As one of the leading exponents of the Jewish return to Ereẓ Israel, he conducted negotiations with Laurence *Oliphant to obtain support for Jewish settlement there. Finally his health broke under the strain of so strenuous a life. Stricken with pulmonary tuberculosis in 1883, he continued writing to the end of his life, and completed his last novel, *Ha-Yerushah*, shortly before his death.

As Novelist

An impassioned defender of Israel's cause and a ferocious critic of its failures, Smolenskin poured his talent wholesale into articles and stories alike. The latter, indeed, frequently serve as vehicles for the conveyance of his ideas. The attempt to combine an attractive tale with the propagation of ideas and social criticism resulted in a hybrid novel, whose major elements are frequently at odds with each other, and which at best are forced to nestle uncomfortably within a single framework. The belief that it is the task of literature to perform a positive service for society is responsible for the bitter satire and didactic moralizing which permeate the stories. Of all his novels, *Ha-To'eh be-Darkhei ha-Ḥayyim* ("The Wanderer in the Paths of Life," 1876; first three parts originally published in *Ha-Shaḥar*, 1 [1868/69] and 2 [1871]), remains, perhaps, the most important. Picaresque and autobiographical in flavor, the story reflects contemporary Jewish life, mainly in Eastern but also in Western Europe, in vivid colors. In spite of the crudities and exaggerations, the tortuous plot and melodramatic villainies, the kaleidoscopic nature of the work, bolstered by the author's obvious sincerity and personal experience, exerts a considerable appeal even for the modern reader. By the end of part three, however, the story has worn itself out, so that the final part, written many years later, has little organic connection with the rest of the novel. It is important only for its penetrating analysis of, and proposed solutions for, the problems of Jewish life. Nowhere else in Smolenskin's novels is the storyteller so completely ousted by the publicist. Much the same applies to *Simḥat Ḥanef* ("The Joy of the Godless" in *Ha-Shaḥar*, 3 [1872]), the flimsy plot of which serves only to house the long philosophical and critical discussions comprising the core of the book. Linguistically the novel displays traces of a simpler and clearer mode of expression, and some of the conversations are quite lively. Many of the epithets, however, are stock-phrases, and the style is frequently stilted and artificial. At many points the author's vitality and power of thought come through the story. But the work exhibits signs of carelessness and over-hasty composition, which are offset only in part by the author's spontaneity and verve. The opening chapters of *Kevurat Ḥamor* ("A Donkey's Burial," in *Ha-Shaḥar*, 4 [1873]) are excellent; the humor is uproarious, and the plot original. While the half-mocking style is fairly consistent, the level is not maintained throughout, and the limitations of language are still painfully obvious. The novel is permeated with bitter social criticism, while fierce invective is leveled against the Jewish community leaders; but the author does produce very moving arguments in extenuation. The characters develop little and suffer from the author's fondness for exaggerated emotionalism. The hero is neither convincing nor consistent, but the principal villain is far from being merely a melodramatic scoundrel, even though his final sanctification is more effective as satire than as story. There is, however, much powerful writing, and the climate of superstition, bigotry, and persecution is outlined with considerable skill. In spite of a promising beginning, the narrative framework of *Ga'on va-Shever* ("Pride and Fall," in *Ha-Shaḥar*, 5 [1874]) is painfully naive, while the clumsily contrived "happy ending," with its deus ex machina in the shape of an inheritance of 15 million rubles, is in keeping with the general low level. The novel is not so much a continuous narrative as it is a number of short stories related by a group of ten fugitives on their way to the United States following the collapse of the Viennese stock exchange in 1873. Some of the individual stories are well related, and contain many points of similarity with *Ha-To'eh be-Darkhei ha-Ḥayyim*. There are also a number of interesting attempts at characterization; but many of the people are mere personifications of a single quality. The fact that some remain nameless throughout the story is indicative of their shadowy existence. The novel is loosely concluded by a brief reference to the ultimate destinies of the respective travelers. The first part of *Gemul ha-Yesharim* ("The Reward of the Righteous," in *Ha-Shaḥar*, 6 [1875]) far outstrips the previous novels in artistry, dramatic techniques, dramatic tension, and characterization; even the dialogue is more natural at times. The main didactic themes are handled skillfully, without obtruding too awkwardly into the plot. The second part (in *Ha-Shaḥar*, 7 [1876]) is interesting for its ideas on nationalism as well as for its severe condemnation of the Poles for their maltreatment of the Jews. The literary quality of the third part (*ibid.*) is much inferior. The author seems almost to have become bored with his story and to be making sporadic attempts to tie up the loose ends. Smolenskin's last great novel, *Ha-Yerushah* ("The Inheritance"), takes place, for the most part, in Romania, where the author had spent three months in 1874 on behalf of the Alliance Israélite Universelle, following a wave of pogroms against Romanian Jewry. *Ha-Yerushah* reflects the growing maturity of Smolenskin's art. While the first part (in *Ha-Shaḥar*, 8 [1876/77]) of the novel is even better than its predecessor in structure, artistry, characterization, and dialogue, in the middle of the second part (in *Ha-Shaḥar*, 10 and 11 [1880/82, 1883]) probability and cohesion are suddenly lost in a burst of melodramatic nonsense. Although the story is brought to a close, the denouement of the plot in the third and final part (in *Ha-Shaḥar*, 12 [1884]), hastily composed during his last illness, is premature and forced. The story clearly remains unfinished, with the main theme of "the inheritance" left hanging in mid-air. The novel illustrates Smolenskin's remarkable talent as well as his inconsistency and lack of critical awareness. There is no marked linguistic development, and the gap between his writings and the Hebrew versions of Mendele's (S.Y. *Abramovitsh) stories, which appeared within a decade of Smolenskin's death, is very great. He was, nevertheless, the leading Hebrew novelist in the 20 years following the death of Abraham *Mapu, whose influence is clearly recognizable in his novels.

Philosopher of Jewish Nationalism

Smolenskin was less a publicist than a philosopher of Jewish nationalism. His understanding of the nature of Judaism and the Jewish people was unfolded and developed in copious and often loosely repetitive articles in *Ha-Shaḥar*, which included: *Am Olam*, his first major study on this subject (in *Ha-Shaḥar*, 3 [1872]); *Et La'asot*, which may be regarded as a continuation of *Am Olam* and which makes a number of practical suggestions for putting the theories of the earlier work into effect (in *Ha-Shaḥar*, 4 [1873]); and *Et Lata'at* (in *Ha-Shaḥar*, 6, 8, 9 [1875, 1876/77, 1878]). Convinced that Jewish nationalism was progressive and not reactionary, he regarded it primarily as a matter of the spirit. The Jewish people had received its Torah in the wilderness before conquering its land and founding a polity. Apart from Torah, however, Israel had always been sustained by its messianic hope and its loyalty to the Hebrew language. The nation's present plight demanded a strengthening of its spiritual forces and national awareness in order to bolster its self-respect. Hence his hostility toward the kind of Enlightenment propagated by the disciples of Moses *Mendelssohn, the so-called Berlin Haskalah, which reduced Judaism to a mere religion and advocated assimilation. Smolenskin discerned the roots of antisemitism in the contempt felt by the nations for the inferior national status of the Jews, a situation that could be reversed only by a real affirmation of Jewish nationhood. The pogroms of 1881 convinced Smolenskin not only that the hope of emancipation was chimerical, but that spiritual nationalism alone was not enough. Henceforward, he became an ardent advocate of a physical return to the homeland, as expressed in 25 articles published in the last three volumes of *Ha-Shaḥar* (vols. 10–12, 1880/82, 1883, 1884). The time had come to establish a political, economic, and spiritual center in Ereẓ Israel in preparation for a future Jewish state. Agricultural settlement by itself would not be able to support mass immigration. Industry was essential, if the stream of refugees from antisemitism and persecution was to be directed successfully toward the homeland. But at the same time Torah and a knowledge of Hebrew literature must be disseminated throughout the people, so that Israel might become once more a free and highly cultured nation in its ancestral land. In great measure, Smolenskin laid the foundations for the Zionist movement which gradually took shape in the following two decades. At the same time he anticipated the concept of a spiritual center, which was later to be argued so forcibly by *Aḥad Ha-Am. Smolenskin's percipience may be discerned in the repeated warnings expressed, in both his articles and stories, that the pogroms in Russia and the antisemitism in Germany were no temporary aberrations, but merely the first manifestations of worse horrors to come. He foresaw danger threatening the entire people, and maintained that only Ereẓ Israel could offer a real refuge, where all the tribes of the dispersion could be gathered into a single nation. *Nekam Berit* (in *Ha-Shaḥar*, 11 [1883]), a story describing the return of an assimilated youth to his people following the Russian pogroms, remains a veritable testament to Smolenskin's nationalism.

General Evaluation

Admittedly, many of Smolenskin's ideas concerning nationalism and the particular qualities of Judaism may be discovered in the writings of S.D. *Luzzatto, Nachman *Krochmal, S.J. *Rapoport, Leopold *Zunz, Abraham *Geiger, and Moses *Hess, although Smolenskin denied any indebtedness to Hess. But Smolenskin endowed their concepts with new life and vigor, refashioning them and adding to them until they became his own. Moreover, through his journal he was able to give them wider currency than had previously been possible. It was not without reason that Smolenskin claimed that he had implanted a love of nation and a new spirit in many a heart and mind. Not merely a thinker, but somewhat of a visionary, Smolenskin's strength lay in his imagination, intuitive foresight, and breadth of perspective. In retrospect, much of what he wrote seems tinged with prophecy. There is something prophetic, too, about his determination and his fire. One of the great fighters of all time in Hebrew literature, he argued his beliefs passionately and with conviction. As an observer of contemporary Jewish life, he remains an important source of information, while his place in the history of Hebrew literature and the growth of Jewish nationalism is equally secure. Of the numerous collections of Smolenskin's writings, the most laudable are *Kol Sifrei Perez Smolenskin* (6 vols., 1905–10, the first of which includes a biography of Smolenskin by R. *Brainin) and *Ma'amarim* (4 vols., 1925–26; 1975). A new edition of the works appeared in 1975.

BIBLIOGRAPHY: C.H. Freundlich, *Peretz Smolenskin* (Eng., 1965); D. Patterson, *The Hebrew Novel in Czarist Russia* (1964); Waxman, Literature, index: D. Weinfeld, in: P. Smolenskin, *Kevurat Ḥamor* (1968, incl. bibl.); Z. Fishman, in: *Hadoar*, 2 (1922), nos. 215–9; Lachower, Sifrut, 4 (1948), index; Klausher, Sifrut, passim (bibl. in: 5 (1955^2), 177–231); Kressel, Leksikon, 2 (1967), 515–21 (incl. bibl.); S. Breiman, in: *Shivat Ẓiyyon*, 314 (1953), 138–63. **ADD. BIBLIOGRAPHY:** M. Ungerfeld, "*Li-Dmuto shel P. Smolenskin*," in: *Moznayim*, 21 (1966), 535–38; D. Weinfeld, "*Ha-Mesapper bi-Yẓirato shel P. Smolenskin*," in: *Halkin* (1975), 503–32; Y. Barzilai, "*Bein P. Smolenskin u-Moshe Hess*," in: *Biẓaron*, 49–51 (1992), 57–79; G. Shaked, "*Hitbadut ha-Ẓippiyyah: Smolenksin ve-Mendele ve-ha-Narativ shel Tekufat ha-Haskalah*," in: *Mi-Vilnah li-Yerushalayim* (2002), 327–40.

[David Patterson]

SMOLI (formerly **Smoler**), **ELIEZER** (1901–1985), Hebrew writer. Born in Volhynia, Smoli immigrated to Palestine in 1920 with a group of pioneers, and graduated from a teachers' seminary in Jerusalem (1923). From 1948 he was supervisor of schools for the Sharon region. Smoli was encouraged by Asher *Barash to write fiction instead of poetry, and his stories were published in the daily *Davar* and in *Davar li-Yladim*.

His books, which manifest his love for the land and for the early pioneers, were the first of their kind. Notable among them is *Anshei Bereshit* (1933; 1963[7]); an English translation entitled *Frontiersmen of Israel* appeared in 1964. Smoli also wrote *Or ba-Galil* (1939; 1956[7]); *Bein Sheki'ah li-Zeriḥah* (1946); *Bein Ḥermon ve-Gilbo'a* (1946; *Between the Hermon and Gilboa*, 1946); *Yafah at Arẓenu* (1948; 1963[5]); *Laylah ba-Mishlat* (1951); *Olam ha-Ḥayyot* (1952); and several works on plant and animal life in Israel.

BIBLIOGRAPHY: Kressel, Leksikon, 2 (1967), 945.

[Getzel Kressel]

SMORGON (Pol. **Smorgonie**), town in Grodno district, Belarus, passed from Poland to Russia in 1793; between 1921 and 1945 within independent Poland. From the 16th century until the second half of the 19th century, the town was the private property of the princes of Radziwill. Jewish settlement in Smorgon is believed to date from the early 17th century. From 1628 the Jews of Smorgon paid their taxes to the community administration of Grodno. In 1631 the community of Smorgon became the center of a *galil* (province) within the framework of the Council of Lithuania (see Councils of the *Lands). The autonomous status of the community was confirmed in 1651. In 1765 there were 649 Jews in the community of Smorgon who paid the poll tax. During the 1830s a Jewish agricultural settlement, Karka, with 30 farmsteads, was established near the town (on the eve of World War I, 40 Jewish families there worked on the land). In 1847 there were 1,621 Jews living in Smorgon. In the 1860s a tanning industry was begun in the town as a result of Jewish initiative. In addition to this, the Jews of the town earned their livelihoods from carpentry, the knitting of socks, the baking of bagels (which were famous throughout Russia), retail trade, and peddling. The *Bund gained many adherents among the workers in Smorgon. From 1899 a Zionist organization was active in the town and in 1905 a branch of the SS (Zionist Socialist Workers' *Party) was established. In 1897 there were 6,743 Jews living in Smorgon (76% of the population). On the eve of World War I, there were two *battei midrash*, seven synagogues, three elementary yeshivot, and a Jewish hospital in the town. A section of the town's Jewish population were *Ḥabad Ḥasidim. In 1915, during World War I, many of the Jews in Smorgon were expelled to the Russian interior. Jewish refugee tanners from Smorgon founded the tanning industries in Kharkov, Rostov, and Bogorodsk. When Smorgon reverted to independent Poland after World War I the Jewish refugees began to return to their destroyed houses. Between the two world wars, a Hebrew *Tarbut school, a drama circle (Bamati), sports clubs, Zionist youth circles, and branches of Po'alei *Zion, *He-Ḥalutz and *Betar functioned in the town.

The spiritual leaders of the community during the early second half of the 18th century included the rabbi of the community Ḥayyim Cohen. In 1827–28 the town rabbi was the renowned Manasseh b. Joseph of *Ilya, a native of Smorgon. Subsequently, a dynasty of rabbis descended from R. Leib Shapira established themselves in the town. From 1910 to 1917 Judah Leib Gordin, the author of *Teshuvat Yehudah*, held rabbinical office in the town. Nahum *Slouschz, the author Aaron Abraham *Kabak, the Yiddish poet Moshe *Kulbak, and David *Raziel, commander of the Irgun Ẓevai *Le'ummi, were natives of Smorgon.

[Arthur Cygielman]

Holocaust Period

In September 1939 the Red Army entered the town and a Soviet administration was established until the outbreak of the German-Soviet war in June 1941, when the Germans occupied the town. The Germans established two ghettos in different places there. In the summer of 1942 some Jews were sent to Kovno (*Kaunas) and shared the fate of that community while the others were sent to Ponary near Vilna, and were killed there. After the war, the Jewish community of Smorgon was not reconstituted. An organization of former residents of Smorgon was formed in Israel.

BIBLIOGRAPHY: *Smorgon, Meḥoz Vilna: Sefer Edut ve-Zikkaron* (1965); S. Dubnow, *Pinkas ha-Medinah* (1925), index; Y. Rivlin, in: *Yahadut Lita*, 1 (1959), 459; A. Tartakower, *Toledot Tenu'at ha-Ovedim ha-Yehudit*, 1 (1929), 36.

SMORGON, Australian business dynasty. The Smorgon family, one of the most successful in contemporary Australia, lived in the Ukraine. Poor before the 1917 Revolution, they temporarily became prosperous during the NEP era under Lenin but immigrated to Melbourne, Australia, in 1926 as collectivization took hold. There GERSHON SMORGON, the head of the family, opened a kosher butcher shop in Carlton, Melbourne. By the start of World War II the family had developed a successful meat-exporting and food-canning business. They became major business leaders in the late 1940s, developing a rabbit-meat exporting business to the United States and also a large-scale paper manufacturing business, chosen by the family's new head VICTOR SMORGON (b. 1913) as being virtually recession-proof. By the 1960s Smorgon Consolidated Industries, the family's private holding company, had also become one of Australia's largest steel manufacturers and, later, large-scale glass manufacturers. The family, located in Melbourne, is also noted for its philanthropy. Australia's *Business Review Weekly*, publishers of the country's annual "rich list," estimated the family's collective wealth at $150 million in 1983, $650 million in 1992, and $2.37 billion (about U.S. $1.8 billion) in 2004, making them the richest family ranked on the list.

BIBLIOGRAPHY: R. Ostrow, *The New Boy Network* (1987), 157–61; W.D. Rubinstein, *Jews in Australia II*, index.

[William D. Rubinstein (2nd ed.)]

°SMUTS, JAN CHRISTIAAN (1870–1950), South African statesman, soldier, and philosopher. In the first half of the 20th century Smuts was a dominant figure in South African public life, both in war and peace; he occupied a place in world history for his part in the two great wars and in the creation of the League of Nations and of the United Nations. As a member of Britain's Imperial War Cabinet in World War I and a long-standing supporter of the Zionist cause (he was a personal friend of Chaim *Weizmann), he helped to formulate the Balfour *Declaration on the Jewish National Home as well as the Palestine Mandate. On many subsequent occasions he manifested his concern for the proper fulfillment of the mandate and used his influence with the British government to defend Jewish rights in Palestine. When the State of Israel was founded in 1948, the South African government, of which Smuts was then prime minister, immediately accorded de facto recognition. Shortly after, Smuts was defeated in a general election by the Nationalists. A settlement established with the help of the South African Zionist Federation, *Ramat Yohanan, was named after Smuts. Smuts was on friendly terms with prominent Jews and showed a deep understanding and love of the Bible. He strongly condemned the Nazi-inspired antisemitic agitation in South Africa in the 1930s. He criticized immigration restrictions on Jews under the Quota Act (1930), though in 1937 the Hertzog government, in which he was deputy prime minister, under political pressures imposed further immigration restrictions under the Aliens Act (see *South Africa). In 1945, Smuts was the author of the Preamble of the United Nations Charter.

BIBLIOGRAPHY: S.G. Millin, *General Smuts*, 2 (1936), 103–22 and index; J.C. Smuts, *Jan Christian Smuts* (1952), index; C. Weizmann, *Trial and Error* (1949), index; L. Stein, *Balfour Declaration* (1961), 473–82 and index; G. Saron and L. Hotz, *The Jews in South Africa – A History* (1955), index. **ADD. BIBLIOGRAPHY:** ODNB; P. Beukes, *The Religious Smuts* (1994); N. Rose, *The Gentile Zionists* (1973).

[Louis Hotz]

SNAKE (Heb. נָחָשׁ, *naḥash*), a generic name for various species of snake, poisonous and harmless. Both in the Bible and generally in rabbinical literature it is mentioned with ignominy as harmful. It already appears at the dawn of history in the Bible as the enemy of man, enticing Eve. Its punishment was that it would have to crawl upon its belly and lick the earth, and enmity would prevail between it and man: "they shall bruise thy head, and thou shalt bruise their heel" (Gen. 3: 13–15). Slander and speaking evil is compared to the venom of the snake (cf. Ps. 140:4), and it has even been suggested that the Hebrew term for this, *lashon ha-ra*, is an abbreviation of *leshon ha-naḥash ha-ra* ("the tongue of the evil snake"). Simeon b. Yohiai stated: "Even with the best of snakes, crush its head" (TJ, Kid. 4:11, 66c). It is permitted to slay "the snake of Israel," apparently the viper common in inhabited localities, even on the Sabbath (Shab. 121b). On the other hand, it was recognized that in the ordinary way even the poisonous snake does not attack man unless it is afraid of being attacked. Hence the directive that the recital of the *Amidah* may not be interrupted "even if a snake is coiled around one's heel" (Ber. 5:1). According to the Jerusalem Talmud, however (Ber. 9a), one may defend oneself against it even when praying, if it appears about to bite. Despite the hatred in general toward snakes, their value in destroying mice was recognized. Some even raised "house snakes" for this purpose (Gen. R. 19:10; this is the "house snake" referred to in TJ, Ter. 8:7, 46a).

Only a few of the species of snakes in Israel are poisonous. Eighteen species of nonpoisonous snakes are to be found, seven whose poison kills small creatures only, and seven which are dangerous to man. In addition to the comprehensive term *naḥash* there is mentioned the *saraf* which appears to be the general name for poisonous snakes whose poison, so to speak, *soref* ("burns") the body. Four individual snakes are mentioned in the Bible: צֶפַע or צִפְעוֹנִי (*ẓefa* or *ẓifoni*), אֶפְעֶה (*efeh*), שְׁפִיפוֹן (*shefifon*), and פֶּתֶן (*peten*), all of which are poisonous. The *ẓefa-ẓifoni* is identified with the Palestine viper, *Vipera palaestinae*, recognizable by the two dark brown wavy stripes extending along the length of the light brown skin. This is the only poisonous snake dwelling in the inhabited regions of Israel. The Bible notes that the *ẓifoni* "excretes" its poison while the snake "bites" (Prov. 23:32), i.e., the latter bites with all its teeth while the poisonous snake only pricks with the anterior teeth, thus excreting the poison, The genus *Viper* is also found in northern countries, while other poisonous snakes dwell in hot regions. The Israeli viper is unique in that it lays eggs, while the other species are viviparous. Isaiah (59:5) already notes that the *ẓifoni* lays eggs and whoever eats them is liable to die from the bite of the serpents breaking out of them. A closely related species, black in color, *Atractaspis eingadensis*, is found in En-Gedi and its vicinity.

Efeh is mentioned in the Bible as a dangerous desert snake (Isa. 30:6). According to the Midrash, this is the *ekhes* (Mekh. Va-Yassa, 1), apparently a snake of the genus *Echis* being meant, two species of which are found in the desert areas of Israel. It can be recognized by the white bands breadthways upon its light brown body. It makes a noise by the rubbing of its scales that sounds like a cry and this may be the origin of its name (פעה; "to cry"). Its poison is very dangerous though it very rarely does harm as it is not found near inhabited places. *Shefifon* is identified by the Septuagint with *Cerastes*, a genus of poisonous snakes of which the species *Pseudocerastes fieldi*, recognizable by glands like protrusions above its eyes, is found in the Negev. It digs into the sand, only its "horns" protruding.

The birds, taking them to be worms, peck at them, whereupon the snake strikes, killing them. This apparently is referred to in the verse: "Dan shall be … a *shefifon* in the path, that biteth the horse's heels" (Gen. 49:17). Its name appears to be connected with the rustling made by its scales. *Peten* has been identified with the Egyptian cobra, *Naja haje*. It is not found in Israel though there are indications that solitary specimens may exist in the southern Negev and in Sinai. It is the most dangerous snake of the region. Even outward contact with it can be dangerous (cf. Job 20:14–16). The *peten* was used by charmers, as is the Indian cobra today, and it is noted that it does not always obey charmers (Ps. 58:5–7). The words (Ps. 58:7), "Break their teeth, O God, in their mouth," may be a reference to the fact that the charmers used to extract the poisonous teeth of the *peten*. The black *peten, Walterinnesia aegyptia*, is found in the Judean desert. It is a dangerous poisonous snake in appearance similar to the nonpoisonous black snake. Rabbinical literature mentions poisonous snakes called *havarvar, arvad*, and *akhnai*, whose identity has not been established.

BIBLIOGRAPHY: Lewysohn, Zool, 234ff.; F.S. Bodenheimer, *Animal and Man in Bible Lands* (1960), 200; A. Barash and J.H. Hoofien, *Zoḥalim* (1961²); J. Feliks, *The Animal World of the Bible* (1962), 102ff. **ADD. BIBLIOGRAPHY:** Feliks, Ha-Ẓome'aḥ, 250, 262.

[Jehuda Feliks]

SNEERSOHN, ḤAYYIM ẒEVI (1834–1882), proto-Zionist. Sneersohn settled in Ereẓ Israel with his family in childhood. He was one of the first *maskilim* in Jerusalem, and arrived at the conclusion that redemption would come gradually and naturally. He left Ereẓ Israel on public missions a number of times. In 1861 he traveled to India and Australia on behalf of the Jerusalem committee for the establishment of Houses of Shelter and Hospices (Battei Maḥaseh ve-Hakhnasat Oreḥim). On this trip he succeeded in winning the support not only of heads of Jewish communities and rabbis, but also of Christians, among them senior ecclesiastics and statesmen. In his speeches in the large towns of Australia, Sneersohn described the project as the beginning of the return to Zion, the redemption of Israel, and the redemption of the world. He spoke in Hebrew, and his speeches were translated into English (his speech in Melbourne was printed in a pamphlet, 1862). He traveled to Paris and London and from there to the United States (1869) in order to gain assistance for the agricultural settlement of Jews of Tiberias. As a result of his representations to the U.S. government, the American consul in Jerusalem was changed, and a Jewish consul (Benjamin P. Peixotto) was sent to Romania (1870). In a letter (printed in the paper *Ha-Ivri*, 1872, 47–50) Sneersohn called on the *Alliance Israélite Universelle to convene a world congress in order to discuss the condition of the Jewish people and the establishment of a Jewish state. In New York he published a selection of his lectures and articles on Ereẓ Israel and Romania entitled *Palestine and Roumania, a Description of the Holy Land, and the Past and Present State of Roumania and the Roumanian Jews* (New York, 1872). In 1875 he returned to Ereẓ Israel. His activities aroused the opposition of the heads of the Ashkenazi community in Jerusalem, who banned, cursed, and persecuted him. As a U.S. citizen, he requested the protection of the American consuls. He later left Ereẓ Israel for South Africa, where he died.

BIBLIOGRAPHY: I. Klausner, in: *Herzl Year Book*, 6 (1965), 25–51; idem, *Rabbi Ḥayyim Ẓevi Sneersohn* (Heb. 1943).

[Israel Klausner]

SNEH (Kleinbaum), MOSHE (1909–1972), Israeli politician and publicist, member of the First to Fifth, and Seventh Knessets. Born in Radzyn, Poland, Sneh received a traditional Jewish education and then graduated from the University of Warsaw in medicine. He took part in the Jewish students' movement in Poland and belonged to the "radical" wing of the *General Zionists led by Yitzhak *Gruenbaum. In 1935 he was one of the founders of the General Zionists A. After the outbreak of World War II he managed to flee from Warsaw to Vilna and from there to Palestine, where he settled in 1940. Sneh was co-opted to the *Haganah command, becoming chief of the national command in 1941. After World War II Sneh was one of the protagonists of the violent struggle against the British anti-Zionist policy and the British Administration in Palestine, and in 1945 joined the *Jewish Agency Executive. On June 29, 1946 (Black Saturday), he managed to escape arrest and left clandestinely for Europe. As he objected to the restriction of the struggle against the British, he resigned from his post as chief of the Haganah command. At the end of 1946 he was appointed head of the European Political Branch of the Jewish Agency, and head of the Illegal Immigration Department in it. Around the time of the publication of the UN partition plan, at the end of 1947, Sneh underwent an ideological change that led to his resignation from the Jewish Agency Executive and his joining the newly formed *Mapam party in 1948 as a member of its more extreme Left wing. He was elected to the First Knesset in 1949 on the Mapam list, but following the *Slansky trial in Prague left the party in February 1952 and formed the Left Faction with two other former Mapam members, later joining the Israel Communist Party (Maki) in November 1954. In his book *Sikkumim ba-She'elah ha-Le'ummit: Le-Or ha-Marksizm- Leninizm* ("Conclusions concerning the Jewish Problem in the Light of Marxism-Leninism"), which he published in 1954, Sneh explained the change in his political views. When the Arab members and some of the Jewish members of the Israel Communist Party broke away to form Rakah, Sneh remained in Maki, which was now predominantly Jewish, and became editor of its daily *Kol Ha'am* – a position he held until 1969. After the *Six-Day War, he became increasingly critical of the anti-Israel policy of the Soviet Union, supporting negotiations between Israel and the Arab states while insisting on the Palestinian right for self-determination in the territories occupied by Israel during the Six-Day War.

Among his other publications are *Li-Ve'ayot ha-Komunizm, ha-Demokratyah ve-ha-Am ha-Yehudi: Rashei Perakim*

("The Problems of Communism, Democracy and the Jewish People: Headings," 1968); *Aḥarit ki-Bereishit: Mivḥar Devarim 1967–72* ("The End like the Beginning: A Selection of Speeches, 1967–1972," 1982); and *Ketavim* ("Writings"), edited by Emanuel Melter, in four volumes (1995–2002).

Moshe's son EPHRAIM (1944–), a physician who served in the IDF until 1987, reaching the rank of brigadier general, served in the Knesset on behalf of the Labor Party from 1992 and served as minister of health from April 1994 until after the elections to the Fourteenth Knesset in 1996. In July 1997 he ran against Ehud *Barak for the *Israel Labor Party leadership, but lost.

BIBLIOGRAPHY: B. Balti, *Ba-Ma'avak al ha-Kiyyum ha-Yehudi: Li-Demuto shel Moshe Sneh* (1981); E. She'alti'el, *Tamid be-Meri: Moshe Sneh, Biographyah* (2000).

[Susan Hattis Rolef (2nd ed.)]

SNEH, SIMJA (1914–1999), Argentinean author. Born in Pulawy, Poland, Sneh received a Jewish education in his youth and later studied history and philosophy at the Free University of Warsaw. He worked as a teacher and journalist. With the emergence of Nazism and Hitler's military aggression, Sneh joined the Polish army and fought under General Anders and with the Jewish Brigade of the British Army in Italy. He arrived in Argentina under precarious circumstances and without papers. Nevertheless, he had an active career as a teacher of Yiddish and Hebrew in the Jewish school system of Buenos Aires. In addition, he worked as a journalist for a variety of Jewish and mainstream newspapers and periodicals. He wrote in Yiddish, Hebrew, and Spanish and his works earned him recognition, praise, and several prestigious awards. Sneh worked for many years in the Department of Culture of the Asociación Mutual Israelita Argentina – AMIA, the Ashkenazi community in Buenos Aires. He was present in the community building on July 18, 1994, when a terrorist bomb destroyed it, killing over 80 people. Sneh survived the attack and died of natural causes in April 1999.

Sneh's *El pan y la sangre* (1977) contains 12 short stories, which are remarkable for the way they recreate specific moments and events. Perhaps the most outstanding quality in Sneh's texts is the fact that they are not merely the stuff of fiction. His writing comes from his own experience, which makes the horrific realism contained in them all the more penetrating. That is not to say that all the stories in the collection are literal recreations of actual events he lived through and witnessed. However, his experience as a Shoah survivor serves as the inspiration for the characters, places, and circumstances of which he writes.

Sneh's true masterpiece is to be found in his subsequent work completed just two years prior to his death. *Sin rumbo* constitutes a truly monumental undertaking. Published between 1993 and 1997 (in Spanish), the six-volume text is over 1,600 pages in length. It was originally written in Yiddish as a trilogy and published in serial form in the Yiddish periodical *Di Presse* in Buenos Aires. One-hundred fifty weekly chapters appeared between 1947 and 1952. The first volume was published as a book under the title of *Na' Venad* (1952). It is part testimonial narrative, part memoir, part novel, and part historical document. It comprises a substantial social and historical record of the Holocaust, and is certainly the single most important Holocaust work written in Spanish. Together, *El pan y la sangre* and *Sin rumbo* constitute a remarkable legacy of an even more remarkable human being who overcame incredible odds and who left the world a gift of momentous significance.

[Darrell B. Lockhart (2nd ed.)]

SNYATYN (Pol. **Śniatyń**), city in Ivano-Frankovisk district, Ukraine; incorporated in 1340 into Poland, passed to Austria in 1772, and reverted to Poland from 1919 to 1939. Jewish merchants from Poland and the east visited the Snyatyn fairs from the 15th century. An organized community was formed in the mid-16th century; in 1572 Jews owned 11 houses in the town. In 1578 King Stephen Báthory accorded the Jews in Snyatyn the right to trade freely there. In 1628, to strengthen its economy, King Sigismund III Vasa authorized members of all nations to settle in Snyatyn. At that time the customs collection at the border station was leased by Jews (see *Naḥmanovich). In 1650, after the devastations by the Cossacks under *Chmielnicki (1648–49), the king granted the community a privilege to produce and sell liquor to facilitate their rehabilitation. There were 1,111 Jews living in the town in 1765; 2,333 (22% of the total) in 1880; and 4,386 (36%) in 1910. In 1894 a Jewish school was established, financed by the Baron de Hirsch *Fund; in 1910 it had 186 pupils. The Jewish population numbered 3,248 (31%) in 1921. After World War I, during the period of independent Poland, the Jews in Snyatyn were severely affected by antisemitic agitation and the economic boycott against them. They were compelled to seek the assistance of Jewish relief institutions.

[Shimon Leib Kirshenboim]

Holocaust Period

When the German-Soviet war broke out, Snyatyn was captured by the Hungarian allies of Germany (July 1941). They imposed economic restrictions on the Jews, but prevented violent attacks by the Ukrainian population. In September 1941 the city was transferred to German administration, and the systematic murder of the Jews began. From September to December, hundreds were killed in the nearby Potoczek forest. A ghetto was established in Snyatyn. In April 1942 the first deportation to the *Belzec concentration camp took place. The Jews began to construct bunkers in the hope of taking shelter there during the coming deportations. On Sept. 7, 1942, the ghetto was liquidated and the last of the Snyatyn Jewish community were sent to Belzec. Jewish life was not revived in the city after the war.

[Aharon Weiss]

BIBLIOGRAPHY: Halpern, Pinkas, index; R. Mahler, *Yidn in Amolikn Poyln in Likht fun Tsifern* (1958), index; M. Bersohn, *Dyplomataryusz dotyczący Żydów w Polsce* (1910), nos. 152–275, 365; B.

Wasiutyński, *Ludność żydowska w Polsce w wiekach XIX i XX* (1930), 124, 131, 155, 157; I. Schiper, *Dzieje handlu żydowskiego na ziemiach polskich* (1937), index.

SNYDER, LOUIS LEO (1907–1993), U.S. historian. Born in Maryland, Snyder's academic career was spent at the City College and City University of New York, where he was professor of history. A most productive author, he wrote textbooks, children's books, and popular history, and edited the Anvil series of more than 100 volumes. Snyder's scholarly studies have centered in the fields of nationalism and German history.

Among his major works are *Hitlerism* (1932), *Race* (1939), *German Nationalism* (1969²), *The Meaning of Nationalism* (1954), *The War: A Concise History, 1939–45* (1960), *Hitler and Nazism* (1967), *The New Nationalism* (1968), *Great Turning Points in History* (1971), *Encyclopedia of the Third Reich* (1976), *National Socialist Germany* (1984), *Diplomacy in Iron: Bismarck* (1985), *Hitler's Elite* (1990), *Encyclopedia of Nationalism* (1990), and *Hitler's German Enemies* (1992). He also edited *Human Rights: Meaning and History* (with M. Palumbo, 1982).

BIBLIOGRAPHY: M. Palumbo and W. Shanahan (eds), *Nationalism: Essays in Honor of Louis L. Synder* (1981).

SO (Heb. סוא), according to the received text of II Kings 17:4 the name of the king of Egypt with whom King *Hoshea of Israel entered into relations in approximately 725 B.C.E. when he discontinued the annual payment of tribute to his Assyrian suzerain.

Whereas סוא-*sw'* does not correspond to the name of any known Egyptian prince or general, it can very well be equated with Egyptian *s3w*, cuneiform *Sa-a-a*, and Greek *Sais*, the name of the city in the western Delta which was the residence of the pharaoh Tefnakhte; and since it now appears that the latter was already reigning over Lower and Middle Egypt at this time, H. Goedicke has suggested that this is the Pharaoh in question. After Goedicke, W.F. Albright has proposed for the pertinent clause in II Kings 17:4 a reconstruction which yields the required sense. But it can be achieved more simply: the mere inversion of the words *so* and *el*, without any addition, makes the clause mean, "For he had sent a mission to Sais, to the king of Egypt" (cf. I Sam. 23:3b; II Sam. 3:20b; I Kings 2:26ab). R. Sayed has suggested that סוא-*sw'* is shortened from *Si3-jb*, which is now known to have been Tefnakhte's Horus-name; but he observes that the normal thing is for a foreign document to refer to Pharaoh by his name or (in the *el-Amarna correspondence) his praenomen (or merely by the title Pharaoh), not by his Horus name. Most recent scholarship (contrast Green) has accepted Goedicke's 1963 identification of "So" as a place name, and the identification of the Pharaoh ruling there as Tefnakhte.

BIBLIOGRAPHY: S. Yeivin, in: VT, 2 (1952), 164–68; H. Goedicke, in: BASOR, 171 (1963), 64–66; W.F. Albright, *ibid.*, 66; R. Sayed, in: VT, 20 (1970), 116–18. **ADD. BIBLIOGRAPHY:** M. Cogan and H. Tadmor, *II Kings* (AB; 1988), 196; B. Becking, *The Fall of Samaria* (1991), 47 n. 2; J. Day, in: VT, 42 (1992), 289–301; A. Green, in: JNES, 52 (1993), 99–108; P. Galpaz-Feller, in: RB, 107 (2000), 338–47.

[Harold Louis Ginsberg]

SOAP. It would appear that in the biblical period soap was derived almost exclusively from plants. Many such plants grow in Israel. They contain chiefly potash and soda, and their ash, dissolved in oil, was used until as late as a generation ago for making a liquid soap. Most of these plants grow in the salty regions of the Arabah, in the Negev, and on the seashore. These belong to the botanical genera *Salicornia, Salsola, Mesembryanthemum, Saponaria. Statice*, and *Atriplex*. In the Bible these washing materials are referred to as *bor, borit*, and *sheleg. Borit* is mentioned in apposition to *neter* ("soda") in the Bible as a material for cleansing stains (Jer. 2:22). The messenger of the covenant will purify the people on the day of the Lord as "with fuller's soap" (*borit*, Mal. 3:2). In other places in the Bible the term *bor* is used for material for the cleansing of hands and clothes (Job. 9:30), and metaphorically for cleanness of hands (Job. 22:30; II Sam. 22:21). *Bor* and *borit* are connected with the word *baroh* ("clean"). According to the Tosefta, *borit* and *ahal* are perennial plants that disappear from the field at the end of the season (Shev. 5:6) and the Jerusalem Talmud (Shev. 7:2, 37b) characterizes them as "species of laundering plants." According to the Babylonian Talmud (Nid. 62a), "*borit* is identical with *ahal*," i.e., both are species of aloe. *Ahal*, in Akkadian *uhulu*, Syrian *ahala*, and Arabic *gasul*, are soap-producing plants containing soaping matter such as *Salicornia*, and in particular the genus *Mesembryanthemum*, called in modern Hebrew *ahal*. One species, *M. crystalinum*, grows on walls and rocks facing the Mediterranean Sea, and it is grown in some countries in order to extract the soda it contains. In the Arabah other species of *Mesembryanthemum* are widespread. These can be recognized by their finger-like thick leaves. After the rains they spread widely.

In rabbinical literature *ashlag* is mentioned together with washing materials (Shab. 9:5; Nid. 9:6). According to the Jerusalem Talmud (Shab. 9:5, 12b), a plant called *oẓerot ru'aḥ* ("wind collector") is meant. It seems that the reference is to the plant *Vaccaria* (*Saponaria*) *segetalis* which contains saponin. In fields of cereal it grows as a weed whose calyx expands when the fruit ripens as if it is "collecting wind." It is called *ashlag* also in Arabic. Perhaps the *shaleg* ("snow water") of Job 9:30 is actually *ashlag*, as suggested by the parallel with *bor* ("soap").

BIBLIOGRAPHY: Loew, Flora, 1 (1926), 637–50; G. Dalman, *Arbeit und Sitte in Palaestina*, 2 (1932), 263; 5 (1937), 155; J. Feliks, *Olam ha-Ẓome'aḥ ha-Mikra'i* (1968²), 298–300. **ADD. BIBLIOGRAPHY:** Feliks, Ha-Tzome'aḥ, 35.

[Jehuda Feliks]

SOARE (Sonnenfeld), IULIA (1920–1971), Romanian author. Soare's semi-autobiographical novel, *Familia Calaff* ("The Calaff Family", 1956), was a sober appraisal of middle-class Jewish life in a Romanian provincial town during the years

1910–20. Her other works include a fictionalized biography of *Stendhal* (1957) and *Vîrsta de bronz* ("The Age of Bronze", 1969), a collection of historical novellas.

SOAVE, MOISE (1820–1882), Italian scholar and teacher in Venice. Soave contributed to *Il Vessillo Israelitico, Il Corriere Israelitico*, and to Geiger's *Juedische Zeitschrift fuer Wissenschaft und Leben*. Apart from studies such as *L'Israelitismo Moderno* (1865), he wrote mostly on the history of Jews in Italy, biographies, and on Italian Jewish literature. One of his works on the *Soncino family (*Dei Soncini celebri tipografi italiani…*, 1878) includes a list of books they printed. Soave corresponded with major Jewish scholars of his time, among them S.D. Luzzatto, E. Renan, and M. Steinschneider.

BIBLIOGRAPHY: M. Coen Porto, in: *Vesillo Israelitico*, 51 (1883), 22–24; G. Gabrieli, *Italia Judaica* (1924), index; I. Luzzato, *Catalogo Ragionato…* (1881), index.

[Alfredo Mordechai Rabello]

SOBEDRUHY (Czech **Sobědruhy**; Ger. **Soborten**), town in N. Bohemia, Czech Republic. Jews are first recorded there in 1334. In 1500 the wooden synagogue was replaced by a stone structure; a lamp there is inscribed with the year 1553. The earliest tombstone inscription dates from 1669; the cemetery served many communities, including Dresden (until 1751). At times Sobedruhy was exclusively inhabited by Jews. In 1750 Empress *Maria Theresa donated a tower clock for the synagogue. There were anti-Jewish riots in Sobedruhy in 1744. The burial of a Frankist from Sobedruhy in Prague in 1800 caused communal disturbances there. In the 19th century Sobedruhy remained an Orthodox community, in contrast to the nearby community of Teplice which was liberal. A community building was opened in Sobedruhy in 1900. There were 120 Jewish families living in Sobedruhy in 1724, 245 persons in 1842, and 393 in 1893. The community numbered 376 persons living in 17 localities in 1902, and 51 in 1930 (3.2% of the total population). Most of the Jews left Sobedruhy at the time of the Sudeten crisis (1938), and the community was dissolved. The congregation was not reestablished after World War II. The synagogue building was demolished and the clock placed in the custody of the municipality. The cemetery, damaged under Nazi rule, continued to exist.

BIBLIOGRAPHY: Herzl, in: H. Gold (ed.), *Die Juden und Judengemeinden Boehmens in Vergangenheit und Gegenwart* (1934), 601–7; JE, 11 (1895), 418 s.v. Soborten.

[Jan Herman]

SOBEL, BERNARD (1887–1964), U.S. theater historian and publicist. Sobel, who began his career as an English teacher, was drama critic for the New York *Daily Mirror*, 1932–35. He wrote *Burleycue: An Underground History of Burlesque Days* (1931), *A Pictorial History of Burlesque* (1956), and *A Pictorial History of Vaudeville* (1961). As a theatrical press agent he represented Florenz Ziegfeld, Metro-Goldwyn-Mayer, and many famous producers and actors. His memoirs, *Broadway Heartbeat*, appeared in 1953.

SOBEL, JACOB ẒEVI (**James H. Soble**; 1831–1913), U.S. Hebrew writer. Born in Lithuania, Sobel was ordained as rabbi and headed a yeshivah, but, influenced by the Haskalah, broke with orthodoxy, and criticized it in his *Ha-Ḥozeh Ḥezyonot be-Arba'ah Olamot* (1872). In 1876 he arrived in New York, and later moved to Chicago where he earned his living as a Hebrew teacher. He contributed to Hebrew periodicals in Russia and the United States but also wrote for the Yiddish and American press. Some of his satire he directed against Gershon *Rosenzweig and signed with the pseudonym "Binocle." His *Shir Zahav li-Khevod Yisrael ha-Zaken* (1877), although of slight literary merit, is historically significant as the first book of Hebrew poetry published in the United States. A paean to Jewry, Hebrew language, and American democracy, it also condemns the ignorance and spiritual emptiness of Jewish immigrants.

BIBLIOGRAPHY: R. Malachi, in: *Sefer ha-Shanah li-Yhudei Amerikah* (1935), 303–9; J. Kabakoff, *Ḥaluẓei ha-Sifrut ha-Ivrit ba-Amerikah* (1966), 23–75.

[Eisig Silberschlag]

SOBEL, RONALD (1935–), U.S. Reform rabbi, interfaith activist. Sobel was born in Cleveland, Ohio, and received his B.A. from the University of Pittsburgh in 1957. He was ordained at *Hebrew Union College in 1962 and earned a Ph.D. from New York University in 1980. He was awarded an honorary D.D. from HUC-JIR in 1987, an honorary D.H.L. from Long Island University in 1983, and an honorary D.L. from St. John's University in 1994. Immediately following his ordination, he was appointed assistant rabbi at New York City's Temple Emanu-El and elevated to associate rabbi in 1968. In 1973, at the age of 37, he became the youngest senior rabbi in the history of the world's largest Jewish house of worship. By the time he became emeritus, in 2002, he had served in that position longer than any of his predecessors.

In the Reform movement, Sobel served as chairman of the Board of Rabbinic Alumni Overseers of HUC-JIR as well as a member of the college's board of governors. He was also a member of the board of governors of the American Jewish Committee (1972–75); chairman of the National Program Committee of the Anti-Defamation League; chairman of the Commission on Jewish Life and Culture of the American Jewish Congress (1982–84); chairman of the Synagogue Council of America's Commission on International Affairs (1975–77); and a trustee of the Jewish Braille Institute.

Sobel has been particularly active in interfaith affairs. In 1975, he was the first rabbi to preach from the high pulpit of Manhattan's St. Patrick's Cathedral, as part of a dialogue he initiated between Temple Emanu-El and the Cathedral. From 1977 to 79, he was chairman of the International Jewish Committee for Interreligious Consultation, the organization that represents the interests of world Jewry vis-à-vis the Vatican and the World Council of Churches. He also served on the boards of governors of the National Conference of Christians and Jews, the Religious News Service, the Association for Religion and Intellectual Life, and the Institutes of Religion and

Health, in addition to serving as a vice chairman of the National Board of Religion in American Life. He also co-founded two grass-roots interfaith coalitions in New York City: the Yorkville Emergency Alliance on the upper East Side (1982) and A Partnership of Faith in New York (1991), a coalition of congregational clergy throughout the five boroughs.

In 2002, Sobel was the recipient of the annual Clergy Person of the Year Award from the Religion in American Life organization. He was appointed chairman of the New York Civil Rights Coalition in 2003.

[Bezalel Gordon (2nd ed.)]

SOBELOFF, ISIDOR (1899–), U.S. social worker and community leader. Sobeloff, who was born in Baltimore, Maryland, and was the brother of Simon E. *Sobeloff, became the city editor of the Cumberland (Md.) *Daily News* in 1920. He subsequently worked as director of the Jewish Community Center in Jersey City, New Jersey (1922–25), then joined the Federation of Jewish Philanthropists in New York (1925–30) and the Travelers' Aid Society (1930–34). While serving as director of public education for the Welfare Council of New York (1934–37), Sobeloff was also managing editor of the *Jewish Social Service Quarterly* (1932–36) and editor of *Better Times*, a social-work publication (1934–37). As executive vice president of the Jewish Welfare Federation of Detroit from 1937 to 1964, Sobeloff made the Jewish philanthropic campaigns in that city among the most effective in the United States. He attempted to do likewise as director of the Jewish Federation Council of Greater Los Angeles (1964–69). In other social-work activity, he was president of the National Conference of Jewish Social Welfare (1945) and a lecturer at the Training Bureau for Jewish Social Work. Sobeloff's many Jewish community positions included secretary of the allotment committee of the United Jewish Appeal (1944).

SOBELOFF, SIMON ERNEST (1894–1973), U.S. jurist. Sobeloff was city solicitor of Baltimore from 1943 to 1947. He became chief judge of the Maryland Court of Appeals in 1952. He was appointed solicitor-general by President Eisenhower in 1954. In this capacity he played a significant role in helping to formulate the government's stand in regard to the Brown v. Board of Education cases (1954). As a result, the U.S. Supreme Court ruled that separate but equal facilities for blacks in public schools did not meet the constitutional requirement of equal protection by the law. Sobeloff broke with precedent by refusing, although solicitor-general, to sign the brief in a case before the Supreme Court in which the government attempted to support the blacklisting of a professor. The court later vindicated his position. In 1956 he became a judge of the fourth circuit U.S. Court of Appeals and its chief judge in 1958. A prominent figure in Jewish communal circles, Sobeloff was a national vice president of the American Jewish Congress and a member of many other Jewish philanthropic and educational organizations.

[Morris D. Forkosch]

SOBIBOR (**Sobibór**), one of the six Nazi death camps situated in German-occupied Poland, three miles west of the Bug River and five miles south of Wlodawa in the General Gouvernment. It was situated in a wooded area near a small village by the same name in the Lublin District. It was built along the Chel-Wlodawa railway line. The camp measured 1,312 by 1,969 feet. Barbed wire – some 9.5 feet high – interspersed among the trees for concealment, surrounded the camp and the outer perimeter was mined.

In March 1942 the Germans began construction work on the camp in preparation for the mass murder of Polish and other Jews. Jewish slave workers were employed on the site. It was the second camp in *Aktion Reinhard* to be built. *Belzec preceded it and was functioning before it was built, and *Treblinka followed. The camp functioned from May 1942 until October 1943, but the largest transport of victims arrived during June–October 1942, the peak period of killing. Sobibor was used mainly for the murder of Jews from German-occupied eastern Poland and occupied parts of the Soviet Union. Non-Jewish prisoners of war as well as Jews from *Czechoslovakia, *Austria, *Holland, *Belgium, and *France were also put to death at Sobibor. The total number of victims is estimated at 250,000. The victims usually arrived by train and their belongings were immediately taken away. They were then ordered to undress, the women's hair shorn, and the naked mass of people was forced into five gas chambers, which had a total capacity of 500 persons. The gassing lasted 15 minutes. Various systems for the disposal of the dead were used: at first mass graves were dug; later the corpses were burned in heaps, and in the last stage the Nazis burned the bodies on disused iron rails. The ashes were usually taken away by train to an unknown destination. The victims' belongings were carefully sorted and sent to Germany. Women's hair was also crated to Germany.

The camp was divided into three sections. Sector I was for administrative functions. Sector II, or the Reception area, was where Jews, who would arrive by train, were received; it was there that their valuables were confiscated, their hair shorn, and their clothes removed. Sector III was the killing center in the northwest area of the camp, equipped with gas chambers and mass graves. A 492-foot path 9–13 feet wide led from Sector II to Sector III. Victims were marched naked from one camp to the other. The gas chambers were powered by a 200 horsepower engine which produced carbon monoxide. Special accommodations were made for those too weak to walk; a narrow gauge railway was used from the station to the gas chambers to take these Jews to their destination. Those who could not manage the final steps, including infants, were shot. The camp staff consisted of approximately 30 SS men and about 100 Ukrainians, under the command of Richard Thomalla and afterward of Franz Stangl. Most of the German guards as well as Stangl were veterans of the killing process; they had participated in the T-4 *Euthanasia program. The Ukrainians were mostly Soviet prisoners of war trained at Trawniki. A few were ethnic Germans. The number of Jew-

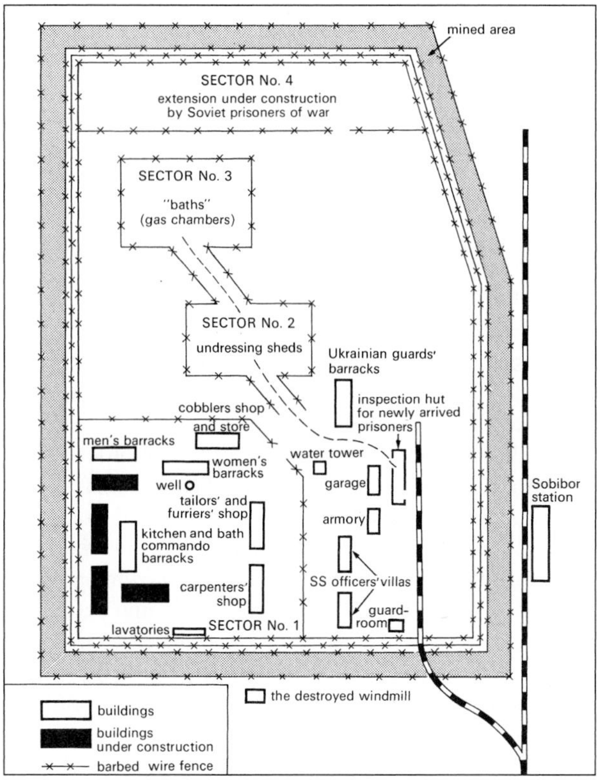

Plan of the Sobibor extermination camp, reconstructed from a drawing by A.A. Pechersky. Courtesy Jewish Observer and Middle East Review, *London.*

ish laborers never exceeded 1,000. Those who weakened were killed and were continually replaced by stronger persons from the new transports. About 200 laborers worked near the gas chambers and in connection with the disposal of corpses. The others were employed in the administrative and economic sections of the camp, especially in sorting out the victims' belongings. Artisans and specialists were usually treated better than other workers.

There were two stages to the killing. The first, from May–July 1942, utilized the gas chambers, which proved inadequate under the strain of massive deportations. Then, as at Belzec, Sobibor camp operations were halted while three more gas chambers were created under the same roof. The capacity was doubled from 600 to 1200.

At the beginning of October 1943, some 300 *Arbeitsjuden* (Jewish laborers) were employed in the camp; most had spent 10–16 months there. Having learned what was in store for them they decided to kill the camp commandant and escape. Poorly armed, they revolted on Oct. 14, 1943, led by Alexander *Pechersky, a Soviet Jewish prisoner of war, and his deputy, Leon Feldhendler, who had been chairman of the Judenrat at Zolkiew in Eastern Galicia. Several German supervisors and Ukrainian *Hiwis* (*Hilfswillige*, "volunteers") were killed. The German supervisors and the *Hiwis* opened fire on the Jews fleeing and prevented them from reaching the exit of the camp. The Jews then came into the area of barbed wire fences and minefields. Some 300 Jews escaped, but most were later killed by the Germans. In the end only 50 survived. Immediately after the revolt, Sobibor was closed down and a grove of trees planted over the site. This was done by some 30 Jewish laborers brought from the General Gouvernment, who were all shot in November 1943. No lists of the victims are extant, possibly because the Germans did not conduct any registration at the camp, or perhaps these lists, with all the other files of the camp, were removed when the camp was closed.

In 1965 a trial was conducted in Krasnodar, U.S.S.R., at which a number of functionaries from Sobibor were tried. A year later, at Hagen, Germany, 11 functionaries were tried: one committed suicide, one was sentenced to life imprisonment, five were given relatively light sentences, and four were acquitted. After the war a monument was erected on the site in memory of the 250,000 victims murdered there.

BIBLIOGRAPHY: Y. Suhl (ed.), *They Fought Back* (1967), 7–50; Ainsztein, in: JSOS, 28 (1966), 19–24; G. Reitlinger, *Final Solution* (1968^2), index; J. Tenenbaum, *Underground* (1952), 261–64, index; Lukaszkiewicz, in: *Biuletyn Glownej Komisji Badania Zbrodni Hitlerowskich w Polsce*, no. 3 (1947). **ADD. BIBLIOGRAPHY:** Y. Arad, *Belzec, Sobibor, Treblinka: The Operation Reinhard Death Camps* (1987); T. Blatt, *From the Ashes of Sobibor: A Story of Survival,* foreword by C.R. Browning (1997); G. Sereny, *Into the Heart of Darkness* (1974); C. Lanzmann, *Shoah* (1985).

[Danuta Dombrowska / Michael Berenbaum (2nd ed.)]

SOBOL, ANDREY MIKHAILOVICH (1888–1926), Russian novelist and playwright. Sobol was born in Saratov of wealthy parents. He joined the revolutionary movement at 16 and in 1906 was jailed and sentenced to hard labor in Siberia. In 1909 he escaped from prison and wandered throughout Europe in poverty, returning to Russia illegally in 1915. He began writing for both liberal and radical periodicals under the pseudonyms of Konstantin Vinogradov and Andrey Nezhdanov. Sobol had misgivings about Bolshevism and retained his faith in humanistic socialism, but, in an open letter published in *Pravda* in 1923, he recanted his "errors." Three years later, disillusioned with the Soviet regime, he committed suicide.

Many of Sobol's semi-autobiographical books, impressionistic and often despairing in tone, depict political émigrés. His most important novel, *Pyl'* ("Dust," 1915), describes the Jewish émigrés in Paris as people who "graze in foreign fields" and have no land or roots. To Sobol, Jews were strangers everywhere, even within the Russian revolutionary movement, which he regarded as riddled with antisemitism. Other works of Jewish interest written by Sobol are *Nechayanno* ("Inadvertently," 1916), which deals with an apostate Jew who finds no peace in his new life; *Rasskazy v pis'makh* ("Tales in the Form of Letters," 1916), satirical sketches of Jewish intellectuals who convert in order to further their careers; and *Pereryv* ("Intermission," 1923), a picture of a Paris Yiddish theater from the inside. Sobol's collected works, in four volumes, appeared in 1926 and 1928.

BIBLIOGRAPHY: Rodin, in: S.M. Ginzburg (ed.), *Yevreyskii Vestnik* (1928), 69–73; Shteynman, in: A. Sobol, *Sobraniie Sochineniia*, 1 (1928), 7–30.

[Yitzhak Maor]

SOBOL, MORDECHAI (1951–), *ḥazzan*. Born in Ḥaderah, Sobol's musical abilities were evident at an early age. When only eight, he was accepted as a pupil by the venerable cantor Solomon Rawitz, who considered him one of his best pupils. In addition to the basics of the prayer services, Cantor Rawitz taught him the principles of sight-reading, harmony, and counterpoint. Sobel was the lead soloist of the Oneg Shabbat choir of Ohel Shem in Tel Aviv. At the age of 12 he began to study with the conductor Samuel Rivlin and sang in his choir, gaining fame throughout Israel for his renditions of cantorial works, particularly those sung by Cantor Mordecai Hirschman. When 16, for the first time he led High Holiday services accompanied by a 40-person choir conducted by Cantor Solomon Rawitz. He served in the Israeli army as a member of the choir of the Army Chief Rabbinate. He arranged and orchestrated melodies for choir and orchestra and wrote original works for passages from the prayer services. Sobol established the Yuval ensemble for cantorial and Jewish music, which had 50 singers and 30 instrumentalists. In 1985 he began a special series of concerts in which the greatest cantors of the world participated. These concerts proved so popular that subscription series were offered to the public annually. The Yuval ensemble also promoted recordings of their concerts.

[Akiva Zimmerman]

SOBOL, YEHOSHUA (1939–), Israeli playwright, prose writer, and director. Sobol was a well known theatrical figure in Israel and abroad. He wrote more than 40 plays, many of which were translated into various languages and performed in theaters around the world. From 1992 he directed his plays, as well as plays by others, in Israel, Switzerland, and the U.S. Between 1984 and 1988 he served as Co-Artistic Director of Haifa Municipal Theater, together with Gedalia Besser. Sobol taught playwriting and conducted drama workshops at the department of theater studies at Tel Aviv University, at the department of Hebrew Literature at Ben-Gurion University of the Negev, and at Wesleyan University in Middletown, Connecticut. He published two novels: *Shetikah* ("Silence," 2000) and *Whisky ze beseder* ("Whisky's Fine," 2005).

After studying literature and history at Oranim College, Sobol received a degree in philosophy from the Sorbonne, Paris, in 1969. His theatrical career started at the Haifa Municipal Theater, in 1971, where he collaborated with director Nola Chilton and wrote the text for *The Days to Come,* a performance based on monologues he collected in an old age home in Haifa. The plays of his playwrighting decade – *Leyl ha-Esserim* ("Status Night of the 20th," 1976), "The Last Worker" (1980), and "Wars of the Jews" (1981) – exposed his inclination toward historical drama. In these plays the intrigue revives a historical moment in the history of the Jewish community or Israeli society; by analyzing its socio-political components. Sobol displays the conflicts involved, the process of cause and effect, the outcome and its influence on present reality. His plays have direct socio-political messages and are written with a clear didactic aim, namely to further spectators' understanding of the complexity of contemporary state of affairs and to promote tolerance and compassion toward minorities.

In the 1980s, Sobol continued to probe the past as a tool for understanding the present. In *Nefesh Yehudi* (*Weininger's Night*, 1982), *Ghetto* (1984), *Adam* (1989), and *Underground* (1991), he went back to European history, analyzed the complexity of "Jewish Fate," and demonstrated past conflicts and events that brought about the transformation of Jews from victims into persecutors. In *The Palestinian Girl* (1985) he reflected upon the unjust conduct of Israelis toward Arabs, and in *Jerusalem Syndrome* (1987) he went back to the events that had led to the destruction of the Temple, showing how the conduct of Jewish extremists fueled conflict and hatred between Jews. *Jerusalem Syndrome* received bad reviews in the press, and its reception by religious audiences was violent and tumultuous: performances were stopped by demonstrations and manifestations during the show and outside the theater. *Solo* (1991), performed in Habimah, Israel's National Theater, echoed Sobol's reflections on the reception of *Jerusalem Syndrome*. For the plot of this play he turned to the life story of Baruch Spinoza and demonstrated a closed, paranoid society that rejected his innovative way of thinking.

Sobol's international career began in 1983, when the Haifa production of his play *Weininger's Night* was invited to participate in the Edinburgh Festival. This was followed by *The Ghetto Triptych* (*Ghetto, Adam, Underground*). *Ghetto* became world famous shortly after its premiere in Haifa in May 1984. The play won the Israeli David's Harp Award for Best Play. The Israeli opening was followed by Peter Zadek's much acclaimed German premiere of the play in Berlin in July 1984. The play and the production were chosen by the leading German theater journal, *Theater Heute*, as the best production and the best foreign play of the year. By 2006 the play had been translated into over 20 languages and had been performed by leading theaters in more than 25 countries throughout the world. Following Nicholas Hytner's production of the play at the Royal National Theatre of Great Britain in 1989, the play won the Evening Standard and the London Critics Award for Best Play of the Year, and was nominated for the Olivier Award in the same category.

From 1995 Sobol cooperated with director Paulus Manker on a number of projects exploring new forms of the theatrical experience. In 1996 the two created the polydrama *Alma*, based on the life of Alma Mahler, for the Wiener Festwochen. It was performed in Purkersdorf, Austria, for six successive seasons. *Alma* was taken to Venice, Italy, and was performed at the Palazzo Zenobio in August and September 2002.

Sobol received many important Israeli awards for his plays and productions. Among these are the David's Harp Award (five times), the David Pinski Award, the Meskin Award, and the Issam Sartawi Award. In 2001 he received the Sapir Award for his prose debut, *Silence*, as best novel of the year, and in 2003 the Rosenbaum Award for his contribution to Israeli theater.

BIBLIOGRAPHY: M. Zur, "Notes on the Night of the Twentieth," in: *Shedemot*, 9 (1978), 9–14; G. Ofrat, "Modern Hebrew Drama: Sobol's Night of 1903," in: *Modern Hebrew Literature*, 9:1–2 (1983), 34–41; Y.S. Feldman, "Zionism – Neurosis or Cure? The "Historical" Drama of Y. Sobol," in: *Prooftexts*, 7:2 (1987), 145–62; M. Handelsaltz: "The Levin-Sobol Syndrome: Two Faces of Modern Hebrew Drama," in: *Modern Hebrew Literature*, 1 (1988), 21–24; L. Lichtenstein, "Rushdie, Steiner, Sobol and others: Moral Bounderies," in: *Encounter*, 73:3 (1989), 34–42; F. Rokem, Y. "Sobol – Between History and the Arts: A Study of *Ghetto* and *Shooting Magda* (The Palestinian Woman)," in: L. Ben Zvi (ed.), *Theatre in Israel* (1996), 201–24; E. Fischer Lichte, "Theater der Erinnerung oder Ritual einer Totenbeschwörung? Anmerkungen zu Peter Zadeks Inszenierung von Sobols Ghetto an der Freien Volksbuehne in Berlin 1984," in: *Theatralia Judaica*, 2 (1996), 164–87; M. Taub, "The Challenge to Popular Myth and Conventions in Recent Drama," in: *Modern Judaism*, 17:2 (1997), 133–62; G. Steindler Moscati, "Revising the Past: The Image of the Idyllic 'Village'," in: *History and Literature* (2002), 319–28.

[Nurit Yaari (2nd ed.)]

SOBOTKA, HARRY HERMAN (1899–1965), U.S. biochemist. Born in Vienna, Sobotka joined Rockefeller Institute for Medical Research, New York (1924), and Bellevue Hospital Medical College, New York University (1926). He was appointed director of the chemical department, Mount Sinai Hospital, New York (1928). He wrote papers on chemistry of steroids and other organic chemicals of pharmaceutical significance.

SOCHACZEW (Rus. **Sokhachev**), city in Warszawa province, central Poland. There is evidence of a Jewish settlement in Sochaczew in 1427, when the city was under the jurisdiction of the princes of Mazovia. An organized Jewish community existed from the end of the 15th century, after the city had been annexed to the kingdom of Poland in 1476. In that era the Jews of Sochaczew engaged in moneylending and trading in cloth and spices. In the first quarter of the 16th century a Jewish physician, Felix, practiced in the city. In 1556, during the Catholic synod of Lowicz, the local authorities, and heads of the church, incited by the entourage of the papal nuncio, L. Lippomano (1500–59), accused Sochaczew Jews of *Host desecration. The three Jews condemned to death were immediately executed although it was evident that the accusation was false and despite the fact that King Sigismund II Augustus had ordered a retrial. Those responsible for the hasty execution, the governors of Rawka province and of the cities of Sochaczew and Plock, were subsequently sued by the heads of the community. By 1599 the Jews of Sochaczew owned 20 houses, a synagogue, hospital, *mikveh*, and cemetery, and engaged in commerce in livestock, leather, and wool, and in such crafts as tailoring and carpentry.

A *blood libel in 1619 resulted in the death at the stake of one Jew. After the Jewish quarter burned down the following year, the burghers opposed its reconstruction and the Jewish community temporarily came to an end. In 1749 King Augustus III granted permission to certain Jewish merchants and craftsmen from Warsaw to renew the settlement in Sochaczew. They established a tannery, a distillery, and tailoring and shoemaking workshops, and traded in agricultural produce. In 1765, there were 1,349 Jews who paid the poll tax in the city and surrounding villages. A new synagogue was built in 1793, which remained standing till World War II. During the *Kosciuszko rebellion (1794) the Jews of Sochaczew donated considerable sums to his cause. In 1800, 52 of the 91 craftsmen in the town were Jews. In 1808 the 1,085 Jews of Sochaczew formed 81% of its population; there were 2,322 Jews (74%) in 1827; and 2,936 (76%) in 1857. During the uprisings of 1863 several Jews fought on the side of Polish rebels in the local battles. In the latter years of the 19th century the Jews established various industrial enterprises and transport firms. In 1883 the rabbi, Abraham Bornstein of *Sochaczew, founded a ḥasidic court and later a large yeshivah. Rabbi Samuel Isaac Landau served the community from 1902 to 1912. From 3,776 (66%) in 1897 the Jewish population had grown to 4,520 (71%) by 1908. In World War I, during the battles of 1915 many Jews left the city and by 1921 their number had dwindled to 2,419 (48%). Between the world wars all the various Jewish parties were active in the city and established educational and cultural institutions. Half of the 24 members of the city council were Jews in 1925 and Moshe Szwarc (*Folkspartei) was vice mayor. During the 1930s a biweekly periodical, *Sokhatshever Tsaytung*, was published. At that time Rabbi A. Zisha Frydman, general secretary of *Agudat Israel, and the writer O. Varshavsky lived in the city.

On the outbreak of World War II there were about 4,000 Jews in Sochaczew. In February 1941 all the Jews were deported to the *Warsaw ghetto and shared the fate of that community. After the war the Jewish community of Sochaczew was not reconstituted.

BIBLIOGRAPHY: Halpern, Pinkas, index; S.A. Bershadski (ed.), *Russko-yevreyskiy arkhiv*, 3 (1882), 140; idem, in: *Voskhod*, 14:11 (1894), 53; P. Mojecki, *O żydowskich oknicieństwach, mordach y zabobonach* (1598), 18; L. Lewin, *Die Landessynode der grosspolnischen Judenschaft* (1926), 27, 29, 45; J. Shatzky, *Geshikhte fun Yidn in Varshe*, 1 (1947), 133; A. Eisenbach et al. (eds.), *Żydzi a powstanie styczniowe, materiały i dokumenty* (1963), index; I. Schiper, *Dzieje handlu żydowskiego na ziemiach polskich* (1937), index; A.S. Stein and G. Weisman (eds.), *Pinkes Sokhatshev* (1962); Dubnow, Hist Russ, index; R. Mahler, *Toledot ha-Yehudim be-Polin* (1946), index.

[Arthur Cygielman]

SOCHACZEW, ABRAHAM BEN ZE'EV NAHUM BORNSTEIN OF (1839–1910), Polish rabbi, head of the *bet din* of Sochaczew. He became famous as a child prodigy. At the age of 14 he married the daughter of Menahem Mendel of

*Kotsk, in whose home he remained for ten years studying Torah and Ḥasidism. Upon his father-in-law's death, he occupied rabbinical posts in *Parczew (1862), Krosniewice (1866), *Nasielsk (1876), and *Sochaczew (1883–1910). In 1870, following the death of Ḥanokh Henyekh, leader of the *Aleksandrow Ḥasidim, he was appointed his successor, but was harassed by slanderers. Abraham founded a yeshivah and was one of the great halakhic authorities of his generation. He originated a special approach to halakhic studies and educated in his yeshivah a generation of disciples who became scholarly ḥasidic leaders. Interested in the settlement of Ereẓ Israel, he sent his son and son-in-law there in 1898 to acquire land for a religious colony, but negotiations fell through on account of the Turkish land laws. Abraham's halakhic works are *Eglei Tal* (1905), including a study of the laws of the Sabbath, and *Avnei Nezer* (1912–34), a collection of responsa on the four parts of the Shulḥan Arukh. He was succeeded as head of the Aleksandrow Ḥasidim by his only son, SAMUEL (1856–1926), who edited his father's writings and responsa on the Shulḥan Arukh, and wrote *Shem mi-Shemu'el* (1928–34) which sets forth many of his father's ideas on Ḥasidism.

BIBLIOGRAPHY: Z.J.H. Mameluk, *Abbir ha-Ro'im*, 2 vols. (1935–38); Y. Raphael, *Sefer ha-Ḥasidut* (1955), 491–5; A.I. Bromberg, *Mi-Gedolei ha-Ḥasidut*, 5 (1955).

[Abraham Isaac Bromberg]

SOCIALISM.

Introduction

The words socialism and socialist were first used about the year 1830 but the origin of the ideas which led to the establishment of the modern labor movement goes back to the time of the French Revolution. For a variety of reasons Jews were attracted to socialism as it developed in Western Europe. Some regarded it as the building of a "just society" based on the teachings of the Bible and the Prophets, while others were attracted by its revolutionary nature. Thus, while some Jews saw socialism as a reply to antisemitism, there were also Jews who saw in it a way of getting rid of their Jewish heritage and serving the cause of the "Brotherhood of Man." Socialism was particularly attractive for Jews anxious to leave the ghetto behind them and who, disappointed with the slow progress of 19th-century liberalism, were keen to embrace a new universal faith.

France

The forerunners of modern socialism were two Frenchmen, Count Henry Claude de Rouvroy de Saint-Simon (1760–1825; see *Saint-Simonism) and Charles *Fourier (1772–1837). Saint-Simon was impressed by Jewish messianic ideals and, referring to the persecution of the Jews, wrote that he looked forward to the time when all men would be brothers. Two of his followers, Barthélemy Prosper Enfantin (1796–1864) and Armand Bazard (1791–1832), considered the *emancipation of the Jews as being one of the preconditions for the liberation of humanity. They believed that Jewish monotheism foreshadowed the approaching unity of mankind and their supporters included many French Jews, among them the poet Léon *Halévy, the bankers Emile and Isaac *Péreire, and the financier Olinde Rodrigues (1794–1851). On the other hand, Charles Fourier identified Jews with capitalism and opposed their emancipation on the grounds that they were "parasites, merchants, usurers." Nevertheless, in his last writings he argued that the Jews should be helped to escape from persecution in Europe by returning to Palestine and once more become a recognized nation with their own king, their own flag, their own consuls, and their own currency. A number of Fourier's followers were Jews who rejected their master's antisemitism. Thus Alexander Weil wrote in 1845 that it was unfair to blame one section of the population for what he regarded as the iniquities of Catholicism and capitalism. He also described the serious condition of the Jews in Eastern Europe, in order to draw the attention of the public to their plight. Similarly, Jean Czynsky, a Polish refugee of Jewish origin, wrote that freedom for Poland and the emancipation of Polish Jews were concepts for which all socialists must strive.

Great Britain

The early development of socialism in Britain at the beginning of the 19th century had little to do with the Jews, who numbered only 20,000 in the country. Nevertheless, Robert Owen (1771–1858), "the father of British socialism," actively campaigned for equality for the Jews and in 1830 submitted a petition to the House of Commons urging the abolition of religious disabilities. His example was followed by a number of leaders of the Chartist movement. Jews first became prominent in British socialism in the latter half of the 19th century and in May 1876 the *Aguddat ha-Soẓyalistim ha-Ivrim was formed in London, its founders including A.S. *Liebermann and Lazar *Goldenberg. German radical groups were also active in London and largely influenced the ideology of Jewish socialists in Britain. They kept in contact with the Russian revolutionary Peter Lavrov (1823–1900), who published the socialist organ, *Vpered*, in London. Toward the end of the 19th century an increasingly large number of Russian Jews became active in British socialism. Theodor Rothstein was a leader of the Marxist Social Democratic Federation, founded by H.M. Hyndman in 1884. Rothstein, who was shocked by an antisemitic outburst by Hyndman, later played an important part at the congress of the Russian Social Democratic Party in London in 1907, and after the Bolshevik seizure of power in 1917 was their unofficial representative in London. Later he helped found the British Communist Party, in which his son Andrew Rothstein was a prominent figure for many years. He was anti-Zionist, as were Joe Finberg, and Boris and Zelda Kahn, all refugees from Russia who played a major part in the British socialist movement. An outstanding figure of the British socialist movement was Eleanor Marx-Aveling (1855–1898), Karl Marx's youngest daughter, who felt a close affinity with the Jewish people and affirmed that "my happiest moments are when I am in the East End of London amid Jewish workpeople."

Germany

In Germany, many of the pioneers of socialism were Jewish. Among them was Moses *Hess, whose study *Die Philosophic der Tat* ("The Philosophy of Action"), linked the ideas of the German philosophical school with the concept of historical materialism on which communism was based. Hess largely influenced the thinking of Karl *Marx and Friedrich Engels but differed from them in that his brand of socialism was based upon ethical concepts. The course of socialism in Germany, however, was dominated not by Hess but by Marx and Ferdinand *Lassalle, the former as the founder of the school of economic materialism and the latter as the father of German Social Democracy. But while Marx was the great theoretician who set out to revolutionize international politics, Lassalle was the political strategist who brought socialism into German political life. Both showed a marked hostility to Judaism. On the other hand, Marx's non-Jewish colleague Friedrich Engels, who at first equated Jews with capitalists, later took a stand against antisemitism which he described as the weapon of the German governing class.

The First International

A number of Jews became prominent during the 19th century in the International Working Men's Association, formed in 1864 by Marx and Engels, which became known as the First International. Among them were several French Jews, including E.E. Fribourg, an opponent of Marx, who was a disciple of the non-Jewish anarchist writer Pierre *Proudhon (1809–1865). Fribourg advocated membership in the association only to people engaged in physical work, a move against Marx, whereas Lazare Lévy, another leading member of the French section of the First International, was a strong supporter of Karl Marx. Jews were also prominent in the workers' uprising in the Paris Commune in March 1871, one of the leaders being Léo *Frankel.

The Second International

The Second International set up at the Paris Congress of 1889 was largely dominated by German socialists, whose delegates represented a strong socialist party in effective control of the trade unions. They included August Bebel, William Liebknecht, Clara Zetkin, and Eduard *Bernstein, the son of a Jewish worker, who had a profound influence on the development of socialism in Germany and elsewhere. Bernstein combined Marxist ideology with British pragmatism in a concept which became known as "Revisionism." He considered assimilation the best solution to the Jewish problem but Jewish suffering in World War I made him a supporter of Jewish settlement in Palestine and of *Po'alei Zion. His non-Jewish colleague August Bebel was also sympathetic to the Jewish cause, describing antisemitism as "socialism of the fools," and, while there were antisemites among the German socialists, the party was committed to fight against discrimination. By 1912 there were 12 Jews among the 100 Social Democrats in the German Parliament. Many other Jews were prominent in the party, the majority of them favoring assimilation, especially after Karl Kautsky's book, *Race and Judaism*, was published in 1914. Most members of the Social Democratic Party were hostile to Zionism, as was the party organ *Die Neue Zeit*, but the Revisionists showed understanding of the labor Zionist cause and their newspaper *Sozialistische Monatshefte*, edited by Joseph *Bloch, was pro-Zionist. In Austria, many prominent figures in the Socialist Party were Jews, among them Victor *Adler, Friedrich Adler, Otto *Bauer, Max *Adler, Hugo *Breitner, and William *Ellenbogen. They all supported assimilation and opposed Jewish national aspirations. In particular, Otto Bauer's work *Die Nationalitaetenfrage und die Sozialdemokratie* (1907), which denied that the Jews were a separate nationality, had considerable influence in socialist circles. On the whole, Jewish socialists in Austria avoided discussion of the Jewish question and were hostile to Zionism, but a notable exception was Julius *Braunthal, who supported the labor Zionist movement.

1914–1939

During World War I several Jewish socialists were among the most outspoken critics of the war, among them Rosa *Luxemburg and Hugo *Haase in Germany, Friedrich *Adler in Austria, Julius *Martov and Lev (Leon) *Trotsky from Russia, and Angelica Balabanov in Italy. In the chaotic conditions after World War I, Jewish socialists held top cabinet posts in socialist administrations in Germany, Austria, Hungary, and Russia. Thus Haase and O. *Landsberg joined the German provisional government following the collapse of imperial Germany, Hugo *Preuss became minister of the interior in the Weimar Republic, Paul Hirsch (1868–1938) was prime minister of Prussia, Kurt Rosenfeld was Prussian minister of justice, and Kurt *Eisner was prime minister of "Soviet" Bavaria. In Austria, Victor Adler, Otto Bauer – who became foreign minister – and Friedrich Adler all played a major part in the Austrian revolution of 1918, and following the Hungarian revolution of 1919 Bela *Kun became dictator in a "Soviet" Hungarian government containing 14 Jewish commissars. In Russia, many Jews held senior posts in the first Bolshevik administration and the Communist Party (see *Communism; *Russia).

Between 1918 and 1939 individual Jewish socialists held prominent positions in several European countries, but their importance tended to be exaggerated by antisemites. Thus in Germany, the Nazis represented the few Jewish socialists as having far greater influence than they actually had. In Austria, Otto Bauer was foreign minister from 1919 to 1920, Oscar Pollak was editor of the party organ *Arbeiter-Zeitung*, and Matilda Pollak was leader of the Social Democratic women. Léon *Blum was prime minister of France and Jules *Moch was minister of public works. In Czechoslovakia Ludwig *Czech was minister of social welfare, while in Holland Saloman Rodrigues de *Miranda was minister of housing, and in Britain Emanuel *Shinwell was secretary of mines. The socialist movement in continental Europe gradually weakened as the pace of the Nazi advance increased.

After the outbreak of World War II, socialist parties survived only in Britain, Sweden, and Switzerland. Most of the socialist refugees fled to England, where the British Labor Party took the initiative in convening regular meetings to discuss matters of common concern. Among them were several Jewish socialists, including Oscar Pollak and Karl Czernitz from Austria and Claudio Treves from Italy.

Post-World War II

After World War II, Jews continued to be prominent in the socialist movements of France and Great Britain. In France, Léon Blum, Jules Moch, Pierre *Mendes-France, and Daniel *Mayer emerged as leading French socialists and all held posts in French coalition governments. All four were active in Jewish affairs and supporters of the State of Israel. In Britain, Jewish participation in the Labor movement considerably increased in the postwar years. There were four Jewish cabinet ministers in the Labor government of 1945–51: Emanuel Shinwell, Harry *Nathan, Lewis *Silkin, and George *Strauss, and the Labor government of 1964–70 at various times included Jews in senior or junior offices, among them Austen Albu (1903–1994), John *Diamond, Harold *Lever, Reginald Freeson (1926–), Baroness Serota, Edmund Dell (1921–1999), and John *Silkin. In addition, Harold *Laski was chairman of the Labor Party from 1945 to 1946, Emanuel Shinwell was chairman of the Parliamentary Labor Party and Ian Mikardo (1908–1993), Frank Allaun (1913–2002), and Sydney *Silverman were members of the Labor Party national executive. One particularly noticeable feature of the growth of Jewish participation in the Labor movement was the sharp increase in the number of Jewish Labor members of Parliament, from four in 1935 to 26 in 1945, around 36 in 1966, and 30 in 1970. Many of the Jews prominent in the Labor Party were associated with the British Po'alei Zion and a Zionist group formed in 1956 called Labor Friends of Israel.

In the British Commonwealth, too, Jews have played an increasingly important part in socialist politics. In Canada a number of Jews were actively associated with the leadership of the socialist New Democratic Party formed in 1961. The most prominent of them was David *Lewis – leader of the parliamentary party. Other Jewish MPs representing the NDP were Max Saltsman (Toronto) and David *Orlikow (Winnipeg). In Manitoba, five Jews were members of the Provincial Legislature: Saul Cherniak, C. Gonick, Sidney Green, Saul Miller, and Sidney Spivak. In British Columbia, too, a number of Jews were prominent in the party, but not in Montreal where the NDP was, generally, a weak body. While the Canadian Labor Zionist movement was not affiliated to the party, there was close cooperation in a number of provinces. Leading personalities of the NDP, which is a member of the Socialist International, visited Israel and showed a friendly attitude to its socialist party. The Canadian Congress, formed in 1956, had a close association both with the Histadrut in Israel and local Jewish labor bodies. In Australia, too, Jews played an increasingly active part in socialist politics. Sidney Einfeld and Senator Sam *Cohen were Labor Party parliamentarians for a number of years. In 1969, three Jewish socialist candidates were elected to the Australian House of Representatives: Joe Berison (Perth), Moses Cass (Melbourne), and Barry Cohen (Robertson Constituency – near Sydney). In 2005, the only Jewish member of the Australian Parliament was the Labor MP Michael *Danby. In recent decades the participation of Jews in left-of-center parties has probably declined sharply, while socialism as a viable ideology would seem to be a thing of the past. The movement of most Jews into the upper middle class, the diminution of right-wing antisemitism, and, above all, the hostility of much of the extreme left to Israel's post-1967 policies, have made it difficult for many Jews to identify as socialists in the old sense. Events such as the end of the Soviet Union in 1991 have also made it difficult for many to see what socialism might be like in the 21st century, especially any such ideology entailing widespread nationalization or sympathy for the radical enemies of Israel.

While many Jews, especially in the United States, remain committed to the value system of liberalism, it would seem clear that the engagement of the Jewish people with socialism is increasingly a thing of the past.

By contrast, the Holocaust and the Communist takeover in part of Europe reduced the Jewish participation in socialist politics to a mere fraction of what it had been before 1939. Nevertheless, a small number of Jews held important posts in European socialist parties after 1945, among them Ludwig *Rosenberg, who was president of the German Confederation of Trade Unions, Siegfried Aufhauser (1884–1962), president of the German Federation of Labor in Berlin, Bruno *Kreisky, who in 1970 became chancellor of Austria, and Karl Czernetz, who was international secretary of the Austrian Social Democratic Party.

Eastern Europe

RUSSIA. Socialism developed in Russia later than in Western Europe, in the second half of the 19th century. The death of Nicholas I and the accession of Alexander II in 1855 led to the emancipation of the serfs in 1861 and a relaxation of the repressive regime. Jews became less isolated from the general stream of Russian public life, and the number of Jewish children in Russian secondary schools rose from 8 to 2,362 between 1840 and 1872. Many Jewish socialists came from traditional homes and were influenced by the writings of Russian philosophers, whose works they studied at secondary schools. They were largely in favor of assimilation, since they regarded Judaism as obsolete and believed that Jewish emancipation would come about through the liberalization of the Russian people with whom the Jews should integrate. Thus, most of the early Jewish socialists regarded the growth of Russian socialism as more important than Jewish emancipation. Many young Jews chose to join the revolutionaries and "go to the people." A number of Jewish socialists converted to Christianity to facilitate their activities among the people, while Jewish women socialists became estranged from Judaism by marriage to non-

Jewish revolutionaries. Though the persecution of Jews was an important motivating force in bringing Jews into the revolutionary camp, the pogroms of 1881 came as a great shock to many Jewish revolutionaries. Particularly disappointing were the antisemitic trends in the Populist movement and the indifference of non-Jewish revolutionaries to violent outbreaks against Jews. In addition Jewish socialists who neglected their own people because they believed them to be tradesmen and middlemen discovered the existence of Jewish workers who were facing oppression and social exploitation.

Some of the first Jewish socialists were prominent in revolutionary uprisings outside the borders of Russia. Robert Feinberg fought in the German revolution of 1848 and was later deported to Siberia, where he died, and Nicolai Utin, son of a rich Jewish contractor, was a liaison officer for the Polish revolutionaries in 1863. Utin fled to Germany, where he became a colleague of Karl Marx and established the Russian section of the First International. However, others were prominent in the ideological movements of the 1860s and 1870s which grew up in the wake of the acute poverty of the Jews. Marc Natanson (1849–1920), son of a Jewish merchant from Grodno, was the organizer of the Zemlya i Volya ("Land and Liberty") group from which emerged some of the famous non-Jewish revolutionary figures, such as Prince Peter Kropotkin, Vera Zasulich, and Georg Plekhanov. Joseph Aptekman (1850) and Lev Deitsch (1855–1941) were leaders of the Narodniki (Populists), a movement which developed among the intelligentsia to redress the injustices done to the Russian peasants. The revolutionaries dressed like peasants and lived with the peasants in the countryside. They soon exposed themselves to ridicule and many were arrested and imprisoned. The failure of the Populists led the revolutionaries to attempt fresh measures. In 1878 the terrorist group known as the Narodnaya Volya ("People's Will") was formed to combat oppression by violence. A number of Jews joined the organization. Many were made desperate by their increasing poverty resulting from the emancipation of the serfs, which enabled the latter to enter trades which had previously been mostly occupied by Jews. Several Jewish members of the Narodnaya Volya were captured and executed, among them Aaron Gobet, who had participated in a plot to assassinate Czar Alexander II in 1879, Solomon Wittenberg, Meir Mlodetsky, a yeshivah student from Slutsk, and Grigori Goldenberg (1855–1880), who committed suicide in the fortress of Petropavlovsk after being arrested for assassinating the governor-general of Kharkov. Other Jewish revolutionaries included Aaron Zundelevich (1850–1923) and Saveli Zlatopolsky, who were members of the executive committee of Narodnaya Volya. The assassination of Czar Alexander II in 1881 led to a reign of terror against the revolutionaries, but the latter continued to work against the regime and many joined the underground socialist organizations that sprang up toward the end of the 19th century.

Jews were exceptionally prominent in the Social Democratic movement and some eventually became leaders of the Russian Social Democratic Party, such as Julius Martov and Lev Trotsky. Others were active in Jewish workers' groups which united in 1897 as the *Bund and by 1904 numbered 23,000 Jews from Lithuania, Russia, and Poland. The Bund and the Russian Social Democrats were united in their opposition to Zionism, but while the Social Democrats insisted that the Jews should assimilate with the general Russian population, the Bund campaigned for recognition of a separate Jewish nationality within a federation of nationalities. After the 1903 split in the Social Democratic Party into Bolsheviks and Mensheviks, some Jewish members of the two groups were particularly vociferous in their opposition to Jewish national aspirations. The Bolsheviks argued that the revolution would solve the Jewish question by giving Jews complete equality and thus lead to their assimilation with the rest of the population.

A third organization in which Jews of Russia played a prominent part was the Russian Social Revolutionary Party formed in Switzerland in 1901. A successor party to the terrorist Narodnaya Volya, the party advocated agrarian reform by violence and the establishment of a Russian federation. Among the forerunners of the movement were Chaim *Zhitlowsky, who later settled in the United States, Mendel Rosenbaum, who immigrated to Israel, and Charles *Rappoport, who became an important figure in the French Communist Party. The movement included a terrorist "fighting organization" in which Mikhail Gots (1866–1906), Abraham Gots (1882–1937), Grigori *Gershuni, and Yevno *Azeff were prominent. Unlike the Social Democratic Party, they were not hostile to Zionism and did not actively struggle for assimilationism. The ultimate success of the Bolsheviks under *Lenin eventually brought about the end of Jewish participation in the socialist movement in Russia. Those Jewish socialists who were opposed to the Bolsheviks were forced to go into exile, and while many other Jews held prominent positions in the Communist Party, they were ultimately purged from the party hierarchy either between 1936 and 1939 or between 1948 and 1953.

POLAND AND ROMANIA. In Poland, Jews were among the pioneers of the socialist movement in the latter part of the 19th century. The first socialist group, Proletariat, was an underground organization responsible for numerous workers' strikes. It included a number of Jews, among them Zigmund Dering and Szymon *Dickstein. Proletariat gave way to the Social Democratic Party (SDKP), a Marxist party which rejected Polish independence and advocated partnership with the Russian socialist movement. Among its leading members were Rosa Luxemburg, Leo Yogiches and Adolf *Warski-Warshawski, all of whom opposed the Bund and the nationalist Polish Socialist Party (PPS). Nevertheless, the Bund and the PPS attracted considerable support from prominent Jewish socialists such as Herman *Diamand, Herman *Liebermann, and Boleslaw *Drobner. In Romania, too, Jews were among the founders of the socialist movement. Thus Constantin Gherea-Dobrogeanu (1855–1920) organized a peasants' revolutionary group in Russia and later settled in Romania, where he advocated universal suffrage. The Romanian Socialist Party was largely antisemitic, however, and when the Jewish Social Democratic group, Lamina, submitted a memorandum to the international Socialist Congress (1896) on the plight of the Jews in Romania, the Romanian socialists defended their party's inimical attitude to the Jewish question. The New Social Democratic Party formed in 1910 urged equality for the Jews but had little influence on the reactionary governments of Romania during the first half of the century.

[Schneier Zalman Levenberg]

United States

Jews played little part in the brand of American socialism which derived from agrarian and populist discontent with the social order. Nor did they appear in the numerous short-lived utopian communities which sprang up early in the 20th century or in the proletarian constituency of the revolutionary syndicalist Industrial Workers of the World which flourished from about 1908 to 1920. The role of Jews in American socialism lay within the urban, industrial environment where the movement had its main strength, and whose ideology was more or less Marxist. They were most prominent in the American Socialist Party from about 1915 until the 1930s, the period when ethnic minorities generally played a key role in the socialist movement. Socialism developed among industrial workers and intellectuals during the 1870s, when the Socialist Labor Party was founded (1877) with one of its strongest bases in the largely Jewish International Cigar Makers Union. Adolph Strasser (1844–1939), a leader of that union, had been secretary of its predecessor, the Social Democratic Party, in 1874. However, he and Samuel *Gompers, also a cigar maker, as founders and leaders of the American Federation of Labor (1886), firmly led it away from socialist involvements and toward "pure and simple" trade unionism. During the 1880s, Jews were among the leaders of short-lived municipal labor or socialist parties in such cities as Detroit, Milwaukee, and New York. After 1890, the Socialist Labor Party was dominated by Daniel *De Leon who maintained the SLP's doctrinal purity by expelling all dissenters and losing practically all influence in the socialist and trade-union movements.

American socialism reached its climactic years between 1900 and 1920. Although Eugene V. Debs was the party's orator, presidential candidate, and moral symbol, its real leaders were Victor *Berger, the first Socialist Party congressman, and Morris *Hillquit. Louis Boudin was a leading Marxist scholar and theoretician. One socialist stronghold was the Jewish labor movement which had begun among East European immigrant proletarians during the 1880s. Their weak, unstable unions were fervently socialist and revolutionary in temper. After 1910, trade unionism, which was overwhelmingly Jewish in membership and leadership, won control of labor conditions in the garment industry by means of a series of dramatic strikes. The International Ladies Garment Workers Union and the Amalgamated Clothing Workers of America remained explicitly socialist, but the revolutionary content of their socialism was relegated to rhetorical flourishes about a vague, ultimate end. The unions' socialist activity emphasized the creation of a comradely environment for their members, who included perhaps 200,000 Jews. The tone of Yiddish-speaking fraternal orders, literature, and theater was also socialist. Abe *Cahan's prosperous **Jewish Daily Forward*, with a maximum circulation of about 150,000 in 1917, wielded great influence, and the monthly **Zukunft* was a notable organ of socialist letters. It was the Jewish East Side which sent the Socialist Party's Mayer *London to Congress in 1914 for the first of three terms, and elected socialists to the state legislature.

Although the Socialist Party had a very high proportion of Jews among its followers and leaders, it took no position on Jewish problems as such. Its general view was that Jewish problems did not exist, being imaginary constructs to divert attention from the true problems of all oppressed. Thus, Jews would achieve a full and final solution with the ultimate social revolution. The existence of the Jews as a people, it was tacitly assumed, might then end. American socialism had nativist elements who pushed it into an anti-immigration policy for several years after 1908, but perceptible antisemitism such as in some European socialist movements did not exist. Nevertheless, it was charged that some of the opposition in 1932 to Hillquit's leadership was antisemitic. In 1908 a Jewish Agitation Bureau was established in order to spread socialism among Yiddish-speaking Jews. Stimulated by immigrants with experience in the East European Bund, the Bureau developed into the Jewish Socialist Federation (JSF) from 1912, over strong opposition from Abe Cahan and other Yiddish-speaking stalwarts opposed to such "separatism." Actually the JSF disavowed any distinct Jewish purpose and attempted only to spread socialism, while it vigorously combated Zionism. Its membership was drawn mainly from immigrants of Bundist background. American socialism was greatly weakened by its opposition to American entry into World War I and by the Communist split in 1919. Among Jews it remained strong, although racked by savage quarrels with Communists. However, as the Democrats from 1928 became the party of urban liberalism, ethnic groups, and social reform, they drew increasing numbers of Jews and other socialists into their ranks. Jewish unions and voters moved en masse to the Democrats during the 1930s as F.D. *Roosevelt's New Deal enacted social legislation and provided national political recognition for Jews and other urban ethnic groups. Such Jews as Gus Tyler, Max and Robert Delson, Sidney *Hook, and J.B.S. Hardman were significant Socialist leaders during the 1930s. The American Socialist Party, led after Debs' death in 1925 by Norman Thomas, turned toward pacifism and isolationism in the face of Nazism and did not change its view on Jewish problems. The magnet of the New Deal and the inadequacies of the Socialist Party left the latter with very little Jewish or other following by the time of World War II.

[Lloyd P. Gartner]

The years after World War II, with their combination of economic prosperity, cold war, and political conformism, witnessed the near total collapse of the socialist movement as a serious political force in the U.S. Many older Jewish socialists joined this trend by moderating their criticisms of American society so as to be reabsorbed into the American political mainstream. Typical of this process was the emergence in New York City and State of the mildly reformist Liberal Party, which was dominated by Jewish labor leaders such as David *Dubinsky and Alex *Rose, nearly all of whom had been active socialists in the 1920s and 1930s.

Nevertheless, although socialist politics remained moribund in America for two decades after World War II, a community of influential socialist thinkers, many of them Jews, continued to exist and to sustain a tradition of radical political critique that served as an intellectual seedbed for the radical revival of the late 1960s. The individuals who composed this community held a wide divergence of views, ranging from the revolutionary Marxism of Herbert *Marcuse to the anarchism of Paul *Goodman and the social democratic humanism of Irving *Howe. All joined in rejecting both Soviet communism and American capitalism as viable social models for the future, though most openly expressed their preference for the latter as the less malign of the two evils and the more amenable to structural change. Other prominent figures from these years whose approach to public issues was socialist in tenor, were academicians such as Lewis A. *Coser and Daniel Bell, writers and journalists like Norman *Mailer, Harvey Swados, Paul Jacobs, and I.F. *Stone, and the psychoanalyst Erich *Fromm. Many socialists published in the pages of the journals *Dissent*, edited by Irving Howe, and *Partisan Review*, edited by Philip Rahv, and a number were identified with the League for Industrial Democracy directed by Tom Kahn.

As in earlier decades, the majority of American Jewish socialists tended to regard specifically Jewish issues as peripheral to broader social and economic problems, but many supported the establishment of the State of Israel both as a result of the Holocaust and as a legitimate expression of Jewish national aspirations. The revival of radical politics in the U.S. toward the end of the 1960s led to profound differences of opinion among socialist intellectuals. Some, such as Marcuse, supported the *New Left despite reservations about its ideological unclarity and tendencies to violence. Others, such as Howe, strongly attacked it for its contempt of intellectual values and climate of "left fascism." Among the points of contention in this debate was the State of Israel, particularly after the Six-Day War (1967). Many New Left supporters tended to side with the anti-Israel position, while its socialist detractors generally defended the Jewish state, though often with noticeably more ambivalence than in former years.

[Hillel Halkin]

Latin America

Jewish work for socialism in Latin America was mainly the result of the efforts of various Jewish labor organizations established by immigrants from Europe. However, in Argentina, where the socialist movement is one of the oldest in the world, Jewish workers played a part in the development of the General Labor movement and were active in both general politics and the trade unions. Enrique Dickmann was one of the outstanding socialist leaders in the early 1940s. The establishment of the military regime in Argentina greatly limited the activities of the Socialist Party, which nonetheless retained its long-standing association with the Socialist International, its representatives including persons of Jewish origin. In Chile, where the socialist movement had deep roots in the country's history, individual Jews played a part within the various left-wing groups. Jews were active, to a lesser degree, in Uruguay, where the socialist groups were weaker than in Chile. In other Latin American countries with a sizable Jewish population, the socialist movement was either very weak or its development was hampered by totalitarian regimes and the contribution of individual Jews was marginal.

Asia and Africa

Of special significance was the impact made by Israeli socialism in Asia and Africa, where it often served as an example for post-colonial development. The achievements of the *Histadrut, the unique character of the *kibbutz and the *moshav, the development of Israel's people's army and the industrial and scientific progress of the Jewish state, were greatly admired in many developing countries. In 1960, the Histadrut established the Afro-Asian Institute. By 1970, about 2,000 students from the "Third World" had attended its various courses conducted alternatively in English or French. The number of visitors to Israel from African and Asian countries increased substantially during the 1960s and the Histadrut sent many technical advisers to developing countries.

In the political field, the Israel Labor Party played an active part in the establishment of the Asian Socialist Conference (1953). Its activities were suspended after the establishment of totalitarian governments and the suppression of socialist groups in a number of Asian countries. A new attempt at setting up a center for the socialist movement in Asia and Oceania was made at a conference held in Wellington, New Zealand, in 1969; the Israel Labor Party was elected as a member of the secretariat established in Singapore. In Africa, the Israel labor movement established close contact with the socialist parties in power in Madagascar and Mauritius.

Within the Socialist International, the Israeli party *Mapai pressed for greater understanding of the specific conditions and needs of Asian and African countries, and was instrumental in the formation of the special committee for underdeveloped countries within the organization. The Israel Labor Party made clear on a number of occasions that it would welcome the affiliation of genuine Arab socialist groups to the International but it opposed cooperation with semi-Fascist or semi-Communist parties using the label "socialist" for political purposes.

Anarchism

The modern anarchist movement emerged during the 19th century. Some of its leaders believed in violent action, others confined themselves to putting forward their own highly individualistic theories on the transformation of authoritarian societies into free cooperation between individuals and groups. The impact of anarchist ideas has differed from country to country.

Famous anarchists had an indirect influence on the development of Jewish radical thought. The ideas of Proudhon, *Bakunin, Elisée Reclus (1830–1905), Kropotkin (1824–1906), Enrico Malatesta (1853–1932), and other libertarian writers were studied in Jewish revolutionary circles, but the impact of socialism on the Jewish labor movement was incomparably stronger than that of anarchism. Political action had a greater appeal to Jewish workers than the belief in the possibility of a violent and sudden transformation of society. Some of the "giants" of anarchism had a friendly attitude to Jews but others, such as Proudhon and Bakunin, showed clear antisemitic tendencies. Bakunin's antipathy to Jews was considerably influenced by his struggle with Karl Marx for the leadership of the First International. The greatest impact of anarchism was in Mediterranean countries – Spain, Italy, and southern France; and in Mexico, Cuba, Argentina, and southern Russia. In all these countries Jewish participation in the movement was of a minor character; of greater significance was the part played by Jews in the development of libertarian ideas in America and Britain.

Anarchism as an organized movement among Jewish immigrants began in the United States in 1886. A new organization, The Pioneers of Liberty, attracted a number of Jewish radical thinkers, among them the poets David Edelstadt and Morris Rosenfeld, the journalist S. *Janovsky, Emma *Goldman, and Alexander *Berkman. At first, Jewish supporters of the new creed were influenced by German immigrants, but they gradually began to make a direct appeal to Jewish workers and to issue literature in Yiddish. Violent clashes with Jewish socialists and religious elements soon followed. During World War I the number of Jewish anarchists fell; some returned to Russia after the Revolution or otherwise departed. Nevertheless, small groups continued their activities.

The Jewish anarchists in the United States kept in close touch with those in Britain, where the movement found a strong foothold among Jewish workers in Whitechapel. One of the leaders of the British group was Rudolf *Rocker, a German non-Jewish anarchist who lived in London from 1895 to 1914. He was a colorful figure among the Jewish supporters of the libertarian ideas and became editor of Yiddish publications. After 1917, anarchism declined as an active force among Whitechapel Jews, although it still retained a small group of adherents in Britain, including a number of Jews.

On the continent of Europe, anarchism attracted support among the Jewish socialist leaders. Thus in Germany, Moses Hess, who knew both Proudhon and Bakunin, was for a short time influenced by their ideas. He adopted the title "anarchy" for his own social philosophy developed in *Die Philosophie der Tat* (1843). A prominent anarchosocialist intellectual in Germany with an international reputation was Gustav Landauer. In France, Léon Blum in his early years was influenced by anarchist ideas, as was Bernard *Lazare, who combined his social revolutionary ideas with belief in Zionism.

In Russia, the anarchists were a marginal factor in the development of the Jewish labor movement. While their ideas influenced some of the Jewish revolutionaries, anarchism played only a minor part among Jewish radical elements. During the years 1918–21, peasants of the southern Ukraine joined the anarchist guerrilla leader Nestor Makhno, whose Revolutionary Insurrection Army was responsible for some of the most brutal pogroms against the Jewish population. Makhno had a number of Jewish supporters and denied responsibility for the brutalities. Toward the end of 1918, Aaron and Fanya Baron helped form the Confederation of Anarchist Organizations in Ukraine. In September 1921, Fanya Baron and eight of her comrades were shot in a Moscow prison. Alexander Shapiro – another Jewish anarchist – hoped to bring about an amelioration of conditions through working with the Soviet regime. But Jewish anarchism, and the movement as a whole, ceased to exist as a vital force in Russia after the "purge" of its supporters in the early 1920s. A number of former anarchists were attracted by kibbutz life in Israel, but after World War II anarchism virtually ceased to exist as an organized force in Jewish life. Nevertheless, "revolt against authority" and belief in libertarian ideas can be found among Jewish New Left intellectuals and students in various countries.

SOCIALISM AND THE JEWS

The first socialists were greatly divided about their attitude to the Jewish problem. Some ignored the issue because of ignorance, indifference, or the small number of Jews in their respective countries. Others were imbued with the general antisemitic prejudices prevailing in both Western and Eastern Europe during the 19th century. Another group – among the pioneers of socialism – was sympathetic to the Jews and championed their right to freedom and equality. Moses Hess, who was the first Zionist among the socialist theoreticians, was an exceptional case. The First International (1864–76) never adopted resolutions on the Jewish problem; the views expressed by its various leaders were of a personal nature. However, three official representatives from Jewish labor organizations were present at the first congress of the Second International (1889): Philip Kranz from London's Jewish International Workers' Educational Club, and Joseph Barsky and Louis Miller from the New York's United Hebrew Trades. The latter submitted a report on the activities of Jewish trade unions; this was the first time that an international socialist conference received information about the existence of an independent Jewish labor movement. The Jewish issue was raised at the second congress of the International (Brussels, 1889) by Abraham Cahan, who represented 30,000 "Yiddish-speaking workers" from the U.S.; he did it against the private advice of Victor Adler and Paul Singer and a number of other leading figures in the organization, who believed that a public discussion on antisemitism was both unnecessary and harmful. After a debate in the course of which two delegates from France made reference to the exploitation of workers by Jewish capitalists and denounced "philo-Semitic agitation," the congress adopted the following resolution:

> Considering that the socialists and workers' parties have always affirmed that there cannot exist for them racial or national antagonism, but only the class struggle of the proletariat of all races and countries against the capitalists of all races and countries;
>
> Considering that for the proletariat of the Jewish race and Yiddish language there exists no other way to achieve emancipation than to join the workers' organizations of their respective countries;
>
> Condemning antisemitic and philo-Semite outbursts as one of the means by which the capitalist class and the reactionary circles seek to divert the Socialist movement from its purpose and divide the workers;
>
> The Congress decides that the question raised by the delegation of the Yiddish-speaking group of American comrades was superfluous and passes to the next item on the Agenda.

The Russian socialists were not represented at the congress, but the resolution on the Jewish problem was sharply attacked for its lack of understanding in an article written by Georg Plekhanov in *Sotsial-Demokrat* (Geneva, 1892). In 1903, the Second International condemned the *Kishinev pogrom but refused to take a clear stand on the Jewish question. Jewish Social Democratic groups had been represented at congresses of the International from 1893, when Jacob Stechenberg represented both Lemberg and Cracow, but the Bund was allotted 12 out of the 29 mandates of the Russian Social Democratic Party. On the other hand Jews also represented the Russian Social Revolutionary Party at congresses of the International, Chaim Zhitlovsky and Ilya Rubanovich representing the party at the congress of 1904. The World Confederation of Po'alei Zion applied for membership of the International in March 1907. It submitted a special memorandum to the bureau of the organization, in the course of which attention was drawn to the unique nature of the Jewish problem which, it claimed, was primarily a result of the abnormal class-structure of the Jewish people and the special economic conditions of the Jewish working masses. The specific character of Jewish emigration was stressed as was the need for a territorial solution of the Jewish problem through the establishment of a Jewish National Home in Palestine. The Zionist socialist memorandum ended with the following request for admission:

> According to the latest resolution of the International Socialist Bureau, representation will henceforth be determined not on the basis of states but of nationalities. The Jewish Socialist Labor Party – Po'alei Zion – which numbers more than 19,000 organized Jewish workers in Russia, Austria, America, England, and Palestine requests the International Socialist Bureau to grant it – as a socialist party of proletarians of Jewish nationality – representation in the Bureau.

In October 1908, the Po'alei Zion Confederation put forward the idea of the creation of a Jewish section within the Socialist International which would comprise all the existing socialist parties of the Jewish proletariat: the Bund, the Po'alei Zion Confederation, the *Jewish Socialist Workers' Party ("Sejm") of Russia, and the *Zionist Socialists (SS) Party of Russia. The request was renewed in May 1911. Po'alei Zion's efforts to obtain admission to the International did not produce any tangible results – ostensibly on account of objections on organizational grounds. Actually, the request was not granted because of the opposition by the majority of socialist leaders – especially of the large parties – to Jewish national aspirations and labor Zionism. Prior to World War I, the large majority of socialist leaders believed in assimilation as the solution of the Jewish problem. Even those of them who recognized that the Jews were a people, either failed to see any justification for their separate existence or did not believe that they would survive as an independent entity. Many socialist leaders of Jewish origin favored assimilation, and for some the Jewish problem was a personal embarrassment. Others were sincere in their belief that socialism would solve the problem of all minorities and that there was no need for the Jews to be singled out as a special issue. There were also individual socialist spokesmen of Jewish origin who suffered from "self-hatred" and expressed antisemitic sentiments. Nevertheless, even prior to 1914, there were leading socialists who showed understanding of Jewish national aspirations and were sympathetic to the Zionist cause. Toward the end of World War I, Jewish socialists renewed their demands for recognition in the world socialist movement. In 1917, *Po'alei Zion submitted a detailed memorandum on the Jewish situation to the Dutch-Scandinavian Socialist Committee, and presented concrete demands on behalf of the Jewish labor movement. In the same year the committee, whose secretary was the pro-Jewish leader, Camille Huysmans (1871–1968), issued its peace manifesto to the warring powers and urged an international solution to the Jewish problem, involving autonomy for the Jews living in compact masses in parts of Poland, Russia, Austria, and Romania. In December 1917, a special conference of the British Labor Party and Trades Union Congress approved a memorandum on war aims which was later endorsed by a meeting of all the socialist parties in allied countries. The memorandum included, inter alia, the following section on the Jewish question:

> The conference demands for the Jews equal elementary rights in the sense of freedom of conscience, residence and trade, and the same political rights that ought to be extended to all citizens. But the conference further maintains that Palestine ought to be set free from the harsh and oppressive government of the Turk and ought to be transformed into a free state, under international guarantee, to which the Jewish people may return if they desire to do so, and where they may develop their own civilization free from the influence of alien races and religions.

During 1919 a number of international socialist conferences were held to discuss problems of a peace settlement. One of them, held in Amsterdam in April, adopted a special resolution dealing with Jewish rights. Beside the demands for equal civil rights, freedom of immigration and settlement in all countries, national autonomy, and representation of the Jewish people in the League of Nations, the motion contained the following clause:

> Recognition of the right of the Jewish people to build their National Home in Palestine, and the establishment of conditions favorable thereto under the protection and control of the League of Nations, which shall also safeguard the rightful interests of the existing non-Jewish population.

These resolutions showed a radical change in the attitude of a number of socialist parties to the Jewish problem. The Po'alei Zion Confederation was permitted to take an active part in the various socialist consultations dealing with a peace settlement and the reconstitution of the International. After the war, the Second International was reconstituted in February 1921 from among the socialist parties which did not join the Communist International. Po'alei Zion accepted an invitation to attend as a separate group and, at the Hamburg conference in May 1923, was represented by seven delegates. In the following year the position of the Po'alei Zion within the International was finally settled by a resolution of the executive in February 1924:

> 1. Palestine is included in the list of nationalities.
> 2. The only Palestinian party who has so far declared its readiness to affiliate is the Po'alei Zion Confederation.
> 3. The Po'alei Zion Confederation also has members in countries other than Palestine and demands – in accordance with article 10 of the bylaws relating to factions and parties – that these members be accredited to the Palestinian party. Accordingly, the members of the Confederation who do not belong to other affiliated parties will be accredited to Palestine.
> 4. Palestine is granted two votes at Congresses. These votes are allotted to the Po'alei Zion Confederation with the understanding that there will have to be a reallotment in case other parties in Palestine will affiliate to the International.

There was still considerable opposition to the Po'alei Zion within the Second International, largely from Jewish assimilationists such as Friedrich *Adler and members of the Bund among the Polish delegation. However, the Po'alei Zion succeeded in forming a representative Socialist Committee for Palestine, whose sponsors included Emil Vandervelde, Léon Blum, and Eduard Bernstein. In addition, 40 leading socialists representing ten European states responded to an invitation to attend a conference in Brussels in August 1928 to extend moral and political support for the labor movement in Palestine.

The persecution of the Jews in Nazi Germany, and the extermination of the Jewish population on the continent of Europe during World War II, finally made the socialist movement alive to the Jewish problem. This, in turn, led to an increasing understanding of Zionist aspirations. The British Labour Party led the campaign for increased Jewish immigration into Palestine and against the anti-Zionist *White Paper introduced by the Conservative government (May 1939), and its program of postwar aims envisaged the establishment of a Jewish state. The reversal of the party's pro-Zionist platform by the Labour government after 1945 came as a shock to many socialists in both Britain and elsewhere. A number of European socialist parties – while deeply sympathetic to the plight of Jewish refugees – were reluctant to criticize the policy of the British Labour government. The situation changed after the UN Partition resolution of 1947 and the establishment of the State of Israel (1948), whose emergence was greeted by many socialist leaders in various parts of the world. From its revival in 1951, the Socialist International gave consistent support to Mapai and later to the Israel Labor Party, which played an active part in the meetings of the bureau, council conferences, and congresses of the organization. The Socialist International, mainly on the initiative of Israeli delegates, took an active interest in the problem of Soviet Jewry and several times officially demanded its positive solution. (See *Russia, Struggle for Soviet Jewry.) The 11th Congress of the Socialist International (June 1969) adopted a resolution which expressed deep concern that two years after the war of the Arab states against Israel, no advance had yet been made toward a settlement based on security and lasting peace in the area. It stated that flagrant violations of the cease-fire agreement and senseless acts of terrorism threatened to lead to an escalation toward a new war. It also pledged full support for the mission of the UN representative Gunnar Jarring and directly negotiated peace treaties between Arab states and Israel. The International appointed a special working group to study the situation of Soviet Jewry and actively identified itself with the struggle for the attainment of its legitimate rights; it also urged Arab governments to allow Jews to emigrate.

Conclusion

Summarizing the Jewish contribution to the Socialist movement the following picture emerges regarding the situation at the end of 1970.

(1) The Nazi-Fascist period and the Holocaust led to a decline both of the Jewish population in Central Europe and in its contribution to the socialist movement; individual Jews, however, continued to play their part in the various labor parties.

(2) The establishment of Communist regimes in Eastern European countries led to the suppression of socialist parties and thus brought to an end the long chapter of Jewish participation in the struggle for democratic socialist ideas in Russia, Poland, Romania, and other countries of the region.

(3) The period of Gaullism in France was followed by both a decrease in the strength of the socialist movement and the part of Jews in its leadership.

(4) A feature of the postwar period was a considerable increase in Jewish participation in the activities of the British Labour Party, and a parallel process, on a smaller scale, was discernible in the Canadian New Democratic Party. A tendency to greater Jewish participation in labor politics was also felt in Australia where the Jewish community was still comparatively small. Similar currents were noticeable in South American countries but the outlook was unclear due, on the one hand, to military dictatorships and, on the other, to the possibility of revolutionary upheavals.

(5) The major center of the Jewish socialist movement with wide links in many parts of the world was Israel. It was the Israel Labor Party and the Histadrut which attracted the interest of both international labor circles and non-aligned countries in the "Third World." The center of gravity of Jewish socialist thought and actions shifted from Diaspora countries to Israel. During the 19th century, the world was mainly familiar with the contribution to socialism made by individuals of Jewish origin, but it is now aware of the collective Jewish contribution created by Jewish labor in the Jewish state.

[Schneier Zalman Levenberg]

SOCIALISM AND WOMEN

Jewish women's involvement with socialism began in 19th-century Europe with the emergence of modern Jewish political movements that sought to address the dislocations caused by industrialization, urbanization, and the breakdown of traditional religious structures. Socialists aspired to create a just society, often conceived in utopian, classless terms. Some Jewish women who worked within socialist movements, parties, trade unions, and causes added gender to their class and national analyses of modernity's problems, insisting on an amalgam of socialism and feminism.

The first Jewish socialists, including female intelligentsia such as Rosa *Luxemburg in Germany, Angelica *Balabanov in Italy, and Matilda Pollak of Austria, put their energies into general socialist movements. However, by the end of the 19th century, the composition and nature of Jewish involvement with socialism was transformed by the growth of a massive Jewish artisanal working-class in Eastern Europe. As Jewish women flocked into light industry, primarily the needle trades, but also tanning, bristle making, and cigar and cigarette production, many began to organize as workers and as Jews to protest their exploitative working conditions. Jewish women joined the socialist-oriented Bund when it formed in Vilna in 1897, comprising one-third of its membership, and occupied many of its middle rank leadership roles. Esther Frumkin (b. 1880), despite being born to a life of privilege, devoted herself to the Bundist cause.

Emigration from Eastern Europe stimulated socialist activism. Jewish immigrant communities in Europe, the Americas, Palestine, and elsewhere, were deeply sympathetic to socialist ideals, many of which were expressed through trade unionism. Women played an important role in realizing many of these aspirations. Although Jews comprised 40 percent of New York's garment workers in the early 20th century, Jewish women often found themselves in less skilled, lower-paying positions, and were viewed skeptically by the labor establishment. Yet, the American and American Jewish trade union movements only became secure when galvanized by labor activities spearheaded by young Jewish women workers in the first decade of the 20th century.

The most important female labor action of the period, the so-called Uprising of the Twenty Thousand (also known as the 1909 Shirtwaist Strike; see *International Ladies Garment Workers Union), involving thousands of Jewish and Italian working girls, began a series of strikes that spread to Philadelphia, Chicago, Cleveland, and Kalamazoo – later called "The Great Revolt" – and emboldened the American labor movement. By 1919, half of all garment workers were members of a union. Fannia M. *Cohn, Rose *Schneiderman, Pauline *Newman, and Clara Lemlich *Shavelson, all East European-born, experienced the shirtwaist strike as the formative event of their activist youth, as did Theresa *Malkiel, who later became an important Socialist Party activist and immortalized her experiences in the novel *Diary of a Shirtwaist Striker* (1910). Many female Jewish trade unionists continued their socialist-inspired activism through progressive and reform politics in the New Deal. Most notable was Bessie Abramowitz *Hillman, who at 21 led a walkout with 16 other young women against a Chicago clothing firm that began the 1910 strike and later became an organizer for the Women's Trade Union League (WTUL). Similar narratives are told of other young Jewish women raised in immigrant communities, such as Rose Kerrigan, whose socialist activism informed her earliest years as a rent striker and her later years as a pension activist in Glasgow, Scotland. While most female Jewish socialists felt loyalty foremost to the working-class from which they came, they also supported middle-class feminist issues, such as suffrage, in disproportionate numbers.

Socialism's strength on the New York Jewish street before World War I made the Jewish Socialist Federation (JSF), established in 1912, the third largest foreign-language federation within the Socialist Party. When the 1917 October Revolution radicalized and split the international socialist and trade union movement, Jewish women joined the ranks of both the Socialist Party (and the nascent Communist Party). Many others became fellow travelers who worked for socialist ideals through the expansive Jewish immigrant fraternal, educational, and cultural networks that included the Yiddish press, supplementary Yiddish schools, theater, and housing and consumer cooperatives.

Socialist activism also informed the Zionist movement and as early as 1907 the Po'alei Zion applied for membership in the Socialist International, asserting that the needs of the Jewish proletariat merited a special Jewish organization. Opposition to Zionism ran strong in the international socialist community, and labor and social Zionists found their successes in the Israeli kibbutz and labor movements. *The Plough Woman* (1931; rep. 2002) recorded the testimonies of female pioneers, such as Rachel *Katznelson-Shazar and Yael Gordon among many others, who were imbued with the socialist ideals that underpinned labor Zionism.

Because socialism was so intimately tied to immigrant labor, culture, and community life, post-World War II suburbanization and upward mobility led to the decline of socialist activism among Jews, including women. An exception was the prominence of certain Jewish women activists in "Second Wave" feminism, which as a movement criticized society chiefly through the lens of gender. Individuals such as Clara

Goodman Fraser, a Jewish feminist from East Los Angeles, believed that resolution of class conflict was necessary to ameliorate the condition of women in a patriarchal society. She combined socialism and feminism on behalf of the Freedom Socialist Party (FSP) and Radical Women (RW) throughout the 1960s and 1970s. In Latin America, many Jewish women, such as the socialist Alicia Portnoy, suffered as leftists under the Argentinean junta in the 1970s.

[Nancy Sinkoff (2nd ed.)]

BIBLIOGRAPHY: E. Silberner, *Western European Socialism and the Jewish Problem* (1955), incl. bibl.; idem, *Ha-Sozyalism ha-Ma'aravi u-She'elat ha-Yehudim…* (1955); idem, in: HJ, 15 (1953), 3–48; 16 (1954), 3–38; idem, in: HUCA, 24 (1953), 151–86; idem, in: JSOS, 8 (1946), 245–66; 9 (1947), 339–62; idem, in: *Scripta Hierosolymitana*, 3 (1955); O. Bauer, *Die Nationalitaetenfrage und die Sozialdemokratie* (1924²); G.D.H. Cole, *A History of Socialist Thought*, 5 vols. (1953–60), index; J. Braunthal *In Search of the Millennium* (1945); idem, *Geschichte der Internationale*, 2 vols. (1961–63); J. Joll, *The Second International* (1966); D.A. Chalmers, *The Social Democratic Party of Germany* (1964); E. Mendelsohn, *Class Struggle in the Pale* (1970); J.L.H. Keep, *The Rise of Social Democracy in Russia* (1963); K. Landauer, *European Socialism: A History of Ideas and Movements from the Industrial Revolution to Hitler's Seizure of Power*, 2 vols. (1959). IN THE U.S.: D. Bell, in: D.D. Egbert and S. Persons, *Socialism and American Life*, 2 vols. (1952), 215–425; A. Goren, *New York Jews and the Quest for Community: The Kehillah Experiment 1908–1922* (1970), 186–96; A. Gorenstein (Goren), in: AJHSP, 50 (1960/61), 202–38; R. Rockaway, in: *Detroit Historical Society, Bulletin* (Nov. 1970), 4–9; D.A. Shannon, *The Socialist Party of America* (1955); J.S. Hertz, *Di Yidishe Sotsialistishe Bavegung in Amerike* (1954); R. Schwarz, in: Fraenkel (ed.), *The Jews of Austria* (1967), 445–66; M. Jarblum, *The Socialist International and Zionism* (1933). **ADD. BIBLIOGRAPHY:** SOCIALISM AND WOMEN: H. Davis-Kram, "The Story of the Sisters of the Bund," in: Contemporary Jewry, 5:2 (1980), 7–43; P.S. Foner, *Women and the American Labor Movement: From Colonial Times to the Eve of World War I* (1979); S. Glenn, *Daughters of the Shtetl: Life and Labor in the Immigrant Generation* (1990; P.E. Hyman, *Gender and Assimilation in Modern Jewish History* (1995); N. Levin, *Jewish Socialist Movements, 1877–1917* (1978); E. Mendelsohn, *Class Struggle in the Pale: The Formative Years of the Jewish Workers' Movement in Tsarist Russia* (1970); T. Michels, "Socialism and the Writing of American Jewish History: World of Our Fathers Revisited," in: *American Jewish History*, 88:4 (December 2000), 521–46; idem, "Socialism with a Jewish Face: The Origins of the Yiddish-Speaking Communist Movement in the United States, 190–1923," in: G. Estraikh and M. Krutikov (eds.), *Yiddish and the Left* (2001), 24–55; A. Orleck, *Common Sense and a Little Fire: Women and Working-Class Politics in the United States, 1900–1965* (1995); G. Sorin, "Socialism," in: P.E. Hyman and D.D. Moore (eds.), *Jewish Women in America* (1997), 2:1269–73.

SOCIALISM, JEWISH. This article refers to specifically Jewish movements and parties which envisaged the creation of a socialist society as an essential aspect of the solution to the Jewish question. This definition, while far from perfect, has the virtue of excluding Jews who happened to be socialists, as well as socialist movements in which many Jews were active but which had no specifically Jewish content or aims (for which see *Socialism).

The Beginnings of the Movement

Jewish socialism, so understood, could originate only in Eastern Europe, and above all in the *Pale of Settlement. In distinction to Western and Central European Jewries, which were largely middle class, East European Jewry included hundreds and thousands of workers, the Yiddish-speaking "masses" so evident in the cities of western and southern Russia. Moreover, by the late 19th century a secular Jewish intelligentsia had developed in the Pale, consisting of students and professionals, many of whom were influenced by radical Russian ideologies. That they should be so was quite predictable, given the all-pervasive antisemitism which awakened their demands for social justice and made public activity, outside radical circles, impossible. These Jewish intellectuals, children of the *Haskalah ("Enlightenment"), were in revolt against the values and traditions of the ghetto. In many cases socialism, the acceptance of which in itself was a sign of assimilation, led them to discover the Jewish proletariat; this discovery, in turn, led them back to the Jewish people, to whom they preached the new doctrine.

The alliance of the radical Jewish intelligentsia with the Jewish masses made Jewish socialism possible. This alliance occurred first and foremost in the area of Jewish settlement in Lithuania (Lithuania-Belorussia, corresponding to the six provinces of the northwest region of the Pale), where the Jewish working class was numerically dominant in the cities and the Jewish intelligentsia was less subject to assimilationist pressures than in Poland or Ukraine. It is no accident that so many of the pioneers of Jewish socialism were "Litvaks" (that is, of Lithuanian origin) and that the *Bund, the first great Jewish socialist party, was founded in Vilna. Indeed, Jewish socialism may be seen as expanding from its Lithuanian base first to Poland and the Ukraine, and then beyond Russia's borders to Austrian Galicia. It took root, too, in the major centers of the Russian Jewish emigration: London, New York, Buenos Aires, and, of course, Palestine.

Russian Jewish socialism may be said to begin with A.S. *Liebermann. Born in Lunna, a student at the celebrated rabbinical seminary in Vilna, Liebermann became a confirmed Populist, influenced in particular by the doctrines of Peter Lavrov. It was in the pages of Lavrov's London journal *Vpered* that Liebermann published in 1875 a series of articles on the Jewish proletariat. Having taken the first vital step in his discovery of the poverty-stricken workers of Bialystok and Vilna, the author went one step further. These workers, he argued, lived under special conditions and spoke a distinct language of their own; they required, therefore, a special organization of their own, a Jewish section within the Russian revolutionary movement. This suggestion was questioned by V.N. Smirnov, secretary of *Vpered*, and Liebermann was accused of having deviated from socialist internationalism. He replied that recognition of the Jewish proletariat's special needs was far from nationalism, and that he himself despised "Jewry," believing only in individuals and in classes. This is the first exposition of what was to become a familiar pattern: the discovery of the

Jewish proletariat is followed by the demand for a specifically Jewish organization, justified on technical grounds by reference to the obvious empiric differences between Jewish and Russian workers. Liebermann went no further than this, and his organizational schemes left no lasting impression in Russia, though he succeeded in establishing a Jewish workers' union in London. He was, however, a true pioneer, not only because he edited the first Jewish socialist journal, **Ha-Emet*, but because his conception of the needs of the Jewish proletariat was accepted by all his successors. His career offered a point of departure, while his quarrel with Smirnov hinted at what was to become a major dilemma for generations of Jewish socialists.

During the 1880s and 1890s socialist circles (*kruzhki* in Russian) were founded in the major cities of Lithuania. These circles succeeded, for the first time, in joining together members of the Jewish intelligentsia and the Jewish working class. The leaders were russified Jews, to a far greater extent than Liebermann, who had retained the characteristics of a *maskil* and published his socialist organ in Hebrew. There were both Populists and Marxists among them, though Marxism was more attractive (after all, Populism placed its hopes on the peasants and there was no Jewish peasantry) and eventually won the day. The aim of the circle was to produce cadres of trained revolutionaries who would dedicate their lives to the Russian revolution. It was, in accordance with both Populist and Marxist teachings, essentially a school for socialism. The worker participants were first taught Russian and then studied economics, literature, and even the natural sciences, the purpose being to make them "class conscious." There was nothing particularly Jewish about these circles except that all the participants were Jews. This was the result not only of the preponderance of Jewish workers in the cities of Lithuania and Belorussia (Vilna, Minsk, Gomel, Dvinsk, etc.) but also of the gulf which separated Jews from Christians, the "estrangement" felt even by russified Jewish intellectuals when they sought to make contact with non-Jews. The all-Jewish character of the circles, therefore, reflected necessity rather than the desire to establish a Jewish movement, a practical example of Liebermann's view that special conditions dictated the creation of a special movement.

The idea of creating a special Jewish movement, however, as apart from circles dedicated to supplying revolutionaries for the Russian movement, was not formulated by the circle leaders until the circles themselves were transformed into trade unions. This transformation, the famous transition from cultural "propaganda" to economic "agitation," occurred in the early 1890s, by which time the circle movement had reached a point of crisis. While the circle was intended to be a school for socialism, a significant number of worker participants used it as a means to attain secular education and to escape the poverty of proletarian existence. Some emigrated, some became students, and others even opened their own shops, thus becoming, in the eyes of the leadership, "exploiters." Searching for a way out of this impasse the intellectual leadership resolved to appeal to the economic interests of the Jewish masses, an idea which came to them partly as a result of new developments within Russian Marxist thought, partly from the example of Polish socialism, and partly from their own experience of early Jewish strikes. Thus the educational circle made way for the strike, and the dominant figure of the circle movement, the teacher, gave way to the labor leader, the "agitator." Class consciousness would be achieved not through studying economics but through the hard school of the strike movement, which would demonstrate to the workers the alliance between the boss and the regime. The new slogan was "through economics to politics." Rather than concentrating on the elite of the circles, the intellectuals went "into the streets, to the masses."

The transition from propaganda to agitation was accompanied by the ideological formulation, expressed in the writings of A. *Kremer, S. *Gozhansky, and J. *Martov, of the need for a specifically Jewish socialist organization. These men, who formerly thought only in terms of Russian socialism, now argued that the Jewish proletariat, miserably exploited and extremely responsive to the slogans of the agitation campaign, was a worthy member of the international working class. Its struggle for better economic conditions was fully justified by the tenets of international Marxism, for the organization of Jewish workers into trade unions would ultimately contribute to the struggle to make Russia into a socialist state. The leaders then went one step further. The struggle of the Jewish proletariat, they argued, was also a national struggle for equal rights for Russian Jewry, a struggle which the assimilated and cowardly Jewish bourgeoisie was incapable of waging and which non-Jewish movements were liable to ignore. Thus the connection was made between the social role of the Jewish proletariat, whose mission was to lead the way to socialism, and its national role as defender of Jewish rights in the Russian Empire. This conception was to be developed into a full blown socialist-nationalist ideology which virtually all Jewish socialist movements came to accept.

The Bund

This way of thought became the organizational and ideological basis for the General Jewish Workers' Union in Russia and Poland (the *Bund), founded in 1897 as the result of the unification of various local movements in the major cities of Lithuania. The new ideology, as well as the new trade union organization, encountered stiff opposition: Russian Marxists, who organized the Russian Social Democratic Workers' Party in 1898, refused to admit the need for an autonomous Jewish organization, a position consistently affirmed by *Lenin in his polemics with the Bund. Certain members of the old circles, who prized the cultural work carried on by the intellectuals, denounced the tactics of agitation as a plot to keep the workers ignorant and therefore incapable of leadership roles in the revolutionary movement. The various opposition movements which emerged in Vilna, Minsk, and other centers advanced an additional argument which was to have considerable weight among Jewish socialists. The Jewish working class, they claimed, could not wage a meaningful class struggle because it consisted almost entirely of artisans, with little if any difference between employers and employees. Those artisans, who for various reasons could gain entrance to the great factories, had nothing in common with the Russian factory proletariat, not to mention the great proletariats of Western Europe. Agitation, therefore, could only lead to the farcical struggle of the "poverty-stricken against the indigent."

The formulators of the agitation program rejected this argument. The Jewish artisan, they wrote, was a particularly apt subject for the slogans of economic action, since he was better educated than the factory worker and was the heir to a long tradition of guild organization. The fact that 90% of the Jewish workingmen in Lithuania were craftsmen who labored in tiny shops might therefore be advantageous, and in the end a Jewish factory proletariat would doubtless develop. Indeed, the outbreak of strikes in the Pale, from 1892 on, and the remarkable organizational achievements of the Jewish proletariat under the leadership of the Bund (achievements which placed the Jewish movement, in Plekhanov's words, in the vanguard of the Russian proletarian army) would appear to bear out the correctness of the agitation tactics. Certainly the opposition movements were swept away by the Jewish workers' massive response to the agitation program. On the other hand, there is considerable evidence that the strike movement was unable to cure the economic troubles of the Jewish artisan class, which were caused to a certain extent by its inability to enter the factories. The Bund's assumption that the Jewish proletariat was essentially no different from any other was to come under heavy attack in the early years of the 20th century.

As already noted, as early as the 1890s the socialists had attributed both a social and a national role to the Jewish proletariat. The success of the agitation tactics gave impetus to the formulation by the leaders of the Bund of a Jewish national program. The development from Liebermann's disavowal of all interest in the Jews as a national entity to the Bund's adoption of the demand for national-cultural autonomy, presented in 1903, is of great importance. It is explicable in terms of the fact that the Jewish proletariat, bearer of the Marxist mission, was also seen as the bearer of the Jewish national tradition as against the assimilated, russified or polonized Jewish middle class. This became clear to the socialists only with the inauguration of the agitation tactics, when they came face to face with the masses for the first time. In order better to serve the cause of the Yiddish-speaking Jewish workers the movement forged a natural alliance with the Yiddish literary renaissance – Jewish workers were now offered *Peretz instead of Turgenev. The interest in all things Yiddish, glorified as the language of the laboring class (in contrast to Hebrew, the language of the reactionary yeshivot), remained a hallmark of the Bund throughout its existence. Moreover, the tactics of agitation brought to the fore a new leadership, a "popular" one often drawn from the so-called "semi-intelligentsia" (meaning the Jewish youth without diplomas), which was less russified and closer to the Jewish masses than the Kremers and Martovs. Both these factors caused Bundists to advance from the attitude that a Jewish organization was justified basically on technical grounds to the attitude that the Jewish people, represented by its proletariat, presented national characteristics of a positive nature which should be fostered. This new assumption was strengthened by the growth of Jewish nationalism in Russia as a competing ideology to Bundism. It was also strengthened by the development, within the Austrian Social Democratic Party, of the theory of national self-determination on a personal rather than a territorial basis. By demanding national rights for the Jews, which meant mainly the right to foster Yiddish cultural activities, the Bund embarked on a course taken by many other socialist parties representing the oppressed nationalities of the Russian and Austrian empires. It was also following trends within the European socialist movement, which during the period of the Second International increasingly came to recognize and encourage the liberation movements of subject peoples. The Bund's combination of socialism and nationalism was therefore in line with tendencies in East European Marxism, though the Jewish case was more difficult to defend since it was by no means clear that the Jews were, in fact, a nationality. Thus Otto *Bauer, chief theoretician of the Austrian Marxists and the author of a famous book on Marxism and nationalism, specifically excluded the Jews from the community of nations. This was the background to the long polemics between the Bund and Lenin, who never doubted that the solution to the Jewish question lay in assimilation. Neither Lenin nor Bauer, however, could convince the Bundists that the defense of the Jewish workers' national needs was any less vital than the defense of their economic and political needs.

In the early years of its existence the Bund ruled, virtually unchallenged, as the party of the politically active Jewish working class. Even its greatest enemies within the Jewish socialist camp have never failed to grant the Bund credit for its role in awakening this class, in which it inspired new hopes for a society based on social justice and democracy. The Bund, in short, put the East European Jewish working class on the map of modern Jewish history. However, a fundamental weakness of the party was its assumption that the condition of the Jews in Russia was not greatly different from the condition of the other nationalities of the empire, except that the Jews lacked a territory and therefore required national cultural autonomy on a personal basis. The task of the Jewish proletariat was to struggle, side by side with the proletariats of the other nationalities, for a socialist Russia. Antisemitism was regarded as a manifestation of capitalism alone; socialism would abolish it, along with all other iniquities, and would solve the Jewish question once and for all. Zionism was therefore regarded as a bourgeois ideology, a brand of utopianism dangerous because it might lure workers away from their proper mission. Zionists were seen as working hand-in-hand with antisemites, the classic example being Herzl's meeting with Von *Plehve.

Zionist Socialism

These views were rejected by a new type of Jewish socialism, Zionist Socialism, which challenged the hegemony of the Bund in the years immediately preceding the first Russian revolution. The ideologists of this new movement were from various backgrounds: there were former "bourgeois" Zionists, such as Nachman *Syrkin, who were unable to withstand the great influence of Russian radicalism and moved to the left but without abandoning their Zionist principles; and former Russian socialists, such as Ber *Borochov, whose encounters with Russian antisemitism, including the proletarian variety, helped to push them into the Zionist camp. The *Zionist Socialists agreed with the Bund in recognizing the predominant role of the Jewish proletariat in modern Jewish history, and in recognizing the dual nature of this role – both social and national. However, they were also in fundamental agreement with the Zionist analysis of the Jewish predicament, namely that antisemitism was endemic to the Diaspora and that the reversal of class relationships through revolution, however desirable, did not constitute a solution. Their problem was to create an ideology which, rejecting both the Bund's russo-centrism and the all-class character of bourgeois Zionism, would combine the revolutionary determinism of the former with the doctrine of territorialism articulated by the latter.

The early *Po'alei Zion circles found it easier to attack the Bund than to formulate a clear alternative. Their attack was based on the theory that the Jewish working class did not constitute a proletariat, a theory somewhat reminiscent of the views of those who opposed the agitation tactics of the early 1890s. The Jewish working class, it was argued, was incapable of transforming itself into a proletariat because of the very nature of the Diaspora, which precluded the possibility of a normal Jewish existence. It was, and would remain, incapable of a meaningful class struggle, and therefore the entire Bundist program was based on a class with no future. Thus the failure of Jewish workers to enter the great factories was not a temporary phenomenon but a symptom of the Jewish people's abnormal situation, which no social revolution could alter. The Jewish strike movement, while perhaps of psychological value, was a palliative rather than a cure. The peculiar nature of the Jewish proletariat, cited by the circle's participants in their polemics with Kremer and Gozhanky, and by the Bundists as proof that the Jewish artisans would be particularly amenable to the class struggle, was presented as proof of the bankruptcy of the Bund's position. Thus the emotional argument against the Bund, the rising tide of antisemitism symbolized by the *Kishinev pogrom (1903), was given "scientific" backing by studies proving the absurdity of Jewish strikes and the absence of Jewish workers from the great factories.

As socialists, however, the Bund's critics were also obliged to base their hopes on the Jewish proletariat (or at least on the "laboring masses"). Therefore they evolved the concept that the Jewish question could be solved only through the territorial concentration of the Jewish working class, where a meaningful class struggle would be feasible and would lead to a Jewish socialist society. This territorial concentration, however, would not come about as the result of the will of the Jewish people – Herzl's famous slogan, "If you will it, it is no dream" was unacceptable to the Marxist and semi-Marxist intelligentsia – but as the inevitable result of the Jewish proletariat's search for a base from which to conduct the class struggle. Thus both the Bund's error and Zionism's ultimate victory were proven in "scientific" terms, as was the pioneering role of the Jewish proletariat in the Zionist movement. Marxist determinism was introduced to lend certainty to the Zionist ideal, a fact of great psychological significance to those who had previously suspected Zionism of being Utopian. Herzl's slogan was turned on its head; since it was proved that "it is no dream," therefore "we shall will it."

While Zionist Socialists (see below) agreed that the abnormal situation of the Jewish working class, itself symptomatic of the incurable disease of the Diaspora, ruled out a Diaspora solution to the Jewish question, there was no agreement on a number of extremely difficult problems inherent in the basic ideology. There was, for example, the problem of the "two levels." Should the Zionist Socialists participate in the political and economic struggle in Russia, or should they concentrate solely on efforts to obtain a territory? The latter alternative was not particularly attractive, since it was not clear exactly how a political party, with its base in Russia, might work to hasten the territorial solution. On the other hand, if the Jewish question could not be solved in Russia, and if the Jewish proletariat was incapable of waging the class struggle, what was the point of organizing a party in the Diaspora at all? It was logical that, despite the "negation of the exile" implied in the theses of the Zionist Socialists, their involvement in the Diaspora should nonetheless increase as their popularity among Jewish workers and intellectuals grew. From a practical point of view it was clear that the territorial solution, especially after the episode of the Uganda *scheme, was far off, and that the Jewish masses would remain in Russia for the foreseeable future. Along with this was the fact that the rising revolutionary storm in Russia, which reached its peak in 1905–06, could not be ignored by the Jewish socialists, whether Zionists or not. Thus Zionist Socialists, revealing an apparent contradiction between their theory and their practice, often became as involved in the Russian struggle as their antagonists, the Bundists. This was particularly true during great upheavals in Russia, when the temptation to participate and therefore to prove one's revolutionary worth was too great to withstand. The problem of the "two levels" remained crucial for all Zionist Socialists, just as the peculiar composition of the Jewish proletariat and the participation of workers in pogroms remained a problem for the Bund. This problem helped split the socialist Zionist camp in 1917 and during the civil war, the greatest Russian upheaval of them all.

Another basic problem was the question in which territory the Jews were to be concentrated. For many Zionist Socialists, who believed along with Herzl in the imminent collapse of Diaspora Jewry (a belief naturally strengthened by the Kishinev pogrom), any territory would do, and therefore they supported the Uganda scheme, an issue which divided the Zionist movement from 1903 on. Moreover, it was difficult for socialists to accept the Palestinian orientation of bourgeois Zionism, since it seemed to be based on mysticism and was unsupported by any scientific, socialist analysis. The eternal bond between the Jewish people and Ereẓ Israel appeared to be a fitting slogan for the *Mizrachi movement but not for Marxists. It is therefore paradoxical that the most consistent Marxist of all, Ber Borochov, nonetheless insisted on Palestine, though he too justified his choice on utilitarianism rather than on appeals to Jewish tradition. The problem of "why Palestine," like the problem of Hebrew versus Yiddish, remained a difficult one for Zionist Socialists, especially for Marxists torn between their loyalty to the national movement and their adherence to scientific socialism.

Other issues also separated the various socialist Zionist groups, which included strict Marxists, semi-Marxists, and Populists. To cite one example, some rejected the "catastrophe" approach to the Jewish Diaspora and insisted that the territorial solution, though necessary, could be achieved only after a long process of development in the Diaspora. During the first Russian Revolution three distinct parties formed out of the ideological confusion: the Marxist, Palestinian Po'alei Zion, the *Zionist Socialist Workers' Party (known as S.S.), which despite its name was territorialist, and the *Jewish Socialist Workers' Party, also known as the "Sejmist" party, which called for the nurturing of Jewish national life in the Diaspora (under the aegis of a Jewish parliament, or Sejm) until the time was ripe for a territorial solution. Together, these parties spelled a serious challenge to the hegemony of the Bund. Unlike the Bund, all suffered from the tension between the ultimate goal, a territorial solution, and the inescapable need to participate in the struggle for socialism, Jewish national rights in the Diaspora, and the improvement of the economic lot of the Jewish masses. The three parties, all claiming to represent the Yiddish-speaking, economically and culturally deprived Jewish laboring masses, found that their activities overlapped. It is significant that the objective situation led all of them to champion national cultural autonomy for Russian Jewry, a stand also taken by the Bund. In fact, though kept alive by polemics between party leaders, ideological distinctions tended to be blurred in the daily struggle. Thus Bundists, socialist Zionists, and socialist territorialists all cooperated in the establishment of Yiddish schools, seen as the mainspring in the creation of Jewish national autonomy. While the gulf between the Bundist and Zionist Socialist analysis of the Jewish question remained as wide as ever, so long as the Jewish masses remained concentrated in the Pale and elsewhere in Eastern Europe, the practical platforms of the various Jewish socialist parties were bound to grow more and more similar.

Europe Outside Russia

In Eastern Europe, beyond Russia's borders, Galicia offered the most fertile ground for Jewish socialism. Both the Bund and the Zionist Socialists made inroads in this Austrian province, which combined economic conditions even worse than those in the Pale with a much more moderate political system. Vienna, a magnet for Galician Jewish intellectuals, became an important Po'alei Zion center, though the absence of a substantial Jewish proletariat made Bundist incursions impossible. The great emigration from Eastern Europe did produce a Jewish proletariat in England, chiefly in London's East End, which became an important Jewish socialist and trade union center in the 1880s. In London, as in the cities of the Pale, there was a profusion of both radical Jewish intellectuals and Jewish artisans, but different conditions made for a very different development in Jewish socialism. One issue, the path to Yiddish, which was complicated in Russia, was much easier in London. Having left Russia behind and not having yet become anglicized, the intellectuals turned to Yiddish to fill the vacuum. Thus Morris *Vinchevsky, Liebermann's contemporary, abandoned his mentor's Hebrew and published in London the first socialist paper in Yiddish, the *Poylishe Yidl*. The English capital became a training ground for Yiddish socialist journalists, whose writings were read in both Russia and America. Trade union activities were central to the Jewish movement from the very beginning, natural in a country which, unlike Russia, boasted an advanced and legal trade union movement. The Jewish unions were often founded by socialists (or anarchists), and for as long as Jewish workers were clearly differentiated from non-Jews it is possible to speak of a Jewish movement. However, on the eve of World War I specifically Jewish unions were on the wane, a result of growing assimilation and the absorption of Jewish workers by English unions. The Yiddish socialist press and Jewish socialist and anarchist groups, deprived of leadership and subjects for organization, were also in decline. The careers of such Jewish socialists as Vinchevsky, Philip *Krantz, and Benjamin *Feigenbaum, who were active in London and then left for the new world, illustrate both the importance of London as a center of early Jewish socialist activity and its rather swift eclipse by New York.

The United States

The history of U.S. Jewish socialism is not unlike that of English Jewish socialism, though incomparably richer and more important. In the United States Russian-Jewish radicals, arriving from the early 1880s onward, found themselves estranged from the mainstream of American political life: even American Marxism, whose main practitioners were German immigrants in New York, was too reformist for them. Leaving Russia behind, but not the Russian radical tradition, they plunged hopefully into the Yiddish-speaking milieu of New York, editing socialist newspapers, writing Yiddish pamphlets and poetry, and above all organizing Jewish workers into trade unions. These unions, unlike most American labor organizations, were socialist in ideology; there were no greater enemies of S. *Gompers' nonpolitical unionism, embodied in the American Federation of Labor, than the Jewish unions led by former Russian radicals. The various waves of immigration brought to the U.S. numerous East European Jewish socialists, including illustrious Bundists and Zionist Socialists, who formed groups of their own. Such organizations, aside from their local activities, were of great importance for their sister organizations in Eastern Europe and Palestine, since they were in a position to offer both political and financial support. Thus just as the significance of American Zionism within the world Zionist movement increased, so did that of the American Po'alei Zion within world labor Zionism, all the more so since most of the prominent Po'alei Zion leaders were at one time or another active in America. Equally important was the cultural work accomplished by Jewish socialists among the Yiddish-speaking immigrants. If the Russian movement had its circles, and later its Yiddish secular schools, American Jewish socialism created the Arbeter Ring ("Workmens' *Circle"), a fraternal organization which combined economic and cultural activities. In the United States, as in Eastern Europe, socialism was the means whereby great numbers of the Jewish poor received an education.

In the United States, as in Russia, the organization of Jewish unions and the use of Yiddish were justified on technical grounds. Thus A. *Cahan, perhaps the dominant figure in American Jewish radicalism, a former student at the same Vilna rabbinical seminary which Aaron Liebermann attended, used Yiddish in his speeches to the Jewish workers in America simply because they understood no other language. Unlike Russia, however, where the tendency was from Russian to Yiddish, in the United States the tendency was from Yiddish to English. The mainstream of the U.S. Jewish socialist movement, represented by Cahan and his newspaper *Jewish Daily Forward*, favored the Americanization of the Jewish masses. National cultural autonomy was regarded as a justified demand for East European Jewry but was clearly absurd in the United States, the land of democracy, where the all-pervasive influence of English soon made itself felt among the immigrant masses. Moreover, if Russian conditions favored the creation of mass socialist parties, like the Bund, which were of a pronounced Marxist, revolutionary character, in the United States the mass Jewish organization was the union, whose socialist character was clear at the outset but which tended to leave socialism behind with the passage of time. It is interesting to note that in Russia, where Jewish workers were not particularly successful in improving their economic situation, the Jewish labor movement and Jewish socialism remained more or less identical. In the United States, where major breakthroughs were made in the Needle Trade Union relations with management in the years immediately preceding World War I, this identity was not maintained. The career of David *Dubinsky, a former Bundist who became the leader of the International Ladies Garment Workers' Union and left Bundism behind, illustrates this process. Thus American soil nourished neither the national nor the radical sides of East European Jewish socialism, though both Yiddishists and Jewish Marxists remained active on the American scene.

Relations with the Communist Party

The Bolshevik October (1917) Revolution and the establishment of the Communist International inaugurated a period of schisms within the Jewish socialist movement, as within virtually all socialist parties. It became necessary to choose between affiliation to the victorious Communist movement and continued adherence to democratic socialism. For the Jewish parties this choice was particularly difficult; the Russian Communist Party, while clearly opposed to antisemitism, inherited an assimilationist attitude toward the Jewish question and was hostile to both Zionism and Bundism. Hence to join the Communist movement meant, essentially, to abandon a specifically Jewish program (though not the use of Yiddish to reach the Jewish workers). In the Soviet Union, of course, there was no freedom to choose. The Bund, which was anti-Bolshevik during the revolution, was not tolerated by the new regime. After the failure of efforts to maintain organizational autonomy as the so-called "Kombund" ("Communist Bund"), the Bund was forced out of existence by 1921. The various Zionist socialist movements, though they lasted longer than the Bund, were finally crushed in the Soviet Union during the later 1920s. It should not be imagined that the collapse of autonomous Jewish socialist parties in the U.S.S.R. was solely the result of repression. In 1918 many Bundists began to opt for Communism, reflecting, among other things, the Jewish reaction to pogroms in the Ukraine. Many members of Po'alei Zion, favorably inclined toward the Bolshevik coup from the beginning, also declared their adherence to the Communist movement, as did the United Jewish Socialist Workers' Party, the left faction of the so-called Fareynikte ("United," e.g., the unified S.S.-Sejmist Party, which had amalgamated in 1917). Such erosion indicates that, at least among certain Jewish socialists, the Jewish content was less important than the hopes for a new society in which all national problems would be automatically solved. If many Jewish radicals had been led to Jewish territorialism by the atmosphere of antisemitism so prevalent in czarist Russia, the victory of Communism, transforming Russia from the most backward to the most enlightened country in Europe, led them back to the ideals of pure internationalism. Moscow for them appeared to be a surer Zion than Jerusalem. As for the Bundists, the attraction of participating in building the new socialist state in Russia, along with the hope that their national program might, after all, be implemented by the Communists, led large numbers to break with the anti-Bolshevik tradition of their party. All Jewish socialists in Russia, moreover, were influenced by their fear of the counter-revolution, which had revealed its antisemitic character in the terrible pogroms in the Ukraine. Clearly it was necessary to fight these forces of reaction, and in the polarized atmosphere of the civil war in Russia the Bolsheviks appeared to many Jewish socialists to be the lesser of the two evils.

Defectors from the various Jewish socialist parties constituted the backbone of the so-called "Jewish Sections" (**Yevsektsiya*) which existed until 1930 as Jewish Communist organizations designed to propagate Communism among the

Soviet Jewish masses. Their creation was in fact a concession to reality on the part of the Communist leadership, whose antipathy to autonomous Jewish organizations was tempered by the fact, "discovered" so many times in the history of Jewish socialism, that the Jewish masses were not yet assimilated and that propaganda would have to be carried on in their language. There was no question of going further, since the Soviet regime saw to it that "national deviations" did not appear. Nonetheless the leaders of the *Yevsektsiya*, though doubtless they were made use of by the regime in its war with Zionism and other "reactionary" Jewish ideologies, saw themselves as defenders of the interests of the Jewish masses. Inevitably, as the regime consolidated itself, and as its policy toward the national minorities became more inflexible, the *Yevsektsiya* came increasingly under attack. Their demise in 1930 meant the end of the history of Jewish proletarian organizations in Russia.

During the interwar period the newly constituted Polish Republic, which included both Galicia and large areas of the former Pale of Settlement, became the center of Jewish socialism. Here the Bund withstood the blandishments of Communism, and despite a sharp move to the left which included the readiness to accept much of the Communist platform, remained intact, though factionalized. In the end its inner solidarity, the fruit of decades of conflict with the Russian and Polish socialist movements, its firm organizational base among Jewish workers, and the failure of the Bolsheviks to conquer Poland, allowed the Bund to flourish until 1939. The Bund retained its hold over the majority of Jewish trade unions, played a dominant role in the Yiddish secular school movement, and succeeded in winning general acclaim as a champion of Jewish rights against the omnipresent Polish antisemitism. The party benefited from the general trend to the left within Polish Jewry, itself the result of the worsening economic and political situation, and became far more than merely the strongest Jewish working class party. Despite the Bund's failure to improve the conditions of the Jewish masses, which deteriorated during the interwar period, it became, by the later 1930s, the strongest Jewish party in Poland. It was the Bund's tragedy that evidence of this strength, its victories in local elections in such cities as Warsaw and Lodz, occurred only a few years before the German conquest, which destroyed East European Jewry and with it the great socialist party which thought only in terms of a Diaspora solution to the Jewish question.

The world Po'alei Zion movement, which had come to overshadow the socialist territorialist parties after the failure of the Uganda project and which naturally benefited from the *Balfour Declaration, split in 1920 over the issues of whether or not to adhere to the Communist International and of their relations with the Zionist movement. The left faction, drawing its strength chiefly from Russia and Poland, actually accepted *Zinoviev's celebrated 21 points for admission to the Comintern, while the right, based mainly on delegations from the United States and Palestine, refused to go that far (though it too took a positive attitude toward the Bolshevik revolution). However, the Left Po'alei Zion did not join the Comintern, not because it decided against this step but because the world Communist movement could not accept its program for Palestine. It thus existed, mainly in Poland, as a Zionist party too far left to have anything to do with the official Zionist movement and as a revolutionary Marxist party unacceptable to the Comintern. This unenviable position, complicated still further by the party's ambivalent attitude toward Hebrew and toward *aliyah* (emigration to Palestine), reduced its appeal and its ability to compete both with the Bund and with the more moderate Zionist socialist movements. No other organization illustrated more clearly the inherent contradictions of a Diaspora-based Marxist Zionist party. On the other hand the Right Po'alei Zion, identifying with *Aḥdut ha-Avodah in Palestine, with the pioneering movement, and generally with progressive Zionism, became ever stronger within the world Zionist movement. In Poland, for example, by the 1930s the moderate socialist Zionist faction had become the strongest force within the Zionist movement. Generally speaking Right Po'alei Zion became less socialist and more nationalist, following the lead of party developments in Palestine, where Syrkin's non-Marxist ideology was more influential than Borochov's strictures. If to Left Po'alei Zion Palestine appeared less important than world revolution and Yiddish more important than Hebrew, Right Po'alei Zion broadened its national base. It thereby followed the course taken by so many other socialist parties which, once they had gained a certain degree of power (in this case in Palestine), spoke less and less of the proletariat and the class struggle.

Pioneering Youth Movements

A striking feature of Jewish socialism in the interwar period was the rise of pioneering youth movements. To a certain extent these movements followed in the footsteps of the *Ẓe'irei Zion ("Youth of Zion") circles, whose history began in Russia in the early 20th century. A fervent supporter of settlement in Palestine, nationalistic, at the outset non-socialist, and even nonpolitical, the Ẓe'irei Zion rejected the Marxist determinism and intense involvement in the Diaspora of the various Jewish socialist parties. Their voluntarism and emphasis on personal salvation through *aliyah*, which established an alternative for Jewish youth to the existing parties, whether Bundist or Zionist, was also the hallmark of the pioneering youth movements established during and after World War I. Thus *Ha-Shomer ha-Ẓa'ir, founded in Galicia during the war by middle-class youths seeking their way between the Polish world which rejected them and the Jewish bourgeois existence they found so distasteful, turned not to Marxism and not to party organization but to self-fulfillment through pioneering, through an act of will which would make them productive proletarians building a just society in Palestine. Both Ẓe'irei Zion and Ha-Shomer ha-Ẓa'ir shared a natural sympathy for socialism, and neither was able to withstand the pressure to organize into political groups. In 1920 the left faction of Ẓe'irei Zion created the Zionist Socialist Party (*ZS), which later merged with Right Po'alei Zion, while the right faction merged with the Palestinian nonsocialist party, *Ha-Po'el ha-Ẓa'ir, to form the *Hitaḥadut. Both these parties offered a moderate labor Zionist alternative to the radical Left Po'alei Zion. As for Ha-Shomer ha-Ẓa'ir, it developed from a self-styled vanguard of romantic idealists into a Marxist movement based on the organizational structure of the Ha-Kibbutz ha-Arẓi, founded in Palestine in 1927. The attraction of Marxism for the Zionist Socialists of the early 20th century had been that it could make Zionism appear determined rather than a mere dream. For the voluntaristic members of Ha-Shomer ha-Ẓa'ir, on the other hand, it functioned as a cement which held the movement together in Palestine, guarding against internal collapse and amalgamation with other elements. The history of both Ẓe'irei Zion and Ha-Shomer ha-Ẓa'ir demonstrates that organizational and ideological consolidation could not be avoided by groups whose initial mission was personal redemption through proletarianization. The acceptance by the Ẓe'irei Zion, for example, of the principle of Jewish national autonomy in Russia, and their active struggle for Jewish rights in the Diaspora, is reminiscent of the history of Po'alei Zion. But the political offshoots of Ẓe'irei Zion, active in an era when *aliyah* was a clear possibility, were firmly centered on Palestine and less subject to the dilemma of the "two levels." The problem of "which territory," of course, had completely disappeared.

This also held for the various pioneering youth movements, Ha-Shomer ha-Ẓa'ir, He-Ḥalutz ha-Ẓa'ir, etc., whose major problem in the Diaspora concerned the likelihood of *aliyah* and the impact of *aliyah* on the local organization. What tied the youth movements of the 1920s and 1930s, whether Marxist or not, to the Jewish socialist tradition, was their preoccupation with the necessity to create a just Jewish society based on productive labor. If Liebermann and later the Bundists and Zionist Socialists discovered the Jewish proletariat, members of the pioneering movements proposed to turn themselves into proletarians in Palestine, an extreme solution which reflected the crisis of East European Jewry in the period between the two world wars.

Later Developments

In the United States in the interwar period, as elsewhere, the Jewish socialist and trade union movement was rent by dissension between communists and socialists, the former mounting a serious and at least partly successful challenge within the Jewish union membership. Here, as in Eastern Europe, former Bundists and socialist Zionists lent their talents to the formation of a Jewish federation within the Communist Workers' Party. More important, however, was the steady decline of the American Jewish proletariat and of Yiddish. To a certain extent this was a function of America's immigration laws, for the children of the Jewish needle trades' workers did not, as a rule, follow the professions of their parents, but entered areas which would have been closed to them in the old world. The striking feature of the Jewish proletariat in the United States was that it was a one-generation phenomenon. If the Jewish unions remained Jewish, they remained so only in terms of their leadership. Similarly, the decline of Yiddish dealt a blow to the socialist press and to the cultural activities of Jewish labor institutions. Thus the ideology of A. Cahan, who believed that the Jewish labor movement's goal was to make good Americans of its members, was achieved, but the movement itself naturally declined once americanization was completed. While certain white collar unions in America, such as the Teachers' Union in New York, were still predominantly Jewish in membership in 1971, they were neither socialist in content nor Jewish in any meaningful form.

The Jewish socialist tradition was eliminated in Eastern Europe by the Holocaust, and in America by the unparalleled opportunities offered by American society. Its chief impact was in Israel, where ideas formed in Eastern Europe were molded to fit the task of building the *yishuv*. The Jewish socialist movement, in the old world and the new, was of enormous significance to countless numbers of Jews, to whom it offered new vistas of education, the ideals of democratic socialism, and the chance to obtain a decent standard of living. The vision of men as different as Liebermann, Kremer, Borochov, and Cahan – that the Yiddish-speaking Jewish masses needed special organizations in order to better their economic and cultural conditions, whether in the Diaspora or in Palestine, and that the task of the radical Jewish intelligentsia was to devote itself to these masses – produced one of the most fruitful of modern Jewish political movements.

BIBLIOGRAPHY: A.L. Patkin, *The Origins of the Russian-Jewish Labour Movement* (1947); M. Epstein, *Jewish Labor in the U.S.A.* (1950); N. Levin, *While Messiah Tarried: Jewish Socialist Movements, 1871–1917* (1977); L.P. Gartner, *The Jewish Immigrant in England* (1960); J. Frankel, *Socialism and Jewish Nationalism in Russia* (dissertation, Cambridge University, 1961); B. Johnpoll, *The Politics of Futility* (1967); E. Mendelsohn, *Class Struggle in the Pale* (1970); M. Rischin, *The Promised City: New York's Jews, 1870–1914* (1964); R. Abramovich, in: *The Jewish People Past and Present*, 2 (1948); B. Borochov, *Ketavim*, ed. by L. Levite et al., 3 vols. (1955–66): M. Mishkinsky, in: YIVOA, 14 (1969); idem, *Yesodot Le'ummiyyim be-Hithavvutah shel Tenu'at ha-Po'alim ha-Yehudit be-Rusyah* (dissertation, Hebrew University, 1965); idem, in: Zion, 31:1–2 (1966); I. Kolatt, *"Ideologyah u-Meẓi'ut bi-Tenu'at ha-Avodah be-Ereẓ Yisrael"* (dissertation, Hebrew University, 1964); Y. Ritov, *Perakim be-Toledot Ẓe'irei Ẓiyyon – Ẓ.S.* (1964); Y. Peterseil (comp.), *Ha-Ma'avak ba-Zirah ha-Proletarit ha-Bein-Le'ummit*, 2 vols. (1954–55); M. Altshuler, *Reshit ha-Yevsektsiya, 1918–21* (1966); M. Minc, *Ber Borochov* (Heb.; dissertation, Hebrew University, 1968); idem, in: *Ba-Derekh*, 5 (1970); N.A. Buchbinder, *Istoriya yevreyskogo rabochego dvizheniya v Rossii* (1925): E. Margalit, in: *Ha-Ẓiyyonut* (1969); *Sotsialistisher Teritorializm, Zikhroynes un Materialn* (1934); *YIVO Historishe Shriftn*, 3 (1939); A. Libermann, *Briv*, ed. by K. Marmot (1951); *Geshikhte fun der Tsionistisher Arbeter Bavegung in Tsofen Amerike*, 2 vols. (1955); A. Cahan, *Bleter fun Mayn Lebn*, 5 vols. (1928–31).

[Ezra Mendelsohn]

SOCIÉTÉ DES ÉTUDES JUIVES, society founded in 1880 by Isidore *Loeb, Zadoc *Kahn, and Israël *Levi to revive interest in the history of French Jewry and spread knowledge of Judaism. From its inception, the Société des Études Juives published the quarterly *Revue des Etudes Juives*, which became one of the leading learned periodicals of modern Jewish scholarship, in which reports on the society's meetings and activities appeared; they were also published in its *Annuaire* (1881–85). In addition, the society sponsored the publication of works such as H. Gross's *Gallia Judaica* (1897), Th. Reinach's (ed.) *Josephus* (7 vols., 1900–32), and Loeb's *Les Tables du Calendrier Juif* (1886). Its activities were suspended during the two world wars; after World War II the society, on the initiative of its president G. *Vajda, renewed its cycle of lectures and the publication of its journal. Among its presidents were J. *Derenbourg, A. *Darmstetter, and members of the *Rothschild family. Th. *Reinach was its secretary for many years and E. *Renan was a member and lecturer. In the early 21st century, the SEJ maintained its tradition of monthly conferences, despite the challenge of a much larger range of Jewish cultural offerings in which the scholarly, historico-philological approach is but one option. Apart from the REJ, the SEJ publishes the "Collection de la Revue des études juives," a very prolific series of monographs (17 titles published between 1980 and 1997; 20 between 1998 and 2004).

[Colette Sirat / Jean-Pierre Rothschild (2nd ed.)]

SOCIETIES, LEARNED. Learned societies among Jews, whose prototypes existed in the talmudic period, flourished in the late Middle Ages and were particularly widespread in Eastern Europe even into the 20th century. They were conceived on a broad basis. Unlike societies formed during the 17th and 18th centuries such as the Académie Française and the Royal Society of London, which operated under royal or government sponsorship and support and consisted of a small, aristocratic element of the general population, Jewish learned societies were democratic and open to all. Workers, merchants, and businessmen joined together in their own localities and formed semiprivate organizations, often with their own dues, structure, and book of statutes, for the study of some aspect of traditional Jewish literature. Among the most common of these groups was the *ḥevra shas* (Talmud; see *Study).

EARLY 19TH-CENTURY SOCIETIES. With the advent of the 19th century and the achievement of civil equality, West European Jewry began a process of self-examination. Although there had been individuals earlier who applied critical methods to traditional study, such as *Elijah, the Gaon of Vilna, and Naḥman *Krochmal, it was Moses *Mendelssohn who initiated new types of learned societies within the Jewish community. Beginning with Mendelssohn there was an increased interest in Hebrew and Bible study. In 1783 Isaac *Euchel established Ḥevrat Doreshei Leshon Ever (Society for the Proponents of the Hebrew Language) in *Koenigsberg, where, later that year, the first secular periodical in Hebrew, *Ha-Me'assef*, began its appearance. In 1819, reacting to riots, a group of young university students led by Leopold *Zunz, Edward *Gans, and Moses *Moser formed the Verein fuer Kultur und Wissenschaft der Juden. Zunz, coining the term **Wissenschaft des Judentums* ("Science of Judaism"), continued to research facets of Jewish literature after the society disbanded in 1824, and nearly all subsequent learned societies were indebted to him for initiating a systematic study of Judaism.

LATTER 19TH-CENTURY SOCIETIES. The greatest period of growth of the learned societies was during the second half of the 19th century, due to an increase in academic specialization along with an expanding teaching profession and a growing awareness of the social sciences. Within the Jewish community the cultural scholarly functions of the learned society were sometimes part of a larger organization. Thus, the Alliance Israélite Universelle, founded in 1860 with the goal of defending civil and religious liberties and alleviating disabilities of Jews, collected valuable demographic and ethnographic materials and sponsored scholarly publications in addition to its own house organs.

The Society for the Promotion of Culture among the Jews of *Russia, founded in 1863, subsidized Jewish scholarly publications despite its russianization aims. Among its more notable journals was *Yevreyskaya Biblioteka* ("Jewish Library"), an annual begun in 1871 containing articles on the nature of the Jewish past and present. Another example of a society sponsored by a larger organization was the Historische Commission, established by the *Deutsch-Israelitischer Gemeindebund in 1885. The commission collected historical data on German Jewry and published the *Zeitschrift fuer Geschichte der Juden in Deutschland* (1887–92; reestablished by I. *Elbogen and A. *Freimann 1929–37).

Publishing Scholarly Works

Some societies were formed in response to a particular aspect of the learned society, such as the publishing of scholarly works. In 1864 the *Mekiẓe Nirdamim Society was established in Germany with the express purpose of publishing Hebrew works of Jewish classical literature, especially unpublished manuscripts. The society, which was transferred to Ereẓ Israel in 1934, had published about 100 books in all by 1970.

Attempts to organize a publishing society in the United States included the American Jewish Publication Society in Philadelphia (1845) and another bearing the same name in 1873, both short-lived. In 1888 the *Jewish Publication Society of America was founded and by 1970 had published over 600 volumes. Among these works were an English translation of the Bible (1917, and a translation beginning in 1962) and the annual American Jewish Year Book starting in 1899. **Monatsschrift fuer Geschichte und Wissenschaft des Judentums* was a scholarly periodical founded by Zacharias *Frankel, published under different editors (including H. Graetz and I. Heinemann) and in different places, but primarily in Breslau. It was published consistently from 1851 until 1939, except for a short interlude in 1887–92. In 1904 the newly founded *Gesellschaft zur Foerderung der Wissenschaft des Judentums financed the publication of the journal. This same organization had undertaken to print a historical encyclopedia of German Jewry, *Germania Judaica* (vol. 1, 1934; vol, 2, 1968).

Germany was the scene of frequent attempts to establish learned societies. In 1841 M. Joel, S. Stern, and L. Zunz founded the Kulturverein, which tried to encourage investigation of contemporary problems by conducting essay contests. Many of its leaders were active in the Reform movement. In 1855 Ludwig Phillippson, along with Jost and A. *Jellinek, founded the Institut zur Foerderung der Israelitischen Literatur, which published over 80 works during its 18-year existence. The *Juedisch-Literarische Gesellschaft, established in 1902 in Frankfurt on the Main, was primarily interested in investigations into aspects of traditional Judaism.

The most important learned society in France, the *Société des Etudes Juives, was founded in 1880 by Zadoc Kahn, Isidore Loeb, and Theodore Reinach. The Société has concentrated on French Jewry, and over 100 volumes of its scholarly journal *Revue des Études Juives* have appeared, extending over 75 years, with a brief interruption during World War II. It has also published such basic works as H. *Gross's *Gallia Judaica* (1897) and Reinach's *Textes*.

20TH-CENTURY SOCIETIES. In response to the need for proper research tools for the investigation of the Holocaust, the Centre de Documentation Juive Contemporaine was established by Isaac *Schneersohn in France in 1943. The organization has encouraged scholars in individual research and has published numerous volumes, including the periodical *Le Monde Juif* (1946). Also devoted to Holocaust research is the Central Jewish Historical Society, founded in 1944 in Lublin by Philip Friedman, which moved to Warsaw in 1948 and became the *Jewish Historical Institute. Among the most notable books it published was Emanuel Ringelblum's *Notits fun Varshever Geto* (1952, fuller edition 1961–63). It also published the quarterly *Bleter far Geshikhte*. With the death of its director, Berl Mark, in 1967, and faced with increasing Polish Jewish emigration and government restrictions, the institute, despite its Marxist orientation, found it increasingly difficult to continue its work.

The end of the 19th century witnessed the birth of a learned society in England, the *Jewish Historical Society of England, founded in 1893 by Lucien Wolf, Albert Hyamson, Israel Abrahams, and Claude Montefiore. It has concentrated its efforts upon the history of the Jews in England and Anglo-Jewry throughout the world. Its scholarly periodicals are *Transactions* (from 1893) and *Miscellanies* (irregularly from 1925).

Though not strictly a learned society, the *Wiener Library and Institute for Contemporary History, established by Alfred *Wiener in 1934 in Amsterdam and moved to London in 1939, specializes in material relating to Nazism, antisemitism, and minority problems, as well as contemporary European history and the State of Israel. It publishes the *Wiener Library Bulletin* and is one of the sponsors of the *Journal of Contemporary History*.

In 1908 Maxim *Vinaver organized the Russian Jewish Historical Ethnographic Society in St. Petersburg and became its first president. Simon *Dubnow, the historian who had issued a call for such a society in 1891, became vice chairman of the society and served as editor of its scholarly journal *Yevreyskaya Starina*. Among the contributors were Meir *Balaban, Isaac (Ignacy) *Schiper, Moses *Schorr, and Mark *Wischnitzer.

Related Institutions in the United States

The 20th century witnessed two major demographic shifts within the Jewish community as the United States and Israel increasingly became the major centers of Jewish scholarly activity. The relative profusion of groups interested in various aspects of Jewish life denied the learned societies any exclusive claim to *Wissenschaft des Judentums*, especially on the contemporary scene. Educational institutions (e.g., Hebrew Union College) and professional societies, such as rabbinical organizations (e.g., Central Conference of American Rabbis), the Association of Jewish Libraries (founded 1966), and the National Council for Jewish Education (founded 1926) have engaged, in part, in activities similar to those of learned societies. They publish journals (*Hebrew Union College Annual, Jewish Education*, etc.) and share the camaraderie associated with such groups (e.g., Society of Jewish Bibliophiles, founded 1961). The sophistication of professional studies in the area of communal needs led to the early formation of the *National Conference of Jewish Communal Services (1898), which publishes the *Journal of Jewish Communal Services*.

Several research institutes are almost exclusively dedicated to the work of learned societies. Among these are the *YIVO Institute for Jewish Research, founded in Vilna in 1925 and moved to New York in 1940, which is a major source of research and information on modern Jewry. It has published most of its work in Yiddish. The *Leo Baeck Institute (founded 1959) serves as a research center for the history of the Jews in German-speaking countries from the enlightenment to the rise of Nazism and publishes a yearbook (from 1956). There are also libraries and archives which engage in scholarly research and publish journals (e.g., *Studies in Bibliography and Booklore* and *American Jewish Archives*, both of Hebrew Union College) although they do not constitute learned societies even in its broadest definition.

However, learned societies in the more classical form do exist. Among those in the United States are the *American Academy for Jewish Research and the *American Jewish Historical Society (founded 1892). The latter collects and publishes material relating to U.S. Jewry, issues the *American Jewish Historical Society Quarterly*, and has published individual monographs relating to the Jews in the United States. The *Conference on Jewish Social Studies (founded 1933) aims to promote a better understanding of the position of the Jews in the modern world through scientific research. Its scholarly journal is *Jewish Social Studies*.

SOCIETIES AND INSTITUTES IN ISRAEL. Especially since its creation the State of Israel has become home to numerous learned societies, research institutes, and academies. The traditional patterns (e.g. *ḥevra shas*) have been infused with new life. Bible study groups flourish; the largest is the Israel Society for Biblical Research, which also publishes the *Beth Mikra*. There is hardly an area of research from archaeology to poetry to Zionism which is not under investigation by some institution, be it under governmental, university, or private auspices. Among those that were established prior to 1948 is the *Israel Exploration Society (founded 1913), which engages in excavations and related research into the history and geography of Israel. It publishes a quarterly in English, a Hebrew quarterly, *Qadmoniot*, and an annual, *Eretz-Israel*. The Historical Society of Israel (founded 1925) promotes the study of Jewish history. The Palestine Historical and Ethnographical Society, as it was originally called, issued a journal, *Me'assef* (6 vols.), and a quarterly, *Zion*, which began to appear regularly in 1935. In 1942 the Israel Folklore Society was founded with the aim of preserving Jewish folklore by recording customs, traditions, folk songs, tales, and proverbs of the various Jewish communities in the Diaspora. It publishes a Hebrew biannual journal, *Yeda Am* ("Folklore").

Several societies have received official government recognition since the establishment of the state. The *Academy of the Hebrew Language, founded at the turn of the century by Eliezer *Ben-Yehuda, was reestablished in 1953 by Knesset law. It studies the vocabulary, structure, and history of the Hebrew language and is the official authority for its development. Among the academy's publications is *Leshonenu*, a journal for the study of the Hebrew language and cognate subjects. Yad Vashem, formally established by the Knesset in 1953, publishes numerous studies relating to the Holocaust. Another academy established by the Knesset is the Israel Academy of Sciences and Humanities (1961), which promotes work in these areas and brings together the most eminent Israel scholars.

Among the many institutes in Israel are the Harry Fischel Institute for Research in Talmud and Jewish Law (founded 1932) and the Institute for Research in Jewish Law (founded 1963), which are both concerned with responsa literature and the codification of Jewish law. The *Ben-Zvi Institute (founded 1948) sponsors research in the history of Jewish communities from the tenth century to the present, with primary interest in Oriental communities. *Sefunot* (starting 1956) is one of its most important publications. The Asher Barash Bio-Bibliographical Institute (founded 1951) gathers documentary material on Hebrew writers and aims at bibliographical registration of all Hebrew literature published since the Mendelssohn era. It publishes an annual anthology, *Genazim* (1961).

There are also many archives in Israel interested in preserving various aspects of Jewish life (see *Archives). The Israel Archives Association (founded 1956) was established to promote cooperation among them and to coordinate their activities. The Association for Jewish Demography and Statistics was established (1958) in cooperation with the Institute of Contemporary Jewry at the Hebrew University to promote the collection, arrangement, and analysis of pertinent data relating to the demography of the Jewish people. The professionalization of Jewish scholarship, the sophistication of research tools, the tragedy of the Holocaust, and the birth of Israel have all given impetus to *Juedische Wissenschaft* in its broadest definition.

BIBLIOGRAPHY: AJYB (1899–), passim; *Scientific and Technical Associations and Institutes in Israel* (1966[2]); *Encyclopedia of Associations* (1968); *The Middle East and North Africa* (1967/68[14]); *The World of Learning* (1968/69[19]); JE, 11 (1905), 421–3; A. Wein, in: *Yad Vashem Studies*, 7 (1970), 203–13.

[Simcha Berkowitz]

SOCIETY FOR THE ATTAINMENT OF FULL CIVIL RIGHTS FOR THE JEWISH PEOPLE IN RUSSIA (Rus. "**Soyuz dlya dostizheniya polnopraviya yevreyskogo naroda v Rossii**"), a non-party organization which existed from 1905 to 1907, whose aim was declared in its name. The society organized the participation of Jews in the elections of the First and Second *Duma, also obtaining legal aid for Jews after the pogroms of October 1905. At the founding convention in Vilna in April 1905, where representatives of the Jewish intelligentsia of all parties took part (with the exception of those on the left), Simon *Dubnow defined the aims of the society. A central committee was elected, whose headquarters were to be in St. Petersburg. Maxim *Vinaver was chosen as chairman of this committee, which he led until the dissolution of the society. The historian Julius *Hessen became its secretary. Three further conventions were held in St. Petersburg, the second in December 1905, following the October *pogroms, when the 1905 Russian revolution had been at its height. It was decided: (1) to appoint a committee in which a delegate of the non-Jewish public would participate to investigate the pogroms and to demand that the guilty officials be dismissed and brought to justice; (2) to claim economic reparation from the government; and (3) to demand the release of Pinḥas *Dashewski who was in prison for attacking the organizer of the *Kishinev pogroms.

The third convention, held in February 1906 on the eve of the elections to the First Duma, was devoted to the elections. Jewish delegates standing for election to the Duma were instructed on how to fight for equal rights for Russian Jewry. The fourth and last conference took place in May 1906, ten days after the opening of the First Duma. Largely by virtue of the society's activities, 12 Jewish delegates had been elected to the Duma. On the question of whether a Jewish national group should be established in the Duma, Vladimir *Jabotinsky (speaking for the Zionists) and Dubnow were in favor of the proposal, but Vinaver and his followers opposed it violently. Political polarization of Jewish life broke up the society; Dubnow and M. *Kreinin founded their party in 1906, and the Russian Zionist conference at *Helsingfors decided that Zionists should contest elections under their own party banner. At a committee meeting in the spring of 1907 it was decided to abolish the society.

BIBLIOGRAPHY: YE, 14 (c. 1910), 515–7; S. Dubnow, *Kniga zhizni*, 2 (1935), 19–29; J.G. Frumkin (ed.), in: *Russian Jewry 1860–1917* (1966), 18–84.

[Baruch Shohetman]

SOCIETY FOR JEWISH FOLK MUSIC, society founded in St. Petersburg in November 1908 by a group of Jewish students at the conservatory there and their friends, among them Solomon *Rosowsky, Lazare *Saminsky, A. Zhitomirsky, and A. Niezwicski (Abileah). It was originally intended to be a "Society for Jewish Music," but the commanding general of the district refused to license it under this title because he doubted whether true Jewish music existed, although he conceded that there must be Jewish folk music. The word folk was therefore inserted in the name and constitution. An important circle of Jewish musicians with similar interests had already formed in Moscow c. 1894 around Joel *Engel, and the first concert of the material they had collected and arranged was held there in 1900. This and similar groups now coalesced with the society in St. Petersburg. Joseph *Achron, Moses *Milner, Mikhail *Gnesin, Joseph *Yasser, Alexander *Veprik, and Alexander *Krein soon joined its ranks. In 1912 the Society already had 389 members with chapters in Moscow, Kiev, Kharkov, and Odessa. In 1918 it was disbanded by the Soviet government as "not conforming to the spirit of the time," but the influence of its ideology and actions persisted both among the members who remained in Russia and among those who left to settle in Western Europe, the United States, and Palestine. The Society's constitution did not fully reflect its unwritten ideology, and its provisions were never carried out in full. These are quoted here because all subsequent organizations for the promotion of Jewish music followed the same basic pattern. The aim of the society was "to promote the research and development of Jewish folk music – religious and secular – by the collection of folk songs and their harmonization, and to aid Jewish composers…." For this purpose the Society was to issue publications of music and musical research; to organize meetings, concerts, operatic performances, and lectures; to form a choir and orchestra of its own; to found a library; to publish a periodical; and to organize competitions and award prizes for "musical works of Jewish character." An ensemble of singers and instrumentalists was founded which undertook many concert tours. Expeditions went to the Vitebsk and Kherson regions, and the melodies they collected were given to various composers for harmonization. Dozens of these works were published. Kisselgoff, Zhitomirsky, and Lvow also published the *Lider Zamlbukh* with arrangements of folk and art material "for school and home use." In 1915 the society was stirred up by the controversy between Saminsky and Engel, in which Saminsky questioned whether the indiscriminate gathering and propagation of any and every tune taken from the "folk" really represented Jewish music, and pressed for a more discerning search as well as for the recognition of the greater authenticity of the liturgical traditions. Saminsky's visits to the Jewish communities in the Caucasus and Turkey confronted him with the reality of a Jewish musical tradition outside the Ashkenazi culture which he had already surmised was neither less and perhaps even more authentic than that of Eastern Europe. Another controversy arose between Engel and *Shalom Aleichem – Engel denying and Shalom Aleichem advocating the recognition of the songs of Mark *Warshawski as true folk songs. Discussions of what constituted Jewish music were also frequent and there was an intense nationalistic spirit (although most of the society's leading members, with the exception of Engel, did not identify directly with the Zionist movement). Engel's foundation of the Juwal-Verlag in Berlin was the last (actually posthumous) direct result of the society's endeavors. Its ideals were carried to the United States, where they were propagated by Saminsky, Yasser, Rosowsky, and Achron, and to Palestine where this was done by Engel himself. After his death in 1927, they continued to exert a strong influence on musical developments in the *yishuv* through Menashe Ravina and Joachim *Stutschewsky.

BIBLIOGRAPHY: L. Saminsky, *Music of the Ghetto and the Bible* (1934), 227–54; Idelsohn, Music, 461–8; M. Ravina (ed. and tr.), *Mikhtavim al ha-Musikah ha-Yehudit me'et Yo'el Engel, M.M. Warshawksi, Shalom Aleichem* (1942); A. Soltes, in: I. Heskes and A. Wolfson (eds.), *The Historic Contribution of Russian Jewry to Jewish Music* (1967), 13–27; J. Yasser, in: *ibid.*, 31–42; B. Bayer, in: *Ha-Ḥinnukh ha-Musikali*, 17 (1931), 39–43.

[Bathja Bayer]

SOCIETY FOR THE PROMOTION OF CULTURE AMONG THE JEWS OF RUSSIA, a society aimed at uniting advanced groups among Russian Jewry for the purpose of practical, organized, and planned activities to promote popular education; founded in St. Petersburg in 1863 on the initiative and with the financial support of wealthy Jews active in the community the majority of whom were residents of the city.

Foundation

Leon *Rosenthal, one of the founders of the society and its treasurer for a long time, stated that the motive for setting it up was the accusation, constantly leveled by government representatives and members of the Russian public in general, that the religious, social, and cultural separatism of the Jews was the chief obstacle to their being granted civic equality. These circles exerted pressure on the leaders of the Jewish community in St. Petersburg to employ their standing to influence the internal regeneration of their people in accordance with the spirit of the times. The Jewish leaders decided to respond to this demand, which seemed to them justified. To set up a countrywide association of supporters of education, they proceeded immediately to work out a set of regulations for the organization. The project encountered numerous difficulties on several sides: the Orthodox sector dissociated themselves from it for fear of adverse consequences to the Jewish religion, while the free-thinking *maskilim* in the capital were of the opinion that it was necessary to introduce more extreme and quicker measures. High government officials, who feared that the society might develop into a broad-based popular association, opposed the establishment of branches throughout the country.

Only after exhausting negotiations with the interested parties for almost a year was a definition of the aims agreed upon, namely, to spread and promote culture among the Jews of Russia, to support Jewish literature and authors, and to assist young students. The means to achieve this would be by teaching Russian to the Jewish masses, and by the publication of original books, translations, and periodicals in Russian and Hebrew. It was laid down that the society should operate under the auspices of the ministry of education and should accept members without distinction of sex, status, or religion.

The first members who agreed to set up the initial fund of the society were mainly representatives of the Jewish financial aristocracy in various cities, particularly St. Petersburg; only a small minority belonged to the intelligentsia. At the first general meeting (December 1863) J.Y. *Guenzburg was elected chairman of the society's committee. The committee energetically recruited new members among wealthy businessmen, well-known scholars, and authors. Special efforts were made to bring into the ranks of the society liberal Christian scholars, writers, and personalities active in public affairs. In the first year of its existence the Jewish members of the society included – in addition to a group of philanthropists – writers and scholars such as Abraham Dov *Lebensohn, A. *Mapu, S.J. *Fuenn, Joshua *Steinberg, H.S. *Slonimski, A. *Zederbaum, Y.L. *Gordon, S.J. Abramowitsch (*Mendele Mokher Seforim), J.L. *Pinsker, L. *Levanda, A.A. *Harkavy, and D. *Chwolson. The various projects of the society were financed by individual contributors headed by J.Y. Guenzburg and his son H. *Guenzburg, and L. Rosenthal. This left its mark on the character of the society and its orientation, which were determined by the personal endeavors of its chief supporters. Another serious setback to its democratic organization was the refusal of the government to permit the society to establish branches in the centers of the *Pale of Settlement; this would have enabled it to influence the masses more closely. After the establishment of a branch in Odessa in 1867, about 31 years passed before a second branch in Riga was authorized.

Ideological Differences

From the beginning differences arose within the committee as to the methods for spreading useful knowledge among the masses, especially the language to be used. The moderate wing, as represented by Rosenthal, regarded it as an association of intellectuals who aimed at building something new and not destroying the traditional, being convinced that religion and knowledge were closely linked. It was, therefore, the duty of the society to provide a "neutral" education for the masses so as not to arouse feelings of distrust, to refrain from offending accepted beliefs and opinions, and by publishing popular articles on science, geography, and general history to expand the Jewish reader's horizon and spur him to constant mental improvement. Rosenthal advocated the Hebrew language for propagating culture among Jewish youth, and proposed giving priority to the society's publication of Hebrew books and periodicals. On the society's committee there was also a group that included Chwolson and Harkavy, which emphasized promoting among the Jewish public a knowledge of the Russian language and the creation of a Russian-Jewish literature, to assist in removing the barriers between Jews and the rest of the population, and to rebut the false accusations leveled at the Jews and Judaism. A small group within the society, represented by S.A. *Schwabacher, rabbi of the Odessa community, and A. Neuman, rabbi of St. Petersburg, demanded that a special department for the education of the younger generation should be devoted to the study of German as a means of understanding fundamental works of Judaism, which had been written mainly in that language, and to becoming acquainted with general European culture. Finally the society's committee approved in February 1864 the view that spreading Russian among Jews was to be the basis for all its activities, since that alone was likely to prepare them gradually to take a direct part in the life of Russian society. The extreme "Russification" group in the society was concentrated in the Odessa branch. Among them were O. *Rabinovich, J.L. Pinsker, and E. Soloveichik.

In 1872, when J.L. Gordon became secretary of the society, he reformulated its operative principles which he had published as a manifesto in the Hebrew press. The innovations in this document were an appeal to those devoted to education in the Pale of Settlement to assist the development of vocational training institutions for young people, which would assure them an honorable and suitable livelihood; a declaration of the society's readiness to help Jewish artisans to settle throughout the Russian Empire; a firm demand to introduce changes in the existing administration of the Jewish communities; and, above all, the credo of Jewish *maskilim* which identified them with the government stand – that the Jews would be deserving of emancipation after their spiritual and moral "improvement" had been achieved. The rights already given to certain classes of Jews in Russia were, in the society's opinion, a forerunner and pledge of general civic equality in the not too distant future if the Jews carried out their duty to themselves and their country by acquiring an education.

Publishing Activities

To help Jews acquire a knowledge of Russian it was resolved to publish primers with suitable exercises and Jewish history in Russian. To encourage Jewish authors in this language they were allotted grants, and it was planned to issue scholarly and literary annuals in which their works would be published. These projects also had the apologetic aim of presenting the Russian reader with authentic information on the history and culture of the Jewish people. The project for publishing the annuals ran into numerous difficulties through lack of sufficient literary talent, censorship restrictions, and internal inhibitions, i.e., apprehension about publishing criticism of the Jewish religion or way of life. After the appearance of the first collection, which had taken about four years to prepare, the society decided to abandon its plans in this area. The heads of the society were interested in issuing a periodical in Russian on Jewish affairs, but did not dare to carry out this aim themselves, contenting themselves with support of the weeklies *Den* (1869–71); *Vestnik Russkikh Yevreyev* (1871–73), issued by A. Zederbaum, and a Russian supplement to the weekly **Ha-Karmel*, edited by S.J. Fuenn (1865, 1866, and 1868).

The most successful literary undertaking of the society in this period was a collection on the views of the Talmud sages, initiated by D. Chwolson. The Hebrew text by Ẓevi Hirsch *Katzenellenbogen and S.J. Fuenn was completed in 1871. The Russian translation, edited by L. Levanda with the comments by J.L. Gordon, was published in three volumes in 1874 and 1876. The publication of the book was aimed both to serve as a textbook for rabbis to prepare their sermons in the language of the country, and to explain to the non-Jewish public the foundations of the Talmud which had determined the national character of the Jews. The latter, apologetic intention, apparently predominated in the 1870s when antisemitism increased in Russia under the influence of J. *Brafman's *Kniga Kagala* ("Book of the Kahal").

The society devoted much effort to a new undertaking to which it ascribed a decisive importance in bringing the Jews of Russia closer to Haskalah – the translation of the Bible into Russian. This approach was naturally based on the revolutionary results achieved in Jewish life of a similar project in German on the initiative and with the participation of Moses *Mendelssohn. In 1873 the society brought out a new translation of the Torah by J. Gerstein ("The Learned Jew"), adviser on Jewish matters to the governor-general of Vilna, and J.L. Gordon, which achieved a wide circulation. The society also allocated large sums as a subvention for translation into Russian of the *siddur* and the *maḥzorim* for the festivals, and for composition of a series of textbooks in Russian to publishers of periodicals, such as the *Yevreyskaya Biblioteka* edited by A. *Landau, and to Jewish scholars undertaking research into Jewish history, such as I. *Orshanski and others. The society allotted grants to the authors of Hebrew books on mathematics, physics, astronomy, biology, chemistry, geology, etc., including the writers H.S. Slonimski, Z.H. *Rabinowitz, S.J. Abramowitsch, and J. *Syrkin. It supported the periodicals **Ha-Ẓefirah* and **Ha-Meliẓ*, which devoted special sections to the natural sciences, and distributed popular Hebrew books on general and Jewish history and biography; in 1866–70 the society published four parts of the history by Georg Weber translated by K. *Schulman, who added chapters on Jewish history in different periods. At the invitation of the society Schulman also wrote a book on Russian geography which appeared in 1870 to serve as a reader for adults to further their acquaintance with their native country. A similar patriotic need was to be met by S. *Mandelkern's Russian history printed in 1895, which incorporated chapters on Jewish history.

Both wings of the society's committee – the protagonists of Hebrew and of Russian – were united in their negative attitude toward Yiddish, which they regarded as an anachronism, symbolizing an obsolete order. Despite this, it expressed readiness to support the Yiddish weekly **Kol Mevasser* for disseminating basic facts among the mass of Jews. The committee allocated modest sums for publishing Yiddish books on Jewish and Russian history. However, in view of severe criticism in the general Russian press and Russian-Jewish press, it later desisted from taking such steps.

Educational Activities

The largest item of expenditure in the society's budget was assistance to Jewish students in Russian institutions of higher education, especially in St. Petersburg, whom the *maskilim* regarded as ideal candidates for leading the nation. At the end of the 1870s the society decided to send several graduates of rabbinical institutes to Breslau for further education in the *Juedisch-Theologisches Seminar and the local university, on the assumption that on their return they would serve as examples of rabbis on the German pattern. However, in eight years not more than three candidates were found suitable. In December 1879 the government banned the grant of scholarships to Jewish students from Russia who were studying at foreign universities, since this was opposed to the regulations of the society.

After the reform in the government educational network for Jews which led to the closure of many schools, and under pressure of appeals for the establishment of improved schools, the society decided to form a special fund to meet the most urgent needs in regard to secondary and elementary schools. Its policy in this field of activity was to refrain from setting up schools, and to support private initiative, without intervening in the internal affairs of these institutions. It also proposed to introduce reading and writing in Russian as a compulsory subject, to set up a special department of Hebrew subjects, to extend aid to the organizers of handicrafts classes attached to the schools, to help establish general teaching institutes in the Pale of Settlement, and to admit several pupils without charge with an allocation from the society. The rabbis of the communities and the authorized representatives of the society would frequently engage in establishing libraries for the use of the public at large.

Membership

The membership of the society numbered 175 in 1864; 287 in 1873, and 740 in 1888. In the first decade of the society's existence, its total income, mainly derived from contributions by the barons Guenzburg and L. Rosenthal, was 120,000 rubles. In its first 25 years it distributed 268,000 rubles to Jewish students in general schools, particularly of higher education; 31,000 rubles in cash, and 25,000 in form of grants of books to private schools; 32,000 rubles for supporting literature; and 24,000 rubles in aid to the needy.

From the 1890s

A new spirit invaded the society from the early 1890s. Educated youths who sought ways to serve their people joined the society and were influential in introducing new methods. In 1891 the society founded a "historical committee" for research in the history of the Jews of Russia. The committee published collections of documents dealing with Jewish history in Russia, and in 1908 became the Jewish Historical and Ethnographic Society. In 1894 a committee for Popular Education was established and in its framework the younger intelligentsia was active (L. *Bramson, J. *Brutzkus, A. *Kahnstam, etc.). The committee made a survey of Jewish schools, and advocated the support of old and new institutions, especially schools including Hebrew studies, in their curricula. The society sent delegates to visit educational institutions. Hebrew teachers were organized, a teachers' convention being held in Orsha (Belorussia) in 1903, and young teachers trained. The "Grodno courses" opened in 1907, and under A. Kahnstam's guidance a new generation of teachers with pedagogical training came into being. The new trends found expression in the society's revised statutes of 1901, which fixed the membership fee at 5 rubles (outside St. Petersburg). Branches were opened in Moscow (1894), Riga (1898), and Kiev (1908), each of which developed independent local activity. From 1902 the society organized councils where delegates of the branches met, as well as Jewish educationalists and cultural workers. In 1900 membership reached 3,010. In 1908 the society's statutes were changed again. It was entitled to open schools, libraries, courses for training teachers, and to give lectures. The membership fee was fixed at 3 rubles annually. Branches were to be opened wherever the number of members reached 25. In 1912 there were 30 branches throughout Russia with 7,000 members. The Moscow branch was particularly active, also being responsible for activity in the districts of Mogilev and Vitebsk. The Kiev branch became a center of activities in the southwestern area of the Pale of Settlement. In 1910 the society maintained ten schools, and partially supported 98 schools, as well as libraries in various Jewish communities. Its yearly budget in 1911 was 378,000 rubles. In 1910 the society began to publish its organ *Vestnik* OPE (later named *Vestnik yevreyskogo Prosveshcheniya*) dealing with education, culture, and libraries. In 1912 a committee was established to find ways to reform and improve the existing traditional *ḥeder*. This problem was debated by the society's council in 1912.

Since the society was the only legal body for educational and cultural activities in Russia, it was joined in the early 20th century by national and Zionist leaders, such as Aḥad *ha-Am, Ḥ.N. *Bialik, S. *Dubnow, etc., and after the failure of the 1905 revolution also by members of the Jewish socialist parties. A struggle evolved in the society's councils between three trends: the initial trend of the assimilationists who advocated closer ties with Russian culture, the Hebrew-Zionist trend, and the Yiddishist *Bund trend. During World War I the society opened 215 schools with 30,000 pupils for Jewish refugee children from the battle zones. The struggle between the trends became even more accentuated. After the Russian February Revolution the Zionists established their own federation for education and culture, *Tarbut, and the Yiddishists established their society, Kultur-Lige (in Kiev). The Bolshevik Revolution of October 1917 put an end to this development. The society's branches in the provincial towns were liquidated, the schools were closed, and all educational activities were prohibited. The center in Petrograd remained in existence, maintained its library, and published three literary-scientific collections. The society was finally disbanded by the authorities in 1930. The library, which contained 50,000 books and about 1,000 manuscripts, was given to the Institute for Proletarian Jewish Culture in Kiev.

BIBLIOGRAPHY: Y.L. Rosenthal, *Toledot Ḥevrat Marbei Haskalah be-Yisrael be-Ereẓ Rusyah*, 2 vols. (1885–90); I.M. Tcherikower, *Istoriya obshchestva dlya rasprostraneniya prosveshcheniya mezhdy yevreyami v Rossii*, 1 (1913); Kritikus (S. Dubnow), in: *Voskhod*, 11:10 (1891), 41–45; Z. Scharfstein, *Toledot ha-Ḥinnukh be-Yisrael*, 1 (1948), 313–23, 389–96.

[Yehuda Slutsky]

SOCIOLOGY. Sociology as a field of intellectual endeavor is much older than sociology as an academic discipline. Modern sociology can be traced to the Scottish moralists such as Adam Ferguson, David Hume, Adam Smith, and possibly to Thomas Hobbes. The word "sociology" was coined by Auguste Comte, and the study of sociology powerfully promoted by Herbert Spencer; but the first chairs of sociology were those of Albion Small in Chicago (1892) and Emile *Durkheim in Bordeaux (1896). Thus, one may say that sustained interest in the structure and processes of society arose when the *ancien régime* toppled and a new social order was painfully ushered in. At the same time, the emancipation set free Jewish intellectual energies on a vast scale. It is a moot question whether the interest of Jewish authors was directed toward the social sciences, including sociology among them, chiefly (as Martin *Buber surmised) because of a long and deep-rooted proclivity of the Jewish mind to think in relations rather than in substance, or because of the opportunity that was offered by the social sciences of a frankly critical stance toward the existing social order, coupled with a perceived chance of improving it. But it is certain that the Jewish condition, placing as it did the Jewish community, and especially the Jewish intellectual, at the margin of society, was ideally designed to make both incentives historically effective. Consequently, Jews were prominent both among the founding fathers of academic sociology and among the spokesmen of that particular brand of social science which sprang from the Socialist movement.

Not all Marxist writers qualify as sociologists, but Karl *Marx does. Armed with a thorough knowledge of Hegelian dialectics and Ricardian economics and buttressed by data of experience from the industrial revolution in England and the political revolution in France, he based his sociology in the first place on the analysis of social stratification. However, his was not a static rank order, as in an Aristotelian world view, but, rather, incessantly exposed to internal contradiction and ensuing transformation until, after a final and decisive class struggle, the moment was reached where a classless society would come into view. The second contribution of Marx to modern sociology was what Max *Scheler and Karl *Mannheim, neither of them Marxian partisans, later called the sociology of knowledge. If the catchword for what was wrong with the working class was "alienation," meaning estrangement from the means of production, so the catchword for what was wrong with intellectuals was "ideology," meaning the erection of a false "superstructure" which was hiding, rather than laying bare, the roots of thought as well as of institutions in the material realm of life.

The comprehensiveness as well as the simplicity of the Marxian sociology, coupled with its polemic emphasis and its action orientation, have made Marxism the prevailing social philosophy not only in the communist countries but also in the "third world," and have gained adherents among intellectuals everywhere, but its universal aim has militated against its development as a specific sociology. Scientifically, the influence of Marxism was much more pronounced within the mainstream of academic sociology than among orthodox Marxists. By way of argument and counterargument, adaptation and refutation, Marx is present in the main body of sociological writing. This is true about Ferdinand Toennies, Werner *Sombart, Max Weber, Ludwig *Gumplowicz, and Karl Mannheim among the classic authors in Europe; and about such U.S. Jewish sociologists as Louis *Wirth and Alvin Gouldner (1920–1980). The same applies for representatives of conflict theory like Lewis *Coser; of the sociology of knowledge, like Kurt Wolff; for race relations specialists like Max Wolff; and a development specialist like Irving Louis Horovitz (the editor of *Trans-Action*, a magazine aimed at popularizing the findings of activist social scientists); for political sociologists and stratification specialists like Reinhard *Bendix and S.M. *Lipset; and urban sociologists and community theorists like Herbert Gans (1927–), Joseph Bensman (1922–), and Maurice Stein (1926–). All those in this latter group are more or less influenced by Marx-derived concepts, but hardly any one of them would consider himself a strict Marxist or even a profound student of Marx. Exceptions might include Bernhard *Stern and Daniel Bell (1919–), both of Columbia University. The latter is best known for his contributions to the understanding of "post-industrial" society.

A sharply profiled group are the founders of the Institut fuer Sozialforschung and leaders of the influential Frankfurt school of sociology, Max *Horkheimer and Theodor W. *Adorno, as well as Herbert *Marcuse; they combined Marxian and, even more so, Hegelian dialectics with Freudian depth psychology, but opposed a party-bound Russian Marxism as much as the U.S. form of ideology-blind positivism. In the case of Herbert Marcuse, once the idol of "New Left" students in two continents, a new kind of "hastening the end" attitude appeared, which cast away the classical Marxian idea of the proletariat as the bearer of the revolution and the redeemer of mankind, in favor of a dynamic interplay of the free intellect and the free eros. This is a species of anarchism, the very contradiction to the dogmatic Marxian approach related to it.

In comparison to these profound ramifications of Marxian influence in sociology, which are traced here only insofar as its major Jewish proponents are concerned, Marxian sociology proper does not seem to have been overly fruitful. Even here, some scholars, such as the Italian Achille *Loria and the Viennese Paul Wiesengruen can only be placed on the periphery of Marxian thought. On the other hand, the sociological significance of those authors who were active participants in socialist and communist partisan movements is blunted by the fact that they were primarily social philosophers, ideologists, polemicists, interpreters rather than researchers or sociological theorists, supplying a comprehensive philosophy of historical development for the faithful. Among those that should be mentioned here because of their advancement of Marxian sociology are Eduard *Bernstein, the leader of the revisionist trend in European socialism, the Austro-Marxists Max *Adler, who strove to combine Marxism and Kantianism, and Otto *Bauer, who created a Marxian theory of nationality and nationality struggles. This approach was a forerunner of those protagonists of the "third world" who, like Frantz Fanon, cast the colored peoples in the role originally designed for the industrial proletariat. Even more in this direction were Rosa *Luxemburg's and Rudolf *Hilferding's assertion that the internal contradictions of capitalism made its expansion into colonialism and imperialism an inescapable necessity. However, Rosa Luxemburg thought that nationalities would disappear in this gigantic expansion of exploitation, a belief which was not shared by the "third world" protagonists. The Hungarian György *Lukacs, more a social philosopher than a sociologist, shared with Rosa Luxemburg the opposition to positivistic and deterministic versions of Marxism and an emphasis on personal spontaneity and historical dialectics. Leo Kofler (1907–1995), Fritz Sternberg (1895–1963), Siegfried *Landshut, and George Lichtheim (1912–1973) were related to that position. The outstanding name among the Russians was Lev *Trotsky, whose concept of "combined development" serves to justify a proletarian revolution in an industrially underdeveloped country.

Jews figure prominently among the founding fathers of academic sociology. The great names here are Ludwig Gumplowicz, Emile Durkheim, and Georg *Simmel. Their backgrounds were in law, economics, history, and philosophy, but their fame rests with their achievements in sociology. Of these, Gumplowicz is the least known today because he spent his adult life, bitter with the frustrations of the Austro-Hungarian nationality struggles, in an academic backwater at the University of Graz. His embracement of a pessimistic brand of social determinism, derived from Darwinian notions, seemed justified by the circumstances. According to Gumplowicz, the individual was nothing except as a member of a group, and groups, in turn, were engaged in a fierce struggle for survival in which the bigger dog usually emerges victorious and imposes his law on the vanquished. This gloomy view of race and ethnic relations contrasted sharply with the only other serious theory of race relations, which was later developed in the

U.S. by Robert E. Park and his disciples. Emile Durkheim is an entirely different figure. Agreeing with Gumplowicz that social phenomena are *sui generis* and more than an aggregate of individual wills, his emphasis was not so much on conflict but on solidarity. Solidarity can be of a "mechanical" nature, as in homogeneous societies, or of an "organic" character, as in societies based on the division of labor, or it can, when individualism is carried too far, be endangered by normlessness, or "anomie." But, although reflected in individual minds, society always remains supreme. As a Jew, Durkheim would provide a fascinating case study, even more than Gumplowicz. The Austrian-Pole Gumplowicz considered the Jews an anachronistic irritant because, having lost language and territory, they had ceased to be a nationality and were doomed to disappear as a separate entity. Durkheim, scion of a rabbinical family turned *libre penseur*, was fond of quoting the biblical sources of Hebraic law as one of the most primitive manifestations of "mechanical solidarity," but he went further than that when he demonstrated in his often quoted book, *Les formes elémentaires de la vie religieuse*, that religion was a social phenomenon of the first order, a deification, as it were, of the solidarity of past, present, and future generations; the totem animal was the powerful ancestor of the tribe, the personification of its strength and endurance. Religion was thus brought down to earth and placed in a historical, and yet generally valid, context. Surely, Durkheim would not have needed to travel around the globe to the Australian Arunta to prove that the Jewish people was the *corpus mysticum* of the Jewish religion and the God of Abraham, Isaac, and Jacob the guarantor of its existence. Durkheim was prevented from stating the matter clearly in this fashion by his desire to strengthen, through his equation of religion and society, the embattled forces of *la république laïque*. However, as Gumplowicz would have had to revise his negative evaluation of a Jewish nationality if he had lived to see the establishment of a Jewish state, so Durkheim's theory of the social nature of religion may well serve to sanctify Israel nationalism as known today.

Georg Simmel, like Durkheim often quoted, especially among U.S. sociologists, asked the Kantian question: "How is sociology at all possible?" He arrived at the conclusion that sociology is a distinctive science because it is not so much concerned with the varying contents of social phenomena but with the forms that they have in common wherever they occur. But these forms are not forms of substance or patterns of behavior; they manifest themselves in interpersonal relations and as such are located in the minds of men. This relational emphasis has struck many readers of Simmel as lacking in concreteness, even in commitment, but it agrees with the Buberian formula about the relational inclination of Jewish thinking, the I-Thou encounter "between man and man," which for Buber must be understood as construed in the image of the encounter between man and the Creator. Indeed, Buber and Simmel were personal friends. More specifically speaking, Simmel made a significant contribution to the sociology of the Jews in his concept of the "stranger," one of his numerous formal concepts that serve to elucidate a variety of actually occurring phenomena. The "stranger," according to Simmel, is not so much the man who comes today and goes tomorrow, but the man who comes today and stays tomorrow; and the Jew throughout the ages, but especially the medieval Jew, is the prototype of the species.

From then on the role that Jews as persons and Jews as a topic have played in sociology becomes ramified and diffuse. Perhaps the most convenient way of coming to grips with it is to differentiate between the European and the U.S. scene, with Israel a possible third partner. In Europe, partly because of the Holocaust, partly for other reasons, only a few outstanding names come to mind. Franz *Oppenheimer, a follower of Gumplowicz and a student of Marx and, like Durkheim, the son of a rabbi, turned the pessimistic and cataclysmic views of his masters into evolutionary optimism by attempting to prove that exploitation and domination will cease once the monopolistic grip on landed estate is loosened. From this point of departure, Oppenheimer became interested in Zionism and was one of the initial promoters of rural cooperatives in Palestine. The Hungarian-born Karl Mannheim combined influences stemming both from Karl Marx and Max Weber in his elaboration of a "sociology of knowledge" which comprehends knowledge as embedded in the situational experience of the man of knowledge, that is, a relational, although not necessarily a relativistic, phenomenon.

Emile Durkheim, more than any other European sociologist, formed a "school"; his disciples were almost all Jews, but few of them were sociologists. One might mention here Maurice *Halbwachs, primarily a demographer, Marcel *Mauss, Durkheim's son-in-law and his successor as editor of *L'Année Sociologique*, Lucien *Lévy-Bruhl and his son Henry *Lévy-Bruhl; all these, going beyond Durkheim, tried to combine sociology and psychology, but their published works fall more in the fields of ethnology, social anthropology, and the history of law and institutions than in the field of sociology proper. Perhaps the most renowned disciple of Durkheim was Marc *Bloch, an economic historian and one of the initiators of a sociological school of historiography. René *Worms, on the other hand, more important as organizer than as scholar, was an adversary of Durkheim. Later French-Jewish sociologists, such as Georges *Gurvitch, Raymond *Aron, and Georges *Friedmann, were less influenced by Durkheim than by idealistic and phenomenological philosophy and by the sociological approach of Max Weber. Georges Friedmann, a specialist in industrial sociology, contributed a brilliant analysis of contemporary Israel and the impact which it might have on the future of the Jewish people. Among the U.S. interpreters of Durkheim (as well as of Simmel, Mannheim, Weber, and Toennies) are such Jewish sociologists as Louis Wirth, Kurt Wolff, Harry Alpert (1912–1977), Reinhard Bendix, Lewis Coser, and Werner J. *Cahnman. Jeffrey Alexander (1947–), a leader in the neo-functionalist tradition, revitalized the understanding of the classic theorists, including Durkheim, Weber, and Marx. His work has been associated with what he calls the "late-Durkheimian" approach, or the "strong program" in cultural sociology (as compared to the "weak" program of the sociology of culture).

In England, Morris *Ginsberg developed a comparative sociological approach, based on evolutionary and social-psychological components; he was the editor of the *Jewish Journal of Sociology*. In pre-Hitlerian Germany and Austria, one encounters, apart from Oppenheimer and Mannheim, a number of interesting Jewish sociologists whose impact, however, was not far-reaching, partly because they were more social philosophers than sociologists, such as Rudolph *Eisler, Wilhelm *Jerusalem, Hermann *Kantorowicz, David *Koigen, Eugen *Rosenstock-Huessy, and the somewhat diffuse Ludwig *Stein (1859–1930), and partly because they were specialized, such as Friedrich Hertz and Walter *Sulzbach, who were students of nationalism, or Siegfried *Kracauer, whose careful analysis of white-collar employees and the social impact of the movies was not sufficiently appreciated. Rudolf *Goldscheid, one of the initiators of the Deutsche Gesellschaft fuer Soziologie, is remarkable because of his ethically motivated opposition to Max Weber's impassioned emphasis on a "value-free" social science. It should be added in this context that Germany, along with the countries of Eastern Europe, gave birth to the sociology of the Jews. In Eastern Europe, the writings of Leon *Pinsker, *Aḥad Ha-Am, and Ber (Dov) *Borochov, although sociological in content, are essayistic in form, while the publications emanating from the Yiddish Scientific Institute (YIVO), first in Vilna, later in New York, are more in the area of social history than sociology. The German effort, on the other hand, in connection with the Verein fuer die Statistik der Juden, was demographic and therefore at least pre-sociological in nature. The foremost name is Arthur *Ruppin; others are Felix Theilhaber, Arthur *Cohen, and Jacob *Lestchinsky; the latter lived in Germany, and later in the U.S., but was at first with the YIVO circle.

The story of the participation of the Jews in U.S. sociology is entirely different from the one in Europe. Among the founding fathers of sociology in the U.S., that is, the first post-Spencerian generation, were no Jews. The same is true about the second generation. As late as the 1930s only two Jewish sociologists of some importance were on the scene, Samuel *Joseph at the predominantly Jewish New York City College, and Louis Wirth, who was soon to rise to prominence at the oldest and most prestigious department of sociology in the country, the University of Chicago. There may be a variety of reasons for this tardy development, but one of them becomes clear if one compares what happened in sociology with the corresponding data in the related field of anthropology. The founding father of cultural *anthropology, as it is known today in the U.S., undoubtedly is Franz *Boas and beside him Edward *Sapir, both German-Jewish immigrants. In the second generation, Jews are prominently represented by such students of Boas as A.A. *Goldenweiser, Robert *Lowie, Paul *Radin, L. *Spier, all of them Austrian, Polish, and Russian immigrants, as well as by the U.S.-born Ruth Benedict and Melville J. *Herskovitz. What is involved is an apparently negative reaction in academic circles to entrusting "foreigners" with the teaching of such sensitive topics as U.S. history, U.S. literature, and especially sociology, while they were "allowed" to safely concern themselves with the analysis of remote cultures such as, for instance, the ones of the Crow, Klamath, and Winnebago Indians. Nor was this negative reaction politically of a predominantly conservative flavor, as one might assume if one were to conclude from European antecedents. Rather, it was radical "progressives" among older U.S. sociologists, like Henry Pratt Fairchild, Edward A. Ross, and Robert Faris who, in Fairchild's terminology, reminded immigrants that as "guests" they must adapt themselves to their "hosts," if they wished to be "accepted" as equals. This attitude amounted to a formidable psychological barrier, especially for aspiring Jewish intellectuals.

This state of affairs totally changed after 1948 when, apart from a limited number of European refugee scholars, a great many native-born Jews entered the ranks of U.S. sociologists. By 2005, of the 50 preeminent sociologists listed at the website http://www.kfunigraz.ac.at/sozwww/agsoe/lexikon/klassiker, approximately one-third were, or are, Jews (www.jinfo.org/Sociologists.html). About the same percentage have served as presidents of the American Sociological Association, including the president as of 2005 (Cynthia Fuchs Epstein, 1933–).

Several scholars of Jewish descent who have been aloof to Jewish life, or even baptized, played a prominent role in U.S. sociology, especially Robert K. *Merton, the foremost structural-functional theoretician in U.S. sociology, whose striking formulations have been widely accepted, Paul F. *Lazarsfeld, the recognized leader in quantitative sociology, Neil J. *Smelser, the most prolific writer among the students of Talcott Parsons, and David *Riesman, a Unitarian, who gained fame with a sociological best seller, *The Lonely Crowd*. Of these, Merton and Lazarsfeld were presidents of the American Sociological Association, as were Philip M. *Hauser, a former deputy director of the U.S. Bureau of the Census and an internationally known demographer, and Reinhard Bendix, a German-born theorist and a specialist in stratification theory. Arnold *Rose, a race-relations specialist, the assistant to Gunnar Myrdal's trailblazing study of the U.S. black, *An American Dilemma* (1944), passed away before he could occupy the office to which he was elected. The three latter scholars were graduates of the University of Chicago and students of Louis Wirth, while Merton represented a school of thought more prominent on the Eastern seaboard. Lazarsfeld was, by training, a mathematical psychologist. Louis Wirth himself, the first Jew to be elected to the presidency of the A.S.A., never fully reconciled his intense interest in Jewish affairs with his conviction that total assimilation was both inevitable and desirable, but his importance rests chiefly with his interest in urbanism, his interpretation of major figures in European sociology, and his passionate espousal of the cause of racial equality and social reform.

Up to the mid-20th century, one can say that a historical and phenomenological trend in U.S. sociology became more pronounced, along with a continuing and major trend of quantitative and positivistic emphasis. To the former trend belonged the Jewish sociologists Cahnman, Coser, and Kurt Wolff, as well as the scholars Albert *Salomon, Bernard Rosenberg (1923–1996), Norman Birnbaum (1926–), Sigmund *Diamond, Benjamin *Nelson (1911–1977), the urbanist Herbert Gans (1927–), and the political sociologist, Amitai Etzioni, an Israeli-American famous for his work on socioeconomics and as founder of the Communitarian movement in the early 1990s; to the latter chiefly some of the students of Paul F. Lazarsfeld, such as Bernard R. Berelson (1912–1979), David Caplovitz (1928–1992), and Herbert Hyman (1918–1985). Mathematical and statistical sociology was furthered by Leo Goodman (1928–) and Mark Granovetter (1943–). The structional-functional school in sociological theory, whose major representatives among Jewish scholars are Marion J. Levy, Jr. (1918–2002) and Neil J. Smelser, represented a third trend. Other scholars occupied a variety of intermediary positions in this regard, such as the criminologists Herbert *Bloch and Albert K. Cohen (1918–), the political sociologists Seymour M. Lipset and Walter B. Simon (1918–), the urban sociologist Alvin *Boskoff, and the industrial sociologists Peter Blau (1918–2002), Robert Dubin (1916–), Philip Selznick (1919–), and Rosabeth Moss Kanter (1943–).

In the second half of the 20th century, sociology developed in several directions in which Jewish sociologists played significant roles. These included challenges to the hegemony of both functionalist (Parsons) and conflict (Marxist) theory in the development of phenomenology, symbolic interactionism and postmodernism; the development of global macrosociology, the concept of "multiple modernities" and the impact of world systems; population studies on both the macro (demography) and micro (networking) levels; the rejection of the notion of "value-free" sociology and the awareness of the influence of social position on the development and impact of sociology, and its extension to the sociology of race, gender, and class relations, their intersections and especially the development of feminist and queer theory; and the developing field of the sociology of Jewry.

Symbolic interactionism, a term coined by Herbert Blumer, grew out of the "Chicago school" and was developed by a number of prominent Jewish sociologists, including the ethnomethodologist Harold Garfinkel (1917–); Erving Goffman (1922–1982), whose dramaturgical approach to impression management and contributions to role theory became a classic of sociology, most famously through his *The Presentation of Self in Everyday Life*. It incorporated Simmelian micro-perspective on interaction with a macro-level analysis of Durkheimian ritual behavior (Adams, 2003). Alfred Schutz contributed the idea of "multiple realities" in a phenomenological perspective contributing to the sociology of knowledge and knowing. Stanley Milgram (1933–1984) had a major impact on social science with what came to be known as the "Milgram experiments," which demonstrated that authority figures could command obedience to extraordinary measures even in the United States by virtue of their position; he also developed the concept of the six degrees of separation, an early development of networking theory.

Bridging macro- and micro-perspectives, and theory and empiricism, Norbert Elias (1890–1990) developed "process" or "figurational" sociology, his most prominent contribution being *The Civilizing Process*. Synthesizing German, American, French, and British social scientific advances through the 1930s, he explored the historical development of "civilized" identity and habitus, the history of emotions, the part played by state formation in that development, and the dynamics of national identity-formation. National identity-formation has also been explored by Erik Erikson (1902–1999) and Alex *Inkeles (1920–), who has focused on the manifestation of "modern" identity as well as convergence and divergence in "modern" societies. Other Jews contributing to such global sociology include Immanuel Wallerstein (1930–), who furthered the concept of the world system and global economic and political stratification; Lewis *Feuer (1912–2002), who began his career as a radical Trotskyist, a scholar of Marx and Hegel, with a major focus on the study of imperialism (http://frm.nationalreview.com/archives/week_2002_11_24.asp); and Shmuel Noah Eisenstadt (1923–), whose concept of "multiple modernities" challenged the linear and unified concept of modernity. Edward Shils (1910–1995), distinguished service professor in the Committee on Social Thought and in Sociology, was internationally renowned for his research on the role of intellectuals and their relations to power and public policy, following in a Weberian tradition. This cultural sociology was echoed in other Jewish sociologists, including Neil Postman (1931–2003), a media theorist, who studied how culture was affected by technology (or "Technopoly" as he called one of his books). One could also say that Thomas Kuhn (1922–1996) was a cultural sociologist in that he studied the impact of shifts in scientific culture or paradigms on society and science.

Jews figured among some of the most prominent demographers in the last half of the 20th century, including Ronald Freedman (1917–), who established and directed the Population Studies Center at the University of Michigan, and with Howard Schuman helped establish the on-going Detroit Area Study (DAS) to analyze social trends in the area; Sidney Goldstein (1927–), generally recognized as the "dean of demographers of American Jewry" and who like Freedman was president of the Population Association of America; Calvin Goldscheider (1941–); Nathan Keyfitz (1913–), who has made significant contributions to fertility, aging, and environmental impacts of population growth and who founded the International Institute for Applied Systems Analysis in Austria; Robert Hauser (1942–), director of the Center for Demography of Health and Aging at the University of Wisconsin-Madison and collaborator on the Wisconsin Longitudinal Study of life course and aging; and Harriet Presser (1936–), founding director of the Center on Population, Gender and

Social Inequality at the University of Maryland. Both Freedman and Presser were presidents of the Population Association of America. Jewish sociologists have also been among the leaders in the field of applied sociology, including Daniel Yankelovich (1924–), founder of the first private firm to measure and analyze shifting trends in American social and cultural values, Ross Koppel (1948–), president of the Social Research Corporation; and Judith Auerbach (1956–), vice president of the American Foundation for AIDS Research, who also served as director of the Behavioral and Social Science Program of National Institutes of Health (U.S.).

Several U.S. Jewish sociologists have made their mark in race and intercultural relations studies, or more generally, studies of inequality, partly because the field explicitly or implicitly includes Jewish topics, but chiefly because, for a variety of reasons, the problems of all minorities appeal to them. Early names to be mentioned here are Leo Srole (1908–1993), a collaborator with W. Lloyd Warner in the ethnic aspects of the much-discussed "Yankee City" studies; Melvin *Tumin (1919–1994), whose monographs deal with situations in North Carolina, Puerto Rico, and Guatemala; Milton *Gordon (1918–) and Nathan *Glazer, profound students of the processes of assimilation and ethnic identification in U.S. life; Milton Barron (1918–) and Stanley Bigman (1915–), authors of pioneering studies on intermarriage; Seymour Leventman (1930–), coauthor of *Children of the Gilded Ghetto* (1961); Arnold Rose; Peter Rose (1933–); Raymond Mack (1927–); and Immanuel Wallerstein in his Africanist studies. Oscar Lewis (1914–1970) focused his attention on the culture of poverty, through ethnographic portrayals of peasant communities in Mexico, Latin America, and Northern India, as well as poor Hispanics in the United States. Stanley Lieberson (1933–) received the Distinguished Contribution to Scholarship Award for his *A Piece of the Pie: Blacks and White Immigrants since 1880*. His work has focused on language usage and conflict, fashion, naming customs, and other nuances of cultural diversity. One of his latest books, *A Matter of Taste: How Names, Fashions, and Culture Change*, included a section on Jewish naming customs.

Other sociologists, like Sophia *Robison, Morris *Janowitz, and Werner J. Cahnman, made contributions in the field of race and intercultural relations, but their main interests are in other fields: Sophia Robison's in criminology, Janowitz' in military sociology, Cahnman's in the development of typological theory, especially in connection with historical studies.

One would be remiss to discuss the field of inequality without its more recent developments in terms of the intersections of race, class, and gender, feminism, and queer theory. Gender studies and feminism began with Betty Friedan (1921–2006), and continued through Jessie Bernard (1903–1996), who helped established the scholastic foundations of modern feminism, Nancy Chodorow (1944–) on the reproduction of mothering, and Judith Butler (1956–), among others. The latter, who credits her first realized interest in social philosophy to her early synagogue experiences, is chief representative of a body of intellectuals who have contributed to the reformulation of social theory in relationship to the "new" social movements such as the 1960s' student movements, the women's movements rekindled in the 1970s and beyond, race and ethnic pride movements stemming from the Civil Rights era of the late 1960s, and the gay and lesbian liberation movements of the 1980s and beyond. Uncovering the sexual politics of the private sphere, and protesting the exclusion of women from the public sphere, state, and economy, her work (most famously *Gender Trouble*), as well as that of others, has initiated debate over the relationships of culture, identity and representation.

Out of reluctance by many sociologists to publicize their own Jewish identity for fear of reprisal in the academy, studies of the Jewish minority were not commonly undertaken until the 1960s legitimized ethnic roots and attention. In the focus on multiculturalism, however, Jews were often obscured as part of the white majority (aptly captured in a study by Karen Brodkin (1941–), *How Jews Became White Folks and What That Says about Race in America*). Therefore, the study of American Jews became essentially a parochial pursuit rather than part of the more mainstream study of ethnic, racial, and religious minorities.

As far as the image of the Jew and the treatment of Jewish topics in sociological literature are concerned, there are differences to be observed as one moves from Europe to the U.S., but also continuities. In Europe the scholarly interest in Jewish matters was predominantly socioeconomic in nature, and it was cultivated primarily by Christian authors. Albert Schaeffle (1831–1903), writing about the Viennese stock exchange crash in 1873, considered the Jews as "naturally belonging to the financial faction." Werner *Sombart's related but historically buttressed thesis that the calculating spirit of the Jews was one of the prime factors in the rise of modern capitalism was contested by Max Weber, who characterized the Jewry of the dispersion as a "*Pariavolk*" whose economic activities were peripheral, not central, to significant occidental developments. Jewish traders, Weber maintained, were not instrumental in bringing about the modern factory as a rationally conceived and continuing enterprise. However, Weber analyzed the "ethical," or "missionary," Hebrew prophecy as the first step on the way to the rational "disenchantment of the world" which later culminated in the Puritan ethic and its secular aftermath. Ferdinand Toennies (1855–1936) occupies middle ground between Sombart and Weber inasmuch as he sees the Jews internally as the remnant of a former "Gemeinschaft," but in their external relations as one of the forces promoting the expanding modern *Gesellschaft*. This discussion has not been continued in the U.S., but Georg Simmel's concept of the "stranger" has led to an interesting elaboration in Robert E. Park's and Everett Stonequist's concept of the "marginal man" as "one who is poised in psychological uncertainty between two or more social worlds; reflecting in his soul the discords and harmonies, repulsions and attractions of these worlds." Park had in mind cultural as well as physical hybrids, emancipated Jews as well as light-skinned blacks. One of Park's disciples, Howard Becker (1899–1960) applied the "marginal man" concept to structural situations in talking about "marginal trading peoples" while Park's Jewish student Louis Wirth analyzed the ghetto as a state of mind marked by marginality; an extended controversy has followed in which a number of Jewish authors, among them Amitai Etzioni and Aaron Antonovsky (1923–1994), participated.

Last, but certainly not least in the present context, ought to be mentioned scholars whose major if not exclusive interest is in the Jewish field. Jewish topics have occupied a place in U.S. sociological literature; however, research on Jews tends to be isolated in Jewish publications rather than well-integrated in appropriate mainstream journals. However, some trends are ascertainable. While an analysis of papers published in three leading sociological journals (*American Sociological Review, American Journal of Sociology, Social Forces*) in the years 1929–64 showed that 74 of the published papers dealt with topics referring to intergroup relations (acculturation, assimilation, intermarriage, prejudice, discrimination, antisemitism, etc.), 51 papers dealt predominantly, although not exclusively, with internal topics of Jewish life (23 with family and youth, 15 with socioeconomic and demographic topics, 13 with Jewish religion and institutions). A comparable analysis of dissertations on Jewish topics (cf. Isacque Graeber, *Jewish Themes in American Doctoral Dissertations*, 1933–64) yielded 53 intergroup relations studies against 47 internal and, in part, structural studies, but the total figures include, along with those in sociology, historical, anthropological and psychological studies, thus impairing comparability. A review of sociological work on American Jewry that was published 1970–80 (Heilman, 1982) lamented the parochialism of the sociology of American Jewry. A later analysis of social science papers appearing in the electronic database JSTOR and dealing with topics related to American Jews (Burstein, 2004) revealed 129 articles, 19 dealing with politics, 29 with family (including fertility and intermarriage), and 26 with educational and economic attainment. Only nine articles dealt with (internal) Jewish religious practices or organizational life. However, the articles tended to cite research written by and for other Jews more than mainstream theories or problematics, indicating a persistent parochialism.

The review was incomplete, since it did not include some of the primary sources for publishing social science research on Jewry (which are not indexed in JSTOR): *Jewish Social Studies*, a publication of the Conference on Jewish Relations which began in 1938; *Commentary*, established in 1946, which aims to present intelligent and accessible analysis of the social character of American Jews; *Judaism*, begun in 1951 and including many sociological articles; *Midstream*, started in 1954; *The Jewish Journal of Sociology*, published bi-annually since 1958 out of the United Kingdom; *Contemporary Jewry*, the official journal of the Association for the Social Scientific Study of Jewry, which began publishing in 1974 as *Jewish Sociology and Social Research*, taking its present name in 1976; or the major journals of sociology of religion (such as *Sociology of Religion, Review of Religious Research, Journal of the Social Scientific Study of Religion, Journal of Contemporary Religion*) and ethnicity (such as *Ethnic and Racial Studies, Ethnicities, Social Identities*). While analyses of Jewish institutional life and identification are rarer in the latter journals than comparisons of Jews to other religious and U.S. denominations, sociological topics focusing on Jews are often included.

The analysis of Jewish institutional life and of the changing factors in Jewish identification has developed considerably in the last several decades. Three surveys of American Jews (the 1971, 1990, and 2000–01 National Jewish Population Studies) have resulted in serious analysis of American Jews, often in comparison to the wider American population and Israeli Jews. The 1990 National Jewish Population Studies resulted in 11 monographs, seven of which were published as a special series by SUNY Press. Topics included denominationalism, gender roles, Jewish and American culture, Jewish Baby Boomers and children, internal migration. Further, an impressive body of community studies has been collected (over 90), summaries of 45 of which have been collected by Ira Sheskin and published under the auspices of the North American Jewish Data Bank, currently housed at the University of Connecticut under the directorship of Arnold Dashevsky.

Early scholars of Jewish sociology included Nathan Goldberg (1903–1979), Erich *Rosenthal, Oscar Janowsky (1900–1993), Bernard Lazerwitz, C. Bezalel Sherman (1896–1971), Benjamin F. Ringer (1920–), Victor Sanua (1920–), Benjamin *Halpern, Will Herberg (1907–1977), Albert Vorspan (1924–), Mannheim Shapiro (1913–1981), Charles S. Liebman (1934–2003), and Albert Gordon (1901–1968); the last was a rabbi turned sociologist. Building on these early foundations, and incorporating new data and approaches, American Jewish sociology has developed along several lines, including: general analyses or theories of American Jewish life (Marshall *Sklare, Charles Silberman (1925–), Calvin Goldscheider (1941–), Seymour Martin Lipset, Charles Liebman (1934–2003); acculturation and assimilation (Steven Cohen, Calvin Goldscheider); ethnicity (Steven Steinberg (1944–); Herbert Gans, especially with his development of the concept "symbolic ethnicity" and, later, "symbolic religiosity")); social history and especially portraits of particular communities and groups of Jews (Samuel Heilman (1946–); Jack Wertheimer (1948–); Lynn Davidman (1955–); Debra Kaufman (1941–)); denominational studies and Jewish pluralism (Bernard Lazerwitz, Arnold Dashefsky (1941–)); American Zionism (Chaim Waxman (1941–); Jonathan Woocher (1946–), who suggested that Israel-oriented sentiment and activity formed the basis of American Jewish "civil religion"); Jewish politics and social movements (Daniel *Elazar (1934–1999); Jewish feminism (see more detail in Women in Sociology below); Jews and economics (Eva Etzioni-Halevy (1934–); Barry Chiswick (1942–)); family, gender roles, intermarriage (Moshe (1936–) and Harriet Hartman (1948–), Rela Mintz Geffen (1943–)); intermarriage (Rodney Stark (1934–) and Charles

Stember (1916–1982), participants in studies on antisemitism that were sponsored by the ADL (Anti-Defamation League) and the AJC (American Jewish Committee), respectively; Egon Mayer (1944–2004), Bruce Phillips, E. Rosenthal, Sylvia Barack Fishman); education (Walter Ackerman (1918–); Steven Steinberg; Harold Himmelfarb (1944–)); demography (Calvin Goldscheider (1941–); Sidney and Alice *Goldstein (1936–)); language and Jewish culture (Max Weinrich, Elihu Katz (1926–), and Sylvia Barack Fishman).

The sociology of Jewish religion began, perhaps, with Mordecai M. Kaplan's *Judaism as a Civilization*, continued with myriad publications of Jacob Neusner, Stephen Sharot's (1943–) focus on Jewish religious movements in comparative perspective, and S.N. Eisenstadt's *Jewish Civilization: The Jewish Historical Experience in a Comparative Perspective* (1992). The contribution of the Diaspora to the development of Jewish life has been explored by Daniel Boyarin (1946–) and Jonathan Boyarin, and the comparative perspective within Judaism, surveying the various Diasporas as well as Israel, has been greatly developed by Eliezer Ben-Raphael (1938–) and colleagues (e.g., *Contemporary Jewries: Convergence and Divergence*, 2003).

The beginnings of sociology in Israel were European. One trend was clearly demographic, starting with Arthur Ruppin and competently continued by the scientific director of the Israel Central Statistical Bureau, Roberto *Bachi, but, another, more descriptive than analytic, and represented by Zvi Rudy (1900–1972) and Aryeh *Tartakower, had East European antecedents. Structural-functionalism dominated Israeli sociology as it was established at Hebrew University's department of sociology, founded in 1948 by Martin Buber, followed as chair by Shmuel N. *Eisenstadt (1923–), Jacob Katz (1904–1998), Joseph Ben-David (1920–1986), and Yonina Talmon (1923–66), later joined by Judith Shuval (1926–), Simon Herman (1912–), and Henry Rosenfeld (1911–1986). The first student to complete her studies in the department, Rivka Bar-Yosef, later became a faculty member and chair. Chaim Adler (focusing on education), Dov Weintraub (1926–85), Erik Cohen (1932–), Moshe Lissak (1928–), and Elihu Katz joined in the next few years, rounding out a major cross-institutional research plan on the emerging Israeli society, including the absorption of immigrants (Eisenstadt), youth movements (Ben-David), kibbutz (Talmon), education (Reuven Kahane), and the moshav (Weintraub). A macrosociological and theoretical emphasis allowed the work to transcend the small-scale case study, and continues to characterize some of its most renowned members, such as Victor Azarya (1946–), Baruch Kimmerling (1939–), Nachmun Ben-Yehuda (1948–), and Erik Cohen. Katz went on to found Hebrew University's Communications Institute, as well as to head the task force charged with the introduction of television broadcasting in the late 1960s. Along with this institutional emphasis, Uriel Foa (1916–1990), Judith Shuval, and Louis *Guttman, the latter of which founded the Israel Institute of Applied Social Research, were early representatives of a positivistic and quantitative sociology, some of which continues at the Institute of Contemporary Jewry at Hebrew University, where Sergio DellaPergola is a chief demographer of Jewry worldwide. Tel Aviv University's Faculty of Social Sciences was founded in the late 1950s with a challenge to the dominant functionalist approach of studying Israeli society, starting with its first chair, Yonaton Shapiro. Applying sociology to some of the country's greatest dilemmas, it developed such foci as the Institute of Labor Relations and a Public Policy Program. Its faculty have studied democracy in Israeli society (Ephraim Yuchtman-Yaar (1935) and Yochanan Peres) and other aspects of political sociology (Hanna Herzog), work and labor markets (Rina Shapira (1932–), Moshe Semyonov (1946–), Noah Lewin-Epstein, and Haya Stier), education and stratification (Hanna Ayalon, Yossi Shavit) as well as ethnicity and Jewish identity in Israel and globally (Eliezer Ben-Rafael). The challenge to the functionalist perspective was further developed at Haifa University, with one of its major proponents Sammy Smooha (1941–), whose research focus on the disadvantaged Asian-African immigrants and Israeli Arabs showed the lack of unity and consensus in the society. A Marxist perspective was further developed at Haifa University with such researchers as Shlomo and Barbara Swirski, Deborah Bernstein (1956– , focusing on gender), and Shulamit and Henry Rosenfeld (focusing on the kibbutz). Israeli feminism developed in the mid-1980s with such scholars as Dafna Izraeli (1937–2003), Deborah Bernstein, and Barbara Swirski. More recently, a post-Zionist perspective incorporating the effects of "colonization" after the 1967 war on Israeli society and the Palestinians has developed in Israel. The establishment of the Israel Sociological Society in 1967 marked a turning point in the development of the sociological occupation in Israel, moving it beyond the confines of academic institutions and setting up its own nationwide community for professional as well as academic purposes. In addition to five major universities in Israel and their faculty and research staff, numerous non-Israeli social scientists have done studies in Israel, especially in and about kibbutzim. A number of Israeli faculty have joint appointments abroad and/or spend sabbaticals abroad, which further connects Israeli sociology to global conferences and developments.

[Werner J. Cahnman / Harriet Hartman (2nd ed.)]

Women in Sociology

Few women, Jewish or otherwise, were among the founders of sociology. Perhaps the earliest Jewish American woman sociologist was Fay Karpf (1893–1981); a preeminent social psychologist, she was the first chair of the Division of Social Psychology of the American Sociological Association, later chairing a department in the Graduate School for Jewish Social Work. Marie *Jahoda (1907–2001), a British social psychologist and researcher at the American Jewish Committee, Columbia University, and the University of Sussex, was also influential in the development of the field. Like many of the first sociologists, some of the Jewish women who made early inroads in the field were intellectual Marxists; these include

Rosa *Luxemburg, who studied the role of women in revolution, and Alexandra Kollontai (1872–1952). Hannah *Arendt (1906–1975) had a deep sense of Jewish identity that shaped her writings and world view, including critical examination of alienation, political power and authority. Rose Laub *Coser (1916–1994) became an international expert on women, work and leadership, focusing on the bureaucratic settings of medical institutions as well as the family.

Jewish women have played major roles in sociological research and leadership. Seven of 18 scholars who contributed to a volume of autobiographical essays by female leaders in the field (ed. A. Goetting and S. Fenstermaker) clearly indicate their Jewishness, including Beth Hess, Suzanne Keller, Helen Mayer Hacker, Janet Lever, Shulamit Reinharz, Gaye Tuchman, and Hannah Scheller Wartenberg. For some, like Hannah Arendt, Shulamit Reinharz, Gaye Tuchman, and Deborah Lipstadt, Jewish identity was always integral to their scholarship; for others, its role has been mixed. Lenore Weitzman became well known for her work on the "divorce revolution" and later focused on the Holocaust. Jewish women who have been active as applied sociologists include Judith Auerbach (1956–), vice president of Public Policy and Program Development at the American Foundation for AIDS Research, and Felice Levine, former executive director of the American Sociological Association.

The contributions of Jewish women have perhaps been most notable in the field of gender studies both generally and as applied to the study of Jews. Among the first feminist scholars was Jessie *Bernard (1903–1996), whose work on "his and her" marriages became a staple of both family and feminist studies. Mirra Komarovsky (1905–1999), the second woman to be president of the American Sociological Association (1972–73), brought out the cultural parameters and contradictions in gender roles. Viola Klein (1908–1973), an Austrian social theorist who fled the Nazis to Great Britain, focused on the social construction of women's nature and attributes, as well as on *Women's Two Roles: Home and Work* (with Alva Myrdal). Cynthia Fuchs Epstein (1933–), current president of the American Sociological Association as of 2005, applied the study of gender to professions; Rosabeth Moss Kanter (1943–) focused on *Men and Women of the Corporation*, in addition to many other contributions to organizational theory and behavior. In what Hester Eisenstein has termed the first phase of women's studies scholarship, the contributions of Carolyn *Heilbrun (1926–2003), Florence Howe (1929–), and Barbara Haber (1934–) stand out, as does Janet Saltzman Chafetz's (1942–) work on gender role socialization, Debra Renée Kaufman's (1941–) application of gender analysis to achievement, and Shulamit Reinharz's (1946–) feminist perspective on social research methods.

In the second phase of feminist scholarship, which concentrated on the strength and power of women, such social scientists as Phyllis Chesler (1940–), Gerda *Lerner (1920–), and Adrienne Rich (1929–) are prominent. Nancy Chodorow's (1944–) *The Reproduction of Mothering* (1978) infused a neo-Freudian understanding into persisting gender difference. Carol *Gilligan's (1936–) *In a Different Voice* (1982) focused on the moral development of women. In such books as *Gender Trouble*, Judith Butler (1956–) contributed to the reformulation of social theory by uncovering the sexual politics of the private realm, and protesting the exclusion of women from the public sphere, state, and economy.

Jewish women were among the founders of Sociologists for Women in Society and continue to be active in it and the National Women's Studies Association. Judith Lorber (1931–), as an example, was a founding editor of *Gender and Society* and president of SWS and the Eastern Sociological Society. Women have also been active in the professional societies devoted to social science research in Jewish studies, including the Association for the Social Scientific Study of Jewry (ASSJ), of which four of the 12 presidents have been women; the Women's Caucus of the Association for Jewish Studies (AJS); and the Jewish Women's Caucus of the National Women's Studies Association.

In their 1994 critique of the application of feminist sociology to American Jews, Lynn Davidman and Shelly Tenenbaum note that the first full-length sociological studies of Jewish women did not appear until 1991; they also point out that few articles in the primary journals for Jewish studies (*American Jewish Year Book, Contemporary Jewry, Jewish Journal of Sociology* and *Jewish Social Studies*) included a focus on women or gender prior to the 1990s. Women's family and economic roles received attention in Goldscheider's *Jewish Continuity and Change* (1984), and were enlarged upon by Moshe and Harriet Hartman's analysis of the 1990 National Jewish Population Study (*Gender Equality and American Jews*, 1996). Women's participation in voluntary Jewish organizations has been the subject of some study (B'nai B'rith (1985), and others reviewed in a report by the National Commission on American Jewish Women (1995), which also reviews other scholarship on Jewish women). Sylvia Barack Fishman has provided in-depth analysis of women's roles and feminism among American Jews. Barbara Schreier shows how the immigrant experience affected Jewish women's fashion, while Riv-Ellen Prell's (1947–) work studies how cultural images of Jews have permeated the interaction between American Jewish men and women. Women's religious identity received attention from Marion Kaplan's work on Jews in imperial Germany; more contemporary work on Jewish identity by Bethamie Horowitz has identified different "journeys" taken by both men and women. Several works have provided ethnographic insights into women's role in Orthodox Judaism, beginning with M. Danzger's general study of the revival of Orthodox Judaism (1989), and including Davidman's and Kaufman's respective studies of newly Orthodox women.

Israeli women have also been the focus of sociological study. Susan Starr Sered and Tamar El-Or have provided especially interesting studies of Israeli religious women; Harriet Hartman's (1948–) dissertation discussed ethnic differences among Israeli women; and Deborah Bernstein's

(1956–) research focuses on Jewish women's roles in pre-state Israel.

While women have been active in Israeli sociology practically since the founding of the first Sociology Department at Hebrew University in 1948, they are underrepresented in leadership and professional positions. Rivka Bar-Yosef, the first student to complete Ph.D. Sociology studies at the Hebrew University, became the third department head. After Bar-Yosef, it took 30 years for another woman to chair that department (Amalya Oliver), and only one woman, Judith Shuval (1926–), has been president of the Israel Sociological Society.

The work of Israeli women sociologists has been diverse, including work on immigration and healthcare (Judith Shuval), Israeli bureaucracy and sociolinguistics (Brenda Danet (1937–), work and occupations (Dafna Izraeli (1937–2003), education (Rina Shapira (1932–), and the kibbutz (Yonina Talmon (1923–1966), Michal Palgi (1944–).

[Harriet Hartman (2nd ed.)]

BIBLIOGRAPHY: American Sociological Association's Committee on the Status of Women in Sociology, 2004. *Final Report.* (L. Davidman and S. Tenenbaum); L. Davidman and S. Tenenbaum, "Towards a Feminist Sociology of American Jews," in: L. Davidman and S. Tenenbaum (eds.), *Feminist Perspectives on Jewish Studies* (1994); M.J. Deegan (ed.), *Women in Sociology* (1991); A. Goetting and S. Fenstermaker (eds.), *Individual Voices, Collective Visions: Fifty Years of Women in Sociology* (1995). S.R. Reinharz, *A Contextualized Chronology of Women's Sociological Work* (1993); idem, "Sociology," in: P.E. Hyman and D.D. Moore (eds.), *Jewish Women in America* (1997), 2:1273–78.

SOCOH OR SOCO (**Sokhko**; Heb. שׂוֹכֹה, שׂוֹכוֹ).

(1) Town in the Shephelah of Judah, situated between Adullam and Azekah (Josh. 15:35). The Philistines camped between Socoh and Azekah prior to the encounter of David and Goliath (I Sam. 17:1). Rehoboam fortified the place (II Chron. 11:7). It was one of the cities occupied temporarily by the Philistines in the time of Ahaz (II Chron. 28:18). In that period it served as an administrative or storage center, being one of the four cities named on the *la-melekh* stamps of the Judean monarchy. In Byzantine times, the name applied to a double village (Eusebius, Onom. 156:18ff.), which was still a center for pottery manufacture. The scholar *Antigonus of Sokho (Avot 1:3) was probably from this village or from the Judean town listed. It is identified with the twin mounds of Khirbat ʿAbbād (the site of the earlier occupation) and Khirbat Shuwayka (occupied in the Iron Age), overlooking Wadi-al-Samt (the valley of Elah), E. of Azekah.

(2) Judean town, situated in the southernmost mountain district (Josh. 15:48). It is the present-day Khirbat Shuwayka, W. of Eshtemoa.

(3) Canaanite town in the Sharon near Yaham, mentioned in the inscriptions of Thutmosis III (no. 67), Amenhotep II (15th century B.C.E.) and Shishak (no. 41; c. 920 B.C.E.). It was included in Solomon's third district (I Kings 4:10). In talmudic times it was a Samaritan settlement and under the crusaders it was known as Casal Soque. It is the present-day Khirbat Shuwaykat al-Ra's, north of Tūlkarm.

BIBLIOGRAPHY: M. Noth, in: PJB, 30 (1934), 35; M. Avi-Yonah, in: QDAP, 10 (1944), 169; Aharoni, Land, index; I. Ben-Zvi, *Sefer ha-Shomronim* (1935), 93; Alt, in: PIB, 25 (1929), 33; 28 (1932), 27.

[Michael Avi-Yonah]

SODERBERGH, STEVEN (1963–), U.S. film director. Soderbergh was born in Atlanta, Georgia, the second of six children. The family moved to Baton Rouge, Louisiana, where Peter Soderbergh, his father, was a professor and dean of Louisiana State University's College of Education. As a teenager, Soderbergh enrolled in film classes at Louisiana State. In 1978, at age 15, he made a short film titled *Janitor.* After graduation from high school in 1980, he skipped college and went directly to Hollywood, where he worked as a freelance film editor. He wrote scripts and made short films, including a documentary about the rock group Yes. Soderbergh was asked to direct a concert film for the band, *Yes: 9012 Live* (1986), which earned him a Grammy nomination. His next project, the Southern drama *sex, lies and videotape* (1989), debuted at the Sundance Film Festival and earned Soderbergh the Palm d'Or at the Cannes Film Festival and an Oscar nod for best original screenplay; the film would go on to earn $100 million worldwide. Soderbergh followed his acclaimed debut with *Kafka* (1991), *King of the Hill* (1993), and *The Underneath* (1995). After Soderbergh filmed the Spalding Gray performance piece, *Gray's Anatomy* (1996), and the low-budget *Schizopolis* (1996), he returned to the mainstream with Elmore Leonard's *Out of Sight* (1998), starring George Clooney and Jennifer Lopez. Following the Terence Stamp-Peter Fonda thriller *The Limey* (1999), Soderbergh received Academy Award nominations for his Julia Roberts vehicle *Erin Brockovich* (2000) and the illegal drug trade thriller *Traffic* (2000); it was the first time a director had received a double nomination since 1938, and Soderbergh took the Oscar for *Traffic.* In 2000, Soderbergh and Clooney founded their production company, Section Eight. Soderbergh's next film was an all-star, big-budget remake of the Rat Pack film *Ocean's Eleven* (2001), which he juxtaposed with the remake of the Russian art film *Solaris* (2002) and the more independent-minded *Full Frontal* (2002), an unofficial sequel to *sex, lies and videotape* for which stars like Roberts, Clooney, and Brad Pitt agreed to work union scale. In March 2002, Soderbergh was elected the first vice president of the Directors Guild of America. He married a second time to model and TV host Jules Asner in 2003, and one year later reunited the *Ocean's Eleven* cast for the sequel *Ocean's Twelve.*

BIBLIOGRAPHY: "Soderbergh, Steven," in: *Encyclopedia of World Biography Supplement,* vol. 25 (Gale, 2005); "Soderbergh, Steven," in: *International Dictionary of Films and Filmmakers, Vol. 2: Directors* (2005[4]). **WEBSITE:** www.imdb/name/nm0001752.

[Adam Wills (2nd ed.)]

SODOM (modern **Sedom**) **AND GOMORRAH** (Heb. סְדֹם וַעֲמֹרָה), two cities in the "plain" of the Jordan, usually mentioned together and sometimes with Admah, Zeboiim, and Bela, which is identified with Zoar. The first biblical reference to them is in the account of the boundaries of Canaan (Gen. 10:19). They were situated in the well-watered Jordan Valley, east of Beth-El (13:10–11). Lot, Abraham's nephew, chose to dwell in Sodom; he was captured in the campaign of the four kings led by Amraphel of Shinear against the five kings of the plain (ch. 14), in which the forces of Sodom and Gomorrah were defeated and their people and chattels taken as booty, until eventually rescued by Abraham. The story of the fall of Sodom and Gomorrah is related in Genesis 18–19: God decided to destroy them because of the grievous sins of their inhabitants. In spite of Abraham's pleas not to punish the just with the wicked, the judgment was executed, as not even ten just men could be found there. The visit of the two angels to Lot and the inhospitable behavior of the people of Sodom occurred on the occasion of the destruction. Finally, Lot and his family were led out of Sodom, and the city, together with three of the others in the plain, only Zoar being saved, was destroyed by a rain of brimstones and fire until "the smoke of the country went up as the smoke of a furnace." In later books of the Bible, the fall of Sodom and Gomorrah is cited as an example of God's wrath and as a warning of future destruction (Deut. 29:22; Isa. 13:19; Amos 4:11). Jerusalem is compared to them (Jer. 23:14; Ezek. 16:49ff.) as are Edom (Jer. 49:18), Babylon (Jer. 50:40), and Moab (Zeph. 2:9). In all these cases, their names indicate the extent of the destruction to come as punishment for a people's sins.

The geographical and historical problems connected with the fate of these two cities are related to the tectonic nature of the Dead Sea. The creation of the Jordan rift certainly antedates Abraham, but local upheavals are by no means excluded. Sodom and Gomorrah are usually assumed to be beneath the southern part of the Dead Sea, south of the *lisān*, the peninsula jutting into the sea, which is shallow and more recent than the rest of the depression. Local tradition, as represented in the Arabic name of the salt mountain, Jebel al-Sudūm or mountain of Sodom, favors the southern site. Some scholars, however, have looked for the two cities at the northern end of the Dead Sea or near Bāb al-Dhrāʿ, east of the *lisān*. No clear archaeological evidence has yet been produced in favor of either theory, although the location of Zoar indicates that ancient tradition placed the five cities at the southern end of the Dead Sea.

[Michael Avi-Yonah]

In the Aggadah

Sodom was the incarnation of wickedness, but wickedness of a special type. It was an evil-mindedness and hard-heartedness which consisted of the inhabitants basing their actions on the strict letter of the law. For instance, when a stranger passed through their territory, he was besieged and robbed of whatever he possessed. However, each Sodomite was careful to take only a trifle, so that when the victim remonstrated with the thieves each would claim that he had taken a mere pittance (less than a *perutah*) which was not worth discussion. After a while, they decided entirely to discourage wayfarers whom they felt were only coming to deplete their wealth, which God had lavished upon them to the extent that even their wheat contained gold dust (Job 28:6; Sanh. 109a). If a lost soul did occasionally wander into Sodom, they fulfilled the dictates of hospitality by giving lodging to the stranger. They had standard-sized beds on which travelers slept. If the stranger was too long for the bed, they shortened him by lopping off his feet – if too short, they stretched him out (a parallel to the Procrustean bed of Greek mythology). If a poor man happened to come there, every resident gave him charity, bricks of gold and silver, upon which he had written his name, but no bread was given to him. When he died of starvation, each came and took his gold and silver back.

There were four judges in Sodom who meted out justice in a unique fashion. Their names were Shakrai ("liar"), Shakurai ("awful liar"), Zayyafi ("forger"), and Mazle Dina ("perverter of justice"). If a man assaulted his neighbor, the judges required the victim to pay the assailant a medical fee for the "bleeding" he received. The judges also ruled that a man had to pay eight *zuzim* for crossing through the waters of a river although the fee was only four *zuzim* when he crossed by ferry. On another occasion they ruled in favor of a Sodomite who stole a carpet from a traveler, and insisted that the stranger had only dreamed that he possessed it. In addition, the outsider was charged three pieces of silver for having his dream interpreted. If a man assaulted his neighbor's wife and caused her to miscarry, the judges ruled that the woman had to be given to the assailant so she would become pregnant from him to compensate for the lost child (Sanh. 109a–b; *Sefer ha-Yashar*, Va-Yera). Charity was forbidden on penalty of death, since it was felt that its practice encouraged the proliferation of beggars. Paltit, the daughter of Lot, secretly sustained a wandering beggar. The Sodomites could not understand why the beggar did not perish and they suspected that he was being given food in secret. Three men concealed themselves near the beggar and Paltit was caught in the act of giving him sustenance. She was put to death by being burned upon a pyre. The doom of Sodom was sealed when a young maiden was caught giving bread, which she had hidden in her pitcher, to a poor man. Once her crime became known, they daubed her with honey and placed her on the parapet of the wall and the bees came and consumed her. The cries of the unfortunate girl finally made God resolve to destroy these sinners (Sanh. 109b; *Sefer ha-Yashar*; Va-Yera; Gen. R. 49:6). God destroyed the city at dawn of the 16th day of Nisan when both the moon and sun were in the heavens, since there were both moon and sun worshipers in Sodom (Gen. R. 50:12).

This attitude of firmly sticking to the letter of the law is reflected in the *halakhah* of *Middat Sedom*, "acting in the manner of Sodom," (Ket. 103a; BB 12b) about a man who refuses to confer a benefit which costs him nothing (BB 12b). The meaning of the sin of Sodom perpetuated in the English language by applying the word sodomy to homosexuality, though based on the Bible (Gen. 19:5–8), is not overstressed in the Midrash.

[Aaron Rothkoff]

Modern Times

In the 20th century the name Sedom was given to the site at the northwestern corner of the Dead Sea and at the foot of the huge salt plug of Mount Sodom (see *Land of Israel, Physiography), where the auxiliary installations of the Palestine Potash Company were set up in 1937. Lying 1,295 ft. (395 m.) below sea level, Sedom has the world's lowest-situated industrial plant. The Palestine Potash Co. was established in 1929, and its Kallia plant, at the northern end of the Dead Sea, began production of potash and bromides in 1932. The opening of the Sedom branch works was necessitated by the lack of room for evaporation pans at Kallia. The carnallite extracted at Sedom was ferried over the Dead Sea north to Kallia, where, during World War II, potash production reached an approximate 100,000 tons annually, thus supplying about half of Great Britain's requirements at the time. The relatively small quantities of bromide also constituted an important contribution to the Allied war effort. The 1947 UN partition plan provided for the inclusion of Sedom and the Dead Sea shore from there north to En-Gedi in the proposed Jewish state. During the Israel War of Independence, the Sedom Works, accessible only by boat, were completely cut off for many months. Reinforced by the workers and settlers from Kallia and *Bet ha-Aravah, who had to evacuate those two places in May 1948 and could only be transferred to Sedom, the core of laborers held out under severe hunger and thirst until contact with the rest of Israel was renewed in "Operation Lot" (December, 1948). The Kallia works remained in Jordanian hands and were completely razed by the Arab Legion; thus the renewal of production at Sedom had to be deferred until 1954, after the Beersheba-Sedom road was built. In the intervening years, existing machinery had become useless through corrosion, and a new plant had to be built. In 1955, the Bromide Company was founded, and it set up its factory near the Sedom Potash Works. Soon after, both enterprises were integrated into the Dead Sea Works. In the initial years, however, output at both plants did not progress satisfactorily, because only part of the evaporation pans had remained accessible (the rest were included in Jordanian territory) and the labor force was unstable. It was therefore decided to replace the system of having laborers live at the spot in temporary quarters and then take home leave for seven to ten days by having a labor force composed only of inhabitants of *Dimonah (and later also *Arad), who could go home every evening. Only in 1957/58 was the previous potash output of 100,000 tons again attained, 151,000 tons were produced in 1962/63 and 188,000 tons in 1963/64. Two steps led to a considerable expansion: the turning of most of the Israel half of the southern Dead Sea basin, an area of 50 sq. mi. (130 sq. km.), into evaporation pans through the construction of a huge containing dike and 25 mi. (40 km.) of other dikes; and the construction in 1964 of a second potash plant which used the hot leaching instead of the cold flotation method (for technical details see *Israel, State of: Economic Affairs, Mineral Resources). In 1964/65, potash output reached 320,000 tons and in 1970 approached 1,000,000 tons after a third plant with a 400,000 tons annual capacity was begun in 1969. From 1970, potash production and exports regained their profitability after a price slump on the world market was overcome. In 2001, potash production stood at 1.77 million tons. Bromine output rose from 5,120 tons in 1964/65 to 206,000 tons in 2001. Another plant at Sedom produces table salt of high purity and industrial salts. The simultaneous progressive mechanization and introduction of electronic devices made feasible the reduction of the labor force.

[Shlomo Hasson]

In the Arts

The interconnected biblical accounts of Lot, the nephew of Abraham, and the wicked "Cities of the Plain" have inspired a number of writers and artists, but relatively few composers. One of the rare medieval treatments in literature is the English mystery play, *Histories of Lot and Abraham* (in MS). Thereafter interest waned until the late 16th century with the publication of an anonymous English ballad, *Of the Horrible and Woeful Destruction of Sodome and Gomorra* (London, 1570). This was followed by *Conflagratio Sodomae* (1607), a five-act neo-Latin tragedy by Andreas Saurius, who also published a German version of the drama (Strasbourg, 1607); and G. Lesley's English verse play, *Fire and Brimstone; or the Destruction of Sodom* (London, 1675). Some of the most significant treatments of the theme have been written by 20th-century authors. Perhaps the most brilliant – and certainly the most disturbing – dramatic interpretation of the subject was Jean Giraudoux's *Sodome et Gomorrhe* (1943), first staged in 1946. Here the French playwright broadened the sweep of the original account and reduced the biblical quorum of ten righteous persons needed to preserve the cities from their overthrow to a single couple, whose inability to maintain normal sexual harmony results in the final catastrophe. Other 20th-century treatments include Robert Brendel's German tale, *Die grosse Hure* (1920); Maria Ley-Piscator's novel, *Lot's Wife* (1954); and Nikos Kazantzakis' Greek drama, *Sodhoma kye Ghomorra* (1956), which attempts to establish a parallel between the biblical past and the menacing present.

In art, the chief episodes treated are Lot's flight from Sodom and his incestuous relationship with his daughters. The flight from Sodom (Gen. 19:16ff., 29) is a favorite choice of artists, the burning city (Gen. 19:24ff.) often being shown in the background, although (unlike the Flood) it seldom formed a subject in itself. The transformation of Lot's wife into a pillar of salt (Gen. 19:26) was sometimes also incorporated in the flight. The pillar occasionally appears as a column with the head of Lot's wife as a capital. In some medieval representations, a goat is shown licking the salt at the base of the pillar, because Lot's wife represents the man who, having been delivered from sin, returns, and "the man who returns to sin is hardened like a rock and is licked by infernal wild beasts" (*Speculum Humanae Salvationis*). The subject is found in the sixth-century *Vienna Genesis* and in the 12th-century mosaics at Monreale. It figures in medieval carvings, stained glass, and manuscripts, including the 13th-century *St. Louis Psalter* (Bibliothèque Nationale) and Sarajevo *Haggadah, where the burning of Sodom and the transformation of Lot's wife appear as separate episodes. In the Renaissance, the subject appears in a fresco by Benozzo Gozzoli in the Campo Santo, Pisa; in the Raphael Loggia in the Vatican; and in a painting by Paolo Veronese in the Louvre. There is also a painting of the subject (Kress Collection, National Gallery of Art, Washington) attributed to Duerer. The subject was later treated in paintings by Rubens (Louvre) and Guido Reni (National Gallery, London). *Rembrandt made a pen-and-ink drawing of Lot's departure. The salacious theme of the elderly, drunken Lot making love to his daughters (Gen. 19:30–38) appealed especially to German, Dutch, and Flemish artists of the Renaissance, and to Italian artists of the 17th century. In many pictures, the elder daughter is shown sitting on his knees, while the younger plies him with wine. The subject appears in the *Vienna Genesis* and in a few other medieval sources; and in paintings by Lucas Cranach (Pinakothek, Munich), Albrecht Altdorfer and Quentin Massys in the Vienna Museum, and Lucas van Leyden (Louvre). The last artist also made a copper engraving of the subject. Other treatments include that by Rubens in the Louvre, a pen-and-ink sketch by Rembrandt, paintings by David Teniers (Pinakothek, Munich), Simon Vouet (Strasbourg Museum) and by Italian artists of the period, including Guercino-Goya and Gustave Courbet who also painted the subject.

In Music

Only slight interest in the subject has been displayed in this field. Beethoven's teacher, Simon Sechter, wrote a two-part oratorio, *Sodoms Untergang* (1840), which was apparently never performed. Other settings are few and forgotten. For Giraudoux' drama, *Sodome et Gomorrhe* (1943), the incidental music was written by Arthur Honegger.

[Bathja Bayer]

BIBLIOGRAPHY: F.M. Abel, *Une Croisière autour de la Mer Morte* (1911), 78ff.; E. Powe, in: *Biblica*, 11 (1930), 23ff. (Eng); R. Koeppel, *ibid.* 13 (1932), 6ff. (Ger.); Clapp, in: *American Journal of Archaeology*, 40 (1936), 335ff.; M.J. Lagrange, in: RB, 41 (1932), 489ff. (Fr.); J.P. Harland, in: BA, 5 (1942), 17ff.; 6 (1943), 41ff.; P. Lapp, in: RB, 73 (1966), 556ff. (Fr.); EM, s.v. (incl. bibl.). IN THE AGGADAH: Ginzberg, Legends, index.

SOEST, town in Germany. The Jewish settlement in Soest is continuous from its beginning in the 13th century until the Holocaust. Jews must have been present in the city during the first half of the 13th century, since a mid-13th century source attests that Jews from Soest were house owners in Cologne. At the beginning of the 14th century, Soest Jews paid a sum of eight marks yearly to the archbishop of Cologne as *Schutzgeld* ("protection money"). From 1330 onward jurisdiction over the Jews passed to the city, which did not allow more than two Jewish families to reside there. Among the Jews of Soest in the Middle Ages were a number of municipal physicians, a very unusual phenomenon for Westphalian Jews at the time. Among these were Master Solomon (1510) and Benedictus (1540). Another remarkable event was the conversion to Judaism of a scholar and canon named Robert, who died in Frankfurt in 1298.

From the beginning of Prussian rule, in the mid-17th century, the Jews of Soest belonged to the duchy of Mark. A family named Stern moved from Frankfurt and around 1700 settled in Soest, where their descendants lived until the Holocaust. Even in the 18th century the number of Jewish families was restricted to two. Only after Soest was included in the grand duchy of Berg (1807–14) did the number increase (70 people in 1822). At that time a synagogue was built, which was expanded in 1882. In addition to the medieval cemetery, a new one was purchased in 1832. Under the influence of the *Obervorsteher* ("senior warden"), L. Hellwitz, changes inspired by the concepts of "radical Reform" were introduced into the liturgy during the first half of the 19th century. The private Jewish primary school, founded in 1828, was converted into a municipal school in 1855. Due to the inclusion of nearby communities, the membership of the Soest community rose to 323 Jews by 1880. After that there was a steady decline: in 1933 there were 162 Jews in Soest, while in 1939 only 64 Jews remained. Deportations to concentration camps brought the community to an end. The four Jews residing there in 1971 belonged to the community of *Paderborn. In 2005, eight Jews from Soest were affiliated with the Paderborn Jewish community. There are commemorative plaques at the Jewish cemetery and the site of the former synagogue.

BIBLIOGRAPHY: *Germania Judaica*, 2 (1968), 769f.; vol 3 (1987), 1376–78; B. Brilling and H. Richtering, *Westfalia Judaica*, 1 (1967), s.v. *Soest*; S. Katzenstein, in: *Soester Heimatkalender* (1930), 60–62; *Mitteilungen des Gesamtarchivs der deutschen Juden*, 3 (1911/12), 26–53. **ADD BIBLIOGRAPHY:** M. Brocke, *Der juedische Friedhof in Soest.* Eine Dokumentation in Text und Bild; G. Koehn, *Die juedische Gemeinde Soest. Ihre Mitglieder von 1700 bis zur Vertreibung und Ermordung im Dritten Reich* (Soester Beitraege, vol. 50) (1993); W. Buss, *Sosatia Judaica. Ein Beitrag zur Geschichte der Juden in Soest* (1994); U. Sasse-Voswinckel and G. Koehn, *Juedische Nachbarn in Soest bis 1942* (2001).

[Bernhard Brilling]

SOFAER, ABRAHAM (1896–1988), British actor. Born in Rangoon, Burma, Sofaer was a schoolmaster before going on the London stage in 1921. He toured in Shakespeare for four years and subsequently appeared in Jewish roles such as Cohen in G.B. Stern's *The Matriarch* (London and New York, 1930), the title role in Schnitzler's *Professor Bernhardi* (1936), Disraeli in Laurence Housman's *Victoria Regina* (which he performed 750 times in the U.S. starting in 1936), and Samson in Milton's *Samson Agonistes* (1951). In the 1930s and 1940s Sofaer appeared in many British films and, from about 1950 until 1970, in more than 20 Hollywood films, always in supporting roles.

SOFAER, ABRAHAM (1939–), U.S. scholar and jurist. After serving in the U.S. Air Force from 1956 to 1959, Sofaer attended Yeshiva University, receiving his bachelor's degree in 1962. He graduated in 1965 from New York University School of Law, where he was editor-in-chief of the *Law Review* and a Root-Tilden scholar. He clerked with Judge Skelly Wright of the U.S. Court of Appeals in 1965 and 1966, then with the Honorable William J. Brennan, Jr., an associate justice of the U.S. Supreme Court, in 1966 and 1967. Sofaer served as an assistant U.S. Attorney for the Southern District of New York from 1967 to 1969.

From 1969 to 1976 Sofaer was professor of law at Columbia University School of Law. In 1975 and 1976 he served as a New York State administrative judge, and was hearing officer for the first major environmental action involving PCBs, the *New York Department of Environmental Conservation v. General Electric Company*, concerning the discharge of PCBs into the Hudson River. Sofaer was appointed U.S. district judge for the Southern District of New York in 1979. He presided over several high-profile cases, including the libel action against *Time* magazine by Israeli general Ariel Sharon, in which Sharon prevailed.

In 1985 Sofaer became legal adviser to the U.S. Department of State. He was the principal negotiator in various international matters, including the dispute between Egypt and Israel over Taba; the U.S. claim against Iraq for its attack on the USS *Stark*; claims against Chile for the assassination of diplomat Orlando Letelier; sovereign immunity in Soviet-U.S. relations; the Iran-U.S. Claims Tribunal; and extradition and mutual legal assistance treaties. In 1989 he received the Distinguished Service Award, the highest State Department award for a non-civil servant.

After leaving the Department of State in 1990, Sofaer entered private practice as a partner in the firm of Hughes, Hubbard, and Reed in Washington, D.C. Two years later he was retained to represent Libya in matters pertaining to the 1988 bombing of Pan Am Flight 103 over Lockerbie, Scotland. Though Sofaer maintained that his role was to seek "consensual resolutions" and that during his tenure at the State Department the investigation of the bombing was focused on Iran, not Libya, he was nevertheless charged with violating Rule 1.11 of the Rules of Professional Conduct by the District of Columbia Bar. Rule 1.11 prohibits a lawyer formerly employed by the federal government from working on a matter in which the lawyer participated while in government employ. Sofaer and his firm subsequently dropped the case. In an appeal of the charges, a three-judge panel of the D.C. Court of Appeals ruled in the bar's favor.

In 1994 Sofaer was named the first George P. Shultz Distinguished Scholar and Senior Fellow at the Hoover Institution of Stanford University. The focus of his work as a legal scholar has included the separation of powers in the American system of government, international law, terrorism, national security, and conflicts in the Middle East. He was a member of the American Bar Association, the American Law Institute, the American Arbitration Association, and the Council on Foreign Relations.

[Dorothy Bauhoff (2nd ed.)]

SOFER (Schreiber), rabbinical family, descendants of Moses *Sofer. ABRAHAM SAMUEL BENJAMIN WOLF (1815–1871), oldest son of Moses Sofer, succeeded his father on his death in 1839 as rabbi and *rosh yeshivah* of Pressburg. During the 32 years he occupied this post, he continued his father's policies in all matters. He was one of the active organizers of Hungarian Orthodoxy for the Jewish Congress which took place in 1869, and subsequently carried on his activity in this sphere (see *Hungary). Though not at first an extremist, he later joined their ranks and finally gave the religious approval of the Sofer dynasty to the schism in Hungarian Jewry. He published responsa and expositions of the Torah under the title *Ketav Sofer* (1873–1938).

His brother SIMEON SOFER (1820–1883) was appointed rabbi of Mattersdorf in 1848 and in 1861 of Cracow, where he served until his death. He founded *Maḥzike Hadas, the Orthodox organization in Galicia, to battle the *maskilim*. With this end in view he strengthened relations with the ḥasidic rabbis of Belz and Zanz. From 1878 he was a member of parliament in Vienna. His books on *halakhah* and homiletics were published under the title *Mikhtav Sofer* (2 vols., 1952–55).

SIMHAH BUNEM SOFER (1842–1906), son and successor of Abraham Wolf, continued to maintain the large yeshivah, to organize Orthodoxy, and to accentuate the differences between it and other sectors of Hungarian Jewry. For this purpose, he strengthened relations with ḥasidic rabbis in Hungary. He expressed his opposition to the *Mizrachi conference which took

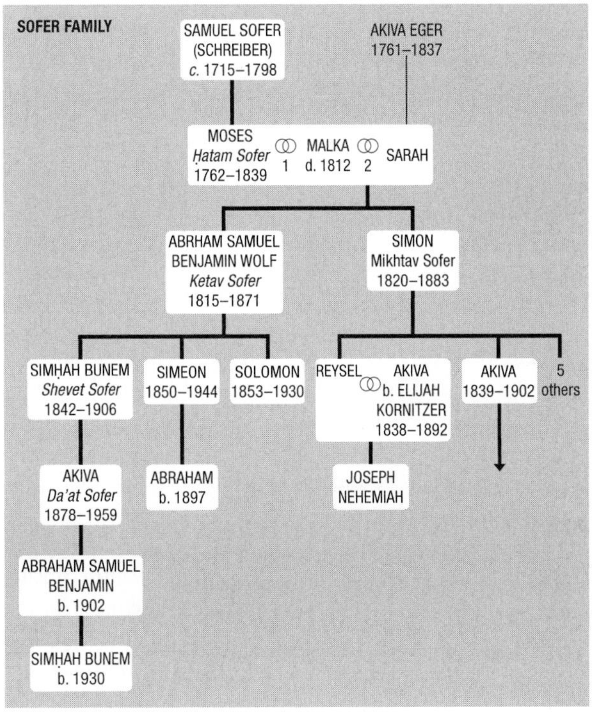

place in Pressburg in 1904. His publications are: *Shevet Sofer,* responsa (1909) and novellae on talmudic tractates (1938–56); and *Sha'arei Simḥah,* on the Pentateuch (1923).

SIMEON (1850–1944), son of Abraham Wolf, founded in 1881 the well-known yeshivah in Erlau (Hung., Eger), where he was rabbi, and taught there until the day he was taken to Auschwitz extermination camp where he perished. He had been in favor of agricultural settlement in Ereẓ Israel. He published the responsa, *Hitorerut Teshuvah* (4 vols., 1912–34).

SOLOMON SOFER (1853–1930), son of Abraham Wolf, was a distinguished preacher and writer. He is the author of *Ḥut ha-Meshullash* (1887), biographies of famous members of the family; and edited the *Iggerot Soferim* (1928), containing letters of his family, the Sofers and the Egers. He served as rabbi of Beregszasz until his death.

AKIVA SOFER (1878–1959), son of Simḥah Sofer, succeeded his father as rabbi and *rosh yeshivah* of Pressburg. In 1940 he settled in Israel where he reestablished the yeshivah of Pressburg (Jerusalem), acting as its head until his death. His publications are *Da'at Sofer* (1963) on Torah, and responsa (2 vols., 1965).

ABRAHAM SOFER (SCHREIBER; 1897–), son of Simeon Sofer, served as rabbi in many communities in Greece and in Italy. He immigrated to Ereẓ Israel in 1939, settling in Jerusalem. From 1948 to 1966 he was a teacher at the Jewish Theological Seminary of New York. As a fruitful rabbinic author, his main activity was preparing the works of Menahem *Meiri, as well as of other rishonim for publication.

BIBLIOGRAPHY: Solomon Sorer, *Ha-Ḥut ha-Meshullash* (1887); idem, *Iggerot Soferim* (1928); Simeon Sofer, *Mikhtav Sofer,* ed. by J.N. Stern (1952), 3–86; A.S.B. Sofer, *Ketov Zot Zikkaron* (1957); Kressel, Leksikon, 2 (1967), 481.

[Moshe Shraga Samet]

SOFER, ḤAYYIM BEN MORDECAI EPHRAIM FISCHEL (1821–1886), Hungarian rabbi. An outstanding pupil of Ḥatam Sofer in Pressburg and of Meir Eisenstaedter in Ungvar, Ḥayyim was appointed head of the yeshivah at Mattersdorf in 1844. He served as rabbi of Gyömrő in 1852, of Sajoszentpeter in 1859, and of Munkacs in 1867. Persecuted by the Ḥasidim despite his religious extremism, he left Munkacs in 1880 and was appointed the chief rabbi of the Orthodox community in Pest. He was one of the leading extreme Orthodox rabbis in Hungary, a signatory of "the infamous excommunication" of the *maskilim* in Michalovce, and a central figure of the Shomerei ha-Dat organization. He demanded that adherents of the Reform movement be excommunicated and that their sons be refused circumcision.

He was the author of the following works: *Peles Ḥayyim* (1854), novellae on the first chapter of *Gittin; Maḥaneh Ḥayyim* (1879–85), responsa arranged according to the order of the Shulḥan Arukh; *Sha'arei Ḥayyim* (1869), admonitions against the Reformers; *Kol Sofer* (2 pts., 1881–82), on the Mishnah; and *Sha'arei Ḥayyim* (1892), a commentary on Psalms.

BIBLIOGRAPHY: A. Stern, *Meliẓei Esh al Ḥodesh Sivan* (n.d.), 1179; S. Weingarten, in: *Arim ve-Immahot be-Yisrael*, 1 (1946), 3535; A. Fuerst, *ibid.*, 2 (1948), 162; J.Z. Sofer, *Toledot Soferim* (1963).

[Itzhak Alfassi]

SOFER, MOSES (known as **Ḥatam Sofer**; 1762–1839), rabbi, halakhic authority, and leader of Orthodox Jewry. Sofer was born in Frankfurt and his two most important teachers there were Phinehas *Horowitz and Nathan *Adler. When, as a result of the opposition to his innovations and departure from accepted custom, Adler was forced to leave Frankfurt, Sofer, his loyal disciple, then 19 years of age, accompanied him on his wanderings. Although Sofer never returned to his native town, he was always proud of it, and used to sign himself "Moses ha-Katan [the insignificant] of Frankfurt on the Main." He served first as rabbi of Dresnitz (Moravia) and of Mattersdorf, and in 1806 was appointed rabbi of Pressburg, at that time the most important community in Hungary, where he remained for the rest of his life. His appointment to this high office came as a result of the reputation he had acquired by virtue of his outstanding scholarship, moral character, talent and leadership, and a mystical religious fervor which he had acquired under the influence of Adler. There already existed in Pressburg an appreciable minority of *maskilim* who unsuccessfully opposed his appointment. However, the opposition was not completely silenced, and Moses Sofer did not have a tranquil time.

During his 33 years there Sofer founded his famous yeshivah, the largest since the Babylonian yeshivot, and made it the center from which to organize Orthodox Jewry in its struggle against the Reform movement. Despite the expansion of his yeshivah and his great influence, which spread far and wide, he was continuously conscious of the growing tension between the traditionalists and the groups which sought a more liberal interpretation of Judaism in order to come to terms with the "spirit of the times." His qualities enabled Sofer to become the undisputed religious authority in his own town. As a result, unlike the case in other large European cities, the innovators were not triumphant. He declared total war with no concessions in the battle against modernity. Though it gave him no pleasure to engage in conflict ("There are no quarrels without wounds," Response, pt. 6, no. 35), he waged the battle of Orthodoxy vigorously, resourcefully, and with diplomatic skill. He adopted the long-range plan of strengthening educational and communal institutions and disseminating Torah study ("It is a time to act for the Lord, increase your Torah," ethical testament, see below); the appointment of his best disciples to rabbinic posts and the strengthening in general of the status of the rabbinate; the formation of a joint front with the ḥasidic movement; and the winning of the confidence of the government in the loyalty of Orthodox Jewry. Nevertheless, when the need arose he did not abstain from also utilizing the methods of propaganda and even demagoguery, by witty epigrams and slogans with which he mercilessly belabored his opponents. These methods were decisive for the Jews of Central Europe, sharpening the division and creating an irreparable breach between the Orthodox and the non-Orthodox sectors. Although he was one of the few rabbis who foresaw this consequence, he nevertheless deliberately adopted this policy. Among the many pungent and pointed epigrams which Sofer coined, and which became the slogans of the Orthodox, the best known is his application of the talmudic dictum "*Ḥadash asur min ha-Torah*" to mean that any innovation, even though from the point of view of *halakhah* it is unimportant, is strictly forbidden simply because it is an innovation.

This extreme view had its source in his profound and unstinted admiration for the classic rabbinic literature to its most minute detail, including every hallowed custom, as it existed in the German-Polish way of life at the end of the 18th century. He was convinced of the inner perfection of that way of life, and of its essential superiority to the prevalent culture, despite the tremendous resurgence of this culture and its massive achievements. Since modernism by its very nature nurtured within itself a distinct threat to every type of traditional institution, he instinctively shrank from it a priori. As a result he obstinately opposed the new type of school founded by the *maskilim* in particular and the doctrine of Moses *Mendelssohn in general, although in principle he was not opposed to secular studies where they were undertaken purely for the needs of the traditional way of life or for the sake of livelihood. Similarly he dissociated himself from the battle for emancipation, not merely because he feared the heavy price that would be exacted for it at the cost of tradition, but because he viewed the very aspiration for equality as a sign of dissatisfaction with the traditional way of life of the community and a desire for partial assimilation with gentile culture. He finally brought to an end the debate which was being hotly waged as to whether the Shulḥan Arukh was still to be regarded as the final authoritative code. The principle of complete submission to the Shulḥan Arukh became one of the fundamental doctrines of Orthodoxy. In addition he ruled that from then onward no distinction existed from the point of view of their religious importance between an insignificant custom and an explicit biblical prohibition. Sofer's attitude made him the undisputed leader of the rabbis of Europe who organized themselves between 1817 and 1821 to frustrate the first efforts of the Reform movement in Berlin, Hamburg, and Vienna. From this struggle which, as a result of his direction, ended in partial success, Sofer emerged as the recognized leader of Orthodoxy, a status which he maintained until the end of his life.

Sofer's first wife died childless in 1812. Some months later he married the daughter of Akiva *Eger, later rabbi of Posen, who was considered the greatest talmudist of his time. Their children formed one of the best-known rabbinic families (see *Sofer family). In his will, Sofer appointed his eldest son, Abraham Samuel Benjamin Wolf, to succeed him as *rosh yeshivah*. Shortly before his death he indicated to the community his desire that Abraham be appointed his successor in the rabbinate during his own lifetime. Although his son was only 24 at the time, Moses Sofer's request was granted. Thenceforth the Pressburg community became the heritage of the Sofer family dynasty. Simeon, his second son, was apointed rabbi of Cracow where he founded the Orthodox organization, Maḥzike Hadas. Solomon Zalman Spitzer, his son-in-law, was rabbi of the Orthodox congregation in Vienna.

Another manner in which he wielded great influence was through his voluminous writing. During his lifetime hardly anything was published. Immediately after his death, however, the family began to publish his writings. They comprise seven volumes of responsa (1855–1912; *Ḥatam Sofer*), sermons (2 vols. 1829), novellae on the Talmud, commentaries on the Torah, letters, poems, and a diary. They all bear the imprint of his Orthodox trend. His ethical testament, of which many editions have been published, is especially worthy of mention. It is wholly devoted to the battle for religion. *Ha-Lev ha-Ivri* (1864) of Akiva Joseph Schlesinger, a book popular among the ultra-Orthodox, of which many editions have appeared (first ed. Vienna, n.d., 2nd 1863), is written in the form of a commentary on this will. Moses Sofer and his sons and disciples played an important part in the growth of the Jewish settlement in Ereẓ Israel in the 19th century until the Zionist immigration. He also made great use of nationalist sentiment in his campaign against the Haskalah and Reform. He fought for the Hebrew language and for the idea of the return to Zion.

BIBLIOGRAPHY: S. Ehrmann, in: L. Jung (ed.), *Jewish Leaders* (1953), 117ff.; J. Katz, in: *Meḥkarim… Muggashim le-G. Scholem* (1968), Heb. pt. 115–48; Berdyczewski, in: *Ha-Asif*, 4 (1888), "*Oẓar ha-Sifrut*," 55–61; B. Dinaburg, *Ḥibbat Ẓiyyon*, 1 (1932), 15ff.; D. Zahavi, *Me-ha-Ḥatam Sofer ad Herzl* (1966); Schischa, in: *Ha-Ma'yan*, 7:4 (1967), 49–70 (a critique of Zahavi); Weingarten, in: *Sinai*, 60 (1967), 77–85 (a critique of Zahavi).

[Moshe Shraga Samet]

SOFERIM (Heb. סוֹפְרִים; "scribes"). Although the word *soferim* is identical with the biblical word translated scribes and dealt with under that heading, during the Second Temple period the word came to denote a specific class of scholars. The exact meaning and delineation of the group involved is a matter of controversy. According to Nachman Krochmal (*Moreh Nevukhei ha-Zeman*, section 11), Frankel (Mishnah pp. 3ff.), Weiss (Dor, 1 (1904^4), ch. 6ff.), and others, the era of the *soferim* of the Talmud commenced in the time of Ezra and continued until the time of Simeon the Just, who was the last of the men of the Great Synagogue. These scribes, whose names are not known and who were active during the time of the Persian rule, laid the foundations of the *Oral Law: they instituted regulations in the social and religious spheres, explained to the people the Torah and its precepts distinctly and gave the sense (Neh. 8:8). They taught the *halakhot* and the traditions in close connection with the study of the Bible and deduced new *halakhot* through the interpretation of the written text. They read the Written Law, interpreted its content, and integrated into it the traditional *halakhot* as well as the laws that had been derived from it. As a result of the activities of the *soferim* the Torah ceased to be the heritage of the priests and levites alone. From among the many pupils they educated, scholars arose from all classes.

Several of these scholars considered the *soferim* also to be the founders and members of the Great Synagogue, and attribute to the period between Ezra the Scribe and Simeon the Just all those traditions and *halakhot* designated as *mikra soferim* ("scribal reading"), *ittur soferim* ("scribal embellishment," Ned. 37b), **tikkun soferim* ("scribal emendation," Gen. R. 49:7; Theodor-Albeck p. 505), *dikdukei soferim* ("details of the scribes," Suk. 28a), and *divrei soferim* ("the words of the scribes," Sanh. 88b). They find support for their views in the talmudic statement, "The early scholars were called *soferim* because they used to count [*sofer* also means 'to count'] all the letters of the Torah. Thus they said that the *vav* in *gaḥon* (Lev. 11:42) marks the middle letter of the Torah" (Kid. 30a); i.e., the scribes scrutinized and were meticulous with the text of the Bible and its transmission. Similarly: "Why are they called *soferim*? Because they enumerated the laws according to numbers [*sefurot*], e.g., five may not separate *terumah*; five are obliged to take **ḥallah*," etc. (TJ, Shek. 5:1). The passage which follows combines two meanings: that the scribes counted the letters of the Bible and taught the *halakhot* or *mishnayot* in numerical form (cf. also Ḥag. 15b, Sanh. 106b). Kaufmann in his *Toledot ha-Emunah ha-Yisre'elit* (vol. 4 pt. 1, 276ff. and 481ff.), however, has proved beyond question that there is no evidence in the Talmuds for an era of the *soferim*, and talmudic tradition does not attribute a single law to this era. The first Mishnah of *Avot* has no reference whatsoever to *soferim* or to generations of *soferim*. Though the Talmud does mention regulations by Ezra and by the men of the Great Synagogue, it does not attribute any decrees or *halakhah* to scribes between Ezra and the tannaitic era. The word *sofer* in both talmudic and later literature is used as a general designation for Torah scholars and copyists from various eras and of different categories. In Ben Sira (39:1–11) the honorable status of the scribe is described. In the Apocrypha and in the New Testament, scribes appear side by side with other notables (see I Macc. 7:12–13; Test. Patr. Levi 8:17; Jos. Ant. 12:142; Luke 11:42–52; etc.). The designation scribes is equivalent to sages and elders, but in several places it alludes to holders of offices in the Temple and in the courts. The meaning of the term varies similarly in talmudic literature. Thus, from the passage in *Sotah* (15a) where Rabban Gamaliel said to the scholars, "Scribes! permit me and I shall expound it allegorically like a jewel," scribes are identical with the scholars. In another passage, however, R. Eliezer the Great says: "Since the day the Temple was destroyed, the scholars began to be like scribes, and the scribes like **ḥazzanim*," etc. (Sot. 9:15), and from this it seems that the status of the scribes was regarded as being lower than that of scholars. In *Leviticus Rabbah* 9:2 (and parallels) the *soferim* are referred to as teachers of Bible in contrast to *mashnim*, teachers of the Mishnah. The phrase "the words of the scribes" in the talmudic sources always refers to the statements of earlier scholars of the Oral Law, and can refer to statements from those attributed to Moses to those of the generation immediately preceding the compilation of the Mishnah (cf. e.g., Yev. 2:4 with Yev. 21a; Or. 3:9 with Kid. 38a; Tosef. Ta'an. 2:6; and Maim. Comm. Kel. 17:12). The sages emphasized the need to heed the words of the *soferim*: "My son! Be more heedful of the words of the *soferim* than of those of the Written Law[Torah]. For the words of the Torah contain positive and negative injunctions (for the transgression of which there is no death penalty) but whoever transgresses the words of the scribes incurs the penalty of death" (Er. 21b; cf. TJ, Ber. 1:5, 3b). The purpose of stringency was to prevent their doctrines being regarded as of secondary importance (cf. Tosef. Ta'an. 2:6, and parallels): "These are the words of the Torah, and the words of Torah do not need strengthening, but those are the words of the *soferim* and the words of the *soferim* require strengthening." They even went so far as to state that God showed Moses the *dikdukei Torah* and the *dikdukei soferim* and the innovations which the *soferim* would introduce in the future (Meg. 19b).

BIBLIOGRAPHY: Schuerer, Hist, index; Halevy, Dorot, passim; Graetz, Hist, index.

[Yitzhak Dov Gilat]

SOFERIM (Heb. סוֹפְרִים), one of the *minor tractates printed in the Talmud editions at the end of the order of *Nezikin*. Its first main division (chs. 1–5) treats the writing of *Sifrei Torah*. The tosafists call it one of the "outside books" (Pes. 40b s.v. *avel*). Another of these tractates is *Sefer Torah*, to which *Soferim* bears a close relationship. *Soferim* contains 21 chapters divided into 255 paragraphs, which, like the *mishnayot* in the Jerusalem Talmud, are called *halakhot*.

Chapters 1–9 cover writing materials; qualifications required in the writer; language and translation of the Bible and laws governing the mode of writing, particularly in reference to the names of God; sewing and repairing the parchment; preservation of scrolls that have become ritually unfit for use; textual variants; and readings of particular words and passages. Chapters 10–17 include regulations for reading on general and particular occasions; reading of particular passages; requirements of a quorum; some further regulations in writing, particularly the Hagiographa, with special attention to the Book of Esther; benedictions for reading these; qualifications for reading; sanctity of religious writings and appurtenances; *tefillin* and *mezuzot*; Torah study; the *Haggadah*; and readings for festivals and New Moon. Chapters 18–21 address daily and festival psalms and other liturgical matters; observances for the Day of Atonement; prayers for Tishah be-Av; blessings and readings on Ḥanukkah, and laws in connection therewith; rejoicing in Nisan; Purim observances; and various *aggadot*.

This division is one of convenience but does not follow the dates of compilation, in which scholars see very much disorder. It is also not regarded as a unity but as a compilation of three distinct works belonging to different dates, with various interpolations. Most scholars regard the work as of Palestinian origin, though it is generally dated about the middle of the eighth century. In various matters the regulations of *Soferim* are accepted in practice as against the Talmud, e.g., reading

Exodus 32:11–14, 34:1–10 on fasts (17:7), whereas the Mishnah prescribes "the Curses and Blessings" (Lev. 26:3–end). *Soferim* appeared in English translation in the Soncino minor tractates (1965).

BIBLIOGRAPHY: J. Mueller, *Massekhet Soferim* (1878); Weiss, Dor, 2 (1903), 217–8; M. Higger, *Soferim* (1937).

[Harry Freedman]

SOFIA, capital of Bulgaria. Jews lived in Sofia from the first centuries of the Christian era under Roman rule. Later they were known as *Romaniots. Their synagogue ("Kahal de los Griegos"; the Greek Synagogue) stood until 1898. When Jews were expelled from Hungary in 1376, some of them came to Sofia. A second wave of Hungarian Jews was brought by Sultan Suleiman the Magnificent, after the short-lived conquest of Buda in 1526. After the expulsion from Bavaria in 1470, Ashkenazi Jews arrived in Sofia, where they established their own community. The refugees from Spain also established a new community. During the 16th century, there were three separate communities – the Romaniot, the Ashkenazi, and the Sephardi. Eventually they amalgamated into a single Sephardi community. Even though the Ashkenazi Jews integrated with the Sephardi Jews, their synagogue was, until in recent times, known as the Kehillat Ashkenazim in order to distinguish it from that of the newer Ashkenazim, who came from Russia, Romania, Hungary, Germany, and Galicia.

During the 16th and 17th centuries, the Jews of Sofia worked as craftsmen and businessmen. The town was a transit center for goods which were sent from Salonika to Bucharest, Belgrade, and other cities. After an abortive rebellion against the Turkish rule, the merchants of *Dubrovnik (Ragusa), who held an important place in the economic life of Sofia, were compelled to cede their position to their Jewish rivals, in whose hands the whole of the commerce became concentrated during the 17th century. At the time the community of Sofia numbered 2,000. When Bulgaria became independent in 1878, the Jews saved the city from pillage and fire. The largest Jewish population of the country was then located in Sofia (according to the official census of 1880, numbering 4,146). Two Jews were appointed to the municipal council. The Jews lived in a quarter which was known as Hagada, situated in the center of the present city. In 1884–85 there were 6,000 Jews in Sofia and in 1920, 16,196. During the Serbo-Bulgarian war in 1885, the community set up a hospital which treated the war casualties. The Jews of the town engaged in commerce, crafts, and brokerage. Three-quarters of them barely earned enough to sustain themselves.

During World War II, in May 1943, an expulsion decree was issued against the Jews of Sofia. At that time they numbered some 25,000. The project to exterminate them, however, was not carried out. After the mass immigration of Bulgarian Jewry to Israel (until 1949), 5,000 Jews remained in Sofia. In 1951 there were 5,259 Jews, in 1964 4,000, and in 2004 around 3,000. (For the postwar period, see also *Bulgaria.)

BIBLIOGRAPHY: Rosanes, Togarmah, passim; S. Mézan, *Les Juifs espagnols en Bulgarie* (1925), 19, 75; E. Condurachi, in: REJ, 1 (1937), 90f.; A. Hananel and E. Eškenazi, *Fontes hebraici ad res oeconomicas socialesque balcanicarum*, 1 (1958), 47–48.

[Simon Marcus]

SOISSONS, town in the Aisne department, N. France. There was a large Jewish community in Soissons by the beginning of the 12th century at the latest. At this time Guibert de Nogent produced his treatise, *De incarnatione contra Judaeos*, with the aim of severing the good relations between the Jews and Count John I of Soissons. At a later date Count Raoul granted the convent of Notre Dame an annual income of six gold bezants for as long as the Jews remained in the town; they were thus untouched by the expulsion of 1182. The community possessed a synagogue, probably in the center of the Juiverie, which was situated under the castle walls, a first cemetery close to the early enclosure of the town (where an early 13th-century gravestone of one Hannah was found), and a second cemetery near St. Christopher's Gate. Jews lived in many of the villages around Soissons. The medieval community came to an end with the expulsion in 1306. Jewish scholars in the town included the commentator Shemaiah, probably a relative and pupil of Rashi. At the beginning of World War II about 80 Jews lived in Soissons but no community was reestablished after the war.

BIBLIOGRAPHY: Gross, Gal Jud, 647f.; A. de Montaiglon, in: *Bulletin de la Société Historique et Archéologique de Soissons*, 2nd series, 4 (1873), 328f.; G. Bowgin, *La Commune de Soissons* (1908), index; J. Saincir, *Le Diocèse de Soissons*, 1 (1935), 144; Z. Szajkowski, *Analytical Franco-Jewish Gazetteer* (1966), 152.

[Bernhard Blumenkranz]

SOKAL, town in Lvov district, Ukraine; within Poland until 1772 and between the two world wars. Jews first settled there in the middle of the 16th century. In 1578 the municipality restricted the number of Jews in the town to two families, who were authorized to occupy two houses. In 1609 the Jews reached an agreement with the townsmen authorizing them to erect 18 houses and a synagogue, and to acquire land for a cemetery. In 1613 the houses of the Jews were destroyed by a fire which broke out in the town; Sokal was devastated by the Cossacks under *Chmielnicki in 1648. In the 17th and 18th centuries Sokal was among the important communities in the province (*galil*) of Chelm-Belz within the framework of the Councils of *Lands. A printing press was established there around 1755. During the period of Austrian rule, from 1772 to 1918, the Jews were mainly occupied in small-scale commerce, crafts, and transportation. *Ḥasidism had considerable influence within the community. The Jewish population numbered 2,408 (36% of the total) in 1880; 3,272 in 1890; 3,778 (41%) in 1900; 4,516 (39%) in 1910; 4,360 (43%) in 1921; and 5,520 in 1931. Between the two world wars, Sokal was within Poland and Zionism played an important role in community life.

[Shimon Leib Kishenboim]

Holocaust Period

After the outbreak of World War II Jewish refugees from Belzec, Krystynopol, and from cities in western Poland arrived in Sokal, and during the period of Soviet rule (1939–41) the Jewish population increased to more than 6,000. The refugees were lodged in synagogues as well as private homes and a special committee was established to aid them. Because of Sokal's proximity to the German border, the Jews of the town witnessed the tragedy of the Jews of Chelm and Hrubieszow in November 1939 when they were brought by the Germans to the Bug River, but the Soviet border patrol prevented the survivors of the "death march" from crossing the river to the Soviet side. In the summer of 1940, refugees in Sokal from western Poland were deported to the Soviet interior. On June 23, 1941, a day after the outbreak of the German-Soviet war, the Germans captured Sokal. Eight persons were shot the same day. On June 30, 1941, the Ukrainian police killed 200 Jews near a brick factory in the neighborhood of Sokal. In the winter of 1941 and early in 1942, the Jews were subjected to forced labor, economic restrictions, and physical attacks. On Sept. 17, 1942, an *Aktion* took place in which 2,000 Jews were deported to the death camp at *Belzec. On Oct. 15, 1942, a ghetto was set up in Sokal into which more than 5,000 Jews, including Jews from Steniatyn, Radziechow, Lopatyn, Witkow, Tartakow, and Mosty Wielkie were concentrated. The ghetto had only four wells and its inhabitants suffered from a severe water shortage. On Oct. 24–28, 1942, 2,500 Jews from Sokal were deported to Belzec. On May 27, 1943, a final *Aktion* took place. The ghetto was liquidated and the town was declared *judenrein*. Some 30 persons survived in forests and hideouts.

[Aharon Weiss]

BIBLIOGRAPHY: Halpern, Pinkas, index; B. Wasiutyński, *Ludność żydowska w Polsce w wiekach XIX i XX* (1930), 118, 147, 152; K. Lepszy (ed.), *Polska w okresie drugiej wojny północnej* (1957), index.

SOKOLKA, town in Bialystok province, N.E. Poland; until 1795 within Poland; until 1807 under Prussia; subsequently until 1915 the town belonged to Russia, reverting to Poland after World War I. Jews settled in Sokolka in the latter half of the 17th century. In 1698 they were granted a royal privilege giving them rights to engage in commerce and own property. There were 522 Jewish poll-tax payers in Sokolka and its surroundings in 1765. The Jewish population of the town numbered 1,454 in 1847; 2,651 (52% of the total) in 1897; and 2,821 (46.4%) in 1921. Jews there earned their livelihood from trade in agricultural produce, hides, and crafts. Jewish contractors developed the tanning industry in Sokolka from 1868, which before the outbreak of World War I employed 700 workers. The Jewish workers' movement began to organize locally in the late 19th century; Zionists began activity in the early 20th century. All Jewish parties were active there between the two world wars. Jews from Sokolka joined the Third Aliyah and helped to found *Kefar Malal in Ereẓ Israel. Jews were occupied in over 80% of the businesses and crafts in the town. The American Jewish Joint Distribution Committee helped to set up a tanning cooperative. Community institutions included schools of the Yavneh, *Tarbut, and CYSHO, a Maccabi sports club, and two libraries.

[Dov Rabin]

Holocaust Period

After the outbreak of World War II a large number of refugees from the surrounding areas and western Poland reached the town. By the end of 1939 there were some 9,000 Jews in Sokolka after it passed to Soviet rule (1939–41), and the activities of the Jewish community institutions and other Jewish bodies ceased. After the outbreak of the German-Soviet war, the town was captured by the Germans (June 27, 1941), and the Jewish population subjected to forced labor, restrictions on movement, and financial payments. In the fall of 1941 a ghetto was established. On Nov. 5, 1942, all the Jews in the town were assembled, a *Selektion* was carried out, and most were deported to the camp at Kelbasin, where all the Jews of the surrounding area were taken. A few weeks later the Jews from Sokolka were transported to the death camp of *Treblinka. Over 200 remained in the ghetto in Sokolka and worked in a factory for felt boots. These few were murdered on Jan. 18, 1943. The town was declared *judenrein*. Isaac Goldstein from Sokolka headed the unit of Ha-No'ar ha-Ẓiyyoni in the Warsaw ghetto uprising of April 1943. Also from Sokolka was Leah Perlstein, a leader of He-Ḥalutz in Poland who distinguished herself by acting as a liaison officer between the Warsaw ghetto and the Polish underground movement to obtain arms for the uprising; she was killed during her mission.

[Aharon Weiss]

BIBLIOGRAPHY: Z.Honik, in: *YIVO Bleter*, 2 (1931), 454; *Sefer Sokolka* (1968); J. Shleymkovich, in: *Folkshilf*, no. 9 (1937); B. Wasiutyński, *Ludność żydowska w Polsce w wiekach XIX i XX* (1930), 83, 87, 89.

SOKOLOF, PHIL (1921–2004), U.S. health crusader. Sokolof, who was born in Omaha, Nebraska, went into home building after four years with a band as a song-and-dance man. He found a way to produce certain construction components less expensively and started producing them himself. He founded the Phillips Manufacturing Company in 1955 and became a millionaire several times over. But in 1966, after a heart attack, he educated himself to the dangers of high cholesterol and began bombarding food manufacturers and others. His campaign gained ammunition from evidence linking cholesterol with clogged arteries and heart disease. He founded the nonprofit National Heart Savers Association in 1985 and supported free cholesterol screenings around the country. His organization's tests of cholesterol levels helped to persuade Congress to proclaim a National Know Your Cholesterol Month and to persuade food processors to cut down on the use of highly saturated coconut and palm oils. The foundation was also credited with helping to pass legislation strengthening requirements for listing cholesterol content on food labels. He wrote *Add Years to Your Life* (2002).

[Stewart Kampel (2nd ed.)]

SOKOLOW, ANNA (1915–2000), U.S. choreographer, teacher, and one of the outstanding figures in American modern dance. She grew up on New York's Lower East Side and began experimenting while a soloist with the Martha Graham Company (1930–38). Her first group work, *Anti-War Cycle*, was presented in 1933 by the Workers' Dance League. As a soloist, she toured Russia in 1934, and her first company, the Dance Unit, gave concerts in the U.S. and Mexico during the 1930s. Under Mexican government auspices, she formed the first Mexican modern dance company, *La Paloma Azul*. Her work reached an artistic turning point in 1953, when she choreographed *Lyric Suite* (to music by Alban Berg) in Mexico. It was performed in New York by nine dancers from the New Dance Group, which became her new company. Other works included *Rooms* (1955), a study of urban loneliness, *Dreams* (1961), an "indictment of the Nazi concentration camps," and *Déserts* (1967). Anna Sokolow made frequent visits to Israel, where she acted as teacher. In 1953 she was invited to Israel to work with the *Inbal dance group. Following this, she was invited yearly until the 1990s and choreographed for the major companies in Israel, including *Bat-Sheva and the Kibbutz Dance Company. Her most important contribution was the creation of the Lyric Theater in Tel Aviv (1962) with the best available dancers of the time, thus creating the first professional dance company in Israel. With them she created 11 original works in four programs. Sokolow introduced new performing standards and educated a new generation of dancers who became active in all major Israeli dance companies.

ADD. BIBLIOGRAPHY: IED, vol. 5, 637a–638b.

[Marcia B. Siegel / Bina Shiloah (2nd ed.)]

SOKOLOW, NAHUM (1859–1936), Hebrew writer, pioneer in modern Hebrew journalism, and president of the World Zionist Organization. Sokolow was born in Wyszogrod, near Plock, Poland, into a family with deep roots in Poland that had produced many rabbis and public figures. He received a fundamental Jewish education and he also acquired a general education. This mixture of Jewish and world culture marked him later in life as one of the few Hebrew authors with a command (both written and oral) of a number of other languages. He also had a command of the treasures of non-Jewish literature and culture, and this contributed to the charm he had for leading personalities of the Western world. After his marriage at the age of 17 he lived in his father-in-law's house in Makow, and pursued his studies. He began to write in a variety of fields – commentaries on Jewish topics, poetry, stories, plays, scientific articles, etc. His first literary effort was a report from Plock to the Hebrew weekly *Ivri Anokhi* (1874).

Sokolow continued sending reports to the newspaper *Ha-Ẓefirah* (1876) and soon became its regular columnist on scientific affairs, a subject that was close to the heart of the editor, Ḥ.Z. *Slonimski. In a short while, Sokolow became one of the paper's most famous writers. His first book also dealt with the natural sciences, geography and geology (*Maẓẓukei Ereẓ*, 1878). At the same time, he developed his writings in other languages (Yiddish, German, and Polish). Finally, Sokolow moved to Warsaw (1880), where his writing took a decisive turn with the publication of the first of a series of articles in *Ha-Ẓefirah* entitled "*Ẓofeh le-Veit Yisrael*," which became most popular. The column treated current affairs in a feature-writing ("feuilleton") style in a rich and sparkling Hebrew. From that time he was the regular columnist for *Ha-Ẓefirah* and gradually transformed the paper into a lively publication, finally becoming its acting editor (his name appeared among the list of editors only from 1886).

Sokolow was the first in the history of the Hebrew press and literature to create a vast reading public, which was an unusual mixture encompassing *maskilim* (Western-oriented secularists), extreme Orthodox rabbis, and religious Jews. He knew how to direct the style of his writing at a variety of different circles because he was close to all of them. Sokolow expressed reservations about the Ḥibbat Zion movement when it first appeared, although he was simultaneously drawn toward it emotionally. He wished to restrain the enthusiasm of the early 1880s and even attacked J.L. *Pinsker's *Autoemancipation*, continuing in this line until the First Zionist Congress (1897). In the meantime, he published books in the fields of history and belles lettres. His textbook on the English language for Yiddish-speakers was widely distributed at the beginning of the great wave of migration to the United States, after the pogroms in southern Russia (1881). He also published an adaptation of Laurence *Oliphant's book on Ereẓ Israel entitled *Ereẓ Ḥemdah* (1885). When he began to feel confined by his position with *Ha-Ẓefirah*, Sokolow started to publish the voluminous yearbooks *Ha-Asif* (6 published, 1885–94), in which all types of literature were presented. These collections had a success unprecedented in the annals of Hebrew literature in the scope of their distribution. These collections marked the beginning of Hebrew literature as a public medium and not only as a vehicle for personal entertainment.

In the spring of 1886 *Ha-Ẓefirah* became a daily, and Sokolow himself filled practically every issue, in addition to his many writings in other periodicals and other languages. With the aid of Y.H. Zagorodski, he also published the first lexicon of Hebrew authors (including some scholars on Judaism who wrote in other languages) entitled *Sefer ha-Zikkaron* (1889). A decisive turn took place in his life with the appearance of Theodor *Herzl. At first he received Herzl's *Jewish State* with reservations. But after his participation in the First Zionist Congress as the correspondent for *Ha-Ẓefirah* and his meeting with the Zionist leader, he became one of Herzl's greatest admirers, and turned *Ha-Ẓefirah* into his most loyal and dedicated Hebrew organ. Through this transformation, Sokolow's writing became even more ramified, and there was almost no literary genre that he did not attempt, especially in his efforts to bring Orthodox circles closer to Zionism through a series of articles that grew into entire volumes (*Le-Maranan u-le-Rabbanan*, 1901).

Sokolow translated Herzl's Zionist novel *Altneuland* into Hebrew under the title *Tel Aviv* (a site mentioned in Ezek.

3:15), by which he meant to symbolize the original name of the book (old-new land; *tel* meaning a hill of ruins, *aviv* meaning spring), and thereby inspired the name for the first Jewish city in Ereẓ Israel. During the controversy over the *Uganda Scheme, his newspaper was the most devoted to Herzl and the plan, although it also published articles against the Scheme. Above all, Sokolow wanted to preserve the unity of the Zionist Organization. As part of his program to combine public activities with literary endeavor, he became involved in the plan to publish a general encyclopedia in Hebrew, which never materialized because of the upheaval surrounding the 1905 revolution in Russia.

At the beginning of 1906, *Ha-Ẓefirah* ceased publication, and in the same year Sokolow was invited by David *Wolffsohn to serve as the general secretary of the World Zionist Organization. His first act in this position was to establish the official Hebrew weekly of the Zionist Organization, **Haolam* (1907), which continued to be published up to and after the establishment of the State of Israel. From that point on, Sokolow's life was intimately connected with the history of the Zionist movement (see *Zionism). From his position as general secretary he rose to become a member of the Zionist Executive in 1911 and was reelected in 1913. He continued to write throughout this period, especially after *Ha-Ẓefirah* was renewed in 1910. He won the esteem of his readers and the Hebrew literary world with the publication of a selection of his articles (1902) and a jubilee book in his honor (1904), as well as by his editing of a literary collection to commemorate the 50th anniversary of the publication of *Ha-Ẓefirah* (1912).

During his period of service as general secretary of the Zionist Organization, Sokolow began meeting with European personalities, an activity which continued until the end of his life. During his first visit to the United States and Canada (1913) he won the support of many Jews and non-Jews for the Zionist cause. Close to the outbreak of World War I, Sokolow visited Ereẓ Israel as head of an investigating committee of the Zionist Organization, and after the trip he published for the first time his impressions of the country and continued to do so after his succeeding visits. With the outbreak of World War I, he moved to London and, together with Weizmann, was involved in Zionist political activity in England and in other countries (France, Italy, etc.). After Herzl, Sokolow was the first Zionist to have an audience with the pope (and the first Jew to have an audience with Pope Benedict XV) whom he informed on the affairs of the Zionist movement (1917). He played an important role in the efforts which eventually achieved the *Balfour Declaration, and was the head of the committee which prepared the wording of the declaration, in addition to procuring the approval of statesmen from other countries for it. His name thus became linked to that of Weizmann, and he became one of the most outstanding figures in the Zionist movement both through his connections with diplomats of many nations and his deep roots in the Jewish world.

During the period of political work for the Balfour Declaration, Sokolow was also involved in preparing his monumental work entitled *History of Zionism, 1600–1918*, which came out in two volumes in 1919 (a shorter German edition came out in 1921). The work not only provides a comprehensive description of the Jewish people's attachment to Ereẓ Israel but also describes the relationship of non-Jews to the idea of the return of the Jews to Ereẓ Israel, and this made it a pioneering endeavor. He revealed a mass of new material, all but unknown until his time, especially on the personalities in England who had preached the return of the Jews to their homeland for hundreds of years. Sokolow wished to prove indirectly that the Balfour Declaration grew out of a rich tradition in England. In his introduction to the book, Lord Balfour expressed his own credo through a defense of the Zionist idea against opposition from a number of viewpoints. In his comprehensive introduction, Sokolow defined the foundations of Zionism in the following points:

A home for Jews who are materially or morally suffering; a home for Jewish education, learning, and literature; a source of idealism for Jews all over the world; a place in which Jews can live a healthy Jewish life; a revival of the language of the Bible; the resurrection by civilization and industry of the old home of our fathers, long neglected and ruined; the creation of a sound, strong Jewish agricultural class.

Thus Sokolow combined all three aspects of the practical, political, and cultural Zionism. Although he himself was involved in political activity throughout the years, he always emphasized the other two aspects as well.

After World War I, when the solution of all problems, including the Jewish problem, was the prevailing mood toward peace, Sokolow headed the Jewish delegation to the Paris Peace Conference. His appearance before the conference on Feb. 27, 1919, was most impressive. Weizmann described Sokolow's speech in *Trial and Error* (1949, p. 243): "… without being sentimental, it was as if two thousand years of Jewish suffering rested on his shoulders. His quiet, dignified utterance made a very deep impression on the assembly." From that time on, Sokolow appeared at every general Jewish and Zionist assembly, and was chairman of most of them. When the Zionist Executive was consolidated after the war, he was elected as its head. He was also the head of the Comité des Délégations Juives, the representative of world Jewry at the League of Nations, succeeding Julian *Mack and Louis *Marshall. In this position he formulated the Jewish claims, especially that of European Jewry, most notably in the field of securing Jewish rights in the new countries created after the conflict. At the Zionist London Conference (1920), which adjusted Zionist policy and organization to the post-war reality, Sokolow was not only one of the principal speakers, but also the one who named the new Zionist fund *Keren Hayesod. From that time until the end of his life he traveled throughout the Jewish world on behalf of the fund. He again visited Palestine in the spring of 1921, at the same time that Winston *Churchill was there, as head of the Zionist Commission (instead of M. *Ussishkin, who was then in the United States). He succeeded in undoing the effect of the Arab memoranda sent to Churchill, and took the opportunity to participate in the founding of the Hebrew Writers' Union in Ereẓ Israel. He also did much to encourage the *yishuv* after the anti-Jewish riots that had taken place at the time. Sokolow was chosen chairman of the 12th Zionist Congress (the first congress to convene after the war; Carlsbad, 1921) and was chairman of every succeeding congress until his death, continuing the tradition of Max *Nordau by speaking on the situation of the Jews of the Diaspora. Although he could not match Nordau's eloquence, he was far more knowledgeable than Nordau about what was happening throughout the Diaspora, in the East as well as the West. At the congresses he proved his skill in cajoling the conflicting factions, and his concluding motto, "It was a difficult Congress but a good one," became famous. He was in great demand as a public speaker. During his trips he would constantly meet with public leaders and heads of government and would obtain pro-Zionist statements from them.

When the enlarged *Jewish Agency was established in 1929, Sokolow became chairman of its Executive. At that time, Arab riots again broke out in Palestine, and opposition, headed by Weizmann, grew in the Zionist movement against the policy of the Zionist Executive toward the Mandatory government. This subject created a storm at the 17th Zionist Congress (1931) and resulted in Weizmann's failure to be reelected president of the Zionist Organization. Sokolow was chosen in his place. He was reelected at the 18th Congress (1933), and continued in the presidency until Weizmann was again elected president at the 19th Congress (1935). During Sokolow's term as president, the Nazis rose to power in Germany, and the United States, which was the main source of Zionist funds, underwent a financial crisis. Sokolow again set out on a series of trips and mobilized a substantial amount of capital to meet the pressing needs of the Zionist endeavor. In 1935, when his last term as president of the organization ended, he was chosen honorary president of the Zionist Organization and the Jewish Agency and chairman of its Department of Education and Culture and of Mosad Bialik. He died in London. In 1956 his remains were reinterred on Mount Herzl in Jerusalem.

With all his dedicated and ramified activity in the Zionist movement for two generations, Sokolow was above all a Hebrew author and journalist (in his case it is sometimes difficult to draw an exact dividing line between these two areas of literary activity). He was also a skilled writer in a number of other languages (notably Yiddish, Polish, German, English, and French). Sokolow was the idol of the Hebrew reading public for almost three generations, and his writings are a unique example of the development of Hebrew literature from the 1870s until the end of his life in the 20th century. The reading public that Sokolow created was not attracted to the Hebrew language by romanticism and nostalgia, but by the response provided by the new Hebrew literature to their actual cultural and social needs. Sokolow created a specific personal genre of writing in each generation, at first as a writer on current affairs and afterward in other roles, especially as a journalist writing what is called in Europe the "feuilleton." He knew the secret of how to be innovative in every new generation and was thus constantly surprising and refreshing, as, for example, in his last years with his endeavors in the field of belles lettres and in his famous series of articles *Ishim* ("Personalities"), which were begun many years before, and only reached their climax late in his life. His works covering his impressions of his travels are also outstanding. His mosaic style added much to the magic of his writings, which no other Hebrew author could match. At the end of his life he worked on the preparation of a lexicon on the history of the Hebrew language (chapters of which were printed in his lifetime).

Sokolow was Hebrew literature's most prolific author for many years, and Bialik said: "If someone were to be found to collect all of Sokolow's writings – his articles, essays, feuilletons, impressions of travels, studies, stories, etc. – and bring them together in one spot, he would need 300 camels." Over the years he published many books in installments in *Ha-Ẓefirah* and *Haolam*, only a small portion of which was later published in book form: *Barukh Spinoza u-Zemanno* (1929), *Ha-Ani ha-Kibbuẓi* (1930), and *Ishim* (3 vols., 1935). A large portion of these works, however, is still buried in periodicals in Hebrew and in other languages. Shortly before his death he published in English the book *Hibbath Zion* (1935) dealing with the Zionist idea in the modern period. After his death *Sefer Sokolow*, edited by S. *Rawidowitz, was published, containing a selection of his early writings with an evaluation and bibliography of his works (1943). A selection of all types of his works was published in three volumes with a comprehensive monograph on him by G. Kressel (1958–61), who also put out a similar selection in Yiddish (1966).

Sedeh Naḥum, a kibbutz in the Jezreel Valley, is named after Sokolow, as is Bet Sokolow, the journalists' house in Tel Aviv. The Tel Aviv municipal council offers an annual prize in journalism in his honor.

BIBLIOGRAPHY: S. Kling, *Nahum Sokolov, Scholar and Statesman. A Biography* (1957); idem, *Nahum Sokolov, Servant of His People* (1960), includes bibliography; C. Weizmann, *Trial and Error* (1949), index; L. Stein, *The Balfour Declaration* (1961), index; Kressel, Leksikon, 2 (1967), 481–7; LNYL, 6 (1965), 318–25. **ADD. BIBLIOGRAPHY:** F. Sokolov, *Avi: N. Sokolov* (1970); idem, *Nahum Sokolov: Life and Legend* (1975); S. Stiftel, *Darko shel N. Sokolov min ha-Pozitivizm ha-Yehudi-Polani el ha-Tenu'ah ha-Ẓiyyonit* (1994).

[Getzel Kressel]

SOKOLOW PODLASKI, town in Warszawa province, Poland. A Jewish community was first organized there at the end of the 16th century. In 1665 the owner of the town, Jan Kazimierz Krasiński (1607–1669), granted the Jews judicial powers among other rights, and accorded Jewish craftsmen the same status as that of the Christians. In the 18th century many Jews engaged in such crafts as weaving, tailoring, furriery, and tanning; they also engaged in wholesale commerce of agricultural produce and cloth. There were 163 Jews who paid the poll tax living in Sokolow in 1765. The Jewish population numbered 1,186 (37% of the total population) in 1827; 2,275 (62%) in 1857; 4,248 (59%) in 1897; 4,430 (55%) in 1921; and 5,027 in 1931.

Sokolow became noted as a center of *Ḥasidism. During the middle of the 19th century R. Elimelech was rabbi of Sokolow, and during the 20th century, the *ẓaddik* Isaac Zelig Morgenstern (d. 1940), a great-grandson of Menahem Mendel the ẓaddik of *Kotsk, held rabbinical office and acted as leader of the Ḥasidim.

After World War I, the economy of the town was disrupted as a result of antisemitic activities. In 1937–38 there were attacks on Jews accompanied by bloodshed.

[Shimshon Leib Kirshenboim]

Holocaust Period

At the outbreak of World War II there were 4,000 Jews in Sokolow. The German army entered the town on Sept. 20, 1939, and immediately began terrorizing the Jewish population. On Sept. 23, 1939 (the Day of Atonement), the Germans set the local synagogue on fire. In the summer of 1941 a ghetto was established in Sokolow. The Jews there were deported to Treblinka death camp on Sept. 22, 1942. They offered considerable passive resistance, some hiding themselves, but about 500 of those found in hiding were shot on the spot. Another 700 succeeded in fleeing into the surrounding forests, but most of them were shot by German armed units who searched the forests. Groups of young Jews joined small partisan units operating in the vicinity. One group entered the Bialystok region and joined the guerrillas there.

The Jewish community was not reconstituted in Sokolow Podlaski after the war. Organizations of former residents were established in Israel, the United States, France, and Argentina.

[Stefan Krakowski]

BIBLIOGRAPHY: R. Mahler, *Yidn in Amolikn Poyln in Likht fun Tsifern* (1958), index; B. Wasiutyński, *Ludność żydowska w Polsce w wiekach XIX i XX* (1930), 35, 65, 182, 201; S. Bronsztejn, *Ludność żydowska w Polsce w okresie międzywojennym* (1943), 278; *Yevreyskaya Starina*, 4 (1911), 286–8; M. Gelbart (ed.), *Sefer ha-Zikkaron, Sokolov Podlask* (Heb. and Yid., 1962); P. Granatstein, *Mayn Khoyrev Shtetl Sokolov* (1946).

SOLA, ABRAHAM DE (1825–1882), rabbi and *ḥazzan*. Born in London, de Sola was the sixth child of the renowned Dutch ḥazzan David Aaron de *Sola, leader of the English Sephardim. Abraham graduated from London Jews' College, where he was a student of the Oriental scholar, Louis *Loewe. He immigrated to Canada via New York in 1847 to begin his ministry at Sheerith Israel in Montreal (a position he obtained through correspondence). Until his death in New York, where he was visiting with his sister, he served his congregation with honor and distinction for 35 years. In many of his sermons and scholarly writings, he expressed his views on the reconciliation between the natural sciences and religion. His long association with McGill University, beginning as a Hebrew lecturer in 1848 and later as professor of Hebrew and Oriental Literature from 1853, earned him, in 1858, an honorary doctor of laws degree (the first to be awarded to a Jewish minister in both America and England). He was also elected as an honorary member of the Natural History Society, before which he gave many lectures. In 1878, he completed his revision of the Sephardic liturgy (based on the respective multivolume editions of his father and Isaac Lesser). His prayer books became the basis for the liturgy of Sephardic synagogues throughout North America, until superseded by David de Sola *Pool's more recent revision in the late 1930s. Like his father and ḥazzanic forebears, whose musical tradition he preserved, he combined "modernism" with "uncompromising Orthodoxy," and mindful of his Sephardi heritage, his life and works served as an "unsurpassed model" well into the 20th century. His writings include *Sermons in Manuscript* (Canadian Jewish Congress Archives, Montreal); *A Jewish Calendar for Fifty Years: Montreal* (1854, with Jacques J. Lyons); *The Sanatory Institutions of the Hebrews as Exhibited in the Scriptures and Rabbinical Writings and as Bearing upon Modern Sanatory Regulations* (1861).

BIBLIOGRAPHY: E. Miller, *Abraham de Sola Papers. A Guide to the Microfilm* (Montreal, 1970).

[Israel J. Katz (2nd ed.)]

SOLA, DE, Sephardi family in Holland, Britain, and North and South America. After 1492 the family dispersed from Spain to Portugal (where some survived as Marranos, were martyred under the Inquisition, or fled overseas), and Holland. From AARON DE SOLA (18th century), who fled to London and settled in Amsterdam, the various branches in England, Canada, the West Indies, and Holland are directly descended.

The descendants of Aaron's second son, ISAAC DE SOLA (b. 1728), who settled in Curaçao, include General JUAN (ISAAC) DE SOLA (c. 1795–1860), a hero of the South American war of liberation against Spain; BENJAMIN DE SOLA (1818–1882), a leader of the Jewish community in Curaçao; an earlier BENJAMIN DE SOLA (1735–1816) who was physician to the Dutch king William V and published medical works; Abraham de Sola (d. 1753), rabbi, preacher, and *ḥazzan* of the Spanish and Portuguese congregation in London (1722–49); and RAPHAEL SAMUEL MENDES DE SOLA (d. 1761), *ḥakham* of Curaçao from 1749.

Staunch adherence to Orthodoxy particularly distinguishes the descendants of Aaron's eldest son, DAVID DE SOLA (1727–1797). Outstanding among these was David's grandson, DAVID AARON DE SOLA (1796–1860). Born in Amsterdam, he was appointed *ḥazzan* of the London Sephardi community in 1818. He was an able assistant to Haham Raphael *Meldola, whose daughter he married in 1819. After Meldola's death in 1828 De Sola virtually assumed the rabbinical leadership of the English Sephardim and in 1831 delivered the first English sermons authorized by the *Ma'amad, which later published several of his addresses. His *Seder Berakhot* (1829), a manual on the blessings, received the support of Moses *Montefiore, who also encouraged De Sola's work on a new prayer book.

Published as *Forms of Prayer According to the Custom of the Spanish and Portuguese Jews* (5 vols., 1836–38; 1852^2), and with a new English translation, this is generally regarded as his finest work and is still used by the English Sephardim. In collaboration with Morris J. *Raphall, De Sola then prepared *Eighteen Treatises of the Mishnah* with the aim of arming his fellow-opponents of the budding Reform movement (1842; 1845^2, a pirated edition was repudiated by the coauthors). De Sola's other works include an English-Hebrew edition of Genesis, published in collaboration with Raphall and I.L. Lindenthal (1844) and intended to form part of a complete Bible ("The Sacred Scriptures") which, however, never appeared; and a new edition, with English translation, of Wolf *Heidenheim's *Ashkenazi maḥzor, The Festival Prayers, according to the custom of the German and Polish Jews* (5 vols., 1860). This *maḥzor* was often reprinted.

David Aaron de Sola also entered into an ill-fated partnership with M.J. Raphall as coeditor of an Orthodox periodical, *The Voice of Jacob* (1841), later taken over by *The *Jewish Chronicle* which it slightly preceded. One of his best-known works, *The Ancient Melodies of the Liturgy of the Spanish and Portuguese Jews* (1857), written in collaboration with the composer Emanuel *Aguilar, was a pioneering attempt to establish the dates of the Sephardi liturgical compositions. De Sola himself composed tunes for the Sephardi synagogue, and an appendix to *The Ancient Melodies* contains his well-known setting of the **Adon Olam* hymn, which has become popular in Ashkenazi as well as Sephardi congregations of Great Britain. He was influential in organizing the Association for the Promotion of Jewish Literature and other similar bodies. Of his 15 children, Abraham *de Sola became a rabbi in Montreal and a leader of Canadian Orthodoxy.

BIBLIOGRAPHY: A. de Sola, *Biography of David Aaron de Sola…* (1864); JC (Nov. 2, 1860), 4; JE, s.v.; J. Picciotto, *Sketches of Anglo-Jewish History* (1956), 36; R.D. Barnett, in: JHSET, 21 (1968), 1–38 esp. 10ff.; A. de Sola Lazaron, *De Sola Odyssey* (1966).

[Godfrey Edmond Silverman]

SOLAL (Kohen-Solal, Shulal, Sholal), family of North African origin which settled in Majorca toward the close of the 13th century and returned to *Algeria as a result of the Spanish persecutions of 1391. MAIMON SOLAL (Xullel), the son-in-law of the famous physician Leon Masconi, was one of the most influential members of the community of Majorca. Due to his intervention the ancient privileges of the Jews on the island were confirmed in 1385. DAVID KOHEN-SOLAL, a correspondent and colleague of Isaac b. Sheshet Perfet (Ribash), assumed the leadership of the community of Mostaganem as soon as he arrived in Algeria. His son, ABRAHAM (I) Kohen-Solal, a disciple of Simeon b. Ẓemaḥ Duran, was regarded as an important rabbinical authority and a scholar of logic and other religious and secular sciences. He had settled in *Honein, where his son ḤAYYIM KOHEN-SOLAL and his descendant NATHAN (I; D.C. 1460) became wealthy merchants. SAADIAH SOLAL was a rabbi in Tlemcen in the first half of the 15th century. NATHAN (II) (also called also Yehonatan) ben Saadiah was born in 1437 and immigrated to Jerusalem before 1471. He left Jerusalem because he suffered from the Musta'arab leaders of the Jerusalem community and settled in Egypt in 1481. In Egypt he served as spiritual leader and between 1484 and 1502 was the Jewish **nagid* of the *Mamluk Sultanate. He established himself in *Cairo, where he headed the Jewish community and renewed its importance. He died in 1602. He had a special court of law for which the *dayyanim* were appointed by him. Spanish scholars had a high opinion of him. He sometimes returned to Jerusalem but still did not get along with the local Musta'arab leaders. He had seven children: Saadiah, Ephraim, Abraham, Dolca, Masoda, Simah, and Isaac. His son Abraham died in 1482. His nephew Isaac ben Abraham ha-Kohen *Sholal (Solal) was the last *nagid* of Egyptian Jewry, from 1502 until 1517. He was a rich grain merchant and held an important position in the mint of the Mamluk sultan. He was also a scholar. Between 1502 and 1508 or between 1509 and 1513 he resigned from his position, but returned after a time. He was a great philanthropist and founded three yeshivas, one in *Egypt and two in Ereẓ Israel. He had a court of law in Cairo and had an important library with many manuscripts. After the Ottoman conquest of Egypt he lost his rank and settled In Jerusalem, and was active there in *Kabbalah in order to bring about the *ge'ulah* (redemption). He issued new regulations in Jerusalem to develop the community, one of which was the exemption of scholars from taxes. He died on Rosh Ḥodesh Kislev 5285 (1524) in *Jerusalem. His wife, Kamar, was the daughter of R. Abraham ben Ḥayyim (d. 1545). When Isaac died his only son, Abraham, was a little boy. He lived many years in Jerusalem, but because of the difficult economic situation he immigrated to Egypt after 1560. The documents of the Muslim court of law in Jerusalem mention several persons of the Sulal family in the 16th century, including Musa Sulal and Salmon ben Musa Sulal. There are many important **Genizah* and other sources for the Sulal family.

The members of the family who had remained in Algeria continued to rank among its Jewish leaders. MOSES BEN ISAAC KOHEN-SOLAL (d. 1788) was one of the principal merchants of Algiers and an esteemed philanthropist. He established an important commercial branch of his business in *Mogador, *Morocco, where his sons had settled. From 1808 Marseilles became the center of the family's activities. In 1835, after having taken into account his economic and political influence, the sultan requested that the French government accept NISSIM KOHEN-SOLAL as Moroccan consul.

BIBLIOGRAPHY: I. Bloch, *Inscriptions tumulaires…* (1888), 72–74; M. Kayserling, in: REJ, 42 (1901), 278–9; I. Epstein, *Responsa of Rabbi Simon b. Zemah Duran* (1930), 100–1; A. Hershman, *Rabbi Isaac Ben Sheshet Perfet and his Times* (1943), 170; Miège, Maroc, 2 (1964), 61, 89, 95, 141. **ADD. BIBLIOGRAPHY:** S. Assaf, in: *Zion*, 2 (1937), 121–24; 6 (1941), 113–18; A. Rivlin, *Ha-Nagid Rav Yehonatan Sulal Birushalayim* (1927); A. David, in: A. Mirsky, A., Grossman, and Y. Kaplan (eds), *Galut Aḥar Golah* (1988), 374–414.

[David Corcos / Leah Bornstein-Makovetsky (2nd ed.)]

SOLARZ, STEPHEN (1940–), U.S. congressman 1974–94, leading Democratic foreign policy expert. Born and educated in Brooklyn, Solarz is the son of an attorney and Tammany Hall captain. He is a product of the New York public schools and a graduate of Midwood High School. He attended Brandeis University (B.A. 1962), where he edited the student newspaper.

He then went on to Columbia Law School but found law school uninteresting and switched to the graduate school in international affairs. Among others, he studied with Zbigniew Brzezinski, who was to become Jimmy Carter's national security advisor while Solarz was a congressman. He also worked with famed columnist Max *Lerner at the *New York Post* and as national news editor of *Newsfront*. He taught political science at Brooklyn College before running for the State Assembly in 1968 and defeating a 15-term incumbent. He served in the Assembly for five years and ran for Congress in 1974 in the most heavily Jewish district in the nation, serving such areas as Brighton Beach, Sheepshead Bay, and Coney Island. His successor in the State Assembly was Charles *Schumer, destined to be his colleague, ally, and sometimes rival in the years ahead.

Solarz asked for a seat on the House Foreign Affairs Committee. His opening salvo in Congress marked him as an ambitious and aggressive comer with a keen interest in foreign policy. In his first six months he gave 12 speeches and co-sponsored 370 bills. Even his most ardent critics could never call him lazy. He conferred with world leaders and set out to make a name for himself in international relations. As one staff member put it: "Steve is only interested in two things: Brooklyn and the rest of the world."

In the 1980s, he chaired the Asian and Pacific Affairs Subcommittee of the House Foreign Affairs Committee, an area of growing interest to the American people in that decade. He is remembered for his leadership on the Philippines. He left Manila just as Benigno S. Aquino was coming home to challenge President Ferdinand Marcos. Following Aquino's assassination, Solarz returned to Manila for the funeral and proceeded to push the Reagan administration to distance itself from the Marcos government. Shortly after Marcos left for exile in Hawaii, Solarz was at one of the opulent palaces and publicized Imelda's massive shoe collection. He worked closely with Aquino's widow, Corazon, who became president.

In his years of service, Solarz became known as one of the most important and informed members of the House. A world traveler, he conducted himself as a future secretary of state. An ardent defender of Israel, he introduced legislation barring U.S. firms from complying with the boycott of Israel. He freed Jewish women from Syria, enabling them to join the Syrian community in Brooklyn. His performance was, to say the least, impressive. Kurt Stone reports that he was one of the first to back the Afghan rebels, created a plan adopted by the UN to resolve the civil war in Cambodia, was the first American government figure to visit North Korea in 30 years, co-sponsored the resolution to allow President George H.W. Bush to use force in the Persian Gulf and help plan a nuclear freeze strategy.

He introduced the Religious Freedom Restoration Act, designed to permit Orthodox Jews to keep their head covered while on public service, which only passed the House after Solarz was no longer a member.

With the redistricting of New York and its diminished congressional representation, Solarz was forced to run as a white man in a mixed hispanic and black district and was defeated in a 1992 primary. His political influence was weakened by the loss of a key ally in Albany – responsible for redistricting – and because he was caught up in the House Banking scandal when it became known that he and his wife had written 743 overdrafts, which hurt his reelection bid as well. Schumer remained in a safe district and soon became a U.S. senator. Solarz was nominated to serve as ambassador to India, where his expertise would have been of service to the Clinton Administration, but the nomination was withdrawn without explanation. Shortly thereafter his wife, Nina, was found guilty of stealing funds from a charity. She was given probation.

Solarz maintained his interest in foreign policy and has extensive ties to both the Middle East and the Pacific rim. His intelligence and diligence served to make him a diminished but important voice in U.S. foreign policy.

BIBLIOGRAPHY: K.F. Stone, *The Congressional Minyan: The Jews of Capitol Hill* (2000); L.S. Maisel and I.N. Forman, *Jews in American Politics* (2001)

[Michael Berenbaum (2nd ed.)]

SOLDI (Soldi-Colbert), EMILE-ARTHUR (1846–1906), French medalist of Danish descent whose real name was Soldyck. At the age of 23 Soldi received the *Grand Prix de Rome* in medal engraving. An amazingly versatile man, he was an archaeologist and sculptor as well, being also noted in his time as a writer and translator from Danish. The best-known medal by Soldi is his "Homage to the Victims of the Invasion," which refers to the Franco-Prussian War of 1870–71. This medal is still being issued by the French mint. He executed many commemorative and portrait medals.

[Daniel M. Friedenberg]

SOLEL BONEH, *Histadrut concern for building, public works, and industry. Solel Boneh developed out of organized groups of Third Aliyah pioneers that contracted to do road building and quarrying. In 1920 the first agreement was signed between the Agricultural Workers' Union and the Public Works Department of the Mandatory government for the building of a road between Tiberias and Ẓemaḥ. The two existing labor parties ran separate contracting offices, which were merged in 1921 into the Histadrut's Public Works and Building Office, renamed Solel Boneh in 1924. The concern carried out a variety of works throughout the country; it worked for British army camps and helped to lay railroad lines and to build Tel Aviv and Jewish quarters in Jerusalem and Haifa. Its resources were scanty, however, and it went bankrupt during the economic crisis of 1927, renewing its activities only in 1935.

During the Arab riots (1936–39) Solel Boneh was responsible for a number of large-scale pioneering operations: the building of *stockade and watchtower settlements, fortifications in Jewish areas, and police stations in outlying spots. It organized Jewish laborers for work in the ports of Tel Aviv and Haifa and was responsible for the erection of the security fence along the northern frontier (the "Tegart Wall") by hundreds of Jewish workers accommodated in a camp that stretched for miles. During World War II Solel Boneh made an important contribution to the war effort, erecting army camps in many parts of the country. It also built airfields, bridges, roads, and factories abroad in Egypt, Syria, Iraq, Cyprus, Iran, and Bahrain.

On the establishment of the State of Israel (1948), Solel Boneh played a large part in the building of thousands of homes, as well as hospitals, schools, factories, roads, and airfields. In 1958, on the initiative of Pinḥas *Lavon, Solel Boneh was reorganized into three companies: Building and Public Works, Overseas and Harbors Works, and Industry, with subsidiary companies for building materials (Even va-Sid – "Stone and Lime"), sanitary installations (Herouth), and tiles and cement products (Hemar). Among Solel Boneh's outstanding projects were the construction of the atomic research center at Naḥal Sorek; the Hadassah-Hebrew University Medical Center at Ein Kerem, Jerusalem; and the 268-foot chimney of the Haifa power station. As part of the reorganization, workers' representatives were co-opted onto the managements: three out of ten in the Building and Public Works Company, the same proportion in Even va-Sid, and two out of 11 in Herouth. The Overseas and Harbors Works Company has carried out extensive projects in Asia, Africa, and non-Arab countries of the Middle East. At the end of 1970 Solel Boneh employed about 25,000 workers and had a turnover of some $230 million.

With the Histadrut selling off its assets in the 1980s and 1990s, Solel Boneh became part of the Housing and Construction Holding Company Ltd., Israel's largest construction group. In the early 2000s Solel Boneh's turnover exceeded $400 million, and it was involved in building the $1.3 billion Trans-Israel Highway.

BIBLIOGRAPHY: I. Bar-Razon, *Solel Boneh, Darko u-Mahuto* (1958); *Solel Boneh, Hitpatteḥuto u-Mifalav* (n.d.); H. Dan, *Be-Derekh Lo Selulah* (1963).

[Moshe Allon.]

SOLIELI (Soloveichik), MORDECAI (Max; 1883–1957), public figure and biblical scholar. Born in Kovno, Lithuania, Solieli was one of the founders of the Russian-language Zionist newspaper, *Yevreyskaya Zhizn* (later **Razsvet*), in 1904. During the Russian Revolution he left Russia for Lithuania. Solieli was elected to the Lithuanian Sejm (parliament) and served as minister for Jewish affairs (1919–21). In 1921 he was elected to the Zionist executive, but as a result of differences of opinion with Weizmann on the question of establishing a Jewish Agency and because of other problems, he resigned in 1922/23. Solieli (along with Yiẓhak *Gruenbaum, Nahum *Goldmann, and others) was a leader of the "radical faction." From 1923 to 1933 he contributed to the (German) *Encyclopaedia Judaica* in Berlin and edited its Bible and Ancient Near-East section. In 1933 he emigrated to Palestine, where he settled in Haifa and was active in public life there. From 1944 to 1948 he served as the head of the department of education for the *yishuv*. When the State of Israel was established he was made director of its broadcasting service Kol Israel and later became chairman of the public council attached to the broadcasting service. His works include *Toledot Bikkoret ha-Mikra* (with Zalman Rubashov-Shazar, 1925); *Sekhiyyot ha-Mikra* (illustrations and documents in biblical research, 1925); and *Lexicon Biblicum* (Hebrew; posthumous, edited by M. Borochov, 1965).

BIBLIOGRAPHY: Y. Gruenbaum, *Penei ha-Dor* (1957), 306–11.

[Yehuda Slutsky]

°**SOLINUS, CAIUS JULIUS** (third century C.E.), Latin grammarian who wrote a work containing geographical and historical tidbits culled from earlier authors. He paraphrased *Pliny the Elder on Judea (*Natural History*, 5:71ff.; 7:65), sometimes borrowing the exact words of his source. Solinus does not seem to have a clear picture of the material he deals with: he mentions a Lake Sara, probably an error for Pliny's Genasara (Kinneret). Though Pliny comments on the Tiberias hot springs, Solinus overlooks this natural phenomenon and refers only to Lake Tiberias. Besides, in repeating Pliny's views on the *Essenes, he used the present tense, although that sect had long been extinct.

[Jacob Petroff]

SOLIS, family name of 17th-century Portuguese Marranos. A young Lisbonite SIMÃO PIRES SOLIS was accused in 1630 of stealing the sacramental elements from the church of Santa Engrácia and he was condemned to the stake. His hands were chopped off and he was dragged through an incensed mob and burned. For weeks thereafter bands of Old Christians rioted against the New *Christians. Solis's brother, the Franciscan HENRIQUE SOLIS, left Portugal, where he was burned in effigy on March 11, 1640. He made his way to Amsterdam and took the name Eleazar, remaining a leading member of Dutch Jewry until 1656. Other bearers of the Solis name are descendants of the Portuguese court financier DUARTE DA SILVA (1596–1688), whose son ISAAC (DIOGO) DA SILVA SOLIS of Hamburg and grandson ISAAC (FERNANDO) DA SILVA SOLIS of the Low Countries adopted their new names upon re-embracing Judaism. Fernando's father FRANCISCO, reconciled at an auto-da-fé in 1652, became treasurer general to Queen Catherine. He was credited with planning the Spanish victory over the Duke of Crequi in 1673, and in 1682 he was named Marquis de Montfort. The Marrano economist DUARTE GOMES DE SOLIS was a financial authority for the Portuguese crown during the early 1600s. His often reprinted and translated *Discourse on the Commerce of the Two Indies* (Lisbon, 1622) projected a scheme for the development of the territorial lands. The volume *Mémoires Inédits* (ed. by Léon Bourdon, 1955) contains GOMES DE SOLIS's economic reports to the crown for 1621. The proceedings of Madrid's inquisitorial court for 1634 record that an otherwise unknown DIEGO DA SOLIS of Lisbon appeared in the defense of Bartolomé Febos.

The Solis name was carried to the New World as well. One JOSEPH DE SOLIS resided at Pernambuco, Brazil, in 1645–50. During the same time BENJAMIN DE SOLIS was a member of the first synagogue in Dutch Brazil. The U.S. family of *Solis-Cohen traces its ancestry back to SOLOMON DA SILVA SOLIS, who fled to Amsterdam from Spain in about 1665 and married Isabel da Fonseca, daughter of the marquis of Turin, count of Villa Real and Monterey.

BIBLIOGRAPHY: Roth, Marranos, index; A. Wiznitzer, *Jews in Colonial Brazil* (1960), 50 (on Duarte Gomes de); 110 (on Joseph de); 138 (on Benjamin de); R.J.H. Gottheil, in: JQR, 15 (1902/03), 231 (on Diego Rs S.).

SOLIS-COHEN, U.S. family founded by JACOB DA SILVA SOLIS who emigrated to the U.S. in 1803. Jacob's grandfather is reported to have refused succession to the marquisate of Turin, since it would have required his defection from Judaism. Most of Jacob's descendants were born and lived in Philadelphia.

JACOB DA SILVA SOLIS-COHEN (1838–1927), grandson of Jacob da Silva Solis, was a surgeon. During the Civil War he served as surgeon to the Union army, and later did pioneering research work in laryngology which led to an honorary professorship at the Jefferson Medical College, Philadelphia. He founded and edited the *Archives of Laryngology*. His brother LEON DA SILVA SOLIS-COHEN (1840–1884) was a writer of stories and verse often based on old Jewish legends. Another brother, DAVID DA SILVA SOLIS-COHEN (1850–1928) was a lawyer. Born in Philadelphia, he settled in Portland, Oregon, where he was active in Jewish organizations, including the Zionist society. He served as Portland police commissioner (1892–94 and 1898–1902) and mayor (1896–98), and also wrote several books for children.

SOLOMON DA SILVA SOLIS-COHEN (1857–1948), another brother, was a physician and poet. A professor of clinical medicine at Jefferson Medical College (1904–27), he was a fellow of the American Association for the Advancement of Science and a trustee of the U.S. Pharmacopoeia Convention. His basic research in medicine was widely noted. He was active in Jewish affairs, attending the Third Zionist Congress in Basle (1899) and later serving as a (non-Zionist) member of the Jewish Agency. He published a volume of original verse, *When Love Passed By* (1929), and translated many Hebrew poems into English, including Ibn Ezra's *Selected Poems* (trans. 1934). A full bibliography is included in his *Judaism and Science* (1940).

JUDITH DA SILVA (1876–1927), daughter of the second Jacob da Silva Solis-Cohen, was a fashion editor. She wrote

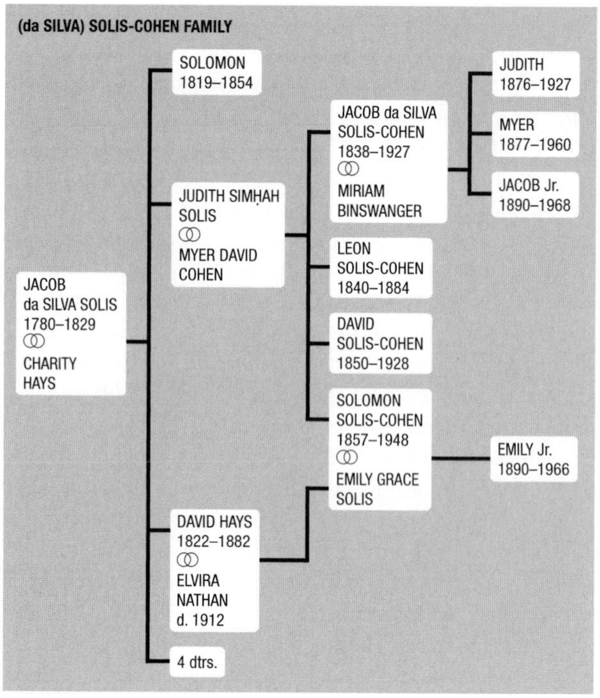

numerous articles and stories on dressmaking and fashion as well as on nature subjects. Her brother MYER DA SILVA (1877–1960), became a physician and later he served on the staff of the graduate school of the University of Pennsylvania and wrote numerous articles on medical subjects. Another brother, JACOB DA SILVA SOLIS-COHEN JR. (1890–1968), was a realtor and genealogist. He served as president of the Jewish Publication Society of America and honorary president of Congregation Mikveh Israel, Philadephia. He wrote a paper on the founder of the family, "Jacob S. Solis: Traveling Advocate of American Judaism" (AJHQ, 52 (1962–63), 310–9). EMILY DA SILVA SOLIS COHEN JR. (1890–1966), daughter of Solomon, was an author and welfare worker. She wrote and translated several popular books for children on Jewish themes, and numerous articles.

BIBLIOGRAPHY: J. Solis-Cohen Jr., in: *The Jewish Experience in America*, 2 (1969), 335–86 (on Jacob da Silva).

[Alan D. Corre]

SOLODAR, ABRAHAM (1890–1936), U.S. Hebrew poet and teacher. Born in Russia, Solodar went to Ereẓ Israel in 1911, and emigrated to the United States in 1926. At an early age he was encouraged in his literary efforts by Bialik in Odessa, and by *Brenner in Tel Aviv.

His volume of lyrical poems, *Shirim*, abounding in folk-motifs, was published posthumously by Menahem *Ribalow (1939) He published *Ba-Teva* (1925), a textbook on natural sciences in Hebrew, a *Hebrew Reader*, and edited the children's weeklies *Alummot* (1922–23) and *Olam ha-Yeladim* (1927–28). Toward the end of his life he edited a Hebrew literary quarterly *Dorenu* (1934) in Chicago.

BIBLIOGRAPHY: H. Bavli, *Ruḥot Nifgashot* (1958), 150–4; Kressel, Leksikon, 2 (1967), 478.

[Eisig Silberschlag]

SOLOMON (Heb. שְׁלֹמֹה; tenth century B.C.E.), son of *David, king of Israel. Born of Bath-Sheba, Solomon was so named by David (II Sam. 12:24; according to the *keri*, Targ. Jon., and according to the Pesh., by his mother), while Nathan called him Jedidiah (Heb. יְדִידְיָה; II Sam. 12:25). Apparently his principal name was Solomon, analogous to the similar Phoenician names שלמין and בעל שלם (cf. the interpretation of the name in I Chron. 22:9), Jedidiah being an affectionate or honorable appellation "because of the Lord" or, according to the Septuagint, "by word of the Lord" (II Sam. 12:25; cf. Deut. 33:12; II Kings 22:1). Following the intervention of Nathan and Bath-Sheba, David decided to have Solomon anointed king in his own lifetime, and not his son *Adonijah the son of Haggith who, supported by some army commanders and a section of "the king's servants" led by Joab son of Zeruiah and Abiathar the priest, was proclaimed king by them beside En-Rogel without David's knowledge (I Kings 1:7, 9, 18, 19, 24, 25, 41, 44). David's mighty men and the Cherethites and the Pelethites, later joined by "the king's servants," sided with Solomon (1:8, 10, 33, 38, 47), who was inducted at the Gihon spring. He was brought down there riding on a mule, and, in the presence of Nathan the prophet and Benaiah son of Jehoiada, was anointed king by Zadok the priest, to the sound of the blowing of the ram's horn and of the people's shout of "Long live King Solomon" (1:32–40). The account does not mention Solomon's qualities by virtue of which he was found worthy of the kingship despite his being one of the king's younger sons (I Chron. 3:1–10). This is ascribed to David's vow to Bath-Sheba, not mentioned in II Samuel, that Solomon would succeed to the throne (I Kings 1:13, 17, 30). Solomon's succession was accompanied by the destruction or banishment of rivals: Joab and Adonijah were killed; Abiathar the priest was banished to Anathoth; the killing of Shimei son of Gera, however, may be explained as a measure taken against potential rebels among survivors of the former royal house.

The Kingdom of Solomon

Already at the outset of his reign Solomon was distinguished as a king who took vigorous action against opponents and did not shrink from a blood vengeance. David's last testament to Solomon should not necessarily be regarded as a tendentious projection by the author of the narrative in order to attribute the bloodshed by the newly crowned king to the instructions of the founder of the royal house. First, David's hostility to Joab was well known. Second, it was certainly unnecessary to ascribe the matter of the sons of Barzillai the Gileadite to David's last testament (2:5–9). Third and primarily, the account of Solomon's elevation contains no exaggerated praise of him. In any event, the bloodshed, associated as it was with a blood vengeance, reflects the upheavals that afflicted the royal court of David, in consequence of which Solomon became king even during his father's lifetime, as emphasized again by the Chronicler in his idealistic, apologetic explanation of Solomon's second, public induction ("And they made Solomon the son of David king the second time," I Chron. 29:20–25; cf. 23:1; 28:1–11, 20–21). Solomon reigned jointly with his father apparently from 967 to 965 B.C.E. and on his own from 965 to 928 B.C.E. According to the biblical account, it was from David that Solomon inherited a kingdom which extended from "beyond the (Euphrates) river to the border of Egypt" (I Kings 5:1). The verse is a late gloss, defining Solomon's territory anachronistically, and attempting to raise Solomon to the status of the great imperialists of the Neo-Assyrian, Neo-Babylonian, and perhaps Persian periods. "Beyond the river" (Heb. *ever ha-nahar* is the equivalent of Akkadian *eber nāri*, first used two centuries after Solomon in Neo-Assyrian sources for the territory west of the Euphrates (Cogan, 213)). Indeed, in the time that has transpired since the appearance of the first edition of the *Encyclopaedia Judaica*, both archaeological evidence and critical study of the biblical texts have undermined the confidence of scholars about the greatness of Solomon. Some scholars despair of recovering the historical Solomon, while others call his very existence into question. J.M. Miller (apud Handy 1–24) has framed the basic issues involved in separating the historical Solomon from the Solomon of legend: (1) The Davidic–Solomonic empire of the magnitude described in the Bible does not seem to fit the circumstances following the collapse of the international system of the Bronze age ca. 1200. (2) Some have argued that the collapse of the Hittite Empire and the withdrawal of Egypt from Asia would have enabled the rise of an empire centered in Palestine. But if that is the case such an empire should have left some epigraphical sources. (3) The biblical descriptions of Solomon's territorial holdings are not of a piece. Close examination reveals that some of the passages point to a relatively modest, and therefore more credible, realm. (4) Archaeological evidence available at present has not revealed anything like an empire centered in the Palestinian hill country in the 10th century. The land of the Philistines was certainly not included in his kingdom, it being clearly stated that Solomon had dominion "to Gaza" (I Kings 5:4 [4:24]), and hence the translation "to the land of the Philistines" (5:1 [4:21]) is correct. It is unlikely that Solomon's dominion extended north over the neo-Hittite kingdom of Hamath, where, according to Chronicles, he built (or reconstructed) store-cities, and reached as far as Tadmor (Palmyra) in the wilderness, where he also fortified himself (II Chron. 8:3–5). More likely is the account in I Kings 9:18 where the *ketiv* reads Tamar, which fits the geographic horizon of the chapter as an important point of the southern border (Cogan, 302). In addition, if Rezon held Damascus, Solomon could not have held much Aramean territory. Similarly, if he handed 20 cities over to Hiram, he did not have dominion in *Phoenicia.

Solomon may have had some share in the exchange of merchandise between the northern and southern countries, as indicated by the obscure passage (I Kings 10:28, 29) which tells of "the king's traders" and that "Solomon's import of

Solomon's division of Israel into districts. The small map shows the boundaries of his kingdom at its greatest extent. Based on Atlas of Israel, *Jerusalem, 1970.*

horses was from… Que" – according to the Septuagint and the Vulgate in Cilicia (cf. II Chron. 1:16 which has קְוֵא instead of קְוֵה as in I Kings 10:28; see *Que). From Anatolia Solomon imported horses which he sold in Egypt; he sold chariots from Egypt to the Aramean and neo-Hittite kingdoms in Syria, "to all the kings of the Hittites and the kings of Aram." However, Na'aman (apud Handy, 71) points out that it was in the eighth–seventh century that Egypt and Que were export centers of horses and chariots, and that the role of Solomon's traders is anachronistically borrowed from that of the *tamkāru* traders of the Neo-Assyrian empire. More likely is some control by Solomon of the commercial route that passed through

Jordan on the way from Arabia to Damascus. Associated with this economic activity of Solomon is the story of the *Queen of Sheba, who came to Jerusalem "with a very great retinue, with camels bearing spices, and very much gold, and precious stones" (I Kings 10:2). "Never again came such an abundance of spices" (10:10; II Chron. 9:1–9) as those which she gave to Solomon. That the queen came to test Solomon's wisdom smacks of legend. The use of the term *ḥiddot*, "riddles" (I Kings 10:1), an Aramaic loan whose shape points to a sound shift no earlier than the sixth century, indicates a late origin for the present text. Nonetheless, early South Arabian trade with Mesopotamia involving wood and spices transported by camels is attested in the early ninth century and may have begun as early as the tenth (Na'aman apud Handy, 72–3). In addition, queens are well attested in Arabia, though according to Kitchen (apud Handy, 141), not after 690 B.C.E. In sum, the story is not to be dismissed as utter anachronistic fantasy.

The Bible speaks of close relations between Solomon and *Hiram (son of Abibaal according to Josephus, king of Tyre), who, according to quotations cited by Josephus (Apion 1:113–5; Ant. 8:144–7), was also renowned for buildings he erected and royal projects he undertook. There is probably some basis to the biblical account that Israel cooperated with Tyre in sailing in the Red Sea. The servants of Hiram, "seamen who were familiar with the sea," sailed with Solomon's servants to Ophir, from which, as also from southern countries as a whole and perhaps from Africa, too, they brought gold and silver, sandalwood and ivory, apes and peacocks (I Kings 9:26–28; 10:11, 22). The port from which the ships put to Sea was *Ezion-Geber (Jazirat Faraun in the gulf south of Elat?). Alongside Solomon's ships (9:26) the Bible mentions "the fleet of Hiram." (10:11, 22). The reference to "a fleet of ships of Tarshish" is to a type of large ship adapted for transporting metal and for sailing great distances (Isa. 2:16; Ezek. 27:25; Ps. 48:8). In the barter trade between Hiram and Solomon, Israel provided Tyre with wheat and oil, while Tyre supplied Israel with cedar and cypress wood and with gold (I Kings 5:22–25 [8–11]; 9:11). The builders of Hiram and of Solomon cooperated in constructing the Temple (5:32 [18]). Apparently the execution by Hiram, the metal craftsman (not the king of the same name) of the bronzework in the Temple (7:13–15) was not an isolated or exceptional circumstance. The cooperation with Hiram in shipping, in work, and in barter provided Solomon with the opportunity of importing metal – copper and iron – from Anatolia and Cyprus and of establishing bronze foundries for the needs of the Temple in the plain of the Jordan (7:46). Another source of copper was Edom, where there is evidence of major copper smelting from Feinan in Jordan from the tenth–ninth century (Cogan, 273; Muhly, 1501, Levy). Based on mutual advantage and on the resulting economic prosperity, special relations apparently developed between Israel and Tyre, which, commencing already in the days of David and perhaps in those of Abibaal, culminated in a treaty between the two kingdoms. These relations explain the biblical account which tells of the personal friendship between Solomon and Hiram ("for Hiram always loved of David") and which refers in particular to Solomon's wisdom (I Kings 5:15–26 [1–12]: cf. the exaggerated phraseology in II Chron. 2:2–15).

Solomon's relations with the other kingdoms, too, were peaceful, while his marriage to foreign women – Moabites, Ammonites, Edomites, Sidonians, and neo-Hittites – led to the establishment of close ties between Israel and the neighboring peoples. The marriage of the daughter of Pharaoh king of Egypt to the king of Israel is a special case, treated at length by the Bible, which states that Solomon brought her to the city of David (I Kings 3:1), built a house for her (7:8; 9:24; II Chron. 8:11), and received Gezer from Pharaoh "as dowry to his daughter" (I Kings 9:16). The father-in-law was undoubtedly a pharaoh of the 21st Dynasty (Siamon or Psusennes II, both of whom reigned in the days of Solomon). There is indeed some basis for conjecturing that the marriage of the daughter of Pharaoh to the king of Israel – an exceptional event in the annals of the pharaohs – reflects a period of Egyptian weakness. Note that Hadad the Edomite was married to the sister of a Pharaoh (I Kings 11:15–22). Though Solomon's marriage into the Egyptian royal family is condemned in I Kings 11:1, it was probably a matter of pride for the Hebrew writer of I Kings 3:1 and 9:16, who wished to preserve the tradition that a parvenu dynast had managed to acquire a bride from a kingdom both ancient and renowned for its wisdom (I Kings 5:10).

Economy and Society

The ancient figurative description of every man dwelling safely under his vine and under his fig tree within Israel's borders "from Dan even to Beer-Sheba" (I Kings 5:5 [4:25]) depicts a flourishing agricultural situation. The passages which tell of the huge quantity of bronze (7:47), the gold and the silver, the luxuries and other precious articles (9:28; 10:10, 11, 12, 14, 22, 25), as well as the statements that silver was regarded as stones (or "it was not considered as anything in the days of Solomon," 10:21) and that cedars were as common as sycamore trees (10:27), exaggerated though they may be, yet reflect a prosperous situation.

The wealth and of the initiative of the kingdom expressed itself primarily in building, as is evident from the Bible and from archaeological finds: the magnificent buildings of the Temple and the king's house together with their appurtenances and ornamentations, the plans of which were apparently based on those of northern Syrian temples (a very close parallel to Solomon's Temple, and contemporary with it, was found in Ain Dara in Syria; see Monson); the extension of Jerusalem to the north; the erection of cities for chariots and horsemen and of store-cities within the kingdom; the special construction of the Israelite house (four-roomed house, in archaeological terminology); the construction in hewn stone and the ornamentation of buildings with proto-Eolithic capitals; public buildings like those brought to light at Beth-Shemesh and at Tell Belt Mirsim, and regarded by some as storehouses; a casemate wall characteristic of, though not exclusive to, this period in the fortification of cities, such as that uncovered at

Hazor, Megiddo, Beth-Shemesh, and Tell Belt Mirsim; the impressive and similar, almost identical, four-pillared gateways at Hazor, Megiddo, and Gezer, built apparently according to a uniform, well-devised, royal plan (these three cities are mentioned in the Bible alongside Jerusalem as an example of the building executed by Solomon, I Kings 9:15). Archaeologists differ over the question of whether this building activity is to be assigned to Solomon in the tenth century or whether it is of a later date (see survey in Dever apud Handy, 217–51; Finkelstein, Rainey, 2001). The peace which reigned in Palestine in the days of Solomon was based not only on political relations but also on chariot cities and principally on fortified cities at the approaches to the mountains of Judah and Jerusalem, at the entrance to the valley of Jezreel, and in Galilee, some of which – Hazor, Megiddo, Gezer, Beth-Horon, Baaloth – are mentioned in the Bible. The defense of Jerusalem was apparently of the greatest importance to Solomon.

The organization of the internal administration, begun in the days of David, was further advanced under Solomon, as can be seen from the list of his officials, among whom are included scribes, the recorder, the commander of the army, priests, the officer in charge of the district officers, the minister over the household, the king's friend, and "Adoniram in charge of the forced labor" (I Kings 4:1–7). The division into districts (see Rainey, 174–79), the inception of which may date from David's reign, was consolidated and stabilized in the days of Solomon, when each of the officers had to make provision for the king's household "for one month in the year" and supply not only "Solomon's provision" (4:7; 5:2–8 [4:22–28]) but also the needs of the court in general, such as horses and swift steeds (= *rekhesh*, רֶכֶשׁ, but perhaps *rekhev* רֶכֶב, "chariots," 5:8 [4:28]). This division, deviating partially from the boundaries of the tribes, reflects the administration that, alongside the ancient tribal division (4:15–18), was based on new territorial units, which differed from the earlier tribal grouping and some of which may have been inhabited also by the surviving Canaanite population (4:8–14, 19; cf. 9:20, 21). Even though Judah had its own special officer (4:19), it was not included among the 12 districts on an equal footing with the rest, for not only did it constitute a special political unit alongside Israel (4:20; 5:5 [4:25]), but it was apparently exempted from the economic obligations to the royal household laid on the other parts of the country.

The construction of buildings, the splendor of the royal court, and the economic expansion involved the duty not only of providing supplies for the court but also "a levy of forced labor," i.e., compulsory service (*corvée), the *mas*, well known from the Amarna letters of the 14th century, imposed both on the surviving Amorites and on the Israelites (5:27–30 [13–16]; 9:20–23). Solomon, it is stated with much exaggeration, had 70,000 "burden-bearers," 80,000 "hewers of stone in the hill country," and a levy of 30,000 men of whom 10,000 a month were sent "by courses" to Lebanon (5:27–29 [13–15]). Alongside them are mentioned 3,300 chief officers "who had charge of the people who carried on the work" (5:30 [16]; cf. the figure of 550 "who had charge of the people," 9:23; these may have been in charge of the non-Israelite workers, or of the king's work in a limited sense, or may represent a different tradition). The men of the levy worked in Lebanon, at building in Israel, and at the copper foundry, such as that in the plain of the Jordan between Succoth and Zarethan (5:31 [17], 32 [18], 7:46 and see above). The revolt against the House of David which broke out at the outset of Rehoboam's reign specifically because of the onerous burden of service (I Kings 12) had its roots in various features that marked Solomon's reign. The people were embittered not only by the heavy taxation, which was an innovation in the kingdom that had come into being against the background of a lengthy tribal regime, but also by the contrast between the heavy burdens on the one hand and the splendor and luxury of the royal court on the other. Likewise the barrier between Israel and Judah, which enjoyed special privileges, alienated the northern tribes from the Davidic kingdom. *Jeroboam son of Nebat, who was "in charge over all the forced labor of the house of Joseph" (11:28), probably revolted against the king not only in his capacity as the officer in charge of the compulsory service but as the standard bearer of the antagonism between the House of Joseph and the northern tribes in general on the one hand and Judah on the other. The divorce from the tribal tradition expressed, for example, in the geographical division of the districts and perhaps also in the fostering of a sacred center in Jerusalem, lacking though it did an ancient tradition, incited the tribes, in an attachment to time-honored centers such as Beth-El, Penuel, Shechem, and Dan, to rebel against the House of David. Thus the kingdom of Solomon, although characterized by economic development and by internal political security, provoked both a social revolt and tribal opposition or a general conservative tribal antagonism, the spokesman of which was the Yahweh prophet Ahijah the Shilonite. But in the days of Solomon the kingdom was still at the height of its power and Jeroboam was compelled to flee to Egypt. The author of the Book of Kings, in keeping with his religious conceptions, ascribes the revolt and the division to the idolatry of the king, in which he was influenced by his foreign wives.

The Wise King and Judge

The Bible attributes the peace and prosperity reigning in the country to the wisdom of Solomon, a literary topos already present in the prologue to the Code of *Hammurapi (COS II, 336–37. King Asshurbanipal of Assyria (669–627) boasts of his own wisdom (Streck Asb. 256 I. 17). Solomon's wisdom is mentioned already in that part of David's last testament which is not formulated in the style of the Book of Deuteronomy (I Kings 2:6, 9). The Bible describes the king as wiser than all men, as uttering proverbs and songs, solving riddles, and speaking of trees and beasts, of fowl, creeping things, and fishes, this being the type of wisdom renowned in eastern lands. His wisdom was essentially part of the totality of the wisdom of the East and the wisdom of Egypt, although it was higher in degree (5:9–14 [4:29–34]; 10:1, 3). Outside the book of I Kings, Prov. 25:1 speaks of "proverbs of Solomon collected by King Hezekiah and his circle." According to the Bible, Solomon was held in high esteem and extolled among other peoples too. Primarily, however, Solomon was considered a wise judge, as is evident from the dream at Gibeon and from the case of the two harlots. Solomon's wisdom was manifested mainly in connection with his royal authority as conceived both in modern times and in the Ancient East. It expressed itself in the function of dispensing justice to individuals and principally of establishing a just and righteous regime for the people as a whole. More precisely, it expressed itself in a capacity for leadership that distinguishes between good and evil ("Give Your servant therefore an understanding mind to govern Your people, that I may discern between good and evil; for who is able to govern this Your great people?" 3:9). The account of the dream at Gibeon likewise associates the king's riches and honor with his understanding ("a wise and discerning mind," 3:12, 13). The other passages, too, which mention the king's wisdom in connection with his political acts apparently refer to a quality of leadership (5:21 [7], 26 [12]; 10:6, 7, 9: "He has made you king, that you may execute justice and righteousness," *ibid.* 23, 24). One of the most important halls in the king's house which was near the Temple was called "the Hall of the Throne" or "the Hall of Judgment" (7:7), symbolizing the decisive quality of leadership as conceived already in the days of the Judges (on David's judicial function, cf. II Sam. 8:15; 12:1–6; 14:5–21).

In addition to this "wisdom," Solomon's royal authority was enhanced by his status as a sacral king, who supervised the religious rites, himself offered sacrifices, blessed the people after the manner of the priests, and took a decisive part in the dedication of the Temple, the sanctification of the court, and the celebration of the Feast of Tabernacles (I Kings 3:15; 8:1–5, 14, 22, 54–56, 62–66). The proximity of the king's house to the Temple, to which no explicit parallel has been found in the Ancient East, also set the seal of divine election and perhaps even of divine favor on the royal authority which produced a decisive change in the regime in Israel. The transition from the Tabernacle to the Temple apparently also symbolized the transition from a tribal to a monarchical regime. Henceforth associated with the Temple, which was conceived in the ancient part of Solomon's prayer as the house of God's habitation (8:13), the kingdom of the House of David was bound up with the city, which as early as in the days of Solomon may have begun to assume a holy character. Yet on the basis of the experience of generations, this close proximity of the royal palace to the Temple provoked the anger of Ezekiel (43:7–10), while the Chronicler saw fit to omit a description of the king's house, the building of which took 13 years, from the account of the Temple.

It is this variegated conception of the quality of leadership informed with a divine inspiration which brought such renown to the wise king that succeeding generations ascribed to him the composition of such widely different poetry and wisdom works as the Song of Songs, Proverbs, and Ecclesiastes, which contain numerous motifs characterizing the attribute of kingship. In assessing the reign of Solomon, it is important to distinguish the main narrative, in which Solomon rules a peaceful and prosperous kingdom, from the details which tell us of the burdensome yoke he laid on the people (I Kings 12:4), of the internal opposition by one of his most talented officials, Jeroboam, who was able to build on northern resentment, and of the opposition of the prophet Ahijah. Most telling of all is the fact that the kingdom did not survive his death.

See also *History: Kingdoms of Israel and Judah.

[Samuel Abramsky / S. David Sperling (2nd ed.)]

In the *Aggadah*

Solomon succeeded to the throne at the age of 12 (SOR 14). His original name, Jedidiah, the "beloved of God," was superseded by that of Solomon (*Shelomoh*) because of the peace (*shalom*) that prevailed throughout his reign. He was also known as Koheleth (Eccles. 1:1), Lemuel (Prov. 31:1), Agur, Jakeh, and Ithiel (Prov. 30:1; Eccl. R. 1:2). Solomon chose wisdom, knowing that once he possessed it all else would come of itself (PR 14:59; Song R. 1:1, no. 9). This God-granted wisdom made him the wisest of mankind. His 800 proverbs are equal to 3,000 since each verse in his book may be interpreted in two or three different ways (Song R. 1:1, nos. 10, 11). He was an expert horticulturist, and he succeeded in growing all types of foreign plants in Ereẓ Israel (Targ. Eccles. 2:4–6; Eccl. R. 2:5). He understood the language of the beasts and birds and they submitted to his judgment (Song R. 1:1, no. 9; Tanh. B., Introd., 157). The two women who claimed the child were really spirits who were sent by God to reveal Solomon's wisdom. All doubt about the fairness of his verdict was dispelled when a heavenly voice proclaimed: "This is the mother of the child" (Mak. 23b). Other perceptive judgments of Solomon are recorded in the case of the slave who claimed he was the master's son (A. Jellinek, *Beit ha-Midrash*, 4 (1967), 145–6); the double-headed son who claimed a double inheritance (*ibid.*, 151–2); and the three men who could not find the money they hid before the commencement of the Sabbath (*ibid.*, 1 (1967), 86–87). He had such confidence in himself that he would have dispensed judgment without resort to witnesses, had he not been prevented by a heavenly voice (RH 21b). Many came to seek his advice (Jellinek, *op. cit.*, 4 (1967), 148–50). The most famous of those who consulted him was the Queen of Sheba (Targ. Sheni 1:3, 8–10). She asked numerous riddles of Solomon, all of which he answered promptly and correctly (Ms. *Midrash ha-Ḥefez*, tr. by S. Schechter in *Folk-Lore*, 1 (1890); 349–58).

Solomon, however, is regarded as the prototype of the rationalist who ultimately is led to sin by his rational approach. He was determined to find reasons for all the divine precepts and succeeded until he came to the law of the Red Heifer, which he was unable to fathom (Eccles. R. 7:23, no. 4). He finally transgressed the biblical laws in that he possessed too many horses, amassed an overabundance of gold and silver, and above all in that he married more than the 18 wives permitted to a monarch (Deut. 17:16–7; Sanh. 21a), because he thought that with his wisdom he would not be affected by his transgression. At this God declared, "As thou livest, Solomon and a hundred of his like shall be annihilated before a single letter of the Torah will be obliterated" (TJ, Sanh. 2b, 20c), and in fact Scripture records that his many wives finally "turned away his heart after other gods" (I Kings 11:4). The rabbis declare that "It would have been better for Solomon to have cleaned sewers than to have this verse written of him" (Ex. R. 6:1). When he married the daughter of Pharaoh, the archangel Gabriel descended from heaven and inserted a reed in the sea around which accumulated silt and on which the city of Rome was ultimately built (Sanh. 21b). On the nuptial night she brought him a thousand musical instruments. Although each one was dedicated to a different idol, Solomon neglected to stop her (Shab. 56b). She spread over his bed a tapestry studded with diamonds and pearls which gleamed like constellations in the sky and created an illusion of stars. Solomon slept on until the fourth hour of the morning, causing deep sorrow among the people since the daily sacrifice could not be offered because the Temple keys lay under Solomon's pillow (Lev. R. 12:5).

The most important of Solomon's acts was his building of the Temple, in which he was assisted by angels and demons. Indeed, the edifice was throughout miraculously constructed, the large, heavy stones rising and settling in their proper places by themselves (Ex. R. 52:4). Solomon split the stone by means of the *shamir*, a worm whose mere touch cleft rocks. He was informed of the worm's location by the chief of the demons, Ashmedai, who was captured by Benaiah, Solomon's chief minister (Git. 68a). Solomon was so assiduous in this task that the Temple's erection took only seven years, about half the time for the erection of the king's palace, despite the greater magnificence of the sanctuary. In this respect, he was the superior of his father, King David, who first built a house for himself, and then thought about a tabernacle for God. Indeed, it was Solomon's meritorious work in connection with the Temple that saved him from being reckoned by the sages as one of the impious kings, among whom his sins might rightfully have placed him (Sanh. 104b; Song R. 1:1, no. 5). Second only to the Temple in beauty was Solomon's throne. None before or after him could construct a similar work of art, and when his vassal-kings saw its beauty they prostrated themselves and praised God. Jewels and gold adorned the throne and animals guarded its approach. These animals also lifted Solomon from step to step when he ascended the throne (Targ. Sheni 1:2, 5–7). The throne did not long remain in the possession of the Israelites. During the life of Rehoboam, the son of Solomon, it was taken to Egypt. Shishak, the father-in-law of Solomon, appropriated it as indemnity for his widowed daughter. Ultimately, the throne was taken to Babylonia, Greece, and finally to Rome (Esth. R. 1:12).

Because of his sins, Solomon gradually lost his throne, his wealth, and even his wisdom. At first he ruled over the inhabitants of the upper world as well as over those of the lower; then only over the inhabitants of the earth; later over Israel alone; then he retained only his bed and his staff; and finally only his staff was left to him (Sanh. 20b). There is a difference of opinion on whether Solomon returned to his throne. He "saw three worlds" which, according to one opinion, means that he was successively a private person, a king, and again a private person. According to another, however, he was king, private person, and again king (Sanh. 20b; Git. 68b). For three long years, he journeyed about as a mendicant from city to city and from country to country, atoning for his sins. While a beggar, during his old age, he wrote Ecclesiastes, saying wherever he went, "I Koheleth was king over Israel in Jerusalem" (Eccles. 1:12). Previously, in his youth, he had written the Song of Songs, and in his middle age Proverbs (Song R. 1:1, no. 10).

[Aaron Rothkoff]

In Islam

From various allusions, which are found in the works of Arab poets, it is evident that tales concerning King Solomon (Sulaymān) were circulated in the Arabian Peninsula even before the appearance of *Muhammad. In the *Koran Solomon is not only the successor of King David (Sura 27:1b) but also the faithful servant of Allah (38:29). He did not even momentarily abandon the service of Allah; it was rather the devils who negated it and taught the people sorcery, thus estranging them from the worship of the Creator (2:96). Once, however, when gazing at his horses, Solomon overlooked the recital of the evening prayer at its proper time; but as a sign of repentance, he killed his beloved horses (38:31–33). In the most positive description of the character of Solomon, one recognizes Christian influence. As a faithful servant, Solomon requests that eternal kingship be granted to him (38:34). He is awarded wisdom and intelligence, understands the speech of the birds, and rules over the wind which blows with strength (27:15, 16, 81; 31:11), as well as over the spirits (21:82; 34:11, 12; 38:35–38). It is no wonder that Solomon's fame reached distant lands and that the Queen of Saba (Sheba) came to visit him (27:20–45). No one was aware of his death until a worm ate away the staff which supported his body, the staff broke, and his body collapsed (34:14).

There are certain characteristics common both to David and Solomon (see *David, in *Islam), Some have been transferred from David to Solomon (the invention of armor), while others have been transferred from Solomon to David, such as the domination of animals and birds (38:17, 18). Solomon participated in the judgment decided by his father concerning the pastureland on which sheep grazed (21:78). David was as wise as Solomon (21:79–82).

Following Jewish *aggadah* and ancient legends, some of which originated in Persia, the Muslim commentators on the Koran and legend writers devote an important place to Solomon's character, birth, wisdom, intelligence as a judge and investigator of complicated affairs, his rule over the jinn (spirits) who obeyed his commands and built palaces, fortresses, bath houses, and dams for him, and his mastery of sorcery and mysticism. Solomon's chief counselor, Aṣāf b. Barakhyā, also made use of the king's magic ring (*khatam Sulaymān*). Solomon lost his kingdom because he listened to the voice of his wife Tarāda, the daughter of the king of Sidon; he was punished by being exiled from his kingdom. Solomon died at the age of 58, after having ruled Israel for 40 years (as did his father David).

[Haïm Z'ew Hirschberg]

In the Arts

IN LITERATURE. As the king of Israel appointed to build the Temple and as the legendary embodiment of wisdom, Solomon became a prototype of Jesus in the medieval Christian world. Treatment of the subject in literature, art, and music involves not only Solomon himself but also the sub-themes of the Queen of Sheba and the Shulammite of the Song of Songs. In literature, one of the earliest surviving works on the theme is an Anglo-Saxon legend, the poetical *Dialogue of Solomon and Saturn* (manuscript at Cambridge; ed. R.J. Menner, 1941). There is also a 15th-century *Dyalogus Salomonis et Marcolfi* (Cologne, 1473); but from this period, beginning with the anonymous German mystery, *Das Spil von Kunig Salomon mit den zweyen Frawen* (1461), most writing on the theme was in dramatic form. One unusual medieval work was the 15th-century Russian "Tale of the Centaur," based on the midrashic account of Solomon's construction of the Temple. During the Renaissance era plays included a Spanish *Farsa de Salomón* (c. 1530) by Diego Sanchez; a *Fastnachtspiel* by the *Meistersinger* Hans Sachs (1550); an anonymous Italian *Rappresentatione del Re Salomone* (Florence, 1562), apparently preceded by an earlier work on the subject (c. 1512); and a drama celebrating the Danish heir to the throne, written by H.J. Ranch of Viborg (1584). However, the outstanding treatment was probably the German neo-Latin playwright Sixtus Birck's *Sapientia Salomonis* (1547), a performance of which by the boys of Westminster School was given before Elizabeth I of England in 1565. Although the 17th century produced further dramas – notably Joost van den Vondel's *Salomon* (1648) in Holland, the *Auto del Rey Salamo* (1612) by Balthasar Dias in Portugal, and Pedro Calderón de la Barca's *La Sibila del Oriente y Gran Reina de Sabá* (Madrid, 1682) in Spain – a more philosophical and pessimistic note was struck by writers emphasizing Solomon's outlook as the traditional author of Ecclesiastes. Two examples are the anonymous German *Schau-Platz der Eitelkeit…* (1668), a five-act prose drama, and the English poet Matthew Prior's verse soliloquy, *Solomon on the Vanity of the World*, written in the 1690s but published only in 1718; works of this type were common throughout the following century. Apart from the texts of various oratorios, such as Thomas Morell's *Solomon* (1749) which was set to music by Handel, the two outstanding 18th-century treatments were both in German: Friedrich Gottlieb Klopstock's tragedy, *Salomo* (1764), and Johann Jacob Bodmer's religious drama, *Die Thorheiten des weisen Koenigs* (Zurich, 1776).

The subject proved even more attractive to some of the major writers of the 19th century, who often displayed greater ingenuity in their use of the legendary material made accessible by modern scholarship; and Jews were prominent for the first time among these authors. Lippmann Moses Bueschenthal's five-act German tragedy, *Der Siegelring des Salomo* (Berlin, 1820), was followed by Kornel Ujejski's Polish biblical poem, *Pieśni Salomona* (1846) and Heinrich *Heine's romantic poem, "Salomo" (in *Romanzero*, 1851). Among works on the theme published in the second half of the century were "Azrael," the Spanish Jew's first tale in the third part of Henry Wadsworth Longfellow's *Tales of a Wayside Inn* (1872), on the Angel of Death's encounter with Solomon; Victor Hugo's grandiose poem "Salomon" (in *La légende des siècles*, 1877); the U.S. poet John Greenleaf Whittier's "King Solomon and the Arts" (1877); Robert *Browning's poem, "Solomon and Balkis" (1883); Paul *Heyse's five-act drama, *Die Weisheit Salomos* (1887); and Károly Szász's Hungarian biblical play, *Bölcs Salomon* (1889). Others who turned to the subject included the Portuguese dramatist Eugénio de Castro e Almeida (*Belkiss, Rainha de Sabá, d'Axum e do Hymiar*, 1894), the English poet Arthur Symons (*The Lover of the Queen of Sheba*, 1899), and the Czech poet Julius *Zeyer. Among 20th-century authors the theme has, if anything, enjoyed even greater popularity. Works which it has inspired include the U.S. poet Vachel Lindsay's "King Solomon and the Queen of Sheba" (in *The Chinese Nightingale and Other Poems*, 1917); Alfons Paquet's German drama, *Markolph; oder Koenig Salomo und der Bauer* (1924); the Irish poet W.B. Yeats' "Solomon and the Witch" (1924); and "Solomon's Parents" (in *Poems of Thirty Years*, 1925) by the English writer Gordon Bottomley.

Some of the outstanding modern interpretations of the story have been written by Jews. The Danish poet Oscar Ivar *Levertin's works on Jewish themes include *Kung Salomo och Morolf* (1905). Three other important works were Edmond *Fleg's biography, *Salomon* (1929); Ḥayyim Naḥman *Bialik's *Va-Yehi ha-Yom…* (English version by Herbert Danby, *And It Came to Pass…* 1938), a collection of legends; and Sammy *Gronemann's biblical comedy, *Der Weise und der Narr; Koenig Salomo und der Schuster* ("The King and the Cobbler," 1942), Nathan *Alterman's Hebrew version of which (1942) was staged in Israel both as a play and as a successful and pioneering Hebrew musical comedy. Gronemann also wrote a comedy entitled *Die Koenigin von Saba* (1951). Three treatments in Yiddish are Abba Isaac Buch's *Ashmedai…* (1911), a drama about Solomon and Jeroboam; Saul Saphire's historical novel, *Shlomo Hamelekh* (1931); and Jerakhme'el Steigman's *Mayse-hlekh vegn Shlomo Hamelekh* (1931), tales for children.

IN ART. In art, too, Solomon is a major biblical theme. Scenes from his life are often found in Byzantine manuscripts, and his figure is sculpted on medieval cathedrals and appears in stained glass; several scenes are also portrayed in the Raphael Loggie in the Vatican. Solomon is also an important figure in art of the Islamic world. The main scenes treated are the anointing and coronation of Solomon, the judgment of Solomon, the construction of the Temple, the visit of the Queen of Sheba, and Solomon worshiping idols. The anointing and crowning of Solomon (I Kings 1:39 and Song of Songs 3:11) appear in medieval sculpture, stained glass, and in manuscripts – notably the ninth-century Bibles of Charles the Fat and St. Paul-Without-the-Walls and the 15th-century *Hours of Turin* by Hubert and Jan Van Eyck (now destroyed). Bath-Sheba sitting at the right hand of Solomon (I Kings 2:19) was regarded as a type of the coronation of the virgin. This interpretation is explicit in the sumptuous *Tapestry of the Three Coronations* in Sens Cathedral, France. The judgment of Solomon (I Kings 3:16–28) has generally been popular with artists. It appears in several French and German Hebrew manuscripts, such as the 13th-century *British Museum Miscellany* and *Bibliothèque Nationale Pentateuch*, the Second *Nuremberg Haggadah*, and the *Tripartite Maḥzor* from the Kauffman Collection, Budapest. In the Middle Ages the judgment of Solomon was regarded as an example of justice and was often depicted in lawcourts. There is a 15th-century sculpture of the subject at the Palace of the Doges, Venice. Among Renaissance treatments are a drawing of the school of Mantegna (Louvre) and a painting by Giorgione (private collection, England). The subject was also popular in the 17th century, particularly with the French school. There are paintings by Rubens (Copenhagen State Museum), Jacob Jordaens (Prado, Madrid), and Nicolas Poussin (Louvre). In the 18th century it was included by Tiepolo in his ceiling for the Archbishop's palace, Udine. Solomon constructing the Temple (I Kings 6:1ff. and 2 Chron. 3:1ff.) is a subject found in 15th-century French manuscripts, notably the *Jewish Antiquities* of Josephus in the Bibliothèque Nationale illustrated by Jean Fouquet. As the real appearance of the Temple was unknown, Fouquet visualized it as a French Gothic cathedral of his own time, and other artists such as Giotto and Taddeo Gaddi imagined it in the form of the Dome of the Rock, i.e., as a circular or octagonal building surmounted by a cupola.

King Solomon and the Queen of Sheba was not a common subject until the 12th century. From that time onward, however, they often appeared as a pair. The two episodes treated in medieval art are the meeting of Solomon and Sheba (I Kings 10:1ff. and 2 Chron. 9:1ff.) and Sheba enthroned beside the king. In Christian iconography Solomon was the type of Jesus and Sheba represented the gentile Church; hence Sheba's meeting with Solomon bearing rich gifts foreshadowed the adoration of the Magi. On the other hand, Sheba enthroned represented the coronation of the virgin. Sculptures of the Queen of Sheba are found on great Gothic cathedrals such as Chartres, Rheims, Amiens, and Wells, and the reception of the queen was a popular subject during the Italian Renaissance, as it appealed to the contemporary taste for pageantry and display. It appears in the famous bronze doors to the Florence Baptistery by Lorenzo Ghiberti, in frescoes by Benozzo Gozzoli (Campo Santo, Pisa) and in the Raphael Loggie (Vatican). The Venetians predictably exploited the decorative possibilities of the subject. There are examples by Tintoretto (Prado) and Veronese (Pinacotheca, Turin). In the 17th century, Claude Lorrain (1600–1682) painted one of his peaceful landscapes of harbors at sunset, representing the queen embarking on her journey to Solomon (National Gallery, London). Depictions of the idolatry of Solomon (I Kings 11:4ff.) are found in medieval art, where the elderly monarch is shown kneeling before an idol to which a woman is pointing. This was also quite a common subject in the 16th and 17th centuries.

IN MUSIC. Two early musical works are Josquin de Pré's motet, *Stetit autem Salomon* (1538), and a curiosity – a canon for 96 voices by Pietro Valentini called *Nodus Salomonis* ("Solomon's Knot"), first published in 1631 and republished and analyzed in 1650 by Athanasius Kircher in his *Musurgia Universalis*; the entire canon is nothing but a kind of "change ringing" on the G major chord. Early oratorios on the theme include Carissimi's *Judicium Salomonis* (1669) and F.T. Richter's *L'incoronazione di Salomone* (Vienna, 1696). The subject is taken up by northern composers: G.C. Schuermann's "spiritual opera," *Salomon* (Brunswick, 1701), J.G. Keiser's opera, *Salomon* (Hemburg, 1703), and M.A. Charpentier's oratorio, *Judicium Salomonis* (Paris, 1702). Porsile's *L'esaltazione di Salomone* (Barcelona, 1711) is held to be the first oratorio performed in Spain (in honor of the emperor Charles III). *Zadok the Priest* (the description of Solomon's coronation) is the first of a set of four coronation anthems composed by Handel for George III (1727) and is still sung at every British coronation. Handel's oratorio, *Solomon*, was first performed at Covent Garden on March 17, 1749; the "Entry of the Queen of Sheba" from this work is often performed as a concert piece, and the oratorio was reedited by *Mendelssohn with cuts and the addition of an organ part. Solomon's judgment again appears as an oratorio subject in I. Holzbauer's *Il Giudizio di Salomone* (Mannheim, 1766), and in a Polish work, *Sad Salomona*, by Chopin's teacher Elsner (tragedy with dances and incidental music; Warsaw, 1806). The 19th century gave new prominence to the Queen of Sheba. Gounod's four-act opera, *La Reihe de Saba* (text by M. Carré and J. Barbier, after Gérard de Nerval), had its premiere at the Paris Opera in 1862; but a more lasting success was gained by Karl *Goldmark's *Die Koenigin von Saba* (text by S.H. *Mosenthal, première in Vienna, 1875). Some of the melodic material is supposed to have been based on synagogal motifs. Ernest *Bloch's *Schelomo, Rhapsodie Hébraïque*, for cello and orchestra, was inspired by a figurine of Solomon sculpted by the wife of the cellist Alexander Barjanski. Bloch's work was composed in 1915 and first performed in 1917 with Barjanski as soloist and the composer conducting. Later works on the subject are Reynaldo *Hahn's *La Reine de Scheba* (1926; text by Edmond *Fleg); *Belkis, Regina di Saba*, a ballet by O. Respighi (1932); and Randall Thompson's *Solomon and Balkis*, an opera in one act, based on Kipling's *The Butterfly that Stamped* (1942). The music for Sammy Gronemann's *Shelomo ha-Melekh ve-Shalmai ha-Sandelar* was written by Alexander Argov.

Ashmedai, an opera based on the talmudic legend of Satan assuming the appearance of the king by Yosef *Tal (to a libretto by Israel Eliraz), had its première at the Hamburg State Opera in autumn 1971; the score includes electronic effects.

See also: *Song of Songs, in the Arts; *Temple, in the Arts.

[Bathja Bayer]

BIBLIOGRAPHY: F. Thieberger, *King Solomon* (1947); J.A. Montgomery, *The Books of Kings* (1951), 67–248 (incl. bibl.); Bright, Hist, 190–208 (incl. bibl.); Alt, Kl Schr, 2 (1953), 1–62; idem, in: VT, 1 (1961), 2–22; A. Malamat, in: *Sefer N.H. Tur-Sinai* (1960), 77–85; idem (ed.), in: *Bi-Ymei Bayit Rishon* (1962), 24–46, incl. bibl. (Eng. sect., 8–9); idem, in: JNES, 22 (1963), 1–17; Y. Yadin, in: BA, 23 (1960), 62–68; idem, in: A. Malamat (ed.), *Bi-Ymei Bayit Rishon* (1962), 66–109 (Eng. sect. 11); idem, in: *Qadmoniyot*, 3 (1970), 38–56; Y. Aharoni, in: A. Malamat (ed.), *Bi-Ymei Bayit Rishon* (1962), 110–31 (Eng. sect. 12); Aharoni, Ereẓ, 258–64; S. Abramsky, *Leksikon Mikra'i*, 2 (1965), 840–4; J.A. Soggin, *Das Königtum in Israel* (1967); M. Noth, *Geschichte Israels* (1950), 187–99 (incl. bibl.). IN THE AGGADAH: Ginzberg, Legends, index; M. Aberbach and L. Smolar, in: JQR (1968), 118–32. IN ISLAM: ʿUmāra, Ms. fol. 58v–82v; Thaʿlabī, *Qiṣaṣ* (1356 A.H.), 244–77; Kisāʾī *Qiṣaṣ* (1356 A.H.), 278–95; G. Salzberger, *Salomons Tempelbau und Thron in der semitischen Sagenliteratur* (1912); H. Speyer, *Die biblischen Erzählungen im Qoran* (1931, repr. 1961), 383–402; H.Z. Hirschberg, in: *Eretz-Israel*, 3 (1954), 213–20; J. Walker, in: *Shorter Encyclopedia of Islam* (1953), s.v. (includes extensive bibliography). **ADD. BIBLIOGRAPHY:** T. Ishida (ed.), *Studies in the Period of David and Solomon and Other Essays* (1982); L. Handy (ed.), *The Age of Solomon: Scholarship at the Turn of the Millennium* (1997); J. van Seters, in: CBQ, 59 (1997), 45–57; J. Muhly, in: CANE, 3:1501–21; R. Hess, in: G. Young (ed.), *Crossing Boundaries and Linking Horizons Studies… Astour* (1997), 279–93; I. Finkelstein, in: NEA 62 (1999), 35–42; M. Cogan, *I Kings* (AB; 2000); J. Monson, in: BAR, 26 (Ain Dara Temple, well illustrated; 2000), 20–35, 67; A. Rainey, in: NEA, 64 (2001), 140–49; T. Levy et al, *Antiquity*, 302 (2004), 865–79; A. Rainey, in: A. Rainey and R.S. Notley, *The Sacred Bridge* (2006), 157–89.

SOLOMON, family of Australian pioneers and statesmen. EMMANUEL SOLOMON (1800–1873) was born in London and transported to Sydney as a convict in 1818 for housebreaking. After being pardoned, he went into business as a merchant in Sydney with his brother and settled in Adelaide, the capital of South Australia, in 1838, two years after it was founded. He was a general merchant and auctioneer and in 1840 opened the city's first theater. Well known for his philanthropic gifts, Solomon helped finance the building of large apartment blocks for the colonists to replace the primitive homes of the early settlers. He served in the South Australian parliament in 1862–65 and 1867–71.

His nephew, JUDAH MOSS SOLOMON (1818–1880), who was born in London and arrived in Sydney in 1831, became Emmanuel Solomon's partner in business in Adelaide. Judah Moss Solomon played an active part in municipal affairs. He was elected to the town council in 1852 and in 1869–71 served as mayor. From 1858 to 1874 he represented Adelaide in the South Australian Parliament and played an important part in introducing a public health act. When a small Jewish community was established in 1848, Judah Moss Solomon was elected first president of the congregation.

Judah Moss Solomon had two sons. The elder, BENJAMIN SOLOMON (1844–1922), was appointed chief censor of Australia on the outbreak of World War I. His brother, VABIAN LOUIS SOLOMON (1853–1908), born in Adelaide, settled in Darwin in the Northern Territory in 1874 and worked as a merchant and shipping agent. He founded the *Northern Territory Times*, the first newspaper in the region, and became mayor of Darwin. Vabian Solomon was prominent in the development of the mining and pearl-fishing industries and on his return to Adelaide became the representative of the Northern Territory in the South Australian Parliament, serving from 1890 to 1901. An expert on financial matters, he was an important political figure in South Australian politics and was premier for a short time in 1899, the first Jew to become premier of an Australian colony or state. Vabian Solomon represented South Australia at the convention which framed the federal Australian constitution. In deference to his religious beliefs, the convention did not meet on Saturdays. He was elected to the first federal Parliament in 1901 and served for two years. In 1905 he was again elected and remained in Parliament until his death. His daughter Esther was the first woman elected to the Adelaide City Council.

BIBLIOGRAPHY: H. Munz, *Jews in South Australia (1836–1936)* (1936). **ADD. BIBLIOGRAPHY:** ADB, 6, 163–64; 12, 11–12; H.L. Rubinstein, Australia I, 394–96; E. Richards, "The Fall and Rise of the Brothers Solomon," in: AJHSJ, 8:2 (1975), 1–28.

[Isidor Solomon]

SOLOMON, family of English origin which won distinction in St. Helena and South Africa. The founder was NATHANIEL SOLOMON (1735–1800), a merchant with interests in the East India trade, who married Phoebe Mitz (or De Mitz) of Leiden in 1774, when she was 14 years old. She was widowed at 40, had 21 children, and lived to a great age. The eldest son, SAUL SOLOMON (I; 1775–1850), left for India at the age of 20, but, on becoming dangerously ill, was put ashore at St. Helena. On his recovery he started trading with passing ships and in time acquired almost a monopoly in the provisioning of ships and the wholesale trade. His brothers JOSEPH and BENJAMIN joined him and by 1815 he had become a wealthy man, noted for his hospitality. He became sheriff of St. Helena and was appointed consul for the Netherlands and France. He kept in touch with the earliest Cape Town congregation. His brother Benjamin (1786–1877) settled in Cape Town where for many years he was usher of the court. SAUL SOLOMON (II; d. 1892), their nephew, was educated in Cape Town. Apprenticed to a bookseller and printer, he eventually became a partner and finally took over the business with his brothers. They printed the *Government Gazette* and in 1863 became proprietors of the newspaper, *The Cape Argus*, which remained a leading daily and was the start of the largest chain of newspapers in South Africa. On the grant of parliamentary government to the Cape in 1854, Saul Solomon was elected a member of the Assembly. He played a leading part in securing responsible government for the Colony in 1872, but because of a physical infirmity declined office. He was a powerful debater, brilliant in repartee, liberal in outlook, and a spokesman for the African population. Like other of the Solomons who settled at the Cape, he became a Christian and married a Christian, but retained an interest in Jews and Jewry. Of his sons SAUL SOLOMON (III; 1875–1960) became a judge of the Transvaal Supreme Court, and WILLIAM EWART GLADSTONE SOLOMON (1880–1966), a painter, was principal of the Government Art School in Bombay. EDWARD SOLOMON, son of Joseph Solomon and nephew of the first Saul, became a Congregational minister. His three sons were all knighted: SIR EDWARD PHILIP SOLOMON (1845–1914), minister of public works in the Transvaal under General Botha; SIR RICHARD SOLOMON (1850–1913), first high commissioner of the Union of South Africa in London (1910–13); and SIR WILLIAM HENRY SOLOMON (1852–1930), chief justice of the Union (1927–29).

BIBLIOGRAPHY: I. Abrahams, *Birth of a Community* (1955), index.

[Lewis Sowden]

SOLOMON (né **Solomon Cutner**; 1902–1988), British pianist. Solomon was born in London and made his first public appearance at the Queen's Hall at the age of eight. Up to the age of 16 he continued to give concerts, after which he studied in London and Paris. His London reappearance in 1921 marked the beginning of a great career, which included world tours and important American appearances in 1926 and 1939. He was made a Commander of the British Empire in 1946. Solomon, as he always called himself, was considered one of the finest pianists Britain ever produced. After suffering a stroke in 1956, he was forced to retire prematurely from the concert platform.

[Max Loppert]

SOLOMON, BERTHA (1892–1969), South African lawyer and politician. Born in Minsk, Russia, she was taken to South Africa at the age of four to join her father Idel Schwarz, a Zionist pioneer. She was the second South African woman to be admitted to the bar, practicing in Johannesburg. She was elected to the Transvaal provincial council in 1933 and from 1938 to 1958 sat in the Union Parliament as a member of the United Party. A vigorous champion of women's rights, she was prominent in the campaign for votes for women in 1930. Through her persistent efforts she was responsible for the Matrimonial Affairs Act of 1953 which removed some of the disabilities of women resulting from the marriage laws. She was also a leading figure in the National Council of Women and was a founder of the South African Women's Auxiliary Air Force in World War II. Her autobiography, *Time Remembered*, appeared in 1968.

[Louis Hotz]

SOLOMON, ELIAS LOUIS (1879–1956), U.S. Conservative rabbi. Solomon was born in Vilna, Lithuania, and after childhood sojourns in England, Cyprus, and Palestine, he immigrated with his family to the United States in 1888. He earned a B.A. from the City College of New York in 1900 and was ordained in 1904 at the *Jewish Theological Seminary, where he earned a D.H.L. in 1910. After heading the Barnett Memorial Hebrew School in Paterson, New Jersey, he served as rabbi of Congregation Beth Mordechai in Perth Amboy, New Jersey (1905–07); Kehillath Israel in the Bronx, New York (1907–18); and associate rabbi of Kehillath Jeshurun in Manhattan, New York (1918–21), before becoming rabbi of Congregation Sha'arei Zedek on New York City's West Side, where he remained until his death.

Solomon was an early leader of Conservative Judaism. His first role was as president of the Alumni Association of the Jewish Theological Seminary of America (1914–16), the forerunner to the *Rabbinical Assembly. In 1913, together with Solomon *Schechter, he helped found the United Synagogue of America, serving as one of the organization's first presidents (1918–24). During his tenure in office, the United Synagogue's Women's League and Young People's League were established, the *United Synagogue Recorder* was launched, and plans were made to build the Yeshurun Synagogue in Jerusalem. Solomon remained the organization's honorary lifetime president, stepping in to serve briefly as its acting executive vice president following Samuel *Cohen's retirement. In 1926, he helped form another umbrella organization for congregations, the Synagogue Council of America, for which he also served as president from 1930 to 1932.

Solomon brought his leadership skills to a wide variety of regional and national Jewish organizations, serving as president of the New York Board of Rabbis (1929–30), chairman of the America Pro-Falasha Committee, honorary president of the American Biblical Encyclopedia, and treasurer of the Jewish Braille Society of America. He was also active in the Hebrew Free Loan Society and the National Council of Christians and Jews. During World War II, he was appointed by President Harry S. Truman to serve on the Selective Service Panel and received a presidential citation.

[Bezalel Gordon, (2nd ed.)]

SOLOMON, EZEKIEL (d. 1806), Michigan's first-known Jewish settler. Born in Berlin, Germany, Solomon was among the first Jewish merchants to go to Montreal, Canada, at the time of the British occupation. Solomon was a partner with Chapman Abraham, Gershon Levy, Benjamin Lyon, and Levi Solomons, who were originally army purveyors and who later figured prominently as pioneer fur traders in Michigan. In 1761 Solomon went to Fort Michilimackinac, today's Mackinaw City in Michigan. He was captured by the Indians during their 1763 massacre, but gained his freedom by being ransomed. He was a partner of the Mackinaw Company enterprise, which was organized in 1779 by some 30 traders and companies and which is believed to be the first example of a department store operation in the United States. He was also one of the organizers, in 1784, of Michigan's first Board of Trade. Although married to a Christian, Solomon remained a

Jew and was an officer and active member of Montreal's Congregation Shearith Israel.

BIBLIOGRAPHY: I.I. Katz, *Beth El Story* (1955), index; J.R. Marcus, *Early American Jewry*, 2 (1953), index; idem, *American Jewry-Documents, Eighteenth Century* (1959), index; Rosenbloom, Biogr Dict, 162; M.H. Stern, *Americans of Jewish Descent* (1960), index.

[Irving I. Katz]

SOLOMON, HANNAH GREENEBAUM (1858–1942), founder and first president of the National Council of Jewish Women (NCJW). The fourth of ten children born to Sarah Spiegel and Michael Greenebaum, a successful Chicago merchant, she married Henry Solomon in 1879 and the couple had three children. Solomon brought leadership and ideological vision to the NCJW, helping it become the premier Jewish women's organization in late 19th and early 20th century America. Representative of a generation of middle-class Jewish women who paved the way for giving women a voice in the public affairs of the Jewish community, Solomon made a career out of voluntarism and social reform. A member of Chicago's most prominent Reform synagogue, Temple Sinai, Solomon had a strong commitment to Jewish life and the larger community; she and her sister, Henrietta Frank, became the first Jewish members of the prestigious Chicago Women's Club in 1876. Already well known, Solomon emerged as an obvious choice to chair the Jewish Women's Congress that convened when Chicago hosted the 1893 World's Fair. At the conclusion of the four-day Congress, delegates founded the National Council of Jewish Women and unanimously elected Hannah Solomon as president.

In the NCJW's early years, Solomon and other leaders often confounded expectations about proper gendered behavior. As Council president, Solomon was the first woman to speak from several synagogue pulpits throughout the country. Through her presidency of the NCJW and directorship of the Bureau of Personal Service, an agency that served Jewish immigrants in Chicago's seventh ward, Solomon established herself as one of the premier community leaders of Chicago. She served for years as the only woman on the Executive Board of the Associated Jewish Charities. Under her leadership, the Chicago NCJW chapter created a Sabbath School for girls in order to inculcate Jewish values and provide young women with educational opportunities. Solomon's support for an initiative within Reform Jewry to move the Saturday Sabbath to Sunday as a means of conforming with American standards and encouraging greater Sabbath observance within the Jewish community created dissension within the NCJW and motivated an attempt to remove her as president. During the contentious debate, Solomon issued her often quoted statement, "I do consecrate the Sabbath. I consecrate every day in the week." Solomon and her allies managed to keep the opposition from ousting her as president and steered the NCJW toward a pluralistic position that supported Sabbath observance without taking an official position on the Sunday Sabbath issue. However, Solomon's stance on Sabbath observance remained a source of divisiveness through her years as president, which concluded in 1905. She wrote the autobiographical *Fabric of My Life* (published posthumously in 1946) and *A Sheaf of Leaves* (1911), a privately printed collection of essays, speeches, and other writings.

BIBLIOGRAPHY: F. Rogow, *Gone to Another Meeting: The National Council of Jewish Women, 1893–1993* (1993); J. Sochen, *Consecrate Every Day: The Public Lives of Jewish American Women, 1880–1980* (1981), 48–61; B.S. Wenger, "Jewish Women and Voluntarism: Beyond the Myth of Enablers," in: *American Jewish History* 79 (Autumn 1989), 16–36.

[Beth S. Wenger (2nd ed.)]

SOLOMON, HAROLD (**"Solly"**; 1952–) U.S. tennis player. Growing up in Silver Spring, Maryland, Solomon proved his tennis abilities early, being ranked the No. 2 youth player in America at 14 before winning the US National Clay Court Championship for 18-year-olds. Solomon attended Rice University and was twice an All-American, establishing himself as a patient and accurate volleyer. Solomon's patented shot, the "moonball" – a deep, high, top-spin lob – kept his opponents from attacking the net, and forced them to maintain their concentration during long rallies, Solomon's forte. As a member of the Association of Tennis Professionals (ATP), Solomon enjoyed a successful 16-year career, won 64 percent of his 879 singles matches, and was selected to four American Davis Cup teams, including two championship teams in 1972 and 1978. From 1975 to 1980, Solomon was one of the top professional tennis players in the world, winning 20 of his 22 singles titles, and being ranked as high as fifth in the 1980 ATP standings before finishing in seventh place. Solomon also finished in the top ten of the ATP in 1976 (8th), 1978 (9th), and 1979 (8th), and maintained a top-20 ranking from 1974 to 1980. Solomon paired with another Jewish player, Eddie Dibbs, to form a doubles team which was referred to affectionately in the press as "The Bagel Twins"; the duo was ranked in the top ten from 1974 to 1976. After retiring in 1986, Solomon went on to become an equally effective coach, helping Mary Joe Fernandez maintain a top-ten ranking from 1994 to 1998, and then managing Jennifer Capriati's celebrated 1999 comeback, when she climbed from 101st to 23rd in the world, while winning her first titles in over six years. Seeking to devote more time to his family, Solomon ended his stretch as a traveling full-time coach in November 2000, serving instead as an adviser to players on the women's circuit. In January 2006 Solomon opened the Harold Solomon International Tennis Academy in Ft. Lauderdale, Florida, to develop young, promising tennis players, with special emphasis on sportsmanship and character building. Apart from his tennis work, Solomon and his wife, Jan, have been active in organizations addressing the problem of world hunger.

[Robert B. Klein (2nd ed.)]

SOLOMON, ODES OF, a collection of early Christian poems of the first century C.E. which might have some bearing on Jewish sectarian literature. The poems were discovered by

J. Rendel Harris, who published them (1909) and gave them the name Odes of Solomon to distinguish them from the better-known *Psalms of Solomon contained in the same manuscript. The Odes were known to some of the Church Fathers: the combination of Odes and Psalms of Solomon was probably quite common in the early Church, but there is no claim to authorship by Solomon in the text. The extant version is a Syriac translation from the Greek. A Hebrew or Aramaic original is possible, but difficult to prove. Of the 41 Odes, 15 are unmistakably, even sharply, Christian, 11 probably Christian, and 14 not necessarily so; none contains positively Jewish material. They can, however, be classed with the *Hodayot* (Qumran *Thanksgiving Psalms) in a loose literary genre, by the common features of a highly poetic record of deeply personal religious experience, centered on the themes of election and salvation, a poetic structure of loose *parallelismus membrorum*, and some figures of style and some unusual metaphors (the firm foundation, the trees planted by God, the lifting to the heights). On the strength of these common metaphors, it has been suggested that some Odes are of Jewish sectarian origin, but this is not likely. However, the doctrinal type of the Christianity expressed by the Odes is not easy to classify (there are some affinities to gnosticism); it is certainly early and, therefore, the possibility that the Odes represent some group of Christians which was influenced by the Dead Sea sect (or some similar Jewish sect) cannot be denied. Even so, the influence of the Dead Sea sect is less pronounced than in other Christian writings. Fragments of the Greek version were published in M. Testuz, *Papyrus Bodmer X–XII* (1959).

BIBLIOGRAPHY: J.R. Harris, *The Odes and Psalms of Solomon* (1909); idem and A. Mingana, *The Odes and Psalms of Solomon* (1916–20; facsimile ed., fuller treatment of text); M. Philonenko, *Les Odes de Salomon* (Dissert., 1960); A. Adam, in: ZNW, 52 (1961), 141–56; J. Carmignac, in: *Revue de Qumran*, 3 (1961), 71–102; 4 (1963), 429–32.

[Jacob Licht]

SOLOMON, PSALMS OF, a collection of 18 pseudepigraphical psalms, extant in Greek and Syriac, but seemingly written in Hebrew. The ascription to Solomon, which stems from the Greek version, has no historical basis, and indeed the psalms themselves make no reference to Solomon. The psalms deal with a number of diverse subjects which include a personal poem, a lament on the nation's troubles, and a hymn of messianic hope, while others deal with social, religious, and political themes.

Psalm 1 speaks of an unexpected war that came to a prosperous nation because of its sins. Psalm 2 relates an attack by gentiles on Jerusalem and the Temple. Although this evil befell the Jews because of their shameful practices, the wicked one who attacked them would receive his deserts. In Psalm 3 the poet discusses the fate of the wicked, who, unlike the righteous, will forfeit the world to come. Psalm 4 attacks the godless who associate with the righteous, censures their transgressions, and looks forward to their destruction by God. (Attempts have been made to equate this with historical situations, but suggestions made so far are without any firm basis.) Psalms 5, 6, and 7 describe God's greatness and His help for the righteous, and entreat Him to help His people. Psalm 8 again describes the tumult of war in sinful Jerusalem and the treatment the city receives at the hands of the conqueror. Psalm 9 again asks God to defend His people. Psalm 10 praises God who rebukes and chastises but who has pity upon the righteous. Psalm 11 contains a vision of the redemption and of the return of the Jewish exiles to Jerusalem. Psalms 12, 13, and 14 praise the righteous and their deliverance, while censuring the wicked and describing their punishment. Psalm 15 presents a description of the crimes of the wicked and of their punishment on the Day of Judgment. In Psalm 16, the poet begs God to keep him from sin, and to show him kindness and deliver him. In Psalm 17 the poet awaits God's judgment and the restoration of the promised kingdom of David, which had been usurped by sinners. However, these are punished by a foreigner (apparently Pompey, see below) who inflicts evils upon Jerusalem, after which, at the end of days, God's salvation will be shown. Psalm 18, the last one, is also filled with messianic hope.

The historical meaning and value of the psalms depends upon the determination of the date of composition. The generally accepted view is that they were compiled about the middle of the first century B.C.E., the political allusions in them reflecting the conquest of Judea by Pompey (63 B.C.E.) and the events connected with it. These can be explained in the light of certain contemporary events, like the verses in Psalm 17 that speak of the promise of the kingdom of David, of its plunder by sinners (the *Hasmoneans), and their punishment by a foreigner (Pompey) who exiled them to the West (Italy). The first verses of the second psalm, which depict a wicked man who broke into Jerusalem and defiled the Temple, refer to a similar situation. Most commentators think that verses 25–29 allude to the fate of Pompey who was murdered in 48 B.C.E. when he went to Egypt after being defeated by Julius Caesar. This interpretation attaches great significance to the criticism of the sins of the Hasmoneans which stigmatizes them as having stolen the kingdom from the dynasty of David. This leads many scholars to believe that the author of the psalms was a *Pharisee, although one must remember that hostility to the Hasmoneans was not restricted to the Pharisees.

There is also considerable historical importance in the eschatological spirit prevalent in the psalms, and in the description of the pious, the righteous, and the God-fearing, who are possibly a collective group that included the author himself. The chief eschatological teaching of the book is found in Psalms 17–18, which give an extensive description of the hoped-for Messiah of the House of David. This section was greatly influenced by Isaiah, chapter 11. The author also preached the doctrine of resurrection (16:12; 15:13). J. Ephron attempted to reject this interpretation completely and postulated that the psalms are Christian. The psalms became known only at the beginning of the 17th century, when the Greek text was published by J.L. de la Cerda from a manuscript. Since then, additional Greek manuscripts have been discovered and further editions have appeared. A Syriac translation has also been discovered but it is of limited value since it was made from the Greek text, not from the Hebrew original.

BIBLIOGRAPHY: O. Gebhardt, *Die Psalmen Salomo's* (1895); Gray, in: Charles, Apocrypha, 2 (1913), 625–52; H.B. Swete, *An Introduction to the Old Testament in Greek* (1914), 282–3, 288; M. Aberbach, in: JQR, 41 (1950–51), 379–96; Ephron, in: Zion, 30 (1964/65), 1–46; O. Eissfeldt, *The Old Testament – An Introduction* (1965), 610–3 (contains bibliography); A. Rahlfs (ed.), *Septuaginta-Studien* (1965^8), 471–89.

[Uriel Rappaport]

SOLOMON, SERVANTS OF (Heb. עַבְדֵי שְׁלֹמֹה). The "Servants of Solomon" are mentioned in I Kings 9:27 (cf. II Chron. 8:18) in an annalistic section (I Kings 9:15–28) that records the grandiose projects undertaken by King Solomon. These included construction within the country and commercial enterprises on an international scale, undertaken in conjunction with Solomon's Phoenician ally, Hiram of Tyre. Solomon's work force, organized to implement his projects, consisted of two major components: corvée labor – large numbers of workers conscripted mainly from the non-Israelite population; and an official, managerial class of army commanders, and some skilled technicians, mostly Israelites. Many scholars assign the "Servants of Solomon" to the non-Israelite corvée, and classify them as royal slaves, hence their name. Supporters of this view cite a later source, the list of returning exiles in the days of Zerubbabel (Ezra 2:2ff.), where "the Sons of the Servants of Solomon" are listed together with the *Nethinim, usually assumed to be Temple slaves (*ibid.* 2:43–58). The slave status of both the Nethinim and the "Servants of Solomon" is to be questioned, however. It is probable that the "Servants of Solomon" were the official class (I Kings 9:27), and not part of the corvée (*ibid.* 9:20–21). They are, after all, mentioned in connection with the trade in gold, brought from *Ophir (location uncertain). Together with Phoenician sea captains provided by Hiram, they set forth on large sailing ships from the port of Elath (Ezion-Geber). The Hebrew term for "slave, servant," *eved*, can also mean "courtier, royal official" (Ex. 8:20; Esth. 3:2).

BIBLIOGRAPHY: Levine, in: JBL, 82 (1963), 207–12 (incl. bibl.).

[Baruch A. Levine]

SOLOMON, SIMEON (1840–1905), British artist. Born in London, he was the son of Michael Solomon, a prosperous hat importer and the second Jew to be made a freeman of the city of London. The young Simeon was encouraged by his brother, Abraham Solomon (1823–1862), a highly gifted but conventional genre artist, who died the very day he was elected an associate of the Royal Academy, and by his sister, Rebecca Solomon (1832–1886), also a Pre-Raphaelite artist whose work was widely exhibited in her lifetime; she had a stabilizing effect on Simeon during the latter's childhood. Simeon, a child prodigy, entered the Royal Academy before he was 15 and exhibited at 18, the youngest artist ever to have been shown there. He created a stir with a picture of the infant Moses set adrift on the Nile and another entitled "Habet," inspired by a contemporary novel, *The Gladiators*. At one Royal Academy exhibition, works by all three Solomons were on show. Simeon Solomon was influenced by the aesthetics of the pre-Raphaelites, Millais and Burne-Jones, with both of whom he was friendly (Burne-Jones said Solomon was the greatest artist in the pre-Raphaelite Brotherhood) and who had a profound effect on his work, which some critics felt to be unmanly and sentimental. In 1871 Simeon also published a prose poem *A Vision of Love Revealed in Sleep* which expresses the ideals of his later paintings and drawings. His public career ended in 1873 when he was arrested in a public lavatory and jailed for a short term for a homosexual offense. At the age of 44, he was admitted to a workhouse. To pay for liquor and drugs, he went on making drawings which he sold to dealers very cheaply. These drawings betray nothing of the degraded circumstances under which he was living. Forgotten for several decades, Solomon's work was rediscovered in the 1960s. His painting, with its soft and subtle gradations, evokes haunting visions. The half-naked angels, somber rabbis, Greek Orthodox priests, and delicately outlined heads of dreamers fail to give any clue to the artist's strange personality. In recent years his reputation has risen, in part because of his status as an ethnic and sexual outsider in Victorian society.

BIBLIOGRAPHY: J.E. Ford, *Simeon Solomon* (Eng., 1908); Werner, in: *Arts Magazine*, 40 (May 1966), 49–51; Lambourne, in: JHSET, 21 (1962–67), 274–86; A. Rubens, *A Jewish Iconography* (1954), nos. 1368 A–K. **ADD. BIBLIOGRAPHY:** ODNB on line; J. Daniels et al., *Solomon: A Family of Painters* (1985); S. Reynolds, *The Vision of Simeon Solomon* (1985).

[Alfred Werner]

SOLOMON, SOLOMON JOSEPH (1860–1927), English painter. Solomon was born in London where he settled and attained considerable social and professional popularity. When in 1918 he was appointed president of the Royal Society of British Artists, he wrote to a Jewish friend: "I feel I ought to accept the presidency of the RBA, because I am a Jew." During World War I, Solomon developed an interest in camouflage and as a result was made lieutenant colonel (1916) and was sent to France on a special mission. On his return he established a camouflage training school. He wrote *Strategic Camouflage* (1920). He was active in Jewish social life, was a founder and the first president of the Maccabean Society (1891), and was an active supporter of the Ben Uri Art Society.

Solomon painted portraits of many eminent people, including Queen Victoria, Israel *Zangwill (1894), Heinrich *Graetz (1887), and Solomon *Schechter (1902). In his fashionable paintings of Edwardian society, he revived the grand manner of the great English portrait painters, employing in addition certain Impressionist devices. He established his reputation with a series of Old Testament subjects with backgrounds inspired by his visit to the Middle East. He painted decorative panels for the Royal Exchange and the House of Lords and mythological and allegorical scenes in the taste of the period. *Allegory* (1904) has been interpreted as representing the ultimate triumph of Judaism as the world religion. He wrote one theoretical work, *The Practice of Oil Painting* (1910).

Solomon's sister, LILY DELISSA JOSEPH (1863–1940), pioneer cyclist, motorist, and airplane pilot, was also a painter.

BIBLIOGRAPHY: O.S. Phillips, *Solomon J. Solomon* (Eng., 1933); DNB, 795–6 (incl. bibl.); Naményi, in: Roth Art, 586–7; M. Buber (ed.), *Juedische Kuenstler* (1903), 141–53.

SOLOMON, TESTAMENT OF, pseudepigraphic work written in Greek, of uncertain date. King Solomon, the narrator, states that during the construction of the Temple his overseer was plagued by the demon Ornias. In answer to the king's prayers, the angel Michael appeared and gave Solomon a ring with which he exorcized the demon. He then summoned up one spirit after another, both male and female, subdued each, and compelled them to assist in the building of the Temple. The queen of the south visited him and marveled. Aderes, king of the Arabs, turned to him when his people were plagued by a demon, and Solomon sent a servant with the ring to subdue and remove it. Solomon then relates his transgressions – how he took many wives; how he sacrificed five locusts to *Moloch in order to obtain the hand of the Jebusite girl; how she persuaded him to build temples to Baal and other gods – which caused him to lose his supernatural powers. In his encounters with the demons Solomon asks each his name, his powers, the angel to whom he is subject, and the means by which he is subdued. The stress on a knowledge of the name and particulars of a demon is common in the demonology of many cultures and is especially pertinent to exorcism. Some of the demons, such as Abezethibod (אב עצות אובד, *Av Eẓot Oved?*), the demon of the Red Sea, Asmodeus, and Beelzebub (Beelzebul; a Greek variant of Beelzebub) are of Oriental origin. Most bear Greek names. Of these, some are concretized evil traits such as are found in classical myths (e.g., Phtonos, jealousy; Eris, strife). Others show affinities to figures of Greco-Roman myth and cult: Obizouth with her dragon-like hair is a Medusa type; Cynopaston, a sea demon, is reminiscent of Poseidon; Onoscelis seems to be the empousa; the dog-shaped Rhabdos and the three-headed serpent are similar to creatures such as Cerberus, the dog of Hades, and the multi-headed Hydra.

Parallel material on Solomon's encounters with demons in Josephus (Ant., 8:45ff.) and midrashic sources (e.g., Git. 68) shows that the Testament contains elements which are considered Jewish; mention of the crucifixion and like references point to Christian elements. Such a syncretistic blend of Jewish, Christian, Oriental, and Hellenic motifs is typical of the demonological and magical literature and papyri emanating from Egypt in the first centuries of the common era. Scholars suggest between c. 100 C.E. and c. 300 C.E. as possible dates of composition. Editions of the Testament of Solomon were published in *Patrologia Graeca* (122 (1899), 1315–58), and by C.C. Mc-Cown (ed.), *The Testament of Solomon* (1922).

BIBLIOGRAPHY: F.C. Conybeare, in: JQR, 11 (1898/99), 1–45; JE, 11 (1907), 448f.; Ginzberg, Legends, 4 (1913), 150–4; 6 (1928), 292f.

[Jacob Petroff]

SOLOMON, WISDOM OF (Gr. Σοφία Σαλωμῶνος (or Σ. Σαλωμῶντος) or, ἡ Σοφία; ἡ πανάρετος Σοφία, "the wisdom of all the good precepts" – a title sometimes given also to Proverbs and Ben Sira), an apocryphal work. The ascription of the book to Solomon is mentioned explicitly in chapters 7–9 (particularly in 9:7), but such early writers as Jerome (*Praefatio in libros Solomonis*), and Augustine (*De Civitate Dei*, 17:20), already were skeptical about this ascription, and attributed the work to Philo despite the fact that its viewpoint differs from his.

The book can be divided into three parts. Chapters 1–5 deal with eschatology, 6–11 deal with wisdom, and 11–19 are a Midrash on the Exodus from Egypt with a Hellenistic presentation. The first part discusses the fate of the righteous and the wicked. The wicked man regards all acts as accidents, and is thus not deterred from doing whatever he wishes; he is unaware that in the end man's life will be judged by his good deeds. Although the wicked man appears to prosper, eternal life and happiness is reserved for the righteous. Thus the righteous man, though he appears not to prosper, is the truly wise man. By its very nature wisdom is unlikely to enter the soul of the wicked (1:4).

The second part describes wisdom as a metaphysical reality, as "a breath of the power of God" (7:25). It exists forever and through its power all knowledge and every virtue is created. It determines the history of Israel. Without expressly mentioning their names, the author exemplifies wisdom's role in the life of biblical "heroes" (Cain, Noah, the men of Sodom, Jacob, and Joseph) and in important events (the Exodus from Egypt and the crossing of the Red Sea).

In the third part the author deals at length with the plagues in Egypt and the redemption. The miracle is regarded not as a change in nature but as a change in the principles that constitute nature, and whether as reward or as punishment always takes the form of measure for measure (e.g., the waters of the Nile were changed to blood because the Egyptians first sinned with water when they cast the Hebrew children into the Nile; on the other hand, the Israelites were rewarded by receiving water from the rock). Punishment itself comes after all possibilities have been exhausted, since it is God's nature to wait for the repentance of the wicked. While discussing Pharaoh's rebelliousness the author incidentally discusses the origin of idolatry in general. It lies in man's bad habit of not seeking for the first cause, and in the fashioning of images which were indeed first created for a specific occasion (e.g., a father mourning for his only son erected an image of him), but then spread through the desire to flatter tyrants and their ambition to exalt themselves. Through idolatry man also found a way of realizing his desires by assigning a different god to each of his vices.

The purpose of the book is to strengthen the Jewish believer against the seduction of idolatry. The problem of the sufferings of the righteous, already discussed in the Bible, is dealt with here against the background of Hellenistic thought. The punishment of the righteous serves the purpose of "testing" or "educating," but his reward is granted in the world to come. God is the God of the living and He intended man to be immortal. However, Satan's jealousy brought death into the world (2:23f.) but only the men of vanity experience it (2:24). The punishment of the righteous is fleeting but his hope everlasting (4:3), while "the memory of the wicked shall perish on the day of reckoning" of their iniquities, i.e., on the eschatological Day of Judgment. Like Proverbs and Ben Sira this work compares wisdom to a creative principal through which God acts in the world (18:15). Idolatry, which is the opposite of wisdom, is regarded as fetishism. The author scorns in particular the worship of "contemptible" beasts (cats, snakes, monkeys), a cult common in Egypt.

Many influences have entered into the book. Besides that of the Bible, the book's view is similar to the view of the sages that evil does not come from the Lord (1:13 – Sifra Be-Ḥukkotai, ch. 4:1); that the soul preexisted (8:20 – Ḥag. 12b): that there is a heavenly temple (9:18 – Gen. R. 1:4); that everything is judged measure for measure (Sot. 1:7); and that the soul is a trust (Yalk Pr. 935). Like the rabbinic *aggadot* it mentions the singing of *Hallel* at the time of the Exodus from Egypt (Pes. 117a). Other views, however, are Platonic and Stoic, e.g., the idea that the world was created from primeval matter (9:9); that the body serves as a hindrance to the influence of God in man (9:15); that there are four virtues (8:7); and that spirit is preexistent. As in Platonism, the wise are the beloved of God, and as in Stoicism the spirit is compared with fire (2:2). The author mentions several other views (that right is might; that man dies but once) only in order to refute them.

As far as the language is concerned, a conscious effort is made to imitate biblical style, including parallelism, but construction of the sentences is Greek and is polished. There is a tendency toward alliteration, paranomasia, and complex words rare even in Greek. Opinions differ as to the composition of the book. Some are of the opinion that the first part was written in Hebrew, others consider the whole book to have been written in Hebrew, while yet others divide it among various authors all of whom wrote in Greek. However, the composition of the Greek words, the use of assonance, the rhythmic construction and the imagery (crowning the head with flowers, the victory processions of athletes, etc.) in all parts of the work alike support the view that it was written in Greek by one person, apparently in Alexandria. The date of composition is uncertain. Since the author opposes the deification of kings, some ascribe it to the era of Caligula. However, the Ptolemaic kings also compared themselves to gods. A 16th-century manuscript was found (now in Hechal Shlomo in Jerusalem) which is a translation of the whole apocryphon, seemingly from the Latin, into a corrupt Hebrew.

BIBLIOGRAPHY: C.L.W. Grimm, *Das Buch der Weisheit erklaert*, in: *Kurzgefasstes exegetisches Handbuch zu den Apokryphen des Alten Testamentes* (1860); W.J. Deane, *The Book of Wisdom* (1881); Charles, Apocrypha, 1 (1913), 518–60; A.T.S. Goodrick, *The Book of Wisdom* (1913); A. Kahana, *Ha-Sefarim ha-Ḥiẓoniyyim*, 1 (1937), 463ff.; J. Reider, *The Book of Wisdom* (1957); E.S. Artom, *Ha-Sefarim ha-Ḥiẓoniyyim*, 2 (1962), 171ff.; Graetz, Gesch, 3 (1906[5]), 382–5; 613–5; D.S. Margoliouth, in: *Journal of the Royal Asiatic Society*, 22 (1890), 263–97; J. Freudenthal, in: JQR, 3 (1890/91), 722–53; DB, 5 (1912), 1351–60; F. Focke, *Die Entstehung der Weisheit Salomos* (1913); H.B. Swete, *Introduction to the Old Testament in Greek* (1914), 267–9; I. Heinemann, *Die griechische Quelle der Weisheit Salomos*, in: *Jahresbericht des juedisch-theologischen Seminars Frankelscher Stiftung fuer das Jahr 1920* (1921), vii–xxv; E.A. Speiser, in: JQR, 14 (1923/24), 455–82.

[Yehoshua M. Grintz]

SOLOMON BEN AARON (**Solomon Yedidya**; 1670(?)–1745), prominent Karaite scholar, author, and spiritual leader from Lithuania. Born in Poswol, he moved after 1707 to Troki. He was a teacher of Torah and had many disciples. In 1710 as a result of a plague, which annihilated more than half of the Karaite population of Lithuania, he lost his wife and children and moved to Vilna, which had become the temporary residence of Karaites during the plague and where he served as the head of the Karaite *bet din*. In Vilna he was friendly with Rabbanite Jews, such as Joshua Heschel and Aryeh Leib Shapira, with whom he corresponded. In 1719 he returned to Troki and became head of the community until the end of his life. He knew Latin, Polish, and Rabbanite literature. Solomon corresponded with Karaite worthies and community leaders from Jerusalem, Constantinople, Damascus, and Lithuania-Poland on learned and community subjects. In 1696/7 Solomon was invited by Prof. Puffendorf, rector of Riga University (then under Swedish control), to come there to expound the Karaite doctrines. He was also asked to write a work about the schism between Karaites and Rabbanites. He wrote a book *Apiryon Asah Lo*, which explains in its first part the commandments according to the doctrines of the Karaites and their differences from those of Rabbanites. The second part contains an anti-Rabbanite polemic. Without any critical approach Solomon introduces the traditional apologetic Karaite claim that the split between Rabbanism and Karaism had begun in the period of the Second Temple. The shortened version of this book was first published by A. Neubauer, *Aus der Petersburger Bibliothek*, Leipzig, (1866), 4–29 (later edition: J. Algamil (ed.), 2000). He wrote several works: *Ḥanokh la-Na'ar* and *Rakh va-Tov* (preserved in mss in various libraries) – grammatical treatises; *Leḥem She'arim* (IOS A 3, JNUL mic. 52475) – polemics between Karaites and Rabbanites by way of questions and answers; *Migdal Oz* (IOS A 162; JNUL mic. 52389) – anti-Christian polemics, a kind of guide for those, who are forced to dispute with Christians. He wrote also liturgical poems in Hebrew and the Karaite language, of which some were incorporated in the Karaite *siddur*.

BIBLIOGRAPHY: G. Akhiezer and D. Shapira, *Peamim*, 89 (2001), 41–42; A. Gottlober, *Bikkoret le-Toledot ha-Kara'im* (1865), 201; A. Neubauer, *Aus der Petersburger Bibliothek* (1866), 78–79; Mann, Texts, 2 (1935), index, 1588; M. Polliack (ed.), *Karaite Judaism: A Guide to Its History and Literary Sources*, (2003), index.

[Golda Akhiezer (2nd ed.)]

SOLOMON BEN ABRAHAM OF MONTPELLIER (13th century), talmudic scholar, initiator of the Maimonidean controversy that took place in the third decade of the 13th century (see *Maimonidean Controversy and Criticism). While he admired Maimonides as a talmudist and always spoke of him with respect, Solomon opposed his philosophic views, and in his fear that they would lead to heresy, began to campaign against the study of the *Guide of the Perplexed* and *Sefer ha-Madda*, the first book of the *Mishneh Torah*, in which Maimonides set down some of his philosophic views. Together with his two disciples, *David ben Saul and Jonah b. Abraham *Gerondi, Solomon enlisted the support of the rabbis of northern France, who in 1232 pronounced a ban against the study of the philosophical works of Maimonides and the secular sciences. The supporters of Maimonidean philosophy in Provence retaliated by excommunicating Solomon and his two disciples. With the deepening of the controversy Solomon was accused by David *Kimḥi, a supporter of the Maimonists, of informing to the Franciscans and the Dominicans concerning the heretical nature of the *Guide*, thus initiating the burning of the work, which is thought to have taken place in Marseilles around 1232. Modern scholars, however, maintain that it is extremely unlikely that either Solomon himself or his two disciples actually did inform to the non-Jewish authorities, for they continued to be respected within the Jewish community as individuals and scholars, and it is difficult to believe that they would have been had they actually informed on the Maimonists.

Cited by Menahem b. Solomon *Meiri in one of his responsa, Solomon was spoken of favorably by *Naḥmanides, Judah *Alfakar, Meshullam b. Solomon, and Joseph b. Todros ha-Levi *Abulafia. From extant sources such as Abraham b. Moses b. *Maimon's *Milḥamot Adonai*, Solomon emerges not as a simple man nor as an extreme fanatic but as a learned talmudist who was uneducated in the realm of philosophy and did not understand the complexities of Maimonidean philosophy. While it is not clear exactly what he opposed in Maimonides' philosophy, it appears that he objected to Maimonides' allegorical interpretation of talmudic passages that described the afterlife in a material fashion and to his interpretation of many biblical laws. He opposed the view that the activation of the intellect was the prerequisite for attaining immortality, maintaining that the observance of the divine law was more important. He criticized Samuel ibn *Tibbon, the translator of the *Guide*, rather than Maimonides himself, for interpreting all biblical narratives allegorically.

BIBLIOGRAPHY: Baer, Spain, index; D.J. Silver, *Maimonidean Criticism and the Maimonidean Controversy* (1965), index; Guttman, Philosophies, 185; Graetz, Hist, 6 (1902), index.

SOLOMON BEN ELIJAH HA-KOHEN (late 11th and early 12th century), founder of an academy in *Damascus in the early 12th century. His father, the *gaon* *Elijah b. Solomon (d. 1083), was head of the Palestinian academy in Tyre. Elijah appointed his elder son, ABIATHAR, as his successor and his second son, SOLOMON, as *av* ("father") of the academy. However, after the dispute which broke out between the members of the academy and *David b. Daniel b. Azariah, who demanded that the Jews of Palestine and *Syria also recognize him, Abiathar was forced to escape to Tripoli in Syria. Solomon also left Tyre. It seems that he remained for some time in one of the villages of Galilee and later settled in *Ḥadrak. There he founded an academy which was considered as a continuation of the Palestinian one. He also assumed the title of *gaon*. A letter that he wrote in 1116, while *gaon* in Ḥadrak, was found in the **Genizah*.

BIBLIOGRAPHY: Mann, Egypt, index; Mann, Texts, 1 (1931), 249ff.; S. Assaf (ed.), *Sefer ha-Yishuv*, 2 (1944), 93–94; Braslavi, in: *Eretz Israel*, 5 (1958), 220f.

[Eliyahu Ashtor]

SOLOMON BEN ḤASDAI, exilarch in Babylonia, 733–c. 759, grandson of the *exilarch *Bustanai. Solomon was a scholar and leader. During his period of office he appointed three *geonim* to the academies of *Sura and *Pumbedita; one of these was his brother-in-law, Natronai Kahana of Pumbedita, who was also a member of the Bustanai family. When the academy of Sura lost its leader and a suitable *rosh yeshivah* could not be found, he appointed R. Yehudai b. *Naḥman of Pumbedita as *Gaon* of Sura. His brother David was the father of *Anan, the founder of the *Karaite sect. His son Isaac Iskoi succeeded him as exilarch.

BIBLIOGRAPHY: Tykocinski, in: *Devir*, 1 (1923), 174–9; Goode, in: JQR, 31 (1940/41), 156–7.

[Abraham David]

SOLOMON BEN JUDAH (d. 1051), Palestinian *gaon* and academy head in Jerusalem and in Ramleh from 1025 to 1051. It appears that R. Solomon was the son of a family of scholars from Fez. He married into the family of Solomon b. Joseph ha-Kohen, who preceded him in the gaonate. He was the father of three sons and a daughter, including Abraham who held the position of "fourth" in the yeshivah, and Yaḥya who studied under R. Hai Gaon.

At first R. Solomon was *ḥazzan* in Jerusalem, then a member of the academy, then *av bet din*, and finally head of the academy. The members of his *bet din* were Nathan b. Abraham as *av bet din*, Tobiah b. Daniel, and Joseph ha-Kohen and Elijah ha-Kohen of the family which held positions in the Ereẓ Israel gaonate. More of his letters have been preserved than of any other Palestinian *Gaon*, and many were published. His Hebrew had a figurative style, and his particular concluding blessing was "great salvation." He also wrote in Arabic. Most of the letters were sent to Egypt. A document of his *bet din* from 1044/45 – evidence of the receipt of a pledge in Jerusalem and signed by the *gaon* and Elijah ha-Kohen – has been preserved. A letter of recommendation written by him for a Jew of Khurasan, who traveled to Egypt to collect funds, is also extant. He also wrote *piyyutim*, some of which were published. These include a *kerovah* for Ḥanukkah, a section of a *piyyut* for Shavuot, and a poem expressing yearning for the redemption of Jerusalem. A *piyyut* in his honor was written by the *ḥazzan* Eli ha-Kohen b. Ezekiel of Fostat, and Ephraim he-Ḥaver b. Shemariah wrote a *kinah* in his memory.

A peaceful man, his judgments were lenient and inclined toward making concessions. His approach to the Karaites was also tolerant; he attempted to abolish the ban which was issued against them every year on Hoshana Rabba on the Mount of Olives. In spite of the authorities' prohibition, the ban was once issued against the Karaites without his consent. As a result, several scholars were arrested and imprisoned in Damascus. The sufferings he endured at the hands of his adversaries are echoed in his letters. He was accused of having taken for himself a contribution which was sent from Mahdīyya to the yeshivah. His relations with Elhanan b. Shemariah were strained and he was compelled to leave Jerusalem after he was declared guilty of not helping certain prisoners. It is also possible that pressure from the local Karaites brought about his departure from Jerusalem to Ramleh. His principal adversary was Nathan b. Abraham, the disciple of Samuel ("the Third") b. Hoshana, and R. Ḥushi'el of Kairouan. After the death of his uncle Bar Yoḥai, the *av* of the academy, Nathan was appointed, with the support of influential circles in Egypt, as *av* in Ereẓ Israel. While R. Solomon was in Jerusalem and Nathan in Ramleh, Nathan proclaimed himself academy head (*rosh yeshivah*). The *Gaon* then went to Ramleh and issued a ban against him for overstepping his bounds. Both factions engaged in polemics and sent letters of accusation to Egypt. The representatives of the Fatimid government in Jerusalem and Ramleh supported R. Solomon, according to instructions received from Egypt. The dispute continued for three years and in 1043 an agreement was reached between the adversaries. According to this, Nathan was to remain *av* and after the death of the *gaon*, he would assume the position of *rosh yeshivah*. During R. Solomon's time the economic situation in Ereẓ Israel, especially in Jerusalem, was poor; heavy taxes were imposed. In 1024 bedouin of the Jarāḥ tribe attacked the country and plundered Ramleh and the rest of the centers. A plague raged through Jerusalem, and in 1033 the country was struck by an earthquake. The pilgrimage from the Diaspora, on which the incomes of the academy and the Jewish population were to a great extent dependent, declined. In his letters to Egypt, R. Solomon described the distressing situation and appealed for support for maintenance of the Jews. He maintained relations with the communities of Damascus, Aleppo, and Tyre; they requested that he pray for them and give them his blessing, and they contributed to his academy. A letter from distant Spain was brought to him "from the merchants in Seville." The *nagid* Jacob b. Amram of Mahdīyya (near Kairouan) sent a contribution to his academy. The *gaon* also exchanged letters with R. Hai Gaon. Relations with Babylonia deteriorated as a result of the rivalry for the support of Egypt, the wealthiest contributor to the academies in Babylonia and Ereẓ Israel. Egypt was the political and financial pillar of Ereẓ Israel and the majority of the academy's income came from there. In 1026–27 R. Solomon sent a *ḥazzan* named Solomon and his own son Abraham in order to raise funds in Egypt. He also maintained a correspondence with personalities in the inner circles of the royal court and the heads of the Egyptian communities, such as the communal leader Samuel b. Talyon and the "chief of the congregation" Abraham b. Isaac ha-Kohen. Most of his letters were addressed to three personalities: Abraham b. Sahlan and his son Sahlan, leaders of the Babylonian community in Fostat who also supported the Ereẓ Israel academy, and Ephraim b. Shemariah of Gaza, a member of the "Great Sanhedrin" and leader of the Ereẓ Israel community in Fostat. The Jerusalemite community in Egypt was subject to the authority of R. Solomon, who also intervened in its internal affairs.

BIBLIOGRAPHY: A. Epstein, in: REJ, 25 (1892), 272–6; A. Marmorstein, in: JQR, 8 (1917–18), 1–29; Mann, Egypt, 1–2 (1920–22), index s.v. *Solomon b. Yehudah*; idem, in: HUCA, 3 (1926), 269–76; Mann, Texts, 1–2 (1931–35), index; R. Gottheil and W.H. Warrel, *Fragments from the Cairo Genizah in the Freer Collection* (1927), 196–201; S. Assaf, in: *Zion*, 2 (1927), 115–6; idem, in: *Mi-Sifrut ha-Geonim* (1933), 208–9; idem and L.A. Mayer, *Sefer ha-Yishuv*, 2 (1944), index; Marx, in PAAJR, 16 (1946–47), 195f.; M. Zulay, in: *Sinai*, 25 (1949), 41f.; A. Scheiber, in: *Tarbiz*, 22 (1951), 171–3; B. Shapira, in: *Yerushalayim*, 4 (1953), 118ff.; H.Z. Hirschberg, in: *Eretz Israel*, 5 (1958), 216–7; A.M. Habermann, in: *Sinai*, 53 (1963), 183–92.

[Eliezer Bashan (Sternberg)]

SOLOMON BEN JUDAH HA-BAVLI (mid-tenth century), Hebrew poet. One of the first Hebrew hymnologists in Europe. He appears to have lived in northern Italy though his family was of Oriental origin. Little is known of him apart from some semilegendary allusions to him as an esteemed *paytan*, and as one of those who conveyed the Oriental "Secrets of Prayer" from Italy to Germany. The limited literary remains now extant consist of a few hymns for the Sabbath and festivals, as well as about 25 *seliḥot*. His best-known production is a *yoẓer* for Passover, *Or Yesha Me'usharim*, the pattern of which is taken from one of Eleazar Kallir's works, and later served as a model for many other Italian and German hymnologists, such as his pupil *Meshullam b. Kalonymus. His *Avodah for the Day of Atonement, *Adderet Tilboshet*, is one of the most puzzling of its kind. The *seliḥot* of Solomon are often referred to as *shalmoniyyot*, a term possibly derived from his name. His poetry is remarkable for its rich, polished rhyme; only his *Avodah* is unrhymed. His style is heavy and murky and his works often raise difficult problems of commentary which the early sages, including Rashi, tried to solve. His *piyyutim* had a great influence on the works of the first Italian and Ashkenazi *paytanim* who took him as a model. In 1865 L. Zunz prepared a list of Solomon ha-Bavli's poems. E. Fleischer published the first critical edition of his poems, with introduction and commentary, in 1973.

BIBLIOGRAPHY: Zunz, Poesie, 100–4; 232–5; Elbogen, Gottesdienst, 325f.; Davidson, Oẓar, 4 (1933), 470, s.v. *Shelomo ha-Bavli*; Roth, Dark Ages, 259–62. **ADD. BIBLIOGRAPHY:** E. Fleischer, *The Poems of Shelomoh ha-Bavli* (Hebrew; 1973); idem, *The Yoẓer* (Hebrew; 1984), 647–53, passim.

[Ezra Fleischer]

SOLOMON BEN JUDAH "OF DREUX" (or Rouen; 12th–13th centuries), French scholar and tosafist. Solomon was one of the eminent pupils of *Isaac b. Samuel of Dampierre. He was regarded as one of the leaders of French Jewry in his time, and was one of the seven French scholars to whom Meir *Abulafia addressed his letter of complaint against the Provençal scholars because of their attitude to Maimonides' view of the resurrection. He is called Solomon ha-Kadosh ("the saintly"), and sometimes simply "Ha-Kadosh," apparently because of his piety and asceticism. Both contemporary and later scholars relied on his customs. Solomon is mentioned in the standard *tosafot* to a number of tractates, in those of a pupil of Rabbenu Perez to *Bava Kama* and *Bava Mezia*, and to a considerable extent in the works of the tosafists of England, which have been discovered during recent years. There is also mention of *tosafot* by Solomon himself which are no longer extant. He also apparently engaged in biblical exegesis since, in addition to quotations from him occurring in the collections of the commentaries of the tosafists to the Pentateuch, he is known to have been the teacher of Meir of Etoile, who engaged exclusively in biblical exegesis. Another of his pupils was *Samuel b. Solomon of Falaise.

Findings of the 1970s on indicate that R. Solomon was associated with Rouen and not Dreux.

BIBLIOGRAPHY: Gross, Gal Jud, 171–3, 626; Urbach, Tosafot, index.

[Israel Moses Ta-Shma]

SOLOMON BEN JUDAH OF LUNEL (Solomon Vivas; 1411–?), Provençal philosopher. At the age of 13, under the direction of his teacher, Solomon ben Menahem (Frat Maimon), Solomon composed a commentary on Judah *Halevi's *Kuzari*, entitled *Ḥeshek Shelomo*, which is extant in manuscript (Bodleian Library, Opp. Add. 114). At times, Solomon quotes his teacher word for word – for example, in the section on the 53rd chapter of Isaiah. While the author claims to have based his commentary on Judah b. Isaac Cardinal's Hebrew translation of the *Kuzari*, it appears that the translation he used was, apart from a few variations, that made by Judah ibn *Tibbon.

The work reflects a considerable knowledge of the philosophical literature of the period. Solomon quotes Shem Tov *Falaquera, *Levi b. Gershom's commentary on Ecclesiastes, a section on physics from Levi's *Milḥamot Adonai*, and portions of Levi's commentary on the Pentateuch. He also refers to *Moses of Narbonne's commentary on al-*Ghazali's "Intentions of the Philosophers", Solomon b. Menahem's commentary on *Levi b. Abraham's *Battei ha-Nefesh*, and *Ru'aḥ Ḥen*, a philosophical work of disputed authorship which was meant to serve as a kind of introduction to the philosophic ideas of Maimonides' *Guide*. In one portion of his commentary, Solomon attributes *Ru'aḥ Ḥen* to Moses ibn *Tibbon, while in another portion, he holds that the work was written by Samuel ibn *Tibbon. He implies that he himself wrote a commentary to the work. Toward the end of *Ḥeshek Shelomo* he refers to *Sefer ha-Sod* by Joseph ibn *Kaspi.

BIBLIOGRAPHY: Steinschneider, in: HB, 16 (1876), 127; Renan, Ecrivains, 412; Gross, Gal Jud, 290.

SOLOMON BEN MEIR (12th century), northern French scholar, grandson of *Rashi and younger brother of Jacob *Tam and *Samuel b. Meir. Very little is known about him. He was born after Rashi's death and was apparently named after him. He occupied himself mainly with exegesis, grammar, and punctuation, and was called "the father of the grammarians." Only fragments of his work have survived in the *Arugat ha-Bosem* of *Abraham b. Azriel, who is the only scholar to cite him. Solomon may possibly have compiled a book of halakhic rulings (Ḥul. 116b, Rashi end of commentary to Mishnah 8:5).

BIBLIOGRAPHY: Gross, Gal Jud, 162, 234; Urbach, Tosafot, 54, 56; S. Poznański, *Perush al Yeḥezkel ... le-Rabbi Eliezer mi-Belganzi* (1913), xxxix ff.

[Israel Moses Ta-Shma]

SOLOMON BEN SAMSON (11th century), scholar of Worms, a contemporary of Rashi's teachers. He used to sign himself ששו"ן and as a result is referred to as "Sason." His teachers were *Jacob b. Yakar and, apparently, *Eleazar of Worms, and he was a colleague of *Isaac b. Judah ha-Levi, the teacher of Rashi. Many of Solomon's rulings are quoted in the *Ma'aseh ha-Ge'onim* (1910) in reply to questions raised by the sons of *Machir b. Judah. It is stated there that he and *Kalonymus of Rome disagreed with Isaac b. Moses of Mainz as to whether a minor male could exercise the equivalent of *me'un* (see *child marriage) with regard to his wife. Some of his responsa were collected in the *Teshuvot Ḥakhmei Ẓarefat ve-Loter*, (ed. by J. Mueller (1881), nos. 43–56).

His responsa are written in the style of Rashi, in a spirit of humility, and are based on the traditions of his teachers. Statements of his are found among various works of the school of Rashi, such as *Shibbolei ha-Leket*, *Sefer ha-Pardes*, and *Sefer ha-Roke'aḥ*. He was also one of the first of the commentators on *piyyut* in Germany. Additional fragments of his work were discovered recently in the manuscript of a prayer book. A *paytan* called Solomon b. Samson b. Eliakim is mentioned by L. *Zunz in his *Literaturgeschichte der synagogalen Poesie*.

BIBLIOGRAPHY: J. Mueller (ed.), *Teshuvot Ḥakhmei Ẓarefat ve-Loter* (1881), xxx; E.E. Urbach (ed.), *Arugat ha-Bosem*, 4 (1963), 15–16; M. Hershler, in: *Hadarom* 25 (1967), 171–6.

[Israel Moses Ta-Shma]

SOLOMON BEN SAMUEL (14th century), scholar living in Urgench, Transoxania (Uzbekistan). In 1339 he compiled a Hebrew-Persian dictionary, *Sefer ha-Melizah*, comprising over 1,000 alphabetical entries on the vocabulary of the Bible, Targum, Talmud, and Midrash. The author knew Turkish, Persian, Arabic, and Aramaic and was well acquainted with the works of Jewish scholarship of the West, including *Rashi, whom he called "Solomon the Frenchman." There are manuscripts of *Sefer ha-Meliẓah* in the *Firkovitch and E.N. *Adler Collections.

[Walter Joseph Fischel]

SOLOMON SULIMAN BEN AMAR (ninth or tenth century), liturgical poet. Solomon was also called Solomon Alsingari, from which it follows that he came from Sindjar, west of *Mosul in Kurdistan. He may possibly have lived in Babylon, but it is not impossible that he lived in Ereẓ Israel or in *Egypt. Many hundreds of his *piyyutim* were discovered in the Cairo **Genizah*. Since many of them do not bear his signature, some of them were attributed in error to other *paytanim*, whose names were also Solomon, as for example Solomon ibn Gabirol.

His important *piyyutim* are *kerovot* for all the Jewish festivals; *yoẓerot*, for all the portions of the Torah; and a *ma'amad* for the order of the Temple service on the Day of Atonement. Only a few of his *piyyutim* have been published, about seven by I. Davidson in *Ginzei Schechter*, 3 (1928), others by various scholars. Fragments of the *ma'amad* were published, without his name being given, by I. Elbogen in his *Studien zur Geschichte des juedischen Gottesdienstes* (1907), 176–82.

BIBLIOGRAPHY: M. Zulay, in: *Sinai*, 17 (1945), 296–304; 25 (1949), 41–44; J. Schirmann, *Shirim Ḥadashim min ha-Genizah* (1965), 46–52; E. Fleischer, in: *Sinai*, 66 (1970), 234–7.

[Abraham David]

SOLOMONS, ADOLPHUS SIMEON (1826–1910), U.S. leader in social welfare programs. Solomons, who was born in New York, as a young man helped found Mount Sinai Hospital. Moving to Washington in 1859, he did government printing, ran a bookstore, and maintained a photograph gallery. In 1871 he was elected to Washington D.C.'s House of Delegates. His greatest achievement was in the service of the American Red Cross, which he helped Clara Barton establish in 1881. While she was absent from Washington in 1883, he conducted the young organization's affairs from its Washington headquarters as second vice president and was described by her as "my good vice president and kind counselor." Solomons held this office for 12 years and represented the U.S. at the Red Cross conference in Geneva in 1884. Sent by President Chester A. Arthur as the U.S. representative to the International Red Cross convention in 1887, he was elected vice president of the convention. For 20 years Solomons was director of Columbia Hospital and Living In Asylum, also serving as an executive of many other health institutions. Of a religious bent, he was concerned with Jewish survival and served as acting president of the Jewish Theological Seminary Association (1902) and as a member of the central committee of the Alliance Israélite Universelle. Solomons became the champion of the new immigrants from Eastern Europe, and was appointed by Baron de Hirsch as general agent for the Baron de Hirsch Fund in the U.S.

BIBLIOGRAPHY: A.V. Goodman, in: AJHSQ, 59, no. 3 (1970), 331–56.

[Abram Vossen Goodman]

SOLOMONS, JACK (1900–1979), British boxing promoter. Born in London's East End, Solomons became a professional fighter at the age of 17, but after three bouts he left the ring and entered the fish business. In 1931 he returned to boxing as a promoter, and following World War II promoted the sport in Great Britain with the 1945 British heavyweight championship match between Jack London and Bruce Woodcock. The event was a huge success and made Solomons the premier boxing promoter in Britain. He staged boxing shows all over the world, and in 1962 put on the first professional bout in Israel. Solomons promoted numerous world title fights including the 1951 middleweight match between Ray Robinson and Randy Turpin and the heavyweight meeting of Cassius Clay and Brian London in 1966. He is the author of the book *Jack Solomons Tells All* (1956).

[Jesse Harold Silver]

SOLOTAROFF, THEODORE H. (1928–), critic and editor. Solotaroff was on the editorial staff of *Commentary* in the early 1960s and subsequently edited the literary quarterly *New American Review*, which published many of the leading young American prose writers of the 1960s. Solataroff's own literary essays were collected in his book *The Red Hot Vacuum* (1970), most of which was devoted to studies of American writing in the years after World War II. He edited, with Nessa Rapoport, *Writing Our Way Home: Contemporary Stories by American Jewish Writers* (1992), later republished as *The Schocken Book of Contemporary Jewish Fiction* (1996). He also wrote two autobiographical works, *Truth Comes in Blows: A Memoir* (1998) and *First Loves: A Memoir* (2003).

SOLOVEICHIK, Lithuanian rabbinical family. (See Chart: Soloveichik Family). It is first heard of in Slobodka. (1) JOSEPH HA-LEVI SOLOVEICHIK was the *parnas* of the community and strove to have the 1758 prohibition forbidding Jews to live in Kovno rescinded. His son, (2) ISAAC, had two sons, (3) Moses and Abraham, who built the great synagogue of Williampol-Slobodka in 1772. MOSES was appointed rabbi of Williampol-Slobodka. Moses' son, (4) JOSEPH, became the son-in-law of Ḥayyim of Volozhin and was rabbi of Kovno. Joseph's son, (5) ISAAC ZE'EV, was appointed the official rabbi of Kovno. (6) Joseph Baer *Soloveichik was the son of Isaac Ze'ev, as was (7) ḤAYYIM SIMḤAH, whose only daughter married Feivel Holzberg, the father of Isaac Raphael Holzberg. (8) SIMḤAH HA-LEVI SOLOVEICHIK, son of Elijah Ẓevi, a son of (4), immigrated to Jerusalem, where he was known as Simḥah of London. (9) Ḥayyim *Soloveichik was the son of (6). (10) SIMḤAH, also a son of (6), was appointed rabbi of Mogilev in 1911. (11) ZALMAN, son of (8), was a well-known Jerusalem communal worker. (12) MOSES, son of (9), was rabbi in a number of Lithuanian towns and then *rosh yeshivah* at the Rabbi Isaac Elchanan Theological Seminary (see *Yeshiva University) in New York. (13) JOSEPH DOV, son of (8), was appointed rabbi of Spring Valley in 1933. (14) MOSES, son of (8), was a *rosh yeshivah* and rabbi in Switzerland. (15) Isaac Ze'ev ha-

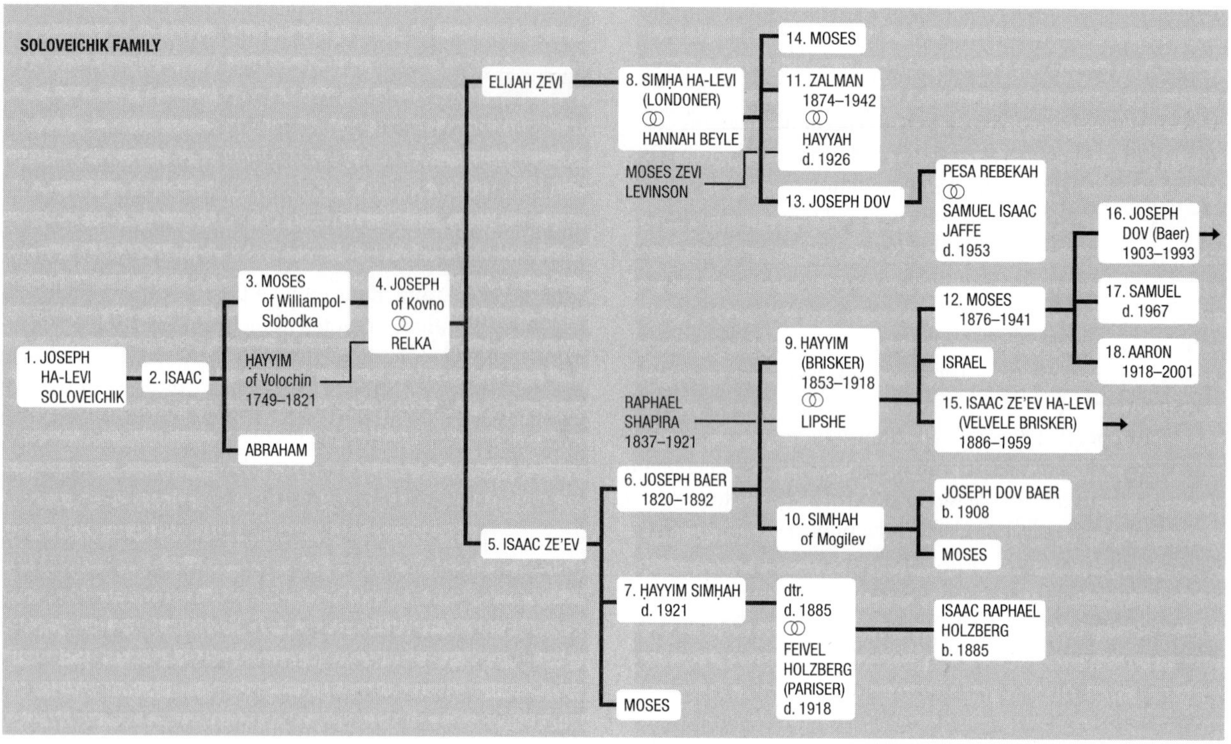

Levi *Soloveichik (1886–1959), son of (9), was a *rosh yeshivah* in Warsaw, succeeded his father at Brisk, and on immigrating to Jerusalem in 1941, founded a yeshivah for exceptional students. He was known as Velvele Brisker. He was regarded as the supreme halakhic authority by the extreme Orthodox section of the community. (16) Joseph Dov *Soloveitchik, (17) SAMUEL SOLEVEICHIK, a prominent chemist, and (18) AARON *SOLOVEICHIK were sons of (12). The literary output of this distinguished family has been remarkably meager, the result of a family tradition against publishing writings except under special circumstances.

BIBLIOGRAPHY: *Yahadut Lita – Temunot ve-Ẓiyyunim* (1959), index; *Sefer Yahadut Lita*, 1 (1959), index; 3 (1967), index.

[Mordechai Hacohen]

SOLOVEICHIK, AARON (1917–2001), U.S. *rosh yeshivah* and noted Orthodox rabbinical personality. Born in Khaslavichy, Belarus, he was taken to Warsaw in 1920 where his father Rabbi Moshe *Soloveichik became head of the Talmud department of the Taḥkemoni rabbinical seminary. In 1930, right after his bar mitzvah, Soloveichik and his family immigrated to the United States, where his father had become the senior *rosh yeshivah* at the Rabbi Isaac Elchanan Theological Seminary. Soloveichik graduated from the high school (Talmudical Academy), and the college (Yeshiva College) affiliated with the Rabbi Isaac Elchanan Theological Seminary. He received his rabbinical ordination from the latter institution and also attained a legal degree from the New York University Law School. Soloveichik first taught Talmud at Mesivtha Tifereth Jerusalem and then at the Rabbi Chaim Berlin Yeshiva. In 1960 he joined the Talmudic faculty of the Rabbi Isaac Elchanan Theological Seminary, where his older brother, Rabbi Joseph Baer *Soloveitchik, was the dominant spiritual and intellectual figure. Rabbi Aaron Soloveichik moved to Chicago in 1966, where he became *rosh yeshivah* and dean of the faculty at the Hebrew Theological College in Skokie, Illinois.

In 1974 he left this school and founded Yeshivas Brisk in Chicago. In 1986 he began commuting weekly to New York to also teach at the Rabbi Isaac Elchanan Theological Seminary, where he became the successor to his ailing brother, Joseph. In addition to Talmud and cognate texts, Soloveichik also taught the philosophy of Judaism, lectured on contemporary issues, and devoted much time to student guidance. He became a beloved and focal rabbinic figure on the American Torah scene. Despite suffering a debilitating stroke in 1983, he courageously continued his teaching responsibilities. Soloveichik was quoted in the New York Times (January 4, 1987), "I try to elevate myself through my suffering. I'm in constant pain. But when I give a *shi'ur*, I don't feel it as much."

Soloveichik was forthright in expressing his opinions and took strong positions on contemporary issues. He opposed the war in Vietnam, which was unusual at the time for an American *rosh yeshivah*. Soloveichik strongly supported the settlement of all of the Land of Israel. He was opposed to the Oslo Accords and lobbied Israeli political and spiritual leaders on both political and theological grounds. Soloveichik declared that the Land of Israel belonged solely to the Jewish people and that compromise would not bring peace.

A portion of his teachings was published by Soloveichik, aided by his students. *Logic of the Heart, Logic of the Mind*, consisting of "reflections on topics of our times" appeared in 1991. Three volumes of his rabbinic novellas were published. *Od Yisrael Yosef Beni Ḥai*, in memory of a grandson, appeared in 1993. Two volumes, entitled *Peraḥ Matteh Aharon*, consisting of insights on the first two divisions of Maimonides' *Mishneh Torah*, were published in 1997 and 1999. In editing these volumes, Soloveichik was assisted by his disciple David Applebaum, who was both a rabbi and medical doctor and resided in Jerusalem. Applebaum was to be murdered in a suicide bombing at the Hillel Café together with his daughter, Naava, on the eve of her wedding (2003).

BIBLIOGRAPHY: S.S. Meiselman, *The Soloveitchik Heritage: A Daughter's Memoir* (1995).

[Aaron Rothkoff (2nd ed.)]

SOLOVEICHIK, ḤAYYIM (known as **R. Ḥayyim Brisker**; 1853–1918), talmudist and predominant figure in Orthodox Jewry in his time. Soloveichik was born in Volozhin where his father Joseph taught at the yeshivah. At the age of 20, he married a daughter of Raphael Shapiro, one of the heads of the yeshivah at Volozhin, and he remained there pursuing his studies with great diligence. He was accustomed to discuss talmudic problems with a small circle of outstanding students and before long his influence was felt throughout the yeshivah. In 1880 he was appointed to the staff and became renowned as a stimulating teacher.

Soloveichik was the initiator of a new trend in Talmud study. Possessed of remarkable analytic powers, he would carefully analyze the subject under discussion into its categories and component parts. He evolved a suitable terminology with which to describe the different concepts and showed that the differences in the Talmud itself and among its authoritative interpreters derived from them. The method spread and was adopted in yeshivot throughout the world. Thousands of students flocked to hear him; many of them became distinguished teachers. Naphtali Ẓevi Judah *Berlin, head of the yeshivah, would consult him before making any change in its administration. After the Volozhin yeshivah closed in 1892, Soloveichik went to live with his father, the rabbi of Brisk (Brest-Litovsk). His father died that same year and Soloveichik succeeded him. He at once threw himself into communal activity, using his great talents to improve existing religious and social services and to establish new ones. His reputation grew; rabbis and laymen of the surrounding district consulted him on all matters. His opinion was always asked for and heeded, his leadership never being taken for granted. He participated in every important rabbinical and communal council. Of a friendly disposition, he kept open house for all, whether talmudists or scientists, learned or ignorant, religious or irreligious. He was ready to help everyone, sympathizing, comforting, and advising. Scholars would bring him their difficulties; even unmarried mothers came to him for assistance and advice. None left him empty-handed and without renewed courage. Most of his salary was given to the needy, and as a result he was frequently in debt. In the winter he left his wood store unlocked so that the poor might help themselves. The lay leaders complained they could not afford the cost involved, but he replied that he would have to instruct his wife not to light his fire since it was impossible for him to sit in a warm room knowing that the poor were freezing.

In 1895 Brisk was swept by a fire which destroyed many homes. All Soloveichik's energies were devoted toward the rebuilding. He slept in the synagogue porch among those who had lost everything in the fire, and the stream of scholars and lay leaders who wanted to consult him came to him there. Stringent personally in the observance of religious precepts, he was always lenient when applying them to others. In public religious practice, however, he was firm and uncompromising, and did all he could to stem the erosion of Jewish life. Because of his sincerity, great knowledge, and personal piety, he invariably prevailed against those who wished lightly to introduce changes into communal institutions or places of learning. Many of his novellae on talmudic tractates have been published, (3 vols., 1952–66), as well as his novellae on Maimonides *Mishneh Torah* (1936).

BIBLIOGRAPHY: B.Z. Eisenstadt, *Ẓaddik li-Verakhah* (1919); D. Feuchtwanger, *Righteous Lives* (1965), 107–9; S.J. Zevin, *Ishim ve-Shittot* (1966^3), 38–85; I. Frenkel, *Men of Distinction*, 1 (1967), 177–85.

[Mordechai Hacohen]

SOLOVEICHIK, ISAAC ZE'EV HA-LEVI (1886–1959), rabbi of Brisk (Brest-Litovsk), halakhist, and talmudist. Born in Volozhin, Isaac was the son of Ḥayyim *Soloveichik, who was his only teacher and regarded him as his spiritual heir, who would continue that tradition of study which originated in Volozhin. Isaac's erudition and acumen were evident from his early youth, and his father stated that in insight he resembled his grandfather Joseph Baer, the founder of the Brisk dynasty of great talmudists. On the death of his father in 1918, Isaac Ze'ev was appointed by the community to succeed him as rabbi of Brisk. He soon became renowned as a central figure in the world of Torah and was popularly known as "R. Velvel." He did not establish a yeshivah at Brisk but gave lessons to a group of the best students of yeshivot as well as other select individuals who assembled in his *bet midrash*. Admission to his circle of students was regarded as a great privilege, to which every student who wished to perfect his knowledge aspired. Despite his youth, the great contemporary talmudists, well-known rabbis, and heads of yeshivot, acknowledged his superiority and paid respectful attention to his words, his *ḥiddushim* ("original deductions") passing from mouth to mouth.

On the conquest of Poland in World War II, he fled from Brisk to Vilna together with five sons and two daughters (his wife and another four children were murdered in Brisk). Soloveichik was saved from the destruction of Polish Jewry and in 1941 went to Ereẓ Israel, settling in Jerusalem. He established there a *kolel* of select young men. A yeshivah was founded and administered by his eldest son Joseph Dov.

There was a great difference between Soloveichik's activities as rabbi of Brisk and his conduct in Jerusalem. During his 20 years as rabbi of Brisk he had been in the center of communal and congregational life, while in Jerusalem he confined himself to his studies, firmly refusing any official appointment and avoiding any public appearance or participation in daily public life. He even refrained from giving halakhic rulings, maintaining that "Jerusalem has a rabbi to whom problems should be addressed." Only in cases where he saw danger to the foundations of religion and faith did he break silence and give his ruling in the most vigorous of terms. He belonged to no party and did not intervene in political affairs, but as an outstanding halakhist he exercised great influence over extensive circles of Orthodox Jewry, especially after the death of Avraham Karelitz (Ḥazon Ish). In Jerusalem, as in Brisk, he lectured daily and his novellae were noted down or transmitted by his pupils. "R. Velvel" loved the Holy Land and believed wholeheartedly in the *mitzvah* of living there.

BIBLIOGRAPHY: I. Goldschlag, in: *Shanah be-Shanah* (1961), 358f.; EG, 2 (1954), index; L. Jung (ed.), *Men of the Spirit* (1964), 195–41.

[Itzhak Goldshlag]

SOLOVEICHIK, JOSEPH BAER, OF VOLOZHIN (1820–1892), talmudist and *rosh yeshivah*. Soloveichik was educated by his father, Isaac Ze'ev *Soloveichik of Kovno, and his great-uncle, Isaac, son of Ḥayyim of Volozhin. While in Volozhin, he married into a wealthy family, but was shortly thereafter forced by his father-in-law to divorce his wife when he failed to give the correct order of the recitation of some minor prayers on a festival. This so embittered him that he left Volozhin and subsequently studied under S. *Kluger in Brody and J.N. Orenstein in Lemberg. His reputation spread, and he was appointed successor to Gershon Menahem of Minsk at the yeshivah there. He finally returned to Volozhin in 1849 to serve as joint *rosh yeshivah* with Naphtali Ẓevi Judah *Berlin (the "Neẓiv"), the son-in-law of Isaac of Volozhin. With the passage of time, the two found it increasingly difficult to agree. It was impossible for them to work in harmony, particularly since both exercised considerable spiritual influence on the students. Their differences caused such a complete break between them that they could not act jointly in the administration of the school or in the planning of the curriculum. They were different in their temperaments and in their approach, to talmudic studies. Berlin was patient and temperate, modest and sober in his ways, preferring erudition to subtlety, while Soloveichik was a dynamic personality, sharp-witted, preferring acumen to erudition in talmudic studies and in wordly matters. Soloveichik respected no person in argument and deferred to no one. They presented their dispute before four outstanding scholars, who decided in favor of Berlin. Soloveichik left Volozhin and became rabbi of Slutsk. He later restored harmony in his relations with Berlin when his son, Ḥayyim, married Berlin's granddaughter. In Slutsk he found scope for his energies, both in Torah teaching and in communal organization. He deployed his abilities and his industry for the community's needs, devoting himself wholeheartedly to helping the poor and the needy. During the severe famine of 1866, he founded a society to help the poor, put himself at its head, and collected subscriptions from door to door. He was devoted to the needs of the community and was an outstanding humanitarian. Even when fighting those who wished to change or undermine Jewish religious life and values, he retained the love and respect of all. With his fiery spirit he could not continue in the rabbinate and in 1875 relinquished his position, settling in Warsaw where he lived privately and in great poverty, devoting himself to study and deeds of benevolence. In 1878, when invited to become rabbi of Brest-Litovsk, he agreed on condition that he would be obeyed in all communal matters and that aid for the poor would be under his direction. In 1890 he was associated with a group which bought land in Ereẓ Israel.

The following of his works have been published, all under the title *Beit ha-Levi: Novellae on the Talmud, 102 responsa and sermons* (2 vols., 1863–64), sermons on Genesis and Exodus (2 vols., 1884), and halakhic novellae (1891). He contributed to I. Lipkin's (Salanter) periodical *Tevunah* in 1861.

BIBLIOGRAPHY: M. Berlin, *Mi-Volozhin ad Yerushalayim* (1939), 23f.; B. Epstein, *Mekor Barukh* (1954); S.K. Mirsky, (ed.), *Mosedot Torah be-Eiropah* (1956), 39–41; *Yahadut Lita*, 1 (1960), index; 2 (1967), 72f.

[Mordechai Hacohen]

SOLOVEICHIK, MOSHE (1879–1941), Orthodox rabbi. The son of a distinguished father, Rabbi Ḥayyim *Soloveichik, and the father of distinguished sons, Rabbi Joseph Dov *Soloveitchik and Rabbi Aaron *Soloveichik, learning was an essential component of his family life. Born in Volozhin and raised in Brest-Litovsk (Brisk), young Moshe studied with his father the talmudic methodology that was the mark of the Soloveichik family. He married the daughter of Rabbi Elihu Feinstein and studied with his father-in-law until his 30th birthday, when he became the communal rabbi of Rassin in the Kovno Province. He established a *kolel* there and in 1913 moved to Chaslovitz, where he was a communal rabbi. He was there during World War I and in 1921 was invited to succeed his father as the rabbi of Brisk. He declined and instead became a Talmud teacher at Taḥkemoni Gevo'a in Warsaw, a school at which both Jewish and secular studies were taught. According to his daughter, Rabbi Moshe was disturbed by the increasing secularization of the curriculum and of the students. There were significant tensions between Soloveichik and Professor *Balaban, the distinguished secular history teacher. Thus when in 1929 he was invited to Rabbi Isaac Elchanan Theological Seminary in New York to replace the recently deceased Rabbi Shlomo Polachek, the offer was accepted with great enthusiasm. His recruitment by Rabbi Bernard Dov Revel enhanced the prestige of the seminary and Moshe Soloveichik became a supporter of Revel's efforts to build an Orthodox Jewish university. His prestige was also enhanced at RIETS, where his *shi'ur* became the gateway to ordination. As Gilbert Klaperman wrote: "To weather Reb Moses Soloveichik's exacting standard and then earn his signature on the semicha was the highest accolade that could come to any student." He had rigorous standards and enforced them, teaching the methodology that had been taught to him by his forebears and the one he had taught to his sons and his students. He died in 1941 and his son Joseph was invited to be his successor as *rosh yeshivah*. He did not publish much during his lifetime in keeping with family tradition, but his legacy was in his teaching, his sons and his students.

BIBLIOGRAPHY: M.D. Sherman, *Orthodox Judaism in America: A Biographical Dictionary and Sourcebook* (1996); S.S. Meiselman, *The Soloveichik Heritage: A Daughter's Memoir* (1995); G. Klaperman, *The Story of Yeshiva University* (1969).

[Michael Berenbaum (2nd ed.)]

SOLOVEITCHIK, JOSEPH BAER (1903–1993), U.S. rabbinic scholar and religious philosopher, preeminent spiritual leader of Modern Orthodoxy in the last half of the 20th century. Scion of a distinguished Lithuanian rabbinical family, Soloveitchik was born in Pruzhana, where his maternal grandfather, Elijah Feinstein, was the rabbi. Soloveitchik spent his formative years in Khaslavichy, Belorussia, where his father Moses served as the rabbi from 1913 until after the Communist takeover in 1918. The Khaslavichy community included a large number of Lubavitcher Ḥasidim. Soloveitchik later integrated their lifestyle and theological stance into his own philosophical lectures and publications. Until his family's relocation to Warsaw, Poland, in 1920, Soloveitchik devoted himself almost exclusively to the study of the Talmud and the Codes. Under his father's tutelage, he mastered his paternal grandfather's (see Hayyim *Soloveitchik) "Brisker Derekh." This method of rabbinic study stressed incisive analysis, exact classifications, critical independence, and emphasis on Maimonides' *Mishneh Torah*.

In his late teens, Soloveitchik received the equivalent of a high school education from private tutors. In Warsaw, he entered the Free Polish University in 1924, studying political science. In 1926, he commenced his studies at the University of Berlin. Soloveitchik majored in philosophy and was attracted to the neo-Kantian school. In 1932, he received his doctorate, after the acceptance of his dissertation on the epistemology and metaphysics of Hermann Cohen.

In his dissertation *Das reine Denken und die Seinskonstituierung bei Hermann Cohen* (Berlin, 1933), Soloveitchik analyzes Cohen's cognitive idealism, according to which objective existence has only cognitive being. The extra-cognitive world, represented by the senses, exists only chaotically and lacks order; its function is to present problems and questions to cognition. Cognition, in turn, creates objects within itself, generating them from the infinitesimal to their objective existence. It should be noted that objective existence in cognition means the existence of scientific objects, subject to Newtonian causality. Soloveitchik expands on these determinations and discusses their development in the thought of his own doctoral advisor, Heinrich Maier, and Paul Natorp, who followed in Cohen's footsteps.

In 1931 Soloveitchik married Tonya Lewit (1904–1967). Her background was similar to that of her husband, in that she had been raised in eastern Europe (Vilna), and sought higher education in western Europe. She received a doctorate in education from Jena University and was to ably assist her husband in all his endeavors until her death. In 1932 they immigrated to the United States, where Rabbi Moses Soloveichik had been the head of the talmudic faculty of the Rabbi Isaac Elchanan Theological Seminary in New York City, since 1929. A few months after his arrival, the younger Soloveitchik became the rabbi of a segment of the Orthodox Jewish community of Boston. This city was to remain his home until his death.

In 1937 he founded the Maimonides School, the first Jewish day school in the New England area. With the influx of European yeshivah students during the late 1930s, Soloveitchik organized the Heikhal Rabbenu Haym ha'Levi and Yeshivath Torath Israel. On May 13, 1941, he succeeded his father as professor of Talmud in New York City at the Rabbi Isaac Elchanan Theological Seminary, which achieved university status in 1945 and became known as Yeshiva University. RIETS, or the Yeshiva, as it was popularly known, was an integral subdivision of the school. Soloveitchik also lectured at the university's Bernard Revel Graduate School, where he served as professor of Jewish philosophy. He was to continue his weekly Talmud lectures at the school until illness forced his retirement in 1985. Soloveitchik gradually became the dominant spiritual personality on the Yeshiva University scene. He was popularly designated "The Rav" or the rabbi par excellence. In this setting he remained the quintessential *rosh yeshivah*, and his lectures were in the classic Brisk tradition. Essentially, the Talmud, Maimonides, and the basic early commentaries were the core of his classes in the yeshivah for 44 years. The Rav thus became the spiritual mentor of the majority of the American-trained Orthodox pulpit rabbis. His position at Yeshiva University was paramount in projecting Soloveitchik into prominence upon both the national and international Jewish scenes. From 1953, Soloveitchik also exerted a decisive influence on Orthodoxy, in his capacity as chairman of the Halakhah Commission of the Rabbinical Council of America. Among his rulings was his unequivocal opposition to mixed seating in synagogues. He went so far as to prohibit listening to the *shofar* on Rosh Hashanah in such synagogues. The Rav advised praying at home without hearing the *shofar* rather than worshipping in such a synagogue. Nevertheless, he did not advocate a total break with the Reform and Conservative movements. Soloveitchik differentiated between "external affairs" and "internal issues." On issues involving relations with the non-Jewish world, he held that cooperation with all Jewish organizations was desirable. Regarding internal matters such as *halakhah* and synagogue ritual, there was less capacity for joint viewpoints.

Soloveitchik questioned aspects of the dialogue initiated by the Catholic Church with Jewish leaders as part of the Church's ecumenical movement during the 1960s.

He encouraged Jewish-Christian dialogue on social, political and ethical issues – even terming it "essential" ("Statement on Interfaith Relations," in *Record of Rabbinical Council of America* (Feb. 1965)). Soloveitchik himself delivered his most famous religious paper, "The Lonely Man of Faith," to an interfaith audience at a Catholic seminary in Brighton, Massachusetts, and he later stated that all discussions of ethics and social values are necessarily "religious." In his essay "Confrontation" (*Tradition* 6:2, Spring–Summer 1964) he espoused a nuanced position regarding interfaith dialogue on religious matters (Eugene Korn, *Modern Judaism* (October 1965), 290–315).

Soloveitchik was originally a devotee of Agudath Israel and served as the chairman of the national executive committee of its American branch. He also was a member of its initial Council of Torah Sages, which was constituted in 1941. As the tragedy of European Jewry became known, the Rav became an advocate of the Mizrachi movement. Following World War II, he became the honorary president of Mizrachi, which was later renamed the Religious Zionists of America. In 1935, Soloveitchik journeyed to Palestine, in what was his only visit to the Holy Land, where he was a candidate for the post of Ashkenazi chief rabbi of Tel Aviv. He was not selected. In 1959, Soloveitchik declined to be a candidate to succeed Chief Rabbi Isaac Herzog. At the time, the Rav's election was assured since he enjoyed a wide spectrum of support.

Soloveitchik represented the entire Jewish community as a member of the advisory committee on humane slaughter of the United States Department of Agriculture, established 1958. In 1958–59 he delivered a series of classes on Jewish social philosophy to a group of social workers in New York. Soloveitchik also was the principal Jewish representative in Yeshiva University's Institute of Mental Health Project, undertaken in 1960, in conjunction with Harvard and Loyola Universities. Its goal was to study religious attitudes toward psychological problems. The lectures delivered to these groups later served as the basis for a portion of his published philosophical writings, particularly "The Lonely Man of Faith." Soloveitchik conducted weekly classes at Congregation Moriya on the upper west side of Manhattan. He also taught in Boston and every Saturday night gave a public lecture on the Torah portion at the Maimonides School. Sunday mornings he conducted a Talmud class under the auspices of the Hevra Shas of Boston. In addition, there were the Rav's annual Teshuvah lectures, delivered under the aegis of the Rabbinical Council of America. There were also a large number of discourses delivered before the Rabbinical Council and the Yeshiva University Rabbinical Alumni. The high point of every annual convention and midwinter conference was generally the Rav's lecture. At these venues, the themes varied and stressed halakhic, philosophical, theological, homiletical, and aggadic insights.

In addition, Soloveitchik's broad knowledge of general culture – philosophy, mathematics, science, literature – was integrated into these public discourses.

Soloveitchik was regarded by the Jewish world as the unchallenged leader of what has been designated as Modern Orthodoxy. Although never totally at home in the world of American Modern Orthodoxy, it was in this universe that the Rav's leadership was widely accepted. While Soloveitchik's brilliant scholarship was acknowledged in all Torah circles, his influence on the masses was through his disciples and the rabbis who followed his teachings. In addition, his public lectures and discourses enabled a wider audience to be inspired by his instruction. As a talmudic and halakhic expositor, the Rav possessed unusual dexterity in exploring difficult technical concepts. He was a remarkable orator in his native Yiddish, and an effective speaker in English and Hebrew. The annual halakhic and aggadic discourse which the Rav delivered at Yeshiva University, on the anniversary of his father's death, attracted thousands of listeners. These Yahrzeit *derashot* lasted from four to five consecutive hours. They were regarded as the major yearly academic event for American Orthodoxy.

Soloveitchik was reluctant to publish due to his family's tradition of perfectionism. Albeit, he wrote much, since all his public lectures were delivered from and preserved in manuscripts. For many decades his main publication was a lengthy essay "*Ish ha-Halakhah*" ((1944), 651–735) which was later translated into English by L. Kaplan and published as *Halakhic Man* (Jewish Publication Society, 1983).

This essay describes the dynasty of Brisk-method scholars. Written during the Shoah, the essay thus manifested a double purpose. First, to constitute a memorial to the type of yeshivah scholarship which was destroyed, and second, to describe this scholarly archetype in modern philosophical categories, so that it might be reconstituted in America. The term "*halakhah*" as used in this essay means primarily scholarship in the Brisk method of study, and not *halakhah* in its practical application. Soloveitchik describes the "Halakhic man" as cognitive man – a mixture of *homo religiosus* and scientist. A careful reading, however, reveals that halakhic man is essentially cognitive man. His cognition is described in line with Hermann Cohen's cognitive idealism, and in accordance with the conventionalistic trend in the philosophy of science. It should be noted that the *halakhah* is not merely a substitute for the laws of science. In the view of the halakhic man (i.e., the *rosh yeshivah*), yeshiva scholarship includes knowledge of scientific law. Since halakhic man's cognition is pervaded by Cohen's neo-Kantianism, and for him the only objective existence is that of the halakhic objects of cognition, it cannot be tolerant of other cognitions. The only experience halakhic man recognizes is the experience of scholarship and the emotions it arouses. Some critics claim, with a large degree of justification, that Soloveitchik himself did not identify with the image of the *rosh yeshivah* described in "Halakhic Man," but that he personally identified with the mixture of scholarship and religious experience, as suggested by his two other great works of this period, "The Halakhic Mind" and "*U-Vikashtem mi-Sham*."

"The Halakhic Mind" (which is understood as depicting Soloveitchik's own orientation), written in 1944 but published only in 1986, differs completely from "Halakhic Man" (which is understood as depicting the *rosh yeshivah* of Brisk) and its cognitive-halakhic idealism. In "The Halakhic Mind," Soloveitchik employs the method which would characterize his writings for the rest of his life: phenomenology of the religious mind. Soloveitchik sought by this approach to point to the need for essentialist research of religious consciousness in general, and of Jewish religious consciousness in particular. His working assumption is cognitive pluralism: just as, for example, there is scientific cognition, so there is also religious cognition. He therefore ignored historic and ontological existence. God's immanence, for instance, is of interest not from a factual perspective (God is or is not immanent), but from its being a factor of the religious mind. Soloveitchik made use of diverse and contradictory sources (philosophy, Kabbalah), because they all construct the essential religious consciousness mind. From this time on, Soloveitchik focused only on research of the religious mind. He added to the phenomenological method another method: reconstruction, namely, that in order to uncover the depths of the religious mind, one must reconstruct its practical and normative dimension. In his terminology, in order to reveal the subjective, one must reconstruct it out of the objective. Soloveitchik divided the Jewish religious mind into three parts: the subjective part (emotions and intellectual or mystical theories); the practical objective part (actions and behavior, such as performing the Torah's commandments); the normative objective part (norms underlying actions and behavior). The subjective part should be reconstructed out of the practical and normative objective parts. Soloveitchik especially emphasized the *halakhah* as a structured component of the religious mind. Accordingly, the halakhic man, namely the *rosh yeshivah* whose cognition is constructed in accordance with cognitive idealism, does not regard the subjective dimension as significant, nor does he recognize cognitive pluralism.

"The Halakhic Mind" thus calls for research into the Jewish religious mind and establishes guidelines for the phenomenological method, but does not fully apply these guidelines, especially not in the relatively small section dealing with Judaism.

The application would come in another work from the same period, namely "*U-Vikashtem mi-Sham*," written in 1944 but only published in 1978. Here Soloveitchik presented, step by step, the construction of the Jewish religious consciousness mind, in three stages. The first two stages are characterized by dialectic, and the third stage by a resolution of the dialectical tension. In the first stage, there is a tension between scientific accomplishments, which empower the person, and divine revelation, which undermines his self-confidence. In the second stage the tension is between love and fear of God. In the third and highest stage, the tension disappears, and is replaced by cleaving to God, in Maimonides' Aristotelian epistemological terms of the unity of intellect, intellection and intelligized object, which Soloveitchik compares with Hermann Cohen's cognitive idealism. Soloveitchik reconstructed these three stages out of the *halakhah*, thus reinforcing his position that the phenomenology of Judaism cannot be separated from Judaism's practical foundation, the *halakhah*.

In 1956 Soloveitchik delivered a sermon in honor of Israel's Independence Day, which was then published as a Hebrew essay, "*Kol Dodi Dofek*" ("Hark! My beloved is knocking" – cf. Song of Songs 5:2). Originally published in 1961 (in Simon Federbush (ed.), *Torah u-Melukhah*, 11–44), this essay was republished many times and was translated into several languages. Here, for the first time, Soloveitchik presented an overtly existentialist approach. Thereafter he would write in an existentialist style, such as his "Lonely Man of Faith," while at the same time continuing to write phenomenological works. The two kinds of works differ regarding the role of distress, metaphysics, the other and the purpose of the work. Regarding suffering, in his phenomenological writings, suffering is one of the dialectical poles, but in his existentialist writings suffering is the central point. Moreover, in the phenomenological writings the dialectical tension is resolved and the suffering disappears, but in the existentialist writings the polarity and suffering remains, but the person learns to live with it and endow it with meaning. Regarding metaphysics, in Soloveitchik's phenomenological works religious metaphysics is of interest and exists as a component of consciousness cognition, i.e., theoretical approaches are important because they reflect the structure of religious "cognition." Conversely, in the existentialist works metaphysics is no longer of interest. The problem of the other first arises in Soloveitchik's existentialist writings. The purpose of his phenomenological works was intellectual curiosity and religious need, but the purpose of his existentialist works is, first and foremost therapeutic: the very act of writing them eased his distress.

Soloveitchik rejected any metaphysical solution to the problem of suffering. The *halakhah* does not pretend to solve the problem; indeed, any solution would be an illusion. What the *halakhah* does is to endow suffering with meaning, thus enabling the suffering person to control his fate, rather than to be controlled by it. This is also the significance of Soloveitchik's dealing with the Shoah and the State of Israel in the same essay: the question of the reason for the Shoah is meaningless, and the only question worthy of discussion is that of meaning. "*Kol Dodi Dofek*," one of Soloveitchik's Zionist homilies, emphasizes the existential foundations of the State of Israel and the exclusive question of meaning. Only the *halakhah* can simultaneously endow with meaning the national catastrophe of the Shoah and the national revival of sovereign statehood.

Soloveitchik's existentialist approach is also reflected in several other works published in a pamphlet "Out of the Storm," but the apex of his existentialist writing is his "Lonely Man of Faith," which focuses on the problem of the other. In the modern world, faith is unique and subjective. Only divine intervention can make communication between two lonely people possible, and at a later stage, create a community. The suffering of loneliness does not disappear, but community life makes it possible to live with suffering and to endow it with meaning.

During the last decade or so of his active endeavors, Soloveitchik softened, somewhat, his resistance to the publication of his works. Subsequently, many volumes appeared under his name, including some that the Rav authorized and others that were edited from his public discourses. This trend intensified after Soloveitchik's death, as students and family published many volumes dedicated to both his Talmudic novellas and philosophical discourses. His son established the Morasha Foundation and his daughters inaugurated The Toras HoRav Foundation. Both were devoted to the publication of their father's manuscripts. Since thousands of recordings and many manuscripts remain unpublished, definitive studies of Soloveitchik and his era will wait for decades.

Soloveitchik was unique among his contemporary rabbinical colleagues. While continuing the intensive Torah scholarship, exemplary piety and dedicated leadership of his forebears, he additionally embraced western civilization. While there was no synthesis between these divergent visions, they co-existed harmoniously in his personality and lifestyle. In a lecture delivered to the Yeshiva University Rabbinic Alumni in 1956, the Rav contrasted his outlook with that of Rabbi Samson Raphael Hirsch. The latter advocated a greater synthesis between Torah and the civilization of a given epoch. Soloveitchik viewed them as separate disciplines and held that each world would lose its uniqueness if integration were attempted. He praised Yeshiva University since the yeshivah division continued the traditions of the classic Lithuanian yeshivot. Alongside the yeshivah, the university operated as a separate academic institution. Soloveitchik felt that both divisions functioned without synthesis and compromise.

Soloveitchik has remained the dominant spiritual leader for the Modern Orthodox world in the years since his death. No single rabbinical figure has emerged to inherit the Rav's mantle of leadership. Often many divergent and even contradictory viewpoints were ascribed to the Rav by his numerous disciples. Few perceived the totality of the Rav's spiritual gestalt. His lack of synthesis and the harmonious coexistence of numerous disciplines and quests that characterized his outlook added to the quandary.

The Soloveitchiks had three children. The eldest, Dr. Atarah Twersky, was chairman of the school committee of the Maimonides School, and thus continued the tradition established by her mother. Her husband, Rabbi Dr. Isadore *Twersky, was both a professor at Harvard University and The Talner Rebbe of Boston. Dr. Tovah Lichenstein resided in Jerusalem and taught at Bar-Ilan University's School of Social Work. She was married to Rabbi Dr. Aharon Lichtenstein, *rosh yeshivah* of Yeshivat Har Etzion in Alon Shvut. The youngest, Rabbi Dr. Haym Soloveitchik, was professor of Jewish history at The Bernard Revel Graduate School of Yeshiva University.

BIBLIOGRAPHY: A. Rakeffet-Rothkoff, *The Rav: The World of Rabbi Joseph B. Soloveitchik* (1999), 2 vols.; S.S. Meiselman, *The Soloveitchik Heritage: A Daughter's Memoir* (1995); M.D. Genack (ed.), *Rabbi Joseph B. Soloveitchik: Man of Halacha, Man of Faith* (1998); A. Sagi (ed.), *Faith in Changing Times: On Rabbi J.B. Soloveitchik's Thought* (Heb., 1996); D. Schwartz, *Rabbi Soloveitchik's Philosophic Thought* (Heb., 2004); M.D. Angel (ed.), *Exploring the Thought of Rabbi Joseph B. Soloveitchik* (1997); D. Hartman, *Love and Terror in the God Encounter: The Theological Legacy of Rabbi Joseph B. Soloveitchik* (2001); L. Kaplan, "Rabbi Joseph B. Soloveitchik's Philosophy of Halakha," in: *The Jewish Law Annual*, 7 (1987), 139–97; Z. Kulitz, *Confrontation: The Existential Thought of Rabbi J.B. Soloveitchick* (1993); R. Munk, *The Rationale of Halakhic Man: Joseph B. Soloveitchik's Conception of Jewish Thought* (1996); A. Rakeffet-Rothkoff, *The Rav: The World of Rabbi Joseph B. Soloveitchik* (1999); D. Singer and M. Sokol, "Joseph Soloveitchik: Lonely Man of Faith," in: *Modern Judaism*, 2 (1982), 227–72.

[Aaron Rothkoff and Dov Schwartz (2nd ed.)]

°SOLOVIEV, VLADIMIR (1853–1900), Russian philosopher and theologian. Born in Moscow, he was the son of S.M. Soloviev, professor of Russian history at Moscow University. Vladimir Soloviev also lectured at this university but suffered the criticism of reactionaries for the liberal character of his Christianity. From 1877 to 1881 he held a post at the Ministry of Education in St. Petersburg, and later devoted himself to writing. His mystical vision, high intelligence, and religious tolerance made him one of the most outstanding men in Russia, and his philosophical and theological writing were influential. He vainly tried to reunite the Russian Orthodox Church and the Roman Catholic Church, and in 1896 he himself was received into the latter.

An interesting component of Soloviev's thought is his theological and practical philo-Semitism. In this he was almost alone in Russian mystical Christian circles and differed from his friend, Feodor Dostoyevski. Soloviev even wrote a small book about Judaism and another about the Talmud. His positive evaluation of Judaism resulted not only from his appreciation of Judaism's "religious materialism," that is, its avoidance of abstract theology. In addition, he opposed Christian missionary activities among the Jews. Soloviev learned Hebrew and on his deathbed he recited a Hebrew psalm for the sake of the Jews.

BIBLIOGRAPHY: D. Stremoukhov, *Vladimir Soloviev et son Oeuvre Messianique* (1935).

[David Flusser]

SOLOW, ROBERT MERTON (1924–), U.S. economist, Nobel Prize laureate. Born in Brooklyn, Solow was educated at Harvard University from which he received his Ph.D. in 1951. From 1949 he was on the faculty of the Massachusetts Institute of Technology, becoming a professor of economics in 1958 and Institute Professor in 1973.

He was also affiliated with the Council of Economic Advisers, as senior economist (1961–62) and consultant (1962–68), and was a consultant to the RAND corporation (1952–64). He served as a director of the Boston Federal Reserve Bank from 1975 to 1980 and was chairman of the bank in 1979–80.

Among Solow's other activities, he was a member of the President's Commission on Income Maintenance (1968–70), served on the board of directors and as a member of the executive committee of the National Bureau of Economic Research, served as a trustee of the Institute for Advanced Studies of Princeton University (1972–78), and was president of the American Economic Association (1979). In 1961 he received the AEA's John Bates Clark Award, given to the best economist under age 40.

A fellow of the American Academy of Arts and Sciences and the recipient of the Seidman award in Political Economics (1983), he was awarded the Nobel Prize in economic sciences in 1987 for his significant contributions to the theory of economic growth.

In 1995 he retired from teaching at MIT. He served as chairman of the board of the nonprofit research group Manpower Demonstration Research Corporation, which he helped establish in the 1970s. He was also Foundation Fellow of the Russell Sage Foundation.

Solow authored a number of works, which include *The Source of Unemployment in the United States* (1964), *Growth Theory* (1970), *The Behavior of the Price Level* (1970), *Made in America* (with M. Dertouzos and R. Lester, 1989), *Learning from "Learning and Doing"* (1997), *Work and Welfare* (1998), *An Almost Practical Step toward Sustainability* (1998), *Monopolistic Competition and Macroeconomic Theory* (1999), and *Structural Reform and Economic Policy* (2005).

BIBLIOGRAPHY: P. Diamond, *Growth/Productivity/Unemployment* (1990).

[Ruth Beloff (2nd ed.)]

SOLTI, SIR GEORG (1912–1997), conductor. Born in Budapest, Solti studied at the Liszt Academy with Dohnanyi, Bartok, and Kodaly and became an accomplished pianist. From 1930 to 1939 he was répétiteur at the Budapest Opera; he worked with Toscanini at Salzburg Festivals, making his debut as a conductor at Budapest (1938). As a Jew facing professional restrictions, he left Hungary in 1939. He spent the war years in Switzerland as a concert pianist, gaining the first prize at the 1942 Geneva competition. Solti's international conducting career began after the war. In 1946 he directed the Munich Opera and then in Frankfurt (1952–61), the Dallas SO (1960–61), and the Covent Garden Opera, London (1961–71). He was appointed director of the Chicago Symphony Orchestra (1969–1990), transforming it to one of the most celebrated orchestras in the world. He subsequently took additional posts as "conseiller musical" at the Paris Opera (1971–73), music director of the Paris Orchestra (1972–75), principal conductor of the LPO and artistic director of the Salzburg Festival. Solti also appeared regularly with the Vienna Staatsoper, and from 1956, he frequently conducted the *Israel Philharmonic Orchestra, with which he also made several recordings. His dynamic and vibrant conducting style, and his preference for huge sound, demanded the outmost professional performance from the players and reflected his charismatic and powerful personality. Solti became known for his wide-ranging concert and operatic repertoire, and his special competence in conducting for recordings. He gave a large number of first performances, made more than 250 recordings, among them the major works of Strauss, Wagner, Mozart, and Verdi. Solti made the first complete *Ring* recording (1958–1966) and conducted it in Bayreuth in commemoration of the one hundredth anniversary of Wagner's death (1983). Outstanding among his other recordings is a Mahler cycle (with the Chicago SO). He was honored with 32 Grammy awards – more than any other artist. In 1971 Solti was knighted; in 1972 he took on British nationality and was entitled Sir Georg. In 1974 he was made a Commandeur of the Légion d'Honneur. He has received many other major honors from many countries. He wrote a memoir, *Solti on Solti* (1997).

BIBLIOGRAPHY: Grove Music Online; P. Dawson-Bowling, "Sir Georg Solti KBE (1912–1997): His Achievement in Wagner," in: *Wagner News*, 123 (Oct. 1997), 14–18; J. Breuer, "Sir Georg Solti (1912–1997)," in: *Hungarian Music Quarterly*, 9:1–2 (1998), 2–4.

[Max Loppert / Naama Ramot (2nd ed.)]

ABBREVIATIONS

GENERAL ABBREVIATIONS

This list contains abbreviations used in the Encyclopaedia (apart from the standard ones, such as geographical abbreviations, points of compass, etc.). For names of organizations, institutions, etc., in abbreviation, see Index. For bibliographical abbreviations of books and authors in Rabbinical literature, see following lists.

*	Cross reference; i.e., an article is to be found under the word(s) immediately following the asterisk (*).
°	Before the title of an entry, indicates a non-Jew (post-biblical times).
‡	Indicates reconstructed forms.
>	The word following this sign is derived from the preceding one.
<	The word preceding this sign is derived from the following one.

ad loc.	*ad locum*, "at the place"; used in quotations of commentaries.
A.H.	*Anno Hegirae*, "in the year of Hegira," i.e., according to the Muslim calendar.
Akk.	Addadian.
A.M.	*anno mundi*, "in the year (from the creation) of the world."
anon.	anonymous.
Ar.	Arabic.
Aram.	Aramaic.
Ass.	Assyrian.
b.	born; *ben, bar.*
Bab.	Babylonian.
B.C.E.	Before Common Era (= B.C.).
bibl.	bibliography.
Bul.	Bulgarian.
c., ca.	Circa.
C.E.	Common Era (= A.D.).
cf.	*confer*, "compare."
ch., chs.	chapter, chapters.
comp.	compiler, compiled by.
Cz.	Czech.
D	according to the documentary theory, the Deuteronomy document.
d.	died.
Dan.	Danish.
diss., dissert,	dissertation, thesis.
Du.	Dutch.
E.	according to the documentary theory, the Elohist document (i.e., using Elohim as the name of God) of the first five (or six) books of the Bible.
ed.	editor, edited, edition.
eds.	editors.
e.g.	*exempli gratia*, "for example."
Eng.	English.
et al.	*et alibi*, "and elsewhere"; or *et alii*, "and others"; "others."
f., ff.	and following page(s).
fig.	figure.
fl.	flourished.
fol., fols	folio(s).
Fr.	French.
Ger.	German.
Gr.	Greek.
Heb.	Hebrew.
Hg., Hung	Hungarian.
ibid	*Ibidem*, "in the same place."
incl. bibl.	includes bibliography.
introd.	introduction.
It.	Italian.
J	according to the documentary theory, the Jahwist document (i.e., using YHWH as the name of God) of the first five (or six) books of the Bible.
Lat.	Latin.
lit.	literally.
Lith.	Lithuanian.
loc. cit.	*loco citato*, "in the [already] cited place."
Ms., Mss.	Manuscript(s).
n.	note.
n.d.	no date (of publication).
no., nos	number(s).
Nov.	Novellae (Heb. *Ḥiddushim*).
n.p.	place of publication unknown.
op. cit.	*opere citato*, "in the previously mentioned work."
P.	according to the documentary theory, the Priestly document of the first five (or six) books of the Bible.
p., pp.	page(s).
Pers.	Persian.
pl., pls.	plate(s).
Pol.	Polish.
Port.	Potuguese.
pt., pts.	part(s).
publ.	published.
R.	Rabbi or Rav (before names); in Midrash (after an abbreviation) – *Rabbah.*
r.	recto, the first side of a manuscript page.
Resp.	Responsa (Latin "answers," Hebrew *She'elot u-Teshuvot* or *Teshuvot*), collections of rabbinic decisions.
rev.	revised.

Rom.	Romanian.
Rus(s).	Russian.
Slov.	Slovak.
Sp.	Spanish.
s.v.	*sub verbo, sub voce*, "under the (key) word."
Sum	Sumerian.
summ.	Summary.
suppl.	supplement.
Swed.	Swedish.
tr., trans(l).	translator, translated, translation.
Turk.	Turkish.
Ukr.	Ukrainian.
v., vv.	*verso*. The second side of a manuscript page; also verse(s).
Yid.	Yiddish.

ABBREVIATIONS USED IN RABBINICAL LITERATURE

Adderet Eliyahu, Karaite treatise by Elijah b. Moses *Bashyazi.

Admat Kodesh, Resp. by Nissim Ḥayyim Moses b. Joseph |Mizraḥi.

Aguddah, Sefer ha-, Nov. by *Alexander Suslin ha-Kohen.

Ahavat Ḥesed, compilation by *Israel Meir ha-Kohen.

Aliyyot de-Rabbenu Yonah, Nov. by *Jonah b. Avraham Gerondi.

Arukh ha-Shulḥan, codification by Jehiel Michel *Epstein.

Asayin (= positive precepts), subdivision of: (1) *Maimonides, *Sefer ha-Mitzvot;* (2) *Moses b. Jacob of Coucy, *Semag.*

Asefat Dinim, subdivision of *Sedei Ḥemed* by Ḥayyim Hezekiah *Medini, an encyclopaedia of precepts and responsa.

Asheri = *Asher b. Jehiel.

Aeret Ḥakhamim, by Baruch *Frankel-Teomim; pt, 1: Resp. to Sh. Ar.; pt2: Nov. to Talmud.

Ateret Zahav, subdivision of the *Levush*, a codification by Mordecai b. Abraham (Levush) *Jaffe; *Ateret Zahav* parallels Tur. YD.

Ateret Ẓevi, Comm. To Sh. Ar. by Ẓevi Hirsch b. Azriel.

Avir Ya'akov, Resp. by Jacob Avigdor.

Avkat Rokhel, Resp. by Joseph b. Ephraim *Caro.

Avnei Millu'im, Comm. to Sh. Ar., EH, by *Aryeh Loeb b. Joseph ha-Kohen.

Avnei Nezer, Resp. on Sh. Ar. by Abraham b. Ze'ev Nahum Bornstein of *Sochaczew.

Avodat Massa, Compilation of Tax Law by Yoasha Abraham Judah.

Azei ha-Levanon, Resp. by Judah Leib *Zirelson.

Ba'al ha-Tanya – *Shneur Zalman of Lyady.

Ba'ei Ḥayyei, Resp. by Ḥayyim b. Israel *Benveniste.

Ba'er Heitev, Comm. To Sh. Ar. The parts on OḤ and EH are by Judah b. Simeon *Ashkenazi, the parts on YD AND ḤM by *Zechariah Mendel b. Aryeh Leib. Printed in most editions of Sh. Ar.

Baḥ = Joel *Sirkes.

Baḥ, usual abbreviation for *Bayit Ḥadash*, a commentary on Tur by Joel *Sirkes; printed in most editions of Tur.

Bayit Ḥadash, see *Baḥ*.

Berab = Jacob Berab, also called Ri Berav.

Bedek ha-Bayit, by Joseph b. Ephraim *Caro, additions to his *Beit Yosef* (a comm. to Tur). Printed sometimes inside *Beit Yosef*, in smaller type. Appears in most editions of Tur.

Be'er ha-Golah, Commentary to Sh. Ar. By Moses b. Naphtali Hirsch *Rivkes; printed in most editions of Sh. Ar.

Be'er Mayim, Resp. by Raphael b. Abraham Manasseh Jacob.

Be'er Mayim Ḥayyim, Resp. by Samuel b. Ḥayyim *Vital.

Be'er Yizḥak, Resp. by Isaac Elhanan *Spector.

Beit ha-Beḥirah, Comm. to Talmud by Menahem b. Solomon *Meiri.

Beit Me'ir, Nov. on Sh. Ar. by Meir b. Judah Leib Posner.

Beit Shelomo, Resp. by Solomon b. Aaron Ḥason (the younger).

Beit Shemu'el, Comm. to Sh. Ar., EH, by *Samuel b. Uri Shraga Phoebus.

Beit Ya'akov, by Jacob b. Jacob Moses *Lorberbaum; pt.1: Nov. to Ket.; pt.2: Comm. to EH.

Beit Yisrael, collective name for the commentaries *Derishah, Perishah*, and *Be'urim* by Joshua b. Alexander ha-Kohen *Falk. See under the names of the commentaries.

Beit Yizḥak, Resp. by Isaac *Schmelkes.

Beit Yosef: (1) Comm. on Tur by Joseph b. Ephraim *Caro; printed in most editions of Tur; (2) Resp. by the same.

Ben Yehudah, Resp. by Abraham b. Judah Litsch (ליטש) Rosenbaum.

Bertinoro, Standard commentary to Mishnah by Obadiah *Bertinoro. Printed in most editions of the Mishnah.

[Be'urei] Ha-Gra, Comm. to Bible, Talmud, and Sh. Ar. By *Elijah b. Solomon Zalmon (Gaon of Vilna); printed in major editions of the mentioned works.

Be'urim, Glosses to Isserles *Darkhei Moshe* (a comm. on Tur) by Joshua b. Alexander ha-Kohen *Falk; printed in many editions of Tur.

Binyamin Ze'ev, Resp. by *Benjamin Ze'ev b. Mattathias of Arta.

Birkei Yosef, Nov. by Ḥayyim Joseph David *Azulai.

Ha-Buẓ ve-ha-Argaman, subdivision of the *Levush* (a codification by Mordecai b. Abraham (Levush) *Jaffe); *Ha-Buẓ ve-ha-Argaman* parallels Tur, EH.

Comm. = Commentary

Da'at Kohen, Resp. by Abraham Isaac ha-Kohen. *Kook.

Darkhei Moshe, Comm. on Tur Moses b. Israel *Isserles; printed in most editions of Tur.

Darkhei No'am, Resp. by *Mordecai b. Judah ha-Levi.

Darkhei Teshuvah, Nov. by Ẓevi *Shapiro; printed in the major editions of Sh. Ar.

De'ah ve-Haskel, Resp. by Obadiah Hadaya (see *Yaskil Avdi).*

Derashot Ran, Sermons by *Nissim b. Reuben Gerondi.
Derekh Ḥayyim, Comm. to *Avot* by *Judah Loew (Lob., Liwa) b. Bezalel (Maharal) of Prague.
Derishah, by Joshua b. Alexander ha-Kohen *Falk; additions to his *Perishah* (comm. on Tur); printed in many editions of Tur.
Derushei ha-Ẓelaḥ, Sermons, by Ezekiel b. Judah Halevi *Landau.
Devar Avraham, Resp. by Abraham *Shapira.
Devar Shemu'el, Resp. by Samuel *Aboab.
Devar Yehoshu'a, Resp. by Joshua Menahem b. Isaac Aryeh Ehrenberg.
Dikdukei Soferim, variae lections of the talmudic text by Raphael Nathan*Rabbinowicz.
Divrei Emet, Resp. by Isaac Bekhor David.
Divrei Ge'onim, Digest of responsa by Ḥayyim Aryeh b. Jeḥiel Ẓevi *Kahana.
Divrei Ḥamudot, Comm. on *Piskei ha-Rosh* by Yom Tov Lipmann b. Nathan ha-Levi *Heller; printed in major editions of the Talmud.
Divrei Ḥayyim several works by Ḥayyim *Halberstamm; if quoted alone refers to his Responsa.
Divrei Malkhi'el, Resp. by Malchiel Tenebaum.
Divrei Rivot, Resp. by Isaac b. Samuel *Adarbi.
Divrei Shemu'el, Resp. by Samuel Raphael Arditi.

Edut be-Ya'akov, Resp. by Jacob b. Abraham *Boton.
Edut bi-Yhosef, Resp. by Joseph b. Isaac *Almosnino.
Ein Ya'akov, Digest of talmudic *aggadot* by Jacob (Ibn) *Habib.
Ein Yiẓḥak, Resp. by Isaac Elhanan *Spector.
Ephraim of Lentshitz = Solomon *Luntschitz.
Erekh Leḥem, Nov. and glosses to Sh. Ar. by Jacob b. Abraham *Castro.
Eshkol, Sefer ha-, Digest of *halakhot* by *Abraham b. Isaac of Narbonne.
Et Sofer, Treatise on Law Court documents by Abraham b. Mordecai *Ankawa, in the 2nd vol. of his Resp. *Kerem Ḥamar.*
Etan ha-Ezraḥi, Resp. by Abraham b. Israel Jehiel (Shrenzl) *Rapaport.
Even ha-Ezel, Nov. to Maimonides' *Yad Ḥazakah* by Isser Zalman *Meltzer.
Even ha-Ezer, also called *Raban* of *Ẓafenat Pa'ne'aḥ,* rabbinical work with varied contents by *Eliezer b. Nathan of Mainz; not identical with the subdivision of Tur, Shulḥan Arukh, etc.
Ezrat Yehudah, Resp. by *Isaar Judah b. Nechemiah of Brisk.

Gan Eden, Karaite treatise by *Aaron b. Elijah of Nicomedia.
Gersonides = *Levi b. Gershom, also called Leo Hebraecus, or Ralbag.
Ginnat Veradim, Resp. by *Abraham b. Mordecai ha-Levi.

Haggahot, another name for *Rema.*
Haggahot Asheri, glosses to *Piskei ha-Rosh* by *Israel of Krems; printed in most Talmud editions.
Haggahot Maimuniyyot, Comm,. to Maimonides' Yad Ḥazakah by *Meir ha-Kohen; printed in most eds. of Yad.
Haggahot Mordekhai, glosses to *Mordekhai* by Samuel *Schlettstadt; printed in most editions of the Talmud after *Mordekhai.*
Haggahot ha-Rashash on Tosafot, annotations of Samuel *Strashun on the Tosafot (printed in major editions of the Talmud).
Ha-Gra = *Elijah b. Solomon Zalman (Gaon of Vilna).
Ha-Gra, Commentaries on Bible, Talmud, and Sh. Ar. respectively, by *Elijah b. Solomon Zalman (Gaon of Vilna); printed in major editions of the mentioned works.
Hai Gaon, Comm. = his comm. on Mishnah.
Ḥakham Ẓevi, Resp. by Ẓevi Hirsch b. Jacob *Ashkenazi.
Halakhot = Rif, *Halakhot.* Compilation and abstract of the Talmud by Isaac b. Jacob ha-Kohen *Alfasi; printed in most editions of the Talmud.
Halakhot Gedolot, compilation of *halakhot* from the Geonic period, arranged acc. to the Talmud. Here cited acc. to ed. Warsaw (1874). Author probably *Simeon Kayyara of Basra.
Halakhot Pesukot le-Rav Yehudai Ga'on compilation of *halakhot.*
Halakhot Pesukot min ha-Ge'onim, compilation of *halakhot* from the geonic period by different authors.
Ḥananel, Comm. to Talmud by *Hananel b. Ḥushi'el; printed in some editions of the Talmud.
Harei Besamim, Resp. by Aryeh Leib b. Isaac *Horowitz.
Ḥassidim, Sefer, Ethical maxims by *Judah b. Samuel he-Ḥasid.
Hassagot Rabad on Rif, Glosses on Rif, *Halakhot,* by *Abraham b. David of Posquières.
Hassagot Rabad [on Yad], Glosses on Maimonides, *Yad Ḥazakah,* by *Abraham b. David of Posquières.
Hassagot Ramban, Glosses by Naḥmanides on Maimonides' *Sefer ha-Mitzvot;* usually printed together with *Sefer ha-Mitzvot.*
Ḥatam Sofer = Moses *Sofer.
Ḥavvot Ya'ir, Resp. and varia by Jair Ḥayyim *Bacharach
Ḥayyim Or Zaru'a = *Ḥayyim (Eliezer) b. Isaac.
Ḥazon Ish = Abraham Isaiah *Karelitz.
Ḥazon Ish, Nov. by Abraham Isaiah *Karelitz
Ḥedvat Ya'akov, Resp. by Aryeh Judah Jacob b. David Dov Meisels (article under his father's name).
Heikhal Yizḥak, Resp. by Isaac ha-Levi *Herzog.
Ḥelkat Meḥokek, Comm. to Sh. Ar., by Moses b. Isaac Judah *Lima.
Ḥelkat Ya'akov, Resp. by Mordecai Jacob Breisch.
Ḥemdah Genuzah, , Resp. from the geonic period by different authors.
Ḥemdat Shelomo, Resp. by Solomon Zalman *Lipschitz.
Ḥida = Ḥayyim Joseph David *Azulai.
Ḥiddushei Halakhot ve-Aggadot, Nov. by Samuel Eliezer b. Judah ha-Levi *Edels.
Ḥikekei Lev, Resp. by Ḥayyim *Palaggi.
Ḥikrei Lev, Nov. to Sh. Ar. by Joseph Raphael b. Ḥayyim Joseph Ḥazzan (see article *Ḥazzan Family).
Hil. = Hilkhot … (e.g. *Hilkhot Shabbat).*
Ḥinnukh, Sefer ha-, List and explanation of precepts attributed (probably erroneously) to Aaron ha-Levi of Barcelona (see article **Ha-Ḥinnukh*).
Ḥok Ya'akov, Comm. to Hil. Pesaḥ in Sh. Ar., OḤ, by Jacob b. Joseph *Reicher.
Ḥokhmat Sehlomo (1), Glosses to Talmud, *Rashi* and Tosafot by Solomon b. Jehiel "Maharshal") *Luria; printed in many editions of the Talmud.
Ḥokhmat Sehlomo (2), Glosses and Nov. to Sh. Ar. by Solomon b. Judah Aaron *Kluger printed in many editions of Sh. Ar.
Ḥur, subdivision of the *Levush,* a codification by Mordecai b. Abraham (Levush) *Jaffe; *Hur* (or *Levush ha-Hur)* parallels Tur, OḤ, 242–697.
Ḥut ha-Meshullash, fourth part of the *Tashbeẓ* (Resp.), by Simeon b. Zemaḥ *Duran.

Ibn Ezra, Comm. to the Bible by Abraham *Ibn Ezra; printed in the major editions of the Bible *("Mikra'ot Gedolot").*
Imrei Yosher, Resp. by Meir b. Aaron Judah *Arik.
Ir Shushan, Subdivision of the *Levush,* a codification by Mordecai b. Abraham (Levush) *Jaffe; *Ir Shushan* parallels Tur, ḤM.
Israel of Bruna = Israel b. Ḥayyim *Bruna.
Ittur. Treatise on precepts by *Isaac b. Abba Mari of Marseilles.

Jacob Be Rab = *Be Rab.
Jacob b. Jacob Moses of Lissa = Jacob b. Jacob Moses *Lorberbaum.
Judah B. Simeon = Judah b. Simeon *Ashkenazi.
Judah Minz = Judah b. Eliezer ha-Levi *Minz.

Kappei Aharon, Resp. by Aaron Azriel.
Kehillat Ya'akov, Talmudic methodology, definitions etc. by Israel Jacob b. Yom Tov *Algazi.
Kelei Ḥemdah, Nov. and *pilpulim* by Meir Dan *Plotzki of Ostrova, arranged acc. to the Torah.
Keli Yakar, Annotations to the Torah by Solomon *Luntschitz.
Keneh Ḥokhmah, Sermons by Judah Loeb *Pochwitzer.
Keneset ha-Gedolah, Digest of *halakhot* by Ḥayyim b. Israel *Benveniste; subdivided into annotations to *Beit Yosef* and annotations to Tur.
Keneset Yisrael, Resp. by Ezekiel b. Abraham Katzenellenbogen (see article *Katzenellenbogen Family).
Kerem Ḥamar, Resp. and varia by Abraham b. Mordecai *Ankawa.
Kerem Shelmo. Resp. by Solomon b. Joseph *Amarillo.
Keritut, [Sefer], Methodology of the Talmud by *Samson b. Isaac of Chinon.
Kesef ha-Kedoshim, Comm. to Sh. Ar., ḤM, by Abraham *Wahrmann; printed in major editions of Sh. Ar.
Kesef Mishneh, Comm. to Maimonides, *Yad Ḥazakah,* by Joseph b. Ephraim *Caro; printed in most editions of *Yad Ḥazakah.*
Keẓot ha-Ḥoshen, Comm. to Sh. Ar., ḤM, by *Aryeh Loeb b. Joseph ha-Kohen; printed in major editions of Sh. Ar.
Kol Bo [Sefer], Anonymous collection of ritual rules; also called *Sefer ha-Likkutim.*
Kol Mevasser, Resp. by Meshullam *Rath.
Korban Aharon, Comm. to *Sifra* by Aaron b. Abraham *Ibn Ḥayyim; pt. 1 is called: *Middot Aharon.*
Korban Edah, Comm. to Jer. Talmud by David *Fraenkel; with additions: *Shiyyurei Korban;* printed in most editions of Jer. Talmud.
Kunteres ha-Kelalim, subdivision of *Sedei Ḥemed,* an encyclopaedia of precepts and responsa by Ḥayyim Hezekiah *Medini.
Kunteres ha-Semikhah, a treatise by *Levi b. Ḥabib; printed at the end of his responsa.
Kunteres Tikkun Olam, part of *Mispat Shalom* (Nov. by Shalom Mordecai b. Moses *Schwadron).

Lavin (negative precepts), subdivision of: (1) *Maimonides, *Sefer ha-Mitzvot;* (2) *Moses b. Jacob of Coucy, *Semag.*
Leḥem Mishneh, Comm. to Maimonides, *Yad Ḥazakah,* by Abraham [Ḥiyya] b. Moses *Boton; printed in most editions of *Yad Ḥazakah.*
Leḥem Rav, Resp. by Abraham [Ḥiyya] b. Moses *Boton.
Leket Yosher, Resp and varia by Israel b. Pethahiah *Isserlein, collected by *Joseph (Joselein) b. Moses.
Leo Hebraeus = *Levi b. Gershom, also called Ralbag or Gersonides.
Levush = Mordecai b. Abraham *Jaffe.
Levush [Malkhut], Codification by Mordecai b. Abraham (Levush) *Jaffe, with subdivisions: *[Levush ha-] Tekhelet* (parallels Tur OḤ 1–241); *[Levush ha-] Ḥur* (parallels Tur OḤ 242–697); *[Levush] Ateret Zahav* (parallels Tur YD); *[Levush ha-Buẓ ve-ha-Argaman* (parallels Tur EH); *[Levush] Ir Shushan* (parallels Tur ḤM); under the name *Levush* the author wrote also other works.
Li-Leshonot ha-Rambam, fifth part (nos. 1374–1700) of Resp. by *David b. Solomon ibn Abi Zimra (Radbaz).
Likkutim, Sefer ha-, another name for *[Sefer] Kol Bo.*

Ma'adanei Yom Tov, Comm. on *Piskei ha-Rosh* by Yom Tov Lipmann b. Nathan ha-Levi *Heller; printed in many editions of the Talmud.
Mabit = Moses b. Joseph *Trani.
Magen Avot, Comm. to *Avot* by Simeon b. Ẓemaḥ *Duran.
Magen Avraham, Comm. to Sh. Ar., OḤ, by Abraham Abele b. Ḥayyim ha-Levi *Gombiner; printed in many editions of Sh. Ar., OḤ.
Maggid Mishneh, Comm. to Maimonides, *Yad Ḥazakah,* by *Vidal Yom Tov of Tolosa; printed in most editions of the *Yad Ḥazakah.*
Maḥaneh Efrayim, Resp. and Nov., arranged acc. to Maimonides' *Yad Ḥazakah* , by Ephraim b. Aaron *Navon.
Maharai = Israel b. Pethahiah *Isserlein.
Maharal of Prague = *Judah Loew (Lob, Liwa), b. Bezalel.
Maharalbaḥ = *Levi b. Ḥabib.
Maharam Alashkar = Moses b. Isaac *Alashkar.
Maharam Alshekh = Moses b. Ḥayyim *Alashekh.
Maharam Mintz = Moses *Mintz.
Maharam of Lublin = *Meir b. Gedaliah of Lublin.
Maharam of Padua = Meir *Katzenellenbogen.
Maharam of Rothenburg = *Meir b. Baruch of Rothenburg.
Maharam Shik = Moses b. Joseph Schick.
Maharash Engel = Samuel b. Ze'ev Wolf Engel.
Maharashdam = Samuel b. Moses *Medina.
Maharḥash = Ḥayyim (ben) Shabbetai.
Mahari Basan = Jehiel b. Ḥayyim Basan.
Mahari b. Lev = Joseph ibn Lev.
Mahari'az = Jekuthiel Asher Zalman Ensil Zusmir.
Maharibal = *Joseph ibn Lev.
Mahariḥ = Jacob (Israel) *Ḥagiz.
Maharik = Joseph b. Solomon *Colon.
Maharikash = Jacob b. Abraham *Castro.
Maharil = Jacob b. Moses *Moellin.
Maharimat = Joseph b. Moses di Trani (not identical with the Maharit).
Maharit = Joseph b. Moses *Trani.
Maharitaẓ = Yom Tov b. Akiva Ẓahalon. (See article *Ẓahalon Family).
Maharsha = Samuel Eliezer b. Judah ha-Levi *Edels.
Maharshag = Simeon b. Judah Gruenfeld.
Maharshak = Samson b. Isaac of Chinon.
Maharshakh = *Solomon b. Abraham.
Maharshal = Solomon b. Jeḥiel *Luria.
Mahasham = Shalom Mordecai b. Moses *Sschwadron.
Maharyu = Jacob b. Judah *Weil.
Maḥazeh Avraham, Resp. by Abraham Nebagen v. Meir ha-Levi Steinberg.
Maḥazik Berakhah, Nov. by Ḥayyim Joseph David *Azulai.

*Maimonides = Moses b. Maimon, or Rambam.
*Malbim = Meir Loeb b. Jehiel Michael.
Malbim = Malbim's comm. to the Bible; printed in the major editions.
Malbushei Yom Tov, Nov. on *Levush*, OḤ, by Yom Tov Lipmann b. Nathan ha-Levi *Heller.
Mappah, another name for *Rema.*
Mareh ha-Panim, Comm. to Jer. Talmud by Moses b. Simeon *Margolies; printed in most editions of Jer. Talmud.
Margaliyyot ha-Yam, Nov. by Reuben *Margoliot.
Masat Binyamin, Resp. by Benjamin Aaron b. Abraham *Slonik
Mashbir, Ha- = *Joseph Samuel b. Isaac Rodi.
Massa Ḥayyim, Tax *halakhot* by Ḥayyim *Palaggi, with the subdivisions *Missim ve-Arnomiyyot* and *Torat ha-Minhagot.*
Massa Melekh, Compilation of Tax Law by Joseph b. Isaac *Ibn Ezra with concluding part *Ne'ilat She'arim.*
Matteh Asher, Resp. by Asher b. Emanuel Shalem.
Matteh Shimon, Digest of Resp. and Nov. to Tur and *Beit Yosef,* ḤM, by Mordecai Simeon b. Solomon.
Matteh Yosef, Resp. by Joseph b. Moses ha-Levi Nazir (see article under his father's name).
Mayim Amukkim, Resp. by Elijah b. Abraham *Mizraḥi.
Mayim Ḥayyim, Resp. by Ḥayyim b. Dov Beresh Rapaport.
Mayim Rabbim, , Resp. by Raphael *Meldola.
Me-Emek ha-Bakha, , Resp. by Simeon b. Jekuthiel Ephrati.
Me'irat Einayim, usual abbreviation: *Sma* (from: *Sefer Me'irat Einayim*); comm. to Sh. Ar. By Joshua b. Alexander ha-Kohen *Falk; printed in most editions of the Sh. Ar.
Melammed le-Ho'il, Resp. by David Ẓevi *Hoffmann.
Meisharim, [*Sefer*], Rabbinical treatise by *Jeroham b. Meshullam.
Meshiv Davar, Resp. by Naphtali Ẓevi Judah *Berlin.
Mi-Gei ha-Haregah, Resp. by Simeon b. Jekuthiel Ephrati.
Mi-Ma'amakim, Resp. by Ephraim Oshry.
Middot Aharon, first part of *Korban Aharon,* a comm. to *Sifra* by Aaron b. Abraham *Ibn Ḥayyim.
Migdal Oz, Comm. to Maimonides, *Yad Ḥazakah,* by *Ibn Gaon Shem Tov b. Abraham; printed in most editions of the *Yad Ḥazakah.*
Mikhtam le-David, Resp. by David Samuel b. Jacob *Pardo.
Mikkaḥ ve-ha-Mimkar, Sefer ha-, Rabbinical treatise by *Hai Gaon.
Milḥamot ha-Shem, Glosses to Rif, *Halakhot,* by *Naḥmanides.
Minḥat Ḥinnukh, Comm. to *Sefer ha-Ḥinnukh,* by Joseph b. Moses *Babad.
Minḥat Yiẓḥak, Resp. by Isaac Jacob b. Joseph Judah Weiss.
Misgeret ha-Shulḥan, Comm. to Sh. Ar., ḤM, by Benjamin Ze'ev Wolf b. Shabbetai; printed in most editions of Sh. Ar.
Mishkenot ha-Ro'im, Halakhot in alphabetical order by Uzziel Alshekh.
Mishnah Berurah, Comm. to Sh. Ar., OḤ, by *Israel Meir ha-Kohen.
Mishneh le-Melekh, Comm. to Maimonides, *Yad Ḥazakah,* by Judah *Rosanes; printed in most editions of *Yad Ḥazakah.*
Mishpat ha-Kohanim, Nov. to Sh. Ar., ḤM, by Jacob Moses *Lorberbaum, part of his *Netivot ha-Mishpat;* printed in major editions of Sh. Ar.
Mishpat Kohen, Resp. by Abraham Isaac ha-Kohen *Kook.
Mishpat Shalom, Nov. by Shalom Mordecai b. Moses *Schwadron; contains: *Kunteres Tikkun Olam.*
Mishpat u-Ẓedakah be-Ya'akov, Resp. by Jacob b. Reuben *Ibn Ẓur.
Mishpat ha-Urim, Comm. to Sh. Ar., ḤM by Jacob b. Jacob Moses *Lorberbaum, part of his *Netivot ha-Mishpat;* printed in major editons of Sh. Ar.
Mishpat Ẓedek, Resp. by *Melammed Meir b. Shem Tov.
Mishpatim Yesharim, Resp. by Raphael b. Mordecai *Berdugo.
Mishpetei Shemu'el, Resp. by Samuel b. Moses *Kalai (Kal'i).
Mishpetei ha-Tanna'im, Kunteres, Nov on *Levush,* OḤ by Yom Tov Lipmann b. Nathan ha-Levi *Heller.
Mishpetei Uzzi'el (Uziel), Resp. by Ben-Zion Meir Hai *Ouziel.
Missim ve-Arnoniyyot, Tax *halakhot* by Ḥayyim *Palaggi, a subdivision of his work *Massa Ḥayyim* on the same subject.
Mitzvot, Sefer ha-, Elucidation of precepts by *Maimonides; subdivided into *Lavin* (negative precepts) and *Asayin* (positive precepts).
Mitzvot Gadol, Sefer, Elucidation of precepts by *Moses b. Jacob of Coucy, subdivided into *Lavin* (negative precepts) and *Asayin* (positive precepts); the usual abbreviation is *Semag.*
Mitzvot Katan, Sefer, Elucidation of precepts by *Isaac b. Joseph of Corbeil; the usual, abbreviation is *Semak.*
Mo'adim u-Zemannim, Rabbinical treatises by Moses Sternbuch.
Modigliano, Joseph Samuel = *Joseph Samuel b. Isaac, Rodi (Ha-Mashbir).
Mordekhai (Mordecai), halakhic compilation by *Mordecai b. Hillel; printed in most editions of the Talmud after the texts.
Moses b. Maimon = *Maimonides, also called Rambam.
Moses b. Naḥman = Naḥmanides, also called Ramban.
Muram = Isaiah Menahem b. Isaac (from: Morenu R. Mendel).

Naḥal Yiẓḥak, Comm. on Sh. Ar., ḤM, by Isaac Elhanan *Spector.
Naḥalah li-Yhoshu'a, Resp. by Joshua Ẓunẓin.
Naḥalat Shivah, collection of legal forms by *Samuel b. David Moses ha-Levi.
*Naḥmanides = Moses b. Naḥman, also called Ramban.
Naẓiv = Naphtali Ẓevi Judah *Berlin.
Ne'eman Shemu'el, Resp. by Samuel Isaac *Modigilano.
Ne'ilat She'arim, concluding part of *Massa Melekh* (a work on Tax Law) by Joseph b. Isaac *Ibn Ezra, containing an exposition of customary law and subdivided into *Minhagei Issur* and *Minhagei Mamon.*
Ner Ma'aravi, Resp. by Jacob b. Malka.
Netivot ha-Mishpat, by Jacob b. Jacob Moses *Lorberbaum; subdivided into *Mishpat ha-Kohanim,* Nov. to Sh. Ar., ḤM, and *Mishpat ha-Urim,* a comm. on the same; printed in major editions of Sh. Ar.
Netivot Olam, Saying of the Sages by *Judah Loew (Lob, Liwa) b. Bezalel.
Nimmukei Menaḥem of Merseburg, Tax *halakhot* by the same, printed at the end of Resp. Maharyu.
Nimmukei Yosef, Comm. to Rif. *Halakhot,* by Joseph *Ḥabib (Ḥabiba); printed in many editions of the Talmud.
Noda bi-Yhudah, Resp. by Ezekiel b. Judah ha-Levi *Landau; there is a first collection *(Mahadura Kamma)* and a second collection *(Mahadura Tinyana).*
Nov. = Novellae, Ḥiddushim.

Ohel Moshe (1), Notes to Talmud, *Midrash Rabbah,* Yad, *Sifrei* and to several Resp., by Eleazar *Horowitz.

Ohel Moshe (2), Resp. by Moses Jonah Zweig.
Oholei Tam. Resp. by *Tam ibn Yaḥya Jacob b. David; printed in the rabbinical collection *Tummat Yesharim.*
Oholei Ya'akov, Resp. by Jacob de *Castro.
Or ha-Me'ir Resp by Judah Meir b. Jacob Samson Shapiro.
Or Same'aḥ, Comm. to Maimonides, *Yad Ḥazakah,* by *Meir Simḥah ha-Kohen of Dvinsk; printed in many editions of the *Yad Ḥazakah.*
Or Zaru'a [the father] = *Isaac b. Moses of Vienna.
Or Zaru'a [the son] = *Ḥayyim (Eliezer) b. Isaac.
Or Zaru'a, Nov. by *Isaac b. Moses of Vienna.
Orah, Sefer ha-, Compilation of ritual precepts by *Rashi.
Oraḥ la-Ẓaddik, Resp. by Abraham Ḥayyim Rodrigues.
Oẓar ha-Posekim, Digest of Responsa.

Paḥad Yiẓḥak, Rabbinical encyclopaedia by Isaac *Lampronti.
Panim Me'irot, Resp. by Meir b. Isaac *Eisenstadt.
Parashat Mordekhai, Resp. by Mordecai b. Abraham Naphtali *Banet.
Pe'at ha-Sadeh la-Dinim and Pe'at ha-Sadeh la-Kelalim, subdivisions of the *Sedei Ḥemed,* an encyclopaedia of precepts and responsa, by Ḥayyim Hezekaih *Medini.
Penei Moshe (1), Resp. by Moses *Benveniste.
Penei Moshe (2), Comm. to Jer. Talmud by Moses b. Simeon *Margolies; printed in most editions of the Jer. Talmud.
Penei Moshe (3), Comm. on the aggadic passages of 18 treatises of the Bab. and Jer. Talmud, by Moses b. Isaiah Katz.
Penei Yehoshu'a, Nov. by Jacob Joshua b. Ẓevi Hirsch *Falk.
Peri Ḥadash, Comm. on Sh. Ar. By Hezekiah da *Silva.
Perishah, Comm. on Tur by Joshua b. Alexander ha-Kohen *Falk; printed in major edition of Tur; forms together with *Derishah* and *Be'urim* (by the same author) the *Beit Yisrael.*
Pesakim u-Khetavim, 2nd part of the *Terumat ha-Deshen* by Israel b. Pethahiah *Isserlein' also called *Piskei Maharai.*
Pilpula Ḥarifta, Comm. to *Piskei ha-Rosh, Seder Nezikin,* by Yom Tov Lipmann b. Nathan ha-Levi *Heller; printed in major editions of the Talmud.
Piskei Maharai, see *Terumat ha-Deshen,* 2nd part; also called *Pesakim u-Khetavim.*
Piskei ha-Rosh, a compilation of *halakhot,* arranged on the Talmud, by *Asher b. Jehiel (Rosh); printed in major Talmud editions.
Pitḥei Teshuvah, Comm. to Sh. Ar. by Abraham Hirsch b. Jacob *Eisenstadt; printed in major editions of the Sh. Ar.

Rabad = *Abraham b. David of Posquières (Rabad III.).
Raban = *Eliezer b. Nathan of Mainz.
Raban, also called *Ẓafenat Pa'ne'aḥ* or *Even ha-Ezer,* see under the last name.
Rabi Abad = *Abraham b. Isaac of Narbonne.
Radad = David Dov. b. Aryeh Judah Jacob *Meisels.
Radam = Dov Berush b. Isaac Meisels.
Radbaz = *David b Solomon ibn Abi Ziumra.
Radbaz, Comm. to Maimonides, *Yad Ḥazakah,* by *David b. Solomon ibn Abi Zimra.
Ralbag = *Levi b. Gershom, also called Gersonides, or Leo Hebraeus.
Ralbag, Bible comm. by *Levi b. Gershon.
Rama [da Fano] = Menaḥem Azariah *Fano.
Ramah = Meir b. Todros [ha-Levi] *Abulafia.
Ramam = *Menaham of Merseburg.
Rambam = *Maimonides; real name: Moses b. Maimon.
Ramban = *Naḥmanides; real name Moses b. Naḥman.
Ramban, Comm. to Torah by *Naḥmanides; printed in major editions. ("Mikra'ot Gedolot").
Ran = *Nissim b. Reuben Gerondi.
Ran of Rif, Comm. on Rif, *Halakhot,* by Nissim b. Reuben Gerondi.
Ranaḥ = *Elijah b. Ḥayyim.
Rash = *Samson b. Abraham of Sens.
Rash, Comm. to Mishnah, by *Samson b. Abraham of Sens; printed in major Talmud editions.
Rashash = Samuel *Strashun.
Rashba = Solomon b. Abraham *Adret.
Rashba, Resp., see also; *Sefer Teshuvot ha-Rashba ha-Meyuḥasot le-ha-Ramban,* by Solomon b. Abraham *Adret.
Rashbad = Samuel b. David.
Rashbam = *Samuel b. Meir.
Rashbam = Comm. on Bible and Talmud by *Samuel b. Meir; printed in major editions of Bible and most editions of Talmud.
Rashbash = Solomon b. Simeon *Duran.
*Rashi = Solomon b. Isaac of Troyes.
Rashi, Comm. on Bible and Talmud by *Rashi; printed in almost all Bible and Talmud editions.
Raviah = Eliezer b. Joel ha-Levi.
Redak = David *Kimḥi.
Redak, Comm. to Bible by David *Kimḥi.
Redakh = *David b. Ḥayyim ha-Kohen of Corfu.
Re'em = Elijah b. Abraham *Mizraḥi.
Rema = Moses b. Israel *Isserles.
Rema, Glosses to Sh. Ar. by Moses b. Israel *Isserles; printed in almost all editions of the Sh. Ar. inside the text in Rashi type; also called *Mappah* or *Haggahot.*
Remek = Moses Kimḥi.
Remakh = Moses ha-Kohen mi-Lunel.
Reshakh = *Solomon b. Abraham; also called Maharshakh.
Resp. = Responsa, *She'elot u-Teshuvot.*
Ri Berav = *Berab.
Ri Escapa = Joseph b. Saul *Escapa.
Ri Migash = Joseph b. Meir ha-Levi *Ibn Migash.
Riba = Isaac b. Asher ha-Levi; Riba II (Riba ha-Baḥur) = his grandson with the same name.
Ribam = Isaac b. Mordecai (or: Isaac b. Meir).
Ribash = *Isaac b. Sheshet Perfet (or: Barfat).
Rid= *Isaiah b. Mali di Trani the Elder.
Ridbaz = Jacob David b. Ze'ev *Willowski.
Rif = Isaac b. Jacob ha-Kohen *Alfasi.
Rif, *Halakhot,* Compilation and abstract of the Talmud by Isaac b. Jacob ha-Kohen *Alfasi.
Ritba = Yom Tov b. Abraham *Ishbili.
Riẓbam = Isaac b. Mordecai.
Rosh = *Asher b. Jehiel, also called Asheri.
Rosh Mashbir, Resp. by *Joseph Samuel b. Isaac, Rodi.

Sedei Ḥemed, Encyclopaedia of precepts and responsa by Ḥayyim Ḥezekiah *Medini; subdivisions: *Asefat Dinim, Kunteres ha-Kelalim, Pe'at ha-Sadeh la-Dinim, Pe'at ha-Sadeh la-Kelalim.*
Semag, Usual abbreviation of *Sefer Mitzvot Gadol,* elucidation of precepts by *Moses b. Jacob of Coucy; subdivided into *Lavin* (negative precepts) *Asayin* (positive precepts).
Semak, Usual abbreviation of *Sefer Mitzvot Katan,* elucidation of precepts by *Isaac b. Joseph of Corbeil.

Sh. Ar. = *Shulḥan Arukh,* code by Joseph b. Ephraim *Caro.
Sha'ar Mishpat, Comm. to Sh. Ar., ḤM. By Israel Isser b. Ze'ev Wolf.
Sha'arei Shevu'ot, Treatise on the law of oaths by *David b. Saadiah; usually printed together with Rif, *Halakhot;* also called: *She'arim of R. Alfasi.*
Sha'arei Teshuvah, Collection of resp. from Geonic period, by different authors.
Sha'arei Uzzi'el, Rabbinical treatise by Ben-Zion Meir Ha *Ouziel.
Sha'arei Ẓedek, Collection of resp. from Geonic period, by different authors.
Shadal [or Shedal] = Samuel David *Luzzatto.
Shai la-Moreh, Resp. by Shabbetai Jonah.
Shakh, Usual abbreviation of *Siftei Kohen,* a comm. to Sh. Ar., YD and ḤM by *Shabbetai b. Meir ha-Kohen; printed in most editions of Sh. Ar.
Sha'ot-de-Rabbanan, Resp. by *Solomon b. Judah ha-Kohen.
She'arim of R. Alfasi see *Sha'arei Shevu'ot.*
Shedal, see Shadal.
She'elot u-Teshuvot ha-Ge'onim, Collection of resp. by different authors.
She'erit Yisrael, Resp. by Israel Ze'ev Mintzberg.
She'erit Yosef, Resp. by *Joseph b. Mordecai Gershon ha-Kohen.
She'ilat Yavez, Resp. by Jacob *Emden (Yaveẓ).
She'iltot, Compilation arranged acc. to the Torah by *Aḥa (Aḥai) of Shabḥa.
Shem Aryeh, Resp. by Aryeh Leib *Lipschutz.
Shemesh Ẓedakah, Resp. by Samson *Morpurgo.
Shenei ha-Me'orot ha-Gedolim, Resp. by Elijah *Covo.
Shetarot, Sefer ha-, Collection of legal forms by *Judah b. Barzillai al-Bargeloni.
Shevut Ya'akov, Resp. by Jacob b. Joseph Reicher.
Shibbolei ha-Leket Compilation on ritual by Zedekiah b. Avraham *Anav.
Shiltei Gibborim, Comm. to Rif, *Halakhot,* by *Joshua Boaz b. Simeon; printed in major editions of the Talmud.
Shittah Mekubbeẓet, Compilation of talmudical commentaries by Bezalel *Ashkenazi.
Shivat Ẓiyyon, Resp. by Samuel b. Ezekiel *Landau.
Shiyyurei Korban, by David *Fraenkel; additions to his comm. to Jer. Talmud *Korban Edah;* both printed in most editions of Jer. Talmud.
Sho'el u-Meshiv, Resp. by Joseph Saul ha-Levi *Nathanson.
Sh[ulḥan] Ar[ukh] [of Ba'al ha-Tanyal], Code by *Shneur Zalman of Lyady; not identical with the code by Joseph Caro.
Siftei Kohen, Comm. to Sh. Ar., YD and ḤM by *Shabbetai b. Meir ha-Kohen; printed in most editions of Sh. Ar.; usual abbreviation: *Shakh.*
Simḥat Yom Tov, Resp. by Tom Tov b. Jacob *Algazi.
Simlah Ḥadashah, Treatise on *Sheḥitah* by Alexander Sender b. Ephraim Zalman *Schor; see also *Tevu'ot Shor.*
Simeon b. Ẓemaḥ = Simeon b. Ẓemaḥ *Duran.
Sma, Comm. to Sh. Ar. by Joshua b. Alexander ha-Kohen *Falk; the full title is: *Sefer Me'irat Einayim;* printed in most editions of Sh. Ar.
Solomon b. Isaac ha-Levi = Solomon b. Isaac *Levy.
Solomon b. Isaac of Troyes = *Rashi.

Tal Orot, Rabbinical work with various contents, by Joseph ibn Gioia.
Tam, Rabbenu = *Tam Jacob b. Meir.
Tashbaẓ = Samson b. Zadok.
Tashbeẓ = Simeon b. Zemaḥ *Duran, sometimes also abbreviation for Samson b. Zadok, usually known as Tashbaẓ.
Tashbeẓ [*Sefer ha-*], Resp. by Simeon b. Ẓemaḥ *Duran; the fourth part of this work is called: *Ḥut ha-Meshullash.*
Taz, Usual abbreviation of *Turei Zahav,* comm., to Sh. Ar. by *David b. Samnuel ha-Levi; printed in most editions of Sh. Ar.
(Ha)-Tekhelet, subdivision of the *Levush* (a codification by Mordecai b. Abraham (Levush) *Jaffe); *Ha-Tekhelet* parallels Tur, OḤ 1-241.
Terumat ha-Deshen, by Israel b. Pethahiah *Isserlein; subdivided into a part containing responsa, and a second part called *Pesakim u-Khetavim* or *Piskei Maharai.*
Terumot, Sefer ha-, Compilation of *halakhot* by Samuel b. Isaac *Sardi.
Teshuvot Ba'alei ha-Tosafot, Collection of responsa by the Tosafists.
Teshjvot Ge'onei Mizraḥ u-Ma'aav, Collection of responsa.
Teshuvot ha-Geonim, Collection of responsa from Geonic period.
Teshuvot Ḥakhmei Provinzyah, Collection of responsa by different Provencal authors.
Teshuvot Ḥakhmei Ẓarefat ve-Loter, Collection of responsa by different French authors.
Teshuvot Maimuniyyot, Resp. pertaining to Maimonides' *Yad Ḥazakah;* printed in major editions of this work after the text; authorship uncertain.
Tevu'ot Shor, by Alexander Sender b. Ephraim Zalman *Schor, a comm. to his *Simlah Ḥadashah,* a work on *Sheḥitah.*
Tiferet Ẓevi, Resp. by Ẓevi Hirsch of the "AHW" Communities (Altona, Hamburg, Wandsbeck).
Tiktin, Judah b. Simeon = Judah b. Simeon *Ashkenazi.
Toledot Adam ve-Ḥavvah, Codification by *Jeroham b. Meshullam.
Torat Emet, Resp. by Aaron b. Joseph *Sasson.
Torat Ḥayyim, , Resp. by Ḥayyim (ben) Shabbetai.
Torat ha-Minhagot, subdivision of the *Massa Ḥayyim* (a work on tax law) by Ḥayyim *Palaggi, containing an exposition of customary law.
Tosafot Rid, Explanations to the Talmud and decisions by *Isaiah b. Mali di Trani the Elder.
Tosefot Yom Tov, comm. to Mishnah by Yom Tov Lipmann b. Nathan ha-Levi *Heller; printed in most editions of the Mishnah.
Tummim, subdivision of the comm. to Sh. Ar., ḤM, *Urim ve-Tummim* by Jonathan *Eybeschuetz; printed in the major editions of Sh. Ar.
Tur, usual abbreviation for the *Arba'ah Turim* of *Jacob b. Asher.
Turei Zahav, Comm. to Sh. Ar. by *David b. Samuel ha-Levi; printed in most editions of Sh. Ar.; usual abbreviation: *Taz.*

Urim, subdivision of the following.
Urim ve-Tummim, Comm. to Sh. Ar., ḤM, by Jonathan *Eybeschuetz; printed in the major editions of Sh. Ar.; subdivided in places into *Urim* and *Tummim.*

Vikku'aḥ Mayim Ḥayyim, Polemics against Isserles and Caro by Ḥayyim b. Bezalel.

Yad Malakhi, Methodological treatise by *Malachi b. Jacob ha-Kohen.

Yad Ramah, Nov. by Meir b. Todros [ha-Levi] *Abulafia.
Yakhin u-Vo'az, Resp. by Ẓemaḥ b. Solomon *Duran.
Yam ha-Gadol, Resp. by Jacob Moses *Toledano.
Yam shel Shelomo, Compilation arranged acc. to Talmud by Solomon b. Jehiel (Maharshal) *Luria.
Yashar, Sefer ha-, by *Tam, Jacob b. Meir (Rabbenu Tam); 1st pt.: Resp.; 2nd pt.: Nov.
Yaskil Avdi, Resp. by Obadiah Hadaya (printed together with his Resp. *De'ah ve-Haskel).*
Yaveẓ = Jacob *Emden.
Yehudah Ya'aleh, Resp. by Judah b. Israel *Aszod.
Yekar Tiferet, Comm. to Maimonides' *Yad Ḥazakah,*by David b. Solomon ibn Zimra, printed in most editions of *Yad Ḥazakah.*
Yere'im [ha-Shalem], [Sefer], Treatise on precepts by *Eliezer b. Samuel of Metz.
Yeshu'ot Ya'akov, Resp. by Jacob Meshullam b. Mordecai Ze'ev *Ornstein.
Yiẓhak Rei'aḥ, Resp. by Isaac b. Samuel Abendanan (see article *Abendanam Family).
Ẓafenat Pa'ne'aḥ (1), also called *Raban* or *Even ha-Ezer,* see under the last name.
Ẓafenat Pa'ne'aḥ (2), Resp. by Joseph *Rozin.
Zayit Ra'anan, Resp. by Moses Judah Leib b. Benjamin Auerbach.
Ẓeidah la-Derekh, Codification by *Menahem b. Aaron ibn Zerah.
Ẓedakah u-Mishpat, Resp. by Ẓedakah b. Saadiah Huẓin.
Zekan Aharon, Resp. by Elijah b. Benjamin ha-Levi.
Zekher Ẓaddik, Sermons by Eliezer *Katzenellenbogen.
Ẓemaḥ Ẓedek (1) Resp. by Menaham Mendel Shneersohn (see under *Shneersohn Family).
Zera Avraham, Resp. by Abraham b. David *Yiẓḥaki.
Zera Emet Resp. by *Ishmael b. Abaham Isaac ha-Kohen.
Ẓevi la-Ẓaddik, Resp. by Ẓevi Elimelech b. David Shapira.
Zikhron Yehudah, Resp. by *Judah b. Asher
Zikhron Yosef, Resp. by Joseph b. Menahem *Steinhardt.
Zikhronot, Sefer ha-, Sermons on several precepts by Samuel *Aboab.
Zikkaron la-Rishonim . . ., by Albert (Abraham Elijah) *Harkavy; contains in vol. 1 pt. 4 (1887) a collection of Geonic responsa.
Ẓiẓ Eliezer, Resp. by Eliezer Judah b. Jacob Gedaliah Waldenberg.

BIBLIOGRAPHICAL ABBREVIATIONS

Bibliographies in English and other languages have been extensively updated, with English translations cited where available. In order to help the reader, the language of books or articles is given where not obvious from titles of books or names of periodicals. Titles of books and periodicals in languages with alphabets other than Latin, are given in transliteration, even where there is a title page in English. Titles of articles in periodicals are not given. Names of Hebrew and Yiddish periodicals well known in English-speaking countries or in Israel under their masthead in Latin characters are given in this form, even when contrary to transliteration rules. Names of authors writing in languages with non-Latin alphabets are given in their Latin alphabet form wherever known; otherwise the names are transliterated. Initials are generally not given for authors of articles in periodicals, except to avoid confusion. Non-abbreviated book titles and names of periodicals are printed in *italics.* Abbreviations are given in the list below.

AASOR	*Annual of the American School of Oriental Research* (1919ff.).
AB	*Analecta Biblica* (1952ff.).
Abel, Géog	F.-M. Abel, *Géographie de la Palestine,* 2 vols. (1933-38).
ABR	*Australian Biblical Review* (1951ff.).
Abr.	Philo, *De Abrahamo.*
Abrahams, Companion	I. Abrahams, *Companion to the Authorised Daily Prayer Book* (rev. ed. 1922).
Abramson, Merkazim	S. Abramson, *Ba-Merkazim u-va-Tefuẓot bi-Tekufat ha-Ge'onim* (1965).
Acts	Acts of the Apostles (New Testament).
ACUM	*Who is who in ACUM [Aguddat Kompozitorim u-Meḥabbrim].*
ADAJ	*Annual of the Department of Antiquities, Jordan* (1951ff.).
Adam	Adam and Eve (Pseudepigrapha).
ADB	*Allgemeine Deutsche Biographie,* 56 vols. (1875–1912).
Add. Esth.	The Addition to Esther (Apocrypha).
Adler, Prat Mus	1. Adler, *La pratique musicale savante dans quelques communautés juives en Europe au XVIIe et XVIIIe siècles,* 2 vols. (1966).
Adler-Davis	H.M. Adler and A. Davis (ed. and tr.), *Service of the Synagogue, a New Edition of the Festival Prayers with an English Translation in Prose and Verse,* 6 vols. (1905–06).
Aet.	Philo, *De Aeternitate Mundi.*
AFO	*Archiv fuer Orientforschung* (first two volumes under the name *Archiv fuer Keilschriftforschung)* (1923ff.).
Ag. Ber	*Aggadat Bereshit* (ed. Buber, 1902*).*
Agr.	Philo, *De Agricultura.*
Ag. Sam.	*Aggadat Samuel.*
Ag. Song	*Aggadat Shir ha-Shirim* (Schechter ed., 1896).
Aharoni, Ereẓ	Y. Aharoni, *Ereẓ Yisrael bi-Tekufat ha-Mikra: Geografyah Historit* (1962).
Aharoni, Land	Y. Aharoni, *Land of the Bible* (1966).

Ahikar	Ahikar (Pseudepigrapha).
AI	*Archives Israélites de France* (1840–1936).
AJA	*American Jewish Archives* (1948ff.).
AJHSP	*American Jewish Historical Society – Publications* (after vol. 50 = AJHSQ).
AJHSQ	*American Jewish Historical (Society) Quarterly* (before vol. 50 =AJHSP).
AJSLL	*American Journal of Semitic Languages and Literature* (1884–95 under the title *Hebraica*, since 1942 JNES).
AJYB	*American Jewish Year Book* (1899ff.).
AKM	Abhandlungen fuer die Kunde des Morgenlandes (series).
Albright, Arch	W.F. Albright, *Archaeology of Palestine* (rev. ed. 1960).
Albright, Arch Bib	W.F. Albright, *Archaeology of Palestine and the Bible* (1935^{3}).
Albright, Arch Rel	W.F. Albright, *Archaeology and the Religion of Israel* (1953^{3}).
Albright, Stone	W.F. Albright, *From the Stone Age to Christianity* (1957^{2}).
Alon, Meḥkarim	G. Alon, *Meḥkarim be-Toledot Yisrael bi-Ymei Bayit Sheni u-vi-Tekufat ha-Mishnah ve-ha Talmud*, 2 vols. (1957–58).
Alon, Toledot	G. Alon, *Toledot ha-Yehudim be-Ereẓ Yisrael bi-Tekufat ha-Mishnah ve-ha-Talmud*, I (1958^{3}), (1961^{2}).
ALOR	Alter Orient (series).
Alt, Kl Schr	A. Alt, *Kleine Schriften zur Geschichte des Volkes Israel*, 3 vols. (1953–59).
Alt, Landnahme	A. Alt, *Landnahme der Israeliten in Palaestina* (1925); also in Alt, Kl Schr, 1 (1953), 89–125.
Ant.	Josephus, *Jewish Antiquities* (Loeb Classics ed.).
AO	*Acta Orientalia* (1922ff.).
AOR	*Analecta Orientalia* (1931ff.).
AOS	American Oriental Series.
Apion	Josephus, *Against Apion* (Loeb Classics ed.).
Aq.	Aquila's Greek translation of the Bible.
Ar.	*Arakhin* (talmudic tractate).
Artist.	Letter of Aristeas (Pseudepigrapha).
ARN^{1}	*Avot de-Rabbi Nathan*, version (1) ed. Schechter, 1887.
ARN^{2}	*Avot de-Rabbi Nathan*, version (2) ed. Schechter, 1945^{2}.
Aronius, Regesten	I. Aronius, *Regesten zur Geschichte der Juden im fraenkischen und deutschen Reiche bis zum Jahre 1273* (1902).
ARW	*Archiv fuer Religionswissenschaft* (1898–1941/42).
AS	*Assyrological Studies* (1931ff.).
Ashtor, Korot	E. Ashtor (Strauss), *Korot ha-Yehudim bi-Sefarad ha-Muslemit*, 1(1966^{2}), 2(1966).
Ashtor, Toledot	E. Ashtor (Strauss), *Toledot ha-Yehudim be-Miẓrayim ve-Suryah Taḥat Shilton ha-Mamlukim*, 3 vols. (1944–70).
Assaf, Ge'onim	S. Assaf, *Tekufat ha-Ge'onim ve-Sifrutah* (1955).
Assaf, Mekorot	S. Assaf, *Mekorot le-Toledot ha-Ḥinnukh be-Yisrael*, 4 vols. (1925–43).
Ass. Mos.	Assumption of Moses (Pseudepigrapha).
ATA	Alttestamentliche Abhandlungen (series).
ATANT	Abhandlungen zur Theologie des Alten und Neuen Testaments (series).
AUJW	*Allgemeine unabhaengige juedische Wochenzeitung* (till 1966 = AWJD).
AV	Authorized Version of the Bible.
Avad.	*Avadim* (post-talmudic tractate).
Avi-Yonah, Geog	M. Avi-Yonah, *Geografyah Historit shel Ereẓ Yisrael* (1962^{3}).
Avi-Yonah, Land	M. Avi-Yonah, *The Holy Land from the Persian to the Arab conquest (536 B.C. to A.D. 640)* (1960).
Avot	*Avot* (talmudic tractate).
Av. Zar.	*Avodah Zarah* (talmudic tractate).
AWJD	*Allgemeine Wochenzeitung der Juden in Deutschland* (since 1967 = AUJW).
AZDJ	*Allgemeine Zeitung des Judentums.*
Azulai	Ḥ.Y.D. Azulai, *Shem ha-Gedolim*, ed. by I.E. Benjacob, 2 pts. (1852) (and other editions).
BA	*Biblical Archaeologist* (1938ff.).
Bacher, Bab Amor	W. Bacher, *Agada der babylonischen Amoraeer* (1913^{2}).
Bacher, Pal Amor	W. Bacher, *Agada der palaestinensischen Amoraeer* (Heb. ed. *Aggadat Amora'ei Ereẓ Yisrael)*, 2 vols. (1892–99).
Bacher, Tann	W. Bacher, *Agada der Tannaiten* (Heb. ed. *Aggadot ha-Tanna'im*, vol. 1, pt. 1 and 2 (1903); vol. 2 (1890).
Bacher, Trad	W. Bacher, *Tradition und Tradenten in den Schulen Palaestinas und Babyloniens* (1914).
Baer, Spain	Yitzhak (Fritz) Baer, *History of the Jews in Christian Spain*, 2 vols. (1961–66).
Baer, Studien	Yitzhak (Fritz) Baer, *Studien zur Geschichte der Juden im Koenigreich Aragonien waehrend des 13. und 14. Jahrhunderts* (1913).
Baer, Toledot	Yitzhak (Fritz) Baer, *Toledot ha-Yehudim bi-Sefarad ha-Noẓerit mi-Teḥillatan shel ha-Kehillot ad ha-Gerush*, 2 vols. (1959^{2}).
Baer, Urkunden	Yitzhak (Fritz) Baer, *Die Juden im christlichen Spanien*, 2 vols. (1929–36).
Baer S., Seder	S.I. Baer, *Seder Avodat Yisrael* (1868 and reprints).
BAIU	*Bulletin de l'Alliance Israélite Universelle* (1861–1913).
Baker, Biog Dict	*Baker's Biographical Dictionary of Musicians*, revised by N. Slonimsky (1958^{5}; with Supplement 1965).
I Bar.	I Baruch (Apocrypha).
II Bar.	II Baruch (Pseudepigrapha).
III Bar.	III Baruch (Pseudepigrapha).
BAR	*Biblical Archaeology Review.*
Baron, Community	S.W. Baron, *The Jewish Community, its History and Structure to the American Revolution*, 3 vols. (1942).

Baron, Social	S.W. Baron, *Social and Religious History of the Jews,* 3 vols. (1937); enlarged, 1-2(1952^2), 3-14 (1957–69).
Barthélemy-Milik	D. Barthélemy and J.T. Milik, *Dead Sea Scrolls: Discoveries in the Judean Desert,* vol. 1 *Qumram Cave* I (1955).
BASOR	*Bulletin of the American School of Oriental Research.*
Bauer-Leander	H. Bauer and P. Leander, *Grammatik des Biblisch-Aramaeischen* (1927; repr. 1962).
BB	(1) *Bava Batra* (talmudic tractate). (2) *Biblische Beitraege* (1943ff.).
BBB	Bonner biblische Beitraege (series).
BBLA	*Beitraege zur biblischen Landes- und Altertumskunde* (until 1949–ZDPV).
BBSAJ	*Bulletin,* British School of Archaeology, Jerusalem (1922–25; after 1927 included in PEFQS).
BDASI	*Alon* (since 1948) or *Hadashot Arkhe'ologiyyot* (since 1961), bulletin of the Department of Antiquities of the State of Israel.
Begrich, Chronologie	J. Begrich, *Chronologie der Koenige von Israel und Juda* (1929).
Bek.	*Bekhorot* (talmudic tractate).
Bel	Bel and the Dragon (Apocrypha).
Benjacob, Oẓar	I.E. Benjacob, *Oẓar ha-Sefarim* (1880; repr. 1956).
Ben Sira	see Ecclus.
Ben-Yehuda, Millon	E. Ben-Yedhuda, *Millon ha-Lashon ha-Ivrit,* 16 vols (1908–59; repr. in 8 vols., 1959).
Benzinger, Archaeologie	I. Benzinger, *Hebraeische Archaeologie* (1927^3).
Ben Zvi, Eretz Israel	I. Ben-Zvi, *Eretz Israel under Ottoman Rule* (1960; offprint from L. Finkelstein (ed.), *The Jews, their History, Culture and Religion* (vol. 1).
Ben Zvi, Ereẓ Israel	I. Ben-Zvi, *Ereẓ Israel bi-Ymei ha-Shilton ha-Ottomani (1955).*
Ber.	*Berakhot* (talmudic tractate).
Beẓah	*Beẓah* (talmudic tractate).
BIES	Bulletin of the Israel Exploration Society, see below BJPES.
Bik.	*Bikkurim* (talmudic tractate).
BJCE	Bibliography of Jewish Communities in Europe, catalog at General Archives for the History of the Jewish People, Jerusalem.
BJPES	Bulletin of the Jewish Palestine Exploration Society – English name of the Hebrew periodical known as: 1. *Yedi'ot ha-Ḥevrah ha-Ivrit la-Ḥakirat Ereẓ Yisrael va-Attikoteha* (1933–1954); 2. *Yedi'ot ha-Ḥevrah la-Ḥakirat Ereẓ Yisrael va-Attikoteha* (1954–1962); 3. *Yedi'ot ba-Ḥakirat Ereẓ Yisrael va-Attikoteha* (1962ff.).
BJRL	*Bulletin of the John Rylands Library* (1914ff.).
BK	*Bava Kamma* (talmudic tractate).
BLBI	*Bulletin of the Leo Baeck Institute* (1957ff.).
BM	(1) *Bava Meẓia* (talmudic tractate. (2) *Beit Mikra* (1955/56ff.). (3) British Museum.
BO	*Bibbia e Oriente* (1959ff.).
Bondy-Dworský	G. Bondy and F. Dworský, *Regesten zur Geschichte der Juden in Boehmen, Maehren und Schlesien von 906 bis 1620,* 2 vols. (1906).
BOR	*Bibliotheca Orientalis* (1943ff.).
Borée, Ortsnamen	W. Borée *Die alten Ortsnamen Palaestinas* (1930).
Bousset, Religion	W. Bousset, *Die Religion des Judentums im neutestamentlichen Zeitalter* (1906^2).
Bousset-Gressmann	W. Bousset, *Die Religion des Judentums im spaethellenistischen Zeitalter* (1966^3).
BR	*Biblical Review* (1916–25).
BRCI	*Bulletin of the Research Council of Israel* (1951/52–1954/55; then divided).
BRE	*Biblical Research* (1956ff.).
BRF	*Bulletin of the Rabinowitz Fund for the Exploration of Ancient Synagogues* (1949ff.).
Briggs, Psalms	Ch. A. and E.G. Briggs, *Critical and Exegetical Commentary on the Book of Psalms,* 2 vols. (ICC, 1906–07).
Bright, Hist	J. Bright, *A History of Israel* (1959).
Brockelmann, Arab Lit	K. Brockelmann, *Geschichte der arabischen Literatur,* 2 vols. 1898–1902), supplement, 3 vols. (1937–42).
Bruell, Jahrbuecher	*Jahrbuecher fuer juedische Geschichte und Litteratur,* ed. by N. Bruell, Frankfurt (1874–90).
Brugmans-Frank	H. Brugmans and A. Frank (eds.), *Geschiedenis der Joden in Nederland* (1940).
BTS	*Bible et Terre Sainte* (1958ff.).
Bull, Index	S. Bull, *Index to Biographies of Contemporary Composers* (1964).
BW	*Biblical World* (1882–1920).
BWANT	*Beitraege zur Wissenschaft vom Alten und Neuen Testament* (1926ff.).
BZ	*Biblische Zeitschrift* (1903ff.).
BZAW	*Beihefte zur Zeitschrift fuer die alttestamentliche Wissenschaft,* supplement to ZAW (1896ff.).
BŻIH	*Biuletyn Zydowskiego Instytutu Historycznego* (1950ff.).
CAB	*Cahiers d'archéologie biblique* (1953ff.).
CAD	*The* [*Chicago*] *Assyrian Dictionary* (1956ff.).
CAH	*Cambridge Ancient History,* 12 vols. (1923–39)
CAH^2	*Cambridge Ancient History,* second edition, 14 vols. (1962–2005).
Calwer, Lexikon	*Calwer, Bibellexikon.*
Cant.	Canticles, usually given as Song (= Song of Songs).

Cantera-Millás, Inscripciones	F. Cantera and J.M. Millás, *Las Inscripciones Hebraicas de España* (1956).
CBQ	*Catholic Biblical Quarterly* (1939ff.).
CCARY	Central Conference of American Rabbis, *Yearbook* (1890/91ff.).
CD	*Damascus Document* from the Cairo *Genizah* (published by S. Schechter, *Fragments of a Zadokite Work*, 1910).
Charles, Apocrypha	R.H. Charles, *Apocrypha and Pseudepigrapha . . .*, 2 vols. (1913; repr. 1963–66).
Cher.	Philo, *De Cherubim.*
I (or II) Chron.	Chronicles, book I and II (Bible).
CIG	*Corpus Inscriptionum Graecarum.*
CIJ	*Corpus Inscriptionum Judaicarum*, 2 vols. (1936–52).
CIL	*Corpus Inscriptionum Latinarum.*
CIS	*Corpus Inscriptionum Semiticarum* (1881ff.).
C.J.	Codex Justinianus.
Clermont-Ganneau, Arch	Ch. Clermont-Ganneau, *Archaeological Researches in Palestine*, 2 vols. (1896–99).
CNFI	*Christian News from Israel* (1949ff.).
Cod. Just.	Codex Justinianus.
Cod. Theod.	Codex Theodosinanus.
Col.	Epistle to the Colosssians (New Testament).
Conder, Survey	Palestine Exploration Fund, *Survey of Eastern Palestine*, vol. 1, pt. I (1889) = C.R. Conder, *Memoirs of the . . . Survey.*
Conder-Kitchener	Palestine Exploration Fund, *Survey of Western Palestine*, vol. 1, pts. 1-3 (1881–83) = C.R. Conder and H.H. Kitchener, *Memoirs.*
Conf.	Philo, *De Confusione Linguarum.*
Conforte, Kore	D. Conforte, *Kore ha-Dorot* (1842^2).
Cong.	Philo, *De Congressu Quaerendae Eruditionis Gratia.*
Cont.	Philo, *De Vita Contemplativa.*
I (or II) Cor.	Epistles to the Corinthians (New Testament).
Cowley, Aramic	A. Cowley, *Aramaic Papyri of the Fifth Century B.C.* (1923).
Colwey, Cat	A.E. Cowley, *A Concise Catalogue of the Hebrew Printed Books in the Bodleian Library* (1929).
CRB	*Cahiers de la Revue Biblique* (1964ff.).
Crowfoot-Kenyon	J.W. Crowfoot, K.M. Kenyon and E.L. Sukenik, *Buildings of Samaria* (1942).
C.T.	Codex Theodosianus.
DAB	*Dictionary of American Biography* (1928–58).
Daiches, Jews	S. Daiches, *Jews in Babylonia* (1910).
Dalman, Arbeit	G. Dalman, *Arbeit und Sitte in Palaestina*, 7 vols.in 8 (1928–42 repr. 1964).
Dan	Daniel (Bible).
Davidson, Oẓar	I. Davidson, *Oẓar ha-Shirah ve-ha-Piyyut*, 4 vols. (1924–33); Supplement in: HUCA, 12–13 (1937/38), 715–823.
DB	J. Hastings, *Dictionary of the Bible*, 4 vols. (1963^2).
DBI	F.G. Vigoureaux et al. (eds.), *Dictionnaire de la Bible*, 5 vols. in 10 (1912); Supplement, 8 vols. (1928–66)
Decal.	Philo, *De Decalogo.*
Dem.	*Demai* (talmudic tractate).
DER	*Derekh Ereẓ Rabbah* (post-talmudic tractate).
Derenbourg, Hist	J. Derenbourg *Essai sur l'histoire et la géographie de la Palestine* (1867).
Det.	Philo, *Quod deterius potiori insidiari solet.*
Deus	Philo, *Quod Deus immutabilis sit.*
Deut.	Deuteronomy (Bible).
Deut. R.	*Deuteronomy Rabbah.*
DEZ	*Derekh Ereẓ Zuta* (post-talmudic tractate).
DHGE	*Dictionnaire d'histoire et de géographie ecclésiastiques*, ed. by A. Baudrillart et al., 17 vols (1912–68).
Dik. Sof	*Dikdukei Soferim*, variae lections of the talmudic text by Raphael Nathan Rabbinovitz (16 vols., 1867–97).
Dinur, Golah	B. Dinur (Dinaburg), *Yisrael ba-Golah*, 2 vols. in 7 (1959–68) = vols. 5 and 6 of his *Toledot Yisrael*, second series.
Dinur, Haganah	B. Dinur (ed.), *Sefer Toledot ha-Haganah* (1954ff.).
Diringer, Iscr	D. Diringer, *Iscrizioni antico-ebraiche palestinesi* (1934).
Discoveries	*Discoveries in the Judean Desert* (1955ff.).
DNB	*Dictionary of National Biography*, 66 vols. (1921–222) with Supplements.
Dubnow, Divrei	S. Dubnow, *Divrei Yemei Am Olam*, 11 vols (1923–38 and further editions).
Dubnow, Ḥasidut	S. Dubnow, *Toledot ha-Ḥasidut* (1960^2).
Dubnow, Hist	S. Dubnow, *History of the Jews* (1967).
Dubnow, Hist Russ	S. Dubnow, *History of the Jews in Russia and Poland*, 3 vols. (1916 20).
Dubnow, Outline	S. Dubnow, *An Outline of Jewish History*, 3 vols. (1925–29).
Dubnow, Weltgesch	S. Dubnow, *Weltgeschichte des juedischen Volkes* 10 vols. (1925–29).
Dukes, Poesie	L. Dukes, *Zur Kenntnis der neuhebraeischen religioesen Poesie* (1842).
Dunlop, Khazars	D. H. Dunlop, *History of the Jewish Khazars* (1954).
EA	El Amarna Letters (edited by J.A. Knudtzon), *Die El-Amarna Tafel*, 2 vols. (1907 14).
EB	*Encyclopaedia Britannica.*
EBI	*Estudios biblicos* (1941ff.).
EBIB	T.K. Cheyne and J.S. Black, *Encyclopaedia Biblica*, 4 vols. (1899–1903).
Ebr.	Philo, *De Ebrietate.*
Eccles.	Ecclesiastes (Bible).
Eccles. R.	*Ecclesiastes Rabbah.*
Ecclus.	Ecclesiasticus or Wisdom of Ben Sira (or Sirach; Apocrypha).
Eduy.	*Eduyyot* (mishanic tractate).

EG	*Enziklopedyah shel Galuyyot* (1953ff.).
EH	*Even ha-Ezer.*
EHA	*Enẓiklopedyah la-Ḥafirot Arkheologiyyot be-Ereẓ Yisrael,* 2 vols. (1970).
EI	*Enzyklopaedie des Islams,* 4 vols. (1905–14). Supplement vol. (1938).
EIS	*Encyclopaedia of Islam,* 4 vols. (1913–36; repr. 1954–68).
EIS²	*Encyclopaedia of Islam, second edition (1960–2000).*
Eisenstein, Dinim	J.D. Eisenstein, *Oẓar Dinim u-Minhagim* (1917; several reprints).
Eisenstein, Yisrael	J.D. Eisenstein, *Oẓar Yisrael* (10 vols, 1907–13; repr. with several additions 1951).
EIV	*Enẓiklopedyah Ivrit* (1949ff.).
EJ	*Encyclopaedia Judaica* (German, A-L only), 10 vols. (1928–34).
EJC	*Enciclopedia Judaica Castellana,* 10 vols. (1948–51).
Elbogen, Century	I Elbogen, *A Century of Jewish Life* (1960²).
Elbogen, Gottesdienst	I Elbogen, *Der juedische Gottesdienst ...* (1931³, repr. 1962).
Elon, Mafte'aḥ	M. Elon (ed.), *Mafte'aḥ ha-She'elot ve-ha-Teshuvot ha-Rosh* (1965).
EM	*Enẓiklopedyah Mikra'it* (1950ff.).
I (or II) En.	I and II Enoch (Pseudepigrapha).
EncRel	*Encyclopedia of Religion,* 15 vols. (1987, 2005²).
Eph.	Epistle to the Ephesians (New Testament).
Ephros, Cant	G. Ephros, *Cantorial Anthology,* 5 vols. (1929–57).
Ep. Jer.	Epistle of Jeremy (Apocrypha).
Epstein, Amora'im	J N. Epstein, *Mevo'ot le-Sifrut ha-Amora'im* (1962).
Epstein, Marriage	L M. Epstein, *Marriage Laws in the Bible and the Talmud* (1942).
Epstein, Mishnah	J. N. Epstein, *Mavo le-Nusaḥ ha-Mishnah,* 2 vols. (1964²).
Epstein, Tanna'im	J. N. Epstein, *Mavo le-Sifruth ha-Tanna'im.* (1947).
ER	*Ecumenical Review.*
Er.	*Eruvin* (talmudic tractate).
ERE	*Encyclopaedia of Religion and Ethics,* 13 vols. (1908–26); reprinted.
ErIsr	*Eretz-Israel,* Israel Exploration Society.
I Esd.	I Esdras (Apocrypha) (= III Ezra).
II Esd.	II Esdras (Apocrypha) (= IV Ezra).
ESE	*Ephemeris fuer semitische Epigraphik,* ed. by M. Lidzbarski.
ESN	*Encyclopaedia Sefaradica Neerlandica,* 2 pts. (1949).
ESS	*Encyclopaedia of the Social Sciences,* 15 vols. (1930–35); reprinted in 8 vols. (1948–49).
Esth.	Esther (Bible).
Est. R.	*Esther Rabbah.*
ET	*Enẓiklopedyah Talmudit* (1947ff.).
Eusebius, Onom.	E. Klostermann (ed.), *Das Onomastikon* (1904), Greek with Hieronymus' Latin translation.
Ex.	Exodus (Bible).
Ex. R.	*Exodus Rabbah.*
Exs	Philo, *De Exsecrationibus.*
EẒD	*Enẓiklopeday shel ha-Ẓiyyonut ha-Datit* (1951ff.).
Ezek.	Ezekiel (Bible).
Ezra	Ezra (Bible).
III Ezra	III Ezra (Pseudepigrapha).
IV Ezra	IV Ezra (Pseudepigrapha).
Feliks, Ha-Ẓome'aḥ	*J. Feliks, Ha-Ẓome'aḥ ve-ha-Ḥai ba-Mishnah* (1983).
Finkelstein, Middle Ages	L. Finkelstein, *Jewish Self-Government in the Middle Ages* (1924).
Fischel, Islam	W.J. Fischel, *Jews in the Economic and Political Life of Mediaeval Islam* (1937; reprint with introduction "The Court Jew in the Islamic World," 1969).
FJW	*Fuehrer durch die juedische Gemeindeverwaltung und Wohlfahrtspflege in Deutschland* (1927/28).
Frankel, Mevo	Z. Frankel, *Mevo ha-Yerushalmi* (1870; reprint 1967).
Frankel, Mishnah	Z. Frankel, *Darkhei ha-Mishnah* (1959²; reprint 1959²).
Frazer, Folk-Lore	J.G. Frazer, *Folk-Lore in the Old Testament,* 3 vols. (1918–19).
Frey, Corpus	J.-B. Frey, *Corpus Inscriptionum Iudaicarum,* 2 vols. (1936–52).
Friedmann, Lebensbilder	A. Friedmann, *Lebensbilder beruehmter Kantoren,* 3 vols. (1918–27).
FRLT	*Forschungen zur Religion und Literatur des Alten und Neuen Testaments* (series) (1950ff.).
Frumkin-Rivlin	A.L. Frumkin and E. Rivlin, *Toledot Ḥakhmei Yerushalayim,* 3 vols. (1928–30), Supplement vol. (1930).
Fuenn, Keneset	S.J. Fuenn, *Keneset Yisrael,* 4 vols. (1887–90).
Fuerst, Bibliotheca	J. Fuerst, *Bibliotheca Judaica,* 2 vols. (1863; repr. 1960).
Fuerst, Karaeertum	J. Fuerst, *Geschichte des Karaeertums,* 3 vols. (1862–69).
Fug.	Philo, *De Fuga et Inventione.*
Gal.	Epistle to the Galatians (New Testament).
Galling, Reallexikon	K. Galling, *Biblisches Reallexikon* (1937).
Gardiner, Onomastica	A.H. Gardiner, *Ancient Egyptian Onomastica,* 3 vols. (1947).
Geiger, Mikra	A. Geiger, *Ha-Mikra ve-Targumav,* tr. by J.L. Baruch (1949).
Geiger, Urschrift	A. Geiger, *Urschrift und Uebersetzungen der Bibel* 1928²).
Gen.	Genesis (Bible).
Gen. R.	*Genesis Rabbah.*
Ger.	*Gerim* (post-talmudic tractate).
Germ Jud	M. Brann, I. Elbogen, A. Freimann, and H. Tykocinski (eds.), *Germania Judaica,* vol. 1 (1917; repr. 1934 and 1963); vol. 2, in 2 pts. (1917–68), ed. by Z. Avneri.

GHAT	*Goettinger Handkommentar zum Alten Testament* (1917–22).
Ghirondi-Neppi	M.S. Ghirondi and G.H. Neppi, *Toledot Gedolei Yisrael u-Ge'onei Italyah ... u-Ve'urim al Sefer Zekher Ẓaddikim li-Verakhah . . .*(1853), index in ZHB, 17 (1914), 171–83.
Gig.	Philo, *De Gigantibus.*
Ginzberg, Legends	L. Ginzberg, *Legends of the Jews,* 7 vols. (1909–38; and many reprints).
Git.	*Gittin* (talmudic tractate).
Glueck, Explorations	N. Glueck, *Explorations in Eastern Palestine,* 2 vols. (1951).
Goell, Bibliography	Y. Goell, *Bibliography of Modern Hebrew Literature in English Translation* (1968).
Goodenough, Symbols	E.R. Goodenough, *Jewish Symbols in the Greco-Roman Period,* 13 vols. (1953–68).
Gordon, Textbook	C.H. Gordon, *Ugaritic Textbook* (1965; repr. 1967).
Graetz, Gesch	H. Graetz, *Geschichte der Juden* (last edition 1874–1908).
Graetz, Hist	H. Graetz, *History of the Jews,* 6 vols. (1891–1902).
Graetz, Psalmen	H. Graetz, *Kritischer Commentar zu den Psalmen,* 2 vols. in 1 (1882–83).
Graetz, Rabbinowitz	H. Graetz, *Divrei Yemei Yisrael,* tr. by S.P. Rabbinowitz. (1928 1929^2).
Gray, Names	G.B. Gray, *Studies in Hebrew Proper Names* (1896).
Gressmann, Bilder	H. Gressmann, *Altorientalische Bilder zum Alten Testament* (1927^2).
Gressmann, Texte	H. Gressmann, *Altorientalische Texte zum Alten Testament* (1926^2).
Gross, Gal Jud	H. Gross, *Gallia Judaica* (1897; repr. with add. 1969).
Grove, Dict	*Grove's Dictionary of Music and Musicians,* ed. by E. Blum 9 vols. (1954^5) and suppl. (1961^5).
Guedemann, Gesch Erz	M. Guedemann, *Geschichte des Erziehungswesens und der Cultur der abendlaendischen Juden,* 3 vols. (1880–88).
Guedemann, Quellenschr	M. Guedemann, *Quellenschriften zur Geschichte des Unterrichts und der Erziehung bei den deutschen Juden* (1873, 1891).
Guide	Maimonides, *Guide of the Perplexed.*
Gulak, Oẓar	A. Gulak, *Oẓar ha-Shetarot ha-Nehugim be-Yisrael* (1926).
Gulak, Yesodei	A. Gulak, *Yesodei ha-Mishpat ha-Ivri, Seder Dinei Mamonot be-Yisrael, al pi Mekorot ha-Talmud ve-ha-Posekim,* 4 vols. (1922; repr. 1967).
Guttmann, Mafte'aḥ	M. Guttmann, *Mafte'aḥ ha-Talmud,* 3 vols. (1906–30).
Guttmann, Philosophies	J. Guttmann, *Philosophies of Judaism* (1964).
Hab.	*Habakkuk* (Bible).
Ḥag.	*Ḥagigah* (talmudic tractate).
Haggai	*Haggai* (Bible).
Ḥal.	*Ḥallah* (talmudic tractate).
Halevy, Dorot	I. Halevy, *Dorot ha-Rishonim,* 6 vols. (1897–1939).
Halpern, Pinkas	I. Halpern (Halperin), *Pinkas Va'ad Arba Araẓot* (1945).
Hananel-Eškenazi	A. Hananel and Eškenazi (eds.), *Fontes Hebraici ad res oeconomicas socialesque terrarum balcanicarum saeculo XVI pertinentes,* 2 vols, (1958–60; in Bulgarian).
HB	*Hebraeische Bibliographie* (1858–82).
Heb.	Epistle to the Hebrews (New Testament).
Heilprin, Dorot	J. Heilprin (Heilperin), *Seder ha-Dorot,* 3 vols. (1882; repr. 1956).
Her.	Philo, *Quis Rerum Divinarum Heres.*
Hertz, Prayer	J.H. Hertz (ed.), *Authorised Daily Prayer Book* (rev. ed. 1948; repr. 1963).
Herzog, Instit	I. Herzog, *The Main Institutions of Jewish Law,* 2 vols. (1936–39; repr. 1967).
Herzog-Hauck	J.J. Herzog and A. Hauch (eds.), *Real-encyklopaedie fuer protestantische Theologie* (1896–1913^3).
HḤY	*Ha-Ẓofeh le-Ḥokhmat Yisrael* (first four volumes under the title *Ha-Ẓofeh me-Ereẓ Hagar)* (1910/11–13).
Hirschberg, Afrikah	H.Z. Hirschberg, *Toledot ha-Yehudim be-Afrikah ha-Zofonit,* 2 vols. (1965).
HJ	*Historia Judaica* (1938–61).
HL	*Das Heilige Land* (1857ff.)
ḤM	*Ḥoshen Mishpat.*
Hommel, Ueberliefer.	F. Hommel, *Die altisraelitische Ueberlieferung in inschriftlicher Beleuchtung* (1897).
Hor.	*Horayot* (talmudic tractate).
Horodezky, Ḥasidut	S.A. Horodezky, *Ha-Ḥasidut ve-ha-Ḥasidim,* 4 vols. (1923).
Horowitz, Ereẓ Yis	I.W. Horowitz, *Ereẓ Yisrael u-Shekhenoteha* (1923).
Hos.	Hosea (Bible).
HTR	*Harvard Theological Review* (1908ff.).
HUCA	*Hebrew Union College Annual* (1904; 1924ff.)
Ḥul.	*Ḥullin* (talmudic tractate).
Husik, Philosophy	I. Husik, *History of Medieval Jewish Philosophy* (1932^2).
Hyman, Toledot	A. Hyman, *Toledot Tanna'im ve-Amora'im* (1910; repr. 1964).
Ibn Daud, Tradition	Abraham Ibn Daud, *Sefer ha-Qabbalah – The Book of Tradition,* ed. and tr. By G.D. Cohen (1967).
ICC	International Critical Commentary on the Holy Scriptures of the Old and New Testaments (series, 1908ff.).
IDB	*Interpreter's Dictionary of the Bible,* 4 vols. (1962).
Idelsohn, Litugy	A. Z. Idelsohn, *Jewish Liturgy and its Development* (1932; paperback repr. 1967)
Idelsohn, Melodien	A. Z. Idelsohn, *Hebraeisch-orientalischer Melodienschatz,* 10 vols. (1914 32).
Idelsohn, Music	A. Z. Idelsohn, *Jewish Music in its Historical Development* (1929; paperback repr. 1967).

IEJ	*Israel Exploration Journal* (1950ff.).
IESS	*International Encyclopedia of the Social Sciences* (various eds.).
IG	*Inscriptiones Graecae,* ed. by the Prussian Academy.
IGYB	*Israel Government Year Book* (1949/50ff.).
ILR	*Israel Law Review* (1966ff.).
IMIT	*Izraelita Magyar Irodalmi Társulat Évkönyv* (1895 1948).
IMT	International Military Tribunal.
INB	*Israel Numismatic Bulletin* (1962–63).
INJ	*Israel Numismatic Journal* (1963ff.).
Ios	Philo, *De Iosepho.*
Isa.	Isaiah (Bible).
ITHL	Institute for the Translation of Hebrew Literature.
IZBG	*Internationale Zeitschriftenschau fuer Bibelwissenschaft und Grenzgebiete* (1951ff.).
JA	*Journal asiatique* (1822ff.).
James	Epistle of James (New Testament).
JAOS	*Journal of the American Oriental Society* (c. 1850ff.)
Jastrow, Dict	M. Jastrow, *Dictionary of the Targumim, the Talmud Babli and Yerushalmi, and the Midrashic literature,* 2 vols. (1886 1902 and reprints).
JBA	*Jewish Book Annual* (19242ff.).
JBL	*Journal of Biblical Literature* (1881ff.).
JBR	*Journal of Bible and Religion* (1933ff.).
JC	*Jewish Chronicle* (1841ff.).
JCS	*Journal of Cuneiform Studies* (1947ff.).
JE	*Jewish Encyclopedia,* 12 vols. (1901–05 several reprints).
Jer.	Jeremiah (Bible).
Jeremias, Alte Test	A. Jeremias, *Das Alte Testament im Lichte des alten Orients* 1930^4).
JGGJČ	*Jahrbuch der Gesellschaft fuer Geschichte der Juden in der Čechoslovakischen Republik* (1929–38).
JHSEM	Jewish Historical Society of England, *Miscellanies* (1925ff.).
JHSET	Jewish Historical Society of England, *Transactions* (1893ff.).
JJGL	*Jahrbuch fuer juedische Geschichte und Literatur* (Berlin) (1898–1938).
JJLG	*Jahrbuch der juedische-literarischen Gesellschaft* (Frankfurt) (1903–32).
JJS	*Journal of Jewish Studies* (1948ff.).
JJSO	*Jewish Journal of Sociology* (1959ff.).
JJV	*Jahrbuch fuer juedische Volkskunde* (1898–1924).
JL	*Juedisches Lexikon,* 5 vols. (1927–30).
JMES	*Journal of the Middle East Society* (1947ff.).
JNES	*Journal of Near Eastern Studies* (continuation of AJSLL) (1942ff.).
J.N.U.L.	Jewish National and University Library.
Job	Job (Bible).
Joel	Joel (Bible).
John	Gospel according to John (New Testament).
I, II and III John	Epistles of John (New Testament).
Jos., Ant	Josephus, *Jewish Antiquities* (Loeb Classics ed.).
Jos. Apion	Josephus, *Against Apion* (Loeb Classics ed.).
Jos., index	*Josephus Works,* Loeb Classics ed., index of names.
Jos., Life	Josephus, *Life* (ed. Loeb Classics).
Jos, Wars	Josephus, *The Jewish Wars* (Loeb Classics ed.).
Josh.	Joshua (Bible).
JPESB	Jewish Palestine Exploration Society Bulletin, see BJPES.
JPESJ	Jewish Palestine Exploration Society Journal – Eng. Title of the Hebrew periodical *Kovez ha-Ḥevrah ha-Ivrit la-Ḥakirat Erez Yisrael va-Attikoteha.*
JPOS	*Journal of the Palestine Oriental Society* (1920–48).
JPS	Jewish Publication Society of America, *The Torah* (1962, 1967^2); *The Holy Scriptures* (1917).
JQR	*Jewish Quarterly Review* (1889ff.).
JR	*Journal of Religion* (1921ff.).
JRAS	*Journal of the Royal Asiatic Society* (1838ff.).
JHR	*Journal of Religious History* (1960/61ff.).
JSOS	*Jewish Social Studies* (1939ff.).
JSS	*Journal of Semitic Studies* (1956ff.).
JTS	*Journal of Theological Studies* (1900ff.).
JTSA	Jewish Theological Seminary of America (also abbreviated as JTS).
Jub.	Jubilees (Pseudepigrapha).
Judg.	Judges (Bible).
Judith	Book of Judith (Apocrypha).
Juster, Juifs	J. Juster, *Les Juifs dans l'Empire Romain,* 2 vols. (1914).
JYB	*Jewish Year Book* (1896ff.).
JZWL	*Juedische Zeitschift fuer Wissenschaft und Leben* (1862–75).
Kal.	*Kallah* (post-talmudic tractate).
Kal. R.	*Kallah Rabbati* (post-talmudic tractate).
Katz, England	*The Jews in the History of England, 1485-1850 (1994).*
Kaufmann, Schriften	D. Kaufmann, *Gesammelte Schriften,* 3 vols. (1908 15).
Kaufmann Y., Religion	Y. Kaufmann, *The Religion of Israel* (1960), abridged tr. of his *Toledot.*
Kaufmann Y., Toledot	Y. Kaufmann, *Toledot ha-Emunah ha-Yisre'elit,* 4 vols. (1937 57).
KAWJ	*Korrespondenzblatt des Vereins zur Gruendung und Erhaltung der Akademie fuer die Wissenschaft des Judentums* (1920 30).
Kayserling, Bibl	M. Kayserling, *Biblioteca Española-Portugueza-Judaica* (1880; repr. 1961).
Kelim	*Kelim* (mishnaic tractate).
Ker.	*Keritot* (talmudic tractate).
Ket.	*Ketubbot* (talmudic tractate).

Kid.	*Kiddushim* (talmudic tractate).
Kil.	*Kilayim* (talmudic tractate).
Kin.	*Kinnim* (mishnaic tractate).
Kisch, Germany	G. Kisch, *Jews in Medieval Germany* (1949).
Kittel, Gesch	R. Kittel, *Geschichte des Volkes Israel,* 3 vols. (1922–28).
Klausner, Bayit Sheni	J. Klausner, *Historyah shel ha-Bayit ha-Sheni,* 5 vols. (1950/512).
Klausner, Sifrut	J. Klausner, *Historyah shel haSifrut ha-Ivrit ha-Ḥadashah,* 6 vols. (1952–582).
Klein, corpus	S. Klein (ed.), *Juedisch-palaestinisches Corpus Inscriptionum* (1920).
Koehler-Baumgartner	L. Koehler and W. Baumgartner, *Lexicon in Veteris Testamenti libros* (1953).
Kohut, Arukh	H.J.A. Kohut (ed.), *Sefer he-Arukh ha-Shalem,* by Nathan b. Jehiel of Rome, 8 vols. (1876–92; Supplement by S. Krauss et al., 1936; repr. 1955).
Krauss, Tal Arch	S. Krauss, *Talmudische Archaeologie,* 3 vols. (1910–12; repr. 1966).
Kressel, Leksikon	G. Kressel, *Leksikon ha-Sifrut ha-Ivrit ba-Dorot ha-Aḥaronim,* 2 vols. (1965–67).
KS	*Kirjath Sepher* (1923/4ff.).
Kut.	*Kuttim* (post-talmudic tractate).
LA	Studium Biblicum Franciscanum, *Liber Annuus* (1951ff.).
L.A.	Philo, *Legum allegoriae.*
Lachower, Sifrut	F. Lachower, *Toledot ha-Sifrut ha-Ivrit ha-Ḥadashah,* 4 vols. (1947–48; several reprints).
Lam.	Lamentations (Bible).
Lam. R.	*Lamentations Rabbah.*
Landshuth, Ammudei	L. Landshuth, *Ammudei ha-Avodah* (1857–62; repr. with index, 1965).
Legat.	Philo, *De Legatione ad Caium.*
Lehmann, Nova Bibl	R.P. Lehmann, *Nova Bibliotheca Anglo-Judaica* (1961).
Lev.	Leviticus (Bible).
Lev. R.	*Leviticus Rabbah.*
Levy, Antologia	I. Levy, *Antologia de liturgia judeo-española* (1965ff.).
Levy J., Chald Targ	J. Levy, *Chaldaeisches Woerterbuch ueber die Targumim,* 2 vols. (1967–68; repr. 1959).
Levy J., Nuehebr Tal	J. Levy, *Neuhebraeisches und chaldaeisches Woerterbuch ueber die Talmudim . . .,* 4 vols. (1875–89; repr. 1963).
Lewin, Oẓar	Lewin, *Oẓar ha-Geonim,* 12 vols. (1928–43).
Lewysohn, Zool	L. Lewysohn, *Zoologie des Talmuds* (1858).
Lidzbarski, Handbuch	M. Lidzbarski, *Handbuch der nordsemitischen Epigraphik,* 2 vols (1898).
Life	Josephus, *Life* (Loeb Classis ed.).
LNYL	*Leksikon fun der Nayer Yidisher Literatur* (1956ff.).
Loew, Flora	I. Loew, *Die Flora der Juden,* 4 vols. (1924 34; repr. 1967).
LSI	*Laws of the State of Israel* (1948ff.).
Luckenbill, Records	D.D. Luckenbill, *Ancient Records of Assyria and Babylonia,* 2 vols. (1926).
Luke	Gospel according to Luke (New Testament)
LXX	Septuagint (Greek translation of the Bible).
Ma'as.	*Ma'aserot* (talmudic tractate).
Ma'as. Sh.	*Ma'ase Sheni* (talmudic tractate).
I, II, III, and IVMacc.	Maccabees, I, II, III (Apocrypha), IV (Pseudepigrapha).
Maimonides, Guide	Maimonides, *Guide of the Perplexed.*
Maim., Yad	Maimonides, *Mishneh Torah (Yad Ḥazakah).*
Maisler, Untersuchungen	B. Maisler (Mazar), *Untersuchungen zur alten Geschichte und Ethnographie Syriens und Palaestinas,* 1 (1930).
Mak.	*Makkot* (talmudic tractate).
Makhsh.	*Makhshrin* (mishnaic tractate).
Mal.	Malachi (Bible).
Mann, Egypt	J. Mann, *Jews in Egypt in Palestine under the Fatimid Caliphs,* 2 vols. (1920–22).
Mann, Texts	J. Mann, *Texts and Studies,* 2 vols (1931–35).
Mansi	G.D. Mansi, *Sacrorum Conciliorum nova et amplissima collectio,* 53 vols. in 60 (1901–27; repr. 1960).
Margalioth, Gedolei	M. Margalioth, *Enẓiklopedyah le-Toledot Gedolei Yisrael,* 4 vols. (1946–50).
Margalioth, Ḥakhmei	M. Margalioth, *Enẓiklopedyah le-Ḥakhmei ha-Talmud ve-ha-Ge'onim,* 2 vols. (1945).
Margalioth, Cat	G. Margalioth, *Catalogue of the Hebrew and Samaritan Manuscripts in the British Museum,* 4 vols. (1899–1935).
Mark	Gospel according to Mark (New Testament).
Mart. Isa.	Martyrdom of Isaiah (Pseudepigrapha).
Mas.	Masorah.
Matt.	Gospel according to Matthew (New Testament).
Mayer, Art	L.A. Mayer, *Bibliography of Jewish Art* (1967).
MB	*Wochenzeitung* (formerly *Mitteilungsblatt*) *des Irgun Olej Merkas Europa* (1933ff.).
MEAH	*Miscelánea de estudios árabes y hebraicos* (1952ff.).
Meg.	Megillah (talmudic tractate).
Meg. Ta'an.	*Megillat Ta'anit* (in HUCA, 8 9 (1931–32), 318–51).
Me'il	*Me'ilah* (mishnaic tractate).
MEJ	*Middle East Journal* (1947ff.).
Mehk.	*Mekhilta de-R. Ishmael.*
Mekh. SbY	*Mekhilta de-R. Simeon bar Yoḥai.*
Men.	*Menaḥot* (talmudic tractate).
MER	*Middle East Record* (1960ff.).
Meyer, Gesch	E. Meyer, *Geschichte des Alterums,* 5 vols. in 9 (1925–58).
Meyer, Ursp	E. Meyer, *Urspring und Anfaenge des Christentums* (1921).
Mez.	*Mezuzah* (post-talmudic tractate).
MGADJ	*Mitteilungen des Gesamtarchivs der deutschen Juden* (1909–12).
MGG	*Die Musik in Geschichte und Gegenwart,* 14 vols. (1949–68).

MGG^{2}	*Die Musik in Geschichte und Gegenwart, 2nd edition (1994)*
MGH	*Monumenta Germaniae Historica* (1826ff.).
MGJV	*Mitteilungen der Gesellschaft fuer juedische Volkskunde* (1898–1929); title varies, see also JJV.
MGWJ	*Monatsschrift fuer Geschichte und Wissenschaft des Judentums* (1851–1939).
MHJ	*Monumenta Hungariae Judaica,* 11 vols. (1903–67).
Michael, Or	H.Ḥ. Michael, *Or ha-Ḥayyim: Ḥakhmei Yisrael ve-Sifreihem,* ed. by S.Z. Ḥ. Halberstam and N. Ben-Menahem (1965^{2}).
Mid.	*Middot* (mishnaic tractate).
Mid. Ag.	*Midrash Aggadah.*
Mid. Hag.	*Midrash ha-Gadol.*
Mid. Job.	*Midrash Job.*
Mid. Jonah	*Midrash Jonah.*
Mid. Lek. Tov	*Midrash Lekaḥ Tov.*
Mid. Prov.	*Midrash Proverbs.*
Mid. Ps.	*Midrash Tehillim* (Eng tr. *The Midrash on Psalms* (JPS, 1959).
Mid. Sam.	*Midrash Samuel.*
Mid. Song	*Midrash Shir ha-Shirim.*
Mid. Tan.	*Midrash Tanna'im* on Deuteronomy.
Miége, Maroc	J.L. Miège, *Le Maroc et l'Europe,* 3 vols. (1961 62).
Mig.	Philo, *De Migratione Abrahami.*
Mik.	*Mikva'ot* (mishnaic tractate).
Milano, Bibliotheca	A. Milano, *Bibliotheca Historica Italo-Judaica* (1954); supplement for 1954–63 (1964); supplement for 1964–66 in RMI, 32 (1966).
Milano, Italia	A. Milano, *Storia degli Ebrei in Italia* (1963).
MIO	*Mitteilungen des Instituts fuer Orientforschung* 1953ff.).
Mish.	Mishnah.
MJ	*Le Monde Juif* (1946ff.).
MJC	see Neubauer, Chronicles.
MK	*Mo'ed Katan* (talmudic tractate).
MNDPV	*Mitteilungen und Nachrichten des deutschen Palaestinavereins* (1895–1912).
Mortara, Indice	M. Mortara, *Indice Alfabetico dei Rabbini e Scrittori Israeliti ... in Italia ...* (1886).
Mos	Philo, *De Vita Mosis.*
Moscati, Epig	S, Moscati, *Epigrafia ebraica antica* 1935–1950 (1951).
MT	Masoretic Text of the Bible.
Mueller, Musiker	[E.H. Mueller], *Deutisches Musiker-Lexikon* (1929)
Munk, Mélanges	S. Munk, *Mélanges de philosophie juive et arabe* (1859; repr. 1955).
Mut.	Philo, *De Mutatione Nominum.*
MWJ	*Magazin fuer die Wissenshaft des Judentums* (18745 93).
Nah.	Nahum (Bible).
Naz.	*Nazir* (talmudic tractate).
NDB	*Neue Deutsche Biographie* (1953ff.).
Ned.	*Nedarim* (talmudic tractate).
Neg.	*Nega'im* (mishnaic tractate).
Neh.	Nehemiah (Bible).
NG^{2}	*New Grove Dictionary of Music and Musicians* (2001).
Nuebauer, Cat	A. Neubauer, *Catalogue of the Hebrew Manuscripts in the Bodleian Library ...,* 2 vols. (1886–1906).
Neubauer, Chronicles	A. Neubauer, *Mediaeval Jewish Chronicles,* 2 vols. (Heb., 1887–95; repr. 1965), Eng. title of *Seder ha-Ḥakhamim ve-Korot ha-Yamim.*
Neubauer, Géogr	A. Neubauer, *La géographie du Talmud* (1868).
Neuman, Spain	A.A. Neuman, *The Jews in Spain, their Social, Political, and Cultural Life During the Middle Ages,* 2 vols. (1942).
Neusner, Babylonia	J. Neusner, *History of the Jews in Babylonia,* 5 vols. 1965–70), 2nd revised printing 1969ff.).
Nid.	*Niddah* (talmudic tractate).
Noah	Fragment of Book of Noah (Pseudepigrapha).
Noth, Hist Isr	M. Noth, *History of Israel* (1958).
Noth, Personennamen	M. Noth, *Die israelitischen Personennamen.* ... (1928).
Noth, Ueberlief	M. Noth, *Ueberlieferungsgeschichte des Pentateuchs* (1949).
Noth, Welt	M. Noth, *Die Welt des Alten Testaments* (1957^{3}).
Nowack, Lehrbuch	W. Nowack, *Lehrbuch der hebraeischen Archaeologie,* 2 vols (1894).
NT	New Testament.
Num.	Numbers (Bible).
Num R.	*Numbers Rabbah.*
Obad.	Obadiah (Bible).
ODNB online	*Oxford Dictionary of National Biography.*
OḤ	*Oraḥ Ḥayyim.*
Oho.	*Oholot* (mishnaic tractate).
Olmstead	H.T. Olmstead, *History of Palestine and Syria* (1931; repr. 1965).
OLZ	*Orientalistische Literaturzeitung* (1898ff.)
Onom.	Eusebius, *Onomasticon.*
Op.	Philo, *De Opificio Mundi.*
OPD	*Osef Piskei Din shel ha-Rabbanut ha-Rashit le-Ereẓ Yisrael, Bet ha-Din ha-Gadol le-Irurim* (1950).
Or.	*Orlah* (talmudic tractate).
Or. Sibyll.	Sibylline Oracles (Pseudepigrapha).
OS	*L'Orient Syrien* (1956ff.)
OTS	*Oudtestamentische Studien* (1942ff.).
PAAJR	*Proceedings of the American Academy for Jewish Research* (1930ff.)
Pap 4QS^{e}	A papyrus exemplar of IQS.
Par.	*Parah* (mishnaic tractate).
Pauly-Wissowa	A.F. Pauly, *Realencyklopaedie der klassichen Alertumswissenschaft,* ed. by G. Wissowa et al. (1864ff.)

PD	*Piskei Din shel Bet ha-Mishpat ha-Elyon le-Yisrael* (1948ff.)
PDR	*Piskei Din shel Battei ha-Din ha-Rabbaniyyim be-Yisrael.*
PdRE	*Pirkei de-R. Eliezer* (Eng. tr. 1916. (1965^{2}).
PdRK	*Pesikta de-Rav Kahana.*
Pe'ah	*Pe'ah* (talmudic tractate).
Peake, Commentary	A.J. Peake (ed.), *Commentary on the Bible* (1919; rev. 1962).
Pedersen, Israel	J. Pedersen, *Israel, Its Life and Culture,* 4 vols. in 2 (1926–40).
PEFQS	*Palestine Exploration Fund Quarterly Statement* (1869–1937; since 1938–PEQ).
PEQ	*Palestine Exploration Quarterly* (until 1937 PEFQS; after 1927 includes BBSAJ).
Perles, Beitaege	J. Perles, *Beitraege zur rabbinischen Sprach- und Alterthumskunde* (1893).
Pes.	*Pesaḥim* (talmudic tractate).
Pesh.	Peshitta (Syriac translation of the Bible).
Pesher Hab.	Commentary to Habakkuk from Qumran; see 1Qp Hab.
I and II Pet.	Epistles of Peter (New Testament).
Pfeiffer, Introd	R.H. Pfeiffer, *Introduction to the Old Testament* (1948).
PG	J.P. Migne (ed.), *Patrologia Graeca,* 161 vols. (1866–86).
Phil.	Epistle to the Philippians (New Testament).
Philem.	Epistle to the Philemon (New Testament).
PIASH	*Proceedings of the Israel Academy of Sciences and Humanities* (1963/7ff.).
PJB	*Palaestinajahrbuch des deutschen evangelischen Institutes fuer Altertumswissenschaft,* Jerusalem (1905–1933).
PK	*Pinkas ha-Kehillot,* encyclopedia of Jewish communities, published in over 30 volumes by Yad Vashem from 1970 and arranged by countries, regions and localities. For 3-vol. English edition see Spector, *Jewish Life.*
PL	J.P. Migne (ed.), *Patrologia Latina* 221 vols. (1844–64).
Plant	Philo, *De Plantatione.*
PO	R. Graffin and F. Nau (eds.), *Patrologia Orientalis* (1903ff.)
Pool, Prayer	D. de Sola Pool, *Traditional Prayer Book for Sabbath and Festivals* (1960).
Post	Philo, *De Posteritate Caini.*
PR	*Pesikta Rabbati.*
Praem.	Philo, *De Praemiis et Poenis.*
Prawer, Ẓalbanim	J. Prawer, *Toledot Mamlekhet ha-Ẓalbanim be-Ereẓ Yisrael,* 2 vols. (1963).
Press, Ereẓ	I. Press, *Ereẓ-Yisrael, Enẓiklopedyah Topografit-Historit,* 4 vols. (1951–55).
Pritchard, Pictures	J.B. Pritchard (ed.), *Ancient Near East in Pictures* (1954, 1970).
Pritchard, Texts	J.B. Pritchard (ed.), *Ancient Near East Texts* ... (1970^{3}).
Pr. Man.	Prayer of Manasses (Apocrypha).
Prob.	Philo, *Quod Omnis Probus Liber Sit.*
Prov.	Proverbs (Bible).
PS	*Palestinsky Sbornik* (Russ. (1881 1916, 1954ff).
Ps.	Psalms (Bible).
PSBA	*Proceedings of the Society of Biblical Archaeology* (1878–1918).
Ps. of Sol	Psalms of Solomon (Pseudepigrapha).
IQ Apoc	The *Genesis Apocryphon* from Qumran, cave one, ed. by N. Avigad and Y. Yadin (1956).
6QD	*Damascus Document* or *Sefer Berit Dammesk* from Qumran, cave six, ed. by M. Baillet, in RB, 63 (1956), 513–23 (see also CD).
QDAP	*Quarterly of the Department of Antiquities in Palestine* (1932ff.).
4QDeut. 32	Manuscript of Deuteronomy 32 from Qumran, cave four (ed. by P.W. Skehan, in BASOR, 136 (1954), 12–15).
4QEx^{a}	Exodus manuscript in Jewish script from Qumran, cave four.
4QEx$^{\alpha}$	Exodus manuscript in Paleo-Hebrew script from Qumran, cave four (partially ed. by P.W. Skehan, in JBL, 74 (1955), 182–7).
4QFlor	*Florilegium,* a miscellany from Qumran, cave four (ed. by J.M. Allegro, in JBL, 75 (1956), 176–77 and 77 (1958), 350–54).).
QGJD	*Quellen zur Geschichte der Juden in Deutschland* 1888–98).
IQH	*Thanksgiving Psalms* of *Hodayot* from Qumran, cave one (ed. by E.L. Sukenik and N. Avigad, *Oẓar ha-Megillot ha-Genuzot* (1954).
IQIs^{a}	Scroll of Isaiah from Qumran, cave one (ed. by N. Burrows et al., *Dead Sea Scrolls* ..., 1 (1950).
IQIs^{b}	Scroll of Isaiah from Qumran, cave one (ed. E.L. Sukenik and N. Avigad, *Oẓar ha-Megillot ha-Genuzot* (1954).
IQM	The *War Scroll* or *Serekh ha-Milḥamah* (ed. by E.L. Sukenik and N. Avigad, *Oẓar ha-Megillot ha-Genuzot* (1954).
4QpNah	Commentary on Nahum from Qumran, cave four (partially ed. by J.M. Allegro, in JBL, 75 (1956), 89–95).
IQphyl	Phylacteries *(tefillin)* from Qumran, cave one (ed. by Y. Yadin, in *Eretz Israel,* 9 (1969), 60–85).
4Q Prayer of Nabonidus	A document from Qumran, cave four, belonging to a lost Daniel literature (ed. by J.T. Milik, in RB, 63 (1956), 407–15).
IQS	*Manual of Discipline* or *Serekh ha-Yaḥad* from Qumran, cave one (ed. by M. Burrows et al., *Dead Sea Scrolls* ..., 2, pt. 2 (1951).

IQS[a]	The *Rule of the Congregation or Serekh ha-Edah* from Qumran, cave one (ed. by Burrows et al., *Dead Sea Scrolls* ..., 1 (1950), under the abbreviation IQ28a).
IQS[b]	*Blessings* or *Divrei Berakhot* from Qumran, cave one (ed. by Burrows et al., *Dead Sea Scrolls* ..., 1 (1950), under the abbreviation IQ28b).
4QSam[a]	Manuscript of I and II Samuel from Qumran, cave four (partially ed. by F.M. Cross, in BASOR, 132 (1953), 15–26).
4QSam[b]	Manuscript of I and II Samuel from Qumran, cave four (partially ed. by F.M. Cross, in JBL, 74 (1955), 147–72).
4QTestimonia	Sheet of Testimony from Qumran, cave four (ed. by J.M. Allegro, in JBL, 75 (1956), 174–87).).
4QT.Levi	*Testament of Levi* from Qumran, cave four (partially ed. by J.T. Milik, in RB, 62 (1955), 398–406).
Rabinovitz, Dik Sof	See Dik Sof.
RB	*Revue biblique* (1892ff.)
RBI	*Recherches bibliques* (1954ff.)
RCB	*Revista de cultura biblica* (São Paulo) (1957ff.)
Régné, Cat	J. Régné, *Catalogue des actes . . . des rois d'Aragon, concernant les Juifs* (1213–1327), in: REJ, vols. 60 70, 73, 75–78 (1910–24).
Reinach, Textes	T. Reinach, *Textes d'auteurs Grecs et Romains relatifs au Judaïsme* (1895; repr. 1963).
REJ	*Revue des études juives* (1880ff.).
Rejzen, Leksikon	Z. Rejzen, *Leksikon fun der Yidisher Literature,* 4 vols. (1927–29).
Renan, Ecrivains	A. Neubauer and E. Renan, *Les écrivains juifs français* ... (1893).
Renan, Rabbins	A. Neubauer and E. Renan, *Les rabbins français* (1877).
RES	*Revue des étude sémitiques et Babyloniaca* (1934–45).
Rev.	Revelation (New Testament).
RGG[3]	*Die Religion in Geschichte und Gegenwart,* 7 vols. (1957–65[3]).
RH	*Rosh Ha-Shanah* (talmudic tractate).
RHJE	*Revue de l'histoire juive en Egypte* (1947ff.).
RHMH	*Revue d'histoire de la médecine hébraïque* (1948ff.).
RHPR	*Revue d'histoire et de philosophie religieuses* (1921ff.).
RHR	*Revue d'histoire des religions* (1880ff.).
RI	*Rivista Israelitica* (1904–12).
Riemann-Einstein	*Hugo Riemanns Musiklexikon,* ed. by A. Einstein (1929[11]).
Riemann-Gurlitt	*Hugo Riemanns Musiklexikon,* ed. by W. Gurlitt (1959–67[12]), Personenteil.
Rigg-Jenkinson, Exchequer	J.M. Rigg, H. Jenkinson and H.G. Richardson (eds.), *Calendar of the Pleas Rolls of the Exchequer of the Jews,* 4 vols. (1905–1970); cf. in each instance also J.M. Rigg (ed.), *Select Pleas* ... (1902).
RMI	*Rassegna Mensile di Israel* (1925ff.).
Rom.	Epistle to the Romans (New Testament).
Rosanes, Togarmah	S.A. Rosanes, *Divrei Yemei Yisrael be-Togarmah,* 6 vols. (1907–45), and in 3 vols. (1930–38[2]).
Rosenbloom, Biogr Dict	J.R. Rosenbloom, *Biographical Dictionary of Early American Jews* (1960).
Roth, Art	C. Roth, *Jewish Art* (1961).
Roth, Dark Ages	C. Roth (ed.), *World History of the Jewish People,* second series, vol. 2, *Dark Ages* (1966).
Roth, England	C. Roth, *History of the Jews in England* (1964[3]).
Roth, Italy	C. Roth, *History of the Jews in Italy* (1946).
Roth, Mag Bibl	C. Roth, *Magna Bibliotheca Anglo-Judaica* (1937).
Roth, Marranos	C. Roth, *History of the Marranos* (2nd rev. ed 1959; reprint 1966).
Rowley, Old Test	H.H. Rowley, *Old Testament and Modern Study* (1951; repr. 1961).
RS	*Revue sémitiques d'épigraphie et d'histoire ancienne* (1893/94ff.).
RSO	*Rivista degli studi orientali* (1907ff.).
RSV	Revised Standard Version of the Bible.
Rubinstein, Australia I	*H.L. Rubinstein, The Jews in Australia, A Thematic History, Vol. I (1991).*
Rubinstein, Australia II	*W.D. Rubinstein, The Jews in Australia, A Thematic History, Vol. II (1991).*
Ruth	Ruth (Bible).
Ruth R.	*Ruth Rabbah.*
RV	Revised Version of the Bible.
Sac.	Philo, *De Sacrificiis Abelis et Caini.*
Salfeld, Martyrol	S. Salfeld, *Martyrologium des Nuernberger Memorbuches* (1898).
I and II Sam.	Samuel, book I and II (Bible).
Sanh.	*Sanhedrin* (talmudic tractate).
SBA	Society of Biblical Archaeology.
SBB	*Studies in Bibliography and Booklore* (1953ff.).
SBE	*Semana Biblica Española.*
SBT	*Studies in Biblical Theology* (1951ff.).
SBU	*Svenkst Bibliskt Uppslogsvesk,* 2 vols. (1962–63[2]).
Schirmann, Italyah	J.Ḥ. Schirmann, *Ha-Shirah ha-Ivrit be-Italyah* (1934).
Schirmann, Sefarad	J.Ḥ. Schirmann, *Ha-Shirah ha-Ivrit bi-Sefarad u-vi-Provence,* 2 vols. (1954–56).
Scholem, Mysticism	G. Scholem, *Major Trends in Jewish Mysticism* (rev. ed. 1946; paperback ed. with additional bibliography 1961).
Scholem, Shabbetai Ẓevi	G. Scholem, *Shabbetai Ẓevi ve-ha-Tenu'ah ha-Shabbeta'it bi-Ymei Ḥayyav,* 2 vols. (1967).
Schrader, Keilinschr	E. Schrader, *Keilinschriften und das Alte Testament* (1903[3]).
Schuerer, Gesch	E. Schuerer, *Geschichte des juedischen Volkes im Zeitalter Jesu Christi,* 3 vols. and index-vol. (1901–11[4]).

Schuerer, Hist	E. Schuerer, *History of the Jewish People in the Time of Jesus*, ed. by N.N. Glatzer, abridged paperback edition (1961).
Set. T.	*Sefer Torah* (post-talmudic tractate).
Sem.	*Semaḥot* (post-talmudic tractate).
Sendrey, Music	A. Sendrey, *Bibliography of Jewish Music* (1951).
SER	*Seder Eliyahu Rabbah.*
SEZ	*Seder Eliyahu Zuta.*
Shab	*Shabbat* (talmudic tractate).
Sh. Ar.	J. Caro Shulḥan Arukh. OḤ – *Oraḥ Ḥayyim* YD – *Yoreh De'ah* EH – *Even ha-Ezer* ḤM – *Ḥoshen Mishpat.*
Shek.	*Shekalim* (talmudic tractate).
Shev.	*Shevi'it* (talmudic tractate).
Shevu.	*Shevu'ot* (talmudic tractate).
Shunami, Bibl	S. Shunami, *Bibliography of Jewish Bibliographies* (1965²).
Sif.	*Sifrei Deuteronomy.*
Sif. Num.	*Sifrei Numbers.*
Sifra	*Sifra* on Leviticus.
Sif. Zut.	*Sifrei Zuta.*
SIHM	Sources inédites de l'histoire du Maroc (series).
Silverman, Prayer	M. Silverman (ed.), *Sabbath and Festival Prayer Book* (1946).
Singer, Prayer	S. Singer *Authorised Daily Prayer Book* (1943¹⁷).
Sob.	Philo, *De Sobrietate.*
Sof.	*Soferim* (post-talmudic tractate).
Som.	Philo, *De Somniis.*
Song	Song of Songs (Bible).
Song. Ch.	Song of the Three Children (Apocrypha).
Song R.	*Song of Songs Rabbah.*
SOR	*Seder Olam Rabbah.*
Sot.	*Sotah* (talmudic tractate).
SOZ	*Seder Olam Zuta.*
Spec.	Philo, *De Specialibus Legibus.*
Spector, Jewish Life	*S. Spector (ed.), Encyclopedia of Jewish Life Before and After the Holocaust (2001).*
Steinschneider, Arab lit	M. Steinschneider, *Die arabische Literatur der Juden* (1902).
Steinschneider, Cat Bod	M. Steinschneider, *Catalogus Librorum Hebraeorum in Bibliotheca Bodleiana,* 3 vols. (1852–60; reprints 1931 and 1964).
Steinschneider, Hanbuch	M. Steinschneider, *Bibliographisches Handbuch ueber die . . . Literatur fuer hebraeische Sprachkunde* (1859; repr. with additions 1937).
Steinschneider, Uebersetzungen	M. Steinschneider, *Die hebraeischen Uebersetzungen des Mittelalters* (1893).
Stern, Americans	M.H. Stern, *Americans of Jewish Descent* (1960).
van Straalen, Cat	S. van Straalen, *Catalogue of Hebrew Books in the British Museum Acquired During the Years 1868–1892* (1894).
Suárez Fernández, Docmentos	L. Suárez Fernández, *Documentos acerca de la expulsion de los Judios de España* (1964).
Suk.	*Sukkah* (talmudic tractate).
Sus.	Susanna (Apocrypha).
SY	*Sefer Yeẓirah.*
Sym.	Symmachus' Greek translation of the Bible.
SZNG	*Studien zur neueren Geschichte.*
Ta'an.	*Ta'anit* (talmudic tractate).
Tam.	*Tamid* (mishnaic tractate).
Tanḥ.	*Tanḥuma.*
Tanḥ. B.	*Tanḥuma.* Buber ed (1885).
Targ. Jon	Targum Jonathan (Aramaic version of the Prophets).
Targ. Onk.	Targum Onkelos (Aramaic version of the Pentateuch).
Targ. Yer.	Targum Yerushalmi.
TB	Babylonian Talmud or Talmud Bavli.
Tcherikover, Corpus	V. Tcherikover, A. Fuks, and M. Stern, *Corpus Papyrorum Judaicorum,* 3 vols. (1957–60).
Tef.	*Tefillin* (post-talmudic tractate).
Tem.	*Temurah* (mishnaic tractate).
Ter.	*Terumah* (talmudic tractate).
Test. Patr.	Testament of the Twelve Patriarchs (Pseudepigrapha). Ash. – Asher Ben. – Benjamin Dan – Dan Gad – Gad Iss. – Issachar Joseph – Joseph Judah – Judah Levi – Levi Naph. – Naphtali Reu. – Reuben Sim. – Simeon Zeb. – Zebulun.
I and II	Epistle to the Thessalonians (New Testament).
Thieme-Becker	U. Thieme and F. Becker (eds.), *Allgemeines Lexikon der bildenden Kuenstler von der Antike bis zur Gegenwart,* 37 vols. (1907–50).
Tidhar	D. Tidhar (ed.), *Enẓiklopedyah la-Ḥalutẓei ha-Yishuv u-Vonav* (1947ff.).
I and II Timothy	Epistles to Timothy (New Testament).
Tit.	Epistle to Titus (New Testament).
TJ	Jerusalem Talmud or Talmud Yerushalmi.
Tob.	Tobit (Apocrypha).
Toh.	*Tohorot* (mishnaic tractate).
Torczyner, Bundeslade	H. Torczyner, *Die Bundeslade und die Anfaenge der Religion Israels* (1930³).
Tos.	*Tosafot.*
Tosef.	Tosefta.
Tristram, Nat Hist	H.B. Tristram, *Natural History of the Bible* (1877⁵).
Tristram, Survey	Palestine Exploration Fund, *Survey of Western Palestine,* vol. 4 (1884) = *Fauna and Flora* by H.B. Tristram.
TS	*Terra Santa* (1943ff.).

TSBA	*Transactions of the Society of Biblical Archaeology* (1872–93).
TY	*Tevul Yom* (mishnaic tractate).
UBSB	United Bible Society, *Bulletin.*
UJE	*Universal Jewish Encyclopedia*, 10 vols. (1939–43).
Uk.	*Ukẓin* (mishnaic tractate).
Urbach, Tosafot	E.E. Urbach, *Baʿalei ha-Tosafot* (1957^{2}).
de Vaux, Anc Isr	R. de Vaux, *Ancient Israel: its Life and Institutions* (1961; paperback 1965).
de Vaux, Instit	R. de Vaux, *Institutions de l'Ancien Testament,* 2 vols. (1958 60).
Virt.	Philo, *De Virtutibus.*
Vogelstein, Chronology	M. Volgelstein, *Biblical Chronology (1944).*
Vogelstein-Rieger	H. Vogelstein and P. Rieger, *Geschichte der Juden in Rom,* 2 vols. (1895–96).
VT	*Vetus Testamentum* (1951ff.).
VTS	*Vetus Testamentum* Supplements (1953ff.).
Vulg.	Vulgate (Latin translation of the Bible).
Wars	Josephus, *The Jewish Wars.*
Watzinger, Denkmaeler	K. Watzinger, *Denkmaeler Palaestinas,* 2 vols. (1933–35).
Waxman, Literature	M. Waxman, *History of Jewish Literature,* 5 vols. (1960^{2}).
Weiss, Dor	I.H. Weiss, *Dor, Dor ve-Doreshav,* 5 vols. (1904^{4}).
Wellhausen, Proleg	J. Wellhausen, *Prolegomena zur Geschichte Israels* (1927^{6}).
WI	*Die Welt des Islams* (1913ff.).
Winniger, Biog	S. Wininger, *Grosse juedische National-Biographie ...,* 7 vols. (1925–36).
Wisd.	Wisdom of Solomon (Apocrypha)
WLB	*Wiener Library Bulletin* (1958ff.).
Wolf, Bibliotheca	J.C. Wolf, *Bibliotheca Hebraea*, 4 vols. (1715–33).
Wright, Bible	G.E. Wright, *Westminster Historical Atlas to the Bible* (1945).
Wright, Atlas	G.E. Wright, *The Bible and the Ancient Near East* (1961).
WWWJ	*Who's Who in the World Jewry* (New York, 1955, 1965^{2}).
WZJT	*Wissenschaftliche Zeitschrift fuer juedische Theologie* (1835–37).
WZKM	*Wiener Zeitschrift fuer die Kunde des Morgenlandes* (1887ff.).
Yaari, Sheluḥei	A. Yaari, *Sheluḥei Ereẓ Yisrael* (1951).
Yad	Maimonides, *Mishneh Torah (Yad Ḥazakah).*
Yad	*Yadayim* (mishnaic tractate).
Yal.	*Yalkut Shimoni.*
Yal. Mak.	*Yalkut Makhiri.*
Yal. Reub.	*Yalkut Reubeni.*
YD	*Yoreh Deʿah.*
YE	*Yevreyskaya Entsiklopediya,* 14 vols. (c. 1910).
Yev.	*Yevamot* (talmudic tractate).
YIVOA	*YIVO Annual of Jewish Social Studies* (1946ff.).
YLBI	*Year Book of the Leo Baeck Institute* (1956ff.).
YMḤEY	See BJPES.
YMḤSI	*Yediʿot ha-Makhon le-Ḥeker ha-Shirah ha-Ivrit* (1935/36ff.).
YMMY	*Yediʿot ha-Makhon le-Maddaʿei ha-Yahadut* (1924/25ff.).
Yoma	*Yoma* (talmudic tractate).
ZA	*Zeitschrift fuer Assyriologie* (1886/87ff.).
Zav.	*Zavim* (mishnaic tractate).
ZAW	*Zeitschrift fuer die alttestamentliche Wissenschaft und die Kunde des nachbiblishchen Judentums* (1881ff.).
ZAWB	*Beihefte* (supplements) to ZAW.
ZDMG	*Zeitschrift der Deutschen Morgenlaendischen Gesellschaft* (1846ff.).
ZDPV	*Zeitschrift des Deutschen Palaestina-Vereins* (1878–1949; from 1949 = BBLA).
Zech.	Zechariah (Bible).
Zedner, Cat	J. Zedner, *Catalogue of Hebrew Books in the Library of the British Museum* (1867; repr. 1964).
Zeitlin, Bibliotheca	W. Zeitlin, *Bibliotheca Hebraica Post-Mendelssohniana* (1891–95).
Zeph.	Zephaniah (Bible).
Zev.	*Zevaḥim* (talmudic tractate).
ZGGJT	*Zeitschrift der Gesellschaft fuer die Geschichte der Juden in der Tschechoslowakei* (1930–38).
ZGJD	*Zeitschrift fuer die Geschichte der Juden in Deutschland* (1887–92).
ZHB	*Zeitschrift fuer hebraeische Bibliographie* (1896–1920).
Zinberg, Sifrut	I. Zinberg, *Toledot Sifrut Yisrael,* 6 vols. (1955–60).
Ẓiẓ.	*Ẓiẓit* (post-talmudic tractate).
ZNW	*Zeitschrift fuer die neutestamentliche Wissenschaft* (1901ff.).
ZS	*Zeitschrift fuer Semitistik und verwandte Gebiete* (1922ff.).
Zunz, Gesch	L. Zunz, *Zur Geschichte und Literatur* (1845).
Zunz, Gesch	L. Zunz, *Literaturgeschichte der synagogalen Poesie* (1865; Supplement, 1867; repr. 1966).
Zunz, Poesie	L. Zunz, *Synogogale Posie des Mittelalters,* ed. by Freimann (1920^{2}; repr. 1967).
Zunz, Ritus	L. Zunz, *Ritus des synagogalen Gottesdienstes* (1859; repr. 1967).
Zunz, Schr	L. Zunz, *Gesammelte Schriften,* 3 vols. (1875–76).
Zunz, Vortraege	L. Zunz, *Gottesdienstliche vortraege der Juden ...* 1892^{2}; repr. 1966).
Zunz-Albeck, Derashot	L. Zunz, *Ha-Derashot be-Yisrael*, Heb. Tr. of Zunz Vortraege by H. Albeck (1954^{2}).

TRANSLITERATION RULES

HEBREW AND SEMITIC LANGUAGES:

	General	*Scientific*
א	not transliterated[1]	ʾ
בּ	b	b
ב	v	v, b̲
גּ	g	g
ג		ḡ
דּ	d	d
ד		d̲
ה	h	h
ו	v – when not a vowel	w
ז	z	z
ח	ḥ	ḥ
ט	t	ṭ, t
י	y – when vowel and at end of words – i	y
כּ	k	k
כ, ך	kh	kh, k̲
ל	l	l̲
מ, ם	m	m
נ, ן	n	n
ס	s	s
ע	not transliterated[1]	ʿ
פּ	p	p
פ, ף	f	p, f, ph
צ, ץ	ẓ	ṣ, ẓ
ק	k	q, k
ר	r	r
שׁ	sh[2]	š
שׂ	s	ś, s
תּ	t	t
ת		t̲
ג׳	dzh, J	ğ
ז׳	zh, J	ž
צ׳	ch	č
—ָ		å, o, ȯ (short) â, ā (long)
—ַ	a	a
—ֲ		a, ^{a}
—ֵ		e, ẹ, ē
—ֶ	e	æ, ä, ę
—ֱ		œ, ě, ^{e}
—ְ	only *sheva na* is transliterated	ə, ĕ, e; only *sheva na* transliterated
—ִ —ִי	i	i
—ֹ וֹ	o	o, o, o
—ֻ וּ	u	u, ŭ û, ū
—ֵי	ei; biblical e	
‡		reconstructed forms of words

1. The letters א and ע are not transliterated.
An apostrophe (') between vowels indicates that they do not form a diphthong and are to be pronounced separately.
2. *Dagesh ḥazak* (forte) is indicated by doubling of the letter, except for the letter שׁ.
3. Names. Biblical names and biblical place names are rendered according to the Bible translation of the Jewish Publication Society of America. Post-biblical Hebrew names are transliterated; contemporary names are transliterated or rendered as used by the person. Place names are transliterated or rendered by the accepted spelling. Names and some words with an accepted English form are usually not transliterated.

YIDDISH

א	not transliterated
אַ	a
אָ	o
ב	b
בֿ	v
ג	g
ד	d
ה	h
וּ ,ו	u
וו	v
וי	oy
ז	z
זש	zh
ח	kh
ט	t
טש	tsh, ch
י	(consonant) y (vowel) i
יִ	i
יי	ey
ײַ	ay
כּ	k
ך ,כ	kh
ל	l
ם ,מ	m
ן ,נ	n
ס	s
ע	e
פּ	p
ף ,פֿ	f
ץ ,צ	ts
ק	k
ר	r
שׁ	sh
שׂ	s
תּ	t
ת	s

1. Yiddish transliteration rendered according to U. Weinreich's Modern *English-Yiddish Yiddish-English* Dictionary.
2. Hebrew words in Yiddish are usually transliterated according to standard Yiddish pronunciation, e.g., חזנות = *khazones.*

LADINO

Ladino and Judeo-Spanish words written in Hebrew characters are transliterated phonetically, following the General Rules of Hebrew transliteration (see above) whenever the accepted spelling in Latin characters could not be ascertained.

ARABIC

ء ا	a[1]	ض	ḍ
ب	b	ط	ṭ
ت	t	ظ	ẓ
ث	th	ع	c
ج	j	غ	gh
ح	ḥ	ف	f
خ	kh	ق	q
د	d	ك	k
ذ	dh	ل	l
ر	r	م	m
ز	z	ن	n
س	s	ه	h
ش	sh	و	w
ص	ṣ	ي	y
ـَ	a	ـَا ى	ā
ـِ	i	ـِي	ī
ـُ	u	ـُو	ū
ـَو	aw	ـِيّ	iyy[2]
ـَي	ay	ـُوّ	uww[2]

1. not indicated when initial
2. see note (f)

a) The EJ follows the *Columbia Lippincott Gazetteer* and the *Times Atlas* in transliteration of Arabic place names. Sites that appear in neither are transliterated according to the table above, and subject to the following notes.

b) The EJ follows the *Columbia Encyclopedia* in transliteration of Arabic names. Personal names that do not therein appear are transliterated according to the table above and subject to the following notes (e.g., Ali rather than ʿAlī, Suleiman rather than Sulayman).

c) The EJ follows the *Webster's Third International Dictionary, Unabridged* in transliteration of Arabic terms that have been integrated into the English language.

d) The term "Abu" will thus appear, usually in disregard of inflection.

e) Nunnation (end vowels, *tanwīn*) are dropped in transliteration.

f) Gemination (*tashdīd*) is indicated by the doubling of the geminated letter, unless an end letter, in which case the gemination is dropped.

g) The definitive article *al-* will always be thus transliterated, unless subject to one of the modifying notes (e.g., El-Arish rather than al-ʿArīsh; modification according to note (a)).

h) The Arabic transliteration disregards the Sun Letters (the antero-palatals (*al-Ḥurūf al-Shamsiyya*).

i) The *tā-marbūṭa* (o) is omitted in transliteration, unless in construct-stage (e.g., *Khirba* but *Khirbat Mishmish*).

These modifying notes may lead to various inconsistencies in the Arabic transliteration, but this policy has deliberately been adopted to gain smoother reading of Arabic terms and names.

GREEK

Ancient Greek	Modern Greek	Greek Letters
a	a	*Α; α; ᾳ*
b	v	*Β; β*
g	gh; g	*Γ; γ*
d	dh	*Δ; δ*
e	e	*Ε; ε*
z	z	*Ζ; ζ*
e; e	i	*Η; η; ῃ*
th	th	*Θ; θ*
i	i	*Ι; ι*
k	k; ky	*Κ; κ*
l	l	*Λ; λ*
m	m	*Μ; μ*
n	n	*Ν; ν*
x	x	*Ξ; ξ*
o	o	*Ο; ο*
p	p	*Π; π*
r; rh	r	*Ρ; ρ; ῥ*
s	s	*Σ; σ; ς*
t	t	*Τ; τ*
u; y	i	*Υ; υ*
ph	f	*Φ; φ*
ch	kh	*Χ; χ*
ps	ps	*Ψ; ψ*
o; ō	o	*Ω; ω; ῳ*
ai	e	*αι*
ei	i	*ει*
oi	i	*οι*
ui	i	*υι*
ou	ou	*ου*
eu	ev	*ευ*
eu; ēu	iv	*ηυ*
–	j	*τζ*
nt	d; nd	*ντ*
mp	b; mb	*μπ*
ngk	g	*γκ*
ng	ng	*νγ*
h	–	ʽ
–	–	ʼ
w	–	*Ϝ*

RUSSIAN

А	A
Б	B
В	V
Г	G
Д	D
Е	E, Ye[1]
Ё	Yo, O[2]
Ж	Zh
З	Z
И	I
Й	Y[3]
К	K
Л	L
М	M
Н	N
О	O
П	P
Р	R
С	S
Т	T
У	U
Ф	F
Х	Kh
Ц	Ts
Ч	Ch
Ш	Sh
Щ	Shch
Ъ	omitted; see note [1]
Ы	Y
Ь	omitted; see note [1]
Э	E
Ю	Yu
Я	Ya

1. Ye at the beginning of a word; after all vowels except ***Ы***; and after ***Ъ*** and ***Ь***.
2. O after ***Ч***, ***Ш*** and ***Щ***.
3. Omitted after ***Ы***, and in names of people after ***И***.

A. Many first names have an accepted English or quasi-English form which has been preferred to transliteration.
B. Place names have been given according to the *Columbia Lippincott Gazeteer.*
C. Pre-revolutionary spelling has been ignored.
D. Other languages using the Cyrillic alphabet (e.g., Bulgarian, Ukrainian), inasmuch as they appear, have been phonetically transliterated in conformity with the principles of this table.

GLOSSARY

Asterisked terms have separate entries in the Encyclopaedia.

Actions Committee, early name of the Zionist General Council, the supreme institution of the World Zionist Organization in the interim between Congresses. The Zionist Executive's name was then the "Small Actions Committee."

***Adar**, twelfth month of the Jewish religious year, sixth of the civil, approximating to February–March.

***Aggadah**, name given to those sections of Talmud and Midrash containing homiletic expositions of the Bible, stories, legends, folklore, anecdotes, or maxims. In contradistinction to **halakhah.*

***Agunah**, woman unable to remarry according to Jewish law, because of desertion by her husband or inability to accept presumption of death.

***Aharonim**, later rabbinic authorities. In contradistinction to **rishonim* ("early ones").

Ahavah, liturgical poem inserted in the second benediction of the morning prayer *(*Ahavah Rabbah)* of the festivals and/or special Sabbaths.

Aktion (Ger.), operation involving the mass assembly, deportation, and murder of Jews by the Nazis during the *Holocaust.

***Aliyah**, (1) being called to Reading of the Law in synagogue; (2) immigration to Ereẓ Israel; (3) one of the waves of immigration to Ereẓ Israel from the early 1880s.

***Amidah**, main prayer recited at all services; also known as *Shemoneh Esreh* and *Tefillah.*

***Amora** (pl. **amoraim**), title given to the Jewish scholars in Ereẓ Israel and Babylonia in the third to sixth centuries who were responsible for the **Gemara.*

Aravah, the *willow; one of the *Four Species used on *Sukkot ("festival of Tabernacles") together with the **etrog, hadas,* and **lulav.*

***Arvit**, evening prayer.

Asarah be-Tevet, fast on the 10th of Tevet commemorating the commencement of the siege of Jerusalem by Nebuchadnezzar.

Asefat ha-Nivḥarim, representative assembly elected by Jews in Palestine during the period of the British Mandate (1920–48).

***Ashkenaz**, name applied generally in medieval rabbinical literature to Germany.

***Ashkenazi** (pl. **Ashkenazim**), German or West-, Central-, or East-European Jew(s), as contrasted with *Sephardi(m).

***Av**, fifth month of the Jewish religious year, eleventh of the civil, approximating to July–August.

***Av bet din**, vice president of the supreme court (*bet din ha-gadol*) in Jerusalem during the Second Temple period; later, title given to communal rabbis as heads of the religious courts (see **bet din*).

***Badḥan**, jester, particularly at traditional Jewish weddings in Eastern Europe.

***Bakkashah** (Heb. "supplication"), type of petitionary prayer, mainly recited in the Sephardi rite on Rosh Ha-Shanah and the Day of Atonement.

Bar, "son of ..."; frequently appearing in personal names.

***Baraita** (pl. **beraitot**), statement of **tanna* not found in *Mishnah.

***Bar mitzvah**, ceremony marking the initiation of a boy at the age of 13 into the Jewish religious community.

Ben, "son of ...", frequently appearing in personal names.

Berakhah (pl. **berakhot**), *benediction, blessing; formula of praise and thanksgiving.

***Bet din** (pl. **battei din**), rabbinic court of law.

***Bet ha-midrash**, school for higher rabbinic learning; often attached to or serving as a synagogue.

***Bilu**, first modern movement for pioneering and agricultural settlement in Ereẓ Israel, founded in 1882 at Kharkov, Russia.

***Bund**, Jewish socialist party founded in Vilna in 1897, supporting Jewish national rights; Yiddishist, and anti-Zionist.

Cohen (pl. **Cohanim**), see Kohen.

***Conservative Judaism**, trend in Judaism developed in the United States in the 20th century which, while opposing extreme changes in traditional observances, permits certain modifications of *halakhah* in response to the changing needs of the Jewish people.

***Consistory** (Fr. *consistoire*), governing body of a Jewish communal district in France and certain other countries.

***Converso(s)**, term applied in Spain and Portugal to converted Jew(s), and sometimes more loosely to their descendants.

***Crypto-Jew**, term applied to a person who although observing outwardly Christianity (or some other religion) was at heart a Jew and maintained Jewish observances as far as possible (see Converso; Marrano; Neofiti; New Christian; Jadīd al-Islām).

***Dayyan**, member of rabbinic court.

Decisor, equivalent to the Hebrew *posek* (pl. **posekim*), the rabbi who gives the decision (*halakhah*) in Jewish law or practice.

***Devekut**, "devotion"; attachment or adhesion to God; communion with God.

***Diaspora**, Jews living in the "dispersion" outside Ereẓ Israel; area of Jewish settlement outside Ereẓ Israel.

Din, a law (both secular and religious), legal decision, or lawsuit.

Divan, diwan, collection of poems, especially in Hebrew, Arabic, or Persian.

Dunam, unit of land area (1,000 sq. m., c. ¼ acre), used in Israel.

Einsatzgruppen, mobile units of Nazi S.S. and S.D.; in U.S.S.R. and Serbia, mobile killing units.

***Ein-Sof**, "without end"; "the infinite"; hidden, impersonal aspect of God; also used as a Divine Name.

***Elul**, sixth month of the Jewish religious calendar, 12th of the civil, precedes the High Holiday season in the fall.

Endloesung, see *Final Solution.

***Ereẓ Israel**, Land of Israel; Palestine.

***Eruv**, technical term for rabbinical provision permitting the alleviation of certain restrictions.

***Etrog**, citron; one of the *Four Species used on *Sukkot together with the **lulav, hadas,* and *aravah.*

Even ha-Ezer, see Shulḥan Arukh.

***Exilarch**, lay head of Jewish community in Babylonia (see also *resh galuta*), and elsewhere.

***Final Solution** (Ger. *Endloesung*), in Nazi terminology, the Nazi-planned mass murder and total annihilation of the Jews.

***Gabbai**, official of a Jewish congregation; originally a charity collector.

***Galut**, "exile"; the condition of the Jewish people in dispersion.

*Gaon (pl. geonim), head of academy in post-talmudic period, especially in Babylonia.

Gaonate, office of *gaon.

*Gemara, traditions, discussions, and rulings of the *amoraim*, commenting on and supplementing the *Mishnah, and forming part of the Babylonian and Palestinian Talmuds (see Talmud).

*Gematria, interpretation of Hebrew word according to the numerical value of its letters.

General Government, territory in Poland administered by a German civilian governor-general with headquarters in Cracow after the German occupation in World War II.

*Genizah, depository for sacred books. The best known was discovered in the synagogue of Fostat (old Cairo).

Get, bill of *divorce.

*Ge'ullah, hymn inserted after the *Shema* into the benediction of the morning prayer of the festivals and special Sabbaths.

*Gilgul, metempsychosis; transmigration of souls.

*Golem, automaton, especially in human form, created by magical means and endowed with life.

*Ḥabad, initials of *ḥokhmah, binah, da'at*: "wisdom, understanding, knowledge"; ḥasidic movement founded in Belorussia by *Shneur Zalman of Lyady.

Hadas, *myrtle; one of the *Four Species used on Sukkot together with the *etrog*, **lulav*, and *aravah*.

*Haftarah (pl. haftarot), designation of the portion from the prophetical books of the Bible recited after the synagogue reading from the Pentateuch on Sabbaths and holidays.

*Haganah, clandestine Jewish organization for armed self-defense in Ereẓ Israel under the British Mandate, which eventually evolved into a people's militia and became the basis for the Israel army.

*Haggadah, ritual recited in the home on *Passover eve at seder table.

Haham, title of chief rabbi of the Spanish and Portuguese congregations in London, England.

*Hakham, title of rabbi of *Sephardi congregation.

*Hakham bashi, title in the 15th century and modern times of the chief rabbi in the Ottoman Empire, residing in Constantinople (Istanbul), also applied to principal rabbis in provincial towns.

Hakhsharah ("preparation"), organized training in the Diaspora of pioneers for agricultural settlement in Ereẓ Israel.

*Halakhah (pl. halakhot), an accepted decision in rabbinic law. Also refers to those parts of the *Talmud concerned with legal matters. In contradistinction to *aggadah*.

Ḥaliẓah, biblically prescribed ceremony (Deut. 25:9–10) performed when a man refuses to marry his brother's childless widow, enabling her to remarry.

*Hallel, term referring to Psalms 113-18 in liturgical use.

*Ḥalukkah, system of financing the maintenance of Jewish communities in the holy cities of Ereẓ Israel by collections made abroad, mainly in the pre-Zionist era (see *kolel*).

Ḥalutz (pl. ḥalutzim), pioneer, especially in agriculture, in Ereẓ Israel.

Ḥalutziyyut, pioneering.

*Ḥanukkah, eight-day celebration commemorating the victory of *Judah Maccabee over the Syrian king *Antiochus Epiphanes and the subsequent rededication of the Temple.

Ḥasid, adherent of *Ḥasidism.

*Ḥasidei Ashkenaz, medieval pietist movement among the Jews of Germany.

*Ḥasidism, (1) religious revivalist movement of popular mysticism among Jews of Germany in the Middle Ages; (2) religious movement founded by *Israel ben Eliezer Ba'al Shem Tov in the first half of the 18th century.

*Haskalah, "enlightenment"; movement for spreading modern European culture among Jews c. 1750–1880. See *maskil*.

*Havdalah, ceremony marking the end of Sabbath or festival.

*Ḥazzan, precentor who intones the liturgy and leads the prayers in synagogue; in earlier times a synagogue official.

*Ḥeder (lit. "room"), school for teaching children Jewish religious observance.

Heikhalot, "palaces"; tradition in Jewish mysticism centering on mystical journeys through the heavenly spheres and palaces to the Divine Chariot (see Merkabah).

*Ḥerem, excommunication, imposed by rabbinical authorities for purposes of religious and/or communal discipline; originally, in biblical times, that which is separated from common use either because it was an abomination or because it was consecrated to God.

Ḥeshvan, see Marḥeshvan.

*Ḥevra kaddisha, title applied to charitable confraternity (**ḥevrah*), now generally limited to associations for burial of the dead.

*Ḥibbat Zion, see Ḥovevei Zion.

*Histadrut (abbr. For Heb. **Ha-Histadrut ha-Kelalit shel ha-Ovedim ha-Ivriyyim be-Ereẓ Israel**). Ereẓ Israel Jewish Labor Federation, founded in 1920; subsequently renamed Histadrut ha-Ovedim be-Ereẓ Israel.

*Holocaust, the organized mass persecution and annihilation of European Jewry by the Nazis (1933–1945).

*Hoshana Rabba, the seventh day of *Sukkot on which special observances are held.

Ḥoshen Mishpat, see Shulḥan Arukh.

Ḥovevei Zion, federation of *Ḥibbat Zion, early (pre-*Herzl) Zionist movement in Russia.

Illui, outstanding scholar or genius, especially a young prodigy in talmudic learning.

*Iyyar, second month of the Jewish religious year, eighth of the civil, approximating to April-May.

I.Ẓ.L. (initials of Heb. ***Irgun Ẓeva'i Le'ummi**; "National Military Organization"), underground Jewish organization in Ereẓ Israel founded in 1931, which engaged from 1937 in retaliatory acts against Arab attacks and later against the British mandatory authorities.

*Jadīd al-Islām (Ar.), a person practicing the Jewish religion in secret although outwardly observing Islām.

*Jewish Legion, Jewish units in British army during World War I.

*Jihād (Ar.), in Muslim religious law, holy war waged against infidels.

*Judenrat (Ger. "Jewish council"), council set up in Jewish communities and ghettos under the Nazis to execute their instructions.

*Judenrein (Ger. "clean of Jews"), in Nazi terminology the condition of a locality from which all Jews had been eliminated.

*Kabbalah, the Jewish mystical tradition:
Kabbala iyyunit, speculative Kabbalah;
Kabbala ma'asit, practical Kabbalah;
Kabbala nevu'it, prophetic Kabbalah.

Kabbalist, student of Kabbalah.

*Kaddish, liturgical doxology.

Kahal, Jewish congregation; among Ashkenazim, *kehillah*.

*__Kalām__ (Ar.), science of Muslim theology; adherents of the Kalām are called *mutakallimūn*.

*__Karaite__, member of a Jewish sect originating in the eighth century which rejected rabbinic (*Rabbanite) Judaism and claimed to accept only Scripture as authoritative.

*__Kasher__, ritually permissible food.

Kashrut, Jewish *dietary laws.

*__Kavvanah__, "intention"; term denoting the spiritual concentration accompanying prayer and the performance of ritual or of a commandment.

*__Kedushah__, main addition to the third blessing in the reader's repetition of the *Amidah* in which the public responds to the precentor's introduction.

Kefar, village; first part of name of many settlements in Israel.

Kehillah, congregation; see *kahal*.

Kelippah (pl. **kelippot**), "husk(s)"; mystical term denoting force(s) of evil.

*__Keneset Yisrael__, comprehensive communal organization of the Jews in Palestine during the British Mandate.

Keri, variants in the masoretic (*masorah) text of the Bible between the spelling (*ketiv*) and its pronunciation (*keri*).

*__Kerovah__ (collective plural (corrupted) from **kerovez̧**), poem(s) incorporated into the **Amidah*.

Ketiv, see *keri*.

*__Ketubbah__, marriage contract, stipulating husband's obligations to wife.

Kevuz̧ah, small commune of pioneers constituting an agricultural settlement in Erez̧ Israel (evolved later into *kibbutz).

*__Kibbutz__ (pl. **kibbutzim**), larger-size commune constituting a settlement in Erez̧ Israel based mainly on agriculture but engaging also in industry.

*__Kiddush__, prayer of sanctification, recited over wine or bread on eve of Sabbaths and festivals.

*__Kiddush ha-Shem__, term connoting martyrdom or act of strict integrity in support of Judaic principles.

*__Kinah__ (pl. **kinot**), lamentation dirge(s) for the Ninth of Av and other fast days.

*__Kislev__, ninth month of the Jewish religious year, third of the civil, approximating to November-December.

Klaus, name given in Central and Eastern Europe to an institution, usually with synagogue attached, where *Talmud was studied perpetually by adults; applied by Ḥasidim to their synagogue ("*kloyz*").

*__Knesset__, parliament of the State of Israel.

K(c)ohen (pl. **K(c)ohanim**), Jew(s) of priestly (Aaronide) descent.

*__Kolel__, (1) community in Erez̧ Israel of persons from a particular country or locality, often supported by their fellow countrymen in the Diaspora; (2) institution for higher Torah study.

Kosher, see *kasher*.

*__Kristallnacht__ (Ger. "crystal night," meaning "night of broken glass"), organized destruction of synagogues, Jewish houses, and shops, accompanied by mass arrests of Jews, which took place in Germany and Austria under the Nazis on the night of Nov. 9–10, 1938.

*__Lag ba-Omer__, 33rd (Heb. **lag**) day of the **Omer* period falling on the 18th of *Iyyar; a semi-holiday.

Leḥi (abbr. For Heb. *__Loḥamei Ḥerut Israel__, "Fighters for the Freedom of Israel"), radically anti-British armed underground organization in Palestine, founded in 1940 by dissidents from *I.Z.L.

Levir, husband's brother.

*__Levirate marriage__ (Heb. *yibbum*), marriage of childless widow (*yevamah*) by brother (*yavam*) of the deceased husband (in accordance with Deut. 25:5); release from such an obligation is effected through *ḥaliz̧ah*.

LHY, see Leḥi.

*__Lulav__, palm branch; one of the *Four Species used on *Sukkot together with the **etrog*, *hadas*, and *aravah*.

*__Ma'aravot__, hymns inserted into the evening prayer of the three festivals, Passover, Shavuot, and Sukkot.

Ma'ariv, evening prayer; also called **arvit*.

*__Ma'barah__, transition camp; temporary settlement for newcomers in Israel during the period of mass immigration following 1948.

*__Maftir__, reader of the concluding portion of the Pentateuchal section on Sabbaths and holidays in synagogue; reader of the portion of the prophetical books of the Bible (**haftarah*).

*__Maggid__, popular preacher.

*__Maḥzor__ (pl. **maḥzorim**), festival prayer book.

*__Mamzer__, bastard; according to Jewish law, the offspring of an incestuous relationship.

*__Mandate, Palestine__, responsibility for the administration of Palestine conferred on Britain by the League of Nations in 1922; mandatory government: the British administration of Palestine.

*__Maqāma__ (Ar. pl. **maqamāt**), poetic form (rhymed prose) which, in its classical arrangement, has rigid rules of form and content.

*__Marḥeshvan__, popularly called Ḥeshvan; eighth month of the Jewish religious year, second of the civil, approximating to October–November.

*__Marrano(s)__, descendant(s) of Jew(s) in Spain and Portugal whose ancestors had been converted to Christianity under pressure but who secretly observed Jewish rituals.

Maskil (pl. **maskilim**), adherent of *Haskalah ("Enlightenment") movement.

*__Masorah__, body of traditions regarding the correct spelling, writing, and reading of the Hebrew Bible.

Masorete, scholar of the masoretic tradition.

Masoretic, in accordance with the masorah.

Meliz̧ah, in Middle Ages, elegant style; modern usage, florid style using biblical or talmudic phraseology.

Mellah, *Jewish quarter in North African towns.

*__Menorah__, candelabrum; seven-branched oil lamp used in the Tabernacle and Temple; also eight-branched candelabrum used on *Ḥanukkah.

Me'orah, hymn inserted into the first benediction of the morning prayer (*Yoz̧er ha-Me'orot*).

*__Merkabah__, *merkavah*, "chariot"; mystical discipline associated with Ezekiel's vision of the Divine Throne-Chariot (Ezek. 1).

Meshullaḥ, emissary sent to conduct propaganda or raise funds for rabbinical academies or charitable institutions.

*__Mezuzah__ (pl. **mezuzot**), parchment scroll with selected Torah verses placed in container and affixed to gates and doorposts of houses occupied by Jews.

*__Midrash__, method of interpreting Scripture to elucidate legal points (*Midrash Halakhah*) or to bring out lessons by stories or homiletics (*Midrash Aggadah*). Also the name for a collection of such rabbinic interpretations.

*__Mikveh__, ritual bath.

*__Minhag__ (pl. **minhagim**), ritual custom(s); synagogal rite(s); especially of a specific sector of Jewry.

*__Minḥah__, afternoon prayer; originally meal offering in Temple.

*__Minyan__, group of ten male adult Jews, the minimum required for communal prayer.

*__Mishnah__, earliest codification of Jewish Oral Law.

Mishnah (pl. **mishnayot**), subdivision of tractates of the Mishnah.

Mitnagged (pl. *__Mitnaggedim__), originally, opponents of *Ḥasidism in Eastern Europe.

*__Mitzvah__, biblical or rabbinic injunction; applied also to good or charitable deeds.

Mohel, official performing circumcisions.

*__Moshav__, smallholders' cooperative agricultural settlement in Israel, see moshav ovedim.

Moshavah, earliest type of Jewish village in modern Ereẓ Israel in which farming is conducted on individual farms mostly on privately owned land.

Moshav ovedim ("workers' moshav"), agricultural village in Israel whose inhabitants possess individual homes and holdings but cooperate in the purchase of equipment, sale of produce, mutual aid, etc.

*__Moshav shittufi__ ("collective moshav"), agricultural village in Israel whose members possess individual homesteads but where the agriculture and economy are conducted as a collective unit.

Mostegab (Ar.), poem with biblical verse at beginning of each stanza.

*__Muqaddam__ (Ar., pl. **muqaddamūn**), "leader," "head of the community."

*__Musaf__, additional service on Sabbath and festivals; originally the additional sacrifice offered in the Temple.

Musar, traditional ethical literature.

*__Musar movement__, ethical movement developing in the latter part of the 19th century among Orthodox Jewish groups in Lithuania; founded by R. Israel *Lipkin (Salanter).

*__Nagid__ (pl. **negidim**), title applied in Muslim (and some Christian) countries in the Middle Ages to a leader recognized by the state as head of the Jewish community.

Nakdan (pl. **nakdanim**), "punctuator"; scholar of the 9th to 14th centuries who provided biblical manuscripts with masoretic apparatus, vowels, and accents.

*__Nasi__ (pl. **nesi'im**), talmudic term for president of the Sanhedrin, who was also the spiritual head and later, political representative of the Jewish people; from second century a descendant of Hillel recognized by the Roman authorities as patriarch of the Jews. Now applied to the president of the State of Israel.

*__Negev__, the southern, mostly arid, area of Israel.

*__Ne'ilah__, concluding service on the *Day of Atonement.

Neofiti, term applied in southern Italy to converts to Christianity from Judaism and their descendants who were suspected of maintaining secret allegiance to Judaism.

*__Neology; Neolog; Neologism__, trend of *Reform Judaism in Hungary forming separate congregations after 1868.

*__Nevelah__ (lit. "carcass"), meat forbidden by the *dietary laws on account of the absence of, or defect in, the act of **sheḥitah* (ritual slaughter).

*__New Christians__, term applied especially in Spain and Portugal to converts from Judaism (and from Islam) and their descendants; "Half New Christian" designated a person one of whose parents was of full Jewish blood.

*__Niddah__ ("menstruous woman"), woman during the period of menstruation.

*__Nisan__, first month of the Jewish religious year, seventh of the civil, approximating to March-April.

Niẓoẓot, "sparks"; mystical term for sparks of the holy light imprisoned in all matter.

Nosaḥ (nusaḥ) "version"; (1) textual variant; (2) term applied to distinguish the various prayer rites, e.g., *nosaḥ Ashkenaz*; (3) the accepted tradition of synagogue melody.

*__Notarikon__, method of abbreviating Hebrew works or phrases by acronym.

Novella(e) (Heb. **ḥiddush (im)*), commentary on talmudic and later rabbinic subjects that derives new facts or principles from the implications of the text.

*__Nuremberg Laws__, Nazi laws excluding Jews from German citizenship, and imposing other restrictions.

Ofan, hymns inserted into a passage of the morning prayer.

*__Omer__, first sheaf cut during the barley harvest, offered in the Temple on the second day of Passover.

Omer, Counting of (Heb. *Sefirat ha-Omer*), 49 days counted from the day on which the *omer* was first offered in the Temple (according to the rabbis the 16th of Nisan, i.e., the second day of Passover) until the festival of Shavuot; now a period of semi-mourning.

Oraḥ Ḥayyim, see Shulḥan Arukh.

*__Orthodoxy__ (Orthodox Judaism), modern term for the strictly traditional sector of Jewry.

*__Pale of Settlement__, 25 provinces of czarist Russia where Jews were permitted permanent residence.

*__Palmaḥ__ (abbr. for Heb. *peluggot maḥaẓ*; "shock companies"), striking arm of the *Haganah.

*__Pardes__, medieval biblical exegesis giving the literal, allegorical, homiletical, and esoteric interpretations.

*__Parnas__, chief synagogue functionary, originally vested with both religious and administrative functions; subsequently an elected lay leader.

Partition plan(s), proposals for dividing Ereẓ Israel into autonomous areas.

Paytan, composer of **piyyut* (liturgical poetry).

*__Peel Commission__, British Royal Commission appointed by the British government in 1936 to inquire into the Palestine problem and make recommendations for its solution.

Pesaḥ, *Passover.

*__Pilpul__, in talmudic and rabbinic literature, a sharp dialectic used particularly by talmudists in Poland from the 16th century.

*__Pinkas__, community register or minute-book.

*__Piyyut__, (pl. **piyyutim**), Hebrew liturgical poetry.

*__Pizmon__, poem with refrain.

Posek (pl. *__posekim__), decisor; codifier or rabbinic scholar who pronounces decisions in disputes and on questions of Jewish law.

*__Prosbul__, legal method of overcoming the cancelation of debts with the advent of the *sabbatical year.

*__Purim__, festival held on Adar 14 or 15 in commemoration of the delivery of the Jews of Persia in the time of *Esther.

Rabban, honorific title higher than that of rabbi, applied to heads of the *Sanhedrin in mishnaic times.

*__Rabbanite__, adherent of rabbinic Judaism. In contradistinction to *Karaite.

Reb, rebbe, Yiddish form for rabbi, applied generally to a teacher or ḥasidic rabbi.

*__Reconstructionism__, trend in Jewish thought originating in the United States.

*__Reform Judaism__, trend in Judaism advocating modification of *Orthodoxy in conformity with the exigencies of contemporary life and thought.

Resh galuta, lay head of Babylonian Jewry (see exilarch).

Responsum (pl. ***responsa**), written opinion (*teshuvah*) given to question (*she'elah*) on aspects of Jewish law by qualified authorities; pl. collection of such queries and opinions in book form (*she'elot u-teshuvot*).

***Rishonim**, older rabbinical authorities. Distinguished from later authorities (**aḥaronim*).

***Rishon le-Zion**, title given to Sephardi chief rabbi of Ereẓ Israel.

***Rosh Ha-Shanah**, two-day holiday (one day in biblical and early mishnaic times) at the beginning of the month of *Tishri (September–October), traditionally the New Year.

Rosh Hodesh, *New Moon, marking the beginning of the Hebrew month.

Rosh Yeshivah, see *Yeshivah.

***R.S.H.A.** (initials of Ger. *Reichssicherheitshauptamt*: "Reich Security Main Office"), the central security department of the German Reich, formed in 1939, and combining the security police (Gestapo and Kripo) and the S.D.

***Sanhedrin**, the assembly of ordained scholars which functioned both as a supreme court and as a legislature before 70 C.E. In modern times the name was given to the body of representative Jews convoked by Napoleon in 1807.

***Savora** (pl. **savoraim**), name given to the Babylonian scholars of the period between the **amoraim* and the **geonim*, approximately 500–700 C.E.

S.D. (initials of Ger. *Sicherheitsdienst*: "security service"), security service of the *S.S. formed in 1932 as the sole intelligence organization of the Nazi party.

Seder, ceremony observed in the Jewish home on the first night of Passover (outside Ereẓ Israel first two nights), when the *Haggadah is recited.

***Sefer Torah**, manuscript scroll of the Pentateuch for public reading in synagogue.

***Sefirot, the ten**, the ten "Numbers"; mystical term denoting the ten spheres or emanations through which the Divine manifests itself; elements of the world; dimensions, primordial numbers.

Selektion (Ger.), (1) in ghettos and other Jewish settlements, the drawing up by Nazis of lists of deportees; (2) separation of incoming victims to concentration camps into two categories – those destined for immediate killing and those to be sent for forced labor.

Seliḥah (pl. ***seliḥot**), penitential prayer.

***Semikhah**, ordination conferring the title "rabbi" and permission to give decisions in matters of ritual and law.

Sephardi (pl. ***Sephardim**), Jew(s) of Spain and Portugal and their descendants, wherever resident, as contrasted with *Ashkenazi(m).

Shabbatean, adherent of the pseudo-messiah *Shabbetai Ẓevi (17th century).

Shaddai, name of God found frequently in the Bible and commonly translated "Almighty."

***Shaḥarit**, morning service.

Shali'aḥ (pl. **sheliḥim**), in Jewish law, messenger, agent; in modern times, an emissary from Ereẓ Israel to Jewish communities or organizations abroad for the purpose of fund-raising, organizing pioneer immigrants, education, etc.

Shalmonit, poetic meter introduced by the liturgical poet *Solomon ha-Bavli.

***Shammash**, synagogue beadle.

***Shavuot**, Pentecost; Festival of Weeks; second of the three annual pilgrim festivals, commemorating the receiving of the Torah at Mt. Sinai.

***Sheḥitah**, ritual slaughtering of animals.

***Shekhinah**, Divine Presence.

Shelishit, poem with three-line stanzas.

***Sheluḥei Ereẓ Israel** (or **shadarim**), emissaries from Ereẓ Israel.

***Shema** ([Yisrael]; "hear… [O Israel]," Deut. 6:4), Judaism's confession of faith, proclaiming the absolute unity of God.

Shemini Aẓeret, final festal day (in the Diaspora, final two days) at the conclusion of *Sukkot.

Shemittah, *Sabbatical year.

Sheniyyah, poem with two-line stanzas.

***Shephelah**, southern part of the coastal plain of Ereẓ Israel.

***Shevat**, eleventh month of the Jewish religious year, fifth of the civil, approximating to January–February.

***Shi'ur Komah**, Hebrew mystical work (c. eighth century) containing a physical description of God's dimensions; term denoting enormous spacial measurement used in speculations concerning the body of the **Shekhinah*.

Shivah, the "seven days" of *mourning following burial of a relative.

***Shofar**, horn of the ram (or any other ritually clean animal excepting the cow) sounded for the memorial blowing on *Rosh Ha-Shanah, and other occasions.

Shoḥet, person qualified to perform **sheḥitah*.

Shomer, *Ha-Shomer, organization of Jewish workers in Ereẓ Israel founded in 1909 to defend Jewish settlements.

***Shtadlan**, Jewish representative or negotiator with access to dignitaries of state, active at royal courts, etc.

***Shtetl**, Jewish small-town community in Eastern Europe.

***Shulḥan Arukh**, Joseph *Caro's code of Jewish law in four parts:
Oraḥ Ḥayyim, laws relating to prayers, Sabbath, festivals, and fasts;
Yoreh De'ah, dietary laws, etc;
Even ha-Ezer, laws dealing with women, marriage, etc;
Ḥoshen Mishpat, civil, criminal law, court procedure, etc.

Siddur, among Ashkenazim, the volume containing the daily prayers (in distinction to the **maḥzor* containing those for the festivals).

***Simḥat Torah**, holiday marking the completion in the synagogue of the annual cycle of reading the Pentateuch; in Ereẓ Israel observed on Shemini Aẓeret (outside Ereẓ Israel on the following day).

***Sinai Campaign**, brief campaign in October–November 1956 when Israel army reacted to Egyptian terrorist attacks and blockade by occupying the Sinai peninsula.

Sitra aḥra, "the other side" (of God); left side; the demoniac and satanic powers.

***Sivan**, third month of the Jewish religious year, ninth of the civil, approximating to May–June.

***Six-Day War**, rapid war in June 1967 when Israel reacted to Arab threats and blockade by defeating the Egyptian, Jordanian, and Syrian armies.

***S.S.** (initials of Ger. *Schutzstaffel*: "protection detachment"), Nazi formation established in 1925 which later became the "elite" organization of the Nazi Party and carried out central tasks in the "Final Solution."

***Status quo ante** community, community in Hungary retaining the status it had held before the convention of the General Jewish Congress there in 1868 and the resultant split in Hungarian Jewry.

***Sukkah**, booth or tabernacle erected for *Sukkot when, for seven days, religious Jews "dwell" or at least eat in the *sukkah* (Lev. 23:42).

***Sukkot**, festival of Tabernacles; last of the three pilgrim festivals, beginning on the 15th of Tishri.

Sūra (Ar.), chapter of the Koran.

Ta'anit Esther (Fast of *Esther), fast on the 13th of Adar, the day preceding Purim.

Takkanah (pl. ***takkanot**), regulation supplementing the law of the Torah; regulations governing the internal life of communities and congregations.

***Tallit (gadol)**, four-cornered prayer shawl with fringes (*ẓiẓit*) at each corner.

***Tallit katan**, garment with fringes (*ẓiẓit*) appended, worn by observant male Jews under their outer garments.

***Talmud**, "teaching"; compendium of discussion on the Mishnah by generations of scholars and jurists in many academies over a period of several centuries. The Jerusalem (or Palestinian) Talmud mainly contains the discussions of the Palestinian sages. The Babylonian Talmud incorporates the parallel discussion in the Babylonian academies.

Talmud torah, term generally applied to Jewish religious (and ultimately to talmudic) study; also to traditional Jewish religious public schools.

***Tammuz**, fourth month of the Jewish religious year, tenth of the civil, approximating to June-July.

Tanna (pl. ***tannaim**), rabbinic teacher of mishnaic period.

***Targum**, Aramaic translation of the Bible.

***Tefillin**, phylacteries, small leather cases containing passages from Scripture and affixed on the forehead and arm by male Jews during the recital of morning prayers.

Tell (Ar. "mound," "hillock"), ancient mound in the Middle East composed of remains of successive settlements.

***Terefah**, food that is not **kasher*, owing to a defect on the animal.

***Territorialism**, 20th century movement supporting the creation of an autonomous territory for Jewish mass-settlement outside Ereẓ Israel.

***Tevet**, tenth month of the Jewish religious year, fourth of the civil, approximating to December–January.

Tikkun ("restitution," "reintegration"), (1) order of service for certain occasions, mostly recited at night; (2) mystical term denoting restoration of the right order and true unity after the spiritual "catastrophe" which occurred in the cosmos.

Tishah be-Av, Ninth of *Av, fast day commemorating the destruction of the First and Second Temples.

***Tishri**, seventh month of the Jewish religious year, first of the civil, approximating to September–October.

Tokheḥah, reproof sections of the Pentateuch (Lev. 26 and Deut. 28); poem of reproof.

***Torah**, Pentateuch or the Pentateuchal scroll for reading in synagogue; entire body of traditional Jewish teaching and literature.

Tosafist, talmudic glossator, mainly French (12–14th centuries), bringing additions to the commentary by *Rashi.

***Tosafot**, glosses supplied by tosafist.

***Tosefta**, a collection of teachings and traditions of the *tannaim*, closely related to the Mishnah.

Tradent, person who hands down a talmudic statement on the name of his teacher or other earlier authority.

***Tu bi-Shevat**, the 15th day of Shevat, the New Year for Trees; date marking a dividing line for fruit tithing; in modern Israel celebrated as arbor day.

***Uganda Scheme**, plan suggested by the British government in 1903 to establish an autonomous Jewish settlement area in East Africa.

***Va'ad Le'ummi**, national council of the Jewish community in Ereẓ Israel during the period of the British *Mandate.

***Wannsee Conference**, Nazi conference held on Jan. 20, 1942, at which the planned annihilation of European Jewry was endorsed.

Waqf (Ar.), (1) a Muslim charitable pious foundation; (2) state lands and other property passed to the Muslim community for public welfare.

***War of Independence**, war of 1947–49 when the Jews of Israel fought off Arab invading armies and ensured the establishment of the new State.

***White Paper(s)**, report(s) issued by British government, frequently statements of policy, as issued in connection with Palestine during the *Mandate period.

***Wissenschaft des Judentums** (Ger. "Science of Judaism"), movement in Europe beginning in the 19th century for scientific study of Jewish history, religion, and literature.

***Yad Vashem**, Israel official authority for commemorating the *Holocaust in the Nazi era and Jewish resistance and heroism at that time.

Yeshivah (pl. ***yeshivot**), Jewish traditional academy devoted primarily to study of rabbinic literature; *rosh yeshivah*, head of the yeshivah.

YHWH, the letters of the holy name of God, the Tetragrammaton.

Yibbum, see levirate marriage.

Yiḥud, "union"; mystical term for intention which causes the union of God with the **Shekhinah*.

Yishuv, settlement; more specifically, the Jewish community of Ereẓ Israel in the pre-State period. The pre-Zionist community is generally designated the "old yishuv" and the community evolving from 1880, the "new yishuv."

Yom Kippur, Yom ha-Kippurim, *Day of Atonement, solemn fast day observed on the 10th of Tishri.

Yoreh De'ah, see Shulḥan Arukh.

Yoẓer, hymns inserted in the first benediction (*Yoẓer Or*) of the morning **Shema*.

***Ẓaddik**, person outstanding for his faith and piety; especially a ḥasidic rabbi or leader.

Ẓimẓum, "contraction"; mystical term denoting the process whereby God withdraws or contracts within Himself so leaving a primordial vacuum in which creation can take place; primordial exile or self-limitation of God.

***Zionist Commission (1918)**, commission appointed in 1918 by the British government to advise the British military authorities in Palestine on the implementation of the *Balfour Declaration.

Ẓyyonei Zion, the organized opposition to Herzl in connection with the *Uganda Scheme.

***Ẓiẓit**, fringes attached to the **tallit* and **tallit katan*.

***Zohar**, mystical commentary on the Pentateuch; main textbook of *Kabbalah.

Zulat, hymn inserted after the **Shema* in the morning service.

ISBN-13: 978-0-02-865946-6
ISBN-10: 0-02-865946-5
90000
9 780028 659466